INOUE'S SMALLER JAPANESE-ENGLISH DICTIONARY

INOUE'S SMALLER JAPANESE-ENGLISH DICTIONARY

BY

JUKICHI INOUE

CHARLES E. TUTTLE COMPANY

RUTLAND, VERMONT

& TOKYO, JAPAN

Published by the Charles E. Tuttle Company, Inc.
of Rutland, Vermont & Tokyo, Japan
with editorial offices at
Suido 1-chome, 2-6, Bunkyo-ku, Tokyo, Japan

Library of Congress Catalog Card No. 81-52936
International Standard Book No. 0-8048-1440-6

First Tuttle edition, 1983
Ninth printing, 1993

PRINTED IN JAPAN

PUBLISHER'S FOREWORD

This dictionary's presentation of copious information in a convenient format makes it an eminently practical reference work, for foreigners who wish to use the Japanese language as well as Japanese who are learning English. It was written near the end of the distinguished life of its compiler, Jukichi Inoue. In his youth Inoue was sent to England for study, returning to Japan to serve at Tokyo University and later the Ministry of Foreign Affairs, which posted him to Belgium and America. The years before his death in 1929 were spent in compiling a series of Japanese-English and English-Japanese dictionaries, of which this is one, and writing books introducing things Japanese to the West. He also was associated with the Inoue English Correspondence School, which first published this work in 1926. The pages that follow retain the romanization Inouye for the compiler's name, which he himself used. His work's many virtues have hardly been diminished by the passage of time.

FOREWORD

This Smaller Japanese-English Dictionary completes my series of dictionaries and with its publication closes the period of over twenty years which I have devoted to the compilation of my dictionaries. The compilation has been hard work; but it has by no means been unpleasant as some people imagine. In looking for words and phrases in the one language which correspond to words and phrases in the other, one comes across many interesting instances and thereby adds to one's knowledge of both languages. Only the research requires a very retentive memory; and of that age is depriving me and I have decided to give up the compilation of dictionaries, especially as the present dictionary completes the series I meant to bring out. I intend, however, to labour in other fields; for I have been so used to working that to cease to labour would be to cease to live.

I take this final occasion to tender my thanks for the favour shown to all my dictionaries and to express my hope that they will be of service to all who use them.

Jukichi Inoue

凡　例

1. 本書は主として中等學校竝に高等程度の學生諸子の使用に充てんが爲に特殊の用意を以て編纂したものである．包容語句は吾人の日常生活に必要なるものを百科に亙つて豐富に採集し，特に新時代の要求に應ずる爲め努めて外來語・新造語をも收めた．且つ各種高等學校入學試驗問題の如きも適宜に之を參酌加味してある．
2. 見出語の排列はすべてアルファベット順にしてある．
3. 合成語は一々之を見出語にするの煩を避け，主要語の見出中に ¶ を以て蒐集してある．
4. 字音は漢音を主とし，特殊のもの通俗のものは呉音又は慣用音をも採用した．
5. 同一の見出語で品詞を異にする時は　——, *a*.　—— **-ni,** *ad*. の如く略書し，成句中にあつては ① [*a*.] ② [*vt*.] の如く示してある．
6. 動詞に附屬する前置詞は特にイタリックを以て示してある．尙譯語中未だ英語化せぬ他國語も亦イタリックを用ひ〔伊〕〔羅〕等を以て其の何國の語たるかを區別してある．
7. 熟語又は文例中　—入國禁止《許可》, prohibition 《permission》 of entry. などある《　》は　—入國禁止, prohibition of entry. —入國許可, permission of entry. とすべきを節約したものなるを示す．
8. 同じく　—滿點を取る, to get [obtain] a full mark. などある [　] は to get a full mark. とするも to obtain a full mark. とするも同義なることを示す．
9. 同じく the Minister of (State for) Justice. などある (　) は其の中の語の有無に拘らず同義なることを示す．但し burning (of a temple) ; to lodge (a person) overnight の如く後又は間に來る字句を示すに用ひた場合も尠くない．
10. 各譯語の間は ; を以て分ち同一語で綴字の異なるものは , を以てし，意義の稍〻異なる譯語の間又は學術語と普通語との間は : を用ひてある．
11. 見出語の次に Ⓢ あだ花．などあるは其の語が見出語の類語なるを示す．

12. 漢字の類語を擧げる場合は〔 〕を用ひてある.

13. ☞ は參照の符號. ＝ は同一の符號.

14. 外來語の音は主として原語音によつたが一般に通用せられて居る訛りの程度をも參酌してある.

15. fa, fi, fe, fo 又は va, vi, vu, ve, vo 等の音は既に我が國語辭書にも採用せられたるものあり, 本書に於てはその性質上特に必要なるを認めて之を新設することにした.

16. 字音の kwa, kwō と發音すべきものは便宜上 ka, kō を用ひることにした.

17. ローマ字 b, m, p の前に來る ン は本書に於ては凡て n を用ひてある.

18. ハイフェンを要する語が二行に跨る時は self- -interest の如く之を重用してハイフェンなき語と區別してある.

ローマ字綴方表

ア a	イ i	ウ u	エ e	オ o	—	—	—	—	—
カ ka	キ ki	ク ku	ケ ke	コ ko	ガ ga	ギ gi	グ gu	ゲ ge	ゴ go
サ sa	シ shi	ス su	セ se	ソ so	ザ za	ジ ji	ズ zu	ゼ ze	ゾ zo
タ ta	ティ(チ) ti(chi)	トゥ(ツ) tu(tsu)	テ te	ト to	ダ da	ディ(ヂ) di(ji)	ドゥ(ヅ) du(zu)	デ de	ド do
ナ na	ニ ni	ヌ nu	ネ ne	ノ no	バ ba	ビ bi	ブ bu	ベ be	ボ bo
ハ ha	ヒ hi	—	ヘ he	ホ ho	パ pa	ピ pi	プ pu	ペ pe	ポ po
マ ma	ミ mi	ム mu	メ me	モ mo	ファ fa	フィ fi	フ fu	フェ fe	フォ fo
ヤ ya	—	ユ yu	—	ヨ yo	—	—	—	—	—
ラ ra	リ ri	ル ru	レ re	ロ ro	—	—	—	—	—
ワ wa	ウィ wi	—	ウェ we	ウォ wo	ヴァ va	ヴィ vi	ヴ vu	ヴェ ve	ヴォ vo
キャ kya	—	キュ kyu	—	キョ kyo	ギャ gya	—	ギュ gyu	—	ギョ gyo
シャ sha	—	シュ shu	シェ she	ショ sho	—	—	—	—	—
チャ cha	—	チュ chu	チェ che	チョ cho	ジァ ja	—	ジュ ju	ジェ je	ジョ jo
ツァ tsa	—	—	ツェ tse	ツォ tso	—	—	—	—	—
ニャ nya	—	ニュ nyu	—	ニョ nyo	ビャ bya	—	ビュ byu	—	ビョ byo
ヒャ hya	—	ヒュ hyu	—	ヒョ hyo	ピャ pya	—	ピュ pyu	—	ピョ pyo
ミャ mya	—	ミュ myu	—	ミョ myo	—	—	—	—	—
リャ rya	—	リュ ryu	—	リョ ryo					
	ン n		ン ṅ						

【備考】

1. 長音の場合は母音の上に長音符 ー を施すこと ā, ī, ū, ē, ō, の如し.
2. 母音の前の n は ṅ を用ひて次の母音と別に發音すべきを區別せり.
3. 邦音アッ, エッの如き發聲は單獨文字にて示す能はず. 已むを得ず à, è の如く文字にアクセントを施して之を分てり.
4. ti, tu, di, du は外來語音を表はす時に限り用ひ普通の場合はそれぞれ chi, tsu, ji, zu を用ひたり.
5. 促音は sotchi (其方), sekkan (折檻), ippen (一遍), kesshin (決心), ittan (一旦) 等の如く子音を重ねて表はす.

略 語 符 號

【動】	動物	【哲】	哲學	【腔腸】	腔腸動物
【植】	植物	【繪】	繪畫	【棘皮】	棘皮動物
【數】	數學	【寫】	寫眞	【甲殼】	甲殼類
【音】	音樂	【印】	印刷	【爬蟲】	爬蟲類
【論】	論理	【博】	博物	【瓣鰓】	瓣鰓類
【心】	心理	【史】	歷史	【地質】	地質學
【文】	文法	【齒】	齒科	【地文】	地文學
【商】	商業	【軍】	軍事	【聲音】	聲音學
【航】	航海	【修】	修辭	【野球】	野球戲
【建】	建築	【電】	電氣	【佛】	佛教
【法】	法律	【美】	美術	〔梵〕	梵語
【經】	經濟	【藥】	藥學	〔羅〕	羅典語
【政】	政治	【倫】	倫理	〔希〕	希臘語
【醫】	醫學	【光】	光學	〔英〕	英國專用語
【生】	生理	【陸】	陸軍	〔米〕	米國專用語
【解】	解剖	【海】	海軍	〔佛〕	佛蘭西語
【理】	物理	【鑛】	鑛物	〔伊〕	伊太利語
【化】	化學	【冶】	冶金	〔獨〕	獨逸語
【天】	天文	【劇】	演劇	〔露〕	露西亞語
【宗】	宗教	【工】	工學	〔西〕	西班牙語
【神】	神學	【獸】	獸醫	〔葡〕	葡萄牙語
【蟲】	蟲類	【彫】	彫刻	〔蘭〕	和蘭語
【魚】	魚類	【農】	農業	〔蘇〕	蘇格蘭
【貝】	貝類	【機】	機械	〔日〕	日本語
【鳥】	鳥類	【紋】	紋章	〔卑〕	卑語
【昆】	昆蟲	【飛】	飛行機	〔俗〕	俗語
【蛾】	蛾類	【詩】	詩形學	〔詩〕	詩用語
【蝶】	蝶類	【生物】	生物學	〔諧〕	諧謔語
【菌】	細菌	【哺乳】	哺乳動物	〔小兒〕	小兒語

品 詞 符 號

a.	adjective.
ad.	adverb.
conj.	conjunction.
fem.	feminine.
int.	interjection.
n.	noun.
pl.	plural.
pref.	prefix.
prep.	preposition.
pron.	pronoun.
suf.	suffix.
v.	verb.
v. aux.	auxiliary verb.
vi.	intransitive verb.
vt.	transitive verb.

INOUYE'S SMALLER JAPANESE-ENGLISH DICTIONARY

A

a, ā, (唯, 諾), *ad.* yes; well. —あーそれでよい, Yes, that will do. —あー勝手におし, Well, do as you please.

à (あッ), *int.* ☞ *atto.* —あッ, 來た, There he comes.

ā (ああ), *int.* ❶ (嗚呼) (嘆息·悲痛·嘆賞など) oh; alas; ah. ❷ (噫, 吁) (驚愕·哀傷·痛恨など) ah; good God [heaven]; good [goodness] gracious. ❸ (言ひ詰まッた時) er—. —ああ嬉しい, Oh, how glad I am! —ああさうさう, Ah, yes, yes. —ああ何とか云ッたけなア, Er—what was his name? —ああ可哀想に, Ah, poor fellow!

aa (彼樣), *ad.* so; in that manner [way]; like that. —ああいふ人達, such people. —ああは言ふものの, though he says so.

abaku (發く), *vt.* ❶ (發掘) to break open; open. ❷ (摘發) to expose; disclose; divulge. —墓を發く, to open a grave. —他人の非を訐(あば)く, to expose other people's faults.

abara (肋), *n.* the ribs; a side of the chest. ¶ 肋骨, a rib.

abaraya (荒屋), *n.* ❶ (茅屋) a hovel. ❷ (廢屋) a dilapidated [ramshackle; tumble-down] house. —荒屋ですがどうぞお上り下さい, Please enter my humble home.

abareru (暴れる), *vi.* to act violently; kick up a row [shindy]. **——,** *a.* rough; rowdy; restive (馬など). —暴れ出す, to become disorderly; turn [grow] restive (馬が). —暴れ込む, to burst into. —暴れ廻る, to rampage; run amuck. —座敷で暴れる, to romp about in the parlour. ¶ 暴れ者, a rowdy; a rough.

abata (痘痕, 菊石), *n.* a pockmark. ¶ 痘面(づら), a pitted [pockmarked] face.

abayo (あばよ), *int.* 〘小兒〙 bye-bye; ta-ta.

abazure (阿婆摺の), *a.* impudent; saucy. ¶ 阿婆摺女, a minx (諧謔的に); a vixen.

abekobe (あべこべに), *ad.* the other way (about); topsy-turvy; *vice versa* 〘羅〙. —あべこべにする, to put the other way about. (上下 (裏表) あべこべにする, to turn upside down (turn inside out).) —箸をあべこべに持つ, to hold chopsticks the other way about. —あべこべに毆られる, to be on the contrary struck oneself. **——-no,** *a.* opposite; contrary; topsy-turvy. —あべこべの方向へ行ッた, He went in the opposite direction.

abiru (浴びる), *vt.* ❶ (かぶる) to pour upon oneself (水など). ❷ (入浴) to take a bath; have [take] a bathe (河·海等で); take a dip (ちょッと浴びる). ❸ (蒙る) to be blamed *for*; bear the blame *for* (罪など). —水 (湯) を浴びる, to take a cold (warm) bath; dash cold (warm) water upon oneself. —罪を浴びる, to bear the blame (for another's fault). —酒を浴びる程飲む, to drink wine in excess. —砲火を浴びる, to be under fire. —子供に湯を浴びさす, to give a child a warm bath. —喝采を背に浴びて, with loud cheers behind him.

abiseru (浴びせる), *vt.* ❶ (かぶらす) to pour (水など); dash *upon*; rain (雨の樣に). ❷ (蒙らす) to lay on. —水を浴びせる, to dash cold water *on*. —敵に砲火を浴びせる, to rain shells upon the enemy. —嘲罵の聲を浴びせる, to cover a person with aspersions. —他人に罪を浴びせる, to lay the blame upon another.

abu (虻), *n.* 【昆】 the gad-fly; the horse-fly. —虻蜂取らずになる, to fall between two stools.

abuku (泡沫), *n.* a bubble; a foam; a froth. ☞ *awa* (泡). ¶ 泡錢, unearned gain [money].

abumi (鐙), *n.* a stirrup. —鐙をふんばッて立つ, to rise in the stirrups.

abunagena (危げな), *a.* dangerous; perilous.

abunai (危い), *a.* ❶(不安心, 危險) dangerous; risky; unsafe. ❷(危篤) in danger; in a critical condition. ❸(不確か, 疑はしい) doubtful; questionable; uncertain. ❹(信用出來ぬ) unreliable; untrustworthy. —あぶない(注意), Look out!; Take care! —危い瀬戸際に, on the verge of danger. —地位が危い, One's position is unsafe. —彼の命が危い, His life is in danger. —あの病人は危い, The patient is in a critical condition. —君の受合は危いもんだ, Your assurance is not to be relied upon.

abunaku (危く), *ad.* ❶(危險) dangerously; perilously. ❷(殆ど) almost; on the point *of*; very nearly. —危くなる, to become dangerous; be in danger. —危くする, to endanger; compromise. —あぶなくつかまる所だッた, I just missed being caught. —あぶなく殺される所だッた, I was on the point of being killed. —彼はあぶなく坑におちる所だッた, He came near falling into the pit.

abunasōna (危なさうな), *a.* dangerous-looking. —危なさうな橋, a rickety bridge.

abura (油), *n.* ❶〔油〕oil. ❷〔脂, 膏〕fat; grease. —油で炒〔い〕る, to fry with fat. —脂が乘る, ①(魚·鳥等が) to become oily; be in season. ②(氣乘りする) to warm to (one's work). —油を塗る, to grease; oil. —油をさす, to oil; lubricate. —膏を絞る, ①(精力を盡す) to exert one's utmost. ②(油を取る) to call over the coals. —油を賣る, to waste time in small talk; talk away one's hours. —油ッ濃い, ①〔油〕oily. ②〔脂〕fatty; greasy. ¶膏汗, greasy sweat. —油紙, oil-paper; oiled paper. —油糟, oil-cake. —脂肉〔ミ〕, fat (lean の對). —油さし, ①(器) an oil-can; an oiler; a lubricator. ②(人) an oiler; a lubricator. —油壺, an oil-cup; a font (洋燈の). —油屋, an oil-dealer[-man; -merchant].

aburae (油繪), *n.* an oil-painting. ¶油繪具, ① oil (往々 oils); oil paint. ②(顏料) oil-colour. —油繪師, an oil-painter.

aburage (油揚), *n.* fried bean-curd (豆腐の); fried food.

aburagiru (油ぎる), *vi.* to be oily; be covered with oil; become oily [greasy]. —油ぎッた, ①〔油〕oily. ②〔脂〕fat; fatty; greasy.

aburamushi (油蟲), *n.* ❶(ごきぶり) the black-beetle; the cockroach. ❷(蚜蟲) the aphis; the plant-louse. ❸(人に附き纏ふ奴) a hanger-on; a parasite.

aburana (油菜), *n.* the cole-seed; the rape.

aburiko (炙子), *n.* a gridiron; a grill.

aburu (炙·焙る), *vt.* to expose to heat. ❶(燒く) to roast (特に肉を); broil (炙子で); toast (パン·輕燒等を). ❷(乾かす) to dry. ❸(暖める) to warm. —炙ッた, roast; broiled. —魚を焙る, to broil fish. —手を焙る, to warm one's hands before [at] a fire.

āchi (綠門, 拱門), *n.* an arch.

achikochi (彼方此方), *ad.* = *achira-kochira.*

achira (彼方), *pron.* that; the other; the other party [side]. ——, *ad.* (位置, 方向) there; over there; away (他方). —彼方へ, away; off; yonder. —彼方の, yonder. —彼方に見える山, the hill I see yonder.

achira-kochira (彼方此方), *ad.* about; here and there (此處彼處に); to and fro (彼方此方に); up and down. —彼方此方走り廻る, to beat up and down. —彼方此方に散ばる紙屑, waste paper scattered about.

ada (仇), *n.* ❶(敵) a foe; an enemy. ❷(怨憤) hatred; grudge; enmity. ❸〔寇〕invasion. ❹(禍, 災害) injury; harm. —仇を報いる, to avenge oneself upon; take revenge (on a person for an injury). —身の仇となる, to lead to one's undoing.

ada (徒), *n.* ❶(無用) uselessness. ❷(空) nothing; naught. ❸(はかないこと) emptiness; vanity. —徒になる, to come to naught. ——**-na**, *a.* ❶ useless; barren. ❷ empty; vain. ——**-ni**, *ad.* in vain; vainly. —時間を徒に費す, to waste time. —徒疎かに思はぬ, not to think lightly of; be grateful. ¶あだ心, a fickle heart. —あだ波, a ripple.

ada (婀娜な), *a.* charming; lovely; coquettish (なまめかしい).

adakamo (恰も), *ad.* = ***atakamo.***

adana (渾名, 綽名), *n.* a nickname; a by-name; a sobriquet. —互に綽名で呼び合ふ, to call each other by nickname. —人に綽名をつける, to give a person a nickname.

adashi (あだし), *a.* ❶(他の) another; any other; other. ❷(無駄の) vain; useless. ¶あだし人, another; others; other people. —あだし言〔ゴ〕, idle talk; gossip; chitchat. —あだし名, a bad name; an ill repute.

adauchi (仇討), *n.* revenge. —仇討する, to revenge; avenge.

adokenai (仇氣ない), *a.* childlike; artless; innocent. —あどけなく, innocently; artlessly; childlike. —あどけない子供, an innocent [artless] child. —あどけない時から, from childhood; from a child. —彼にはまだ何處か仇氣ない所がある, There is still something childlike about him.

aegu (喘ぐ), *vi.* to pant; gasp; puff. —喘ぎながら云ふ, to speak gaspingly. —喘ぎ喘ぎ何か云ふ, to gasp out something.

aen (亞鉛), *n.* 【鑛】zinc. ——, *a.* zinc. ¶ 亞鉛版, 【印】half-tone; zincotype; zincograph. —亞鉛板, a zinc-plate. —亞鉛引鐵鈑, galvanized sheet-iron. —亞鉛鍍金(ﾒｯｷ), galvanization. —亞鉛凸版, an anastatic plate.

aenai (敢ない), *a.* sad; pitiful. —敢ない最後を遂げる, to come to a pitiful [sad] end. —敢なく斷られる, to be bluntly refused.

aete (敢て), *ad.* ❶ (づかづかと) boldly; daringly. ❷【肯】(得心して) willingly. —敢てする, to dare; venture; make so bold as *to.* —敢て云ふ, I venture to say; I dare say. —敢て內閣に列しようとしない, He does not insist upon a seat in the Cabinet.

aezu (敢へず), *ad.* without giving ...time *to*; instantly

afureru (溢れる), *vi.* to overflow; run over. —溢れさす, to deluge; flood; glut. —溢れ出る, to brim over; overflow. —愛嬌溢れるばかりの目許, eyes brimming with charm. —品が市場に溢れてる, The article gluts the market. —目には涙が溢れて居た, Her eyes were swimming with tears.

Afurika (阿弗利加), *n.* Africa. —阿弗利加の, African. ¶ 阿弗利加人, an African.

agaki (足掻), *n.* ❶(馬の) pawing. ❷(藻掻) flounder. —足掻が取れない, to be unable to struggle out.

agaku (足掻く), *v.* ❶(馬が) to paw. ❷(もがく) to flounder. —何をそんなに足掻くのか, Why are you floundering so?

agameru (崇める), *vt.* to revere; look up *to*; worship (崇拜). —英雄を崇める, to worship a hero. —師と崇める, to revere as one's teacher.

aganai (贖, 償), *n.* atonement; expiation; reparation. —贖金を出す, to pay an indemnity.

aganau (購ふ), *vt.* to buy; purchase.

aganau (贖·償ふ), *v.* ❶(賠償) to repay; indemnify; compensate. ❷(贖罪) to atone; expiate. —損害を償ふ, to compensate for [make good] a loss. —前日の罪を贖ふ, to atone for one's former misdeeds.

agari (上り), *n.* ❶(上達) progress; improvement. ❷(騰貴) rise; advance. ❸(完成, 出來ばえ) completion; finish. ❹(雙六等にて競技者の終り) finish. ❺ =*agaridaka.* ¶巡査上り(の人), an ex-policeman. —上り段, an entrance. —上り口, an entrance; a front door (戸口).

agaridaka (上り高), *n.* ❶ receipts (收入); proceeds (賣上高); takings; turnover. ❷(收穫) yield; produce.

agariori (上り下り), *n.* going up and down; ascent and descent. —上り下りする, to go up and down; ascend and descend. —二階の上り下りが厄介だ, It is troublesome going up and down the stairs.

agarisagari (上り下り), *n.* rise and fall.

agaru (上る), *vi.* to rise; go up; come up (上より云ふ時). Ⓢ 登る, 昇る, 達する, 昂る, 騰貴する, 昇進する. ❶(持ち上げて) to lift. ❷(上達) to improve; progress. ❸(參上) to call on (at); visit. ❹ to enter (學校·家に); come (go) in. ❺(捕まる) to be caught. ❻(成績·實が) to appear; come out. ❼(奉納) to be offered. ❽(止む) to stop. ❾(とれる) to be produced. ❿(證據が) to be produced; come up. ⓫(死ぬ, 枯れる) to die. ⓬(陸へ) to land. —手が上る, to become skilful. —學校へ上る, to enter a school. —頗る上らぬ風彩, a very poor appearance. —旗があがってる, A flag is up. —水が床まで上った, The water reached the floor. —どうぞお上り下さい, Please come in. —一反步から一石あがる, A *tan* yields a *koku* (of rice).

age (上), *n.* lift; uptake.

age (揚), *n.* ❶ = *aburage.* ❷ fry; fried food. ¶揚鍋, a frying-pan.

age (褶), *n.* a tuck. —褶をする, to tuck; make a tuck *in.* —褶をおろす, to undo [let out] the tuck.

ageashi (擧足とる), *vt.* to trip.

ageba (揚場), *n.* a landing; a wharf; a quay. ¶ 揚場人足, a wharf-hand; a wharf-labourer.

agehachō (鳳蝶), *n.* the swallow-tail.

ageku (擧句, 揚句), *n.* the end; the conclusion. —擧句の果に, in the end; finally. —失敗の擧句に, to complete one's failure. —その擧句に一度行きました, After that I went again.

agemaku (揚幕), *n.* 【劇】 a (drop-)curtain.

ageoroshi (上下), *n.* ❶(上下) raising and lowering. ❷(荷物の) shipping and unlading.

ageru (上げる), *vt.* ❶(持上げる) to raise; lift. ❷(揭揚) to fly (凧·氣球·旗等); hoist (帆·旗等); set up (旗); put up (同上). ❸(高くする) to raise; lift up (目·頭·手·足等); put up (値段). ❹(擧示) to give; mention; produce (證據). ❺(成績·實·效果·利益を) to produce; bring; yield. ❻(進呈, 獻納) to give; present; offer. ❼(選任, 登庸) to raise; appoint (任命); elect (選擧). ❽(擧行) to hold; perform; keep. ❾(生む) to give birth *to*; be delivered *of*. ❿(捕縛) to catch. ⓫(沒收) to confiscate; deprive *of*. ⓬(終了) to finish; complete. ⓭(嘔吐) to vomit; spew out. ⓮(遣る) to send. —花火を揚げる, to let off fireworks. —床をあげる, to put away a bed. —兵を擧げる, to raise an army. —荷を揚げる, to land the cargo. —お髮(ぐし)をあげる, to dress [do up] her hair. —子供を學校にあげる, to send [put] a boy to school. —一例を擧げれば, to cite an instance; to give an example. —...の健康を祝して杯を擧げる, to raise one's glass *to*—. —人を上げたり下げたりする, to praise and blame a person in turn.

ageru (揚げる), *vt.* to fry (油で).

agesage (上下), *n.* ❶(上下) raising and lowering. ❷(褒貶, 毀譽) praise and blame. ❸(抑揚) intonation. —潮の上げ下げ, ebb and flow of the tide. —箸の上げ下げにも小言を並べる, to find fault with me for the least trifles.

ageshio (上潮), *n.* the flood-tide; the rising [flowing] tide.

agesoko (上底), *n.* a false [raised] bottom; the kick (罎の).

agete (擧げて), *ad.* all; wholly; altogether. —擧げて數ふ可らず, to be too numerous to mention; be incalculable. —一家を擧げて旅行してる, He is travelling with the whole family.

agezu (上げず), in less than; within.

agi (阿魏), *n.* ❶【植】 the asafœtida plant. ❷(藥品) asafœtida.

agito (顋, 腮), *n.* ❶(魚の) the gills (of a fish). ❷=*ago* の❶

ago (頤, 顎), *n.* ❶(動物の) the jaw; the chin. ❷(機械などの) jaws; cheeks. ❸(鐖)(矢鏃·釣針等の) a barb. —頤が干上る, to starve. —顎を外す, to dislocate one's jaw. —人を頤で扱ふ, to treat others superciliously. ¶二重(ふた)顎, a double chin. —上(下)顎, the upper (lower) jaw.

agumu (倦む), *vi.* to be weary; get [grow] tired *of*; be sick *of* (厭になる). —待ち(聞き)あぐむ, to be tired of waiting (hearing).

agura (胡坐), *n.* crossed legs. —胡坐をかく, to sit cross-legged. ¶胡坐鼻, a pug-nose; a turned-up nose.

aha (アハヽ), *int.* aha; ha-ha.

ahen (阿片), *n.* opium. —阿片を吸ふ, to smoke opium. ¶阿片丁幾, laudanum; tincture of opium. —阿片中毒, opiumism. —阿片常用, the opium habit. —阿片劑, opiate.

ahiru (鶩, 家鴨), *n.* the duck; the drake (牡); the duckling (子).

ahisan (亞砒酸), *n.* arsenious acid.

ahitsu (堊筆), *n.* a crayon. ¶堊筆畫, a crayon; a picture in crayon.

ahō (阿呆), *n.* a fool (痴愚); a dunce; a goose. ☞ ***baka.*** —阿呆な, foolish.

ahōdori (信天翁), *n.* the albatross.

ai (藍), *n.* ❶(植物) the indigo-plant. ❷(染料) indigo. ❸(色) blue colour. ¶人造藍, artificial indigo. —藍玉, an indigo-ball; (洗濯用) a thumb-blue.

ai (相), *n.* (相手) company. ——, *ad.* each other (兩者); one another (三人以上); mutually (互に); together (共に). —相向ッて, face to face; opposite each other.

ai (間), *n.* ❶ a distance (距離); an interval (間隔). ❷(中間) the middle. ❸(切り) a pause; a break. ☞ ***aida.***

ai (愛), *n.* love; affection. —夫婦の愛, conjugal love. —親子の愛, love between parent and child. —愛の神, the god of love; Cupid (羅馬); Eros (希臘).

aiai (靄靄たる), *a.* ❶(雲氣のたなびく貌) trailing. ❷(情の濃かな貌) harmonious. —和氣靄々の間に, in harmony.

aiban (間判), *n.* medium-sized paper.

aibetsu (哀別), *n.* ❶ sorrowful parting. ❷(悲しみ) sorrow of parting.

aibiau (歩合ふ), *v.* to compromise; make mutual concessions.

aibiki (相引), *n.* ❶(交綏) mutual withdrawal; draw. ❷(媾曳) a secret meeting of lovers. —媾曳する, to meet secretly.

aibo (愛慕), *n.* adoration. —愛

慕する, to adore.

aibō (相棒), *n.* a mate; a partner; a pal 〔卑〕.

aibore (相惚), *n.* mutual love.

aibu (愛撫する), *vt.* to caress; love; nurse (嬰兒など). —蝶よ花よと愛撫した, He loved her as the apple of his eye.

aichaku (愛著), *n.* =*aijaku*.

aida (間), *n.* ❶(距離) a space; a distance; an interval (間隔). ❷(時間) time. ❸(中間) the middle. ❹(切り) a pause; a break. ❺ =*naka* (仲). ——, *prep.* for; pending; during. ——, *conj.* while (する間); as (により). —長い間, for a long time. —間をあける, to leave a space between. —間を取る, to split the difference. —二尺の間を置いて, at an interval of two feet. —二人の間を割く, to cause ill-feeling between them. —木立の間を拔る, to slip through a copse. —明日參上仕るべく候間, As I shall call on you to-morrow. —三日の間お待ち下さい, Please wait (for) three days. —汽車の出るまでにはまだ間がある, There is still time before the train starts. ——-**no**, *a.* half-way; intermediate. ——-**ni**, *prep.* (…の) between; among; amongst; during. ——, *conj.* (…する) while. —其間に, meanwhile; in the meantime. —留守の間に, in one's absence. —僕の寢てる間に, while I was asleep. —停車場まで行く間に, on the way to the station. —二人の間に出來た子供, a child born to the couple. ——-**wa**, *conj.* while; as (so) long as. —私の生きてる間は, while I live; as long as I live.

aidagara (間柄), *n.* ❶(關係) connection; relation. ❷(交誼) terms; relations. —親子の間柄, relations of parent and child. —友達の間柄, friendly relations; friendship.

aideki (愛溺する), *v.* to dote *on*; love to distraction. ——, *a.* tender; fond.

aidoku (愛讀する), *vt.* to read with pleasure; enjoy reading. —彼の作を愛讀してる, I read his work with pleasure. ¶愛讀者, a reader. —愛讀書, a favourite book.

aien-kien (愛緣機緣), *n.* ❶ dependence of all things upon karma-relations. ❷(合緣奇緣) mysterious [inscrutable] karma-relations.

aifuda (合札), *n.* a check; a tally. ¶合札法, the check-system.

aigamo (間鴨), *n.* the duck.

aigan (哀願), *n.* supplication; entreaty. —哀願する, to implore; supplicate (a person *for* a thing); entreat. ¶哀願者, a suppliant.

aigan (愛玩する), *vt.* to fondle; make a pet *of*; pet.

aigi (間著), *n.* a spring (an autumn) suit; a *demi-saison* 〔佛〕.

aigo (愛護する), *vt.* to patronize; favour; befriend.

aihan (合判), *n.* ❶(契印) a counter-seal; a counter-stamp. ❷(連帶判) a joint seal. —合判する, to counterseal.

aihan-suru (相反する), *v.* to oppose; contradict; be opposed [opposite; contrary] *to*. —相反せる, opposed; (diametrically) opposite; contrary. —相反して, contrarily; oppositely; antithetically.

aiiku (愛育する), *vt.* to rear [breed] carefully.

aiirenu (相容れぬ), *vi.* to be opposed *to*; be incompatible *with*; be at variance *with*. ——, *a.* opposite; contrary; incompatible. —水と油とは相容れぬ, Water and oil do not mix.

aiiro (藍色), *n.* indigo; blue. —藍色の, blue.

aijaku (愛著), *n.* attachment; love. —愛著さす, to win the heart [affections] *of*; make a conquest *of*. —愛著する, to be attached *to*; love.

aiji (愛兒), *n.* a beloved [darling] child.

aijin (愛人), *n.* a sweetheart (男女); a love (女); a lover; a darling.

aijirushi (合印), *n.* a check mark; a tick.

aijō (愛情), *n.* love; affection. —愛情ある, affectionate; loving. —愛情なき, loveless; cold.

aika (哀歌), *n.* an elegy; a dirge.

aikagi (合鍵), *n.* a fellow [false] key; a skeleton-key.

aikata (相方), *n.* a mate; a partner.

aikawarazu (不相變), *ad.* as ever; as usual.

aikei (愛敬する), *vt.* to revere; esteem; respect.

aiken (愛犬), *n.* a pet [favourite] dog.

aiko (相子, 互角), even; quits. —相子だよ, We are quits! —これで相子になる, This makes us even.

aiko (愛顧), *n.* patronage; favour; grace. —愛顧する, to patronize; favour; take under one's wing [patronage]. —…の愛顧を蒙る, to be in a person's (good) graces.

aikō (愛好する), *v.* to relish; be fond *of*; have a liking [fancy] *for*.

aikoku (哀哭する), *v.* to wail; bewail; lament.

aikoku (愛國), *n.* love of one's country; patriotism. —愛國の, patriotic. ¶愛國婦人會, the

Ladies' Patriotic League. —愛國者, a patriot. —愛國心, patriotism; patriotic spirit.

aikotoba (合言葉), *n.* a password; a watchword; the word.

aikuchi (合口), *n.* ❶(匕首) a dagger; a dirk; a poniard. ❷(話の合ふ) good company.

aikumu (相組む), *vi.* ❶(連合, 提携) to unite *with*; combine *with*; co-operate *with*. ❷(とッ組む) to grip [grasp] each other. —相組んで仕事する, to work in co-operation. —相組んで倒れた, They fell in each other's grip.

aikurushii (愛くるしい), *a.* charming; lovely. —愛くるしい顔, a charming face.

aikyō (愛嬌, 愛敬), *n.* amiableness; attractiveness; charm. —愛嬌のある, amiable; attractive; charming. —愛嬌のない, unattractive; unamiable. —愛嬌をふりまく, to be amiable to everybody. —何處かに愛嬌がある, There is something attractive about her. ¶ 愛嬌日,【商】days of grace. —愛嬌者, an attractive person; a winsome woman. —愛嬌商賣, a trade which requires attractive manners.

aima (合間), *n.* an interval. —合間に, in the intervals *of*.

aimai (曖昧), *n.* vagueness (淡然); ambiguity (疑はしい). **—— -na,** *a.* vague; ambiguous; doubtful. —曖昧な返答をする, to answer vaguely [ambiguously]; give a vague [an ambiguous] answer. **—— -ni,** *ad.* vaguely; ambiguously. —曖昧にする, to mystify; obscure; equivocate.

aimatsu (相待つ), *v.* to correlate; be brought together. —相待って, correlatively; in co-operation *with*.

aimochi (相持ち), *n.* mutual aid. —世間は相持ちだ, In this world we help one another.

aimusubu (相結ぶ), *vi.* to combine; associate. —相結んで, in combination; in association.

ainarabu(相並ぶ), *v.* =*narabu.*

ainiku (生憎), *ad.* unluckily; unfortunately. —生憎の, unlucky; unfortunate. —お生憎樣です, Sorry to disappoint you; That is unlucky; Sorry we are out of stock (商品なき時). —生憎不在でお氣の毒でした, I am sorry I was unfortunately out.

ainoko (合子), *n.* ❶(混血兒) a half-breed; a half-caste; a mulatto (白人と黑人との); a Eurasian (歐洲人と亞細亞人との). ❷(間生) a half-blood; a hybrid; a mongrel. —混種(ざつ)の, mongrel; hybrid. ¶ 合子辨當, a luncheon half Japanese and half foreign.

ainori (相乘りする), *v.* to ride double [together].

ainu (アイヌ), *n.* an Ainu, Aino.

aioi (相生の), *a.* growing together; aging together.

airashii (愛らしい), *a.* pretty; winsome; lovely. —愛らしい人よ, O dear one; O beloved; my darling.

airo (隘路), *n.* a pass; a defile; a gorge.

airon (火熨斗), *n.* an iron. —アイロンをかける, to iron.

Airurando (愛蘭), *n.* Ireland. —愛蘭の, Irish; Hibernian. ¶ 愛蘭語, Irish. —愛蘭人, an Irishman; the Irish. —愛蘭自由國, Irish Free State.

aisa (あいさ), *n.* 【鳥】the merganser.

aisanshiki (愛餐式), *n.* a love-feast.

aisatsu (挨拶), *n.* ❶(會釋) compliments; greeting; salutation. ❷ an answer (回答); an advice (通知); a notice (同上). —挨拶する, ① to greet; pay [make; send] one's compliments; pass the time of day. ② to answer; reply *to*; give notice *of*; announce. —朝晩の挨拶をする, to salute morning and night; say good-morning and good-night. —まだ何の挨拶もない, I have not yet had an answer. —彼は挨拶なしに出發した, He started without taking leave.

aiseki (愛惜する), *vt.* to grudge; be reluctant [unwilling; loath] to part *with* (物) [*from* (人)].

aiso (哀訴する), *v.* to entreat; supplicate; plead (*with* a person *for* [*against*]).

aiso (愛想), *n.* amiableness; courtesy; affability. —愛想のよい, amiable; affable; courteous. —愛想よく, affably; courteously. —愛想のない, unamiable; grumpy; surly. —愛想が盡きる, to become disgusted.

aisukurīmu (氷菓子), *n.* ice-cream.

Aisurando (氷蘭), *n.* Iceland. ¶ 氷蘭人, an Icelander.

ai-suru (愛する), *vt.* to love; favour; be fond *of*. **——,** *a.* dear. —愛すべき, lovable.

aita (愛他心), *n.* altruism. —愛他的, altruistic.

aita (明いた), *a.* =*aiteru.* —開いた口が塞がらぬ, to stand [remain] agape with amazement.

aità (あ痛ッ), *int.* it hurts; ouch! —あいたッ, 足踏んだね, Ouch! You've stepped on my foot.

aitade (藍蓼), *n.* 【植】the water-pepper.

aitagai (相互に), *ad.* =*tagai*(互に).

aitai (相對で), *ad.* by mutual [common] consent; by mutual agreement.

aitai-suru (相對する), *vt.* to oppose; confront; face. —相對して, antithetically; face to face.

aitaka (あいたか), *n.* =*ajisashi.*

aite (相手), *n.* ❶ (共勞者) a co-operator; a companion; a fellow. ❷ (對手) a match; an opponent; the other party; a party (一對の片方). —相手なき, unrivalled; matchless; unequalled. —相手する, to bear (a person) company. —相手どる, to set oneself *against*. —喧嘩なら相手にならう, If you want to fight, I'm your man.

aiteru (明いてる), *a.* ❶ (空) empty; vacant; blank. ❷ (開) open; unclosed. ❸ (手隙) free; disengaged. ☞ *aku* (明く). —明いてる席, a vacant seat. —今手があいてる, I am disengaged just now.

aitō (哀悼), *n.* grief; sorrow; lamentation. —哀悼する, to lament; grieve *for*; sorrow *for*. —哀悼の意を表する, to offer condolence; express one's sympathy.

aitsu (彼奴), *n.* that [the] fellow; that chap.

aitsuide (相次で), *ad.* one after another; in succession.

aiyūsen (隘勇線), *n.* an anti-aborigines defence-line; a picket-line against aborigines.

aizō (愛憎), *n.* likes and dislikes. —愛憎なく, fair field and no favour.

aizu (合圖), *n.* a signal; a sign; a cue. ¶ 合圖言葉, a watchword; a catchword.

aizuchi (相槌打つ), *v.* ❶ to strike alternately. ❷ (調子合はす) to chime in *with*; fall in *with*.

aji (鰺), *n.* the horse-mackerel.

aji, ajiwai, (味), *n.* ❶ taste; flavour; relish. ❷ (おつなこと) zest. ❸ (趣味) taste; interest. —味のある, ① savoury; tasty. ② (趣味) tasteful; interesting. —味のない, insipid; tasteless; flavourless. —味のよい, savoury; palatable. —味のわるい, unsavoury; unpalatable; flat. —味がする, to smack *of*; savour *of*; taste. —味を占める, to get the taste *of*; experience the pleasure *of*. —味を附ける, to flavour; relish; point (話等に). —熱があるから食物に味がない, As fever has set in, food has no relish.

Ajia (亞細亞), *n.* Asia. —亞細亞の, Asian; Asiatic. ¶ 亞細亞人, an Asiatic.

ajikinai (味氣ない), *a.* unhappy; wretched; miserable. —味氣なく, unhappily. —味氣なさ, unhappiness; misery; bitterness.

ajina (味な), *a.* quaint; curious; queer. —味なことをいふ, to say quaint things.

ajiro (足代), *n.* scaffolding.

ajiro (網代), *n.* a split-bamboo fish-basket.

ajisai (紫陽花), *n.* 【植】the hardy hydrangea.

ajisashi (鰺刺), *n.* 【鳥】the Daurian tern.

ajitsukeru (味附ける), *vt.* to flavour; spice; season. —味附け海苔, flavoured laver.

ajiwai (味), *n.* ☞ *aji* (味).

ajiwau (味ふ), *vt.* ❶ to taste. ❷ (翫味) to appreciate; enjoy. ❸ (經驗) to experience. —貧苦を味はふ, to experience poverty.

aka (赤), *n.* red (赤, 紅); crimson (緋); rouge (赭). —赤の, ① (色) red. ② =*akano* (眞の).

aka (垢), *n.* dirt; filth. —垢だらけの, filthy; covered with filth. —垢の附いた, filthy; soiled; dirty. —垢がつく, to become dirty [filthy].

aka (淦), *n.* bilge(-water). —淦を汲(く)む, to bail out a boat. ¶ 淦取, a bail; a bailer (器又は人).

aka (閼伽), *n.* lustral water.

akabamu (赤ばむ), *vi.* to redden; grow red; crimson.

akabō (赤帽), *n.* a (luggage-) porter (鐵道の).

akacha (赤褐色), *n.* light reddish-brown.

akaei (赤鱝), *n.* 【魚】the sting-ray.

akagaeru (赤蛙), *n.* 【兩棲】the brown frog.

akagai (赤貝), *n.* 【貝】the bloody-clam.

akagane (銅), *n.* copper. —銅色の, copper-coloured.

akagera (赤啄木鳥), *n.* 【鳥】the Japanese great spotted woodpecker.

akagetto (赤毛布), *n.* ❶ a red blanket. ❷ (田舍者) a countryman; a bumpkin; a rustic.

akagire (皹), *n.* chap.

akago (赤子), *n.* a baby; an infant. —赤子の樣な, babyish; babylike.

akaguma (赤熊), *n.* the brown bear.

akaguroi (赤黑い), *a.* reddish-black.

akagutsu (赤靴), *n.* russet boots; russet shoes.

akahada (赤膚), *n.* an abrasion; a scratch.

akahadaka (赤裸の), *a.* naked; stark-naked. —赤裸にする, to strip naked.

akahaji (赤恥), *n.* deep disgrace;

open shame. 一人前で赤恥かく, to be put to shame in public.

akahara(赤腹), *n.* 【鳥】the Japanese brown ouzel; 【魚】the dace.

akahige (赤髯), *n.* ❶ a red beard. ❷【鳥】Temminck's robin.

akahoṅya (赤本屋), *n.* a red-story-bookseller; a dealer in cheap books.

akai (赤い), *a.* red; ruddy (顔色); flushed (赧い). 一赧い顔をする, to blush.

akake, akakke, (赤髮), *n.* red hair; carrot hair.

akako (孑孑), *n.* 【蟲】the river-worm.

akaku (赤く), *ad.* redly. 一赤くなる, ① to redden; become red. ② (顔が) to flush; colour. 一赤くする, ① to redden. ② (顔を) to flush.

akameru (赤める), *vt.* ❶ to redden. ❷ (赧) to flush.

akameshi (赤飯), *n.* rice boiled with red beans.

akami (赤味), *n.* redness; a tinge [tint] of red. 一赤味がかッた, rubicund; reddish.

akami (赤身), *n.* ❶ lean; lean flesh. ❷ (心材) heartwood.

akamuke (赤剝), *n.* the raw.

akanasu (蕃茄), *n.* 【植】the tomato.

akanbei (あかんべい), (赤目の轉化) "Wouldn't you like it?"

akanbō (赤ん坊), *n.* a baby. 一僕は赤ん坊ぢやない, I was not born yesterday.

akane (茜), *n.* 【植】the Bengal madder. ¶ 茜色, madder red.

akanishi (紅螺), *n.* 【貝】the whelk.

akano (眞の), *a.* utter; perfect; complete; absolute. 一眞の他人, an utter stranger; a person in no way related.

akanu (飽かぬ), *a.* unwearied; untired. 一あかぬ眺め, an ever-fresh prospect.

akanuke (垢拔のした), *a.* polished; refined.

akaragao(赤顔), *n.* a red [blowzy] face; a flushed face.

akarameru (赧らめる), *vt.* to blush; flush; redden. 一顔を赧らめる, to blush; colour. 一顔を赧らめさす, to put to the blush.

akaramu (赤らむ), *vi.* ❶ (赤くなる) to crimson; redden. ❷ (熟する) to ripen; redden. ❸ (赧) to blush; flush.

akarasama (明樣の), *a.* frank; candid; open; plain. 一明樣に, frankly; plainly. 一明樣な話が, to speak plainly.

akari (明り), *n.* ❶ (光明) light; fire-light (爐の). ❷ (燈火) a light. ❸ (潔白の證明) proof of one's innocence. 一明りを消す, to put out the light. 一明りをつける, to light a candle (a lamp; the gas). 一明りを立てる, to clear oneself; prove one's innocence. 一明り先に立つ, to stand in a person's light. ¶ 消燈器 (ｱｶﾘｹｼ), an extinguisher.

akarimado (明窓), *n.* a sky-light (屋根の); a dormer-window; 【航】a companion (後甲板の).

akarui (明るい), *a.* bright; light. **——,** *vi.* to be learned *in*; be versed *in*; be well-posted *in*. 一その事情に明るい, to be well versed in the affair.

akaruku (明るく), *ad.* brightly; clearly. 一明るくなる, ① (夜明ける) to dawn. ② (光明となる) to brighten; light up; kindle. ③ (曉通する) to become versed *in*; gain knowledge *of*. 一明るくする, to make light; light; lighten. 一もッと明るくして頂戴, Please turn up the light.

akarumi (明るみ), *n.* ❶ (光明) light. ❷ (公開) publicity. ❸ (明るい場所) a light place. 一明るみで, in the light. 一明るみに出す, to bring to light; make public.

akashi (明し), *n.* ❶ (燈火) a light; a lamp. ❷ (潔白の證明) proof of one's innocence. ☞ *akari.*

akasu (明す), *vt.* ❶ (告げる) to disclose; divulge; reveal. ❷ (過ごす) to spend [pass] (a whole night *in*); sit up (all night). ❸ =*akeru* (明ける). 一秘密を明かす, to break [divulge] a secret. 一一晩泣き明かす, to pass a night in tears.

akasu (飽かす), *vt.* to satiate; cloy; pall. 一金に飽かして, regardless of expense.

akasuri (垢擦), *n.* a wash-rag; a wash-cloth.

akatonbo(赤蜻蛉), *n.* 【昆】Sympetrum (學名).

akatsuki (曉), *n.* ❶ (夜あけ) dawn; daybreak. ❷ (その時) time; occasion. 一曉の鐘, the dawn-bell. 一私が歸朝の曉には, when I return to Japan.

akaza (藜), *n.* 【植】the white goose-foot; the figweed.

ake(明), *n.* ❶ (滿期) expiration; expiry. ❷ (曉) daybreak; dawn.

akebi (通草), *n.* 【植】Akebia.

akebono (曙), *n.* dawn; daybreak.

ākēdo(アーケード), *n.* an arcade.

akegarasu (明烏), *n.* ❶ the morning crow. ❷ (嗜聲) the

morning caw of a crow.

akehanashi (開放), *n.* ❶ (明けて置く) leaving open. ❷ (隠さぬ) openness; frankness; candour. —開放しに, openly; frankly. —開放し無用, Shut the door after you.

akehanasu (明放す), *vt.* ❶ (はね明ける) to throw open. ❷ (明けて置く) to leave open.

akekure (明暮), *n.* & *ad.* morning and evening; day and night. —年の明暮に, at the beginning and end of a year.

ake-no-myōjō (曉の明星), *n.* the morning star.

akeru (開·明ける), *vt.* ❶ (開く) to open; unseal (開封). ❷ (空にする) to empty (容器を); vacate (家屋·場所等を); drain (盃等を). ❸ (隙かす) to leave (a space); space; leave disengaged (手を). —蓋を開ける, ① to open a lid. ② (始める) to open; commence. —席をあける, to make room. —家をあける, ① (留守) to leave home. ② (立退) to move from a house. —穴を開ける, ① to make a hole. ② (缺損) to make a gap. —通り道をあける, to make way.

akeru (明ける), *vi.* ❶ (明るくなる) to dawn. ❷ to (come to an) end; expire. —明けても暮れても, day and night; at all hours; always. —夜が明けた, The day has dawned.

aketate (開閉), *n.* opening and shutting. —開閉する, to open and shut.

akewatashi (明渡し), *n.* vacation; making over; surrender (城などの).

akewatasu (明渡す), *vt.* to make over; hand over; surrender (城など). —家を明け渡す, to vacate a house.

aki (秋), *n.* autumn; fall 〔重に米〕. —秋の, autumn; autumnal. —秋日和, a fine autumn day. —秋向きの品, fall goods. —秋風を吹かす, to make one tired *of*; grow nauseating.

aki (空), *n.* ❶ (間隙) a gap; an opening; a break. ❷ (空位, 空職) a vacancy; a vacant post. ❸ (暇) leisure. —空椅子を狙ふ, to have one's eye on the vacant post.

aki (飽), *n.* tiredness; weariness. —飽きの來る, tiresome; wearisome. —今に直ぐ飽きが來るだらう, He will soon get tired of it.

akiaki (飽飽する), *vi.* to be sick *of*; be utterly weary *of*; get thoroughly tired *of*. —飽々さす, ① [*vt.*] to satiate; make sick *of*. ② [*a.*] tedious; tiresome.

akichi (空地), *n.* a blank space; an open [a vacant] ground.

akima (明間), *n.* a vacant [an empty; unoccupied] room. —明間あり, Rooms to let.

akimekura (明盲), *n.* ❶ (清盲) amaurosis; a blind person with open eyes. ❷ (文盲) an ignoramus; an illiterate.

akinai (商), *n.* a trade. —商向きの, merchantable; suitable for selling. —商をする, to trade; do trade [business]. (日に五百圓の商をする, to turn over 500 *yen* a day.) —今日はさッぱり商がない, I have done no trade at all to-day.

akinau (商ふ), *v.* to sell; deal *in*; trade *in*.

akindo (商人), *n.* a merchant (特に大商人); a shopkeeper (小賣商人); a tradesman (同上). ¶ 商人根性, the tradesman's spirit; trade spirit.

akkippoi (厭きッぽい), *a.* easily tired; unpersevering.

akirakana (明かな), *a.* ❶ (明白な) clear; plain; distinct (はッきりした). ❷ (光る) bright. —明かな區別, a sharp distinction. —明かな事實, a plain fact.

akirakani (明かに), *ad.* ❶ (明白に) clearly; plainly; distinctly. ❷ (輝く) brightly. —明かになる, ① to become clear; come to light. ② to brighten. —明かにする, ① to make clear; clear up; elucidate. ② (顯彰) to show.

akirame (諦), *n.* resignation. —諦めのよい人, one who readily resigns himself to fate.

akirameru (諦める), *v.* to give up [over]; resign oneself *to*; reconcile oneself *to*. —諦めた世の中, the world in which I have given up all hopes. —無いものと諦める, to give up for lost.

akireru (呆れる), *vi.* to be astonished *at*; be amazed *at*. —呆れさす, to amaze; astonish; strike dumb. —呆れ顔する, to look amazed [astonished]. —呆れて物が言へぬ, to be dumb with astonishment.

akiru (飽きる), **aku** (飽く), *vi.* ❶ (滿足) to be satiated *with*; have had enough *of*. ❷ (あぐむ) to get [be] tired *of*; grow [be] weary *of*. —厭きさす, to cloy; glut; satiate: make tired. —飽くを知らぬ; 飽くなき, insatiate.

akisu (空巣), *n.* ❶ an empty nest. ❷ (留守の家) a house whose inmates are away. ¶ 空巣狙ひ, a sneak-thief.

akitaranu (飽き足らぬ, 慊らぬ), *a.* ❶ dissatisfied; unsatisfactory. ❷ insatiate. ——, *vi.* to feel dissatisfied *with.*

akiya (空家), *n.* a vacant house.

akka (惡化する), *v.* to degenerate; deteriorate; become [grow] worse.

akkan (惡漢), *n.* a blackguard; a rascal; a villain.

akkan (惡感-情), *n.* ill feeling; bad [ill] blood. —惡感を懷く, to harbour ill-feelings.

akkanka (惡感化), *n.* baneful influence. —惡感化を及ぼす, to have baneful influence.

akke (呆氣に取られる), *v.* to be taken aback [by surprise]; be struck all of a heap; be astonished.

akkei (惡計), *n.* an evil design; a plot. —惡計する, to plot; form a plot; make evil designs.

akkenai (飽氣ない), *a.* brief; abrupt; sudden. —飽氣なく, abruptly; suddenly. —それでは餘りあっけない, That is too abrupt.

akki (惡鬼), *n.* a demon; a fiend; an evil spirit.

akkō (惡口), *n.* vilification; abuse. —惡口する, to vilify; abuse; use abusive language.

akō (榕樹), *n.* the banian-tree; the Indian fig.

akogare, akugare, (憧憬), *n.* ❶ (浮立つ) entrancement; rapture. ❷ (思ひ焦る) longing; yearning. ❸ (心落ちつかぬ) absent-mindedness; absence of mind.

akogareru (憧れる), *v.* ❶ to be entranced; be enraptured. ❷ to long *for*; pine *for*; yearn *for* [*after*]. ❸ to be absent-minded; be lost *in* (迷ひ込む). —憧れあるく, to walk with one's head in the clouds. —英雄に憧れる, to yearn after heroes.

akoyagai (阿古屋貝, 珠母), *n.* 【貝】 the pearl-oyster.

aku (あく), *n.* ❶ (灰汁) lye. ❷ (植物の澁味ある液) an astringent juice. —灰汁拔けのした, freed from gawkiness.

aku (惡), *n.* evil; ill; vice. —惡に陷る, to fall into evil ways. —惡をなす, to do evil.

aku (明く), *vi.* ❶ (開く) to open. ❷ (始まる) to open; begin; commence. ❸ (不用, 手隙) to have done *with*; be disengaged. ❹ (滿了) to expire; come to an end. —手があいたら, when you are disengaged. —その本があいたら, if you have done with the book. —四時に幕があく, The curtain rises at four.

aku (飽く), *vi.* ☞ *akiru* (飽きる).

akuba (惡罵), *n.* abuse; slander. —惡罵する, to abuse; slander; speak ill *of.*

akubi (欠伸), *n.* a yawn; yawning. —欠伸する, to yawn; gape. —欠伸を噛み殺す, to smother [suppress] a yawn.

akudoi (あくどい), *a.* ❶ (濃厚にすぎる) heavy; oppressive. ❷ (煩らはしい) tedious; tiresome. ❸ (しつこい) persistent; mulish. ❹ (重苦しい) heavy; loud (色彩·衣裳·文體等の); gaudy (服裝などの). —あくどい料理, heavy dishes.

akudoku (あくどく), *ad.* heavily; tediously; persistently. —あくどく尋[*]く, to ask persistently.

akueki (惡疫), *n.* an infectious disease; an epidemic.

akuen (惡緣), *n.* an evil lot; an evil affinity.

akufū (惡風), *n.* vice; evil customs [ways]. —惡風に染まる, to be infected with vice.

akugi (惡戯), *n.* a practical joke; a prank; mischief.

akugyō (惡行), *n.* evil deeds; an evil [a vicious] course; wicked ways.

akuhei (惡弊), *n.* an abuse; an evil.

akuheki (惡癖), *n.* a bad habit; a vice.

akuhitsu (惡筆), *n.* bad writing; poor penmanship; a bad hand.

akui (惡意), *n.* ❶ (敵意) ill-will; malice. ❷ (故意) malicious intent; bad faith. —惡意を以て, with malicious intent; in bad faith. —に對し惡意を懷く, to bear ill-will against; bear malice towards.

akuji (惡事), *n.* an evil deed [act]; an ill-deed; a wrong. —惡事を働く, to do evil; commit a crime. —惡事千里を走る, "Ill news flies apace."

akujo (惡女), *n.* ❶ (毒婦) a bad [wicked] woman. ❷ (醜婦) an ugly woman; a fright.

akuma (惡魔), *n.* a devil; an evil spirit; a demon. —惡魔の樣な, devilish; fiendish; diabolical. —惡魔を拂ふ, to expel evil spirits; drive out the devil. —いい惡魔拂ひをした, We are well rid of the devil.

akumade (飽く迄), *ad.* ❶ (最後迄) to the end; to the last. ❷ (極力) to the utmost; to the best of one's abilities [power]. ❸ (思ふ存分) to one's heart's content. —飽くまでやる, to go with it to the end; go all lengths. —飽くまで反對する, to oppose to the bitter end.

akumei, akumyō, (悪名), *n.* a bad name; a bad reputation; disrepute.

akumu (悪夢), *n.* a bad dream; a nightmare. —悪夢に魘はれる, to be oppressed by a nightmare.

akunen (悪念), *n.* an evil intention; an evil thought [mind].

akunichi (悪日), *n.* an unlucky day; a black day.

akunin (悪人), *n.* a bad man; a knave; a villain.

akuratsu (悪辣な), *a.* crafty; subtle; wily.

akurei (悪例), *n.* ❶ (悪慣例) a bad precedent. ❷ a bad example.

akuru (翌る), *a.* next; following. —翌る朝(日; 年), next [the following] morning (day; year).

akuryō (悪靈), *n.* the evil spirit of the dead.

akuryoku (握力), *n.* (the strength of) grip (of the hand); grasping power. ¶ 握力計, a hand-dynamometer.

akusaku(齷齪), *ad.* =*akuseku*.

akusei(悪性), *n.* ❶(疾病) malignancy. ❷ (性質) evil [ill] nature [disposition]. —悪性の, ① malignant. ② ill-disposed; evil-natured; vicious. —悪性感冒に罹る, to catch a malignant cold.

akusei(悪政), *n.* misgovernment; misrule.

akusei (悪聲), *n.* ❶ (悪評) a bad report; abuse. ❷ (悪音) a harsh note.

akuseku (あくせく), *ad.* hard; diligently. —あくせく働く, to work hard.

akusen (悪錢), *n.* ill-gotten money. —悪錢身につかず, "Evil got, evil spent."

akusen (悪戰), *n.* a desperate [hard] fight; a hard struggle. —悪戰苦鬪する, to fight desperately.

akusento (アクセント), *n.* an accent. —第一(第二)アクセント, primary (secondary) accent.

akushin (悪心), *n.* malevolence; an evil mind [thought].

akushitsu (悪疾), *n.* ❶ a malignant disease. ❷(癩病) leprosy. —悪疾に罹る, to catch a malignant disease.

akushitsu (悪質), *n.* baseness; bad [inferior] quality. —悪質の, base; bad; inferior.

akushu (握手), *n.* handshake; concert (提携); reconciliation (仲直り). —握手する, to shake hands; act in concert (提携); be reconciled.

akushū (悪臭), *n.* a bad [foul] smell; stench; an offensive odour. —悪臭ある, stinking; rancid. —悪臭を放つ, to emit an offensive smell.

akushū (悪習), *n.* a vice; a bad habit; a bad custom. —悪習に染む, to contract a bad habit.

akusō (悪相), *n.* a gallows look; an unprepossessing appearance; a forbidding look.

akuta (芥), *n.* garbage; refuse; rubbish.

akutai (悪態), *n.* abuse; calumny; foul [abusive] language. —悪態をつく, to abuse; use foul language.

akutare (悪たれ), *n.* ❶ (悪態口) abuse; abusive [scurrilous] language. ❷ (悪漢) a blackguard; a villain; a rascal. —悪たれな, foul-mouthed; blackguardly.

akutareru (悪たれる), *vi.* ❶ (悪戯する) to do mischievous things; be up to mischief. ❷ (亂暴する) to make [kick up] a row. ❸ (悪態口をきく) to use abusive language.

akutarō(悪太郎), *n.* a bad [mischievous] child. ¶ 悪太郎時代, the most mischievous age.

akuto (悪徒), **akutō** (悪黨), *n.* a blackguard; a scoundrel; a ruffian.

āku-tō (アーク燈), *n.* an arc-lamp.

akutoku (悪徳), *n.* vice; wickedness. —悪徳の, vicious; wicked. ¶ 悪徳記者, an unprincipled journalist.

akuun (悪運), *n.* ❶(不運) doom; ill-luck. ❷ (悪事の運) luck in an evil course. —悪運の强い奴, a fellow lucky in his evil course.

akuyō (悪用), *n.* abuse; perversion. **—— -suru**, *vt.* to abuse; pervert. —才を悪用する, to abuse one's talent.

akuyū (悪友), *n.* a bad [an evil] friend. —悪友を遠ざける, to shun bad company.

ama (尼), *n.* ❶ a nun; a priestess. ❷ (婦人を罵って) a hussy. —尼になる, to take the veil. ¶ 尼寺, a convent; a nunnery.

ama (蜑, 海人), *n.* a fisherman [*fem.* -woman]; a diver.

ama (亞麻), *n.* 【植】 the flax.

amaagari (雨上り), after rain. —雨上りの空, the sky after rain.

amabō (雨帽), *n.* a rainproof hat; a sou'wester; a southwester.

amacha (甘茶), *n.* ❶【植】(土常山) Hydrangea hortensis (學名). ❷ (土常山の莖葉煎汁) an infusion of Hydrangea hortensis.

amadai (甘鯛), *n.* 【魚】 the tile-fish.

amadaoshi (亞麻倒), *n.* 【植】 the flax dodder; the wild-flax.

amadare (雨垂, 雨滴), *n.* an eavesdrop; a rain-drop.

amado (雨戸), *n.* a shutter; a rain-door. —雨戸を閉める, to put

· up the shutters; shut the rain-doors.

amaeru (甘·嬌える), *vi.* ❶ to get spoilt; behave like a spoilt child. ❷ (人の深切などに) to avail oneself *of*; take advantage *of*. —深切に甘える, to avail oneself of another's kindness.

amaettare (嬌狎兒), *n.* a spoilt child.

amagaeru (雨蛙), *n.* the tree-frog.

amagaitō (雨外套), **amagappa** (雨合羽), *n.* a rain-coat; a mackintosh; an oil-coat.

amagakoi (雨圍), *n.* a shelter from rain.

amagasa (雨傘), *n.* an umbrella.

amagi (雨衣), *n.* an oil-coat; a rain-coat.

amagoi (雨乞する), *v.* to pray for rain; offer prayers for rain.

amagu (雨具), *n.* rain articles.

amagumo (雨雲), *n.* 【氣象】the nimbus; a rain-cloud.

amagumori (雨曇), *n.* a cloudy [threatening] weather.

amai (甘い), *a.* ❶ (甘味) sweet; sugary; mellow (果實): insufficiently flavoured [salted]. ❷ (刀·刃等の鈍い) blunt; dull. ❸ (魯鈍) dull; slow: (嚴ならぬ) indulgent; linient: (やさしい) soft. —子に甘い親, an indulgent parent. —刃のあまい小刀, a soft-edged knife. —甘い物を好く, to have a sweet tooth. —甘くする, to sweeten; sugar. —人を甘く見る, to consider a person soft-headed. —まだ鹽が甘い, The flavour is still sweet. —彼は人間が少し甘い, He is of a rather indulgent disposition.

amajio (淡鹽の), *a.* under-salted.

amake (甘氣), *n.* sweetness; a sweet flavour [taste].

amake (雨氣), *n.* a sign [an indication] of rain. —雨氣を催す, to threaten rain; show signs of rain.

amakuchi (甘口), *n.* ❶ (甘味を好むこと) fondness for sweet food; a sweet tooth. ❷ (口前の上手) flattery; cajolery; wheedling. —甘口に乘せる, to dose a person with cajolery.

amami (甘味), *n.* sweet flavour; sweetness.

amamoyō (雨模樣), *n.* threatening of rain; a sign of rain.

amana (山慈姑), *n.* 【植】*Tulipa edulis* (tulip の一種·學名).

amanattō (甘納豆), *n.* sugared red bean.

amaneki (普·遍き), *a.* universal; all-round; general.

amaneku (普·遍く), *ad.* universally; everywhere; all over. —遍く日本を經巡る, to travel throughout [all over] Japan. —遍く天下に知らる, to be known the world over; be universally known. —普く賞讃を博する, to meet with universal applause.

amanin (亞麻仁), *n.* the flax-seed; the linseed. ¶ 亞麻仁油, linseed oil.

amanjiru (甘んじる), *vi.* =*amanzuru.*

amanogawa (天の川), *n.* the Milky Way; the Galaxy.

amanojaku (天邪鬼), *n.* the dog in the manger.

amanzuru (甘んずる), *vi.* to be [rest; remain] contented *with*; be satisfied *with*. —甘んじて, willingly; readily. (甘んじて制裁を受ける, to submit willingly to punishment.) —現在の位置に甘んずる, to be contented with one's present position.

amaōi (雨覆), *n.* a screen [covering] against rain.

amapan (甘麵麭), *n.* a bun.

amari (餘), *n.* ❶ (殘餘) the remainder; the rest; the remnant. ❷ (過剩分) the balance; the excess; the surplus.

amari (餘り), *ad.* ❶ (過度に 法外に) too; too much; to excess; over-. ❷ (左程) very; particularly. ❸ (…の餘り) in the excess *of*; in the fulness *of*; overcome *with*. ❹ (約) about; some; or so. ❺ (以上, 强) more than; over. —悲しさの餘り, in (the excess of) one's grief; overcome [overwhelmed] with grief. —四十餘りの男, a man forty odd years old; a man in the forties. —餘り勉强する(飲む)と, if you study (drink) too much. —そりゃあんまりだ, That is too bad of you. —近頃は餘り見えません, I have not lately seen much of him.

amaru (餘る), *v.* ❶ to remain; be left over [behind]. ❷ to exceed. —手に餘る, to be beyond one's control; be too much for one (敵し難い). —力に餘る, to be beyond one's power. —身に餘る光榮, honour too great for one; honour beyond one's deserts. —思案に餘って, overcome with anxiety. —餘る程金を持ってる, He has money enough and to spare.

amarugamu (アマルガム), *n.* amalgam.

amassae (剩へ), *ad.* =*amatsusae.*

amasu (餘す), *v.* ❶ (餘分) to leave; leave over. ❷ (殘る) to leave behind. —餘す所なし, to leave nothing over.

amata (數多の), *a.* many; a good [great] deal of; abundant. —數多の船, many vessels. —許多の金,

a large sum of money.
amatarui (甘たるい), *a.* ❶ (味の) sweetish; sugary. ❷ (言葉の) smooth; honeyed; oily.
amaterasu (天照す), *a.* heaven-shining: ruling from heaven. —天照大神, the Sun-Goddess.
amatsu (天津), —天津日嗣, the Imperial Throne. —天津神, the gods of heaven.
amatsubame (雨燕), *n.* 【鳥】 the white-rumped swift; the swift (通俗に).
amatsusae (剰へ), *ad.* moreover; besides; in addition.
amattare (嬌羿兒), *n.* =*amaettare.*
amattarui (甘ッたるい), *a.* =*amatarui.*
amayadori (雨宿する), *vi.* to take shelter from rain. —軒下に雨宿りする, to take shelter from rain under the eaves.
amayakasu (甘やかす), *vt.* to coddle; spoil; indulge.
amayoke (雨除), *n.* ❶ 【建】 a drip. ❷ (雨宿り) taking shelter from rain.
amazake (甘酒), *n.* a sweet drink made from glutinous rice.
amazarashi (雨曝にする), *vt.* to expose to rain. —雨曝しになる, to be exposed to rain; stand in the rain.
ame (雨), *n.* ❶ rain. ❷ (…の雨) a rain; a shower. —彈丸の雨, a rain of shells. —雨降る, It rains. —雨が漏る, The rain leaks in. —雨に逢ふ, to be caught in a rain. ¶ 大 (小) 雨, a heavy (light) rain.
ame (飴), *n.* glutinous rice-jelly.
ameagari (雨上り), after rain.
amefurashi (雨虎), *n.* 【軟體】 the sea-hare.
amefuri (雨降), *n.* rainfall; rain; rainy weather (雨天). —雨降りに出掛ける, to go out into the rain.
amegachi (雨勝ちの), *a.* rainy; moist.
ameiro (飴色), *n.* reddish yellow.
amenbō (水黽), *n.* 【昆】 the pond-skater.
amendō (巴旦杏, 扁桃), *n.* 【植】 the almond.
Amerika (亞米利加), *n.* America. —亞米利加の, American. ¶ 亞米利加人, an American. —亞米利加土人 [印度人], an American Indian.
ami (網), *n.* a net. —網にかかる, to be caught in a net. —網を打つ, to cast a net. —網を曳く, to draw a net. —網を張る, to spread [set] a net (漁網を); put up the net (テニスの網を); form a cordon (非常線を). (網を張ッて待つ, to wait with nets spread out.)
amiagegutsu (編上靴), *n.* laced boots; bootees (嬰兒の).
amiawasu (編合はす), *vt.* to interknit; intertwine; plash (枝等).
amība (アミーバ), *n.* amœba [*pl.* amœbæ].
amibari (編針), *n.* a knitting-needle.
Amida (阿彌陀), *n.* Amitabha (梵). —帽子を阿彌陀に被る, to wear a hat on the back of the head.
amidana (網棚), *n.* a rack; a cart-ladder (車などの).
amidasu (編出す), *vt.* to work out; think out.
amigasa (編笠), *n.* a wattle-hat.
amigata (網形), *n.* reticulation. —網形の, reticulate; reticular.
amihiki (網引), *n.* net-drawing; a net-drawer (人).
amijiban (網襦袢), *n.* a netted underwear [undershirt].
amime (網目), *n.* a mesh. ¶ 網目版, a half-tone (process).
amimono (編物), *n.* knitting; knitwork.
amiuchi (網打), *n.* net-casting; cast of a net.
amizaiku (網細工), *n.* meshwork; network.
amu (編む), *vt.* (絲·藤など) to knit; weave; crochet (鉤針で) —髮を編む, to braid [plait] the hair. —眞田紐を編む, to weave straw-braids.
an (案), *n.* ❶ (机) a table; a desk. ❷ a proposal (提案); a draft (草案); a plan (計畫); expectation (豫期). —案に相違して, contrary to expectation. —案に違はず; 案の如く, sure enough; as was expected. ☞ *annojō.* —案を立てる, to draw up a plan.
an (庵), *n.* a hermitage; a retreat.
an (餡), *n.* bean-jam (小豆の); arrowroot condiment (葛溜り).
ana (穴), *n.* a hole. ❶ a hollow (凹んだ); a den (獅子等の). ❷ (隱れ遊びする所) a den; a haunt. ❸ (缺損) a gap. —穴だらけの, full of holes; honeycombed. —穴に逐ひ込む, to earth; chase into a hole. —穴をあける, ① to make a hole; bore a hole (錐等で). ② (缺損を來たす) to make a gap [hole]. —穴を埋める, ① to fill up a hole. ②(缺損塡補) to fill up a gap. —人の顏を穴のあく程見詰める, to stare a person dead. —耳の孔を掘ッて能ッく聞け, Prick up your ears and listen. ¶ 穴塞ぎ, a stop-gap.
anadori (侮), *n.* ❶ (輕蔑) contempt; slight; disdain. ❷ (慢) conceit.
anadoru (侮る), *vt.* to despise; disdain; make light *of.* —自ら侮る者, a conceited person. —侮り

難き敵手, an antagonist not to be despised.

anagachi (强ち), *ad.* necessarily; altogether; always.

anago (あなご), *n.* the conger (-eel); the sea-eel.

anaguma (貛), *n.* the badger; the brock.

anagura (穴藏), *n.* a cellar; a cave.

anamichi (穴道), *n.* an underground way; a subway; a tunnel.

ananasu (鳳梨), *n.* the ananas; the pine-apple.

ańanri (暗暗裏に), *ad.* indirectly; tacitly.

anasagashi (穴探しする), *vt.* to find fault *with*; pick a hole.

anata (貴方), *pron.* you; sir.

anaume (孔塡め), *n.* a stop-gap.

anbai (鹽梅, 按排), *n.* ❶ (身體の調子) condition. ❷ (風, 工合) way; manner; condition. ❸ (調味) taste; flavour. ❹ (配列) arrangement. —鹽梅する, ① (配置) to group; arrange. ② (調味) to dress; flavour; season. ③ (適度) to moderate; qualify. —この鹽梅では, at this rate. —よい鹽梅に, luckily; fortunately. (萬事よい鹽梅にいッた, All went well.) —そいつはいい鹽梅だ, That is lucky. —少し鹽梅が惡い, He is not in good condition; he is indisposed.

anbako (暗箱), *n.* a camera.

anbun (按分する), *vt.* to proportion. ¶ 按分比例, proportion. (按分比例で, in proportion; proportionately.)

anchaku (安著), *n.* safe arrival. —安著する, to arrive safely [in safety].

anchi (安置する), *vt.* to ensconce; enshrine.

anchimon(i) (安質母尼), *n.* antimony.

anchoku (安値な), *a.* cheap; of low [moderate] price; inexpensive. —安値に, cheaply; inexpensively.

anchū (暗中に), *ad.* in the dark. ¶ 暗中飛躍, ① a leap in the dark. ② secret intrigues; a dark plot. (暗中飛躍を試みる, ① to take a leap in the dark. ② to intrigue secretly; make dark plots.) —暗中摸索, groping [fumbling] in darkness.

anda (安打), *n.* 【野球】 a base-hit; a safe hit. ¶ 直安打, a line drive.

andārain (字下線), *n.* an under line. —字下にアンダーラインを引く, to underline [underscore] a word.

ando (安堵), *n.* ease; relief. —安堵さす, to set a person's mind at rest. —安堵する, to feel easy; be [feel] relieved.

andō, andon, (行燈), *n.* a (paper-framed) night-light; a night-lamp. ¶ 行燈袴, an undivided *hakama*; a skirt.

ane (姉), *n.* an elder sister. ¶ 姉婿, an elder sister's husband; a brother-in-law. —姉娘, an elder daughter.

anehazuru (姉羽鶴), *n.* the demoiselle crane.

ańei (暗影), *n.* a dark shadow. —暗影を投ずる, to cast a dark shadow.

anemone (アネモネ), *n.* 【植】 the anemone; the wind-flower.

anga (安臥), *n.* repose; rest. —安臥する, to repose.

angai (案外), *ad.* unexpectedly; contrary to expectation. —案外の, unexpected; unforeseen. —案外早く片附く, to be settled sooner than we expected.

angō (暗合), *n.* accidental agreement; a (mere) coincidence. —暗合する, to coincide.

angō (暗號), *n.* ❶ (符號) a cipher. ❷ (合圖) a signal; a sign. ❸ (合ひ詞) a watchword; a password; a code (暗號規定). —暗號する, to give a signal; make a sign. —暗號で通信する, to communicate by signs. ¶ 暗號帳, a code book. —暗號電報, a cipher [code] telegram. (暗號電報を打つ, to telegraph in cipher. —暗號電報を譯す, to decode a cipher telegram.) —暗號解, a cipher-key.

angū (行宮), *n.* a temporary palace.

anguri (あんぐり), *ad.* vacantly; agape. —あんぐり口をあいて, with one's mouth agape. —(あきれて)あんぐり明いた口が塞らなかッた, I remained agape with astonishment.

angya (行脚), *n.* travelling on foot; pilgrimage (on foot). —行脚する, to make a pilgrimage on foot. ¶ 行脚僧, a palmer; an itinerant priest.

ani (兄), *n.* an elder brother.

ani (豈), *ad.* how. —豈圖らんや, to my great surprise; most unexpectedly. —豈それ然らんや, How can it be so?

anirin (アニリン), *n.* 【化】 aniline. ¶ アニリン染料(色素), aniline dyes (colouring matter).

ańitsu (安逸, 安佚), *n.* living in ease [idleness]; living free from care. —安逸を貪る, to live in indolence.

aniyome (嫂), *n.* an elder brother's wife; a sister-in-law.

anjaberu (アンジャベル), *n.* 【植】 the carnadine; the carnation.

anjin (按針), *n.* a pilot (船の).
anjiru (案じる), *vt.* ❶ (心配する) to be anxious *about* [*for*]; be [feel] uneasy *about*. ❷ (工夫する) to think out; work out; devise. ❸ (考へる) to think. —案じ出す, =*anjiru* の ❷ —案じすぎる, to be overanxious *about*. —案じ煩ふ, to be oppressed with anxiety. —子の行末を案じる, to be anxious about one's child's future. —非常に案じて問ふ, to ask with deep concern. —案じるより生むが易い, The reality often belies our fears.
anka (行火), *n.* a foot-warmer.
anka (安價な), *a.* cheap; low-priced; inexpensive. —極く安價な, dog-cheap.
ankan (安閑たる), *a.* leisured; leisurely; idle; indolent. —安閑として日を送る, to pass one's days in indolence.
ankasshoku (暗褐色), *n.* dark brown.
ankensatsu (暗劍殺), *n.* a fatal direction. —あの方面は暗劍殺だ, That direction is fatal to me.
anki (安危), *n.* fate; welfare. —國家安危の懸る所, upon which the fate of the country depends.
anki (安氣な), *a.* easy; tranquil; peaceful.
anki (諳記する), *vt.* to commit to memory; learn [get] by heart; learn; memorize. ¶ 諳記力, memory; retentiveness.
anko (安固な), *a.* secure; firm.
ankō (鮟鱇), *n.* 【魚】 the devil-fish; the angler.
ankoku (暗黒の), *a.* black; dark; pitch-dark. ¶ 暗黒時代, a dark age; the dark ages (歐洲中古の). —暗黒面, the dark side; the shady [seamy] side.
ankōru (再演所望), *n.* *encore* 【佛】.
ankōshoku (暗紅色), *n.* dark crimson; garnet.
ankuru (アンクル), *n.* an anchor.
ankyo (暗渠), *n.* an under-drain; a covered ditch.
anma (按摩), *n.* shampooing; a shampooer (人). —按摩する, to shampoo.
anmin (安眠), *n.* a quiet rest [sleep]. —安眠する, to repose; sleep quietly.
anmoku (暗默の), *a.* implied; tacit. —暗默の承諾, tacit consent.
anmonia (安母尼亞), *n.* 【化】 ammonia.
anmonyūmu (安母尼謨), *n.* 【化】 ammonium.
anna (彼樣な), *a.* such (a); like that; of that sort. —あんな奴, such a fellow. —あんな所で, in a place of that sort. —彼樣に, so; like that; in such a manner. (あんなに金がありながら, though he has so much money.)
annai (案內), *n.* ❶ (導き) guidance; lead; conduct. ❷ (勝手) one's way. ❸ (通知) advice; notice; invitation (招待). ❹ (入門, 手引) a guide; an introduction. —彼の案內で, under his guidance. —案內もなく, ① without any notice. ② (取次も乞はずに) without being shown in. —案內も待たずに, without waiting to be shown in. —御案內の通り, as you are aware. —案內を知ってる, to be familiar [acquainted] with the place. —園遊會に案內を受ける, to receive an invitation to a garden-party. **—— -suru**, *vt.* ❶ to guide; conduct; lead. ❷ (招待する) to invite. —書齋へ案內する, to show a person into the study. —道を案內する, to show a person the way; conduct a person over the road. —途中まで案內する, to set a person on his way. —先に立って案內しろ, Lead on! ¶ 案內狀, ① an [a letter of] advice; a notice. ② an invitation. —案內記 [書], a guide; a guide-book. —案內者, a guide; an usher (取次).
annei (安寧), *n.* (public) peace; tranquillity. —安寧を亂す (保つ), to disturb (maintain) the public peace. ¶ 安寧秩序, public peace and order.
an-ni (暗に), *ad.* darkly; covertly; by hint.
annojō (案の定), *ad.* sure enough; as was expected; as we expected.
ano (彼の), *a.* that. —あの人, ① he (she). ② (指しながら) that man there. —あの山, the mountain over there.
anō (あのう), *int.* well; dear me.
an'on (安穩に), *ad.* peacefully; calmly.
anoyo (あの世), *n.* the other world; the world to come.
anpaia (審判官), *n.* an umpire.
anpan (餡麵麭), *n.* a bean-jam bun.
anpera (茭蓙), *n.* ❶ 【植】 the Chinese mat-rush. ❷ (同上編蓆) the rush-mat.
anpi (安否), *n.* safety; welfare. —安否を問合はす, to ask after a person's welfare [health].
anpō (罨法), *n.* 【醫】 poultice; cataplasm.
anpuku (按腹する), *vi.* to shampoo [massage] the abdomen.
anraku (安樂な), *a.* easy; comfortable; snug. —安樂に暮す, to live in ease [comfort]. ¶ 安樂椅子, an easy-chair.

anryū (暗流), *n.* an undercurrent.
ansatsu (暗殺), *n.* assassination. —暗殺する, to assassinate. —總督が暗殺されんとした, An attempt was made on the Viceroy's life. ¶ 暗殺者, an assassin.
ansei (安靜な), *a.* peaceful; quiet; tranquil. —患者は安靜にして置かねばならぬ, The patient must be kept quiet. ¶ 安靜療法, rest-cure.
ansha (暗車), *n.* a screw-propeller.
ansha (暗射する), *v.* to point out a position on a skeleton map. ¶ 暗射地圖, a skeleton map.
anshi (暗示), *n.* suggestion; a hint; allusion. —暗示する, to hint; imply; insinuate. —暗示を與へる, to give a hint.
anshin (安心), *n.* freedom from care [anxiety]; ease (of mind); relief. —安心さす, to ease; set a person at ease; put a person at his ease. —安心する, to feel easy [at ease]; breathe again; feel relieved. ¶ 安心立命, calmness and resignation.
anshitsu (暗室), *n.* a dark-room.
anshō (暗礁), *n.* a reef; a (sunken) rock; a breaker. —暗礁に乘り上げる, to run [strike] on a rock. (暗礁に乘り上げて破碎する, to split on a rock.)
anshō (諳誦), *n.* ❶ recitation; repetition. ❷ =*anki* (諳記). —諳誦する, ① to recite. ② =*anki* (諳記する).
anshutsu (案出する), *vt.* to devise; contrive; think out. —邦文タイプライターを案出する, to invent a typewriter for Japanese characters.
ansoku (安息する), *vi.* to rest; repose. ¶ 安息日, the Sabbath (day); the Lord's Day. —安息香, 【植】 the gum-benzoin shrub.
antai (暗體), *n.* 【光】 a black body.
antai (安泰な), *a.* peaceful; secure; free from care.
antan (暗澹たる), *a.* ❶ (暗く靜な) gloomy; dark. ❷ (物凄い) dismal; lurid; blue; black. —暗澹として, ① gloomily; darkly. ② dismally; luridly; blackly. —暗澹たる失望, black despair.
antei (安定), *n.* ❶ (落つき) stableness. ❷ (重心の) stability; equilibrium. —安定を失ふ〔保つ〕, to lose [maintain] equilibrium. ¶ 安定狀態, settled state. —安定翼, an aileron; a balancing plane.
antō (暗鬪), *n.* ❶ a fight in the dark; a secret faction. ❷ 【劇】 dumb show. —暗鬪する, to fight in the dark; fight in secret.
an'un (暗雲), *n.* dark clouds; storm-clouds. —暗雲低迷す, Dark clouds hang low.
an'ya (暗夜), *n.* a dark night. —暗夜に乘じて, under cover of night.
anza (安坐する), *vi.* to sit (cross-legged).
anzan (安產), *n.* an easy delivery.
anzan (暗算), *n.* mental arithmetic. —暗算する, to calculate mentally.
anzanshi (案山子), *n.* (かかし) a scarecrow; (木偶) a dummy.
anzen (安全), *n.* safety; security. —安全な, safe; secure; riskless; free from danger. —安全に到著する, to arrive safely [in safety]. ¶ 安全瓣, a safety-valve. —安全地帶, a safety zone. —安全第一, safety first. —安全自轉車, a safety-bicycle; a safety 〔俗〕. —安全剃刀, a safety-razor. —安全球, a safe hit. —安全マッチ, a safety-match. —安全ピン, a safety-pin. —安全ランプ, a safety-lamp. —安全週, a safety week. —安全島, an island refuge; a safety island 〔米〕.
anzu (杏), *n.* the apricot.
an-zuru (案ずる), *vt.* ☞ *anjiru.*
anzuruni (按ずるに), it appears [seems] to me that; to my thinking.
ao (靑), *n.* blue; green (綠). —靑々と, in green.
aobachi (靑蜂), *n.* the burnished wasp.
aobae (靑蠅), *n.* the bluebottle-fly.
aobamu (靑ばむ), *vi.* to grow green.
aogaeru (靑蛙), *n.* the green frog; the edible frog.
aogai (靑貝), *n.* the mother-of-pearl.
aogera (靑啄木鳥), *n.* the Japanese great woodpecker.
aogiri (梧桐), *n.* the sultan's [Chinese] parasol.
aogu (仰ぐ), *vt.* ❶ (仰ぎ見る) to look up (at). ❷ (敬ふ) to revere; look up *to.* ❸ (飮む) to take. ❹ (乞ふ, 求む) to ask *for*; rely upon (賴る). —師と仰ぐ, to revere as one's teacher. —毒を仰ぐ, to take poison. —裁判を仰ぐ, to lay before the court; submit (a case) to the court. —人の助力を仰ぐ, to look to a person for assistance.
aogu (扇ぐ), *vt.* to fan; 〔詩〕 winnow (翼で). —火を下から扇ぐ, to fan the fire from under.
aoi (葵), *n.* the hollyhock.
aoi (靑い), *a.* ❶ blue; green (綠); pale (蒼白). ❷ (不熟) green; unripe. ❸ (黃口) inexperienced; raw.
aoiki (靑息), *n.* gasp. —靑息吐息を吐く, to pant and gasp. —借

金で青息を吐く, to pant under a heavy debt.

aoku (青く), *ad.* blue; green. —青くなる, ① to turn blue [green]. ② (顔色が) to lose colour; turn blue [pale].

aomono (青物), *n.* vegetables; greens; greengrocery. ¶ 青物市場, a vegetable market. —青物屋, a greengrocer: a greengrocery.

aomukeru (仰向ける), *vt.* to face (骨牌を); upturn; lay a person on his back.

aomuki (仰向の), *a.* supine; upward. —仰向に寝る(泳ぐ), to lie (swim) on one's back. —仰向に倒れる, to fall backwards.

aomuku (仰向く), *vi.* to look up [upward]; turn one's face up.

aomushi (螟蛉), *n.* the green caterpillar.

aonisai (青二才), *n.* a stripling; an unlicked cub, a chicken.

aonori (青海苔), *n.* Enteromorpha compressa (green laver の一種·學名).

aori (煽), *n.* ❶ incitement; instigation. ❷ the force of a wind.

aoru (煽る), *v.* ❶ (扇ぎ立てる) to fan; incite; instigate. ❷ (鼓揺) to flap; bang; slam. ❸ (呷る) to quaff at a draught; gulp down. —相場を煽る, to boom. —火の手を煽る, to fan the flame. —ビールを呷る, to gulp down ale.

aosagi (青鷺), *n.* the heron.

aosuji (青筋), *n.* blue veins. —青筋を立てて爭ふ, to quarrel with blue veins starting.

aotenjō (青天井), *n.* the blue sky [heavens]. —青天井の下で一夜を明かす, to pass a night under the blue sky.

aoyagi (青柳), *n.* the green willow.

aozameru (青ざめる), *vi.* to pale; turn pale; grow pallid. —青ざめた, pale; pallid; ghastly.

aozora (青空), *n.* the blue sky.

appaku (壓迫), *n.* pressure; press; oppression. —壓迫する, to press; oppress. —壓迫を加へる, to bring pressure *upon*.

appare (天晴, 適), *ad.* admirably; splendidly. ——, *int.* bravo!; well done! ——-**na**, *a.* admirable; splendid; fine. —天晴な人物, a man of fine [splendid] character. —天晴な勝利, a splendid victory.

appuku (壓服·壓伏する), *vt.* to suppress; keep down; overwhelm.

ara (粗), *n.* ❶ (魚等の) guts; entrails. ❷ (缺點) a fault; a flaw. —人のあらを探す, to pick holes in another's coat; look for defects in others.

ara (新), *n.* a new thing. ——, *a.* new; raw; fresh.

ara (あら), *int.* oh!; why; good gracious!; O dear! —あらまア, [*int.*] Dear, dear!; Dear me!; O dear! (あらまアさう, Dear, dear!; Is that true?). —あら嫌だ, Oh, don't! [How horrid!]. —あらどうかしたの, Oh, what's the matter?

araara (粗粗), *ad.* approximately; in the rough; in brief. —あらあらかしく, yours affectionately.

araarashii (荒荒しい), *a.* rough; violent; rude. —荒々しく扱ふ, to handle (a thing) roughly.

Arabiya (亞剌比亞), *n.* Arabia. ¶ 亞剌比亞人, an Arab. —亞剌比亞數字, an Arabic figure [character]; cipher.

aradateru (荒立てる), *vt.* ❶ (心氣を) to excite; agitate. ❷ (事を) to aggravate.

aradatsu (荒立つ), *vi.* ❶ (氣を) to be excited; be agitated. ❷ (浪など) to rise high.

aragyō (荒行), *n.* ascetic penance; religious austerities.

arai (洗), *n.* wash; rinse.

arai (荒い), *a.* ❶ (粗) coarse; rough. ❷ (暴) violent; rough. ❸ (疎) sparse; scattered. —粗い木理, coarse grain.

araiba (洗場), *n.* a lavatory; a wash-place.

araidate (洗立する), *vt.* =*arai-tateru.*

araigami (洗髮), *n.* hair let down after washing.

araiguma (浣熊), *n.* the racoon.

araihari (洗張する), *vt.* to wash and stretch; full (布を).

araiko (洗粉), *n.* washing-powder.

araitateru (洗立てる), *vt.* to rake up; make inquiry *into.* —昔のことを洗立てる, to rake up the bygones.

araizarai (洗浚), *ad.* entirely; completely.

araizarashi (洗晒の), *a.* faded after repeated washing; washed-out.

arakabe (粗壁), *n.* the first coating on a wall. —粗壁を塗る, to give the first coating; rough-coat.

arakajime (豫め), *ad.* beforehand; previously; in advance. —豫め通告する, to give previous notice *of*; inform beforehand.

arakanna (粗鉋), *n.* a jack-plane.

arakata (粗方), *ad.* for the most part; mostly; practically. —粗方出來上った, It is almost completed. —試驗ももう粗方濟んだ, The examination is now practically over.

arakezuri (荒削), *n.* rough planing. —荒削りする, to rough-hew; rough-plane.

araku (荒く), *ad.* ❶ (粗) coarsely; roughly. ●〔暴〕violently; vehemently; roughly. ●〔疎〕sparsely. —粗くなる, to roughen; become rough. —粗くする, to roughen; coarsen; make coarse.

aramahoshii (あらまほしい), *v.* to be desirable; be desired to be.

aramashi (粗増), *n.* the greater part; the most part; an outline. —, *ad.* =*arakata*. —粗増の, general; rough. —粗増を話す, to give a rough account; give an outline. —水は粗増退いて了ッた, The flood has mostly receded.

aramono (荒物), *n.* kitchenware. ¶ 荒物屋, a kitchenware-dealer.

aranami (荒浪), *n.* rough waves; stormy waves; high seas.

arankagiri (あらん限り), *ad.* with utmost; with all possible; to the best (of one's ability). —力のあらん限り, to the best of my ability. —命のあらん限り, as long as life lasts. **—-no,** *a.* utmost; all; every possible. —あらん限りの力を以て, with all one's might; with one's utmost energy. —あらん限りの聲を出して, at the top of one's voice. —有らん限りの手段を盡す, to try every possible means. —有らん限りの財力を盡す, to exhaust all one's resources. —有らん限りの智慧を絞る, to cudgel one's brains to the utmost.

aranui (疎縫), *n.* =*karinui.*

aranuri (荒塗), *n.* rough coat; rough-cast. —荒塗する, to rough-coat; rough-cast.

arappoi (荒ッぽい), *a.* ●〔暴〕rough; rough-mannered. ●〔疎〕(まばら) sparse; scattered. —荒ッぽいことをする, to behave roughly. —荒ッぽく扱ふ, to handle [treat] roughly.

ararageru (荒らげる), *vt.* to roughen; make harsh. —聲を荒らげて, in a harsh tone.

araraka (荒かに), *ad.* roughly; gruffly.

arare (霰), *n.* ● hail. ●(餅の一種) a small dumpling cube. —霰が降る, It hails.

araremonai (あられもない), *a.* ●(ありさうもない) impossible. ●(似合はぬ) unbecoming.

araryōji (荒療治), *n.* ●(手術の) rough operations; rough remedies. ●(厳酷の處置) desperate measures. —荒療治する, ①(ひどくする) to treat roughly; take desperate measures. ②(殺す) to put to death; kill.

arasagashi (瑕探し), *n.* fault-finding; picking holes. —人の瑕探しをする, to find fault with others; pick holes in another's coat. —貰ひ物のあら探しをする, to look a gift-horse in the mouth.

araseitō (紫羅欄花), *n.* the queen's stock.

arashi (嵐, 暴風雨), *n.* a storm; a tempest. —嵐の夜, a stormy night. —嵐の海上に, on the stormy sea.

arasoi (爭), *n.* ●(爭論) a dispute; a quarrel; a squabble. ●(爭闘) strife; struggle. ●(不和) discord; dissension. ●(競爭) a competition; a contest. —爭好きの, disputatious; quarrelsome. —階級間の爭, class strife. —金錢上の爭, a quarrel about money matters. —内輪の爭, a family quarrel; internal dissension. —爭の種を蒔く, to sow the seed of discord. —爭を調停する, to adjust [settle] a dispute. ¶ 勢力爭, a struggle for power.

arasotte (爭ッて), *ad.* contentiously; in competition.

arasou (爭ふ), *vi.* ●(爭論する) to dispute *with*; contend *with*. ●(競爭) to compete *for*; contend *for*; strive *for*. —爭ふべからざる; 爭はれぬ, indisputable; undeniable (否認し難き). —得意を爭ふ, to compete for custom. —雌雄を爭ふ, to strive for mastery. —場所を爭ふ, to scramble for a place.

arasu (荒す), *vt.* ●(害する) to lay waste; ravage. ●(騒がす) to overrun; infest. ●(掠める) to pillage. ●(破壞) to ruin; spoil. —皮膚を荒す, to roughen the skin. —田畑を荒し廻る, to overrun [ravage] fields.

arasuji (荒筋), *n.* ● an outline. ●(脚本等の) scenario.

arata (新な), *a.* new; fresh. —そは吾人の記憶に新なる所である, It is fresh in our memory. **—-ni,** *ad.* newly; afresh. —新にする, to renew; make anew. —新に建てた家, a newly-built house. —新に買入れた土地, a newly-bought plot of land. —を新に註文する, to give fresh orders *for*.

arataka (灼な), *a.* efficacious; marvellous.

aratamaru (改·革まる), *vi.* ●(變更) to change; alter; be revised (改正). ●(改善) to mend; improve. ●(病氣が) to become serious; change for the worse. —事態大に改まッた, Things have greatly improved.

aratameru (改める), *vt.* ●(變更) to change; alter; revise (改正). ●(檢査) to examine; inspect. ●(改悛) to correct; mend;

reform. —規則を改める, to amend [revise] rules. —切符を改める, to examine tickets. —過を改める, to correct one's faults; reform. —語調を改める, to change one's note. —言葉を改めて語る, to speak in a serious tone. —名を太郎と改める, to change one's name to Tarō.

aratamete (改めて), *ad.* anew; afresh; formally (正式に). —何れ改めて伺ひます, I will call again some day.

arau (洗ふ), *vt.* ❶ to wash; scour; rinse. ❷ (調べる) to inquire *into*; examine. —瓶を濯ふ, to rinse a bottle. —汗を洗ひ流す, to wash away the sweat. —汚染を洗ひ落す, to wash off [out] stains.

arauma (悍馬), *n.* an unbroken horse.

araumi (荒海), *n.* a rough sea; an open sea; the ocean (大洋).

arawa (陽な), *a.* ❶ (むき出しの) frank; candid. ❷ (公然) open; public. ——**-ni**, *ad.* ❶ frankly; candidly. ❷ publicly; openly. —陽に云へば, to speak candidly.

arawareru (表れる), *vi.* ❶ 【現】 (出現する) to appear; make its appearance; come in sight (見えて來る). ❷ 【露】 (露顕する) to come to light; be out. ❸ 【著】 (著名になる) to become known [famous]. ❹ 【表】 (表面に出る) to find expression; appear. —正直が顔に表れてゐる, He has honesty written in his face.

arawasu (表はす), *vt.* ❶ (顯出) to show; display; reveal. ❷ (著作) to write; publish. ❸ (露現) to expose; bare. ❹ (著名) to make famous. ❺ (表現) to express; manifest. —言語に表はす, to express in words. —姿を現はす, to make its appearance. —一書を著はす, to write a book; publish a book. —腕前を顯はす, to show [display] one's ability. —名を顯はす, to make one's name; make oneself famous. —肌を露はして, with her shoulders bared.

arayuru (有らゆる), *a.* all; every. —あらゆる點に於て, in all respects. —あらゆる手段を盡す, to exhaust every possible [available] means.

arazareba (非ざれば), **arazunba** (非ずんば), *conj.* unless; if ...not. —大資本を擁するに非ざれば, unless we have a large capital. —Aに非ずんばBなり, If it is not A, it is B.

arazukuri (荒造), *n.* rough make. —荒造の, rough; crude.

arazumori (粗積), *n.* a rough estimate. ☞ *gaisan* (概算).

are (荒), *n.* ❶ (時化) a storm; a stormy weather. ❷ (荒廢) ravages; dilapidation. ❸ (皮膚の) coarseness; roughness. ¶ 荒模樣, a threatening [lowering] sky; signs of coming storm.

are (彼), *pron.* ❶ (人) he (she). ❷ (事物) it; that. —あれからこちらへ, since then.

are (あれ), *int.* there; I say; look! —あれ危い, I say, look out! —あれ鐘が鳴る, There goes the bell!

areato (荒跡), *n.* ravages (荒らした跡); ruins (廢跡).

arechi (荒地), *n.* waste land (蕪地); poor soil (瘠地); barren land (不毛の地). —蕪地(ぶち)を起す, to bring waste land into cultivation.

aredake (あれだけ), =*arehodo.*

aregiri (あれぎり), =*arekkiri.*

arehodo (彼程), *ad.* such; so much; so many; to such a degree.

arei (啞鈴), *n.* a dumb-bell. ¶ 啞鈴體操, dumb-bell exercise.

arekkiri (あれッきり), *ad.* after that; since. ——, *n.* all (全部); the last (最後). —あれッきりよしました, After that I left it off completely. —あれッきり逢ひません, I have not seen him since.

arekurai (あれ位), *ad.* so; so much; that much.

arenari (あれなり), *ad.* ❶=*arekkiri.* ❷ as it (he) is. —あれなりにしても置けない, We cannot leave it as it is.

areno (荒野), *n.* a wilderness; wilds.

areru (荒れる), *vi.* ❶ (荒廢する) to run to waste; become waste; be dilapidated (家屋が); be overgrown with weeds (庭園が). ❷ (あばれる) to rage; storm. ❸ (皮膚などのあらびる) to become red [rough; coarse]. —荒れ果てた, desolate; waste; dilapidated.

areshiki (あれしきの), *a.* such; like that.

areta (荒れた), *a.* ❶ (荒廢) waste (土地); dilapidated (家屋). ❷ 【暴】 rough; stormy. ❸ 【粗】 coarse; rough; red. —荒れた航海, a rough passage.

areumi (荒海), *n.* a rough sea; a stormy sea; high seas.

areya-koreya (彼此), this and that; with one thing or another. —あれやこれやで心配する, to be anxious now for this and now for that.

ari (蟻), *n.* ❶ the ant. ❷ 【鎹】 dovetail. —蟻の穴から堤も崩れる, "A little leak will sink a great ship." ¶ 蟻の塔; 蟻塚, an ant-hill.

Āria-jin (アーリア人), *n.* an Aryan.

ariake (有明), *n.* ❶ (殘月) daybreak; dawn. ❷ (有明行燈) a night-light [-lamp].

ariamaru (有餘る), *vi.* to be in excess; be more than enough. **——**, *a.* overflowing; profuse. —有餘る人口, surplus population. —有餘る程の金を持ッて, having enough money and to spare.

ariari (歴然と), *ad.* clearly; plainly; vividly.

ariawase (有合せの), *a.* ready; at hand. —有合せの物を食べる, to take pot-luck.

ariawaseru (有合せる), *vi.* to happen to be; happen to be at hand.

aridaka (有高), *n.* the total amount; the amount in hand. —在庫品の有高を調べる, to examine the quantity of goods in store.

arifureta (有觸れた), *a.* common; commonplace; trite. —有觸れた話, a common story.

arigachi (有勝ちの), *a.* common; of common occurrence; apt to occur. —そんな事は有勝ちだ, Such things are of common occurrence.

arigane (有金), *n.* cash [money] in hand.

arigatai (有難い), *a.* thankful; grateful; obliging. —(大きに) 有難う, Thank you (very much); (many) Thanks. —有難がる, to be thankful *for*; feel grateful *for*. —親の有難味が分る, to appreciate the beneficence of one's parents. —…なし下され有難く奉存候, I beg to thank you *for*. ¶ 有難迷惑, a misplaced kindness.

arigeni (有りげに), as if; as though. —心ありげに見える, to appear as if he had an inclination *for*.

arihozo (蟻枘), *n.* 【建】 dovetail tenon.

arijigoku (蟻地獄), *n.* 【昆】 the ant-lion.

arika (所在), *n.* the place where ... is; whereabouts (大凡の); locality (正確な). —所在を尋ね歩く, to go in search *of*. —未だに所在が分らぬ, His whereabouts is still unknown.

arikitari (在來の), *a.* conventional; traditional; usual. —在來の方法, conventional method. —在來の例に倣ふ, to follow the tradition.

arikui (食蟻獸), *n.* 【哺乳】 the ant-eater.

arinagara (ありながら), though ...is; in spite of; notwithstanding. —女でありながら, a woman as she is.

arini (在荷), *n.* stock (in hand); goods in stock. —在荷を調べる, to take stock. ¶ 在荷調べ, stock-taking.

arinomama (有の儘), *n.* the (exact) truth. —有の儘を云ふ, to tell the exact truth; say without concealment. **——-no**, *a.* naked; bare; ungarbled. —有の儘の話, an ungarbled account. —有の儘の事實, the bare facts; the naked truth. **——-ni**, *ad.* without concealment; just as it is.

arinotowatari (會陰), *n.* 【解】 the perineum.

arisama (有樣), *n.* ❶ (光景) appearance; sight. ❷ (狀態) state; condition. ❸ (境遇) circumstances; situation. —かかる有樣で, in [under] these circumstances.

arisōmonai (有りさうもない), *a.* improbable; unlikely. —有りさうもない事, an improbability; a thing unlikly to happen.

arisōna (有りさうな), *a.* probable; likely. —有りさうなこと, a probable thing; a likely event.

arisui (蟻吸), *n.* 【鳥】 the wryneck.

aritake (有りたけ), all; all that there is; whole. —有りたけここへ出せ, Chuck out all you have.

aritei (有體), =*arinomama.*

aritewa (在りては), *prep.* ❶ (取ては) in the case of; to. ❷ (於ては) in. —支那にありては, in the case of China.

aritsugi (蟻繼), *n.* 【建】 the dove-tail.

aritsuku (有りつく), *vt.* to get; find; come *upon*. —仕事(飯)に有りつく, to get work (a meal).

ariuru (有得る), *vi.* may be; can be; to be possible. —有り得べからざる, impossible. —幽靈などと云ふものはあり得ない, There can be no such things as ghosts.

arizarin (アリザリン), *n.* alizarin.

arizashi (蟻差), *n.* 【建】 dovetail (joint).

arizuka (蟻塚), *n.* an ant-hill; an ant-mound.

arō (あらう), ❶ (未來) will (三人稱); shall (一人稱). ❷ (想像) I think; I suppose. —君ともあらうものが, you, of all persons. —さぞ悲いであらう, How sad you must be! —明日は雨であらう, I think it will rain to-morrow.

aru (有·在る), *vi.* ❶ (存在) to be; there is [are]; exist: (發見) to be found; occur: (所在) to be; stand; be situated; be located; lie. ❷ (所有) to have; possess. ❸ (擧行) to take place; be held. ❹ (發生) to take place; happen;

occur; break out. ❺(測定上) to stand (丈け); weigh (重さ); measure (寸法). —手のある桶, a pail with a handle. —有るかなきかの財產, very slender means. —事あれかしと祈る, to pray for a disturbance. —今日は議會がある, The House meets to-day. —偶にはさういふ事もある, Such things sometimes happen. —そんな事はありやうがない, That cannot be. —寺は高臺の東方にある, The temple stands east of the hill.

aru (或), *a.* a [an]; one; a certain; some. —或る程度まで, to a certain degree. —或日, one day. —或人, a certain man (さる人); some one (或者); somebody (誰かが). —或所, a certain place.

arubamu (アルバム), *n.* an album.

arufabetto (アルファベット), *n.* the alphabet. —アルファベット順に列べる, to arrange alphabetically [in alphabetical order].

aruhei (有平), *n.* hardbake.

aruiwa (或は), *ad.* (多分) perhaps; possibly. —, *conj.* or. —或は曰く, some say; according to some. —それ或は然らん, Perhaps (it is) so; It may be so.

aruji (主人), *n.* a master; a host (主人役). —主人顏する, to lord it like a master.

arukari (アルカリ), *n.* alkali.

arukaroido (アルカロイド), *n.* an alkaloid.

arukasu (歩かす), *vt.* to make walk; walk. —歩けなくなるまで歩かす, to walk a person off his legs.

aruki (歩き), *n.* walking; walk. —庭を一歩きする, to take a turn in the garden. 「き方. gait; pace.」

arukiburi (歩態, 歩容), *n.* Ⓢ 歩

arukōru (酒精), *n.* alcohol. ¶ 純アルコール, absolute alcohol. —酒精中毒, alcoholic poisoning; alcoholism. —酒精ランプ, an alcohol-lamp; a spirit-lamp.

aruku (歩く), *vi.* to walk. —歩き廻る, to walk about; tramp about; wander about. —歩き通す, to walk all the way. —歩いて行く to go on foot. 「not; I am not.」

arumaishi (あるまいし), it is

arumajiki (あるまじき), *a.* improper; unbecoming; unworthy. —男子にあるまじき行爲, an act unworthy of [unbecoming to] a man.

arumiryūmu (アルミニゥム), *n.* aluminium.

arumono (或物), *n.* something; some (若干); some one (或者).

arupaka (アルパカ), *n.* 【動】the alpaca (又其の毛·其の毛の織物)

Arupusu (アルプス), *n.* the Alps.

arutoki (或時), *ad.* once (upon a time); one time; on one occasion.

Aruzenchin (アルゼンチン), *n.* the Argentine Republic; Argentina.

arya (ありァ), *int.* Oh dear; dear me; Heavens!

aryū (亞流), *n.* ❶(二流人士) a second-rate man. ❷(流を汲む人) a man of the school of....

aryūsan (亞硫酸), *n.* sulphurous acid.

asa (麻), *n.* (大麻) the hemp; (麻布) hemp-cloth. —麻につれる蓬, "With the good we become good." ¶ 麻綱, a hempen rope.

asa (朝), *n.* morning. —朝に, in the morning. (十日の朝に, on the morning of the 10th.) —朝から晩まで, from morning to [till] evening.

asaame (朝雨), *n.* morning rain; the cry of the morning.

asaban (朝晩), *n.* & *ad.* morning and evening; night and morning.

asaborake (朝開), *n.* daybreak; dawn; peep of day. 「a scratch.」

asade (淺手), *n.* a slight wound;

asagao (朝顏), *n.* ❶【植】the morning-glory. ❷【建】splay.

asagi (淺葱), *n.* light blue.

asagiri (朝霧), *n.* a morning mist.

asagumori (朝曇), *n.* morning cloudiness. —朝曇の空, a cloudy morning sky.

asaguroi (淺黑い), *a.* brunette (皮膚の); dark; brown.

asahakana (淺はかな), *a.* shallow; shallow-minded; thoughtless (思慮なき). —淺はかな人, a shallow-minded man. 「ing] sun.」

asahi (朝日), *n.* the rising [morn-

asai (淺い), *a.* ❶(水深·容器·智慮の) shallow. ❷(交際·關係の) slight. ❸(時日の) short (短い); early (早い). ❹(色·眠·吃水の) light. ❺(傷·知識の) shallow; slight. —淺からぬ, close; deep. (淺からぬ因緣, a deep affinity.) —淺い眠り, light sleep. —傷は淺い, The wound is slight. —春がまだ淺い, The spring is still early.

asajie (淺智慧の), *a.* shallow-minded; shallow-brained.

asakoki (麻扱), *n.* a ripple; a hackle.

asaku (淺く), *ad.* shallowly; slightly; lightly; early. —淺くなる, to (become) shallow. —春なほ淺く, in the early spring.

asakusanori (淺草海苔), *n.* 【植】the laver.

asamadaki (朝まだき), *ad.* before sunshine. —, *n.* (early) morning.

asamashii (浅ましい), *a.* ❶(浅はか) shallow; shallow-minded. ❷(みすぼらしい) miserable; wretched. ❸(さもしい) mean. —浅ましい姿をする, to make a miserable appearance. —さてさて浅ましい世の中だ, Well, well, it is a mean world.

asameshi (朝飯), *n.* breakfast. —朝飯を食ふ, to breakfast. —そんな事は朝飯前だ, That is the easiest thing in the world.

asamidori (淺綠), *n.* light green.

asane (朝寢), *n.* late rising. —朝寢する, to sleep till late in the morning. ¶ 朝寢坊, a late riser; a lie-a-bed.

asaoki (朝起), *n.* early rising; an early riser (人). —朝起する, to rise [get up] early. —朝起は三文の得, "The early bird catches the worm."

asari (淺利貝), *n.* Tapes philippinarum.

asaru (漁る), *vt.* ❶(すなどる) to fish. ❷(探求) to search *for*; look *for*. —餌を漁る, to search for food.

asase (淺瀬), *n.* a shallow; a shoal. —淺瀬を渡る, to ford [wade] a stream. —淺瀬に乘り上げる, to run aground [ashore].

asatte (明後日), *n.* & *ad.* the day after to-morrow.

asayake (朝紅), *n.* the morning glow (of the sky).

asayu (朝湯), *n.* a morning bath. —朝湯に入る, to have a morning bath.

asayū (朝夕), *n.* & *ad.* morning and evening.

asazake (朝酒), *n.* morning draught; morning drink.

ase (汗), *n.* sweat; perspiration. —汗だらけの; 汗みづくの, sweaty. —汗染みる, to be stained with sweat. —汗をかいて, in a sweat. —珠の汗を流す, to sweat in beads. —汗びッしょりになる; びッしょり汗をかく, to perspire [sweat] profusely. ¶ 汗の珠, a sweat-bead; beads of sweat.

asebamu (汗ばむ), *vi.* to sweat; perspire.

asebi (梫木), *n.* the Japanese andromeda.

asebo, asemo, (汗疹), *n.* sweat-rash; prickly heat.

asechirin (アセチリン), *n.* acetylene.

aseino (阿世の), *a.* time-serving. —阿世の徒, a time-server.

asejuban (汗襦袢), *n.* a sweater; an undershirt.

asemizu (汗水), *n.* sweat. —汗水垂らして, by the sweat of one's brow.

aseñyaku (阿仙藥), *n.* the catechu (-tree).

aseru (焦る), *vi.* to hurry; grow impatient. —あせるな, Keep your hair on!; Keep cool!

aseru (褪せる), *vi.* to fade. ☞ *sameru.*

ashi (葦), *n.* the reed.

ashi (足, 脚), *n.* ❶〔足〕a foot; a paw (犬猫などの鋭爪ある). ❷〔脚〕a leg (人・動物・器物の). ❸(步調) step; pace. —足の早い, ① swift-footed. ② (腐り易い) perishable. —足の達者な人, a good walker. —足がつく, to be tracked; be traced. —足が遠くなる, His visits become rare. —足を留める, to stop; stay. —足をとる, to catch a person's leg. —足を引きずる, to drag one's foot. —足を速める, to quicken one's pace. —足を出す, ① to put out one's feet. ② (醜態を露はす) to show the cloven foot. ③ (金が足らなくなる) to run short. —足を踏み外す, to miss [lose] one's footing. —足が棒のやうになッた, My legs are stiff as a poker. —足序に之を出して來て吳れないか, Will you, while on foot, post this letter?

ashiato (足跡), *n.* a footprint; a footmark; trace. —足跡をつける, to follow up footmarks.

ashiba (足場), *n.* a footing; a scaffolding (足代); staging. —足場をかける, to set up a scaffolding; erect a scaffold. —足場を得る, to gain a footing. (…に堅固な足場を得る, to secure a firm footing *on*.)

ashibaya (足早の), *a.* fast; quick (-footed); swift (-footed). —足早に步く, to walk quickly [at a quick pace].

ashibumi (足踏), *n.* ❶(足を踏むこと) stamping; treading. ❷(足を踏み入れること) access; visit. ❸【軍】marking time. —足踏する, ① to tread; stamp. ② to visit; come (go). ③【軍】to mark time. —足踏オイ!, Mark time!

ashibyōshi (足拍子とる), *v.* to beat time with the feet.

ashida (足駄), *n.* high clogs. —足駄の齒, supports of high clogs. —足駄を穿く, to put on high clogs.

ashidassha (足達者の), *a.* strong-footed; strong-legged.

ashidome (足止, 足留), *n.* confining indoors. —三日間の足留をくふ, to be ordered to keep indoors for three days.

ashidori (足取り), *n.* pace; gait.

ashigakari (足掛り), *n.* a foothold; a footing.

ashigaru (足輕), *n.* a foot-soldier (of the old régime).

ashige (足蹴にする), *v.* to kick;

trample (on). 「馬の).
ashihibiki(足響), *n.* tramp (人・
ashika (海驢), *n.* Steller's sea--lion; the sea-lion.
ashikake (足掛け), *n.* a pedal (自轉車などの); a foot-rest (椅子等の); a foot-board; a stretcher (短艇の); a step. —足掛け三年になる, It spreads over three calendar years.
ashikarazu (不惡), *ad.* not ill; not bad. —どうぞ惡しからず, Please don't take it amiss [ill].
ashikase(足械), *n.* fetters; irons; shackles. —足械をかける, to fetter; put in irons.
ashiki (惡しき), *a.* =*warui.*
ashiko (彼處), ☞ *asoko.*
ashikoshi (足腰), *n.* legs and loins [waist]. —足腰の立たぬ樣にする, to make a person unable to stand.
ashiku (惡しく), *ad.* =*waruku.*
ashikubi (足首), *n.* the ankle.
ashimatoi (足纏), *n.* =*ashitematoi.*
ashimoto (足下), *n.* ❶ (脚下) one's feet. ❷ (歩調) step; pace. ❸(弱點) a weak point. —足もとに, at one's feet. —足もとの確な, sure-footed. —足下の明るい中に, ① (暗くならぬ中に) while it is still light. ② before the game is up. —人の足下を見る [に附込む], to take advantage of a person's weak point. —足下へも寄りつかぬ, not to be compared with. —足下に氣をつけよ, Mind your footing! 「lame man.
ashinae (蹇), *n.* a cripple; a
ashinami (足竝), *n.* pace; step. —足竝を揃へて, keeping pace *with.* —足竝を亂す, to break step; walk out of step.
ashioto (足音), *n.* a step; a footfall; a footstep; a tramp (大きな). —足音を立てずに, without any sound of footsteps; with silent footsteps.
ashirai (扱ひ), *n.* ❶ (もてなし) treatment. ❷(操縦) management; handling. ❸ (配合) garnishing.
ashirau (扱ふ), *vt.* ❶ (もてなす) to treat. ❷(操縦) to manage; handle. ❸(配合) to arrange; garnish (食品を). —鼻で扱ふ, to sniff at others. —顧で扱ふ, to treat superciliously.
ashita(明日), *n.* & *ad.* to-morrow.
ashita (朝), *n.* morning; morn [詩]; (旦) dawn; break of day; daybreak. —朝に紅顏あッて夕に白骨, "To-day red, to-morrow dead."
ashitematoi (足手纏), *n.* a hindrance; a drag; an encumbrance (係累). —足手纏が多いから, as I have many encumbrances.
ashitsuki (足附), *n.* gait; walk.
ashiura (蹠), *n.* the sole.
ashiyowa (足弱の), *a.* weak--legged.
ashiyubi (趾), *n.* a toe. —趾の腹, the ball of the toe.
ashizama(惡様に), *ad.* ill; spitefully; disparagingly. —人の事を惡様に云ふ, to speak ill [evil] of a person. 「pace.
ashizoroe (足揃へ), *n.* keeping
ashizuri (足摺する), *v.* to scrape one's feet. —足摺して辯士を沈默さす, to scrape down a speaker.
ashura (阿修羅), *n.* [梵] Asura.
asobasu(遊ばす), *v.* ❶ (遊ばせる) to make play; amuse. ❷ [敬語] to be pleased *to.* —子供を遊ばす, to amuse children. —金を遊ばせて置く, to let money lie idle. ¶ あそばせ言葉, respectful language.
asobi (遊), *n.* ❶ (遊戲, 娯樂) play; sport; game; amusement. ❷ (遊興) pleasures. ❸(遊行) diversion; a trip; an excursion. —遊びがてら, for diversion; by way of diversion. —遊に耽る, to be given up [be addicted] to pleasures. —遊に餘念がない, to be engrossed in play. —鎌倉へ遊びに行く, to make a pleasure trip to Kamakura. ¶ 遊相手; 遊仲間; 遊友達, a playmate; a playfellow. —遊仕事, work done at leisure; work done to beguile time.
asobiba (遊場), *n.* ❶ (遊戲場) a playground. ❷ (遊樂地) a pleasure-ground; a pleasure-resort.
asobidōgu (遊道具), *n.* a plaything; a toy.
asobidoki(遊時), *n.* ❶ (休憩時) playtime. ❷ (遊樂季節) pleasure season.
asobikin (遊金), *n.* =*yūkin.*
asobinin(遊人), *n.* ❶(破落戶, 賭博師) a rogue; a gambler. ❷(遊民) the idle; the unemployed (失業者).
asobizuki(遊好きの), *a.* ❶ playful; sportive; frolicsome. ❷ (道樂な) pleasure-loving; dissipated.
asobu (遊ぶ), *v.* ❶ (遊戲) to play; amuse oneself. ❷ (弄ぶ) to play *with*; make fun *of.* ❸(遊興, 放蕩) to carouse; take to loose pleasures. ❹ (遊行) to take a stroll (散步); make a trip *to*; visit. ❺(遊惰, 無職) to be idle; idle away; be without employment. —遊んで居る, to be at play (遊戲); lie idle (資本がねてる); be doing nothing (無爲); be without em-

ployment (無聊); be out of work (同上). —遊び暮らす, to drone away; idle away. —遊び戯れる, to sport; gambol; frolic. —遊び廻る, to gad about. —支那に遊ぶ, to make a trip to China. —仁齋の門に遊ぶ, to study under Jinsai. —かるた(鬼ごッこ)をして遊ぶ, to play cards(tag). —一週間ぶッ通しに遊ぶ, to carouse for a week. —よく勉めよく遊べ, Work hard, play hard.

asoko (彼處), *pron.* that place [part]; that; there. —彼處に, there; yonder; over there.

assaku (壓搾する), *vt.* to press; compress. ¶ 壓搾器, a press; a compressor. —壓搾空氣, compressed air.

assari (あッさり), *ad.* lightly; simply; neatly (清楚に). —あッさりした, light; plain; frank. —あッさりした返事, a neat reply. —あッさりした氣質, frank disposition. —あッさりした食物, light [simple] food. —あッさり小言を云ふ, to scold lightly. —氣があッさりする, to feel refreshed.

assatsu (壓殺する), *vt.* to crush to death.

assei (壓制), *n.* oppression; despotism; coercion. —壓制的, oppressive; despotic; coercive. —壓制する, to oppress; coerce. ¶ 壓制者, an oppressor; a despot.

assen (斡旋), *n.* good offices; mediation; agency. —斡旋する, to mediate; use one's good offices. —(誰の)斡旋で, by [through] the agency of —; by —'s good offices. ¶ 斡旋者, a mediator.

assetsu (壓接する), *vt.* to impact.

asshi (壓死する), *vi.* to be crushed [squeezed] to death. ¶ 壓死者, a person crushed to death.

asshuku (壓縮する), *vt.* to compress; press; constrict.

assui-ponpu (壓水ポンプ), *n.* a force-pump.

as-suru (壓する), *vt.* ❶ (押しつける) to press. ❷ (壓倒) to overwhelm; overbear; overawe. —指を以て壓する, to press it with one's finger.

asu (明日), *n.* & *ad.* to-morrow. —明日の晩, to-morrow evening.

asufaruto (地瀝青), *n.* asphalt.

asunaro (羅漢柏), *n.* the hatchet-leaved arbor-vitæ.

asuparagasu (アスパラガス), *n.* the asparagus.

astorakan (アストラカン), *n.* astrakhan.

atae (與), *n.* a gift. —天の與, Heaven's gift.

ataeru (與へる), *vt.* ❶ to give; grant. ❷ (授ける) to confer; bestow; impart. ❸ (蒙らす, 加へる) to deal; inflict. —與へられた, given. (與へられた點Aより, from a given point A.) —惡感情を與へる, to breed bad feelings. —便宜を與へる, to give [afford] facilities. —知識を與へる, to impart knowledge. —影響を與へる, to exert influence *upon*; affect; have effect *upon*. —權能を與へる, to confer powers *on*. —問題を與へる, to give [set] a question. —賞を與へる, to award a prize. —彼に本を與へる, to give a book to him; give him a book.

atafuta (あたふた), *ad.* hurry-scurry; in a hurry. —あたふた飛出す, to rush out helter-skelter.

atai (價, 値), *n.* ❶ (價値) value; worth. ❷ (代價) price. —するだけの値がない, It is not worth doing. —一顧の値もない, It is not even worth consideration.

atai-suru (値する), *v.* to be worth; deserve; be worth while. —賞讃に値する, to be worthy of praise. —其罪確に死に値す, The crime certainly deserves death.

atakamo (恰も), *ad.* just (丁度); as it were (云はば); so to speak (同上). —恰もよし, just at the time; just then. —恰も…の如し, to be (look) (just) like —; be (just) as — as. (堅きこと恰も岩石の如し, to be just as firm as a rock.) —恰も…なるかの如く, as if; as though. —恰も眠れるが如く, just as if in sleep.

atama (頭), *n.* the head. ❶ (頭髮) the hair. ❷ (物の端) tip; top. —釘の頭, the head of a nail. —指の頭, the tip of a finger. —頭へ來る酒, a heady wine. —頭の黑い鼠, a thief in the house; a dishonest inmate. —頭の善(惡)い人, a clear-(muddle-)headed man. —頭のある, ① headed. ② clear-headed; clever. —頭のない, ① headless. ② muddle-headed; dull-headed. —頭がよい; よい頭を持つ, to have a clear [good] head. —頭が痛い, to have a pain in the head. —…の頭がある, to have a head *for*. —頭に浮ぶ, to come into one's head. —頭を上げる, to raise one's head; come to the front (擡頭する). —頭を下げる, ①(叩頭する) to bow; bow the head. ②(屈服する) to bow the neck; submit. (頭を下げて詫びる, to apologize with one's head bowed). —頭をはる, ①(頭をはねる)to squeeze. ②(頭を毆る) to give a person a crack [whack] on the head. —頭を押へる, ① to hold one's head with hands. ② (制壓) to keep a person under. —頭を痛める, to feel great anxiety (心痛); rack [cudgel; beat] one's brains (苦心). —頭を刈る, ① to cut one's hair. ② (刈ッて貰ふ) to have one's hair cut. —頭を掻く, to scratch one's head. —頭のぎりぎりから爪尖まで, from the crown of the head to the tip of the toes. —人に頭が上らぬ, I can not hold up my head before others. —頭の悪い奴だな, What a muddle-head! —何にでもよく頭を突込む男だ, He has a finger in every pie.

atamagonashi (頭ごなしに), *ad.* severely; unsparingly. —頭ごなしにする, ① (叱りつける) to rate severely; abuse roundly. ② (酷評する) to pull to pieces; pull down.

atamakabu (頭株), *n.* leadership; (人) chief men; leaders.

atamakara (頭から), *ad.* ❶ (初めから) from the first [outset]. ❷ (一も二もなく) flatly; point-blank. —頭からはねつける, to refuse flatly [point-blank]. —頭から呶鳴りつける, to rate a man point-blank.

atamakazu (頭數), *n.* the number of persons.

atamaōi (頭被ひ), *n.* a head-dress; a head-gear.

atamashigoto (頭仕事), *n.* headwork.

atamawari (頭割に), *ad.* per head. —頭割にする, to divide equally among them; put so much per head.

atan (亞炭), *n.* brown coal.

atara (可惜), *a.* ❶ (貴重) precious; valuable. ❷ (殘念) regrettable; deplorable. —可惜好機を逸する, to miss [let slip] the best opportunity.

atarashii (新しい), *a.* new; fresh (新鮮な); novel (嶄新な); up-to-date (近頃の). —新しい女, the new woman. —新しい魚, a fresh fish. —新しがる, to believe oneself up-to-date.

atari (あたり), *n.* the neighbourhood (邊); time (頃). ——, *ad.* & *prep.* about. —あのあたり, ① at that time; in those days. ② (あの邊) that part; that quarter. —東京あたり, about Tōkyō. —ここらあたりに, about here; hereabouts. —あたり構はず, regardless of the people about one; regardless of the neighbours. —入口のあたりの涼しい風, the cool air about the door. —あたりに人なきが如く, as if there were no one about. —あたりを見廻す, to look around. —あたりに氣を配る, to look carefully about one. —そこらあたりが本當だらう, That is about the truth.

atari (當), *n.* ❶ (豐作) a good crop; a rich harvest. ❷ (的中, 成功) a hit; a success. ❸ (果物の損傷) damage. ❹ (目當) a clue. ❺ (仕向) treatment. ¶ 大當り, a great hit [success]. (今度の狂言は大當りだ, The new play has made a great hit.) —當り年, ① (豐年) a year of good crop; a fruitful [abundant] year. ② (多幸な又は思ひ通りになる年) a good year *for*; a lucky [successful] year. —當り籤, a prize ticket. —當り狂言, a successful play; a play that makes a hit. —當り外れ, hit or miss.

atari (當り), **atatte** (當ッて), *prep.* at; in; on; to; towards. —この時に當ッて, at this juncture; at the time.

atarimae (當前), *n.* Ⓢ 割前, a share.

atarimae (當前の), *a.* ❶ (當然) natural; reasonable; proper. ❷ (通常の) usual; ordinary. —當前の事さへして居れば, if you only behave like an ordinary man. —當前に行けば, in the ordinary course.

atarisawari (當障のない), *a.* non-committal; neutral. —當り障りのない挨拶をする, to give a non-committal answer.

ataru (當る), *v.* ❶ (相當) to correspond *to*; answer *to*: be equivalent *to*. ❷ (的中) to hit; tell (彈丸); strike (同上): come true. ❸ (中毒) to disagree *with*; be poisoned; become ill from eating. ❹ (ぶッつかる) to strike *against*; collide *with*. ❺ (探る, 試みる) to sound: make a try *at*: ask. ❻ (方角) to bear; lie *to*. ❼ (量る) to measure. ❽ (暖を取る) to warm oneself. ❾ to be exposed *to* (日光·風雨に); shine *upon* (日が); beat *upon* (雨が窗等に). ❿ (敵·事等に) to engage; face: take in hand. ⓫ (該當) to fall [come] under; fall *on*. —當らず障らず, to leave it as it is. —當ッて見る, ① (探る) to sound. ② (やッて見る) to try; have a try *at*. —當り散らす, to fall foul of (everybody); vent one's anger at random. —靴があたる, The shoe pinches (my toes). —籤が當る, ① to win in a lottery; draw a prize. ② The lot falls upon one. —火にあたる, to warm oneself at the fire. —日にあたる, to bask in the sun (ひなたぼッこ); be exposed to the sun. —的 [圖] に中る, to hit the mark. —難局に

當る, to deal with a difficult situation. —冷い空氣にあたる, to expose oneself to the cold air. —敢然事に當る, to face matters bravely. —顔をあたる, to shave one's face. —値段をあたる, to ask the price. —長さをあたる, to measure its length. —彈が頭に中ッた, A bullet hit him on the head. —剃刀が少しあたる, The razor drags a little. —祭日が日曜に當る, The holiday falls on a Sunday. —雨が窗硝子にあたる, The rain beats upon the window-pane. —彼の豫言が中ッた, His prophecy has turned out true. —彼は陽氣に中ッた, The season disagreed with him. —中らずと雖も遠からず, It does not hit the truth, but is not far from it. —何もそんなに騒ぐに値らぬ, There is no need to be so excited.

atatakai (暖·温い), *a.* warm; mild; genial. —暖に, warmly. —暖かさうな著物, warm-looking clothes. ¶ 温味, warmth; heat.

atatamaru (暖·溫まる), *vi.* to (become) warm; warm up; warm oneself. —懐が暖まると, when one's purse grows heavy.

atatameru (暖·溫める), *vt.* to (make) warm. —舊交を溫める, to revive old friendship.

atatte (當·方ッて), *prep.* ☞ *atari* (當り).

atau (能ふ), *v. aux.* can. —, *vi.* to be able to. —能はしめる, to enable (a person to do something). —能はざらしめる, to disable (a person from doing something). —能ふべくんば, if possible. —能ふ限り, as far as possible.

atchi (彼方), *pron.* =*achira*.

ate (當), *n.* ❶ (目的) an object; an aim. ❷ (希望, 見込) hope; expectation. ❸ (信賴) reliance; dependence; security (擔保). ❹ (當てるもの) a pad; a bolster; a skid. —當になる, [*a.*] reliable; trustworthy. —當にならぬ, ① [*a.*] unreliable; untrustworthy. ② [*v.*] not to be relied upon; not to be counted [reckoned] upon. —當にする, to trust *to*; rely [depend] *upon*; count *upon*. —...を當にして, ① (頼みにして) on the strength *of*; on the faith *of*. ② (見越して) in anticipation [expectation] *of*. —(家をあてにして金を借る, to borrow money on the house.) —これと云ふ當もなく, without any definite object in view. —どこへと云ふ當もなく, without having any place to go to. —金の出來る當がない, to have no hope of making money [finding the money]. —當が外れた, My hopes were crushed [frustrated].; My expectations were falsified.

ate (宛), *n.* address. —A氏宛の手紙, a letter addressed to Mr. A. —一人四つ宛に配る, to distribute four to each. —誰宛に出すのですか, To what address shall I send it?

atedo (當途), *n.* an aim; an object. —當途もなく探す, to search aimlessly.

ategai (宛行), *n.* allowance; ration (兵士·馬等にやる一日分の). ¶ 宛行扶持, ① an allowance of rice. ② (當方の料簡で與へるもの) money, etc. given at discretion.

ategau (宛行ふ), *vt.* ❶ (與へる) to allow; give; provide *with*; supply. ❷ (割當) to allot; assign. ❸ (充當) to apply; appropriate; devote. ❹ (當てる) to apply. —午前を讀書にあてがふ, to devote the forenoon to reading.

ategoto (當事), *n.* a thing relied [counted] upon; anticipation.

atehamaru (當嵌る), *v.* ❶ (適用) to apply *to*; hold good. ❷ (該當) to come under; fall within the purview *of*. ❸ (恰當) to fit; suit. —地位に當嵌る人物, a person fitted for the post. —この場合はその條文に當嵌らない, The present case does not come under the article.

atehameru (當嵌める), *vt.* to apply; fit. —文章に語を當嵌める, to fit a word into a sentence.

atehazure (當外れさす), *v.* to disappoint; frustrate; falsify.

ateita (當板), *n.* 【航】 a skid.

ateji (當字), *n.* a phonetic equivalent.

atekko (當事), **attekkura** (當競), *n.* guessing; a guessing game. —當事をする, to make a guess; compete in guessing.

atekomu (當込む), *vt.* to count [reckon] upon; expect; anticipate. —櫻時を當込みに, counting upon the cherry-season. —戰爭を當込んで, in anticipation [expectation] of a war. —政府は其議席を當込んで居る, The Government count on the seat.

atekosuri (當擦), *n.* an insinuation; an innuendo; a hint. —當擦りを云ふ, to make insinuating remarks; make an insinuation.

atekosuru (當擦る), *v.* to insinuate; make an insinuation; hint a fault.

atemi (當身), *n.* a knock with the fist at a vital point.

atemono (あてもの), *n.* ❶ (中物) guessing. ❷ (當物) a pad; a bolster.

atena (宛名), *n.* an address. —手紙の宛名を書く, to address a letter. ¶ 宛名印刷器, an addressing-machine. —宛名不明信書, a blind letter.

aterareru (中てられる), *v.* ❶ (判じあてられる) to be guessed. ❷ (毒・暑さ等に) to be poisoned *by* (毒に); be affected *by* (暑さに). ❸ (困らされる) to be disgusted; be tormented.

ateru (當・中・充てる), *vt.* ❶ (充當) to apply; allot; devote. ❷ (あてがふ) to apply; put. ❸ (的中) to hit; guess. ❹ (さらす) to expose; subject. ❺ (接觸) to touch; strike. —中て損ふ, to guess wrong; make a wrong guess; make a bad shot. —當ててご覽, (give a) guess! —日光に當てる, to expose to the sun. —雨にあてて曝す, to expose to the rain. —補布をあてる, to patch; put a patch on. —すッかり當てられた, You have hit [guessed] it exactly.

ateru (宛てる), *vt.* to address; direct.

atetsuke (當附), *n.* an insinuation; a (sly) dig [hint] *at*; a pointed reference *to*.

atetsukeru (當附ける), *v.* to insinuate; hint *at*. —當附けたことを云ふ, to make a pointed reference *to*. —彼の言は僕に當附けたのだ, His remark was intended for me.

ateyaka (艶美な), *a.* charming; bewitching. —艶美に, charmingly; bewitchingly.

atezuiryō (當推量), *n.* a random conjecture; a random guess; a haphazard supposition.

atezuppō (當寸法), *n.* a random [rough] guess; a random speech (でまかせ). —當寸法に, by guess; at random; (at) haphazard. —當寸法を云ふ, to hazard a conjecture; talk at random (出任せ).

ato (跡, 後), *n.* ❶ (殘痕) a mark: (通ッたあと) a trace: (遺跡) site; remains: (形跡) marks; traces; vestiges. ❷ (殘餘) the remainder; the rest. ❸ (血統, 子孫, 家督) line; offspring; headship (of a family). ❹ (うしろ) the back; the rear. ❺ (結果, 將來) consequences; the future. —足の跡, =*ashiato*. —歯 (靴) の痕, print of a tooth (shoe). —十年あと, ten years ago. —後で, ① afterwards; later on. ② (何々した後で) after. —後から, ① from behind. ② (後程) later on. —後へ, ① back; backwards; astern. ② after. —後の始末をする, to settle the matter; set things right. —跡を絶つ, to come to an end. —跡を晦ます, to cover one's traces. —あとを弔ふ, ① to pray for the dead. ② (戰跡等を) to visit the site. —後を引受ける, to take up what one has left; take over a business; answer for the consequences. —後をつける, to follow (up); follow the track *of*; dog the steps *of*. —後を慕ふ, to run after; follow. —後を追ふ, to run after; follow; pursue. —叔父の後を繼ぐ, to succeed one s uncle. —後から後からと, in rapid succession; one after another. —後はどうならうと, whatever the consequences may be. —後は云はんでよい, The rest needs no telling. —それから後のことは知らぬ, I don't know what followed. —後は野となれ山となれ, "After us the deluge." ——ni, *ad.* after; behind; back; astern. —後に殘す, to leave behind. —後にする, ① (後廻) to postpone *to*; put off *till*. ② to leave behind. —後になる, to drop [fall] behind; drop [fall] astern. (後になり先になりして sometimes going before and sometimes falling behind.). —人の後について行く, to follow at another's heels.

āto (アート), *n.* art.

atoashi (後足), *n.* hind legs. —後足で立つ, to stand on hind legs; rear (馬・鳥など).

atoato (あとあと), *n.* the future; matters arising hereafter.

atobarai (後拂), *n.* after-payment; deferred payment.

atogaeri (後歸), *n.* =*atomodori.*

atogai (尾棹), *n.* a stroke-oar (漕艇の).

atogama (後釜), *n.* the successor (後繼者); the second wife (後妻). —後釜に据わる, to step into another's shoes; settle as successor (second wife).

atogetsu (後月), *n.* & *ad.* last month; ultimo (ult. と略す).

atohara (後腹), *n.* ❶ (產後痛) after-pains. ❷ (後妻の子) a child by the second wife. ❸ (出來事にいふ) the after-part.

atohiku (後引く), *v.* ❶ (永く殘る) to trail. ❷ (貪る) to long for more. ❸ (再發) to recur.

atojie (後智慧), *n.* an after-thought; after-wit; being wise after the event.

atojisari (後退する), *vi.* ❶ (背進) to step [walk] backwards; back. ❷ (尻込) to shrink back; draw back. —馬 (船) を後退さす, to back a horse (boat).

atokata (跡形), *n.* trace; vestige; evidence. —跡形もない, traceless; unfounded; baseless. —跡形もないことだ, It is quite groundless [There is no trace of truth in it].

atokin (後金), *n.* after payment (後拂); the balance (殘金).

atokuchi (後口), *n.* ❶ (後味) after-taste. ❷ (殘り分) the remainder; the rest. ❸ (申込の後れた分) a late application; later consignment.

atomawashi (後廻しにする), *vt.* to defer; put off; leave (a thing) till later on.

atome (跡目), *n.* ❶ (家督) the headship of a family. ❷ (家督相續人) the family heir. —跡目を相續する, to succeed to the headship of the family.

atomodori (後戻り), *n.* ❶ (後步) backing; backward movement. ❷ (退步) retrogression. ❸ (引返) going back. ❹ (病の) relapse. —後戻りする, ① to back. ② to retrograde. ③ to go back; retrace one's steps [way]. ④ (病氣が) to have a relapse.

atonomatsuri (後の祭), the day after the fair.

atooi (後追する), *vt.* to run after; follow.

atooshi (後押), *n.* ❶ pushing from behind (後から押すこと); backing (後援). ❷ (人) a pusher; a backer; a supporter. —後押する, ① to push (a *kuruma*). ② (後援) to back; support. ③ (煽動) to abet; egg on. —立派な後押がある, to have a fine backer. —英國と云ふ後押がある, She has England at her back.

atori (花雞), *n.* 【鳥】the brambling.

atorie (アトリエ), *n.* an atelier.

atosaki (後先), *n.* before and behind; before and after [since]; front and rear; both ends (兩端); consequences (結果). —後先の考なき, thoughtless; improvident; reckless (無鐵砲な). —後先も考へずに, without considering the consequences. —後先に巡査がついて, with policemen before and behind one. —話が後先になってる, The talk is topsy-turvy [out of order]. ¶ 後先見ず, ① (事) thoughtlessness; recklessness. ② (人) an unthinking person; a reckless person.

atoshiranami (跡白波), *n.* —跡白波と失せる, to make oneself scarce; flee no one knows where.

atoshimatsu (後始末), *n.* ❶ (處置) settlement (of an affair). ❷ (整頓) setting to rights; putting in order. —後始末する, ① to settle (an affair). ② to set [put] to rights; put [set] in order.

atotori (跡取), *n.* an heir [*fem.* heiress]; a successor; an inheritor.

atouma (後馬), *n.* a wheeler (leader の對); a wheel-horse.

atoyure (餘震), *n.* after-shocks.

atozuke (後附), *n.* (食後の) dessert; the dessert course.

atsubottai (厚ぼったい), *a.* very thick.

atsugami (厚紙), *n.* pasteboard; cardboard.

atsugaru (暑がる), *vi.* to be sensitive to heat; feel the heat; complain of the heat.

atsugeshō (厚化粧), *n.* heavy toilet.

atsugi (厚著する), *v.* to be thickly clothed.

atsui (厚い), *a.* ❶ thick. ❷ (深切, 手厚い) cordial; warm; hearty. ❸ (危篤) critical; serious. —二人は熱い仲だ, They are both very thick. —彼の病今や篤し, His illness is now worse.

atsui (熱・暑い), *a.* ❶ hot. ❷ (熱中) mad.

atsukai (扱), *n.* ❶ (待遇) treatment. ❷ (物の使用・取扱) use; handling; management. ❸ (處理) conduct; transaction. ❹ (調停) mediation; good offices; a mediator (人). —患者の扱がいい, Patients are well treated.

atsukainin (扱人), *n.* ❶ (仲裁人) a mediator. ❷ a person in charge (係り); a person who has the care *of* (世話人・監督人).

atsukamashii (厚かましい), *a.* impudent; brazen-faced. —厚かましさ, impudence. —厚かましくも...する, to have the face [cheek] *to*.

atsukau (扱ふ), *vt.* ❶ (人を) to treat. ❷ (機械・器具を) to handle; manage; use. ❸ (商品を) to deal *in*; handle. ❹ (問題・材料・事件を) to treat; handle; deal *with*. ❺ (事務を) to conduct; manage; carry on. ❻ (喧嘩を) to mediate; intervene. —扱ひ易い, handy; easy to handle; easy to deal *with*. —扱ひにくい, unwieldy; hard to handle; hard to deal *with*. —私の扱ってる機械, machinery under my care. —客を扱ふ, to treat guests. —機械を扱ふ, to manage a machine.

atsukawa (厚皮), *n.* ❶ a thick skin. ❷ (鐵面皮) a brazen face. —厚皮の, ① thick-skinned. ② brazen-faced; impudent.

atsuke (暑氣), *n.* heat fever.

atsuku (厚く), *ad.* ❶ thick(-ly). ❷ (深切に) kindly; warmly. —

厚くな(す)る, to thicken; become (make) thick. —厚くもてなす, to treat kindly. —篤く禮を云ふ, to express one's heartfelt thanks; thank heartily.

atsuku (熱·暑く), *ad.* hotly; burning. —熱くな(す)る, to heat; become (make) hot.

atsukurushii (暑苦しい), *a.* sultry; sweltering; close. —暑苦しい天氣, sultry weather; close weather.

atsumari (集), *n.* ❶ (集合) a gathering; a collection; a crowd. ❷ (會合) an assembly; a meeting.

atsumaru (集る), *vi.* ❶ (集合) to gather (together); collect; centre *upon* (集中). ❷ (會合) to meet; assemble. —集れ!, Fall [close] in! —類を以て集る, to gather in kind.

atsumeru (集める), *vt.* to collect; bring together; concentrate *upon* (集中). —額を聚める, to put (their) heads together. —材料を蒐める, to collect materials.

atsumono (羹物), *n.* soup; broth.

atsurae (誂), *n.* an order. —誂への, made to order.

atsuraemuki (誂向の), *a.* fit [suitable] *for*; just the right. —それこそ誂向だ, That is the very [just the] thing I want. —兵士には誂向に出來てる, He is cut out for a soldier. —天氣は誂向だッた, The weather was all that could be desired.

atsuraeru (誂へる), *vt.* to order. —…を…へ誂へる, to order something *from*; give an order for something *to*.

atsureki (軋轢), *n.* friction; discord (不和); collision (衝突). —軋轢する, to clash *with*; discord *with* [*from*]; jar *with*.

atsuryoku (壓力), *n.* pressure. —大氣の壓力, the atmospheric pressure. ¶ 壓力計, a pressure-gauge; a manometer.

atsusa (厚さ), *n.* thickness. —厚さ二吋の板, a board two inches thick.

atsusa (暑さ), *n.* heat; hotness. —暑さに中る; 暑さに負ける, to be affected with the heat; suffer from summer heat.

atsuyoku (壓抑する), *vt.* to repress; keep down.

atto (呀と), *int.* —呀と言はせる, to utter [give] a startled cry.

attō (壓倒する), *vt.* to overwhelm; overpower; crush. —天下を壓倒する, to overwhelm the world. —輸入品を壓倒する, to drive out imported articles. —壓倒的多數を制する, to control the overwhelming majority.

au (合ふ), *v.* ❶ (一致) to agree *with*; accord *with*; answer [correspond] *to* (符合). ❷ (適合) to fit; suit; become (似合ふ). ❸ (調和) to agree *with*; tune *with*. ❹ to be right (正しい); pay (割に合ふ). —合はぬ仕事, a work which does not pay. —ほめ合ふ, to praise each other. —調子が合ふ, to harmonize *with*; tune *with*. —見本に合ふ, to come up to the sample. —人相書に合ふ, to answer [correspond] to the description. —きちんと體に合ふ, to fit one to a nicety. —僕の時計は合ッてゐる, My watch is right. —この服はよく體に合ふ, This coat is a good fit.

au (遇ふ), *v.* ❶ 〔逢,會〕(豫期して) to meet; see (面會). ❷ 〔遭〕(不圖) to meet *with*; come *across*; chance *upon*: (經驗) experience; suffer. —亂世に遭ふ, to fall upon [be born in] a turbulent age. —災難に遭ふ, to meet with an accident; suffer a misfortune. —曲り角で友達に遇ふ; to come across [meet with] a friend at the corner. —度々火事に遭ッた, I have suffered from several fires.

auto (アウト), *n.* 【競技】 out. —競技者をアウトにする, to put out a player.

awa (粟), *n.* 【植】 the Italian millet. —肌に粟を生ずる, to make one's hair stand on end.

awa (泡), *n.* bubble; foam; froth. —泡を食ふ, to be flurried; be flustered. —泡を吹く, to foam (at the mouth); froth. (口から泡を吹いて, with a foaming mouth.) —水の泡となる, to come to naught.

awabi (石決明,鮑), *n.* 【貝】 the ear-shell; the sea-ear.

awadatsu (泡立つ), *vi.* to bubble; foam; froth. ——, *a.* bubbling; foaming; frothy.

awadatsu (粟立つ), *vi.* to make one's hair stand on end; have the goose-flesh; feel chill from cold (fear).

awai (淡い), *a.* light; pale; thin.

awaku (淡く), *ad.* lightly; palely; tastelessly.

awamori (泡盛), *n.* a spirit made from sweet potato.

aware (あはれ), *n.* ❶ 〔哀〕(悲哀) sadness; sorrow. ❷ 〔憐,憫〕(不愍) pity; compassion. —憐と思ふ, to feel pity *for*; take pity *on*. —あはれを催す, to be moved to pity.

aware (あはれ), *int.* alas.

awaremi (憐), *n.* ❶ 〔憫〕 pity; compassion; sympathy. ❷ (救恤) alms; charity. —人に憐をかける,

to treat another with compassion.

awaremu (憐む), *v.* to pity; feel pity *for*; have [take] pity on; sympathize *with*. —憐むべき, ① pitcous; pitiful; miserable. ② (可愛らしい) lovely. —貧民を恤む, to pity the poor; give alms to the poor.

awarena (哀·憐な), *a.* ❶ (哀) sad. ❷ (憫,憐) pitiful; touching. ❸ (貧弱な) poor; sorry.

awareppoi (哀れッぽい), *a.* sad; pitiful; touching. —哀れッぽく持ちかける, to try to work upon another's compassion.

awase (袷), *n.* a lined garment.

awaseme (合せ目), *n.* a joint; a seam.

awasemono (合せ物), *n.* ❶ two things joined together. ❷ (混合物) a mixture.

awaseru (合せる), **awasu** (合す), *v.* ❶ (結合) to unite; combine; match (配する). ❷ (混合, 調合) to mix. ❸ (加へる) to add; put together. ❹ (適合, 調整) to adapt; suit: tune to. ❺ (引會はす) to bring together; introduce. —三味線に合はす, to tune to the *samisen*. —手を合して, with folded hands. —力を合はす, to co-operate [unite] *with* (a person *in* ...). —色を合はす, to match colours. —に時計を合はす, to set a clock right (by ...). —帳尻を合はせる, to adjust [square] accounts. —剃刀を合はせる, to set a razor. —誰が行っても合はせない, They deny him to all callers. ——目でよいから會はしてくれ, Let me see him even for a moment. —AはBとCとを合はせた位ある, A is as large as B and C put together.

awasete (合せて), ❶ (合して) altogether; in all; put together. ❷ (つれて) to the accompaniment *of*. ❸ (に從ッて) according to. ❹ (併せて) also; and. —雛形に合せて作る, to make according to pattern.

awatadashii (惶しい), *a.* confused; flurried; agitated. —惶しく, in confusion; in a flurry; hurriedly. —惶しい人の足音, confused sounds of feet.

awatemono (狼狽者), *n.* one easily bewildered.

awateru (慌てる), *vi.* to be confused; be flurried; be bewildered. —慌てて, in confusion; in bewilderment; in a flurry. —慌てさす, to flurry; confuse. —さう慌てるな, Don't be so flurried. —餘程慌てたものと見える, He appears to have been in a great fluster.

awaya (あはや), *int.* —あはやと見る間に, while I looked on in amazement.

awayokuba (あはよくば), *ad.* if opportunity offered [served]; if it be timely.

awayuki (沫雪, 淡雪), *n.* light snow.

aya (文), *n.* ❶ (模樣, 色彩) figure; design: colour; embellishment. ❷ (區別) distinction. ❸ (仕組) a design. —彼の言には文がない, His speech is unadorned.

aya (綾), *n.* ❶ (模樣) figure; design. ❷ (織物) damask; twill. ¶ 綾絹; sarsenet; sarcenet. —綾金巾, figured [twisted] shirtings.

ayabumu (危ぶむ), *vt.* to apprehend; fear; be afraid *of*; doubt (疑ふ). —前途を危ぶむ, to be apprehensive of the future.

ayadoru (操る), *vt.* =***ayanasu***, ***ayatsuru***.

ayafuya (あやふやの), *a.* vague; ambiguous.

ayakarimono (肖者), *n.* a lucky person.

ayakaru (肖る), *vt.* to resemble; take after.

ayamachi (過), *n.* ❶ (過失) a fault; an error; a mistake. ❷ (不慮の災難) an accident; a mishap. —過の功名, an accidental achievement; a lucky mistake. —過を悛める (再びする), to correct (repeat) one's error. —過を悔いる (謝する), to regret (apologize for) a fault.

ayamari (謬), *n.* a mistake; an error; a fault (過失). —謬を正す, to correct an error.

ayamari (謝罪, 詫), *n.* an apology. ¶ 謝罪狀; 謝罪證文, a letter of apology; a written apology.

ayamaru (誤る), *v.* ❶ to make a mistake; commit [make] an error; err. ❷ (誤をさす) to mislead; misguide; lead astray. —誤ることなき, unerring; unfailing. —讀み誤る, to make a mistake in reading; misread. —身を誤る, to make a slip (女が); go astray; ruin [wreck] oneself. —道を誤る, to take the wrong road. —處置を誤る, to mismanage [misconduct] the affair. —法の解釋を誤る, to misconstrue the law. —外國人と誤られる, to be mistaken for a foreigner. —過ッて改むるに憚る勿れ, Do not hesitate to correct your error.

ayamaru (謝·詫る), *v.* to apologize; beg (another's) pardon; express one's regret.

ayamatsu (過つ), *v.* to commit [make] a fault [a mistake; an error]; err; slip. —君の方が過ッて居る,

You are in the wrong.

ayamatta (誤·過ッた), *a.* wrong; incorrect; mistaken.

ayamatte (誤·過ッて), *ad.* by mistake (間違へて); by accident (過失で). —過ッて人を殺す, to kill a person by accident. —過ッて人の部屋に入る, to enter another's room by mistake.

ayame (菖蒲), *n.* 【植】the sweet-flag. —六日の菖蒲十日の菊, the day after the fair.

ayame (文目), *n.* ❶ (模樣) figures; stripes; form. ❷ (區別, 條理) distinction; reason.

ayanasu (操す), *vt.* ❶ (操る) to play *upon*; make a puppet *of*. ❷ (修飾) to embellish. —人をいい加減に操す, to play upon a man as one pleases.

ayaori (綾織), *n.* twill (綾羅紗); figured cloth; damask.

ayashibi (怪火), *n.* Jack-o'-lantern (鬼火); incendiarism (放火).

ayashige (怪しげな), *a.* suspicious-looking; doubtful-looking; questionable. —怪しげな家, a suspicious-looking house; a house of suspicious character.

ayashii (怪しい), *a.* ❶ (不思議, 奇怪) wonderful; unaccountable. ❷ (異常, 異例) unearthly; weird; strange. ❸ (疑はしい, 信じ難い) doubtful; incredible. ❹ (賤しい, 胡散な) suspicious. —怪しい空模樣, a doubtful appearance of the sky. —怪しい外國船, a strange foreign vessel.

ayashimi (怪み), *n.* suspicion; doubt; wonder (不思議がること).

ayashimu (怪·異む), *vt.* ❶(不思議がる) to wonder [marvel] *at*; wonder [marvel] (if, how, why, etc.). ❷ (疑ふ) to suspect; doubt. —警官に怪まれる, to be suspected by the police. —彼の成功は怪むに足らぬ, His success is not to be wondered at.

ayasu (あやす), *vt.* to amuse; dance (膝の上で踊らして); dandle (同上).

ayatori (綾取), *n.* (遊戯) cat's-cradle. —綾取する, to play at cat's-cradle.

ayatsuri (操り), *n.* ❶【劇】a puppet-show; a puppet-play. ❷ (操機) working puppet. ¶ 操人形, a puppet; a marionette.

ayatsuru (操る), *vt.* ❶ (人形を) to move; work. ❷ (機械·船·櫓等を) to manage; handle; work. ❸(人を) to make a puppet *of*; manipulate. —船を操る, to manage a ship. —綠を操る; 陰で人を操る, to pull the strings [wires]. —人形を操る, to move [work] a puppet; pull the wires [strings]. —櫓を操る, to handle an oar; row [work at] an oar.

ayaui (危い), *a.* **ayauku** (危く), *ad.* =*abunai* (危い), ***abunaku*** (危く).

ayu (鮎, 香魚), *n.* 【魚】 Plecoglossus altivelis (學名).

ayu (阿諛), *n.* flattery; adulation; sycophancy. —阿諛する, to flatter; adulate; truckle. ¶ 阿諛者, a flatterer; a sycophant.

ayumi (歩), *n.* ❶ walking; stepping: pace; step. ❷=***ayumiita*** (歩板). —牛の歩 (で), (at) a slow pace; (at) a snail's pace. —歩がのろい, to have leaden feet; be slow of foot.

ayumiau (歩合ふ), *v.* =***aibiau*** (歩合ふ).

ayumiita (歩板), *n.* a plank for stepping over; 【航】a gang-plank.

ayumu (歩む), *v.* to walk. ☞ ***aruku*** (歩く).

aza (痣), *n.* ❶ a birth-mark; a macula [*pl.* -læ]. ❷ (紫斑) a bruise; a discolouration. —打たれて痣になる, to be discoloured by a blow. —打たれて紫斑だらけになる, to be beaten black and blue.

azakeri (嘲), *n.* ridicule; scorn; derision. —嘲りの喝采, derisive cheers. —世の嘲りを受ける, to be scorned by the world.

azakeru (嘲る), *v.* to deride; ridicule; scoff *at*.

azami (薊), *n.* 【植】the thistle.

azamuku (欺く), *v.* ❶ (だます) to deceive; dupe; impose upon. ❷ (と見違へる, と競ふ) to be taken for; be as...as; rival. —雪を欺く肌, a skin as white as snow.

azana (字), *n.* ❶ (字) a common name. ❷ (綽名) a nickname.

azanau (糾ふ), *vt.* to twist.

azarashi (海豹), *n.* 【動】 the (common) seal. —海豹漁業, seal-fishery.

azawarai (嘲笑), *n.* ridicule; derision; mockery.

azawarau (嗤ふ), *v.* to ridicule; deride; mock *at*.

azayaka (鮮な), *a.* fresh (記憶など); clear (印刷·手蹟など); bright (色·花など). **——-ni,** *ad.* clearly; brightly. —鮮に晴れた天氣, a fine [bright; clear] weather.

aze (畔), **azemichi** (畔道), *n.* a ridge between rice-fields; a foot-path between rice-fields.

azen (啞然として), *ad.* dumbfounded. —啞然たらしめる, to dumbfound; strike dumb.

azoku (亞族), *n.* a subfamily; a subtribe.

azoku (亞屬), *n.* 【生物】a sub-genus.

azuchi(射垜), *n.* a target-mound; a butt.

azukari (預り), *n.* taking charge *of*; receiving in charge. ¶ 預り金, a deposit; money received in charge. —預り物, a thing received in charge; a thing under one's care; a deposit; a charge. —預り人, a depositary; a trustee. —預り證, a deposit receipt. —預證券, a warehouse receipt.

azukaru (預る), *v.* ❶ (受託) to take charge *of*; take in charge; be entrusted *with*. ❷ (享受) to be favoured *with*; enjoy. —御贔屓に預る, to enjoy patronage [favour]. —娘を預る, to take charge of his daughter. —…を預ッて居る, to have charge *of*; have custody *of*; be in charge *of*.

azukaru (與る), *v.* ❶ (參與, 關係) to take part *in*; participate *in*; be concerned *in*. ❷ (享ける) to partake of (饗應に); share *in* (恩惠·利益等に). —計畫に與る, to participate in the plan. —その相談に與る, to be consulted in it. —利益の分配に與る, to share the profits. —僕の與り知る所でない, That is none of my business.

azukekin (預け金), *n.* deposit (money). ☞ *yokin* (預金).

azukemono (預け物), *n.* a deposit; a charge; a thing given in charge.

azukenin (預け人), *n.* a depositor.

azukeru (預ける), *v.* to deposit; give charge *of*; give in charge. —に預けてある, to be in the custody *of*. —人に金を預ける, to entrust [trust] a person with one's money; entrust one's money to a person. —金を銀行へ預ける, to deposit money in a bank. —荷物を倉庫會社へ預ける, to deposit goods with a warehouse company.

azuki (赤小豆), *n.* 【植】the hairy-podded kidney-bean; the red [Indian] bean. ¶ 赤小豆色, russet.

azuma (東國), *n.* the Eastern provinces.

azuma-kōto (東コート), *n.* a lady's overcoat.

azumaya (四阿), *n.* a summer-house: an arbour; a bower.

azusa(梓), *n.* 【植】the catalpa.

B

ba (ば), ❶ (假定又は條件の意) if. ❷ (接續の用をなす) and. —すればする程, the more..., the more .... (考へれば考へる程むづかしい, The more I think, the more difficult it is.) —買はないのならば賣らない, If you won't buy, I won't sell.

ba (場), *n.* ❶ (場所), a place; a seat (席); room (空所); space (同上). ☞ *basho* (場所). ❷=*baai* (場合). ❸【劇】(場面) a scene. —其場で, on the spot. —場に出す, ① to play (骨牌札を); turn up (切札を). ② (取引所) to bring [report] to the House (註文を). —場を塞ぐ, to take up space. —いい場を取ッて置く, to take [reserve] a good seat; book a good seat (劇場で).

bā (バー), *n.* ❶ (酒場) a bar. ❷ (簡易飲食店) a coffee-house; a cheap eating-house. ☞ *sakaba* (酒場). —バーの給仕女, a barmaid; a waitress.

baai (場合), *n.* ❶ (折) a case; an occasion. ❷ (事態) a situation; an event; circumstances (事情). —場合により, as the case may be. —場合によっては, according to circumstances. —…の場合には, when; in case (*of*); in the event *of*. —場合が場合だから, the circumstances being what they are. —どんな場合も…せぬ, in [under] no circumstances; in no case. —如何なる場合に於ても, in all circumstances; in any case whatever.

baatari (場當り), *n.* 【劇】a gag; a stage effect. —場當りをやる, to play to the gallery.

baba (婆), *n.* ❶ (老婆) an old woman. ❷(祖母) a grandmother; a grandmamma, grandma; a granny (おばあさん).

baba (馬場), *n.* a riding-ground; a riding-course; a race-course.

babiso (馬鼻疽), *n.* glanders.

bachi (罰), *n.* retribution; divine punishment (神罰). —罰があたる, to incur a curse; suffer punishment. —罰をあてる, to curse; inflict a punishment. ¶ 罰當り, ① curse. ② (人) an accursed man. (此の罰當り奴(め), Damn you!)

bachi (撥), *n.* ❶(撥) (三味線·琵琶等の) a plectrum. ❷(桴) (太鼓の) a drum-stick.

bachirusu(バチルス), *n.* a bacillus [*pl.* -li].

bafun (馬糞), *n.* horse-dung. ¶ 馬糞紙, strawboard; millboard.

bāgen-dē (廉賣日), *n.* a bargain-day.

bagu (馬具), *n.* horse-gear; harness; trappings (裝飾). —馬具を

附ける, to harness. —馬具を解く, to unharness. ¶ 馬具屋, a saddler.
bahifū (馬脾風), *n.* 【醫】 diphtheria; croupous [diphtheric] laryngitis.
bahitsu (馬匹), *n.* horses. ¶ 馬匹共進會, a horse-show.
bai(海贏), *n.* 【貝】 the ivory-shell.
bai (倍), ❶ (二倍) double; twice; again. ❷ (何倍) times; -fold. —二倍にする《になる》, to double. **—-no,** *a.* ❶ double. ❷ -fold. —十倍の, tenfold. —倍の大きさ, double the size. —二百倍のレンズ, a lens magnifying 200 times.
baiai (奪合), *n.* scramble. —場所を奪合ふ, to scramble for a place.
baibai (賣買), *n.* sale; sale and purchase; trade; business; traffic. —賣買を取り極める, to close [strike] a bargain. —賣買する, [*vt.*] to sell and purchase; sell; deal *in*. ¶ 賣買契約, a bargain; a sale-contract; the contract of sale. —賣買總額, a turn-over; the proceeds (of sale). —賣買約定高, the amount of sales contracted.
baiboku (賣卜), *n.* fortune-telling; divination. ¶ 賣卜者, a fortune-teller; a diviner.
baibun (賣文), *n.* hack-work; literary work done by contract. —賣文する, to write by contract [at a special rate of charge]. ¶ 賣文業者, a hack; a ghost; a hodman.
Baiburu(バイブル), *n.* the Bible; the Scripture(-s).
baidai (倍大の), *a.* double. —新年の倍大號, the New Year's double-number.
baidoku (黴毒), *n.* 【醫】 syphilis. —黴毒性の, syphilitic. ¶ 黴毒病院, a lock-hospital.
baien(煤煙), *n.* soot; lampblack; smoke-black.
baigō (媒合する), *vi.* to pander; pimp.
baihin (陪賓), *n.* a guest invited with [to meet] the guest of honour.
baihin (賣品), *n.* an article for sale. —賣品として提供する, to offer for sale.
baijō (陪乗する), *v.* to attend on ...in the same carriage.
baijū (陪從), *n.* attendance. —陪從する, to attend (*on* [*upon*]); wait *upon*. ¶ 陪從者, an attendant; suite (集合).
baika (梅花), *n* a plum-blossom.
baika (賣價), *n.* the sale-price.
baikai (媒介), *n.* ❶ (仲介) agency; medium. ❷ (媒妁) match-making; acting as go-between. —媒介する, to mediate; act as a medium. ¶ 媒介物, a medium; an instrument; a vehicle. —媒介者, a go-between; a middleman; an agent.
baikan(陪觀), *n.* sight-seeing with a superior. —陪觀する, to go sight-seeing with a superior. (陸軍大演習を陪觀する, to attend the grand military manœuvres in the Imperial train.)
baikin (黴菌), *n.* a bacterium [*pl.* -ria]; a bacillus [*pl.* -li].
baikoku (賣國的), *a.* traitorous. ¶ 賣國奴, a traitor(to his country); a betrayer of his country.
baikyaku (賣却), *n.* sale; disposal (by sale). —賣却する, to sell; dispose *of*. ¶ 賣却代金, sale-price.
baikyū (倍舊の), *a.* twice the former quantity; more than before.
baimashi (倍增する), *vt.* to double; redouble. —賃錢を倍增しする, to double the fare; charge double the fare.
baimei (賣名), *n.* striving for publicity. —賣名の徒, men who strive to gain publicity.
baion (陪音), *n.* 【音】 overtone; harmonic.
baiorin(ヴァイオリン), *n.* a violin; a fiddle.
bairin (梅林), *n.* a plum-orchard.
bairitsu (倍率), *n.* 【理】 magnification; magnifying power.
baisei (陪星), *n.* 【天】 a satellite.
baiseki (陪席する), *vi.* to attend [be present at] as an assistant. ¶ 陪席判事, an associate judge; an assessor.
baisenzai (媒染劑), *n.* a mordant.
baishaku (媒妁), *n.* acting as go-between; making a match; match-making. —媒妁する, to act as go-between; make a match *between*. ¶ 媒妁人, a match-maker; a go-between.
baishin (陪臣), *n.* a rear vassal; a vavasour.
baishin (陪審), *n.* a jury; trial by jury (陪審裁判). ¶ 起訴陪審(官), 大陪審(官), a grand jury; a grand juror (員). —陪審長, the foreman of the jury. —陪審員, a juror; a juryman. —陪審(官)席, the jury-box. —陪審制度, the jury system.
baishō (賠償), *n.* compensation; indemnification; reparation. —賠償する, to indemnify (損害·費用等を); compensate; make reparation *for*. ¶ 賠償金, (*a*) a compensation: (*b*) 【法】 an indemnity; damages.
baishoku (陪食する), *v.* to eat with a superior.
baishū (買收する), *vt.* ❶ to buy; buy over. ❷ to bribe; buy off; corrupt. —土地を買收する, to

purchase land. —議員を買收する, to buy off the members.

baisū (倍數), *n.* a double; a multiple.

bai-suru (倍する), *v.* to double; multiply. —二を倍すれば四となる, Twice two makes four.

bai-suru (陪する), *v.* to attend; wait *on*; escort. —乘輿に陪する, to escort the Imperial car.

baitai (媒體), *n.* 【生·化】a mediator; a medium.

baiten (賣店), *n.* a shop; a stand (勸工場等の); a store 〖重に米〗. —博覽會へ賣店を出す, to set a stand at the Exhibition.

baitokukin (賣得金), *n.* the proceeds (of a sale).

baiu (梅雨), *n.* ❶ the rain (of the rainy season). ❷ (時季) the rainy season. —鬱陶しい梅雨, the gloomy rainy season. —梅雨が明ける《に入る》, The rainy season comes to an end 《sets in》.

baiyaku (賣約), *n.* a contract of sale. —賣約をする, to bargain. ¶ 賣約濟, "Sold."

baiyaku (賣藥), *n.* a patent [proprietary] medicine. —賣藥的廣告, a puff; an advertisement like that of a patent medicine.

baiyō (培養), *n.* culture; cultivation. —葡萄を培養する, to grow [cultivate] grapes.

baji-tōfū (馬耳東風), utter indifference; perfect nonchalance. —馬耳東風に, like water off a duck's back. (人の言を馬耳東風に付する, to treat a person's words with utter indifference).

bajō (馬上で), *ad.* on horseback. ¶ 馬上像, an equestrian statue.

bajū (馬銃), *n.* a carabine.

bajutsu (馬術), *n.* horsemanship; equestrianism. ¶ 馬術家 [師], an equestrian; the master of horsemanship. —馬術敎師, a riding-master.

baka (馬鹿, 莫迦), *n.* ❶ (人) a fool; a blockhead; a dunce. ❷ (事) foolishness; silliness; nonsense (たはけた言ひごと又仕打). —馬鹿な, foolish; stupid (間抜けの); absurd; silly. —馬鹿に, awfully 〖俗〗; devilish 〖俗〗; extra 〖俗〗; extremely. —馬鹿げきった, preposterous; utterly absurd. —馬鹿云へ, Nonsense! —馬鹿野郎!, Fool! ; Idiot! ; Stupid! —馬鹿にする, to make a fool *of*; dupe; play *upon* [*on*]; make light *of* (輕視する). —馬鹿の大連れ, "Fools go in throngs." —馬鹿につける藥なし, "Who is born a fool is never cured." —彼奴と一緒に行って馬鹿を見た, I was a fool to have gone with that fellow. ¶ 馬鹿話, flummery; trash; a silly talk. —馬鹿强情, pig-headedness. —馬鹿力, enormous strength. (馬鹿力を出す, to put forth all one's strength; strain oneself to the utmost.) —馬鹿眞似, foolery; tomfoolery; buffoonery. —馬鹿騷ぎ, uproar; hubbub; racket; high jinks. (馬鹿騷ぎをする, to paint the town red 〖米·俗〗; raise Cain 〖卑〗.) —馬鹿正直, strict [stubborn] honesty.

bakabakashii (馬鹿馬鹿しい), *a.* stupid; ridiculous; absurd.

bakagai (馬鹿貝, 痴蛤), *n.* 【貝】 the trough-shell.

bakari (ばかり), ❶ (程度) about; or so. ❷ (のみ) only; alone. ❸ (やっと) just (now). —三十人許りの人, about [some] thirty persons. —と云はぬばかり, as much as to say; as if to say. —家の内にばかり居る, to remain always indoors. —骨と皮ばかりだ, He is all skin and bones. —今來たばかりだ, He has just come. —十分ばかり待って下さい, Please wait just ten minutes. —勉强ばかりして少しも遊ばぬ, It is all work and no play with him.

bakasu (魅す), *vt.* ❶ (迷はす) to bewitch; enchant; fascinate. ❷ (たばかる) to delude; befool. —人を魅す, to bewitch men. —女に魅される, to be fascinated by a woman.

bakazu (場數), *n.* the number of places; experience. —場數を履む, to gain experience.

bakemono (化物), *n.* ❶ (妖怪, 幽靈) a ghost; a spectre; a bogy. ❷ (顏·姿の怪物然たる人) a fright; a guy; a scarecrow. ¶ 化物屋敷, a haunted house.

baken (馬券), *n.* a pari-mutuel ticket.

bakenokawa (化の皮), *n.* pretence; disguise. —化の皮を露す, to give the show away; show the cloven foot.

bakeru (化ける), *v.* to assume [take] the form *of*; change [transform] itself *into*. —美人に化ける, to change itself into a beautiful woman. —羊羹色に化ける, to fade into a dark brown.

baketsu (バケツ), *n.* a bucket.

bakken (拔劍), *n.* a drawn sword. —拔劍する, to draw the sword.

bakkin (罰金), *n.* a fine; a penalty; a forfeit, forfeiture. —罰金に處する to fine; mulct. —罰金を出し給へ, Pay your forfeit.

bakko (跋扈), *n.* rampancy; domination. —閥族の跋扈, the domination of clannism. —跋扈する,

to be rampant; dominate.
baku (貘), *n.* 【哺乳】the tapir.
baku (縛), *n.* arrest. —縛に就く, to be arrested.
bakuchi (博打), *n.* gambling; gaming. —博打に負ける, to lose in gambling. —博打する; 賭博を打つ, to gamble; game; play. (大賭博を打つ, to play for heavy [high] stakes.) ¶ 博打場, a gambling place; a gambling-hell [-den]. —賭博打, a gambler; a gamester.
bakuchiku (爆竹), *n.* a (fire-) cracker; a squib.
bakuchin (爆沈), *n.* blowing up; sinking by explosion. —爆沈する, to blow up.
bakudai (莫大な), *a.* immense; huge; enormous.
bakudan (爆彈), *n.* a bomb. —爆彈を投ずる, to throw a bomb *at*; drop a bomb *on* (投下). ¶ 爆彈襲擊, a bombing-raid.
bakuden (幕電), *n.* sheet lightning.
bakufu (幕府), *n.* feudal government; the shogunate. —德川幕府時代に, under [during] the shogunate of Tokugawa.
bakufu (瀑布), *n.* a waterfall; a fall; a cataract.
bakuga (麥芽), *n.* malt.
bakugeki (莫逆の), *a.* very intimate; on cordial [intimate] terms. —莫逆の友, a bosom friend.
bakugeki (駁擊), *n.* attack (攻擊); refutation (駁論). —駁擊する, to attack; controvert; refute.
bakugeki (爆擊する), *vt.* to bomb (特に空中より). ¶ 爆擊(用飛行)機, a bomber.
bakuha (爆破する), *vt.* to explode; blast; blow up; destroy by explosion.
bakuhatsu (爆發), *n.* explosion; burst; detonation. —爆發する, ① [*vt.*] to explode; blast; blow up. ② [*vi.*] to explode; burst. ¶ 爆發物, an explosive. —爆發藥, fulminate; fulgurite.
bakumatsu (幕末), *n.* the end [last days] of the feudal government [shogunate].
bakuon (爆音), *n.* explosion.
bakuretsu (爆裂), *n.* detonation explosion. —爆裂する, to burst; explode; blow up. —ダイナマイトで巖石を爆裂さす, to blast rocks with dynamite. ¶ 爆裂彈, a bomb; a bomb-shell.
bakuro (暴露), *n.* ❶ (曝晒) exposure. ❷ (露顯) disclosure; divulgation. **——-suru,** ❶ [*vi.*] to be exposed; come to light. ❷ [*vt.*] to disclose; expose; bring to light. —風雨に暴露する, to expose to wind and rain. —醜態を暴露する, to disclose its disgraceful condition. —內部の腐敗を暴露する, to expose the internal corruption.
bakurō (博勞, 伯樂), *n.* a horse-coper; a horse-dealer.
bakuron (駁論), *n.* retort; refutation. —駁論する, to refute; retort; rebut.
bakuryō (幕僚), *n.* ❶ the staff; a staff-officer. ❷ (股肱) a right-hand man.
bakusei (爆聲), *n.* report; crackle; crack. —爆聲を發する, to crack; crackle.
bakushin (驀進する), *vi.* to rush; plunge; dash forward.
bakusho (曝書), *n.* airing of books.
baku-suru (駁する), *vt.* to attack; assail. —他人の說を駁する, to attack other's views.
baku-suru (縛する), *vt.* to bind; arrest; apprehend. ☞ ***hobaku*** (捕縛する). —强盜を縛する, to arrest an armed burglar.
baku-taru (漠たる), *a.* ❶ (廣漠) wide; extensive; vast. ❷ (空漠) vague; indefinite; ambiguous.
bakuteria (バクテリア), *n.* a bacterium [*pl.* -ria].
bakuto (博徒), *n.* a gambler.
baku-to (漠と), *ad.* =***bakuzen.***
bakuyaku (爆藥), *n.* an explosive; blasting-powder.
bakuzen (漠然), *ad.* vaguely; ambiguously; indefinitely. **——-taru,** *a.* vague; indefinite; ambiguous. —漠然たる記憶, dim memory. —漠然たる證言, ambiguous testimony.
bakyaku (馬脚を露はす), *v.* to show the cloven foot.
bamen (場面), *n.* a scene.
ban (判), *n.* size.
ban (晚), *n.* evening (夕); night (夜).
ban (番), *n.* ❶ (番號) number. ❷ (順番) turn; order. ❸ (見張) guard; watch. ❹ (回) a time; a round; a bout. —番をする, to watch; keep watch *over*; keep [stand] guard *over*.
ban (萬), *ad.* most likely; very probably. —萬已むを得ざる場合は, in an unavoidable case.
ban (鷭, 田鷄), *n.* 【鳥】the moorhen; the waterhen.
banana (バナナ), *n.* 【植】the banana (木叉實); the plantain-tree.
banareta (場馴れた), *a.* experienced; veteran.
banban (萬萬), *ad.* ❶ certainly; surely; very well. ❷ (打消の場合) by no means; never.
banbutsu (萬物), *n.* the creation; all things; nature. —萬物の靈長,

the lord of the creation.
bancha (番茶), *n.* coarse tea.
banchi (番地), *n.* (house) number. —本郷區西片町十番地ロ三號, No. 10, B 3, Nishikatamachi, Hongō-ku.
banchi (蕃地), *n.* the aborigines' land.
bandai (番臺), *n.* the watch-stand.
bandai (萬代), *n.* eternity; all ages. ☞ *bansei.*
bando (礬土), *n.* 【化】alumina.
bane (彈機), *n.* a spring. —彈機仕掛けの, worked by a spring; spring- (例へば spring-mattress); snap- (例へば snap-hook).
bangai (番外), *n.* & *a.* extra. —番外である, ①(普通でない) to be out of the ordinary. ②(競技等で) to be nowhere; come in nowhere.
bangata (晩方), *ad.* towards evening; in the evening.
bangō (番號), *n.* a number. —番號,(號令) Number! —番號をつける, to number.
bangoya (番小屋), *n.* a gate-house; a watch-box.
bangumi (番組), *n.* a program; a card.
bangusai (萬愚祭), *n.* (四月一日) All Fools' Day.
bañi (蠻夷), *n.* a savage; a barbarian; a vandal.
bañichi (萬一), *ad.* by any chance. —萬一に備へる, to prepare against accidents. —萬一を慮って, for fear of the worst. —萬一の場合には, if the worst comes to the worst. —萬一火事でもあったら, if a fire breaks out by any chance.
baniku (馬肉), *n.* horse-flesh.
banjaku (磐石), *n.* a rock. —磐石のやうに堅固である, to be firm as a rock.
banji (萬事), *n.* everything; all; all things. ——, *ad.* all; in everything; in all things. —萬事を放擲して, throwing away [setting aside] everything.
banjin (蕃人), *n.* a savage; a barbarian; aborigines.
banjō (盤狀の), *a.* discoid(-al).
banka (挽歌), *n.* a dead-march; a dirge; a requiem.
bankai (挽回), *n.* recovery; revival; retrieval. —挽回する, to revive; retrieve. —挽回し難い, to be beyond [past] retrieve.
bankara (蠻カラ), *n.* an unfashionable person; one indifferent to personal appearance (social conventions).
banken (番犬), *n.* a watch-dog; a house-dog.
banki (萬機), *n.* all state affairs. —萬機公論に決する, to discuss and decide publicly upon all affairs of state.
bankin (輓近), *n.* recent times. —輓近の, recent.
bankō (蠻行), *n.* (an act of) barbarity; vandalism.
bankoku (萬國), *n.* the world; all nations [countries]. —萬國共通の, international; universal. ¶ 萬國平和會議, an international peace conference. —萬國郵便聯合, the Universal Postal Union. —萬國聯合郵便葉書, a universal postcard.
bankon (晩婚), *n.* a late marriage.
bankuruwase (番狂はせ), *n.* ❶(不順番) putting out of order; disarranging. ❷(期待外なること) being contrary to expectation; upsetting one's calculation. —番狂はせの勝負, a match [game] which upsets their calculation. —飛んだ番狂はせをする, to put them terribly out of order; disarrange things fearfully.
banmeshi (晩飯), *n.* a supper; the evening meal. —晩飯を食ふ, to have supper; sup. —晩飯に間に合ふやうにする, to get home (have a thing made) in time for supper.
banmin (萬民), *n.* the whole nation; all (the) people.
bannan (萬難), *n.* innumerable difficulties. —萬難を排して, through fire and water.
bannen (晩年), *n.* the decline of life; last [closing] years; the close (of life).
bannin (番人), *n.* a watchman (見廻り人); a watcher (見張り人); a keeper (守人).
bannin (萬人), *n.* all people; all men; all. —天下萬人の視る所, the cynosure of the whole nation.
bannō (萬能), *n.* omnipotence. —萬能の, omnipotent; almighty; all-powerful. (萬能の神, the Almighty (God). —萬能の金, the almighty dollar [gold].)
banpan (萬般の), *a.* all. —萬般の準備, all preparations.
banpei (番兵), *n.* a guard; sentinel; a sentry. —番兵の勤務をして, on guard duty. —番兵を置く, to post a guard.
banpuku (萬福), *n.* all happiness; all blessings.
banri (萬里), *n.* ten thousand … a long distance. —萬里の長… the Great Wall of China.
banryoku (萬綠), *n.* a myr… green leaves; universal verdure. 萬綠叢中紅一點, one red strea… the vast green foliage.
bansan (晩餐), *n.* a dinner.

sword.

baute (場打), *n.* stage-fright.

bāya (婆や), *n.* ❶ (老女) an old woman. ❷ (乳母) a (wet) nurse; an amah.

bazā (慈善市), *n.* a bazaar.

bazoku (馬賊), *n.* the mounted bandits; the Chunchuses.

bechabecha (べちゃべちゃ), *n.* prattle; tattle; gibber. ——, *ad.* tattlingly. —ベチャベチャ喋る, to prattle; tattle; gibber.

beika (米貨), *n.* ❶ American currency; an American coin. ❷ American goods.

beika (米價), *n.* the price of rice. —米價を調節する, to regulate the price of rice.

Beikoku (米國), *n.* America. —米國化する, to Americanize. ¶ 米國風, Americanism. —米國人, an American; a Yankee. —米國國旗, the American [star-spangled] flag; the stars and stripes. —米國政府, the United States [American] Government; Uncle Sam.

beikoku (米穀), *n.* rice; cereals. ¶ 米穀問屋組合, the rice-merchants' association. —米穀取引所, the rice exchange. [a rice-dealer.]

beishō (米商), *n.* a rice-merchant;

beishoku (米食), *n.* feeding on rice; rice-eating. —米食する, to eat rice; feed on rice.

beiton (米噸), *n.* the short ton (二千封度, 我が二百四十二貫弱).

bekarazu (べからず), *v. aux.* ❶ (不可) must not; shall not; should not; do not (命令). ❷ (不可能) cannot. —境内の樹木を折るべからず, The trees in the grounds must not be broken.

bekkakkō (眼元興), "Wouldn't you like it?"; 'Catch me!'

bekkaku (別格の), *a.* special. ¶ 別格官幣大社, a special government shrine.

bekke (別家), *n.* a branch house; a cadet family. —別家する, to found a branch house.

bekken (瞥見する), *vt.* to catch a glimpse *of*; glance *at*; have [take] a glance *at*.

bekko (別戶), *n.* =*bekke* (別家). —別戶を構へる, to keep (a) house independently [separately].

bekko (別個の), *a.* different; another. —それは別個の問題である, That is another question.

bekkō (別項), *n.* a separate paragraph; another section [clause]. —別項記載の如く, as mentioned [stated] in a separate [another] clause [section].

bekkō (鼈甲), *n.* tortoise-shell. ¶ 鼈甲の櫛, a tortoise-shell comb.

bekkyo (別居), *n.* living in a separate house; living separately *from*; 【法】judicial separation. —別居する, to separate from one's husband (wife); live separately.

ben (便), *n.* ❶ (便利) convenience; facilities. ❷ (糞便) excreta; dejecta; fæces. —互の便を計る, to consult mutual convenience. —多大の便を得る, to obtain very great facilities. **—— - nisuru,** *vt.* to facilitate; make convenient. —交通を便にする, to facilitate communication.

ben (瓣), *n.* a petal (花瓣); a valve (機械の); a ventil (樂器の).

ben (辯), *n.* speech; tongue (口舌); eloquence (能辯). —辯に任せて, setting loose his tongue. —辯が旨い, to have a fluent [glib] tongue.

benbaku (辯駁), *n.* refutation; confutation; 【法】rejoinder. —辯駁する, to refute; confute; rejoin. —辯駁書を送る, to send a letter of refutation.

benben (便便と), *ad.* idly. —便々と日を送る, to pass one's days in idleness. **—— - taru,** *a.* ① (肥滿) huge; protruding; bulging. ② idle; slow; dilatory. —便々たる腹, a huge paunch; a pot-belly.

benbetsu (辨別), *n.* discrimination (識別); discretion (分別). **—— - suru,** *vt.* to discriminate (*between*; A *from* B); distinguish *between*; A *from* B); tell (A *from* B). —理非を辨別する, to discriminate between reason and unreason.

benbu (抃舞する), *vi.* to leap with joy; jump for joy.

benchara (辯茶羅), *n.* flattery; honeyed words; blarny; soft sawder.

benchi (腰掛), *n.* a bench. ¶ 共同ベンチ, a public bench.

benchū (鞭蟲), *n.* 【蟲】the threadworm; the whipworm.

benden (便殿), *n.* an Imperial resting-room. [inguinal adenitis.]

bendoku (便毒), *n.* 【醫】bubo;

beneki (便益), *n.* convenience (便宜); advantage (利益); benefit (同上). —相互の便益を謀る, to consult mutual convenience.

bengaku (勉學), *n.* (diligent) study. —勉學の爲め東京に遊ぶ, to stay in Tōkyō for study.

bengi (便宜), *n.* convenience; expediency; facility. —便宜の爲め; 便宜上, for convenience' sake. —自己の便宜上より, from personal convenience. —便宜の處置を

執る, to take expedient measures. —便宜を計る, to consult a person's convenience. —便宜を與へる, to give [afford] facilities *for*.

bengo (辯護), *n.* advocacy; defence; plea. **—— -suru,** *vt.* to advocate; plead; defend. —被告の爲に辯護する, to defend the accused; plead for the accused. —人を辯護する, to defend [plead for] a person. ¶ 辯護人, a counsel (for the defence). —辯護者, a defender; an advocate.

bengoshi (辯護士), *n.* a lawyer. ❶ [英] (*a*) (上級) a counsel (a barrister; an advocate 之に入り, 英蘭の barrister は蘇格蘭では advocate と稱す): (*b*) (下級) an attorney(-at-law); a solicitor. ❷ [米] a counsel; a counsellor; an attorney (-at-law). —辯護士に鑑定さす, to take legal [counsel's] advice. —辯護士に依頼する, to take one's case to an advocate. —辯護士を業とする, to practise law. —(高等)辯護士の免許を受ける, to be called to the bar. ¶ 辯護士協會, the bar association.

beni (紅), *n.* ❶ rouge. ❷ (色) deep-red; crimson.

benigara (紅殼), *n.* rouge; red ochre.

benihiwa (紅鶸), *n.* 【鳥】 the mealy redpoll.

benimasu (紅鱒), *n.* 【魚】 the blue-back [sawqui] salmon.

benisashi (べにさし), *n.* 【魚】 the goat-fish.

benjo (便所), *n.* a water-closet [W.C.]; a privy; a latrine (學校·病院等の公衆便所). —便所に行く, to go to stool; go to wash one's hands. ¶ 共同便所, a public latrine.

benkai (辯解), *n.* vindication; explanation; excuse. —辯解する, to vindicate; explain; excuse. —辯解の餘地がない[が立たない], to admit of no excuse. ¶ 辯解者, an apologist; a pleader; a vindicator.

benkeijima (辨慶縞), *n.* checks; chequers; checkers. —辨慶縞の服地, chequered cloth.

benki (便器), *n.* a chamber(-pot); a commode.

benkyō (勉强), *n.* ❶ (勉學) study. ❷ (勉勵) diligence; industry. ❸ [俗·商] (割引) reduction. —勉强な, studious; sedulous; diligent. —試驗前の俄か勉强, cramming for examination. **—— -suru,** *v.* ❶ to study. ❷ to reduce. —學課を勉强する, to do one's lessons. ¶ 勉强家, a studious person; a hard student [worker]. —勉强室, a study.

benmaku (瓣膜), *n.* 【解·動】 the valve; the valvula [*pl.* -læ] (小瓣); the valves of the heart.

benmei (辯明), *n.* explanation; vindication; demonstration. —辯明する, to explain; vindicate; demonstrate. —辯明を求める, to call another to account. ¶ 辯明書, a written explanation; a vindication.

benpaku (辯駁), *n.* =*benbaku.*

benpatsu (辮髮), *n.* a pigtail; a queue; a braid.

benpi (便祕), *n.* 【醫】 costiveness; constipation. —便祕する, to be constipated.

benran (便覽), *n.* a handbook; a handy-book; a manual.

benrei (勉勵), *n.* industry; diligence; assiduity. —勉勵する, [*a.*] industrious; diligent; assiduous; hard-working.

benri (便利), *n.* convenience; expediency; handiness (使用上の便利). 便利な, convenient; expedient; handy. —衆人の便利の爲め, for public convenience. —一層便利にする爲に, for greater convenience.

benri (辨理), *n.* management; administration; conduct. —辨理する, to manage; administer; conduct. ¶ 辨理士, an attorney at patent.

benron (辯論), *n.* debate; argument; 【法】 pleadings. —辯論する, to debate; argue; plead. ¶ 辯論家, a debater. —辯論期日, the day for pleadings.

bensai (辨濟), *n.* repayment; acquittance; performance. **—— -suru,** *vt.* to repay; make good. —債務を辨濟する, to repay [discharge] a debt.

bensai (辯才), *n.* (the gift of) eloquence.

bensei (鞭聲), *n.* the smack (of a whip). —鞭聲肅々, quietly urging their horses.

benshi (辯士), *n.* an orator; a speaker.

benshō (辨償), *n.* payment; repayment; indemnification; compensation. **—— -suru,** *vt.* to pay; repay; indemnify. —金錢で辨償する, to repay with money. ¶ 辨償金, an indemnity; damages.

benso (辯疏する), *vt.* to plead; excuse; explain. ☞ *benkai* (辯解する).

ben-suru (便する), *v.* to make convenient; facilitate; be of service *to.* —初學の士を便する, to be of service to beginners.

bentatsu (鞭撻する), *vt.* ❶ to lash; horsewhip; chastise. ❷ to incite; spur. —下僚を鞭撻する, to spur on one's subordinates.

benten (辨天), *n.* ❶ [B-]=*Ben-*

zaiten (辯才天). ❷ a beautiful woman; a beauty. 一後辯天前板額, Fair behind, foul before.
bentō (辨當), *n.* a luncheon; a tiffin. 一辨當を食ふ, to have tiffin. 一當日は各自辨當持參の事, Every one to bring his own luncheon on that day. ¶ 辨當箱, a luncheon-box.
bentsū (便通), *n.* evacuation; stool. 一便通する, to stool; ease oneself; ease [relieve] nature. 一便通を催す, The bowels begin to act.
Benzaiten (辯才天), *n.* 〔梵〕 ⌈Sarasvatī.⌉
benzetsu (辯舌), *n.* tongue; speech. 一立板に水を流すやうな辯舌, a tongue [speech] of wonderful fluency [eloquence].
ben-zuru (辨ずる), *v.* ❶ (辨別) to distinguish; discriminate; discern. ❷ (やッて行く, 處辨する) to do; get on; transact. 一用を辨ずる, to transact business. 一…無しに辨ずる, to do [manage] without; dispense with; get on without. 一彼が居なくちゃ事が辨じない, I cannot get on without him.
ben-zuru (辯ずる), *v.* ❶ to speak. ❷ (辯論) to controvert. ❸ (辯護) to advocate; defend; plead *for*; speak *for*. 一滔々と辯じ立てる, to explain fluently.
beppa (別派), *n.* a different [separate] sect 《party》. 一別派を立てる, to form a separate party.
beppai (別杯), *n.* a parting-cup; a stirrup-cup. 一別杯を酌む, to quaff a parting-cup.
beppin (別嬪), *n.* a beauty; a beautiful woman.
beppō (別報), *n.* another report.
beppū (別封), *n.* ❶ (別封物) a separate cover. ❷ (封中の別箇の手紙) the accompanying letter. 一別封の書類, documents under separate cover.
beppyō (別表), *n.* a separate [the accompanying] table.
berabō (篦棒), *n.* a fool; a rascal. 一篦棒め, you fool; you rascal; hang you; deuce take you. **—— -ni**, *ad.* deucedly; devilish 〔俗〕; awfully 〔俗〕. 一篦棒に高い値段, an extra high price.
beru (鈴, 鐘), *n.* a bell; a call-bell (呼鈴). 一戸のベルを押す, to ring the door-bell. 一ベルを(押して)鳴らす, to give the bell a ring; push the bell-button. 一ベルを鳴らして珈琲《召使》を呼ぶ, to ring for coffee 《a servant》.
Berugī (白耳義), *n.* Belgium. ¶ 白耳義人, a Belgian. 一白耳義皇帝, the King of the Belgians.

beruto (調帶), *n.* a belt.
beshi (可し), *v. aux.* ❶ (未來) shall; will. ❷ (命令) must; shall (二·三人稱); will (同上); should; ought to. 一人の取るべき道を辿る, to follow the path which men should take.
beso (べそをかく), *v.* to sob; snuffle; make a wry face.
bessatsu (別冊), *n.* another book; a separate book.
bessei (別製の), *a.* specially-made; of special make.
bessekai (別世界), *n.* another world; a different world.
besseki (別席), *n.* another seat; a separate [special] seat; another room; a separate [special] room.
besshi (別紙), *n.* an annexed paper; an enclosure. 一別紙雛形の通り, according to the form annexed hereto.
besshi (別使), *n.* a special [an express] messenger. ¶ 別使配達, express delivery (電報等の).
besshi (蔑視する), *vt.* to despise; scorn; hold in contempt; look down *upon*. 一主人を蔑視する, to slight one's master.
besshite (別して), *ad.* especially; particularly; above all (就中). 一今日は別して多忙だ, I am especially busy to-day.
besshitsu (別室), *n.* another [a separate] room; a special room (特別室).
besshō (別稱), *n.* an alias; ⌈another name.⌉
besshu (別種), *n.* another [a different] species; another [a different] kind. 一別種の, different; of different kind.
bessō (別莊), *n.* a villa. 一別莊番を置く, to put a care-taker in charge of a villa.
bēsu (ベース), *n.* a base (壘); baseball (野球).
besuto (最善), *n.* best. 一ベストを盡す, to do one's best.
beta (全體), *ad.* all over. 一べた一面の水, water all over. 一べた一面に塗る, to paint [smear] all over.
betabeta (べたべた), *ad.* ❶ (粘りつく樣) stickily; adhesively. ❷ (惡丁寧に塗る樣) thickly. ❸ (なまめかしく寄添ふ樣) flirtingly. ❹ (一面に) all over. 一べたべた紙を貼りつける, to stick paper all over. 一べたべた手にくッつく, It makes the hand sticky.
betatsuku (べたつく), *vi.* ❶ (粘著) to be sticky; feel sticky; be clammy. ❷ (狎戲) to flirt.
betsu (別), *n.* distinction (區別); difference (相異). 一別の, other;

different; separate; distinct. —別なの, [*pron.*] another. —男女の別なく, without distinction of sex; irrespective of sex. —晝夜の別なく勉强する, to study day and night [at all hours]. —暫くそれは別として, setting that aside [apart] for the present.

betsubetsu (別別の), *a.* separate; respective; individual. —別別の部屋に住居する, to live in separate rooms. **—-ni,** *ad.* separately; respectively; individually; one by one. —別々になる, to become separate; be separated.

betsubin (別便), *n.* another post; another messenger.

betsudan (別段), *ad.* especially; specially; particulary. **—-no,** *a.* especial; special; particular. —別段の規程, special regulations. —別段の用事, particular business. —別段の定めなきときは, unless otherwise provided.

betsudōtai (別働隊), *n.* ❶【軍】a flying column [party]. ❷ (別派) another party.

betsuen (別宴), *n.* a farewell dinner.

betsugyō (別行), *n.* a new line; another line. —これより別行にせよ, Begin a new line here.

betsuhaitatsu (別配達), *n.* special delivery.

betsuji (別事), *n.* ❶ (出來事) an incident; an event; an occurrence. ❷ (他事) another [a different] matter [affair; thing].

betsujō (別條), *n.* an unusual matter; an accident; casualty. —別條なく, without accident [mishap]; safely; well.

betsuma (別間), *n.* another [a different] room (別室); a special room (特別室).

betsumei (別名), *n.* a by-name; another name.

betsumondai (別問題), *n.* another [a different] question.

betsumono (別物), *n.* a different thing; an exception. —別物扱ひする, to treat differently; discriminate *against*.

betsu-ni (別に), *ad.* ❶ (別段) specially; particularly; in particular. ❷ (分離して) separately; independently. ❸ (餘分に) additionally. —別になる, to become separate. —別にして置く, to set aside [apart]. —別に五圓やる, to give five *yen* extra.

betsuri (別離), *n.* parting; separation. —別離の情[悲み], the sorrow of parting. —別離の涙に暮れる, to be sunk in tears of parting.

bettaku (別宅), *n.* a separate house; a villa.

bettari (べッたり), *ad.* fast (粘りつく); all over (一面に); thickly (こてこて). —彼方へべッたり此方へべッたり, He sucks up now to this man and now to that.

betto (別途), *n.* another [a different; a separate] path; a special use (別用). —別途に出る, to appear in a different way; take a different direction (別の方向を取る). ¶ 別途積立金, special reserve (fund).

bettō (別當), *n.* ❶ (執事) a steward; an intendant. ❷ (馬丁, 厩丁) a groom (馬飼); an ostler; a stable-man; a (running) footman.

bi (美), *n.* ❶ (美麗) beauty; handsomeness; goodness. ❷ (美味) sweetness; good flavour.

bi (微), *n.* minuteness (微細); poorness (貧弱); slightness (少し). —微を穿ち過ぎた, fine-spun; hair-splitting. —微に入り細に渉る, to go [enter] into minute details.

bibi (微微として), *ad.* pettily; in a very small way. —國威微々として振はず, The national power is too slight to make itself felt. **—-taru,** *a.* small; insignificant; slight; poor. —微々たる供給, poor [scanty] supply. —微々たる一漁村, a small fishing village.

bibishiku (美美しく), *ad.* beautifully; splendidly; magnificently.

bibō (美貌), *n.* a beautiful face; good looks.

bibōjin (未亡人), *n.* a widow; a relict.

bibōroku (備忘錄), *n.* a memorandum; a minute-book; *aide-mémoire*〔佛〕.

bibun (美文), *n.* belles-lettres; elegant prose. ¶ 美文學, polite literature; belles-lettres.

bibun (微分), *n.*【數】a differential; the differential calculus.

bibunshi (微分子), *n.* an atom; a corpuscle.

bidan (美談), *n.* a fine [beautiful] story.

bifū (美風), *n.* a fine custom [habit]. —淳朴の美風, the fine habit of honest simplicity. —婦人の美風, a fine womanly quality.

bifū (微風), *n.* a (light) breeze; a gentle [light] wind.

bifuku (微服), *n.* disguise. —微服する, to disguise oneself.

bifuteki (ビフテキ), *n.* beefsteak.

bigaku (美學), *n.* æsthetics.

biganjutsu (美顔術), *n.* the art of beauty; beauty-culture. ¶ 美顔術所, a beauty shop (店); a beauty parlour (室).

bihin (備品), *n.* supplies; furniture; equipment.

bihō (彌縫), *n.* patchery; patchwork; temporary remedy. —彌縫する, to patch up; stop a gap; make a shift. —彌縫策を講ずる, to devise makeshifts.

bii (微意), *n.* ❶ (微志) a humble desire [opinion]. ❷ (祕密の意志) a secret intention. —微意を寓する, to hint one's secret intention.

bijaku (微弱な), *a.* feeble; weak.

biji (美事), *n.* a fine deed; a praiseworthy act. —聖代の美事, a fine action of His Majesty's reign.

biji (美辭), *n.* rhetoric; oratory. ¶ 美辭法, rhetoric.

biji (鼻茸), *n.* =*bijō* (鼻茸).

bijin (美人), *n.* a beauty; a beautiful [pretty] woman; a belle 〔佛〕. —美人薄命, "Over the greatest beauty hangs the greatest ruin." —美人といふも皮一重, "Beauty is only skin-deep."

bijō (鼻茸), *n.* a nasal polypus [*pl.* -pi].

bijogane (鉸具金), *n.* a buckle; a clasp.

bijutsu (美術), *n.* art; the fine [elegant] arts. ——**-teki**, *a.* artistic. —美術的鑑識, artistic discernment. ¶ 造形美術, formative arts; *Bildende Künste* 〔獨〕. —美術學校, a school of design [art]; an [a fine] art school. —美術品, an object [a work] of art; an *objet d'art* 〔佛〕; an article of virtu. —美術家, an artist. —美術工藝品, industrial art work. —美術展覽會, an art exhibition. —美術通, a virtuoso; a connoisseur. —帝國美術院, the Imperial Academy of Art.

bika (美化する), *vt.* to beautify; refine.

bikataru (鼻加答兒), *n.* 【醫】 nasal catarrh; coryza.

bikko (跛), *n.* ❶ (跛行) limp; lameness. ❷ (跛者) a lame person; a cripple. ❸ (不對) unevenness. —跛の, ① lame; crippled; halt. ② (不對の) uneven. —跛を引く, to limp; hobble; halt.

bikkuri (喫驚), *n.* fright; surprise; amazement. —喫驚さす, ① [*vt.*] to surprise; startle; give (a person) a turn. ② [*a.*] surprising; amazing; startling. —喫驚する, to be surprised; be amazed; be taken aback. —喫驚仰天する, to be struck all of a heap; be lost in amazement; be thunderstruck. —喫驚した, [*a.*] startled; amazed; frightened. —喫驚して, in amazement; in surprise; in a fright. (喫驚して氣絕する, to faint from fright. —びっくりして目を丸くする, to stare with astonishment.) ¶ びっくり箱, a jack-in-a-box.

bikō (尾行する), *v.* to follow; dog; shadow. —見え隱れに尾行する, to follow by concealing oneself at times. —角袖を尾行さす, to send a plain-clothes detective to shadow him.

bikō (微光), *n.* a glimmer; twilight. —希望の微光, a glimmer of hope.

bikō (微行), *n.* incognito. —微行する, to travel incognito; go in disguise.

bikō (備考), *n.* a note; a remark. ¶ 備考欄, the remarks column.

bikō (備荒), *n.* provision against famine. ¶ 備荒貯蓄, a famine fund; an emergency fund. —備荒貯蓄米, the rice stored against famine.

bikō (鼻孔), *n.* the nostril. —鼻孔の, nasal.

bikō (鼻腔), *n.* the nasal passage. ¶ 鼻孔粘膜, a nasal mucous membrane.

bikotsu (尾骨), *n.* the coccyx; the rump.

bikotsu (鼻骨), *n.* 【解】 the nasal bone.

biku (比丘), *n.* 〔梵 Bhiksu, 淨乞食〕 a priest; a Buddhist priest.

biku (魚籠), *n.* a fish-pot; a creel; a small fish-basket.

bikubiku (びくびく), *ad.* tremblingly; in fear; in trepidation. —びくびくする, to be afraid; tremble with fear; have one's heart in one's boots. —びくびく試驗を受けた, I went through examination trembling.

bikuni (比丘尼), *n.* 〔梵 a Bhiksunī, 乞士女〕 a nun; a priestess.

bikuto, bikurito, (悸と), *ad.* wincingly; flinchingly. —びくりとする, to wince; flinch; start. (びくりとした, My heart gave a leap.) —びくともせぬ, ① [*v.*] to remain unmoved [calm]; not to turn a hair; not to move a muscle. ② [*a.*] unflinching. (びくともせぬ面魂, a face unmoved by fear.) —天地が引っくり返らうがびくともせぬ, He would not turn a hair even if the heavens fell.)

bikutsuku (びくつく), *vi.* to start; wince; flinch. ——, *a.* jumpy; wincing; flinching. —矢鱈にびくつく, to tremble constantly with fear.

biman (彌漫), *n.* diffusion; pervasion; spread. —彌漫する, to spread; diffuse; extend all around.

bimei (美名), *n.* honour; reputation; good [fair] name. —慈善の美名の下に, under the fine name of charity.

bimi (美味), *n.* ❶ (旨いこと) a good flavour; savouriness; daintiness. ❷ (美食) a delicacy; a dainty; good things. —美味に飽かす, to pamper. —美味に飽く, to be sated with dainties.

bimyō (美妙), *n.* exquisiteness; delicacy. **—-na,** *a.* exquisite; delicate. —美妙な音樂に酔ふ, to be intoxicated with exquisite music.

bimyō (微妙), *n.* delicacy; subtlety; nicety. —造化の微妙, the subtlety of creation. **—-na,** *a.* delicate; nice; subtle. —微妙な作用で動く, to move [work] by delicate action.

bin (便), *n.* ❶ (方便) means. ❷ (機會) an opportunity; an occasion. ❸ (郵便) mail; post. ❹ (音信) a message; a communication. —第一(二)便, the first (second) post.

bin (瓶, 罎), *n.* ❶ (びん) a bottle; a phial; a flask (フラスコ). ❷ (かめ) a jar; a vase. —罎に入れる, to bottle.

bin (鬢), *n.* the side-lock. —鬢を掻き上げる, to comb up the side-locks.

binben (黽勉), *n.* industry; diligence; assiduity. —黽勉な, industrious; diligent.

binbō (貧乏), *n.* poverty; penury; indigence. —貧乏な, poor; penurious; indigent. —貧乏神に取りつかれる, to be overtaken by poverty. —貧乏籤を抽く, to draw a blank; be unlucky. —貧乏子寶, "Children are poor men's riches." —稼ぐに追ひつく貧乏なし, "No poverty can overtake industry." ¶ 貧乏町, a slum; a rookery. —貧乏人, a poor man; a pauper; the poor.

bindome (鬢留), *n.* a side-lock fastener.

binjō (便乘する), *v.* to go on board; be on board. —御用船に便乘する, to go on board [go by] a transport.

binkan (敏感), *n.* irritability; sensibility; susceptibility. —敏感な, sensitive; irritable.

binkatsu (敏活), *n.* alacrity; briskness; promptitude. —敏活に, promptly; with promptitude. —事務の敏活を計る, to promote promptitude in business. **—-na,** *a.* prompt; brisk; alert. —敏活な處置を執る, to take prompt measures.

binnaga (鬢長), *n.* 【魚】the long-finned albacore.

bin-naru (敏なる), *a.* sharp; quick; acute.

binran (紊亂), *n.* disorder; disorganization; derangement. **—-suru,** *vt.* to disorganize; throw into confusion; derange. —風紀を紊亂する, to throw public morality into disorder. —社會の秩序を紊亂する, to derange social order.

binrō(ji) (檳榔子), *n.* the catechu [betel-nut] palm-tree. —檳榔子黑に染める, to dye deep black.

binsai (敏才), *n.* alertness; adroitness.

binsatsu (憫察する), *vt.* to consider; take into account [consideration].

binsen (便船), *n.* a ship leaving for one's destination.

binsen (便箋), *n.* a memo (memorandum の略).

binshō (敏捷), *n.* ❶ (才智の) sharpness; shrewdness; astuteness. ❷ (動作の) promptitude; quickness; agility. —敏捷な, sharp; smart; shrewd; prompt. —敏捷に, sharply; shrewdly; promptly. (敏捷に立廻る, to act very promptly.) —事務は敏捷でなければならぬ, Business must be smartly done.

bintsuke (鬢附), *n.* pomade; pomatum.

binwan (敏腕), *n.* ability; cleverness. —敏腕な, able; clever; capable. —敏腕を揮ふ, to exercise one's ability. ¶ 敏腕家, a man of ability.

binzen (憫然な), *a.* pitiful; poor; affecting. —憫然な奴, poor fellow. —憫然に思ふ, to take pity *on*; be affected with pity.

binzume (罎詰の), *a.* bottled. —罎詰にする, to bottle.

bion (微溫), *n.* lukewarmness; tepidity. —微溫的態度を執る, to take a lukewarm attitude. ¶ 微溫湯, tepid [lukewarm] water.

bira (披露), *n.* a handbill; a placard; a poster. —披露を貼る, [*vt.*] to post; placard.

biran (糜爛), *n.* ❶ (ただれ) inflammation. ❷ (腐爛) ulceration; fester; decomposition (死體など). ❸ (紊亂) disorder; confusion. —糜爛する, ① to be inflamed. ② to fester; ulcerate; be decomposed. ③ to be disordered [confused].

birei (美麗な), *a.* beautiful; lovely.

biri (びり), *n.* the last; the bottom; the tail. —一番になったよ, びりから, I am now the first, that is, counting backward.

birō (尾籠な), *a.* indelicate; improper; indecent. —尾籠な話だが, though I appear to speak with indelicacy.

birōdo (天鵞絨), *n.* velvet. ¶ 天鵞絨まがひ, velveteen.

biroku (微祿), *n.* a small [poor] salary [stipend]. —微祿する, to be impoverished; be in reduced circumstances.

biroku (美祿), *n.* a good [large] stipend. —天の美祿, the meat of

the Gods; the ambrosia; the nectar.
biruburōkā (ビルブローカー), *n.* a bill-broker.
biru (麥酒), *n.* beer; ale. ¶ 氣拔けビール, flat beer. —黒ビール, black beer; stout; porter. —ミュンヘンビール, Munich beer. —麥酒店, a beer-house; a beer-hall.
birudingu (ビルディング), *n.* a building.
Biruma (緬甸), *n.* Burma. ¶ 緬甸人, a Burmese.
biryō (鼻梁), *n.* the bridge of the nose.
biryoku (微力), *n.* slight [small] power; slight strength. —微力を顧みず, without considering the smallness of one's power. —微力を致す, to do what little one can; do all in one's power.
bisai (微細な), *a.* minute; fine; delicate. —微細に, minutely; in detail. —微細な區別, nice distinction. —意味の微細な相違, delicate shades of meaning; *nuance* 〔佛〕. —微細な點に渉って説明する, to explain by going into details.
bisan (彌散), *n.* diffusion.
biseibutsu (微生物), *n.* a microbe; a micro-organism.
bisen (微賤), *n.* humbleness; lowliness; obscurity. —微賤な, humble; lowly; obscure. —微賤から身を起す, to rise in the world from a humble position.
Bishamonten (毘沙門天), *n.* 〔梵〕 Vaisramana (多聞); the god of treasure.
bishin (微震), *n.* microseism; a slight shock (of earthquake); an earth tremor (地球回轉の).
bishō (微小), *n.* an iota; minuteness. —微小の, minute.
bishō (微少), *n.* a jot; a whit. —微少の, little; slight
bishō (微笑), *n.* a smile. —微笑する, to smile; beam. —顔に微笑を浮べて, with a smile in one's face. —獨りで微笑を洩す, to smile to oneself.
bishō (微傷), *n.* a scratch (掻傷); a slight wound [injury]. —微傷を蒙る, to be slightly injured.
bishobisho (びしょびしょ), *ad.* drizzling (微雨が); thoroughly drenched (濡れて). —びしょびしょ降る, to drizzle. —びしょびしょになって歩く, to walk drenched [wet] to the skin.
bishoku (美食), *n.* delicious food; delicacy; rich diet; high living [feeding]. —美食する, to regale; live on rich diet. ¶ 美食家, an epicure; a *gourmet* 〔佛〕.
bishonure (びしょ濡れ), *n.* drench; soaking. —びしょ濡れになる, to be soaked to the bone; be wet [drenched] to the skin. (びしょ濡れになって, wet like a drowned rat.)
biso (鼻祖), *n.* a founder; a father; an originator.
bisō (美裝), *n.* array; elegant attire. —美裝する, to attire oneself elegantly; dress richly. —美裝した, finely arrayed; elegantly attired; richly dressed.
bisoku (鼻息), *n.* a superior's pleasure. —他人の鼻息を窺ふ, to consult another's pleasure; hang on another's smiles.
bisshori (びっしょり), wet; streaming; profusely. —汗をびっしょりかく, to perspire profusely.
bisui (微睡), *n.* a nap; a doze; drowse. —微睡する, to take a nap; doze; drowse.
bisuketto (ビスケット), *n.* a biscuit.
bita(sen) (鐚錢), *n.* a small iron coin.
biteikotsu (尾骶骨), *n.* 【解】the coccyx.
biteki (美的), *a.* æsthetic(-al).
biten (美點), *n.* a beauty; an excellence; a virtue. —美點を擧げる, to name its points of beauty [excellences; virtues].
bitoku (美德), *n.* a virtue; mental grace. —本然の美德, the natural virtues. —美德を傷ける, to injure a man's virtue.
biu (眉宇), *n.* the eyebrows. —眉宇の間に溢る, to show itself in his face.
biwa (枇杷), *n.* 【植】the Japanese medlar; the loquat.
biwa (琵琶), *n.* a lute. ¶ 琵琶法師, a (professional) lute-player.
biyahōru (ビヤホール), *n.* a beer-hall.
biyō (微恙), *n.* a slight indisposition [illness].
biyōyanagi (未央柳), *n.* the Chinese St. John's-wort.
bizai (微罪), *n.* a peccadillo; a small [slight; petty] offence.
bō (妄), *n.* falsity; untruthfulness. —妄を辯する, to point out the falsity.
bō (某), *n.* some one; a certain person. ——, *a.* some; a certain. —某日, one day; some day; on a certain day. —林某, a (certain) Mr. Hayashi.
bō (帽), *n.* =*bōshi*.
bō (棒), *n.* ❶ a rod (竿); a pole (竿); a staff (杖); a cudgel (棍棒); a club (同上). ❷ (線) a line; a dash. —棒で毆る[打つ], to beat with a cudgel; cudgel; give a beating. —棒に振る, to waste; lose. (身代を棒に振る, to squander one's fortune.) —棒をひく, ①(線引く) to line through; draw a line.

② =*chōkeshi* (帳消にする).

bō (暴), *n.* violence. —暴を以て暴に代ふ, to meet violence with violence. **—-na;** *a.* violent; outrageous. —暴な事をする, to act violently.

bōatsu (防遏), *n.* prevention; obstruction. —防遏手段を執る, to take preventive measures. **—-suru,** *vt.* to prevent; obstruct; check. —敵の侵入を防遏する, to check the enemy's invasion.

bōbi (防備), *n.* defences; defensive preparations. —防備する, to arm *against*; defend; guard. —防備を施す, [*vt.*] to fortify. —防備なき都市を襲ふ, to attack defenceless cities.

bōbiki (棒引), *n.* ❶ drawing a line through. ❷【商】writing-off. —棒引にする, to write off.

•**bōbō** (蓬蓬), *ad.* ❶ shaggily (頭髪が); thickly (草木が). ❷ (焔が燃えるさま) flamingly; in flames. —(火が)ぼうぼう燃える, to burn in flames. —蓬々と生える, to grow in profusion (草・髯が).

bochi (墓地), *n.* a burial-ground; a cemetery; a grave-yard. ¶ 共同墓地, a public cemetery.

bōchō (傍聴), *n.* attendance. —傍聴禁止で, *in camera* (法廷の)〔羅〕; with closed doors. —傍聴を禁止する, to clear the court. **—-suru,** *vt.* to hear; attend. —帝國議會を傍聴する, to attend a sitting of the Imperial Diet. ¶ 傍聴筆記, a shorthand report. —傍聴券, an admission-ticket. —傍聴無料, admittance free. —傍聴人, the audience; the general public admitted. —傍聴料, the admission-fee. —傍聴席, seats for the public; the auditorium; the (strangers') gallery (議會の).

bōchō (膨脹), *n.* expansion; inflation; dilatation. —通貨の膨脹, inflation of the currency. —膨脹する, to dilate; inflate; expand. ¶ 膨脹瓣, an expansion valve. —膨脹機關, an expansion engine.

bodai (菩提), *n.* 〔梵 Bodhi, 正覺〕 supreme knowledge. —菩提の爲め, for salvation. —菩提の道に志す, to be converted to Buddhism. —先祖代々の菩提を弔ふ, to pray [have prayers read] for the spirits [souls] of one's ancestors. ¶ 菩提樹, ① the bo-tree; the sacred fig-tree. ② Tilia Miqueliana (lime-tree の一種). —菩提心, the desire for [spirit of] salvation; a devotional spirit. —菩提所, the family temple (cemetery).

bōdai (厖大な), *a.* mammoth; prodigious; enormous. —厖大な軍備, bloated armaments.

bōdan (妄談), *n.* a baseless tale; an idle talk.

bōdan (防彈の), *a.* bomb-proof; bullet-proof. ¶ 防彈室, a bomb-proof chamber.

bōdara (棒鱈), *n.* a dried cod.

bōdō (妄動する), *vi.* to act heedlessly; behave heedlessly [thoughtlessly].

bōdō (暴動), *n.* a riot; a disturbance; a rising. —暴動を起す(鎭壓する), to cause (quell) a riot. ¶ 食糧暴動, food-rioting. —暴動者, a rioter; a mutineer (軍).

bōei (防衛), *n.* defence; protection; safeguard. **—-suru,** *vt.* to defend; protect; safeguard. —自己の利益を防衛する, to protect [safeguard] one's interests.

bōeki (防疫), *n.* prevention of infectious diseases. ¶ 防疫官, an officer for the prevention of infectious diseases.

bōeki (貿易), *n.* trade; commerce. —貿易する, to trade; commerce; carry on trade. ¶ 發動(受動)貿易, active (passive) commerce. —自由貿易, free trade. (自由貿易論者, free traders.) —保護貿易, protection; protective trade. (保護貿易主義, protectionism. —保護貿易主義者, protectionists.) —外國(內國)貿易, foreign (inland; home; domestic) trade. —貿易中心地, the trade-centre. —貿易風, the trade; the trade-wind. —貿易銀, a trade doller. —貿易品, trade goods; merchandise. —貿易事務官, a commercial agent. —貿易場, a trading-post. —貿易均衡, balance of trade. —貿易港, a trade-port; a commercial port. —貿易商, a merchant; a trader. —貿易商會, a trading firm [company].

bōenkyō (望遠鏡), *n.* a telescope; a glass. —望遠鏡で月を見る, to look at the moon through a telescope. ¶ 反射望遠鏡, a reflecting telescope. —屈折望遠鏡, a refracting telescope. —天體望遠鏡, an astronomical telescope. —(月蝕の)望遠鏡的觀測, telescopic observation (of a lunar eclipse).

bōfu (亡父), *n.* the late [deceased] father; my late [departed] father.

bōfu (防腐的), *a.* antiseptic; aseptic. —防腐的手術, an aseptic operation. —防腐する, to prevent putrefaction; disinfect. ¶ 防腐法, antisepsis. —防腐劑, an antiseptic; a preservative; an aseptic.

bōfu (暴富), *n.* sudden wealth; rapidly-made fortune.

bōfū (暴風), *n.* a wind-storm; a gale (强風); a stormy [wild; heavy; violent] wind.

bōfūu (暴風雨), *n.* a storm; a tempest; stress of weather. —暴風雨の爲め, under stress of weather. —暴風雨の中心, a storm-centre. —暴風雨の夜, a wild [roaring] night. ¶ 暴風雨眼, the eye of a storm; a storm-centre. —暴風雨警報, a storm warning. —暴風雨帶, a storm-belt; a storm-zone.

bōfura, bōfuri, (孑孑), *n.* 【蟲】 the river-worm.

bōgai (妨害, 妨碍), *n.* ❶ (阻止) disturbance (治安·安眠·占有等); impediment (進行·進歩等); hindrance (同上). ❷ (障害) obstacle; obstruction. —妨害を除去する, to abate a nuisance. **——-suru,** *vt.* to disturb; obstruct; hinder; impede. —苗の發育を妨害する, to retard the growth of a sprout. ¶ 妨害物, an obstruction; an obstacle; a hindrance.

bōgen (妄言), *n.* ❶ (虛言) a lie; a falsehood. ❷ (無暗の言) an idle talk.

bōgen (暴言), *n.* violent [abusive; strong] language. —暴言する; 暴言を吐く, to use [resort to] violent language; speak violently.

bōgi (謀議), *n.* consultation; deliberation; conference. —謀議を凝らす, to deliberate *on*; consult *about*; discuss fully.

bogi-sha (ボギー車), *n.* a bogie; a bogie-car.

bogo (母語), *n.* the mother-tongue.

bōgui (棒杭), *n.* a post; a pile; a stake. —棒杭を打ッて境界を明にする, to mark the boundary with stakes.

bōgumi (棒組), *n.* ❶ (仲間) a fellow-bearer; a mate; a pal〖卑〗. ❷【印】(setting in) a galley. ¶ 棒組盤,【印】a galley; a slip-galley.

bōgyaku (暴虐), *n.* tyranny; outrage; oppression. —暴虐な, tyrannical; outrageous; oppressive.

bōgyo (防禦), *n.* ❶ defence. ❷【野球】cover. —防禦なき, unguarded; defenceless; undefended. —防禦する, to defend; shield; guard *against*. —防禦の位置に立つ, to stand on the defensive. —防禦線を突破する, to break through a line of defence. ¶ 防禦砲火, defensive fire. —防禦工事, defence-works. —防禦戰, a defensive war (battle).

bohan (母斑), *n.* a birth-mark; a mother's mark; a mother-mark.

bōhan (謀判), *n.* ❶ a false [counterfeit] seal. ❷ forging [counterfeiting] of a seal. ¶ 謀判人, a counterfeiter [forger] of a seal.

bōhatei (防波堤), *n.* a break-water; a mole.

Bohemia (ボヘミア), *n.* Bohemia. ¶ ボヘミア人, a Bohemian; a Czech.

bohi (墓碑), *n.* a gravestone; a tombstone. —墓碑銘, an epitaph.

bohyō (墓標), *n.* a grave-post.

bōhyō (妄評), *n.* ❶ (無暗の評) shallow [poor] criticism. ❷ (謙辭) my criticism.

bōi (暴威), *n.* abuse of power; excessive [extreme] rigour; great violence. —暴威を振ふ [逞しうする], to abuse power; act with great violence; exercise excessive rigour.

bōi (ボーイ), *n.* a boy; a waiter. ¶ ボーイスカウト, boy scouts.

boikotto (ボイコット), *n.* a boycott; boycotting. —獨貨をボイコットする, to boycott German goods.

boin (母音), *n.* a vowel; a vocal; a vowel sound.

boin (拇印), *n.* a thumb-print.

bōin (暴飲), *n.* heavy drinking. —暴飲する, to drink deep; drink hard [like a fish].

bōjaku-bujin (傍若無人の), *a.* shameless; outrageous. —傍若無人の振舞をする, to behave outrageously.

bōji (榜示), *n.* a public notice; a notification. —榜示する, to notify; give public notice; put up a notice. ¶ 榜示杭, a notice-post.

bōjin (傍人), *n.* a bystander; a looker-on.

bōka (防火), *n.* protection against fire; prevention of fires. ¶ 防火壁, a fire-wall. —防火金庫, a fire-proof safe. —防火栓, a fire-plug; a fire hydrant. —防火設備, arrangements for prevention of fires.

bokan (母艦), *n.* a dépôt-ship; a mother-ship. ¶ 飛行機母艦, a seaplane carrier; a seaplane tender〖米〗.

bōkan (坊間に), *ad.* in the streets; on the market.

bōkan (防寒), *n.* protection against cold. ¶ 防寒服, winter clothes; clothes for cold weather.

bōkan (傍觀する), *v.* to look on; stand by. —傍觀的態度を執る, to take the attitude of a looker-on. ¶ 傍觀者, a bystander; a looker-on; a spectator.

bokashi (暈), *n.* 【美】gradation; shading off. ¶ 暈畫, a vignette.

bokasu (暈す), *vt.* to grade; shade off; vignette (遠景·周圍を).

boke (木瓜), *n.* 【植】Pyrus japonica (學名); the Japan quince.

bokei (母系の), *a.* on the maternal side; maternal. ¶ 母系先祖, a maternal ancestor.

bōkei (傍系), *n.* a collateral line.

bōken (冒險), *n.* an adventure; a risk; a hazard. —冒險的, adventurous; risky; hazardous. —冒險する, ① [*vi.*] to adventure; run a risk; make a venture. ② [*vt.*] to venture; risk; hazard. —冒險を試みる, to venture upon a hazardous enterprise. ¶ 冒險事業, a hazardous enterprise. —冒險家, an adventurer. —冒險小說, an adventure novel.

bōken (剖檢する), *vt.* to dissect; hold an autopsy *on.*

bokeru (ぼける), *vi.* ❶ (耄ける) to grow mentally weak; dote. ❷ (褪める) to fade.

boki (簿記), *n.* book-keeping. —簿記をつける, to keep books. ¶ 家計 (商用; 銀行) 簿記, domestic (commercial; bank) book-keeping. —單 (複) 式簿記, book-keeping by single (double) entry. —簿記棒, a ruler. —簿記帳, an account book. —簿記方, a book-keeper; a ledger clerk.

bokka (牧歌), *n.* a bucolic; a pastoral.

bokkō (勃興), *n.* rise; sudden rise. —勃興する, to arise suddenly; spring into existence.

bokkusu (ボックス), *n.* ❶ (席) a box. ❷ (靴革) box-calf.

bokkyaku (沒却する), *vt.* to destroy; ignore; sink. —自己の利益を沒却する, to sink oneself [one's own interests]; rise above self.

bokō (母校), *n.* the alma mater (羅).

bōkō (膀胱), *n.* the (urinary) bladder. ¶ 膀胱炎, cystitis; the inflammation of the bladder.

bōkō (暴行), *n.* violence; outrage; a violent conduct; an act of violence. —暴行する, to outrage; behave [act] violently; offer violence. —暴行を加へる, to do violence *to*; be violent *with.*

bokoku (母國), *n.* the home-land; the fatherland; the mother country. ¶ 母國語, the mother tongue.

bōkoku (亡國), *n.* ❶ a ruined [doomed; fallen] country. ❷ (國家の滅亡) national ruin.

bōkon (亡魂), *n.* an apparition; a ghost; a spirit. —亡魂を弔ふ, to pray for the spirits of the dead.

Bōkotō (澎湖島), *n.* the Pescadores.

boku (僕), *n.* ❶ (家僕) a (man-) servant. ❷ [*pron.*] (私) I.

bokuchiku (牧畜), *n.* stock-farming; cattle-raising (牧牛); graziery (業). ¶ 牧畜者, a stock-farmer; a stock-breeder; a grazier.

bokuchoku (樸直), *n.* artlessness; simplicity; straightforwardness. —樸直な, simple; straightforward.

bokudō (牧童), *n.* a herdboy; a cowboy; a shepherd boy.

bokugū (木偶), *n.* ❶ a wooden image. ❷ (木偶漢) a puppet; a dummy.

bokugyū (牧牛), *n.* cattle-breeding [raising].

bokujō (牧場), *n.* a pasture; a stock-farm; a ranch (米). —牧場へやる, to put [send; turn; turn out] to grass.

bokumetsu (撲滅), *n.* destruction; extirpation; extermination. **—— -suru,** *vt.* to destroy; extirpate; exterminate. —惡疫を撲滅する, to stamp out a plague.

bokunenjin (木念仁), *n.* a blunt [an awkward] fellow; a stock.

bokusatsu (撲殺する), *vt.* to beat to death; kill with a blow; slaughter (牛等を).

bokusha (牧者), *n.* a stockman; a herdman; a ranchman.

bokushi (牧師), *n.* a pastor; a minister; a clergyman. ¶ 牧師館, a parsonage; a vicarage. —牧師管區, a pastorate.

bokushu (墨守する), *v.* to keep *to*; stick *to*; adhere *to.* —舊慣を墨守する, to adhere to old customs.

bokusō (牧草), *n.* the feed; the grass; the pasturage.

boku-suru (卜する), *vt.* ❶ (占ふ) to augur; divine; prognosticate. ❷ (住居を極める) to fix [take up; settle] (one's abode). —天氣を卜する, to read the sky. —運命を卜する, to cast a horoscope [nativity].

boku-suru (牧する), *vt.* ❶ (牧畜) to shepherd (羊を); summer (牛を); pasture. ❷ (統治) to govern. —民を牧する, to govern [care for] the people.

bokutaku (木鐸), *n.* ❶ a bell with a wooden tongue. ❷ (師表) a proclaimer; an instructor; a guide.

bokuteki (牧笛), *n.* a reed; an oaten pipe.

bokutō (木刀), *n.* a wooden sword.

bokutotsu (樸訥な), *a.* artless; simple; simple and honest.

bokuyō (牧羊), *n.* sheep-breeding. ¶ 牧羊者, a sheep-farmer [-master]; a shepherd.

bōkyaku (忘却), *n.* forgetfulness; oblivion. —忘却する, to forget; bury in oblivion; commit [consign] to oblivion. —忘却される, to be buried in oblivion; go [pass] out of another's mind.

bōkyo (暴擧), *n.* rowdyism; tumult; disturbance. —暴擧を謀る, to plan a disturbance.

bōkyōbyō (望郷病), *n.* homesickness; nostalgia.

bōman (暴慢), *n.* insolence; contumely; overbearing contempt. —暴慢な, insolent; contumelious. —暴慢を挫く, to crush a person's insolence.

bōmei (亡命), *n.* flight. —亡命する, to flee; take to flight; take [seek] refuge. ¶ 亡命者, a fugitive; a refugee; an exile.

bōmin (暴民), *n.* a mob; rioters; a lawless crowd.

bon (凡), *n.* mediocrity; average; the average [medial] standard. —凡なる, commonplace; mediocre; ordinary. —凡を拔く, to be above mediocrity; be extraordinary.

bon (盆), *n.* ❶ a tray; a salver. ❷ (盂蘭盆) the Feast of Lanterns. —大雨盆を覆す, to rain in torrents.

bōnasu (賞與), *n.* a bonus.

bonbon (ボンボン), *n.* a bonbon.

bonbon (ぼんぼん), *ad.* tick-tick (of a wall-clock); bang (銃聲等). ¶ ぼんぼん時計, a wall-clock.

bonbori (雪洞), *n.* a hard-lantern.

bonbu (凡夫), *n.* ❶ (俗人) a layman. ❷ (平凡人) a common man; an ordinary man. —凡夫のあさましさ, the shallowness of a common man.

bonchi (盆地), *n.* 【地文】a basin; a hollow.

bōne (棒根), *n.* 【植】the taproot.

bōnenkai (忘年會), *n.* a social gathering to speed the parting year.

bongo (梵語), *n.* Sanskrit.

bonjin (凡人), *n.* ❶ a man of mediocrity; an ordinary [average] man; everyday people. ❷ (素人) a layman.

bonkei (盆景), *n.* tray-landscape.

bonmatsuri (盆祭), *n.* the Feast of Lanterns.

bonnō (煩惱), *n.* 〔梵 Tanha〕the worldly passions; lust (色慾). —煩惱心を斷ち切る, to free oneself from worldly passions.

bon-no-kubo (盆窪), *n.* the nape; the back [scruff] of the neck.

boṅodori (盆踊), *n.* the dance of the Feast of Lanterns.

bonsai (盆栽), *n.* a dwarf [dwarfed] tree; a potted plant.

bonshō (梵鐘), *n.* a temple-bell.

boṅyari (ぼんやり), *ad.* ❶ (朦朧) indistinctly; hazily; dimly. ❷ (放心) absent-mindedly; abstractedly; vacantly. ——, *n.* (魯鈍者) an absent-minded person; a dullard; a doodle. —ぼんやりして, with a vacant look [air]. —ぼんやり考へ込んでゐる, to be in a brown study. ——-**shita**, *a.* ❶ dim; faint; hazy; indistinct. ❷ listless; vacant; absent-minded. ❸ (魯鈍) dull; stupid. —ぼんやりした色, faint [dim] colour. —ぼんやりした燈火, a dim light.

boṅyō (凡庸の), *a.* common; mediocre; banal.

bonyū (母乳), *n.* mother's milk. ¶ 母乳兒, a breast-fed baby; a baby brought up on the mother's milk.

bonyū (募入), *n.* allotment. ¶ 募入法方, method of allotment. —募入通知書, an allotment letter.

bonzoku (凡俗), *n.* ❶ (平凡) commonplace; mediocrity; vulgarity. ❷ (平凡人) an ordinary man; the vulgar [集合]. ❸ (僧と區別して俗人) a layman; the laity [集合]. —凡俗の, ① (世俗の) lay; secular. ② (平凡の) common; ordinary.

bōon (忘恩の), *a.* ungrateful; unthankful. ¶ 忘恩漢, an ungrateful person; an ingrate.

boppatsu (勃發), *n.* outbreak; outburst. —革命の勃發, revolutionary outbreak. —勃發する, to break out; burst out.

bora (鯔), *n.* 【魚】the gray mullet.

bōraku (暴落), *n.* a sudden fall; a heavy fall; a slump (株式等の) 〔俗〕. —株式の暴落, a slump in stocks; a heavy fall in the prices of stocks. —暴落する, to fall suddenly; go down with a run.

bōrei (亡靈), *n.* an apparition; a ghost; a shade.

bōrei (暴戾な), *a.* atrocious; violent; outrageous.

bōri (暴利), *n.* ❶ (高利) usury; excessive interest. ❷ (法外の利益) excessive [excess; undue] profits. —暴利を貪る, to make excessive profits; profiteer (特に戰時などに). ¶ 暴利商人, a profiteer. —暴利取締令, the ordinance for control of excessive profits.

boro (襤褸), *n.* ❶ rags; tatters. ❷ a fault (缺點); a weak point (弱點). —ぼろの, ragged; tattered. —ぼろになる, to be reduced to rags. —ぼろを出す, ① to show one's true colours; show the cloven foot [hoof]. ② to betray one's ignorance. ¶ ぼろ着物, ragged clothes; tattered [threadbare] clothes; rags. —ぼろ屋, ① a rag-shop; a dolly shop. ② (人) a rag-merchant; a ragman.

bōrō (望樓), *n.* a watch [an observation]-tower; a look-out; a signal station (海軍の) ¶ 望樓手, a watchman; a signalman; a look-out (man).

bōrō (暴浪), *n.* 【地文】 a swell.

boroboro (ぼろぼろの), *a.* ❶ (脆い) light; crisp; crumbly. ❷ ragged; tattered; threadbare. —ぼろぼろになる, to crumble; be torn to ribbons. —ぼろぼろに裂く, to tear to shreds.

boroi(ぼろい), *a.* money-making; profitable; lucrative: excessive; undue. —ぼろい儲け口, an opportunity for making money; a source of profit.

boru (ぼる), *vt.* to overcharge; charge unreasonably. ¶ 暴利屋, a dear shop.

bōru (ボール), *n.* ❶ (球) a ball. ❷ (野球) a baseball. ❸ (舞踏會) a ball. ❹ (板紙) board; pasteboard. ¶ ボール箱, a pasteboard-box; a carton.

bōrudo (黒板), *n.* a blackboard.

bōruto (ボールト), **bōto** (ボート), *n.* a bolt. —ボールトで締める, to bolt; fasten with a bolt.

bōryaku (謀略), *n.* stratagem; artifice. —謀略に長ずる, to be skilled in stratagem.

bōryoku (暴力), *n.* violence; force; brute [physical] force. —暴力に訴へる, to appeal [resort] to brute force. —暴力を加へる, to lay violent hands *on*.

bosai (募債), *n.* the raising [flotation] of a loan. —募債する, to raise [float] a loan.

bōsai(亡妻), *n.* the late [deceased] wife.

bōsaki (棒先), *n.* ❶ (うはまへ) a commission; a squeeze. ❷ (駕籠の) the front-bearer (of a palanquin). —棒先を切る, to take a commission; squeeze.

bosan (墓参する), *vi.* to visit a grave; worship at the grave.

Bosatsu (菩薩), *n.* 〔梵〕 Bodhisattva.

bōsatsu (忙殺される), *v.* to be worked to death; be extremely busy; be pressed *with* (business).

bōsatsu (謀殺), *n.* murder; premeditated [wilful] murder. —謀殺する, [*vt.*] to murder. ¶ 謀殺者, a murderer.

bosei (母性), *n.* motherhood.

bōsei (暴政), *n.* tyranny; tyrannical government; despotism.

bōseki (紡績), *n.* spinning. —紡績する, [*vi.*] to spin. ¶ 紡績業, cotton-spinning industry. (紡績業者, a cotton-spinner.) —紡績所, a cotton mill; a cotton-spinnery; a spinning-mill.

bōsen (防戰する), *vi.* to fight in defence; make a stand.

bōsetsuen (傍切圓), *n.* 【數】 an escribed circle; an excircle.

boshi (拇指), *n.* 【解】 the pollex; the thumb.

boshi (蹈趾), *n.* 【解】 the hallux; the big toe.

bōshi (防止する), *vt.* to prevent; check; thwart. —防止的, preventive. —弊害を防止する, to check the evils *of*.

bōshi (帽子), *n.* ❶ (縁ある) a hat. ❷ (縁なき) a cap; a bonnet (婦人用の). —帽子の山, crown. —帽子の儘で, with one's hat on. —帽子を被る, to put on a hat; put one's hat on. —帽子を脱ぐ, to take off one's hat; uncap. ¶ 高帽子, a tall hat. —疊み(高)帽子, an opera-hat. —帽子掛, a hat-peg; a hat-rack; a hat-rail (壁に打附けた小形のもの); a hat-stand. —帽子屋, a hatter.

bōshin (妄信), *n.* ❶ superstition. ❷ (輕信) credulity. —妄信する, to believe unquestioningly; be easy of belief.

bōshitsu(亡失する), *v.* to lose; be deprived *of*.

bōsho (謀書), *n.* a forged document. —謀書謀判の罪, forgery of a document and seal. —謀書する, to forge a document.

bōshō (帽章), *n.* the badge (of a cap or hat).

bōshō (謀將), *n.* a strategist; a general skilled in strategy.

boshoku (暮色), *n.* evening scenery; evening shades.

bōshoku (暴食), *n.* excessive eating; gluttony; voracity. —暴食する, ① [*v.*] to gorge; overeat; raven. ② [*a.*] intemperate; ravenous; voracious. ¶ 暴食家, a great eater; a glutton; a gourmand.

boshū (募集), *n.* levy (兵士·軍隊等); collection(人員·寄附金等); flotation (公債等). **——-suru,** *vt.* to levy [recruit] (兵士·軍隊などを); collect; raise (公債·金員等を). —懸賞小說を募集する, to open a prize contest for novels. —寄附金を募集する, to collect contributions. ¶ 募集係, a collector.

bōshu (防守), *n.* defence. —防守的, defensive. —防守する, to defend; act on the defensive.

bōshu (謀主), *n.* a leader; an arch-plotter.

bōshū (防臭する), *vt.* to deodorize. ¶ 防臭瓣, a trap; a gas-trap; a stench-trap. —防臭劑, a deodorizer.

bōsō (妄想), *n.* chimera; craze; moonshine. —妄想的, chimerical. —妄想に耽る, to be addicted to

moonshining; be given to crazes.
bossho (沒書), *n.* ❶ (寄稿の) a rejected contribution. ❷ (配達不能郵便) a dead letter. ―沒書する, [*vt.*] to reject. ¶ 沒書籠, a waste-paper basket.
bosshū (沒收), *n.* confiscation; forfeiture. ―沒收する, to confiscate. ¶沒收物, a confiscated article [property]; a forfeit.
bosshumi (沒趣味の), *a.* tasteless; insipid; dry.
bos-suru (沒する), *vi.* ❶ (沈む) to sink; go down; set (日・月等の). ❷ (隱れる) to disappear; merge in (something else). ―, *vt.* ❶ (隱す) to sink; hide; drown *in.* ❷ (沒却) to destroy; sink (個性等を). ―太陽地平線下に沒す, The sun dips [sinks] below the horizon.
bos-suru (歿する), *vi.* to die; pass away.
bōsui (防水の), *a.* waterproof. ¶ 防水布, waterproof cloth. ―防水外套, a waterproof coat; a mackintosh; an oilskin. ―防水隔室, a watertight compartment. ―防水組合, an association for protection against floods.
bōsui (紡錘), *n.* a spindle.
bōtakatobi (棒高跳), *n.* 【競技】 pole-vault [-jump]; pole-vaulting.
botamochi (牡丹餅), *n.* a rice-cake covered with bean-jam.
botan (牡丹), *n.* 【植】 the peony; the tree-peony.
botan (鈕, 扣鈕), *n.* a button; a stud (シャツの胸鈕及びカフス鈕等); a sleeve-link (鎖で繋ぎ合はせるカフス鈕). ―扣鈕を外す, to unbutton; undo one's buttons. ―扣鈕を掛ける, to button (up). ―扣鈕をつける, to sew on a button. ¶ 鈕孔, a buttonhole; an eyelet. ―扣鈕掛, a button-hook.
bōtan (妄誕の), *a.* absrud; baseless; groundless.
botankyō (巴旦杏), *n.* 【植】 the almond.
botchan (坊ちゃん), *n.* ❶ a boy. ❷ a baby.
botefuri (棒手振), *n.* a huckster; a pedlar; a hawker.
bōtetsu (棒鐵), *n.* bar-iron.
bōto (暴徒), *n.* a mob; rioters; a rabble. ―暴徒を鎭定する, to quell a riot. ¶ 暴徒嘯集罪, the offence of incitement to riot.
bōto (ボート), *n.* ❶ a boat. ❷ (漕艇) boating. ボートに行く, to go a-boating. ―端艇の練習を始める, to commence boat-training. ¶ 端艇懸け, 【航】 a davit. ―ボートレース, a boat-race; a regatta. ―ボート漕手, a boatman.
bōtō (冒頭), *n.* the opening; the exordium (特に論說等の); the beginning (of a composition or speech).
bōtō (暴投), *n.* 【野球】 a wild pitch.
bōtō (暴騰), *n.* a jump; a sudden rise; 物價の暴騰, a steep rise of prices. ―暴騰する, to (make a) jump; rise suddenly; shoot up.
bōtoku (冒瀆する), *vt.* to defile; pollute; debase. ―尊嚴を冒瀆する, to debase another's dignity.
botsubotsu (勃勃として), *ad.* spiritedly; animatedly. ―勇氣勃々として, his courage being aroused.
botsuga (沒我), *n.* non-egotism; self-effacement. 沒我の域に達する, to rise above self.
botsugo (歿後), *ad.* after death.
botsujōshiki (沒常識), *n.* lack of common sense. ―沒常識な, senseless; wanting common sense.
botsukōshō (沒交涉), *n.* unconnectedness; unconcern. ―沒交涉である, to have nothing to do *with*; have no connection *with*; have no hand *in.*
botsuraku (沒落), *n.* fall; ruin; wreck. ―沒落さす, to ruin; shipwreck; sink. ―沒落する, to fall; be wrecked; be ruined.
botsuryō (沒了する), *v.* ❶ (なくなる) to disappear; vanish. ❷ (盡きる) to be exhausted; come to an end.
botsuzen (勃然), *ad.* ❶ (突然) suddenly. ❷ (憤然) in a flare; firing up. ―勃然挑みに應する, to flash back defiance.
bottō (沒頭する), *v.* to dive *into*; plunge *into*; be engrossed *in.*
bot-to, bōt-to, (茫乎), *ad.* ❶ (朦朧) dimly; hazily. ❷ (茫然) abstractedly; absent-mindedly. ❸ (赧顏) blushingly; flushily. ❹ (火の) flaming up. ―ぼーッと燃え上る, to flame up.
bōu (暴雨), *n.* a heavy [hard] rain.
boya (小火), *n.* a small fire.
bōya (坊や), *n.* sonny; my boy; my darling.
bōzai (防材), *n.* a boom. 河に防材を置く, to boom a river.
bōzatō (棒砂糖), *n.* a sugar-loaf; loaf sugar.
bōzen (茫然), *ad.* ❶ (渺漠) extensively; boundlessly. ❷ (放心) absent-mindedly; vacantly; aghast. ―茫然たる, ① wide; extensive; boundless. ② absent-minded; vacant. ―茫然と立つ, to stand aghast. ―茫然自失する, to be entranced.
bōzen (厖然たる), *a.* large; bulky; extensive.
bōzu (坊主), *n.* ❶ a priest; a

bonze (日本の). ❷ (坊主頭) a tonsure, a shaven head. —坊主になる, ① to become [turn] a priest; ② to shave the head. ¶ 三日坊主, a person of a changeful mind.

bu(分), *n.* ❶ (厚さ) thickness. ❷ (百分の一) per cent. ¶ 五分利公債, the five per cents; fives.

bu (歩), *n.* ❶ a *tsubo* (坪). ❷ (歩割) rate; percentage; a share.

bu (武), *n.* ❶ (武藝) military arts. ❷ (武威) military power; military glory. —武を輝かす, to raise military power. —武を學ぶ, to study military arts.

bu (部), *n.* ❶ (部分) a part; a portion; a region. ❷ (部屬) a bureau; a department; a division. ❸ (書物の) a copy. ¶ 收稅部, the tax-collection department.

buai (歩合), *n.* ❶ (割合) rate. ❷ (百分比例) percentage. ❸ (歩口錢) a percentage. —賣高に應じ歩合を出す, to give a percentage on the proceeds of sale. ¶ 歩合算, (the calculation of) percentage.

buaikyō (無愛嬌の), *a.* charmless; unamiable; disobliging.

buaisō (無愛想), *n.* unsociability; crustiness; surliness. —人に無愛想をする, to be surly to a person. **—-na**, *a.* unsociable; surly; crusty. —無愛想な返事, a short [curt] answer.

bubarai (賦拂), *n.* payment by instalment. ¶ 賦拂込金, instalment.

bubaru(武張る), *vi.* to be soldierlike.

bubetsu (侮蔑), *n.* scorn; insult; contempt. —露骨な侮蔑, open contempt. —侮蔑的, scornful; contemptuous. —侮蔑する, [*vt.*] to scorn; despise; treat with contempt.

bubiki (歩引), *n.* discount. ☞ *waribiki.*

būbū (ぶうぶう), *ad.* ❶ (豚などの鳴聲) gruntingly. ❷ (不平など) grumblingly. —ブウブウ云ふ, [*vi.*] to grumble; growl; grunt.

bubun (部分), *n.* a part; a portion; a section. —部分的, paratil; sectional; divisional. ¶ 部分蝕,【天】a partial eclipse. —部分所有者,【法】a part-owner.

buchi(斑), *n.* ❶ mottles; patches; spots. ❷=*aza* (紫斑). —斑の, pied; dappled; spotted; brindled; mottled. —全身斑だらけである, to have patches all over the body. ¶ 斑猫, a tabby (cat). —斑馬, a dappled horse.

buchikowashi (打壞し), *n.* smash; crash. —打壞しをやる, to mess matters; make a mess of it. ¶ 打壞し屋, a damper; a marplot; a wet blanket.

buchikowasu (打壞す), *vt.* to smash; crash; spoil. —洒落(計畫)を打壞す, to spoil a joke (plot).

buchō (部長), *n.* the head [chief] of a section [division, &c.].

buchōhō (不調法), *n.* ❶ (不束) awkwardness; clumsiness. ❷ (過失) fault; carelessness. ❸ (酒など好まぬこと) inability to drink wi[ne] [or] smoke, &c.]. —不調法の, aw[k]ward; clumsy. ¶ 不調法者, a clumsy person.

budai(ぶだひ), *n.*【魚】the parrot-wrasse.

budan (武斷), *n.* militarism. ¶ 武斷派, a militarist party. —武斷主義, militarism. (武斷主義者, a militarist.)

budō (葡萄), *n.*【植】the grape-vine; the vine; the grape (實). ¶ 葡萄棚, a grape-vine trellis. —葡萄液, grape-juice. —葡萄園, a grapery; a vineyard. —葡萄色, dark purple. —葡萄核, a grape-stone. —葡萄栽培, viticulture. —葡萄酒, wine; vintage wines. —葡萄糖, grape-sugar; fruit-sugar.

budō (無道), *n.* wickedness; viciousness. —無道の, wicked; vicious; unprincipled.

buen (無鹽の), *a.* fresh; unsalted. ¶ 無鹽バタ, fresh butter.

buenryo (無遠慮の), *a.* forward; obtrusive; unreserved. —無遠慮に, forwardly; obtrusively; unreservedly.

bufūryū (無風流), *n.* inelegance; want of taste. —無風流な, inelegant; tasteless.

bugei (武藝), *n.* military arts; military accomplishments (嗜み).

bugen (分限), *n.* ❶=*bungen* (分限)の❶. ❷ (物持) a man of wealth; a rich man. ¶ 一代分限, a parvenu; an upstart. —分限者, a man of wealth.

bugu (武具), *n.* armoury; arms; weapons of war.

bugyo (撫馭), *n.* gentle management; mild control; lenient rule. —撫馭する, to manage gently; control mildly; rule leniently.

bugyō (奉行), *n.* a magistrate; a governor; a high commissioner (of the feudal government).

bui (武威), *n.* military glory [prestige]; military power.

bui (部位), *n.*【醫】a region.

bui (無異), *n.* peace; tranquillity; calmness. —無異の, uneventful; peaceful; quiet.

bui (無爲), *n.* doing nothing. —無爲に苦しむ, to be tired of doing nothing.

bui(浮標), *n.* a buoy; a life-buoy (救命浮標).

buiki(無意氣), *n.* rusticity; gawkiness; ungainliness. —不意氣な, rustic; gawky; ungainly.

buiku(撫育する), *vt.* to bring up; rear; govern leniently (撫馭).

buin, buon, (無音), *n.* not writing (calling). —無音に過ぎる, to neglect to write (call); not to write for a long time. —無音を謝する, to apologize for not writing (calling).

buji (無事), *n.* ❶ (安全) safety. ❷ (平安, 無異) peace; tranquillity; calm. ❸ (閑散) leisure. ❹ = *bunan* の ❷ —無事の, safe; tranquil; peaceful; uneventful. —無事で居る, to be well; be in good health. —無事息災に, safe and sound. **—— ni,** *ad.* safely; in safety; peacefully; without mishap; without any accident. —無事に濟む, to go off without mischance. —無事に暮らす, to live in peace; lead a quiet [an eventless] life.

bujin (武人), *n.* a military man; a man of arms; a soldier.

bujin (無人の), *a.* uninhabited; deserted.

bujoku (侮辱), *n.* insult; affront; indignity (侮辱的待遇). —侮辱する, [*vt.*] to insult; affront; treat with contempt. —侮辱を忍ぶ, to pocket [put up with] insult.

bujutsu (武術), *n.* military arts. ¶ 武術修業, travelling to improve one's military skill; knight-errantry.

buka (部下), *n.* an adherent; a follower; a subordinate; (one's) men. —部下の兵士, soldiers under one's command; one's men. —多くの部下を有する, to have a large following. —部下の勇氣を稱揚する, to praise the bravery of his men.

bukakkō (不恰好な), *a.* clumsy; uncouth; unshapely.

bukan (武官), *n.* an officer; a military (naval) officer. ¶ 侍從武官, an aide-de-camp to His Majesty. —公使館附武官, a military (naval) attaché to a legation.

buke (武家), *n.* ❶ (武門) the military caste (階級); a military family. ❷ (武士) a *samurai*; a knight; a warrior.

buki (武器), *n.* arms; a weapon. —武器を執る, to take up arms. —涙は女の武器, Tears are the woman's weapon.

bukimi (不氣味の), *a.* eerie; uncanny; repulsive.

bukiryō (不器量), *n.* ❶ (醜貌) ugliness; plainness; homeliness. ❷ (不才) want of ability; inability. —不器量の, ① plain; homely; ugly. ② unable; untalented.

bukitchō, bukiyō, (不器用), *n.* awkwardness; clumsiness; unskilfulness. —不器用の, awkward; clumsy; unskilful. ¶ 不器用者, a bungler; a botcher.

bukka (物價), *n.* prices (of commodities). —物價の變動, fluctuation of prices. —物價の騰貴, rise in prices; appreciation of prices. ¶ 物價表, prices current. —物價指數, an index-number of prices.

bukka (物貨), *n.* goods; commodities; articles.

bukkaku (佛閣), *n.* a Buddhist temple.

bukken (物件), *n.* an object; a thing; *res* [羅].

bukken (物權), *n.* 【法】 a real right; rights of things.

bukkirabō (打切棒), *n.* ❶ plainness; unaffectedness; bluntness. ❷ (人) a blunt person; a plain-spoken man. —ぶきッら棒の口のききやうをする, to talk bluntly.

bukku (ブック), *n.* a book (書物); an album (寫眞帖など).

bukkyō (佛教), *n.* Buddhism. ¶ 佛教傳來, the introduction of Buddhism. —佛教青年會, the Young Men's Buddhist Association. —佛教徒, a Buddhist.

bukō (武功), *n.* military achievement [merit]; distinguished military services. —武功を樹てる, to render high military services.

bukoku (誣告), *n.* 【法】 a false charge. —誣告する, to accuse falsely; make a false charge. —誣告の訴を起す, to bring an action on a false accusation.

bukotsu (無骨な), *a.* blunt; churlish; rustic. ¶ 無骨者, a blunt person; a churl.

bukubuku (ぶくぶく), *ad.* ❶ (膨れる貌) dropsically; fatly; plumply. ❷ (沈み行く貌) bubblingly. ❸ (柔な貌) softly. —ブクブク沈む, to sink with bubbles.

bukyō (武俠), *n.* gallantry; chivalry. —武俠的, chivalrous; gallant.

bukyoku (舞曲), *n.* a ballet; a dance; dancing and mosic.

bumon (武門), *n.* ❶ a military family. ❷ (階級) the military class [caste].

bumon (部門), *n.* a branch; a class; a group; a section; a department. —部門分けする, to departmentalize.

bun (文), *n.* ❶ a sentence; a composition (文章); a prose (散文); style (文體); literature (文學); learning (學藝). ❷ (儀禮) ceremony. ❸ (文事) civil affairs. —文を賣る, to write by contract. ¶ 單 (混; 複) 文, a simple (complex; compound) sentence.

bun (分), *n.* ❶ (本分) duty; part. ❷ (分限, 分際) social position [standing]; station (in life). ❸ (區分) part; 【數】 segment (直線の). ❹ (持分) a part; a portion; a share. ❺ (等級) rate; kind. —分相應の, suited to one's position. —この分では, at this rate. —分に安んずる, to be contented with one's lot. —分を守る, to keep to one's sphere in life. —分を辨へる, to know one's place (in the world). —分を盡す, to do one's part [duty]. —半學期分の學費を納付する, to pay a half-term's school fee.

būn (ぶーん), *n.* ❶ (蜂等の鳴聲) hum; drone. ❷ (投石・弦等の唸) tang; twang. —ブーンと唸る, to hum (蜂・獨樂などが): whirr (翼・齒車などが).

buna (山毛欅), *n.* 【植】 Fagus Sieboldi (beech-tree の一種・學名).

bunai (部內), *n.* the circles; the service. ¶ 陸(海)軍部內, military (naval) circles.

bunan (無難), *n.* ❶ (安全) safety; security. ❷ (無缺點) blamelessness; faultlessness. —無難の, ① safe; secure. ② blameless; faultless; free from reproach. —無難に, ① safely; without accident; without a hitch. ② with impunity.

bun'an (文案), *n.* a draft; a sketch. —廣告の文案を作る, to make a draft of an advertisement.

bunben (分娩), *n.* delivery; parturition. —分娩する, to give birth *to*; be delivered *of*; be brought to bed *of*.

bunbetsu (分別), *n.* discrimination (辨別); separation (分離), division (分割).

bunbo (分母), *n.* 【數】 a denominator. ¶ 最小公分母, the least common denominator.

bunbōgu (文房具), *n.* stationery. ¶ 文房具入, a writing-case. —文房具商, a stationer.

bunbu (文武), *n.* ❶ (文學と武藝) literature and military arts. ❷ (文事と兵事) civil and military affairs. ¶ 文武百官, all the civil and military officers. —文武兩道, the arts of war and peace.

bunbun (ぶんぶん), *n.* (蜂・蚊などの) buzz; hum. —ブンブン云ふ, to buzz; hum.

bunbutsu (文物), *n.* ❶ (文學と技藝) learning and arts. ❷ (文明) civilization. ❸ (事物) things. —泰西の文物, things western; western civilization.

bunchi (聞知する), *v.* to learn (*that, how* 等); hear (*that, of, about* 等); be informed *of*. —余輩の聞知する所によれば, it appears from what we hear that....

bunchiha (文治派), *n.* the civilian party.

bunchin (文鎭), *n.* a letter [paper]-weight.

bunchō (文鳥), *n.* 【鳥】 the paddy-bird.

bundan (文壇), *n.* the literary world. —文壇に立つ, to take one's stand [have a footing] in the literary world.

bundoki (分度器), *n.* a protractor.

bundō (綠豆), *n.* 【植】 the hairy-podded kidney bean.

bundori (分捕), *n.* ❶ (鹵獲) capture; seizure. ❷ (私奪) plunder. ¶ 分捕品, a prize (海上の); a loot; a booty; spoils; plunder.

bundoru (分捕る), *vt.* to capture; loot; spoil; plunder.

bunen (無念の), *a.* careless; thoughtless; inconsiderate.

bungai (分外の), *a.* undeserved (賞讃など); undue (望など).

bungaku (文學), *n.* literature; letters. —文學の; 文學的, literary. —文學上, literarily. ¶ 純[美]文學, polite literature; belles-lettres. —軟[輕](硬)文學, light (serious) literature. —文學博士, a doctor of literature (D. Lit. 又は Lit. D. と略す). —文學界, the literary world; the world of letters. —文學者, a literary man; a man of letters. —文學士, a Bachelor of Literature (B. A. と略す).

bungei (文藝), *n.* ❶ (文學) literature. ❷ (文學と藝術) literature and art; the Muses. ❸ (文學的技能) literary accomplishments. ¶ 文藝復興, renaissance; the revival of learning [literature]. —文藝欄, literary column.

bungen (分限), *n.* ❶ (身分) social position [standing]; station of life; ❷ (物持) a man of wealth.

bungo (文語), *n.* the written language; literary language; literary words.

bungō (文豪), *n.* a great writer.

bungyō (分業), *n.* division of labour [work].

bun'i (文意), *n.* the meaning (of a passage); the literary significance.

bunin (無人), *n.* want of persons [hands].

bunjaku (文弱), *n.* literary effeminacy; effeminacy arising from pursuit of literature. —文弱に流れる, to sink into literary effeminacy.

bunji (文事), *n.* literature (文學); learning (學問).

bunka (文化), *n.* culture; civilization. ¶ 文化政策, cultural policy.

—文化主義者, a culturist.
bunka (文科), *n.* the faculty of literature. ¶ 文科大學, the College of Literature.
bunka (分化する), *vi.* to differentiate; specialize.
bunka (分科), *n.* a (branch) department; a faculty. ¶ 分科競漕, an intercollegiate boat-race.
bunka (分課), *n.* a section; a department: formation of sections.
bunkai (分界), *n.* the boundary; the border; demarcation. —分界を立てる, to mark the bounds. ¶ 分界線, a boundary line; the line of demarcation.
bunkai (分解), *n.* analysis; dissolution; resolution; 【文】parsing. —力の分解, resolution [decomposition] of a force. **—— -suru,** *v.* to analyse; decompose; dissolve; resolve; take to pieces; 【文】parse. —化合物を元素に分解する, to resolve [dissolve] a compound into its elements. —機械を分解する, to break up [take to pieces] a machine.
bunkaku (分劃する), *vt.* to graduate; mark off.
bunkan (文官), *n.* a civil official [officer]; a civil servant; a civilian. —文官登用試驗, the civil service examination.
bunkatsu (分割), *n.* partition; division. —分割する, to partition; divide. ¶ 分割拂, payment in [by] instalments.
bunke (分家), *n.* a branch [collateral] family; a cadet house. —分家する, to set up a branch family.
bunken (文獻), *n.* authority.
bunken (分遣する), *vt.* 【軍】to detach; detail. ¶ 分遣艦隊, a detached squadron. —分遣隊, a detachment; a party.
bunki (分岐する), *vi.* to diverge (*from*); branch off; 【電】shunt. ¶ 分岐點, a branching point; the turning point (場所·時間·發達等の); the parting of the ways.
bunko (文庫), *n.* ❶ (手文庫) a box; a casket. ❷ (書庫·圖書館) a library; archives (記錄保存所). ❸ (叢書) a library; a series; collected works. ¶ 巡回文庫, a travelling library.
bunkō (分校), *n.* a branch school.
bunkōjō (分工場), *n.* a branch factory.
bunkōki (分光器), *n.* a spectroscope.
bunkyō (文敎), *n.* (secular) education.
bunkyoku (分極), *n.* 【電】polarization.
bunmawashi (筆規), *n.* a pair of compasses.
bunmei (文名), *n.* literary fame.
bunmei (文明), *n.* civilization. —文明の利器, an effective instrument [a weapon] of civilization. ¶ 文明批評家, a civil critic. —文明國, a civilized country [power].
bunmyō (分明な), *a.* clear; plain; evident; obvious. —分明に, clearly; plainly; evidently.
bunnaguru (打毆る), *vi.* to punch; knock down; thrash.
bunnin (分任), *n.* the division of work; taking charge of work in portions.
bunpa (分派), *n.* a sect; a ramification; a branch. —分派する, ① to form a sect; ramify. ② (分遣する) to detail; detach; draft.
bunpai (分配), *n.* distribution; allotment (割當); partition (分割). —富の分配, distribution of wealth. —分配する, to distribute; allot; partition. —分配に與る, to get a share *of*.
bunpan (文範), *n.* a model composition.
bunpi, bunpitsu, (分泌), *n.* secretion. —分泌する, [*vt.*] to secrete. ¶ 分泌物, a secretion.
bunpitsu (文筆), *n.* literature; letters; the literary art. —文筆に從事する, to pursue literature. —文筆に衣食する, to live by the pen. ¶ 文筆業, pursuit of literature; the profession of letters.
bunpō (文法), *n.* grammar. —文法的, grammatical. —文法上, grammatically. (文法上の誤(意味), grammatical errors (meaning).) ¶ 文法家, a grammarian; a grammatist. —文法書, a grammar.
bunpu (分布), *n.* 【博】distribution. —地理的分布, geographical distribution. —分布する, to be distributed.
bunrei (文例), *n.* an example; a model.
bunretsu (分列), *n.* file-off; filing off. —分列する, to file off. —分列式を行ふ, to have a march-past; march past the reviewing officer.
bunretsu (分裂), *n.* disruption; disintegration; split (黨派等の). —分裂する, to disunite; split; be disrupted.
bunri (文理), *n.* ❶ (木理) the grain. ❷ (文脈) a line of thought; context. —文理解釋, grammatic interpretation.
bunri (分利), *n.* 【醫】crisis. ¶ 分利狀態, a critical condition. —分利期, a critical period.
bunri (分離), *n.* separation; secession; split (黨派等の); severance. —分離する, ① [*vi.*] to separate; secede; split. ② [*vt.*] to separate; segregate; disintegrate.

bunritsu (分立する), *vi.* to separate *from*; secede *from*.
bunro (分路), *n.* 【電】 a shunt.
bunrui (分類), *n.* classification; arrangement; assortment. —分類する, to classify; sort; assort.
bunryō (分量), *n.* quantity; measure. —一定の分量まで, up to a definite quantity.
bunryoku (分力), *n.* 【理】 a component (force; of a force).
bunsai (文才), *n.* literary ability; literary genius. —文才を恃む, to rely upon one's literary ability.
bunsan (分散), *n.* ❶ dispersion; dissipation. ❷ (破產) bankruptcy; insolvency. ❸ 【天】 disintegration. —分散する, to disperse; disintegrate: become insolvent.
bunsatsu (分冊), *n.* a livraison 【佛】; a (serial) part; a separate volume.
bunsei (文勢), *n.* strength; force; literary spirit.
bunseki (文責), *n.* responsibility for the language. —文責記者に在り, The responsibility for the language lies with the writer.
bunseki (分析), *n.* analysis; assay (鑛石の) —分析する, to analyze; assay. ¶ 定量(性)分析, 【化】 quantitative (qualitative) analysis. —分析化學, analytical chemistry. —分析者, an analyst; an assayer. —分析所, an assay office.
bunsen (文選), *n.* ❶ picking out of characters; a character-picker (文選工). ❷ a selection.
bunsha (分社), *n.* a branch office; a branch company (firm).
bunshi (文士), *n.* a literary man; a man of letters. ¶ 文士社會, literary circles.
bunshi (分子), *n.* ❶ 【數】 a numerator. ❷ 【理·化】 a molecule. ❸ (構成要素) an element; an ingredient; a component. ¶ 分子量, molecular weight. —分子式, a molecular formula.
bunshi (分詞), *n.* 【文】 the participle. —現在(過去)分詞, the present (past) participle.
bunshin (文身), *n.* tattoo; tattooing (事).
bunsho (文書), *n.* ❶ (書いたもの) writing; documents; papers. ❷ (記錄) a record; archives. ❸ (書籍) a book. —文書を以て遺言する, to make a will in writing. ¶ 文書僞造, forgery of documents. —文書課, the section of archives [correspondence].
bunsho (分署), *n.* a substation; a branch station; a branch office. ¶ 日比谷警察分署, the Hibiya police substation.
bunshō (文相), *n.* the Minister of Education.
bunshō (文章), *n.* a sentence (文法上の); a composition (作文); an essay (論文). —文章がうまい(拙い), to write a good (poor) style. —文章を書く, to write a composition. ¶ 文章家, a finished [good] writer. —文章論, syntax.
bunshū (文集), *n.* a collection of works; collected works.
bunshutsu (分出する), *vi.* to diverge *from*; branch off; ramify. ——, *a.* divergent; ramifying.
bunso (分疏する), *v.* to explain; apologize.
bunson (分損), *n.* 【商】 partial loss. ¶ 分損擔保, with average. —特擔分損不擔保, free from particular average.
bunsū (分數), *n.* 【數】 a (vulgar) fraction. ¶ 假[帶]分數, an improper fraction. —複分數, a compound fraction. —分數式(方程式), a fractional expression (equation).
bunsuikai (分水界), **bunsuisen** (分水線), **bunsuirei** (分水嶺), *n.* a divide; a watershed; water-parting.
buntai (分隊), *n.* a squad. ¶ 分隊長, the commander of a squad.
buntai (文體), *n.* style. —弱い(强い; 雄健な) 文體, weak (strong; energetic) style.
buntan (分擔), *n.* divided [partial] charge; contribution. ——**-suru**, *vt.* to share *in*; take a share *of*; take over a portion *of*. —費用を分擔する, to bear the expenses in common.
bunten (文典), *n.* grammar (文法); a grammar (文法書).
bunten (分店), *n.* a branch shop [store]; a branch office.
buntsū (文通), *n.* correspondence; exchange of letters. —文通する, to correspond *with*.
buṅun (文運), *n.* the trend (advance) of civilization.
buṅya (分野), *n.* a field (of operations): distribution (of seats).
buṅyo (分與する), *vt.* to distribute (*among*); portion; parcel out.
bunzai (分際), *n.* social standing; condition.
buppin (物品), *n.* an article; a commodity; goods. ¶ 物品陳列場, a bazaar. —物品切手, a presentation ticket. —物品引換拂, cash on delivery (C. O. D. と略す).
buppō (佛法), *n.* Buddhism.
buppōsō (佛法僧), *n.* 【鳥】 the broad-billed roller.
burabura (ぶらぶら), *ad.* ❶ (浮搖) to and fro; danglingly. ❷ (漫步) ramblingly. ❸ (徒食) idly; lazily. ❹ (慢性) lingeringly. —

ぶらぶら歩く, to ramble; stroll; saunter. —ぶらぶら公園を歩き廻る, to take a stroll in a park. —(定職なく)ぶらぶらして居る, to loll about without employment. —一生ぶらぶらして暮す, to saunter through life. ¶ ぶらぶら病, a lingering disease.

burai (無頼の), *a.* knavish; roguish; abandoned. ¶ 無頼漢, a knave; a rascal; a hooligan.

Burajiru (伯剌西兒), *n.* Brazil. ¶ 伯剌西兒人, a Brazilian.

buraku (部落), *n.* a village; a community; a countryside.

burandē (ブランデー), *n.* brandy.

buranko (鞦韆), *n.* a swing; swinging. —ぶらんこに乘る, to get on a swing.

burari-to (ぶらりと), *ad.* ❶(さがる) danglingly; in a dangle. ❷(あてどなく) aimlessly; purposelessly.

burasagaru (ぶら下がる), *vi.* to dangle; hang. —ぶらさげる, to dangle; hang; suspend. —吊革にぶら下がる, to hang by straps.

burashi (ブラシ), *n.* a brush. —ブラシをかける, to brush.

buratsuku (ぶらつく), *vi.* to saunter; ramble; stroll.

burei (無禮), *n.* insolence; disrespect; insult. —無禮な, insolent; impolite; impudent. ¶ 無禮講, a free and easy party.

burēki (制動機), *n.* a brake. —ブレーキを掛け[締め]る, to put on the brake. —ブレーキを緩める, to take off the brake. ¶ 手動ブレーキ, a hand-brake.

buri (鰤), *n.* 【魚】 the yellow-tail.

buri (部理の), *a.* partial; limited. ¶ 部理代(理)人, a special agent.

-buri (振), ❶ (樣子) condition; appearance; manner. ❷ (經て) after; on; in; for. ❸ (分) a portion. —男振り, (a man's) personal appearance. —三日振りの藥, medicine for three days. —十年振りで歸る, to return after ten years' absence. —三人振り誂へる, to order for three.

burikaeshi (ぶり返し), *n.* a relapse.

burikaesu (ぶり返す), *vi.* to relapse; have [suffer] a relapse.

buriki (鉽力, 白葉鐵), *n.* 〔蘭 blik〕 tin-plate. ¶ ブリキ罐, a tin (can). —ブリキ屋, a tinman; a tinsmith. —ブリキ細工, tinware.

Buriten (不列顚國), *n.* Britain; Great Britain. ¶ 不列顚人, a Briton; a Britisher 〔俗〕.

burōkā (仲買人), *n.* a broker.

buromaido (ブロマイド), *n.* a bromide ¶ ブロマイド寫眞, a bromide photograph.

buru (振る), *v.* to affect; assume [put on] the airs *of*; pretend. —, *a.* would-be. —紳士ぶる, to affect the gentleman.

buruburu (戰戰), *ad.* shiveringly; tremblingly. —ぶるぶるする, ① [*vi.*] to shiver; tremble; quiver. ② [*a.*] shivering; trembling.

burudoggu (ブルドッグ), *n.* 【動】 the bulldog.

Burugaria (ブルガリア), *n.* Bulgaria. ¶ ブルガリア人, a Bulgarian; a Bulgar.

burui (部類), *n.* a class; an order; a group. —部類分けする, to classify; divide into groups. —の部類に入る, to come [fall] under the head of.

burujoa (ブルジョア), *n.* (中產階級) the *Bourgeoisie* 〔佛〕.

buryō (無聊), *n.* loneliness; ennui 〔佛〕. —無聊に苦しむ, to feel very much ennuyé; be overcome with ennui. —無聊を慰める, to while away one's loneliness; beguile time.

buryoku (武力), *n.* military power; force of arms. —武力に依って, by force of arms; by military power. —武力に訴へる, to appeal [resort] to arms. ¶ 武力解決, solution by force. —武力干涉, armed intervention.

busahō (無作法), *n.* awkwardness; uncouthness; ungainliness. —無作法な, awkward; uncouth; ungainly. —不作法に, awkwardly; ungracefully.

busaiku (不細工), *n.* botch; bungle; clumsiness. —不細工な, botchy; bungling; clumsy.

busata (無沙汰する), *vi.* to neglect to write 〔call〕.

busei (無勢), *n.* few persons (troops).

bushi (武士), *n.* a *samurai*; a knight; a warrior. —武士の情, a *bushi's* sympathy; knightly fellow-feeling. ¶ 武士道, *bushidō*; chivalry; the way of knighthood. (武士道を立てる, to show the *bushidō* spirit.) —武士氣質, chivalry.

bushitsuke (不躾), *n.* impertinence; ill-breeding; bad [ill] manners. —不躾な, impertinent; ill-mannered; rude; ill-bred. —不躾ながら, though it is rude [unmannerly]; pardon me, but....

busho (部署), *n.* post; quarters (海軍). —部署に就く, to take one's allotted post. (戰鬪部署に就かす, to beat to quarters.)

bushō (無精·不精な), *a.* lazy; indolent; slothful. ¶ 無精者, a sluggard; a lazybones; a slut (女).

bushukan (佛手柑), *n.* 【植】the horned orange.

busō(武裝), *n.* armament; arming oneself. —武裝する, to arm (oneself). ¶ 武裝中立 (平和), armed neutrality (peace). —武裝解除, disarmament. (武裝解除する, [*vt.*] to disarm.) —武裝商船, an armed merchantman; an auxiliary cruiser (補助巡洋艦).

busō (無雙の), *a.* unparalleled; incomparable; peerless.

bussan (物產), *n.* a product; a production. ¶ 主要物產, staple products. —物產地, the land of production. —物產陳列所, a products museum.

busshi (物資), *n.* goods; commodities; resources (資源).

busshi (佛師), *n.* a maker of Buddhist images.

busshitsu (物質), *n.* matter; a substance. —物質的(文明), material (civilization). —物質化する, to materialize. ¶ 物質不滅, the indestructibility of matter. —物質界, the material world. —物質主義, materialism.

bussho (佛書), *n.* a Buddhist book; the Buddhist scriptures.

busshoku(物色する), *v.* to cast about *for*; search *for*; look *for*. ㇾ候補者を物色中, to be looking for the candidate.

busshukaku (物主格), *n.* 【文】 the possessive [genitive] case.

busso (佛祖), *n.* the founder of Buddhism.

bussō (物騷な), *a.* dangerous; unsafe.

bussō (佛葬), *n.* Buddhist burial rites. —佛葬にする, to bury according to Buddhist rites.

busū (部數), *n.* number (of copies, &c.); circulation (新聞發行の); issue (同上)

busui (不粹), *n.* inelegance. —「不粹の, inelegant.

bu-suru(撫する), *vt.* ❶(なでる) to stroke; pat (輕打). ❷ (愛撫) to caress.

buta (豚), *n.* the pig; the hog (特に去勢した); the swine (總稱); the boar (去勢せぬ); the sow (牝豚). ¶ 豚小舍, a pigsty. —豚肉, pork.

butai(部隊), *n.* a force; a party; a detachment.

butai (舞臺), *n.* the stage. —舞臺に出る, to come on [upon] the stage; enter the scene. —脚本を舞臺に上ぼせる, to stage a play. ¶ 舞臺監督, a stage-manager. —舞臺效果, stage-effect. —舞臺指揮, a stage-direction.

butchigai (打違に), *ad.* crosswise. —打違ひにする, to cross.

butchōzura (佛頂面), *n.* a scowl; a sulky [surly] look. —佛頂面する, to scowl; look surly.

butō (舞踏), *n.* dance; dancing. —舞踏する, to dance. ¶ 舞踏病, chorea; St. Vitus's dance. —舞踏服, a dancing dress; a ball-dress. —舞踏會, a ball; a dancing party. (舞踏會を催す, to give a ball.) —舞踏教師, a dancing master. —舞踏室, a ball [dancing]-room.

butsu (佛), *n.* ❶ (佛陀) the Buddha; Gautama (釋迦). ❷ (佛教) Buddhism.

butsubutsu (ぶつぶつ), *n.* (吹出物) a pustule. ——, *ad.* ❶ (囁く) grumblingly; growlingly. ❷ (沸然) simmeringly; pipingly. ❸ (點々) here and there; in patches. —ぶつぶつ云ふ, ① to grumble; mutter. ② [*a.*] grumbling; growling.

butsuda (佛陀), *n.* the Buddha; Sakya (釋迦).

butsudan (佛壇), *n.* the family Buddhist shrine.

butsuden (佛殿), *n.* the Buddhist sanctum.

butsudō (佛道), *n.* Buddhism; Buddhist doctrines. —佛道に入る, to be converted to Buddhism.

butsuga (佛畫), *n.* a Buddhist picture [painting].

butsugaku (佛學), *n.* Buddhist studies. ¶ 佛學者, a Buddhist scholar.

butsugi (物議), *n.* public discussion [controversy]; public criticism [agitation]. —物議を生ずる, to give rise to public discussion.

butsuji (佛事), *n.* Buddhist mass [ceremony]. —佛事を營む, to hold Buddhist mass.

butsujō (物上の), *a.* 【法】real. ¶ 物上擔保, real security.

butsujō (物情), *n.* the state of affairs; things; the public feeling.

butsuma (佛間), *n.* a room for Buddhist services; a prayer-room.

butsumon (佛門), *n.* Buddhism (佛教); priesthood (僧門).

butsuri (物理), *n.* ❶ (物の道理) the law of nature; physical law. ❷ (學) physics. —物理的變化, physical change. ¶ 物理學, physics; natural philosophy. —物理化學, physical chemistry. —物理學者, a physicist.

butsuyoku (物慾), *n.* worldliness; the world. —物慾の, worldly-minded.

butsuzen (佛前), ❶ before the Buddhist shrine. ❷ before the tablet of a deceased person.

butsuzō (佛像), *n.* a Buddhist image.

buttai(物體), *n.* a body; a substance; matter.

buttsukaru (打附かる), *v.* ❶

(衝突) to bump *against*; clash *with* (刀・時間・利益など); knock *against*. ❷ (直接交渉) to negotiate *with*; treat *with*. ❸ (出會ふ) to run *across*; come *across* [*upon*]. —思はず打ッ附かる, to blunder *upon*. —今度の日曜は大祭とぶッつかる, Next Sunday falls on a national holiday.

buttsuke (打附けに), *ad.* ❶ (いきなり) suddenly; abruptly. ❷ (最初に) first. ❸ (卒直に) plainly; unreservedly; roundly.

buttsukeru (打附ける), *vt.* ❶ to throw; fling; shy. ❷ (當てる) to knock *against*; strike *against*; dash *against*. —...に...を打ッ附ける, to dash a thing *against* [*on*].

buun (武運), *n.* military fortune. —武運拙く, ill-starred in war.

buwake (部分け), *n.* classification; sorting. ☞ ***bunrui.***

buyōjin (不用心), *n.* ❶ (不注意) want of caution; carelessness. ❷ (不安心) unsafeness; insecurity. —不用心の, ① incautious; careless. ② insecure; unsafe. —火事の時に不用心だ, It is unsafe when there is a fire.

buyu (蚋), *n.* 【昆】 the saw-fly; the gnat.

buyū (武勇), *n.* valour; bravery; a brave deed.

buzama (無様な), *a.* uncouth; ungainly; unsightly.

byakudan (白檀), *n.* 【植】 the (white) sandalwood. ¶ 白檀油, oil of santal [sandalwood].

byakurō (白鑞), *n.* solder —白鑞で接ぐ, to solder.

byō (秒), *n.* a second.

byō (鋲), *n.* a tack. —鋲止めする, to tack.

byō (廟), *n.* an ancestral shrine; a shrine; a mausoleum (陵). —廟に納める, to enshrine.

byōbō (渺茫たる), *a.* vast; boundless; limitless. —渺茫として, vastly; expansively.

byōbu (屏風), *n.* a (folding) screen. —屏風で仕切る, to screen off. —逆屏風を立てる, to stand a screen upside down.

byōchi (錨地), *n.* a berth; an anchor ground; an anchorage. —錨地に就く, to take up a berth. —錨地を變へる, to shift berth.

byōdō (平等), *n.* equality; evenness. —平等にする, to make equal; equalize; level. **—— -no,** *a.* equal; even. —平等無差別の, equal and without discrimination.

byōdō (廟堂), *n.* the Cabinet; the Ministry.

byōdoku (病毒), *n.* the virus. —病毒を受ける, to be tainted

byōei (苗裔), *n.* a descendant; lineage; the stock.

byōga (病臥する), *vi.* to lie sick [ill].

byōga (描畫), *n.* drawing; copying; painting. —描畫する, to draw; copy; paint.

byōgen (病源), *n.* the cause [origin] of a disease. ¶ 病源菌, pathogenic bacteria; a pathogen(e).

byōgi (廟議), *n.* a cabinet council.

byōin (病院), *n.* a hospital; an infirmary. ¶ 私立病院, a private hospital. —一般病院, a general hospital; a polyclinic. —病院船, a hospital-ship.

byōjaku (病弱の), *a.* weak; infirm; valetudinarian.

byōjō (病狀), *n.* condition (of a disease *or* a patient).

byōjoku (病褥), *n.* the bed of sickness; the sick-bed.

byōka (病家), *n.* a sick family (病人ある家); a patient's house (加療患者の家). —病家を廻る (醫者が), to go one's rounds.

byōki (病氣), *n.* illness; sickness; indisposition. —病氣で引籠る, to be confined by illness. —病氣がなほる, to recover from illness. —病氣に罹る, to be taken ill; fall [get] sick. —病氣のため歸らす, to invalid a person home. —病氣見舞に行く, to visit a sick person; inquire after a sick person. ¶ 病氣缺席, absence on account of sickness. —病氣賜暇, sick-leave. —病氣屆, a report of illness.

byōkin (病菌), *n.* a germ; a disease-germ.

byōkon (病根), *n.* ❶ the cause [origin] of a disease. ❷ (弊害の源) the cause [root] of an evil.

byōku (病苦), *n.* pains of sickness; anguish. —病苦を冒して, in spite of the pains of sickness.

byōku (病軀), *n.* a sick body; a diseased body.

byōmei (病名), *n.* the name of a disease.

byōnin (病人), *n.* a patient; an invalid; a sick person.

byōri (病理の), *a.* pathological. ¶ 病理學, pathology. (病理學者, a pathologist.)

byōsa (錨鎖), *n.* an anchor chain; a (chain-)cable; a hawser (小さな). ¶ 錨鎖孔, a hawse-hole.

byōsei (病勢), *n.* the condition of a disease. —病勢募る, His condition becomes worse. —病勢革る, The illness takes a serious turn.

byōsha (病舍), *n.* an infirmary (學校・救貧院などの); a ward (病院の).

byōsha (描寫), *n.* delineation; representation; portrayal. —描寫

する, to depict; delineate; portray.
byōshi (病死する), *vi.* to die of sickness; succumb to a disease.
byōshin (病身), *n.* ❶ sickliness; infirmity. ❷ a weak [sickly] constitution. —病身の, sickly; invalid; infirm. —病身である, to be in poor health; be sickly.
byōshitsu (病室), *n.* a sick--bay (船中の); a sick-room.
byōshō (病床), *n.* a sick-bed. —病床につく, to be confined to bed; keep one's bed. ¶ 病床日記, a sick-bed record; the nurse's report.
byōshō (病症), *n.* symptoms (of a disease).
byōshō (病傷の), *a.* sick and wounded. ¶ 病傷兵, the sick and wounded soldiers.
byō-taru (眇たる), *a.* little; small.
byōteihō (鋲釘法), *n.* rivetting.
byōteki (病的), *a.* diseased; morbid. ¶ 病的素質, diathesis.
byūken (謬見), *n.* an error; a fallacy. —謬見を固持する, to uphold an error.
byūron (謬論), *n.* 【論】 fallacy.
byūsetsu (謬說), *n.* a mistaken opinion; a false view; a false report (誤報, 誤傳).

C

cha (茶), *n.* ❶【植】 the (Chinese) tea-tree; the tea-plant. ❷ tea. ❸ (茶の湯) tea-ceremony. ❹ = *chairo* (茶色). —濃(薄)い茶, strong (weak) tea. —茶を飲む, to take tea. —茶を淹(い)れる, to make tea. —茶を出す(客に), to serve tea. —お茶を濁す, to get out of a fix. —そんな事はお茶の子だ, Such a thing is very easily done.
chabako (茶箱), *n.* a tea-chest.
chabishaku (茶柄杓), *n.* a tea--ladle.
chaban (茶番), *n.* ❶ an attendant; a waiter. ❷ (茶番狂言) a farce; a burlesque. ¶ 茶番役者, a low comedian.
chabanashi (茶話), *n.* table--talk; tea-talk; tea-gossip.
chabatake (茶畑), *n.* a tea--plantation.
chabo (矮雞), *n.* ❶ a bantam. ❷ (矮身者) a manikin; a pigmy.
chabon (茶盆), *n.* a tea-tray.
chabudai (卓袱臺), *n.* a tea--table; a dining-table[-stand].
chabuya (卓袱屋), *n.* an eating--house, a chop-house.
chacha (茶茶を入れる), *v.* to obstruct; hinder; check; put a spoke in another's wheel.
chadachi (茶斷する), *vi.* to abstain from tea.
chadai (茶代), *n.* a tip. —茶代を遣る, to give a tip; tip.
chadai (茶臺), *n.* a saucer; a presentoir (高い茶臺).
chadansu (茶簞笥), *n.* a tea--cabinet.
chadōgu (茶道具), *n.* a tea-set (一組); a tea-service (同上).
chadokoro (茶所), *n.* ❶ (茶の產地) a tea-growing district. ❷ (葉茶屋) a tea-dealer's.
chagama (茶釜), *n.* a pot for tea-making; a tea-urn.
chagashi (茶菓子), *n.* tea-cake. —客に茶菓子を出す, to offer tea--cake to a visitor.
chagyō (茶業), *n.* tea-dealing; tea-business. ¶ 茶業組合, a tea guild [association].
chahōji (茶焙), *n.* a tea-firing pan (器); tea-firing (事).
chaire (茶入), *n.* a tea-caddy; a tea-canister (罐).
chairo (茶色), *n.* tea-colour; light brown (褐色を帶びた).
chajin (茶人), *n.* ❶ (茶事通) an expert tea-maker. ❷ (好事者) an eccentric.
chaka (茶菓), *n.* tea and cake; refreshments.
chakasshoku (茶褐色), *n.* light brown.
chakasu (茶化す), *vt.* to rally; banter; make fun *of*.
chaki (茶氣), *n.* humour; pleasantry.
chakichaki (嫡嫡), *n.* a pure breed. —部内のちゃきちゃき, the ablest men of the circle.
chakiki (茶試味), *n.* ❶ tea-tasting. ❷ (人) a tea-taster.
chakin (茶巾), *n.* a tea-cloth; a tea-napkin.
chakkō (著港する), *vi.* to arrive in port; make port. —著港の筈, to be due *at*. —船舶著港次第, upon arrival of the vessel.
chakoshi (茶漉), *n.* a tea--strainer.
chaku (著), *n.* (到著) arrival. —, *numeral.* a suit. —著次第, immediately upon arrival. —第一著に, first; in the first place; first of all. —衣服一著, a suit of clothes.
chakuchaku (著著), *ad.* steadily; swimmingly. —著々歩を進める, to make steady progress.
chakuden (著電), *n.* a telegram received.

chakufuku (著服), *n.* ❶ (著衣) dressing. ❷ (私竊) embezzlement; peculation. —著服する, ① (著衣) to clothe oneself; dress; put on clothes. ② (私竊) to pocket; embezzle; peculate.

chakugan(著眼), *n.* aim; observation; attention. —著眼する, to aim *at*; observe; turn one's attention *to*. ¶ 著眼點, the point aimed at; the point of observation.

chakugyo (著御), *n.* arrival. —著御あらせらる, to arrive *at*.

chakui (著衣), *n.* one's clothes. —著衣する, to dress; put on clothes.

chakujitsu (著實な), *a.* steady; trustworthy. —著實に, steadily; honestly. —穩健著實な方針を執る, to take a moderate and steady direction.

chakumoku (著目), *n.* =*chakugan.*

chakuni (著荷), *n.* the arrival of goods [cargo]; arrival (到著荷). ¶ 著荷拂, payment on arrival.

chakuriku (著陸), *n.* 【飛】 reaching the ground; alighting; landing. —著陸する, to reach the ground; alight; land. ¶ 著陸場, a landing-ground [-place].

chakuseki (著席する), *vi.* to take a seat [chair]; sit down.

chakusha (著車), *n.* arrival. ¶ 著車場, the arrival platform.

chakushi (嫡子), *n.* ❶ (嫡嗣) the heir; the eldest son (總領). ❷ (嫡出子) a legitimate child.

chakushoku (著色), *n.* colouring; painting; facing (茶の); tint. —著色する, [*vt.*] to colour; paint; tint; face (茶を). —著色せる, coloured. ¶ 著色畫, a coloured picture; a painting.

chakushu (著手), *n.* commencing; setting about; setting to work. **——-suru,** *v.* to begin; commence; set about; set to work; set one's hand *to*; undertake; start. —事業に著手する, to embark in an undertaking.

chakushutsu (嫡出), *n.* legitimacy. —嫡出の, legitimate; lawful; born in lawful wedlock. ¶ 嫡出子, a legitimate child.

chakusō (著想), *n.* conception.

chakusui (著水する), *vi.* to take to the water (飛行機が).

chaku-suru (著する), *v.* ❶ (被る) to wear (著てゐる); have on (同上); put on (瞬間の動作). ❷ (到る) to arrive *at* [*in*]; get *to*; reach. ❸ (執著) to be deeply attached *to*; be infatuated *with*.

chakuyō (著用する), *v.* to wear.

chame(茶目), *n.* a wag; a joker.

chamise (茶店), *n.* a tea-booth; a resting-booth (掛茶屋). —茶店に憩ふ, to rest at a tea-booth.

chan (瀝青), *n.* pitch; tar. —瀝青を塗る, to tar; coat with pitch.

chanoma (茶の間), *n.* ❶ a sitting-room; a morning-room; a living-room. ❷ a tea-room.

chanoyu (茶の湯), *n.* tea-ceremony. —茶の湯の稽古, lessons in tea-ceremony.

chanpion (選手), *n.* a champion.

chanpon (ちゃんぽん), *n.* mixture; medley. —日本酒とビールとちゃんぽんに飲む, to take *sake* and beer mixed [promiscuously].

chanto (ちゃんと), *ad.* ❶ (整然) in good order; neatly; tidily. ❷ (正確) correctly; precisely. ❸ (完全) perfectly; completely; quite. ❹ (適當) properly. ❺ (歷然) clearly; distinctly. —ちゃんと耳を揃へて金を返す, to return the money in full. **——-suru,** *vt.* to tidy (室·卓·證等を). —ちゃんとした, ① tidy; neat; trim; spruce; smug. ② correct; precise. ③ proper. (ちゃんとした證據を握る, to hold a sure proof.)

chari (茶利), *n.* humour; buffoonery; pleasantry. —茶利を交せる, to put in buffoonery.

charyō (茶寮), *n.* a tea-cottage; a tea-ceremony building.

chashitsu (茶室), *n.* a tea-room.

chashō (茶商), *n.* a tea-merchant; a tea-dealer.

chātā (チャーター), *n.* charter. ¶ チャーター船, a chartered ship.

chataku (茶托), *n.* a saucer.

chatsubo (茶壺), *n.* a tea-pot; a tea-canister; a tea-caddy.

chatsumi (茶摘), *n.* tea-picking.

chauke (茶請), *n.* refreshment; tea-cake; collation; snack.

chawakai (茶話會), *n.* a tea-party; a tea-fight.

chawan (茶碗), *n.* a teacup (喫茶用); a rice-bowl (喫飯用).

chaya (茶屋), *n.* ❶ (葉茶屋) a tea-shop; a tea-dealer's. ❷ (掛茶屋) a (wayside) resting-booth. ❸ (酒樓) a restaurant; a tea-house. ¶ 芝居茶屋, a tea-house attached to a theatre.

chazutsu (茶筒), *n.* a tea-can[-canister].

che (ちェ), **ché** (ちェッ), *int.* (舌打) pooh; tchick; tush.

Chekku (チェック), *n.* a Czech.

chi (血), *n.* ❶ (血液) blood; gore. ❷ (血の道) dizziness. —血あり涙ある, sympathetic. —血に汚れた, blood-stained. —血に渴した, blood-thirsty. —血に塗れる, to be smeared with blood [gore]. —血の附いた, bloody; blood-stained; gory. —血の涙を流す, to weep tears of pain [bitter tears]. —血の雨を降らす, to shower blood. —血の出る様な金, money which is as flesh and blood to one. —血を出す[取る], to bleed; let out blood. —血を湧かせる, to turn the blood. —血を分けた兄弟, a brother german. —血で血を洗ふ, to wash blood with blood; quarrel with blood relations; settle strife by strife. —血を以て購へる, blood-bought.

chi (地), *n.* ❶ the earth (大地); land (陸地); ground (地面). ❷ (位地) position. —地に投げる, to fling down to the ground. —地の利を占める, to have the ground on one's side (試合等で); be on favourable ground. —地を易へて視れば, if we change our position. —道義地を拂ふ, Morality has passed out of this world. —彼の名聲は地に墜ちた, His reputation entirely fell off.

chi (治), *n.* peace; good government.

chi (乳), *n.* a loop.

chi (知), *n.* ❶ (知識) knowledge. ❷ (知合ひ) acquaintance.

chi (智), *n.* ❶ (智力) intellect; understanding. ❷ (智慧) wisdom. ¶ 智仁勇, wisdom, benevolence, and valour. —智を磨き徳を勵む, to sharpen wisdom and stimulate virtue.

chian (治安), *n.* the peace; the public peace. —治安を妨害する(守る), to break (keep) the peace. ¶ 治安妨害, breach of the peace. —治安判事, a justice of the peace. —治安警察法, the peace police law.

chibamu (血含む), *vi.* to turn blue; become livid.

chiban (地番), *n.* a lot number.

chiban (地盤), *n.* the ground. ☞ *jiban.*

chibanare (乳離), *n.* weaning. —乳離れする, to be weaned. ¶ 斷乳兒, a weanling; an infant past the breast.

chibashiru (血走る), *vi.* to be bloodshot. —血走った眼, bloodshot eyes.

Chibetto (西藏), *n.* Tibet, Thibet. ¶ 西藏人, a Thibetan.

chibi (ちび), *n.* a midge; a tot.

chibichibi (ちびちび), *ad.* ❶ (少しづつ) by [in] driblets; in small quantities; little by little. ❷ (吝嗇) scantly; stingily. —ちびちび飲む, to bib; tipple.

chibiru (禿びる), *vi.* to wear out; waste away. —禿びた, worn-out.

chibō (智謀), *n.* craftiness; shrewdness.

chibungaku (地文學), *n.* physiography; physical geography. ¶ 地文學者, a physiographer.

chibusa (乳房), *n.* the breast(s). —赤兒に乳房を含ませる, to give the breast to an infant.

chibusu (窒扶斯), *n.* 【醫】 typhus; typhoid fever. —窒扶斯性の, typhous; typhoid.

chichi (父), *n.* a father. —父らしい, paternal; fatherlike; fatherly.

chichi (乳), *n.* ❶ (乳汁) milk. ❷ =*chibusa, chikubi.* —乳の涸れた牝牛, a dry cow. —嬰兒に乳を飲ます, to give the breast to an infant; suckle [give suck to] a child; give milk to a child. —牝牛の乳を搾る, to milk a cow.

chichi (遲遲), *ad.* ❶ (緩かで迫らぬ) slowly; tardily. ❷ (日永くして暖か) lingering. ❸ (遲く, のろく) languidly; ploddingly. —遲々として進まず, to progress at snail's pace; make slow progress.

chichikata (父方の), *a.* on the father's side; paternal; agnate. —父方の祖母, a paternal grandmother.

chichikubi (乳首), *n.* =*chikubi.*

chichikusai (乳臭い), *a.* ❶ smelling of milk; unweaned. ❷ (黄口の) unfledged; callow; green. —乳臭い少年, a green youth.

chichishibori (乳搾り), *n.* ❶ (搾乳) milking. ❷ (搾乳人) a milkmaid; a dairymaid; a milker.

chichū (地中), underground. —地中の, ① (陸に圍まれた) mediterranean. ② (地の中の) underground; subterranean [-neous]. —地中に埋藏する, to bury in the ground. ¶ 地中海, the Mediterranean (Sea).

chidarake (血だらけの), *a.* bloody; gory. —血だらけになる, to be covered with blood.

chidatsu (褫奪する), *vt.* to strip *of*; deprive *of*; oust. —官位を褫奪する, to deprive a person of his office and rank.

chidome (血止の), *a.* stanching; styptic. —血止めする, [*vt.*] to stanch. ¶ 血止藥, a styptic.

chidon (遲鈍), *n.* ❶ slowness. ❷ dull wit. —遲鈍な, slow; sluggish; slow-witted; dull-witted.

chidori (千鳥), *n.* ❶【鳥】 the plover. ❷【建】 zigzag. —千鳥足に歩く, to walk zigzag.

chie (智慧), *n.* wisdom; wit; intelligence. —智慧の環, the Chinese rings [puzzle]; a puzzle-ring. —智慧ある, (人の) wise; intelligent;

resourceful. —智慧づく, to grow intelligent. —智慧を磨く, to sharpen one's wits. —智慧をつける, to instigate; egg on; incite. —無い智慧を絞る, to cudgel an empty brain. —三人寄れば文殊の智慧, Two heads are better than one. ¶ 智慧齒, a wisdom-tooth.

chieki (地役), *n.* 【法】easement; (predial) servitude.

chien (遲延), *n.* delay; procrastination; 【法】laches. ☞ *entai* (延滯). —遲延する, ① [*vi.*] to delay; be in arrear *with*; be behindhand *with*. ② [*a.*] procrastinating; delaying; dilatory.

chigaeru (違へる), *v.* ❶ (異にする) to change; vary; alter. ❷ (背く) to break (約束等). ❸ (交叉さす) to cross; make (things) overlap each other. ❹ (誤る) to mistake; make a mistake. 足の骨を違へる, to put one's foot out of joint. —路を違へて行く, ① to go by a wrong road. ② (他の道から行く) to take another [a different] path.

chigai (違ひ), *n.* ❶ (差) difference; dissimilarity. ❷ (誤) a mistake; an error. —違ひない, ① [*a.*] certain; sure. ② there is no doubt; I am sure *of* [sure that]; must. —それに違ひない, There is certainly no mistake about it.

chigaidana (違棚), *n.* a pair of shelves overlapping at different levels.

chigai-hōken (治外法權), *n.* extraterritoriality; extraterritorial jurisdiction.

chigaku (地學), *n.* geography. ¶ 地學協會, a geographical society.

chigatana (血刀), *n.* a bloody sword.

chigau (違ふ), *vi.* ❶ (異る) to differ *from*; be different *from* [*to* 【俗】]; be unlike. ❷ (背く) to act (be) contrary *to*. ❸ (交叉する) to cross. ❹ (誤る) to go [be] wrong; be mistaken; be erroneous. ❺ (不一致) to disagree. ❻ (離れる) to deviate; diverge.

chigi (遲疑する), *vi.* to hesitate; vacillate; waver.

chigirechigire (ちぎれちぎれ), *ad.* in pieces; in shreds.

chigireru (捥斷れる), *vi.* to come off; be torn off.

chigiri (契), *n.* ❶ a pledge (誓約); faith (同上); a promise (契約); an engagement (婚約). ❷ 【建】=*chikiri* (袵). —二世の契, marriage troth. 夫婦の契を結ぶ, to be betrothed; plight one's troth *with*.

chigiru (契る), *vt.* ❶ (約束する) to promise; pledge; agree. ❷ (言ひかはす) to engage; engage oneself *to*. 末を契る, to pledge oneself till death.

chigiru (捥切る), *vt.* ❶ (もぎる) to pluck; pick; tear off. ❷ (手で細かに切る) to tear to pieces. 花をちぎる, to pluck [pick] a flower. 袖をちぎる, to tear off a sleeve.

chigo (稚兒), *n.* ❶ (乳呑兒) a baby; an infant; a nursling. ❷ (行童) a temple page.

chigū (知遇), *n.* friendship; acquaintance. —知遇を受ける, to be favoured with friendship.

chiguhagu (ちぐはぐの), *a.* uneven; ununiform; irregular. 揃ってるものをちぐはぐにする, to break what is made in a set.

chigyō (知行), *n.* a fief; a feudatory; a stipend. ¶ 知行取, a stipendiary; a feoffee.

chihā (字華), *n.* the Chinese word-guessing lottery.

chihai (弛廢), *n.* slackening; relaxation. 弛廢する, to slacken; relax.

chihan (池畔), *n.* pond-side.

chihei (地平), *n.* the horizon; the level. —地平の, horizontal. ¶ 地平線, the horizon; the horizontal line. (地平線上(下), above (below) the horizon. —地平線に沿って, horizontally. 地平線下に沒する, to vanish below the horizon.)

chihiro (千尋の), *a.* fathomless; bottomless. —千尋の海, the fathomless sea.

chiho (地步), *n.* ground; stand; standing. 地步を占める, to take one's stand; gain ground. 地步を進める, to make progress. —從來の社會的地步を保つ, to retain one's former social standing.

chihō (地方), *n.* ❶ (一地方) a district; parts; neighbourhood. ❷ (田舍) the country; the provinces. ❸ (國郡) a province. 地方の人, country people. ¶ 仙臺地方, Sendai and neighbourhood. 東北地方, the North-eastern Provinces. —地方病, an endemic. 地方廳, a local government office; a prefectural office. 地方長官, a local governor. 地方行政, local administration. —地方官, a local official [officer]. —地方官廳, the local authorities. 地方裁判所, a local (law) court. —地方新聞, the local press. —地方色, local colour (興論・小說等の). —地方的偏見, localism. —地方稅, rates; a local tax.

chihō(治法), *n.* treatment; method of treatment.

chihō (痴呆), *n.* 【醫】 dementia.

chihyō (地表), *n.* the surface of the ground. —地表に露出する, to appear above (the) ground.

chii (地衣), *n.* 【植】 the lichen.

chii(地位), *n.* ❶ (位置) position; situation. ❷(身分) standing; position; condition; station; caste (階級). —地位ある人, a person of position [condition]. —地位の低い人, a person of humble position.

chiiki(地域), *n.* a district; a tract; an area. —地域を限って許す, to permit within a certain area.

chiiku (智育), *n.* mental training; intellectual culture.

chiisai (小さい), *a.* ❶ (小形の さい) small; little; tiny; minute. ❷ (幼い) juvenile; little; young. ❸ (狭い) narrow. ❹ (微細) fine. ❺ (けちな) petty; insignificant; slight; trifling. —一番小さい, ① (最小) the smallest; the least. ② (最幼) the youngest. —小さい事, little things; a trifle. —小さい時から, from infancy; from childhood. —小さく (小規模に), on a small scale. —小さくなる, to decrease; diminish; shrink; (人前で) sing small [low].

chiji (知事), *n.* a governor; a prefect. ¶ 府縣知事, a prefectural governor. —京都府知事, Governor of Kyōto Prefecture.

chijiki (地磁氣), *n.* terrestrial [earth] magnetism.

chijiku(地軸), *n.* the earth's axis.

chijimaru (縮まる), *vi.* Ⓢ 縮かまる. ❶ (短減) to shorten; contract; dwindle. ❷ (皺寄る) to crumple; wrinkle; shrivel. ❸ (畏縮) to wince; shrink; cower. —縮みあがる, to shrink up. —縮かまって居る, to huddle oneself up.

chijimeru (縮める), *vt.* Ⓢ 縮ます. ❶ (短縮, 減縮) to contract; condense; shorten. ❷ (皺にする) to crumple; wrinkle; shrink. ❸ (引込める) to draw in. —壽命を縮める, to shorten one's life; drive a nail into one's coffin. —首を縮める, to draw in one's head.

chijimi (縮), *n.* (織物) corrugated cloth; crepon; (cotton) crape.

chijimu (縮む), *vi.* ☞ ***chijimaru.***

chijin (地神), *n.* an earthly deity.

chijin (知人), *n.* an acquaintance; a friend.

chijin(痴人), *n.* a fool; a simpleton; an idiot.

chijirasu(縮らす), *vt.* to frizzle; crimp; curl.

chijireke (縮毛), *n.* frizzled [wavy] hair; curl; friz.

chijireru (縮れる), *vi.* to frizzle up; crisp; curl. —縮れた, curly; curled; frizzled.

chijō (地上), *n.* ❶ (地面表) the surface of the ground. ❷ (現世) this world. —地上の, ① on the ground; overground. ② (現世) earthly; terrestrial. ¶ 地上權,【法】 superficies.

chijō (痴情), *n.* a blind passion; foolish [blind] love.

chijoku (恥辱), *n.* shame; disgrace; dishonour. —恥辱を雪ぐ, to clear oneself of shame.

chijutsu (治術), *n.* ❶ medical treatment. ❷ (治國術) statecraft.

chika (地下), *n.* ❶ (土地の下) underground. ❷ (黃泉) the infernal regions; the other world. —地下の,【地質】 subterranean; underground. —地下を通して流れる, to flow underground. ¶ 地下室, a cellar; a basement. —地下水, underground water; ground water. —地下鐵道, an underground railway; the tube(倫敦地下電氣鐵道).

chika (地價), *n.* ❶ (法定の) the assessed value of land. ❷ (賣買上の) the value of land; a land-value. ¶ 地價割, land-rate.

chika (治下), under government. —彼の治下に, under him [his rule].

chikagoro (近頃), *ad.* lately; of late; recently; latterly; in these days (此節); nowadays (同上).

chikai (誓), *n.* ❶ a vow; an oath. ❷ (盟) (二人以上互の) a pledge; engagement; league. —誓を立てる, to take [make; swear] an oath.

chikai (地階), *n.* 【建】 a ground storey [floor].

chikai (近い), *a.* ❶ near; close. ❷ (親しい) intimate. ❸ (時・距離等) short. ——, *vi.* to border [verge] *on*; be near [hard] *upon*; be getting on *for* (年齢, 時間). —近い間柄, close relations; intimacy. —ぢき近い處に, quite close by. —耳が近い, to be quick of hearing. —詐欺に近い, to verge [border] on fraud. —五十に近い, to be near [hard] upon fifty.

chikajika (近近に), *ad.* shortly; in a short time; one of these days.

chikaku (地殼), *n.* the earth's crust.

chikaku (知覺), *n.* ❶ (知り覺ること) consciousness; sensation. ❷ 【心】 perception. —知覺を失ふ, to lose consciousness. ¶ 知覺神經, the sensory nerve.

chikaku (近く), *ad.* ❶ near; close. ❷ (近頃) recently; lately. ❸ (近々) shortly; in a short time.

——, *prep.* by; near; about. —この近くに, in this neighbourhood; near here. —近くにある, to lie (close) *by*. —近くから見る, to take a near view *of*.

chikame (近眼), *n.* ❶ (近視) near-sightedness. ❷ (近視者) a short-sighted [near-sighted] person. —近眼の, near-sighted.

chikamichi (近路), *n.* ❶ (捷路, 捷徑) a short cut [way]; a cut; a cross-cut. ❷ (早道) a royal road *to*. —近道する, to take a short cut; cut off a corner; cut across.

chikan (痴漢), *n.* an ass; a fool; an idiot.

chikan (置換), *n.* 【化】 metathesis: substitution; transposition. —置換する, to substitute; transpose; replace.

chikan (遲緩の), *a.* tardy; dilatory.

chikara (力), *n.* ❶ (筋肉力) strength; might. ❷ (根氣, 精力) spirit; energy; vigour. ❸ (能力) power; capacity; ability. ❹ (威力, 權力) power; force; authority. ❺ (效力) virtue; effect; efficacy. ❻ (助力) aid; help; assistance. —蒸氣の力, the power of steam. —力ある, powerful; energetic; vigorous. —力なき, powerless; forceless; weak. —力の强い, strong; of great strength. —...の力で, by dint *of*; by force *of*; by [in] virtue *of*. —力に任せて, =力任せに. —力が盡きる, to spend itself (暴風等の). —英語の力がつく, to become proficient in English. —...に力を入れる, ① (肩を持つ) to take the part *of*; take another's side. ② (重きを置く) to lay stress *on*. —力の及ぶ限り, to the best of one's ability. —力のあらん限りを爲す, to do one's utmost [best]. —力を落す, to lose one's spirit; lose heart. —力を盡す, =盡力する.

chikaradameshi (力試し), *n.* an essay (試みること); a trial of strength.

chikarakobu (力瘤), *n.* the protuberance caused by the biceps-flexor. —力瘤を入れる, to put energy *into*; do one's utmost.

chikarakurabe (力競べ), *n.* a trial of strength; a passage of [at] arms.

chikaramakase (力任せに), with all one's strength [might]; with might and main; by sheer force.

chikaramochi (力持), *n.* (事) lifting heavy weights: (人) a Titan; the strong man (見世物の).

chikaranuke (力拔), *n.* despondency; dispiritedness; dejection. —力拔けがする, to feel dispirited [dejected].

chikaraotoshi (力落し), *n.* discouragement; disappointment; dispiritedness; despondency; dejection. —力落しする, to lose courage [heart]; be disheartened.

chikarawaza (力業), *n.* ❶ (勞働) labour; rough work. ❷ (力技) a feat of strength.

chikarazukeru (力附ける), *vt.* to encourage; nerve (心身に).

chikarazuku (力附く), *vi.* to recover [gather] strength; convalesce.

chikarazuku (力盡で), by force; by main force; by sheer strength.

chikashii (親しい), *a.* close; near; familiar; intimate. —親しく, closely; intimately.

chikatte (誓ッて), *ad.* by God; by Heaven; by Jove; upon my word; honour bright 〔俗〕. —誓ッて酒を絕つ, to swear off drink.

chikau (誓ふ), *v.* ❶ (神等に) to swear; vow; make [take] an oath. ❷ 〔盟〕 [相互的に] to engage *to*; undertake *to*; pledge oneself. —誓ひ絕つ, to forswear; swear off. —從順を誓ふ, to vow obedience.

chikayoru (近寄る), *v.* ❶ (接近) to approach; come near; draw near. ❷ (交る) to associate *with*. —近寄り難い, inaccessible; unapproachable; difficult of access.

chikayoseru (近寄せる), *v.* Ⓢ 近づける. ❶ (接近) to allow [cause] to come near [approach]. ❷ (昵近) to become intimate; be on intimate terms *with*.

chikazuki (近附), *n.* an acquaintance. —近附きになる, to become acquainted *with*; make another's acquaintance. —どうかお近附きを願ひます, I beg for the pleasure of your acquaintance.

chikazuku (近づく), *v.* ❶ (接近) to approach; draw near; come near. ❷ (交際) to become intimate *with*; associate *with*. —近づき難い, unapproachable; inaccessible. —終りに近づく, to draw to an end [a close].

chikei (地形), *n.* natural features; configuration; topography. ¶ 地形圖, a topographical map.

chikei (笞刑), *n.* whipping; the rod; castigation.

chikemuri (血煙立てて), reeking with blood.

chiken (地券), *n.* a title-deed. ¶ 地券面, the area inscribed in a title-deed.

chiki (知己), *n.* ❶ (己を知ッて與れる者) an appreciative friend. ❷ (知人) an acquaintance; a friend. —知己の榮を辱うする, to be

honoured with his acquaintance.
chiki (稚氣), *n.* boyishness; childishness; puerility.
chikin (鷄肉), *n.* chicken. ¶ チキンカツレツ, chicken cutlet.
chikken (畜犬), *n.* ❶ keeping a dog. ❷ a house-dog. ¶ 畜犬税, dog-tax.
chikketto (チッケット), *n.* a ticket.
chikki (チッキ), *n.* a check. —手荷物をチッキにする, to have one's luggage checked.
chikkō (築港), *n.* harbour-construction. —築港する, to construct a harbour.
chikkyo (蟄居), *n.* ❶ (潜み隱れ) hibernation; seclusion. ❷ (籠居) confinement. —蟄居する, ① to hibernate. ② to sit at home; keep one's [the] house; keep indoors.
chikoku (治國), *n.* the government [rule] of a country. ¶ 治國術, statecraft.
chikoku (遲刻), *n.* lateness; being behind time; being late. **——suru**, *vi.* to be late. —學校を遲刻する to be late at (for) school. ¶ 遲刻簿, a late book (學校の). —遲刻日數, the number of days late. —遲刻點, a late mark.
chikotsu (恥骨), *n.* 【解】 the pubis; the pubic bone. ¶ 恥骨筋, the pectineal muscle.
chiku (麻栗樹), *n.* 【植】 the teak.
chikuba (竹馬), *n.* stilts. —竹馬の友, a friend from childhood; an old playfellow.
chikubi (乳頭), *n.* a nipple; a pap; a teat (人間の); a rubber nipple (ゴム製の).
chikuchiku (ちくちく), *ad.* prickingly; sorely. —ちくちくする, ① [*vi.*] to prick; tingle; ache. ② [*a.*] sore; prickly.
chikudeki (搐搦), *n.* spasm; cramp. —搐搦する, [*vi.*] to vellicate; twitch.
chikuden (蓄電), *n.* charge. ¶ 蓄電池, 【電】 an accumulator; a storage [secondary] battery [cell]. —蓄電瓶, a Leyden jar. —蓄電器, an electric condenser.
chikugo (逐語的に), *ad.* word for [by] word; verbally; verbatim. —逐語的に譯す, to translate verbally [word for word]; metaphrase. ¶ 逐語譯, a verbal [literal] translation; metaphrase.
chikuhaku (竹帛), *n.* a history; a historical record. —名を竹帛に垂る, to leave a name on record.
chikuichi (逐一), *ad.* ❶ (一々) one after another; one by one. ❷ (詳に) minutely; in detail; in full. —逐一陳べる, to specify.
chikuji (逐次), *ad.* successively; in order; step by step. —逐次的, successive. ¶ 逐次配列, seriation; serial formation. —逐次除法, 【數】 successive division. —逐次出版, serial publication.
chikujō (逐條的に), *ad.* article by article. —逐條審議を遂げる, to discuss article by article.
chikujō (築城), *n.* 【軍】 fortification. —築城する, [*vi.*] to fortify. ¶ 築城學 [術], fortification.
chikunen (逐年), *ad.* year by year; annually.
chikuonki (蓄音器), *n.* a phonograph; a graphophone; a gramophone. —蓄音器の針, the recording stylus [needle]; the recorder. —蓄音器の圓盤樂譜, a disk-record of a gramophone.
chikuroku (逐鹿), *n.* contest; competition. —逐鹿場裡の人となる, to become a candidate; appear in the field.
chikurui (畜類), *n.* ❶ (家畜) domestic animals. ❷ (獸類) beasts.
chikusan (畜産), *n.* ❶ live stock. ❷ stock-breeding; stock-farming. ¶ 畜產學, zootechny; zootechnics.
chikuseki (蓄積), *n.* ❶ (貯へること) accumulation; storing up. ❷ (貯へ) (*a*) store: (*b*) hoard; savings. —蓄積する, to store; accumulate; hoard.
chikushō (畜生), *n.* a brute; a beast. **——**, *int.* Hang it!; Damn it! —畜生同樣の, beast-like; brute-like.
chikushō (蓄妾), *n.* concubinage.
chikuten (逐電する), *vi.* to abscond; decamp; run away.
chikutei (築堤), *n.* embankment. —築堤する, to embank; dike, dyke.
chikuzai (蓄財), *n.* ❶ (ためた財) a store of money; a hoard; accumulated wealth. ❷ (ためること) thrift; amassment of money. —蓄財する, to lay up money; save up (儉約して). ¶ 蓄財家, a thrifty person; a money-maker. —蓄財主義, thriftiness.
chikuzō (築造), *n.* construction; erection. —築造する, to construct; erect; build.
chikyō (地峽), *n.* an isthmus; a neck.
chikyōdai (乳兄弟), *n.* a foster-brother; a foster-sister.
chikyū (地球), *n.* the earth; the globe. ¶ 地球儀, the globe; the sphere; the terrestrial globe.
Chikyūsetsu (地久節), *n.* the Empress's birthday.
chimamire (血塗れの), *a.* blood-stained; bloody; smeared with

blood. —血塗れになる, to be smeared with blood.

chimanako (血眼), *n.* a blood-shot eye; a red eye. —血眼になッて探す, to search for it with blood-shot eyes.

chimata (巷), *n.* ❶ (岐路) a cross-way. ❷ (街) a street.

chimatsuri (血祭), *n.* blood-offering.

chimayou (血迷ふ), *vi.* to run [go] mad; be out of one's senses; be in a frenzy. —血迷へる群集, a frenzied crowd.

chimei (地名), *n.* a place-name; the name of a place. ¶ 地名辭書, a gazetteer.

chimei(知名の), *a.* noted; famous; celebrated. —知名の士を聘する, to engage a person of note.

chimei(致命), *n.* fatalness; mortalness. **——-teki,** *a.* fatal *to*; mortal *to*; vital; deadly. —致命的打擊, a death [mortal] blow. ¶ 致命症, a fatal disease. —致命傷, a death-wound; a mortal [vital] wound. (致命傷を負ふ, to be mortally wounded.)

chimi(地味), *n.* fertility (of soil). —肥えた地味, a fertile [rich] soil.

chimitsu (緻密な), *a.* delicate; minute; subtle. —緻密な細工, an elaborate work. **——-ni,** *ad.* minutely; closely; subtly; elaborately. —緻密に調査する, to make a close examination.

chimu (團, 組), *n.* a team (野球·蹴球などの). ¶ チームレース, a team race.

chin(狆), *n.* the lap-dog; the pug-dog; the Japanese spaniel [pug].

chin(亭), *n.* an arbour; a summer-house.

chin (珍), *n.* ❶ curiousness; strangeness. ❷ (珍奇物) a curiosity. —珍な, curious; odd; strange.

chin (朕), *n.* We. —朕惟ふに, it seems to Us.

chin (賃), *n.* hire (借り賃, 雇ひ賃); wages (勞銀); fare (乘車·乘船賃); freight (運賃). —賃を拂ふ, to pay one's fare.

chinamagusai (血腥い), *a.* ❶ (血の香がする) bloody; smelling of blood. ❷ (殺伐な) bloody; sanguinary.

chinami(因), *n.* connection; relation. —因に, by the way; in this connection; in passing.

chinamu (因む), *vi.* to be connected *with* (關係); call [name] after(命名). —地名に因み斯く名づく, It is so called after the name of the place.

chinatsu (鎭壓), *n.* suppression; subjugation. —鎭壓する, to subjugate; suppress; subdue.

chinba (跛), *n.* ❶ (跛行) lameness; limp. ❷ (跛行者) a lame man [person]. ❸ (片方の不足) an odd pair. —跛の, ① lame; limping. ② (片方の不足せる) odd. —跛にする, to cripple. —跛に足駄を穿く, to wear an odd pair of clogs. ¶ 跛行抜き(水泳), trudgen stroke.

chinbotsu (沈沒), *n.* sinking; foundering (浸水沈沒). —沈沒する, to sink; go down; founder. (碇泊中に沈沒する, to founder at her anchors.) ¶ 沈沒船を引揚げる, to raise a sunken ship.

chinbu(鎭撫する), *vt.* to pacify; quell; appease; tranquillize. —ストライキを鎭撫する, to quell a strike.

chinbun (珍聞), *n.* a curious news [story].

chinchaku (沈著), *n.* calmness; composure; self-possession. —沈著な, self-possessed; composed; serene. —沈著に, composedly; serenely.

chinchikurin (ちんちくりんの), *a.* short; short-statured; dwarfish.

chinchin (ちんちん), *n.* (小鈴·鍵等の鳴る響) clang-clang; jingle. —チンチン云ふ, to clang; chink.

chinchō (沈重), *n.* (愼重) care; prudence. —沈重に處理する, to manage with prudence.

chinchō (珍重する), *vt.* to set a high value *upon*; set store *by*; make much *of*; prize.

chindai (鎭臺), *n.* a garrison.

chindan (珍談), *n.* a news; an interesting story.

chindeki (沈溺する), *v.* to be addicted *to*; abandon oneself *to*; give oneself up.

chinden (沈澱), *n.* 【化】 precipitation; deposition; sedimentation. —沈澱する, to precipitate; deposit. ¶ 沈澱物, 【化】 a precipitate; a sediment; a deposit. —沈澱池, a settling-pond.

chinetsu (地熱), *n.* the heat of the earth.

chingaiyaku (鎭咳藥), *n.* a cough-cure; a cough remedy.

chingara (珍柄), *n.* (織物) a fine [rare] pattern.

chingin (沈吟する), ❶ to ponder; meditate. ❷ (小聲で歌ふ) to hum.

chingin (賃銀), *n.* wages; pay; fare (乘賃). —相當の賃銀に對する相當の勞働, a fair day's work for a fair day's wages. ¶ 時間(出來高)拂賃銀, time (piece) wages. —實價(呼價)賃銀, the real (nominal) wages. —最低賃銀, minimum wages. —生活賃銀, living wages. —賃銀基金說, the wages-fund theory. —賃銀支拂表, a pay-bill; a pay-sheet. —賃銀鐵則, the iron law of wages.

chingo (鎮護), *n.* guard; protection. —鎮護する, to guard; protect.

chinji (椿事, 珍事), *n.* ❶ an accident; a tragedy; a disaster. ❷ (珍らしい出來事) a curious event.

chinjō (陳情する), *vi.* to state one's views [opinions]. ¶ 陳情者, a memorialist; a spokesman. —陳情書, a memorial; a petition.

chinju (鎮守), *n.* a local deity; a tutelary deity. ¶ 鎮守祭, the fête of the local deity.

chinjufu (鎮守府), *n.* an admiralty (port); a naval station. ¶ 橫須賀鎮守府, the Yokosuka Admiralty Port.

chinjutsu (陳述), *n.* a statement; a declaration; deposition (證人の). —陳述する, to state; declare; set forth; depose. —陳述書を發する, to issue a written statement.

chinka (沈下), *n.* sinking; subsidence; sag. —沈下する, to sink; subside; sag.

chinka (鎮火する), *vi.* to be put out; be extinguished.

chinki (丁幾), *n.* a tincture. ¶ 規那丁幾, tincture of quinine. —丁幾劑, a tincture.

chinki (珍奇), *n.* novelty; rarity; curiosity. —珍奇の, novel; curious; rare.

chinkoro (狗兒), *n.* a pup, puppy; a doggy, doggie.

chinkyaku (珍客), *n.* a rare guest; a welcome visitor.

chinmari (ちんまりした), *a.* snug; cosy; compact.

chinmi (珍味), *n.* a dainty; a delicacy; a titbit. —珍味の, dainty; delicate.

chinmochi (賃餅を搗く), to pound rice-cake on contract.

chinmoku (沈默), *n.* silence; reticence; taciturnity. —沈默の, silent; taciturn; close-tongued; reticent. —沈默する, to hold one's tongue. —沈默さす, to silence; tie a person's tongue; put to silence. —沈默を破る, to break the silence. —沈默を守る, to observe [keep] silence; remain mute [silent]. ¶ 沈默家, a man of few words; a taciturn person.

chinmurui (珍無類の), *a.* most curious; quaintest; queerest.

chinne (珍値), *n.* a fancy price.

chinnyū (闖入), *n.* intrusion; trespass. —闖入する, to break [burst] *into*; trespass *into*; intrude *upon*.

chinō (智能), *n.* intellect; talent. ¶ 智能犯, intellectual crime. —智能考査, mental test.

chinō (智囊), *n.* brain.

chinomiba (乳齒), *n.* a milk-tooth.

chinomigo (乳呑兒), *n.* a baby; a suckling; an infant at the breast.

chinpin (珍品), *n.* a curio; a rare article.

chinpon (珍本), *n.* a rare book.

chinpu (陳腐な), *a.* stale; commonplace; trite. —陳腐な洒落, a stale joke; a chestnut.

chinpunkan (陳糞漢), *n.* ❶ gibberish; jargon. ❷ one who talks gibberish.

chinretsu (陳列), *n.* exhibition; display; show. —陳列する, to exhibit; display. —陳列して, on view. ¶ 陳列箱; 陳列棚, a glass-case; a show-case. —陳列品, exhibited articles. —陳列館, a museum. —陳列窓, a show-window. —陳列室, a show-room.

chinrin (沈淪する), *vi.* to sink *into*; be ruined. —不幸に沈淪する, to be steeped in misery; sink into the depth of misery.

chinsei (沈靜), *n.* ❶ (平靜) placidity; calmness; stillness. ❷ (商況不振) flatness; dulness; slackness. —沈靜する, to be still; abate (苦痛・風等が); settle (騷が).

chinsen (賃錢), *n.* wages; fare (乘賃); carriage (運賃). ¶ 賃錢表示器, a taximeter. —賃錢先拂, carriage forward.

chinsetsu (沈設する), *vt.* to lay. ¶ 沈設水雷, a submarine mine.

chinsha (陳謝する), *v.* to apologize *for*; express one's regret. ¶ 陳謝狀, a written apology; a letter of apology.

chinshaku (賃借), *n.* hire; lease (土地の). —賃借する, to lease; rent; hire. ¶ 賃借地, leased land. —賃借權, (the right of) lease. —賃借人, 【法】a lessee; a hirer.

chinshi (沈思), *n.* meditation; reflection; contemplation. —沈思する, to meditate; ponder over; reflect.

chinshigoto (賃仕事), *n.* a job; jobwork; piece-work.

chinsho (珍書), *n.* a rare book. ¶ 珍書狂, bibliomania; a bibliomaniac (人).

chintai (沈滯), *n.* dulness; stagnation. —沈滯する, to stagnate. —商業を沈滯さす, to depress trade; cause stagnation of trade.

chintai (賃貸), *n.* hire; letting out; lease. —賃貸する, to lease

(土地を); rent (土地・家屋などを); charter (船舶を); job (馬・馬車などを). ¶ 賃貸價格, a rental value. —賃貸契約, a lease. —賃貸人,【法】a lessor; a letter.

chintei (鎮定), *n.* suppression; quelling; tranquillization. —鎮定する, to suppress; quell; tranquillize.

chintō (枕頭に), *ad.* at the bed-side; by one's bedside.

chintsū (沈痛な), *a.* painful; agonizing; racking.

chintsū (鎮痛の), *a* soothing; paregoric. —鎮痛する, to alleviate [mitigate; assuage] pain. ¶ 鎮痛劑, an alleviative; a lenitive; an anodyne; a paregoric.

chin̓utsu (沈鬱), *n.* melancholy; gloom; depression. —沈鬱な, melancholy; gloomy; depressed.

chin̓yū (沈勇), *n.* cool courage.

chinza (鎮座する), *vi.* to take up an abode; dwell.

chin-zuru (陳ずる), *vt.* ❶ (陳述) to state; set forth. ❷ (辯明) to explain.

chion (地溫), *n.* underground temperature.

chippokena (ちっぽけな), *a.* very small; very little; minute; tiny; wee.

chippu (チップ), *n.* (纏頭) a tip.

chippuku (蟄伏), *n.* ❶ (冬眠) hibernation; dormancy; winter sleep. ❷ (潜伏) (lying in) concealment. —蟄伏する, to hibernate; conceal oneself.

chirabara (ちらばら), *ad.* scatteringly; stragglingly; here and there.

chirabaru (散ばる), *vi.* ❶ to be scattered about; straggle. ❷ (弘まる) to spread; circulate; diffuse.

chirachira (ちらちら), *ad.* ❶ (霏々) fluttering. ❷ (明滅) flickering. ❸ (眩惑) dazzling. ❹ (定まりなく) fitfully; by fits. —ちらちらする, ① (光・星等) to twinkle; wink. ② (灯・焰等) to waver; flicker. ③ (眩惑) to be dazed; be dazzled.

chirahora (ちらほら), *ad.* here and there; by twos and threes. —ちらほら咲く, to bloom here and there; bloom by twos and threes.

chirakaru (散らかる), *vi.* to be in disorder; be scattered about. —散らかす, to scatter.

chirari (瞥りと), *ad.* at a glance; hastily; a little. —ちらりと見る, to glance at; catch a glimpse *of*; cast a look [an eye; a glance] *at*. —ちらりと耳にする, to catch the ear; hear it whispered.

chirashi (散らし), *n.* ❶ (散亂) scattering. ❷ (亂雜) disorder. ❸ (鮨) loose *sushi*. ¶ 散らし髮, loosened hair. —散らし藥,【醫】a resolvent; a dissolvent. —散らし廣告, a handbill; a leaflet.

chirasu (散らす), *vt.* ❶ (散落) to scatter; shed. ❷ (散布) to scatter; strew; sprinkle (灰・水等を). ❸ (離散) to disperse; dissolve; break up. ❹【醫】to resolve (腫物を). ❺ (髮を) to loosen; let down. —蕾の花を散らす, ① to scatter a flower in the bud. ② (夭折) to go [be cut off] before one's bloom. —蜘蛛の子を散らす如くに逃げ去る, to run away in all directions.

chiratsuku (ちらつく), *vi.* ❶ (眩惑) to be dazed; be dazzled. ❷ (彷彿) to flitter. ❸ (明滅) to flicker. ❹ (きらきらする) to twinkle; wink.

Chiri (智利), *n.* Chili. ¶ 智利人, a Chilian. —智利硝石, Chili [cubic] saltpetre.

chiri (塵), *n.* ❶ (塵埃) dust; grime. ❷ (塵芥) rubbish; garbage. —塵にまみれた, dusty; covered with dust; grimy. —塵を拂ふ, to shake off the dust; dust. —塵っぱ一つないやうにする, to clean a room so that there is not a speck of dust in it. —塵も積れば山と成る, "Little and often make a heap in time."

chiri (地利), *n.* advantage of position; a vantage-ground; a strategic advantage.

chiri (地理-學), *n.* geography. —地理的, geographic(-al). (地理的位置, geographical position.) ¶ 政治地理, political geography. —世界[萬國]地理, universal geography. —商業地理, commercial geography. —地理學者, a geographer. —地理哩, a geographical mile. —地理書, a geography.

chiriakuta (塵芥), *n.* rubbish; litter; garbage. —金錢を塵芥の様に浪費する, to make ducks and drakes of one's money; throw [fool] away one's money.

chiribameru (鏤める), *vt.* to set; mount (寶石等を); inlay. —金剛石を鏤める, to set diamonds. —眞珠を鏤めた指環, a pearl ring.

chirigami (塵紙), *n.* toilet-paper.

chirige, chirike, (身柱), *n.* the nape (of the neck).

chiriharai (塵拂), *n.* a dust-brush; a duster.

chirijiri (散散に), *ad.* scattered; here and there; straggling. —散り散りばらばらになる, to scatter; straggle; disperse.

chirikemuri (塵煙), *n.* a cloud of dust.

chirimen (縮緬), *n.* silk crape; crêpe. ¶ 縮緬紙, crêpe-paper.
chirinchirin (ちりんちりん), *n.* ting; tinkle; clink (鐸の音). —, *ad.* ting-ting. —チリンチリン鳴る, to tinkle; jingle (鈴など); ting.
chirirenge(散蓮華), *n.* an earthenware spoon.
chiritori (塵取), *n.* a dust-pan.
chiriyoke(塵除), *n.* a dust-cloth; a dusting-sheet. ¶ 塵除服, a dust--cloak; a dust-coat; a dust-wrap. —塵除眼鏡, goggles.
chiru (散る), *vi.* ❶ (散落) to fall; scatter. ❷ (離散) to scatter; disperse. ❸ (浸出) to spread; diffuse. ❹ (放散) to be distracted. ❺ (消散) to disperse; be resolved. —散りも初めず咲きも殘らず, in full bloom; with no blossom yet scattered or left unopened.
chiryaku (智略), *n.* craft; resources.
chiryo (智慮), *n.* prudence; wisdom; thought. —智慮の深《淺》い人, a man of great《little》prudence.
chiryō (治療), *n.* ❶ (醫術を施すこと) medical treatment. ❷ (治療すること) cure; remedy. —治療中, (under) medical treatment. —治療する, to treat; cure. —治療し難い, irremediable; incurable; remediless. —治療の見込が無い, to have no hope of recovery. ¶ 治療所, an infirmary.
chiryoku (知力, 智力), *n.* intellect; mental capacity [power]; intellectual power.
chisa (萵苣), *n.* 【植】the garden lettuce.
chisan (遲參), *n.* lateness; being behind time. —遲參する, to come [arrive] late; be behind time. ¶ 遲參者, a late comer.
chisei(地勢), *n.* physical features.
chisei (治世), *n.* ❶ (治まれる世) the (piping) time of peace. ❷ (在位間) reign. —ヴィクトーリア女皇の治世, the reign of Queen Victoria.
chisha(知者, 智者), *n.* a sage; a wise man; a man of resource.
chisha (治者), *n.* the ruler; the governing.
chishi (地誌), *n.* a geography; a topography.
chishi (智齒), *n.* a wisdom-tooth. —智齒を生ずる, to cut one's wisdom-tooth.
chishiki(知識), *n.* ❶ knowledge; information; learning (學識). ❷ (智識)(名僧) a learned priest. —知識ある, learned; well-informed. —知識を擴める, to improve one's knowledge. ¶ 知識階級, the intellectual class; intelligentsia. —知識慾, passion for knowledge.
Chishima (千島), *n.* the Kurile Islands; Kuriles. ¶ 千島海流 (親潮) the Kurilian current.
chishio (血汐), *n.* blood; gore. —血汐に染まる, to be stained with blood.
chishitsu (地質), *n.* geology; the nature of soil. ¶ 地質學, geology. (地質學者, a geologist.)
chishitsu (知悉する), *vt.* to know completely; be fully informed *of*; be fully aware *of*.
chiso (地租), *n.* land-tax. ¶ 地租委讓, assignment of land-tax. —地租割, land-rate.
chisō (地層), *n.* 【地質】a stratum [*pl.* -ta]; a layer.
chisō (馳走), *n.* dinner; feast; entertainment. —馳走する, to entertain; treat; feast; regale.
chisoku(遲速), *n.* speed; velocity; progress.
chisso (窒素), *n.* nitrogen. ¶ 窒素瓦斯, nitrogen gas. —窒素肥料, nitrogenous manure.
chissoku (窒息), *n.* suffocation; asphyxia; asphyxiation. —窒息さす, to suffocate; choke; asphyxiate; smother. —窒息する, to choke; suffocate; smother. ¶ 窒息瓦斯, asphyxiating gas. —窒息性蒸氣, suffocating vapours.
chisui (治水), *n.* river-improvement. ¶ 治水工學, hydraulic engineering. —治水工事, embankment works; riparian works.
chisuji(血筋), *n.* lineage; stock; blood.
chi-suru(治する), *vt.* ❶ to cure; heal. ❷ (匡正) to correct; reform. ❸ (支配) to govern. —病を治する, to cure a person of his disease; heal a person's disease.
chitai(地帶), *n.* a zone; a belt; a region.
chitai (遲滯), *n.* delay; retard; arrear. —遲滯なく, without delay; forthwith; promptly. —遲滯さす, to delay. —遲滯する, ① [*vi.*] to delay. ② [*a.*] dilatory.
chitchana(小っちゃな), *a.* wee; tiny.
chitchoku (黜陟), *n.* promotion and degradation. —黜陟する, to promote or degrade.
chitei (治定), *n.* decision. —治定する, [*vt.*] to fix; decide.
chiteki (知的), *a.* intellectual.
chiten(地點), *n.* a point; a spot. —豫定の地點, the intended spot.
chitoku(知得する), *vt.* to learn; be informed *of*; become acquainted *with*. —事實を知得する, to acquaint oneself with facts.
chitsu (帙), *n.* a case [cover] for books.

chitsujo (秩序), *n.* order; discipline. —秩序的, orderly; methodical. —秩序のない, disordered. —秩序を亂して, out of order; in disorder. —秩序整然として, in perfect order. —社會の秩序を亂す, to subvert social order.

chitsuzuki (血續), *n.* blood-relationship; blood-kindred.

chitto (些と), *ad.* ❶ (僅少) a few (數); a little (量,度). ❷ (暫時) for a while; a bit. ❸ (稍) somewhat; rather; slightly. —ちッと大き過ぎる, It is a little too large. —ちッとお休みなさい, Rest a while. —ちッとお待ち下さい, Please wait a bit.

chittomo (ちッとも), *ad.* (否定的に) ❶ at all; a bit; in the least. ❷ for a moment [an instant]. ☞ *sukoshimo* (少しも). —ちッとも知りませんでした, I had not the slightest knowledge of it. ちッとも痛いことはない, I do not feel any pain.

chiwa (痴話), *n.* lovers' talk; love-talk. ¶ 痴話喧嘩, lovers' quarrel.

chiyahoya (ちやほやする), *v.* to make much *of*; pay assiduous attentions *to*.

chiyo (千代), *n.* a thousand ages. —千代に八千代に, for ever (and ever); for aye.

chizu (地圖), *n.* ❶ a map; a chart (海圖). ❷ (書物) an atlas. —地圖で(捜し)見る, to look up on a map. ¶ 掛地圖, a wall-map. —折地圖, a folding-map.

cho (著), *n.* work. —マコーレーの全著, the complete works of Macaulay.

cho (緒), *n.* the beginning; the end (of a thread). —緒に就く, to come to the beginning (of a thing).

chō (丁), *n.* ❶ (偶數) an even number. ❷ (書物の紙數にいふ) a leaf. ❸ (豆腐の切數にいふ) a block.

chō (疔), *n.* 【醫】 a carbuncle; a furuncle.

chō (町), *n.* ❶ (距離) a *chō* (120 yards). ❷ (面積) a *chō* (2.45 acres). ❸ (市街) a street. ❹ (都會) a town.

chō (兆), *n.* 【數】 a billion 〔英〕; a trillion 〔米〕.

chō (兆,徵), *n.* a sign; a symptom; an omen.

chō (長), *n.* ❶ (上長) a head; a chief; a principal. ❷ (長所) merits; best. —長を取り短を捨てる, to utilize the strong points and disregard the weak ones.

chō (挺), *numeral.* a pair (鋏など); a block (墨など); a piece (墨·銃など). —錨二挺, two anchors.

chō (朝), *n.* ❶ (朝廷) the court. ❷ (治世年間) a reign; an epoch. ❸ (政を聽くこと) holding court. ❹ (朝見) a levée. ❺ (王朝) a dynasty. ¶ 平安朝, the Heian epoch. —清朝, the Tsin dynasty.

chō (腸), *n.* ❶ 【解】 the intestines. ❷ (臟腑) the bowels; the entrails.

chō (蝶), *n.* the butterfly.

chō (調), *n.* ❶ (調子) tune; pitch; key. ❷ (樂譜) a note. ❸ 【文】 the voice (態). ❹ (曲) a mode; a song. ❺ (句調) a tone.

chō (寵), *n.* favour. —寵を受ける, to be in a person's favour.

chō (廳), *n.* an office; a government.

chōai (帳合), *n.* account; balance of accounts; stock-account. —帳合する, to balance the accounts.

chōai (寵愛), *n.* favour. —寵愛の, pet; favourite; darling. —寵愛する, to favour; caress; pet.

chōba (丁場), *n.* ❶ a station; a stage. ❷ a *jinrikisha*-house.

chōba (帳場), *n.* a counter.

chōba (調馬), *n.* horse-training; horse-breaking. —調馬する, to train horses; break in horses. ¶ 調馬師, a horse-breaker.

chōba (嘲罵), *n.* taunt; jeer; sneer. —嘲罵する, to taunt (*with*); laugh *at*; jeer *at*.

chōbatsu (懲罰), *n.* chastisement; punishment; penalty. —懲罰する, to chastise; punish. —懲罰に付せられる, to be referred to the disciplinary committee. ¶ 懲罰委員, a disciplinary committee.

chōbi (掉尾の), *a.* active towards the end; final. —掉尾の勇を鼓する, to make a final brave effort.

chōbo (帳簿), *n.* an account-book; a book. —帳簿上の貸(借), book credit (debt). —帳簿へ記入する, to enter in an account-book; enter accounts. —帳簿を締切る, to close the books. —帳簿を檢査する, to audit accounts. ¶ 帳簿方[係], a book-keeper.

chōbo (徵募), *n.* enlistment.

chōbō (眺望), *n.* prospect; view. —眺望する, to take a view *of*; look *upon*. —眺望絶佳である, to command a most beautiful view.

chōbon (張本), *n.* (事件の起因) the origin [cause] of an affair. ¶ 張本人, a leader; a chief.

chōbun (弔文), *n.* a funeral address.

chōbun (長文の), *a.* lengthy; long.

chōchaku (打擲), *n.* thrashing; hiding. —打擲する, to thrash; beat; maul; give a hiding.

chōchibusu (腸窒扶斯), *n.* typhoid (fever); enteric [gastric] fever.

chochiku (貯蓄), *n.* ❶ (蓄へること) storing up; saving; laying by. ❷ (蓄へ) store (物品等の); savings (金錢). —貯蓄する, [*vt.*] to store; save; lay by [aside]. ¶ 貯蓄銀行, a savings-bank. —貯蓄心, a thrifty spirit; thriftiness. —貯蓄預金, savings deposit.

chōchin (提燈), *n.* a lantern. ¶ 提燈競走, a lantern race. —提燈持ち, ① a lantern carrier. ②(他人のお先になる人) a bottle-holder; a candle-holder; a puffer. ③ (空讚) puff; puffery. (提燈持ちをする, to hold the candle *for*; puff.)

chōchō (町長), *n.* a town-headman.

chōchō (喋喋), *ad.* garrulously; volubly; fluently. —喋々する, to prate; chatter; talk at length.

chōchō (蝶蝶), *n.* the butterfly.

chōchū(腸蟲), *n.* the enterozoon; an intestinal worm.

chō-chū-seppō (帳中說法), *n.* a curtain-lecture.

chodai (著大な), *a.* great; vast; immense.

chōdai (頂戴), *n.* (貰ふこと) receipt; acceptance. —...頂戴, please; be good enough *to*. —頂戴する, ① (貰ふ) to receive; accept; take; have. ② (懇請) to ask *for*; beg *for*. —それを借して頂戴な, Do lend it me, please.

chōdaisoku (長大息する), *vi.* to heave [give] a deep [heavy] sigh.

chōdatsu (調達), *n.* supply; purveyance (食料の); provision (同上). **—— - suru,** *vt.* to raise (調金); supply (供給); purvey; provide. —資金を調達する, to raise a fund *for*.

chōden (弔電), *n.* a telegram of condolence. —弔電を發する, to send a telegram of condolence.

chōdo (丁度), *ad.* ❶ (宛然) as if; as though. ❷ (きちんと) just; precisely; sharp; flat (距離, 時間勘定, 重量). —丁度眞中に, right in the middle. —丁度五時に, at five sharp; just [exactly] at five.

chōdo (調度), *n.* supply; service, ¶ 調度課, the supplies section.

chōdokyū(超弩級艦), *n.* a super-dreadnought.

chōeki(懲役), *n.* penal servitude. ¶ 有(無)期懲役, penal servitude for a term of years (for life). —懲役人, a convict.

chōetsu (超越), *n.* ❶ (すぐれたこと) superiority; excellence. ❷ (世俗を脫すること) transcendence. ❸ (踰越) exceeding one's powers; acting *ultra vires*. ☞ *chōzetsu*. —超越的, transcendental. —超越する, ① to be superior *to*; excel; surpass. ② to transcend; rise above. ③ to exceed [go beyond] one's powers; act *ultra vires*.

chōfu (貼附する), *vt.* to affix *to*; stick *on*. —印紙を貼附する, to affix a revenue-stamp.

chōfuku (重複), *n.* repetition; redundancy; pleonasm. —重複の, repeated; redundant; pleonastic. —重複する, [*vi.*] to be repeated; be redundant.

chōfun (鳥糞), *n.* guano.

chōga (朝賀), *n.* offering congratulations to the Emperor.

chōga (潮河), *n.* a tidal river.

chōgai (蝶貝), *n.* 【貝】 the pearl-oyster.

chogen (緒言), *n.* an introduction; a preface; a foreword.

chōgenbō (ちゃうげんばう), *n.* 【鳥】 the kestrel; the merlin.

chōgi (長技), *n.* a speciality.

chōgi (朝儀), *n.* an Imperial [a cabinet] council.

chōgō (調合), *n.* mixture; preparation; composition. **—— - suru,** *vt.* to mix; compound; prepare. —藥を調合する, to make up medicine. ¶ 調合劑, a mixture; a preparation.

chōgū(寵遇), *n.* special favour; patronage.

chōgyo(釣魚), *n.* angling. —釣魚の友, a brother of the angle.

chōhan (丁半), *n.* ❶ (采の目の奇數と偶數) odd and even numbers. ❷ (賭博) gambling. —丁半を爭ふ, to gamble.

chōhatsu(挑發), *n.* 【法】 provocation; incitement. —挑發的, provocative; suggestive (色情の). —挑發する, to provoke; incite; suggest. (劣情を挑發する, to excite low passions.)

chōhatsu (徵發), *n.* requisition; commandeering; forage. —徵發する, to requisition; commandeer; impress. (馬匹を徵發する, to requisition horses.) ¶ 徵發令, a requisition order.)

chōhei (徵兵), *n.* conscription; a conscript. —徵兵を免れる, to be exempted from conscription. ¶ 徵兵忌避, evasion of military service. —徵兵檢查, medical examination for conscription. —徵兵令, the conscription law. —强制(志願)徵兵制度, the compulsory (voluntary) conscription system.

chōhen (長篇), *n.* a long work.

chōhō (弔砲), *n.* a minute gun.

chōhō (重寶な), *a.* serviceable; convenient; handy. ¶ 重寶者, a handy-man.

chōhōkei(長方形), *n.* a rectangle; an oblong.

chōi (弔慰), *n.* condolence. —弔慰の爲め, for condolence. —弔慰金, condolence-money.
chōi (弔意), *n.* condolence. —弔意を表する, to express condolence.
chōi (重圍), *n.* a siege; an investment. —敵の重圍に陷る, to be besieged [invested] by the enemy.
choichoi (ちょいちょい), *ad.* occasionally; now and then; at times. —ちょいちょい出て行く, to go out at times.
chōikataru (腸胃加答兒), *n.* gastro-enteric catarrh.
chōin (調印), *n.* affixing a seal; sealing. —調印する, to set a seal (捺印); sign and seal (記名調印). ¶ 調印國, signatory powers.
choito (ちょいと), ❶ (呼掛け) I say; please. ❷ (稍) just; slightly; a little bit. ❸ with a (sudden) jerk (ぐいと); quickly (ひらりと); suddenly. —ちょいと見る, to glance *at*. —ちょいと跳び退く, to jump away quickly.
chōja (長者), *n.* ❶ (目上) (*a*) a senior; an elder: (*b*) one's betters; one's superiors. ❷ (身分の高い人) a man of position. ❸ (族長) a chief; a headman. ❹ (素封家) a man of wealth; a wealthy person.
chōjakumono (長尺物), *n.* a long film; a long picture.
chōji (丁子), *n.* ❶【植】the cloves; the clove pink. ❷ (黑味を帶びた淡黃色) dusky yellow. ❸ (燈心の先に出來る黑い塊) snuff. ¶ 丁子油, oil of cloves.
chōji (弔辭), *n.* (an expression of) condolence; a funeral oration (葬式の時の). —弔辭を陳べる, to express one's condolence.
chōji (停止), *n.* (差止) suspension; temporary prohibition. ¶ 御停止, suspension of musical performances during Imperial mourning.
chōji (寵兒), *n.* a pet; a favourite.
chōji (懲治), *n.* correction; chastisement; castigation. —懲治的, penitentiary; corrective. —懲治する, to chastise; correct. ¶ 懲治監, a house of correction; a penitentiary.
chōjin (超人), *n.* 【哲】a superman; an overman.
chōjin (鳥人), *n.* a bird-man; an aviator.
chōjiri (帳尻), *n.* balance; balance-account. —日本銀行の今週の帳尻, this week's balance-account of the Bank of Japan. —帳尻を誤魔化す, to cook accounts.
chō-jiru (長じる), *v.* Ⓢ 長ずる. ❶ (生長) to grow. ❷ (熟達) to be versed *in*; excel *in*; be expert *in*. ❸ (耽る) to indulge *in*; be addicted *to*.
chōjo (長女), *n.* the eldest daughter.
chōjō (長上), *n.* one's betters; one's superiors; one's senior.
chōjō (重疊), *n.* ❶ (重なること) being piled up; being placed one upon another; superposition. ❷ (滿足) excellence; admirableness. —重疊する, [*vi.*] to be piled up; rise one upon another.
chōjō (頂上), *n.* ❶ (いただき) the summit; the top. ❷ (極點) height; zenith; climax. —小山の頂上, a hill-top. —頂上に達する, ① to reach the summit. ② to rise to the highest pitch.
chōju (長壽), *n.* a long life; longevity. —長壽を保つ, to live long; reach old age.
chōjū (鳥銃), *n.* a fowling-piece.
chojutsu (著述), *n.* ❶ (著作) writing a book. ❷ (著作物) a work; writings. —著述する, to write a book. ¶ 著述業, authorship; profession of letters. —著述家, an author; a writer.
chōka (町家), *n.* a tradesman's house; business quarter.
chōka (超過), *n.* excess. —超過する, [*vt.*] to exceed. ¶ 超過額, balance; excess.
chōkai (町會), *n.* at own assembly. ¶ 町會議員, a town assembly-man.
chōkai (潮解), *n.* 【化】deliquescence. —潮解する, to deliquesce; deliquate.
chōkai (懲戒), *n.* discipline; reprimand. —懲戒する, to reprimand, discipline. ¶ 懲戒處分, a disicplinary disposition.
chōkaku (頂角), *n.* a vertical angle.
chōkaku (聽覺), *n.* (sense of) hearing; audition.
chōkan (長官), *n.* a chief; a president. ¶ 北海道長官, the Governor of Hokkaidō.
chōkanmaku (腸間膜), *n.* 【解】the mesentery.
chōkanzu (鳥瞰圖), *n.* a bird's-eye view.
chōkataru (腸加答兒), *n.* intestinal catarrh.
chōkei (長兄), *n.* the eldest brother.
chōkei (長計), *n.* a plan [design] for a many years' undertaking. —百年の長計を立てる, to make a plan for a century.
chōkekkaku (腸結核), *n.* intestinal tuberculosis.
chōken (朝憲), *n.* the constitution. —朝憲を紊亂する, to defy [act in defiance of] the constitution.
chōkeshi (帳消), *n.* ❶ (帳簿の取消) cancelling an account; writing-off. ❷ (相殺) quitting scores; making even. —帳消にする, to

write off; strike a balance; cancel (square) an account; quit scores. 一死ねばすべて帳消し, "Death quits all scores."

chōki (弔旗), *n.* a flag at half-mast. —弔旗を揭げる, to hoist the flag half-mast high.

chōki (長期), *n.* a long date; maximum term (刑等の). —長期の, long; long-dated. ¶ 長期貸付, a long-term loan.

chōki (聽器), *n.* the organ of hearing.

chokin (貯金), *n.* savings. —貯金する, to save money; lay aside [by; up] money. ¶ 日掛貯金, daily savings. —貯金箱, a money-box; a savings-box. —貯金通帳, a (savings) deposit pass-book. —貯金局, a savings-office.

chokka (直下する), *vi.* to plunge (瀧など); fall perpendicularly. —直下一千二百丈, a perpendicular fall of 12,000 feet.

chokkai (ちょっかいを出す), *vi.* ❶ to snatch. ❷ (横合から手を出すこと) to meddle; put in one's oar; put out a hand.

chokkaku (直角), *n.* a right angle. —直角の, rectangular; right-angled. —直角をなして, at right angles. ¶ 直角三角形, a right-angled triangle.

chokkaku (直覺), *n.* 【心】 intuition. —直覺的に, intuitively; instinctively. ¶ 直覺判斷, intuitive judgment.

chokkatsu (直轄), *n.* direct control. ¶ 文部省直轄學校, a school under the direct control of the Education Department.

chokkei (直系), *n.* a direct line. ¶ 直系卑(尊)屬, a lineal descendant (ascendant). —直系親, a lineal relative.

chokkei (直徑), *n.* a diameter; direct distance.

chokki (チョッキ), *n.* a waistcoat; a vest 米

chokkin (直近の), *a.* immediate; nearest.

chokkiri (ちょっきり), *ad.* ❶ (短く) shortly. ❷ (正しく) just; exactly. ❸ (物を切る時) quickly.

chokkō (直行), *n.* ❶ (正しい行) honesty; uprightness. ❷ going direct; (列車) a through train. —直行する, to go direct *to*; come streight *from*.

chokkō (直航), *n.* a direct voyage. —孟買に直航する, to sail direct to Bombay. ¶ 直航船, a direct steamer.

chokkura (ちょっくら), *ad.* ❶ (速に) quickly; in a short time; in a hurry. ❷ (暫時) for a while. ❸ (ちょっと) just.

chokkyo (勅許), *n.* royal charter; Imperial permission. —勅許を仰ぐ, to beg for Imperial sanction.

chokkyū (直球), *n.* 【野球】 a line drive.

choko, choku, (猪口), *n.* a *sake*-cup.

chōkō (朝貢), *n.* bringing a tribute to the country. —朝貢する, to bring a tribute.

chōkō (潮港), *n.* a tidal harbour.

chōkō (潮候), *n.* a tide period.

chōkō (潮紅), *n* reddening of the face. —潮紅する, to flush; redden; crimson.

chōkō (徵候), *n.* a symptom; an indication; an omen. —徵候を呈する, [*vt.*] to betray; omen; augur.

chōkō (聽講), *n.* attendance (at a lecture). —聽講する, to attend. ¶ 聽講券, an attendance [lecture]-ticket. —聽講料, a lecture fee. —聽講生, a student attending a lecture.

chokochoko (ちょこちょこ), *ad.* ❶ (頻々)=*chokuchoku* (ちょくちょく). ❷ (せせこましく) bustling; in a hurry. —ちょこちょこする, ① (せせこまし) to bustle about; hurry about. ② (ひょろひょろ) to toddle along; totter.

chōkoku (彫刻), *n.* engraving; carving; sculpture. —彫刻する, to engrave; carve; sculpture. ¶ 彫刻物, a carving; an engraving; a statue. —彫刻術, engraving; sculpture. —彫刻師, a carver; an engraver; a sculptor. —彫刻刀, a burin (銅版の); a graver.

chokorēto (チョコレート), *n.* chocolate.

chōkotsu (腸骨), *n.* 【解】 the ilium.

chokozai (猪口才な), *a.* ❶ shallow; superficial. ❷ conceited; impertinent.

chōkōzetsu (長廣舌), *n.* a long tongue; garrulity; loquacity. —長廣舌を揮ふ, to give loose to [set loose] one's tongue.

choku (直), *n.* ❶ (正直) right; integrity. ❷ (眞直) uprightness. ❸ (當直) duty. ❹ (廉價) cheapness. —直な, ① (氣輕な) lively; airy; open-hearted. ② (廉價の) cheap; low-priced. —直に, ① airily; light-heartedly. ② cheaply; at a low price.

choku (勅), *n.* an Imperial order.

chōku (長軀), *n.* a tall body; high stature.

chōku (白墨), *n.* chalk.

chokuchō (直腸), *n.* the rectum.

chokuchoku (ちょくちょく), *ad.* now and then; at times; often. —ちょくちょく出掛ける, to go out now and then.

chokudai (勅題), *n.* the subject

of the ode to be presented to the Imperial Court.

chokuei (直營する), *vt.* to manage directly. 一政府の直營事業, enterprises under direct government management.

chokugen (直言), *n.* outspokenness; plain speaking; bluntness. 一直言する, to speak bluntly. ¶ 直言直行, plain speaking and straightforward action. 一直言家, a plain-spoken man.

chokugo (勅語), *n.* an Imperial rescript [speech]. ¶ 教育勅語, the Imperial Rescript on Education.

chokugo (直後に), immediately after.

chokuhitsu (直筆), *n.* ❶ (筆を眞直にして書く) writing with an upright hair-pen. ❷ (有の儘書く) unadorned writing; plain writing.

chokujō (直情の), *a.* impulsive. 一直情の人, a man of impulse. 一直情徑行の, straightforward; simple-hearted

chokujō (勅諚), *n.* an Imperial order.

chokunin (勅任), *n.* direct Imperial appointment. ¶ 勅任官, an official directly appointed by the Emperor. 一勅任敎授, a professor of the *chokunin* rank.

chokurei (直隷), *n.* being under direct control. 一直隷する, to be under direct control.

chokurei (勅令), *n.* an Imperial edict; an Imperial ordinance. 一勅令を以て發布する, to issue by Imperial order; promulgate as an Imperial ordinance.

chokuritsu (直立), *n.* ❶ (眞直に立つ) standing erect [straight]; perpendicularity. ❷ (高度) height. 一直立せる, erect; upright; perpendicular. 一直立する, to stand; stand erect; stand bolt-upright (棒立). 一直立一千尺, a height of 1000 feet; 1000 feet in height. 一直立不動の姿勢を取る, to assume an erect and immobile posture; stand at attention.

chokuryū (直流), *n.* 【電】 a direct current. ¶ 直流發電機, a direct current dynamo.

chokusai (勅裁), *n.* Imperial decision. 一勅裁を仰ぐ, to submit to Imperial decision.

chokusen (直線), *n.* a straight line. 一直線の, straight; rectilinear. 一一直線に, in a bee [crow; straight] line; as the crow [stork] flies. 一一直線に行く, to take [make] a bee-line. ¶ 直線形, a rectilinear figure.

chokusen (勅選), *n.* Imperial nomination. ¶ 勅選議員, a member (of the House of Peers) nominated by His Majesty.

chokuseppō (直說法), *n.* 【文】 the indicative (mood).

chokusetsu (直接の), *a.* direct; immediate; first-hand (傳聞など). 一直接に, immediately; direct; directly; at first-hand. ¶ 直接談判, direct negotiation. 一直接行動, a direct action. 一直接(國)稅, a direct (national) tax.

chokusha (直射), *n.* a direct shot [hit]; a direct fire. 一直射する, to fire direct *upon* (砲火); shine directly *upon* (光線が). 一日光の直射を受ける, to be exposed to the direct light of the sun.

chokushi (勅使), *n.* an Imperial messenger.

chokushi (勅旨), *n.* an Imperial order.

chokushin (直進), *n.* direct advance. 一直進する, to go right on; follow one's nose.

chokutsū (直通), *n.* direct communication. 一直通する, to communicate directly. ¶ 直通列車, a through train.

chokuyaku (直譯), *n* a literal [word for word] translation. 一直譯する, to translate literally [word for word].

chokuyu (勅諭), *n.* an Imperial mandate.

chokuzei (直稅), *n.* a direct tax.

chokuzen (直前の), *a.* forward. 一直前する, to come forward without hesitation.

chōkyo (聽許), *n.* permission; grant. 一聽許する, to permit; grant.

chōkyori (長距離), *n.* a long [great] distance. ¶ 長距離電話, a long-distance telephone. 一長距離飛行, a long-distance flight. 一長距離砲, a long-range gun.

chōkyū (長久), *n.* continuance; permanence. 一武運長久を祈る, to pray for continuance of military fortune.

chōmaku (腸膜), *n.* 【解】 the peritoneum. ¶ 腸膜炎, peritonitis.

chomei (著名な), *a.* prominent; noteworthy; noted. 一著名な人, a person of note; a celebrity.

chomei (著明な), *a.* clear; evident; obvious. 一著明な證據, clear evidence.

chōmei (長命), *n.* a long life; longevity. 一長命の, long-lived; longeval. 一長命する, to be long-lived; live long.

chōmen (帳面), *n.* an account-book (計算帳); a ledger (臺帳); a register (記錄, 登記簿). 一帳面につける, to keep account *of*; enter in the book. 一帳面をつける, to

keep accounts. [ing; seasoning.
chōmi (調味), *n.* flavouring; dress-
chōmin (町民), *n.* a townsman; townspeople; townsfolk; the town.
chōmon (弔問), *n.* a visit of condolence. —弔問する, to pay a visit of condolence; call to express condolence.
chōmon (聽聞), *n.* listening; hearing; audience. —聽聞する, to listen *to*; hearken *to*; give ear *to*.
chōna (釿), *n.* an adze.
chōnai (町内の), *a.* within the town (ward); of the town. —町内の噂, town-talk.
chōnan (長男), *n.* the eldest son.
chonbori (ちょんぼり), *ad.* a bit; a little; a drop.
chōniku (鳥肉), *n.* fowl; flesh [meat] of fowl.
chōnin (町人), *n.* a citizen; a tradesman; townsfolk.
chonmage (丁髷), *n.* a top-knot; a queue.
chōon (長音), *n.* a prolonged sound; 【聲音】 a long vowel [syllable]. —長音の, 【音】 major; 【聲音・詩】 long. ¶ 長音階, 【音】 major scale.
chōon (調音), *n.* intonation; harmonic; tuning. —調音する, to harmonize; modulate.
chōonki (聽音器), *n.* an audiphone; an acousticon. [slightly.
choppiri (少許), *ad.* a little;
chōraku (凋落), *n.* ❶ (凋枯) withering; fading. ❷ (落魄) ruin; decay; decline. —凋落する, ① to fade; wither. ② to decay; be ruined; fall into decay; decline.
chōrei (潮齡), *n.* the age of the tide.
chōrei (廳令), *n.* an office ordinance. ¶ 警視廳令, an ordinance [order] of the Metropolitan Police Department.
chōren (調練), *n.* drill; parade; military exercise. —調練する, to drill; parade. ¶ 調練場, a parade ground.
chōri (重利-法), *n.* compound interest. —重利で計算する, to compute at compound interest.
chōri (超理的), *a.* supernatural; mystic.
chōri (調理), *n.* ❶ (處理) arrangement; putting in order. ❷ (割烹) cooking. —調理する, ① to put in order; put straight; manage. ② to cook; dress. ¶ 調理臺, a dresser. —調理法, the method of cooking; cookery; cuisine. [still.
choritsu (佇立する), *vi.* to stand
chōro (朝露), *n.* morning dew.
chōrō (長老), *n.* ❶ (老年者) an elder; a father. ❷ (高德の老僧) a father. ❸ 【宗】 (長老教會の) a presbyter; an elder. ❹ (佛寺の) a superior. —市の長老, the Father of the city. ¶ 長老派, 【宗】 Presbyterianism. —長老教會, the Presbyterian Church.
chōrō (嘲弄), *n.* derision; scoff; mockery. —嘲弄する, to deride; scoff *at*; jeer *at*. ¶ 嘲弄者, a scoffer.
chorochoro (ちょろちょろ), *ad.* tricklingly. —ちょろちょろ流れる, to trickle.
choromakasu (瞞著す), *vt.* ❶ (欺く) to cheat; bamboozle; hoodwink. ❷ (私儉) to pilfer; make free *with*. —人の金をちょろまかす, to cheat a man out of his money.
choron (緒論), *n.* introduction.
chōrui (鳥類), *n.* the birds; the feathered tribe.
chōryō (跳梁), *n.* gambolling; frisking; strutting. ☞ *bakko* (跋扈). —跳梁する, to gambol; frisk about; strut about. [boid.
chōryōkei (長菱形), *n.* a rhom-
chōryoku (張力), *n.* 【理】 tension; tensile force.
chōryoku (聽力), *n.* hearing; the power of hearing. ¶ 聽力計, an acoumeter; an audimeter.
chōryū (潮流), *n.* ❶ (海流) a tide; a tidal current; a stream. ❷ (風潮) tendency; trend; drift; stream; current. —世の潮流に從ふ, to follow the fashion; go with the stream; swim with the tide.
chōsa (調査), *n.* examination; inquiry; investigation. —調査する, to examine; investigate; inquire *into*. —其の筋の調査に據れば, according to inquiry made by the authorities. —調査の方針を定める, to fix upon the plan of investigation. ¶ 調査委員, a commission [commitee] of inquiry.
chosaku (著作), *n.* a literary work; a work; a production. ¶ 著作權, copyright. (著作權登錄, copyright registered; entered at Stationers' Hall 【英】)
chōsan (朝餐), *n.* breakfast. —朝餐をする, to (take) breakfast.
chōsei (長生), *n.* longevity. —長生する, to live long.
chōsei (長逝), *n.* death; decease. —長逝する, to pass away; die.
chōsei (鳥聲), *n.* a bird-call; a bird-cry.
chōsei (調製), *n.* preparation; concoction. —調製する, ① (作成) to draw up; get up. ② (製造) to concoct (藥など); prepare; make.
chōsei (調整), *n.* adjustment;

putting in order; regulating. —調整する, to regulate; adjust; put in order. ☞ *chōsetsu.*

chōseki(長石), *n.* 【鑛】feldspar; felspar; felstone(岩石中に混じた).

chōseki (朝夕), *n.* morning and evening.

chōseki (潮汐), *n.* a tide.

Chōsen (朝鮮), *n.* Chōsen; Korea. ¶ 朝鮮語, Korean. —朝鮮人, a Korean; a Corean. —朝鮮人參, ginseng. —朝鮮總督(府), the Governor-General (Government-General) of Chōsen.

chōsen (挑戰), *n* challenge; defiance. —挑戰する, to challenge; call to combat; offer [bid; give] battle; call out; fling [throw] down the gauntlet. —挑戰的態度に出る, to take a provocative attitude.

chōsetsu(調節), *n.* ❶ (事物の) regulation; adjustment; accommodation. ❷ (精神の) attemperment. —調節する, ① to accommodate; regulate (機械·時計を); adjust. ② to attemper. ¶ 調節器, 【工】a regulator; a governor.

chosha (著者), *n.* an author; a writer.

chōsha (長者), *n.* ❶ (年長者) a senior; an elder. ❷ (長上) one's superiors; one's betters. ❸ (高德者) a man of virtue. ☞ *chōja.*

chōsha(諜者), *n.* a spy; a police-spy; a secret agent.

chōsha (聽者), *n.* a listener; the audience (聽衆).

chōshi (弔詞), *n.* condolence. —弔詞を讀む, to read out an address of condolence.

chōshi (銚子), *n.* a *sake*-holder; a bottle.

chōshi(調子), *n.* ❶ (音調) strain; note; tune. ❷ (語調) tone; strain; accent (抑揚). ❸ (論調) tone. ❹ (工合) rate (分). ❺ (はずみ) chance; impetus; spur. —調子の好い, sociable; companionable. —調子の低い, low-pitched. —調子の高い, high-pitched. —調子外れの, out of tune; tuneless; discordant; disharmonious. —調子づく, to get into the way; catch the infection; work oneself up. —調子が外れる [狂ふ], to get out of tune. —調子に乘る, to let oneself go. —調子を上げる, to raise the tune; tone up. —調子を下げる, to lower one's tone. —調子を變へる, to change one's tune [note]. —調子よく運轉する, to work smoothly. ¶ 調子外れ, ① (調子不整)【音】discord. ② (脫線) disharmony.

chōshin (長針), *n.* the long [minute-] hand.

chōshin (朝臣), *n.* a courtier; the court (全體).

chōshin (調進), *n.* purveyance; catering; supply. —調進する, to purvey (食物を); serve (料理などを); supply.

chōshin (寵臣), *n.* a favourite (retainer).

chōshin(聽診), *n.* 【醫】auscultation; stethoscopy. —聽診する, to auscultate. ¶ 聽診器, a stethoscope.

chōshinkei (聽神經), *n.* the auditory nerve.

chōshizen (超自然的), *a.* supernatural; preternatural.

chosho (著書), *n.* a work. ¶ 歷史的著書, an historical work. —著書短評, a book notice.

chōsho (長所), *n.* an excellence; a strong point; merit. —長所と短所, strong and weak points; the strength and the weakness; excellences and defects; merits and faults.

chōsho(調書), *n.* 【法】a record; a protocol; minutes of (legal) proceedings. —調書を作成する, to draw up a protocol.

chōshō (嘲笑), *n.* ridicule; derision; sneer. —嘲笑する, to laugh *at*; scorn; sneer [jeer] *at*; ridicule. —嘲笑すべき, ludicrous; ridiculous. —嘲笑を買ふ, to make an exhibition of oneself; make oneself a laughing-stock; expose oneself to ridicule. ☞ *chōsan* (朝餐).

chōshoku (朝食), *n.* breakfast.

chōshoku (調色-法), *n.* mixing colours. —調色板, a palette; a tablet.

chōshū (長袖), *n.* long sleeves. ¶ 長袖武士, a carpet-knight.

chōshū (徵集), *n.* ❶ (徵し集めること) collection. ❷ (現役兵の召集) levy. —徵集する, to collect; call out; levy.

chōshū(徵收), *n.* collection; imposition; levy. —租稅を徵收する, to collect [levy] a tax. ¶ 徵收額, levy; amount levied.

chōshū (聽衆), *n.* the audience; hearers; attendance. ¶ 聽衆席, auditorium; auditory.

chōso(彫塑), *n.* modelling; plastic art (術).

chōsoku (長足の), *a.* rapid; swift. —長足の進步を爲す, to make very rapid progress; make long strides *in*.

chōson (町村), *n.* towns and villages. ¶ 町村制, the town and village organization.

chosui (貯水), *n.* storage; pondage. ¶ 貯水池, a reservoir; a tank.

chō-suru (弔する), *v.* to mourn *for*; condole *with*.

chō-suru (潮する), *vi.* to rise; set *in*; flow *in*.

chō-suru (徵する), *v.* ❶ (徵集)

to collect. ❷ to induce (歸納); judge *from* (判斷); compare (照らす). —從來の經驗に徵すると, judging from past experience.

chōtai (調帶), *n.* a belt; a band.

chōtan (長短), *n.* ❶ long and short; length (長さ). ❷ (優劣) merits and defects; good and evil (善惡); excess and deficiency (不過足). —人の長短を彼此する, to criticize others' merits and defects.

chōtei (朝廷), *n.* the Imperial [Royal] court (宮廷); the government.

chōtei (調停), *n.* reconciliation; mediation. **—-suru,** *vt.* to mediate (*between*); reconcile; settle. —爭議を調停する, to settle [compose] a dispute. —兩國の間を調停する, to mediate between the two powers.

chōteki (朝敵), *n.* a rebel; a traitor; the king's enemy.

chōten (頂點), *n.* a climax; a culmination; a summit. —頂點に達する, to culminate; reach the summit.

chōtō (朝禱), *n.* the matins.

chototsu (猪突する), *vi.* to rush headlong; make a headlong rush.

chōtsū (腸痛), *n.* 【醫】 enteralgia; (intestinal) colic.

chōtsugai (蝶番), *n.* ❶【機】 a knee-joint; a hinge; a hinge-joint. ❷ (關節) the ginglymus. —蝶番で接合する, to hinge.

chotto (一寸, 鳥渡), *ad.* ❶ (暫し) just; a short time; for a moment. ❷ (少し) just; slightly; a little. —一寸した感冒, a slight cold. —一寸した誤謬, a trifling error. —一寸したことから, from a trifle; from a slight affair. —ちょっとの間に, in no time; in a moment. —一寸見た所で, at first sight [view]. —一寸お待ちなさい, Wait a moment [a bit].

chōwa (調和), *n.* ❶ harmony (音·色·人の); reconciliation (異說などの); accord (一致). ❷ (好釣合) symmetry; keeping; adjustment (配合). —調和する, ① [*vi.*] to harmonize *with*; accord *with*; agree *with*. ② [*vt.*] to harmonize; reconcile; adjust. —色の調和を缺く, to lack the harmony of colours.

chōya (朝野), *n.* the government and people; the nation. —朝野の名士, distinguished persons in government service and private life.

chōyaku (跳躍), *n.* jump; spring; skip. —跳躍する, to jump; spring; prance (馬が).

chōyō (長幼), *n.* the young and the old.

chōyō (重陽), *n.* (九月九日) the chrysanthemum fête-day.

chōyō (貼用する), *v.* to paste; apply *to* (膏藥など); affix (印紙).

chōza (長坐する), *v.* to sit long; stay long.

chōzai (調劑), *n.* preparation. —調劑する, to prepare [make up] medicine. ¶ 調劑法, pharmacy; pharmaceutics.

chōzame (鰉), *n.* 【魚】 the sturgeon.

chōzei (徵稅), *n.* tax-collection.

chōzen (超然), *ad.* ❶ (卓然) out and away; pre-eminently. ❷ (離脫) standing aloof; unconcernedly. —超然として俗外に立つ, to stand aloof from the world. ¶ 超然內閣, a non-party [super-party] government.

chōzetsu (長舌), *n.* chatter; babble; rattle; prattle.

chōzetsu (超絕的), *a.* transcendental; pre-eminent; markedly superior. —超絕する, to transcend; surpass.

chozō (貯藏), *n.* preservation; storage; store. —貯藏する, to store; preserve. ¶ 貯藏品勘定, store account. —貯藏室, a store-room.

chōzō (彫像), *n.* a statue; a carved statue.

chōzoku (超俗的), *a.* unworldly.

chōzu (手水), *n.* (水) washing-water; (事) washing; cleaning. —手水を使ふ, to wash oneself. ¶ 手水場, a privy; a water-closet [W. C.]. —手水鉢, a washhand-basin; a wash-basin.

chōzuke (丁附), *n.* pagination. —丁附する, to paginate; page.

chōzume (腸詰), *n.* sausage.

chū (中), *n.* ❶ (中央) the middle; the centre. ❷ (中間) medium. **—,** *prep.* ❶ (間) during; pending. ❷ (到る處) throughout. ❸ (進行中) under; in the course *of*. ❹ (以內) within; in the course *of*. ❺ (數に云ふ) among; of. ❻ (場所に云ふ) in. **—,** *conj.* (間) while. **—,** *ad.* (到る處) all over; in all (Tōkyō など). —旅行中, ① during [in] one's journey. ② (で不在) being away on a journey. —そこら中, all over the place. —試驗中, under examination. —建造中, under construction; in process [course] of construction. —一年中, throughout the year. —百中の一, one in a hundred. —中を取る, to take the mean; split the difference.

chū (忠), *n.* ❶ (忠義) loyalty. ❷ (忠信) fidelity; faithfulness; honesty; single-heartedness. —職に忠なる人, a man faithful in the performance of his duties.

chū (宙), *n.* atmosphere; the air.

—宙で, by heart; by rote; from memory. (宙で讀む, to read by rote.) —宙にぶらさがる, to be suspended in mid-air. —宙を飛んで行く, to go off like a shot; fly on the wings of the wind.

chū (註), *n.* gloss; comment; annotation. —註を入れる, to annotate.

chūai (忠愛な), *a.* loyal and loving.

chūbaika (蟲媒花), *n.* 【植】 an entomophilous flower.

chūbei (駐米), *a.* resident in America; accredited to the United States Government. ¶ 駐米大使, the ambassador at Washington [in the United States].

chūbō (廚房), *n.* a kitchen; a cuisine; a cook-house (船中の).

chūboku (忠僕), *n.* a trusty [faithful] servant.

chūbu (中部), *n.* the central [middle] portion. ——, *a.* middle; medial; mid. ¶ 中部鐵道管理局, the Central Railway Superintendence Bureau.

chūburari (宙ぶらり), *n.* hanging; suspension; poise. —宙ぶらりの, hanging; in suspense; unsettled. —宙ぶらりである, to be suspended; be in suspense; be unsettled.

chūburu (中古の), *a.* slightly old; clean second-hand.

chūcho (躊躇する), *vi.* to hesitate; waver; vacillate. —毫も躊躇することなく, without the least hesitation.

chūchū (ちゅーちゅー鳴く), *vi.* ❶ (雀等が) to twitter; chirp. ❷ (鼠が) to squeak.

chūdan (中段), *n.* the landing (階段のたまり); half-way up.

chūdan (中斷), *n.* ❶ (中絶) interruption (時效の); abatement (訴訟の); discontinuance. ❷ (中央切斷) breaking in the middle. ——**suru**, *vt.* to interrupt; abate; cut in two. —時效を中斷する, to interrupt the prescription.

chūdō (中道), *n.* (半途) a half way; (中を得た道) the middle way.

chūdoku (中毒), *n.* poisoning. —中毒する, to be poisoned.

chūdoku (駐獨), *a.* resident in Germany; accredited to the German Government.

chūei (駐英), *a.* resident in England; accredited to the Court of St. James's. ¶ 駐英日本大使, the Japanese Ambassador in London [accredited to the Court of St. James's].

chūfu (廚夫), *n.* a ship's cook. ¶ 廚夫長, a steward.

chūfū (中風), *n.* 【醫】 (a light attack of) apoplexy.

chūfuku (中腹), *n.* half-way up; mountain-side.

chūfutsu (駐佛), *a.* resident in France; accredited to the French Government.

chūgaeri (宙返り), *n.* a somersault; a loop (飛行機の); looping the loop (同上). —宙返りする, to turn a somersault; loop the loop.

chūgai (中外), *n.* the internal and external; home and abroad (國の). —中外の眼を驚かす, to cause amazement at home and abroad.

chūgai (蟲害), *n.* damage done by insects; a blight.

chūgaku (中學-校), *n.* a middle school; an intermediate school. —中學程度の學校, a school of the middle-school grade; a secondary school.

chūgata (中型), *n.* a medium size.

chūgen (中元), *n.* the last day of the Feast of Lanterns; the fifteenth day of the seventh month of the lunar calendar.

chūgen (中原), *n.* ❶ (國の中央部) the midland. ❷ (競爭場裏) the field of contest. —中原の鹿を逐ふ, to run after the great prize; enter the field as competitor.

chūgen (忠言), *n.* faithful advice.

chūgi (忠義), *n.* loyalty; faithfulness; allegiance. —忠義の, loyal; faithful. —忠義を誓ふ, to swear allegiance.

chūgoku (中國), *n.* the central [middle] provinces.

chūgoshi (中腰), *n.* half-sitting. —中腰になって聞く, to listen in a half-sitting posture.

chūi (中位), *n.* mean; medium; the middle position (中位置). —(中位の) medium; middle; middle-sized (大さの).

chūi (中尉), *n.* a lieutenant (陸軍); a sub-lieutenant (海軍).

chūi (注意), *n.* ❶ (留意) attention; heed; care. ❷ (警戒) caution; vigilance; guard. ❸ (警告) warning; advice (忠告). —注意!, "with care". —注意深い, careful; attentive; cautious. —注意する, ① to pay attention; attend *to*. ② to take care; look out; beware *of*. ③ to warn; caution. —注意を惹く, to attract [draw; arrest] attention. —注意を促す, to call attention *to*. ¶ 注意事項, matters to be attended to; precautions. —注意人物, a marked man; a person watched by the police; a suspect.

chūji (中耳), *n.* 【解】 the tympanum; the drum; the middle ear. ¶ 中耳炎, tympanitis; otitis media.

chūjiki (晝食), *n.* a midday meal;

lunch; luncheon; tiffin. —晝食する, to lunch; tiffin.

chūjitsu (忠實), *n.* honesty; fidelity; faith. **—-na,** *a.* honest; faithful; trusty. —忠實な友, a staunch friend. —自己の言に忠實な, true to one's words.

chūjō (中將), *n.* a lieutenant-general (陸); a vice-admiral (海).

chūjō (衷情), *n.* one's true heart; one's inmost feelings. —衷情に於て, in one's inmost heart.

chūjun (中旬), *n.* the second ten days (of a month); the middle of a month.

Chūka (中華), *n.* China. ¶ 中華民國, the Chinese Republic.

chūkai (仲介), *n.* mediation; intermediation; agency. —仲介する, ① to mediate (between persons). ② (介在する) to lie *between*; be hemmed in.

chūkai (註解), *n.* annotation; an explanatory note; a comment.

chūkaku (中核), *n.* the kernel. —議論の中核, the kernel of the argument.

chūkan (中間), *n.* ❶ (眞中) the middle; the midway. ❷ (間) medium; mean. —中間に挾まる, to be hemmed in. —中間に位する, to lie *between*. ¶ 中間貿易, intermediate trade. —中間驛, an intermediate station; a way-station. —中間判決, 【法】 interlocutory judgment. —中間國, a buffer state.

chūkan (晝間), *n.* the daytime. —晝間の, diurnal; daytime.

chūkansetsu (肘關節), *n.* the elbow-joint.

chūkei (中景), *n.* the middle ground [distance] (畫).

chūken (中堅), *n.* ❶ the main body; the centre. ❷ 【野球】 the centre (field); (人) a centre-fielder; 【蹴球】 a half-back. —國民の中堅たる人物, men who are the backbone of the nation.

chūki (中氣), *n.* (a light attack of) apoplexy.

chūkin (忠勤), *n.* loyal service; faithful discharge of one's duties. —忠勤する, to serve faithfully. — —忠勤を勵む, to be zealous in the discharge of one's duties.

chūko (中古), *n.* the Middle Ages. —中古の, mediæval.

chūkō (中項), *n.* 【數】 the mean.

chūkō (忠孝), *n.* loyalty and filial piety. —忠孝兩全の道, a way to perfection in both loyalty and filial piety.

chūkō (鑄工), *n.* a caster; a founder.

chūkō (鑄鋼), *n.* cast-steel.

chūkoku (忠告), *n.* ❶ (勸告) advice; counsel; recommendation. ❷ (警告) warning; caution. ❸ (訓戒) admonition; expostulation; remonstrance. —忠告する, ① to advise; counsel. ② to warn; caution. ③ to admonish; expostulate; remonstrate. —醫師の忠告に從ふ, to follow medical advice.

chūkon (忠魂), *n.* a loyal soul (忠義心); the loyal dead (忠死者). ¶ 忠魂記念碑, a monument to the loyal dead.

chūkū (中空), *n.* the air; mid-air.

chūkun (忠君), *n.* loyalty. —忠君の, loyal. ¶ 忠君愛國主義, loyalism and patriotism.

chūkyū (誅求する), *vt.* to exact; extort.

chūmitsu (稠密な), *a.* dense; thick. —人口稠密な國, a densely [thickly] populated country.

chūmoku (注目する), *vt.* to note; observe; watch. —注目すべき, noticeable; noteworthy.

chūmon (註文), *n.* ❶ (誂) an order. ❷ (希望) a request; a wish. ❸ (期待) expectation. —註文に應ずる, to take up an order. —註文通りになる, to be as one expected; be according to one's expectation. —御註文は直に調進可仕候, Orders punctually attended to. **—-suru,** *vt.* to order; bespeak; request (要求). —船を米國へ註文する, to order a ship from America. ¶ 大口 (小口) 註文, a large (small) order. —註文控帳, an order-book. —註文係, an order-clerk. —註文品, ① an article made to order (既製). ② goods on order (未製). —註文取り, (人) a canvasser; a drummer. —註文用紙, an order-form.

chūnen (中年), *n.* prime of manhood; early manhood. —中年の, of [in] early manhood. ¶ 中年者, a grown-up person.

chūnichi (中日), *n.* ❶ the middle day. ❷ (日支) Japan and China.

chūnichi (駐日), *a.* resident in Japan; accredited to the Court of Tōkyō. ¶ 駐日支那公使, the Chinese Minister in Tōkyō.

chūniku (中肉), *n.* ❶ (程よき肉附き) medium flesh. ❷ (並肉) meat of medium quality. —中肉中背の人, a person of medium height and flesh.

chūnin (仲人), *n.* ❶ (媒妁者) a go-between. ❷ (仲裁者) a mediator; an intermediary. ❸ (仲介者) a middle-man.

chūnori (宙乘), *n.* a mid-air performance.

chūnyū (注入する), *v.* to instil *into*; infuse *into*; impregnate (思想・感情を); cram *into* (詰込む); pour *into*.

chūō (中央), *n.* the centre. —中央の, central; mid; middle. —中央に, in the centre; in the middle. ¶ 中央政府, the central government. —中央市場, an emporium. —中央集權, centralization (of power). —中央黨, the centre.

chūon (中音), *n.* 【音】 alto. ¶ 中音部記號, alto clef.

chūritsu (中立), *n.* neutrality. —中立の, neutral. ¶ 嚴正中立, strict neutrality. —中立地帶, a neutral zone. —中立違反, violation of neutrality. —中立貨, neutral goods. —中立權, neutral rights. —中立國, a neutral power. (永世中立國, a permanent neutral state.) —中立船, a neutral ship. —中立主義, neutralism.

chūritsu (中率), *n.* 【數】 the mean.

chūro (駐露), *a.* resident in Russia; accredited to the Russian government. ¶ 駐露日本大使, the Japanese Ambassador at Moscow.

chūrō (中老), *n.* ❶ middle age (四十歲から五十歲まで). ❷ (中老人) a middle-aged person; an elderly person (五十から六十迄).

chūrui (蟲類), *n.* worms; insects.

chūryō (忠良の), *a.* good and loyal.

chūryū (中流), *n.* ❶ (河の) mid-stream. ❷ (社會の) the middle class; the *bourgeoisie* 〖佛〗. —中流の, middle-class; *bourgeois* 〖佛〗.

chūsa (中佐), *n.* a lieutenant-colonel (陸軍); a commander (海軍).

chūsai (仲裁), *n.* arbitration; mediation. —仲裁する, to arbitrate. —仲裁裁判に付する, to submit to arbitration. ¶ 仲裁判決, an arbitration award. —仲裁條約, an arbitration treaty. —仲裁人, an arbiter; an arbitrator; a mediator (調停者). —仲裁裁判所, the court of arbitration.

chūsan (中產), *n.* medium-sized property; moderate means [wealth]. ¶ 中產階級, the *bourgeoisie* 〖佛〗.

chūsatsu (駐劄), *a.* resident; accredited *to*. ¶ 日本駐劄英國大使, the British Ambassador in Tōkyō [in Japan; accredited to the Court of Tōkyō].

chūsei (中世), *n.* the middle age. ¶ 中世紀, the Middle Ages.

chūsei (中性), *n.* ❶ 【文】 the neuter gender. ❷ 【理】 the mean; 【化】 neutrality. —中性の, 【文】 neuter; 【化】 neutral; indifferent.

chūsei (忠誠), *n.* integrity; single-mindedness.

chūseki (沖積の), *a.* 【地質】 alluvial. ¶ 沖積層, wash; alluvium.

chūseki (柱石), *n.* the foot-stone; the corner-stone; the foundation-stone. —國家の柱石, the pillar of the state.

chūsen (抽籤), *n.* lot; drawing. —抽籤で, by (means of) drawings. ¶ 抽籤償還, redemption by drawing.

chūsetsu (忠節), *n.* loyalty; allegiance (忠順).

chūsha (注射), *n.* injection. —注射する, to inject; syringe. ¶ 注射器, an injection-syringe; an injector; a syringe. —注射藥, an injection.

chūshaku (註釋), *n.* =*chūkai* (註解).

chūshi (中止), *n.* suspension; discontinuance; stay. **—-suru,** *vt.* to discontinue; suspend; stay (判決など). —俄に中止する, to break off short.

chūshi (中指), *n.* the middle finger.

chūshi (注視する), *vt.* to observe closely; gaze steadily *at*; contemplate. —擧動を注視する, to watch closely another's behaviour.

chūshi (駐支), *a.* resident in China; accredited to the Chinese Government. ¶ 駐支日本公使, the Japanese Minister at Peking [in China].

chūshin (中心), *n.* ❶ (中點) the centre; the pivot; the heart (中央). ❷ (心中) heart. —工業の中心(地), an industrial centre. —中心を失ふ, to lose balance. ¶ 中心人物, the central figure. —中心點, a central point; a pivot; a focus.

chūshin (忠臣), *n.* a loyalist; a loyal subject; a faithful retainer.

chūshin (忠信), *n.* loyalty; fidelity; faithfulness.

chūshin (衷心), *n.* one's inmost heart. —衷心の, hearty; heart-felt; cordial. —衷心から, heartily; from the bottom of one's heart.

chūshin (注進する), *vt.* to report.

chūsho (中暑), *n.* ❶ midsummer. ❷ (暑氣あたり) heat-stroke.

chūshō (中傷する), *vt.* to calumniate; defame; slander. —中傷的報道, a slanderous report.

chūshō (中稱), *n.* 【文】 the neuter.

chūshō (抽象的), *a* abstract. —抽象的に, in the abstract. ¶ 抽象名詞, an abstract noun.

chūshū (仲秋), *n.* mid-autumn. —仲秋の月, the harvest moon.

chūshutsu (抽出する), *vt.* to derive; extract; abstract.

chūsū (中樞), *n.* the centre; the pivot; the focus. —中樞の, central; pivotal. ¶ 中樞院, (朝鮮の) the Chōsen Privy Council.

chū-suru (誅する), *vt.* to punish with death; put to death.

chūtai (中隊), *n.* a company. ¶ 歩兵一箇中隊, an infantry company. —砲兵一箇中隊, an artillery battery. —騎兵一箇中隊, a cavalry squadron. —中隊長, a company commander.

chūtai (中帶), *n.* the temperate zone. ¶ 寒(暖)中帶, the cold (warm) temperate zone.

chutchoku (黜陟), *n.* promotion and degradation.

chūten (中點), *n.* the middle (point).

chūten (冲天の), *a.* rising up the sky; ascending the heavens; sky-high.

chūtetsu (鑄鐵), *n.* ❶ cast-iron. ❷ iron-founding. ¶ 鑄鐵所, an iron-foundry.

chūto (中途), *n.* the mid-course; midway; half-way. —中途から引返す, to return [retrace one's steps] before reaching one's destination.

chūtō (中東), *n.* the Middle East.

chūtō (中等), *n.* the middle class; medium; mediocrity. ¶ 中等教育, secondary education —中等社會, the middle class.

chūto-hanpa (中途半端の), *a.* unfinished; incomplete.

chūton (駐屯する), *vi.* to be stationed. ¶ 駐屯軍, an army of occupation (占領軍); a garrison.

chūwa (中和する), *vt.* ❶ (緩和) to moderate. ❷ (相殺) to counteract; neutralize.

chūya (晝夜), *n.* night and day. —, *ad.* night-and-day. —晝夜兼行で働く, to work double tides. ¶ 晝夜平分時, the equinox.

chūyō (中庸), *n.* the mean; the middle course [way]. —中庸の, moderate (行爲·言語の); mean.

chūyū (忠勇), *n.* loyalty and bravery.

chūzai (駐在), *n.* residence. —駐在する, to reside; be in residence. ¶ 駐在官, an officer [official] resident in a country; a resident. —駐在國, the country of residence.

chūzei (中背), *n.* medium height. —中背の男, a man of medium height.

chūzetsu (中絶), *n.* interruption; intermission; interception. —中絶する, to come to a standstill; fall into abeyance.

chūzō (鑄造), *n.* ❶ cast; casting. ❷ (鑄貨) minting; coinage. —鑄造する, ① (活字·鐵器を) to cast; found. ② (貨幣を) to coin; mint. ¶ 鑄造所, a foundry. —鑄造貨幣, a metallic coin.

D

daba (駄馬), *n.* a pack-horse; a sumpter-horse; a hack (劣等馬).

daben (駄辯), *n.* balderdash; trash; twaddle. —駄辯を弄する, to talk trash.

dabi (荼毘), *n.* cremation. —荼毘に付する, to cremate.

dabō (打棒), *n.* a bat.

daboku (打撲), *n.* a blow; contusion. —打撲する, to strike; thrash. —打撲傷を負ふ, to be bruised; suffer a contused wound.

dabora (駄法螺), *n.* bunkum; bounce; gas; big talk.

dabudabu (だぶだぶの), *a.* loose; baggy.

daburu (ダブる), *v.* to double.

daburu-kara (ダブルカラ), *n.* a double-collar.

daburu-purē (ダブルプレー, 複殺), *n.* 【野球】 double play.

dabutsuku (だぶつく), *vi.* ❶ to be loose. ❷ (過多) to be glutted.

dachin (駄賃), *n.* ❶ (駄馬賃) a pack-horse charge. ❷ (使などの報酬) reward.

dachō (駝鳥), *n.* 【鳥】 the ostrich.

dada (駄駄), *n.* peevishness; petulance; pettishness. —駄々をこねる, to fret; be peevish.

dadakko (駄駄子), *n.* a spoilt child; a fretful child.

dadappiroi (徒廣い), *a.* large and clumsy.

daden (打電する), *v.* to telegraph (*to*); wire (*to*) 〔俗〕; cable (*to*) (海底線で); send a telegram *to*.

daeki (唾液), *n.* sputum; saliva. ¶ 唾液腺, a salivary gland.

daen (橢圓-形), *n.* an ellipse; an oval. —橢圓形の, elliptical; oval. ¶ 橢圓軌道, 【天】 an elliptic orbit. —橢圓體, an ellipsoid; an ovoid.

dafu (懦夫), *n.* ❶ (臆病者) a coward; a dastard; a poltroon. ❷ (怠惰者) a drone. —懦夫を起たせる, to make a dastard rise.

daga (だが), *conj.* (...であるが) but; however; yet.

dagashi (駄菓子), *n.* coarse confectionery; inferior cake.

dageki (打撃), *n.* ❶ (打敲くこと) a hit; a percussion; a stroke. ❷ (傷害, 惡影響) a blow; a shock. —打擊を加へる, to strike; deal a blow. —大打撃を受ける, to be hard hit; suffer a heavy blow.

daha (打破する), *vt.* to break down (破壞); do away *with* (廢棄); defeat (打負かす). —現狀を打破

する, to break down the present condition; destroy the *status quo*.

dahei (舵柄), *n.* a tiller; a helm.

daho (拿捕), *n.* capture; seizure. —拿捕する, to capture; seize.

dai (大), *n.* ❶ (大月) a month of thirty-one days. ❷ (大形) large size. ❸ (大きいこと) largeness; greatness. ——, *a.* large; great (偉大); grand (壯大). ¶ 大事業《人物》, a great enterprise 《character》. —大規模, a large scale. —大東京, Greater Tōkyō.

dai (代), *n.* ❶ (代金) price. ❷ (世代) time; generation. ❸ (治世) reign. ❹ (時代) age; period; dynasty (王朝); lifetime (生存中). ❺ (代理) a proxy. ❻ (年齢の十年範圍) the —s. —二十代で, in one's twenties.

dai (題), *n.* ❶ (題目, 表題) subject; title; heading. ❷ (問題) a problem; a question. ❸ (詩文等の課題) a subject; a theme; a thesis; a topic. —題を出す, to give out problems.

dai (臺), *n.* ❶ (置物臺) a stand; a rest; a holder. ❷ (小丘) a hill. —二十圓臺を割る, to exceed [go beyond] twenty *yen* odd.

daiba (臺場), *n.* a battery; a fort.

daibakari (臺秤), *n.* a weigh-bridge; a platform-scale.

daibanjaku (大磐石), *n.* a great rock. —大磐石の如く確(ジカ)と, firm as a rock.

daiben (大便), *n.* human excretion; stool. —大便に行く, to go to the W. C. —大便をする, to (go to) stool; ease nature [oneself].

daiben (代辨する), *vt.* to represent; act *for*. ¶ 代辨業, agency.

daibu (大分), *ad.* =***daibun***.

daibubun (大部分), *n.* a greater part; a better part. —地球表面の大部分, a large proportion of the earth's surface.

daibun (大分), *ad.* much; considerably; greatly; largely; to a great extent. —大分賣れる, to have a large sale; sell well. —大分氣分がよい, to feel very much better.

daibutsu (代物), *n.* a substitute.

daichi (大地), *n.* earth; ground.

daichi (臺地), *n.* a terrace.

daichō (大腸), *n.* the colon; the large intestine. ¶ 大腸加答兒, catarrh of the colon.

daichō (臺帳), *n.* ❶ (元帳) a ledger. ❷ (脚本) a play-book. ¶ 土地臺帳, a cadastre.

daidai (臭橙), *n.* 【植】 the Seville [bitter; bigarade] orange.

daidai (代代), *ad.* for generations; from father to son. —代々の, successive; hereditary; family.

daidaiteki (大大的), *a.* great; grand; gigantic. —大々的に, on a grand [gigantic] scale.

daidaṅen (大團圓), *n.* the catastrophe; the grand finale.

daidō (大同), *n.* great similarity; general resemblance. —大同小異である, to be substantially the same; be much alike.

daidō (大道), *n.* ❶ (道路) a highway; a (high) road; a street. ❷ (正義, 公道) the right; great principles. —人倫の大道, the great principles of morality. ¶ 大道店, street stalls. —大道商人, a street-vendor.

daidokoro (臺所), *n.* a kitchen.

daidōmyaku (大動脈), *n.* the aorta [*pl.* -tæ].

daigaku (大學), *n.* a university (學位授與の權ある); a college (分科·單科大學); an academy. —大學を卒業する, to graduate from a university 〔英〕; be graduated at a university 〔米〕. ¶ 法科大學, the college of law; the law college. —綜合大學, a university. —東京帝國大學, the Imperial University of Tōkyō. —大學帽, a college cap; a mortar board. —大學院, a university hall. —大學教授, a university professor. —大學生, a collegian; a university student. —大學總長, the rector; the president of a university.

daigan (大願), *n.* an earnest prayer; a great desire. ¶ 大願成就, an earnest prayer granted; a great desire fulfilled.

daigawari (代替), *n.* succession to the family estate; a change of headship.

daigensui (大元帥), *n.* the generalissimo; the commander-in-chief of sea and land forces [the army and navy].

daigi (代議的), *a.* representative. ¶ 代議政體, representative government.

daigi (臺木), *n.* a stock; a string-piece.

daigishi (代議士), *n.* a representative; a member of parliament [a diet, &c.]; a deputy; an assemblyman. —本縣選出代議士某氏, Mr. ..., Member of the Diet [M. P.] for this prefecture.

daigo (大悟), *n.* light; perfect knowledge. —大悟の域に達する, to reach the borders of perfect knowledge [light].

daigyaku (大逆), *n.* (high) treason.

daihai (代拜する), *v.* to worship as another's proxy.

daihitsu (代筆する), *v.* to write for another.

daihoñei (大本營), *n.* the Imperial headquarters; the High Command.
daihyō (代表), *n.* ❶ representation. ❷ (代表者) a representative. —代表的, representative; typical. —代表する, to represent; stand for; typify. —...を代表して, in [on] behalf *of*. (我國を代表して會議に列する, to represent our country at the conference.) —代表者を出す[送る], to send up a representative.
daiichi (第一), *n.* first; the first. —第一に, first; firstly; primarily; in the first place; first of all; to begin with. —第一位を占める, to be at the head *of*. ¶ 第一列, the front rank. —第一人者, the first; the (one) man of the age. (第一人者である, to stand alone [have no equal].)
daiichiryū (第一流), *n.* the first; the first grade [rank; class]. ——-**no**, *a.* the first; the foremost; of the first rank [rate]. —我國第一流の人士, the first [foremost] men of our country.
daiikki (第一期), *n.* the first term [period]; the primary stage (病の).
daiin (代印する), *v.* to seal [set a seal] by proxy.
daiippo (第一步), *n.* the first step.
daiissen (第一線), *n.* the first line.
daiisshin (第一審), *n.* the first instance; the first trial [hearing]. ¶ 第一審裁判所, the court of first instance.
daiitchaku (第一著), *n.* ❶ the first step. ❷ the first arrival. —第一著に, in the first instance; in the first place; first of all. —第一著となる, to come (in) first.
daiittō (第一等), *n.* the first; the first class; the first grade [俗].
daija (大蛇), *n.* a big snake; a huge serpent.
daiji (大事), *n.* ❶ (重大事) a serious matter; a matter of importance; great affairs. ❷ (大事業) a great enterprise. ❸ (大切) importance. ❹ (用心, 愼重) prudence; a great care. —大事にする, to make much *of*; think much *of*; take great care *of*. —大事に至らぬ前に, before the matter grows serious. —大事を取る, to use prudence; be prudent. —お大事に, Take care of yourself. ——-**na**, *a.* important; cherished (慈愛); beloved (愛好). —大事な細君[女房], the wife of one's bosom.
daijin (大臣), *n.* a minister; a secretary (of state) [英]. —大臣の, ministerial; secretarial. ¶ 大臣官房, the minister's secretariate. —大臣席, the minister's seat; the Treasury benches [英]. —大臣職, the portfolio.
daijin (大盡), *n.* ❶ (富者) a rich [wealthy] man; a man of property. ❷ (豪遊者) one given to extravagant pleasures. —大盡風を吹かす, to give oneself the air of a rich man.
daijinbutsu (大人物), *n.* a great man [character].
daijingū (太神宮), *n.* the shrine of the Sun-Goddess.
daijiri (臺尻), *n.* the butt-end (of a gun).
daijōbu (大丈夫の), *a.* safe; secure; right.
daijōfu (大丈夫), *n.* a man; a heroic man; a manly fellow.
daijushō (大綬章), *n.* (勳章) the Grand Cordon. ¶ 旭日大綬章, the Grand Cordon of the Order of the Rising Sun.
daika (代價), *n.* price.
daikagura (大神樂), *n.* a street performance with a lion's mask.
daikako (大過去), *n.* 【文】 the pluperfect tense; the past perfect.
daikan (大寒), *n.* severe cold; hard frost.
daikan (代官), *n.* 【史】 a deputy.
daikantoku (大監督), *n.* 【宗】 an archbishop.
daikin (代金), *n.* price; purchase-money. ¶ 代金引換郵便, cash-on-delivery post. —代金引換賣, C.O.D. sale.
daikōbutsu (大好物), *n.* a delight; a thing which one is very fond *of*.
daikoku (大黑), *n.* ❶ the god of wealth. ❷ (梵妻) a Buddhist priest's wife. ¶ 大黑帽子, a flat cap. —大黑柱, ① (支持者) a prop; a pillar. ② (柱石) the central pillar (of a house). (彼は家の大黑柱だ, He is the prop (and stay) of his family.)
daikon (大根), *n.* 【植】 the (garden) radish. ¶ 大根卸, ① (器具) a radish-grater. ② grated radish.
daiku (大工), *n.* a carpenter; a wood-worker; carpentry (業). ¶ 大工道具, a carpenter's tools. (大工道具箱, a carpenter's chest.)
daikuñi (大勳位), *n.* the grand order; the Order of the Chrysanthemum.
daikyū (大弓), *n.* a long bow; archery (射法). ¶ 大弓場, an archery ground.
daima (大麻), *n.* 【植】 the hemp.
daimai (大枚), *ad.* as much as; to the tune of. —大枚壹萬圓を拂ふ, to pay to the tune of ten thousand *yen*.
daimeishi (代名詞), *n.* the pro-

noun. —代名詞狀の, pronominal. ¶ 不定代名詞, the indefinite pronoun.

daimoku (題目), *n.* ❶ (題號) a title. ❷ (問題, 表題) a subject; a theme; a subject matter. —お題目を唱へる, to chant the Nichiren prayer.

daimyō (大名), *n.* a *daimyō*; a feudal lord. ¶ 大名行列, a *daimyō's* procession.

dainamaito (ダイナマイト), *n.* dynamite.

dainan (大難), *n.* a great calamity; a disaster. —大難が小難で濟む, to escape a great calamity by falling into a small misfortune.

dainashi (臺なしにする), *vt.* to spoil; mar; make a muddle *of*.

daini (第二), *n.* the second. —第二の, the second; another; the other (the one の對). —第二に, secondly; in the second place.

dainin (代人), *n.* a proxy; an attorney; a substitute. —代人で, by deputy; by proxy. —代人を遣はす, to send a substitute [proxy].

Dai-Nippon-Teikoku (大日本帝國), *n.* the Empire of Japan. ¶ 大日本帝國政府, the Imperial Japanese Government.

dainō (大腦), *n.* the cerebrum.

dainō (大農), *n.* ❶ a wealthy farmer. ❷ *grande culture*.

dainō (代納する), *vt.* to pay by proxy.

dainoji (大の字), —大の字なりに臥す, to sprawl; lie sprawling.

daiō (大黃), *n.* 【植】the (medicinal) rhubarb.

daiōjō (大往生), *n.* euthanasia; an easy [a painless] death. —大往生を遂げる, to die painlessly.

daionjō (大音聲に), *ad.* aloud; in a loud voice.

dairi (內裏), *n.* 【史】the Imperial palace.

dairi (代理), *n.* 【法】agency; proxy; procuration. —代理の, vicarious; vicegerent; acting. —代理する, to represent; act *for*; take the place *of*. ¶ 代理委任狀, the power [letter; warrant] of attorney. —代理人, 【法】a representative; an agent; an attorney. (部理(總)代理人, a partial (universal) agent.) —代理領事, an acting consul. —代理商, a commercial agent. —代理大使(公使), the *chargé d'affaires* of an embassy (a legation). —代理店, an agency.

dairinkusho (大林區署), *n.* a local forestry office.

dairiseki (大理石), *n.* marble.

dairyō (大漁, 大獵), *n.* a great [good] catch (魚); a great [large] take (鳥獸).

daisai (大祭), *n.* a great festival. ¶ 大祭日, a national holiday.

daisaku (代作), *n.* composing for another (事); a composition written by another. —代作する, to compose [write] for another.

daisan (第三), *n.* the third. ¶ 第三者, a third person [party].

daisharin (大車輪), *n.* ❶ (機械體操) a giant-swing. ❷ (一生懸命) all one's might; might and main. —大車輪になる, to exert oneself to the utmost.

daishi (臺紙), *n.* pasteboard; mounting; stub (小切手の). —寫眞を臺紙に貼る, to mount a photograph.

daishikyū (大至急に), *ad.* urgently; post-haste.

daishin (代診), *n.* a doctor's assistant.

daishiñin (大審院), *n.* the Supreme Court; the Court of Cassation.

daisho (代書する), *vt.* to write for another. ¶ 代書所, a scribe's office; a writer's office. —代書人, a scribe; a writer for another.

daishō (大小), *n.* ❶ (大と小) the large and small. ❷ (大さ) the size. ❸ (大小刀) the two swords.

daishō (代償), *n.* compensation; indemnification. —...の代償として, in payment [compensation] *for*.

daisōjō (大僧正), *n.* an archbishop; a primate.

daisoreta (大それた), *a.* insolent; atrocious; impudent.

daisōtō (大總統), *n.* (支那) the president. ¶ 大總統府, the president's office.

daisū (代數・學), *n.* algebra. —代數的, algebraic(-al). ¶ 代數學者, an algebraist [-brist].

daitai (大隊), *n.* a battalion. ¶ 大隊長, a battalion commander.

daitai (大體), *n.* (大要) general principles; outline; substance. —大體に於て, on the whole; in (the) gross; generally [roughly] speaking. —大體に通ずる, to have a general knowledge *of*.

daitaibutsu (代替物), *n.* fungibles.

daitaikotsu (大腿骨), *n.* 【解】the femur; the femoral bone; the thigh-bone.

daitan (大膽), *n.* ❶ daring; audacity; intrepidity. ❷ (鐵面皮) impudence. —大膽な, ① audacious; daring; intrepid. ② impudent. —大膽不敵の大賊, a great robber of bold and fearless disposition. —大膽に, fearlessly; boldly; audaciously. (大膽に構へる, to present a bold front.)

daitasū (大多數), *n.* the (great) majority (of the company); the (great) mass (of the audience). —

大多數は, for the most part; mostly. —大多數を占める, to hold a large majority.

daitō(大統), *n.* the Imperial Line [Throne]. —大統を繼ぐ, to succeed to the (Imperial) Throne.

daitō (大纛), *n.* ❶ a great military standard. ❷(天皇の軍旗) the Imperial Military standard. ❸(大本營) the grand headquarters.

daitōryō(大統領), *n.* a president. —大統領の職, presidency; presidentship. —大統領改選の年, a presidential year (米).

daiya(mondo)(金剛石), *n.* diamond.

daiyō (代用), *n.* substitution. —...の代用になる, to do duty *for*; serve *for*. —A を B に代用する, to use A as a substitute for B; substitute A for B. ¶ 代用教員, a substitute teacher. —代用食, substitute food.

daiyoku (大慾), *n.* avarice; greed; cupidity. —大慾は無慾に似たり, "Avarice overreaches itself."

daiyūsei (大熊星), *n.* the Great Bear; the Plough; Charles's Wain.

daizai (大罪), *n.* a great [heinous] crime; a high [grave; serious] offence. ¶ 大罪人, a great offender [criminal].

daizai (題材), *n.* a material. —評論の題材, the material for criticism.

daizenshiki (大膳職), *n.* the Bureau of Imperial Cuisine.

daizu (大豆), *n.* 【植】 the soy-bean; the soja-bean. ¶ 大豆粕, bean-cake; bean oil-cake.

dajaku (惰弱な), *a.* indolent; effeminate.

dajare (駄洒落), *n.* a poor pun [[joke]; a witticism.

dakan (兌換), *n.* conversion. —兌換する, to convert. ¶ 兌換銀行, a bank of issue. —兌換準備, conversion reserve. —兌換紙幣, convertible paper-money [-note].

dakara (だから), *ad.* therefore; consequently; accordingly. ——, *conj.* because; as; for. ——, *prep.* on account of; because of.

dakatsu(蛇蝎), *n.* vipers; adders. —蛇蝎視する, to abhor; loathe; abominate.

dake (だけ), *particle.* ❶ (分量·程度を示す) only; just; but. ❷ (事物·分量·程度を限示す) at least; as much (many) as; as [so] far as; as...as. ❸ (ばかり, のみ) only; alone. —私だけの, my own. —稼ぐだけ食ふ, to eat up all that one earns. —私の知ッてるだけでは, so far as I know. —それだけの事さ, That is all. —これだけは本當だ, This much is true. —これだけしかない, This is all I have. —彼は私より二つだけ年上だ, He is my senior by two years.

daki (抱き), *n.* embrace; incubation. ¶ 抱き子, an infant [a baby] in arms.

daki (唾棄する), *vt.* to reject; discard; cast away.

daki (舵機), *n.* a rudder (舵); steering-gear (操舵機); helm (同上) ¶ 舵機室, a steering-room.

daki (惰氣), *n.* ❶ (厭氣) being bored; tiredness; disinclination. ❷ (怠り心) indolence; inactivity; sluggishness.

dakiau (抱合ふ), *vi.* to interlock; hug [embrace] each other; be locked in each other's arms.

dakikomu (抱込む), *vt.* ❶ (抱く) to embrace; hug; cuddle. ❷ (籠絡) to draw in; win over; bring (a man) over to one's side.

dakishimeru (抱締める), *vt.* to hug; embrace closely; hold [press] to one's breast.

dakitsuku (抱附く), *vi.* to cling to; fold in one's arms [to one's breast]. —頸に抱きつく, to throw one's arms around another's neck.

dakkai (脫會する), *vi.* to leave [resign from] a society; secede [withdraw] from an association.

dakkaku (脫殼する), *v.* to exuviate; slough; shed [cast off] the shell [skin].

dakkan (脫監), *n.* prison-breaking; jail-breaking. —脫監する, to break jail [prison]; escape from prison; break out of prison. ¶ 脫監者, a prison-breaker; a jail-breaker.

dakkan(脫艦する), *vi.* to desert (from a warship); desert one's ship. ¶ 脫艦兵, a deserter from a warship; a runaway marine.

dakkan (奪還する), *vt.* to recover; recapture; take back.

dakkō(脫肛), *n.* 【醫】 proctocele; prolapsus ani 【羅】.

dakkō (脫稿する), *vi.* to be completed; be brought to completion.

dakkyaku (脫却する), *vt.* to quit; get away *from*; shake *off*. —風塵を脫却する, to quit the city; seek solitude.

dakkyū (脫臼), *n.* dislocation; luxation. —脫臼する, to be dislocated; be luxated; be out of joint.

daku(抱く), *vt.* ❶ (人が) to embrace; hug; hold [fold] in one's arms. ❷ (鳥が卵を) to hatch; incubate. —抱き上げる, to lift up in one's arms. —抱き起す, to raise in one's arms; pick [catch] up. —抱き止める, to stop by throwing one's arms round another. —子供を抱く, to embrace a child. —卵

を抱く (抱かす), to sit on eggs (set a hen).

dakudaku (だくだく), *ad.* in streams. —だくだく流れ出る, to flow in streams; gush out.

dakuhi (諾否), *n.* yes or no; acceptance or rejection; an answer.

dakuon (濁音), *n.* sonancy; a sonant.

dakuryū (濁流), *n.* a muddy stream; a turbid current.

daku-suru (諾する), *v.* to consent *to*; assent *to*.

dakyō (妥協), *n.* mutual concession; composition; compromise. 妥協點を見出す, to find the basis for compromise. **——-suru,** *v.* to compromise; make terms *with*; meet a person halfway. —民黨と妥協する, to come to terms with the popular party.

dakyū (打球), *n.* polo (打毬戯); drive (croquet 戯の); batting (野球・クリケットの打法).

damaru (默る), *vi.* to shut up; hush up; hold one's tongue. —默れ!, Hold your tongue! ; Shut up!, Silence! —默らす, to silence; stop a person's mouth; shut a person's mouth; shut a person up. —默ッて, (默して) silently; (斷りなく) without leave (notice). —默ッてゐる, to be silent; remain silent.

damashikomu (瞞込む), *vt.* to inveigle; insnare; entrap.

damashiuchi (騙打), *n.* an assault by surprise; a surprise attack. —騙打ちにする, to assault a person unawares.

damasu (瞞・騙・欺す), *vt.* to deceive; cheat; impose *upon*. —人を瞞して金を取る, to take a person's money by fraud; cheat person of his money.

dame (駄目の), *a.* useless; of no use; hopeless (望なき). —駄目と知りつつ, knowing that it would be in vain. —駄目を押す, to question to make sure. —これでは駄目だ, This will never do.

damigoe (濁聲), *n.* a hoarse [gruff] voice.

damin (惰眠), *n.* a dull slumber; lethargy. —地方人の惰眠を驚かす, to awake the people of the provinces from their dull slumber.

dan (段), *n.* ❶ (階段) (*a*) a step; a stair; a rung [round (of a ladder)]: (*b*) a staircase; a flight of steps: (*c*) a stage. ❷ (區分) a division. ❸ (品等) a grade. ❹ (條) a paragraph; a passage; a chapter; a column (段欄); a matter (箇條). ❺ an act (劇のくぎり). —段が違ふ, to be of a different grade *to*; stand on different levels; outclass. —石の段を下る, to walk down [descend] the stone steps.

dan (煖), *n.* warmth. —煖を取る, to get warm; warm oneself.

dan (團), *n.* a group; a college; a team (野球・蹴球等の); a party; an association.

dan (談), *n.* a story; a tale. —談偶々…に及ぶ, the conversation turned *upon*.

dan (壇), *n.* ❶ (壇階) a platform; a dais (一段高い座); a terrace. ❷ (…社會) the circle; the world.

danan (斷案), *n.* ❶ a decision; the last word. ❷【論】consequence; a conclusion. —斷案を下す, to make a decision; decide.

danbashigo (段梯子), *n.* stairs; a staircase; a flight of steps. —段梯子を登る, to go up [climb] a flight of steps.

danbira (段平, 闊劍), *n.* a broad sword.

danbō (煖房), *n.* a stove. ¶ 煖房器, a steam-heater. —煖房裝置, a heating apparatus.

danbukuro (駄荷袋), *n.* ❶ (荷袋) a large cotton bag. ❷ (ズボン) pantaloons; trousers.

dancha (磚茶), *n.* tile [brick] tea.

danchaku-kyori (彈著距離), *n.* the gunshot (-reach); arrival distance; the range of a projectile.

danchō (斷腸), *n.* heart-break; the rending of the heart. **——-no,** heart-breaking; heart-rending. —斷腸の思あらしめる, to break the heart *of*; go to a person's heart.

dandan (段段), *ad.* gradually; by degrees; little by little. —段段…なる, to grow in (beauty; strength; wisdom *etc.*). (段々面白くなる, to get more and more interesting.) —段々に骨を呑込む, to get gradually into the knack.

dandara (段段), *n.* cross stripes; coloured stripes. —紅白だんだらの幕, a curtain of red and white stripes.

dandō (彈道), *n.* a trajectory.

dandori (段取), *n.* a programme; a plan; an arrangement.

dangai (彈劾), *n.* impeachment. —彈劾する, to impeach.

dangai (斷崖), *n.* a cliff; a bluff; a precipice.

dangan (彈丸), *n.* ❶ (總稱) shot (屢〻複數); a ball; a projectile. ❷ (小銃の) a bullet; a shot. ❸ (破裂彈) a shell; a bullet-shell. —彈丸の通らぬ, bullet-proof; shot-proof. —彈丸雨下の中に, under a hail [shower] of shots.

dangen (斷言), *n.* an assertion; a positive statement; an affirmation.

——**-suru,** *vt.* to assert; asseverate; state [declare] positively. —少しも憚る所なく斷言する, to assert without the least compunction.

dangi (談義), *n.* ❶ (評定) deliberation. ❷ (說敎) a sermon; a lecture (小言)

dango (團子), *n.* a dumpling. ¶ 團子鼻, a potato-nose; a bottle-nose.

dangō (談合), *n.* consultation; conference. —談合する, to consult *with*; confer *with*; lay heads together.

dangoku (暖國), *n.* a warm country.

dani (蜱), *n.* 【節足】 the tick.

dani (だに), *particle.* only; even.

dańi (暖衣), *n.* warm clothes [clothing]. —暖衣飽食の徒, men in comfortable circumstances; men of affluence.

danji (男兒), *n.* (男の子) a boy; a man-child; (丈夫) a man.

danjiau (談合ふ), *vi.* to consult *with*; confer *with*; talk *with*.

danjiki (斷食), *n.* fast; fasting. —斷食する, to fast. ¶ 斷食療法, fast-cure.

dan-jiru (談じる), *vi.* ❶ (話す) to speak; say; talk. ❷ (論談) to discourse. ❸ (詰る) to reason [argue] *with*. —...と同日を以て談ずべからず, not to be named on [in] the same day *with*.

danjite (斷じて), *ad.* certainly; positively; never (打消).

danjo (男女), *n.* man and woman. ¶ 男女同權, the equality of the sexes. —男女混合教授學校, a mixed school.

danjō (壇場), *n.* ❶ an altar-place; the service-room. ❷ a stage. ❸ a platform. —得意の壇場である, to be on one's own ground.

danka (檀家), *n.* a supporter of a Buddhist temple.

dankai (段階), *n.* steps; a stage.

dankei (男系), *n.* male side; male lineage; the father's side. ¶ 男系親, an agnate; a relative on the father's side. —男系相續, succession in the male line.

danketsu (團結), *n.* combination; union; organization. —團結する, to unite; combine; organize. —團結せる, combined; united; corporate. —團結して, in combination [union]. —團結を固くする, to strengthen the union. ¶ 團結力, power of combination.

danki (暖氣), *n.* warmth; warm weather.

danko (斷乎たる), *a.* determined; decisive; firm. —斷乎たる處置を執る, to take a decisive step. ——**toshite,** *ad.* firmly; positively; resolutely. —斷乎として動かぬ, to stand [remain] firm.

dankō (男工), *n.* a male hand [operative].

dankō (彈孔), *n.* a shot-hole.

dankō (斷行する), *vt.* to execute; carry into effect; put in practice.

dankō-kyōsō (斷郊競走), *n.* a cross-country race.

dankon (彈痕), *n.* a shot mark.

danmari (默), *n.* ❶ (無言) silence. ❷ (默り芝居) a dumb show; a pantomime. ❸ (默り役者) a mute; a mummer. ❹ (沈默者) a taciturn person.

danmatsuma (斷末魔), *n.* the last breath; the last moment; the last gasp. —斷末魔の苦しみ, the agony of death.

danmen (斷面), *n.* a section. ¶ 水平(縱; 橫; 直立)斷面, horizontal (longitudinal; cross; vertical) section.

danna (旦那), *n.* ❶ (夫) a husband. ❷ (主人) a master; a governor. ❸ (呼びかけ) Sir. —もし旦那, Please, your honour [Sir].

danna (檀那) *n.* a supporter of a Buddhist temple.

dannen (斷念する), *vt.* to give up; renounce; abandon; relinquish.

dano (だの), *particle.* ❶ (事物を竝列する場合) and; or; what with ...and what with. ❷ (似たるもの) and the like. —百合だの, ダリアだの, lilies, dahlias, and the like.

danpan (談判), *n.* negotiation; parley. —談判する, to negotiate (*with*); treat *with*; parley *with* (休戰·條件等). —談判破裂するや, upon rupture of the negotiations. —談判を開始する, to open negotiations.

danpatsu (斷髮する), *vi.* to cut the queue [top-knot].

danpei (談柄), *n.* a topic; a subject of conversation; a talk.

danpen (斷片), *n.* a fragment; a piece; a scrap. —斷片的, fragmentary. (斷片的に, in fragments; disconnectedly.)

danpen (彈片), *n.* a (shell-) splinter.

danpingu (ダンピング, 不當廉賣), *n.* 【商】 dumping.

danraku (段落), *n.* ❶ (文段) a paragraph; a section. ❷ (落着) a stage; a conclusion; a period; a full stop. —段落がつく, to come to a full stop [to conclusion]. ¶ 段落點, a period; a full stop.

danran (團欒), *n.* making a group; sitting in a circle. —團欒する, to sit around; sit in circle; be in harmony. —一家團欒の樂しさを缺く, to lack the pleasures

of a (harmonious) home.
danro (煖爐), *n.* a stove; a fire-place. —煖爐を焚く, to light a stove.
danron (談論する), *vt.* to talk; discuss. —政事を談論する, to talk [discuss] politics.
danryoku (彈力), *n.* elastic force; elasticity. —彈力ある, elastic.
danryū (暖流), *n.* a warm current.
dansei (男生), *n.* a male scholar [pupil]; a boy; a male student.
dansei (男性), *n.* ❶ the male sex. ❷【文】the masculine gender. —男性の, male; masculine; virile. —男性的, manly; masculine.
dansei (彈性), *n.* elasticity. ¶ 彈性護謨, gum elastic; india-rubber. —彈性體, an elastic body.
dansen (斷線), *n.* snapping of a wire (lamp-filament).
danshaku (男爵), *n.* a baron. ¶ 男爵夫人, a baroness.
danshi (男子), *n.* ❶ (男の子) a boy; a son (息). ❷ a man; a male; the sterner [male] sex. —男子たる者, one who calls himself a man.
danshō (談笑), *n.* chat; chatting; merry talk.
danshū (男囚), *n.* a male prisoner.
dansō (男裝する), *vi.* to wear male attire; be disguised as a man. —男裝して, in male attire; in male disguise.
dansō (彈奏する), *vt.* to play (on). ¶ 彈奏者, a player.
dansō (斷層), *n.* 【地質】dislocation; a fault. ¶ 斷層地震, dislocation earthquake.
danson-johi (男尊女卑), *n.* predominance of man over woman.
dansu (舞踏), *n.* a dance; dancing. —ダンスする, to dance; galop.
dansui (斷水する), *vi.* ❶ (渴水) to run short (of water). ❷ (給水止め) to cut [shut] off the water.
dantai (團體), *n.* a body; a party; a corporation. —團體で來る, to come in parties. ¶ 團體乘車券, ticket for parties. —團體旅行, a tour of a party; a party tour. —團體割引, discount for parties.
dantei (斷定), *n.* dictum; judgment (判斷); decision (決定). —斷定する, to judge; decide; conclude.
dantōdai (斷頭臺), *n.* the scaffold; the block. —斷頭臺の露と消える, to be brought to the block.
dantsū (段通), *n.* a cotton carpet [rug].
danu (彈雨), *n.* a hail [shower; rain] of bullets.
danwa (談話), *n.* conversation; talk; speech; word. —食卓上の談話, table-talk. —談話を止める, to break off [cut short; drop] the conversation. ¶ 談話體, a conversational [colloquial] style.
danyaku (彈藥), *n.* ❶ ammunition. ❷ (資力) means; resources; the wherewithal. ¶ 彈藥縱列, an ammunition column. —彈藥庫, a powder magazine.
danzai (斷罪), *n.* judgment; condemnation; (斬罪) decapitation.
danzen (斷然), *ad.* positively; resolutely; flatly. —斷然たる, positive; resolute; flat. —斷然拒絕する, to refuse flatly.
danzetsu (斷絕), *n.* ❶ (絕滅) extinction. ❷ (切斷) rupture; interruption; break. —斷絕する, ① [*vi.*] to become extinct; rupture (決裂). ② [*vt.*] to break [cut] off; sever.
danzoku (斷續する), *vi.* to intermit. —斷續的に, intermittently; off and on.
dan-zuru (彈する), *vt.* to play. —琴を彈ずる, to play (on) the *koto*.
dan-zuru (斷する), *vt.* to judge; decide.
dappi (脫皮), *n.* ecdysis; the casting [shedding] of skins. —脫皮する, to cast [shed] skins.
daradara (だらだら), *ad.* ❶ (滴滴) in drops. ❷ (漸々) gradually. ❸ (緩徐) slowly; sluggishly. —だらだら坂, a gentle slope. —涎をだらだら流す, to let saliva stream down. —彼はいつもだらだらとしてゐる, He is always inert.
daraiban (旋盤), *n.* a lathe. —旋盤に掛ける, to turn.
darake (だらけの), *a.* full *of*; covered *with*; smeared *with*. —血だらけの手, a bloody hand.
darakeru (だらける), *vi.* to feel languid; loosen [slacken] one's effort; flag. —だらけた, languid; sluggish; dull.
daraku (墮落), *n.* depravity; fall; corruption. —人類の墮落, the Fall (of man). —墮落する, to degrade; fall. ¶ 墮落書生, a depraved student.
darari-to (だらりと), *ad.* ❶ (ぶらりと) dangling; lollingly. ❷ (勢なく) languidly.
darashi (檢束ない), *a.* negligent (怠慢な); slovenly; slipshod (文體の). —だらしない女, a slattern; a slut. —だらしない風をする, to be slovenly dressed.
dare (誰), *prop.* ❶ (何人) who (が); whose (の); whom (に, を). ❷ (誰かが, 或人が) some; some one; somebody. ❸ (誰でもが, 何人でもが) any; anyone; anybody; whoever. ❹ (誰も皆) everyone;

all. ●(誰もない) no one; none. —誰だか, some one or other. —誰が來た, Who came? —誰か來たか, Did any one call? —誰が何と言っても, Whatever anybody may say. —誰の番だ, Whose turn is it? —誰か知ってる者は手を上げ, Any one who knows, hold up your hand.

dareru (撓れる), *vi.* ❶(興味がへる) to grow listless. ●(活氣がなくなる) to flag; droop.

daria(ダリア), *n.* 【植】the dahlia.

darin (舵輪), *n.* a steering-wheel.

darō (だらう), shall be; will be; (と思ふ) I think; I suppose: (か知ら) I wonder.

darui (怠るい), *a.* languid; listless; tired (疲勞). —足がだるい, My legs feel heavy.

daruma (達磨), *n.* ❶(菩提達磨) Bodhidharma. ●(不倒翁) a tumbler. ●(一種の船) a cargo boat; a lighter.

daryoku (惰力), *n.* (force of) inertia.

dasan (打算する), *vt.* to calculate; count; reckon. —打算的, calculating; calculative; prudential.

dasei(惰性), *n.* (force of) inertia.

dashi(だし), *n.* ❶(煮汁) broth; stock. ●(香餌) a stalking-horse; a blind; a cloak. —人をだしに遣ふ, to use a man as a blind; make a stalking-horse of a man. —宗教をだしに使って, under the veil of religion.

dashi(山車), *n.* a procession-car; a float.

dashiau (出合ふ), *vt.* to contribute jointly. —費用を出し合ふ, to club the expense.

dashimae (出し前), *n.* a share; the amount (to be) contributed.

dashin(打診する), *vt.* to percuss; sound; tap. ¶ 打診器, a plexor.

dashinuke (出拔に), *ad.* all of a sudden; suddenly; abruptly. —後から出し拔けになぐる, to hit a person suddenly from behind.

dashinuku (出拔く), *vt.* to steal a march *on*; forestall; outwit.

dashippanashi (出放しにする), *v.* to leave (the gas or water) flowing [turned on]; leave (things) about; leave (things) lying about.

dashishiburu (出澁る), *vt.* to grudge; be unwilling to pay.

dashu (打手), *n.* a batter. ¶ 强打手, a hard hitter; a heavy batter.

dashu (舵手), *n.* a coxswain (端艇の); a cox (同上); a steersman; a helmsman; a quartermaster.

dasoku (蛇足), *n.* a superfluity; a redundancy. —蛇足の, superfluous; redundant.

dassen (脫線), *n.* ❶ derailment. ●(横道へそれること) digression; deviation. ——**-suru,** *v.* ❶ to run off the metals [rails; track]. ● to wander; digress; fly [go] off at a tangent (話など). —主題から脫線する, to wander from the subject.

dassen (脫船する), *vi.* to desert (from) a ship. ¶ 脫船者, a deserter; a runaway seaman.

dasshimen (脫脂綿), *n.* absorbent cotton.

dasshinyū (脫脂乳), *n.* skim-milk.

dasshu (奪取する), *vt.* to capture; seize; take; carry.

dasshutsu (脫出), *n.* ❶ escape. ●【醫】prolapse (子宮·直腸等の). —脫出する, ① to escape *from*; get away *from*. ② to prolapse.

dasso (脫疽), *n.* 【醫】gangrene; mortification.

dassō (脫走), *n.* desertion; escape. ——**-suru,** *v.* to desert; escape; run away; flee; abscond. —隊を脫走する, to desert (from) one's regiment. ¶ 脫走者, a deserter; a runaway.

dassui (脫水する), *vt.* 【化】to dehydrate.

das-suru (脫する), *v.* ❶(遺脫) to leave out; omit; drop. ●(脫ぐ) to take off; doff. ●(免る) to escape *from*; get rid [out] *of*; free oneself *from*. —舊慣を脫する, to shake off old habits. —危險區域を脫する, to escape from the danger zone. —肝心の語を脫する, to leave out an important word.

dasu (出す), *vt.* to put (手·足·舌·力·精·本·芽など); bring out. ●(取出す) to take out; pull out (短銃等を). ●(露出) to expose (胸·脛等). ●(發行, 發刊) to publish. ●(差出す) to send in; bring forward; present. ●(拂ふ) to pay. ●(解任) to discharge; turn out. ●(開業) to open; start; set up. —賣物に出す, to display [put up] for sale. —力を出す, to put forth one's strength. —茶を出す, to offer tea. —店を出す, to open a shop. —證據を出す, to produce evidence. —願書を出す, to present a petition. —辭表を出す, to tender [send in] one's resignation. —旗(掲示)を出す, to put up a flag (notice). —樽から酒を出す, to draw wine from a cask. —手紙を出す, to send a letter by post.

-dasu(出す), to begin; commence. —降り出す, to begin to rain.

dāsu (打), *n.* a dozen. —打賣り, sold in dozens [by the dozen].

datai (墮胎), *n.* abortion. —墮胎する, to have an abortion; procure an abortion. ¶ 墮胎罪, the crime of abortion; criminal abortion.

datchō (脱腸), *n.* 【醫】 hernia; rupture. ¶ 脫腸帶, a truss.

date (伊達), *n.* dandyism; foppery. ¶ 伊達者, a dandy; a fop.

datō (妥當), *n.* propriety; appropriateness; fitness. —妥當な, proper; appropriate; suitable.

datsubō (脫帽する), *vi.* to doff a hat; pull [take] off one's hat (cap); uncover. —脫帽!, Hats off!

datsuei (脫營する), *vi.* to desert (from) barracks. ¶ 脫營兵, a deserter; a runaway soldier.

datsugoku (脫獄), *n.* prison [jail]-breaking. ☞ *dakkan.*

datsuji (脫字), *n.* ❶ omission of a word. ❷ an omitted word.

datsumō (脫毛), *n.* ❶ (脫落) falling out [off] of hair; loss of hair. ❷ (拔くこと) depilation. ¶ 脫毛藥, a depilatory.

datsuraku (脫落する), *vi.* to slough (皮·殼等); fall off (毛髮等).

datsurō (脫漏), *n.* omission. —脫漏する, to be omitted; be left out.

datsurui (奪壘), *n.* 【野球】 base-running.

datsuryaku (奪掠), *n.* plunder; pillage; loot. —奪掠する, to plunder; pillage; loot.

datsuzei (脫稅), *n.* evasion of taxes. —脫稅する, to evade taxes. ¶ 脫稅者, an evader of taxes; a tax-dodger.

datsuzoku (脫俗), *n.* being above the world; unworldliness. —脫俗の, unworldly.

dattai (脫退する), *v.* to secede *from.*

Dattan (韃靼), *n.* Tartary. ¶ 韃靼人, a Tartar.

datte (だッて), *conj.* (と云ッたッても) but; yet; still. ——, *ad.* (でも, にても) even. —さうだッて, So he says (they say). —何だッて歸ッて來た, Why on earth have you come home? —だッて極りが惡いんですもの, Still I felt so abashed.

dattō (脫黨), *n.* defection; secession; 【政】 cave (脫黨組にも云ふ). —脫黨する, to secede from a party; desert [leave] one's party. ¶ 脫黨者, a seceder; a rat; a turncoat.

de (で), *particle.* ❶ (時間, 年齡) in; at. ❷ (場所) in; at; on. ❸ (材料) from; of. ❹ (原因) with; of; from; by; for; owing to; on account of. ❺ (方便) (*a*) through; by: (*b*) by; on: (*c*) in; with. ❻ (價) for; at. ❼ (割合) by. ❽ (推定) from; by. ❾ (依據) by; according to...; on. —インキで, in ink. —ペンで, with a pen. —時間で雇ふ, to hire by the hour. —五十錢で買ふ, to buy it for fifty sen. —年金で暮らす, to live on an annuity. —肺病で死ぬ, to die of consumption. —八十八で死ぬ, to die at eighty-eight. —ミルクで育てる, to bring up on milk. —鐵で出來て居る, to be made of iron. —十日で讀切る, to read it though in ten days.

de (で), *conj.* and; so; then. —で私は行かなかッた, And so I did not go.

de (出), *n.* ❶ coming out; supply (供給); appearance (出願). ❷ (出身, 素性) birth; origin. ❸ (出費) outlay; outgoings. ❹ (出勤) attendance. ❺ (出發) start. ❻ (太陽·月の上り) rise. ❼ (人出) turnout. —出がある, to go a long way; last long. —此急須は出が惡るい, This tea-pot does not pour out well.

deai (出會), *n.* a meeting (會合); a love-meeting (密會); blending (色彩などの配合). —出會ひ頭に, upon encountering; on meeting suddenly. ¶ 出會ひ場所, a trysting-place; a meeting-place.

deakinai (出商), *n.* hawking; peddling.

dearuku (出步く), *vi.* to go about; gad about.

deau (出會ふ), *v.* ❶ (遭遇) to encounter; meet *with*; come across [upon]. ❷ (會合) to meet; gather; meet clandestinely (密會). —雨に出會ふ, to be caught in a rain. —困難に出會ふ, to meet with a difficulty.

deba (出刃-庖丁), *n.* a kitchen-knife.

deba (出齒), *n.* a buck-tooth; a projecting tooth.

debana (出花), *n.* the first infusion of tea.

debana (出鼻), *n.* ❶ dash. ❷ (始め) the beginning; the outset; the start.

debaru (出張る), *vi.* ❶ (突出) to project; protrude. ❷ (出向く) to go to a place on business. —出張ッた, projecting; protruding; beetling.

debeso (出臍), *n.* a started [prominent] navel.

debitai (出額), *n.* a projecting forehead; beetle-brows.

debu (肥滿漢), *n.* a fatty.

debudebu (でぶでぶの), *a.* plump; plumpy.

dechigai (出違ひになる), *vi.* to miss a visitor.

deddobōru (死球), *n.* 【野球】 a dead-ball.

defune (出船), *n.* an outgoing vessel. —出船入船, incoming and outgoing vessels.

degake (出掛に), on going out.

degara (出柄), *n.* tea-grounds; coffee-grounds.

degeiko (出稽古), *n.* teaching

out of one's house; giving lessons at a pupil's house.

degirai (出嫌の), *a.* reluctant to go out; home-keeping; stay-at-home. —出嫌ひの人, a stay-at-home; one who keeps indoors.

degiwa (出際に), *ad.* just as one was going out; when one was on the point of going out.

deguchi (出口), *n.* the way out; the exit; the outlet; the gateway. —出口を塞ぐ, to shut up the outlet [exit].

dehairi (出入), *n.* ❶ going in and out. ❷ (親しく出入すること) access. —出入する, ① to go in and out. ② to have access (to a house); frequent (a place or house).

dehazure (出外れ), *n.* the far end (of a place). —出外れる, to come *out of*; leave.

dehōdai (出放題), *n.* random; offhandedness. —出放題に, at random. (口から出放題にしゃべる, to jabber whatever comes to mind.) —出放題を云ふ, to talk at random; say whatever comes uppermost.

deichi (泥地), *n.* a moss; a bog; a fen.

deinei (泥濘), *n.* mire; mud; quagmire. —泥濘の, muddy; boggy; sloughy.

deiri (出入), *n.* ❶ going in and out; entrance and exit. ❷ (出納, 收支) receipts and payments; incomings and outgoings. ❸ (定雇) a regular employee. —出入の醫者, the family doctor. —出入の職人, workmen regularly employed in one's house. —出入を差止める, to forbid the house. ¶ 出入口, a doorway; a gateway; a gate. —金銀出入帳, a cash-book.

deisui (泥醉する), *vi.* to be dead drunk.

deitan (泥炭), *n.* peat. ¶ 泥炭地, bog-land; peat-moss.

dekakeru (出掛ける), *vi.* to go out; start; set out. —一寸散步に出掛ける, to go out for a stroll.

dekasegi (出稼), *n.* being at work in another country [region]; emigration (移住). ¶ 出稼人, an emigrant.

dekasu (出來す), *vt.* ❶ (生じさす) to do; bring forth; bring to pass. ❷ (旨くやる) to succeed. ❸ (仕上げる) to complete; (bring to a) finish. —借金を出來す, to run into debt; contract a debt. —大變な事を仕出來す, to bring on a frightful thing [new trouble]. —出かした出かした!, Well done! Well done!; Bravo!

dekadan (デカダン), *n.* ❶ decadence; *décadence* 【佛】. ❷ (人) a decadent; a *décadent* 【佛】.

deki (出來), *n.* ❶ (製作) the make. ❷ (出來榮) performance; effect; yield (農作物の). —一箱の出來, the make of a box.

dekiagari (出來上り), *n.* completion; finish. —出來上る, to be completed; be finished.

dekiai (出來合), *n.* a ready-made one. —出來合の, ready-made; ready-built (家に云ふ). —出來合で間に合はす, to put up with a ready-made one. ¶ 出來合服, ready-made clothes; slops. —出來合品, a ready-made article; a ready-made 【俗】.

dekibae (出來榮), *n.* success; turn-out; result.

dekidaka (出來高), *n.* crop (收穫); yield (同上); output (生產); a day's dealings (一日の取引高).

dekigokoro (出來心), *n.* a sudden impulse; a (passing) fancy; a caprice. —出來心の, impulsive; carried by a sudden impulse. —一時の出來心から, from a moment's impulse.

dekigoto (出來事), *n.* an accident; an event; an occurrence. —悲慘な出來事, a tragical event.

dekimono (腫物), *n.* 【醫】 a sore; a tumour; a boil.

dekiru (出來る), *vi.* ❶ (能否) to be able; be in a position *to.* ❷ (秀でる) to be proficient; be versed *in*; be skilled. ❸ (仕上がる) to be done; be finished. ❹ (發生する) to happen; occur. ❺ (農作物などが) to grow; be produced; be raised; yield. ❻ to be made (製造); be built (築造); be brewed (釀造). —, *a.* ❶ (可能) possible. ❷ (秀でた) proficient; able; clever. —出來ない, ① [*v.*] to be impossible; be unable; cannot. ② [*a.*] impossible (不可能な); dull (遲鈍な); backward (進步せぬ). (それは出來ない相談だ, It is an impossible proposal. —惡い事は出來ないものだ, One cannot do evil with impunity.) —出來る限り, as far as possible. (出來る限り早く, as soon as one can; with all speed. —出來る限り働く, to do one's best.) —出來るだけ早く, as soon as possible; at your earliest convenience. —出來るだけのことをする, to do one's best possible. —出來るならお出なさい, Come if possible. —御飯が出來ました, Dinner is served [ready]. —私に出來ることなら何なりとも致します, I shall be pleased to do anything for you that is in my power.

dekishi (溺死), *n.* drowning. —溺死する, to be drowned; drown oneself (故意に).

dekisokonai (出來損ひ), *n.* ❶ a failure; a bad make. ❷ (人) a deformed person; a freak of nature. —出來損ふ, to fail.

dekitate (出來立ての), *a.* just made; newly-made; brand-new. —出來立ての著物, newly-made clothes. —出來立てのほやほや, hot from the oven.

deko (凸額), *n.* a projecting forehead; beetle-brows.

dekobō (凸坊), *n.* a mischievous boy; an imp.

dekoboko (凸凹), *n.* unevenness; jaggedness; ruggedness. —凸凹の地面, broken [rugged] ground.

deku (木偶), **dekunobō** (木偶坊), *n.* ❶ (人形) a puppet. ❷ (罵語) a blockhead; a dunce.

demae (出前), *n.* sending dishes to order.

deme (出眼), *n.* a protruding eye; a goggle eye.

demise (出店), *n.* a branch shop.

demizu (出水), *n.* a freshet; a flood. ☞ *shussui.*

demo (でも), *particle.* (「にても」の約) if; though; even if; also. —雨天でも, even if it rains. —子供でも分る, Even a child can understand it. —誰でも宜しい, Anybody will do. —學者でもあるかの樣に, as if he were a scholar. —馬鹿でも利口でもない, He is neither a fool nor a wise man.

demo (でも), *conj.* (それでもの約) but; still; yet.

demo- (でも), ❶ (拙) poor; unskilled. ❷ (自分免許の) would-be. ❸ (僞) pseud-, pseudo-. ¶ でも醫者, an unskilled doctor. —でも紳士, a would-be gentleman.

demodori (出戻), *n.* ❶ coming home without reaching one's destination. ❷ (離緣で歸ること) coming home after a divorce: (その女) a divorced wife come home.

demono (出物), *n.* ❶ (賣物) an article on [for] sale. ❷ (腫物) a tumour; a boil.

demukae (出迎へ), *n.* meeting; going to meet a person. —出迎へる, to meet; come out to meet. —停車場で出迎を受ける, to be met at the station.

den (傳), *n.* ❶ (傳記) a biography; a life. ❷ (傳說) a tradition. ❸ (傳授) initiation. ❹ (方法) a method; a way; a secret (秘傳).

de-nakereba (でなければ), *conj.* if...not; unless; (or) else.

denaosu (出直す), *vi.* to come again.

deṅatsu (電壓), *n.* electric pressure.

denbu (臀部), *n.* the buttocks; the posteriors; the rump.

denbun (傳聞), *n.* hearsay; a report. —傳聞する, to hear (from others); know by hearsay.

denchi (電池), *n.* a trough-battery; an electric battery; a (an electric) cell.

denchū (電柱), *n.* a telegraph (telephone)-pole [-post]; an electric pole. ¶ 電柱廣告, an advertisement on an electric pole.

dendō (殿堂), *n.* a palace; a temple.

dendō (傳道), *n.* propagandism; mission work. —傳道する, [*vi.*] to preach; propagandize. ¶ 傳道師, a missionary; a propagandist; an evangelist.

dendō (傳導), *n.* transmission; conduction. —傳導する, [*vt.*] to transmit; 【理】 conduct. ¶ 傳導體, a conductor; a transmitter.

dendōki (電動機), *n.* an electric motor; an electromotor.

deṅen (田園), *n.* fields and gardens; the country (田舍). ¶ 田園生活, country [rural] life. —田園都市, a garden-city.

dengaku (田樂), *n.* baked bean-curd served with *miso.*

dengeki (電擊), *n.* an electric shock.

dengon (傳言), *n.* ❶ (a verbal) message; word. ❷ remembrances; compliments; regards. —傳言する, to send a message; send a person word (that). —傳言を言ひ置く, to leave word.

dengun (殿軍), *n.* the rear-guard.

dengurikaeshi (でんぐり返し), *n.* a somersault. —でんぐり返る, to go head over heels; turn somersault. —でんぐり返しに落ちる, to fall head over heels.

deṅi (電位), *n.* 【電】 electric potential.

denji (田地), *n.* a rice-field; a rice-paddy.

denjiki (電磁氣), *n.* electromagnetism.

denju (傳授), *n.* instruction; initiation into a secret process [art]. **——suru,** *vt.* to instruct; initiate. —秘術を傳授する, to induct [initiate] a person into a mystery [secret].

denka (殿下), *n.* Highness; Royal Highness; Imperial Highness; Serene Highness. ¶ 李王殿下, His Highness Prince Li. —故有栖川宮殿下, His Imperial Highness the late Prince Arisugawa. —英國皇太子殿下, His Royal Highness the Prince of Wales.

denka (電化), *n.* electrification. —鐵道を電化する, to electrify a railway.

denkai (電解), *n.* electrolysis.

denki (電氣), *n.* electricity. —電氣の; 電氣的, electric(-al). —電氣に打たれて死ぬ, to die from an electric shock. ¶ 陰(陽)電氣, negative (positive) electricity. —電氣時計, an electric clock. —電氣學, the electric science; electricity; electrology. —電氣學者, an electrician. —電氣技師, an electric(-al) engineer. —電氣火花, an electric spark. —電氣事業, electric enterprise. —電氣仕掛, being operated [worked] by electricity; an electric device. —電氣化學, electrochemistry. —電氣感應, electric induction. —電氣工學, electrical engineering. —電氣死刑, electrocution. —電氣鍍金, galvanization; electroplating. (電氣鍍金する, to electroplate; galvanize.) —電氣鐵道, an electric railway.

denki(傳奇), *n.* romance. —傳奇的, romantic.

denki (傳記), *n.* a biography; a life; a memoir.

denki(傳騎), *n.* a mounted orderly.

denkō (電光), *n.* a flash of lightning; a bolt. —電光石火の如く, like a flash of lightning; with lightning speed; quick as lightning.

denkun (電訓), *n.* telegraphic instructions.

denkyoku (電極), *n.* an electrode; a pole.

denkyū (電球), *n.* the bulb of an electric lamp; an electric bulb. ¶ 金屬(炭素)線電球, an electric bulb with a metallic (carbon) filament.

Denmāku (丁抹), *n.* Denmark. ¶ 丁抹人, a Dane.

dennetsu(電熱), *n.* electric heat. ¶ 電熱器, an electric heater.

denpa (電波), *n.* an electric wave.

denpa(傳播), *n.* circulation; diffusion; dissemination. —— **-suru,** *v.* to circulate; disseminate; spread; get abroad; be propagated. —人から人へと傳播する, to spread from one person to another.

denpata (田畑), *n.* ploughland; land under cultivation.

denpō (電報), *n.* a telegram; a wire; a cablegram (海底電報). —電報で知らす, to inform by wire. —電報を打つ, to telegraph; wire; cable (海底電報を打つ); send one a wire [telegram]. ¶ 暗號電報, a cipher telegram. —外(內)國電報, a foreign (domestic) telegram. —間送電報, a deferred telegram. —至急電報, an urgent telegram. —電報配達夫, a telegraph messenger. —電報頼信紙, a message [telegram] form. —電報料, a telegram charge.

denpu (田夫), *n.* a bumpkin; a rustic; a peasant. ¶ 田夫野人, illiterate persons; rude men.

denpun(澱粉), *n.* 【化】 dextrine; starch.

denpyō (傳票), *n.* an advice slip; a voucher; a docket.

denrai(傳來), *n.* transmission (相傳); introduction (渡來). —傳來の, hereditary; traditional. —傳來する, [*vi.*] ① to be transmitted; be handed down; descend. ② to be introduced; be brought over.

denrei (電鈴), *n.* an electric bell.

denrei (傳令), *n.* 【軍】 an orderly; a messenger.

denri (電離), *n.* electrolytic dissolution; electric dissociation.

denryaku (電略), *n.* a telegraphic address; a cable-address.

denryoku (電力), *n.* electric power. ¶ 電力計, a wattmeter.

denryū (電流), *n.* an electric current. —電流を通ずる, to electrify; pass an electric current through.

densatsu (電殺), *n.* electrocution. —電殺する, to electrocute.

densen (電線), *n.* ❶ telegraph wire; electric wire. ❷ a telegraph-line. ¶ 電線工夫, a lineman.

densen (傳染), *n.* contagion (接觸); infection(間接). —— **-suru,** *v.* to be infected; catch; take. —虎列剌に傳染する, to be infected by cholera. ——, *a.* (傳染的, 傳染性の) contagious; infectious; taking; catching. ¶ 傳染病, an infectious [a contagious] disease. (傳染病研究所, an infectious diseases investigation laboratory.) —傳染病院, an infectious diseases hospital.

densetsu (傳說), *n.* tradition.

densha(電車), *n.* an electric car; an electric tram-car. —電車が滿員だ, The car is full. ¶ 電車停留場, an electric-car [a tram] station; a tram-car stop.

denshi (電子), *n.* electron; electrum.

denshin (電信), *n.* ❶ telegraphy; telegraph. ❷ =*denpō*. ¶ 電信柱, a telegraph pole. —電信符號, a telegraph code. —電信係, a telegraph operator [clerk]. —電信技手, a telegraph operator; a telegrapher; a telegraphist. —電信爲替, a telegraphic money order; a telegraph transfer. —電信機, a telegraph; a telegraphic instrument. —電信局, a telegraph office. —電信隊, a telegraph corps.

denshobato(傳書鳩), *n.* a carrier-pigeon.

denshoku (電飾), *n.* (electric) illumination.

denshū (傳習する), *v.* to be trained [instructed]. ¶ 傳習所, a training-school.

densō (電送する), *vt.* to telegraph; wire; cable. ¶ 電送寫眞, a telephotograph. —寫眞電送機, a telephote.

dentatsu(傳達する), *vt.* to transmit; convey; communicate; deliver.

dento (電鍍), *n.* electroplating; galvanization. —電鍍する, [*vt.*] to electroplate; galvanize.

dentō (電燈), *n.* an electric light [lamp]. —電燈を點ける, to turn [switch] on the electric lamp. —電燈を消す, to turn [switch] off the electric lamp. ¶ 電燈會社, an electric light company.

dentō(傳統), *n.* ❶ (因襲的信仰·慣例等) tradition. ❷ (系統をつぐこと) succession; descent. —傳統的友國, a traditional friendly power.

denwa (電話), *n.* ❶ a telephone message; a phone [俗]. ❷ (電話機) a telephone; a phone [俗]. ❸ (電話術) telephony. —電話で話す, to telephone (a person); phone. —電話をかける, to ring up (呼出す); telephone; phone. —電話を切る, to ring [switch] off. —電話をつなぐ, to put one person through to another. —電話番號 (本局) 一番, telephone No. 1 (Head). —お電話ですよ, You are rung up. ¶ 卓上電話, a desk-telephone. —取附電話, a wall-telephone. —呼出電話, a call telephone. —電話便, telephone-post. —電話帳, a telephone directory. —電話加入者, a telephone subscriber. —電話交換局, a telephone exchange [call] office. —電話交換手, a telephone operator [girl]. —電話室, a telephone-booth. —電話料, a telephone (message) fee.

depātomento (デパートメント·ストア), *n.* a department store.

deppuri (でっぷり肥えた), *a.* stout; plump; corpulent.

deru (出る), *v.* ❶ (外へ出る) to go out; come out. ❷ (出現) to come out; appear; be out (星など); rise (太陽など). ❸ (出發) to start; leave; sail (出帆). ❹ (出席) to go *to*; attend; appear before. ❺ (起因) to originate *in* [*from*]; spring *from*. —出て行け!, Get out! —出て見る; 見に出る, to turn out to see. —幽靈が出る, A ghost appears [walks]. —十番は未だ出ません, No. 10 is not connected yet. —停車場前へ出る, to find oneself before the station.

desakari (出盛), *n.* appearing in the largest number; the season. —蜜柑の出盛り, the season for oranges; the orange season.

desaki (出先), *n.* the place one has gone to. —出先が分らない, We do not know where he has gone.

deshabari (出しゃばり), *n.* ❶ (行爲) intrusion; forwardness. ❷ (人) an intruder; a whipper-snapper. —出しゃばる, ❶ [*vi.*] to intrude; chop in; put oneself forward. ❷ [*a.*] forward; intrusive.

deshi (弟子), *n.* ❶ (門人) a disciple; a pupil; a follower. ❷ (徒弟) an apprentice. —弟子入りする, to enter as a pupil; become an apprentice. —弟子にする, to take in as a pupil. —弟子をとる, to take apprentices.

desorou (出揃ふ), *vi.* to appear all together.

desu (です), *v. aux.* to be. —...ですからね, you see.

desugimono (出過ぎ者), *n.* an intruder; a busybody.

desugiru (出過ぎる), *vi.* ❶ (過出) (*a*) to be too far out: (*b*) (茶など) to be too strong; be overdrawn. ❷ (僭越) to intrude upon; be too forward.

detarame (出鱈目), *n.* random; haphazard; off-handedness. —出鱈目の, random; haphazard; off-hand. —出鱈目に, at random; haphazard. (出鱈目に話す, to talk wild [at random].)

detchi (丁稚), *n.* a boy; an apprentice. —丁稚奉公する (にやる), to serve (send out for) apprenticeship.

dewa (では), *particle.* ❶ (にては) in the case of; as to; as for. ❷ (であるならば) if so; then; in that case. —私の考へる所では, to my mind [thinking]; in my opinion.

deyō (出様), *n.* ❶ (出具合) the way one [a thing] comes out. ❷ (仕向方) overtures; the way one is addressed; attitude. —先方の出様によって, by their behaviour towards us. —出様は先方次第だ, Our attitude will depend entirely upon the other party's.

dezomeshiki (出初式), *n.* the New Year's parade (of the fire-brigades).

do (ど), **domo** (ども), *particle.* but; yet.

do (度), *n.* ❶ degree; extent; measure; graduation (目盛); 【理】 intensity (强度). ❷ (たび) times; instances. —度の强い眼鏡, spectacles of a high degree. —度を失ふ, to be frightened out of one's wits; lose presence of mind. —度を過ごす, to go beyond bounds. —度を計る, to measure.

dō (同), *a.* the same; the said.

dō (胴), *n.* the trunk (身體の); the body (同上又は衣服の).

dō (堂), *n.* a temple; a shrine (祠); a hall (室, 講堂). —堂に入る, to be skilled in; be master of.

dō (銅), *n.* copper.

dō (どう), *int.* (馬を留める時) ho!; whoa!; so!

dō (何樣), *ad.* how. **——,** *pron.* what. —どうあッても; どうしても, in any case; in any circumstances; come what may. (どうあッてもせぬ, on no account.) —どう見ても, in every respect; from every point of view. —どうでもかうでも, by hook or by crook. —どうでもよろしい, I don't care. —それはどうでもよい事だ, It is a matter of indifference. —何う致しまして, Not at all. —芝居に行ッてはどうだ, What say you to a theatre?

doa (扉), *n.* a door.

doai(度合), *n.* degree; rate; measure.

doba (駑馬), *n.* a hack; a jade.

doban (土蕃), *n.* aborigines.

dōban (銅版), *n.* copper-plate.

dobashi (土橋), *n.* an earthen bridge.

dobato(鳩), *n.* 【鳥】 the house-pigeon.

dobei (土塀), *n.* a plaster-wall; a mud-wall.

dobin (土瓶), *n.* a [an earthen] teapot.

doboku (土木), *n.* engineering works; public works; works. ¶ 土木技師, a civil engineer. —土木課, section of public works. —土木工學, civil engineering.

doboku (奴僕), *n.* servants; menials; domestics.

dobu(泥溝), *n.* a ditch; a gutter; a sewer. ¶ 溝泥(水), ditch-mud (-water). —溝浚へ, scavengering; a scavenger (人).

dobun(どぶんと), *ad.* (with a) plop.

dōbun (同文), *n.* identity of scripts (同字なること); the same [identical] scripts (同文字). ¶ 同文電報, a multiple telegram. —同文通牒, an identical note.

dōbunbo (同分母), *n.* the same denominator.

dōbutsu (動物), *n.* an animal; fauna (一地方又は一時代の). —動物(性)の, animal. ¶ 高等(下等)動物, the higher (lower) animals. —動物園, the zoological gardens; a menagerie; the Zoo (特に倫敦の) 〔俗〕. —動物學, zoology. —動物虐待防止會, a society for the prevention of cruelty to animals (S.P.C.A. と略す)

dobyakushō (土百姓), *n.* a peasant; a clodhopper.

dochaku (土著の), *a.* native; native-born; indigenous. ¶ 土著人, natives.

dōchaku(撞著), *n.* contradiction; clash; conflict. —自家撞著の, self--contradictory. **——-suru,** *v.* to be contradictory *to*; be in conflict *with*. —前後撞著する, to contradict itself.

dochira (何方), *pron.* ❶ (場所) where. ❷ (孰) which. —何方でも, either; whichever. (何方でもよい, Either will do. —何方でもすきなのをお取り, You may choose whichever you like.) —何方へ, ① where. ② Where are you going? [Whither bound?] —何方の(を), which.

dōchū(道中), *n.* a journey; travelling. **——,** *ad.* in one's journey; while on a journey. ¶ 道中案內, the travellers' guide; a guide-book. —道中日記, an itinerary; a record of a journey.

dodai(土臺), *n.* foundation; groundwork: 【建】 groundsill; ground-plate. **——,** *ad.* from the outset; from the base; fundamentally. —事實を土臺とした小說, a novel based upon facts. ¶ 土臺石, a foundation-stone.

dōdan (同斷), *n.* the same; ditto.

dodanba (土壇場), *n.* (斷頭場) the scaffold; the block. —土壇場に坐る, to be prepared for the worst.

dōdentai(導電體), *n.* an electric conductor.

dōdō (堂堂), *ad.* stately; in a dignified manner. —堂々と爭ふ, to contend [dispute] in a dignified manner. **——-taru,** *a.* imposing; dignified; stately. —堂々たる肩書, a sounding title. —堂々たる邸宅, a stately mansion.

dōdōmeguri (どうどうめぐりする), *vi.* to go round and round.

dōfū (同封する), *vt.* to enclose. —外の手紙と同封する, to enclose with another letter.

dōfubo (同父母の), *a.* german; consanguineous. ¶ 同父母兄弟, a full brother; a brother german.

dogai(度外視する), *vt.* to ignore; disregard; neglect. —之を度外に置く, to leave it out of account.

dōgane (胴金), *n.* a metal clasp.

dōgi (胴衣), *n.* an underwear; a waistcoat.

dōgi (動議), *n.* a motion. —動議を提出する, to present [make] a motion. ¶ 動議通告簿, an order--book.

dōgi (道義), *n.* moral principles; morality. —道義の念; 道義心, moral sense. —道義を重んずる, to set value upon morality.

dogimagi (周章する), *vi.* to be in a flurry [flutter]; lose one's head. —どぎまぎさす, to flurry; flutter.

dogo(土語), *n.* a dialect; a patois; a native tongue.

dogū(土偶), *n.* an earthen image; a clay image.

dōgu (道具), *n.* a tool; an implement; an instrument. ¶ 臺所道具,

• kitchen utensils. —學校道具, school things. —道具箱, a tool-box. —道具部屋, (劇場の) a property-room. —道具立, ① a scene; *mise en scène* [佛]. ② (準備) preliminary arrangements. —道具屋, an upholsterer (家具商); a tool-dealer.

dōgyō (同行), *n.* ❶ (道連れ) a road-companion; a fellow-traveller. ❷ (同じ修行者) a brother [*pl.* brethren].

dōgyō (同業), *n.* ❶ the same calling [profession; trade; occupation]. ❷=同業者. ¶ 同業組合, a craft-guild; a guild; a trade association. (同業組合聯合會, the union of trade associations [guilds].) —同業者, a person of the same trade [profession; calling]; a fellow-trader. —同業社會, the profession; the trade.

dōhai (同輩), *n.* an [a social] equal; a comrade; a colleague.

dōhan (同伴する), *v.* to accompany; go (in company) *with.*

dohazure (度外れの), *a.* inordinate; excessive.

dohi (土匪), *n.* rebellious natives; local rebels.

dōhō (同胞), *n.* a brother; a compatriot; a countryman. —我が在外同胞, our countrymen abroad.

dohyō (土俵), *n.* ❶ a sand-bag; a gabion. ❷ (土俵場) a ring; an arena. —土俵入, a display of wrestlers on the ring.

dōhyō (道標), *n.* a sign-post; a finger-post; a way-mark [-post]; a guide-stone (道標碑).

dōi (同意), *n.* ❶ assent; agreement; concurrence. ❷ (同意義) the same meaning. —同意する, to assent *to*; concur (*with* a person); agree (*to* a proposal; *with* a person). —同意を表する, to express agreement [concurrence]. —兩親の同意を得て, with one's parents' consent. ¶ 同意語, a synonym. —同意者, an assentient; an assentor. —同意書, a written consent.

dōin (動員), *n.* mobilization. —動員令を下す, to issue mobilization orders. —軍隊を動員する, to mobilize troops. ¶ 工業動員, industrial mobilization.

Doitsu (獨逸), *n.* Germany. —獨逸製の, of German make; made in Germany. ¶ 獨逸帝國(共和國), the German Empire (Republic). —獨逸語, German. —獨逸人, a German.

dōitsu (同一), *n.* identity; sameness. —同一の, the same; the identic(-al). —同一人の所爲, the act of the same person. —社會主義と無政府主義とを同一視する, to identify socialism with anarchism.

dōiu (どう云ふ), *a.* what; what kind [sort; manner] of. —どういふ譯で, why; for what reasons. —どう云ふものか, somehow; for some reason or other. —どう云ふことがあらうとも, come what may; whatever may happen.

dōjaku (瞠若する), *vi.* to stare with astonishment; be struck dumb. —有髯男子をして後に瞠若たらしむ, to make bearded men stare with astonishment.

dōji (同時), *n.* the same time. —同時の, simultaneous; contemporaneous. —同時に, simultaneously; at the same time; concurrently; contemporaneously.

dōji (童子), *n.* a boy; a child.

dōjidai (同時代の), *a.* contemporary; contemporaneous; of the same age. —同時代の人, a contemporary. —同時代に, in the same age; contemporaneously.

dojin (土人), *n.* a native; an aboriginal; aborigines [*pl.*].

dōjin (同人), *n.* comrades; companions. ¶ 社中同人, the comrades in the company.

dō-jiru (動じる), *v.* to be agitated; be perturbed; be confused.

dōjitsu (同日), *n.* the same day. —同日の論に非ず, not to be spoken of in the same breath.

dojō (泥鰌), *n.* the loach. —いつも柳の下に鰌は居らぬ, "A fox is not caught twice in the same snare."

dojō (土壤), *n.* soil; mould; loam.

dōjō (同上), the same as the above; ditto; do. (ditto の略).

dōjō (同情), *n.* sympathy; fellow-feeling. —同情ある, sympathetic; feeling. —同情する, to sympathize *with*; feel sympathy *for*; feel *for*. —同情に訴へる, to appeal to one's sympathy. —同情に値する, to deserve one's sympathy. ¶ 同情罷工, a sympathetic strike.

dōjō (同乘する), *v.* to ride together. ¶ 同乘者, a fellow rider.

dōjō (道場), *n.* ❶ (僧侶の) a cloister; a religious house. ❷ (武術の) a hall for military exercises; an exercise-hall. ¶ 町道場, a private fencing-school.

dōka (どうか), ❶ (どうぞ) please; if you please. ❷ if; whether (or not). —行くかどうか聞いて見ろ, Ask him if he will go; Ask him whether he goes or not.

dōka (同化-作用), *n.* assimilation. —同化する, to assimilate.

dōka (桐花), *n.* a paulownia flower. ¶ 桐花大綬章, the Grand Cordor of the Paulownia.

dōka (銅貨), *n.* a copper (coin); copper coinage.

dōka (導火), *n.* ❶ (口火) a fuse. ❷ (動機) an incentive; a stimulus. ¶ 導火索, a (safety-) fuse; a quick-match. —導火線, ① (a safety-) fuse; a blasting-fuse. ②(誘因, 動機) an incentive (*to*).

dokai(土塊), *n.* a lump of earth; a clod.

dōkakōka (何うか斯うか), *ad.* somehow or other; in one way or another; by hook or by crook. —どうかかうか暮して行く, We manage to keep body and soul together.

dōkaku (同格), *n.* 【文】apposition: the same rank; equality. —同格に附合ふ, to associate on an equal footing [on equal terms]. ¶ 同格名詞, a noun in apposition.

dokan (土管), *n.* a drain pipe; an earthen pipe.

dōkan (同感する), *v.* to sympathize *with*; see eye to eye *with*; agree *with*. —僕も同感だ, I agree [am at one] with you.

dōkan (導管), *n.* a pipe; a conduit-pipe; a duct.

dōka-shite (何樣かして), *ad.* somehow; in some way; by all means (是非とも).

dōka-suru (何樣かする), *v.* ❶ to do something *with*. ❷ to be something the matter *with*. ❸ to manage somehow. —何樣かすると, ①(時として) sometimes; in some cases. ②(仕方に云ふ) in some way. —彼奴餘程どうかして居るよ, He is not quite himself.

dokata (土方), *n.* a navvy. —土方の親分, a coolies' boss.

dōkatsu (恫喝), *n.* bluster; intimidation. —恫喝する, to bluster; intimidate.

dōke (道化), *n.* buffoonery; drollery; farce. —道化る, to play the buffoon; jest. —道化た人だ, He is a funny man. ¶ 道化形, 【劇】 a clown; a buffoon; a funny man. —道化者, a buffoon; a joker. —道化芝居, a farce; a burlesque.

dōkei (憧憬), *n.* =*shōkei.*

dōken (同權), *n.* the same right; equality of rights.

doki (土器), *n.* an earthen vessel; earthenware; crockery.

doki (怒氣), *n.* anger; passion; displeasure. —怒氣を含んで, in an angry tone.

dōki (同氣), *n.* the same turn of mind; the same spirit. —同氣相求む, "Birds of a feather flock together."

dōki(同期), *n.* the same period. ¶ 同期生, a student of the same year.

dōki (銅器), *n.* a copper [bronze] utensil [implement]. ¶ 銅器製造者, a coppersmith.

dōki(動悸), *n.* 【醫】palpitation of the heart; throb. —動悸する, to palpitate; throb.

dōki (動機), *n.* a motive; an incentive; a spring.

dokidoki (悸悸), *ad.* pit-a-pat; pitpat. **——-suru**, *v.* to throb; palpitate; go pit-a-pat. —どきどきする胸を押へる, to press the throbbing breast.

dōkin (同衾する), *vi.* to sleep *with*; lie together; share the bed. ¶ 同衾者, a bedfellow.

dokki (毒氣), *n.* noxious vapour [gas]; mephitis: (惡心) malice.

dokku (船渠), *n.* a dock. —ドックに入れる, to dock. —ドックに入る(から出る), to come into (out of) dock.

dokkyo(獨居), *n.* solitude; living alone. —獨居する, to live alone [in solitude]; live a solitary life.

dokkyō (讀經), *n.* chanting the Buddhist sacred books; Sutra-chant. ¶ 讀經者, a reader; a chanter.

doko (何處), *pron.* where; what place; what part. —何處でも, wherever. —何處へ, where; whither. (どこへ行って來たのか, Where have you been?) —何處から, whence; wherefrom. —どこか此のあたり, somewhere about here. —何處までも, to the last [end]; through thick and thin. —何處に, where; in what place. —何處にか, somewhere; anywhere. —何處らに, whereabouts. —どこにも見えない, I cannot find it anywhere. —何處か[何處となく]をかしい, There is something funny about it.

dokō (土工), *n.* ❶ earthwork; entrenchments. ❷=*dokata.*

dōko (銅壺), *n.* a (copper) boiler.

dōkō (同行する), *vi.* to go (take) *with*, accompany; go along *with*. ¶ 同行者, a fellow-traveller; a (road-) companion.

dōkō (瞳孔), *n.* the pupil.

dōkoku (同國), *n.* the same country (province). ¶ 同國人, ① (同邦人) a fellow-countryman; one's countryman. ②(同縣人) a person from the same province. ③ (同郷人) a person from the same place.

dokoroka (どころか), far from: not to speak *of*; to say nothing *of*. —壹圓どころか五十錢もない, I haven't 50 *sen*, to say nothing of one *yen*. —己の過を悔悟するどころか却ってそれを誇って居る, So far from repenting of his error, he glories in it.

dōkotsu (橈骨), *n.* 【解】 the radius.

doku (毒), *n.* poison; harm (害); virus (病毒). —毒になる, to do harm. —毒を仰ぐ, to take poison. —毒を入れる, to poison. —からだに毒である, to be bad for health. —全身に毒が廻ッた, The virus penetrated the whole body. —毒を食はば皿まで, "In for a penny, in for a pound."

dokuaku(毒惡な), *a.* venomous; virulent.

dokuannai (獨案内), *n.* a cab; a crib [俗]; a pony [米]. —獨案内を使ふ, to use a crib. ¶ 法律獨案内, Every Man His Own Lawyer. —ナショナルリーダー獨案内, a guide to the National Readers.

dokudan (獨斷), *n.* ❶ dogmatism; a dogma. ❷(專斷) self-decision; arbitrary decision. —獨斷する, ① to dogmatize. ② to decide for oneself; decide arbitrarily. —獨斷的處置, an arbitrary measure. —彼の獨斷で, by his own decision; at his own discretion. ¶ 獨斷家, a dogmatist.

dokudokushii (毒毒しい), *a.* virulent; vicious; envenomed. —毒々しく, viciously; virulently.

dokueki (毒液), *n.* venom; poisonous fluid.

dokufu(毒婦), *n.* a wicked woman; a Jezebel.

dokuga (毒牙), *n.* a poison-fang; a fang. —毒牙に罹る, to be bitten by the poison-fang. —毒牙を逞うする, to use his poison-fangs; display one's virulence.

dokugaku (獨學), *n.* self-education; self-study; self-tuition. —獨學の, self-educated; self-taught. —獨學する, to study by oneself; teach oneself. —獨學で英語を勉强する, to study English without a teacher.

dokugasu (毒瓦斯), *n.* poison-gas; poisonous gas. ¶ 毒瓦斯彈, a poison-gas shell. —毒瓦斯攻擊, a gas attack. —毒瓦斯戰, a (poison-) gas warfare.

dokugo (獨語), *n.* ❶ soliloquy. ❷=獨逸語. —獨語する, to talk [say] to oneself; soliloquize.

dokuha (讀破する), *v.* to read through.

dokuhaku (獨白), *n.* 【劇】 a monologue; a soliloquy. —獨白する, to soliloquize.

dokuhitsu (毒筆), *n.* a venomous pen. —毒筆を揮ッて攻擊する, to attack with rancour.

dokuja (毒蛇), *n.* a poisonous [venomous] snake; a viper; an adder.

dokukai (讀會), *n.* reading. —第一讀會を通過する, to pass the first reading.

dokumi (毒試する), *vt.* to taste.

dokumushi(毒蟲), *n.* a poisonous insect.

dokuritsu (獨立), *n.* independence. —獨立の, independent; absolute; free. (獨立の生計を營む, to live independently.) —獨立で, on one's own account; for oneself; in itself. (獨立で商賣を始める, to commence business on one's own account.) —獨立獨步である, to live independently; be one's own man. —獨立する, to become independent. —獨立獨行する, to stand on one's own foot [bottom]. ¶ 獨立國, an independent [a free; a sovereign] state. —獨立句,【文】 an absolute infinitive phrase. —獨立祭, the Independence Day.

dokuro (髑髏), *n.* the cranium; the skull. —髑髏の舞, the dance of death; *danse macabre* [佛].

dokuryoku(獨力で), *ad.* single-handed; by oneself.

dokusai (獨裁), *n.* absolutism; despotism; autocracy. —獨裁的, absolute; despotic; autocratic. ¶ 獨裁君主 [主權者], an autocrat; a despot; an absolute ruler.

dokusatsu (毒殺する), *vt.* to poison; kill by poisoning.

dokusei (毒性の), *a.* poisonous; virulent.

dokusen (獨占), *n.* monopoly; exclusive possession. —獨占する, to monopolize; possess exclusively. ¶ 獨占(的)價格, monopoly price. —獨占權, monopoly; exclusive right. —獨占(的)企業, a monopolistic undertaking [enterprise].

dokusenjō(獨擅場), *n.* =***hitoributai.***

dokusha (讀者), *n.* readers.

dokushin (獨身), *n.* celibacy; bachelorhood. —獨身で暮す, to lead a bachelor's life; live singly. ¶ 獨身生活, a single life. —獨身者, (男) a single man; a bachelor; a celibate; (女) a [an old] maid; a spinster.

dokusho (讀書), *n.* reading. ☞ ***tokusho.***

dokushō (獨唱), *n.* solo.

dokushu (毒手), *n.* an evil design; a murderous [fell] hand. —毒手に倒れる, to fall under another's hand.

dokushū(獨習する), *vt.* to study by oneself; practise by oneself. 外國語を獨習する, to study a foreign language by oneself. ¶ 獨習書, a book for self-study; a self-educator.

dokusō (獨奏), *n.* 【音】 solo.

dokusō(獨創), *n.* originality. —

獨創の才に富む, to have a great talent for originality.

doku-suru (毒する), *vt.* to poison. —社會を毒する, to poison society.

dokutoku (獨得の), *a.* peculiar *to*; special · characteristic. —獨得の妙技, a great special talent [capacity].

dokutoru (ドクトル), *n.* ❶ a doctor. ❷ [俗] (名人) an adept; an old hand.

dokuyaku (毒藥), *n.* a poison. —毒藥を飲む, to take poison.

dokuzetsu (毒舌), *n.* a malicious tongue; an evil tongue. —毒舌を揮ふ, to attack with rancour.

dokyō (度胸), *n.* courage; spirit; mettle. —度胸のよい, courageous; spirited; mettlesome. —度胸を据ゑる, to summon [screw up] one's courage. —度胸を試めす, to put one's courage to the test.

dōkyo (同居する), *vi.* to lodge; live *with*; live in the same house. ¶ 同居人, an inmate; persons living in the same house.

dōkyō (道敎), *n.* Taoism.

dokyū (弩級艦), *n.* a Dreadnought; a ship of the Dreadnought class. ¶ 弩級型戰艦, a Dreadnought type battleship. —弩級前戰艦, a pre-Dreadnought battleship.

dōkyū (同級), *n.* the same grade [class; form]. ¶ 同級生, a class-fellow; a class-mate.

doma (土間), *n.* ❶ (劇場の) the pit; the parterre. ❷ 【建】 an unfloored space [part]; earthen floor.

dōmaki (胴卷), *n.* a sack-belt.

dōmei (同盟), *n.* an alliance; a league; a union. —同盟する, to ally *with*; form an alliance *with*. ¶ 日英同盟, the Anglo-Japanese Alliance. —三國同盟, the Triple Alliance. —中歐同盟軍, the Central Allied Army. —同盟國, an allied power; an ally.

dōmei-higyō (同盟罷業), *n.* Ⓢ 同盟罷工 a strike. —同盟罷業中である, to be on strike. —同盟罷業中の職工, workmen on strike. —同盟罷業を宣言する, to declare a strike. —賃銀値上げの爲め同盟罷業する, to (go on) strike for a higher pay. ¶ 同盟罷業者, a striker.

dōmei-kyūkō (同盟休校), *n.* a school strike.

dōmei-taigyō (同盟怠業), *n.* go slow; ca' canny; (誤ッて) sabotage.

dōmo (どうも), *ad.* very; quite: somehow. —どうも困ッた, I am in great straits. —どうも致方がない, There is no help for it.

dōmō (獰猛な), *a.* ferocious; fierce.

domori (吃, 吶), *n.* stutter; a stutterer (人). —吃を矯正する, to remedy stuttering.

dōmori (堂守), *n.* a shrine-keeper.

domoru (吃る), *vi.* to stutter.

dōmyaku (動脈), *n.* 【解】 an artery. ¶ 肺動脈, a pulmonary artery. —動脈血, arterial blood. —動脈硬化, arterial sclerosis. —動脈瘤, an aneurysm.

don (どん), *n.* ❶ (砲聲) boom bang (銃聲). ❷ (午砲) the noon-gun.

donabe (土鍋), *n.* an earthen pot.

donaru (呶鳴る), *vi.* to roar; shout; bawl. —呶鳴り込む, to go in, roaring with anger.

dōnarikōnari (何うなり斯うなり), *ad.* somehow; anyhow. —何うなり斯うなり口を糊す, to keep alive somehow.

donata (誰方), *pron.* who. —誰方か, some gentleman (lady); somebody.

donburi (丼), *n.* a bowl; a porringer (小丼).

donchan (どんちゃん), *ad.* very noisily; in great confusion. ¶ どんちゃん騷ぎ, a great noise; an uproar.

donchō (緞帳), *n.* a drop-curtain. ¶ 緞帳芝居, a low-class theatre.

dondo (呑吐する), *vt.* to take in and send out; take in and drop.

dondon (どんどん), *n.* (太鼓の) rub-a-dub; dub-a-dub. ——, *ad.* ❶ noisily. ❷ (どしどし) rapidly; quickly.

dōnen (同年), *n.* the same age; the same year. —彼と僕とは同年だ, He and I are of the same age.

donguri (團栗), *n.* an acorn. —團栗の背較べだ, There is nothing [little] to choose between them.

dōnika (何うにか), *ad.* somehow. ☞ *dōkakōka, nantoka.*

dōnimo (何うにも), *ad.* Ⓢ 何うにも斯うにも. in any way. —どうにも仕樣がない, There is no help for it in any way. —どうにも手の出し樣がない, I can in no way interfere.

dōnin (同人), *n.* ❶ the same [said] person. ❷ =*dōshi* (同志).

donkaku (鈍角), *n.* 【數】 an obtuse angle.

donna (何樣な), *a.* what; what kind [sort] of; what...like. —どんな譯で, why; for what reason; on what ground. —どんな人でも, any person. —どんな事があッても, at all hazards. —どんなにしてでも, by all (manner of) means. —どん

なに嬉しいだらう, How glad he must be! —どんな馬鹿でもそんなことは知ッて居る, The veriest simpleton knows that.

dono (殿), *n.* Mister (Mr. と略す); Esquire (Esq. と略す). —内田康殿, Yasushi Uchida, Esq.

dono(何の), *a.* what (不定數中); which(定數中). —どの…も, any; every. —淺草のどの邊にお住ひですか, In what part of Asakusa do you live? —どの道を行ッても上野に出る, Every road leads to Uyeno.

donokurai (何の位), *ad.* Ⓢ何れ位. ❶ (時間) how long. ❷ (距離) how far. ❸ (數量) how many; how much (量); what (同上). ❹ (程度) how; to what extent. ❺ (大・長・深・厚さ) how large (long; deep; thick). —どれ位心配したか分らない, I can't tell you how anxious I was.

donomichi (何の道), *ad.* anyhow; anyway. —どの道明日迄には歸る, Anyhow I shall be back by to-morrow. —どの道多少の紛擾は免れない, Anyway we cannot avoid some trouble.

donshoku (貪食する), *vt.* to devour; eat greedily.

donshū(呑舟の魚), *n.* ❶ (大魚) a great fish. ❷ (傑物) a great man; a notorious man. —網, 呑舟の魚を洩らす, "Laws catch flies, but let hornets go free."

donsu (緞子), *n.* damask silk.

donten (曇天), *n.* cloudiness; cloudy weather; an overcast sky.

don-to (どんと), *ad.* with a bang.

doṅyoku (貪慾), *n.* avarice; rapacity; cupidity. —貪慾な, avaricious; rapacious. ¶ 貪慾者, a cormorant; a harpy.

doṅyori (どんより), *ad.* colourlessly; dully. —どんよりした, lack-lustre (眼の); fishy (同上); dull (眼・空・光・色の).

donzei (呑噬する), *vt.* to encroach *upon*; devour; swallow up.

donzoko (極底), *n.* the very bottom. —極底の生活, bottom life. —不運の極底に, at the bottom of fortune's wheel.

dōo (堂奥), *n.* the mysteries; the esoteric principles. —堂奥を究める, to study the mysteries.

dora (銅鑼), *n.* a gong; a tom-tom.

dōraku (道樂), *n.* ❶ (好事) a hobby; a toy. ❷ (放蕩) dissipation; profligacy; debauchery. —道樂をする, to be dissipated; take to loose pleasures. ¶ 食道樂, epicurism; good living: (人) an epicure; a *gourmet* [佛]. —釣道樂, the angling hobby; an inveterate angler (人). —道樂者, a profligate; a libertine; a debauchee. —道樂息子, a prodigal [profligate] son.

dorama (演劇), *n.* a drama.

dōran (動亂), *n.* disturbance; commotion; turbulence. —歐洲の大動亂, the great European war.

dore(どれ), *int.* come; well. —どれ一服しよう, Well, let's have a whiff.

dore (何れ, 孰れ), *pron.* ❶ (孰が) which? ❷ (何れか) any; some one. —どれでも, whichever; whichsoever; any. —どれも, any; every; all.

dorei(奴隸), *n.* a slave; a bondman. —流行の奴隸, the slaves of fashion. ¶ 奴隸賣買, slave-trade; slave traffic.

dorekisei (土瀝靑), *n.* asphalt.

dōri (道理), *n.* reason (條理); right; justice. —道理に適ふ, to be reasonable; accord with reason. —道理に適ッた, reasonable; rational. —…も道理だ, it is no wonder; no wonder (that). —道理で來なかッた, No wonder he did not come. —無理が通れば道理が引ッ込む, "Where might is master, justice is servant."

doro (泥), *n.* mud; mire; slush. —泥だらけの, muddy; covered with mud; miry. —親の顏に泥を塗る, to bring disgrace upon one's father. ¶ 泥靴, muddy boots.

dōro (道路), *n.* a road; a highway; a street. —道路を塞ぐ(開く; 通る), to obstruct (open; pass) a road. ¶ 道路妨害, the obstruction of a public highway. —道路工夫, a roadman. —道路修繕, road repairs. —道路掃除人, a scavenger; a street-orderly; a street-sweeper.

dorobō (泥棒), *n.* ❶ a robber; a thief (特に竊盜); a burglar (夜中家宅侵入盜賊). ❷ robbery; theft; burglary. —泥棒する, to thieve; steal; rob (a person) of (a thing). —泥棒に這入る, to break into a house. —泥棒をつかまへて繩を綯ふ, to shut the stable-door after the steed is stolen.

dorodoro(どろどろ), *n.* (粘體) sloppiness; sludge. —どろどろの, sloppy; sludgy; thick.

dorogame (泥龜), *n.* the terrapin; the snapping-turtle.

doromamire (泥塗れの), *a.* miry; muddy. —泥塗れになッて, covered with mud.

doromizu (泥水), *n.* muddy water.

doron(どろん), *n.* disappearance;

elopement (駈落). —どろんを極める, to disappear; abscond; elope; make oneself scarce.

doroppu (ドロップ), *n.* ❶ (菓子) drops. ❷=*rakudai* (落第). ❸【野球】drop. —チョコレート(製)ドロップ, chocolate drops.

dorosarai (浚泥機), *n.* a mud-drag; a dredger.

doroyoke (泥除), *n.* a mud-guard; a splash-board.

doru (弗), *n.* a dollar. ¶ 弗箱, ① a strong-box. ② (弗旦) a patron; a protector. —弗相場, exchange rate of a dollar.

dōrui (同類), *n.* ❶ (同種類) the same class [order; kind]. ❷ (共謀者) a confederate; an accomplice; a partner. ❸ (黨人) a partisan. ¶ 同類意識, consciousness of kind. —同類項,【數】a similar term; like terms.

doryō (度量), *n.* ❶ capacity (for tolerance). ❷ (寛容) generosity; liberality; broad-mindedness. —度量ある, broad-minded; generous; liberal. —度量なき, narrow-minded; ungenerous.

dōryō (同僚), *n.* a colleague; an associate.

doryōkō (度量衡), *n.* weights and measures.

doryoku (努力), *n.* (utmost) effort; exertion; strain. ——**suru,** *v.* to exert oneself to the utmost; do one's best [utmost]; make utmost efforts. —出來る限り努力する, to strain every nerve.

dōryoku (動力), *n.* 【機】motive power; motor power. —動力を變更する, to change the motive power. ¶ 動力計, a dynamometer.

dōsa (礬沙水), *n.* a glaze (of alum and glue). —礬沙水を引く, [*vt.*] to glaze.

dōsa (動作), *n.* ❶ action; movement. ❷ (擧止) behaviour; deportment; demeanour.

dosakusa (どさくさ), *n.* bustle; confusion; tumult. —どさくさ紛れに附け込む, to take advantage of the bustle.

dōsan (動產), *n.* ❶ (獨法系) movable property [thing]; movables. ❷ (英法系) personal estate [property]; personal effects; chattels. ¶ 動產稅, a movable property tax.

dōsatsu (洞察), *n.* discernment; penetration; insight. —洞察する, to discern; penetrate *into*; see *into*; have an insight *into*.

dōse (どうせ), *ad.* anyway; anyhow.

dosei (土星), *n.* Saturn.

dosei (土製の), *a.* earthen.

dōsei (同性の), *a.* ❶ congenial; cognate. ❷ homosexual. —同性の愛, homosexual love.

dōsei (同姓), *n.* the same surname. ¶ 同姓同名, the same family and personal name. —同姓者, a namesake; a person of the same name.

dōsei (同棲する), *vi.* to cohabit; live together.

dōsei (動靜), *n.* ❶ motion and rest; movements. ❷ (狀態) state; condition; situation. —政界の動靜, the condition of the political world. —敵の動靜を監視する, to watch the movements of enemy troops.

dōseki (同席する), *vi.* to sit together.

dōsen (同船する), *vi.* to board [be in] the same ship; be a fellow passenger *with*. ¶ 同船者, ① a shipmate; a fellow sailor. ② a fellow passenger.

dōsha (同車する), *vi.* to ride together; take [be in] the same car.

doshaburi (土砂降), *n.* a heavy [pouring] rain; a downpour. —どしゃ降りに降る, to pour down; rain in torrents; rain cats and dogs.

dōshi (同士), *n.* —すいた同士, lovers. —同士討を始める, to begin fighting with (those of) their own side. —兩人は敵同士だ, The two are enemies.

dōshi (同志), *n.* ❶ the same mind [opinion]. ❷ (同志者) a person of the same mind [opinion]. —同志の, of the same mind; like-minded. —同志を糾合する, to call together persons of the same mind.

dōshi (導師), *n.* an officiating priest.

dōshi (動詞), *n.* 【文】the verb. ¶ 規則(不規則)動詞, a regular (an irregular) verb. —他(自)動詞, a transitive (an intransitive) verb. —動詞狀名詞, a verbal (noun); the gerund.

-dōshi (通し), all through; throughout; all the time. —步き(泣き; 立ち)通しである, to walk (cry; stand) all the time. —夜通し働く, to work all night.

doshidoshi (どしどし), *ad.* ❶ (續々迅速に) in rapid succession; rapidly. ❷ (絕え間なく) unceasingly; constantly.

doshin (どしんと), *ad.* heavily; with a thud [bump].

dōshin (道心), *n.* ❶ (道義心) moral spirit. ❷【佛】(菩提心) religious spirit. ❸ (僧) a priest.

dōshińen (同心圓), *n.* a concentric circle.

dōshita (どうした), what. —してそれがどうした, And what o that?

dōshite (どうして), *ad.* ❶ (如何

にして) how; in what manner. ❷ (何故に) why; how is [comes] it that.... ❸ (反對に) on the contrary. —どうしてそれどころか, No, far from it. —どうしてでも; どうしても, in any case; by any means; at any rate. (どうしても思ひ出せない, I cannot for the life of me recall it.)

doshitsu (土質), *n.* the nature and condition of the soil; the soil. —土質に適せぬ, not to agree with [suit] the soil.

dōshitsu (同質), *n.* the same nature [quality]; homogeneity; homogeneousness; cognateness.

dōshitsu (同室), *n.* the same room [chamber]. —同室する, to live in the same room *with*; chum *with*; share a room *with*. ¶ 同室者, a chum; a chamber-fellow.

dōsho (同處), *n.* the same place the above-mentioned place. —同處同番地何某, So and So, of the same street and number.

doshoku (怒色), *n.* an angry face [look]; anger.

dōshoku (銅色), *n.* copper colour. ¶ 銅色人種, the copper-coloured race.

dōshu (同種の), *a.* similar; of the same kind.

dōshuku (同宿する), *vi.* to live in the same hotel *with*; lodge in the same house *with*. ¶ 同宿人, the household (家中全部); the inmates of the same hotel [lodging-house]; a fellow-lodger.

dōshumi (同趣味), *n.* the same taste; the same interest.

dōshūmi (同臭味), *n.* the same party; the same set [clique; clan].

dosō (土葬), *n.* inhumation; interment. —土葬する, to inter; bury in the ground.

dōsō (同窓-生), *n.* a fellow-student; a school-fellow; an alumnus [*pl.* alumni]. ¶ 同窓會, a gathering of alumni; a meeting of old boys.

dosoku (土足), *n.* (泥足) muddy feet; dirty feet. —土足の儘(履物の儘), without taking off one's foot-gear; with foot-gear on. —土足にかける, to tread under foot.

dossari (どッさり), *n.* plenty; lots; heaps; power.

dosshiri (どッしりした), *a.* massive; substantial; weighty. —どッしりした人物, a dignified character. —どッしりした柱, a massive pillar.

dosu- (どす), *pref.* dark. —どす黒い, dusky; dark.

dosū (度數), *n.* the number of times. ¶ 度數料金, message rate. —度數制度, the time-charge system. —通話度數計(電話), a service-register.

do-suru (度する), *vt.* to save; redeem from sin. —度し難い, beyond redemption; past reclaim; past praying for.

dōsuru (如何する), *vi.* ❶ what to do. ❷ how to do. —どうする積りか, What do you mean to do? —どうすればよからう, What had I better do? —君が居ないとどうする事も出來ない, We can do nothing without you.

dotabata (どたばた), *ad.* noisily.

dōtai (同體), *n.* the same body. —同體に落つ, to have a dog-fall.

dōtai (動態), *n.* movement. —人口の動態統計, statistics of movements of the population.

dōtai (動體), *n.* a moving body; a body in motion.

dōtai (導體), *n.* 【理】 a conductor.

dotchi (何方), *pron.* ❶ (選擇) either (二者其の一); neither (二者打消); which (どれ). ❷ (方角) where; in which direction; which way [road]. —どッち道, anyway. —どッちでもよい, Either will do. —どッちも欲しくない, I want neither. —どッちもどッちである (相伯仲する), There is little to choose between them.

dote (土手), *n.* (堤) a bank; a dyke; an embankment. —土手を繞らす(築く), to surround with (construct) a bank. —土手に登るべからず, Keep off the bank. ¶ 土手道, a bank path.

dōtei (童貞), *n.* chastity (男女の); virginity (女の). —童貞を破る, to lose one's chastity.

dōtei (道程), *n.* ❶ (距離) the distance; the length (of a road). ❷ (旅程) the distance of a journey. ❸ (旅途) course; route; itinerary.

dōteki (動的), *a.* dynamic; kinetic.

dotera (褞袍), *n.* a dressing-gown.

dotō (怒濤), *n.* raging billows; angry waves; high seas.

dōto (道途), *n.* ❶ the road; the street ❷ (進程) the tenor; the course. —己の生活の道途, the tenor of one's life.

dōtō (同等), *n.* equality; par. —同等の權利, equal rights. —と同等である, to be on a par *with*; be on a level *with*. ¶ 同等者, an equal.

dōtoku (道徳), *n.* morality. —道徳的觀念, moral sense. —道徳的制裁, moral sanction. —道徳上の罪人, a moral offender. ¶ 道徳家, a moralist (宗教家の對); a virtuous person (有徳の人).

dotto (どッと), *ad.* ❶ (哄然) all together. ❷ (どすんと) plump; flop. ❸ (遽に) suddenly; all of a sudden; all at once. —どッと吹き出す, to burst out laughing.

dōwa (道話), *n.* a moral discourse.

dōwa(童話), *n.* a story for children; a fairy tale.

dōwasure (胴忘れする), *v.* to forget for the moment; let slip from one's memory.

doyadoya (どやどや), *ad.* in confusion; in crowds.

doyaki (土燒), *n.* earthen ware.

dōyara (どうやら), *ad.* likely. —どうやら天氣になりさうだ, The weather promises [is likely; bids fair] to be fine.

doyō (土用), *n.* dog-days. ¶ 土用干, summer airing. —土用太(二; 三)郎, the first (second; third) day of *doyō*.

dōyō (同樣), *n.* similarity; sameness; parity. —同樣の, similar (to); same. —同樣に, similarly; in a similar way; in the same manner [way] *as*; uniformly. —死んだと同樣, as good as dead. —兄弟同樣にする, to treat like a brother.

dōyō (動搖), *n.* shock; disquiet; unrest; agitation. —動搖する, to shake; sway; swing; be agitated. —民心の動搖, shock of the national thought. —浪に動搖せる船, a ship rocked by the waves.

dōyō (童謠), *n.* a children's song.

doyōbi (土曜日), *n.* Saturday.

dōyoku (胴慾な), *a.* ❶ avaricious; greedy. ❷ selfish.

doyomeku (どよめく), *vi.* to rumble; reverberate.

dōyōshō(桐葉章), *n.* a decoration of the Paulownia Leaf. ¶ 靑色(白色)桐葉章, a decoration of the Blue (White) Paulownia Leaf.

dōza (同座する), *v.* =*dōseki.*

dozaemon (土左衛門), *n.* a drowned person [body].

dōzai (同罪), *n.* the same offence [crime]. —雙方とも同罪だ, Both are equally to blame.

dōzan (銅山), *n.* a copper mine.

dōzei (同勢), *n.* a party; followers; companions.

dōzen (同然), *n.* being the same. —新しいも同然である, to be as good as new. —乞食も同然である, to be no better than a beggar.

dozō (土藏), *n.* a godown; a storehouse.

dōzo (何卒), pray; please; if you please. —どうぞお食(あが)り下さい, Please take it. —どうぞ戶をしめて下さい, Oblige me by shutting the door.

dōzō (銅像), *n.* a bronze statue; a copper image. —銅像を建てる, to set up [erect] a bronze statue.

dōzoku (同族), *n.* ❶ the same family. ❷ (同族籍) the same class [caste].

dō-zuru (動ずる), *v.* =*dō-jiru.*

E

e (え), **ē** (えー), *int.* ❶ well. ❷ (疑問) eh; what. —どうでせうか, えー, What do you think, eh? —えー, 一番やり直せ, Well, do it over again.

e (へ), *prep.* ❶ for; to; towards. ❷ in; into; on. ☞ *ni* (に). —東方へ進み行く, to make for the east.

e (柄), *n.* a handle; a haft. —柄をすげる, ① to mend a handle. ②(ない事をある樣に云ふ) to tell specious untruths; exaggerate.

e, eba, esa, (餌), *n.* ❶ (餌食) bait (釣魚の); food (飼餌). ❷(餌誘) a decoy; a decoy-bird (囮); an allurement. ☞ *ejiki* (餌食). —鳥の餌, food for a bird. —人を瞞す餌にする, to use it to decoy people. —鷄に餌を遣る, to feed the fowl. —釣針に餌を附ける, to bait an angling-hook.

e(繪), *n.* a painting(彩色あるもの); a picture (繪畫); a drawing (圖畫). —繪の樣な景色, a picturesque view. —繪を畫く, to draw; paint. —...の繪を畫く; を繪に畫く, to paint; draw; make a picture *of*.

eba (餌), *n.* a bait. ☞ *e* (餌).

ebi (蝦,海老), *n.* the lobster. —蝦で鯛を釣る, to throw a sprat to catch a whale.

ebicha (海老茶), *n.* maroon.

ebira (箙), *n.* a quiver.

ēbīshi (エービーシー), *n.* ABC; alphabet. —エービーシー順に配列する, to alphabetize; arrange alphabetically.

Ebisu (惠比須), *n.* a god of wealth. ¶ 惠比須紙, a loose leaf (in a book); a dog's-eared leaf. —惠比須顏, a smiling face. (借りる時の惠比須顏返す時の閻魔顏, "In borrowing an angel, in repaying a devil.")

ebonaito(硬化護謨), *n.* ebonite; vulcanite.

eboshigai (烏帽子貝), *n.* 【貝】 the ship-barnacle.

ebukuro (餌袋), *n.* a crop; a craw.

eda (枝), *n.* ❶ (樹枝) a branch; a bough (大枝). ❷ (支派) a branch; an offshoot. —枝を出す, to shoot out branches. —枝を下ろす[切る], to lop off [away] branches. ¶ 枝振り, the shape of a branch.

edaha (枝葉), *n.* ❶ branches and leaves. ❷ (支派) ramifications. —枝葉に入る, [*vi.*] to diverge; branch off. —枝葉に渉る, to run into ramifications; digress.

edatsugi (枝接), *n.* grafting; cleft-grafting.

efuda (繪札), *n.* a court-card.

efude (繪筆), *n.* a paint-brush.

egakidasu (描出す), *vt.* to delineate; represent. —當時を腦裏に描き出す, to call that time to mind; picture the scene of the time to oneself.

egaku (畫·描く), *v.* ❶ (繪畫を) to draw; paint (著色して); portray. ❷ (寫述) to depict; delineate; describe. —花鳥を描く, to paint birds and flowers. —大圏を畫く, to describe great circles.

egami (繪紙), *n.* a print; a picture-sheet.

egao (笑顏), *n.* a smiling [beaming] face. —笑顏で人を迎へる, to greet a person with a smile. —笑顏が急に脹れる, to laugh on the wrong side of the mouth.

egao (得顏に), *ad.* with elated looks.

eginu (繪絹), *n.* silk-canvas.

egoi (蘞い), *a.* acrid.

egokoro (繪心), *n.* an artistic taste; a taste for pictures.

eguru (抉·刳る), *vt.* to gouge (特に眼を); scoop out; scrape out. —木を刳る, to scoop a piece of wood. —壁を刳り拔く, to scrape a hole through a wall. —人の腸を刳る, to cut to the heart.

ehagaki (繪葉書), *n.* a picture postcard; a pictorial postcard.

ehen (えへん), *int.* ahem; hem. —エヘンと咳拂ひする, to clear one's throat (with a hem).

ehō (惠方), *n.* the lucky direction (for the year). ¶ 惠方詣, visiting a shrine or temple in the lucky direction.

Ehoba (耶和華), *n.* Jah; Jehovah.

ehon (繪本), *n.* a picture-book; an illustrated book (繪入本). ¶ 繪本三國志, the Illustrated *Sangokushi*.

ei (鱝魚), *n.* 【魚】 the ray.

ei (榮), *n.* ❶ (榮譽) honour. ❷ (盛榮) splendour. —晩餐に御臨席の榮を得度候, I beg to be honoured with your company at dinner.

ei (裔), *n.* a descendant; the seed.

ei (嬰), *n.* 【音】 a sharp (樂鍵の). —嬰ろ調, B sharp.

Eibei (英米), *n.* England and America. —英米の, Anglo-American.

eibin (穎敏), *n.* sagacity; discernment; penetration. **—— -na,** *a.* sagacious; discerning; penetrating. —穎敏な頭腦, a clear brain.

eibin (銳敏), *n.* smartness; keenness; acuteness. —銳敏に感じる, to feel keenly. **—— -na,** *a.* keen; sharp; acute. —銳敏な耳, a sharp [quick] ear.

eibun (英文), *n.* an English sentence (writing; composition); English. —英文で書く, to write in English. —英文を上手に書く, to write English well; be a good writer of English. ¶ 英文和譯, translation from English into Japanese.

eibun (叡聞), *n.* the hearing of His Majesty. —叡聞に達する, to reach His Majesty's ears; be reported to His Majesty.

eibungaku (英文學), *n.* English literature.

eichi (叡智), *n.* intelligence; wisdom.

eidan (英斷), *n.* decisive judgment; wise decision. —英斷する, to give a decisive judgment; decide wisely.

eiei (營營), *ad.* strenuously; earnestly. ☞ ***akuseku.***

eien (永遠), *n.* eternity; perpetuity; permanence. —永遠に, eternally; permanently; for ever. **—— -no,** *a.* perpetual; eternal; permanent. —永遠の計を定める, to make permanent plans.

eiga (映畫), *n.* ❶ a picture thrown upon the screen; a reflection. ❷ a film. ¶ 映畫劇, a film-drama.

eiga (榮華), *n.* prosperity; glory; splendour. —榮華に誇る, to be proud of one's prosperity. —浮世の榮華の果敢なさよ!, How transient are the glories of this world!

eigaku (英學), *n.* the study of English. ¶ 英學生, an English student. —英學者, an English scholar.

eigo (英語), *n.* English; the English language. —現代式の英語, current English. —英語で話す(書く), to speak (write) in English. —英語を話す, to speak English. ¶ 純正英語, the King's [Queen's] English.

eigō (永劫), *n.* perpetuity; eternity. ☞ ***eikyū*** (永久).

eigyō (營業), *n.* (regular) business; trade; occupation. ¶ 營業案內, a business-guide; a catalogue. —營業妨害, obstruction of business. —營業部, business department. —營業費, working [trade; business] expenses. —營業報告, a business report. —營業時間, business [office] hours. —營業所, an office; the place [seat] of business. —營業稅, business tax.

eihei (衛兵), *n.* a guard; a post. —衛兵を置く, to post a guard. —衛兵勤務番になる(上番), to mount [go on] guard. —衛兵勤務に交代する, to relieve guard.

eihō(銳鋒), *n.* a sharp point; the brunt. —銳鋒を挫く, to blunt the edge *of*.

eii (銳意), *ad.* zealously; eagerly; diligently. —銳意其事に從ふ, to apply oneself with zeal to it.

Eiin (英印の), *a.* Anglo-Indian.

eiji (英字), *n.* an English letter; English.

eiji(嬰兒), *n.* a nursling; a baby; an infant.

eijin (英人), *n.* an Englishman; a Britisher; the English (英國民); the British (同上).

eijoku (榮辱), *n.* honour and disgrace; dignity; reputation.

eiju (衛戍), *n.* a garrison. ¶ 衛戍病院 (監獄), a garrison hospital (prison). —東京衛戍總督, the commander of the Tōkyō garrison.

eijū (永住する), *vi.* to reside [live] permanently.

eika (英貨), *n.* English currency. ¶ 英貨公債, a sterling loan

eikaku (銳角), *n.* an acute angle.

eikan (榮冠), *n.* the crown; laurels. —勝利の榮冠を戴く, to be crowned with victory.

eiketsu (英傑), *n.* a great man; a hero; a master mind.

eiki (銳氣), *n.* an animated spirit; high spirits; energy. —銳氣を養ふ, to foster a high spirit.

eikin (英斤), *n.* a pound.

eiko (榮枯), *n.* vicissitudes; ups and downs; the rise and fall. ¶ 榮枯盛衰, the ups and downs [vicissitudes] of life.

eikō (榮光), *n.* ❶ sun-glow; corona. ❷(光背) a glory; a halo; an aureole, aureola.

Eikoku (英國), *n.* England; Great Britain (英·威及び蘇); the United Kingdom (英本國). ¶ 英國軍艦, a British warship; H. M.'s ship. —英國人, =*eijin* (英人). 英國國旗, the British flag; the Union Jack. —英國國教, the (Established) Church of England. —英國宮廷, the Court of St. James's. —英國政府, the British Government; H. (B.) M.'s Government.

eikyo (盈虛する), *vi.* to wax and wane.

eikyō (影響), *n.* influence; effect; consequence. —影響する, to influence; affect; have an effect *upon*.

eikyū (永久), *n.* permanence; eternity; perpetuity. —永久の, permanent; perpetual; eternal. —永久に, perpetually; permanently; for ever. —永久不變に存する, to remain unchanged for ever. ¶ 永久齒, a permanent [second] tooth.

eimai (英邁な), *a.* wise; sagacious.

eimin (永眠する), *vi.* to pass away; take one's last sleep.

einai (營內), *ad.* within barracks. ¶ 營內生活, a barrack life.

eiran (叡覽), *n.* the Emperor's personal inspection. —叡覽を賜はる, to be honoured with His Majesty's inspection.

eiri(營利), *n.* money-making. —營利に汲々たり, to be engrossed in money-making. ¶ 營利會社, a company established for profit.

eiri (銳利な), *a.* sharp; keen; acute. —銳利な刃物, a sharp edge-tool.

eiri (繪入の), *a.* illustrated; pictorial. ¶ 繪入日刊新聞, an illustrated daily (paper).

eiryo (叡慮), *n.* the Emperor's mind (pleasure; anxiety). —叡慮を安んじ奉る, to set His Majesty's mind at ease.

eiryō(英領), *n.* a British dominion. ¶ 英領印度, British India.

eisai (英才, 穎才), *n.* ❶(才) high intelligence; great ability; talent. ❷ a talented man; a man of high intelligence.

eisei (衛星), *n.* a satellite; a secondary planet.

eisei(衛生), *n.* sanitation; hygiene; health. —衛生的, hygienic; sanitary; wholesome. —衛生に注意する, to attend to sanitation. ¶ 公共衛生, public health. —衛生係, a health-board: a health-officer. —衛生學, hygienics; sanitary science. —衛生家, a sanitarist. —衛生組合, a sanitary association. —衛生局, the Sanitary Bureau; the Board of Health. —衛生試驗所, a hygienic laboratory. —衛生材料, medical stores.

eisha (映射する), *vt.* to reflect.

eisha (映寫する), *vt.* to project [throw] on a screen. ¶ 映寫機, a kinematograph. —映寫幕, a screen.

Eishi (英支の), *a.* Anglo-Chinese. ¶ 英支關係, Anglo-Chinese relations.

eishi (英姿), *n.* a gallant form.

eisho (英書), *n.* an English book.
eisho (營所), *n.* barracks; a station; an encampment.
eisō (營倉), *n.* ❶ a guard-house; a guard-room. ❷ detention. —營倉に入れられる, to be confined in the guard-room. ¶ 輕(重)營倉, light (heavy) imprisonment.
eison (永存する), *vi.* to last; remain perpetually.
eitai (永代), *n.* perpetuity. ¶ 永代借地權, a perpetual lease; a lease in perpetuity.
eitatsu (榮達), *n.* promotion; rise. —榮達する, to be promoted to a high post; rise in the world.
eiten (榮典), *n.* distinction; honours; a mark of distinction.
eiten (榮轉), *n.* promotion. —榮轉する, to be promoted (*to*).
Eiwa (英和), *a.* English-Japanese; Anglo-Japanese.
eiyaku (英譯), *n.* an English translation [version]; translation into English. —英譯する, to translate [render; turn] into English.
eiyo (榮譽), *n.* honour; distinction; glory. —榮譽とする, to take [consider] it as an honour *to*; feel honoured.
eiyō (榮耀-榮華), *n.* luxury. ☞ *eiga* (榮華). —榮耀榮華に暮す, to live in great luxury.
eiyō (榮養), *n.* nutrition; nourishment; aliment. —榮養に富む, to be very nutritive. —榮養物を攝取する, to take nutritious food in moderation. ¶ 榮養不良, innutrition; malnutrition. —榮養價値, nutritive value; food value. —榮養管, the alimentary canal. —榮養研究所, an institute for the study of alimentation.
eiyū (英雄), *n.* a hero; a great man. ¶ 英雄崇拜, hero-worship.
eizen (營繕する), *vt.* to build and repair. ¶ 營繕係, an official builder.
eizō (映像), *n.* a reflection; a reflex.
eizō (影像), *n.* ❶ a shadow; a phantom. ❷ (形像) an image.
eizōbutsu (營造物), *n.* a structure; public works. —市の營造物, municipal works. —營造物破壞を行ふ, to carry out sabotage.
eizoku (永續する), *vi.* to continue; last long; remain permanently.
ei-zuru (咏·詠ずる), *vt.* (作歌) to compose; (朗詠) sing; chant.
ei-zuru (映ずる), *vi.* to be reflected *in*; mirrored *in*; strike [shine] *upon*. ——, *a.* reflective. —外人の眼に映じた日本, Japan as she appears to foreign eyes.
ejiki (餌食), *n.* ❶ bait (魚の); food (鳥などの); prey (肉食動物の). ❷ (犧牲) a victim. ☞ *e* (餌). —魚の餌食となる, to become food for fishes.
Ejiputo (埃及), *n.* Egypt. ¶ 埃及人, an Egyptian.
ēkā (エーカー), *n.* an acre.
ekaki (畫工), *n.* an artist; a painter.
eki (役), *n.* ❶ (戰役) a war; a battle (war 中の); a campaign. ❷ (勞役) labour; service.
eki (易), *n.* ❶ (易經) Yi-King; the Book of Changes. ❷ (易占) divination. —易を立てる, to divine; augur.
eki (益), *n.* ❶ (便益) advantage; use. ❷ (ため) benefit; good. ❸ (收益) profit; gain. —益ある, advantageous; beneficial; profitable. —學生に益を與へる, to benefit students.
eki (液), *n.* ❶ (液體) liquid. ❷ (液汁) juice; sap; liquor (化學作用から得た).
eki (驛), *n.* ❶ (宿驛) a post-town; a stage. ❷ (停車場) a station; a depot [米].
ekibyō (疫病), *n.* an infectious disease; an epidemic; a plague.
ekichō (益鳥), *n.* a useful [beneficial] bird.
ekichō (驛長), *n.* a station-master.
ekiden (驛傳), *n.* ❶ (宿次) a post-town; a post-station. ❷ (驛馬) a post-horse. ¶ 驛傳競走, a relay race.
ekifu (驛夫), *n.* a porter; a rail-way-porter.
ekijū (液汁), *n.* sap (植物の); juice (動·植·果實などの).
ekika (液化する), *v.* to liquefy.
ekika (液果), *n.* a berry.
ekika (腋下, 腋窩), *n.* 【醫】 the axilla; the armpit.
ekikin (益金), *n.* profit; gains.
ekirei (驛鈴), *n.* ❶ (驛路の鈴) a bell given by the Court for use in official errands. ❷ (發車のベル) the starting bell.
ekiri (疫痢), *n.* 【醫】 cholera infantum; summer diarrhœa (of children).
ekiro (驛路), *n.* ❶ a journey. ❷ a postal road.
ekiryō (液量), *n.* a liquid measure. ¶ 液量オンス, a fluid ounce (我が一勺五七五に當る).
ekisha (易者), *n.* a diviner; an augur; a fortune-teller.
ekisu (越幾斯), *n.* an extract. ¶ 牛肉エキス, extract of beef.
eki-suru (益する), *vt.* to profit; benefit. ——, *vi.* to profit [benefit] *by*. —何の益する所があるか, What good will it do?
ekitai (液體), *n.* 【理】 liquid. ¶ 液體空氣 (燃料), liquid air (fuel).

ekken (越權), *n.* going beyond [exceeding] one's powers. —越權の處置をする, to act [take steps] *ultra vires*; override one's commission.

ekken (謁見), *n.* an Imperial audience. —謁見の榮を得る, to be honoured with an audience by His Majesty.

ekkisu (エッキス), *n.* X; x; an unknown quantity. ¶ エッキス光線, X-rays; Röntgen rays.

eko (依估-贔屓), *n.* partiality; favouritism; one-sidedness. —依估贔屓する, to show partiality *to*; be one-sided.

ekō (回向する), *v.* to say mass for the dead; have mass said *for*.

ekoji (依估地な), *a.* obstinate; stubborn; refractory.

ekubo (靨), *n.* a dimple.

ema (繪馬), *n.* a votive picture [tablet] (of a horse); an *ex-voto* [羅].

emakimono (繪卷物), *n.* a picture-scroll.

emi (笑), *n.* a smile. —口許に笑を浮べて, with a smile about the mouth.

emiwareru (笑割れる), *vi.* to burst open (栗等が); split open.

emo-iwarenu (得も云はれぬ), *a.* indescribable; unspeakable. —得も云はれぬ景色, a view beautiful beyond description.

emoji (畫文字), *n.* a pictograph; a picture-word.

emon (衣紋), *n.* clothes; a dress. —衣紋を繕ふ, to adjust one's dress; sleek up. ¶ 衣紋留, a brooch; a hook and eye. —衣紋掛, a clothes-horse; a clothes-rack.

emono (得物), *n.* a (suitable) weapon.

emono (獲物), *n.* a prize (戰の); game (獸獵の); a catch (漁獵の); booty. —獲物を追ふ, to follow [pursue] game.

emu (笑む), *vi.* ❶ (笑顏になる) to smile. ❷ (花咲く) to open; bloom. ❸ (果實が) to split; burst open.

en (宴), *n.* a feast; a banquet; a dinner. —…君の爲に送別の宴を張る, to give a farewell dinner in honour *of* Mr….

en (冤), *n.* a false charge [accusation]. —冤を雪ぐ, to clear oneself of a false charge.

en (圓), *n.* ❶ (貨幣單位) *yen.* ❷ (圓形) a circle. —圓を描く, to draw a circle. ¶ 武藏一圓, the whole of Musashi.

en (緣), *n.* ❶【建】a verandah; a portico. ❷ (端) a margin; a border; an edge.

en (緣), *n.* ❶ (關係) blood-relationship (血族の); conjugal relations (夫婦の); ties (親子・夫婦の); affinity. ❷ (宿緣) fate; karma-relations. —緣が遠い, to have little prospects of marriage. —緣もゆかりもない奴, a fellow in no way related. —緣にひかれる, to be drawn together by affinity. —夫婦の緣を切る, to divorce; sever conjugal ties. —緣は異なもの, "Marriages are written in heaven."

ena (胞衣), *n.*【解】the placenta.

enameru (エナメル), *n.* enamel.

enazo (繪謎), *n.* a rebus; a picture puzzle.

enbaku (燕麥), *n.* oats.

enban (鉛版), *n.* a stereotype.

enban (圓盤), *n.* a disk, disc; a discus. ¶ 圓盤投げ, throwing the discus.

enbi (艶美な), *a.* beautiful; charming.

enbifuku (燕尾服), *n.* a swallow-tail; a swallow-tailed coat; an evening dress.

enbō (遠望), *n.* a distant view [prospect].

enbō (遠謀), *n.* a long-sighted [far-seeing] plan.

enbun (艶聞), *n.* a love affair.

enbun (鹽分), *n.* salinity. —鹽分ある(水・泉等の), saline; saltish.

enchaku (延著), *n.* arrival (delivery) after delay; delayed arrival (delivery). —延著する, to arrive late; be delayed in delivery.

enchō (延長), *n.* protraction (時間); extension (鐵道・時間等); prolongation (物・事・時等); length (長さ). **—— -suru**, *vt.* to prolong; extend. —會期を延長する, to prolong the session.

enchoku (鉛直の), *a.* perpendicular; vertical.

enchū (圓柱), *n.* a column.

endai (遠大な), *a.* far-reaching; grand. —遠大の計を立てる, to make a far-reaching plan.

endai (緣臺), *n.* a bench.

endai (演題), *n.* a subject; the subject [title] of an address.

endan (演壇), *n.* a platform; a pulpit; a rostrum. —演壇に立つ, to stand on the platform.

endan (緣談), *n.* a proposal of marriage. 緣談を申込む, to make a proposal of marriage.

enden (鹽田), *n.* a salt-pond; a salt-field; a saltern.

endō (豌豆), *n.*【植】the (common) garden pea.

endō (沿道), *n.* the route; the road.

endoku (鉛毒), *n.* lead-poisoning; 【醫】plumbism; saturnism.

eṅeki (演繹的), *a.* deductive; *a-priori* [羅]. —演繹する, to deduce. ¶ 演繹法, deduction.

eṅen (蜿蜒), *n.* winding; meander; sinuosity. **——,** *ad.* sinuously; windingly. —蜿蜒として平野を流る, to wind [meander] through the plains.

eṅen (燄燄・炎炎たる), *a.* flaming; blazing. —燄々として, in flames; in a blaze.

enerugī (エネルギー), *n.* energy.

engan (沿岸), *n.* the coast. ¶ 沿岸貿易, coasting-trade. —沿岸防禦, coast defence. —沿岸航海船, a coaster; a coasting-vessel.

engawa (緣側), *n.* a verandah.

engei (園藝), *n.* gardening. ¶ 園藝術, horticulture. —園藝家, a horticulturist.

engei (演藝), *n.* performance; entertainment. ¶演藝場, an entertainment hall; a variety hall. —演藝者, an artiste; a performer.

engeki (演劇), *n.* a play; a drama; a theatrical performance.

engen (淵源), *n.* a source; a fountain. —法律の淵源, the source of law.

engi (演技), *n.* performance; representation.

engi (緣起), *n.* ❶ (由來) history; origin. ❷ (前表) luck; omen. ❸ (吉兆) a good omen; a lucky sign. —緣起よき, lucky; auspicious; of good omen. —緣起直しに, in order to change the luck. —緣起を祝ふ, to celebrate a lucky event.

engo (掩護), *n.* cover; covering; protection. —掩護する, to cover; protect. —砲兵の掩護の下に, under the cover of the artillery. ¶ 掩護砲火, covering fire. —掩護隊, a covering party [force].

engoku (遠國), *n.* a far [distant] country; a far-off land.

engumi (緣組) *n.* ❶【法】(養子緣組) adoption (of a son). ❷ (婚姻) marriage; match; union. —緣組する, ① to adopt; be adopted. ② to marry.

engun (援軍), *n.* reinforcements.

eṅin (延引), *n.* ❶ (延期) postponement; prolongation. ❷ (遲滯) delay. —延引する, ① [*vt.*] to postpone; put off; retard; delay. ② [*vi.*] to delay *in*; be behind time *with*; procrastinate.

eṅin (遠因), *n.* a remote cause.

enishida (金雀枝), *n.* 【植】 the common broom.

enja (緣者), *n.* a relative; a relation; a connection.

enjaku (燕雀), *n.* small birds; the humble. —燕雀安ぞ鴻鵠の志を知らんや, How can the humble know the ambitions of the great?

enji (臙脂), *n.* cochineal.

enjin (エンヂン), *n.* ❶ an engine. ❷ (齒科用) a dental engine.

enjitsuten (遠日點), *n.* 【天】 aphelion; apsis.

enjo (援助), *n.* assistance; aid; support. —援助する, to assist; support; aid.

enju (槐), *n.* 【植】 the Japanese [Chinese] pagoda-tree.

enjuku (圓熟する), *vi.* to mellow, mature; ripen. —圓熟せる, mature; mellow (性質); ripe; perfect.

enka (煙火), *n.* ❶ kitchen fire. ❷ (花火) fireworks.

enka (嚥下), *n.* deglutition. —嚥下する, to ingest (食物を); swallow.

enka (鹽化の), *a.* muriatic (現今は商業用のみ). ¶ 鹽化物, a chloride. —鹽化加里, potassium chloride. —鹽化水素, hydrogen chloride

enkai (沿海), *n.* the inshore. ¶ 沿海漁業, inshore fishery; longshore fishing. —沿海州, Primorskaya; the Maritime Province.

enkai (宴會), *n.* a dinner-party (晩餐會); an entertainment; a banquet. —宴會の主人役, the host (私宴の); the toast-master (公宴の). —宴會を開く, to hold a dinner-party; give a party.

enkai (遠海), *n.* deep sea. ☞ *eṅyō*. ¶ 遠海魚, pelagic fish.

enkaku (沿革), *n.* ❶ history. ❷ (發達) development; progress.

enkaku (遠隔の), *a.* distant; remote; far; far-off. —遠隔の地, a remote place.

enkan (鉛管), *n.* a leaden pip ¶ 鉛管工, a plumber.

enkatsu (圓滑), *n.* ❶ (滑か) smoothness. ❷ (融和) harmony. —圓滑な, smooth; harmonious. —圓滑に纏める, to settle smoothly.

enkei (圓形), *n.* a circle; circularity. —圓形に切拔く, to cut out in a circle; cut out a circle.

enkei (遠景), *n.* a distant view; a perspective.

enken (延見する), *vt.* to receive (in audience).

enki (延期), *n.* postponement; deferment. —延期する, to postpone; put off; defer. —來る二十日迄延期, postponed until the 20th.

enki (鹽基), *n.* a base. —鹽基性の, basic. ¶ 鹽基性酸化物, a basic oxide.

enkin (遠近), *n.* distance; far and near. —路の遠近を問はず, irrespective of the distance of the road. ¶ 遠近法, 【畫】 perspective; perspective representation. (線條遠近法, linear perspective.)

enkiri (緣切), *n.* ❶ (離婚) divorce. ❷ (關係を斷つ) breaking

off of relations; severing of connection.

enko (縁故), *n.* connection; relation. —縁故ある, connected; related.

enkō (猿猴), *n.* the long-armed monkey.

enkon (怨恨), *n.* enmity; animosity; rancour. —怨恨を懐く, to harbour enmity [ill-blood].

enkyoku (婉曲な), *a.* circumlocutional; roundabout; periphrastic; euphemistic. —婉曲に言ふ, to speak in a roundabout way; euphemize. ¶ 婉曲法,【修】euphemism; periphrasis.

enkyori (遠距離), *n.* a long distance; a long range.

Enma (閻魔), *n.* 【梵】Yama; the judge of Hades. ¶ 閻魔帳,【學生·俗】the teacher's mark-book. —閻魔堂, the Yama's shrine.

enmaku (煙幕), *n.* a smoke-screen [-curtain].

enman (圓滿), *n.* ❶ (完全無缺) perfection. ❷ (圓滑) smoothness; harmony. —圓滿な, perfect; harmonious; smooth. —圓滿に事を納める, to settle the matter smoothly [peacefully].

enmei (延命), *n.* lengthening of life; a long life; longevity. ¶ 延命菊,【植】the (common) daisy.

enmusubi (縁結), *n.* the wedding-knot; the marriage-tie.

ennetsu (炎熱), *n.* extreme [severe] heat. —炎熱の, torrid; sweltering; sultry.

ennichi (縁日), *n.* the fête-day (of a local deity). —縁日の露店, a fête-day street-stall.

ennin (延引), *n.* ☞ *enin.*

ennoshita (縁の下), under the verandah. —縁の下の力持をする, to make ineffective efforts *for*.

eñō (鴛鴦), *n.* 【鳥】the mandarin duck. —鴛鴦の契, a life-long pledge; a marriage-pledge.

enogu (繪具), *n.* painting materials; a paint; a pigment. —繪具を溶く, to dissolve colours. ¶ 繪具箱, a colour-box. —繪具刷毛, a paint-brush. —繪具皿, a palette.

enoki (榎), *n.* 【植】the Chinese nettle-tree.

enpei (援兵), *n.* reinforcements; relief; a relieving force. —援兵を送る, to send reinforcements.

enpei (掩蔽する), *vt.* to mask (兵力等を); occult; cover up. —罪跡を掩蔽する, to cover up the traces of a crime.

enpen (緣邊), *n.* ❶ (へり) an edge; a margin; a border. ❷ (緣附口) an offer of marriage. ❸ (緣故) relatives.

enpitsu (鉛筆), *n.* a pencil; a lead pencil. —鉛筆を削る, to sharpen a pencil. ¶ 色(青; 赤)鉛筆, a coloured (blue; red) pencil. —鉛筆挾, a pencil-case; a porte-crayon. —鉛筆畫, a pencil-sketch [-work]; a line-drawing. —鉛筆削, a pencil-sharpener.

enpō (遠方), *n.* a great distance; a long way. —遠方の, distant; remote; far-away [-off]. —遠方から, from a distance; from afar —遠方に, in the distance; far off.

enpu (怨府), *n.* the focus of hatred.

enpukuka (艶福家), *n.* one fortunate in love; a ladies' pet.

enrai (遠來の), *a.* coming from a distance. —遠來の客, a guest from a distant part.

enrai (遠雷), *n.* a distant thunder. —遠雷の響, the boom [rumbling] of distant thunder.

enraku (宴樂), *n.* mirth; conviviality; merry-making.

enrei (艶麗な), *a.* beautiful; charming.

enreisō (延齡草), *n.* 【植】the wake-robin.

enro (遠路), *n.* a long road [way]; a long journey.

enrui (鹽類), *n.* 【化】salts.

enryo (遠慮), *n.* ❶ (遠い考) forethought; long-sightedness. ❷ (差控) reserve; diffidence; constraint. ❸ (忌服令) retirement during mourning. —遠慮なく, without reserve (ceremony). (遠慮會釋なく, without making any bones about it.) —遠慮する, ① [*vi.*] to stand upon ceremony; be reserved; keep one's distance. ② [*a.*] reserved; diffident; constrained. —御遠慮なさるな, Don't stand on ceremony. —喫煙は御遠慮被成下度候, Passengers are requested to refrain from smoking.

ensaki (緣先), *n.* the ledge of a verandah.

ensan (鹽酸), *n.* hydrochloric acid. ¶ 鹽酸加里, potassium chlorate.

ensei (遠逝), *n.* death; decease. [=*chōsei* (長逝).]

ensei (遠征), *n.* ❶ (遠くへ行く) an expedition; an out-match (競技の). ❷ (遠く征討する) an expedition. —遠征する, to go on an expedition. —萬里遠征の客を送る, to see off one who sets out on a long journey. ¶ 遠征軍, an expeditionary army [force].

ensei (厭世), *n.* weariness of the world. —厭世的, world-weary.

enseki (宴席), *n.* a banquet hall; a dining-hall.

enshigan (遠視眼), *n.* long [far]-sightedness; hyperopia. —遠視眼

の人, a long-sighted person; a hypermetrope.
enshin (圓心), *n.* the centre (of a circle).
enshin (遠心的), *a.* centrifugal. ¶ 遠心力, centrifugal force.
ensho (艶書), *n.* a love-letter.
enshō (炎症), *n.* inflammation. —炎症を起す, to become inflamed; cause inflammation.
enshō (延燒する), *vi.* to be burnt down (by a spreading fire). —延燒を防ぐ, to prevent the spread of the fire.
enshoku (艶色), *n.* beauty.
enshū (圓周), *n.* the circumference. ¶ 圓周率, 【數】 the ratio of the circumference of a circle to its diameter; perimetric ratio; π (希. 發音 pi).
enshū (演習), *n.* practice; exercise; manœuvres. —演習に召集される, to be called out for manœuvers. ¶ 大演習, grand manœuvres. —發火演習, firing-practice. —射擊演習, target practice; rifle practice.
enso (鹽素), *n.* chlorine. ¶ 鹽素酸カリウム, potassium chlorate; chlorate of potash.
ensō (燕巢), *n.* a bird's-nest; a swallow's nest.
ensō (淵叢), *n.* a centre; a flower-garden (*of*); a place where...flourishes.
ensō (演奏), *n.* a musical performance. —演奏する, to perform; render. ¶ 演奏會, a concert.
ensoku (遠足), *n.* a walking tour; an excursion on foot. —遠足する, to take a long walk; go on [make] an excursion; tour on foot [*through*; *about*].
ensui (圓錐-形), *n.* a cone. ¶ 圓錐曲線法, conic sections.
ensui (鉛錘), *n.* a plumb.
ensui (鹽水), *n.* brine.
entai (延滯), *n.* delay; procrastination. ¶ 延滯金, arrears. —延滯利子, interest for delay.
entan (鉛丹), *n.* 【化】 minium; red lead.
entarō (圓太郎馬車), *n.* a rattle-trap. —圓太郎自動車, a rattle-autobus.
entei (園丁), *n.* a gardener.
enten (炎天), *n.* sweltering heat; hot weather; broiling weather. —炎天に曝される, to be exposed to the blazing sun.
enten-katsudatsu (圓轉滑脫), *n.* suavity; blandness. —圓轉滑脫の妙を得る, to master the art of suavity.
entō (鉛糖), *n.* sugar of lead; lead acetate.
entō (圓筒, 圓壔), *n.* a cylinder.
entō (遠島), *n.* banishment to a distant island; transportation; exile.
entotsu (煙突), *n.* a chimney; a funnel (汽船の); a chimney-stack; a stove-pipe (暖爐の). ¶ 煙突掃除夫, a chimney-sweep (-er); a sweep.
entsuzuki (緣續), *n.* relationship.
eṅyō (遠洋), *n.* a deep sea; an ocean. —遠洋の, pelagic; deep-sea. ¶ 遠洋漁業, deep-sea [pelagic] fishery. —遠洋航海, ocean navigation. —遠洋航路, an ocean line.
eṅyūkai (園遊會), *n.* a garden-party. —園遊會を催す, to hold a garden-party.
enzai (寃罪), *n.* a false charge. 「☞ *en* (寃).」
enzan (演算), *n.* 【數】 operation.
enzei (鹽稅), *n.* salt-duty; tax on salt; *gabelle* (佛).
enzen (宛然), *ad.* just; exactly; as if. ☞ *sanagara*. —宛然別世界に來たやうだった, I felt as if I had come into another world.
enzetsu (演說), *n.* a speech; an address; an oration. —演說する, to speak; make [deliver] a speech; give an address. ¶ 卓上演說, a table speech. —即席演說, an off-hand [extempore] speech. —演說筆記, a report of a speech. —演說家, a public speaker; an orator. —演說會, a speech [an address] meeting.
enzō (醃藏, 鹽藏), *n.* preserving in salt; corning. —醃藏する, to salt; corn. ¶ 醃藏物, corned food.
enzui (延髓), *n.* 【解】 medulla oblongata.
enzukeru (緣附ける), *vt.* to give in marriage; marry (a girl *to*); wed; dispose of (one's daughter).
enzuku (緣附く), *vi.* to marry; be given in marriage.
en-zuru (演ずる), *vt.* to perform; play; render; act. —活劇を演ずる, to make a scene. —失態を演ずる, to commit a blunder.
eppei (閱兵する), *vt.* to review; parade; muster. ¶ 閱兵式, a review (of troops).
era (鰓), *n.* a gill.
erabu (選·撰ぶ), *vt.* ❶ to choose; select; pick. ❷ (えり分け分類す) to sort; assort. ❸ (選擧) to elect. —朋友を選ぶ, to choose a friend. —人の撰ぶままに任す, to leave to the discretion of a person.
eragaru (偉がる), *vi.* to think highly of oneself; have a high opinion of oneself. ——, *a.* snobbish; pretentious.
erai (偉い), *a.* ❶ great (偉大な); fine (立派な); famous (名高い). ❷ (ひどい) severe; violent; awful; extraordinary.
erasōna (偉さうな), *a.* remark-

able-looking; important-looking. —偉さうな風をする, to look big. —偉さうなことを云ふ, to talk big. —偉さうに見せる, to carry it off well.

erevētā (昇降機), *n.* an elevator; a lift.

eri (襟), *n.* ❶ (頸) the neck. ❷ (衣襟) the neck-band. ❸ (カラー) a collar (洋服の). —襟を掴む, to collar; seize [take] by the collar.

eridasu (擇出す), *vt.* to sort out; pick out.

eridome (襟止), *n.* a brooch; a breast-pin.

eridoru (選取る), *vt.* to pick out; take one's choice.

erigami (襟髮), *n.* the back-hair. —襟髮を掴む, to seize a person by the back-hair [neck].

erijirushi (襟章), *n.* 【陸軍】 a collar-badge.

erikazari (襟飾), *n.* a necktie; a cravat. ¶ 襟飾止め, a scarf-pin.

erikonomi (選好する), *v.* to have one's choice; be fastidious [particular; nice] *about*.

erikubi (襟首), *n.* the nape; the scruff (of the neck). —襟首を捉へる, to seize a person by the scruff of his neck.

erimaki (襟卷), *n.* a scarf; a neck-cloth; a comforter (長い羊毛製の).

erinuki (選拔), *n.* pick; choice; selection; the pick [choice] *of*. —選拔きの, picked; choice; selected. —擇り拔く, to choose; select; pick out.

eriwakeru (選分ける), *vt.* to sort; sift; pick.

eru (得る), *vt.* ❶ (獲得) to get; obtain; procure. ❷ (可能) to be able to; can. ☞ *uru* (得る). —...せざるを得ず, cannot but; cannot help —ing. —愛を得る, to win her heart. —勝利を獲る, to gain [win] a victory.

eru (擇る), *vt.* to choose; select; pick out. ☞ *erabu* (選ぶ).

esagashi (繪探し), *n.* a picture puzzle; a hidden picture. —繪探しを判じる, to solve a picture puzzle.

esashi (餌差), *n.* a bird-catcher.

ese (似而非), *a.* & *pref.* false; pseud-, pseudo-; would-be. ¶ 似而非學者, a sciolist; a charlatan.

eshaku (會釋する), *vt.* to salute; accost; greet. —丁寧に會釋する, to salute carefully.

eshi (繪師), *n.* a painter; an artist.

eshiki (會式), *n.* a religious fête; a religious ceremony.

eso (壞疽), *n.* mortification; necrosis; gangrene. —壞疽性の, necrotic; gangrenous.

es-suru (謁する), *v.* to have an audience *of*; be received in audience.

Esu (耶蘇), *n.* Jesus.

esukarētā (自動階段), *n.* an escalator.

Esukimō (エスキモー), *n.* an Eskimo; an Esquimau [*pl.* -maux.].

Esuperanto (萬國共通語), *n.* Esperanto.

eta (穢多), *n.* an outcast; a pariah.

etai (得體), *n.* form; shape; nature. —得體の知れぬ, nondescript; neither flesh nor fowl.

etari (得たり), *int.* coming pat *to*; being according to expectation. —得たり賢しと...する, to jump [catch] *at* (an offer).

ete (得手), *n.* ❶ (得意) skill; excellence. ❷ (得手物) a forte; speciality. —得手勝手な, self-willed; egotistic. —得手勝手を云ふ, to say things to suit one's convenience.

ēteru (エーテル), *n.* ether.

etoku (會得), *n.* understanding; comprehension; grasp. —會得する, to understand; comprehend; grasp.

etsu (悦に入る), to be much pleased; to rejoice *at*.

etsu (閱), *n.* revision. —某氏閱, revised by Mr. ...

etsubo (笑壺, 笑局), *n.* a smile of satisfaction [gratification]. —獨り笑局に入る, to smile to oneself with satisfaction.

etsudoku (閱讀する), *vt.* to peruse; run through; run over.

etsunen (越年), *n.* ❶ passing from the old year to the new. ❷ (越冬) hibernation. —越年する, to pass into the new year; hibernate.

etsuran (閱覽), *n.* reading; perusal; inspection. —閱覽する, to read over; peruse; inspect. ¶ 閱覽券, a library admission-ticket. —閱覽料, a library admission-fee. —閱覽室, a reading-room.

etsureki (閱歷), *n.* a personal history; a career.

ētto (えーっと), **ēto** (えーと), *int.* eh; er; well; let me see.

eyasui (得易い), *a.* easily-obtained. —得易からざる品, an article hard [not easy] to obtain.

eyō (榮燿), *n.* =*eiyō*.

ezogiku (翠菊), *n.* 【植】 the China aster.

ezōshi (繪草紙), *n.* a picture-book; a print; a picture sheet.

ezu (繪圖), *n.* ❶ (設計圖) a plan; a design. ❷ (地圖) a map. ❸ a drawing (畫); an illustration (圖解).

F

fauru (ファウル), *n.* 【野球】 a foul. —ファウルを主張する, to claim a foul.

feruto-bō(フェルト帽), *n.* a felt hat.

firumu (フィルム), *n.* 【寫】 a film. —フィルムに撮る, to film. ¶ 封切フィルム, a released film [reel].

fito (呎), *n.* feet (foot の複數).

fōku (肉叉), *n.* a fork.

forumarin (フォルマリン), *n.* formalin.

fu (歩), *n.* (將棋の) a pawn. —歩を打つ(つき出す), to place (move forward) a pawn.

fu (府), *n.* ❶ (行政區劃の名) an urban prefecture. ❷ (官廳) a government office. ❸ (集る處, 中心) a centre; a focus.

fu (負の), *a.* negative; minus.

fu (訃), *n.* a report of another's death. —訃に接する, to be informed of a person's death.

fu (腑), *n.* ❶ (臟腑) the viscera; the bowels. ❷ (心) the heart. —腑に落ちぬ, not to go down with one.

fu (斑), *n.* ❶ (斑點) a speckle; a spot; a mottle. ❷(斑條) stripes. —斑のある, speckled; spotted; mottled.

fu (譜), *n.* ❶ (圖表) a table; an album. ❷ (系譜) a family record. ❸ (樂譜) a score; a setting; a record (蓄音器の).

fū (風), *n.* ❶ (風體, 風貌) an appearance; a style; an air. ❷ (風儀, 風習) manners; customs; morals. ❸ (流, 式, 型) a style; a fashion; a type (型). —こんな風の物, things of this kind. —かういふ風に, in [after] this manner; like this. —日本風に暮らす, to live in the Japanese style. —學者(道德家)の風をする, to set up for a scholar (moralist).

fū (封), *n.* seal; closing. —封を開く[切る], to unseal; break the seal.

fuan(不安), *n.* uneasiness; anxiety; insecurity; unrest. —良心の不安を感ずる, to feel the pangs of conscience. **—-no,** *a.* uneasy; anxious; insecure. —不安の(裡に)一夜を明かす, to pass an uneasy night. —不安の念に驅られる, to be pursued by uneasiness.

fuannai (不案內), *n.* ❶ (未知) ignorance. ❷ (不慣) unfamiliarity. —不案內の, ignorant *of*; unfamiliar *with*. —土地不案內である, to be unfamiliar with the locality. —この邊は全く不案內だ, I am quite a stranger hereabouts.

fuanshin (不安心), *n.* anxiety; apprehension; uneasiness. —不安心の, apprehensive; anxious; uneasy. —不安心にする, to cause uneasiness *to*; make a person anxious.

fūatsu(風壓), *n.* ❶ wind-pressure. ❷ (航差) leeway drift(-age).

fūbaika (風媒花), *n.* 【植】 an anemophilous flower.

fubako (文筥), *n.* a letter-case; a dispatch-box.

fubarai (賦拂), *n.* payment by instalments. ¶ 賦拂買入, hire-purchase.

fubatsu(不拔の), *a.* unswerving; steadfast; indomitable. —確固不拔の決心を以て, with firm and indomitable determination.

fuben(不便), *n.* ❶ inconvenience; inexpediency. ❷ (扱ひにくいこと) unwieldiness. **—-na,** *a.* ❶ inconvenient; inexpedient. ❷ unwieldy. —不便な土地, an inconvenient locality.

fubenkyō (不勉强の), *a.* idle.

fubi (不備), *n.* deficiency; defect; imperfection. **—-no** (不備の), *a.* defective; imperfect. —不備の點を補正する, to correct [remedy] the defects.

fubin(不敏), *n.* unworthiness. —予不敏なりと雖も, unworthy as I am.

fubin (不憫), *n.* ❶ (不束) ignorance; rudeness. ❷(氣の毒) deserving compassion. ❸ (憫然) piteousness; pitifulness. —不憫の, piteous; pitiful; poor. —不憫と思召して, for pity's sake. —不憫に思ふ, to take pity *on*; feel pity *for*.

fubo(父母), *n.* father and mother; parents.

fubuki (吹雪), *n.* a snow-storm; a blizzard (烈雪風).

fubun (不文の), *a.* ❶ (學問なき) illiterate; uneducated. ❷ (文字に表さぬ) unwritten. ¶ 不文律, the unwritten law; the common law (英米の).

fūbun (風聞), *n.* a report; a rumour; hearsay.

fubunmei(不分明の), *a.* unclear; ambiguous; obscure.

fūbutsu(風物), *n.* scenery; natural objects; natural features of the season.

fuchaku (不著), *n.* non-arrival.

fuchaku(附著する), *vi.* to attach *to*; adhere *to*; stick *to*. ¶ 附著

力, adhesion.

fuchi (淵), *n.* ❶ (深淵) an abyss. ❷ (河の) a pool.

fuchi(緣, 邊), *n.* ❶ (端) an edge; a brink (崖などの); a brim (茶碗·帽子などの). ❷ (外緣) a margin; a hem (手巾など); a rim (眼鏡·車·帽子などの). ❸ (枠) a frame. ❹ (周圍, 近邊) a border; a hem; side. —盆の緣, the brim [rim] of a tray. —河の邊, the river-side. —眼鏡の緣, the frame [rim] of spectacles.

fuchi (不治の), *a.* incurable. —不治の病に惱む, to be afflicted with an incurable disease.

fuchi (布置), *n.* arrangement.

fuchi (扶持), *n.* support; upkeep. —他人より扶持を受ける, to be supported by another.

fūchi (風致), *n.* taste; elegance. —風致ある, tasteful; elegant. —風致を害する, to injure the view.

fuchin (浮沈), *n.* ups and downs; rise and fall; vicissitudes. —人生の浮沈, vicissitudes of life; ups and downs of life. —浮沈常なき運命, chequered lot [fortunes]. —浮沈を共にする, to share the smiles and frowns of fortune. —世と共に浮沈する, to swim with the world.

fuchitsujo(不秩序), *n.* disorder; disarray; disarrangement.

fuchō (不調), *n.* break-off; rupture. —不調に歸する[終る], to end in rupture.

fuchō (府廳), *n.* an urban prefectural office. ¶ 東京府廳, the Tōkyō Prefectural Office.

fuchō (符牒), *n.* ❶ (しるし) a sign; a mark; a token. ❷ (暗號) cryptogram; a cipher. ❸【商】a price-mark.

fūchō (風鳥), *n.* 【鳥】the bird of paradise.

fūchō (風潮), *n.* ❶【航】the lee-tide. ❷(時流) the tide; the stream; the current; the drift; the fashion. —世の風潮に隨ふ, to go with the tide [times; stream]; swim with the current. —世の風潮に逆ふ, to run counter to the fashions of the world; go [run] against the stream.

fuchōwa (不調和), *n.* disharmony; dissonance; discord. —不調和の, disharmonious; discordant.

fuchū (不忠), *n.* disloyalty; undutifulness; infidelity. —不忠の, disloyal; undutiful; unfaithful.

fuchūi (不注意), *n.* carelessness; heedlessness; negligence. —不注意の, careless; heedless; negligent. —不注意に, carelessly; heedlessly; neglectfully.

fuchūjitsu (不忠實), *n.* disloyalty; faithlessness. —不忠實の, disloyal; unfaithful.

fuda (札), *n.* ❶ (附札) a label; a tag. ❷ (貼札) a placard; a label. ❸ (護符) a charm. ❹ (門標) a door-plate; a name-plate. ❺ (カルタ札) a card. ❻ a chit (票); a ticket (切符); a check (合札). —札を貼る, to paste a card [label]; label.

fudan(不斷), *ad.* always; usually; habitually; at other times. —不斷の, ① (恆久) constant; endless; incessant. ② (平常) everyday; usual; habitual. —不斷著で, in everyday clothes; in morning dress (女).

fudansō (不斷草), *n.* 【植】the red beet.

fudasho (札所), *n.* a temple at which a charm is given to a pilgrim.

fudatsuki (札附の), *a.* ❶ (正札つきの) with marked price; guaranteed (保證附の). ❷ (知れ渡ッてる) well-known; notorious. —札附きの惡漢, a notorious rascal.

fude (筆), *n.* ❶ a hair-pen; a hair-pencil; a (writing) brush (刷筆). ❷(筆寫, 描畫) writing; painting. ❸ (同上の作品) a production; a work. —仕上の筆, the finishing touch [stroke]. —名家の筆に成る畫, a picture by a master. —筆を擱く, to lay aside one's pen; stop writing. —筆を入れる, (訂正) to correct. —生活の爲に筆を執る, to write for a living.

fudebushō (筆不精), *n.* ❶ laziness with the pen. ❷ (人) a lazy writer; a bad correspondent.

fudeire (筆入), *n.* a brush-case; a pen-case.

fudekake (筆架), *n.* a brush-rack; a pen-rack.

fudeki (不出來), *n.* bad make; failure. —不出來の, unsatisfactory; poor; badly made (製作物に云ふ). —此畫は彼にしてはちと不出來だ, This picture is not quite up to the mark for him.

fudemame (筆まめ), *n.* (事) readiness with the pen; (人) a ready writer.

fudetate (筆立), *n.* a pencil-vase; a pen-stand; a brush-stand.

fudezukai (筆遣), *n.* command of the pen.

fudō (不同), *n.* dissimilarity; inequality; unlikeness. —不同の, dissimilar; unequal; unlike.

fudō(不動), *n.* ❶ firmness; steadiness; immobility. ❷ [F-] (不動明王の略) Acara (阿遮羅). —不動の, firm; steadfast; immobile; immovable.

fudō (浮動する), *vi.* ❶ to float; waft. ❷ (ぐらつく) to totter; fluctuate. ¶ 浮動票, a floating vote.

fudō(婦道), *n.* womanhood. —婦道を全うする, to perform the duties of womanhood.

fūdo (風土), *n.* climate; natural features (of a region). —風土的, climatic. —風土に馴らす, to acclimate (人を); acclimatize (重に動植物を). —風土に馴れる, to become acclimated; be acclimatized. ¶ 風土病, an endemic.

fudōi (不同意), *n.* disagreement; dissent. —不同意を唱へる, to object *to*; raise an objection *to*.

fudōri (不道理), *n.* unreason; irrationality; unreasonableness. —不道理の, irrational; unreasonable.

fudōsan (不動產), *n.* immovable property; immovables; real estate.

fudōtoku(不道德), *n.* immorality. **——-na,** *a.* immoral; unvirtuous. —不道德な人, a man lost to virtue; a reprobate. —不道德な事をする, to act immorally; be guilty of immorality.

fue (笛), *n.* ❶ (横笛) a flute; a fife(軍樂用の). ❷(呼子) a whistle; a pipe. ❸ (縱笛) a clarionet; a pipe. —笛の孔, the finger-holes of a flute. —笛を吹く, to pipe; (play a) flute; play on the flute; (blow a) whistle.

fue (鰾), *n.* (魚の) a fish-maw; a fish-sound.

fueisei (不衞生), *n.* insanitation; insanitary condition. —不衞生の, unhealthy; insanitary.

fueki (不易の), *a.* invariable; unchangeable; immutable.

fueki (扶掖する), *vi.* to assist; help; lead (指導).

fuen (敷衍, 布演), *n.* amplification; enlargement; expatiation. —敷衍する, to amplify; expatiate *on*; enlarge *on*

fueru (殖える), *vi.* to increase (增加); multiply (增殖, 繁殖); swell.

fuete (不得手), *n.* ❶ (不得意) unskilfulness; inexpertness. ❷ (好まぬこと) dislike; want of taste. ❸ (弱點) a weakness; a weak point. **——-na,** *a.* ❶ unskilful; inexpert. ❷ having no taste *for*. —不得手な事をする, to do something out of one's line.

fuetsu (斧鉞), *n.* ❶ a battle-axe. ❷ (重き制裁) a heavy punishment. —斧鉞を加へる, to cut down heavily.

fūfu (夫婦), *n.* man [husband] and wife; a couple. —似合った夫婦, a well-matched couple. —夫婦の愛情, conjugal affection. —夫婦になる, to become man and wife. ¶ 若夫婦, a young couple. —夫婦喧嘩, conjugal quarrels. —夫婦約束, engagement; betrothal. (夫婦約束する, to engage oneself *to*.)

fufuku (不服), *n.* ❶ (不納得) objection; disagreement. ❷ (不滿足) disaffection; dissatisfaction. —不服を唱へる, to grumble; express dissatisfaction.

fūga (風雅), *n.* elegance; refinement; grace. **——-na,** *a.* elegant; refined; graceful. —風雅な人, a man of elegance.

fūgai (風害), *n.* damage done by wind.

fugainai (腑甲斐ない), *a.* poor-spirited; spiritless.

fūgawari (風變り), *n.* ❶ (異樣, 變態) eccentricity; peculiarity; oddity. ❷ (變人) an original; an eccentric; an oddity. —風變りの, odd; peculiar, eccentric.

fugen (不言), *n.* silence. ¶ 不言實行, silence and practice; action before words.

fugen (附言する), *v.* to add; say in addition.

fugen(富源), *n.* sources of wealth; natural resources (天然の). —富源に饒かである (乏しい), to be rich (poor) in natural resources. —富源を開拓する, to develop natural resources.

fugen (誣言), *n.* a false accusation [charge].

fūgetsu (風月), *n.* scenery; nature. —風月を友とする, to make nature one's companion.

fugi(不義), *n.* ❶ (不正) iniquity; injustice; perfidy. ❷ (私通) fornication; adultery (姦通). —不義の快樂, improper [illicit] pleasures. —不義の富貴, ill-gotten wealth and power. —不義をする, to commit adultery *with*.

fūgi (風儀), *n.* ❶ (行儀) morals; behaviour. ❷ (風習) manners; customs; habits. —世間の風儀, public morals. —學生の風儀, the manners of students. —風儀のわるい, of bad customs; of lax morals.

fugiri (不義理), *n.* dishonesty (不信實); dishonour (不面目); ingratitude (忘恩). —不義理の借金, dishonourable debts. —不義理をする, to act dishonestly (ungratefully).

fugō (符合する), *vi.* to accord *with*; coincide *with*; correspond *to*. —事實と符合する, to agree with the facts.

fugō(符號), *n.* a symbol; a sign; a mark. —符號を附ける; to affix a private mark.

fugō (負號), *n.* 【數】a negative [minus] sign.

fugō (富豪), *n.* a man of wealth; a wealthy man; a rich man.

fugōkaku(不合格), *n.* disqualification; failure. —不合格となる, to fail to come up to the standard [mark]; fail in an examination. ¶ 不合格者, a disqualified person.

fugōri (不合理), *n.* illogicality; irrationality; unreason. —不合理の, illogical; irrational; unreasonable.

fugu (河豚), *n.* 【魚】 the globe-fish.

fugu (不具), *n.* deformity. ☞ *katawa.* —不具の, deformed (畸形の); crippled (手又は足を損じたる); maimed. ¶ 不具者, a cripple.

fugū (不遇), *n.* ❶ (不幸) misfortune. ❷ (落魄) obscurity. **——-no,** *a.* ill-fated; unfortunate; obscure. —不遇の人, an ill-fated person. —不遇の中に一生を送る, to spend one's whole life in obscurity. ¶ 不遇時代, one's dark days.

fugutaiten (不倶戴天の), *a.* deadly; irreconcilable; mortal. —不倶戴天の仇, a deadly foe; a sworn enemy.

fugyō (俯仰天地に恥ぢず), I stand unashamed before God and man.

fugyōgi (不行儀), *n.* bad manners; misbehaviour. —不行儀の, ill-mannered; misbehaved.

fugyōseki (不行跡), *n.* misconduct; profligacy. —不行跡を働く, to misconduct oneself.

fūha(風波), *n.* ❶ (風と波) wind and wave. ❷ (荒浪) raging billows; a storm; a tempest. ❸ (葛藤) a quarrel; a dispute; a discord. —家庭の風波, family dissensions. —風波を凌ぐ, to brave the winds and waves.

fuhai (腐敗), *n.* corruption (道徳の); decay; putrefaction. —腐敗する, to spoil; putrefy; decay; corrupt. —腐敗した, putrid; rotten; corrupt.

fuhaku (浮薄), *n.* unfeelingness; frivolity. —浮薄の行爲, a frivolous [unfeeling] act.

fuharai (不拂), *n.* non-payment.

fuhatsu (不發), *n.* misfire. ¶ 不發彈, a blind shell.

fuhei (不平), *n.* ❶ (不滿) discontent; dissatisfaction; disaffection. ❷ (苦情) grievance; complaint. —不平を懐く, to be disaffected *towards.* —...に對して不平を鳴らす, to raise a complaint *against.* ¶ 不平黨, malcontents.

fuheikin (不平均), *n.* disproportion; inequality. —不平均の, unequal; disproportionate.

fuheikō (不平行), *n.* non-parallelism.

fuhen (不偏), *n.* impartiality; equitableness; fairness. —不偏不黨の, impartial; neutral.

fuhen (不變の), *a.* unchangeable; invariable; inalterable. ¶ 不變色, a grain [fast; permanent] colour.

fuhen (普遍), *n.* universality; ubiquity. —普遍的, universal; omnipresent; ubiquitous.

fūhi (風靡する), *vt.* to sweep over; overwhelm.

fuhinkō(不品行), *n.* ❶=*fugyōgi.* ❷ (放埒) profligacy; dissoluteness; loose conduct. —不品行の, dissolute; profligate.

fuhitsuyō (不必要の), *a.* unnecessary; needless.

fuhō (不法), *n.* ❶ (違法) illegality; unlawfulness. ❷ (無法) lawlessness (理不盡); exorbitance. ❸ (不正) iniquity; wrong; wrongfulness. **——-no,** *a.* ❶ illegal; illicit; unlawful. ❷ lawless; wrongful; iniquitous. —不法な事をする, to act unlawfully. ¶ 不法行爲, a tort 【法】; an unlawful act; a wrongful act.

fuhoṅi(不本意), *n.* unwillingness; reluctance. —不本意ながら, unwillingly; reluctantly.

fuhyō (浮氷), *n.* a floe(-ice).

fuhyō (浮評), *n.* a baseless [an unfounded] rumour.

fuhyō (浮標), *n.* a buoy. ¶ 繋船浮標, mooring-buoy. —救命浮標, a life-buoy.

fuhyō(譜表), *n.* 【音】 staff; score.

fūhyō (風評), *n.* a rumour; a report.

fuhyōban (不評判), *n.* a bad reputation; disrepute; unpopularity. —不評判の, disreputable; unpopular.

fui (ふい), *n.* ❶ (皆無) nothing; naught. ❷ (不成就) failure. —ふいになる, to come to naught; end in failure. —ふいにする, to lose; bring to naught.

fui (不意), *n.* ❶ (意外) unexpectedness. ❷ (突然) suddenness; abruptness. ❸ (偶然) fortuitousness. —不意を襲ふ, to catch a person napping; take by surprise. —不意を打たれる, to be taken by surprise; be struck off one's guard; be taken at a disadvantage. **——-no,** *a.* ❶ unforeseen; unexpected. ❷ sudden; abrupt. ❸ fortuitous; accidental. —不意の訪問, a surprise visit. **——-ni,** *ad.* unexpectedly; (at) unawares; suddenly; abruptly. —不意に出會ふ, to chahce [happen] upon; come [drop] across.

fuichō (吹聽する), *vt.* to make public; recommend (推擧); announce (披露).

Fuifuikyō (回回教), *n.* Mohammedanism; Islam. ¶ 回回教徒, a Mohammedan; a Mussulman [*pl.* -s]; a Moslem.

fuigo (鞴), *n.* a bellows.

fuiku (傅育), *n.* bringing up; teaching; tuition.

fuin (父音), *n.* a consonant.

fuin (訃音), *n.* a report [notice] of death. ☞ *fu* (訃).

fūin (封印), *n.* a stamped seal; a seal. 一封印する, to seal.

fuiri (不入), *n.* a thin house; a small audience.

fuitchi (不一致), *n.* disharmony; discord; disaccord; disagreement. 一内部の不一致を醸す, to lead to internal disaccord.

fuiuchi (不意打), *n.* ❶ a sudden attack; a surprise. ❷ (不意の訪問) a surprise visit. 一不意打を喰ふ, to be taken unawares [by surprise].

fūja (風邪), *n.* a cold. 一風邪に罹る [冒される], to take [catch] cold.

fuji (藤), *n.* 【植】 the wistaria.

fuji (不次の), *a.* ❶ out of order; in irregular order. ❷ unusual; exceptional; special.

fuji (不時の), *a.* untimely; unexpected; contingent; unlooked-for. 一不時の出來事 a contingency; an emergency. 一不時の入費, incidental expenses. ¶ 不時著陸, untimely [emergency] landing.

fujidana (藤棚), *n.* a wistaria-trellis.

fujiiro (藤色の), *a.* lilac; lilac-coloured.

fujikō (不時候の), *a.* unseasonable. ☞ *fujun* (不順).

fujimame (藤豆), *n.* 【植】 the Egyptian kidney-bean.

fujimi (不死身), *n.* invulnerability; insensibility to pain.

fujimurasaki (藤紫), *n.* (色) powder-blue.

fujin (夫人), *n.* ❶ (妻女) a wife; a married lady. ❷ (敬語) lady; madam (手紙の初に於ける sir の對); *madame* [佛]. ¶ 新夫人, the bride. 一田中夫人, Mrs. Tanaka.

fujin (婦人), *n.* a woman; a lady. 一貞操な婦人, a woman of virtue; a chaste woman. 一婦人の龜鑑, a mirror [pattern] of womanhood. 一婦人らしい, womanly; ladylike. ¶ 婦人傍聽席, the ladies' gallery (衆議院内の). 一婦人科, 【醫】 gynæcology. 一婦人參政權, woman [female] suffrage. (婦人參政權論者, a suffragette.)

fujinbō (不人望), *n.* unpopularity. 一不人望の, unpopular.

fū-jiru (封じる), *vt.* ❶ (封をなす) to seal; enclose (封込む). ❷ (神佛の力にて閉込む) to seal in by divine power. ❸ (使用を禁ず) to bar. ❹ (封鎖する) to blockade. 一封じられた手, (相撲にて) a barred chip. 一手紙を封じる, to seal a letter. 一子供の蟲を封じる, to work a charm against infantile eclampsia.

fujisshi (不實施), *n.* suspension; abeyance; non-operation.

fujitsu (不日), *ad.* shortly; before long; at no distant date.

fujitsu (不實), *n.* ❶ (虛僞) untruth; falsehood. ❷ (不誠意) faithlessness; perfidy; insincerity. ❸ (薄情) cold-heartedness. ——**no**, *a.* ❶ untruthful; false. ❷ insincere; faithless; perfidious. ❸ cold-hearted; heartless. 一不實の申立をなす, to make a false statement.

fujitsubo (藤壺), *n.* 【貝】 the acorn-shell.

fujiyū (不自由), *n.* =*fujū*.

fujo (扶助), *n.* ❶ (補助) assistance; aid; help. ❷ (扶養) support; relief (救恤). 一扶助する, ① to assist; help; aid. ② to support; relieve (救恤する). 一他人の扶助を仰ぐ, to look to others for assistance. ¶ 遺族扶助料, a compassionate allowance to the (surviving) family.

fujo (婦女 -子), *n.* a woman; womenfolk.

fujō (不淨), *n.* ❶ (不清潔) impurity; unholiness; uncleanness. ❷ (大小便) filth. 一不淨の, impure; unholy; unclean.

fujōri (不條理), *n.* unreasonableness.

fuju (腐儒), *n.* a pedant.

fujū (不自由), *n.* ❶ (不如意) want; privation; discomfort (不快). ❷ (不便利) inconvenience. 一不自由の, ① uncomfortable; comfortless. ② inconvenient. 一不自由する, to want *for*. (金に不自由する, to be hard up for money. 一金に不自由せぬ, to have no lack of money.) 一手足が不自由だから, as my limbs are crippled. 一何不自由なく暮す, to live in comfort [in easy circumstances].

fujūbun (不十分), *n.* insufficiency; inadequacy; imperfection (不完全). 一不十分の, insufficient; inadequate; imperfect. 一證據不十分により, through insufficiency of evidence; on account of insufficient evidence.

fujuku (不熟の), *a.* unripe; immature; raw. 一不熟の文字を羅列する, to set down immature expressions.

fujukuren (不熟練の), *a.* inexperienced; unskilful; inexpert. ¶

不熟練勞働, unskilled labour.
fujun (不純), *n.* impurity. **——-no,** *a.* impure. —不純な思想, mixed ideas.
fujun (不順), *n.* unseasonableness (天候の); irregularity(不規則). —不順の陽氣, unseasonable weather.
fuka (鱶), *n.* 【魚】 the shark.
fuka (不可な), *a.* bad; wrong. —不可とする, to disapprove; disfavour. —…と云ふは不可なり, it would not do to say that….
fuka (附加する), *vt.* to add; annex; append; supplement. —に附加して, in addition to. ¶ 附加刑, 【法】 an additional [accessory] penalty. —附加稅, a surtax; an additional tax. (附加稅を課する, to surtax; put [levy] a surtax *on.*)
fuka (負荷), *n.* ❶【理】 load. ❷(負擔) a burden.
fuka (浮華), *n.* vanity; love of display; ostentation. —浮華の, vain; ostentatious; showy. ¶ 浮華輕佻, fickleness; frivolity.
fuka (賦課する), *vt.* to levy *on*; impose *upon.*
fuka (孵化), *n.* hatch; hatching; incubation. —孵化する, to hatch; incubate. ¶ 孵化場, a hatchery. —孵化器, an incubator.
fūka (風化), *n.* ❶【化】 efflorescence. ❷【地質】 weathering; deflation. —風化する, to effloresce; weather.
fukabun (不可分), *n.* indivisibility. —不可分の, indivisible; impartible.
fukade (深手), *n.* a severe [deep] wound. —深手を負ふ, to be severely [badly] wounded.
fūkaden (フーカデン), *n.* (西洋料理) fricandeau [*pl.* -x].
fukai (不快), *n.* ❶ (不愉快) discomfort; disagreeableness; displeasure. ❷ (微恙) an indisposition; a slight illness. —不快な, ① indisposed; ill; unwell. ② unpleasant; disagreeable; displeased. —不快に思ふ, to be displeased *with*; take umbrage [offence] *at.* —不快で引籠る, to be confined by an indisposition.
fukai (府會), *n.* a prefectural assembly.
fukai (附會), *n.* a forced analogy; catachresis. —附會せる, far-fetched; forced; distorted. —附會する, to distort; twist; strain.
fukai (深い), *a.* ❶ deep. ❷ (親密, 密接) intimate; close. ❸ (濃厚) heavy (霧); thick (霧などの). —深い知識, deep knowledge. —深い交り[仲]である, to be on intimate terms *with.*
fukairi (深入する), *vi.* to go deep *into*; be taken up *with*; be entangled *in.*
fukakai (不可解), *n.* mystery; inscrutability. —不可解の, mysterious; inscrutable; enigmatic.
fukakōryoku (不可抗力), *n.* an act of God [nature]; *vis major* 〖羅〗; *force majeure* 〖佛〗.
fukaku (不覺), *n.* ❶ (覺えぬこと) unconsciousness. ❷ (覺悟なきこと) negligence. ❸ (失策) a mistake. ❹ (敗) a defeat. —不覺の, ① unconscious. ② negligent. —不覺を取る, to suffer an unexpected defeat.
fukaku (俯角), *n.* an angle of depression [declination]; dip; 【天】 depression.
fukaku (深く), *ad.* deep; deeply. —深くなる(する), to deepen. —深く感謝する, to thank heartily. —深く研究する, to go deep into a subject. —深く遺憾とする, to regret deeply.
fukakujitsu (不確實な), *a.* uncertain; unreliable. —不確實な事業に手を出す, to engage in a shaky business.
fukakutei (不確定の), *a.* undecided; undetermined; unfixed; indefinite; uncertain.
fukameru (深める), *vt.* to deepen.
fukami (深み), *n.* a deep place; a depth.
fukan (俯瞰する), *vt.* to command; overlook. ¶ 俯瞰圖, a bird's-eye view.
fūkan (封緘), *n.* a seal. —封緘する, to seal. ¶ 封緘葉書, a letter-card. —封緘紙, wafer; seal.
fukanō (不可能), *n.* impossibility. —不可能の, impossible. —殆ど不可能である, to be hardly possible. ¶ 不可能事, an impossibility; an impossible thing.
fukan-shihei (不換紙幣), *n.* inconvertible paper-money.
fukanshō (不干涉), *n.* non-interference [intervention]; *laissez-faire* 〖佛〗 (特に商工業に對する放任).
fukanzen (不完全), *n.* imperfection; incompleteness. —不完全の, imperfect; incomplete; defective.
fukappatsu (不活潑), *n.* ❶ inactivity; lifelessness. ❷ (商況) stagnation; depression; slackness. —不活潑の, ① dull; inactive; spiritless. ② stagnant; slack; flat.
fukasa (深さ), *n.* depth. —深さ六呎の水, water 6ft. deep.
fukashin (不可侵), *n.* inviolability. ¶ 不可侵權, an inviolable right.
fūkasu (吹す), *vt.* to smoke; puff.
fukasu (更す), *v.* to sit up late.

fukasu (蒸す), *vt.* to steam.

fuke (頭垢, 雲脂), *n.* scurf; dandruff.

fukei(父兄), *n.* a father or an elder brother.

fukei (父系), *n.* paternity; the paternal lineage. —父系の, on the paternal side; paternal.

fukei (不敬), *n.* disrespect; irreverence. —不敬の, disrespectful; irreverent. ¶ 不敬罪,【法】lese-majesty.

fūkei (風景), *n.* a landscape; scenery (一地方の); a view. ¶ 風景畫, a landscape. (風景畫家, a landscape-painter.)

fukeiken (不敬虔), *n.* impiety; irreverence. —不敬虔の, impious; irreverent.

fukeiki (不景氣), *n.* stagnation; dulness; depression. **——-na,** *a.* ① stagnant; dull. ② (陰氣な) gloomy; dismal; cheerless. —不景氣な時節, a time of trade depression.

fukeizai (不經濟), *n.* want of economy; extravagance. —不經濟の, uneconomical; wasteful; extravagant.

fukekka (不結果), *n.* failure; unsuccess. —不結果の, unsuccessful; abortive. —不結果に終る, to end in failure; prove abortive; bring on untoward consequences.

fuken (府縣), *n.* a prefecture. ¶ 府縣社, a prefectural shrine.

fukenkō (不健康), *n.* unhealthiness; insalubrity; sickliness. **——-na,** *a.* unhealthy; insalubrious; sickly. —不健康な氣候, a sickly climate. ¶ 不健康狀態, unhealthy condition.

fukenkō (不權衡), *n.* inequality; want of balance; disproportion. —不權衡の, disproportionate; ill-balanced; inequal.

fukenshiki (不見識の), *a.* ❶ without knowledge; unlearned. ❷ offensive; shabby.

fukenzen (不健全の), *a.* ❶ unsound; unhealthy; unwholesome. ❷ =*fukenkō* (不健康な). —不健全な思想, unhealthy ideas.

fukeru (耽る), *vi.* to be addicted *to*; be given *to*; indulge *in*. —讀書に耽る, to give oneself up to reading. —遊戲に耽る, to be addicted to sports.

fukeru(ふける), *vi.* ❶〔更〕(夜が) to grow late; advance. ❷〔老〕(年が) to look old; advance in years; age. —年よりも老けて見える, to look older than one's years.

fukeru (風化る), *vi.* to mildew; mould; weather.

fuketsu (不潔な), *a.* filthy; foul; dirty. —不潔な場所, a filthy place. —不潔な町, a dirty street. —不潔な水, foul water.

fuketsudan (不決斷の), *a.* undecided; indecisive; irresolute.

fukettei (不決定の), *a.* undecided; unsettled.

fuki(蕗), *n.* the bog-rhubarb; the butter-bur.

fuki (袘), *n.* the out-turned skirt of the lining.

fuki (不歸の), *a.* unreturning; gone for ever. —不歸の客となる, to pass away; leave this world.

fuki (不羈), *n.* liberty; freedom; independence. —不羈の, unrestrained; free; independent. —不羈獨立の精神に富む, to be rich in unrestrained and independent spirit.

fuki (附記する), *vt.* to write [put down] in addition; add.

fūki (風紀), *n.* morale; discipline; public morality. —風紀嚴肅な軍隊, a well-disciplined army. —風紀を紊る, to be injurious to public morality. —風紀を振肅する, to reestablish public morality. ¶ 風紀紊亂, demoralization.

fūki (富貴), *n.* ① wealth and rank; the wealthy and noble (人).

fukiage(吹上げ), *n.* ❶ a fountain. ❷ (相場騰貴) rise. —吹き上げる, to blow up; spout.

fukiburi (吹降), *n.* rain with wind; windy rain; rain and wind.

fukichigiru (吹きちぎる), *vt.* to blow off.

fukichirasu (吹散らす), *vt.* to overblow; blow about; scatter.

fukidasu (吹出·噴出す), *vi.* Ⓢ 吹出·噴出る. ❶〔噴出〕(*a*) (水·血など) to spout; spurt out; gush out: (*b*) (瓦斯·蒸氣など) to blow off: (*c*) (火山など) to erupt. ❷〔吹出〕(腫物·蕁など) to break out; exude (樹脂·汗). ❸ (噴飯) to burst out laughing; burst into laughter. **——,** *vt.* ❶ (*a*) (水·血など) to spout; spurt: (*b*) (瓦斯·蒸氣など) to blow off. ❷ (*a*) (息を) to breathe forth: (*b*) (火·煙·灰など) to emit; send out: (*c*) (芽など) to put [send] forth. ☞ *funshutsu* (噴出する).

fukidemono (吹出物, 腫物), *n.* a rash; a pimple; an eruption.

fukigen (不機嫌), *n.* displeasure; ill [bad] humour; glumness. —不機嫌の, displeased; glum; sulky. —不機嫌である, to be in a pet; be out of humour [temper; sorts].

fukiharau (吹拂ふ), *vt.* to blow away. —雲を吹き拂ふ(風が), to clear the sky from clouds.

fukikaeru (葺替へる), *vt.* to reroof; rehatch; retile.

fukikaesu (吹返す), *v.* to come to oneself. —息を吹き返す, to come to life [oneself] again.

fukikakeru (吹掛ける), *v.* ❶ to blow *upon.* ❷(價格を大きく言ふ) to ask a high price. ❸(喧嘩など) to provoke; challenge. —息(霧)を吹き掛ける, to breathe (spray) *upon.* —大きく吹き掛ける, to make an exorbitant demand [a tall order]. —人に喧嘩を吹きかける, to pick a quarrel with another; provoke another to a quarrel.

fukikesu (吹消す), *vt.* to blow out (燈火を).

fukikomu (吹込む), *v.* ❶ (蓄音器などへ) to sing [speak] *into.* ❷(鼓吹する) to prompt; quicken (元氣を); inspire (同上). —魂を吹き込む, to breathe a spirit *into.* —蠟管に唄を吹き込む, to sing into a wax roller. —隙間から風が吹き込む, The wind blows in through the crevices.

fukikomu (拭込む), *vt.* to wipe thoroughly. —拭き込んだ縁側, the verandah rubbed bright.

fukimari (不極の), *a.* unfixed; undecided; irregular (不規則).

fukimekuru (吹剝る), *vt.* to blow off. —屋根を吹き剝る, to blow off the roof.

fukin (布巾, 拭布), *n.* a towel; a napkin (特に食卓用の); a dish-cloth (皿拭).

fukin (附近), *n.* neighbourhood; vicinity; environs (あまはり). —東京附近, the environs of Tōkyō. —この附近に, in this neighbourhood.

fukin (賦金), *n.* ❶ (賦拂) (an) instalment. ❷ (公課) a tax; an imposition.

fūkin (風琴), *n.* an organ; an accordion (手風琴); a harmonica (口風琴).

fukinagashi (吹流), *n.* a streamer; a pennon; a pennant (檣頭の).

fukin'itsu (不均一の), *a.* ununiform; unequal.

fukinsei (不均齊の), *a.* asymmetrical.

fukinshin (不謹愼な), *a.* imprudent; indiscreet; immodest. —不謹愼な行爲, imprudent conduct.

fukintō (不均等の), *a.* unequal.

fukiorosu (吹下す), *v.* to blow down.

fūkiri (封切), *n.* ❶ (封を切ること) unsealing; breaking a seal. ❷ (始めてのこと) opening; the first presentation. ¶ 封切(活動)寫眞, released films [reels].

fukiritsu (不規律), *n.* indiscipline; want of discipline. —不規律の, undisciplined; irregular.

fukiryō (不器量), *n.* =*bukiryō.*

fukisarashi (吹曝), *n.* bleakness; draughtiness; exposure to weather. —吹曝しの, bleak; draughty; wind-swept.

fukishikiru (吹頻る), *vi.* Ⓢ 吹荒む. to bluster; rage; blow violently [hard; heavily]. **——,** *a.* blusterous; boisterous; raging.

fukiso (不起訴), *n.* 【法】 non-prosecution; dropping a case. —不起訴になつた, The case was dropped.

fukisōji (拭掃除), *n.* house-work; sweeping and wiping.

fukisoku (不規則), *n.* irregularity. **——-na,** *a.* irregular; snatchy; fitful. —不規則な生活, irregular life. ¶ 不規則變化, 【文】 irregularity.

fukitaosu (吹倒す), *vt.* to blow down; blow over.

fukitobasu (吹飛す), *vt.* ❶ (風が) to blow off. ❷ (法螺で) to blow up.

fukitōshi (吹通), *n.* passage of wind; ventilation. —吹通しの好い座敷, a well-ventilated room.

fukitoru (拭取る), *vt.* to wipe out; wipe up.

fukitsu (不吉), *n.* unluckiness; an ill omen; inauspiciousness. **——-na,** *a.* unlucky; ill-omened; inauspicious. —不吉な夢, an unlucky dream. —不吉の兆, an ill [evil; unlucky] omen.

fukitsukeru (吹附ける), *vt.* to blow *against*; sweep *against.* —岸に吹き附けられる, to be blown [driven] ashore. —火焰を吹き附ける, to blow the flames *upon.*

fukiwakeru (吹分ける), *vt.* ❶ (簸る) to winnow. ❷【冶金】(製錬) to smelt. ❸ (分析) to assay.

fukiya (吹矢), *n.* a blow-gun.

fukiyamu (吹止む), *vi.* to cease to blow; blow itself out; rage itself out; blow over.

fukiyose (吹寄せ), *n.* a drift; a snow-drift. —吹き寄せる, to drift (風が雪を); drive [blow] together.

fukkatsu (復活), *n.* ❶ (蘇生) revival; resurrection. ❷ (再興) resuscitation; restoration. —復活さす, ① (蘇生) to revive; resuscitate; bring [restore] to life. ② (再興する) to resuscitate; restore. —復活する, (蘇生する) to revive; return to life; be restored. ¶ 復活祭, the Resurrection; the Easter.

fukkiru (吹切る), *vi.* to open; burst.

fukko (復古), *n.* restoration; revival of the ancient régime.

fukkō (復校; 復興; 腹稿), *n.* =

fukukō. ⌈*koku.*⌉
Fukkoku (佛國), *n.* =*Futsu-*⌋
fukkyū (復舊), *n.* =*fukukyū.*
fukō (不孝), *n.* unfiliality; undutifulness [to one's parents]. —不孝の, undutiful; unfilial. ¶ 不孝者, an unfilial [undutiful] child
fukō (不幸), *n.* ❶ (心の) unhappiness. ❷ (不運) (a) misfortune. ❸ (災難) a disaster. ❹ (死去) death. —重ね重ねの[打續く]不幸, a series of misfortunes. —不幸中の幸, a piece of fortune [luck] in one's misfortune. —不幸な, unhappy; unfortunate. —不幸にも; 不幸にして, unhappily; unfortunately. (不幸にも息子を失ッた, He had the misfortune to lose his son.) —不幸と見える幸福, a blessing in disguise. —不幸に遇ふ, to meet with a misfortune; have a misfortune; suffer a reverse.
fūkō (風光), *n.* natural beauties; scenery. ¶ 風光明媚, enchanting views [scenery].
fukōhei (不公平な), *a.* one-sided; unfair; partial. —不公平な審判, an unfair decision. —不公平に, one-sidedly; unfairly; partially.
fukōi (不行爲), *n.* omission; inaction; a negative act.
fukoku (布告), *n.* a decree; a proclamation; an edict. —布告する, to decree; proclaim.
fukoku (富國), *n.* ❶ enriching a country. ❷ (富める國) a rich country. ¶ 富國策, a plan for national enrichment.
fukōsei (不公正), *n.* inequity; injustice; partiality. —不公正の, inequitable; unjust; partial.
fukotsu (跗骨), *n.* 【解】 the tarsus; the foot-bone.
fuku (服), *n.* ❶ (衣服) clothes; a garment; a dress. ❷ (服裝) dress; costume. ❸ (洋服) foreign clothes; a foreign suit. —服を代へる, to change one's clothes. ¶ 服地, cloth.
fuku (副), *a.* assistant; auxiliary, secondary. ——, *pref.* vice-; sub-.
fuku (福), *n.* ❶ (幸福) good fortune; luck; happiness. ❷ (福貴) fortune; wealth. —福を降す, to bless.
fuku (吹·噴く), *v.* ❶ (吹) to blow. ❷ (噴) to spout; emit. ☞ *fukidasu.* ❸ (出息) to breathe out. ❹ (吹き鳴らす) to blow (喇叭·笛などを); play *on* (管樂器を); whistle (口笛·汽笛など). ❺ (萌す) to sprout. ❻ (鑄る) to coin; mint. ❼ (吹分ける) to smelt. —笛を吹く, to play (on) the flute. —芽を吹く, to send up a shoot. —煙を噴く, to emit smoke.
fuku (拭く), *vt.* to wipe; wipe away [off; out] (拭取る). —手を拭く, to wipe one's hands. —ハンケチで涙を拭く, to wipe away tears with a handkerchief.
fuku (葺く), *vt.* to cover; thatch (藁·藺等で); tile (瓦で). —草で葺いた屋根, a grass-thatched roof.
fukuan (腹案), *n.* the general plan in one's mind. —腹案ある演說, a set speech.
fukube (匏瓜), *n.* ❶ 【植】 the bottle-gourd. ❷ (瓢) a gourd.
fukubiki (福引), *n.* a lottery; a tombola. ⌈founder.⌉
fukubotsu (覆沒する), *v.* to⌋
fukubu (腹部), *n.* 【解】 the abdomen; the abdominal region.
fukubukuro (福袋), *n.* the lucky bag.
fukubukushii (福福しい), *a.* fortunate-looking; happy-looking.
fukuchō (副長), *n.* ❶ (副艦長) a commander. ❷ a vice-principal [-director].
fukudairi (復代理), *n.* ❶ subagency. ❷ (復代理人) a subagent.
fukudaitōryō (副大統領), *n.* a vice-president.
fukueki (服役), *n.* ❶ (兵役に服す) service (in the army or navy). ❷ (苦役に服す) servitude. ——**-suru**, *v.* ❶ to serve in the army (or navy). ❷ to serve a sentence. —滿期服役する, to serve one's full time.
fukugichō (副議長), *n.* a vice--president; a deputy speaker.
fukugō (複合の), *a.* compound; complex; composite. ¶ 複合名詞, 【文】 a compound noun. —複合語, a compound (word.)
fukugyō (副業), *n.* subsidiary work [business]; by-business.
fukugyō (復業する), *vi.* to resume [return to] one's work.
fukuhai (腹背), *n.* the front and rear. —腹背に敵を受ける, to have the enemy in front and rear.
fukuhei (伏兵), *n.* an ambuscade; an ambush; troops in ambush. —伏兵を置く, to make [construct; lay] an ambush. ⌈the throne.⌉
fukuheki (復辟), *n.* restoration to⌋
fukuheki (腹壁), *n.* abdominal wall. ⌈a counterpart.⌉
fukuhon (複本), *n.* a duplicate;⌋
fokuhoṅisei (複本位制), *n.* 【經】 bimetallism; bimetallic system.
fukuiku (馥郁たる), *a.* fragrant; odorous; sweet-scented. —馥郁たる淸香, delicate fragrance.
fukuin (幅員), *n.* ❶ (幅) breadth; width. ❷ (廣袤) area; extent.

fukuin (福音), *n.* ❶ (基督教の) the [Christian] gospel. ❷ (喜びの音づれ) a godsend; glad tidings. ¶ 福音傳道, evangelism; evangelization. (福音傳道者, a minister; an evangelist.) —四福音書, the four gospels.

fukuin (復員する), *vt.* to demobilize. ¶ 復員令, demobilization orders.

fukujū (服從), *n.* obedience; submission; subordination. —服從的, submissive; obedient. —服從する, to obey; submit *to*; bend *to*.

fukujusō (福壽草), *n.* 【植】 Adonis amurensis (pheasant's eye の類·學名).

fukukaichō (副會長), *n.* a vice-chairman.

fukukan (副官), *n.* (將官附) an aide-de-camp [*pl.* aides-de-camp] (A.D.C. と略す); an adjutant. ¶ 高級副官, a senior adjutant. —副官部, the adjutant's office.

fukukanchō (副艦長), *n.* a commander.

fukukantoku (副監督), *n.* a dean; an archdeacon.

fukuken (復權), *n.* rehabilitation.

fukuki (復歸する), *vi.* to return *to*; revert *to*.

fukukō (復校), *n.* return to school. —復校を許される, to be allowed to return to school; be readmitted into school.

fukukō (復航), *n.* return [homeward] voyage.

fukukō (復興), *n.* revival; resuscitation. —復興する, to revive. —國文學の復興, the revival of the national literature. —復興事業, revival works.

fukukō (腹腔), *n.* the abdominal cavity.

fukukōshin (匐行疹), *n.* 【醫】 herpes; serpigo.

fukukyū (匐球), *n.* a grounder (野球); a daisy-cutter (クリケット).

fukukyū (復仇), *n.* reprisal; retaliation.

fukukyū (復舊), *n.* restoration; recovery; restitution. —復舊さす, to restore (to the original state). —復舊する, to be restored. —復舊工事を起す, to commence repairs [restoration works].

fukumaden (伏魔殿), *n.* a pandemonium; an enchanted palace.

fukumaku (腹膜), *n.* 【解】 the peritoneum. ¶ 腹膜炎, peritonitis.

fukumei (復命する), *vi.* to report the result (of a mission).

fukumen (覆面), *n.* covering the face; a mask (假面); a veil (面被). —覆面の强盜, a masked burglar. —覆面する, to mask oneself; veil oneself; muffle the face. ¶ 覆面頭巾, a domino; a muffler.

fukumeru (含める), *vt.* ❶ (籠める) to include; put *into*. ❷ (云ひ含める) to give private instructions; give a person to understand (that). ❸ (口に入れさす) to feed from the mouth.

fukumu (服務), *n.* (public) service. ¶ 服務時間, hours of service; business [office] hours. —服務規律, the public service regulations.

fukumu (含·銜む), *vt.* ❶ (口に入れる) to keep [hold] in one's mouth. ❷ (心に) (*a*) (留意) to bear in mind: (*b*) (懷く) to bear; harbour; entertain: (*c*) (怨を) to bear malice [grudge] *against*. ❸ (內在) (*a*) (含有) to hold; contain: (*b*) (含蓄) to imply: (*c*) (包含) to include; comprise; embrace. —鹽分を含む, to contain a salt. —顏に笑を含んで, with a smile in his face. —其他の雜費を含む, [*a.*] including other sundries. —此事をお含み置き下さい, Please bear this matter in mind.

fukurahagi (腓), *n.* 【解】 the calf.

fukuraka (脹かな), *a.* stout; corpulent; fat; plump.

fukuramu (脹む), *vi.* to bulge; swell (out); rise (麵麭が). ☞ *fukureru.*

fukureru (脹れる), *vi.* ❶ to swell; bulge; puff (up). ❷ (帆が風で) to belly; draw. ❸ (俗)(怒る) to be sulky; sulk. —脹れた, baggy; plump; bulgy. —脹れ出す, to bulge; swell. ¶ 脹れ面, ① (ふくれた顏) a swollen face. ② (憤怒の面色) sulky looks; sulks. (脹れ面をする, to be in the sulks; look sulky.)

fukuri (福利), *n.* prosperity; welfare; well-being. —國民の福利を增進する, to promote national prosperity.

fukuri (複利), *n.* compound interest. —複利で計算する, to reckon at compound interest.

fukurin (覆輪), *n.* a border; an ornamental border [rim].

fukuro (袋, 囊), *n.* ❶ a bag; a sack; a pouch. ❷ (巾著) a purse. ❸ (蜜柑·橙等の中の房の外包) a loculus. —袋の中の鼠, a mouse in a trap. —袋に入れる, to (put into a) bag.

fukurō (梟), *n.* 【鳥】 the owl.

fukurogumo (袋蜘蛛), *n.* the wolf-spider.

fukuroji (袋地), *n.* ❶ (袋の布地) bagging. ❷ (袋地所) a land-locked piece of land.

fukurokuju (福祿壽), *n.* ❶ (福·祿·壽) wealth, happiness and long life. ❷ [F-] the God of longevity.

fukuromachi (袋町), *n.* a blind alley [lane]; a *cul-de-sac.*
fukuromono (袋物), *n.* pouches. ¶ 袋物商, a dealer in pouches.
fukuronezumi (袋鼠), *n.* 【哺乳】 the kangaroo.
fukurotataki (袋叩にする), *vt.* to drub; maul; give (a person) a drubbing.
fukuryō (服量), *n.* dosage; a dose.
fukuryōji (副領事), *n.* a vice-consul.
fukusa (袱紗), *n.* a small cloth-wrapper. —袱紗に包む, to wrap up in a small wrapper.
fukusanbutsu (副產物), *n.* a by-product.
fukusatsu (複殺), *n.* 【野球】 a double play.
fukusayō (副作用), *n.* secondary reaction.
fukusei (服制), *n.* the uniform system. —服制を一定する, to adopt a definite uniform.
fukusei (複製), *n.* reproduction; reprint. —複製する, to reprint; reproduce. —複製を許さず, reproduction [reprint] prohibited.
fukuseki (復席する), *vi.* to resume [return to] one's seat.
fukuseki (復籍する), *vi.* to return to one's original family.
fukusen (伏線), *n.* ❶ an under-plot. ❷ =*yobōsen.* ❸ (奸策) an intrigue. —伏線を張る, to lay an under-plot.
fukusen (複線), *n.* 【鐵道】 a double track. ¶ 架空複線式, the double trolley system.
fukusha (伏射), *n.* lying-down fire. —伏射する, to fire lying.
fukusha (複寫), *n.* reproduction; reprint; facsimile. —複寫する, to reproduce; copy. ¶ 複寫版, a mimeograph; a papyrograph.
fukusha (輻射), *n.* radiation. ☞ *hōsha* (放射). —輻射する, to radiate.
fukushachō (副社長), *n.* a vice-president.
fukushi (副使), *n.* a vice-ambassador; an assistant envoy.
fukushi (副詞), *n.* 【文】 the adverb. —副詞的に, adverbially. ¶ 副詞句, an adverbial phrase.
fukushi (福祉), *n.* welfare; well-being; happiness.
fukushihainin (副支配人), *n.* a sub-manager.
fukushiki (複式), *n.* 【數】 a compound expression. ¶ 複式機關, a compound engine.
fukushiki-kokyū (腹式呼吸), *n.* abdominal respiration.
fukushin (腹心), *n.* ❶ (心の奥底) the bottom of one's heart. ❷ (股肱) a confidential [faithful] follower. —腹心の人, a right-hand man. —腹心の友, a bosom-friend; a confidant.
fukushin (覆審), *n.* reconsideration; review. —覆審する, to reconsider; review. ¶ 覆審法院, a court of review.
fukushin (唐紅), *n.* fuchsine.
fukusho (副書), *n.* a copy.
fukusho (副署), *n.* a counter-signature. —副署する, [*vt.*] to countersign.
fukushō (副章), *n.* (勳章の) a decoration attached to another.
fukushoku (復職), *n.* resumption of office; reappointment; reinstatement. —復職さす, to reinstate. —復職する, to resume one's office; return to one's former post.
fukushokubutsu (副食物), *n.* supplementary food; relish (おかず).
fukushū (復習), *n.* review. —復習する, [*vt.*] to review; go over.
fukushū (復讐), *n.* revenge; vengeance; retaliation. —人に復讐する, to revenge oneself on [upon] a person; be revenged on [upon] a person. —復讐心に燃える, to burn with revenge. ¶ 復讐戰, a war of vengeance; a return match.
fukusō (伏奏する), *v.* to report to the Throne.
fukusō (服裝), *n.* dress; costume. —服裝を改める, to change one's dress.
fukusō (輻湊), *n.* assembling; gathering; crowding. —輻湊する, to assemble; crowd; gather.
fukusōri (副總理), *n.* Ⓢ 副總裁. a vice-president.
fukusū (複數), *n.* 【文】 the plural (number).
fukusui (覆水盆に返らず), "Lost happiness never returns."
fukusuke (福助), *n.* a big-headed manikin.
fuku-suru (服する), *v.* ❶ (從ふ) to obey; submit *to*; yield *to.* ❷ (從へる) to subdue; subjugate. ❸ (役に) to serve. ❹ (藥を) to take. —理に服する, to submit [yield] to reason.
fuku-suru (復する), *vi.* to be restored *to*; return *to.* ——, *vt.* to recover; restore; resume. —座に復する, to resume [return to] one's seat.
fukutetsu (覆轍), *n.* another's failure. —覆轍を履む, to repeat another's failure.
fukutō (復黨する), *vi.* to return to [rejoin] one's former party.
fukutōdori (副頭取), *n.* a vice-president.
fukutsu (不屈の), *a.* indomitable; inflexible; unyielding.

fukutsū (腹痛), *n.* gastralgia; a pain in the abdomen.

fukuyaku (服藥する), *vi.* to take medicine. —服藥さす, to administer medicine.

fukuyō (服用する), *vt.* to take. —鑛泉を服用する, to drink the mineral waters.

fukuyō (服膺する), *vt.* to keep in mind; lay to heart; treasure up (in memory).

fukuyō (複葉), *n.* ❶【植】a compound leaf. ❷ (複葉飛行機) a biplane.

fukuzai (伏在する), *vi.* to lie concealed.

fukuzai (服罪する), *vi.* ❶ (服罪) to submit to a sentence; serve a sentence. ❷ (自白) to confess guilt; plead guilty.

fukuzatsu (複雜な), *a.* complicated; intricate. —複雜する, to be complicated.

fukuzō (腹藏なき), *a.* unreserved; frank; candid. —腹藏なく, unreservedly; without reserve; frankly.

fukyō (不況), *n.* dulness; slackness; depression. —貿易の不況, trade depression.

fukyō (不興), *n.* displeasure; ill-humour. —不興を蒙る, to incur displeasure; fall into disgrace.

fukyō (布教), *n.* mission; propagandism. ¶ 布教師, a missionary; a propagandist.

fukyō (富强), *n.* wealth and power; greatness.

fūkyō (風敎), *n.* public morals. —風敎に害がある, to be injurious to public morals.

fukyū (不朽), *n.* incorruption【聖書】; immortality; perpetuity. —不朽の, deathless; immortal; imperishable. —名を不朽に傳ふ, to hand down one's name for ever.

fukyū (不急の), *a.* unurgent; unpressing.

fukyū (普及), *n.* diffusion (新說·敎育など); spread (敎育など); propagation (新說など). —普及する, to spread; diffuse.

fukyū (腐朽), *n.* decay; decomposition. —腐朽する, to decay; decompose; grow rotten; rot.

fumajime (不眞面目の), *a.* frivolous; unserious.

fuman (不滿-足), *n.* dissatisfaction; discontent; displeasure. —に不滿である(を懷く), ①(不滿足) to be dissatisfied [discontent] *with*. ②(不快) to be displeased *at* [*with*]. —不滿の色をあらはす, to betray discontent.

fumei (不明), *n.* ❶ (不分明) obscurity; indistinctness. ❷(不敏) lack of sagacity. **——-no,** *a.* ❶ dark; obscure; indistinct. ❷ unwise; unworthy. —意味不明の文字, an obscure word. —余の不明の致す所である, to be due to lack of sagacity on my part. —彼の行方は今尙不明である, His whereabouts is still unknown.

fumeisū (不名數), *n.*【數】an abstract number.

fumeiyo (不名譽), *n.* dishonour; ignominy; discredit.

fumenboku (不面目), *n.* disgrace; opprobrium; shame. —さうするのを不面目に思ふ, to think it a shame to do so.

fumetsu (不滅の), *a.* immortal; imperishable; indestructible.

fumi (文), *n.* ❶ (書物) a book. ❷ (手紙) a letter. ❸ (艶書) a *billet-doux*【佛】; a love-letter.

fūmi (風味), *n.* flavour; taste; relish. —風味ある; 風味のよい, savoury; tasty; spicy. —薄荷の風味がある, to taste [savour] of mint. —...に風味を附ける, to flavour; season.

fumidai (踏臺), *n.* a stool; a footstool; a step. —人を踏臺にする, to use a man as a stepping-stone.

fumidasu (踏出す), *v.* to step forward; take a step forward.

fumidokoro (踏處), *n.* a spot to step on; a stepping-place.

fumihazusu (踏外す), *v.* to miss one's foot [footing]; make a false step.

fumiishi (踏石), *n.* a stepping-stone; a step-stone.

fumikatameru (踏固める), *vt.* to stamp [tread] down.

fumikesu (踏消す), *vt.* to stamp [tread] out.

fumikiri (踏切), *n.* ❶【鐵道】a crossing. ❷【相撲】stepping out of bounds. ❸【競技】the scratch; the take-off. ¶ 踏切板, (競技) the take-off plank. —踏切番, a gateman (at a crossing).

fumikiru (踏切る), *vt.* to step out of (bounds).

fumiko (踏子), *n.* a pedal; a treadle.

fumikoeru (踏越える), *vt.* to step over.

fumikomu (踏込む), *vt.* ❶ (踏入る) to step into. ❷ (侵入) to rush into; break into. ❸ (警官の手入) to raid *into* (賭場等に).

fumikorosu (踏殺す), *vt.* to trample to death.

fumikosu (踏越す), *vt.* to step across. —人の頭の上を踏み越す, to step over a man's head.

fumikotaeru (踏堪へる), *vi.* to hold out; keep one's ground.

fumimochi (不身持), *n.* profligacy; misbehaviour; loose conduct.

fumin (不眠の), *a.* sleepless; wakeful; insomnious. —不眠不休で, without rest and sleep. ¶ 不眠症, 【醫】 insomnia; vigilance; sleeplessness.

fuminarasu (踏均らす), *vt.* to tread down; beat. —踏み均らした道, the beaten track.

fuminijiru (踏みにじる), *vt.* to trample under foot. ☞ *jūrin.*

fumitaosu (踏倒す), *vt.* ❶ to trample down. ❷ (不拂) to evade payment; cheat of. ❸ (輕蔑的評價) to beat down unreasonably. —借金を踏み倒す, to evade the payment of one's debts. —踏み倒した値段をつける, to put a ridiculously low price (*upon*).

fumitodomaru (踏止まる), *vi.* to take one's stand; make a stand; stand [hold] one's ground. —踏み止まって抵抗する, to make a stand (against an enemy).

fumitsubusu (踏潰す), *vt.* to crush [smash] by treading on.

fumitsukeru (踏附ける), *vt.* ❶ to trample *on*; tread [trample] under foot. ❷ (輕蔑) to scorn; spurn; treat with contempt.

fumō (不毛), *n.* barrenness; infertility; sterility. —不毛の地, a sterile [barren] land.

fumon (不問に付する), *v.* to let pass; pass over; leave unnoticed.

fumoto (麓), *n.* the foot; the bottom.

fumu (踏む), *v.* ❶ (踏附ける) to tread *on*; stamp *on*. ❷ (評價) to appraise; estimate; value. ❸ (履行) to keep; make good; fulfil. ❹ (韻字を) to rhyme. ❺ (拂はぬ) to cheat of; evade payment. —私の踏んだ所では, according to my valuation. —實地を踏んで來た人, one who has been through the mill. —踏んだり蹴たりする, to add insult to injury. —薄氷を履む, to step on thin ice. —約を履む, to make good [fulfil] one's promise; be true to a contract.

fumuki (不向の), *a.* unsuitable; unmarketable; unsalable. —不向の品, an unsuitable [unmarketable] article; an article in no demand. —當世に不向な, unsuited to the present age.

fun (分), *n.* ❶ a minute (時·度の). ❷ one-tenth of a *monme* (秤の). —十五分, fifteen minutes; a quarter of an hour (a degree). —一時四十五分, one forty-five; a quarter to two. —三時三十分, three thirty; half past three. —四時四十分, twenty minutes to five. —東經十度二十分, 10 degrees 20 minutes east longitude (10° 20′ E. Long.)

fun (糞), *n.* excrement; dung; droppings (鳥·獸の) 〔俗〕.

funa (鮒), *n.* 【魚】 the crucian; the Prussian [crucian] carp.

funaaka (船淦), *n.* bilge(-water).

funaashi (船脚), *n.* (船の速力) headway; speed; (吃水) draught.

funaasobi (舟遊), *n.* boating; outing in a pleasure-boat.

funabashi (船橋), *n.* a pontoon (-bridge); a bridge of boats.

funabin (船便で), by ship.

funachin (船賃), *n.* ❶ (乘客の) passage; fare. ❷ (荷物の) freight; freightage. ❸ (貸船料) boat-hire.

funadoiya (船問屋), *n.* a shipping agent. 「company.」

funagaisha (船會社), *n.* a ship

funahiki (船曳), *n.* towage. ¶ 船曳路, a tow-path; a towing-path.

funakaji (船火事), *n.* a ship fire a fire on a ship.

funani (船荷), *n.* cargo; freight; lading. —船荷を卸す, to unload cargo. ¶ 故障(無故障)船荷證劵, a foul (clean) bill of lading.

funanori (船乘), *n.* a boatsman; a sailor; a seaman. —船乘となる, to take to the sea; go to sea. ¶ 船乘業(生活), seafaring profession (life).

funaoroshi (船卸), *n.* ❶ (進水) the launching of a ship; the launch. ❷ (荷卸) discharge. —船卸しする, [*vt.*] ① to launch. ② to discharge; unship; unload.

funare (不慣の), *a.* unaccustomed; inexperienced; unused. —勞働に不慣れの, unaccustomed to labour. —不慣れの土地で, in a strange land.

funawatashi (船渡), *n.* ❶ (船で人馬等を渡すこと) ferry; ferriage. ❷ (渡船場) a ferry.

funayado (船宿), *n.* ❶ (船客荷物取扱所) a shipping agent. ❷ (遊船宿) a place for letting pleasure-boats; a boat-keeper's. ❸ (船乘宿) an inn for sailors.

funayoi (船暈), *n.* seasickness. —船暈する(せぬ)人, a bad (good) sailor.

funazumi (船積), *n.* shipping; shipment. ¶ 船積港, a port of shipping. —船積荷物, shipping goods. —船積送狀, a shipping invoice. —船積取扱人, a shipping-agent.

funbaru (踏張る), *v.* ❶ (股を張る) to straddle; stride. ❷ (飽くまで主張する) to insist *upon*; maintain stubbornly; hold fast *to*.

❷ (力を入れる) to exert oneself. —踏張り通す, to stand out; hold out.

funben (糞便), *n.* dejecta; night-soil.

funbetsu (分別), *n.* discretion; judgment; discernment. —分別のない人, a man without discretion. —分別がつく, to cut one's wisdom [eye] -tooth. —分別盛りの年で, at the age of mature discernment.

funbo (墳墓), *n.* a tomb; a grave; a sepulchre. —墳墓の地, home; one's birthplace.

fundakuru (奪取る), *vt.* to snatch; switch.

fundo (憤怒), *n.* anger; rage; wrath.

fundō (分銅), *n.* a counterweight; a counterpoise; a poise.

fundoshi (褌), *n.* a loin-cloth; a waist-cloth. —褌を締める, to gird up one's loins.

fune (舟, 船), *n.* (a) craft. ❶ (小舟) a boat. ❷ (大船) a vessel (普通漕ぎ船より大きなもの), a ship (航海大船, 又マストのある大小船). ❸ (槽) a tank; a trough. —船に乗る, to take boat; get [go] on board [a vessel]. —船から海中に落ち込む, to fall overboard.

funegai (船貝), *n.* 【貝】 the ark-shell.

funenshitsu (不燃質の), *a.* incombustible.

funesshin (不熱心), *n.* want of zeal; lukewarmness. —不熱心な, half-hearted; lukewarm.

fungai (憤慨する), *vi.* to burn with indignation; be indignant *at*. —, *vt.* to resent.

fungeki (憤激する), *vi.* to flash up [out]; be enraged. —憤激さす, to stir a person's blood.

fungi (紛議), *n.* dispute; dissensions; complication. —紛議を醸す, to lead to dissension. —紛議を調停する, to mediate in a dispute.

fungō (吻合する), *vi.* to conform *to*; agree *with*; harmonize *with*.

funiai (不似合の), *a.* ❶ unsuitable; unbefitting; unbecoming. ❷ ill-matched; ill-assorted. —不似合の夫婦, an ill-matched couple. 學者に不似合の態度, an attitude unbecoming to a scholar.

fuñiki (雰圍氣), *n.* the atmosphere.

funin (赴任する), *vi.* to start [leave] for one's post; proceed to one's post.

funinjō (不人情), *n.* unkindness (不深切); heartlessness (無情). —不人情の, unkind; heartless; unfeeling.

funinka (不認可), *n.* disallowance; disapprobation; rejection. —不認可となる, to be rejected; be disallowed.

funinki (不人氣), *n.* unpopularity. —不人氣の, unpopular.

funinshō (不姙症), *n.* sterility.

funjō (紛擾), *n.* complication; disturbance; disorder.

funka (噴火), *n.* an eruption. —噴火する, to erupt; burst out. ¶ 噴火口, a crater. —噴火山, a volcano.

funkei (刎頸の), *a.* most intimate; lifelong. —刎頸の友, a devoted friend; a bosom friend; a most intimate friend. —刎頸の交を結ぶ, to contract a lifelong friendship.

funki (奮起), *n.* excitement; stirring up. —奮起する, to arouse oneself; stir up; brace oneself up.

funkotsu (粉骨碎身する), *vi.* to exert oneself to the utmost; do one's utmost; make one's best exertions.

funkyū (紛糾), *n.* complication; entanglement; disorder. —紛糾さす, to throw into confusion [disorder]; complicate; entangle. —ますます紛糾する, to become more complicated.

funman (憤懣), *n.* indignation; resentment.

funmatsu (粉末), *n.* powder; dust. —粉末にする, to pulverize; powder; reduce to powder.

funmuki (噴霧器), *n.* a spray; an atomizer; a vaporizer.

funnyō (糞尿), *n.* night-soil. ☞ *funben*. ¶ 糞尿汲取人, a night-man.

funō (不能), *n.* ❶ (不可能) impossibility. ❷ (無能) inability; incompetence [-cy].

funori (布海苔), *n.* ❶ 【植】 Gloiopeltis furcata (學名). ❷ gloiopeltis glue.

funpan (噴飯する), *vi.* to burst out laughing. —噴飯の至りである[に堪へない], to be most ludicrous.

funpatsu (奮發), *n.* exertion; vigorous effort. —奮發する, to exert oneself; make an effort.

funpon (粉本), *n.* 【畫】 a study; a sketch.

funpun (紛紛), *ad.* confusedly (混亂); in disorder; pell-mell (紛亂). —紛々たる, confused; disordered. —落花紛々として飛ぶ, Fallen flowers fly pell-mell.

funran (紛亂さす), *vt.* to confuse; muddle up [together].

funrei (奮勵), *n.* endeavour; exertion; effort; push. —奮勵する, to endeavour *to*; strive *to*; make an effort [a push] *to*; get up steam.

funrin (分釐), *n.* a grain; a little.

—分釐もたがはぬ, not to differ in the least.

funsai (粉碎する), *vt.* to break to pieces; comminute; pulverize. —敵を粉碎する, to crush the enemy. —一擊の下に粉碎する, to shatter with a blow.

funsen (噴泉), *n.* a fountain (噴水); a geyser (間歇泉).

funsen (奮戰), *n.* a desperate fight. —奮戰する, to fight desperately.

funshi (憤死する), *vi.* to die with indignation; die in a fit of anger.

funshin (分針), *n.* the minute-hand.

funshin (奮進する), *vi.* to push; make a push *for*.

funshitsu (紛失), *n.* loss. —紛失する, to lose. —紛失屆を出す, to report a loss. ¶ 紛失物, a lost [missing] article. —紛失主, the loser; the owner of a lost article.

funshoku (粉飾する), *vt.* to paint; ornament; adorn.

funshutsu (噴出), *n.* eruption (火山の); gush (水・石油など); spouting (水・血など). —噴出する, ① [*vi.*] to erupt; jet; spurt. ② [*vt.*] to spout; vomit (火山・煙突が); emit. ☞ *fukidasu.* ③ [*a.*] eruptive; salient (水等の) [詩].

funsō (扮裝), *n.* impersonation; make-up; disguise (變裝). ——**suru,** *vt.* to disguise; dress up; impersonate; play [act] the part *of*; support the character *of*. —女子に扮裝する, to be disguised [dressed up] as a woman.

funsō (紛爭), *n.* dissension; dispute; complication. —紛爭の渦中に投ずる, to throw oneself into [embroil oneself in] a strife.

funsui (噴水), *n.* a fountain; a jet (水の). ¶ 噴水井戸, an Artesian well.

fun-suru (扮する), *vt.* to act [play] the part *of* (役に); impersonate. ☞ *funsō* (扮裝する). —豐太閤に扮する, to impersonate the Taikō.

funtan (粉炭), *n.* slack (煉炭用石炭粉末); dust-coal.

funtō (奮鬪), *n.* struggle; hard fight. —奮鬪する, to fight; struggle; battle. ¶ 奮鬪生活, a strenuous life.

fuňun (紛紜), *n.* dissension; dispute; complication.

funyoi (不如意), *n.* ❶ going contrary to one's wishes. ❷ (手許の逼迫) narrow circumstances; straits. ——**-no,** *a.* straitened; poor. —不如意の生活を送る, to lead a life of poverty.

fūnyū (封入する), *vt.* to enclose; inclose. —彼の手紙封入御送附申候, I send you his letter under cover.

funzen (憤然), *ad.* indignantly; angrily.

funzen (奮然), *ad.* energetically; strenuously.

funzorikaeru (踏反り返る), *vi.* to fall [bend oneself] backward.

fuon (不穩), *n.* ❶ unrest; disquiet; disorder. ❷ =*fuontō.* ——**-no,** *a.* disquieting; unquiet; threatening; disorderly; unsettled. —不穩の言辭を弄する, to use violent [strong] language. —形勢頗る不穩である, The situation is extremely threatening.

fuontō (不穩當), *n.* ❶ (不適當) inappropriateness. ❷ (過激, 亂暴) immoderateness; violence. ——**-no,** *a.* ❶ inappropriate. ❷ immoderate; violent. —不穩當の語を削る, to strike out inappropriate words.

furachi (不埒), *n.* ❶ (無禮) insolence; rudeness. ❷ (不法) lawlessness; outrageousness. ❸ (不正) villainy; iniquity. ——**-na,** *a.* ❶ insolent; rude. ❷ lawless; outrageous. ❸ reprehensible; wicked; villainous. —不埒な奴, a vicious [an unprincipled] fellow. —不埒な行をする, to misconduct oneself.

furafura (ふらふらする), *vi.* ❶ to be giddy; be dizzy; swim. ❷ to totter; reel; stagger. ——, *a.* ❶ unsteady; shaky. ❷ (眩暈) dizzy; faint; giddy. —足がふらふらする, not steady on his legs.

furai (フライ), *n.* ❶【料理】fry. ❷【野球】(飛球) a fly (ball). ¶ フライ鍋, a frying-pan.

fūraijin (風來人), *n.* ❶ a wanderer; a vagabond. ❷ =*kimagure.*

furan (腐爛), *n.* putrefaction; putridity; ulceration (腫物等の). —腐爛する, to putrefy; decay.

furan (法), *n.* (佛國貨幣) a franc (f. 又は fr. と略す).

furanki (孵卵器), *n.* an incubator; a (an artificial) mother.

furanneru (フランネル), *n.* flannel.

Furansu (佛蘭西), *n.* France. ¶ 佛蘭西大革命, the great French Revolution. —佛蘭西語, French. —佛蘭西人, the French (全體); a Frenchman [*fem.* -woman].

furareru (振られる), *vi.* to be rejected; get the mitten; be shown the cold shoulder.

furarito (ふらりと), *ad.* without notice (だまって); suddenly (ふいと); aimlessly (あてもなく).

furashi-ten (フラシ天), *n.* (織物) plush.

furasu (降らす), *vt.* to make fall. —黃金の雨を降らす, to send a

shower of gold.

furasu (觸らす), *vt.* to spread; make public. —世間へ觸らす, to spread in all quarters; make widely public.

furasuko (フラスコ), *n.* a flask.

furatsuku (ふらつく), *vi.* to feel dizzy [giddy]; swim.

fure (觸), *n.* ❶ (周知) promulgation. ❷ [布令] an official notice; a government proclamation. ❸ (呼報) cry. —布令を出す, to give an official notice. —布令を廻す, to send round an official notice.

furedashi (觸出), *n.* announcement.

furei (不例), *n.* indisposition.

furekomi (觸込), *n.* announcement. —觸れ込む, to announce.

furemawaru (觸廻る), *v.* to cry about; circulate; noise abroad; spread abroad.

furen (不廉の), *a.* dear; high-priced; expensive; costly.

fureru (振れる), *vi.* ❶ (動搖) to shake. ❷ (擺動) to swing. ❸ (偏差) to deflect.

fureru (觸れる), *vi.* ❶ (接觸) to touch. ❷ (牴觸) to conflict *with*; violate; infringe. ❸ =*furasu*. ❹ (狂ふ) to go [run] mad; get crazy. —怒に觸れる, to incur another's anger. —目に觸れる, to meet the eye. —耳に觸れる, to reach the ear. —規則に觸れる, to infringe the rules. —國禁に觸れる, to conflict with the law of the land. —手を觸れるな!, Hands off!; Keep your hands off!

furi (振), *n.* ❶ (振動) (*a*) swing: (*b*) shake. ❷ (舞の仕方) posture (of a dance). ❸ [風] (容子, 顏色, 態度) air; manners; way. ❹ (見せかけ) feint; pretence. —振をつける, (舞踊) to design the postures. —助力する風をして, under the pretence of helping. **——-suru,** *vt.* to affect; pretend; feign. —寢た振する, to feign sleep. —見ぬ (聽かぬ)振する, to shut one's eyes (ears) *to*. —知らぬ振する, to pretend [feign] ignorance.

furi (不利), *n.* disadvantage; unfavourableness. —不利の條件, an unfavourable condition. —不利の地位に立つ, to stand in a disadvantageous position. —不利を來す, to prove disadvantageous.

furi (不理), *n.* unreasonableness; unreason. ☞ *muri.*

furiageru (振上げる), *vt.* to raise; lift. —手を振り上げる, to lift one's hand.

furiai (振合), *n.* comparison (比較); common practice (慣例).

furidashi (振出), *n.* ❶ (藥) an infusion. ❷ (出發點) the starting-point; a throw (雙六の). ❸ (發行) issue; drawing; remittance. —振り出す, ① (振ッて出す) to shake out. ② (藥を) to infuse. ③ (手形を) to draw; issue; remit. ¶ 振出局, the office of issue. —振出人(手形の), a drawer (of a bill); a remitter (of a money order).

furieki (不利益), *n.* disadvantage. —自己の不利益を顧みず, regardless of the disadvantage to himself.

furigana (振假名), *n.* the *kana* attached to an ideograph.

furiharau (振拂ふ), *vt.* to shake off; whisk off (塵など). —引留める手を振り拂ふ, to shake off the hand that stops him.

furikae (振替), *n.* transfer; change. —振替へる, to transfer; change. ¶ 振替貯金, giro-transfer [book-transfer] savings. (振替貯金口座, giro-transfer [book-transfer] savings account.) —振替傳票, a transfer slip.

furikaeru (振返る), *vi.* ❶ (返顧) to turn one's head; turn backward; turn round. ❷ (回想) to recall; recollect; call to mind. —後を振り返る, to look over one's shoulder. —過去を振り返り見る, to look back upon the past.

furikakaru (降りかかる), *vi.* ❶ (泥水・雨など) to spatter; splash *on*; fall *on*. ❷ (災難など) to come *on*; fall *on*; befall.

furikakeru (撒掛ける), *vt.* to sprinkle *on* [*over*].

furikō (不履行), *n.* 【法】 non-performance; non-fulfilment; default. —契約不履行の訴を起す, to bring an action for non-fulfilment of a contract.

furikomerareru (降籠められる), *vi.* to be kept indoors by rain.

furikomu (降込む), *vi.* to blow [in; rain *into*.]

furimaku (振撒く), *vt.* to distribute (分配); sprinkle (水・鹽など); strew (花など). —水を振り撒く, to sprinkle water. —多分の金を振り撒く, to distribute a large sum of money. —愛嬌を振り撒く, to have a smile for everybody; make oneself amiable *to*.

furimawasu (振廻す), *vt.* to brandish; flourish; swing. —棒を振り廻す, to brandish a stick. —官權を振り廻す, to abuse the official authority.

furimi-furazumi (降りみ降らずみ), *ad.* raining at intervals; raining off and on.

furimuku (振り向く), *vi.* to turn;

turn one's face; turn about [round]. —振り向く途端に, just as I turned round.

furin (不倫), *n.* immorality. —不倫の行爲, an immoral act.

fūrin (風鈴), *n.* a bell that rings in the wind. ¶ 風鈴草,【植】the Canterbury bells.

furiotosu (振落す), *vt.* to shake off; spill (馬が乗手を).

furishikiru (降頻る), *vi.* to rain incessantly; fall thick and fast.

furisode (振袖), *n.* long sleeves; a long-sleeved garment.

furisuteru (振捨てる), *vt.* ❶(振放す) to shake off. ❷(遺棄する) to abandon; desert.

furitsu (府立の), *a.* prefectural. —東京府立第一中學校, the First Tōkyō Prefectural Middle School.

furo (風呂), *n.* a bath. —風呂に入る[を使ふ], to have [take] a bath. ¶ 蒸風呂, a vapour [Turkish] bath. —風呂場, a bath-room. —風呂番, a bath-keeper; a bath attendant.

furō (不老), *n.* eternal youth. —不老不死の藥を求める, to seek the elixir of life.

furō (浮浪する), *vi.* to vagabondize; wander about; tramp. ¶ 浮浪人, a tramp; a vagabond; a vagrant.

fūrō (風浪), *n.* wind and waves; heavy seas. —風浪險惡の爲め, on account of the heavy seas.

fūrō (封蠟), *n.* sealing-wax; seal.

furokku (フロック), *n.*【撞球】a fluke.

furokkukōto (フロックコート), *n.* a frock-coat.

furoku (附錄), *n.* an appendix; a supplement. ¶ 日曜附錄, a Sunday supplement.

furoku (浮肋), *n.* a floating rib.

furonzai (不論罪), *n.* a non--punishable [non-indictable] offence.

furoshiki (風呂敷), *n.* a cloth--wrapper. —風呂敷に包む, to wrap in a cloth-wrapper. —大風呂敷をひろげる, to draw the long bow; talk big [tall].

furu (古, 舊), *a.* old; second-hand. ☞ *furui* (古い). —古の値段, second-hand price. —古で買ふ, to buy second-hand.

furu (降る), *vi.* to fall; come down. —強く降る, to fall heavily; pelt. —降り續く, to fall continually. —降ッても照ッても, rain or shine. —降ッたり止んだりする, to rain fitfully [off and on]. —雨(雪; 霰)が降る, It rains (snows; hails).

furu (振る), *vt.* ❶(振り動かす) to wag (尾など); wave (旗·手·布など); shake; swing (振子など). ❷【俗】(擯斥す) to reject; repulse; refuse; give the mitten *to*; show the cold shoulder. —首を振る, ① to shake one's head. ②(拒絶) to refuse. —帽を振る, to wave one's hat. —腕を振ッて歩く, to swing one's arms.

furubiru (古びる), *vi.* to age; look old.

furubokeru (古惚ける), *vi.* to look old [antiquated; musty]. —古惚けた antiquated; musty.

furudōgu (古道具), *n.* ❶ old furniture; a second-hand article. ❷(骨董品) a curio; bric-à-brac. ¶ 古道具屋, a dealer in second-hand articles.

furueru (震へる), *vi.* to shake; tremble; shiver (特に寒さで); shudder (ぞッとする). ——, *a.* shaky; trembly; tremulous. —寒くて震へる, to shiver with cold.

furugi (古著), *n.* old clothes; cast--off clothes. ¶ 古著屋, ①(店) a second-hand clothing shop. ②(人) an old-clothes dealer; an old clothes--man.

furuhon (古本), *n.* a second-hand book; an old book. ¶ 古本屋, a second-hand bookseller (book-shop).

furui (篩), *n.* a sieve.

furui (古い), *a.* old. ❶[古] aged; ancient. ❷[舊, 陳] old; stale. —舊い理論(偏見), a crusted theory (prejudice). —彼は頭が舊い, His head is antiquated.

furuiagaru (震上る), *vi.* to tremble. —(を)見て震ひ上る, to tremble at the sight *of*.

furuigoe (震聲), *n.* a tremulous [trembling] voice; quaver.

furuiokosu (振起す), *vt.* to rouse up (勇氣などを); arouse; stir up. —勇氣を振ひ起す, to screw up [pluck up] one's courage.

furuiotosu (篩落す), *vt.* to throw out; weed out.

furuitatsu (奮起つ), *v.* =*funki* (奮起する).

furuiwakeru (篩分ける), *vt.* ❶ to sift; winnow. ❷(選擇) to select; sift out. —良否を篩ひ分ける, to sift the good from the bad.

furukizu (舊創), *n.* ❶ an old wound. ❷(舊惡) a former misdeed; an old offence.

furuku (舊·古く), *ad.* anciently; from old; of old. —舊くから, from old; from old times. (古くからの友人, an old friend.)

furukusai (舊臭い), *a.* ❶(ふるびた) old; antiquated. ❷(陳腐な) stale; hackneyed. ❸(舊式な) antiquated; old-fashioned. —舊臭い話, a hackneyed story; a chestnut; a twice-told tale. —舊臭くなる, to become antiquated [stale hackneyed].

furumai (振舞), *n.* behaviour;

deportment; conduct. —他人に對する振舞, behaviour to [towards] others.
furumau (振舞ふ), *vi.* to behave oneself; act; conduct oneself. —, *vt.* (馳走) to entertain; treat. —公明正大に振舞ふ, to play fair (and square).
furumono (古物), *n.* a second-hand (article); second-hand goods.
furusato (故郷), *n.* ❶(家郷) one's home; one's birth-place. ❷(故棲) the old home.
furusu (古巣), *n.* the old nest; the old haunt [home].
furusukyappu (フルスキャップ), *n.* foolscap.
furute (古手), *n.* a second-hand. —官吏の古手, a superannuated official. —洋服の古手を買ふ, to buy cast-off foreign clothes.
furutte (奮ッて), *ad.* strenuously; with energy; of one's own accord. —奮ッて事に當る, to buckle oneself to a task. —奮ッて御出席有之度候, We hope you will make every effort to attend.
furutteru (振ッてる), *a.* ❶(盛な) fine; high; splendid. ❷(優れた) superior. ❸(目覺しい) admirable; astonishing. ❹(奇異) bizarre. —この繪はなかなか振ッてる, This picture is rather bizarre [*outré*].
furuu (振ふ), *vi.* ❶〔震〕(ゆるぎ動く) to shake; quake. ❷(顫震) to tremble; shiver; shudder (戰慄する). ☞ *furueru.* ❸(振作) to be in high spirits; be elated; become active [prosperous] (市況など). ❹〔奮〕(はげます) to rouse oneself; bestir oneself. —, *vt.* to shake; rock; flourish (振廻す). —武器を揮ふ, to wield a weapon. —權力を振ふ, to exercise [wield] power.
furuu (篩ふ), *vt.* to sieve; sift; screen. —砂利を篩ふ, to riddle [screen] gravel.
furyo (不慮の), *a.* contingent; unexpected; unforeseen. —不慮の變に備へる, to provide against contingencies.
furyo (俘虜), *n.* a captive; a prisoner (of war). —俘虜となる, to be taken prisoner [captive]. ¶ 俘虜情報局, the Prisoners' Intelligence Bureau. —俘虜交換船, a cartel (-ship). —俘虜收容所, an internment camp (英); a detention camp (米).
furyō (不良の), *a.* bad; depraved (惡化せる). —不良の徒, the depraved. —天候不良の爲め, owing to bad [inclement] weather. ¶ 不良品, articles of inferior quality. —不良少年, a depraved youth.
furyō (不獵, 不漁), *n.* a lack of game; a poor bag; a poor catch [take].
furyō (負量), *n.* 【數】 a negative; a minus [negative] quantity.
furyōdōtai (不良導體), *n.* a non-conductor.
furyōken (不料簡), *n.* (誤ッた考) indiscretion; wrong-headedness. —不料簡を出す, to harbour indiscreet intentions.
furyoku (富力), *n.* wealth; resources.
furyoku (浮力), *n.* ❶【理】 buoyancy. ❷【飛】 lift.
fūryoku (風力), *n.* the force of the wind. —風力次第に加はる, The wind gradually gains in force. ¶ 風力計, an anemometer; a wind-gauge.
furyū (浮流する), *vi.* to float about; drift about. —浮流水雷に觸れる, to strike a floating mine.
fūryū (風流な), *a.* elegant; tasteful; refined. ¶ 風流人, a man of (refined) taste.
furyūtsū (不流通の), *a.* non-negotiable (商券など).
fusa (房), *n.* ❶〔房〕(花・實が一莖に簇生するもの) a bunch; a cluster. ❷〔總〕(絲で作ッたもの) a tassel; a tuft; a fringe. ❸(髮の) a lock; a tuft of hair.
fūsa (封鎖), *n.* blockade. —封鎖する, to blockade; bottle [block] up. —封鎖を侵破する(打破する; 解く), to run (break; raise) a blockade. ¶ 封鎖侵破船(者), a blockade-runner.
fusafusa (總總した), *a.* flocculent; fleecy. —總々した髮, fleecy hair.
fusagaru (塞がる), *vi.* ❶(閉塞) to choke (管など); clog (水管など); be blocked (up) (通路など). ❷ to be occupied (時・室・職・席など); be filled (時・缺員・場所など); be full. ❸ (從事中, 使用中) to be engaged. —悲しくて胸が塞がる, to be choked with sorrow. —金融が塞がッた, The circulation of money has stopped. —今手が塞がッてる, I am engaged [occupied] now.
fusagikomu (鬱込む), *vi.* to be in low spirits.
fusagu (塞ぐ), *vt.* ❶ to block (通路を); clog (流水等を); choke (隙などを); close (目・口などを); shut (同上). ❷(占有) to occupy; fill. —漏口を塞ぐ, to stop a leak. —後進の路を塞ぐ, to obstruct the promotion of younger men.
fusagu (鬱ぐ), *vi.* to be in low [poor] spirits; be depressed; be out of spirits.

fusai (負債), *n.* a debt; dues; liabilities. —負債を拂ふ, to pay one's dues.

fūsai (風采), *n.* appearance; presence. —風采の揚らぬ人, a person of vulgar appearance. —風采堂々として人を威壓する, to overawe others by the dignity of his presence.

fusaku (不作), *n.* a bad [poor] harvest [crop]; failure (of crops). —不作の年, a lean year.

fusan (不參), *n.* absence; non-attendance; non-appearance (特に法廷に於ける當事者又は證人としての). —不參屆を出す, to give notice of one's absence [non-attendance]. ¶ 不參者, an absentee.

fusanjikai (府參事會), *n.* a prefectural council.

fusansei (不贊成), *n.* disapproval; disagreement.

fusawashii (相應しい), *a.* suitable; becoming; fitting. ——, *vi.* to suit; become. —相應しい良緣, a suitable match. —紳士に相應しからぬ行爲, an act unbecoming a gentleman.

fuse (布施), *n.* an offering (at a temple); alms.

fusegu (防·拒ぐ), *vt.* ❶(豫防) to prevent; guard *against*. ❷(眼前の敵を) to defend *against*; resist. —災害を防ぐ, to ward off disaster. —敵を拒ぐ, to keep off the enemy. —來襲を禦ぐ, to repel an attack. —霜害を防ぐ, to prevent injury by frost.

fusei (不正), *n.* injustice; wrong; illegality (違法). —不正の金, ill-gotten money. —不正の儲け, dishonest gains. —不正を働く, to do a dishonest thing. ¶ 不正品, a fraudulent article; an adulterated article; an article unlawfully obtained. —不正手段, improper [unlawful] means.

fusei (不齊の), *a.* irregular; 【解】 scalene.

fuseijitsu (不誠實), *n.* Ⓢ 不誠意. insincerity; untrustworthiness; bad faith. —不誠實の, insincere; untrustworthy; dishonest.

fuseikaku (不正確な), *a.* inaccurate; inexact; uncertain; incorrect. —不正確な調査, an inaccurate investigation.

fūsei-kakurei (風聲鶴唳に驚く), to be frightened by the rustling of leaves.

fuseiki (不正規), *n.* irregularity. ¶ 不正規軍, the irregular army [troops]. —不正規兵, an irregular.

fuseikō (不成功), *n.* unsuccess; failure; ill success. —不成功の, unsuccessful. —不成功に終る, to end in failure.

fuseiri (不整理), *n.* maladjustment; disorder; derangement; disarrangement.

fuseiritsu (不成立), *n.* failure; non-fulfilment; miscarriage. —不成立となる, to fail; fall through; prove abortive [a failure].

fuseisan (不生產的), *a.* unproductive; unfruitful. —不生產的勞働, unproductive labour.

fuseishutsu (不世出の), *a.* unparallelled (in the world).

fuseiton (不整頓), *n.* disorganization (會社などの); disorder; disarrangement. —不整頓の, disorganized; disorderly.

fusen (附箋), *n.* a tag; a slip; a label. —附箋する, [*vt.*] to tag; label (作文等に).

fuseru (伏せる), *vt.* ❶(逆倒) to invert; reverse; turn down (カルタ札を). ❷(潛伏さす) to ambush (兵を). ——, *vi.* ❶(就寢) to go to bed; turn in. ❷(橫臥) to lie down. ❸(引籠る) to be confined; be laid up. —皿を伏せる, to turn a plate upside down. —本を伏せる, to lay a book face down. —土管を伏せる, to lay an earthen pipe. —眼をふせて見る, to look with downcast eyes.

fusessei (不節制), *n.* immoderateness; intemperance.

fusessō (不節操な), *a.* unchaste; inconstant; unfaithful.

fusetsu (浮說), *n.* a rumour. —浮說を信ずる, to believe [give credit to] a rumour.

fusetsu (符節を合する), to put together the two halves of a seal.

fusetsu (敷設), *n.* construction; laying. ——-**suru**, *vt.* to construct; lay. —海底電線を敷設する, to lay a cable. ¶ 敷設水雷, a (submarine) mine. —鐵道敷設權, the right of railway construction.

fūsetsu (風雪), *n.* a snow-storm. —風雪を冒す, to defy the snow-storm.

fūsetsu (風說), *n.* a rumour; a report; a hearsay. —風說を立てる, to start a rumour. —...との風說あり, It is rumoured that...; Rumour says that...

fuseya (伏屋), *n.* a humble [poor] cottage.

fusha (府社), *n.* a prefectural shrine.

fusha (富者), *n.* a rich [wealthy] man; a man of means [property]; the rich.

fūsha (風車), *n.* a windmill; wind-wheel.

fushi (節), *n.* ❶(節瘤) a knot; a knob; a node. ❷(樹節) a gnarl; a knar. ❸(關節) a joint; a knuckle (指の). ❹【顏】(絲のふし) a burl. ❺(曲調) a tune; an air. —節な

しの, knotless; clean. —節だらけの, knotty. —節面白く歌ふ, to sing a charming air.
fushi (不死の), *a.* deathless; immortal; undying.
fushi (父子), *n.* father and son (daughter).
fūshi (諷示する), *vt.* to suggest; hint.
fūshi (諷刺), *n.* satire; sarcasm; irony. —諷刺的喜劇, a burlesque. —軍閥の跋扈を諷刺する, to caricature the domination of militarism. ¶ 諷刺畫, a caricature.
fushiana (節穴), *n.* a knot-hole.
fushiawase (不仕合), *n.* misfortune. ☞ *fuun* (不運).
fushidara (不爲體), *n.* misconduct; slovenliness; untidiness.
fushiito (節絲), *n.* knotted silk.
fushigi (不思議), *n.* ❶ mystery; marvellousness; strangeness. ❷ a mystery; a wonder; a miracle. —世界の七不思議, the seven wonders of the world. —不思議中の不思議, the mystery of mysteries. —不思議がる, to wonder *at*; marvel. —不思議にも, for a wonder; to a wonder. —不思議に助かる, to escape by a miracle. —…は不思議でない, It is no wonder that.... **——-na,** *a.* mysterious; strange; wonderful; marvellous; miraculous; supernatural. —不思議な事には, What is wonderful is that...; The wonder of it is that.... —不思議な夢を見る, to dream [have] a strange dream.
fushikobu (節瘤), *n.* a gnarl; a knot. ☞ *fushi* (節).
fushimarobu (伏轉ぶ), *vi.* to fall and roll about.
fushimatsu (不始末), *n.* ❶ (不取締) mismanagement; irregularity; misconduct. ❷ (不節儉) wastefulness; unthriftiness.
fushimawashi (節廻し), *n.* intonation.
fushime (伏目になる), *v.* to droop; cast down one's eyes. —伏目勝ちに, droopingly; with drooping eyes.
fushin (不信), *n.* ❶ (不誠實) insincerity; perfidy. ❷ (疑) mistrust; discredit (不信用). ❸ (宗敎上の) unbelief. —不信を責める, to reproach a person for insincerity.
fushin (不振), *n.* inactivity; depression; dulness. —不振の, inactive; flat; dull. —市場不振なり, The market is flat.
fushin (不審), *n.* ❶ (疑念) doubt; doubtfulness; suspicion (嫌疑). ❷ (疑問) a question. ❸ (怪異) strangeness. —不審に思ふ, to feel strange; be suspicious *about*. **——-no,** *a.* ❶ doubtful; suspicious. ❷ strange. —不審の念を起さす, to excite suspicion.
fushin (浮心), *n.* 【理】 the centre of buoyancy.
fushin (普請), *n.* building; repairs (修繕). —普請中, in course of [under] construction (建築中) under repair (修繕中). —住宅を普請する, to build a residence. ¶ 普請小屋, a building-shed.
fushin (腐心する), *vi.* to tax one's ingenuity; rack one's brains. —自家廣告に腐心する, to rack one's brains for self-advertisement.
fushinjin (不信心), *n.* unbelief; infidelity; impiety. —不信心の, unbelieving; infidel; undevout; impious. ¶ 不信心者, an unbeliever.
fushinkō (不信仰), *n.* =*fushinjin.*
fushinnin (不信任), *n.* want [lack] of confidence; discredit; distrust. ¶ 不信任案, a bill for a vote of want of confidence. —不信任投票, no confidence vote; vote of censure.
fushinsetsu (不深切な), *a.* unkind; disobliging.
fūshinshi (風信子), *n.* 【植】 the hyacinth. ¶ 風信子石, 【鑛】jacinth; hyacinth.
fushinyō (不信用), *n.* discredit; distrust.
fushiogamu (伏拜む), *vt.* to fall down and worship.
fushite (伏して), *ad.* humbly; bowing down. —伏して願上候, I implore you; I humbly beg you.
fushizen (不自然), *n.* unnaturalness; artificiality (人爲的); affectedness (衒った). —不自然の, unnatural; affected; artificial.
fushō (不肖), *n.* ❶ unworthiness; incapacity. ❷ (謙辭として *pron.*) I; myself. —予不肖ながら, unworthy as I am. —不肖を顧みず, without a due sense of my unworthiness.
fushō (不祥), *n.* an ill-omen; inauspiciousness; unpropitiousness. —國家の不祥事, an ill omen to the state.
fushō (不詳の), *a.* unknown; not known. —姓名不詳の男, a man, name unknown; a man whose name is unknown.
fushō (負傷), *n.* a wound; an injury; a hurt. —負傷を免かる, to escape with a whole skin. **——-suru,** *vi.* to receive a wound; be [get] wounded; be injured. —少しも負傷せずに, without any wound. ¶ 負傷者, a wounded [injured] person.
fūsho (封書), *n.* a sealed letter.
fushō-bushō (不承不承に), *ad.* reluctantly; unwillingly; with a bad grace. —不承不承に承知する, to

consent with reluctance.
fushōchi (不承知), *n.* refusal; objection; disapproval.
fushōjiki (不正直), *n.* dishonesty. —不正直の, dishonest.
fushōka (不消化), *n.*【醫】apepsia: indigestion. —不消化の, indigestible; undigested (未消化の). ¶ 不消化物, indigestible food. —不消化病, dyspepsia.
fushoku (扶植する), *vt.* to plant; implant. —勢力を扶植する, to establish one's influence (確定); extend one's influence (擴張).
fushoku (腐蝕), *n.* corrosion. —腐蝕さす, to canker; erode (酸類などが). —腐蝕する, to corrode; rust (金屬が).
fūshū (風習), *n.* manners; custom; usage (慣例). ☞ ***fūzoku, shūkan.***
fushubi (不首尾), *n.* ❶(失敗) failure; unsuccess. ❷(よく受けられぬ) disapproval; disfavour.
fuso (父祖), *n.* an ancestor; a forefather.
fusoku (不足), *n.* ❶(缺乏) want; scarcity; dearth. ❷(不十分) shortage; deficiency; deficit. ❸(不滿) dissatisfaction; discontent. ❹(差額) a difference. ❺【商】(缺量) ullage. —不足税の信書, ①(切手貼用なき) unstamped [unpaid] letter. ②(貼用不足の) an insufficiently stamped letter. —不足する, to lack; want; come [fall; run] short. —不足をいふ, to complain of a thing [person] to a person [another]; express dissatisfaction *with.* —不足を補ふ, to make good [up] a deficiency. —手不足の場合だから, as we are short of hands. —何不足なく暮らしてゐる, to live comfortably. —何一つ不足の點なき樣にする, to leave nothing to be desired.
fusoku (不測の), *a.* ❶ immeasurable; fathomless. ❷(豫測し難い) unforeseen; unlooked-for. —不測の禍に罹る, to meet with an unforeseen disaster.
fusoku (附則), *n.* additional [supplementary] rules [provisions].
fūsoku (風速), *n.* velocity of the wind.
fuson (不遜), *n.* haughtiness; insolence; arrogance. **——-no,** *a.* haughty; arrogant; insolent. —不遜の態度, haughty deportment.
fusōō (不相應の), *a.* unsuited; inappropriate; out of keeping. —身分不相應の奢りをする, to live in extravagance unsuited to one's means.
fusoroi (不揃の), *a.* irregular; uneven; ununiform.
fusso (弗素), *n.*【化】fluorine.
fusu (伏す), *vi.* ❶(隱伏) to ambush. ❷(うつむく) to bow down; bend the face down. —机に俯して, with one's face on the desk. ⌈*fuseru* (伏せる).⌉
fusu (臥す), *vi.* to lie. ☞
fusū (負數), *n.*【數】a negative [number]; a minus.
fusuma (衾), *n.* a coverlet; a quilt.
fusuma (襖), *n.* a sliding-door. —襖を開ける(閉ぢる), to open (close) a sliding-door.
fusuma (麩), *n.* bran (小麥など碾いた皮屑).
fu-suru (付する), *vt.* to commit *to*; refer *to*; put *to.* —投票に付する, to put (the matter) to the vote. —委員會に付する, to refer to a committee. —事件を公判に付する, to commit a case for trial.
fū-suru (諷する), *vt.* ❶(諷示) to suggest; hint; give [drop] a hint. ❷(諷刺) to satirize; insinuate; hint *at.* —詩を以て諷する, to satirize in verse.
futa (蓋), *n.* a lid (机·箱·釜等の); a cover. —蓋をする, to put on the lid; close; cover. —蓋を明ける, ① to open; uncover; take off the lid. ②(開始) to open; commence; begin.
futaba (嫩, 二葉), *n.* a bud. —嫩のうちに摘む, to nip in the bud.
futae (二重), *n.* ❶(二重ね) two layers. ❷(折れ重なること) fold. —二重の, double; twofold. ¶ 二重瞼, folded eyelids.
futago (雙子), *n.* a twin (一人); twins. —雙子の兄弟(姉妹), twin brother(-s) (sister(-s)).
futagokoro (貳心), *n.* ❶(異心) duplicity; perfidy; treachery. ❷(孰れにするか迷へる心) dilemma; perplexity. —貳心ある, double-hearted; perfidious; treacherous. —貳心を懷く, to harbour treachery.
futai (附帶の), *n.*【法】accessory; incidental; collateral. ¶ 附帶條件,【法】a condition collateral; a rider. —附帶私訴,【法】an incidental private action.
fūtai (風袋), *n.* ❶【商】tare. ❷(包裝) a package; packing. ¶ 普通(平均)風袋, customary (average) tare. —實際[正味]風袋, real [actual; particular; open] tare.
futaishō (不對稱の), *a.* unsymmetrical.
futaitō (不對等の), *a.* unequal.
futakoto (二言目には), *ad.* whenever one opens one's mouth.
futaku (付託する), *vt.* to commit *to*; refer *to.*

futamata (二股の), *a.* forked. ¶ 二股膏藥, a trimmer; a waverer.

futame (二目と見られぬ), *v.* to be unable to look a second time; be piteous to look at again. ——, *a.* repulsive; disgusting.

futame (不爲), *n.* being bad; being unbeneficial; harm (害); disadvantage (不利益).

futamichi (二道をかける), to have two strings to one's bow.

futan (負擔), *n.* a burden. —重税の負擔, the burden of a heavy tax. —負擔になる, to be a burden *on*. —負擔に堪へぬ, to be unable to bear burden. —費用を負擔する, to bear the expenses. —人民に租税を負擔さす, to burden the people with taxes.

futaoya (兩親), *n.* both parents. —兩親に夙く死別れる, to be parted early by death from both parents.

futashika (不確), *n.* uncertainty. ——**-na**, *a.* uncertain; indefinite. —不確な返事, an indefinite answer.

futatabi (再び), *ad.* ❶(二度) twice. ❷(くりかへして) again; afresh. —過を再びせぬやうにする, to take care not to repeat the offence.

futatōri (二通の), *a.* twofold; duplicate. —證書を二通り作る, to draw up a certificate in duplicate.

futatsu (二つ), *n.* two (2; II) —二つながら, [*ad.*] both. —二つとない, [*a.*] ①(唯一つの) unique; only. ②(比べものない) peerless; matchless; unequalled (二つとない命, this one life.) —二つに切る, to cut in two. —二つに見える, to see double. —價を二つにする, to give two prices. —二つ宛數へる, to count two by two. —林檎を二つ宛貰ふ, to receive two apples each.

futatsu (布達する), *v.* to notify; issue a notification.

futegiwa (不手際), *n.* clumsiness; awkwardness; unhandiness. —不手際の, clumsy; awkward; unhandy.

futei (不貞), *n.* Ⓢ 不貞節, 不貞操. unchastity; unfaithfulness; (conjugal) infidelity. —夫に不貞な妻, a wife false to her husband.

futei (不逞の), *a.* insubordinate; rebellious. —不逞の徒を集める, to collect [gather] insubordinate men. ¶ 不逞鮮人, an insubordinate Korean.

futei (不定), *n.* uncertainty; indefiniteness; indeterminateness. ——**-no**, *a.* uncertain; indefinite; indeterminate. —住所不定の惡徒, rogues without settled homes. ¶ 不定法, 【文】 the infinitive. —不定冠詞, 【文】 the indefinite article. —不定期間, uncertain duration.

fūtei (風體), *n.* appearance. —風體怪しき男, a suspicious-looking man. —怪しむべき風體をする, to have a suspicious appearance.

futeiki (不定期), *n.* an irregular period. ¶ 不定期航海, irregular service. —不定期船, a tramp (steamer).

futeisai (不體裁の), *a.* unseemly; unsightly; unbecoming. —不體裁な服裝, shabby clothes.

futeki (不敵の), *a.* fearless; daring; dauntless; intrepid; audacious. —不敵の振舞, daring [fearless] conduct.

futekihō (不適法の), *a.* unlawful; illegal.

futekinin (不適任の), *a.* unfit. —金の番には不適任である, to be unfit for guarding money. ¶ 不適任者, an unsuitable person.

futekitō (不適當な), *a.* ❶(ふさはしからぬ) inappropriate (*to*); unsuitable; unsuited. ❷(不十分) insufficient; inadequate. —不適當な例, an inapt example.

futekusare (不貞腐), *n.* the sulks; sulkiness. —不貞腐になる, to go into the sulks. —不貞腐を言ふ, to use sulky language.

futen (普天の下率土の濱), every place under the heavens; all the corners of the earth.

fūten (瘋癲), *n.* lunacy; madness insanity. ¶ 瘋癲病醫, an alienist —瘋癲病院, a lunatic hospital [asylum]; a madhouse; an insane asylum. (瘋癲病院へ送る, to put into a lunatic asylum.) —瘋癲者, a lunatic; a madman.

futettei (不徹底の), *a.* inconsistent; illogical; unconvincing (透徹しない); imperfect (不十分な).

futo (不圖), *ad.* ❶(思ひがけず) unexpectedly; unintentionally (何氣なく); suddenly (突然). ❷(偶發的に) by chance; accidentally. —不圖した事から, from a slight affair [matter]; from a trifle. —不圖胸に浮ぶ, to come into one's head; occur to one. —不圖(何々)する, to happen [chance] to....

futō (不撓の), *a.* inflexible; tenacious; unyielding. —不撓の精神を以て, with an untiring spirit.

futō (不當), *n.* unreasonableness; injustice. ——**-no**, *a.* ❶ wrongful; unjust; unwarranted. ❷ inappropriate; improper. ❸ (過當の) undue; excessive. —不當な事をする, to act unreasonably. ¶ 不當利得, ① 【法】 unjustified benefits

unjust enrichment. ② profiteering (暴利取得). —不當廉賣, dumping. —不當支出, improper disbursement.
futō (不等の), *a.* unequal.
futō (埠頭), *n.* a pier; a wharf; a quay.
fūto (呎), *n.* (英國尺度) a foot [*pl.* feet].
fūtō (封筒), *n.* an envelope.
futodoki (不屆の), *a.* badly-managed; insolent; reprehensible. —不屆千萬な奴, a most insolent fellow.
futōhen (不等邊三角形), *n.* a scalene (triangle).
futoi (莞), *n.* 【植】 the bulrush.
futoi (太い), *a.* big; thick (頸など); burly (肥大); fat (活字). —太い聲, a deep voice. —太い奴, a shameless fellow. —太い料簡を出す, to grow audacious.
futōitsu (不統一), *n.* disunion; want of uniformity. —不統一の, disunited; ununiform. —內部の不統一を暴露する, to bring to light the internal disunion.
futōkō (不凍港), *n.* an ice-free port.
futokoro (懷), *n.* the breast; the bosom; the pocket. —懷に入れる, to put in one's bosom. —懷を暖める, to line one's pocket. —短刀を懷にして, with a short sword in his bosom.
futokorode (懷手), *n.* hand in the bosom. —懷手して暮らす, to live with hands in one's pockets.
futokorogatana (懷刀), *n.* ❶ a dagger; a poniard. ❷ (腹心の人) a confidant; a chief adviser.
futoku (太く), *ad.* ❶ (大きく) thickly. ❷ (大膽に) boldly. ❸ (橫著に) audaciously; shamelessly. —太くする, to make thick; thicken.
futoku (不德), *n.* ❶ (德を具へ居らぬ) want [lack] of virtue; unworthiness. ❷ = ***futokugi***. —私の不德の致す所である, It is due to my unworthiness.
futokugi (不德義), *n.* vice; wickedness; viciousness. ¶ 不德義漢, a vicious [wicked] man.
futokusaku (不得策), *n.* inexpediency; unadvisability; an unwise course. —不得策の, inexpedient; unwise; unadvisable.
futokutei (不特定の), *a.* unspecified; indefinite; non-specific.
futokuyōryō (不得要領), *n.* irrelevance; inconclusiveness; pointlessness. —不得要領の返事, an irrelevant answer; a non-committal answer. —不得要領な事を云ふ, to speak from the purpose; talk round.
futōmei (不透明の), *a.* opaque.
futomomo (太股), *n.* the thigh. —太股を出す, to expose one's thighs.
futomono (太物), *n.* piece-goods; dry-goods; cotton goods.
futon (蒲團), *n.* ❶ (夜具) bedclothes; bedding. ❷ a quilt (掛蒲團); a coverlet (同上); a mattress (敷蒲團); a cushion (座蒲團). —蒲團を畳む, to fold up the bedding.
futoppara (太腹の), *a.* audacious.
futorishimari (不取締), *n.* mismanagement; misconduct; neglect of supervision.
futoru (太る), *vi.* to grow fat [plump]; fatten; gather [put on] flesh. —太ッた人と痩せた人, a fat man and a thin one. —彼は見違へる様に太ッた, He has grown stout beyond recognition.
futosa (太さ), *n.* thickness; size.
futōsoku-undō (不等速運動), *n.* ununiform motion.
futotcho (太ッちョ), *n.* a fatty.
futsū (不通), *n.* interruption of communications; no communication; no intercourse (交際せぬ). —不通となる, to be cut off; be interrupted; be suspended. —言語不通の爲に生ずる間違, mistakes arising out of ignorance of a language. ¶ 電信(電話; 鐵道)不通, interruption of telegraphic communication (telephone service; railway traffic).
futsū (普通), *ad.* generally; commonly; usually. —普通の, common; ordinary; general; usual. ¶ 普通學, ordinary [general] knowledge. —普通語, a common word. —普通教育, common education. —普通選擧, manhood suffrage; universal suffrage.
futsugo (佛語), *n.* French; the French language.
futsugō (不都合), *n.* ❶ (不便) inconvenience; trouble. ❷ (不埒) impropriety; reprehensibleness. **—— -no**, *a.* ❶ inconvenient; troublesome. ❷ improper; reprehensible. —不都合な箇所, an objectionable point. —無斷で持ッて行くとは不都合千萬だ, It was most unwarrantable to take it away without notice.
futsujin (佛人), *n.* a Frenchman; the French.
futsukayoi (宿酔), *n.* overnight drunkenness. —二日酔する, to have a mouth on 〔俗〕.
Futsukoku (佛國), *n.* France. ¶ 佛國大統領, the President of the French Republic. —佛國翰林院, the French Academy.
futsuriai (不釣合の), *a.* disproportionate; out of place [keeping]; ill-matched. —不釣合の緣組, an ill-sorted match. —不釣合の夫婦, an ill-matched couple.

futsutsuka (不束な), *a.* ❶ incapable. ❷ rude; ill-bred.
futsuzen (怫然), *ad.* in anger; in a passion. —怫然色を作す, to change colour with anger.
futtei (拂底), *n.* scarcity; dearth; shortage. —小錢(人物)の拂底, scarcity of small coins (men of character). —拂底する, to show a deficiency; run short.
futtō (沸騰する), *vi.* ❶ to boil; seethe; effervesce. ❷ to seethe; become animated [excited]. —議論が沸騰した, The discussion became heated. ¶ 沸騰酒(水), an effervescent wine (drink). —沸騰點, the boiling-point.
futtobōru (蹴球), *n.* (a) foot-ball.
futtsuri (ふっつり), *ad.* (斷念) decisively; definitely; absolutely. —(絲などが)ふっつり切れる, to snap.
fūu (風雨), *n.* ❶ (風と雨) wind and rain; weather. ❷(暴風雨) a tempest; a storm. —風雨に曝す, to weather; expose to the weather. —雨風を凌ぐ, to weather out a storm.
fuun (不運), *n.* misfortune; ill-luck; adverse circumstances. —不運に生れる, to be born under an unlucky star. —不運のどん底に居る, to be at the bottom of Fortune's wheel.
fuun (浮雲), *n.* a cloud-drift; a floating cloud.
fūun (風雲), *n.* the state of affairs; the situation; the cloud. —東亞の風雲, the situation in (the) Eastern Asia.
fuwa (不和), *n.* discord; disharmony; dissension. —不和の種を蒔く, to sow dissension; make mischief; sow the seeds of discord *between*. —一家の不和を來す, to bring about disunion in a family.
fuwa (附和(雷同)する), *vi.* to follow another blindly; echo another's views.
fuwafuwa (浮浮した), *a.* ❶(物に云ふ) soft; fluffy. ❷(精神に云ふ) giddy; fickle; unsteady. —浮浮した蒲團に坐る, to sit on a soft cushion.
fuwarito (ふはりと), *ad.* lightly; softly.
fuwatari (不渡), *n.* dishonour(手形の); non-payment. (不拂). ¶ 不渡小切手, a dishonoured cheque.
fuyakasu (ふやかす), *vt.* to soak; sodden; steep.
fuyakeru (ふやける), *vi.* to sodden; grow sodden.
fuyasu (殖す), *vt.* to increase; propagate (動·植物を); raise (給料など). —人數を殖す, to increase the number of men.
fuyo (付與する), *vt.* to give; issue; grant (特權など). —人に權能を付與する, to invest a person with power [authority].
fuyo (賦與する), *vt.* (特に上帝から) to dispense; endow *with* (能力等を); bestow *on*. —才能を賦與する, to endow with talent.
fuyō (芙蓉), *n.* 【植】❶(もくふよう) Hibiscus mutabilis (rose-mallow の一種·學名). ❷ (蓮) the lotus.
fuyō (不用), *n.* uselessness; inutility. —不用の, useless; unnecessary; unneedful. —不用に歸する, to become useless [unnecessary]. —不用品を拂ふ, to sell unnecessary articles. ¶ 不用書類, waste papers.
fuyō (扶養), *n.* maintenance; support. —扶養の義務, the duty of [to furnish] support. —扶養する, to maintain; support.
fuyō (浮揚), *n.* floating. —浮揚する, to float off (坐礁船などが); fly. —中空に浮揚せる輕氣球, a balloon suspended in mid-air.
fuyōi (不用意), *n.* unpreparedness; improvidence.
fuyōjō (不養生の), *a.* careless of health; intemperate.
fuyōkoku (附庸國), *n.* a dependency.
fuyu (冬), *n.* winter. —暖い冬, a mild [an open] winter. —嚴しい冬, a hard [severe] winter. —冬の最中, mid-winter.
fuyū (浮游する), *vi.* to waft; float. —浮游する塵, suspended particles of dust; floating dust.
fuyū (富裕の), *a.* wealthy; affluent; opulent. —富裕に暮らす, to live in affluence; be well off.
fuyufuku (冬服), *n.* winter-clothing [clothes; suit].
fuyugare (冬枯の), *a.* winter-stricken. —冬枯の野景, a view of the winter-stricken field.
fuyugomori (冬籠), *n.* hibernation; winter sleep [confinement]. —冬籠する, to hibernate; winter (*in*; *at*); be confined in winter.
fuyugoshi (冬越), *n.* passing the winter; hibernation. —冬越しする, [*vi.*] to winter.
fuyukai (不愉快), *n.* unpleasantness; cheerlessness; discomfort. —不愉快な天氣, unpleasant weather.
fuyukitodoki (不行屆), *n.* ❶(過怠) neglect; remissness; mismanagement (不取締). ❷ (不才) want of ability [talent]. ❸ (不十分) insufficiency. —不行屆の, ① negligent; remiss. ② untalented. ③ insufficient. —職務不行屆の爲め, for the neglect of one's duties.
fuyumono (冬物), *n.* winter clothing [wear].

fuyumuki(冬向の), *a.* for winter use. —冬向の品, articles for winter use; winter goods.

fuzai (不在), *n.* absence; being away from home. —不在を狙ふ, to take advantage of one's absence. ¶ 不在者, an absentee.

fuzakeru (巫山戯る), *vi.* ❶(いちゃつく) to flirt, coquet *with* (a man); dally *with* (a woman; a girl). ❷(跳廻る) to romp; gambol; play pranks (いたづらする). ❸(冗談云ふ) to jest; trifle. —猫と巫山戯る, to play with the cat. —若い男女の巫山戯合ひ, the flirting of a young man and woman. **——,** *a.* flirtatious; pankish; frisky.

fuzei (風情), *n.* (風趣) taste; elegance. —丁稚風情, fellows like apprentices. —私風情のもの, the likes of me〔俗〕; such as I.

fuzen (不全の), *a.* incomplete; imperfect. ¶ 不全麻痺,【醫】paresis; partial paralysis.

fuzen(不善), *n.* evil; vice; wickedness.

fūzen (風前の燈である), to hang by a thread.

fuzoku (附屬の), *a.* adjunctive; appendant; appurtenant; accessory; subsidiary; subordinate. —附屬する, to belong *to*; be attached *to*. ¶ 附屬品, appurtenances; accessories; fittings. —附屬書類, an annex. —高等師範學校附屬中學校, the middle school attached to the Higher Normal School.

fūzoku(風俗), *n.* ❶(習俗) manners; custom; usage. ❷(風儀) popular (public) morals. —善良の風俗, good morals. —風俗を亂す, to deprave [corrupt] manners. ¶ 風俗壞亂, demoralization.

fuzoroi (不揃の), *a.* =*fusoroi.*

fuzu (附圖), *n.* an appended map.

fuzui (不隨), *n.* paralysis. —半身が不隨になる, to be paralyzed on one side. ¶ 半身不隨, paraplegia (下部); hemiplegia (片側). —全身不隨, general paralysis; holoplexia.

fuzui (附隨の), *a.* attendant; accompanying; concomitant. —附隨の出來事, dependent events. —附隨の弊害, accompanying evils [abuses]. —附隨する, to go *with*; follow; accompany.

fuzuii(不隨意), *n.* involuntariness. ¶ 不隨意筋,【生】an involuntary muscle.

fū-zuru (封ずる), *vt.* =*fū-jiru.*

G

ga (が), *conj.* ❶(然し乍ら) but; however; yet. ❷(と雖も) though; although; as. ❸(接續) and; who; which.

ga (蛾), *n.* a moth.

ga (我), *n.* ❶【哲】(自家の存在) ego; the subject. ❷ self-will (我意); selfishness (我儘); egoism (利己). —我を折る, to yield (to pressure); give in; bend. —我を通す, ① [*v.*] to hold one's own; carry one's will through. ② [*a.*] self-willed; masterful. —我を張る, ① [*v.*] to carry one's will. ② [*a.*] self-asserting; opinionated. (我を張り通す, to carry one's will through to the end.)

ga (駕), *n.* a carriage. —駕を迎へる, to welcome [go out to meet] a carriage [a man of rank]. —駕を枉げる, to call *on*; visit.

ga (畫), *n.* a picture; a painting (著色畫); a drawing (圖畫).

gaban(畫板), *n.* a drawing-board; a panel.

gabato (Q破と), *ad.* suddenly; quickly.

gabei (畫餅に歸する), to fall to the ground; come to nothing [naught].

gabi (蛾眉), *n.* ❶(美人の眉) an arched eyebrow. ❷(美人) a beautiful woman.

gabugabu (がぶがぶ飲む), *v.* to quaff; swill.

gachagacha (がちゃがちゃ), *n.* =*kutsuwamushi.* **——,** *ad.* (金屬等の觸れる音) clang. —ガチャガチャさす, to clatter; rattle. (錢をガチャガチャさせる, to tingle one's money.) —ガチャガチャと響く, to go crack.

gachi (雅致), *n.* elegance; (good) taste. —頗る雅致に富む, to be extremely tasteful.

-gachi (勝), *suf.* ❶(傾向) to be apt *to*; be liable *to*. ❷(優勢) to prevail; predominate. —留守勝ち, mostly away from home; seldom at home. **——-no,** *a.* prone; apt. —病氣勝ちの, prone to sickness.

gachō (鵞鳥), *n.* the goose [*pl.* geese]; the gander (雄).

gaden-insui (我田引水の), *a.* self-seeking; self-profiting.

gādo (ガード), *n.*【鐵道】a girder-bridge; a railway arch.

gaen (賀筵), *n.* a banquet in congratulation.

gaenzuru (肯んずる), *v.* to consent *to*; assent *to*; agree *to*. —肯んずる樣子がない, to show no disposition to agree.

gafu (畫布), *n.* canvas.

gaga (峨峨たる), *a.* craggy; rugged; steep.

gāgā (があーがあー鳴く), *vi.* to quack (家鴨が); croak (蛙が).

gagaku (畫學), *n.* drawing. ¶ 畫學紙, drawing-paper.

gaganbo (大蚊), *n.* 【昆】 the daddy-long-legs.

gagō (雅號), *n.* a pen-name; a pseudonym; a *nom de guerre* 〖佛〗.

gahaku (畫伯), *n.* a great painter [artist]; a master.

gahitsu (畫筆), *n.* a brush; a brush-pencil.

gaho (牙保), *n.* brokerage. ¶ 贓物牙保, brokerage of stolen goods.

gahō (畫法), *n.* drawing. —畫法に適ってゐる (ゐない), to be in (out of) drawing.

gahō (畫報), *n.* a pictorial. ¶ 演藝畫報, the Dramatic Pictorial.

gahyō (賀表), *n.* a congratulatory address. —賀表を奉る, to present a congratulatory address.

gai (外), *prep.* ❶ (以上) besides; in addition to. ❷ (以外) outside; without. —文明の範圍外に, without [outside] the pale of civilization. —三里外に放逐せらる, to be expelled outside the three-*ri* limit.

gai (害), *n.* ❶ (害惡) evil; bane; ill. ❷ (傷害) injury; harm. ❸ (妨害) obstruction; obstacle; impediment. ❹ (損害) damage; loss; detriment. —健康の害になる, to be injurious [harmful] to health. —學生の害になる書物, a book harmful to students. —害多くして益少し, to do more harm than good. —(人から)害を蒙る, to suffer injury. —洪水の害を免かれる, to escape damage from floods.

gai (該), *a.* the...in question [under consideration]; (the) said; the above-mentioned. —該問題, the matter in question. —該時代, the period under consideration [review].

gai (我意), *n.* self-will; obstinacy.

gaiaku (害惡), *n.* injury; mischief; harm. —害惡を除く, to remove the harm.

gaibu (外部), *n.* the exterior; the outside. —外部の樣子, the external condition.

gaibun (外聞), *n.* publicity; reputation. —外聞の惡い, disreputable; discreditable; scandalous.

gaibutsu (外物), *n.* an (external) object; outward things; 【哲】 non-ego.

gaichō (害鳥), *n.* an injurious [a noxious] bird.

gaichū (害蟲), *n.* an injurious [noxious] insect; the blight; vermin. 害蟲を驅除する, to exterminate noxious insects.

gaiden (外電), *n.* (外國電報の略) a foreign telegram.

gaido (案内者), *n.* a guide; a cicerone. ¶ ガイドブック, a guide-book.

gaidoku (害毒), *n.* evil; poison; virus. —社會に害毒を流す, to poison [taint] society.

gaien (外延), *n.* 【論】 denotation; extension.

gaihaku (外泊する), *vi.* to stop out.

gaihaku (該博な), *a.* exhaustive; erudite; profound. —該博な知識を有する, to possess exhaustive knowledge.

gaihin (外賓), *n.* a foreign guest. —外賓を招待する, to entertain a foreign guest.

gaihō (外方に), *ad.* outwards.

gaihō (外報), *n.* foreign news; a foreign report.

gaiji (外耳), *n.* 【解】 the auricle; the external ear. ¶ 外耳炎, 【醫】 otitis externa; inflammation of the outer ear.

gaijin (外人), *n.* a foreigner. ¶ 在留外人, foreign residents. —外人社會, a foreign community.

gaii (害意), *n.* malevolence; malice; ill-will.

gaika (外貨), *n.* foreign goods.

gaika (凱歌), *n.* a triumphal song. —凱歌を奏する, to sing in triumph; sing a triumphal song.

gaikai (外界), *n.* outward things; the external world. —外界の事情, externals.

gaikai (外海), *n.* the main sea. —外海に出る, to go out to (come upon) the sea.

gaikaku (外角), *n.* 【數】 an external [exterior] angle.

gaikaku (外郭), *n.* the contour; the outline.

gaikaku (外殼), *n.* a shell; a crust.

gaikan (外患), *n.* foreign invasion foreign evil.

gaikan (外觀), *n.* outward [external] appearance; outward form; shape (形狀). —外觀の宏壯, the magnificence of outward appearance. —外觀を繕ふ, to save [keep up] appearances.

gaikatsu (概括する), *vt.* to generalize; sum up; summarize. —概括的の議論, a generalized argument. —概括して云へば, to sum up; the long and the short of the matter is....

gaikei (外形), *n.* exterior; shape; outward [external] form. —事物の外形と內容, the external form and internal state of things.

gaiken (外見), *n.* appearance; look; face. ☞ *gaikan* (外觀).

—外見より判斷すれば, on the face of it.

gaiki(外氣), *n.* open air. —外氣に當る[觸れる], to be exposed to air.

gaikin (外勤), *n.* being on outside duty; duty abroad. ¶ 外勤巡査 a patrol; a patrolman [米]. —外勤員, a person on outside duty; a canvasser (勸誘員).

gaikō (外交), *n.* ❶ (外國との關係) foreign [diplomatic] relations. ❷ diplomacy. —外交的辭令に嫻れる, to be skilled in diplomatic language. —外交の機宜を誤る, to miss a diplomatic opportunity. —外交關係を斷絶する, to break off diplomatic relations. ¶ 外交部, (支那) the Waichiao-pu. —外交文書, a diplomatic note [document; paper]. —外交團, the diplomatic corps [body]; the *corps diplomatique* [佛]. —外交談判, diplomatic negotiations. —外交員, a canvasser. —外交家, a diplomat; a diplomatist. —外交官, a diplomatic officer [official]; a diplomatic agent; diplomatic service (全體). —外交官補, an *attaché* [佛]; a diplomatic probationer. —外交問題, a diplomatic question.

gaikō (外光), *n.* 【畫】 *plein air.* [佛]

gaikō(外項), *n.* 【數】 the extremes; extreme terms.

gaikō(外寇), *n.* a foreign invasion; an alien [a foreign] enemy (外敵).

gaikoku (外國), *n.* a foreign country [power; state]; foreign parts. —外國行の, outward-bound; foreign-going. —外國產の, foreign; foreign-produced. —外國製の, foreign-made; of foreign make [manufacture]. —外國へ行く (から歸る), to go (return from) abroad. ¶ 外國貿易, foreign trade. —外國電報, a foreign telegram. —外國語學校, a foreign language school. —外國人, a foreigner. —外國爲替相場, foreign exchange rate. —外國航路, a foreign (service) route. —外國公使, a foreign minister. —外國米, foreign rice. —外國船, a foreign vessel; a foreign bottom. —外國商館, a foreign firm.

gaikotsu(骸骨), *n.* the skeleton; bones. —骸骨の樣に痩せ衰へる, to be reduced to a skeleton [shadow]. —骸骨を乞ふ, to tender one's resignation.

gaikyō (概況), *n.* general condition.

gaimai (外米), *n.* foreign rice.

gaimaku (外膜), *n.* 【解】 the involucre; a mantle.

gaimen (外面), *n.* outside; exterior; outward appearance.

gaimu (外務), *n.* foreign affairs. —外務大臣 [卿], the Minister for Foreign Affairs; the Foreign Minister: the (Principal) Secretary of State for Foreign Affairs (英國); the Foreign Secretary. —外務次官, the Vice-Minister for Foreign Affairs; the Under-Secretary for Foreign Affairs. —外務省, the Department [Ministry] of Foreign Affairs; the Foreign Office.

gainen (概念), *n.* 【哲】 concept; general idea.

gairai (外來の), *a.* foreign; exotic; imported. ¶ 外來患者, an out-patient. —外來者, a person from abroad; a stranger; an immigrant (移住); a denizen (歸化).

gairo (街路), *n.* a street; a road. —街路を行く, to go down the street. ¶ 街路樹, roadside trees. —街路公園, a roadside garden.

gairon (概論), *n.* the general argument; general remarks; an introduction (*to*).

gairyaku(概略), I. *n.* an outline; an epitome; a summary. **——**, II. *ad.* in the main; for the most part; in the rough; roughly. —概略の飜譯, rough translation.

gaisai (外債), *n.* a foreign loan [debt]. —外債を起す, to raise a foreign loan.

gaisaku (外柵), *n.* a bail (城の).

gaisan (概算), *n.* a rough estimate [calculation]. **——-suru,** *vt.* to make a rough estimate *of*; estimate roughly. —收容人員を五百人と概算する, to reckon the persons taken in roughly at 500. ¶ 概算額, an approximate sum.

gaisei (碍性), *n.* 【理】 impenetrability.

gaiseki (外戚), *n.* the wife's relation; a maternal relation; a relation on the mother's side.

gaisen (凱旋), *n.* a triumphal return. —凱旋式を行ふ, to celebrate the triumphal return. ¶ 凱旋行列, a triumphal progress. —凱旋軍, an army [troops] returned in triumph. —凱旋軍人, a returned hero. —凱旋門, a triumphal arch.

gaisetsu (概說する), *vt.* to give an outline *of*.

gaisetsuen (外接圓), *n.* 【數】 a circumscribed circle.

gaishi (外資), *n.* foreign capital. ¶ 外資輸入, introduction of foreign capital.

gaishi (碍子), *n.* 【理】 an insulator.

gaishite(概して), *ad.* generally; in general; in the main. —概して云へば, roughly [generally] speaking.

gaishō (外相), *n.* the Foreign Minister; the Minister for Foreign Affairs. —外相の夜會, the Foreign Minister's Ball.

gaishō (外商), *n.* a foreign merchant.

gaishutsu (外出), *n.* going out; outing. ¶ 外出日, a leave-day. —外出時間, the leave-time; the hours for going out. —外出證, a pass.

gaiso (外祖), *n.* ❶ (外祖父) a maternal grandfather. ❷ (外祖母) a maternal grandmother.

gaisō (咳嗽), *n.* a cough. —咳嗽する, to cough.

gaisoku (外側), *n.* outside.

gaison (外孫), *n.* a grandchild by a daughter.

gaisū (概數), *n.* approximate numbers (近數); round numbers (端數を切捨てた數).

gai-suru (害する), *vt.* ❶ (損傷) to harm; injure; damage. ❷ (妨害) to obstruct; impede; check. ❸ (殺害) to kill; slay. ——, *a.* harmful *to*; injurious *to*; hurtful *to*; detrimental *to*. —田畑を害する, to damage a field. —青年を害する, to be harmful to youths. —風致を害する, to spoil [mar] the beauty of a place. —(彼の)感情を害する, to hurt his feelings. —他人の利益を害する, to prejudice another's interests.

gaitan (骸炭), *n.* coke.

gaitan (慨歎する), *vt.* to deplore; lament. —慨歎の至りだ, to be most deplorable.

gaiteki (外的), *a.* external; outward.

gaiteki (外敵), *n.* a foreign enemy.

gaitō (外套), *n.* a cloak; a mantle; an overcoat. ¶ 外套室, a cloak-room. —外套掛け, an overcoat stand [rack].

gaitō (街燈), *n.* a street-lamp; a road-lamp〔米〕. —街燈をつける, to light a street-lamp. ¶ 街燈柱, a lamp-post.

gaitō (街頭), *n.* a street. —街頭に立つ, to stand in a street.

gaitō (該當する), *vi.* to come [fall] *under*; fall [come] within the purview *of*; be applicable *to*; correspond *to* (照應する); deserve (賞罰に云ふ). —刑法第九十五條に該當する, to come under Art. 95 of the Criminal Code.

gaiya (外野), *n.* 【野球】 outfield. ¶ 外野手, an outfielder.

gaiyō (外用), *n.* external application. ¶ 外用水藥, a wash; a lotion. —外用藥, a medicine for external application; an external medicine.

gaiyō (外洋), *n.* the ocean; the high sea. —外洋へ乘り出す, to sail far out on the ocean. —外洋を航行する, to sail on the ocean.

gaiyō (概要), *n.* an epitome; an outline; a summary. —概要の記述, a compendious statement. —概要を擧ぐれば, if we give an epitome.

gaiyū (外遊), *n.* a foreign travel; a trip abroad. —外遊する, to travel abroad; take a trip abroad. —外遊の途に上る, to set out on a foreign travel.

gaizen (蓋然-性), *n.* probability. —蓋然の結果, the probable result.

gaji (賀辭), *n.* congratulations. —賀辭を呈する, to offer congratulations.

gajō (賀狀), *n.* a congratulatory letter.

gajō (畫帖), *n.* a picture-album.

gaka (畫架), *n.* an easel; a painter's easel.

gaka (畫家), *n.* an artist; a painter.

gakai (瓦解), *n.* breakdown; collapse; fall. —內閣(德川幕府)の瓦解, the fall of a cabinet [ministry] (the Tokugawa feudal government). ——**-suru**, *vi.* to fall; break down; collapse. —將に瓦解せんとす, to stand on the brink of ruin.

gake (崖), *n.* a bluff (海邊の); a cliff; a precipice. —崖下に落ちる, to fall down a precipice. ¶ 崖崩れ, falling [crumbling; sliding] of a cliff; a landslip.

-gake (掛), ❶ (序) while; when; on the way. ❷ (賭) a risk. ❸ (倍) times; (百分の十) ten per cent. ❹ (著けて) in; with...on. —行掛けに, on one's way *to*. —脚袢掛けで, with gaiters on. —定價の八掛で, at eighty per cent of the published price. —襷がけで働く, to work in shirt-sleeves.

gaki (餓鬼), *n.* ❶ a hungry devil. ❷ (子供) a brat; an imp; an urchin. ¶ 餓鬼大將, the leader of mischievous boys; the cock of the walk [school].

gakka (學科), *n.* ❶ (科目) a faculty (學部, 分科); a study; a subject of study (一科). ❷ (課程) a curriculum; a course (of study).

gakka (學課), *n.* a lesson; a task. ¶ 學課時間表, a table [schedule] of lesson-hours.

gakkai (學界), *n.* the learned world; the scholastic world. —學界の權威, the authority of the learned world.

gakkai (學會), *n.* an academy; an institution; a (learned) society. ¶ 東洋學會, the Oriental Society.

gakkan (學監), *n.* a school su-

perintendent. ⌈a school.⌉
gakkan (學館), *n.* an institution; ⌋
gakkari (がッかりした), *a.* ❶ (落膽) disheartened; dejected; downcast. ❷ (失望) disappointed; in despair. ❸ (疲勞) weary; tired; exhausted. —がッかりした樣子, ① a disappointed look; a look of despair. ② a tired look. —がッかりさす, ① to dishearten; dispirit. ② to disappoint. ③ to fatigue; weary. —がッかりする, ① to be disheartened. ② to be disappointed. ③ to be tired [worn] out; be exhausted; be fatigued. —がッかり力を落す, to be thoroughly disheartened; lose heart completely.
gakki (樂器), *n.* a (musical) instrument.
gakki (學期), *n.* a (school) term; a session 〖米〗. ¶ 學期試驗, a term examination.
gakkō (學校), *n.* a school; a college (高等の學校又は大學); an academy (中學乃至高等學校程度の). —學校へ行く, to go to school. —學校へ出す, to send [put] to school. —學校から歸る, to come home from school. —學校に入學する, to enter a school. —學校を休む, to be absent from school. ¶ 市町村立學校, a communal school. —學校時代, one's school-days. —學校友達, a schoolmate; a schoolfellow. —學校用品, school requisites.
gakkotsu (顎骨), *n.* the maxillary bone; the jaw-bone.
gakkyū (樂弓), *n.* 【音】 a bow.
gakkyū (學究), *n.* a student; a scholar. —學究的態度, scholastic attitude.
gakkyū (學級), *n.* a form; a class; a grade. ¶ 第三學級, the third grade [class]. ⌈artist.⌉
gakō (畫工), *n.* a painter; an⌋
gakōsō (鵞口瘡), *n.* ❶ 【醫】 aphthæ; thrush. ❷ (獸醫) the foot-and-mouth disease.
gaku (樂), *n.* music. —樂を奏する, to perform music; play (on a musical instrument); touch the strings.
gaku (學), *n.* ❶ (學問) learning; study. ❷ (知識) knowledge; attainment. ❸ (科學) a science.
gaku (萼), *n.* the calyx.
gaku (額), *n.* ❶ (ひたひ) the forehead. ❷ (額面) a tablet; a panel. ❸ (たか) a sum; an amount; quantity. —額を揭げる, to hang a framed picture; hang up a tablet.
gakubatsu (學閥), *n.* an academical clique; academical cliquism.
gakuboku (學僕), *n.* a servant-student; a servitor. ⌈の).⌉
gakubu (學部), *n.* faculty (大學⌋
gakubuchi (額緣), *n.* a picture-frame.
gakuchō (樂長), *n.* a conductor.
gakuchō (學長), *n.* a president; a dean; a director.
gakudō (學童), *n.* a school-child.
gakufu (岳父), *n.* the father of one's wife; a father-in-law.
gakufu (樂譜), *n.* 【音】 a score; a staff.
gakufu (學府), *n.* a çentre [seat] of learning. ¶ 最高學府, the highest centre [seat] of learning.
gakufū (學風), *n* a school; a method of study.
gakugei (學藝), *n.* ❶ sciences and arts. ❷ (修得せる) literary accomplishments.
gakugo (學語), *n.* a scientific term; a technical term.
gakugyo (鰐魚), *n.* 【爬蟲】 the crocodile; the alligator.
gakugyō (學業), *n.* school (-work); studies. —學業を勵む, to devote oneself to one's studies. —學業を廢する, to give up one's studies.
gakuha (學派), *n.* a school. ¶ エピキュラス學派, the School of Epicurus; the Epicureans.
gakuhi (學費), *n.* school [college] expenses. —學費に窮する, to be hard up [straitened] for school expenses.
gakui (學位), *n* a degree; an academical [a university] degree. —學位を授ける, to grant [confer] a degree. ¶ 學位授與式, ceremony for conferring degrees.
gakuji (學事), *n.* ❶ (學務) school [college] affairs; educational affairs. ❷ (學業) school-work; one's studies.
gakujutsu (學術), *n.* ❶ arts and sciences. ❷ (學問) learning; study. ❸ (學業) school-work. ¶ (通俗)學術講演會, a (popular) science lecture meeting. —學術試驗, examination in proficiency.
gakumen (額面), *n.* ❶ = *gaku* (額の)❷. ❷ (券面記載額) face-value; face. —額面以上で, above par; at a premium. —額面以下で, below par; at a discount. ¶ 額面價格, face par; nominal par.
gakumon (學問), *n* ❶ (學ぶこと) learning; study. ❷ = ***gakushiki***. ❸ a science (科學); a study (科目). —學問を好む, to be fond of study [learning].
gakumu (學務), *n.* school [college] affairs. ¶ 學務委員, a school-board (全體); a member of a

school-board (個人). —普通(専門)學務局, the Bureau of Common (Special) School Affairs.

gakunen (學年), *n.* an academical year; a school year. —學年試驗を終る, to finisn the annual examination.

gakurei (學齢), *n.* school age. —學齢に達する(達せぬ), to reach [be under] the school age. ¶ 學齢兒童, children of school age; schoolable children.

gakureki (學歴), *n.* an educational course; the course of studies pursued.

gakuri (學理), *n.* scientific reason [principle]; theory. —學理を應用する, to put a theory in practice.

gakuryō (學寮), *n.* ❶ (寄宿舍) a dormitory. ❷ (僧侶の修學所) a priests' seminary.

gakuryoku (學力), *n.* scholarship; knowledge. —中學卒業以上の學力ある者, a person possessing at least the proficiency of one who has completed the middle school course. —學力考査試驗を行ふ, to hold an examination for testing proficiency.

gakusei (學生), *n.* a student (中學以上); a scholar; a pupil. ¶ 學生帽, a school [college] cap. —學生服, school [college] uniform.

gakusei (學制), *n.* an educational system. ⌈administration.⌉

gakusei (學政), *n.* educational

gakuseki (學籍-簿), *n.* a school [college] register. —學校の學籍簿に名を列する, to keep one's name on the school register.

gakusetsu (學說), *n.* a theory; a doctrine. —學說を樹てる, to set up a theory.

gakusha (學者), *n.* a scholar; a learned man; a man of learning. —學者ぶる人, a pedant.

gakushi (學士), *n.* a university graduate; a bachelor. ¶ 學士會, a society of (university) graduates; a university club. —帝國學士院, the Imperial Academy.

gakushi (學資), *n.* ❶ (教育資金) an education fund; means for education. ❷ (學費) school expenses.

gakushi (樂師), *n.* a musician; a performer.

gakushiki (學識), *n.* learning; scholarship; erudition. —學識ある, learned; erudite. —學識に乏しい, defective in scholarship. —學識に富む, to possess high scholarship.

gakushu (樂手), *n.* a bandsman.

gakushū (學習する), *vt.* to study; learn. ☞ ***manabu***.

Gakushūin (學習院), *n.* the Peers' School. ¶ 女子學習院, the Peeresses' School.

gakusoku (學則), *n.* school rules [regulations].

gakutai (樂隊), *n.* a band; a musical band; an orchestra. ¶ 海(陸)軍樂隊, a naval (military) band. —樂隊長, a bandmaster. —樂隊員, a bandsman.

gakuto (學徒), *n.* ❶ a scholar; a student. ❷ (門下) disciples [followers] (of an eminent scholar).

gakuya (樂屋), *n.* ❶【劇】the green-room. ❷ (內幕) behind the scenes; the inside.

gakuyū (學友), *n.* ❶ (同窓) a school-fellow [-mate]; a fellow-student. ❷ (學問上の友) a literary friend. ¶ 學友會, the old boys' society; a meeting [gathering] of old boys.

gakuzen (愕然), *ad.* in amazement; amazedly; aghast. —愕然として色を失ふ, to turn pale with amazement. —愕然として爲す所を知らず, to be amazed out of one's wits.

gama (香蒲), *n.*【植】the cat-o-nine-tails; the cat-tail.

gama (蝦蟇), *n.*【兩棲】the bull-frog; the toad. =***hikigaeru.***

gamaguchi (蟇口), *n.* a pouch; a purse.

gaman (我慢), *n.* ❶ (忍耐) patience; endurance. ❷ (容赦) forbearance. ❸ (自制) self-denial; self-restraint. —我慢强い, patient; of great endurance. —我慢する, ① to endure; persevere; bear; stand. ② to put up *with*; bear *with*. ③ to restrain oneself; control oneself. —我慢しきれない, to be beyond endurance; be past bearing.

-gamashii (がましい), *suf.* looking like; appearing to be. —嫉妬がましい素振り, jealous-looking behaviour. —晴がましく著飾る, to be dressed out as for a holiday.

gamigami (がみがみ), *ad.* shrewishly; snappishly; snarlingly. —人をがみがみ叱り飛ばす, to blow a fellow up sky-high.

gamusha (我武者), *n.* a dare-devil; a devil-may-care fellow.

gan (雁), *n.*【鳥】the wild goose.

gan (願), *n.* a vow; an invocation. —願をかける, to make an invocation. —願にかけて毎朝早起する, to make it a point to get up early every morning.

gan (癌), *n.*【醫】a cancer.

ganbaru (頑張る), *vi.* to insist *upon*; persist *in*; keep a stiff upper lip; stand firm. ——, *a.* insistent; persistent.

ganbyō (眼病), *n.* ophthalmia; an eye-affection [disease].

ganchiku (含蓄), *n.* implication; comprehension; inclusion. —含蓄的, implicative; implicit. —含蓄する, to imply; comprise; include.

ganchū (眼中), *ad.* in the eye. —彼等の眼中に置かれない, to count for little in their eyes.

gandōjōchin (强盗提燈), *n.* a dark lantern.

gańen (岩鹽), *n.* rock-salt.

gangan (がんがん), *ad.* clang-clang; clangorously. —耳がガンガン鳴る, to have a buzzing [ringing] in the ear.

gangasa (雁瘡), *n.* ecthyma.

gangi (雁木), *n.* ❶ (犬牙の如く入れ違ったもの) zigzag. ❷ (段段) steps; tiers.

gangu (玩具), *n.* a toy; a plaything. ¶ 玩具商, a toy-dealer.

gangu (頑愚), *n.* pig-headedness; obstinacy. —頑愚な, pig-headed.

ganjitsu (元日), *n.* the New Year's Day.

ganjō (頑丈, 岩乗), *n.* ❶ (强壯) browniness; sturdiness; stoutness. ❷ (堅牢) solidity; strength. ——**-na,** *a.* ❶ brawny; strong; robust. ❷ solid; strong (-built); sturdy. —岩乗な身體, a strong constitution. —頑丈な杖, a stout stick.

ganka (眼下に), *ad.* beneath the eye. —眼下に見る, ①(見下ろす) to command; overlook; have under vision. ②(蔑視する) to look down *upon.*

ganka (眼科), *n.* ophthalmology. ¶ 眼科醫, an oculist; an ophthalmologist.

ganka (眼窩), *n.* 【解】 the orbit of the eye; the eye-socket.

gankai (眼界), *n.* the field of vision; eyeshot; view. —眼界に入り來る, to come into one's field of vision; come in sight. —眼界を大にして宇內を視る, to extend the field of vision and see the universe.

ganken (眼瞼), *n.* 【解】 the palpebra [*pl.* -ræ]; the eyelid.

ganken (頑健), *n.* vigorous health. —頑健な, healthy.

gankin (元金), *n.* the principal.

ganko (頑固), *n.* obstinacy; stubbornness; bigotry. —— **-na,** *a.* obstinate; stubborn; bigoted. —頑固な心, a stubborn heart. ¶ 頑固爺, an obstinate old fellow.

gankō (眼孔), *n.* the eyehole; the orbit of the eye; the eye-socket.

gankō (眼光), *n.* ❶ (眼の光) the glitter of the eye. ❷ (眼力) light; penetration; insight. —眼光の鋭い, lynx-eyed; sharp-sighted; eagle-eyed.

gankō (雁行), *n.* the flight of wild geese. —雁行する, to walk abreast; go side by side; keep up *with.*

gankubi (雁首), *n.* the bowl (of a pipe).

gankutsu (巖窟), *n.* a cave; a cavern; a grotto.

gankyō (頑强な), *a.* headstrong; unbending; stubborn. —頑强な抵抗, a stubborn [stout; vigorous] resistance. —頑强に抵抗する, to offer stubborn resistance.

gankyū (眼球), *n.* 【解】 the ball [bulb] of the eye; the eyeball. ¶ 眼球炎, ophthalmitis.

ganmei (頑迷な), *a.* bigoted; pig-headed; obstinate.

ganmen (顏面), *n.* the face. ¶ 眼面神經痛, face-ache; facial neuralgia.

ganmi (翫味する), *vt.* ❶ to taste. ❷ to appreciate.

ganmō (願望), *n.* a wish; a desire. —願望を遂げる, to fulfil one's wishes.

ganmoku (眼目), *n.* the (main) point; the pith; the essence. —眼目とする所, the principal object in view. —問題の眼目を閑却して枝葉に走る, to overlook the point of the question and digress into side issues.

gannen (元年), *n.* the first year.

ganpeki (岸壁), *n.* a sea-wall; a quay.

ganpi (がんぴ), *n.* 【植】 ❶ (剪夏羅) Lychnis coronata (campion の一種・學名). ❷ (雁皮) Wickstrœmia sikokianum (native daphne の類・學名). ¶ 雁皮紙, thin rice-paper.

ganrai (元來), *ad.* originally; primarily; in the first place (第一). —元來の, real; original; primary.

ganri (元利), *n.* the principal and interest. —元利耳を揃へる, to bring both the principal and interest. ¶ 元利合計, amount with interest added.

ganrō (玩弄する), *vt.* to play *with*; dally *with*; trifle *with.* —他人の玩弄物となる, to become another's plaything. ¶ 玩弄紙幣, toy paper-money.

ganryō (顏料), *n.* ❶ cosmetics; face-paints. ❷ (繪具) a colour.

ganryoku (眼力), *n.* ❶ (視力) eyesight; sight; power of vision. ❷ (洞察力) insight; penetration. —鋭い眼力, sharp insight; acute penetration.

ganseki (巖石, 岩石), *n.* a rock.
ganshiki (眼識), *n.* discernment; penetration; insight.
ganshoku (顏色), *n.* the face; complexion; countenance. —顏色を變やる, to change one's countenance; change colour. —顏色を失ふ, to lose colour; turn pale. —顏色を和げる, to soften one's features. —人をして顏色なからしめる, It leaves tae others nowhere.
ganshu (癌腫), *n.* 【醫】a cancer.
ganso (元祖), *n.* the originator; the founder; the father.
gansō (含嗽), *n.* =*ugai* (含嗽).
gansui (含水の), *a.* 【化·鑛】hydrous.
gantan (元旦), *n.* the New Year's Day. ¶ 元旦試筆, the trial writing of the New Year's Day.
gan-toshite (頑として), *ad.* obstinately; stubbornly. —頑として聽き入れぬ, He stubbornly refuses to hear of it.
gaṅyaku (丸藥), *n.* a pill.
gaṅyū (含有する), *vt.* to contain; hold; have...*in*.
ganzen (眼前に), *ad.* before one's eyes; in one's sight; in one's presence. ☞ *mokuzen.* —(危險・死などが)眼前に迫る, to stare one in the face. —眼前で起る, to happen in one's sight.
ganzenai (頑是ない), *a.* innocent; artless.
ganzō (贋造する), *vt.* to counterfeit; forge; fabricate. —贋造の, counterfeit; forged; spurious; false. ¶ 贋造物, a forgery; a counterfeit. —贋造貨幣, base [counterfeit; spurious] coin; counterfeit money. (贋造貨幣を行使する, to utter base coin.) —贋造者, a counterfeiter; a forger; a fabricator.
ga-pen (鵞ペン), *n.* a quill(-pen).
gappei (合併), *n.* ❶ (打ッて一丸とすること) union; combination; amalgamation. ❷ (一方が他方を併す) annexation (領土など); affiliation (會社など). —合併する, ① to unite; combine; amalgamate. ② to annex; affiliate.
gappi (月日), *n.* the date. —月日の知れぬ, dateless; undated. —月日を記す, to put down [enter; give] the date; date.
gappon (合本する), *vt.* to bind together; bind in one volume. ¶ 講義錄合本, a bound volume of lectures.
gara (柄), *n.* ❶ (模樣) pattern; design. ❷ (體格) build; stature (身長). —良(惡)い柄, a good (poor) pattern. —澁い[凝ッた]柄, a tasteful pattern. —柄にない事をする, to do a thing at variance with one's appearance; go out of one's character.
-gara (柄), *suf.* situation; standing; nature. —商賣柄, the nature of one's trade. —時節柄, ① the time of the season. ② (時の形勢) in view of the times.
garagara (がらがら), *ad.* ❶ (物が觸れ合ひ鳴るさま) with a rattle [clatter]. ❷ (愼ましからぬさま) flightily. ——, *n.* (がらんがらん) a rattle. —ガラガラ鳴る, to rattle; clatter; crash. —ガラガラ落ちる, to clatter down.
garakuta (がらくた), *n.* lumber; rubbish; odds and ends. ¶ がらくた道具, odd articles.
garan (伽藍), *n.* a Buddhist temple. ¶ 大伽藍, a cathedral; a minster.
garanchō (塘鵝), *n.* 【鳥】the pelican.
garandō (空洞), *n.* void; emptiness; hollowness.
garanten (ガランテン), *n.* 【料理】galantine.
garari (がらりと), *ad.* entirely; quite; completely. —がらりと變る, to change [alter] completely. —がらりと晴れる, to turn fine; turn into bright weather. —がらりと當が外れる, to have one's expectation completely falsified.
garasu (硝子), *n.* glass. —窓に硝子を嵌める, to put a pane in the window. ¶ 擂[艶消]硝子, frosted [ground] glass. —(著)色硝子, coloured glass; stained glass. —剪嵌め彩色硝子, mosaic glass. —硝子箱, a glass-case; a case (標本又は器物等の). —硝子壜, a glass bottle, a phial; a vial. —硝子戶, a sash-door. —硝子紙, glass-paper (布製は glass-cloth). —硝子板, a sheet of glass; a plate glass; a (window-)pane. —硝子切り, (切斷器又は人) a glass-cutter. —硝子工, a glass-blower. —硝子工場, a glass manufactory; glass-works. —硝子窓, a glass window; a sash-window. —硝子障子, a glass [glass-windowed] sliding door. —硝子屋, a glass-man; a glazier.
gareki (瓦礫), *n.* rubble; trash; rubbish.
garon (瓩), *n.* a gallon (容量單位・英國では我が二升五合二勺に當り米國では約二升一合に當る).
-garu (がる), ❶ (せんと欲す, と感ず) to want *to*; long *for*; feel like. ❷=*buru* (振る). —惜しがる, to be loath to part *with*. —痒がる, to feel itchy. —痛がる, to complain of pain. —氣の毒がる, to feel sorry *for*. —行きたがる,

to wish to go. —獨りで偉がッて居る, to think oneself great.

garyō (雅量), *n.* generosity; magnanimity; broad-mindedness. —雅量ある, generous; magnanimous; broad-minded. —雅量を示す, to show one's broad-mindedness. —人を容れる雅量がない, He has no capacity for tolerance.

garyū (我流), *n.* one's own style [method; way].

gasagasa (がさがさ), *ad.* rustlingly.

gasatsu (我雜な), *a.* bearish; rude; rough. ¶ 我雜者, a rude [bearish] fellow; an unmannerly person; a bear.

gashi (餓死する), *vi.* to die of starvation; die from [of] hunger; starve to death.

gashin-shōtan (臥薪嘗膽), *n.* suffering privations; enduring hardships. —臥薪嘗膽十年の後, after ten years of great hardships.

gashitsu (畫室), *n.* an *atelier* 〔佛〕; a studio.

gashō (臥床), *n.* lying in bed.

gasorin (ガソリン), *n.* gasoline.

gassai (合切), *ad.* all; all together. ¶ 合切袋, a grab-all; a hold-all; a travelling sack. —合切籠, a hamper.

gassaku (合作), *n.* a joint production [work]; collaboration.

gassan (合算する), *vt.* to add up [together]; sum up; cast up.

gasshiri (がッしり), *ad.* ❶ (物のよく合ふさま), exactly; to a nicety [T]. ❷ (充滿するさま) fully. —がッしりした, sturdy; stout; vigorous.

gasshō (合唱), *n.* chorus. —合唱する, to sing in chorus; chorus. ¶ 合唱團, a chorus; a choir.

gasshūkoku (合衆國), *n.* a federal state; the United States (U. S. と略す). ¶ 北米合衆國, the United States of America (公稱にして U. S. A. と略す); America (俗稱). (北米合衆國大統領, the President of the United States of North America. —合衆國政府, the United States Government.

gasshuku (合宿する), *vi.* to board [lodge] together. ¶ 巡查合宿所, a police boarding-house.

gassō (合奏), *n.* a concert. —合奏する, [*vi.*] 【音】 to score; play [sing] in concert. ¶ 二部合奏, a duet, duette. —三部合奏, a trio. —四部台奏, a quartet. (絃樂四部合奏, a string quartet.)

gas-suru (合する), *v.* ❶ (合併) to combine *with*; unite *with*; join. ❷ (一致) to agree *with*; be at one *with*; accord *with*. ❸ (合算) to add [put] together; sum up. —目的に合する, to accord with one's object. —合して一となる, to combine into one.

gasu (瓦斯), *n.* gas; coal-gas. —瓦斯の漏れぬ, gas-tight. —瓦斯を引く, to lay on gas. —瓦斯をつける, to light [turn on] the gas. —瓦斯を消す, to turn off the gas. ¶ 瓦斯エンヂン, a gas-engine. —瓦斯發動機, a gas-motor. —瓦斯會社, a gas company. —瓦斯火口, a gas-burder; a gas-jet. —瓦斯竈, a gas-oven; a gas-range. —瓦斯管, a gas-pipe; a gas-main. —瓦斯檢出器, a gas-indicator. —瓦斯マントル, a gas-mantle. —瓦斯メートル, a gas-meter. —瓦斯ストーヴ, a gas-stove. —瓦斯體, a gaseous body. —瓦斯タンク, a gas-tank. —瓦斯燈, a gas-light; a gas-lamp. —瓦斯用器具, gas-fittings.

gasuito (瓦斯絲), *n.* gassed yarn.

ga-suru (賀する), *vt.* to celebrate (式典を擧げて); congratulate another *upon*; wish a person joy (of the occasion).

gatagata (がたがた), *ad.* with a rattling sound. —がたがたする, I. [*vt.*] ① (音) to chatter; rattle. ② (搖れる) to shake (家など); jolt (馬車が); be shaky (梯子段など); shiver [shake] (with cold); tremble (with fear). II. [*a.*] shaky; crazy; rickety.

-gatai (難い), *suf.* hard; difficult; impossible. —到底行はれ難い, to be quite impossible to carry out. —二度とあり得難い機會, an opportunity which is not likely to come again.

gātā-kunshō (ガーター勳章), *n.* the Garter (英國ナイトの最高勳章, 同國民中受勳者は二十五名に限る); the Order of the Garter. ¶ ガーター勳爵士, Knight of the Garter (K. G. と略す).

gatakuribasha (我多馬車), *n.* a rattle-trap; a shandrydan.

gatapishi (がたぴし), *ad.* with a bang; with a rattle.

gatchi (合致), *n.* agreement; coincidence; accordance. —意志の合致, agreement of intentions. —合致する, to agree *with*; coincide *with*; accord *with*.

gateki (畫的), *a.* picturesque; scenical.

gaten (合點する), *v.* to understand; comprehend; grasp; catch; see; take in. —能く合點が行くまで, until you thoroughly understand it. —おッと合點だ, All right; I see.

-gatera (がてら), *suf.* =*-katagata.*

gatsugatsu (がつがつ食ふ), *v.* to devour; stodge; eat greedily [ravenously].

gayagaya(がやがや), *ad.* noisily; clamorously.

gāze(ガーゼ), *n.* 〔獨 gaze〕 lint; charpie.

gazen (俄然), *ad.* suddenly.

gazō (畫像), *n.* a likeness; a portrait. —人の畫像を描く, to paint a person's portrait.

gazoku(雅俗), *n.* ❶ the classical and the common. ❷ (雅人と俗物) the refined and the vulgar.

ge (下), *n.* inferiority. —下の下, the lowest (poorest) of all. —甲の下, the lowest (lower) class of the first grade.

-ge (げ), *suf.* as if; having the appearance *of.* —怪しげな家, a suspicious-looking house. —心ありげに, as if one had something in one's mind. —意味ありげな口振り, a significant way of speaking. —心地よげに眠る, to sleep with a snug look.

geba (下馬), *n.* ❶ (下乘) dismount. ❷ (乘馬通行禁止) order to dismount. ¶ 下馬評, an outside comment.

geban (下番する), *vi.* to come off guard.

gedai (外題), *n.* the title [name] of a play; the play; the piece. —狂言の外題, the title of the play.

gedatsu (解脫), *n.* 〔梵 Vimokcha〕 deliverance; salvation; emancipation. —煩惱を解脫する, to be delivered from worldly passions.

gedō (外道), *n.* ❶ (己の信敎外の敎) heathenism. ❷ (同上敎徒) a heathen.

gedoku (解毒の), *a.* antidotal; anti-poison. ¶ 解毒劑, an antidote; a counterpoison.

gehin (下品な), *a.* mean; vulgar; coarse. —下品な言葉, coarse [vulgar] language. —下品な生ひ立ち, low-breeding.

gei (藝), *n.* ❶ (技能) ability; capacity. ❷ (技術) arts; crafts. ❸ (演技) a performance. ❹ (遊藝) an accomplishment. ❺ (藝當) a feat; a trick. —藝を仕込む, to have accomplishments taught. —藝盡しをやる, to show off one's accomplishments in turn.

geigi (藝妓), *n.* a *geisha*; a singing girl.

geigō (迎合する), *v.* to truckle *to*; cringe *to*; cultivate; chime in *with.*

geiin (鯨飲する), *v.* to drink deep [hard]; drink like a fish [sponge].

geijutsu (藝術), *n.* art; the arts.

——-teki, *a.* artistic. —藝術的作品, a work of art. ¶ 低級藝術, art of low order; low-class art. —藝術家, an artist. —藝術衝動, art impulse.

geika(猊下), *n.* His Holiness (羅馬法王); His Eminence (君牧師).

geimei (藝名), *n.* a professional name.

geinin (藝人), *n.* an artiste; a public performer.

geisha (藝者), *n.* a *geisha*; a singing-girl.

geishu(迎珠), *n.* 【解】the tragus.

geitō (藝當), *n.* a trick; a feat; a performance. —あぶない藝當をする, to do dangerous feats.

geiyu (鯨油), *n.* train-oil (特に脊美鯨の); whale-oil.

geji (下知する), *vt.* to command; order; give orders. —下知を傳へる, to deliver a command.

gejigeji (蚰蜒), *n.* 【多足】the milliped. —蚰蜒のやうに嫌はれる, to be hated like a viper.

gejo (下女), *n.* a maid-servant; a servant-girl; a maid. —下女奉公に出る, to go out to service as a maid-servant. —下女を雇入れる, to engage a maid-servant.

gejun (下旬), *n.* the last ten days (of a month).

geka (外科-學), *n.* surgery. —外科手術を施す, to operate; perform a surgical operation. ¶ 整形外科學, plastic surgery. —外科手術室, a surgery; an operating room. —外科用機械, surgical instruments.

gekai(下界), *n.* the lower world; this world.

gekan (下疳), *n.* chancre. ¶ 軟性下疳, a chancroid.

geki (隙), *n.* ❶ (すきま) a crevice; a chink; a crack. ❷ (不和) enmity; a quarrel. —彼等の間に隙を生じた, A quarrel arose among them.

geki (劇), *n.* drama; a play; theatricals. ¶ 劇文學, drama; dramatic literature.

geki (檄-文), *n.* a declaration; a manifesto. —檄を四方に飛ばす, to scatter manifestos in all directions.

gekichin(擊沈する), *vt.* to sink; send to the bottom.

gekidan (劇壇), *n.* the stage. —劇壇に立つ (を去る), to come [go] on (go off; leave) the stage.

gekido(激怒), *n.* fury; rage; wrath; exasperation. —激怒する, to blaze [flare] up; rage; fly into a passion [rage]; boil with rage.

gekidō (激動さす), *vt.* ❶ to excite; agitate; ferment. ❷ to convulse; shake violently.

gekigakki(擊樂器), *n.* an instrument of percussion.

gekiha (撃破する), *vt.* ❶(物を) to blow up; crush. ❷(敵を) to defeat; rout; crush. —敵軍を物の見事に撃破する, to inflict a crushing defeat upon the enemy.

gekihen (劇變), *n.* revolution(社會などの); revulsion (感情の); 【地質】convulsion. —劇變する, to change violently [suddenly].

gekihyō (劇評), *n.* dramatic criticism. ¶ 劇評家, a dramatic critic.

gekijin (劇甚な), *a.* intense; vehement; vigorous; keen; sharp. —競爭劇甚を極む, The competition is most severe.

gekijō (劇場), *n.* a theatre; a playhouse. ¶ 帝國劇場, the Imperial Theatre.

gekijō (激情), *n.* fury; flame; passion. —激情に驅られる, to be carried away by a fit of passion.

gekijō(撃攘する), *vt.* to dislodge; expel; drive away.

gekika (劇化する), *vt.* to dramatize.

gekikai (劇界), *n.* the theatrical world; the stage.

gekikō (激昂), *n.* excitement; agitation. —激昂さす, to excite; incense; infuriate. —激昂する, to be excited; be infuriated; flame [blaze; fire] up.

gekimetsu (撃滅する), *vt.* to annihilate; exterminate; destroy.

gekimu (劇務), *n.* an onerous [burdensome] duty; the press of business. —劇務に斃れる, to succumb to the strain of overwork; fall victim to the press of business.

gekirei(激勵する), *vt.* to encourage; incite; stimulate; spur on; stir up.

gekiretsu (激烈な), *a.* severe; vehement; intense. —激烈な競爭, a keen competition; a sharp contest. —激烈な地震, a severe [violent] earthquake. —激烈な寒さ, intense cold.

gekirin (逆鱗), *n.* Imperial [Royal] wrath. —逆鱗に觸れる, to incur another's displeasure.

gekirō (激浪), *n.* angry waves; raging billows; heavy [high] seas. —天を拍つ激浪, the raging billows that beat against the sky. —激浪に浚はれる, to be swept away by angry waves.

gekiron (激論), *n.* a violent dispute [controversy]; a heated argument [discussion]. —激論する, to dispute angrily; have high words; discuss hotly; argue with warmth.

gekiryū(激流), *n.* a rapid [swift] current; a rapid.

gekisaku (劇作), *n.* dramatization; a drama. ¶ 劇作家, a dramatist; a playwright.

gekisei (劇性の), *a.* acute (急性の); violent (劇烈の); malignant (惡性の). ¶ 劇性病, an acute [a virulent] disease.

gekisei(激成する), *vt.* to intensify; aggravate; heighten. —變亂を激成する, to aggravate the disturbance.

gekisen(激戰), *n.* a severe fight [battle]; a bloody battle. —激戰する, to fight furiously.

gekishin (激震), *n.* a severe [violent] shock (of earthquake).

gekishō (激賞する), *vt.* to extol [praise] to the skies; praise highly; speak of (a person) in high terms.

gekishoku (劇職), *n.* a busy office; a burdensome post. —劇職に就く, to assume [take up] a busy office.

geki-suru (激する), *vi.* ❶ (激昂) to be excited; be infuriated; be enraged. ❷ (激流など) to dash *against*. —激して, furiously; in a passion; in hot blood. —激し易い, excitable; hot-headed [-brained]; inflammable. —急流の巖石に激する音, the noise of the rapid current dashing against the rocks.

gekitai (撃退), *n.* ❶ (撃攘) repulse. ❷ [錯] (拒絶) refusal; rejection. **——-suru**, *vt.* ❶ to repulse; repel; drive back. ❷ to refuse; reject. —撃退される, to meet with [suffer] a repulse. —敵の來襲を撃退する, to repel the enemy's assault [attack].

gekitaku (撃柝), *n.* beating of clappers. —第一の撃柝, the first beat [stroke] of clappers.

gekitetsu(撃鐵), *n.* a gun-lock; a hammer; a cock. —撃鐵を上げる, to cock; raise the cock.

gekitsū (劇痛), *n.* a sharp [an acute] pain; a severe [violent] pain.

gekitsū (劇通), *n.* an expert in dramas.

gekitotsu(激突), *n.* a shock; a violent collision.

gekiyaku (劇藥), *n.* a powerful medicine. —劇藥往生を企てる, to plan a suicide by taking a powerful medicine.

gekkan(月刊), *n.* monthly publication. ¶ 月刊雜誌, a monthly (magazine).

gekkei(月經), *n.* 【醫】catamenia; the courses; menses. ¶ 月經期, the menstrual [catamenial] period.

gekkeiju (月桂樹), *n.* 【植】the bay-laurel; the bay-tree.

gekkeikan (月桂冠), *n.* ❶ a laurel crown [wreath]; the bays. ❷

(優勝又はその名譽) honours; laurels. —勝利の月桂冠, the laurel of victory —月桂冠を戴く, to reap [win] laurels.

gekken (擊劍), *n.* fencing. ¶ 擊劍道場, a fencing-school; a fencing-hall. —擊劍家, a fencer. —擊劍試合, a fencing-match. —擊劍師範, a fencing-master.

gekkin (月琴), *n.* a *yukin*〔支那〕; a moon-guitar.

gekkō (月光), *n.* the moonbeam; moonlight; moonshine. —月光を浴びる, to be flooded by the moonlight; bathe in the moonlight.

gekkyū (月給), *n.* a monthly salary. —百圓の月給を取る, to receive a monthly salary of 100 *yen*; draw [take] a salary of 100 *yen* a month. ¶ 月給日, a salary [pay-] day. —月給取, a salaried person.

geko (下戸), *n.* a temperate person; a non-drinker.

gemen (外面), *n.* the face; the outward appearance. —外面如菩薩內心如夜叉, beauty without and foulness within; a fair face with a foul heart.

gēmu (ゲーム), *n.* a game. ¶ ゲーム取り, a marker.

gen (言), *n.* a word; a speech; a remark. —言を俟たず, to go without saying; be needless to say. —言を食む, to eat one's own words; eat the leek. —言を左右に託す, to equivocate.

gen (弦), *n.* ❶ (弓づる) a bow-string. ❷ (曲線上の二點を結ぶ直線) a chord. ❸ (斜線) the hypotenuse. ❹ (月の) a quarter.

gen (舷), *n.* the gunwale; the gunnel. —舷々相摩して, board and [by] board; on even board *with*.

gen (絃), *n.* a string;【音】a chord (琴などの).

gen (現), *a.* present; actual. ¶ 現皇帝, reigning sovereign. —現戶主, the present head of the family.

gen (嚴), *n.* strictness; severity. —嚴に過ぎず寬に失せず, to be neither too strict nor too indulgent.

gen (驗), *n.* virtue; efficacy; effect.

genan (下男), *n.* a male [man-] servant.

geńan (原案), *n.* the original bill [motion; draft; proposal]. —原案通り可決する, to pass a bill in its original form; pass a bill as drafted. —原案に贊成する, to support the original proposal. —原案を提出する, to produce a draft proposal.

genba (現場), *n.* =*genjō* (現場).

genbatsu (嚴罰), *n.* a severe punishment. —嚴罰に處する, to punish severely; inflict a severe punishment.

genbo (原簿), *n.* a ledger; an original register.

genbun (原文), *n.* ❶ (本文) the text. ❷ (原作) the original.

genbuńitchi (言文一致), *n.* unification of (a style unifying) the spoken and written languages.

genbutsu (現物), *n.* ❶ the article; the thing. ❷ spot-goods. ❸ stocks. ¶ 現物問屋 [仲買], a spot-broker.

gendai (現代), *n.* to-day; the present time [day]; the day [the age; the period]. —現代化する, to modernize. ¶ 現代語, a living language. —現代人, a modern. —現代思想, modern ideas.

gendan (嚴談), *n.* a strong protest (抗議); a strong demand for explanation (詰問). —嚴談を持ち込む, to enter a strong protest.

gendo (限度), *n.* a limit. —限度を超す(に達する), to exceed (reach) the limit.

gendō (言動), *n.* speech and conduct. ☞ *genkō* (言行). —言動を愼む, to be circumspect in speech and conduct.

gendō (原動的), *a.* motive. ¶ 原動機, a prime mover; a motor. —原動力, motive power [force]; generative power.

geńei (幻影), *n.*【心】an illusion; a vision; a phantasm; a phantom; phantasmagoria.

geńeki (現役), *n.* active service; commission (軍艦の). —現役中の, in commission (軍艦の); in active service. —現役に服する, to enter active service. ¶ 現役兵, a soldier [a private] in active service. —現役艦, a commissioned vessel; a vessel in commission.

genetsuzai (解熱劑), *n.* an antifebrile: an antipyretic; a febrifuge.

gengai (言外の), *a.* unexpressed. —言外の意味を掛(ク)む, to read between the lines.

gengaku (絃樂), *n.* string music. ¶ 絃樂器, a stringed instrument.

gengaku (減額する), *vt.* to abate; reduce; cut down.

gengaku (衒學), *n.* pedantry; bookishness. —衒學的文體, a pedantic style. ¶ 衒學者, a pedant.

genge (紫雲英), *n.*【植】the Chinese milk-vetch. =***rengesō.***

gengetsu (弦月), *n.* the crescent moon; the sickle moon.

gengi (原義), *n.* the original [primary] meaning.

gengo (言語), *n.* a language; a speech; a word. —言語を愼む,

to be careful in speech; weigh one's words. ¶ 言語學, philology. (言語學者, a philologist.)

gengo (原語), *n.* the original word [language].

gengō (元號), *n.* the name of an era.

gengō (減號), *n.* 【數】 a negative [minus] sign.

gengorō (龍蝨), *n.* 【昆】 the Japanese water-beetle.

gengyōin (現業員), *n.* an operative.

geñin (原因), *n.* a cause (結果に對する根本原因); a reason (理由); the origin (根原). —出火の原因, the origin of the fire. —原因に溯れば, to go back to the cause.

geñin (現員), *n.* the actual staff.

genji (現時), *ad.* at present; nowadays. —現時の, present; present-day; modern.

genjin (原人), *n.* the primitive man. ¶ 原人時代, the primitive age.

genjitsu (現實), *n.* the actuality; the reality. **——-no,** *a.* actual; real; existent. —現實の社會, the real world. —現實化する, to actualize; realize.

genjō (原狀), *n.* the original state; *status quo ante* 〔羅〕. ¶ 原狀回復, 【法】 *restitutio in integrum*; recovery of the original state; revivor (訴訟上の).

genjō (現狀), *n.* the actual condition; the (present) situation [state]; the existing state of affairs; the *status quo.* ¶ 現狀維持, the maintenance of the *status quo.*

genjō (現場), *n.* the spot; the scene (of action); the actual place (築建場等の). —現場で, on the spot; (*in*) *flagrante delicto* 〔羅〕. —現場へ驅け著ける [急行する], to hurry to the scene. —現場を目撃する, to see the scene [actual spot].

genjū (嚴重な), *a.* strict; stringent; rigorous; severe; secure (堅固). —嚴重な規則, a strict rule. —嚴重に取締る, to manage [control] strictly. (門の內外を嚴重に取締る, to guard the gate strictly within and without.)

genjutsu (幻術), *n.* magic; sorcery; the black art. ¶ 幻術者, a magician; a sorcerer [*fem.* sorceress].

genka (言下に), *ad.* at the word; promptly.

genka (原價, 元價), *n.* the original price [cost]; the cost price. ¶ 原價販賣, sale at cost price. —原價計算, cost-accounting.

genka (現下), *ad.* at present; at the moment. —現下の問題, the question of the hour.

genka (減價), *n.* reduction of price; abatement; discount. —一割の減價で賣る, to sell at ten per cent. discount. ¶ 特別減價販賣, a special discount sale.

genkai (限界), *n.* bounds; confines; limits; limitation. —限界する, to limit; bound; 【醫】 localize. ¶ 限界線, a boundary line; line of demarcation.

genkaku (幻覺), *n.* 【哲】 hallucination.

genkaku (嚴格), *n.* strictness; severity; rigour. —嚴格に云へば, strictly speaking; in the strict sense of the word. **——-na,** *a.* strict; severe; rigorous. —嚴格な規律, strict discipline. —嚴格な檢查, strict inspection. —嚴格な敎師, a strict schoolmaster.

genkan (玄關), *n.* ❶ an entrance; a front door; a street-door. ❷ an entrance-hall; a hall; a portico. —玄關拂ひを食ふ, to be driven from the door. ¶ 玄關番, a janitor; a door-keeper; a hall-keeper.

genkan (嚴寒), *n.* sharp frost; severe [intense] cold.

genkei (原形), *n.* original form. —原形に復する, to return to the original form. —殆ど原形を止めず, with hardly a trace of the original form. ¶ 原形質, 【生物】 protoplasm.

genkei (減刑), *n.* commutation (of penalty); mitigation (of penalty). —減刑する, to commute a sentence; mitigate a punishment.

genki (元氣), *n.* energy (精力); spirit (氣力); vigour. —元氣な, spirited; high-spirited; lively. —元氣よく, spiritedly. —元氣づく, to rally one's strength; recruit oneself; recover one's spirits. —元氣である, to be in good [high] spirits; be of good cheer. —元氣がない, to be out of sorts [spirits]; be in low spirits. —元氣を出す, to cheer up; show spirit; brace oneself up. —元氣をつける, to cheer up; hearten up.

genki (衒氣), *n.* flauntiness; ostentatiousness. —衒氣滿々, to be flaunty all over.

genkin (現金), *n.* (卽金) cash; ready money. —現金で買ふ, to buy outright. —現金で賣る, to sell for cash (down). **——-na,** *a.* venal; mercenary; calculating. ¶ 現金拂, cash payment. —現金勘定, cash account. —現金値段, cash price. —現金取引, cash [ready money] transaction; cash trade. —現金取立郵便, C. O. D. [cash on delivery] post.

genkin (嚴禁する), *vt.* to prohibit strictly; interdict; ban.

genkō (言行), *n.* saying and doing; words and deeds; speech and action. —言行一致の人, a man of his word. —言行一致する, to be as good as one's word.

genkō(原稿), *n.* a manuscript; a copy. ¶ 原稿料, copy-money. —原稿用紙, copy paper.

genkō (現行), *n.* ❶ (犯罪の) being in the commission of the crime; being in the act *of.* ❷ (事の) being actually in force [operation]; being now in use. —現行の教科書, the text-books now in use. —現行條約の上では, according to the existing treaty. —現行中捕へらる, to be caught in the act; be caught red-handed [*flagrante delicto*]. ¶ 現行犯, a flagrant offence. —現行法, the existing law; the law in force.

genkoku (原告), *n.* 【法】 the plaintiff; the complainant. ¶ 原告代理人, the plaintiff's attorney; the complainant's counsel.

genkoku (嚴酷な), *a.* severe; rigorous; stern.

genkon (現今), *ad.* nowadays; at present; at this day. ——**-no,** *a.* present; current. —現今の趨勢より察すれば, judging from the present tendency [trend of affairs].

genkotsu (拳骨), *n.* a fist. —拳骨を喰はす, to punch; thump; fetch a blow; (strike with the) fist. —拳骨を固める, to clench [clinch] one's fist.

genkun (元勳), *n.* a veteran [elder] statesman. —維新(國家)の元勳, a veteran statesman of the Restoration (nation).

genkyō(元兇), *n.* an arch-villain; a ringleader; the head of a gang (of evil-doers).

genkyō (現況), *n.* the present condition; the situation.

genkyū (言及する), *v.* to advert to; make mention *of*: refer *to*; allude *to*; touch *upon*.

genkyū (原級), *n.* 【文】 the positive (degree).

genmai (玄米), *n.* unhulled rice.

genmei (言明), *n.* declaration; announcement. —言明する, to declare; announce. —政府が先きに言明せる通り, as was lately declared by the government.

genmei (嚴命する), *v.* to give strict orders.

genmen (減免), *n.* ❶ (刑の) mitigation and remission. ❷ (租税の) reduction and exemption.

genmetsu (幻滅), *n.* disillusion; disillusionment. —幻滅の悲哀, sorrow of disillusionment.

genmin(原民), *n.* aborigines; aboriginals.

genmitsu (嚴密な), *a.* strict; exact; scrupulous. —嚴密に, strictly; to the letter. —嚴密な注意(檢査), strict attention (examination).

genmoku (眩目する), *v.* to daze; dazzle. —人をして眩目せしめる, to dazzle people.

genmon (舷門), *n.* gangway.

genmyō(玄妙な), *a.* mystic(-al); mysterious; miraculous; occult.

gen-ni (現に), *ad.* ❶ actually; with one's own eyes. ❷ (言ッて見れば) for instance.

gen-ni (嚴にする), *vt.* to make strict. —戸締りを嚴にする, to look carefully after the door fastenings. —監視(防備)を嚴にする, to make the supervision (defences) strict.

gennin (現任), *n.* the present post [office]. ¶ 現任者, the actual [present] holder of the post.

gennō (玄翁), *n.* a bush-hammer; a stone-hammer.

genpan (原板), *n.* 【寫】 the negative.

genpi (嚴秘), *n.* strict secret. —嚴秘に付する, to make strictly secret.

genpin (現品), *n.* the goods (in stock). —現品不足の爲め, through deficiency of goods.

genpō (減法), *n.* 【數】 subtraction.

genpō (減俸), *n.* reduction of a salary.

genpon (元本), *n.* the principal.

genpon (原本), *n.* ❶ (最初に作製せられた文書) the original; the original bill (手形の). ❷ (原文) the text.

genpu (原符), *n.* a counterfoil; a stub.

genpyō (元標), *n.* the starting-point of mile-posts.

genri (原理), *n.* the fundamenta. truth; a principle. —原理を究める, to inquire into the principles *of*.

genrō (元老), *n.* ❶ an elder [veteran; senior] statesman; *genrō*. ❷ (古顏, 功勞者) an elder; a veteran; a patriarch. ¶ 元老院, the senate. (元老院議員, a senator.)

genron (言論), *n.* speech; discussion. —言論の力, power of speech. —一部の言論界, a section of the press —言論の自由を拘束する, to restrict the liberty of speech. ¶ 言論戰, a speech-making campaign.

genryō (原料), *n.* (raw) materials. —原料を海外より仰ぐ, to obtain raw materials from abroad.

gensai (減殺する), *vt.* to deaden (勢など); cut down; reduce.

gensai-kikin (減債基金), *n.* the sinking-fund.

gensanchi (原產地), *n.* the country of origin; the provenance. ¶ 原產地證明書, a certificate of origin.

gense (現世), *n.* this life [world]; the land of the living. —現世の, earthly; worldly; mundane.

gensei-dōbutsu (原生動物), *n.* the protozoa.

gensei (現勢), *n.* the present condition.

gensei (嚴正な), *a.* strict; rigid; rigorous. —嚴正な裁判, rigid justice. ¶ 嚴正中立, strict neutrality. —嚴正科學, exact sciences (數學等).

genseki (言責), *n.* responsibility for one's word. —言責を重んずる, to bear the responsibility for one's word; be faithful to one's word.

genseki (原籍), *n.* the (original) domicile. —原籍地役場へ照會する, to inquire of the office at the place of domicile.

gensen (源泉), *n.* ❶ (水源) a fountain; a headspring; a well-spring. ❷ (淵源) a fountain; a source. ¶ 源泉課稅, taxation [taxing] at the source.

genshi (原子), *n.* 【理】 an atom. —原子化する, to atomize. ¶ 原子價, atomic value. —原子熱, atomic heat. —原子量, atomic weight. —原子說, atomic theory.

genshi (原始的), *a.* primitive; primeval; original. —原始的生活, primitive life. —原始的取得, original acquisition. ¶ 原始時代, the primitive age.

Genshisai (元始祭), *n.* the National Fête of the Third of January.

genshitsu (言質), *n.* a pledge; commitment. —言質を與へる, to pledge [plight] one's word; commit oneself. —言質を取る, to take a person's pledge.

gensho (原書), *n.* the original. —原書で讀む, to read in the original.

genshō (現象), *n.* a phenomenon [*pl.* -mena]; an appearance. —空中の現象, an appearance in the sky. —注目すべき現象, a notable phenomenon.

genshō (減少), *n.* decrease; diminution; reduction. —減少する, ❶ [*vi.*] to decrease; diminish; fall off. ❷ [*vt.*] to decrease; reduce; remit. ❸ [*a.*] decreasing; diminishing. —多少の減少を見る, to suffer a slight decrease.

genshoku (原色), *n.* primary [fundamental] colours. ¶ 原色寫眞, a heliochrome.

genshoku (現職), *n.* the present post (職務); the present occupation (職業). —現職を擲つ, to give up the present occupation (post).

genshoku (減食する), *vi.* to reduce one's diet.

genshu (元首), *n.* the chief of a state; the chief executive.

genshu (嚴守する), *vt.* to observe [keep] strictly. —時間を嚴守する, to be punctual to the minute. —秘密を嚴守する, to keep a secret strictly.

genshuku (減縮する), *vt.* to reduce; curtail; cut down. ——, *vi.* to shrink; grow less. —滯在日數を減縮する, to curtail the duration of one's stay.

genshuku (嚴肅), *n.* gravity (眞面目); dignity (嚴か); solemnity (同上). —嚴肅な, grave; dignified; solemn. —嚴肅に舉行される, to be held with great solemnity.

genshutsu (現出する), *vi.* to appear; emerge (into view); be revealed.

genso (元素), *n.* 【化】 an (a chemical) element; an elementary body.

gensō (幻想), *n.* a vision; a phantasm; a day-dream. —少年の幻想に囚はれる, to be lured by dreams of youth.

gensoku (原則), *n.* a principle; a fundamental principle [rule]. —原則として, as a (general) rule.

gensoku (舷側), *n.* 【航】 the side (船首から船尾まで); the broadside (船首から船尾部まで).

genson (玄孫), *n.* a great-great-grandchild.

genson (現存), *n.* (actual) existence. —現存する, to exist (actually); be in existence; subsist. —現存の人物で當時を知る者は稀だ, There are few persons living who remember those times. ¶ 現存者, the living; a survivor (生殘者).

genson (減損する), *v.* to detract (價値など); deteriorate (同上); decrease; diminish; lessen. ¶ 減損補塡準備金, depreciation reserve.

gensū (原數), *n.* the original number.

gensū (減數), *n.* 【數】 a subtrahend.

gensui (元帥), *n.* 【陸】 a marshal; field-marshal (英): 【海】 an admiral of the fleet; a fleet admiral. —元帥府に列せらる, to be appointed to the Board of Marshals and Fleet Admirals. ¶ 元帥刀, the marshal's (fleet admiral's) sword.

gensui (減水), *n.* the decrease [fall] of water. —減水する, to decrease; fall; subside; recede.

gensun (原寸), *n.* full size.

gentai (減退する), *vi.* to fall off; recede; subside; ebb; diminish; be on the wane. —貿易の減退, depression of trade.

gentei(舷梯), *n.* an accommodation ladder.

gentei(限定), *n.* definition; limitation (制限); determination. —限定する, ① [*vt.*] to define; determine; limit. ② [*a.*] defining; determinative; limitative; qualifying.

gentō (幻燈), *n.* a magic lantern.

gentō (舷燈), *n.* 【航】 running lights; side-lights.

gentō (厳冬), *n.* a hard [severe; rigorous] winter.

gen̄un (眩暈), *n.* 【醫】 vertigo; dizziness; giddiness.

genwaku (眩惑する), *vt.* to dazzle; blind. ——, *vi.* to be dazzled; be blinded. —外觀の美に眩惑される, to be dazzled by the splendour of its appearance.

genya (原野), *n.* a field; a waste land; a wilderness.

genyu (原油), *n.* crude petroleum.

genzai(現在), *n.* the present time; 【文】 the present tense. ——, *ad.* actually; before one's eyes. —現在に於て未來を判じる, to read the future in the now. —現在今見て來たのだ, I actually saw it just now. ¶ 現在完了, 【文】 the present perfect. —現在會員, the actual members.

genzei (減税), *n.* reduction of taxes.

genzen (儼然), *ad.* authoritatively; solemnly; gravely. —儼然と構へる, to assume a grave air.

genzō (幻像), *n.* a vision; an illusion; a phantom; a phantasm.

genzō (現像), *n.* 【寫】 development. —現像する, to develop. ¶ 現像液, a developer. —現像皿, a developing tray.

genzoku (還俗する), *vi.* to return to secular life; become a layman.

gen-zuru (減ずる), *vt.* ❶ (差引く) to deduct; reduce (代價を); discount. ❷ (減少) to abate; decrease; diminish (少く或は小さくする). ❸ (輕減) to allay (苦痛などを); mitigate (刑·苦痛などを); commute (刑などを). ——, *vi.* to abate; decrease; diminish. —一死一等を減ずる, to mitigate the sentence of death by one degree.

geppō(月俸), *n.* a monthly salary. —月俸一千圓, a monthly salary of one thousand *yen*.

geppō (月報), *n.* a monthly report [review].

geppu (月賦), *n.* a monthly payment [instalment]. —五圓宛の月賦で拂ふ, to pay by monthly instalments of five *yen*. ¶ 月賦販賣, sales on monthly instalment.

geppu (噯氣), *n.* belch; eructation.

geraku (下落), *n.* ❶ (相場などの) fall; decline; depreciation. ❷ (品質·品性の) deterioration; depreciation. —米價の下落, a fall in the price of rice. —下落さす, ① to depreciate; sink; lower. ② to degrade; deteriorate. —下落する, ① to depreciate; decline; fall [go] off. ② to degrade; deteriorate; degenerate.

geretsu (下劣な), *a.* mean; vulgar; base; ignoble; low.

geri (下痢), *n.* 【醫】 diarrhœa; loose bowels. —下痢を起す, to suffer from diarrhœa; have loose bowels. —下痢を止める, to stop loose bowels.

gesaku (戯作), *n.* a novel; a romance; fiction. ¶ 戯作者, a writer of fiction; a novelist; a playwright.

gesen (下賤の), *a.* ❶ humble; low; mean. ❷ vulgar; low; base. —下賤の生れ, humble birth.

gesha(下車), *n.* alighting. —下車する, to alight (from a car); get out [down; off]. ¶ (途中)下車驛, a stop-over station.

geshi (夏至), *n.* the summer solstice; midsummer.

geshuku (下宿する), *vi.* to lodge; board. ¶ 下宿人, a lodger; a boarder; a (paying) guest. —下宿料, lodging; the charge for lodging. —下宿屋, lodgings; a lodging-house.

geshunin (下手人), *n.* the murderer.

gesoku(下足), *n.* foot-gear; foot-wear; clogs and sandals. ¶ 下足番, a care-taker of clogs and sandals. —下足料, the charge for taking care of clogs and sandals.

gessekai(月世界), *n.* the moon; the lunar world.

gessha (月謝), *n.* a monthly (school; tuition) fee.

gesshoku (月蝕), *n.* a lunar eclipse; an eclipse of the moon.

gesshū (月收), *n.* a monthly income.

gesu (下種, 下司), *n.* a churl; a mean fellow. —下種ばッた, churlish; mean; low. —下司の智

慧は後から出る，"After-counsel is a fool's counsel."

gesu (解す), *vt.* ❶ (了解) to understand; comprehend; take in; make out; twig〔俗〕. ❷ (消化) to digest.

gesui (下水), *n.* a sewer; a drain; a gutter. ¶ 下水口, a gully-hole; an outfall. —下水渠, a sewer; a gully-drain.

geta (下駄), *n.* wooden clogs. —下駄を穿く, to wear [put on] clogs. ¶ 下駄屋, a clog-shop.

gētoru (ゲートル), *n.* gaiters. ¶ 卷ゲートル, puttees; putties.

getsugaku (月額), *n.* the monthly amount [sum].

getsumatsu (月末に), at the end of a month.

getsumei (月明に), *ad.* in moonlight.

getsurei (月齡), *n.* age of the moon.

getsuyōbi (月曜日), *n.* Monday.

gettan (月旦), *n.* ❶ the first (day) of the month. ❷ (人物批評) criticism of persons.

gezai (下劑), *n.* a purgative; a laxative. —下劑をのむ, to take a purgative.

gi (技), *n.* art (技術); craft (同上); ability (手腕). —未熟の技, unskilled art.

gi (義), *n.* ❶ (正義) justice; righteousness; probity. ❷ (君臣·父子等の道及び關係) relations; ties. —義の爲に死する, to die for righteousness' sake. —君臣の義を重んずる, to respect the relations of lord and retainer. —義に於て見るに忍びず, to be unable for reasons of humanity to look on.

gi (儀), *n.* a ceremony. —神前に參拜の儀を行ふ, to hold the ceremony of worship at the shrine.

gi (議), *n.* ❶ (議論) discussion; debate. ❷ (相談, 協議) consultation; deliberation. ❸ (會議) a council. —總會の議に付する, to submit to the discussion of a general meeting.

gian (議案), *n.* a bill; a measure; a proposal; a project. —議案を提出する, to introduce [file] a bill. —議案を撤回する, to withdraw a bill. —議案を通過さす, to pass [carry] a bill. —議案を修正 (變更) する, to revise (alter) a bill.

gibōshi (紫萼), *n.* 【植】 the savannah-wood.

gibōshi (擬寶珠), *n.* the ornamental tops of railings.

gibutsu (僞物), *n.* a forgery; a spurious article; a counterfeit. —僞物を賣りつける, to palm off a false article upon a person.

gichō (議長), *n.* the president; the speaker; the chairman. —議長[座長]に選ぶ, to put in the chair. —議長を呼ぶ, to address the chair. ¶ 議長席, the chair. (議長席に就く, to take the chair.)

gidai (議題), *n.* a subject for discussion [debate]. —議題に上る[となる], to come up [be brought up] for discussion [debate]; come on the tapis.

gidan (疑團), *n.* a doubt. —疑團を懷く(解く), to harbour (dispel) a doubt.

gidayū (義太夫), *n.* a (form of) ballad-drama. ¶ 義太夫語り, a *gidayū*-singer.

gien (義捐する), *vt.* to subscribe; contribute. ¶ 義捐金, a contribution; a subscription. (義捐金を募る, to invite subscriptions; collect contributions.) —義捐者, a subscriber; a contributor.

gifun (義憤), *n.* righteous indignation.

gigei (技藝), *n.* arts; crafts (手工). ☞ *gei* (藝). ¶ 技藝學校, a crafts [technical] school.

gigi (疑義), *n.* a doubt; a question. —疑義を質す, to ascertain doubtful points.

gīgī (ぎーぎー), *ad.* gratingly. —ギーギーさす(する), to grate; rasp.

gigochinai (ぎごちない), *a.* ❶ (固苦しい) stiff; stiff-mannered. ❷ (身體に恰當せぬ) ill-fitting.

gigoku (疑獄), *n.* a scandal; a great criminal case. —疑獄を起す, to raise a scandal.

gihan (僞版), *n.* a piracy; a pirated edition (of a book).

gihei (疑兵), *n.* dummy troops.

gihitsu (僞筆), *n.* a forged handwriting (picture).

gihyō (儀表), *n.* a model; a pattern; a good example.

giin (僞印), *n.* a forged seal.

giin (議院), *n.* ❶ (一院) the chamber; the House. ❷ = *gikai* (議會). ¶ 議院法, parliamentary procedure; the parliamentary law. —議院政治, parliamentary government.

giin (議員), *n.* an assembly man; a member (of an assembly); (國會の) a Member of Parliament (M. P. と略す); a congressman〔米〕; a member of the Diet. —議員の特權, the privilege of members of Parliament. —議員の任期, the term of membership. —議員に選ばれる, to be elected [returned] a member of.... —議員を辭する, to resign one's membership [seat] in... ¶ 議員席, floor.

giji (議事), *n.* (parliamentary) proceedings. —議事を開く(閉じる), to open (close) a sitting. —議事の進行を計る, to plan the progress of proceedings. —議事日程を變更する, to alter the order of the day. / ¶ 議事妨害, obstruction of proceedings. —議事堂, an assembly-hall; the Houses of the Diet [of Parliament](國會議事堂) —議事錄, the proceedings [transactions] (協會等の); the minutes.

gijin (擬人), *n.* personification; impersonation.

gijishō (疑似症), *n.* a suspected case.

gijō (儀仗), *n.* a *cortège* 〔佛〕. ¶ 儀仗兵, a guard of honour. (儀仗兵を附せらる, to be escorted by a guard of honour.)

gijō (議場), *n.* an assembly-hall; a chamber. —議場を整理する, to maintain order in the assembly [chamber].

gijutsu (技術), *n.* art; technique (音樂·繪畫等の); technics. —技術上の手腕, technical skill. ¶ 技術家, a technician; a technical expert.

gikai (議會), *n.* ❶ (合議制機關) the Diet (日); the Congress (米); the Parliament (英, 伊). —議會の協贊を得る, to obtain the approval of both Houses of the Diet. ¶ 帝國議會, the Imperial Diet. —第四十八議會, the forty-eighth session of the Diet. —特別(臨時)議會, a special (an extraordinary) session of the Diet.

gikan (技監), *n.* a chief engineer; an engineer-in-chief.

gikei (義兄), *n.* an elder sister's husband; the wife's elder brother; a brother-in-law.

giketsu (議決), *n.* a decision (of a meeting). —議決する, to decide *on*; pass a vote *of*; vote *for*.

giki (義氣), *n.* ❶ (義俠心) chivalry. ❷ (正義心) right-mindedness.

gikō (技工), *n.* an artisan; a mechanic.

gikō (技巧), *n.* art; technics, technique. —技巧を弄する, to give play to one's art.

gikokkai (擬國會), *n.* a parliamentary debating society.

gikunshi (僞君子), *n.* a hypocrite. —僞君子的, hypocritical.

gikyo (義擧), *n.* a heroic [chivalrous] deed; a philanthropic work.

gikyō (義俠-心), *n.* chivalry; gallantry; generosity; public spirit. —義俠心に富む, to be full of chivalry. ¶ 義俠家, a chivalrous [gallant; generous] person.

gikyōdai (義兄弟), *n.* a brother-in-law; a step-brother.

gikyoku (戲曲), *n.* a drama; a play. ¶ 戲曲作家, a dramatist; a playwright.

gimei (僞名), *n.* a false [fictitious; an assumed] name; an *alias* 〔羅〕. —僞名で, under a false name.

gimon (疑問), *n.* ❶ (問題) a question; a problem. ❷ (疑念) a doubt. ¶ 間接疑問, 【文】 an indirect [oblique] question. —疑問文, an interrogative sentence. —疑問代名詞, the interrogative pronoun. —疑問標, a question mark; an interrogation mark [point]. —疑問詞, an interrogative. —疑問點, a point at issue; a moot point; a doubtful point.

gimu (義務), *n.* duty; obligation; liability; debt (債務); responsibility (責任). —法律上の義務, legal obligation. —義務に背く, to swerve from one's duty. —義務を盡す, to perform [do] one's duty. —義務を履行する, to meet one's engagements; pay one's debt. —義務を怠る, to fail in one's duty. —...を己の義務とする, to make it one's duty *to*.... —德義上...の義務あり, to be on one's honour *to*. —その人の義務なり, It is for [up to 〔俗〕] a person *to*. ¶ 義務敎育, compulsory education. —義務年限, an obligatory term of service.

gin (銀), *n.* silver. —銀の, silver; silvered.

ginbae (青蠅), *n.* the green bottle-fly.

ginen (疑念), *n.* doubt; mistrust; suspicion. —疑念を懷く, to harbour suspicion. —疑念を起さす, to incur [excite] suspicion.

ginga (銀河), *n.* the Galaxy; the Milky Way.

gingami (銀紙), *n.* silvered paper.

ginka (銀貨), *n.* a silver coin.

ginkai (銀塊), *n.* a silver ingot; bar silver.

ginkise (銀被の), *a.* silver; silvered; silver-plated.

ginkō (銀行), *n.* a bank. —銀行に預ける, to bank; deposit in a bank. ¶ 組合銀行, an associated bank. —親銀行, the parent bank. —土地抵當銀行, a land-bank; a land mortgage bank. —特殊[特許]銀行, a chartered bank. —銀行簿記, bank book-keeping. —銀行團, a bank association. —銀行營業時間, banking hours. —銀行日步, the bank-rate. —銀行員, the staff of a bank; a bank clerk [employee]. —銀行家, a banker. —銀行株, the bank-stock. —銀行爲替(手形), a bank-draft. —銀行通帳, a bank-book. —銀行定休日, a bank-holiday.

ginkonshiki (銀婚式), *n.* a silver wedding.

ginmekki (銀鍍金する), *vt.* to silver; plate [coat] with silver.

ginmi (吟味), *n.* examination; investigation. —吟味に吟味する, to examine searchingly.

ginmigaki(銀磨), *n.* (粉) plate-powder. —銀磨きをかける, to polish with plate-powder.

ginmōru (銀モール), *n.* silver lace; silver braid.

ginnan (銀杏), *n.* 【植】 ❶ the gingko-tree; the maiden-hair tree. ❷ the fruit of the maiden-hair tree.

ginō (技能), *n.* ability; capacity.

ginpai (銀杯), *n.* a silver cup.

ginpai (銀牌), *n.* a silver medal.

ginpaku (銀白の), *a.* silvery.

ginpaku (銀箔), *n.* silver-leaf; [foil]; silver-paper.

ginpō(銀寶), *n.* 【魚】 the gunnel.

ginpun(銀粉), *n.* powdered silver; silver powder.

ginsei (吟聲), *n.* recitation.

ginsei (銀製の), *a.* silver. ¶ 銀製器具, a silver utensil; a silverware.

ginsekai (銀世界), *n.* a silver world; snow scenery.

ginshoku (銀色の), *a.* argent; silvery.

ginteki (銀笛), *n.* a flageolet.

ginzan (銀山), *n.* a silver-mine.

gin-zuru (吟ずる), *v.* to chant; recite. —詩を吟ずる, to recite a poem.

giragira (ぎらぎらする), *vi.* ❶ (燦爛) to glitter; glisten. ❷ (まぶしい) to dazzle; glare. ——, *a.* glittering; dazzling.

giretsu (義烈), *n.* heroism; gallantry. —義烈の, heroic; gallant.

giri (義理), *n.* duty; obligation; a sense of duty [honour]. —義理ある兄弟, a brother-in-law. —義理一遍で, from a sheer sense of duty. —義理にからまれる, to be influenced [swayed] by one's sense of obligation. —義理を知らぬ, to be blind to one's duty; have no sense of justice. —この金は義理にも取れぬ, I cannot, in honour, accept this money.

girigiri (ぎりぎり), *ad.* ❶(軋る音) gnashingly. ❷ (きびしく) severely; violently; by force. —ぎりぎり決著の値, the lowest (possible) price; the bottom price. —絲をぎりぎり卷きつける, to wind the thread round and round.

Girisha (希臘), *n.* Greece. ¶ 希臘語, Greek. —希臘人, a Greek. —希臘敎, the Eastern [Greek] Church; the Orthodox Church.

giron (議論), *n.* ❶ (論辯) argument. ❷ (討論) debate. ❸ (論議) discussion. ❹ (論爭) controversy; contest; dispute. —机上の議論, academic argument. —議論好きの, argumentative; contentious; disputatious. —議論を戰はす, to join issue *with*; bandy argument *with*. —反對(贊成)の議論をする, to argue against (for) a thing. —議論は姑く措いて, laying aside the argument for the moment. —最早議論の餘地なし, to admit of no further discussion. ¶ 議論家, a controversialist; an argumentative person.

giryō (伎倆, 技倆), *n.* ability; talent; capacity. —技倆ある人, a man of parts [talent]; a talented man. —平日の技倆を示す, to display his usual ability.

giryō (議了する), *v.* to close a discussion.

gisan (蟻酸), *n.* 【化】 formic acid.

gisei (擬制), *n.* a fiction.

gisei (擬製の), *a.* imitative; spurious. ¶ 擬製品, an imitation.

gisei (擬勢), *n.* bluff. —擬勢を示す, to bluff.

gisei (犧牲), *n.* ❶ (いけにへ) a sacrifice; a victim. ❷(獻身) self-sacrifice; self-immolation. ❸ (餌食, 遭難者) a victim; a prey. ❹ (身代り) a scapegoat. —健康を犧牲として, at the cost of health. —如何なる犧牲を拂ッても, at any price [cost]. —自分の貪慾の犧牲となる, to fall a victim to one's own avarice. —國の爲に身を犧牲にする, to sacrifice oneself [lay down one's life] for one's country. —自國語を犧牲にして他國語を學ぶ, to learn a foreign language at the expense of one's own. —自由を犧牲にして平和を求める, to purchase peace at the price of liberty. ¶ 犧牲球,【野球】a sacrifice hit.

giseki (議席), *n.* a seat. —議席に著く, to take one's seat in the chamber.

gishi (技師), *n.* an engineer (土木·機械·鑛山·電氣等の); an architect (建築の); an (a technical) expert (專門家). ¶ 技師長, the engineer-in-chief; the chief expert.

gishi (義士), *n.* ❶ (節義の高い人) a righteous person. ❷ (忠義の人) a loyal retainer; a patriot. ¶ 義士銘々傳, the Lives of the Loyal Retainers.

gishi (義子), *n.* an adopted son; a foster-child.

gishi(義齒), *n.* an artificial tooth; a false tooth.

gishiki (儀式), *n.* ❶ (式典) a ceremony; a rite; a solemnity. ❷ (禮儀, 禮式) etiquette; form; formality. —儀式ばッた待遇, stiff reception. ¶ 儀式係, a marshal.

gishimai (義姉妹), *n.* a sister--in-law.
gishin (疑心), *n.* suspicion. —疑心暗鬼を生ず, Suspicion will raise phantoms.
gishō (僞證), *n.* 【法】 perjury; false evidence (虚僞の證言); false testimony (同上). —僞證する, to perjure oneself; bear false witness; give false evidence. —僞證罪に問はれる, to be charged with perjury.
gishu (技手), *n.* =*gite*.
gishu (義手), *n.* an artificial arm.
gisō (儀裝), *n.* ceremonial equipage. ¶ 儀裝馬車, a state carriage.
gisō (艤裝), *n.* equipment (of a ship); equipage; outfit. —艤裝する, to equip (ship); rig; fit out [up].
gisoku (義足), *n.* an artificial leg [foot].
gisshiri (ぎッしり), *ad.* closely; to the full; to the utmost (capacity). —ぎッしり詰る, to be full; be closely packed; be packed to the full. —器にぎッしり詰め込む, to pack it tightly in a vessel; fill to the utmost; pack to the full.
gi-suru (擬する), *vt.* to imitate; copy; personate (扮す). —外國製に擬して造る, to make in imitation of the foreign article. —外務大臣に擬する, to put him down for the Minister for Foreign Affairs. —刀を咽喉に擬する, to point a sword at his throat.
gi-suru (議する), *vt.* ❶ (論議) to discuss; debate. ❷ (相談, 熟議) to consult; deliberate. ❸ (非議) to criticize. —國事を議する, to deliberate on the affairs of state.
gite (技手), *n.* an assistant-engineer [-expert]; an operator.
gitei (義弟), *n.* the wife's younger brother; a younger sister's husband; a brother-in-law.
gitei (議定する), *vt.* to confer and agree *upon*; concert. ¶ 議定官, a councillor. —議定書, a protocol.
giten (疑點), *n.* a doubtful point; a moot point.
giun (疑雲), *n.* a cloud of doubt.
giwaku (疑惑), *n.* doubt; distrust; suspicion. ☞ *utagai*. —疑惑を起さす, to arouse suspicion. —衆人から疑惑を受ける, to incur the suspicion of the people.
giyū (義勇), *n.* ❶ (義心と勇氣) uprightness and courage. ❷ (義の爲にする勇) heroism; courage. —義勇公に奉ずる, to sacrifice oneself courageously to the public good. ¶ 義勇兵, 【軍】 a volunteer. —義勇艦隊, a volunteer fleet [squadron].

gizagiza (ぎざぎざ), *n.* zigzag; indent; mill (貨幣の); notches.
gizen (僞善), *n.* hypocrisy. —僞善的, hypocritical. ¶ 僞善者, a hypocrite.
gizen (巍然として), *ad.* loftily; conspicuously.
gizō (僞造する), *vt.* to conterfeit; forge. ¶ 僞造者, a forger.
go (五), *n.* five.
go (後), *ad.* afterwards (あとで); later on; subsequently. ——, *prep.* & *conj.* after; behind [*prep.*].
go (期), *n.* occasion; time; moment. —その期に及んで, on that occasion.
go (碁), *n.* *go.* ¶ 西洋碁, checquers; draughts.
go (語), *n.* ❶ (言葉) a word; a language; a term (專門語). ❷ a proverb. —語に曰く, says the proverb. —語を强めて云へば, to put it more strongly.
gō (業), *n.* ❶ 【梵】 karma (身・口・意の三に作す行爲). ❷ =*gōhō* (業報). —業が深い, to be past [beyond] redemption.
gō (號), *n.* ❶ (番號) number (雜誌などの). ❷ (雅號) a pen--name; *nom de plume* 【佛】. —第一號, No. I; number one. —本鄉西片町十番地への三號, Lot C 3, No. 10, Nishikatamachi, Hongō. —號を逐うて掲載する, to publish serially.
gō (鄉), *n.* a village; a district; the country. —鄉に入っては鄉に從へ, "When at Rome, you must do as the Romans do."
goba (後場), *n.* (取引市場) the afternoon market.
gobaishi (五倍子), *n.* galls; gall-nuts.
goban (碁盤), *n.* a checker-board. —碁盤の目, checkers; squares. ¶ 西洋碁盤, a draught-board.
gōben (合辦), *n.* joint management. —日支合辦の事業, an enterprise under joint Sino-Japanese management.
gobi (語尾), *n.* a termination; a suffix. ¶ 語尾變化, 【文】 inflection. —形容詞の語尾に ly を附して, by suffixing "ly" to adjectives.
gobō (牛蒡), *n.* 【植】 the burdock.
gobu (五分), *n.* ❶ (半分) a half. ❷ (平等) evenness. ❸ (百分の五) 5 per cent. —五分五分の勝負, a draw; a drawn game. —五分利附公債, a five-percent public loan; five-percents.
gobugari (五分刈), *n.* crop; short cropping (of hair). —五分刈にする, to crop short.
gobyū (誤謬), *n.* an error; a mistake; a blunder. —誤謬を生ずる, to make an error. —誤謬を正す, to correct errors.

gochagocha (ごちゃごちゃ), *n.* ❶ (亂雜) higgledy-piggledy; confusion. ❷=*monchaku.* —ごちゃごちゃに入れる, to put in pell-mell; huddle together.

gōchin (轟沈する), *v.* to sink by explosion; blow up and sink.

gochisō (御馳走), *n.* a dinner; an entertainment. ☞ *chisō.* —御馳走になる, to be entertained (at dinner).

gochō (伍長), *n.* a corporal; a foreman (職工の). ¶伍長勤務上等兵, a lance-corporal.

gochō (語調), *n.* 【修】the tone; accent. —怒った語調で, in an angry tone.

gōchoku (剛直の), *a.* inflexible; staunch; unbending.

gōdan (强談), *n.* persistent [importunate] demand; intimidation (恐喝). —强談する, to demand importunately; intimidate.

godatsu (誤脫), *n.* an oversight; a slip; an omission.

gōdatsu (强奪する), *vt.* to rob *of*; despoil *of*; extort *from.*

gōdō (合同), *n.* combination; union; amalgamation. —合同する, to unite *with*; combine *with*; amalgamate. ¶合同企業, a trust.

goei (護衛する), *vt.* to escort; guard; convoy. —護衛を附する, to place under escort. ¶護衛兵, an escort; a guard; a body-guard. —護衛巡查, a policeman on guard.

gofu (護符), *n.* a charm; an amulet.

gofuku (吳服), *n.* cloth; drapery; dry [piece] goods. ¶吳服太物類, cloths of all kinds. —吳服屋, a draper; a cloth-dealer; a dry-goods store〔米〕.

gōfuku (剛愎な), *a.* headstrong; obdurate; obstinate.

gofun (胡粉), *n.* whitening; chalk; whitewash.

gōgai (號外), *n.* ❶ (新聞の號外) an extra; a special. ❷(番外) an extra. ¶號外賣り, an extra-vendor; a seller of extras.

gogaku (語學), *n.* linguistics; language study. —語學の素養[知識], linguistic knowledge. —語學の才がある, to have an aptitude for languages. ¶語學敎師, a language-master (現今の外國語の). —語學者, a linguist.

gogan-kōji (護岸工事), *n.* embankment works.

gogatsu (五月), *n.* May. —五月の節句, the fête of May; the Feast of Flags.

gogen (語原), *n.* an etymon; the derivation of a word. ¶語原學, etymology.

gōgi (合議), *n.* consultation; conference. —合議する, to consult together; confer *with.* ¶合議(制)裁判所, a collegiate court.

gōgi (强氣な), *a.* grand; splendid; tremendous. —强氣な構へ, a fine [magnificent] house.

gogo (午後), *n.* afternoon; p. m. (*post meridiem*〔羅=after midday〕の略). —木曜日の午後に, (on) Thursday afternoon; on Thursday in the afternoon.

gōgo (豪語する), *vt.* to rant; talk big.

gōgō (轟轟たる), *a.* thundering; rumbling; roaring. —轟々たる砲聲, thundering artillery. —轟々たる爆音を立てて, with a thunderous explosion.

gōgō (囂囂), *ad.* uproariously; clamorously; boisterously. —世論囂々, The world is in uproar.

gohan (御飯), *n.* ❶ boiled rice. ❷ a meal; a repast. —御飯を出せ, Bring in dinner.

gōhara (業腹), *n.* vexation; mortification; resentment. —業腹で堪らない, to be vexed beyond endurance.

gohei (御幣), *n.* cut-paper hung in a Shintō shrine. ¶御幣擔ぎ, superstitious person (人).

gohei (語弊), *n.* misuse of words; an inapt expression [term].

gohō (午砲), *n.* the midday-gun; the noon-gun.

gohō (誤報), *n.* misinformation; a misreport; an erroneous report.

gohō (語法), *n.* ❶ (言法) expression; diction; phraseology. ❷ (文法) grammar. —簡單な語法で, in simple phrase. —語法を誤る, to use bad grammar.

gōhō (合法), *n.* lawfulness; legality. —合法的, lawful; legal.

gōhō (業報), *n.* Ⓢ業果. a karma effect.

gōhō (號砲), *n.* a signal gun. ¶非常號砲, (號砲五發) an emergency signal gun.

gōhō (豪放な), *a.* Bohemian; bold.

gōhyakushi (合百師), *n.* a street [curbstone] rice-broker.

goi (語彙), *n.* a vocabulary; a glossary.

gōi (合意), *n.* mutual agreement; mutual consent. —一般の合意, general compact.

goisagi (五位鷺), *n.* 【鳥】the night-heron.

goishi (碁石), *n.* go-stones; checker-stones.

gōitsu (合一する), *vt.* to combine; unite; unify; consolidate. ——, *vi.* to unite; become one.

goji (誤字), *n.* an erratum [*pl.* -ta]; a misprint; a wrong word;

a clerical error (書誤り).
gojin (吾人), *pron.* we.
gojippo-hyappo (五十歩百歩), to be six of one and half a dozen of the other.
gojitsu (後日), *n.* the future; another day. —後日の爲め, for future reference. —後日の證據に, as a future proof. —後日の戒めに, as a warning for the future. —後日の禍を貽(のこ)す, to leave evils to spring up in the future. ¶ 後日譚, later records; reminiscences.
gojo (互助), *n.* mutual aid.
gojō (五常), *n.* the five cardinal virtues.
gojō (互讓), *n.* mutual concession; give-and-take; compromise.
gojō (御諚), *n.* a command. —有難き御諚を拜す, to be honoured with gracious words.
gōjō (强情), *n.* obstinacy; doggedness; refractoriness; pertinacity; mulishness. —强情を張る, to persist *in*; be obstinate. ¶ 强情張り, (人) an obstinate [a stubborn] fellow.
gojū (五十), *n.* fifty. —五十代の人, a quinquagenarian. ¶ 五十音, the Japanese syllabary. —五十年祭, a jubilee; a semi-centenary [-centennial].
gojū (五重の), *a.* five-fold; quintuplicate. —五重の塔, a five-storied pagoda.
gōka (豪家), *n.* a family of wealth and influence.
gokai (沙蠶), *n.* 【環蟲】 the lobworm; the lugworm.
gokai (五戒), *n.* the five commandments (against murder, theft, lust, lying, and intemperance).
gokai (誤解), *n.* misunderstanding; misapprehension. —誤解を防ぐ爲に, to prevent misunderstanding. —誤解を招く虞がある, to be liable to cause misunderstanding.
gokaku (五角), *n.* a pentagon.
gokaku (互角の), *a.* equal; even; well-matched. —互角である, to be equally balanced (in power).
gokaku (語格), *n.* diction; grammar; 【文】 the case. ¶ 語格論, 【文】 accidence.
gōkaku (合格), *n.* pass; eligibility. —體格檢査に合格する, to pass a physical [medical] examination. ¶ 合格者, a person who has passed an examination; a successful candidate.
gokan (五官), *n.* Ⓢ五官器 the five organs (of sense) (即ち nose, eye, skin, ear, and tongue).
gokan (五感), *n.* the five senses.
gokan (語幹), *n.* 【文】 a stem.
gōkan (强姦), *n.* rape; violation. —强姦する, [*vt.*] to rape; ravish; violate.
goke (後家), *n.* widow.
gokei (互惠の), *a.* reciprocal. ¶ 互惠條約, a reciprocal treaty; a treaty of reciprocity. —互惠主義, reciprocity (principle).
gōkei (合計), *n.* the sum (total); the total. —合計で, in all; in the aggregate; in the total. —合計する, to sum [reckon; count; add] up; total. (合計して…となる, to foot [come] up *to*; amount *to*; total.) ¶ 總合計, grand total.
gokeiji (御慶事), *n.* a happy event in the Imperial family; an Imperial wedding (結婚); a birth in the Imperial family (出產).
goken (護憲運動), *n.* movement for the defence of constitution.
gōken (剛健な), *a.* vigorous; sturdy; manly. —剛健な文體, a vigorous style. —剛健な發育を遂げる, to undergo vigorous development.
gōketsu (豪傑), *n.* a great man; a hero. —豪傑肌の人, a heroic-minded person.
goki (語氣), *n.* ❶ (物の云ひぶり) a way of speech. ❷ (語勢) tone.
gōki (剛毅な), *a.* sturdy; firm; manly.
gōki (豪氣), *n.* sturdy spirit; valour; manliness.
gokigen-yō (御機嫌よう), good-day; good evening; good-bye!; farewell!
gōkin (合金), *n.* an alloy.
gokō (後光), *n.* a glory (放光); an aureole; a halo (佛像等の背光); a nimbus (神佛等の體周の).
gokoku (五穀), *n.* the five cereals.
gokoku (後刻), *ad.* later on.
gokoku (護國), *n.* guardianship of a country. —護國の干城, the bulwark of his country.
gokon (語根), *n.* the root (form) of a word; the radical.
goku (極), *ad.* extremely; exceedingly; strictly. —ごく高くッても, at the highest; at most. —ごく内輪に見積ッても, even at the lowest estimate. —ごく內所にする, to keep it strictly secret.
goku (語句), *n.* words and phrases.
gokuaku (極惡の), *n.* atrocious; most wicked; fiendish. 極惡の罪, a crime of the blackest [deepest] dye. —極惡非道の人, a fiend; a devil.
gokudōmono (極道者), *n.* a scoundrel; a villain; a devil; a profligate (放蕩者).
gokui (極意), *n.* the secret; the mysteries. —極意を究める, to master the mysteries.

gokuin (極印), *n.* a stamp; a die; a hall-mark.

gokujōhin (極上品), *n.* an article of the highest [finest] quality; an A 1 article; the first-rate article.

gokumon (獄門), *n.* ❶ (獄屋の門) a prison-gate. ❷ (梟首) exposure of a head before a prison-gate. —獄門に梟す, to expose before a prison-gate.

gokuraku (極樂), *n.* Ⓢ 淨土 ❶ the paradise (of the Buddhists); heaven; the abode of the blessed. ❷ (極安樂) bliss; happiness. —極樂往生を遂げる, to enter paradise; die happily [painlessly; peacefully]. ¶ 極樂鳥, the bird of paradise.

gokuri (獄吏), *n.* a jailer, gaoler; a turnkey.

gokusho (極署), *n.* extreme [intense] heat.

gokutsubushi (穀潰し), *n.* a drone; a good-for-nothing; a person not worth his salt.

gokuzaishiki (極彩色), *n.* minute [brilliant] colouring. —極彩色に化粧する, to bedizen in full toilet.

gōkyū (號泣する), *vi.* to cry; wail; lament.

goma (胡麻), *n.* 【植】 the East Indian sesame; the gingili, gingelly; —胡麻を摺る, to flatter; toady; suck up *to.* ¶ 胡麻油, gingili [gingelly] oil. —胡麻摺り, a flatterer; a sycophant; a toady.

goma (護摩), *n.* 〚梵 Homa〛 holy fire for invocation; an invocation made during the burning of the holy fire. —護摩を焚く, to light a holy fire.

gomakasu (誤魔化す), *v.* ❶ (人を) to hoodwink; bamboozle; gammon. ❷ (金品等を) to peculate (着服); cook (勘定などを); fudge (仕事を). ❸ to shift; shuffle; quibble. —過失を誤魔化す, to cover up [smooth over] a fault. —教師を誤魔化す, to hoodwink a teacher. —人の目を誤魔化す, to gammon a person. —帳面を誤魔化す, to manipulate [cook] accounts.

gomame (鱓), *n.* dried sardines.

gōman (傲慢), *n.* arrogance; pride; haughtiness. **——na,** *a.* arrogant; proud; haughty. —傲慢な風, an arrogant manner; high airs. —傲慢な顔, a haughty [proud] look.

gomanohai (護摩の灰), *n.* a disguised footpad.

gōmei-gaisha (合名會社), *n.* an ordinary [unlimited] partnership.

gomen (御免), *n.* ❶ (免許) permission; licence. ❷ (免職) dismissal; discharge. ❸ (許容) permission; leave. ❹ (勘辨) pardon; excuse. —御免下さい, I beg your pardon (詫びる時); Pardon [excuse] me (同上); May I come in? (訪問の時) —少々御免なさい (除けて通る時), Please let me by [pass]. —一寸御免下さい (座を外す時), Excuse me a moment. —御免を蒙りたい, I beg to be excused. —そんな話はもう御免だ, I would rather not hear such tales.

gomi (芥, 塵), *n.* dust; dirt; rubbish. ¶ 芥箱, a dust-bin. —芥捨場, a tip; a dump〚米〛. —芥取, a dust-pan.

gomigomi (埃埃した), *a.* dusty. —埃埃した市中の住居, residence in a dusty city.

gō-mo (毫も), *ad.* in the least; at all; in the slightest degree. —毫も…なし, not a little [jot]. —毫も關係がない, to be utterly [absolutely] unconnected *with*; be entirely cut off *from*. —…には毫も關係しない, to have nothing to do *with*. —毫も意に介せず, not to care a pin [farthing].

gōmō (剛毛), *n.* 【生】 a seta; a bristle.

gomokunarabe (五目竝), *n.* *gobang* (日本の碁盤の訛).

gōmon (拷問), *n.* torture; examination by torture. —拷問に掛ける, to put to the torture for examination.

gomu (護謨), *n.* ❶ (彈性護謨) caoutchouc; rubber; India-rubber. ❷ (樹膠) gum. ❸ (硬化護謨) ebonite; vulcanite. ❹ (人造護謨) celluloid. ¶ 赤護謨, gutta-percha. —護謨判, a rubber-stamp. —護謨引外套, a mackintosh; a rubber-coat. —護謨靴, elastic boots; rubber shoes. —護謨櫛, a celluloid comb. —護謨管, an India-rubber tube. —護謨毬, an India-rubber ball. —護謨人形, a rubber doll. —護謨糊, gum arabic; mucilage. (護謨糊附封筒, an adhesive envelope.) —護謨の樹, the India-rubber tree; the gum-tree. —護謨輪, a rubber tire [tyre]; a rubber wheel.

gonge (権化), *n.* Ⓢ 権現 incarnation; personification. —惡魔の権化, the devil incarnate; the incarnate fiend.

gongo-dōdan (言語道斷の), *a.* unspeakable; abominable; outrageous. —言語道斷の所爲, an abominable act.

gongyō (勤行), *n.* (divine) service; church-service.

gonin (誤認する), *v.* to misconceive; mistake *for*; take *for*.

沙塵を火煙と誤認する, to take a cloud of dust for smoke.

gōnō (豪農), *n.* a wealthy [rich] farmer; a wealthy and powerful farmer.

gō-no-mono (剛の者), *n.* a strong man; a brave man.

goraku (娛樂), *n.* pleasure; amusement; recreation. —娛樂的氣分, the amusive mood. —娛樂の鄕, the abode of pleasure. —公衆の娛樂, public amusements. —娛樂的に讀まれる, to be read for amusement. ¶ 娛樂場, a casino; a place of amusement [entertainment]; a pleasure resort.

goran (御覽), ❶ [*n.*] sight; inspection. ❷ [*vi.*] (見よ) see!; look! ❸ [*particle*] see; try. ❹ [*int.*] there! —御覽に入れる, to show you; bring before you. —御覽の通り, as you see. —見て御覽, Look at it. —今一度言ッて御覽, Try and say it again. —一寸著て御覽, Just try it on.

gōrei (號令), *n.* an order; the word of command (特に軍隊の). —號令に從ふ, to obey the command. —號令をかける, to give an order [command]; give the word of command. —天下に號令する, to rule the whole country.

gōri (合理的), *a.* rational; reasonable. —合理的性質, rational nature. ¶ 合理主義, rationalism.

gōriki (强力), *n.* ❶=*kyōryoku*. ❷ (登山人夫) a mountain guide. —强力を雇ふ, to engage a (mountain) guide.

gorimuchū (五里霧中に), in utter bewilderment; at sea; in a maze. —五里霧中に彷徨ふ, to be in utter bewilderment; lose one's bearings.

gorin (五倫), *n.* the five human relations (of father and son, master and servant, husband and wife, friends, and brothers.)

gorira (大猩猩), *n.* 【哺乳】the gorilla.

gōritsu-hirei (合率比例), *n.* 【數】multiple proportion.

goro (ごろ), *n.* ❶ (匍球) a grounder; a bounder; a daisy-cutter (クリッケット). ❷ (輾子) a roller; a roll. ❸ (破落戶) a vagabond.

goro (語呂), *n.* the sound; euphony.

gorogoro (ごろごろする), *vi.* ❶ (ころげる) to roll. ❷ (なまけて居る) to knock about; idle; loaf. —ゴロゴロ轉がす, to roll about. —猫が喉をゴロゴロ鳴らす, The cat purrs.

gorone (轉寢する), *vi.* to roll asleep; lie asleep in one's clothes.

gorotsuki (破落戶), *n.* a vagabond; a rogue; a scamp. —ごろつきの群, a pack of rogues.

gorufu (ゴルフ戲), *n.* golf. —ゴルフ戲をなす人, a golfer. ¶ ゴルフ棒, a driver; a golf-club; a lofter (高打の). —ゴルフ倶樂部, a golf club.

goryō (御料), *n.* Imperial property (財產); Imperial use (使用). —御料の馬車, an Imperial carriage. ¶ 御料地, an Imperial estate; a crown [royal] demesne. —御料局, the Bureau of Imperial Estates. —御料林, a crown forest; an Imperial estate forest.

gōryoku (合力), *n.* ❶ (協力) co-operation. ❷【理】resultant (of forces). ❸ (施與) charity; alms; aids. —他人の合力を受ける, to receive alms; live on charity.

gosa (誤差), *n.* an error.

gosai (後妻), *n.* a second wife.

gosan (午餐), *n.* lunch; luncheon. —午餐を供する, to give [offer] lunch. ¶ 午餐會, a luncheon party.

gosan (誤算する), *vt.* to miscalculate; miscount. —年齡を誤算する, to miscount one's age.

gose (後世), *n.* the future life [state]; the world to come. —後世を祈る, to pray for a future life.

gosei (悟性), *n.* 【心】understanding.

gosei (語勢), *n.* emphasis; stress. —…の語勢を强める, to emphasize; stress; lay stress *on*.

gōsei (合成), *n.* 【理】composition; 【化】synthesis (analysis の對). ¶ 合成語, a compound word. —合成金, a composition metal; an alloy.

gōsei (剛性), *n.* 【理】rigidity.

gosen (互選), *n.* mutual election. —互選の結果, the result of mutual election. ¶ 互選議員, a member elected by mutual vote. —互選投票, mutual vote.

gosetsu (誤綴), *n.* bad [erroneous] spelling.

gosha (誤寫する), *v.* to miscopy; make a clerical error.

gōsha (鄕社), *n.* a village shrine.

gōsha (豪奢), *n.* luxury; extravagance; sumptuousness. —豪奢に耽る, to repose in the lap of luxury. —豪奢に暮らす, to live like a lord [in luxury].

-goshi (越し), ❶ (場所) on the other side; across; over. ❷ (時限) over; after. —壁越しに, through [over] a wall. —三年越しに歸る, to return after three years. —山越しに行く, to go over a mountain.

gōshi (合祀する), *vt.* to enshrine together; dedicate collectively *to*.

—靖國神社に合祀する, to enshrine together at the Yasukuni Shrine.

gōshi (合資), *n.* joint stock. ¶ 合資會社, a limited partnership; a joint-stock partnership.

goshigoshi (ごしごし擦る), to rub hard.

goshiki (五色), *n.* the five colours (red, blue, yellow, black, and white); various colours. ¶ 五色眼鏡, a kaleidoscope.

gōshiki (合式の), *a.* formal; in due form; regular; correct.

goshikku (ゴシック), *n.* Gothic. —ゴシック體活字, Gothic type. —ゴシック式建築法, the Gothic style.

goshin (誤信する), *vt.* to misbelieve.

goshin (誤診), *n.* 【醫】 erroneous diagnosis.

goshin (護身), *n.* self-protection; self-preservation. ¶ 護身刀, a sword for self-protection. —護身用ピストル, a life-preserver; a revolver.

goshiṅei (御眞影), *n.* an Imperial portrait. —御眞影を拜する, to make an obeisance [to bow] before the Imperial portrait.

gosho (御所), *n.* a palace; the Imperial palace.

goshō (後生), *n.* the future life; the future life of happiness; happiness in the next life. —後生ですから, for pity's [mercy's] sake. —後生を願ふ, to pray for a happy future; pray for future happiness. —後生大事に仕舞ひ込む, to put it away with the greatest care.

gōshō (豪商), *n.* a wealthy merchant; a merchant prince.

goshoku (誤植), *n.* an erratum; a misprint; a typographical [printer's] error. —誤植だらけである, to teem with [be full of] misprints. —誤植を校正する, to correct misprints.

Gōshū (濠洲), *n.* Australia. ¶ 濠洲人, an Australian. —濠洲聯邦, the commonwealth of Australia. —濠洲產, an Australian product. —白人濠洲主義, the White Australia principle.

gosō (護送する), *vt.* to convoy; escort; send under guard. —監獄に護送する, to send under guard to prison. ¶ 護送自動車, a prison motor-van. —護送船, a convoy; an escort.

gosogoso (ごそごそ), *ad.* ❶ with a rustle. ❷ (滑かでないさま) roughly. —鼠か何かごそごそする, I hear the rustling of rats or something.

go-suru (伍する), *v.* ❶ (列する) to range *with*; rank *with* (*among*); take one's seat *among*. ❷ (交る) to associate *with*.

gō-suru (號する), *vt.* ❶ (稱する) to name; style. ❷ (聲言する) to declare.

gotagota (ごたごた), *n.* (紛擾) quarrel; dispute; trouble. ——, *ad.* in confusion; in a muddle; in a tumble; pell-mell. —ごたごたを惹き起す, to make [raise] a dust. —品物をごたごた入れる, to put things in anyhow. —家の中がごたごたして居る, We are in confusion at home.

gōtai (剛體), *n.* 【理】 a rigid body.

gotaisō (御大葬), *n.* an Imperial funeral.

gōtan (豪膽な), *a.* daring; dauntless; fearless; stout-hearted.

gote (後手になる), *v.* to be forestalled.

gōteki (號笛), *n.* a horn; a siren; a whistle. —號笛を鳴らす, to hoot; whistle.

goten (御殿), *n.* a palace; an Imperial palace.

gōtenjō (格天井), *n.* 【建】 a tessellated [coffered; compartment] ceiling.

-goto (每), *suf.* every; each. —田每の月, the moon reflected in every paddy-field. —國每に, in every country. —三十分每に, every half-hour. —二(三)日目每に, every other [second] (third) day.

gōtō (强盜), *n.* robbery (行爲); a robber (人). —强盜に這入られる, to be robbed by burglars. —强盜を働く, to commit robbery. ¶ 强盜殺人, robbery and murder.

gotoki (如き), *a.* like; such as; such...as. —我々如き貧乏人, poor men like us. —夢の如き人生, dreamlike human life.

gotoku (如く), *ad.* as; as...as (肯定); so...as (否定). …の如くに, as if; as though; after the fashion *of*. —仰せの如く, as you (are pleased to) say. —君の言の如くんば, were it as you say. —水を離れた魚の如く, like fish out of water. —恰も…の如し, it is as if.... —例へば…など云ふ如し, as, for instance, ...

gotta (ごッた), *n.* ❶ (錯雜) jumble. ❷ (ませ物) salmagundi; olla podrida. —ごッたまぜの, jumbled; mixed-up. —ごッたまぜにする, to jumble; mix up. ¶ ごッた煮, hotchpotch.

gōu (豪雨), *n.* a heavy rain.

gouchi (碁打), *n.* *go*-playing (事); a *go*-player (人).

goyaku (誤譯), *n.* mistranslation;

misrendering; misinterpretation. —誤譯する, to mistranslate; misinterpret. —誤譯を指摘する, to point out mistakes in a translation.

goyō (御用), *n.* ❶(用事) business. ❷(公用) official business; service; public service. ❸(註文) an order. —御用始め, opening of government offices in the New Year. —御用納め, closing of government offices at the year-end. —宮內省御用, patronized by the Imperial Household. —御用有之英國へ出張を命せらる, He is ordered to proceed to Great Britain on official business. ¶ 御用掛, (a person in) government service without official rank. (東宮御學問所御用掛, a tutor without official rank to the Crown Prince.) —御用聞き, a roundsman. —御用記者, a government journalist. —御用船, a vessel chartered by the government. —御用新聞, a government organ. —御用商人, a purveyor to the government. —御用邸, a detached palace.

goyō (誤用する), *vt.* to misuse; misapply; misemploy. —文字を誤用する, to misuse words.

gōyoku (强慾), *n.* avarice; rapacity; greediness. —强慾の, avaricious; greedy; rapacious.

gōyū (豪遊), *n.* extravagant pleasures. —一夜千金の豪遊を試みる, to indulge in pleasures that cost a thousand *yen* in one night.

goza (茣蓙), *n.* a mat; matting.

gozasho (御座所), *n.* the sitting-room (of a high personage); the presence-chamber.

goze (瞽女), *n.* a blind female street-singer.

gozen (午前), *n.* the forenoon; morning. ——, *ad.* before noon; a. m. 〖羅 *ante meridiem* の略〗.

gozen (御前), *n.* ❶(貴人の前) the presence of a high personage. ❷(特に帝王の前) the Imperial presence. —御前を退出する, to retire from the presence. ¶ 御前演劇, a command-performance. —御前會議, a council in the Imperial presence.

gōzen (傲然), *ad.* proudly; arrogantly; haughtily.

gōzen (轟然), *ad.* with a great noise; with a loud report. —轟然たる, uproarious; thunderous.

gozō (五臟), *n.* the viscera (肝·心·脾·肺·腎臟). —五臟六腑に沁み渡る, to sink [penetrate] to one's heart's core.

gozonji (御存じ), *n.* knowledge; being aware. —御存じの方, your acquaintance. —兼て御存じの通り, as you already know.

gozume (後詰), *n.* the rear; reserves. —後詰の大將, the general in the rear.

gu (具), *n.* ❶(一揃) a suit. ❷(道具) a tool. —の具に供する, to make it a tool *for*; use it *for*.

gu (愚), *n.* ❶ folly; stupidity. ❷(愚物) a fool; a dunce. ❸(自分) I. —愚にもつかぬことを言ふ, to say preposterous things; talk sheer nonsense. —自ら高ぶり人を愚にする, to give oneself airs and fool others.

gū (ぐう), *n.* squeak; squeal. —ぐうの音も出させぬ答 (出ぬ負), a crushing reply (defeat).

guai (具合), *n.* ❶(合ふさま) order (整調); condition (狀態); state (同上). ❷(配合の趣) harmony; fitness. ❸(方法) manner; way; method. —具合のよい, snug; cosy; comfortable. —具合の惡い, uncomfortable; unfavourable. —身體の具合がよくない, I do not feel very well.

gubi (具備する), *vt.* to be furnished *with*; possess; be complete.

gubijinsō (虞美人草), *n.* = ***hinageshi.***

gubu (供奉する), *vt.* to attend *on*; follow. —鸞輿に供奉する, to follow in the Imperial train. ¶ 供奉員, the suite; the retinue.

gubutsu (愚物), *n.* a fool; a blockhead.

guchi (愚痴), *n.* an idle complaint; querulousness. —愚痴っぽい, given to complaining; querulous. —愚痴をこぼす, to make complaints; grumble; mutter.

guchoku (愚直な), *a.* disinterestedly honest; simple and honest.

gudenguden (ぐでんぐでんに), *ad.* senselessly; helplessly. —ぐでんぐでんに酔ふ, to be dead drunk.

gudon (愚鈍な), *a.* stupid; dull; muddle-headed.

gufū (颶風), *n.* a hurricane. —颶風に遇ふ, to encounter a hurricane.

gugansha (具眼者), *n.* an intelligent [keen] observer.

gūgen (寓言), *n.* an allegory; a parable; an apologue. —寓言的 allegorical.

gūhatsu (偶發する), *vi.* to occur happen; chance. ¶ 偶發原因 an occasional cause.

gūi (寓意), *n.* a hidden meaning a moral; an allegory. ¶ 寓意畫 an allegorical picture.

guigui (ぐいぐい), *ad.* with grea strength; with all one's strength with a strong pull (飲酒に云ふ)

—ぐいぐい綱を引く, to give strong pulls to a rope; pull a rope with all one's strength.

guito (ぐいと), *ad.* with an effort. —ぐいと引く, to pull with a jerk; pluck; twitch. —ぐいと押し出す, to push out at a go. —ぐいと一息に飲み干す, to empty at a draught; drain the cup at a gulp.

gūji (宮司), *n.* the chief priest of a government [national] shrine. ¶ 大宮司, the chief priest of the Ise Shrine.

gujin (愚人), *n.* a fool; a block-head.

gujō (具狀する), *vt.* to make a full report; report fully [in detail]. —其の理由を具狀する, to present a full statement of the reasons therefor.

gūkyo (寓居), *n.* a temporary residence; an abode.

gumai (愚昧), *n.* stupidity; imbecility. —愚昧の, stupid; imbecile; ignorant.

gumi (茱萸), *n.* 【植】 Elæagnus pungens.

gumin (愚民), *n.* ignorant people; the populace; the rabble.

gun (軍), *n.* ❶ a force; an army. ❷ (戰) a war; a battle. —軍を旋(かへ)らす, to return with one's forces. —軍を進める(率ゐる), to march (lead) an army.

gun (郡), *n.* district; subprefecture.

gun (群), *n.* a crowd (集團); a throng (狹き所に集ッた); a group (人・物の少數の). —一群の山賊, a gang of brigands. —鷄群の一鶴, a Triton among minnows. —群をなす, to herd together. (群をなす鳥, social birds. —群をなして來る, to come in swarms [crowds].) —群を拔く, to be above the common run.

gunba (軍馬), *n.* a war-horse; a charger.

gunbaiuchiwa (軍配團扇), *n.* ❶ (軍扇) a war-fan. ❷ 【植】 the penny-cress; the wild cress.

gunbi (軍備), *n.* armaments; military preparations; preparedness. —軍備を擴張する, to increase armaments. —軍備を縮少する, to reduce armaments. ¶ 軍備縮少論, the argument for the reduction of armaments.

gunbō (軍帽), *n.* a (military) cap.

gunbu (郡部), *n.* a district section (of the prefecture). ¶ 郡部選擧區, a rural electoral district. —郡部選出議員, a member for [representative of] a rural district.

gunchō (郡長), *n.* a district headman; a subprefect.

gundan (軍團), *n.* an army-corps. ¶ 軍團長, the commander of an army-corps.

gungaku (軍樂), *n.* military music. —軍樂を奏する, to play military music. ¶ 軍樂隊, a military band (陸); a naval band (海).

guṅi (軍醫), *n.* an army (a naval) surgeon; a medical officer. ¶ 軍醫部, the army medical corps; the medical department.

gunji (軍事), *n.* military affairs. ¶ 軍事行動, military action. —軍事敎育, military education. —軍事參議院, the high military council. —軍事參議官, a member of the high military council; a high military councillor. —軍事探偵, a (military) spy. —軍事通信員, a military (naval) correspondent.

gunjin (軍人), *n.* (陸軍) a soldier; a military man; (海軍) a marine; (將校) a military (naval) officer. —軍人の職, the military profession. —軍人となる, to go [enlist] for a soldier.

gunjin (軍陣), *n.* ❶ (陣立) a battle formation. ❷ (戰場) a battle-field; the field of battle. —軍陣に臨む, to be present at the field of battle.

gunjō (群靑), *n.* ultramarine.

gunjuhin (軍需品), *n.* munitions of war; military stores.

gunka (軍歌), *n.* a war-song. —軍歌を奏する, to sing a war-song.

gunkan (軍艦), *n.* a man-of-war; a warship. —軍艦を派遣する, to dispatch a warship. ¶ 軍艦旗, a man-of war's flag; an ensign. —軍艦乘組員, a man-of-war's man.

gunki (軍紀), *n.* military discipline. ¶ 軍紀弛廢 (振肅), relaxation (strict maintenance) of military discipline.

gunki (軍旗), *n.* the (regimental) colours; a banner; a standard. —軍旗に敬禮する, to salute the colours. ¶ 軍旗護衞兵, a colour party 〔英〕; a colour guard 〔米〕. —軍旗祭, the celebration of the presentation of colours.

gunki (軍機), *n.* a military secret. —軍機を洩らす, to betray [disclose] military secrets. ¶ 軍機保護法, law for the preservation of military secrets.

gunkō (軍港), *n.* a naval port; a naval station. —横須賀軍港, Yokosuka naval port.

gunkoku-shugi (軍國主義), *n.* militarism. ¶ 軍國主義者, a militarist.

gunkyo (群居する), *vi.* to live gregariously; hive.

gunmu (軍務), *n.* military affairs [business]. ¶ 軍務局, the Bureau of Military (Naval) Affairs.

gunpō (軍法), *n.* ❶ (兵術) the

art of war. ❷(陸海軍刑法) military law; articles of war. ¶ 軍法會議, a court-martial; a court of inquiry. (高等軍法會議, a general court-martial. —軍法會議に付する, to court-martial.)

gunpu(軍夫), *n.* a military coolie.

gunpuku (軍服), *n.* a uniform; regimentals.

gunri (軍吏), *n.* a military (naval) paymaster; an accountant(-officer).

gunritsu (軍律), *n.* ❶ (軍紀) military discipline. ❷ (軍法) military law.

gunryaku (軍略), *n.* strategy.

gunsei(軍制), *n.* military organization [system].

gunsei (軍政), *n.* military administration.

gunsei (群棲·群生する), *vi.* to hive; live gregariously; grow in clusters (果實など).

gunseki (軍籍), *n.* the military register. —軍籍に入る, to enlist; enter the army (navy).

gunshi(軍使), *n.* a *parlementaire* (佛); the bearer of a flag of truce.

gunshi (軍資), *n.* a war-fund; the sinews of war. —軍資を獻納する, to contribute the war-fund.

gunshin (軍神), *n.* the war-god; the god of war; Ares (希臘); Mars (羅馬).

gunshireibu (軍司令部), *n.* military headquarters.

gunshireikan (軍司令官), *n.* an army commander.

gunshoku(軍職), *n.* the military profession; the profession of arms.

gunshū(群集, 群衆), *n.* a crowd; a multitude; a throng; a concourse; a flock. —群集する, to crowd together; assemble; gather; flock together; swarm. (群集して來る, to come in flocks.) ¶ 群衆心理, psychology of the mob; mob mind.

gunsō (軍曹), *n.* a sergeant.

guntai (軍隊), *n.* an army; troops; a corps; forces. —軍隊的敎育を施す, to give military training. ¶ 軍隊衛生, military sanitation. —軍隊輸送, transportation of troops.

guntō (軍刀), *n.* a sabre; a (service) sword.

guntō (群島), *n.* an archipelago; a group of islands. —馬來群島, the Malay Archipelago.

gunyagunya (ぐにゃぐにゃの), *a.* soft; flabby; limp.

guṅyakusho (郡役所), *n.* a district office.

guṅyō (軍用の), *a.* military. ¶ 軍用鳩, a military carrier-pigeon. —軍用飛行機, a war-plane. —軍用金, a war-fund. —軍用旅館, an inn for billeting troops. —軍用鐵道, a military railway.

gunzoku (軍屬), *n.* a civilian attached to the army (navy); a civilian in military employment.

guragura (ぐらぐらする), *vi.* to swim; whirl; totter; shake; wobble. —ぐらぐらする机 (家), a shaky table (house). —頭がぐらぐらする, One's head grows dizzy.

guramu (瓦), *n.* gramme, gram.

gurasu (狂らす), *vt.* ❶ (狂はす) to put out of order. ❷ (惑はす) to mislead: lead astray. —順を狂らす, to put out of order. —人目を狂らす, to deceive people's eyes.

gureru (狂れる), *vi.* ❶ (迷ふ) to go astray. ❷ (狂ふ) to get out of order; go wrong.

guretsu (愚劣な), *a.* foolish; absurd.

guriguri (ぐりぐり), *n.* a hard lump under the skin.

Gurinitchi (グリニッチ), *n.* Greenwich. —グリニッチ子午線の平均時, Greenwich time.

gurō (愚弄する), *vt.* to mock; deride; make sport *of*. ——, *a.* derisive; derisory. —人の愚弄する所となる, to come to be an object of derision.

guron (愚論), *n.* a foolish argument.

gurosu (グロス), *n.* a gross.

guru (共謀になる), *v.* to conspire *with*; collude *with*.

guruguru (ぐるぐる), *ad.* round and round; in a circle. —帶をぐるぐる巻にする, to wind the sash round the body. —水車がぐるぐる廻る, The water-mill turns round and round.

-gurumi (くるみ), *suf.* inclusive *of*; with; including; ...and all.

gururi (ぐるりと), *ad.* ❶ (一周するさま) round. ❷ (向を反すさま) opposite; contrary. ❸ (全く) completely. —ぐるりと廻る, to turn round; go round about. —ぐるりと取卷く, to surround completely. —ぐるりと向を變へる, to shift the direction completely. —身體をぐるりとまはす, to turn right round.

gusaku (愚策), *n.* a foolish plan.

gushin(具申する), *vt.* to report; refer to a superior officer.

gushō (具象), *n.* embodiment; concreteness. ¶ 具象名詞, 【文】 the concrete noun.

gussuri (ぐッすり), *ad.* sound; fast. —ぐッすり眠る, to sleep soundly. —ぐッすり寢込む, to fall into deep sleep; fall fast [sound] asleep.

gūsū (偶數), *n.* an even number.

gū-suru (寓する), *vt.* (寓意) to

allude *to.* ——, *vi.* (寄寓) to live temporarily. —教訓的意味を寓する, to possess a didactic meaning.

gū-suru (遇する), *vt.* to treat; use. —敬して師の禮を以て遇する, to treat a person with respect due to a teacher.

gutai (具體的), *a.* concrete. —具體的說明, a concrete explanation. —具體的に, concretely; in the concrete. —具體化する, to take (concrete) shape.

gutto (ぐッと), *ad.* ❶ (力を入れて) with an effort. ❷ (一氣に) at once; at a gulp. —ぐッと(言葉に)行き詰まる, to be at a loss for words. —目をつぶッてぐッと飲む, to close the eyes and drink at a gulp.

gūwa (寓話), *n.* an allegory; a fable; a parable.

guyū (具有する), *vt.* to possess; have; be armed *with*; be furnished *with.*

gūzen (偶然), *ad.* casually; by chance [accident]; unexpectedly; fortuitously. —偶然の友, a chance companion. —偶然に出逢ふ, to chance [happen] *upon*; meet by chance; happen [chance] to meet. —偶然露店で之を見出す, to chance upon this in a street stall.

gūzō (偶像), *n.* an idol (神・佛の); an image; an effigy. —偶像を崇拜する, to worship idols. ¶ 偶像破壞, iconoclasm. —偶像崇拜, idolatry. (偶像崇拜者, an idolater [*fem.* -tress].)

guzuguzu (愚圖愚圖), *ad.* ❶ (鈍く) tardily; sluggishly. ❷ (なまけて) idly; lazily. —ぐづぐづして時間を費す, to dally away time. —ぐづぐづして好機を逸する, to dally away opportunity.

guzuru (愚圖る), *v.* ❶ (ねだる) to importune *for*; tease *for*; pester (with requests). ❷ (ぐづぐづ云ふ) to grumble *at*; complain *of.* ❸ (だだをこねる) to fret.

gyafun (ぎゃふんと參る), *v.* to be non-plussed; be squashed.

gyāgyā (ぎゃーぎゃー泣・鳴く), *vi.* to squall (小兒が); squawk (鳥が).

gyakkō (逆行する), *vi.* to retrogress; move backward. ——, *a.* 【天】 retrograde; retrogressive. —時勢に逆行する, to run counter to the spirit of the time; swim against the stream.

gyakkyō (逆境), *n.* adverse situation; adverse circumstances; adversity. —逆境に陷る, to be driven to extremity; fall upon evil days. —逆境と鬪ふ, to struggle with adversity.

gyaku (逆), *n.* ❶ (さかしま) inverse. ❷ (反對) oppositeness; contrariness; reverse. ❸ (不道理) irrationality; unreason. ❹ 【數】 converse. ☞ *gyaku-ni.* —逆の仕方, backward process.

gyakuchō (逆調), *n.* unfavourable condition.

gyakufū (逆風), *n.* a contrary [an adverse] wind; a head-wind.

gyakujō (逆上), *n.* dizziness. —— **-suru**, *vi.* to have a rush of blood to the head; be dizzy; be crazy (發狂). —嬉しさの餘り逆上する, to be transported [beside oneself] with joy.

gyakumodori (逆戻りする), *vi.* to retrograde; go back; retrace one's steps; have a relapse (病が). —五十年許り逆戻りする, to be set back fifty years.

gyaku-ni (逆に), *ad.* in the opposite direction; backwards; reversely. —逆に始める, to begin at the wrong end. —逆に手をねぢる, to twist one's hand the wrong way. —順序を逆にする, to reverse the order.

gyakuryū (逆流), *n.* ❶ (逆に流れること) flowing upstream; refluence (潮・血の). ❷ (逆に流れる水) back current.

gyakusatsu (虐殺), *n.* massacre; slaughter; carnage. —— **-suru**, *vt.* to massacre; slaughter. —女子供を虐殺する, to massacre women and children.

gyakusei (虐政), *n.* tyranny; oppressive government.

gyakusetsu (逆說), *n.* a paradox.

gyakushi (虐使する), *vt.* =***kokushi*** (酷使する). —雇人を虐使する, to maltreat one's employés.

gyakushū (逆襲), *n.* a counter-attack. —逆襲する, to counter-attack. —逆襲を受ける, to receive a counter-attack. —逆襲的態度に出る, to assume the attitude of counter-attack.

gyakutai (虐待), *n.* ill-treatment; cruelty; persecution. —虐待する, to ill-treat; treat with cruelty; persecute.

gyakute (逆手), *n.* a counter-chip; foul play.

gyakutegata (逆手形), *n.* 【商】 a redraft.

gyakuten (逆轉), *n.* ❶ (逆戻) reversion; retrogression. ❷ 【飛】 a loop. —逆轉する, ① to reverse; retrograde. ② to loop the loop; turn somersault. —數回逆轉を試みた, The airman reversed the machine several times.

gyakuyō (逆用する), *vt.* to turn *upon*; pervert.

gyakuyunyū (逆輸入する), *vi.* to reimport.

gyakuyushutsu (逆輸出する), *vt.* to reexport.

gyakuzoku (逆賊), *n.* a rebel; a traitor. —逆賊を誅する, to punish traitors with death.

gyō(行), *n.* ❶(くだり) a line. ❷(修行) austerities. —二頁の五行目, the fifth line of the second page; page 2, line 5. —行を揃へて書く, to write in regular lines. —行を改めて書く, to begin a new line. —無言の行をする, to perform silent austerities.

gyō (業), *n.* ❶(學業) studies. ❷(所業) an act; conduct. ❸(職業) business; trade(大工·鍛冶屋など); occupation; profession (知識的の). ❹(功業) (meritorious) service. ❺(事業) an enterprise (企業); industry (產業); service (概して交通業); interests. —業とする, [*vt.*] to follow; pursue; engage *in*; practise (醫師·辯護士などを); make a profession [business] *of*. (醫を業とする, to practise medicine; be a doctor by profession.) —業を勵む, to work diligently at one's business.

gyoba(漁場), *n.* a fishing ground [place]; a fishery.

gyōchū(蟯蟲), *n.* the seat-worm; the threadworm.

gyoen (御苑), *n.* an Imperial garden. —御苑の拜觀を許される, to be permitted to visit the Imperial garden.

gyoen(御宴), *n.* an Imperial dinner. —御宴に陪する, to attend an Imperial dinner.

gyofu(漁夫, 漁父), *n.* a fisherman. —漁父の利を占める, to play off one person against another.

gyofuku (魚腹に葬られる), to feed the fishes.

gyōgi (行儀), *n.* manners; behaviour; deportment. —行儀のよい(わるい), well(ill)-behaved; well(ill)-mannered. —行儀見習の爲め, to learn manners.

gyogu (漁具), *n.* fishing implements.

gyogun(魚群), *n.* a school [shoal] of fish.

gyogyō(漁業), *n.* fishery; fishing industry. ¶ 漁業場, =*gyoba*. —漁業權, fishery right. —漁業區, a fishery lot.

gyōgyōshii (仰仰しい), *a.* exaggerated; ostentatious.

gyōja (行者), *n.* an ascetic; a fakir; an itinerant performer.

gyoji (御璽), *n.* the Imperial seal; the Privy seal [signet].

gyōji (行司), *n.* an umpire; a wrestling umpire.

gyōjō (行狀), *n.* ❶ (品行) behaviour; demeanour; deportment. ❷ (言行錄) *memorabilia*〖羅〗.

gyoka(漁火), *n.* a fishing fire (to attract fish).

gyokaku (漁獲する), *v.* to fish; catch fish. ¶ 漁獲高, catch (of fish).

gyōkaku (仰角), *n.* an angle of elevation.

gyokan (御感), *n.* Imperial admiration [appreciation]. —御感斜ならず, His Majesty highly admired it.

gyōkei (行啓), *n.* the going out (of the Empress or the Crown Prince). —東宮殿下の行啓を仰ぐ, to beg for the visit of H. I. H. the Crown Prince.

gyokei-suirai (魚形水雷), *n.* a torpedo; a fish-torpedo. ☞ *gyorai* (魚雷).

gyōketsu(凝結する), *v.* to congeal; coagulate; freeze; condense.

gyoki (漁期), *n.* a fishing season.

gyōki (澆季), *n.* degeneration; *fin de siècle* 〖佛〗. —澆季の世に生れる, to be born in degenerate times.

gyōko (凝固する), *vi.* to condense; solidify; congeal.

gyōkō (行幸), *n.* the going out (of the Emperor); the Imperial Progress. —行幸あらせられた, His Majesty was pleased to go.

gyōkō (僥倖), *n.* good fortune; (good) luck; a godsend; a fluke; a windfall (僥倖收益). —僥倖にも[にして], by luck; by good fortune; by a fluke. (僥倖にも成功した, I had the luck [good fortune] to succeed.) **—— -suru,** *vt.* to pray for luck. —萬一を僥倖する, to trust to luck; chance it.

gyokuseki-konkō(玉石混淆), *n.* a medley of the good and the bad; a web of good and evil; thread and thrum. —玉石を混淆する, to mix the good and the bad together.

gyokutai (玉體), *n.* the person of an Emperor.

gyokuza (玉座), *n.* the throne; the Imperial throne.

gyokuzui (玉髓), *n.* 【礦】 chalcedony, calcedony.

gyomei (御名), *n.* the Imperial Name; His Majesty's Name. —御名御璽, the Imperial Sign Manual and Imperial Seal.

gyomō (漁網), *n.* a fishing-net.

gyōmu(業務), *n.* business; affairs. —人の業務を妨害する, to hinder another's business. ¶ 業務執行, conduct [management] of business. (業務執行社員, 【法】 a managing [working] partner.)

gyoniku (魚肉), *n.* fish-meat.

gyorai (魚雷), *n.* =*gyokei-suirai*. ¶ 魚雷發射管, a torpedo-tube; a launching-tube.

gyōretsu (行列), *n.* a procession; a parade; *cortège* 〔佛〕. —行列する, to go in procession; parade.

gyorogyoro (ぎょろぎょろ), *ad.* ⑤ ぎょろりと. with eyes wide open. —ぎょろぎょろした目で人を睨める, to stare at a person with goggle-eyes.

gyorui (魚類), *n.* the fishes; the finny tribes.

gyoryō (漁獵), *n.* hunting and fishery.

gyōsan (仰山な), *a.* ❶ (大袈裟な) exaggerated. ❷ (澤山の) much (many); plentiful. —仰山な人, a large crowd of people; a great [large] number of people. —つまらない事を仰山にいふ, to talk exaggeratingly of trifles; make a mountain out of a molehill.

gyosei (御製), *n.* Imperial composition; an Imperial ode.

gyōsei (行政), *n.* administration. ¶ 行政法, administrative law. —行政官, an administrative [executive] officer. —行政官廳, an administrative office. —行政警察, the administrative police. —行政機關, an administrative organ. —行政裁判所, the Court of Administrative Litigation. —行政處分, an administrative disposition [measure].

gyōseki (行跡), *n.* conduct; behaviour.

gyosen (漁船), *n.* a fisher-boat; a fishing boat [vessel].

gyosha (馭者, 御者), *n.* a driver; a coachman; a carter (荷車の); a waggoner (同上). ¶ 御車臺, a driving-box; a box; a driver's seat.

gyōshi (凝視する), *vt.* to stare *at*; fix one's eyes *on*; gaze *on*; scrutinize; regard.

gyōshō (行書), *n.* the intermediate style of writing (between the running and square styles).

gyōshō (行商), *n.* ❶ (行爲) peddling; huckstery. ❷ (人) a pedlar; a packman; a hawker. —行商する, [*vi*] to peddle; hawk.

gyōshō (驍將), *n.* a brave general; a leader; a master writer (文學の).

gyoshoku (魚食), *n.* ichthyophagy; fish-eating. ¶ 魚食者, a fish-eater; an ichthyophagist.

gyōshū (凝集する), *vi.* to cohere. ——, *a.* coherent; cohesive.

gyōshuku (凝縮する), *v.* to condense.

gyoson (漁村), *n.* a fishing village.

gyo-suru (御·馭する), *vt.* ❶ (乘御) to ride; drive. ❷ (統御) to control; manage; handle. —御し難い, intractable; unmanageable; unruly. —御し易い, amenable; manageable; tractable. —馬を馭する, to manage [control] a horse.

gyōten (仰天する), *vi.* to be amazed; be taken aback; be wonder-struck.

gyōten (曉天), *n.* the morning sky. —曉天の星の如く, like the stars at dawn.

gyōtsū (曉通する), *v.* to be at home *in*; be versed *in*.

gyotto (ぎょッとする), *vi.* to be startled; get a start.

gyounsha (魚運車), *n.* 【鐵道】 a fish-van (鮮魚輸送貨車); a fish-car.

gyoyu (魚油), *n.* fish-oil (特に肝油·鯨油).

gyōzui (行水), *n.* tub-bathing. —行水を使ふ, to bathe in a tub.

gyūeki (牛疫), *n.* cattle-plague; rinder-pest.

gyūgyū (ぎューぎュー), creak; squeak. —ぎューぎュー押し込む, to squeeze *into*. —ギューギュー云はせる, to make a person squeal.

gyūhi (牛皮), *n.* ❶ ox-hide; cowhide. ❷ (菓子) Turkish delight.

gyūin-bashoku (牛飲馬食する), *vi.* to gorge and swill.

gyūji (牛耳), *n.* leadership. —牛耳を執る; 牛耳る, to take the command *of*.

gyūnabe (牛鍋), *n.* a beef-pan

gyūniku (牛肉), *n.* beef. ¶ 牛肉屋, ① a butcher; a beef-shop. ② (牛肉料理屋) a beef-restaurant; a beef eating-house.

gyūnyū (牛乳), *n.* (cow's) milk. —牛乳で育てる, to bring up on the bottle; feed on cow's milk. ¶ 無菌(消毒)牛乳, sterilized milk. —牛乳壜, a milk-bottle. —牛乳配達夫, a milkman. —牛乳店, a milk-shop. —牛乳屋, a dairyman (人) a dairy (搾取所); a milk-shop (販賣店).

gyūraku (牛酪), *n.* butter.

gyūtō (牛刀), *n.* a butcher's knife. —牛刀を以て鷄を割く, to break a butterfly on the wheel; employ a steam-engine to crack a nut.

gyūtō (牛痘), *n.* 【醫】 cow-pox. —牛痘を接種する, to vaccinate.

gyūtto (ぎューッと), *ad.* ❶ tightly; firmly; closely. ❷ with a creak. —ギューッと握る (手を), to give him a squeeze (of the hand). —ギューッと押す, to push with a jerk. —ギューッと開く (閉まる), to swing open (to).

H

ha (は), *n.* 【音】C; do [伊]; I.
ha (刃), *n.* an edge; bit (錐・鉋の).
ha(派), *n.* ❶(學派, 流派) a school. ❷(分派) a sect. ❸(黨派) a party. —眞宗本願寺派, the Honganji section of the Shinshū. —官學派と私學派, the government school and private school coteries.
ha (葉), *n.* a leaf; foliage (叢葉); a blade (長い). —葉の茂ッた, leafy. —葉のない, leafless; naked.
ha (齒), *n.* ❶ a tooth [*pl.* teeth]. ❷(齒車の) a cog; a rim. —齒のない, toothless. —齒が生える, to teethe; cut one's teeth. —齒をうかす, to set (a person's) teeth on edge. —齒を磨く, to clean [brush] one's teeth. —齒を喰ひしばる, to clench [gnash] one's teeth. —齒が痛んでたまらぬ, I suffer terribly from toothache.
ha (霸), *n.* ❶(霸權) hegemony; supremacy; leadership. ❷(首領) a chief. —霸を天下に爭ふ, to contend for supreme power in the country.
haba (幅, 巾), *n.* breadth; width. —幅四呎, four feet in width. —幅を利かす, to lord it *over*; be influential.
habakari (憚りながら), *ad.* ❶ (恐れ多いが) may I trouble you *to*. ❷(廣言ながら) allow me to tell you that. —憚りながら君と意見を異にする, I venture to differ from you.
habakaru (憚る), *v.* to dread; be afraid *of*; fear. —憚る所なく, without compunction [reserve]. —人前も憚からずに, regardless of company.
habamu (阻む), *vt.* to oppose; obstruct; thwart; check; stop.
habataki (羽搏する), *vi.* to flutter; clap [flap; beat] the wings.
habatobi (幅跳), *n.* a long jump.
haberu (侍る), *v.* ❶(附添ふ) to attend *on*; wait *upon*; serve *at*. ❷ (である) to be. —酒席に侍る, to serve at a drinking party.
habikoru (蔓る), *vi.* ❶(蔓延) to overgrow; spread; extend. ❷ (跋扈) to grow in power; be rampant; domineer.
habotan (葉牡丹), *n.* 【植】 the (garden) cabbage; the cauliflower.
habuku (省く), *vt.* ❶ (省略) to omit; leave out; dispense *with*. ❷ (節約) to reduce; cut down; curtail. ❸ (除却) to remove; cut away [off]; exclude. —手數を省く, to save trouble. —無用の手續を省く, to do away with useless formalities. —直接關係のない點を省く, to dispense with points which have no direct connection.
habutae (羽二重), *n.* *habutaye.*
hachi (八), *n.* eight.
hachi (蜂), *n.* 【昆】 the bee (蜜蜂); the wasp (黃蜂). —蜂に螫される, to be stung by a bee.
hachi (鉢), *n.* a bowl; a rice-tub (飯櫃); a pot (植木鉢, 壺). —鉢(咲き)の梅, a plum-tree (flowering) in a pot. —鉢に植ゑる, [*vt.*] to pot.
hachiawase (鉢合せする), *vi.* to run [knock] against a person.
hachibungi (八分儀), *n.* an octant.
hachigatsu (八月), *n.* August (Aug. と略す).
hachijū(八十), *n.* eighty.
hachikireru (張切れる), *vi.* to burst.
hachiku (破竹の勢で), with irresistible force.
hachimaki(鉢卷), *n.* a headband; a handkerchief tied round the head.
hachimen (八面體), *n.* 【數】 an octahedron.
hachimitsu (蜂蜜), *n.* honey; comb-honey (巢にあるもの).
hachinosu (蜂巢), *n.* a hive; a bee-hive; a honeycomb. —蜂の巢をつついたやうに, like poking into a hornet's nest.
hachisu (蓮), *n.* ❶ the Chinese water-lily; the lotus (通稱). ❷ (木槿) the rose of Sharon.
hachō (波長), *n.* wave-length.
hachū (爬蟲), *n.* a reptile. ¶ 爬蟲類, the Reptilia.
hada (肌, 膚), *n.* ❶(皮膚) the skin. ❷(肌合ひ) disposition; character; temper. —肌をぬぐ, to be in shirt sleeves; expose [bare] the shoulders (肌を露はす). —大肌ぬぎで, with the body bared to the waist. —肌を刺すやうな寒さ, piercing cold.
hadagi (肌著), *n.* an underwear; an undershirt.
hadaka(裸), *n.* (裸體) the naked body; nakedness. —裸で, in nakedness; in buff; in nature's own clothing. —裸になる, to become naked; take off one's clothes. —裸にする, to bare; denude; strip; uncover; divest *of*. ¶ 裸踊, a naked dance. —裸馬, a barebacked horse; an unsaddled horse (鞍なき馬). (裸馬に乘る, to ride bareback.)
hadakamugi (裸麥), *n.* the rye.
hadami (肌身), *n.* the body. —

肌身を汚す, to defile the body. —肌身離さず持つ, to have always about one.
hadan(破談する), *vt.* to break off.
hadashi (跣足), *n.* barefoot. —跣足になる(で逃出す), to become (run out) barefooted.
hade (派手), *n.* display; flashiness; fineness. —派手好きの, showy; dressy. —派手に著飾る, to dress gaily. **——-na,** *a.* gay; showy; flashy. —派手な著物, a gay dress.
hadō (波動), *n.* a wave; waviness; roll; fluctuation. —波動する, to wave; roll.
hadome (歯止), *n.* a brake; a drag; a pawl(掣手).
hādoru (ハードル), *n.* 【競技】a hurdle-race.
hae (蠅), *n.* the fly. —飯の上の蠅, a source of annoyance.
haechō (蠅帳), *n.* a meat-safe.
haegiwa (生際), *n.* the borders of the hair; the root of the hair. —生際の濃い(薄い)女, a woman with thick (thin) borders of hair.
haeharai (蠅拂), *n.* a fly-whisk.
haenuki (生抜きの), *a.* native--born; true-born.
haeru (生える), *vi.* to grow.
haeru (映・榮える), *vi.* to look well; improve.
haetori (蠅取), *n.* (器) a fly--catcher; a fly-trap; fly-paper (紙). —蠅取草, the lopseed.
haeuchi (蠅打), *n.* a fly-flap; a flapper.
hafu (破風), *n.* 【建】a gable. ¶ 破風窓, a gabled window.
hafu (覇府), *n.* the *shōgunate*; a feudal government.
hagai (羽交), *n.* pinion.
hagaki (葉書), *n.* a postcard; a postal card. ¶ 往復葉書, a return postcard. —私製(官製)葉書, a private (an official) postcard. —萬國聯合郵便葉書, a universal postcard.
hagane (鋼), *n.* steel.
hagareru (剝れる), *vi.* to come off; be stripped off.
hagasu (剝す), *vt.* to strip off; take off; tear off.
hagayui (歯痒い), *a.* impatient; irritated.
hage (禿), *n.* baldness; a bald patch (禿あと).
hageatama (禿頭), *n.* ❶ a bald head. ❷(禿頭者) a baldpate; a baldhead.
hagemasu (勵ます), *vt.* to encourage; urge; stimulate. —聲を勵まして, with a loud voice. —他の者を勵ます, to encourage the others. —自ら氣を勵ます, to pluck [muster; summon] up one's courage.
hagemu (勵む), *v.* to strive at; be diligent [zealous; assiduous] *in.*
hageru (禿げる), *vi.* to grow [become] bald; become bare (山). —禿げた, bald; bare.
hageshii (烈·劇しい), *a.* violent; severe; vehement. —烈しい風, a strong wind. —烈しい風雨, a heavy storm. —潮流が烈しい, The tide runs strong.
hageshiku(烈·劇しく), *ad.* violently; severely; vehemently.
hagetaka (兀鷹), *n.* 【鳥】the vulture.
hagi (萩), *n.* Lespedeza bicolor (bush-clover の一種·學名).
hagi (脛), *n.* the leg. —脛もあらはに, with the legs exposed.
hagi (綴布), *n.* a patch.
hagime (矧目), *n.* a lap-joint; a seam.
hagire(歯切のよい), *a.* powerful; energetic; smart. —歯切れのよい文章, a powerful [an energetic] writing.
hagishiri (歯軋する), *vi.* to grit [grind] the teeth.
hagitori(剝取), *n.* ❶(剝し取り) stripping off; taking off. ❷(剝取帖) a pad; a tear-off block. ❸(强奪) taking away by force; robbing (a person) of (his things). ¶ 剝取り暦, a block calendar. —剝取線, a preforeted line.
hago (黐擌), *n.* a limed twig.
hagoita (羽子板), *n.* a battledore.
hagoku (破獄する), *vi.* to break out of a prison; escape from prison.
hagoromo (羽衣), *n.* a robe of feathers.
hagu(剝ぐ), *vt.* ❶(剝し取る) to strip off; tear off; pull off. ❷(剝奪) to strip [divest; deprive] *of.* —官位を剝ぐ, to deprive a person of office and rank. —木の皮を剝ぐ, to strip a tear; peel off a bark.
hagu (矧ぐ), *vt.* ❶(矢竹に羽を) to fledge. ❷【建】to join; piece. —矢を矧ぐ, to fledge [feather] an arrow.
haguki (歯齦), *n.* the gums.
hagureru (逸れる), *vi.* to lose the way; lose [stray from] one's companion. —逸らかす, to let stray; let go astray. ¶ はぐれ羊, a stray sheep.
haguruma (歯車), *n.* a toothed wheel; a cog-wheel.
haha (母), *n.* a mother. —母の愛, motherly [maternal] love. —母なき, motherless.
hahā (ははー), well; indeed; I see. —ははーなるほど, Ah, yes.
ha-ha, hā-hā, (呵呵), *int.* ha ha; haw-haw.
hahakigi (帚木), *n.* the broom goosefoot.
hahen (破片), *n.* a fragment; a piece.
hai (蠅), *n.* the fly.

hai (灰), *n.* ashes. —灰になるまで, until it is reduced (we turn) to ashes. —灰を篩ふ, to sieve ashes.
hai (杯, 盃), *n.* a cup; a glass.
hai (肺), *n.* the lungs.
hai (敗), *n.* defeat (敗北); failure (仕損). —敗を取る, to be defeated; suffer defeat; fail. —敗を轉じて勝となす, to snatch a victory out of defeat.
hai (はい), ❶ yes; well; here, sir (出席の返事). ❷ (物を渡す時) here it is; here you are. —はいかしこまりました, Very well, sir.
haian (廢案), *n.* the dropping of a proposal; a rejected bill; a draft [proposal] withdrawn [discarded].
haibi (配備), *n.* arrangement; disposition. —配備する, to arrange; dispose; station. ¶ 攻撃(防禦)配備, offensive (defensive) dispositions.
haiboku (敗北), *n.* defeat. —敗北する, to be defeated; sustain a defeat. —總敗北である, to be totally defeated.
haibu (背部), *n.* the back.
haibun (配分), *n.* apportionment; distribution (分配); proportion (割前). **——-suru,** *vt.* to apportion; distribute; divide; share; proportion. —人に配分する, to apportion to a person.
haibutsu (廢物), *n.* a useless article [thing]; a waste product; waste. ¶ 廢物利用, utilization of waste products.
haibutsukyō (拜物敎), *n.* fetishism.
haibyō (肺病), *n.* consumption; a lung-disease. —肺病に罹る, to be attacked by consumption. —肺病をわづらッてる, to suffer from consumption. ¶ 肺病患者, a consumptive (patient).
haichai (はいちゃい), *int.* & *n.* [小兒] bye-bye; ta-ta.
haichaku (廢嫡する), *vt.* to disinherit.
haichi (背馳する), *v.* to be contrary *to*; run counter *to*; contradict.
haichi (配置), *n.* arrangement; disposition. —配置する, to arrange; dispose; station; set.
haichō (廢朝), *n.* suspension of business at (the) Court.
haiden (拜殿), *n.* the hall of worship; the front-shrine.
haiden (配電する), *v.* to distribute electric current. ¶ 配電線, a service-wire. —配電所, a distributing station.
haideru (這出る), *vi.* to crawl out; creep out.
haidō (擺動), *n.* oscillation.
haien (肺炎), *n.* pneumonia; inflammation of the lungs.
haietsu (拜謁), *n.* audience; an audience with the Emperor. —拜謁を許す, to grant an audience *to*.
haifu (配布する), *vt.* to distribute; apportion; give out.
haifuki (灰吹), *n.* a bamboo spittoon.
haifuku (拜復), in reply to your letter.
haifun (ハイフン), *n.* a hyphen.
haifurui (灰篩), *n.* an ash-sieve.
haiga (拜賀), *n.* respectful congratulations; felicitations [congratulations] to superiors.
haigai (排外主義), *n.* exclusionism; the principle of seclusion. ¶ 排外主義者, an exclusionist. —排外思想, an anti-foreign spirit; anti-foreign ideas.
haigaku (廢學する), *vi.* to give up one's studies; abandon study.
haigan (拜顔), *n.* the honour [pleasure] of seeing [meeting] a person. —拜顔を得たく, to desire the pleasure of seeing you.
haigo (背後), *n.* the rear. —彼の背後に, behind him. —敵の背後を衝く, to attack the enemy's rear [the enemy in the rear].
haigo (廢語), *n.* an obsolete word; a disused word.
haigō (配合), *n.* harmony (色); match; mixture (混合). —配合する, to match; couple; pair; conjugate; mix. —色の配合が頗るよい, The colours are very well matched.
haigū (配偶), *n.* conjugality; match. ¶ 配偶者, a spouse; a consort; a couple (兩人).
haigyō (廢業する), *v.* to shut up shop; close [give up] one's business; discontinue business. ¶ 廢業屆, a report of retirement from business.
haihan (背反する), *vi.* to be contrary *to*; be opposed *to*; go *against*. —自己の意思に背反する, to go against one's wishes.
haihei (癈兵), *n.* a disabled [crippled] soldier; an invalid. —癈兵救恤の爲に, for relief of disabled soldiers. ¶ 癈兵院, an asylum [a refuge] for disabled soldiers.
haiiro (灰色の), *a.* grey; ashen; ash-coloured.
haijo (排除する), *vt.* to displace (船體が水を); remove; eliminate. —凡ての故障を排除する, to sweep all obstacles from one's path.
haika (配下), *n.* a subordinate; a follower; an adherent. —配下に屬する, to be under (—'s command).
haika (排貨), *n.* boycotting. ¶ 排貨同盟, a boycott.
haikagura (灰神樂), *n.* a cloud of ashes. 灰神樂を揚げる, to raise a cloud of ashes.
haikai (徘徊する), *v.* to wander,

roam (國·海等を); prowl.
haikan (拜觀), *n.* seeing; having the honour of seeing. —禁苑を拜觀する, to have the honour of seeing the grounds of the Imperial Palace.
haikan (廢刊する), *v.* to cease [stop] publication.
haikan (廢官), *n.* abolition of an office.
haikan (廢艦), *n.* a superannuated vessel.
haikara (高襟), *n.* ❶ (人) a dandy; a swell; a coxcomb. ❷ (風) stylishness; fashionableness; swellishness. —ハイカラの, stylish; fashionable; dressy. ¶ ハイカラ男, a man of fashion; a popinjay.
haikei (背景), *n.* background; setting (劇場). ¶ 背景畫家, a scene-painter.
haikei (拜啓), dear sir (madam); I respectfully state; I beg to say.
haikekkaku (肺結核), *n.* phthisis; pulmonary tuberculosis.
haiken (拜見), *n.* seeing; looking; 【商】 inspection (檢査). —ちよッと拜見, Let me have a look. ¶ 拜見手數料, inspecting commission.
haiki (排汽), *n.* exhaust.
haiki (廢棄する), *vt.* to abrogate; abolish; denounce. —條約を廢棄する, to denounce a treaty.
haikinshū (拜金宗), *n.* (主義) mammonism. ¶ 拜金主義者, a mammonist.
haikishō (排氣鐘), *n.* an air-pump.
haikō (廢校する), *v.* to close [abolish] a school.
haikomu (這込む), *vi.* to crawl *into*; creep *into.* —穴へ這ひ込む, to crawl into a hole.
haikyōsha (背敎者), *n.* an apostate; a renegade.
haikyū (配給する), *vt.* to distribute.
haimawaru (這廻る), *vi.* to crawl about; creep about.
haimei (拜命する), *v.* to receive an official appointment; be appointed.
haimen (背面), *n.* the rear; the back. ¶ 背面砲擊, reverse fire. —背面攻擊 a rear attack.
hainarashi (灰均), *n.* an ash-leveller.
hainichi (排日), *n.* anti-Japanism. —排日運動をする, to make an anti-Japanese movement. ¶ 排日熱, Japanophobia; anti-Japanese sentiment.
hainin (背任), *n.* breach of trust; abuse of office. —背任罪に問はれる, to be charged with breach of trust.
hainō (背嚢), *n.* a knapsack; a bit. —背嚢をつける(おろす), to strap on (take off) a knapsack.
hainoboru (這登る), *vt.* to climb; crawl up; clamber. —蛇の如く這ひ登る, to creep up like a snake.
hai-pesuto (肺ペスト), *n.* pneumonic plague.
haire (齒入), *n.* clog-mending. ¶ 齒入屋, a clog-mender.
hairetsu (排列, 配列), *n.* arrangement; disposition; 【數】 permutation. —語の排列, the arrangement of words. —排列する, to arrange; set [place] in order; dispose.
hairi (背理の), *a.* absurd; reasonless; irrational; preposterous.
hairō (肺勞), *n.* 【醫】 phthisis; consumption.
hairu (這入る), *v.* ❶ (入る) to enter; go *in*; come *in*. ❷ (貫き入る) to penetrate. ❸ (收容) to hold (容器に); contain (同上). ❹ (加入) to join. ❺ (包含) to be included; fall under; be among. —盜賊が這入る, The robber breaks in. —この水差は二パイント這入る, The jug holds two pints. —どうしても頭に這入らない, I cannot get it into my head.
hairyo (配慮), *n.* trouble; anxiety; solicitude.
hairyō (肺量), *n.* lung capacity. ¶ 肺量器, a pulmometer.
haiseki (排斥), *n.* expulsion; exclusion; ostracism. —市長排斥の運動を起す, to raise an agitation for expulsion of the mayor. ——-suru, *vt.* to expel; exclude; ostracize. —不正の徒を排斥する, to expel dishonest persons.
haisen (杯洗), *n.* a basin for wine-cups.
haisen (肺尖), *n.* the apex of the lung. ¶ 肺尖炎, apical pneumonia. —肺尖加答兒, catarrh of the apex.
haisen (敗戰する), *vi.* to lose a battle; lose the day; be defeated.
haisetsu (排泄する), *vt.* to discharge; purge; eject. ——, *a.* excretive; excretory. ¶ 排泄物, the discharges; excreta (尿·汗など); excrement.
haisetsuki (排雪機), *n.* 【鐵道】 a snow-plough; a snow-sweeper [-scraper] (街鐵の).
haisha (齒醫者), *n.* a dentist.
haishaku (拜借する), *vt.* = *karu* (借る).
haishi (稗史), *n.* a fiction; a novel; a romance.
haishi (廢止), *n.* abolition; abrogation; annulment. ——-suru, *vt.* to abolish; abrogate; annul. —舊制を廢止する, to abolish the old system.
haishi (廢址), *n.* ruins. —ポンペイの廢址, the ruins of Pompeii.
haishin (背信), *n.* faithlessness; betrayal. —背信の, faithless.
haishin (背進する), *vi.* ❶ to

countermarch; go astern (船が). ❷ to fall back; retire; retreat. —豫定通り背進する, to retire as pre-arranged.

haishitsu (廢疾), *n.* an incurable disease (不治の病); disablement.

haisho (配所), *n.* a place of banishment; a penal colony. —彼の配所の友, companions of his exile.

haishoku (配色), *n.* 【畫】matching [agreement] colour.

haishutsu (排出する), *vt.* to expel; exhaust (空氣等を). —, *vi.* to transpire (皮膚・肺から).

haiso (敗訴), *n.* losing a suit [case]; a losing suit. —判決は彼の敗訴となった, Judgment was given against him.

haisō (敗走する), *v.* to be routed; take to flight.

haisui (配水する), *v.* to distribute water. ¶ 配水管, a distributing pipe.

haisui (排水), *n.* drainage; bailing (淦の); displacement (水を押し開く). ¶ 排水地域, catchment area. —排水孔, a scupper(-hole) (甲板の). —排水渠, catch-water; drain; gutter. —排水噸數, displacement tonnage.

haisui-no-jin (背水の陣を布く), to burn one's boats; burn the bridges.

hai-suru (拜する), *v.* ❶ (禮拜) to worship; (崇拜) reverence; venerate. ❷ to be appointed (任官); receive (拜受). —命を拜して, in obedience to the order. —龍顏を拜する, to be admitted into the Imperial Presence. —宮城に向って拜する, to bow respectfully in the direction of the Imperial Palace.

hai-suru (配する), *vt.* ❶(夫婦にする) to marry; wed. ❷(添へ合はす) to pair; couple. ❸(くばる) to distribute.

hai-suru (排する), *vt.* ❶ to exclude; expel. ❷ (押開く) to push open. —衆議を排する, to disregard the general opinion. —人を排して自ら進む, to push others aside for one's own advancement.

hai-suru (廢する), *vt.* ❶ to abolish (制度・舊風など); repeal (法律・條令など); abrogate (特に後の法令で); cancel. ❷ =*yameru*. —郡制を廢する, to abolish the district organization. —事業を廢する, to give up one's business.

haita (排他的), *a.* exclusive; cliquish. ¶ 排他主義, exclusivism; cliquism.

haitai (胚胎する), *vi.* to germinate; originate *in*; come of.

haitai (廢頽), *n.* decadence; disrepair; decay. —風俗の廢頽, decay of manners. —廢頽する, to decay; fall into decay.

haitaka (鷂), *n.* 【鳥】the sparrow-hawk.

haitatsu (配達), *n.* distribution (配付); delivery (引渡) —— -**suru**, *vt.* to distribute (くばる); deliver (渡す). —牛乳を配達する, to deliver milk. ¶ 特別配達, express delivery. —配達不能信書, a dead letter. —配達區分別, sorting (郵便物). —配達證明書, a delivery receipt.

haitei (廢帝), *n.* a deposed [dethroned] emperor.

haitō (配當), *n.* distribution; division; 【商】a dividend. —配當する, to distribute; apportion; share; prorate. ¶ 配當額[金], a dividend. (特別配當金, a bonus; an extra dividend). —配當落, ex dividend (ex. div. と略す). —配當附, cum dividend (cum div. と略す).

haitoku (悖德), *n.* corruption; immorality; depravity. ¶ 悖德漢, a depraved fellow. —悖德行爲, a foul deed; immoral conduct.

haiyō (佩用する), *vt.* to wear.

haiyū (俳優), *n.* an actor [*fem.* -tress]. ¶ 新俳優, an actor of the new school; a new-school actor.

haizai (配劑), *n.* ❶ (調劑) prescription; dispensing. ❷ (取合せ) combination; disposition; dispensation. —天の配劑, a dispensation of Providence.

haizara (灰皿), *n.* an ash-pan; an ash-tray.

haizō (肺臟), *n.* the lungs.

haji (恥), *n.* shame; disgrace. —恥の上塗, incurring further shame; adding to one's shame. —恥を雪ぐ, to clear oneself from shame; wipe out one's shame. —恥を忍ぶ, to endure [bear; put up with] shame. —恥を知る(知らぬ), to be sensible [alive] (insensible; lost; dead) to shame. —恥をかく, to bring a disgrace [shame] upon oneself; disgrace oneself. —人に恥をかかす, to put a person to shame. —世間に恥を晒す, to wash one's dirty linen in public. —恥を恥と思はぬ, to think naught of shame. —問ふは一時の恥, To ask is a moment's shame.

haji (把持する), *vt.* to grasp; grip; hold *on*; lay hold *on* [*of*].

hajiiru (恥入る), *vi.* to be ashamed (*of*); be confused; be put out of countenance.

hajikeru (彈ける), *vi.* to pop; split open.

hajiku (彈く), *vt.* ❶ to flip; flick (爪で). ❷ (うけつけぬ) to refuse; repel. —彈き出す, to spring out; burst open. (算盤で儲を彈き出す, to reckon the profit with an abacus.) —彈き返す, to bound back. —油は水を彈く, Oil repels water.

hajimari (始り), *n.* =*hajime*.

hajimaru (始る), *vi.* to begin; commence; open (開く); arise *from* (發生する).

hajime (始, 初), *n.* ❶ the beginning; commencement; outset. ❷ (第一番) the first; the head. —初は[に], (at) first; at the outset [start]; in the beginning. —初より終まで, from first to last; from the beginning to the end. —始が大事, "Well-begun is half done."

hajimeru (始める), *vt.* to begin; commence; open (會など); start; originate; inaugurate; launch; set about; get to (仕事など); enter on [upon]. —商賣を始める, to start in business. —討論を始める, to open the debate. —事業を創める, to embark upon an enterprise. —更に攻撃を始める, to renew the attack.

hajimete (始めて), *ad.* for the first time; for once.

hajinoki (黄櫨), *n.* 【植】the red-lac sumach.

hajirami (葉蚤), *n.* 【昆】the leaf-fly; the leaf-hopper.

hajiru (恥·羞ぢる), *vi.* to feel abashed [shy]. —年にも恥ぢぬ振舞, behaviour shameful in one of his age.

hajisarashi (恥晒し), *n.* shame; exposure of shame.

hajishirazu (恥不知), *n.* shamelessness; (人) a shameless fellow.

hajō (波狀), *n.* wave; waviness.

hajū (把住する), *vt.* to retain.

haka (墓), *n.* a grave; a tomb. —墓に參る, to visit a grave. —墓を建てる, to raise a tomb. —墓を發く(掘る), to open (dig) a grave.

haka (破瓜), *n.* pubescence. ¶ 破瓜期, age of puberty.

hakaba (墓場), *n.* a graveyard; a cemetery (共同墓地).

hakabakashii (捗捗しい), *a.* rapid; quick. —捗々しい進步を見ぬ, not to make rapid progress.

hakadoru (捗る), *vi.* to progress; make progress. —路が捗らない, to make little progress.

hakahori (墓掘り), *n.* a grave-digger.

hakai (破戒する), *vi.* to transgress a commandment; break Buddhist laws. ¶ 破戒者, a transgressor.

hakai (破壞), *n.* destruction; demolition; ruin. —破壞する, ① [*vt.*] to break; destroy; ruin (場所を); make havoc *of*; play havoc *among*. ② [*vi.*] to be destroyed; be smashed. ¶ 破壞力, destructive power. —破壞者, a destroyer; a desolator. —破壞的政略, a destructive policy.

hakaku (破格), *n.* ❶ (異例) being contrary to usage; an exception. ❷ 【文】 irregularity in grammar [metre]; being against grammatical rules; solecism. —破格の拔擢をなす, to make an unprecedented selection.

hakama (袴), *n.* loose trousers; a divided skirt. —袴を穿〔は〕く(脫ぐ), to wear (take off) a *hakama*.

hakanai (果敢ない), *a.* ❶ (暫時の) fleeting; transitory; ephemeral. ❷ (あはれな) miserable; pitiful; sad. ❸ (空な) empty; vain. —果敢ない戀, short-lived love. —果敢ない最期を遂げた, He came to a sad end.

hakarai (計ひ), *n.* management; arrangement; discretion (裁量). —君の計ひで, at your discretion.

hakarau (計ふ), *vt.* to negotiate; manage; arrange. —僕の一存で計ふことは出來ぬ, I cannot do it at my own distretion.

hakarazu (圖らず), *ad.* unexpectedly; unawares; by chance. —圖らずも逢ふ, to chance *upon*.

hakari (秤, 量), *n.* ❶ (器) a weighing beam; a balance (天秤). ❷ (量) measure. —秤にかけてみる, to weigh in a balance. ¶ 衡桿, a beam. —秤皿, a scale.

hakarigatai (計·測り難い), *a.* unfathomable (深さ·意味などの); hard to foresee (豫測し難い).

hakarigoto (計, 謀), *n.* ❶ (計畫) a plan; a scheme. ❷ (謀略) a stratagem; a ruse. ❸ (陰謀) a plot. —謀を運らす, to form a stratagem; plot. —謀の罠に落ちる, to fall into a snare laid for one. —謀の裏を掻く, to countermine; counterplot; outmanœuvre.

hakaru (計·謀·量·測る), *v.* ❶ (數へる) to calculate; estimate; compute. ❷ (長短·輕重を) to weigh; measure. ❸ to sound (水深などを); survey (土地などを); fathom (測量綱にて). ❹ (相談する) to confer *with*; consult *with*. ❺ (推量) to guess; surmise; conjecture. ❻ (*a*) (企らむ) to plot; plan; contrive: (*b*) (欺く) to deceive; impose *upon*: (*c*) (志す) to aim at. —身長を測る, to take one's (another's) measure. —獨立を計る, to aim at independence. —己を以て人を忖〔はか〕る, to measure others' corn by one's own bushel. —他人の胸中を揣〔はか〕る, to guess what is in another's mind.

hakase (博士), *n.* a doctor. —三木博士, Dr. Miki. —博士の學位を取る, to take a doctor's degree. —彼は其道にかけての博士だ, He is a man learned in that line. ¶ 博士號, doctorate. —博士論文, a thesis for a doctorate.

hake (捌), *n.* ❶(賣行) sale; demand. ❷(排水) drain.

hake (刷毛), *n.* a brush. —刷毛でこする, to brush. ¶ 梳刷(ｶﾞﾌﾞ), a comb-card.

haken (派遣), *n.* dispatch; detachment. ——**-suru**, *vt.* to dispatch; send; 【軍】detach (分遣); draft (同上); delegate (代表者として). —軍隊を派遣する, to send an army. —使節(艦隊)を派遣する, to despatch an envoy (a fleet).

haken (霸權), *n.* hegemony; supremacy; leadership. —東洋の霸權を握る, to have the hegemony of the Far East.

hakeru (捌ける), *vi.* ❶(排水) to flow; run out. ❷(捌け) to be in demand; move off; sell.

haki (破棄する), *vt.* to denounce; annul; break (off). —封印を破棄する, to break a seal.

haki (破毀), *n.* ❶ destruction; demolition. ❷【法】reversal (by reason of errors of law); recall (for matters of fact); revocation. ——**-suru**, *vt.* ❶ to destroy; demolish. ❷【法】to set aside; reverse; revoke. —下級裁判所の判決を破毀する, to set aside the judgment of the inferior court.

haki (霸氣ある), *a.* ambitious; high-spirited; vigorous.

hakichigaeru (履違へる), *v.* ❶ to wear another's (clogs, boots, &c.). ❷(誤解) to take (one thing) for (another); understand wrongly.

hakidame (掃溜), *n.* a rubbish heap; a dirt-heap; a dust-hole.

hakidasu (吐出す), *vt.* ❶(嘔吐) to vomit; spew; spue. ❷ to disgorge (呑んだものを); spit out (唾唾を); breathe out (息を). ❸(噴出) to emit; eject; discharge. —黑煙を吐き出す, to vomit black smoke.

hakidasu (掃出す), *vt.* to sweep out; discharge; turn out.

hakihaki (はきはき), *ad.* smartly; briskly; promptly. —はきはき物をやる, to do things smartly.

hakike (嘔氣), *n.* nausea; qualm. —嘔氣を催す, to nauseate; retch; keck. (嘔氣を催して苦しむ, to suffer from nausea.)

hakimono (履物), *n.* footgear; footwear; clogs. ¶ 履物商, a clog-dealer. —履物店, a clog-shop.

hakiyoseru (掃寄せる), *vt.* to sweep up; sweep into a heap. —落葉を掃き寄せる, to sweep fallen leaves into a heap.

hakka (薄荷), *n.* ❶【植】the peppermint. ❷(薄荷精) menthol. ¶ 薄荷腦, menthol. —薄荷油, peppermint oil.

hakka (發火する), *v.* to ignite; catch fire; take fire. —發火し損ふ(銃が), to miss fire. —發火演習の爲め行軍する, to march for rifle practice.

hakkaishiki (發會式), *n.* the opening [inaugural] ceremony; inauguration.

hakkaku (八角), *n.* an octagon

hakkaku (發覺), *n.* detection; discovery; disclosure. —發覺する, to be detected; be discovered; be disclosed; come to light.

hakkan (發刊), *n.* publication; issue. —發刊する, to issue; publish; bring out; start.

hakkan (發汗), *n.* perspiration. —發汗する, to perspire. ¶ 發汗劑, a diaphoretic; a sudorific.

hakke (八卦), *n.* trigrams; (占筮) divination. —當るも八卦當らぬも八卦, The chances are even in divination.

hakkekkyū (白血球), *n.* 【生】a leucocyte.

hakken (發見), *n.* ❶(新に見出す) discovery. ❷(見露はす) detection. —發見する, to discover; detect. ¶ 發見者, a discoverer.

hakki (白旗), *n.* a white flag; a flag of truce. —白旗を揭げる, to display a flag of truce.

hakki (發揮する), *vt.* to display; exhibit; make manifest. —特長を發揮する, to display a strong point. —十分發揮さす(才能などを), to give full play [swing] *to*.

hakkin (白金), *n.* platinum. ¶ 白金寫眞版, a platinotype.

hakkiri (はッきり), *ad.* ❶(明瞭, 分明) clearly; plainly; distinctly. ❷(確然) certainly; for certain; exactly. はッきりした輪郭, a sharp outline. —はッきりせぬ天氣, unsettled weather. —はッきり發音する, to pronounce distinctly. —はッきり聞える, to hear distinctly.

hakkō (發光する), *vi.* to radiate; emit light; ray; gleam. ¶ 發光體, a light; a luminary; a (self-) luminous body.

hakkō (發行), *n.* publication; issue; flotation (債券などの). —發行を禁止(停止)する, to prohibit [suppress] (suspend) publication. ——**-suru**, *vt.* to issue; publish; float. 紙幣を發行する, to issue paper-money. ¶ 發行高, the number of copies published; issue (新聞·紙幣などの); circulation (新聞等の). —發行禁止(停止), suppression

(suspension) of publication. —發行者, a publisher. —發行所, the publishing office.
hakkō (薄倖の), *a.* ill-fated; ill-starred; unlucky; unfortunate.
hakkō(醱酵), *n.* fermentation; ferment; zymosis. —醱醸さす, to ferment. ¶ 醱酵牛乳, sour milk.
hakkutsu (發掘する), *vt.* to unearth; exhume; disinter.
hakkyō (發狂), *n.* madness; insanity; lunacy. —發狂さす, to derange; drive one mad [wild]. —發狂する, to be out of one's mind; become insane; go [run] mad. ¶ 發狂者, a madman; a lunatic; an insane person.
hakkyū (薄給), *n.* a low [slender] salary; scanty pay. ¶ 薄給者, a low-salaried person.
hako (箱), *n.* a box; a case; a chest (櫃); a coffer (同上). —箱に入れる, to put in a box; encase. —箱に詰めて送る, to send in a box. ¶ 箱一杯, a boxful.
hakō (跛行する), *vi.* to hobble; limp.
hakō (爬行する), *vi.* to crawl; creep. ¶ 爬行動物, a reptile.
hakobe(蘩蔞), *n.* 【植】 the chickweed.
hakobi (運び), *n.* ❶ (進捗) progress. ❷ (段取) stage. ❸ (轉移) transfer. —運びをつける, to settle; arrange; bring about.
hakobu (運ぶ), *vt.* (運搬) to carry; convey. ——, *vi.* (進捗) to progress; advance. —すらすら運ぶ, to go on smoothly [swimmingly]. —萬事好都合に運んだ, Everything has gone well.
hakoiri (箱入の), *a.* contained in a box; cased. ¶ 箱入娘, a pet daughter.
hakozume (箱詰にする), *vt.* to enclose in a box; pack in a box.
haku (箔), *n.* foil; leaf (金·銀など); tinsel. —箔をつける, to gild.
haku(吐く), *vt.* ❶ (嘔吐) to spew; spue; throw up; expectorate (唊唾); spit (唾). ❷ (噴出) to puff out; emit. ❸ (口外する) launch out (雑言を); express; speak; utter. —意見を吐く, to express [lay] one's views. —吐きさうな氣持になる, to turn sick. —容易に實を吐かぬ, He does not readily confess the truth.
haku (穿く), *vt.* to wear; put on. —長靴下をはく, to pull on one's stockings. —靴を穿いてゐる, to have one's boots on.
haku (排く), *vt.* (水等を) to draw off; drain off. —水を排き出す, to run the water off.
haku(掃く), *vt.* to sweep (掃除); daub (塗傅). —床を掃く, to sweep the floor. —顔に白粉を薄く刷く, to touch up the face with paint.
hakua (白堊), *n.* chalk. ¶ 白堊館, the White House.
hakuai (博愛), *n.* philanthropy; humanity. ¶ 博愛家, a philanthropist.
hakuboku(白墨), *n.* chalk.
hakubokushitsu (白木質), *n.* sap; sap-wood.
hakubutsu (博物 -學), *n.* natural history. ¶ 博物標本, a natural-history specimen. —博物學者, a naturalist. —博物館, a museum.
hakuchi (白痴), *n.* ❶ idiocy; imbecility. ❷ (人) an idiot.
hakuchō (白鳥), *n.* 【鳥】 the swan.
hakuchū (白晝に), *ad.* in broad [full] daylight.
hakuchū (伯仲する), *vi.* to be equal; be on a par.
hakudatsu (剝脱する), *vi.* to exfoliate; fall [come] off.
hakudatsu (剝奪する), *vt.* to deprive *of*; divest *of*; strip *of*. —人の權利を剝奪する, to divest a person out of his right.
hakudō (白銅), *n.* nickel. ¶ 白銅貨, a nickel (coin).
hakuen (白鉛), *n.* white lead.
hakugai (迫害), *n.* persecution oppression. —迫害する, to persecute; oppress. —宗教上の迫害, religious persecution.
hakugaku (博學), *n.* erudition; extensive [wide] learning; scholarship. —博學多才の人, a man of great learning and ability
hakugeki (迫撃する), *vt.* to attack at close quarters. ¶ 迫撃砲, a trench mortar.
hakuhatsu (白髪), *n.* white [gray] hair.
hakuhei (白兵), *n.* swords and bayonets; side arms. —白兵を交へる, to fight hand to hand. ¶ 白兵戰, a close combat; a hand-to-hand fight.
hakuhen (薄片), *n.* a lamina; a slice; a thin leaf (薄い箔); a foil; lamella.
hakuhyō (薄氷), *n.* thin ice. —薄氷を履む如し, to feel as if (one) wear treading upon eggs.
hakujaku (薄弱な), *a.* flimsy; feeble; slender. —薄弱な論理(議論), a weak logic (argument).
hakujin (白刃), *n.* a naked sword.
hakujinshu (白人種), *n.* the white race; the whites.
hakujitsu (白日), *n.* broad daylight; daytime.
hakujō (白狀), *n.* confession; avowal; acknowledgment. ——**suru**, *vt.* to confess; acknowledge; avow; own. —すッかり白

狀する, to make a clean breast *of*. —無理やりに白狀さす, to force a confession out of a person.

hakujō (薄情な), *a*. inhuman (人又は行ひ); unfeeling; cold-hearted; heartless.

hakumai (白米), *n*. hulled rice. ¶ 白米商, a rice-dealer.

hakumei (薄命な), *a*. ill-fated; ill-starred; unlucky; unfortunate; unhappy.

hakunetsu (白熱), *n*. incandescence; white heat; fervour. —白熱的の試合, an exciting game. —白熱に達する, to reach white heat. ¶ 白熱燈, an incandescent lamp.

hakurai (舶來), *n*. ❶ importation; coming from abroad. ❷ (優良) superior quality. —舶來の, imported; foreign-made; exotic; oversea. ¶ 舶來品, a foreign article.

hakurankai (博覽會), *n*. an exposition; an exhibition. ¶ 內國勸業博覽會, a domestic industrial exposition. —萬國大博覽會, an international exposition, a world's fair. —博覽會出品者, an exposition exhibitor.

hakurenge (玉蘭), *n*. 【植】 the yulan magnolia.

hakuri (薄利), *n*. small profit. ¶ 薄利多賣, small profits and quick returns.

hakurō (白鑞), *n*. solder.

hakusei (剝製する), *vt*. to stuff. ¶ 剝製鳥, a stuffed bird. —剝製標本, a stuffed specimen. —剝製師, a taxidermist.

hakuseki (白晳人種), *n*. the white race.

hakusha (拍車), *n*. spur. —拍車附きの靴, spurred boots.

hakusha (薄謝), *n*. a slight token of thanks.

hakushaku (伯爵), *n*. an earl (英); a count [*fem*. -ess].

hakushi (白紙), *n*. blank paper. ¶ 白紙委任狀, a blank power of attorney. —白紙主義, clean-slate principle.

hakushi (博士), *n*. a doctor. ☞ hakase.

hakushi (薄志弱行の), *a*. infirm of will and weak in action.

hakushiki (博識), *n*. erudition; scholarship; wide knowledge.

hakushoku (白色の), *a*. white; of white colour.

hakushu (拍手), *n*. clap; the clapping of hands. —拍手する, to clap (hands). ¶ 拍手喝采, applause; cheers; plaudits.

hakuso (齒垢), *n*. tartar.

haku-suru (博する), *vt*. to gain; win; obtain. —信用(名聲; 勝利)を博する, to win credit (a reputation; a victory).

hakutaisen (白苔癬), *n*. (小兒の) white-gum.

hakuya (箔屋), *n*. a gilder.

hakuyō (白楊), *n*. the white poplar; the white asp; the Dutch beech.

hakuyō (舶用の), *a*. marine. ¶ 舶用機關, a marine engine.

hakyaku (破却する), *vt*. to destroy; demolish.

hakyō (破鏡), *n*. divorce. —破鏡の歎を見る, to be divorced.

hakyū (波及), *n*. propagation. —波及する, ① to extend; spread. ② (影響) to affect; influence.

hama (濱), *n*. the beach; the shore; the seashore. —濱に, ashore. —濱傳ひに, along the seashore. —濱(邊)に遊べる子供, children playing on the sands.

hamaendō (濱豌豆), *n*. 【植】 the seaside pea.

hamaguri (蛤), *n*. 【貝】 the clam.

hamaki (葉卷煙草), *n*. a cigar. ¶ 葉卷パイプ, a cigar-holder.

hamariyaku (適役), *n*. 【劇】 a suitable character.

hamaru (嵌る), *v*. ❶ (嵌入) to fix in; fit in. ❷ (適合) to fit; apply *to*. ❸ (深入) to go deep *into*; immerse oneself *in*; be addicted *to*. ❹ (陷る) to fall *into*.

hamashion (金盞菜), *n*. 【植】 the blue chamomile.

hame (羽目), *n*. ❶ (壁の) weather-boarding; wainscot. ❷ (窮境) plight; fix; straits. —妙な羽目になって, in a queer plight. —苦しい羽目に陷る, to fall into great straits. —羽目を外して遊ぶ, to be on the loose. ¶ 羽目板, a dado; a wainscot; weather-boarding.

hamekizaiku (嵌木細工), *n*. a parquet; parquetry.

hamekomu (嵌込む), *vt*. to inlay *in*; insert *in*; let *in*. —柱を嵌め込む, to fit in a pillar. —人を適當な地位へ嵌め込む, to put a man in a suitable position.

hameru (嵌める), *vt*. ❶ (差込む) to fix *in*; fit *in*; set (*in*) (寶石などを). ❷ (適合さす) to fit *to*; apply *to*. ❸ (塡充する) to fill in; put in; insert *in* [*into*]. —手袋を嵌める, to pull [put] on one's gloves. —指輪を嵌める, to wear [put on] a ring. —戶を嵌める, to fit in a door. —脫臼を嵌める, to set a dislocation. —障子に硝子を嵌める, to fit panes into a sliding-door.

hametsu (破滅), *n*. ruin; destruction; wreck; fall; overthrow; fate. —破滅する, to come to naught; go to pot; go to (rack and) ruin. —破滅に近き, on one's last legs.

—彼の生涯の破滅, the wreck of his life. —身の破滅を來す, to bring down ruin on oneself.

hami (馬銜), *n.* a bit.

hamidasu (食出す), *vi.* to protrude; bulge out; be forced out.

hamigaki (齒磨), *n.* dentifrice (總稱); tooth-powder (粉齒磨); tooth-wash (水齒磨); tooth-paste (煉齒磨).

hamon (波紋), *n.* rings in water; ripple. —波紋をなす, to ripple.

hamon (破門), *n.* 【宗】 excommunication; interdict (羅馬敎); expulsion (放逐). —破門する, to excommunicate; unchurch; expel.

hamonika (ハモニカ), *n.* a harmonica.

hamono (刃物), *n.* an edged tool; an edge-tool. —刃物三昧をする, to brandish edged tools. ¶ 刃物類, cutlery. —刃物師, a cutler.

hamono (端物), *n.* an odd [incomplete] set.

hamu (食む), *v.* to eat; feed *on.*

hamu (燻腿), *n.* ham.

hamukau (刃向ふ), *vt.* to oppose; resist.

hamushi (羽蟲), *n.* an insect; a bird-louse.

han (半), *n.* ❶ (なかば) half. ❷ (奇數) odd number. ❸ 【音】 mezzo [*ad.*]. ——, *a.* half; odd. ——, *pref.* hemi-; semi-; demi-. —半か丁か, odd or even. —半磅, half a pound. —二磅半, two pounds and a half; two and a half pounds.

han (判), *n.* a stamp; a seal. —判を捺す, to seal; affix [set] a seal.

han (版), *n.* ❶ (木版) a plate. ❷ (活版等) cast; impression. ❸ (印刷) printing. ❹ (出版) an edition.

han (班), *n.* ❶ 【軍】 a squad. ❷ (仲間) a company; a set; a gang. —第二中隊第三班, the third squad of the second company.

han (煩), *n.* worry; trouble. —煩に耐へない, to be unable to stand the worry. —煩を厭うて略する, to leave out to save trouble.

hana (花), *n.* ❶ a flower (花一輪又は草花); a blossom (特に果實の). ❷ (いけ花) flower-arrangement. ❸ (花合せ) playing cards; "flower-cards." ❹ (祝儀) a tip; a gratuity. —花に水をやる, to water the flowers. —花のトンネルを潜る, to pass through an avenue of flowers. —花を咲かす, ① to make a flower bloom. ② to make hearts ache. —はなをやる, to tip. —花を活ける, to arrange flowers (in a vase [basin]). —花を持たす, to let another have the credit (*for*). —花も實もある, fine in appearance and quality [substance]. (花も實もある言葉, refined [elegant] and instructive language.) —若い中が花, Youth is the flower of life. ¶ 花時, the flower [cherry-blossom] season. —花吹雪, a blast of falling cherry-blossoms. —花霞, a cloud of flowers. —花曇, cloudy weather during the cherry-blossom season.

hana (鼻), *n.* ❶ the nose; the snout (豚等の); the muzzle (犬·馬等の口鼻). ❷ (水鼻) snivel. —鼻(の先)であしらふ, to turn up one's nose *at*; snuff [sniff] *at*. —鼻が利く, to have a good nose. —鼻が落ちるやうに臭ふ, to stink like a polecat. —鼻にかける, ① (誇る) to vaunt; plume [pride] oneself *on*; be proud *of*. ② (言葉を) to snuffle out. —鼻につく, to be sick *of*; be tired *of*; be disgusted *with*. —鼻の下が長い, to be spoony on a girl. —鼻の下が干上る, to be starved. —洟をかむ, to blow the nose. —洟を垂らす, to snivel; run at the nose. —鼻をあかす, to put a person's nose out of joint. —鼻を突くやうな, offensive to the smell [nose]. —鼻聲で言ふ, [*vt.*] to twang; snuffle out; nose. —鼻張りの强い奴, a great braggart. ¶ 鼻紙, nose-paper.

hanaabu (花虻), *n.* 【昆】 the drone-fly.

hanaashirai (鼻扱ひにする), *v.* to sniff [snuff] *at*.

hanaawase (花合), *n.* card-playing. —花合をする, to play cards.

hanabanashii (華華しい), *a.* glorious; brilliant; splendid. —華華しい最期, a glorious death.

hanabashira (鼻梁), *n.* the bridge (of the nose). —...の鼻梁を折る, to take (a person) down a peg or two; put a person's nose out of joint.

hanabi (花火), *n.* fireworks. —花火を揚げる, to let off fireworks. ¶ 廻轉花火, a catherine-wheel; a girandole. —仕掛花火, a set piece.

hanabira (花瓣), *n.* a petal.

hanadensha (花電車), *n.* a decorated tram-car.

hanagasutō (花瓦斯燈), *n.* a gaselier.

hanagata (花形), *n.* ❶ (花模様) flourish; festoon (彫刻せる); ornament (印刷の). ❷ (人氣物) a lion; a star. —上流社會の花形, leaders of society.

hanage (鼻毛), *n.* the vibrissa [*pl.* -sæ]; the hairs of the nostrils.—鼻毛を讀まれる, to bemade a fool *of*.

hanagoe (鼻聲), *n.* a nasal voice [sound]; a twang; a snuffling voice.

hanagoza (花座), *n.* a mat with flower patterns; figured matting.

hanagusuri (鼻藥), *n.* ❶ (子供を宥め賺す爲の) a thing to humour a child. ❷ (賄賂) a bribe; *douceur* 〖佛〗; a tip (祝儀). —鼻藥をかがす, to grease the fist [palm]; grease another in the fist.

hanahada (甚だ), *ad.* exceedingly; extremely; nitensely; very. —甚だしく失望した, woefully disappointed.

hanahadashii (甚しい), *a.* extreme; intense; severe. —甚しい臆病者, a sad coward. —甚しきに至ッては, in extreme cases.

hanaiki (鼻息), *n.* breathing through the nose; snort (激しい). —鼻息が荒い, ① to breathe hard through the nose. ② to be on high stilts. —鼻息を窺ふ, to truckle to another; consult another's pleasure; dance attendance on another.

hanaji (鼻血), *n.* nose-bleed; bloody nose.

hanakanzashi (花簪), *n.* a hair-pin with artificial flowers [floral designs in metal].

hanakaze (鼻風邪), *n.* coryza; a cold in the head.

hanakuso (鼻糞), *n.* nasal mucus; snot 〖卑〗.

hanamegane (鼻眼鏡), *n.* a *pince-nez* 〖佛〗; a double eye-glass; eye-glasses.

hanami (花見), *n.* flower-viewing. ¶ 花見時, the flower season. —花見船, a pleasure-boat for flower-viewing. —花見客, a flower-viewing party.

hanamichi (花道), *n.* a stage-passage.

hanamuke (餞), *n.* a parting-present; a souvenir. —餞する, to give a parting-present.

hanamuko (花婿), *n.* a bride-groom.

hanao (鼻緒), *n.* the thong (for clogs or sandals). —鼻緒をすげる, to fix a thong (in a clog).

hanare (離), *n.* =*hanarezashiki.* —錢の離れが綺麗な, open-handed; free-handed; ungrudging with one's money.

hanarebanare (離離になる), *v.* to get separated; be scattered; be dispersed.

hanareru (離·放れる), *vi.* ❶ (分離) to separate *from*; part *from* (*with*); be estranged *from* (疎離する). ❷ (自由になる) to get free; get [break] loose (繫馬が). —陸を離れる (船が), to bear off the coast; clear the land. —手 (床) を離れる, to get out of hand (bed). —餘程離れて, a good distance off. —十呎離れて居る, to be separated ten feet. —離るべからざる密接の關係, inseparably close relations.

hanareuma (放馬), *n.* a runaway horse; a stray horse.

hanarewaza (離業), *n.* a stunt; a brilliant feat.

hanareya (離家), *n.* a solitary house.

hanarezashiki (離座敷), *n.* a detached room; a room under a separate roof.

hanasaki (鼻先), *n.* the tip of the nose. —女の鼻先思案, a woman's short-sighted thoughts. —鼻先であしらふ, to sneer [sniff; snuff] *at*; turn up one's nose *at*.

hanaseru (話せる), *a.* sensible (物の分ッた); companionable (友として面白い). —君はなかなか話せる, You are a very sensible fellow.

hanashi (話, 噺), *n.* ❶ (談話) a talk; conversation (會話); a chat (雜談). ❷ (物語) a story; a tale; a narrative (順序立ッた). —話の種, a topic for conversation. —...とか云ふ話だ, they [people] say; it is said; the story goes that. —話に實が入る, to be engrossed in talk. —彼の話によれば, according to his account. —話をつける, to negotiate; settle (the matter). —人と話を始める, to enter into conversation with a person. —「お話中」です, engaged. ¶ 話振り, the way of talking.

hanashiau (話合ふ), *vi.* to converse [talk] *with*; consult *with* (相談); take counsel together (同上).

hanashijōzu (話上手), *n.* ❶ skill in conversation. ❷ (人) a good talker; a clever [skilful] talker.

hanashika (落語家), *n.* a story-teller.

hanashite (話手), *n.* a speaker; a talker; a reciter.

hanashizuki (話好の), *a.* chatty; talkative.

hanashōbu (花菖蒲), *n.* 【植】 Kaempfer's iris.

hanasu (話す), *v.* ❶ (物言ふ) to say; speak; utter. ❷ (聞かす) to tell; narrate; recount (詳しく). ❸ (語合ふ) to converse *with*; talk *with*; speak (*with, to*, 人; *of, about*, 物). —話しつづける, to speak on. —出放題に話す, to talk at random. —人に話しかける, to address oneself to a person. —友人と話す, to talk with a friend. —...と話し始める, to fall into conversation *with*. —君にちと話したい事がある, There is something I want to talk to you about.

hanasu (離す), *vt.* ❶ (分離) to separate; part; sever. ❷ (自由にする) to set free; let go; turn loose. ☞ ***hanatsu.*** —手を放すな, Don't let go your hold.

hanasuji (鼻筋), *n.* the ridge of the nose. —鼻筋の通ッた女, a straight-nosed woman.
hanataba (花束), *n.* a *bouquet* 〘佛〙; a nosegay.
hanatake (鼻茸), *n.* a nasal polypus.
hanatsu (放つ), *vt.* ❶(手離す) to drop; quit [leave] hold *of*; let go (*of*). ❷(自由にする) to let loose; release; set free. ❸(發射) to shoot; let off (鐵砲·洒落を); let fly...*at* (飛道具を). ❹(香氣·光などを) to emit; give out; give forth. —光を放つ, to emit light. —火を放つ, to set on fire; set fire *to*. —矢を放つ, to shoot an arrow. —鐵砲を放つ, to fire a gun; let [fire] off a gun. —間諜を放ッて敵情を探る, to send a spy to find out the enemy's condition.
hanauri (花賣), *n.* a flower-seller; a florist; a flower-girl (少女).
hanauta (鼻唄), *n.* humming; a hum. —鼻唄を歌ふ, to hum a song.
hanawa (花環), *n.* a wreath; a garland; a chaplet (of flowers).
hanawa (鼻環), *n.* a nose-ring. —牡牛に鼻環つける, to ring the bull.
hanaya (花屋), *n.* a florist.
hanayaka (華やかな), *a.* flowery; gay; gaudy.
hanayashiki (花屋敷), *n.* a flower-garden.
hanayome (花嫁), *n.* a bride.
hanazakari (花盛り), *n.* full bloom. —人生の花盛りに, in the full bloom of life.
hanazono (花園), *n.* a garden; a flower-garden.
hanazuna (花綵), *n.* a festoon. —花綵で飾る, [*vt.*] to festoon.
hanbai (販賣), *n.* sale. —販賣する, to sell; deal *in*. ¶ 販賣價格, the selling price. —販賣係, a salesman; a sales department (販賣課). —販賣人, a salesman; a saleswoman (女).
hanbaku (反駁する), *vt.* to refute; contradict; retort.
hanbatsu (藩閥), *n.* a clan. —藩閥の寵兒, the favoured child of clannism. ¶ 藩閥內閣, a clan cabinet.
hanbetsu (判別する), *vt.* to discriminate; distinguish [tell] *from*. —是非を判別する, to discriminate between right and wrong. —異同を判別する, to discriminate the points of similarity and difference.
hanbō (繁忙), *n.* busyness; press of business. —繁忙に苦しむ, to be pressed with business. —御繁忙中誠に恐入り候へ共, though I am sorry to trouble you when you are so busy.
hanbun (半分), *n.* a half. —半分だけ, by halves. —面白[冗談]半分に, half in joke [jest; fun]. —半分に切る, to cut a thing in half [into halves]. —半分に(だけ)減らす, to reduce to (by) half. —彼が言ふことは半分おまけだ, Half what he says is made up.
hanbun-jokurei (繁文縟禮), *n.* officialism; red-tape[-tapery, -tapism]; vexatious rules and prolix forms.
hanchū (範疇), *n.* category.
handa (半田, 白鑞), *n.* solder. —半田著けする, to solder.
handan (判斷), *n.* judgment; decision. **——-suru**, *vt.* to judge; decide; conclude. —夢を判斷する, to read [interpret] a dream.
handikyappu (ハンディキャップ), *n.* a handicap.
hando (礬土), *n.* 【化】 alumina.
handō (反動), *n.* reaction.
handoku (判讀する), *vt.* to decipher; make out.
handon (半どん), *n.* a half-holiday; Saturday.
handoru (把手), *n.* a handle.
hane (羽), *n.* a quill (翮); a wing (翼); feather (羽毛); plumage. —羽を擴げる(疊む), to spread (fold) wings. —羽根が生えて飛ぶ樣に賣れる, to sell like hot cakes [like fun]. ¶ 羽布團, feather bedding.
hane (跳), *n.* ❶(飛躍) bounce; bound; spring. ❷(飛沫) splashes of mud; spatter; splash. —著物に跳ねをあげる, to spatter [splash] one's clothes with mud.
hane (羽子), *n.* a shuttlecock. —羽子をつく, to play battledore and shuttlecock.
haneagaru (跳上る), *vi.* to jump; jump [spring] up; start to one's feet (びッくりして).
hanebashi (跳橋), *n.* a draw-bridge.
hańei (反映), *n.* a reflection; a reflex. —輿論の反映, the reflex of public opinion.
hańei (繁榮), *n.* prosperity. ¶ 繁榮時代, the day of prosperity.
hańeikyū (半永久的), *a.* semi-permanent.
hanekaeru (跳反る), *vi.* to rebound; spring back; recoil.
hanekaesu (跳反す), *vt.* to bounce; double (撞球戲).
hanekasu (跳かす), *vt.* to spatter (泥等を); bespatter (泥水などを); splatter; splash. —水を跳ねかし合ふ, to splash water at each other.
hanemawaru (跳廻る), *vi.* to frisk; romp; skip. **——**, *a.* frolicsome; frisky. —喜んで跳ね廻る, to skip about with joy.
hanemushi (跳蟲), *n.* 【昆】 the spring-tail.
hańen (半圓), *n.* ❶ a semicircle. ❷(五十錢) half a *yen*. —半圓を

描いて走る, to run in a semicircle.

hanenokeru (撥除ける), *vt.* to throw out; eliminate; reject. —悪いものを撥ね除ける, to throw out bad ones.

haneokiru (跳起きる), *vi.* to jump up; spring up.

hańeri (半襟), *n.* an ornamental neck-band. —半襟をかける, to put on an ornamental neck-band.

haneru (跳·撥ねる), *vi.* ❶ to jump; hop (ぴょんぴょんと); spring. ❷(跳廻る) to romp; skip; caper. ❸(とばしる) to spatter; splash. ❹(反撥) to rebound; recoil; react. —鯉が跳ねた, The carp leapt out of the water.

haneru (刎ねる), *vt.* ❶(斬首) to cut off. ❷(除ける) to reject; strike out; leave out. —首を刎ねる, to strike a person's head off.

hanetobasu (跳飛ばす), *vt.* to send flying; splash (泥など).

hanetsukeru (撥附ける), *vt.* to spurn; refuse; repel; repulse.

hanga (版畫), *n.* a print.

hangaku (半額), *n.* a half-amount; half the sum (price; fare). —半額入場, admission at half-price.

Hangari (匈牙利), *n.* Hungary. ¶ 匈牙利人, a Magyar; a Hungarian.

hangeki (繁劇の), *a.* overbusy.

hangen (半減する), *vt.* to halve; reduce by one half. ——, *vi.* to be reduced to [by] one half. —製造費を半減する, to reduce the cost of manufacture by one half.

hangetsu (半月), *n.* ❶(半輪) the half-moon. ❷(半ケ月) half a month; a fortnight. —半月毎の(に), semi-monthly; fortnightly.

hangi (版木), *n.* a block; a printing-block. ¶ 版木師, a block-cutter.

hango (反語), *n.* irony.

hangoroshi (半殺にする), *vt.* to half-kill.

hangutsu (半靴), *n.* shoes. ¶ 長半靴, half-boots.

hangyaku (叛逆), *n.* treason; insurgency; rebellion. —叛逆心を懐く, to harbour treason. ¶ 叛逆者, a rebel; a traitor.

hanhan (半半に), *ad.* half and half; in halves; in half. —費用を半々に負擔する, to bear the expenses half and half.

hańi (範圍), *n.* sphere (勢力·活動などの); circle (交際などの); scope. —...の範圍外(内), beyond (within) the pale [compass; limits; bounds; scope] *of.* (人智の範圍外, outside the scope of human intellect.) —議論の範圍, the range of discussion. —活動すべき範圍, the sphere of activity.

hanikamu (はにかむ), *vi.* to be abashed; be shy. ——, *a.* bashful; coy; shy.

haniwa (埴輪), *n.* a clay figure [image].

hanji (判じ), *n.* judgment. ☞ *handan.* ¶ 判じ繪, a rebus; a picture puzzle. —判じ物, a puzzle; a riddle.

hanji (判事), *n.* a judge; a justice; a magistrate. ¶ 係判事, a trial judge. —判事職, the bench; judgeship; justiceship. —判檢事登用試驗, an examination for the appointment of judges and procurators.

han-jiru (判じる), *vt.* ❶(判定) to decide; judge. ❷(解明) to interpret (夢等を); solve (謎等を); divine (占ふ). ❸(判讀) to decipher; make out.

hanjō (繁昌), *n.* prosperity. —繁昌する, to prosper; flourish; thrive. —彼等の商賣は大繁昌だ, They drive a roaring trade.

hanjuku (半熟の), *a.* half-ripe (果實); half-boiled (煮物). —半熟の卵, a soft-boiled egg. —半熟にする, to parboil.

hanka (繁華な), *a.* busy; bustling; flourishing.

hankai (半開の), *a.* ❶ half-open [-opened]. ❷ semi-civilized. ¶ 半開國, a semi-civilized country.

hankako (半過去), *n.* 【文】 the imperfect tense.

hankan (反感), *n.* antipathy; ill-feeling. —反感を抱いてる, to harbour antipathy *against.* —他の反感を買ふ, to incur another's ill-feeling.

hankan (半官的), *a.* semi-official. —半官半民の事業, a semi-government enterprise. —半官報の傳ふる所によれば, according to the report of the semi-official press.

hankatsū (半可通), *n.* ❶ sciolism; a smattering of knowledge. ❷ a smatterer; a sciolist.

hankechi (手巾), *n.* a (pocket) handkerchief. —ハンケチを振る, to wave a handkerchief. ¶ 麻ハンケチ, a cambric. —絹ハンケチ, a silk handkerchief.

hankei (半徑), *n.* a radius.

hanken (版權), *n.* copyright; literary property. —版權を侵害する, to infringe copyright; pirate. ¶ 版權所有, "all rights reserved"; "copyrighted."

hanketsu (判決), *n.* judgment; (judicial) decision; adjudication. —判決に服する, to accept [submit to; abide by] a judgment. —判決を破毀する, to reverse a judgment. —事件に判決を下す, to adjudicate upon a case. ——-**suru**, *vt.* to adjudicate; adjudge; decide; judge; find (陪審官が). —の利

(不利)に判決する, to give the case [give it] for (against) a person. ¶ 判決例, an authority; a (judicial) precedent; a leading case. —判決謄本, a copy of the decision.

hanki(半期, 半季), *n.* a half-term; a half year. ¶ 前半期, the former [first] half year. —後半期, the latter [second] half year. —半期配當金, a half-yearly dividend. —半期決算(檢査), half-yearly settlement (audit).

hanki (半旗), *n.* the flag at half-mast. —半旗を揚げる, to half-mast a flag.

hanki (反旗を飜す), *v.* to set up the flag of revolt; revolt [rebel] *against.*

hankichigai (半狂人), *n.* a half-mad man.

hankō (反抗する), *v.* to oppose; resist; be in antagonism *to* [*with*]. —反抗するに至る, to come into antagonism *with.* —輿論に反抗して, in opposition to public opinion. ¶ 反抗心, spirit of insubordination; a rebellious spirit.

hankon (瘢痕), *n.* a scar; a seam (細長き). —瘢痕を生ずる, to leave a scar.

hankyō (反響), *n.* ❶(やまびこ) an echo; resonance; reverberation. ❷(言論の) reflection; echo. ——**suru,** *v.* to echo; re-echo; reflect; resound; reverberate. —反響する ほど喝采する, to applaud to the echo.

hankyū (半弓), *n.* a small bow.

hankyū (半球), *n.* a hemisphere. ¶ 東(西)半球, the Eastern (Western) hemisphere.

hankyūbi(半休日), *n.* a half-holiday.

hanmā (ハンマー), *n.* a hammer.

hanmei(判明する), *vi.* to become clear [plain]; prove [turn out] to be. —彼の所在は今に判明せぬ, His whereabouts is still unknown.

hanmen (反面), *n.* the reverse.

hanmen (半面), *n.* ❶(片面) one side; a half. ❷(一面の半面) half the face. ❸(彫像の) a profile. —半面の識ある, slightly acquainted. (半面の識なき人, an utter stranger).

hanmo(繁茂する), *vi.* to flourish; grow thick [rank].

hanmokku (ハンモック), *n.* a hammock. —木蔭にハンモックを釣る, to hang a hammock in the shade of a tree.

hanmoku (反目する), *vi.* to be at feud [enmity; odds; variance] *with.*

hanmomohiki (半股引), *n.* trunk-drawers.

hanmon (反問), *n.* 【法】 cross-examination; cross-questioning. —反問する, to interrogate [ask] in return; cross-examine; cross-question.

hanmon (煩悶), *n.* agony; anguish. —煩悶する, to be in agony; writhe with pain; fret oneself; worry oneself. —煩悶中に一生を送る, to fret away one's life.

hanmyō(斑猫), *n.* 【昆】 the blister (-beetle).

hanne (半値), *n.* half-price. —半値で買ふ, to buy at half-price. —半値に減(ﾏ)ける, to take half-price.

hannen (半年), *n.* a half-year; half a year. —半年毎の, half-yearly; semi-annual. —半年毎に, half-yearly; semi-annually.

hannichi (半日), *n.* a half-day; half a day.

hannin (犯人), *n.* an offender; a criminal; a culprit. —犯人の行方, the criminal's whereabouts. —犯人をつかまへる, to catch the offender.

hanninkan(判任官), *n.* a *hannin* official; an official appointed at the discretion of the chief official.

hannoki(赤楊), *n.* Alnus japonica (alder の一種).

hannya(般若), *n.* a female demon; a demoness. —般若の面, the female demon's mask.

hannō (反應), *n.* reaction; reflex; response (感應). —反應する, to react; respond. —アルカリ性反應を呈す, to show an alkaline reaction.

hanpa (半端), *n.* ❶(はした) a fragment; a fraction; an odd sum. ❷(未完) imperfection; incompleteness. —半端の, ① fragmentary; odd. ② imperfect; incomplete; uncompleted.

hanpatsu (反撥する), *v.* to repulse; repel; rebound. ¶ 反撥力, repulsion; repellent [repulsive] force.

hanpei (藩屏), *n.* a bulwark. —皇室の藩屏, the bulwarks of the Imperial family.

hanpen (半平), *n.* fish minced and steamed.

hanpirei (反比例), *n.* inverse proportion.

hanpuku (反覆する), *vt.* ❶ to reverse. ❷ (繰返す) to repeat; reiterate; do over again. —反覆常なき, fickle; changeable.

hanpuku (半腹), *n.* half-way up. —山の半腹の町, a town half-way up the mountain.

hanpyaku (凡百の), *a.* all; of all kinds; of every description.

hanran (氾濫する), *vi.* to flood; overflow.

hanran (叛亂), *n.* rebellion; revolt; insurrection. —叛亂を起す, to rise in revolt.

hanrei (凡例), *n.* explanation; explanatory notes; legend (地圖の)

hanro (販路), *n.* a market (for goods); an outlet. —販路を開く, to open a market *for*. —販路を擴張する, to extend the market *for*.

hanrō (煩勞), *n.* trouble; pains.

hanrui (煩累), *n.* troublesomeness; vexatiousness. —家事の煩累なき, without family troubles.

hanryo (伴侶), *n.* a companion; an associate. —學生の好伴侶, a good companion for students.

hansa (煩瑣的), *a.* subtle; scholastic. ¶ 煩瑣哲學, scholasticism.

hansayō (反作用), *n.* reaction.

hansei (反省する), *v.* to reflect *on*; search one's heart; reconsider (再考). —反省を促す, to call for grave reflection.

hansei (半生), *n.* half a life; half a lifetime.

hansei (半晴の), *a.* fair (天氣豫報で).

hanseihin (半製品), *n.* half-finished goods.

hansen (帆船), *n.* a sailing-ship [-vessel]; a sailer.

hansha (反射), *n.* reflex; reflection. —反射する, to reflect; reverberate. ¶ 反射鏡, reflex mirror. —反射爐, a reverberatory (furnace). —反射作用, reflex action. —反射運動, reflex movement.

hanshi (半紙), *n.* (ordinary) rice paper.

hanshi (判士), *n.* 【陸】a member of the court-martial; a judge martial. ¶ 判士長, the president of the court-martial.

hanshi (藩士), *n.* a clan retainer; a clansman.

hanshi-hanshō (半死半生の), *a.* half dead; more dead than alive; all but dead.

hanshin (半身), *n.* half the body. ¶ 半身不隨, 【醫】hemiplegia. —半身像, a half-length; a half figure.

hanshin (半神·半人), *n.* a demigod.

hanshin-hangi (半信半疑), *n.* uncertainty; being half in doubt. —半信半疑で聞く, to listen half in doubt.

hanshinkyō (汎神敎), *n.* Ⓢ 汎神論. pantheism.

han-shite (反して), *ad.* contrary *to*; in violation *of* (違背); in opposition *to* (反對); against [*prep.*] —之に反して, on the contrary; on the other hand. —己の意思に反して, against one's (own) will.

hanshō (反證), *n.* disproof; counter-evidence. —反證を擧げる, to produce disproof.

hanshō (半鐘), *n.* a fire-alarm; a fire-bell. ¶ 半鐘泥棒, a sky-scraper.

hanshoku (繁殖する), *v.* to breed; multiply; propagate.

hanshu (藩主), *n.* the head [chief; lord] of a clan; a *daimyō*.

hanso (反訴), *n.* 【法】cross-action; cross-claim. —反訴を提起する, to bring a cross-action.

hansō (帆走する), *v.* to sail.

hansoku (犯則), *n.* infringement [violation] of regulations. ¶ 犯則者, an offender; 【軍】a defaulter.

hansoku (反則), *n.* irregularity; being against the rules; a foul. —反則の漕法《打方》, a foul stroke 《blow》. —反則をする, to infringe [act against] the rules. ¶ 反則圏, 【蹴球】penalty area.

hansū (半數), *n.* half a number. ¶ 半數改選, re-election of half the members.

hansū-dōbutsu (反芻動物), *n.* a ruminant.

han-suru (反する), *v.* ❶ (叛く) to rebel *against*; revolt *against*. ❷ (反對) to oppose *to*; object *to*. ❸ (違背) to infringe; violate. ❹ (相違) to be contrary *to*; go *against*; run counter *to*. —豫想に反する, to belie [go contrary to] one's expectations. —持論に反する, to run counter to one's theory. —彼の言行は相反する, His word and deed contradict each other.

hantai (反對), *n.* ❶ opposition; antagonism; objection. ❷ (逆) inverse; reverse; contrariety. —反對に解釋する, to interpret by contraries. —反對の方向に行く, to go in an opposite direction. —反對の態度を取る, to assume an attitude of opposition. —反對行動に出る, to resort to a counter-action. —反對を招く, to provoke opposition. —反對を唱へる, to take opposition *to*. **——-suru**, *vt.* to oppose; object; resist; take exception [objection] *to*. —反對せんが爲に反對する, to oppose for opposition's sake. ¶ 反對論者, an opponent; an anti--ist. —反對說, an opposition theory; the opposite view. —反對者, an antagonist; an opponent; an oppositionist. —反對黨, the Opposition. (反對黨員, an oppositionist.) —反對投票, a negative vote. —反對運動, countermotion; countermovement.

hantei (判定する), *vt.* to judge; decide.

hanten (半纏), *n.* a short coat.

hanten (斑點), *n.* a spot; a speck; a patch. —斑點ある豹, a spotted leopard. —斑點を附ける, to dapple; spot.

hanten (飜轉する), *v.* to reverse.

hanto (半途で), *ad.* midway; half-way. ☞ *tochū* (途中で).

hanto (版圖), *n.* dominion; a territory.

hanto (叛徒), *n.* rebels; insurgents.

hantō (半島), *n.* a peninsula.

hantōmei (半透明の), *a.* translucent; semi-transparent. ¶ 半透明體, a translucent body.
hantorichō (判取帳), *n.* a chit-book; a delivery book.
hantsukimai (半搗米), *n.* half-hulled rice.
hanuke (歯抜の), *a.* toothless.
hanuki (歯抜), *n.* a tooth-drawer.
hańyake (半燒の), *a.* half-baked (パン等); half-roasted (肉等); partially burnt (半燒失). —全燒八戸半燒五戸で鎮火した, The fire was put out after burning completely eight houses and partially five.
hanza (反坐する), *vi.* to retaliate.
hanzai (犯罪), *n.* a crime; an offence. —犯罪の形跡が更に認められぬ, to be unable to find any proof of crime. ¶ 犯罪地, a venue; the locality of the commission of a crime. —犯罪嫌疑者, a suspected criminal. —犯罪行爲, a criminal act. —犯罪人, a criminal; an offender. (未決犯罪人, an unconvicted criminal.) —犯罪定型; 犯罪人型, criminal type.
hanzan (半產), *n.* a miscarriage. —半產する, to miscarry; slip 〔俗〕; slip a calf (牛などの).
hanzatsu (繁雜), *n.* complexity. **—— -na,** *a.* complicated; complex. —繁雜な手數, complicated formalities.
hanzen (判然), *ad.* ❶ (確然) definitely. ❷ (明瞭) clearly; distinctly. —判然とした返事, a definite answer.
hanzen (飜然), *ad.* suddenly. —飜然前非を改めた, He suddenly turned away from his former evil ways.
hanzubon (半ズボン), *n.* knee-breeches; knickerbockers; pantalets (自轉車用又は婦人小兒用).
hanzui (伴隨する), *vt.* to accompany; follow. —弊害が伴隨する, to be accompanied by abuses.
haō (霸王), *n.* ❶ (諸侯の旗頭) a suzerain; an autocrat. ❷ (雄長) a king; the mistress. —海運界の霸王, the king of marine transportation business.
haori (羽織), *n.* a coat; a *haori.* ¶ 羽織ごろつき, a well-dressed rogue.
happi (法被), *n.* a livery coat.
happō (八方), *n.* ❶ (四方と四隅) the four sides and four corners. ❷ (各方面) all directions [sides]. —八方に目を配る, to keep an eye on all quarters. ¶ 八方美人, one who speaks fair to every one [is affable to all persons]; everybody's friend.
happō (發泡), *n.* 【醫】 vesication. ☞ *hatsubō.*
happō (發砲する), *vi.* to fire (a gun); discharge a gun; play off artillery *on.* —要塞に向って發砲する, to fire upon a fortification.
happu (發布), *n.* promulgation. —發布する, to promulgate; proclaim; publish.
happun (發憤する), *vi.* to be roused into indignation; be enraged.
happyō (發表), *n.* announcement; publication (公表). —發表する, to announce; publish.
hara (原), *n.* a plain (平野); a field (原野); a wilderness (荒野). —草生ひ茂る原, a wilderness overgrown with weeds.
hara (腹), *n.* ❶ the belly (腹部); the stomach (胃); the bowels (腸). ❷ (內心) the mind; the heart. ❸ (膽力) pluck. —腹一杯に食ふ, to eat one's fill. —腹が大きい, ① to have a big paunch. ② (大度) to be a large-minded; generous [*a.*]. —腹が痛む, to have a stomachache. —腹が減る, to get hungry; feel hungry. —腹が下る, to have loose bowels; suffer from diarrhœa. —腹が立つ, =*haradatsu.* —腹の穢い, mean; base; mean-minded. —腹の黑い奴, an evil-hearted fellow. —腹を肥やす, to feather one's nest. —腹を探る, to enter into another's mind. (痛くない腹をさぐられる, to be suspected where one is innocent.) —腹を据ゑる, to be prepared *for*; be resigned. —腹を立てる, to lose one's temper; take offence; get angry. —腹を抱へて大笑する, to split one's sides (with laughter). —それが卵でないなら腹を切らう, I'll be hanged if it isn't an egg!
harabai (腹這になる), *vi.* to lie down flat.
harachigai (異腹), *n.* half-blood; being born of a different mother. —腹違ひの兄弟, brothers born of different mothers; agnate brothers; half-brothers.
haradachi (立腹), *n.* anger; displeasure. —腹立ちまぎれに, out of spite; in a fit of spleen; in a moment of anger.
haradatsu (腹立つ), *vi.* to become angry; take offence.
haragake (腹掛), *n.* a stomach-cover; a stomach-protector.
harahara (はらはら), *ad.* ❶ (氣づかひ危む貌) with the heart leaping into one's mouth; with the heart going pit-a-pat; all of a twitter. ❷ (淚などの落ちる貌) falling rapidly in big drops. —はらはら

と涕を流して, with tears falling in big drops. —見て居てもはらはらする, to feel the heart leap into one's mouth even as one looks on.

harai (拂), *n.* payment (支拂); disposal (賣拂). —拂ひがきたない, to be unpunctual in paying bills. —拂ひに差支へる, to be unable to meet the bills. —拂ひを受取る, to receive payment.

harai (祓), *n.* purification; exorcism.

haraikomi (拂込), *n.* payment; payment of an instalment (掛金の). —(株式の)第一回拂込の催告, the first call. ¶ 拂込金, subscription. —拂込(未拂込)資本, paid-up (unpaid; uncalled-up) capital. —拂込濟株券, paid-up shares.

haraikomu (拂込む), *vt.* to pay up; pay in. —株金の全額を拂ひ込む, to pay up the shares.

haraimodosu (拂戻す), *vt.* to repay; refund; reimburse. —過剰金を拂ひ戻す, to pay back the amount in excess.

haraimono (拂物), *n.* an article to dispose of.

haraisage (拂下), *n.* sale (of government property). —拂ひ下げる, to sell; dispose *of*.

haraise (腹癒する), *vi.* to vent one's spleen [anger]; have one's revenge *for*; pay a person out. —腹癒せに手痛く一つ毆る, to give a stunning blow to vent one's spleen.

haraiwatashi (拂渡), *n.* payment. —拂ひ渡す, to pay (out). ¶ 拂渡局, the payment [pay-] office.

harakonashi (腹こなしに), *ad.* to help digestion.

harakudari, harakudashi, (腹下,下痢), *n.* 【醫】 diarrhœa.

haramaki (腹卷), *n.* a health-band.

haramu (孕·姙む), *v.* to conceive; become pregnant. —孕んで居る to be with child; be in the family way; be full in the belly 〔俗〕. —帆が風を孕む, The sails fill.

haran (波瀾), *n.* ❶ (波濤) a surge; a billow. ❷ (葛藤) disturbance; storm. ❸ (抑揚變化) movement (小說·詩等の). —變化と波瀾とに富む, to be replete with incidents and movements.

haraobi (腹帶), *n.* ❶ (腹卷) a health-band. ❷ (岩田帶) a bandage used during pregnancy. ❸ (馬絛) a belly-band; a breast-band.

hararago (鮞), *n.* (fish-)roe.

harasu (晴らす), *vt.* ❶ (散らす) to clear up; dispel; dissipate. ❷ (雪ぐ) to wreak; pay off. —恨みを晴らす, to wreak vengeance *upon*. —宿怨を晴らす, to pay off an old score.

harasu (脹·腫らす), *vt.* to swell. —指を腫らす, to swell a finger; have a swollen finger. —眼を泣き腫らす, to have one's eyes swollen with tears.

haratsuzumi (腹鼓打つ), *v.* to drum the abdomen; live in contentment; be happy and contented.

harau (拂ふ), *vt.* ❶ (驅逐) to drive away. ❷ (掃く) to sweep away; clear away; brush (刷毛にて). ❸ (除去) to remove; get rid *of*. ❹ (代價·注意·敬意等を) to pay. —陣營を拂ふ, to strike tents. —敵を攘ふ, to drive away the enemy. —注意を拂ふ, to pay attention *to*. —敬意を拂ふ, to pay one's respects. —…の代價を拂ふ, to pay *for*; pay the price *of*. —竹の枝を拂ふ, to lop [prune] a bamboo of its branches. —風水面を拂ふ, The wind plays on the water.

harau (祓ふ), *vt.* to exorcize. —惡魔災難を祓ふ, to make incantations for immunity from evil influences and calamities.

harawata (腸), *n.* ❶ the intestines. ❷ (臟腑) bowels; entrails. —腸を斷つ, to break one's heart.

hare (晴), *n.* clear [fine] weather. —西の風晴, the weather cleared by the west wind.

hare (腫), *n.* swelling; dropsy (水腫).

harebare (晴晴しい), *a.* ❶ (快晴の) fine; clear; bright; cheerful. ❷ (堂々たる) fine; splendid. ❸ (見映ある) showy; ostentatious. ❹ (心のすがすがしい) light-hearted; free from care; fresh; cheerful. —晴々しく著飾る, to be showily dressed. —氣が晴々する, to feel cheerful; feel refreshed. —氣を晴々さす, to make one's spirit cheerful.

harebottai (腫れぼッたい), *a.* swollen. —泣いて腫れぼッたい眼, eyes swollen with weeping.

haregi (晴衣), *n.* holiday [Sunday] clothes; one's Sunday best.

harema (晴間), *n.* an interval of clear weather (during rain).

haremono (腫物), *n.* a swelling; a boil.

harenchi (破廉恥), *n.* infamy; shamelessness; impudence. ¶ 破廉恥漢, a shameless [an infamous] fellow. —破廉恥罪, an infamous offence [crime].

hareru (晴れる), *vi.* ❶ to become clear; clear up; brighten. ❷ (疑などが) to be dispelled; clear up; disappear. ❸ (氣が) to be enlivened; be refreshed. —氣が晴れる, to feel cheerful. —晴れ渡りて

一塵の雲なき空, a clear sky without a speck of cloud. —天氣は晴れさうだ, The weather looks promising. —それでやッと疑が晴れた, With that my suspicions are at last dispelled.

hareru (脹·腫れる), *vi.* to swell.

harete (晴れて), *ad.* publicly; openly. —晴れて夫婦になる, to become openly man and wife.

haretsu (破裂), *n.* explosion; eruption (火山の); rupture (談判·管等の). —破裂さす, to explode; burst; rupture. —破裂する, to explode; burst (汽罐·鐵管など); erupt. ¶ 談判破裂, the rupture of negotiations.

hareyaka (晴やかな), *a.* ❶ (空の) cloudless; clear; bright. ❷ (快い) fresh; cheerful. ❸ (見映ある) ostentatious; showy; fine-looking. —晴やかに著飾る, to be gaily [showily] dressed.

hari (針), *n.* ❶ a needle (縫針, 編針); a pin (留針); a hook (釣針). ❷【動】a sting (蜂等の螫); a spine (魚の). ❸ (時計の針) a hand. —針のめど, a needle's eye. —針で刺す, [*vt.*] to sting. —針をさす, to prick with a pin; drive a pin (*into*). —針に絲を通す, to thread a needle. —針程の事を棒程に云ふ, to make a mountain of a molehill.

hari (梁), *n.* a beam; a girder.

hari (張), *n.* tension (張力).

hari (玻璃), *n.* crystal (水晶); glass (硝子). ☞*garasu*. ¶ 玻璃器, a glass; glass-ware.

hariageru (張上げる), *vt.* to raise; strain. —聲を張り上げる, to strain one's voice.

hariai (張合), *n.* ❶(競爭) strife; rivalry. ❷ (仕甲斐) being worth while [the trouble]. —互に張合ひになる, to strive with each other; be in rivalry. —張合ひが拔ける, to lose energy; feel it not to be worth while [worth doing].

hariau (張合ふ), *v.* to strive *with*; vie *with*; rival *with*.

haribako (針箱), *n.* a work-box.

hariban (張番), *n.* ❶ watch; guard. ❷ (人) a watchman; the watch; the guard. —張番する, to watch; keep watch. —張番を置く, to set a guard.

haridashi (貼出), *n.* a notice; a placard; a bill. —貼り出す, to bill; placard; put [post] up.

haridashi (張出), *n.* 【建】a gable; a gallery. —張り出す, ① [*vi.*] to jut (out; forth); project; beetle; overhang. ② [*vt.*] to project.

harifuda (貼札), *n.* ❶ (廣告等の) a bill; a poster; a notice (公告の). ❷ (附札) a label; a tag (附箋). —貼札無用, Stick no bills. ¶ 貼札廣告, poster-advertising.

harigami (貼紙), *n.* ❶ (貼附) paper-patching. ❷ a label; a tag (附箋). ❸ =*harifuda* の ❶.

harigane (針金), *n.* wire. ¶ 針金切り, a wire-cutter.

hariganemushi (線蟲), *n.* 【昆】 the wireworm.

harii (鍼醫), *n.* a needle-doctor; an acupuncturist.

hariita (張板), *n.* a board for stretching and drying washed cloth.

harikaeru (張替へる), *vt.* to repaper; recover. —提燈(障子)を張り替へる, to repaper a lantern (sliding-doors). —蝙蝠傘を張り替へにやる, to send an umbrella to be recovered.

hariko (張子), *n.* papier-maché. —張子ぢゃないから濡れたッて大丈夫だ, As I am not made of salt [sugar], I shall be safe even if I get wet.

harikomu (貼込む), *vt.* to paste in. ¶ 貼込帳, a scrap-book.

harikomu (張込む), *v.* ❶ (見張る) to keep watch. ❷(おごる) to put oneself to the expense *of*; go to the expense *of*.

harimogura (はりもぐら), *n.* 【哺乳】the porcupine ant-eater.

harimono (張物), *n.* cloth-stretching. —張物する, to stretch a cloth.

harin (破倫), *n.* immorality; being contrary to morals. —破倫の行爲, an immoral act.

harinezumi (蝟), *n.* 【哺乳】the hedgehog.

harisakeru (張裂ける), *vi.* to burst open; split open. —張り裂ける様な胸, a bursting heart.

harisashi (針刺), *n.* a needle [pin]-cushion; a needle-case.

harishigoto (針仕事), *n.* needle-work; sewing.

haritaosu (張倒す), *vt.* to knock down; floor; send to grass; give a slap on the head.

haritsuke (磔刑), *n.* crucifixion. —磔刑にする, to crucify.

haritsukeru (貼附ける), *vt.* to paste *on*; stick *on*.

haritsumeru (張詰める), *v.* ❶ to strain; stretch; string. ❷ to freeze all over. —張り詰めた氣, a tense spirit. —氷が張り詰めた湖水, a lake frozen all over.

harō (波浪), *n.* a wave. —波浪天を拍つ, The waves dash against the sky.

haru (春), *n.* ❶ spring; spring-time [-tide]. ❷ (春情) love. —

人生の春, the spring-time of life. —春の曙, a spring dawn. —春咲きの花, spring flowers. —春を鬻ぐ, to sell her favours. —春を解する, to attain [arrive at] puberty.

haru (張る), *vt.* ❶(布き延べる) to spread; stretch. ❷(引き張る) (*a*) (繩·綱など) to stretch; tighten: (*b*) (氣を) to strain [stretch] (the (nerves). ❸(開き張る) to stretch (幕等を); pitch (天幕等を); stick [push] out (肘を); open (傘等を). ❹(打つ) to slap (平手で); box. **—**, *vi.* ❶(嵩む) (*a*) (經費) to be great; swell: (*b*) (値段) to be high; be dear; be expensive. ❷(肩などが) to grow stiff. ❸(滿つ) (*a*) (帆が) to draw; swell: (*b*) (腹が) to be full. ❹(たるみなくなる) to tighten; become tight. —ぴんと張った綱,【航】a taut rope. —皮が張る, to skin over. —提燈を張る, to paper lanterns. —肘を張る, to stick out the elbows. —帆を張る, to fill the sail (風を滿たす); set a sail (掛ける). —蝙蝠傘を張る, to cover an umbrella. —目を張る, to strain one's eyes. —店(世帶)を張る, to keep a shop (house). —夜店を張る, to open a night street-stall. —床板を張る, to nail down the floor-boards; board the floor. —池に水を張る, to fill a pond with water. —幕を張り廻す, to hang round a curtain. —肩が張った, My shoulders grew stiff. —乳が張って來た, The breasts began to swell. —値段が少しはる, The price is a little high. —湖水一面に氷が張った, The lake is frozen all over; The ice covered the whole lake.

haru (貼る), *vt.* to apply (膏藥などを); stick; paste.

harubaru(遙遙), *ad.* from a great distance; all the way. —遙々來る, to come from a distance.

harugi(春着), *n.* The New Year's clothes; a spring wear.

haruka (遙に), *ad.* ❶ far; far away; far off. ❷(より甚だしく) by far; by a long way. —遙に良し, to be much better; be far better; be better by far. —遙か海上を眺める, to gaze far out into the sea. —遙に富士が見える, Mt. Fuji is to be seen far off.

harumeku (春めく), *vi.* to look like spring.

harusame (春雨), *n.* the spring rain.

hasai (破碎), *n.* crushing; cracking. —破碎する, to break (to pieces); shatter; fracture (頭蓋等を).

hasaki(刃先), *n.* the edge (of a blade).

hasamaru (挾る), *v.* ❶(介在) to lie between; be in the middle *of*. ❷(ひッかゝる) to get jammed in; be caught *in*; stick *between*. —二人の間に介って, hemmed in between the two.

hasami (鋏), *n.* ❶ (a pair of) scissors. ❷【動】〔螯〕a claw. ❸〔剪〕nip; clip; snip. —切符に鋏を入れる, to punch a ticket.

hasami(挾), *n.* a clip(新聞等の).

hasamibako (耳下腺炎), *n.* the mumps.

hasamimushi (挾蟲), *n.* 【昆】the seaside ear-wig.

hasamiuchi (挾擊), *n.* a simultaneous attack on both flanks. —挾擊になる, to find oneself between two fires. —敵艦を挾擊にする, to double upon an enemy's ship.

hasamu (はさむ), *vt.* ❶〔挾〕to hold *between*. ❷〔插〕to insert *in*; put *between*; jam *into*. ❸〔剪〕to cut; shear; clip. —兩腋に挾む, to hold under both arms. —髮を剪む, to cut one's hair; have one's hair cut. —火箸で挾み上げる, to take a thing up with the tongs.

hasan (破產), *n.* bankruptcy; failure; insolvency. —破產する, to become bankrupt [insolvent]; go into liquidation. —破產の申請をなす, to present a bankruptcy petition. ¶ 詐欺(過怠)破產, fraudulent (negligent) bankruptcy. —破產法, bankruptcy law. —破產者, a bankrupt; an insolvent.

hasei (派生), *n.* derivation. —派生する, to be derived *from*. ¶ 派生語,【文】a derivative (word).

hasen (波線), *n.* wavy lines;【地文】a wave-line.

hasen (破船), *n.* (a) shipwreck; (a) wreck.

haseru (馳せる), *vi.* ❶〔馳〕(馬) to run; gallop. ❷〔駛〕(船) to run; sail (帆走); steam (汽走). **—**, *vi.* to drive (馬車); ride (馬·自轉車など); send in haste (使者など); despatch (同上). —馳せ參じる, to hurry [hasten] *to*. —順風に駛せる, to run before the wind. —使を馳せる, to send a messenger post-haste. —名聲を世界に馳せる, to spread one's name all over the world.

hashagu (はしゃぐ), *vi.* ❶(乾燥) to dry up. ❷(騷ぐ) to romp about; be in high spirits.

hashi (橋), *n.* a bridge; a link (仲介物). —橋の下, below the bridge. —橋の欄干に凭れる, to lean on a bridge-rail. —橋を架ける, to bridge (a stream); build a bridge over (a river); throw a bridge across (a river). —橋を渡

る, to cross the bridge. ¶ 橋賃[錢], bridge-toll. —橋詰; 橋の袂, the approach to a bridge.

hashi (端), *n.* ❶ (終端) an end; a tail end; a tip. ❷ (一片) a morsel; a fragment; a scrap. ❸ (緣) the skirt; the edge (稜); the margin (表面のへり). —端から端まで, from end to end.

hashi (箸), *n.* chopsticks. ¶ 箸箱, a chopstick case.

hashibami (榛), *n.* ❶【植】the Japan hazel. ❷ (果實) a hazel-nut.

hashigo (梯子), *n.* a ladder; stairs (段梯子). —梯子をかける, to put up a ladder. —梯子を登る, to climb [go up] a ladder. ¶ 火事梯子, a fire-ladder. —繩(鎖)梯子, a rope (chain)-ladder. —梯子段, ① (段) a step; a stair. ② (階段) stairs; a staircase; a flight of stairs. (梯子段を踏み外す, to miss one's footing [foot] on the stairs.)

hashika (痲疹), *n.*【醫】measles.

hashike (艀, 艀船), *n.* a lighter; a sampan. —本船まで艀で行く, to go to the steamer by a lighter. ¶ 艀賃, lighterage.

hashikoi (敏い), *a.* sharp; smart; nimble. —はしこく立廻る, to behave [act] smartly.

hashikure (端くれ), *n.* a scrap; odds and ends.

hashinaku (端なく), *ad.* unexpectedly; suddenly. —端なくも物議を醸す, to happen to arouse public discussion.

hashio (齒齦), *n.* tartar of [on] the teeth.

hashira (柱), *n.* ❶ a pillar; a post; a pole (電信·電話等の); a column (圓柱). ❷ (支材) a support; a prop. —柱を立てる, to set up a pillar.

hashiradokei (柱時計), *n.* a wall-clock.

hashiragoyomi (柱暦), *n.* a wall-calendar; a sheet-calendar.

hashirasu (走らす), *vt.* ❶ (馳けらす) to run; sail (舟を). ❷ (敗走さす) to put to flight; rout. —ペンを走らす, to drive a pen.

hashiri (走り), *n.* the first of the season. ¶ 走り手, a runner.

hashirigaki (走書する), *v.* to scribble; scrawl.

hashirihabatobi (走幅跳), *n.*【競技】running long jump.

hashiritakatobi (走高跳), *n.*【競技】running high jump.

hashiru (走る), *v.* ❶ (走) to run. (*a*) (馳ける) to gallop (馬など): (*b*) (駛) to sail (帆走); steam (汽走): (*c*) (滑る) to glide. ❷ (奔) to run away; flee; go over to (他黨へ). ❸ (迸る) to spurt. —走り廻る, to run about. —利慾に走る, to be eager for gains. —極端に走る, to rush into extremes. —一日に一千哩を走る, to run 1000 miles a day. —血が走ッた, The blood spurted.

hashita (端), *n.* odd sum; a fraction; change (釣錢).

hashitagane (端金), *n.* odd money; a petty [small] sum of money. a mere pittance.

hashitanai (はしたない), *a.* mean; ignoble; of low birth. —はしたない口をきく, to talk vulgarly.

hashiwatashi (橋渡する), *v.* to introduce; act as intermediary [go-between].

hashōfū (破傷風), *n.*【醫】tetanus.

hashoru (端折る), *vt.* ❶ (裾を折る) to tuck up. ❷ (省略する) to cut short; shorten. —端折ッて云へば, to cut the matter short. —裾を端折る, to tuck in the skirt.

hashu (播種する), *vi.* to sow seed; seed. ¶ 播種期, the seeding season; the seed-time.

hashutsu (派出), *n.* ❶ sending out; despatch; detachment. ❷ (分れ出る) branching off. ❸ (由來) derivation. —派出する, ①【軍】to detach (船艦·軍隊等を); despatch. ② (派生する) to be derived *from*. ¶ (巡査) 派出所, a police box.

hason (破損), *n.* damage; breakage; dilapidation. —破損する, to damage; dilapidate (家屋等); wear off (磨損する).

hassan (八算), *n.* simple arithmetic; a simple sum. —八算の九九を覺える, to learn the multiplication table.

hassan (發散), *n.* ❶ (液體の蒸發) exhalation; volatilization. ❷ (光·熱等の放出) emanation; radiation. ❸ (香などの) diffusion; exudation. —發散する, to volatilize; emanate *from*; radiate. —臭氣の發散を防ぐ, to prevent the exudation of smell.

hassei (發生する), *vi.* ❶ (起こる) to occur; happen; spring up (新思想等); be generated (熱·電氣·病など). ❷ (起因する) to originate *from*; spring *from*. —事件の發生, happening of an event. —天然痘患者橫濱に發生す, There has been a case of small-pox in Yokohama.

hassei (發聲), *n.* utterance; vocalization; exclamation. —座長の發聲で, at the word of the chairman.

hassha (發車), *n.* the starting (of a train). —發車する, to start; leave. —三番線より發車する, to start from track No. 3. —發車

時間に間に合ふやうに行く, to go to be in time for the train. ¶ 發車信號, a starting signal.

hassha (發射), *n.* ❶ (發砲) discharge; firing. ❷ (放射) radiation (光・熱など); emission (同上); emanation (光). **—-suru,** *vt.* ❶ to discharge; fire. ❷ to radiate; emit. —水雷を發射する, to discharge a torpedo. ¶ 水雷發射管, a (torpedo) tube.

hasshin (發信), *n.* despatch of a message [letter]. —發信する, to despatch [send] a message or letter. ¶ 發信簿, forwarding letter book. —發信機, a sender; a transmitter. —發信局, the original sending office. —發信人, the sender (of a message or letter).

hasshin (發疹), *n.* 【醫】 eruption; exanthema; efflorescence. —發疹する, to effloresce. ¶ 發疹チブス, exanthematous typhus.

hasshōchi (發祥地), *n.* the cradle. —革命思想の發祥地, the cradle of revolutionary ideas.

hassō (發送する), *vt.* to despatch; forward. ¶ 發送係, a forwarding clerk.

hassōhō (發走法), *n.* 【競技】 — [start.]

hassuru (發する), *v.* ❶ (出發) to start *from*; depart *from*; set out [off]. ❷ (派遣, 發送) to despatch. ❸ (出す) (*a*) (命令等) to issue: (*b*) (聲音など) to utter: (*c*) (煙・火など) to emit. ❹ (發生) to originate *from*; arise *from*; spring *from*. ❺ (起點) to flow [rise] *from* (河川); start *from* (火事・線路など). ❻ (放つ) (*a*) (砲など) to discharge; fire: (*b*) (光・熱・香氣等) to radiate (光・熱など); emit. —午前六時三十分に發する, to depart (at) 6. 30 a. m. —香氣を發する, to breathe fragrance. —火を發する, to emit fire. —大聲を發する, to give a great shout. —禮砲を發する, to fire a salute. —照會狀を發する, to send a letter of inquiry. —天龍川は諏訪湖から發す, The Tenryū River rises in Lake Suwa.

hasu (蓮), *n.* 【植】 the lotus 【俗】. ¶ 蓮池, a lotus pond.

hasu (斜), *n.* slant. —斜になる 〔する〕, to slant. —四角を斜に切る, to cut a square slantwise.

hasū (端數), *n.* a fraction; the amount over. —端數を切り捨てる, to cut off fractions.

hasuha (蓮葉な), *a.* loose; wanton. ¶ 蓮葉者, a hoyden; a hussy.

ha-suru (派する), *vt.* to send out; despatch.

hata (側), *n.* ❶ a side; neighbourhood. ❷ (外部, 局外) outside; onlookers. —側で見て居る, to be looking on beside him.

hata (將), *ad.* more. **—,** *conj.* ❶ (それとも, 又は) or. ❷ (且又) both [at once]...and; moreover; again.

hata (旗), *n.* a flag; a banner; a standard. —旗で信號する, to flag. —旗を揭げる, to hoist a flag. —旗を出す, to hang out a flag. —旗を下ろす, to take down the flag; lower [strike] the flag (降參・敬禮の爲に). —旗を振る, to wave a flag. ¶ 旗行列, a flag-procession.

hata (織機), *n.* a loom. —機を織る, to weave.

hataage (旗揚), *n.* ❶ the raising of one's banner [standard]; levy of troops. ❷ (興起) rise. —旗揚げする, to raise [levy] troops; raise one's banner [standard].

hatabako (葉煙草), *n.* leaf-tobacco.

hatabi (旗日), *n.* a national holiday.

hatafuri (旗振り), *n.* a flagman.

hatagashira (旗頭), *n.* a head; a leader; a captain.

hatago (旅籠), *n.* ❶ (旅籠屋) an inn; a tavern. ❷ (旅籠錢) inn [tavern]-charges.

hatairo (旗色), *n.* the movement of the banner; the state of an army; the tide of war (battle); the issue of the day. —旗色を見る, to see how the day goes [which way the cat jumps]; sit on the fence.

hatajirushi (旗章), *n.* the flag-design [-device].

hatake (畑, 畠, 圃), *n.* ❶ a field; a farm. ❷ (特技) speciality. ❸ (雰圍氣) atmosphere. —畑違ひの事, something out of one's line. —畑に種をまく, to sow seeds in a field. —畑をつくる, to till [cultivate] a field (耕作); crop a field *with* (作附).

hatake (波太介), *n.* ❶ (糠粃疹) pityriasis. ❷ (赤糠粃疹) pityriasis rubra. ❸ (鱗屑疹) psoriasis.

hataki (敲), *n.* dusting (事); a duster (塵はたき). —彩配(ざい)をかける, to dust.

hataku (敲く), *vt.* ❶ (打つ) to beat; slap (平手で). ❷ (拂ふ) to dust. —障子をはたく, to dust the sliding-door. —病人の脊中をはたく, to shampoo a patient's back.

hatamoto (旗本), *n.* ❶ (麾下) an adherent. ❷ (德川家直參の士) a direct feudatory of the *shōgun*.

hatan (破綻), *n.* ❶ ruin; failure. ❷ breach; rupture. —破綻する, to fail; be ruined. —破綻を生ずる, to cause failure; bring ruin.

hatankyō (巴旦杏), *n.* 【植】 the almond.

hataori (機織), *n.* weaving (事);

a weaver (人). ¶ 機織機械, a loom. —機織女, a weaver.

hatarakasu (働かす), *vt.* ❶ (勞働) to work; set to work. ❷ (使用, 活動) to employ; use; exercise (筋肉·才能·官能·記憶力などを). ❸ (活用) to conjugate (動詞を); apply (應用). —頭を働かす, to make one's brain work. —機械を働かす, to set a machine to work. —才氣を働かす, to bring one's ability into action; call one's ability into play. —手を自由に働かす, to use hands freely; give free play to hands.

hataraki (働), *n.* ❶ (作用, 活動) function (機能); operation; movement. ❷ (才能) ability; talent; energy. ❸ (勞働) labour; work. ❹【機】power. —働きのある人, a man of resource.

hataraku (働く), *v.* ❶ (作用) to operate *upon*; work *upon*; act *upon*. ❷ (勞働) to labour; work; toil *at*. ❸ (奮鬪) to exert oneself. ❹ (語尾活用) to be conjugated. —働き續ける, to work on. —惡事を働く, to commit crimes. —パン(生計; 主義)の爲に働く, to work for bread (a living; the cause).

hatashite (果して), *ad.* ❶ (案の定) just; just as I thought; as was expected; sure enough. ❷ (本當に) ever; really. —果して然らば, if that be the case —果して事實であった, It proved [turned out] to be true. —果して復た逢ふ事があらうか, Shall we ever meet again?

hatasu (果す), *vt.* ❶ (遂行) to accomplish; perform; carry out. ❷ (履行) to discharge; perform; fulfil. —目的(使命)を果す, to accomplish one's object (mission). —約束を果す, to fulfil a promise.

hatato (礑と), *ad.* ❶ (物の俄に打合ふ貌) with a clapping sound. ❷ (切迫の貌) suddenly. —礑と行き詰まる, to be at a loss for a word (an answer; an excuse). —礑と當惑する, to be at a loss what [how] to do.

hatatori (旗取-競爭), *n.* a flag-race.

hatazao (旗竿), *n.* ❶ a flagstaff. ❷【植】(南芥菜) the glabrous rock-cress.

hatchaku (發著), *n.* departure and arrival. —列車の發著時刻, the arrival and departure hours of trains. ¶ 汽車發著(時間)表, a railway time-table. —發著掲示板, a station-calendar.

hatchi (艙口), *n.* 【航】a hatch.

hate (果), *n.* ❶ (結果) the consequence; the result; the end. ❷ (末端) the end; the termination; the extremity. ❸ (際限) limits; bounds; end. —榮華の果, the consequence of one's prosperity. —議論の果, the end (result) of the discussion. —世界の果, the end of the earth. —果は, in the end; in the long run.

hatena (はてな), *int.* (考へる時) let me see.

hatenkō (破天荒の), *a.* unprecedented.

hateru (果てる), *vi.* ❶ (終る) to conclude; terminate; come to an end. ❷ (死去) to die; meet one's end [fate]. —疲れ果てる, to be dead tired; be tired out.

hateshi (果てしなき), *a.* endless; interminable; limitless.

hato (鳩), *n.* 【鳥】the dove; the pigeon.

hatō (波濤), *n.* billows; surges; high seas.

hāto (ハート), *n.* heart.

hatoba (波止場), *n.* a wharf; a quay (海岸と竝行せる). —船を波止場に横附けにする, to bring a ship alongside a wharf. ¶ 波止場人足, an alongshoreman; a wharfman. —波止場料[稅], wharfage.

hatogoya (鳩舍), *n.* a dove-cot; a pigeonry; a loft.

hatome (鳩目), *n.* an eyelet.

hatomugi (鳩麥), *n.* 【植】the pearl-barley.

hatomune (鳩胸), *n.* a pigeon [chicken]-breast.

hatsu (初), *n.* the outset; the first; the beginning. ——, *a.* first; maiden; early; new. ¶ 初演說(航海), a maiden speech (voyage). —初雪, the first snow (of the season).

hatsu (發), *n.* ❶ (出發) departure; starting; leaving. ❷ [*num.*] a round. —二十發の彈丸, twenty rounds of ball cartridge. —九時三十分發の列車, the train leaving at half past nine.

hatsubai (發賣), *n.* sale. —發賣する, to sell. —新聞の發賣頒布を禁止する, to prohibit the sale and distribution of a newspaper. ¶ 發賣禁止, prohibition of sale.

hatsubō (發泡), *n.* 【醫】vesication. ¶ 發泡膏, a blister-plaster; a blister.

hatsubutai (初舞臺), *n.* *début* [佛]; the first appearance. —初舞臺の人, *débutant* [*fem.* -*e*] [佛]. —初舞臺に立つ, to come out; make a *début*.

hatsubyō (發病する), *vi.* to fall ill [sick]; be taken ill [sick]

hatsudake (初茸), *n.* 【植】Lactarius hatsudake (學名).

hatsuden (發電), *n.* ❶【理】electrification. ❷ sending of a telegram; a telegram *from*. ¶ 發電機,【電】a dynamo; an electric machine; a generator. —發電所, a (an electric) power-house [-station]; a generating station. (汽 (水) 力發電所, a steam (water; hydraulic) power plant.)

hatsudō (發動), *n.* motion; putting in motion. ¶ 發動(的) 貿易, active commerce. —發動機, a motor. (ガソリン發動機, a gasoline motor. —發動機船, a motor-boat.)

hatsuga (發芽する), *vi* to bud; germinate; sprout.

hatsugen (發言), *n.* speech; utterance. —發言する, to speak; utter; open one's mouth; take the floor (議會で)〔米〕. —發言の機會を失する, to lose the opportunity of speaking. ¶ 發言權, the right of speaking; the floor; the voice. (發言權を得る [許さる], (議院で) to catch the Speaker's eye; get [obtain] the floor〔米〕. —に發言權がない, to have no voice *in*.)

hatsugi (發議), *n.* a proposal; a motion. —發議する, to propose; propound; move. ¶ 發議 [案] 權, the initiative. —發議者, a proposer; a mover.

hatsuharu (初春), *n.* the early spring; new spring.

hatsui (發意), *n.* a proposal (發議); an original idea (創意); a plan (計畫). —の發意で, on the initiative *of*.

hatsuiku (發育), *n.* growth; development. —發育する, to grow; develop. (十分發育した, full-grown.) —發育不十分の, undergrown. ¶ 發育初期, an early stage of growth.

hatsukanezumi (二十日鼠), *n.* the mouse [*pl.* mice].

hatsukoi (初戀), *n.* the first love; calf-love.

hatsumei (發明), *n.* ❶ invention. ❷ (怜悧) intelligence. —發明な, intelligent; clever; sagacious. —發明の才, ingenuity; inventive genius. —發明する, to invent; devise. ¶ 發明品, an invention. —發明者, an inventor [*fem.* -tress].

hatsunetsu (發熱), *n.* 【醫】 pyrexia; fever. —發熱する, to grow feverish; have an attack of fever.

hatsuni (初荷), *n.* the first consignment.

hatsuon (發音), *n.* pronunciation; articulation (音節に云ふ); enunciation. —明瞭な發音, clear [distinct] pronunciation. —發音する, [*vt.*] to pronounce; enunciate. ¶ 發音辭典, a pronouncing dictionary. —發音符, phonetics; diacritical marks.

hatsurai-shingō (發雷信號), *n.* 【鐵道】 detonator.

hatsuratsu (潑剌たる), *a.* fresh; sprightly; keen. —潑剌たる才氣, a keen intellect.

hatsuuri (初賣), *n.* the first sale; the handsel.

hatsuyō (發揚する), *vt.* to exalt; raise. —國威を發揚する, to raise the national prestige.

hattatsu (發達), *n.* development; advancement; progress (進步). —人智の發達, advancement of human knowledge. —發達する, to develop; advance; progress. —發達を害する, to impede [arrest] the progress.

hatten (發展), *n.* expansion; enlargement; development. —發展さす, to develop; expand. —發展する, to develop; extend; expand.

hatto (法度), *n.* ❶ (法律) a law; an ordinance. ❷ (禁制) prohibition.

hatto (はッと), *ad.* suddenly. —はッと思ッて四邊を見廻した, In amazement I looked around.

hau (這ふ), *vi.* ❶ to crawl; creep. ❷ (延びからむ) to creep; trail.

hauta (端唄), *n.* a ditty; a short song.

Hawai (布哇), *n.* Hawaii. ¶ 布哇人, a Hawaiian.

haya (早), *ad.* ❶ (既に) already. ❷ (早くも) now. —夢の間に早や五年も經ッた, Five years have already elapsed as in a dream.

hayaashi (早步, 速步), *n.* quick steps; a trot; 【陸】 quick march. —早足進め!, quick march!

hayabusa (隼), *n.* 【鳥】 the peregrine (falcon).

hayade (早出), *n.* early attendance at office.

hayafune (早船), *n.* a clipper; a fly-boat; a fast boat.

hayagane (早鐘), *n.* a fire-bell; an alarm-bell. —早鐘を撞いて警を傳へる, to give warning by tolling the fire-bell.

hayagaten (早合點する), *vi.* to jump at a conclusion.

hayagawari (早變), *n.* a quick [lightning] change. —早變りする, to make a quick change.

hayai (早い), *a.* ❶ (夙) (未明, 時期) early. ❷ (速, 疾) fast; quick; prompt; swift. —早いが勝, The quickest wins. —一刻も早い方がよい, The sooner, the better. —月日の經つは早いものだ, Days and months pass quickly.

hayajimai (早終ひ), *n.* early closing.

hayajini (夭折する), *vi.* to die young.

hayaku (破約), *n.* breach of contract [promise]. —破約する, to break an agreement [a contract]. —破約を申込む, to propose to nullify the contract.

hayaku (早く), *ad.* ❶ early (時間・季節等); soon (間もなく); at once (直ちに). ❷ (速に) quickly; promptly; fast; swiftly. —早くな

る(する), to quicken. —早く起きる, to rise early. —早く起き早く寢る, to keep early hours. —早く親に分れる, to part early from one's parents. —醫者がもっと早く來たなら, if the doctor had come sooner. —早からう惡からう, (諺) "Good and quickly seldom meet."

hayakuchi (早口), *n.* rapid speaking [speech]. —早口で聽きとれない, His talk is so rapid that I cannot take it in.

hayamaru (早まる), *vi.* to be precipitate; be rash; be overhasty. —早まった事をする, to do a hasty [rash] thing; commit a rash act.

hayame (早目に), *ad.* a little early; a little before time; earlier than usual.

hayameru (早める), *vt.* to quicken; hasten; speed. —歩調を速める, to mend [quicken] one's pace. —己の零落を早める, to hasten one's ruin.

hayamichi (早道, 捷徑), *n.* = ***chikamichi.***

hayane (早寢する), *vi.* to go to bed early.

hayanomikomi (早呑込), *n.* a hasty conclusion. ☞ ***hayagaten.***

hayaoki (早起, 夙起), *n.* ❶ early rising. ❷ (人) an early riser; an early bird. —早起は三文の德, "The early bird catches the worm."

hayari (流行), *n.* ❶ (時好) fashion (服裝等の); popularity; the vogue. ❷ (疫病等の) prevalence. ☞ ***ryūkō*** (流行). ¶流行感冒 (ㇳ), an epidemic cold; influenza. —流行ッ兒, a lion; a person much sought after. (文壇の流行ッ兒, a lion of the literary world.) —流行言葉, a word [phrase] in vogue. —流行眼病 (ノ), epidemic ophthalmia. —流行唄, a popular song. —流行病, an epidemic.

hayaru (逸る), *vi.* to be hasty; be impetuous; be rash.

hayaru (流行る), *vi.* ❶ (一般に亙る) to prevail; be prevalent. ❷ (時好) to be in fashion [vogue]; be popular. ❸ (繁昌) to prosper; have a large practice (醫師・辯護士等が). —流行らぬ, out of fashion; unfashionable. —あの店は大層流行る, The shop has a large custom.

hayasa (早さ), *n.* ❶ (朝など) earliness. ❷ (速なること) quickness; rapidity; swiftness. ❸ (速力) speed.

hayase (早瀬), *n.* rapids; a swift current; a shoot.

hayashi (林), *n.* a forest (大林); a wood (森).

hayashi (囃子), *n.* an orchestra; a musical band. ¶囃方, an orchestra; a musician (of a band).

hayashi (はやし), *n.* 【料理】 hash; hashed meat.

hayasu (生やす), *vt.* to grow; sprout; cultivate. —髭を生やす, to grow [sprout] a moustache; cultivate a beard.

hayasu (榮す), *vt.* ❶ (賞めて) to applaud; cheer. ❷ (嗤うて) to jeer *at.* —見物に榮される, to be jeered by spectators.

hayasu (囃す), *v.* to play music; beat time.

hayate (疾風, 颶風), *n.* a squall; a storm.

hayatori (早取する), *vt.* to snap [俗]; snapshot. ¶早取寫眞, a snapshot. (早取寫眞器, a kodak; a snapshot camera.)

hayawaza (早業), *n.* ❶ quick work; a feat. ❷ (手品) sleight of hand. —電光石火の早業, a lightning trick.

hazama (狹間), *n.* ❶ (間) an interval; an interstice. ❷ (銃眼) a loophole; a crenel. ❸ (山峽) a vale; a gorge; a narrow.

haze, hazenoki, (櫨), *n.* 【植】 the red lac [tallow] sumach.

haze (沙魚, 鯊), *n.* 【魚】 the goby.

hazeru (爆る), *vi.* ❶ (炒れてはじける) to decrepitate; burst open. ❷ (肉などの冷水等にはじける) to crinkle.

hazu (筈), *v. aux.* ought to; should; must be. —さうあるべき筈だ, That is as it should be. —そんな筈がない, It cannot be so. —彼が行く筈だ, He is expected to go. —それもその筈だ, That was to be expected. —さう云ふ筈ではなかったんだが, It could not have been so.

hazukashii (恥しい), *a.* shameful; ashamed; abashed. —恥しからぬ敵, a worthy adversary. —恥しがる, ① to be shy; be bashful; be abashed. ② (慚愧) to be ashamed.

hazukashime (辱), *n.* shame; insult; affront. —辱めを忍ぶ, to swallow [pocket] an insult.

hazukashimeru (辱める), *vt.* to put (a person) to shame; insult; disgrace. —父祖の名を辱める, to bring disgrace upon the family.

hazumi (はずみ), *n.* ❶ (反跳) spring; bound. ❷ (機勢) momentum; inertia. ❸ (刺戟) an impetus; an impulse; a stimulus. ❹ (機會) a chance. —最初の反跳で, on the first bound. —時のはずみで, on the impulse [spur] of the moment. —一寸したはずみで, by a mere chance. —どうしたはずみか, by some chance.

hazumu (はずむ), *vi.* ❶ (反跳)

to bound; bounce; spring. ❷ (亢進) to be encouraged; rise in spirit. ❸ (調子づく) to catch the infection; work oneself up. —はずむ毬, a bounding ball. —息を嗤ます, to gather one's voice.

hazure (外), *n.* ❶ (しくじり) miss; failure. ❷ (外端) outskirts. ❸ (不作) failure. —町の外れに, at the end of the town. —僕の云ッたことに外れはない, It does not differ from what I said.

hazureru (外れる), *v.* ❶ (離れる) (*a*) to deviate *from*; swerve *from*; depart *from*: (*b*) to run off; get out *of*: (*c*) to come off; be off; get out of place. ❷ (齟齬) to fail; go wrong; go contrary *to*. ❸ (見當違ひ) to miss. —人並に外れた, out of the ordinary. —人の道に外れる, to deviate from the way of humanity. —道を外れる, to leave the track. —線路を外れる, to run off the metals; be derailed. —針路を外れる, to deviate from the course. —的を遠く外れる, to shoot wide of the mark.

hazusu (外す), *v.* ❶ (取外す) to unfasten; disjoin; disconnect; put out of place [gear]; remove; take off; undo. ❷ (失敗) to fail *in* (試驗などを); miss (的・機會等を); miss one's tip (仕損ず). ❸ (避ける) to avoid; avert; slip. —錠前を外す, to pick a lock. —機會を外す, to miss an opportunity. —機械を外す, to put a machine out of gear. —障子を外す, to take out a sliding-door. —桶の箍を外す, to take off a bucket-hoop.

he (へ), *n.* 【音】E; fa [伊]; 4.

hē (へー), *int.* (驚異・疑問の發聲) hey; dear me; indeed.

hebereke (泥酔の), *a.* sottish. —へべれけに酔ふ, to be dead drunk.

hebi (蛇), *n.* 【爬蟲】the snake; the serpent.

hebī (へビー), *n.* full speed; spurt. —へビー, (力漕・力走の號令) heavy! (競漕・競走で日本學生が用ひる); row faster; pull away [harder]. —へビーを掛ける, to spurt; work hard.

hebo (平凡), *n.* ❶ (拙劣) bungling; a bungler (人). ❷ (野菜等の發育不全) being under-grown. —平凡の, poor; green; bungling. ¶ 平凡畫工, a dauber; a daubster. —へぼ醫者, a bungling doctor. —へぼ職人, a bungler; a cobbler; a poor tool. —平凡役人, a petty official.

hechima (絲瓜), *n.* 【植】Luffa cylindrica (washing-gourd の類).

hedatari (隔り), *n.* ❶ (距離) distance. ❷ (懸隔) gulf; distance.

hedataru (隔る), *vi.* ❶ (仕切) to be partitioned. ❷ (遠隔) to be far *from* [*off*; *away*]; be removed *from* (代); be separated (時代). —距ッた, far; distant. —三哩隔ッて居る, to be three miles off [away].

hedate (隔), *n.* ❶ (仕切) partition. ❷ (差別) difference. ❸ (隔意) reserve. —誰にでも隔なく交る, to be friendly with any one without reserve. —間に隔を附ける, to discriminate between.

hedateru (隔てる), *v.* ❶ (仕切る) to part; separate. ❷ =*hedataru*. —河を隔てて, across a river; on the other side of a river.

heddoraito (前燈), *n.* a headlight.

hedo (反吐つく), *vi.* to vomit; spue; spew.

hedomodo (へどもどする), *vi.* to be confused; be bewildered; be in a quandary.

hegi (折木), **hegiita** (折板), *n.* shingles; splint; slat.

hei (兵), *n.* ❶ (軍人) a soldier. ❷ (軍勢) an army; troops.

hei (塀), *n.* a fence; a wall. —低い塀, a dwarf-wall. —塀を繞らす, to surround with a wall. —塀を跳び越す, to jump over a wall.

hei (諾), *ad.* yes; all right; ay, sir. —へい畏りました, Very well, sir.

heian (平安), *n.* peace; quiet; tranquillity. —心の平安, peace of mind.

heiba (兵馬), *n.* an army (軍隊); a war (戰爭); military affairs (軍事).

heibon (平凡な), *a.* commonplace; ordinary; trivial. —平凡な繪, a picture of average merit. —平凡な顏, a common-looking face; a face without any character.

heichi (平地), *n.* a level; a flat; a plain. —平地に波瀾を起す, to raise a storm in a dead calm.

heidon (併呑する), *vt.* to annex; absorb; merge. —四鄰を併呑する, to absorb all its neighbours.

heiei (兵營), *n.* barracks. ¶ 兵營生活, barrack life.

heieki (兵役), *n.* military service. —兵役を勤め上げる, to serve one's time. ¶ 二年兵役, two years' service. —兵役免除, exemption from military service.

heienban (平圓板), *n.* a disk. ¶ 平圓板音譜, a disk-record.

heifū (弊風), *n.* evil customs [habits].

heifuku (平伏する), *vi.* to prostrate oneself; kiss the ground.

heifuku' (平服), *n.* plain clothes; everyday clothes; an undress. ¶ 平服巡査, a plain-clothes constable [policeman].

heigai (弊害), *n.* an evil; an abuse; a vice. —弊害を伴ふ, to accompany [attend] evils.

heigakkō (兵學校), *n.* a naval (military) college [academy].

heigaku (兵學), *n.* military science.

heigei (睥睨する), *vt.* to look contemptuously *at*; glower *at*.

heigen (平原), *n.* a plain. ¶ 關東平原, the plains of Kantō.

heigō (併合), *n.* ❶ annexation. ❷ amalgamation; union; consolidation. —併合する, to annex; unite; consolidate.

heihaku (幣帛), *n.* an offertory; an offering; a present.

heihatsu (併發), *n.* concurrence. —熱を併發する, to be accompanied [complicated] by fever. ¶ 併發症, a complication.

heihei (へいへいする), *vi.* to fawn *upon*; truckle (*to*); cringe *to*. **—,** *a.* fawning; obsequious.

heihei-bonbon (平平凡凡の), *a.* commonplace. ☞ ***heibon.***

heihō (平方), *n.* ❶ (自乘) the square of a number. ❷ (正方形) a square. —五平方寸, five square inches. —五寸平方, five inches square. —平方に開く, to extract the square root (*of*). ¶ 平方根, a square root. —平方尺, a square foot.

heihō (兵法), *n.* art of war; generalship.

heii (平易), *n.* ❶ (容易) ease; facility. ❷ (平明) plainness; simpleness. **——-na,** *a.* easy; plain; simple. —平易な英語, simple English. —平易に說明する, to give very simple explanations.

heiin (兵員), *n.* 【軍】 strength (of an army); men.

heiin (閉院), *n.* the closing [prorogation] of the Diet.

heiji (平時), *n.* ❶ (常時) ordinary times. ❷ (平和の時) peace-time. ¶ 平時封鎖, a pacific blockade.

heiji (兵事), *n.* military affairs. ¶ 兵事課, the military section.

heijitsu (平日), *n.* ❶ (平素) ordinary times. ❷ (尋常の日) an ordinary day. —平日の通り, as usual; as on ordinary days.

heijō (平常), *ad.* usually; ordinarily; always. —平常に復する, to be oneself again.

heijō (閉場する), *v.* to close. ¶ 閉場式, the closing ceremony.

Heika (陛下), *pron.* His (Her) Majesty (H. M. と略す); Sire (呼掛). ¶ 天皇(皇后)陛下, H. M. the Emperor (Empress).

heika (平價), *n.* ❶【商】par. ❷ (平日の價) an ordinary price.

heikai (閉會), *n.* prorogation (議會); the closing (of a meeting). —閉會する, to prorogue; close.

heikatsu (平滑な), *a.* smooth; flat; even. —平滑にする, to smooth; planish (打って); lubricate (油で).

heikegani (平家蟹), *n.* 【甲殼】 the mask-crab.

heiken (兵權), *n.* military power.

heiki (平氣), *n.* ❶ calmness; composure; coolness. ❷ (無頓著) indifference; coolness; unconcern —平氣の, calm; cool; unconcerned —平氣を裝ふ, to assume a calm [composed] air. —一向に平氣である, to remain as cool as a fish [cucumber].

heiki (兵器), *n.* arms; weapon of war; ordnance. —兵器の改良 improvement of arms. ¶ 兵器庫 ordnance stores. —兵器廠, a depot, an ordnance department.

heikin (平均), *n.* ❶ (ならし) an average; a mean. ❷ (均衡) balance; equilibrium; poise. —平均する, ① [*vt.*] to average (異なれる數個の數量を). ② [*vi.*] to balance; equilibrate; poise. —平均して, on an average. —平均を取る, ① to take the average. ② to balance. —平均を失ふ, to lose one's balance; overbalance. —彼の賣上は一日五十圓平均だ, His sales average fifty *yen* a day. ¶ 國力平均, the balance of power. —平均數, 【數】 average value. —平均點, the average mark; 【數】 mean point.

heikō (平行), *n.* parallelism; parallel. —平行する, to run parallel *to*. ¶ 平行棒, parallel bars. —平行定規, a parallel ruler. —平行線, parallel lines. —平行四邊形, a parallelogram.

heikō (平衡), *n.* balance; equilibrium. ☞ ***heikin.*** —平衡を失する, to lose balance.

heikō (竝行·併行する), *vi.* ❶ (竝び行く) to run *with*; go side by side; go abreast. ❷=***heikō*** (平行する).

heikō (閉口する), *vi.* to be silenced; be discomfited; be stumped. —閉口さす, to discomfit; embarrass; floor. —錢の無いには閉口だ, I am stumped by want of money. —どうも彼奴には閉口した, I could never stand the fellow.

heikyo (屛居する), *vi.* to live retired; seclude oneself; live in retirement [seclusion]. —一室に屛居する, to shut oneself up in a room.

heimen (平面), *n.* a plane; a level; 【數】 a plane (surface). ¶ 平面鏡, a plane mirror. —平面

圖, a ground-plan; a plan; a plane figure (平面形).

heimin (平民), *n.* the (common) people; a commoner; a plebeian. —平民的, popular; democratic. ¶ 平民主義, democratism. (平民主義者, a democratist.)

heimyaku (平脈), *n.* the normal pulse.

heinen (平年), *n.* ❶ (例年) an ordinary [a normal] year. ❷ (閏年の對) the common [civil] year. ¶ 平年作, a normal crop; an average crop.

heion (平穩な), *a.* calm; serene; tranquil. —平穩な航海, a calm voyage. —平穩に日を送る, to pass one's days in peace.

heiran (兵亂), *n.* a war; a disturbance. —兵亂の巷と化する, to change into a scene of war.

heiretsu (竝列する), *vt.* to stand [draw up] in a row.

heiritsu (竝立する), *v.* to stand side by side [together; abreast]; coexist.

heiryaku (兵略), *n.* strategy; generalship.

heiryoku (兵力), *n.* ❶ (武力) military force. ❷ (兵員數) (military) strength. —兵力に依って, by force of arms.

heisa (閉鎖する), *vt.* to close; shut; lock.

heisatsu (併殺), *n.* 【野球】 double play (二人); triple play (三人).

heisei (平靜), *n.* calm; tranquillity; peace. —平靜な, calm; tranquil; peaceful.

heisei (幣制), *n.* monetary system; currency system.

heisei (弊政), *n.* corrupt government; maladministration; misgovernment. —弊政を釐革する, to reform a corrupt government.

heiseki (兵籍), *n.* a military register. —兵籍に入る, to enlist; enter the army. ¶ 兵籍簿, a muster-roll; a muster-book.

heisen (兵燹), *n.* a fire [conflagration] caused by war.

heishi (兵士), *n.* a soldier. ¶ 兵士宿泊所, a billet.

heishiki-taisō (兵式體操), *n.* (military) exercises; drilling.

heishin-teitō (平身低頭する), *vi.* to prostrate oneself before; do obeisance *to*; kiss the ground.

heisho (兵書), *n.* a book on strategy [tactics]; a military work.

heishū (弊習), *n.* corrupt customs [usages]. —多年の弊習, a corrupt usage of long standing.

heiso (平素), *ad.* usually; always. —平素の行狀, daily conduct.

heisō (兵曹), *n.* 【海】 a sergeant. ¶ 上等兵曹, a first-class sergeant. —兵曹長, a sergeant-major.

heisoku (閉塞), *n.* blocking; obstruction. **——-suru,** *vt.* to block up; close up. —港口を閉塞する, to block the harbour-entrance. ¶ 閉塞船, a block-ship. —旅順口閉塞, the blocking-up [bottling-up] of Port Arthur.

heisotsu (兵卒), *n.* 【軍】 a private; a (common) soldier; the ranks; the rank and file. —兵卒より身を起して大將となる, to rise from the ranks to be a general.

hei-suru (聘する), *vt.* to engage. —師を聘する, to engage a teacher.

heitai (兵隊), *n.* a company of soldiers; troops; a soldier (兵士). —玩具の兵隊, toy [tin] soldiers.

heitan (平坦の), *a.* flat; even; level. —平坦にする, to even; roll.

heitan (兵站), *v.* communications; *étapes* 〔佛〕. ¶ 兵站部, communications [*étapes*] dépôt; a supply department; a commissariat.

heitan (兵端), *n.* hostilities; an act of war. —兵端を開く, to open [commence] hostilities.

heitei (平定する), *vt.* to pacify; suppress; put down; tranquillize; subdue. —天下を平定する, to restore peace in the empire.

heiten (閉店する), *vi.* to shut up shop; close shop; give up business.

heitsukubaru (へいつくばる), *vi.* to cringe; prostrate oneself *before*; bow to the ground.

heiwa (平和), *n.* peace. —良心の平和, peace of conscience. —平和保障の防備, peace preparedness. —平和を提議する, to offer peace; hold out the olive-branch. —平和を保持する(破る), to keep (break) the peace. —永遠の平和を確保する, to secure permanent peace. **——-no,** *a.* peaceful; quiet; pacific. —平和的侵入, peaceful penetration. ¶ 平和條約, a treaty of peace. —平和主義, pacifism. —萬國平和會議, an international peace conference.

heiya (平野), *n.* a plain; an open field.

heiyō (併用する), *vt.* to use together [jointly].

heiyu (平癒), *n.* recovery; restoration of health. —平癒する, to be cured *of*; recover *from*; heal. —母の病氣平癒を神に祈る, to pray to God for one's mother's recovery.

heizei (平生), *ad.* usually; ordinarily. —平生通りに, as usual.

heizen (平然たる), *a.* cool; calm; undisturbed. —平然として居る, to remain calm.

heki (癖), *n.* ❶ (片癖) eccentricity; peculiarity. ❷ (習癖) a habit. ❸

(性癖) inclination; propensity. —癖ある, eccentric.

hekichi (僻地), *n.* a retired [an obscure] spot; an out-of-the-way place. —山間の僻地, a retired spot among the mountains.

hekieki (辟易する), *vi.* ❶ (畏縮) to shrink back; flinch; give way. ❷ (喫驚) to be frightened. ❸ (退却) to flee; retreat.

hekiga (壁畫), *n.* a wall-painting; a mural painting; a fresco.

hekigyoku (碧玉), *n.* jasper.

hekiken (僻見), *n.* a prejudice; a bias.

hekireki (霹靂), *n.* ❶ (霹雷) thunder. ❷ (大音) a sudden peal of thunder; a clap. —霹靂一聲, a clap of thunder.

heki-suru (僻する), *vi.* ❶ (心が) to be prejudiced; be biassed. ❷ (土地が) to be secluded. —僻した, ① biassed; partial; prejudiced. ② secluded; out-of-the-way.

hekitō (劈頭に), *ad.* first. —劈頭第一に, the first and foremost; to start [begin] with.

hekomasu (凹ます), *v.* ❶ (窪ます) to depress; dent; hollow. ❷ (閉口させる) to put down; squelch; take the conceit out of a person. —相手を凹ます, to crush [put down] one's opponent.

hekomu (凹む), *vi.* ❶ (くぼむ) to give way; sink; collapse. ❷ (閉口) to come down; yield; be humiliated (凹まさる). ❸ (缺損) to lose.

hekoobi (兵兒帶), *n.* an unlined sash.

hekotareru (へこたれる), *vi.* ❶ to shrink; flinch; show the white feather. ❷ to be entirely exhausted; be dead tired; collapse.

hema (へま), *n.* ❶ (氣がきかない) stupidity; awkwardness. ❷ (へた) a blunder; a bungle. —へまに行く, to go wrong [amiss]; go contrary to one's wishes. —へまをやる, to bungle; make a mess of it; blunder. —貴樣はへまな奴だ, What a bungler you are!

hemeguru (經廻る), *vt.* to travel about; travel *through*; traverse.

hemogurobin (血色素), *n.* hemoglobin.

hen (篇), *n.* ❶ (卷) a book; a volume; a part. ❷ (書中の分類) a section. ❸ (詩の) a canto. —第一篇, Book I; the first volume. —一篇の詩, a piece of poetry; a poem.

hen (遍), *n.* a time. —何遍も何遍も, again and again; repeatedly.

hen (邊), *n.* ❶ (角(ｶｸ)の) a side. ❷ (*a*) (方面) parts; quarters: (*b*) (附近) neighbourhood; vicinity.

hen (變), *n.* ❶ (變化) change; transition. ❷ (變災) a calamity; a disaster; a terrible accident. ❸ (小出來事) an incident; an event. ❹【音】flat. ❺ (緩急) an emergency. —萬一の變に備へる, to provide against emergencies.

henachoko (へなちょこの), *a.* poor.

henatsu (變壓する), *vt.*【電】to transform. ¶ 變壓所, a transformer sub-station. —變壓機, a transformer; a converter. —變壓塔, a transforming tower.

henbutsu (偏物, 變物), *n.* ❶ (偏屈家) a bigot; an obstinate person. ❷ (奇人) an eccentric; an oddity.

henchikirin (變痴奇林な), *a.* queer; odd; curious.

henchō (偏重する), *vt.* to give [attach] too much importance *to.* —事實を偏重する, to lean upon facts.

henchō (變調), *n.* a changed [an altered] tone; irregularity. —財界の變調を來す, to change the tone of the financial world.

henden (返電), *n.* a reply telegram.

hendō (變動), *n.* changes; fluctuation. —著しい變動, marked fluctuations. —變動する, to change; shift; alter. —變動のない, firm (價格·貨物等の); unchanged; unaltered. —政治 (社會) 的大變動, a political (social) cataclysm.

hengaku (扁額), *n.* a tablet.

henge (變化), *n.* a spectre; a phantom; an apparition.

hengen (片言), *n.* ❶ (隻語) a word; a few words. ❷ (片口) a one-sided [an *ex-parte*] statement.

hengen (片舷), *n.* a broadside. —片舷齊發を行ふ, to fire a broadside.

hengen (變幻), *n.* transformation; appearance and disappearance; appearances and transformations. —變幻極まりなき, phantasmagoric.

heni (變異), *n.* ❶ (怪異) a wonder; a prodigy; a marvel. ❷ (天變地異) a catastrophe; a natural calamity.

henji (返事), *n.* a reply; an answer. —返事する, to answer; reply. —の返事に, in answer *to.* —返事として, for answer. —澁々の (快い; 曖昧の; 色よい) 返事, a reluctant (willing; vague; favourable) answer. —返事をやる (認む), to return (write) an answer. —二つ返事で承知する, to give a ready consent.

henji (變事), *n.* a mishap; an accident; a disaster.

henji (片時), *n.* a moment. —

片時も早く, as quickly [soon] as possible.

henjin (偏人,變人), *n.* an eccentric; an original.

henka (變化), *n.* ❶ (かはり) change; mutation; variation. ❷【生物】transformation (變態). ❸ (多樣) variety; diversity. ❹ (變更) modification; alteration; change. ❺ (變遷) change; transition. ❻【文】declension (名詞等の); conjugation (動詞の); inflection (名詞·動詞の). —變化に富む, to be full of variety. —變化のない文章, a monotonous composition. **——-suru,** *vi.* to change; alter; vary; change *into*; turn *into*; transform itself *into*. **——,** *vi.* to change; vary; transform *into*; decline; conjugate. —變化し易い, changeable.

henkaku (變革), *n.* a change; a reform; a revolution.

henkan (返還する), *vt.* to return; restore; retrocede (領土を).

henkan (變換), *n.* change; diversion (水路等の). **——-suru,** *vt.* to change; convert. —方向を變換する, to change front; change the direction *of*.

henkei (變形), *n.* transformation; metamorphosis; variation. —變形する, ① [*vt.*] to transform; change; metamorphose (*to*; *into*). ② [*vi.*] to be transformed [metamorphosed]; change.

henken (偏見), *n.* a biassed [prejudiced] view; prejudice. —偏見のない, impartial; unbiassed; unprejudiced. —偏見を懷く, to harbour prejudice. —偏見を去る, to get rid of [remove] prejudice.

henkin (返金する), *v.* to repay the money; refund the money.

henkō (變更), *n.* change; alteration; amendment (修正). **——-suru,** *vt.* to change; alter; amend; modify. —役割を變更する, to alter the cast. —住所(名前)を變更する, to change one's address (name).

henkutsu (偏屈な), *a.* eccentric; narrow-minded; cross-grained.

henkyaku (返却する), *vt.* to return; repay.

henkyō (偏狹な), *a.* narrow-minded; parochial; provincial.

henmei (變名), *n.* ❶ (異名) an assumed name; a fictitious name; an alias. ❷ (匿名) incognito.

henmu (片務的), *a.*【法】unilateral; one-sided (條約等). ¶ 片務契約, a unilateral contract.

hen-na (變な), *a.* ❶ (異常) unusual. ❷ (怪しい) suspicious; strange. ❸ (奇妙) queer; strange; odd. ❹ (をかしい) funny; droll; ludicrous. —變な(出來)事, a strange event. —變な氣持がする, to feel queer. —變な處で遇ふ, to meet in a strange place. —變な顏をする, to make a queer face. —君は變な事を言ふね, What a strange thing you say! —何だか變な臭ひがする, There is a queer smell about it. —變に暖かい, It is unpleasantly warm.

hennō (片腦), *n.* refined camphor. ¶ 片腦丁幾, tincture of camphor. —片腦油, camphor-oil.

hennō (返納する), *vt.* to return; restore.

hennyū (編入する), *vt.* to admit [put] *into* (學級などに); enroll; incorporate *into*. —第四年級に編入せらる, to be admitted into the fourth year grade. —豫備役に編入する, to transfer to the reserve. —騎兵に編入する, to assign to the cavalry.

henpa (偏頗), *n.* partiality; unfairness; favouritism. **——-no,** *a.* partial; unfair; one-sided. —偏頗の處置, a one-sided measure.

henpei (扁平な), *a.* flat.

henpeki (偏癖), *n.* eccentricity; crankiness; crotchetiness.

henpen (片片と), *ad.* in pieces (きれぎれに); in flakes (一ひらづつに).

henpen (翩翩), *ad.* & *a.* fluttering. —日章旗が翩々と翻る, The sun-flag is fluttering.

henpi (邊鄙な), *a.* out-of-the-way; remote; retired.

henpō (返報), *n.* ❶ (返事) a reply; an answer. ❷ (報復) retaliation; revenge; requital.

henpu (返付する), *vt.* to return.

henpuku (邊幅), *n.* ❶ (緣邊) an edge; a margin. ❷ (外見) outward appearance; get-up. —邊幅を飾る, to adorn the outside.

henran (變亂), *n.* a disturbance; a disorder; a rising. —變亂を釀す, to lead to a disturbance.

henrei (返戾する), *vt.* to return.

henrei (返禮), *n.* ❶ (贈物) a return present. ❷ (答禮) a return call. ❸ (報償) recompense; requital. —返禮に, in acknowledgment of a present.

henreki (遍歷), *n.* travel; tour. —諸國を遍歷する, to travel through many countries.

henro (遍路), *n.* pilgrimage; a pilgrim (人). ☞ *junrei.*

hensa (偏差), *n.*【天】variation.

hensai (返濟), *n.* repayment; refundment. —返濟する, to pay (back); repay; refund. ¶ 返濟期限, the period of repayment. (返濟期限となる, to fall in (負債など); mature.)

hensai (變災), *n.* an accident; a disaster; a calamity.

hensan (編纂), *n.* compilation; editing. —編纂する, to compile; edit. ¶ 國史編纂係, a national history compilation committee.

hensei (編成する), *vt.* to organize; form; compose. 一陸戰隊を編成する, to form a naval brigade. —豫算を編成する, to draw up an estimate; frame a budget.

hensei (編制), *n.* formation; organization. ¶ 平(戰)時編制, peace (war) organization [footing]. —艦隊編制, organization of squadrons.

hensei (變性する), *vt.* to metamorphose; denaturalize; denature. **—**, *vi.* to degenerate.

hensen (變遷), *n.* change; transition (過渡); vicissitudes (浮沈). —人生の變遷, the vicissitude of life. —變遷する, to change; shift.

hensetsu (變節する), *vi.* to apostatize; backslide; turn one's coat. ¶ 變節漢, a backslider; a renegade; a turn-coat.

hensetsu (變說する), *vi* to change one's opinion; recant; veer round in opinion.

hensha (編者), *n.* an editor; a compiler.

henshi (變死), *n.* an unnatural death. —變死を屆出る, to report a violent death.

henshin (返信), *n.* a reply; an answer. ¶ 返信料, a reply charge; return postage.

henshin (變心), *n.* change of mind; inconstancy; backsliding. —變心する, to change [alter] one's mind; backslide.

henshitsu (變質する), *vi.* to metamorphose; transmute; degenerate.

henshoku (變色する), *vi.* to change (colour); become discoloured; discolour. —變色さす, to discolour.

henshu (變種), *n.* 【生物】a variety; a variation. —ダリアの變種, a variety of the dahlia.

henshu (騙取する), *vt.* to swindle. defraud. —人から金を騙取する, to cheat a person out of his money.

henshū (編輯), *n.* compilation; editing. —編輯する, to compile; edit. ¶ 編輯局, the compilation [editorial] bureau. —編輯人, a compiler; an editor.

hensō (返送する), *vt.* to return; send back.

hensō (變裝する), *vi.* to disguise oneself; masquerade. —男に變裝した女, a woman disguised [masquerading] as a man; a woman in a man's garb.

hensoku (變則), *n.* irregularity; anomaly. —變則の英語, ① English studied in an irregular style. ② broken English. —變則の敎育, irregular education.

hen-suru (貶する), *vt.* ❶ (おとす) to reduce *to.* ❷ (けなす, くさす) to belittle; cry down; bring into contempt.

hen-suru (偏する), *vi.* to lean *to* [*toward*]; incline *to* [*toward*].

hentai (變態, 變體), *n.* ❶【生物】metamorphosis. ❷ (違例) anomalous state of things. ¶ 變態心理, abnormal mentality. (變態心理學, abnormal psychology.)

henteko (變挺な), *a.* queer; odd; rummy; rum.

henten (變轉), *n.* change; transition; mutation. —變轉する, to change; pass *from...to.*

hentō (返答), *n.* a reply; an answer. ☞ *henji* (返事). —返答する, to reply; answer. —返答に窮する, to be hard up [at a loss] for an answer.

hentō (扁豆), *n.* 【植】the lentil.

hentōsen (扁桃腺), *n.* 【解】the tonsil. ¶ 扁桃腺炎, tonsillitis.

hentōtsū (偏頭痛), *n.* 【醫】megrim; migraine.

hentsū (變通), *n.* adaptation to circumstances; opportunism. —變通自在の, nimble in adaptation.

henzō (變造), *n.* alteration; defacement (外部變造); debasement (實質變造). **—-suru,** *vt.* ot alter; deface; debase. —貨幣を變造する, to deface a coin. ¶ 變造小切手, an altered cheque.

hen-zuru (變する), *vt.* to change (*into*); alter; transmute *into* (形狀·性質等を). **—**, *vi.* to change (*into*); alter; turn *into.* —變じ易い, changeable; mutable. —變すべからざる, unchangeable; inalterable. —性質を變ずる, to change one's character [nature]. —顏色を變ずる, to change one's countenance; change colour.

hera (篦), *n.* a spatula.

herasagi (篦鷺), *n.* 【鳥】the spoonbill.

herasu (減らす), *vt.* to decrease; reduce; lessen. ☞ *gen-zuru.*

herazuguchi (へらず口を叩く), *v.* to talk impudently.

heri (減), *n.* ❶ (減少, 減少高) decrease; decrement. ❷ (減損) wear. ❸ (損失) loss.

heri (緣), *n.* an edge (涯·本等の); a brim (盃等の); a border (疊などの); a rim (帽子·眼鏡·花壇等の). —疊の緣, the border of a mat. —緣をつける, to border.

herikazari (緣飾), *n.* a fringe

a purl; an edging. —縁飾りある, fringy.

herikudaru (謙る), *vi.* to humble [humiliate] oneself. —人に謙る, to humble oneself before another.

herikutsu (屁理窟), *n.* a cavil; a quibble. —屁理窟を捏ねる, to chop logic; indulge in hair-splitting argument. ¶ 屁理窟家, a caviller; a quibbler; a chop-logic.

herinui (縁縫), *n.* enlacement.

heritoru (縁とる), *vt.* to face (著物を); border; fringe; rim. —縁取りの花, a fringed flower.

heru (減る), *vi.* ❶ (減少) to diminish; dwindle; fall off (得意先等). ❷ (減磨) to wear out. ☞ *gen-zuru* (減ずる).

heru (經る), *v.* ❶ (經過) to pass; elapse. ❷ (通過) to go through; pass through. ❸ (經驗) to see; experience. —一年を經て, after a year. —西伯利亞を經て, *via* [by way of] Siberia. —批准を經ざるべからず, It is subject to ratification.

herumetto (兜帽), *n.* a helmet.

herunia (歇爾尼亞), *n.* 【醫】 hernia.

hesaki (舳), *n.* the bow; the prow.

heso (臍), *n.* 【解】 the navel; a thole (-pin) (櫓·橈などの).

hesokuri (臍繰-金), *n.* secret savings; hoard.

hesonoo (臍緒), *n.* 【解】 the navel-string. —臍の緒切ッて以來, in (all) one's born days.

heta (蔕), *n.* ❶ the stem. ❷ (䕯) operculum (貝の).

heta (下手), *n.* unskilfulness; awkwardness. **——-na**, *a.* unskilful; awkward; bungling. —下手な繪, a poor picture. —下手な英語で話す, to speak in poor English.

hetabaru (へたばる), *vi.* ❶ to fall flat; fall prostrate. ❷ (疲勞) to drop with fatigue; be dead tired. ❸ (屈服) to give in; yield.

hetoheto (へとへとになる), *vi* to be knocked up; be dead tired; be fagged out.

hetsurai (諂), *n.* flattery; toad-eating.

hetsurau (諂ふ), *v.* to fawn *upon*; cringe *to*; truckle *to*. —目上の人に諂ふ, to curry favour with one's superiors.

hetto (ヘット), *n.* fat.

heya (部屋), *n.* a room; an apartment.

hi (日), *n.* the sun (太陽); a day (暦日); date (日附). —日に日に, every day. —日に燒けた顏, a sunburnt face. —日の暮れぬ中に, before dark; before sunset. —日が出[上] (入[沒す])る, The sun rises (sets; goes down; sinks). —日が延びる, The days lengthen. —日がつまる, The days shorten [grow short; draw in]. —日を定める[選ぶ], to fix a day. —日を避ける, to shade against the sun. —無事に日を送る, to spend [pass] one's days in peace.

hi (火), *n.* ❶ fire (火); flame (火焰). ❷ (火災) a fire. ❸ (燈) a light. —火が附く, to catch [take] fire. —火に炙(ア)る, to expose to a fire. —火にかける, to put over the fire. —火に燒けない[耐へる], to be proof against fire. —火を起す[焚く], to make a fire. —火を煽る(吹く), to fan (blow) fire. —火を附ける, ① (放火) to set on fire; set fire *to*. ② (點燈) to light a lamp. ③ to light a cigarette (pipe). —火を失する[出す], to cause a fire; catch fire. —火をいける, to bank up a fire; damp a fire. —火を掻き出す, to rake out the fire.

hi (比), *n.* ❶ (比類) an equal; a peer. ❷ (比較) comparison. ❸ 【數】(割合) ratio; rate (步合). —米國の富は日本の比にあらず, With America's wealth that of Japan is not to be compared.

hi (妃), *n.* a princess (consort). ☞ *hidenka* (妃殿下).

hi (否), *n.* ❶ (可からぬこと) badness; wrong. ❷ (反對) opposition. ☞ *kahi* (可否), *sanpi* (贊否).

hi (非), *n.* ❶ (惡) wrong; badness. ❷ (過失, 罪惡) an error; a misdeed. ❸ (缺點) a defect. ☞ *hito-suru* (非とする). —日に非なり, It is becoming daily worse. —非を鳴らす, to exclaim [cry] *against*. —非を遂げる, to carry through a misdeed. —非を非とし是を是とする, to make a clear distinction between right and wrong.

hi (脾), *n.* 【解】 the spleen.

hi (碑), *n.* ❶ (墓碑) a tombstone; a gravestone. ❷ (記念碑) a monument. —碑を建てる, to raise a tombstone (monument) *to*.

hi (梭), *n.* a shuttle.

hi (緋), *n.* scarlet. —緋の衣, a scarlet robe.

hi (樋), *n.* ❶ (とひ) a water-pipe; a trough. ❷ (水門) a sluice; a flood-gate.

hiaburi (火刑), *n.* the stake; burning at the stake.

hiagaru (干上る), *vi.* ❶ (乾き切る) to dry up; parch. ❷ (食ふことが出來なくなる) to starve.

hiai (悲哀), *n.* sorrow; grief. —人生の悲哀, the sorrows of life. —悲哀の中に日を送る, to pass one's days in sorrow.

hiatari (日當りよき), *a.* sunny. —日當りの側, the sunny side.

hiba(檜葉), *n.* 【植】❶ =*asunaro* (羅漢柏). ❷ (檜屬の總稱) the swamp-cypress. ❸ (檜の葉) a swamp-cypress leaf.

hibachi (火鉢), *n.* a brazier. ¶ 箱 (長) 火鉢, a fire box (an oblong brazier).

hibai-dōmei (非賣(非買)同盟), *n.* a boycott.

hibaihin (非賣品), *n.* an article not for sale; "not for sale." (札書).

hiban (非番), *n.* off-duty; off-guard. ¶ 非番巡査, an off-duty policeman.

hibana (火花), *n.* a spark. —火花を發する, ① [*vi.*] to scintillate; spark. ② [*a.*] sparkling; scintillant. —火花を散らす, to make sparks fly.

hibara (脾腹), *n.* the sides.

hibari (雲雀), *n.* 【鳥】the lark; the skylark.

hibashi (火箸), *n.* tongs; the blacksmith's-tongs (鍛冶屋の).

hibi (ひび), *n.* ❶ (皸) a chap. ❷ (龜裂) a crack; a rift. —皸が切れる, to be chapped.

hibi (日日), *ad.* daily; day by day; day after day; from day to day; every day. —日々の事, a daily occurrence; an everyday affair. —日々に暑さがつのる, It becomes hotter every day.

hibiki (響), *n.* ❶ (音響) a sound; a noise; a report (砲などの). ❷ (反響, 餘韻) an echo. ❸ (影響) influence; effect. ❹ (振動) vibration.

hibiku (響く), *v.* ❶ (反響) to resound; echo; ring. ❷ (影響) to influence; affect. ❸ (振動) to vibrate. ❹ (發音) to sound. —耳に響く, to fall on one's ear. —名聲全國に響き渡る, His fame rings throughout the country.

hibiware (龜裂), *n.* a crack.

hibiyaki (罅燒), *n.* crackle; crack-ware.

hibō (非望), *n.* inordinate ambition. —非望を懷く, to harbour inordinate ambition.

hibō (誹謗), *n.* abuse; calumny; defamation. —誹謗する, to abuse; calumniate; traduce.

hiboku (婢僕), *n.* domestics; servants; menials.

hibon (非凡の), *a.* extraordinary; uncommon.

hiboshi (干乾), *n.* starvation. —干乾になる(する), to starve.

hiboshi (日干にする), *vt.* to dry in the sun. —日干にした, sun-dried.

hibu (日歩), *n.* daily (rate of) interest. —日歩の金, money loaned at daily interest. —日歩を拂ふ, to pay daily interest.

hibukure (火脹), *n.* a blister (caused by fire). —火脹れになる, to blister.

hibun (碑文), *n.* an epitaph; an inscription.

hibunmei (非文明な), *a.* ❶ uncivilized. ❷ (粗野) rude; impolite.

hibusshitsu (非物質的), *a.* immaterial.

hibuta (火蓋), *n.* the apron (of a gun). —火蓋を切る, ① to open fire. ② (開始) to prepare the way; open a way; break the ice.

hibyōin (避病院), *n.* an isolation-hospital; an infectious diseases hospital.

hichiriki (篳篥), *n.* a flageolet.

hichisha (被治者), *n.* the governed; the ruled.

hichō (飛鳥), *n.* a flying bird; a flyer; a bird on the wing. —飛鳥の如く, quick as lightning.

hida (襞), *n.* a plait; gathers (著物の); a pucker. —襞を取る, to gather in; fold; plait; pucker.

hidachi (肥立), *n.* health (after delivery); convalescence (恢復); growth.

hidai (肥大の), *a.* stout; corpulent.

hidara (干鱈), *n.* a dried cod.

hidari (左), *n.* left. —左向け左, (號令) left turn! —左前に著る, to wear a dress the left side under the right [the wrong way].

hidarigawa (左側), *n.* the left side. —左側を通行すべし, "Keep to the left."

hidarigiki (左利の), *a.* left-handed.

hidasso (脾脫疽), *n.* 【醫】anthrax.

hidatsu (肥立つ), *vi.* to grow (daily) better (快方に向ふ); grow up (day by day) (發育).

hiden (祕傳), *n.* a mystery; a traditional secret. —祕傳の妙薬, a secret medicine of great virtue. —祕傳を敎へる, to impart the mystery.

hidenka (妃殿下), *n.* Her Imperial [Royal] Highness.

hideri (旱), *n.* drought; (continued) dry weather. —旱續き, continuous drought; continued dry weather.

hidō (非道), *n.* ❶ (非理) injustice. ❷ (殘忍) cruelty; inhumanity. —非道な, unjust; cruel; inhuman; merciless.

hidoi (ひどい), *a.* ❶ cruel; harsh (待遇, 評など); severe (評など). ❷ (*a*) (烈しい) severe; intense; sharp: (*b*) (恐しい) terrible [俗]; frightful: (*c*) (法外の) exorbitant: (*d*) (重大) gross (誤など); serious (病氣・誤など). —ひどい風, a strong wind. —ひどい寒さ, a severe cold. —ひどい雨, a heavy rain. —ひどい目に逢ふ, to meet with a terrible experience.

hidokei (日時計), *n.* a sun-dial; a dial.

hidoku (ひどく), *ad.* ❶ severely; violently; badly. ❷ excessively; extremely; frightfully; terribly; awfully. ☞ *hijō* (非常に). —ひどく欲しがる, to set one's heart *upon*. —酷く叱られる, to be severely scolded.

hidori (日取), *n.* the date. —日取を定める, to settle the date [day].

hidōtoku (非道徳的), *a.* non--moral; a-moral.

hie (稗), *n.* 【植】 the barn-yard grass.

hiekikan (非役艦), *n.* a vessel out of commission.

hieki (裨益), *n.* benefit; profit. —裨益する, ①[*vt.*] to benefit. ②[*vi.*] to profit [benefit] *by.*

hieru (冷える), *vi.* to grow [get] cold; chill; cool. —冷え切ッた, stone-cold.

hieshō (冷性), *n.* a chilly constitution.

hifu (皮膚), *n.* 【解】 the cutis: the skin. ¶ 皮膚病, a cutaneous [skin] disease.

hifu (被布), *n.* a gown.

hifukidake (火吹竹), *n.* a bamboo blower.

hifuku (被服), *n.* clothing; drapery. —軍隊に被服を給する, to clothe the army. ¶ 被服廠, the clothing department.

hifuku (被覆), *n.* a cover; a mantle. ¶ 被覆線, covered wire.

hifun (悲憤), *n.* indignation; resentment. —悲憤する, to be indignant; one's blood boils; resent [*vt.*]. —悲憤に耐へない, to burst with indignation.

higa (彼我), *n.* self and others; he and I; they and we. —彼我の便を計る, to promote the convenience of all parties.

higaeri (日歸する), *vi.* to go and return in one day [on the same day].

higai (被害), *n.* injury; damage. ¶ 被害地, a damaged district. —被害者, the injured party; a victim; a sufferer.

higake (日掛), *n.* a daily payment [instalment]. ¶ 日掛貯金, daily savings.

higame (僻目), *n.* ❶ (見誤り) an error of sight; a prejudice (偏見). ❷ squint.

higami (僻), *n.* prejudice; warp (心の). —僻みを出す, to show prejudice. ¶ 僻み根性, a warped spirit.

higan (彼岸), *n.* ❶ yonder shore. ❷ (春秋分) the equinoctial week. —彼岸の入り, the beginning of the equinoctial week. —彼岸の中日, the equinoctial day. ¶ 彼岸櫻, 【植】 the early-flowering cherry-tree.

higanakin (緋金巾), *n.* Turkey--red cambric.

higara (日柄), *n.* ❶ (日の吉凶) the kind of day (whether lucky or unlucky). ❷ =*hikazu.* —日柄を擇ぶ, to choose a lucky day.

higarame (僻目, 眇), *n.* squint.

higasa (日傘), *n.* a parasol (婦人用の); a sunshade.

higashi (東), *n.* east. —東の, east; easterly; eastern. —東へ, east; eastward. —東に, in the east (東部に); on the east (東側に); (to the) east (東に當ッて). —東に向ッて進行する, to proceed towards the east. ¶ 東風, an east [easterly] wind.

higashi (干菓子), *n.* dry confectionery.

higata (干潟), *n.* a beach.

hige (鬚), *n.* ❶ (總稱) a beard. ❷ 〔鬚〕(頤ひげ) a beard. ❸ 〔髭〕(上ひげ) a mustache, moustache. ❹ 〔髯〕(頰・動物の) whiskers. —鬚なき顏, a smooth [beardless] face. —髭を生やす, to grow [wear] a mustache (beard). —鬚を剃る, to shave one's beard; have one's beard shaved (剃らせる, 剃ッて貰ふ).

hige (卑下する), *vi.* to humble [depreciate] oneself. ☞ *kenson.*

higeki (悲劇), *n.* a tragedy. ¶ 悲劇役者, a tragedian.

higenkōhan (非現行犯), *n.* a non-flagrant offence.

higensū (被減數), *n.* 【數】 a minuend.

higi (非議する), *vt.* to censure; criticize.

higiri (日限), *n.* fixing the day; a fixed date. —日限りの, of a fixed date.

higo (庇護), *n.* protection; patronage; favour. —庇護する, to protect; harbour (罪人等を); patronize. —神の庇護により, by the grace of God.

higo (卑語), *n.* a slang; a vulgarism.

higo (蜚語, 飛語), *n.* a (groundless) rumour. —蜚語紛々たり, to be full of rumours.

higō (非業の), *a.* unnatural; violent. —非業の死を遂げる, to come to a violent end; die an unnatural death.

higoi (緋鯉), *n.* 【魚】 the red carp.

higoro (日頃), *ad.* ❶ (平素) in ordinary times; usually; always. ❷ (近來) of late; lately. ❸ (久しく) for a long time. —日頃の思ひ, a long-cherished wish.

higoto (日毎に), *ad.* everyday; daily; day by day.

higuchi (火口), *n.* ❶ (砲口, 銃口) the muzzle. ❷ (洋燈・機械の) a burner. ❸ 【工】 a fire-door.

higuma (羆), *n.* 【哺乳】 the ground--bear; the brown bear.

higurashi (日暮し), *n.* ❶ (一日

を暮すこと) spending the whole day. ❷【昆】【蜩】Leptopsaltria japonica(學名). ——, *ad.* all (the) day long.

higure (日暮), *n.* nightfall; evening; sunset.

higuruma (向日葵), *n.* 【植】the sunflower. =*himawari.*

higyō (罷業する), *vi.* to go on strike.

hihan (批判), *n.* criticism. —批判する, to criticize.

hihei (疲弊さす), *vt.* to exhaust.

hihi (狒狒), *n.* ❶【哺乳】the baboon. ❷(好色漢) a satyr.

hihō (悲報), *n.* a heavy [sad] news.

hihō (飛報), *n.* an express message.

hihō (秘法), *n.* a secret recipe [method].

hihogosha (被保護者), *n.* a protégé [*fem.* -gée].

hihoken (被保險の), *a.* insured. ¶ 被保險物, an insured property. —被保險人, the (person) insured.

hihoshōnin (被保證人), *n.* ❶ the principal debtor. ❷ a guarantee.

hihyō (批評), *n.* criticism; comment; review. **——-suru,** *vt.* to criticize; comment *upon*; review. —本を批評する, to review a book. ¶ 批評家, a critic; a reviewer; a commentator. —破壞(建設)的批評, destructive (constructive) criticism.

hiibaba (曾祖母), *n.* a great-grandmother.

hiideru (秀でる), *vt.* to surpass; excel. ——, *vi.* to excel *in.* —秀でた, surpassing; preeminent.

hiijiji (曾祖父), *n.* a great-grandfather.

hiiki (贔屓), *n.* ❶(愛顧) patronage; favour. ❷(偏愛) partiality; favouritism; preference. ❸(顧客) a patron(藝人·商店の); a customer (商店の); clientèle (集合名詞). ❹(味方) a friend; a supporter. —贔屓する, ①(愛顧) to favour; be partial *to*; patronize. ②(味方) to side *with*; take the part *of*; support. —贔屓の引倒し, to injure a person by injudicious favour [partiality]. —贔屓を受ける, to be in another's (good) graces enjoy his favour. ¶ 贔屓相撲(役者), a favourite wrestler (actor).

hiimago (曾孫), *n.* a great-grandson (-granddaughter); a great-grandchild.

hiiragi (柊), *n.* 【植】Osmanthus aquifolius (fragrant olive の類·學名).

hiire (火入), *n.* a fire-pan.

hiji (肘, 肱, 臂), *n.* ❶【解】the elbow. ❷(肱狀のもの) an arm. —肘で押す, to elbow; jostle. (肘で押し退ける, to elbow aside.) —肘で衝く, to jog; nudge. —肘を張る, to push out the elbow. —肘を掣[ヒ]く, to pull the arm; hinder; obstruct.

hijideppō (臂鐵砲), *n.* a set-down; the cold shoulder. —臂鐵砲を喰はす, to give [show] the cold shoulder.

hijigane (肘金), *n.* a hook (of a fastening).

hijigi (肘木), *n.* a bracket.

hijikake (臂掛), *n.* an elbow-rest. ¶ 臂掛椅子, an arm-chair; an elbow-chair.

hijiki (鹿尾菜), *n.* 【植】Cystophyllum fusiforme (學名).

hijimakura (肘枕), *n.* making a pillow of the arm; an arm used as a pillow.

hijiri (聖), *n.* ❶(聖人) a sage. ❷(高徳の僧) a saint.

hijitsubo (肘壺), *n.* a staple; an anchor and collar.

hijitsuki (臂突), *n.* a pad; an arm-rest; an elbow cushion.

hijō (非常), *n.* an extraordinary occasion; an emergency; a contingency. —非常の, extraordinary; exceptional; extreme. —非常に, extraordinarily; exceptionally; uncommonly. —非常(の場合)に備へる, to provide against emergencies [contingencies]. —非常線を張る, to post a cordon. —(兵士の)非常召集を行ふ, to make an extraordinary call to colours. ¶ 非常口, an emergency-exit. —非常報知器, an alarm-signal. —非常警報, urgent warning. —非常汽笛, an alarm-whistle. —非常線通行券, a cordon pass. —非常信號, an emergency signal. —非常特別稅, an extraordinary special tax.

hijōkokunin (被上告人), *n.* 【法】an appellee; a respondent.

hijōshiki (非常識), *n.* lack of (common) sense.

hijosū (被除數), *n.* 【數】the dividend.

hijōsū (被乘數), *n.* 【數】the multiplicand.

hijū (比重), *n.* specific gravity. ¶ 比重計, a hydrostatic balance; a hydrometer(液體の); a stereometer.

hijun (比準), *n.* proportion (割合); standard (標準).

hijun (批准), *n.* ratification. 條約を批准する, to ratify a treaty. ¶ 批准交換, the exchange of ratifications.

hijutsu (秘術), *n.* a secret art.

hika (皮下の), *a.* 【醫】hypodermic; subcutaneous. —の皮下注射する, to make a hypodermic injection *of.*

hika (悲歌), *n.* an elegy; a dirge.

hikae (控), *n.* ❶(控制) stay; restraint; abstention. ❷(支柱) a prop; a stay; a shore. ❸(副本) a duplicate; a copy. ❹(手控) a note (手帳); a memorandum; a memo (備忘錄). ❷ (掛換, 豫備) reserve. —控を取る, to make a copy.

hikaechō (控帳), *n.* a memorandum [*pl.* -da]; a memo; a note-book.

hikaegaki (控書), *n.* minutes; notes.

hikaejo (控所), *n.* a waiting-room.

hikaeme (控目の), *a.* moderate; temperate. **—— -ni,** *ad.* moderately; temperately; in moderation. —控目に云ふ, ① to speak within bounds. ② to speak with reserve. —萬事控目にする, to do all things in moderation.

hikaeru (控へる), *vt.* ❶ (引留める) to stop; hold back; restrain. ❷ (持つ) to have; be situated (位置する). ❸ (待つ) to wait. ❹ (書留める) to jot down; note (down); make a note *of*. ❺ (差控へる) to forbear *from*; hold back; refrain *from*. ❻ (節制) to be moderate *in*; be temperate *in*. —次の間に控へる, to wait in the next room. —手綱を控へる, to draw in the reins. —眼前に敵を控へる, to have the enemy before one [in front].

hikaeshitsu (控室), *n.* an anteroom; a lobby (下院等の).

hikagaku (非科學的), *a.* unscientific.

hikagami (膕), *n.* 【解】 the ham.

hikage (日影, 日蔭), *n.* ❶ (日光) sunshine; light. ❷ (日蔭) the shade. ¶ 日蔭者, ① (埋れ人) one who is unable to appear in the world; an outcast. ② (憚り忍ぶ者) a recluse.

hikaki (火耙), *n.* a fire-hook; a poker.

hikaku (比較), *n.* ❶ (くらべ) comparison. ❷ (釣合ひ) balance —比較的, comparative. —比較する, to compare; contrast; set against. —比較級の形容詞, the comparative adjective. —兩者の比較優劣, the relative merits of the two. —比較にならぬ, to be beyond [without; past] comparison [compare]; not to bear comparison; not to be compared with. (比較にならぬ程, out and away; without [out of; beyond all] comparison.) ¶ 比較研究法, the comparative method.

hikaku (皮革), *n.* skins; hides (生皮); leather (革皮). ¶ 皮革商, a leather-shop; a leather-seller; a dealer in hides and leather.

hikaku (皮殼), *n.* a shell; incrustation.

hikan (悲觀), *n.* pessimism. —悲觀的, pessimistic. —物事を悲觀する, to look upon the dark side of things.

hikan (避寒する), *v.* to go to ... during the winter cold. ¶ 避寒所, winter-quarters (個人の); a winter resort (地).

hikarabiru (干乾びる), *vi.* ❶ (乾枯) to dry up; parch. ❷ (生氣なくなる) to shrivel; be wizened. —干乾びた顔, a wizened face.

hikari (光), *n.* ❶ (光明) light. ❷ (光線) a ray; a beam. ❸ (光輝) brightness; shine. ❹ (光澤) lustre; polish. ❺ (閃光) flash. ❻ gleam (暗中刀等の); glimmer (螢などの).

hikarimono (光り物), *n.* a meteor; a shooting star.

hikaru (光る), *vi.* ❶ (輝く) to shine; gleam (暗中に時々); glitter (金銀等がピカピカする); sparkle (星・寶石等がピカピカする). ❷ (閃く) to flash. ❸ (光澤ある) to polish. **——,** *a.* brilliant; bright; refulgent. —光らす, to make glitter; kindle.

hikasareru (惹かされる), *v.* to be drawn *by*. —夫婦の情にひかされる, to be drawn by conjugal affection.

hikasū (被加數), *n.* 【數】 the summand.

hikazu (日數), *n.* ❶ the number of days. ❷ many days.

hike (引), *n.* ❶ (退散) closing. ❷ (減耗) loss. ❸ (負, おくれ) defeat. —十二時引, office closed at twelve. —負を取る, to be beaten [defeated]; give in; yield the palm *to*.

hikeishiki(非形式的), *a.* informal.

hiken (比肩する), *vt.* to keep pace *with*; take rank *with*.

hiken (披見する), *vt.* to open and read; read.

hiken (卑見), *n.* my (humble) view [opinion].

hikeru (引ける), *vi.* ❶ (退出, 退散) to break up. ❷ (氣おくれする) to lose courage; one's heart fails one. ❸ (閉ぢる) to close.

hikeshi(火消), *n.* ❶ extinguishing fire. ❷ (消防夫) a fireman. ¶ 火消壺, a pot for extinguishing live charcoal.

hiketsu (否決), *n.* rejection; negative. —否決する, to reject; throw out; negative.

hiketsu (秘訣), *n.* a secret; a (secret) recipe; a mystery. —成功の秘訣, the secret of success.

hiketsu (秘結), *n.* costiveness; constipation. —秘結する, ① [*vi.*] to be costive. ② [*a.*] (秘結性の) costive.

hiki (匹, 疋), *n.* ❶ (布二反の單位數) a length of cloth (about 25 yards). ❷ [*numeral*] (*a*) (反物) a piece (of clothing): (*b*) (生物) a head (牛馬). —六匹の猫, six cats.

hiki (引), *n.* ❶ (引力) attraction. ❷ (贔屓) influence; help; backing. ❸ (割引) discount. 一定價の一割引, ten per cent. discount on the price. 一いい引がある, to have a good backing.

hiki (誹譏, 誹毀), *n.* 【法】 libel (書面の); slander (口頭の); defamation. 一誹毀する, to libel; slander; defame.

hiki (避忌する), *vt.* to evade. 一徴兵を避忌する, to evade conscription.

hikiage (引上, 引揚), *n.* ❶ (拔擢) promotion. ❷ (値上げ) raising. ❸ (引張りあげる) hoist; pulling up. ❹ (撤退) withdrawal; evacuation. ❺ (海中から浮ばす) reflotation (沈沒船の).

hikiageru (引揚げる), *vt.* ❶ (引張りあげる) to raise; hoist; draw up. ❷ (拔擢) to promote. ❸ (値上げ) to raise. ❹ (撤退) to withdraw; evacuate. ❺ (海中から浮ばす) to refloat. 一賣價を引上げる, to raise the sale-price. 一二錢銅貨を引揚げる, to withdraw two-*sen* copper coins from circulation. 一沈沒船を引揚げる, to raise a sunken ship.

hikiai (引合), *n.* ❶ (參考) reference; comparison. ❷ (連累者, 引合人) a person involved [implicated] in another's affair; a witness (證人); a reference (參考人). ❸ being involved [implicated] in another's affair.

hikiami (曳網), *n.* a seine; a towing-net; a drag-net.

hikiau (引合ふ), *v.* ❶ (交渉) to negotiate *with*; bargain *with*. ❷ (商利ある) to pay.

hikiawase (引合せ), *n.* ❶ (對照) reference; checking. ❷ (紹介) bringing together; introduction. 一校正刷の引合せ, the checking of the proofs.

hikiawasu (引合す), *vt.* ❶ to compare; control; check. ❷ to bring together; introduce. 一兩人を引合せる, to introduce the two persons to each other.

hikicha (碾茶, 挽茶), *n.* powdered tea.

hikidashi (引出), *n.* ❶ (預金等の拂受) drawing. ❷ (抽斗) a drawer.

hikidasu (引出す), *vt.* ❶ to draw (out); pull out; take out. ❷ (預金などを) to draw; get [obtain] *from*. 一銀行から預金を引出す, to draw one's money from a bank.

hikido (引戸), *n.* a slide-door; a sliding-door.

hikifuda (引札), *n.* a handbill; a circular.

hikifune (曳船), *n.* ❶ (曳く船) a tugboat; a tug; a tow-boat. ❷ (曳かれる船) a tow-boat. ❸ (曳くこと) tow; towing.

hikigaeru (蟇蛙), *n.* 【兩棲】 the toad.

hikigane (引金), *n.* a trigger (鐵砲の); a spring.

hikigeki (悲喜劇), *n.* a tragi-comedy.

hikigoto (引事), *n.* ❶ (引例) an instance; an example; an allusion (引喩). ❷ (引證) an illustration; a quotation; a reference.

hikihagasu (引剝がす), *vt.* to strip off; strip; pull off; tear off; rip off; uncover (蓋物を).

hikihanasu (引離す), *vt.* to pull apart [asunder]; part; separate.

hikiharai (引拂ひ), *n.* vacation; clearing out; withdrawal.

hikiharau (引拂ふ), *vt.* ❶ (立退く) to clear out; vacate; quit. ❷ (取拂ふ) to clear away. 一家を引拂ふ, to vacate a house.

hikihazusu (引外す), *vt.* ❶ to pull out of place; take down; unfasten. ❷ to throw off.

hikiireru (引入れる), *vt.* ❶ (挽込) to draw [drag] into; pull in. ❷ to win [gain] over *to*; bring over [round]; entice in. ❸ (つれこむ) to bring in. 一味方に引入れる, to bring a person over to one's side.

hikiiru (率·將·帥ゐる), *vt.* to lead; head. 一を率ゐて, at the head *of*.

hikikae (引換), *n.* exchange; conversion (兌換). 一引換に, in exchange *for*. ¶ 引換拂, payment on delivery; cash on delivery (C. O. D. と略す). 一引換準備金, a reserve for exchange. 一引換證, a tally.

hikikaeru (引換へる), *vt.* to exchange; convert. 一…に引換へて, on the contrary; on the other hand. 一小切手を正金に引換へる, to cash a cheque.

hikikaesu (引返す), *vi.* ❶ (元へ) to come back; retrace one's steps. ❷ (再發) to have a relapse. 一途中から引返す, to turn back [retrace one's steps] on the way.

hikiko (曳子), *n.* a drawer; a puller.

hikikomisen (引込線), *n.* 【電】 a service-wire.

hikikomoru (引籠る), *vi.* ❶ (外出せぬ) to keep one's [the] house; keep indoors [at home]. ❷ (病で) to be confined to one's bed.

hikikorosu (轢殺す), *vt.* to kill by running over. 一轢き殺される, to be run over and killed.

hikikurumeru (引括める), *vt.* to bring [put] together; make into a bundle; include (包括); summarize (總括); generalize (概括).

—引括めて言へば, in short; to put in a few words; to sum up.

hikimado (引窓), *n.* a skylight (with a sliding shutter); a trap-door.

hikimaku (引幕), *n.* a drawing curtain.

hikimatomeru (引纏める), *vt.* to bring together. —家財を引纏める, to bring together household goods.

hikimawasu (引廻す), *vt.* ❶ (連れ廻す) to lead about. ❷ (幕など) to draw around.

hikimodosu (引戻す), *v.* ❶ = ***hikikaesu.*** ❷ (連れ戻る) to bring back. ❸ (還元する) to reduce; restore. ☞ ***hikinaosu.*** ❹【商】 to react; improve. —舊制に引戻す, to restore to the old system.

hikimono (挽物), *n.* turnery; turned articles. ¶ 挽物工場, a turnery; a turning-shop. —挽物師, a turner.

hikin (卑近の), *a.* superficial; simple; familiar.

hikinobashi (引延し), *n.* ❶ (引いて延ばすこと) drawing out. ❷ (布衍) expressing more fully; expansion. ❸【寫】(擴大) enlargement. ¶ 引伸寫眞, an enlarged photograph.

hikinobasu (引延す), *vt.* ❶ (引いて延ばす) to draw out; stretch; extend (延長). ❷ (布衍する) to express more fully; expand; spin out. ❸ (擴大) to enlarge. ❹ (延引) to postpone; put off; defer. —文章を引延ばす, to expand a composition.

hikinokori (引殘), *n.* a remainder; balance.

hikinuku (引拔く), *vt.* ❶ (拔き取る) to pull [draw] out; extract. ❷ (選拔) to select; pick out.

hikinzoku (非金屬), *n.* 【化】 a non-metal; a metalloid.

hikinzoku (卑金屬), *n.* base metals.

hikiokosu (引起す), *vt.* ❶ (倒れたのを起たす) to raise up; pull up. ❷ (惹起) to lead *to*; give rise *to*; bring on. ❸ (復興) to revive; resuscitate. —不平を惹き起す, to give rise to discontent.

hikiorosu (引卸す), *vt.* to drag [pull] down (旗などを). —坐礁船を引卸す, to tow off a stranded ship.

hikirisutokyō (非基督敎の), *a.* anti-Christian (反對の); non-Christian.

hikisagaru (退下がる), *vi.* to retire; withdraw. —御前を引下がる, to retire [withdraw] from the presence *of*.

hikisageru (引下げる), *vt.* to lower; bring down; reduce (位・値等を). —十錢方引下げる, to bring down about ten *sen*.

hikisaku (引裂く), *vt.* to tear up; tear to [in] pieces; pull to [in] pieces. —手紙を引裂く, to tear up the letter.

hikisaru (引去る), *v.* ❶ (退去) to retire; withdraw. ❷ (控除) to deduct; subtract. —水が引去る, The water subsides. —所得金から一割を引去る, to deduct ten per cent. from the income.

hikishiboru (引絞る), *vt.* to draw aside and fasten (幕など); strain (聲を). —弓を引絞る, to draw the bow to the full. —聲を引絞ッて, at the top of one's voice; at the highest pitch (of one's voice).

hikishimeru (引締める), *vt.* to strain; tighten; brace. —引締ッた顏, a firmly-set face. —引締りの市況, a firm [stiff] market. —心を引締める, to brace up one's spirits; brace oneself; strain one's nerves.

hikishio (退潮), *n.* an ebb; an ebb-tide.

hikitaosu (引倒す), *vt.* to pull down.

hikitate (引立), *n.* ❶ (眷顧) patronage; favour. ❷ (推薦) recommendation. ❸ (奬勵) encouragement. —偏に御引立を願ふ, We sincerely entreat your patronage.

hikitateru (引立てる), *vt.* ❶ (眷顧) to patronize; favour. ❷ (推薦) to recommend. ❸ (奬勵) to encourage. ❹ (作興) to keep up (氣を). ❺ (强制的に連れ行く) to drag off; march off. —後進の士を引立てる, to encourage one's juniors.

hikitatsu (引立つ), *vi.* ❶ (目立つ) to look well; improve. ❷ (人氣・市況が活氣づく) to become active; become flourishing. —額で繪が引立つ, The frame sets off the picture.

hikite (彈手), *n.* a player; a performer.

hikitomeru (引留める), *vt.* ❶ (留置) to detain; take by the button. ❷ (阻止) to keep back; check; pull up. —客を引留める, to detain a guest. —袖にすがッて引留める, to catch another by the sleeve.

hikitorinin (引取人), *n.* one who receives [takes over]; a claimer; a claimant.

hikitoru (引取る), *vt.* ❶ (取戻す) to take back. ❷ (受取る) to receive; claim. ❸ (引下る) to withdraw; retire. ❹ (引受く) to take over. —子供を引取ッて育てる, to take over the child and bring it up.

hikitsugi (引繼), *n.* ❶ (繼承) succession. ❷ (受授) transfer; taking over (受ける).

hikitsugu (引繼ぐ), *vt.* ❶ (繼承) to succeed *to.* ❷ (受授) to take over (受ける). —事務を引繼ぐ, to take over the business.

hikitsukeru (引附ける), *v.* ❶ (引寄せる)【理】to attract; draw; draw *to* [*towards*]. ❷ (魅する) to charm; fascinate; attract. ❸ (痙攣する) to have a convulsive fit; be convulsed. —人を惹きつける, [*a.*] charming; winning; fascinating; attractive. (人を惹きつける魅力, the power of fascinating people.)

hikitsureru (引連れる), *vt.* to take with one.

hikitsuri (引釣), *n.* ❶ (痙攣)【醫】spasm (筋の); twitch; cramp. ❷ (火傷等で生ずる痕) a seam; a scar; a cicatrice.

hikitsuru (引釣る), *vi.* ❶ (緊張) to strain; tighten. ❷ (痙攣) to twitch; be cramped; have a cramp [spasm].

hikitsuzuite (引續いて), *ad.* continually; successively; in succession. —三日間引續いて, for three days running. —當日以後引續いて, from that day on.

hikitsuzuku (引續く), *vi.* to continue. ——, *a.* continual; serial; successive. —引續く災害, a succession [series] of disasters.

hikiuke (引受), *n.* ❶ (受諾) acceptance (爲替手形の). ❷ (保證) guaranty; security. ❸ (擔任) undertaking; assumption; charge. ❹ (後援) espousal. —(爲替手形を)呈示して引受を求める, to present (a bill) for acceptance. ¶ 引受人, an acceptor (爲替手形の).

hikiukeru (引受ける), *vt.* ❶ (受諾) to accept (爲替手形の); honour (同上). ❷ (保證) to guarantee; be responsible *for*; answer *for*. ❸ (擔任) to assume; take in hand; undertake. ❹ (遺傳) to inherit. ❺ (傳染) to catch. —仕事を引受ける, to take on work; undertake a work. —責を引受ける, to assume responsibility *for*; undertake to answer *for*. —店を引受ける (讓受), to take over a business [shop].

hikiusu (碾臼), *n.* a quern (穀粒を碎く); a stone handmill.

hikiutsushi (引寫する), *vt.* to trace.

hikiwake (引分), *n.* a draw; a drawn game [match]. —引分ける, to part; pull [draw] apart. —引分けになる, to end in a draw.

hikiwari (ひきわり), *n.* ❶ (碾割麥) barley meal. ❷ (鋸での) sawing.

hikiwaru (ひきわる), *vt.* ❶ to grind (臼で). ❷ to saw (鋸で).

hikiwatashi (引渡し), *n.* delivery; transfer; surrender. ¶ 引渡日, the day of delivery [transfer]. —引渡人, a transferrer, transferor; a deliverer. —引渡猶豫金,【株式】backwardation. —引渡濟, delivered; transferred.

hikiwatasu (引渡す), *vt.* to transfer; hand over; extradite (逃亡犯人を他國に). —警官に引渡す, to deliver [hand] over to the police; give in charge to the police.

hikiyoseru (引寄せる), *vt.* ❶ (引張りよせる) to draw towards one. ❷ (吸引) to attract; draw. —椅子を引寄せる, to draw a chair towards one. —手を取って引寄せる, to draw a person by the hand to one [one's side].

hikizai (挽材), *n.* lumber. ¶ 挽材工場, a saw-mill.

hikizan (引算), *n.*【數】subtraction.

hikizuna (曳綱), *n.*【建】a sash-cord [-line] (窓の);【航】a tow-line (曳船の); a leading-rein (馬の).

hikizuru (引摺る), *v.* to trail; drag; —引摺り出す, to drag out. —引摺り込む, to drag *into*; bring *into*.

hikka (筆禍), *n.* misfortune [calamity] brought [caused] by one's pen. —筆禍に罹る, to meet with a misfortune from one's pen.

hikkakari (引掛), *n.* ❶ (手掛り) a clue. ❷ (關係) relation; connections. ❸ (累) implication; involvement.

hikkakaru (引掛る), *vi.* ❶ (からみつく) to catch; get caught; be hooked (鉤に). ❷ (關係する) to form relations [connections] *with*. —著物が釘に引掛ッた, My clothes caught on a nail. —凧が木に引掛ッた, The kite caught in a tree.

hikkakeru (引掛ける), *vt.* to hang (a thing) *on*; hook; hitch. —女を引掛ける, to seduce a woman. —著物を肩に引掛ける, to throw clothes over one's shoulders.

hikkaku (引搔く), *vt.* to scratch; claw. —抽斗を引搔き廻はす, to rummage a drawer.

hikkei (必携の), *a.* indispensable. —學生必携の書, a book indispensable to students.

hikki (筆記), *n.* ❶ a note; a report; a note-book. ❷ (海軍の屬吏) a writer. —筆記する, to note down; jot down; report. ¶ 筆記帳, a note-book. —筆記者, an amanuensis; a reporter; a copyist; a writer. —筆記試驗, a written examination.

hikkirinashi (引切なしに), *ad.* without a break; without intermission; continually.

hikkō (筆耕), *n.* ❶ copying for hire. ❷(人) a copyist; an amanuensis. ¶ 筆耕料, copying-fee.

hikkomasu (引込ます), *vt.* Ⓢ 引込める. to take back (出した物を); turn down (洋燈等の心を); draw back (手を); retract (角・爪等を); pull in (首等).

hikkomu (引込む), *vi.* ❶(退き入る) to draw back *into*; retract. ❷(退隱) to retire. ❸(退却) to retreat; fall back. —部屋(田舍)へ引込む, to retire to one's room (into the country).

hikkoshi (引越), *n.* removal; house-moving. ☞ ***iten.***

hikkurikaeru(引繰返る), *vi.* ❶(倒になる) to be overturned; turn upside down. ❷(倒れる) to tumble down; upset; capsize. ❸(裏が出る) to be inside out.

hikkurikaeshi(引繰返しに), *ad.* ❶ upside down; topsy-turvy. ❷ inside out. ❸ on the contrary.

hikkurikaesu (引繰返す), *vt.* ❶(倒にする) to upset; overturn; turn upside down. ❷(倒す) to tumble down; upset; capsize. ❸(裏返す) to turn inside out.

hikkyō (畢竟), *ad.* after all. ☞ ***kekkyoku.***

hiko (曾孫), *n.* a great-grandchild.

hikō (非行), *n.* a misdeed; a misdemeanour; a delict.

hikō (飛行), *n.* flying; flight; aviation (空中). ☞ ***kōkū***(航空). —飛行する, ①(飛ぶ) to fly; wing. ②(航空) to aviate; make a flight. ③(疾行) to go off like a shot; outstrip the wind; put one's best leg foremost. ¶ 冒險(處女)飛行, an adventurous (a maiden) flight. —低空飛行, low flying. —長距離飛行, a long-distance flight. —民間飛行, civil flying [aviation]. —飛行帽, a helmet. —飛行病, aerial sickness. —飛行中尉, a flight-lieutenant. —飛行服, flying uniform; flight dress. —飛行場, an aerodrome; an aviation-station. —飛行術, aviation; airmanship. —飛行家, an aviator; an airman. (女流飛行家, an air-woman.) —飛行俱樂部, an Aero Club. —飛行免狀, a flying certificate. —飛行將校, a flight officer. —飛行隊, a flying corps. —飛行郵便, air-mail; air-post.

hikō (罷工), *n.* stoppage of work. ☞ ***dōmei-higyō.***

hikobae (蘖), *n.* an offset; outgrowth; an offshoot.

hikōkennin(被後見人), *n.* 【法】 a ward; a pupil.

hikōki (飛行機), *n.* an aeroplane; a flying-machine. ¶ 單葉飛行機, a monoplane. —複葉飛行機, a biplane. —郵便飛行機, an air--mail. —飛行機母艦, an aeroplane depôt-ship. —飛行機操縱者, an aeroplane pilot. —飛行機格納庫, a hangar. —飛行機射擊砲, an anti-aircraft gun; an anti-air gun.

hikoku(被告-人), *n.* the defendant (民事); the accused (刑事); the prisoner (at the bar) (同上). ¶ 被告辯護人, the counsel for the defence [accused; prisoner] —被告(訴訟)代理人, the counsel for the defence; the defendant's counsel.

hikōsen (飛行船), *n.* an airship; a dirigible. ¶ 飛行船操縱者, an aeronaut.

hikōshiki (非公式の), *a* un-{official; informal.}

hikōsonin (被控訴人), *n.* 【法】 an appellee; a respondent.

hikōtei (飛行艇), *n.* a flying boat; a hydroplane; a hydro--aeroplane.

hiku (引く), *v.* ❶(引張る) to draw; pull; haul. ❷〔曳, 牽〕 to drag; draw. ❸〔挽〕 to saw (鋸で). ❹〔碾〕 to grind (磨臼で). ❺〔惹〕(人目・注意等) to attract; catch; draw. ❻(架設, 敷設) to instal (電燈・電話等); lay (水道・瓦斯等). ❼(血統等を) to run in the blood; be descended. ❽(引用) to quote; cite. ❾(辭書を) to consult; look up; refer *to*. ❿(圖面等) to draw. ⓫(塗る) to lay on; apply. —人の氣をひく, to test [try] a man's mind. —責を引く, to take the responsibility upon oneself. —線(圖面; 幕)を引く, to draw a line (plan; curtain). —網(車)を引く, to draw a net (carriage). —牛を牽く, to lead an ox. —澁を引く, to varnish with *shibu*. —客を引く, to draw guests [customers]. —譬を引く, to quote an instance. —米を臼でひく, to grind rice in a handmill. —肺病の血筋を引く, to have consumption in the family. —彗星は尾を曳く, A comet trails a tail.

hiku (退く), *v.* ❶ to back; fall back. ❷(減退) to subside (洪水等); abate (熱等); remit (同上); go down (腫・水等). ☞ ***shirizoku.*** —學校を退く, to leave school.

hiku (減く), *vt.* to subtract (引去る); deduct (差引く); bate. —一志に付二片を減く, to allow

twopence in the shilling discount.
hiku (弾く), *vt.* to play; play *on.* —ピアノを弾く, to play (on) the piano.
hiku (轢く), *vt.* to run over. —自動車に轢き倒される, to be knocked down [over] by a motor-car.
hikui (低い), *a.* ❶ low. ❷ (矮)(短軀) short. ❸ (卑)(いやしい) low; humble. —低い調子, a low pitch. —低い鼻, a short [flat] nose.
hikuku (低く), *ad.* low; down.
hikutsu (卑屈), *n.* meanness; servility; obsequiousness. —卑屈な, mean; servile; obsequious.
hikyaku (飛脚), *n.* a postman; a courier. —飛脚を立てる, to send a courier. ¶ 早飛脚, an express messenger.
hikyō (卑怯), *n.* ❶ (臆病) cowardice. ❷ (公明正大ならぬ事) foulness. —卑怯な手段で, by foul means.
hikyō (悲況), *n.* a sad [distressing] state.
hikyō (悲境), *n.* a sad condition; distressing circumstances. —悲境に陷る [沈淪する], to fall into a distressing condition; sink under misfortune.
hikyū (飛球), *n.* 【野球】 a fly ball.
hikyū-kansetsu (髀臼關節), *n.* the hip-joint.
hima (隙), *n.* ❶ (不和) bad terms; ill-feeling. ❷ (間隙) a crevice; a gap; an interval. ❸ (時間) time. ❹ (餘暇) spare time; time to spare; leisure. ❺ (賜暇, 休暇) leave; vacation. ❻ (解雇) dismissal; discharge. ❼ (閑散) dulness; slackness. —ひまがかゝる, to take up time. —暇が出來たら, if I can find time. —お暇でしたら, if you are disengaged [not engaged]. —暇をやる, to dismiss; discharge. —ひまをつぶす, to while away one's time; waste time. —三日間の暇を貰ふ, to obtain three days' leave.
himajin (閑人), *n.* a person of leisure; an idler.
himaku (被膜), *n.* 【生】 the coat; 【解】 the involucre.
himan (肥滿), *n.* corpulence; stoutness; fleshiness. —肥滿する, to get flesh; grow corpulent [stout]. —肥滿した, stout; fleshy; corpulent.
Himaraya (ヒマラヤ), *n.* the Himalayas.
himashi (日増に), *ad.* day by day; daily; every day. —日増しに生長する, to grow day by day.
himashi (蓖麻子), *n.* a castor-bean. ¶ 蓖麻子油, castor-oil.
himatsu (飛沫), *n.* splash; plash. —事件の飛沫は彼にまで及んだ, The consequences of the affair have even involved him.
himatsubushi (消閑), *n.* whiling away one's time; wasting time; kill-time.
himawari (向日葵), *n.* 【植】 the sunflower.
hime (姬), *n.* a young lady of birth.
himei (非命の), *a.* untimely; unnatural. ☞ *higō* (非業の).
himei (悲鳴), *n.* a shriek; a cry of distress; a scream. —悲鳴を揚げる, to cry aloud (in distress); shriek.
himei (碑銘), *n.* an epitaph; an inscription (on a tomb [monument]).
himen (罷免する), *vt.* to dismiss; discharge.
himenori (姬糊), *n.* rice-starch; rice-paste.
himeyuri (姬百合), *n.* 【植】 the Japanese red-star lily. —谷間の姬百合 [鈴蘭], the lily of the valley.
himitsu (秘密), *n.* ❶ (内證) secrecy; confidence; (a) mystery (事); a secret (同上). ❷ (神祕) mystery; occultness. ❸ (奧義) a mystery. —公然の祕密, an open secret. —祕密を明かす, to trust [confide] one's secrets *to.* —祕密を發く, to expose a secret. —祕密を守る, to keep a [the] secret; keep one's (own) (another's) counsel; maintain secrecy. —祕密會を請求する, to demand a secret session. **—— -no,** *a.* secret; confidential; private. —祕密の鍵を握る, to hold the key to a secret. **—— -ni,** *ad.* secretly; in secret; confidentially. —祕密にする, to keep a thing secret; conceal. ¶ 祕密文書, secret documents [despatches]. —祕密結社, a secret assosiation. —祕密藥, a nostrum.
himo (紐), *n.* ❶ (索) a cord; a band. ❷ (打紐) a braid; a tape; a fillet (髮紐). ❸ (革紐) a thong; a strap. ❹ (紙紐) a paper-string (こより). ❺ (リボン) a ribbon; a lace. —紐を締める [結ぶ], to lace (靴の); tie a cord. —紐をとく, to unloosen [untie] a cord.
himojii (饑い), *a.* hungry; keen- [sharp-] set. —饑じい時にまづい物なし, "Hunger is the best sauce."
himoku (費目), *n.* an item of expense.
himono (干物), *n.* a dried fish; a kipper (鮭·鰊の).
himoto (火元), *n.* the origin of a fire.
himotoku (繙く), *vt.* (繙讀) to read.
himuro (氷室), *n.* an ice-house; an ice-room.
hin (品), *n.* (品格) dignity; character. ☞ *shina* (品). —品のよい, dignified; refined; gentle-

manlike (男); ladylike (女).

hin (貧), *n.* poverty. —貧の盗み, theft under the pressure of poverty.

hina (鄙), *n.* the country; the countryside.

hina (雛), *n.* ❶ (雛鳥) a chicken; a fledgling ❷ (雛人形) a doll.

hinagata (雛形), *n.* ❶ (模型) a model. ❷ (標本) a specimen. ❸ (見本) a sample; a pattern. ❹ (様式) form. —別紙雛形の通り, according to the form herein enclosed. —雛形を取る, to take a pattern.

hinageshi (虞美人草), *n.* 【植】 the corn-poppy.

hinagiku (雛菊), *n.* 【植】 the daisy.

hinamatsuri (雛祭), *n.* the Feast of Dolls (the 3rd March).

hinan (非難), *n.* blame; censure; disparagement. —非難する, to censure; blame. —非難の的となる, to become the object of criticism. —非難を免れぬ, to be open to censure. —非難の聲が高かった, Disapproval was loudly expressed.

hinan (避難), *n.* refuge. —避難する, to take refuge; seek safety in flight. ¶ 避難港, a harbour of refuge. —避難者, a refugee. —避難所, an asylum; a haven; a refuge.

hinarazu (日ならず), *ad.* in a few days; before long; shortly.

hinashi (日済貸), *n.* loan of money payable in daily instalments.

hinata (日向), *n.* sunshine; the sun. —日向に干す, to dry in the sun. —日向ぼッこする, to bask in the sun; sun oneself.

hine (陳), *n.* ❶=*okute* (晩稲). ❷ (舊穀) old cereal. ❸ (陳腐) staleness.

hinekure (拗くれた), *a.* ❶ crooked; distorted; crabbed. ❷ eccentric; crotchety.

hinekuru (捻る), *vt.* ❶ to twirl; twiddle; twist. ❷=*moteasobu.*

hinemosu (終日), *ad.* all day; all day long; from morning to [till] night.

hineru (捻る), *vt.* ❶ (摘みひねる) to nip; tweak. ❷ (指先でねぢる) to twist; contort. ❸ (指の間に持ちてねぢつける) to wrench. ❹ (つめる) to pinch. —髭をひねる, to twirl one's moustache. —頰〔口端〕をひねる, to pinch the cheek (mouth).

hinetsu (比熱), *n.* specific heat.

hinhin (馬), *n.* a gee 〔俗〕; a gee-gee 〔小兒〕.

hiñi (品位), *n.* ❶ (品等, 品質) grade; quality. ❷ (品格) dignity. ❸ (金属の性合) standard. —品位ある, dignified. —品位を保つ, to maintain [keep] one's dignity.

hiniku (皮肉), *n.* ❶ (皮と肉) skin and flesh. ❷ (意地惡いこと) malice; spite. ❸ (冷嘲) cynicism; irony. —皮肉に, caustically; cynically. —皮肉(な事)を言ふ, to say spiteful [malicious] things. ☞ *hinikuru.* ¶ 皮肉家, a cynic.

hiniku (髀肉), *n.* the thigh. —髀肉の嘆を發する, to sigh for unquiet times; strain at the leash.

hinikuru (皮肉る), *vt.* to say cynical things *of*; speak caustically *of*.

hinin (否認する), *vt.* to deny; disavow; repudiate.

hinin (非人), *n.* an outcast; a pariah.

hinin (避姙), *n.* prevention of conception; contraception. —避姙する, to prevent conception.

hininshō (非人稱の), *n.* 【文】 impersonal. ¶ 非人稱動詞, the impersonal verb.

hinjaku (貧弱な), *a.* poor; meagre; slight.

hinji (賓辭), *n.* 【文】 the object; 【論】 a predicate.

hinkaku (品格), *n.* dignity; character. ☞ *hiñi.* —品格を墮す, to lower one's dignity.

hinkaku (賓格), *n.* 【文】 the objective case.

hinkei (牝鷄), *n.* a hen.

hinketsu (貧血), *n.* 【醫】 anæmia. —貧血する, to become anæmic.

hinkō (品行), *n.* conduct; behaviour. ¶ 品行方正, good conduct. —品行證明書, a character; a certificate of good conduct. —品行點, a conduct mark.

hinkon (貧困), *n.* poverty; penury; indigence. —貧困の, poor; indigent; penurious.

hinku (貧苦), *n.* the hardship of poverty.

hinkyū (貧窮), *n.* poverty; indigence; destitution.

hinmin (貧民), *n.* the poor; the paupers; proletarians. ¶ 貧民學校, a ragged school; a charity school. —貧民窟, the slums; the slum quarters; the poor district. —貧民救助法, poor-law.

hinmoku (品目), *n.* an item; an article; a list of articles.

hinoban (火の番), *n.* a fire-watchman; a fire-watch [-guard]. —火の番が廻る, The fire-watchman goes his round.

hinobe (日延), *n.* ❶ (日をのべること) extension of time. ❷ (延期) postponement. —雨天に付日延, Postponed on account of rain.

hinode (日の出), *n.* sunrise. —日の出の勢である, to be in the ascendant.

hinoiri (日の入), *n.* sunset; sundown.

hinoki (檜, 扁柏), *n.* 【植】 the Japan cypress.

hinokibutai (檜舞臺), *n.* a stage-board of Japan cypress. —檜舞臺に出る, to appear before the great public.

hinoko (火の粉), *n.* a spark. —火の粉をかぶる, to be covered with sparks.

hinomaru (日の丸), *n.* the sun-flag (旗).

hinomi (火の見), *n.* a fire-lookout. —火の見櫓に登る, to go up the fire-tower.

hinoshi (熨斗), *n.* a flat-iron; a smoothing-iron. —熨斗をする [かける], [*vt.*] to iron.

hinoshita (日の下開山), *n.* the invincible champion wrestler.

hinotama (火の玉), *n.* ❶ a fire-ball. ❷=*ayashibi* (怪火).

hinote (火の手), *n.* the flames; force of a fire. —火の手が揚がる, The fire flames up.

hinpan (頻繁な), *a.* frequent; incessant; busy.

hinpatsu (頻發), *n.* frequency; frequent occurrence.

hinpin (頻頻として), *ad.* frequently; often; in rapid succession.

hinpu (貧富), *n.* wealth and poverty; the rich and the poor (貧者と富者). —貧富貴賤の別なく, without distinction of wealth or rank.

hinpyō (品評), *n.* criticism. —品評する, to criticize. ¶ 品評會, a competitive exhibition; a prize show.

hinsei (品性), *n.* character. —品性の高潔な人, a man of high character. ¶ 品性陶冶, cultivation of character; character formation.

hinseki (擯斥), *n.* rejection; exclusion; scorn. **——-suru,** *vt.* to reject; exclude; treat with scorn [disdain]. —擯斥すべき, contemptible; despicable. —仲間から擯斥する, to exclude a person from company.

hinsen (貧賤), *n.* poverty and humbleness. —貧賤な, poor and humble [low].

hinsha (貧者), *n.* a poor man. —貧者の一燈, the widow's mite.

hinshi (品詞), *n.* 【文】 a part of speech. ¶ 品詞論, etymology.

hinshi (瀕死の), *a.* dying; at death's door; on the verge of death. —瀕死の狀態である, to be brought to the verge of death; be at the point of death.

hinshitsu (品質), *n.* quality.

hinshuku (顰蹙する), *vi.* to frown; scowl; knit [bend] one's brows.

hinsō (貧相の), *a.* meagre; poor-[seedy]-looking.

hin-suru (瀕する), *vi.* to be on the point [verge; brink] *of*.

hinto (ヒント), *n.* a hint. —ヒントを與へる, to (give a) hint.

hinyō (泌尿), *n.* urination. ¶ 泌尿器, 【醫】 the urinary organ.

hiōgi (射干), *n.* 【植】 the blackberry-lily.

hioi (日覆), *n.* ❶ (日除け) an awning (重に布幕); a sunshade; a window-blind; a sun-screen (簾・衝立等). ❷ a havelock (軍帽等の垂布附の); a (cap-)cover (學生帽等の).

hippaku (逼迫), *n.* stringency; tightness. —金融は逼迫せり, Money is tight.

hipparu (引張る), *vt.* ❶ (牽く) to pull; draw; drag. ☞ *hiku* (引く). ❷ (張る) to stretch over; strain. ❸ (延引) to postpone; defer; put off. ❹ (むしる) to pluck. —仲間に引張り込む, to drag him into the set. —警察へ引張られて行く, to be taken to the police station. —彼は雙方から引張り凧だ, He is much sought for by both sides.

hippataku (引敲く), *vt.* to thrash; drub; whack.

hippō (筆法), *n.* ❶ (運筆法) (the style of) penmanship; chirography; a stroke of the pen. ❷ (やりかた) a manner; a method.

hippō (筆鋒), *n.* the point of a pen. —筆鋒鋭利當るべからず, The sharpness of his pen is irresistible.

hippu (匹夫), *n.* ❶ (一人の男) a man. ❷ (卑人) a man of humble position; a common man. ¶ 匹夫匹婦, humble men and women; the common people.

hira (平の), *a.* (なみ) common; ordinary. ¶ 平人足, a common labourer. —平重役, a mere director.

hirachi (平地), *n.* a level ground.

hiradoma (平土間), *n.* 【劇場】 the parterre; the pit.

hiragana (平假名), *n.* the Japanese cursive syllabary.

hirahira (翩翩), *ad.* in a waving manner. 翩々する, to flap; flutter; play.

hiraishin (避雷針), *n.* a lightning-rod [-conductor].

hirakeru (開ける), *vi.* ❶ (開く) to open. ❷ (開發, 開化) to become civilized; be modernized; develop. ❸ (常識的) to become sensible. ❹ (發展) to extend.

hiraketa (開けた), *a.* ❶ (開いた) open; clear. ❷ (開化せる) enlightened; civilized. ❸ (世情に通じた) experienced; tactful; sensible (物の分ッた). —開けた人, a man of the world.

hiraki (開), *n.* ❶ opening. ❷【商】(價の差) margin; difference.
hirakido (開 戸), *n.* a (hinged) door.
hirakifū (開封), *n.* an unfastened [open] envelope. —開き封の書狀, an open letter.
hiraku (開 く), *vt.* ❶ (あける) to open; unfold; lay open. ❷ (拓) =*kaikon* (開墾する). ❸ (開始) to start; commence; open. ❹ (創立) to open; found; set up; establish. ❺【數】to extract. ❻ (開 催) to hold; give. ——, *vi.* ❶ (咲く) to open; bloom; be out. ❷ (始まる) to open. —眼 (口) を開く, to open one's eyes (mouth). —襖を左右に開く, to open the sliding-doors to the right and left. —發見の端を開く, to lead the way [give a clue] to discovery.
hirame (比目魚), *n.*【魚】Paralichthys olivaceus (flat-fishの一種).
hiramekasu (閃かす), *vt.* ❶ to flash; glint. ❷ (振り廻す) to brandish; flourish. —白刃を閃かす, to brandish one's sword.
hirameki (閃き), *n.* ❶ flash; glitter (刃などの); glint. ❷ (翻り) waving (旗などの); play. —希望の閃き, a flash of hope.
hirameku (閃く), *vi.* ❶ to flash; sparkle; glitter. ❷ (翻る) to play; fly; wave.
hirani (平に), *ad.* ❶ (偏に) humbly; earnestly. ❷ (飾なく) plainly; openly. ❸ flat. —平に御容赦被下度候, I humbly beg your pardon.
hirari (翻然), *ad.* nimbly; quickly. —ひらりと樹から跳びおりる, to jump down nimbly from the tree. —ひらりと體をかはす, to dodge.
hiratai (平たい), *a.* Ⓢ 平ッたい. ❶ (平 坦) flat; even; level. ❷ (扁 平) flat. ❸ (平 易) simple; plain. ❹ (率直) plain; blunt. —平たく云へば, in plain language. —潰して平ッたくする, to smash and flatten.
hirate (平 手), *n.* the palm; the open hand. —平手で打つ, to slap; give a slap. (平手で耳を打つ, to box a person's ears.)
hiraya (平 家), *n.* a one-storied house; a one-story building. —木造瓦葺平家一棟, a tile-roofed, single-storied wooden house. ¶ 平家建, a one-storied building.
hirazan (平算), *n.* simple arithmetic.
hire (鰭), *n.* the fin.
hirei (比例), *n.*【數】proportion. —比例する, to proportion; proportionate. —勞力に比例して, in proportion to the labour. —人口に對する出產の比例, the proportion of birth to the population. ¶ 單(複)比例, simple (compound) proportion. —比例中數, [項], mean proportional. —比例代表, proportional representation. —比例式, proportion (formula).
hireki (披瀝する), *vi.* to open; show. —胸中を披瀝する, to open one's bosom [heart; mind] *to*; unbosom oneself *to*.
hire-niku (ヒレ肉), *n.* fillet.
hiretsu (卑劣な), *a.* mean; vile; base.
hiri (非 理の), *a.* unreasonable; irrational.
hirihiri (ひりひりする), *a.* hot; pungent; sharp; smarting; tingling. —ひりひり痛む, to smart; tingle.
hirikken (非立憲的), *a.* unconstitutional.
hirin (比倫), *n.* a peer; a match; an equal.
Hirippin (比 律 賓), *n.* the Philippines. ¶ 比律賓人, a Filipino [*fem.* -na]. —比律賓群島, the Philippine Islands.
hiritsu (比率), *n.* ratio.
hiro (尋), *n.* a fathom.
hirō (疲勞), *n.* fatigue; exhaustion (病人の); weariness. —疲勞さす, to fatigue; weary; exhaust. —疲勞する, to be fatigued; be tired; be exhausted; weary. —疲勞の色を見せる, to betray a tired look. —疲勞を感ずる, to feel fatigue.
hirō (披 露), *n.* announcement; introduction (紹介); advertisement (廣告). —披露の宴, a dinner for making an announcement. —友人を集めて披露する, to call together friends and make an announcement. ¶ 披露會, an inaugural meeting.
hiroba (廣場), *n.* an open space; an open; an esplanade. —廣場へ出る, to come out upon the open.
hirobiro (廣廣した), *a.* extensive; wide; spacious.
hirogari (廣がり), *n.* ❶ (廣衷) expansion; stretch; extension. ❷ (蔓延) spread.
hirogaru (廣・擴がる), *vi.* ❶ (廣く延びる) to expand; stretch (野原等); extend. ❷ (蔓延) to outspread; overspread; run (火事・報知等). —四方に廣がる, to blaze [spread] abroad. —報知は野火の如くに擴がッた, The news spread like wild fire.
hirogeru (廣・擴げる), *vt.* ❶ (廣く延べる) to enlarge; spread; extend. ❷ (開く) to unfold; open; unroll (卷いた物を). ❸ (張る) to stretch. ❹ (流布) to outspread; spread. —翼(地圖)を廣げる, to spread wings (a map). —道路を

廣げる, to widen a road. —運動場(校舍)を擴げる, to enlarge a playground (school-house).

hirohaba (廣幅の), *a.* wide; broad.

hiroi (廣い), *a.* ❶ wide; broad; large. ❷ 〔濶〕 open; broad. ❸ 〔汎〕 (一般的) universal; general. ❹ 〔寛〕 (ゆるやかな) generous. —心の廣い, large-minded. —廣い帶, a broad sash. —廣い見解を取る, to take wide views —あの人は交際が廣い, He has large social relations.

hiroimono (拾物), *n.* ❶ (拾得物) anything picked up [found]. ❷ (意外の見附物・儲物) a piece [stroke] of good luck [fortune]; a lucky find.

hiroinushi (拾主), *n.* the finder of lost property.

hiroiyomi (拾讀する), *vt.* to dip *into* (a book); pick up (chief points [interesting parts] *of*). —新聞紙を拾讀みする, to read interesting parts of a newspaper.

hirokōji (廣小路), *n.* a wide broad] street; an avenue (特に米); a *boulevard* (並木ある) 〔佛〕.

hiroku (廣く), *ad.* ❶ wide(-ly); broad(-ly); largely; on a large scale (大規模に); generally (一般的に). ❷ (公然) publicly; broad and wide. —廣くする (なる), to widen; enlarge. —廣く云へば, broadly speaking. —廣く交際する, to have a wide circle of friends. —博く書を讀む, to read a large number of books.

hiroma (廣間), *n.* a hall; a saloon.

hiromaru (廣まる), *vi.* ❶ (普及) to spread; diffuse. ❷ (流布) to circulate; take air; get wind. ❸ (流行) to be in fashion [vogue].

hirome (披露目), *n.* an announcement; advertisement (廣告). —結婚の披露目をする, to hold a party to announce a marriage; hold a wedding party. ¶ 披露目屋, an advertiser.

hiromeru (廣める), *vt.* ❶ (擴大する) to extend; widen. ❷ (傳播さす) to diffuse; propagate. ❸ (披露する) to announce. —宗旨を廣める, to propagate a religion.

hironriteki (非論理的), *a.* illogical; irrational.

hirosa (廣さ), *n.* ❶ (廣袤) dimension; extent; area. ❷ (幅) width; breadth. —廣さ六呎, six feet broad [wide]. —廣さ三萬平方哩, 30,000 square miles in extent.

hirou (拾ふ), *vt.* ❶ to pick up (落ちたるを); gather (採集); glean (落穗を). ❷ (選拔) to select; pick out. —拾ひ上げる, ① to pick up. ② (拔擢) to select; pick out. —拾ひ集める, to pick up; gather. —拾ひ出す, to pick out; select. —松葉(落穗)を拾ふ, to gather pine-leaves (gleanings). —蟇口を拾ふ, to pick up [find] a purse. —途を拾ッて歩く (雨降りなどに), to pick one's steps.

hiru (蛭), *n.* 【環蟲】 the (medicinal) leech. —蛭をつける, to apply a leech.

hiru (蒜), *n.* 【植】 the Spanish garlic.

hiru (晝), *n.* ❶ (白晝, 晝間) the daytime; daylight. ❷ (午時) noon. ❸ =*hirumeshi*. ¶ 晝休み, midday rest [recess].

hiru (干る), *vi.* ❶ to dry (乾く); ebb (海水が). ❷ (盡きる) to be exhausted.

hiru (簸る), *vt.* to winnow; fan.

hirugaeru (翻る), *vi.* ❶ (裏返しになる) to turn over. ❷ 〔飄, 飜, 翻〕 to stream; fly; flutter. —翻ッて考へれば, upon reconsidering the matter.

hirugaesu (翻す), *vt.* ❶ (裏返へらす) to turn over. ❷ (風になびかす) to fly; wave. ❸ (改變する) to change; turn. —前說を翻す, to change one's former opinion. —國旗を高く飜す, to wave high the national flag.

hirugao (旋花), *n.* 【植】 the larger bindweed.

hirui (比類なき), *a.* matchless; peerless; unparallelled.

hiruma (晝間), *n.* the daytime; day.

hirumeshi (晝飯), *n.* a midday meal; a luncheon; a dinner.

hirumu (怯む), *vi.* 【軍】 to waver; wince; flinch. —敵を見て怯む, to flinch before the enemy.

hirune (晝寢), *n.* a siesta; a midday nap. —晝寢する, to take siesta; take a midday nap.

hiryō (肥料), *n.* a manure; a fertilizer. —肥料を施す, to (apply) manure; dung. ¶ 人造肥料, artificial manure. —窒素 (燐酸; 加里) 肥料, nitrogenous (phosphatic; potassic) manure.

hisago (瓢), *n.* a gourd.

hisagu (鬻ぐ), *vt.* to sell; deal *in*.

hisan (砒酸), *n.* arsenic acid.

hisan (飛散する), *vi.* to scatter; disperse; fly (急に). —風の爲に飛散する, to be scattered by the wind.

hisan (悲慘な), *a.* sad; miserable; tragical. —悲慘な出來事, a tragedy; a tragic event.

hisan (悲酸), *n.* bitterness; misery; affliction. ☞ *hisan* (悲慘な). —悲酸を嘗める, to experience misery; taste bitterness.

hisashi (廂), *n.* ❶ (家の) the

eaves; a roof; a pent-roof. ❷ 〔庇〕 a drip; a canopy; a peak (帽子の).

hisashiburi (久振に), *ad.* after a long time [interval]; a long time since. —久振りで晴れ上る, to clear up after a long spell of rain.

hisashii (久しい), *a.* long; long--continued; of long standing; old. —久しく, long; for a long time.

hisei (秕政), *n.* misgovernment; misrule; maladministration.

hiseki (砒石), *n.* 【化】 arsenic; white arsenic.

hisen (卑賤), *n.* humbleness; meanness (of position); obscurity. —卑賤から起る, to rise from obscurity.

hisenkyo (被選擧權), *n.* Ⓢ 被選權. the right to be [of being] elected. ¶ 被選擧人, a person having the right to be elected; a person who may be elected; an eligible person. ¶ 被選擧資格, eligibility; qualification for election.

hisenron (非戰論), *n.* anti-war argument. ¶ 非戰論者, an anti--war speaker.

hisentōin (非戰鬪員), *n.* 【軍】 a non-combatant.

hisha (飛車), *n.* 【將棋】 a rook; a castle.

hishaku (柄杓), *n.* a ladle; a dipper. —柄杓で汲む, to ladle.

hishi (菱), *n.* ❶ 【植】 the water caltrops. ❷ (菱形) a lozenge; a rhomb. ❸ (商標) a diamond.

hishigata (菱形の), *a.* lozenge; diamond; rhombic.

hishigeru (拉げる), *vi.* ❶ (押潰される) to be crushed; be flattened; collapse. ❷ (挫ける) to collapse; give away. —, *a.* collapsible.

hishigu (拉ぐ), *vt.* ❶ (挫く) to break; crush. ❷ (押潰す) to squash; crush. —相手の勢を取りひしぐ, to break the opponent's power.

hishihishi (犇犇), *ad.* pushingly; overwhelmingly. —犇々つめかける, to come on in crowds.

hishiko (鯷), *n.* 【魚】 the anchovy.

hishimeku (犇めく), *vi.* to push about; clamour; make an uproar.

hishinshi (非紳士的), *a.* ungentlemanlike.

hishio (醬), *n.* jelly.

hishio (干潮), *n.* =*hikishio*.

hishito (犇と), *ad.* firmly; tightly; fast. —犇と子を抱き締める, to press the child tightly to her bosom.

hisho (秘書), *n.* ❶ (秘藏の本) a secret book. ❷ =秘書役. ¶ 秘書課, a secretariat. —秘書官, a private [confidential] secretary. —秘書役, a confidential clerk; a private secretary.

hisho (避暑), *n.* avoiding the heat of summer; going to a summer resort. ¶ 避暑地, a summer resort. —避暑客, a summer visitor; a visitor at a summer resort.

hishō (飛翔する), *vi.* to fly; take one's [a] flight. —高空に飛翔する, to fly through the high air.

hishō (費消する), *vt.* to spend; use up; consume.

hishō-jiken (非訟事件), *n.* a non-contentious case.

hishoku (非職), *n.* being on the retired list. —非職にする, to put on the retired list.

hishu (匕首), *n.* a dagger; a dirk.

hiso (砒素), *n.* arsenic.

hisō (皮相), *n.* ❶ =*gaimen*, ❷ (淺薄) shallowness; superficiality. —皮相の見(觀察), a superficial view(observation). —事物の皮相のみを觀察する, to look only at the surface of things.

hisō (悲壯の), *a.* tragic(-al); touching.

hisohiso (密密), *ad.* secretly; in secret. —密々話す, to speak in the ear; (talk in a) whisper.

hisokani (密・私・竊に), *ad.* secretly; in private; in secret. —密に計を敵に通ずる, to betray the plan to the enemy.

hisomeru (潛める), *vt.* ❶ (密にする) to subdue; depress. ❷ (忍ばす) to conceal; hide; bury. —聲を潛める, to depress one's voice. —物蔭に身を潛める, to conceal oneself in a shadow. —心を潛めて書を讀む, to read a book with a calm mind.

hisomeru (顰める), *vt.* to knit; wrinkle; contract. —眉を顰める, to knit [bend] the brows; contract the eyebrows; wrinkle one's forehead; frown.

hisomu (潛む), *vi.* ❶ (潛在) to lurk. ❷ (忍びかくれる) to hide; conceal oneself; bury oneself in oblivion. —空家に潛む, to conceal oneself in an unoccupied house.

hissageru (提げる), *vt.* to carry; take up; take along *with*.

hissan (筆算), *n.* ❶ (書く事と算術) writing and arithmetic. ❷ (洋算) foreign arithmetic.

hissei (畢生の), *a.* lifelong. —畢生の事業, a life-work. —畢生の勇を鼓す, to call forth all one's courage.

hissei (筆生), *n.* a copyist; an amanuensis.

hisseki (筆蹟), *n.* penmanship; handwriting.

hissha (筆者), *n.* a writer. —不明の筆者, an unknown writer.

hisshi (必至), *n.* necessity; the inevitable; inevitability. —必至的歸結, a necessary conclusion.
hisshi (必死), *n.* desperation. —必死の場合, a desperate case. —必死になッて働く, to work for dear [one's] life. —必死になッて奔走する, to exert oneself with desperation.
hisshi (筆紙), *n.* pen and paper. —筆紙に盡しがたい, to baffle description.
hisshō (必勝), *n.* certain victory. —必勝を期して戰ふ, to fight in sure expectation of victory.
hisshoku (筆觸), *n.* 【美】a touch.
hisshu (必須の), *a.* necessary; indispensable. ¶ 必須科目, an indispensable subject.
hissori (ひッそり), *ad.* silently; quietly; still. —ひッそり(閑と)して居る, to be as silent as the grave.
his-suru (必する), *vt.* to be sure [certain; secure] *of.* —勝利を必する, to be secure of victory.
hi-suru (比する), *v.* ❶ (喩へる) to compare *to*; liken *to.* ❷ (比べる) to compare *with.* —に比すれば[して], as compared *with*; in comparison *with.* —に比して毫も遜色がない, not to fear (from) comparison *with.*
hi-suru (祕する), *vt.* to hide *from* (事柄を); keep secret; keep back. —事實を祕する, to sink [suppress] a fact. —喪を祕する, to keep the mourning secret.
hisuterī (ヒステリー), *n.* hysteria; hysterics. —ヒステリー性の人, a hysteriac.
hitai (額), *n.* the forehead; the brow(-s). —額を鳩める, to lay their heads together.
hitaki(ひたき), *n.* 【鳥】the fly-catcher.
hitan (悲歎), *n.* sorrow; lamentation; grief. —悲歎の涙に暮れる, to weep with sorrow; be drowned in tears of sorrow.
hitasu (浸す), *vt.* to soak; steep; immerse. —に浸る, to be dipped *in*; be submerged *in*; be steeped *in.*
hitasura (只管, 一向), *ad.* earnestly; intently. 只管學問を勉强する, to devote oneself earnestly to one's studies.
hitato (直と), *ad.* ❶ tightly; closely. ❷ (うちつけに) bang; slap. —ひたと寄り添ふ, to approach close *to.*
hitch (筆致), *n.* style; touch (筆觸).
hitchū (匹儔), *n.* a peer; a match; an equal.
hitchū (筆誅), *n.* castigation with the pen. —筆誅を加へる, to castigate with the pen.
hitei (否定的), *a.* negative; 【文】privative. —否定する, to deny; negative. ¶ 否定語, a negative.
hiten (批點), *n.* ❶ (評點) marks made in criticism or for correction. ❷ (缺點) a defect; a fault.
hito (人), *n.* ❶ (人間,人類) man; a person (男女ともに). ❷ (世人) people. —人らしい, like a man; humanly. —人の惡い, ① (惡性) bad; bad [ill]-natured; wicked; evil; cross. ② (狡猾) cunning; crafty; sly. ③ (憎らしい) mischievous; up to tricks. —人の好い, good-natured. —人は病の器 "Sickness is every man's master." —人の噂も七十五日, "A wonder lasts but nine days."
hito(匪徒), *n.* insurgents; bandits; brigands.
hito (費途), *n.* expenditure; expenses. —費途を明かにする, to make clear how the money was spent.
hitō (避逃する), *vi.* to decamp; fly away; abscond.
hitoashi (一足), *n.* a step; a pace. —一足お先へ失敬しよう, I will just go before you.
hitobarai (人拂する), *vi.* to clear (a room; a place) of persons. —人拂して密議する, to clear the room [place] and consult in secret.
hitobito (人人), *n.* people; men; folks.
hitochigai (人違する), *vi.* to mistake [take] a person for another.
hitodachi (人立), *n.* Ⓢ 人だかり. a crowd [throng] of people.
hitodama (人魂), *n.* a spirit of the dead; a death fire.
hitodanomi (人賴), *n.* dependence [reliance] upon another.
hitode (海盤車, 海扇), *n.* 【動】the star-fish.
hitode (人手), *n.* ❶ (働き手) hands. ❷ (助力) help; assistance. ❸ (他人の手) another's hand. —人手が足りない, to be short of hands. —人手に渡る, to pass into other hands. —人手を借りる, to get help.
hitode (人出), *n.* coming [going] out of people; a turnout (見物人).
hitodenashi (人でなし), *n.* a miscreant; a vile wretch.
hitodōri (人通), *n.* the passing of people on the road. —人通りの劇しい町, a crowded street; a bustling street.
hitoe (一重), *n.* a single-fold. —壁一重のお鄰り, a neighbour separated by [on the other side of] a wall.
hitoemono (單物), *n.* an unlined garment.
hitoeni (偏に), *ad.* ❶ humbly;

earnestly. ❸ wholly; entirely.

hitofude (一筆), *n.* ❶ a line. ❷(書畫の) a stroke; a touch. —一筆書き送る, to drop a line.

hitofuri(一降), *n.* a fall. —一降り欲しいものだ, I wish we could have a fall of rain.

hitogaki (人垣), *n.* a crowd in a row; a living wall.

hitogara (人柄), *n.* ❶(品格) personal character; personality. ❷(容貌)appearance; person. —人柄の著物, a presentable dress. —人柄の良い娘, a genteel-looking girl.

hitogiki (人聞), *n.* ❶(他聞) the hearing of others. ❷(又聞) hearing at second-hand. —人聞きの惡いことを云ふ, to say things that sound bad.

hitogokoro (人心), *n.* consciousness. —人心がつく, to come to oneself; be oneself again.

hitogomi (人込), *n.* a crowd; a throng. —人込みにまぎれ込む, to disappear [be lost] in the crowd. —人込みを押分けて通る, to push one's way through a crowd.

hitogoroshi (人殺), *n.* murder (行爲): a murderer (人).

hitōha (非黨派の), *a.* non-party. ¶ 非黨派問題, a non-party question.

hitoharago (一腹子), *n.* a farrow (豚の); a litter (豚・犬等の); a hatch (鷄等の); a brood (同上).

hitoiki (一息), *n.* ❶(一呼息) a breath. ❷(暫時) a while. ❸(一氣呵成) an effort. —一息に飲み干す, to drain at one gulp; empty at a draught.

hitoikire (人熅), *n.* stuffiness; closeness (of a crowded room).

hitojichi (人質), *n.* a hostage. —人質に取る, to take as a hostage. —人質を遣る, to give a hostage.

hitojini (人死), *n.* death; loss of life. —澤山人死を出す, to cause many deaths.

hitokado (一廉), *ad.* fairly. ——**no,** *a.* tolerable; passable; fair; fine. —一廉の人, a somebody; a person of importance. —一廉の功を樹てる, to render a great service.

hitokage(人影), *n.* ❶(映る影) the shadow of a man. ❷(開の) a figure; a form.

hitokarage (一紮), *n.* a bundle; a lump. —一紮げにする, to summarize (概括する); lump together; bundle up [together].

hitokata (一方ならぬ), *a.* great; immense. —一方ならぬ厄介を掛ける, to be a very great trouble *to.*

hitokiwa (一際), *ad.* especially; particularly; remarkably. —一際目に立つ大男, a conspicuously big man.

hitokoe (一聲), *n.* a voice; a cry.

hitokoro (一頃), *ad.* at one time; once. ☞ *ichiji* (一時).

hitokuchi (一口), *n.* ❶(一口の分量) a mouthful; a bite; a morsel; a draught. ❷(一言) a word. —一口に云へば, in a word; in short. —一口に頰張る, to cram one's mouth. ¶ 一口噺, a joke; a short tale [story].

hitokumi (一組), *n.* a set (道具の); a pack (カルタ等の); a team (駿人等の).

hitokuse (一癖ある), *a.* uncommon.

hitomachigao (人待顔で), *ad.* looking as if waiting for another; with an expectant look.

hitomae (人前), *n.* company. —人前を憚る, to be reserved in company. —人前を繕ふ, to keep up appearances before company.

hitomakase (人任せにする), *vt.* to entrust [leave] (everything) to others.

hitomakumono (一幕物), *n.* a one-scene piece; a one-act play.

hitomane (人眞似), *n.* imitation; mimicry. —人眞似をする, to play the ape; mimic another.

hitomazu (一先), *ad.* for the present; for a while; for a short time. —一先づ打切りにする, to end it for the present.

hitome (一目), *n.* a glance. ☞ *ikken* (一見). —一目で見拔く, to see through at a glance.

hitome (人目), *n.* the eyes of others; public sight; the world. —人目を偸んで, by stealth; stealthily. —人目を憚る, to fear being seen; shun notice. —人目を恥ぢる, to be ashamed to be seen.

hitomi (瞳子), *n.* the pupil; the apple of the eye.

hitomigokū (人身御供), *n.* ❶ a human sacrifice; a victim. ❷(犧牲) a scapegoat.

hitomishiri (人見知りする), *a.* bashful; shy. —人見知りする子, a child shy in company.

hitomoshigoro (火燈し頃), *n.* the time of candle-lighting [lamp-lighting].

hitonadare (人頽), *n.* a swarming crowd.

hitonaka (人中), *n.* ❶(稠座) company. ❷(世間) the world. —人中で恥をかく, to be put to shame in company. —人中へ出る, to appear in the world; go into society.

hitonami (人竝), *n.* the generality of men; the common run. —人並外れて丈高い, tall beyond the common run. —人並の目鼻立ち, ordinary features. —人並の口を利く, to talk like an ordinary man.

hitonami (人波), *n.* a surging crowd. —人波打つ(群衆が), to surge.

hitonareru (人馴れる), *vi.* to be used to company [society]; become familiar with others.

hitonatsukoi (人懐こい), *a.* warm-hearted; tender-hearted. —人懐こい目で人を見る, to look at another with a warm heart.

hitoomoi (一思に), *ad.* with one effort; outright. —一思ひに殺して了ふ, to kill outright. —苦(にが)い藥を一思ひに飲む, to take a bitter medicine with one effort.

hitori (一人), *n.* ❶ a person; a man; one. ❷ 〔獨〕 (自分だけなること) being alone. —獨りで, by oneself (單身で); of oneself (自然に); of its own accord (自發的に). (獨りでやれ, Do it by yourself. —燈火が獨りで消えた, The light went out of itself.) —一人も殘らず, without exception; every one of them; to the last man. —一人一人呼び出す, to call up one by one. —獨り取殘されて了ッた, I was left alone [to myself]. ¶ 一人子(息子; 娘), an only child (son; daughter).

hitori (獨, 啻), *ad.* ❶ (單に) alone. ❷ (取別け) only; merely; solely. —獨り…のみならず尙又, not only [merely]..., but (also).

hitoriannai (獨案內), *n.* a cab; a crib; a guide. ☞ *dokuannai.*

hitoribotchi (獨法師の), *a.* lonely. —獨法師になる, to be left alone [to oneself].

hitoributai (獨舞臺), *n.* having the stage to oneself; being the master (mistress) *of* (the situation).

hitorigime (一人決), *n.* self-decision; having settled [decided] by oneself alone.

hitorigoto (獨言), *n.* a monologue; a soliloquy; talking to oneself. —獨言を云ふ, to soliloquize; monologize; talk [say] to oneself.

hitorigurashi (獨暮し), *n.* celibacy; a bachelor [single] life.

hitorijime (獨占), *n.* monopoly. —利益を獨占めにする, to take all the profit to oneself.

hitorimono (獨身者), *n.* an unmarried person; a single man (woman); a bachelor(男); a spinster (未婚女); an old maid(老孃).

hitorimushi (燈蛾), *n.* 【蛾】 the tiger-moth.

hitoritengu (獨天狗), *n.* a self-sufficient person.

hitoriyogari (獨好がり), *n.* self-satisfaction; self-complacency. —獨好がりの, self-satisfied; self-complacent.

hitorizumai (獨住居), *n.* living alone [by oneself].

hitosarai (人攫ひ), *n.* ❶ (行爲) abduction; kidnapping. ❷ (人) a kidnapper.

hitosashiyubi (人差指), *n.* the index(-finger); the forefinger.

hitoshii (等·均·齊しい), *vi.* to be equal *to*; be equivalent *to*; amount *to*.

hitoshikiri (一頻), *ad.* at one time; for a while. —一頻りの雨, a shower.

hitoshiku (等·均·齊しく), *ad.* equally; evenly; alike. —均しく利益を分つ, to divide the profit equally. —名を等しくする, to be of equal fame.

hitoshio (一入), *ad.* still [much] more; especially.

hitoshio (一鹽の), *a.* lightly salted.

hitoshirenu (人知れぬ), *a.* unknown to others. —人知れぬ苦勞をする, to bear hardships unknown to others.

hitosoroi (一揃), *n.* a set (道具); a suit (服); a stand (武具).

hitosuji (一筋に), *ad.* earnestly; with the whole heart. —一筋に思ひ詰める, to love with all one's heart; love to distraction; be madly in love *with*. —一筋繩ではいかぬ奴だ, He is a fellow very hard to manage.

hi-tosuru (非とする), *vt.* to disapprove; deprecate.

hitotabi (一度), *ad.* once; one time.

hitotamari (一堪りもなく), *ad.* without any resistance.

hitotonari (爲人), *n.* character; disposition. —爲人溫厚篤實である, to be gentle and sincere in character.

hitotōri (一通り), *ad.* generally; in the main (大體); once (一度). —一通り知ッてる, to have a fair knowledge *of*. —一通り目を通す, to pass the eyes *over*; glance *through*.

hitotsu (一), *n.* ❶ (一箇) one; a unit. ❷ (同一) the same. —一つ宛; 一つ一つ, one by one. (一つ一つ擇り分ける, to pick one by one.) —一つとして見るに足る物がない, There was not a thing worth seeing.

hitotsuana (一穴の狐), *n.* the foxes of the same complexion.

hitotsubu (一粒), *n.* a grain. ¶ 一粒種, the only child (一人子). —一粒選り, ① (事) careful selection [picking]. ② (物) the pick of the basket. (一粒選りの人物, a carefully selected person.)

hitotsukami (一摑), *n.* a handful; a grasp. —一摑みに, at one swoop.

hitotsuki (一突), *n.* a push; a stroke. —一突きに突き破る, to break through at one stroke.

hitotsume (一目の), *a.* one-eyed. ¶ 一目小僧, a one-eyed bogie [monster].

hitotsunabe (一つ鍋の物を食ふ), to live in the same house (*with*).

hitotsuniwa (一つには), *ad.* ❶ (第一に) first; first of all; firstly. ❷ (部分的) partly.

hitotsuoki (一つ隔に), *ad.* alternately. —赤と白とを一つ置きに並べる, to range red and white alternately.

hitoyasumi (一休みする), *v.* to take a rest; rest oneself a while.

hitoyoshi (好人), *n.* ❶ (性質) good nature. ❷ (人) a good-natured man.

hitozato (人里), *n.* a human dwelling; a village.

hitozuki (人好きする), *a.* amiable; genial; companionable. —人好きのする繪, a picture that catches one's fancy. —人好きのする婦人, an amiable lady.

hitozureta (人擦れた), *a.* knowing; canny; artful.

hitozute (人傳に), *ad.* through another. —人傳に聞いて知ってゐる, to know by hearsay.

hitsu (櫃), *n.* a box; a chest (函); a coffer.

hitsū (悲痛), *n.* grief; sorrow; sadness; pang. —悲痛な, grievous; sad; pathetic.

hitsuboku (筆墨), *n.* pen and ink; writing materials; stationery.

hitsudan (筆談), *n.* written conversation. —筆談する, to converse on paper (*with*); converse by writing.

hitsudoku (必讀), *n.* indispensable reading. —學生必讀の書, a book which students should not miss reading.

hitsugi (柩), *n.* a coffin.

hitsuji (羊), *n.* ❶【哺乳】the sheep; the lamb (仔羊); the wether (去勢した羊); the ewe (牝); the ram (牡). ¶ 牧羊者 (ひつじかひ), a shepherd.

hitsujuhin (必需品), *n.* a necessary; a necessity; a requisite.

hitsuke (火附), *n.* ❶ (放火) incendiarism; arson. ❷ (放火者) an incendiary; a fire-fiend〔俗〕.

hitsumetsu (必滅), *n.* perishableness; certainty of destruction.

hitsuyō (必要), *n.* necessity; need; requirement. —必要の場合には, in case of necessity; if needs be. —…する必要がない, There is no need to…. —實際の必要に應する, to meet a practical need. —必要は發明の母, "Necessity is the mother of invention." ¶ 必要品, a necessary; a requisite; a necessity. (生活必要品, the necessaries of life.)

hitsuzen (必然の), *a.* necessary; inevitable; certain. —必然の結果として, as a necessary consequence.

hittateru (引ッ立てる), *vt.* ❶ = ***hikitateru*** (引立てる). ❷ (持上げる) to lift; raise. —漸く腰を引ッ立てる, to rise at last from his seat.

hitteki (匹敵する), *vt.* to be a match *for*; be on a par *with*; be equal *to*; equal; match. —匹敵するものなし, to be without a match; have no equal *in*.

hitto (ヒット), *n.*【野球】a hit.

hittō (筆頭), *n.* the first (in a roll or list); the doyen.

hiuchi (火打箱), *n.* a tinder-box. ¶ 燧石, a flint (for striking fire); a fire-stone.

hiuragakinin (被裏書人), *n.* an endorsee, indorsee.

hiwa (鶸), *n.* ❶【鳥】the siskin. ❷ (色) light green.

hiwai (卑猥な), *a.* coarse; indecent; obscene. —卑猥な話, obscene [broad] talk.

hiwari (日割), *n.* ❶ daily rate. ❷ programme. —日割で勘定する, to pay [settle] by the day. —試験の日割を發表する, to announce the days fixed for examination.

hiya (冷), *n.* ❶ (冷酒の略) cold *sake*. ❷ (冷水の略) cold water. ❸ (冷飯の略) cold boiled-rice.

hiyaase (冷汗), *n.* cold sweat [perspiration]. —冷汗をかく, to be in cold sweat.

hiyahiya (ヒヤヒヤ), *int.* hear! hear!

hiyahiya (冷冷する), *vi.* ❶ to be cool. ❷ (危ぶんで) to be in great fear [trepidation].

hiyakashi (冷かし), *n.* ❶ (冷評) banter; chaff; raillery; jest; *badinage*〔佛〕. ❷ (素見) having a look without intending to buy. ❸ (冷却) cooling. ❹ (浸漬) steeping.

hiyakasu (冷かす), *vt.* ❶ (冷評) to chaff; banter; rally. ❷ (素見) to shop (店を); amuse one's self by looking *at*. ❸ (冷却する) to chill; cool. ❹ (浸漬) to steep; soak.

hiyaku (非役), *n.* being out of office; being out of commission. ☞ ***hieki*** (非役). —非役の軍人, a retired officer.

hiyaku (飛躍), *n.* a leap. —大飛躍を試みる, to try a bold leap [a flying jump].

hiyaku (秘薬), *n.* a secret [an efficacious] medicine [remedy]; a nostrum.

hiyameshi (冷飯), *n.* cold boiled-rice.

hiyari (冷りとする), ❶ (寒氣立つ) Blood runs chill. ❷ (冷たく思ふ) to feel cold.

hiyashigusuri (冷却藥), *n.* a cooling draught; a cooler.

hiyasu (冷す), *vt.* to cool.

hiyayaka (冷かな), *a.* ❶ (つめたい) chilly; cold; cool. ❷ (冷淡な) cold-hearted; cold. —冷かに考へる, to think coolly.

hiyazake (冷酒), *n.* unheated [cold] *sake.*

hiyō (日傭), *n.* daily employment (事); a day-labourer (人). ¶ 日傭賃, daily wages. —日傭稼, working for daily wages. —日傭取, a dayman; a day-labourer.

hiyō (飛揚), *n.* a flight. ——**suru,** *v.* to fly. ——, *a.* 【動】volitant; volant. —空中に飛揚する, to fly in [through] the air.

hiyō (費用), *n.* expense; expenditure; outlay. —莫大(僅少)の費用で, at a great (little) expense. —費用お構ひなしに, regardless of expense. —如何に費用がかゝらうとも, at any expense. —費用を拂ふ, to meet an expense. —費用を節減する, to curtail [cut down] expenses.

hiyodori (鵯), *n.* 【鳥】the brown-eared bulbul.

hiyoke (日除), *n.* a sun-blind; a sun-screen. —日除をする, to screen from the sun.

hiyokko (雛鷄), *n.* a chicken; a chick.

hiyoku (肥沃の), *a.* fertile; rich.

hiyokuzuka (比翼塚), *n.* a lovers' mound.

hiyori (日和), *n.* ❶ (晴天) fine weather. ❷ (天氣模様) weather. ❸ (形勢) condition; situation; the state of affairs. ☞ ***tenki*** (天氣). —日和を見る, ① to forecast the weather. ② to see how the land lies [the wind blows; the cat jumps]. ¶ 日和下駄, low-supported clogs (worn in dry weather).

hiyu (比喩), *n.* a metaphor (暗比); a simile (明比). —比喩的, figurative; metaphorical.

hiza (膝), *n.* the knee; the lap. —膝までの深(高)さの, knee-deep (-high). —膝を組む, to cross one's legs. —膝を崩す, to squat crookedly. —膝を容るゝ餘地なし, to have no room for any more person.

hizagashira (膝頭), *n.* Ⓢ 膝株. the bend of the knee.

hizakake (膝掛), *n.* a rug; a wrapper.

hizakurige (膝栗毛で), *ad.* on shanks' mare.

hizamazuku (跪く), *vi.* to kneel; drop [fall] on one's knees. —跪いて, on one's knees.

hizamoto (膝下), near one's knee; beside oneself. —父母の膝下を離れる, to leave one's parents' side.

hizeme (火攻), *n.* 【軍】an attack with fire.

hizeme (火責にする), *v.* to torture with fire.

hizen (疥癬, 皮癬), *n.* itch; mange (犬·牛·馬等の); scabies. —皮癬をかく, to suffer from the itch. ¶ 皮癬かき, an itchy person.

hizō (秘藏する), *vt.* to prize; treasure (up); enshrine.

hizō (脾臟), *n.* the spleen.

hizoku (卑俗の), *a.* vulgar; gross; coarse.

hizuke (日附), *n.* date. —本月十日の日附の貴翰, your letter of the 10th instant [dated the 10th instant; under date (of) the 10th instant]. —日附をする, to date.

hizume (蹄), *n.* the hoof [*pl.* -s]. —蹄にかける, to kick; trample under foot.

hizumi (歪), *n.* 【理】strain; distortion.

hizumu (歪む), *vi.* to be bent; be crooked; be warped.

ho (ほ), *n.* 【音】E; mi (伊); 3.

ho (帆), *n.* a sail; a canvas (木綿の). —帆を揚げる(おろす), to hoist [spread] (lower) a sail. —追手に帆を揚げて駛る, to speed with the sail hoisted in the fair wind; sail before the wind.

ho (歩), *n.* a step; a pace; march (軍隊の). —歩を進める, ① to make progress. ② to step forward. —歩を速(緩)める, to quicken [mend] (slow down) one's pace. —一歩を誤れば, if we take a false step.

ho (穗), *n.* ❶ an ear; a head; a spike (小麥の). ❷ (物の穗先) the head (刃物の); the spike.

hō (方), *n.* ❶ (方角, 方面) a direction; a quarter. ❷ (側) a side; a part. ❸ (方法) a method; a way. ❹ (四角) a square.

hō (法), *n.* ❶ (方法) a method; a manner; a way. ❷ (法律) a

law. ● (法則) a rule; a law. ● (儀式) a ceremony; religious rites [practices] (佛法). ● (宗教) religion. ● (除數) a divisor. ● (動詞の) the mood. —法を曲げる, to pervert the law. ¶ 普通法, general law (一般法); common law (慣習法).

hō (苞), *n.* 【植】 a bract.

hō (砲), *n.* a gun; a cannon (大砲); ordnance.

hō (報), *n.* ● (むくい) recompense; reward (報酬, 應報). ● (報知) a report; information. —近著の報によれば, according to a late report.

hō (頰), *n.* the cheek. —こけた頰, hollow cheeks. —ポチャポチャした頰, chubby [plump] cheeks.

hoan (保安), *n.* preservation of peace. ¶ 保安課 (警察), the peace preservation section (police).

hōan (法案), *n.* a bill; a measure. —法案を否決する, to reject [throw out] a bill. —法案を通過さす, to pass a bill.

hōbai (朋輩), *n.* one's mates [comrades; companions].

hobaku (捕縛する), *vt.* to arrest; seize; apprehend.

hōbaru (頰張る), *vt.* to stuff into one's mouth; fill the mouth *with*; cram [stuff] the mouth. —餅を頰張る, to fill the mouth with rice-cake.

hobashira (檣), *n.* a mast.

hōben (方便), *n.* ● 【佛】 (權智を以て下根の衆生を導くこと) a pious fraud. ● (手段) means. ● (權宜) a shift (臨機の計); an expedient; a contrivance (工夫). — 一時的方便, a temporary expedient.

hōbeni (頰紅), *n.* cheek rouge.

hōbi (褒美), *n.* a prize; a reward. —褒美を貰ふ, to receive a prize [reward].

hobo (粗, 略), *ad.* nearly; almost; about. —ほぼ同年配 (である), to be much of an age. —ほぼ出來上る, to be nearly completed. —ほぼ似てゐる, to resemble fairly.

hobo (保姆), *n.* a nurse; a dry-nurse; a nursery governess.

hōbō (魴鮄), *n.* 【魚】 the gurnard.

hōbō (方方), *n.* all sides; every direction. —方々歩き廻る, to walk about everywhere. —方々から電話がかゝる, to be called up by telephone from everywhere.

hōbō (鋒鋩), *n.* the sword-point. —鋒鋩を露はす, to betray sharpness.

hōboku (放牧する), *vt.* to graze; put [send; turn; turn out] to grass.

hōbone (頰骨), *n.* 【解】 the cheek-bone.

hōbun (法文), *n.* ● the wording of the law; the letter of the law. ● the law.

hōbutsusen (拋物線), *n.* a parabola.

hōchi (封地), *n.* a fief; a feud.

hōchi (報知), *n.* information; intelligence; report. ☞ *hō* (報). —報知する, to inform; report; send word; let know. ¶ 報知艦, an advice-vessel. —報知器, an alarm; a communicator (汽車の).

hōchikoku (法治國), *n.* a law-governed country.

hōchiku (放逐), *n.* ● (逐ひ出すこと) ejection; expulsion; exclusion. ● (追放) deportation; banishment. —— **-suru**, *vt.* ● to eject; expel; drive out. ● to deport; banish. ● (解雇) to dismiss; discharge; turn out. —惡魔を放逐する, to exorcise the devil.

hochō (步調), *n.* ● (足竝) pace; step. ● (行動) action. —步調を亂す, to break stop. —步調を取る, to mark time. —步調を揃へる, to keep step (with a person). —步調を共にする, to act in concert *with*.

hōchō (庖刀), *n.* a kitchen-knife. ¶ 魚庖刀, a fish-knife.

hōdai (放題), at will; as one pleases; without restraint. —したい放題なことをする, to do as one pleases. —金を遣ひ放題に遣はせる, to let a person spend as much money as he pleases.

hōdai (砲臺), *n.* a battery; a fort (要塞).

hōdan (砲彈), *n.* a shell; a projectile. —砲彈を冒して進む, to advance under a hail of the enemy's shells.

hodasareru (絆される), *vi.* to be fettered; be encumbered; be hindered. —子に絆される, to be hindered by a child. —深切に絆されて從ふ, to be subdued by kindness.

hodashi (羈絆), *n.* bonds; ties; encumbrance. ☞ *kizuna* (絆).

hodatsu (逋脫する), *vt.* to evade; escape. —稅金の逋脫を謀る, to attempt to evade the payment of taxes.

hōden (放電), *n.* (electric) discharge. ¶ 火花 (聲無) 放電, a spark (silent) discharge.

hodo (程), *n.* ● (程度) limit; bounds; extent. ● (中庸) moderation. ● (分限) social standing; station of life; position. ● (時間) time; interval. ● (人あしらひ)

address. ——, *ad.* ❶(比較) as [so]...as; so...that; like. ❷(概略) about; some. —程經て, some time after [later]; after a lapse of time; later *on*. —二十分程, some [about] twenty minutes. —彼れ程正直な男, such an honest man as he is. —大砲の音が聞えぬ程の聾, so deaf that he cannot hear a cannon. —冗談にも程がある, There is a limit to a joke.

hodō (步道), *n.* a footway; a footpath; a walk; a sidewalk.

hodō (鋪道), *n.* a pavement; a flagging (板石の).

hodō (輔導する), *vt.* to lead; guide.

hōdō (報道), *n.* news; information; a report. ☞ *hōchi* (報知).

hodobashiru (迸る), *vi.* to gush out; rush out; spurt.

hodokoshi (施), *n.* ❶(施與) alms-giving; charity. ❷(施物) (an) alms; a charity; a dole. —施を乞ふ(受ける), to beg (receive) alms. —貧乏人に施をする, to give alms to the poor.

hodokosu (施す), *vt.* ❶(施與) to give; give alms; dispense. ❷(彩色等を加へる) to apply. ❸(用ひ行ふ) to practise; carry out; perform. —藥を施す, to dispense medicine. —恩惠を施す, to show favours; confer a favour on a person. —敎育を施す, to give (an) education. —あらゆる手段を施す, to use every means.

hodoku (釋く), *vt.* ❶ to untie; unbind; unfasten; unloosen; undo; open (開く). ❷(はぐす) to take to pieces; unravel. ☞ *toku* (解く). —釋ける, to come [get] loose; get untied.

hodonaku (程なく), *ad.* soon; presently; ere [before] long. —程なく全快した, It was not long before he recovered.

hodoyoi (程よい), *a.* moderate; fair; temperate (飲食家など). —程よく, moderately; fairly. —程よい時分に, opportunely; in season.

hōe (法會), *n.* a mass; a Buddhist service.

hoegoe (吠聲), *n.* bark; bay; howl (狼・犬の).

hōen (砲煙), *n.* (cannon) smoke. —砲煙彈雨の間に戰ふ, to fight amid cannon smoke and under a hail of shots.

hoeru (吠える), *vi.* ❶(吠)(主に犬) to bark; bay. ❷(吼)(牛其他猛獸) to bellow; brag(驢の); roar (虎・獅子等の). ❸(海・風等の) to roar; howl; rave.

hōetsu (法悅), *n.* ecstasy; transport; rapture.

hōfu (抱負), *n.* aspiration; ambition; plan. —大きな抱負, very high aspirations.

hōfu (豐富な), *a.* rich; plentiful; abundant. —豐富な供給, ample [copious; plentiful] supply. —音量の豐富な聲, a rich voice.

hofuku (匍匐する), *vi.* to crawl; creep; trail (蔓が地を). ——, *a.* 【博】reptant (主に植物); reptile; creeping.

hōfuku (法服), *n.* a robe; a gown; the long robe.

hōfuku (報復), *n.* revenge; requital; retaliation. —報復する, to revenge; take vengeance; retaliate.

hōfuku (捧腹する), *vi.* to burst out laughing; burst into a loud laugh. —捧腹絶倒する, to scream; burst into a fit of laughter; shake [hold; split] one's sides with laughter. —捧腹絶倒さす, to throw into convulsions.

hofuru (屠る), *vt.* ❶(屠殺) to butcher (主に牛馬に云ふ); slaughter. ❷(慘殺) to massacre.

hōfutsu (髣髴・彷彿する), *vi.* ❶ to resemble closely; be very like. ❷ to appear dimly.

hōga (萌芽), *n.* ❶(芽の出ること) germination; pullulation. ❷(めばえ) a germ; a shoot; a sprout. —萌芽する, to germinate; sprout; pullulate.

hōgai (法外の), *a.* excessive; unreasonable; exorbitant. —法外の價で, at a fancy price. —法外の要求をする, to make an excessive demand.

hōgaku (方角), *n.* a direction; a quarter. —方角違ひの, in the wrong direction.

hōgaku (法學), *n.* the law; jurisprudence. ¶ 法學博士, a doctor of law. —法學士, a bachelor of law.

hōgan (包含する), *vt.* to include; comprise; comprehend; contain.

hōgan (砲丸), *n.* a cannon-ball. ¶ 砲丸投げ, putting the shot.

hogaraka (朗かな), *a.* ❶ bright; clear; serene. ❷(聲) clear; sonorous. —朗かな天氣, a bright day. —朗かな音聲で, in a clear voice.

hogei (捕鯨), *n.* whale-fishing [-fishery]; whaling. ¶ 捕鯨船, a whale-boat; a whaler.

hōgei (奉迎する), *vt.* to welcome (the Emperor, *etc.*). ¶ 奉迎門, a gate (an arch) to welcome His Majesty.

hōgeki (砲擊), *n.* bombardment; cannonade; artillery attack. ——**suru**, *vt.* bombard; cannonade; fire *on*. —要塞を砲擊する, to fire on a fort.

hōgen (方言), *n.* a dialect; a provincialism (地方詞).

hōgen (放言), *n.* random speech; unreserved talk. —放言する, to speak at random; talk unreservedly [without reserve].

hogo (保護), *n.* protection; shelter; care. —法律の保護の下に, under the guardianship of the laws. —警察に保護願を出す, to apply to the police station for protection. **—-suru,** *vt.* to protect; guard; shelter. —産業を保護する, to protect industries. —身體を保護する, ① to protect one's body. ② (身體を大事にする) to take care of oneself [one's health]. —文藝を保護する, to patronize literature. ¶ 保護預り, safety deposit. —保護貿易, protective trade; protection. —保護鳥, a protected bird. —保護國, a protecting state; a protected state (被保護國); a protectorate (同上). —保護者, a protector [*fem.* -tress]; a guard, guardian; a patron [*fem.* -ess]. —保護司, a probation officer —保護色, protective colouring. —保護税率, protective tariff.

hogu, hōgu, (反古), *n.* waste paper. —反古になる, to become waste-paper. —反古にする, to throw into the waste-paper basket. (約束を反古にする, to break one's promise.) ¶ 反古籠, a waste-paper basket.

hogusu (釋す), *vt.* ❶ (組立てたもの又は縫物を) to take to pieces; pick to pieces. ❷ (編物又は縺れたものを) to unravel; unknit (編物を); disentangle (縺れたものを). —絲を釋す, to unravel a thread. —著物をほぐす, to take a dress to pieces.

hōgyo (崩御), *n.* demise (of the crown).

hōgyoku (寶玉), *n.* a jewel; a gem; a precious stone. —寶玉入りの指環, a jewelled ring. —寶玉で飾る, [*vt.*] to jewel. ¶ 寶玉商, a jeweller.

hohei (歩兵), *n.* ❶ (軍人の) the infantry; foot (horse の 對); a foot-soldier (個人). ❷ (將棋の) a pawn. ¶ 歩兵中隊, a (an infantry) company. —歩兵大隊, an infantry battalion. —歩兵第四聯隊, the 4th infantry regiment.

hōhei (砲兵), *n.* ❶ (隊) artillery. ❷ (兵) an artilleryman; a gunner. ¶ 砲兵中隊, a (an artillery) battery. —砲兵彈藥車, a caisson; an artillery ammunition waggon. —砲兵縦列, an artillery train. —砲兵工廠, an arsenal; an ordnance factory. —砲兵聯隊, an artillery regiment.

hōheishi (奉幣使), *n.* an official sent (by the Emperor) to make offerings at a shrine.

hōheishi (報聘使), *n.* a messenger (to return courtesies).

hōhen (襃貶), *n.* praise and censure; criticism.

hōhige (頰鬚, 髯), *n.* whiskers.

hohitsu (輔弼する), *vt.* to assist; give advice *to.* —輔弼の臣, ministers of state; advisers to the Throne.

hōhō (方法), *n.* a method; a plan; a device. —方法を見出す, to find a way. —方法を廻らす, to think of a way.

hōhō (這這の體で), *ad.* precipitately; hurriedly; in haste. —這々の體で逃げ出した, He ran precipitately out of the house.

hohoemu (微笑む), *vi.* to smile. —微笑みながらいふ, to say [speak] smiling [with a smile].

hoi (補遺), *n.* a supplement; an addendum.

hōi (方位), *n.* a direction; a course; bearings. ☞ *hōgaku* (方角). —方位を定める, ① to find one's way. ② to find one's position. ¶ 方位主點, cardinal points.

hōi (包圍), *n.* siege; investment. —包圍する, to besiege; lay siege *to*; invest. —包圍を解く, to raise the siege *of.* ¶ 包圍軍, an investing army. —包圍攻撃, a siege.

hōi (法衣), *n.* a sacerdotal robe; canonicals; a vestment.

hōigaku (法醫學), *n.* medical jurisprudence; forensic medicine.

hoiku (保育), *n.* bringing up; nursing.

hoiro (焙爐), *n.* a drier. —焙爐に掛ける, to dry in a drier.

hōitsu (放逸の), *a.* unrestrained; unbridled. —放逸な生活をする, to lead a fast life; live without restraint.

hoji (保持), *n.* holding; maintenance; preservation. **—-suru,** *vt.* to hold; preserve; maintain. —健康を保持する, to preserve one's health.

hōji (邦字), *n.* a Japanese word. ¶ 邦字新聞, a vernacular [Japanese] paper; a paper in Japanese.

hōji (法事), *n.* a Buddhist mass. —法事を營む, to hold mass.

hojikuru (穿る), *vt.* ❶ (穿つ) to dig up; grub. ❷ (耳·齒など) to pick; clean. ❸ (探す) to ferret out; pry *into.* 齒(耳)をほじくる, to pick one's teeth (ear). —人の缺點[?]を穿くる, to ferret

out people's defects.
hōjin (法人), *n.* 【法】 a juristic [juridical] person; a corporate body. ¶ 法人所得, the income of a corporation.
hōjiro (頰白), *n.* 【鳥】 the Japanese bunting.
hojiru (穿る), *vt.* = ***hojikuru.***
hojo (補助), *n.* ❶ (補足) supplement. ❷ (援助) assistance; aid; help. ❸ (補給) grant-in-aid. —補助する, to aid; assist; support. —補助を受ける, to have a grant; be subsidized. ¶ 補助貨幣, subsidiary coin. —補助金, a subvention; a subsidy; a grant-in-aid.
hōjo (幇助する), *vt.* 【法】 to assist; help; aid and abet; back up. —惡事を幇助する, to abet an evil deed.
hōjō (方丈), *n.* ❶ (和倘の居間) a monastery; a superior's quarters. ❷ (寺の主僧) a superior; an abbot; a prior.
hōjō (褒狀), *n.* an honourable mention; a certificate of merit.
hōjō (豐饒な), *a.* fertile; rich; fruitful. —豐饒な土地, fertile land.
hojū (補充), *n.* complement; replenishment; recruitment. **——-suru,** *vt.* to complement; recruit; replenish *with.* —缺員を補充する, to fill up vacancies. ¶ 補充兵, a recruit.
hōjū (放縱), *n.* indulgence; self-indulgence; licence; *abandon* 《佛》. —放縱な, self-indulgent; loose; free; Bohemian.
hōjuku (豐熟する), *vi.* to ripen; mature.
hōjutsu (砲術), *n.* artillery; gunnery.
hoka (外), *n.* ❶ (他處) some other place. ❷ (外部, 戸外) outside; without. —外に, [*ad.*] (*a*) besides (の外に); in addition to (同上); elsewhere (餘所に): (*b*) otherwise. ☞ ***tani*** (他に). —の外(は), [*prep.*] except; save; outside. —彼の外皆, all save him. —某陸軍大尉外二十一名, Captain ...and twenty-one others. —外ならぬ, to be nothing but; be no other than. —これ外ない, This is all I have [all there is]. —泣くよりほかはない, She can do nothing but weep. —外に何が《か》要るか, What else do you want? 《Is there anything else you want?》. —彼の外には適任者がない, There is no suitable person except him. 英語の外に外國語を知らぬ, to know no other foreign language than English.
hōka (法科), *n.* the law department. ¶ 法科大學, the law college.
hōka (法貨), *n.* legal tender.
hōka (放火する), *vt.* to set fire *to.* —明家に放火する, to set fire to an empty house. ¶ 放火犯, arson.
hōka (放課), *n.* the end of a lesson-hour. ¶ 放課後, after school. —放課時間, playtime; recess.
hōka (苞裹), *n.* a wrapper; a covering; a package.
hōka (砲火), *n.* fire; gun-fire. —敵の猛烈な砲火の下に, under the enemy's heavy fire. —砲火を浴びる, to be under fire. —砲火を集中する, to concentrate the fire *on.* ¶ 障壁砲火, barrage; a curtain-fire.
hōkaburi (頰冠り), *n.* covering one's cheeks with a towel.
hōkai (崩壞), *n.* collapse; dissolution; breakdown; disintegration. —崩壞する, to collapse; give way; crumble (岩石など); disintegrate (同上).
hōkaiseki (方解石), *n.* calcite; calc-spar.
hokakebune (帆掛船), *n.* a sailing-ship [-vessel; -boat]; a sailer.
hokakeru (帆掛ける), *vi.* to hoist a sail; set sail.
hokaku (捕獲), *n.* seizure; capture. —捕獲する, to capture; seize. ¶ 捕獲物, a prize. —捕獲審檢所, a prize court. (國際《高等》捕獲審檢所, the international 《higher》 prize court. —捕獲審檢所評定官, a prize court assessor.) —捕獲賞金, prize money.
hokan (保管), *n.* custody; keeping; safe-keeping. —保管する, to take charge *of*; take custody *of.* ¶ 保管物, an article in custody. —保管金, money in one's custody. —保管人, 【法】 a depositary; a custodian. —保管料, a charge for custody; custody-fee.
hōkan (法官), *n.* judiciary (全體); a judge; a judicial officer. ¶ 法官部, 【陸】 the judicial department.
hōkan (放還する), *vt.* to discharge; release; set free.
hōkan (奉還する), *vt.* to return [restore] to the Emperor. —大政を奉還する, to return the administrative authority to the Throne.
hōkan (砲艦), *n.* a gun-boat [-vessel].
hōkan (幇間), *n.* a buffoon; a professional jester.
hōkanshō (寳冠章), *n.* the Order of the Sacred Crown.
hōkatsu (包括する), *vt.* to include; comprise; cover; embrace; take *in.* —包括的, 【法】 universal; inclusive *of.*
hōkei (方形), *n.* squareness; a square(物).
hoken (保險), *n.* ❶ insurance; assurance (生命保險に用ふ). ❷ (保證) warranty. —保險を附す

る, to effect an insurance; insure. —保險を解除する, to cancel an insurance. —保險を勸誘する, to canvass for insurance. —生命を保險する, to assure a life. ¶ 物品保險, goods insurance. —勞働(者)保險, workingmen's insurance. —保險物, a thing [property] insured. —保險代理業, insurance agency. —保險會社, an insurance company [office]. —保險業者, an insurer; an underwriter. —保險勸誘人, an insurance agent. —保險契約者, an insurance-taker; an insurant. —保險金, insurance money. (保險金受取人, a beneficiary.) —保險人, an insurer; an underwriter. (被保險人, the insured; the assured.) —保險率, a premium rate. —保險證券, a (an insurance) policy.

hoken (保健), *n.* sanitation. —國民の保健狀態, sanitary [health] condition of the nation. ¶ 保健大臣, Health Minister. —保健衞生調査會, the Board for the Investigation of National Hygiene. —保健課, the health-preservation section. —保健省, Health Ministry. —保健食物, sanitary food. —保健運動, a constitutional (walk).

hōken (封建-制度), *n.* feudalism; the feudal system. ¶ 封建時代, the feudal age [times].

hōken (奉獻), *n.* dedication; consecration; oblation. —奉獻する, to devote; dedicate; consecrate.

hōken (寶劍), *n.* the sacred sword.

hoketsu (補缺), *n.* supply of deficiency; filling a vacancy; an emergency man (野球の). ¶ 補缺募集, an invitation for filling vacancies. —補缺入學, admission (into a school) to fill up a vacancy. —補缺選擧, a by-election.

hōki (箒), *n.* a broom. —箒で掃く, to sweep with a broom.

hōki (法規), *n.* laws and regulations. —法規に牴觸する, to contravene [infringe] laws and regulations.

hōki (放棄する), *vt.* ❶ (權利·要求等) to renounce; waive; relinquish. ❷ (計畫等) to give up; abandon. ❸ (物等) to throw away.

hōki (蜂起する), *vi.* to rise in arms [rebellion].

hōkiboshi (彗星), *n.* a comet. ☞ *suisei* (彗星).

hōkigi (地膚), *n.* 【植】 Ⓢ はうきぐさ. the broom goosefoot.

hokinsha (保菌者), *n.* a bacilli-carrier; a bacillus-carrier.

hokkai (北海), *n.* ❶ the north [northern] sea. ❷ [K-] the North Sea; the German Ocean.

hokkē (ホッケー), *n.* 【遊戲】 hockey.

hokki (發起), *n.* ❶ (發議) promotion (會社等の); instance; proposal. ❷ (發心) a suggestion. —...の發起で, at the instance *of*; under the auspices *of*. —發起する, [*vt.*] to promote; propose; project. ¶ 發起人, ① a promoter. ② an originator.

hokkoku (北國), *n.* the north; a northern country; the northern provinces.

hokku (發句), *n.* ❶ (連歌の第一句) the first line of a long ode. ❷ (俳句) a seventeen-syllabled verse; a *hokku*.

hokku (ホック), *n.* hook-and-eye. —ホックで留める, [*vt.*] to hook.

hokkyoku (北極), *n.* the North Pole. ¶ 北極熊, the polar bear. —北極圈, the Arctic circle; the Arctic. —北極星, 【天】 the pole-star; the north star; the lodestar. —北極探檢, an Arctic expedition.

hoko (矛, 鋒), *n.* a halberd; a spear; arms (武器). —鋒を向ける, to turn one's arms *against*. —戈を執って起つ, to take up arms.

hokō (步行), *n.* walk; tramp. —步行する, ① [*vi.*] to walk; tramp; go on foot. ② [*a.*] 【動】 gressorial; ambulatory; pedestrian. ¶ 步行動物, an ambulatory animal. —步行者, a walker; a foot-passenger; a pedestrian.

hōko (寶庫), *n.* a treasure-house; a treasury.

hōkō (方向), *n.* ❶ (向) a direction; bearings. ❷ (方針, 針路) a course; a line. —潮流の方向, the set [drift] of current. —方向を取る(轉ずる), to take (change) one's course. —方向を保つ, to hold one's course; keep to one's line. —方向を誤る, to take a wrong course.

hōkō (芳香), *n.* fragrance; aroma; perfume. ¶ 芳香劑, an aromatic.

hōkō (彷徨する), *vi.* to wander [roam] about; ramble; stroll; straggle; saunter.

hōkō (放校する), *vt.* to expel from school.

hōkō (奉公), *n.* ❶ public service. ❷ service. —奉公に行く, to go into service; go out to serve. —子供を奉公に出す, to send [put] out a child to service. —...に奉公してゐる, to be in —s' service. —女中奉公をする, to enter into domestic service; serve as a maidservant. —奉公口を探す, to look for employment [a position]. —奉公の精神に乏しい, to be lacking [wanting] in patriotic

(public) spirit. ⌈howl; bellow.⌉
hōkō (咆哮する), *vi.* to roar;⌋
hōkō (砲工), *n.* a gunman. ¶ 砲工學校, the Artillery and Engineering School.
hōkō (縫工), *n.* 【軍】 an army-tailor. ¶ 縫工長, a master tailor.
hōkoku (報告), *n.* ❶ (報知) a report; a return. ❷ (報告書) a report; returns. —報告する, to report. —報告を作る, to make a report. —報告書を差出す, to hand in one's report. ¶ 報告者, a reporter. —報告筒, 【軍】 a message tube.
hōkoku (報國の), *a.* patriotic. ¶ 報國心, patriotism.
hokori (埃), *n.* dust. —埃が立つ, to be dusty. —埃を立てる, to raise [kick up] dust. —埃を濕す, to lay the dust.
hokori (誇), *n.* pride (矜恃); glory (名譽); credit (同上). —處女の誇, pride of maidenhood. —誇とする, to be proud *of*; take pride *in*; glory *in*.
hokorobi (綻), *n.* a rent; a rip; an opening of a seam. —綻びを切らす, to rent.
hokorobiru (綻びる), *vi.* ❶ (縫目) to be rent; rip. ❷ (開花) to (burst) open.
hokoru (誇る), *vi.* ❶ (誇張) to boast (*of*); brag *of*; vaunt. ❷ (心に恃む) to be proud *of*. ❸ (功など高ぶる) to pride oneself *upon*; plume oneself *upon*. —世界に誇るべき美擧, a fine deed one may well be proud of before the world.
hokosaki (鋒尖), *n.* ❶ the point of a spear. ❷ (論鋒) the force of an argument. —鋒先を鈍らす, to take the edge off an argument.
hōku (ホーク), *n.* a fork.
Hokubei (北米), *n.* North America. ¶ 北米土人, the Red Indians. ⌈the northern part.⌉
hokubu (北部), *n.* the north;⌋
hokuchi (引火奴), *n.* tinder; touchwood. ⌈Arctic Ocean.⌉
Hokuhyōyō (北氷洋), *n.* the⌋
hokui (北緯), *n.* north latitude.
hokuro (黒子), *n.* a mole. —黒子を拔く, to remove a mole.
Hokushin (北清), *n.* North China. ¶ 北清事件, the Boxer Troubles.
hokutosei (北斗星), *n.* the Great Bear; the Plough; Charles's Wain. ⌈aside; omit.⌉
hōkyaku (放却する), *vt.* to set⌋
hokyū (補給する), *vt.* to grant to meet a deficit; replenish (coal, *etc.*).
hōkyū (俸給), *n.* a salary; a pay. ☞ gekkū (月給). —一月三百圓の俸給を取る, to draw [take; receive] a monthly salary of 300 *yen*. ¶ 俸給生活者改善同盟團, the Salaried Men's Union.
homaesen (帆前船), *n.* a sailing-ship; a sailing-vessel; a sailer.
hōmairu (方哩), *n.* a square mile.
hōman (放漫な), *a.* loose; lax; profligate.
homare (譽), *n.* honour (名譽); glory (光榮); fame (名聲). —一國の譽, national honour [glory].
hōmatsu (泡沫), *n.* a bubble; a foam; a froth. ¶ 泡沫會社, a bubble company.
hōmei (芳名), *n.* a good name; a fair fame. —芳名を千載に遺す, to leave a good name forever behind one.
homen (鋪面), *n.* pavement.
hōmen (方面), *n.* a direction; a quarter; parts. —各方面から, from all quarters. —倫敦方面へ, in the direction of London. ¶ 關西方面, the Kansai districts. —方面委員, a district-visitor.
hōmen (放免), *n.* release; discharge; acquittal (無罪放免). —放免する, to release; discharge; acquit.
homeru (褒める), *vt.* to praise; speak highly *of*; applaud (喝采). —其徳を頌めたゝへる, to praise his virtue.
hōmō (法網), *n.* the net [grip] of the law. —巧に法網を潛る, to slip skilfully from the grip of the law; escape the law cleverly.
homomen (帆木綿), *n.* sail-cloth; canvas.
hōmon (砲門), *n.* ❶ (軍艦の) a gun-port; a port-hole. ❷ (要塞の) a crenelle; an embrasure. ❸ (砲口) the muzzle.
hōmon (訪問), *n.* a visit; a call. —訪問を受ける, to receive a call. —— **-suru**, *vt.* to visit; call *at* (a place); call *on* (a person). —訪問する暇がない, to have no time to visit; have no spare time for visiting. ¶ 訪問記者, an interviewer. —訪問者, a visitor; a caller.
hōmotsu (寶物), *n.* a treasure. ¶ 寶物展覧會, an exhibition of treasures.
hōmu (法務), *n.* ❶ (宗務) ministerial [clerical] duty. ❷ (法律事務) law business. ¶ 法務局, Bureau of Judicial Affairs.
hōmu (ホーム), *n.* ❶ (家庭) a home. ❷ 【競技】 the home. ❸

【鐵道】a platform. ¶ ホームラン, 【野球】a home run. —ホームシック, home-sickness; nostalgia.

hōmuru (葬る), *vt.* to bury; inter; consign to the grave. —葬られる, ① to be buried. ② (忘れられる) to be forgotten; be buried in oblivion. ③ (議案が) to be shelved; be smothered up. —父の死骸を葬る, to commit the father's body to the grave.

hōmyō (法名), *n.* a Buddhist name.

hon (本), *n.* a book.

hon- (本), *pref.* ❶ (現前の) the present; this; the (same). ❷ (主たる) the head; the main; the principal. ❸ (眞正の) real; true; genuine.

hoṅan (翻案), *n.* adaptation. —沙翁の劇を翻案する, to adapt a play by Shakespeare.

honba (本場), *n.* ❶ (眞の產地) the original place; the best place; the home (動植物等の). ❷ (中心) the centre. ❸ =*honmono*.

honba (奔馬), *n.* a runaway (horse).

honbako (本箱), *n.* a book-case.

honbu (本部), *n.* the head office; the head department; the headquarters; the mainland (本土). ¶ 支那本部, China Proper.

honbun (本分), *n.* (proper) duty; function; part. —軍人の本分, the proper duty of a military man. —本分を盡す, to perform [fulfil] one's duties; do one's part. —働くことは人の本分である, Labour is man's true vocation.

honchōshi (本調子), *n.* 【音】 the normal key; the key note.

hondana (本棚), *n.* a book-shelf.

hondawara (馬尾藻), *n.* 【植】 the gulf-weed.

hondo (本土), *n.* the mainland (本部); our country (我國). ¶ 日本本土, Japan Proper.

hondō (本堂), *n.* the main temple.

hondō (本道), *n.* the highway; the high road; the trunk-road.

hone (骨), *n.* ❶【解】the bone. ❷ (扇・障子等組立材料) a frame (障子などの); a rib (傘などの); a stick (扇の). —骨が折れる, to require great efforts. —骨まで徹る, to pierce to the bone. —骨と皮ばかりになる, to be reduced to a skeleton; be worn to a shadow; be all skin and bones. —骨を休める, to take rest after toil. —骨を違へる, [*vt.*] to dislocate. —骨を接ぐ, to set a bone. —骨を挫く, to sprain a bone. —骨を折る, =*honeoru*. —骨を惜む, to spare oneself.

honegumi (骨組), *n.* ❶ (骨骼) the bony frame; the skeleton. ❷ (體格) the physique; the build. ❸ (基本組織) the framework; the structure. —骨組のしっかりした人, a man strongly knit together; a man of strong build.

hoṅei (本營), *n.* the headquarters (hdqrs. と略す).

honemi (骨身), *n.* ❶ (骨と身) flesh and bones. ❷ (骨髓) the marrow; the heart. —骨身にこたへる, to go deep into one's heart; touch to the quick; penetrate to the heart.

hōnen (豐年), *n.* a fruitful [an abundant] year. ¶ 豐年祝, the harvest-festival [feast].

honenuki (骨拔), *n.* being deprived of bones; being unboned. ¶ 骨拔き泥鰌, an unboned loach. —骨拔き議案, a mutilated bill.

honeori (骨折), *n.* an effort; exertion; painstaking. —骨折損をする, to toil [labour] for nothing. ¶ 骨折仕事, a toilsome [laborious] work; a drudgery.

honeoru (骨折る), *vi.* to labour; toil; take pains. —少しも骨折らずに, without taking any pains.

honeoshimi (骨惜する), *vi.* to grudge pains. —骨惜みせずに働く, to labour without stint; work without sparing oneself.

honetsugi (骨繼, 接骨), *n.* ❶ bone-setting. ❷ (接骨醫) a bone-setter.

hongan (本願), *n.* a long-cherished desire.

hongen (本源), *n.* ❶ (根本義) a principle; an element; a cause. ❷ (根本) source; fountain; origin.

hongetsu (本月), *n.* this [the current] month; instant (inst. と略す). —本月六日, the 6th inst. —本月分の月謝, this month's fee.

hongi (本義), *n.* ❶ (原義) the original meaning [signification]. ❷ (眞義) the proper meaning [signification]. ❸ (本旨) the (fundamental) principle.

hongoku (本國), *n.* ❶ (國籍を置く國) one's own country; the home; the fatherland (祖國). ❷ (古鄉) one's native place [country]. ¶ 本國政府, the home government.

hongyō (本業), *n.* the principal occupation [business]. —本業とする, to make it one's principal occupation.

hoṅi (本位), *n.* the (monetary) standard. ¶ 複(單)本位, the double (single) standard. (複(單)本位制, bimetallism (monometallism).)

hōnin (放任する), *vt.* to leave alone; let alone; not to interfere. ¶ 放任主義, the laissez-faire principle; the let-alone policy.

honjitsu (本日), *n.* this day; to-day. ——, *ad.* to-day.

honka (本科), *n.* the regular course. ¶ 本科生, a regular-course student.

honkai (本懐), *n.* ❶ (本意) a long-cherished desire. ❷ (滿足) satisfaction. —本懐を達する, to carry out [fulfil] a long-cherished desire.

honkaigi (本會議), *n.* a full-dress debate [meeting] (議會の).

honkan (本官), *n.* ❶ (本務の官職) the principal official business. ❷ (文官任用によれる官吏) a duly-appointed government official.

honkan (本管), *n.* the main (水道·瓦斯等の).

honke (本家), *n.* ❶ the principal family; the head house. ❷ the original manufacturer (元祖). ¶ 總本家, the head family. —本家本元, ① the original home. ② the true originator.

honki (本氣), *n.* ❶ (正氣) senses; sanity; soberness. ❷ (眞面目) seriousness; earnestness. —本氣の沙汰である, to be in his senses.

honkō (本校), *n.* ❶ the principal school. ❷ this school.

honkoku (翻刻), *n.* reprint; republication. —翻刻する, to reprint; republish. ¶ 翻刻物, a reprint.

honkyo (本據), *n.* the headquarters; the base (根據地).

honkyoku (本局), *n.* the head office. —電話本局二十五番, Telephone, Head [Main] No. 25.

honmaru (本丸), *n.* the inner citadel.

honmatsu (本末), *n.* cause and effect (本と末); the beginning and the end (始と終); the relative importance (輕重). —本末を顚倒する, to reverse the order; put the cart before the horse.

honmō (本望), *n.* ❶ (宿望) a long-cherished wish [desire]. ❷ (大志望) a great object; the principal object. ❸ (滿足) satisfaction. —本望を遂げる, to obtain one's desire; realize one's wish.

honmon (本文), *n.* (原文) the text (註·插畫等に對する); the original (原本); a body (手紙·書類の). ¶ 本文引用, a contextual quotation.

honmono (本物), *n.* a genuine article; a real thing. —本物らしい (貨幣·人物が), to ring true; have the true ring.

honmu (本務), *n.* ❶ (本分) duty. ❷ (本來の務) proper [regular] business.

honne (本音), *n.* undisguised speech; one's real intention (眞意); the truth (眞實). —本音を吐く, to disclose one's real intention.

honnin (本人), *n.* ❶ (自身) oneself. ❷ (當人) (the) said person; the person in question. ❸ (代理人·保證人に對し) the principal. —本人自身で, in person; personally.

honno (ほんの), *a.* mere. ——, *ad.* just; but; only; nothing but. —ほんの少し, just a little bit. —ほんの名ばかりの國王, a king only in name.

honnō (本能), *n.* instinct. —本能的道德, instinctive morality. —本能を滿足する, to satisfy the instinct. —本能的に風雨を感ずる, to feel the wind and rain instinctively.

hōnō (奉納する), *vt.* to offer; dedicate. ¶ 奉納物, an offering; an oblation; an *ex-voto* 〔羅〕. —奉納額, a votive [dedicated] tablet; a votive offering. —奉納者, a dedicator; an offerer. —奉納踊 (相撲), a dedicatory dance (wrestling).

honobono (仄仄と), *ad.* dimly; faintly.

honogurai (仄暗い), *a.* dim; dusky; sombre.

honoka (仄に), *ad.* dimly; faintly; indistinctly. —仄に聞く, to hear indistinctly; hear say.

hōnoki (厚朴), *n.* 【植】 Magnolia hypoleuca (學名).

honomekasu (仄かす), *vt.* to hint (*at*); allude *to*; give [drop] a hint *to*.

honoo (炎, 焰, 燄), *n.* a flame; a blaze. —怒の焰, a blaze of anger. —焰に包まれる, to be wrapped in flames.

honpō (本邦), *n.* our country; this country.

honpō (本俸), *n.* regular pay [salary].

honrai (本來), *n.* ❶ (由來) origin. ❷ (順當) the natural course. ——, *ad.* ❶ originally; primarily. ❷ naturally; by nature; essentially. ❸ (初めから) from the first. —本來の, original; natural; essential; proper.

honrō (飜弄する), *vt.* to fool; trifle *with*; play *with*; make fun *of*. —波に飜弄される, to be at the mercy of waves; be tossed about by the sea.

honron (本論), *n.* the main discourse (subject).

honrui (本壘), *n.* ❶【野球】 the home base. ❷ (根據) the base. ¶ 本壘打, the home run (hit).

honryō (本領), *n.* ❶ (本分) province; sphere. ❷ (特色) a

special character. —本領を發揮する, to display one's speciality.

honryū (本流), *n.* ❶ (幹流) the main stream. ❷ (正統) the true lineage.

honryū (奔流する), *vi.* to flush; rush; dash along.

honsai (本妻), *n.* a legal wife; ⌈a wife.⌉

honsei (本性), *n.* the original nature; the true nature.

honseki (本籍), *n.* 【法】 the permanent domicile; the place of register.

honsen (本線), *n.* the main line.

honsha (本社), *n.* the head office.

honshi (本旨), *n.* the fundamental principle; the main object.

honshin (本心), *n.* ❶ (良心) conscience; right mind; heart. ❷ (正氣) oneself; senses. —本心に立ちかへる, to return to one's right mind; recover oneself; reform one's life. —本心を失ふ, to lose one's mind.

honshitsu (本質), *n.* 【哲】 essence; (real) substance.

honsho (本初), *a.* prime. ¶ 本初子午線, the prime [standard] meridian.

honshō (本性), *n.* ❶ (正氣) senses; sobriety. ❷ =*honsei* (本性). —本性を顯はす, to show oneself [come out] in one's true colours. —醉うて本性を失ふ, to lose one's senses through drunkenness.

honshoku (本色), *n.* the true character; a characteristic.

honshoku (本職), *n.* ❶ (本業) the principal business [occupation]; the regular occupation. ❷ (黒人) a professional.

honsō (奔走する), *vi.* ❶ to run about. ❷ to be busily engaged; exert oneself; bustle. —國事に奔走する, to busy oneself with national affairs. —政界に奔走する, to be busily engaged in the political world.

hontai (本隊), *n.* the centre (兩翼に對して); the main body (of an army).

hontai (本體), *n.* ❶ 【哲】 substance; a thing in itself. ❷ (眞のすがた) the true form; real substance.

hontaku (本宅), *n.* the (principal) residence.

hontate (本立), *n.* a book-stand.

honten (本店), *n.* the head [principal] office [shop].

hontō (本當の), *a.* true; real; actual. —本當に, truly; really; actually; very. —本當は, in fact; in reality; properly speaking. —本當の狂氣 stark madness. —本當の兄弟, full [true] brothers. —本當の惡黨, a regular rascal.

hoṅya (本屋), *n.* a bookseller; a book-shop (店) [-store 〚米〛]; a publisher (出版業者).

hoṅyaku (翻譯), *n.* translation; version; rendering. **—-suru,** *vt.* to translate *into*; render *into*; turn *into*; put *into*; do *into*. —それを英語に翻譯する, to put it into English. ¶ 翻譯課, the section of translation. —翻譯官, a translator; a secretary-translator (外務省の). —翻譯者, a translator.

honyū (哺乳動物), *n.* a mammal. ¶ 哺乳類, 【動】 Mammalia (學名).

honzan (本山), *n.* the head temple; the cathedral church.

honzen (本膳), *n.* 【料理】 the principal table at a dinner.

honzen (本然の), *a.* natural; inborn; intrinsic. —本然の性に歸る, to return to one's natural character.

honzen (翻然), *ad.* suddenly. ⌈☞ *hanzen.*⌉

honzōgaku (本草學), *n.* botany. ¶ 本草學者, a herbalist; a botanist.

honzon (本尊), *n.* ❶ (主として祭る佛像) the principal image. ❷ (衆の仰ぐ人物) the idol.

hōō (鳳凰), *n.* the (Chinese) phœnix. —宮中鳳凰の間に於て, in the Phœnix Hall of the Palace.

hōō (法王), *n.* a pope (羅馬法王). ¶ 法王廳, the Vatican.

hōon (報恩), *n.* gratitude; returning kindness. ⌈northward.⌉

hoppō (北方), *n.* the north; the

hoppu (忽布), *n.* 【植】 the hop.

hora (法螺), *n.* ❶ (法螺貝) the trumpet-shell. ❷ (大言壯語) exaggeration; boast; tall talk. —法螺を吹く, ① (貝を) to blow a trumpet-shell. ② (大言す) to blow one's own trumpet; draw a [the] long bow; brag. ¶ 法螺吹き, a boaster; a bouncer; a braggart.

horaana (洞穴), *n.* a hollow; a cave; a cavern; a den.

hōraku (崩落), *n.* (取引市場) a break. —大崩落を來す, to bring about a great break.

hōran (放卵する), *vi.* to lay eggs; spawn.

hōratsu (放埓), *n.* ❶ =*hōtō* (放蕩). ❷ =*hōjū* (放縱).

horebore (惚惚させる), *vt.* to charm. —惚々するやうな姿(笑), a charming figure (smile).

hōrei (法令), *n.* laws and ordinances; laws and regulations. ¶ 法令全書, a complete collection of laws and regulations.

hōren (鳳輦), *n.* an Imperial car

(palanquin); a state carriage.

hōrensō (菠薐草), *n.* 【植】 the (garden) spinach.

horeru (惚れる), *vi.* to fall in love *with*; be fascinated [enamoured; smitten] *with*. —惚れられる, to win the heart *of*. —女に惚れ込んで, gone on a woman. —人の氣前に惚れる, to fall in love with a person's spirit.

hōretsu (砲列), *n.* a line of guns; a firing-line. —砲列を布く, to range guns in a line; come into action (砲兵が).

hori (堀, 濠), *n.* ❶ (堀割) a canal. ❷ (濠) (城池) a moat; a fosse. —堀を掘る, to dig a moat.

hōri (方里), *n.* a square *ri*.

hōri (法理), *n.* law philosophy.

hōri (鳳梨), *n.* a pine-apple; an ananas.

hōribanashi (抛放しにする), *vt.* to leave (things) about; leave (a person) to oneself; neglect. ☞ *hōnin* (放任する).

horidashimono (掘出物), *n.* a find; a treasure-trove (地中からの). —掘出物をする, to pick up a bargain; make a find.

horidasu (掘出す), *vt.* to dig out; unearth.

hōridasu (抛出す), *vt.* to throw out; fling out; cast out.

horiido (掘井戸), *n.* a well; an Artesian well (掘抜井戸).

hōrikomu (抛込む), *vt.* to throw *into*; cast *into*.

horimono (彫物), *n.* ❶ (彫刻) a carving; an engraving. ❷ (文身, 刺靑) a tattoo; tattooing. ¶ 彫物師, ① (彫刻師) a carver; a sculptor. ② (文身師) a tattooer.

horinukiido (掘拔井戸), *n.* an Artesian well.

hōritsu (法律), *n.* ❶ law. ❷ (命令の對) a statute (law); an act of Parliament [Congress 〔米〕]. —法律の字面, the letter of the law. —法律を犯す[破る], to infringe [break; violate] the law. —法律を執行する, to put a law in force. ¶ 法律案, a bill. —法律學, law; jurisprudence. —法律語, a law term. —法律事務所, a law-office. —法律家, a lawyer; a jurist; a jurisconsult. —法律顧問, a legal adviser [counsellor].

horiwari (堀割), *n.* a canal; a moat.

horo (幌), *n.* ❶ (幌) (車等の) an owning; a folding top [hood]; a calash-top. ❷ (母衣) (武具) a hood. ¶ 幌馬車, a carriage with a hood [calash-top]; a covered carriage.

horō (歩廊), *n.* ❶ a platform. ❷ a corridor; a passage.

hōrō (放浪する), *vi.* to wander about; rove; roam. ¶ 放浪生活, a wandering life.

hōrō (琺瑯-質), *n.* enamel. —琺瑯をかける, [*vt.*] to enamel.

horobiru (亡・滅びる), *vi.* to perish; be destroyed; be ruined.

horobosu (亡ぼす), *vt.* to destroy; ruin; overthrow (覆へす).

horogaya (母衣蚊帳), *n.* a small mosquito-net (for children).

horohorochō (珠鷄), *n.* 【鳥】 the guinea-fowl.

hōroku (焙烙), *n.* a shallow parching pan.

horori (ほろりとする), *v.* to be moved to tears.

horoyoi (微醉), *n.* slight intoxication.

horu (彫る), *vt.* to carve; engrave; chisel.

horu (掘る), *vt.* ❶ to dig; cut (運河・塹壕・溝等); sink (井戸・竪坑等). ❷ (刳る) to scoop; hollow out. —掘り下げる, to dig down; sink. —石油を掘り當てる, to strike oil. —敷居の溝を鑿る, to cut a groove in the sliding-door sill.

hōru (抛る), *vt.* ❶ (投げる) to throw; hurl; fling. ❷ (放棄) to throw away; give up; abandon. —抛ッて置く, to neglect; leave alone.

hōrui (堡壘), *n.* a fort; a battery.

Horutogaru (葡萄牙), *n.* Portugal. ¶ 葡萄牙人, a Portuguese.

hōryaku (方略), *n.* a plan; a scheme; a stratagem (軍略). —敵の方略の裏を搔く, to meet [oppose] the enemy's plan with a counter-plan.

horyo (捕虜), *n.* a prisoner of war; a captive. ☞ *furyo*.

horyū (蒲柳の質), *n.* delicate health; weak constitution.

horyū (保留), *n.* reservation. ☞ *ryūho* (留保).

hosa (輔佐, 補佐), *n.* aid; assistance; support. —補佐する, to aid; assist. ¶ 輔佐人; 保佐人, an assistant; a curator (保佐人).

hosaki (穗先), *n.* ❶ (芒) an ear. ❷ (鋒鋩) a point; a head; a spear-head (槍の).

hōsaku (豐作), *n.* a heavy [good; rich] crop; good [rich; abundant] harvest.

hōsan (放散する), *v.* to radiate; diffuse.

hōsan (硼酸), *n.* boracic acid. ¶ 硼酸軟膏, boracic ointment.

hōsei (方正な), *a.* ❶ (正しい) good; righteous; upright. ❷ (方形の) square.

hōsei (法制), *n.* laws (法律);

legislation (立法); legal organization. ¶ 法制經濟, laws and economy. —法制局, the Bureau of Legislation.

hōsei (砲聲), *n.* the sound of firing; the report (of a gun); roar; boom (遠い).

hōseki (寶石), *n.* a (precious) stone; a gem; a jewel. —指環に寶石を鏤める, to set a gem in a ring. ¶ 寶石商, a jeweller.

hosen (保線), *n.* maintenance of way (鐵道の). ¶ 保線係, a patrolman (電線等の); a trackman (鐵道). —保線工夫, a lineman (線路·電線等の修繕係), a surface-man (鐵道).

hōsen (放線), *n.* radiation. —放線狀の, radiant (植物等); stellate. ☞ *hōsha* (放射).

hōsen (砲戰), *n.* an artillery duel; a cannonade.

hōsenka (鳳仙花), *n.* 【植】 the (common) garden balsam; the lady's slipper.

hōsha (放射), *n.* emission (光·熱·香·臭等の); radiation (光·熱の); ejection. ☞ *fukusha* (輻射). —放射する, ① [*v.*] to radiate; emit. ② [*a.*] emissive; radiant. ¶ 放射道路, a radiating road. —放射熱, radiant heat.

hōsha (砲車), *n.* a gun-carriage; a gun detachment.

hōsha (硼砂), *n.* borax.

hoshaku (保釋), *n.* bail; bailment. —保釋中の被告人, a prisoner released on bail. —保釋する, [*vt.*] to bail. —保釋になる, to be released on bail. ¶ 保釋金, bail (money).

hōshaku (方尺), *n.* a square *shaku.*

hoshi (星), *n.* ❶ (星辰) a star. ❷ (點) a spot; a speck; a dot. ❸ (的の中心) a bull's-eye. ❹ (目印) a mark. —星が飛ぶ, A star shoots.

hōshi (放資), *n.* investment (of capital). ☞ *tōshi* (投資).

hōshi (法師), *n.* a bonze; a Buddhist priest.

hōshi (奉仕), *n.* attendance; service. —奉仕する, to attend *on*; serve.

hoshiakari (星明), *n.* starlight.

hoshiba (干場), *n.* a drying-ground [place].

hoshibudō (乾葡萄), *n.* raisins; plums.

hoshidaikon (干大根), *n.* a dried radish.

hoshigaru (欲しがる), *v.* to wish *for*; long *for*; crave *for*.

hoshii (欲しい), *vt.* to want; like; wish. ☞ *hos-suru.* ——, *a.* desirable.

hoshii (糒), *n.* dry boiled-rice.

hoshiimama (恣·縦·肆な), *a.* ❶ (恣, 縦) wayward; selfish. ❷ (專橫) arbitrary; despotic. —肆に, ① waywardly; selfishly. ② arbitrarily. **——-nisuru,** *v.* to do as one pleases; indulge; give loose *to.* —國の政權を擅にする, to usurp the government of a country.

hōshiki (方式), *n.* ❶ a form; a formula; a method (方法); 【論】 mood. ❷ (手續) formalities; process. —方式に從ふ, to follow the established form [usage].

hoshikusa (乾草), *n.* hay. —乾草にする, [*vt.*] to hay.

hoshimono (干物), *n.* clothes for drying; things set for drying. ¶ 干物竿, a clothes-drying pole.

hōshin (方針), *n.* a course; a policy (政策). —方針を誤る, to take a wrong course. —方針を立てる, to fix one's aim [policy]; shape one's course.

hōshin (放心), *n.* ❶ (安心) freedom from care [anxiety]. ❷ (うつとり) absent-mindedness; absence of mind; abstraction. —放心する, to be absent-minded.

hōshin (砲身), *n.* the (gun-) barrel.

hōshin (疱疹), *n.* 【醫】 herpes; shingles.

hoshinori (乾海苔), *n.* dried laver.

hoshizukiyo (星月夜), *n.* a starlight night; a bright starry night.

hoshō (步哨), *n.* 【軍】 a sentry; a sentinel; a picket (一團の). —步哨に立つ, to be on sentry.

hoshō (保障), *n.* security; guarantee. —保障する, to secure; guarantee. —憲法の保障により, by the guarantee of the constitution. ¶ 保障占領, guarantee occupation.

hoshō (保證), *n.* 【法】 suretyship; security; pledge. —保證する, to guarantee; warrant; certify; pledge. —保證(人)に立つ, to stand surety *for*; become surety. —保證(人)を立てる, to give surety; give security; give bail. ¶ 保證金, security; caution money. —保證人, 【法】 a surety (特に連帶保證人); a guarantor (普通の保證人); a security (概して訴訟上の). —保證附銀行小切手, a certified cheque.

hoshō (補償), *n.* compensation; indemnity; indemnification. —損害を補償する, to indemnify losses [damages]; pay damages. ¶ 補償金, an indemnity.

hōshō (法相), *n.* the Minister of

Justice.

hōshō (褒章), *n.* a medal (for merit).

hōshō (褒賞), *n.* a prize; a reward. —褒賞を授ける(貰ふ), to give (receive) a prize. ¶ 褒賞受領者, a prize-man. —褒賞授與, distribution of prizes; prize-giving.

hoshoku (補色), *n.* 【理】a complementary colour.

hōshoku (奉職する), *vi.* ❶ (在職) to be in office; serve *in* [*at*]. ❷ (就職) to enter the service *of*. ¶ 奉職口, a post; a position; a berth. —奉職者, a person in office [service].

hōshoku (飽食する), *vi.* to be sated with food; overeat; surfeit.

hoshu (保守), *n.* conservation; unprogressiveness; reaction. —保守する, to conserve; uphold. ¶ 保守家, a conservative; a reactionary. —保守主義, conservatism. —保守的精神, a conservative spirit. —保守黨, 【政】the conservative party; the right. (保守黨員, a conservative.)

hoshu (捕手), *n.* 【野球】a catcher.

hoshū (補習), *n.* supplement. ¶ 補習學校, a continuation school. —補習科, a supplementary class [course].

hōshu (法主), *n.* a high-priest; an archbishop.

hōshu (砲手), *n.* a gunner; an artillerist; an artilleryman.

hōshu (寶珠), *n.* ❶ a gem; a treasure. ❷ (寶珠の玉) a cordate ball with flammules around.

hōshū (報酬), *n.* remuneration; recompense; reward; honorarium.

hōshuku (奉祝), *n.* celebration. —奉祝する, to celebrate.

hosō (鋪裝), *n.* pavement. ——**suru**, *vt.* to pave. —路面を鋪裝する, to pave a road.

hōso (硼素), *n.* boron.

hōsō (包裝), *n.* packing; package. —包裝する, to pack.

hōsō (放送), *n.* (radio-)broadcasting (無線電話の). —放送する, to (radio-)broadcast. ¶ 放送辯士, an announcer. —放送機, a (radio-)broadcaster. —放送局, a (radio-)broadcasting station. —放送無線電話, radiophone. —放送室, a (radio-)broadcasting room.

hōsō (奉送する), *vt.* to see off (the Emperor).

hōsō (疱瘡), *n.* ❶ (天然痘) small-pox. ❷ =*shutō* (種痘). —疱瘡にかゝる, to be attacked by small-pox.

hōsō (法曹), *n.* judiciary; lawyers; the bench and the bar. ¶ 法曹界, the judicial world [circles]; the legal world.

hosobiki (細引), *n.* a cord.

hosoi (細い), *a.* ❶ (幅狹い) narrow. ❷ thin; slender; fine. —細い聲, a thin voice. —細い道, a narrow road [path]. —細い線, a fine line.

hosoku (細く), *ad.* slenderly; thinly. —次第に細くなる, to fine away; taper.

hosoku (捕捉する), *vt.* to catch; grasp; seize.

hosoku (補足する), *v.* to supplement; complement; supply; make good. ¶ 補足語, 【文】the complement (of the predicate).

hōsoku (法則), *n.* a law; a rule.

hosome (細目), *n.* ❶ (細い眼) eyes slightly open. ❷ (細い網目) fine meshes. ❸ narrowishness. —戸を細目に開ける, to open the door a little.

hosomeru (細める), *vt.* to make fine; make thin; make slender. —聲を細めていふ, to speak in a low voice.

hosomi (細身の), *a.* narrow-edged. —細身の刀, a narrow-edged sword.

hoson (保存), *n.* preservation; conservation. —保存する, to preserve; conserve; maintain. ¶ 永久保存, permanent preservation.

hosonagai (細長い), *a.* slender; slim; lanky. —細長く, slenderly; as thin as a lath.

hosonawa (細索), *n.* 【航】a marline; a bobbin.

hosoomote (細面), *n.* an oval face.

hosoru (細る), *vi.* ❶ to become small; dwindle. ❷ (瘦せる) to become thin [slender]; lose flesh; become emaciated.

hosotsu (步卒), *n.* a foot-soldier; an infantryman.

hossa (發作), *n.* 【醫】a paroxysm; an attack; an access. ——**teki**, *a.* paroxysmal. —發作的に, by fits; paroxysmally.

hosshin (發心する), *vi.* to be converted; regenerate; reform. ¶ 發心者, a regenerate man; a reformed person.

hossoku (發足する), *v.* to start on foot; set off on foot.

hossori (細ッそりした), *a.* slight; thin; slender; slim.

hossu (拂子), *n.* a brush of long white hair (carried by priest).

hos-suru (欲する), *vt.* ❶ (願望) to desire; wish. ❷ (意志) to intend; purpose. —平和を欲する, to wish (for) peace.

hosu (干す), *vt.* to dry; desiccate.

hōsu (蛇管), *n.* a hose.

hōsun (方寸), *n.* ❶ (一寸四方) a square *sun*. ❷ (心) mind; heart.

一方寸の中に, in the mind.
ho-suru (補する), *vt.* to appoint.
hōtai (奉戴する), *v.* to have (a prince) for the president; be presided over by (a prince). 一宮家を總裁に奉戴する, to have a prince for the president.
hōtai (繃帶), *n.* dressing; bandage. 一手に繃帶して居る, to have one's hand in bandage. 一傷を繃帶する, to bind up [dress] a wound. ¶ 卷繃帶, a roller-bandage.
hōtan (放膽の), *a.* bold; daring.
hotaru (螢), *n.* 【昆】 the firefly. 一螢の光, the glow [glimmer] of a firefly. ¶ 螢狩, firefly-catching. 一螢籠, a firefly-cage.
hotarugusa (螢草), *n.* 【植】 Bupleurum sachalinense (hare's ear の一種・學名).
hotaruishi(螢石), *n.* fluor spar; Derbyshire spar.
hotategai(帆立貝), *n.* 【貝】 the scallop-shell.
hote (帆手), *n.* the clew-lines of a sail.
hōtei (法定の), *a.* 【法】 legal; statutory. ¶ 法定價格, the legal price. 一法定速度, the legal limit (自轉車・自動車等の). 一法定相續人, an heir-at-law.
hōtei (法廷), *n.* a court; a law court; a court of justice; a tribunal; a judgment-hall. 一法廷に出る, ① (出廷) to appear in court. ② to go into court. 一法廷に持ち出す, to bring before the [into] court.
hōtei (奉呈, 捧呈), *n.* presentation; offer. 一國書を捧呈する, to present credentials.
hoteibara(布袋腹), *n.* a pot-belly.
hōteishiki(方程式), *n.* 【數】 an equation. 一方程式を解く, to solve an equation. ¶ 一次方程式, an equation of the first degree; a simple equation. 一二次方程式, an equation of the second degree; a quadratic equation.
hōteki (拋擲する), *vt.* ❶ to throw away. ❷ (放棄) to abandon; discard. ❸ (閑却) to lay aside.
hōten (法典), *n.* (單行法の對) a code.
hōten (寶典), *n.* a treasury; a thesaurus.
hoteru (旅館), *n.* a hotel.
hoteru (火照る), *vi.* to feel hot; burn; flush.
hōtō (奉答), *n.* a reply to the Throne. 一御下問に奉答する, to reply to an Imperial question. ¶ 奉答文, the text of the reply to the Throne.
hōtō (放蕩), *n.* dissipation; debauchery; a fast life. 一放蕩する, to be dissipated; live fast. 一放蕩に身を誤る, to be ruined by dissipation. ¶ 放蕩者, a debauchee; a libertine; a rake.
hōtō (朋黨), *n.* a faction; a clique. ¶ 朋黨心, party spirit; cliquism.
hōtō (砲塔), *n.* a turret.
hōtō (寶刀), *n.* a precious sword.
hotoke (佛), *n.* the Buddha. 一知らぬが佛, "Ignorance is bliss."
hotokenoza (佛耳草), *n.* 【植】 the hen-bit; the lion's snap.
hotondo (殆ど), *ad.* almost; all but; nearly. 一殆ど…ない, hardly ever; hardly [scarcely] any. 一殆ど常に, almost always.
hotoori(餘熱), *n.* ❶(熱心) ardour; fervour. ❷ (熱) heat; hotness.
hotori (ほとり), *n.* ❶ (邊, 畔) (附近) neighbourhood; vicinity. ❷ (側) (傍) a side. 一河の畔に臨む家, a house by the river.
hototogisu (杜鵑), *n.* 【鳥】 the (little) cuckoo.
hotsugan (發願), *n.* invocation. 一發願する, to invoke; enteart with a vow.
hotsui(發意), *n.* = ***hatsui***(發意).
hotsureru (紕れる), *vi.* to be frayed (絲等が); ravel; become loose.
hottan (發端), *n.* the beginning; the opening; the origin. 一發端に溯る, to trace back to the beginning [origin].
hottategoya (掘立小屋), *n.* a thatch barn; a hut.
hotto (ほッと), *ad.* with relief. 一ほッと息をつく, to breathe again; breathe freely.
hottōnin (發頭人), *n.* a ringleader; an originator.
hōwa(法話) *n.* a sermon; a homily. ☞ ***sekkyō*** (說敎).
hōwa (飽和), *n.* 【化】 saturation. 一飽和さす, to saturate. ¶ 飽和溶液, saturated solution.
hoya (火屋), *n.* ❶ (香爐・手あぶり等の上覆) a perforated lid [cover]. ❷ (洋燈の) a (lamp-) chimney.
hoyahoya (ほやほやの), *a.* steaming; smoking; hot *from*; fresh *from*. 一出來たてのほやほやの, hot from the oven; hot and hot. 一學校出たてのほやほやの, fresh from school.
hoyō (保養), *n.* recreation; recuperation. 一保養する, to recreate oneself; recruit (one's health). 一保養の爲め, for the benefit of one's health.
hōyō (包容), *n.* ❶ (包括) comprehension. ❷ (寬容) tolerance.
hōyō (抱擁する), *vt.* to embrace; clasp.
hōyō (法要), *n.* Buddhist service [mass].
hōyō (蜂腰), *n.* a slender waist.

hoyoku (補翼する), *vt.* to assist.
hoyū (保有する), *vt.* to hold; possess.
hōyū (朋友), *n.* a friend; a companion. ☞ *tomo* (友).
hōza (砲座), *n.* a gun-platform.
hozei (保税), *n.* bond. ¶ 保税貨物, bonded goods; goods in [under] bond. —保税倉庫, a bonded warehouse. (保税倉庫にある, in bond.)
hozen (保全), *n.* integrity; preservation. —保全する, to keep [preserve] intact. ¶ 領土保全, integrity of territory; territorial integrity.
hozo (臍), *n.* ❶【解】(へそ) the umbilicus; the navel. ❷【植】the hilum. ❸ (枘) (接合凸部) the tenon; the thole, thole-pin (櫓の); a cog. —臍を噛む, to repent bitterly. (臍を噛むの悔, unavailing repentance.)
hōzō (包藏する), *vt.* ❶ to contain; embody. ❷ to cherish; harbour; entertain.
hōzō (保藏する), *vt.* to preserve; conserve.
hōzō (寶藏), *n.* a storehouse of treasures; a treasury.
hozon (保存), *n.* =*hoson* (保存).
hōzue (頰杖をつく), *v.* to rest the cheek on the arm.
hōzuki (酸漿), *n.*【植】the winter-cherry. ¶ 酸漿提燈, a small round red-lantern.
hō-zuru (奉する), *vt.* ❶ (奉獻) to dedicate; present. ❷ =*hōtai* (奉戴する). ❸ (從ふ) to obey; observe; follow; believe *in* (信奉). —命令を奉する, to obey orders.
hō-zuru (封する), *vt.* to set up.
hō-zuru (崩する), *vi.* to pass away.
hō-zuru (報する), *vt.* ❶ (知らせる) to inform; report; announce. ❷ (返事する) to reply; answer. ❸ (むくいる) to revenge (復讐); repay; requite. —恩を報する, to repay kindness. —出火を報する, to give an alarm of a fire. —死去を報する, to report a person's death; inform A of B's death.
hyakka (百花), *n.* innumerable flowers; all flowers. —百花爛漫, countless flowers in bloom.
hyakkanichi (百箇日), *n.* the hundredth day. —亡父の百箇日, the hundredth day after my father's death.
hyakkaten (百貨店), *n.* a department store.
hyakka-zensho (百科全書), *n.* a cyclopedia [cyclopædia]; an encyclopædia [encyclopedia].
hyakkei (百計), *n.* all plans; all resources. —百計盡きたり, We are at the end of our resources.
hyakki-yakō (百鬼夜行), prowling of demons at night.
hyaku (百), *n.* a hundred.
hyakubai (百倍), *n.* a hundredfold; a centuple.
hyakubun (百分), *n.* a hundredth part. —百分の一, a hundredth; one-hundredth, 1/100. —百分の五, 5 per cent. —百分一の圖, a diagram one-hundredth of the natural size. ¶ 百分算,【數】percentage.
hyakudo (百度-參), *n.* a hundred tramps in prayer (over a definite distance). —お百度を踏む, ① to make the hundred tramps. ② to visit him a hundred times *for*.
hyakuhatsu (百發百中), unfailing shot. —百發百中であつた, Every shot told.
hyakuiromegane (百色目鏡), *n.* (玩具) a kaleidoscope.
hyakujikkō (百日紅), *n.*【植】=*sarusuberi*.
hyakuman (百萬), *n.* a million. ¶ 百萬長者, a millionaire.
hyakunen (百年), *n.* a century. ¶ 百年祭, a centenary.
hyakunichizeki (百日咳), *n.*【醫】whooping-cough.
hyakuseki (百尺竿頭一歩を進める), to make a further advance; go a step further.
hyakusen (百戰百勝), *n.* unfailing victory.
hyakushō (百姓), *n.* ❶ (農夫) peasantry (農民); a peasant; a farmer. ❷ (田舍者) a rustic; a bumpkin; a clodhopper. —百姓一揆を起す, to cause a peasant riot. ¶ 百姓家, a farm-house; a farmer's cottage.
hyakushutsu (百出する), *vi.* to arise in numbers [confusion].
hyakuten (百點), *n.* the full mark (滿點).
hyappan (百般の), *a.* all; every; of all kinds.
hyappō (百方), *ad.* ❶ in all directions. ❷ in every way. —百方手を盡す, to use every possible means; leave no stone unturned.
hyō (豹), *n.*【哺乳】the leopard.
hyō (表), *n.* ❶ (作表) a table; a schedule; a list; a chart (溫度表等). ❷ (君主又は官府等に奉る書) a memorial. —表に作る, to tabulate.
hyō (俵), *n.* a bag. ¶ 米百俵, a hundred bags of rice.
hyō (票), *n.* ❶ =*fuda* (札). ❷ (投票) a vote. —清き一票を投ず る, to give a clean vote.
hyō (評), *n.* ❶ (批評) a criticism; a notice. ❷ (取沙汰) a rumour; a report; (common) talk (話柄);

popularity (人氣). 「It hails.
hyō (雹), *n.* hail. —雹が降る,
hyōban (評判), *n.* ❶ (世評) the world's opinion. ❷ (取沙汰) a rumour; a report; (common) talk (話柄); a sensation (大評判). ❸ (名聲) fame; reputation; repute; name; character; credit; notoriety (惡評判); popularity (人氣). —評判の孝行息子, a son noted for his filial piety. —大評判の犯人, a notorious offender. —評判が好(惡)い, to have a good (ill) name; stand high (low) in the opinion of the public; be well (ill) spoken *of*; be popular (unpopular). —...との評判だ, It is reported [rumoured] that...; rumour has it that.... —評判になる, to be talked about; become the talk of the town; take [get] wind. —評判を落す, to fall into disrepute.
hyōbō (標榜する), *vt.* to adopt as a platform; profess. —正義を標榜して, clothed with righteousness. 「grave-post (墓標).
hyōboku (標木), *n.* a post; a
hyōchaku (漂著する), *vi.* to be cast [thrown; washed] ashore; drift [float] ashore.
hyōchū (氷柱), *n.* an icicle.
hyōchū (標註), *n.* a note; a top-note.
hyōchūtō (表忠塔), *n.* a memorial tower for the faithful dead.
hyōdai (表題, 標題), *n.* ❶ (書物等の外題) a title. ❷ (作品の題目) a heading (章・表等の); a superscription (文章の). ¶ 表題紙, the title-page (書物の).
hyōga (氷河), *n.* a glacier. ¶ 氷河時代, the glacial epoch; the ice age.
hyōgen (氷原), *n.* an ice-field.
hyōgen (表現), *n.* 【藝術】 expression; presentation. —表現する, to manifest (性質・感情等を); express.
hyōgeru (剽戯る), *vi.* to play the fool; jest; fool. —剽戯た, droll; humorous; funny.
hyōgi (評議), *n.* discussion; council; conference. —評議する, to confer *with*; deliberate (*on*); consult *with* (*about*). ¶ 評議員, a councillor; a board (團體). —評議室, a council-chamber.
hyōgo (評語), *n.* an epithet.
hyōgo (標語), *n.* a motto.
hyōgō (表號), *n.* a sign; a symbol; an emblem.
hyōgu (表具), *n.* mounting (of a picture). —表具する, [*vt.*] to mount (a picture). ¶ 表具師, a mounter.
hyōhaku (表白する), *vt.* to express; manifest; confess.
hyōhaku (漂白), *n.* decolorization. —漂白する, to bleach; decolorize. ¶ 漂白粉(液), bleaching lime [powder] (liquor). —漂白劑, a decolorizing [bleaching] agent; a decolorant.
hyōhaku (漂泊), *n.* ❶ (漂流) drifting. ❷ (流浪) roving; vagrancy. ☞ *rurō* (流浪). —漂泊する, [*vi.*] to drift; rove; roam.
hyōhen (豹變する), *vi.* to reform [change] suddenly.
hyōhi (表皮), *n.* 【解】 the cuticle; the epidermis; the scarf-skin.
hyōhon (標本), *n.* ❶ (博物) a specimen. ❷ (商品見本) a sample. ❸ (代表物) an example; a type. ¶ 動物標本, zoological specimens. —標本臺紙, a setting-board.
hyoihyoi (ひょいひょい), *ad.* ❶ (折節) by fits; by snatches; at times. ❷ (手輕く繰返して) lightly and repeatedly.
hyoito (ひょいと), *ad.* ❶ (不意に) all of a sudden; suddenly. ❷ (思はず) unexpectedly. ❸ (はずみで) by chance; by accident. —ひょいと椅子を立つ, to bob up from one's chair.
hyōji (表示), *n.* =*hyōshi* (表示).
hyōjō (表情), *n.* expression. —表情ある眼, talking [expressive] eyes.
hyōjō (評定), *n.* deliberation; conference. ☞ *hyōgi* (評議). ¶ 評定官, a councillor.
hyōjun (標準), *n.* ❶ a standard; a basis; a criterion (批判の). ❷ (段階) a level (社會的, 道德的, 智的). —價格の標準, the standard of value. ¶ 標準壓(溫), normal pressure (temperature). —萬國標準時, universal time.
hyōka (評價), *n.* valuation; appraisal; assessment. —評價する, to value; appraise; assess. ¶ 評價價格, an appraisement; an appraised value. —評價人, an assessor; an appraiser.
hyōkai (氷海), *n.* a frozen sea.
hyōkai (氷塊), *n.* a mass of ice; a block of ice.
hyōkai (氷解する), *vi.* ❶ to thaw; melt. ❷ (氷釋) to vanish; melt away; clear away.
hyōkan (剽悍な), *a.* impetuous; daring; intrepid.
hyōkei (標型), *n.* a type.
hyōketsu (氷結), *n.* freezing; congelation. —氷結する, to freeze; congeal.
hyōketsu (表決), *n.* vote. —表決する, [*vt.*] to vote.

hyōketsu (評決), *n.* a verdict (陪審官); an adjudication. —評決する, [*vt.*] to find (陪審官が); adjudicate.

hyōki (表記する), *vt.* to declare; inscribe [mark; mention] (on the face). ¶ 表記價格, the declared value.

hyōkin (剽輕な), *a.* facetious; funny; droll. ¶ 剽輕者, a witty [funny] person; a droll.

hyokkuri (ひょっくり), *ad.* accidentally; by chance; casually. —ひょっくり出會ふ, to meet by accident; knock *against*.

hyokohyoko (ひょこひょこ), *ad.* ❶ (ぴょこぴょこ) in jumps. ❷ (ぺこぺこ) bobbing the head. —ひょこひょこ頭を下げる, to bob the head up and down.

hyōmei (表明する), *vt.* to express; show; manifest.

hyōmen (表面), *n.* ❶ (外面) the surface; the face; the outside. ❷ (外見) appearance. —表面を飾る, to make a brave show. —彼の表面の用向, his ostensible errand.

hyōnō (氷嚢), *n.* an ice-bag.

hyōri (表裏), *n.* the face and the back; the outside and inside. —表裏反覆がある, to carry two faces (under one hood).

hyōrō (兵糧, 兵粮), *n.* military provisions. —兵糧を絕つ, ① (來らぬ) to have no more provisions; have provisions cut off. ② (送らぬ) to send no more provisions. —兵糧攻めにする, to starve (the garrison) into surrender; starve (a person) into submission.

hyōrō (漂浪する), *vi.* to wander about. ¶ 漂浪者, a wanderer; a nomad; a tramp.

hyorohyoro (ひょろひょろ), *ad.* ❶ (蹌踉) staggeringly; totteringly; reelingly. ❷ (細く高く) lankily. —ひょろひょろする, ① [*vi.*] to stagger; totter; reel. ② [*a.*] trembly; tottery; shaky; rickety.

hyōron (評論), *n.* a criticism; a review; a commentary. —評論する, to review; criticize. ¶ 評論家, a reviewer; a critic.

hyoronagai (ひょろ長い), *a.* lanky; slender; elongated.

hyorotsuku (ひょろつく), *vi.* ❶ (蹌踉) to stagger; totter; reel. ❷ (漂泊) to wander.

hyōryō (秤量する), *vt.* to weigh. ¶ 秤量臺, a weigh-bridge.

hyōryū (漂流する), *vi.* to drift about; float about; be adrift. ¶ 漂流人, a person adrift on the sea; a castaway (難船者).

hyōsatsu (表札), *n.* a door-plate; a name-plate. —表札を掲げる, to put up a door-plate.

hyōsen (票箋), *n.* a label.

hyōsetsu (拍節), *n.* 【音】 beat. ¶ 拍節鞭, a baton.

hyōsetsu (剽竊), *n.* piracy; plagiarism. —剽竊する, to pirate; plagiarize; lift. ¶ 剽竊者, a plagiarist.

hyōsha (評者), *n.* a critic.

hyōshaku (評釋), *n.* critical annotation [notes]. —評釋する, to annotate critically.

hyōshi (表示), *n.* expression; demonstration; indication. **——suru**, *vt.* to express; demonstrate; indicate. —意志を表示する, to express [declare] one's intention.

hyōshi (表紙), *n.* a cover; binding. —表紙を附ける, to cover *with*; bind *in*. ¶ 紙表紙, a paper cover [binding]. —革表紙, a leather cover [binding].

hyōshi (拍子), *n.* ❶ (聲調) tune; rhythm; beat (太鼓の). ❷ (はずみ) (*a*) chance: (*b*) impulse. —...する拍子に, in the act [instant] *of*; as.... —拍子を合はせる, to keep time; chime in *with*. —拍子抜けがする, to be out of time [tune]; be discouraged. ¶ 拍子木, wooden clappers.

hyōshiki (標識), *n.* a mark; a sign; a land mark.

hyōshitsu (氷室), *n.* an ice-room; an ice-house.

hyōshitsu (漂失する), *vi.* to drift away.

hyōshō (表象), *n.* ❶ presentation. ❷ (象徵) a symbol; an emblem.

hyōshō (表彰する), *vt.* to commend officially; recognize officially; reward (in recognition of his services).

hyōshutsu (表出する), *vt.* to express.

hyōso (瘭疽), *n.* 【醫】 paronychia; whitlow.

hyōsō (表裝), *n.* ❶ (表具) mounting. ❷ (裝釘) way of binding. ❸ 【商】 make-up. —表裝する, to mount (繪等を).

hyōsoku (平仄), *n.* ❶ 【詩】 the metre. ❷ (辻褄) consistency.

hyō-suru (表する), *vt.* to express; make known; show. —同情を表する, to show sympathy *for*. —謝意を表する, to express thanks.

hyō-suru (評する), *vt.* to criticize; estimate.

hyōtan (瓢簞), *n.* ❶ 【植】 the bottle-gourd. ❷ 〔瓢〕 a gourd. —瓢簞鯰である, to be slippery as an eel.

hyōtan (氷炭相容れず), *v.* to be as opposed to each other as fire and water.

hyōteki (標的), *n.* a mark; a target. —標的を外れて, beside [wide of] the mark.

hyōten (氷點), *n.* the freezing point. —氷點を降る, to fall below (the) freezing-point. ¶ 氷點以下十度, ten degrees of frost.

hyōten (評點), *n.* a point; a mark.

hyotto (ひよつと), *ad.* by any chance; by accident. —ひよつとして...たら, if by any chance.

hyottoko (彥德), *n.* ❶ a goblin. ❷ (男子を罵る語) an ugly fellow.

hyōzan (氷山), *n.* an ice-berg; an ice-mountain.

hyōzen (飄然), *ad.* excursively; abruptly.

hyū (ひゆー), *n.* ping (銃彈); whiz (砲彈·矢等). —ヒューと鳴る, to whiz; whistle.

hyūhyū (ひゆーひゆー), *n.* ❶ (風音) sough. ❷ (鞭など振廻す音) swish. —ヒューヒュー吹く, [*vi.*] to whiffle; whistle.

I

i (い), *n.* 【音】A; la【伊】; 6.

i (猪), *n.* 【哺乳】the wild boar.

i (藺), *n.* 【植】Juncus effusus (rushの一種·學名).

i (井), *n.* a well. —井の中の蛙大海を知らず, (諺) "He who is in hell knows not what heaven is."

i (位), *n.* ❶ (官位) court rank. ❷ (位置) rank; position; place. ¶ 正(從)四位, the first (second) grade of the fourth court rank.

i (胃), *n.* the stomach; the crop (鳥の餌袋); the craw (鳥·昆蟲の). —胃が丈夫である(弱い), to have a good (weak) digestion.

i (威), *n.* ❶ (威嚴) dignity. ❷ (勢力) authority; power; influence. ❸ (武力) arms; force. ☞ *iryoku* (威力). —威を振ふ, to exercise authority (*over*); show one's power (*over*); exert influence.

i (意), *n.* ❶ (意志) will; volition. ❷ (意向) intention; purpose. ❸ (心) mind; thought (思想); idea (觀念); heart (衷情). ❹ (願望) wish; desire. ❺ (意義) meaning; sense; purport. —意に適する, to be to one's liking [mind]; suit one's fancy. —意に介する, to pay [give] heed *to*; take to one's heart. —意に介せぬ, ① [*a.*] indifferent; nonchalant. ② [*v.*] not to care *about*; not to take (it) to heart. —人の意に忤(さか)ふ, to act contrary to another's will. —意を用ひる, to be careful *about*; pay attention *to*.

i (偉), *n.* greatness.

i (膽), *n.* the gall-bladder; the gall.

iai (居合), *n.* drawing a sword sitting. ¶ 居合拔き, sword-play.

iaku (帷幄), *n.* ❶ (帷幄) a curtain; a tent; a tent-curtain. ❷ (作戰計畫をする所) the headquarters; the staff office. —帷幄に參する, to attend the council of war.

ian (慰安), *n.* ❶ consolation; solace; comfort. ❷ (休養) relaxation; recreation. —慰安する, to solace; console; comfort. —慰安を與へる, to give comfort *to*; afford solace. —讀書に慰安を求める, to find solace in reading.

iatsu (威壓する), *vt.* to overawe; overbear; treat with a high hand.

iawasu (居合はす), *vi.* to happen [chance] to be present; be present by chance.

ibara (茨), *n.* ❶ (荊棘) a thorn; a bramble. ❷ (薔薇) the rose. —茨の垣, a thorn hedge. —茨を拓く, to rear roses; reclaim a waste land.

ibariya (威張屋), *n.* a swaggerer; a vain man; a bully.

ibaru (威張る), *vi.* to be haughty; swagger; hold one's head high. ——, *a.* lordly; pretentious; lofty; uppish; overbearing; stuck-up.

ibi (萎靡する), *vi.* to droop; decline; decay.

ibiki (鼾), *n.* snore. —鼾をかく, to snore.

ibitsu (飯櫃の), *a.* wry. —いびつに, awry.

ibo (疣), *n.* ❶ 【植】a papula; a papilla. ❷ a wart.

ibokeitei (異母兄弟), *n.* an agnate brother; a half-brother; a stepbrother.

ibō (威望), *n.* influence and popularity.

ibogaeru (疣蛙), *n.* the toad.

iboji (疣痔), *n.* blind piles.

ibota (水蠟), *n.* ❶ 【植】the Chinese wax-tree. ❷ (疣取蠟) tree-wax; pehláh (白蠟).

ibu (慰撫する), *vt.* to solace; console; soothe.

ibukaru (訝る), *v.* to doubt; suspect; wonder.

ibukashii (訝しい), *a.* doubtful; questionable; suspicious. —訝しく思ふ, to consider suspicious [strange].

ibuki (檜柏), *n.* 【植】the Chinese juniper.

ibukuro (胃嚢), *n.* the stomach. ☞ *i* (胃).

ibunshi (異分子), *n.* a foreign [an alien] element; heterogeneous elements.

iburu (燻る), *vi.* to smoke;

smoulder. ——, *a.* smoky; smouldering.

ibushi (燻), *n.* ❶ fumigation. ❷ oxidization. ¶ 燻肉, smoked meat. —いぶし銀, oxidized silver.

ibusu (燻す), *vt.* ❶ (くすぶらす) to smoke; make smoky. ❷ (燻蒸する) to fumigate. ❸ (金屬を) to oxidize. —蜂を燻し殺す, to smoke out wasps.

ibutsu (遺物), *n.* ❶ (死後の) relics. ❷ (遺贈物) a legacy; a bequest. ❸ (生殘の人・物) survivals; a relic. —太古の遺物, remains of the palæozoic age.

ibyō (胃病), *n.* dyspepsia; disorder of the stomach.

ichi (一, 壹), *n.* ❶ (ひとつ) one. ❷ (最上, 最初) the first. ❸【數】unity. ❹ (骨牌又は骰子の目など) an ace. —一から十まで, in everything. —一も二もなく承諾する, to jump at another's proposal; give a ready consent. —一を知って二を知らぬ, to look only on one side of the shield. —一か八か遣って見る, to run a risk; risk it; run the hazard.

ichi (市), *n.* a market; a fair. —市に出す, to market; take to market. —市を開く, to open a fair. —門前市を成す, A large crowd gathers before the gate.

ichi (位置, 位地), *n.* ❶ (所在) position; situation; location; site. ❷ (立場) stand; station. ❸ (身分) situation; position; standing. ❹ (位, 職) a position; a post; a rank. —困難の位置を脱する, to come out of a difficult situation.

ichiba (市場), *n.* a market; a bazaar (東洋の). ¶ 公設市場, a public market. —魚(青物)市場, a fish (vegetable) market.

ichiban (一番), *n.* ❶ (第一) the first. ❷ (一回) a game; a round; a bout (相撲などの). ——, *ad.* ❶ (最も) most. ❷ (試みに) on trial. —東京一番の大建物, the largest building in Tōkyō. —一番綺麗である, to be the most beautiful of all. ¶ 一番列車, the first train. —一番勝負, contest decided by a single round [bout; game].

ichibetsu (一別), *n.* parting. —一別以來, since I saw you last; since we last met.

ichibetsu (一瞥), *n.* a glance; a glimpse. —一瞥する, to glance (*at*); have [catch] a glimpse *of*; take a glance *at*.

ichibi (市日), *n.* a market day.

ichibō (一望, 一眸), *n.* a look. —一望の平野, a stretch of open country.

ichibu (一部), *n.* ❶ (一部分) a part; a portion; a section. ❷ (書物の) a copy; a volume (一卷); a set. —…の一部をなす, to form a part *of*.

ichibu-shijū (一部始終, 一伍一什), *n.* the (full) particulars; all the details. —一部始終を物語る, to tell all *about*; give the full particulars.

ichida (一駄), *n.* a load; a horse-load.

ichidai (一代), *n.* a generation; a life. —一代の名優, the greatest actor of the age [day]. —一代身上を作る, to make a fortune in a lifetime.

ichidan (一團), *n.* a party; a group; a gang. —一團の和氣, the harmony of a party [circle]. —一團をなして, in a body; in a group.

ichido (一度), *ad.* once; one time. —一度に, ① (同時に) at the same time; together (一緒に). ② (一時に) at once; at a time; at a stretch (一氣に). —皆が一度にどっと笑ひ出した, They all burst out laughing.

ichidō (一同), *n.* all the persons concerned; all. —一同承諾する, to accept unanimously. —我々一同を招く, to invite all of us.

ichien (一圓), *n.* ❶ (一帶) the whole. ❷ (貨幣の) a *yen*. —關東一圓の不作, crop failure in all the Eastern Provinces.

ichigai (一概に), *ad.* ❶ (概して) in general; generally. ❷ (一度に) at once. ❸ (無差別に) indiscriminately; absolutely; unqualifiedly (無條件に).

ichigatsu (一月), *n.* (第一月) January.

ichigeki (一擊), *n.* a blow; a hit. —一擊の下に, at one blow; with a single blow.

ichigenron (一元論), *n.*【哲】monism. ¶ 一元論者, a monist.

ichigo (苺), *n.*【植】the strawberry; the raspberry. ¶ 蝦夷苺, the common raspberry.

ichigo (一期), *n.* the limit of life. —一期の思ひ出に, as last act of one's life.

ichigon, ichigen, (一言), *n.* a word. —男子の一言, a man's word. —一言にて云へば, in a word. —一言をも出さぬ, not to utter a word. —一言半句も出ぬ, not to have a word to say.

ichihatsu (鳶尾), *n.*【植】the wall iris.

ichii (一位), *n.* ❶ (一位置) unit's place. ❷ (第一位) the first rank; the first rate. ❸【植】(水松) Toxus cuspidata (yew-tree の一種.

學名); the yew(-tree). —第一位を占める, to stand first; take the first place; be in the first rank.

ichii (一意), *ad.* single-heartedly; with all one's heart. —一意事に從ふ, to engage in an affair with all one's heart.

ichiichi (一一), *ad.* ❶ (一つ一つ) one by one; singly. ❷ (精細に) at large; in full; in detail. —一々話して聞かす, to tell it in detail. —一々呼び出す, to summon them one after another.

ichiin (一員), *n.* a member.

ichiinsei (一院制), *n.* the unicameral system.

ichii-taisui (一衣帶水), *n.* a narrow strip of water.

ichiji (一次の), *a.* primary; first; 【數】linear. ¶ 第一次桂內閣, the first Katsura Cabinet [Ministry].

ichiji (一事), *n.* one thing; an affair. ¶ 一事狂, monomania.

ichiji (一時), *ad.* ❶ (或時) once time; once. ❷ (暫時) for a time; for a while; for the present. —一時の考, a passing fancy. —一時的建築, a temporary building. —一時を凌ぐ(金策など), to tide over a crisis. ¶ 一時金, ① (一時に拂ふ金) money paid in a lump. ② (一時賜金) a grant in a single sum. —一時借入金, a floating debt; an unfunded debt (政府の).

ichijiku (無花果), *n.* ❶【植】the fig-tree. ❷ (果) a fig.

ichijin (一陣), *n.* a blast; a gust. —一陣の風, a blast; a gust of wind.

ichijirushii (著しい), *a.* remarkable; conspicuous; distinguished. —著しい成功, a signal success. —著しい產業の發達, the remarkable development of industries. —著しく, remarkably; strikingly; in a marked degree.

ichijitsu, ichinichi, (一日), *n.* ❶ (第一日) the first day; the first. ❷ (一晝夜) a whole day; a day and a night. ❸ (晝) a day; the daytime. ❹ (只の一日) one day; a single day. **—,** *ad.* ❶ (一日につき) a day; per day. ❷ (終日) all day. ❸ (或日) one day (過去); some day (未來). —一日二回, twice a day. —一日置きに, every other day. —一日千秋の思ひをなす, to feel as if one day were years.

ichijō (一帖), *n.* a quire. —洋紙一帖, a quire of foreign paper.

ichijō (一場), *n.* a place; a scene. —一場の夢と化する, to become a momentary dream. —一場の演說を試みる, to make a speech.

ichiko (市子), *n.* a witch (女).

ichimai (一枚), *n.* a pane (板硝子などの); a sheet (紙の); a leaf (書物の). —紙一枚, a sheet of paper.

ichimatsu (市松), *n.* chequer-work. ¶ 市松模樣, a chequered [checkered; plaid] pattern.

ichimei (一命), *n.* a life. —一命を擲って國家に盡す, to serve the state at the risk of one's life; throw away one's life in the service of the state.

ichimen (一面), *n.* ❶ (片面) one side. ❷ (一帶) the whole surface. —新聞の一面, the first page (of a newspaper). —座敷一面に, all over the room. —一面の火となる, to be in a blaze; be (enveloped) in flames.

ichimenshiki (一面識), *n.* meeting once; slight acquaintance. —一面識がある, to be slightly acquainted.

ichimi (一味), *n.* partisans; the same party; conspirators. —一味徒黨を集める, to gather [muster] their gang [crew; band].

ichimin (一眠), *n.* 【養蠶】the first moulting.

ichimō-dajin (一網打盡する), *v.* to catch at one cast; make a wholesale arrest.

ichimoku (一目), *n.* ❶ an [one] eye (隻眼); a glance (一見). ❷ (碁) a square; a checker-stone (一石子). —一目置く, ① 【碁】to put a stone in advance. ② (遜る) to yield the palm *to*; be inferior *to*. —一目瞭然たる, as clear as day; as plain as the nose in one's face.

ichimokusan (一目散に), *ad.* at full [top] speed; as fast as his legs could carry him. —一目散に逃出す, to scamper away; take to one's heels; run away for one's life.

ichimon (一文), *n.* one *mon*; a farthing. ¶ 一文無, being without a penny; pennilessness. —一文吝みの百損, "Penny wise, pound foolish."

ichimon (一門), *n.* the whole family; a clan.

ichimonji (一文字に), *ad.* in a straight line; in a bee-line; as the crow flies.

ichimotsu (一物), *n.* ❶ (一つの物) a thing. ❷ (企み) a deep design. —胸に一物ある, designing; with designs in his heart; having an axe to grind.

ichimotsu (逸物), *n.* ❶ (勝れたもの) a thing of surpassing quality; a paragon. ❷ (快馬) a courser; a gallant horse.

ichinan (一難), *n.* a hardship;

a difficulty. —一難を經る每に, with every difficulty overcome.

ichinen (一年), *n.* ❶ one year; a twelvemonth. ❷ (或年) one year (過去); some year (將來). —一年中, throughout the year; all the year round (年百年中). ¶ 一年生 (學校の), a first-year grade boy. —一年生草木,【植】the aunual herb. —一年志願兵, a one-year's volunteer.

ichinen (一念), *n.* concentrated thought; concentration; an ardent desire. —一念天に通ず, "Faith will move mountains."

ichini (一二), *n.* ❶ (最高に近いこと) the highest; the first. ❷ (僅少なこと) a few. —一二度, once or twice. —一二を爭ふ, to contend for the first place [position]; be competitors.

ichinin (一人), *n.* one person; one; a head. —一人につき五志(シリング), 5s. per man [head]. —一人乘の, single-seated. (一人乘の乘物 a single-seater.) —一人一人に, man by man. ¶ 一人一票, one man, one vote.

ichinin (一任する), *vt.* to leave entirely *to*; leave to another's discretion; place in a person's care [hand].

ichiō (一應), *ad.* ❶(一度) once; one time. ❷ (一通り) generally; in outline. —今一應, once more; again. —念の爲め一應, again, to make sure.

ichiran (一覽), *n.* ❶(一讀) a perusal; sight; a look. ❷ (一覽表其他) a brief summary (綱要); a calendar. —一覽する, to see; take [have] a look *at*; peruse. —讀者の一覽に供する, to offer for the reader's perusal. ¶ 一覽拂爲替手形, a bill [draft] at sight; a sight bill (S/B と略す). —一覽表, a table; a list; a conspectus.

ichirei (一例), *n.* an instance; an example. —一例を擧げれば, for instance; for example; to cite an instance; to give an example.

ichiren (一連), *n.* ❶ a string. ❷ (洋紙の) a ream (of paper).

ichiretsu (一列), *n.* ❶【軍】a file (縱); a rank (橫) (前列を front rank, 後列を rear rank といふ); a line. ❷ a line; a row. —一列に並ぶ, to stand in a row; aline. ¶ 一列橫隊, a single rank. —一列縱隊, a (single) file [line].

ichiri (一理), *n.* a reason. —君の言ふ所にも一理ある, There is a reason in what you say.

ichiri-ichigai (一利一害), *n.* an advantage and a disadvantage.

ichirin (一輪), *n.* a wheel. ¶ 一輪花, a single flower. ¶ 一輪插し, a small vase for a single flower.

ichiritsu (一律の), *a.* uniform. —一律に, uniformly.

ichirizuka (一里塚), *n.* a milestone.

ichiroku-shōbu (一六勝負), *n.* ❶ (賭博) gambling. ❷ (運任せ) a speculation; a hazard; the last cast. —一六勝負をやる, to run a risk; take chances; stake one's all.

ichiru (一縷), *n.* a thread; a hair. —一縷の望, the last straw; a gleam of hope.

ichiryōnichi (一兩日), *n.* a day or two. —一兩日中に, within a day or two.

ichiryū (一流の), *a.* ❶ (一流の) of the first rank [rate; order]; leading. ❷ (獨得の) special; characteristic; favourite (お得意の). —一流の人士, a person of the first rank. —氏一流の皮肉演說, a sarcastic speech characteristic of [peculiar to] him.

ichiwari (一割), *n.* ten per cent; [10 %.]

ichiya (一夜), *n.* ❶ (一晩) one night. ❷ (終夜) all night. —一夜の宿を乞ふ, to ask for a night's shelter [lodging].

ichiyaku (一躍), *ad.* at one [a] [bound.]

ichiyō (一樣), *n.* ❶ (同一) sameness; equality (同等, 均一). ❷ (類似) similarity. ❸ (一律) uniformity. —一樣に, similarly; equally; uniformly. —— **-no**, *a.* same; equal; similar; uniform. —一樣の取扱, indiscriminate treatment.

ichiyō-raifuku (一陽來復), *n.* return of good fortune.

ichiza (一座), *n.* ❶ (藝人の一團隊) a theatrical company; a troupe. ❷ the whole company (全同席者); the whole assembly (同上). —玉乘一座, a company [troupe] of ball-walkers. —一座する, to be in company *with*; sit *with*; assemble. —一座を見下ろす, to look down upon those present.

ichizen (一膳), *n.* a bowl; a cup. —飯(吸物)一膳, a bowl of boiled rice (soup). —箸一膳, a pair of chopsticks. ¶ 一膳飯屋, a chophouse.

ichizoku (一族), *n.* ❶ (一家族) the whole family. ❷ (一門, 親戚) a clan; kin; relatives.

ichizon (一存), *n.* one's own discretion [judgment]. —私の一存にはまゐりません, I cannot deal with it at my own discretion.

ichizu (一途に), *ad.* with a whole

heart; with all one's heart. —一途に思ひ込む, to be so possessed with the idea.

icho (遺著), *n.* a posthumous work; (literary) remains.

ichō (公孫樹, 銀杏), *n.* 【植】 the gingko(-tree); the maiden-hair-tree.

ichō (胃腸), *n.* the stomach and intestines. ¶ 胃腸病院, a gastroenteric diseases hospital.

ichō (移牒する), *vt.* to transmit; forward; communicate.

ichū (意中), *n.* one's thoughts [intention]; one's mind. —意中の人, a sweetheart; a lady-love (女); a lover (男). —人の意中を探る, to sound another's mind [intentions]; feel another's pulse. —互に意中を語る, to lay bare each other's thoughts.

idai (偉大), *n.* greatness; mightiness; grandeur. —偉大な, great; mighty (有力の); grand.

idaku (抱・懐く), *vt.* ❶ to fold in one's arms [to one's breast]; embosom; hug. ❷ 【懐】 to harbour; entertain. —子を抱いて, with a child in one's arms. —不安を懐いて, in trembling uncertainty. —惡意を懐く, to harbour malice. —前に灣を抱く, to enclose a bay in front.

idasu (出す), *vt.* ❶ (取出す) to take out; bring forth. ❷ (產出す) to yield; produce. ☞ *dasu* (出す) —候補者を出す, to run a candidate. —人物を出す, to produce [give birth to] men of character.

Idaten (韋駄天), *n.* Veda 【梵】; the guardian god of Buddhism. ¶ 韋駄天走り, running at lightning speed.

iden (遺傳), *n.* heredity; transmission. —遺傳的, hereditary; transmittable. **——-suru,** *v.* to be hereditary; transmit. —子孫に病氣を遺傳する, to transmit the disease to his descendants.

ideru (出でる), *v.* = *deru* (出る). —其の右に出でる, to excel [surpass] him; be his superior. —一週を出でずして, within [inside of] a week.

idetachi (打扮), *n.* ❶ (扮裝) clothes; attire; garment. ❷ (旅裝) travelling clothes; outfit; equipment.

ido (井戸), *n.* a well. —井戸を掘る, to dig [sink] a well. ¶ 井戸端會議, a well-side gossip. —井戸側, the well-tube. —井戸掘り, ① well-sinking. ② a well-borer. —井戸水, well-water. —井戸流し, a well-curb. —井戸浚へ, well-clearing.

ido (緯度), *n.* 【地】 latitude. ¶ 高(低)緯度, high (low) latitudes.

idō (異同), *n.* difference. —異同を辨ずる, to distinguish [know] one from another; discriminate between things.

idō (異動), *n.* change.

idō (移動), *n.* transition; motion; movement. —移動する, to move; pass; shift; travel (機械に云ふ). ¶ 移動警察, travelling police. —移動起重機, a travelling crane.

idokoro (居所), *n.* an address (宿所); whereabouts (所在); a seat (席).

idomu (挑む), *vt.* ❶ (仕かける) to challenge; defy; dare. ❷ (誘ふ) to entice; tempt. —爭を挑む, to assume the aggressive.

ie (家), *n.* a house; family; home. —家の外(內)に, out-of-doors (indoors). —家にゐる, to stay [*be*] at home. —家の方へ歸る, to make for home. —家を興す, to restore one's family to fortune. —家を相續する, to succeed to a family estate.

iebato (家鳩, 鴿), *n.* 【鳥】 the domestic [house] pigeon.

iede (家出する), *vi.* to leave one's house; run away from home.

iedomo (雖), *conj.* though; although; notwithstanding. —三歲の小兒と雖も, even a little child. —吾れ貧なりと雖も, poor as I am; though I am poor.

iegamae (家構), *n.* the structure [plan] of a house. —立派な家構へ, a fine-looking house.

iegara (家柄), *n.* ❶ (門閥) a noble family; a family of high standing. ❷ (血筋) blood; descent. ❸ (家系) lineage; parentage; stock. ❹ (家格) the standing of a family. —家柄から出る, to come of a good stock [family].

iegoto (家毎に), *ad.* at every house; from door to door; from house to house.

ieji (家路), *n.* the homeward road. —家路を指して歸る, to bend one's steps homeward; return on the road to home.

ieki (胃液), *n.* gastric juice.

iemoto (家元), *n.* ❶ (自家) one's (own) house. ❷ (妻の里) the wife's home. ❸ (遊藝等で流儀の本家) the head-house.

ienami (家竝), *n.* (家ならび) a row of houses. —家竝に, house by house.

ienushi (家主), *n.* a house-owner; a landlord.

ieru (癒える), *vi.* ❶ to be healed; heal; be cured. ❷ (憤などの晴れる) to recover one's temper. —

病が癒える, to recover from sickness.

iesagashi (家探し), *n.* house-hunting.

Iesu (耶蘇), *n.* = ***Esu*** (耶蘇).

ietsuki (家附の), *a.* ❶ (家傳來の) hereditary; family. ❷ (家で生れた) born in the house. —家附の娘, a daughter of the house; an heiress (嗣女).

ietsuzuki (家續), *n.* a continuous row of houses.

ieyashiki (家屋敷), *n.* 【法】 messuage; a house and its curtilage.

ifu (委付する), *vt.* 【法】 to abandon.

ifu (畏怖), *n.* fear; fright. —畏怖する, to fear; be frightened.

ifū (威風), *n.* dignity; an imposing [a majestic] air; dignified manner. —威風堂々と, majestically; in a dignified manner.

ifū (遺風), *n.* a survival; a relic; remains.

ifukeitei (異父兄弟), *n.* a uterine brother; a stepbrother; a half-brother.

ifuku (衣服), *n.* clothes; clothing; dress; garments.

ifuku (畏服する), *vi.* to submit out of fear; be overawed; be overpowered.

iga (毬, 毬彙), *n.* a bur, burr.

igaguri (毬栗), *n.* chestnuts in burs. ¶ 毬栗頭, a close-cropped head.

igai (貽貝), *n.* 【貝】 the sea-mussel; dried mussels (商品).

igai (以外), *prep.* ❶ except; outside (*of*); beyond. ❷ besides; in addition *to*. —學課以外, outside our lessons. —土曜以外には, except on Saturday(s).

igai (意外の), *a.* ❶ (不測の) unexpected; unlooked-for; unanticipated. ❷ (偶然の) incidental; accidental. ❸ (驚くべき) surprising; amazing. —意外の愉快, an unlooked-for pleasure. —意外の結果, an unexpected result. —意外の知らせ, a surprising report. —意外に捗どる, to progress beyond expectation. —此處で遇ふとは意外だ, I did not expect to see you here.

igai (遺骸), *n.* remains; a corpse; a dead body.

igaku (醫學), *n.* medicine; medical science. ¶ 醫學博士, a doctor of medicine (M. D. と略す). —醫學生, a medical student. —醫學專門學校, a medical college. —醫學士, a bachelor of medicine.

igami (歪), **igamu** (歪む), = ***yugami*** (歪), ***yugamu*** (歪む).

igamiai (啀合), *n.* snarling [growling] at each other.

igamu (啀む), *vi.* to snarl; growl.

igan (胃癌), *n.* 【醫】 gastroscirrhus; cancer of the stomach.

igata (鑄型), *n.* a mould; a cast. —鑄型に流す, to pour into a mould.

igen (威嚴), *n.* dignity; stateliness; grandeur. —威嚴のある, dignified; stately; majestic. —威嚴を保つ, to keep [maintain] one's dignity.

igeta (井桁), *n.* a well-crib. —井桁に積む, to pile crosswise in two parallels.

igi (威儀), *n.* dignity; majestic appearance. —威儀ある人, a man of noble presence.

igi (異議), *n.* demurrer 【法】; dissent; objection. —異議がない, to have no objection *to*; have nothing to say *against*. —異議を唱へる, to demur; object *to*; dissent *from*.

igi (意義), *n.* meaning; signification; import. —意義の深い謎, a riddle of deep significance. —意義を誤解する, to mistake the meaning; misconstrue.

Igirisu (英吉利), *n.* England; Great Britain. ☞ ***Eikoku.***

igo (以後), *ad.* ❶ after; since. ❷ (將來は) henceforth; in future; from this time forward. **—— -no,** *a.* subsequent (其後の); future (今後の). —以後の見せしめに, as a warning for the future.

igo (圍碁), *n.* *go*-play.

igokoro (居心よい), *a.* comfortable (to live in); cosy; snug. —居心よい家, a snug house to live in.

igon (遺言), *n.* = ***yuigon*** (遺言).

iguchi (缺唇), *n.* a hare-lip.

igyō (異形の), *a.* monstrous; grotesque; fantastic.

igyō (偉業), *n.* an achievement; a great undertaking.

igyō (醫業), *n.* medicine; the medical profession; medical practice.

ihai (位牌), *n.* an ancestral tablet (祖先の); a family tablet.

ihai (違背), *n.* violation; infringement; transgression. ☞ ***ihan*** (違反). —違背する, to violate; infringe; transgress.

ihaku (威迫する), *vt.* to threaten; menace; intimidate. —敵を威迫する, to threaten the enemy.

ihan (違犯, 違反), *n.* infringement; violation; transgression. **—— -suru,** *vt.* to offend *against*; infringe; violate. —契約に違反する, to act contrary to contract.

ihatsu (遺髮), *n.* the deceased's hair.

ihen (異變), *n.* a change; a catastrophe; an accident (事變).

ihō (違法の), *a.* illegal; unlawful; illicit. —違法處分をなす, to take measures contrary to law.

ihoku (以北), *ad.* & *n.* north *of*; and north. —函館以北では, at Hakodate and northwards.

ihyō (意表), *n.* unexpectedness. —意表に出づる, to turn out contrary to expectation.

ii (いい), *a.* ❶〔善, 良, 好, 美〕good; excellent; beautiful. ❷〔吉〕(めでたい) auspicious; happy. ❸〔宜〕(判斷的に用ふ) good. ☞ *yoi* (よい), *umai* (旨い). —いい天氣, pleasant [fine] weather. —いい鹽梅に, I am happy to say. —いいか, 投げるよ, Ready? I'll throw it. —それは無くてもいい, I can do without it. —出京した方がいいさ, You had better go to Tōkyō.

ii (易易たる), *a.* easy; simple.

ii (唯唯), *ad.* yes. —唯々諾々と, quite willingly; in ready compliance. (唯々諾々として從ふ, to submit willingly).

iiai (言合ひ), *n.* ❶ bandying words. ❷ (口論) a dispute; a quarrel. —言ひ合ふ, ① to bandy words *with*. ② to quarrel; dispute.

iiarasou (言爭ふ), *vi.* to dispute; quarrel; altercate; squabble.

iiarawashi (言表し -方), *n.* expression. —言ひ表はす, to express; put; couch; describe; represent.

iiateru (言當てる), *vt.* ❶ to guess (correctly); hit. ❷ (豫言) to prophesy; foretell.

iiawaseru (言合せる), *vi.* to make a previous agreement; preconcert. —言ひ合せた樣に, as if prearranged.

iiayamari (言誤り), *n.* a misstatement; a slip of the tongue. —言ひ誤る, to make a mistake [slip] in saying; misstate; missay.

iibun (言分), *n.* ❶ (申譯) an excuse; an explanation. ❷ (辭柄) a pretext. ❸ (非難) criticism; objection. ❹ (主張) a claim; what one has to say; one's say.

iichigaeru (言違へる), *vt.* to mistake; say by mistake.

iichigai (言違ひ), *n.* a mistake; a misstatement.

iichirasu (言散らす), *v.* ❶ (言觸らす) to make public; spread. ❷ (勝手に喋る) to say all sorts of things. —好きな事を言ひ散らす, to say whatever one pleases.

iidako (飯蛸), *n.* 【頭足】 Octopus ocellatus (學名).

iidasu (言出す), *v.* ❶ to begin to speak; start a talk; broach. ❷ (口外) to utter; speak out; pronounce. ❸ (發議) to propose; bring forward.

iie (否), *ad.* no; nay; not at all. —いいえどう致しまして, Oh no, not at all.

iifukumeru (言含める), *v.* to instruct; inculcate; tell.

iifurasu (言觸らす), *vt.* to make public; spread; circulate ☞ *fuichō* (吹聽する).

iifurusu (言古す), *vt.* to make stale.

iifuseru (言伏せる), *vt.* to silence; confute. —議論で相手を言ひ伏せる, to silence [defeat] an antagonist in argument.

iigai (言甲斐ある), *a.* worth speaking. —言甲斐なき奴, a poor-spirited fellow.

iigakari (言掛), *n.* ❶ (一旦言出した關係) connection from having spoken out. ❷ (口實) a pretext. ❸ (無根のことを口實にする强要) a false charge. —少しの事を言掛りにする, to trump up charges on the slightest pretext.

iigatai (言難い), *a.* hard [difficult] to say [speak]; unspeakable.

iigusa (言種), *n.* ❶ (言ふこと) words; remarks. ❷ (話の種) a topic [subject] for conversation [talk]. ❸ (辭柄) an excuse; a pretext; a plea. ❹ (不平) complaints; grumble.

iiharu (言張る), *vt.* to persist *in*; declare persistently; assert. —我儘を言ひ張る, to persist in wilfulness.

iihiraki (言開), *n.* vindication. —言ひ開く, to vindicate oneself; exculpate oneself; clear away charges; justify oneself.

iikaeru (言換へる), *vt.* to say in another way. —言ひ換へれば, in other words; that is to say.

iikaesu (言返す), *vt.* to answer back; retort; repeat (繰返す). —言ひ返す言葉もない, to have no words to answer back with.

iikagen (好加減の), *a.* ❶ appropriate; suitable; moderate. ❷ (申譯だけの) perfunctory. —好い加減に, perfunctorily; slovenly. —好い加減な事を云ふ, to say things to humour a person (氣に入りさうな); speak at random (出鱈目). —好い加減な返事をする, to give a vague answer (瓢箪鯰); answer at random. —好い加減な(仕)事をする, to do things by halves; do a work slovenly.

iikakeru (言掛ける), *vt.* ❶ (言始める) to begin to speak. ❷ (話掛ける) to speak *to*; address; accost. ❸ (持出す) to bring forward. ❹ (誣ひる) to accuse (a person of theft); charge (a person with theft).

iikaneru(言兼ねる), *v.* to hesitate to say; be unable to say [speak].

iikata(言方), *n.* the way of speaking; expression; language.

iikawasu (言交す), *v.* to promise mutually; vow each other; exchange vows. —言ひ交した仲, the relations of a plighted couple. —言ひ交した言葉を反古にする, to throw a mutual promise to the winds.

iiki (好氣), *n.* self-conceit. —好い氣な, ①(得意) conceited; proud; vain. ②(呑氣) easy-going; light-hearted; slovenly (だらしない). —默ッてゐれば好い氣になりあがる, He has the cheek to presume upon my silence.

iiki (異域), *n.* a foreign [strange] land. ☞ *ikyō* (異鄕).

iikikasu (言聞かす), *vt.* ❶ (敎へる) to instruct; inculcate; tell. ❷(訓戒する) to admonish; remonstrate (with a person) *on.* —如何に言ひ聞かしても, try hard as I may to instruct him.

iikiru (言切る), *vt.* ❶ to finish saying; say all. ❷(斷言する) to say positively; declare; assert.

iikitari (言來り), *n.* tradition; an old saying. —言ひ來りの, traditional.

iiko (好子), *n.* a pretty child; a dear little thing. —好い子だからおよしなさい, Don't do it, there's a dear.

iikomeru (言籠める), *vt.* to talk down; silence. —言ひ籠められる, to be argued into silence; be driven into a corner.

iikurumeru (言ひくるめる), *vt.* Ⓢ 言黑める. to dupe; argue into consent. —白を黑と言ひ黑める, to prove that black is white and white black.

iimae (言前), *n.* an excuse; a pretence; a pretext.

iimagirasu (言紛らす), *vt.* to explain away. ——, *vi.* to quibble; shuffle. —他の事に言ひ紛らす, to put off by referring to other things. —話を轉じて言ひ紛らす, to wrap it up by changing the topic.

iimakasu (言負す), *vt.* to defeat in argument; refute. ☞ *iikomeru* (言籠める).

iimakuru (言捲る), *vt.* to talk down; corner. —相手を言ひ捲くる, to talk down one's opponent.

iimawashi (言廻し), *n.* expression; a way of speaking; diction.

iimorasu (言漏らす), *vt.* ❶ (言ひ落す) to omit to say; leave untold [unsaid]; skip. ❷(漏洩) to disclose; let slip; let out.

iin (委員), *n.* ❶ (個人) a member of a committee; a committee-man; a commissioner; a commissar (勞農露國の). ❷(團體) a committee; a commission; a board. ¶ 常任[常置]委員, a standing committee. —委員長, the chairman (of a committee). —委員付託, reference to a committee; commitment. —委員會, ① a meeting of a committee. ② =*iin* (委員)の❷. —委員室, a committee-room.

iin (醫員), *n.* a medical assistant; the medical staff (全體). ¶ 當直醫員, the physician on duty.

iin (醫院), *n.* a dispensary. ¶ 齒科醫院, a dental office. —醫院長, the head of a dispensary; the head physician.

iinamaru(言訛る), *vi.* to corrupt.

iinaosu (言直す), *vt.* to re-say; restate; correct. —今一度言ひ直して御覽, Now re-say it once more.

iinarawashi (言慣はし), *n.* ❶ (口癖) the habit of saying. ❷ (口碑) a saying; a proverb. ❸ (語法) a usage; an idiom. —言ひ慣はす, ① to accustom a person to say. ② to become proverbial. —多年言ひ慣はしの言葉, the language one has long been used to.

iinareru (言馴れる), *vi.* to become used [accustomed] to say; be familiarized *with.*

iinari (言ひなりに), *ad.* as one says; as one wishes. —言ひなり次第になる, to submit readily; be led by the nose. (言ひなり次第になる人, an accommodating man; a nose of wax.) —某の言ひなりになッてる, to be under a person's thumb.

iinazuke (許嫁), *n.* ❶ (事) betrothal; affiance. ❷ (人) the betrothed; the affianced; the intended. —許嫁の夫(女), a betrothed [affianced] husband (wife); the *fiancé* (*fiancée*) 〔佛〕. —と許嫁の仲である, to be affianced *to.*

iine (言値), *n.* the price asked; the seller's price. —言ひ値で買ふ, to buy at the price asked [at the seller's price]. —言ひ値から二割減(げ)く, to reduce the price asked by 20 per cent.

iinikui (言難い), *a.* ❶ (言ふに困難なる) hard [difficult] to say. ❷ (言ふを憚る) that one hesitates to say; delicate. —言ひにくさうにもぢもぢする, to fidget as if he hesitated to speak.

iinobasu (言延す), *v.* to postpone with excuses.

iinuke (言抜け), *n.* an excuse; an evasion; an evasive answer. —罪を言ひ抜ける, to slip out of a charge by talk; talk down a charge.

iioki (言置), *n.* ❶ leaving word. ❷ =*yuigon* (遺言). —言ひ置く, to leave word [direction]. (彼は何か言ひ置いて行ッたか, Has he left any message with you?)

iiokuru (言送る), *vt.* to communicate *to*; inform *of*; apprise *of*.

iiotosu (言落す), *vt.* to omit to say. ☞ *iimorasu*.

iioyobu (言及ぶ), *vt.* to refer to; make reference to; allude to.

iishiburu (言澁る), *v.* to hesitate to speak.

iisokonai (言損ひ), *n.* a mistake [slip] in speaking; a misstatement. —言ひ損ふ, ①=*iiayamaru* (言誤る). ② to fail to tell.

iisugiru (言過ぎる), *v.* to speak too much [severely]; go too far. —君は言ひ過ぎた, You went too far in your talk.

iisuteru (言捨てる), *vt.* to say and leave without waiting for an answer; say over one's shoulder; make a parting remark.

iitai (言度い), *a.* wishing to say. —言ひたいことがある, I have a word to say. —言ひたい事を言ふ, to have one's say.

iitasu (言足す), *v.* to say in addition; add.

iitate (言立て), *n.* an allegation; an assertion.

iitateru (言立てる), *v.* ❶ (申立てる) to allege; assert; report; ❷=*fuichō* (吹聽する). —病氣と言ひ立てて缺勤する, to report oneself ill and be absent from duty.

iitoshi (好い年), *n.* a good age. —好い年をして, at one's age.

iitōsu (言通す), *v.* to persist *in* (saying); insist *on* [*upon*]. —何處までも知らぬと言ひ通さうとする, He persists to the end in professing ignorance of it.

iitsu (唯一の), *a.* =*yuitsu* (唯一の).

iitsuke (言附け), *n.* bidding; directions (指圖); instructions (同上). —言附け通りに, according to instructions.

iitsukeru (言附ける), *vt.* ❶ (申附ける) to direct; instruct; bid. ❷ (告口, 吩咐) to tell; sneak 〔學校·俗〕. —或る事を爲せと言ひ附ける, to direct a thing to be done.

iitsukurou (言繕ふ), *v.* to gloze; gloss over; palliate.

iitsukusu (言盡す), *v.* to exhaust (a subject); say all (one wishes to say); say that can be said. —言ひ盡されぬ, inexhaustible; impossible to describe fully.

iitsumeru (言詰める), *vt.* to silence; out-talk.

iitsunoru (言募る), *v.* to come to high words.

iitsutae (言傳へ), *n.* ❶ (口碑) a tradition. ❷ (傳言) a (verbal) message. —言ひ傳へる, ① to hand down by tradition. ② to give a message; send word. ③ (言ひふらす) to spread; circulate.

iiwake (言譯), *n.* ❶ (詫) an excuse; an apology. ❷ (辯解) an explanation; vindication; defence (辯護). —苦しい言譯, a pitiful [sorry] excuse. —まづい言譯, a poor [clumsy; an awkward] excuse. —言譯する, [*vt.*] to apologize; (make an) excuse; plead; defend; vindicate. —言譯として, by way of excuse. —ほんの言譯に, as a mere excuse; for mere form's sake (形式一偏に).

iiwatashi (言渡), *n.* sentence. ¶ 言渡日, the day for sentence. —言渡書, a sentence; an order; written judgment.

iiwatasu (言渡す), *vt.* ❶ (言附) to order; tell. ❷ (宣告) to sentence; award (審判·審査·損害賠償額を). —判決を言ひ渡す, to give [render; deliver; pronounce] judgment (upon); pass [pronounce; give] sentence (upon). —死刑を言ひ渡す, to sentence a person to death.

iiyō (言樣), *n.* the way of speaking; expression; phraseology. —言ひ樣なき, indescribable; unutterable.

iiyoru (言寄る), *vt.* to court; woo; make suit *to*; make love *to*; make up *to*.

ijaku (胃弱), *n.* 【醫】 dyspepsia; a weak stomach. ☞ *ibyō* (胃病).

iji (意地), *n.* ❶ (根性) temper; disposition. ❷ (我意) egotism; self-will. ❸ (執拗) obstinacy; stubbornness. —意地の惡い, ill-tempered; ill-natured; spiteful. ☞ *ijiwaru* (意地惡い). —意地になる, to become obstinate. (意地になッて他人の邪魔をする, to obstruct others from obstinacy.) —意地を張る, to grow implacable.

iji (維持), *n.* maintenance; support. **——-suru**, *vt.* to maintain; support; keep up. —一國の體面を維持する, to maintain the dignity of a nation. —原案を維持する, to maintain [support] the original bill. ¶ 維持費, upkeep [maintenance] expenses. —維持員會, the board of supporters.

ijiiji (いぢいぢする), *vi.* ❶ to be timid; be shrinking. ❷ to be greedy.

ijikeru (いぢける), *vi.* to shrink (with fear); shrug (with cold); be stunted. —いぢけた, stunted (木などの); cramped. (いぢけた字を書く, to write a cramped hand.)

ijikitanai (意地穢い), *a.* ❶ (食ひたがる) greedy. ❷ (卑劣の) mean; base.

ijikuneta (いぢくねた), *a.* distorted.

ijikuru (弄る), *vt.* to monkey *with* [俗]. ☞ *ijiru* (弄る).

ijimeru (窘める), *vt.* ❶ to tease; worry; bully. ❷ (じらす) to irritate. —小作人を窘める, to oppress tenant farmers. —弱い者を窘める, to bully the weak.

ijin (異人), *n.* a foreigner (外國人); a westerner (西洋人).

ijin (偉人), *n.* a great man; a hero; a master spirit. —絕代の偉人, the greatest man that ever lived. ¶ 偉人傳, a biography of great men [heroes].

ijirashii (いぢらしい), *a.* lovely (愛らしい); pitiful (憫むべき).

ijiru (弄る), *vt.* to finger; play *with*; fidget *with*; meddle *with*; fool *with* [米·卑]. —火(刃物)を弄る, to play with fire (edged tools). —口鬚を弄る, to twiddle one's moustache.

ijiwaru (意地惡), *n.* ❶ (性質) cross temper; crabbedness. ❷ (人) a spiteful thing; a crab; a (she-) cat (女). —意地惡い, ① (根性曲りの) cross-tempered; crabbed; ill-natured. ② (生憎) unfortunate; unlucky. —意地惡く, ① ill-naturedly; crabbedly; crossly. ② (不幸に) unluckily; unfortunately.

ijō (以上), ❶ (上記) the above; the above-stated [-mentioned]; the said. ❷ (書翰の結文) yours respectfully [truly; sincerely, &c.]. ❸ (より以上) more than; over; above. ❹ (からは) since; now that. —二哩以上, two miles or more. —十錢以上の額, a sum of not less than ten *sen*. —六歲以上の子供, children six years old and upwards. —三分の二以上の多數, a majority of at least two-thirds. —以上述ぶる如く, as above stated.

ijō (異狀), *n.* change (變動); derangement (狂ひ); abnormal symptoms (變徵候). —異狀がある, to be abnormal (脈搏など); be affected (精神·器官など); be deranged (精神など); be out of order (機械·組織等の). —異狀が無い, to be normal; be in good order; show no abnormal sign [symptom] (徵候を認めず). —異狀を呈する, to show abnormal symptoms.

ijō (異常の), *a.* abnormal; unusual; extraordinary.

ijō (委讓), *n.* assignment; transfer. —委讓する, to assign; transfer.

ijō (圍繞する), *vt.* to surround; encircle; enclose.

ijōfu (偉丈夫), *n.* a great man; a hero; a giant.

ijū (移住), *n.* ❶ emigration (外國へ); immigration (外國より). ❷ (轉住) migration; transmigration. —移住さす, to emigrate; immigrate; settle. —移住する, ① [*vi.*] to emigrate *from*; immigrate *to*; settle *in*. ② [*a.*] emigrant; immigrant. ¶ 移住地, a settlement. —移住民, an emigrant; an immigrant; a settler.

ijutsu (醫術), *n.* medicine; the healing [medical] art. ¶ 醫術開業免狀, a medical practitioner's license. —醫術開業試驗, an examination for medical practitioners.

ika (烏賊), *n.* 【頭足】the cuttle-fish. —烏賊の甲, the cuttle bone; the sepiost. ¶ 槍烏賊, the squid. —烏賊胸 (ワイシャツの), a shirt-front; a dickey.

ika (以下), ❶ (下記) the following. ❷ (より下) less than; under; below. ❸ (其餘) and the rest; etc. —中流以下, below the middle class; from the middle class downwards (中流をも含めて). —六歲以下, children under six years of age. —以下次號, to be continued (in our next). —首相以下の陪從者, the prime minister and others in attendance. —厘位以下は之を切捨つ, Fractions of a *rin* to be disregarded.

ika (醫科), *n.* a medical department. ¶ 醫科大學, a medical college; a college of medicine. (醫科大學附屬病院, a hospital attached to the medical college; a medical college hospital.)

ikabakari (如何許り), *ad.* how; how great; how much. —, *pron.* what.

ikada (筏), *n.* a raft. —筏に組んで流す, to make a raft of it and float it down. ¶ 筏乘り, a raftsman; a rafter.

ikade (爭で), *ad.* how.

ikaesu (射反す), *vt.* ❶ (反射) to reflect. ❷ to shoot back.

ikaga (如何), *ad.* how. —, *pron.* what. ☞ *dō* (何樣). —明日では如何です, Will to-morrow suit you?

ikagawashii (如何はしい), *a.* ❶ (訝しい) doubtful; questionable; suspicious. ❷ (淫猥) obscene; indecent. ❸ (後暗い) shady (行

爲等の). 一如何はしい人物, a questionable character.

ikahodo (如何程), *ad.* ❶ how much; how many; what [*pron.*] ❷ however. 一如何程有り餘る身代でも, However large a fortune may be.

ikai (位階), *n.* a court rank.

ikaiyō (胃潰瘍), *n.* 【醫】❶ gastrelcosis; ulceration of the stomach. ❷ an ulcer of the stomach; peptic ulcer.

ikakeru (鑄掛ける), *vt.* to tinker; mend. ¶ 鑄掛屋, a tinker.

ikaku (威嚇), *n.* menace; intimidation; bluff. 一威嚇的, minacious; threatening; intimidatory. 一威嚇する, to menace; intimidate; scare; bluff.

ikakuchō (胃擴張), *n.* 【醫】gastrectasia; dilatation of the stomach.

ikameshii (嚴しい), *a.* ❶ (威嚴ある) dignified; stately; solemn. ❷ (嚴肅な) grave; stern. 一嚴しい軍裝をする, to put on a dignified military uniform. 一嚴しく威儀を飾る, to make a dignified appearance.

ikamono (僞物), *n.* a spurious article; a sham; a fake〔卑〕. ¶ 僞物師, a swindler; a faker〔卑〕.

ikan (如何), *pron.* what. ——, *ad.* how. 一如何となれば, [*conj.*] because; for. 一如何ともし難き事, what cannot be helped. 一…の如何による, to depend *upon*. 一事の如何を問はず, regardless of the nature of the matter.

ikan (尉官), *n.* 【陸】a company officer; 【海】lieutenants and sub-lieutenants.

ikan (偉觀), *n.* a wonderful [remarkable] sight; a grand sight.

ikan (遺憾), *n.* regret. 一遺憾な, regrettable; regretful; deplorable. 一遺憾なく, thoroughly; to perfection; satisfactorily. 一遺憾ながら, to my regret; I regret [am sorry] to say *that*; much as I regret it. 一遺憾とする(に思ふ), to regret; feel sorry *for*. 一…のは[とは]遺憾である, it is to be regretted *that*. 一遺憾の意を表す, to express one's regret.

ikan (醫官), *n.* a medical officer.

ikanago (王筋魚), *n.* 【魚】the (sand-)lance; the sand-eel.

ikanaru (如何なる), *a.* what; what kind of; whatever (…も). ☞ *donna*. 一如何なる結果にならうとも, whatever results may follow. 一如何なる手段を執っても, by fair means or foul.

ikani (如何に), *ad.* how. ——, *int.* how now. 一如何にしても, by all means; at any cost; by some means or other. 一如何にあらうとも, however that may be. 一如何に働いても, however hard you may work; work as hard as you may [will].

ikanimo (如何にも), *ad.* ❶ (確に) certainly; indeed; to be sure. ❷ (甚だ) very; extremely. ❸ (さう) yes; quite so.

ikaraseru (怒らせる), *vt.* ❶ (おこらせる) to anger; offend; provoke. ❷ (聳えさす) to square (肩などを). 一肩を怒らして, with shoulders perked up. 一眼を怒らして, with angry eyes.

ikari (怒), *n.* anger; rage (烈怒); fury (狂氣の如き). 一怒りの餘り, in a fit of passion [fury]; in a paroxysm of rage. 一怒りに觸れる, to arouse another's anger. 一怒りに任せる, to give way to anger; become blind with fury. 一怒りを宥める, to soothe [appease] another's anger. 一怒りを抑へる, to repress anger; bridle wrath.

ikari (錨, 碇), *n.* an anchor. 一錨を卸す, to cast anchor; come to anchor. 一錨を揚げる, to heave up the anchor; weigh anchor. ¶ 錨索, a hawser; an anchor-rope.

ikaru, ikaruga, (桑鳫, 斑鳩), *n.* 【鳥】the Japanese hawfinch.

ikaru (怒る), *vi.* ❶ to get [grow] angry (*at* は物; *with* は人); be offended. ❷ (肩の) to draw up. 一怒り易い, irritable; quick-tempered; hot-tempered. 一容易に怒らぬ, slow to wrath. 一青く(眞赤に)なって怒る, to be pale (red) with anger.

ikasu (活かす), *vt.* ❶ (復活さす) to revive; restore. ❷(蘇生さす) to bring a person to life [his senses]. ❸ (生々さす) to vivify; give life [vividness] *to*. 一學問を活かして使ふ, to put one's learning into practical use. 一魚を活かして置く, to keep the fish alive.

ikataru (胃加答兒), *n.* 【醫】catarrh of the stomach; gastric catarrh.

ikatsui (嚴い), *a.* ❶ (いかめしい) dignified; imposing. ❷ (威張った) haughty; arrogant.

ikayō (如何樣に), *ad.* ❶ (方法) how; in what way. ❷ (程度) how; how much; however (…も). ☞ *donnani* (何樣に). 一如何樣にも, in any way [manner].

ikazuchi (雷), *n.* =***kaminari.***

ike (池), *n.* a pond; a pool (小池); a basin (溜池). 一池の端, the side of a pond; the pond-side.

ikebana (活花), *n.* flower-arrangement (術); flowers arranged in a vase (花).

ikedori (生捕), *n.* ❶ (擒ること) taking prisoner; capture; catching alive. ❷ (生捕られてゐること) captivity. ❸ (人) a captive; a prisoner. —生捕る, ① to take (a person) prisoner; take (a person) captive; capture. ② (生物を) to catch [take; caputure] alive.

ikegaki (生垣), *n.* a (quickset; set) hedge. —生垣を作る, to plant a hedge.

ikei (畏敬する), *vt.* to revere; venerate; hold in reverence.

ikeiren (胃痙攣), *n.* 【醫】gastralgia; gastrodynia.

ikeizai (違警罪), *n.* a police offence.

iken (意見), *n.* ❶ opinion; view. ❷ (警告) advice; admonition; remonstrance. —意見の合致, consonance [coincidence] of opinions. ¶意見する, to admonish; give counsel; remonstrate [expostulate] *with*. —私の意見では, in my opinion. —意見を異にする, to dissent from a person; differ in opinion. —意見を交換する, to compare notes; exchange views. —私は…といふ意見だ, I am of opinion that.

iken (威權), *n.* power; authority. —威權を揮ふ, to exercise one's authority.

iken (違憲), *n.* unconstitutionality. ¶違憲行動, unconstitutional action.

ikenai (いけない), *aux.* ought not *to*; must not; will [shall] not. **—**, *a.* ❶ (惡しき) bad; inferior (劣等). ❷ (無效の) useless; of no use. —(…すると)いけないから, lest; for fear of; so as not *to*. (降るといけないから, lest it should rain.) —もう病人はいけない, The patient is now hopeless.

ikenie (生贄, 犧牲), *n.* a victim; a sacrifice; a prey. —犧牲にする, to victimize; sacrifice. —犧牲となる, to become sacrifice *to*; be sacrificed; fall a victim *to*.

ikeru (生ける), *a.* live; living. —生きとし生けるもの, all living things. —生けるが如く, as if living; vividly.

ikeru (活ける), *vt.* ❶ (花を) to arrange (flowers); set (flowers) in water; put (a flower) in a vase. ❷ (魚を) to keep alive. ❸ (埋める) to bank up (火を); cover up; bury.

ikesu (生洲), *n.* ❶ a fish-pond; a fish-preserve. ❷ =*ike* (池). ❸ a well (魚舟の).

iketsuhō (移血法), *n.* transfusion.

iki (生), *n.* ❶ (魚等の) liveliness. ❷ (簿記·校正用語, 復活) *stet* 〖羅〗. —生のいい魚, a lively [fresh] fish.

iki (息), *n.* breath; wind; breathing (呼吸). —息ある中に, while I still breathe. —息が詰まる, to be suffocated; be choked. —息が續く(續かぬ), to have a good [long] (bad) wind. —息がくさい, to have a foul breath. —息が絶える, to breathe one's last; expire. —息をする, to breathe; respire. —息をつく, to fetch a breath; recover [get] one's wind (切らした息を回復する); pause (休む); take [draw] breath. —息を切らす, to lose one's breath [wind]. (息を切らして馳ける, to run out of breath.) —息を殺して, with bated breath. —息の根を止める, to put an end to his life.

iki (域), *n.* limits; bounds; confines. —名人の域に達する, to make oneself master *of*; attain perfection (in an art).

iki (位記), *n.* a diploma of court rank. —位記を賜ふ, to confer a court rank. —位記を剝奪する, to deprive a person of his court rank.

iki (意氣), *n.* ❶ (心立) mind. ❷ (氣勢) high spirits. —意氣揚々と, in good spirits; elated; in exultation. —意氣相投ずる, to be like-minded. —意氣相投合せる人々, persons of congenial temper. —意氣當るべからず, to be irresistibly high-spirited. —意氣銷沈[沮喪]する, to be depressed [dispirited]; be disheartened; be out of spirits; droop; despond. —意氣に感ずる, to catch a person's spirit.

iki (遺棄), *n.* desertion; abandonment (妻子·武器·死傷者·船等の). —遺棄する, to desert; abandon.

ikibaru (息張る), *vi.* to hold one's breath and distend the stomach; strain (oneself).

ikibotoke (活佛), *n.* a distinguished priest; a living Buddha.

ikichi (生血), *n.* blood of a living person or animal; heart-blood; life-blood.

ikichigai (行違), *n.* =***yukichigai***.

ikidaore (行倒), *n.* =***yukidaore***.

ikidomari (行止), *n.* =***yukidomari***.

ikidōri (憤), *n.* ❶ (憤怒) indignation; resentment; anger. ❷ (奮發心) energetic spirit.

ikidōru (憤る), *v.* to be indignant *at*; be enraged *at*; resent.

ikigai (生甲斐ある), *a.* worth living.

ikigake (行掛に), *ad.* =***yukigake***.

ikigami (生神), *n.* a living god

ikigimo (生膽), *n.* gall; gall-bladder.

ikigire (息切れ), *n.* short wind; shortness of breath; gasp; pant. —息切れがする, to gasp; be short of breath; be short-winded.

ikigomi (意氣込), *n.* highspiritedness (元氣); intentness (熱心). —非常な意氣込みで, with great eagerness.

ikigurushii (息苦しい), *a.* stifling; oppressive; close.

ikihaji (生恥), *n.* a life shame. —生恥を曝らす, to expose oneself to shame in life; outlive one's honour.

ikiiki (生生), *ad.* lively; vividly. —生々した花, fresh flowers.

ikiji (意氣地), *n.* an unyielding spirit; spirit. ☞ *ikuji.* —意氣地のない, spiritless; faint-hearted.

ikijibiki (活字引), *n.* a walking [living] dictionary.

ikijiki (生食する), *a.* 【動】predatory. ——, *v.* to prey *upon.*

ikikaeru (生返る), *vi.* to revive; return to life; come to oneself. —生返らす, to revive; resuscitate; bring [restore] to life.

ikiki (往來), *n.* =*yukiki.*

ikimaku (敦圍く), *vi.* to fume; rave; flash up.

ikimono (生物), *n.* a living thing; a living creature [animal].

ikimu (息む), *vi.* to strain oneself; bear up.

ikina (粋な), *a.* stylish; smart; spicy〖俗〗. —粋な男, a stylish fellow; a spark. —粋な姿で, in a stylish figure.

ikinagara (生ながら), *ad.* living; alive. —生きながら葬られる, to be buried alive.

ikinagaraeru (生長らへる), *vi.* to survive; live out; live on.

ikinari (突然), *ad.* suddenly; abruptly; all at once. —いきなり飛びつく, to fly into a person's arms. —いきなり席につく, to take a seat without any greeting.

ikiningyō (生人形), *n.* a life-size figure; a waxwork (蠟製の).

ikinobiru (生延びる), *vt.* ❶ (存命) to survive (another); outlive; overlive. ❷ (逃出) to escape alive.

ikinokori (生殘), *n.* ❶ survival. ❷ (生殘者) a survivor. —戰場の生殘り, survivors of the war. —生き殘る, to survive; outlive.

ikinuki (息拔き), *n.* ❶ (通氣孔) a breathing-hole. ❷ (骨休め) rest. —息拔きする, to rest; take a rest.

ikioi (勢), *n.* ❶ (元氣, 活氣) energy; spirit; vigour. ❷ (勢力, 力) influence; power; strength. ❸ (成行) course of things [events]. ❹ (語勢) emphasis; stress. ❺ (はずみ) momentum; impetus. ❻ (趨勢) tendency; trend (of things). —非常な勢で, with great force 〖energy〗. —勢ひ已むを得ず, by force of circumstances. —勢に驅られて, compelled by circumstances. —勢に乘じて, taking advantage of force 〖favourable circumstances, &c.〗. —多數の勢を恃んで, relying upon the force of number. —天下の勢を察する, to understand the general tendency of the world. —勢ひああ出ねばならなかった, I was forced (by circumstances) to act as I did.

ikire (熅), *n.* ❶ (むしあつきこと) sultriness; closeness; oppressiveness. ❷ (いきまくこと) fume; passion.

ikireru (熅れる), *vi.* ❶ to be sultry; be close; be oppressive. ❷ to fume.

ikiru (活・生る), *vi.* ❶ (生活する) to live. ❷ (蘇生する) to revive; be restored to life. ❸ (活躍) to become vivid; be vivified. —生きた證據, a living witness. —百まで生きる, to live to be one hundred. —生きた錢を使ふ, to make best use of one's money; know when to spend money. —生きる爲に働く, to work to live.

ikisaki (行先), *n.* =*yukisaki.*

ikisatsu (經緯), *n.* ❶ ins and outs; circumstances. ❷ =*funnun.*

ikiseki (息急き), *ad.* gaspingly; pantingly. —息急き切って, in great haste; out of breath; breathlessly.

ikitodoku (行屆く), *vi.* =*yukitodoku.*

ikitsuku (行著く), *v.* ❶ (到著) to arrive *at* [*in*]; reach; get *to.* ❷ (精力・資力が盡きる) to be exhausted. ❸ (死ぬ) to die.

ikiume, ikiuzume, (生埋めにする), *vt.* to bury alive.

ikiutsushi (生寫), *n.* a copy of a living being; a double; a living image. —親に生寫しである, to be an exact copy of its parent.

ikiwakare (生別), *n.* a life-long separation [parting]. —生き別れる, to part for life [forever].

ikiwataru (行渡る), *v.* =*yukiwataru.*

ikizukai (息遣), *n.* (the manner of) breathing.

ikizumaru (息詰る), *vi.* to suffocate; choke. ——, *a.* oppressive; close; suffocating.

ikka (一家), *n.* ❶ (一軒の家) a house. ❷ (一家族) a family. ❸ (流派) a school. —彼の一家言, his personal opinion. —一筆を以て

一家を成す, to rise to eminence by one's pen.

ikkai (一介の), *a.* mere. —一介の貧書生, a poor student.

ikkai (一回), *n.* & *ad.* once; one time. 今一回, once more; once again. ¶ 一回分, an instalment (月賦などの); a doze (藥).

ikkai (一階), *n.* the ground-floor.

ikkaku (一角-獸), *n.* 【哺乳】 the (sea) unicorn; the narwhale, narwhal.

ikkaku-senkin (一攫千金), *n.* a thousand pieces of gold at a grasp [with one scoop]. —一攫千金を夢みる, to dream of wealth got at a stroke.

ikkan (一貫する), *v.* ❶ to be consistent. ❷ to run *through*.

ikkanbari(一閑張), *n.* papier-maché; lacquered papier-maché ware. —一閑張の机, a papier-maché table.

ikkanen (一箇年の), *a.* yearly; annual; one year's. —一箇年の產出, the annual [yearly] yield [output]. —滿一箇年で修了する, to complete in one full year.

ikkatsu (一括する), *vt.* ❶ (一にくゝる) to make into a bundle; lump together. ❷ (概括する) to sum up; summarize; generalize. —一括して, in the lump [gross]; in block.

ikkatsu (一喝), *n.* a shout; a roar. —一喝する, to browbeat [*vt.*]; shout [*vi.*].

ikken (一件), *n.* ❶ (一事件) an affair; a matter. ❷ (例の件) that thing [affair]. ¶ 一件書類, papers relating to an affair [a case].

ikken (一見), *n.* a sight; a glance; a glimpse. —, *ad.* apparently; seemingly; at first sight. —一見する, to take a look *at*; glance *at*; catch [get] a glimpse *of*. —一見して, at a [one] sight; at a glance.

ikkenya (一軒家), *n.* a solitary house [cottage].

ikketsu (一決する), *v.* to come to a decision.

ikketsu (溢血), *n.* extravasation (of blood).

ikki (一氣に), *ad.* at a stretch; at a breath; at a heat; at a blast. —一氣呵成に, at one effort; at a heat. (一氣呵成に仕事を仕上げる, to finish work at a stretch.) —城を一氣に攻め落す, to take a castle by assault.

ikki (一揆), *n.* ❶ a riot; a rising; a revolt. ❷ (暴徒) rioters; a mob. —一揆が起る, A revolt breaks out. —一揆を起す, to rise *against*; raise a riot.

ikki (一騎), *n.* a single horseman. —大將と大將の一騎打, a single combat between the generals. —一騎當千の勇を振ふ, to display matchless bravery.

ikko (一己), *n.* oneself. —私一己としては, for my (own) part; as for me. —私一己の考へでは, in my own opinion.

ikko (一戶), *n.* a house; one household. —一戶を構へる, to keep house.

ikko (一箇), *n.* one. —一箇の, individual (各箇の); one; single. —一箇につき, each; apiece. ¶ 一個人, an individual. (一個人の資格で, in the capacity of a private person.)

ikko (一顧), *n.* notice; consideration. —一顧の價値なき, not worth consideration; beneath notice.

ikkō (一行), *n.* a party; a company; the suite (隨員). —雁次郎一行, Ganjirō's company. —公使一行を乘せた列車, the train carrying the minister and his suite.

ikkō (一向), *ad.* at all; in the least; quite. —一向知らぬ, to know nothing *of*.

ikkō (一考), *n.* consideration. —一考する, to give a thought; take into consideration. —一考の餘地がある, to leave room for consideration.

ikkoku (一刻), *n.* ❶ (瞬時) a moment; a short space of time. ❷ (頑固) obstinacy; stubbornness. — -**no**, *a.* ❶ momentary. ❷ obstinate; stubborn. —一刻の間も爭ふ, to be a question of moments. ¶ 一刻者, a stubborn person; a touchy person (怒り易い人). —一刻千金, a moment of utmost value [importance].

ikkyo (一擧), *n.* one effort; a single stroke. — -**ni**, — -**shite**, *ad.* by one effort; at a single stroke; at one swoop; at one coup. —一擧に事を決める, to decide a matter by one effort. ¶ 一擧一動, every movement; every motion. —一擧兩得, killing two birds with one stone.

ikkyoshu (一擧手), *n.* a slight effort. —一擧手一投足の勞を吝む, to grudge the least trouble.

iko (遺孤), *n.* an orphan; a posthumous child (遺腹).

ikō (以降), *ad.* after; since. ☞ igo(以後).

ikō (衣桁), *n.* a clothes-rack; a clothes-horse [-stand].

ikō (威光), *n.* ❶ (尊嚴) dignity; majesty. ❷ (勢力) influence; power; authority. —親の威光で, through the influence of one's parents.

ikō (偉功), *n.* a great service; a

brilliant achievement. —偉功を奏する, to render great services.

ikō (意向, 意嚮), *n.* mind; inclination; disposition. —意向を探る, to sound another's opinion; feel another's pulse.

ikō (遺稿), *n.* remains.

ikoku (異國), *n.* a foreign country. ¶ 異國情調, an exotic mood. —異國人, a foreigner; an alien; a stranger.

ikomu (鑄込む), *vt.* to cast. —金を型に鑄込む, to cast gold in a mould.

ikon (遺恨), *n.* ❶ (怨) resentment; grudge; hatred; enmity; spite. ❷ (殘念) regret; mortification; chagrin. —遺恨を晴らす, to give vent to one's enmity; pay off old scores.

ikorosu (射殺す), *vt.* to shoot dead.

ikotsu (遺骨), *n.* ashes.

ikou (憩ふ), *vi.* to take a rest.

iku (行く), *v.* to go. ☞ *yuku.*

iku- (幾), how many (much, &c.). —幾萬, tens of thousands *of*.

ikubaku (幾何), *ad.* how many (much). —幾何もなく, before long; shortly; in a little while.

ikubi (猪首), *n.* a bull-neck.

ikubun (幾分), *n.* a part; a portion; something [*pron.*]. —幾分の, some. —幾分か, partly; more or less; to a certain degree.

ikudo (幾度), *ad.* how often; how many times. —幾度となく, many a time; ever so often. —幾度も幾度も, very often; again and again; over and over again.

iku-dōon (異口同音に), *ad.* with one voice [accord]; unanimously; in a breath.

ikue (幾重にも), *ad.* repeatedly; earnestly. —幾重にも賴む, to request most earnestly.

ikuei (育英), *n.* education. —育英事業に力を盡す, to devote oneself to education.

ikuji (育兒 -法), *n.* infant-rearing. ¶ 育兒院, an orphan asylum; an orphanage.

ikuji (意氣地), *n.* spirit. —意氣地ない, poor-spirited; spiritless; faint-hearted. —意氣地がない, to have no spirit. ¶ 意氣地無し, ① (性質) pusillanimity; spiritlessness. ② (臆病者) a spiritless person; a coward; a faint heart.

ikun (偉勳), *n.* a great merit [achievement]. —偉勳を樹てる, to accomplish a brilliant achievement [exploit].

ikun (遺訓), *n.* a testament; dying injunctions.

ikunen (幾年), *ad.* how many years. —幾年立っても, after ever so many years; after the lapse of countless years.

ikunichi (幾日), *ad.* what day (月の); how many days (何日の間). —幾日も經たずに, before many days were past.

ikunin (幾人), *ad.* how many persons. —幾人となく; 幾人も幾人も, any number of persons.

ikura (幾何), *ad.* ❶ (どのやうに) however. ❷ (何程) what; how much (量); how many (數); how far (距離); how long (時). —幾らでも, any amount; any sum (金額など); as many (much) as a person wants. —幾らかの, a little; some. —幾ら高くとも, at the dearest. —一時間(一日)幾らで借す, to lend by the hour (day).

ikusa (軍, 戰), *n.* ❶ (鬪) a battle; a fight. ❷ (戰) a war; warfare. ☞ *sensō* (戰爭). —激しい戰, a severe battle. —軍に勝つ(負ける), to gain [win] (lose) a battle [the day]; be victorious (defeated) in a war.

ikuta (幾多の), *a.* many; numerous; various (色々の).

ikutsu (幾つ), *ad.* how old (幾歲); how many (幾個). —お幾歲ですか, How old are you?

ikyō (異教), *n.* foreign religion; paganism; heathenism. ¶ 異教徒, a heretic; a heathen; a pagan.

ikyō (異郷), *n.* a strange land; a foreign country (外國). —異郷の鬼となる, to die in a strange land.

ikyoku (委曲), *n.* details; particulars. —委曲を悉(つく)す, to give full particulars; go into (minute) details.

ima (今), *ad.* ❶ (現今) now; at present; at this time. ❷ (直に) at once; soon; immediately. ——, *n.* the present time; this (very) moment. —たった今, ① this very moment. ② just now; just; a moment ago. —今直ぐ, immediately; at once; in a moment. —今暫し, a little longer [more]. —今一つ, one more. —今一人, another person; the other person (二人のとき). —今一度, once more [again]; again; *encore* 〔佛〕 [*n.* & *int.*]. —今でも, even now. —今(も)尙, still to this day; even now. —今に, ① (まだ尙) yet (否定と共に); as yet; still; to this day. ② (やがて) before long; presently; some day. —今の所, for the present; at present; for the time being. —今の今まで, till this moment. —今の總理大臣, the present premier [prime minister]. —今は昔, once upon a time; long ago. —今より五年後に, five years hence. —今か今かと待つ, to expect every moment. —今の内だ, Now is the time. —今にも降り出しさうだ, It threatens to rain every moment. —病人は今にも知れない, The patient may succumb at any moment.

ima (居間), *n.* a sitting-room; a living room; a parlour [英].

imada (未), *ad.* yet; as yet. ☞ *mada.*

imadoki (今時), *ad.* nowadays; in these days.

imagoro (今頃), *ad.* ❶ (現下) at this moment. ❷ (今時分) at this time of day (night; the year). —來年の今頃, this time next year.

imaimashii (忌忌しい), *a.* ❶ (忌み嫌ふ) disgusting; abominable. ❷ (腹立しい) provoking; vexing. —忌々しがる, to be vexed *at*; feel vexation *at.*

imamata (今又), *ad.* further.

imamekashii (今めかしい), *a.* modern in style; fashionable. —今めかしく裝ふ, to dress oneself in the present fashion.

imasara (今更), *ad.* now; at this hour. —今更どうにも仕樣がない, Nothing can be done now.

imashigata (今し方), *ad.* just; just now; a moment ago.

imashime (誡, 戒, 警), *n.* ❶ (戒心) caution; guard. ❷ (訓戒) precept; admonition. ❸ (譴責) reproof; reprimand. ❹ (警備) guard; defence. —一の戒となる, to be a lesson *to.*

imashimeru (戒·警める), *vt.* ❶ (用心さす) to caution; warn; ❷ (警備) to guard. ❸ (訓) (教へ戒める) to admonish. ❹ (譴責) to reprove; correct (折檻); talk *to* [俗]. —不心得を戒める, to reprove a person for misconduct. —將來を戒める, to caution [warn] a person for the future. —夜を警める, to keep guard at night. —酒を戒める, to prohibit the use of *sake*; prohibit drink; ban *sake.*

imawa (今はの際に), on the brink [point] of death; on one's death-bed; at the last moment.

imawashii (忌はしい), *a.* disagreeable; disgusting; abominable.

imayō (今樣), *n.* ❶ (現代風) the (modern) style; modernism. ❷ (一種の歌體) the latter-day style. —今樣の, modern; up-to-date; latter-day. —今樣に, in the present fashion.

imi (忌), *n.* ❶ (嫌忌) dislike; aversion; repugnance. ❷ (喪期) mourning. —父の忌, mourning on the death of one's father. —忌がかゝる, to be in mourning.

imi (意味), *n.* ❶ (意義) meaning; sense; signification. ❷ (主旨) import; purport; effect. —意味する, to mean; signify. —意味ありげの, significant. —意味なき言葉, a senseless [an empty] word. —嚴格なる意味に於て, in the strict sense. —意味の微妙なる差異, a nice shade of meaning. —意味深長である, to be pregnant with meaning; have a deep meaning [significance]. —意味を取り違へる, to mistake the meaning; misconstrue

imijiki (いみじき), *a.* ❶ (すぐれた) excellent; exquisite; admirable. ❷ (甚しい) extraordinary. —いみじく, ① excellently; exquisitely; splendidly. ② very; exceedingly.

imikirau (忌嫌ふ), *vt.* to loathe; abhor; detest.

imikotoba (忌語), *n.* a word tabooed by superstition.

imin (移民), *n.* ❶ (人) an emigrant (往住者); an immigrant (來住者). ❷ (事) emigration (往住); immigration (來住). ¶ 契約移民, a contract emigrant. —移民會社, an emigration company. —移民制限法, an immigration restriction law. —移民取扱人, an emigration-agent.

imina (諱), *n.* ❶ (謚) a posthumous name. ❷ (實名) the true name.

imo (芋), *n.* 【植】 ❶ (さといも) the taro. ❷ (やまいも) the Japanese [Chinese] yam. ❸ (馬鈴薯) the potato. ❹ (甘藷) the sweet potato.

imogara (芋莖), *n.* the stems of the taro plant.

imohori (芋掘), *n.* ❶ potato-digging (事); a potato-digger (人, 器). ❷ (田舍漢) a rustic; a clodhopper.

imomushi (芋蟲), *n.* the green caterpillar.

imon (慰問), *n.* inquiry after another's health; consolation; condolence (弔慰). —慰問する, to inquire after another's health; console; condole *with* (弔慰). ¶ 慰問袋, a comfort bag.

imono (鑄物), *n.* a moulding; a casting. ¶ 鑄物師, a founder; a caster

imori (井守, 蠑螈), *n.* 【兩棲】 Triton pyrrhogaster (newt の一種).

imose (妹背), *n.* husband and wife; a couple. —妹背の緣, conjugal affinity.

imoto, imōto, (妹), *n.* a younger sister. —義理の妹, a sister-in-law.

imu (忌む), *vt.* ❶ (嫌忌) to abhor; loathe; detest. ❷ (忌憚) to dread;

shun (忌避); avoid (同上). —忌むべき, loathsome; abhorrent; detestable.

imu (齋む), *v.* to restrain oneself; purify.

imukyoku (醫務局), *n.* the bureau of medical affairs; the medical bureau.

imushiro (藺莚), *n.* a rush-mat.

imyō (異名), *n.* another name (別名); a nickname (渾名); a sobriquet (同上).

in (印), *n.* a seal; a stamp. —印を押す, to affix [stamp] a seal; seal; stamp.

in (院), *n.* ❶ a house; an institute; a hall. ❷ (先帝) an ex-Emperor. ❸ (寺) a Buddhist temple.

in (陰), *n.* ❶ (支那哲學) negative. ❷ (山, 北) the north of a mountain. ❸ (裏面) secrecy. —陰に陽に, secretly and ostensibly.

in (員), *n.* a member.

in (韻), *n.* a rhyme; a rhyming word; the Chinese sound of an ideograph. —韻を押(フ)む, to rhyme; use a rhyme at the end of a line.

ina (鯔), *n.* 【魚】 the grey mullet.

ina (否), *ad.* no; nay. —否と答へる, to return a negative; answer with a No; answer in the negative.

iña (瘖瘂), *n.* deaf-mutism; deaf-dumbness [-muteness]. ¶ 瘖瘂者, a deaf-mute.

inabikari (稻光, 電), *n.* (a flash of) lightning. —稻光がする, Lightning flashes.

inada (鰍), *n.* 【魚】 the yellow-tail.

inagara (坐ながら), *ad.* sedentarily; seated. —坐ながら天下を制する, to rule the country from his seat.

inago (蝗), *n.* 【昆】 the locust.

inaho (稻穗), *n.* an ear of rice.

inai (以內), *ad.* inside of; within (未滿). —拾圓以內, not exceeding ten *yen*. —一週間以內に, inside of a week; within a week.

inai-inai-bā (居ない居ないばー), *n.* (兒戯) bo-peep.

inaka (田舍), *n.* the country; the provinces (地方). —田舍じみた; 田舍めいた, rural; rustic; provincial; country-looking; country-like; countrified; boorish. —田舍育ちの, country-bred. —田舍びさす, to countrify; ruralize; rusticate. —田舍へ引込む, to retire into the country. —田舍に孤棲して, in rural seclusion. —田舍を廻る, to tour in the provinces. ¶ 田舍氣質, rusticity; provincialism. —田舍町, a country town. —田舍者, a countryman; a rustic; a provincial. —田舍紳士, a country gentleman. —田舍家, a country house; a rural house. —田舍住居, country [rural] life; rustication.

inamu (否·辭む), *vt.* ❶ (辭退) to decline. ❷ to refuse (拒絕); deny (否認, 否定). —否むべからざる事實, an undeniable fact.

inamura (稻叢), *n.* a rick; a stack.

inamushi (稻蟲), *n.* the locust; the rice insect.

inan (以南), south *of*.

inanaku (嘶く), *vi.* to neigh; whinny (靜かに又は嬉しげに).

inaorigōtō (居直强盜), *n.* a thief changed into an armed robber.

inaoru (居直る), *vi.* ❶ (坐り直す) to sit upright. ❷ (態度硬化する) to assume suddenly a strong attitude; come out strong.

inaosu (鑄直す), *vt.* to recast, recoin (貨幣を).

inarabu (居竝ぶ), *vi.* to sit in a row.

Inari (稻荷), *n.* the god of cereals. ¶ 稻荷鮨, a *sushi* covered with fried bean-curd.

inasaku (稻作), *n.* rice-crop.

inase (鯔背な), *a.* gallant; dashing; gay.

inataba (稻束), *n.* a shock; a sheaf.

inaya (否や), *ad.* ❶ (…するや直に) no sooner…than; scarcely [hardly] …when; the moment; directly [*conj.*]. ❷ (…かどうか) whether [*conj.*]. —否やの返事, a definite answer. —聞くや否や, as soon as I heard it. —それが眞なりや否や(を, は), whether it is true or not. —私が彼を見るや否や彼は逃げた, The moment I saw him, he ran away; No sooner did I see him than he ran away.

inazuma (稻妻), *n.* lightning. —稻妻の如く疾く, with lightning speed; as quick [swift] as lightning.

inban (印判), *n.* a seal; a stamp. ¶ 印判師, a seal-engraver.

inbanesu (インバネス), *n.* an inverness; an inverness coat [cloak].

inbi (隱微の), *a.* occult; latent.

inbō (陰謀), *n.* a (secret) plot; a conspiracy; an intrigue. —陰謀を企てる, to plot secretly; intrigue; conspire. ¶ 陰謀者, a plotter; a conspirator.

inbun (韻文), *n.* a verse. —韻文に作る, to compose in verse.

inchi (吋), *n.* an inch.

inchi (引致する), *vt.* to take into custody; take *to* (the police station); bring (before a judge).

inchō (院長), *n.* ❶ (大審院·控訴院等の長官) the president (of a court, *etc.*). ❷ (病院長) the director of a hospital; the head physician.

indenki (陰電氣), *n.* negative (electricity).

Indo (印度), *n.* India; Hindustan. ¶ 東印度, the East Indies. —後印度, Further India. —西印度諸島, the West Indies. —印度支那, Indo-China. —印度語, Hindoo; Hindustani (官話). —印度人, an Indian; a Hindu. —印度敎, Hinduism; Hindooism. —印度洋, the Indian Ocean.

indō (引導), *n.* ❶ (導くこと) guidance. ❷ (死者を彼岸に導くこと) guiding the soul of the dead to the other world. —引導を渡す, ① to read the prayer for the passage of the dead to the other world. ② (往生せしめる) to put an end *to*; kill; do *for*; give warning (解雇などの豫告).

ine (稻), *n.* 【植】 the (cultivated) rice; the rice-plant; the paddy. —稻を刈る, to mow [cut] down the rice-plant.

inei(陰影), *n.* shadow; shade (繪畫などの). ¶ 陰影描法, shading.

inekabu (稻株), *n.* a rice stubble.

inekari (稻刈), *n.* mowing of rice-plants; rice-mowing.

inekoki (稻扱), *n.* ❶ rice-hackling. ❷ (道具) a rice-hackle.

inemuri (居睡り), *n.* a doze; a drowse. —居睡りする, ① to doze (off); drowse. ② to fall [drop] into a doze; drop asleep.

ineru (寢る), *vi.* ❶ (臥床に入りてやすむ) to go to bed; retire; turn in. ❷ 〔寐〕 (寢入り込む) to go to sleep; sleep.

infuruenza (流行性感冒), *n.* influenza; *grippe* 〔佛〕.

inga (因果), *n.* ❶ (原因と結果) cause and effect. ❷ = *gōhō* (業報). ❸ (不運) misfortune; ill-luck. —因果な, unfortunate; unlucky; ill-starred. —親の因果が子に報ふ, "The sins of the father are visited upon the children." ¶ 因果關係, causation; causality. —因果應報, retribution for a deed done in a previous life; retributive justice. —因果律, the law of causation; (principle of) causality.

inga (印畫), *n.* ❶ (寫眞) a print. ❷ (板畫) an engraving.

inga (陰畫), *n.* 【寫】 a negative picture.

ingai (院外の), *a.* outside the Diet; extra-Parliamentary; outside. ¶ 院外團, non-Parliamentary members. —院外運動, an outdoor agitation.

ingenmame (隱元豆), *n.* 【植】 the kidney-bean; the haricot.

ingi (院議), *n.* the decision of the House. —院議を重んじて, in deference to the decision of the House.

ingin (慇懃), *n.* ❶ (懇切) politeness; courtesy; civility. ❷ (よしみ) friendship; comity (主として國際上の). ❸ (情交) intimacy. —慇懃な, courteous; obliging; gallant (特に婦人に). —慇懃に挨拶する, to salute courteously. —慇懃を通ずる, to be intimate *with*; be on familiar terms *with*.

ingo (隱語), *n.* a secret language; an enigma (謎の如き); a cant (同業者間などの).

ingō (因業な), *a.* a hard-hearted; merciless. —因業なことを言ふ, to say heartless things. ¶ 因業親爺, a crusty old fellow; an old screw.

ingyō (印形), *n.* a seal; a signet.

inin (委任), *n.* mandate 【法】; charge; commission. —委任する, to entrust [charge] a person *with*; commit to the charge *of*; commission. (萬事僕に委任し給へ, Leave everything to me.) ¶ 委任狀, a letter [power] of attorney; a (letter of) procuration. —委任者, the mandator; the mandant. —委任統治, mandatory rule. (委任統治國, a mandatory power.)

inin (殷殷たる), *a.* rumbling; roaring. —殷々たる砲聲, the roar of guns.

inishie (古), *n.* antiquity; ancient [former; old] times. —遠く古へに溯れば, going back to the distant past.

inja (隱者), *n.* a hermit; a recluse.

inji (陰事), *n.* a secret; a hidden affair. —人の陰事を摘發する, to expose another's secrets.

injun (因循な), *a.* dilatory; vacillating; indecisive. —因循な奴, a vacillating [dull and sluggish] fellow. —因循姑息な手段を取る, to temporize.

inka (姻家), *n.* a connection by marriage.

inkan (印鑑), *n.* a seal-impression; impression of a legal seal. —印鑑屆を出す, to report a seal-impression. —印鑑證明を請求する, to apply for a certificate of a seal--impression.

inkan (殷鑑), *n.* an example. —殷鑑遠からず, An example is not far to seek.

inkaten(引火點), *n.* 【化】 flashing [flash]-point.

inken (引見する), *vt.* to see; grant an interview *to*; give audience *to*.

inken (陰險な), *a.* subtle; crafty; insidious. —陰險な男, a crafty fellow; a snake. —陰險な手段を弄する, to take subtle expedients.

inken (隱顯·隱見する), *vi.* to appear and disappear; recur. —隱見出沒自在である, to appear and disappear at pleasure. ¶ 隱顯砲, a disappearing gun.

inketsu (引決する), *v.* ❶ (覺悟を定める) to be prepared *for.* ❷ (自殺) to commit suicide; kill oneself. —引決を迫る, to urge a person to (acknowledge his responsibility and) resign.

inki (インキ), *n.* ink. —インキで消す, to ink out. —ペン先にインキをつける, to dip a pen in ink. ¶ 文房インキ, writing ink. —インキ消, an (ink-)eraser. —インキ壺, an ink-bottle; an ink-pot; an inkstand.

inki (陰氣), *n.* gloominess; dismalness; cheerlessness. **——·na,** *a.* gloomy; dismal; cheerless. —陰氣な話, a dismal talk. —陰氣な室, a gloomy room. —陰氣な聲, a sepulchral voice.

inkin (陰金·田蟲), *n.* the ring-worm.

inko (鸚哥), *n.* 【鳥】 the macaw.

inkō (咽喉), *n.* the throat; 【解】 the fauces. —內海の咽喉を扼す, to command the gate of the Inland Sea. ¶ 咽喉カタル, catarrh of the throat; pharyngeal catarrh.

inkurain (インクライン), *n.* an inclined plane.

inkyaku (韻脚), *n.* a foot; rhymed verse.

inkyo (隱居), *n.* ❶ (*a*) 【法】 resignation of headship: (*b*) retirement; retreat; seclusion. ❷ (退隱し居る所) a retreat; a seclusion. ❸ (同上の人) a person who retires from the headship of a house; a retired person; an old man (老翁); an old woman (老媼). —隱居する, to retire [abdicate] from the headship of a family; retire from active life; go into retirement.

inkyoku (陰極), *n.* 【電】 the negative pole; the cathode.

inmetsu (堙滅), *n.* destruction; extinction. —堙滅する, to bury in [consign to] oblivion; destroy; make away *with.*

innai (院內), within the chamber. ¶ 院內總務, the whip; the whipper-in.

innen (因緣), *n.* ❶ (宿命) fate; destiny (緣). ❷ (由緒) origin; cause. —因緣と諦める, to accept as fate.

in-ni (陰に), *ad.* in secret; secretly.

inniku (印肉), *n.* the ink for a seal; a seal-pad; a tampion (石版用). ¶ 印肉入れ, a seal-pad case.

innin (隱忍), *n.* endurance; patience. —隱忍する, to be patient; endure; put up *with.*

inningu (インニング), *n.* innings (競技で).

inochi (命), *n.* life. —命の親, the preserver of one's life. —命乞ひする, to plead [ask] for one's life; ask for [cry] quarter. —命冥加がある, to be saved from death by Providence. —命からがら逃れる, to escape with bare life. —命に關はる, ① [*v.*] to endanger one's life. ② [*a.*] fatal; deadly; mortal. —命のあらん限り働く, to work as long as life lasts. —命を拾ふ, to have a narrow escape. —命を繫ぐ, to keep body and soul together. —命を縮める, to shorten one's days [life]; drive a nail into one's coffin. —命を的にかける, to risk one's life.

inochigake (命懸けの), *a.* desperate; perilous. —命懸けで, at the risk of one's life; for one's life; for dear life. —命懸けの仕事, a desperate undertaking; a work undertaken at the risk of one's life.

inochishirazu (命知らず), *n.* ❶ (丈夫で長く保つこと) lasting long. ❷ (無分別で命を輕んずる者) a dare-devil; a desperado.

inogo (瘰), *n.* lymphadenitis.

inoko (豕), *n.* a pig.

inokori (居殘り), *n.* remaining behind; a person left (behind). —居殘る, to remain behind; be left (behind). —居殘り番をする, to take one's turn for remaining behind.

inori (祈), *n.* ❶ (祈禱) prayer; supplication; invocation. ❷ (呪詛) imprecation. —朝の祈り, the morning prayer [service]; the matins. —夕の禱り, the evening prayer; the vespers. —祈りを捧げる, to offer prayers; say grace (食事の前後に).

inoru (祈る), *vt.* ❶ (祈禱) to pray; supplicate. ❷ (呪ふ) to imprecate. ❸ (こひねがふ) to wish. —神に祈る, to pray to God [to the gods]. —君の成功を祈ッて, with hearty wishes for your success.

inoshishi (猪), *n.* the wild boar. ¶ 猪武者, a soldier of reckless valour.

inpei (隱蔽する), *vt.* to conceal; cover; suppress. —罪跡を隱蔽する, to cover the traces of crime.

inpon (院本), *n.* a drama; the book of a play.

inrei (引例), *n.* an instance; an example.

inreki (陰曆), *n.* the lunar calendar.

inritsu (韻律), *n.* a rhythm; a metre; a measure.

inrō (印籠), *n.* an *inro* 〖日〗; a seal-case; a medicine-case (藥籠).

inryō (飲料), *n.* a drink; a beverage (主として清涼飲料). ¶ 飲料水, drinking water.
inryoku (引力), *n.* 【理】 gravitation (地球の); attraction (物質間の). —引力ある, attractive; magnetic.
insatsu (印刷), *n.* printing. —印刷中, (to be) in (the) press. —印刷に付する, to send [put] to (the) press. —印刷の誤りを校正する, to correct the press. ¶ 印刷物, printed matter. —印刷術, (the art of) printing; typography. —印刷機械, a printing machine [press]; a press. —印刷局, the Printing Bureau. —印刷者, a printer; a typographer. —印刷所, a printing office; a press. (端物印刷所, a jobbing house.) —印刷職工, a pressman.
insei (隕星), *n.* a meteor; a falling star; a shooting star (光輝薄弱な).
inseki (姻戚), *n.* a relative by marriage [affinity]; affinity.
inseki (隕石), *n.* an aerolite; a meteorite.
insekiyaku (引赤藥), *n.* a rubefacient.
inshi (因子), *n.* 【數】 a factor ☞ *insū* (因數).
inshi (印紙), *n.* a stamp. —印紙を貼る, to affix [put on] a stamp. ¶ 印紙蒐集家, a philatelist; a stamp-collector. —印紙賣捌所, a stamp-office; "stamps on sale." —印紙稅法, the stamp-duty law.
inshin (音信), *n.* communication; tidings; news. —何の音信もない, There have been no tidings from him.
inshō (引證), *n.* a quotation (引用); a citation (同上); a reference (參照). —引證する, to quote *from*; cite; refer *to*. ¶ 引證文, a quotation.
inshō (引照), *n.* reference. —引照する, to refer *to*.
inshō (印章), *n.* ❶ (印顆) a seal; a stamp. ❷ (印影) an impression; a mark; a seal; a stamp.
inshō (印象), *n.* an impression. —印象する, to impress *on*; print *on*. —聽衆に深き印象を與へる, to make a deep impression upon one's hearers. ¶ 印象派, 【文藝】 the impressionist school.
inshoku (飲食), *n.* eating and drinking. —飲食する, to eat and drink; fare. —飲食を節する, to eat and drink in moderation. ¶ 飲食物, food and drink; diet (規定の). —飲食器, table-service; table-ware. —飲食店, an eating-house.
inshu (飲酒), *n.* drinking. —飲酒に耽る, ① [*a.*] intemperate; crapulent. ② [*vi.*] to be given to drinking; give oneself up to drinking.
inshū (因襲), *n.* a long-established custom; convention; tradition. 因襲的道德, conventional morality. —因襲に從ふ, to follow a long usage; succumb to conventionalism. —因襲を破る, to break a long-established usage; depart from convention. ¶ 因襲主義, conventionalism.
insotsu (引率する), *vt.* to lead.
insū (因數), *n.* 【數】 a factor. ¶ 公因數, a common factor. —因數分解法, factoring; factorization.
insū (員數), *n.* the number.
insupirēshon (靈感), *n.* inspiration.
in-suru (淫する), *vi.* to indulge *in*. —書に淫する, to be engrossed in books.
intai (引退), *n.* retirement; resignation (辭職). —引退する, to retire *from*; resign.
intai (隱退する), *vi.* to retire (from the world); seclude oneself from the world.
intō (咽頭), *n.* 【解】 the pharynx. ¶ 咽頭炎, 【醫】 pharyngitis.
intoku (陰德), *n.* private kindness; a secret act of charity. —陰德を人に施す, to do a person private kindness.
intoku (隱匿する), *vt.* to conceal; secrete; harbour.
inton (隱遁), *n.* retirement from the world; seclusion. —隱遁する, to retire from the world; seclude oneself from the world; renounce the world. —隱遁生活を送る, to live a retired life; live retired [in retirement]. ¶ 隱遁者, a hermit; a recluse.
inu (犬), *n.* ❶ the dog; the bitch (牝). ❷ (諜者) a spy; a secret agent. —犬の頸輪, a dog-collar. —犬の遠吠, a distant bark [bay]. —犬と猿の仲, "They agree like cats and dogs." —犬を飼ふ, to keep a dog. —犬骨折って鷹の餌食, "One beats the bushes and another catches the birds."
inugoya (狗舍), *n.* a kennel.
inuhariko (犬張子), *n.* a papier-maché dog.
inujini (犬死する), *vi.* to die to no purpose.
inuki (居拔), *n.* quitting a house without touching its fixtures and furniture. —居拔きのまゝ店を讓る, to transfer a shop with its stock and goodwill.
inukoro (狗兒), *n.* a pup; a puppy.
inukoroshi (犬殺), *n.* a dog-killer.
inuku (射貫く), *vt.* to pierce by shooting; pierce with a shot; shoot *through*.

inutsu (陰鬱), *n.* ❶ (曇ッて) gloominess; cloudiness. ❷ (氣ふさぎ) melancholy; gloom; dismalness. —陰鬱にする, to gloom; overcloud; cast [throw] a chill over. **——-na**, *a.* gloomy; dismal; melancholy. —陰鬱な顔, a melancholy [glum] face.

inwai (淫猥な), *a.* obscene; indecent.

inyō (引用), *n.* quotation; citation. —引用する, to quote; cite; make reference *to*. ¶ 引用文, a quotation. —引用符, a quotation mark; inverted commas. —引用書, reference books.

inyō (陰陽), *n.* ❶ (男と女) the male and female principles. ❷ (日と月) the sun and the moon. ❸ (積極消極) the positive and negative. —繪畫の陰陽, the lights and darks of a picture.

inyō (飲用), *n.* ❶ (飲料用) drinking purposes. ❷ (內服用) internal use. —飲用に供する, to supply for drinking purposes.

inyoku (淫慾), *n.* carnal passion; sexual appetite; lust.

inyu (引喩), *n.* an allusion.

inyu (隱喩), *n.* 【修】 a metaphor.

inyū (移入), *n.* importation (from oversea territories). —移入する, to import; introduce (文物制度など); bring in.

inzei (印稅), *n.* ❶ (印紙稅) stamp duty. ❷ (書籍の) a royalty.

inzen (隱然たる), *a.* virtual; practical.

iō (硫黃), *n.* =*yuō*.

ion (イオン), *n.* 【電】 ion. ¶ 陰(陽)イオン, negative (positive) ion.

iori (庵), *n.* a hermitage; a cell; an anchorage. —庵を結ぶ, to build a hermitage.

iotosu (射落す), *vt.* to bring down. —飛行船を射落す, to bring down an airship.

ippai (一杯), *n.* ❶ (一さかづき) a cup; a glass. ❷ (充滿) fulness. ❸ (全部) the whole. —力一杯引ッ張る, to pull with all one's strength. —コップに一杯注ぐ, to fill a cup to the brim. —手一杯に擴げる, to extend as far as one can manage.

ippaku (一泊), *n.* a night's lodging. —一泊する, to put up for a night *at* (a hotel); pass a night *at*. —一泊二等五圓, five *yen* for second class per night.

ippan (一般の), *a.* ❶ (普通の) common; ordinary. ❷ (全般の) general. —一般に, commonly; generally; universally. —一般の承認, common consent. ¶ 一般投票, referendum.

ippan (一班), *n.* a class; a section.

ippan (一斑), *n.* a part; a portion. —一斑を見て全豹を知る, "You may know the lion by his claw."

ippatsu (一發), *n.* a shot; one round. —一發の砲聲, a roar of cannon.

ippatsu (一髮), *n.* a hair. —一髮千鈞を引くが如し, to hang (over) like the sword of Damocles.

ippen (一片), *n.* a bit; a piece; a flake. —一片の反古, a scrap of paper. —一片の同情, a bit of sympathy.

ippen (一遍), *ad.* once. —通り一遍の挨拶, a greeting for form's sake. —一遍行ッて見る, to go once.

ippen (一變), *n.* a complete change. —形勢一變する, The situation completely changes.

ippin (一品), *n.* a course; a dish; an article. ¶ 一品料理, one-course dinner.

ippin (逸品), *n.* a rarity. —繪畫の逸品, a fine piece of painting.

ippo (一步), *n.* one step; a pace. —一步一步, step by step. —一步進んで, [*ad.*] further. —一步退いて考へると, if we think again. —一步も讓らぬ, not to yield a step. —一步を誤る, to take a false step.

ippō (一方), *n.* ❶ one; one side; a party. ❷ (他の一方) the other; the other side; the other party. —一方では…又他の一方では, on the one hand…on the other (hand).

ippon (一本), *n.* a copy (書物一部). —鉛筆一本, a pencil. —白墨一本, a piece of chalk. —一本立になる, to become independent. ¶ 一本調子, (音聲等の) monotone; monotony. (一本調子の, monotonous.) —一本道, a straight road.

ippu-ippu (一夫一婦), *n.* monogamy. ¶ 一夫一婦主義者, a monogamist.

ippuku (一服), *n.* ❶ (藥の) a dose; a draught (水藥の); a potion (特に水藥・毒藥の). ❷ (煙草の) a smoke; a whiff; a pipe. ❸ (茶の) a sip. —一服やる, to take a rest (一休み); have a smoke. —一服つける, to light a pipe.

ippūryū (一風流の), *a.* original; eccentric.

ippu-tasai (一夫多妻), *n.* polygamy. ¶ 一夫多妻(主義者), a polygamist.

ira (刺), *n.* ❶ (草のとげ) stinging hairs. ❷ (魚の背鰭) the spine.

iradatsu (苛立つ), *vi.* to be excited [irritated]; grow impatient;

chafe. —苛立てる, to excite; irritate; rasp.

irai (以來), *ad.* ❶ (其後) since; since then; ever since. ❷ (今後) in future; henceforth. ☞ *igo.*

irai (依頼), *n.* ❶ (たのみ) a request. ❷ (あてにすること) confident expectation. ❸ (たよること) dependence; reliance. —依頼に應じて, in compliance with a request. **——-suru,** *v.* ❶ (たのむ) to (make a) request; ask; apply. ❷ (あてにする) to trust; count *on*; reckon *on*. ❸ (たよる) to depend *upon*; lean *on* [*upon*]; resort *to* (手段等に); have recourse *to* (同上). —人に依頼する, to rely upon others. ¶ 依頼人, a client (辯護士等の).

iraira (いらいらする), *vi.* ❶ to sting. ❷ to be vexed; be irritated; be in a chafe. **——,** *a.* ❶ stinging. ❷ irritating; vexing.

irakusa (蕁麻), *n.* 【植】 Urtica Thunbergiana (nettle の一種·學名).

iranu (要らぬ), **irazaru** (要らざる), *a.* unwanted; unneeded; uncalled-for. —いらぬ心配をする, to feel needless anxiety. —いらざる世話をやく, ① [*v.*] to meddle in the affairs of another. ② [*a.*] meddlesome; officious.

irassharu (いらッしゃる), *vi.* ❶ (居る, 在る) to be. ❷ (行く) to go. ❸ (來る) to come. —いらッしゃい, いらッしゃい, "Walk up! Walk up!"

ireba (入齒), *n.* an artificial [a false] tooth. —金の入齒をして居る人, a man with a gold-plugged tooth. —入齒を入れる, to have a false tooth put in. ¶ 總入齒, a set of false teeth.

irege (入髮), *n.* false hair; toupee (禿隱し). —入毛をする, to use false hair.

irejie (入智慧), *n.* suggestion (暗示); instigation (敎唆). —入智慧する, to suggest; put up *to*; instigate (敎唆する).

irekae (入換へ), *n.* change; replacement; 【鐵道】 shunting. —入れ換へる, to replace; interchange; shunt. —疊を入れ換へる, to replace the old mats with new ones.

irekake (入掛け), *n.* suspending before time (芝居·寄席等の).

ireko (入子), *n.* a nest of boxes. ¶ 入子箱, a nest-box.

ireme (義眼), *n.* a glass [false] eyes; an artificial eye.

iremono (入物, 容器), *n.* a receptacle; a vessel; a case.

ireru (入れる), *vt.* ❶ to put in; pour in (注ぐ); insert *in* (插む). ❷ (這入らす) to admit; let in; take in. ❸ (聽きいれる) to listen *to*; grant; accede *to*. —入れ違へる, to misplace; place [put] in a wrong place; put in by mistake. —入れ直す, to put in afresh; reinsert; reset. —御耳に入れる, to inform; bring to a person's knowledge. —御覽に入れる, to submit it for your inspection. —風を入れる, to admit air; air (a room). —光を入れる, to let in light. —諫を容れる, to listen to remonstrances. —利息を入れる, to pay interest. —賄賂を納れる, to accept a bribe. —一萬人を容れ得る會堂, a hall capable of accommodating 10,000 people.

irezumi (入墨), *n.* a tattoo (物); tattooing (事). ☞ *horimono* (文身). —入墨する, to tattoo.

iri (入), *n.* ❶ (入場者數) attendance; audience; a house (劇場等にいふ). ❷ (容量) content; capacity. ❸ (收入) income. ❹ (入費) expenses. ❺ (始まること) entering; the beginning (開始). ❻ (沒すること) set; setting. —二斗入りの米櫃, a rice-box capable of holding two *to*. —一斤入りの茶筒, a tea-canister holding one *kin*. —金五圓入りの蟇口, a purse with five *yen* in it. —入りがある(ない), to have a large (small) audience; draw a full (poor) house.

iri (炒, 煎), *n.* parching; roasting. ¶ 煎り玉子, scrambled eggs. —炒立て豆, fresh parched beans.

iriai (入相), *n.* sunset; evening. —入相の鐘の音, the sound of the evening bell.

iribitaru (入浸る), *vi.* to stay continually.

irichigau (入り違ふ), *vt.* to be put in each other's place (互の場所に); enter and pass each other (行違ふ).

irie (入江), *n.* an inlet; a creek; a cove.

irigome (炒米), *n.* parched rice.

irigomi (入込), *n.* ❶ (混同) coming in [entering] together. ❷ (集會場の共同席) public seats.

irijūmu (イリヂュム), *n.* iridium.

irikawari (入替), *n.* change; rotation (官職等の). —入替りに, one after another; in turn. —入り換はる, to enter by turns; take another's place; change places.

iriko (海參), *n.* a dried sea-slug.

irikomu (入込む), *v.* ❶ (這入る) to enter; go [come] in; penetrate (*into*). ❷ =*irikumu.*

irikuchi (入口), *n.* an entry; an entrance; a way in. —部屋の入口, the door of room. —港の入口, a harbour-entrance.

irikumu (入組む), *vi.* to be complicated. —入り組んだ, complicated; intricate. (入り組んだ事件, a tangled affair. —入り組んだ細工, an inwrought work.)

irimajiru (入交る), *vi.* to be mixed; be mingled together.

irimame (炒豆), *n.* parched peas.

irimidareru (入亂れる), *v.* to be confused; be mixed [jumbled] together. —入り亂れて鬪ふ, to fight in confusion.

irimuko (入婿), *n.* a husband who assumes his wife's surname [enters his wife's family]; an adopted husband. —入婿になる, to marry an heiress.

irinabe (炒鍋), *n.* a frying [roasting] pan.

irini (入荷), *n.* goods received; arrivals.

iritsuku (煎附く), *vi.* to sizzle. —煎り附ける, to boil down. —煎り附くやうに暑い, sizzling hot.

iriumi (入海), *n.* an inlet; an arm of the sea; a bay.

iriyō (入用), *n.* ❶ (必要) need; want; necessity. ❷ (出費) expenses.

iro (色), *n.* ❶ (色彩) colour; hue (混色); dye (染色). ❷ =*shikitaku* (色澤). ❸ (顏色) complexion; countenance. ❹ (情事) love. ❺ (情人) a lover (男); a sweetheart. ❻ (種類) a kind; a sort. —褪り《褪め》易い色, a fickle 《fugitive; fading》 colour. —永持ちする色, a fast colour. —色が白い《黑い》, to be white 《dark》; have a light 《dark》 complexion. —色に迷ふ, to be lost in love. —感情を色に表はす, to betray [show] one's feeling. —色を失ふ, to lose colour; turn pale.

irō (慰勞), *n.* acknowledgment of services rendered. —慰勞する, to express one's obligations; thank for another's services. —慰勞會を開く, to hold [give] a party in acknowledgment of services. ¶ 慰勞金, a bonus; a gratuity for services rendered.

irō (遺漏), *n.* omission (脫漏); neglect (手落). —遺漏なく, thoroughly; without omission.

iroage (色揚する), *v.* to heighten colour; redye.

iroai (色合), *n.* colouring; shade (濃淡); tone (色調).

irodori (色取), *n.* ❶ (彩色) painting; colouring. ❷ (裝飾) colour; decoration.

irodoru (彩る, 色取る), *vt.* to colour; paint; decorate.

iroenpitsu (色鉛筆), *n.* a colour pencil; a crayon (墨筆).

irogami (色紙), *n.* coloured paper.

irogarasu (色硝子), *n.* stained glass; coloured glass; flashed glass.

iroha (伊呂波), *n.* ❶ the Japanese syllabary. ❷ (初步) the rudiments; A. B. C. —伊呂波順に, in *i-ro-ha* order.

iroiro (色色), *ad.* in various ways; variously; manifoldly. —色色考へて見る, to think it over in various ways. **——-no**, *a.* various; miscellaneous; of different kinds. —色々な費用, sundry expenses.

iroka (色香), *n.* beauty; charms. —色香に迷ふ, to be smitten with a woman's charms.

iroke (色氣), *n.* ❶ (色合) colour; hue; shade. ❷ (春情) love. —頗る…に色氣がある, to have a good [great] mind *to*.

irokeshi (色消), *n.* ❶ (色收差を消すこと) achromaticity; achromatism. ❷ (興をさますこと) inelegance. ¶ 色消レンズ, an achromatic lens.

irome (色目), *n.* a love glance; sheep's eyes. —色目を使ふ, to make eyes *at*; cast sheep's eyes *at*.

iromegane (色眼鏡), *n.* coloured spectacles. —色眼鏡で見る, to see through coloured glasses.

iromeku (色めく), *v.* ❶ (色づく) to be tinged; be coloured. ❷ (なまめく) to charm; fascinate. ❸ (負け色だつ) to begin to waver. ❹ (景色だつ) to begin to stir; become excited; become active (活氣づく).

iron (異論), *n.* an objection; a dissent; a difference (of opinion). —異論を唱へる, to dissent from (another's view); make objection *to*.

iroonna (色女), *n.* a sweetheart; a lady-love; a mistress.

irootoko (色男), *n.* ❶ (情郞) a lover; a paramour (密夫). ❷ (好男子) a gallant; a spark 〔俗〕.

irori (圍爐裏), *n.* a hearth; a fireplace. —圍爐裏を圍んで坐す, to sit around the hearth.

irotsuke (色附, 著色), *n.* colouring; staining.

irotsuya (色澤), *n.* ❶ (光澤) gloss; polish; lustre. ❷ (血色) complexion. —色澤の好い顏をして, with a fresh complexion.

irozameru (色褪める), *vi.* ❶ (褪色する) to fade. ❷ (血色を失ふ) to lose colour; grow pale. —色褪めた, ① decolourized; faded. ② pale; colourless.

irozashi (色差), *n.* ❶ (血色) complexion. ❷ (色合) colour; hue.

irozuku (色著く), *vi.* to put on colour; gain colour.

irozuri (色摺), *n.* colour-printing. —色摺にする, to print in colours. ¶ 色摺板畫, colour-prints.

iru (入る), *v.* ❶ to enter; come [go] in; get in. ❷ (沒す, 隱れる) to set; sink; go down. ❸ (加入) to join. —梅雨に入る前に, before the rainy season sets in. —主題に入るに先ち, before entering into the subject. —新世紀に入るに方り, on the threshold of a new century. —惡徒の仲間に入る, to join a gang of villains.

iru (炒・煎る), *vt.* to roast; parch. ❷ [煎・熬] (油いりにする) to fry. —豆を炒る, to roast [parch] peas.

iru (居る), *vi.* ❶ (狀態を示す) to be. ❷ (現在の行動を示す) to be -ing. ❸ (現在する) to be; be in (在宅). ❹ (住んで居る) to inhabit; live. —じッと默ッて居る, to remain silent. —風をひいてゐる, to have a cold.

iru (要る), *v.* to require; need; want.

iru (射る), *v.* to shoot (弓・鐵砲を); let fly.... —利を射る, to make a venture for profit; aim at profit-making.

iru (鑄る), *vt.* ❶ to found; cast. ❷ (貨幣を) to mint; strike. —銅像を鑄る, to cast a bronze statue.

irui (衣類), *n.* clothing; dresses; one's wardrobe (衣裳全部).

iruka (海豚), *n.* 【哺乳】 the dolphin.

iruminēshon (電飾), *n.* illumination. —イルミネーションを施す, to illuminate.

iryō (醫療), *n.* medical treatment. ¶ 醫療器械, medical instruments [appliances].

iryoku (威力), *n.* power; authority; might. —金錢の威力, the power of money. —威力を示す, to show one's power.

iryoku (偉力), *n.* great power [influence]; efficiency (有效). —偉力を發揮する, to prove highly efficient; play an important role *in*.

iryū (遺留する), *vt.* to leave behind; bequeath. ¶ 遺留分, 【法】 a legal portion. —遺留品, a thing left behind.

isagiyoi (潔い), *a.* ❶ (廉潔) pure; chaste. ❷ (未練なき) manful; brave. —潔い討死, a brave death in battle. —...するを屑しとせぬ, to disdain *to*; be too proud *to*.

isagiyoku (潔く), *ad.* manfully; bravely; with a good grace. —潔く白狀する, to confess frankly. —潔く屈服する, to yield with a good grace.

isaha (斑葉の), *a.* spotted.

isai (委細), *n.* particulars; details. —委細に物語る, to narrate minutely [in detail]. —委細を話す, to tell all the details. —委細構はずに立去る, to leave regardless of consequences.

isai (異彩), *n.* brilliance. —異彩を放つ, to shine; be conspicuous; stand out.

isakai (諍), *n.* a quarrel; a squabble; a dispute; high words.

isaki (鷄魚), *n.* 【魚】 Pristipoma japonicum (學名).

isakusa (葛藤), *n.* a quarrel; a dispute; a dissension; troubles.

isamashii (勇しい), *a.* gallant; valiant; heroic. —勇しく, gallantly; valiantly; heroically.

isame (諫), *n.* ❶ (諫諍) remonstrance; expostulation. ❷ (忠告) admonition; warning (警告). —諫を更に聽かぬ, to turn a deaf ear to another's counsel.

isameru (諫める), *vt.* to remonstrate *with*; expostulate *with*; warn.

isamu (勇む), *vi.* to be emboldened; be inspired with courage.

isan (違算), *n.* miscalculation; an error (in calculation).

isan (遺算), *n.* a slip; an oversight; an omission.

isan (遺產), *n.* ❶ 【法】 an estate; a property left behind; an inheritance. ❷ a bequest; a legacy. ¶ 遺產相續人, an inheritor; an heir to a property.

isao(shi) (勳), *n.* an exploit; a meritorious deed.

isaribi (漁火), *n.* a fishing-fire.

isasaka (聊か), *ad.* a little; slightly; somewhat. —聊かの路銀, a trifling sum for travelling expenses.

isayoi (十六夜), *n.* the sixteenth (night) of the moon. —十六夜の月, the moon on its sixteenth night.

iseebi (伊勢蝦), *n.* the spiny lobster.

isei (以西), west *of*.

isei (威勢), *n.* ❶ (威力) power; authority; influence. ❷ (元氣) spirits. ❸ (威名) prestige. —威勢のよい, powerful; mighty; spirited.

isei (異性), *n.* ❶ the opposite [other] sex. ❷ different character [nature]. ❸ 【化】 metamerism; isomerism. —異性の愛, sexual love.

iseki (遺跡), *n.* remains; ruins; relics. —太古の遺跡, the remains [relics] of an ancient age.

isen (緯線), *n.* a parallel of latitude.

iseru (寄襲る), *vt.* to gather.

isetsu (異說), *n.* ❶ (異端) a

heterodoxy; a heresy. ❷ a different opinion.

isha (慰藉), *n.* comfort; consolation; solace. —慰藉する, to comfort; console. ¶ 慰藉料, a solatium.

isha (醫者), *n.* a doctor; a physician; a medical man. —醫者に見て貰ふ, to consult a doctor; see a doctor. —醫者にかゝって居る, to be under medical treatment. —醫者を呼ぶ, to send for a doctor; call in a doctor.

ishi (石), *n.* (石塊) a stone. —石の如く堅い, as hard as a stone. —石を切り出す, to quarry stones.

ishi (意志, 意思), *n.* will; volition; intention (意向). —意志の强固な人, a man of strong will. —意志の疏通を計る, to make plans for mutual understanding —意志を決定する, to make up one's mind.

ishi (縊死), *n.* self-strangulation; death by hanging. —縊死する, to hang oneself; kill oneself by hanging.

ishi (遺子), *n.* a posthumous child; an orphan.

ishi (遺志), *n.* the intention of a deceased person. —遺志に背く, to act contrary to (be against) the deceased's wishes

ishi (醫師), *n.* a medical practitioner. —醫師の免許狀, a medical licence. ¶ 醫師會, a medical association.

ishibai (石灰), *n.* lime.

ishibashi (石橋), *n.* a stone bridge. —石橋を叩いて渡る, to be too cautious.

ishibotoke (石佛), *n.* a stone Buddhist image [idol].

ishibumi (碑), *n.* a stone monument. ☞ *hi* (碑).

ishidan (石段), *n.* a stone step. a stone-stair; a stone platform.

ishidatami (石疊, 甃), *n.* ❶【建】stone-flooring; stone-pavement. ❷ (市松模樣) a chequered pattern.

ishidōrō (石燈籠), *n.* a stone-lantern.

ishigake (石崖), *n.* a stone-wall.

ishigaki (石垣), *n.* a stone-wall; a stonework; a dry stone-dyke. —石垣を繞らす, to surround with a stone-wall.

ishigame (水龜), *n.*【爬蟲】the Japanese terrapin.

ishihajiki (石彈), *n.*【遊戲】marbles; taw. —石彈きする, to play marbles.

ishikeri (石蹴り), *n.*【遊戲】hopscotch.

ishiki (居敷), *n.* ❶ (臀) the bottom; the posteriors. ❷ (衣服の臀部) the seat.

ishiki (意識), *n.* consciousness. —意識する, to be conscious *of*. —意識を回復する, to recover consciousness; come to one's senses [oneself].

ishiki (違式), *n.* informality; breach of etiquette.

ishikiri (石切), *n.* ❶ quarrying; stone-cutting. ❷ (石切工) a quarryman. ¶ 石切場, a (stone-) quarry; a stone-pit.

ishikoro (石塊), *n.* a small stone; a pebble.

ishiku (石工), *n.* a stone-mason; a stone-cutter.

ishimochi (石首魚), *n.*【魚】Sciæna Schlegelii (學名).

ishin (威信), *n.* prestige; dignity; authority. —我が帝國の威信, the prestige of our Empire. —威信を保つ (損する), to maintain [keep up] (impair) one's dignity.

ishin (維新), *n.* the Imperial Restoration. —維新の改革, the reforms of the Restoration period.

ishinage (石投), *n.* ❶ (投石) stone-throwing. ❷ (投石機) a stone-sling; a catapult. —石投げで投げる, [*vt.*] to sling; catapult.

ishinagi (石投), *n.*【魚】the bass.

ishin-denshin (以心傳心), *n.* telepathy; mind [thought]-transference.

ishin-dōtai (異身同體), *n.* one flesh.

ishitsu (遺失), *n.* loss. —遺失する, to lose. —遺失せる, lost. ¶ 遺失物, a lost property; a lost article. (遺失物保管所, a lost-property office.)

ishiusu (石臼), *n.* a quern; a stone-mill.

ishiwara (石原), *n.* a stony place.

ishiwata (石綿), *n.* asbestos; amianth; amiantus.

ishiya (石屋), *n.* ❶ (石商) a stone-merchant. ❷ (石工) a stone-cutter; a stone-mason.

ishiyama (石山), *n.* a quarry.

ishizue (礎), *n.* ❶ (土臺石) a foundation-stone; a corner-stone; a foot-stone. ❷ (基礎) the foundation; the basis; groundwork. ❸ (柱石) a pillar. —礎を据ゑる, to lay the foundation. —國の礎として仰ぐ, to look upon as the corner-stone of the state.

ishizuka (石塚), *n.* a stone-mound; a cairn.

ishizuki (石突), *n.* the butt-end (槍等の); a ferrule (杖等の).

ishizukuri (石造), *n.* stone-building; masonry. —石造りの, stone; stone-built.

ishizuri (石摺), *n.* a print from stone. —石摺りにする, to print from stone.

isho (遺書), *n.* a will; a testament.

ishō (衣裳), *n.* dress; costume; clothes.

ishō (意匠), *n.* (a) design. —意匠を凝らす, to apply oneself exclusively to designing. ¶ 意匠登錄, registration of a design.

ishoku (衣食), *n.* ❶ (衣と食) clothes and food. ❷ (生計) means of subsistence. —衣食する, to feed and be clothed; live. ¶ 衣食住, food, clothing and habitation; the necessaries of life.

ishoku (移植), *n.* transplantation. —移植する, ① (植物を) to transplant; naturalize. ② (皮膚などを) to transplant; graft.

ishu (意趣), *n.* ❶ (意向) intention. ❷ (遺恨) malice; a grudge. —意趣返しに, in revenge; in retaliation. —意趣返しする, to pay a person out; revenge oneself *on*; retaliate.

ishū (蝟集する), *vi.* to throng; crowd together; swarm.

ishū (遺臭), *n.* ❶ scent. ❷ an ill name left to posterity. —(獵犬が)遺臭をつけ失ふ(再び嗅ぎ當てる), to lose (recover) the scent.

ishuku (萎縮), *n.* shrinkage; contraction; 【醫】 atrophy. —萎縮さす(する), to shrink; contract; atrophy; wither.

iso (磯), *n.* a beach; a shore; a strand. —磯近く, inshore.

isō (意想), *n.* thought; conception. —意想外の, unanticipated; unthought-of; unexpected.

isogani (磯蟹), *n.* 【甲殼】 the sand-crab.

isogashii (忙しい), *vi.* to be busy. ——, *a.* busy. —忙しく, busily. —商賣上で忙しい, to be pressed with business.

isogasu (急がす), *vt.* to hasten; hurry up; urge. —工事を急がす, to hurry up the works. —馬車を急がす, to drive in haste.

isogi (急ぎ), *n.* haste; hurry. ——**-no**, *a.* urgent; pressing; hasty. —急ぎの註文(用), an urgent order (business).

isoginchaku (磯巾著), *n.* 【珊瑚】 the sea-anemone.

isogu (急ぐ), *vi.* to make haste; hasten; hurry; be in a hurry. —出來るだけ急ぐ, to hurry as much as possible. —家路を急ぐ, to hasten on one's way home. —急がば廻れ, "The more haste, the less speed."

isoide (急いで), *ad.* hurriedly; hastily; in a hurry. —急いで持ッて來い, Make haste and bring it.

isoiso (いそいそ), *ad.* cheerfully; blithefully; with a light heart.

isōrō (居候), *n.* a hangar-on; a dependant.

isoshimu (勤む), *v.* to work [labour] diligently; be diligent *in*.

issai (一切), *ad.* all; altogether; absolutely; wholly; at all; whatever. ——**-no**, *a.* whole; all; every. —一切(の)關係を絕つ, to cut off all relations; wash one's hands completely *of*.

issai-tafu (一妻多夫), *n.* polyandry.

issaku (一昨日), *n.* & *ad.* the day before yesterday. —一昨々日, three days ago. —一昨年, the year before last. —一昨夜[晚], the night before last.

issan-ni (逸散に), *ad.* at full [top] speed; at the top of one's speed.

issei (一世), *n.* ❶ (一代) an age. ❷ (一生) a life-time. ❸ (同名第一代の王者の稱) the first. —那翁一世, Napoleon I [the First]. —一世の英雄, the hero of his age. —一世一代の大出來, the greatest success of his life.

issei (一齊の), *a.* simultaneous. —一齊に, simultaneously; in chorus; all together. ¶ 一齊射擊, a volley; volley-firing; fusillade.

isseimen (一生面を開く), to find a new phase [departure].

issekigan (一隻眼), *n.* an eye. —一隻眼を具する, to have a special eye *for*.

issen (一洗する), *vt.* to wash away; efface.

issetsu (一切), *ad.* =*issai*.

issetsu (一說), *n.* ❶ (意見) another opinion [view]. ❷ another version. —一說によれば, according to another opinion.

issha-senri (一瀉千里に), *ad.* with great rapidity; in a hurry.

isshi (一矢), *n.* an arrow. —一矢を酬いる, ① to shoot back an arrow. ② to give a smart reply.

isshi (一視する), *vt.* ❶ to see once; take a glance. ❷ (同一視) to regard [treat] in the same way. ¶ 一視同仁, universal brotherhood; loving all equally.

isshiki (一式), *n.* a complete set.

isshin (一心), *n.* a whole mind; a whole heart; one mind. —一心に, whole-heartedly; absorbedly; intently. —一心不亂に, with all one's mind [heart]; with heart and soul. —一心になる, to devote oneself *to*; give all one's mind *to*; be absorbed [immersed; lost] *in*.

isshin (一身), *n.* ❶ (自身) oneself. ❷ (全身) the whole body. —一身を立てる, to make one's way in the world. —一身上の都合で辭職する, to resign for personal reasons.

isshin (一新する), *vt.* to renew; renovate; reform. 一面目を一新する, to make a complete change; change its appearance completely. —一新紀元を劃する, ① [*v.*] to make an epoch. ② [*a.*] (劃時代的) epoch-making.

isshin (一審), *n.* the first instance.

isshinkyō (一神教), *n.* monotheism.

isshi-sōden (一子相傳の), *a.* transmitted from father to one son. —一子相傳の妙藥, an efficacious medicine transmitted to one son in each generation.

issho (一緒に), *ad.* ❶ (共に) together; with; in company *with.* ❷ (同時に) at the same time. —一緒にする, ① (混同する) to mix up *with*; confound *with.* ② (一所に置く) to put together. ③ (結合さす) to unite. —一緒に住む, to live together. —一緒に行って貰ふ, to get a person to go with one.

isshō (一生-涯), *n.* a whole life; all one's life; lifetime. ☞ *shūsei* (終生). ——, *ad.* for life; during one's life. —一生に一度, once in a lifetime. —一生の仕事, one's life-work. —私の一生の望, my one and only hope.

isshō (一笑), *n.* a laugh; an amusement. —一笑に付する, to laugh a thing off.

isshō-kenmei (一生懸命に), *ad.* ❶ (全力を以て) with all one's might [strength]; with might and main. ❷ (懸命に) for dear life; for one's life. —一生懸命になる, to get up steam; be up to the eyes *in.* —一生懸命に働く, to work with all one's might. —一生懸命に逃げる, to run for one's (dear) life.

isshoku (一食), *n.* a meal.

isshu (一首), *n.* an ode; a piece.

isshu (一種), *n.* ❶ (同種類の一) one of a kind; a species. ❷ (一いろ) a kind; a sort. ——**-no,** *a.* a kind [sort] *of*; of a kind. —一種特別の, peculiar; special. —一種の珈琲, a sort of coffee.

isshū (一周), *n.* (一めぐり) one round; one revolution; a lap (徒歩競走の). ——**-suru,** *vt.* to come full circle (運動場などを); go (travel; sail) round; make one revolution. —ベースを一周する, to make a round of the bases. ¶ 一周忌, the first anniversary of a death. —一週年, a full year (滿一年); an anniversary. —世界一周旅行, a tour round the world.

isshū (一週-間), *n.* a week. —一週一回の, weekly. —一週後の火曜日, Tuesday week.

isso (寧そ), *ad.* rather; preferably; better. ☞ *mushiro* (寧ろ).

issō (一掃する), *vt.* to sweep off [away]; make a clean sweep *of*; drive off. —暗雲を一掃する, to clear the air.

issō (一層), *ad.* more; much more; still more. —一層の困難を來す, to lead to further hardships.

issō (一艘), *n.* a vessel; a ship.

issō (逸走する), *vi.* to scamper; scuttle; run away.

issoku (一足), *n.* a pair. —一足跳びに, at a bound; at a jump; with one bound.

issui (一睡する), *vi.* to take a nap.

issun (一寸), *n.* a *sun*; a Japanese inch. ¶ 一寸法師, a dwarf; a pigmy; a midget. —一寸の蟲にも五分の魂, "Even a fly has its spleen."

is-suru (逸する), *vi.* ❶ (逃げる) to scamper; run away; slip (機會). ❷ (散失する) to be lost; disappear. ——, *vt.* ❶ (逃がす) to let slip (機會); let escape (敵軍, 敵艦). ❷ (それる) to miss (的); deviate [swerve] *from* (針路, 正路). ❸ (遺脱す) to omit (日附·姓名等). —常軌を逸する, to be off the beaten track.

isu (椅子), *n.* ❶ a chair. ❷ (地位) a post; a chair. —椅子に著く, to sit in [on] a chair; take a seat. —大臣の椅子に就かす[据ゑる], to give a portfolio; appoint minister. —椅子を狙ふ, to aim at a post. ¶ 三脚椅子, a three-legged stool. —揺り椅子, a rocking chair.

isū (異數), *n.* rareness; uncommonness. —異數の拔擢, rare [unusual] selection.

isuka (鶍交喙), *n.* 【鳥】 the crossbill.

isukumaru (居竦まる), *vi.* to crouch.

i-suru (醫する), *vt.* to heal; cure; quench. —渴を醫する, to slake [quench] one's thirst.

isuwari (居据りの), *a.* ❶ (坐り居る) sedentary. ❷ (不動の) stationary. —居据りの仕事, sedentary work. —居据る, ① (定住) to settle down. ② (不動) to remain stationary; remain in office.

ita (板), *n.* ❶ a board; a plank (厚板). ❷ (金屬板) a plate. —板を張り詰める, to board *over.*

itabari (板張りする), *vt.* to board; plank. —天井を板張りする, to board the ceiling.

itabasami (板挾), *n.* ❶ (板と板の間に挾まること) being pressed between two boards. ❷ (中間に立って困ること) a dilemma; a fix. —板挾みにあふ, to be put in a fix; be in a dilemma.

itabashi (板橋), *n.* a wooden bridge.

itabei (板塀), *n.* a board fence; a wooden wall.

itabuki (板葺), *n.* shingle-roofing. ¶ 板葺屋根, a shingle [board] roof.

itachi (鼬鼠), *n.* 【哺乳】 the Japanese weasel.

itachigokko (鼬ごっこ), *n.* ❶ (兒戲) laying hand upon hand. ❷ (互に同じことを反覆すること) repeating the same thing.

itadaki (頂), *n.* ❶ (頭上) the crown. ❷ (山巔) the top; the summit; the peak. ❸ (最高所) the head; the top. —小山の頂に, on [at] the top of a hill.

itadaku (戴く), *vt.* ❶ (冠る) to put on; wear. ❷ (奉戴する) to have *over*. ❸ (貰ふ) to accept; receive. ☞ ***chōdai, morau.*** —雪を戴く山巓, peaks surmounted [capped] with snow. —總裁に戴く, to install as president.

itade (痛手), *n.* ❶ a severe wound. ❷ (大打擊) a heavy blow. —痛手を負ふ, to be severely wounded; suffer a heavy blow.

itado (板戶), *n.* a wooden door.

itadori (虎杖), *n.* 【植】 the giant knotweed.

itagakoi (板圍), *n.* a board enclosure; boarding; hoarding. —板圍ひする, to board up; enclose with boarding.

itagami (板紙), *n.* board; pasteboard; cardboard (薄い).

itagane (板金), *n.* a metal plate; a sheet-metal; a planchet (鑄貨用).

itagarasu (板硝子), *n.* plate-glass; sheet-glass; pane (窓の).

itago (板子), *n.* a plank. —板子一枚下は地獄, "Those who go to sea are only four inches from death."

itai (痛い), *a.* painful; sore. —痛い所, a sore; a sore point. —腹(頭)が痛い, I have a pain in my stomach (head).

itajiki (板敷), *n.* boarding; a board-floor.

itakedaka (居丈高になる), *vi.* to draw oneself up.

itaku (甚·痛く), *ad.* very much; exceedingly; severely. —いたく夜も更けたり, The night is far gone [spent; advanced].

itaku (委託), *n.* 【商】 consignment; commission; trust. —委託する, to consign; entrust; commit; give charge *of*; give in charge. —委託を受ける, to be entrusted. ¶ 委託販賣, consignment [commission] sale; sale on commission. (委託販賣人, a commission merchant; a factor.) —委託品, consignment (goods); an article consigned; trust; charge. —委託金, trust-money; money in trust. (委託金費消, embezzlement. —委託金費消者, an embezzler.) —委託者, a consignor; a truster.

itamashii (傷·痛ましい), *a.* painful; pitiful; piteous. —傷ましく, painfully; sadly; piteously.

itame (板目), *n.* ❶ the grain (of a board). ❷ (板と板との合目) a joint.

itameru (傷·痛める), *vt.* ❶ (傷ける) to injure; hurt; harm. ❷ (こはす) to injure; damage; spoil. ❸ (惱ます) to trouble; pain; grieve.

itameru (煠める), *vt.* to fry. —葱を油で煠める, to fry stone-leek in oil.

itami (痛, 傷), *n.* ❶ (痛苦) pain; ache; smart (ひりひりする). ❷ (悲傷) pain; grief; distress. ❸ (損傷) damage; injury; wear (and tear).

itamiiru (痛入る), *vi.* to be extremely obliged. —お禮では却て痛入ります, You embarrass me by thanking me.

itamu (痛·傷む), *vi.* ❶ (痛苦) to hurt; pain; be painful. ❷ = *itamu* (傷·悼む). ❸ (損傷) to be hurt; be broken; be injured; be damaged; wear off [away; out] (服·靴·機械等). —傷んだ林檎, a damaged apple. —痛がる, to complain of pain; be in pain. —針を刺すやうに痛む, to hurt like a pin-prick.

itamu (傷·悼む), *vi.* ❶ (悲傷) to grieve; be grieved *at* (*for*). ❷ (哀悼) to lament; mourn regret. —友人の死を悼む, to lament [mourn] the death of a friend. —果敢なき人生を傷む, to mourn for [lament] the frailty of life.

itan (異端), *n.* heresy. ¶ 異端者, a heretic; a heathen.

itanoma (板の間), *n.* a wooden floor. ¶ 板の間稼ぎ, a bath-house thief.

itari (至), the utmost limit; the height; the climax. —欣喜の至りである, It gives me the greatest pleasure.

Itari(a) (伊太利), *n.* Italy. ¶ 伊太利語, Italian; the Italian language. —伊太利人, an Italian. —伊太利ネル, cotton flannel.

itarikku (伊太利體), *n.* & *a.* 【印】 Italic.

itaru (至る), *vi.* ❶ (往く) to go; proceed; repair. ❷ (到著する) to arrive *at* [*in*]; reach [*vt.*]; lead *to.* ❸ (極度) to go so far *to*; go (to) the length *of*. ❹ (結果) to come *to*; grow *to*; become. —知るに至る, to get [come] to know. —發狂に至らしむ, to drive one mad. —召使に至るまで, even to one's servants. —一月より三月に至るまで, from January till March. —古より今に至るまで, from old times up to now.

itarutokoro (到處), *ad.* everywhere; all over; far and wide.

itashikata (致方), *n.* help; a way. ☞ *shikata.* —何とも致し方がない, There is no help for it.

itashikayushi (痛し痒し), to be in a quandary [dilemma]; be in an awkward predicament.

itasu (致す), *vt.* ❶ (效) (盡す) to render; do. ❷ (輸) to carry; transport; send. ❸ (爲す) to do. ❹ (招來) to invite; bring; lead *to.* —力を致す, to render service. —賢者を致す, to invite intelligent men. —不敏の致す所である, to be due to my unworthiness. —どう致しまして, Not at all; Don't mention it. —どう致しませう, What shall I do?

itatamaranu (居たたまらぬ), *a.* unable to remain. —居たたまらなくする, to make the place too hot for a person.

itatte (至ッて), *ad.* very; exceedingly; extremely. —至ッて腕白者, a very wilful child. —至ッて厳格な, extremely severe.

itaura (板裏-草履), *n.* wooden-soled sandals.

itawaru (勞はる), *vt.* ❶ (同情する) to pity; sympathize *with.* ❷ (大事にする) to care *for*; treat kindly. —病人をいたはる, to sympathize with (take care of) a patient. —弱者をいたはる, to pity the weak. —老人を勞はる, to car for the old.

itaya (板屋), *n.* a house with a shingle roof; a board yard.

itazura (徒), *n.* ❶ (徒爲) uselessness. ❷ (惡戲) mischief; a trick; a prank. ❸ (淫行) (an) immorality. —理(?)もない惡戲, a wanton mischief. —いたづら盛りの男兒, a boy in his most mischievous age. —徒をする, to play a trick [prank] *on*; be mischievous; play *with* (弄ぶ). ——**no,** *a.* ❶ (徒爲) useless; vain. ❷ (惡戲) mischievous; naughty. ❸ (淫行) immoral; wanton. ——**ni,** *ad.* ❶ (無益) needlessly; in vain; for nothing. ❷ (安閑) idly. ❸ (惡戲) in fun; out of mischief. —徒らに抵抗する, to resist in vain. —徒らに一生を送る, to lead a useless life; pass a life in idleness. ¶ 惡戲者, a naughty [mischievous] boy; a person fond of playing practical jokes.

itchaku (一著), *n.* ❶ (第一著) the first arrival. ❷ (衣服等の一揃) a suit.

itchi (一致), *n.* ❶ (協同) co-operation; concert. ❷ (同意) agreement; unanimity. ❸ (統一) unity; uniformity. ❹ (調和) harmony; concord. ❺ (符合) coincidence; conformity. —一致する, ① (同意) to agree; assent; concur. ② (統一) to be unified. ③ (調和) to harmonize *with*; accord *with*; concur *with*. ④ (符合) to coincide *with*. ⑤ (共同, 和合) to unite; co-operate; be united. —一致行動に出る, to act in concert. —一致を缺く, to lack unanimity. —一致の歩調をとる, to move in harmony. —一致して共同の敵に當る, to meet in concert [union] the common enemy. —議論の一致點を見出す, to find the point of agreement in the arguments.

itchi-hankai (一知半解), *n.* smattering; sciolism. —一知半解の徒, men with smattering of knowledge; a sciolist.

itchō (一朝), *ad.* in a day; one day; suddenly. —一朝事あらば, should a disturbance arise one day.

itchokusen (一直線), *n.* a straight line. —一直線に行く, to go straight; go in a bee line.

itchōra (一張羅), *n.* the sole holiday suit.

iten (移轉), *n.* ❶ transfer. ❷ (引越) removal; moving. —所有權(占有)の移轉, transfer of ownership (possession). —移轉を通知する, to inform a person of one's change of address. —移轉先をくらます, to keep secret where one has removed (to). —移轉屆をする, to report one's removal. ——**-suru,** *v.* ❶ to transfer [*vt.*]; pass *to.* ❷ (引越す) to remove; move. —本郷から本所へ移轉する, to remove from Hongō to Honjo.

itetsu (鑄鐵), *n.* cast-iron.

ito (絲), *n.* ❶ a thread (縫絲); a yarn (織絲, 編絲); a filament (纖細な); a string (紙鳶などの). ❷ (絃) (樂器の) a string; a gut (ヴァイオリンの). ❸ (釣絲) a line. —絲に通す, to thread (數

珠玉等を). —絲を繰る, to reel thread. —絲を紡ぐ, to spin thread. —(陰で)絲を引く, to pull the wires. —縺れた絲を解く, to unloose [unravel] tangled thread.

ito (最), *ad.* very; most; exceedingly. —いと面白く日を送る, to pass the day delightfully.

ito (意圖), *n.* a design; a purpose.

itō (以東), east *of.*

itodo (いとど), *ad.* more; more and more; still more.

itoguchi (緒, 絲口), *n.* ❶ (絲端) the end of a thread. ❷ (端緒) a clue (手掛り); the beginning. —緒があく, to find a clue. —出世の緒となる, to become the beginning of one's rise in the world.

itoguruma (紡車), *n.* a spinning-wheel.

itohiku (絲引く), *vi.* to string (膠等が).

itokenaki (幼き), *a.* young; little; tender. —幼き時親に別れる, to be parted from one's parents in infancy [childhood].

itokiriba (絲切歯), *n.* the eye-tooth; the dog-tooth.

itoko (從兄弟, 從姉妹), *n.* a cousin (german); a first cousin. ¶ 從兄弟違ひ, a cousin once removed. —從兄弟同士, cousins; cousinhood; cousinship.

itokuri (絲繰), *n.* reeling. ¶ 絲繰機械, a reeling-machine.

itokuzu (絲屑), *n.* waste thread; silk waste.

itoma (暇), *n.* ❶ (閑暇) leisure; spare time; time. ❷ (賜暇) leave of absence. ❸ (雇傭契約解除) discharge; dismissal. ❹ (辭去) leave-taking. —五日間の暇, five days' leave of absence. —讀書の暇さへない, to have no time for reading. —枚擧に遑あらず, to be too numerous to mention.

itomagoi (暇乞), *n.* leave-taking; a parting call. —暇乞ひする, to take leave *of*; say good-bye *to*; bid farewell *to* (嚴肅に). —暇乞ひに出る, to pay a farewell call. —暇乞ひの爲め, to take leave.

itomaki (絲卷), *n.* a spool; a bobbin; a reel.

itome (絲目), *n.* the strings of a kite.

itomeru (射留める), *vt.* to shoot dead; bring down.

itonami (營), *n.* business; occupation. —佛事の營みをする, to hold Buddhist mass. —其日の營みに差支へる, to be unable to keep body and soul together.

itonamu (營む), *vt.* ❶ (爲す) to do; make. ❷ (從事) to carry on; engage *in*; pursue. ❸ (取行ふ) to perform; hold. —私利を營む, to work for personal profit. —商業を營む, to carry on business. —辯護士の業を營む, to practise law.

itoori (絲織), *n.* a soft and smooth sort of silk cloth.

itoshigo (愛し子), *n.* a darling; a beloved child.

itoshii (愛しい), *a.* darling; beloved; dear; near one's heart.

itōsu (射通す), *vt.* ❶ (射貫く) to shoot (an arrow) *through.* ❷ (透徹する) to pierce through.

itotori (絲取), *n.* ❶ (製絲) silk-spinning. ❷ (製絲女工) a silk-spinner. ¶ 絲取場, a filature.

itou (厭ふ), *vt.* ❶ (きらふ) to dislike; hate; loathe; grudge (to do something); be disgusted *with.* ❷ (自愛する) to take care (of oneself). —厭ふべき惡臭, a disgusting smell. —身を厭ふ, to take care of oneself. (身を厭はずに, without sparing oneself.) —仕事を厭ふ, to dislike work. —人は生來艱難を厭ふ, Man has a natural aversion to misery.

itowashiki (厭はしき), *a.* disagreeable; unpleasant; unpleasing; hateful; offensive; nauseous.

itoyanagi (絲柳), *n.* the weeping willow.

itoyori-kikai (絲撚機械), *n.* a twiner.

itoyū (絲遊), *n.* gossamer; gossamer-webs. ☞ *kagerō.*

itsu (一), *n.* ❶ (ひとつ) one. ❷ (同一) the same; identity. —一の, ① (一つの) one; a, an. ② (同一の) same; identical.

itsu (何時), *ad.* when; at what time. —何時でも; 何時だって, at any time; whenever; always (常に). —何時頃, when; about what time. —何時から, from what time; from when; how long. (いつとも知れぬ古い時代から, from time unknown [immemorial].) —何時まで, till when; how long. —何時までも, long; for a long time; for ever. —何時の年も, every year. —何時でも宜しい, Any time will do. (何日でも私はよろしい, Any day will suit me.)

itsū (胃痛), *n.* 【醫】gastralgia.

itsubi (溢美), *n.* overpraise. —...といふも溢美に非ず, It is not overpraising to say that....

itsubusu (鑄潰す), *vt.* to melt down (old coins, 舊貨を).

itsuji (逸事), *n.* an anecdote.

itsuka (何時か), *ad.* ❶ (早晩) sooner or later. ❷ (いつともなく) before one is aware. ❸ (曾て) (過去) once; one day; some time ago. ❶ (未來) some day; some time; some other day. —何時か彼處へ連れて行かう, I will take you there one day.

itsuki (居附), *n.* living at the place. —居附きの家庭敎師, a resident-tutor.

itsukeru (告ける), *vt.* to tell; sneak [俗]. ☞ ***iitsukeru.***

itsuku (居附く), *vt.* ❶ (定住する) to be settled in a place. ❷ (家に落つく) to get used (to a house).

itsukushimi (慈), *n.* love; affection.

itsukushimu (慈む), *vt.* ❶ (愛する) to love; cherish; care *for.* ❷ (憐む) to pity.

itsumo (何時も), *ad.* ❶ (何時でも) always (常に); usually (平常); whenever (每度). ❷ (永久) for ever; evermore; eternally. —いつも云ふ通り, as I say usually. —いつも柳の下に鰌は居らぬ, "A fox is not caught twice in the same snare." **——-no,** *ad.* usual; accustomed; habitual; wonted; ordinary; regular. —いつもの通り, as usual. —いつもの洋服, everyday clothes.

itsu-ni (一に), *ad.* solely; entirely; completely.

itsuraku (逸樂), *n.* pleasure. —逸樂を事とする, to make pleasure one's business.

itsutsu (五つ), *n.* five.

itsuwa (逸話), *n.* an anecdote; anecdotage.

itsu-wa (一は), *ad.* (部分的に) partly; what with. —一は世辭一は袖の下で今の位地を占めたのだ, What with soft sawder and what with palm-grease, he rose to his present position.

itsuwari (僞), *n.* ❶ (詐)(虛言) a lie; a falsehood; a pretence. ❷ (詐謫) a deceit; a fraud. —詐を云ふ, to tell a lie [falsehood]; lie.

itsuwaru (僞·詐る), *v.* ❶ (虛言) to lie; tell a falsehood. ❷ (空事) to pretend; feign; dissemble. ❸ (欺く) to deceive. —僞ッて, falsely; deceitfully; fraudulently; under pretence *of.* —佯り狂する, to feign madness. —名を僞る, to give a false name.

itsuya (乙夜の覽), *n.* Imperial perusal. —乙夜の覽を賜はる, to be honoured with His Majesty's perusal.

itsuyara, itsuzoya, (日外), *ad.* ❶ (過日) the other day. ❷ (何時なりしか) some time ago; once; one day.

itsuzuke (居續する), *vi.* to stay on.

ittai (一帶), *n.* a region; a tract.

ittai (一體), *n.* one body. **——,** *ad.* ❶ (一體全體) (共に who, what, where 等に伴ふ) on earth; in the world. ❷ (元來) in fact; really. —佛像一體, a Buddhist image. —一體に, ① (到る處) all over (the country). ② (總じて) generally; on the whole. —一體となッて行動する, to act as one man [body]. —一體君は何者だ, What on earth [in the world] are you? —一體君が惡いよ, You are really to blame.

ittan (一旦), *ad.* once. —一旦…した以上は, (when; if) once.

itte (一手に), *ad.* by oneself; alone. —一手に引受ける, to undertake single-handed. (敵を一手に引受ける, to face the enemy alone.) ¶ 一手販賣, sole agency; monopoly (專賣). (一手販賣人, a sole agent.)

ittei (一定の), *a.* fixed; regular; invariable (不變の); uniform (一樣の). —一定する, to fix; standardize; unify (畫一にする). —一定の職業 (收入), a fixed [regular] occupation (income). —一定不變の法則, a fixed and unchangeable rule; a fixed law. —一定の資格ある者, persons with a definite qualification.

itteiji (一丁字), *n.* a letter; a word. —目に一丁字なき, unlettered; illiterate.

itteki (一滴), *n.* a drop.

itten (一天), *n.* the whole sky; the whole heavens. —一天萬乘の君, a sovereign.

itten (一點), *n.* ❶ (一つの點) a point. ❷ (一箇) one; an article (一品). ❸ (すこし) a speck; a dot. —一點の私心もない, I have not the least selfish motive.

ittenbari (一點張りで), *ad.* concentrating one's energies *upon*; sticking to one bush; by sheer …; solely by dint *of.* —知らぬの一點張りで押通した, He persisted in denying any knowledge of it.

ittetsu (一徹), *n.* stubbornness. —老の一徹, stubbornness of age. ¶ 一徹者, a stubborn person.

itto (一途), *n.* a way.

ittō (一刀), *n.* a sword. —一刀の下に斬り殺す, to cut down at a single stroke of a sword. —一刀兩斷の處置を執る, to take a decisive measure.

ittō (一等), *n.* the first rank [grade](官職階級の); the first class. —刑一等を減ずる, to reduce a penalty by one degree. —さうするのが一等だ, It is best to do so. ¶ 一等巡洋艦, a first-class cruiser.

——一等國, a first-class power [state]. ——一等船客, a first-class [cabin] passenger. ——一等船室, a saloon. ——一等車, a first-class car. ——一等賞, the first-class prize.

ittō (一統), *n.* ❶ (一血統) a line; lineage. ❷ (統一) subjugation of the whole country; unification. ❸ = *ichidō* (一同). ——一統する, to bring under one rule; unify; subjugate.

ittōbiki (一頭牽の), *a.* Ⓢ 一頭立. one-horse. ——一頭牽の馬車, a one-horse carriage; a gig; a buggy.

ittōchi (一頭地を抜く), to rise to eminence; tower [rise] above one's fellows.

ittoku-isshitsu (一得一失), *n.* an advantage and a disadvantage; "no rose without a thorn."

ittsū (一通), *n.* a copy; one document. —副本一通, a copy.

ittsui(一對), *n.* a pair; a couple; a brace.

iu (言: 云ふ), *v.* ❶ (口に出す) to say; speak; talk. ❷ (謂) (人にいふ) to tell; say *to.* ❸ (と噂す) it is said; they say; people say. ❹ (稱す) to name; call. —スミスと云ふ人, one Smith; a man named Smith. —謂ふ所の, the so-called. —言ふ迄もなく, not to mention; needless to say. —言ふに言はれぬ, ① (言表し能はざる) indescribable; inexpressible. ② (言ふことを憚る) delicate. —(と)云はぬばかりに, as much as [as if] to say. —言ふと同時に實行する, to suit the action to the word. —言ふことを聽く, ① (耳を傾ける) to listen to another's words. ② to do as another says [tells one]. ③ (忠告を容れる) to listen to a person's advice. —と云はざるべからず, It must be pronounced that; It must be considered to be. —言ふは易く行ふは難し, "Easier said than done." —言はずして明かなり, It goes without saying. —誰であったかは言ひ難い, It is hard to say who it was. —貴樣は己を馬鹿と云ったな, You called me a fool, didn't you?

iwa (岩, 巖), *n.* a rock. —岩の多い, rocky.

iwaba (言はば), *ad.* ❶ (一言せば) in a word; in short. ❷ (言ふもよくば) may well be called. ❸ (喩へば) so to speak [say]; as it were; in a manner.

iwabotan (岩牡丹), *n.* 【植】 the sun-plant.

iwaeru(結へる), *vt.* to tie; bind. —手足を結へる, to bind the hands and feet.

iwai (祝), *n.* congratulation; celebration. (記念の). —七つのお祝をする, to celebrate the attainment of the seventh year.

iwaibi (祝日), *n.* a national holiday; a fête day. —七五三の祝日, the gala day for children who are 3, 5, and 7 years old.

iwaimono (祝物), *n.* a congratulatory present. —祝物を贈る, to send a congratulatory present.

iwaku (曰く), *vi.* to say. —聖書に曰く, It says in the Bible; The Bible says. ——, *n.* ❶ (わけ, 仔細) a cause; reasons. ❷ (來歷) a story; a past. —曰く附きの女, a woman with a past.

iwana (嘉魚), *n.* 【魚】 the char; the bull-trout.

iwankatanaki (言はん方なき), *a.* unspeakable; unutterable. —その混雜言はん方なし, The confusion was indescribable.

iwan̄ya (況や), *ad.* how much more (less); much more (less); still more (less). —況や...に於てをや, much [still] more (less) is it the case with....

iwao (巖), *n.* a rock.

iware (謂), *n.* ❶ (理由) a reason. ❷ (原因) a cause. ❸ (由緒) history; story. —謂れなき, motiveless; causeless. —謂れなく, without any reason [cause]. (謂れなく人を打つ, to strike a person without any provocation. —何の謂れもなく, without any reason.)

iwashi (鰯), *n.* 【魚】 the sardine.

iwau (祝ふ), *vt.* to celebrate (祝賀); commemorate (記念); congratulate (慶賀). —紀元節を祝ふ, to celebrate the Anniversary of the Founding of the Empire. —開業十年を祝ふ, to celebrate the tenth anniversary of the opening of the business.

iwaya(巖窟), *n.* a cave; a cavern; a grotto (主として裝飾せる).

iwayuru (所謂), *a.* the so-called. ——, *ad.* so to speak. —眞に所謂, the properly [truly] so-called. —法律上に所謂, in legal parlance. —所謂一般の讀者, what is called the general reader.

iya (いや), *int.* ❶ (驚き又は嘆息の發聲) oh; ah. ❷ (呼掛の發聲) hi; hallo. —いや今日は, Hallo, good morning. —いや驚いた, Well, I am surprised.

iya (否), *ad.* (いな) no; nay; not so.

iya (否, 嫌, 厭), *n.* ❶ (嫌惡) dislike; disgust. ❷ (倦厭) weariness. —否でも, even against one's will. (否でも應でも, whether he will or no; willy-nilly.) —いやな心持, an unpleasant sensation. —いやな臭ひ, an offensive [a bad] smell. —いやな天氣, disagreeable [nasty] weather! —厭な仕事, an ugly job; a horrible task. —いやにじめじめした, unpleasantly moist. —いやに氣取ッた奴, a disagreeably prim fellow. —厭な顔をする, to make a wry face. —嫌ならおよし, You needn't if you don't want to. —厭だと云ッてしない, He refuses to do it. **——-ninaru,** *vi.* ❶ (嫌ふに至る) to become disgusted *with.* ❷ (倦みあきる) to get weary [tired] *of.* —厭になりかける, to begin to feel disgusted. —この世が厭になる, to become disgusted with life; become sick of life.

iyagaru (嫌がる), *vt.* to dislike; hate; be unwilling [reluctant] *to*; be loath *to*; be averse *to.*

iyahaya (いやはや), *int.* (意外の驚を示す發聲) oh dear; dear.

iyaiya (否否), *ad.* ❶ no, no. ❷ (否々ながら) reluctantly; unwillingly; with a bad grace. —いやいや我慢する, to put up *with* against one's will; bear reluctantly.

iyaki (否氣, 厭氣), *n.* repugnance; dislike; aversion. —嫌氣がさす, to begin to feel repugnance [aversion] *for*; begin to get tired *of.*

iyaku (意譯), *n.* free translation; paraphrase. —意譯する, to translate freely; paraphrase.

iyaku (違約), *n.* breach of promise [contract]. —違約する, to break a promise [contract]; break one's word. ¶違約金, a penalty; damages for breach of contract.

iyaku (醫藥), *n.* a medicine; medical treatment (醫療).

iyami (否味, 厭味), *n.* a cutting remark; an irony; a sarcasm. —厭味を云ふ, to say sarcastic things.

iyaōnashi (否應なしに), *ad.* willy-nilly; whether willing or not. —否應なしに承諾さす, to wring consent. —否應なしに連れて行く, to take a person with one by force.

iyarashii (否・厭らしい), *a.* ❶ (きらはしい) disagreeable; unpleasant; offensive. ❷(みだりがましい) obscene; indecent. ❸ (下卑た) vulgar. —いやらしく飾る, to bedizen [*vt.*]; be vulgarly dressed.

iyashii (卑しい), *a.* ❶ (下賤) humble; low; mean. ❷ (卑劣) base; vile; ignoble. ❸ (卑むべき) contemptible; despicable. ❹ (野卑) vulgar; rude; gross. ❺ (吝な) stingy; miserly.

iyashikumo (苟も), *ad.* at all; in the least; ever. —苟もする, to waste; trifle away; make light of. —苟もやるなら, if you do it at all. —苟も紳士なら, if he is anything of a gentleman. —一分時たりとも苟もせぬ, not to trifle away even a minute. —一言半句も苟もせぬ, not to waste a word.

iyashimi (卑, 賤), *n.* contempt; scorn. —人の賤みを受ける, to incur the contempt of others.

iyashimu (賤む), *vt.* to scorn; despise; disdain. —賤むべき, contemptible; despicable.

iyasu (癒す), *vt.* ❶ (醫す) to cure; heal; restore. ❷ (晴らす) to wreak; soothe; quench. —傷を癒す, to heal a wound. —病を癒す, to cure a disease.

iyō (異樣の), *a.* strange; queer; singular. **——-ni,** *ad.* strangely; singularly. —異樣に感ずる, to strike one as strange.

iyoiyo (愈), *ad.* ❶ [漸] (次第に) more and more; still more. ❷ (遂に) at last. ❸ (何樣しても) in any way; anyway. ❹ (屹度) certainly; really; assuredly. —愈〻となれば, if the time comes. —愈〻承知しないか, Do you refuse anyway? —愈〻出でて愈〻奇なり, The more it appears, the more strange it is.

iyū (畏友), *n.* a respected friend; a venerated friend.

iza (いざ), *int.* (誘ひ立つる時の發聲) come; now. —いざとなれば, if compelled [forced]. —いざ鎌倉といふ時, when an emergency arises; in case of emergency.

izaisoku (居催促する), *v.* to wait and dun for the payment of money.

izakaya (居酒屋), *n.* a grog-shop; a public-house; a pot-house.

izanau (誘ふ), *vt.* ❶ to invite. ☞ *sasou.* ❷ (誘惑) to entice; lure. ❸ (導く) to lead; guide. —敵を誘ふ, to entice the enemy. —花に誘はれて蝶が來る, The butterfly comes lured by flowers.

izari (居行), *n.* a cripple (躄). —躄の乞食, a crippled beggar.

izaru (居行る), *vi.* to crawl *along*; creep *on.* —居行り寄る, to crawl over.

izasaraba (いざさらば), *int.* ❶ come; now. ❷ (訣別) adieu; farewell.

izayoi (十六夜), *n.* =*isayoi.*

izen (以前), *ad.* ❶ (今より前) before; ago. ❷ (往時) formerly; in former times; once (曾て).

——, *conj.* before. —…以前に, [*ad.*] previous [prior] *to.* —彼の以前の友人, his former friend.

izen (依然), *ad.* as before; as it was; still. —依然としてある, to remain unchanged.

izeru (畫架), *n.* an easel.

izō (遺贈), *n.* 【法】 legacy; bequest (動產の). —遺贈する, to devise (不動產を); bequeath (動產を). ¶遺贈者, a legator; a devisor.

izoku (遺族), *n.* a surviving [bereaved] family; the survivors. ¶遺族扶助料, a compassionate allowance; an allowance to a surviving family.

izon (異存), *n.* an objection. ☞ *igi* (異議). —毛頭異存無之候, I have not the least objection.

izuko, izuku, (何處), *pron.* where. —何處も, everywhere; anywhere. —何處へ(に), where. —何處より, whence; from where.

izukumaru (居竦まる), *vi.* = *isukumaru.*

izukunzo (焉・安・惡んぞ), *ad.* why (なぜ); how. —焉んぞ知らん, How should we know?

izumai (坐樣), *n.* sitting posture. —坐樣を崩す(直す), to sit easy (upright).

izumi (泉), *n.* a spring; a fountain; a spring-head.

izure (何れ), *pron.* which; where. ☞ *dochira, dore, dotchi.* ——, *ad.* ❶ (いづれにせよ) anyhow; at any rate; in any case. ❷ (早晚) sooner or later. ❸ (いづれ其の中) some day; one of these days; shortly; before long. ——**-ka,** *pron.* which; whichever. —孰れかの一つ, [*conj.*] either…or. —甲か乙か孰れかの中, either A or B. ——**-mo,** [*conj.* & *pron.*]. both…(and). —孰れも…せず, [*conj.* & *pron.*] neither…(nor). ——**-no,** *a.* what; which. —何れの日か, ① some day. ② when.

izuru (出づる), *vi.* = *ideru,* = *deru,*

J

ja (邪), *n.* ❶ (不正) wrong; unrighteousness. ❷ (邪惡) evil; vice.

ja (蛇), *n.* a snake; a serpent. —蛇の道は蛇(へび), "Set a thief to catch a thief."

jaaku (邪惡の), *a.* wicked; vicious; evil.

jabara (蛇腹), *n.* 【建】 a cornice; close parallels. ¶蛇腹附カメラ, a bellows-camera.

jabon (ジャボン), *n.* 〔蘭 zamboa〕 【植】 the shaddock; the pompelmous (大形の); the pomelo (小形の); the grape-fruit 〔米〕; the forbidden fruit.

jabujabu (じゃぶじゃぶさす), *vt.* (水を) to plash (water); dabble (in water).

jachi (邪智), *n.* craft; guile; perverted talent. —邪智深い人, a very crafty person.

jadō (邪道), *n.* vice; evil courses; heretical doctrines (邪說). —邪道に陷る, ① (邪說) to lapse into heresy; pervert. ② (墮落) to go wrong; be led astray; deviate from the path of duty.

jagataraimo (馬鈴薯), *n.* 【植】 the (common) potato.

jaguchi (蛇口), *n.* a mouth-pipe; a mouth-piece.

jahō (邪法), *n.* ❶ (邪敎) heresy; heterodoxy. ❷ (魔法) black arts; sorcery.

jajauma (じゃじゃ馬), *n.* a restive horse.

jakago (蛇籠), *n.* a bamboo case of stone used for embankments.

jakan (蛇管), *n.* a hose.

jaken (邪慳), *n.* ill-nature; cruelty. —邪慳な, ill-natured; cruel; harsh. —邪慳にする, to ill-treat; treat harshly; be hard *upon.*

jaketsu (ジャケツ), *n.* a jacket.

jaki (邪氣), *n.* ❶ (瘴氣) miasma; poisonous air; pestilential vapours. ❷ (風邪) a cold. —邪氣を拂ふ, to clear away poisonous vapours.

jakkan (若干), *n.* & *pron.* a number; a sum (額); some. —若干の砂糖, some quantity of sugar.

jakkan (弱冠), *n.* twenty years of age; youth.

jakki (惹起する), *vt.* to give rise [occasion] *to*; lead *to*; cause. —騷動を惹起する, to raise [create; make] a disturbance.

jakku (ジャック), *n.* the knave; the jack.

jakō (麝香), *n.* musk. ¶麝香入石鹼, a musk-soap. —靈猫(じゃかうねこ), the civet (-cat). —(宮中)麝香の間, the Musk Chamber.

jaku (弱), *n.* weakness; the weak (弱者); the young (若者). ——, *ad.* (不足) a little less than; a little under. —七パーセント弱, less than 7 %. —弱を助け强を挫く, to help [side with] the weak and crush [break] the strong.

jakuhai (弱輩), *n.* ❶ young people; a young fellow; a youngster. ❷ (未熟者) a novice; an inexperienced person.

jakumetsu (寂滅), *n.* ❶ (涅槃)

Nirvāna. ❷ (死去) death; entering Nirvāna; annihilation. —寂滅する, to die; enter Nirvāna.

jakunen (弱年), *n.* youth; adolescence.

jakuniku-kyōshoku (弱肉强食), *n.* the strong preying on the weak.

jakura (雀羅), *n.* a sparrow-net. —門前雀羅を張る, to have few callers; be deserted by the world.

jakusha (弱者), *n.* the weak.

jakushin (弱震), *n.* 【地文】a weak shock (of earthquake).

jakusotsu (弱卒), *n.* a poor [cowardly] soldier.

jakuten (弱點), *n.* a weakness; a weak point [side]; a defect. —人の弱點に乘ずる, to take advantage of others' weak points.

jakuyaku (雀躍する), *vi.* to dance [leap] for joy.

jakyō (邪敎), *n.* a heretical religion; heresy. ¶ 邪敎徒, a heretic; a heathen; an infidel.

jakyoku (邪曲), *n.* wickedness; viciousness; iniquity.

jama (邪魔), *n.* ❶【佛】the Devil; the Satan. ❷ (障礙) a hindrance; an obstruction; an obstacle. ❸ (干涉) interference; prevention. —邪魔な, inconvenient; obstructive; burdensome. —邪魔になる, to stand [be] in the way *of* [in a person's way]. —邪魔にする, to regard it as an encumbrance. ——**suru**, *vt.* to hinder; obstruct; interrupt; disturb; thwart. —往來の邪魔(を)する, to obstruct the road; interrupt the traffic.

jamonseki (蛇紋石), *n.* 【鑛】ophite; serpentine.

jamu (ジャム), *n.* jam.

janjan (じゃんじゃん), *n.* clash; clang-clang (鐘聲). —ジャンジャン鳴らす(鳴る), to clash; jangle.

janken (じゃん拳), *n.* (a kind of) mora.

janku (戎克), *n.* a junk.

janome (蛇の目), *n.* a double-ring; a bull's eye. —蛇の目から傘, an umbrella with the bull's eye design [a broad border].

jarajara (じゃらじゃら), *ad.* ❶ (鐵·錢などの鳴る音) with a jingle. ❷ (女のなまめき戯れる樣) coquettishly; flirtingly. —じゃらじゃらした, coquettish; frivolous.

jaratsuku (じゃらつく), *v.* to philander; flirt *with*; dally *with*. ——, *a.* coquettish; flirty; flirtish.

jarasu (調弄す), *v.* to play *with*; flirt (男を). —猫をじゃらす, to play with a cat.

jareru (戯れる), *vi.* to play; frisk; gambol. ——, *a.* frisky; frolicsome. —よく戯れる猫, a very playful [frolicsome] cat.

jari (砂利), *n.* gravel; ballast. —砂利を敷く, to (cover with) gravel; ballast. ¶ 砂利置場, a gravel-yard.

jasetsu (邪說), *n.* a heresy; a wrong view.

jashin (邪神), *n.* the devil; the demon.

jashū (邪宗), *n.* =*jakyō*.

jasui (邪推), *n.* unjust [groundless] suspicion; distrust. —邪推する, to suspect; distrust; be distrustful *of*. —邪推深い人, a distrustful man. —邪推を廻はす, to entertain unjust suspicions.

Jawa (瓜哇), *n.* Java. ¶ 瓜哇人, a Javan; a Javanese.

jerachin (ジェラチン), *n.* gelatine.

jeri (ジェリ), *n.* jelly.

ji (字), *n.* ❶ a letter; a character; an ideograph (漢字などの). ❷ (筆蹟) handwriting; penmanship. ❸ (語) a word. —字が旨い(下手), to write a good (poor) hand.

ji (次), *n.* ❶ (次第) order. ❷ (度) time. ❸【數】dimension. ——, *a.* next; the following; the ensuing. —第四次,【數】the fourth dimension. —次を逐ふ, to go in order.

ji (地), *n.* ❶ (土地) ground; land. ❷ (素地) ground; field (繪·貨幣·旗等の). ❸ (織地) texture; fabric; material. —赤い地に菊の御紋章, the Imperial crest of chrysanthemum on a red ground.

ji (柱), *n.* (琴の) a bridge.

ji (時), *n.* time; hour (時間); o'clock (時刻). —三時半, half past three. —何時に, at what time [hour]. —八時に, at 8 o'clock.

ji (痔), *n.* piles; hemorrhoids.

ji (辭), *n.* a word; a term; an address (挨拶).

jiai (地合), *n.* texture; fabric; stuff.

jiai (自愛), *n.* self-love; looking after oneself [one's health]; taking care of oneself. —自愛する, to take care of oneself.

jiai (慈愛), *n.* affection; love. —慈愛深い, affectionate.

jiarinsan (次亞燐酸), *n.* hypophosphorous acid.

jiasutāze (ヂアスターゼ), *n.* diastase.

jibachi (地蜂), *n.* the wasp.

jiban (地盤), *n.* ❶ the foundation; the ground; the base. ❷ (勢力範圍, 根據) the sphere (of influence [activity]); foothold. —地盤を固める, to harden the foundation.

jibara (自腹切る), *v.* to pay for a thing oneself; untie one's purse-strings. —自腹を切って, at one's own expense.

jiben(自辨で), *ad.* at one's own expense. —自辨する, to pay oneself; provide oneself (被服など).

jibeta, jibita, (地下), *n.* the ground; the earth. —地下に手をついて謝まる, to apologize with one's hands on the ground.

jibi-inkō-ka(耳鼻咽喉科), *n.* otorhinolaryngology.

jibiki (字引), *n.* a dictionary; a lexicon (古語·外國語の). —字引を引く, to look up in a dictionary; consult [refer to] a dictionary. —字引と首引きする, to struggle (through) with a dictionary.

jibiki (地引), *n.* seining. ¶ 地引網, a seine; a drag-net.

jibin (次便で), *ad.* by the next mail [post]. —次便に讓る, to leave to the next mail [post].

jibo (字母), *n.* ❶ (音標字) a letter; a syllabic. ❷ (活字の) a matrix.

jibo (慈母), *n.* a kind [an affectionate] mother.

jibō-jiki(自暴自棄), *n.* desperation; despair. —自暴自棄に陷る, to grow desperate; abandon oneself to despair.

jibun(自分), *n.* self; ego. ——, *pron.* oneself. —自分勝手な, selfish; self-seeking; self-centred. (自分勝手の理窟を捏ねる, to trump up reasons for one's own convenience.) —自分の都合を計る, to consult one's own convenience. —自分免許の大學者だ, He is a great scholar in his own estimation. —自分ながら愛想が盡きた, I am quite disgusted with myself.

jibun (時分), *n.* ❶(季節) season. ❷ (時機, 時期) a proper time. ❸ (時刻) time; hour. —去年の今時分に, this time last year. —よい時分を窺ふ, to watch for a proper time.

jibun (時文), *n.* contemporary writing; the writing of a period. —時文體で書く, to write in current style.

jibutsu (事物), *n.* things.

jibyō (持病), *n.* ❶ (痼疾) a chronic disease [ailment]. ❷ (癖好) a hobby; a weakness.

jichi (自治), *n.* self-government; home rule. ¶ 模範自治村, a model self-governed village. —自治團體, a self-governing community; a municipality (市町村などの). —自治權, autonomy. —自治機關, an organ of self-government; a municipality (市·町·村などの); a self-governing body. —自治制, a system of self-government; autonomy.

jichō (次長), *n.* a vice-chief; a vice-director.

jichō (自重 -心), *n.* ❶ (自尊) self-respect; amour-propre; pride. ❷ (自愛) care for oneself. —自重する, to respect oneself; take care of oneself (自愛).

jida (耳朶), *n.* (耳たぶ) the ear-lobe. —耳朶に觸れる, to reach [come to] one's ears.

jidai (地代), *n.* rent; ground[land]-rent.

jidai (時代), *n.* ❶ (時勢) the times; the time. ❷ (年代) a period; an age; an epoch; an era. ❸ (代) a generation. —時代の要求, the demands of the age. —時代の新傾向, the new tendency of the times. —其時代に, in those days. —時代後れの, behind the times; antiquated. —時代後れとなる, to go out of date. —時代の推移につれて, with the changes of the times. ¶ 明治時代, the Meiji era. —時代錯誤, anachronism. —時代精神, the spirit of the age [times]. —時代思潮 [思想], the current thoughts.

jidai (事大的), *a.* trusting to a stronger power. ¶ 事大主義, the policy of truckling to a stronger power.

jidan(示談), *n.* private settlement; amicable arrangement; compromise. —示談にする, to settle privately; settle out of court; compromise. —示談を申込む, to propose amicable arrangement.

jidanda (地團駄踏む), *vi.* to stamp; stamp with rage [impatience] (癇癪を起して). —地團駄踏んで口惜しがる, to stamp with mortification.

jidaraku (自墮落な), *a.* slovenly; slatternly. ¶ 自墮落女, a slovenly woman; a slattern; a draggle-tail.

jiden (自傳), *n.* an autobiography.

jidenki (磁電氣), *n.* magneto-electricity.

jidō (自動, 自働), *n.* self-motion; automatism; self-action. —自動的, self-moving; self-acting; automatic. —自動する, to act of itself; move automatically. ¶ 自動電話, an automatic [a public] telephone. —自動販賣器, a slot-machine. —自動自轉車, a motor-cycle; a cycle-car; an autobi. —自動階梯, an escalator. —自動機械, an automatic machine. —自動人形, an automaton. —自動詞, 【文】 the intransitive verb. —自動艇, a motor-boat; an auto-boat 〔俗〕. —自動鐵道, a switch-back railway.

jidō (兒童), *n.* a child [*pl.* children]. ¶ 兒童敎育, education of children.

—見童心理學, child-psychology.
jidoko (地床), *n.* a bed; a road-bed.
jidori (地取), *n.* (土地の區畫) ⌈laying out.⌋
jidōsha (自動車), *n.* an automobile; a motor-car; an autocar. ¶ 配達自動車, a delivery-truck. —乘合自動車, a motor-bus; an autobus〔俗〕. —辻(待)自動車, a taxicab; a taxi〔俗〕. —運搬[貨物]自動車, a motor-truck; a motor-lorry. —自動車車庫, a garage. —自動車運轉手, a chauffeur (男); a chauffeuse (女).
jiei (自營), *n.* self-support. —自營する, to support oneself.
jiei (自衞), *n.* self-defence; self-preservation. ¶ 自衞權, right of self-defence. —自衞策, a self-protecting policy. ⌈epidemic.⌋
jieki (時疫), *n.* a plague; an
jifu (自負), *n.* self-conceit; self-glorification; vaingloriousness. —自負する, to be self-conceited; boast *of*; vaunt. ⌈theria.⌋
jifuteria (實布的里亞), *n.* diph-
jiga (自我), *n.* the I: self; ego. ¶ 自我主義, egoism. —自我主義者, an egoist.
jigai (自害する), *vi.* to die by one's own hand; commit suicide.
jiga-jisan (自畫自讚), *n.* self-admiration; self-praise.
jigane (地金), *n.* ❶ (土臺の金) metal underneath. ❷ (本性) true character. ❸ (原料金) metal; bullion (金・銀貨の). —地金を現はす, to show the cloven foot; show [come out in] one's true colours. ⌈現する, to reveal.⌋
jigen (示現), *n.* revelation. —示
jigen (次元), *n.* dimension.
jigen (時限), *n.* the limit of time.
jigi (字義), *n.* the meaning of a word; acceptation. —字義通りの翻譯, literal translation.
jigi (兒戲), *n.* a child's play; childishness; puerility. —兒戲に類する, to be like child's play.
jigi (時宜), *n.* circumstances; opportunity. —時宜に適した, opportune; timely. —時宜によッては, according to circumstances; as the case may be; as circumstances require.
jigi (時儀), *n.* ❶ the compliments of the season. ❷ = *jigi* (辭儀) の❶. —時儀を述べる, to present the compliments of the season.
jigi (辭儀), *n.* ❶ (お辭儀) a bow; a salute. ❷ (遠慮) ceremony. —辭儀する, ① to bow; greet; make a bow [courtesy]. ② (遠慮) to stand on ceremony; decline (辭退).
jigitarisu (ジギタリス), *n.* ❶ (藥) digitalis. ❷【植】the fox-glove; Digitalis purpurea (學名).
jigo (耳語する), *vi.* to whisper; talk in a whisper; whisper in one's ears.
jigo (事後の), *a.* after the fact. —事後承諾を求める, to ask for *ex post facto* consent.
jigo (爾後), ❶ (其後) since then; since. ❷ (此後) henceforth; hereafter.
jigō (自業-自得), *n.* the natural consequence of one's misdeed. —自業自得で苦しむ, to fry in one's own grease. —自業自得で仕方がない, to have only oneself to blame.
jigō (次號), *n.* the next number [issue]. —以下次號, to be continued (in our next). ⌈voice.⌋
jigoe (地聲), *n.* one's natural
jigoku (地獄), *n.* Naraka (奈落迦)〔梵〕; the Hades; Hell; the lower [under] world. —地獄に墮とす, to send into Hades. —地獄の沙汰も金次第, "Money is the key that opens all doors."
jiguchi (地口), *n.* 【修】a pun: a word-play. —地口をいふ, to make a pun; play on words.
jigyō (地形), *n.* groundwork. —地形をする, to prepare the ground for a building.
jigyō (事業), *n.* ❶ (企業) an undertaking; an enterprise; business. ❷ (仕事) a work; a task; a deed. ❸ (實業) an industry. —事業の繰延べ, postponement of work. —事業を起す, to commence an undertaking. ¶ 事業家, an enterpriser. —事業界, the industrial world. —事業年度, a business year [term].
jiha (自派), *n.* one's own party.
jihaku (自白), *n.* confession. —自白する, to own; confess.
jihatsu (自發-性), *n.* spontaneity; spontaneousness. —自發的, spontaneous. —自發的に, spontaneously; of one's own accord.
jihei (時弊), *n.* the evils of the times; the existing evils; the abuses of the age.
jihei (辭柄), *n.* a pretext; an excuse. —辭柄を設けて, on the [under] pretext [plea] *of*.
jihen (事變), *n.* ❶ (變亂) a disturbance; an emergency (急變). ❷ (變災) an accident; an incident; a disaster.
jihi (自費), *n.* private expense. —自費で洋行する, to go abroad at one's own expense. ¶ 自費生, a private student.
jihi (慈悲), *n.* mercy; benevolence; compassion. —慈悲深い, com-

passionate; merciful; charitable. —慈悲も情もなく, without mercy or pity. —慈悲をかける, to have [take] compassion *on*.

jihibiki (地響), *n*. a thud. —地響を打ッて倒れる, to fall with a thud on the ground.

jihishinchō (慈悲心鳥), *n*. 【鳥】 the Amoor cuckoo.

jihitsu (自筆), *n*. ❶ (自ら書く) autography; writing with one's own hand. ❷ (本人の手蹟) an autograph; one's own writing. —自筆の履歴書, one's curriculum vitæ written in one's own hand.

jihyō (時評), *n*. criticisms of current events; editorial notes (新聞紙の).

jihyō (辭表), *n*. a (letter of) resignation. —辭表を提出する, to tender [give in; send in] one's resignation; send in one's papers.

jii (侍醫), *n*. a court physician; a royal physician; a physician in ordinary. ¶ 侍醫局, the Bureau of Court Physicians.

jii (辭意), *n*. one's intention to resign. —辭意を仄かす, to hint one's intention to resign.

jii (辭彙), *n*. a dictionary; a lexicon.

jiin (寺院), *n*. a Buddhist temple; a church.

jiishiki (自意識), *n*. self-consciousness.

jijaku (自若たる), *a*. self-possessed; composed; calm. —自若として, composedly; calmly.

jiji (爺), *n*. ❶ (祖父) a grandfather. ❷ (老爺) an old man.

jiji (時事), *n*. current events [affairs]; the events of the day. —時事に通ずる, to be well-posted in current events. ¶ 時事漫評, current criticism; current gossip. —時事問題, a current question.

jiji (時時), *ad*. from time to time; at times; occasionally. —時々の, occasional. —危險は時々刻々に迫る, Danger threatens us every moment.

jiji (事事-物物), *n*. everything.

jijin (自刃), *n*. suicide. —自刃する, to commit suicide; kill oneself.

jijin (時人), *n*. the people of the time; the contemporaries.

jijitsu (事實), *n*. a fact; the truth; a matter of fact. —事實上, actually; practically; as a matter of fact. —赤裸々の事實, a plain [naked] fact. —事實無根に付, as the statement is unfounded. —事實に反する, to be contrary to the facts. —事實を調査する, to inquire into the facts. ¶ 事實問題, a question of fact.

jijitsu (時日), *n*. the time; the date; the day. —時日が切迫する, to have little time left; be pressed for time.

jijo (自助), *n*. self-help.

jijo (兒女), *n*. ❶ (女兒) a young girl. ❷ (子供) children.

jijo (侍女), *n*. a waiting woman; a lady-in-waiting.

jijō (自乘), *n*. 【數】 square. —自乘する, to square. ¶ 自乘數, a square number.

jijō (事情), *n*. circumstances; condition; state. —家の事情で, for one's family reasons. —事情の許す限り, as far as circumstances permit. —如何なる事情があッても, in [under] any circumstances; on any account; by all means. —事情を打明ける, to reveal the whole affair.

jijoden (自敍傳), *n*. an autobiography.

jijō-jibaku (自繩自縛), *n*. being hoist on one's own petard; falling into one's own trap.

jijū (侍從), *n*. a chamberlain; a lord in waiting. ¶ 侍從武官, an army (a naval) aide-de-camp to His Majesty; a gentleman-at-arms. (侍從武官長, the chief aide-de-camp to His Majesty.) —侍從長, the Grand Chamberlain; the Lord Chamberlain. —侍從職, the Board of Chamberlains; the Lord Chamberlain's department.

jika (自家), *n*. one's own house; home; one's self (自己). —自家用の, for home (one's personal) use. —自家撞著の, self-contradictory. ¶ 自家保險, self-insurance. —自家廣告, self-advertisement.

jika (耳科), *n*. 【醫】 otology. ¶ 耳科醫, an aurist; an otologist.

jika (時價), *n*. the current [ruling] price; the prevailing price.

jika (磁化), *n*. magnetization.

jikai (次回), *n*. next time. —次回に讓る, to postpone to next time.

jikai (次會), *n*. the next meeting; the next sitting; the next session (議會などの).

jikaku (耳殼), *n*. the auricle; concha.

jikaku (字畫), *n*. the strokes (of an ideograph).

jikaku (自覺), *n*. (self-)consciousness; self-awakening. —自覺的に, consciously. —自覺する, to be conscious *of*; be awakened *to*.

jikaku (持格), *n*. 【文】 the possessive case; the genitive (case).

jikan (次官), *n*. a vice-minister; an undersecretary (英); an assistant secretary (米). ¶ 外務次官, the Vice-Minister for Foreign Affairs.

jikan (時間), *n.* time; hour. —規定の時間, regular hours. —時間通りの, punctual. —時間が掛かる, to take time. —時間に遅れる, to be late (for school); come late; be behind time. —時間を守る, to be punctual. ¶ 時間表, a schedule; a time-table (學校·汽車の); a time-book (執務などの). —時間登錄器, a time-register [-recorder].

jika-ni (直に), *ad.* =*chokusetsu.*

jikasen (耳下腺), *n.* 【解】the parotid (gland). ¶ 耳下腺炎, parotiditis; mumps.

jikatsu (自活), *n.* self-support. —自活の道, means of self-support. —自活する, ① [*vi.*] to support [sustain] oneself. ② [*a.*] self-supporting; independent.

jikei (自警), *n.* self-warning. ¶ 自警團, a vigilance committee; a self-organized body for the maintenance of order.

jikei (慈惠), *n.* charity. ¶ 慈惠病院, a charity hospital.

jiken (事件), *n.* ❶ (事柄) a matter; an affair. ❷ (出來事) an event; an incident; an occurrence. ❸ (爭訟) a case; a cause; a suit. —小さな(訴訟)事件, a petty case. —最も重大な事件, a matter of the utmost concern. ¶ 極東事件, the Far Eastern Affairs.

jikeshi (抹字器), *n.* an eraser. ¶ 字消護謨, an India-rubber.

jiketsu (自決), *n.* ❶ self-determination. ❷ (辭職) resignation. —自決する, to decide by oneself; resign.

jiketsu (痔血), *n.* 【醫】bleeding piles.

jiki (直に), *ad.* ❶ (直接) directly; personally. ❷ (間もなく) soon; presently; immediately. —直き近く, close by; near by. —直に覺えられる, to be easy to learn; be easily learnt. —ぢき十二時になる, It is very close upon twelve.

jiki (次期), *n.* next term. —次期の議會, the next session of the Diet.

jiki (自記の), *a.* ❶ (自筆) autographical. ❷ (器械等の) self-registering [-recording]. —自記する, ① to write with one's own hand. ② to register automatically. ¶ 自記寒暖計, a self-registering thermometer.

jiki (時期), *n.* ❶ time; period. ❷ (時季) season.

jiki (時機), *n.* an opportunity; an occasion. —時機を待つ, to wait for an opportunity; bide one's time. —時機を逸する, to (let) slip an opportunity.

jiki (磁氣), *n.* magnetism. ¶ 磁氣感應(抵抗), magnetic induction (reluctance).

jiki (磁器), *n.* porcelain; china.

jikidan (直談), *n.* direct negotiation; personal consultation; a personal account (直話). —直談する, to consult personally *with*; have a personal interview *with*.

jikiden (直傳), *n.* direct transmission.

jikihitsu(直筆), *n.* an autograph; a holograph.

jikisan (直參), *n.* immediate vassalage; an immediate vassal [attendant; follower] (人).

jikiso (直訴), *n.* a direct appeal. —直訴する, to make a direct appeal; appeal directly.

jikitarisu (ジキタリス), *n.* = *jigitarisu.*

jikitorihiki (直取引), *n.* a bargain on spot; a spot bargain; a direct transaction [dealing].

jikiwa (直話), *n.* personal talk.

jikiyunyū (直輸入), *n.* driect importation. —直輸入する, to import direct.

jikiyushutsu (直輸出), *n.* direct exportation. —直輸出する, to export direct.

jikka (實科), *n.* a practical course. ¶ 實科女學校, a girls' practical school.

jikka (實家), *n.* the family in which one was born; the original house.

jikka (實價), *n.* the intrinsic value; the real [actual] value; the money value (公債等の額面に對する).

jikkakukei(十角形), *n.* a decagon.

jikkan (十干), *n.* the ten calendar signs; the ten stems of the sexagenary cycle.

jikkan (實感), *n.* ❶ actual sensation; experience. ❷ (觀者に與ふる效果) effect.

jikkei (實兄), *n.* one's own elder brother.

jikkei (實景), *n.* the actual view; nature.

jikken (實見する), *vt.* to observe [see] actually. ¶ 實見者, a witness; an eye-witness.

jikken (實檢する), *vt.* to inspect (調査する); identify (異物に相違なきを確む).

jikken (實驗), *n.* ❶ an experiment. ❷(經驗) (practical) experience. —化學の實驗, a chemical experiment. —實驗する, to make an experiment; experiment *on*; experience (經驗). ¶ 實驗科學, an empirical science. —實驗室, a laboratory.

jikken (實權), *n.* real power.

jikkō (實行), *n.* practice (實踐);

execution (遂行); performance (履行); enforcement (實施). ——**suru,** *vt.* to practise; carry into effect; carry into execution. —計畫を實行する, to execute a plan —約束を實行する, to perform [carry out] a promise. ¶ 實行委員, an executive committee.

jikkō (實效), *n.* a practical result; efficacy; effect. —實效ある, efficacious; effective. —實效を擧げる, to produce the desired result; prove effective.

jikkon (昵懇), *n.* intimacy; familiarity. —昵懇の, intimate; familiar. (と昵懇の間柄である, to be on familiar terms *with.*)

jikkyō (實況), *n.* the real [actual] condition; the actual state of things.

jiko (自己), *n.* self; ego. ——, *pron.* oneself. ☞ *jika* (自家). —自己流の, of one's own style. —自己中心の, self-centred. —自己本位の, egoistic. —自己滿足の, self-satisfied. —自己の體面に關する, to affect one's reputation. ¶ 自己保存, self-preservation. —自己崇拜, autolatry. —自己修養, self-culture.

jiko (事故), *n.* ❶ (事件) an accident; an incident. ❷ (事情) circumstances; reasons; cause. ❸ (故障) a hitch; an obstacle.

jikō (事項), *n.* matters; items (項目); particulars (同上).

jikō (時好), *n.* the current fashion; the style. ☞ *ryūkō.* —時好を追うて, after the fashion. —時好に投ずる, to follow the current fashion.

jikō (時效), *n.* 【法】 prescription. —時效の中斷(停止; 完成; 期間); interruption (suspension; completion; period) of prescription. ¶ 消滅時效, extinctive [negative] prescription. —取得時效, acquisitive [positive] prescription.

jikō (時候), *n.* ❶ (季節) season. ❷ (氣候) climate. —時候外れの, unseasonable; out of season. ¶ 時候不順, unseasonable weather.

jikoku (自國), *n.* one's (own) country; one's native land; home. —自國の, home; domestic; native. ¶ 自國語, the vernacular (language); the mother tongue.

jikoku (時刻), *n.* time; hour. ☞ *jikan* (時間). —時刻通りに, punctually.

jikon (自今), *ad.* henceforth; in future; from this time forward.

jiku (軸), *n.* ❶ 【機】 an arbor; a spindle; a shaft; (中心棒) an axis [*pl.* axes]; an axle; a pivot. ❷ (中心) a centre; a pivot. ❸ (莖) the stem; the stalk. ❹ (卷物) a roll. —地球の軸, the axis of the earth. —マッチの莖木〔ぢく〕, a match-splint.

jiku (字句), *n.* wording; phraseology; letter. —字句に拘泥する, to adhere too closely to the wording.

jikuro (舳艫), *n.* the stem and stern. —舳艫相銜んで進む, to advance in an end-on line.

jikyo (辭去する), *v.* to leave; take leave.

jikyōki (持兇器の), *a.* armed. ¶ 持兇器强盜, armed robbery (事); an armed robber (人).

jikyoku (事局), *n.* affairs; matters. —事局に當る者, those charged with the affairs.

jikyoku (時局), *n.* the situation. —時局に對する當局の態度, the attitude of the authorities towards the situation.

jikyoku (磁極), *n.* a (magnetic) pole.

jikyū (自給), *n.* self-supply; self-support (自活自營). —自給する, to support oneself. —自給自足の, self-sufficient; self-sufficing.

jikyū (持久する), *vi.* to endure; hold out; persevere. —持久策を立てる, to form a plan for holding out. ¶ 持久力, staying powers; stay. —持久戰, a protracted struggle; a position-war (陣地戰).

jimae (自前), *n.* one's own mistress. —自前になる, to become one's own mistress; set up on one's own account.

jimama (自儘), *n.* self-will; wilfulness. ☞ *wagamama.* —自儘に, wilfully.

jiman (自慢), *n.* pride; boast; self-praise; vanity. —(何)自慢の, proud *of*; vain *of*. —自慢らしく, boastfully; conceitedly; vauntingly. —自慢する, to be proud [boastful] *of*; boast *of*; brag *of*. —自慢ではないが, without boasting, I may say. —自慢話をする, to blow one's own trumpet. ¶ 自慢家, a boaster; a vaunter; a braggart.

jimawari (地廻り), *n.* ❶ (近在よりの廻送) coming from neighbouring districts. ❷ (其の近傍を常に廻り歩く人) a prowler in the neighbourhood. ❸ (船につき) coasting.

jimei (自明の), *a.* self-evident; axiomatic(-al); self-explaining. —自明の理, an axiom; a self-evident truth; a truism.

jimejime (じめじめした), *a.* damp; wet; sodden. —じめじめする, to feel damp.

jimen (地面), *n.* ❶ (土地表面) the surface (of land); the ground

❸ (地所) land; ground.

jimetsu(自滅), *n.* self-destruction; self-ruin; suicide. —自滅する, to destroy [ruin] oneself.

jimi (地味な), *a.* plain; quiet; sober. —地味な色, quiet colour. —地味な人, a sober man. —地味な服裝をする, to be plainly [quietly] dressed.

jimi(滋味), *n.* ❶ savouriness; richness. ❷ delicacies; delicious food.

-jimiru (染る), to look like. —汗染みた著物, dirty-looking clothes. —氣違じみた男, a mad-looking fellow.

jimoku (耳目), *n.* ❶ the eyes and ears; eye and ear. ❷ (見聞) observation. —耳目に觸れる, to be seen and heard; meet the eye and ear. —世間の耳目を惹く, to attract public attention.

jimon (自問する), *v.* to ask oneself; question oneself. —自問自答する, to answer one's own question.

jimu (事務), *n.* business; work; office. —事務を執る, to engage in business. —事務を引繼ぐ, to take over business. —事務を管理する, to manage [conduct] the business. —事務的才幹を有する, to possess business ability. ¶ 事務長, a purser (船舶の); *c.* head official. —事務費, office expenses. —事務員, a clerk. —事務次官, a permanent undersecretary. —事務家, a man of business [affairs]; a business man. —事務所, an office.

jimu (時務), *n.* current [social] affairs. —時務に通ずる, to be versed in current affairs.

jimushi(蠐螬), *n.* 【昆】 the grub.

jin(仁), *n.* ❶ (仁愛) benevolence; humanity; philanthropy. ❷ (種子などの) a nucleus; a kernel. ❸ a person. —身を殺して仁を爲す, to sacrifice one's life for others.

jin(陣), *n.* a position; a camp; formation (陣形). —陣を引拂ふ, to strike camp; evacuate a position.

jin (腎), *n.* 【解】 the kidney.

jin (ジン酒), *n.* gin.

jinai(仁愛), *n.* charity; humanity; philanthropy. —仁愛なる, benevolent; philanthropic.

jinai (塵埃), *n.* dust; dirt. ☞ *jinkai.* —塵埃の巷, a crowded [bustling] street.

jinan(次男), *n.* the [one's] second son.

jinarashi (地均), *n.* ❶【建】 (ground-)levelling. ❷ (修道ローラー) a roller.

jinari (地鳴), *n.* rumbling of the ground.

jinbaori (陣羽織), *n.* a coat (worn over an) armour.

jinbō (人望), *n.* popularity. —人望ある, popular. —人望を博する, to gain popularity; win good opinion. —人望を失ふ, to lose popularity.

jinbun (人文), *n.* civilization. ¶ 人文地理, descriptive geography.

jinbutsu (人物), *n.* ❶ (人) a person; a character (小說作中の); a figure (繪などの). ❷ (人格) personality; character. ❸ (人材) a man of talent [ability]. —末頼母しい人物, a man of great promise. —人物を畫く, to paint human figures. ¶ 人物評, personal criticism; a character sketch.

jinchi (人智), *n.* human understanding; human intellect; human knowledge.

jinchi (陣地), *n.* a position. —陣地を奪還(固守; 撤退)する, to recover (hold; evacuate) a position.

jinchiku (人畜), *n.* men and beasts [cattle].

jinchōge (沈丁花), *n.* 【植】 the sweet-scented daphne.

jindai (甚大の), *a.* very great; extraordinary; enormous; heavy; serious.

jindai (神代), *n.* the age of gods; the mythological age.

jindaiko (陣太鼓), *n.* a war-drum.

jindate (陣立), *n.* battle-array. —陣立をする, to form an army in battle-array.

jindō (人道), *n.* ❶ humanity. ❷ (步道) a side-walk; a footway; a foot-path. —人道を無視する, to ignore humanity. ¶ 人道問題, the question of humanity. —人道主義, humanism; humanitarianism.

jindoru (陣取る), *vi.* to encamp; (pitch a) camp. —高地に陣取る, to take up a position on high ground [on a hill].

jin'ei (人影), *n.* a human shadow. —人影を絕つ, to be completely deserted. —人影を認める, to see the shadow of a man; catch sight of a man.

jin'ei (陣營), *n.* quarters; an encampment.

jin'en(人煙), *n.* human habitation; population. —人煙稠密(稀薄)の地, a densely (sparsely) populated district.

jinenjo (自然薯), *n.* 【植】 Dioscorea japonica (yam の一種・學名); the Japanese yam.

jinezumi (地鼠), *n.* 【哺乳】 Sorex dsinezumi (shrew-mouse の一種).

jingasa (陣笠), *n.* ❶ a camp-hat (worn by common soldiers). ❷ (雜兵) the rank and file; common soldiers; soldiery. ¶ 陣笠連, the rank and file (of a party);

members below the gangway 〔英〕.

jingi (仁義), *n.* ❶ humanity and justice. ❷ (人道) humanity. ¶ 仁義忠孝, humanity, justice, loyalty, and filial piety.

jingi (神祇), *n.* the deities of heaven and earth.

jingi (神器), *n.* a sacred treasure. ☞ *shinki.*

jingo (人後に落ちる), to fall behind others.

jingū (神宮), *n.* a Shintō shrine. ¶ 伊勢太神宮, the Great Shrine of Ise. —明治神宮, the Meiji Shrine.

jiñi (人爲), *n.* man's handiwork; artificiality; human power (人力). **—-teki,** *a.* artificial; unnatural. —人爲的の市況, manipulated [artificial] market. ¶ 人爲相場, manipulated [artificial] market price. —人爲淘汰, artificial selection.

jiñi (人意), *n.* the public mind. —人意を强うするに足る, to go far to strengthen the public mind.

jinin (自任する), *v.* to charge oneself *with*; pretend *to*; make [have] pretension *to*. —學者を以て自任する, to fancy [look upon] oneself a scholar.

jinin (自認する), *vt.* to acknowledge; admit.

jinin (辭任), *n.* resignation. —辭任する, to resign (one's post).

jiñin (人員), *n.* ❶ (職員) the staff; the personnel. ❷ (人數) the number of men. —人員不足の, short-handed; short of hands. ¶ 人員點呼, roll-call.

jinja (神社), *n.* a shrine. ¶ 神社局, the Shrine Bureau.

jinji (人事), *n.* ❶ (人の業) human work. ❷ (世俗の事) human affairs; the world. ❸ (身上に關する事) personal affairs. —人事不省となる, to become unconscious; lose one's senses. ¶ 人事課, the section of personnel.

jinji (仁慈の), *a.* benevolent; charitable.

jinjō (尋常の), *a.* ❶ (普通) common; ordinary; average. ❷ normal (異常なき); gentle (やさしい); shapely (鼻・口などの). —尋常一樣の事をする, to do the usual common things. **—-ni,** *ad.* commonly; ordinarily; obediently; gently (素直に). —尋常に白狀する, to confess without concealment. ¶ 尋常兒(童), a normal child. —尋常小學校, an ordinary primary [elementary] school.

jinjutsu (仁術), *n.* a benevolent [healing] art.

jinka (人家), *n.* a house; a human dwelling [habitation]. ☞ *jinen.* —人家の絶えた, desolate.

jinkai (塵芥), *n.* dust; rubbish; garbage. —此處塵芥捨つべからず, No rubbish allowed here. ¶ 塵芥車, a dust-cart; a tip-cart. —塵芥掃除人, a dustman.

jinkaku (人格), *n.* ❶【法】personality. ❷ (品性) character. ❸ (個性) personality; individuality. ¶ 二重人格, a double character; 【心】double personality. —人格化, personification; impersonation. (人格化する, to personify; impersonate.) —人格敎育, character-building. —人格者, ①【法】a person (自然人と法人). ② (人格の人) a man of (high) character.

jinkan (人寰, 塵寰), *n.* the world. —人寰を遠ざかる, to keep aloof from the world.

jinkei (仁惠), *n.* benevolence; charity.

jinkei (陣形), *n.* 【軍】formation.

jinken (人權), *n.* rights of man; human rights; personal rights. —人權蹂躪を叫ぶ, to allege encroachment upon personal rights.

jinketsu (人傑), *n.* a remarkable man; a hero.

jinkō (沈香), *n.* 【植】the agila-wood; the aloes-wood.

jinkō (人工), *n.* artificiality; human work [labour]. —人工的, artificial. —人工を加へる, to apply work *to*; work *upon*. ¶ 人工受胎, artificial fertilization. —人工呼吸, 【醫】artificial respiration.

jinkō (人口), *n.* ❶ population. ❷ (衆口) the world; gossip. —農村人口の減退, rural depopulation. —人口の都市流入, the drift of population to the cities. —人口に膾炙する, to be in everybody's mouth. ¶ 人口統計, vital statistics. —人口增殖率, the rate of increase of population.

jinmashin (蕁麻疹), *n.* 【醫】urticaria; nettle-rash.

jinmei (人名), *n.* names of persons. ¶ 人名簿, a directory; a list [register] of names; a roll (特に點呼用). —人名辭書, a biographical dictionary. —人名口座 [勘定], personal accounts.

jinmei (人命), *n.* human life. —人命救助の賞として, in reward for saving life. —多大の人命を犧牲にして, at a great sacrifice of life.

jinmen-jūshin (人面獸心), *n.* a demon in human shape; a human monster.

jinmin (人民), *n.* the people; the public (公衆); the populace (衆庶). ¶ 人民控所, a public waiting-room.

jinmoku (人目), *n.* others' eyes; public attention. —人目を驚かす, to astonish the public.

jinmon (訊問), *n.* 【法】 an examination; an inquiry; interrogation. —證人を訊問する, to interrogate [examine] a witness.

jinmon (尋問), *n.* question; asking; query. —尋問する, to question; inquire; ask; query. ☞ *tazuneru, tou.*

Jinmutennō-sai (神武天皇祭), *n.* the Anniversary of (the Death of) the Emperor Jinmu.

jinniku (人肉), *n.* human flesh. —人肉を食む人, a cannibal.

jinpin (人品), *n.* personal character; personal appearance (人相). —人品の悪い, ill-favoured; ugly-looking. —人品のよい, fine-looking; personable. —人品卑しからぬ人, a man of no mean appearance.

jinpun (人糞), *n.* human fæces; night-soil.

jinrai (迅雷), *n.* a sudden peal of thunder; a thunderclap.

jinrikisha (人力車), *n.* a *jinrikisha*; a rickshaw (外人の訛り). ¶ 人力車賃, *jinrikisha*-fare. —人力車夫, a *jinrikisha*-man. —人力車停車場, a *jinrikisha*-stand.

jinrin (人倫), *n.* ❶ (道義) morality; moral principles. ❷ (人道) humanity; human relations (人と人との關係). —人倫の道, human duties; moral principles; moral law.

jinrui (人類), *n.* mankind; the humankind; the human race. ¶ 人類學, anthropology. (人類學者, an anthropologist.)

jinryoku (人力), *n.* human power. —人力の及ばぬ, beyond human power. —人力では如何ともし難い, No human effort will avail.

jinryoku (盡力), *n.* effort; exertion; endeavour. —盡力する, to endeavour; exert oneself; make every effort. —御盡力に依り, through your exertions.

jinsai (人材, 人才), *n.* a capable man; a man of talent [ability]. —人才を登用する, to employ men of ability.

jinsei (人生), *n.* life; human life; man's life. —人生の行路, the road of life. —人生僅か五十年, Man's span of life is but fifty years. ¶ 人生觀, a view of life.

jinsei (人性), *n.* human nature; humanity.

jinsei (人世, 塵世), *n.* the world.

jinsei (仁政), *n.* benevolent government. —仁政を施す, to govern with benevolence.

jinseki (人跡), *n.* human footsteps. —人跡未到の, untrodden. —人跡絕えたる, trackless.

jinsen (人選), *n.* selection of a suitable person. —人選する, to select a suitable person (for a post).

jinsha (仁者), *n.* a philanthropist; a humane [benevolent] person; a kind-hearted person. —仁者に敵なし, "Virtue, the safest defence."

jinshaku (人爵), *n.* human honours; nobility conferred by man.

jinshin (人心), *n.* men's minds; the public feeling; the popular sentiment. —人心の歸嚮を察する, to perceive the tendency of men's mind. —人心を統一する, to unify the public feeling. —都下人心恟々たり, The public mind in the capital is agitated.

jinshin (人身), *n.* the human body. ¶ 人身賣買, flesh-traffic. —人身攻擊, a personal attack; a personal abuse; personalities.

jinshin (人臣), *n.* a subject. —位人臣を極める, to reach the highest rank open to a subject.

jinshin (甚深の), *a.* profound; deep. —甚深の注意を拂ふ, to pay profound attention.

jinshō (人證), *n.* testimony [evidence] of witnesses.

jinshu (人種), *n.* a race. —人種的感情, racial feeling. ¶ 人種學, ethnology. —人種改良學, eugenics. —人種差別撤廢, abolition of racial discrimination.

jinsoku (迅速), *n.* rapidity; swiftness; promptitude. —迅速な, rapid; swift; prompt. —迅速に事を運ぶ, to despatch business rapidly.

jinsui (盡瘁する), *v.* to devote oneself entirely *to*; devote all one's energies *to*. —職務に盡瘁する, to devote oneself to one's duty.

jintai (人體), *n.* the human body. ¶ 人體解剖, human anatomy.

jintai (靱帶), *n.* 【解】 the ligament.

jinteihō (人定法), *n.* 【法】 a positive [an artificial] law.

jintōzei (人頭稅), *n.* poll-tax; capitation tax. —人頭稅を取る, to levy a poll-tax.

jintō (陣頭), *n.* the head of an army.

jintoku (仁德), *n.* benevolence; humanity.

jintsū (陣痛), *n.* 【醫】 labour-pains; throes.

jintsūriki (神通力), *n.* divine powers.

jinushi (地主), *n.* a landlord; a landowner; a landed proprietor.

jiñyō (陣容), *n.* camp formation; battle-array. —陣容を整へる, to array the camp formation.

jiṅyoku (人慾), *n.* human passions; human want.

jinzen (荏苒), *ad.* putting off from day to day. —荏苒日を移す, to waste days by delay.

jinzō (人造の), *a.* artificial. ¶ 人造肥料, artificial manure. —人造絹絲, artificial silk thread. —人造金, artificial [imitation] gold. —人造氷, artificial ice. —人造石, artificial stone. —人造眞珠, a fish-pearl; an artificial pearl; a paste-pearl.

jinzō (腎臟), *n.* 【解】 the kidney. ¶ 腎臟炎, 【醫】 nephritis.

jion (字音), *n.* the sound of a word [a character].

jippa (十把一括に), in a lump; in the gross; taken altogether. —十把一括の評, a sweeping [wholesale] remark. —十把一括に言ふ, to say in a word.

jippi (實否), *n.* the truth; the real facts. —能く實否を質す, to ascertain the truth carefully.

jippi (實費), *n.* actual expenses. —印刷實費にて頒つ, to distribute at the cost price of printing. ¶ 實費診療所, an office for medical treatment at cost price.

jippō (實包), *n.* a ball-cartridge.

jippu (實父), *n.* the true [real] father.

Jipushii (ジプシイ), *n.* a gipsy, [gypsy.]

jirafu (麒麟), *n.* 【動】 the giraffe; the camelopard.

jirai (地雷-火), *n.* a mine; a fougasse 〔佛〕. —地雷火を伏せる [埋設する], to lay [charge] a mine.

jirai (爾來), *ad.* since (then); ever since.

jirasu (焦らす), *vt.* to irritate; [fret; provoke.]

jirei (辭令), *n.* ❶ (言葉遣ひ) manner of speaking. ❷ (敍任辭令) a government order. —辭令に巧である, to be skilful in adressing people. —辭令を受取る, to receive a written order. ¶ 辭令書, a written order; a commission; an order.

jirenma (ヂレンマ), *n.* a dilemma. —ヂレンマに陷る, to fall into a dilemma.

jireru (じれる), *vi.* to fret; get irritated; get vexed [annoyed]. —じれ易い, fretful; irritable.

jirettai (じれッたい), *a.* vexatious; irritating; provoking. —ああじれッたい, 早くお歩きよ, How provoking! Walk quickly.

jiri (自利), *n.* ❶ self-interest; one's own interest; self-profit. ❷ (利己) self-seeking. —自利を圖る, to pursue [seek] one's own interest; make plans for personal profit; look to the main chance.

jiri (事理), *n.* reason. —事理に暗い人, a person unamenable to reason. —事理を解する(解せぬ), to be (un-)reasonable.

jirijiri (じりじり), *ad.* little by little; gradually; step by step; slowly and steadily. —じりじり(弱ッて)死ぬ, to die by inches.

jiriki (自力), *n.* one's own power; one's own exertion; one's own ability. —自力で, by one's own [unaided] power; unaided; independently.

jiritsu (自立), *n.* independence; self-support. —自立する, to establish [support] oneself; become independent; stand on one's own [legs.]

jirō (耳漏), *n.* otorrhœa.

jirō (痔瘻), *n.* 【醫】 fistula ani; fistula in ano.

jirojiro (じろじろ), *ad.* staringly. —人をじろじろ見る, to stare a man in the face; look a man up and down; measure a man with one's eyes.

jiron (持論), *n.* a cherished opinion [view]; an opinion; a stock argument. —余の持論の一, one of my pet theories.

jiron (時論), *n.* a current view.

jirori (じろりと), *ad.* with a glance. —じろりと見る, to glance *at*; cast a suspicious glance *at* (うさん臭げに).

jiryoku (磁力), *n.* magnetism; magnetic force. ¶ 磁力線, a line of magnetic force.

jiryū (時流), *n.* the fashion; the current of the times. —時流を拔く, to tower above one's contemporaries.

jisa (時差), *n.* equation of time.

jisai (自裁), *n.* =*jisatsu.*

jisaku (自作の), *a.* of one's own making 〔writing (書いた)〕. ¶ 自作農, a peasant proprietor.

jisan (自讃する), *v.* to praise oneself; sing one's own praises.

jisan (持參する), *v.* to bring; bring [take] with one. ¶ 持參金, 【法】 a dowry; a (marriage) portion. —持參人, a bearer. (持參人拂手形, a bill [note] (payable) to bearer.)

jisatsu (自殺), *n.* suicide. —自殺する, to commit suicide; kill oneself; die by one's own hand. —自殺を企てる, to attempt suicide. ¶ 自殺未遂, an attempted suicide. —自殺(的)論法, suicidal logic. —自殺者, a suicide.

jisei (自制), *n.* self-control; self-restraint; self-command. —自制する, to control [restrain] oneself.

jisei (自製の), *a.* of one's own

making; home-made.

jisei (時制), *n.* 【文】 the tense.

jisei(時勢), *n.* ❶ (時世) the times; the age. ❷ (時代の趨勢) the tendency [spirit] of the age [times]; the times. —時勢後れの, behind the times; old-fashioned: *passé* 〔佛〕. (時勢後れの人, an antediluvian; an old fogy; a man behind the times.) —時勢に伴ふ, to follow the spirit of the times; go [float] with the stream; keep abreast of [with] the times(時勢と竝進する). —時勢に逆ふ, to run counter to the spirit of the times; swim against the stream. —時勢に後れる, to be [fall] behind the times.

jisei (辭世), *n.* the dying words; a death-song; a swan-song.

jiseki (耳石), *n.* otolith.

jiseki (次席), *n.* the next seat; being next in position [rank].

jiseki(事蹟, 事迹), *n.* an evidence; a vestige.

jisen (自選する), *v.* to elect oneself. ¶ 自選投票, self-vote.

jisetsu (自說), *n.* one's own view [opinion].

jisetsu (時節), *n.* ❶ (季節) season. ❷ (時機) time; occasion; season. —時節柄, in these times; in view of the times.

jisha (侍者), *n.* an attendant; a page; a valet.

jishaku (磁石), *n.* ❶ a magnet. ❷ (羅針盤) a compass. —磁石の引力, magnetic attraction.

jishin (自身), *n.* self; oneself [*pron.*]. —彼女の自身の財產, property of her own. —自身でやる, to do it oneself. —自身(で)出頭する, to appear in person.

jishin (自信), *n.* self-confidence; assurance. —自信ある, self-confident. —自信する, to have self-confidence.

jishin (地震), *n.* an [a shock of] earthquake. ¶ 斷層(陷落)地震, a dislocation (downfall) earthquake. —破壞的地震, a destructive earthquake. —海底(火山)地震, a submarine (volcanic) earthquake. —地震日和, an earthquake weather. —地震地帶, an earthquake belt [zone]. —地震學, seismology. —地震計, a seismometer; a seismograph. —地震圖, an earthquake country.

jishin (磁針), *n.* a (magnetic) needle.

jishitsu (自失する), *vi.* to be self-abstracted; be dazed; be in a brown study. —自失せる, distracted; vacant.

jishitsu(痔疾), *n.* hemorrhoids; piles.

jisho (地所), *n.* land; ground. —地所附き賣家, a house and lot for sale.

jisho (自署), *n.* signature; sign manual. —自署する, to sign one's name; affix one's signature.

jisho (辭書), *n.* a dictionary; a lexicon; a word-book. ¶ 佛英辭書, a French-English dictionary. —辭書編纂法, lexicography. —辭書編纂者, a lexicographer.

jishō (自稱), *a.* self-styled; self-assumed; would-be. —自稱する, to call [style] oneself; profess. ¶ 自稱紳士, a self-styled gentleman.

jishoku (辭色), *n.* words and looks.

jishoku (辭職), *n.* resignation. —辭職する, to resign (one's office [post]; quit office; lay down one's duties; throw up one's appointment; abdicate one's office. —辭職を迫る, to urge resignation.

jishu (自主), *n.* independence. —自主的, independent (獨立的); active (主動的). ¶ 自主權, (right of) autonomy.

jishu (自首する), *v.* to surrender oneself to justice; give oneself up to the authorities.

jishū (自修する), *v.* to study oneself; practise by oneself. ¶ 英作文自修書, a self-taught English composition. —自修時間, study-hours.

jison (自存の), *a.* self-existent. —自存する, to exist of [by] itself.

jison (自尊の), *a.* self-respecting. ¶ 自尊心, the spirit of self-respect; (proper) pride. (人の自尊心を傷ける, to wound a person's *amour propre.*)

jissa (實査する), *vt.* to inspect actually. —實査を經たる後, after it has been actually inspected.

jissai (實際), *n.* ❶ (眞實) the truth; a (matter of) fact. ❷ (實狀) the actual state [condition]. ❸ (現實) reality; actuality. —, *ad.* ❶ (眞實に) actually; really; in fact. ❷ (事實上) practically; virtually; as a matter of fact. —實際的, ① (眞實の) true; real; actual. ② practical; matter-of-fact. —實際のところでは, as it is. —實際に行はれぬ議論, an impracticable argument. ¶ 實際家, a practical man; a matter-of-fact man.

jisseikatsu (實生活), *n.* a real [an actual] life; the realities of life.

jisseken (實世間), *n.* the every-day [actual] world.

jisseki (實跡), *n.* actual traces; an evidence.

jisseki (實績), *n.* actual results. —實績を擧げる, to give actual results.

jissen (實踐), *n.* practice. —實踐(躬行)する, to practise; perform; act up *to*. ¶ 實踐的理性, 【倫】practical reason.

jissen (實戰), *n.* an actual fight. —實戰に臨む, to see service; serve in a campaign.

jissetsu (實說), *n.* a true story; a real fact (事實).

jisshi (實子), *n.* the real [true] child. —彼は實子がない, He has no child of his own.

jisshi (實施), *n.* enforcement; execution. —實施する, to enforce; put in operation; carry into effect. —實施し得べき, enforceable; practicable. —新條約の實施, coming into operation of the new treaties.

jisshin (十進の), *a.* decimal; denary. ¶ 十進法, the decimal system.

jisshitsu (實質), *n.* ❶ (本質) substance; essence. ❷ (內容) contents; matter (材料). —實質上, substantially; materially. —實質的進步, substantial progress.

jisshō (實證), *n.* an actual proof. —實證を握る, to hold actual proofs. ¶ 實證哲學, positive philosophy; positivism.

jisshū (實收), *n.* actual receipts; actual income; actual yield.

jisshū (實習), *n.* practice; exercise. —實習する, to practise.

jissoku (實測), *n.* (actual) survey; measure. —山林を實測する, to survey a forest.

jissū (實數), *n.* 【數】real quantity.

jisuberi (地辷), *n.* 【地質·鑛山】dislocation; landslip; landslide.

jisui (自炊する), *vi.* to cook food for oneself; do one's own cooking.

ji-suru (治する), *vt.* ❶ (政治) to govern; rule. ❷ (癒やす) to heal; cure. ❸ (救治) to help; relieve. —病を治する, to cure a disease.

ji-suru (侍する), *vi.* to attend *on*; wait *on*. —君側に侍する, to attend [wait] upon one's lord.

ji-suru (持する), *vt.* to observe (守る); hold (保持する). —固く持する, to stand one's ground; stand firm; hold one's own.

ji-suru (辭する), *vt.* ❶ (辭職) to resign; lay down. ❷ (辭退) to decline. ❸ (辭去) to take leave; leave. —死をも辭せず, not to hesitate even to die.

jisutoma (ヂストマ), *n.* 【扁蟲】a distoma.

jita (自他), *n.* self and others; 【哲】subject and object.

jitabata (じたばたする), *vi.* to flounder; struggle. —じたばたしても追ッつかない, It is no use, struggle as we may.

jitai (字體), *n.* the form of a character; style; type.

jitai (事態), *n.* things; matters; the state of affairs [things].

jitai (辭退する), *v.* to decline.

jitaku (自宅), *n.* one's house; home. ¶ 自宅教授, home-teaching; private lessons. —自宅療養, home treatment [remedy]. —自宅診察, office consultation.

jitan (事端), *n.* the origin [cause] of an affair. —事端を滋くする, to complicate the affair.

jitchaku (實著な), *a.* steady. ☞ *chakujitsu.*

jitchi (實地), *n.* practice. ☞ *jissai.* —實地を踏む, to pass through practical work. —實地に應用する, to apply to practice. ¶ 實地調査, actual investigation. —實地試驗, a practical examination.

jitchoku (實直), *n.* honesty; uprightness; sincerity. —實直な, honest; upright; sincere. —實直に, honestly; sincerely.

jiteki (自適), *n.* suitability to oneself; self-enjoyment. —悠々自適する, to live in free and easy retirement.

jiten (次點), *n.* the next mark [number]. ¶ 次點者, a person with the next number of marks; the next candidate; *proxime accessit* 【羅】.

jiten (自轉), *n.* rotation. —自轉する, to rotate.

jiten (辭典), *n.* = *jisho* (辭書).

jitensha (自轉車), *n.* a bicycle (二輪, 略して bike); a tricycle (三輪). —自轉車に乘る, to ride a bicycle; bicycle; bike 【俗】.

jitetsu (磁鐵), *n.* magnetic iron.

jitojito (じとじとする), *a.* wet; moist; damp.

jitoku (自得する), *v.* ❶ (自ら滿足する) to be (self-)satisfied; be contented with oneself. ❷ (解する) to apprehend; appreciate. ❸ (自ら取得する) to acquire by oneself. —其の妙味を自得する, to appreciate its delicate taste.

jitsu (實), *n.* ❶ (眞實) the truth; the reality. ❷ (誠實) sincerity; kindness (深切). ❸ 【數】a dividend. ❹ (實質) substance; essence. —實は, [*ad.*] ① (眞實) really; in fact. ☞ *jissai* (實際). ② (實を云へば) to tell [speak] the truth; to confess the truth. —實の兄, one's own elder brother. —實の名, the real name. —實の無い, ① insincere; heartless; cold-hearted. ② nominal. —實の所は, the truth is that.... —實を明かす, to reveal the truth. —改革の實を擧げる, to achieve the reality of reform.

jitsu- (實), *a.* actual; real; true. ¶ 實尺, true measure.

jitsubo (地坪), *n.* area.

jitsubo (實母), *n.* the true [real] mother.

jitsubutsu (實物), *n.* the real thing; reality; life. —實物大の, life-size. —實物の樣に描いてある, to be drawn (painted) to the life. ¶ 實物敎授, an object-lesson; object-teaching.

jitsudan (實彈), *n.* a live-shell; a ball-cartridge. ¶ 實彈射擊, target practice.

jitsueki (實益), *n.* utility; use.

jitsugen (實現), *n.* realization; fruition. —實現する, to realize; materialize.

jitsugetsu (日月), *n.* ❶ (日と月) the sun and the moon. ❷ (時) time. ¶ 日月星辰, the host [hosts] of heaven.

jitsugyō (實業), *n.* business; industry (生產業). —實業に從事する, to engage in business. —實業界に投ずる, to enter [go into] the business world. ¶ 實業團體, a business organization. —實業學校, an industrial school. —實業家, a business-man. —實業敎育, industrial [technical] education.

jitsui (實意), *n.* sincerity; faithfulness. —實意のない, insincere; unfaithful; unkind.

jitsuin (實印), *n.* the legal seal.

jitsujō (實情), *n.* the true circumstances. —實情を打明ける, to put a person in possession of the true circumstances.

jitsumei (實名), *n.* the true [real] name.

jitsumeishi (實名詞), *n.* 【文】 a substantive.

jitsumu (實務), *n.* (practical) business. —實務の才, business ability. ¶ 實務家, a business man; a man of business ability (實務の才ある).

jitsu-ni (實に), *ad.* ❶ (眞に) really; indeed; truly. ❷ (甚だ) very; much; exceedingly. —實に美しい景色だ, It is a very beautiful view.

jitsurashii (實らしい), *a.* likely; probable. —さも實らしく, as if it were quite true.

jitsurei (實例), *n.* an example; an instance; an illustration. —實例を示す, to cite an instance; set a person an example.

jitsureki (實歷), *n.* actual experiences.

jitsuri (實利), *n.* utility; material interests (物質的利益). —實利的, utilitarian; practical; useful. ¶ 實利主義, utilitarianism

jitsuroku (實錄), *n.* an authentic record.

jitsuryoku (實力), *n.* real power; real ability. —實力を養成する, to foster real ability.

jitsuyō (實用), *n.* practical use. ¶ 實用英語, practical English. —實用品, a useful article; an article of practical use. —實用新案, a utility model. —實用主義, ① practicality; practicalness. ② 【哲】 pragmatism.

jitsuzai (實在), *n.* (actual) existence; being; reality; actuality. —實在的, real; actual; existent. —實在する, to exist really.

jitsuzuki (地續の), *a.* contiguous *to*; adjacent *to*.

jittai (實體), *n.* 【哲】 noumenon; substance; entity. —實體的, noumenal; substantial; material. —實體なき, insubstantial. ¶ 實體鏡, a stereoscope.

jitte (十手), *n.* a metal truncheon.

jitto (じッと), *ad.* ❶ (熟々) fixedly; steadily; firmly. ❷ (靜かに) still; quietly; patiently (忍耐して). —じッと堪へる, to bear firmly. —じッとして居る, to keep still; remain quiet; stand stockstill. —じッと人の顏を看まもる, to stare fixedly at a person.

jiyaku (持藥), *n.* one's usual medicine [tonic].

jiyo (自餘), *n.* the rest; the remainder; the others.

jiyō (自用の), *a.* for private [personal] use.

jiyō (時樣), *n.* the fashion; the style.

jiyō (滋養), *n.* nourishment; nutrition. —滋養になる, ① [*v.*] to be nutritious. ② [*a.*] (滋養分のある) nourishing; nutritious. —多量の滋養分を含む, to contain a great deal of nutriment [nutritious matter]. ¶ 滋養物, nourishing [nutritious] food.

jiyū (自由), *n.* freedom; liberty. —自由な, free; unrestricted. —身體の自由, personal liberty. —自由行動を執る, to take free action. —自由の身である, to be one's own master. —人の自由を拘束する, to restrict a person's liberty. **——-ni**, *ad.* freely; at liberty; without restraint. —自由自在に, freely; with freedom; unrestrictedly; as one pleases [wishes]. —英語を自由に話す, to speak English fluently. —人を自由にする, to do with another as one pleases. —どうぞ御自由に(なさい), Please yourself; Make yourself at home. ¶ 自由貿易, free trade. —自由畫, free drawing. —自由放任主義,

the *laissez-faire* principle. —自由移民, free immigrants. —自由意思, free will. —自由結婚, a free marriage. —自由港, a free port. —自由國(市), a free state (city). —自由教育, free education. —自由競爭, free [unrestricted] competition. —自由勞働者, casual labourers. —自由思想家, a free-thinker. —自由主義, liberalism (宗教の); the principle of freedom. —自由黨, the liberal party.

jiyū (事由), *n.* a cause; a ground. —正當の事由なく(して), without just cause.

jizai (自在), *n.* ❶(自由) freedom; freeness. ❷(自在鉤) a hanger; a pothook. ¶ 自在畫, free-hand drawing.

jizen (次善の), *a.* next best.

jizen (事前の·に), *a.* & *ad.* before the fact.

jizen (慈善), *n.* charity; benevolence. ¶ 慈善箱, a poor-box; an alms-box [-chest]. —慈善舞踏會, a charity ball. —慈善病院, a charity hospital. —慈善學校, a charity school. —慈善市, a charity fair [bazaar]. —慈善事業, works of charity. —慈善家, a charitable person; a philanthropist. —慈善鍋, a charity-pot.

Jizō (地藏-菩薩), *n.* Jizō (the guardian deity of children). ¶ 地藏顏, a plump, cheerful face.

jizoku (持續的), *a.* durable; standing. —持續する, ① [*vt.*] to continue; sustain; maintain. ② [*vi.*] to endure; last; stand out; remain; hold out; keep up.

jizoku (時俗), *n.* the manners of the age. —時俗に染まる, to become conventional.

jo (序), *n.* ❶(はしがき) a preface; a foreword. ❷(順序) order. ❸(端緒) an opening; a beginning.

jō (上), *n.* ❶(うへ) the above. ❷(優等) the first; the superior; the best. ❸(書物の) the first volume. —上の上, the highest; the very best; the superfine. —…上の事は, as regards; as *to*.

jō (丈), *n.* ❶(尺度) ten *shaku*. ❷(長さ) length.

jō (帖), *n.* (紙を數へる語) a quire (of paper).

jō (狀), *n.* ❶(有樣) condition; state. ❷(書狀) a letter.

jō (條), *n.* ❶(箇條) an article. ❷(線) a line; a streak (電光などの), a stripe (縞などの). —條を逐うて討議する, to discuss article by article.

jō (情), *n.* ❶ feeling; sentiment (情操); affection (情愛). ❷(事情) circumstances. —情がある, ① to have feeling; be friendly. ② to be affectionate. —情に脆い, susceptible; sentimental. —情の深い, affectionate; warm-hearted. —情を通ずる, to become intimate *with*. —情を明かす, to disclose [confide] the truth [circumstances]. —情に於ては許すべきだが, It may be permitted from personal feelings; but....

jō (尉), *n.* white ashes (of burnt charcoal).

jō (錠), *n.* ❶ a lock. ❷(錠劑) a pastille; a tablet, tabloid. —錠を下ろす, [*vt.*] to lock; lock up. —錠をねぢきる, to wrench (away; open) the lock.

jō (孃), *n.* a young lady; an unmarried lady; Miss.

jō (疊), *n.* number of mats. —六疊の間, a six-mat room.

jōai (情愛), *n.* affection. ☞ jō (情).

jōba (乘馬), *n.* ❶(乘ること) horse-riding; riding. ❷(乘る馬) a saddle-horse; a riding horse. —乘馬する, to ride a horse; mount [get on] a horse; take horse. ¶ 乘馬服, a riding-dress; a riding-habit (婦人用). —乘馬隊, a mounted corps. —乘馬用長靴, riding-boots. —乘馬像, an equestrian statue.

jōban (上番), *n.* being on guard; 【軍】guard-mounting.

jōbeki (乘冪), *n.* 【數】power. ¶ 一(二; 三)乘冪, 【數】the first (second; third) power.

jōbi (常備の), *a.* standing. ¶ 常備軍, a standing army. —常備兵役, service with the colours and in the first reserve. —常備艦隊, a standing squadron.

jōbu (上部), *n.* the upper part; the top; the upside.

jōbu (丈夫な), *a.* ❶(壯健) healthy; strong; robust. ❷(鞏固) strong; solid; firm. —丈夫さうな, (身體の) stout-looking; sturdy-looking. —丈夫になる, to become healthy; improve [gain] in health; grow strong. —氣を丈夫に持つ, to keep up one's spirit.

jōbukuro (狀袋), *n.* an envelope.

jobun (序文), *n.* a preface; a foreword.

jōbun (條文), *n.* ❶(箇條) the text (of regulations, &c.). ❷(斑條) a stripe; a streak.

jōbutsu (成佛する), *vi.* to become a Buddha; enter Nirvāna; rest in peace.

jōchi (常置の), *a.* standing; permanent.

jochō (助長する), *vt.* to promote; further; foster; conduce *to*; facilitate. —惡弊を助長する, to promote [aggravate] evils.

jōcho (情緒), *n.* emotion; heart-strings. —情緒纏綿として, being overcome with emotions.

jōchō (上長), *n.* a superior; a senior; an elder (年長者). ¶ 上長官, a field-officer (陸); a captain. a commander (海); a superior officer (上官).

jōchō (冗長な), *a.* diffuse; redundant; prolix.

jōchō (情調), *n.* mood. ¶ 詩的情調, poetical mood.

jochū (女中), *n.* ❶ (下婢) a maidservant; a housemaid; a waitress. ❷ (侍婢) a waiting-woman. ¶ 女中部屋, the maidservants' room. —女中奉公, domestic service (of a woman). —女中頭, the head-servant; the housekeeper.

jōchū (絛蟲), *n.* the tape-worm.

jochūgiku (除蟲菊), *n.* 【植】 a vermifuge-chrysanthemum.

jōdan (戯談, 冗談), *n.* ❶ (戯事) a sport; a trick; a prank. ❷ (戯言) a joke; a jest. —戯談に, jestingly; in fun; in jest. —戯談半分に, half in joke [play]. —戯談を言ふ, to jest; joke; crack a joke. —戯談はさて措き, joking [jesting] apart. —御戯談でせう, You are joking.

jōdo (淨土), *n.* paradise; Elysium.

jōdō (常道), *n.* the universal rule [duty]; the common way [path]; the beaten track.

jodōshi (助動詞), *n.* 【文】 the auxiliary verb.

jōen (上演), *n.* performance; presentation. —上演する, to perform; put on the stage; present.

jōfu (上布), *n.* superior grass-cloth; cambric (白麻の).

jōfu (丈夫), *n.* a hero; a man.

jōfu (情夫), *n.* a lover.

jōfu (情婦), *n.* a mistress.

jofuku-shusshi (除服出仕), *n.* an appearance at office after mourning.

jogai (除外する), *vt.* to except; eclude. —原則に除外例を設く, to make an exception to the rule.

jōgai (場外に), *ad.* outside a hall [room]; outside. —場外に溢れる, to flow outside.

jogakkō (女學校), *n.* a girls' school. ¶ 高等女學校, a girls' high school.

jogaku (序樂), *n.* 【音】 a prelude; an overture.

jōgaku (上顎), *n.* the upper jaw. ¶ 上顎骨, 【解】 the maxillary (bone); the upper jaw-bone.

jogakusei (女學生), *n.* a school-girl; a girl-student.

jōge (上下), *n.* ❶ the upper and lower sides. ❷ (尊卑) superiors and inferiors; high and low. ❸ (官民) the government and the people. —上下に, up and down; above and below; high and low. —上下四方に, in every direction. —上下する, to fluctuate (相場などの); rise and fall. —上下顛倒して, upside down. —上下心を一にして, all classes being unanimous. ¶ 上下動, vertical shock.

jogen (助言), *n.* =*jogon.*

jōgen (上弦), *n.* the first quarter.

jōgi (定木, 定規), *n.* a ruler; a rule; a square. ¶ 雲形定木, a French curve. —丁字定木, a T-square.

jōgi (情誼), *n.* ties of friendship; friendship; friendly feelings. —情誼に厚い, to be warm-hearted; be friendly.

jōgiin (常議員), *n.* a permanent member (of a council).

jogō (除號), *n.* 【數】 the sign of division (÷).

jōgo (上戸), *n.* a drinker; a tippler; a toper. —怒 (笑; 泣) 上戸, one who fumes (laughs; is maudlin) in his cups.

jōgo (冗語), *n.* a redundant [superfluous] word; a redundancy. —冗語を省く, to dispense with redundant expressions.

jōgo (漏斗), *n.* a funnel.

jōgō (定業), *n.* a fixed fate [doom]; predestination; Karma (梵).

jōgō (乘號), *n.* 【數】 the sign of multiplication (×).

jogon (助言), *n.* advice; counsel. —助言する, to advise; give advice; counsel. ¶ 助言者, an adviser.

jōhakukotsu (上膊骨), *n.* 【解】 the humerus.

jōhatsu (蒸發), *n.* 【化】 vaporization; evaporation; volatilization. —蒸發する, ① [*v.*] to evaporate; vaporize. ② [*a.*] vaporable; vaporific. ¶ 蒸發氣, vapour; steam (蒸氣); exhalation.

jōheki (城壁), *n.* a castle-wall; a rampart.

jōhi (上皮), *n.* 【植·解】 the epithelium; the epidermis; the tegument.

jōhi (冗費), *n.* dead [useless] expenses; superfluous expenses.

jōhin (上品な), *a.* refined; polished; genteel. —上品に, gracefully; genteelly. —上品ぶる, to give oneself airs.

joho (徐歩する), *vi.* to saunter; walk slowly.

johō (除法), *n.* 【數】 division.

jōho (讓步), *n.* concession. —讓步する, to concede; make a concession; give way. —讓步的態度をとる, to take a conciliatory attitude.

jōhō (上方), *n.* the upper part. —上方へ動く, to move upwards.

jōhō (乗法), *n.* 【數】multiplication.
jōhō (情報), *n.* an intelligence; a report. —…の旨情報あり, It is reported that.... ¶ 情報局, the intelligence bureau.
joi (女醫), *n.* a lady-doctor; a woman-doctor. ¶ 女醫學校, a women's medical college.
joi (敍位), *n.* conferment of [conferring] a rank.
jōi (上位), *n.* a superior rank; precedence. —…の上位に立つ, to be higher in rank than; take precedence [rank] *of*.
jōi (情意), *n.* sentiment. ¶ 情意投合, unity of sentiment; mutual understanding.
jōi (攘夷), *n.* exclusion of foreigners.
jōi (讓位), *n.* abdication (of the Throne). —讓位する, to abdicate (the crown; the Throne).
jōin (上院), *n.* the Upper House; the Senate (佛國及び北米合衆國). ¶ 上院議員, a member of the Upper House; a senator.
jōin (冗員), *n.* superfluous officials; supernumeraries. ¶ 冗員淘汰, the dismissal of superfluous officials.
joji (女兒), *n.* a girl; a daughter.
joji (序次), *n.* order; sequence.
joji (敍事), *n.* 【修】narration; description. —敍事的, narrative; descriptive. —敍事體に書く, to write in narrative style. ¶ 敍事文, a narrative; a description.
jōji (情事), *n.* an intrigue; a love affair.
jōjin (常人), *n.* an ordinary [a common] man; the run of people (集合的に).
jōjin (情人), *n.* a lover; a love; a sweetheart.
jōjitsu (情實), *n.* ❶ private circumstances [considerations] ❷ (實情) the real facts (of a case). —情實に動かされる, to be influenced by private [personal] considerations.
jojo (徐徐に), *ad.* slowly; gradually; by degrees.
jōjō (上乘), *n.* the best; a masterpiece. —上乘な, the very best.
jōjō (上場する), *vt.* to present; produce; put on the stage.
jōjō (情狀), *n.* circumstances. —情狀を酌量する, to take the (extenuating) circumstances into consideration.
jojōfu (女丈夫), *n.* a heroine; an Amazon.
jojōshi (抒情詩), *n.* lyric poetry; a lyric; a lyrical poem.
jōju (成就), *n.* accomplishment; completion; success. **——-suru**, *vt.* to accomplish (自己の計畫など); complete (完成する); succeed *in*. —目的を成就する, to attain one's object.
jōjun (上旬), *n.* the first ten days (of a month).
jojutsu (敍述), *n.* description; delineation; narration. —敍述する, to describe; narrate; delineate. ¶ 敍述(的)形容詞, the predicative adjective. —敍述者, a relater; a narrator; a delineator.
jōjutsu (上述の), *a.* the above; the above-mentioned; aforesaid. —上述の如く, as above-stated [aforesaid].
jōka (上下), *n.* =*jōge* (上下).
jōka (城下), *n.* a castle-town.
jōka (情火), *n.* a fire of passion.
jōka (情歌), *n.* a love-song; a love-ode.
jōka (蒸化する), *vt.* to evaporate; vaporize.
jōkaku (城郭), *n.* a castle; a stronghold.
jōkaku (乘客), *n.* =*jōkyaku*.
jokan (女官), *n.* a court lady; a maid of honour; a lady-in-waiting.
jōkan (上官), *n.* a chief; a superior officer; a senior (officer).
jōkan (條款), *n.* articles; provisions; clauses.
jōkan (鑲嵌), *n.* 【齒科】inlay.
jokei (女系), *n.* the female side.
jokei (敍景), *n.* description of scenery; a scenery sketch.
jōkei (情景), *n.* ❶ a scene; a prospect. ❷ (心的作用と自然現象) nature and sentiment.
joken (女權), *n.* woman's [women's] rights; woman [female] suffrage (女子參政權). ¶ 女權擴張論, feminism. (女權擴張論者, a feminist; a (woman-) suffragist (女子參政權主張者); a suffragette (參政權獲得運動をなす女子).
jōken (條件), *n.* 【法】a condition; terms. —…の條件の下に; の條件附きで, under [on] condition that.... —條件を附ける, to make conditions; annex conditions *to*; tie up. ¶ 條件法, 【文】the conditional mood. —條件句, 【文】a conditional clause.
jōki (上記の), *a.* =*jōjutsu*.
jōki (上氣する), *vi.* to be dizzy; have vertigo.
jōki (條規), *n.* provisions; articles.
jōki (常規), *n.* a groove; a beaten track [path]. —常規に拘泥する, to move along the old groove. —常規を逸する, to be off the rails; go off the track.
jōki (蒸氣), *n.* ❶ steam (水蒸氣); a vapour (蒸發氣). ❷ (蒸氣船) a steamer; a steamship. —蒸氣を起す, to generate steam. ¶ 蒸氣機關, a steam-engine. —蒸氣喞筒, a steam-pump; a steam fire-engine (消防用).
jōkigen (上機嫌), *n.* high spirits;

good humour; cheerfulness. —上機嫌で, good-humouredly; in high spirits.

jokō (女工), *n.* a factory girl; a factory hand.

jokō (女皇), *n.* an empress; a queen.

jokō (徐行する), *vi.* to walk slow; go slowly; crawl; creep. —最徐行 (電車), "Run very slowly."

jōkō (條項), *n.* articles; provisions; stipulations; clauses.

jōkō (情交), *n.* friendship; intimacy. —情交を結ぶ, to become intimate *with.*

jōkō (常衡), *n.* avoirdupois.

jōkoku (上告), *n.* 【法】an appeal; a demand for revision. —上告する, to appeal; demand revision. 上告を破毀(棄却)する, to quash (reject) the appeal. ¶ 上告人, 【法】an appellant; a demandant; an applicant for revision.

jōkon (條痕), *n.* a stria; a streak.

jōkū (上空), *n.* the upper regions; the sky.

jokuchi (辱知諸君), *n.* my friends.

jokun (敍勳), *n.* conferment of a decoration.

jokusho (溽暑), *n.* sultriness.

jokusō (褥瘡), *n.* a bed-sore.

jōkyaku (乘客), *n.* a passenger; a fare. ¶ 乘客案內所, an inquiry office. —乘客係, a passenger agent. —乘客手荷物, a luggage.

jōkyaku (常客), *n.* a regular customer; a patron; a habitué.

jokyo (除去する), *vt.* to remove; clear; eliminate.

jokyō (助敎), *n.* an assistant teacher [master]; an usher.

jōkyō (上京する), *vi.* to go [come] (up) to town [Tōkyō]. —上京の途に上る, to start [leave] for Tōkyō.

jōkyō (狀況, 情況), *n.* circumstances; conditions; situation. —目下の狀況では, under existing conditions; in the present state of things.

jokyōju (助敎授), *n.* an assistant-professor.

jokyōshi (女敎師), *n.* a female teacher; a schoolmistress.

jokyū (女給), *n.* a waitress.

jōkyū (上級), *n.* a high class [grade]. ¶ 上級官廳, the superior authorities. —上級裁判所, a superior court. —上級生, a higher-grade student; an advanced student; a senior student.

jōmae (錠前), *n.* a lock. ☞ *jō* (錠). ¶ 錠前屋, a locksmith.

jomaku (序幕), *n.* the opening [first] act; a prelude.

jomaku (除幕する), *v.* to unveil. ¶ 除幕式, the (ceremony of) unveiling.

jōman (冗漫), *n.* diffuseness; prolixity. —冗漫な, diffuse; prolix.

jomei (助命), *n.* sparing a life; quarter (俘虜の). —助命する, to spare another's life; give quarter.

jomei (除名), *n.* expulsion; striking off a name. —除名する, to expel *from*; take [strike] a person's name off the book [list].

jōmi (情味), *n.* charm; relish.

jōmon (定紋), *n.* a family crest; a coat of arms.

jōmu (常務), *n.* ordinary [regular] business. ¶ 常務委員, a standing committee. —常務取締役, a managing director.

jōmuin (乘務員), *n.* a man on car service; a trainman; employees serving on a train (*etc.*).

jōmyaku (靜脈), *n.* the vein. ¶ 靜脈血, venous blood.

jōmyō (定命), *n.* fatality; the destined duration of life.

jōnai (場內), *n.* enclosure; the inside of a hall (會場內). ——, *ad.* in the enclosure; in the grounds; in the hall.

jōnetsu (情熱), *n.* passion.

jonin (敍任), *n.* conferment and appointment.

jōnin (常任), *a.* standing; in ordinary. ¶ 常任書記, a permanent clerk.

joō (女王), *n.* ❶ (女皇) a queen. ❷ (五世以下の女皇族) a princess.

jōran (上覽), *n.* Imperial inspection.

jōran (擾亂), *n.* agitation; disturbances; riot. —擾亂する, to agitate; throw into disorder [confusion].

jorei (女禮), *n.* female etiquette.

jōrei (條例), *n.* an act; regulations.

jōrei (常例), *n.* usage; cutsom; convention.

joren (鋤簾), *n.* a dredge; a scoop; a trowel (園丁用の).

jōren (定連), *n.* regular patrons [customers].

jōri (條理), *n.* reason. —條理ある(なき), reasonable (unreasonable). —條理に適ふ, to accord [square] with reason.

jōri (情理), *n.* sentiment and reason.

jōriku (上陸), *n.* landing; disembarkation. —上陸する, to land; disembark; go ashore. ¶ 上陸地, a landing; a landing-place. —上陸地點, the point of disembarkation; the landing spot. —上陸軍, a landing force.

joro (如露), *n.* a watering-pot.

joron (序論), *n.* introduction.

jōrui (城壘), *n.* a fortress (城寨); a rampart (壘壁).

jōruri (淨瑠璃), *n.* a (kind of) ballad-drama.

jōryō (丈量-法), *n.* measurement; gauging. —丈量する, to measure (土地を); gauge (桝など).

joryoku (助力), *n.* assistance; help; aid. —助力する, to help; aid; assist. —他の助力を籍らずに, without another's help; unaided.

jōryokuju (常綠樹), *n.* an evergreen (tree).

joryū (女流), *n.* a female; the fair sex ¶ 女流文學者, a woman of letters. —女流作家, a woman [lady] writer.

jōryū (上流), *n.* ❶ (川上) the upper stream. ❷ (上流社會) the higher [upper] classes. ¶ 上流人士, gentlefolks; people of quality. —上流社會, (high) society; the higher classes.

jōryū (蒸溜-法), *n.* distillation. ¶ 蒸溜器, a still; a pot-still (汽套なき). —蒸溜酒, spirituous liquors. —蒸溜裝置, distillatory apparatus. —蒸溜水, distilled water.

jōsai (城砦, 城寨), *n.* a fortress; a stronghold.

josainai (如才ない), *a.* smart; tactful; adroit. —如才なく立廻る, to move about with great adroitness.

josanpu (助產婦), *n.* a midwife. ☞ *sanba.*

jōsashi (狀插), *n.* a letter-file; a letter-rack.

josei (女性), *n.* ❶ womanhood; the female [fair; gentle; soft; weaker] sex. ❷【文】the feminine gender. —女性的, feminine; effeminate.

josei (女婿), *n.* a son-in-law.

josei (助成する), *vt.* to aid; assist; foster. ¶ 助成金, a subsidy.

josei (助勢する), *vt.* to help; assist; second.

jōsei (上製), *n.* superior make; superior get-up (本の).

jōsei (情勢), *n.* situation; condition; the state of affairs.

jōsei (醸成する), *vt.* to brew; arouse; cause; breed.

joseito (女生徒), *n.* a girl-student; a schoolgirl.

joseki (除籍する), *vt.* to remove from a census-register.

jōseki (上席), *n.* seniority; precedence; an upper seat (上座). ☞ *shuseki.* —の上席を占める, to take precedence [rank] *of.*

jōsen (乘船), *n.* embarkation. —乘船する, to embark; go aboard (a ship); go on board. ¶ 乘船賃, (passage) fare; passage-money. —乘船切符, a passage-ticket.

josetsu (絮說する), *vt.* to dwell *on*; enlarge *upon*; expatiate *on.*

jōsetsu (常設の), *a.* standing; permanent. —常設する, to establish permanently. ¶ 常設館, a permanent hall.

josetsusha (除雪車), *n.* a snow-ploughing car; a snow-plough.

jōsha (乘車する), *vi.* to take a train (tram-car, *etc.*); ride in a train (car; carriage, *etc.*). ¶ 乘車賃, fare; railway [car] fare. —乘車券, a ticket; a railway (tram-car) ticket. (割引 (回數; 定期) 乘車券, a cheap (commutation; season) ticket. —急行乘車券, an express ticket. —鐵道無賃乘車券, a railway pass.)

jōsha (淨寫), *n.* a fair [clean] copy. ☞ *jōsho.*

joshaku (敍爵), *n.* ennoblement; conferring a peerage.

joshi (女子), *n.* ❶ (女兒) a girl; a daughter. ❷ (婦人) a female; a woman. ¶ 女子大學, the Women's [Ladies'] University. —女子敎育, female education; education of women. —女子參政權, woman [female] suffrage. (女子參政權論者, a (woman-)suffragist; a suffragette (獲得運動をなす女).)

joshi (女史), *n.* Mrs.; Miss (未婚者に); Madame.

jōshi (城址), *n.* the remains of a castle; the site of castle.

jōshi (情死), *n.* a love suicide. —情死する, to die together for love.

jōshiki (常識), *n.* common sense; good sense; mother-wit. —常識ある人, a man of sense. —常識に富む, to be full of common sense; be very sensible.

joshin (女神), *n.* a goddess.

jōshin (上申), *n.* a report. —上申する, to report. ¶ 上申書, a written report.

joshō (女將), *n.* a mistress; a landlady. ☞ *okami.*

jōsho (淨書), *n.* a fair copy. —淨書する, to write out fair; make a fair [clean] copy *of.*

jōshō (上昇する), *vi.* to rise; ascend; climb.

jōshō (常勝の), *a.* ever-victorious.

joshoku (女色), *n.* a woman's beauty; a fair face.

jōshoku (常食), *n.* diet; usual food.

joshu (助手), *n.* an assistant.

joshū (女囚), *n.* a female prisoner.

jōshū (常習), *n.* a common custom (社會の); a habit (個人の). ¶ 常習犯, habitual crime: (人) a habitual criminal. —賭博常習者, a confirmed gambler.

josō (女裝する), *vi.* to put on a female [woman's] dress [garb]; dress up as a woman.

jōso (上訴する), *vi.* to appeal (to a higher court).

jōsō (上奏する), *vt.* to report to the Throne [His Majesty]; memorialize the Throne. ¶ 上奏案, a draft memorial to the Throne.
jōsō (上層), *n.* superstratum (地層などの); upper regions (上空). —社會の上層, the upper crust; the upper stratum of society.
jōsō (情操), *n.* sentiment.
joson (女尊男卑), *n.* respect for woman at the expense of man.
josū (序數), *n.* an ordinal (number) (cardinal の對).
josū (除數), *n.* 【數】 a divisor.
jōsū (乘數), *n.* 【數】 a multiplier.
jōsū (常數), *n.* ❶ (自然の運命) the natural course (of things); destiny; fate. ❷【數・理】 a constant; an invariable.
jōsui (上水), *n.* water-supply; waterworks.
jōsui (淨水), *n.* ❶ (清水) clean water. ❷ water for cleaning. ¶ 淨水場, a cleaning bed.
jo-suru (敍する), *vt.* ❶ (敍位) to create; invest *with*; confer *on*. ❷ (敍述) to describe.
jo-suru (恕する), *vt.* to forgive; pardon; overlook.
jotai (除隊), *n.* 【軍】 discharge from military service. ¶ 除隊兵, time-expired soldiers; discharged soldiers.
jōtai (上腿), *n.* 【解】 the femur; the thigh.
jōtai (狀態), *n.* state; condition. —現在の狀態では, as the case stands at present; in the present state of affairs.
jōtai (常態), *n.* the normal state [condition].
jōtan (上端), *n.* the top; the head; the upper end.
jōtatsu (上達する), *v.* to progress; advance (*in*); improve (*in*); attain proficiency.
jotei (女帝), *n.* an empress (-regnant); a queen(-regnant).
jōtei (上帝), *n.* God; the Lord.
jōtei (上程する), *vt.* to put on the orders of the day; put on the calendar; bring up for discussion; lay before the Diet.
jōto(讓渡), *n.* =*yuzuriwatashi.*
jōtō (上等の), *a.* first-rate; first-class. —最上等の; 上等飛切りの, of the finest [highest] quality. ¶ 上等兵, a superior private. —上等席 (室), the first-class seat (cabin).
jōtō (常套), *n.* commonplace; triteness. ¶ 常套語, a household word; a hackneyed word; a trite saying. —常套手段, worn-out measures.
jōtokui (定得意), *n.* a regular customer.
jōtōshiki (上棟式), *n.* a celebration of the completion of the framework (of a house).
jōwa (情話), *n.* a love-story.
joya (除夜), *n.* the watch-night; the New Year's Eve.
jōyado (定宿), *n.* one's usual hotel.
joyaku (助役), *n.* ❶ (市の) a deputy-mayor; (町村の) the headman's assistant. ❷ (驛の) an assistant station-master.
jōyaku (條約), *n.* a treaty; a convention. —條約上の權利, treaty rights. —條約を締結(破棄)する, to conclude (denounce) a treaty. ¶ 條約國, a treaty-power. —條約締結權, treaty-making powers.
jōyatoi, jōyō, (常傭), *n.* regular employ. ¶ 常傭人夫, a regular employee.
jōyo (剩餘), *n.* 【數】 remainder; surplus. ¶ 剩餘金, a surplus fund. —剩餘價值, surplus value.
jōyo (讓與), *n.* cession (領土等の); concession (特權・利權等の); transfer (讓渡). —讓與する, to cede; concede; transfer.
jōyō (常用), *n.* permanent use; common use. —常用の器具, utensils for daily use. ¶ 常用語, common words; everyday words.
jōyoku (情慾), *n.* passions; desire. —情慾の奴隸, a slave of passions.
joyū (女優), *n.* an actress.
jōza (上座), *n.* the top-seat; the upper seat; the chief seat.
jōzai (淨財), *n.* 【宗】 offertory; offerings.
jōzai (淨罪), *n.* purgation from sins.
jōzai (錠劑), *n.* a lozenge; a pastille; a tablet, tabloid.
jōzetsu (饒舌), *n.* talkativeness; chattiness; garrulity. —饒舌を弄する, to wag the [one's] tongue. ¶ 饒舌家, a talkative person; a chatterbox.
jōzō (釀造), *n.* brewing; brewage. —釀造する, to brew. ¶ 釀造者, a brewer. —釀造所, a brewery.
jōzu (上手), *n.* ❶ (熟練) skill; dexterity. ❷ (上手な人) an expert; an adept; a good hand. —上手な, skilful; dexterous; expert; proficient. —上手に出來てる, to be cleverly done; be skilfully made. —お上手を云ふ, to make compliments *to*; say nice things; flatter. —なんでも上手である, to be skilful in [a good hand at] everything.
jō-zuru (乘ずる), *v.* ❶【數】 to multiply. ❷ =*noru* (乘る). ❸ (つけこむ) to avail oneself *of*; take advantage *of*. —怒りに乘じて, in the heat of passion. —勝に乘じて, flushed with victory.

ju (從), *a.* secondary; subordinate; junior. —從一位, the first court rank, junior grade.
ju (綬), *n.* a ribbon; a cordon.
ju (壽), *n.* ❶ (祝賀) congratulation; felicitation. ❷ (長命) longevity; long life. ❸ (年齡) age; natural life (壽命).
ju (儒), *n.* ❶ (孔子の道) Confucianism. ❷ (學徳秀でた人) a Confucian scholar; a Confucianist.
jū (十), *n.* ten. —十中の九まで, nine (times) out of ten; in nine cases out of ten.
jū (從たる), *a.* 【法】 accessory (principal の對); secondary; subordinate. —從たる原因, a secondary cause.
jū (銃), *n.* a gun; a musket; a rifle (施條銃). —銃の肩を代へる, to change arms. —銃を組む(解く), to pile (unpile) arms; stack (unstack) arms. —銃を捧げる, to present arms.
-jū (中に), all over; in all ...; throughout. —世界中に, all the world over.
jūbai (十倍の), *a.* tenfold. —十倍にして返す, to return it tenfold.
jūbako (重箱), *n.* a nest of boxes.
juban (襦袢), *n.* an underwear; an undershirt; a chemise (女の肌著).
jūboku (從僕), *n.* a servant; a valet; a lackey.
jūbun (十分, 充分), *ad.* enough; fully; sufficiently. ——**-na,** *a.* enough; sufficient; full. —十分な報酬, an adequate return (for).
jūbun (十分の), *a.* (十に分けた) decimal. —十分の一, a tenth. —十分の九, nine-tenths.
jūbutsu (從物), *n.* 【法】 an accessory (thing).
jūbyō (重病), *n.* a serious illness.
jūchin (重鎭), *n.* a leader; a man of influence; an authority.
jūchū-hakku (十中八九), *ad.* in eight or nine cases out of ten; in a vast majority of cases. ☞ *jū.*
jūdai (十代), *n.* teens (十三より十九までの年齡). —十代に, in one's teens.
jūdai (重大な), *a.* serious; grave; important —重大な過失, a gross negligence. —重大な結果, grave consequences. —重大な任務を帶びて, on an important mission. —重大視する, to regard as serious; take a serious view *of.* ¶ 某重大事件, a certain serious affair.
jūdai (重代の), *a.* for (of) successive generations. —先祖重代の寶, a treasure handed down from one's ancestors.
judaku (受諾する), *vt.* to accept. —招請を受諾する, to accept an invitation.
jūdan (縱斷する), *v.* to cut [divide] vertically. ¶ 縱斷面, a longitudinal section.
judō (受動的), *a.* passive (active の對). —受動的反抗, passive resistance. ¶ 受動調[態], 【文】 the passive (voice).
jūdō (柔道), *n.* jūdō〔日〕; jū-jutsu; jiu-jutsu. ¶ 柔道師範, an instructor [teacher] of *jūdō;* a jiu-jutsian. —柔道家, an expert in *jūdō.*
jūdon (重鈍の), *a.* dull.
juei (樹瘿), *n.* a wart.
jueki (樹液), *n.* sap; milk.
jūeki (汁液), *n.* juice.
jūeki (獸疫), *n.* a cattle-disease [-plague].
juekisha (受益者), *n.* 【法】 a person enriched (利得者); a beneficiary (受益權者).
jūen (重緣), *n.* cross-marriages.
jufu (呪符), *n.* an amulet; a charm; a periapt.
jūfuku (重複), *n.* =*chōfuku.*
jufun (授粉), *n.* 【植】 pollination.
jugaku (儒學), *n.* Confucianism.
jūgan (銃丸), *n.* a bullet.
jūgan (銃眼), *n.* 【軍】 a loophole; a crenel; a crenelle.
jūgatsu (十月), *n.* October.
jūgo (十五), *n.* fifteen; the fifteenth (第十五). ¶ 十五分, a quarter of an hour. —十五夜, the night of the full moon.
jūgun (從軍する), *v.* to join the army; take part in a campaign. —從軍を願ひ出る, to apply for attachment to the army. ¶ 從軍記者, a war-correspondent. —從軍記章, a war-medal.
jugyō (授業する), *vt.* to teach; instruct; give lessons. ¶ 授業時間, school-time; lesson [school] hours. —授業料, school-fee(-s); tuition-fee.
jūgyō (從業する), *vi.* to be in employment. ¶ 從業時間, working hours. —從業員, an operative; an employee; a servant.
jūhachi (十八), *n.* eighteen; the eighteenth (第十八). ¶ 十八番, ① the eighteenth. ② (おはこ) a favourite trick [performance]; a hobby; speciality. (十八番をやる, to ride one's horse [hobby].)
jūhan (從犯), *n.* ❶ being accessory. ❷ (從犯者) an accessory (to a crime).
juhi (樹皮), *n.* the bark; the cortex.
jūhi (鞣皮), *n.* ❶ tanning. ❷ (柔皮) tanned leather. ¶ 鞣皮業, tannery.
jūhi (獸皮), *n.* hide; skin; fell. ¶ 獸皮商, a fell-monger; a skin-merchant.

jūhō (什寶), *n.* a treasure.
jūhō (重砲), *n.* a heavy gun.
jūhō (重寶), *n.* a precious treasure.
jūhō (銃包), *n.* a cartridge.
jūhō (銃砲), *n.* guns; fire-arms. ¶ 銃砲商, a dealer in fire-arms; a gun-merchant.
jūi (重圍), *n.* a siege; an investment. —重圍に陷る, to be invested by the enemy.
jūi (獸醫), *n.* a veterinary (surgeon). ¶ 獸醫學, veterinary science. —獸醫學校, a veterinary school.
jūichi (十一), *n.* eleven; the eleventh (第十一).
jūichigatsu (十一月), *n.* November.
jūin (充員), *n.* the reserve; drafts. ¶ 充員召集, general levy; levy in mass [*en masse*]; calling out of the reserve.
juisha (受遺者), *n.* 【法】 a legatee; a devisee (不動產の).
jūjaku (柔弱), *n.* effeminacy; weakness; feebleness. —柔弱な, effeminate; weak; feeble.
jūji (十字 -形), *n.* a cross. ¶ 十字街, cross-roads. —十字軍, crusaders. —十字火, a cross-fire. —十字架, a cross; a crucifix.
jūji (住持), *n.* an abbot; the superior (of a temple).
jūji (從事する), *v.* to engage *in*; pursue; devote oneself *to*.
jūjin (柔靱な), *a.* elastic; flexible. —柔靱な皮, soft leather.
jūjitsu (充實), *n.* abundance; fulness; completion. —充實する, to complete; perfect; fill up. —內容が充實してゐる, to be full of matter.
juju (授受), *n.* transfer; delivery and receipt. —授受する, to transfer; deliver.
jūjū (重重), *ad.* repeatedly. —重重申譯がありません, I have absolutely nothing to say in excuse.
jūjun (柔順), *n.* gentleness; meekness. —柔順な, gentle; meek; obedient; submissive.
jūjun (從順), *n.* obedience; docility; tractability. —從順な, obedient; docile; tractable.
jūjutsu (柔術), *n.* jū-jutsu; jiu-jutsu. ☞ *jūdō* (柔道).
jūka (銃火), *n.* rifle-fire.
jūkan (縱貫する), *vi.* to run lengthwise.
jūkazei (從價稅), *n.* an *ad valorem* duty. ¶ 從價稅率, *ad valorem* tariff.
jūkei (銃刑), *n.* punishment of death by shooting. —銃刑に處する, to sentence a person to be shot.
jukeisha (受刑者), *n.* a convict; a convicted person.
jūkeitei (從兄弟), *n.* a cousin.
juken (受驗), *n.* undergoing an examination. ¶ 受驗科目, subjects for examination. —受驗料, an examination-fee. —受驗者, an examinee; a candidate for an examination. —受驗資格, qualifications for examination.
juken (授權する), *vt.* to authorize [empower] (a person to do ...).
jūken (銃劍), *n.* ❶ (銃と劍) a rifle and a sword. ❷ (銃用劍) a bayonet. ¶ 銃劍術, bayonet exercise. —銃劍突擊, a bayonet charge.
jūketsu (充血), *n.* 【醫】 congestion; hyperæmia. —充血する(さす), to congest. —充血した, congested; bloodshot (眼に云ふ).
jūki (什器), *n.* utensils; household furniture; fittings.
jūki (銃機), *n.* a gun-lock.
jukkei (術計), *n.* a stratagem; an artifice.
jukkō (熟考), *n.* mature [careful] consideration; deliberation. —熟考の上, after careful consideration. —熟考する, to consider carefully; ponder (*over*); think *over*; deliberate.
jūkō (銃工), *n.* a gunsmith.
jūkō (銃口), *n.* the muzzle.
jūkon (重婚), *n.* bigamy. —重婚する, to commit bigamy. ¶ 重婚者, a bigamist.
juku (塾), *n.* a boarding-school; a private school.
jūku (十九), *n.* nineteen; the nineteenth (第十九).
jukuchi (熟知する), *vt.* to be familiar *with*; be acquainted *with*; have full knowledge *of*.
jukudan (熟談), *n.* careful consultation. —熟談する, to consult carefully; talk over fully.
jukudoku (熟讀する), *vt.* to read carefully; peruse.
jukugi (熟議), *n.* careful [mature] deliberation. —熟議する, to deliberate fully.
jukugo (熟語), *n.* ❶ (熟字) a Chinese compound word. ❷ (慣用熟語) a phrase; an idiomatic phrase; an idiom. ¶ 新熟語, a new-coined phrase.
jukuhi (熟皮), *n.* tanned hide; leather.
jukuren (熟練), *n.* skill; dexterity; mastery. —熟練な, skilful; skilled; practised. —熟練して居る, to be experienced *in*; be skilled [practised] *in*. ¶ 熟練家, an expert; a man of experience.
jukushi (熟柿), *n.* a ripe [mellowed] persimmon. ¶ 熟柿主義, a waiting policy.

jukushi (熟視する), *vt.* to gaze *at*; look steadily *at*; scrutinize.

jukusui (熟睡), *n.* deep [sound] sleep. —熟睡する, to sleep soundly [fast].

juku-suru (熟する), *vi.* ❶ to ripen; mature; mellow. ❷ (熟錬) to become skilful; acquire skill. —熟した果物, ripe fruits. —業務に熟する, to be matured in one's business.

jukutatsu (熟達), *n.* mastery; proficiency; skill. —熟達せる, skilled; proficient. —熟達する, to master; attain proficiency *in*; be versed *in*. ¶ 熟達者, an adept; a master.

jukyō (儒教), *n.* Confucianism; the teaching of Confucius.

jūkyo (住居), *n.* dwelling; residence. —住居する, to live *in*; dwell *in*; reside *in*. —住居を定める, to take up one's residence *in*. ¶ 住居人, a resident; an occupant; an inhabitant.

jūman (十萬), *n.* a hundred thousand.

jūman (充滿), *n.* fulness; abundance; repletion. —充滿さす, to fill. —充滿する, to be full *of*; be filled *with*; teem with.

jūmen (澁面), *n.* a wry face; a grimace. —澁面する, to make a wry face.

jūmentai (十面體), *n.* a decahedron.

jūmin (住民), *n.* inhabitants; population; residents.

jūmō (獸毛), *n.* animal hair.

jumoku (樹木), *n.* a tree.

jumon (呪文), *n.* a spell; a charm; an incantation. —呪文を唱へる, to make an incantation; chant a spell.

jūmonji (十文字), *n.* a cross. 十文字の, cross-shaped; cruciform. —十文字に, crosswise; in a cross.

jūmotsu (什物), *n.* = *jūki.*

jumyō (壽命), *n.* life; the destined length of life; (one's) natural life. —壽命が縮まる (延びる), to shorten (lengthen) one's life.

jun (旬), *n.* ❶ (十日) a period of ten days. ❷ (時として十年) ten years; a decade.

jun (純), *n.* purity. **——**, *a.* ❶ (金銀につき) pure; fine; solid. ❷ (利益などにつき) clear; net. —純な, pure. ¶ 純量 (收入; 能率), net weight (income; efficiency).

jun (順), *n.* ❶ (順番) order. ❷ (順當) favourableness; seasonableness; naturalness. —順を變へる, to change the order. —順を逐うて, in order; in regular sequence. **——-ni**, *ad.* in (regular) order; one by one. —身長の順に竝ぶ, to stand in order of height.

junan (受難), *n.* sufferings. ¶ 受難劇, a passion play.

jūnan (柔軟な), *a.* soft; flexible; supple. ¶ 柔軟體操, free gymnastics; callisthenics.

junban (順番), *n.* order; turn (輪番). —順番に, in order; in turn. (順番に入り換る, to change [take one's turn] in order.) —順番を狂はす, to disturb the order.

junbi (準備), *n.* preparation; arrangement; outfit. —準備する, to prepare; arrange *for*; get ready *for*. —準備中である, to be getting ready *for*; be in course of preparation. —試驗準備をする, to prepare oneself for examination. ¶ 準備金, a reserve fund. (法定 (責任) 準備金, legal (liability) reserve.)

junboku (淳朴な), *a.* simple; homely; simple-hearted [-minded]; naïve.

junbun (純分 -度), *n.* fineness (金・銀の).

junchi (馴致する), *v.* ❶ to habituate *to*; naturalize; domesticate. ❷ (來たす) to give rise *to*; lead *to*; bring *on*.

junchō (順調), *n.* ❶ (順よく調ふこと) favourableness; smoothness (すらすら); satisfactoriness (滿足); seasonableness (陽氣の). ❷ (平穩な工合) normality. —順調の, favourable; prosperous. —順調に復する, to resume its normal condition. —順調に進む [行く], to proceed favourably (談判等が); go smoothly.

juṅeki (純益), *n.* net [clear] profit (gross profit の對).

juṅen (順延), *n.* postponement (in order). —雨天順延, in case of rain, to be postponed till the next fine [fair] day.

jūnen (十年), *n.* ten years; a decade. —十年一日の如く, with unswerving fidelity; without intermission for ten years.

jungetsu (閏月), *n.* an intercalary month.

junguri (順繰に), *ad.* in order. —順繰りに出る, to appear in turn.

jungyaku (順逆), *n.* ❶ right and wrong. ❷ (外國貿易外國爲替相場の) favourableness and unfavourableness.

jungyō (巡業), *n.* a provincial tour (of strolling players, &c.). —巡業する, to stroll (田舍を).

juṅi (順位), *n.* order; rank. ☞ *jun* (順).

jūni (十二), *n.* twelve; a dozen; the twelfth (第十二). ¶ 十二支, the twelve zodiacal signs; the twelve branches of the sexagenary cycle. —十二指腸, 【醫】 the duodenum. (十二指腸蟲, Dochmius duodenalis; the hook-worm.)

jūnigatsu (十二月), *n.* December.

jūniku (獸肉), *n.* (animal) flesh; meat (食用の).

jūnin (十人), *n.* ten men. —十人十色, so many men, so many minds. —十人竝の器量, ① (才) ordinary ability. ② (容) ordinary personal appearance.

jūnin (住人), *n.* an inhabitant; a resident; a dweller.

jūnin (重任), *n.* ❶ (重き任) a heavy responsibility; a responsible position [post] (地位). ❷ (再任) reappointment. —重任する, to be reappointed. —重任を負ふ, to shoulder a heavy responsibility.

junji (順次), *n.* order. ☞ *junjo.* ——, *ad.* in order; successively; one by one.

junjitsu (旬日), *n.* a period of ten days; a decade. —旬日を出でずして, within ten days.

junjo (順序), *n.* ❶ (次第) order; sequence. ❷ (手續) procedure; process; method. —順序不同, not in order. —順序よく, in good order; methodically. —順序を誤る, to follow a wrong order. —順序書を作る, to form a programme.

junjun (順順に), *ad.* in order; in turn.

junjun (諄諄と), *ad.* carefully; earnestly.

junkai (巡回, 巡廻), *n.* ❶ (巡行) a tour; a round. ❷ (巡視) a tour of inspection. —巡廻する, ① [*v.*] to patrol (巡査·番兵·番人等が); make the round *of*; make [go] one's rounds. ② [*a.*] circulatory; itinerant. ¶ 巡廻敎師 (講演者), an itinerant teacher (lecturer). —巡廻裁判所, a circuit court.

junkan (循環), *n.* circulation; rotation; cycle. —循環する, to circulate; recur; rotate. ¶ 循環小(級)數, recurring decimals (series). —循環論法, 【論】 circular reasoning; reasoning in a circle; begging the question. —循環數, repetend.

junken (巡檢), *n.* a round; a visit. =*junsatsu.*

junketsu (純血の), *a.* pure; full-blooded; thorough-bred (馬の).

junketsu (純潔), *n.* purity; pure-mindedness. —純潔な, pure; pure-minded; chaste. —純潔無垢の處女, a chaste [virtuous] maiden.

junkin (純金), *n.* pure [solid] gold.

junkinjisan (準禁治產), *n.* 【法】 quasi-incompetence. ¶ 準禁治產者, a quasi-incompetent (person).

junkō (巡幸), *n.* an Imperial tour; a Royal progress.

junkō (巡航), *n.* a cruise. —巡航する, to cruise.

junkoku (殉國), *n.* sacrifice of one's life for one's country.

junkyo (準據する), *v.* to be based *upon*; conform *to*; comply *with*. —に準據して, in conformity *with* [*to*]; in accordance *with*; in pursuance *of*.

junkyō (順境), *n.* a favourable condition; favourable circumstances; prosperity. —順境に向ふ, to take a favourable turn.

junkyō (殉敎), *n.* martyrdom. ¶ 殉敎者, a martyr.

junkyōin (准敎員), *n.* an assistant-teacher (in an elementary school).

junnan (殉難), *n.* martyrdom. —殉難する, to sacrifice [lay down] one's life for one's country [sovereign]. ¶ 殉難者, a martyr; a victim (遭難者).

junnen (閏年), *n.* a leap year.

junō (受納する), *v.* to accept.

jun'ō (順應), *n.* adaptation; respondency. —順應する, to accommodate [adapt] oneself *to*; respond *to*.

jūnō (十能), *n.* a fire-shovel.

jūnō (重農主義), *n.* 【經】 physiocracy. ¶ 重農主義者, a physiocrat.

junpai (巡拜する), *v.* to make a pilgrimage.

junpaku (純白の), *a.* pure-white; pearly.

junpitsu (潤筆料), *n.* a fee for writing (painting).

junpō (遵奉する), *vt.* to observe; follow; obey.

junpū (順風), *n.* a fair [favourable] wind. —順風に駛す[帆を揚げる], to sail with [before] the wind.

junpū (淳風美俗), *n.* good morals or manners.

junra (巡邏), *n.* patrol. ¶ 巡邏船, a guardboat; a patrol-ship; a revenue-cutter [-cruiser] (密輸監視の).

junran (巡覽する), *v.* to go sight-seeing; go *over* (a factory or ship).

junrei (巡禮), *n.* ❶ (巡拜) a pilgrimage. ❷ (巡拜者) a pilgrim; a palmer. —巡禮する, to make a pilgrimage.

junreki (巡歷する), *v.* to itinerate; journey [travel; tour] *through*; make a tour *round*.

junretsu (順列), *n.* 【數】 permutation.

junri (純理的), *a.* rational.

junro (順路), *n.* the usual route.

junroku (馴鹿), *n.* 【哺乳】 the reindeer.

junryō (純良な), *a.* pure; genuine. ¶ 純良品, a genuine article.

junryō (順良な), *a.* obedient; gentle; meek.

junsa (巡査), *n.* a policeman; a police officer; a (police) constable. ¶ 巡查部長, a police sergeant; the chief of the police section.

junsai (蓴菜), *n.* 【植】 Brasenia purpurea (American water-shield の類·學名).

junsatsu (巡察する), *v.* to patrol; go the rounds; go a round of inspection.

junsei(純正な), *a.* pure; genuine. ¶ 純正經濟學 (科學), pure economics (science). —純正哲學, metaphysics.

junshi (巡視する), *v.* to make a tour [go a round] of inspection.

junshi (殉死), *n.* suicide upon death of one's lord. —殉死する, to immolate oneself on the death (at the funeral) of one's lord; follow one's lord to the other world.

junshikan (准士官), *n.* 【陸】 a sub-officer; 【海】 a warrant officer.

junshoku (殉職する), *v.* to die at one's post.

junshoku (潤色する), *vt.* to adorn; ornament; embellish.

junshu(遵守する), *vt.* to observe; follow; obey.

junsui (純粹), *n.* purity; genuineness; pureness. —純粹の, pure; genuine; true; unmixed.

jun-suru (殉する), *v.* to die *for*; sacrifice oneself *for*; die a martyr *to*. —國難に殉する, to die [lay down one's life] for the country.

juntaku (潤澤), *n.* ❶ (色澤) gloss; lustre. ❷ (恩澤) favour. ❸ (濕潤) moisture. ❹ (澤山) abundance. —潤澤な, abundant; ample; exuberant; plenteous. —潤澤に, plentifully; in abundance.

juntō(順當の), *a.* regular; normal; seasonable (陽氣に). —順當に行けば, if all goes well; if things go right (*with*); if nothing goes amiss (*with*).

juṅyō (巡洋), *n.* a cruise. —巡洋する, to cruise. ¶ 巡洋艦, a cruiser. —一等巡洋艦, a first-class cruiser. —戰鬪巡洋艦; 巡洋戰艦, a battle-cruiser.

juṅyō (準用する), *v.* 【法】 to apply correspondingly; apply *mutatis mutandis*.

juṅyōshi (順養子), *n.* a young brother adopted as the son.

junyū (授乳する), *vt.* to suckle; give suck *to*. ¶ 授乳期, lactation.

juṅyū(巡遊する), *v.* to go [travel] about; make a tour [trip].

junzen (純然たる), *a.* pure; perfect; absolute.

jun-zuru (準ずる), *v.* to apply correspondingly (準用); be proportionate *to* (比例). —…に準じて, according *to* (*as*); in proportion *to* (*as*). —以下之に準ず, It applies correspondingly to the following cases.

jūō (縱横に), *ad.* ❶ (横と縱) vertically and horizontally; in all directions; throughout the length and breadth (*of*). ❷ (思ふまゝ) as one pleases; at will. —縱横(無盡)に切り捲る, to slash about in all directions.

jūoku (十億), *n.* a thousand million; a milliard; a billion (佛·米).

Jupitā (ジュピター), *n.* Jupiter.

juppei (恤兵), *n.* the relief of soldiers. ¶ 恤兵金, the war relief-fund.

jūrai (從來), *ad.* hitherto; heretofore; up to this time. —從來の惡習, the existing evils.

jūran (縱覽), *n.* ❶ (見ること) inspection. ❷ (讀むこと) reading. —縱覽する, to inspect; go over (a house); visit. —縱覽に供する, to be on view; be open to the public. ¶ 縱覽者, a reader (閲覽者); a visitor. —縱覽謝絕 (隨意), "Inspection declined (invited)."

jūretsu (縱列), *n.* 【陸】 a column; a file.

juri (受理する), *vt.* to accept; receive; take up.

jūrin (蹂躙する), *vt.* to trample *upon*; tread down; outrage. —人權を蹂躙する, to infringe upon personal rights.

juritsu (樹立する), *vt.* to establish; plant.

jūroku (十六), *n.* sixteen; the sixteenth (第十六). ¶ 十六むさし, the fox and geese.

jūrui (獸類), *n.* beasts; animals.

juryō (受領する), *vt.* to accept; receive.

jūryō (重量), *n.* weight. ¶ 總重量, gross weight.

jūryō (銃獵), *n.* shooting; hunting (獸獵). ¶ 銃獵期, the shooting [hunting] season. —銃獵免狀, a shooting license. —銃獵者, a hunter; a huntsman; a sportsman.

jūryoku (重力), *n.* 【理】 (attraction of) gravitation; gravity.

jūryōzei (從量稅), *n.* a specific duty. ¶ 從量稅率, a specific tariff.

jusan (授產), *n.* giving employment; providing with work. ¶ 授產學校, an industrial school.

jūsan (十三), *n.* thirteen; the thirteenth (第十三).

jūsatsu (重殺), *n.* 【野球】 a double play.

jūsatsu (銃殺する), *vi.* to shoot dead [to death]; kill by shooting.

jusei (授精-作用), *vi.* 【植】 fertilization.

jūsei (銃聲), *n.* a gun-report.

jūsei (獸性), *n.* ❶ (動物性) animality. ❷ (人間の) bestiality; the beast (in man).

jūsen (縱線), *n.* a longitudinal line.

jusha (儒者), *n.* a Confucian (scholar). ⌈follower; a servant.⌉
jūsha (從者), *n.* an attendant; a
jushaku (授爵), *n.* ennoblement; conferment of [raising to] a peerage.
jushi (樹脂), *n.* resin; rosin; vegetable tallow. ⌈teenth (第十四).⌉
jūshi (十四), *n.* fourteen; the four-
jūshi (重視する), *vt.* to value much; think much *of*; attach importance *to.* ⌈fat.⌉
jūshi (獸脂), *n.* grease; animal
jūshichi (十七), *n.* seventeen; the seventeenth (第十七). ⌈cousin.⌉
jūshimai (從姉妹), *n.* a (female)
jushin (受信), *n.* receipt of a message. —受信する, to receive a message. ¶ 受信機, a receiver; a recorder. —受信局, the receiving office; the office of receipt. —受信人, an addressee.
jūshin (重心), *n.* 【數·理】 the centre of gravity. —重心を保つ, to maintain the equilibrium.
jūshin (銃身), *n.* a barrel; a gun-barrel.
jushō (受賞), *n.* receiving a prize [reward]. ¶ 受賞詩, a prize poem. —受賞者, a prizeman. (受賞者人名表, a prize-list.)
jushō (綬章), *n.* a cordon.
jūsho (住所), *n.* a domicile【法】; residence; an address (所番地). ¶ 住所姓名, one's name and address. (住所姓名簿, a directory; an address book.)
jūshō (重傷), *n.* a serious wound [injury]. —重傷を負ふ, to be seriously [badly] wounded. —重傷を蒙らす, to inflict a serious wound [injury] *upon.* ¶ 重傷者, a seriously wounded [injured] person.
jūshoku (住職), *n.* the superior (of a temple); an abbot.
juso (呪詛), *n.* 【宗】 curse; malediction; anathema. —呪詛する, to curse; anathematize.
jūsō (重曹), *n.* bicarbonate of soda.
jūsō (銃創), *n.* a bullet [gunshot] wound.
jūsō (銃鎗), *n.* a bayonet.
jūsoku (充塞する), *v.* to fill up; be blocked up; be congested.
jūsotsu (從卒), *n.* an officer's servant; a soldier-servant.
jussū (術數), *n.* a policy; a device; a stratagem.
jū-suru (住する), *vi.* to live; reside; dwell. ☞ *jūkyo.*
jutai (受胎), *n.* conception. —受胎する, to conceive.
jutai (授胎する), *vt.* to impregnate; fecundate; fertilize.
jūtai (縱隊), *n.* a column; a file.
jūtai (重態), *n.* a serious [critical] condition. —重態に陷る, to fall into a critical condition.
jutaku (受託), *n.* trust. ¶ 受託販賣, sales on consignment. —受託人, a trustee; a consignee. —受託裁判所, a court of requisition.
jūtaku (住宅), *n.* a house; a residence; a dwelling house. 住宅難に苦しむ, to suffer from scarcity of houses. ¶ 住宅區域, a residential quarter. —住宅組合, a building-society; a building and loan association. —住宅問題, the housing problem.
jūtan (絨氈), *n.* a carpet; a rug (粗毛にして小さい). —絨氈を敷く, to spread a carpet.
jūtansan (重炭酸-鹽), *n.* 【化】 a bicarbonate. ¶ 重炭酸曹達, bicarbonate of soda; baking soda.
jutchū (術中に陷る), to fall into another's trap; be caught in a trap. —術中に陷れる, to entrap; ensnare.
jūtei (從弟), *n.* a (younger) cousin.
jūteki (獸的), *a.* animal; bestial.
jūten (充塡する), *vt.* to plug; fill up. —齲齒をゴムで充塡する, to plug a decayed tooth with gum.
jūten (重點), *n.* a colon (:).
jūtō (充當する), *vt.* to appropriate *for*; allot *to*; assign *to.*
jutsu (術), *n.* ❶ (すべ) means. ❷ (技術) art. ❸ (術計) artifice; craft. ❹ (妖術) magic. —術を使ふ, to practise magic.
jutsugo (術語), *n.* a technical term; technics; terminology.
jutsugo (述語), *n.* 【文】 the predicate.
juwaki (受話器), *n.* a receiver. —受話器を手に執る, to take the telephone receiver in one's hand.
jūyaku (重役), *n.* ❶ (要職) an important [a high] office. ❷ (要職にある人) a high officer. ❸ 【商】 a director. —重役會議を開く, to open a meeting of directors. ¶ 重役會, a board of directors. —重役連, the directorate; the management.
jūyaku (重譯), *n.* retranslation; double translation. —重譯する, to retranslate; translate again.
juyo (授與する), *vt.* to grant; award; confer *on* [*upon*]. —學位を授與する, to confer a degree. ¶ 卒業證書授與式, the ceremony of the award of diplomas.
juyō (需要, 需用), *n.* demand【經】; request. —需要に應ずる, to meet a demand. —大に需要がある, to be in great demand; there is a great demand *for.* ¶ 需要供給, demand and supply. —需要者, a demander; a consumer (消費者).

jūyō (充用する), *vt.* to appropriate *to* (*for*); apply *to*; devote *to*.

jūyō (重用する), *vt.* to promote a person to a responsible post.

jūyō (重要), *n.* importance; consequence; weight. **—— -na,** *a.* important; weighty; of consequence. —重要な人, a man of importance [weight]. —重要な位地を占める, to hold an important position. ¶ 重要物產, staple products. —重要問題, a serious [an important] question. —重要書類, valuable documents [papers].

jūyoku (獸慾), *n.* animal passion; carnal desires. —獸慾を遂げる, to satisfy [gratify] one's animal desires.

jūyu (重油), *n.* crude petroleum; heavy oil.

jūzai (重罪), *n.* ❶【法】a felony: a grave [serious] crime. ❷ (大なる過誤) a grave [serious] fault. ¶ 重罪犯人, a felon. —重罪裁判, a trial for felony [a grave crime].

jūzei (重稅), *n.* a heavy tax; heavy taxation (課稅).

jūzen (十全), *n.* perfectionism【宗】; perfection. —十全の, perfect.

jūzen (從前), *ad.* hitherto. —從前の通り, as before; as heretofore.

jūzoku (從屬), *n.* subordination; dependency. —從屬さす, to subordinate. —從屬する, to be subject *to*; be dependent *upon*; be subordinate *to*; be under control *of*.

juzōsha (受贈者), *n.*【法】a donee; a presentee.

juzu (珠數), *n.* a rosary; beads. —珠數を爪操る, to tell [count; say; recite] one's beads. —珠數繫ぎにする, to wire (南京玉を); tie (persons or things) in a row. ¶ 珠數玉, ① a bead. ②【植】Job's tears (川穀).

juzukakebato (斑鳩), *n.*【鳥】the (common) Indian dove.

K

ka (蚊), *n.*【昆】the mosquito.

ka (か), *particle.* ❶ (疑問) ? ❷ (不定又は疑念) if (通例 wonder; doubt の次に來る); whether (同上); can. ❸ (反語) how; who; what. ❹ (語句を重ねる場合) or; either...or; whether...or not.

ka (可), ❶ (よろし) good; right; well. ❷ (差支なし) may. —可もなく不可もなき, indifferent; middling. —孰れにても可, Either will do.

ka (香), *n.* scent; perfume. ☞ *nioi* (香).

ka (科), *n.* ❶ (學術上の分類)【動】order;【植】family. ❷ (分科) a section; a department; a division.

ka (課), *n.* (事務分擔區分) a section.

kaba (河馬), *n.*【哺乳】the hippopotamus.

kaba (樺), *n.* ❶【植】(香蒲) the birch-tree. ❷ = *kabairo* (樺色).

Kabafuto (樺太), *n.* Karafuto; Saghalien; Sakhalin.

kabairo (樺色), *n.* orange (colour); reddish-yellow.

kaban (鞄), *n.* a trunk (大形); a (travelling) bag; a portmanteau (旅行鞄); a hand-bag (手提鞄). —鞄を提げる, to carry a bag.

kabane (屍), *n.* a dead body; a corpse; a carcass (鳥獸の). —屍を山野に曝す, to lie dead in the open air.

kabari (蚊鉤), *n.* a fly; a hackle; a fly-hook. —蚊鉤で釣る, to fly-fish; fish with a fly.

kabau (庇ふ), *vt.* Ⓢ庇護する. to excuse *from*; screen *from*; shelter *from*.

kabayaki (蒲燒), *n.* broiled eels (鰻の); spitchcock.

kabe (壁), *n.* a wall. —壁を塗る, to plaster a wall. —壁越しに話す, to talk through a wall. —壁一重隔てて, with a wall between. —壁に耳あり障子に目あり, "Hedges have eyes and walls have ears."

kabegami (壁紙), *n.* wall-paper; paper-hangings (普通複數).

kaben (花瓣), *n.*【植】a petal.

kabetsuchi (壁土), *n.* plaster; stucco.

kabi (黴), *n.* mould; mildew. —黴臭い, ① [*a.*] frowzy; fusty; musty. ② [*v.*] to smell musty. —黴臭くなる, to grow musty. —黴がはえる, = *kabiru*.

kabi (華美), *n.* showiness; splendour; gorgeousness. —華美に流れる, to be [become] showy.

kabin (花瓶), *n.* a vase; a flower-vase.

kabin (過敏な), *a.* oversensitive; nervous (神經が); irritable. —過敏な市場, a sensitive market. —過敏な神經, high-strung nerves; highly sensitive nerves.

kabiru (黴る), *vi.* to mould; mildew; become mouldy. —黴びた醬油, mouldy soy.

kabocha (南瓜), *n.*【植】the (great) pumpkin.

kabu, kabura, (蕪菁), *n.* the turnip.

kabu (株), *n.* ❶ (株根) a stump; a stub. ❷ (商業取引關係) goodwill; business (營業); practice (辯護士·醫師等の); interest (in a business). ❷ (會社株) shares (株式); stocks (同上); a share-certificate (株券). ❸ (慣用手段) a trick; one's hobby. —株を募る, to invite subscription for shares. —お株を出す, to ride [mount] one's hobby. —米屋の株を讓る, to transfer a rice-dealer's goodwill.

kabu (下部), *n.* the lower part.

kabuken (株券), *n.* a share-certificate; a share.

kabuki (歌舞伎 -芝居), *n.* the theatre; play. ¶ 歌舞伎役者, an actor (男); an actress (女).

kabukimon (冠木門), *n.* a gate with a cross-bar.

kabukin (株金), *n.* a share; share-capital.

kabun (下文), *n.* the writing given below; the following. —下文に示す如く, as (is) shown [stated; given] below [hereunder]; as follows.

kabun (可分の), *a.* divisible; separable.

kabun (過分の), *a.* ❶ (過大) excessive; immoderate. ❷ (不相當) undue; unmerited; undeserved.

kabunushi (株主), *n.* a shareholder; a stockholder. ¶ 株主名簿, a list of shareholders. —株主總會, a general meeting of shareholders.

kabureru (氣觸れる), *vi.* ❶ to be bitten *with*; have a skin-eruption; be poisoned *with*. ❷ to be influenced *by*; be infected *with*. —漆にかぶれる, to be poisoned by lacquer. —政治熱にかぶれる, to be influenced by the political fever.

kaburi (頭), *n.* the noddle; the head. —頭を掉る, to shake one's head. —否と頭を縱に掉る, to refuse with a nod.

kaburimono (冠物), *n.* ❶ (頭被) head-gear. ❷ (帽子) a hat.

kaburu (被·冠る), *v.* ❶ (かんむる) to wear; put on. ❷ (上へ著る) to cover oneself *with*; be covered *by*. ❸ (身に引受ける) to take upon oneself. —浪をかぶる, to ship a sea (船が); to be washed by the sea [waves]. —手拭を被る, to cover one's head with a towel.

kabusaru (かぶさる), *vi.* to hang over (崖など); lap (二物が半ば重り合ふ).

kabuseru (被せる), *vt.* ❶ (上から蔽ふ) (*a*) to cover; put over: (*b*) to coat; overlay; plate. ❷ (瞞ます) to palm off *upon*; foist *upon*; put [impose] *upon*. ❸ (轉嫁する) to impute *to*; charge *with*; lay *on*. ❹ (水等を) to dash *on*; pour *on*. —蓋を冠せる, to put the lid on it. —人にかぶせる, to palm off a thing on a person; foist a false article upon a person. (人に罪をかぶせる, to lay [put] the blame on another; charge a person with an affence.)

kabushiki (株式), *n.* shares; stocks. ¶ 株式申込證, an application for shares; an application slip. —株式申込人, an applicant for shares. —株式賣買, stock-jobbing, stock-jobbery. —株式會社, a joint-stock company. —株式仲買人, a stockbroker. —株式市場, the stock-market. —株式取引所, a stock exchange; a *bourse* [佛].

kabuto (冑, 兜), *n.* a helmet. —勝って兜の緒を締める, to be cautious after a success. —兜を脫ぐ, ① to take off one's helmet. ② (降參する) to lay down arms; throw up the sponge.

kabutobana (烏頭), *n.* 【植】 the Japanese monk's-hood.

kabutogani (兜蟹), *n.* 【甲殼】 the king-crab; the horseshoe-crab.

kabutomushi (兜蟲), *n.* 【昆】 a beetle.

kabutsu (貨物), *n.* ❶ (財貨) goods (廣義); commodities. ❷ (運送貨物) freight; goods; cargo.

kabuya (株屋), *n.* a speculator in stocks; a stock-jobber.

kachi (勝), *n.* victory; winning. —勝に乘ずる, to take advantage of a victory. —勝を得る[占める], to have [win] the battle; gain [win] a victory; carry [win] the day. —勝を制する, to gain the upper hand *of*; get the better *of*.

kachi (徒步で), *ad.* on foot.

kachi (價値), *n.* ❶ (人物の) merit; worth; excellence. ❷ (事物の) value; worth. —價値ある, ① meritorious; worthy; excellent. ② valuable; worth. ¶ 價値なき, ① worthless; unworthy. ② valueless; poor (つまらぬ). ¶ 價値判斷, valuation; estimation.

kachiau (搗合ふ), *vi.* ❶ (衝突) to clash *with*; collide *with*; knock [strike; dash] *against*. ❷ (矛盾) to conflict *with*; contradict. ❸ (祭日などが) to fall *on*.

kachidoki (勝鬨を揚げる), to give [raise] a shout of victory; crow *over*.

kachiguri (搗栗), *n.* dried chestnuts.

kachihokoru (勝誇る), *vi.* to crow over; be proud of one's victory; be puffed up with success.

kachikachi (かちかち), *n.* & *ad.* ❶ (柱時計の音) tick-tick; tick-tack. ❷ (固き物を叩く音) click; click-clack.

kachiki (勝氣の), *a.* unyielding; spirited; stout-hearted.

kachiku (家畜), *n.* domestic animals; cattle; live stock. ¶家畜病院, a hospital for domestic animals.

kachiwataru (徒渉る), *v.* to wade; ford.

kachō (家長), *n.* the head of a family; a paterfamilias; a patriarch.

kachō (課長), *n.* the chief [head] of a section.

kachū (花柱), *n.* 【植】a style.

kachū (渦中に投ずる), to plunge into a whirlpool; entangle oneself *in*; be embroiled [entangled] *in*. —渦中に捲き込まれる, to be drawn into the vortex.

kachū (華冑), *n.* Ⓢ貴族. nobility; aristocracy. ¶華冑界, the aristocratic world; the nobility.

kadai (過大の), *a.* exaggerated (誇大の); excessive (過度の). —過大に云ふ, to exaggerate. —歲入を過大に見積る, to overestimate the revenue [annual income]. —過大の要求をする, to make an excessive demand.

kadai (課題), *n.* a thesis; a subject; a theme. —課題を出す, to give the subject (for work).

kadan (花壇), *n.* a flower-bed; a parterre.

kadan (果斷), *n.* (prompt) decision. —果斷(決行)の人, a man of prompt decision; a strong man. —果斷の處置を執る, to take drastic [decisive] measures.

kaden (家傳), *n.* a thing handed down in a family. —家傳の妙藥(妙法), a sovereign remedy (a secret process) handed down in a family.

kaden (訛傳), *n.* a false rumour [report].

kado (角), *n.* ❶ a corner; an angle; an edge (稜角). ❷ (曲り角) a corner; a turn. —角の取れない, angular. —角を取る, to round off the angles; trim the corners. —角を曲る, to turn the corner; go [come] round the corner. (角を曲って二軒目, the second house after turning the corner.) —さう云っては物に角が立つ, It would sound harsh to say so.

kado (門), *n.* ❶ (もん) a gate. ❷ (入口) an entrance; a door. —門に立つ, to stand at the gate [door]. —門を通る, to pass another's door.

kado (廉), *n.* ground (理由); charge (罪科); a point (點). —職務怠慢の廉に依り, on the ground of neglect of duty. —不審の廉を糺す, to examine suspicious points.

kado (過度の), *a.* excessive; immoderate; inordinate. —過度の勉强, excessive work [study]. —過度に酒を飲む, to drink to excess.

kadō (可動の), *a.* movable; mobile.

kādo (カード), *n.* ❶ (歌留多) (playing) cards. ❷ (紙札) a card; a name-card; a slip. ¶通信用カード, correspondence card. —カード式簿記, book-keeping by card system.

kadochigai (門違), *n.* ❶ mistaking a door. ❷ (かんちがひ) a false impression [idea]. —門違ひする, to knock at a wrong door.

kadodatsu (角立つ), *vi.* to be harsh; sound harsh. —角だった, angular (石など); rough; harsh.

kadode (門出, 首途), *n.* departure; setting out. —軍の門出, departure for the war. —門出の盃, a stirrup-cup; a parting-cup.

kadofuda (門札), *n.* a door-plate; a name-plate.

kadoguchi (門口), *n.* a gate; an entrance; a door.

kadomatsu (門松), *n.* pine-trees set up for the New Year's decorations. —門松を立てる, to set up pine-trees for the New Year.

kadomise (角店), *n.* a corner-shop.

kadonami (門並に), *ad.* ❶ (軒別に) from door to door. ❷ (毎戶に) at every house.

kadowakashi (勾引), *n.* ❶ (誘拐) abduction; kidnapping. ❷ (誘拐者) an abductor; a kidnapper. —勾引す, to kidnap; abduct.

kadozuke (門附), *n.* a strolling musician; a piper. —門附をする, to sing [thrum the *samisen*] from door to door [from house to house].

kae (替), *prep.* 【商】at (簿記記號 @); for.

kaedama (替玉), *n.* a substitute; a dummy. —替玉になる, to become a substitute *for*. —替玉を使ふ, to use a dummy; employ a substitute.

kaedasu (汲出す), *vt.* to bail (特に船の淦を); pump (ポンプで); drain. —船の淦を汲へ出す, to bail (out) a boat; pump a ship.

kaede (楓, 槭), *n.* 【植】the maple-tree; the Japanese maple.

kaehosu (汲干す), *vt.* to draw off; drain. —井戶を汲へ干す, to empty a well.

kaen (火焰, 火炎), *n.* a blaze; a flame. —火焰に包まれる, to be wrapped [enveloped] in flames. —火焰の中から救ひ出す, to rescue from the flames.

kaeri (反り), *n.* (襟の) lapel.
kaeri (歸り), *n.* return; coming home; going back. —歸り(しな)に, on one's way home [back]. —歸り仕度する, to prepare to go back; make preparations for return. —歸りを急ぐ, to hurry back.
kaerimichi (歸途), *n.* the way home.. —歸り途に, on one's way home [back].
kaerimiru (顧る), *vt.* ❶ (ふりかへり見る) to look back; turn. ❷ (目をかける) to favour; care *for.* ❸【省】(反省) to consider; review; reflect *on.* ❹ (回想) to reflect *upon*; retrospect; retrace. —かへりみて, ①【顧】(ふりかへッて) on looking back. ②【省】(反省して) upon reflection. —顧みない, to disregard; neglect; ignore. —淺學非才をも顧みず, in spite of my superficial learning.
kaerishō (返り證), *n.* a cross-deed; a counter-deed; a bond of defeasance. —返り證を取る, to take the bond of defeasance.
kaeriuchi (返討), *n.* being killed by the object of one's vengeance. —返討ちにする, to kill a person who comes to wreak vengeance on one; kill the avenger.
kaerizaki (返咲), *n.* Ⓢ 狂ひ咲. reflorescence [reflowering] (in the same year).
kaeru (蛙), *n.* 【兩棲】 the frog. —蛙の子は蛙. "Vipers breed vipers."
kaeru (代·變·換へる), *vt.* ❶【變】 to change; alter; transform. ❷【代】(交代) to substitute; alternate. ❸【換】(交換) to exchange (交換, 兩替); barter (物々交換); cash (現金に換へる). —金に換へる, to convert into money. —...に代ふるに, in place *of.* —金を換へる, to change money. —着物を更へる, to change clothes.
kaeru (孵へる), *vi.* to be hatched.
kaeru (歸·還·回·返る), *vi.* ❶(復歸) to return; come [get] back. ❷ (歸去) to leave; go away; drop away. ❸【反】 to reverberate (反射); reflect (同上); spring back (反跳). —歸らぬ旅, one's last journey. —歸れ!, (去れ) Off with you! —お歸りなさい, Welcome home!
kaeruoyogi (蛙泳), *n.* breast-stroke.
kaerutobi (蛙跳), *n.* 【遊戲】 leap-frog. —蛙跳びをする, to play at leap-frog.
kaesu (返·反す), *vt.* ❶ (返却, 酬いる) to return (返却, 還付); pay (返濟); revenge (復讐). ❷ (覆す) to overturn; upset. ❸ (耕す) to till; cultivate. ❹ (戻らせる) to send back; let go back. ❺ (復舊) to restore; resuscitate. —客を歸す, to dismiss one's guests. —使を返す, to send back a messenger. —インキ瓶を覆す, to upset an ink-bottle. —借りた金を返す, to return borrowed money; repay [pay back] a debt. —もと來た道を取ッて返す, to go back the same way; retrace one's steps. —返す言葉がない, I have no word to say in answer.
kaesu (孵す), *vt.* to breed, hatch.
kaesugaesu (返す返すも), *ad.* deeply; really; extremely; earnestly.
kaette (却ッて), *ad.* ❶ (反對に) on the contrary. ❷ (寧ろ) rather; all [only] the more. —智慧があるので却ッてしくじる, His very sagacity will mislead him. —子供らしいから却ッて好きだ, I like him all the more for being so childish [childlike].
kafē (カフェー), *n.* a café【佛】; a coffee-house. ¶ カフェーテリア, a cafeteria.
kafu (下附), *n.* grant; issue. —下附する, to grant; issue.
kafu (火夫), *n.* a fireman; a stoker.
kafu (家扶), *n.* a steward.
kafu (家婦), *n.* a housewife (主婦).
kafu (寡婦), *n.* a widow; a relict.
kafū (下風), *n.* a subordinate position. —下風に立つ, to play second fiddle *to.*
kafū (家風), *n.* a family custom.
kafū (歌風), *n.* poetical style.
kafuku (禍福), *n.* a misfortune and a blessing; fortune and misfortune; weal or [and] woe. —禍福は糾へる繩の如し. "Fortune and misfortune are neighbours."
kafukubu (下腹部), *n.* 【解】 the hypogastric region.
kafukyū (過不及なく), *ad.* (過不足なく) in exact quantities.
kafun (花粉), *n.* 【植】 pollen.
kafuri (過振), *n.* 【商】 overdraft. ¶ 過振小切手, an overdrawn cheque.
kafusu (カフス), *n.* cuffs. ¶ カフス釦, cuff-button [-link].
kagai (加害), *n.* assault; injuring. ¶ 加害者, an assailant; an injurer.
kagai (課外の), *a.* extraordinary. ¶ 課外講義, a special lecture.
kagaku (下顎), *n.* the lower jaw. ¶ 下顎骨, 【解】 the mandible; the lower jaw-bone.
kagaku (化學), *n.* chemistry. ¶ 化學反應, a chemical reaction. —化學方程式, a chemical equation. —化學記號, a chemical symbol. —化學器械, chemical apparatus.

—化學工業, chemical industry. —化學(製)品, a chemical (article). —化學(的)變化, a chemical change. —化學(的)作用, a chemical action. —化學者, a chemist. —化學式, a chemical formula.

kagaku (科學), *n.* science. —科學的に, scientifically. ¶ 純正(應用)科學, pure (applied) science. —科學的研究, scientific study [researches]. —科學的經營法, scientific management. —科學者, a scientist; a man of science.

kagamaru (屈まる), *vi.* to bend; stoop; crouch (踞む).

kagameru (屈める), *vt.* ❶ (折曲げる) to bend; bow. ❷ (縮こめる) to draw in. —身を前へ屈める, to bend forward.

kagami (鏡), *n.* ❶ (姿見) a mirror; a looking-glass; a glass. ❷ (樽の蓋) a barrel-head. —鏡の樣に靜かな海, a glassy [calm] sea; a sea calm as glass [as a mirror]. —鏡に向ふ, to face the looking-glass; look in a mirror. —酒樽の鏡を拔く, to take out the head of a barrel.

kagami (鑑), *n.* a mirror; a paragon. —武士の鑑, a mirror of knighthood. —人の鑑となる, to become a pattern to others.

kagamimochi (鏡餅), *n.* a rice-dumpling offering (in January).

kagamitate (鏡立), *n.* a looking-glass stand.

kagamu (屈む), *vi.* ❶ (傴) (背が曲る) to be hunchbacked [humpbacked]. ❷ (屈) (折曲がる) to stoop; bow; crouch.

kaganbo (大蚊), *n.* 【昆】 the daddy-long-legs.

kagaribi (篝火), *n.* a watch-fire; a camp-fire; a bonfire. —篝火を焚く, to light a watch-fire.

kagaru (縢る), *vt.* to darn; cross-stitch; knit. —毬を縢る, to work figures on a ball.

kagashi (案山子), *n.* a scarecrow. ☞ *kakashi*.

kagato (踵), *n.* =*kakato*.

kagayakasu (輝かす), *vt.* to light up; kindle; shed light on. —國威を輝かす, to raise the national prestige. —名を世界に輝かす, to make one's name shine throughout the world.

kagayaku (輝く), *vi.* to shine; beam; brighten. —喜びに輝ける眼, eyes sparkling with joy.

kage (かげ), *n.* ❶ (陰) (光の當らぬ物蔭) shade; dark. ❷ (裏面) the back; the other side; the reverse (side). ❸ (蔭) (庇護) favour; patronage. ❹ (影) (投影) a shadow; a phantom. ❺ (景) (ひかり) light. —障子に映る人の影, a human shadow falling on the sliding door. —蔭で惡口を云ふ, to backbite; speak ill of a person behind his back. —蔭で凄いことをやる, to do dreadful things in private. —影も形もなくなる, to be clean gone; not to leave a shadow behind. —樹木の蔭に, under a tree (樹下); in the shade of a tree (樹陰); behind a tree (背後に). —蔭に隱れる, to lie concealed in a shadow. —陰になり陽(ひ)になり, both openly and secretly; in public and in private. —影の形に隨ふ如く, as the shadow follows the substance. —壁に影を投ずる, to cast a shadow on the wall.

kage (鹿毛), *n.* fawn colour (色); a bay horse (馬).

kagebenkei (影辨慶), *n.* a blusterer; a braggart. —影辨慶を使ふ, to play the braggart at home.

kageboshi (陰干), *n.* drying in the shade.

kagehōshi (影法師), *n.* a shadow.

kagee (影繪), *n.* a shadowgraph; a shadow-picture.

kagegoto (陰言), *n.* Ⓢ 陰口. backbiting. —陰言を云ふ, to backbite; speak ill of a person behind his back.

kagehinata (陰日向), *n.* ❶ (陰と日向) light and shade. ❷ (表裏) doubleness. —陰日向のある人, a double-dealer. —陰日向のある召使, an eye-servant. —陰日向をする, to work only under a master's eye. —彼は陰日向がある, He plays a double game.

kageki (過劇の), *a.* extreme; excessive; violent. —過劇の運動, excessive exercise.

kageki (過激な), *a.* extreme; radical; red; ultra; violent (激烈な). ¶ 過激派, ① Bolsheviki; Maximalists: radicals. ② (一員) a Bolshevist, Bolshevik; a Maximalist: a radical. —過激思想, dangerous thoughts (危險思想); Bolshevist thoughts.

kageki (歌劇), *n.* an opera; a lyric drama. ¶ 歌劇團 (女優), an opera company (dancer).

kagemi (影身に添って), keeping close behind a person.

kagemusha (影武者), *n.* a dummy general [soldier].

kagen (下弦), *n.* the last quarter; the last phase of the moon.

kagen (加減), *n.* ❶ (加と減) addition and subtraction. ❷ (健康狀態) health condition. ❸ (程度) degree; measure. ❹ (鹽梅)

flavour. ● (斟酌) qualification; modification. —加減する, ①(鹽梅) to flavour; season. ②(量定) to moderate; qualify; modify. ③(調節) to regulate; adjust. ④(斟酌) to make allowance *for*. —加減が惡い, to feel indisposed. —加減を惡くする, to lose tone; get out of sorts.

kagen, kagon, (過言), *n.* ●(誇張) exaggeration; saying too much. ●(失言) a slip of the tongue. —...と謂ふも過言ではあるまい, it would not be too much [it would be no exaggeration] to say that....

kagen (寡言の), *a.* taciturn. —寡言の人, a man of few words; a taciturn person.

kagerō (蜉蝣), *n.* 【昆】 a day-fly; a may-fly.

kagerō (陽炎, 絲遊), *n.* a gossamer; a gossamer-web. —陽炎が立つ, A gossamer floats.

kageru (陰る), *vi.* ●(日陰になる) to be obscured; be darkened. ●(曇る) to dim; cloud. —陰り始める, to begin to throw shadows.

kagi (鉤), *n.* a hook; a catch; a clasp. —鉤で引掛ける, to hook; catch with a hook. —鉤で引上げる, to draw up with a hook.

kagi (鍵), *n.* a key. —鍵を掛ける, to turn the key on; lock.

kagiri (限), *n.* ●(制限, 限度) a limit; a bound; an end. ●(劃) a line; a boundary. ●(涯)(境界) a boundary. ——, *ad.* & *conj.* ●(間は) so [as] long as; until. ●(及ぶ限り) as far as; in so far as; to the utmost. ●(非ずんば) unless; without. ●(何日限り) not later than. ●(のみ) only. —限りある, limited; finite. —限りなき, limitless; boundless; infinite. —今日を限りの命, the life that ends with to-day. —私の生きてる限り, as long as I live; while my life lasts. —予の知る限りでは, to the best of my knowledge; as far as I know; for aught I know. —事情の許す限りは, as far as circumstances permit. —此度限り許す, to permit this once [this time only] —聲を限りに叫ぶ, to cry at the top of one's voice. —力の及ぶ限りを盡す, to do one's utmost [best]; do as well as one can. —學生に限り入場を許す, Admission to students only.

kagiru (限る), *vt.* to limit; bound; restrict. ——, *vi.* to be limited *to*; be peculiar *to*. —時間を限って, within a prescribed time. —その日に限って, on that particular day. —貸間あり, 但し學生に限る, Rooms to let; only students need apply. —彼に限ってそんな事はせぬ, He, of all others, never does such a thing. —そんな事がないとも限らぬ, It is not impossible for it to happen; One cannot say that it is impossible.

kagitabako (嗅煙草), *n.* snuff.

kagitsukeru (嗅附ける), *vt.* ● to smell (out); scent (out). ●(探知する) to get wind *of*, scent. —陰謀を嗅ぎ附ける, to scent treachery.

kagizaki (鉤裂), *n.* a rent; an L-shaped tear.

kago (籃, 籠), *n.* a basket (編籃); a coop (漁獵用又は鷄など を入れる); a cage (鳥籠). —籠の中の雲雀, a caged lark; a captive lark. —籠の鳥を放す, to let the bird out of the cage. ¶ 籠屋, a basket-maker. —籠細工, basketwork; basket-ware.

kago (駕籠, 轎), *n.* a palanquin; a sedan-chair (轎). ¶ 駕籠舁, 轎夫, a palanquin-bearer; a (chair-) bearer.

kago (加護), *n.* blessing; divine protection. —神の加護の下に, under divine protection.

kagō (化合), *n.* (chemical) combination. —化合する, to combine. ¶ 化合物, 【化】a compound body; a (chemical) compound.

kagō (加號), *n.* a plus (sign) (+).

kagome (籠目), *n.* ● woven-bamboo pattern. ●(商標) a double triangle.

kagu (家具), *n.* (household) furniture; utensils (小道具). ¶ 洋式 [西洋] 家具, foreign furniture. 家具陳列所, a pantechnicon. —家具屋, upholstery (業); an upholsterer (人); a furniture-store (店).

kagu (嗅ぐ), *vt.* to smell; sniff; scent. —嗅ぎなれぬ香, an unfamiliar smell.

kagura (神樂), *n.* a sacred music and dance; a *Kagura* (日本古代の). ¶ 神樂堂, a hall [stage] for sacred dances.

kagyō (家業), *n.* ●(商工) a business; a trade. ●(職業) an occupation; a calling; a profession (知識的). ● =*kagyō* (稼業).

kagyō (稼業), *n.* means of living; livelihood. —稼業に精出す, to work hard for one's livelihood.

kagyō (課業), *n.* a lesson; a task.

kagyū (蝸牛), *n.* the snail. —蝸牛角上の爭をする, to raise a storm in a tea-cup.

kahaku (假泊する), *vi.* to anchor for a while; lie for a while at anchor.

kahan (河畔), *n.* riverside.
kahan (過半), *n.* the better part; the greater part; the majority. **——,** *ad.* mostly; more than half.
kahan (過般), *ad.* the other day; some time ago. 一過般來, of late; for some time past.
kahansū (過半數), *n.* a majority of the members. 一過半數を占める, to be in the majority; have a majority.
kahei (貨幣), *n.* a coin; coinage; metallic currency. 一貨幣の表(裏) the obverse (reverse) of a coin. ¶ 貨幣鑄造, mintage; coinage. 一貨幣地金, bullion. 一貨幣制度, monetary [currency] system.
kahi (下婢), *n.* a maid; a maid-servant; a domestic (servant).
kahi (可否), *n.* ❶ (良否) good or bad; right or wrong. ❷ (贊否) for and against; *pro* and *con.* 一可否の論, *pros* and *cons.* 一可否同數の場合には, in case of a tie. 一投票に依って可否を決する, to decide by vote.
kahitsu (加筆する), *v.* ❶ to insert [add] a character. ❷ (添削) to correct.
kahō (加法), *n.* addition.
kahō (加俸), *n.* additional salary. 一年功加俸を受ける, to receive an additional salary for long service.
kahō (果報), *n.* ❶ (善果) retribution; reward. ❷ (幸福) a good fortune. ❸ (僥倖) a luck; a windfall. ¶ 果報者, a fortunate person; a child of fortune.
kahō (家寶), *n.* a family treasure.
kahodo (斯程), *ad.* so: such. 一斯程の, such.
kai (貝, 介), *n.* ❶【動】a shell-fish. ❷ (殼) a shell.
kai (囘), *n.* ❶ (度) a time. ❷ (競技・勝負の) a bout; a heat; a game. 一月に三四囘, three or four times a month.
kai (快), *n.* pleasure; merriment. 一頻りに快を貪る, to indulge in pleasures.
kai (戒, 誡), *n.* a commandment. 一戒を持する[守る](破る), to observe (break) the commandments. 一戒を受(授)ける, to become (make a person) a disciple.
kai (界), *n.* ❶ a zone; a field. ❷ (社界) world; circles. ❸ (舞臺) the stage; the field; the arena.
kai (海), *n.* the sea; waters. ¶ 日本海, the Sea of Japan; the Japan Sea. 一支那海, the Chinese waters.
kai (會), *n.* ❶ (會合) a meeting; an assembly; a party (宴會の類). ❷ (議會) a congress; a conference. ❸ (團體) an association; a society; a club. 一會を開く, ① to open a meeting. ② (會を催す) to hold a meeting. 一會を閉ぢる, to close a meeting.
kai (棹, 櫂), *n.* an oar; a paddle. 一棹で漕ぐ, to oar; paddle. 一棹を漕ぐ, to pull an oar. 一棹を漕ぎ外す, to catch a crab. 一棹を納める, to boat [lay in the ship] oars. 一棹を(棹架に)はめる, to ship oars. 一棹を立てる, to toss oar.
kai (下位), *n.* inferiority; subordinariness.
kai (甲斐, 效), *n.* ❶ (效果) effect; fruit; result. ❷ (價値) worth. ❸ (益) avail; advantage; use. ☞ *kainai.* 一甲斐ある, available; worth; worth while.
kaiage (買上), *n.* purchase. 一買上げる, to purchase. 一宮內省御買上品, an article purchased by the Household Department.
kaiaku (改惡する), *vt.* to disimprove; deteriorate.
kaiaoru (買煽る), *vt.* to bull.
kaiba (海馬), *n.* ❶【魚】(龍落子) the hippocampus [*pl.* -pi]; the sea-horse. ❷【哺乳】(海象(セイウチ)) the walrus.
kaiba (飼糧), *n.* feed (馬一囘の); fodder; forage. 一飼糧をやる, to fodder; feed.
kaibashira (貝柱), *n.* a ligament; a shell-ligament.
kaibatsu (海拔), above the sea-level. 一海拔三千尺に達する, to reach 3000 feet above the sea-level.
kaibō (海防), *n.* coast defence. ¶ 海防艦, a coast-defence ship.
kaibō (解剖), *n.* ❶ (解體) dissection. ❷ (分析) analysis. ❸ (分解)【文】parsing; analysis. **—— -suru,** *vt.* to anatomize; dissect: 【文】parse; analyze. 一屍體を解剖する, to dissect a body. 一文章を解剖する, to analyze a sentence. ¶ 解剖學, anatomy. 一解剖室, a dissecting-room.
kaibotan (貝鈕釦), *n.* a shell-button.
kaibun (怪聞), *n.* the marvellous; a scandal (醜聞).
kaibushi (蚊燻), *n.* a mosquito-fumigator; a smudge.
kaibutsu (怪物), *n.* ❶ a monster; a prodigy. ❷ = *bakemono.* 一政界の怪物, a prodigy of the political world.
kaibyaku (開闢), *n.* ❶ (天地創造) the creation. ❷ (一國の成立) foundation. 一開闢以來, since creation [the beginning of the world]; since the foundation of the country (一國の).
kaichiku (改築), *n.* rebuilding

(再建); reconstruction (河川・港灣等の). ¶ 改築工事, reconstruction works.

kaichin (開陳する), *vt.* to state; set forth.

kaichō (海鳥), *n.* a sea-bird; a sea-fowl.

kaichō (廻腸), *n.* 【解】 the ileum.

kaichō (開帳する), *v.* ❶ to expose a Buddhist image to public view; raise [open] the curtain. ❷ (賭場を) to keep (a gambling-house).

kaichō (會長), *n.* the president (of a society); the chair; the chairman. —會長席に就く, to take the chair.

kaichoku (戒飭する), *vt.* to caution; admonish; warn.

kaichū (蛔蟲), *n.* 【蟲】 the round-worm; the intestinal worm(蚘蟲); the thread-worm.

kaichū (改鑄する), *vt.* to recoin; remint; recast (大砲等を).

kaichū (海中に), *ad.* in the sea. —海中に漂ふ, to drift in the sea. —海中に投棄する, to throw overboard; throw into the sea.

kaichū (懷中), *n.* ❶ (ふところ) a breast-pocket; the bosom. ❷ (金入) a purse; a pocket-book. ❸ (所持金) money in hand. —懷中する, to pocket; put in one's bosom. —懷中物御用心, "Beware of pickpockets." ¶ 懷中電燈, a pocket-lamp. —懷中時計, a watch. —懷中鏡, a pocket-glass. —懷中日記, a pocket diary.

kaidai (海内に), *ad.* in the whole country; within the four seas. —海内に冠絶する, to be unique in the whole country.

kaidaku (快諾する), *v.* to consent readily. —快諾を與へる(得る), to give (gain one's) ready consent.

kaidan (廻段), *n.* 【建】 winding stairs; circular stairs.

kaidan (階段), *n.* ❶ 【地質】 a terrace; an ascent (段々). ❷ (階子段) steps; stairs; a staircase. ❸ (等差) a grade; a scale.

kaidan (快談する), *v.* to talk pleasantly [cheerfully].

kaidan (怪談), *n.* a ghost story.

kaidan (會談する), *v.* to converse *with*; confer *with*.

kaidanshi (快男子), *n.* a fine-spirited fellow.

kaidashi (買出), *n.* ❶ (仕入れ) wholesale purchase; laying-in. ❷ (買ひに行くこと) going for purchase.

kaidō (海棠), *n.* 【植】 the many-flowered aronia.

kaidō (街道), *n.* a road; a highway. ¶ 木曾街道, the Kiso Highway. —本街道, the main road; the high road.

kaidō (會同), *n.* an assemblage; a meeting; a gathering. —會同する, to meet; gather; assemble.

kaidō (會堂), *n.* ❶ (集會場) a meeting-house; an assembly-hall [-room]. ❷ (禮拜堂) a chapel; a church.

kaidoku (回讀する), *vt.* to read in turn. ¶ 雜誌回讀會, the magazines circulating association.

kaien (開演), *n.* the commencement [opening] of a performance. —晝夜二度開演する, to give two performances a day; give morning and evening performances.

kaifu (廻付する), *vt.* to send up; forward; transmit.

kaifū (海風), *n.* a sea-wind; a sea-breeze (海軟風).

kaifū (開封), *n.* an unfastened [open] envelope. —開封する, to unseal (a letter); break (a seal); open (a letter). —開封にて, under flying seal; in an unfastened envelope. —開封の手紙, an unsealed [open] letter.

kaifuku (回復, 恢復), *n.* ❶ (恢復) (もとへもどる) restoration; reestablishment; revival. ❷ (快復) (病氣の) recovery; convalescence; recuperation. ❸ (取戻) recovery; restitution; retrieval. —回復の見込なき, beyond recovery; hopeless (病人など). **——-suru**, *vt.* to recover; regain; retrieve. ——, *vi.* to revive; be restored to health; convalesce. —健康を回復する, to recover [regain] one's health. —元氣を回復する, to recover one's spirits. —昔日の信用を恢復する, to recover one's former credit. ¶ 快復期, convalescence.

kaiga (繪畫), *n.* paintings; pictures. ¶ 繪畫陳列館, a picture-gallery. —繪畫展覽會, an art exhibition.

kaigai (海外), *n.* foreign countries. —海外の領土, an oversea(s) dominion; a dominion beyond the seas. —海外に遊ぶ, to travel [go] abroad. —海外視察の途に上る, to start [go] on a tour of inspection abroad. ¶ 海外出稼[移住], emigration. —海外諸國, foreign countries.

kaigan (海岸), *n.* the coast; the sea-coast; the seashore; the seaboard; the seaside. —海岸近く, inshore. —海岸傳ひに, alongshore. —海岸の方に, coastward. —海岸に沿うて航行する, to sail along the coast; sail coastwise. ¶ 海岸通り, the bund (the bluff の對). —海岸局, a coast-station. —海岸線, ① the coast-line. ② (海岸の鐵道線) a coast-line; a coast railway.

kaigara (貝殼), *n.* a shell.
kaigarabone(肩胛骨), *n.* =*ken-kokotsu.*
kaigaramushi (貝殼蟲), *n.* the scale-insects.
kaigen (改元する), *v.* to change the name of an era.
kaigenrei (戒嚴令), *n.* martial law. —戒嚴令を施く(解く), to proclaim (withdraw) martial law.
kaigi (會議), *n.* a meeting; a conference; a convention. —會議に付する, to submit [refer] to the council; lay before the council. —會議に列する, to attend a conference. —會議を開く[始める], to open a conference [meeting, &c.]. ¶ 會議場; 會議室, a council-chamber; a council-house.
kaigi (海技), *n.* seamanship. ¶ 海技免狀, a certificate of competency.
kaigi (懷疑), *n.* doubt; incredulity. —懷疑の, sceptical; incredulous. ¶ 懷疑說, scepticism.
kaigo (改悟), *n.* repentance; reform. **——-suru,** *v.* to repent; reform. —前非を改悟する, to repent (of) one's misdeeds [sins].
kaigo (悔悟), *n.* penitence; contrition; repentance. —悔悟の自殺, penitential suicide.
kaigo (海語), *n.* a sea-term; a nautical term.
kaigō (會合), *n.* a meeting; a gathering; an assembly. —會合する, to meet; gather; assemble.
kaigoroshi (飼殺し), *n.* keeping for life; supporting till death. —一生飼殺しにする, to support a person for life.
kaigui (買食), *n.* buying and eating confectionery between meals.
kaigun (海軍), *n.* the navy; the naval forces; the fleet. ¶ 海軍武官, a naval officer. (大使館附海軍武官, a naval attaché to an embassy.) —海軍部內, the naval circles. —海軍病院, a naval hospital. —海軍大學校, the higher naval college (日). —海軍大臣; 海軍卿, the Minister of the Navy; the First Lord of the Admiralty(英); the Secretary of the Navy (米); the Minister of Marine(佛). —海軍演習, naval manœuvres. —海軍軍人, the navy(全體); a naval man. —海軍軍令部, the Naval General Staff. —海軍次官, the Vice-Minister of the Navy (日); the Assistant Secretary of the Navy(米). —海軍艦政本部, the Department of the Matériel of the Navy. —海軍下士, a petty officer. —海軍經理部, the Direction of Accounts and Supplies. —海軍旗, a naval flag; an ensign. —海軍國, a naval Power. —海軍根據地, a naval base. —海軍競爭, naval race. —海軍休日, a naval holiday. —海軍力, naval power; sea-power; naval strength. —海軍省, the Navy Department; the Admiralty (英). —海軍造兵廠, a naval arsenal.
kaigyaku (諧謔), *n.* a joke; drollness; facetiousness. —諧謔の言を弄する, to crack jokes. ¶ 諧謔家, a humourist [humorist]; a man of humour.
kaigyō (開業), *n.* opening of a business [trade]. —開業する, to commence business; open a business; start a business. —開業十週年, the tenth anniversary of the opening of a business [trade]. —商店の開業式を行ふ, to perform [celebrate] opening a shop. ¶ 開業費, the expenses of opening a business. —開業醫, a medical practitioner.
kaigyū (海牛), *n.* 【哺乳】 the manatus; the sea-cow.
kaihai (改廢), *n.* revision and abolition.
kaihai (壞敗), *n.* ❶ (墮落) corruption; perversion. ❷ (廢頹) dilapidation; ruin. —壞敗する, ① to pervert; corrupt; injure. ② to dilapidate; ruin; go to ruin.
kaihaku(灰白の), *a.* ash-coloured; ashen; hoary.
kaihan (改版), *n.* a new[revised] edition. —改版する, to issue a new edition (改正版發行); revise the old edition (舊版改正).
kaihan (解版), *n.* 【印】 decomposition; distribution(復室を含む).
kaihatsu (開發), *n.* ❶ (開くこと) cultivation (土地・人德など); enlightenment (知識など); development (同上). ❷ (展開, 發展) development; evolution. —開發的, evolutionary; developmental. —開發する, to cultivate; develop; open (土地を); exploit (鑛山・土地など).
kaihei (海兵), *n.* a marine; a sailor. ¶ 海兵團, a marine division.
kaihei (開平), *n.* 【數】 extraction of a square root.
kaihei (開閉), *n.* opening and closing. —開閉する, to open and close. ¶ 開閉器, 【電】 a switch.
kaihen (改變), *n.* alteration; change; conversion (信仰・主義等).
kaihen (海邊), *n.* the seashore; the seaside; the beach.
kaihi (回避), *n.* avoidance; evasion; put-off. —回避する, to avoid; evade; shun.
kaihi (會費), *n.* ❶ (會の維持費) tax. ❷ (集會の分擔金) the subscription [fee] for a meeting.
kaihin (海濱), *n.* the seashore; the seaside; the sea-coast. ¶ 海濱

病院, a seaside hospital.

kaihō (介抱する), *vt.* to nurse; tend; take care *of*. ¶ 介抱者, a nurse; a sick-nurse.

kaihō (快方), *n.* 【醫】 convalescence; recovery. —快方に赴く, to get on well; become convalescent; be in a fair way to recovery. —快方に向へる患者, a convalescent.

kaihō (快報), *n.* glad tidings; a joyful report; welcome news.

kaihō (海法), *n.* maritime law.

kaihō (海堡), *n.* a sea-fort; a coast battery.

kaihō (開方), *n.* 【數】 evolution; extraction (of roots).

kaihō (開放), *n.* opening; openness (性質などの). **—-suru,** *vt.* to open; throw open. —國を開放する, to throw open the country (to foreigners). —庭園を公衆に開放する, to open one's garden to the public. ¶ 開放主義, the open-door principle.

kaihō (解放), *n.* release; liberation; emancipation. —婦人(奴隷)の解放, emancipation of women (slaves). **—-suru,** *vt.* to release; set free; set at liberty; emancipate. —罪人を解放する, to release [discharge] a prisoner (from custody).

kaihō (會報), *n.* a report; transactions; proceedings; minutes.

kaihō (懐抱する), *vt.* to entertain; harbour; cherish.

kaihyō (海豹), *n.* 【哺乳】 the seal; the sea-leopard.

kaihyō (海標), *n.* a sea-mark.

kaihyō (開票), *n.* the opening of the ballot. —開票する, to open the ballot.

kaihyō (解氷), *n.* melting (away) of ice.

kaii (介意する), *vi.* to trouble oneself *about*; be concerned; concern oneself; take to heart.

kaii (怪異), *n.* ❶ (不思議) strangeness; mystery. ❷ (ばけ物) a monster; a prodigy.

kaiin (改印する), *v.* to change one's seal. ¶ 改印届, a notice of the change of one's seal.

kaiin (海員), *n.* a seaman; a mariner; a sailor.

kaiin (開院), *n.* the opening of the Diet. —開院する, to open the Diet. ¶ 開院式, the ceremony of opening the Diet; the opening (ceremony) of the Diet.

kaiin (會員), *n.* a member (of society, &c.). ¶ 準會員, an associate-member. —正會員, a regular member. —終身會員, a life-member. —會員章, the badge of membership.

kaiinu (飼犬), *n.* a house-dog. —飼犬に手を噛まれる, to be bitten by the viper in one's bosom.

kaiire (買入), *n.* purchase. —買入れる, to buy; purchase. ¶ 買入帳, a purchases book; bought books.

kaija (海蛇), *n.* a sea-snake; a sea-serpent.

kaiji (怪事), *n.* an extraordinary thing; a marvellous thing.

kaiji (海事), *n.* marine affairs [matters]. ¶ 海事局, the Marine Bureau. —海事審判所, a naval [admiralty] court. —海事思想, a maritime [seafaring] spirit.

kaijin (灰燼に歸する), to be reduced to ashes.

kaijo (刈除), *n.* removal; cutting off; mowing. —刈除する, to mow; cut off; cut down; do away *with*; weed.

kaijo (解除), *n.* 【法】 rescission; release; acquittance. **—-suru,** *vt.* to rescind; release; cancel (取消); acquit. —契約を解除する, to rescind a contract.

kaijō (回狀), *n.* Ⓢ 回章. a circular (letter). —回狀を廻す, to send a circular letter; circulate a note.

kaijō (海上の), *a.* marine. —海上の危險, perils of the sea (狹義の); maritime perils. —海上の覇者, the mistress of the sea [seas]. ¶ 海上保險, marine insurance. (海上保險者, an underwriter; a marine insurer. —海上保險を附する, to insure against sea-perils.) —海上權, command of the sea; sea-power. —海上勤務, sea-service; service afloat. —海上生活, life afloat; seafaring [sea] life.

kaijō (階上に), *ad.* upstairs; overhead; in an upper storey [floor].

kaijō (開城), *n.* surrender [capitulation; evacuation] of a fortress. —開城する, to surrender a fortress; capitulate (條件附で); deliver up a fortress (明渡す). ¶ 開城條約, the capitulations; the terms of surrender.

kaijō (開場), *n.* opening. —開場する, to open. ¶ 開場式, the opening ceremony.

kaijō (會場), *n.* ❶ (會合所) a meeting-place; an assembly-room; an assembly-hall. ❷ (博覧會等の場所) site (敷地); a building; a section.

kaijō (塊狀の), *a.* massive.

kaijū (海獸), *n.* a marine animal.

kaijū (懐柔する), *vt.* to conciliate. ¶ 懐柔策, a conciliatory policy; conciliating measures.

kaika (怪火), *n.* ❶ Jack-o'-lantern; the will-o'-the-wisp; *ignis fatuus*

〔羅〕. ❷ (放火) arson; incendiarism.
kaika (階下に), *ad.* downstairs; below stairs.
kaika (開化), *n.* civilization; enlightenment; culture. —開化する, to civilize [*vt.*]; be civilized.
kaika (開花), *n.* bloom; blow; efflorescence. —開花する, to flower; effloresce; bloom; blow. ¶ 開花期, florescence; efflorescence.
kaikaburu (買被る), *vt.* ❶ (眞價より高く買ふ) to buy dear; pay too much *for*. ❷ (眞價以上に信ずる) to overestimate; overrate; think too highly of.
kaikai (開會), *n.* ❶ opening of a meeting; opening of the session (議會など). ❷ (會期) a session; a sitting. —開會する, to open a meeting; sit (議事を開く). —議會の開會中, during the session; during the sitting of Parliament. —開會の辭を述べる, to deliver an opening address.
kaikaku (改革), *n.* reform. —官制を改革する, to reform the government organization. ¶ 改革案, a reform bill. —改革者, a reformer.
kaikaku (海角), *n.* a promontory; a headland; a cape.
kaikan (快感), *n.* pleasure; sense of pleasure.
kaikan (海關), *n.* the (maritime) customs. ¶ 海關稅, a customs-duty. ☞ *kanzei* (關稅).
kaikan (開館), *n.* opening of a hall. ☞ *kaijō* (開場).
kaikan (會館), *n.* a hall; a club; an institute.
kaikata (買方), *n.* a buyer; a bull (取引市場).
kaikatsu (快活な), *a.* lively; cheerful; sprightly.
kaikei (會計), *n.* accounts (出納計算); finance (財政); a bill (勘定書). ¶ 物品(金錢)會計, a goods (cash) account. —一般(特別)會計, a general (special) account. —會計係, an accountant; a paymaster; a treasurer (團體・俱樂部・會社等の). —會計法, the financial law. —會計課, the section of accounts. —會計檢查, audit. (會計檢查官, a public auditor; an auditor of public accounts. —會計檢查院, the Board of Audit. —會計檢查をする, to audit accounts.) —會計年度, the financial [fiscal 〔米〕] year. —(免許)會計士, a chartered accountant; a certified public accountant 〔米〕.
kaikei-no-haji (會稽の恥を雪ぐ), to clear oneself of the shame of a former defeat.
kaiken (會見), *n.* an interview; a meeting. —會見する, to have an interview *with*; meet.
kaiken (懷劍), *n.* a dagger; a poniard; a dirk. —懷劍で刺す, to stab with a dagger.
kaiketsu (解決), *n.* settlement; solution. —解決する, to settle; solve; decide (爭論など).
kaiketsubyō (壞血病), *n.* 【醫】 scorbutus; scurvy.
kaiki (回忌), *n.* an anniversary of a death.
kaiki (回歸), *n.* a revolution. —回歸する, to revolve. ¶ 回歸熱, 【醫】 relapsing [recurrent] fever. —回歸線, the tropics. (南(北)回歸線, the tropic of Capricorn (Cancer).)
kaiki (皆既-蝕), *n.* a total [absolute] eclipse.
kaiki (海氣), *n.* sea-air.
kaiki (開期), *n.* 【法】 a term (開廷期); a session.
kaiki (開基), *n.* the foundation (of a temple).
kaiki (會期), *n.* a session; a sitting.
kaiki (甲斐絹), *n.* lustring.
kaikin (戒禁), *n.* a commandment.
kaikin (皆勤), *n.* regular attendance.
kaikin (解禁), *n.* removal of a prohibition; release from prohibition.
kaikiri (買切), *n.* purchase; buying up. —買切りの汽車, a special train. —買ひ切る, to buy up; engage the whole *of*. (棧敷を買ひ切る, to engage [book] all the boxes.)
kaiko (蠶), *n.* the silkworm; 【蛾】 the true silkworm-moth. —蠶を飼ふ, to rear [breed] silkworms. ¶ 蠶時, the season for silkworm-rearing.
kaiko (回顧する), *vt.* to look back; reflect *on*; review. —往事を回顧する, to reflect [look back] on the past. ¶ 回顧錄, reminiscences.
kaiko (解雇), *n.* discharge; dismissal. —解雇する, to discharge; dismiss.
kaikō (回航する), *vt.* to bring out (a ship). —, *vi.* to navigate; sail.
kaikō (海口), *n.* the entrance of a bay [channel; harbour].
kaikō (海光), *n.* sea-fire.
kaikō (海港), *n.* a sea-port. ¶ 海港檢疫, port-quarantine.
kaikō (開校する), *vi.* to open a school. ¶ 開校式, the opening ceremony of a school.
kaikō (開港), *n.* ❶ (外國貿易の爲の) opening of a port. ❷ (開港場) an open port.
kaikō (邂逅する), *v.* to meet *with*; come across [upon]; encounter.
kaikoku (戒告), *n.* warning. —戒告する, to warn; give warning.
kaikoku (廻國), *n.* ❶ going round [wandering about] the country. ❷ (廻國巡禮) pilgrimage (事); a pilgrim (人).

kaikoku (海國), *n.* a maritime country [power]; a sea-girt land (四面海の). ¶ 海國民, a maritime nation. —海國主義, navalism.

kaikoku (開國), *n.* ❶ (建國) foundation of a state; establishment of an empire. ❷ (外國と交通を開くこと) opening of a country.

kaikomu (買込む), *vt.* to buy in; buy up (買占める).

kaikomu (掻込む), *vt.* ❶ (掻寄せる) to collect; rake in. ❷ (脇へ抱へる) to hold under an arm. ❸ (液體を汲入れる) to scoop in.

kaikon (悔恨), *n.* contrition; regret; remorse; repentance.

kaikon (塊根), *n.* a tuberous root. ¶ 塊根植物, a tuberous plant.

kaikon (開墾), *n.* bringing under cultivation; reclamation of waste-land; disafforestation (山林の). —開墾する, to reclaim; open; bring under cultivation. ¶ 開墾地, reclaimed land; land brought under cultivation.

Kaikōsha (偕行社), *n.* the Army [Military] Club.

kaiku (化育する), *vt.* to develop.

kaikyo (快擧), *n.* a fine [splendid] undertaking.

kaikyō (改鋏する), *vt.* to punch (a ticket).

kaikyō (海峽), *n.* a strait; straits (固有名詞と共に用ひる時); a sound; a belt (狹きもの). ¶ 海峽植民地, the Straits Settlements (馬剌加及び新嘉坡).

kaikyōbyō (懷鄉病), *n.* homesickness; nostalgia.

kaikyū (階級), *n.* rank; class; grade. —階級的感情, class-feeling. ¶ 第三階級, the third estate. —階級意識, class consciousness. —階級制度, the class system. —階級戰 [鬪爭], class struggle [strife].

kaikyū (懷舊), *n.* recollection; retrospection; retrospect. —懷舊の涙に暮れる, to be bathed in tears by recollections. ¶ 懷舊談, reminiscences; recollections.

kaimaki (掻卷), *n.* a quilt; a sleeved bed-covering.

kaimamiru (垣間見る), *v.* to peep; take a peep.

kaimei (改名する), *vi.* to change one's name.

kaimei (開明), *n.* enlightenment; civilization.

kaimen (海面), *n.* ❶ the sea-surface; the sea-level. ❷ (海に面したる側) the sea-front.

kaimen (海綿), *n.* a sponge.

kaimodosu (買戻す), *vt.* to repurchase; buy back; redeem.

kaimoku (皆目), *ad.* utterly; absolutely; entirely; at all. —皆目分らぬ, ① (解らぬ) to be completely incomprehensible; not to understand at all. ② (知れぬ) to be utterly unknown.

kaimono (買物), *n.* ❶ (物を買ふこと) bargain; purchase; shopping. ❷ (買ったもの) a purchase. ❸ (買ふべきもの) things to purchase [buy]; purchases to be made. —買物する, to make a purchase. —買物に行く, to go (out) shopping.

kaimu (皆無), *n.* nothing; naught; nil. ——, *ad.* entirely (打消文に用ふ); utterly (同上). —殆ど皆無, next to nothing.

kaimu (海霧), *n.* sea-fog.

kaimyō (戒名), *n.* a posthumous Buddhist name.

kain (下院), *n.* the Lower Chamber [House]. ☞ *shūgiin*. ¶ 下院議員, a member of the Lower House [Chamber]; a Congressman (米); a Representative (米).

kain (禍因), *n.* a cause of evil.

kainai (甲斐ない), *a.* ❶ (詮なし) unavailing; inoperative (利き目なき); vain; useless. ❷ (未熟) green; inexperienced; callow. ☞ *kai* (甲斐). —甲斐なく, to no purpose [effect]; in vain; without success. —生きて甲斐ない身の上, this life which is not worth living. —後悔するも甲斐なし, to be of no avail to repent.

kainan (海難), *n.* perils of the sea; a casualty [disaster] at sea. ¶ 海難救助, salvage. —海難屆, a protest.

kainanpū (海軟風), *n.* 【地文】 a sea-breeze.

kainarasu (飼馴す), *vt.* to domesticate; tame.

kaine (買値), *n.* cost price; prime cost.

kaineko (飼猫), *n.* a domestic cat.

kainin (解任する), *vt.* to recall; release from office.

kainin (懷妊), *n.* pregnancy; conception (受胎). ☞ *ninshin* (姙娠). —懷妊する, to conceive; become pregnant.

kainushi (買主), *n.* a buyer; a purchaser.

kainushi (飼主), *n.* the master; the owner.

kaioki (買置), *n.* ❶ (事) buying and keeping. ❷ (品) articles bought and kept. —買ひ置く, to buy and keep.

kaiōsei (海王星), *n.* 【天】 Neptune.

kairai (傀儡), *n.* a doll; a puppet. ¶ 傀儡師, a puppet-man; a wire-puller (黑幕).

kairaku (快樂), *n.* ❶ (樂しみ) pleasure; enjoyment. ❷ (喜悅) mirth; merriment. —快樂を求める, to pursue pleasure; gather (life's) roses. ¶ 快樂主義, hedonism; epicureanism.

kairan (解纜する), *vi.* to weigh

anchor; sail *from*; set sail. —神戸を解纜する, to sail from Kōbe.

kairan (壞亂), *n.* subversion (秩序の); corruption (風俗の); demoralization (同上). —壞亂する, to subvert; corrupt; demoralize.

kairei (廻禮), *n.* a round of complimentary visits. —廻禮に行く, to go [pay; make] a round of complimentary calls [visits].

kaireki (改曆), *n.* ❶ (曆法改正) correction of the calendar. ❷ (改年) the change of the year; the new year.

kairi (海狸), *n.* 【哺乳】the beaver.

kairi (海里), *n.* a sea-mile; a knot; a nautical mile.

kairiku (海陸), *n.* land and sea. —海陸にて, by sea and land.

kairitsu (介立する), *vi.* to intervene [stand; lie] *between*.

kairitsu (戒律), *n.* commandments; precepts; Buddhist precepts.

kairo (回路), *n.* 【電】a circuit. ¶ 再生回路, regenerative circuit.

kairo (海路), *n.* a sea-route. —海路で, by sea.

kairo (懷爐), *n.* a pocket-warmer; a pocket-stove.

kairō-dōketsu (偕老同穴), *n.* 【海綿】Venus's flower-basket. —偕老同穴の契を結ぶ, to pledge mutual fidelity.

kairō (廻廊), *n.* a corridor; a gallery; a passage.

kairyō (改良), *n.* improvement; amelioration; reform. —改良する, to improve; ameliorate; reform; make better. ¶ 改良服, a reformed dress. —改良者, an improver; a reformer.

kairyō (飼料), *n.* provender; fodder.

kairyoku (怪力), *n.* Herculean strength; remarkable strength; mysterious power.

kairyoku (海綠-色), *n.* sea-green.

kairyū (海流), *n.* an oceanic [ocean] current.

kairyū (會流する), *v.* confluent. ¶ 會流點, a confluence.

kairyū (開立), *n.* 【數】extraction of a cube root.

kaisai (快哉を叫ぶ), to utter a cry of joy.

kaisai (皆濟する), *vt.* to pay off [up]; pay in full. —借金を皆濟する, to pay up [off] the debts.

kaisai (開催する), *vt.* to hold; give; open. —開催中の會議, council in session.

kaisaku (開鑿), *n.* cutting; excavation; digging. —開鑿する, to cut; excavate; dig. ¶ 開鑿工事, excavation works.

kaisan (海產-物), *n.* marine products. ¶ 海產動物, marine animals. —海產物問屋, a wholesale dealer in marine products.

kaisan (開山), *n.* the founder of a Buddhist temple [sect]; a founder.

kaisan (解散), *n.* dissolution (議會·會社等の); disbandment (軍隊の); dispersion (集會の); 【軍】the dismiss (休む時の). —議會を解散する, to dissolve the Diet.

kaisatsu (改札する), *vi.* to examine [punch] tickets. ¶ 改札係, a ticket examiner; a ticket collecter. —改札口, a (platform) wicket.

kaisatsu (開札する), *vi.* to open tenders.

kaisei (回生-起死), *n.* restoration of the dead to life. —回生起死の妙藥, a wonderful medicine for restoring the dead to life.

kaisei (改正), *n.* ❶ (變更) alteration; change. ❷ (改善) improvement; reform. ❸ (修正) revision; amendment. **—— -suru,** *vt.* ❶ to alter; change. ❷ to improve; reform. ❸ to revise; amend. —市區を改正する, to improve the streets of the city. —汽車時間表を改正する, to alter [change] the railway time-table. ¶ 改正規則, revised regulations.

kaisei (快晴の), *a.* fine; clear; cloudless. —本日天氣快晴, The weather is fine to-day.

kaisei (海生の), *a.* 【植】salt; marine.

kaiseki (解析), *n.* analysis; anatomy; dissection. —解析する, to analyze; anatomize. ¶ 解析幾何學, 【數】analytical geometry.

kaiseki (會席), *n.* a meeting.

kaisen (回旋), *n.* involution; convolution. —回旋する, to revolve; rotate.

kaisen (疥癬), *n.* itch; scabies; mange (馬·犬等の).

kaisen (改選), *n.* re-election. —改選する, to re-elect.

kaisen (海戰), *n.* a naval action [engagement]; a sea-fight. ¶ 海戰術, naval tactics. —海戰記念日, the Naval Battle Commemoration Day; the Navy Day.

kaisen (開戰), *n.* outbreak of war [hostilities]. —開戰の詔勅, Imperial proclamation of war. —開戰する, to open war; commence [open] hostilities.

kaisen (會戰), *n.* an encounter; a battle. —會戰する, to fight; fight a battle; encounter; meet.

kaisetsu (廻折), *n.* 【光】diffraction. —廻折する, to diffract.

kaisetsu (開設), *n.* establishment. —開設する, to establish; found; open.

kaisetsu (解說), *n.* explanation; illustration; a key.

kaisha (會社), *n.* a company; a corporation. —會社組織にする,

to organize into a company; change into the company system. —會社を解散する, to dissolve a company; wind up a company (清算を済まして). ¶會社法, a company act; a company law. —會社員, an employé of a company.

kaisha (膾炙する), *v.* to be well known *to*; be in everybody's mouth; be familiar *to*.

kaishaku (介錯する), *v.* to cut off a person's head when he commits suicide by disembowelment. ¶介錯人, an assistant; a second at *harakiri*.

kaishaku (解釋), *n.* ❶ (解明) explanation; elucidation; exposition (法律など). ❷ (註解) note; commentary; annotation. —解釋する, ① to explain; elucidate; expound (法律·經典など); construe; interpret. ② to annotate; comment; gloss. —嚴格な解釋から云へば, strictly interpreted; if we put a strict construction upon it. ¶英文解釋法, a key to English translation. —解釋者, ① an explainer; an elucidator; an exponent. ② an annotator; a commentator.

kaishi (開示する), *vt.* to display; unroll; disclose; open *to*; lay before.

kaishi (開始), *n.* commencement; opening; inauguration. —開始する, to commence; open; start (事業·談話など).

kaishi (懐紙), *n.* toilet-paper; paper carried in the bosom.

kaishiki (解式), *n.* a key.

kaishime (買占), *n.* 【商】 corner; rig; buying up. —買ひ占める, to corner; buy up.

kaishin (改心), *n.* conversion; reform. —改心さす, to convert; reclaim; reform. —改心する, to reform (oneself); amend; turn over a new leaf. —改心の見込なし, to be beyond [past] reclamation.

kaishin (改進的), *a.* progressive. ¶改進黨, the Progressive Party.

kaishin (廻診する), *v.* to visit; go one's round (病家を).

kaishin (海神), *n.* the sea-god; Neptune (羅馬).

kaishin (海深), *n.* the depth of a sea.

kaishin (開進), *n.* evolution; development. —開進する, to evolve; develop.

kaishin (會心の), *a.* congenial; agreeable; satisfactory. —會心の友, a congenial friend. —會心の作, a work after one's fancy [heart]. —會心の笑みを浮べる, to give a smile of satisfaction.

kaisho (楷書), *n.* the square style of Chinese character-writing.

kaishō (改稱する), *v.* to change (a) name [title]; rename.

kaishō (海相), *n.* =*kaigun* (海軍大臣).

kaishō (海嘯), *n.* 【地文】 a tidal bore; a tidal wave.

kaishō (會商), *n.* negotiation. —會商する, to negotiate *with*.

kaishōhō (海商法), *n.* the law of maritime commerce.

kaishoku (解職), *n.* dismissal; release from office [a post]. —解職する, to dismiss; release from office [a post].

kaishoku (會食), *n.* mess; dining together. —會食する, to dine together [with]; mess together [with]; take meal together.

kaishu (會主), *n.* the promoter [convener] of a meeting (發起者); the chairman (座長).

kaishū (回收する), *vt.* to collect; withdraw; retire. —貸金を回收する, to withdraw loans.

kaishū (改宗), *n.* conversion; proselytism. —改宗さす, to convert; proselytize. —佛教に改宗する, to be converted to Buddhist; turn a Buddhist. ¶改宗者, a convert; a proselyte.

kaishū (改修), *n.* repairs; improvement. —改修する, to repair; improve (a river).

kaishū (晦澁の), *a.* obscure; crabbed.

kaishun (回春), *n.* recovery.

kaishun (改悛), *n.* penitence; repentance; reform. —改悛する, to mend; reform.

kaiso (開祖), *n.* the founder; the originator.

kaisō (回想), *n.* recollection; reminiscence; review. —回想する, to recollect; review; call [bring] to mind.

kaisō (廻送する), *vt.* to transport; forward.

kaisō (廻漕), *n.* transportation; shipping; carriage by sea. —廻漕する, to transport by sea. ¶廻漕問屋, a shipping-agent. —廻漕業, shipping [carrying] trade; marine transportation business.

kaisō (改葬), *n.* reburial; reinterment. —改葬する, to rebury; reinter.

kaisō (海草, 海藻), *n.* the seaweeds.

kaisō (海葬), *n.* burial at sea. —海葬する, to bury at sea.

kaisō (潰走さす), *vt.* to rout; put to rout; put to flight; scatter. —潰走する, to stampede; scatter.

kaisō (會葬する), *vi.* to attend a funeral. ¶會葬者, a mourner; persons attending a funeral.

kaisoku (快速な), *a.* fast; speedy; swift. ¶快速力, high speed. (快速力を出す, to develop high speed.)

kaison (海損), *n.* an average. ¶ 單獨(共同)海損,【商】particular (general) average. —海損不擔保, free of all average (f.a.a. と略す). —海損契約書, an average agreement (bond).

kaisū (回數), *n.* the number of times; frequency. ¶ 回數券, a commutation [season] ticket.

kaisui (海水), *n.* sea-water.

kaisuiyoku (海水浴), *n.* sea-bathing. ¶ 海水浴場, a bathing-place; a sea-bathing place.

kai-suru (介する), *v.* to interpose *between*; insert; get a person to mediate (仲人にする). —友人某を介して, through (the agency of) a friend.

kai-suru (解する), *vt.* ❶(理解) to understand; make out; comprehend; appreciate. ❷ (解釋) to take; accept; interpret. —文學を解する, to understand literature.

kaitai (拐帶する), *v.* to abscond *with*; make off *with*. ¶ 拐帶者, an absconder.

kaitai (解隊), *n.* 【軍】disbandment.

kaitai (解體), *n.* dismemberment; dissection; decomposition. ——-**suru**, *vt.* to dismember; dissect; decompose. —飛行機を解體する, to take an aeroplane to pieces.

kaitai (懈怠), *n.* neglect; negligence; omission.

kaitai (懷胎), *n.* pregnancy; conception.

kaitaku (開拓), *n.* bringing under cultivation; reclamation of waste land; colonization (植民). ——-**suru** (開拓する), *vt.* to bring under cultivation; reclaim; colonize. —新販路を開拓する, to open a new market. ¶ 開拓地, a tract of land cleared for cultivation; a clearing. —開拓者, a cultivator; a pioneer; a colonist.

kaitate (買建), *n.* (取引市場) a bull order.

kaite (買手), *n.* a purchaser; a buyer. —買手がつく(を探す), to find (look for) a purchaser.

kaitei (改訂), *n.* revision. —改訂する, to revise (書物·條約など). ¶ 改訂版, a revised edition.

kaitei (海底), *n.* the sea-bed; the bottom of a sea; the sea-bottom. —海底の沈積物, a marine deposit. —海底に沈む, to go to the bottom. ¶ 海底電報, a cable despatch; a submarine telegram; a cablegram. —海底電線, a submarine cable. —海底電信, submarine telegraph.

kaitei (海程), *n.* distance by sea.

kaitei (階梯), *n.* ❶(階段) a step; stairs; a ladder. ❷ (手引) a primer; ABC; an elementary book.

kaitei (開廷), *n.* sitting of a court; opening of a court [law-court]. —開廷する, to open a court; hold a court; sit.

kaitei (解停), *n.* release from suspension.

kaiten (廻轉), *n.* revolution (周行); rotation (軸を中心として); gyration. —廻轉する, to revolve; rotate; gyrate. ¶ 廻轉臺, a turn-table (鐵道の). —廻轉木馬, a giddy-go-round; a merry-go-round; a roundabout; a whirligig.

kaiten (開店), *n.* opening a shop. —開店する, to open a shop; set up in trade.

kaiten (開展), *n.* ❶ extension; expansion. ❷(發達) development; evolution. —開展する, ① to extend; expand. ② to evolve; develop.

kaitetsuro (塊鐵爐), *n.* 【冶金】a bloomery.

kaitō (回答), *n.* an answer; a reply. —回答する, to answer; give an answer [a reply]; reply *to*. —回答を待つ, to wait for an answer.

kaitō (快刀), *n.* a sharp sword [blade]. —快刀亂麻を斷つ, to cut the Gordian knot.

kaitō (解答), *n.* an answer;【數】a solution. —解答する, to answer; solve. ¶ 解答者, a solver.

kaitō (會頭), *n.* the president (of a society).

kaitsū (開通), *n.* opening; opening for traffic. —開通する, to open; be opened for traffic. ¶ 開通期, the date of opening. —運河開通式, the opening (ceremony) of a canal.

kaitsuburi (かいつぶり), *n.*【鳥】the little grebe. =**nio** (鳰).

kaitsuke (買附の), *a.* accustomed; customary. —買附けの店, a shop where one is a regular customer; a shop where one has been accustomed to make purchases.

kaitsumamu (掻摘む), *vt.* to summarize; abridge; sum up. —掻い摘んで云へば, in short; briefly stated; to sum up. —大意を掻い摘む, to make a summary of the main points.

kaiukenin (買受人), *n.* a purchaser; a buyer.

kaiukeru (買受ける), *vt.* to buy over; take over; buy.

kaiun (海運), *n.* shipping; marine transportation; carriage [transportation] by sea. ¶ 海運業, carrying [shipping] trade; marine transportation business; shipping business; shipping interests. —海運界, the shipping world. —海運政策, shipping policy.

kaiun (開運), *n.* improvement of one's fortune. —開運の護符, an amulet for bettering one's fortune. —開運の日を待つ, to wait for a better fortune [for fortune's smiles].

kaiusagi (飼兎), *n.* 【哺乳】the rabbit.

kaiwa (會話), *n.* conversation; dialogue (對話). —會話體で書く, to write in a colloquial [conversational] style.

kaiwai (界隈), *n.* vicinity; neighbourhood. —界隈の人々, neighbours; the neighbourhood.

kaiyaku (解約), *n.* the termination [dissolution] of a contract. —解約する, to terminate [dissolve] a contract.

kaiyō (海洋), *n.* an ocean. —海洋の自由, the freedom of the sea.

kaiyō (解傭), *n.* dismissal; discharge. ☞ ***kaiko*** (解雇).

kaiyū (回遊), *n.* an excursion; a trip; a circular tour. —回遊する, to make an excursion; make a tour. ¶回遊切符, an excursion ticket; a circular ticket. —回遊列車, an excursion train. —回遊者, an excursionist.

kaiyū (洄游), *n.* migration. —洄游する, to migrate.

kaizai (介在する), *vi.* to intervene *between*; lie *between*; stand *between*.

kaizaiku (貝細工), *n.* ❶ shell-work. ❷【植】the winged everlasting.

kaizan (改竄), *n.* revision; correction. —改竄する, ①(訂正) to revise; correct; amend. ②(改變) to change; tamper *with* (勝手に書類・遺言狀などを); dabble *with* (勝手に本文などを). ¶改竄者, a corrector.

kaizen (改善), *n.* improvement; betterment; amelioration. ——**-suru,** *vt.* to improve; better; ameliorate. ——, *vi.* to improve; ameliorate; mend. —道路を改善する, to improve the road.

kaizeru (カイゼル), *n.* Kaiser.

kaizō (改造), *n.* reconstruction; reorganization; rebuilding. —社會の改造, the reorganization [regeneration] of society. ——**-suru,** *vt.* to reorganize; reconstruct; rebuild. —社會(內閣)を改造する, to reorganize society (the cabinet).

kaizoe (介添), *n.* help; chaperonage (公會の席で貴婦人の); tending (病人の). ¶介添人, a second (決鬪の); a sick-nurse (病人の); a bridesmaid (花嫁の); one's best man (花婿の); a bottle-holder (拳鬪の); a chaperon (貴婦人の).

kaizoku (海賊), *n.* ❶ (行爲) piracy. ❷ (人) a pirate; a sea-robber; a (sea-)rover. ¶海賊船, a pirate-ship; a sea-rover.

kaizu (海圖), *n.* a (sea-)chart.

kaizuka (貝塚), *n.* a shell-mound; a (kitchen-)midden.

kaji (舵, 梶), *n.* ❶ (船の舵) a rudder (舵板); a helm (特に舵柄). ❷ (車の梶棒) the shaft; the thill ❸ (楫) (櫂) an oar. —舵とる, [*vt.*] to steer; helm; manage; control. ☞ ***omokaji, torikaji.***

kaji (火事), *n.* a fire; a conflagration (大火). —火事に遭ふ, to suffer from a fire. —火事を出す, to cause a fire. —火事だ! 火事だ!, Fire! Fire! ¶火事場, the scene of a fire; a place in flames (燃えて居る所); the ground burnt down (燒跡). (火事場泥棒する, ① to thieve at a fire. ② (どさくさ紛れに私利を得る) to fish in troubled waters.) —火事裝束, a fire-dress.

kaji (加持), *n.* incantation. ¶加持祈禱, faith-cure; incantations and prayers.

kaji (家事), *n.* domestic [family] affairs; household matters; *menage* 〔佛〕. —家事の都合により, for family reasons. ¶家事費, domestic expenses. —家事經濟, domestic [household] economy.

kaji (鍛冶), *n.* a smith; a blacksmith (鐵工). ¶鍛冶場, a forge; a smithy.

kajibō (梶棒), *n.* the shaft; the thill.

kajika (鰍), *n.* 【魚】the sculpin.

kajika (河鹿), *n.* 【兩棲】Hyla (學名); the singing frog.

kajikamu (龜屈む), *vi.* Ⓢかじける. to be numb with cold; be benumbed; be chilled.

kajiki(maguro) (旗魚), *n.* 【魚】the spearfish.

kajiku (花軸), *n.* 【植】the rachis, rhachis; the flower-stalk.

kajin (佳人), *n.* a beauty. ¶才子佳人, the wit and beauty.

kajin (家人), *n.* ❶ (妻子眷族) the family; one's people; the inmates (of a house). ❷ (家臣, 家隸) retainers; followers; one's people 〔俗〕. —家人の隙を窺ふ, to watch for a chance to slip into (out of) a house.

kajiritsuku (齧附く), *vi.* ❶ to fasten one's teeth *in*. ❷ (絡みつく, 離れまいとする) to cling (fast) *to*; cleave *to*; stick *to*. —頸に齧り附く[取り附く], to hang on another's neck.

kajiru (齧る), *vt.* ❶ to gnaw; nibble *at* (少々づつ). ❷ (部分的に知る) to smatter; get a smattering *of*. —齧り取る, to bite off; gnaw away [off]. —佛

語を少し齧る, to get a smattering of French.

kajitori (舵取), *n.* a steerer; a steersman; a helmsman; a coxswain (ボートの).

kajitsu (果實), *n.* ❶ (植物の實) a fruit; fruitage (總稱); a nut (堅果); a berry (漿果). ❷【法】fruits. ¶ 果實酒, fruit-liquor[-drink].

kajitsu (過日), *ad.* the other day; a few days ago.

kajiya (鍛冶屋), *n.* = *kaji* (鍛冶).

kajo (花序), *n.* 【植】inflorescence.

kajō (下情), *n.* the condition of people. —下情に通じる, to possess knowledge of the condition of the people.

kajō (過剩の), *a.* excessive; surplus; superfluous. ¶ 過剩人口, surplus population.

kajō (箇條), *n.* an article (條目); a condition (條件); a provision (規定). —箇條を擧げる, to give the articles. ¶ 箇條書, the articles; stipulations (約束の). (箇條書にする, to itemize; put down article by article.)

kaju (果樹), *n.* a fruit-tree. ¶ 果樹園, an orchard. —果樹栽培, pomiculture.

kajū (苛重の), *a.* heavy; burdensome.

kajū (加重), *n.* aggravation.

kajū (家従), *n.* a lower official in a household; a lower household official.

kajū (過重の), *a.* overburdensome; too heavy. —過重視する, [*vt.*] to overestimate; set too much value *upon*; attach too much importance *to*.

kaka, kakā, (嬶), *n.* ❶ (母の賤稱) a mammy. ❷ (家婦の賤稱) (my) old woman [俗]; a wife. ¶ 嬶天下, petticoat government; smock-rule; henpeckery.

kakae (抱), *n.* ❶ (抱へること) holding in arms. ❷ (容積) an armful *of*. ❸ (扶養し置くこと) maintenance. ❹ (雇ひ置くこと) employment. ❺ (抱へてある人) an employee. ¶ 抱へ車, ① a private *jinrikisha*. ② (抱車夫) a *jinrikisha*-man in private employ. —抱へ運轉手, a chauffeur in one's employ; one's chauffeur.

kakaenushi (抱主), *n.* the master [*fem.* mistress]; the employer.

kakaeru (抱へる), *vt.* ❶ (抱きかゝへる) to hold in arms (抱く); hold under one's arms (脇に抱へる); embrace (人を抱く). ❷ (雇入れる) to engage; keep (抱へ置く). —車夫を抱へ入れる, to engage a *jinrikisha*-man.

kakageru (揭げる), *vt.* ❶ (高く上げる) to lift up; raise; hoist; hang up (高く吊す). ❷ to insert *in*. —衣を褰げて小川を渉る, to tuck up the skirts and wade a brook.

kakaku (家格), *n.* family rank.

kakaku (價格), *n.* price; value. —價格を一定する, to fix the prices. —價格を附する, to valuate; appraise. ¶ 市場價格, market price. —價格表記郵便物, mail matter with declared value. —價格消却法, the method of depreciation.

kakan (花冠), *n.* ❶【植】the corolla. ❷ (花にて造れる冠) a coronal; a chaplet; a wreath.

kakan (果敢の), *a.* resolute; determined. —果敢の氣に富む, to possess a very resolute spirit.

kakan (禍患), *n.* misfortune (不幸); a calamity (災難); an evil (禍).

kakao (カカオ), *n.* cacao (木又は其實); the cocoa-tree (木); a cocoa-bean (實).

kakari (掛, 係), *n.* ❶ (關係) relation; connection. ❷ (擔任) charge; business (職務); a department (部屬). ❸ (擔當者) the person in charge *of*; the person responsible *for*. ❹ (費用) expenses; expenditure. ❺ (負擔) burden; charge; taxes. —係の役人, the official in charge. —掛りを拂ふ, to pay the expenses. —掛り負けになる, The expenses exceed the earnings; The income runs short of the expenses.

kakari (懸), *n.* hanging; suspension. —懸りの點, the centre of suspension.

kakariai (係合, 掛合), *n.* implication; involvement. —係合ひになる, to be involved in (the affair). —係り合ふ, to be involved *in*; be implicated *in*; be mixed up *in*.

kakariba (繫船場), *n.* an anchorage; a roadstead (沖の).

kakaribito, kakariudo, (掛人), *n.* Ⓢ 寄食者. a dependant; a hanger-on. —掛人となる, to sponge [hang] *on*.

kakarimusubi (係結), *n.* 【文】concord.

kakaritsuke (掛りつけの), *a.* regular. —掛りつけの醫者, one's family physician.

kakaru (掛かる), *vi.* ❶ (懸) (つりさがる) to hang *on* [*upon*]; be suspended; hang *over* (疑惑·危難など). ❷ (目方がある) to weigh. ❸ (如何に依る) to depend *on*; hang *on*. ❹ (架) (橋梁·鐵道等) to be built; be laid. ❺ (投錨) to cast anchor. ❻ (罹) (病氣) to suffer *from*; be attacked; be seized *with*. ❼ (引掛る) (網・枝・釘・係蹄(ワナ)等) to be caught *in* (網・係蹄に); be caught *on* (釘・枝・電線などに); fall *into* (陷る). ❽ 〔要〕(費す) to take; require; cost (金が). ❾ (著手) to set *to*; go about; begin *to*. ❿ (水・雨など) to be splashed *with* (water); be exposed *to* (rain); be in (the rain). ⓫ (係はる) to concern (名譽・一身などに). ⓬ (課稅) to be imposed *upon*; be levied. —罹り易い, [*a.*] liable (不幸・災難等に); subject *to* (病氣に). —いくら掛ッても, at any expense; cost what it may. —醫者にかゝる, to consult a doctor. —ベンチに凭る, to sit on a bench. —詐欺にかゝる, to be swindled. —盗難に罹る, to be robbed. —誰でも掛ッて來い, Come on, any one of you. —この帽子は十圓かゝッた, This hat cost me ten *yen*; I gave [paid] ten *yen* for this hat. —上野まで三時間かゝる, It takes three hours to reach Uyeno.

kakaru (斯かる), *a.* such; this; that. —斯かる狀態, such a state [condition]. —斯かる折しも, at this time [junction].

-kakaru (かかる), *suf.* to begin *to*; be going *to*; be about *to*. —しかゝる, to set [begin] doing. —死にかゝッて居る, to be on the point [verge] of death.

kakasazu (缺かさず), *ad.* regularly. —一夜も缺かさず, without missing a night.

kakaseru (書かせる), *vt.* to cause to write; (書いて貰ふ) have (a letter) written (字を); have (a picture) painted (繪を).

kakashi (案山子), *n.* ❶ a scarecrow. ❷ (看板の人) a scarecrow; a lay-figure; a man of straw. ❸ (人おどし) a bogie; a bugbear.

kakato (踵), *n.* the heel (人の). ¶ 踵摺れ, a heel-sore.

kakawarazu (拘らず), *prep.* ❶ (にも拘らず) in spite *of*; notwithstanding; with [for] all. ❷ (關係なく又は如何を問はず) regardless *of*; irrespective(-ly) *of*; without regard *to*. ——, *conj.* (それにも拘らず) however; notwithstanding that; though; although. —晴雨に拘らず, whether it be [is] fine or not; rain or shine. —多少に拘らず, no matter how small; irrespective of the quantity. —男女に拘らず, irrespectively of the sex; without regard to sex. —友人の諫めるにも拘らず, notwithstanding the remonstrances of one's friends.

kakawaru (拘・關・係はる), *v.* ❶ (拘泥) to adhere *to*; keep *to*. ❷ (影響) to affect; concern. ❸ (關與) to be concerned *in*; have to do *with*; have a hand [finger] *in*. ❹ (從事) to engage [concern] oneself *in*; deal *with*. —名譽に關はる, to affect one's honour [reputation]. —一身上に關はる, to concern one's welfare. —命に關はる大事件, a serious affair which may endanger one's life.

kake, kakera, (片, 缺), *n.* a fragment; a piece; a bit. —硝子の缺け, a fragment [bit] of glass.

kake (掛), *n.* ❶ (信用) credit; trust. ❷ = *kakedaikin*. ❸ =*kakene*. ❹ (計算歩合) per cent. —掛で, on credit [trust]; on account. (掛で賣買する, to deal on credit.) —一割掛で賣る, to sell at 10 per cent. profit.

kake (驅), *n.* run; gallop (馬の).

kake (賭), *n.* a bet; a wager; a stake. —賭する, to lay a wager; make a bet; bet.

-kake (掛), ❶ unfinished. ❷ about *to*; on the point *of*. ☞ *-kakeru*. ❸ (架) a rack; a stand. —吸(食)ひ掛けの, half-smoked(-eaten).

kakeagaru (驅上る), *vi.* to run up.

kakeai (掛合), *n.* ❶ (談判) negotiation; consultation. ❷ (交互) alternation. ❸ (交互に語ること) alternate speeches. —掛合ひに, alternately; by turns. ¶ 掛合ひ人, a negotiator.

kakeami (掛網), *n.* ❶ (漁具) a wall-net. ❷ (ストーヴ用) a fire-guard.

kakeashi (驅足), *n.* 【軍】double; double-quick; double-time; canter (馬の緩漫な). —驅足する,【軍】to double; march at double-quick; have a run. —驅足進め!, Double march!

kakeau (掛合ふ), *v.* to negotiate *with*; treat *with*. —値段を掛け合ふ, to bargain with a person over a price.

kakeawasu (掛合はす), *vt.* to multiply. ☞ *kakeru* (掛ける).

kakebarai (掛拂), *n.* payment on account.

kakebuton (掛蒲團), *n.* a coverlet; a coverlid.

kakedaikin (掛代金), *n.* an account; a bill; money due for goods sold on account.

kakedashi (驅出), *n.* ❶ (走り出すこと) start (競走の); bolting (馬など突然の); scampering. ❷ (始) beginning. ❸ (新參) a person fresh *from*; a greenhorn. —驅け出す, to start; bolt; scamper.

kakedokei (掛時計), *n.* a clock; a wall-clock.
kakefu (掛布), *n.* a cover; a cloth-covering.
kakegae (掛替), *n.* a substitute; a reserve; a spare (thing). —掛替へのない, the sole; the only. (掛替へのない命, the life which cannot be replaced.)
kakegai (掛買), *n.* purchase on account.
kakegami (懸紙, 附箋), *n.* a tag; a slip; a label.
kakegane (掛金), *n.* =*kakigane.*
kakego (掛子), *n.* a tray.
kakegoe (掛聲), *n.* ❶ a shout; a call. ❷ (聲援) shouts of encouragement. ❸ (拍子聲) a shout to mark time. —掛聲勇ましく, with tremendous shouts.
kakegoto (賭事), *n.* betting. —賭事する, to bet; lay; gamble. ¶賭事師, a better.
kakehanareru (掛離れる), *vi.* to be far apart; be far off [away]; be at a distance. —掛け離れた時代, distant [remote] ages.
kakehashi (懸橋), *n.* ❶ (棧道) a bridge over a gorge. ❷ =*hashigo* (梯子). ❸ (媒介) an intermediary; mediation —戀の懸橋, love-broking.
kakehazushi (懸外), *n.* hanging and unhanging.
kakehedate (懸隔), *n.* estrangement; distance; a gulf.
kakehi (筧), *n.* a water-pipe; a spout.
kakehiki (掛引, 駈引), *n.* ❶ (進退) advance and retreat. ❷ (値段の掛引) bargain(-ing); haggling; chaffering. ❸ (策略) tactics. —値段の掛引をする, to bargain about the price.
kakei (火刑), *n.* the stake; fire and fagot. ☞ *hiaburi* (火刑).
kakei (河系), *n.* a river system.
kakei (家計), *n.* family circumstances; housekeeping. —家計不如意, straitened family circumstances. ¶家計簿, a domestic account-book.
kakei (家系), *n.* lineage; ancestry; stock.
kakejaya (掛茶屋), *n.* a (wayside) resting-booth.
kakeji (掛字), *n.* Ⓢ 懸軸, 懸物. a *kakemono*; a hanging picture.
kakekaeru (掛替へる), *vt.* to substitute; replace; change. —橋を架け替へる, to rebuild a bridge.
kakekin (掛金), *n.* ❶ (賣掛代金) money due for goods sold on credit. ❷ (賦金) an instalment. —五十錢宛掛金する, to pay in instalments of fifty *sen.*
kakekin (賭金), *n.* a bet; stakes.
kakekko (駈事), *n.* a race. —駈事する. to run a race.
kakekomu (駈込む), *vi.* to run into.
kakekotoba (掛詞), *n.* a play upon words; a word-play; a *jeu de mots* [佛].
kakemawaru (駈廻る), *vi.* ❶ (走り廻る) to run about; gambol; skip. ❷ (奔走する) to bustle about. —あちこち駈け廻る, to beat up and down.
kakeme (掛目), *n.* weight; measure. —掛目が輕い, to be light in weight.
kakemochi (掛持する), *v.* to do business in two or more places. —三校掛持ちする, to teach at three schools.
kakemono (掛物), *n.* ❶ (懸軸) a *kakemono*; a hanging picture. ❷ (菓子) coating. ❸ (衾衣) a bed-covering; a coverlet.
kakemono (賭物), *n.* a bet; stakes; a wager. ☞ *kake* (賭).
kaken (家憲), *n.* the rules [constitution] of a house; household regulations. —家憲を定める, to establish the rules of a house.
kakenaosu (掛直す), *vt.* ❶ (改めてかける) to rehang. ❷ (量り直す) to reweigh; weigh again.
kakene (掛値), *n.* ❶ (二價) an overcharge. ❷ (誇張) an exaggeration. —掛値なき, ① net; clear. ② unexaggerated. —掛値を言ふ, to ask two prices; ask a fancy price. —現金掛値なし, Cash and one price only.
kakenukeru (駈拔ける), *vi.* to outrun; run past; run through.
kakeochi (駈落), *n.* ❶ (道行) elopement. ❷ (逐電) decampment; abscondence. —男と駈落する, to elope [run away] with a lover. ¶駈落結婚, a runaway match. —駈落者, a runaway; an eloper.
kakeru (翔る), *vi.* to soar. —天を翔る雲雀, a soaring skylark; a lark in the air.
kakeru (掛ける), *vt.* ❶〔懸〕(吊す) to hang; suspend; hook (鉤に). ❷ (計量する) to weigh. ❸〔架〕(かけ渡す) to bridge (a river); span (a river with a bridge); build (a bridge). ❹ (課す) to impose [lay; put] (a tax) *on.* ❺ (迷惑・心配などを) to give; cause. ❻〔要〕(費す) to spend (金・時などを); lay out (金). ❼〔乘〕【數】 to multiply. ❽ (注ぎかける) to pour *on*; sprinkle *on*; throw *on.* ❾ [*vi.*] (腰掛ける) to sit down; take a seat. ❿ (掛金を) to pay in. ⓫ (交尾さす) to put *to.* ⓬ (著せる) to cover; wrap; lay (繪具など). —(に)かけては, in; in the point *of*; in the way *of.* —馬の蹄にかける, to

trample under (the horse's) hoof. —專門家の鑑定にかける, to submit it to an expert for examination; submit it for expert opinion. —卓布を掛ける, to put the table-cloth *on*; lay cloth; spread a cloth on (a table). —資本をかける, to spend money *on*; invest capital *in*. —四に三を掛ける, to multiply 4 by 3.

kakeru (缺ける), *vi.* ❶ (不足する) to lack; be missing; be wanting *in*. ❷ (損じる) to be broken [flawed]; chip (石などへげる). ❸ (不行屆になる) to be neglected. ❹ (虧) (月が) to wane. ——, *a.* lacking; wanting; destitute *of*; defective *in*. —一圓に參錢缺ける, to be three *sen* short of one *yen*. —禮儀に缺ける, to be lacking in manners [respect].

kakeru (驅ける), *vi.* to run; 【軍】 double; gallop (馬が). —驅け戻る, to run back.

kakeru (賭ける), *vt.* to bet; stake; wager. —馬に金を賭ける, to put [bet; stake] money on a horse. —命を賭けて爲す, to do at the risk of one's life.

-kakeru (かける), *suf.* to begin to; be going to; be on the point *of*. ☞ *-kakaru* (かかる). —手紙を書きかける, to begin writing a letter.

kakesaki (掛先), *n.* credit-customers.

kakesen (掛錢), *n.* an instalment.

kakeshōbu (賭勝負), *n.* a (betting) game; betting.

kakesu (懸巣), *n.* 【鳥】 the Japan [Japanese] jay.

kakete (驅手), *n.* a runner.

kakete (賭手), *n.* a better, bettor; a layer.

kakete (かけて), *particle.* ❶ (一帶に亙って) all over. ❷ (及びて) (from...) to [till]; between. ❸ (關して) as to; as regards; in the way of. ❹ (祈念して) by (God, 神かけてなど).

kaketobi (驅跳), *n.* flying jump [leap]; running jump.

kaketori (掛取), *n.* a (bill-) collector; bill-collecting. —掛取りに廻る, to go (round) bill-collecting.

kaketsu (可決する), *vt.* to pass; vote (投票により); agree to (a bill) (原案通りに). —可決確定, passed and decided on.

kaketsukeru (驅附ける), *vi.* to run up *to*; hasten *to*. —醫者へ驅け附ける, to run for a doctor.

kaketsunagi (掛繫), *n.* hedging.

kakeuri (掛賣), *n.* sale on credit; credit (sale). —掛賣する, to sell on credit; give credit. ¶ 掛賣帳, (小賣店) a credit sales book.

kakeya (掛矢, 大槌), *n.* a beetle; a large mallet; a wooden sledge-hammer.

kakeyoru (驅寄る), *vi.* to run up *to*; run close.

kakezan (掛算), *n.* multiplication.

kakezao (掛竿), *n.* a drying-pole.

kakezu (掛圖), *n.* a wall-map.

kakezuru (驅ずる), *vi.* Ⓢ 驅ずり廻る. to run about; busy oneself about; bustle about.

kaki (柿), *n.* 【植】 the persimmon.

kaki (牡蠣), *n.* 【貝】 the (edible) oyster. —牡蠣のフライを食ふ, to eat fried oysters. ¶ 牡蠣田; 牡蠣床, an oyster-bank [-bed; -field]. —牡蠣殼, an oyster-shell.

kaki (垣, 墻), *n.* a fence. —垣を以て繞らす, to enclose with a fence; fence round [in]. —兄弟墻に鬩ぐ, Brothers quarrel among themselves.

kaki (下記の), *a.* the following; the undermentioned.

kaki (火器), *n.* firearms.

kaki (火氣), *n.* heat; fire; flame.

kaki (花卉), *n.* a flower; a flowering plant; a bedder (花壇に適した). ¶ 花卉品評會, a flower-show.

kaki (花期), *n.* the flower-season.

kaki (夏季, 夏期), *n.* summer; summer-time; the summer season. ¶ 夏季學校, a summer-school. —夏季講習會, a summer lecture-class. —夏季休業[休暇], a summer vacation; summer holidays.

kaki (嫁期), *n.* nubility; the nubile [marriageable] age.

kāki (カーキー色), *n.* khaki. ¶ カーキー服, a khaki dress [uniform].

kakiatsumeru (書集める), *vt.* to compile.

kakiatsumeru (掻集める), *vt.* to glean; scrape together; rake together. —落葉を掻き集める, to rake together the fallen leaves.

kakiawasu (掻合はす), *vt.* to adjust. —着物の前を掻き合はす, to adjust one's dress.

kakichigaeru (書違へる), *vt.* to miswrite; make a mistake in writing; make a clerical error. —番地を書き違へる, to write down the wrong number.

kakichin (書賃), *n.* a charge [fee] for writing.

kakichirasu (書散らす), *vt.* to scribble.

kakidashi (書出), *n.* ❶ (筆頭) the first (in a list); the head of a list. ❷ (起筆) the beginning; the outset. ❸ (勘定書) a bill; an account bill. ❹ (掲示) a notice.

kakidasu (掻出す), *vt.* to rake out. —火を掻き出す(爐から), to rake out the fire.

kakigane (掛金), *n.* a catch; a latch; a staple. —掛金を掛ける [下ろす], to latch; fasten a staple. —掛金を外す, to unfasten a staple.

kakigoshi (垣越しに), *ad.* over a hedge [fence].

kakihajimeru(書始める), *v.* to begin to write.

kakihan (書判), *n.* a signature; a written seal-mark; a monogram.

kakiire (書入), *n.* ❶ (記入) entry; inscription; insertion. ❷ (財產の抵當) mortgage; hypothecation. ❸ (當込み) anticipation. —書き入れる, to write in (手形などに); inscribe *in*; en- (*in*); mortgage. ——年一度の書入日, the busiest [most profitable] day of the year. —地所を書入れにして金を借りる, to borrow money by mortgaging land.

kakiireru(搔入れる), *vt.* to rake in. ¶搔入時, the money-making season.

kakiiro (柿色), *n.* yellowish-brown.

kakikae (書換), *n.* rewriting; renewal (更新); transfer (名義書換へ). —書き換へる, to rewrite; renew; transfer. (看板を書き換へる, to repaint a signboard.)

kakikata (書方), *n.* ❶ (運筆) the manner [method] of writing; a style. ❷ (措辭) phraseology. ❸ (習字) penmanship.

kakikesu (搔消す), *vt.* to scratch out; wipe out.

kakikieru (搔消える), *vi.* to vanish; disappear. ☞ *kieru.*

kakikizu (搔痕), *n.* a scratch.

kakikomi (書込み), *n.* insertion; entry (載). —書き込む, to insert *in*; enter *in*; write *in*.

kakikomi (搔込主義), *n.* the principle of taking everything into one's lap; the raking-in principle.

kakikomu (搔込む), *vt.* to rake *in*. —食物を口に搔き込む, to shovel food into one's mouth.

kakikuwae (書加へ), *n.* addition; addendum. —書き加へる, to add.

kakimawasu (搔廻す), *vt.* ❶ (攪拌) to stir (up; about); churn. ❷ (搔探す) to rummage (about); ransack. ❸ (紛亂さす) to disturb; throw in confusion. ❹ (切廻す) to manage affairs arbitrarily [as one pleases]. —火を搔き廻す, to stir the fire; poke the fire (棒で). ——人で家を搔き廻す, to manage the whole household as one pleases.

kakimazeru (搔混せる), *vt.* to mix [mingle] by stirring; mix up. —卵を搔混せる, to beat up eggs.

kakimidasu (搔亂す), *vt.* to confuse; throw into confusion; disarrange. —搔亂した身裝を繕ふ, to adjust disarranged dress. —髮を搔亂して, with dishevelled hair.

kakimochi (缺餅), *n.* dried rice-cake.

kakimono(書物), *n.* (a) writing; a document.

kakimorasu (書漏らす), *vt.* to omit in writing. ☞ *kakiotosu.*

kakimushiru (搔挘る), *vt.* to scratch; tear. —髮をかきむしる, to tear one's hair.

kakin (家禽), *n.* the poultry; domestic fowls; a barn-door fowl. ¶家禽商, a poulterer.

kakin(瑕瑾), *n.* a flaw; a blemish; a defect. ☞ *kizu* (瑕).

kakinaosu (書直す), *vt.* to rewrite; write afresh.

kakinarasu (搔均らす), *vt.* to level; rake smooth [clean]. —灰を搔き均らす, to level ashes (with an ash-leveller); rake ashes level.

kakine (垣根), *n.* ❶ (垣のもと) the foot of a fence. ❷ (垣) a fence; a hedge.

kakinikui (書惡い), *a.* ❶ (運筆) awkward (筆など使ひにくい); difficult [hard] to write. ❷(作文) hard; difficult.

kakinokeru (搔退ける), *vt.* to rake aside. —人を搔き退けて見る, to see by pushing one's way through a crowd.

kakinokosu (書遺す), *vt.* to leave in writing. —後世に書き遺す, to leave in writing for future generations.

kakinoseru (書載せる), *vt.* ❶ (記入) to enter; record; book. ❷ (掲載) to give; insert.

kakinuki (書拔), *n.* an abstract. —書き拔く, to make an abstract (大要を); extract from (章句など); select from (善い所だけを).

kakioki (書置), *n.* a writing left behind; a written will (遺言狀). —書置をして家出する, to run away from home leaving a note behind.

kakiokuru(書送る), *vt.* to write *to*; send a letter *to*.

kakiotosu (書落す), *vt.* to omit in writing; omit to write.

kakiotosu (搔落す), *vt.* ❶ (切落) to cut off. ❷(ひっかき落す) to scratch off; scrape off. —靴の泥を搔き落す, to scrape off [away] mud from shoes.

kakiowaru (書終る), *v.* to finish writing; have done writing.

kakishirusu (書記す), *vt.* to write down; put down; set down.

kakisokonau (書損ふ), *v.* ❶ to make a mistake in writing; miswrite. ❷ to write wrong.

kakitasu (書足す), *v.* ❶ to write a postscript. ❷ to add (in writing); write in addition. ❸ to supplement; enlarge.

kakitateru (掻立てる), *vt.* to stir up; beat; poke (火など). —火を掻き立てる, to give the fire a stir; stir the fire. —行燈を掻き立てる, to feed up the square lantern.

kakite (書手), *n.* ❶ (筆者) a writer; a penman. ❷ (能筆家) a calligrapher. ❸ (作者) an author; a writer.

kakitome (書留), *n.* registration. —書留にする, to register. ¶ 書留料, registration-fee [-charge]. —書留郵便, a registered letter.

kakitomeru (書留める), *vt.* to make a note [memorandum; minute] *of*; write [put] down; take down. —住所姓名を書留める, to take down the name and address.

kakitori (書取), *n.* ❶ (筆記) taking down. ❷ (朗讀筆記) dictation. —書き取る, ①=*kakitomeru.* ② to write from dictation.

kakitsubata (燕子花), *n.* 【植】 the smooth iris.

kakitsuke (書附), *n.* ❶ (文書) a document. ❷ (覺書) a memorandum; a note. ❸ (勘定書) a bill.

kakitsukeru (書附ける), *vt.* = *kakitomeru.* —明細に書き附ける, to write down in detail. —忘れぬ様に書き附けて置く, to make a memorandum [take a note] of it so as not to forget it.

kakiwakeru (掻分ける), *vt.* to make one's way through. —群衆を掻き分けて進む, to make one's way through the crowd.

kakiwari (書割), *n.* 【劇】 scenery; set scene; scene-painting.

kakiyoseru (掻寄せる), *vt.* to rake together; scratch [scrape] up [together].

kakizome (書初), *n.* the first writing of the year.

kakka (閣下), *n.* your (his) excellency; your (their) excellencies; your (his) lordship (貴族に對し). —閣下及び諸君, Your Excellency and Gentlemen.

kakkaku (斯斯), *ad.* so; so and so; such and such. —斯々の次第で, for such and such reasons; in such various ways.

kakkaku (赫赫たる), *a.* brilliant; illustrious; glorious.

kakkan (客觀), *n.* 【哲】 an object. —客觀的研究 (描寫), an objective study (description).

kakke (脚氣), *n.* beri-beri 〔錫蘭〕. —脚氣が起る, to have an attack of beri-beri. ¶ 脚氣衝心, heart failure through beri-beri.

kakkei (活計), *n.* livelihood; living; subsistence. ☞ *seikei.*

kakketsu (喀血, 咯血), *n.* 【醫】 hemoptysis; blood-spitting. —喀血する, to vomit blood.

kakki (活氣), *n.* animation; vigour; spirit. —活氣のある, animated; spirited; vigorous. —活氣のない, unanimated; spiritless; dull. —活氣に富む (乏しい), to be full of (wanting in) spirit.

kakki (客氣), *n.* animal spirits; impetuosity; passion. —少年の客氣に驅られる, to be driven [urged] by the animal spirits of youth.

kakki (劃期的), *a.* epoch-making.

kakkiri (かっきり), *ad.* exactly; precisely; just. —かっきり七時に, at just 7 o'clock; at 7 o'clock sharp; precisely at 7 o'clock. —かっきり十三歳, to be thirteen years old to a day. —かっきり時間に間に合ふ, to be just in time.

kakko (括弧), *n.* 【印・數】 brackets; a parenthesis [*pl.* -theses]. —括弧に包む, to bracket; parenthesize; put in brackets [parenthesis]. ¶ 二重括弧, double parentheses.

kakko (確乎たる), *a.* steady; firm; positive. —確乎たる信念, a strong [firm] conviction. —確乎たる證據, an absolute proof; a strong evidence. —確乎不抜の精神, an unyielding spirit.

kakkō (郭公), *n.* 【鳥】 the (little) cuckoo.

kakkō (恰好), *n.* ❶ (形) shape; form; figure. ❷ (風態) appearance; fashion. ❸ (頃合) suitableness; moderateness (値頃); reasonableness (同上). —恰好よく, in (good) shape; fitly. —恰好のよい, shapely; well-formed; well-made; fine. —恰好の惡い, ill-formed; unshapely; ill-shaped; clumsy. —恰好の品, a likely article. —恰好を直す, to adjust the shape [form]. —恰好を惡くする, to deform; disfigure.

kakkoku (各國), *n.* every country [state]; all countries [powers; states]; various countries (諸國). —各國使臣, the chiefs of foreign missions.

kakkyo (割據する), *vi.* to hold one's own (ground).

kako (水夫), *n.* a boatman; a waterman.

kako (過去), *n.* ❶ the past; a previous life (前世). ❷ 【文】 the past (tense); the preterite. —過去の出來事, past events; bygones. ¶ 過去分詞, 【文】 the past participle. —過去帳, a necrology (寺院の); a register of the dead members of a family. —過去完了, 【文】 the past perfect; the pluperfect.

kakō (火口), *n.* ❶ (噴火口) a crater. ❷ (火焚口) the fire-door.

kakō (加工する), *vt.* to work up;

add work *to*. ¶ 加工費, cost [expense] of work done (on a material). —加工品, an article worked.

kakō (河口), *n.* the mouth (of a river); the river-mouth; the estuary.

kakōgan (花崗岩), *n.* 【鑛·地質】 granite. =***mikageishi.***

kakoi (圍), *n.* ❶ (かこみ) an enclosure; a fence; a casing (機械等保護の). ❷ (保藏) preservation; store; storage. ❸ (獸檻) a pen (家畜·家禽等の); a run (家禽など の); a cot(羊の). —圍ひの梨子, stored pears. —圍ひ込む, to build *in*; fence *in*; enclose. (板塀で圍ひ込む, to fence round with boards.)

kakoku (苛刻, 苛酷), *n.* ❶ (殘酷) cruelty; mercilessness; relentlessness. ❷ (嚴酷) severity; rigour; sternness. ❸ (暴虐) tyranny; oppressiveness. —苛刻な, ① cruel; merciless; relentless. ② severe; rigorous; stern. ③ oppressive; tyrannical. (苛酷な評(言), a severe [harsh] criticism (remark).) —苛刻に取扱ふ, to treat cruelly [severely].

kakomi (圍), *n.* ❶ an enclosure. ❷ (攻圍) a siege; an investment.

kakomu (圍む), *vt.* ❶ (圍繞) to enclose (*in*; *with*); surround *with*; beset. ❷ (攻圍) to besiege; lay siege *to*; invest. —食卓を圍んで, seated round the table. —碁を圍む, to play *go*; have a game of *go*. —城を濠で圍む, to surround a castle with moats.

kakōseki (花崗石), *n.* 【鑛】 granite.

kakotsu (化骨), *n.* 【生】 ossification. —化骨する, to ossify.

kakotsuke (假託), *n.* a pretence; a pretext; an excuse.

kakotsukeru (託つける), *vt.* to pretend; make an excuse [a pretext] *of*. —慈善事業に託つけて, under the cloak of charitable works. —用事に託つけて遊びに來る, to come for pleasure on the pretext of business.

kakou (圍ふ), *vt.* ❶ (圍む) to enclose; fence (*with*); fence in [about; round]; surround *with*. ❷ (保藏) to preserve; keep; store. ❸ (蓄へ養ふ) to keep. —梨を冬期まで圍ッて置く, to keep pears until winter.

kaku (各), *a.* every; each; respective; several. **——,** *ad.* respectively; severally.

kaku (客), *n.* a guest; a customer (顧客); a visitor (來客). =***kyaku.*** —此の地に客となりてより, since I came to this place.

kaku (格), *n.* ❶ (格式) standing; rank. ❷ (資格) character; capacity. ❸ 【文】 the case. —...の格で, in the capacity *of*; in the character *of*. —支配人格に取扱ふ, to treat him on the standing of a manager.

kaku (額), *n.* an amount; a sum.

kaku (角), *n.* ❶ (角度) an angle. ❷ (方形) a square. ❸ (角材) squared timber. ❹ (將棋の) the bishop. —角張ッた顔, a square face. —角に切る, to cut square.

kaku (核), *n.* 【植】 a nucleus; a stone (桃·桃胡などの堅核).

kaku (隔), *a.* every other [second] alternate. —隔年(月), every other year (month); alternate years (months).

kaku (翮), *n.* (鳥の) the calamus; the quill.

kaku (殼), *n.* a palet (植物の); a shell (果物·卵·動物等の); a husk (穀物·果物·種子等の).

kaku (畫, 劃), *n.* a stroke.

kaku (斯く), *ad.* thus; in this manner [way]; like this; so. —斯く云へばとて, even if we say so.

kaku (缺く), *v.* ❶ (欠缺) to lack; be wanting *in*. ❷ (怠る) to neglect; fail *in*. ❸ (毀損) to break; chip (石·瀨戶物などの端を). —缺くべからざる, necessary (*to*; to do; *for*); indispensable; requisite *to*. —判斷力を缺く, to want judgment. —義理を缺く, to fail in propriety.

kaku (舁く), *vt.* to bear; carry on the shoulder. —擔架で舁いて行く, to convey [carry] on a stretcher.

kaku (書く), *vt.* ❶ to write. ❷ (描く) to draw; paint (繪具にて); describe (描寫). ❸ (作成す) to make (書物·遺言·證書を); make out (表·證書·小切手等を); compose (文章·詩を).

kaku (搔く), *vt.* ❶ (引ッ搔く) to scratch (爪で); claw (猫などが爪で); rake (熊手などで). ❷ (梳る) to comb. —頭を搔く, to scratch one's head. —雪を搔く, to rake away the snow. —松葉を搔く, to rake the fallen pine-needles together.

kakū (架空の), *a.* ❶ (空中に架せる) overhead; aerial. ❷ (空想的) imaginary; visionary; fanciful. —架空的計畫, castles in the air; castles in Spain. ¶ 架空線, overhead wires; an aerial line. (架空電力線, overhead electric power lines.)

kakuban (隔番に), *ad.* by turns; alternately.

kakubeijishi (角兵衞獅子), *n.* a street-tumbler with a lion's mask.

kakubetsu (格別), *ad.* especially; particularly; exceptionally. —格別の, especial; particular; special; exceptional.

kakubō (角帽), *n.* a (square) college cap; a mortar-board; a trencher-cap (大學の).

kakuchiku (角逐する), *vi.* to compete *with*; strive *with*. —國際場裏に角逐する, to strive in the international world. —選擧場裏に角逐する, to compete at the elections; contest an election.

kakuchō (擴張), *n.* expansion; enlargement; extension. **——-suru,** *vt.* to expand; extend; enlarge. —領土(貿易)を擴張する, to extend territory (trade). —校舍(工場)を擴張する, to enlarge a school-building (factory).

kakudai (擴大する), *vt.* to enlarge; magnify; dilate. —事件は益〻擴大する模様である, The affair threatens to expand still further. ¶擴大器, an amplifier. —擴大鏡, a magnifier; a magnifying glass.

kakudan (格段の), *a.* especial; particular; special; marked.

kakudo (角度), *n.* an angle; degrees of an angle. —角度を測る, to measure an angle.

kakugai (格外の), *a.* exorbitant; extravagant; unreasonable; extraordinary. —格外に, exorbitantly; unreasonably; excessively. —格外の値を貪る, to charge an exorbitant price.

kakugan (擱岸する), *vi.* to run ashore [aground].

kakugari (角刈), *n.* a square cut. —角刈の頭, a square-cropped head.

kakugen (格言), *n.* a proverb; an aphorism; a maxim.

kakugen (確言する), *vt.* to affirm; assert; assure.

kakugi (閣議), *n.* a Cabinet council [meeting]. —閣議に付(提出)する, to submit to (lay before) the Cabinet council. ¶定例閣議, an ordinary Cabinet council.

kakugo (客語), *n.* 【文】❶(目的語) an object. ❷(賓辭) the predicate.

kakugo (覺悟), *n.* ❶(悟ること) perception. ❷(用意) preparedness. ❸(豫期) anticipation; expectation. ❹(決心) resolution; resolve; decision. **——-suru,** *v.* ❶(悟る) to perceive; apprehend; realize. ❷(用意) to be ready [prepared] *for*. ❸(豫期) to anticipate; expect. ❹(決心) to be resolved; be determined; make up one's mind. —萬一を覺悟してゐる, to be prepared for the worst.

kakuhan, kōhan, (攪拌する), *vt.* to stir up; churn; whisk.

kakuheki (隔壁), *n.* a partition (-wall); 【航】a bulkhead; 【植・動】a dissepiment; 【生】a septum.

kakuhi (革皮), *n.* leather and skins. ¶革皮商, (店) a leather shop: (人) a dealer in leather.

kakuho (確保する), *vt.* to guarantee; secure; assure. —東洋永遠の平和を確保する, to secure the permanent peace of the East. —支那の領土保全を確保する, to guarantee the integrity of China.

kakuhō (確報), *n.* a definite [reliable] report.

kakui (隔意), *n.* reserve; estrangement; alienation. —隔意なく意見を交換する, to compare notes without reserve; exchange views frankly.

kakuin (客員), *n.* a person treated as a member.

kakuji (各自の), *a.* each; every; respective. —各自に, each; individually; respectively.

kakujin (各人), *n.* every person; each (person); all persons.

kakujitsu (隔日に), *ad.* every other [second] day; on alternate days. ¶隔日熱, tertian.

kakujitsu (確實), *n.* reliability; authenticity; validity. **——-na,** *a.* reliable; authentic; valid. —確實な方法, a safe [sure] method. —確實な報道, an authentic [reliable] information.

kakujū (擴充する), *vt.* to amplify; 【論】distribute; generalize.

kakuka (核果), *n.* 【植】a drupe; a stone-fruit; a drupaceous fruit.

kakumaku (角膜), *n.* 【解】the cornea (of the eye). ¶角膜炎, 【醫】keratitis.

kakumau (匿ふ), *vt.* to harbour; shelter; screen. —罪人を匿ふ, to shelter [harbour] a criminal.

kakumei (革命), *n.* a revolution. —革命的, revolutionary; red. —革命を起す, to cause a revolution. ¶反革命運動, a counter-revolutionary movement. —革命軍, a revolutionary army. —革命家, a revolutionist. —革命黨, the revolutionary party.

kakunin (確認する), *vt.* to confirm; validate; certify; acknowledge firmly.

kaku-no-gotoki (斯の如き), *a.* such. —斯の如く, thus; in this way [manner]. —事情斯の如くなるを以て, such being the case.

kakunōko (格納庫), *n.* a hangar; a garage; an aviation-shed; an aero-shed. ¶格納庫係り, a hangar-man.

kakuran (霍亂), *n.* summer [European] cholera.

kakuran, kōran, (攪亂する), *vt.* to throw into confusion [disorder]; denrage; disturb. —平和を攪亂する, to disturb the peace.

kakure (隠れなき), *a.* open; well-known; famous. —隠れなき醜聞, an open scandal.

kakurega (隠所), *n.* ❶ (隠遁所) a hermitage; a retreat; a refuge. ❷ (潜伏所) a hiding [lurking] place.

kakurei (閣令), *n.* a Cabinet ordinance.

kakurenbō (隠坊), *n.* hide-and-seek (兒戯); hy-spy. —隠ん坊をする, to play hide and seek.

kakureru (隠れる), *vi.* ❶ (*a*) to hide; hide [conceal] oneself; lurk *in* (潜む): (*b*) (見えなくなる) to be lost sight *of*; disappear from sight. ❷ [匿] (逃げて) to abscond (逐電); make off (同上); make oneself scarce [俗]. ❸ =*uzumoreru.* ❹ (隠遁) to retire from the world; seclude oneself from society. —隠れた同情者, a private sympathizer. —隠れて事をする, to do a thing in secret. —樹蔭に隠れる, to hide behind a tree. —山に隠れる, to retire among the mountains. —隠れたるより見はるゝはなし, "Nothing comes fairer to light than what has been hidden."

kakuri (隔離する), *vt.* to isolate; segregate; seclude. ¶ 隔離病院, an isolation hospital. —隔離病舎, an isolated ward. —隔離患者, an isolated patient.

kakurihin (獲利品), *n.* winnings.

kakuritsu (確立する), *vt.* to establish; settle. —根本を確立する, to settle the basis.

kakuron (各論), *n.* a special treatise.

kakuron (確論), *n.* an infallible argument; an indisputable opinion.

kakuryō (閣僚), *n.* (his) cabinet colleagues.

kakusaku (畫策), *n.* a plan; a project; a scheme. —畫策する, to plan; project; scheme. —畫策を誤る, to make a bad scheme.

kakusan (擴散), *n.* 【理】diffusion.

kakusei (隔世), *n.* a different age; another age [world]. —隔世の感がある, We feel as if we were really in another world. ¶ 隔世遺傳, atavism.

kakusei (廓淸), *n.* purification; expurgation. —社會の廓淸を圖る, to plan the purification of society.

kakusei (覺醒), *n.* awakening; disillusion. **——-suru,** *vi.* to awake [awaken] *from*; wake up; come to one's senses. **——,** *vt.* to awake [awaken]; arouse. —社會の惰眠を覺醒する, to arouse society from its torpor.

kakuseiki (擴聲器), *n.* a loud-speaker.

kakusha (客車), *n.* a passenger-car; a railway carriage.

kakushaku (矍鑠たる), *a.* vigorous; vigorous [hale] in old age. —矍鑠として居る, to retain one's vigour.

kakushi (衣兜, 衣嚢), *n.* a pocket. —衣嚢に入れる, to pocket; put in one's pocket.

kakushidate (隠立する), *v.* to conceal matters *from*; keep a matter secret [dark]; keep a thing from others. —隠立てなき, straightforward; frank; open-hearted.

kakushigei (隠藝), *n.* (private) accomplishments. —隠し藝を出す, to exhibit [make a display of] one's accomplishments.

kakushiki (格式), *n.* ❶ (身分の) status; grade; station in society. ❷ (法式) etiquette; convention; established rules.

kakushin (革新), *n.* reform; renovation. —革新する, to reform; renovate. —政界革新の旗, the standard of government reform.

kakushin (核心), *n.* a kernel; a nucleus. —核心に觸れる, to touch the core; refer to the main point.

kakushin (確信), *n.* ❶ (a strong) conviction; firm belief. ❷ (自信) confidence; assurance. —確信ある, confident. **——-suru,** *vt.* to believe (firmly); be confident *of*; be assured [convinced] *of*. —成功を確信する, to be sure [confident] of success.

kakushite (斯くして), *ad.* thereby; thus; in this way [manner].

kakushitsu (客室), *n.* a drawing-room; a parlour; a cabin (商船の一等); a saloon (特等室).

kakushitsu (確執), *n.* (不和) discord; disharmony; feud. —確執する, to be at enmity [feud; variance] *with*. —兩者の間に確執を生ずる, to breed discord between the two.

kakusho (各所に), *ad.* everywhere; on all sides [hands]; in various places; *passim* (書物などの) [羅]. —各所の賣藥店にあり, It is sold at druggists' everywhere.

kakushō (確證), *n.* corroboration; a positive [conclusive] proof; a strong evidence. —確證を握る, to possess positive proof.

kakushu (各種), *n.* various kinds; every kind; all sorts [kinds]. —各種の品, all descriptions of goods. —各種の人物, all sorts [manner] of men.

kakushu (恪守・確守する), *vt.* to adhere *to*; cling *to*; stick *to*; observe strictly. —時間を確守する, to be punctual. —主義を確守する, to stick to one's colours.

kakushu (馘首する), *vt.* ❶ (斬首) to behead; cut off a head. ❷ (免職) to dismiss; discharge.

kakushu (鶴首する), *v.* to crane [stretch out] one's neck; look forward eagerly; wait with an outstretched [a craned] neck (待つ).

kakushū (隔週), *ad.* every other [second] week; biweekly; fortnightly. ¶ 隔週評論, the fortnightly review.

kakusode (角袖), *n.* square sleeves; bag sleeves. ¶ 角袖巡査, a detective; a plain-clothes constable; a policeman in plain clothes.

kakusu (隠す), *vt.* ❶ to hide; conceal; secrete. ❷ (秘す) to keep (the matter) secret; keep (anything back) *from*; keep (a person) in the dark *about*. ❸ (匿まふ) to shelter; screen; harbour. ❹ (見えなくする) (*a*) to put out of sight; keep back: (*b*) (覆ひて) veil; cloak; cover: (*c*) (遮りて) screen. —隠して, in secret; in private. ☞ ***hisokani.*** —年を隠す, to suppress a part of one's age. —姿を隠す, to abscond (逐電); conceal oneself. —感情をかくす, to pocket [conceal] one's feelings.

kakusui (角錐), *n.* 【數】 a pyramid.

kaku-suru (畫・劃する), *vt.* ❶ (引く) to draw (線を). ❷ (區劃する) to divide; mark off. ❸ (畫策する) to plan; scheme; plot. —線を劃する, to draw a line. —時期を劃する, to make an epoch.

kakutai (客體), *n.* 【哲・法】 an object.

kakutan (咯痰), *n.* expectoration; sputum.

kaku-taru (確たる), *a.* definite; positive; decisive. ☞ ***kakko.***

kakute (斯くて), *ad.* thus; so. ——, *conj.* and thus; so; then.

kakutei (確定), *n.* conclusion; settlement; confirmation. —確定する, ① [*vt.*] to fix; settle; establish (事實等を). ② [*vi.*] to be settled; become final (判決が). —確定の事實, an established fact. —確定の收入, a fixed income. ¶ 確定判決, a final judgment.

kakutei (畫定・劃定する), *vt.* to define; mark out (方針を): demarcate (境界を). —境界を劃定する, to demarcate the boundary.

kakuto (客途), *n.* travel (特に他國に於ける). —客途に上る, to set out on a travel.

kakuto (殼斗), *n.* 【植】 a cupule; the acorn-cup.

kakutō (角燈), *n.* a (square) hand-lantern; a policeman's lantern; a bull's-eye lantern.

kakutō (格鬪), *n.* a scuffle; a grapple; fisticuffs. —格鬪する, to scuffle; grapple; fight hand to hand.

kakutō (確答), *n.* a definite answer [reply]. —確答を促す, to press a person for a definite answer; demand a definite answer of a person.

kakutoku (獲得), *n.* acquisition. —利權の獲得, acquisition of a right. —獲得する, to acquire.

kakuza (擱坐する), *vi.* to strand; run [go; strike] aground; run ashore. ¶ 擱坐船, a stranded ship.

kakuzai (角材), *n.* square timber; a balk; a scantling (小角材).

kakuzatō (角砂糖), *n.* cube sugar.

kakuzetsu (隔絶する), *vi.* to be remote [distant; far] *from*; lie far *from*; be isolated.

kakuzuke (格附), *n.* 【商】 grading.

kakyō (佳境), *n.* a delightful [an interesting] portion. —佳境に入る, to reach the height of pleasure [enjoyment]; thicken (話などが).

kakyō (架橋), *n.* ❶ bridge-building [-construction]. ❷ a bridge.

kakyoku (歌曲), *n.* an air; a tune; a melody.

kakyū (下級), *n.* a low class [grade]; a lower class [grade]; inferiority. —下級の, low-class; low; inferior. ¶ 下級人民, the lower classes; the populace. —下級裁判所, an inferior [a lower] court. —下級生, a low-class [low-grade] student; a lower boy 〔英〕. —下級社會, the lower classes; the lower orders.

kakyū (火急に), *ad.* urgently; hastily; in hot haste. —火急の用事, an urgent [a pressing] business.

kama (釜), *n.* ❶ a kettle; an iron pot; a copper (炊事又は洗濯用の). ❷ 〔罐〕 a boiler. ❸ 〔窯〕 an oven; a kiln. —釜の下を焚きつける, to make [kindle] a fire under a pot.

kama (鎌), *n.* a sickle; a reaping-hook; (時計の) a detent.

kamabisushii (喧・譁しい), *a.* noisy; clamorous; uproarious. —喧しく, noisily; clamorously. —耳に喧しい, to sound noisily to the ear.

kamaboko (蒲鉾), *n.* hashed fish; boiled fish-paste. —蒲鉾形の, semicircular; semioval.

kamachi (框), *n.* 【建】 a frame; a frame-work; a window-frame (窓の); a door-frame (戸の).

kamado (竈), *n.* ❶ an oven; a furnace; a kitchen-range. ❷ = ***kama*** (釜). ❸ (世帶) house-keeping.

kamae (構), *n.* ❶ (構造) construction; appearance (外觀). ❷ (身構へ) posture; position; attitude. —身法(しんぽう)を正しくする, to correct one's posture.

kamaeru (構へる), *v.* ❶ (造る) to build; construct. ❷ (用意) to make ready *for*; put oneself in a posture. ❸ (僞構) to feign; pretend. —待ち構へる, to wait ready; be ready *for*. —言を構へる, to quibble; shuffle. —槍を構へる, to couch a lance. —一戸を構へる, to keep house.

kamakiri (螳螂), *n.* 【昆】 the mantis; the praying-mantis.

kamakubi (鎌首), *n.* a goose-neck. —鎌首を立てる(蛇が), to raise its head ready to dart.

kamakuraebi (鎌倉蝦), *n.* 【節足】 the spiny lobster.

kamasu (魳), *n.* 【魚】 the barracuda.

kamasu (叺), *n.* a straw-bag.

kamau (構ふ), *v.* ❶ (頓著, 介意) to mind; heed; care [trouble oneself; concern oneself] *about*. ❷ (干渉) to interfere *in*. ❸ (からかふ) to tease; annoy; make fun *of*. ❹ (もてなす) to entertain; treat. —構はぬ, ① [*v.*] not to mind; be indifferent [careless] *about*; take no notice [heed] *of*. ② [*a.*] heedless; unmindful; unconcerned. —結果に構はず, irrespective of the consequences. —費用構はず, without regard to [regardless of] expenses. —雨の降るのも構はず, in spite of rainy weather [the rain].

kame(龜), *n.* 【爬蟲】 the tortoise; the turtle (海龜). —龜の甲, turtle-shell; tortoise-shell.

kame (甁), *n.* ❶ (淺深とも口の開きたる) a jar; an urn. ❷ (口開き形大なる) a pot. ❸ (形も口も小なる) a crock.

kamei (下名), *n.* ❶ the undersigned (署名にいふ); the undermentioned. ❷ [*pron.*] I.

kamei (下命), *n.* ❶ (申附) a command; an order. ❷ (註文) an order.

kamei (加盟), *n.* accession; entrance; joining. —加盟を申込む, to apply for entrance [admission]. ——**-suru**, *v.* to accede *to*; join; become a member *of*. —組合に加盟する, to join an association. ¶ 加盟者, an associate.

kamei(家名), *n.* the family name; the reputation of a family. —家名を揚げる, to raise the family name. —家名を辱しめる, to stain the family name; bring disgrace on one's family.

kamemushi (椿象), *n.* 【昆】 the shield-bug.

kamen (假面), *n.* a mask; a disguise; a veil. —假面を被る, to wear a mask; play the hypocrite. (宗教の假面を被って, under the cloak [veil] of religion.) —假面を脱ぐ, to unmask; throw off the mask; show one's true colours. —人の假面を剝ぐ, to unmask a person.

kamenoo (尾閭骨), *n.* the coccyx.

kamera (カメラ), *n.* a camera. ¶ カメラマン, a camera-man.

kamereon (カメレオン), *n.* 【爬蟲】 the chameleon.

kami (上), *n.* ❶ (上部) the upper part; the head; the top. ❷ (上流) the upper stream. ❸ (長上) one's superiors; one's betters. ❹ (政府) the government; the authorities. —人の上に立つ, to stand above others. —上は王公より下は庶民に至る迄, from the princes above to the common people below; from the princes down to the common people. —上を見習ふ下, "Like master, like man."

kami (神), *n.* ❶ (一神敎で) God; the Lord; Almighty; the Creator (造物主). ❷ (多神敎で) a *kami* [日]; a god; a deity. —神の業, to divine [supernatural] act. —神の恵により, by God's grace. —神に捧げる, to sanctify; consecrate to God. —神に祀る, to apotheosize; deify. —神にあらざる限り何人も…ぬ, no one short of a god….

kami (紙), *n.* paper. —紙に包む, to wrap in paper.

kami (髮), *n.* ❶ (頭髮) hair. ❷ (髮の結方) coiffure. —髮を結ふ, to do [put] up her hair; tie the hair. —髮を解く, to let down one's hair. —髮を分ける (捲る), to part (tear) the hair.

kami (加味する), *vt.* to flavour; season; tinge; add.

kamiaraiko (髮洗粉), *n.* hair-wash powder.

kamiau(嚙合ふ), *vi.* ❶ to bite [fight] each other. ❷ to engage (捿目など); mesh (歯・輪など); tooth (同上).

kamibasami (紙挾), *n.* a clip; a paper-clip; a paper-holder.

kamidana (神棚), *n.* a shelf (niche) for *Shintō* tablets.

kamideppō(紙鐵砲), *n.* a pop-gun.

kamifuda (紙牌), *n.* a card; a card-board; a slip of paper.

kamigamishii (神神しい), *a.* venerable; solemn; holy.

kamiire (紙入), *n.* a pocket-book.

kamikaesu (嚙返す), *vi.* to ruminate; chew the cud.

kamikazari (髮飾), *n.* adorning

the hair (事); hair-ornaments (物).
kamikire (紙片), *n.* a slip of paper.
kamikiri (紙刀), *n.* a paper-knife [-cutter].
kamikirimushi (天牛), *n.* 【昆】 the longicorn beetle.
kamikiru (嚙切る), *vt.* to bite off; cut off with the teeth. —舌を嚙み切って死ぬ, to commit suicide by biting off one's tongue.
kamikonasu (嚙みこなす), *vt.* ❶ (咀嚼) to masticate; chew. ❷ (理解) to appreciate; digest.
kamikorosu (嚙殺す), *vt.* ❶ to worry [bite] to death. ❷ (欠伸·笑·感情等を) to choke; stifle; smother; keep back.
kamikudaku (嚙砕く), *vt.* to grind [crush] with the teeth; crunch; bite and break.
kamikuzu (紙屑), *n.* waste-paper. ¶紙屑拾ひ, a rag-picker; a rag-man; a chiffonier. —紙屑籠, a waste(-paper)-basket. —紙屑買, a ragman.
kamimakitabako (紙巻煙草), *n.* a cigarette.
kaminari (雷), *n.* a thunder; a thunderbolt (雷電). —雷が鳴る, It thunders; The thunder rolls [roars]. —雷が落ちる, Lightning strikes; The thunderbolt falls.
kamirure (加密爾列), *n.* 【植】 =*kamitsure.*
kamisabiru (神さびる), *v.* to excite feelings of reverence. —神さびた, solemn; venerable; holy.
kamishimo (上下), *n.* ❶ (上と下) above and below; the upper and lower classes; the governing and the governed; inferiors and superiors. ❷ (裃) a *kamishimo*; a ceremonial dress.
kamisori (剃刀), *n.* a razor. —剃刀のやうな, sharp as a razor; smart; shrewd. ¶剃刀砥, a razor-grinder.
kamitabako (嚙煙草), *n.* plug tobacco; cake tobacco.
kamitsu (花蜜), *n.* 【植】 nectar.
kamitsuku (嚙附く), *vt.* to lay hold *of* with the teeth; bite (犬が). —嚙み附かうとする, to bite *at*; snap *at*.
kamitsure (加密爾列), *n.* 【植】 the dog's [German] chamomile.
kamiya (紙屋), *n.* a paper-store.
kamiyasuri (紙鑢), *n.* emery-paper.
kamiyo (神代), *n.* the age of the gods.
kamiyui (髪結), *n.* ❶ toilet, toilette. ❷ (女髪結) a female hair-dresser.
kamizaiku (紙細工), *n.* paper-work.
kamizutsumi (紙包), *n.* a paper parcel. —紙包みにする, to wrap [pack] in paper; make a paper parcel *of*.
kamo (鴨), *n.* ❶ 【鳥】 the wild duck. ❷ (素人客) a lamb 〔英〕; a countryman 〔米〕.
kamoi (鴨居), *n.* the door-head; the upper sliding-groove; the lintel.
kamoji (髢), *n.* a toupee; a toupet; a switch. —髢を入れる, to put in a switch.
kamoku (科目), *n.* 【動·植】 (事物の區分) a genus; a branch; an item (項目); a subject (研究·試驗の). —豫算の科目, the items of a budget. —科目を分つ, to divide into genera; give the items.
kamoku (課目), *n.* a lesson; a course. —日々の課目に追はれる, to be urged on by daily lessons.
kamoku (寡默の), *a.* taciturn; reticent; silent. —寡默の人, a man of few words.
kamome (鷗), *n.* 【鳥】 the (common) gull; the sea-gull.
kamon (家門), *n.* one's family [clan]. —家門の矜, pride of birth.
kamonaku (可もなく不可もなき), *a.* indifferent; mediocre; neither good nor bad. —可もなく不可もなく, betwixt and between.
kamonohashi (鴨嘴獸), *n.* 【哺乳】 the duckbill; the platypus.
kamoshika (羚羊), *n.* 【哺乳】 the antelope.
kamoshirenu (かも知れぬ), *v. aux.* may; might; may possibly.
kamosu (醸す), *vt.* ❶ (醸造) to brew. ❷ (惹起) to give rise *to*; bring about; breed. —紛擾を醸す, to give rise to disturbance. —禍を醸す, to breed misfortune.
kamotsu (貨物), *n.* goods; freight. ¶重量貨物, 【航】 dead weight. —容積貨物, measurement goods. —貨物驛, a goods-station. —貨物係, a freight clerk. —貨物自動車, a motor-truck (大形); a motor-waggon (小形). —貨物列車, a goods-train; a freight-train 〔米〕. —貨物船, a cargo-boat; a freighter. —貨物車, a goods-waggon; a freight-car 〔米〕. —貨物收入, goods earnings [income]. —貨物取扱所, a goods office.
kamu (嚙む), *vt.* ❶ (かみつく) to bite; nip; nibble (魚などが餌に). ❷ (かじる) to gnaw. ❸ (咀嚼) to chew; masticate; munch (ポリポリ, ムシャムシャ). ❹ (かみしめる) to grit with one's teeth. —草を嚙む, to chew grass.
kamu (擤む), *vt.* to blow. —鼻を擤む, to blow one's nose.
kan (官), *n.* ❶ (官府) the government (政府); an office (役所); the

authorities (當局). ❷ (官職) a government post. ❸ (器官) an organ. —官に就く, to obtain a government post. —官を辭する, to resign a government post.

kan (棺), *n.* Ⓢ 棺桶. a coffin. —棺側の附添人, a pall-bearer. —棺に納める, to coffin. ¶ 棺昇き, a coffin-carrier.

kan (管), *n.* 【解】 a meatus; a duct; a pipe.

kan (館), *n.* a building; a mansion; a hall.

kan (卷), *n.* ❶ (卷物) a roll. ❷ (書籍) a book. ❸ (冊) a volume (vol. と略す).

kan (冠), *n.* a crown; a coronet; a ceremonial hat. —冠を挂(か)ける, to resign one's post. —天下に冠たり, to be the first in the country.

kan (貫), *n.* *kan* (8.2673 pounds).

kan (勘), *n.* perception; intuition. —勘のよい盲人, a quick-witted blind man.

kan (款), *n.* ❶ (誠心) goodwill. ❷ (項目) a section. —款を敵に通ずる, to betray to the enemy.

kan (寒), *n.* ❶ (寒氣) cold. ❷ (小寒より節分まで) the cold season. —寒の入, the beginning of the cold season.

kan (間), *n.* ❶ (時間) interval; space; during (一期間). ❷ (距離) from...to; for (里數など). ❸ (中間) between (二者); among (三者以上). ❹ (不和) discord; feud. —過去四十年間, during the past forty years. —東京大阪間の距離, the distance between [from] Tōkyō and [to] Ōsaka. —三時間で, in three hours. —間髮を容れず, quicker than thought; quick as lightning.

kan (閑), *n.* ❶ (閑暇) leisure; spare time. ❷ (閑靜) quietness. —半日の閑を得て, having got a spare half-day. —...せんとして未だ閑を得ず, not to have time yet to do....

kan (燗), *n.* heating [warming] *sake*; warmed [heated] *sake* (燗酒). —燗する, to heat; warm. ¶ 燗德利, a bottle for warming *sake*.

kan (簡), *n.* simplicity; brevity, conciseness. —簡にして要を得てる, to be brief and to the point. —成るべく簡に從ふ, to make it as concise as possible.

kan (癇), *n.* ❶ (癇癖) irritability; peevishness. ❷ (癇の病) meningitis. —癇に障る, to irritate. —癇を起す, to become peevish; be convulsed.

kan (感), *n.* feeling; sensation (感覺); sense (感念). —愉快の感あらしめる, to give pleasure; impart a pleasant feeling [sensation]. —感極まつて泣く, to be moved to tears.

kan (寬), *n.* generosity; leniency; indulgence. —寬に失する, to be too lenient *to* [*with*] (處分など); be too indulgent (甘い).

kan (驛), *n.* restiveness; unruliness.

kan (環), *n.* a ring; a circle.

kan (歡,驩), *n.* pleasure; joy; delight. —驩を交へる, to exchange courtesies. —歡を盡す, to revel (痛飲して); enjoy oneself to the full [to one's heart's content].

kan (觀), *n.* ❶ (所見) a view; an opinion. ❷ (外觀) an appearance; look. ❸ (光景) a spectacle; a sight; a scene. ❹ (眺望) a sight; a view; scenery.

kan (鑵), *n.* a can; a tin; a canister (茶などを入れる). —鑵に詰める, to pack (肉・果物等を保存する爲に); tin; can [米].

kana (假名), *n.* the Japanese syllabary. —假名を振る, to give *kana*.

kanaami (金網), *n.* a wire-gauze; a wire-netting; a fire-netting. —金網を張る, to cover with a wire-netting.

kanabera (金箆), *n.* ❶ (金屬製のへら) an iron spatula. ❷ (鏝の一種) a trowel (左官の).

kanabō (鐵棒), *n.* ❶ (棍棒) a metal rod [pole]; a crowbar; a billet (短き). ❷ (器械體操) a horizontal bar. —鐵棒を曳く, to gad about. ¶ 金棒曳, ① (金棒を突鳴らして行く夜番) a night-watchman (with an iron pole). ② (噂を觸れ廻る者) a gad-about; a gossip; a news-monger.

Kanada (加奈陀), *n.* Canada.

kanadarai (金盥), *n.* a metal [brass] basin.

kanaderu (奏でる), *vt.* ❶ (音樂を奏す) to perform; play *on*. ❷ (琴を彈く) to play.

kanae (鼎), *n.* a tripod; a tripod kettle. —鼎の沸くが如くである, to seethe like a kettle; be in a ferment. —鼎の輕重を問はれる, to be weighed in the balance; be put to the test.

kanaeru (叶へる), *vt.* ❶ (滿足さす) to grant; answer [hear] (祈願などを). ❷ [諧] (和合さす) to harmonize; accord. ☞ *kanau* (叶ふ). ——, *a.* fit *for*; suitable *for*; answerable.

kanagashira (金頭), *n.* 【魚】 Lepidotrigla alata (gurnard の一種).

kanagu (金具), *n.* metal fittings. —金具を附ける, [*vt.*] to shoe; tag.

kanahebi (金蛇), *n.* 【動】 Tachydromus tachydromides (學名).

kanahibashi (鐵火箸), *n.* iron tongs.

kanai (家内), *n.* ❶ (家族) a family; a household. ❷ (妻) one's wife. ¶家内安全, safety of the family. —家内一同, the whole family. —家内工業, house [home] industry.

kanakana (かなかな蟬), *n.* 【昆】Leptopsaltria japonica (學名).

kanake (金氣), *n.* ❶ (金屬の氣) a trace of metal. ❷ (金澁) a metallic taste; an iron flavour.

kanakin (金巾), *n.* shirtings; calico. ¶色金巾, dyed shirtings.

kanakirigoe (金切聲), *n.* a shrill [piping] voice; a piercing cry; a scream. —金切聲を立てる, to scream; shriek; raise a shrill voice.

kanaku (姦惡な), *a.* villainous; knavish; rascally.

kanakugi (金釘), *n.* a (metal) nail.

kanakuso (金屎, 鐵屎), *n.* ❶ (鐵の銹) iron rust. ❷ (金滓) slag; dross; scoria.

kanakuzu (鐵屑), *n.* filings; scrap-iron; scrap-metal.

kaname (金目, 要冬青), *n.* 【植】 the Chinese hawthorn.

kaname (要), *n.* ❶ (扇眼) a rivet; a pivot. ❷ (要點) an important point; the point; a pivot; main points. —肝心要の所で, at the critical point.

kanameishi (要石), *n.* a head-stone; a key-stone.

kanamono (金物), *n.* ❶ (鐵器類) hardware; a metal utensil. ❷ (金具) metal fittings. ¶金物屋, an ironmonger; a hardware-dealer; a hardwareman; a hardware-shop.

kanarazu (必ず), *ad.* ❶ (きッと) certainly; surely; without fail. ❷ (是非とも) by all means. ❸ (いつも) always; ever; invariably (不相變). ❹ (必然的に) needs; necessarily; of necessity. —必ずしも, (部分的打消) not always (時・場合にいふ); not all; not necessarily (必然). —必ずなし遂げる, to carry through without fail.

kanari (可成り), *ad.* fairly; tolerably; moderately. **——-no,** *a.* fair; tolerable; passable. —可成りの畫, a passable picture. —可なりの出來, a fair make. —可なりの旅館, a decent hotel. —可なりの畫家, a respectable painter.

kanaria (金絲雀), *n.* 【鳥】 the canary (bird).

ka-naru (可なる), *a.* fair; good; right.

kanashii (悲しい), *a.* ❶ (心情) (*a*) (悲) sad; sorrowful; mournful: (*b*) (哀) piteous; pathetic; touching. ❷ (事狀) (歎はしい) lamentable (悲しむべき); deplorable (慨歎すべき); regrettable. ❸ (憫むべき, 悲慘なる) pitiable; poor; miserable. —悲しい話, a sad [tragic] tale; a sorrowful tale. —悲しい出來事(報知), a sad event (news). —悲しげに泣く, to weep sorrowfully. —悲しいかな, ① [*int.*] alas!; ah me!; woe is me! (悲哀・痛恨の發聲). ② (悲しい事には) sad to say; I am sorry to say that...; it is a pity that.... —悲しく, sorrowfully; pathetically; lamentably.

kanashiki (鐵敷), *n.* Ⓢ鐵床. an anvil.

kanashimi (悲, 哀), *n.* grief; sorrow; sadness. —哀みの極み, (軍曲) the dead march.

kanashimu (悲・哀む), *vt.* ❶ (悲痛) to grieve ❷ (哀悼) to deplore; mourn. ❸ (悲歎) to bewail; lament; rue. ❹ (殘念) to regret; rue; be chagrined. —悲むべき, sorrowful; mournful; lamentable. —別離を悲む, to sorrow at parting. —友人の死を哀む, to lament [mourn] the death of a friend. —聞く人をして悲ましむ, to sadden every man who hears it.

kanashisa (悲しさ), *n.* sadness; sorrowfulness; mournfulness.

kanata (彼方), *pron.* = ***achira.***

kanateko (鐵梃), *n.* a crow; a crowbar.

kanatsunbo (金聾), *n.* stone-deafness: a stone-deaf person (人).

kanau (かなふ), *v.* ❶ [適] (適合, 一致) to comply *with*; accord *with*; be compatible *with*. ❷ [稱, 副] (相應) to correspond; answer; meet. ❸ [敵] (匹敵) to be a match *for*; be equal *to*; be up *to*. —叶はぬ戀, unrequited love. —道理に適ふ, to accord [square] with reason. —意に適ふ, to please [suit] one's fancy; be agreeable to one. —方式に適ふ, to be according to form. —衆望に叶ふ, to accord with popular wishes. —職に稱ふ, to be equal to the task. —かう暑くては敵はない, This heat is too much for me.

kanawa (鐵輪), *n.* ❶ (金屬の輪) a metal hoop; a metal ring; a tyre (車の). ❷ (石突) a ferrule; a shoe. ❸ (鐵環戯) a quoit.

kanazuchi (鐵槌), *n.* a hammer; a claw-hammer(釘拔附).

kanba (樺), *n.* 【植】 the white birch.

kanban (看板), *n.* a sign-board; a sign; a placard. —看板になる, to serve as a figure-head. —看板

を出す, to set up a sign-board; open a shop. ¶看板娘, a show-girl. —看板屋, a sign-painter.

kanbase (顔), *n.* face; complexion; countenance.

kanbashii (芳·香ばしい), *a.* sweet-scented; fragrant; balmy. —芳ばしき名を後世に遺す, to leave behind an honourable name.

kanbashitta (甲走ッた), *a.* shrill; sharp. —甲走ッた聲で叫ぶ, to shout in a shrill voice.

kanbasu (畫布), *n.* canvas.

kanbatsu (旱魃), *n.* a drought; continual dry weather.

kanben (勘辨), *n.* pardon; excuse; forbearance (我慢). —勘辨する ① (寬恕) to pardon; excuse. ② (我慢) to forbear; put up *with*; have patience *with*.

kanben (簡便), *n.* simplicity; convenience; expediency. **——-na,** *a.* simple; expedient; convenient; handy. —簡便な機械, a simple [handy] machine.

kanbi (完備せる), *a.* perfect; complete.

kanbō (官房), *n.* the secretariate. ¶官房長, the chief of the secretariate.

kanbō (感冒), *n.* cold. —感冒に罹る, to catch [take] (a) cold.

kanbō (監房), *n.* a cell; a ward.

kanbō (觀望), *n.* watchful waiting. **——-suru,** *vt.* to watch; wait and watch. —兩端を持して觀望する, to sit on the fence. —形勢(の推移)を觀望する, to wait and watch the development; watch which way the wind sets. ¶觀望政策, watchful waiting; wait and see policy.

kanboku (肝木), *n.* 【植】the marsh [water] elder; the cranberry-tree.

kanboku (灌木), *n.* 【植】a frutex; a shrub.

kanbotsu (官沒する), *vt.* to confiscate.

kanbotsu (陷沒), *n.* sinking; subsidence; depression. —陷沒する, to sink; subside; become hollow.

kanbu (患部), *n.* the affected part. —患部を冷やす(洗滌する), to cool (wash) the affected part.

kanbu (幹部), *n.* the management; the managing staff; the governing body (學校·病院等の); the machine (政黨などの); leaders.

kanbun (漢文), *n.* ❶ (文學) Chinese classics. ❷ (文章) Chinese composition; Chinese writing.

kanbunsho (官文書), *n.* an official document.

kanbutsu (奸物, 姦物), *n.* a villain; a knave; a rascal; a ruffian.

kanbutsu (官物), *n.* government property.

kanbutsu (乾物), *n.* dried vegetables. ¶乾物類, groceries. —乾物屋, a grocer.

kanbutsue (灌佛會), *n.* the fête of the Buddha's birthday.

kanbyō (看病), *n.* nursing; tending a sick person. —看病する, to nurse; tend; attend on (an invalid). ¶看病人, a nurse; a sick-nurse.

kanchi (奸智, 姦智), *n.* cunning; craft; guile. —奸智に長けた男, a cunning [crafty] fellow.

kanchi (閑地), *n.* ❶ (空地) a vacant land; an unoccupied lot. ❷ (閑靜な所) a retired [secluded] place; a quiet region. —冠を挂けて閑地に就く, to retire to private life; resign one's post and retire.

kanchō (干潮), *n.* ebb-tide; ebb; low-tide.

kanchō (官廳), *n.* a government office (役所); the authorities (當局). ¶上級命令官廳, 【法】the authority in command. —官廳簿記, government bookkeeping.

kanchō (管長), *n.* the superintendent priest (of a sect); the administrative head (of a sect).

kanchō (館長), *n.* the governor; the superintendent.

kanchō (間諜), *n.* a spy; a secret emissary. —間諜を放つ, to send out a spy.

kanchō (灌腸), *n.* 【醫】rectal injection. —灌腸する, to clysterize; administer an enema *to*. ¶滋養(リスリン)灌腸, nutrient (glyceline) enema. —灌腸器, an enema-syringe. —灌腸劑, a clyster; an enema.

kanchō (艦長), *n.* 【海】the commander (of a warship); the captain; ¶艦長室, the cabin.

kanchū (寒中), *n.* the cold season, the depth [dead] of winter.

kandai (寬大), *n.* ❶ (寬裕) generosity; magnanimity; large-mindedness [-heartedness]. ❷ (嚴ならざること) liberality; leniency (刑などの); clemency. —寬大な, ① large-minded [-hearted]; magnanimous; generous. ② liberal; tolerant; lenient. —寬大に扱ふ, to treat leniently [generously]. —寬大に處置する, to deal leniently (with a person).

kandan (寒暖), *n.* ❶ (寒と暖) heat [hotness] and cold; temperature (溫度). ❷ (時候) season. ¶寒暖計) a thermometer.

kandan (間斷), *n.* intermission; interruption. —間斷なき, incessant; ceaseless; unremitting. —間斷なく, ceaselessly; incessantly; without intermission.

kandan (閑談), *n.* ❶ (靜な話) quiet conversation [talk]. ❷ (無駄話) a chat; a gossip; a chit-chat. —閑談する, ① to converse quietly. ② to (have a) chat *with*; gossip. —閑談に耽る, to give oneself up to [indulge in] gossip.

kanden (感電), *n.* electrification; electrization; an electric shock. —感電する, to be struck by electricity; get an electric shock; be electrified.

kandenchi (乾電池), *n.* a dry cell; a dry pile; a dry battery.

kanden-denki (感傳電氣), *n.* faradism.

kandō (勘當), *n.* disowning; disinheriting. —勘當する, to disinherit; disown. —親から勘當を受ける, to be disowned [disinherited] by one's parent.

kandō (間道), *n.* a bypath; a secret path; a by-road. —間道より進む, to march by a secret path.

kandō (感動), *n.* impression; emotion; excitement. —感動さす, to impress; move; affect. —感動し易い, emotional; impressionable; sensitive; impressible. —深く感動する, to be deeply [greatly] moved. —大なる感動を與へる, to make a great impression.

kane (金), *n.* ❶ (金屬) metal. ❷ (金錢) money. —金で買はれぬ, not to be had for money. —金のある, rich; wealthy. —金の奴隸, a slave to mammon. —金の蔓, means of making money. —金の生る木, the pagoda tree; the veritable mine of gold; the goose that lays the golden eggs. —金の轡をはめる, to gag a man with a golden bit; give hush-money. —金の爲に節を賣る, to sell one's honour for money. —金にする, to make money out of; turn into money; realize; convert into cash. —金になる仕事, a profitable [lucrative] work. —金に目のない; 金次第の, mercenary; venal. —金に詰まる, to be short of money; be hard up (for money). —金に困って[窮して; 詰って], pressed for money. —金に目が眩む, to be blinded by money. —金を儲ける, to make [earn] money. —金を寢かす[遊ばす], to let money lie idle. —金の世の中, "Gold rules the world." —金が金を呼ぶ[產む], "Money begets [breeds] money."

kane (鉦), *n.* (叩きがね) a gong.

kane (鐘), *n.* a bell (鐘, 半鐘); a time-bell (時の鐘); a school-bell (學校の). —鐘を撞く, to strike [toll] a bell. —鐘が鳴る, The bell rings [tolls].

kane (鐵漿), *n.* a black tooth-dye.

kańei (官營の), *a.* government; state. ¶官營事業, state [government] enterprise.

kaneire (金入), *n.* ❶ (金匣) a money-box. ❷ (財布) a purse; a money-bag; a pocket-book (紙入).

kanejaku (曲尺), *n.* ❶ (曲尺) the common *shaku* (=11.91 inches). ❷ (大工の指金) a carpenter's square; a trying square.

kanekashi (金貸), *n.* (業) money-lending: (人) a money-lender.

kanemawari (金廻), *n.* circulation of money.

kaneme (金目), *n.* value. —金目の物, a valuable (article).

kanemochi (金持), *n.* a rich [wealthy] man; a millionaire. —金持の嫁を貰ふ, to marry a fortune. ¶金持階級, the moneyed class.

kanemōke (金儲), *n.* money-making; earning money; gain. —金儲けが旨い, to be clever at making money. —金儲けをする, to make money.

kane-no-te (曲尺の手), *n.* a right angle.

kanensei (可燃性), *n.* combustibility; inflammability. ¶可燃(性の)物, a combustible; an inflammable.

kaneru (兼ねる), *v.* ❶ to combine (兼備); be used for two or more purposes (兼用); discharge two or more offices (functions) at the same time (兼務). ❷ (憚る) to be diffident (遠慮); be afraid of. —兩職を兼ねる, to discharge two offices. —人前をかねる, to be diffident in company. —御無沙汰お詫を兼ねて, to apologize at the same time for my neglect to pay my respects.

-kaneru (兼ねる), *v.* to be unable; cannot; be difficult [hard]; hesitate. —行き兼ねる, cannot go; to be unable to go. —泥棒もし兼ねぬ, to dare even to rob. —甚だ申し兼ねますが, though I say it with great hesitation.

kanete (豫て), *ad.* already; previously; some time ago. —豫てお約束をした通り, as I have already promised.

kanetsu (火熱), *n.* heat; caloric.

kanetsu (加熱する), *v.* to heat. —加熱壓搾する, to hot-press.

kańetsu-tenko (簡閱點呼), *n.* inspection of reservists. —簡閱點呼の召集に應ずる, to respond to the calling off for the inspection of reservists.

kańetsuki (鐘撞), *n.* a bell-ringer (寺院等の). ¶鐘撞堂, a belfry; a bell-tower.

kanezukai (金遣), *n.* money-spending. —金遣ひの荒い, prodigal; extravagant; spendthrift; free with one's money.

kanezuku (金盡で), *ad.* for money. —金盡で得られぬ, not to be had for money.

kanga (官衙), *n.* a government office.

kanga (嫻雅な), *a.* ❶ refined; elegant; polished. ❷ (靜にして風趣に富む) quiet and tasteful.

kangae (考), *n.* ❶ thought; idea; a conception. ❷ (思慮) prudence; thought; discretion. ❸ (熟考) consideration; deliberation. ❹ (沈思) meditation; contemplation. ❺ (判斷) judgment; discretion. ❻ (目論見) intention; plan. —旨い考, a happy thought; an excellent [a capital] idea. —私の考では, in my opinion; to my thinking; as far as I can see. —前後の考もなく, without regard to the consequences; thoughtlessly. —考へ事をして居る, to be wrapped in thought. —やっと考がついた, At last I hit upon it.

kangaebukai (考深い), *a.* thoughtful; prudent; judicious.

kangaechigai (考違), *n.* misapprehension; misunderstanding; misconception. —私の考違ひでなければ, if I remember aright; if my memory does not fail me.

kangaedasu (考出す), *vt.* ❶ (想起) to call to mind; recall; recollect. ☞ *omoidasu.* ❷ (案出) to think out; conceive; strike [hit] upon. —名案を考へ出す, to think out [conceive] a capital plan.

kangaekata (考方), *n.* the way of thinking (考へ樣); how to solve (a problem) (解き方).

kangaekomu (考込む), *vi.* to be absorbed [lost] in thoughts; brood over; meditate.

kangaemono (考物), *n.* ❶【遊戲】a puzzle. ❷ (思案を要する) a matter for consideration; a puzzler.

kangaenaosu (考直す), *vt.* to reconsider; think over again; unthink (考へ變へる). —今一度考へ直す, to reconsider it once more.

kangaeru (考へる), *vt.* ❶ to think; consider; deem. ❷ (意見) to think; be of opinion that.... ❸ (心算) to intend; mean; think *of.* ❹ (熟考) to consider; think over. ❺ (考量) to take into account; take account *of*; take into consideration (酌量). ❻ (憂慮) to apprehend; take to heart; have thought *for.* ❼ (判斷) to judge; think. ❽ (回想) to reflect *on.* ❾ (想像) to think *of*; imagine; fancy. ❿ (豫想) to expect; contemplate. —考へた丈でも, at the bare thought *of.* —予の考へる所では, to my mind; to my thinking; in my opinion. —よくよく考へた揚句, after racking my brains to the utmost. —篤と考へる, to think seriously *of.* —後先を考へる, to weigh the consequences. —物事を眞面目 (呑氣) に考へる, to take things seriously (easy). —よく考へろ, Turn it over in your mind. —私は之を諷刺だと考へる, I take this to be ironical. —考へれば考へる程愈〻分らなくなる, The more I think, the more incomprehensible it becomes.

kangaetsuku (考附く), *v.* ❶ (想起) to recollect; call to mind; recall. ❷ (思浮ぶ) to think *of*; strike [hit] upon; occur to [strike] one. —何と答へて宜しいか考へ附かぬ, I am at a loss for an answer.

kangai (管外), *ad.* outside the jurisdiction *of.* ¶ 管外旅費, expenses for travelling outside the jurisdiction.

kangai (感慨), *n.* deep emotion; pensive reflection. —感慨措く能はず, I was bursting with emotion.

kangai (灌漑), *n.* irrigation; watering. —灌漑する, to irrigate; water. —灌漑を便にする, to facilitate irrigation. ¶ 灌漑工事, irrigation works.

kangaku (官學), *n.* a government school [college]; a government educational institution. ¶ 官學派, the government school coterie.

kangaku (管樂), *n.* piping; the music of wind-instruments. ¶ 管樂器, a wind-instrument.

kangaku (漢學), *n.* Chinese literature [learning]; Chinese classics. ¶ 漢學者, a Chinese scholar.

kangamiru (鑑みる), *v.* to take warning *by*; take example *by*; consider. —前人の失敗に鑑みて, in view of another's failure in the past.

kangan (汗顔), *n.* abashment; shame. —汗顔の至りに堪へず, I am covered with shame.

kangarū (カンガルー), *n.*【哺乳】the kangaroo.

kangei (歡迎), *n.* welcome; reception. —歡迎する, to welcome; receive warmly; bid welcome. —歡迎される, to have favourable reception; be in popular favour; be welcomed *by.* —熱心な歡迎をする, to give a warm [hearty; cordial] welcome. ¶ 歡迎會, a reception; a welcome meeting. —歡迎者, a welcomer.

kangeki (間隙), *n.* ❶ (空隙) a crevice; a chasm; an interstice. ❷ (不和) a breach of friendship; estrangement; alienation. ❸ (閑暇) interspace; interval. —間隙を生ずる, to lead to estrangement.

kangeki (感激), *n.* deep emotion; excitement; sensation. **——-sasu,** *vt.* to excite; impassion; put in emotion. —感激さして泣かせる, to move to tears. **——-suru,** *vi.* to be deeply moved [affected] *by*; be excited *by*. —優渥なる聖旨に感激する, to be deeply moved by His Majesty's gracious words.

kangeki (觀劇), *n.* play-going. ¶ 觀劇會, a playgoers' society.

kangen (甘言), *n.* honeyed words [tongue]; fair words; flattery. —甘言を以て誘ふ, to wheedle; entice by coaxing. —甘言に乘せられる, to yield to another's cajolery.

kangen (換言する), *vt.* to restate; reword; say in other words. —換言すれば, in other words; that is to say; or.

kangen (管絃), *n.* Ⓢいとたけ. ❶(管樂器と絃樂器) wind and string instruments. ❷ (音樂) music. ¶ 管絃樂, orchestra.

kangen (諫言), *n.* remonstrance; admonition; expostulation. —諫言する, to remonstrate *with*; expostulate *with*; admonish.

kangen (還元), *n.* reduction; deoxidation. —還元する, to reduce; deoxidize; resolve (a compound) into its elements. ¶ 還元劑, a reducing agent; a deoxidizing agent.

kangezai (緩下劑), *n.* 【醫】 a lenitive; a laxative.

kangiku (寒菊), *n.* 【植】 the winter-flowering chrysanthemum.

kangiku (觀菊), *n.* chrysanthemum-viewing. —觀菊の御宴, an Imperial chrysanthemum party.

kango (看護), *n.* ❶ nursing; sick-nursing. ❷ 【軍】 a sick-berth attendant. —看護する, to nurse; tend; take care *of*. ¶ 看護長, 【海】 the chief sick-berth steward. —看護婦, a nurse; a sick-nurse. (看護婦長, a matron. —看護婦會, a nurses' association.) —看護人, a medical orderly; a nurse. —看護卒, a hospital orderly; a private of the army medical corps.

kango (監護する), *vt.* to confine; keep in custody.

kango (漢語), *n.* a Chinese word; the Chinese written language.

kangoku (監獄-署), *n.* a prison; a gaol; a jail. =***keimusho*** (刑務所). ¶ 海(陸)軍監獄, a naval (military) prison.

kangun (官軍), *n.* a government [the Imperial] army; government forces.

kangyo (還御), *n.* the return of His Majesty.

kangyō (官業), *n.* a government enterprise; state [government] industry. —官業より民業に移す, to transfer from government to private management; convert from a government into a private enterprise.

kangyō (勸業), *n.* encouragement of industry. ¶ 勸業銀行, the Hypothec Bank. —勸業課, the section of industries. —勸業債券, a hypothec debenture. —內國勸業博覽會, a national industrial exhibition.

kani (蟹), *n.* the crab. —蟹の橫這ひ, the side-crawl of a crab.

kańi (官位), *n.* office [official post] and court rank.

kańi (敢爲の), *a.* undaunted; intrepid; gallant.

kańi (換位), *n.* 【文】 inversion; 【論】 conversion.

kańi (簡易), *n.* simplicity; easiness. —簡易な, simple; easy; plain. ¶ 簡易保險, simple insurance; industrial (life) insurance; national insurance. —簡易生活, a simple life. —簡易食堂, a people's luncheon-room. —簡易圖書館, a common library.

kańin (官印), *n.* a stamp; the seal of an office; a chop [支那].

kanja (患者), *n.* a patient; a sufferer; a case.

kanja (間者), *n.* a spy. =***kan-chō*** (間諜).

kanji (莞爾として), *ad.* with a smile. —莞爾として笑ふ, to smile.

kanji (幹事), *n.* a manager; a director; a secretary.

kanji (監事), *n.* ❶ a supervisor. ❷ =***kensayaku*** (檢査役).

kanji (漢字), *n.* a Chinese character [ideograph; letter].

kanji (感じ), *n.* ❶ (感覺) feeling; sense; sensation. ❷ (印象) impression; effect. ❸ (感應) induction; influence. ❹ (效果) effect; efficacy; virtue. ❺ (觸覺) touch; feel. —感じの早(鈍)い, sensitive (dull). —感じがなくなる, to be benumbed; become insensible.

kanjiki (樏), *n.* snow-shoes.

kanjiku (卷軸), *n.* a scroll; a roll.

kanjin (肝心な), *a.* important; essential; material; momentous.

kanjin (閑人), *n.* a man of leisure.

kanjin (寬仁), *n.* magnanimity; generosity; liberality. —寬仁大度の, noble-minded; benignant and magnanimous.

kanjin (勸進する), *v.* to solicit contributions for pious purposes. ¶

勧進元, a promoter.

kan-jiru (感じる), *vt.* =kan-zuru.

kanjitsugetsu (閑日月), *n.* ❶ (ひまな時) spare time; leisure. ❷ (悠然として迫らぬこと) serenity; composure.

kanjiyasui (感じ易い), *a.* ❶ (鋭敏の) sensitive; susceptible; tender. ❷ (感傷的) sentimental; emotional; easily moved [affected]. ❸ (良導性の) conductive. —病毒に感じ易い, to be readily accessible to [affected by] virus.

kanjo (官女), *n.* a court lady; a maid of honour.

kanjō (感狀), *n.* a letter of approbation [praise] for meritorious services.

kanjō (感情), *n.* feelings; susceptibilities; emotion (情緒). —感情に走る, to give way to feelings [sentiment]. —一時の感情に驅られて, carried away by a sudden impulse; driven by a passing emotion. —人の感情を害する, to hurt [wound] another's feelings; offend another's susceptibilities. —感情的に物を判斷する, to judge things sentimentally. ¶ 感情家, a sentimentalist; a man of emotional disposition.

kanjō (勘定), *n.* ❶ bill; charge. ❷ (計算) (*a*) accounts: (*b*) calculation; counting; reckoning. ❸ (決算) settlement of accounts; balance. —勘定する, ① (計算) to count; number; reckon. ② (決算) to settle; balance (清算する); square [settle] accounts with a person. ③ (支拂ふ) to pay. ④ (加算する) to add up; cast up; sum up; count up. —勘定に入れる, to take (a thing) into account; take account of (a thing). —の勘定に組入れる, to place [pass] to account *of*. —勘定を拂ふ, to pay the bill [one's shot; one's score]. —勘定を濟ます, to settle accounts; pay one's score. —勘定を取る, to collect bills; get one's pay. —勘定を誤魔化す, to cook accounts. ¶ 勘定日, a pay-day; a settlement-day; the day of reckoning. —勘定違ひ, miscalculation; a mistake in calculation. —勘定書, a bill; an account.

kanjō (環狀), *n.* annulation. —環狀の, circled; annular. ¶ 環狀道路, a circular [ring-shaped] road.

kanju (甘受する), *vt.* to submit *to*; acquiesce *in*; accept. —侮辱を甘受する, to submit to insult.

kanju (感受する), *v.* to be impressed; receive; receive an impression. ¶ 感受性, susceptibility; sensibility.

kanka (干戈), *n.* arms; weapons. —干戈に訴へる, to appeal [resort] to arms. —干戈を交へる, to wage war *with*; open hostilities.

kanka (坎坷, 轗軻), *n.* neglect by the world. —轗軻落魄する, to live in poverty, neglected by the world.

kanka (看過する), *vt.* to overlook; look over; pass over.

kanka (乾果), *n.* 【植】 dry fruits.

kanka (閑暇), *n.* leisure; spare time. ☞ *hima* (隙). —御閑暇も御座候はば, if you have any time to spare.

kanka (感化), *n.* reform; conversion; influence. —感化する, to influence; reform; convert. —感化を受ける, to be influenced *by*; feel a person's influence. —感化を受け易い, amenable to influence. ¶ 感化院, a reformatory; a reform school.

kanka (瞰下する), *vt.* to command; overlook. —湖水を瞰下する, to command a view of the lake.

kankai (官海), *n.* the official world; government circles.

kankaku (間隔), *n.* ❶ a space; an interval. ❷ (懸隔) a distance; a gap; a gulf. —一定の間隔を置いて, at regular intervals.

kankaku (看客, 觀客), *n.* a spectator; the audience. ¶ 低級觀客, the gallery.

kankaku (感覺), *n.* 【心】 sensation; sense. —感覺的快樂, the pleasures of sense. —感覺鋭敏の, high-strung. —感覺を失ふ, to become insensible [senseless]; lose sensibility. —感覺が鈍い (鋭い), The senses are dull (keen). ¶ 感覺中樞, the sense-centre. —感覺器, a sense-organ; the sensorium (全體). —感覺力, sensibility. —感覺神經, a sensory nerve.

kankan (看貫), *n.* a weigh-bridge; a platform-scale; a weighing machine. —看貫を試(い)る, to weigh.

kankan (かんかん), ❶ (銅・鐵等を打つ音) clangour. ❷ (火が) at red heat. ❸ (太陽の照るさま) brightly.

kankanshiki (觀艦式), *n.* a naval review.

kankatsu (管轄), *n.* jurisdiction; control; competence. —管轄する, to have jurisdiction *over*; have competence *over*; control. —管轄內(外), within (outside) the jurisdiction. —管轄に屬する, to fall within the jurisdiction *of* (管轄內); be subject to the jurisdiction *of* (管轄を受く). —管轄官廳へ願出る, to make application to the competent authorities. ¶ 管轄違ひ, error of jurisdiction. —管轄區域, compass of competency; (extent of) jurisdiction.

kankei (奸計, 姦計), *n.* wiles; crafty designs; sharp practices.

kankei (換刑), *n.* commutation. —換刑する, to commute.

kankei (關係), *n.* ❶ (關聯) relation; connection; bearing. ❷ (關與) participation; concern; implication. ❸ (間柄) (*a*) (交際關係) relations; terms: (*b*) 【法】 privity; relation. ❹ (利害關係) interest; concern. ❺ (影響) influence; affection; effect. ❻ = *jōkō* (情交). —…に關係なく, independently *of*; irrespective *of* (拘らず). —…と關係がある, to have to do *with*; have relations *with*. —關係を結ぶ, to enter into a connection *with*; form a connection *with*. —と關係を絶つ, to wash one's hands *of*; break off [cut] a connection *with*; sever connection.
——-suru, *v.* ❶ (關聯) to relate *to*; be connected *with*; refer *to*; concern; regard; have respect *to*; have relation *to*; bear *upon*. ❷ (影響) to affect; influence; have influence *on*; have effect *upon*. ❸ to matter; concern. ❹ (關與) to participate *in*; take part *in*; have to do *with*; have a hand [finger] *in*. —余に何等關係する所なし, It does not concern me. ¶ 關係代名詞, 【文】 the relative (pronoun). —關係副詞, 【文】 the relative adverb. —關係者, a participant, participator; the parties concerned; the interested parties (利害關係者).

kankei (還啓), *n.* (皇太后・皇后・皇太子の) return (of the Empress Dowager; the Empress; the Crown Prince).

kanken (官憲), *n.* the authorities.

kanken (管見), *n.* ❶ (見る所の小なる) a narrow view. ❷ (己の意見の謙辭) one's view [opinion].

kanken (關鍵), *n.* ❶ bolt and key. ❷ (要訣) the key; the secret. —祕密の關鍵を握る, to grasp [hold] the key to the secret.

kanketsu (完結), *n.* ❶ (完成) completion. ❷ (終結) finish; conclusion; end. —完結する, ① to complete. ② to be concluded; be completed; (come to an) end.

kanketsu (奸譎), *n.* craftiness; subtlety; guile. —奸譎な, crafty; subtle; guileful; wily. ¶ 奸譎手段, sharp practices.

kanketsu (間歇), *n.* intermission; intermittence. —間歇する, to intermit (熱・痛・脈搏等に云ふ). ¶ 間歇熱, ague; intermittent fever; chills and fevers. (三日間歇熱, 【醫】 tertian fever.) —間歇泉, a geyser; an intermittent fountain.

kanketsu (簡潔な), *a.* terse; pithy; succinct. —簡潔にする, to make it terse. —簡潔に書く, to write tersely.

kanki (官紀), *n.* official discipline. —官紀を振肅 (紊亂) する, to enforce (subvert) official discipline.

kanki (寒氣), *n.* the cold. —寒氣に負ける, to suffer from cold. —寒氣を凌ぐ, to endure [brave] the cold.

kanki (勘氣), *n.* displeasure; anger.

kanki (換氣-法), *n.* ventilation. —換氣する, to ventilate.

kanki (喚起する), *vt.* to awaken; evoke; arouse. —輿論を喚起する, to arouse public opinion. —國民の注意を喚起する, to evoke the attention of the country.

kanki (歡喜), *n.* joy; delight; gladness. —歡喜する, to be delighted; rejoice. —歡喜に充つ, to be in high glee; be in an ecstasy [transports] of joy.

kankin (官金), *n.* a government fund; public money. ¶ 官金費消, peculation of government [public] funds; malversation. (官金費消者, a peculator.)

kankin (看經), *n.* reading of the [sutras.]

kankin (監禁), *n.* confinement; imprisonment; detention. —監禁する, to confine; imprison; incarcerate. ¶ 不法監禁, unlawful detention; false imprisonment.

kankiri (罐切), *n.* a tin-cutter; a can-opener.

kanko (乾涸する), *vi.* to dry up.

kanko (歡呼), *n.* jubilation; a cheer; an acclamation. **——-suru,** *vi.* to jubilate; give cheers; acclaim. —萬歲を歡呼する, to cry out *banzai*; give cheers.

kankō (刊行), *n.* publication; edition. —刊行する, to publish; print. ¶ 刊行物, a publication. (定期刊行物, a periodical.)

kankō (甘汞), *n.* calomel.

kankō (敢行する), *vt.* to dare [venture] to do.

kankō, kenkō, (箝口する), *vt.* to gag; impose silence; muzzle. ¶ 箝口具, a gag; a muzzle (動物の). —箝口金, hush-money.

kankō (感光), *n.* 【寫】 exposure to light. —感光さす, to expose; sensitize to light. ¶ 感光紙, sensitive [sensitized] paper.

kankō (慣行の), *a.* habitual; customary. —慣行する, to practise habitually.

kankō (緘口する), *v.* to hold one's tongue; be silent; say nothing.

kankō (還幸), *n.* the return of His Majesty.

kankō (觀光), *n.* sightseeing; visit. ¶ 觀光團, a tourist party. —觀光者, a visitor; a sightseer.

kankōba (勸工場), *n.* a bazaar; a co-operative department store.

kankodori (閑子鳥), *n.* 【鳥】the Himalayan cuckoo.

kankōgyō (官工業), *n.* government manufacturing industry.

kankoku (勸告), *n.* ❶ (助言) advice; counsel. ❷ (訓誡) exhortation; admonition; warning. ❸ (諫言) remonstrance; expostulation. —醫者の勸告に依り, upon medical advice. **——-suru,** *v.* ❶ to advise; counsel; recommend. ❷ to exhort; admonish; warn. ❸ to remonstrate *with*; expostulate *with*. —辭職を勸告する, to urge a person to resign. ¶ 勸告者, ① an adviser; a counsellor. ② an admonisher; an admonitor. ③ a remonstrant.

kankōri (官公吏), *n.* public officers; government and municipal officials.

kankōsho (官公署), *n.* (government and other) public offices.

kankotsu (顴骨), *n.* Ⓢ 頰骨. 【解】the malar (bone); the zygoma. ¶ 顴骨突起, the zygomatic process.

kankotsu-dattai (換骨脫胎), *n.* adaptation. —換骨脫胎する, to adapt.

kanku (管區), *n.* a district; a command.

kanku (艱苦), *n.* hardships; privations. ☞ ***kannan.***

kankyaku (閑却する), *vt.* to neglect; ignore; disregard. —閑却される, to pass out of mind; be neglected.

kankyo (官許), *n.* government permission; (government) licence; legalization. —官許の, licensed.

kankyo (閑居), *n.* ❶ (逸居) being at leisure. ❷ (退隱生活) living in seclusion; a retired life. ❸ (靜な住居) a retreat. —閑居する, to live in retirement; live in seclusion.

kankyō (感興), *n.* ❶ (興味) interest. ❷ (文學的の) inspiration. —感興を殺ぐ, to destroy interest.

kankyō (環境), *n.* environment; surroundings.

kankyō (艦橋), *n.* a bridge.

kankyū (官給), *n.* governmental supply. ¶ 官給品, articles supplied by the government.

kankyū (感泣する), *vi.* to be moved to tears; shed tears of gratitude.

kankyū (緩急), *n.* ❶ urgency. ❷ (危急の場合) an emergency. —緩急に備へる, to provide against emergencies. —緩急宜しきを得る, to treat [meet] a case according to its urgency. ¶ 緩急機, a brake. —緩急車, a brake-van.

kanman (干滿), *n.* (潮の) ebb and flow; flux and reflux; tide.

kanman (緩慢), *n.* ❶ (緩やか) laxity (處分などの); slackness (金融などの). ❷ 【音】*andante* 〔伊〕. ❸ (のろいこと) slowness; dilatoriness. **——-na,** *a.* ❶ lax; slack (金融·市況などの); dull (市況などの). ❷ slow; dilatory; remiss. —緩慢な商況, slack trade [business]; dull trade.

kanme (貫目), *n.* ❶ (重量) weight. ❷ (重量の單位) *kan* (3.75キログラム又8.2673封度に相當す). ❸ (貫祿) dignity; authority; importance.

kanmei (官名), *n.* an official title.

kanmei (官命), *n.* government orders (官の命令); an official mission (公用). —官命を帶びて, on an official mission.

kanmei (感銘), *n.* ❶ (印象) a (deep) impression. ❷ (感謝) deep gratitude. ❸ (感動) impression; affection. —感銘する, ① to be deeply impressed on one's mind; be engraved on one's mind. ② to feel grateful [thankful] *for*. ③ to be deeply impressed *with*; be deeply moved *by*.

kanmei (簡明), *n.* terseness; neatness; conciseness. —簡明な, terse; concise; short and clear.

kanmi (甘味), *n.* ❶ (あまみ) a sweet taste; sweetness. ❷ (美味) a good flavour; savouriness; delicacy.

kanmi (鹹味), *n.* a salt taste; saltiness.

kanmin (官民), *n.* the government and the people; officials and private persons. —官民一致して, with the unanimity of officials and private persons.

kanmoku (緘默), *n.* silence; dumbness; speechlessness. —緘默する, to hold one's tongue; keep one's mouth shut; be silent.

kanmon (喚問), *n.* summons and examination. —喚問する, to summon and examine.

kanmon (關門), *n.* a barrier; a gate; a barrier-gate. —うまく試驗の關門を通過する, to pass successfully the barrier of examination.

kanmonji (閑文字), *n.* irrelevant words; a cheap writing.

kanmuri (冠), *n.* a crown; a coronet. —冠をつける, to put on a crown.

kanna (鉋), *n.* a plane. —鉋をかける, to plane.

kannakuzu (鉋屑), *n.* shavings.

Kannamesai (神嘗祭), *n.* the Harvest Thanksgiving Day.

kannan (艱難), *n.* ❶ (辛苦) hardship; tribulation; privation. ❷ (窮境) misery; adversity; difficulties. —艱難する, to suffer hardships [privations] —艱難に打勝つ, to overcome difficulties. —艱難辛苦を嘗め盡す, to go through trials and tribulations.

kannei (奸佞), *n.* subtlety; craftiness; cunning. —奸佞な, crafty; subtle; cunning.

kannen (觀念), *n.* ❶【佛】meditation; contemplation. ❷【哲】idea; conception (概念); notion (想念). ❸ (覺悟) resolution (決心); resignation (諦め). —觀念する, ① (想念する) to meditate; contemplate. ② (覺悟) to resolve; be convinced *of* (確信). ¶ 觀念聯合, association of ideas.

kannetsu (寒熱), *n.* ❶ heat and cold. ❷ chillness and fever. —寒熱往來す, Chillness and fever succeed each other.

kannin (堪忍), *n.* patience; forgiveness; pardon. —堪忍する, to have patience *with*; bear *with*; put up *with*. —堪忍袋の緒が切れる, One's patience is exhausted.

kanningu (カンニング), *n.* 【學生・俗】a dishonest [cunning] trick.

kan-nisuru (寛にする), *vt.* to relax (規律・規則などを); mitigate (刑を); moderate. —規則を寛にする, to relax rule.

kan-nisuru (簡にする), *vt.* to simplify. —手續を簡にする, to simplify the procedure.

kannō (完納する), *vt.* to pay in full.

kannō (官能), *n.* function. —官能的, functional.

kannō (堪能), *n.* =*tannō* (堪能).

kannō (感應), *n.* ❶【佛】(*a*) response; answer: (*b*) (靈感) inspiration. ❷ (心の) feeling; response. ❸【理】induction (電氣, 磁氣); influence (電氣). ❹ (藥の) efficacy; effect; virtue. ——**suru**, *v.* ❶ (*a*) to answer; respond: (*b*) to be inspired. ❷ to influence; induce. ❸ to feel; respond. ❹ to take effect. —電氣に感應する, to induce electricity. ¶ 感應電流, an induced current. —感應コイル, an induction-coil.

kannoki (閂), *n.* a gate-bar; a cross-bar.

Kannon (觀音), *n.* the goddess of mercy. ¶ 觀音開, a double door.

kannushi (神主), *n.* a *Shintō* priest.

kannyū (嵌入する), *vt.* to inlay; insert; put in.

kanō (化膿), *n.* 【醫】suppuration; maturation; purulence. —化膿さす, to draw; suppurate. —化膿する, to suppurate; gather; mature.

kanō (可能性), *n.* possibility; potentiality. —可能的, possible; potential. ¶ 可能法,【文】the potential (mood).

kanō (假納する), *vt.* to deposit. ¶ 假納金, cover. —假納關稅, a deposited duty.

kanō (嘉納する), *vt.* to sanction; accept with pleasure; appreciate.

kańō (感應), *n.* =*kannō* (感應).

kańō (觀櫻), *n.* cherry-viewing. ¶ 觀櫻會, a cherry-party; a cherry-viewing party.

kanogotoku (…かの如く), *ad.* as though; as if.

kanojo (彼女), *pron.* she. —彼女の《に; を》, her.

kańōi (棺被), *n.* a (funeral) pall.

kanoko (鹿の子), *n.* a fawn. ¶ 鹿の子絞り, dappled cloth.

kańon (感恩), *n.* gratefulness; gratitude.

kanpa (看破する), *vt.* to penetrate; see *through*; fathom. —胸中を看破する, to read a person's heart; penetrate into another's heart. —祕密を看破する, to pierce into the secret.

kanpai (乾杯), *n.* a toast; pledge. —乾杯する, to toast; drink a toast; drink to another's health (健康のために). —乾杯の辭を述べる, to propose a toast.

kanpai (感佩する), *v.* to be deeply impressed *with*; be deeply grateful *for*; remember with gratitude.

kanpan (甲板), *n.* a deck; a board. —甲板を一掃する, to sweep the deck. ¶ 上甲板, the upper [spar] deck; the tonnage-deck (二甲板を有する船の上甲板). —中甲板, a middle deck (三層甲板船にありては upper deck と lower deck の中間); a main deck (軍艦にては upper [spar] deck の次, 商船にありては poop deck と forecastle の中間の場所). —下甲板, a lower deck. —甲板室, a deck-house; a round-house.

kanpan (乾板), *n.* a dry plate.

kanpatsu (煥發), *n.* ❶ (輝き顯はれる) flash; spark (機才等の); coruscation. ❷ (渙發の誤用) promulgation; proclamation. —煥發する, ① to flash. ② to promulgate; proclaim.

kanpeisha (官幣社), *n.* a government shrine. ¶ 官幣大社, a great government shrine.

kanpeishiki (觀兵式), *n.* 【軍】a parade; a (military) review.

kanpeki (完璧), *n.* ❶ a perfect [flawless] jewel. ❷ (完全) perfection.
kanpeki (癇癖), *n.* irritability; testiness; irascibility. ¶ 癇癖家, a short-tempered person.
kanpi (官費), *n.* government expense; public cost. ¶ 官費留學生, a student sent abroad by the government.
kanpo (緩歩する), *vi.* to pace; walk slowly; stroll.
kanpō (官報), *n.* ❶ the Official Gazette. ❷ (電信) a government telegram.
kanpō (漢方), *n.* Chinese medicine [medical art]. ¶ 漢方醫, a doctor of the Chinese school.
kanpon (完本), *n.* a complete set of books.
kanpu (姦夫), *n.* an adulterer.
kanpu (姦婦), *n.* an adulteress.
kanpu (還付), *n.* restoration; return; retrocession. —還付する, to return; restore; retrocede.
kanpū (寒風), *n.* a cold wind. —身を劈くが如き寒風, a cutting [sharp; piercing] wind.
kanpuku (官服), *n.* (an official) uniform.
kanpuku (感服する), *v.* to admire; esteem (敬服); have a high opinion *of* (同上). —感服さす, to strike with wonder [admiration].
kanpun (感奮する), *vi.* to be deeply moved *by*; be inspired *by*; be excited. —感奮さす, to rouse; stir; inspire.
kanraku (乾酪), *n.* cheese.
kanraku (陷落), *n.* ❶【地質】depression; fall; subsidence. ❷ (城の) fall; surrender. —陷落する, ① to fall in; subside; depress. ② to surrender (城が); fall.
kanraku (歡樂), *n.* pleasure; merriment; mirth. —歡樂を極める, to quaff the full meed of pleasure; drink the cup of joy to the dregs. —人生の歡樂を盡す, to exhaust the pleasure of life. ¶ 歡樂鄕, a lotus-land; a Utopia.
kanran (甘藍), *n.* the colewort.
kanran (橄欖), *n.* 【植】the Chinese olive. ¶ 橄欖石, 【鑛】peridote. —橄欖油, olive-oil; sweet-oil.
kanran (觀覽), *n.* sight; viewing; inspection. —觀覽する, to see; inspect; view. —觀覽に供する, to present [submit] for inspection; put on view. ¶ 觀覽料, entrance-money; admission-fee. —觀覽席, a stand. —觀覽者, a spectator; a visitor. —觀覽車, a big wheel. —觀覽稅, tax on admissions.
kanrei (寒冷), *n.* coldness; cold; chillness.
kanrei (慣例), *n.* custom; usage; practice. —一定せる慣例, an established custom. —慣例を破る, to act contrary to custom; break the custom. —將來に惡慣例を貽す, to leave a bad precedent behind.
kanrei (緩冷する), *vt.* to anneal.
kanreisha (寒冷紗), *n.* victoria lawn.
kanreki (還曆), *n.* ❶ the sexagenary cycle. ❷ (六十歲) the sixty-first year. ¶ 還曆祝, celebration of the sixty-first birthday.
kanren (關聯する), *vi.* to be related *to*; be connected *with*. —…に關聯して, in connection *with*; in relation *to*.
kanri (官吏), *n.* a government official. ¶ 官吏社會, official circles [class]. —官吏收賄罪, official corruption.
kanri (管理), *n.* administration; management; control. —管理する, to administer; manage; control. —鐵道の管理を解く, to release railways from control. ¶ 食糧管理, food control. —管理人, an administrator (遺產·相續財產等の); a manager; a controller.
kanri (監吏), *n.* an overlooker; an inspector (稅關の); a tide-waiter (入港船に至ッて監視する者); a landing [coast]-waiter (沿岸貿易船の荷物積卸しの).
kanrin (官林), *n.* a government [state] forest.
kanritsu (官立の), *a.* government. ¶ 官立學校, a government school.
kanro (甘露), *n.* nectar; honey-dew; manna.
kanrui (感淚), *n.* tears of gratitude (sympathy). —感淚に咽ぶ, to be choked with tears of gratitude. —感淚を催す, to shed tears of gratitude.
kanryaku (簡略), *n.* brevity; simplicity; conciseness. —簡略な, brief; simple; concise. —簡略に, briefly; concisely.
kanryō (完了), *n.* completion; finish; 【文】the perfect. —完了する, to complete; finish; accomplish. ¶ 完了時, 【文】the perfect tense.
kanryō (官僚), *n.* bureaucracy (全部); a bureaucrat (一人). ¶ 官僚政治, bureaucracy; bureaucratic government. —官僚主義, bureaucratism.
kanryū (貫流する), *vt.* to run [flow] *through*.
kanryū (寒流), *n.* a cold current.
kansa (監査), *n.* inspection; audit (會計の). —監査する, to inspect; audit. ¶ 監査役, an inspector (會社等の); an auditor.
kansai (完濟する), *vt.* to meet [pay] in full.
kansai-suirai (艦載水雷-艇), *n.*

a torpedo-launch; a vedette-boat.

kansaku (奸策, 姦策), *n.* machination; intrigue; wiles.

kansan (閑散な), *a.* ❶ leisurely; quiet (閑靜な). ❷ (取引の) dull. —閑散な時期, a dull [slack] season. —閑散である, to be out of work; be at leisure; be slack.

kansan (換算), *n.* conversion; exchange. —換算する, to convert; change. ¶ 換算率, exchange rates.

kansatsu (監察する), *vt.* to inspect; look over. ¶ 方面監察, a patrolman. —監察官, an inspector; a censor.

kansatsu (鑑札), *n.* a licence, license. ¶ 鑑札料, licence-fee.

kansatsu (觀察), *n.* observation; survey. —觀察する, to observe; see; view. —觀察を誤る, to commit an error in observation; make an erroneous observation. —觀察點を異にする, to differ in points of view.

kansei (完成), *n.* completion; perfection. —完成する, ① [*vt.*] to complete; perfect; mature (計畫等を). ② [*vi.*] to be completed.

kansei (官制), *n.* government organization.

kansei (官製の), *a.* of government manufacture; manufactured by the government. ¶ 官製葉書, a government postcard. —官製刻み煙草, cut-tobacco of government manufacture; government cut-tobacco.

kansei (陷穽), *n.* a snare; a trap; a pitfall.

kansei (閑靜な), *a.* quiet; restful.

kansei (瞰制する), *vt.* to command.

kansei (喚聲), *n.* a war-cry; a battle-cry.

kansei (歡聲), *n.* a shout of joy; a hurrah; a huzza. —歡聲を發する, to shout for joy.

kansei (鼾聲), *n.* snoring; a snore.

kansei-honbu (艦政本部), *n.* 【海】 the Department of Materiel of the Navy.

kanseki (艦籍), *n.* forum of a man-of-war.

kanseki (漢籍), *n.* a Chinese book; a book in the classical Chinese style.

kansen (汗線), *n.* 【解】 a sweat gland.

kansen (官線), *n.* a government [state] line.

kansen (官選の), *a.* chosen by the authorities. ¶ 官選辯護人, a designated advocate.

kansen (幹線), *n.* a trunk-line (鐵道・運河の); a trunk (同上); a main [stock] line (of railway).

kansen (感染), *n.* infection; contagion. —— **-suru**, *v.* ❶ (病が人に) to infect. ❷ (人が病に) to be infected; taint; be affected; catch. —病毒に感染する, to be infectetl by virus. —流行性感冒に感染する, to catch influenza.

kansen (艦船), *n.* ships; vessels. ¶ 艦船行商人, a bumboat-man.

kansen (觀戰), *n.* witnessing a battle. ¶ 觀戰武官, an officer attached to a field army.

kansenkyoku (管船局), *n.* the Mercantile Marine Bureau.

kansetsu (官設の), *a.* government. ¶ 官設鐵道, a government [state] railway.

kansetsu (間接の), *a.* ❶ indirect; mediate. ❷ circuitous; oblique (迂曲の). —— **-ni**, *ad.* ❶ indirectly; mediately. ❷ circuitously; obliquely. —間接に影響を受ける, to be indirectly affected. ¶ 間接稅, an indirect tax.

kansetsu (關節, 關接), *n.* ❶ (ふし) a joint; an articulation; an article. ❷ (繼ぎ目) a joint. ¶ 關節僂麻質斯, articular rheumatism.

kansetsu (環節), *n.* a segment.

kan-sezu (關せず), *v.* no matter how (when; what); regardless *of*; irrespective(-ly) *of*. —人物の如何に關せず交はる, to associate with a person irrespective of his character [no matter who he may be].

kansha (官舍), *n.* an official residence.

kansha (感謝), *n.* thanks; gratitude (感謝の心); 【宗】 thanksgiving. —感謝する, to thank; return thanks; express gratitude; make acknowledgments *to*. —心からの感謝, hearty thanks. ¶ 感謝狀, a letter of thanks.

kanshaku (癇癪), *n.* quick-[short-] -temper; passion; spleen. —癇癪を起す, to lose one's temper; fly into a passion. —癇癪を抑へる, to check one's temper [anger]. ¶ 癇癪玉, a (fire-)cracker; a squib; a bang. —癇癪持ち, ① (人) a testy [choleric] person; a spitfire; a pepper-pot 【俗】. ② (性) testiness; tetchiness.

kanshi (干支), *n.* the sexagenary cycle.

kanshi (冠詞), *n.* 【文】 the article. —冠詞の用法を誤る, to misuse the articles.

kanshi (監視), *n.* ❶ observation; watch; lookout; custody; superintendence. ❷ (稅關の) water-guard; a tide-waiter. —監視する, to watch; oversee; superintend. —監視を嚴にする, to make the surveillance strict. ¶ (稅關)監視部長, the superintendent of water-guard. —監視哨所, a lookout.

kanshi (諫止する), *vt.* to dissuade.

kanshi (瞰視する), *v.* to look down *upon*; command a view *of*. —市街を瞰視する, to command a view of city.

kanshi (環視), *n.* concentration of looks; concentrated attention. —環視する, to concentrate looks [attention] *upon*. —衆人環視の中に, with all eyes fixed upon it (him). —列國環視の的となる, to become the focus of the world's attention; have the world's attention concentrated upon one.

kanshiki (鑑識), *n.* ❶ (鑑別) judgment; discernment. ❷ (鑑賞) appreciation; taste (文學・美術の). ❸ (評價) criticism; estimate. —鑑識する, ① to judge; discern; measure. ② to appreciate; taste. ③ to criticize; estimate. —書畫の鑑識に長ずる, to have an eye for [be a good judge of] writings and pictures. ¶ 鑑識家, a judge; a connoisseur.

kanshin (奸臣, 姦臣), *n.* a villainous [treacherous; wicked] retainer.

kanshin (寒心する), *vi.* to shudder *at*; one's blood runs cold. —寒心さす, to make one shudder; make one's blood run cold.

kanshin (感心な), *a.* admirable; praiseworthy; commendable. —感心する, to admire; wonder *at*; approve *of* (贊成). —感心して聞く, to listen with admiration.

kanshin (歡心), *n.* good will; favour. —婦女の歡心を買ふ, to ingratiate oneself with a woman [into a woman's favour]; pay one's court to a woman. —俗衆の歡心を求める, to curry favour with the public.

kan-shite (關して), in connection *with*; relative *to*; with [in] regard *to*; with respect *to*. —此事に關して, in this connection.

kansho (甘蔗), *n.* the sugar-cane. ¶ 甘蔗糖, cane sugar.

kansho (甘薯), *n.* sweet potato.

kansho (官署), *n.* a government office.

kansho (寒暑), *n.* heat and cold; temperature.

kansho (漢書), *n.* a Chinese book.

kanshō (干涉), *n.* interference; intervention; interposition. **—suru**, *v.* to interfere *in*; intervene *in*; meddle *in*. —他人の事に干涉する, to meddle in another's concerns. ¶ 選擧干涉, interference in election.

kanshō (奸商), *n.* a dishonest [crafty] merchant.

kanshō (官省), *n.* a government department.

kanshō (管掌), *n.* management; conduct; administration. —管掌する, to manage; conduct; administer.

kanshō (感傷的), *a.* sentimental; pathetic(-al).

kanshō (緩衝), *n.* deadening [neutralizing] a shock. ¶ 緩衝地帶, a neutral zone. —緩衝國, a buffer state.

kanshō (環象), *n.* environment.

kanshō (環礁), *n.* 【地質】 an atoll; a lagoon island.

kanshō (簡捷), *n.* simplification.

kanshō (觀象), *n.* observation (of the weather); meteorological observation. ☞ *kansoku*.

kanshō (觀賞する), *vt.* to admire; praise. ¶ 觀賞植物, an ornamental plant.

kanshō (觀照), *n.* contemplation. —觀照する, to contemplate.

kanshō (鑑賞), *n.* appreciation; taste. —鑑賞する, to appreciate.

kanshoku (官職), *n.* a government [an official] post.

kanshoku (寒色), *n.* a cold colour.

kanshoku (間色), *n.* a compound [secondary] colour.

kanshoku (間食する), *vi.* ❶ to eat between meals. ❷ to eat [take food] at intervals.

kanshoku (感觸), *n.* ❶ (感覺) sensation; touch (觸感). ❷ (感情) feelings; susceptibilities.

kanshu (看守), *n.* ❶ (見まもる) oversight; surveillance. ❷ (監獄の) a warder; a jailer; a turnkey. ❸ (航路標識所の) a lighthouse-keeper; a light-keeper. —看守する, to guard; watch. ¶ 看守長, a chief warder.

kanshu (看取する), *vt.* to see *through*; perceive. —人の性格を看取する, to study a person's character.

kanshu (貫主), *n.* the chief abbot.

kanshu (監守), *n.* custody; charge; safe-keeping. —監守する, to have charge [custody] *of*; keep. ¶ 監守人, a keeper; a custodian.

kanshū (慣習), *n.* custom; usage; convention. ☞ *shūkan* (習慣). ¶ 商慣習, the mercantile usage; the custom of merchants.

kanshū (監修する), *v.* to superintend a compilation.

kanshudan (慣手段), *n.* = *kan̈yō* (慣用手段).

kansō (乾燥), *n.* ❶ (乾くこと) drying; desiccation; aridity; 【醫】 exsiccation. ❷ (無趣味) dryness; baldness (文體の). —乾燥する, ① [*vi.*] to season; dry. ② [*vt.*] to desiccate; dry. —乾燥せる, dry; arid (土地又は氣候につき). —乾燥極まる, dry-as-dust ¶ 乾燥期, the dry season (rainy season

の對). —乾燥室, a drying-room.
kansō (感想), *n.* impression; thoughts; feeling. —彼の感想を叩く, to ask for his impressions. ¶感想錄, a record of impressions.
kansō (諫諍する), *vi.* to remonstrate (fearlessly) *with*; expostulate *with*.
kansō (觀想), *n.* contemplation. —觀想する, to contemplate.
kansoku (觀測), *n.* observation; survey. ——**-suru,** *vt.* to observe; sight (星などを); survey. —氣象を觀測する, to observe the weather; make an observation of the weather. ¶觀測氣球, an observation-balloon (敵狀); a sounding balloon (氣象). —觀測所, an observatory; an observing station; an observation-post (砲火の). —觀測者, an observer.
kanson-minpi (官尊民卑), *n.* respect for the government and contempt for the people.
kansū (完數), *n.* an integer.
kansū (函數), *n.* 【數】 a function.
kansui (鹹水), *n.* salt-water; brine. ¶鹹水魚, a salt-water fish. —鹹水湖, a salt-lake.
kan-suru (冠する), *vt.* to cap; crown; surmount.
kan-suru (管する), *v.* ❶ (管轄) to control; have competence *over*; exercise jurisdiction *over*. ❷ (取締る) to oversee; supervise; control. ❸ (司る) to administer; manage; conduct; take charge *of*; rule.
kan-suru (緘する), *vt.* ❶ (閉ぢる) to shut; close. ❷ (封ずる) to seal.
kan-suru (關する), *v.* ❶ (關係) to be connected *with*; concern; relate *to*. ❷ (影響) to affect; influence. ☞ ***kankei*** (關係する). ——, *prep.* regarding; concerning; respecting.
kantai (款待), *n.* welcome; a warm reception; hospitality. —款待到らざるなし, to receive with open arms. ——**-suru,** *vt.* to welcome; receive; give a warm welcome [reception]. —下にも置かず款待する, to overwhelm with welcome.
kantai (寒帶), *n.* a frigid zone. ¶北(南)寒帶, the Arctic (Antarctic) zone.
kantai (艦隊), *n.* a squadron (小); a fleet (大). ¶艦隊司令官, a commander of a squadron.
kantai (艦體), *n.* the hull of a warship.
kantaku (官宅), *n.* an official residence.
kantan (肝膽), *n.* ❶ (きも) the liver; the gall-bladder (膽嚢). ❷ (眞心) one's innermost heart. —肝膽相照らす, ① [*a.*] (意氣相投する) congenial. ② to lay open each other's innermost heart. —肝膽を碎く, to exert oneself with great zeal.
kantan (感歎), *n.* admiration; exclamation. —感歎する, ① [*vi.*] to admire; cry out [exclaim] with admiration. ② [*vt.*] to admire; applaud; praise. ¶感歎符, the exclamation mark [point]; the note of exclamation (!).
kantan (簡單), *n.* shortness; brevity; conciseness. —簡單な, short; brief; concise. —簡單にする, to simplify; cut short. —簡單に話す, to speak briefly; have a word *with*.
kantei (官邸), *n.* an official residence.
kantei (鑑定), *n.* (expert) opinion; appraisal (價格の); judgment (物品の). —鑑定する, to give one's opinion; appraise; judge; criticize. ¶鑑定官, (關稅の) a customs appraiser. —鑑定人, an expert witness (裁判所から命ずる); an appraiser. —鑑定書, an opinion in writing; a written opinion.
kanteki (灌滴), *n.* embrocation. ¶灌滴療法, treatment by embrocation.
kanten (旱天), *n.* ❶ (旱魃) drought; (continuous) dry weather. ❷ (炎天) hot [broiling] weather.
kanten (寒天), *n.* ❶ (寒空) cold weather. ❷ (食品の名) the Bengal [Japanese] isinglass; the agar-agar 〘印度〙.
kanten (寛典), *n.* clemency; leniency. —寛典に處する, to treat with leniency.
kantera (カンテラ-燈), *n.* a metal hand-lantern; a lantern. ¶カンテラ行列, a lantern-procession.
kantetsu (貫徹), *n.* ❶ (貫通) penetration. ❷ (成就) accomplishment. —貫徹する, ① to penetrate; pierce. ② to accomplish; carry through.
kanto (官途), *n.* government service. —官途に就く, to enter (the) government service.
kantō (官等), *n.* an official grade [rank].
kantō (款冬), *n.* 【植】 the bull's foot; the colt's foot.
kantoku (監督), *n.* ❶ supervision; superintendence. ❷ (人) a supervisor; a superintendent; a presiding officer (試驗場の); a foreman (職工などの); a bishop (耶蘇教の). —監督する, to supervise; superintend; preside over. ¶大監督, an archbishop. —現場監督, supervision of works. —監督判事, 【法】 a superintending judge. —監督官廳, the competent authorities

(當該官廳); the intendant office (下級官廳を監督するもの). —監督教會, the Episcopal Church. —監督局, a superintendence office. —監督者[人], =*kantoku* の❷.

kantōshi (間投詞), *n.* 【文】 the interjection.

kantsū (姦通), *n.* adultery; illicit intercourse. —姦通する, to have illicit intercourse *with*; commit adultery *with*. ¶姦通者, an adulterer (男); an adulteress (女).

kantsū (貫通), *n.* penetration. —貫通する, ① [*vt.*] to penetrate; perforate; pierce. ② [*vi.*] to pierce *through*; pass [run] *through*.

kantsubaki (寒椿), *n.* 【植】 the winter-flowering camellia.

kanwa (閑話), *n.* gossip; chit-chat; quiet talk. —閑話休題, to return to our subject.

kanwa (緩和), *n.* moderation; relaxation; alleviation. ——**-suru,** *vt.* to relieve; alleviate; assuage; moderate. —惡感情を緩和する, to soften ill-feeling. —形勢を緩和する, to relieve the situation.

kan̓ya (寒夜), *n.* a cold night.

kan̓yo (干與する), *v.* to participate *in*; take part *in*; be implicated (かゝり合ふ). —陰謀に干與する, to take part [be implicated] in the intrigue. ¶干與者, a participant; a party concerned.

kan̓yō (肝要な), *a.* important; essential; necessary.

kan̓yō (官用), *n.* ❶ (官務) government [official] business. ❷ (官の使用) official use.

kan̓yō (涵養), *n.* fostering; cultivation. ——**-suru,** *vt.* to foster; cultivate. —國力を涵養する, to foster national power.

kan̓yō (寛容する), *vt.* to tolerate; pardon; put up *with*.

kan̓yō (慣用の), *a.* common; customary; conventional. ¶慣用語 an idiom. (慣用語法, idiom.) —慣用手段, an old trick; a usual dodge.

kan̓yu (肝油), *n.* cod-liver oil. ¶無臭肝油, inodorous cod-liver oil.

kanyū (加入), *n.* subscription; entrance; admission. ——**-suru,** *v.* to enter (*into*); join. —長距離電話に加入する, to subscribe to the long-distance telephone. ¶加入金, entrance fee; entry-money. —加入者, an entrant; a subscriber; a member.

kan̓yū (官有の), *a.* government [state]-owned. ¶官有物, a government property. —官有地, state demesne; government land [estate].

kan̓yū (奸雄, 姦雄), *n.* a great villain.

kan̓yū (勸誘), *n.* ❶ (寄附・選擧等の) canvassing; canvass. ❷ (說き勸め) exhortation; persuasion. ❸ (誘引) invitation; inducement. —勸誘する, ① to canvass *for*. ② to exhort; persuade. ③ to invite; induce. ¶勸誘員, a canvasser; a canvassing agent.

kanzainin (管財人), *n.* 【法】 an administrator [*fem.* -trix]; a manager.

kanzashi (簪), *n.* a (an ornamental) hair-pin.

kanzei (間稅), *n.* an indirect tax.

kanzei (關稅), *n.* customs; a customs-duty; custom-dues; (佛國等の) *douane* [佛]. ¶關稅自主權, tariff autonomy. —關稅改革, a tariff reform. —關稅局, the Customs Bureau. —關稅率, the customs tariff.

kanzen (完全), *n.* completeness; perfection; integrity. —完全な, perfect; complete; consummate; integral; whole; entire; unbroken; thorough; full; plenary; faultless (瑕なき); free from blemish (同上). —完全の域に達する, to attain perfection. ¶完全無缺, absolute perfection. —完全燃燒器, a smoke-consumer; a smoke-consuming apparatus.

kanzen (間然する), *vt.* to criticize; find fault *with*. —間然する所なし, to be above reproach; leave nothing to be desired; be faultless.

kanzen-chōaku (勸善懲惡), *n.* morality; poetical justice. ¶勸善懲惡劇, a moral play.

kanzenyori (簡箋縒), *n.* Ⓢ 紙縒[こより]. a string of twisted paper.

kanzetsu (冠絕する), *v.* to surpass; be matchless; be peerless.

kanzō (甘草), *n.* 【植】 the liquorice (-plant); (根) liquorice (-root).

kanzō (萱草), *n.* 【植】 the yellow day-lily.

kanzō (肝臟), *n.* the liver. ¶肝臟病, a liver disease. —肝臟炎, hepatitis; inflammation of the liver.

kanzuku (感附・勘附く), *vt.* to get scent *of*; scent; suspect.

kanzume (罐詰), *n.* ❶ (物) a tinned [canned [米]] goods; tinned [canned [米]] food. ❷ (事) tinning; canning. —牛肉 (豚肉) の罐詰, tinned [canned] beef (pork). —罐詰にする, to can [米]; tin; pack. ¶罐詰業者, a packer; a canner. —罐詰所, a packing [can]-house; a cannery; a canning-factory.

kan-zuru (感ずる), *v.* ❶ (感知) to feel; be conscious; experience (不便・困難などを); be impressed *with* (事の重大・必要などを). ❷

(感動) to be moved by; be impressed *by*; be struck *by*. ❷ (影響される) to be affected; be influenced *by*. —說に感ずる, to be impressed by another's views. —困難を感ずる, to find difficulty *in*. —不便を感ずる, to experience inconvenience. —感ずる所ありて, for certain convincing reasons.

kan-zuru (觀する), *vt.* to look *at*; view; observe; contemplate (觀照). —世事を觀ずる, to look at the world's affairs.

kao (顏), *n.* ❶ (顏面) the face. ❷ (顏貌) looks. ☞ *kaotsuki* (顏附). ❸ (面目) countenance; honour. —何喰はぬ顏をして, with an unconcerned look. —顏を背ける, to turn away one's face; look away. —顏を潰す, to dishonour a person; put a person out of countenance.

kaō (花押), *n.* a signature; a monogram.

kaobure (顏觸), *n.* ❶ (關係連名) the list (of men composing a party); personnel; members. ❷ (披露) introduction.

kaodachi (顏立), *n.* features; looks.

kaoiro (顏色), *n.* ❶ (顏の色合) complexion; colour. ❷ (顏附) a face; a countenance. —顏色が惡い, to look off colour. —顏色を讀む, to read another's face. —顏色を窺ふ, to hang on another's smiles; study the pleasure of others.

kaoku (家屋), *n.* a house; a building. ¶家屋周旋業者(管理人), a house-agent. —家屋稅, a house-duty; a house-tax.

kaomuke (顏向), *n.* showing one's face; turning one's face *to*. —世間へ顏向けもならぬ, He cannot show his face in the world.

kaori (馨, 薰), *n.* aroma; perfume; fragrance.

kaoru (薰る), *vi.* to smell; be fragrant.

kaotsuki (顏附), *n.* looks; a countenance; a face.

kaoyaku (顏役), *n.* a chief; a leader; a boss (親分).

kaozoroi (顏揃), *n.* a complete set of men; a gathering of men of a certain set [profession, &c.]

kappa (合羽, 雨衣), *n.* a raincoat; a waterproof; an oilskin.

kappa (河童), *n.* a imaginary river animal (supposed to drown people). —河童の河流れ, "The best horse stumbles."

kappan (活版), *n.* typography; movable type printing. —活版に付する, to put into type; put to press. ¶活版機械, a printing-press. —活版製造所, a type-foundry. —活版職工, a pressman. —活版屋, a printer; a printing-office (活版所).

kapparai (攫拂), *n.* a snapper-up; a purloiner. —攫拂ふ, to snap up; make off *with*; filch.

kappatsu (活發), *n.* briskness; activity; vigour. **——-na**, *a.* brisk; active; vigorous. —活發な女, a brisk [vivacious] woman.

kappo (濶歩), *n.* stride; stalk. —濶歩する, to stalk along; stride; swagger about.

kappō (割烹), *n.* cookery; *cuisine* 〔佛〕. —割烹する, to cook. ¶割烹學校, a cookery school. —割烹著, a cookery-apron. —割烹書, a cookery-book; a cook-book 〔米〕. —割烹店, a restaurant; an eating-house.

kappuku (恰幅), *n.* figure; presence; physique. —恰幅のよい, portly; of fine presence.

kara (空), *n.* ❶ (空虛) emptiness; vacancy. ❷ (空洞) a hollow. —空の, empty. —空にする, to empty (容器等を); make empty.

kara (殼), *n.* ❶ (穀物の) a husk; a hull. ❷ (貝類・卵・堅果の) a shell; a nutshell (堅果の). ❸ 〔雪花菜〕(豆腐の) bean-curd refuse. ❹ (脫殼) a slough (蛇の); a cast-off skin [shell].

kara (から), *particle.* from. ❶ (場所) (*a*) out of (中・奧から); (*b*) through; by; at. ❷ (時) since (このかた). ❸ (原料) out of; of. ❹ (原因) because. —枝から枝へ, from branch to branch. —...からである, to be due to. —病氣だから, because [as] one is ill; on account of [owing to; because of] illness. —梯子から落ちる, to fall off a ladder. —舊家から出る, to come of an old family. —彼の目から見ると, in his eyes. —雲間から洩れ輝く, to shine through a rift in the cloud. —此の見地からすれば, from this point of view. —五時から七時までの間に, between five and seven. —其樣な振舞があってからは, after such behaviour.

kara (カラ), *n.* a shirt-collar; a collar.

kara (から), *ad.* quite; completely; wholly. —から意氣地のない奴だ, He has no spirit at all.

karada (體), *n.* ❶ (身體) body; person. ❷ (體格) constitution; build; physique. ❸ (健康) health. —體一面に, all over the body. —體を休める, to rest [recreate] oneself. —體を大切にする, to take great care of oneself.

Karafuto (樺太), *n.* Karafuto; Saghalien.

karagara (辛辛), *ad.* barely;

narrowly. ―からがら間に合ふ, to be barely in time. ―命からがら逃げる, to escape with bare life.

karage (紮, 捆), *n.* ❶ (からげること) packing; binding. ❷ (一に束ねたもの) a bundle; a sheaf (稲などの); a packet (包裝せるもの). ―荷物を一捆げにする, to tie goods into one bundle.

karagenki (空元氣), *n.* bluster; Dutch courage〔俗. 酒の上での〕.

karageru (紮・捆げる), *vt.* ❶ (からむ) to tuck up. ❷ (結束) to tie up; pack up; bind. ―絲でからげる, to fasten with a thread. ―裾をひッからげる, to tuck up the skirt.

karai (辛い), *a.* ❶ (味の) hot; pungent; salty (鹽辛い). ❷ (つらい) hard. ❸ (嚴しい) severe. ―辛い葡萄酒, dry wine.

karaibari (空威張), *n.* bluster; empty boast; bluff. **――-suru,** *vi.* to bluster; bluff. ―陰で空威張する, to bluster behind another's back.

karakai (揶揄), *n.* banter; chaff; raillery.

karakau (揶揄ふ), *vt.* to banter; chaff; make fun *of.* ―子供にからかふ, to tease [chaff] children.

karakami (唐紙), *n.* Ⓢ 襖. a sliding-door; a sliding-screen.

karakane (唐金, 靑銅), *n.* bronze.

karakara (からから), *ad.* ❶ (呵呵) loudly; aloud. ❷ (戶など開閉の音) with a rumble. ―カラカラ笑ふ, to laugh aloud.

karakara (からからになる), *vi.* to dry up; shrivel. 〔☞ *kasa.*〕

karakasa (傘), *n.* an umbrella.

karaki (唐木), *n.* foreign wood (of value). ¶ 唐木細工, ware made with foreign wood.

karaku (辛く), *ad.* ❶ (味) pungently. ❷ (つらく) hard. ❸ (嚴しく) severely.

karakuji (空籤), *n.* a blank (ticket). ―空籤を引く, to draw a blank.

karakumo (辛くも), *ad.* narrowly; barely; with difficulty.

karakuri (絡繰), *n.* ❶ (しかけ) machinery; works; device (工夫). ❷ (覗眼鏡) a peep-show; a show-box. ❸ =*kontan* (魂膽). ¶ 絡繰人形, a marionette.

karakusa (唐草-模様), *n.* a vine pattern; an arabesque; flourish.

karamaru (絡まる), *vi.* ❶ (捲附く) to twine *round*; get twisted *round*; wind *round*. ❷ (縺れる) to get entangled; foul (錨索等が); ravel. ❸ (絆される) to be entangled. ☞ *karamu*. ―朝顔の蔓を垣に絡ませる, to trail the tendrils of the morning-glory on the fence.

karamatsu (落葉松), *n.* 【植】 Larix leptolepis (larch-tree の一種).

karamawari (空轉する), *vi.* to race (機關・推進機・外輪などの).

karamete (搦手), *n.* the postern (城などの). ―搦手から攻め寄せる, to assault from the rear.

karametoru (搦取る), *vt.* to arrest; apprehend; seize.

karami (辛味), *n.* an acrid taste; a pungent ingredient (藥味).

karamiau (絡合ふ), *vi.* to intertwine; be interlaced; get entangled.

karamu (絡む), *v.* ❶ (捲附く) to twine [coil; wind] *round.* ❷ (縺れる) to get entangled. ☞ *karamaru.* ―絡み附ける, to entwine [twine] (one thing) round another; wind a thing round another. ―人の首に絡みつく, to clasp a person round the neck.

karamushi (苧麻), *n.* 【植】 the China-grass; the grass-cloth-plant; the ramie.

karankaran (からんからん), *ad.* ding-dong; with a clang. ―カランカランと鳴る, to ring with a clang.

karareru (驅られる), *vi.* ❶ (動かされる) to be carried away *by*; be devoured *with*; be stricken *with.* ❷ (强ひられる) to be prompted; be actuated; be spurred on. ―野心に驅られた, devoured with ambition. ―熱情に驅られて, under the influence [sway] of passion.

kararito (からりと), *ad.* Ⓢ からッと. ❶ (戶など開く音) with a bang. ❷ (一變する樣) completely (全々); suddenly (忽然). ―からりとした, ① (心の) open-hearted; frank; candid. ② (空の) clear. ③ (室の) open.

karasawagi (空騷), *n.* great cry and little wool; much ado about nothing. ―空騷ぎをする, to fuss; make a fuss about trifles.

karashi (芥子), *n.* mustard. ¶ 芥子泥, mustard-plaster; 【醫】 sinapism. ―芥子入れ, a mustard-pot (食卓の).

karashina (芥), *n.* 【植】 Brassia cernua (cabbage の一種・學名).

karashishi (唐獅子), *n.* the lion.

karasu (烏, 鴉), *n.* ❶ the crow; the raven (大鴉). ❷ (健忘者) a forgetful person.

karasu (枯らす), *vt.* ❶ (枯れさす) to let wither; blight; blast. ❷ (貯藏して熟さす) to season.

karasu (涸らす), *vt.* to dry up; exhaust (井戶・財源など); drain (財源など). ―資源を涸らす, to drain [dry up] the source of capital.

karasu (嗄らす), *v.* to get hoarse. —聲を嗄らして呶鳴る, to roar with a hoarse voice.
karasugai (烏貝), *n.* the swan mussel.
karasuguchi (烏口), *n.* a drawing pen.
karasumugi (燕麥), *n.* the oat.
karasuuri (烏瓜), *n.* 【植】 Trichosanthes cucumeroides (snake-gourd の一種・學名).
karatachi (枳殼), *n.* 【植】 Aegle sepiaria (Bengal quince の類・學名).
karate (空手), *n.* an empty hand. —空手で戻る, to go home empty-handed. —空手で商賣を始める, to start business without capital.
karazao (連枷), *n.* a flail. —連枷で打つ, to flail; thresh.
kare (彼), *pron.* ❶ (男性) he; (女性) she. ❷ (あれ) that. —彼か是か, either...or. —彼も此も…ならず, neither...nor.
kare (枯), *a.* dead; dry; withered.
karē (カレー), *n.* curry. ¶ カレー粉, curry-powder. —カレーライス, curried rice.
kareba, kareha, (枯葉), *n.* a dead [withered] leaf. ¶ 枯葉色, filemot; yellowish-brown.
karegoe (嗄聲), *n.* a hoarse [husky] voice.
karei (鰈), *n.* 【魚】 the halibut.
karei (家令), *n.* a steward; a controller.
karei (家例), *n.* family practice [usage].
karei (華麗な), *a.* splendid; magnificent; florid.
kareki (枯木), *n.* a dead [withered] tree.
karekore (彼此), *pron.* this and that (彼と此れ). ——, *n.* one thing and [or] another. ——, *ad.* about; some; nearly. —彼れ此れ云ふ, ① (評判) to talk about. ② (異議) to raise objections. ③ (苦情) to make complaints; grumble. —彼れ此れする中に, in the meantime; meanwhile; in the interim. —彼れ此れと手を出す, to try several things.
karekusa (枯草), *n.* ❶ dry grass. ❷ (乾草) hay.
karen (可憐な), *a.* ❶ (憐れな) pitiful; poor. ❷ (可愛らしい) pretty; lovely; tiny (小さな).
kareno (枯野), *n.* a withered field; a barren moor.
karera (彼等), *pron.* they.
kareru (枯れる), *vi.* ❶ to wither; wilt; perish. ❷ (熟する) to mature; mellow; season. —枯れた, ① dry; dead; withered. ② mellow; matured. —枯れかゝった葉, the yellowing leaves.
kareru (涸れる), *vi.* to be exhausted; dry (up) (河など); run dry (水など).
kareru (嗄れる), *vi.* to get [grow] hoarse. —嗄れた, hoarse; husky.
kari (雁), *n.* the wild goose.
kari (加里), *n.* potassium; potash.
kari (狩, 獵), *n.* ❶ (鳥獸獵) chase; hunting; shooting (銃獵). ❷ (漁獵) fishing. ❸ (尋ね探すこと) search; hunting. ¶ 獵小屋, a hunting-box.
kari (借), *n.* a loan; a debt; borrowing. —借りがある, to have a debt; owe money. —借りを拵へる, to fall [run] into debt. —君に十圓借りがある, I owe you ten *yen*.
kari (假の), *a.* ❶ (一時的の) temporary; provisional; interim. ❷ (果敢ない) transient; evanescent; ephemeral. ❸ (僞はれる) assumed; false. —假の世, a frail life; the evanescent world. ¶ 假橋, a temporary bridge. —假普請, a temporary building. —假營業所, a temporary place of business. —假住所, provisional domicile. —假入學, admission on probation.
kariatsumeru (驅集める), *vt.* to muster; gather together; round-up (牛馬を); beat up (鳴物を叩き).
kariba (獵場), *n.* a hunting ground; a preserve (個人所有の); a chase.
karichin (借賃), *n.* hire (動產の); rent (不動產の).
karidasu (獵出す), *vt.* to put up; hunt out [up]; round up. —有權者を獵り出す, to hunt up those possessing the right.
karigi (借著), *n.* borrowed clothes. —借著をする, to wear borrowed clothes.
karigoya (假小屋), *n.* a shed; a booth.
kariho (刈穗), *n.* harvested rice-ears.
kariire (刈入), *n.* harvest. —刈入れる, to reap; get in; harvest. ¶ 刈入れ時, the harvest-time.
kariireru (借入れる), *vt.* to hire; rent (家又は土地を); lease (土地を); borrow (金を); take (家を); charter (汽船を). ¶ 一時借入金, a temporary loan; floating debt.
karikabu (刈株), *n.* a stubble.
karikaeru (借換へる), *vt.* to convert; renew. —公債に借換へる, to convert into a public loan.
karikata (借方), *n.* debit; debtor (Dr. と略す); debit side. ☞ *kashikata* (貸方).
karikomi (刈込), *n.* cutting (頭髮の); clipping (同上); pruning (樹木の). —刈込五十錢, hair-cutting, fifty *sen*.
karikomu (刈込む), *vt.* to crop; trim; prune. —頭を短く刈込む, to cut hair close.

karikoshi (借越), *n.* an outstanding debt; overdraft (過振り). —借越しをする, [*vi.*] to overdraw. ¶ 借越金, overdraft.

karima (借間), *n.* lodgings; a hired room.

karin (花梨), *n.* 【植】 the Chinese quince.

karina (假名), *n.* a pseudonym; a *nom de guerre* [佛]; an assumed [a false] name (僞名); a provisional name (新聞等にある).

karini (假に), *ad.* ❶ (一時的) provisionally; for the time being; for the present. ❷ (假定的) hypothetically; supposing. ❸ (便宜上) for convenience sake; by way of experiment (試に). —假にさうとしても, even supposing that it is so.

karinimo (假にも), *ad.* even for a time [moment]; even in sport (戯れにも); at all. ☞ ***karisome*** (假初にも).

karintō (花林糖), *n.* fried dough-cake.

karinui (假縫する), *vt.* to baste; tack.

karinushi (借主), *n.* a borrower (借用者); a debtor (負債者); a renter (借家人); a lessee (借地人).

kariokiba (假置場), *n.* an entrepôt; a temporary depot (税關の).

kariru (借りる), *vt.* ❶ (*a*) to borrow: (*b*) (借り料を拂ッて) to lease (土地); rent (土地·家屋などを); hire (座敷など). ❷ (藉) (かこつける) to make a pretext *of*. —手を借りる, to get help. —智慧を借りる, to borrow another's brain; ask another's advice. —名を慈善に藉りて, under the veil [cloak] of charity.

karisashiosae (假差押), *n.* 【法】 provisional seizure [attachment]. —假差押をする, to attach provisionally; make provisional attachment.

karishikkō (假執行), *n.* 【法】 provisional execution.

karishobun (假處分), *n.* 【法】 provisional disposition.

karishōzoku (狩裝束), *n.* hunting dress.

karishutsugoku (假出獄), *n.* provisional release. —假出獄になる, to be released on ticket of leave. ¶ 假出獄者, a ticket-of-leave man; a provisionally-released prisoner.

karisome (假初·苟且の), *a.* ❶ (一時の) provisional; transient; transitory. ❷ (些細の) trivial; trifling; slight. —假初の病, a slight indisposition. —假初にも, ever; for a moment; on any account; even in sport (戯談にも). —假初にする, to make light *of*; slight; neglect.

karitateru (獵立てる), *vt.* to drive; chase; hunt up.

karitateru (驅立てる), *vt.* ❶ (勵ます) to drive hard; urge on; speed. ❷ (逐ひやる) to drive away.

karite (刈手), *n.* a mower (草の); a reaper (麥等の).

karite (借手), *n.* a borrower; a tenant (土地·家屋の).

karitoji (假綴), *n.* temporary binding; paper binding. —假綴ちにする, to bind temporarily; bind in paper.

kariudo (獵人), *n.* a hunter [*fem.* -tress]; a huntsman.

kariukeru (借受ける), *vt.* = ***kariireru*** (借入れる).

kariuzume (假埋), *n.* temporary burial.

karizumai (假住居), *n.* a temporary residence [abode].

karō (過勞), *n.* over-exertion; overwork; excessive labour. —過勞する, to overwork oneself; overtax one's powers; work too hard.

karogaro (輕輕と), *ad.* lightly; easily.

karogaro-shii (輕輕しい), *a.* heedless; rash; hasty. **——shiku**, *ad.* heedlessly; rashly; hastily. —輕々しく扱ふ, to trifle with; treat heedlessly. —輕々しく臆斷する, to jump to a hasty conclusion; conclude without due consideration.

karōjite (辛うじて), *ad.* barely; with difficulty; narrowly. —辛うじて通過する, to scrape through (試驗などを). —辛うじて逃げる, to escape by the skin of one's teeth. —辛うじて間に合ふ, to be barely in time.

karonzuru (輕んずる), *vt.* to make light *of*; attach little importance *to*; hold cheap. ☞ ***anadoru***. —生命を輕んずる, to make light of life. —人を輕んずる, to slight a man.

karori (カロリー), *n.* a calorie (熱量單位).

karu (刈る), *vt.* to cut (down); mow (草·穀物を); reap (穀物を); crop (穀物·髮などを); prune (枝を). —頭髮[?]を刈りに行く, to go to have one's hair cut.

karu (狩る), *vt.* to hunt; chase; course. —乞食を狩る, to round up beggars.

karu (借る), *vt.* =***kariru.***

karu (驅る), *v.* ❶ to drive (馬車など); ride (馬など). ❷ (追ひ立てる) to drive away. ❸ (せき立てる) to drive; spur on; press.

karuhazumi (輕忽), *n.* rashness; hastiness. ☞ ***keisotsu*** (輕率).

karui (輕い), *a.* light. ❶ (輕微) slight (病·傷·食事など). ❷ (淡白) mild (食物·煙草など); plain (食物). ❸ (輕易) easy. —輕い罰 (荷), light punishment (goods).

—輕い食物, light [plain] food. —輕い手傷, a slight wound.

karuishi (輕石), *n.* a pumice; a pumice-stone.

karuko (輕子, 擔夫), *n.* a porter; a coolie.

karuku (輕く), *ad.* lightly; slightly; easily (すらすらと). —背を輕く叩く, to tap on the back. —輕くなる, to lighten; ease off (負擔などが). —輕くする, to lighten; mitigate (刑罰など).

karushūmu (カルシゥム), *n.* calcium.

karuta (骨牌), *n.* ❶ (札) cards; playing-cards. ❷ (遊び) cards; a game of [at] cards; card-playing. —骨牌を配る, to deal cards. —骨牌を切る, to shuffle (the) cards. ¶ 歌留多會, ① (團體) a card party. ② (競技) card-playing.

karuwaza (輕業), *n.* acrobatism; acrobatic feats. ¶ 輕業師, an acrobat.

karuyaki (輕燒), *n.* a cracknel.

karyō (下僚), *n.* subordinates; a (clerical) staff.

karyō (佳良), *n.* goodness; fairness.

karyō (科料), *n.* 【法】 a fine; a penalty. —科料に處する, to fine.

karyoku (火力), *n.* caloric force; heating power.

karyū (下流), *n.* the down stream (川の); the lower classes (社會の). —テムズ河の下流に位せる, situated down the Thames.

karyū (花柳-界), *n.* *demi-monde* 【佛】; the frivolous [gay] society. ¶ 花柳病, a venereal disease.

kasa (かさ), *n.* ❶【笠】(かぶりかさ) a sedge-hat (菅笠); a bamboo-hat (竹子笠). ❷【傘】(さし傘) an umbrella; a parasol; a sunshade (日傘). ❸【蓋】(笠又は傘形のもの) a shade; a lamp-shade (ランプの). ❹【暈】(日・月の)【理】a halo; a corona (日・月の). ❺ (茸類の)【植】a pileus; a cap. —傘を翳(+)す, to put up an umbrella. —傘を擴げる, to open an umbrella. —人の威光を笠に被る, to make use of another's influence.

kasa (嵩), *n.* (容積) bulk; volume; size.

kasabaru (嵩張る), *vi.* to bulk; take up space; be bulky. ——, *a.* bulky; voluminous. ☞ *kasamu.*

kasabuta (痂), *n.* a scab; a slough. —痂を生ずる, to scab; slough.

kasai (火災), *n.* a fire. ¶ 火災報知器, a fire-alarm. —火災保險, fire insurance. ¶ 火災準備金, fire reserve.

kasaku (家作), *n.* a house; a building.

kasamu (嵩む), *vi.* to grow bulky; mount up (ふえる); swell (同上). —借金が嵩む, to run up debts.

kasan (加算), *n.* addition. —加算する, to add.

kasan (家產), *n.* family property.

kasanaru (重なる), *vi.* ❶ (重積) to be piled up; overlap. ❷ (累加) to accumulate. —重り合って, one above the other.

kasanegasane (重重), *ad.* again and again; repeatedly; frequently. —重ね重ねの, repeated; frequent. —重ね重ね失敗をする, to fail repeatedly.

kasanegi (重著), *n.* wearing a set of garments.

kasaneru (重ねる), *vt.* ❶ (重疊) to pile on [upon;] heap up. ❷ (累加) to accumulate. ❸ (繰返す) to repeat. —倫落を重ねて, ruin on ruin. —五版を重ねる, to run into [go through] five editions.

kasasagi (鵲), *n.* 【鳥】 the magpie; the pie.

kasatate (傘架), *n.* an umbrella-stand.

kase (枷), *n.* shackles; irons; fetters (足枷).

kase (桛, 綛), *n.* a reel; a skein; a hank.

kasegu (稼ぐ), *v.* to labour; work (for a living); earn (儲ける). —稼ぐに貧乏追ひつかず, "No poverty can overtake industry."

kasei (火星), *n.* 【天】Mars.

kasei (火勢), *n.* the force of a fire.

kasei (加勢), *n.* reinforcements (援兵); assistance; support. —加勢する, to back; reinforce; support.

kasei (苛性), *n.* causticity. ¶ 苛性曹達, caustic soda.

kasei (煆性の), *a.* calcined (煆燒せる). ¶ 煆性石灰, quicklime.

kasei (家政), *n.* housekeeping; household management; domestic economy. —家政に巧な人, a good housekeeper. ¶ 家政婦, a housekeeper.

kaseigan (火成岩), *n.* igneous rock.

kaseki (化石), *n.* ❶ (化石すること) petrifaction; petrification; fossilization. ❷ (化石) a fossil. —化石する, to fossilize; petrify. ¶ 化石動物, a zoolite.

kaseki (呵責), *n.* =*kashaku* (呵責).

kasen (河川), *n.* rivers. ¶ 河川改修工事, river repair-works.

kaseru (かせる), *vi.* ❶ (乾く) to dry up; scab (疥癬等が). ❷ (感染して發疹する) to break out.

kasetsu (佳節), *n.* an auspicious occasion.

kasetsu (架設), *n.* construction; installation. ——**-suru,** *vt.* to construct; build; lay (電線など). —電線を架設する, to lay an electric wire. ¶ 電話架設工事, telephone installation work.

kasetsu (假設), *n.* 【論】 a hypothesis; an assumption.

kasezue (拐杖), *n.* a crutch.

kasha (貨車), *n.* a truck; a goods-waggon. ¶ 有蓋貨車, a covered waggon. —無蓋貨車, an open truck [waggon]; a truck.

kashaku (呵責), *n.* torture; pang; prick. —呵責する, to torment; torture. —良心の呵責, a twinge of conscience; qualms [prick] of conscience; compunction.

kashaku (假借なき), *a.* unsparing; implacable; scathing. —假借なく, unsparingly; without mercy; scathingly. —假借する, to pardon; allow; extenuate.

kashi (樫), *n.* 【植】Quercus myrsinæfolia (oak の一種・學名); the oak【俗】.

kashi (貸), *n.* lending; a loan. —貸しになる, to become a loan. ¶ 貸地, land to let. —貸自轉(自動)車, bicycles (motor-cars) on hire.

kashi (下士-官), *n.* 【陸】a non-commissioned officer (N.C.O. と略す); 【海】a warrant officer; a petty officer. ¶ 下士卒, non-commissioned officers and men.

kashi (下肢), *n.* a lower limb; a leg.

kashi (下賜), *n.* an Imperial grant [donation]. **——-suru,** *vt.* to bestow; grant; confer. —御手許金を御下賜される, to grant out of the Privy Purse.

kashi (河岸), *n.* ❶ a bank; a river-bank; a river-side. ❷ (魚河岸) the river-side fish-market. —舟を河岸につける, to put a boat alongside a river-bank.

kashi (家資), *n.* family property. ¶ 家資分散, insolvency.

kashi (菓子), *n.* cake; confectionery; sweets. ¶ 西洋菓子, foreign confectionery. —菓子パン, cake; fancy bread. —菓子屋, a confectioner; a confectionery (店).

kashichin (貸賃), *n.* rent; hire.

kashidaore (貸倒), *n.* a bad debt. —貸倒れになる, to become a bad debt.

kashidori (樫鳥), *n.* 【鳥】the Japanese jay.

kashigu (炊ぐ), *vt.* to cook; boil.

kashigu (傾ぐ), *v.* to incline; careen (船); list (同上). ☞ *keisha* (傾斜する).

kashihon (貸本), *n.* a loaned book. ¶ 貸本屋, a lending [circulating library (人).

kashikata (貸方), *n.* 【簿記】credit; the creditor side; a creditor; a lender. —貸方に記入する, to enter [put] to a person's credit; credit to a person.

kashikin (貸金), *n.* a loan. —貸金を催促する, to dun for a debt. ¶ 恩給立替貸金, a loan on pensions.

kashikiri (貸切の), *a.* reserved. ¶ 貸切車, a reserved carriage.

kashiko (彼處), *pron.* there; yonder. ☞ *asoko* (あそこ).

Kashikodokoro (賢所), *n.* the hall in the Imperial palace where the Yata Mirror is installed.

kashikoi (賢い), *a.* clever; sensible; intelligent; wise; sagacious. —賢く, cleverly; intelligently; sensibly.

kashikoki (畏き), *n.* reverend; august; awe-inspiring. —畏きあたりの思召, the intention in Exalted Quarters.

kashikomaru (畏る), *v.* ❶ (畏敬) to reverence; revere; obey with respect. ❷ (端坐) to sit straight. ❸ (謹承) to understand; agree *to*; assent *to*. —畏りました, Very well, sir.

kashikoshi (貸越), *n.* outstanding account; overdraft. —貸越しになる, to remain unpaid [outstanding]; be carried over as unpaid.

kashikosōna (賢さうな), *a.* intelligent-looking; clever-looking.

kashima (貸間), *n.* a room [an apartment] to let. —貸間あり, A room [An apartment] to let.

kashimia (カシミア), *n.* cashmere (ショール用毛織物); cassimere (男服用).

kashin (花信), *n.* tidings of flowers.

kashin (花神), *n.* Flora (古羅馬の); the goddess of flowers.

kashin (禍心), *n.* malice (惡心); treachery (叛心); evil intention. —禍心を包藏する, to harbour malice [treacherous designs].

kashin (過信する), *vt.* to place too much confidence [trust] *in*; overtrust; trust too much.

kashinagaya (貸長屋), *n.* a row of undetached rented houses.

kashinushi (貸主), *n.* a lender; a creditor (債權者); a landlord (地主,家主).

kashira (頭), *n.* ❶ (あたま) the head. ❷ (長) a head; a chief; a leader (首領); a foreman (職工の); a master. ❸ (上座) the top. —頭を擡(もた)げる, to raise the head; come to the fore.

-kashira (かしら), I wonder. —今日彼は來るかしら, I wonder if he will come to-day.

kashiraji (頭字), *n.* ❶ (花文字) a capital (letter). ❷ (首字) an initial letter; initials (姓名の).

kashiseki (貸席), *n.* an assembly room on hire.

kashite (貸手), *n.* =*kashinushi.*

kashitsu (過失), *n.* fault. ❶【法】negligence; default. ❷ an error; a mistake. ¶ 過失殺傷, accidental homicide or wounding. —過失者, a person guilty of negligence [a fault].

kashitsuke (貸附), *n.* loaning. —金を貸附ける, to lend [put] out money at interest. ¶ 金錢貸附業, money-lending. —貸附金, a loan.

kashiuma (貸馬), *n.* a hack; a horse for hire. ¶ 貸馬屋, a job-master.

kashiwa (槲), *n.*【植】the Mongolia oak.

kashiwa (黄鷄), *n.* (羽毛の黄褐色な鷄, 主に牝), a (domestic) fowl.

kashiwade (柏手打つ), *vi.* to clap hands (before a shrine).

kashiwamochi (柏餅), *n.* a rice-cake wrapped in *kashiwa*-leaf.

kashiya (貸家), *n.* a house to let. ¶ 貸家探し, house-hunting.

kashizuku (傅く), *v.* to wait *upon* [*on*]; attend *on*; nurse (傅育).

kasho (箇所), *n.* a place (所); a passage (文章の); a part (部分). —落雷の箇所, a spot struck by lightning.

kashō (煆燒), *n.* scorification; calcination.

kashō (過稱する), *vt.* to over-praise; reward excessively.

kashoku (貨殖), *n.* money-making.

kashoku (過食する), *vi.* to over-eat; eat to excess; surfeit oneself.

kashoku (華燭の典を擧げる), to celebrate a wedding; perform a marriage ceremony.

kashu (火酒), *n.* fire-water; spirituous liquors; ardent spirits.

kashū (歌集), *n.* a collection of odes; a poetical collection.

kasō (下層), *n.* an under [a lower] layer; a substratum. —社會の最下層, the lowest stratum of society. ¶ 下層社會, the lower classes. 下層民, the common people.

kasō (火葬), *n.* cremation. —火葬する, to cremate. ¶ 火葬場, a crematorium; a crematory.

kasō (家相), *n.* aspect of a dwelling-house.

kasō (假裝), *n.* disguise; masque. —假裝する, to disguise (oneself as); masquerade. ¶ 假裝行列, a fancy procession. —假裝巡洋艦, a converted cruiser.

kasō (假想の), *a.* imaginary. ¶ 假想敵國, an imaginary enemy.

kasoku (加速-度), *n.* acceleration.

kassai (喝采), *n.* applause; cheers; plaudits. —喝采を博する, to win applause. (滿堂の喝采を博する, to carry [bring down] the house.) ¶ 大喝采, ovation.

kassarai (攫浚), *n.* a snapper-up. —攫浚ふ, to snatch; whisk; swoop up〖俗〗.

kasseki (滑席), *n.* a slider; a sliding seat.

kasseki (滑石), *n.*【鑛】talc.

kassen (合戰), *n.* a battle; a fight; an engagement.

kassha (滑車), *n.* a pulley; a block;【解】a trochlea.

kasshoku (褐色), *n.* & *a.* brown. ¶ 褐色人種, the brown race.

kassō (滑走), *n.* glide. —滑走する, to slide; glide. ¶ 滑走(飛行)機, a glider.

kas-suru (渇する), *v.* ❶ (咽喉が渇く) to be thirsty; be dry. ❷ (渇望) to thirst [hunger] *for* [*after*].

kasu (滓, 糟), *n.* ❶ grounds (特に珈琲の); dregs; lees. ❷ (魚類の締粕) cake; oil-cake; fish-cake. —人間の糟, the dregs of the population; the scum of society.

kasu (貸す), *vt.* ❶ (*a*) to lend; loan: (*b*) (賃貸) to hire; let (on hire); lease (家屋・土地など); rent (同上). ❷ (假) (許す) to allow; tolerate. —地所を貸す, to let out land on [to] lease. —家屋を貸す, to rent [lease] a house. —時間を假す, to allow time.

kasugai (鎹), *n.* an (iron) clamp; a cramp; a cramp-iron.

kasui (下垂する), *vi.*【植】to nutate: droop; hang down.

kasuka (微・幽な), *a.* ❶ (微少) scanty. ❷ (不分明) dim; faint; indistinct. ❸ (憐むべき) poor; wretched; miserable. —— **-ni**, *ad.* faintly; dimly; indistinctly. —幽かに記憶する, to have a faint recollection.

kasumeru (掠める), *vt.* ❶ (そッと知らぬ樣に盜む) to steal; filch. ❷ (掠奪) to plunder; despoil; pillage. ❸ (輕く觸れて過ぎる) to graze; shave. —村落を掠める, to plunder a village. —水面を掠める風, a wind sweeping the surface (of the water). —他人の目を掠める, to do a thing by stealth.

kasumi (霞), *n.* ❶ a haze; a mist. ❷ (翳) glaze (眼の); mist (同上); fog. —霞に包まれる, to be veiled [wrapped] in a mist; be covered with mist. —霞棚引く山々, the hills over which the mist trails. ¶ 夕霞, the evening haze.

kasumu (霞む), *vi.* ❶ to mist; be hazy. ❷ (翳) to mist (眼が); cloud; dim. —霞ます, ① to haze; mist. ② (眼を不明ならす) to blear; blur; dim; glaze. —霞み渡る, to be covered with mist.

kasureru (掠れる), *v.* ❶ (輕く觸れる) to graze; shave; scrape.

❷ (薄切れる) to thin and break. ❸ (聲の嗄れ出る) to grow hoarse.

kasuri (絣, 飛白), *n.* scattered figures; a cloth with scattered figures.

kasurikizu (擦傷), *n.* a graze; an abrasion.

kasuru (擦る), *vt.* ❶ (輕く觸れる) to graze; shave; scrape. ❷ (上前をはねる) to squeeze. —袖を擦る, to graze the sleeve.

ka-suru (化する), *v.* ❶ (變化) to change [turn] *into*; become; transform *into*. ❷ (導化) to reduce *to* (物を); be reduced *to*; influence (人を); be influenced *by*. —人の徳に化する, to be influenced by another's virtue. —小數を分數に化する, to convert a decimal into a vulgar fraction.

ka-suru (架する), *vt.* to construct; bridge (河に橋を). ☞ *kasetsu* (架設する).

ka-suru (科する), *vt.* to inflict; impose.

ka-suru (課する), *vt.* ❶ (税など) to levy; impose (税・義務など); charge. ❷ (仕事を) to assign; impose. —仕事(問題)を課する, to set a person a task (problem). —日課として英語を課する, to assign English as a daily lesson.

ka-suru (嫁する), *vt.* ❶ (嫁ぐ) to marry (a man); be married *to*. ❷ (なすりつける) to lay on; impute *to* (過失などを); charge *to*. —責任を他人に嫁する; to shuffle off responsibility upon others; shift responsibility on another's shoulders.

kasutera (カステラ), *n.* sponge-cake.

kata (方), *n.* ❶ (方向) direction. ❷ (側) a side; a party; part. ❸ (方法) a manner; a way; a method. ❹ (處置) steps; settlement (解決). ❺ (係) a person in charge; duty (役目). ❻ (人) a person. —乙方甲, A, c/o B; A, care of B. —方をつける, to settle (the matter).

kata (形, 型), *n.* ❶ (形狀) form; shape. ❷ (樣式) type; fashion; style. ❸ (方式) form; formality; formula. ❹ (模樣) a pattern; a figure. ❺ (模型) a model; a pattern. ❻ (鑄型) a mould; a matrix. ❼ (抵當) security; pledge. —型に嵌(は)める, to mould after a pattern; put into the same mould. —型に入れて鑄る, to cast in a mould. —柔道の型を示す, to show the forms [chips] in *jūdō*.

kata (肩), *n.* the shoulder. —肩を持つ, to stand by; take a person's part; side *with*. (...の肩を持って, in favour *of*.) —肩を竝べる, to hold hand *with*; compare *with*; stand abreast *of*. —肩をすくめる, to shrug one's shoulders. —肩を怒らす, to perk up the shoulders. —肩で風を切って歩く, to strut; swagger; walk with a swagger.

kata (潟), *n.* ❶ (干潟) a beach. ❷ (入江) a bay; an inlet; a lagoon (海と相通ずる湖).

kata (過多), *n.* excess; overabundance; superabundance. —過多の, excessive; overabundant.

kataage (肩揚), *n.* a tuck at the shoulder. —肩揚げをする, to tuck at the shoulders.

kataashi (片足), *n.* one foot; one leg; one shoe (clog, *etc.*). —片足で跳ぶ, to hop.

katabami (酢漿草), *n.* 【植】 the yellow-flowered wood-sorrel.

katabira (帷子), *n.* a (summer) garment of hemp.

katachi (形), *n.* ❶ (形體) form; shape; figure. ❷ 〔貌〕 (面貌) looks; countenance; the cut of one's face. ❸ 〔狀〕 (有樣) state; condition. ❹ 〔容, 姿〕 (すがた) personal appearance; style; figure. ❺ 〔像〕 (肖像) an image. —原(もと)の形を存する, to retain the original form. —聞く者は皆容を改めた, All who heard sat up straight.

katachinba (片跛), *n.* =*chinba* (跛).

katachizukuru (形作る), *v.* ❶ (形成) to form; give shape *to*; cast. ❷ 〔容〕 (姿を飾る) to adorn [bedeck] oneself. —團體を形作る, to form a corporate body.

katadoru (象る), *vt.* to model; imitate; fashion. —...に象って作る, to fashion according *to* [*after*].

katagaki (肩書), *n.* a title; a handle to one's name. —博士の肩書がある醫者, a physician with a doctorate. —肩書で人を驚かす, to amaze others with one's titles.

katagarasu (片硝子の), *a.* open-faced (時計の). —片硝子の時計, a half-hunter.

katagata (旁), at the same time; while; both...and. —見物旁々, partly for sight-seeing.

katageru (擔げる), *vt.* to shoulder; carry [lay] on the shoulder. —荷を擔げる, to carry a burden on the shoulder.

katagi (氣質), *n.* character; spirit; manners. ¶ 雇人氣質, the employee spirit. —當世女學生氣質, manners of the present-day girl-students.

katagi (堅氣), *n.* ❶ (律氣) honesty. ❷ (正業) a respectable calling; a legal [legitimate] occupation. **——-no,** *a.* honest; steady (and honest); of good morals. —堅氣の奉公, service in a respectable house. —堅氣の商賣, a respectable calling. —堅氣の商人, an honest merchant.

katagi (堅木), *n.* ❶ hard wood. ❷【植】(血槠) the Japanese silkworm-oak.

kataguruma (肩車), *n.* riding (pick-a-back) on another's shoulders. —肩車に乘る, to ride (pick-a-back) on another's shoulders. —子供を肩車に乘せる, to carry a child pick-a-back on one's shoulders.

katahada (片肌脫ぐ), ❶ to bare one shoulder. ❷ (助力する) to render assistance; set [put] one's shoulder to the wheel.

katahaji (片端), *n.* =*katahashi.*

katahara (片腹痛い), *a.* ridiculous; laughable; side-splitting. —片腹痛く思ふ, to feel like laughing; think it ridiculous.

katahashi (片端), *n.* an edge; an end; a side. —片端に避ける, to step aside. —片端から仕事を片附ける, to dispose of one's tasks in rapid succession.

katahima (片暇), *n.* odd moments; leisure. —片暇の內職, private leisure-hour work.

katahiza (片膝), *n.* one knee. —片膝を崩す, to relax a knee. —片膝立てて詰め寄る, to press close with one knee on the ground.

kataho (片帆), *n.* a reefed sail. —片帆を揚げる, to reef a sail.

katahō, katappō, (片方), *n.* one party; one side. —靴が片方見えない, I have lost the fellow of my shoe.

katahō (片頰), *n.* one cheek. —片頰に笑む, to smile on one side of the face.

katahotori (片邊), *n.* a corner.

katai (堅·固い), *a.* ❶ hard; solid. ❷ (硬) hard; tough. ❸ (剛) stiff; rigid. ❹ (堅固,鞏固,確實) firm; solid; sound. ❺ (正直) honest; upright; steady (實著な). —堅い頭, a hard head. —堅い人, an honest [steady] man; a man of good morals (品行方正な人). —固い意志, a strong [an iron] will. —固い結目, a tight knot. —固い約束をする, to make a firm promise.

katai (過怠), *n.* negligence. ¶ 過怠金, penalty for neglect.

katai (難い), *a.* ❶ (困難) difficult; hard. ❷ (不可能) impossible. —近寄り難い, to be difficult of access.

kataiji (片意地), *n.* obstinacy; stubbornness. —片意地な, obstinate; stubborn. —片意地を張る, to be stiff-necked; be obstinate.

katainaka (片田舍), *n.* a remote village [country-place]; an out-of-the-way corner.

katajikenai (忝い), *a.* grateful; thankful; obliged. —忝く, gratefully; thankfully; with thanks; with gratitude.

katajikenōsuru (辱うする), *vt.* Ⓢ 辱くする. to be favoured *with.* —愛顧を辱うする, to enjoy [be favoured with] the patronage *of.* —天覽を忝うする, to be honoured with Imperial inspection.

katakage (片蔭), *n.* a shade. —片蔭に潛む, to steal into [conceal oneself in] a shade.

katakake (肩掛, 肩巾), *n.* a shawl; a cape; wraps.

katakata (片方), *n.* ❶ (一方) one side; one party. ❷ (相手) one of a pair; the other.

katakawa (片側), *n.* one side. —片側の時計, a single-cover watch; a half-hunter. —片側車馬通行止, (揭示) No thoroughfare for horses and vehicles on this side (of the road).

kataki (敵), *n.* ❶ (讐敵) an enemy; a foe. ❷ (敵手) an adversary; an opponent; a rival (in love or trade). ❸ (復讐) revenge. —敵としてつけ覘ふ, to shadow another as one's enemy. ¶ 敵同士, mutual enemies. (敵同士の會社, rival companies.)

katakiuchi (敵討), *n.* revenge.

katakiyaku (敵役), *n.* 【劇】the villain's part. —敵役を勤める, to play the villain.

katakoto (片言), *n.* ❶ (片口) one side; one-sided statement. ❷ (不完全の言) babble; lisp; imperfect language. —片言を言ふ, to babble; prattle; lisp. —片言交りに物を言ふ, to babble out something.

kataku (固く), *ad.* ❶ (緊密) tightly; fast; firmly. ❷ (嚴重に) strictly; rigidly. ❸ (鞏固に) firmly; strongly; solidly. ❹ (一徹に) stubbornly; obstinately. ❺ (きッぱりと) positively; flatly; resolutely; decisively. ❻ (著實に) honestly; steadily. —固く約束をする, to promise firmly [positively]. —堅く斷る, to refuse positively. —堅く禁ずる, to prohibit strictly. —固く握る, to squeeze it tight.

kataku (花托), *n.* 【植】the receptacle; the torus; the thalamus.

kataku (家宅), *n.* a house; premises; a homestead. ¶ 家宅侵入, trespass on another's premises;

forcible entry. (家宅侵入者, a trespasser.) —家宅捜索, a domiciliary visit [search].

kataku (假託), *n.* pretext; pretence. —假託する, to make a pretence [pretext] *of*.

katakuchi (片口), *n.* ❶ a lipped bowl. ❷ (片言) an *ex-parte* statement.

katakuna (頑な), *a.* stubborn; obstinate; pig-headed.

katakuri (片栗), *n.* ❶【植】the dog's tooth [dog-tooth] violet. ❷ (片栗粉) the starch of the dog-tooth violet.

katakurushii (固苦しい), *a.* ❶ (儀式張った) formal; punctilious; stiff. ❷ (打解けぬ) strait-laced; stiff (-mannered); starchy. —固苦しい挨拶をする, to greet punctiliously. —固苦しくする, to stand on [upon] ceremony.

katamari (塊), *n.* ❶ a lump; a clot (血などの); a clod (土の). ❷ (聚團) a cluster; a bunch; a group. —虚言(うそ)の塊, a web of lies; a mass of falsehood. —不良少年の團, a group [gang] of depraved boys.

katamaru (固・凝る), *vi.* ❶ (硬化) to harden; solidify; consolidate; stiffen; set. ❷ (凝結) to congeal; coagulate; freeze; curdle; bind (雪など). ❸ (集合) to assemble; gather; crowd. ❹ (塊となる) to mass; lump; agglomerate. ❺ (凝る) to be engrossed [absorbed; lost] *in*; be given up *to*. —天氣が固まる, The weather sets fair. —信仰に固まる, to be engrossed in religious practices; be devoted to religion.

katame (固め), *n.* ❶ (堅くする事) hardening; fortifying; strengthening. ❷ (警備, 防備) defence; guard. ❸ (約束) a promise; an engagement; a plight; a pledge.

katame (片目, 隻眼), *n.* one eye: (人) a one-eyed man.

katamen (片面), *n.* one side [face].

katameru (固める), *v.* ❶ (堅くする) to harden; solidify; consolidate. ❷ (固結) to tighten; compact. ❸ (凝結) to congeal; freeze; coagulate. ❹ (警備) to defend; guard; fortify. ❺ (强固) to confirm; strengthen; solidify. ❻ (集中) to collect; mass; concentrate. ❼ (身を) (*a*) (用意) to make ready *for*: (*b*) (婚嫁) to marry: (*c*) (鎧裝) to arm oneself *with*; equip oneself *with*: (*d*) (落ちつく) to settle down; settle oneself. —拳固を固める, to clench the fist. —基礎を固める, to consolidate the basis [foundation; groundwork.] —身を固める, to settle oneself; be settled. —土を固める, to harden the ground.

katami (片身), *n.* one side.

katami (形見), *n.* a keepsake; a memento; a relic. —親の形見にする, to keep it as a memento of a parent. —形見分けに貰ふ, to receive as a memento.

katami (肩身), *n.* one's condition. —肩身が狭い, It makes one feel small [cheap].

katamichi (片道), *n.* one way. ¶片道切符, a single ticket.

katamukeru (傾ける), *vt.* ❶ (傾斜) to lean; slant; slope; tilt. ❷ (傾注) to devote oneself *to*; concentrate (one's powers; energies; attention) *on*. ❸ (亡ぼす) to destroy; ruin (國・家・産等を); bring to ruin. ❹ (杯を) to drink; drain.

katamuki (傾), *n.* ❶ (傾斜) lean; slant; slope; tilt. ❷ (傾向) tendency; trend. ❸ (性向) disposition; propensity; predilection. —...する傾きがある, (人) to be apt *to*; be prone *to*: (物) there is a tendency *to*.

katamuku (傾く), *vi.* ❶ (傾斜) to lean; slant; slope. ❷ (傾向) to trend; tend; be disposed. ❸ (衰微) to decline; fall; be reduced. ❹ (日・月が) to decline *toward*; slant *toward*.

katan (荷擔), *n.* ❶ (味方すること) assistance; support. ❷ (加はること) participation; combination; conspiracy (共謀). **——-suru,** *v.* ❶ to assist; support; side *with*. ❷ to participate *in*; take part *in*; join *in*. —惡人に荷擔する, to side with a villain.

katana (刀), *n.* a sword. —刀を拔く, to draw [unsheathe] a sword. —刀を納める, to sheathe a sword. ¶刀鍛冶, a swordsmith. —刀傷(きず), a sword-cut.

katanashi (形無), *n.* naught. —形無しになる, to come to naught; fail. —形無しにする, to bring to naught; spoil.

katanito (カタン絲), *n.* machine cotton.

kataomoi (片思), *n.* unreturned [unrequited; one-sided] love. —片思をする, to love without return.

kataoya (片親), *n.* a parent. —片親を失(な)す, to lose a parent.

katarau (語らふ), *v.* ❶ (談合) to talk together; consult together. ❷ (約束) to promise; engage. ❸ (誘(さ)き入れる) to gain over; win over. —不良の輩を語らひ集める, to gather a number of evil-disposed men.

katari (騙), *n.* ❶ (騙取) fraud;

swindling; imposition. ❸ (騙兒) a swindler; an impostor.

kataroku (型錄), *n.* a catalogue.

kataru (語る), *vt.* ❶ (話す) to speak *with* [*to*]; tell (告げる); relate (物語る). ❷ (節つけて歌ふ) to recite; chant.

kataru (騙る), *vt.* to defraud; cheat; swindle.

kataru (加答兒), *n.* catarrh.

katashiro (形代), *n.* ❶ an image; an icon. ❷ a substitute. ❸ (形跡) vestiges; traces. —形代もなくなる, to leave not a trace behind.

katasumi (片隅), *n.* a corner; an angle. —片隅に寄る(寄せる), to draw to (put in) a corner.

katate (片手), *n.* ❶ (隻手) one hand; a single hand. ❷ (片手桶) a piggin. —片手の, one-handed.

katatema (片手間に), *ad.* in spare time [hours]; at leisure [odd] hours. —片手間に翻譯する, to do translation at odd hours.

katateochi (片手落), *n.* partiality; one-sidedness. —片手落ちの裁判, a one-sided judgment.

katatoki (片時), *n.* a moment; an instant.

katatsumuri (蝸牛), *n.* the snail.

katatsunbo (片聾), *n.* deafness in one ear.

kataude (片腕), *n.* ❶ one arm. ❷ (助手) a right-hand man; a right arm; a helper.

katawa (片端, 片輪), *n.* ❶ (畸形) deformity. ❷ (不具者) a deformed [an invalided] person; a maimed person; a cripple. ❸ (不揃物) an incomplete [odd] set. —片端の, ① (畸形の) deformed; maimed; crippled. ② (不揃の) odd; incomplete. —片端にする, to maim; disable; cripple.

katawaki (片脇), *n.* ❶ (腋) one arm. ❷ (一方) one side. —片脇に抱へる, to hold under one arm.

katawara (傍), *n.* the side (わき, そば). ☞ ***katahara.*** **——**, *ad.* =***katagata*** (旁). **——-ni,** *ad.* ❶ (側に) by; by the side of; beside. ❷ (他に) besides (別に); aside (脇へ). —傍に除ける, to set aside. —傍に人無きが如く, outrageously.

katayoru (片寄る), *vi.* ❶ (片方に寄る) to step [move] aside. ❷ (偏在する) to be nearer *to*. ❸ (傾く) to lean *to*; incline towards; trend *to*. ❹ (偏向する) to be biassed; be partial; be prejudiced.

katazu (固唾を呑んで), *ad.* with bated breath; with breathless interest (anxiety). —固唾を呑んで見物する, to look on with bated breath.

katazukeru (片附ける), *vt.* ❶ (整頓する) to put in order; set [put] to rights; tidy up. ❷ (仕舞ひ込む) to put away; lay aside. ❸ (始末する) to settle; dispose of; work off. ❹ (了る) to finish; make an end *of*; bring to a conclusion [an end]. —娘を片附ける, to marry off one's daughter. —借金を片附ける, to pay [clear; work] off one's debts. —食卓を片附ける, to clear the table.

katazuku (片附く), *vi.* ❶ (整然となる) to be put in order. ❷ (落著) to be settled; come to a conclusion; be disposed *of*. ❸ (終了) to be finished; end; come to an end. ❹ (嫁す) to marry; get married.

katazumi (堅炭), *n.* hard charcoal.

katazumu (偏ずむ), *vi.* =***katayoru*** (片寄る).

katchikatchi (かつちかつち), *n.* tick; tick-tack. —カッチカッチいふ, to tick (特に時計に云ふ).

katchū (甲冑), *n.* a helmet and armour; an armour; panoply.

kate (糧), *n.* bread; food; provisions. —心(頭)の糧, mental (intellectual) food.

katei (課程), *n.* a course, a curriculum; a routine. —學校の課程, a school course. —日々の課程, a daily routine.

katei (過程), *n.* process.

katei (家庭), *n.* a home; a family; a household. —家庭の樂み, domestic [fireside] pleasure; home comfort. —嚴格な家庭に育つ, to be brought up in a strict family. ¶ 家庭醫學, domestic medicine. —家庭工業, household industry. —家庭教師, a tutor [*fem.* -ess]; a (resident) governess (女); a daily governess (女で通ひの). —家庭生活, home life; domestic life.

katei (假定), *n.* supposition; assumption; fiction (擬制). —假定する, to suppose; assume; take for granted. ¶ 假定文, 【文】a conditional sentence. —假定法, 【文】the subjunctive mood.

kato (過渡), *n.* transition. ¶ 過渡期, a transition period [stage].

katō (下等な), *a.* ❶ (劣等) inferior; low; coarse. ❷ (下品) mean; low; vulgar; coarse. —下等な品, an inferior article. —下等な人物, a man of low character. ¶ 下等社會, the lower classes; the proletariat.

katō (過當の), *a.* excessive; exorbitant; extravagant. —過當の要求を爲す, to make an exorbitant demand.

katoku (家督), *n.* ❶ (跡目) the headship of a family. ❷ =家督相續人. —父の家督を相續する, to succeed to one's father's house. ¶ 家督相續,【法】succession to a house; succession to the headship of a house. —家督相續人, an heir; an heir [a successor] to a house. (法定家督相續人, an heir at law; a legal heir; an heir apparent. —推定家督相續人, an heir presumptive.)

ka-tosuru (可とする), *vt.* to approve; assent *to*; be in favour *of*.

katsu (且), *ad.* also; moreover; again; besides; furthermore; at the same time. **——,** *conj.* and; also; as well; both...and; at the same time...and; at once...and.

katsu (活), *n.* resuscitation. —活を入れる, [*vt.*] to resuscitate; revive; reanimate.

katsu (渇), *n.* thirst. —渇を醫する, to slake [quench] one's thirst. —渇を覺える, to feel thirsty.

katsu (勝つ), *v.* ❶ (勝利) to conquer; win; gain a victory *over*. ❷ (優る) to outdo; surmount; exceed. ❸ (克) (抑止) to command; control; overcome (困難などに). —樂々と勝つ, to walk over (the course); have a walk-over [俗]; ride over (競馬で); win at a canter; gain an easy victory. —困難に克つ, to conquer [overcome; surmount] difficulties. —戰に勝つ, to have [win] the battle; gain [win] a victory; carry [win] the day.

katsuai (割愛する), *vt.* to part reluctantly *with*; spare.

katsuben (活辯), *n.* Ⓢ 活動辯士. a cinema-speaker; a film-interpreter; a movie talker.

katsubō (渇望する), *v.* to thirst *for* [*after*]; long *for* [*after*]; pant *for* [*after*].

katsubushi (鰹節), *n.* =*katsuobushi.*

katsubutai (活舞臺), *n.* a living stage; the stage of (one's) activity. —外交の活舞臺に躍出する, to make his appearance on the diplomatic stage.

katsubutsu (活物), *n.* a thing of life; a living being; life (集合).

katsudatsu (豁達な), *a.* ❶ (大度) magnanimous; large-minded. ❷ (開豁) broad; open.

katsudō (活動), *n.* ❶ activity; operation; animation. ❷ =*katsudō-shashin* (活動寫眞). —活動的生活をする, to lead an active [a stirring] life. **——-suru,** *v.* to move actively; be active; take an active part *in*. —今日の社會に活動する, to take an active part in the present-day world. ¶ 活動俳優, a photoplay-actor [-performer]; a photo-player; a film-actor [*fem.* -actress]; a movie-actor [*fem.* -actress]. —活動範圍, the sphere of one's activity [action]. —活動家, a man of action; an active man.

katsudō-shashin (活動寫眞), *n.* ❶ a motion-picture; a moving picture; a movie [米・俗]. ❷ a kinematographic entertainment; the pictures [俗]; the movies [米・俗]. ¶ 活動寫眞映寫機, a kinematograph, cinematograph; a vitascope; a kinetoscope; a moving-picture machine. —活動寫眞劇, a cinema [film; picture]-drama; a photoplay; a motion-picture play. —活動寫眞界, the cinema [film; screen] world. —活動寫眞館, a cinema; a picture-hall [-house; -palace; -theatre]; a picturedrome; a movie(-hall). —活動寫眞檢閲部, the board of film censors. —活動寫眞狂, a movie fan; a film fan; a kinema fan. —活動寫眞撮影技師, a kinetographer. —活動寫眞撮影術, kinetography. —活動寫眞撮影機, a kinetograph. —活動寫眞製作會社, a (film-)producing company.

katsueru (餓ゑる), *vi.* ❶ (うゑる) to be hungry; be starved; starve. ❷ =*katsubō* (渇望する). —名譽に餓ゑる, to hanker after honour [fame]. —功名に餓ゑる, to thirst for fame.

katsugan (活眼), *n.* perspicacity; piercing [penetrating] eyes; quick discernment. —活眼を開いて世界の大勢を見る, to see the world situation with penetrating eyes.

katsukatsu (且且), *ad.* ❶ (先づ先づ) so much. ❷ (辛うじて) narrowly; barely.

katsugeki (活劇), *n.* a scene. —活劇を演ずる, to make a scene.

katsugu (擔ぐ), *vt.* ❶ (荷ふ) to carry; shoulder; carry [bear] on the shoulder. ❷ (欺く) to hoax; quiz; make game *of*. ❸ (迷信) to be superstitious. —候補者に擔ぎ上げる, to bring a person forward as a candidate. —最寄りの病院にかつぎ込む, to take to the nearest hospital.

katsuiro (勝色), *n.* a grey colour.

katsuji (活字), *n.* 【印】a movable type; a (printing) type. ☞ *kappan.* —活字を拾ふ, to pick up types. ¶ 活字鑄造者, a type-founder. —活字鑄造所, a type-foundry. —活字金, type-metal.

katsujinga (活人畫), *n.* a living picture; a *tableau* (*vivant*) [佛].

katsujō (割讓), *n.* cession; alienation. —割讓する, to alienate; cede.

katsumoku (刮目する), *vi.* to watch eagerly; watch with keen interest. —刮目して, on the *qui vive*; with dilated eyes.

katsuo (鰹), *n.* 【魚】 the bonito.

katsuobushi (鰹節), *n.* a dried bonito.

katsura (桂), *n.* 【植】 Cercidiphyllum japonicum (學名).

katsura (鬘), *n.* a wig; a periwig. ☞ *kazura.*

katsuretsu (カツレツ), *n.* a cutlet.

katsuro (活路), *n.* a means of escape; the way out of a difficulty. —活路を開く, to cut one's way through. —活路を得る, to find the way of escape.

katsute (嘗て), *ad.* ❶ (前に) formerly; before; already. ❷ (曾)(一度) once; on one occasion; at one time.

katsuyaku (活躍する), *vi.* to rouse oneself to action; take an active part *in*. —經濟界に活躍する, to be active in the economic world.

katsuyakukin (括約筋), *n.* 【解】 a sphincter.

katsuyō (活用), *n.* ❶ (應用) practical use; application; utilization (利用). ❷ 【文】 conjugation (動詞の); declension (格の). —活用する, ① to put to practical use; apply; utilize. ② to inflect; conjugate; decline.

kattai (癩), *n.* (病) leprosy: (人) a leper.

kattan (褐炭), *n.* 【鑛】 lignite; brown coal.

kattarui (かったるい), *a.* tired; weary; languid.

katte (勝手), *n.* ❶ (*a*) (我儘) self-will; waywardness; arbitrariness: (*b*) (自由) voluntariness (任意); liberty. ❷ (臺所) a kitchen. ❸ (便利) convenience. ❹ (事情, 樣子) circumstances; condition. —勝手な, ① (我儘) selfish; self-willed; wilful. ② (自由) voluntary (自發的); free. —勝手に, ① selfishly; as one pleases. ② voluntarily (自發的に); of one's own accord (同上); without leave (無斷に); at will; at choice. —勝手次第である, to be at liberty to do as one pleases [likes]. —勝手を知ってる, to know the ropes [俗]. —どうしようと俺の勝手だ, I'll do as I please. —勝手にし給へ, Please yourself; Do as you please. ¶ 勝手道具, kitchen-ware; kitchen things; kitchen utensils. —勝手口, the kitchen-door; the servants' entrance; the back-entrance. —勝手向, circumstances; means.

katto (赫と), *ad.* with a burst. —赫と怒る, to flare up; flash up [out]; burst into a passion. —赫と逆上する, to become suddenly dizzy; be seized with dizziness.

kattō (葛藤), *n.* complication; dissension; dispute. —葛藤を起す, to give rise to complications; breed discord.

kau (支ふ), *vt.* to set (a prop) obliquely *against*. —倒れぬやうに支材(㊫)をかふ, to prop it up to prevent its falling.

kau (買ふ), *vt.* ❶ (購求) to buy; purchase; get. ❷ (招致) to incur; bring upon oneself; provoke (起さす). ❸ (喧嘩に應ずる) to accept; take up. ❹ (藝妓を) to hire. ❺ (人の長所を認める) to appreciate; approve; acknowledge. —買ひ過ぎる, to overbuy; buy too much. —人の歡心を買ふ, to win [gain] another's favour. —人の怒りを買ふ, to bring anger upon oneself. —其の點は買ってやる, I give you credit on that point.

kau (飼ふ), *vt.* ❶ to breed; raise; rear. ❷ to keep. —蠶を飼ふ, to rear silkworms. —猫を飼ふ, to keep a cat.

kawa (川, 河), *n.* a river; a stream. —野を流れる川, a brook running through the fields. —川の上(下)流, the upper (lower) stream of a river. —川傳ひに行く, to go along a river.

kawa (皮, 革), *n.* ❶ skin; fur (毛皮); hide (重に牛馬の生皮又は鞣し皮); leather (鞣革). ❷ bark (樹皮); rind (果物の); peel (橙・レモン等の). —饅頭の皮, the covering of a jam-dumpling. —猫の皮, a cat-skin. —西瓜の皮, the rind of the water-melon. —馬の皮, a horse-hide. —木の皮を剝く, to peel off a bark. ¶ 革細工, leather work.

kawa (側), *n.* ❶ (物の一方面) a side; a row (列). ❷ (外包) a case. —東側の家, a house on the east side.

kawabata (河端), *n.* Ⓢ 河邊. ❶ (河畔) riverside. ❷ (岸) a river-bank.

kawabiraki (川開), *n.* the opening of the river season.

kawabukuro (革嚢), *n.* a leather bag; a skin (酒又は水を入れる).

kawadoko (河床), *n.* a bed; a river-bed; a channel.

kawaebi (川海老), *n.* 【甲殼】 the crayfish; the crawfish.

kawafune (川舟, 河船), *n.* a river-boat; a sampan; a barge.

kawagishi (河岸), *n.* a bank; a river-bank; a riverside.

kawagoromo (裘), *n.* furs; a fur-robe; fur-clothes.

kawagoshi (川越), *n.* fording; wading. —川越しをする, to ford [wade] a river.

kawaguchi (河口), *n.* a river-mouth; the mouth of a river.

kawahagi (鱗魚), *n.* 【魚】 the leather-fish.

kawahimo (革紐), *n.* a leather [a thong; a leash.]

kawahone, kōhone, (河骨), *n.* 【植】 Nuphar japonicum (yellow water-lily の一種・學名).

kawaigaru (可愛がる), *vt.* to love; caress; fondle; pet.

kawaii (可愛い), *a.* ❶ dear; darling; pet. ❷ =*kawairashii.* ——, *v.* to be dear *to*; be fond *of*.

kawairashii (可愛らしい), *a.* lovely; pretty; sweet. —可愛らしい少女, a sweet [pretty] girl. —可愛らしい人形, a lovely doll.

kawairo (革色), *n.* bluish green.

kawaisō (可哀想な), *a.* ❶ (憐むべき) poor; piteous; wretched. ❷ (無慈悲な) cruel; merciless; pitiless. —可哀想な老人, a poor old thing. —可哀想な目に逢はせる, to treat cruelly. —可哀想に思ふ, to take [have] pity *on*; feel pity *for*.

kawaita (乾いた), *a.* ❶ dry; parched. ❷ (渴) thirsty.

kawajōki (川蒸氣), *n.* a river-steamer.

kawakami (川上), *n.* the upper part of a river. —川上に上る, to go up the river.

kawakasu (乾かす), *vt.* ❶ to dry; drain off [away] (池の水などを); parch (土地などを). ❷ (渴) to make thirsty.

kawaki (乾き), *n.* ❶ drying. ❷ (渴) thirst. ❸ (旱魃) drought.

kawaku (乾く), *vi.* ❶ to dry (up); drain off [away]; parch. ❷ (渴) to be thirsty; feel thirsty; be dry. —口が渴く, to have a dry throat; feel thirsty. —喉が渴いて堪らない, I am dying of thirst.

kawamukai, kawamukō, (川向), *n.* the opposite side of a river. —川向ひの火事, a fire across the river.

kawamuki (皮剝), *n.* ❶ (皮をむくこと) paring; skinning. ❷ (器具) a parer; a fruit-knife; a paring-knife.

kawaobi (革帶), *n.* a leather-belt.

kawaoso (川獺), *n.* the otter.

kawara (瓦), *n.* a tile (粘土製の); a terra-cotta (陶瓦). —瓦葺の, tiled; tile-roofed. ¶ 瓦屋, ① a tiler (製造人); a tile-dealer (商人). ② (瓦葺家) a tile-roofed house.

kawara (河原), *n.* a dry river-bed; a river-beach.

kawarake (土器), *n.* ❶ unglazed earthen ware. ❷ an earthen cup.

kawari (代), *n.* ❶ (交替) alternation. ❷ (代理) procuration; agency. ❸ (代理人) a deputy; a proxy; an agent. ❹ (代用物) a substitute (人, 物); a shift (物の). ❺ (代償) compensation; return (報酬); remuneration (同上); rewards (同上); amends (損害の). ❻ (食物の) a second help [helping]. —代りとして, by way *of*; as a substitute *for*. —一飯のお代りをする, to ask for [have] a second helping. ——**-ni,** *ad.* ❶ in place *of*; on [in] behalf *of* (代表). ❷ instead of (せぬ代りに). ❸ (代償として) in return; in consideration *of*; to make up *for*. ❹ (その代りには) (but) on the other hand; but (at the same time). —代りになる[をする], to do duty *for*; serve the purpose *of*; serve *for*.

kawari (變), *n.* ❶ (變化) change; variation. ❷ (變更) alternation; change. ❸ (異變) an accident. ❹ (差異) difference. —皆樣お變りはありませんか, Are they all well?; How are your people?

kawariau (代合ふ), *v.* to alternate *with*; take turns.

kawariban (代番に), *ad.* Ⓢ 代り代り. by turns; turn and turn about; alternately. —代番に見張する, to watch by turns.

kawarime (替目, 變目), *n.* turn; turning (-point); change. —月の替り目, the end of the month.

kawarimono (變者), *n.* an eccentric; a character; a crank.

kawariyasui (變り易い), *a.* changeable; fickle (心, 天候); inconstant (心). —變り易い風, a variable wind. —變り易い天氣, broken [unsettled] weather.

kawaru (代る), *v.* to replace; take the place *of*; change. —…に代る, to take the place (*of*). —…に代って, in [on] behalf *of*; for; in (the) place *of*.

kawaru (變る), *vi.* ❶ (變化) (*a*) to change; alter; vary (種々に): (*b*) (變って…と成る) to change *into*; turn *into*; become. ❷ (推移) to pass over. ❸ (移轉) to remove. ❹ (相違) to be different; differ (意見・性質等). —渝らざる信義, abiding [unchangeable; constant] faith. —變れば變る世の中だね, What a changeable world it is!

kawaryō (川漁), *n.* river-fishing.

kawase (川瀨), *n.* a shallow part of a river; a river-shallow.

kawase (爲替), *n.* exchange; an

(a money-)order. —爲替を組む, to draw a money order; draw a bill. ¶ 爲替振出人, a drawer. —爲替相場, the rate [course] of exchange. —爲替手形, a bill; a draft; a bill of exchange. —爲替取扱局, a money-order office. —爲替受取人, a payee.

kawasemi (魚狗, 翡翠), *n.* 【鳥】 the eastern [Indo-Malay] kingfisher.

kawashimo (河下), *n.* the lower part of a river. —河下へ[に], down a river.

kawasu (交す), *vt.* ❶ (交へる) to exchange. ❷ (躱す) to avoid; dodge; parry. —言葉を交はす, to exchange words *with.* —體を躱して避ける, to evade by dodging.

kawato (革砥), *n.* a strop. —革砥で研ぐ, to strop (剃刀などを).

kawauso (川獺), *n.* the otter.

kawaya (厠), *n.* a latrine; a water-closet; a privy.

kawaya (皮屋), *n.* a fell-monger; a skinner; a furrier.

kawayanagi (川柳), *n.* 【植】 the bitter [purple] willow.

kawayugaru (可愛がる), *vt.* to love. ☞ ***kawaigaru.***

kawayui (可愛い), *a.* =***kawaii.***

kawazu (蛙), *n.* 【兩棲】 the frog.

kaya (芒, 萱), *n.* 【植】 Miscanthus sinensis (學名).

kaya (榧), *n.* 【植】 Torrega nucifera (stinking-yew の一種・學名)

kaya (蚊張), *n.* a mosquito-curtain [-net]. —蚊張の吊手, a mosquito-net hanger. —蚊張を吊る(外す), to hang (take down) a mosquito-net.

kayabuki (茅葺), *n.* miscanthus-roofing.

kayaku (火藥), *n.* powder; gunpowder. —火藥を裝塡する, to prime gunpowder. ¶ 火藥庫, a (powder-) magazine.

kayaribi (蚊遣火), *n.* a smudge; a mosquito fire.

kayatsurigusa (蚊屋釣草), *n.* 【植】 Cyperus japonicus (galingale の一種・學名).

kayō (斯樣な), *a.* such; of this kind; of the kind [sort]. —斯樣に, thus; in this way; so.

kayōbi (火曜日), *n.* Tuesday.

kayoi (通), *n.* ❶ (通ふこと) going back and forth; plying (船などに云ふ); running (同上); frequenting (足繁く); circulation (循環). ❷ (通勤) attending [going to] office from home; living out. ❸ (通帳) a pass-book; a chit-book. —横濱通ひの汽船, a steamer plying between here and Yokohama; a Yokohama liner. —通ひで品物を買ふ, to buy things on account. ¶ 學校通ひ, daily attendance at school. —通ひ番頭, a clerk who lives out of the house; a daily clerk. —通船, a sampan.

kayoke (蚊除), *n.* a mosquito-fumigator; a smudge.

kayoku (寡慾の), *a.* uncovetous; indifferent to money; unselfish.

kayou (通ふ), *v.* ❶ (往來) to go back and forth; ply [run] between (交通機關に云ふ). ❷ (通勤) to attend; go *to.* ❸ (足繁く行く) to frequent; haunt. ❹ (通じる) to communicate *with.* ❺ (出入) to go in and out (空氣などが孔から). ❻ (循環) to circulate. —通ひ馴れた途, a familiar road. —學校へ通ふ, to go to school. —遠くて通ひ切れない, It is too far to attend regularly.

kayowai (かよわい), *a.* feeble; weak; fragile; delicate. ☞ ***yowai*** (弱い).

kayu (粥), *n.* (rice-)gruel; mash.

kayui (痒・癢い), *a.* itchy. ——, *vi.* to itch; feel itchy. —痒い所に手が屆く, to leave nothing to be desired.

kazagoe (風聲), *n.* a voice hoarse from a cold.

kazaguruma (風車), *n.* ❶ a windmill. ❷ 【植】 (鐵線蓮) the large-flowered clematis.

kazagusuri (風藥), *n.* a medicine [cure] for cold. —風藥を飲む, to take medicine for cold.

kazahioi (風日覆), *n.* a jalousie.

kazai (家財), *n.* ❶ (家の道具) household furniture. ❷ (家の財產) household [family] effects [goods; property]; goods and chattels. —家財を取纏めて引越す, to remove with all one's chattels.

kazakami (風上), *n.* the windward; the weather-side. —風上に向く, to look to windward. —風上に向いて, in the wind's eye. —彼奴は風上に置けぬ人間だ, The fellow is not fit for our company.

kazami (風見), *n.* a (weather-) cock; a (weather-) vane.

kazamuki (風向), *n.* the direction of the wind. —風向を見る, to observe the direction of the wind.

kazan (火山), *n.* a volcano. ¶ 活(休; 死)火山, an active (a dormant; a dead) volcano. —火山灰, volcanic ashes. —火山岩, volcanic rocks. —火山地震, volcanic earthquake. —火山脈, a volcanic chain. —火山島, a volcanic island.

kazaochi (風落), *n.* windfall. —栗の風落ちを拾ふ, to pick up the chestnuts blown down by the wind.

kazari (飾), *n.* ❶ (裝飾) (*a*) decoration; adornment: (*b*) a decoration; an ornament; finery (身體·衣服等の). —店頭の飾, shop decoration; shop-dressing. —飾のない, plain; artless; homely. —飾をつける, to furnish with ornaments; adorn; decorate.

kazarike (飾氣のない), *a.* plain; simple; artless.

kazarimono (飾物), *n.* ❶ (飾るもの) ornamental articles; ornaments. ❷ (裝飾的人物) a dummy; a figure-head.

kazaritateru (飾立てる), *vt.* to trick out; decorate; adorn. ☞ *kazaru.* —店の窓を飾り立てる, to dress a (shop-)window.

kazaritsuke (飾附), *n.* arrangement; decoration; adornment. ☞ *sōshoku.*

kazariya (錺屋), *n.* a goldsmith; a silversmith (銀細工屋).

kazaru (飾る), *v.* ❶ (裝飾) to ornament; decorate; adorn. ❷ (立派にする) to enrich; trim (著物等を); beautify.

kazashimo (風下), *n.* the lee; the leeward; the lee side. —風下の海岸, a lee shore. —風下に在る, to lie leeward; lie on the leeward *of.* —風下に流れる,【航】to sag.

kazasu (簪す), *vt.* to stick in the hair; adorn the hair. —花を簪す, to stick a flower in the hair.

kazasu (翳す), *vt.* to hold up; shade. —扇を翳す, to screen the face [shade one's eyes] with a fan. —額に手を翳す, to shade the eyes with the hand on the forehead. —火鉢に手を翳す, to hold the hand over the brazier. —刀を振り翳す, to hold up a sword.

kazatori (風取), *n.* a ventilator (通風器); a wind-sail (風取帆).

kazatōshi (風通し), *n.* ventilation; airing; a ventilator (通風器). —風通しの惡い, airless; close; stuffy; ill [badly] ventilated. —風通しのよい室, an airy room.

kazayoke (風除), *n.* a wind-screen; a wind-shield.

kaze (風), *n.* ❶ a wind; a breeze (輕風). ❷ (風邪) a cold. —强い(弱い)風, a strong (gentle) wind. —暖い(寒い; 冷かな; 涼しい)風, a warm (chilly; cold; cool) wind. —風の神, the god of wind; Æolus【羅】. —風の便り, a rumour. —風の强い夜, a windy night. —風が起る (吹く; 靜まる; 變る), The wind rises (blows; lulls; changes). —風に向[逆]って, in the wind's eye; in the teeth [eye] of the wind. —風を引いて居る, to have (a) cold. ¶ 風模樣, ① indications [signs] of wind. ② = *kazamuki.*

kazedatsu (風起つ), *vi.* to be windy [blowy].

kazei (苛税), *n.* a heavy tax.

kazei (課税), *n.* imposition; taxation. —課税する, to tax; levy [impose; assess] a tax *on*; levy duties *on.* ¶ 課税品, a taxed article; a taxable [dutiable] article.

kazakiri (風切-羽), *n.* (鳥の) the remex [*pl.* remiges].

kazen (果然), *ad.* as was expected.

kazenuki (風拔), *n.* an air-hole; a vent.

kazetōshi (風通), *n.* =*kaza-tōshi.*

kazetsu (佳絕な), *a.* exquisite; excellent; matchless.

kazoekirenu (數へ切れぬ), *a.* numberless; innumerable; countless.

kazoeru (數·算へる), *v.* to count; reckon; calculate. —數へ違へる, to miscount; miscalculate. —數へ難くなる, to lose count *of.* —百(千)を以て數へる, to be counted by the hundred (thousand). —數ふるに足らない, not worth consideration [taking into account].

kazoku (家族), *n.* a family; members of a family; a household. —八人の家族, a family of eight. ¶ 家族制度, the family system.

kazoku (華族), *n.* ❶ (一人) a noble; a nobleman; a peer. ❷ (集合) the nobility; the peerage; the aristocracy. —華族の禮遇を停止する, to deprive temporarily of the honours of peerage. ¶ 大名華族, a peer of the *daimyō* descent. —一代華族, a life-peer; a paper peer【英·俗】. —公卿華族, a peer of the *kuge* descent. —世襲華族, a hereditary peer. —華族會館, the Peers' Hall [Club].

kazu (數), *n.* number. ☞ *sū.*

kazukazu (數數の), *a.* many; numerous.

kazukeru (かづける), *vt.* ❶ (託(カヅ)ける) to pretend; make a pretence [pretext] *of.* ❷ (被(カ)せる) to lay *on*; put *upon*; shift (off) *on.* —託けて, under pretence [pretext; plea] *of*; on the pretence [pretext; plea] *of*; under the cloak [mask; veil] *of.* (用事にかづけて, on the pretence of having business; under the cloak of business.)

kazunoko (數子), *n.* herring roe.

kazura (葛), *n.* the vine.

kazura (鬘), *n.* a wig; a periwig. ¶ 鬘師, a wig-maker.

kazutori (數取), *n.* counters; check (竹牌の); tally.

ke (毛), *n.* ❶ a hair. ❷ (羽毛) feather; down (綿毛). ❸ (獸毛) fur; wool (羊毛). —柔(剛)い毛,

soft (coarse; bristly) hair. —毛だらけの, hairy; pilose; pilous. —毛のない, hairless; bald. —毛が生える(抜ける), The hair grows (falls off). —鳥の毛をむしる, to pluck a bird. —毛を吹いて疵を求める, to bring misfortune upon oneself by too close searching.

ke (氣), *n.* ❶ (樣子) appearance; a sign. ❷ (氣味) a touch; a smack; a symptom (症徵). —火の氣もない家, a house where there is no sign of fire burning; a deserted [lonely] house. —肺病の氣はない, There is no symptom of consumption.

keageru (蹴上げる), *vt.* to kick up; send up with a kick.

keai (蹴合), *n.* spar; cock-fighting (鷄の). —蹴合ひする; 蹴合ふ, to spar.

keana (毛孔), *n.* pores (of the skin).

keba (毳), *n.* ❶ nap (布面又は植物), fluff; floss; pile (特に天鵞絨等の); *duvet* (生絲の) [佛]. ❷ (地圖の線影) hatching; *hachure* [佛]. —毳立たす, to fluff; nap.

kebakebashii (けばけばしい), *a.* ❶ (華麗な) gaudy; showy; flashy. ❷ (きらきらした) glaring; glittering; dazzling.

kebayaki (毳燒する), *vt.* to singe. —木綿絲を毳燒きする, to singe cotton yarn.

kebōki (毛箒), *n.* a whisk; a feather-brush.

kebukai (毛深い), *a.* hairy; shaggy.

keburi (氣振), *n.* ❶ (素振) behaviour; bearing. ❷ (樣子) look; air; appearance. ❸ (けはひ) a sign; an indication.

kebyō (假病, 虛病), *n.* feigned sickness; malingering (特に軍人の). —假病を使ふ, to feign sickness; sham illness; malinger.

kechi (けち), *n.* ❶ (不吉) ill luck; inauspiciousness; an ill omen (兆). ❷ (怪しいこと) strangeness. ❸ (吝嗇) niggardliness; stinginess; miserliness. ❹ (卑賤) meanness; shabbiness. —人にけちをつける, to bring ill-luck upon a person.
——-na, *a.* ❶ niggardly; stingy; miserly. ❷ mean; paltry; shabby; poor. —けちな奴, a curmudgeon; a stingy fellow.

kechikechi (けちけちする), *vi.* to be stingy [miserly].

kechinbō (吝嗇漢), *n.* a niggard; a curmudgeon; a stingy fellow.

kedakai (氣高い), *a.* noble; dignified; lofty. —氣高い人品, noble [lofty] character.

kedamono (獸), *n.* ❶ =*kemono* (獸). ❷ (人を罵る語) a beast; a brute.

kedashi (蓋), *ad.* (多分) probably; perhaps.

kedoru (氣取る), *vt.* to scent; smell; perceive. —素振で氣取る, to perceive from another's gesture.

kega (怪我), *n.* ❶ (負傷) a hurt; a wound; an injury. ❷ (過ち) a mistake; an accident. —怪我の功名, fame won by accident; an accidental achievement; a lucky hit. —怪我をする, to get [be] hurt; be injured [wounded]. —怪我をさす, to injure; wound; inflict a wound. ¶ 怪我負け, an accidental defeat. —怪我人, ① an injured person; a wounded person. ② (複數) the injured; the wounded.

kegarawashii (穢·汚はしい), *a.* ❶ (きたない) unclean(-ly); filthy; foul. ❷ (いまはしい) loathsome; disgusting; abominable —穢はしい話, filthy talk; a foul affair.

kegare (汚, 穢), *n.* ❶ (不淨) impurity; uncleanliness; pollution. ❷ (汚點) a stain; a soil. —家名の汚れ, a stain upon the family honour. —衣の汚れを洗ふ, to wash the stain on the clothes.

kegareru (汚れる), *vi.* ❶ (よごれる) to be defiled [soiled]. ❷ (辱めらる) to be put to shame; be polluted.

kegareta (汚れた), *a.* ❶ (よごれた) filthy; foul; unclean. ❷ (不神聖の) unholy. ❸ (女の不淨な) defiled; unclean. —汚れた名譽, tarnished [sullied] honour. —汚れた布, foul linen.

kegasu (汚·瀆す), *vt.* ❶ (よごす) to stain; taint; pollute. ❷ (傷つける) to bring reproach *upon*; disgrace; corrupt; sully (名聲·品性等を). ❸ (瀆す) (*a*) (處女等を) to dishonour; defile; deflower; violate: (*b*) (神聖を) to profane; desecrate; defile. —名を汚す, to stain one's reputation. —神を汚す, to profane a deity; blaspheme God.

kegawa (毛皮), *n.* fur (飾用又は裏用の); pelt; skin. —毛皮の襟卷 (婦人の), a victorine; a boa.

kegawari (更毛する), *vi.* to moult.

kegen (怪訝な), *a.* dubious; suspicious; doubtful.

kegirai (毛嫌ひする), *v.* to be prejudiced *against*; dislike instinctively.

kegoromo (毛衣), *n.* a fur (-robe); a fur-coat.

kehaegusuri (毛生藥), *n.* a hair-restorer; a hair-invigorator; a hair-grower.

kehai (氣配, 氣色), *n.* ❶ (素振) behaviour; bearing. ❷ (樣子) look; appearance; air. ☞ *kihai.*

kehanasu (蹴放す), *vt.* to kick

open; kick away.

kei (兄), *n.* ❶ (あに) an elder brother. ❷ (敬稱) Mr.; my dear .... ❸ (君) you. —兄たり難く弟たり難し, There is little to choose between them.

kei (刑), *n.* a punishment; a penalty. —刑に處する, to sentence a person; condemn to a penalty [punishment]. —刑に服する, to submit to a punishment. —刑を減する, to mitigate a punishment.

kei (系), *n.* ❶ (系統) a system. ❷ (血統) a line; lineage. ❸【數】a corollary.

kei (計), *n.* ❶ (計略) a stratagem; a plan. ❷ (計器) a meter; a gauge, gage. ❸ (合計) the amount; the sum (total). —計三十, thirty in all; total, 30.

kei (徑), *n.* 【數】diameter.

kei (景), *n.* a view; a scene; a prospect. ☞ *keshiki.*

kei (罫), *n.* 【印】rule: a line; ruled lines. —罫を引く, to rule [draw] a line.

keiai (敬愛), *n.* respect and affection; veneration. —敬愛する, ① to venerate; respect. ② [*a.*] respectful; venerable.

keian (桂庵), *n.* a servants' registry (office); a servants' agency; an employment office; a register-office〔米〕; an intelligence office〔米〕.

keiba (競馬), *n.* a horse-race [-running]; a race. ¶ 競馬番組, a fixture-card; a race-card. —競馬場, a race-ground; a race-track; a race-course. —競馬觀覽席, a race-stand. —競馬騎手, a jockey. —競馬馬, a racer; a racing horse.

keibatsu (刑罰), *n.* punishment; a penalty.

keiben (輕便な), *a.* ❶ handy; convenient; portable (携帶に便な). ❷ simple; plain. ¶ 輕便鐵道, a light railway.

keibetsu (輕蔑), *n.* scorn; contempt; disdain. —輕蔑する, to despise; disdain; treat with contempt. —輕蔑的態度を執る, to take up a contemptuous attitude.

keibi (輕微な), *a.* slight; trivial; insignificant.

keibi (警備), *n.* defence; guard. —警備する, to defend; guard. ¶ 警備艦, a guard-ship. —警備隊, a garrison.

keibiki (罫引), *n.* ❶ line-ruling. ❷ (道具) a ruler; a gauge.

keibo (景慕·敬慕する), *vt.* to esteem; adore.

keibo (繼母), *n.* a stepmother.

keibu (警部), *n.* a police inspector. ¶ 警部補, an assistant police inspector.

keibutsu (景物), *n.* ❶ (風物) (natural) features of the season; the scenery. ❷ (景品) a premium. ❸ (餘興) an entertainment.

keichō (輕佻な), *a.* imprudent; light-minded; fickle. —輕佻の舉動, light behaviour. —輕佻浮薄の徒, fickle and unfeeling fellows.

keichō (傾聽する), *vt.* to listen *to*; give ear *to*; hearken *to*.

keichoku (痙直), *n.* 【醫】spasm; cramp.

keichū (閨中), *n.* a bed-chamber [-room].

keichū (傾注する), *vt.* to concentrate; devote; bend. —全力を傾注する, to devote one's utmost energies *to*; devote oneself entirely.

keidai (境內), *n.* the precincts.

keido (硅土), *n.* 【化】silica.

keido (傾度), *n.* obliquity; inclination.

keido (經度), *n.* 【地】longitude (long. と略す).

keidoki (計度器), *n.* a meter.

keidōmyaku (頸動脈), *n.* the carotis; the carotid (artery).

keiei (經營), *n.* ❶ administration; management; conduct. ❷ (計畫) a programme; a plan; an undertaking (企圖). ❸ (造營) construction; building; erection. ——**-suru**, *vt.* ❶ to administer; manage; conduct; run. ❷ to plan; undertake. ❸ to construct; build; erect. —鐵道を經營する, to manage a railway. ¶ 經營者, ① a constructor; an erector. ② an administrator; a manager.

keiei (警衞する), *vt.* to escort; convoy; guard.

keien (敬遠する), *vt.* to keep at a respectful distance; give a wide berth *to*.

keifu (系譜), *n.* pedigree; genealogy; a family-tree. ☞ *keizu.*

keifu (繼父), *n.* a stepfather.

keifuku (敬服する), *vt.* to pay deference *to*; respect; reverence.

keiga (慶賀する), *v.* to congratulate *on*; felicitate; offer [tender] one's congratulation [felicitations].

keigai (形骸), *n.* ❶ (からだ) a body; a skeleton (骨組). ❷ (殘骸) ruins; a wreck. —形骸の奴隸となる, to become the slave of one's body.

keigai (謦咳), *n.* ❶ (笑ひつ語りつすること) merry talk. ❷ (しはぶき, せきばらひ) clearing the throat; coughing. —謦咳に接する, to have the pleasure [honour] of one's acquaintance.

keigan (炯眼), *n.* ❶ (炯々たる眼光) glittering eyes. ❷〔慧眼〕(鋭き眼力) quick [piercing] eyes; penetration; clear-sightedness. —炯

眼の, quick-sighted; clear-sighted; penetrating.

keigen (輕減), *n.* mitigation; alleviation; palliation. **——-suru,** *vt.* to mitigate; alleviate; palliate. —國民の負擔を輕減する, to lighten the burden of the people.

keigo (敬語), *n.* an honorific; a term of respect; a salutation (手紙等の).

keigo (警護, 警固), *n.* escort; convoy; guard. —警護する, to escort; convoy; guard.

keigō (契合する), *vi.* to coincide.

keigu (敬具), yours sincerely; yours faithfully; yours (very) truly.

keihaku (輕薄), *n.* ❶ (不信) perfidy; insincerity. ❷ (變り易いこと) fickleness; frivolity; flippancy. ❸ (佞諛) flattery; obsequiousness. —輕薄な, ① perfidious; insincere. ② fickle; flippant; frivolous. ③ obsequious. ¶ 輕薄才子, an able man of frivolous disposition.

keihatsu (啓發する), *vt.* to develop; enlighten; cultivate.

keihi (桂皮), *n.* (藥種用) cinnamon; cassia bark.

keihi (經費), *n.* expenses; expenditure; outlay. —經費を節約する, to retrench (expenses); curtail expenses [expenditures].

keihin (景品), *n.* a premium. ¶ 景品券, a premium ticket. —景品附賣出し, opening sales with premiums.

keihō (刑法), *n.* the criminal [penal] law; the criminal [penal] code. —刑法上の責任, penal responsibility.

keihō (警砲), *n.* an alarm-gun [-cannon]; a signal-gun.

keihō (警報), *n.* an alarm-signal; an alarm; a warning. —警報する, to give the alarm; give warning. ¶ 警報器, an alarm; an alarum; 【鐵道】 a communication cord.

keihokyoku (警保局), *n.* the Police Bureau.

keii (敬意), *n.* respect; homage; duty. —敬意を表する, to pay [do] homage *to*; pay one's respects *to*; show respect.

keii (經緯), *n.* ❶ (織絲の縱·横) the warp and woof. ❷ (横縱) length and breadth. ❸ (經度緯度) latitude and longitude. ❹ (いきさつ) ins and outs; circumstances. —經緯する, to regulate. ¶ 經緯儀, an altazimuth; a theodolite.

keii (輕易な), *a.* easy; light; simple. —輕易な條件で, on easy terms.

keiin (契印), *n.* a seal over the joint of two sheets of paper; a tally.

keiji (刑事), *n.* ❶ criminal matters; a criminal case (事件). ❷ (刑事巡査の略) a detective. ¶ 刑事部, the Department of Criminal Cases. —刑事被告人, the accused; the prisoner (at the bar). (刑事被告人席, the bar; the dock.) —刑事問題, a crown-case [英]; a criminal case. —刑事裁判所, a criminal court. —刑事訴訟, a criminal suit [action]. (刑事訴訟法, the Code of Criminal Procedure.)

keiji (啓示), *n.* revelation. ☞ *mokushi*.

keiji (揭示), *n.* a notice; a notification; a placard. —揭示する, to post [put] up a notice; notify; placard; post. ¶ 揭示場, a place for posting notices. —揭示板, a notice-board.

keiji (慶事), *n.* a happy event; an auspicious event; a matter for congratulation; a wedding (婚禮).

keiji (繫辭), *n.* a copula.

keijijō (形而上の), *a.* metaphysical; spiritual; abstract. ¶ 形而上學, metaphysics; philosophy.

keijika (形而下の), *a.* physical; concrete; corporeal. ¶ 形而下學, a physical [concrete] science.

Keijō (京城), *n.* Seoul.

keijō (刑場), *n.* an execution-ground. —刑場の露と消えた, He breathed his last on the scaffold.

keijō (形狀), *n.* shape; form; figure. ☞ *katachi* (形).

keijō (計上する), *vt.* to add [sum] up. —豫算に計上された經費, the expenditures given in the Budget.

keijō (經常の), *a.* ordinary. ¶ 經常費, ordinary expenditure [expenses]. —經常歲入(出), ordinary annual revenue (expenditure).

keiju (繼受する), *vt.* =*uketsugu*.

keijū (輕重), *n.* relative importance [gravity]; weight. —事の輕重を計る, to weigh the importance of an affair. —人物を輕重する, to weigh his character.

keika (傾下する), *vi.* to slope down; bend downward.

keika (經過), *n.* ❶ (進行) progress; process; course (成行). ❷ (通過) passage; transit. ❸ (時間の) lapse. —經過する, ① to progress; proceed. ② to pass; pass over [through; off]. ③ to elapse; go; pass (away); run by; wear *on* (段々と); expire (滿了); run out (同上). —事件の經過を報告する, to report the course of an affair.

keikai (境界), *n.* a boundary; a border; bounds. —境界を定める, to fix the boundary; draw the line of demarcation. ¶ 境界標, a landmark. —境界線, a boundary line; a line of demarcation.

keikai (輕快な), *a.* ❶ (氣輕) light-hearted; cheerful; buoyant. ❷ (身輕) light; nimble. ❸ (快方) convalescent. —輕快な扮裝をする, to be lightly dressed.

keikai (警戒), *n.* ❶ (警告) warning; caution; admonition. ❷ (警備) watch; outlook; guard. ❸ (用心) caution; precaution; guard. —警戒する, ① to warn; caution. ② to guard *against*; watch; look out *for*. ③ to take care; caution. —沿岸の警戒を解く, to withdraw the coast warning. ¶ 警戒線, a cordon; a guarded line. —警戒色, a warning colour.

keikaku (計畫), *n.* ❶ a plan; a design; a project. ❷ (企圖) an undertaking; an enterprise. —五年計畫, a five years' programme; a project extending over [covering] five years. —計畫する, ① to plan; design; project. ② to undertake. ③ (志す) to intend; contemplate. —計畫を立てる, to make [form] a plan; draw up a plan. ¶ 計畫者, a projector; a designer.

keikan, kaikan, (挂冠), *n.* resignation. —挂冠する, to resign.

keikan (桂冠), *n.* a laurel. —桂冠を戴かしめる, to laurel.

keikan (警官), *n.* a policeman; a police constable [officer]; the police. ¶ 警官隊, the police band.

keikan (鷄冠), *n.* a cock's comb.

keikei (烱烱たる), *a.* fiery; glittering; glaring.

keikei (輕輕に), *ad.* carelessly; heedlessly; lightly. —輕々に看過する, to pass over lightly. —輕々に事を處する, to deal with an affair carelessly.

keiken (敬虔), *n.* piety; devoutness; devotion. —敬虔な, pious; devout; reverential.

keiken (經驗), *n.* experience. —經驗ある, experienced. —經驗なき, inexperienced; callow; raw. —經驗する, to experience; pass *through*. —經驗から話す, to speak from experience. —經驗がある, to have experience *in*. (日本語を教へた經驗がある, to have experience of teaching Japanese.) —經驗に富む, to be highly experienced; have wide experience. —經驗に乏しい, to lack experience; be lacking [wanting] in experience. —苦い經驗を嘗める, to have [undergo] a bitter experience. ¶ 經驗談, a narrative of personal experience. (經驗談をする, to relate one's experiences.) —經驗家, a man of experience.

keiki (刑期), *n.* the term of penalty [service].

keiki (計器), *n.* a meter; a gauge; a measure.

keiki (景氣), *n.* ❶ (景況) state; condition; appearance. ❷ (商況) the condition of trade [market]; tone of the market. ❸ (元氣) animation; high spirits. ❹ (人氣) popularity. —景氣のよい, high-spirited (元氣); prosperous. —景氣を恢復する, to recover the normal condition (of trade).

keiki (繼起), *n.* 【論】 sequence; succession.

keikihei (輕騎兵), *n.* the light horse [cavalry] (輕騎隊); a light horseman.

keikikyū (輕氣球), *n.* a balloon. [☞ *kikyū*.]

keiko (稽古), *n.* study (學ぶこと); practice (練習); lesson (課業). —稽古する, to learn; study; take lessons *in*; practise. ¶ 下稽古, a rehearsal; preparation. —稽古著, a practice [exercise] dress.

keikō (傾向), *n.* tendency; inclination; disposition. —傾向がある, to be disposed *to*; have an inclination; have a tendency.

keikō (螢光), *n.* fluorescence.

keikō (鷄口), *n.* the beak of a fowl. —鷄口となるも牛後となる勿れ, "Better be the head of a dog than the tail of a lion."

keikoku (經國の), *a.* administrative. —經國の才, administrative ability; statesmanship. ¶ 經國策, a state policy.

keikoku (警告), *n.* warning; caution; admonition. —警告する, to warn; caution *against*; admonish.

keikotsu (頸骨), *n.* the malar bone; the neck bone.

keikotsu (輕忽), *n.* carelessness; heedlessness; imprudence. —輕忽な, careless; heedless; imprudent. —輕忽に, carelessly; heedlessly; imprudently.

keiku (警句), *n.* ❶ (奇警の句) an epigram; a witty remark; a pithy saying. ❷ (格言) an aphorism; an apophthegm. —警句を吐く, to make a witty remark.

keikyo (輕擧), *n.* a heedless undertaking; a rash action; an inconsiderate [a thoughtless] conduct. ¶ 輕擧盲動, a rash and unconsidered action.

keikyō (景況), *n.* ❶ (狀況) a state; a condition; circumstances. ❷ (見込) a prospect; a promise.

keikyoku (荊棘), *n.* thorns; brambles. —荊棘を拓(ひら)く, to make a way through brambles.

keikyū (警急), *n.* alarm. —警急喇叭を吹く, to sound the alarm. ¶警急集合所,【軍】an alarm-post.

keima (桂馬), *n.* the knight (將棋の).

keimei (鷄鳴), *n.* ❶(cock-)crow. ❷(曉) early dawn.

keimō (啓蒙), *n.* enlightenment; illumination; instruction of the ignorant. ¶啓蒙時代(運動), the period of (movement for) enlightenment.

keimon (閨門), *n.* a bed-chamber [-room] (寢室); home (家庭).

keimu (警務), *n.* police affairs. ¶警務總長, (朝鮮) the superintendent-general of police.

keimusho (刑務所), *n.* a prison; a gaol; a jail.

keimyō (輕妙な), *a.* ❶ light-handed; light (and delicate). ❷ (巧妙な) skilful; dexterous; tactful. —輕妙な文章, a light composition.

keiniku (鷄肉), *n.* fowl; chicken; light [white] meat.

keiran (鷄卵), *n.* an egg; a hen's egg. ¶鷄卵紙,【寫】albuminized paper.

keiransō (けいらんさう), *n.* 【植】the wall-flower.

keirei (敬禮), *n.* salutation; a salute; an obeisance. —敬禮!, (命令) salute! —敬禮する, to do [make] an obeisance *to*; salute; make a respectful salutation. —敬禮に對して答禮する, to acknowledge a salute. ¶海軍敬禮, a naval salute. —最敬禮, a most respectful salutation.

keireki (經歷), *n.* career; personal history; one's story; antecedents. —學校の經歷, school history [career].

keiren (痙攣), *n.*【醫】a spasm; convulsion; a cramp. —痙攣を起す, to have a convulsive [spasmodic] fit; have a cramp; be convulsed.

keiri (經理), *n.* dealing; intendance; management. ¶經理學校, the Paymasters' School. —經理局, the Bureau of Accounts and Supplies (海軍); the Intendance Bureau (陸軍); the Bureau of Accounts (遞信・鐵道省).

keirin (經綸する), *vt.* to rule; govern.

keiro (毛色), *n.* the colour of the hair. —毛色の變つた人間, ① (外國人) a foreigner; a stranger. ② (一風變つた人) a man out of the common run.

keiro (徑路), *n.* a path; a course; a process (過程). —…の踏める徑路を辿る, to walk in the path traced by… .

keirui (係累), *n.* ❶ dependants; an encumbrance【俗】. ❷ (まきぞへ) implication; complicity. —係累なき, unencumbered.

keiryaku (計略), *n.* ❶ (策略) a stratagem; an artifice; a ruse. ❷ (計畫) a plan; a scheme; a design. —計略にかける, [*vt.*] to entrap. —敵の計略にかゝる, to fall into the enemy's snare. —計略の裏をかく, to out-manœuvre. —計略を以て, by stratagem.

keiryōki (計量器), *n.* a meter; a gauge; a measure; a scale.

keiryū (繫留する), *vt.* to moor. ¶繫留氣球, a moored [captive] balloon. —繫留所, a moorage.

keiryū (溪流), *n.* a brook; a mountain stream.

keisai (掲載), *n.* insertion; publication. —掲載する, to insert; publish (in a paper); set up. —掲載を見合せる, to withhold publication.

keisan (卦算), *n.* Ⓢ 文鎭. a paper-weight.

keisan (計算), *n.* ❶ (勘定) calculation; reckoning; computation. ❷(會計) account. **——-suru**, *v.* ❶ to calculate; reckon; compute. ❷ to cipher (算術で); do a sum. —損益を計算する, to calculate the profit and loss. —點數を計算する, to add up the marks. ¶計算日, settling [account] day. —計算貨幣, money of account. —計算器, an adding-machine; an arithmometer. —計算書, an account note; a statement of account.

keisan (硅酸), *n.* silicic acid.

keisatsu (警察), *n.* ❶ police (抽象); the police (集合). ❷ = 警察署. —警察に引渡す, to hand over a person to the police. ¶地方警察, the local police. —警察部, the constabulary; the police department. —警察犯, a police offence. (警察犯所罰令, law for punishment of contraventions of police regulations.) —警察法規, police laws and regulations. —警察醫, a police medical officer; a police surgeon. —警察事故, a police case. —警察官, a police officer; a policeman; the police. —警察權, police authority [power]. —警察犬, a police-dog. —警察署, a police office; a police station; a station-house (建物). (警察署長, the chief of a police station. 警察分署, a branch police-station.) —警察處分, police disposition.

keisei (形成する), *vt.* to form; shape; frame.

keisei (形勢), *n.* ❶ (狀態) the state of things [affairs] (事情); condition; situation (局面). ❷ (情勢) the course of events; progress [development] of affairs. —形勢を觀望する, to watch the course of events. ¶形勢觀望者, a trimmer.

keisei (警世の), *a.* warning; premonitory. —警世の大文字を草する, to write words of warning.

keisei (警醒する), *vt.* to awake; rouse; warn; caution *against*; disillusion.

keiseki (形跡), *n.* ❶ (痕跡) a trace; a vestige; a shadow. ❷ (證跡) signs; evidence.

keiseki (硅石, 珪石), *n.* 【鑛】 silex; silica; millstone grit.

keisen (經線), *n.* 【地】 circles of longitude; 【天】 a meridian.

keisen (繫船), *n.* ❶ (碇泊) mooring; laying-up (艤裝を解いての). ❷ (繫留船) a moored ship; a laid-up ship. —繫船する, to moor a vessel; lay up a ship. ¶繫船場, moorings; moorage. —繫船浮標, a mooring [anchoring] buoy. —繫船料, pier dues.

keisetsu (螢雪), *n.* diligence in study. —螢雪の功を積む, to gather the fruits of diligent study.

keisha (傾斜), *n.* ❶ inclination; slant; bent; grade (道路等の). ❷ 【地質】 dip (地層の). —傾斜さす, to slope; slant; incline. —傾斜する, ① to incline; slant; lean; list. ② 【地質】 to dip. —地層の傾斜, dip of a stratum. ¶傾斜度, rake; gradient; pitch.

keishi (啓示), *n.* revelation. ☞ ***mokushi*** (默示).

keishi (罫紙), *n.* ruled paper.

keishi (輕視する), *vt.* to disregard; slight; make light *of*.

keishi (警視), *n.* a police superintendent. ¶警視廳, the Metropolitan Police Department. —警視總監, the Inspector-General of the Metropolitan Police.

keishiki (形式), *n.* form; formality; ceremony. —形式的に, formally; ceremonially. —形式的訪問, a formal call [visit].

keishin (敬神の), *a.* pious; devout; religious.

keishin (輕信する), *vt.* to believe heedlessly; give ready credence *to*. ——, *a.* credulous.

keisho (經書), *n.* the canons. ☞ ***keiten*** (經典).

keishō (形勝), *n.* ❶ (景色) a picturesque spot. ❷ (要害) a vantage-ground.

keishō (敬稱), *n.* a title of honour; a honorific.

keishō (警鐘), *n.* a tocsin; an alarm-bell; a fire-alarm[-bell].

keishō (輕少の), *a.* slight; trifling; small. —輕少ながら, such a trifle as it is.

keishō (輕症), *n.* a slight illness [attack].

keishō (輕傷), *n.* a slight wound [injury]; a scratch. —輕傷を負ふ, to be slightly wounded [injured].

keishō (繼承), *n.* succession; inheritance. —繼承する, to succeed *to*; inherit; take over. ¶繼承者, a successor; an inheritor; an heir.

keishoku (景色), *n.* a view; scenery; prospect. ☞ ***keshiki.***

keishu (計手), *n.* an intendant; an accountant.

keishu (警手), *n.* a palace guard (皇宮の).

keishū (閨秀), *n.* an eminent woman. ¶閨秀歌人, a poetess. —閨秀作家, a female writer; an authoress.

keiso (硅素), *n.* 【化】 silicon.

keisō (係爭), *n.* contention; dispute. ¶係爭問題, an issue.

keisō (輕裝), *n.* a light dress. —輕裝する, to be lightly dressed.

keisō (輕躁の), *a.* light-minded; thoughtless; heedless.

keisotsu (輕率な), *a.* heedless; thoughtless; rash.

keisū (係數), *n.* 【數】 a coefficient.

kei-suru (刑する), *vt.* to punish.

kei-suru (敬する), *vt.* to respect; honour; venerate (老人などを). —神を敬する, to reverence God. —人を敬する, to respect a man.

kei-suru (慶する), *v.* to rejoice; congratulate.

keitai (形體, 形態), *n.* form; shape; figure. —形態を變ずる, to transform; transfigure.

keitai (携帶), *n.* carrying with one. —携帶する, to take; carry; bring. —携帶に便な, portable; convenient to carry. ¶携帶品(一時)預り所, a cloak-room; a left-luggage office. —携帶口糧, 【軍】 field ration.

keitei (逕庭), *n.* a gap; a difference; a gulf.

keiteki (勁敵), *n.* a formidable [powerful] enemy.

keiteki (警笛), *n.* an alarm-whistle; a honk (自動車・自轉車の).

keiten (經典), *n.* the scripture; the canons; classics (Chinese).

keito (毛絲), *n.* Berlin wool; woollen yarn; worsted. —毛絲の編物をする, to knit with Berlin wool. ¶毛絲細工, woolwork.

keitō (鷄頭), *n.* 【植】 the cock's comb.

keitō (系統), *n.* ❶ a system. ❷ (系圖) lineage; genealogy; family-line. ❸ (出身) descent; extraction. ❹ (派) a party; a clique. ❺ 【地】 formation. —系統的, systematic.

—系統を引く, to be descended *from* (後裔); be inheritable (遺傳); be transmitted by heredity (同上). ¶消化器系統, the digestive system.

keitō (傾倒する), *vt.* to devote; concentrate; squander away (蕩盡). —精神を傾倒する, to give all one's mind *to*.

keitō (鷄闘), *n.* cock-fighting; spar.

keitsui (頸椎), *n.* 【解】the cervical vertebra.

keiyaku (契約), *n.* a contract; an agreement. —契約する, to contract; agree; make a contract [an agreement]. —契約を結ぶ, to conclude [make] a contract; make an agreement. —契約書を取交はす, to exchange deeds of contract. ¶物(債)權契約, real (obligatory) agreement. —契約違反, breach of contract. —契約移民, indentured immigrants. —契約期限, the term of contract. —契約者, a contractor.

keiyō (形容), *n.* ❶ (形狀) figure; form; appearance. ❷ (比喩, 修飾) a metaphor; a figure of speech. ❸【文】qualification; modification. —形容する, to qualify; modify; express figuratively. ¶形容詞, 【文】the adjective.

keiyu (經由), *prep.* *via* [羅. =by way]; by way *of*; through. —經由する, to pass through; go by way *of*. —沙港經由桑港行, bound for San Francisco *via* Seattle. —上海經由ロイテル通信, a Reuter message coming through Shanghai.

keiyu (輕油), *n.* light oil.

keizai (經濟), *n.* economy. —經濟向きの品, an economical article. ¶經濟封鎖, economic blockade. —經濟學, economics; political economy. —經濟事情, economic circumstances [condition]. —經濟家, a good economist; a man of economy. —經濟界, economic circles; the economic world. —經濟思想, economic ideas [thoughts].

keizai (輕罪), *n.* 【法】a misdemeanour; a delict; a minor crime.

keizoku (繼續), *n.* continuation; succession; maintenance (持續). —繼續する, ① [*vt.*] to continue; maintain; go on *with*. ② [*vi.*] to continue; last; run on. ¶繼續事業, a continuing undertaking. —繼續日數, running days.

keizu (系圖), *n.* lineage; genealogy; a family tree.

keizukai (系圖買), *n.* fencing; a fence (人). ☞ ***kobai*** (故買).

kejirami (毛蝨), *n.* the crab-louse.

kejusu (毛繻子), *n.* sateen; Italian cloth.

kekka (結果), *n.* result; consequence; effect; product; outcome; issue; end. —熟慮の結果, after mature consideration. —…の結果として, as a result *of*; as a consequence *of*. —豫め結果を考察する, to weigh [consider] the consequences. —同一の結果を來す, to lead to the same result. —意外の結果を生ずる, to bring about unexpected results; lead to unexpected consequences.

kekka (結痂する), *vi.* to scab.

kekkai (血塊), *n.* gore; a clot of blood.

kekkai (決潰する), *vi.* to break down; give way; ulcerate (膿潰).

kekkaku (缺格), *n.* disqualification.

kekkaku (結核), *n.* ❶【醫】a tubercle. ❷【地質】concretion. ¶結核病, 【醫】tuberculosis. —結核菌, 【菌】Bacillus tuberculosis; a tubercle bacillus.

kekkan (血管), *n.* a blood-vessel.

kekkan (缺陷), *n.* a defect; a gap; deficit.

kekki (血氣), *n.* mettle; animal spirit; physical vigour. —少年の血氣, the ardour [animal courage] of youth. —血氣の若者, a vigorous youth. —血氣の勇, brute [animal] courage. ¶血氣盛り, prime; bloom of youth.

kekki (蹶起する), *vi.* to spring up; rouse oneself to action.

kekkin (缺勤), *n.* absence from office; non-attendance. **——-suru,** *v.* to absent oneself from duty [office]; be absent from duty [office]. —無屆缺勤する, to be absent without leave. ¶缺勤者, an absentee.

kekkō (決行する), *vt.* to execute; carry out; carry [put] into effect.

kekkō (結構), *n.* (組立) plot (戯曲等の); frame (社會·法律·天地等の); structure (建物·文章などの). **——-na,** *a.* ❶ (立派な) magnificent; fine; beautiful. ❷ (美味な) delicious; dainty; sweet. —結構な品, (立派な品) an exquisite article; a nice [fine; beautiful] present [gift] (贈物).

kekkon (血痕), *n.* a blood-stain. —血痕のある, blood-stained.

kekkon (結婚), *n.* marriage; wedding. —結婚する, to marry; get married; wed. —結婚の怡樂, wedded bliss. —結婚の羈絆, the marriage tie. —結婚を約する, to engage to marry. —結婚を申込む, to make an offer of marriage; propose (to a lady). —結婚を諾する, to consent to marriage. ¶結婚媒介業[所], matrimonial agency. —結婚日, the wedding-day (當日

記念日). —結婚披露, a wedding-reception. —結婚祝, wedding presents. —結婚期, nubility; marriageable age. —結婚年齢, marriageable age. —結婚生活, married life. —結婚式, a marriage (ceremony); a wedding; nuptials. —結婚指環, a wedding ring.

kekkōso (血紅素), *n.* hæmoglobin.

kekku (結句), *ad.* (結局) after all; in the end; in the long run.

kekkyo (穴居), *n.* troglodytism; cave-dwelling. —穴居する, to dwell in a cave.

kekkyoku (結局), *n.* the conclusion; the final result [issue]; the end. ——, *ad.* eventually; in the end; in the long run. —結局の勝利, the final victory.

kekkyū (血球), *n.* 【解】 a blood-corpuscle.

kekomu (蹴込む), *vt.* to kick in [into].

kemari (蹴毬), *n.* ❶ (遊) football. ❷ (毬) a football.

kemisuru (閲する), *vt.* ❶ (検閲) to examine; inspect; survey (検分); see; review (兵を). ❷ (閲讀) to read; peruse; look over. ❸ (經過) to elapse; pass; go by. —兵を閲する, to review troops.

kemono (獸), *n.* a brute; a beast. —獸の様な, beastly; brutal; bestial.

kemu (煙), *n.* smoke. ☞ ***kemuri.*** —煙の様な話, a tale that one cannot make head or tail of. —人を煙に卷く, to bewilder; mystify.

kemui (煙い), *a.* Ⓢ 煙たい. smoky. —親爺を煙たがる, to be afraid of one's father.

kemudashi (煙出), *n.* a chimney; a stove-pipe (ストーヴの) a funnel (汽船の). ☞ ***entotsu.***

kemukujara (毛むくぢゃらの), *a.* hairy; shaggy.

kemuri (煙), *n.* smoke. —濛々たる煙, a cloud of smoke. —煙を吐き出す, to emit smoke; puff out smoke. —細い煙を起てる, to eke out a scanty livelihood.

kemuru (煙る), *vi.* to smoke; smoulder; be smoky. ——, *a.* smoky. —煙れる火, a smoky fire.

kemushi (毛蟲), *n.* a hairy caterpillar; a grub.

ken (件), *n.* a matter; an affair; a case.

ken (拳), *n.* ❶ (こぶし) the fist. ❷ (遊) Japanese mora; *ken* 〔日〕.

ken (圏), *n.* a sphere; a circle; a province (學圏). ¶ 勢力(利益)圏, the sphere of influence (interests). —圏内(外), within (out of) the sphere *of*.

ken (兼), *conj.* and; and in addition. —總理大臣兼外務大臣, Minister President and Minister for Foreign Affairs.

ken (軒), *n.* a house; a door. —軒別に, house by house; from door to door; to [at] each house. —隣から三軒目の, three doors off.

ken (間), *n.* six *shaku*; a *ken*.

ken (險, 嶮), *n.* ❶ (難所) a precipice; a dangerous path; an impregnable pass (難攻不落の). ❷ (險相) a sinister look. —顔に險がある美人, a beautiful woman with a sinister expression.

ken (螫), *n.* (蟲の) the aculeus; the sting.

ken (劍, 劍), *n.* ❶ a sword(刀劍); a bayonet (銃劍); a sabre. ❷ (針) a needle; a pointer; a hand (示針). —劍で刺し通す, to spit a man with a sword. ¶ 劍附鐵砲, a musket with a bayonet.

ken (驗), *n.* ❶ (效驗) effect; efficacy; virtue. ❷ (徵(しるし)) a sign. —驗が見えない, to have no effect; not to take effect.

ken (腱), *n.* 【解】 a tendon; a sinew.

ken (縣), *n.* a prefecture. ¶ 縣知事, a prefectural governor; the governor of a prefecture.

ken (權), *n.* authority (權力); power (同上); right (權利).

kenage (健氣な), *a.* ❶ (男らしい) gallant; heroic; manly. ❷ (敏捷な) brisk; smart. ❸ (殊勝な) praiseworthy. —健氣な振舞, manly behaviour.

keṅaku (險惡な), *a.* dangerous; perilous; threatening (空模様・態度などの). —險惡な空模様, a lowering [threatening] sky. —險惡な天候, rough [ugly; stormy] weather.

kenami (毛竝), *n.* the lie of hair.

keṅan (檢案する), *vt.* to examine.

keṅan (懸案), *n.* a pending question.

kenasu (貶す), *vt.* to disparage; depreciate; cry down.

kenban (鍵盤), *n.* a keyboard; a clavier; a manual-key (風琴の).

kenbi (兼備する), *v.* to combine; unite; be equally versed *in*. —才色を兼備する, to combine wit and beauty.

kenbikyō (顯微鏡), *n.* a microscope. —百倍の顯微鏡, a microscope with ten diameters magnification. ¶ 顯微鏡的檢査, microscopical examination. —顯微鏡使用法, microscopy.

kenbō (健忘), *n.* forgetfulness; loss of memory. —健忘症に罹る, to suffer from amnesia. ¶ 健忘家, a forgetful person.

kenbō (權謀), *n.* craft; artifice;

intrigue. ¶ 權謀家, an intriguer; a crafty person.

kenbu (劍舞), *n.* a sword-dance.

kenbun (見聞), *n.* experience; information; observation. —見聞を博くする, to add to [extend] one's experience [knowledge].

kenbun (檢分), *n.* inspection; examination; survey. —檢分する, to inspect; examine; survey.

kenbutsu (見物), *n.* sight-seeing; visit. **—-suru,** *vt.* to visit; see the sight *of*; see. —京都を見物する, to see the sights of Kyōto; do Kyōto [俗]. —芝居を見物する, to go to a theatre; see a play. ¶ 見物人, audience (觀客); a sightseer (遊覽客); a looker-on (傍觀者). (黑山の様な見物人, a large crowd of spectators.)

kenchi (見地), *n.* a view; a standpoint; a point of view. —見地を異にする, to differ in the [have a different] point of view. —此の見地よりすれば, viewed in this light.

kenchi (軒輊), *n.* difference; disparity; distance.

kenchiku (建築), *n.* ❶ construction; building; erection. ❷ (建築物) a building; a structure; an edifice (大廈). —建築する, to build; erect; construct. —建築中である, to be under construction; be in course of construction. ¶ 建築學, architecture. —建築技師, an architect. —建築家, a (master) builder; an architect. —建築借用地, a building-lease. —建築請負, building contract. (建築請負師, a (master) builder.)

kencho (顯著な), *a.* ❶ (著しい) conspicuous; remarkable; striking. ❷ (明白な) patent; manifest; obvious. —顯著な事實である, to be an obvious fact.

kenchō (縣廳), *n.* a prefectural office; the prefectural authorities.

kenchū (繭紬), *n.* pongee.

kendai (見臺), *n.* a reading-desk a book-rest.

kenden (喧傳する), *v.* to be noised abroad; get about; be circulated; spread.

kendenki (驗電器), *n.* a rheoscope; an electroscope.

kendō (劍道), *n.* (the art of) fencing; swordsmanship.

kendō (獻堂), *n.* dedication [consecration] of a church. ¶ 獻堂記念日, the dedication day.

kendō (權道), *n.* policy; an expedient; a ruse.

kendon (慳貪), *n.* ❶ (貪慾) covetousness; avarice. ❷ (冷酷) harshness; cruelty. —慳貪な, ① covetous; avaricious. ② cruel; harsh.

keṅeki (檢疫), *n.* quarantine; medical inspection. —檢疫停船中, in quarantine. —檢疫する, to quarantine; inspect. ¶ 海(陸)上檢疫, marine (land) inspection. —檢疫員, (a member of) the medical inspection staff. —檢疫官, a quarantine officer; a health-officer. —檢疫許可證, a pratique. —檢疫港, a quarantine port. —檢疫船, a quarantine-ship; a lazaretto. (檢疫船旗, the yellow flag; the quarantine-flag.)

kenen (懸念), *n.* anxiety; uneasiness; apprehension. —懸念する, to be anxious *about*; be uneasy *about*; apprehend.

keṅen (慊焉たる), *a.* unsatisfied; discontented.

keṅen (嫌厭), *n.* abhorrence; dislike; detestation. —嫌厭する, to dislike; abhor; detest.

keṅetsu (檢閱), *n.* ❶ inspection; examination. ❷ (軍隊) review; parade. ❸ (出版物, 映畫) censorship. —新聞の檢閱, censorship of the press [newspapers]. —檢閱を經る, to pass muster [inspection]; pass censorship. **—-suru,** *vt.* ❶ to inspect; examine. ❷ to review. ❸ to censor. —軍隊を檢閱する, to pass troops in review; review troops. ¶ 檢閱係, an inspector; an examiner; a censor. —檢閱使, an inspector. —檢閱濟, "passed inspection."

kengai (嶮崖, 懸崖), *n.* a cliff; a precipice.

kengaku (見學), *n.* study by inspection. —工場を見學する, to visit a factory for study; inspect a factory. ¶ 見學旅行, a tour of study.

kenganhō (檢眼法), *n.* 【醫】 ophthalmoscopy.

kengankyō (檢眼鏡), *n.* 【醫】 an ophthalmoscope.

kengen (建言), *n.* a proposition; a proposal; a suggestion. —建言する, to memorialize; propose; propound.

kengen (權限), *n.* 【法】 competency; competence; powers; authority. —權限內に於て, within the scope of authority. —權限を付與する, [*vt.*] to empower; authorize. —權限を越える, to exceed one's competence; act *ultra vires*.

kengi (建議), *n.* ❶ (申出) a proposal; a proposition; an overture. ❷ (建白) a memorial; a representation. **—-suru,** *v.* ❶ to propose; make a proposal. ❷ to memorialize; make a representation. —政府へ建議する, to make a representation to the government.

¶建議者, a proposer; a memorialist. —建議書, a memorial.

kengi (嫌疑), *n.* suspicion. —嫌疑を受ける, to come [fall] under suspicion. —嫌疑を招く, to incur suspicion. ¶嫌疑者, a suspect; a suspected person.

kengo (堅固な), *a.* ❶ (强固) steady; firm; rigid. ❷ (堅牢) strong; hardy; solid. ❸ (不拔) impregnable (難攻不落の); well-fortified. ❹ (健全) healthy; sound; strong; vigorous; of good health; robust; sturdy. —用心堅固な人, a most cautious man. —堅固な家屋, a substantial house; a house of substantial build. —堅固にする, ① to steady; season (錬る). ② to strengthen.

kengō (喧囂), *n.* noise; din; uproar (大騷).

kengu (賢愚), *n.* ❶ ability; wisdom. ❷ the wise and the foolish. —賢愚の差, difference in ability. —賢愚を問はず一様に, to all equally irrespective of their ability.

kengun (懸軍), *n.* a detached [flying] army.

kengyō (兼業), *n.* by-work; by-occupation; subsidiary business.

keṅi (權威), *n.* power; authority; influence (勢力); dignity (威嚴); an authority (泰斗). —學界の權威, an authority in science. —權威ある言葉, cathedral [authoritative] utterance.

keṅin (檢印), *n.* a stamp; an official seal of approval. ¶檢印濟, "approved and sealed."

keṅin (牽引する), *vt.* to pull; draw; drag (ひきずる). ¶牽引機, a tractor(-plane). —牽引力, tractive power; pulling power.

keṅizai (健胃劑), *n.* a stomachal; a stomachic; a peptic.

kenji (檢事), *n.* a procurator; a public prosecutor; a director of public prosecutions; a procurator-fiscal [蘇]; a district attorney [米]. ¶檢事長, a chief procurator (of a court of appeal). —檢事局, the procurator's office. —檢事正, a chief procurator of a local court. —檢事総長, the procurator-general; the attorney-general [英].

kenji (健兒), *n.* a spirited boy; a vigorous youth.

kenjin (賢人), *n.* a sage; a wise man; a philosopher (哲人).

kenjin (縣人), *n.* an inhabitant [a native] of a prefecture. ¶同縣人, a person from [native of] the same prefecture.

kenjitsu (堅實な), *a.* solid; steadfast; reliable. —堅實に, steadily; solidly; reliably. —堅實な會社, a substantial firm.

kenjō (謙讓), *n.* modesty; humility; diffidence.

kenjō (獻上する), *vt.* to present; make a present *of*; dedicate.

kenjū (拳銃), *n.* a pistol; a revolver (連發の).

kenjutsu (劍術), *n.* (the art of) fencing; fence; swordsmanship. —劍術の達人, a master of fence; a skilful fencer; a master swordsman.

kenka (堅果), *n.* 【植】 a nut.

kenka (喧嘩), *n.* ❶ (口論) a dispute; a quarrel; a squabble. ❷ (爭鬪) a fight; a scuffle; a struggle. —喧嘩好きの, quarrelsome. —喧嘩さす, to set (people) by the ears; set (dogs) fighting. —喧嘩する, ① to quarrel; dispute; squabble. ② to fight; scuffle; exchange blows (撲り合ふ). —喧嘩を仕かける, to pick a quarrel *with*; force [fit; fasten] a quarrel *upon*. —喧嘩を買ふ, to take up a quarrel. —喧嘩兩成敗, "When two quarrel, both are in the wrong."

kenka (鹼化する), *vt.* to saponify.

kenkai (見解), *n.* an opinion; a view. —余の見解を以てすれば, in my opinion.

kenkai (縣會), *n.* a prefectural assembly. ¶縣會議長, the president of a prefectural assembly. —縣會議員, a member of a prefectural assembly. —縣會議事堂, a prefectural assembly-hall.

kenkaku (懸隔), *n.* a difference; a disparity (位·年等); a gap; a gulf.

kenkan (兼官), *n.* an additional government post (兼ねてる官職).

kenkan (顯官), *n.* a high (government) official; a dignitary.

kenka-shokubutsu (顯花植物), *n.* 【植】 Phanerogamæ (學名); flowering plants.

kenken (拳拳), *ad.* respectfully; carefully; dutifully. —拳々服膺する, to bear carefully in mind.

kenketsu (欠缺), *n.* absence.

kenkin (兼勤), *n.* additional duties; holding an additional post. —校長を兼勤する, to hold the additional post of headmaster.

kenkin (獻金), *n.* contribution. ¶獻金者, a contributor.

kenko (眷顧), *n.* favour; patronage. —眷顧する, to favour; patronize. —眷顧に報いる, to return favours.

kenkō (軒昂), *ad.* rising high; toweringly; soaringly. —意氣軒昂たり, to be in high spirits.

kenkō (健康), *n.* health. —健康の, healthy; sound; well-conditioned. —健康が勝れぬ; 健康でない, to be in poor spirits; be out of health;

be unhealthy. —健康に適する, to suit one's health; be healthy; be salubrious. —健康を回復する, to recover one's health. —健康を祝する, to toast; drink (to) another's health. ¶ 健康狀態, healthy [health] condition. —健康診斷, health examination. —健康證明書, a certificate of health; a (clean) bill of health.

kenkō (權衡), *n.* ❶ (はかり) a balance; scales; a weighing beam. ❷ (釣合) balance; equilibrium; proportion. —權衡を取る, to balance. —權衡を失ふ, to lose balance.

kenkōkotsu (肩胛骨), *n.* the scapula; the shoulder-blade.

kenkoku (建國), *n.* the foundation [establishment] of a state.

kenkon (乾坤), *n.* ❶ (天地) heaven and earth; the universe (宇宙). ❷ (陰陽) positive and negative. —乾坤一擲の大賭博, a gamble for the throne.

kenkyaku (健脚), *n.* strong legs. —健脚な, sure-footed. ¶ 健脚家, a good walker; a pedestrian.

kenkyo (檢擧する), *vt.* to hunt up; take up; run in; take into custody.

kenkyō (檢鏡), *n.* microscopical examination.

kenkyō-fukai (牽强附會), *n.* sophistication; distortion. —牽强附會の, sophistic(-al); far-fetched. (牽强附會の說, forced view; sophistry.) —牽强附會する, to strain (the meaning or explanation of); force (an analogy); give a strained meaning *to*.

kenkyū (研究), *n.* study; researches (學術上の); investigation; inquiry. —數學の研究, study of mathematics. —研究する, [*vt.*] to study; investigate; inquire *into*; engage in researches. —研究に沒頭する, to be engrossed in researches [study]. —研究心に乏しい, to lack [be wanting in] the spirit of inquiry. ¶ 研究科, the post-graduate course; the seminar (大學等の). —研究科目, a (subject of; course of) study. —研究者, a student; an investigator. —研究室, a laboratory (實驗室). —研究所, a (research) laboratory; an investigation institute.

kenma-kokugeki (肩摩轂擊), *n.* jostling of men and vehicles.

kenmaku (權幕, 劍幕), *n.* a look; an attitude. —恐ろしい權幕で, with a threatening look [countenance].

kenmei (賢明), *n.* wisdom; intelligence; sagacity. —賢明な, wise; intelligent; sagacious.

kenmen (劵面), *n.* the face of a bill [note]. ¶ 劵面額, face value; par value.

kenmō (絹毛), *n.* silk and cotton. ¶ 絹毛交織物, silk-and-cotton cloth.

ken-mo-hororo (權もほろろの), *a.* curt; tart; snappish. —權もほろろの挨拶をする, to answer curtly; give a tart reply.

kenmon (權門), *n.* an influential [a powerful] family. —權門に媚びる, to truckle to men of influence.

kenmu (兼務), *n.* =*kenkin* (兼勤), *kennin* (兼任).

kennan (劍難の相), *n.* a physiognomy presaging danger by steel.

kennin (兼任), *n.* an additional post (兼ねた任務); holding an additional post (兼ねること).

kennin (堅忍-不拔), *n.* perseverance; fortitude. —堅忍不拔の, persevering; indomitable; indefatigable.

kennō (權能), *n.* 【法】competency; competence; power; authority. —權能を與へる, [*vt.*] to authorize; empower; enable.

kennō (獻納), *n.* presentation; contribution; offering. —獻納する, to offer; present; contribute. ¶ 獻納品, an offering; a present.

kennon (險呑な), *a.* dangerous; risky; hazardous.

kennyō (檢尿), *n.* uroscopy; examination of the urine.

kennyūki (檢乳器), *n.* a lactoscope; a lactometer.

ken'o (嫌惡), *n.* dislike; aversion; loathing. —嫌惡する, to hate; dislike; loathe.

ken'onki (檢溫器), *n.* a clinical thermometer.

kenpaki (檢波器), *n.* 【無電】a (wave-)detector.

kenpaku (建白), *n.* a memorial. —建白する, to address a memorial *to*; memorialize; present one's view *to*. ¶ 建白書, a memorial.

kenpei (兼併), *n.* annexation. —兼併する, to annex.

kenpei (憲兵), *n.* a gendarme; gendarmerie (全體); the military police. ¶ 憲兵司令部, the gendarmerie [military police] headquarters. —憲兵隊, the gendarmerie [military police] corps. —憲兵屯所, a gendarmerie [military police] station.

kenpei (權柄), *n.* power; authority. —權柄を振ふ, to wield power; domineer *over*; lord it *over*.

kenpen (權變), *n.* opportunism; trimming.

kenpitsu (健筆), *n.* ❶ a powerful pen; a ready pen. ❷ a skilful hand; skilful penmanship. —健筆

を揮ふ, to wield a powerful pen. ¶ 健筆家, a ready writer; a skilful penman.

kenpō (憲法), *n.* a constitution; constitutional law; organic law. —憲法の制定, establishment of a constitution. —憲法上の, constitutional. ¶ 憲法違犯, an unconstitutional act; an unconstitutionality. —憲法政治, constitutional government.

kenpō (縣報), *n.* a prefectural bulletin.

kenpon (獻本), *n.* a presentation copy. —獻本する, to present a copy.

kenponashi (枳椇), *n.* 【植】the Japanese raisin-tree.

kenpu (絹布), *n.* a silk fabric; silk stuff [tissues]. ¶ 絹布商, a mercer.

kenran (絢爛), *n.* gorgeousness; brilliancy; floweriness. —絢爛たる, gorgeous; brilliant; flowery.

kenren (眷戀する), *v.* to be attached *to*; yearn [long] *after*; stick [adhere; cling] *to* (執著).

kenri (權利), *n.* 【法】a right; a title; a privilege (特權). —他人の權利を蹂躙(侵害)する, to trample on (infringe; trespass on) another's rights. ¶ 權利者, an obligee; a claimant (請求權ある人).

kenritsu (縣立の), *a.* prefectural. ¶ 縣立學校, a prefectural school.

kenrō (堅牢), *n.* solidity; substantiality; stability. —品質の堅牢, the solidness of quality. —堅牢な, solid; substantial; stable.

kenryaku (權略), *n.* tactics; shrewdness.

kenryō (見料), *n.* a fee; charge for inspection. —貸本の見料, charge for reading a book.

kenryō (賢良), *n.* the wise and virtuous. —賢良を擧げる, to take the wise and virtuous into service.

kenryoku (權力), *n.* power; authority; sway. —權力の均衡を失ふ, to lose the balance of power.

kensa (檢査), *n.* inspection; examination; scrutiny (精査); audit (會計の). —檢査する, to inspect; examine; scrutinize; audit. ¶ 檢査官; 檢査人; 檢査役, an inspector; an examiner; an auditor. (度量衡檢査官, a surveyor of weights and measures.) —檢査濟, "examined."

kensai (賢才), *n.* a wise man; a man of ability.

kensaku (建策, 獻策), *n.* a suggestion; an advice. —建策する, to advise.

kensaku (檢索), *n.* search; an index (索引).

kensan (研鑽), *n.* study; prosecution of one's study. —研鑽する, to study; prosecute (one's study).

kensatsukan (檢察官), *n.* a public prosecutor [procurator].

kensei (牽制する), *vt.* ❶ (制止する) to check; hold in check; restrain. ❷ (誘致する) to divert. ¶ 牽制運動, diversion.

kensei (憲政), *n.* constitutional government; constitutionalism. ¶ 憲政黨, the constitutional party; the constitutionalists. —憲政擁護, the defence of constitution.

kensei (權勢), *n.* power; influence.

kensei-chōsa (縣勢調査), *n.* prefectural census-taking.

kenseki (譴責), *n.* reprimand; admonition; censure. —譴責する, to reprimand; admonish; censure.

kensetsu (建設), *n.* establishment; construction; erection. —建設する, to establish; found; construct; build; erect. ¶ 建設費, the cost of construction. —建設者, a constructor; a founder.

kensha (賢者), *n.* a wise man; a sage. —賢者は一語にして足る, *verbum* (*sat*) *sapienti* [羅. =a word (is enough) to the wise].

kensha (縣社), *n.* a prefectural shrine.

kenshi (犬齒), *n.* 【解】a canine tooth; a dog-tooth. ¶ 上(下)犬齒, an eye (stomach)-tooth.

kenshi (檢屍), *n.* an inquest; a post-mortem examination; autopsy. —檢屍する, to examine a corpse; hold an inquest *over*. ¶ 檢屍官, a coroner.

kenshi (繭絲), *n.* a silk-thread. ¶ 繭絲取引所, a silk exchange.

kenshiki (見識), *n.* ❶ (意見) an opinion; a view. ❷ (識見) knowledge; discernment. ❸ (氣位) airs. —見識ばる, to stand on one's dignity; give oneself airs. —見識がある, to have knowledge; be possessed of discernment. —見識が高い, to be far-sighted.

kenshin (檢診), *n.* medical examination.

kenshin (獻身的), *a.* self-sacrificing. —獻身的にやる, to devote oneself *to*. —獻身する, to consecrate oneself *to*; devote oneself *to*; sacrifice oneself *for*.

kenshitsuki (檢濕器), *n.* a hygrometer.

kenshō (肩章), *n.* a shoulder-strap [-knot]. ¶ 正服肩章, an epaulette.

kenshō (檢證), *n.* 【法】verification; evidence by inspection; inspection of locality.

kenshō (懸章), *n.* 【軍】a sash. ¶ 副官懸章, the adjutant's sash.

kenshō (懸賞), *n.* (事) a prize contest; offering a prize: (品) a prize; a reward. —懸賞する, to offer a prize [reward]. —懸賞で人

を探す, to search for a person by offering a reward. ¶ 懸賞募集(課題), an advertisement (a subject) for a prize contest. —懸賞金, a prize; stakes (特に競馬の); a purse. —懸賞論文, a prize-essay.

kenshuku (牽縮), *n.* retraction.

kenso (嶮岨, 険阻), *n.* ❶ (嶮崖) a steep; a precipice. ❷ (峻嶮) steepness; precipitousness. —険阻な, steep; precipitous; abrupt.

kensō (険相), *n.* a sinister look [appearance].

kensō (喧噪), *n.* clamour; tumult; uproar. —喧噪な, clamorous; tumultuous; uproarious. —喧噪を極める, to become extremely tumultuous; be in an uproar.

kensoku (検束), *n.* restraint; restriction; check. —検束する, to restrain; put under restraint; restrict; check. ¶ 検束者, a restrainer.

kenson (謙遜), *n.* modesty; diffidence; self-depreciation. —謙遜な, modest; diffident; self-depreciating. —謙遜する, to be modest [diffident]; depreciate oneself. —謙遜に過ぎる, to carry modesty to excess.

kensui (懸垂する), *v.* to hang; overhang.

ken-suru (検する), *vt.* to inspect; examine. ☞ *kensa* (検査する).

ken-suru (験する), *vt.* ❶ (試験) to try (良否·成分を); test (同上); examine. ❷ (経験する) to experience.

kentai (倦怠), *n.* weariness; fatigue; languor. —倦怠する, to become weary [fatigued; tired]; feel languid. —倦怠を覚える, to feel languor; feel dull.

kentai (兼帯), *n.* (兼用) the use of one thing for two or more purposes; (兼任) discharging the duties of two different offices at the same time. —洋傘と杖と兼帯になる, to serve as both an umbrella and a walking stick.

kentan (健啖), *n.* gluttony; voracity; gormandism. —健啖の, gluttonous; voracious; gourmand. ¶ 健啖家, a gormand; a glutton.

kentei (検定), *n.* ❶ official approval [sanction]; certification. ❷ (捕獲審検所の判決) judgment. ❸ =検定試験. —検定する, to give official approval *to*; certify. ¶ 文部省検定済, "approved by the Educational Department." —検定試験, an official qualification-examination. (教員検定試験委員, the (examining) committee for teachers' qualification-examination.)

kenten (圏點), *n.* a small circle for emphasis.

kentō (犬闘), *n.* a dog-fight.

kentō (見當), *n.* ❶ (狙ひ) aim; mark. ❷ (見込) expectation. ❸ (標準) a standard; the mark. ❹ (方角) a way; a direction. —二千圓見當で, at about [in the neighbourhood of] ¥ 2000; at 2000 *yen* or thereabouts. —見當をつける, ① (狙ふ) to take aim *at*. ② (見込む) to see one's way *to*. —見當を外れる, to miss the mark. ¶ 見當違ひ, irrelevancy; being wide of the mark.

kentō (拳闘), *n.* boxing; pugilism. —拳闘する, to box. ¶ 拳闘家, a boxer; a pugilist. —拳闘試合, a boxing-match; a spar.

kentō (健闘する), *vi.* to fight strenuously [with might and main].

kentsuku (劒突), *n.* scolding; rating. —劒突を食はせる, to scold; rate; blow up.

kenuki (鑷, 毛拔), *n.* hair-tweezers.

keṅyaku (儉約), *n.* economy; thrift; frugality. —儉約する, to economize; spare *of*; practise [use] economy. ¶ 儉約家, an economist; a thrifty person.

keṅyō (兼用する), *vt.* to use for double purposes; use for both... and.... ☞ *kentai.*

keṅyō (顕要の), *a.* prominent; distinguished; important. —顕要の地位を占める, to hold a prominent post; occupy an important position.

keṅyōsui (懸壅垂), *n.* 【醫】 the uvula.

kenzai (健在する), *vi.* to be in good [sound; excellent] health. —幸に健在なれ, May you be in good health!

kenzan (見參), *n.* interview; meeting. —見參する, to see; have an interview *with*. ¶ 初見參, the first interview.

kenzan (檢算する), *vt.* 【數】 to prove; test; check.

kenzen (健全), *n.* healthiness; sound health; wholesomeness.
—-na, *a.* healthy; sound; wholesome. —健全な讀物, wholesome reading. —健全な思想を涵養する, to foster healthy ideas.

kenzen (顯然), *ad.* evidently; manifestly; clearly.

kenzō (建造する), *vt.* to build; construct.

kenzoku (眷屬), *n.* a family; a household; belongings.

ken-zuru (獻ずる), *vt.* to present; offer; dedicate (神殿·著書等を); devote [consecrate] oneself *to* (身を).

keori (毛織-物), *n.* a woollen fabric; woollen cloth; woollen goods. —毛織の, woollen.

keotosu (蹴落す), *vt.* to kick down.

keppaku (潔白), *n.* purity; integrity; spotlessness. **——-na,** *a.* pure; spotless; stainless. —潔白な人, a man of spotless integrity; an incorruptible person (賄賂等の利かぬ人).

keppan (血判), *n.* sealing with (a clot of) blood; a seal of blood. —血判する, to seal with (a clot of one's) blood. (血判して誓ふ, to pledge with a seal of (one's) blood.)

keppeki (潔癖), *n.* a marked habit of cleanliness; fastidiousness. —潔癖な, dainty; fastidious.

keppyō (結氷する), *vi.* to freeze; be frozen.

kera (螻蛄), *n.* 【昆】 the African mole-cricket.

kera (啄木鳥), *n.* 【鳥】 the wood-pecker.

kerai (家來), *n.* a retainer; a follower; a servant. —家來にする, to take another into one's service.

keredo (けれど-も), *conj.* although; but; however.

keri (鳬), *n.* ❶【鳥】 the grey-headed wattled lapwing. ❷ (結末) end; close. —鳬がつく, to come to an end [a close]; come to a conclusion; be brought to an end.

keri (蹴), *n.* a kick.

kerihajime (蹴始), *n.* 【蹴毬】 kick-off.

kerite (蹴手), *n.* a kick; a kicker.

keru (蹴る), *v.* to kick; foot; spurn. —蹴り始める, to kick off (蹴毬戯). —蹴り返す, to kick back. —蹴り込む, to kick in. —埃を蹴立てる, to kick up a dust.

kesa (今朝), *n.* & *ad.* this morning.

kesa (袈裟), *n.* a scarf; a scapular; a stole. —袈裟掛けに斬る, to cut aslant in the shoulder.

keshi (罌粟), *n.* 【植】 the (opium; white) poppy. —罌粟粒ほどの大きさ, the size of a poppy-seed.

keshigomu (消護謨), *n.* an india-rubber; an eraser.

keshiin (消印), *n.* a (cancelling) stamp; a post-mark (郵便物の); a date-mark (同上). —消印をする, to cancel with a stamp.

keshikakeru (嗾ける), *vt.* to set on; egg on; instigate. —犬を嗾ける, to set on a dog; set a dog *at.*

keshikaranu (怪しからぬ), *a.* ❶ (奇怪) strange; extraordinary; absurd. ❷ (無禮) insolent; impudent; impertinent. ❸ (無法な) lawless; violent; outrageous. ❹ (猥りな) indecent; improper; unbecoming (ふさはしからぬ). —怪しからぬ噂, a scandalous rumour. —怪しからぬ奴, an insolent [impertinent; outrageous] fellow.

keshiki (氣色), *n.* ❶ (氣配) a sign; an indication; an appearance. ❷ (顏色) appearance; look; expression. —毫も恐るゝ氣色もなく, without showing the slightest sign of fear.

keshiki (景色), *n.* scenery (一地方の); a scene (眼前の); a view (眺望). —雄大な景色, magnificent [imposing] scenery.

keshin (化身), *n.* incarnation; personification; avatar. —惡魔の化身, the devil [fiend] incarnate.

keshitomeru (消止める), *vt.* to put out; put down; quench. —大事に至らぬ中に消し止める, to put out [extinguish] a fire before it becomes serious.

keshizumi (消炭), *n.* charcoal cinders.

keshō (化生), *n.* an apparition; a phantom; a spectre.

keshō (化粧), *n.* toilet; toilette; make-up. —化粧する, ① to make one's toilet; make up [劇]; dress; paint (紅粉で). ② to ornament; adorn. ¶ 厚化粧, heavy toilet; thick paint. —薄化粧, light toilet. —化粧部屋, a dressing [toilet]-room. —化粧臺, a toilet-table; a toilet-stand. —化粧品, toilet articles [goods]. —化粧廻し, an ornamental apron (角力の). —化粧石鹼, a toilet-soap.

kesō (懸想する), *v.* to fall in love *with*; lose one's heart *over.*

kessai (決濟する), *v.* to settle accounts; square accounts.

kessai (決裁), *n.* sanction; approval; decision. ¶ 決裁權, a casting-vote [-voice].

kessai (潔齋), *n.* purification; abstinence.

kessaku (傑作), *n.* a masterpiece; a master-work.

kessan (決算), *n.* settlement; settlement of accounts; settled accounts. —決算する, to settle an account [a bill]; balance an account. ¶ 決算日, a settling [settlement] day. —決算報告, a settled-account report. —決算表, a balance sheet. —決算期, a settlement term.

kessei (血清), *n.* 【醫】 the (blood-) serum. —血清注射, serum injection. —血清療法, serotherapy.

kesseki (結石), *n.* 【醫】 stone; concretion; calculus.

kesseki (缺席, 闕席), *n.* ❶ absence; non-attendance. ❷【法】 non-appearance; default. —缺席する, ① to be absent; absent oneself *from.* ② to default; make a default. ¶ 闕席判決, 【法】 judgment by default. —缺席屆, a notice of non-attendance [absence].

kessen (血栓), *n.* 【醫】 a thrombus [*pl.* -bi].

kessen (血戰する), *vi.* to fight desperately.

kessen (決戰), *n.* a decisive battle. —決戰する, to fight a decisive battle.

kessen(決選), *n.* a final election. ¶ 決選投票, a decisive [final] ballot; second ballot.

kessetsu (結節), *n.* nodulation; protuberance; 【解】 a tubercle; 【植】 a node.

kessha(結社), *n.* an association; a society; a guild.

kesshi (決死), *n.* braving [courting] death; desperation. —決死の覺悟で, prepared to die fighting. ¶ 決死隊, a forlorn hope.

kesshin (決心), *n.* resolution; determination; will. —決心する, to make up one's mind; resolve; determine. —決心を飜へす, to reconsider one's resolution; give up one's resolution.

kes-shiru (結しる), *vi.* to be constipated; be costive.

kesshite (決して), *ad.* (否定語と共に) never; by no means; on no account. —決して嘘を云ふな, Never tell a lie. —そんな事は決してない, There is no such (a) thing.

kessho (血書する), *vt.* to write in blood.

kesshō (決勝), *n.* the decision of a contest; a final (運動・競技の). ¶ 決勝線, the goal-line. —決勝戰, ① a final contest. ② a decisive battle. —決勝點, the goal; the winning post; the home.

kesshō (結晶), *n.* crystal [crystalline] structure; crystallization (作用); a crystal (物). —結晶する, to crystallize.

kesshoku (血色), *n.* the colour of the face; complexion. —血色が惡い, to look unwell [sallow]. —血色が好く(惡く)なる, to gain (lose) colour. —血色の勝れぬ, wan; pale; sallow.

kesshutsu (傑出する), *vi.* to excel; be pre-eminent; surpass others.

kessō (血相), **kissō** (氣相), *n.* a look; countenance. —血相を變へる, to change (one's) countenance; change colour.

kessoku (結束), *n.* ❶ (括る) tying up; binding up. ❷ (團結) combination; union. —結束する, ① to bind up; tie. ② to unite; combine. ¶ 結束品[具], bindings.

kesson (缺損), *n.* ❶ (不足) shortage; deficit; default. ❷ (毀損) damage; injury. —缺損する, ① to be short (in number or quantity). ② to damage; injure. —缺損になる, to be short (不足する); result in a loss (損失に終る); suffer a loss *of*; amount to a loss *of*. ¶ 缺損額, shortage.

kes-suru(決する), *vt.* ❶(決定) to decide; resolve; determine. ❷ (判定) to decide; judge; find (陪審官が). ❸ (決壞) to break down. —, *vi.* ❶ to determine *on*; fix *on*; settle *on*; come to a decision; be decided (勝敗等). ❷ (陪審官が) to find. ❸ (決潰) to give way. —雌雄を決する, to decide a contest. —訴訟を決する, to judge [decide] a case.

kesu(消す), *vt.* ❶ (火·燈火等を) to put out; extinguish; quench. ❷ (文字などを) (*a*) (拭ひ消す) to erase; rub out; wipe out: (*b*) (刪除, 抹消) to strike out [off]; cancel; cross out [off]. ❸ (毒などを) to counteract (解毒劑が); 【化】 neutralize (酸性·毒性等を). —燈火を消す, to put out a light. —棒を引いて消す, to score off [out]; cross out [off]; strike out [off]. —消し難き印象を殘す, to leave a permanent impression *upon*.

kēsu (活字盤), *n.* 【印】 a case.

keta (桁), *n.* ❶ (橋又は家の) a cross-beam; a girder. ❷ (船の) a yard. ❸ (十露盤の) a reed of an abacus. —橋の桁, a bridge-girder. —一桁間違へる, to mistake the unit [place].

ketai(懈怠), *n.* =*kaitai*.

ketaosu (蹴倒す), *vt.* to kick down.

ketatamashii (けたたましい), *a.* ❶ (騷々しい) noisy; clamorous; wild. ❷ (慌しい) flurried; confused; agitated. —けたゝましい音をさせる, to make a great noise.

ketchaku (決著, 結著), *n.* settlement; end; conclusion. —決著をつける, to settle; bring to a conclusion [an end].

ketchō(結腸), *n.* 【解】 the colon.

ketobasu (蹴飛す), *vt.* to kick away.

ketsu (穴), *n.* ❶ =*ana* (穴). ❷ =*shiri*(尻).

ketsu (決), *n.* decision. —決を採る, to take the decision; divide.

ketsu (闕), *n.* ❶ (缺けること) deficiency; shortage; defect. ❷ (宮城) the Imperial palace.

ketsuatsu (血壓), *n.* blood pressure. ¶ 血壓計, a hemadynamometer.

ketsuban (缺番), *n.* a missing number (番號落ち); a vacant number (明き番).

ketsubetsu (訣別), *n.* ❶ (別離) parting; separation. ❷ (告別) leave-taking; farewell. —訣別する, to part [separate] *from*; bid farewell; take leave *of*.

ketsubi(結尾), *n.* the conclusion;

the end; the finis (本の).

ketsubō (缺乏), *n.* ❶ (皆無) want; lack; absence. ❷ (不足) deficiency; shortage; scarcity. —資金の缺乏, shortness of fund; scarcity of capital. —缺乏する, to lack; be short *of*; run short *of* [low; out]. —缺乏に應する, to meet a want. —缺乏を來す, to cause a shortage.

ketsubun (結文), *n.* ❶ an epilogue. ❷ (手紙の) complimentary close; terminal salutation.

ketsubun(闕文), *n.* a lacuna; a hiatus.

ketsubutsu (傑物), *n.* an extraordinary character; a master spirit [mind].

ketsudan (決斷), *n.* decision; determination; resolution. —決斷する, to decide; determine. —決斷力のある人, a man of decision; a man of high resolve.

ketsueki(血液), *n.* blood. —血液の循環をよくする, to stimulate the circulation of blood. —血液を淨化する, to purify the blood.

ketsuen (血緣), *n.* kinship; ties of blood. ☞ ***ketsuzoku.***

ketsugi (決議), *n.* a resolution; a decision. —總會の決議, a resolution of a general meeting. —決議する, to resolve; decide. —決議案を提出する, to move a resolution.

ketsugō (結合), *n.* union; combination; conjunction. —結合する, ① [*vi.*] to combine [unite] *with*; join together; incorporate *into*. ② [*vt.*] to combine [unite]; connect; weld; consolidate; cement; join. ¶ (加減)結合器,【電】a (vario-) coupler.

ketsugyokuzui (血玉髓), *n.* 【鑛】heliotrope.

ketsui (決意), *n.* resolution; determination. ☞ ***kesshin.***

ketsuin (缺員), *n.* a vacancy; a vacant post [office]. —缺員を生ずる, to cause a vacancy. —缺員を補ふ, to fill a vacancy.

ketsumaku (結膜), *n.* 【解】the conjunctiva. ¶ 結膜炎,【醫】conjunctivitis. (顆粒狀結膜炎, granular conjunctivitis; trachoma.)

ketsumatsu (結末), *n.* ❶ (終末) a conclusion; a termination. ❷ (結果) a result; consequence; an outcome. ❸ (大團圓) a catastrophe; *denouement* 【佛】. —結末の, final. —結末をつける, to bring to a conclusion [an end].

ketsumazuku (蹴躓く), *vi.* to stumble; trip. ☞ ***tsumazuku.***

ketsumyaku (血脈), *n.* ❶ (血管) a blood vessel. ❷ (血統) a family line; lineage; consanguinity.

ketsunyō (血尿), *n.* 【醫】red urine. ¶ 血尿病, hematuria.

ketsuon (血溫), *n.* blood-heat.

ketsurei (缺禮), *n.* breach of etiquette; neglect [failure; omission] to pay one's compliments [to offer one's greetings].

ketsuretsu (決裂), *n.* rupture. —決裂する, to rupture; break down. ¶ 決裂點, breaking point.

ketsuro (血路), *n.* a way cut through the enemy's ranks. —血路を求める (切り開く), to find (carve out) a way through (the enemy's ranks).

ketsuron (結論), *n.* 【論】conclusion; judgment. —結論する, to conclude. —結論に達する, to come to a conclusion; arrive at a conclusion.

ketsuroten (結露點), *n.* the dew-point.

ketsurui(血涙), *n.* tears of blood; bitter tears.

ketsuryō (缺量), *n.* 【商】ullage.

ketsuryō (結了する), *v.* to finish; conclude; terminate.

ketsuzei (血稅), *n.* blood-tax.

ketsuzen (決然), *ad.* in a determined manner; firmly. —決然たる, determined (attitude; look).

ketsuzoku (血族), *n.* a blood-relation; a blood-relative; a kinsman (a kinswoman); kinsfolk. ¶ 血族關係, blood-connection; blood-relationship. —血族結婚, consanguineous marriage.

kettai (結滯), *n.* pause (脈搏の).

kettaku (結託), *n.* conspiracy. —結託する, to conspire *with*. —結託して, in conspiracy [league] *with*.

kettan (血痰), *n.* blood phlegm.

kettei (決定), *n.* decision; conclusion; settlement. —決定的勝利, a decisive victory. **——·suru**, *vt.* to determine; decide; resolve; conclude; fix (價·日時·場所を); mark out (方針を). **——**, *vi.* to come [be brought] to a conclusion. —日を決定する, to settle the day; fix the date. ¶ 決定書, a written decision.

ketteishiki (結締織), *n.* 【解】a connective tissue.

ketten (缺點), *n.* ❶ (弱點) a weak point; a weakness; a failing. ❷ (瑕疵) a flaw; a defect; a blemish. —缺點を見出す, to pick holes *in*.

ketto (毛布), *n.* a blanket.

kettō (血統), *n.* lineage; descent; a family-line.

kettō(決答), *n.* a definite answer; a decisive reply.

kettō (決鬪), *n.* a duel; a single combat. —決鬪する, to duel; fight a duel. —決鬪を申込む, to challenge a person to a duel; cast

[fling] (out) the glove [gauntlet].
kettō (結黨する), *vi.* to form [organize] a party.
keu (稀有の), *a.* rare; uncommon; unusual.
keura (毛裏), *n.* fur lining. —毛裏の外套, a fur-lined overcoat.
kewashii (險・嶮しい), *a.* steep; precipitous; abrupt. —嶮しい崖, an abrupt cliff. —嶮しい小山, a steep hill.
keyaki (欅), *n.* 【植】 Zelkowa serrata (zelkowa-tree の一種・學名).
kezuru (削る), *vt.* ❶ (刃物で) to shave (鉋で); plane (同上); sharpen (尖らす). ❷ (刪除) to strike out; erase; expunge. ❸ (減らす) to curtail; cut down; retrench. ❹ (取上げる) to confiscate.
ki (木), *n.* a tree (樹木); wood (木材); (wooden) clappers (拍子木). —木の股, a fork of a tree. —木から落ちた猿, a fish out of water. —木の繁ッた山, a woody hill. —木で作る, to make of wood. —木に竹を接ぐ, to sew the fox's skin to the lion's.
ki (生の), *a.* raw; undiluted; unmixed. —生一方の人, a simple-minded man. —生で賣る, to sell pure [undiluted]
ki (季), *n.* ❶ (季節) a season. ❷ (年少) the youngest. —銃獵季に入る, to enter the shooting season.
ki (忌), *n.* ❶ = **mo** (喪). ❷ (年忌) an anniversary of a death; a death-day.
ki (奇), *n.* ❶ (珍奇) curiousness; oddity. ❷ (不思議) strangeness; wondrousness. ❸ (奇數) an odd number. —奇なる, curious; strange; queer. —奇を好む, to be fond of curious things.
ki (騎), *n.* (騎兵の略) a horseman; cavalry (總稱).
ki (記), *n.* ❶ an account; a narrative; a record. ❷ (記念) memory.
ki (軌), *n.* ❶ (軌間) gauge. ❷ (軌條) a rail. ❸ (轍) a rut; a wheel-track. ❹ (軌範) a norm; a standard.
ki (氣), *n.* ❶ (精神) spirit; soul; mind. ❷ (氣質) temper; disposition; turn of mind. ❸ (氣分) mood; humour; frame of mind. ❹ (感情) feelings; sentiment; susceptibilities. ❺ (意向) an inclination; a bent; a desire; an intention. ❻ (注意) care; heed; attention. ❼ (呼吸) breath. ❽ (氣體) (*a*) (精氣) ether: (*b*) (空氣) air; atmosphere: (*c*) (蒸發氣) vapour; exhalation. —氣が狂ふ, to become mad; go off one's head 【俗】. —氣が違ッて居る, to be of unsound mind; be out of one's mind [senses]. —氣がふれる, to go mad. —氣が塞ぐ, to have the blues; be gloomy; be in the blues [dumps]; be depressed in spirits. —氣が詰まる, ① [*v.*] to be suffocated; be choked. ② [*a.*] fusty; suffocating; choking. —氣が進む, [*a.*] willing. —氣がつく, ☞ ***kigatsuku***. —氣が利いた, ☞ ***kigakiita***. —氣が濟まぬ, to be ill at ease. —氣が遠くなる, to feel faint; faint. —氣が咎める, to feel uneasy at heart; feel compunction; suffer from self-reproach. —氣が向いた時に, when one feels inclined. —(する)氣がある, to have inclination *for*. —(する)氣がない, to be in no mood (for a thing; to do). —氣に障る, to offend; displease; hurt other's feelings; offend another's susceptibilities. —氣に入る, ☞ ***kiniiru***. —氣にする, ☞ ***kinisuru***. —氣にかける, ☞ ***kinikakeru***. —氣になる, ☞ ***kininaru***. —氣の無い, ☞ ***kinonai***. —氣の拔けた, ☞ ***kinonuketa***. —氣の強い, plucky; stout-hearted. —氣の長い, good-tempered; patient; deliberate (悠長). —氣の荒い男, a man of rough temper. —氣の小さい男, a chicken-hearted fellow. —氣を廻す, to grow suspicious. —氣を揉む, to bother [worry] oneself *about*; fret (oneself). —氣を取り直す, to recover oneself. —氣を失ふ, to faint away; swoon. —氣を落ち著ける, to collect one's wits; calm [compose] oneself. —氣を落す, to be cast down; lose one's spirits [heart]; be dispirited [disheartened]. —氣を惡くする, to take in bad part; take exception *to*. —氣を散する [晴らす], to divert [distract] one's mind from care; divert oneself. —氣を利かせる, to take the hint. —氣をゆるす, to relax attention. —勉强に氣を取られる, to be engrossed in study. —やる氣なら, if one means to do it. —氣をしッかり持て, Keep up your spirits. —それで氣が濟んだ, That lifts a weight off my mind.
ki (期), *n.* ❶ (時代) a period; an age; an epoch. ❷ (期間) a term; a period. ❸ (定時) an appointed hour; a fixed time. ❹ (段階) a stage. ❺ (時期) season (季節); time. —期を定める, to fix the term. —期をあやまる, to miss the opportunity; be at a wrong time; be inopportune.
ki (黄), *n.* yellow.
ki (機), *n.* ❶ (機會) an opportunity; a chance; an occasion. ❷ (機械) a machine (又飛行機); an apparatus (器械); an engine (機關).

—機に乗ずる, to take occasion; seize [take advantage of] an opportunity. —機に臨みて, upon [on] occasion; when occasion comes. —機の到るを待つ, to wait for a favourable opportunity; bide one's time. —機を得たる(得ざる), opportune (inopportune); in (out of) season. —機を逸する, to miss an opportunity [a chance].

ki (器), *n.* ❶ (器具) a utensil; a tool; an apparatus. ❷ (器量) capacity; ability.

kiai (木藍), *n.* 【植】 the dyer's indigo-plant.

kiai (氣合), *n.* ❶ (氣持) feelings; disposition (性質); temper (同上). ❷ (呼吸) breath. ❸ (掛聲) a shout; a yell. —氣合の面白い人, a man of pleasant disposition. ¶ 氣合術, art of mesmerizing by will-power.

kiatsu (氣壓), *n.* atmospheric pressure. ¶ 氣壓計, a barometer; a manometer. —氣壓低下,【氣象】 depression.

kiawasu (來合はす), *vi.* to come by chance; happen to come.

kiba (牙), *n.* a fang (特に犬及び狼の); a tusk (象·海象(せいうち)等の); a canine tooth (犬齒).

kiba (木場), *n.* a timber-yard.

kiba (騎馬), *n.* equitation; horse-riding. —騎馬で行く, to go on horseback. ¶ 騎馬行列, a cavalcade. —騎馬巡査, the mounted police; a mounted policeman. —騎馬旅行, a journey on horseback.

kibachi (黃蜂), *n.* 【昆】 the Japanese tailed-wasp.

kibamu (黃ばむ), *vi.* to be tinged with yellow. —黃ばんだ木の葉, yellowish leaves.

kibarashi (氣晴し), *n.* distraction; diversion; recreation; relaxation. —氣晴しになる, to serve as a diversion. —氣晴しする, to recreate oneself; divert oneself.

kibaru (氣張る), *v.* ❶ (いきむ) to strain oneself. ❷ (*a*) (努力) to exert oneself [one's powers]: (*b*) (はずむ) to treat oneself *to*. ❸ (見榮張る) to make a display.

kibasami (木鋏), *n.* a trimmer; (a pair of) pruning-shears.

kibashiri (木走), *n.* 【鳥】 the (common) creeper.

kibatsu (奇拔な), *a.* original; extraordinary. —奇拔な思ひ附, an original idea.

kibaya (氣早な), *a.* hasty; impetuous; quick-tempered.

kiben (詭辯), *n.* sophistry; sophism. —詭辯を弄する, to sophisticate; quibble. ¶ 詭辯家, a sophist; a quibbler.

kibi (黍), *n.* 【植】 the (true) millet.

kibi (機微), *n.* secrets; inner working. —人心の機微に立入る, to dive into the secrets of the human heart.

kibi (驥尾に附す), *v.* to play second fiddle; follow the lead.

kibikibi (きびきびした), *a.* smart; spirited; vigorous.

kibin (機敏な), *a.* ❶ smart; shrewd; quick-witted. ❷ (迅速な) quick; prompt; ready. —機敏に, ① smartly. ② quickly; promptly.

kibiru (生麥酒), *n.* draught beer; beer on draught.

kibishii (嚴·酷しい), *a.* severe. ❶ (嚴重) strict; rigid; stern. ❷ (峻烈) harsh; bitter; sharp. —嚴しい寒さ, severe [intense; bitter] cold. —嚴しく, severely; strictly; rigidly, sternly. (門の出入を嚴しくする, to be strict in letting people pass through the gate.)

kibisho (急須), *n.* a small teapot.

kibisu (踵), *n.* the heel. —踵を接して, in the wake *of*; in rapid succession (續々). —踵を回す, to turn on one's heels; turn back; retrace one's steps. —踵を翹(ア)げて待つ, to be on the tiptoe of expectation.

kibo (規模), *n.* scale (仕掛); a plan (設計). —大(小)規模に, in large (little); on a large (small) scale. —規模を擴張する, to enlarge the plan.

kibō (希望, 冀望), *n.* a hope. ❶ (期望) a prospect; an expectation. ❷ (願望) a desire; intention. —多年の希望, a long-cherished desire. —一縷の希望, a gleam [ray] of hope. —希望する, ① to hope; expect; look forward *to*. ② to desire; wish. —希望に副ふ, to meet [come up to] one's expectation. —希望通りに行く, to proceed [go on] as one expected. —希望を懷く, to cherish [entertain] a hope [desire]. —希望を棄てる, to give up one's hope. —希望を達する, to get [realize] one's wish. —希望が全く絶えた, All hope is gone.

Kibōhō (喜望峯), *n.* the Cape of Good Hope. ¶ 喜望峯植民地, the Cape Colony.

kibone (氣骨), *n.* care; anxiety; mental strain. —氣骨が折れる, to be a great strain on one's mind.

kibori (木彫), *n.* wood-carving.

kibuku (忌服), *n.* mourning.

kibun (奇聞), *n.* a strange news.

kibun (氣分), *n.* ❶ (健康狀態) state of health. ❷ (情調) mood; humour; atmosphere (雰圍氣). ❸ (感情) feelings; sentiment 〔俗〕.

❸ =*kishitsu.* —氣分が惡るい, to feel bad [ill; unwell]; feel out of sorts; be off colour. —氣分が變だ, I don't feel myself.

kiburushi (著古し), *n.* ☞ *kifurushi.*

kibutsu (奇物), *n.* a curiosity (物); an oddity (人・物など); an odd character (人).

kibutsu (器物), *n.* a vessel (容器); a utensil (器具); furniture.

kichaku (歸著), *n.* ❶ (歸來) arrival; return; coming back. ❷ (歸結) conclusion; result; consequence. —歸著する, ① to arrive *at*; return; come back. ② to reach [arrive at; come to] a conclusion; end [result] *in.* —同じ事に歸著する, to come to the same thing in the issue [in the end; after all].

kichi (吉), *n.* fortune; good luck.

kichi (危地), *n.* ❶ (危險) peril; danger; hazard. ❷ (危き地位) a dangerous condition [position]. ❸ (危險な土地) a dangerous place. —危地に陷る, to fall into danger. —危地に出入する, to pass through dangers. —危地を脫する, to find one's way out of danger; get out of danger.

kichi (旣知の), *n.* known; already-known. ¶ 旣知數, 【數】 a known quantity.

kichi (機智), *n.* wit; acumen; resource. —機智に富む, to possess great acumen; be resourceful.

kichigai (氣違, 狂), *n.* ❶ (狂氣, 狂者) (*a*) madness; insanity; lunacy: (*b*) a lunatic; a madman; an insane [crazy] person. ❷ (熱狂, 熱狂家) (*a*) mania: (*b*) a fanatic; an enthusiast; a maniac. —純然たる氣違, stark madness. —氣違ひになる, =*ki*(氣が狂ふ). —氣狂ひの樣に騷ぐ, to rave about like a madman. ¶ 芝居狂, an inveterate playgoer. —野球狂, a baseball fan. —氣違ひ雨(天氣), fitful [capricious] rain (weather).

kichinichi (吉日), *n.* a lucky [an auspicious] day; a red-letter day.

kichinto (きちんと), *ad.* accurately; precisely; exactly. ☞ *kakkiri, kitchiri.* —きちんとした, trim; neat; tidy. —きちんと合ふ, to fit like a glove; fit to a nicety; suit to a T. —きちんと時間を守る, to be punctual to the minute.

kichinyado (木賃宿), *n.* a doss-house.

kichirei (吉例), *n.* an auspicious custom. ¶ 吉例歲暮大賣出し, the customary year-end sale.

kichō (記帳), *n.* ❶ (直接記入) register. ❷ (轉記) posting. —記帳する, to enter in an account-book; enter [post] accounts.

kichō (基調), *n.* the key-note.

kichō (貴重な), *a.* precious; valuable; costly. —貴重する, to treasure; value; prize. ¶ 貴重品, valuables.

kchō (歸朝する), *vi.* to come home; return [come back] to Japan. ¶ 歸朝者, one lately returned to Japan.

kichōmen (几帳面な), *a.* regular; precise; punctilious. —几帳面な男, a precise man.

kichū (忌中), *n.* mourning. —忌中に付, being in mourning.

kidai (稀代の), *a.* rare. ☞ *kitai.*

kidan (奇談), *n.* a strange story; an interesting incident.

kidate (氣立), *n.* disposition; temper; spirit. —氣立てのよい, well-conditioned; well-natured; tender-hearted.

kiden (起電機), *n.* an electric machine.

kido (木戶), *n.* ❶ (小門) a wicket. ❷ (城戶) a gate. ❸ (興行物の入口) an entrance. ❹ =木戶錢. —木戶御免である, to have free entrance (at the theatre). ¶ 木戶番, a door-keeper. —木戶札, an admission ticket. —木戶口, a gate-way; a door-way. —木戶錢, an admission fee; gate-money; door-money.

kido (喜怒), *n.* joy and anger; feelings.

kidō (軌道), *n.* ❶ (天體の) an orbit. ❷ (鐵道の) a track; a line (of rails). ❸ =*jōki* (常規). —軌道を布設する, to lay a line. ¶ 軌道車, a tramway-car; a tram.

kidō (氣道), *n.* 【解】 the respiratory tract.

kidō-enshū (機動演習), *n.* manœuvres.

kidoku (奇特), *n.* ❶ (殊勝) praiseworthiness; laudability. ❷ 【佛】(靈現) efficacy; special grace. —奇特な, ① praiseworthy; laudable. ② (信心深い) devout; pious.

kidoru (氣取る), *v.* ❶ (容態ぶる) to give oneself [assume; put on] airs; strike an attitude; attitudinize; mince. ❷ (樣子をまねる) to affect; play. —氣取ッた, affected; perky; mincing. (いやに取氣ッた女學生, a school-girl of very affected manners.) —役者を氣取る, to assume [put on] the airs of an actor.

kie (歸依する), *v.* to become a believer *in*; be converted *to.* —基督敎に歸依する, to embrace [be converted to] Christianity.

kiei (氣銳の), *a.* spirited; vigorous. —年少氣銳の徒, young and spirited fellows; spirited young bloods.

kiei (歸營する), *vi.* to return [go back] to barracks. ¶ 歸營喇叭, 【軍】 retreat.

kien (奇緣), *n.* irony of fate; a strange affinity [relation].

kien (氣焰), *n.* big words; a tall [big] talk. —氣焰が昂らぬ, to be in low spirits. —氣焰を吐く, to talk big.

kiensan (稀鹽酸), *n.* 【化】 diluted hydrochloric acid.

kieru (消える), *vi.* ❶ (火・灯などの) to go out; burn (itself) out (燃え切る); be blown out (吹消さる). ❷ (雪などの) to melt away; thaw; disappear. ❸ (噂などの) to die out; fall away; blow over. ❹ (字などの) to be worn out. ❺ (影・姿・形などの) to vanish; disappear. ❻ (泡などの) to burst; break. —消え殘る雪, the snow remaining unthawed. —消えかゝる, to be on the point of disappearing; be going out (燈が). —消えてなくなる, to vanish into the void [air]; fade away to nothing. —徐々に消える, to swoon (音樂など); die away (音響など); burn low [down] (火が). —雲の中に消え去る, to disappear into the cloud.

kietsu (喜悅), *n.* joy; gladness; delight.

kifu (寄附), *n.* ❶ contribution; donation; subscription. ❷ (奉納) offering; dedication. —寄附を乞ふ, to ask for a contribution. —及ばずながらも應分の寄附をする, to contribute what little one can. **—-suru**, *vt.* ❶ to contribute *to*; subscribe *to*; donate; endow. ❷ to offer; dedicate. —鳥居を寄附する, to dedicate a shrine-gate. —十磅を慈善事業に寄附する, to contribute £10 to a charity. ¶ 寄附金, a contribution; a donation; a subscription. (寄附金を勸誘する, to canvass for contributions.) —寄附者, a contributor; a subscriber.

kifu (碁布する), *vi.* to lie scattered about.

kifū (氣風), *n.* disposition; tone; atmosphere.

kifujin (貴婦人), *n.* a lady; a gentlewoman; a dame. —貴婦人らしい, ladylike; gentlewomanly; gentlewomanlike. ¶ 貴婦人團, a ladies' association.

kifuku (起伏), *n.* undulation; ruggedness; ups and downs (道路等の). —起伏する, ① [*v.*] to undulate; stand high and low; rise and fall. ② [*a.*] undulating; rugged; rolling (原野などの).

kifuku (歸服), *n.* submission; surrender; obedience. —歸服する, to submit; surrender; yield; obey.

kifurushi (著古し), *n.* old [worn-out] clothes. —著古す, to wear out. —著古した, worn-out; old; shabby.

kiga (饑餓), *n.* hunger; starvation. —饑餓に迫って, under the pressure of hunger; goaded by hunger.

kigae (著替), *n.* a spare suit of clothes; a change of clothes.

kigai (危害), *n.* injury; harm. —人に危害を加へる, to injure [hurt] another. ¶ 危害品, dangerous goods.

kigai (氣槪), *n.* spirits; mettle; a firm mind. —氣槪のある人, a man of mettle; a man of firm mind.

kigakari (氣懸り), *n.* suspense; auxiety; concern. —氣懸りになる, to lie heavy on one's mind (事が); feel anxious [uneasy] *about*.

kigake (來掛に), *ad.* on coming; on the way hither. —來掛けに寄った, I have called on my way.

kigakiita (氣が利いた), *a.* smart; sensible; quick-witted. —氣が利いた人, a smart person; a man of sense; a sensible man. —氣が利かぬ奴, a dull-witted fellow.

kigaku (器樂), *n.* instrumental music.

kigan (祈願), *n.* prayer; supplication; invocation. —祈願する, to invoke; pray; supplicate. —…に祈願を籠める, to make supplications *to*. ¶ 祈願者, a suppliant.

kigane (氣兼), *n.* constraint; scruple. —氣兼せぬ, unconstrained; unreserved. —氣兼する, to feel constraint; be afraid of giving trouble; stand on scruple.

kigaru (氣輕), *n.* light-heartedness; ease; buoyancy. —氣輕な, light-hearted; cheerful; buoyant.

kigatsuku (氣が附く), *v.* ❶ (正氣づく) to recover one's senses; come to oneself. ❷ (さとる) to become aware *of*; notice; perceive. ❸ (用意周到) to be attentive; be prudent. —よく氣がつく人, a very tactful man.

kigawari (氣變り), *n.* whimsicality; flightiness; fickleness. —氣變りする, to change one's mind; divert one's mind.

kigeki (喜劇), *n.* a comedy. —一場の喜劇を演ずる, to act a comic scene. ¶ 樂喜劇, a musical comedy. —小喜劇, a comedietta. —喜劇女優, a comedienne. —喜劇役者, a comedian.

kigen (紀元), *n.* ❶ an emergent year. ❷ an era; an epoch. —神武紀元二千五百八十六年卽ち西暦一千九百二十六年, the 2586th year after the Accession of the Emperor Jimmu, that is to say, 1926th year of the Christian Era.

—西暦紀元前, B. C. (=Before Christ); A. C. [羅 *Ante Christum*]. —西暦紀元後, A. D. [羅 *Anno Domini.* =in the year of our Lord]. —一新紀元を開く事件, an epoch-making event.

kigen (起原), *n.* the origin; the rise; the beginning. —起原する, to derive its origin *from*; originate *in*; take rise *in*. —起原を探る, to look for [search] the origin.

kigen (期限), *n.* ❶【法】(期日) time. ❷ (期間) a term; a period. —期限内に, within a fixed term. —期限を經過すると, when the term expires. ¶ 有效期限, the term of validity.

kigen (機嫌), *n.* ❶ (氣持) humour; spirits; mood; temper. ❷ (起居) state of health. —機嫌よく, good-humouredly; well; in good part; in good humour. —機嫌を取る, to pay court *to*; flatter; humour; soothe (宥める). —機嫌を損ふ, ① (他人の) to give umbrage; hurt the feelings *of*; give offence. ② (自分が) to take umbrage *at*; take offence. —御機嫌を伺ふ, to pay one's respects *to*; ask [inquire] after another's health. —御機嫌よう, (別辭) good-bye; farewell; *adieu*; *bon voyage* [佛]. —御機嫌は如何です, How do you find yourself?; How do you do?

Kigensetsu (紀元節), *n.* the Anniversary of the Accession of the Emperor Jimmu.

kigi (機宜), *n.* an occasion; an opportunity; a chance. —機宜を得ざる, untimely; inopportune. —機宜の處置を取る, to act as the occasion may require; take measures according to circumstances.

kigō (記號), *n.* a sign; a symbol; 【音】 notation.

kigō (揮毫), *n.* (書の) writing: (繪の) painting; drawing.

kigokoro (氣心), *n.* character; disposition. ☞ *kishitsu.* —氣心の知れた (知れぬ), of known (unknown) disposition.

kigokochi (著心地), *n.* the feeling of a dress. —著心地のよい著物, a comfortable dress.

kigomi (氣込), *n.* =*ikigomi.*

kigu (危惧), *n.* apprehension; dread; fear. —危惧する, to dread; apprehend; fear. —危惧の念を抱く, to entertain apprehensions.

kigu (器具), *n.* utensils; things; an implement; a tool (道具).

kigū (奇遇), *n.* an unexpected meeting; a strange connection.

kigū (寄寓), *n.* lodging; sojourn. —寄寓する, to lodge; live *with*; sojourn.

kigurai (氣位), *n.* self-conceit; vanity. —氣位の高い, proud; vain; self-conceited.

kigusuri (生藥), *n.* a drug. ¶ 生藥屋, (人) a druggist: (店) a drug-shop; a druggist's (shop).

kiguya (木具屋), *n.* a dealer in wooden ware.

kigyō (企業), *n.* an enterprise; an undertaking. ¶ 企業家, an entrepreneur; an enterpriser. —企業組合, a syndicate. —企業心, the spirit of enterprise.

kigyō (起業), *n.* flotation; promotion. —起業する, to start an enterprise; embark in [enter on] an enterprise. ¶ 起業公債, an industrial loan.

kigyō (機業), *n.* textile industry. ¶ 機業家, a textile manufacturer.

kihai (氣配), *n.* ❶ =*kikubari.* ❷【商】tone. —市場の氣配, the tone of the market.

kihaku (稀薄な), *a.* ❶ (薄弱な) rare; weak; dilute. ❷ (稀少な) thin; sparse. —稀薄な空氣, thin air; rarefied air. —人口稀薄の地, a thinly [sparsely] populated district. —稀薄にする, to rarefy; weaken; dilute.

kihan (軌範), *n.* a model; an example; a standard.

kihan (羈絆), *n.* fetters; bonds; shackles. —の羈絆を脫する, to shake off the yoke *of*.

kihatsu (揮發), *n.* volatilization. —揮發する, to volatilize. ¶ 揮發油, a volatile oil; an essential oil; naphtha (揮發石油).

kihei (奇兵), *n.* a strategic detachment; troops detailed for special service; a surprise force.

kihei (騎兵), *n.* a horseman; a cavalryman; a trooper; cavalry (總稱). ¶ 騎兵銃, a carbine. —騎兵監, a cavalry inspector.

kiheki (奇癖), *n.* eccentricity; an eccentric habit; a kink. ¶ 奇癖家, an eccentric (person); a character.

kihi (忌避), *n.* ❶ (徵兵の) evasion. ❷ (裁判上の) challenge; refusal. **—— -suru**, *vt.* to evade; challenge; refuse; take exception *against* [*to*]. —陪審員を忌避する, to challenge a juror. —判事を忌避する, to refuse a judge.

kihin (氣品), *n.* tone; dignity. —氣品のある, dignified. —國民の氣品を高める, to raise the tone of the nation.

kihin (貴賓), *n.* an honoured guest. ¶ 貴賓席, seats reserved for special guests.

kihiroi (木拾ひ), *n.* a faggot-gatherer.

kihō (季報), *n.* a quarterly report.

kihō (氣泡), *n.* a bead; a bubble (硝子等の); a blowhole (鑄物の).
kihō (既報の), *a.* already reported. —既報の如く, as already reported.
kihōheitai (騎砲兵隊), *n.* horse artillery.
kihon (基本), *n.* a foundation; a basis; standard (基準). ¶ 基本金, a fund; a foundation(-fund). —基本單位, a standard [fundamental] unit. —基本財產, fundamental property.
kii (奇異), *n.* peculiarity; oddity; strangeness. —奇異な, strange; odd; singular.
kiichigo (木莓), *n.* 【植】 the raspberry.
kiin (氣韻), *n.* spirit. —氣韻ある, (人·美術品等につき) spirited. —氣韻の高い, of high spirit.
kiin (基因する), *v.* to issue *from*; be owing *to*; originate *in*.
kiiro (黄色), *n.* yellow. —黄色い, yellow. (黄色い聲を出す, to speak in a shrill voice.)
kiishibai (生石灰), *n.* quicklime.
kiito (生絲), *n.* raw silk. ¶ 生絲檢查所, a silk conditioning-house [office]. —生絲組合, the raw silk merchants' association; the raw silk guild. —生絲商, a raw-silk merchant.
kiitsu, kiichi, (歸一), *n.* unification. —歸一する, to unify.
kiji (雉), *n.* 【鳥】 the Japanese green pheasant; the pheasant [俗]. —雉の草隱れ, the ostrich policy.
kiji (木地, 生地), *n.* ❶ (木理) the grain (of wood). ❷ (素地) plain wood (塗らぬ); ground (面); body (陶器等の). —生地の, plain; unvarnished.
kiji (記事), *n.* ❶ (記述) description. ❷ (記載事項) a paragraph; an article; an account. ¶ 社會記事, social [sensational] news. —新聞記事, a newspaper account [paragraph]. —記事文, a descriptive composition.
kijibato (雉鳩), *n.* 【鳥】 the (eastern) turtle-dove.
kijiku (機軸), *n.* ❶ (機械の中軸) an axle; an axis. ❷ (工夫) a plan; a method; a device. ☞ *shinkijiku.*
kijin (奇人), *n.* ❶ (かはり者) an odd [a strange] person; an original; an eccentric (person). ❷ (非凡な人) an extraordinary man.
kijin (貴人), *n.* a dignitary; a man of (exalted) station; a person of rank.
kijin-no-urei (杞人の憂), *n.* =*kiyū* (杞憂).
kijitsu (奇日), *n.* an odd day.
kijitsu (期日), *n.* a fixed date; an appointed day; a due date.
kijo (鬼女), *n.* a demoness; a she-devil.
kijo (貴女), *n.* a lady; a dame; a gentlewoman. ——, *pron.* you.
kijō (机上の), *a.* academical; impracticable; paper. —机上の空論, an academical argument [discussion]. ¶ 机上問題, a problematic question.
kijō (氣丈の), *a.* firm; resolute; stout-hearted.
kijūki (起重機), *n.* a crane; a jack; a derrick.
kijun (歸順する), *v.* to submit; renew allegiance *to*.
kijutsu (奇術), *n.* prestidigitation; jugglery; curious tricks [feats]. —奇術を行ふ, to juggle. ¶ 奇術師, a juggler.
kijutsu (記述), *n.* description; an account. —記述的, descriptive. —記述する, to describe; give an account *of*.
kika (奇禍), *n.* a calamity; an accident. —奇禍に遭ふ, to meet with a calamity.
kika (奇貨), *n.* a rarity (奇品); a good opportunity (好機). —(を)奇貨として, seizing [taking] the advantage *of*.
kika (氣化), *n.* 【化】 vaporization; gasification. —氣化する, to vaporize; gasify. ¶ 氣化器, a carburetter.
kika (稀化), *n.* attenuation.
kika (幾何-學), *n.* geometry.
kika (麾下, 旗下), *n.* (troops under) one's command. —麾下の, under one's command. —旗下に加はる, to enlist under the standard *of*.
kika (歸化), *n.* naturalization. —日本に歸化する, to be naturalized in Japan. ¶ 歸化人, a naturalized subject [citizen]. (歸化日本人(日本へ歸化せる人), a naturalized Japanese.)
kika (歸嫁する), *v.* ❶ to marry. ❷ (轉嫁) to attribute *to*; impute *to*.
kikaeru (著更へる), *v.* to change one's clothes [things].
kikageki (喜歌劇), *n.* a comic opera.
kikai (奇怪な), *a.* ❶ (不思議な) strange; mysterious; singular. ❷ (けしからぬ) insolent; impudent; outrageous.
kikai (氣界), *n.* the atmosphere.
kikai (器械), *n.* an instrument; an apparatus; a tool (道具); an implement (同上) —器械的, instrumental. ¶ 器械體操, heavy gymnastics.
kikai (機械), *n.* machinery (機械類); a machine; an engine (機關). —時計の機械, the works of a watch. —機械的, mechanical; automatic. —機械的に, mechanically; automatically. (機械的に職務を執る, to perform one's duties in a mechanical fashion.) —機械を据附ける, to fit up [set up; install]

machinery. ¶ 機械油, machine-oil. —機械場, a mill; a factory; a machine-room; an engine-room (機關室). —機械學, mechanics. —機械工學, mechanical engineering. —機械工場, a machine-shop. —機械師, a mechanist; a mechanician.

kikai (機會), *n.* an opportunity; a chance; an occasion. —機會を捉へる, to seize an opportunity. —機會のあり次第, on the first occasion; on the earliest possible opportunity. ¶ 機會均等主義, the principle of equal opportunity.

kikaku (規格), *n.* a gauge, gage.

kikan (奇觀), *n.* a wonder; a singular spectacle; a wonderful sight. —奇觀を呈する, to present a wonderful sight.

kikan (軌間), *n.* Ⓢ 軌幅. (railway) gauge.

kikan (氣管), *n.* the windpipe; the trachea [*pl.* -cheæ].

kikan (汽管), *n.* a steam-pipe.

kikan (汽罐), *n.* a (steam-)boiler.

kikan (飢寒), *n.* hunger and cold. —飢寒を忍ぶ, to endure [stand] hunger and cold.

kikan (期間), *n.* a term; a period. —期間の經過 [滿了], expiration of a term. ¶ 法定期間, a (stated) period fixed by law.

kikan (旗艦), *n.* a flagship.

kikan (器官, 機官), *n.* an organ.

kikan (機關), *n.* ❶ (機械) an engine; a machine. ❷ (手段的に設置せられるもの) an organ; a machine (政治組織などの); means (交通などの). ¶ 海軍機關少將, an engineer rear-admiral. —海軍機關學校, the Naval Engineering College. —機關兵, a stoker〔英〕; a fireman〔米〕. —機關兵曹, an engine-room artificer. —機關銃, a machine-gun; a maxim gun. —機關官,【海】a naval engineer; an engineer officer. —機關車, an engine; a locomotive (engine). —機關士, an engineer. —機關新聞, an organ (paper). —機關室, an engine-room. —機關手, an engine-driver〔英〕; an engineer〔米〕; an engine-runner; an engine-man.

kikan (龜鑑), *n.* a mirror; a pattern; a paragon.

kikanshi (氣管支), *n.* bronchus [*pl.* -chi; -chia]; bronchial tubes. ¶ 氣管支炎,【醫】bronchitis. —氣管支肺炎, bronchopneumonia. —氣管支加答兒, bronchial catarrh.

kikasu (利かす), *vt.* to wield; exert; sway. —氣を利かす, to have one's wit about one; act with tact; take the office.

kikasu (聞かす), *v.* ❶ (知らす) to explain; inform a person *of*; let another know *of*. ❷ (承知さす) to make a person agree; persuade (another).

kikatsu (飢渴), *n.* hunger and thirst. —飢渴を醫する, to satisfy one's hunger and thirst.

kikei (奇計), *n.* a cunning plan; an ingenious scheme.

kikei (奇警な), *a.* ❶ epigrammatic; pointed; shrewd. ❷ (奇拔な) original.

kikei (畸形), *n.* monstrosity; malformation; deformity. ¶ 畸形兒, a malformed child; a monstrosity.

kiken (危險), *n.* danger; peril; risk. —前途に横はる危險, breakers ahead. —危險を冒す, to run a risk [the risk]; face a danger. (如何なる危險を冒しても, at all hazards; at any risk.) **—-na,** *a.* dangerous; perilous; risky. —危險な生活, a precarious life. ¶ 危險物, dangerous goods. —危險事業, a dangerous [hazardous] enterprise. —危險人物, a dangerous character. —危險區域, a danger-zone. —危險思想, dangerous thoughts.

kiken (貴顯), *n.* a man of rank [position]; a dignitary; a (high) personage.

kiken (棄權), *n.*【法】waiver; quitclaim; abstention (投票權放棄). —棄權する, ① to waive [abandon; relinquish] a right. ② to waive one's right to vote; refrain [abstain] from voting. ¶ 棄權者, a releasor【法】; an absentee (缺席による).

kiketsu (既決の), *a.* already decided; settled; convicted (罪の). ¶ 既決事項, a matter settled. —既決囚, a convict; a convicted prisoner.

kiketsu (歸結), *n.* result; conclusion; end. —歸結する, to conclude; end; come to a conclusion.

kiki (危機), *n.* a crisis; a critical moment. —危機一髮の際に, at a critical moment. —危機一髮の所で助かる, to have a narrow escape; escape by a hair's breadth [by the skin of one's teeth]. —危機に瀕す, to reach a critical point.

kiki (毀棄), *n.* destruction; demolition; damage. —毀棄する, to demolish; destroy; damage.

kiki (歸期), *n.* the time of return.

kiki (きーきー), *n.* squeak; squeal; creak. —キーキーいふ, to squeal; squeak; creak.

kikiakiru (聞飽きる), *vi.* to be tired [sick] of hearing.

kikiawase (聞合せ), *n.* reference; inquiry. —聞き合せる, to inquire *about*; refer *to*; make inquiries *about.* ☞ *toiawaseru.*

kikichigai (聞違ひ), *n.* mishearing; hearing incorrectly. —聞き違へる, to mishear; make a mistake in hearing.

kikidasu (聞出す), *v.* to hear; find out; get wind of. —人から聞き出す, to pump [get] (something) out of a person (消息など).

kikigaki (聞書), *n.* a note taken down from another's lips.

kikigurushii (聞苦しい), *a.* disagreeable to hear; offensive to the ear. —聞き苦しい事を話す, to talk of disagreeable things.

kikiireru (聽入れる), *vt.* ❶ (聽許) to grant; hear; answer (祈願を); assent *to*; comply *with*. ❷ (聽從) to listen *to*; follow; obey; accept. —いくら忠告しても聽き入れぬ, He was deaf to all advice.

kikikajiru (聞嚙る), *vt.* to get a smattering *of*; catch a part *of*.

kikikomu (聞込む), *v.* to hear; come to [reach] one's ears; come to one's knowledge.

kikime (利目, 效驗), *n.* virtue; effect; efficacy. —利目のある, efficacious; effective. —利目が少ない, to be of little effect.

kikimorasu (聞洩らす), *v.* to miss hearing; escape one's ears; fail to hear.

kikin (基金), *n.* a fund.

kikin (饑饉), *n.* famine; scarcity; dearth. ¶ 饑饉地, a famine-stricken district. —饑饉年, a famine year; a lean year. —饑饉救濟資金, a famine relief fund.

kikinagasu (聞流す), *vt.* ❶ to take no notice *of*; give no attention *to*. ❷ to pass over [by] in silence.

kikinaosu (聞直す), *vt.* to inquire [ask] again.

kikinareru (聞慣れる), *v.* to become used to hearing; be accustomed to hear.

kikinikui (聞惡い), *a.* ❶ (容易に耳に入らぬ) difficult [hard] to hear. ❷ =*kikigurushii.*

kikinokosu (聞殘す), *vt.* to leave unheard. —肝心の點を聞き殘す, to leave an important point unheard.

kikinzoku (稀金屬), *n.* 【化】 a rare metal.

kikinzoku (貴金屬), *n.* the precious metals; the noble metals.

kikioboeru (聞覺える), *v.* to learn by ear [hearing].

kikiotosu (聞落す), *vt.* to miss hearing; fail to hear; omit to hear.

kikisokonau (聞損ふ), *vt.* ❶ (聞落す) to fail to hear; lose; miss. ❷ (聞誤る) to misapprehend; hear incorrectly; mishear.

kikisute (聞棄てにする), *vt.* to pass over [by] (in silence); pass unnoticed. —聞棄てにならぬ, not to be passed over.

kikitadasu (聞質す), *vt.* to inquire; ascertain. —料簡を聞き質す, to ascertain another's intention.

kikitagaru (聞きたがる), *vi.* to be inquisitive; be curious to hear.

kikitodokeru (聞屆ける), *vt.* to grant; entertain; hear.

kikitogameru (聞咎める), *vt.* to reprove; bear in mind.

kikitoreru (聞蕩れる), *vt.* to be fascinated *by*; be charmed *by*; be absorbed [lost] *in*.

kikitoru (聞取る), *vt.* to hear; catch. —聞き取れない, inaudible.

kikitsukeru (聞附ける), *v.* ❶ (聞き出す) to hear; overhear; get wind *of*. ❷ (聞き知る) to catch (a voice; a sound). ❸ =*kikinareru.*

kikitsutae (聞傳へ), *n.* hearsay; second-hand news (受賣り話). ☞ *iitsutae.* —聞き傳へる, to hear from others; know by hearsay; hear at second hand.

kikiwake (聞分), *n.* ❶ (理解力) understanding. ❷ (道理に耳を傾けること) listening to reason. —聞分けのない, wilful; stubborn; pig-headed; unreasonable; unamenable to reason. —聞き分ける, to understand; listen *to*. (道理を聞き分ける, to listen to reason.)

kikka (菊花), *n.* the chrysanthemum. ¶ 菊花大綬章, the Grand Cordon of the Chrysanthemum. —菊花章頸飾, the Collar of the Chrysanthemum.

kikkake (切掛), *n.* ❶ (合圖) a sign; a signal. ❷ (初頭) the beginning. ❸ (機會) an opportunity; a chance.

kikkari (きッかり), *ad.* exactly; just; sharp. —きッかり六時に, at six o'clock sharp. —きッかり十人, just [exactly] ten men. —きッかりと合ふ, to fit a person to a T.

kikkō (拮抗する), *vt.* to rival; match; equal. —に拮抗するものなし, to have no equal [rival] *in*; be without a rival *in*; be matchless [peerless] *in*.

kikkō (龜甲), *n.* a tortoise-shell; a carapace.

kikkyo (拮据する), *vi.* to toil hard; labour diligently; work assiduously.

kikkyō (吉凶), *n.* fortune; good or ill luck. —吉凶を占ふ, to tell (another's) fortune.

kikkyō (喫驚), *n.* surprise; amazement. ☞ *bikkuri.*

kikō (奇功), *n.* singular success; miraculous success. —奇功を收め

る, to win [gain] singular success.

kikō (奇效), *n.* a remarkable [marvellous] efficacy. —奇效を奏する, to show remarkable efficacy.

kikō (奇行), *n.* strange conduct; eccentricity. ¶ 奇行家, an eccentric.

kikō (寄港する), *v.* to call [touch] at a port; put in at a port. ¶ 寄港地, a port of call.

kikō (寄稿), *n.* contribution; a contribution (稿). —寄稿する, to contribute *to*; write *for*. ¶ 寄稿家, a contributor.

kikō (紀行), *n.* an account of travels. ¶ 紀行文, narrative style.

kikō (起工), *n.* setting to work; commencement of a work. —起工する, to set to work; start a work. ¶ 起工式, the commencement ceremony (of a work); the turning of the first sod (土木事業の); the laying of the foundation-stone (建築工事の).

kikō (氣孔), *n.* a pore; a breathing-pore.

kikō (氣候, 季候), *n.* climate; weather (天候); season (季節). —氣候になれる, to season to a climate; get [become] acclimated (人); become acclimatized (動植物). ¶ 氣候病, an endemic; a climatic disease.

kikō (歸向), **kikyō** (歸嚮), *n.* trend; tendency. —歸向する, to trend toward [in the direction *of*]; incline *to*.

kikō (歸航), *n.* the homeward [return] voyage. —歸航する, to make a homeward voyage; be homeward bound.

kikoe (聞え), *n.* fame; reputation; publicity (周知).

kikoeru (聞える), *vi.* ❶ to hear; be able to hear; be audible. ❷ (理に叶ふ) to be reasonable. ❸ (名高し) to be well-known; be celebrated; be noted *for*. ❹ (響く) to sound. ❺ (解る) to understand; see. —耳に聞える, to meet the ear. —(呼べば)聞える所[距離]に, within call [cry; hearing].

kikoku (枳殻), *n.* 【植】=*karatachi.*

kikoku (歸國), *n.* home-coming; return to one's country; return from abroad (歸朝). —賜暇歸國中, at home on furlough. —歸國する, to return home; come home; return from abroad (歸朝する).

kikon (氣根), *n.* ❶【植】an aerial root. ❷ (根氣) energy.

kikon (既婚の), *a.* married. ¶ 既婚者, a married person.

kikori (樵夫), *n.* a woodman; a woodcuttr.

kikōshi (貴公子), *n.* a young noble [prince].

kikoshimesu (聞召す), *vt.* ❶ (聞く) to hear; learn. ❷ (飲む) to drink; (食ふ) eat.

kikotsu (氣骨), *n.* spirit; mettle. ☞ *kigai* (氣概). —氣骨ある, spirited; mettled. —稜々たる氣骨, an unbending spirit.

kiku (菊), *n.* 【植】the (common) garden chrysanthemum. —菊の紋, a chrysanthemum crest. —十六瓣の菊, the sixteen-petalled chrysanthemum.

kiku (利く), *v.* ❶ (奏效) to be efficacious [effective] (藥が); be good *for* (同上); act [operate; work] *upon* (同上). ❷ (徹へる) to tell *on*; affect. ❸ (鍵・制動機などが) to act. —眼が利く, to be far-sighted; have a keen insight (眼識がある). —鼻が(よく)利く, to have a keen [fine] sense of smell. —毒はすぐ利く, A poison works immediately. —釘が利かぬ, The nail doesn't catch.

kiku (規矩), *n.* ❶(文廻しと差金) compasses and a rule. ❷ (標準, 規則) a norm; a criterion; a standard.

kiku (崎嶇たる), *a.* rugged; steep; precipitous.

kiku (聞・聽く), *v.* ❶ 〔聞〕 to hear (音・話などを); hear *of* (事柄・事情などを); learn (聞知する). ❷ 〔聽〕 (*a*) (傾聽) to listen *to*; hearken *to*: (*b*) (聽許) to grant; entertain; accede *to*: (*c*) (聽從) to listen *to* (忠告・道理など); follow (忠告など). ❸ 〔尋〕 to ask; inquire *about*; question. —聽き得べき距離内(外), within (out of) earshot; within (out of) hearing. —聞く所によれば, I hear (that); we learn (that); from what I hear. —親の意見も聽かずに, in defiance [in spite] of his father's remonstrance. —彼はよく言ふことを聽く, He always does as I tell him.

kikuban (菊版), *n.* (an) octavo.

kikubari (氣配), *n.* care. —氣配りで氣疲れがする, to become worn out with cares.

kikuimushi (木喰蟲), *n.* 【昆】the wood-eater; the wood-borer.

kikuitadaki (菊戴), *n.* 【鳥】the golden-crested wren; the gold-crest.

kikurage (木耳), *n.* 【植】the Jew's ears; Judas's ear.

kikyaku (棄却する), *vt.* ❶ to abandon; renounce; give up. ❷ 【法】to reject; dismiss.

kikyo (起居), *n.* getting along. —起居を共にする, to eat off the same trencher; live under the same roof; live in the same house (*with*).

kikyō (桔梗), *n.* 【植】the Chinese

bell-flower. ¶ 桔梗色, dark violet.

kikyō (奇矯の), *a.* odd; eccentric.

kikyō (歸京する), *vi.* to return to the capital; be back in Tōkyō.

kikyō (歸鄕する), *vi.* to return to one's native province; go (come; return) home.

kikyoku (歸極), *n.* polarization.

kikyū (企及する), *v.* to attain; be equal.

kikyū (危急), *n.* emergency; crisis; an imminent danger. —危急存亡の秋, a time of emergency; a critical time. —危急の場合, in case of emergency; in the hour of period. —危急を告げる, ① (危急を報ずる) to give [raise] alarm. ② (危險に瀕する) to be in imminent danger; be at a crisis.

kikyū (氣球), *n.* a balloon. ¶ 自由氣球, a free balloon. —測風氣球, a pilot-balloon. —氣球家, an aeronaut; a balloonist. —氣球隊, a balloon corps.

kikyū (歸休する), *v.* to be released before expiration of term of service.

kimae (氣前), *n.* ❶ (氣風) disposition; turn of mind; personality (人格). ❷ (金錢などを惜氣もなく出す風) generosity; liberality. —氣前がよい, to have an open hand; be free with one's money.

kimagure (氣紛れ), *n.* whim; fancy; caprice. —氣紛れな天氣, capricious [fitful] weather. —ほんの氣紛れから, out of mere freak. ¶ 氣紛れ者, a whimsical [capricious] person; a crank.

kimai (期米), *n.* time-bargain rice; rice for future delivery. ¶ 期米相場, rice-option quotation.

kimakase (氣任せに), *ad.* at one's pleasure; as one pleases [chooses]. —氣任せにさせて置く, to let a person take his own course [do as he pleases].

kimama (氣儘), *n.* wilfulness; unrestrainedness; waywardness. —氣儘な, wilful; unrestrained; wayward. —氣儘に, wilfully; unrestrainedly; at will. —氣儘をする, to behave as one pleases. ¶ 氣儘者, a wilful person.

kiman (欺瞞), *n.* trickery; deception. —欺瞞する, to deceive; cheat; defraud; beguile. ¶ 欺瞞術, 【軍】 camouflage.

kiman-menjo (期滿免除), *n.* prescription of penalties. —期滿免除になる, to be barred by prescription.

kimari (極り), *n.* ❶ (取極め) settlement; arrangement; agreement. ❷ (終局) conclusion; end. ❸ (秩序) order; regularity. ❹ (規則) rule; regulation; formula (方式). ❺ (習慣) convention; custom. —極りが惡い, to feel ashamed [awkward]; be abashed; be embarrassed. —極りのない, untidy; slovenly. —極りのよい, (整然たる) neat; trim; tidy. —極りをつける, to settle; bring to a conclusion. ¶ 極り文句, an old expression; a set phrase.

kimaru (極る), *v.* to be settled; be decided; arrive at an agreement. —極ッた業がない, to have no regular occupation; have no fixed work. —極りきッた仕事をする, to do the same old work; do routine work. —極りきッた道を行く, to go the same old [beaten] path.

kimawari (きまはり), *n.* 【鳥】 [the nuthatch.]

kimazui (氣不味い), *a.* disagreeable; unpleasant.

kime (極), *n.* agreement (約定); arrangement (取極め); rule (規定). —時間極め賃銀, time wages.

kime (木目), *n.* grain (木・皮膚・石等の); texture (肌理). —きめの粗い(細かい)肌, a rough (fine) skin.

kimei (記名), *n.* signature; putting down one's name. —記名式の, registered. **——-suru**, *vi.* to sign (one's name); subscribe (one's name); put down one's name. —記名調印する, to sign and seal. ¶ 記名株券, a name-share; a registered share. —記名公債證書, registered [inscribed] public loan bonds. —記名投票, open ballot. (記名投票する, to vote by open ballot.)

kimeru (極める), *vt.* to decide; settle; fix. —腹を極める, to settle one's mind.

kimi (君), *n.* ❶ (君主) a ruler; a sovereign. ❷ (主君) a master; a lord. **——**, *pron.* (貴君) you. —君に忠を盡す, to serve one's lord faithfully. —君, 君, も少し靜かにし給へ, I say, be a little more quiet.

kimi (黄味), *n.* ❶ a yellow tint. ❷ (卵黄) the yolk (of an egg). —黄味を帶びた, yellowish; yellow-tinted.

kimi (氣味 -合), *n.* ❶ (心持) feeling; sensation. ❷ a touch; a spice; a flavour. —少しく肺病の氣味, a slight touch of consumption. —氣味の惡い音, a weird [an unearthly] sound. —氣味の惡い笑, an uncanny laugh. —氣味が惡い, to make one feel nervous; give one a feeling of eeriness. —氣味がよい, to feel easy [comfortable]; be pleasant. —氣味惡く思ふ, to have a vague feeling of uneasiness; have a feeling of eeriness. —高慢の氣味がある, to have a spice of arrogance. —好い氣味だ, Serve you right!

kimigayo (君が代), *n.* the national anthem of Japan; the *Kimigayo*. —君が代は千代に八千代にさゞれ石の巖となりて苔のむすまで, May our Sovereign reign for thousands of ages until pebbles become rocks overgrown with moss.

kimijika (氣短な), *a.* ❶ (せッかちな) impetuous; hasty. ❷ (怒りッぽい) short-tempered; quick-tempered; testy.

kimitsu (機密), *n.* secrecy; a secret. —政治の機密に參與する, to take part in the important affairs of the government. ¶ 機密費, secret-service money [fund]. —機密漏洩, divulgation of a secret.

kimo (肝, 膽), *n.* ❶ (肝臟) the liver; the gall-bladder (膽嚢); gall. ❷ (度胸) courage; spirit; pluck (豪膽). —肝に銘する, to fix deeply in one's mind; print on one's memory [mind]. —膽を冷す, to make one's blood run cold; make one's flesh creep. —膽を潰す, to be amazed; be struck all of a heap; be frightened out of one's wits [senses].

kimochi (氣持), *n.* ❶ (感じ) feeling; sensation. ❷ (氣分) mood; humour; frame of mind. —氣持がよい, to feel comfortable (安樂な); feel well (病人などが); feel refreshed (氣が晴々する). —氣持のよい, comfortable; snug; pleasant. —氣持を惡くする, ① (自分が) to feel hurt; take offence; take in bad part. ② (人の) to make one feel sick. —氣持を直して下さい, Please be yourself again.

kimodama (肝魂), *n.* courage; spirit; pluck (豪膽).

kimoiri (肝煎), *n.* ❶ (周旋者) an assistant; an agent. ❷ (會社等の) a manager; a director. ❸ (斡旋) good offices; assistance; mediation (仲裁).

kimon (鬼門), *n.* ❶ (艮(うしとら)) the north-eastern direction. ❷ (忌み恐れる方角) an unlucky quarter.

kimono (著物), *n.* *kimono* 〔日〕; clothes; dress; clothing (衣類). —著物を著る(著てゐる), to put on (wear) clothes. —僕は著物を濡らした, I got my things wet.

kimusume (生娘), *n.* a maiden; a virgin; a maid.

kimuzukashii (氣むづかしい), *a.* ❶ (機嫌の取りにくい) hard to please; squeamish; queasy. ❷ (擇り好みして) fastidious; particular. —氣むづかしい顔をして, with a sour look.

kimyaku (氣脈), *n.* connection. —氣脈を通じて, in concert *with*. —互に氣脈を通じる, to establish communication *between*.

kimyō (奇妙な), *a.* ❶ (妙な) curious; singular; odd. ❷ (不思議な) wonderful; marvellous. —奇妙な事もあるものだ, Wonders will never cease.

kin (斤), *n.* a catty 〔支〕; a pound 〔英〕 (lb. と略す, 約百二十匁); a *kin* 〔日〕.

kin (金), *n.* ❶ gold. ❷ (金錢) money. —二十二金, gold 22 carats fine. —十八金の時計, a watch of eighteen-carat gold.

kin (筋), *n.* a muscle.

kin (禁), *n.* ❶ (禁令) a (government) prohibition; an interdict. ❷ (つゝしみ) self-restraint. —禁を犯す, to violate [contravene] the interdict.

kina (規那), *n.* quinine. ¶ 規那丁幾, tincture of quinine. —規那皮, cinchona bark.

kinaga (氣長な), *a.* slow; deliberate; leisurely. —氣長な人, a slow-coach. —氣長に待つ, to wait with patience.

kinako (黄粉), *n.* bean-flour.

kinakusai (焦臭い), *v.* ❶ to smell of burnt paper (cloth). ❷ to burn (子供の隠れん坊戯・ごみかくし戯等にて).

kinan (危難), *n.* danger; peril; an accident (災難). —危難を避ける, to avoid danger; keep out of danger.

kinatsu (禁遏する), *vt.* to prohibit; prevent.

kinba (金齒), *n.* a gold-plugged tooth; a gold-covered tooth. —金齒を入れる, to plug with gold.

kinbae (金蠅), *n.* 【昆】 the green-bottle-fly.

kinban (勤番), *n.* being on duty; one's turn for duty.

kinbato (金鳩), *n.* 【鳥】 the green-winged dove.

kinben (勤勉), *n.* diligence; industry; application. —勤勉な, diligent; industrious; hard-working. ¶ 勤勉家, a hard worker.

kinbo (欽慕する), *vt.* to admire; adore; esteem highly; have a high [sincere] regard *for*.

kinbō (近傍), *n.* the neighbourhood; the vicinity; the environs. —近傍の, neighbouring; adjacent.

kinbuchi (金緣), *n.* gilt edges (of a book); gold rims; a gilt frame. —金緣の眼鏡, gold(-rimmed) spectacles. —金線の本, a gilt-edged book.

kinbyōbu (金屛風), *n.* a gold-foiled [-leafed] screen.

kinchaku (巾著), *n.* a purse; a money-bag; a money-pouch. ¶巾著切, a pickpocket; a pickpurse; a cutpurse.

kinchaku (近著の), *a.* new; recently received; to hand. —近著の外字新聞に依れば, according to foreign newspapers to hand.

kinchisan (禁治產), *n.* 【法】 incompetence. ¶禁治產者, an incompetent person.

kinchō (緊張), *n.* strain; tension; tightness. —現代生活の緊張, the strain of modern life. —緊張の頂點に達する, to be strained to the breaking point. **——-suru**, *v.* to strain; stretch; tighten. —精神を緊張する, to strain one's mind.

kinchō (謹聽する), *vt.* to listen *to*; listen with attention; listen [hear] attentively. —謹聽!謹聽!, hear! hear! —謹聽して居る, to be all ears [all attention].

kinchoku (謹直な), *a.* sober; conscientious; scrupulous. —謹直に勤める, to do one's duty conscientiously [scrupulously].

kinda (勤惰), *n.* diligence and idleness; diligence. ¶勤惰表, an attendance-book; a roll(軍隊等の).

kindai (近代), *n.* modern age. —近代的, modern. ¶近代人, a modern (man). —近代史, a modern history. —近代思想, modernism; modern thought.

kindaka (金高), *n.* an amount [a sum] of money; a sum.

kindei (金泥), *n.* gold paint.

kindo (襟度), *n.* capacity; largeness of mind; magnanimity. —大國民の襟度を示す, to show the magnanimity of a great nation.

kindoku (菌毒), *n.* mushroom-poison.

kine (杵), *n.* a pestle; a pounder. —杵で搗く, to pestle.

kinema (キネマ), *n.* cinema. ¶キネマカラー, cinema-colour.

kinen (祈念), *n.* prayer; supplication; invocation. —祈念する, to pray *to*; supplicate; invoke.

kinen (記念), *n.* commemoration; remembrance; memory. —記念する, to commemorate. —記念の爲め; 記念に, in commemoration *of*. (記念の爲め保存する, to keep in remembrance [as a memorial] *of*.) —記念碑を建てる, to raise a monument. —記念祭を擧行する, to keep [celebrate] an anniversary. ¶記念日, an anniversary; the memorial [commemoration] day. —記念物, ① a souvenir; a remembrancer; a memento. ②(形見) a keepsake; a token (交友等の). —記念館, a memorial hall.

kinen (禁煙), *n.* prohibition of smoking. ¶禁煙家, an anti-tobacconist. —禁煙室, (汽車の) a no-smoking compartment.

kinensai (祈念祭), *n.* a fête for praying for an abundant harvest.

kinezumi (木鼠, 栗鼠), *n.* the squirrel. =***risu.***

kinga (謹賀), *n.* congratulations; felicitations. —謹賀新年, (with best wishes for [I wish you]) a happy New Year.

kingaisen (菫外線), *n.* Ⓢ 紫外線. 【理】 an ultra-violet ray.

kingaku (金額), *n.* an amount [sum] of money; a sum.

kingami (金紙), *n.* gold-coloured paper.

kingan (近眼), *n.* myopia; near-sightedness; short sight; short-sightedness. ¶近眼鏡, spectacles for a short-sighted person; concave spectacles. —近眼者, a short-sighted person.

kingawa-dokei (金側時計), *n.* a gold watch.

kingen (金言), *n.* a golden saying; a wise [old] saw; a maxim.

kingen, kingon, (謹嚴な), *a.* grave; sedate; stern. —謹嚴なる口調を以て, in a grave tone.

kingin (金銀), *n.* ❶ gold and silver. ❷ (金錢) money; cash (現金); specie (正金). ¶金銀在高(簿記), cash balance. —金銀手許在高(簿記), cash in [on] hand. —金銀塊, bullion. —金銀出納帳, a cash book.

kingoku (禁獄), *n.* confinement; imprisonment; incarceration. —禁獄する, to confine; imprison; incarcerate.

kingusari (金鎖), *n.* a gold chain.

kingyo (金魚), *n.* the gold-fish. ¶金魚鉢, a gold-fish basin. —金魚藻, the hornwort. —金魚草, 【植】 the snapdragon.

kingyo (禁漁), *n.* prohibition of fishery. ¶禁漁期, close season. ☞ *kinryō.*

kinichi (忌日), *n.* the anniversary of a death.

kiniiri (氣に入り), *n.* a favourite; a pet; a darling. —氣に入りの, favourite; pet; darling.

kiniiru (氣に入る), *v.* to catch [take] a person's fancy; find favour *with*; be to a person's taste [liking] (意に適ふ). —氣に入ッた家, a house after one's fancy. —段々氣に入る, to grow on [upon] a person.

kinikakeru (氣に掛ける), *vt.* to

mind; take to heart. —氣にかけぬ, to take no notice *of*; not to take in bad part. —氣にかゝる, to weigh on one's mind.

kinin (歸任する), *vi.* to return to one's post.

kiṅin (近因), *n.* a proximate [an immediate] cause.

kiṅin (金員), *n.* a sum of money; a sum.

kininaru (氣になる), *v.* to feel uneasy *about*; weigh [prey] on one's mind; lie heavy on one's mind(...が). —する氣になる, to find it in one's heart to; bring oneself *to*; fall into a mood *for*.)

kinine (規尼涅), *n.* cinchona; quinia; quinine.

kinisuru (氣にする), *vt.* to take to heart. ☞ *kinikakeru*. —借金を氣にする, to be anxious [troubled] about one's debt.

kiṅitsu (均一), *n.* uniformity. —十錢均一, a uniform rate (price) of ten *sen*. —均一の, uniform (價などの); equal (税率など). (壹圓均一の店, a one-*yen* shop.) —均一にする, to equalize; make uniform; reduce to uniformity. ¶ 均一制度, the uniform rate system.

kinji (近似の), *a.* approximate; close; almost exact. ¶ 近似値,【數】an approximate value; an approximation.

kinji (近時), *ad.* now; now-a--days; lately. —近時の, recent.

kinjitsu (近日-中に), *ad.* shortly; in a few days.

kinjo (近所), *n.* the neighbourhood. —近所の迷惑, annoyance to the neighbourhood. —直ぐ近所に, close [near; hard] *by*.

kinjō-teppeki (金城鐵壁), *n.* an impregnable fortress; a tower of strength.

Kinjō-heika (今上陛下), *n.* His Majesty the Present Emperor; the reigning sovereign.

kinjū (禽獸), *n.* birds and beasts; the (dumb) animals. —禽獸に等しい行爲, conduct worthy of a beast; bestial conduct.

kinka (近火), *n.* a fire in one's [the] neighbourhood; a near fire.

kinka (金貨), *n.* a gold coin; gold specie. ¶ 金貨本位, the gold standard.

kinkai (近海), *n.* the adjacent seas; the neighbouring waters; the home waters. ¶ 近海魚, a shore fish. —近海漁業, coast [inshore] fishery (三海哩內). —近海航路, a coastwise route.

kinkai (金塊), *n.* an ingot of gold; gold bullion; a gold bar (棒狀の).

kinkaku (巾幗), *n.* ❶ a woman's mourning head-cover. ❷ (婦人) a woman; womanhood. ¶ 巾幗政治, gynarchy; petticoat government.

kinkan (金柑), *n.* 【植】the kumquat.

kinkan (近刊), *n.* a recent publication [issue]. ¶ 近刊書目, a catalogue of recent publications.

kinkanshoku (金環蝕), *n.* an annular eclipse (of the sun).

kinkei (錦鷄), *n.* 【鳥】the golden pheasant.

kinken (近縣), *n.* adjacent [neighbouring] prefectures.

kinken (金權), *n.* ❶ = *kinryoku*. ❷ (金錢出納權) power to dispose of money. —金權を握る, to exercise control over money.

kinken (勤儉な), *a.* thrifty. ¶ 勤儉貯蓄, thrift and saving.

kinketsu (金穴), *n.* ❶ (出資家) a capitalist; a financial supporter [backer]; an oaf-bird【卑】. ❷ (金坑) a gold-mine.

kinki (近畿), *n.* the country around Kyoto.

kinki (欣喜), *n.* joy; gladness; delight. —欣喜雀躍する, to jump for joy; leap with joy.

kinki (錦旗), *n.* a brocade flag; the Imperial standard (天皇旗).

kinkin (近近), *ad.* shortly; before long; in the near future.

kinkin (僅僅), *ad.* only; but; not [no] more than. —僅々たる, few (數); little (量); small.

kinko (近古), *n.* the early modern age.

kinko (金庫), *n.* ❶ (匣) a safe; a strong-box; a coffer. ❷ (國庫に保管出納する現金を取扱ふ所) a cash office; a treasury. ¶ 本(支)金庫, the head (branch) cash office. —耐火金庫, a fire-proof safe.

kinko (海參), *n.* Ⓢ いりこ. a dried sea-slug.

kinko (禁錮), *n.* 【法】imprisonment; confinement. —禁錮する, to imprison; confine; commit (to prison).

kinkō (均衡), *n.* equilibrium; balance. —均衡を保つ, to keep [maintain] equilibrium. —均衡を取る, to balance.

kinkō (欣幸), *n.* joy; delight. —欣幸とする, to rejoice *at*; be delighted *with*.

kinkō (近郊), *n.* suburbs; environs.

kinkō (金工), *n.* Ⓢ 金匠. ❶ (工) metal-work. ❷ (人) a metal--worker; a goldsmith (金細工師).

kinkō (金坑), *n.* a gold-mine.

kinkonshiki (金婚式), *n.* a golden wedding.

kinkotsu (筋骨), *n.* ❶ bones and sinews [muscles]. ❷ (骨格) physique; build; frame. —筋骨逞しき人, a stalwart man; a man of fine physique [stout build].

kinkuchi (金口の), *a.* gold-tipped. ¶ 金口卷煙草, a gold-tipped cigarette.

kinkyō (近況), *n.* the recent state [condition].

kinkyori (近距離), *n.* a close range; a short distance.

kinkyū (緊急), *n.* urgency; emergency; exigency. —緊急の, urgent; pressing; crying. ¶緊急勅令, an urgency Imperial Ordinance. —緊急動議, an urgency motion. —緊急事件, an urgent [a pressing] affair; an emergency.

kinmanka (金滿家), *n.* a millionaire; a rich [wealthy] man; a man of wealth.

kinmekki (金鍍金), *n.* gilding; gold plating. —金鍍金の, gilt; gold-plated.

kinmizuhiki (龍芽草), *n.* 【植】 the agrimony; the liverwort.

kinmokusei (金木犀), *n.* 【植】 the fragrant olive.

kinmōru (金モール), *n.* gold lace [braid].

kinmotsu (禁物), *n.* ❶ (有害物) an injurious [noxious] thing. ❷ (斷物) a thing abstained *from*. ❸ (忌み嫌ふ物) an aversion. ❹ (禁制) a prohibited thing; taboo.

kinmu (勤務), *n.* duty; service. —勤務する, to serve. ¶勤務時間, the hours of service; office hours.

kinnen (近年), *n.* late years; recent years [times].

kinniku (筋肉), *n.* the muscles; brawn (特に腕又は腓の); the sinews. —筋肉の運動, muscular movement [motion]. ¶筋肉勞働者, a physical [manual] labourer.

kinnō (勤王), *n.* loyalty; loyalism. ¶勤王家, a loyalist; a royalist. —勤王主義, loyalism; royalism.

kinō (昨日), *ad.* & *n.* yesterday. —昨日の朝, yesterday morning. —昨日の晩, last evening.

kinō (器能), *n.* ability; faculty.

kinō (機能), *n.* function; power (機械の). ¶生活機能, vital function.

kinō (歸農する), *vi.* to return to the land.

kinō (歸納), *n.* induction. —歸納する, 【論】 to induce; generalize. ¶歸納法, 【論】 induction; the inductive method.

kinodoku (氣の毒), *n.* ❶ (同情して思ひやる情) sorrow; sympathy. ❷ (他人に對して濟まぬと思ふ心) regret. —氣の毒な有様, a painful appearance; a pitiful sight (光景). —氣の毒に思ふ, to be sorry *for*; sympathize *with*. —お氣の毒だがお斷りする, I regret to say that [I am sorry] I must decline it.

kinoko (茸, 蕈), *n.* ❶ (總稱) the fungus [*pl.* -gi]. ❷ (普通の) the mushroom. ❸ (有毒の) the toadstool. —蕈をとる, to pick up [gather] mushrooms.

kinome (木の芽), *n.* the bud of a tree.

kinomi (木の實), *n.* a fruit; a nut (堅果); a berry (漿果).

kinomi-kinomama (著のみ著の儘), ❶ with only the clothes on one's back. ❷ (著替へせずに) without changing one's clothes. —著のみ著のまゝ燒け出される, to be burnt out with only the clothes on one's back.

kinonai (氣の無い), *a.* spiritless; dispirited. —氣の無い返事をする, to give a spiritless answer.

kinonuketa (氣の拔けた), *a.* flat; vapid; stale. —氣の拔けた麥酒, flat beer.

kinori (氣乘), *n.* giving one's mind; interest. —氣乘りする, to give one's mind *to*; interest oneself *in*; warm (up) *to*. —氣乘りがしない, to have no inclination *for*.

kinpai (金杯), *n.* a gold cup [goblet].

kinpai (金牌), *n.* a gold medal. ¶金牌受領者, a gold medallist.

kinpaku (金箔), *n.* gold-foil; gold-leaf; gilding. —金箔附きの惡人, an unadulterated villain. —金箔で塗る, to cover with gold-foil; gild. —金箔を剝ぐ, to strip off the gilt. ¶金箔師, a gold-beater.

kinpatsu (金髮), *n.* golden hair. ¶金髮婦人, a woman with golden hair; a golden-haired lady.

kinpen (近邊), *n.* neighbourhood; vicinity. —此の近邊に, about here; in this neighbourhood.

kinpōge (金鳳花), *n.* 【植】 the buttercup.

kinrai (近來), *ad.* of late; in recent times; nowadays. —近來の, late; recent; modern.

kinran (錦襴), *n.* (gold) brocade. ¶錦襴表裝, brocade mounting.

kinrei (禁令), *n.* a prohibition; an interdict; a ban.

kinri (金利), *n.* interest.

kinrin (近隣), *n.* neighbourhood; vicinity. —近隣の人, a neighbour.

kinrō (勤勞), *n.* ❶【經】(personal) services. ❷ diligence; diligent service [labour]. —勤勞する, to labour; be diligent [faithful] in the discharge of one's duty. ¶勤勞所得, income from service.

kinryō (斤量), *n.* weight.

kinryō (金量), *n.* troy (weight).

kinryō (禁獵), *n.* prohibition of shooting. —禁獵する, to preserve; prohibit shooting. ¶禁獵期, the close season; the close-time for shooting; the fence-season. —禁獵區域, a preserve; a sanctuary.

kinryoku (金力), *n.* the power of money; the influence of wealth.

kinryoku (筋力), *n.* muscular power [strength]; thews; brawn.

kinsaku (金策する), *vi.* to make a plan for obtaining money; raise money [the wind].

kinsei (均勢), *n.* balance of power; equilibrium. —列强の均勢を破る, to destroy the balance of power among the great Powers.

kinsei (均齊), *n.* symmetry.

kinsei (近世), *n.* modern times [age]; recent times. ¶近世史, modern history (十五世紀以後).

kinsei (金星), *n.* 【天】Venus.

kinsei (禁制), *n.* prohibition; interdiction; a ban. —禁制を解く, to lift the ban. ¶禁制品, contraband goods; prohibited goods. (戰時禁制品, contraband of war.)

kinseki (金石), *n.* ❶ (鑛物) a mineral. ❷ (鐘·石碑等の類) stone and metal.

kinsen (金錢), *n.* money. —金錢の奴隷, a slave of Mammon. —金錢上の援助, pecuniary assistance. ¶金錢問題, money matter; a question of money; a pecuniary question. —金錢登錄器, a cash register.

kinsen (金線), *n.* gold wire.

kinsen (琴線に觸れる), to touch a string.

kinseni (筋纖維), *n.* a muscular fibre.

kinsenka (金盞花), *n.* 【植】Calendula arvensis (pot-marigold の一種·學名).

kinsetsu (緊切な), *a.* urgent; pressing.

kinshi (近視), *n.* short [near] sight. ¶近視眼, myopia; near-sightedness; short sight. —近視眼者, a myope.

kinshi (禁止), *n.* prohibition; interdiction; a ban. —禁止的, prohibitive; interdictory. —禁止する, to prohibit; interdict; forbid. —上陸禁止に會ふ, to be prohibited from landing. ¶禁止法, a prohibitory law. —禁止(的)價格, a prohibitive price. —禁止稅, a prohibitive tax.

kinshi-gyokuyō (金枝玉葉), *n.* the Imperial family. —金枝玉葉の御身を以て, being a member of the the Imperial family.

kinshi-kunshō (金鵄勳章), *n.* Order of the Golden Kite.

kinshin (近親), *n.* a near relation [relative].

kinshin (謹愼), *n.* ❶ prudence; discretion; circumspection. ❷ (罰の) home confinement; disciplinary confinement. —謹愼する, to be circumspect; be discreet; be confined at home (罪にて).

kinshitsu (琴瑟), *n.* conjugal harmony. —琴瑟相和する, to live in conjugal harmony.

kinshō (僅少), *n.* a little (量); a few (數); a trifle. ☞ *wazuka.* ——**-no**, *a.* little; few; trifling. —僅少の差を以て, by a slight [small] difference.

kinshō (焮衝), *n.* inflammation. ☞ *enshō* (炎症). —焮衝する, to become [get] inflamed.

kinshoku (金色の), *a.* golden; blond, blonde (髮の).

kinshu (金主), *n.* a capitalist; a financier. —金主は誰ですか, Who is going to finance it?

kinshu (禁酒), *n.* temperance; abstention from drink; (total) abstention. —禁酒する, to abstain [refrain] from wine. —婦人の禁酒運動, women's prohibition movement. —禁酒を誓ふ, to swear off drink. ¶禁酒家, a total abstainer; an abstainer; a teetotaler. (禁酒家の徽章, a blue ribbon.) —禁酒會, a temperance society. —禁酒主義, teetotalism.

kinshuku (緊縮), *n.* ❶ (收縮) contraction; shrinkage; constriction. ❷ (減縮) reduction; retrenchment. —緊縮する, ① to shrink; contract. ② to reduce; retrench; cut down. —財政緊縮の方針を執る, to adopt the policy of financial retrenchment.

kinsoku (禁足), *n.* confinement. —禁足する, to confine; keep indoors.

kinsu (金子), *n.* money.

kintei (欽定の), *a.* established by the Emperor; compiled by Imperial order (書籍の). ¶欽定憲法, a constitution granted by an Emperor.

kinten (均霑する), *v.* to enjoy equally; share (in); participate *in.*

kinten (禁轉の), *a.* non-negotiable. ¶禁轉小切手, a non-negotiable cheque.

kintetsu (金鐵), *n.* ❶ gold and iron. ❷ (堅固) firmness.

kintō (均等), *n.* equality; evenness; parity; balance. —均等の權利を享有する, to enjoy equal rights. —利益を均等にする, to equalize the advantages.

kintō (近東), *n.* the Near East. ¶近東問題, the Eastern Question. —近東諸國, the Near-Eastern states.

kintoki (金時), *n.* 【植】Carpopeltis angusta (學名).

kinu (絹), *n.* ❶ silk. ❷ (絹布) silk stuff; a silk fabric. —絹(製)の, silk; silken; silky. —絹張りの洋傘, a silk umbrella. ¶絹織

物, silk goods; silk tissues; silks. —絹商人, a silk-mercer.

kinuchijimi (絹縮), *n.* corrugated silk.

kinuito (絹絲), *n.* silk; silk-thread.

kinuke (氣拔け), *n.* ❶ (氣落ち) dispiritedness; disappointment; despondency. ❷ (放心) absent-mindedness; abstraction. ❸ (無味) flatness; staleness; vapidity. —氣拔けした, flat; stale; vapid. —氣拔けがする, ① to be dispirited; despond; be cast down. ② to be absent-minded; be abstracted.

kinumono (絹物), *n.* silk fabrics.

kinuta (砧), *n.* a fulling-block.

kinuten (絹天), *n.* silk velvet.

kiṅyō (緊要な), *a.* ❶ (大切) important; weighty; significant. ❷ (必要) necessary; indispensable.

kiṅyōbi (金曜日), *n.* Friday.

kiṅyoku (禁慾), *n.* mortification; continence. ¶ 禁慾主義, Stoicism; asceticism.

kiṅyu (禁輸), *n.* prohibition of [ban on] export.

kinyū (記入), *n.* entry; insertion. **——-suru,** *vt.* ❶ to enter; note down; keep (日記・計算・帳簿などを). ❷ (充塡) to fill up (定所に); insert. —帳簿に記入する, to enter in the books.

kiṅyū (金融), *n.* circulation of money. —金融は緩慢である(逼迫してる), Money is easy (tight). ¶ 金融逼迫, dearness [scarcity] of money; pressure on the money market; monetary stringency. —金融狀態, monetary situation [conditions]. —金融界, financial circles; moneyed interests. —金融機關, banking facilities. —金融市場, the money market.

kinzai (近在), *n.* neighbouring villages; neighbourhood; the surrounding country.

kinzan (金山), *n.* a gold-mine.

kinzan (近算), *n.* approximation; approximate calculation.

kinzen (欣然), *ad.* gladly; willingly; cheerfully.

kinzoku (金屬), *n.* a metal. ¶ 金屬元素, a metallic element.

kinzoku (勤續), *n.* continual service. —勤續する, to serve (for... years). —永年勤續の賞として, in recognition of [in reward for] his long service.

kin-zuru (禁する), *v.* ❶ (禁示) (法令又は威力にて) to prohibit; interdict; forbid. ❷ (抑制) to suppress; repress; forbear. ❸ (禁斷) to abstain *from*; refrain *from*. —出入を禁する, to close one's doors *against*; forbid another (to enter) one's house. —通行を禁ず, "No thoroughfare."

kiō (旣往), *n.* the past; the bygone days. —旣往に溯る, ① to go back to the past. ② [*a.*] retrospective.

kiochi (氣落), *n.* dejection; despondency; dispiritedness. —氣落ちさす, to discourage; dispirit; dishearten. —氣落ちする, to despond; be dejected; be dispirited.

kioku (記憶), *n.* ❶ memory. ❷ (喚想) recollection; reminiscence. —當にならぬ記憶, treacherous memory. —記憶の善(惡)い人, a person with a good (bad) memory. —記憶に新たなる, fresh in one's memory; fresh in the mind. —尙記憶に存する, to remain still in one's memory. —余の記憶にして誤なくば, if I remember right [aright]; if my memory does not fail me. —記憶を辿る, to trace back one's memory. —記憶を新たにする, to brush up one's memory. **——-suru,** *v.* ❶ (覺えて居る) to remember; bear [have; keep] in mind; hold in memory. ❷ (諳記する) to commit to memory; memorize; learn by heart. ❸ (思出す) to remember; recollect; call to mind [memory]. —記憶すべき, memorable. ¶ 記憶術, mnemonics; art of memory. (ペルマン式記憶術, Pelmanism.) —記憶力, memory; rententiveness. (記憶力の減退, failure of memory.)

kiokure (氣後れ), *n.* faint-heartedness. —氣後れする, ① [*vi.*] to lose heart [courage]; one's heart fails one. ② [*a.*] faint-hearted; timorous; dastardly.

kiomoi (氣重い), *a.* gloomy; heavy-hearted; dismal.

kion (氣音), *n.* aspirate; aspiration.

kion (氣溫), *n.* atmospheric temperature.

kiotsukeru (氣をつける), *v.* ❶ (世話) to look after; see after; take care *of*. ❷ (注意) to mind; take heed; pay attention *to*. ❸ (監視) to keep an eye *on*; watch. ❹ (用心, 警戒) to take care; stand [be; lie] upon one's guard; be on the lookout *for*. —氣を附け, Look out!; 【軍】 Attention! —...やうに氣をつける, to see [look] to it that.... —能く氣をつける, to keep a good lookout.

kippan (喫飯), *n.* meal; taking meal. ¶ 喫飯時間, meal-time.

kippari (きッぱり), *ad.* ❶ (明白) clearly; distinctly; explicitly. ❷ (斷然) positively; decisively; flatly. —きッぱり斷る, to decline positively; give a flat refusal.

kippō (吉報), *n.* joyful news; good [glad] tidings; goon news. —吉報

を齎らす, to bring good news.

kippu (切符), *n.* a ticket. ¶ 無賃切符, a free pass. —切符切り, (鋏) a ticket-punch; a punch-pliers: (人) a ticket-puncher. —切符賣, a booking-clerk; a ticket-clerk. —切符賣場, a booking-office; a ticket office; a box-office (劇場の).

kira (浮垢), *n.* oily scum.

kira (綺羅), *n.* fine clothes; a fine dress. —綺羅を飾る, to be finely dressed; be gorgeously attired.

kirabiyaka (きらびやかな), *a.* gaudy; gorgeous; gay.

kirai (嫌), *n.* ❶ (嫌惡) dislike; aversion; hatred. ❷ (疑, 缺點) suspicion; fault; charge (非難). —嫌ひな, which one dislikes. —繁文縟禮の嫌ひがある, to be open to the charge of red-tapism.

kirakira (煌煌), *ad.* glitteringly; brilliantly. —きらきらする, ① to sparkle (光・星等が); glare; glitter. ② [*a.*] brilliant; bright; glistening; twinkling; dazzling.

kiraku (氣樂な), *a.* easy; easy-going; comfortable. ——**-ni,** *ad.* at (one's) ease; comfortably. —氣樂に暮す, to live in comfort [ease]; lead a comfortable life.

kirameki (煌き), *n.* glimmer; sparkle; gleam.

kirameku (煌く), *vi.* (光・星等が) to glare; glitter; glisten.

-kiranai (切らない), cannot all; be unable to; be too...*for* [*to*]. ☞ *-kirenai.*

kirara (雲母), *n.* mica.

kirasu (切らす), *v.* (品物を) to run out *of*; run short *of*; be out of stock. ☞ *kireru.* —小錢を切らす, to run out of small coin.

kirau (嫌ふ), *vt.* to dislike; have a dislike *to*; loathe. —嫌はれる, to fall into disfavour. —勉强を嫌ふ, to dislike study.

kire (切), *n.* ❶ =*kireaji.* ❷ (切れ目) a gap; a rift. ❸ (斷片) a piece; a fragment; a junk; a scrap (小さくちぎった). ❹ (反物, 反物の片端) a cloth; a clout; drapery. ❺ (段落) a close place for leaving off. ❻ (塊) a lump; a block. —鯛一切, a slice of sea-bream. —木の切, a chip [piece] of wood. —パンの切, a scrap [morsel] of bread. —肉の切, a piece [slice] of meat.

kireaji (切味), *n.* sharpness. —切味のよい, sharp; incisive; keen. —刀の切味を試めす, to try (the cut of) one's sword.

kiregire (切切に), *ad.* into [to] pieces; to shreds; to fragments. —切れ切れに裂く, to tear asunder; tear into [to] pieces.

kirehashi, kireppashi, (切端), *n.* a patch; a rag; a snippet.

kirei (綺麗), *a.* ❶ (立派な) beautiful; pretty (少女・花など); tidy. ❷ (清潔な) clean; clear (水などの澄める); neat (着物など). ❸ (潔白な) pure; innocent. ❹ (完全な) complete (勝負・治癒などの); splendid (勝など). —綺麗好きの奴僕, a tidy servant. —綺麗に勘定を濟ます, to settle the accounts completely. —綺麗に負ける, to be fairly beaten. —ペン先を綺麗に拭ふ, to wipe the nib clean. —座敷を綺麗に掃除する, to clean a room.

kireji (切地), *n.* stuff (for clothes).

kireme (切れ目), *n.* ❶ (間隙) an interval (時の); a rent; a gap. ❷ =*danraku.* —雲の切れ目, a rift in the clouds. —切れ目をつなぐ, to close a gap.

kiremono (切物), *n.* (刃物) cutlery; edged tools.

-kirenai (切れない), **-kirenu** (切れぬ), *v.* (不可能) to be unable to; be too much for; cannot... too much. —食ひきれぬ程の食物, food more than one can manage.

kireru (切れる), *v.* ❶ (切り得る) to cut; be sharp (銳利). ❷ (切斷) (*a*) to break; snap (ふッつり切れる); be rent (裂ける): (*b*) (電話) to be cut off; be disconnected. ❸ (絕緣) to be severed; be cut *from*; be separated. ❹ (盡きる) (*a*) (物) to run out; run short *of*: (*b*) (時) to be up; expire; come to an end. ❺ (決潰) to break down give way; collapse. ——, *a.* (銳利な) sharp; keen; incisive. —能く切れる, to cut clean; cut well. —雲が切れる, The cloud is rent. —切ッても切れぬ仲である, to be on too intimate terms to be separated.

kiretsu (龜裂), *n.* cracking; a crack; a chap (特に手の). —龜裂する, to crack; chap.

kiri (桐), *n.* 【植】Paulownia tomentosa (學名); the paulownia (俗稱). —桐一葉のおとづれ, announcing the approach of autumn.

kiri (切), *n.* ❶ (切ること) cutting; cut. ❷ (段落) proper place to leave off. ❸ (際限) a limit; a bound; the end. —...切りがない, there is no end [limit] to... .

kiri (錐, 鑽), *n.* a gimlet (もみぎり); an awl (革等を穿つ錐); a drill (金石等を穿つ錐). —錐で孔をあける, to bore a hole with an awl; drill a hole.

kiri (霧), *n.* mist; fog; spray (飛沫). —霧深い, foggy; misty. —

霧を吹く, [*vt.*] to spray.

kiri (奇利), *n.* a windfall; unexpected gain; good [blind] luck.

-kiri (きり), ❶ (のみ) only; all. ❷ (以來) since. —知ッてるのは私きりだ, I am the only one who knows. —去年別れたきりまだ逢はぬ, Since we parted last year, I have not seen him.

kiriageru (切上げる), *vt.* ❶ (しまひにする) to close; stop; wind up. ❷ (端數を) to raise to units. —五以上の端數を切上げる, to raise fractions not lower than 0.5 to units. —早く仕事を切上げる. ① to bring work quickly to an end. ② to close work earlier than usual.

kiriai (切合), *n.* fighting with swords. —切合ひする; 切合ふ, to cross swords; fight together with swords.

kiriame (霧雨), *n.* a drizzle; a mizzle.

kiribana (切花), *n.* cut-flowers.

kiribari (切張する), *vt.* to paper over (holes); patch with paper.

kirichijimeru (切縮める), *vt.* to shorten; curtail; cut down.

kirichin (切貨), *n.* commission for changing money; brokage. —十圓の切貨に三十五錢も取られる, to be charged 35 *sen* for changing a ten-*yen* note.

kiridashi (切出), *n.* ❶ a knife. ❷ (肉の) scraps of meat.

kiridasu (切出す), *vt.* ❶ (言出す) to open one's mouth; break the ice. ❷ (切ッて出す) to bring down *out of*; quarry (石を山から).

kirido (切戸), *n.* a low garden-gate.

kiridōshi (切通し), *n.* a cut; a cutting; an excavation.

kirifuda (切札), *n.* (トランプ) a trump (card). —切札で取る, [*vt.*] to trump.

kirifuki (霧噴器), *n.* a vaporizer; an atomizer.

kirigirisu (蟋蟖), *n.* 【蟲】 Gompsocleis mikado (green [long-horned] grasshopper の一種・學名).

kirihame (切嵌, 剪嵌), *n.* mosaic. —切り嵌める, to cut and fit into. ¶ 剪嵌細工, tessellation; mosaic-work.

kirihanasu (切離・切放す), *vt.* ❶ to cut; cut off; chop off. ❷ (釋放) to emancipate; set free; set at liberty. —その問題と切り離して, separated from that question.

kiriharau (伐拂ふ), *vt.* to cut away; prune [lop] off [away] (無駄な枝を); clear away (樹木を).

kirihiraku (切開く), *vt.* ❶ (道などを) to cut; open; cleave. ❷ (血路を) to cut one's way *through*; carve out a way *through*. ❸ (山・荒地等を) to clear (樹木等を切り拂ふ); disafforest; open (開拓).

kiriishi (切石), *n.* ❶ a hewn stone; a block (建築用の); ashlar. ❷ (敷石) a paved stone.

kirikabu (伐株), *n.* a stub; a stump; a stock.

kirikae (切替), *n.* ❶ (變更, 取替) change. ❷ (兩替) exchange. ❸ (更新) renewal. —手形の切替へ, renewal of bills. —切替へる, to change; exchange; renew. ¶ 切替畑, 【農】 a forest converted into arable land.

kirikizamu (切刻む), *vt.* to hash (肉を); mince (同上); hackle.

kirikizu (切傷), *n.* a cut; an incised wound; an incision.

kiriko (切子, 切籠), *n.* a facet. ¶ 切籠燈籠, a square *bon* lantern with the corners cut off.

kirikōjō (切口上), *n.* a stiff way of speaking. —切口上に挨拶する, to address in a stiff manner.

kirikomi (切込む), *v.* ❶ (切入る) to cut one's way *into* (敵陣などへ); attack. ❷ (深く切る) to cut deep *into*. —どこ迄も切り込んで質問する, to question to the last details.

kirikorosu (斬殺す), *vt.* to slay; put to the sword.

kirikuchi (切口), *n.* a cut end; a butt-end (木口); the opening of a wound (傷口); a slash (長い).

kirikumi (切組), *n.* 【建】 dovetail; piecing together. —切組む, to piece together.

kirikuzu (切屑), *n.* scraps; ends; parings (芋等の).

kirikuzusu (切崩す), *vt.* ❶ (高い所を切りて低くする) to level down; cut [put] down. ❷ (組織を破る) to disorganize (敵黨など); break (同盟罷業など); to throw (the enemy) into disorder (斬入ッつて敵の陣容を破る).

kirikyōgen (切狂言), *n.* an after-piece; the last piece.

kirimawasu (切廻す), *vt.* ❶ (あちこち切る) to cut here and there; cut in places. ❷ (專擅の處置をする) to carry matters with a high hand. ❸ (巧みに事物を處理する) to manage affairs skilfully.

kirime (切り目), *n.* ❶ notch; a nick; indentation. ❷ an end. —切り目ある, notched; notchy.

kirimi (切身), *n.* fish cut in slices; a slice of fish; a chop (肉の厚い); a cut.

kirimomi (錐揉), *n.* boring. —板に錐揉みする, to bore a board with a gimlet.

kirin (麒麟), *n.* 【動】 ❶ the giraffe; the camelopard. ❷ (支那で想像の動物) kylin, kilin. ¶ 麒麟兒, a wonderful child; a prodigy; an infant prodigy.

kirinukeru (切抜ける), *v.* ❶ (包圍を) to cut one's way *through*; carve out a way *through*. ❷ (困難を) to find one's way out *of*; get [come] out *of*; come safely *through*. —困難を切抜ける, to tide over a difficulty. —危機を切抜ける, to stand out a crisis.

kirinuki (切抜), *n.* ❶ a cutting; a scrap. ❷ (拔萃) an extract; an abstract; an excerpt. —新聞の切抜き, a press-cutting. —切抜く, to cut out; excise; extract. ¶ 切拔帳, a scrap-book. —切拔通信社, press-cutting agency; a press-clipping bureau.

kirisage (切下げ), *n.* (頭髮) hair cut short and let down.

kirisageru (切下げる), *v.* to cut down to.

kirishima(tsutsuji) (石巖), *n.* 【植】 the Indian rhododendron.

kirishitan (切支丹), *n.* 〔葡 Christão〕 a Christian; (天主敎) a (Roman) Catholic.

kirisuteru (切捨てる), *vt.* ❶ to cut off. ❷ (人を) to cut down. ❸ (端數を) to omit. —錢位未滿切捨て, Fractions of a *sen* omitted.

Kirisuto (基督), *n.* (Jesus) Christ. ¶ 基督紀元一千年, the thousandth year of the Christian era; 1000 A. D. (Anno Domini, in the year of our Lord の略). —基督紀元前, Before Christ (B. C. と略す). —基督降誕祭, Christmas. —基督敎, Christianity; the Christian religion [faith]. (基督敎化する, to Christianize.) —基督敎會, a Church. —基督敎青年會, the Young Men's Christian Association (Y.M.C.A と略す). (基督敎青年會館, the Y.M.C.A. Hall.) —基督敎徒, a Christian. —基督新敎, Protestantism.

kiritaosu (切倒す), *vt.* to fell; cut down (木・人を); hew down.

kiritate (切立の), *a.* just cut. —お花切立て!, Fresh-cut flowers!

kiritorisen (切取線), *n.* a dotted line; a perforated line.

kiritoru (切取る), *vt.* ❶ to cut off; amputate (手足などを); trim [lop] off [away] (枝等を). ❷ (人を斬ッて取る) to seize [rob] by cutting down

kiritsu (紀律, 規律), *n.* ❶ (秩序) order; discipline; regularity. ❷ (規定) regulations; laws; rules. —規律のある, regular; orderly; disciplined. —規律のない, irregular; disorderly; undisciplined.

kiritsu (起立), *n.* standing up. —起立する, to rise (to one's feet); stand up. —贊否を起立に問ふ, to ask (those present) to express their approval by standing up.

kiritsugi (切接-法), *n.* grafting.

kiritsukeru (切附ける), *vt.* to chop *at*; cut *at*; attack.

kiritsumeru (切詰める), *vt.* to curtail; cut down; retrench (節約) shorten (短縮). —切詰めた暮し, living in straitened circumstances.

kiriuri (切賣), *n.* selling by pieces.

kiriwara (剉藁), *n.* chaff.

kiro- (基), kilo- (千). ¶ キログラム, a kilogramme (一千グラム). —キロメートル, a kilometre (一千メートル). —キロワット, a kilowatt (一千ワット).

kiro (岐路), *n.* the parting of the ways (路の分れたる處); a branch-road; a fork-way. —岐路に泣く, to cry from uncertainty [be undecided] at the parting of the ways.

kiro (歸路), *n.* the way home [back]; the return journey. —歸路に就く, to start [make] for home; bend one's steps [course] homeward.

kiroku (記錄), *n.* ❶ a record; a document; archives (官府の文書). ❷ (年代記) a chronicle; annals. —記錄破りの, record-breaking. —記錄に存する, to be on record. —記錄を作る, to establish a new record; make a record. —記錄を破る, to break the record. ¶ 記錄係, an archivist; a recorder; a keeper of records; a scorer (試合の). —記錄保持者, a record-holder. —記錄課, the section of archives.

kiru (切・伐・斬・截・斫る), *v.* ❶ (刃物にて) (物を) to cut; chop (細く刻む); slash (長めに). ❷ 絕緣) to cut off; disconnect; sever. ❸ (電話など) to cut off; disconnect; ring off. ❹ 【數】 to cut; intercept (二點間などを). ❺ (割引)【商】 to discount (手形を). ❻ (橫切る) to cross; intersect. ❼ (遮斷) to cut off. ❽ (乾かす) (水などを) to let run off. ❾ (日限などを) to limit (the date); fix (定める). —書き切る, to finish writing. —爪を切る, to cut [pare] a nail. —手を切る, to sever [cut] connections *with*; break *with*. —骨牌を切る, to shuffle cards. —道先を切る, to cross another's path. —身を切るやうな風, a cutting [piercing] wind.

kiru (著・被る), *v.* ❶ (衣類を) to put on (動作); wear (著用). ❷ (罪を) to be charged *with*; be accused *of*. —著て居る, to have on (著物を); wear (同上); be dressed *in*.

kiruku (キルク), *n.* a cork. ☞ *koruku.*

kiryō (器量), *n.* ❶ (才器) ability; talent; capacity. ❷ (標緻) presonal appearance; countenance; looks. —標緻のよい(わるい)女, a pretty (plain) woman. —器量をあげる (下げる), to gain (lose) credit; gain (lose) countenance.

kiryokn (汽力), *n.* steam-power. ¶ 汽力起重機, a steam-crane.

kiryoku (氣力), *n.* ❶ energy; spirit; vigour. ❷ (空氣の力) atmospheric power; pneumatic power. —氣力の盛な人, a man of spirit. —氣力を失ふ, to lose one's spirits.

kiryoku (機力), *n.* 【機】 power. ¶ 機力旋盤, a power-lathe.

kiryū (氣流), *n.* an atmospheric current; an aerial [air] current.

kiryū (寄留), *n.* temporary residence. —寄留する, to reside temporarily *at*. ¶ 寄留地, a place of temporary residence. —寄留替, change of temporary residence. —寄留者, a temporary resident.

kiryūsan (稀硫酸), *n.* 【化】 dilute sulphuric acid.

kisago, kishago, (細螺), *n.* the periwinkle.

kisai (奇才), *n.* ❶ great talent; remarkable ability. ❷ (人) a man of great ability.

kisai (鬼才), *n.* genius; marvellous genius.

kisai (起債), *n.* flotation [raising] of a loan. ¶ 起債額, the amount of a loan floated.

kisai (記載), *n.* mention; statement. —記載する, to mention; state; enter.

kisaki (后), *n.* an empress; a queen. —后に立てる, to make empress.

kisan (起算する), *vt.* to reckon [count] *from*; compute *from*. ¶ 起算日, the day from which time is computed. —起算點, the starting-point of reckoning.

kisan (歸參する), *v.* to return to one's former employer; re-enter one's former master's service.

kise (著せ), *n.* sheathing; sheath (道具の); plating (金・銀等の). —金著せ側時計, a gold-plated watch.

kisei (祈誓), *n.* a vow; a pledge; an oath.

kisei (起誓する), *vi.* to make a vow; vow; pledge oneself; make an oath.

kisei (氣生の), *a.* aerial. ¶ 氣生植物, an air-plant; an aerial plant.

kisei (氣勢), *n.* spirit. —氣勢を示す [張る], to show one's spirit.

kisei (寄生), *n.* parasitism. —寄生する, to live *upon* [*in*]; be parasitic *on*; be a hanger-on. ¶ 寄生蟲, a parasite.

kisei (期成する), *vt.* to resolve to carry out. ¶ 通行稅廢止期成同盟會, an association for effecting the abolition of transit-duty.

kisei (既成の), *a.* already completed; existing. ¶ 既成品, a ready-made article. —既成事實, an accomplished fact. —既成政黨, the existing political parties. —既成鐵道, an already-completed railway.

kisei (歸省する), *vi.* ❶ (故郷に父母を見舞ふ) to go [return; come] home. ❷ (歸鄉する) to return to one's native place.

kiseki (奇蹟), *n.* a miracle; a wonder; a marvel. —奇蹟的, miraculous. —奇蹟を行ふ, to work wonders [miracles].

kiseki (鬼籍), *n.* a register of the dead. —鬼籍に上る, to join the majority; go to one's long home.

kiseki (輝石), *n.* 【鑛】 augite.

kisen (汽船), *n.* a steamer; a steamboat; a steamship. —マニラ行汽船, a steamer for Manilla. ¶ 汽船會社, a steamship company. —汽船宿, an inn for steamship passengers.

kisen (貴賤), *n.* ❶ (尊卑) high and low; gentle and simple; great and small. ❷ (階級) rank. —貴賤男女, all ranks and both sexes; high and low without distinction of sex. —貴賤を論せず, irrespective of rank.

kisen (基線), *n.* 【數】 a base line.

kisen (機先を制する), to get the start *of*; forestall; steal a march *on* [*upon*].

kiseru (煙管), *n.* a pipe; a tobacco-pipe. —煙管をくはへて, with a pipe in one's mouth. —煙管の羅宇をすげかへる, to put a new stem in a pipe. ¶ 煙管筒, a pipe-holder.

kiseru (著・被せる), *v.* ❶ (衣類などを) to put *on*; dress; clothe. ❷ (覆包) to cover; put *over*; veneer (粗材に良材を). ❸ (罪などを) to impute; charge a person *with*; attribute. ❹ (金を) to coat (箔にて); overlay. —外套を著せる, to help a person on with a great coat. —夜具を著せる, to put a quilt over. —罪を被せる, to lay a crime at another's door; impute a crime to another; charge another with a crime. —銅に金を著せる, to overlay copper with gold.

kisetsu (季節), *n.* a season. —野球の季節, the baseball season. —季節向きとなる, to come in; become seasonable. ¶ 季節物, seasonable goods.

kisetsu (既設の), *a.* already-established; existing.

kisezu-shite (期せずして), *ad.* unexpectedly; accidentally (不圖); by accident. —期せずして…する, to happen *to*; chance *to*. —期せずして出會ふ, to happen to meet; meet unexpectedly.

kisha (汽車), *n.* a (railway-)train (列車); a railway-carriage (客車); a railway-car. ☞ *tetsudō* (鐵道). — 一番汽車で, by the first train. —汽車で行く, to go by train [rail]. —汽車に乘る, to take [get into] a train. —汽車に乘り後れる, to miss a train. ¶ 夜汽車, a night-train. —汽車賃, a railway fare. —汽車發著表, a railway time-table. —汽車發著掲示板, a station-calendar. —汽車旅行案內, a railway guide.

kisha (記者), *n.* a writer; an editor (特に主筆); a journalist (新聞記者). —朝日新聞の記者, a journalist on the staff of the *Asahi*. ¶ 記者席, a reporters' gallery (議會に於ける速記者等の); a press-gallery (議會等に於ける新聞記者の); a press-box (クリケット戲その他興行場の).

kisha (喜捨), *n.* alms; voluntary contribution. —喜捨する, to contribute; give alms.

kisha (騎者), *n.* a rider.

kishaku (稀釋する), *vt.* to dilute; attenuate. ¶ 稀釋液, a dilute solution.

kishi (岸), *n.* bank (川の); beach (海の); shore (海·湖等の). —岸打つ波, wash. —岸近く(水上より云ふ), inshore. —岸にうちあげる, to cast ashore.

kishi (旗幟), *n.* ❶ a flag; a banner; a standard. ❷ (立場) stand; attitude. —旗幟を鮮明にする, to show one's colours; define one's position.

kishi (譏刺する), *vt.* to satirize.

kishi (騎士), *n.* ❶ a cavalryman; a horseman. ❷【史】a knight; a cavalier.

kishimu (軋む), *vi.* =*kishiru* 「の❶」

kishin (鬼神), *n.* ❶ (目に見えぬ神靈) gods; deities. ❷ (死者の) spirits of the dead; the manes; a dæmon. ¶ 鬼神學, demonology. —鬼神崇拜, demonolatry.

kishin (貴紳), *n.* men of position; distinguished gentlemen.

kishiri (軋), *n.* ❶ (軋ること) squeak; creak. ❷ (軋轢) jar; friction; collision.

kishiru (軋·轢る), *n.* ❶ (軋む) to creak; squeak (扉など); grate; grind (齒の浮くやうに). ❷ (擦合ふ, 軋轢) to clash *with*; jar *with*; disagree. —戶が軋る, The door grates.

kishitsu (氣質), *n.* disposition; temperament. —氣質のよい(惡い)人, a good (bad) tempered man; a man of good (bad) disposition.

kisho (寄書), *n.* a contribution. —寄書する, to contribute; write. ¶ 寄書家, a contributor.

kishō (奇勝), *n.* a unique [singular] landscape. —天下の奇勝を探る, to look for beautiful views of the country.

kishō (記章), *n.* a medal.

kishō (起床する), *vi.* to rise; get up; leave one's bed. ¶ 起床喇叭,【軍】the reveille; the morning-bugle; the rouse.

kishō (起請), *n.* a vow; an oath; a pledge. —起請を書く, to make a written pledge.

kishō (氣性), *n.* disposition; temper; temperament. ☞ *kishitsu*. —負けぬ氣性, the temper that never acknowledges a defeat. —氣性の勝ッた女, a woman of overpowering spirit.

kishō (氣象), *n.* ❶ atmospheric phenomena; weather (天候). ❷ =*kishō* (氣性). —氣象を觀測する, to make meteorological observations. ¶ 氣象臺, a meteorological observatory. (中央氣象臺, the Central Meteorological Observatory.) —氣象學, meteorology. —氣象觀測部, the weather-service; the Weather-Bureau organization for meteorological observations. —氣象局, the Weather Bureau. —氣象網, (一國の) *réseau* 【佛】.

kishō (稀少な), *a.* sparse (人口等の); scarce; rare.

kishō (旗章), *n.* ❶ (紋) the badge on the flag. ❷ (旗) a flag; colours; an ensign; a banner.

kishō (徽章), *n.* a badge; insigna (勳章などの); an emblem (黨派·團體などの).

kishoku (氣色), *n.* ❶ feelings (感情); humour (氣分). ❷ (やうす) a sign; appearance. —氣色がよい(惡い), to be in good (bad) humour; feel good (bad). —氣色を損ずる, to put a person out of humour.

kishoku (寄食する), *v.* to sponge *upon*; depend *on*; hang *on*. ¶ 寄食者, a sponger; a parasite; a hanger-on.

kishoku (機織), *n.* weaving.

kishōsan (稀硝酸), *n.* 【化】dilute nitric acid.

kishu (寄主), *n.* 【生】the host.

kishu (旗手), *n.* a standard-bearer;

a starter (競馬の); an ensign (陸軍の). ¶ 聯隊旗手, the bearer of regimental colours. —旗手少尉, a sublieutenant with the colours.

kishu (騎手), *n.* a rider; a horseman; a jockey (競馬の).

kishu (機首), *n.* the bow of a flying machine. —機首を西に向ける, to veer to the west.

kishū (奇襲), *n.* a surprise; a sudden attack. —奇襲を食ふ, to be taken by surprise.

kishū (貴衆), *n.* Peers and Commons. ¶ 貴衆兩院, the Houses of Peers and Representatives; both Houses [Chambers].

kishuku (耆宿), *n.* a veteran. —政界の耆宿, a veteran of the political world; a veteran politician.

kishuku (寄宿), *n.* boarding (食卓附の); lodging (間借の); board and lodging. —寄宿する, to lodge *at*; board *with* (賄附で). ¶ 寄宿學校, a boarding-school. (寄宿學校生徒, a boarding-scholar; a boarder. —寄宿料, lodging [boarding] charges; lodging; boarding. ¶ 寄宿舍, a boarding-house; a dormitory.

kiso (起訴), *n.* prosecution; indictment (陪審官よりの). —起訴する, to prosecute; indict.

kiso (基礎), *n.* the foundation; the basis; the base; the substructure; ground-work; fundamental (根本). —基礎を置く, to base *on*. —他日の基礎を作る, to lay the foundation of the future. ¶ 基礎工事, foundation work; ground-making.

kisō (奇想), *n.* a fantasy; a fantastic idea; a conceit.

kisō (起草), *n.* drafting. —起草する, to draft; draw up; make a draft *of*. ¶ 起草者, a drafter; a draftsman.

kisoku (氣息), *n.* breath; breathing. —氣息奄々としてゐる, to be at his last gasp.

kisoku (規則), *n.* a rule; a regulation. —規則正しく, in a regular manner; regularly; methodically. (規則正しくする, to regularize.) —規則に反して [を犯して], out of order; contrary to rule [regulation]. —規則を守る, to observe the rules. —規則を設ける, to establish [lay down] regulations. ¶ 規則書, a prospectus.

kisoku (驥足を展べる), to give full play to one's talents.

kison (毀損), *n.* damage; injury; detriment (人格・名譽など); defamation (同上). **——-suru**, *vt.* to damage; injure; spoil; defame (名譽を). —器物を毀損する, to damage utensils. —名譽を毀損する, to defame one's character.

kisou (競ふ), *vi.* to compete; vie; cope; strive; struggle; contend. **——**, *vt.* to emulate. —勢力を競ふ, to contend for power. —先を競うて馳せる, to vie with one another in running (up to it).

kissa (喫茶), *n.* tea-drinking. ¶ 喫茶會, a tea-party. —喫茶店, a tea-booth.

kissaki (切先, 鋩), *n.* the point of a sword; a sword-point.

kisseki (詰責), *n.* reprimand; rebuke; censure. —詰責する, to reprimand; rebuke; censure.

kisshiri (きッしり), *ad.* tightly; closely. ☞ *gisshiri.*

kissu (接吻), *n.* a kiss. —キッスする, to kiss.

kissui (生粹の), *a.* true-born; genuine; pure. —生粹の英國人, a true-born Englishman.

kissui (吃水), *n.* 【航】 draught. ¶ 吃水線, the water-line. (載貨吃水線, the load-line; the load-water line.)

kis-suru (吃·喫する), *vt.* to take; eat (食ふ); drink (飲む); smoke (煙草を). —一驚を喫する, to be amazed; be astonished; be surprised.

kisu (鱚, 鶏魚), *n.* 【魚】 Sillago japonica (學名). 「—奇數の, odd.

kisū (奇數), *n.* an odd number.

kisū (基數), *n.* 【數】 a simple number (一より九までの數); a cardinal number (序數の對); the base (十進法 10 の如き).

kisūhō (記數法), *n.* notation; the scale of notation; the system of notation.

kisui (既遂), *n.* 【法】 consummation. ¶ 既遂犯, a consummated crime. 「period of heat.

kisuiki (起水期), *n.* rut-time; the

ki-suru (記する), *vt.* to write down; record; take note. —心に記する, to bear in mind; lay to heart. —記するに足る, to be worthy of mentioning.

ki-suru (期する), *v.* ❶ (期待) to expect; look forward *to*; count [reckon] *on* (あてにする). ❷ (約束) to promise; pledge. ❸ (豫定) fix; appoint. ❹ (覺悟, 所信) to be prepared *for* (覺悟); be confident (確信); be sure [certain] (同上). —必勝を期する, to be absolutely certain of victory.

ki-suru (歸する), *v.* ❶ (終る) to result [end; issue] *in*. ❷ (基因) to impute *to*; attribute *to*; ascribe *to*. ❸ (負はす) to impute *to*; lay [put] *on*; lay at a person's door. ❷ (落ちる) to fall *into*; fall *upon*; devolve *on* (財產などが). —期する所, after all; in the issue. —無に歸せしむ, to reduce to nothing.

kita (北), *n.* ❶ the north. ❷ (北風) the north wind. ☞ ***higashi.*** —北の, north; northern; northerly.

kitae (鍛), *n.* ❶ (鍛冶) temper. ❷ (鍛錬) training; practice; drill.

kitaeru (鍛へる), *vt.* ❶ (鍛冶) to temper; forge. ❷ (鍛錬) to drill; train; practise. —鍛へ上げた腕, highly-trained skill. —刀を鍛へる, to temper [forge] a sword. —腕を鍛へる, to improve one's art.

kitai (稀代·希代の), *a.* (世に稀な) rare; extraordinary; uncommon.

kitai (奇態), *n.* ❶ (奇なるさま) a strange [peculiar] style. ❷ (奇妙, 不思議) strangeness; wonderfulness. —奇態な, strange; peculiar; queer; wonderful; marvellous.

kitai (氣體), *n.* gas; a gaseous body.

kitai (期待), *n.* expectation; anticipation. —期待する, to expect; look forward *to*; anticipate. —期待して, in expectation *of*; expectantly. —期待せぬ, [*a.*] unexpected; unlooked-for. —期待以上に, beyond expectation. —期待に反して, against expectation; contrary to one's expectation. —期待を裏切る, to betray one's expectation; go contrary to one's expectation.

kitai (機體), *n.* a chassis (飛行機の); the fuselage (同上); the body.

kitaku (寄託), *n.* 【法】 deposit; trust. —寄託する, to deposit *with*; entrust *with*; give in charge. ¶ 寄託物, a deposit; goods deposited. —寄託者, a depositor.

kitaku (歸宅する), *vt.* to return home; come [go] home; be back.

kitan (忌憚する), *v.* =***habakaru.*** —忌憚なき, unreserved; frank; candid. —忌憚なく云へば, to speak without reserve.

kitanai (汚·穢い), *a.* ❶ (不潔) unclean; soiled; dirty. ❷ (吝嗇) stingy; niggard; close-fisted. ❸ (卑劣, 野卑) mean; low; vulgar. ❹ (卑怯) foul; unfair; dishonourable. ❺ (猥褻) indecent; filthy; smutty. —汚ない敗け, an ignominious defeat. —汚ない家, a filthy [squalid] house. —汚ない金, filthy lucre. —汚ない言葉を使ふ, to use vulgar [coarse] language.

kitanarashii (汚ならしい), *a.* ❶ (見苦しい) dirty-looking; unsightly; squalid (家など). ❷ (破れ汚れた) shabby; ragged. ❸ (猥褻な) indecent; filthy. —汚ならしい風, shabby appearance.

kitaru (來る), *vt.* ❶ to come; arrive. ☞ ***kuru*** (來る). ❷ (生ずる) to come *of*. ——, *a.* coming; next; to come. —來る日曜日, next Sunday. —來て見る, to come; come to see; come and see.

kitasu (來す), *vt.* to produce; bring on; give rise *to* (惹起). ☞ ***maneku.*** —變化を來す, to work a change.

kitate (來立て), *n.* ❶ (新著) a new arrival. ❷ (來た當座) the time immediately following one's arrival; the early days of one's coming. —東京へ來立て, being newly arrived in Tōkyō; one's early days in Tōkyō.

kitcha (喫茶), *n.* =***kissa.***

kitchiri (きッちり), *ad.* ❶ (きッかり) exactly; precisely; to a nicety. ❷ (しッかり) tightly; closely; hard.

kitchō (吉兆), *n.* a lucky sign; a good omen.

kitei (規定), *n.* provisions; prescription. —規定の料金, the regulation fare [charge]. —規定の方法, the prescribed method. —規定する, to provide; prescribe; stipulate.

kitei (規程), *n.* rules; regulations; stipulations. ¶ 條約規程, treaty stipulations.

kitei (既定の), *a.* already-fixed [decided]; established. —既定の歳入, the already-fixed revenue. —既定の法律, an established law.

kiteki (汽笛), *n.* a steam-whistle.

kiten (起點), *n.* the starting-point; the point of departure; the origin.

kiten (氣轉, 機轉), *n.* wit; tact. —氣轉の利く, ready-witted; tactful; quick [sharp-] -witted. —氣轉の利かぬ, slow [dull] -witted. —氣轉を利かす, to act with tact.

kito (企圖), *n.* a plan; a scheme; a project. —企圖する, to plan; scheme; project.

kito (歸途), *n.* the way home; the home route. —歸途に就く, to start for home. —人を歸途に要する, to lie in ambush for another on his way home.

kitō (祈禱), *n.* a prayer; service; grace (食事前後の). —病氣平癒の祈禱, prayers for recovery (from illness). —祈禱を捧げる, to offer up prayers. ¶ 祈禱文, prayer. —祈禱會, a prayer-meeting. —祈禱書, a prayer-book; a service-book.

kitoku (危篤の), *a.* critical; serious. —危篤に陥る, to become critical.

kitokuken (既得權), *n.* an acquired right; vested interests.

kitsuen (喫煙), *n.* smoke; smoking. —喫煙する, to smoke; have a smoke. —禁喫煙, "No smoking."; "Smoking forbidden." ¶ 喫煙家, a smoker. —喫煙車, a smoker; a smoking-car; a smoking compartment. —喫煙室, a smoking room; a divan.

kitsui (きつい), *a.* ❶ (勇健な) brave (勇敢な); strong (力のある); plucky (氣の强い). ❷ (强烈な) strong (飲料など); intense (寒暑など); severe (風·痛·地震·罰など). —きつい シャツ, a tight shirt. —きつい顔(目), fierce look (eyes). —きつい煙草, strong tobacco. —きつい風, a violent [vehement] wind.

kitsuke (氣附), *n.* ❶ (興奮劑) a stimulant; a restorative. ❷ (...方) care of; c/o. —横濱郵便局氣附, c/o the Yokohama Post Office.

kitsukeru (著附ける), *v.* to become used to wearing.

kitsumon (詰問), *n.* cross-examination; interrogation; rigid [searching] inquiry. —詰問する, to interrogate; examine closely; put to the question.

kitsune (狐), *n.* the fox. —赤狐, the common fox. —牝狐, a vixen; a bitch fox. —白狐, the silver fox. —狐の穴, a fox-earth; a fox's earth. —狐の皮, a fox-case; a fox-skin. —狐の尾, a fox-brush [-tail]. —狐の嫁入, the devil beating his wife. —狐につか(魅(つ)さ)れる, to be possessed (bewitched) by a fox. ¶ 狐獵, fox-hunt(-ing); fox-chase. —狐つき, one possessed by a fox.

kitsunebi (狐火), *n.* the will-o'-the-wisp; Jack-o'-lantern; the elf-fire; *ignis fatuus* [羅].

kitsurifune (きつりふね), *n.* 【植】 the yellow balsam; the touch-me-not.

kitsuritsu (屹立する), *vi.* to soar; stand high; tower high. —雲表に屹立する, to rise [tower] above the clouds.

kitsutsuki (啄木鳥), *n.* 【鳥】 the woodpecker.

kitte (切手), *n.* ❶ (郵便切手) a (postage-)stamp. ❷ (小切手) a cheque, check. ❸ (切符) a ticket; a pass. —切手を貼る, to stamp; affix a stamp. —切手を再貼する, [*vt.*] to restamp. ¶ 記念切手, a commemoration-stamp. —切手蒐集, philately; stamp-collecting. (切手蒐集者, a stamp-collector; a philatelist.) —切手賣下所, a stamp-office.

kitte (切ッての), *a.* most. —界隈切ッての美人, the *belle* of the whole neighbourhood. —校内切ッての勉强家, the most diligent student in the whole school.

kitto (屹度), *ad.* ❶ (確かに) surely; certainly; positively. ❷ (決して) on any account; by all means; never (打消). —屹度だね, Honour bright [sure]?

kiuke (氣受), *n.* popularity; vogue. —氣受がよい, to be popular; be favourably received. —氣受が惡い, to be unpopular; be coldly received; be ill spoken *of*.

kiun (機運, 氣運), *n.* ❶ (運勢) fortune; luck. ❷ (機會) chance; opportunity; time. ❸ (傾向) (natural) tendency. —機運が向いて居る(居ない), to be in luck (out of luck).

kiuri (胡瓜), *n.* 【植】 the cucumber. ¶ 胡瓜揉み, sliced cucumber rubbed and seasoned with vinegar.

kiutsu (氣鬱な), *a.* gloomy; melancholy; low-spirited. ¶ 氣鬱症, melancholia; megrims.

kiutsuri (氣移する), *a.* changeable; capricious; fickle.

kiwa (際), *n.* ❶ (端) an edge; a verge; a brink (緣). ❷ (側) a side; a margin (邊). ❸ (間際) critical moment; point of time; a brink (滅亡の). —井戸の際, the margin of the well. —水の際, the edge [border; brink] of the water; the water's edge. —立ち際に, on the point of starting. —仕舞際に, toward [close to] the end.

kiwada (黃蘗), *n.* 【植】 the Siberian cork-tree. —黃蘗の粉, cork-tree powder.

kiwadatsu (際立つ), *v.* to stand out; be conspicuous; strike the eye (建物などが). —際立ッた, sharp-cut; conspicuous; marked. (際立ッた輪郭, a sharp outline.)

kiwadoi (際疾い), *a.* ❶ (*a*) (危機の迫れる) critical; ticklish (質問などの); delicate (同上): (*b*) (さしせまッた) imminent; impending. ❷ (危險な) perilous; dangerous; hazardous. —際どい商賈, hazardous trade. —際どい話, indecent talk. —際どい時に, at the eleventh hour; at the critical moment; in the nick of time. —際どい所まで持ッて行く, to bring a matter to a crisis; strain a matter to the breaking point.

kiwamari (極り), *n.* ❶ (終局) end; extremity; termination. ❷ =***kimari*** (極). ❸ (限界) limit; bound. ❹ (極度) the acme; the extreme. —極りなき, limitless; endless; interminable.

kiwamaru (極·窮·谷まる), *vi.*

❷ (極) to be carried to the extreme; come to the last extremity [utmost point]. ❸ (終る) to end; conclude. ❹ (窮困) to be brought to great straits; become needy. —不埒極まる奴, a most insolent fellow. —極まる所を知らず, to be beyond all bounds.

kiwameru (極・究める), *v.* ❶ (極める) to carry to the utmost; go to extremes. ❷ (決定) to determine; decide; establish. ❸ (研究) to investigate thoroughly; exhaust. —贅澤を極める, to live in greatest luxury. —口を極めて賞める, to praise in the highest terms; praise [laud] to the skies. —學術の蘊奥を究める, to study the most abstruse principles of science.

kiwamete (極めて), *ad.* extremely; excessively; exceedingly. —極めて惡き, shockingly bad〔俗〕; the worst.

kiwamono (際物), *n.* a seasonable article; an article suitable to the season. ¶ 際物商ひ, sale of articles suitable to the season. —際物師, a vendor [seller] of articles suitable to the season.

kiwata (木綿), *n.* 【植】 the herbaceous cotton-plant.

kiyaku (規約), *n.* articles; an agreement; a contract. —規約する, to agree *upon*; enter into agreement; make an agreement. —規約第十八條に依り, according to Art. 8 of the contract.

kiyaku (期約), *n.* fixing of a term. ¶ 期約徒弟, an apprentice.

kiyami (氣病), *n.* hypochondria; depression of spirits; a hypochondriac (人).

kiyari (木遣), *n.* the lumberers' chant; the chant of labourers in laying the foundation of a building. ¶ 木遣唄, the song chanted in laying the foundation of a building.

kiyasume (氣休), *n.* consolation; comfort; solace (不幸などの時に). —氣休めをいふ, to speak soothing words *to*; say things to put [set] a person at ease.

kiyo (寄與), *n.* contribution. —寄與する, to contribute *to* [*towards*]. ¶ 寄與的過失, contributory negligence.

kiyo (毀譽), *n.* praise and censure. —毀譽褒貶を顧みない, to take no note of others' criticism.

kiyō (器用な), *a.* skilful; dexterous; ingenious. —器用な職人, an ingenious workman. —器用に, skilfully; dexterously; ingeniously.

kiyoi (清い), *a.* ❶ (清潔) clean; pure; unstained (無垢な). ❷ (曇なき) clear; limpid; unsullied. ❸ (さわやかな) fresh. ❹ (高潔な) noble; holy. ❺ (貞節な) virgin; chaste. ❻ (潔白な) innocent; pure; cleanly. —清き愛, Platonic love. —清い聲, a liquid voice. —清き一票, a clean vote. —清き流れ, a clear [limpid] stream.

kiyome (清・淨め), *n.* ❶ cleaning; clearing; depuration. ❷ (淨潔) purification (お祓など); exorcism (厄拂などの); ablution (洗淨による);【宗】absolution (罪の).

kiyomeru (清・淨める), *v.*, ❶ to clear; clarify; purify; consecrate (神聖にする). ❷ (罪を) to cleanse *of*; purify *of*; purge *of*. —心(身體)を清める, to purify the heart (body).

kiyowai (氣弱い), *a.* faint-hearted; timid; chicken-hearted.

kiyu (窺窬する), *vt.* ❶ (のぞきみ) to peep; peer; pry *into*. ❷ pretend. —帝位を窺窬する, to have designs upon the Imperial Throne.

kiyū (杞憂), *n.* an imaginary [a blue] fear; a bugbear; a groundless apprehension [foreboding of evil]; scare. —杞憂を懷く, to entertain groundless fears; feel needless anxiety.

kiza (跪坐する), *vi.* to kneel (down); fall on one's knees.

kiza (氣障な), *a.* affected; conceited; disagreeable. —氣障な奴, a conceited [an affected] fellow. —氣障な建物, a building in an affected style.

kizahashi (階, 梯), *n.* stairs; (a) [flight of) steps.

kizamime (刻目), *n.* a notch; an incision; a nick. —刻み目を附ける, [*vt.*] to jag; nick; notch.

kizamitabako (刻煙草), *n.* cut tobacco.

kizamu (刻む), *vt.* ❶ (細かく切る) to cut; chop fine [up]; mince (肉などを). ❷ (彫刻する) to carve; engrave; chisel. ❸ (ぎざぎざをつける) to notch; incise; indent. —佛像を刻む, to carve a Buddhist image. —煙草を刻む, to cut tobacco fine. —腦裏に刻みつける, to engrave into [upon] the mind.

kizashi (兆), *n.* ❶ (徵候) a symptom; a sign; an indication. ❷ (萌芽) a germ.

kizasu (兆す), *v.* ❶ (前兆) to augur; show symptoms [signs] *of*; betoken; ❷ (萌す) to sprout; germinate.

kizetsu (氣絶), *n.* fainting; a (dead) faint; a swoon. —氣絶

さす, to stun; knock a person senseless. —氣絶する, to faint away; swoon away; become insensible. (氣絶する程打つ, to knock one almost out of his senses.)

kizewashii (氣急しい), *a.* restless; fidgety; fussy. —氣急しく, restlessly; fidgetily; fussily.

kizō (寄贈), *n.* contribution; presentation; donation. —寄贈する, to contribute; present; donate. ¶ 寄贈品, a gift; a donation. —寄贈者, a contributor; a donor.

kizoku (貴族), *n.* ❶ (身分, 家柄) the nobility; the peerage; the aristocracy. ❷ (人) a nobleman; a peer [*pl.* -ess]; an aristocrat. —貴族的, aristocratic(-al). —貴族に列する, to ennoble; confer a peerage *on*. ¶ 貴族社會, the nobility; the aristocracy; the peerage.

kizoku (歸屬), *n.* 【法】 reversion. —歸屬する, to revert *to* (財產·官職等が); escheat *to*; become vested *in*.

kizokuin (貴族院), *n.* the House of Peers; the House of Lords (英國). ¶ 貴族院議員, a member of the House of Peers; a Lord of Parliament (英國).

kizu (傷, 創), *n.* ❶ (怪我) a wound; an injury. ❷ (瑕疵) a fault; a defect; a flaw; a stain (しみ); a blotch (同上); a speck (疵又は害蟲による果物の); a bruise (果實のあたり).

kizuato (傷痕), *n.* a scar; a seam; a cicatrice, cicatrix.

kizuchi (木槌), *n.* a mallet; a beetle (大槌).

kizuguchi (傷口), *n.* the opening [the lips] of a wound. —傷口を縫ふ, to put a stitch [stitches] in the lips of a wound.

kizugusuri (傷藥), *n.* an ointment; a salve. —傷藥を塗る, to smear with a salve.

kizui (氣隨な), *a.* wilful; self-willed; wayward.

kizuisen (黃水仙), *n.* 【植】 the jonquil.

kizukai (氣遣), *n.* fear; anxiety; concern. ☞ *shinpai*. —氣遣ひなき, without concern [fear; anxiety]. —死ぬ氣遣ひはない, There is no fear of death.

kizukau (氣遣ふ), *v.* to fear; be [feel] anxious *about*; worry (oneself). —氣遣はしく思ふ, to have fear *for*. —身の上を氣遣ふ, to be concerned on his account; be anxious for his welfare.

kizuku (築く), *vt.* to build; construct; throw up (急造).

kizuku (氣附く), *v.* to become aware; take notice *of*; think *of*.

kizumari (氣詰りな), *a.* fusty; stuffy; gloomy.

kizumono (疵物), *n.* a flawed article; a damaged article (損じ物).

kizuna (絏, 絆), *n.* an encumbrance; ties; chains. —愛の絆, ties of affection. —絆を斷つ, to cut away the fetters.

kizuta (常春藤), *n.* 【植】 the ivy; the bindwood.

kizutsukeru (傷ける), *v.* ❶ (怪我) to wound; injure; hurt. ❷ (*a*) (名譽などを) to defame; disparage; injure: (*b*) (感情などを) to hurt; wound. ❸ (破る) to ruin; spoil; mar. —傷けられた自負心, wounded vanity. —頭を傷ける, to break a head. —己の名を傷ける, to defame oneself.

kizutsuku (傷く), *vi.* to get hurt; be injured; be wounded.

kizuyoi (氣强い), *a.* ❶ brave; stout-hearted; resolute. ❷ (無情) hard-hearted; heartless; unfeeling. —氣强く, ① bravely; resolutely; with a stout heart. ② heartlessly; pitilessly.

ko (小), *a.* little; small; young. —, *ad.* rather; pretty (可なり); somewhat (稍); about (約). —, *suf.* [名詞に附す] -ling (例へば youngling など); -let (例へば leaflet; ringlet など): [adjective に附す] -ish (例へば smartish; prettyish など). —小一哩, a short mile.

ko (子, 兒), *n.* ❶ (人間の) a child. ❷ (動物の) young. ❸ (利子) interest. —子に後れる, to survive a child. —子にひかさるゝ親の情, the feelings of the parent drawn towards the child.

ko (故), *a.* the late; the deceased. —故某氏, the late Mr. —.

ko (湖), *n.* a lake. —琵琶湖, Lake Biwa.

ko (弧), *n.* ❶ (木の弓) a bow. ❷ (弓狀) an arc.

ko (粉), *n.* powder; flour (穀類の細粉); meal (穀類の粗粉). —粉にひく[する], to powder; grind to powder.

ko (格), *n.* ❶ (障子の骨) lattice; cross-laths. ❷ (梯子の段) a stave; a rung; a round.

ko (箇, 個), *n.* —林檎五箇, five apples. —石鹼六箇, six pieces [tablets] of soap.

kō (工), *n.* ❶ (職人) an artisan; a mechanic. ❷ (工業) industry. ❸ (仕事) work; task.

kō (功), *n.* ❶ (手柄) merits; (distinguished) services; a meritorious deed. ❷ (成功) success; achievement. ❸ (效) effect. —金鵄勳章功二級, the Second Class of the (Order of the) Golden Kite. —功

を誇る, to boast of one's meritorious deed. —功を奏する, to take effect (奏效); be successful; succeed.

kō (紅), *n.* red; vermilion; crimson. —雙頰に紅を潮する, to flush her cheeks [face].

kō (公), *n.* ❶ (公爵) a prince; a duke (歐洲の). ❷ (大名, 諸侯) a lord; a prince. ❸ (公共) the public; the state (國家). ❹ (公平) justice. —伊藤公, Prince Itō. —公に奉ずる, to serve the state; labour for the public good.

kō (坑), *n.* a pit. —坑外へ出す, to bring to the pit mouth.

kō (甲), *n.* ❶ (鎧) an armour. ❷ (龜·蟹などの甲羅) a carapace; a shell. ❸ (手足の) the back (手の); the instep (足·靴の). ❹ (乙の對) the one; the former.

kō (䋄), *n.* (鳥の) a web.

kō (行), *n.* ❶ (旅行) a journey; an expedition (征行又は征伐). ❷ (一行) suite; party. —君の萬里の行を送る, to wish you God-speed on your long journey.

kō (好), *n.* =*yoshimi* (好). **——**, *a.* favourable; good; suitable. —好一對, a well-assorted pair; a well-matched couple. —好時期, a favourable time. —好敵手, a good match.

kō (交), *n.* ❶ (交際) intercourse; friendship. ❷ (替り目) about the time. —三四月の交, about March or April.

kō (校), *n.* ❶ (學校の略) a school. ❷ (校正の略) correction; proof-reading; a proof (sheet) (校正刷).

kō (效), *n.* ❶ (效力) effect; force; validity. ❷ (效驗) efficacy; virtue. ❸ (效果) result; fruit. —效ある, of avail; valid; effective. —何の效もなく, of no avail; without avail [result]; without effect.

kō (孝), *n.* filial piety. —父母に孝を盡す, to be dutiful to one's parents.

kō (香), *n.* incense (焚きもの); fragrance (芳香); perfume (同上). —香を焚く, to burn incense.

kō (項), *n.* ❶ (ぼんのくぼ) the nucha【解】; the nape (of the neck); the scruff (of the neck). ❷ (箇條) a clause; a paragraph. ❸【數】a term. —第三條第四項, Art. III, Clause 4. —前項記載の通り, as stated in the preceding clause [foregoing paragraph].

kō (侯), *n.* ❶ (侯爵) a marquis; a marquess. ❷ (大小名) a prince; a lord.

kō (候), *n.* a season.

kō (寇), *n.* the enemy; an invasion.

kō (港), *n.* a harbour; a port.

kō (綱), *n.* ❶ (つな) a rope. ❷ (大別) a group. ❸【動】a class; a group.

kō (稿), *n.* a copy; a draft. —稿を脫する, to be completely drafted.

kō (鴻), *n.* 【鳥】the eastern bean-goose.

kō (斯様), *ad.* thus; so; in this manner [way]; like this.

koakinai (小商), *n.* 【商】trading on a small scale; petty trade; retail (trade). —小商ひする, to trade on a small scale [in a small way]; sell retail.

koakindo (小商人), *n.* a retail-dealer (小賣商人); a small-tradesman; a small shop-keeper.

kōan (公安), *n.* the public peace (and order). ☞ *chian* (治安). —公安を害する, to disturb the public peace; break the peace.

kōan (苟安), *n.* momentary [a moment's] ease. —苟安を偸む, to snatch a moment of ease.

kōan (考案), *n.* a design; a plan; a device.

kōatsu (高壓), *n.* ❶ (高度の壓力) high pressure; high tension. ❷ (壓迫) pressure; coercion; high-handedness. **——-teki**, *a.* high-handed; coercive; oppressive. —高壓的に, high-handedly; with a high hand. ¶ 高壓電氣, a high-tension current. —高壓線, high-pressure lines. —高壓手段, a high-handed [an oppressive] measure.

koba (木羽), *n.* shingles. —木羽で葺く, to shingle. ¶ 木羽葺屋根, a shingle roof.

kōba (工場), *n.* a factory; a workshop; works. ☞ *kōjō.*

kobachi (小鉢), *n.* a server.

kobai (故買), *n.* purchasing stolen goods; fencing〔俗〕. —故買をする, to purchase stolen goods; receive; fence. ¶ 故買者, a purchaser of stolen goods; a receiver; a fence.

kōbai (公賣), *n.* a public sale; a public auction. —公賣する, to sell in public; sell by auction. —公賣に付する, to put to public sale; put up to auction.

kōbai (勾配), *n.* gradient; slope; incline. —屋根の勾配, pitch of a roof. —急な勾配, a sharp [steep] gradient. —緩い勾配, a gentle [an easy] gradient.

kōbai (紅梅), *n.* 【植】the red-flowered *mume* plum.

kōbai (購買), *n.* purchase. —購買する, to purchase; buy. —貨幣の購買力, the purchasing value of money; money value. —農家の購買力, the purchasing power of farmers. ¶ 購買組合, a purchase guild [association].

kōbaisū (公倍數), *n.* 【數】 a common multiple. —最小公倍數を求める, to find the least common multiple.

kōbako (香匣), *n.* a cassolette; an incense-boat (舟形の).

kōbaku (廣漠たる), *a.* vast; extensive; immense.

kobamishōsho (拒證書), *n.* a protest.

kobamu (拒む), *n.* ❶ (阻む) to check; keep away; resist. ❷ (拒絶する) to refuse; decline; repulse. —見る(聽く)ことを拒む, to shut one's eyes (ears) *to*.

koban (小判), *n.* a *koban* [日]; an old gold coin. —小判形の, oval.

kōban (交番), *n.* ❶ (交番所) a police-box; a police-stand. ❷ (交代) spell 【航】; alternation. —交番に, alternately; by turns. ¶ 交番電流,【電】an alternating current.

kōban (絞盤), *n.* a capstan.

kobanzame (小判鮫), *n.* 【魚】 the sucker.

kobaruto (コバルト), *n.* 【化】 cobalt.

kōbashii (芳ばしい), *a* ❶ (香よき) fragrant; sweet; odorous. ❷ (利得ある) profitable; lucrative; favourable. ❸ (令聞ある) famous; well-known. —香しい話でない, It is not a pleasant story.

kōbe (首, 頭), *n.* the head. —頭を垂れ(上げ)る, to hang (raise) one's head. —首を伸べて待つ, to wait with a craned neck.

kōbeki (降冪), *n.* 【數】 a descending series.

kōben (巧辯), *n.* ❶ (詭辯) sophistry; sophism. ❷ (辯才) eloquence; the gift of the gab; a glib tongue.

kōben (抗辯), *n.* ❶ (抗言) dispute; refutation; protest. ❷ 【法】 a plea; a defence. —抗辯する, to dispute *with*; refute; protest *against*.

kobetsu (戶別に), *ad.* house by house; at each house; from door to door. ¶ 戶別訪問, house-to-house visitation; canvassing from door to door.

kobetsu (箇別的), *a.* 【論・文】 individual; distributive. —箇別的に, individually; distributively.

kobi (媚), *n.* flattery; adulation; fawning. —媚を呈する, to curry favour *with*. —媚を賣る, to flatter for money.

kōbi (交尾), *n.* copulation (動物の); tread (雄鷄の). —交尾する, ① [*vi.*] to copulate; pair; couple. ② [*vt.*] to cover (a female); tread (a hen). ¶ 交尾期, the pairing-time [-season].

kōbi (後備), *n.* the second reserve; *kōbi* [日]. ¶ 後備役, service in the second reserve. —後備軍, the second reserve army [forces]. —後備兵, the second reserve; *landwehr* [獨]; a second reservist (個人).

kobihetsurau (媚諂ふ), *v.* to fawn *upon*; flatter; curry favour *with*.

kobiki (木挽), *n.* a sawyer. ¶ 木挽場, a lumber-mill; a saw-mill.

kōbin (幸便), *n.* a good opportunity of sending. —幸便に託する, to take [avail oneself of] this good opportunity to send.

kōbin (後便), *n.* a later mail; a later opportuniy. —詳細は後便, Further details by a later mail.

kobiritsuku (こびりつく), *vi.* to stick *to*; adhere *to*; cling *to*.

kobiru (媚びる), *vt.* to flatter; fawn *upon*; truckle *to*.

kobito (小人), *n.* a dwarf; a pigmy; a Lilliputian. ¶ 小人島, Lilliput; an island of pigmies.

kōbo (公簿), *n.* a public register; a court-roll.

kōbo (公募する), *vt.* to collect [invite] publicly. —志願者を公募する, to invite publicly [advertise for] applicants.

kōbo (皇謨), *n.* an Imperial undertaking [plan]; the Imperial policy.

kōbo (酵母), *n.* zyme; yeast; ferment.

kōbō (好望), *n.* promise; good [bright] prospects. ☞ *yūbō.*

kōbō (廣袤), *n.* area; extent; dimension. ☞ *hirosa.*

kōbō (興亡), *n.* rise and fall (of a nation); vicissitudes. —一國興亡の別るゝ處, the turning point in the fate [rise and fall] of a nation.

koboku (古木), *n.* an old [aged] tree.

koboku (枯木), *n.* a withered tree.

kōboku (校僕), *n.* a college [school] servant.

kōbokushitsu (硬木質), *n.* hard-wood.

kobonnō (子煩惱), *n.* ❶ (子供を切愛すること) excessive love of children. ❷ (子を可愛がる親) a fond father (mother).

koboreru (零・溢れる), *vi.* to spill; run over; brim over; drop (淚が). —零れる程の, full to overflowing.

koboreru (壞れる), *v.* to be nicked; be broken. —刃の壞れた小刀, a knife with a nicked edge.

koborezaiwai (僥倖), *n.* a luck; a godsend. ☞ *gyōkō.*

kobosu (零す), *v.* ❶ (溢れさす) to spill; pour out (つぎ出す); shed (淚を). ❷ (愚痴る) to grumble *at* [*about*; *over*]; complain *of*; murmur *at*. ¶ こぼしや, a grumbler.

kobotsu (毀つ), *vt.* to break [pull] (down); destroy; demolish. —人の徳を毀つ, to calumniate another.
kobōzu (小坊主), *n.* a young priest; an acolyte (番僧); a novice (見習僧).
kobu (瘤), *n.* ❶【醫】a wen; a bump; a protuberance. ❷ (木節) a gnarl; a knur; a knob.
kobu (昆布), *n.* =*konbu.*
kobu (鼓舞する), *vt.* to incite; stimulate; arouse. ——, *a.* stimulant; inspiring; encouraging. —勇氣を鼓舞する, to stir up courage. —士氣を鼓舞する, to stimulate the morale of the troops.
kōbu (後部), *n.* the afterpart; the stern (船の); the rear; the hind part; the back-part.
kōbu (荒蕪), *n.* barrenness; wildness; desolation. —荒蕪の, waste; barren; desert. —荒蕪地を開墾する, to reclaim waste land; bring waste land under cultivation.
kobun (子分, 乾分), *n.* a protegé; a follower.
kobun (古文), *n.* ancient [archaic] writings; classics.
kōbun (公文), *n.* an official document; an official note; archives.
kōbun (行文), *n.* style.
kōbunbo (公分母), *n.* 【數】a common denominator. ¶ 最小公分母, the least common denominator.
kobune (小舟), *n.* a (small) boat; a skiff; a lighter (艀舟).
kobungaku (古文學), *n.* classics.
kobunsho (古文書), *n.* an ancient [old] document.
kōbunsho (公文書), *n.* an official document [note]; a public record; a state paper.
koburi (小降), *n.* a light rain (雨); a slight fall of snow (雪).
kobushi (辛夷), *n.* 【植】Magnolia Kobus (magnolia の一種・學名).
kobushi (拳), *n.* the fist. —拳で打つ, to fisticuff. —拳を固める, to clench one's fist.
kobushi (古武士), *n.* an old-time warrior.
kobutsu (古物), *n.* ❶ (骨董) an antique; antiquities; a curio. ❷ (ふるもの) old things. ¶ 古物商, a second-hand dealer.
kōbutsu (鑛物), *n.* a mineral. ¶ 鑛物學, mineralogy. (鑛物學者, a mineralogist.)
kōcha (紅茶), *n.* black tea.
kochaku (固著する), *v.* to adhere *to*; stick *to*; cleave *to*. —岩に固著する, to stick hard to the rock.
kōchaku (膠著), *n.* agglutination (膠にて); cementation (セメントなどで); adhesion (粘りつくこと). —膠著する, to agglutinate; stick; glue (one thing to another).
kochi (鯒), *n.* 【魚】Platycephalus indicus (flathead の一種・學名).
kochi (東風), *n.* an east [easterly] wind. =*tōfū.*
kōchi (公知の), *a.* well-known; public. —公知の事實, a well-known fact; a matter of public knowledge.
kōchi (巧遲), *n.* the skilful but slow. —巧遲は拙速に如かず, The skilful but slow is inferior to the unskilful but quick.
kōchi (巧緻), *n.* exquisiteness; delicacy. —巧緻な, exquisite; delicate; elaborate.
kōchi (拘置する), *vt.* to confine; detain; keep in custody.
kōchi (高地), *n.* high ground; an upland (一國の); a hill (丘). —二百三高地, the 203-metre Hill.
kōchi (荒地), *n.* a waste; an uncultivated [a waste] land.
kōchi (耕地), *n.* arable land; a cultivated field; a plantation (煙草・砂糖・綿など大規模に作る). —耕地を整理する, to adjust arable land.
kōchin (工賃), *n.* wages (of workmen); pay.
kōchin (交趾), *n.* 【家禽】the cochin.
kochira (此方), ❶ this place (處); this side (側); this way (道); this (gentleman) (人). ❷ (自分) I; we. ❸ (話の相手方) your house; yours. —此方樣は小林樣とおッしゃいますか, Is this Mr. Kobayashi's? ——-e, *ad.* here; this way; on this side. —どうぞ此方へお上り下さい, Please come in this way.
kochō (胡蝶), *n.* a butterfly.
kochō (枯凋), *n.* ❶ (枯れ凋む) withering; fading; decay. ❷ (衰へる) decline; decay. ☞ *chōraku.* —枯凋する, ① to wither; fade. ② to decay; decline.
kochō (誇張), *n.* exaggeration; grandiloquence (言・文などの); turgidity (文體などの). —誇張する, to exaggerate; magnify; overdraw. ——-teki, *a.* exaggerated; grandiloquent; turgid; bombastic; inflated. —誇張的記述, exaggerated description. —誇張的廣告, a puff. —新聞紙上の誇張的記事, exaggerations of a newspaper. ¶ 誇張法, 【修】hyperbole.
kōchō (工長), *n.* a foreman.
kōchō (好調-子), *n.* ❶ (音聲の調子よきこと) tunefulness; melodiousness. ❷ (工合よきこと) smoothness; favourableness.
kōchō (紅潮する), *vi.* to flush.
kōchō (高調), *n.* a high pitch.

—高調する, to accentuate; emphasize; stress; lay stress *upon*.
kōchō (高潮), *n.* ❶ (極度の上汐) the high tide [water]. ❷ (感情又は時勢の高まりし時) the climax; culmination. —歡樂の高潮に達する, to reach the climax of pleasure. ¶ 高潮線, the high-water mark.
kōchō (校長), *n.* a principal; a headmaster (中學·小學校の); a director. ¶ 女校長, a headmistress; a lady principal.
kōchō (候鳥), *n.* a bird of passage; a migratory bird.
kōchoku (硬直な), *a.* sturdy; stout; stiff. —硬直な男子, a stiff man.
kōchū (口中), *n.* the interior of the mouth. —口中の病, a disease of the mouth. ¶ 口中藥, a stomatic.
kōchū (行廚), *n.* a luncheon; a lunch; a tiffin.
kodachi (木立), *n.* a cluster of trees; a clump; a copse.
kodai (古代), *n.* antiquity; ancient [olden] times; the days of yore. **—-no,** *a.* antique; ancient; archaic. —古代の記念物, memorials of remote ages.
kodai (誇大な), *a.* exaggerated; high-flown (語氣など); inflated. ¶ 誇大妄想狂, megalomania; a megalomaniac (人).
kōdai (絞臺), *n.* the gibbet; the gallows.
kōdai (廣大·宏大な), *a.* ❶ great; huge (巨大). ❷ (廣い) vast (平原など); extensive; immense. ❸ (宏壯な) grand; magnificent. —宏大な建物, a magnificent building. —廣大無邊の, boundless; unbounded.
kōdaka (甲高な), *a.* high-backed; with a high instep.
kodakai (小高い), *a.* slightly high. —小高い丘, a low hill.
kodakku (コダック), *n.* a kodak. —コダックで撮影する, to kodak.
kōdaku (肯諾), *n.* approval. —肯諾する, to approve.
kodama (谺,木靈), *n.* ❶ (樹木の精) the dryad. ❷ (反響) an echo; reverberation. —谺に響く, to echo; reverberate; resound. —谺を返す, to reecho.
kodan (古談), *n.* a legend; an old tale.
kōdan (光彈), *n.* 【軍】 a star-shell.
kōdan (降壇する), *vt.* to leave a lecture-platform [platform; rostrum].
kōdan (講談), *n.* ❶ (寄席の) story-telling; a narrative; a narration. ❷ (講話) a discourse. ¶ 講談本, a story-book. —講談師, a story-teller; a narrator.
kodate (小楯), *n.* a small shield. —樹木を小楯にして, shielding oneself behind a tree.
kodawaru (こだはる), *vi.* = kōdei.
kōdei (拘泥する), *vi.* to adhere *to*; cling *to*; stick *to*. —字句に拘泥する, to adhere to the letter.
kodemari (麻葉繡毬), *n.* 【植】 Spiræa cantoniensis (meadow-sweet の一種·學名).
kōden (香奠), *n.* a present made in condolence. ¶ 香奠返し, a return for a condolence present.
kodō (鼓動), *n.* beat; pulse; palpitation. —鼓動する, to beat; pulse; palpitate.
kōdo (光度), *n.* intensity of light; illuminating power 【理】; brightness 【天】. —星の光度, brightness of a star. ¶ 光度計, a photometer.
kōdo (高度), *n.* ❶ altitude; height. ❷ high degree; high power (顯微鏡等の). —高度の眼鏡, a high-power spectacles. —千五百米の高度を保つ, to maintain the height of 1500 metres. ¶ 高度計, an altimeter.
kōdo (硬度), *n.* hardness; solidity.
kōdo (コード), *n.* a cord.
kōdō (公道), *n.* ❶ (正義) justice; right. ❷ (道路) a highway (海陸の); a public road. —天下の公道, a public highway. —公道を踏む, to take the path of justice.
kōdō (坑道), *n.* ❶ (鑛山) a gallery (of a mine); a drift; a tunnel. ❷ 【軍】 a gallery; a mine.
kōdō (行動), *n.* an action; a movement; proceeding. —行動を執る, to take action; make a move. —行動を共にする, to make a common cause. **—-suru,** *vi.* to act; move (in a matter); proceed. —巧みに行動する, to play one's part well. —自由に行動する, to act freely.
kōdō (孝道), *n.* filial piety [duty].
kōdō (黄道), *n.* ❶ 【天】 the ecliptic. ❷ (天子の通路) the route of an Imperial progress.
kōdō (黄銅), *n.* brass. ¶ 黄銅鑛, copper pyrites. —黄銅色, brass yellow.
kōdō (講堂), *n.* a lecture-hall; a hall; a theatre (席が圓形階段の).
kodōgu (小道具), *n.* ❶ fittings. ❷ 【劇】 stage property.
kodoku (孤獨), *n.* ❶ an orphan (孤兒); a solitary person (單獨の人). ❷ singleness (獨身); solitude (獨居); solitariness. ¶ 孤獨生活, a solitary life.
kōdoku (購讀する), *vt.* to take (in); subscribe *to*. —購讀を豫約する, to subscribe *for*. ¶ 購讀者, a reader *of*; a subscriber *to* (新聞·雜誌の).

kōdoku (鑛毒), *n.* mine pollution.

kodomo (子供), *n.* a child [*pl.* -ren] (男女とも). —子供じみた, childish. —子供らしく, childishly; boyishly. —ジョウンズの子供等, the little Joneses. —子供の時から, from a child; from childhood. —子供扱ひにする, to treat like a child. ¶ 子供だまし, a trick to deceive children. —子供服, children's clothes; short clothes [coats] (膝までの). —子供芝居, juvenile theatricals.

koe (肥), *n.* ❶ (肥料) manure. ❷ (大小便) night-soil. ☞ ***koyashi.*** —肥を取る, to clear the night-soil. —肥を施す, to manure.

koe (聲), *n.* a voice (音聲); a sound (音響); a cry (呼聲); a note (鳥の); a cry (蟲の). —雲雀の囀る聲, the lark's note. —聲の屆く所に, within cry *of*. —聲を潜める, to lower one's voice. —聲を立てる, to raise one's voice. —思はず聲を出す, to cry out involuntarily. —聲を呑んで泣く, to weep with a suppressed cry.

koeda (小枝), *n.* a twig; a sprig; a spray (花などの). —梅の小枝, a spray of plum-blossoms.

koegawari (聲變), *n.* 【生】 the change of voice (懷春期の). —聲變りする, The voice is cracked.

kōei (光榮), *n.* honour; glory; lustre. —光榮とする, to feel it a honour *to*; esteem it a high honour. —無上の光榮を擔ふ, to bear the highest honours; be loaded with honours; be covered with glory.

kōei (後裔), *n.* a descendant; a scion; posterity.

kōei (後衞), *n.* ❶ the rear (of an army); the rear-guard. ❷ the back player (庭球); a back (蹴球).

kōeki (公益), *n.* the public [common] good; the public benefit [interest]; the public welfare. —公益に關する事柄, a matter of public interest. ¶ 公益法人, a juridical person for the public benefit.

kōeki (交易), *n.* barter (物々交換); trade (貿易); traffic (同上). —交易する, to trade; traffic; barter.

kōen (口演), *n.* oral statement; oral narration. ¶ 口演者, a speaker.

kōen (公演), *n.* a public performance.

kōen (公園), *n.* a park; a public garden; a square.

kōen (光燄), *n.* brilliancy.

kōen (高遠な), *a.* lofty; elevated; sublime. —高遠の理想(思想), a lofty ideal (idea).

kōen (後援), *n.* backing; support; succour. —後援する, to uphold; support; back up. ¶ 後援者, a supporter; a patron; an upholder; a backer.

kōen (講演), *n.* a lecture; a public address; a speech. —講演する, to lecture; address. ¶ 講演會, a lecture-meeting. —講演者, a lecturer; a speaker.

koeru (肥える), *vi.* ❶ (肥滿) to grow fat [corpulent; plump]; fatten; wax fat. ❷ (肥沃) to grow fertile [rich; productive]. —肥えた土地, a fertile land. —能く肥えた牛, well-conditioned cattle. —目が肥えてゐる, to have a trained eye.

koeru (越·超える), *v.* ❶ (通過) to pass (*through*); go *through*; cross (山川·海などを). ❷ (超過) to exceed; pass; go *beyond*. ❸ (勝る) to surpass; excel; transcend; exceed. —...を越えて, [*prep.*] over; out; out of; beyond; above. —界を越える, to break bounds. —線路を越える, to cross the rails. —百圓を越えぬ, not exceeding 100 *yen*.

kōetsu (校閲), *n.* revision; recension. —校閲する, to revise; look over. ¶ 校閲者, a reviser.

kofū (古風), *n.* old fashion (舊式); antique style (美術などの); old customs [manners] (風俗·習慣など). —古風の, old; old-fashioned; antique (古代風の).

kōfu (工夫), *n.* a workman; a labourer; a navvy. ¶ 工夫長, an overlooker; a ganger; a foreman of workmen [navvies].

kōfu (公布), *n.* official announcement; promulgation; proclamation. —公布する, to proclaim; promulgate; announce officially.

kōfu (交付), *n.* delivery; transfer. —交付する, to deliver; transfer; hand (手交).

kōfu (坑夫, 鑛夫), *n.* a miner; a pitman (炭坑の); a collier (同上). ¶ 坑夫肺炎, the collier's lung [phthisis].

kōfū (校風), *n.* school discipline (校紀); school custom. —校風を紊亂する, to break down school discipline.

kōfuku (口腹), *n.* the mouth and paunch [belly]. —口腹の慾, appetite; craving for food.

kōfuku (校服), *n.* a school uniform.

kōfuku (幸福), *n.* ❶ happiness (心の滿足); welfare; well-being. ❷ (幸運) blessing (特に天與の福); good fortune; good luck. **—— -na**, *a.* happy (滿足せる); blessed; fortunate; lucky. —幸福な生活を送る, to lead a happy life. —幸福な家庭を作る, to make a happy home.

kōfuku (降服,降伏), *n.* surrender; submission. ☞ *kōsan.* —降服する, to surrender *to*; yield *to*; captulate (條件附で). —降服して捕虜となる, to yield oneself as prisoner. ¶降服條件, the terms of surrender.

kōfun (口吻), *n.* the manner of speaking; tone (語調). —口吻を學ぶ, to mimic another's manner of speaking. —不平の口吻を漏らす, to betray a tone of discontent.

kōfun (公憤), *n.* public indignation.

kōfun (紅粉), *n.* rouge and powder. —紅粉を粧ふ, to paint.

kōfun (興奮,亢奮), *n.* excitement; stimulation. —興奮さす, to excite; stimulate. —興奮する, to be excited; be stimulated. ¶興奮劑, a stimulant; a bracer; a cordial.

Kōfūshi (孔夫子), *n.* Confucius.

koga (古雅な), *a.* graceful (體裁よき); elegant; classical (古典的).

koga (古畫), *n.* an ancient [old] picture [painting].

kōga (高雅), *n.* concinnity (文體の); elegance. —高雅な, refined; elegant.

kogai (小買する), *vt.* to buy in small quantities.

kogai(子養,子飼), *n.* bringing up from infancy. —子飼ひの獅子, a lion reared from infancy; a lion caught young.

kogai (戸外), *n.* the open; the open air. —戸外の, out-of-door; outdoor. —戸外で, outdoors; out of doors; in the open air. —戸外に居る, to be in the open air. ¶戸外學校, an open-air school. —戸外生活, the life in the open. —戸外運動, out-of-door exercise. —戸外遊戯, outdoor sports [games; amusement].

kōgai (笄), *n.* (髮の) a bar for the hair.

kōgai (口外する), *v.* to mention; disclose; let out.

kōgai (口蓋), *n.* 【解】 the palate; the roof of the mouth. ¶口蓋骨, the palate [palatine] bone.

kōgai (郊外), *n.* the suburbs; the outskirts (of a town); the environs. ¶郊外散步, a walk in the suburbs. —郊外生活, suburban life.

kōgai (校外), *n.* the outside of a school. ¶校外生, a day-scholar (通學生); a correspondence scholar [pupil] (通信學生).

kōgai (港外に), *ad.* outside the port [harbour]. —港外に碇泊する, to anchor outside the harbour.

kōgai (梗槪), *n.* an outline; a summary; an epitome.

kōgai (慷慨), *n.* indignation; patriotic indignation. —慷慨する, to be indignant; give vent to one's patriotic indignation. ¶慷慨家, a man of spirit; a deplorer (of the evils of the times).

kōgai (構外), *ad.* outside the premises. —停車場構外, outside the station compound.

kōgaku (工學), *n.* engineering. ¶工學博士, a doctor of engineering. —工學者, an engineer. —工學士, a bachelor of engineering.

kōgaku (光學), *n.* optics.

kōgaku (後學), *n.* ❶ (後進生) a junior. ❷ (後の知見) instruction (誡め); information (知識). —後學の爲に, for future instruction; for one's edification [information]; for future reference.

kogamo (小鴨), *n.* 【鳥】 the teal.

kōgan (厚顔), *n.* impudence; effrontery; barefacedness. —厚顔にも…する, to have the impudence [effrontery] *to*. **——no,** *a.* impudent; shameless; brazen [bare]-faced. —厚顔無恥の徒, shameless persons; those lost to shame.

kogane (小錢), *n.* ❶ a small sum. ❷ a small change [coin]. —小錢を溜める, to save up small sums. (彼は大分小錢を溜めて居る, He has (saved) a pretty penny.)

kogane (黄金), *n.* gold. —黄金色の, golden; gold.

koganemushi (金龜子), *n.* 【昆】 Mimela lucidula (學名).

kogara (小雀), *n.* 【鳥】 the Japanese marsh-tit.

kogara (小柄の), *a.* ❶ (小さな縞柄) small-patterned. ❷ (小づくり) of small build.

kogarashi (木枯,凩), *n.* an autumn wind.

kogareru (焦れる), *v.* to long [yearn] *after*; sigh *for*; be smitten with love. —焦れ死にする, to die of love.

kogasu (焦す), *v.* ❶ to burn; scorch; char; singe. ❷ (胸を) to burn; pine *for* [*after*]. —著物を焦す, to scorch one's clothes. —戀に胸を焦す, to pine with love *for*; burn with love.

kogata (小形の), *a.* small-sized; undersized; miniature. ¶小形自動車, a small motor-car.

kogatana (小刀), *n.* a knife; a pocket-knife; a pen-knife. —小刀細工をする, to resort to petty devices; resort to temporizing measures.

kogawa (小川), *n.* a brook; a rivulet; a rill.

kogawase (小爲替), *n.* a postal order; a postal note.

kōge (高下), *n.* ❶ (上下…階級) rank; grade; high and low. ❷ (高低…價格) fluctuations; rise and fall. ❷(優劣…品質) quality; good or bad. —高下する, to fluctuate.

kōge (香華), *n.* incense and flowers; offerings. —香華を手向ける, to offer incense and flowers. ¶香華料, an offering in money to the dead.

kogecha (焦茶), *n.* (繪具) dark brown.

kōgei (工藝), *n.* technology; technics; the industrial arts. ¶工藝學校, a polytechnic school; a technical school; a school of technology. —工藝品, an industrial product. —工藝家, a technologist. —工藝館, the industrial hall.

kōgeki (攻擊), *n.* an attack; an assault. —攻擊する, to attack; assault; assail; fall on. —攻擊的行動, offensive movement. —攻擊的態度に出る, to act on the offensive. —攻擊を受ける, to be attacked. ¶總攻擊, a general attack. —側(背; 正)面攻擊, a flank (rear; frontal) attack. —攻擊側,【野球】the side at bat. —攻擊(用)武器, offensive arms. —攻擊軍, an army of attack; an attacking force.

kōgekika (好劇家), *n.* a play-lover; a play-goer.

kogekusai (焦臭い), *a.* smelling of something burning. ——, *vi.* to give a burning smell. —何だか焦臭い, I smell something burning.

kogen (古諺), *n.* an adage; an old maxim [proverb; saying; say].

kōgen (公言), *n.* open declaration; profession; avowal. —公言する, to declare in public [openly]; profess; avow.

kōgen (巧言), *n.* adulation; fair [honeyed] words; deftness of tongue. —巧言令色の人, a coaxer; a cajoler; a toad-eater; a flatterer.

kōgen (高言, 廣言), *n.* tall talk; grandiloquence; bombast. —片腹痛い廣言, ridiculous boasting. —高言を吐く, to brag *of*; boast *of*; talk tall.

kōgen (高原), *n.* a table-land; a plateau.

kōgen (郊原), *n.* a suburban field.

kōgen (曠原), *n.* a wilderness; a waste land.

kogeru (焦げる), *vi.* to be scorched; burn; be singed.

kogi (漕), *n.* a pull; a stroke. —櫓の一漕ぎ, a stroke of oar.

kogi (狐疑), *n.* doubt; hesitation; vacillation. —狐疑する, to doubt; hesitate; vacillate.

kōgi (公義), *n.* justice; equity.

kōgi (交誼), *n.* friendship; friendly intercourse [relation]. —隣國の交誼を重んずる, to value [set store by] friendly relations with neighbouring countries. —交誼を斷つ, to break friendship *with*; have done *with*.

kōgi (好誼, 厚誼), *n.* intimate friendship; kindness; kind treatment.

kōgi (抗議), *n.* a protest. —抗議する, to protest *against*. —抗議を申込む, to enter [make] a protest *against*. ¶抗議者, a protester, protestor. —抗議書, a written protest.

kōgi (廣義), *n.* a wide [broad] sense. —廣義に解釋する, to put a wide construction *upon*; interpret in a wide sense.

kōgi (講義), *n.* a lecture. —講義する, to lecture *on*. ¶講義錄, a transcript of lectures; a correspondence course (通信講義錄).

kogidasu (漕出す), *v.* ❶ to pull out; row out. ❷(漕始める) to begin to row.

kogikata (漕方), *n.* the manner [style] of rowing; stroke.

kogimodosu (漕戻す), *v.* to row back.

kogire (小切), *n.* a small piece; a strip; a rag.

kogirei (小綺麗な), *a.* prettyish; neat; natty. —小綺麗に, neatly; nattily.

kogite (漕手), *n.* an oarsman; a puller; a rower.

kogitsukeru (漕附ける), *v.* ❶ to get *to*; pull in (陸へ); row up *to*. ❷(やり及ぶ) to contrive; manage; work one's way through.

kogitte (小切手), *n.* a cheque; a check【米】. —小切手を支拂ふ, to cash a cheque. —小切手を現金に引換へる, to cash a cheque. ¶線引小切手, a crossed cheque. —小切手帳, a cheque-book.

kogo (古語), *n.* ❶ an old word; an archaic word. ❷(古諺) an old saying; an old proverb.

kōgo (口語), *n.* an oral [a spoken] language. ¶口語體, colloquial style; colloquialism. (口語體の, colloquial.)

kōgo (交互), *n.* ❶(交番) alternation. ❷(相互) reciprocity. —交互の, ① alternate. ② reciprocal; mutual. —交互に, ① interchangeably; by turns; alternately. ② reciprocally; mutually. —交互する, to alternate; intercross. ¶交互計算, account current.

kōgō (苟合する), *vi.* to temporize; follow another blindly; go with the stream.

kōgō (皇后), *n.* a queen; an empress; an empress-consort (女帝と區別する時); a queen-consort (同上). ¶皇后宮職, the Services to Her Majesty the Empress. —皇后宮太夫, the Lord Steward to

Her Majesty.
kōgō (香盒), *n.* an incense-case.
kogoe (小聲で), *ad.* beneath [under] one's breath; in a low voice; in a whisper.
kogoejini (凍死する), *v.* to be frozen to death.
kogoeru (凍える), *vi.* to freeze; become numb; be benumbed with cold. —凍えた, frozen; numb with cold. —凍えさす, to freeze.
kogome (小米), *n.* broken rice. ¶ 小米櫻,【植】Spiræa Thunbergii (meadow-sweet の一種・學名).
kogomu (踞む), *vi.* to stoop; bend; bow. —腰を踞める, to bend the body.
kogoroshi (兒殺し), *n.* ❶ (事) infanticide; child-murder. ❷ (人) a child-murderer.
kogoru (凝・凍結る), *vi.* to freeze; congeal. —凝らす, to freeze; congeal.
kogoshi (小腰), *n.* a slight bow. —小腰を屈める, to make a slight bow; bow slightly.
kōgōshii (神神しい), *a.* ❶ (かみがみしい) god-like; heavenly. ❷ (莊嚴) solemn; venerable.
kogoto (小言), *n.* ❶ (訓戒の言) a reproof; a lecture; a rebuke. ❷ (叱責) blame; scolding; fault-finding. ❸ (口小言) grumbling; murmur. —小言を食ふ, to be scolded. —小言を言ふ, ① to reprove; rebuke; read another a lecture [lesson]. ② to scold; find fault *with*; blame. ③ to grumble; murmur.
kogoto (戸毎に), *ad.* at every door [house]; from door to door.
kogu (漕ぐ), *vt.* to pull (橈を); row (船を); oar (橈にて); scull (二挺橈で船を). —烈しく(大きく)漕ぐ, to row a fast (long) stroke. —深く(淺く)漕ぐ, to pull deep (shallow). —漕ぎ損じ(て後にひっくりかへ)る, to catch a crab. —一生懸命に漕ぐ, to bend to one's oar. —一分間に三十本の割で漕ぐ, to row 30 to the minute.
kōgu (工具), *n.* a tool.
kōgū (皇宮), *n.* the Imperial Palace. ¶ 皇宮警察, the Imperial Palace police. —皇宮警手, an Imperial Palace policeman.
kōgū (厚遇), *n.* hospitality; kind treatment; warm reception. —厚遇する, to treat kindly; receive warmly; give a warm [cordial] reception. —非常な厚遇を受ける, to be treated royally; be received with great warmth.
koguchi (小口), *n.* ❶ (端緒) the beginning; the inception. ❷ (はし) one end. ❸ (小額) a small sum (of money). ❹【建】header; butt-end (木口). ❺ (書物の) an edge. ¶ 小口註文, a small order. —小口當座, a petty current account.
kogun (孤軍), *n.* an isolated force.
kōgun (行軍), *n.* a march; marching. ¶ 旅次行軍, a route march. —雪中行軍, a snow march.
kōgun (後軍), *n.* the rear-guard.
kogurakaru (こぐらかる), *vi.* to be entangled; get in a tangle. —こぐらかす, to entangle.
kōgushi (香具師), *n.* a mountebank.
kogusuri (粉藥), *n.* powdered medicine; a powder.
kōgyō (工業), *n.* industry; manufacturing industry. —工業的, industrial. —工業用の, for industrial use. ¶ 工業中心地, an industrial centre. —工業地, a manufacturing district. —工業學校, a technical school; a technological school. (高等工業學校, a higher technical school; a higher school of technology.) —工業博覽會, an industrial exhibition. —工業家, an industrialist; a manufacturer. —工業試驗所, an industrial experimental station.
kōgyō (興行), *n.* performance; exhibition. —興行する, to perform; run (a play); show; get up. —晴天十日の興行, performances for ten fine days. ¶ 興行飛行, an exhibition flight. —興業權, a stage-right; a dramatic right; a right of performance; a play-right. —興行師, a show-man; the runner of a show.
kōgyō (鑛業), *n.* mining; mining industry. ¶ 鑛業權, a mining right.
kōgyō-ginkō (興業銀行), *n.* an industrial bank.
kōgyoku (紅玉), *n.* 【鑛】ruby.
kōgyoku (硬玉), *n.* 【鑛】jade.
kōha (光波), *n.* a light-wave.
kōha (硬派), *n.* ❶ (政黨政派の) a stalwart section. ❷ (新聞・雜誌の) a political staff [department]. ¶ 硬派記者, a political writer; a writer on the political staff.
kōhai (光背), *n.* a glory; an aureola; a halo. ☞ *gokō.*
kōhai (向背), *n.* attitude. —向背を決する, to decide upon the attitude to be taken.
kōhai (荒廢, 荒敗), *n.* desolation; devastation; ruin. —荒廢する, to go [run] to waste; go to ruin; lie waste. —荒廢に委する, to let run waste.
kōhai (後輩), *n.* a junior; younger men.
kōhai (興敗), *n.* rise and fall;

fate; vicissitudes.

kōhai (曠廢する), *vt.* to neglect.

kohaku (琥珀), *n.* amber; 【化】 succinite. ¶ 琥珀織, taille; taffeta (薄琥珀).

kōhaku (厚薄), *n.* ❶ thickness. ❷ partiality.

kōhaku (紅白), *n.* red and white.

kōhaku (黄白), *n.* ❶ (黄と白) white and yellow. ❷ (金銀) gold and silver. ❸ (貨幣) lucre; money.

kōhan (公判), *n.* a trial; a (public) hearing. —事件を公判に付する, to put the case on trial; commit the case for trial. ¶ 公判廷, the court of trial.

kōhan (後半), *n.* the latter half; the second half. ¶ 後半生, the latter half [part] of one's life.

kōhan (皓礬), *n.* ❶ 【化】 sulphate of zinc; white vitriol. ❷ 【鑛】 goslarite.

kōhan (廣汎な), *a.* expansive; extensive; vast. —廣汎に亙る, to cover a vast space.

koharu (小春), *n.* an Indian summer; St. Martin's summer.

kohaze (鞐), *n.* a clasp. —鞐を掛ける(外す), to fasten (unfasten) a clasp.

kōhei (工兵), *n.* an engineer; a sapper. ¶ 工兵監, the inspector of engineers.

kōhei (公平), *n.* impartiality; fairness; justice. **——-na,** *a.* impartial; just; unprejudiced; fair. —公平な判斷, impartial judgment. —公平な待遇, a fair field [play]. **——-ni,** *ad.* impartially; fairly. —公平に言へば[評すれば], to do justice *to.*

kōheihō (衡平法), *n.* 【法】 equity.

kōhen (後篇), *n.* a sequel; the latter [second] part.

kōhi (口碑), *n.* (oral) tradition.

kōhi (公費), *n.* public expenditure [expense]. —公費を投ずる, to spend public money *upon.*

kōhi (皇妃), *n.* an empress; a queen; a queen (an empress)-consort.

kōhi (珈琲), *n.* coffee. —珈琲を入れる, to make coffee. ¶ 珈琲店, a coffee-house; a cafe.

kōhi-dōbutsu (厚皮動物), *n.* 【動】 Pachydermata (學名); the pachyderms.

kohitsuji (羔, 小羊), *n.* a lamb. —羔の毛, lamb's-wool.

kōho (候補), *n.* ❶ candidacy; candidateship. ❷ (候補者) a candidate. —...の候補者になる, to put in *for*; stand *for.* —候補者として打って出る, to come forward as a candidate. —候補を辭退する, to decline the candidacy. ¶ 衆議院議員候補者, a candidate for the House of Representatives.

kōhō (公法), *n.* public law.

kōhō (公報), *n.* an official report; a *communiqué* (佛).

kōhō (後方), *n.* rear. ¶ 後方勤務, rear-service.

kōhō (後報), *n.* a later [further] report.

kohon (古本), *n.* an old book; a second-hand book. ¶ 古本商, a second-hand bookseller.

kōbone (河骨), *n.* =*kawahone.*

kohyō (小兵の), *a.* of small build; little.

kōhyō (公表), *n.* an official announcement; publication. —公表する, to make public; announce publicly.

kōhyō (公評), *n.* popular [public] opinion; public view [judgment].

kōhyō (好評), *n.* a favourable opinion [criticism; comment]. —好評嘖々たり, to be wildly welcomed. —好評を博する, to meet with a favourable criticism.

kōhyō (降雹), *n.* a hail-storm.

kōhyō (講評), *n.* criticism. —講評する, to criticize.

koi (鯉), *n.* the carp [*sing.* & *pl.*]

koi (請), *n.* a request; a petition. —(の)請により, at the request *of.*

koi (戀), *n.* love; affections; the tender passion. —戀の神, Cupid (羅馬); Eros (希臘); the god of love. —戀の敵, a rival in love. —戀する, to love; fall in love *with.* —戀の闇路に踏み迷ふ, to be lost in the maze of love. —戀を仕掛ける, to woo; make love *to.* —戀は思案の外, "Love is blind." —戀に上下の差別なし, "Love lives in cottages as well as in courts."

koi (故意), *n.* 【法】 intention; design; purpose. —故意の, 【法】 intentional; wilful; designed (豫謀せる). **——-ni,** *ad.* 【法】 intentionally; deliberately; designedly; purposely. —故意に出でたる行爲, an intentional act.

koi (濃い), *a.* ❶ (濃厚) dark (色); deep (同上); heavy; thick. ❷ (こまやか) close; near; intimate. —濃い髯, a heavy beard. —濃い髮, thick [rich] hair. —濃い茶, strong tea.

kōi (行爲), *n.* ❶ (行動) an act; action. ❷ (行狀) behaviour; conduct; course. ❸ (所業) deed; work; doings.

kōi (好意), *n.* goodwill; friendship. —...の好意(斡旋)により, owing to the good offices *of.* —...に好意を持つ, to wish one well.

kōi (攻圍), *n.* an investment; a siege. —攻圍する, to invest;

besiege; lay siege *to*. ¶ 攻圍軍, an investing [a besieging] army; the besiegers.

kōi (皇位), *n.* the (Imperial) Throne. —皇位繼承の順序, the order of succession to the Imperial Throne.

kōi (高位), *n.* a high rank; eminence; dignity. ¶ 高位高官, persons of high rank and office.

kōi (厚意), *n.* kindness; favour; friendship. ☞ *kōjō* (厚情). —厚意を謝す, to thank another for his kindness.

kōi (校醫), *n.* a school physician [doctor].

koibito (戀人), *n.* a sweetheart (男女); a lover (男); a love (女). —戀人同士の結婚, a love-match.

koibumi (戀文), *n.* a love-letter; a *billet-doux* 〔佛〕.

koika (戀歌), *n.* a love-song.

koiki (小意氣な), *a.* somewhat stylish [chic]; smart; neat (家など); trim (家·座敷など).

koikogareru (戀焦れる), *vi.* to pine *for* (love); be dying *for* (a girl). —戀ひ焦れた, love-sick.

kōin (勾引, 拘引), *n.* arrest; custody. —勾引する, to arrest; take up; take into custody; take *to*; bring (before a preliminary judge); run in 〔俗〕. ¶ 勾引狀, a writ [warrant] of arrest.

kōin (光陰), *n.* time. —光陰人を待たず, "Time and tide tarry for no man." —光陰矢の如し, "Time fleeth away without delay."

kōin (皇胤), *n.* the Imperial lineage; the Imperial descendants.

kōin (後胤), *n.* a descendant; offspring; posterity.

koinegau (希·冀ふ), *vt.* to crave; entreat; beseech.

koinegawakuwa (希·冀·庶幾くは), *ad.* would that; I wish.

koinu (子犬), *n.* a pup; a puppy.

koiru (線輪), *n.* 【電】 a coil.

koishi (小石, 礫), *n.* a pebble; a shingle.

koishii (戀しい), *a.* dear; beloved. 戀しき君へ, to my darling [dearest]. —戀しがる, to long [yearn] *for* [*after*].

koishitau (戀慕ふ), *vt.* to long *for*; yearn *after*.

koisuru (戀する), *v.* ☞ *koi*.

kōiu (斯う云ふ), *a.* such; this; of this kind [sort].

koiwazurai (戀煩), *n.* Ⓢ 戀病. love-sickness.

koji (固持する), *v.* to persist *in*; stand fast [firm]; hold fast.

koji (固辭する), *vt.* to refuse; decline (positively).

koji (居士), *n.* ❶ (仕官せぬ人) a retired scholar. ❷ (信者) a Buddhist layman.

koji (故事), *n.* origin (起原); tradition (口碑). —希臘神話の故事を引く, to cite references [refer] to Greek mythology. ¶ 故事熟語辭典, a dictionary of fables and phrases.

koji (孤兒), *n.* an orphan; orphanhood. ¶ 孤兒院, an orphanage; an orphan asylum.

kōji (麴), *n.* malt; yeast. —麴に作る, [*vt.*] to malt. ¶ 麴屋, a maltster.

kōji (小路), *n.* an alley; a lane; a narrow street.

kōji (工事), *n.* construction; works. ¶ 工事監督, the clerk of the works. —工事請負人, a (works) contractor.

kōji (公示), *n.* exhibition; publication (公表). —公示する, to exhibit; gazette; report; make public. ¶ 公示催告, 【法】 public summons. —公示送達, 【法】 service of publication.

kōji (公事), *n.* public affairs.

kōji (好事), *n.* ❶ a good thing. ❷ (よい行) a good deed. —好事魔多し, "Good things are too often obstructed."

kōji (後事), *n.* future affairs. —後事を人に託する, to give another the charge of future affairs.

kojiki (乞食), *n.* ❶ a beggar. ❷ (乞食すること) mendicancy; begging. —乞食する, ① [*vi.*] to beg; go (about) begging; live as a beggar. ② [*a.*] mendicant. —乞食往生する, to die a beggar. ¶ 乞食坊主, a mendicant friar [priest].

kōjiki (好時機), *n.* a favourable opportunity. —捉ふべき好時機, opportunity ripe to be seized.

kojima (小島, 嶼), *n.* an islet; a small island.

kojin (古人), *n.* the ancients; the men of old [yore].

kojin (故人), *n.* (死者) the deceased; the departed.

kojin (個人), *n.* individual. **——teki**, *a.* individual; personal; private (私的). —個人的權利(自由), personal rights (liberty). ¶ 個人性, personality; individuality. —個人主義, individualism. (個人主義者, an individualist.)

kōjin (公人), *n.* a (public) character; a public man.

kōjin (行人), *n.* a passer-by.

kōjin (幸甚), to be very happy; be highly pleased; be very glad.

kōjin (後人), *n.* posterity.

kōjin (後塵), *n.* the dust raised by a horse or a person. —後塵を拜する, to play second fiddle; follow at another's heels.

kōjin (紅塵, 黃塵), *n.* dust. —紅

塵萬丈, a cloud of dust.

kojinmari (こじんまりした), *a.* snug; trim; neat.

kojio (小汐), *n.* 【天】 the neap (-tide).

kojireru (拗れる), *v.* ❶ (ねぢれる) to twist; be twisted. ❷ (こじける) to relapse; grow worse; become inveterate. ❸ (すねる) to sulk; get peevish.

kojiri (鐺, 鏢), *n.* a crampit; a chape.

kojiru (抉る), *vt.* to wrench; prize; twist violently. —金庫(戶)をこじあける, to wrench open a safe (door).

kō-jiru (嵩じる), *vi.* to grow worse; change for the worse; become inveterate. —嵩じて…となる, to develop *into*…; lead *to*….

kojitsu (故實), *n.* ancient practices. —故實に通ずる, to be versed in ancient practices.

kōjitsu (口實), *n.* an excuse; a pretext; a plea. —口實を見出す, to find a pretext [an excuse]. —口實を設ける, to invent an excuse.

kojitsuke (牽强), *n.* distortion; forced meaning; strained interpretation. —こじつけの, distortioned; far-fetched (說明·比喩等の); strained. —こじつける, to force; distort; strain the meaning.

kojō (孤城), *n.* a solitary castle. ¶ 孤城落日, helpless predicament.

kōjo (工女), *n.* a factory-girl; a female operative; a female [mill-hand].

kōjo (公序), *n.* public welfare [order].

kōjo (皇女), *n.* a royal princess; an Imperial princess; a princess (of the Blood).

kōjo (控除する), *vt.* to deduct; subtract.

kōjō (工場), *n.* works; a factory; a workshop. ¶ 工場長, works [factory] manager. —工場法, the factory law. —工場主, the occupier of a factory. —工場閉鎖, lock-out (同盟罷業の對). —工場管理, factory [workshop] management; factory administration.

kōjō (口上), *n.* ❶ (傳言) a verbal) message. ❷ (口語) word of mouth. ❸ (陳述) statement; speech. ❹ (芝居などの) an introduction; a prologue. —口上で, orally; verbally; by word of mouth. ¶ 口上書, a verbal note.

kōjō (甲狀腺), *n.* the thyroid (gland).

kōjō (向上), *n.* elevation; rise; progress. —向上さす, to raise; elevate (高める); improve (改善する). —向上する, to rise; progress; become higher. ¶ 向上心, aspiration; a progressive spirit.

kōjō (交情), *n.* friendship; intimacy.

kōjō (攻城), *n.* a siege. ¶ 攻城砲, a siege-gun [-piece]. —攻城作業, siege-works.

kōjō (厚情), *n.* kindness; kind treatment.

kojōki (小蒸氣-船), *n.* a steam-launch.

kōju (口授), *n.* oral instruction. [☞ *kuju*.]

kōjū (講中), *n.* a religious association; a pilgrims' club.

kōjun (孝順な), *a.* dutiful; filial; pious.

kojūto (小姑), *n.* the husband's sister; a sister-in-law. ¶ 小姑政策, pin-prick policy.

kōjutsu (口述), *n.* oral statement; delivery; lecture (講義). —口述する, to state orally. ¶ 口述試驗, an oral [*viva voce*] examination.

koka (呼價), *n.* the nominal price.

koka (瓠果), *n.* a pepo; a peponida; a peponium.

kōka (口禍), *n.* misfortunes arising from the tongue.

kōka (工科), *n.* the engineering department; the faculty of engineering. —工科大學, an engineering college.

kōka (公暇), *n.* an officially-granted holiday. —公暇を得て, on leave of absence.

kōka (功過), *n.* deserts; merits and demerits.

kōka (汞和), *n.* amalgamation.

kōka (考課), *n.* consideration [weighing] of results. ¶ 考課狀, a business-report.

kōka (效果), *n.* effect; result; efficacy (藥の). —更に效果なし, to have no effect *upon*; make no impression *on*. —效果を生ずる, to prove efficacious [effective]; produce effect.

kōka (高架), *a.* elevated; high-level. ¶ 高架線, an elevated track. —高架鐵道, an overhead [high-level] railway 〖英〗; an elevated railroad 〖米〗.

kōka (高價), *n.* costliness; expensiveness; a high price. —高價な, costly; expensive; high-priced. —高價に賣れる, to fetch [bring] a high price.

kōka (降嫁), *n.* the marriage of an Imperial princess with one below her rank.

kōka (絞架), *n.* gallows; a gallow-tree; a gibbet.

kōka (黃禍), *n.* the yellow peril.

kōka (硬化), *n.* 【醫】 scleroma; sclerosis; metallization (護謨の). —硬化する, to harden (器官·態度·相場); stiffen (態度·相場); become firm (同上); metallize (護謨を); vulcanize (護謨に硫黃を加へ).

kōka (硬貨), *n.* hard money; coin; metallic currency.

kokabu (子株), *n.* new shares.

kokage (木蔭, 樹蔭), *n.* the shade of a tree; a bower (木蔭の場所).

—樹蔭に憩ふ, to rest under the shade of a tree. —樹蔭に隠れる, to conceal oneself behind a tree.

kōkai (公海), *n.* high seas; the main (sea).

kōkai (公開), *n.* openness; publicity. —公開する, to open to the public; throw open to the public. —公開の席で, in public. ¶ 公開演說(講演), a public speech (lecture). —公開狀, an open letter.

kōkai (公會), *n.* a public assembly; a public meeting.

kōkai (更改), *n.* 【法】 novation. —更改する, to make a novation.

kōkai (後悔), *n.* remorse; repentance; penitence. —後悔する, to rue; repent *of*; be penitent [sorry] *for*. —後悔前に立たず, "Repentance does not bring the lost back." ¶ 後悔者, a penitent.

kōkai (航海), *n.* navigation; a trip. —航海中, on the voyage; at sea. —航海する, to navigate; go (on) a voyage; make [take] a voyage *to*. —航海の安全を祈る, to wish a pleasant voyage. ¶ 航海長, a navigating officer; a navigator. —航海術, (the art of) navigation. —航海日誌, 【航】 a log-book; a journal. —航海者, a navigator; a voyager.

kōkaidō (公會堂), *n.* a town hall; a public hall; an auditorium 〖米〗.

kōkaikotsu (甲介骨), *n.* 【解】 concha; a turbinate bone.

kokain (コカイン), *n.* cocaine. ¶ コカイン注射, cocainization.

kokaku (呼格), *n.* 【文】 the vocative (case).

kokaku (孤客), *n.* a lonely traveller [stranger].

kokaku (顧客), *n.* custom; a customer. ☞ ***tokui.***

kōkaku (口角泡を飛ばして論ずる), to argue with passion.

kōkaku (甲殼), *n.* a shell. ¶ 甲殼類, 【動】 Crustacea (學名); crustaceans.

kōkaku (岬角), *n.* a cape; a headland; a promontory.

kōkaku (高閣), *n.* ❶ (高き置きだな) a high shelf. ❷ (高樓) a great house; a mansion; a palace. —高閣に束ねる, to shelve; lay on the shelf.

kōkakuka (好角家), *n.* a lover of wrestling; a wrestling fan.

kōkan (好感), *n.* good feelings (好感情); good will (好意); favourable impression (好印象). —に對し好感を懷く, to entertain good feelings *toward*. —好感を與へる, to give a person a favourable impression.

kōkan (好漢), *n.* a good fellow; jolly fellow [dog].

kōkan (交換), *n.* exchange; interchange; substitution (置換). —交換する, to change *for*; interchange; substitute *for*; reciprocate; truck *for*; barter *for*. —日本銀行の交換尻, the clearing-house balance of the Bank of Japan. ¶ 交換價値, 【經】 the exchange value. —交換敎授, an exchange-professor.

kōkan (交感), *n.* sympathy. ¶ 交感神經, the sympathetic nerve.

kōkan (交驩), *n.* an exchange of courtesies.

kōkan (後患), *n.* the seed of trouble. —後患を貽(のこ)す, to sow the seed of trouble.

kōkan (高官), *n.* ❶ high office. ❷ (高官者) a high official.

kōkan (浩瀚な), *a.* voluminous.

kōkan (槓杆), *n.* a lever. —槓杆で上げる, to lever.

kokansetsu (股關節), *n.* the coxa; the hip-joint.

Kōkasasu (高加索), *n.* Caucasus. ¶ 高加索人種, the Caucasian race.

kōkasshoku (黃褐色), *n.* yellowish brown; tan.

kokasu (こかす), *vt.* ❶ (轉がす) to tumble; roll over. ❷ (物品を密に他へ移す) to remove [make away] secretly.

kokatsu (涸渇する), *v.* ❶ (水など) to be parched dry; be dried up. ❷ (缺乏) to be exhausted; be drained; run short [low].

kōkatsu (狡猾), *n.* cunning; artfulness. **——-na,** *a.* cunning (惡賢い); crafty (策略ある); artful (同上). —狡猾な親爺, a wily old man. —狡猾に立廻る, to act [behave] craftily.

kōkatsu (廣闊な), *a.* wide; spacious; extensive.

koke (苔), *n.* moss. —苔に埋まる, to be covered with moss.

koke (鱗), *n.* a scale. ☞ ***uroko.***

koke (虛假, 白痴), *n.* a fool; a dunce; an idiot.

kōke (高家), *n.* a high family; a noble house.

kōkei (口徑), *n.* calibre; bore. —十六口徑砲, a gun of sixteen calibres.

kōkei (光景), *n.* a view; scenery; a scene; a spectacle. —慘憺たる光景, a pitiful [wretched] spectacle.

kōkei (肯綮), *n.* a tender point [part]; a vital point. —肯綮に當る, to hit the mark; be to the point.

kōkei (後景), *n.* the background.

kōkei (後繼), *n.* succession. ¶ 後繼內閣, the succeeding ministry [cabinet]. —後繼者, a successor; an heir (嗣子); an inheritor (同).

kōkei (狡計), *n.* a guile; an artifice; a finesse.

kōkei (絞刑), *n.* hanging. —絞

刑に處する, to hang.
kōkeiki (好景氣), *n.* prosperity. ☞ *keiki.* —好景氣に向ふ, to tend to prosperity; look bright.
kokeitai (固形體), *n.* a solid body.
kōkekka (好結果), *n.* a success; a good result. —好結果を收める, to succeed; produce good results.
kokekokkō (こけこッこー), *n.* (鷄の啼聲) cock-a-doodle-doo.
kokemusu (苔蒸す), *vi.* to moss. —苔蒸した墓(屋根), a moss-grown [mossy] grave (roof). —轉石苔蒸さず, "A rolling stone gathers no moss."
koken (沽券), *n.* ❶ (地所賣買の證券) a deed of sale. ❷ (人物の價値) worth; dignity; credit. —沽券を落す, to bring discredit.
kōken (公權), *n.* public rights. ¶ 公權停止, suspension of public rights.
kōken (後見), *n.* ❶【法】guardianship; wardship. ❷ prompting (能又は劇の). —後見する, ① to guard; act as a guardian; have the ward *of.* ② to prompt. —後見を受ける, to be under ward. ¶ 後見人, ①【法】a guardian. ② a prompter.
kōken (效驗), *n.* efficacy; effect. —效驗を奏する, to operate (藥が); work; be efficacious.
kōken (貢獻), *n.* contribution; services. —貢獻する, to contribute *to*; serve; render services *to.*
kokeodoshi (虛假威), *n.* a display to impose upon fools; a claptrap.
kokerabuki (柿葺), *n.* a shingle-roof.
kokeru (憔ける), *vt.* to sink; be emaciated; lose flesh (病氣などにて). —憔けた頰, hollowed [sunken] cheeks.
koketsu (固結する), *vi.* to solidify; consolidate; tighten.
koketsu (虎穴), *n.* ❶ a tiger's den [lair]. ❷ a most dangerous place. —虎穴に入らずんば虎兒を獲ず, "Nothing venture, nothing get."
kōketsu (高潔), *n.* nobleness; integrity; purity. **——-no,** *a.* noble; high-minded; pure. —高潔の士, a man of high [noble] character.
kōketsu (硬結), *n.*【醫】induration; scleroma; callousness (皮膚の).
kōketsu (膏血), *n.* sweat and blood; the sweat of the brow. —人民の膏血を絞る, to put the people under the screw; exact from the people the fruits of their toil [labour].
kōketsu (曠缺), *n.*【法】absence.
koki (古稀), *n.* the seventieth year of age. ☞ *kōfun.*
kōki (口氣), *n.* the way of speaking.
kōki (光輝), *n.* brilliancy; brightness; lustre. —光輝ある, ① (光彩ある) brilliant; lustrous; splendid. ②【鑛・昆】(光りある) luminous. —光輝を發する, to emit lustre; radiate.
kōki (好期), *n.* an opportune [a favourable] time.
kōki (好機-會), *n.* a good [favourable] opportunity; a good chance. —好機に乘ずる [を捉へる], to seize [take advantage of] a good opportunity.
kōki (香氣), *n.* fragrance; perfume; aroma. —香氣を放つ, to emit a perfume.
kōki (後期), *n.* the latter term [period].
kōki (高貴の), *a.* noble; high; dignified. —高貴の人, a man of rank; a high personage.
kōki (校規), *n.* school rules [regulations]; school discipline (校紀).
kōki (校旗), *n.* a school flag.
kōki (降旗), *n.* a white flag; a flag of surrender. —降旗を揭げる, to hoist [put up] a white flag.
kōki (綱紀), *n.* ❶ control; rein. ❷ (國家の大法) the constitution; the organic law; law and order. ❸ (國家の政治) national affairs; affairs of the state; administration. —綱紀紊亂, disorganization of the constitution.
kōki (廣軌), *n.*【鐵道】a broad gauge.
kōki (衡器), *n.* a weighing-machine; a balance.
kōki (興起する), *vi.* to rouse oneself to action; rise.
kōkiatsu (高氣壓), *n.* high barometric [atmospheric] pressure.
kokibutsu (古奇物), *n.* articles [objects] of virtu. ☞ *kottō.*
kokimazeru (扱雜・扱混せる), *vt.* to mix together.
kōkin (公金), *n.* public money. —公金を私消する, to misappropriate [peculate] public money. ¶ 公金私消, peculation.
kōkin (拘禁), *n.* detention; confinement; imprisonment. —拘禁する, to imprison; detain; confine.
kōkishin (好奇心), *n.* curiosity. —好奇心に驅られる, to be impelled by curiosity.
kokitsukau (扱使ふ), *vt.* to work hard; drive hard; keep busy. —牛馬の如く扱き使ふ, to work a person like a horse.
kōkiun (好機運), *n.* turn of luck [fortune]. —好機運に向ふ, to come to a (favourable) turn of fortune.
kokizami (小刻に), *ad.* ❶ in small slice. ❷ with short steps. —小刻みに步く, to walk with short steps; mince (氣取って步く); walk with mincing steps (同上).

kokka (刻下の), *a.* present. —刻下の問題, the question of the hour. —刻下の急務, the most pressing duty of the moment.

kokka (國家), *n.* a state. —國家的事業, a national enterprise. ¶ 國家經濟, state economy.

kokka (國歌), *n.* the national anthem [air].

Kokkai (黑海), *n.* the Black Sea.

kokkai (國會), *n.* the National Assembly; the Diet; the Parliament; the Congress (米). ☞ *gikai.* (議會). ¶ 國會議員, a member of the Imperial Diet (日本); a member of Parliament (an M. P. と略す); a congressman (米). —國會議事堂, the Houses of Parliament (the Diet); the Capitol (米).

kokkaku (骨格), *n.* the build; the frame. —骨格の逞しい人, a well-knit person; a man of stout build.

kokkan (酷寒), *n.* severe cold.

kokkei (滑稽), *n.* ❶ (冗談) a joke; a jest; fun. ❷ (道化) drollery; comicality; facetiousness. —滑稽な, ① (笑ふべき) funny; ridiculous. ② droll; comic(-al); facetious. —滑稽交りの演說, a humorous speech; a speech spiced with jokes. —大いに滑稽を演ずる, to become very comic. ¶ 滑稽本, a comic book; a book of humour [fun]. —滑稽文學, comic [humorous] literature. —滑稽談, a facetious story; a joke; a jest. —滑稽劇, a farce; a burlesque; a comedy. —滑稽家, a joker; a humourist; a droll; a funny man.

kokkeijitsu (國慶日), *n.* a national holiday.

kokken (國憲), *n.* the national constitution.

kokken (國權), *n.* national power.

kokki (克己), *n.* self-denial; self-control; self-restraint. ¶ 克己心, self-denying spirit.

kokki (國旗), *n.* the national flag. —國旗を揭げる, to hoist [hang out; put up] the national flag.

kokkin (國禁), *n.* national interdict; a legal prohibition.

kokko (國庫), *n.* the (national) treasury; the exchequer; the public treasury [purse]. —國庫事務を取扱ふ銀行, a bank conducting the business of the national treasury. ¶ 國庫支辨, defrayment [disbursement] of the national treasury.

kokko (こッこ), *n.* (牝鷄の鳴聲) cluck. —コッコと鳴く, to cluck.

kokkō (國光), *n.* (國の威光) national glory [prestige].

kokkō (國交), *n.* diplomatic relations. —國交の斷絕, rupture of diplomatic relations.

kokkoku (刻刻), *ad.* every moment.

kokku (刻苦), *n.* arduousness; painstaking; hard work [labour]. —刻苦する, to work hard; work diligently; toil hard.

kokku (廚夫), *n.* a cook. ¶ 廚夫部屋, a kitchen; 【航】 the cook-house. —廚夫長, a head cook.

kokkui (極印), *n.* =*kokuin.*

kokkun (國君), *n.* a monarch; a king; a sovereign; a potentate; a prince 〔修〕.

kokkuri (狐狗狸), *n.* table-turning; planchette.

kokkuri (こッくり), *ad.* with a nod. —こッくりこッくり舟を漕ぐ, to rock in a doze.

kokkyō (國敎), *n.* the state [established] religion; the state [established] church (國立敎會).

kokkyō (國境), *n.* the frontier; the border. —國境に迫る, to press upon the frontier. —國境を畫定する, to define the boundaries of a country.

koko (戶戶に), *ad.* at every house.

koko (此處), *ad.* here (場所). —, *n.* & *pron.* this place; this. —こゝ暫く, for the present. —此處を先途と戰ふ, to fight desperately. —此處ぞと思ふところを狙ッて, aiming at what one thought the vital point.

koko (呱呱), *n.* a cry of a baby. —呱々の聲をあげる, to see the light; come into existence.

koko (箇箇), *ad.* each; individually; severally. —箇々の, individual; several; each; particular. —箇々獨立する, to become severally independent.

kokō (戶口), *n.* population; houses and inhabitants. ¶ 戶口調査, census-taking.

kokō (虎口), *n.* the tiger's [lion's] mouth; an extreme danger. —虎口を逃れる, to escape [be snatched] from the jaws of death. (虎口を逃れて龍穴に入る, to jump out of the frying-pan into the fire.)

kokō (股肱), *n.* a right hand (man); a henchman.

kokō (弧光), *n.* arc; arc-light; voltaic light. ¶ 弧光燈, arc-lamp.

kokō (餬口, 糊口), *n.* daily bread; living; livelihood. —糊口する, to line *on* (*by*). —糊口に窮する, to find it difficult to keep the wolf from the door. —糊口の資を得る, to get [earn] a livelihood.

kōko (江湖), *n.* the public; the world. —江湖に問ふ, to appeal to the public.

kōko (考古), *n.* study of ancient arts and customs; study of antiquities. ¶ 考古學, archæology.

kōko (好古), *n.* love of antiquity; antiquarianism. ¶ 好古家, an antiquary; antiquarian.

kōko (好箇の), *a.* fair; best. —好箇の參考書, an excellent book of reference.

kōko (後顧する), *vi.* to look back. —後顧の憂, anxiety for home.

kōkō (口腔), *n.* the oral cavity. ¶ 口腔外科, dental surgery.

kōkō(公行する), *vi.* ❶ (賄賂) to be open; prevail. ❷ (盜賊) to be at large; be rampant.

kōkō (孔口), *n.* 【動】 a stoma; an orifice.

kōkō (坑口), *n.* a pit-mouth.

kōkō (孝行), *n.* filial piety [duty]; obedience to parents. ¶ 孝行息子, an obedient [a dutiful] son.

kōkō(航行), *n.* navigation; voyage; sailing. —航行する, to navigate; voyage; sail.

kōkō (皎皎と), *ad.* brightly. —皎々たる, pale; bright.

kōkō (港口), *n.* a harbour-entrance.

kōkō (膏肓), *n.* the marrow; the inside. —病膏肓に入る, The disease (habit) penetrates to the marrow.

kōkō (鑛坑), *n.* a mine; a mine-shaft.

kōkō (かうかう), *n.* (香の物) vegetables preserved in bran and salt; pickles.

kokoa (ココア), *n.* cocoa.

kokochi (心地), *n.* ❶ (*a*) (感じ) feeling; feel; sensation: (*b*) (氣分) mood; humour. ❷ (考へ) an idea. —心地(が)惡るい, to feel uncomfortable; feel bad [ill]. —心地(が)よい, to feel comfortable [snug]; feel well (病氣などの).

kokoira (此邊に), *ad.* hereabout (-s); (about) here; in this neighbourhood. —こゝいらの家, houses in this neighbourhood.

kokoku (故國), *n.* the native land; the homeland (本國); the fatherland (祖國); the motherland (母國); the old country (移民から).

kōkoku (公告), *n.* public notice; public announcement. —公告する, to give public notice *of*; notify publicly; announce publicly.

kōkoku (抗告), *n.* 【法】 complaint; exception. —抗告する, to complain; make a complaint *against*.

kōkoku (皇國), *n.* the Empire.

kōkoku (廣告), *n.* ❶ an advertisement; a notice; an announcement; publicity. ❷ (廣告札) a poster (ポスター); a bill (ビラ); a hand-bill (引札). —廣告する, to advertise. ¶ 廣告技師, an advertisement builder. —廣告掲示場, a bill-posting station. —廣告欄, an advertisement column. —廣告料, advertising rates; advertisement charge. —廣告者, an advertiser. —廣告塔, an advertisement tower. —廣告取り, an advertising solicitor. —廣告取次人, an advertising agent. —廣告郵便, advertising post.

kokon (古今), *n.* ancient and modern ages. —古今未曾有の大動亂, the greatest disturbance on record; the greatest war that the world has ever seen. —古今其の比を見ず, Its equal is not to be found in any age.

kōkon (黃昏), *n.* nightfall; evening; dusk; twilight.

kokonoe (九重), *n.* the Imperial palace; the Court (宮廷).

kokora (此邊に), *ad.* hereabout (-s); (about) here; in this neighbourhood.

kokoro (心), *n.* ❶ (精神) the mind; the soul; the spirit. ❷ (心情) heart; breast. ❸ (意思) will; intention; (考へ) an idea. ❹ (思慮) thought; consideration. ❺ (意味) meaning; significance; sense. —心に懸る, to weigh upon one's mind. —心に適せる, after one's (own) heart; after one's fancy. —心に浮ぶ, to come into mind; occur to one (ふと); come across one's mind (同上). —心にも無い事を云ふ, to say what is not in one's mind [what one's heart does not approve]. —ものに心を籠める, to have one's heart in a thing; give one's whole mind *to*. —心を奪ふ, to charm; fascinate; captivate. —心を安める, to set one's mind at ease. —…に心を用ひる, to attend *to*; give attention *to*. —心を許す, ① (油斷) to relax one's attention; be off one's guard. ② (信用) to place deep confidence in; trust implicitly.

kokoroarige (心有氣な), *a.* significant; meaning; suggestive. —心有氣な振舞, significant behaviour. —心有氣に, significantly.

kokoroatari (心當り), *n.* a clue; knowledge. —心當りが無い, to have no clue *to*. —心當りを探す, to look for in likely places; search likely places *for*.

kokorobakari(心許りの), *a.* ❶ (僅許りの) trifling; slight. ❷ (形許りの) informal.

kokorobase (心ばせ), *n.* mind; heart; disposition (性質).

kokorobosoi (心細い), *a.* slender (見込など); discouraging (形勢など); helpless; uncertain. —心細くなる, to feel discouraging.

kokorodanomi (心頼み), *n.* reliance; hope. —心頼みにする, to rely [count] *upon*; put hopes *on*.

kokorodate (心立), *n.* heart; disposition; temper. —優しい心立, tender-heartedness; kindly disposition. —心立てのよい人, a good-hearted man.

kokoroe (心得), *n.* ❶ (知識) knowledge; information. ❷ (會得) understanding. ❸ (覺悟) preparedness. ❹ (規則) orders; rules; directions. ❺ (官職の) an acting.... ¶ 局長心得, an acting director. —執務心得, rules for the conduct of business.

kokoroechigai (心得違ひ), *n.* ❶ (誤解) misunderstanding; misapprehension; mistake. ❷ (無作法, 不心得) misbehaviour; misconduct; an indiscretion. —心得違ひをする, ① to misapprehend; misunderstand. ② to misbehave oneself; misconduct oneself.

kokoroeru (心得る), *v.* ❶ (會得する) to know; understand; perceive. ❷ (と思ふ) to consider; take; regard *as*. —萬事心得た, All right; I'll see to it.

kokorogakari (心掛り), *n.* care; concern; anxiety. —心掛りの, causing anxiety. —心掛りになる, to weigh on one's mind.

kokorogake (心掛け), *n.* ❶ (目的) aim; object; purpose. ❷ (用心) attention; prudence. —心掛ける, to aim *at* (目ざす); bear [keep] in mind (留意); be careful.

kokorogamae (心構), *n.* readiness of mind; expectation. —心構へをする, to prepare in mind *for*.

kokorogara (心柄), *n.* ❶ (氣立) heart; disposition; nature; temper. ❷ (自業自得) the result [fruits; consequences] of one's own deed.

kokorogawari (心變), *n.* fickleness; inconstancy; unfaithfulness. —心變りする, ① [*a.*] fickle; inconstant; faithless. ② [*v.*] to change one's mind.

kokorogumi (心組), *n.* design; intention.

kokorogurushii (心苦しい), *a.* ❶ (心配な) anxious; uneasy. ❷ (恥しい) shameful. ❸ (氣の毒な) painful. ——, *v.* ❶ to be uneasy *about*. ❷ to be ashamed of oneself. ❸ to pain oneself.

kokorohisoka (心密に), *ad.* inwardly; mentally; in one's heart; in *petto*. —心密かに思へらく, I thought to myself *that*....

kokoroiki (心意氣), *n.* ❶ (氣立) disposition; nature; temper. ❷ (意向) intention.

kokorokara (心から), *ad.* heartily; with all one's heart; cordially. —心からの歡待, a warm [cordial; hearty] welcome. —心から感謝する, to thank heartily.

kokoromachi (心待), *n.* expectation. —心待ちに待つ, to look forward *to*; wait in expectation *for*.

kokoromakase (心任せに), *ad.* as one pleases; at will. —心任せになる, to be at one's mercy; be in one's power; be at one's disposal. —心任せにさす, to let another have his own way. —お心任せになさい, Just please yourself.

kokoromi (試), *n.* ❶ (ためし) a trial; a test; a try [俗]. ❷ (實驗) an experiment; experimentation. ❸ (誘惑) temptation. ❹ (試圖) an attempt; first endeavour. —新しい試みをする, to make a new attempt; put to a new test. —試みに使ってみる, to employ [take] a man on trial; give a man a trial.

kokoromiru (試る), *vt.* ❶ to try; test; put to proof [the test]. ❷ (企圖) to attempt. ❸ (惑試) to tempt. —...遠征を試みる, to attempt an expedition *to*.

kokoromochi (心持), *n.* ❶ (感じ) feeling; sensation. ❷ (感情) feelings. ❸ (氣分) (*a*) spirits; (*b*) humour; mood. ——, *ad.* (少し) a thought; an idea; a trifle; a shade; slightly. —心持よく, pleasantly; comfortably; agreeably. —心持ち大きくする, to make it a thought larger. —何とも言はれぬよい心持だ, I feel indescribably jolly.

kokoromotonai (心許ない), *a.* ❶ (待ち遠しい) impatient. ❷ (氣遣はしい, 覺束ない) uneasy; apprehensive; precarious. —心許なく思ふ, to feel uneasy; be anxious *for*.

kokoronaki (心なき), *a.* ❶ (無心) innocent. ❷ (無情) heartless; cold [hard]-hearted; cruel. ❸ (無思慮) thoughtless; inconsiderate.

kokoronarazumo (心ならずも), *ad.* ❶ (不本意) against one's will; reluctantly. ❷ (不安) anxiously; uneasily.

kokorone (心根), *n.* ❶ (心底) one's inmost feelings; one's motive; heart. ❷ (根性) disposition; temper. —心根を察する, to enter into another's feelings; sympathize with another's feelings.

kokoronikui (心憎い), *a.* ❶ (奥床しい) enviable. ❷ (心に惡く思はれる) hateful.

kokoronokori (心殘), *n.* regret. —...に心殘りがある, to have

something to regret *in*; have a feeling of regret *for*. —心殘りは一つも無い, I have nothing to regret.

kokoro-no-mama (心の儘に), *ad.* as one pleases; at will.

kokoro-no-soko (心の底), *n.* the heart; one's inmost feelings; the heart of hearts; the heart's core; the bottom of one's heart. —心の(奥)底では, in one's heart of hearts; in the inmost recesses of one's heart.

kokoro-no-take (心の丈), *n.* all one's heart. —心の丈を口說く, to try to persuade with all one's heart.

kokorooboe (心覺), *n.* remembrance; recollection. ☞ ***kioku.*** —心覺えに覺えて居る, to have a faint recollection *of*.

kokorooki (心置なく), *ad.* ❶ without reserve; unreservedly. ❷ without anxiety; easy in mind.

kokorosamishii (心淋しい), *a.* lonesome; pensive; melancholy.

kokorosemai (心狹い), *a.* narrow-minded; ungenerous. —心狹く, narrow-mindedly; ungenerously.

kokoroshizuka (心靜に), *ad.* calmly; tranquilly; composedly; coolly. —心靜かに考へる, to think over [consider] calmly.

kokorouki (心憂き), *a.* sorrowful; sad; melancholy. —心憂き月日を送る, to pass days in sorrow; pass sorrowful days.

kokoroureshii (心嬉しい), *a.* delightful; joyful; glad; gladsome.

kokoroyasudate (心安立), *n.* familiarity. —心安立な, familiar. —心安立に, familiarly; in a familiar manner.

kokoroyasui (心安い), *a.* ❶ (親密) intimate; friendly; familiar. ❷ (安心) free from care [anxiety]. ❸ (容易) easy. ——, *vi.* ❶ to be on familiar [intimate] terms *with*. ❷ to feel easy.

kokoroyoi (快い), *a.* pleasant; cheerful; comfortable. —快からぬ, displeasing; ill-affected (不服な). —前よりは快い, (病氣の) to be better; feel better. —快げに眠ってる, to be lapped in pleasant sleep.

kokoroyoku (快く), *ad.* ❶ (心地よく) pleasantly; cheerfully; comfortably. ❷ (喜んで) willingly; readily; with good grace. ☞ ***kimochiyoku.*** —快く承知する, to give a ready consent. —忠告を快く受ける, to take one's advice in good part.

kokoroyoshi (快しとする), *vt.* to be pleased; be willing.

kokoroyuku (心行くまで), *ad.* to one's heart's content. —心行くまで泣く, to cry one's fill.

kokorozashi (志), *n.* ❶ (意向) will; intention. ❷ (志望) aim; purpose; aspiration. ❸ (深切) kindness; intentions; one's good wishes; a present (贈物). —志を達する, to attain [accomplish] one's aim. —志ある者は事竟に成る, "Where there's a will, there's a way."

kokorozasu (志す), *v.* to purpose; aim *at*; aspire *to* [*after*]. —學問に志す, to make study one's object.

kokorozoe (心添), *n.* advice; counsel; help (助力).

kokorozuke (心附), *n.* ❶ a tip; a gratuity; perquisite. ❷ (注意) advice; counsel. —女中に心附けをやる, to tip the maid.

kokorozuku (心附く), *vi.* to take notice *of*; become aware *of*; occur to one. ☞ ***kizuku.***

kokorozukushi (心盡), *n.* ❶ (深切) kindness. ❷ (苦心) trouble; efforts. —心盡しの饗應, a hearty entertainment. —心盡しの甲斐もなく, in spite of all our efforts.

kokorozuyoi (心强い), *a.* ❶ (無情な) heartless; cold; hard. ❷ (氣丈夫な) stout-hearted; courageous. —心强く思ふ, to feel safe [secure].

kokotsu (股骨), *n.* 【解】 the femur; the femoral [thigh-] bone.

kōkotsu (恍惚たる), *a.* raptured; transported. —恍惚として, in raptures; in ecstasy; transported. —恍惚たらしめる, to enrapture; fascinate; charm. (恍惚たらしめる微笑, a winning smile.)

kōkotsu (硬骨), *n.* ❶ (かたい骨) a hard bone. ❷ (剛强人に屈せぬこと) inflexibility; unbendingness. ¶ 硬骨漢, a man of strong mind; a hard-headed man.

kōkōya (好好爺), *n.* a soft-headed person; a good-natured man.

koku (石), *n.* *koku* (穀類は 4.9629 bushels, 液は 39.7033 gallons).

koku (酷), *n.* ❶ severity; cruelty; harshness. ❷ (酒類の濃味) body. —酷な取扱, harsh treatment. —酷のある酒, wine with body. —酷に失する, to be too severe.

koku (穀), *n.* grain; cereals; corn.

koku (扱く), *vt.* to hackle; thresh. —稻を扱く, to hackle rice.

koku (濃く), *ad.* deeply; thick. —濃くする (なる), to thicken; deepen. —白粉を濃くつける, to paint thick.

kokū (虛空), *n.* the sky; the air; empty space (空間). —虛空を摑

む, to clutch at the air.

kōku (鑛區), *n.* a mine-lot.

kōkū (高空), *n.* a high altitude. —高空を翔ける, to fly in the sky.

kōkū (航空), *n.* aerial navigation; flight. ☞ *hikō* (飛行). ¶ 航空地圖, an aeronautical map; an aero-map; an aerial chart. —航空中尉, a flying-officer [-observer]. —航空大臣, the Minister for Air. —航空學; 航空術, aircraft; aeronautics. —航空法, law of the air; aerial navigation law. —航空家, a flying-man; an airman; an aviator; an aerostat. —航空界, the aerial world. —航空機, ① an airplane; an aeroplane; a flying-machine. ② (總稱) aircraft; aeronef. (航空機射撃砲, an anti-aircraft gun; an aerogun.) —(航空) 機械士, an aeromechanic. —航空根據地, an air-base. —航空日誌, a journey log book. —航空路, an air [aerial] route; an air lane. (航空路圖, a route map.) —航空省, the Air Ministry. —航空隊, a flying [an air] corps; an aviation corps. —航空大佐, a group-captain. —航空用發動機, an aeromotor.

koku-an̄an (黒暗暗たる), *a.* pitch-dark. —黒暗々の裏に消え失せる, to vanish into the darkness.

kokuban (黒板), *n.* a blackboard. ¶ 黒板拭き, a (blackboard-)rubber; an eraser.

kokubetsu (告別), *n.* leave-taking; adieu; farewell. —告別の辭, parting words; a farewell address; valediction. —告別する, to take (one's) leave *of*; bid adieu [farewell] *to*; say good-bye. ¶ 告別會 [宴], a farewell entertainment [dinner]. —告別式, a farewell ceremony.

kokubo (國母), *n.* ❶ (皇后) the Empress; the Queen. ❷ (皇太后) the Empress-Dowager; the Queen-Mother (英).

kokubō (國防), *n.* national defence. ¶ 國防會議, the National Defence Council.

kokubun (告文), *n.* a declaration; a manifesto.

kokubun (國文), *n.* national literature. ¶ 國文學, Japanese literature. (國文學者, a student of Japanese literature.) —國文科, the national literature course.

kokubyaku (黒白), *n.* ❶ (黒白) black and white. ❷ (善惡, 理非) good and bad; rights and wrongs; merits. —黒白をつける, to judge [decide on] the merits of a case. —黒白を爭ふ, to contend as to which is right.

kokuchi (告知), *n.* notice; information; notification. —告知する, to notify; report; inform. ¶ 告知板, a message board (公衆用の). —告知書, a (written) notice; a notification.

kokuchū (國中), *n.* the whole country (province). —國中に, throughout the country; all over the country.

kokudo (國土), *n.* a realm; a territory; a domain.

kokudo (國帑), *n.* national funds.

kokudo (黒奴), *n.* a black; a negro.

kokudō (國道), *n.* a highway; a national road.

kokueki (國益), *n.* national interest [benefit]. —國益を謀る, to promote national interests.

kokuen (黒鉛), *n.* black-lead; graphite; plumbago.

kokuen (黒煙), *n.* black smoke. ¶ 黒煙郷, a black country.

kokufu (國富), *n.* national wealth; national resources (富源). —國富を增進する, to promote national wealth.

kokufū (國風), *n.* ❶ national customs [manners]; nationalism. ❷ (和歌) national poetry; folk-songs (俗曲).

kokufuku (克復), *n.* restoration. —克復する, to restore; be restored.

kokuga (穀蛾), *n.* 【蟲】 the corn-moth.

kokugai (國外に), *ad.* outside a country; abroad; beyond seas (海外). —國外に追放する, to expel [deport] from the country.

kokugaku (國學), *n.* Japanese classical literature; national literature. ¶ 國學者, a Japanese classical scholar.

kokugen (刻限), *n.* time; a time-limit; fixed time.

kokugi (國技), *n.* the national sport. ¶ 國技館, the Wrestling Amphitheatre.

kokugo (國語), *n.* ❶ a language; a tongue. ❷ (自國語) the national language; vernacular; the mother tongue.

kokugū (酷遇する), *vt.* to ill-treat; treat harshly; maltreat.

kokugura (穀倉), *n.* a granary.

kokuhaku (告白), *n.* ❶ (自白) confession. ❷ (公言) profession; avowal; declaration. —告白する, ① to confess; own. ② to profess; avow; declare.

kokuhaku (刻薄, 酷薄), *n.* heartlessness; pitilessness; cold-heartedness. —刻薄な, pitiless; heartless; cold-hearted.

kokuhatsu (告發), *n.* 【法】 accusation; prosecution; indictment. —告發する, to accuse; indict; prosecute. ¶ 告發者, an accuser;

a presecutor; an indictor.

kokuheisha (國幣社), *n.* a national shrine. —國幣大(中; 小)社, a national shrine of the major (middle; minor) grade.

kokuhi (國費), *n.* national expenditure. —國費を擲つ, to expend national fund [public money] *upon.*

kokuhin (國賓), *n.* a guest of the nation [state]; a national guest.

kokuho (國歩), *n.* the fortunes of a country. —國歩艱難の時に際して, in a national crisis; in a time of national stress.

kokuhō (國法), *n.* the law of the land [realm]; national laws.

kokuhō (國寶), *n.* national treasures.

kokuhyō (黑表), *n.* a black list. —黑表に載せる, to blacklist.

kokuhyō (黑票), *n.* a black ball (反對投票). —黑票を投ずる, to black-ball.

kokuhyō (酷評), *n.* a severe [harsh; bitter] criticism. —酷評する, to criticize severely; cut up.

kokui (國威), *n.* national prestige [dignity; glory]. —國威を輝かす, to shed national glory.

kokuin (極印), *n.* a stamp; a die; a stamp-die. —極印を打つ, to stamp with a die.

kokuji (告示), *n.* a notification; an announcement; a bulletin. —告示する, to notify; give notice; announce. ¶ 告示板, a notice [bulletin] board.

kokuji (國字), *n.* Japanese characters.

kokuji (國事), *n.* affairs of state; national affairs. —國事に奔走[盡瘁]する, to exert oneself for [devote oneself to] the country's interests. ¶ 國事犯, ① a political offence; high treason. ② (人) a political offender; a state prisoner. —國事探偵, a political spy.

kokuji (國璽), *n.* the Great Seal; the Seal of the State [Empire].

kokuji (酷似する), *v.* to resemble closely [nearly]; bear a close resemblance *to*; be the very image *of*.

kokujin (國人), *n.* the people; the nation; fellow-countrymen.

kokujin (黑人), *n.* a negro [*fem.* -ress]. ¶ 黑人種, the black race.

kokujō (國情), *n.* the condition of [state of affairs in] a country.

kokujoku (國辱), *n.* national disgrace [dishonour]. —國辱を雪ぐ, to wipe away a national disgrace.

kokuka (槲果), *n.* 【植】 glans; a gland.

kokumei (克明な), *a.* honest; faithful; dutiful; diligent. —克明に守る, to observe [guard] faithfully.

kokumin (國民), *n.* ❶ (一國民) a people; a nation. ❷ (人民) the people. ¶ 國民軍, the militia; a national army. —國民皆兵制, the system of universal military service. —國民教育, national education. —國民性, national character [traits]; nationality. —國民大會, a national meeting; a mass-meeting. —國民黨, the nationalist party; the nationalists.

kokumotsu (穀物), *n.* grain; cereals; corn. ¶ 穀物市場, the corn-market.

kokumu (國務), *n.* state affairs; affairs of state. ¶ 國務大臣, a minister of state. —國務院, (支那) the Cabinet. —國務卿, the Secretary of State (米). —國務省, the State Department (米).

kokunai (國內), *n.* the interior; the whole country (國中). ☞ *naikoku.* —國內の, internal; interior; inland; home; domestic. ¶ 國內法, national law; municipal [territorial] law.

kokunaishō (黑內障), *n.* 【醫】 amaurosis; gutta serena; cataract.

kokunan (國難), *n.* national danger [calamity; crisis]. —國難に殉する, to sacrifice oneself in the national calamity.

kokunetsu (酷熱), *n.* intense heat. ☞ *kokusho.*

kokuniku (黑肉), *n.* a black-ink pad.

kokuō (國王), *n.* a king; a monarch; a sovereign.

kokuon (國恩), *n.* the blessings of one's country.

kokura (小倉-布), *n.* duck cloth.

kokuran (國亂), *n.* a national disturbance [commotion]; a civil war (內亂); an internal agitation [troubles] (同上).

kokuri (國利), *n.* national interests. —國利民福を計る, to promote national welfare and happiness.

kokuri (酷吏), *n.* a tyrannical [cruel; hard] official.

kokuritsu (國立の), *a.* national. ¶ 國立銀行 (公園), a national bank (park).

kokuron (國論), *n.* national opinion [view]; public opinion (輿論).

kokurui (穀類), *n.* cereals; grains.

kokuryoku (國力), *n.* national resources (財力); national power [strength] (勢力).

kokusai (國祭), *n.* ❶ (國の祭) a national festival [fête]. ❷(國祭日) a national holiday.

kokusai (國際), *n.* international intercourse. —國際間の, international. —國際問題を惹起する, to give rise [lead] to an international issue. ¶ 國際貿易, international trade. —國際仲裁裁判(所), international (court of) arbitration. —國際團體, community [family] of nations. —國際紛議, international disputes [complications]. —國際法, international law; law of nations. (國際公(私)法, public (private) international law.) —國際情誼, comity of nations. —國際條約, an international treaty. —國際會議, an international conference [congress]; a council of nations. —國際管理, international control [management]. —國際爲替, international exchange. —國際競技, international games [matches]. —國際聯盟, the League of Nations (理事會は the Council, 總會は the Assembly, 事務局は the Secretariat, 事務總長は the Secretary-General). —國際勞働會議, the International Labour Conference. —國際司法裁判所, the Court of International Justice. —國際市場, international market. —國際證券, interbourse [international] securities; internationals. —國際主義, internationalism.

kokusai (國債), *n.* a national debt [loan]. ☞ *kōsai* (公債). ¶ 國債證券, a national loan bond. —國債整理資金, consolidated funds.

kokusaku(國策), *n.* state [national] policy.

kokusan (國產), *n.* a product of a country; home [domestic; national] products (內國生產物). ¶ 國產獎勵博覽會, an exhibition for the encouragement of national industries.

kokusei (國勢), *n.* ❶ (形勢) the state [condition] of a country. ❷ (勢力) national power. ¶ 國勢調查, census. (國勢調查員, an enumerator. —國勢調查用紙, a census-paper. —國勢調查の執行, the taking of a census.)

kokuseki (國籍), *n.* nationality; citizenship [米]. —國籍不明の船舶, a vessel of unknown nationality. —國籍を離脫する, to expatriate oneself. ¶ 國籍離脫, expatriation.

kokushi (國士), *n.* a celebrity; a man of national reputation.

kokushi (國史, 國志), *n.* ❶ a history of a nation. ❷ (日本史) a history of Japan; a Japanese history.

kokushi (酷使する), *vt.* to overwork; overtask; drive [work] a person hard. —雇人を酷使する, to work one's servant hard.

kokushibyō (黑死病), *n.* black plague. ☞ *pesuto*.

kokusho (國書), *n.* ❶ (元首の文書) credentials. ❷ (書籍) national works [literature].

kokusho(酷暑), *n.* severe summer [heat]; intense [tropical] heat. —酷暑の候 [砌], in this parching hot season.

kokushoku (黑色), *n.* black (colour).

kokushoku (穀食する), *v.* to feed on cereals.

kokushu (國手), *n.* a (skilled) physician; an expert doctor.

kokuso (告訴), *n.* accusation; complaint; information. —告訴する, to accuse; complain; lodge a complaint *against*. —告訴を取下げる, to withdraw a complaint. ¶ 告訴狀, a letter [statement] of complaint; a bill (of information). —告訴人, an accuser; a complainant.

kokusō(國喪), *n.* national mourning.

kokusō (國葬), *n.* a state funeral. —國葬にする, to inter at the state expense.

kōkusu(骸炭), *n.* coke.

kokusui (國粹), *n.* national characteristics; nationality. ¶ 國粹保存, preservation of national characteristics.

koku-suru (哭する), *vt.* to lament; bewail; mourn *for*.

kokutai(國體), *n.* ❶ national constitution; nationality. ❷ (國家の體面) the honour of one's country.

kokutan (黑檀), *n.* 【植】 Diospyros peregrina (ebony-tree の一種・學名); the ebony (俗稱). —黑檀製の, ebony.

kokutei (國定の), *a.* established by the state; state; statutory. ¶ 國定教科書, a school text-book compiled by the state authorities; a state text-book. —國定稅率, general [statutory] tariff.

kokuten(黑點), *n.* a black [dark] spot; a macula (太陽・鑛物・皮膚等の). —太陽の黑點, a solar macula; a sun-spot.

kokuun (國運), *n.* the national fortune; the fate of a country. 國運を賭して戰ふ, to fight with the country's fate at stake; stake country's fortune on a war.

kokuyō (國用), *n.* national expenses [expenditure].

kokuyōseki(黑曜石), *n.* 【地質】 obsidian; volcanic glass.

kokuyu (告諭), *n.* an official notice [announcement].

kokuyū (國有), *n.* nationalization; state [government] ownership. —國有にする, to nationalize; bring under state-ownership. ¶ 國有地 (林; 鐵道; 財產), state land (forest; railway; property).

kokuze (國是), *n.* national [state] policy. —國是を誤る, to take an erroneous [a false; an unwise] national policy; deviate from the true national policy.

kokuzei (國稅), *n.* a national tax.

kokuzō (穀象-蟲), *n.* 【昆】 the rice-weevil; the grain-weevil.

kokuzoku (國賊), *n.* a traitor (to his country); a betrayer (of his country); a rebel.

kokyō (故郷), *n.* one's native place [province]; the birthplace; (one's) home. —故郷へ錦を飾る, to return to one's birthplace in splendour [honour].

kōkyo (公許), *n.* official [government] permission. ☞ *kankyo.*

kōkyo (抗拒する), *v.* to resist; defend *against*; withstand.

kōkyo (皇居), *n.* the Imperial palace.

kōkyo (溝渠), *n.* a ditch; a gap (へだて). ☞ *mizo.*

kōkyo (薨去), *n.* death; decease. —薨去する, to pass away.

kōkyō (口供), *n.* 【法】 testimony; deposition.

kōkyō (口鏡), *n.* a dental mirror; a dentist's mirror.

kōkyō (公共の, 公共的), *a.* public; common. —公共心に訴へる, to appeal to another's public spirit. ¶ 公共團體, a public corporation [body]. —公共事業, a public enterprise.

kōkyō (好況), *n.* a prosperous condition; a favourable aspect. —好況を呈する, to show a favourable market.

kōkyō (廣狹), *n.* ❶ (廣さと狹さ) broadness and narrowness. ❷ (幅, 面積) width; extent; dimensions.

kōkyōgaku (交響樂), *n.* 【音】 symphony.

kokyū (胡弓), *n.* a *kokyū*; a three-stringed fiddle.

kokyū (呼吸), *n.* ❶ (息) breath; breathing; respiration. ❷ (こつ) knack; trick. —呼吸する, to breathe; draw breath; respire. —今に商賣の呼吸が分ッて來るだらう, You will soon get [learn] the trick of the trade. ¶ 呼吸器病, a disease of the respiratory organs. —呼吸器保護器, a respirator. —呼吸切逼, laboured breathing [respiration]. —呼吸測定計, a respirometer.

kokyū (故舊), *n.* an old acquaintance [friend; crony].

kōkyū (考究, 講究), *n.* ❶ (研究) study; research; investigation; inquiry; examination. ❷ (熟慮) consideration; deliberation. —考究する, to investigate; inquire *into*; study. ¶ 考究者, an investigator.

kōkyū (恆久の), *a.* permanent; eternal. ☞ *eikyū.*

kōkyū (後宮), *n.* ❶ the Imperial harem [seraglio]. ❷ (后妃などの稱) the consort of the Emperor.

kōkyū (高級の), *a.* high-class; superior; senior. ¶ 高級參謀 (副官), a senior staff officer (adjuatant).

kōkyū (高給), *n.* high salary [pay]. —高給の, high-salaried.

kōkyū (硬球), *n.* 【庭球】 a hard [regulation] ball.

kōkyū (購求する), *vt.* to (make a) purchase.

kōkyūbi (公休日), *n.* an off-day; a holiday.

koma (駒), *n.* ❶ (馬) a horse. ❷ (子馬) a colt; a pony. ❸ (樂器の) a bridge; a fret. ❹ (棋子) a chessman; a man; a piece.

koma (獨樂), *n.* a top. —獨樂が澄む (くるくる廻る; 味噌する), A top sleeps (whirls; wobbles). ¶ 獨樂遊び, top-spinning. —獨樂廻し, ① top-spinning. ② (曲藝師) a top-spinner.

komadori (駒鳥), *n.* 【鳥】 the Japanese robin.

komageta (駒下駄), *n.* jointless clogs.

komagiri (細切り), *n.* ❶ (細く切ること) cutting fine. ❷ (細切肉) mincemeat; forcemeat; forced meat.

komagoma (細細), *ad.* ❶ (細片) to pieces; finely. ❷ (詳細に) minutely; in detail [full]. ☞ *komakani.* —細々と書き記す, to write down in detail.

komai (木舞), *n.* 【建】 lath. ¶ 木舞搔き, lathing (事); a lather (人).

komai (古米), *n.* old rice.

komainu (狛), *n.* a figure [an image] of a Korean dog.

komakai (細かい), *a.* ❶ (細小) small; minute; fine. ❷ (詳細) detailed; minute; (full and) particular. ❸ (緻密) delicate; elaborate (精巧); careful (細心). ❹ (勘定高い) stingy; niggardly; miserly. —細かい觀察, close observation. —細かい事, a trifling matter.

komakani (細かに), *ad.* Ⓢ 細かく. ❶ (細小) finely; to pieces; into fragments. ❷ (詳細) in detail [full]; minutely; at length. ❸ (綿密) delicately; elaborately (丹念に); carefully; closely (緻密に). —細かに切る, to cut fine. —細かに調べる, to scrutinize; examine closely.

komaku (鼓膜), *n.* 【解】 the tympanum; the tympanic membrane; the ear-drum.

komamono (小間物), *n.* fancy goods [articles]; toilet articles. ¶ 小間物店, a fancy-goods shop; a fancy store. (小間物店を出す, ① to open [set up] a fancy goods shop. ② (嘔吐) to shoot [jerk] the cat; cast up accounts [卑].)

kōman (高慢), *n.* ❶ (自負) pride; self-conceit. ❷ (傲慢) haughtiness; arrogance. ❸ (高言) boast; brag. **——-na,** *a.* ❶ proud; (self-)conceited. ❷ haughty; uppish; arrogant. ❸ boastful; high-flown. —高慢な態度, haughty air.

komanuku (拱く), *vt.* to fold (the arms). —手を拱いて傍観する, to stand looking on with folded arms.

komaraseru (困らせる), *vt.* Ⓢ 困らす, to annoy; embarrass; worry. —人を困らせ抜く, to worry a person to death.

komarimono (困り者), *n.* a ne'er-do-well; a sad dog (放蕩者); a troublesome person (厄介者).

komaru (困る), *v.* ❶ (難儀) to suffer; be afflicted; be distressed. ❷ (當惑) to be perplexed; be embarrassed; be at a loss. ❸ (困窮) to be straitened; be hard up; want *for*. ☞ *komatta.* —困り果てる [切る; 抜く], to be at one's wits' end; be sorely perplexed [greatly embarrassed]. —貧乏で困ッてゐる, to be in reduced [poor; straitened] circumstances. —返答に困ッてゐる, to be at a loss for an answer.

komata (小股), *n.* short steps. —小股に歩く, to walk with short steps. —小股を掬ふ, to trip.

komatchakure (小間瘤奴), *n.* a precocious child; an insolent fellow; a whipper; a snapper. —小間瘤れた, pert; impertinent; forward; precocious (早熟の).

komatsubara (小松原), *n.* a grove of young pines.

komatta (困ッた), *a.* vexatious; troublesome; awkward. **——,** *int.* botheration; the deuce; the devil. —ひどく困ッた様子, a deeply concerned air.

komayaka (細·濃かな), *a.* ❶ (綿密な) fine; close; minute. ❷ (濃い) thick; deep. ❸ (厚い, 親しい) close; intimate; affectionate.

komazukai (小間使), *n.* a lady's maid.

kome (米), *n.* rice.

komebitsu (米櫃), *n.* a rice-chest.

komedawara (米俵), *n.* a straw rice-bag.

kōmei (公明な), *a.* fair; impartial; straight; honest; just. —公明正大な, fair and square. (公明正大な處置, fair dealing [play].)

komekami (顳顬), *n.* the temple.

komemushi (米蟲), *n.* 【昆】the rice-weevil.

komeru (籠·込·罩める), *vt.* ❶ (塡める) to charge; load. ❷ (含ませる) to include; put *into*; force in (插込める). ❸ (集中する) to concentrate *upon*; rivet *upon*; devote. —夜を込めて, before dawn [daybreak]. —心を籠めて, with one's heart and soul; with all one's mind; intently. —彈丸をこめる, to load a gun.

komesōba (米相場), *n.* speculation in rice.

kometsubu (米粒), *n.* a grain of rice.

kometsuki (米搗), *n.* ❶ (動作) rice-cleaning. ❷ (人) a rice-cleaner. ¶ 米搗蟲, 【昆】the click-beetle.

komeya (米屋), *n.* a rice-dealer (人); a rice-shop (店).

komi (込みで), ❶ (...を包含して) included. ❷ (選擇なしで) in a job lot; in the lump; in bulk; in the gross. —込みで買ふ, to buy in the lump [gross]. ¶ 込み値段, all-round [overhead] price.

kōmi (香味), *n.* smack; spice.

komiageru (込上げる), *v.* ❶ (嘔吐を催す) to feel sick; retch. ❷ (迫り來る) to have convulsions. —込上げて來る涙, tears that come surging.

komiau (込合ふ), *vi.* to crowd; throng; jostle. —込合ひますから懐中物御用心, As it is crowded, beware of pickpockets.

komichi (小道, 徑), *n.* a (narrow) path; a lane; a bypath (脇道); a defile (縦列でないと通れぬ程の).

komiiru (込入る), *vt.* ❶ (複雑) to be complicated; be entangled; be intricate. ❷ (精緻) to be elaborate. —込入ッた, ① (複雑) complicated; intricate; entangled. ② (精巧) elaborate; minute. (込入ッた話, a tangled tale.)

kōmin (公民), *n.* a citizen. ¶ 公民權, civic rights; right of citizenship.

komiya (槊杖), *n.* a ramrod; a rammer.

komo (菰, 薦), *n.* ❶ (眞菰) the Canada [Indian] rice. ❷ (荒蓆) a rush-mat; straw matting. ¶ 菰包み, a packing of rush-mat. (菰包みにする, to pack in rush-mat.)

komochi (子持), *n.* ❶ (姙娠) pregnancy. ❷ (子を有すること) motherhood; fatherhood. ❸ (人) a pregnant woman; a mother; a father. ¶ 子持縞, a pattern with thin stripes between thick ones.

komogomo (交), *ad.* ❶ (交互に) alternately; by turns. ❷ (次々に) one after another; in succession.

kōmoku (項目), *n.* a head; a heading; an item. —項目に分ける, to itemize.

kōmoku (綱目), *n.* ❶ (分類) classification. ❷ (要點) the main points; the gist; the outlines (大要).
komon (小紋), *n.* a speckled pattern.
komon (顧問), *n.* an adviser; a counsellor. ¶ 法律顧問, a legal adviser [counsellor]. —顧問官, a councillor; a counsellor.
kōmon (肛門), *n.* 【解】 the anus.
kōmon (後門), *n.* a postern gate; a back [rear]-gate.
kōmon (閘門), *n.* a lock-gate.
komori (子守), *n.* ❶ nursing. ❷ (人) a (dry) nurse; an amah. —子守する, to have charge [care] of a child; look after a baby. ¶ 子守女, a nurse-maid. —子守唄, a lullaby; a cradle-song; a nursery song.
komori(小森), *n.* an underwood; a copse.
kōmori(蝙蝠), *n.* 【哺乳】 the bat.
kōmorigasa (蝙蝠傘), *n.* an umbrella. ¶ 蝙蝠傘屋, an umbrella-dealer (商人); an umbrella-shop (商店); an umbrella-maker (製造人); an umbrella-mender (修繕人).
komoru (籠る), *vi.* ❶ (籠居) to stay; confine oneself *in*; shut oneself up. ❷ (含まる) to be included [implied]. —書齋に籠る, to seclude oneself in one's study. —城に籠る, to shut oneself up in a castle. —情の籠ッた言葉, affectionate [kind] words.
komu (込む), *vi.* ❶ (雜沓) to crowd; throng *about*; press *upon*. ❷ (潮が) to flow; rise.
kōmu (工務), *n.* public works. ¶ 工務監督局, the Board of Works and Public Buildings. —工務局, the Engineering Bureau (鐵道省の); the Bureau of Industry (商工省の).
kōmu (公務), *n.* government service; public service; official business. —公務多端のため, on account of press of official business. ¶ 公務員, a public officer. —公務所, a public office.
kōmu (港務), *n.* port service; harbour service. ¶ 港務部, the port [harbour] office; the harbour department. —港務(部)長, a harbour-master.
komugi (小麥), *n.* 【植】 the wheat; the corn [英]. ¶ 小麥粉, wheat flour; corn-flour.
komura (腓), *n.* 【解】 the calf. —腓が返る, to be seized with a cramp in the calf.
kōmurasu (蒙らす), *vt.* ❶ (受けさす) to inflict *on* (打擊・損害・罰などを); subject a person *to*; visit *with* (天罰などを). ❷ (被せる) to lay [put] *on*; impute *to*; lay at another's door. —人に損害を蒙らす, to inflict losses upon another.
kōmuru (蒙・被る), *v.* ❶ (かぶる) to put on; wear. ❷ (受ける) to receive (恩・侮辱等を); suffer (害・損害・罰・敗北等を); sustain (同上); incur (不興・非難等を). —影響を被る, to be influenced [affected]; be under the influence *of*.
komusō (虛無僧), *n.* a strolling minstrel.
komusume (小娘), *n.* a young girl; a lass; a maid.
kōmyaku (鑛脈), *n.* a mineral vein; a lode; a lead. —鑛脈に掘り當てる, to strike a lode.
kōmyō (功名), *n.* a glorious deed; a great exploit. —功名をなす, to perform a glorious deed; achieve an exploit of great merit. ¶ 功名心, ambition.
kōmyō (巧妙な), *a.* skilful; dexterous; masterly. —巧妙な仕掛, a clever device.
kōmyō (光明), *n.* ❶ (光) light; rays. ❷ (後光) a halo; a glory. ❸ (希望) hope; prospect. —前途の光明を認める, to see the gleam of hope beyond.
kon (根), *n.* ❶ (根氣) patience; perseverance. ❷ 【數】 a root; a radical. ❸ 【化】 a radical.
kon (紺), *n.* dark blue; navy-blue.
kona (粉), *n.* ❶ (穀類の) meal; flour. ❷ (粉末) powder. ❸ (果實・葉等の面に生ずる) bloom. —粉の, floury; powdery. —粉にする, to powder; pulverize. —粉まみれにする, to bepowder; cover with powder.
konacha (粉茶), *n.* broken tea; dust tea.
konagona (粉粉に), *ad.* to [into] pieces; to fragments; to powder. —こなごなに碎く, to break into pieces; smash (to fragments).
konagusuri (粉藥), *n.* powdered medicine; (medical) powder. ☞ *kogusuri.*
konahiki (粉碾), *n.* milling(事); a triturator(器).
konai(戶內へ・に・で), *ad.* indoors; within doors.
kōnai (港內), *n.* the inside of a harbour.
kōnai (構內), *n.* the premises; the compound; the yard. ¶ 學校構內, the school close. —稅關構內, the Custom House compound.
konaida (此間), *ad.* ❶ (先日) the other day; some [a few] days ago. ❷ (近頃) lately; of late; recently. —此間の火事, the late fire.
kōnaien (口內炎), *n.* 【醫】 stomatitis.
konamaiki (小生意氣な), *a.* impertinent; saucy; pert. —小生

意氣な口をきく, to talk impertinently.

konamijin (粉微塵に), *ad.* to [into] pieces; into smithereens; into atoms. ☞ ***konagona.***

kōnan (後難), *n.* future trouble; the consequences. —後難を恐れる, to fear the consequences.

konare (消化), *n.* digestion. —消化の良い(惡い)食物, digestible (indigestible) food.

konareru (こなれる), *vi.* ❶ (消化) to be digested. ❷ (熟) to mature; ripen.

konashabon (粉石鹼), *n.* soap-powder; powdered soap.

konasu (こなす), *vt.* ❶ (粉碎) to reduce to powder; pulverize; powder. ❷ (消化) to digest. ❸ (自由に取扱ふ) to manage [bring] into subjection; do without difficulty. ❹ (處置) to deal *with*; manage. ❺ (誹謗) to deride; treat with ridicule; disparage. —數でこなす, to make up for by number. —頭から人をこなす, to disparage another without compunction.

konata (此方), =***kochira.***

konazumi (粉炭), *n.* ground charcoal; charcoal powder.

konban (今晩), *n.* & *ad.* to-night; this evening. —今晩は, (挨拶) Good evening.

kōn-bīfu (醃藏牛肉), *n.* corned beef.

konbinēshon (コンビネーション), *n.* combinations; combination garment.

konbō (棍棒), *n.* a club; an Indian club (體操用); a cudgel.

konbu (昆布), *n.* 【植】❶ Laminaria (學名). ❷ (眞昆布) the Japanese tangle. ¶ 刻み昆布, sliced tangle.

konchi (根治), *n.* 【醫】eradication; radical cure. —根治する, to effect a radical cure; cure completely.

konchū (昆蟲), *n.* an insect. ¶ 昆蟲學, entomology. (昆蟲學者, an entomologist.)

kondaku (混濁, 溷濁), *n.* ❶ muddiness; turbidity; impurity. ❷ dulness; thickness. —混濁さす, to muddle; make muddy [turbid; foul]. —混濁する, to become turbid [muddy].

kondan (懇談), *n.* close conversation; social consultation. —懇談する, to commune *with*; converse freely [without constraint] *with*; consult without reserve.

kondate (獻立), *n.* ❶ (料理) order of dishes. ❷ (手配) a programme; preparation; arrangements. —獻立する, to prepare; make a programme. ¶ 獻立表, a bill of fare; a menu (card).

kondensu-miruku (煉乳), *n.* condensed milk; Swiss milk.

kondo (今度), *ad.* ❶ (現在) this time; now. ❷ (此の次) next time; another time. ❸ (近々) shortly; in the near future. ❹ (此程) lately; recently. —今度の英語の先生, the new English teacher. —今度言ッたら, if you say it again.

kondō (混同), *n.* confusion; mixing up. **——-suru,** *vt.* to confuse *with*; mix *with* (混合). —目的と手段とを混同する, to confound [confuse] the means with the end.

konebachi (捏鉢), *n.* a kneading-trough.

konekaesu (捏返す), *vt.* to knead; mix together. —下手な理窟をこね返す, to use [bring forward] flimsy arguments.

koneko (小猫), *n.* a kitten.

kōnen (後年), *n.* after [future] years; years to come; later years (近年). ☞ ***bannen.*** —後年に至りて, in after years; in years to come.

koneru (捏ねる), *vt.* to knead; work [mix] together.

kōnetsu (口熱), *n.* fever of the mouth.

kongan (懇願), *n.* entreaty; solicitation; supplication. —懇願する, to entreat; implore; supplicate. —懇願を容れる, to accede to an entreaty.

kongarakaru (こんがらかる), *vi.* to get entangled (絲・事件など縺れる); get complicated (事件など複雜になる); be confused (話など混亂する). —こんがらかす, to entangle; complicate; confuse. —絹絲のこんがらかり, a tangled skein of silk.

kongasuri (紺飛白), *n.* bluish cloth with white scattered figures.

kongen (根源, 根元), *n.* ❶ (原因) the cause. ❷ (根本) the root; the source; the origin. ☞ ***konpon, moto.*** —根源に溯る, to retrace [go back] to the source. —...の根元を究める, to get at the root *of*.

kongetsu (今月), *n.* this month; the present [current] month; instant (inst. と略す). —去年の今月, this month last year. —今月五日に, on the fifth inst.

kongi (婚儀), *n.* marriage (ceremony); wedding (ceremony). —婚儀を調へる, to make preparations for a marriage ceremony. —婚儀を行ふ, to solemnize [celebrate] a marriage.

kongo (今後), *ad.* henceforth; hereafter; in future. —今後もあ

る事だ, It may happen again.

kongō (混合), *n.* 【化·鑛】 mixture (化合の對); medley. —色の混合, mixture of colours. —混合する, to mix; intermix; mingle. ¶ 混合物, 【化】 a mixture; a medley.

kongōgiri (金剛錐), *n.* 【工】 a diamond-drill; a diamond-borer.

kongōriki (金剛力), *n.* Herculean strength. —金剛力を出す, to put forth [exert] enormous strength.

kongōsha (金剛砂), *n.* emery; emery-powder. ¶ 金剛砂布, emery-cloth. —金剛砂紙, emery-paper. —金剛砂回轉砥, an emery-wheel.

kongōzue (金剛杖), *n.* an alpenstock; a pilgrim's staff.

kongyō (今曉), *ad.* early [at daybreak] this morning.

koṅi (懇意), *n.* friendship; intimacy; familiarity. —懇意な間柄, intimate relations [terms]. —非常に懇意にして居る, to live on most familiar terms (*with*).

konimotsu (小荷物), *n.* luggage; baggage [米]. ¶ 小荷物扱所, a luggage-office; a parcel-office [米].

koṅin (婚姻), *n.* marriage. ☞ ***kekkon.*** —婚姻の神, Hymen.

kōnin (公認), *n.* official recognition; authorization; public approval. —公認する, to recognize officially; authorize; approve publicly. ¶ 公認候補者, an approved candidate.

kōnin (後任), *n.* a successor. —後任になる, to succeed a person in his office; take another's place; fill the post vacated by another.

koninzu (小人數), *n.* a small number [party] of men.

koṅiro (紺色), *n.* dark blue.

koṅitsu (渾一), *n.* unity; consolidation. ¶ 渾一體, a complete whole; a unity; an organism.

konjaku (今昔), *n.* ancient and modern. —今昔の感に堪へぬ, to be deeply affected by the thought of the change between the past and present.

konji (恨事), *n.* a matter for regret; a deplorable [regrettable] affair.

konji (根治), *n.* =***konchi.***

konji (紺地), *n.* deep blue texture.

konjiki (金色), *n.* golden colour. ¶ 金色夜叉, a usurer.

kon-jiru (混じる), *vt.* ❶ (混合) to mix; mingle. ❷ (混同) to confound [confuse] *with.*

konjō (今生), *n.* this world; this life. —今生の暇乞, one's farewell in this world.

konjō (根性), *n.* spirit; disposition; temper. —根性の曲がった[惡い], ill-tempered; ill-natured; cross-grained. ¶ 奉公人(商人)根性, the servant (tradesman) spirit.

konjō (紺靑), *n.* azure blue.

konjō (懇情), *n.* kindness; kindly feeling; warm friendship.

konkagiri (根限り), *ad.* with all one's might; to the utmost; as long as one's strength lasts. —根限り働く, to work to the utmost.

konkai (今回), *ad.* this time; lately. ☞ ***kondo.***

konkei (根莖), *n.* 【植】 the rhizome; the rootstock.

konketsu (混血), *n.* half-blood; cross-breed. ¶ 混血兒, a half-blood; a half-caste (特に父が歐洲人で母が印度人の). ☞ ***ainoko.***

konki (根氣), *n.* perseverance; patience; energy. —根氣が竭きる; 根氣負けがする, to give out; one's patience is exhausted. —根氣競べをする, to vie with each other in perseverance; see which can hold out longest. —根氣のよい, patient; persevering; untiring. —根氣よく勉强する, to study perseveringly.

konki (婚期), *n.* marriageable [nubile] age.

konkō (混淆), *n.* a mixture; a medley; hotch-potch. —混淆する, to mix; jumble; medley.

konkoido (螺獅線), *n.* 【數】 a conchoid.

konkon (混混, 滾滾), *ad.* rushing down; gushing. —滾々として湧出する, to gush out.

konkon (懇懇), *ad.* ❶ (懇ろなる狀) earnestly; seriously. ❷ (繰返して說く狀) repeatedly. —懇々說論する, to admonish repeatedly; talk seriously *to.*

konku (困苦), *n.* hardship; tribulation; privation. —困苦する, to suffer; suffer hardships. —困苦を嘗める, to suffer tribulations; undergo hardships.

konkurīto (混凝土), *n.* concrete. —コンクリートで固める, to concrete. ¶ 鐵筋コンクリート, ferro-concrete; re-inforced concrete; armoured concrete. —コンクリート鋪裝, concrete pavement. —コンクリート混合機, a concrete-mixer.

konkyaku (困却), *n.* embarrassment; perplexity; trouble. —困却する, to be embarrassed; be in trouble; be in a fix.

konkyo (根據), *n.* the base; the foundation; the ground; the authority (典據). —薄弱な根據, slight [weak] ground. —根據のない, baseless; unfounded; groundless. —根據を固める, to make the ground firm. —敵の根據を衝く, to attack the enemy's base. ¶ 根

據地, the base (of operations).

konkyū (困窮), *n.* poverty; destitution; penury. —困窮せる, needy; destitute; straitened. —困窮する, to be destitute; be reduced to poverty; be in straitened [reduced] circumstances.

konma (句點), *n.* a comma. —コンマ以下の人間, a man of no account; a nobody. —コンマを切る, to insert a comma.

konmei (昏迷), *n.* stupor; stupefaction; trance. —昏迷する, to be stupefied *with*; be petrified *with*.

konmisshon (コンミッション), *n.* ❶ (口錢) a commission. ❷ (賄賂) a bribe. —コンミッションを拂ふ(貰ふ), to pay (receive) a commission.

konmō (懇望), *n.* earnest desire; entreaty; solicitation. —懇望する, to entreat; solicit; desire [ask] earnestly.

konmori (こんもり), *ad.* thickly; densely. —こんもりした森, a dense grove.

konna (こんな), *a.* such; of this kind [sort]; this kind [sort] *of*. **——-ni,** *ad.* so; like this; in this manner. —こんなに澤山, so many (much).

konnan (困難), *n.* difficulty (困難なこと, 障碍); trouble (面倒); hardship (艱難). —困難する, to suffer; suffer hardships; have a hard time of it. —困難して, with (great) difficulty; after a great struggle. —困難して居る, to be in difficulties; be distressed; be embarrassed. —困難に打勝つ, to overcome [surmount] difficulties. —困難に陷る, to get [fall] into a difficulty; be beset with difficulties. —幾多の困難と鬪ふ, to contend with many difficulties. **——-na,** *a.* difficult; hard; troublesome (うるさい). —困難な事業(仕事), a tough [up-hill] work; a hard task.

konnen (今年), *n.* & *ad.* this year; the present [current] year.

konnichi (今日), *n.* & *ad.* ❶ (本日) to-day; this day. ❷ (當今) nowadays; these days [times]; the present day [time]. —今日まで, until [up to] the present; until [till] to-day. —今日より, from this day (forward). —今日は, (挨拶) Good day!; Good morning (午前又は dinner 前, 夕刻に dinner を喫するならば午後もかく云ふ); Good afternoon (午後).

konnyaku (蒟蒻), *n.* ❶【植】Amorphophallus Rivieri (學名); the devil's tongue. ❷ (食品) *konnyaku*; kneaded devil's tongue root. ¶ 蒟蒻版, a hectograph; a papyrograph.

konnyū (混入する), *v.* to mix; mingle; dash (酒に水を割る). —牛乳に水を混入する, to mix milk with water.

kono (此, 斯, 是), *a.* this; these; present. —此二三日, these two or three days; the last few days. —此數年來, for several years past. —此點までは, so far.

kōnō (行嚢), *n.* ❶ (郵便の) a mail-bag; a post-bag; a mail-sack 〔米〕 ❷ (背嚢, 今は旅行用にも用ふ) a knapsack.

kōnō (效能), *n.* effect; efficacy; virtue (of a medicine). —效能のある, effective; efficacious; good *for*. —多少の效能がある, to have some effect. ¶ 效能書, a statement of the virtues.

kōnō (後腦), *n.* 【解】the metencephalon; the hind-brain.

kōnō (貢納する), *v.* to pay tribute *to*. ¶ 貢納金, tribute-money.

konoaida (此間), =*konaida.*

konobun (此分では), *ad.* at this rate; as things are.

konoe (近衞), *n.* ❶ (皇宮のまもり) the Imperial palace guard. ❷ =近衞兵. ¶ 近衞兵, the Imperial guards; the Household troops [guards]: a guardsman (特に將校). —近衞騎兵, a life-guardsman; a body-guard. —近衞師團, the Imperial Guard Division.

konogoro (此頃), *ad.* ❶ (此間) lately; recently; for some time back [past]. ❷ (此節) now; nowadays; in these days. —つい此頃, only a few days ago. —此頃の寒さ, the present cold weather.

konoha (木葉), *n.* a leaf; fallen leaves (落葉). ¶ 木葉蝶,【蝶】Kallima inachis (學名). —木葉落し, a death drop (飛行機の).

konohen (此邊に), *ad.* hereabouts; in this neighbourhood; in this quarter (of the city).

konohodo (此程), *ad.* =*kono-aida.*

konohoka (此外), *ad.* besides this; in addition; besides; moreover.

konokata (以來), *ad.* since. ☞ *irai.* —十年この方, for ten years past. —先週の月曜この方, ① (今週の日・月曜日に云ふ時) since Monday last. ② (今週の火曜以後に云ふ時) since last Monday week. ③ (今週の月曜日に云ふ時) since to-day week. ④ (今週の火曜日に云ふ時) since yesterday week.

konokata (此方), *n.* & *pron.* this gentleman (lady). —この方が田中さんです, This gentleman is Mr. Tanaka.

konokurai (此位), *ad.* about

this; this much; so much. —此位の大きさです, It is about this size.

konoma (木間), among the trees. —木の間を洩れる月影, the moonlight streaming from among the trees.

konomae (此前), *ad.* last; the last time; before.

kōnōmaku (硬腦膜), *n.* 【解】the dura (mater); the endocranium. ¶ 硬腦膜炎,【醫】endocranitis.

konomashii (好ましい), *a.* pleasant; desirable; agreeable (氣持のよい). —好ましからぬ, unpleasant; undesirable; disagreeable.

konome (木芽), *n.* a bud; a leaf-bud. ☞ *kinome.* —木の芽が出る, to bud; come in leaf.

konomi (好), *n.* ❶ (嗜好) liking; fancy; fondness. ❷ (希望) a request; a wish. ❸ (時好) fashion; style. ❹ (選好) choice; preference. —お好みとあれば, if you wish it. —御註文は御好み次第, Served to order.

konomi (木實), *n.* a fruit (of a tree).

kōnomono (香の物), *n.* radishes pickled in salt and bran; pickled vegetables.

konomu (好む), *vt.* ❶ (好惡) to like; be fond *of*; care *for*. ❷ (選好) to choose; prefer; have a preference *for*. ❸ (嗜好) to have a taste *for*; take delight *in*; relish. —好んで, by choice (選好んで); of one's own will (勝手に).

konosaki (此先), *ad.* ❶ (時) hereafter; in future; for the future. ❷ (距離) beyond this.

konosetsu (此節), *ad.* nowadays; in these days; of late. ☞ *konogoro.*

konoshiro (鰶), *n.* 【魚】Konosirus punctatus (學名).

konotoki (此時), *ad.* then; at this time; at this juncture. —此の時早く彼の時遲く, at this very moment; at this instant.

konotōri (此通り), *ad.* like this; in this manner; (as) you see (御覧の通り). —此通りの有樣です, I am in the condition you see me in.

kōnotori (鸛), *n.* 【鳥】the Japanese stork.

konotsugi (此次の), *a.* next. —此次に, the next time. —此次の日曜, next Sunday; Sunday next.

konoue (此上), *ad.* ❶ (より以外又は以上) besides; moreover; in addition to this. ❷ (斯くなる以上) if this is the case; when things have come to such a pass. —此上ない品, a first-rate article; an article of the very best quality. —此上ない幸福, supreme happiness. —此上ない好天氣, an ideal weather. —此上ない名譽, the highest honour. —此上もなく喜んでる, to be delighted beyond measure. —此上とも御愛顧を乞ふ, I solicit your continued patronage.

konowata (海鼠腸), *n.* the salted entrails of the trepang.

konoyo (此世), *n.* the [this] world; this life; the present life. —此世の, worldly (浮世の); earthly (下界の); temporal (俗世の). —此世を終る迄, to [till] the last [end]. —此世を去る, to leave this world.

konpai (困憊), *n.* exhaustion; fatigue. —困憊する, to be exhausted; be fatigued; be tired to death; be dead tired.

konpaku (魂魄), *n.* the soul; the spirit; the ghost. ☞ *reikon.*

konpan (今般), *ad.* now; this time; lately.

konpasu (コンパス), *n.* ❶ (羅針盤) the mariner's compass. ❷ (兩脚器) (a pair of) compasses. ❸ [譜] (脚) legs; stumps. —コンパスで測る, to calliper; measure with compasses; see in the dial of a compass (羅針盤で).

konpeitō (金米糖), *n.* a sugar-plum; a comfit.

konpeki (紺碧), *n.* & *a.* dull blue.

konpon (根本), *n.* ❶ (根元) the root; the origin; the source (本源). ❷ (基礎) the foundation; the basis. —根本を誤る, to make [take] a wrong start; begin at the wrong end. ——**-teki**, *a.* thorough; radical; fundamental. —根本的に, radically; fundamentally; thoroughly. —根本的に治療をする, to effect a radical cure.

konran (昏亂), *n.* derangement; bewilderment. —昏亂する, to be deranged; be bewildered (面喰ふ).

konran (混亂), *n.* confusion; disorder; chaos (混沌); complication (錯雜); disturbance (擾亂). —火事場の混亂, confusion at a fire. —内部の混亂, internal disorder. —混亂する, to be disordered; be thrown into confusion; be in a mess [tangle].

konrei (婚禮), *n.* marriage; matrimony; wedding. ☞ *kekkon.* —婚禮の祝物, a wedding present.

konrinzai (金輪際), *ad.* never; to the end; on no account. —金輪際放さぬ, I will never let go.

konro (焜爐), *n.* a small portable furnace.

konryō (袞龍), *n.* royal robes. —袞龍の袖に隱れる, to conceal oneself under the Imperial ægis.

konryū (建立), *n.* building;

erection. —建立する, to build; erect.

konryū (混流), *n.* cross currents.

konsamai (混砂米), *n.* rice cleaned [refined] by sand.

konsei (混成), *n.* mixture; medley; composition. —混成する, to mix; put together; be made by mixture *of*. ¶ 混成旅團, a mixed [composite] brigade. —混成酒, mixed *sake* [spirits].

konsei (懇請), *n.* entreaty; solicitation. ☞ ***kongan.***

konseki (痕跡), *n.* a mark; a trace; vestiges. —痕跡を殘す, to leave marks behind. —痕跡を辿る, to follow up the traces.

konsen (混線), *n.* entangled wires. —混線する, to get entangled; be crossed.

konsen (混戰), *n.* a confused conflict; a free fight; a *mêlée* [佛]. —混戰する, to fight in confusion.

konsetsu (懇切な), *a.* kind; cordial; warm-hearted. —懇切に取扱ふ, to treat kindly.

konshin (渾身), *n.* body and soul. ☞ ***zenshin.*** —渾身の力を奮ッて, with whole strength; with might and main; (with) body and soul.

konshin (懇親), *n.* friendship; friendliness; intimacy. —懇親を結ぶ, to enter into friendship; strike up friendship *with*. —懇親會を開く, to open a social meeting.

konshū (今週), *n.* this week. —今週の金曜, Friday this week; next Friday.

konsoru-kōsai (コンソル公債), *n.* consolidated annuities; consols.

konsū (根數), *n.* 【數】 a root; a radical; a surd.

konsui (昏睡), *n.* 【醫】 coma; lethargy. —昏睡狀態に陷る, to fall into coma; fall into a comatose state [condition]; become comatose.

kontan (魂膽), *n.* ❶ (わけがら) meaning; sense. ❷ (計畫) a secret scheme [design].

kontei (根柢), *n.* the root; the bottom; the foundation. ☞ ***konpon.*** —根柢ある議論, a valid [solid; sound] argument. —根柢から改革する, to reform from the foundation; make a radical reform; reform radically.

kontō (昏倒), *n.* swoon; faint. —昏倒する, to swoon; faint away; fall down in a swoon.

kontoku (懇篤な), *a.* kind; cordial. —御懇篤なる示教を蒙る, to receive your kind instruction [advice].

konton (混沌, 渾沌), *n.* chaos; disorder (不秩序の); vagueness. —混沌たる, chaotic; disorderly; vague. —混沌として豫測を許さぬ, to be too vague to forecast.

konuka (小糠), *n.* rice-bran. ¶ 小糠雨, a drizzle; a mizzle.

konusumi (小盜み), *n.* a petty theft; a petty larceny; pilfering. —小盜みする, to pilfer; filch.

konwa (混和), *n.* mixture; confusion of goods. ☞ ***kongō.***

konwa (懇話), *n.* friendly [familiar] talk; a chat. —懇話する, to chat; gossip (閑談する); have a free and easy talk.

koṅya (今夜), *n.* & *ad.* this evening; to-night. —去年の今夜, this evening last year.

koṅya (紺屋), *n.* dyeing (業); a dyer (人); a dyer's (店). —紺屋の白袴, "The tailor's wife is worst clad."

konyakku (コニャック酒), *n.* cognac.

koṅyaku (困厄), *n.* misfortune; hardships; distress. —困厄に逢ふ, to meet with a misfortune.

koṅyaku (婚約), *n.* promise of marriage; engagement; betrothal. —婚約せる人, an affianced lover; a fiancé [*fem.* -cée]; an engaged couple (男女一組). —婚約する, to engage [plight] oneself *to*; betroth. —婚約してゐる, to be engaged *to*; be betrothed *to*.

koṅyoku (混浴), *n.* mixed [promiscuous] bathing. —混浴する, to bathe promiscuously [together].

koṅyu (懇諭する), *vt.* to admonish carefully; talk seriously *to*.

kōnyū (購入する), *vt.* to purchase; buy in.

konzatsu (混雜), *n.* ❶ (混亂) confusion; disorder; mess. ❷ (錯雜) intricacy; complication; entanglement. —混雜の際, in the confusion. —混雜さす, ① to confuse, throw into disorder. ② to complicate; entangle. —混雜する, ① to be confused; be disordered; be jumbled together (ごッちゃになる). ② to be complicated; be entangled.

konzen (渾然), *ad.* ❶ (融合の貌) homogeneously; harmoniously. ❷ (圭角なき又は缺陷なき貌) consummately; perfectly. —渾然たる, ① homogeneous; harmonious. ② perfect; consummate.

konzetsu (根絕), *n.* eradication; extirpation. —根絕する, to eradicate; extirpate; root out.

kon-zuru (混ずる), *vt.* ❶ (混合) to mix; mingle; blend. ❷ (混同) to confound; confuse; mix. —水に酒を混ずる, to dash water with spirit.

koō (呼應する), *vi.* to form connection *with*; establish communication *with*. —相呼應して, in concert *with*; in union.

kōo (好惡), *n.* likes and dislikes; fancy. —好惡によりて人を批判する, to form an estimate of a man according to one's fancy.

koodori (雀躍する), *vi.* to leap for joy; dance with joy.

kooke (小桶), *n.* a keg.

koō-konrai (古往今來), *ad.* since ancient times; in all ages.

kōon (皇恩), *n.* Imperial benevolence [favours]. —皇恩に浴する, to enjoy Imperial favours.

kōon (厚恩), *n.* great favour [kindness]; innumerable blessings. —厚恩を受ける, to be received [meet] with great kindness; be under deep obligation.

kōon (高音), *n.* 【音】 alt; high tone; high-pitch sound.

kōon (喉音), *n.* a guttural (sound).

kōon (鴻恩), *n.* great benevolence.

kōotsu (甲乙), *n.* ❶ A and B. ❷ (差) difference; superiority or inferiority (優劣). —甲乙なき, equal; level. —甲乙を附ける, to grade; discriminate.

kopekku (コペック), *n.* (露貨) a copeck, kopeck.

koppa (木端), *n.* a chip; a piece of wood; a splinter.

koppā-pēnto (コッパー・ペーント), *n.* copper paint.

koppī (コッピー), *n.* ❶ (複寫) copying. ❷ (複寫器) a copying-press. —コッピーに掛ける, to put under press; take copies *of*.

koppu (コップ), *n.* a (wine) cup; a (wine) glass (硝子製の); a tumbler (水呑コップ). —コップに七分目の水, water seven parts full in a tumbler.

koppun (骨粉), *n.* ground bones; bone dust [meal]. ¶ 骨粉肥料, bone manure.

kora (こら), *int.* halloo; hi; I say. —こら! こら! 貴樣は何者か, Hi, I say, who are you?

kōra (甲羅), *n.* a carapace; a shield; a lorica. —甲羅を乾す, to bask in the sun.

koraeru (堪・怺へる), *vt.* ❶(忍ぶ) to bear; stand; put up *with*. ❷ (制する) to control; restrain; repress. ❸ (恕する) to forbear; pardon; have patience *with*. —堪へ兼ねる, unable to bear any longer. —寒さを怺へる, to bear up against cold. —痛さ [苦痛] を堪へる, to bear [stand; endure] pain.

korai (古來), *ad.* from old times; ever. —古來の, old; time-honoured.

kōrai (後來), *ad.* henceforth; hereafter; for the [in] future.

kōraku (行樂), *n.* pleasure; dissipation. —行樂を追ふ, to pursue pleasure

kōran (勾欄), *n.* a balustrade; banisters.

kōran (高欄), *n.* a balustrade on the top of a building.

kōran (高覽), *n.* your inspection [perusal]. —御高覽に供す, to submit it for your inspection.

kōran (攪亂), *n.* =***kakuran.***

kōran (コーラン), *n.* (回々敎の經典) the Koran, Alkoran.

korashime (懲しめ), *n.* punishment; correction; discipline.

korasu (凝らす), *v.* to apply one's whole heart; concentrate; strain. —粧ひを凝らす, to dress up; decorate beautifully. —意匠を凝らす, to think out a design carefully. —瞳を凝らす, to strain one's eyes.

korasu (懲らす), *v.* to chastise; punish; correct.

kōrasu (凍らす), *vt.* to freeze; congeal.

kōrasu (合唱), *n.* chorus.

kore (是, 此, 之), *pron.* this. —是が爲め, on this account; consequently. —之に反して, on the contrary; on the other hand. —是に由ッて之を觀れば, in [under] these circumstances; in view of these facts.

kore (これ), *int.* I say; halloo; hi.

koregiri (此限), ❶ this is all; there is no more; this only. ❷ (唯一度) once for all; this once.

korehodo (此程), *ad.* Ⓢ 此位. this much; so far.

korei (古例), *n.* an old custom. —古例に則る, to follow an old custom.

kōrei (好例), *n.* a good example. —好例を示す, to set an example *to*.

kōrei (恆例), *n.* usage; an established custom; a rule.

kōrei (高齡), *n.* an advanced age; old age. —高齡に達する, to attain [reach] an advanced age. ¶ 高齡者, persons of advanced age; the aged.

kōreihō (皇禮砲), *n.* an Imperial [a Royal] salute. —二十一發の皇禮砲を放つ, to fire an Imperial salute of twenty-one guns.

kōreisai (皇靈祭), *n.* a day for the worship of the Imperial Ancestors. ¶ 春〔秋〕季皇靈祭, the Feast of the Vernal 〔Autumnal〕 Equinox.

korekara (是から), *ad.* ❶ (時) now; in future; from this time forward. ❷ (所) hence; from here [this place]. —是からが面白いのだ, Now comes the fun of it.

korekore (これこれ), *ad.* so and

so. ☞ *kakkaku* (斯斯). ——, *int.* =*kore* (これ).

koremade (是迄), *ad.* ❶ (今迄) hitherto; until now; up to this time. ❷ (此處迄) (up) to this point [place]; so [thus] far. —これ迄に, ① before now; in the past. ② to this (pass). —これ迄の處では, thus [so] far; as yet.

koremiyogashi (これ見よがしに), *ad.* ostentatiously; to attract attention.

korera (此等), *pron.* these; such as these.

korera (虎列剌), *n.* cholera. ¶ 眞性コレラ, Asiatic [epidemic; algid; malignant; serious] cholera. —コレラ菌, a comma bacillus. —コレラ豫防注射液, anticholerin; anti-cholera serum.

koreshiki (此式の), *a.* such a trifling; such a slight; so little. —此れ式の事 (傷), such a trifle (slight wound).

kōretsu (後列), *n.* the rear-rank; the rear.

kori (梱), *n.* a bale; a pack; a package.

kori (凝), *n.* stiffness; hardening. —肩 (頸) の凝り, a crick in the back (neck).

kori (垢離), *n.* lustration; purification by ablution. —水垢離をとる, to purify oneself with water.

kōri (氷), *n.* ice; frozen water. —氷で閉ぢ込める, to freeze in. —氷が張り詰める, to be iced [frozen] over. —氷を滑る, to slide along the ice; skate upon the ice. ¶ ぶッかき氷, chopped ice. —氷製造所, an ice-factory.

kōri (郡), *n.* a (rural) district.

kōri (公吏), *n.* an (a public) official; a municipal official.

kōri (公理), *n.* 【數・論】an axiom.

kōri (功利), *n.* utility. ¶ 功利主義, utilitarianism.

kōri (行李), *n.* ❶ (旅行用) a basket-trunk; a bag; a hamper. ❷ (旅行の荷物) luggage; baggage 〔米〕; a pack. ❸ 【軍】baggage; impedimenta. ¶ 竹行李, a bamboo-trunk.

kōri (高利), *n.* high interest; usury. —高利の金を借る, to borrow money at high interest. —高利を貪る, to charge usurious interest. ¶ 高利貸, a usurer; a blood-sucker 〔卑〕. (高利貸業, usury.)

kōribukuro (氷袋), *n.* an ice-bag; an ice-poultice; an ice-cap (頭に當てる).

kōridōfu (氷豆腐), *n.* frozen bean-curd.

kōrifurawā (コーリフラワー), *n.* 【植】the cauliflower.

kōrigānna (氷鉋), *n.* an ice-cutter an ice-plane.

kōrigashi (氷菓子), *n.* ices; ice-cream.

kōrigura (氷庫), *n.* an ice-house.

korikatamari (凝固), *n.* ❶ = *gyōko* (凝固). ❷ (固信者) a devotee; a bigot; a fanatic. —凝り固まる, ① (凝結) to coagulate; congeal; freeze. ② (熱中) to be absorbed [engrossed] *in*; devote oneself *to*; be devoted *to*. —天理敎の凝固り, a fanatical Tenrikyō believer; a Tenrikyō fanatic.

korikō (小利口な), *a.* smart; clever; sharp.

korikori (懲懲する), *v.* to have had enough *of*.

kōrimakura (氷枕), *n.* an ice-pillow. —氷枕をさせる, to make him rest his head on an ice-pillow.

kōrimizu (氷水), *n.* ice-water; iced water.

kōrimuro (氷室), *n.* an ice-pit (地下の); an ice-house.

kōrin (降臨), *n.* advent; descent. —降臨する, to descend *upon*.

kōrinoko (氷鋸), *n.* an ice-saw.

korinto (コリント式), *n.* 【建】the Corinthian order.

koriru (懲りる), *vi.* to learn [be taught] a lesson; profit by experience. —懲り果てる, to have had enough *of*.

korishō (凝性), *n.* concentrativeness. —凝性の, concentrative.

kōrisuberi (氷滑), *n.* skating (氷靴で); sliding. —氷滑りする, to skate; slide. ¶ 氷滑り場, a skating rink.

koritsu (孤立), *n.* isolation; standing alone; friendlessness. —名譽の孤立, spendid isolation. —孤立する, to be isolated; stand alone; be without a friend.

kōritsu (工率), *n.* 【理】power.

kōritsu (公立の), *a.* public. ¶ 公立學校, a public school.

kōritsu (後率), *n.* 【數】a consequent.

kōritsu (效率), *n.* ☞ *nōritsu.* efficiency.

kōritsuku (凍著く), *vi.* to freeze *to*.

kōriya (氷屋), *n.* an ice-shop (店); an iceman (人).

kōrizatō (氷砂糖), *n.* sugar candy.

kōrizume (氷詰にする), *vt.* to pack with ice; ice up [over]; freeze *in*.

koro (頃), *n.* time. ——, *ad.* when. ——, *prep.* about. —若い頃, when (I was) young. —其頃は, in those days. —來月十日頃, about the tenth of next month.

koro (轆, 轉子), *n.* a roller; a runner.

korō (古老, 故老), *n.* an old man; an elder; an aged man.

korō (固陋の), *a.* conservative; fogyish; bigoted.

korō (虎狼), *n.* an insatiable

person; a brute; a wolf (貪慾者). —虎狼の慾をし逞うする, to give rein to his insatiable greed.

kōro (行路), *n.* ❶ a course; a track. ❷ (旅行) a journey. ¶ 行路病者, a person sick on the road. —行路樹, roadside trees. —行路難, the difficulty of the path of life.

kōro (香爐), *n.* an incense-burner; a thurible; a censer.

kōro (航路), *n.* a sea-route; a course; a steamship line [service]. ¶ 南米航路, South-American line. —航路補助金, navigation subsidy. —航路標識, a beacon.

kōrō (功勞), *n.* merits; services. —功勞ある, meritorious.

kōrō (劫臘, 功老), *n.* long experience; many years' experience. —劫臘を經る, to have a long experience; be old in experience.

kōrō (高樓), *n.* a lofty [high; high-storied] building.

koroai (頃合), *n.* ❶ (適當な程度) moderateness; suitability. ❷ (適當な時機) opportuneness. —頃合ひな讀み物, a suitable book.

korobasu (轉ばす), *vt.* ❶ (まろばす) to roll; roll over; lob (球を). ❷ (倒す) to knock down; tumble over [about; down]. —人を轉ばす, to roll another over. —球を轉ばす, to lob a ball.

korobu (轉ぶ), *vi.* ❶ (轉げる) to roll; roll over. ❷ (倒れる) to fall down; tumble. —轉ばぬ先の杖, "Keep your powder dry."

korogaru (轉·輾がる), *vi.* ❶ (反轉) to roll; tumble; wallow. ❷ (倒れる) to fall down; tumble. ❸ (橫臥) to lie down. —轉がり廻る, to roll; wallow; tumble about.

korogasu (轉がす), *vt.* =*korobasu.* —ころころ轉がす, to roll over and over. —雪を轉がして球にする, to roll snow into a ball.

korogeochiru (轉落ちる), *vi.* to fall over; tumble down.

korogeru (轉げる), *vi.* to tumble; roll.

kōrogi (蟋蟀), *n.* 【昆】 Gryllodes berthellus (學名); the cricket [俗].

korokke (コロッケ), *n.* 【料理】 croquette.

koromo (衣), *n.* ❶ =*kimono* (著物). ❷ (法衣) a (priest's) robe; a gown. ❸ (揚物等の上に著せる) a coat. —墨染の衣, a black robe.

koromogae (衣更), *n.* (季節に應じ衣を著更へる) change of clothes (according to season).

korōmu (コローム), *n.* chromium; chrome.

koron (コロン), *n.* colon (:). —コロンを切る, to insert a colon.

kōron (口論), *n.* a quarrel; a dispute; an altercation. —口論する, to quarrel; dispute; have high words.

kōron (公論), *n.* ❶ (輿論) public opinion. ❷ (公平の論) an impartial opinion (意見); fair criticism (批評). —萬機公論に決す, to refer all state affairs to public opinion.

kōron (抗論する), *v.* to attack; oppose; remonstrate.

korona (コロナ), *n.* a corona.

koroppu (格魯布), *n.* 【醫】 croup. —格魯布性の, croupous, croupy.

koroppu (コロップ), *n.* =*koruku.*

korori (ころり), *ad.* suddenly (突然); completely (全々); easily (苦もなく). —ころりと死ぬ, to die suddenly; pop off.

kororodain (コロロダイン), *n.* chlorodyne.

kororofōmu (コロロフォーム), *n.* chloroform.

koroshimonku (殺文句), *n.* enticing [alluring] words. —殺し文句を竝べる, to talk enticingly.

korosu (殺す), *v.* to kill; put to death. —邪魔ものを殺して了ふ, to make away with those who stand in the way. —それが嘘言なら殺してもよい, Strike me dead if it isn't true.

korotaipu (コロタイプ), *n* collotype. ¶ コロタイプ版, collotype print.

koru (梱る), *vt.* to pack up; tie up.

koru (凝る), *v.* ❶ (熱中) to be absorbed [engrossed; lost] *in.* ❷ (風變り) to be tasteful; be elegant; be elaborate. ❸ (鬱血) to grow stiff. —肩が凝る, to get a crick in the back. —學問に凝る, to be engrossed in study.

kōru (凍る), *vi.* ❶ (氷結) to freeze. ❷ (凝結) to congeal.

kōru (コール), *n.* call-money; call-loan.

kōrubīfu (コールビーフ), *n.* cold beef.

koruku (コルク), *n.* ❶ a cork. ❷ 【植】 the cork-tree; the cork oak-tree. —コルクで塞ぐ, [*v.*] to cork (up). —燒コルクで黑く塗る, to blacken with burnt cork. ¶ コルク拔き, a cork-screw.

korusetto (コルセット), *n.* a corset; stays.

kōrutā (コールター), *n.* coal-tar; gas-tar (瓦斯製造から生ずる).

kōruten (コール天), *n.* coarse velvet.

korya (こりゃ), ❶ (こらの音便) I say; here; look here. ❷ (これはの音便) oh; indeed; dear me.

—こりゃ大變, O my, here's to do. —こりゃたまらぬ, Oh dear, this is awful.

kōryaku (攻略する), *vt.* to capture; carry; reduce (要塞等を); conquer (國を).

koryo (顧慮する), *vt.* to be anxious *about*; concern oneself *about*; pay [have] regard *to*.

kōryo (行旅), *n.* ❶ (旅行) a travel. ❷ (旅人) a traveller.

kōryo (考慮), *n.* consideration; reflection; deliberation. —考慮する, to consider; reflect *upon*; think over.

kōryō (口糧), *n.* ration (一日分の).

kōryō (蛟龍), *n.* ❶ a dragon which ascends to the heavens in rain. ❷ (時を得ざる英雄) a hero out of his time.

kōryō (香料), *n.* ❶ (藥味又は香の材料) spices; perfume; aromatic. ❷ =*kōden* (香奠). —香料を加へる[交せる], to spice.

kōryō (校了), *n.* final proof-reading [-correction]; O. K. (=all correct). —校了になる, to be ready for the press; be returned with "O. K."

kōryō (高粱), *n.* 【植】*kaoliang* 〔支那〕; the tall millet.

kōryō (荒涼たる), *a.* desolate; dreary; bleak.

kōryō (綱領), *n.* a general plan; a digest; synopsis.

kōryōdo (高陵土), *n.* kaolin; China-clay; procelain-clay.

kōryoku (效力), *n.* effect. ❶ (きゝめ) (*a*) (效果) efficiency: (*b*) (效驗) virtue; efficiency. ❷ 【法】(はたらき) operation; force; validity (有效). —效力を失ふ, to lose effect; go out of force (自然に). —效力を生ずる, to take effect; come into effect [force; operation].

koryōriten (小料理店), *n.* a coffee-house.

kōryū (勾留, 拘留), *n.* detention; custody. —拘留中, under arrest; in detention; in custody. —拘留する, to detain; keep in custody. —拘留三日に處せらる, to be sentenced to three days' detention. ¶拘留狀, a warrant of detention [commitment].

kōryū (交流), *n.* 【電】an alternating current.

kōryū (興隆), *n.* rise; prosperity.

kosa (濃さ), *n.* depth (色などの); thickness (髮·眉·毛·糊·汁などの); strength (茶などの).

kōsa (公差), *n.* ❶【數】a common difference. ❷ (造幣の) allowance; remedy (of weight); tolerance.

kōsa (交叉), *n.* decussation【醫】; intersection; crossing. ——**-suru,** *v.* to decussate; intersect; cross. —國旗を交叉する, to cross national flags. ¶交叉點, a point of intersection; a crossing; a junction (鐵道の); a point (轉轍點).

kōsa (考査), *n.* examination; scrutiny. ——**-suru,** *vt.* to examine; scrutinize. —學力を考査する, to look into another's proficiency.

kōsa, kōsha, (膠砂する), *vi.* to ground; go [run; strike] aground.

kosai (小才), *n.* smartness. —小才が利く, ① [*a.*] witty; smart; clever. ② [*v.*] to be smart.

kosai (巨細に), *ad.* minutely; in detail; fully. —巨細に取調べる, to make detailed examination.

kōsai (口才), *n.* lip-wisdom.

kōsai (公債), *n.* a public loan [debt]; the funds. —公債に應募する, to respond to an invitation for a public loan; take up a loan. ¶四(五)分利附公債, the four (five) per cents; the fours (fives). —公債募集, flotation of a public loan. —公債證書, a public (loan) bond; a bond. —公債所有者, a fund-holder.

kōsai (光彩), *n.* lustre; brilliancy; splendour. —光彩陸離たる, lustrous; brilliant; splendid; dazzling. —光彩を添へる, to add lustre; lend brilliancy.

kōsai (交際), *n.* friendly relations; (social) intercourse. —交際する, to have social relations [intercourse] *with*; associate *with*; keep company *with*; deal *with*; have dealings *with*. —交際を結ぶ, to enter into social relations *with*. —交際を避ける, to shun company [social intercourse]; keep oneself to oneself. —交際界の花と謳はれる, to be looked upon as the flower of society. ¶交際費, social expenses. —交際家, a social person; a society lady (女); society people.

kōsai (虹彩), *n.* the iris (眼球の).

kōsai (後妻), *n.* a second wife.

Kosakku (哥薩克), *n.* the Cossacks. ¶哥薩克人 (騎兵), a Cossack.

kosaku (小作), *n.* tenancy. —小作する, to tenant a farm. ¶小作權, tenant-right. —小作米, rice made over (to the landlord) as rent. —小作人, a tenant(-farmer); tenantry (集合). —小作料, farm rent.

kōsaku (工作), *n.* work; engineering work; manufacture (製作); carpentering. —工作する, to work *on*; carpenter; manufacture. ¶工作場, a workshop. —工作物, a structure. —工作船, a workshop-ship; a repair-ship.

kōsaku (交錯), *n.* complication; intricacy; entanglement. —交錯する, to be entangled; be involved; be complicated.

kōsaku (耕作), *n.* ❶ (耕耘) farming; cultivation; tillage. ❷ (農業) agriculture; husbandry; plough. —耕作する, to farm; cultivate; till. —耕作に從事する, to follow the plough. —耕作に適する, arable. ¶耕作物, a farm produce.

kosame (小雨), *n.* a light rain; a drizzle; a fine rain. —小雨が降る, to drizzle (主格 the day; rain; it); mizzle (主格 it).

kosan (古參), *n.* a senior; a doyen. ¶古參兵, a senior private.

kōsan (公算), *n.* possibility.

kōsan (恆產), *n.* fixed property.

kōsan (降參), *n.* ❶ (降服) surrender; submission; capitulation (條件附の). ❷ (閉口) nonplus; perplexity. —降參する, ① to surrender *to*; submit *to*; capitulate. ② to be stumped; be floored; be nonplussed. —降參を勸める, to summon the enemy to surrender.

kosaramono (小皿物), *n.* food piled in a small plate.

kosatsu (古刹), *n.* an old temple.

kosatsu (故殺), *n.* unpremeditated murder; murder in the second degree. —故殺する, to commit unpremeditated murder.

kōsatsu (考察), *n.* consideration. —考察する, to consider; weigh; reflect *upon*.

kōsatsu (絞殺), *n.* strangulation. —絞殺する, to strangle [throttle] to death.

kosei (個性), *n.* individuality; personality; individual character. —個性の發達(自由), development (freedom) of individuality.

kōsei (公正), *n.* ❶ (公平) impartiality; fairness; equity. ❷ (公證力ある事) authenticity. —公正な取扱, fair [impartial] treatment; fair play. ¶公正證書, an authentic document; a notarial deed (公證人の). (公正證書に作成する, to draw it up as a notarial deed.)

kōsei (孔性), *n.* 【理】 porosity.

kōsei (行星), *n.* a planet.

kōsei (攻勢), *n.* the offensive. —攻勢を執る[に出る], to take the offensive.

kōsei (更生), *n.* regenesis; regeneration. —更生する, to regenerate; be born again.

kōsei (更正), *n.* rectification; correction.

kōsei (恆星), *n.* a fixed star.

kōsei (後世), *n.* the future; future generations; posterity.

kōsei (後生), *n.* (後進) juniors. 後生畏るべし, A youth should be respected.

kōsei (後世), *n.* posterity; future (life).

kōsei (校正), *n.* proof-reading; correction (of the press); revision. —校正する, to read proof; correct (the press); revise. ¶校正係, a proof-reader; a reader; a corrector (of the press). —校正刷, a proof; a proof-sheet.

kōsei (高聲), *n.* a loud voice; loudness. —高聲に叫ぶ, to raise one's voice; cry aloud. ¶高聲器, a loud-speaker.

kōsei (硬性の), *a.* hard.

kōsei (構成), *n.* organization; constitution; structure. **——-suru,** *vt.* to organize; constitute; construct; frame. ——, *a.* constituent; component. —犯罪を構成する, to constitute a crime. ¶構成分子, a component (part); an element.

koseidai (古生代), *n.* 【地質】 palæozoic era.

koseki (戶籍), *n.* ❶ (本籍を正しく整へる制度) census registration. ❷ (戶籍簿) a census register. —戶籍に入れる, to enter in a census register. ¶戶籍簿, a census register. —戶籍吏, a registrar; a census officer. —戶籍謄本(抄本), a copy (an abstract) of a census register. —戶籍役場, a census registration office.

koseki (古蹟), *n.* ruins; historic remains; a classic ground (史上有名な土地). —古蹟を探る, to antiquarianize; search for ruins. ¶古蹟保存會, a society for the preservation of historic remains.

kōseki (功績), *n.* an exploit; distinguished service; meritorious deeds [services].

kōseki (鑛石), *n.* an ore; a mineral. ¶鑛石檢波器, a crystal detector.

kōsekido (洪積土), *n.* diluvium.

kosekose (鼠賊), *n.* a sneak-thief.

kosekose (こせこせする), *vi.* to potter; niggle; fuss about trifles. ☞ *kosetsuku.* —こせこせする男, an fussy man.

kosen (古錢), *n.* an ancient [old] coin; a rare coin. ¶古錢學, numismatics.

kosen (孤線), *n.* 【數】 an arc of a circle.

kōsen (口錢), *n.* commission; brokerage. —口錢を取る, to take a commission.

kōsen (公選), *n.* election (by the people). —公選する, to elect.

kōsen (光線), *n.* ❶ (光) light. ❷ (光の筋) a ray; a beam; a

ray of light. —光線の屈折, refraction of light. ¶光線透過診斷,【醫】diagnosis by transillumination.

kōsen (交戰), *n.* ❶ (戰爭) hostilities; war; warfare. ❷ (戰鬪) a battle; an engagement; an action. —交戰的行爲, a belligerent act. —交戰する, to fight; join battle. —交戰中である, ① to be at war *with.* ② to be engaged in battle *with.* ¶交戰團體, a belligerent community. —交戰狀態, state of war. —交戰國, a belligerent.

kōsen (好戰的), *a.* bellicose; warlike; militant. —好戰的國民(態度), a warlike people (attitude).

kōsen (黃泉), *n.* the Hades [希臘神話]; the other world. —黃泉の客となる, to depart this life; pass away.

kōsen (鑛泉), *n.* a mineral spring; a mineral water (鑛水). ¶鑛泉水, table-water (壜詰とせる).

kosenjō (古戰場), *n.* an ancient [old] battle-field.

kōsetsu (公設の), *a.* public. ¶公設市場, a public market.

kōsetsu (巧拙) *n.* skill; dexterity; workmanship (手工の).

kōsetsu (降雪), *n.* snowfall. ¶降雪量, snowfall.

kosetsuku (こせつく), *vi.* to niggle; potter; fuss about. ——, *a.* niggling.

kōsha (巧者な), *a.* clever; ingenious; skilful.

kōsha (後者), *n.* the latter.

kōsha (後車), *n.* the waggon-body (砲車の).

kōsha (校舍), *n.* a school-house [-building].

kōshahō (高射砲), *n.* an anti-aircraft gun; an aerogun.

koshaku (小癪な), *a.* forward; impertinent; saucy.

kōshaku (公爵), *n.* a prince [*fem.* -ss]; a duke [*fem.* duchess] [英]. ¶公爵未亡人, a (dowager-) duchess. —公爵(公爵夫人)閣下, his (her) Grace the Duke [Duchess] [英].

kōshaku (侯爵), *n.* a marquis [*fem.* marchioness].

kōshaku (講釋), *n.* ❶ (講義) a lecture; an explanation; an exposition. ❷ (*a*) (說敎) a sermon; preaching: (*b*) (講話) a lecture; a discourse. ❸ (講談) story-telling. —講釋する, ① (講義) to lecture *on*; give a lecture; expound. ② (講談) to tell a story. ¶講釋師, a story-teller.

koshi (腰), *n.* ❶ the loin; the waist; the haunch (人又は四獸足の). ❷ (衣服の腰に當る所) the hip. ❸ (コップの) a stem. ❹ (障子の) the skirting of a *shōji.* —腰が强い, ① (角力の) to be strong-kneed. ② (談判等の) to be firm. —腰が弱い, ① (角力の) to be weak in knees; be weak-kneed. ② (談判等の) to lack firmness. —腰の曲った老人, an old man bent [bowed] with age. —腰を掛ける, ① (動作) to sit down. ② (一時的) to take up a position [work] temporarily. —腰を延ばす, to straighten [stretch] oneself. —腰を拔かす, ① (病氣又は負傷で) to lose one's legs. ② (驚いて) to remain stock-still; be petrified [paralyzed] with terror [fear]. —話の腰を折る, to interrupt one in speech; spoil a story.

koshi (輿), *n.* a palanquin.

koshi (枯死する), *vi.* to die; be withered. ☞ ***kareru*** (枯れる).

koshi (虎視する), *vi.* to gloat *over* [*upon*].

koshi (誇示する), *vt.* to show off; make a display [parade] *of*; flaunt.

Kōshi (孔子), *n.* Confucius.

kōshi (公私), *n.* public [official] and private (affairs). —公私を混同する, to confuse public and private matters.

kōshi (公使), *n.* a minister; an envoy. —公使を召還する, to recall a minister. ¶支那駐箚日本公使, the Japanese Minister to [resident in] China. —公使館, a legation; a mission [米]. (在中華民國日本帝國公使館, the Japanese Legation in China. —墨國公使館書記官, the Secretary of the Mexican Legation.)

kōshi (行使する), *vt.* to employ; exercise; utter (贋造紙幣などを). —權利を行使する, to exercise one's right. —贋造紙幣を行使する, to utter [make use of] counterfeit paper-money.

kōshi (考試), *n.* =***shiken.***

kōshi (孝子), *n.* a dutiful child (son; daughter).

kōshi (厚志), *n.* kindness; kind wishes.

kōshi (格子), *n.* a lattice (戶・窓などの); a bar (檻格子の); a grating (鐵などの). —格子造りの, latticed; coffered. ¶格子戶, a lattice-door. —格子縞, a plaid; cross stripes.

kōshi (高士), *n.* a man of virtue [high character]; a hermit (隱君子).

kōshi (皇子), *n.* a prince.

kōshi (後肢), *n.* a hind leg.

kōshi (嚆矢), *n.* the first; a pioneer (率先者).

kōshi (講師), *n.* a lecturer; an instructor.

koshiage (腰揚), *n.* a tuck in the skirt. —腰揚げをする, to tuck in the skirt.

koshiben (腰辨), *n.* a petty official; petty-officialdom.
koshibone (腰骨), *n.* the hip-bone; the huckle-bone.
koshigami (漉紙), *n.* filtering paper.
koshiginchaku (腰巾著), *n.* a shadow (うるさく附き纏ふ者); a henchman (從者); a satellite.
koshihame (腰羽目), *n.* a dado.
koshihimo (腰紐), *n.* a waist-band.
koshiire (輿入), *n.* ❶ the bride's entry into the bridegroom's home. ❷ a marriage ceremony. —輿入する, to enter the bridegroom's home.
koshiita (腰板), *n.* ❶ (壁の) a panel; a clapboard. ❷ (袴の) a back-stay.
koshikake (腰掛), *n.* ❶ a seat (汽車などの); a bench (細長い); a chair (椅子); a form (學校などの背無く長い); a stool (背なき一人掛の); a tip-up seat (劇場などの折上式). ❷ (一時的) a temporary [makeshift] work. —腰掛に這入る, to enter it for a stop-gap.
koshikakeru (腰掛ける), *v.* to sit *on* [*in*]; take a seat; be seated.
koshikata (來し方), *n.* the past. =*kako.* —來し方行末を思ひめぐらす, to ponder over the past and future.
koshiki (古式), *n.* a time-honoured [established] rule [form].
koshiki (漉器), *n.* a colander, cullender (料理用の).
kōshiki (公式), *n.* ❶ (おほやけの儀式) formality. ❷ (範則)【數】a formula. —公式の訪問, a formal [an official] visit. —公式に當嵌めて解釋する, to interpret by formal application. ¶ 公式馬車, a state carriage.
koshimaki (腰卷), *n.* a waist-cloth; a loin-cloth.
koshin (コシン), *n.*【撞球】the cushion (of a billiard table).
kōshin (功臣), *n.* a meritorious retainer; subjects with distinguished services. —維新の功臣, the meritorious subjects of the Restoration.
kōshin (行進), *n.* march;【音】progression. ——**-suru**, *vi.* to march. —敵に向って行進する, to march against an enemy. ¶ 行進曲,【音】a march.
kōshin (更新する), *vt.* to renew; renovate.
kōshin (孝心), *n.* filial piety.
kōshin (恆心), *n.* a settled mind; constancy; steadiness.
kōshin (昂進, 亢進), *n.* rise; increase (增進); excitement (神氣·性慾などの); exasperation (病勢などの). —昂進さす, to excite; exasperate; increase; whet. —昂進する, to rise; increase; be excited.
kōshin (後進), *n.* ❶ (後より進むこと) going after; following at another's heels (追隨する). ❷ (逆進) going astern. ❸ (後輩) a junior. —後進の途を開く, to make room for one's juniors.
koshinage (腰投), *n.* throwing at one's loin.
koshinawa (腰繩で送られる), to be sent in bonds.
kōshinbara (庚申薔薇), *n.*【植】the China [monthly] rose.
kōshinjo (興信所), *n.* an inquiry association; a credit bureau; a mercantile agency.
kōshinjutsu (降神術), *n.* spiritism; spiritualism; mediumism.
koshinuke (腰拔), *n.* ❶ (病氣で) a cripple; a crippled man. ❷ (臆病) cowardice; timidity; poltroonery. ❸ (臆病者) a coward; a poltroon; a milksop. ¶ 腰拔け武士, a white-livered *bushi.*
koshio (小潮), *n.* the neap-tide; the neap.
koshiobi (腰帶), *n.* a girdle; a waistband.
koshioshi (腰押), *n.* ❶ (事) instigation; backing. ❷ (人) an instigator; an abettor; a backer.
koshirae (拵へ), *n.* ❶ (製作) make; workmanship (細工); mounting (刀の). ❷ (構造) make; construction. ❸ (型) style; fashion. ¶ 拵へ話, a fabricated story; a made-up story; a cock-and-bull story. —拵へ物, a counterfeit (摸造·贋造·類似品など); a sham (僞物).
koshiraeru (拵へる), *vt.* ❶ (製造, 製作) to make; manufacture; fabricate. ❷ (調達) to raise; make up. ❸ (捏造, 虛構) to fabricate; invent; make up. ❹ (作成) to draw up; make out. ❺ (儲ける) to make; gain; accumulate (ためる). ❻ (調製) to prepare (藥·食料品·辨當など). ❼ (取繕ふ) to palliate; gloss over; smooth over. —金を拵へる, to make money; make a fortune (身代を); raise money (調達する). —口實を拵へる, to invent [make up] an excuse. —二人分の辨當を拵へる, to prepare luncheon for two.
kōshita (かうした), *a.* such.
koshitsu (固執する), *vt.* to persist *in*; adhere *to*; stand firmly.
koshitsu (痼疾), *n.* a chronic [a confirmed; an inveterate] disease.
kōshitsu (皇室), *n.* the Imperial [Royal] House [Family]. —皇室の尊嚴を保つ, to maintain the dignity of the Imperial Court. ¶ 皇室費,

the Imperial Household expenses [allowance]; the civil list. —皇室典範, the Imperial House Law.

kōshitsu (膠質), *n.* colloid. ¶ 膠質物, a jelly; a gelatinoid.

koshiwa (小皺), *n.* wrinkles; furrows. —額に小皺を寄せる, to wrinkle [furrow] one's brows.

koshiyu (腰湯), *n.* a hip-bath; a sitz-bath; a demi-bath. —腰湯をする, to have a sitz-bath.

koshō (小姓), *n.* a page.

koshō (故障), *n.* ❶ (障碍) an obstacle; an impediment; a hitch. ❷ (缺陷) a defect. ❸ (損傷) damage. ❹ (變事) an accident; a mishap. ❺ (異議) a protest; an objection. —故障のある機械, a machine out of order [gear]. —故障なく行く, to come off well; be completed without a hitch. —故障を云ふ, to protest *against*; raise [enter] an objection *to*. —...故障を入れる, to enter an objection *against*. —機關に故障を生じた場合に, in the event of the engine breaking down. ¶ 故障期間, 【法】 term for protest. —故障[危險]信號, a danger signal.

koshō (湖沼), *n.* a lake; a mere.

koshō (胡椒), *n.* ❶ (藥味) pepper. ❷【植】 the black pepper-plant. ¶ 胡椒入れ, a pepper-box [-pot; -castor].

kōsho (公署), *n.* a public office.

kōsho (高所), *n.* a height; an eminence; altitudes.

kōshō (工廠), *n.* a workshop. ¶ 呉海軍工廠, the Kure Naval Arsenal.

kōshō(公證), *n.* ❶ (行爲) a notarial act. ❷ (證據) authentic evidence. —公證する, to authenticate. ¶ 公證人, a notary (public). —公證役場, the office of a notary public.

kōshō (公稱), *a.* nominal. ¶ 公稱資本, nominal capital.

kōshō (考證), *n.* research; investigation. —考證する, to make researches; investigate.

kōshō (交渉), *n.* ❶ (談判) negotiation. ❷ (提案) overture (of peace). ❸ (關係) relation; connection. —交渉する, to negotiate [treat; confer] *with* (a person) *for*; approach with a proposal (提議する). —交渉を開始する, to open negotiations. —交渉不調に終れり, The negotiations proved abortive. ¶ 團體交渉, collective bargaining. —交渉團體, a negotiating body.

kōshō (好尙), *n.* ❶ (嗜好) inclination; fancy; predilection (偏好). ❷ (流行) the fashion.

kōshō (哄笑), *n.* laughter; loud laughter; a loud laugh; a guffaw. —哄笑する, to laugh loud; guffaw.

kōshō (高尙な), *a.* ❶ (上品) noble; lofty; refined. ❷ (高級) high; high-toned; advanced. —高尙な讀物, learned books. —高尙な目的, a high purpose. —高尙な學理, an advanced theory.

kōshō (高唱する), *vi.* ❶ (高調子で歌ふ) to sing loudly [sharp]; sing at a high pitch [in a high tone]. ❷ (唱道する) to advocate; propagate.

kōshōgai (公生涯), *n.* public life; one's career as a public man.

koshoku (古色), *n.* the colour of age; an antique look; hoariness. —古色ある; 古色蒼然たる, antique; time-honoured. —古色を帶びる, to have the note [mark] of antiquity; be sanctified by age.

kōshoku (公職), *n.* a public office [post]; public service. —公職に就く, to take up a public post; enter the government service.

kōshoku (紅色), *n.* red. ¶ 深(淡)紅色, crimson (light red).

kōshoku (黄色), *n.* yellow. ¶ 黄色人種, the yellow race. —黄色新聞, the yellow press.

kōshoku (曠職), *n.* neglect of public duties.

koshōnin (小商人), *n.* a small shopkeeper; a small tradesman; a petty trader.

koshu (戸主), *n.* the head of a house [family].

koshu (古酒), *n.* old wine [*sake*].

koshu (固守する), *vt.* to hold [keep] *to*; adhere [cling] *to*; persist [persevere] *in* (方針などを). —方針を固守する, to persevere [persist] in a course. —舊習を固守する, to cling to old customs.

koshu (鼓手), *n.* a drummer.

kōshu (攻守), *n.* offence and defence; 【野球】 batting and fielding. ¶ 攻守同盟, an offensive and defensive alliance.

kōshu (絞首する), *v.* ❶ to strangle. ❷ (絞罪に處す) to hang; gibbet. ¶ 絞首臺, the gallows; the gibbet. (絞首臺の露と消える, to end one's life on the gallows.)

kōshu (校主), *n.* the owner [proprietor] of a school.

kōshū (公衆), *n.* the (general) public. —公衆の前で, in public. —公衆の利益を保護する, to protect the public interests. —公衆の縱覧を許す, to throw open to the public. ¶ 公衆電話, a public telephone. —公衆衛生, public health. —公衆娯樂場, a public place of amusement.

kōshū (講習), *n.* study; practice (實習). —講習する, to study; learn; practise. ¶ 講習會, a class; a course. —講習生, a student [pupil] of a school [an educational institute; a special course]. —產業講習所, an institute for the study of industries; an industrial institute.

kōshugakkō (工手學校), *n.* an artisan school.

koso (こそ), *a.* the very. ——, *ad.* just. ——, *conj.* as. —彼こそ適任なれ. He is just the man for the post.

kōso (公訴), *n.* public action.

kōso (皇祖), *n.* the founder of the Empire. —我皇祖皇宗, Our Imperial Ancestors.

kōso (皇祚), *n.* the (Imperial) throne. —皇祚を踐む, to accede to the Throne; ascend the Throne.

kōso (高祖), *n.* ❶ (血統の宗主) the founder of a family line. ❷ (五代前の祖) a great-great-grandfather.

kōso (控訴), *n.* an appeal (to a superior [higher] court). ¶ 控訴院, a court of appeal; an appellate court. —控訴期間, the term of appeal. —控訴申立書, a petition of appeal. —控訴人, an appellant.

kōso (酵素), *n.* 【化】 enzyme.

kōsō (公葬する), *v.* to perform a funeral at public expense.

kōsō (宏壯な), *a.* grand; magnificent; lofty. —宏壯を極める, to be at the height of magnificence.

kōsō (抗爭), *n.* ❶ (爭論) dispute; controversy. ❷ (對抗) opposition; rivalry; resistance (抵抗). —抗爭する, ① (爭論) to dispute *with*; wrangle *with*. ② to oppose; resist.

kōsō (後送する), *vt.* ❶ to send to the rear. ❷ (後より送る) to send afterwards.

kōsō (校葬), *n.* a funeral performed at school expense. —校葬にする, to bury [inter] at school expense.

kōsō (航走する), *vi.* to run; sail (帆走); steam (汽走).

kōsō (高僧), *n.* a high priest; an arch-priest (長).

kōsō (高燥の), *a.* high and dry. —高燥の地(敷地), a high and dry land (site).

kōsō (降霜), *n.* the fall of frost.

kōsō (構想), *n.* ❶ (思想の組立) conception. ❷ (趣向) a plan; a design; invention (創意).

kōsobo (高祖母), *n.* a great-great-grandmother.

kosode (小袖), *n.* a wadded silk garment.

kōsofu (高祖父), *n.* a great-great-grandfather.

kosoguttai (擽ッたい), *a.* ticklish. ——, *vi.* to tickle; be ticklish. ☞ ***kusuguttai.***

kosoguru (擽る), *vt.* to tickle. —腋の下を擽る, to tickle under the arm. —擽って笑はせる, to tickle a person into laughter.

kōsōjū (口裝銃), *n.* a muzzle-loading gun; a muzzle-loader.

kosokoso (こそこそ), *ad.* secretly; on the sly; stealthily. ——, *a.* secret; stealthy. —こそこそ盜む, to pilfer; filch. —こそこそ…をする, to do something stealthily [on the sly]. ¶ こそこそ話, a secret talk. —こそこそ泥棒, a sneak-thief; a pilferer.

kosoku (呼息), *n.* expiration.

kosoku (姑息の), *a.* temporizing. ¶ 姑息手段, a makeshift; a temporizing measure; a half-measure.

kōsoku (拘束), *n.* ❶ (束縛) binding; restraint; restriction. ❷ (拘禁) confinement; detention. **——-suru,** *vt.* ❶ to bind; restrain; restrict. ❷ to confine; detain. —自由を拘束する, to restrain another's liberty. ¶ 拘束力, binding force.

kōsoku (高速-度), *n.* high speed. ¶ 高速電車, a high-speed car. —高速(度)鋼, high-speed steel.

kōsoku (校則), *n.* school regulations.

kōsoku (梗塞), *n.* tightness; stringency; stoppage. —金融がはたと梗塞した, The circulation of money suddenly stopped. ¶ 金融梗塞, tight money; stringent money market.

kōson (皇孫), *n.* ❶ an Imperial grandson. ❷ (皇胤) an Imperial descendant.

kossetsu (骨折), *n.* a fracture (of a bone). ¶ 單純骨折, a simple fraction. —骨折整復, 【醫】 diaplasis.

kosshi (骨子), *n.* the essence; the gist; the substance. —議論の骨子, the main point of the argument.

kossho (忽諸に付する), to neglect; disregard; overlook.

kosso (骨疽), *n.* 【醫】 necrosis.

kossō (骨相-學), *n.* phrenology. ¶ 骨相學者, a phrenologist.

kossori (こッそり), *ad.* ❶ secretly; stealthily; on the sly. ❷ (音をたてずに) quictly; noiselessly.

kosu (越す), *vt.* to cross (橫切る); pass (過ごす); exceed (超過する); remove (引越す). ☞ ***koeru*** (越える). —郡部へ越す, to remove to the outskirts of the city. —冬を越す, to keep over the winter (持つ); pass the winter (すごす). —豫定數を越す, to exceed the estimated number. —そ

れに越したことはない, Nothing can be better than that.

kosu (濾·漉す), *vt.* to filter; strain. —砂で水を漉す, filter water through sand.

kosū (戸數), *n.* the number of houses. ¶ 戸數割, a household rate.

kōsu (コース), *n.* a course.

kosui (狡い), *a.* cunning; sly; artful. —狡い奴, an artful fellow. —狡い事をする, to play foul; play a foul game; deal unfairly. —狡く立廻る, to conduct oneself artfully.

kosui (湖水), *n.* a lake.

kosui (鼓吹する), *vt.* to inspire *with*; infuse [instil] *into*; inculcate *on*. —新思想を鼓吹する, to infuse new thoughts *into*.

kōsui (香水), *n.* perfume; scent. ¶ 香水吹き, a scent-atomizer. —香水類, perfumery.

kōsui (硬水), *n.* hard water.

kōsui (鑛水), *n.* mineral water.

kosumechikku (コスメチック), *n.* a cosmetic. —コスメチックをつける, to apply a cosmetic *to*.

kosumosu (コスモス), *n.* 【植】 the cosmos.

kosuru (擦る), *v.* to rub; scrub (強く擦る); chafe (擦りいためる). —眼を擦る, to rub one's eyes. —泥を擦り落す, to scrape away [off] mud.

ko-suru (鼓する), *vt.* ❶ to beat (太鼓など). ❷ (振ひおこす) to rouse; stir up. —勇を鼓する, to stir [pluck] up one's courage.

kō-suru (抗する), *vt.* to oppose; resist. ☞ *hankō*. —輿論に抗する, to oppose [run against] public opinion.

kō-suru (航する), *vi.* to navigate; sail. ☞ *kōkō* (航行).

kotaba (小束), *n.* a small bundle. —小束に束ねる, ① (小束にする) to make into a small bundle. ② (幾個にも縛る) to bind in small bundles.

kotabako (粉煙草), *n.* dust [broken] tobacco.

kotae (答), *n.* ❶ (返答) an answer; a reply; a response (應答). ❷ (解答) an answer; a result. ❸ 〔應〕 efficacy (きゝ目); response (感應); reaction (同上). —適當な答, a suitable [fit] answer.

kotaeru (答へる), *v.* ❶ (返答) to answer; reply; respond. ❷ 〔應〕 (效力) to take effect; tell *on*. ❸ 〔徹〕 (透徹) to penetrate; pierce; impress (感銘). —否(然り)と答へる, to answer in the negative (affirmative). —試驗問題を皆答へる, to clear an examination paper. —ひしひしと胸に應へる, to come to [sink into] one's heart.

kotaeru (堪へる), *vt.* to bear; suffer; endure; stand. ☞ *koraeru.*

kotai (固體), *n.* a solid; a solid body. —固體化する, to solidify.

kotai (個體), *n.* an individual; 【生物】 a person.

kōtai (交代, 交替), *n.* relief; alternation; shift (職工等の); change. —交代に, alternately; by turns. —交代する, to alternate; relieve; take turns.

kōtai (後退する), *vi.* to retreat; fall back.

kōtaigō (皇太后), *n.* the Empress Dowager; the Queen-Dowager; the Queen-Mother.

kōtaishi (皇太子), *n.* the Crown Prince; the Prince Imperial. ¶ 英國皇太子, the Prince of Wales. —皇太子妃, the Crown Princess.

kōtaison (皇太孫), *n.* the eldest grandson of an emperor [a king] in the direct line.

kōtaku (光澤), *n.* gloss; lustre; polish. —光澤ある, gloss; lustrous; polished. —光澤を出す, to burnish (堅きものにて); polish (磨いて); gloss (磨棒などで).

kōtan (降誕), *n.* birth. —降誕する, to be born. ¶ 降誕祭, birthday celebrations.

kotatsu (火燵, 炬燵), *n.* a quilted foot-warmer [hearth]. —火燵にあたる, to warm oneself at a foot-warmer.

kōtatsu (口達), *n.* a verbal [oral] communication; a verbal notification. —口達する, to communicate verbally; notify verbally.

kōtatsu (公達), *n.* an official [a government] notification.

kotchi (此方), =*kochira.*

kotchō (骨頂), *n.* the height; the zenith; the acme. —馬鹿の骨頂, the height of folly.

kote (鏝), *n.* ❶ (左官の) a trowel; a float. ❷ (燒鏝) (*a*) (裁縫用) an iron; a flat-iron; a smoothing-iron: (*b*) (理髮用) a curling-iron; curling-tongs: (*c*) (鑄掛用) a soldering-iron. —鏝をあてる [かける], ① to trowel; dress with trowel. ② to iron.

kote (籠手, 小手), *n.* ❶ a gauntlet (臂鎧); a bracer (弓の); fencing gloves (擊劍の). ❷ (手先) a forearm. —小手をとられる, to be beaten by a stroke on the forearm.

kotei (固定), *n.* lock-up (資本の). **—— -sasu,** *vt.* to fix; lock up (資本を); tie up (同上). —資本を固定させて置く, to keep capital locked up. **—— -suru,** *vi.* to be fixed; be settled (相場·天候など); be locked up (資本が). —固定してゐる, immovable; fixed;

locked-up; stationary. ¶ 固定資本, fixed capital.

kōtei (工程), *n.* the rate [amount] of work; the progress (of the work).

kōtei (公定の), *a.* official; statutory; prescribed. ¶ 公定價格, tax price; official price. —公定相場, an official quotation.

kōtei (行程), *n.* distance; a journey (旅の); a march (軍隊の).

kōtei (肯定), *n.* affirmation. —肯定的, affirmative. —肯定する, to affirm; answer [reply] in the affirmative. ¶ 肯定文,【文】an affirmative sentence.

kōtei (皇帝), *n.* an emperor. ¶ 英國皇帝, the King of Great Britain and Ireland.

kōtei (校庭), *n.* a school court [close]; a school playground.

kōtei (校訂), *n.* revision; revisal; recension. —校訂する, to revise.

kōtei (高低, 昂低), *n.* ❶ (高低) undulation; unevenness (凸凹). ❷ (昂低) fluctuation (相場等の). ❸ (音の) pitch; intonation.

kōtei (高弟), *n.* the best [ablest] pupil [disciple].

kōtei (航程), *n.* the run of a ship.

koteki (公的), *a.* public; official. —公(的)生活, public life.

kōteki (公敵), *n.* a public enemy.

kōtekishu (好敵手), *n.* a good [an excellent] match. —…の好敵手たるを失はず, to prove oneself a match *for*.

kotekote (こてこて), *ad.* ❶ (澤山) profusely; plentifully; abundantly. ❷ (あくどく) heavily; thickly. —こてこて色を塗る, to paint heavily [thickly].

koten (古典), *n.* classics. ¶ 古典學者, a classicist; a classical scholar.

kōten (公轉), *n.* revolution. —公轉する, to revolve.

kōten (交點), *n.* ❶【數・理】a point of intersection. ❷【天】a node.

kōten (好轉する), *vi.* to turn in favour *of*.

kōten (皇典), *n.* Japanese classical literature. ¶ 皇典講究所, a school [an institute] for the study of Japanese classical literature.

kōten (高點), *n.* a high mark. —最高點で當選する, to be elected [returned] with the highest number of votes.

kōtenteki (後天的), *a.* a posteriori【羅】; acquired.

kōtetsu (甲鐵), *n.* armour-plate; armour. ¶ 甲鐵艦, an ironclad; an armoured ship.

kōtetsu (更迭, 交迭), *n.* change; alternation. —地方官の交迭 a gubernatorial change. —交迭する, to change; alternate.

kōtetsu (鋼鐵), *n.* steel. ¶ 鋼鐵船, a steel-ship.

koto (言), *n.* a word. ☞ *kotoba*.

koto (事), *n.* ❶ a thing (云ひ又は爲す); things (物事, 事物). ❷ (事件) a matter; an affair; a case; *res*【羅】. ❸ (事情) circumstances; things; state of things. ❹ (用務) business; task; affairs. ❺ (變事) an accident; an emergency. ❻ (事實) a fact. —事小なりと雖も, slight as the matter is. —敵を事ともせず, making no account of the enemy. —迅速に事を運ぶ, to settle a matter promptly [quickly].

koto (琴), *n.* a *koto*. —琴を彈く, to play *koto*.

koto (糊塗する), *vt.* to gloss over; patch up. —一時を糊塗する, to temporize; gloss over for a time. ¶ 糊塗手段, an expedient; a shift; a shuffle; temporizing methods.

kotō (弧燈), *n.* an arc-lamp.

kotō (孤島), *n.* a solitary island. —絶海の孤島, a solitary island in the farthest seas.

kōto (コート), *n.* ❶ (庭球場) a (tennis-)court. ❷ (上衣) a coat.

kōtō (口頭), *n.* *viva voce*; word of mouth. —口頭で答へる, to answer verbally [by word of mouth]. ¶ 口頭辯論,【法】oral proceedings; oral pleading. —口頭試驗, a *viva voce* [an oral] examination.

kōtō (叩頭), *n.* a bow; obeisance; a ko-tow [kow-tow]【支】. —叩頭する, to bow to the ground; ko-tow.

kōtō (昂騰), *n.* rise; appreciation; ascent. —昂騰する, to rise; appreciate; go up; ascend.

kōtō (皇統), *n.* the Imperial line.

kōtō (後燈), *n.* tail-light (自動車などの).

kōtō (後頭-部), *n.* the occipital region.

kōtō (高等の), *a.* high; advanced; superior. ¶ 高等學校, a high school; an academy. —高等法院, the High Criminal Court for the trial of political offences; the High Court of Justice. —高等科, the advanced course; the higher department. —高等官, a higher official. —高等警察, the high police; the secret service police. —高等敎育, higher education. —高等政策, high politics.

kōtō (高踏する), *vi.* to rise above the vulgar; stand aloof from the crowd. —高踏勇退する, to resign one's post resolutely.

kōtō (喉頭), *n.*【解】the larynx. ¶ 喉頭炎,【醫】laryngitis. —喉頭加答兒, laryngeal catarrh.

kotoba (言葉, 詞), *n.* ❶ (言語) speech; words. ❷ a word; a term. ❸ (國語) language; tongue; speech. ❹ (話) speech; remark. ❺ (方言) dialect. ❻ (言葉遣) language; word; wording; parlance. —言葉の丁寧な, fair-spoken. —言葉に表はす, to word; express in words. —言葉を掛ける, [*vt.*] to accost; address; speak *to*. —言葉を交はす, to speak *with*; exchange words *with*. —言葉を飾る; 言葉に花を咲かす, to adorn one's speech. —無益の言葉を費す, to waste words. —言葉を換へて云へば, in other words. —言葉尻を取る, to catch another in his words; stumble him in his speech. ¶ 田舎言葉, country dialect [brogue]. —言葉遣, ①(語法) parlance; expression; diction. ② (云振り) manner of speaking.

kotobuki (壽), *n.* ❶ (祝賀) congratulation; felicitation. ❷ (長命) longevity; long life. ❸ (齢) age.

kotogara (事柄), *n.* a matter; an affair; circumstances (事情).

kotogoto (事毎に), *ad.* in everything [every matter]. —事毎に失敗(成功)する, to fail (succeed) in everything (one undertakes).

kotogotoku (悉く), *ad.* ❶ (一括的) all; wholly; entirely; completely. ❷ (殘らず) without exception (例外なく); one and all; to a man (一人も殘らず).

kotogotoshii (事事しい), *a.* fussy; exaggerated. —事々しく, fussily; exaggeratingly. (事々しく騷ぎ立てる, to make a fuss.)

kotohajime (事初), *n.* beginning; commencement; setting.

kotohogu (壽・言祝ぐ), *vt.* to congratulate [felicitate] *on* (成功などを); celebrate (勝利などを); drink *to* (健康・成功などを).

kotoji (琴柱), *n.* 【香】a bridge (of a *koto*).

kotokireru (縡・事切れる), *vi.* to breathe one's last; expire.

kotokomaka (事細かに), *ad.* minutely; particularly; fully; in detail. —事細かに述べる, to give the full particulars (of); state in detail [full].

kōtoku (公德), *n.* public morality. —公德を重ずる, to set high value upon public morality. —公德心を涵養する, to foster a public spirit.

kōtoku (高德), *n.* high virtue; high character. ¶ 高德者, a man of high virtue [character].

kōtō-mukei (荒唐無稽の), *a.* wild; fantastic; fabulous. —荒唐無稽の說, a myth; an old wives' tale; a blue wonder.

kotonareru (異れる), *a.* ❶ different (*from*); unlike; dissimilar *to*; strange (並でない); curious (珍奇の); variant (變形の). ❷ = *ayamareru*.

kotonaru (異る), *vi.* to differ *from*; be different *to* [*from*]; vary *from*; be strange (並でない).

kotoni (殊に), *ad.* ❶ (別段に) particularly; especially; exceptionally. ❷ (就中) above all; before all things.

kotonisuru (異にする), *vi.* to differ. —本質を異にする, to differ in substance. —待遇を異にする, to discriminate *between*; make discrimination in treatment. —彼と意見を異にする, to differ from him.

kotoniyoruto (事によると), *ad.* possibly (前に may を附す); maybe; perhaps.

kotonohoka (殊の外), *ad.* ❶ (非常に) exceedingly; unusually; exceptionally. ❷ (案外) unexpectedly; beyond one's expectation.

kotori (小鳥), *n.* a small bird; a dicky-bird.

kotosara (殊更), *ad.* ❶ (故意に) purposely; on purpose; intentionally; knowingly. ❷ (殊に) particularly; especially; above all (就中). —殊更鄭重に, with studied politeness.

kotoshi (今年), *n.* this year; the current year.

koto-tosuru (事とする), *vi.* to indulge *in*; give oneself up *to*; make it a point [rule] *to* (規則とする). —惡事を事とする, to devote oneself solely to evil ways.

kotowari (理), *n.* right; justice; reason (道理).

kotowari (斷), *n.* ❶ (豫告) a notice; a warning. ❷ (辭退, 拒絕) declining; a refusal. ❸ (許可) permission; leave. ❹ (言譯) an excuse; a plea.

kotowarijō (斷狀), *n.* a letter of regret (辭退狀); a letter of refusal (拒絕狀). —斷り狀を出す, to send a letter of regret (refusal).

kotowaru (斷る), *v.* ❶ (豫告する) to warn; give notice *of*. ❷ (拒絕する) to refuse; repulse. ❸ (謝絕・辭退する) to decline; beg off. ❹ (言譯する) to make an excuse; apologize *for*. —體よく斷られた, He was courteously refused.

kotowaza (諺), *n.* a proverb; a saying; an adage; a dictum. ☞ *kakugen*. —諺にもある通り, as the proverb says; as the saying is.

kotoyoseru (事寄せる), *vt.* to pretend; make a pretence *of*; make an excuse *of*. —病氣に事寄せて, on the plea of illness.

kotozukeru (事託ける), *vt.* to entrust; charge.

kotozute (言傳), *n.* ❶ a (verbal) message. ❷ (宜しくとの) remembrances. ☞ *dengon.* —言傳する, to send a message *to*; send word [a verbal message] *to.* —言傳を頼まれる, to be charged with a message; be asked to take a message.

kotsu (骨), *n.* ❶ a bone. ❷ (遺骨) ashes. ❸ (調子) the knack; the trick; the hang 〔俗〕. —死體を骨にして送る, to send the remains cremated. —...の骨を覺える, to learn the knack; get the hang *of.*

kōtsū (交通), *n.* communication (通信, 往來); traffic (運輸); intercourse (交際). —交通の便(不便), the facility (difficulty) of communication. (交通の便をよくする, to improve [increase] the facilities of communication.) —交通する, to have intercourse *with*; communicate *with* (通信・往來する). ¶ 交通兵, line-of-communication troops. —交通巡査, a traffic policeman; a pointsman. —交通勞働者, a transport-worker. —交通遮斷, prohibition of intercourse; isolation (隔離); quarantine (船內檢疫による). (交通遮斷線, a (sanitary) cordon.)

kotsuage (骨上), *n.* gathering of incinerated bones (after cremation).

kotsuban (骨盤), *n.* the pelvis.

kotsubu (小粒), *n.* a granule.

kotsudō (骨堂), *n.* an ossuary; a charnel-house.

kotsuen (骨炎), *n.* 【醫】 ostitis.

kotsugara (骨柄), *n.* constitution; build.

kōtsugō (好都合), *n.* convenience; expediency; opportuneness. —好都合の, convenient; expedient; opportune. —好都合にゆく, to go well [swimmingly].

kotsuka (骨化), *n.* 【生】 ossification. —骨化する, to ossify.

kotsukotsu (矻矻), *ad.* ploddingly; diligently; assiduously. —こつこつ勉强する, to grind; plod.

kotsukotsu (こつこつ), *n.* a tap; a knock. —戶をコツコツ叩く, to tap at the door.

kotsumaku (骨膜), *n.* 【解】 the periosteum. ¶ 骨膜炎, periostitis.

kotsun (こつん), rap; whack. —コツンと打つ, to rap; whack.

kotsuniku (骨肉), *n.* flesh and blood; blood relations; kindred. —骨肉の爭, domestic discord; family dissensions.

kotsutsubo (骨壺), *n.* an ossuary; a cinerary urn; an urn.

kotsuyō (骨瘍), caries.

kotsuzen (忽然), *ad.* all of a sudden; suddenly.

kotsuzui (骨髓), *n.* ❶ medulla (ossium); a (bone-)marrow. ❷ (要點) substance; essence (眞髓); kernel (同上). —骨髓までも, to the bone [core; marrow]. —怨み骨髓に徹す, Hatred penetrates to the marrow. ¶ 骨髓炎, osteomyelitis; inflammation of a bone-marrow.

kotta (凝ッた), *a.* tasteful; artistic; *recherché* 〔佛〕. —凝ッた意匠, a *recherché* design.

kottan (骨炭), *n.* animal charcoal; bone-black.

kotteri (こってり), *ad.* thickly; abundantly; plentifully.

kottō (骨董-品), *n.* curios; objects of virtu; *bric-à-brac* 〔佛〕. —骨董を商ふ, to sell curios. ¶ 骨董癖, virtu. —骨董商, a curio-dealer. —骨董店, a curio shop.

kōtto (こうッと), *int.* why; well; let me see.

kou (乞・請ふ), *vt.* to beg; seek; entreat; pray. —何々せんことを請ふ, to ask [beg; request] a person to do something. —是非御來來を乞ふ, I beg earnestly for your company.

kou (戀ふ), *vt.* to love.

kōu (降雨), *n.* rain; rainfall. ¶ 大降雨, heavy rainfall; downpour of rain. —降雨期, the rainy season. —降雨量, the fall; (the amount of) rainfall.

kouma (仔馬), *n.* a colt; a pony; a fool.

koume (小梅), *n.* 【植】 the Japanese plum.

kōun (幸運, 好運), *n.* (good) fortune; (good) luck. —好運の絕頂に在り, to be at the top of fortune's wheel. —幸運にも, fortunately; luckily; by good luck. ¶ 好運兒, the favourite of fortune.

kōun (皇運), *n.* prosperity of the Imperial Throne. —皇運の隆盛を祈る, to pray for the prosperity of the Imperial Family.

kouri (小賣), *n.* retail. —小賣で, by [at] retail. —小賣する, to retail; sell by retail. ¶ 小賣部, a retail department. —小賣人, a retailer; a retail-dealer. —小賣店, a retail shop. —小賣相場, retail price.

koushi (犢), *n.* a calf. ¶ 犢皮, calf; calfskin. —犢肉, veal.

kōwa (口話), *n.* oral narration.

kōwa (講和, 媾和), *n.* peace; reconciliation (和解). —講和する, to make peace; become reconciled. ¶ 講和談判, peace negotiations. —媾和委員, a peace committee. —

講和會議, a peace conference [congress]. —講和大使, a peace envoy.

kōwa (講話), *n.* a lecture; a discourse. —講話する, to lecture; give [deliver] lectures. ¶ 通俗講話, a popular lecture. —講話者, a lecturer; a speaker.

kowabaru (强ばる), *vi.* to stiffen; become stiff. —こはばったシャツの胸, a stiff shirt-front. —死骸が强ばる, The dead body becomes rigid.

kowagaru (恐がる), *vt.* to fear; dread; be afraid *of*. —恐がらす, ① (恐れさす) to frighten; terrify; scare. ② (脅かす) to threaten; intimidate.

kowagowa (恐恐), *ad.* timidly; with fear; gingerly. —こはごは傍へ行く, to approach with fear.

kowai (恐い), *a.* terrible; fearful; dreadful; frightful. —こはい目に會ふ, to be frightened.

kowai (强·硬い), *a.* hard; tough (肉などの); stiff.

kowaiken (强意見), *n.* severe admonition; remonstrance; expostulation (諫諍). —强意見をする, to admonish [exhort] severely; remonstrate [expostulate] with a person on a matter; give a good talking-to.

kowairo (聲色), *n.* ❶ (音調) the tone of a voice. ❷ (假聲) imitation of a voice. —聲色を使ふ, to imitate [mimic] a voice; speak in an unusual voice. ¶ 聲色使ひ, a professional imitator of actors' voices.

kowake (小別), *n.* subdivision; subsection; items. —小別けする, to subdivide; itemize.

kowaki (小脇に), *ad.* under one's arm. —小脇に抱へる, to hold (anything) under one's arm.

kowameshi (强飯), *n.* steamed rice (mixed with red beans).

kowamote (强持てする), *vi.* to be respectfully treated from fear.

kōwan (港灣), *n.* a harbour. ¶ 港灣防禦艦, a harbour-defence ship.

kowappa (小童), *n.* ❶ (幼童) a youngster. ❷ (惡戲小僧) an urchin; an imp; a whipper-snapper. ❸ (青二才) a green boy; a chicken.

koware (毀れ), *n.* ❶ (破損,破壞) break; breakage; break-down (機械). ❷ (破損物) breakage; wreckage; damaged things. ❸ (破片) a fragment; (broken) pieces. ❹ (崩壞物) debris; *débris* [佛]. ¶ 毀れ椅子, a broken chair.

kowaremono (毀れ物), *n.* a fragile article. —毀れ物注意 (荷印), "Fragile—Handle with care."

kowareru (毀れる), *vi.* to break; be broken; be smashed (微塵になる). —毀れ易い, fragile; brittle; delicate (時計の機械などの). —毀れかゝった, half-ruined [-damaged]; broken-down; rickety (家·車など). —ばらばらに毀れる, to fall asunder.

kowariita (小割板), *n.* a strip.

kowasu (毀·壞·破す), *vt.* to break (down); destroy; smash (破碎). —家を毀す, to pull down [demolish] a house. —計畫を毀す, to mar a plan. —身體をこはす, to impair one's health; undermine one's constitution.

koya (小屋), *n.* ❶ a cottage; a hut; a shed. ❷ (物置小屋) a granary (穀物の); a shed; a garage 自動車など入れる). ❸ (家畜小屋) a pen; a stable (牛馬等の); a pigsty (豚の). ❹ (番小屋) a blockhouse; a box. ¶ 小屋掛け, a booth.

kōya (紺屋), *n.* a dyer. ☞ *końya*.

kōya (荒野), *n.* a wilderness.

kōya (曠野), *n.* a wild plain; a moorland; a moor.

koyagi (野羔), *n.* a kid (皮·肉をも云ふ).

koyaku (子役), *n.* ❶ a child's part (in a play); the rôle of a child. ❷ (役者) an actor playing the rôle of a child.

kōyaku (口約), *n.* verbal promise [contract; agreement]. —口約する, to make a verbal promise.

kōyaku (口譯), *n.* oral translation.

kōyaku (公約), *n.* a public contract (公法上の契約); a public pledge (政黨などが國民への). —公約する, to pledge [commit] oneself publicly; take the pledge openly.

kōyaku (膏藥), *n.* a plaster (硬膏); a salve (軟膏); an ointment (同上). —膏藥を貼る, to stick [apply] a plaster; salve; dress with an ointment. —膏藥張りだらけの障子, a paper sliding-door full of patches.

koyakunin (小役人), *n.* a petty official. ☞ *koshiben*.

kōyakusū (公約數), *n.* 【數】a common measure; a common factor. ¶ 最大公約數, the greatest common measure (G. C. M. と略す).

koyama (小山), *n.* a hill; a hillock; a mound.

kōyamaki (高野槇), *n.* 【植】the whorled-leaved umbrella-pine.

koyami (小歇), *n.* a break; a lull.

koyashi (肥), *n.* manure; a fertilizer; night-soil (人糞). —肥をやる, to manure.

koyasu (肥す), *vt.* ❶ (肥沃) to fertilize; manure; enrich (the soil). ❷ (肥滿) to nourish; fatten. ❸ (富ます) to enrich (oneself). —

地味を肥す, to fertilize land.

koyasugai (子安貝), *n.* 【貝】 Cypræa mauritania (cowry の一種).

koyō (雇用, 雇傭), *n.* employ; engagement; hiring of services. ¶ 雇傭契約, an agreement for services.

kōyō (公用), *n.* official business; public service. —公用を帯びて, on official business.

kōyō (孝養), *n.* filial duties. ☞ *kōkō* (孝行). —父母に孝養を盡す, to discharge one's duties [be dutiful] to one's parents.

kōyō (效用), *n.* use (用途); 【經】 utility. —效用多き(少き), of much (little) use [utility]. ¶ 限界(全部)效用, marginal (total) utility.

kōyō (紅葉), *n.* red [autumn] leaves; crimson foliage; autumn (-al) tints (色). —紅葉する, to turn red; be tinged (with red).

kōyō (綱要), *n.* a summary; an outline; an epitome.

koyoi (今宵), *n.* & *ad.* this evening (今夕); to-night (今夜).

koyōji (小楊枝), *n.* a tooth-pick.

koyomi (暦), *n.* an almanac; a calendar. —暦を繰る, to look up in an almanac. ¶ 剝(は)し暦, a block-calendar.

koyori (紙縒), *n.* a paper-string. —紙縒で綴ぢる, to bind up with paper-strings. —紙縒を撚る, to twist paper into string.

koyū (固有-性), *n.* a peculiarity (特性); a characteristic (同上); individuality (個性). —固有の, ① (特有の) characteristic (*of*); peculiar (*to*); individual. ② (生得の) inherent (*in*); innate. ¶ 固有名詞, 【文】 the proper noun [name].

kōyu (香油), *n.* hair oil; pomatum; pomade.

kōyu (鑛油), *n.* mineral oil.

kōyū (公有の), *a.* public. ¶ 公有財產, public property.

kōyū (交友), *n.* friends; companions; company.

kōyū (校友), *n.* an old boy; a school-fellow; an alumnus [*pl.* -ni]. ¶ 校友會, a students' association; an alumni association; an old boys' meeting. (校友會雜誌, a school magazine; (會報) an alumni bulletin).

koyubi (小指), *n.* the little finger; the ear-finger.

kōza (口座), *n.* an account; a seat of account. —各口座を決算する (簿記), to balance accounts. ¶ 金銀口座, cash account.

kōza (高座), *n.* a platform; a pulpit (說敎の); a dais.

kōza (講座), *n.* ❶ (講義をする席) a chair; a pulpit; a stand. ❷ (大學の特定敎授事務) a (professional) chair. —...の講座を擔任する, to have charge of [hold] the chair *of*. —講座を囑託する, to give charge of a chair.

kōzai (功罪), *n.* merits and demerits; services and crimes.

kōzai (絞罪), *n.* hanging. —絞罪に處する, to hang; gibbet; send to the gallows.

kozaiku (小細工), *n.* artifices; pretty devices.

kozan (故山), *n.* one's native province; home. —故山に起臥する, to live in the retirement of one's native province.

kōzan (高山), *n.* a high [lofty] mountain. ¶ 高山植(動)物, an alpine plant (animal); alpine flora (fauna) (全體).

kōzan (鑛山), *n.* a mine. ¶ 鑛山學, mining engineering. —鑛山學校, a school of mines. —鑛山技師, a mining engineer. —鑛山業, mining industry. —鑛山監督, a mine-captain. —鑛山局, the Mining Bureau; the Bureau of Mines. —鑛山師, a speculator in mines.

kozappari (小ざっぱりした), *a.* ❶ (座敷·服裝などの) neat; trim; tidy. ❷ (人) comely; dapper. —小ざっぱりした座敷, a neat room.

kozara (小皿), *n.* a small plate; a small saucer.

kozei (小勢), *n.* a small force; a small number of persons.

kōzei (港稅), *n.* harbour [port] -dues; port charges.

kōzen (公然), *ad.* ❶ (隱さずに) openly; publicly; in public. ❷ (公式に) officially. —公然の祕密, an open secret. —公然の手續をする, to go through the prescribed formalities.

kōzen (昂然), *ad.* proudly; haughtily; arrogantly. —意氣昂然たり, to hold one's head high; be in high spirits.

kōzen (浩然の氣を養ふ), to foster an unrestricted spirit.

kozeni (小錢), *n.* small coin [change]; loose money [cash]; money of small denominations.

kozeriai (小競合), *n.* a skirmish; a scrimmage, scrummage (football 等遊戲の際の格鬪にも用ふ). —小競合ひする, to skirmish; have a brush (with the enemy).

kōzetsu (口舌), *n.* words; talk; the tongue. —口舌の爭, a verbal contention; high [bitter; hot] words; wordy warfare. —口舌の徒, a controversialist.

kozō (小僧), *n.* ❶ (雛僧) a young Buddhist disciple; a priestling; an acolyte. ● (丁稚) a boy; a shop-boy; a servant-boy. ● (徒弟) an apprentice. ● (孺子) a boy; a child; an urchin. ● (未熟者) a fledgling; a greenhorn. —生意氣な小僧, a conceited pup; a whipper-snapper. —小僧にやる, to apprentice (a boy) *to*; put out (a boy) to service.

kōzo (楮), *n.* 【植】 Broussonetia kasinoki (paper mulberry の一種).

kōzō (構造), *n.* structure; construction; frame (組立). —人體の構造, the structure of the human body. —宇宙の構造, the frame of the universe. —構造する, to construct; frame; form.

kozoku (古俗), *n.* old [time-honoured] customs.

kōzoku (皇族), *n.* the Imperial [Royal] Family; the princes of the Blood; an Imperial [a royal] prince (個人的に). ¶ 皇族會議, an Imperial Family council.

kōzokuryoku (航續力), *n.* endurance; sea endurance.

kozotte (舉ッて), *ad.* all; in a body; as one man. —一家擧ッてブラジルへ移住した, The whole family emigrated to Brazil.

kozoru (擧る), *v.* to bring all together.

kōzu (好事), *n.* virtuosity; dilettantism. ¶ 好事家, a virtuoso; a dilettante [*pl.* -ti].

kozue (梢), *n.* ● a tree-top. ● (小枝) a twig; a bough.

kōzui (洪水), *n.* a flood; an inundation; a deluge (大洪水). —洪水に遭ふ, to suffer from a flood; be flooded; be inundated.

kozuka (小柄), *n.* the knife worn in the sword-sheath; a sword-knife.

kozukai (小使), *n.* ● (雜僕) a servant; an attendant; a man. ● (用たし) an errand-boy; a messenger-boy; a boy.

kozukai (小遣-錢), *n.* pocket-money; pocket expenses; pin-money (妻の). ¶ 小遣帳, a petty cash-book; a book of household expenses.

kozuku (小突く), *vt.* (*a*) (輕く叩く) to pat; push: (*b*) (勵ます) to cheer; spur: (*c*) (搖り當る) to strike [knock; dash] *against*; shake. —人を小突き廻す, to push a man about. —嫁を小突き出す, to tease the wife out of the house.

kozukuri (小作の), *a.* of small stature [build]; short-statured.

kōzuru (鸛), *n.* 【鳥】 the Japanese stork.

kō-zuru (困ずる), *vi.* to be troubled; be perplexed; be at a loss. —困じ果てる, to come to one's wits' end; come to the end of one's tether.

kō-zuru (薨ずる), *vi.* to pass away.

kō-zuru (講ずる), *v.* ● (講義) to lecture *on*; instruct *in*; preach (法話などを). ● (講習) to practise; study. ● (工夫) to devise; project. —方策を講ずる, to devise some means; cast about for some means.

kozutsumi (小包), *n.* a parcel; a packet; a package. ¶ 代金引換小包, C. O. D. (cash on delivery) parcel. —小包郵便料, parcel post charge.

ku (九), *n.* nine; the ninth (第九).

ku (句), *n.* ● a clause (主格あるもの); a phrase (主格なきもの). ● (詩歌の) a line; a verse.

ku (苦), *n.* ● (苦勞) trouble; distress; privation. ● (苦痛) pain; suffering; bitterness. ● (心配) anxiety. —苦になる, to cause anxiety; weigh on one's mind. —苦にする, to take to heart; worry oneself *about* [*over*]; concern oneself about; be anxious *about*; brood *over*.

ku (區), *n.* ● (區域) a division; a section; a district. ● (市の) a (an urban) district; a ward. ● 【動】 series.

kū (空), *n.* ● (虛空) the air; the sky. ● (空虛) emptiness; vacancy; void. ● (眞空) vacuum. ● (幻空) vanity; emptiness; unsubstantiality. —空な, ① (空虛の) empty; vacant; hollow. ② (幻空の) empty; unsubstantial; visionary (空想的). ③ (くだらぬ) idle; empty; vain (無駄な). ④ (抽象的) abstract. —空に, ① (空しく) vainly; in vain. ② (うはの空) abstractedly; absent-mindedly; idly (怠けて). ③ (當途もなく) aimlessly; thoughtlessly (考なしに). —空を摑んで, catching at the air.

kūbaku (空漠たる), *a.* ● vast; extensive; boundless. ● vague; obscure; ambiguous.

kubarimono (配物), *n.* presents distributed among friends.

kubaru (配る), *vt.* ● (配置) to dispose; station; arrange. ● (配分) to distribute; serve out (食物等を); deal (骨牌等を). ● (配達) to deliver. ● (割當) to apportion; assign; parcel out. —新聞を配る, to deliver newspapers. —四方に目を配る, to keep the eyes open in all directions. —近所へ餅を配る, to distribute rice-cakes amongst neighbours.

kuberu (焚べる), *vt.* to put [throw] into the fire; burn. —薪

を焚べる, to burn fuel; feed (a fire) with faggots.

kubetsu (區別), *n.* ❶ (差別) distinction; differentiation. ❷ (分類) classification. ❸ (識別) discrimination. ☞*sabetsu* (差別). —區別を立てる, to distinguish; differentiate; discriminate. ——**suru**, *v.* ❶ (差別) to distinguish; discriminate; make a difference *between*. ❷ (分類) to classify; divide; distinguish. ❸ (識別) to discriminate; discern. —善惡を區別する, to discriminate between the good and the bad.

kubi (首), *n.* the neck (頸); the head (頭); a head cut off (首級). —首になる, to be dismissed [discharged]; get the sack 〖卑〗 — 首にする, to dismiss; discharge; (give the) sack 〖卑〗 —頸を延ばす, to make a long neck; crane out one's neck. (首を延ばして待つ, to wait with a craned neck; be on the tiptoe of expectation.) —首を刎ね [切] る, to cut off the head; behead; decapitate. —首を縊る, to hang oneself. —首を横に振る, to shake one's head. —首を縦に振る, to nod assent. ¶ 首曲り, a wry-necked person.

kubikase (首枷), *n.* ❶〖支那〗 a cangue, cang. ❷ (係累) an encumbrance.

kubikazari (頸飾), *n.* a collar (勳章の); a neck-chain; a necklace; a gorget (同上).

kubiki (軛), *n.* a yoke. —軛をつける, to yoke.

kubikukuri (首縊), *n.* suicide by hanging.

kubimaki (頸卷), *n.* a neck-cloth; a comforter; a muffle, muffler. — 頸卷をする, to put on a neck-cloth; muffle up one's throat.

kubippiki (首引), *n.* ❶ (遊戯) a tugging contest between two persons with an endless cord round their necks. ❷ (互に競ひ合ふ) struggling *with*. —字引と首ッ引, struggling with a dictionary.

kubire (括), *n.* a compressed [constricted] part.

kubireru (縊れる), *vi.* to hang oneself; strangle oneself. —縊られる, to be hanged; be strangled.

kubiru (括る), *vt.* to constrict.

kubiru (縊る), *vt.* to strangle; throttle.

kubisuji (首筋), *n.* the scruff (of the neck); the nape.

kubittake (首ッ丈), *ad.* over head and ears; up to the ears 〖neck〗. —首ッ丈より高い, higher than the neck.

kubittama (頸玉), *n.* ❶ (頸筋) the scruff; the nape; the neck. ❷ (頸輪) a collar (犬などの). —頸玉に噛りつく, to hang on another's neck; throw one's arms round another's neck.

kubiwa (頸環), *n.* a collar (犬などの).

kubo (窪, 凹), *n.* a basin (盆地); a depression; a hollow.

kūbō (空望), *n.* vanity; a vain [an empty] hope. —空望を抱く, to hope against hope; harbour an empty hope.

kubochi (窪地), *n.* a low land; a hollow; a depression.

kuboi (窪い), *a.* hollow; concave; sunken.

kubomasu (凹ます), *vt.* Ⓢ 窪める. to dent; hollow; depress.

kubomi (凹み), *n.* a hollow; a depression; a dent.

kubomime (凹み目), *n.* a score; a notch; an indent. —凹み目を附ける, to score; notch; indent.

kubomu (凹·窪む), *vi.* to subside; be depressed; become hollow. — 凹んだ眼, sunken eyes.

kubu (九分通り), *ad.* nine cases out of ten; ten to one; almost.

kubun (區分), *n.* ❶ (分類) classification; sorting; division. ❷ (區畫) section; division; compartment. —區分する, ① to classify; divide. ② to draw a line of demarcation.

kūbun (空文), *n.* a dead letter; a scrap of paper.

kuchi (口), *n.* ❶ the mouth; jaws (猛獸等の); the spout (鐵瓶等の). ❷=*mikaku*. ❸=*kotoba*. ❹ (就職口) a position; a post; a berth; an opening. ❺ (栓) a stopper; a plug; a tap (樽の). ❻ (種類) kind; sort; description. ❼ (穴) an opening; an aperture; a hole. ❽ (入口) an entrance; a door; a gate. ❾ (分) a share (ひとむき); a lot (競賣品等); a parcel (荷物等); an assortment. ❿ (吸口) a mouthpiece. ⓫ (器物の縁) a lip; an edge; a brim. ⓬ (人數) the number of persons. — 口が旨い, ① [*vi.*] to have a fluent [ready] tongue. ② [*a.*] fair-spoken; persuasive; smooth-tongued; honey-tongued. —口が惡い, to have a sharp [caustic] tongue. —口が利けなくなる, to be deprived of (the power of) speech; lose one's tongue. —口に合ふ, to suit one's taste. —口に慣れる, ① (食ひ慣れる) to become palatable. ② =*iinareru* (言慣れる). —口一杯に頰張る, to fill the mouth *with*. —口に任せて喋る, to talk at random; say what comes uppermost. —口の達者な, fluent; voluble; glib-tongued. —口の惡い, slanderous; sarcastic. —口を探す, to look for a position [berth]; look out for an opening. —口を出す, to put in a word; interpose; obtrude oneself *upon*. —口を噤む, to hold one's tongue; shut [close] one's mouth. —口を揃へて, with one mouth [voice]. —口を極めて褒める, to praise to the skies. —吾々の口を箝するに外ならぬ, to be nothing but to gag our mouths. —口は禍の門, "The mouth is the gate of evils." —口に蜜あり腹に劍あり, "A false friend has honey in his mouth, gall in his heart."

kūchi (空地), *n.* a vacant ground; an unoccupied land; a blank space.

kuchiake (口明け), *n.* opening; the first dealing [transaction]; a hansel, handsel.

kuchiatari (口當), *n.* taste. —口當りのよい, pleasant to the taste; palatable; smooth (酒).

kuchiba (朽葉), *n.* withered [dead; decayed] leaves. ¶ 朽葉色, tawniness; russet; filemot.

kuchibashi (嘴), *n.* ❶ (鳥の) a beak (猛禽等の强く且つ鉤形の) a bill (鳩·鷄·水禽等の). ❷ (管等の) a snout. —嘴の黄色い人, a greenhorn; a fledgling; an unlicked cub. —嘴を入れる, to put in a word; interpose; put one's oar in.

kuchibashiru (口走る), *vt.* to let slip; blurt out; babble. —とんでもない事まで口走る, to let slip even the most indiscreet remarks.

kuchibaya (口速に), *ad.* rapidly; fast. ☞ *hayakuchi.*

kuchibeni (口紅), *n.* rouge. —口紅をさす, [*vt.*] to rouge.

kuchibi (口火), *n.* a train; a fuze; a priming. ☞ *dōka.* —口火をつける, to light a fuze.

kuchibiru (脣), *n.* the lip; 【動】 the peristome. —脣を舐める, to lick one's lips. ¶ 上(下)脣, the upper (lower; under) lip.

kuchibue (口笛), *n.* a whistle; whistling. —口笛吹く, to whistle.

kuchidashi (口出), *n.* obtrusion; obtruding remarks. —口出しする, to meddle *in*; obtrude on self *upon*; put in one's oar. —餘計な口出しをするな, Don't meddle in things that don't concern you.

kuchidassha (口達者な), *a.* glib-tongued; voluble; loquacious.

kuchidome (口留する), *v.* to bribe to secrecy; hush up; muzzle. ¶ 口留金, hush-money. (口留金をゆする, to blackmail a person.)

kuchie (口繪), *n.* a frontispiece.

kuchigane (口金), *n.* a capsule (硝子壜の); a lamp-hoop (洋燈の).

kuchigaru (口輕の), *a.* ❶ talkative; voluble. ❷ apt to disclose secrets; leaky [俗]. —口輕な面白い男, a talkative, amusing man.

kuchigenka (口喧嘩), *n.* a dispute; a quarrel.

kuchigirei (口綺麗な), *a.* innocent; unconcerned. ☞ *keppaku* (潔白な). —口綺麗な事を云ふ, to speak like an innocent person.

kuchigitanai (口穢い), *a.* ❶ (口惡き) abusive; scurrilous; foul-mouthed [-tongued]. ❷ (食物に卑しい) greedy. —口穢く罵る, to abuse in coarse language; use abusive language.

kuchigomoru (口籠る), *vi.* ❶ (吃る) to mumble; stutter; speak indistinctly. ❷ (返事に窮して) to hesitate in speaking; falter; hum and haw. —口籠ッて, stammeringly; hesitatingly.

kuchigōsha (口巧者), *n.* ❶ (事) plausibility. ❷ (人) a clever [good] talker. —口巧者に言ひ拔ける, to get out (of a scrape) with his smooth tongue.

kuchigotae (口答), *n.* a retort; answering back. —口答する, to retort; answer back.

kuchiguchi (口口に), *ad.* among various people; severally.

kuchiguruma (口車), *n.* fair speech; glib talk; cajolery. —口車に乘せる, to cajole; wheedle. —うかと口車に乘る, to allow oneself thoughtlessly to be wheedled.

kuchiguse (口癖), *n.* ❶ a habit in speaking; a way of speaking. ❷ cant. —口癖のやうに云ふ, to harp *on*; babble (of an affair) habitually.

kuchihabattai (口幅ッたい), *a.* big; tall; boastful; grandiloquent. —口幅ッたい言分, tall talking.

kuchihige (髭), *n.* a moustache, mustache. —髭を生やす, to grow a moustache.

kuchiire (口入), *n.* good offices; agency; intermediation. —某の口入で, by the agency [good offices] of Mr.—. ¶ 口入(營)業, employment agency. —口入人, an employment agent; a servants' registry office keeper; a go-between (仲介者). —口入宿, an employment office; a (servants') registry office [英]; an intelligence [a register] office [米].

kuchikazu (口數), *n.* ❶ (言葉數) words. ❷ (人數) the number of persons; heads. ❸ (同種を一纏めにしたる數) a share; a lot; a parcel. —口數の多い, talkative;

loquacious; garrulous. —口數の少い, reticent; taciturn. 「wood.
kuchiki(朽木), *n.* decayed [rotten]
kuchikiki (口利), *n.* ❶ (口巧者) a clever talker. ❷ (勢力家) a man of influence. ❸ (仲裁者) a mediator. ❹ (代辯者) a spokesman; a mouthpiece.
kuchikogoto(口小言), *n.* grumble; murmur.
kuchiku(驅逐する), *vt.* to expel; eject; oust; chase (追擊); dislodge (陣地から): drive away (敵を). —米貨を驅逐する, to drive American goods off the market. —敵を國内より驅逐する, to clear the land of the enemy. ¶ 驅逐艦, a (torpedo-boat) destroyer. (驅逐艦隊, a destroyer-flotilla.) —驅逐機, a chaser.
kuchimae (口前), *n.* a way of speaking (話振); tongue (辯舌). —口前の旨い, fair-spoken; persuasive.
kuchimakase (口任せ), *n.* random talk. —口任せに, at random.
kuchimame(口まめな), *a.* talkative; loquacious; voluble; garrulous.
kuchimane(口眞似), *n.* imitation of another's talk. —口眞似をする, to mimic another's talk.
kuchimoto(口元), *n.* the mouth. —口元の可愛い娘, a sweet-mouthed girl. —口元が締ってゐる(ゐぬ), to have firm (loose) lips.
kuchinaoshi (口直), *n.* taking away the taste; dessert (後附).
kuchinashi (梔子), *n.* 【植】 the Cape jasmine.
kuchi-nisuru(口にする), *v.* ❶ (言ふ) to say; speak; talk. ❷ (食ふ) to eat; drink (飲む); take.
kuchinuki(口拔), *n.* a cork-screw.
kuchiōi(口覆), *n.* (呼吸器保護器) a mask; a respirator. 「speech.
kuchiomoi(口重い), *a.* slow of
kuchioshii (口惜しい), *a.* mortifying; regretful. ☞ *kuyashii.*
kuchiru (朽ちる), *vi.* to rot; decay; putrefy. —朽ち果てる, ① to decay completely; rot. ② (死ぬ) to die; end one's life.
kuchisaganai (口さがない), *a.* censorious; talkative; gossipy. —口さがない京童, the townspeople who are fond of scandals.
kuchisakashii (口賢しい), *a.* fair-spoken; smooth-tongued; clever at talking.
kuchisaki (口先, 口頭), *n.* the lips; the tongue. —口先だけの友人, a mouth-friend. —口先計りの慰め, lip-comfort. —口先ばかり大膽な, bold in word only. —彼の同情は口先計りであつた, His sympathy was only verbal.

kuchisugi (口過), *n.* livelihood; (the means of) living; subsistence. ☞ *seikei* (生計).
kuchisusugu (漱ぐ), *vi.* to cleanse [rinse] the mouth; gargle.
kuchitori (口取), *n.* ❶ (口座) accounts. ❷ (料理) a side-dish.
kuchitsuki (口附), *n.* ❶ = *kuchimoto.* ❷ (言振り) way of speaking. —口附きの煙草, cigarettes with mouthpieces.
kuchiura (口占を引いて見る), to sound another's views; feel another's pulse.
kuchiutsushi (口移), *n.* ❶ (物を含んで他人の口に入れる) transferring from mouth to mouth. ❷ (口授) oral instruction [teaching].
kuchiwa (口輪), *n.* a muzzle. —口輪を嵌める, to muzzle.
kuchiwake(口別), *n.* assortment. —口別けする, to assort; sort.
kuchiyakamashii (口喧しい), *a.* fault-finding; scolding; nagging. —口喧しい女, a termagant; a vixen; a shrew.
kuchiyakusoku (口約束), *n.* a verbal promise; a verbal [oral] agreement [contract]. —口約束する, to give one's word; make a verbal contract [promise].
kuchiyose(口寄), *n.* ❶ (巫術) necromancy; sorcery. ❷ (市子) a necromancer; a sorceress; a witch; a spirit-rapper. 「☞ *kōza.*
kuchiza (口座), *n.* an account.
kuchizusamu (口吟む), *v.* ❶ (漫吟する) to sing to oneself; hum. ❷ (詩歌を作る) to compose (a poem).
kuchizutae (口傳), *n.* Ⓢ 口傳(クデン) ❶ oral delivery. ❷ (口碑) tradition. —口傳へに殘る, to be handed down by tradition.
kuchō (口調, 句調), *n.* tone (語調); euphony (語呂). —口調のよい, euphonious; melodious. —口調よく讀む, to read in a melodious tone. —口調を好くする, [*vt.*] to euphonize; melodize. —人の口調を眞似る, to imitate a person's tone.
kuchō(區長), *n.* the headman of a ward [an urban district]. ¶ 本郷區長, the Headman of Hongō Ward.
kuchū (驅蟲する), *v.* to exterminate the noxious insects (害蟲); expel [destroy] intestinal worms (蛔蟲). ¶ 驅蟲藥, ① an insecticide; an insect powder. ② (蟲下し) an anthelminthic; a vermifuge.
kūchū (空中), *n.* the mid-air; the air; the sky. —空中高く, high up in the air. —空中でとんぼ返りする, to make a somersault in the air.

—空中樓閣を畫く, to build castles in the air. ¶ 空中電氣, atmospheric electricity; strays; statics; X's. —空中魚雷, an aerial torpedo. —空中艦隊, an air-squadron. —空中滑走, 【飛】 volplane. (空中滑走して降る, to plane down; volplane.) —空中線, an aerial (wire); an antenna. —空中戰, a battle in the air; an air battle; an aerial fight; aerial warfare. —空中襲撃, an air-raid; a raid. (空中襲撃機, a raider.) —空中偵察兵, an air-scout. —空中郵便, air-post [-mail].

kuda (管), *n.* ❶ a pipe; a tube; the stem (of a pipe); hose. ❷ 【學】 (絲卷管) a spool.

kudakeru (碎·摧ける), *vi.* ❶ (壞れる) to be broken; go to pieces; smash (粉々に). ❷ (勢力が衰へる) to decline; sink; slacken. ❸ (さばける) to be social [affable]. —碎け易い, fragile; brittle; crisp (煎餅等の). —當ッて碎ける, to run the risk.

kudaku (碎く), *vt.* ❶ (破碎する) to break; smash; crush. ❷ (搗き碎く) to pound. ❸= *kujiku*. —心を碎く, to rack [cudgel] one's brains; tax one's ingenuity. —身を粉に碎く, to work like a slave; toil and moil; slave it. —細かく氷を碎く, to break ice into bits.

kudakudashii (管管しい), *a.* tedious; tiresome; lengthy. —くだくだしく話す, to enter into the smallest details; talk tediously.

kudamono (果物), *n.* a fruit; fruitage (集合的に). ¶ 果物屋, a fruiterer; a fruiterer's (shop).

kudan (件の), *a.* (the) said; above-mentioned; (the matter) in question. —件の人物, the person in question; the said man.

kūdan (空談), *n.* idle [empty; trivial] talk; tittle-tattle; chit-chat. —空談に耽る, to be given to gossiping [idle talk]. —空談に時を費す, to gossip away time.

kudaranai (下らない), *a.* ❶ (無價値な) valueless; worthless; useless. ❷ (馬鹿げた) foolish; stupid; senseless. ❸ (瑣細な) frivolous; trivial; petty. —下らない本, a book of no value; a trashy book. —下らない事で怒る, to get angry at [about] trifles.

kudari (下·降り), *n.* ❶ (おりること) descent; going down. ❷ (衰退) decline. ❸ (田舍下り) going into the country; leaving the capital. —下り列車(線), a down train (line).

kudari (下痢·腹), *n.* loose bowels; diarrhœa. —下痢止めの妙藥, a specific for diarrhœa.

kudarizaka (下り坂), *n.* ❶ (坂道) a downhill; a descent. ❷ (衰運) decline; declining fortune; decadence. —人生の下り坂, the decline [autumn] of life. —下り坂である, to be on the decline [wane; down grade].

kudaru (下·降る), *v.* ❶ (おりる) to come [go] down; get down; descend; dismount (馬から). ❷ (ふる) to fall; drop; come down. ❸ (命令·判決等が) to be given; be issued; be delivered (判決が). ❹ (劣る) to be inferior *to*; fall (off) in quality; depreciate in value. ❺ (下痢する) to be attacked by diarrhœa; have loose bowels. ❻ (降參する) to surrender; submit; yield. ❼ (謙遜する) to humble oneself; condescend. ❽ (都から田舍へ行く) to go into the country; go up country 【米】. —東國へ下る, to go down to the Eastern Provinces. —人に下る, to submit to others. —富士川を舟で下る, to go down [descend] the Fujikawa in a boat.

kudasaru (下さる), *v.* ❶ (與へる) to give. ❷ (依賴の意) to be so kind [good] as *to*; have the goodness *to*. ❸ (敬語として) to condescend; vouchsafe; deign.

kudashi (下し), *n.* evacuation; purging; opening the bowels. —下しをかける, to give a purgative; purge the bowels. ¶ 下し藥, a purgative; a cathartic; an aperient.

kudasu (下·降す), *vt.* ❶ (おろす) to let down; lower. ❷ (降らす) to let fall; visit a person *with* (禍福を). ❸ (與へる) to give; grant; make a present *of*. ❹ (下げる) to abase; degrade; depreciate. ❺ (下痢さす) to open (the bowels); purge [evacuate] the bowels. ❻ (降參さす) to reduce; subdue; subjugate. ❼ (命令·判決·批評等を) to give; issue; render. —自ら手を下して, with one's own hand. —判斷を下す, to pass one's criticism [opinion] *on*. —品質を下す, to lower the quality. —敵を降す, to subdue the enemy.

kuden (口傳), *n.* ❶ (口で傳へる) oral instruction. ❷ (奥義を授ける) oral instruction into a secret [mystery]. —口傳を授ける, to give oral instruction; teach orally.

kūden (空電), *n.* =*kūchū* (空中電氣).

kūdetā (クーデター), *n.* coup d'état 【佛】.

kudo (苦土), *n.* magnesia.

kudoi (諄い), *a.* ❶ (冗長の)

tedious; lengthy; diffuse. ❹(しつこい) importunate. ❺(味等の) thick; heavy; greasy(油こき). —諄い話, a tedious story. —諄く, tediously; diffusely; repeatedly (何度も); importunately.

kudoku(口說く), *vt.* ❶(强請)to solicit; importune; wheedle [coax] *into* (巧言で); make advances *to* (申出る). ❷(こぼす) to complain of; grumble. —口說き落す, to persuade a person into compliance; seduce a woman (女を).

kudoku (功德), *n.* piety; a virtuous action. —功德の爲め, for piety's sake.

Kuēkā-ha(クエーカー派), *n.* 【宗】 the Society of Friends; the Quakers. ¶ クエーカー教, Quakerism.

kueki (苦役), *n.* ❶(勞働) hard toil [labour]; drudgery. ❷(懲役) penal servitude; (imprisonment with) hard labour. —苦役に服する, to serve one's term; serve time.

kuenai (食へない), *a.* Ⓢ 食へぬ. ❶(食に適せぬ) not good to eat; not edible; uneatable. ❷(生活の出來ぬ) hard to live; unable to keep body and soul together. ❸(狡智ある) cunning; crafty; wily. ❹(手におへない) uncontrollable; unmanageable. —食へない奴, a sharp fellow (狡い); a deep one (腹黑い).

kuensan(枸櫞酸), *n.* citric acid.

kufū(工夫), *n.* ❶(考案) device; contrivance; design (意匠). ❷(計畫) a plan; a project; a scheme. ❸(手段) a way; a means; an expedient. —工夫する, ①(考案) to devise; design; contrive. ②(計畫) to plan; project; scheme. 工夫を凝らす, to elaborate a plan.

kūfuku (空腹), *n.* hunger; an empty stomach. —空腹を感ずる, to feel hungry. —空腹を忍ぶ, to stand hunger. —空腹を滿す, to satisfy one's appetite (on some food); appease one's hunger.

kugai (苦界, 苦海), *n.* (苦しみ多き世の中) a bitter world; a life of bitterness.

kugaji (陸路), *n.* overland route; route by land.

kugaku (苦學), *n.* pursuit of knowledge under difficulties [in adversity]; hard study. —苦學する, to study under difficulties [in adversity]. ¶ 苦學生, a self-supporting student; a struggling student.

kugatsu(九月), *n.* September.

kuge(公卿), *n.* a court-noble.

kūgeki(空隙), *n.* ❶(空間) a vacant space; a place unoccupied. ❷(裂目, 綻び) a crevice; a rent; a breach. ❸(戶・壁等の隙) a chink; a crack. ❹(紙の餘白) a blank.

kugen (苦言), *n.* bitter counsel; exhortation; outspoken advice. —苦言を呈する, to offer bitter counsel.

kūgen (空言), *n.* empty words; idle talk.

kugi(釘), *n.* a nail; a rivet (鋲); a peg (木・竹の). —釘が利く(利かぬ), The nail is fast (loose). —釘に引掛ける(衣服等を), to be caught in a nail. —釘を拔く, to pull out a nail. —釘を打ち込む, to drive in a nail. —足に釘を刺す, to run a nail into one's foot. ¶ 釘打器, a nail-driver.

kugin (苦吟する), *v.* to compose laboriously; work out (a poem).

kuginuki(釘拔), *n.* a nail-puller; (鋏式); a nail-extractor (槓杆式); (a pair of) pincers.

kugiri(句切), *n.* ❶(句讀) punctuation (法); stop (點); pause (讀誦の時の). ❷(終止) a place for leaving off; a period. —句切る, ①(句讀點を附す) to punctuate; set off with punctuation marks. ②(分畫する) to divide [cut off] (by a partition); mark off; mark out (線等で). —句切を附ける(事件等の), to settle [decide] a matter.

kugizuke (釘附にする), *vt.* to nail up; fasten with nails. —釘附けの箱, a nailed box; a pegged box (木釘止めの).

kugo (供御), *n.* the Emperor's meal [food].

kuguri(潛), *n.* a wicket.

kugurido(潛戶), *n.* a side-door [-gate]; a wicket-door [-gate].

kuguru (潛る), *v.* ❶(水中に) to dive. ❷(通過する) to pass *through*; creep *through*. ❸(避脫) to evade; escape. —水を潛る, to dive into the water. —垣根を潛る, to creep in through a hedge. —橋の下を潛る, to pass under a bridge. —群衆の間を潛る, to make one's way through a crowd.

kugyō (苦行), *n.* asceticism; ascetic practices [acts]; religious penance [austerities]. —苦行する, to practise asceticism [religious austerities].

kūhaku(空白), *n.* a blank; a blank space; a margin (紙端の).

kūhi(空費する), *vt.* to waste; misemploy; throw [cast; trifle] away.

kuhō (句法), *n.* phraseology; diction; phrase; turn of expression.

kūhō (空砲), *n.* an unloaded gun; a blank cartridge (空包). —空砲を放つ, to fire a blank cartridge.

kui (杭, 杙), *n.* a post; a stake (垣などの); a pile (地中に打込む大杙). —杭を打つ, to drive in a stake [pile]. ¶ 杭打機, a pile

(-driving) engine; a pile-driver.
kui (悔), *n.* =*kōkai* (後悔).
kuiarasu (食荒す), *v.* to eat of every dish; devour (貪食); eat ravenously.
kuiaratame (悔改), *n.* 【宗】 repentance; contrition. —悔改める, to repent *of*.
kuiau (喰合ふ), *vi.* =*kamiau.*
kuiawase (食合せ), *n.* (食物の) eating foods which disagree with one when taken together.
kuibuchi (食扶持), *n.* ❶ (扶持) rations; allowance. ❷ (生活費) cost of living; livelihood. —食扶持を入れる, to pay for one's board and lodging.
kuichigai (喰違ひ), *n.* ❶ (齟齬, 矛盾) contrariety; inconsistency; discordance. ❷ (交叉, 交錯) crossing; being crossed; interlock (歯車等の). —喰ひ違ふ, ① to be in discord *with*; run counter *to*; be inconsistent *with*. ② to cross; interlock.
kuichirasu (喰散す), *vt.* to eat in disorder; eat and spoil.
kuidaore (喰倒れ), *n.* ruin through luxury in food; ruin through extravagant diet.
kuidōraku (食道樂), *n.* ❶ (事) free living; epicurism. ❷ (人) an epicure; a free liver; a *gourmet.*
kuihagureru (食ひはぐれる), *vi.* to lose one's livelihood. —食ひはぐれることはない, It will save you from starving.
kuikajiru (食齧る), *vt.* to eat a bit *of*; dabble *in* (種々の學問・技藝を); learn a little *of*. —何でも少しづつ食ひ齧ッてる, to know a little of everything; have a smattering of everything.
kuikake (食掛の), *a.* left half-eaten. —食ひかけのパン, bread left half-eaten.
kuike (食氣), *n.* an appetite; a stomach. ☞ *shokuyoku.*
kuiki (區域), *n.* ❶ (限界) the limit; the boundary (境界). ❷ (範圍) the extent; the scope; a range. ❸ (區畫) a section; a district (地方). —區域を定める, to fix the boundary.
kuikiru (喰切る), *vt.* ❶ (喰盡す) to eat up. ❷ (嚙切る) to bite off; cut [tear] off with the teeth; crop (動物が草木の端を). —二つに喰ひ切る, to gnaw in two.
kuikomi (喰込み), *n.* ❶ (收入不足) a loss (損失); a deficit (缺損). ❷ (腐蝕) erosion; corrosion. —三百圓の喰込み, a deficit of ¥300. —喰ひ込む, ① (内部へ深く) to bite *in*; eat *into*; bore *into* (蟲が木などに). ② (侵入) to encroach [trespass] *upon*. ③ (資本を損す) to lose part of the capital; leave a deficit; be a drain on one's capital. ④ (腐蝕する) to erode; corrode.
kuimono (食物), *n.* ❶ food; eatables; victuals. ❷ (餌食) a victim; a prey. —食ひ物になる, to fall a victim [prey] *to*; become the victim [prey] *of*. —食ひ物にする, to prey *on* [*upon*]; make a victim *of*. —食物に不自由する, to be lacking [wanting] in food; be short of provisions.
kuin (女王, 皇后), *n.* a queen.
kuina (秧鷄), *n.* 【鳥】 the Eastern [Indian] water-rail.
kuinige (喰逃する), *vi.* to run away without paying for one's food; bilk 〖卑〗.
kuinokoshi (食殘し), *n.* remnants [leavings] of food; broken meat [victuals]. —食ひ殘す, to leave partially eaten.
kuiru (悔いる), *vt.* Ⓢ 悔ゆる. to regret; repent *of*; rue. —...した日を悔いる, to rue the day when. —今更悔いても仕方がない, Repentance now is of no avail.
kuishibaru (喰緊る), *vt.* to clench; set [grind] (one's teeth); gnash (the teeth). —歯を喰ひ緊ッて, with clenched teeth.
kuishinbō (食ひしんばう), *n.* a glutton; a gourmand; a pig 〖俗〗.
kuisugi (食過ぎ), *n.* surfeit; overeating; glut. —食ひ過ぎる, to eat too much; eat to excess; overeat oneself *with*; be surfeited.
kuitaosu (食倒す), *v.* to live at another's expense; sponge *upon*.
kuitaranu (食足らぬ), *vi.* ❶ (まだ欲しい) to want more food; be unsatiated. ❷ (物足らぬ) to be insufficient; be no match *for* (相手・敵として). ☞ *akitaranu.*
kuite (食者), *n.* ❶ an eater; one who eats. ❷ (大食家) a hearty [great] eater; a gourmand; a glutton.
kuitomeru (喰止める), *vt.* to check; hold [keep] in check; keep under; stem; stay. —敵(火)を喰ひ止める, to hold the enemy (fire) in check.
kuitsubushi (喰潰し), *n.* a drone; a hanger-on; a sponge. —喰ひ潰す, to eat (oneself or another) out of house and home. —彼は身代を喰ひ潰した, He squandered away his fortune.
kuitsuku (喰附く), *vt.* ❶ (嚙附く) to bite; fasten one's teeth *on*; snap (ぱくッと). ❷ (執著する) to hold on *to*; stick *to*. —喰ひ附かんとする, to snap *at* (犬などの); show one's teeth (牙を剝く).

kuitsukusu (食盡す), *vt.* to eat up; dispose *of*; devour. —御馳走を喰ひ盡す, to clean the board. —糧食を食ひ盡す, to exhaust provisions.

kuitsumeru (食詰める), *v.* to have no more means of subsistence; be reduced to the last stage of poverty; become unable to subsist. —東京を食ひ詰める, to exhaust one's means in Tōkyō.

kujaku (孔雀), *n.* 【鳥】 the peacock (雄); the peahen (雌); the peafowl (雌雄). ¶ 孔雀草,【植】 the French marigold.

kuji (籤), *n.* a lot; lottery (籤引). ☞ *chūsen* (抽籤). —籤に强い, to be lucky at lotteries. —籤に當る(外れる), to draw a prize (blank). —籤を引く, to draw lots; ballot; draw cuts (棒で).

kuji (公事), *n.* ❶ (訴訟) an action; a lawsuit; a cause. ❷ (政事) government business; state affairs.

kujibiki (籤引), *n.* lot-drawing; lottery. —籤引にする, to decide by lot; draw lots *for*.

kujikeru (挫ける), *vi.* ❶ (挫傷) to be broken; be crushed. ❷ (氣落ちする) to be discouraged; be disheartened; lose heart.

kujiku (挫く), *vt.* ❶ (挫傷) to sprain; break; crush. ❷ (氣落せしむ) to discourage; dishearten; depress. —頸を挫く, to break one's neck; have a wrick in one's neck. —手頸を挫く, to sprain one's wrist. —相手の勢を挫く, to break the opponent's power.

kujinogare (籤逃れ), *n.* escape [being let off] by lottery.

kujira (鯨), *n.* ❶【哺乳】 the whale; the bull whale (牡); the cow whale(牝). ❷【天】Cetus; the Whale. ❸ *kujirajaku* の略. —鯨の骨, whalebone. —鯨の鬚, whale-fin; baleen. ¶ 鯨船, a whaler; a whale-boat; a whaling-schooner.

kujirajaku (鯨尺), *n.* Ⓢ 鯨差 the cloth measure; a cloth *shaku* (=14.91 inches).

kujiru (抉じる), *vt.* to pick; bore; gouge.

kujo (驅除する), *v.* to exterminate; destroy; drive away. —害蟲を驅除する, to exterminate [destroy] the noxious insects.

kujō (苦情), *n.* ❶ (愁訴) a complaint; a grievance. ❷ (紛議) a trouble; a difficulty. —苦情の種, a bone to pick; the seed of grievance; the cause of complaint. —苦情を言ふ, to complain *of*; make a complaint; grumble *at*. —苦情を持出す, to bring forward a grievance.

kuju (口授), *n.* ❶ oral [verbal] instruction [teaching]. ❷ dictation. —口授する, to instruct [teach] orally; dictate.

kujū (九十), *n.* ninety; the ninetieth (第九十). —九十代, the nineties (溫度·年齡等に).

kukai (區會), *n.* a ward [an urban district] assembly.

kukaku (九角 -形), *n.* 【數】 an enneagon; a nonagon.

kukaku (區畫,區劃), *n.* ❶(區分) a section; a division; compartment; a block. ❷(境界) boundary; limits. —區畫する, to divide; partition; mark off. —區畫を設ける, to set up a boundary. ¶ 行政區畫, an administrative division. —區畫整理, boundary adjustment.

kukan (軀幹), *n.* ❶ (胴) trunk; body. ❷ (體格) physique.

kūkan (空間), *n.* ❶ (あき) space; room. ❷【哲】space (time の對); the infinite.

kukei (矩形), *n.* a rectangle. —矩形の, rectangular.

kūkei (空閨を守る), to remain chaste in the spouse's absence.

kūken (空拳), *n.* an empty hand. —徒手空拳を以て, without any capital.

kukenui (絎縫), *n.* blind-stitch.

kukeru (絎ける), *vt.* to blind-stitch; whip.

kuki (莖), *n.* a stalk; a stem.

kūki (空氣), *n.* air; atmosphere (雰圍氣). —新鮮(不潔)な空氣, fresh (foul) air. —空氣入りの護謨輪, a pneumatic tyre. —空氣の流通のよい(惡い), well-(ill-) ventilated. —空氣に暴す, [*vt.*] to air. —空氣を抜く, [*vt.*] to deflate (氣嚢·タイヤ等より). —空氣を入れる, [*vt.*] to inflate (タイヤ等に); let air in. ¶ 空氣傳染, infection. —空氣銃, an air-gun. (室內空氣銃, a pop-gun.) —空氣枕, an air-pillow; an air-cushion. —空氣ポンプ, an air-pump.

kukin (クキン), *n.* =*kōchin.*

kukkiri (くっきり), *ad.* ❶ (分明) clearly; distinctly; sharply. ❷ (著しく) remarkably; markedly; strikingly.

kukkyō (屈强な), *a.* powerful; robust; stalwart. —屈强な若者, a powerful [stalwart] young man.

kukkyoku (屈曲), *n.* indentation (海岸線の); winding (河·道等の); bending (撓曲); refraction (光線の屈折); 【文】(曲折) inflexion. —屈曲する, to bend; be curved; be refracted. —屈曲の多い海岸線, an indented coast-line.

kuko (枸杞), *n.* 【植】 the Chinese box-thorn.

kuku (九九), *n.* multiplication.

—九々の表, the multiplication table.

kuku (區區), *ad.* (まちまちに) variously; diversely. —區々たる, ① (まちまちの) various; diverse; divided. ② (數ならぬ) insignificant; trivial; petty. —區々に渉る, to go into particulars [details].

kūkū (空空), *a.* ❶ (茫然たる) listless; absent-minded; vacant. ❷ (私心なき) unselfish; disinterested. ❸ (煩惱なき) unworldly. —空々寂々, ① (虛無) the null and void; vacuity. ② (無心) listlessness; thoughtlessness; abstraction.

kukumeru (銜める), *v.* to feed from one's mouth.

kukuri (括), *n.* ❶ (結ぶこと) binding; tying; fastening. ❷ (束) a bundle. ❸ (結目) a knot; a tie. ❹ (結末) conclusion; end. —物の括りをつける, to bring to a conclusion [an end]. ¶括り紐, a wrapping-string; a twine. —括り枕, a stuffed pillow. —括り袖, a bag-sleeve.

kukuru (括る), *vt.* ❶ (束にする) to bundle; tie; bind. ❷ (結ぶ) to tie; fasten (結び附ける); brace (締め括る). ❸ (總括する) to summarize; sum up (〆る). ❹ (縛る) to bind. ❺ (縊る) to strangle; throttle. —紐で括る, to tie with a cord. —括弧で括る, to put in parenthesis (丸の) [brackets (角の)]. —包を腰へ括り附ける, to tie a parcel tightly to the hip.

kukyō (苦境), *n.* distressed [adverse] circumstances; a painful position; an adversity. —苦境に陷る, to fall into adverse circumstances.

kūkyo (空虛), *n.* emptiness; vacancy; voidness. —空虛な頭腦, an empty head.

kuma (熊), *n.* 【哺乳】 the bear. ¶日本熊, the Japanese black bear. —熊の油, bear-grease. —熊の膽, the bear's gall.

kuma (曲, 阿, 隈), *n.* ❶ (隅) a corner; a nook. ❷ (奥まった所) a recess; a retired place. ❸ (曲) indentation (海岸などの屈曲); a turn (河の). ❹ (物影になった暗い處) shade; blur; 【彫刻】 tint. ❺ (隈取) make-up. —隈を取る, ① (顏の) to make up the face. ② (畫の) to shade the colours.

kumabachi (熊蜂), *n.* 【昆】 the mandarin paper-wasp.

kumadaka (熊鷹), *n.* 【鳥】 the Indian crested eagle.

kumade (熊手), *n.* a rake; a bamboo-rake (竹製の); a hay-fork (乾草を集める). —熊手で掻きならす, [*vt.*] to rake.

kūmai-sōba (空米相場), *n.* speculation in rice.

kumanaku (隈なく), *ad.* all over; everywhere; universally. —隈なく探す(照る), to look (shine) in every nook and corner.

kumazasa (熊笹), *n.* 【植】 Bambusa Veitchii (bamboo の一種).

kūmei (空名), *n.* an empty name; an empty title.

kumen (工面), *n.* ❶ (工夫) a device; a contrivance; a plan. ❷ (金策) raising money. ❸ (金廻り, 暮し向) pecuniary means [condition]; circumstances. —工面が悪い, to be badly off; be in narrow [straitened] circumstances. ——**suru**, *v.* to devise; contrive; manage. —金を工面する, to raise money.

kumi (組), *n.* ❶ (絲を組むこと) plaiting; braiding. ❷ 【印】 composition (植字); make-up (本組). ❸ (一揃) a set; a pack; a suit; a pair (一對). ❹ (仲間) a class; a company; a circle. ❺ (側) side. —木杯一組, a set of wooden cups. —洋服一組, a suit of foreign clothes. —二番組 (消防の), the second company. —組を分ける, to divide into classes.

kumi (苦味), *n.* a bitter taste; bitterness; gall. ¶苦味丁幾, bitter tincture; stomach-drops.

kumiai (組合), *n.* ❶ 【法】 a partnership; an association. ❷ an association; a union (職工等の); a guild (同業者の). ❸ =*kumiuchi*. —組合外の人, an outsider. ¶組合銀行, an associated bank. —組(合)長, the president of an association. —組合員, a partner; an associate; a member (of an association); an insider. —組合契約, a contract of partnership [association]. —組合教會, the Congregational Church.

kumiau (組合ふ), *vi.* ❶ (組打する) to grapple *with*; fight. ❷ (仲間になる) (*a*) to form a partnership; enter into partnership *with*: (*b*) to unite *with*; combine *with*: (*c*) to associate *with*. —組合って商賣する, to trade in partnership. —手を組合って歩く, to walk arm in arm.

kumiawase (組合せ), *n.* ❶ 【數】 combination. ❷ (取組) match. ❸ (編合せ) intertwinement. —組合せる, ① to join together; put together; unite. ② to braid; plait; intertwine. ③ (取組ます, 配す) to match *against*; pit *against*: pair *with*. (銃を組合はせる, to pile arms.)

kumichō (組長), *n.* a monitor (級長); the head (of a company, association, *etc.*)

kumidasu (汲出す), *vt.* to ladle (柄杓で); drain; bail (淦を).

kumifuseru (組伏せる), *vt.* Ⓢ 組敷く. to hold down; get (a person) under.

kumigashira (組頭), *n.* the head (of a company, *etc.*); a foreman; a captain.

kumihosu (汲干す), *vt.* to drain; dry.

kumiido (汲井戸), *n.* a draw-well.

kumiireru (組入れる), *vt.* to assign; include; incorporate. ☞ *hennyū.*

kumiito (組絲), *n.* plaited thread; silk-braid.

kumikae (組換), *n.* recomposition. —組み換へる, to recompose; rearrange.

kumikawasu (酌交す), *v.* to help one another to wine; drink together; exchange cups.

kumiko (組子), *n.* ❶【建】a frame. ❷ (組下), one's subordinates; one's men.

kumikomu (汲込む), *vt.* to lade *into* (柄杓で); pour *into.* —水を汲み込む, to pour water *into.*

kuminaosu (組直す), *vt.* to reset; recompose.

kumisuru (與する), *v.* to take part *in*; join (*in*); side *with.* —正義に與する, to be on the side of justice.

kumitate (汲立ての), *a.* just [freshly] drawn.

kumitate (組立), *n.* ❶ erection. ❷ (構造) structure; framework; composition. ❸ (組織) system; organization; constitution. ¶ 組立本箱, a sectional bookcase.

kumitateru (組立てる), *v.* to frame; put together; erect. —機械を組立てる, to fit together [up] the machine. (印刷機械を組立てる, to erect a printing-press.)

kumitegata (組手形), *n.* a bill in sets; a set of bills.

kumitoru (汲取る), *vt.* ❶ to draw; dip; ladle. ❷ (酌量) to sympathize *with*; take into consideration [account]; enter into (another's feelings). —事情を汲みとる, to take the circumstances into consideration. —糞尿を汲み取る, to remove night-soil.

kumitsuku (組附く), *vi.* to grapple [close] *with*; seize hold *of.*

kumiuchi (組打), *n.* a close struggle; a grapple; a scrimmage. —組打ちする, to struggle together; grapple *with*; close *with.*

kumiwakeru (汲分ける), *vt.* ❶ to pour separately. ❷ (斟酌する) to consider; weigh. —事情を汲み分ける, to consider the circumstances.

kumo (蜘蛛), *n.* the spider. ¶ 蜘蛛の巣, a spider's web; a cobweb. (蜘蛛の巣だらけの, cobwebby.)

kumo (雲), *n.* a cloud. —雲に隠れる, to hide behind a cloud. —雲を凌ぐ, to rise [soar; tower] above the clouds. —雲を掴む様な話, a vague [misty] story. —雲を衝くやうな大男, a towering giant; a great big fellow.

kumogakure (雲隱する), *vi.* ❶ to hide behind a cloud. ❷ to conceal [hide] oneself. ❸ to pass away; die. —雲隱れの月, the moon (hidden) behind a cloud.

kumogata (雲形), *n.* cloud-form. ¶ 雲形定規, a French curve.

kumogire (雲切), *n.* a break [rift] in the clouds.

kumoma (雲間), *n.* a space between the clouds. —雲間の月, the moon peering through the clouds.

kumon (苦悶), *n.* agony; anguish. —苦悶さす, to agonize. —苦悶する, to be in agony [anguish]; writhe with pain; struggle.

kumonaku (苦もなく), *ad.* easily; readily; without difficulty.

kumonomine (雲峯), *n.* a group of cloudy columns [layers]; a bank of cloud.

kumonoue (雲上), *n.* (禁中) the Imperial court (palace). ¶ 雲の上人, a court-noble.

kumoraseru (曇らせる), *vt.* to cloud; overcast (空を); dim (鏡等を); tarnish (光る物を); darken; render gloomy

kumori (曇), *n.* cloudy weather (曇天); cloudiness; dimness; tarnish (光り物の); cloud (顏・心の). —曇なき心, a clear conscience.

kumoru (曇る), *vi.* ❶ (空が) to become cloudy; overcast. ❷ to (grow) dim (硝子・鏡等); tarnish (刀等); be smoked (火屋等).

kumosuke (雲助), *n.* a palanquin-bearer; a coolie.

kumotsu (供物), *n.* an offering; a sacrifice; an oblation.

kumoyuki (雲行), *n.* ❶ the course of clouds. ❷ (形勢) the course [trend] of events.

kumu (汲・酌む), *vt.* ❶ to draw; ladle (柄杓で); scoop (up). ❷ (酌量する) to consider; sympathize *with.* ❸ (會飲する) to drink together. —情を酌む, to consider the circumstances.

kumu (組む), *vt.* ❶ to unite *with*; cooperate *with*; associate *with.* ❷ (取組む) to grapple; seize. ❸ (編む) to knit; plait; braid. ❹

(交叉する) to fold (腕を); cross; pile (銃を). ● (組立てる) to frame; construct. ● (活字を) to set in type; compose. —膝を組む, to cross the legs.

kun (君), *n.* Mister (略して Mr.).

kun (訓), *n.* ❶ (訓戒) a precept; a lesson. ● (訓讀) metaphrase of Chinese characters into Japanese.

kun (勳), *n.* ❶ (いさを) merit; desert. ● (勳等) class (of an order). ¶ 勳一等瑞寶章, the First Class of the Order of the Sacred Treasure.

kū-na (空な), *a.* vacant; empty.

kunai (宮內), *n.* the Imperial [Royal] Household. ¶ 宮內大臣, the Minister of the Imperial Household Department. —宮內官, an official of the Imperial Household. —宮內省, the (Imperial) Household Department.

kunan (苦難), *n.* suffering; hardships; tribulation. —苦難より救ふ, to relieve a person from hardship.

kunbokushi (君牧師), *n.* a cardinal.

kunden (訓電), *n.* telegraphic instructions. —訓電を仰ぐ, to ask for telegraphic instructions.

kundō (訓導), *n.* (小學校の) a teacher of an elementary school.

kundoku (訓讀する), *v.* to metaphrase [render] Chinese characters into Japanese.

kunekune (曲曲), *ad.* ❶ zigzag; windingly. ● (性惡) ill-naturedly.

kuṅen (薰煙), *n.* smoke.

kunenbo (九年母, 香橙), *n.* 【植】 the common [sweet] orange-tree; the (bergamot) orange.

kuneru (紆る), *vi.* to wind; meander; be bent [crooked]. —紆ッた, crooked; distorted.

kuni (國), *n.* ❶ (國家) a state; a country. ● (國土) realm; territory; domain. ● (州) a province. ● (故鄉) the native country [province]; the home; the fatherland. —國の光, the honour of a country; national glory. —國の者, a man from one's native province. —國の爲に, for (the sake of) one's country. —國を賣る, to betray [sell] one's country.

kuṅi (勳位), *n.* ❶ class of order and court rank. ● (勳功によッて賜る位) court rank conferred for meritorious service. ● (勳等) class of an order.

kunigara (國柄), *n.* the character of a country; nationality.

kunijiman (國自慢), *n.* spread-eagleism; national vanity. —お國自慢をする, to take pride in [be proud of] one's country.

kunikotoba (國言葉), *n.* ❶ (國語) a language; the mother tongue; the vernacular. ● (方言) a dialect; provincialism.

kuniku (苦肉の計), *n.* a plan to deceive others by self-suffering.

kunimoto (國許), *n.* one's native province [place]; home.

kuninamari (國訛), *n.* provincialism; brogue (訛); provincial accent.

kunizakai (國境), *n.* the frontier; the boundary of a country.

kunji (訓示), *n.* instructions; directions. —訓示する, to instruct; issue [give] instructions.

kunjō (薰蒸), *n.* fumigation. —薰蒸する, to fumigate. ¶ 薰蒸消毒器, a fumigator.

kunkai (訓戒), *n.* warning; admonition. ☞ ***imashime.*** —訓戒する, to warn; admonish.

kunkō (勳功), *n.* exploits; distinguished service; meritorious deeds. —勳功を樹てる, to win one's spurs; perform meritorious deeds.

kunmei (君命), *n.* an Imperial command; the command [order] of one's lord. —君命を辱めぬ, not to neglect to carry out one's lord's orders.

kunmō (訓蒙), *n.* instruction of the ignorant; enlightenment.

kunniku (燻肉), *n.* smoked meat.

kunō (苦惱), *n.* ❶ (苦悶) suffering; agony; throes. ● =***hanmon*** (煩悶).

kuṅon (君恩), *n.* Imperial [Royal] benevolence; the favours of the Emperor [King].

kunpū (薰風), *n.* ❶ (軟風) a soft [gentle] breeze. ● (南風) a southerly wind. ● (夏の風) a summer breeze.

kunrei (訓令), *n.* instructions; orders; directions. —訓令する, to instruct; order; direct. —訓令を發する, to issue [give] instructions.

kunren (訓練), *n.* training; drill. —訓練する, to train; drill (人・小兒・動物を). —訓練の足らぬ, insufficiently trained.

kunrin (君臨する), *v.* to reign *over*; rule (*over*).

kunsei (燻製), *n.* bloating; smoking. —燻製の鯡, a bloater; a bloat [bloated; smoked] herring. —燻製にする, to bloat (鯡などを); smoke-dry.

kunshi (君子), *n.* the superior man; a perfect [true] gentleman; a man of character.

kunshin (君臣), *n.* master and servant; sovereign and subject. —

君臣の義, true relations of master and servant.

kunshō (勳章), *n.* an order; a decoration. —勳章を褫奪する, to deprive a person of his decoration(s). —勳章を胸にかける, to fasten a decoration on one's breast.

kunshu (君主), *n.* a sovereign; a ruler; a monarch. ¶ 君主國, a monarchy. —君主政體, monarchy.

kunshu (葷酒), *n.* garlic and wine. —葷酒山門に入るを許さず, It is forbidden to bring garlic and wine within the temple-gate.

kunten (訓點), *n.* marks used in rendering Chinese sentences into Japanese.

kuntō (薰陶), *n.* discipline; training; education. —薰陶する, to discipline; train up; educate. —薰陶を受ける, to be educated; be trained.

kunugi(櫟), *n.* 【植】the Japanese silk-worm oak.

kunwa (訓話), *n.* a moral tale.

kuṅyu (訓諭), *n.* admonition; injunction; instruction.

kun-zuru (薰ずる), *vi.* to send forth fragrance; be fragrant.

kuōruni (加ふるに), *ad.* besides; moreover; in addition.

kuppuku (屈服, 屈伏), *n.* submission; surrender. —屈服さす, to subjugate; humiliate; force into submission. —屈服する, to submit; surrender; yield.

kūpon (クーポン), *n.* a coupon (利札, 切取註文用紙).

kura (倉, 庫, 藏), *n.* a storehouse; a warehouse; a godown (東洋英語); a granary (穀倉).

kura (鞍), *n.* a saddle. —鞍を置く, to saddle; put [load] a saddle. —馬を一鞍責める, to have a ride on a horse.

-kura (競), a match; a race. ¶ 駈け競, a (running) race. —食ひ競, an eating match.

kuraban (倉番), *n.* a warehouse-keeper; a godown watchman.

kurabarai (藏拂), *n.* clearing of a godown; clearance. —藏拂ひ大賣出し, clearance [clearing] sale; selling-off sale.

kurabemono (比物), *n.* comparison. —比べ物にならぬ, not to be compared *with*; not to be able to hold a candle (*to*).

kuraberu(比べる), *vt.* ❶ (比較する) to compare *with*; set *against*. ❷ (なぞらへる) to compare *to*; liken *to*. ❸ (角する) to compete; match; measure. —...に比べれば; 比べて, in comparison *with*; compared *with*. —腕を比べる, to match oneself in ability against another.

kurabu (クラブ), *n.* (骨牌) clubs.

kurabu (倶樂部), *n.* ❶ (團體) a club. ❷ (集合所) a club-house; a club-room. ¶ 富士登山倶樂部, the Fuji Club. —倶樂部員, a member of a club; a club-member; a club-man.

kuradashi (庫出), *n.* taking out of a godown [warehouse]; delivery.

kuragari (暗がりに), *ad.* in the dark [darkness].

kurage (水母), *n.* 【腔腸】the medusa; the jelly-fish.

kurai (位), *n.* ❶ (王位) the throne. ❷ (位置) station; position. ❸ (位階, 階級) grade; rank; order. ❹ (品位) dignity. ❺【數】a place. —位に卽く, to accede to [ascend; mount] the throne; be crowned. —位人臣を極む, to reach the highest rank open to a subject.

kurai (位), *particle.* ❶ (疑問の場合) how much (many; long; far, *etc.*). ❷ (約) about; some; ...or so. ❸ (程度, 比較) insomuch that; so ... that; so ... as; so; like; as. —私位因果の者はない, There is no one so unfortunate as I. —恥を搔く位ならいッそ死ぬ, I would sooner die than disgrace myself.

kurai (暗い), *a.* ❶ (暗黑な) dark; dim; dusky. ❷ (に暗い) ignorant *of*; blind *to*. ❸ (後暗い) shady; underhand. —世事に暗い人, a person ignorant of the world. —不氣味(ぶ)な暗い晩, an uncanny dark night.

kūrai (空雷), *n.* (空中魚雷) an air-bomb; an aerial torpedo.

kuraidori (位取), *n.* a place; putting in a place.

kuraimake (位負けする), *v.* to be unable to live up to one's position.

kuraire (庫入), *n.* storage. —庫入れする, to store; warehouse. ¶ 庫入申告書, warehousing entry.

kuraisuru (位する), *vi.* to lie; stand; be situated *in* (*on*).

kuraku (苦樂), *n.* pleasure and pain. —苦樂を倶にする, to share the pleasures and pains. —苦樂を意に介しない, to be indifferent to pleasure and pain.

kuraku (暗くなる), *v.* to darken; grow dark. —暗くならぬ內に, before dark. —暗くなッてから, after dark. —暗くする, to darken; blacken; shade; obscure. (ランプを暗くする, to turn down the light.)

kurakura (くらくら), *ad.* ❶ (沸騰するさま) seethingly; bubblingly. ❷ =*guragura*. —くらくら煮え立つ, ① [*v.*] to seethe; bubble; boil up. ② [*a.*] seething; bubbling.

kuramasu (くらます), *vt.* ❶ (不明にする) to obscure; cover ❷ (眩) to daze; dazzle; blind. ❸ (欺く) to deceive; impose *upon*; hoodwink. —踪跡を晦ます, to conceal oneself; cover one's traces.

kuramu (くらむ), *vi.* ❶ (暗くなる) to grow dark. ❷ (眩) to be dizzy [giddy]; be dazzled. ❸ (迷はさる) to be blinded (*by*); be dazzled (*by*). —慾に心が眩む, to be blinded by avarice.

kurani (倉荷), *n.* warehoused goods. ¶ 倉荷證券, a (warehouse) warrant; a warehouse certificate.

kuranokami (内藏頭), *n.* the Director of the Bureau of Imperial Treasury.

kurarionetto (クラリオネット), *n.* a clarionette.

kurashi (暮し), *n.* livelihood; living; subsistence. ☞ *seikei*. —身分相當(不相當)の暮し, living within (beyond) one's means. —暮しを立てる, to make the pot boil; get one's living. (暮しを立てて行く, to keep the pot boiling.).

kurashiki (倉敷-料), *n.* storage; warehouse rent.

kurashita (鞍下), *n.* the part of the body under the saddle; sirloin.

kurashikku (古典), *n.* the classics.

kurasu (暮す), *v.* ❶ (月日を送る) to pass time; spend time. ❷ (生活する) to lead a life; live; subsist; get on [along]. —睦じく暮す, to live on good terms. —質素に暮す, to live in a small way. —負債をせずに暮す, to pay one's way; keep one's head above the water. ☞ *kuu*.

kurau (食ふ), *vt.* to eat; devour.

kurawasu (食はす), *vt.* ❶ (くはす) to feed *with*; give food *to*. ❷ (打つ) to strike; thrash; lick [卑]. ❸ (誘惑) to work *upon*. —啗はすに利を以てす, to work upon a man with prospects of profit.

kurawatashi (倉渡), *n.* 【商】 ex warehouse [store].

kurayami (暗闇), *n.* dark; darkness. —暗闇の恥を明るみへ持出すな, "Don't wash your dirty clothes in public."

kurazure (鞍擦), *n.* saddle-gall [sore].

kure (暮), *n.* ❶ (日暮) sunset; dusk; twilight. ❷ (末) the close; the end. ❸ (歲末) the end of a year. —秋(春)の暮に, at the close [end] of autumn (spring). —暮の大賣出し, a great year-end sale.

kuregure (呉呉も), *ad.* repeatedly; again and again; earnestly.

kurenai (紅), *n.* red; deep red (深紅); crimson (同上); scarlet (緋).

kureosōto (クレオソート), *n.* 【化】 creosote.

kureru (呉れる), *vt.* to give. —彼が頭を刈って呉れた, I had my hair cut by him. —さうして呉れるか, Will you please do so? —今日限り暇を呉れる, You (shall) leave my service to-day. —靴を出して呉れ, Please put out my boots.

kureru (暮れる), *vi.* ❶ (夜になる) to grow dark. ❷ (終る) to end; close. —暮れ果てる, to grow quite dark. —年が暮れる, The year closes [comes to an end]. —悲歎の涙に暮れる, to be overcome with bitter tears.

kurēyon (堊筆), *n.* a crayon. ¶ 堊筆挾み, a crayon-holder; a port-crayon. —堊筆畫, a crayon. (堊筆畫法, crayon-drawing. —堊筆畫紙, crayon-board.)

kuri (栗), *n.* 【植】 the chestnut-tree (樹); a chestnut (實); chestnut (栗材). —栗の毬, a chestnut-bur.

kuri (庫裏), *n.* the priests' quarters.

kūri (空理), *n.* doctrinairism, doctrinarianism; an abstract theory.

kūri (苦力), *n.* a coolie, cooly.

kuriageru (繰上げる), *vt.* ❶ to move up; turn up; carry forward. ❷ (豫定の時間・日などを) to make earlier. ❸ (撤退) to retire gradually. —順次繰上げになる, to go up in order.

kuriawase (繰合せ), *n.* arrangement; management. —繰り合はす, ① (時間を) to make [arrange] time. ② (仕事を) to adjust one's business. —繰合せをつける, to make arrangement. —萬障を繰合はす, to make every effort (*to*).

kuridasu (繰出す), *v.* ❶ (絲等を) to draw out; let out; veer away [out] (錨鎖を). ❷ (軍を) to march out; file out. ❸ (槍を) to thrust; let out. —軍隊を繰り出す, to call out troops.

kurigata (刳形), *n.* 【建】 mould; moulding.

kurige (栗毛), *n.* a chestnut horse.

kurigoto (繰言), *n.* tiresome story; repetition; complaint (愚痴). —老の繰言, an old man's (woman's) complaints.

kuriireru (繰入れる), *vt.* to transfer; carry forward; bring over.

kurikae (繰替), *n.* transfer; exchange; change. —繰替へる, to transfer; exchange; change.

kurikaesu (繰返す), *vt.* ❶ to repeat; reiterate; do (say) over. ❷ (製絲) to rereel; reel back. 長々と繰返して話す, to repeat [reiterate] at length.

kuriketto (クリケット), *n.* cricket. ¶ クリケット競技場, a cricket-ground.

kurikomu (繰込む), *vt.* ❶ (編入) to draft *into*; transfer *into*. ❷ (進入) to march in; file in.

kurikoshi (繰越), *n.* transfer. —繰越す, to carry over [forward]; bring over; transfer. —次葉へ繰越, carried forward. —前葉より繰越, brought down [forward; over]; carried down. ¶ 前期繰越金, balance brought forward from the last account.

kurikuri (くりくり), *ad.* ❶ (まろやかな貌) roundly. ❷ (廻轉する貌) round and round. —くりくり肥えた赤ん坊, a fat round baby. —頭をくりくりと剃る, to have one's head clean shaved.

kurimawashi (繰廻), *n.* contrivance; device; shift. —繰廻しをつける, to contrive; shift and contrive; make shift.

kurimono (刳物), *n.* a turnery. ¶ 刳物師, a turner.

kurīmu (クリーム), *n.* cream. —クリーム色の, cream-coloured.

kurinobe (繰延べ), *n.* postponement. —繰延べる, to postpone; put off; defer.

kurinuku (刳抜く), *vt.* to hollow out; excavate; scoop.

kurisageru (繰下げる), *vt.* to carry down; take down; move down.

kurisuchan (基督教信者), *n.* a Christian.

kurisumasu (クリスマス), *n.* Christmas; Noël 【佛】. —クリスマスの贈物, a Christmas present. —クリスマスの前夜, Christmas eve.

kuriya (廚), *n.* a kitchen.

kuro (畔), *n.* =***aze*** の ❶.

kuro (黒), *n.* black; blackness.

kurō (苦勞), *n.* ❶ (心配) care; anxiety; worry. ❷ (難儀) trouble; hardship; trial. ❸ (骨折) labour; toil. —苦勞する, ① to be anxious; worry (oneself). ② to be troubled; suffer hardships; have a hard time of it. ③ to work [labour] hard; struggle with difficulties. —苦勞性の人, one given to worries. —苦勞した事のある人, a man who has suffered hardships. —苦勞を忘れる, to forget one's troubles.

kuroaza (黒痣), *n.* a black macula.

kurobo (黒穗病, 麥奴), *n.* smut; burnt ear; maize-smut (玉蜀黍の).

kuroboshi (黒星), *n.* a black spot [dot].

kurochi (黒血), *n.* dark blood.

kurochiku (紫竹), *n.* 【植】 the wanghee [whanghee]-cane.

kurodai (黒鯛), *n.* 【魚】 the gilt-head.

kurogaki (黒柿), *n.* 【植】 the persimmon heartwood.

kuroguro (黒黒と), *ad.* intensely black; in deep black. —墨黒々と書く, to write down in deep black.

kuroi (黒い), *a.* black.

kuroichigo (黒苺), *n.* 【植】 the thimble-berry; the black American raspberry.

kuroishi (黒石), *n.* ❶ (黒き岩石) a black stone. ❷ (圍碁) black checkers.

kurōke (クローケ), *n.* 【遊戲】 croquet.

kurokemuri (黒煙), *n.* black smoke. —黒煙を吐く, to puff out [emit] black smoke.

kurokoge (黒焦の), *a.* charred. —黒焦げになる, to be charred; be burnt black.

kuroku (黒く), *ad.* black; in black. —黒く塗る, to paint black. —黒くなる, to get [turn; become] black; blacken. —黒くする, to blacken; make black.

kurokumo (黒雲), *n.* a dark [black] cloud.

kuromaku (黒幕), *n.* ❶ a black curtain. ❷ (黒幕策士) a wire-puller. —黒幕となる, to pull the wires [strings]; be behind the scenes.

kuromame (黒豆), *n.* 【植】 a black soy-bean.

kurome (黒目), *n.* the pupil (of the eye).

kuromeru (黒める), *vt.* ❶ to blacken. ❷ (巧に欺く) =***iikurumeru***.

kuromi (黒味), *n.* a black tinge. —黒味勝ちの青色, blue tinged with black. —黒味を帶びる, to be tinged with black; be black-tinted.

kuromoji (黒文字), *n.* ❶ 【植】 (鉤樟) Lindera hypoglauca (wild-allspice の類・學名). ❷ (小楊子) a tooth-pick.

kurōmu (クローム), *n.* chromium; chrome.

kūron (空論), *n.* a futile [an academic] argument; visionary [impracticable] views. —空論を吐く, to state [advance] visionary views. ¶ 空論家, a doctrinaire.

kuronbo (黒奴), *n.* ❶ a negro [*fem.* negress]; a blackamoor; a black. ❷ = ***kurobo***. ❸ 【劇】 a prompter.

kuronuri (黒塗の), *a.* black-varnished; black-lacquered.

kuropan (黒麵麭), *n.* brown [black] bread.

kuroppoi (黒っぽい), *a.* blackish.

kurorasha (黒羅紗), *n.* black (woolen) cloth.

kuroshio (黒潮), *n.* the Black [Japan] Stream [Current]; the Japanese Gulf Stream; the *Kuroshiwo*.

kuroshōzoku (黒装束), *n.* a black dress. —黒装束の, dressed in black.

kurōsu (クロース), *n.* the book-binder's cloth; cloth. —クロース綴の, bound in cloth. ¶クロース表紙, cloth boards.

kurosurēto (クロスレート), *n.* cross rate.

kurosuwādo (クロスワード), *n.* a cross-word puzzle.

kurotegumi (黒手組), *n.* the Black Hands; the Black Hand Association.

kurōto (黒人), *n.* (堪能者) an expert; an adept; a professional (專門家); a (professional) speculator (相場師). ¶黒人の目, a trained eye; an expert eye.

kurowaku (黒枠), *n.* mourning-borders. ¶黒枠附廣告, an advertisement with mourning-borders; a black-edged advertisement; a notice of a death (in a newspaper).

kuroyaki (黒燒), *n.* anything burnt black [to cinders]. —蠑螈の黒燒, a charred newt. —黒燒にする, to char.

kuroyama (黒山), *n.* a black mountain. —黒山の様な人集(だか)り, a dense [closely-packed] crowd.

kurozatō (黒砂糖), *n.* brown sugar.

kurozuishō (黒水晶), *n.* morion.

kurozunda (黒ずんだ), *a.* umber; darkish; dull.

kuru (来る), *vi.* to come. ❶ (来る) (*a*) to arrive *at* [*in*] (到着): (*b*) (手紙が) to come to hand: (*c*) (風雨が) to come on: (*d*) (季節などが) to set in. ❷ (訪問) to visit [*vt.*]; call (on one; at one's house). ❸ (なって来る) to become; get; grow. —来る筈, is to come; be due. —取りに来る; 連れに来る, to come *for*; come to fetch. —聞いて来る, to go and ask. —進んで来る, to come on [forward; forth]. —日本へ来る途中, en route [on one's way] to Japan. —へ往って來た, (I) have been *to*. —汽車(船)が來た, The train (boat) is in. —よし來た, 始めよう, All right! We'll set to. —よく來て與れたね, So good of you to come. —玄關へ誰か來てゐる, Someone is at the door.

kuru (刳る), *vt.* to bore; scoop out; hollow out. —穴を刳る, to bore a hole.

kuru (繰る), *vt.* ❶ (捲く, 紡ぐ) to reel; wind; spin (紡ぐ). ❷ (檢索) to look up; consult; go over (ざっと). —帳面を繰る, to go over one's account-books. —頁を(一枚一枚)繰る, to turn over the pages one after another.

kurubushi (踝), *n.* 【解】 the ankle; the ankle-bone (踝骨).

kurubyō (佝僂病), *n.* 【醫】 rachitis; rickets.

kurui (狂), *n.* ❶ (氣が狂ふ) madness; insanity; derangement. ❷ (順序・位置の變化) disorder; disarrangement; dislocation. ❸ (歪) crookedness; warp.

kurukuru (くるくる), *ad.* round and round. —くるくる廻る, to turn round and round. —山がくるくる廻るやうに見える, The mountains reel before our eyes.

kuruma (車), *n.* ❶ (總稱) a vehicle; a carriage; a car. ❷ (荷車) a cart (二輪車); a wagon (四輪車); a van (大八車). ❸ (俥, 人力車) a *jinrikisha*; a rick-shaw. ❹ (一輪の手車) a barrow; a wheel-barrow. ❺ (車輪) a wheel. —車で運ぶ, to carry in a cart. —車に乗って行く, to go in a carriage [by *jinrikisha*]. —車を降りる, to alight from [get off; get out of] a *jinrikisha*.

kurumachin (車賃), *n.* fare; hire; carriage.

kurumadome (車止), *n.* ❶ (車の通行禁止) "No thoroughfare for vehicles." ❷ (停車場の) a buffer-stop.

kurumaebi (車蝦), *n.* 【甲殼】 the prawn.

kurumahiki (車挽), *n.* ❶ (人力車夫) a *jinrikisha*-puller [-man]. ❷ (荷車挽) a cart-drawer; a carter.

kurumaido (車井戸), *n.* a wheel-well.

kurumaru (包まる), *vi.* to be wrapped [tucked] up *in*.

kurumaya (車屋), *n.* ❶ (製造人) a cartwright; a wheelwright. ❷ =***kurumahiki*** の❶.

kurumayose (車寄), *n.* a drive; a carriage porch [entrance].

kurumaza (車座になる), to sit in a circle.

kurumeru (包める), *vt.* ❶ (概括する) to sum up; summarize (總括). ❷ (籠絡する) to entice; cajole. —(引っ)包めて言へば, to sum up; in a few words; in short. —七頁より十六頁まで包めて, pages 7 to 16 inclusive.

kurumi (胡桃), *n.* the walnut.

kurumu (包む), *vt.* to wrap up *in*; tuck up *in*; lap up.

kuruppu (クルップ砲), *n.* a Krupp gun.

kururito (くるりと), *ad.* around. —くるりと廻る, to turn (around); turn on one's heels.

kururu (樞), *n.* a hinge.

kurushii (苦しい), *a.* ❶ (苦痛) painful; distressing; trying (思など). ❷ (困難) hard; difficult. ❸ (困窮) narrow; straitened. ❹ (窮した) far-fetched; forced; awkward. —苦しい經驗, a bitter [painful] experience. —苦しい息, short breath; panting breath (喘ぐ). —苦しい洒落(言譯), a far-fetched pun (excuse). —苦しい立場, an awkward position (進退に窮する).

kurushimagire (苦し紛れに), *ad.* goaded by pain; driven by desperation.

kurushimasu (苦ます), *vt.* Ⓢ 苦める. ❶ (困らす) to worry; harass; embarrass. ❷ (苛責) to torture; torment. ❸ (苦惱) to inflict pain *on*; distress; mortify. ❹ (虐待) to tease; torture; persecute (迫害). —心を苦める, to cudgel [rack] one's brains.

kurushimi (苦), *n.* ❶ (苦痛) pain; pang (劇痛). ❷ (難儀) hardships; distress; suffering. ❸ (苦悶) agony; anguish; torment. ❹ (苦心) hard [intense] application. —一生の苦み, lifelong pain; torture for life.

kurushimu (苦む), *vi.* ❶ (苦痛) to feel pain; suffer; be afflicted. ❷ (困難) to be troubled; be perplexed [embarrassed]; be at a loss. ❸ (苦悶) to be tortured; be tormented. —渴に苦む, to be distressed by thirst. —病に苦む, to suffer from [be afflicted by] illness. —處分に苦む, to be at a loss how to deal with it. —解決に苦む, to be puzzled for solution.

kuruu (狂ふ), *vi.* ❶ (狂氣) to go [run; become] mad [crazy]; become insane; lose one's head. ❷ (狂亂) to rave; behave wildly; run riot (亂暴する). ❸ (跳ね廻る) to romp about; caper. ❹ (調子を失ふ) to get out of order; fall into disorder; go wrong. ❺ (歪む) to crook; bend; warp. —狙ひが狂ふ, to miss one's aim. —豫算が狂ふ, to expend beyond one's estimate. —(機械が)狂って居る, to be out of order [gear]; be out of working order. —時計が狂った, The clock has gone wrong.

kuruwa (郭), *n.* (城郭) an inclosure, enclosure; a quarter.

kuruwasu (狂はす), *vt.* ❶ (氣を) to make [drive] (one) mad; derange (one's mind). ❷ (機械等を) to put out of order; derange; dislocate (位置を). ❸ (手順を) to disarrange; disturb; upset. ❹ (裏をかく) to frustrate; thwart; discomfit. ❺ (相場等を) to affect. —豫定を狂はせる, to upset the arrangement.

kusa (草), *n.* grass; a weed (雜草). —草の葉, a blade of grass; leaves of the grass. —草の風に靡くが如し, to bend like grass before the wind. —草を食ふ, to graze; pasture. —庭の草を取る, to weed a garden.

kusa (濕疹), *n.* 【醫】eczema.

kusaba (草葉の蔭で), under the sod; in one's grave.

kusabana (草花), *n.* a flower; a flowering-plant.

kusabi (轄, 楔), *n.* a wedge; a cleat; a linchpin (車輪の).

kusabōki (草箒), *n.* a broom; a besom.

kusabue (草笛), *n.* a leaf-whistle; a reed.

kusabukai (草深い), *a.* ❶ grassy; grass-worn; overgrown with grass. ❷ (僻遠の) out-of-the-way; remote. —草深い片田舍, an out-of-the-way village.

kusabuki (草葺の), *a.* (straw-) thatched. ¶ 草葺屋根, a straw-thatched roof.

kusagiru (耘る), *v.* to weed; mow.

kusai (臭い), *a.* ❶ (臭氣) stinking; fetid; rank. ❷ (怪しい) suspicious. ❸ (臭味ある) smelling *of*; savouring *of*; smacking *of*. —耶蘇臭い, to smack of Christianity. —學者臭い, to be pedantic [professorial].

kusaibansho (區裁判所), *n.* a district court (若し地方裁判所を a district court と譯した場合には 區裁判所は a sub-district court と譯するを可とす).

kusaichi (草市), *n.* a grass-market (for the Feast of Lanterns).

kusaichigo (くさいちご), *n.* 【植】Rubus Thunbergii (bramble の一種・學名).

kusairo (草色), *n.* dark green.

kusakagerō (草蜉蝣), *n.* the lace-wing fly.

kusakaki (草搔), *n.* ❶ (器) a rake; a hoe. ❷ (人) a weeder; a mower.

kusakari (草刈), *n.* ❶ (事) mowing. ❷ (人) a mower. ❸ (草刈機) a mower; a mowing-machine; a lawn-mower. ¶ 草刈鎌, a sickle.

kusaki (草木), *n.* plants. —草木の無い(不毛の), bare of vegetation; barren.

kusakusa (くさくさする), *vi.* (氣が) to feel wretched [depressed; oppressed; worried].

kusame, kusami, (嚏), *n.* a sneeze; sneezing. —嚏をする, to sneeze.

kusami (臭味), *n.* stink; offensive smell [odour].

kusamura (叢), *n.* a bush; a thicket; a cover (鳥獸のゐる).

kusarasu (腐らす), *v.* ❶ (腐敗) to corrupt; spoil (害ふ); putrefy (腐爛). ❷ (腐朽) to allow to decay [rot]; decompose.

kusareen (腐緣), *n.* an evil affinity.

kusareta (腐れた), *a.* ❶ (腐敗) corrupted; spoiled; putrid. ❷ (腐朽) rotten; decayed; decomposed. ¶ 腐れ卵, an addle [bad] egg.

kusari (腐), *n.* corruption; rotting. ☞ *fuhai.* —腐りがつく, to begin to rot.

kusari (鎖, 鏈), *n.* a chain; a guard; a tether (犬などの). —鎖で繫ぐ, to enchain; chain up (犬などを); put in chains (囚徒などを). —鏈を外す, to unchain; unlink.

kusarikatabira (鏈帷子), *n.* a chain-armour; a (coat of) mail.

kusaru (腐る), *vi.* ❶ (腐敗) to rot; putrefy; become stale (魚が). ❷ (腐朽) to decay; become rotten; decompose. —腐ッた, rotten; putrid; stale (魚の). ☞ *kusareta.* —腐り易い, perishable. —心(しん)まで腐ッてる, to be rotten to the heart [core]. —腐ッても鯛, "An old eagle is better than a young sparrow."

kusasu (腐・貶す), *vt.* to disparage; decry; cry down; run down; depreciate.

kusatori (草取), *n.* ❶ (事) weeding. ❷ (器具) a weeding-fork; a weeder.

kusawake (草分), *n.* a pioneer.

kusawara (草原), *n.* a place overgrown with weeds.

kusazōshi (草雙紙), *n.* an illustrated story-book.

kusazumi (草堆), *n.* a haystack.

kuse (癖), *n.* ❶ (習慣) a habit; a way; a trick. ❷ (特色, 特性) a characteristic; a peculiarity. ❸ (性癖) a propensity; a predilection; a bias. —癖がつく, to fall [get] into the [a] habit (*of*). —…の癖がある, to have the habit (*of*). —癖をつける, to form a habit; make a thing habitual. —髮の癖直しをする, to straighten out one's hair. ——**-ni,** *conj.* though; when; and yet. —子供の癖に, though he is a child; child as he is. —女の癖に, though she is a woman.

kusei (區制), *n.* (電車等の) distance system.

kūseki (空席), *n.* a vacant seat (席); room (場所); a vacancy (地位の等).

kusemono (曲者), *n.* ❶ (姦物) a ruffian; a villain; a rascal. ❷ (盜賊) a robber; a thief. ❸ (嫌疑者) a suspect; a suspicious person [character]. ❹ (氣の許せぬ者) a treacherous person. —手におへぬ曲者, an ugly customer; a rascal hard to deal with.

kusen (苦戰), *n.* a hard fight; a desperate battle. —苦戰する, to fight hard [desperately].

kusetsu (苦節), *n.* unswerving loyalty. —苦節を守る, to be loyal to the cause to the end; uphold the cause faithfully.

kushakusha (くしゃくしゃにする), *vt.* to crumple; rumple. —くしゃくしゃの, crumpled.

kushi (串), *n.* a skewer; a spit. —串にさす, to spit; skewer.

kushi (櫛), *n.* a comb. —櫛を插す, to stick a comb in one's hair. —櫛で髮を梳く, to comb [dress] the hair.

kushi (驅使する), *vt.* to order about; drive hard. —文字を自由自在に驅使する, to have a good command of words.

kushigaki (串柿), *n.* persimmons dried on skewers.

kushikezuru (梳る), *vt.* to comb (髮を); scribble (羊毛・綿を); dress (髮を). —風に梳る, to be swayed by the wind.

kushin (苦心), *n.* ❶ (苦勞) anxiety; care. ❷ (努力) hard toil; painstaking; labour; trouble. —苦心する, to labour; tax one's ingenuity [energy]; rack [beat] one's brains; make great efforts. ¶ 苦心談, tales of bitter experiences. —苦心慘憺, hard toil and application.

kushō (苦笑), *n.* a sardonic smile; a bitter smile. —(微)苦笑する, to smile bitterly [sardonically]; smile a bitter smile.

kūsho (空所), *n.* blank (space); vacancy; a gap (間隙).

kūshoku (空職), *n.* a vacancy; a vacant post; an unoccupied position.

kuso (糞), *n.* dung; fæces. ——, *int.* Hang it!; Damn it! —糞味噌にけなす, to pull a person to pieces; run him down mercilessly. —糞の役にも立たぬ, to be good for nothing; be of no use. —糞喰へ, Go and be hanged! —えー糞ッ, Damn it!; Hang it!

kūsō (空想), *n.* a fancy; a vision; a day-dream. —空想的, fanciful; dream-like; visionary; imaginary; Utopian. —空想に耽る, ① to be given [addicted] to day-dreams

[-dreaming]. ② [*a.*] visionary; dreamy. —空想を描く, to build castle in the air; make a visionary plan. ¶ 空想家, a fancier; a day-dreamer; a visionary.

kūsōba (空相場), *n.* speculation; a time-bargain; fictitious transaction.

kusobae (糞蠅), *n.* the dung-fly.

kusobenkyō (糞勉强), *n.* diligent [hard] study; swot. —糞勉强する, to swot; grind; dig [米·俗].

kusoochitsuki (糞落著に落著く), to remain cool as a cucumber.

kussaku (掘鑿), *n.* digging; excavation. —掘鑿する, to dig out; excavate. ¶ 掘鑿器, a digger; an excavator.

kussetsu (屈折), *n.* refraction (光線の); 【文】 inflexion. —屈折自在の, refrangible; flexible; pliant. —屈折する, ① [*v.*] to refract; bend. ② [*a.*] refractive; refracting; refrangible; 【文】 inflective. ¶ 屈折望遠鏡, a refracting telescope. —屈折光, refracted light. —屈折能[力], refractive power. (屈折力ある, refractive.) —屈折レンズ, a refractor.

kusshi (屈指の), *a.* preeminent; prominent; leading. —屈指の資產家, a prominent man of wealth. —屈指する, to enumerate; reckon on fingers.

kusshin (屈身する), *vi.* to stoop; [bend the body.]

kusshin (屈伸), *n.* extension and contraction. —屈伸自在の, elastic; flexible. —屈伸する, to extend and contract; be elastic.

kus-suru (屈する), *vi.* ❶ (曲る) to bend. ❷ (衰ふ, 詰まる) to give way; be depressed (in spirits) (氣が). ❸ (屈服する) to bend *to*; yield [submit] *to*; give in *to*. ❹ (沮喪する) to be disheartened; be daunted; lose heart. ——, *vt.* ❶ (曲げる) to bend. ❷ (屈服さす, 挫く) to make submit; bring under; bring down. —力屈する, One's strength fails one. —人に屈する, to yield [submit] to another. —指を屈するに遑あらず, to be countless [innumerable]; be too numerous to count.

kusuberu (燻べる), *vt.* to fumigate; smoke; cure (燻製). —硫黄で燻べる, to fumigate with sulphur.

kusuburu (燻る), *vi.* ❶ (いぶる) to smoke; be smoky; smoulder. ❷ (屏居する) to shut oneself in; remain indoors. ❸ (失意の境遇にゐる) to live in obscurity. —田舍に燻ッて居る, to rust in the country.

kusuguru (擽る), *vt.* to tickle. [=*kosoguru*.]

kusuguttai (擽ッたい), *a.* ticklish; comic; funny. —あゝ擽ッたい, Oh, you tickle me.

kusukusu (くすくす), *ad.* titteringly. —くすくす笑ふ, to titter; giggle; chuckle.

kusumu (くすむ), *vi.* to become sober; become dull. —くすんだ色, a sombre [sober; dull] colour.

kusuneru (くすねる), *vt.* (竊取) to pocket; embezzle; steal.

kusunoki (樟, 楠), *n.* 【植】 the camphor-tree.

kusuri (藥), *n.* ❶ (藥品) a medicine; a drug (藥種); chemicals (化學藥). ❷ (釉藥) glaze; enamel. —藥一服, a dose of medicine. —藥を飲む, to take medicine. —陶器に藥をかける, to glaze earthenware.

kusuribin (藥甁), *n.* a phial, vial; a medicine-bottle.

kusuriya (藥屋), *n.* ❶ (調劑師) an apothecary; a chemist; a pharmacist. ❷ (藥種屋) a druggist: (店) a pharmacy; a chemist's; a drug-store.

kusuriyu (藥湯), *n.* a medicated [[medical] bath.]

kusuriyubi (藥指), *n.* (無名指) the ring-finger (特に左手の).

kutabaru (くたばる), *vi.* to kick the bucket; hop the twig.

kutabire (草臥), *n.* fatigue; weariness; exhaustion. —草臥が出る, The fatigue begins to tell. —草臥が拔ける, to recover from fatigue.

kutabireru (草臥れる), *vi.* ❶ (疲勞) to get tired; be fatigued; be wearied. ❷ (倦怠) to become tired *of*.

kuten (句點), *n.* punctuation [marks [points].]

kutō (句讀), *n.* punctuation; pause. —句讀を切る, [*vt.*] to punctuate; point.

kutsu (靴), *n.* shoes (短靴); boots (深靴). —靴を穿く (脫ぐ), to put on (take off) one's shoes. —靴を穿かす, to shoe; boot. ¶ 婦人靴, a lady's shoes (boots). —兵隊靴, military boots.

kutsū (苦痛), *n.* pain; suffering; agony; pang. —苦痛を與へる, to give pain *to*; torment; cause suffering *to*. —苦痛を感ずる, to suffer pain; feel pain. —苦痛を耐へる, to bear [endure] pain [agony]. —苦痛を和げる, to relieve [ease; soothe] pain.

kutsuarai (靴洗), *n.* a hydraulic [brush.]

kutsubake (靴刷毛), *n.* a shoe-brush; a blacking brush.

kutsubera (靴篦), *n.* a shoe-lift; a shoe-horn.

kutsugaeru (覆る), *vi.* ❶ (顚倒する) to overturn; upset; capsize

(船が). ❸ (滅びる) to fall; be overthrown.

kutsugaesu (覆す), *vt.* ❶ (逆に倒す) to upset; overturn; capsize. ❷ (滅し倒す) to overthrow; subvert. —彼の學說を根柢から覆す, to overturn his theory from the foundation.

kutsuhimo (靴紐), *n.* a boot-lace; a shoe-lace [-string; -tie].

kutsujoku (屈辱), *n.* humiliation; shame; disgrace. —屈辱的媾和, a humiliating peace. —屈辱を忍ぶ, to eat humble-pie; pocket an insult; put up with humiliation. —昔日の屈辱を雪ぐ, to clear oneself of one's former disgrace.

kutsujū (屈從), *n.* humiliation; humbleness; submission. —屈從さす, to bring (a person) to his knees; force into submission; humiliate. —屈從する, to surrender; submit; yield.

kutsuko (口籠), *n.* a muzzle.

kutsumigaki (靴磨), *n.* ❶ (事) shoeblacking; shoe-polishing; shoe-cleaning (艶出し). ❷ (器) a shoe-brush. ❸ (人) a shoeblack; boots (ホテルの); a bootblack.

kutsunaoshi (靴直し), *n.* a cobbler.

kutsunugi (沓脫), *n.* (靴脫器) a bootjack.

kutsunugui (靴拭), *n.* a door-mat (蓆); a (foot-)scraper (鐵製).

kutsurogu (寛ぐ), *vi.* to be at ease; make oneself at home. —打ち寛いで, at home; at ease.

kutsushita (靴下), *n.* socks (短い); stockings (長い); hoses (同上). —靴下一足, a pair of socks [stockings]. ¶靴下留, garters. —靴下吊り, suspenders.

kutsuwa (轡), *n.* a bit; a bridle (-bit); a gag-bit. —轡を竝べて, neck and neck.

kutsuwamushi (轡蟲), *n.* 【昆】 Mecopoda elongata (long-horned grasshopper の一種・學名).

kutsuya (靴屋), *n.* ❶ (靴匠) a shoemaker; a bootmaker. ❷ (店) a shoe-shop; a shoe-factor (問屋).

kutsuzoko (靴底), *n.* a sole; a clump(-sole) (厚きもの). —靴底を附け更へる, to resole.

kutsuzumi (靴墨), *n.* shoe-blacking; blacking; shoe-polish (液體); shoe-dressing (半液體).

kutsuzure (靴擦傷), *n.* a shoe-sore.

kuttaku (屈託), *n.* vexation; trouble; anxiety. —屈託する, to be vexed; be troubled [uneasy] *about*; be anxious *about*.

kuttekakaru (喰ってかかる), *v.* to defy; fall *upon*; go *for* 〘俗〙.

kuttsukeru (くっつける), *vt.* to join; unite; fix; set. —壁にくっつけて, close to the wall. —糊(膠)でくっつける, to paste (glue) together.

kuttsuku (くっつく), *vi.* ❶(附著する) to cleave *to*; stick *to*. ❷ (附隨する) to cling *to*; adhere *to*; follow [*vt.*]. —くっつき合って, close to each other. —僕にくっついてゐろ, Keep close to me.

kuu (食ふ), *v.* ❶ (たべる) to eat; take; feed upon. ❷ (生活する) to live; subsist. ❸ (侵す) to encroach *on*. ❹ (食ひつく) to bite. ❺ (かじる) to nibble; gnaw. ❻ (欺かれる) to be taken in; fall into (a trap). —食ひ盡す; 食って仕舞ふ, to eat up. —一杯食はされる, to be imposed upon; be taken in. —食ひすぎて病氣になる, to eat oneself sick. —食ふに困る人人を助ける, to relieve those who cannot support themselves. —その手は食はぬ, That trick won't do with me.

kuwa (桑), *n.* 【植】 the Indian mulberry; the mulberry-tree 〘俗〙.

kuwa (鍬), *n.* a hoe; a mattock. —鍬を入れる, to hoe; begin hoeing.

kuwadate (企), *n.* ❶ (目論見) a plan; a scheme; a plot (陰謀). ❷ (試み) an attempt; a try 〘俗〙. ❸ (企業) an undertaking; an enterprise.

kuwadateru (企てる), *v.* ❶ (目論む) to plan; scheme; contrive. ❷ (試みる) to attempt; make an attempt; try to; undertake; take in hand. —謀叛(暗殺)を企てる, to plot a rebellion (an assassination).

kuwaeru (加へる), *vt.* ❶ (足す, 增す) to add; augment; increase. ❷ (附加) to add; annex; append. ❸ (加算) to add up; run up; sum up. ❹ (加入, 算入) to add; include (算入する). ❺ (與へる) to give; deliver; inflict. —三に加へる四, to 3 add 4. —打擊を加へる, to deliver a blow. —速力を加へる, to increase speed; gain in velocity. —危害を加へる, to do bodily harm; inflict an injury *upon*.

kuwaeru (銜へる), *vt.* to hold [take] in the teeth [mouth]; hold between the teeth. —指を銜へて見てゐる, to look on with a finger in the mouth; look on longingly.

kuwai (慈姑), *n.* 【植】 (the common) arrowhead [arrow-leaf].

kuwake (區分), *n.* assortment; sorting; division. —區分けする, to assort; sort.

kuwasemono (食せ物), *n.* ❶ (物) a counterfeit; a fraud; a fake;

a take-in. ❷ (人) a hypocrite; a humbug; an impostor.

kuwaseru (食はせる), *vt.* ❶ (食物を與へる) to feed (an animal) *with* [*on*]. ❷ (欺く) to cheat; take in; sell. ❸ (養ふ) to support; provide *for*; feed.

kuwashii (委・詳・精しい), *a.* ❶ (詳細) detailed; minute; particular. ❷ (精通) well-informed *in*; well up *in*; familiar *with*. ❸ (精確) precise; exact; accurate. —詳しい話, a minute [detailed] account; a full and particular account.

kuwashiku (委・詳・精しく), *ad.* ❶ (詳細) minutely; in detail; at length. ❷ (精確) accurately; precisely. —精しく知る(話す), to know (speak; talk) like a book.

kuwatsumi (桑摘), *n.* ❶ (事) mulberry-picking. ❷ (人) a mulberry-picker.

kuwawaru (加はる), *vi.* ❶ (増加) to increase. ❷ (加入) to join; enter; take part [place] *in*. —年が加はる, to advance in years. —討議に加はる, to take part in a debate. —國際聯盟に加はる, to join the League of Nations.

kuyakusho (區役所), *n.* a ward [an urban district] office.

kuyami (悔), *n.* ❶ (後悔) regret; repentance; penitence. ❷ (弔) condolence. —悔を云ふ, to express (one's) condolence. ¶ 悔状, a letter of condolence.

kuyamu (悔む), *v.* ❶ (後悔する) to regret; repent; sorrow (*after*; *for*). ❷ (弔ふ) to lament; condole *with*, express sympathy.

kuyashii (口惜しい), *a.* sorrowful; mortifying; vexatious. —口惜しがる, to be mortified; be chagrined. —口惜しまぎれに, from mortification; from chagrin.

kuyō (供養), *n.* mass. —死者を供養する, to have mass said for the dead.

kuyokuyo (くよくよする), *vi.* to mope; brood *over*; feel melancholy.

kuyurasu (薫らす), *vt.* to smoke; fumigate; burn. —煙草を薫らす, to smoke tobacco.

kuyuru (悔ゆる), *vt.* ☞ **kuiru.**

kūzen (空前の), *a.* unprecedented; record-breaking; unheard-of. —空前絶後, the first and last.

kuzetsu (口說), *n.* ❶ a quarrel; a dispute. ❷ (男女間の) a lovers' (conjugal) quarrel. —口說の絶えない, with incessant quarrels.

kuzu (葛), *n.* ❶【植】Pueraria Thunbergiana (學名); the arrowroot [俗]. ❷ (葛粉) arrowroot powder.

kuzu (屑), *n.* ❶ (廢物) waste; refuse; scraps. ❷ (殘物) remnant; leavings; refuse. ❸ (がらくた) rubbish; trash. —人間の屑, a good-for-nothing; the dross of mankind; the dregs of population. ¶ 木屑, chips. —パン屑, a crumb.

kuzuhiroi (屑拾), *n.* a ragman; a rag-picker; a *chiffonier* [佛].

kuzuito (屑絲), *n.* waste silk.

kuzukago (屑籠), *n.* a waste-basket; a waste-paper basket.

kuzure (崩, 頽), *n.* ❶ breakdown; collapse. ❷ (暴落) a slump.

kuzureru (崩・頽れる), *vi.* ❶ (崩壞) to collapse; crumble; go [fall; break] to pieces. ❷ (形が) to go [get] out of shape; be disfigured (顔などが). ❸ (隊形など) to be thrown into confusion [disorder].

kuzusu (崩す), *vt.* ❶ (破壞する) to pull down; break [tear] down; destroy. ❷ (省略) to simplify. ❸ (兩替) to change; break. —崖(家)を崩す, to pull down the precipice (house). —百圓札を崩す, to change a hundred-*yen* note (into smaller notes). —身を持ち崩す, to lapse into dissipation; abandon oneself to dissipation.

kuzuya (屑屋), *n.* a ragman; a rag-merchant.

kuzuyu (葛湯), *n.* arrowroot gruel.

kyabetsu (甘藍), *n.*【植】the (garden) cabbage. ¶ キャベツ卷, cabbage roll.

kyabine (キャビネ), *n.* a cabinet. ¶ キャビネ型寫眞, a cabinet photograph [photo].

kyahan (脚絆), *n.* gaiters (ゲートル); leggings.

kyakka (却下する), *vt.* to dismiss; reject.

kyaku (客), *n.* a visitor; company (一人又は數人); a guest (賓客); a passenger (旅客); a customer (顧客). —客が減る[さびれる], Customers fall off. —客を好む, to welcome visitors; keep an open door [house]. —客を釣る, to arouse a customer's curiosity. —客を呼ぶ, to draw customers (audience).

kyakuashirai (客扱), *n.* ⑤ 客あつかひ. entertainment; reception; treatment (of guests). —客扱ひのよい, hospitable; affable; genial.

kyakuden (客殿), *n.* a reception-hall.

kyakudome (客止), *n.* turning away guests [customers; spectators].

kyakufu (脚夫), *n.* a postman; a letter-carrier; a courier.

kyakuhiki (客引), *n.* a tout; a barker (店先に居る).

kyakuhon (脚本), *n.* the book

of words; a play-book; (歌劇の) a libretto [*pl.* -ti].
kyakuma (客間), *n.* a drawing-room; a parlour [米]; a guest-chamber (旅館などの). —客間に通す, to usher [show] (a guest) into a drawing-room.
kyakurai (客來), *n.* having company. —客來で大變失禮致しました, As I had a visitor, I have kept you long waiting.
kyakuseki (客席), *n.* guests' seats; auditorium.
kyakusen (客船), *n.* a passenger-boat; a passenger-vessel [-ship].
kyakusha (客車), *n.* a passenger-car; a railway carriage; a coach.
kyakushoku (脚色), *n.* dramatization. —脚色する, to dramatize.
kyakuzashiki (客座敷), *n.* = *kyakuma.*
kyan (俠), *n.* a jade; a hussy; a hoyden.
kyandē (糖菓), *n.* candy.
kyankyan (きゃんきゃん鳴く), *vi.* to yelp; yap.
kyanon (キャノン), *n.* 【撞球】a cannon. —キャノンを突く, to cannon.
kyara (伽羅), *n.* 【植】the aloes-wood; the agila [eagle]-wood.
kyarako (キャラコ), *n.* calico.
kyarameru (キャラメル), *n.* caramel.
kyasha (花車·華奢な), *a.* delicate; slender; slim. —華奢な身體, a slim body; a slight build.
kyatatsu (脚立), *n.* a step; a foot-stool; a trestle.
kyatsu (彼奴), *n.* & *pron.* the fellow; he; she.
kyo (居), *n.* an abode; a residence; a dwelling.
kyo (虛), *n.* ❶ (空虛) emptiness; vacancy; vacuity. ❷ (弱點, 不用意) a weak point; a neglected side; unpreparedness. ❸ (虛言) a lie; a falsehood. —虛を衝く, to take another off his guard.
kyo (擧), *n.* ❶ (行動) action. ❷ (企圖) an undertaking; a project; a scheme. ☞ *kuwadate* (企).
kyō (凶), *n.* ❶ (不吉) ill-luck; evil; misfortune. ❷ (災難) a misfortune; a calamity.
kyō (狂), *n.* ❶ (狂氣) madness; mania. ❷ (狂人) a madman; a maniac. ❸ (熱狂者) a fan.
kyō (强), *a.* (强い) strong; powerful; mighty. —, *ad.* (餘) a little over; and a fraction. —五里强, long five miles. —三十七度强, a little over 37 degrees.
kyō (經), *n.* 【梵】Sutra; the Buddhist scripture.
kyō (興), *n.* amusement; mirth; entertainment. —興に入る, to be amused; take interest *in.* —興に乘じて, in the excess of mirth. —興を催す, to feel interest; become interested. —興を醒す, to kill joy; damp one's pleasure.
kyō (今日), *n.* & *ad.* to-day. —今日中に, in the course of to-day. —今日の四時, to-day at four o'clock.
kyōai (狹隘な), *a.* narrow; limited; confined.
kyōaku (凶惡な), *a.* villainous; fiendish; atrocious.
kyōan (敎案), *n.* a plan for teaching (in the class). —敎案を作る, to make preparations for class work.
kyōatsu (强壓する), *vt.* to oppress; coerce; treat with a high hand. —强壓的, oppressive; coercive; high-handed.
kyōbai (競賣), *n.* auction; public [auction] sale. —競賣する, to put to [sell by] auction; put up [sell] at auction [米]; bring [put; send] to the hammer. —競賣になる, to be put at auction; come under the hammer; go to the hammers. ¶ 强制競賣, compulsory (sale by) auction. —競賣人, an auctioneer. —競賣入札者, a bidder.
kyōben (敎鞭), *n.* the rod. —敎鞭を執る, to teach; be engaged as a teacher.
kyōben (强辯する), *vi.* to quibble (ごまかす); sophisticate (詭辯).
kyobō (虛妄), *n.* falsehood; untruth. —虛妄の, false; untrue; groundless (論據なき).
kyōbo (敎母), *n.* a godmother.
kyōbō (凶暴な), *a.* atrocious; outrageous; ferocious.
kyōbō (共謀), *n.* complicity (in a crime); collusion; conspiracy. —共謀する, to collude *with*; conspire together [*with*]; confederate *with.* —共謀して, in conspiracy *with.* ¶ 共謀者, an accomplice; a conspirator; a confederate.
kyōbō (狂暴な), *a.* wild; furious; fierce; outrageous.
kyōbō (强暴), *n.* violence; outrage.
kyōboku (喬木), *n.* a tree (shrub に對す); a tall [timber; large] tree; a forest tree. —喬木風多し, "Tall trees catch much wind."
kyōbu (胸部), *n.* 【解】the thorax; the thoracic region; the breast.
kyōbun (虛聞), *n.* ❶ (虛傳) a false rumour [report]. ❷ = *kyomei.* —虛聞を傳へる, to spread a false rumour.
kyōchi (境地), *n.* field; state.
kyōchikutō (夾竹桃), *n.* 【植】the rose-bay.
kyōcho (共著), *n.* (*a*) collaboration (仕事): (*b*) a joint work.
kyōchō (協調), *n.* harmony (調

和); cooperation (協同); conciliation (醸和). —協調を保ッて, in concert *with*.

kyōchō (强調), *n.* a strong tone; a strong [an upward] tendency; firmness. —强調する, to accentuate.

kyōchoku (强直), *n.* rigidity; stiffness. ¶ 死後强直, rigor mortis.

kyōchū (胸中), *n.* mind; the bosom; intentions (意向). —胸中を察する, to enter into another's feelings. —深く胸中に藏する, to hide deep in one's heart.

kyochū-chōtei (居中調停), *n.* 【法】 mediation; intermediation. —居中調停の勞を取る, to undertake the task of intermediation.

kyōda (怯懦な), *a.* cowardly; timid; pusillanimous.

kyōda (强打), *n.* ❶ a heavy blow; severe drubbing; a swashing blow. ❷ (遊戯) a heavy [hard] hit (野球); a slog (球の). —强打する, to strike hard; give a heavy blow. ¶ 强打手, a slogger; a heavy [hard] hitter.

kyodai (巨大な), *a.* huge; enormous; immense. 巨大な動物, a huge animal.

kyōdai (兄弟), *n.* ❶ a brother (男); a sister (女). ❷ (同胞) brethren (brother の複數). —兄弟の樣に, brotherly; fraternally; like brothers. ¶ 兄弟喧嘩, a quarrel between brothers.

kyōdai (强大), *n.* mightiness; powerfulness; greatness. —强大な, strong; mighty; powerful.

kyōdai (鏡臺), *n.* a mirror-stand; a toilet-stand; a dressing-table.

kyodaku (許諾), *n.* ❶ (許可) permission. ❷ (承諾) consent.

kyōdan (教壇), *n.* ❶ (學校の) the (teacher's) platform. ❷ 【宗】 the pulpit. —教壇に立つ, to stand on the platform.

kyōdan (教團), *n.* an order; a brotherhood; a fraternity.

kyodatsu (虛脫), *n.* 【醫】 collapse; prostration.

kyodō (擧動), *n.* ❶ (行動) action; movement. ❷ (行爲) conduct; behaviour; demeanour (振舞). —擧動不審の, suspicious. —擧動が變だ, to be strange in his manner. —擧動を窺ふ, to watch a person's movements.

kyōdo (强度の), *a.* intensive; high-grade; intense. —强度の近視眼, extreme near-sightedness.

kyōdo (鄉土), *n.* one's native country [place; province]. ¶ 鄉土藝術, *heimat kunst* [獨].

kyōdō (共同), *n.* union, cooperation (協同). —共同の, joint; common; public; co-. —共同する, to join; unite; cooperate. —共同して, jointly; in cooperation; in common. ¶ 共同企業, a joint enterprise. —共同生活, common life: cohabitation (男女の). —共同責任, joint liability. —共同借家(借地)人, a co-tenant.

kyōdō (協同), *n.* cooperation. —協同一致の精神, cooperative spirit. —協同する, to cooperate; act jointly [in unison]; combine. —一致協同して, in cooperation; in concert. ¶ 協同組合, a cooperation; a cooperative society. —協同作戰, joint operation; 【野球】 team-work [-play].

kyōdō (教導), *n.* instruction; moral instruction. —教導する, to instruct; lead; act as guide. ¶ 教導團, a school for non-commissioned officers. —教導職, a moral instructor.

kyōdō (嚮導), *n.* ❶ guidance; lead; conduct. ❷ 【軍】 a guide; a pivot(-man). —嚮導する, to guide; lead; conduct. —嚮導右(左)!, Pivot! Right (Left)!

kyōdō (驚動する), *vt.* to startle; astonish. —天下の耳目を驚動させる, to startle the world.

kyoei (虛榮), *n.* vanity; vain display. —虛榮を好む, to be fond of vain display. —虛榮心を滿足さす, to gratify one's vanity.

kyōei (胸泳), *n.* breast-stroke.

kyōei (競泳), *n.* a swimming race [match].

kyōeibyō (恐英病), *n.* Anglophobia. ¶ 恐英病者, an Anglophobe.

kyōeki (共益), *n.* common benefit.

kyōekisha (教役者), *n.* a religious worker.

kyōen (饗宴), *n.* a feast; a banquet.

kyōetsu (恐悅), *n.* joy; delight.

kyōfu (恐怖), *n.* dread; dismay; terror. —恐怖さす, to scare; terrify. 恐怖する, to be afraid *of*; be terrified. —恐怖すべき, fearful; terrible; dreadful. —恐怖に襲はれた, terror-stricken; terror-struck. ¶ 恐怖時代, the reign of terror.

kyofu (教父), *n.* ❶ a godfather. ❷ the father; a father of the church.

kyōfū (强風), *n.* ❶ a strong wind; a gale. ❷ 【氣象】 a fresh gale; a gale.

kyōfū (驚風), *n.* = ***nōmakuen.***

kyōfū(kai) (矯風(會)), *n.* (a society for the) reform of manners.

kyōga (恭賀する), *vt.* to congratulate; felicitate. —恭賀新年, A Happy New Year (to you); With New-Year's greetings.

kyōgai (境涯), *n.* circumstances; condition; situation in life (身分).

—安樂な境涯, easy circumstances; an easy life.

kyogaku (巨額の), *a.* enormous; an enormous sum *of.*

kyōgaku (驚愕さす), *vt.* to astonish; dismay. —驚愕する, to be thrown into consternation; be astonished; be amazed. —驚愕色を失ふ, to turn pale with amazement.

kyōgaku (共學), *n.* (男女共學) co-education; mixed education.

kyō-garu (興がる), *vi.* to be amused [diverted]; take interest *in.*

kyōgeki (挾擊する), *v.* to double *upon*; attack both flanks. ☞ ***hasamiuchi.***

kyogen (虛言), *n.* a lie; a falsefood. ☞ ***uso*** (うそ).

kyōgen (狂言), *n.* ❶ a *No* farce; a farce. ❷ (歌舞伎芝居) a play; a performance. ❸ (企みたる言行) a trick; an artifice; a got-off [made-up] affair. ¶ 狂言自殺, a sham suicide. —狂言師; 狂言役者, a *No*-comedian.

kyogetsu (去月), *n.* & *ad.* last month; *ultimo* (ult. と略す)〔羅〕. —去月八日, the eighth of last month; the 8th ult.

kyogi (虛僞), *n.* falsehood; falsity; a lie (虛言). —虛僞の陳述[申立], a false statement.

kyōgi (狹義), *n.* a narrow sense. —狹義に解すれば, if we interpret it in a narrow sense.

kyōgi (協議), *n.* consultation; conference; deliberation. —協議上の離婚, a divorce by mutual consent. —協議する, to confer *with* (a person); consult *with* (a person *about* some matter); consult together; take counsel together. —協議が調ふ, to come to an agreement. ¶ 協議委員, a joint committee; a conference committee. —協議會, a conference; a consultation; a council.

kyōgi (教義), *n.* a doctrine; a tenet (個人・宗派の).

kyōgi (經木), *n.* a chip; wood shavings. ¶ 經木細工, chipware. —經木眞田, a chip [wood-shaving] braid. (經木眞田帽, a chip hat.)

kyōgi (競技), *n.* ❶ a game; a sport; athletic sports [games]. ❷ (試合) a match; a tournament. ¶ 五種競技, pentathlon (走幅跳, 槍投, 二百米突, 圓盤投, 千五百米). —十種競技, decathlon (百米突, 走幅跳, 砲丸投, 走高跳, 四百米突, 百十米突, ハードルレース, 圓盤投, 棒高跳, 槍投, 千五百米突). —競技場, a ground; a field (クリケット・フットボール等の); links (ゴルフの); a stadium (段々になった見物席ある). —競技會, athletic sports [meeting]. —競技精神, sportsmanship. —競技者, an athlete; a contestant.

kyogō (倨傲の), *a.* arrogant; haughty; proud; insolent.

kyōgō (叫號する), *vi* to shout; vociferate; cry violently.

kyōgō (校合), *n.* proof-reading (校正); correction (同上); collation (校訂). —校合する correct (校正する); read proofs (同上); collate (校訂する).

kyōgō (競合), *n.* concurrence.

kyōgū (境遇), *n.* ❶ (生活狀態) conditions; circumstances; situation. ❷ (環境) environment; surroundings. —境遇に束縛せられる, to be controlled by circumstances. —悲慘な境遇に陷る, to fall into a pitiful situation.

kyōgyō (競業), *n.* trade competition.

kyōha (敎派), *n.* a sect; a persuasion; a denomination.

kyohaku (巨擘), *n.* a star; an authority; a great artist.

kyōhaku (脅迫, 强迫), *n.* threat; intimidation; menace. —脅迫する, to intimidate; menace; threaten. ¶ 脅迫狀, a threatening letter. —脅迫者, an intimidator; a threatener.

kyōhan (共犯), *n.* 【法】 complicity. ¶ 共犯者, an accomplice.

kyōheki (胸壁), *n.* ❶ 【解】 the thoracic parietes; the walls of the chest. ❷ 【軍】 a breastwork; a parapet; a breast-wall.

kyōhen (凶變), *n.* a calamity; a disaster. ☞ ***jihen.***

kyohi (巨費), *n.* enormous expenses; stupendous expenditure. —巨費を投じて, at a heavy cost; at enormous expenses.

kyohi (拒否), *n.* rejection; repulse; disapproval. —拒否する, to repulse; reject; decline; veto (議案等を). ¶ 拒否權, veto.

kyohi (許否), permission; consent. —許否を決する, to decide whether to permit or not.

kyohō (巨砲), *n.* a big [great] gun.

kyohō (虛報), *n.* a false report.

kyōho (襁褓), *n.* =***mutsuki.***

kyōhō (敎法), *n.* religion.

kyōhō (凶報), *n.* ill tidings; bad [sad] news. —凶報に接する, to receive sad news.

kyōhon (狂奔する), *vi.* to run madly about; rush about; bustle about (奔走); busy oneself (about something) (同上).

kyoi (虛位), *n.* a nominal rank; a mere title.

kyoi (虛威), *n.* bluff; bluster; vapour. —虛威を張る, to bluff; vapour.

kyōi (胸圍), *n.* the girth [circumference] of the chest.

kyōi (脅威), *n.* menace; threat. *ikaku* (威嚇). —脅威する, to menace; threaten; be dangerous *to*.

kyōi (驚異), *n.* ❶ marvellousness; wonderfulness. ❷ a marvel; a wonder; a prodigy. —驚異の眼を見張る, to look on with wondering eyes.

kyōiku (敎育), *n.* education; teaching; instruction; upbringing (養育); training (訓練); culture (敎養). —敎育ある人, an educated man; a man of culture. —敎育ある中等階級, the educated middle class. —敎育する, to educate; instruct; bring up. —敎育を受ける, to receive education; be educated. ¶ 學校敎育, school education. —高等(社會)敎育, higher (social) education. —敎育勅語, the Imperial Rescript on Education. —敎育學, pedagogics; pedagogy; paideutics. —敎育家, an educationalist; an educator; a teacher. —敎育會, an educational society.

kyōin (敎員), *n.* a teacher; a master; a schoolmaster; an instructor. ¶ 敎員檢定試驗, the teachers' pass [qualification] examination. —敎員免許狀, the teacher's qualification certificate. —敎員養成所, a training college [school].

kyojaku (虛弱な), *a.* delicate; frail; weak.

kyōjaku (强弱), *n.* strength; relative strength (of the two contending parties).

kyōji (凶事), *n.* a calamity; a misfortune; an unlucky affair.

kyojin (巨人), *n.* ❶ a giant; a colossus; a Titan. ❷ (偉人) a great man.

kyōjin (狂人), *n.* a lunatic; a a madman; a maniac.

kyōjin (强甚な), *a.* strong; violent; severe. —强甚な地震, a violent shock of earthquake.

kyōjin (强靱な), *a.* tenacious; stout (紙).

kyojitsu (虛日), *n.* a day of leisure; an idle day.

kyojitsu (虛實), *n.* (眞僞) truth. —事の虛實を探る, to inquire into the truth of a matter.

kyōjitsu (凶日), *n.* an unlucky day; a black [woeful] day.

kyōjiya (經師屋), *n.* a paper-hanger.

kyojō (居常), *ad.* always; usually; ordinarily. ☞ *tsune* (常に).

kyōjo (共助), *n.* mutual aid.

kyōjō (凶狀), *n.* a crime; an offence. ¶ 凶狀持ち, an unarrested criminal; a culprit.

kyōjō (敎場), *n.* a class-room; a school-room.

kyojū (居住), *n.* residence; abode; dwelling. —居住する, ① [*vi.*] to live; dwell (*in*); reside (*at*; *in*). ② [*a.*] resident. ¶ 居住地, a place of residence. —居住者, a resident; a dweller.

kyōju (享受する), *vt.* to enjoy; receive.

kyōju (敎授), *n.* ❶ (敎へる事) teaching; instruction; tuition. ❷ (人) a professor; the faculty (敎授團); professoriate (同上). ❸ (職) professorship; professoriate. —敎授する, to teach; instruct; give lessons *in*. ¶ 名譽敎授, honorary [emeritus] professor. —敎授法, pedagogy; method of teaching. —敎授會, board of professors.

kyōjun (恭順), *n.* submission; obedience. —恭順な, obedient; submissive.

kyōjutsu (供述), *n.* statement (陳述); 【法】deposition (證人の). —供述する, to depose. ¶ 供述書, 【法】 a deposition; an affidavit.

kyoka (炬火), *n.* a torch; a torchlight; a link. ☞ *taimatsu.*

kyoka (許可), *n.* permission; leave; licence. —許可する, to permit; give leave; license. —許可なしに, without leave [permission]. —許可を乞ふ, to ask permission; beg leave; apply for permission (出願する).

kyoka (許嫁), *n.* =*iinazuke.*

kyōka (狂歌), *n.* a comic poem; comic poetry.

kyōka (敎化), *n.* culture; enlightenment; civilization. —敎化する, to culture; enlighten; civilize.

kyōka (敎科), *n.* a course of study; the curriculum (of studies).

kyokai (巨魁), *n.* the ringleader; the chieftain (山賊・蠻人などの).

kyōkai (協會), *n.* an association; a society; an institution.

kyōkai (敎誨), *n.* admonition; counsel. —敎誨する, to admonish; give counsel *to*; show another his errors. ¶ 敎誨師, a prison chaplain; a prison missionary.

kyōkai (敎會), *n.* ❶ (宗敎團體) a religious association; a church. ❷ (敎會堂) a church; a chapel.

kyōkai (境界), *n.* a border; a boundary. ☞ *keikai* (境界).

kyōkaku (俠客), *n.* a man of chivalrous spirit; a man of chivalry. —俠客肌の男, a man of dashing manners.

kyōkaku (恐嚇), *n.* threat; menace; intimidation. —恐嚇の文句, threatening language; a bluff. —— **suru**, *vt.* to threaten; intimidate. —殺すぞと恐嚇する, to threaten with death. ¶ 恐嚇者, an intimidator; a threatener.

kyōkaku (胸廓), *n.* 【解】 the

thorax; the chest. —胸廓の廣い(狭い), broad (narrow) -chested.

kyōkan (凶悍な), *a.* barbarous; savage; ferocious.

kyōkan (凶漢), *n.* ❶ (惡漢) a villain; a ruffian. ❷ (殺人者) a murderer; an assassin (暗殺者).

kyōkan (叫喚), *n.* a shout; a cry; an outcry; a clamour; hue and cry.

kyōkan (教官), *n.* an instructor; a teacher.

kyōkasho (教科書), *n.* a school--book; a text-book; a class-book.

kyōkatabira (經帷子), *n.* a shroud; a cerement; a grave-clothes.

kyokatsu (虛喝), *n.* a bluff; an empty threat. —虛喝する, to bluff; use empty threats.

kyōkatsu (脅喝), *n.* threat; intimidation. —脅喝する, to threaten; intimidate. —脅喝して默らせる, to intimidate [threaten] into silence. ¶ 脅喝取財, blackmail; extortion by threats. (脅喝取財する, to blackmail; extort by threats.)

kyōken (狂犬), *n.* a mad [rabid] dog. ¶ 狂犬病,【獸醫】hydrophobia; rabies.

kyōken (恭儉), *n.* modesty; moderation. —恭儉己を持する, to behave with modesty and moderation.

kyōken (强健な), *a.* healthy; robust; stout; sturdy. —强健な人, a man of robust health [strong physique; stout build]. —强健な身心, a sound body and mind.

kyōken (教權), *n.* ❶ (宗教上の權力) sacerdotal power; church power. ❷ (教授上の威嚴) pedagogical authority.

kyoki (歔欷), *n.* sob; convulsive weeping. —歔欷する, to sob; weep convulsively.

kyōki (凶器, 兇器), *n.* weapons; arms. —兇器を携へて闖入する, to break in with a weapon.

kyōki (狂氣), *n.* madness; insanity; lunacy. ☞ *kichigai.*

kyōki (狂喜する), *vi.* to be mad with joy; be transported with joy; be in ecstasies [raptures]. —狂喜の餘りに, in the excess of his joy.

kyōki (俠氣), *n.* chivalrous spirit; chivalry. —俠氣ある人, a chivalrous person; a man of chivalry.

kyōki (狹軌), *n.* a narrow gauge. ¶ 狹軌鐵道, a narrow-gauge railway. ☞ *kōki* (廣軌).

kyōki (强記), *n.* good [strong; retentive] memory; retentiveness. —强記の人, a man of good [retentive; tenacious] memory.

kyokin (醵金), *n.* a collection; a contribution; a subscription. —醵金する, ① (募金する) to collect contributions [subscriptions]; take up a collection. ② (寄附する) to contribute; subscribe.

kyōkin (胸襟), *n.* the bosom; heart; mind. —胸襟を披く[披いて語る], to speak one's mind; open [lay bare] one's heart *to*; unbosom oneself *to*.

kyokkai (曲解), *n.* a far-fetched [perverted] interpretation [construction] (牽强附會の); a strained [forced] interpretation (無理な); a a biassed [prejudiced] interpretation (偏見ある). —曲解する, to interpret [construe] perversely; put a wrong construction (on another's remark); pervert the meaning (*of*).

kyokkei (極刑), *n.* extreme penalty; maximum punishment; capital punishment (死刑). —極刑に處せらる, to be sentenced [condemned] to capital punishment.

kyokken (極圈), *n.* the polar circle. ¶ 南(北)極圈, the Antarctic (Arctic) Circle.

kyokki (旭旗), *n.* the Flag of the Rising Sun; the Sun-flag.

kyokkō (極光), *n.* the aurora (polaris); the polar lights.

kyokkyū (曲球), *n.* 【野球】a curve; a shoot [卑].

kyokō (虛構), *n.* fabrication; invention; fiction. —虛構の說, a pure fabrication; a canard. —事實を虛構する, to concoct facts.

kyokō (擧行), *n.* holding; performance; solemnization. —— -**suru,** *vt.* to hold; perform; solemnize (嚴肅に). —試驗を擧行する, to hold an examination.

kyōko (鞏固な), *a.* firm; solid; stable; strong. —鞏固な意志, a strong [an iron] will. —基礎を鞏固にする, to make the basis firm; make the foundation solid.

kyōkō (兇行), *n.* violence; an outrage; a murder (殺人); a tragedy (慘劇). —兇行の現場, the spot where the outrage was committed; the scene of the outrage.

kyōkō (恐慌), *n.* a panic; an alarm; a scare. —恐慌に襲はれる[を來す], to be panic-stricken; be struck [seized] with a panic. —恐慌を惹起(助長)する, to create (foster) a panic.

kyōkō (强行), *n.* enforcement. —夜襲を强行する, to force a night attack. ¶ 强行軍, a forced march. —强行法,【法】imperative law. —强行偵察, reconnaissance in force.

kyōkō (强硬な), *a.* strong (反對・抗議・手段など); firm; resolute; unyielding. —强硬な態度を執る, to take a firm attitude *towards*. —

強硬に主張する, to insist obstinately *on*; stick obstinately *to*. —強硬に反對する, to oppose strongly.

kyōkō-kingen (恐惶謹言), Yours most respectfully; I am your most obedient servant (公式に).

kyokoku (擧國), *n.* the whole nation [country; empire]. —擧國一致して强敵に當る, to meet the strong enemy with the whole nation behind us. ¶ 擧國一致內閣, a coalition cabinet; a cabinet of all talents. —擧國皆兵, national service; universal conscription.

kyōkoku (强國), *n.* a great [strong] power; a powerful state. —世界の强國, the Great Powers. —世界的强國, a world-power.

kyokotsu (距骨), *n.* 【解】the astragalus; the ankle-bone.

kyōkotsu (胸骨), *n.* 【解】the sternum; the breast-bone.

kyoku (曲), *n.* ❶ (邪) wrong; blame; fault. ❷ (歌・音樂の) a tune; music; a song. ❸ (興) interest; pleasure. ¶ 曲獨樂, top-spinning tricks.

kyoku (局), *n.* ❶ (官署) an office; a station. ❷ (圍碁・將棋の盤面・勝負) a checker-board; a game of checkers. ❸ (中央官省の部局) a bureau; a department. ❹ situation (時局); the affair (其の事物). ❺ (終局) conclusion. —局に當る, to be in authority; have [take] charge *of* the affair. —局を結ぶ, to come to a conclusion [close; an end]. ¶ 局員(全體), the staff of a bureau (an office).

kyoku (極), *n.* ❶ (頂上) the height; the climax; the summit. ❷ (地球・磁氣などの) the pole. —絕望の極, ① the depth of despair. ② [*ad.*] in one's despair. —悲歎の極, ① the extremity of grief. ② [*ad.*] in (the excess of) one's grief. —榮華の極に達する, to be at the height of one's prosperity.

kyōku (狂句), *n.* a comic poem; a comic verse.

kyōku (恐懼する), *v.* to fear; dread; be overawed. —恐懼措く能はず, to be overawed; be filled with fear [awe].

kyōku (敎區), *n.* a parish; a circuit (メソヂスト敎の說敎區).

kyokuba (曲馬), *n.* a circus; equestrian feats. ¶ 曲馬場; 曲馬館, a circus; a hippodrome. —曲馬師, a circus-rider; an equestrian.

kyokubi (極美), *n.* exquisiteness; super-excellence; beau ideal.

kyokubi (極微な), *a.* atomic; microscopic. ¶ 極微動物, 【動】a microzoon; an animalcule.

kyokubu (局部), *n.* (一部) (*a*) part; a section: (*b*) 【醫】the part affected (患部). ☞ *kyokusho*. —局部の, partial; sectional; local.

kyokuchi (局地の), *a.* local.

kyokuchi (極地), *n.* the pole; the polar region.

kyokuchi (極致), *n.* ❶ (頂上) the climax; the zenith; the culmination. ❷ (理想) ideal perfection; crown. —美の極致に達する, to reach the ideal perfection of beauty.

kyokuchō (局長), *n.* the director of a bureau; the chief of an office.

kyokuchoku (曲直), *n.* good or bad; right or wrong; merits. —理非曲直を爭ふ, to contend on the question of right and wrong.

kyokudai (極大), *n.* the greatest; the maximum. ¶ 極大量, the maximum [*pl.* -ma].

kyokudo (極度), *n.* the extreme; the highest degree [point]; the climax. —極度の, extreme; utmost; supreme. —極度に, extremely; to the utmost.

kyokudome (局留), *n.* ❶ (郵便) *poste restante* [佛]; "to be called for"; c/o postmaster. ❷ (電報) *télégraphe restante*.

kyokugai (局外), *n.* being outside any circle. —局外に立つ, to stand outside. ¶ 局外中立, neutrality. —局外者, an outsider; the man in the street [cars (米)].

kyokugaku (曲學), *n.* prostitution of learning. —曲學阿世の徒, scholars who prostitute their learning to worldly ends.

kyokugei (曲藝), *n.* tricks; feats; (fancy) stunts. —曲藝を演する, to perform stunts. ¶ 曲藝師, an acrobat; a tumbler; a contortionist (關節を自由に歪める).

kyokugen (局限), *n.* restriction; limitation; localization. —局限する, to restrict; limit; localize (一地方だけに).

kyokugen (極言する), *vt.* to speak bluntly [without reserve]; go (to) the length of saying; go so far as to say. —極言すれば, not to mince words.

kyokugen (極限), *n.* a limit; the extremity; the extreme.

kyokuhei (曲柄), *n.* a crank. ¶ 曲柄軸, a crank-shaft.

kyokuhi (曲庇する), *vt.* to shelter; harbour; screen.

kyokuhirui (棘皮類), *n.* 【動】Echinodermata (學名).

kyokuhitsu (曲筆する), *v.* to pervert in writing; give a perverted account.

kyokujiku (極軸), *n.* the polar axis.

kyokujitsu (旭日), *n.* the rising sun. ¶ 旭日桐花大綬章, the Grand Cordon of the Rising Sun with the Paulownia Flowers. —旭日旗, the flag of the Rising Sun; the Sun-flag.

kyokumachi(局待), *n.* waiting at the office (略符號 WT). ¶局待電報, *telegraphe restante.*

kyokumen (曲面), *n.* a curved surface.

kyokumen (局面), *n.* the situation; the aspect [phase; state] of affairs. —局面の轉換, a change in the situation. —局面を一變する, to change the aspect of affairs; turn the tables (急に).

kyōkun (教訓), *n.* ❶ instruction. ❷(教) a lesson; a precept. —教訓的お伽噺, a moral tale for children. —教訓する, to instruct; teach. —教訓を守る, to observe a precept.

kyokunori (曲乘), *n.* circus-riding (馬などの); trick-riding (自轉車等の). —自轉車の曲乘, trick-cycling; a cycling performance. —曲乘りをする, to ride a trick.

kyokuritsu (曲率), *n.* curvature.

kyokuroku (曲彔), *n.* the officiating priest's arm-chair.

kyokuron(極論する), *v.* to argue exhaustively.

kyokuryō (極量), *n.* 【醫】 the maximum dose.

kyokuryoku (極力), *ad.* to the utmost; with all one's might; with might and main.

kyokuryū (極流), *n.* a polar current.

kyokuseki (跼蹐する), *vi.* to crouch; stoop; bend. —小天地に跼蹐する, to be confined in a small country.

kyokusen (曲線), *n.* a curve; a curved line. ¶曲線美, the curve [line] of beauty.

kyokusen (棘線), *n.* barbed wire.

kyokusetsu (曲折), *n.* ❶ (屈曲) winding; bend; meander. ❷ (變化あること) complication. ❸ (詳細) details; particulars. —曲折する, to wind; bend; meander. —多少の波瀾曲折を經て, after some complications.

kyokushaku (曲尺), *n.* the carpenter's foot-measure [square].

kyokusho (局所, 局處), *n.* the affected part (患部); a part (一局部). ☞ ***kyokubu.*** —局所の, local; topical 【醫】. ¶ 局所病, a local disease [affection]. —局所麻酔, local anæsthesia [paralysis].

kyokushō (極小の), *a.* atomic; minimum; inappreciable. ¶極小量, a grain; the minimum.

kyokutan (極端), *n.* ❶ (終端) the end; the extremity. ❷ (中庸を失へる物·事) the extremity; the extreme; the excess. —極端な, extreme (case; measures; views, *etc.*) excessive. —極端に趨る, to run to an extreme. —極端から極端へ趨る, to run from one extreme to the other. ¶極端家, an extremist; an ultraist. —極端主義, extremism.

kyokuten (極點), *n.* the extreme point; the climax; the culmination.

kyokutō (極東), *n.* the Far East. ¶極東問題, the Far Eastern question. —極東オリンピック大會, the Far Eastern Olympic meeting.

kyōkyō (匈匈, 恟恟), *ad.* ❶ (騷擾の貌) greatly excited; filled with alarm. ❷ (喧しく議論する聲) clamorously. —人心匈々たり, The people are in great alarm.

kyōkyō(兢兢), *ad.* cautiously (警戒); tremblingly (びくびく).

kyōkyū (供給), *n.* supply; provision. —供給する, to supply *with*; furnish *with*; provide *for*. —供給を受ける, to be supplied *with*. ¶ 供給不足, deficiency of supply. —供給過多, oversupply; overstock; glut. —供給者, a supplier.

kyōmaku(胸膜), *n.* 【解】 the pleura. ¶胸膜炎, pleuritis, pleurisy.

kyōmaku(鞏膜), *n.* 【解】 the sclera; the sclerotic coat (of the eye).

kyoman (巨萬の), *n.* myriad; enormous. —巨萬の富を作る, to make enormous wealth.

kyōman (驕慢な), *a.* proud; arrogant; haughty.

kyomei (虚名), *n.* an empty name; a false reputation. —虚名を博する, to make for oneself an empty name.

kyōmei (共鳴), *n.* ❶ (共鳴り) resonance. ❷ (同感) sympathy; echo. —共鳴する, ① to be resonant. ② to sympathize *with*; respond *to*; re-echo. ¶共鳴者, a sympathizer.

kyōmi (興味), *n.* interest; zest. —興味を添へる, to add a zest *to*. —興味を殺ぐ, to detract from one's enjoyment; diminish one's interest. —興味を持つ, to take an interest *in*; be interested *in*.

kyomin (居民), *n.* inhabitants; residents; the people.

kyōmō (兇猛の), *a.* barbarous; savage; brutal.

kyōmon (教門), *n.* religion (宗教); a sect (宗派).

kyōmon (經文), *n.* ❶ (經中の文) the (Buddhist) scripture; a text (說教の). ❷ (經典) a Sutra; a sacred book [writing].

kyomu (虚無), *n.* ❶ (空無) nothing; naught; non-existence. ❷

(心に何事をも懐かず) self-annihilation; self-abandonment. ¶ 虛無主義, Nihilism; nothingism. —虛無黨, the Nihilists.

kyōmu (敎務), *n.* ❶ school affairs. ❷ religious affairs. ¶ 敎務課, the section of school affairs.

kyōna (京菜), *n.* 【植】Brassica japonica (cabbage の一種·學名).

kyonen (去年), *n.* & *ad.* last year.

kyōnen (凶年), *n.* ❶ (不作) a lean [bad; sterile] year; a year of bad harvest. ❷ (不祥) an unlucky year; a year of calamity.

kyōnen (享年), *n.* age. —享年四十五, He died in his forty-fifth year.

kyōnichibyō (恐日病), *n.* ❶ (太陽を恐れる) heliophobia. ❷ Japanophobia.

kyōnin (杏仁), *n.* the apricot-stone.

kyōō (饗應), *n.* an entertainment; a banquet (大宴會); a dinner. —饗應する, to entertain; give dinner *to*; banquet. —饗應を受ける, to be invited to dinner.

kyorai (去來する), *vi.* to recur; come and go. —白雲去來す, The white clouds are moving to and fro.

kyōraku (享樂), *n.* enjoyment. —享樂する, to enjoy. ¶ 享樂主義, epicurism; hedonism. (享樂主義者, an epicurean; a hedonist.)

kyōraku (競落する), *vt.* to knock down. ¶ 競落代價, 【法】 the price realized at an auction. —競落人, the successful bidder.

kyōran (狂亂), *n.* ❶ craziness; madness; insanity. ❷ =*kyōbō* (狂暴). —狂亂さす, to drive a person out of his senses. —狂亂する, ① to be driven mad *with*; go [run] mad. ② to rage; rave (波·風等が).

kyōran (狂瀾), *n.* angry waves; furious surges; swelling billows.

kyorei (虛禮), *n.* formalism; empty forms. —虛禮に流れる, to degenerate into mere formalism.

kyōren (敎練), *n.* exercises; drilling; training. —敎練する, to drill; train; exercise. ¶ 各個敎練, individual training.

kyōretsu (强烈な), *n.* strong; severe; violent.

kyori (巨利), *n.* an enormous [a large] profit. —巨利を博する, to make a large profit.

kyori (距離), *n.* distance; range (達度); an interval (間隔). —一定の距離を保つ, to maintain [keep] a fixed distance. —雙方の主張には餘程の距離がある, There is a great gap between their claims.

kyōri (敎理), *n.* a doctrine; a dogma; a tenet.

kyōri (鄕里), *n.* ❶ (村里) a village. ❷ (故鄕) one's native place; one's home.

kyōritsu (共立の), *a.* public; cooperative; joint. ¶ 共立女子職業學校, the public female crafts school.

kyorō (虛勞), *n.* emaciation; tabefaction.

kyorokyoro (きょろきょろ), *ad.* with a startled look; restlessly. —きょろきょろする, to look around restlessly.

kyōryaku (劫掠する), *vt.* to plunder; pillage; spoil. —海岸を劫掠する, to harry the sea coasts.

kyōryō (狹量な), *a.* narrow-minded; illiberal; intolerant.

kyōryō (橋梁), *n.* bridges.

kyōryoku (協力), *n.* cooperation; joint operation [efforts]; combined strength. —協力する, ① [*v.*] to cooperate; combine; unite. ② [*a.*] cooperative. —協力して, in cooperation; shoulder to shoulder. ¶ 協力者, a co-worker; a co-operator.

kyōryoku (强力な), *a.* strong; powerful.

kyoryū (居留), *n.* residence; dwelling. —居留する, to reside *at*; dwell *in*. ¶ 居留民, residents; a colony. (居留民團, a settlement corporation.) —居留外國人, foreign residents. —共同(專管)居留地, a common (an exclusive) settlement.

kyōsa (敎唆), *n.* abetment; instigation; incitement. —敎唆する, to abet; incite; instigate. ¶ 敎唆者, an abettor; an instigator.

kyōsai (共濟), *n.* cooperation; mutual aid. ¶ 共濟組合, a friendly society; a mutual relief [aid] association.

kyōsai (匡濟する), *vt.* to reform; remedy.

kyōsaku (凶作), *n.* a bad crop; a poor harvest; failure of crops.

kyōsaku (狹窄), *n.* 【醫】stenosis; stricture (直腸·尿道·食道等の); constriction. —狹窄する, to constrict.

kyōsan (共產), *n.* community of goods. ¶ 共產主義, communism. (勞働共產主義, syndicalism. —共產主義者, a communist.) —共產黨, the communist party; the communists.

kyōsan (協贊), *n.* consent; approval. —協贊する, to approve; consent *to*. —協贊を經る, to be approved; obtain approval. ¶ 協贊會, a supporters' association.

kyōsan (胸算), *n.* ❶ mental calculation [arithmetic]. ❷ (計畫) a plan. —胸算を立てる, to make a calculation in one's mind; make a plan.

kyosei (去勢), *n.* castration; gelding. —去勢する, to castrate; geld; emasculate; caponize (鷄を). ¶ 去勢馬, a gelding. —去勢鷄, a capon.

kyosei (虚勢), *n.* false show of power [strength]; bluff; bluster. —虚勢を張る, to make a show of power; bluff; bluster.

kyōsei(匡正する), *vt.* to correct; reform; remedy; mend; cure. —惡風を匡正する, to reform evil customs.

kyōsei (强制), *n.* compulsion; constraint; coercion. —强制する, to compel; force; constrain; coerce. —强制されてする, to do it under compulsion. —强制してさせる, to make another do it by compulsion; force another into doing it. ¶ 强制管理, compulsory administration. —强制執行,【法】distraint; forcible [compulsory] execution; execution. —强制手段, a coercive measure.

kyōsei (强請する), *vt.* to extort; exact. ☞ ***nedaru.***

kyōsei (矯正), *n.* reform; correction; reclamation. **——-suru,** *vt.* to reform; correct; redress; reclaim. —吃を矯正する, to cure stuttering. —矯正し得べき, reformable; corrigible; reclaimable. ¶ 矯正院, a house of correction; a reformatory.

kyosetsu (虚說), *n.* a false [ungrounded] report [rumour]; a fabrication (虚構). —虚說を流布する, to spread a false rumour.

kyōsha (强者), *n.* a strong man; a man of power; the strong.

kyōsha (驕奢), *n.* luxury; extravagance. —驕奢を極める, to live in utmost luxury.

kyoshi (鋸齒), *n.* a saw-tooth. —鋸齒狀の, serriform; serrate(d); saw-toothed.

kyoshi (擧示する), *vt.* to give; mention; cite.

kyoshi (擧止), *n.* Ⓢ 擧措. deportment; demeanour; behaviour.

kyōshi (敎子), *n.* a god-child.

kyōshi (敎旨), *n.* ❶ =***kyōri, kyōgi.*** ❷ =***mune*** (旨). —佛敎の敎旨, the teaching of the Buddha [Buddhism].

kyōshi (敎師), *n.* a teacher; a master; a schoolmaster. —音樂の敎師, a music master.

kyoshin (虚心), *n.* composure; indifference; impartiality (無私). —虚心の, composed; indifferent. —虚心平氣で考へる, to think over with perfect composure. ¶ 虚心坦懷, an open mind.

kyōshin (强震), *n.*【地文】a strong shock of earthquake.

kyōshinkai (共進會), *n.* an (a competitive) exhibition; a prize show.

kyoshitsu (居室), *n.* a sitting-[living-; private] room; a parlour.

kyōshitsu (敎室), *n.* a school-room; a class-room; a school. ¶ 化學敎室, a chemistry school.

kyosho (居所, 居處), *n.* a place of residence; a dwelling-place; an abode. —居所不明, (his) whereabouts unknown.

kyosho (據所), *n.* the source; the origin; a reference. —據所不明の, of unknown origin.

kyoshō (巨匠), *n.* a master; a great artist.

kyoshō(擧證), *n.* presentation of proof. —擧證の責[義務], the burden of proof. —擧證する, to adduce [produce] an evidence [a proof]; testify.

kyōsho (敎書), *n.* the President's message (米).

kyōshō (狹小な), *a.* narrow; strait.

kyōshō (協商), *n.* ❶ negotiation ❷ (協約) an agreement; an understanding; *entente* (佛). —協商する, to negotiate *with*; treat *with.* —協商が成立する, to come to an agreement. ¶ 三國協商, the Triple Entente. —協商國, the entente powers.

kyoshoku (虚飾), *n.* ostentation; display; show. —虚飾する, to gloss; gild. —虚飾を避ける, to shun display. ¶ 虚飾家, a coxcomb; a spark; a dandy.

kyōshoku (敎職), *n.* ❶ teachership; mastership; teaching. ❷(布敎者の職) the ministry.

kyoshu (擧手), *n.* holding up one's hand; show of hands (裁決の). —擧手の禮, (military) salute.

kyoshū (去就), *n.* attitude; position. —去就に迷ふ, to be undecided what position [attitude] to assume (in regard to a matter). —去就を決する, to decide upon one's attitude.

kyoshū (醵集する), *vt.* to collect. —義金を醵集する, to collect subscriptions.

kyōshu (兇手), *n.* an evil [a heinous] hand. —刺客の兇手に斃れる, to fall victim to assassination.

kyōshu (拱手する), *vi.* to fold [cross] one's arms. —拱手して, without effort; with folded arms. —拱手傍觀する, to look on with unconcern.

kyōshu (敎主), *n.* the head of the sect.

kyōshu (梟首), *n.* exposure of the head (after execution).

kyōshū (强襲), *n.*【軍】a storm;

an assault; an onslaught. —强襲する, to storm; assault. —强襲によって要塞を拔く, to take a fortress by storm.

kyōshū (鄕愁), *n.* nostalgia; homesickness.

kyōshūjo (敎習所), *n.* a training school. ¶ 巡査敎習所, a police training school.

kyōshuku (恐縮), *n.* ❶ (畏恐) shrinking; recoil. ❷ (恐れ入ること) great obligation; sorrow (氣の毒). —恐縮する, to shrink; recoil; be much obliged; be very sorry. —恐縮の至です, I am deeply grateful to you.

kyoshutsu (醵出), *n.* contribution; subscription. —醵出する, to contribute; subscribe; pay one's share. ¶ 醵出金, a subscription; a contribution. —醵出者, a subscriber; a contributor.

kyōso (敎祖), *n.* the founder of a sect.

kyōsō (强壯な), *a.* strong; robust; healthy. ¶ 强壯劑, 【醫】a restorative; a roborant; a tonic.

kyōsō (競走), *n.* a race; a foot-race (徒歩の). —競走する, to run (a race); race *with.* —競走に勝つ, to win (a race); come in first. ¶ 競走場, a race-ground [-track]; a (race-)course. —競走者, a competitor in a race, a racer; a runner.

kyōsō (競爭), *n.* competition; contest; rivalry. —競爭する, to compete; rival; contest; emulate *with*; vie *with.* —競爭に勝つ, to outrun competition; win in a competition; gain the upper hand. —競爭場裏に打って出る, to come forward as a competitor. ¶ 競爭價格, competitive price. —競爭値下げ, competitive lowering of prices; reciprocal underselling. —競爭制度, the competitive system. —競爭線, a competing line; a rival line. —競爭選擧, a contested election. —競爭者, a competitor; a contestant; a rival. —競爭試驗, a competitive examination. —競爭心, the spirit of emulation; a competitive spirit. —競爭割引, rate-cutting (汽車·汽船·商船等の).

kyōsō (競漕), *n.* a (boat-)race; a regatta. ¶ 競漕艇, a racer.

kyōsoku (脇息), *n.* an arm [elbow]-rest. —脇息に凭(もた)れる, to lean on an arm-rest.

kyōsoku (敎則), *n.* school (class-room) regulations.

kyōson (共存), *n.* coexistence. —共存する, to coexist.

kyōsuibyō (恐水病), *n.* 【醫】 rabies; hydrophobia.

kyō-suru (供する), *vt.* ❶ (供給する) to furnish; supply; provide. ❷ (奉る) to offer; present; dedicate. —天覽に供する, to submit for His Majesty's inspection. —靈前に供する, to offer it to the dead [before the tablet of the dead].

kyō-suru (狂する), *vi.* to become insane; go [run] mad. —狂せんばかりに悲しむ, to lament almost to madness.

kyota (許多の), *a.* numerous; many; a great many.

kyōtai (狂態), *n.* scandalous conduct (醜態).

kyōtai (嬌態), *n.* coquetry; fascinating behaviour.

kyotaku (居宅), *n.* a (dwelling-) house; a residence.

kyōtaku (供託), *n.* 【法】 deposit; lodgment. —供託する, to deposit; lodge. ¶ 供託物, a deposit; a deposited article. —供託金, deposit money. —供託者, a depositor. —供託所, a deposit office; a depository.

kyotan (咗痰), *n.* sputum. ¶ 咗痰劑, an expectorant.

kyōtan (驚嘆する), *vt.* to admire; wonder *at.* —驚嘆に價する, to be worthy of our admiration.

kyōtei (協定), *n.* arrangement; agreement; understanding. —協定する, to arrange; agree *upon*; come to an agreement [understanding]. ¶ 協定稅率, a conventional tariff.

kyōteki (强敵), *n.* a strong [powerful] enemy; a formidable adversary.

kyōten (敎典), *n.* a scripture; a canon; a religious code.

kyōten-dōchi (驚天動地の), *a.* world-shaking [-moving]; tremendous.

kyotō (巨頭), *n.* a leader.

kyōto (兇徒), *n.* ❶ (惡漢) ruffians. ❷ (騷擾者) rioters; insurgents.

kyōto (敎徒), *n.* a believer; a follower 【米】.

kyōtō (敎頭), *n.* a head-teacher.

kyōtō (驚倒さす), *vt.* to astound; astonish; startle.

kyōtō (鄕黨), *n.* ❶ a village (community). ❷ one's native province [country]. ¶ 鄕黨心, parochialism.

kyōtsū (共通), *n.* community. —利害の共通, community of interests. —共通事務を處理する爲め, to conduct their common business. —— **-no,** —— **-suru,** *a.* common; general; mutual. —各國共通の, common to every country. —互に共通する所が多い, They have much in common with each other. ¶ 共通切符, a common ticket.

kyōtsū (胸痛), *n.* 【醫】 pleurodynia; a pain in the chest.

kyōwa (共和の), *a.* republican.

¶ 共和國, a republic. —共和政治, republicanism; republican government. —共和政體, the republican form of government. —共和黨, the republican party.

kyōwa (協和), *n.* harmony; concord; consonance. —協和する, to be in harmony [concord].

kyōyaku (共軛の), *a.* conjugate. ¶ 共軛角,【數】a conjugate angle.

kyōyaku (共譯), *n.* joint translation.

kyōyaku (協約), *n.* an agreement; a convention; *entente*〔佛〕. ¶ 紳士協約, the Gentlemen's Agreement.

kyoyō (許容), *n.* ❶ (許可) permission; grant. ❷ (宥恕) pardon; toleration. —許容する, ① to grant; permit; allow. ② to pardon; tolerate.

kyōyō (共用), *n.* common use. —共用する, to use in common. ¶ 共用栓, a street-pump; a common water-hydrant.

kyōyō (强要する), *vt.* to force; compel. —金錢を强要する, to extort money (from a person).

kyōyō (敎養), *n.* culture; education. —敎養する, to educate. —敎養ある人, a man of culture. —敎養を施す, to culture; educate; give education.

kyōyu (敎諭), *n.* a teacher (of a secondary school).

kyōyū (共有), *n.* co-ownership; joint [common] ownership; community. —共有の, common; joint. —共有する, to hold in common; own jointly. ¶ 共有者,【法】a co-owner; a joint owner [proprietor]. —共有財產, common property.

kyōyū (享有), *n.* enjoyment. —享有する, to enjoy.

kyōyū (俠勇), *n.* chivalry.

kyōzai (敎材), *n.* teaching materials.

kyozetsu (拒絕), *n.* refusal; repulse; rejection. —— **-suru,** *vt.* to refuse; reject; repulse; repel. —入國を拒絕する, to refuse entry into a country. ¶ 拒絕證書, a protest (爲替手形の).

kyōzō (胸像), *n.*【彫刻】a bust.

kyō-zuru (興ずる), *vi.* to be interested *in*; be amused *at* [*with*].

kyū (灸), *n.* ❶ moxa; moxibustion; moxicautery. ❷ (懲しめ) punishment. —灸をすゑる, to burn moxa; cauterize with moxa.

kyū (柩), *n.* a coffin. —柩を送る, to follow the hearse.

kyū (急), *n.* ❶ (緩急) an emergency; a danger (危難); a crisis (危機). ❷ (緊急) urgency; pressing need (火急). ❸ (迅速) hastiness; promptitude. —急の間に合はぬ, to fail in case of sudden need. —急を要する, to admit of no delay. —急を告げる, ① (急を知らす) to inform of urgency *of*; give alarm. ② (事が切迫する) to become critical; impend; be urgent; press. —— **-na,** *a.* ❶ (緊急の) pressing; urgent. ❷ (不時の) sudden. ❸ (險阻の) steep; precipitous. —急な用事, pressing business. —急な坂, a steep slope. ☞ *kyū-ni* (急に).

kyū (級), *n.* ❶ (階級) a grade; a class; an order. ❷ (學年) a grade; a standard (小學校の). ❸ (組) a class; a form (公立學校の). ❹【文】a degree. —次官級の人物, a man of the vice-minister class. —三千噸級の汽船, a steamer of 3000 ton type. —級を分ける, to divide a grade. ¶ 二級俸, the second-class salary.

kyū (球), *n.* ❶ (圓體) a sphere; an orb; a bulb (寒暖計等の). ❷ (毬) a ball.

kyū (舊), *a.* old; ancient; past. —舊の正月, the New Year's Day of the old [lunar] calendar. —舊に復する, to be restored; revert to the former state. ¶ 舊師, one's former teacher.

kyū (撞球棒), *n.*【撞球】a (billiard-) cue. ¶ キュー架〔ﾎﾞﾝ〕, a bridge.

kyūaku (舊惡), *n.* a former misdeed; a past crime. ¶ 舊惡露顯, exposure of a past crime.

kyūba (急場), *n.* an emergency; a crisis. —急場を凌ぐ, to tide over a crisis; meet a pressing need.

kyūbaku (舊幕), *n.* the old feudal government; the shogunate. ¶ 舊幕時代, the old feudal times.

kyūban (吸盤), *n.*【動】a sucker; a sucking-disk; an acetabulum.

kyūbin (鳩便), *n.* ❶ pigeon-post. ❷ (鳩信, 鳩報) a pigeongram.

kyūbō (窮乏), *n.* want; destitution; indigence. —窮乏を告げる, to be depleted; run short.

kyūbun (舊聞), *n.* old [stale] news.

kyūbyō (急病), *n.* a sudden illness. —急病で死ぬ(に罹る), to die of (be seized with) a sudden illness. ¶ 急病人, an urgent case.

kyūchi (救治), *n.* ❶ =*chiryō* (治療). ❷ (救濟) relief; reform. —救治する, ① to cure; remedy. ② to relieve; reform; remedy. ¶ 救治策, relief measures; a remedy.

kyūchi (窮地), *n.* a predicament; an extremity; a sad plight. —窮地に陷る, to go to the wall; be brought to bay.

kyūchi (舊知), *n.* an old friend [acquaintance].

kyūchō (級長), *n.* the head of a class; a monitor.

kyūchū (宮中), *n.* the Imperial court. —宮中喪仰出さる, to proclaim court-mourning. ¶ 宮中顧問官, a court-councillor. —宮中席次, precedence at court.

kyūdai (及第), *n.* passing an examination. —— **-suru**, *vi.* to pass (an examination); be promoted (進級する); satisfy the examiners (大學にて). —どうかかうか及第する, to scrape through. —優等で及第する, to pass the examination with honours. ¶ 及第者, a person passing an examination; a successful examinee [candidate]. —及第點, pass-mark.

kyūden (宮殿), *n.* a palace; a Royal [an Imperial] palace.

kyūden (急電), *n.* an urgent telegram. —急電に接して, upon receipt of an urgent telegram.

kyūden (給電), *n.* supply of (electric) power. ¶ 給電線,【電】a feeder.

kyūdō (舊道), *n.* a former [an old] road. —箱根の舊道, the old Hakone road.

kyūdōsha (求道者), *n.* a seeker after truth.

kyūen (救援), *n.* rescue; relief. 救援する, to rescue; relieve. —救援列車を發する, to despatch a relief train.

kyūen (舊怨), *n.* old enmity; an old score.

kyūfu (給付), *n.* ❶【法】prestation. ❷ (保險給付) a benefit.

kyūgaku (休學), *n.* resting from school. —休學する, to rest from school; miss school.

kyūgeki (急激な), *a.* rapid; sudden; abrupt; radical (過激な). —急激な改革, a radical reform. —急激な變動, a sudden change.

kyūgeki (舊劇), *n.* a play of the old school; a classical drama.

kyūgijō (球戯場), *n.* a billiard saloon.

kyūgo (救護), *n.* relief; protection; salvage (貨物を水火より). —救護する, to relieve; aid; protect. ¶ 救護隊, a relief party; a salvage corps (火災時財産の). —赤十字救護班, a relief contingent of the Red Cross Society.

kyūgō (糾合), *n.* convocation; rally. —— **-suru**, *vt.* to convoke; call together; rally. —同志を糾合する, to call together those of the same mind.

kyūgyō (休業), *n.* ❶ resting from work; taking a holiday; shut-down (鑛山・工場などの). ❷ (休暇) the holidays; the vacation. —本日休業, "closed to-day." —— **-suru**, *vi.* to be closed; rest from work; take [have] a holiday (休暇をとる); shut down. —臨時休業する (商店・學校など), to close temporarily.

kyūgyū (九牛の一毛), an inappreciable [infinitesimal] portion; a drop of the bucket [ocean].

kyūha (急派する), *vt.* to dispatch hastily.

kyūha (舊派), *n.* the old school; the classical school (文學・美術等の). ¶ 舊派俳優, an actor of the old school.

kyūhaku (急迫の), *a.* pressing; urgent; imminent.

kyūhaku (窮迫), *n.* ❶ (貧窮) distress; destitution; straitened [narrow] circumstances. ❷ (處置などの) embarrassment; extremity; dilemma. —窮迫する, ① to be hard up; be in need; be badly off. ② (當惑する) to be at a loss; be at one's wits' end. ③ (窮迫されて) to be driven into a corner; go to the wall.

kyūhan (急坂), *n.* a steep slope.

kyūhan (舊藩), *n.* a former clan.

kyūhei (舊弊), *n.* ❶ (古くからの弊害) a long-standing evil; old abuses. ❷ (古風) an old fashion; conservatism; fogyism. ¶ 舊弊家, an old fogy; an old-fashioned person; an antediluvian.

kyūhen (急變), *n.* a sudden change; an unexpected event [calamity]; an emergency. —急變する, to change suddenly; take a critical turn (病勢が).

kyūhi (給費する), *vt.* to give an allowance (for school expenses). ¶ 給費生, a scholar; an exhibitioner; a foundationer.

kyūhin (救貧), *n.* relief of the poor; poor relief. ¶ 救貧院, a poor-house; a workhouse; an alms-house【米】.

kyūhō (急報), *n.* a dispatch; an urgent message [report]; an express. —急報する, to send an urgen message; report promptly.

kyūhō (臼砲), *n.* a mortar.

kyūin (吸引), *n.* absorption; suction. —吸引する, to absorb; suck in; imbibe; attract (引附ける).

kyūji (給仕), *n.* ❶ (給仕すること) waiting at table. ❷ (小使) an office boy; a footboy; a servant. ❸ (旅館等の) awaiter; a table-servant; an attendant. ❹ (船車の) a cabin [ship]- boy (汽船); a (train-)boy (汽車). ❺ (其他の) a page (小姓); a shop-girl (-boy) (賣子). —給仕する, to wait on [upon]; wait at table; serve (at a dinner). ¶ 給仕頭, a head-waiter. —給仕女, a waitress; a waiting maid.

kyūjin (求人), *n.* seeking for employees.

kyūjitsu (休日), *n.* a holiday; a rest-day; an off-day (暇の日).

kyūjo (宮女), *n.* a court-lady; a maid of honour.

kyūjo (救助), *n.* rescue; succour; relief; aid. —救助を求むる聲, a voice calling for help. —救助の見込なし, to be a total wreck. **—-suru** (救助する), *vt.* to rescue; succour; relieve. —人命を救助する, to save a (human) life. —窮民を救助する, to relieve people in distress. ¶ 救助網, ① (火災時の) a life-net. ② (電車·自動車の) a netting; a safety-net; a tram-car fender. —救助米, rice dealt out to the poor. —救助料, salvage(-money). —救助作業, rescue work; salvage operations (遭難船の). —救助策, a plan for rescuing; a remedial measure (救濟策). —救助船, a salvage vessel; a wrecker; a life-boat (救命艇). —救助隊, a rescue party.

kyūjō (弓狀の), *a.* arched; arch-shaped; arcuate(d); bow-shaped.

kyūjō (休場する), *vi.* to shut (the theatre; the wrestling booth) temporarily: absent oneself from (the stage, 俳優が; the arena, 力士が).

kyūjō (宮城), *n.* the Imperial palace [castle].

kyūjō (球狀の), *a.* spherical; globular; orbicular.

kyūjō (窮狀), *n.* straitened [distressed] circumstances; a sad plight; a wretched [miserable] condition. —窮狀を訴へる, to complain of one's sad plight [wretched condition].

kyūjō (舊情), *n.* old friendship. —舊情を溫める, ① to renew one's old friendship. ② to return to one's first love.

kyūjutsu (弓術), *n.* archery. ¶ 弓術家, an archer.

kyūjutsu (救恤), *n.* relief. —救恤する, to relieve; give [administer] relief. ¶ 救恤金, relief-money; a relief fund.

kyūka (休暇), *n.* ❶ holidays; a vacation. ❷ (賜暇) furlough; leave of absence. —休暇を賜ふ, to grant leave of absence [a furlough]. ¶ 慰勞休暇, a furlough; leave of absence. —休暇日誌, a diary of a vacation.

kyūka (毬果), *n.* 【植】 a cone.

kyūkai (休會), *n.* adjournment. —休會する, to adjourn.

kyūkaku (嗅覺), *n.* the sense of smell; the olfactory sense.

kyūkan (休刊), *n.* suspension; discontinuance. —休刊する, to suspend [discontinue] publication; stop issue. ¶ 年中無休刊, Issued all the year round.

kyūkan (球竿), *n.* a bar-bell. ¶ 球竿體操, bar-bell exercise.

kyūkan (舊慣), *n.* old customs. —舊慣を墨守する, to stick to old customs.

kyūkan (舊觀), *n.* old appearance. —舊觀を留めず, to leave no trace of the former appearance.

kyūkatsu (久闊), *n.* a long neglect in calling (writing). —互に久闊を敍する, to make inquiry of each other after long absence.

kyūkei (弓形の), *a.* crescent-shaped; bow-shaped; arched.

kyūkei (求刑する), *v.* to demand punishment.

kyūkei (休憩), *n.* rest; repose; recess. —休憩する, to rest; repose; take rest. ¶ 休憩時間, recess time. —休憩室, a resting-room; a retiring-room. —休憩所, a resting-place; a pavilion (天幕·假屋などの).

kyukei (球莖), *n.* 【植】 the corm; the solid bulb.

kyūki (窮鬼), *n.* the god of poverty.

kyūki (舊記), *n.* an old chronicle.

kyūkihō (九歸法), *n.* 【數】 the division table (used in calculation with the abacus).

kyūkin (給金), *n.* pay; wages (賃銀); a salary (俸給). —僅かの給金, a mere pittance (of a salary). —多額の給金, good pay. —給金が好い (惡い), to be well [amply] (ill; miserably) paid. —給金を貰ふ, to receive a salary.

kyūkō (休校), *n.* a temporary closure of a school. **—-suru,** *vi.* to close a school temporarily. —同盟休校する, to go on strike.

kyūkō (休講), *n.* absence from one's lecture; rest from one's lecture. —休講する, to absent oneself from one's lecture.

kyūkō (急行), *n.* ❶ going in a hurry. ❷ =急行列車. —急行する, to go in a hury; hasten[hurry] *to*. —急行に乘る, to take the express. ¶ 急行券, an express ticket. —急行列車, an express (train). (最大急行列車, a special express; a limited express [train].) —急行料金, express charges.

kyūkō (急航する), *vi.* to hasten *to*; hurry *to*.

kyūkō (躬行する), *vt.* to act up *to*; practise; carry out.

kyūkō (舊交), *n.* old friendship [acquaintance]. ☞ *kyūjō* (舊情).

kyūkon (求婚), *n.* wooing; courtship; suit. —求婚する, to woo; pay court *to*; pay addresses *to*. ¶

求婚廣告, a matrimonial advertisement. —求婚者, a wooer; a suitor.

kyūkon (球根), *n.* 【植】 a bulb (玉葱などの); a tuber (芋などの).

kyūkutsu (窮屈), *n.* ❶ (嚴重) strictness; rigidity. ❷ (氣がね) uneasiness; discomfort. ❸ (狹隘) narrowness; tightness; limitedness. **——-na,** *a.* ❶ strict; rigid; stiff. ❷ uneasy; constrained; uncomfortable. ❸ narrow; tight; cramped. —窮屈な部屋, a narrow room. —窮屈な服, a tight coat. —窮屈な思ひをする, to feel uncomfortable; feel constrained (固くなる). —窮屈に坐る, to sit in a cramped manner.

kyūkyo (急遽), *ad.* in haste; in a hurry; hastily; hurry-scurry (周章して). —急遽上京する, to go up to Tōkyō in a hurry.

kyūkyō (究竟), *n.* ultimateness; the ultimate result. —究竟の, ultimate; final. —究竟の目的, the ultimate end.

kyūkyō (舊敎), *n.* Roman Catholicism; Romanism. ¶舊敎徒, a Roman Catholic.

kyūkyō (窮境), *n.* ❶ (貧窮) poverty; narrow circumstances; indigence. ❷ (窮地) a predicament; an extremity; a corner. —窮境に陷(おとし)れる, to bring [drive] one to bay; put one in a hole. —窮境に陷ッて居る, to be in extremity.

kyūkyoku (究極の), *a.* ultimate; final; eventual. —究極の勝利, a final victory.

kyūkyū (汲汲たる), *a.* diligent; industrious. —富貴に汲々とする, to pant for wealth and rank. —金儲けに汲々としてゐる, to be bent on gain.

kyūkyū (救急の), *a.* first-aid; emergent; temporary. ☞ *ōkyū.* ¶救急箱, a medicine chest.

kyūmei (救命), *n.* saving lives; life-saving. ¶救命浮標, a life-buoy. —救命具, a life-saving apparatus; a life-preserver (救難用具). —救命ジャケツ, a life-jacket. —救命索, a life-line. —救命帶, a safety [life] -belt. —救命艇, a life-boat.

kyūmen (球面), *n.* a spherical surface. ¶球面角(三角), a spherical angle (triangle).

kyūmin (窮民), *n.* a pauper; the poor; the needy. ¶震災窮民, sufferers from an earthquake.

kyūmon (糺問), *n.* ❶ minute examination. ❷ (裁判上) judicial enquiry; cross-examination (證人に對する反對側よりの糺問, 我國の對質に類す). —糺問する, to examine; cross-examine.

kyūmu (急務), *n.* urgent business; pressing need; a burning question. —刻下の急務, the urgent necessity of the moment; the burning question of the day.

kyūnan (救難), *n.* saving; rescue; salvage (海難救助). ¶救難列車, a breakdown van [英]; a wrecking-car [-train] [米]. —救難(作業)隊, a breakdown gang; a wrecking-crew.

kyūnen (舊年), *n.* last year; the past [old] year.

kyū-ni (急に), *ad.* suddenly; at once; hurriedly. —急に惡くなる (病氣が), to develop a critical turn. —急に騰る (物價など), to rise with a jump. —急にさがる (物價など), to come down with a run. —急に止まる, to come to a sudden stop [standstill].

kyūnyū (吸入する), *vt.* to inhale; suck in. ¶吸入器, an inhaler; an inspirator. (吸入器をかける, to use an inhaler; inhale steam.) —吸入藥, vapour.

kyūnyūki (吸乳器), *n.* a breast-pump.

kyūon (舊恩), *n.* old [former] kindness [favour]. —舊恩に報いる, to repay old favours.

kyūpī (キューピー), *n.* Ⓢ キューピッド. Cupid.

kyūrai (舊來), *ad.* from old times. —舊來の, old; time-honoured; long-established.

kyūrei (舊例), *n.* an old custom; an old precedent; usage. —舊例に仍ッて, in accordance with the old usage.

kyūreki (舊曆), *n.* the old calendar; the old style (卽ちジュリウス曆); the lunar calendar (陰曆). —舊曆の十五日, the 15th day of the moon (according to the old calendar).

kyūri (胡瓜), *n.* 【植】 the cucumber.

kyūri (窮理), *n.* investigation of natural principles.

kyūrō (舊臘), *n.* the end of last year; last December.

kyūryō (給料), *n.* pay; wages (勞銀); a salary (俸給). ¶給料日, a pay-day. —給料取, a salaried man; the salariat (階級).

kyūryū (急流), *n.* a rapid current; a violent [rushing] stream; a torrent.

kyūsai (休載する), *v.* not to appear (in the column); be held over. —小說は本日休載す, The novel will not appear to-day.

kyūsai (救濟), *n.* relief; redress; aid. —救濟する, to relieve; redress; remedy; aid. ¶救濟組合, a mutual relief [aid] association. —救濟策, a relief measure; a remedy. —救濟者, a saviour; a reliever.

kyūsaku (窮策), *n.* the last shift [resort]. —一時の窮策, a temporary shift; a makeshift. —窮策を用ひる, to take to the last shift; appeal to the last resort.

kyūsan (急霰), *n.* a shower of hail. —急霰の如き拍手, a thunderous [deafening] applause.

kyūsei (救世), *n.* salvation (of the world). ¶ 救世軍, the Salvation Army. (救世軍軍人, a Salvationist.). —救世主, the Saviour (of the world); Messiah; the Redeemer.

kyūsei (舊姓), *n.* one's former name; one's maiden name (處女姓). —スミス夫人舊姓ジョウンズ, Mrs. Smith, née Jones.

kyūsei (急性の), *a.* 【醫】 acute. ¶ 急性腦膜炎, acute meningitis.

kyūseki (休戚), *n.* interests; welfare. —國民と休戚を共にする, to have common interests with the people.

kyūseki (求積), *n.* 【數】 mensuration.

kyūseki (舊跡, 舊蹟), *n.* ruins; sites of historic interest; a historic ground. —名所舊蹟が多い, to abound with places of note and historic interest.

kyūsen (休戰), *n.* armistice; truce; cessation of arms [hostilities]. —休戰する, to make [conclude] a truce; suspend hostilities. —休戰を申込む, to make a proposal for armistice. ¶ 休戰條約, an agreement of truce; a truce; an armistice. —休戰旗, a flag of truce.

kyūsenpō (急先鋒), *n.* a leader; the van. —彼はあらゆる社會改良の急先鋒である, He is in the van [forefront] of all social reforms.

kyūsetsu (急設する), *vt.* to install (provide *with*) as soon as possible. —電話の急設, rapid installation of telephones.

kyūsha (柩車), *n.* a hearse.

kyūshi (九死一生の場合), a case [question] of life or death. —九死に一生を得る, to have a narrow [a hairbreadth] escape; be snatched from the jaws of death.

kyūshi (臼齒), *n.* the molar teeth; the molars; the grinders. ¶ 大臼齒, the molars; the large [true] molars. —小臼齒, the small [false] molars; the premolars.

kyūshi (休止), *n.* pause; cessation; suspension. —商賣は休止の姿である, Business is at a standstill. **——-suru,** *v.* to cease; stop; suspend; be suspended; be brought [come] to a standstill. —運轉を休止する, to stop the engine.

kyūshi (急使), *n.* an express messenger.

kyūshiki (舊式), *n.* old style; old fashion. —舊式な帽子, an old-fashioned hat.

kyūshiki (舊識), *n.* an old friend [acquaintance]. ☞ *kyūchi.*

kyūshin (求心的), *a.* centripetal. ¶ 求心力, centripetal force.

kyūshin (急進的), *a.* radical. ¶ 急進主義, radicalism. —急進黨, the radical party; the left (左黨).

kyūshinkei (嗅神經), *n.* 【醫】 the olfactory nerve.

kyūshisō (舊思想), *n.* antiquated thoughts; hackneyed ideas.

kyūsho (急所), *n.* a vital part [point]; the heart. —急所の痛手を受ける, to be mortally wounded. —急所を突く, to strike [charge] another home.

kyūshō (求償), *n.* claim for indemnity. ¶ 求償權, (right of) recourse.

kyūshō (宮相), *n.* the Minister of the Imperial Household.

kyūshoku (休職), *n.* temporary retirement; provisional release from office. —休職を命ずる, to release provisionally from office.

kyūshoku (求職), *n.* seeking employment. —求職の廣告を出す, to advertise for a situation. ¶ 求職者, one who seeks employment.

kyūshu (舊主), *n.* one's former lord [master].

kyūshu (鳩首する), *v.* to lay our (their) heads together.

kyūshū (吸收), *n.* 【法】 merger; 【化】 absorption; suction. **——-suru,** *vt.* ❶ (液體·瓦斯などを) to absorb; suck in [up]; merge. ❷ (吸入する) to inhale; breathe in; take in. —知識を吸收する, to suck in knowledge. ¶ 吸收劑, 【化】 an absorbent.

kyūshū (舊習), *n.* old customs; old usages; old abuses (舊弊).

kyūso (窮鼠), *n.* a cornered rat; a rat at bay. —窮鼠却って猫を咬む, "A trampled worm will turn."

kyūsō (急送する), *vt.* to express; send by express; send by an early mail (郵便で).

kyūsō (急躁), *n.* hastiness; precipitancy.

kyūsodai (窮措大), *n.* a poor student.

kyūsoku (休息), *n.* rest; repose; relaxation. ☞ *kyūkei* (休憩). **——-suru,** *vi.* to rest; repose; take breath (中休みする). —ゆっくり休息する, to take a good [complete] rest. ¶ 休息時間, a recess; breathing time.

kyūsoku (急速の), *a.* rapid; swift; quick. —急速の進歩をする,

to make rapid progress.

kyūsokudo (急速度), *n.* Ⓢ 急速力. high speed. —急速度で, at full speed; at high speed.

kyūsu (急須), *n.* a small china teapot.

kyōsū (級數), *n.* 【數】 progression; series. ¶ 等差[算術]級數, arithmetical progression. —等比[幾何]級數, geometrical progression. —三角級數, trigonometric series.

kyūsui (吸水), *n.* suction. ¶ 吸水ポンプ, a suction-pump.

kyūsui (給水), *n.* water-supply; supply of water; water service. —給水する, to supply water. ¶ 給水驛, a tank-station. —給水管, a service-pipe; a feed-pipe (汽罐の). (給水本管, a supply main; a water-main.) —給水船, a water-boat. —給水塔, a water-tower.

kyū-suru (休する), *vi.* to be ruined; be undone; be all up *with*. —萬事休す, All is up [over]; The game is up.

kyū-suru (給する), *vt.* to supply; provide; allow. —手當を給する, to give an allowance. —彈藥を給する, to serve out ammunition.

kyū-suru (窮する), *vi.* ❶ (貧窮) to be in want [need]; be in narrow [straitened; needy] circumstances; be reduced to poverty. ❷ (當惑) to be troubled [puzzled; perplexed]; be at a loss. ❸ (困却する) to be in a fix; get into a scrape [difficulties]; be driven to the wall. —糧食に窮する, to run short of provisions. —返答に窮する, to be at a loss for an answer. —手段に窮する, to be at one's wits' end. —金に窮してる, to be hard up for money.

kyūtai (舊態), *n.* old order; the former state of things. —舊態に復する, to relapse into the former state of things. —舊態を改める, to be reformed; assume a new aspect.

kyūtaku (舊宅), *n.* the old [former] residence; one's former house.

kyūtan (急湍), *n.* rapids.

kyūtan (給炭), *n.* coal supply. ¶ 給炭所, a coaling-station; a coaling-depot. —給炭船, a collier; a coal-ship.

kyūtei (宮廷), *n.* the Imperial palace (皇居); the court; the royal household. ¶ 宮廷列車, the Imperial train.

kyūteibi (休廷日), *n.* 【法】 *dies non (juridicus)* 【羅. =not a court-day】.

kyūteki (仇敵), *n.* a sworn enemy; a mortal foe. —仇敵視する, to look upon as a mortal enemy.

kyūten (灸點), *n.* moxicautery; moxicausis. ¶ 灸點師, a moxa-burner; a moxicauterist.

kyūten (急轉), *n.* a sudden change. —急轉する, ① to whirl; race (推進機·水極車等に云ふ). ② (形勢など) to change suddenly; take a sudden turn. —急轉直下の勢で, with sudden energy [force].

kyūto (舊都), *n.* an old capital; a former seat of government.

kyūtō (球燈), *n.* a round [glove] lantern.

kyūtō (舊冬), *n.* last winter [December].

kyūtō (舊套), *n.* convention; old customs. —舊套を脫する, to throw off conventions; be free from conventions. —舊套を脫せず, to stick to conventions.

kyūtsui (窮追する), *vt.* ❶ (追ひ詰める) to drive (another) into a corner; press (the fugitive) close. ❷ (問ひ詰める) to cross-question; press (a person) hard with questions.

kyūu (急雨), *n.* a shower; a sudden fall of rain.

kyūyaku (窮厄), *n.* ❶ (困窮) distress; hardship; misery. ❷ (不運) adversity; misfortune. ❸ (貧困) poverty; destitution; indigence; penury.

kyūyaku (舊約), *n.* the old covenant. ¶ 舊約全書, the Old Testament.

kyūyo (給與), *n.* grant; supply; allowance. —給與する, to grant; supply; allow; provide *with* (食料など). ¶ 現品給與, an allowance in kind. —給與金, an allowance.

kyūyo (窮餘の策), *n.* a makeshift; the last resort.

kyūyō (休養), *n.* rest; repose; relaxation. —戰後の休養, the post-bellum recuperation. —休養する, to rest; repose; recuperate. ¶ 休養室, a resting-room.

kyūyō (急用), *n.* urgent [pressing] business. —急用で呼びにやる, to send for a person on urgent business. —急用電報を打つ, to send a telegram on an urgent matter.

kyūyō (給養), *n.* supply; allowance; maintenance. —給養する, to supply; allow; maintain; sustain; support. ¶ 戰時給養, field supplies. —給養係, 【軍】 a quartermaster. —給養班, 【軍】 a squad.

kyūyū (級友), *n.* a class-mate; a class-fellow.

kyūyū (舊友), *n.* an old friend [acquaintance].

kyūyusen (給油船), *n.* a tanker; a tank-ship [-vessel].

kyūzō (急造する), *vt.* to construct hurriedly; run [throw] up.

M

ma (眞), *n.* truth. ——, *a.* (眞面目な) serious (look); (眞實な) true (man); (純な) pure (white). ——, *ad.* (丁度) just (behind); due (west); right (under). —眞に受ける, to take for truth; take [accept] as true.

ma (間), *n.* ❶ (部屋) a room; a chamber; an apartment. ❷ (をり, 運) chance; luck. ❸【音】(休止) a rest. ❹ =*aida, hima.* —間が悪い, to be abashed; be awkward; be embarrassing. —勉强する間がない, to have no time for study. —忙しくて飯を食ふ間もない, I am too busy even for meals.

ma (魔), *n.* an evil spirit; a demon; a devil. —魔がさす, to be under the influence of an evil spirit. —魔を除ける, to keep out of harm's way.

mā (まあ), *ad.* (一寸) just. ——, *int.* ❶ (驚の叫) dear me!; oh dear!; fancy! ❷ (先づ) well. —まあ驚いた, Well, I'm surprised. —まあ一寸お上りなさい, Dear me, do just step in.

maai (間合), *n.* ❶ (時機) opportunity; chance. ❷ =*hima.*

maaji (眞鰺), *n.* 【魚】 the saurel horse-mackerel.

mabara (疎の), *a.* sparse (人口等の); thin; scattered. ——-**ni,** *ad.* sparsely; thinly; scattered about. —疎らに散在してゐる, to be scattered here and there.

mabataki (瞬), *n.* a wink; blinking; twinkling. —瞬する; 瞬く, to wink; blink; twinkle. ☞ *matataku.*

mabayui (目映い), *a.* dazzling; glaring. ☞ *mabushii.*

mabireru (塗れる), *vi.* to be smeared [covered] *with.* ☞ *mamireru.*

mabisashi (眉庇), *n.* ❶ a visor, vizor; a frontlet (冑の). ❷ (帽の) a peak; an eye-shade.

maboroshi (幻), *n.* ❶ (幻影) an apparition; a phantom; a vision. ❷ (幻覺) hallucination; illusion (錯覺). —幻の如き人生, a visionary life.

mabu (間夫), *n.* a secret lover; a fancy-man (賣笑婦の) [卑].

mabuchi (眼緣, 眶), **mabuta** (眼瞼), *n.* the eyelid. ¶ 一(二)重瞼, a foldless (folded) eyelid. —上(下)瞼, the upper (lower) eyelid.

mabuka (眼深に), *ad.* shading the eyes. —帽子を眼深に被る(被って), to pull (with) one's hat over one's eyes.

mabushii (眩い), *a.* ❶ (目映い) dazzling; glaring; blinding. ❷ (面羞かしい) abashed. —眩しくする, to dazzle. —眩しい程美しい, of dazzling beauty.

mabusu (糝·塗す), *vt.* to cover with flour; roll in flour.

machi (町), *n.* ❶ (都會) a town. ❷ (通り) a street; a road. ¶ 町役場, the town office.

machi (襠), *n.* a gusset; a gore.

machiagumu (待倦む), *vi.* to grow tired with waiting; tire of waiting.

machiai (待合), *n.* Ⓢ 待合茶屋. an assignation-house; a house of accommodation. ¶ 待合室, (停車場の) a waiting-room; a *salle d'attente* [佛].

machiakasu (待明かす), *vt.* to wait all night; wait till daybreak.

machiawasu (待合はす), *v.* ❶ (約束して待つ) to rendezvous; meet at an appointed place. ❷ (來るのを待つ) to wait *for.* —上り汽車を待合はす, to wait for the arrival of the up-train.

machibito (待人), *n.* an expected person; a person waited *for.*

machibōke (待惚けを食はす), to keep a person waiting in vain.

machibuse (待伏), *n.* ambush; ambuscade; lying in ambush [wait]. —待伏する, to ambush; ambuscade; lie in ambush.

machidōshii (待遠しい), *a.* tired of waiting; waiting impatiently. —お待遠様, Sorry to have kept you waiting.

machigaeru (間違へる), *vt.* to mistake; make a mistake *in.* —列車に乘り間違へる, to take a wrong train. —夜盗と間違へられる, to be mistaken for a burglar. —人を間違へる, to take [mistake] a person (*for*). —道を間違へる, to miss one's way [road]; take a wrong road. —計算を間違へる, to make an error in calculation.

machigai (間違), *n.* ❶ (誤謬) a mistake; an error. ❷ (失錯) a failure; a blunder; a slip. ❸ (過失) a fault; a mistake. ❹ (喧嘩) a collision; a quarrel. ❺ (男女の間の) an indiscretion. ❻ (不慮の出來事) an accident. ☞ *ayamari.* —間違なく, without fail; for certain. —間違だらけの, very faulty; full of faults. —間違がない, to be free from mistakes. —それに間違ない, There is no mistake about it. —何かの間違だらう, It must be some mistake.

machigau (間違ふ), *vi.* to mistake; err; blunder. —間違ッて, by mistake. —間違ッた考へ, a mistaken [an erroneous] idea. —間違ッた事を云ふ, to say wrong things; blunder. —此の事實たるや間違ふべくもない, The fact is not to be mistaken.

machihazure (町外れ), *n.* ❶ the suburbs; the outskirts; environs. ❷ the end of a street [road]. —町外れの掛茶屋, a tea-booth on the outskirt of the town.

machikamaeru (待構へる), *vt.* to be ready *for*; wait *for*; watch *for*. —其日の來るのを待ち構へる, to wait for the day to come.

machikaneru (待兼ねる), *vt.* to wait impatiently; wait on tiptoe *for*. —返事を待ち兼ねて, too impatient to wait for an answer.

machikogareru (待焦れる), *v.* to be dying *for* [to do]; wait anxiously; long *for*. —君の來るのを待ち焦れてゐた, He was dying to see you.

machikurasu (待暮す), *v.* to wait all day *for*; pass the whole day in waiting.

machikutabireru (待草臥れる), *v.* to tire of waiting; grow tired with waiting.

machimachi (區區の), *a.* diverse; different; various. —意見がまちまちだから, as the views are diverse.

machimōkeru (待設ける), *vt.* to expect; anticipate; look forward *to*.

machin (馬錢子), *n.* 【植】 the nux-vomica tree; (實) nux-vomica.

machinē (晝間興行), *n.* a matinée; a morning performance.

machiukeru (待受ける), *vt.* to wait *for*; expect.

machiwabiru (待侘びる), *v.* = ***machiagumu***.

mada (まだ), *ad.* ❶ (今に) yet; as yet; still. ❷ (その上) moreover; still; yet (比較級と共に). ❸ (やッと) only; merely. —まだあるか, Are there any left? —まだ來たばッかりだ, I have only just come. —まだ時間がある, There is still time.

madai (眞鯛), *n.* 【魚】 Pagrus major (sea-bream の一種·學名).

madai (間代), *n.* charge for a room; a room-rent.

madake (苦竹), *n.* 【植】 Phyllostachys bambusoides (whangee cane の類·學名).

madako (海蛸), *n.* 【軟體】 the poulp(e); the octopus.

madara (斑), *n.* spots; specks; speckles. —斑の, spotted; mottled; speckled.

madarukoi (間怠こい), *a.* Ⓢ 間怠い. slow; dull; sluggish.

madashimo (まだしも), *ad.* rather; preferably. ☞ ***mushiro***. —この方がまだしもだ, This is less objectionable.

made (迄), ❶ (範圍, 程度) as far as; so far as; to. ❷ (時, 場所) till; to; up to; by (迄に). —今月まで, down 《up》 to this month. —百圓迄, up to 100 *yen*. —彼の歸りまで, till his return. —最後の一人になる迄, to the last man. —晩まで待つ, to wait till evening. —命までも, even one's life. —來週迄に, by next week. —こゝ[そこ] 迄はよい, So far, so good.

mado (窓), *n.* a window; a port (船の); a light (明取り). —窓を覗く, ① (内から) to look out of the window. ② (外から) to look in at the window. —窓を開ける《閉める》, to open [raise] 《shut; let down》 the window. ¶ 窓硝子, window-pane; window-glass.

madō (魔道), *n.* ❶ (邪敎) heterodoxy; heresy; diabolism. ❷ (邪道) evil ways. —魔道に陷る, to fall into evil ways.

madoakari (窓明), *n.* window light.

madogamachi (窓框), *n.* a window-sash.

madoguchi (窓口), *n.* a window; a counter (切符賣口).

madoi (惑), *n.* = ***mayoi***.

madoi (團居), *n.* sitting in a circle; the hearth; a family gathering; a home-circle. —家族の樂しき團居, the pleasant [happy] family circle.

madoka (圓かな), *a.* ❶ (圓い) round. ❷ (安かな) quiet [calm] (眠り); pleasant [sweet] (夢).

madokake (窓掛), *n.* a window-curtain; a sun-blind (日除).

madonna (聖母), *n.* Madonna.

madori (間取), *n.* the plan of a house; house-planning; arrangement of rooms. —間取の良い《惡い》家, a house with well 《badly》-arranged rooms.

madoromu (微睡む), *vi.* to doze; drowse; drop into a nap.

madorosu (マドロス), *n.* ❶ 〔蘭 matroos〕 (船乘) a sailor; a seaman. ❷ (のろま) a dunce; a blockhead.

madou (惑ふ), *v.* ❶ (當惑する)

to puzzle; be at a loss; be perplexed. ❷ (勘違ひする) to misconstrue; misapprehend. ☞ *madowasu.*

madowaku (窓枠), *n.* a window-frame.

madowasu (惑はす), *vt.* ❶ (惑亂) to perplex; distract; bewitch. ❷ (誘惑) to mislead; tempt. ❸ (欺き惑はす) to deceive; delude; cheat.

mae (前), *n.* ❶ (正面) the front. ❷ (眼前, 手近) the presence; being at hand. ❸ (先立, 先行) precedence; antecedence. ❹ (以前, 昔) a former time. ❺ (何人前) a share; a portion. ——, *ad.* ago (過去); since (現在迄); before. ☞ *maeni* (前に). —牛肉三人前, beef for three (persons). —五年前, five years ago [since]. —三時に十五分前, a quarter to three. —前同様, to be the same as before; be unchanged; be no better than before. —人の前で, in the presence of a person; in [before] a person's face. —前へ出る, to come forward; step up. —四五日前から, for the last four or five days. —僕の家のすぐ前だ, It stands just opposite our house. ——**-no,** *a.* ❶ (時間) previous to (より前の); preceding (以前の); last (此前の). ❷ (場所, 位置) front; facing. ❸ (前面の) front; opposite (向側の). ❹ (前述の) foregoing; above-mentioned. —前の頁を參照して下さい, Please refer to the preceding page. ——**-ni,** *prep.* & *ad.* ❶ (時間) before; ago; back; previously (前以て); formerly (以前に). ❷ (正面に) before; in front *of.* ❸ (前方に) ahead; onward; forward. ❹ (先立って) before. ❺ (順序) before; anteriorly. —餘程前に, long before [ago].

maeashi (前足), *n.* a foreleg; a forefoot.

maeba (前齒), *n.* a front tooth; an incisor.

maebarai (前拂), *n.* advance; payment in advance; cash with order (C. W. O. と略す). —前拂ひする, to pay in advance.

maebi (前日), *n.* the day before; the preceding [previous] day.

maebure (前觸), *n.* ❶ (豫報) a preliminary announcement. ❷ (先驅) a forerunner; a herald. —前觸れする, to announce in advance.

maedare (前垂), *n.* an apron; a pinafore (涎掛).

maedate (前立), *n.* a plume; a pompon; a crest. —前立附きの軍帽, a plumed military cap.

maegaki (前書), *n.* a preface (例言); a prelude (同上); a preamble (條約文の前文).

maegami (前髮), *n* a forelock.

maegari (前借する), *vt.* to borrow in advance. —給金を前借りする, to get one's salary in advance.

maegashi (前貸), *n.* advancement; advance; payment in advance. —前貸しする, to advance; make advance; pay in advance.

maegashira (前頭), *n.* 【相撲】 a first-grade wrestler.

maegeiki (前景氣), *n.* forecast; prospect.

maeiwai (前祝), *n.* celebration in anticipation.

maejirase (前知せ), *n.* ❶ (前兆) an omen; a presage; a sign. ❷ (蟲の知せ) a presentiment; a foreboding (凶事の). ❸ = *maebure.*

maekata (前方), *ad.* some time ago. ☞ *katsute.*

maekin (前金), *n.* advance (money); earnest money (手金); bargain money (同上). —前金を出す《借る》, to pay 《borrow》 in advance.

maekōjō (前口上), *n.* an introductory remark; a prologue (特に劇の); an exordium (講話等の).

maemotte (前以て), *ad.* in advance; in anticipation; beforehand. ☞ *arakajime.*

maeoki (前置), *n.* an introduction; preparatory remarks; a premise (前提). —前置きに, by way of introduction; as a preliminary. —前置きする, to make preparatory remarks; preamble; premise.

maeuri (前賣), *n.* an advance sale (of tickets).

maewatashi (前渡), *n.* advance. ¶ 前渡し金, advance (money).

mafu (麻布), *n.* linen.

mafugu (河豚), *n.* the globe-fish.

mafura (マフラ), *n.* a muffler.

mafutatsu (眞二つに), *ad.* right [just] in two; exactly in half [two]. —眞二つに切る, to cut right [exactly] in two [half].

magaeru (擬へる), *vt.* ❶ to imitate; make in imitation. ❷ (贋造) to counterfeit; forge; make a spurious copy *of.*

magai (擬), *n.* an imitation (摸造品); a sham (僞物); a counterfeit (贋造物). —金剛石擬ひの指輪, a ring set with an imitation diamond.

magaki (籬), *n.* a hedge; a bamboo fence (竹の).

magamo (眞鴨), *n.* 【鳥】 the wild duck; the mallard.

magana-sukigana (間がな隙がな), *ad.* whenever one has time;

at all spare moments.

magao (真顔), *n.* a sober [serious] look [countenance]; a grave face. —真顔で, with a straight [grave] face; with a serious look; in sober earnest (真剣に).

magari (曲り), *n.* crookedness; a bend; a turn (轉向); a curve.

magari (間借), *n.* renting [living in] a room. —間借りする, to rent a room; engage a room.

magarikado (曲角), *n.* a corner (町角); a turning; a turn (in a road). —第二番目の曲り角を左へ曲る, to take the second turning to the left.

magarikuneru (曲りくねる), *vi.* to wind; be crooked; meander (川などの). —曲りくねった川, a meandering [winding] brook.

magarime (曲り目), *n.* a bend; a turning.

magarinari (曲りなりに), *ad.* anyhow; somehow or other.

magaru (曲る), *v.* ❶ (屈曲) to bend; be bent [crooked]; curve. ❷ (轉向) to turn; round; make a turn. ❸ (心が) to be crooked. —歳で腰が曲る, to be bent with age. —右の方に曲る, to strike [turn] to the right. —角を曲る, to turn a corner.

magatama (曲玉), *n.* a bead.

magatta (曲った), *a.* ❶ (屈曲) bent; crooked; curved. ❷ (不正) crooked; dishonest. ❸ (曲解) forced; distorted; twisted. —曲った道, a winding [crooked] road. —心の曲った人, a man with a crooked mind.

magau (紛ふ), *vi.* ❶ (混淆する) to be confounded; be confused. ❷ (見違ふ) to be mistaken *for*; be taken *for*. —紛ふ方なき彼の肉筆, a signature which is unmistakably his.

mage (髷), *n.* ❶ a chignon (女の); a queue (辮髮); a top-knot (丁髷). ❷ =***marumage*** の略. —髷に結ふ, to gather [dress] the hair into a chignon.

magemono (曲物), *n.* a round [circular] box of chip-wood.

mageru (曲·枉げる), *v.* ❶ to bend (屈曲); crook; curve (彎曲). ❷ (意志·主義·說·法などを) to bend; give up; submit; depart *from*. ❸ (解釋を) to distort; twist; wrench (理を非に) —主義を曲げる, to depart [make a departure] from one's principles. —法律を曲げる, to strain the law. —意志を曲げる, to yield [submit] to another's opinion; act against one's will.

magete (枉げて), *ad.* against [one's will.]

magirasu (紛らす), *vt.* ❶ (混同) to confuse; obscure; render uncertain. ❷ (心·氣など) to divert; distract; beguile. —戯談に紛らす, to turn it off as a joke. —笑ひに紛らす, to laugh it off. —退屈を紛らす, to beguile monotony; beguile the time; kill time.

magirawashii (紛らはしい), *a.* ❶ (混同し易い) confusing; liable to be confused. ❷ (曖昧な) equivocal; ambiguous; obscure; vague; doubtful. —紛らはしい名, names liable to be confused.

magirekomu (紛込む), *vi.* to get mixed; be lost among other things. —群集の中へ紛れ込む, to be lost in the crowd.

magiremonai (紛れもない), *a.* unmistakable; the very; veritable. —紛れもなく, unmistakably.

-magireni (紛れに), in; in excess *of*. —口惜し紛れに, in one's mortification. —醉った紛れに, under the influence of liquor [wine].

magireru (紛れる), *vi.* ❶ (混同) to be mistaken *for*; be confounded *with*. ❷ (他に心を奪はれる) to be diverted; be beguiled; be distracted. ❸ (混入) to be mixed *among*; be lost *among*.

magiru (間切る), *vi.* 【航】 to beat about; tack; board. ——, *vt.* (部屋を仕切る) to partition; divide.

magiwa (間際), *n.* the eve; the verge; the point. —選擧の間際に, on the eve of an election. —今出發と言ふ間際に, when I am on the point of starting.

mago (孫), *n.* a grandchild; a grandson; a granddaughter.

mago (馬子), *n.* a packhorse driver. —馬子にも衣裳髮形. "Fine feathers make fine birds."

magoi (眞鯉), *n.* the black carp.

magokoro (眞心), *n.* sincerity; single-heartedness; the true heart. —眞心を籠めて, with one's whole heart; from the bottom of one's heart.

magomago (間誤間誤), *ad.* being embarrassed; being bewildered; being frustrated. —まごまごする, =***magotsuku***.

mago-no-te (孫の手), *n.* a back-scratcher; a skin-scraper.

magotsuku (間誤つく), *vi.* ❶ (當惑) to be perplexed [puzzled; bewildered]; be embarrassed; be at one's wits' end. ❷ (狼狽) to be confused; be upset; be flurried. ❸ (下手をやる) to bungle; do clumsily. ❹ (徘徊) to hang about; knock about; wander about. —返事にまごつく, to be at a loss for an answer.

maguchi (間口), *n.* frontage. —間口五間奥行七間の家, a house with 5 *ken* frontage and 7 *ken* depth.

maguneshia (マグネシア), *n.* 【化】 magnesia.

maguneshūmu (マグネシゥム), *n.* 【化】 magnesium.

magureatari (紛中り), *n.* a lucky hit [shot]; a fluke; a lucky guess (特に當事に云ふ). —紛れ中りに, by a fluke.

magureru (迷れる), *vi.* ❶ = *mayou.* ❷ = *magireru.*

magurezaiwai (僥倖), *n.* blind luck; a lucky chance.

maguro (鮪), *n.* 【魚】 the tunny.

magusa (秣), *n.* fodder; forage; provender. ¶ 秣袋, a nose-bag. —秣槽, a manger; a crib.

maguso (馬糞), *n.* horse-dung.

magusodaka (馬糞鷹), *n.* 【鳥】 the kestrel.

maguwa (馬鍬, 耙), *n.* a harrow; a rake; a drag (重き); a brake-harrow (大耙).

mahi (痲痺), *n.* ❶【醫】paralysis; anæsthesia (痲醉). ❷ paralysis; (moral) stupor. —痲痺する, to be paralyzed; be anæsthetized.

mahiru (眞晝), *n.* mid-day; noonday; broad daylight (白晝).

mahiwa (金翅雀), *n.* 【鳥】 the siskin.

maho (眞帆), *n.* full sail.

mahō (魔法), *n.* magic; witchcraft; sorcery. —魔法を使ふ, to practise sorcery; conjure. ¶ 魔法壜, a thermos (flask); a vacuum flask. —魔法使ひ, a wizard; a magician; a sorcerer.

mahogani (桃花心木), *n.* 【植】 mahogany (其の材をも云ふ).

Mahometto (マホメット敎), *n.* Mahomedanism; Islamism. ¶ マホメット敎徒, a Mohammedan; a Mahometan; a Mussulman [*pl.* -mans]; a Moslem; an Islamite.

mai (枚), *n.* ❶ = *bai* (枚). ❷ a piece (片); a sheet (紙の); a leaf (書物の一葉). —紙十五枚, fifteen sheets of paper. —三錢切手十枚, ten three-*sen* stamps.

mai (舞), *n.* dancing (舞踏); a dance (一舞ひ). —舞を舞ふ, to dance.

mai (まい), *v. aux.* ❶ (決心) I will not; I would not; I am determined not to.... ❷ (想像, 推測) I am afraid; I dare say [suppose] not; I do not think. —そんな事は萬あるまい, It can not possibly happen.

mai- (毎), *a.* every; each. —毎日曜日, every Sunday.

maiagaru (舞上る), *vi.* to fly high [upward]; soar (飛鳥が); be whirled up [aloft] (吹き上げらる). —空中高く舞ひ上る, to fly high up into the sky.

maiasa (毎朝), *ad.* every morning.

maiban (毎晩), *ad.* every evening [night]; night after night.

maibotsu (埋沒), *n.* burial. —埋沒する, to be buried; be buried under [beneath] the debris.

maichimonji (眞一文字に), *ad.* straight; in a straight [bee-] line; as the crow flies. —眞一文字に突進する, to rush straight forward.

maido (毎度), *ad.* ❶ (毎回) each time; every time. ❷ (度々) (very) often; frequently; repeatedly.

maifuku (埋伏する), *vi.* to be in ambush *for*; lie concealed *for*.

maigetsu (毎月), *ad.* every month; each month. —毎月の, monthly.

maigiri (舞錐), *n.* a bow-drill.

maigo (迷子), *n.* a stray child; a lost child. —迷子になる, to go astray; be lost. ¶ 迷子札, a child's (identification) tag.

maihada (槍皮), *n.* oakum.

maika (烏賊魚), *n.* 【軟體】 the cuttlefish.

maiko (舞子), *n.* a dancing girl.

maikomu (舞込む), *vi.* ❶ (人など) to drop in; call unexpectedly; come *into*; fly *into* (鳥が). ❷ (事物など) to come upon; fall upon; befall.

maikurofōn (送話器), *n.* 【電】 a microphone.

maikyo (枚擧する), *vt.* to count; enumerate; reckon. —枚擧に遑あらず, to be too many to enumerate [mention].

maimodoru (舞戻る), *vi.* to come back; come again; return.

mainai (賂), *n.* = *wairo.*

mainasu (マイナス), *n.* ❶ (減號) minus (符號 −). ❷ (負債) a minus (asset); a debt. —, *a.* (零度以下の) minus. —, *prep.* 【數】(引く) minus. —マイナス五度, minus 5 degrees. —八マイナス五, eight minus five; 8 − 5.

mainen (毎年), *ad.* yearly; annually; every year. —毎年の, annual; yearly. —毎年起る問題, a question of annual occurrence; a hardy annual.

mainichi (毎日), *ad.* every day; daily. —毎日毎日, day by day; day after day; from day to day. —毎日の, everyday; daily.

mairasu (參らす), *vt.* ❶ (降參さす) to beat; beat a person all to sticks; beat a person hollow. ❷ (與へる) to give; send.

mairi (詣), *n.* ❶ visit. ❷ (巡禮) pilgrimage; a pilgrim (人). ¶ 伊勢詣り, pilgrimage (a pilgrim) to the Ise Shrine.

mairu (参る), *v.* ❶ (行く) to come; go; visit. ❷ (詣) to visit; make [go on] a pilgrimage *to*; pay homage *to*. ❸ (敗北) to be defeated [beaten]; have [get] the worst; suffer a defeat. ❹ (閉口) to be dumbfounded; be nonplussed; be put out; be floored. —只今参ります, (I am) coming, sir. —参ッた!, You have me!

mairu (哩), *n.* ❶ a mile; a statute mile (=760 yards, 即 5280 feet 我が 14 町 45 間强に當る). ❷ (海里) a knot; a nautical mile; an admiralty knot (即 6080 feet 我が 16 町 59 間に當る).

mairuka (眞海豚), *n.* 【哺乳】the dolphin.

maisetsu (埋設する), *vt.* to lay (underground). ¶ 地下埋設管, underground [subterranean] pipes.

maishin (邁進する), *v.* to dash forward; make a push; make a dash *at*.

maishū (毎週), *ad.* every week; weekly. —毎週の, weekly.

maisō (埋葬), *n.* burial; interment; inhumation. —埋葬する, to bury; inter; inhume. ¶ 埋葬式, the burial-service; the obsequies. —埋葬證, a burial permit.

maisu (賣僧), *n.* a degenerated [corrupt] bonze [monk]; an apostate (priest).

maiwashi (鰯), *n.* 【魚】the sardine.

maizō (埋藏する), *vt.* to hide underground; bury in the earth. ¶ 埋藏物,【法】treasure trove.

majieru (交へる), *vt.* ❶ (混ぜる) to mix; alloy. ❷ (交換, 交叉) to exchange (fire, 砲火; words, 言葉); join (battle, 戰); cross (swords, 刃). —兵を交へる, to go to war [make war] *with*; open hostilities. —膝を交へて語る, to have a heart-to-heart talk; have a tête-à-tête (密談).

majika (間近の), *a.* very near; near by; close by. —間近く, at hand; close [near] at hand; (very) soon. —間近くなる, to be (fast) drawing near (試験など).

majimaji (瞠瞠), *ad.* with winking [blinking] eyes. —瞠々と見る, to blink *at*.

majime (眞面目), *n.* earnestness; seriousness; soberness. —眞面目腐って, with solemn looks. —眞面目である, to be in earnest. **—-na,** *a.* serious; earnest (本氣); sober (素面). —眞面目な問題, a serious subject. **—-ni,** *ad.* in earnest; seriously. —眞面目に働く, to do one's duty faithfully; work honestly.

majinai (呪, 禁厭), *n.* charm; spell; enchantment. —呪ひをする, to charm; enchant; bind by a spell. ¶ 呪符, a talisman; a charm; an amulet.

majiri (雜, 交, 混), *n.* ❶ (まじること) mixture; medley. ❷ (まじりもの) a mixture; a motley; a blend. —白髮交り, grizzled [grizzly] hair. —雜りのない, pure; genuine; neat (酒などの).

majirogu (瞬ぐ), *vi.* =*mabataku*.

majiru (雜·交·混る), *vi.* ❶ to be mixed; be blended; be adulterated (質の惡い物が). ❷ (加はる) to join *in*. —婦人も大分雜ってゐた, There was a fair sprinkling of ladies.

majiwari (交), *n.* ❶ (交際) intercourse; relations (交際關係); association. ❷ (交情) intimacy; friendship. —交を結ぶ, to contract [strike; cement] friendship; grow intimate *with*. —交を絶つ, to break *with*; break off [sever] friendship *with*.

majiwaru (交る), *vi.* ❶ (交際) to associate *with*; keep [bear] company *with*; have intercourse *with*. ❷ (交叉) to cross; intersect; cut (each other). ❸ (混入) to mix; mingle. —善《惡》い人と交る, to keep good 《bad》 company. —兩河の交る所に, at the confluence of the two rivers.

majo (魔女), *n.* a witch; a wise woman.

majutsu (魔術), *n.* magic; conjuring; witchcraft. ¶ 魔術師, a magician; a conjuror.

makai (魔界), *n.* hell; the infernal regions; the nether world.

makanai (賄), *n.* ❶ (行爲) preparing food; catering; purveyance. ❷ (人) a cook; a purveyor; a victualler. ❸ (食事) board; food. —賄附き間貸, board and lodging. —賄無しの下宿, dry lodging.

makanau (賄ふ), *vt.* ❶ (食事) to board; cater *for* (a person). ❷ (調達) to supply *with*; furnish.

makareru (卷かれる), *v.* to be wound [twisted] round. —煙に卷かれる, ① to be wrapt by smoke. ② to be mystified; be bewildered.

makarideru (罷出る), *vi.* to come; present oneself; wait *on*.

makarimachigaeba (罷間違へば), *ad.* if the worst comes to the worst; if things come to the worst; in case of failure.

makaroni (マカロニ), *n.* macaroni.

makaru (負かる), *v.* can be lowered; can bate. —これ以上は負かりません, I cannot come down any further.

makaseru (任せる), *vt.* Ⓢ任す. ❶ (委託) to leave (anything to a person); trust (a person) *with*; give (anything) in charge *of*. ❷ (忍從) to resign [submit; surrender] oneself *to*. ❸ (放任) to leave [let] alone. —力任せになぐる, to strike with all one's strength. —金に任せて, without regard to cost; regardless of expense. —金と暇とに任せて as long as one's money and time permit. ——身を他人に任せる, to submit [surrender; give up] oneself to another's care [will]. —他人の判斷に委せる, to leave to another's judgment. —運を天に委せる, to abandon [resign] oneself to fate; trust to chance [luck]; submit to one's fate. —足に任せて疾走する, to run as fast as one's legs can carry one. —僕に任し給へ, Leave the matter to me.

makasu (負かす), *vt.* ❶ (勝つ) to beat; defeat; vanquish. ❷ (値切る) to beat down; get (the price) reduced. —競走で負かす, to beat another in a race.

make (負), *n.* ❶ (敗北) defeat; loss. ❷ (減價) reduction. —負ッ腹を立てる, to become angry from losing; be angered by loss.

makegirai (負嫌の), *a.* Ⓢ負けず嫌ひの; 負けぬ氣の. unyielding; stubborn. —負嫌ひの人, a man of unyielding spirit.

makeiro (敗色), *n.* a sign of defeat. —敗色が見える, to show signs of defeat.

makejidamashii (負けじ魂), *n.* an obstinate [unyielding] spirit.

makeoshimi (負惜), *n.* unwillingness to acknowledge defeat; an excuse (for failure). —負惜みの强い人, a man who does not acknowledge a defeat.

makeru (負ける), *v.* ❶ (敗北する) to be defeated; be beaten; lose the day. ❷ (屈する) to yield; give way; submit. ❸ (減價) to reduce; abate; come down. ❹ (劣る) to be inferior *to*; fall behind. ❺ (かぶれる) to be poisoned. —十錢負ける, to bate ten *sen*. —競走《裁判》に負ける, to lose a race《lawsuit [case]》. —負ければ賊, "The conquered are the wrong." —五圓に負けろ, Come down to 5 *yen*.

makezu-otorazu (負けず劣らずの), *a.* evenly [well] matched.

maki (槇), *n.* 【植】 the Chinese yew-tree.

maki (卷), *n.* ❶ (書冊) (a) volume; (a) book; a scroll (古代の卷物式の本). ❷ (絹・紙などの卷軸) a roll; a scroll. ❸ 【料理】 a roll.

maki (薪), *n.* firewood; wood faggots (粗朶).

makiagaru (卷上がる), *vi.* to roll up; curl up.

makiageki (捲揚機), *n.* a winch; a windlass: a hoist; a lift.

makiageru (捲上げる), *vt.* ❶ to roll up; wind up (捲上げる). ❷ (計略で取上げる) to take away. —金を捲上げる, to clean a person of his money; clean a person out; cheat [wheedle] a person out of his money. —帆を捲上げる, to stow [furl] a sail. —錨を捲上げる, to heave up an anchor.

makiba (牧場), *n.* a meadow; a pasture. ☞ *bokujō*.

makichirasu (撒散らす), *vt.* ❶ to scatter about; sprinkle; strew (花等を). ❷ (浪費する) to squander; waste; lavish. —廣告を撒き散らす, to distribute advertisement cards.

makie (蒔繪), *n.* relief lacquer. —金《銀》蒔繪の硯箱, a gold 《silver》-lacquered ink-stone-case. ¶ 蒔繪師, a lacquerer.

makigami (卷紙), *n.* a roll of paper (一卷の紙); rolled letter-paper (手紙用); letter-scroll.

maki-gētoru (卷ゲートル), *n.* puttees.

makijaku (卷尺), *n.* a tape-measure.

makijita (卷舌), *n.* a rolled tongue; roll. —卷舌を使ふ, to roll; trill.

makikomu (捲込む), *vt.* ❶ (捲入れる) to roll up; infold (捲き包む). ❷ (渦が船などを) to suck in; swallow up; engulf. ❸ (捲添にする) to involve *in*; implicate *in*. —波に捲き込まれる, to be swallowed up by a wave. —機械に捲き込まれる, to be caught in a machine.

makimodosu (卷戻す), *vt.* to unwind; unreel; uncoil.

makimono (卷物), *n.* ❶ a roll; a scroll; a *makimono*; a roll-picture (繪卷物). ❷ (古の本) a scroll. —卷物を展げる, to unfold a roll.

makinaoshi (蒔直し), *n.* renewal; renovation. —蒔直す, to renew; renovate. —新規蒔直しを試みる, to do it all over again.

makitabako (卷煙草), *n.* a cigar (葉卷); a cigarette (紙卷).

makitorigami (卷取紙), *n.* roll-paper.

makitsuke (蒔附), *n.* sowing. ¶ 蒔附け時, the sowing season.

makitsukeru (捲附ける), *vt.* to wind [twine] round; tie [wrap] around; twist; coil.

makitsuku (捲附く), *v.* to coil [wind] around; twine round; twist about. —針金が足に捲きついた, A wire caught my leg.

makiwari (薪割), *n.* ❶ an axe; a wood-cleaver. ❷ (事) firewood-chopping.

makiya (薪屋), *n.* a dealer in firewood; a faggot-seller.

Makiyaverizumu (マキャヴェリズム), *n.* Machiavellism.

makizoe (捲添), *n.* involvement; implication; entanglement. —捲添へにする, to involve; implicate; entangle. —捲添へを喰ふ[になる], to be involved *in*; be implicated *in*; be entangled *in*.

makka (眞赤), *n.* deep-red; crimson. ——**-na**, *a.* ❶ deep [bright] red; crimson. ❷ (眞實の) pure; full. —眞赤な虚言, a downright [barefaced] lie. —羞かしくて眞赤になる, to blush for shame.

makki (末期), *n.* a later period; the end.

makkō (抹香), *n.* incense (powder).

makkō (眞向に), *ad.* right in the face. —太刀を眞向に振り翳す, to brandish a large sword in his face. —眞向から切りつける, to cut at another in front.

makkōkujira (抹香鯨), *n.* 【哺乳】the sperm whale; the cachalot.

makkura (眞暗 -闇), *n.* pitchy [pitch-; utter] darkness. —眞暗になる, to become pitch-dark.

makkuro (眞黒), *n.* pitch-black; deep [jet] black; coal-black. —眞黒な, coal-black; jet-black. —眞黒に塗る, to paint perfectly black. —眞黒に焦げる, to be scorched black [to blackness].

makogarei (まこがれひ), *n.* 【魚】the dab.

makomo (眞菰), *n.* 【植】the water-oat; the Indian rice.

makoto (眞, 實, 誠), *n.* ❶ (眞實) truth; reality; a fact (事實). ❷ (正直) honesty; uprightness. ❸ (忠實) loyality; fidelity; faithfulness. ❹ (誠意) sincerity; true-heartedness. —眞の, real; true. —誠のある, sincere; true-hearted. —眞らしい話, a story that sounds true; a plausible story.

makotoni (誠に), *ad.* ❶ (實際) really; truly; verily; in truth [fact]; indeed. ❷ (實に) very; awfully; exceedingly. ❸ (心から) heartily.

makotoshiyaka (誠しやかな), *a.* plausible; specious; seeming. —誠しやかに, plausibly; speciously; with a show of truth.

maku (幕), *n.* ❶ (帳) a curtain; a veil. ❷ (天幕) a tent. ❸ (劇の) an act (齣); a scene (段). —夜の幕, the cope of night; the night's curtain. —通し幕, one play all through. —幕を下す, to drop the curtain. —幕を張る[引く], to draw the curtain. —吾々の出る幕でない, It is not for us to show ourselves.

maku (膜), *n.* a tunic (外膜); a film (薄膜); 【解】a membrane.

maku (卷·捲く), *vt.* ❶ (ぐるぐる卷く) to wind; roll; reel. ❷ (纏ふ, 包む) to wrap; lap; tuck up. ❸ (捲く) to wind (a clock). —絲を卷く, to reel thread. (絲を卷いて玉にする, to wind thread into a ball.) —新聞紙で物を卷く, to roll up a thing in a newspaper.

maku (蒔·播く), *vt.* to sow. —種を蒔く, to sow seed. —蒔かぬ種は生えぬ, "He who sows little reaps little."

maku (撒く), *vt.* ❶ (撒散らす) to scatter about; strew (花など); spread (花札·乾草など). ❷ (振撒く, 振掛ける) to sprinkle (水·灰·鹽など); spatter (水). ❸ (伴をはぐらかす) to give (a person) the slip [guy]; escape stealthily from (company). —道路に水を撒く, to sprinkle [spatter] water on the pavement; water the street.

māku (標章), *n.* a mark. —マークを打つ, to stamp a mark *on*.

makuai (幕間), *n.* an interval between acts. —幕間に, between the acts.

makuaki (幕開), *n.* raising of the curtain; opening.

maku-no-uchi (幕の内), *n.* 【相撲】the first grade; a first-grade wrestler.

makura (枕), *n.* a pillow; a bolster (長い括り枕); a neck-rest (日本·支那等の). —枕する, to rest one's head *on*. —枕を竝べる, to lie side by side. —枕を高うして眠る, to sleep on a calm conscience; sleep in peace. —城を枕に打死する, to die in defence of a castle.

makurabyōbu (枕屏風), *n.* a bed-screen; a small screen at the bed-head.

makuragi (枕木), *n.* (鐵道などの) a sleeper.

makuramoto (枕頭, 枕元), *n.* the bedside. —死人の枕元に集る, to gather about the death-bed.

makurasagashi (枕探し), *n.* (事) bedroom theft: (人) a bedroom thief.

makurereru (捲れる), *vi.* to turn (up).

makuri (海人草, 海仁草), *n.* 【植】Digenea Simplex (學名).

makuru (捲る), *vt.* ❶ (端折る) to turn up; tuck up; roll up. ❷ (めくる) to turn over (the leaves);

turn up (a trump-card). —袖 [腕] を捲る, to turn [tuck] up one's sleeves.

makushita (幕下), *n.* 【相撲】 the second grade; a second-grade wrestler.

makutsu (魔窟), *n.* ❶ (惡魔の巣窟) a pandemonium. ❷ (不正漢の巣窟) a nest; a den. ¶ 魔窟狩, raid on disreputable quarters.

makuwauri (甜瓜), *n.* 【植】 the melon; the musk-melon 〔米〕.

mama (儘, 随, 任), *ad.* ❶ (思ふ通り) as one pleases; as one likes; at one's will. ❷ (通り) as; just as; as it is. ❸ (故に) as. —御意の儘に, as you please. —靴の儘で上る, to enter with the shoes on. —もとの儘である, to be [remain] as it was. —聞いた儘を話す, to tell a story as one heard it. —其の儘にして置け, Leave it just as it is. —不斷著の儘で來た, I have come without dressing.

mama (間間), *ad.* (every) now and then; at times; from time to time. ☞ *tokidoki*.

mama (ママ), *n.* ❶ (母) mamma; mama. ❷ (乳母) a nurse.

māmā (まあまあ), *int.* Well, well. —まあまあ (靜まり給へ). Now calm yourself; Do be quiet!

mamagoto (飯事), *n.* playing at housekeeping.

mamahaha (繼母), *n.* a step-mother.

mamako (繼子), *n.* a stepchild; a stepson (男); a stepdaughter (女). —繼子扱ひにする, to treat like a stepchild.

mamayo (ままよ), *int.* never mind!

mame (豆), *n.* ❶【植】 a bean (そら豆); a pea (豌豆). ❷ (小なるもの) a miniature.

mame (まめな), *a.* ❶ (忠實な) honest; faithful. ❷ (達者な) healthy; robust; hale. ❸ (よく働く) industrious; busy. —まめな主婦, a busy housewife. —まめに働く, ① to serve honestly; ② to work hard. —まめに暮す; まめで居る, to be quite well.

mame (肉刺), *n.* a blister; a water-blister; a corn (底豆).

mamedeppō (豆鐵砲), *n.* (玩具) a pea-shooter.

mamegaki (豆柿), *n.* 【植】 the European date-plum.

mamejidōsha (豆自動車), *n.* a baby-car; a toy auto.

mamekasu (豆糟), *n.* bean-cake.

mamemaki (豆撒), *n.* scattering of peas (for luck).

mameranpu (豆ランプ), *n.* a miniature lamp.

mamesoppu (豆ソップ), *n.* pea soup.

mametsu (磨滅), *n.* defacement; attrition; wear and tear. —磨滅さす, to batter; wear out by friction. —磨滅する, to wear (off; out; away; down); be defaced; be worn out.

mamezō (豆藏), *n.* ❶ a clown. ❷ (小人) a dwarf. ❸ (饒舌な人) a chatterbox.

mamezōmushi (豆象蟲), *n.* 【昆】 the Chinese pea-weevil.

mami (貒), *n.* 【哺乳】 (a variety of) the Japanese raccoon-dog.

mamieru (見える), *vt.* to have an audience *with*; be received in audience; have an interview *with*; see; meet.

mamireru (塗れる), *vi.* to be smeared *with*; be daubed *with*.

mamizu (淡水), *n.* fresh water.

mamonaku (間もなく), *ad.* soon; before long; in a short time.

mamono (魔物), *n.* a spirit; a spectre.

mamori (守), *n.* ❶ (守護) protection; guard (警護). ❷ (防禦) defence. ❸ (守札) an amulet; a charm; a talisman.

mamorigami (守神), *n.* a genius; a tutelary deity; a guardian (god).

mamoru (守·護る), *vt.* ❶ (守護) to protect; guard; watch (見守る); watch *over*. ❷ (防禦) to defend. ❸ (遵守) to obey; observe; follow. —門を守る, to guard a gate. —規律を守る, to keep good order. —規則を守る, to observe the regulations. —己の說を守る, to hold to one's own opinion.

mamukō (眞向の), *a.* just [directly] opposite. **—— -ni,** *ad.* (right) in front of; right over against; straight ahead. —家の眞向うに, over against a house.

mamushi (蝮蛇), *n.* 【爬蟲】 the halys-viper. —蝮蛇のやうに執念深く, as spiteful as a viper.

man (萬, 万), *n.* ten thousand; a myriad. —何萬といふ星, myriads of stars; tens of thousand of stars.

man (滿), *n.* ❶ fulness. ❷ (酒をなみなみとつぐ) being brimful. —ビールの滿を引く, to empty a full cup of beer at a draught. —滿を持して放たず, to keep the bow bent to the full. —滿は損を招く, "A flow will have an ebb."

manabi (學), *n.* study. —學びの窓, a class-room; a school-room. —學びの道, a guide to knowledge; the road to knowledge; learning; study.

manabu (學ぶ), *vt.* to practise (習ふ); learn (修める); study (硏

究する). —劍術を學ぶ, to practise fencing. —英語を學ぶ, to learn English.

manaita (俎), *n.* a block; a dresser (肉屋の); a chopping-board (臺所用).

manajiri (眥), *n.* the outer canthus; the outer corner of the eye.

manatsu (眞夏), *n.* midsummer.

manazuru (眞名鶴), *n.* 【鳥】the white-naped crane.

manben (滿遍なく), *ad.* evenly (平等に); without exception (漏れなく); generally (一般に).

manbiki (萬引), *n.* a shop-lifter (人); shop-lifting (事). —萬引する, to steal [lift] from a shop.

manbō (翻車魚), *n.* 【魚】the sun-fish.

manbyō (萬病), *n.* all kinds of diseases [maladies]. ¶ 萬病藥, a panacea; a cure-all; a universal medicine.

manchaku (瞞著的), *a.* tricky; fraudulent; deceptive. —— **-suru,** *vt.* to delude; impose *upon*; practise *on* [*upon*]. —世間を瞞著する, to impose upon the world. ¶ 瞞著手段, a trick.

manchō (滿潮), *n.* high-tide.

mandō (萬燈), *n.* ❶ (多くの燈) many lanterns. ❷ a paper lantern.

mandō (滿堂), *n.* the whole company [assembly]; the whole audience (聽衆). —滿堂の諸君, ladies and gentlemen.

mandorin (マンドリン), *n.* a mandolin(e); a mandola (大形).

mane (眞似), *n.* imitation; mimicry (嘲弄的の). —馬鹿な《の》眞似をする, to act 《play》 the fool. —死んだ眞似をする, to feign death. —人の眞似をする, to follow another's example; take a leaf out of another's book: mimic another.

maneku (招く), *vt.* ❶ (招待) to invite; ask. ❷ (招來する) to bring [draw] upon oneself; incur; occasion. ❸ (呼寄せる) to call in; send for (使で); beckon (手で). —手で招く, to beckon with the hand. —醫者を招く, to send for [call in] a doctor. —危險を招く, to court a danger (求める); incur danger (來たす). —誤解を招く, to cause [lead to] misunderstanding. —晩餐に人を招く, to invite [ask] a person to dinner.

mañen (蔓延), *n.* spread; propagation; diffusion. —蔓延する, to spread (*over*); diffuse; scatter about; overrun (雜草など).

maneru (眞似る), *vt.* to imitate; mimic; ape; copy; pretend (僞る). —知らざる眞似をして, under pretence of ignorance. —西洋風を眞似る, to imitate European manners.

mañetsu (滿悅), *n.* great joy; exultation. —頗る滿悅の態であった, He appeared highly delighted.

manga (漫畫), *n.* a sketch; a caricature (ポンチ繪); a cartoon (大諷刺畫). ¶ 漫畫家, a caricaturist; a cartoonist.

mangan (滿俺), *n.* 【化】manganese.

mangan (滿願), *n.* completion of a vow.

mangen (漫言), *n.* stray notes; jottings; gossip. ¶ 時事漫言, comments on current events.

mangetsu (滿月), *n.* a full moon. —滿月の夜, a full-moon night.

maniai (間合), *n.* a makeshift; a temporary expedient.

maniau (間に合ふ), *vi.* ❶ (役に立つ) to serve [answer] the purpose; serve one's purpose [turn; need]; serve; do. ❷ (時間に後れぬ) to be in time *for* 《to》; catch (the train). —今から行けば間に合ふ, You will be in time if you start now. —金は間に合ふ丈けある, I have enough money for the purpose.

maniawase (間に合せの), *a.* temporizing; makeshift; temporary (一時的); extemporary (無準備).

maniawasu (間に合す), *v.* ❶ to make (it) serve one's purpose; do [manage; make shift] *with* 《without》 (…で又は…なしで). ❷ (調へる) to get [have] (it) ready.

mañichi (萬一), *ad.* by any chance. ☞ *bañichi.*

manimani (まにまに), *ad.* in accordance *with* (從ひ); just as (通りに); at the mercy *of* (他のなす儘に). —風のまにまに漂ふ, to float on the wind (香); drift at the mercy of the wind (船).

mañin (滿員), *n.* no vacancy; a full house; "Full up." (揭示札). —滿員である, to be (all) full; be full up; be crowded [packed]. —每夜滿員の盛況であった, Night after night it drew full houses. ¶ 滿員札, a full-car notice.

maningen (眞人間), *n.* a true [an honest] man. —眞人間になる, to become an honest [a true] man; turn over a new leaf.

Manira (マニラ), *n.* Manila. ¶ マニラ葉卷煙草, a Manila (cigar).

manji (卍字), *n.* a fylfot, filfot 【梵】; a gammadion; Svastika 【梵】.

manjiri (まんじりともせぬ), not to have a wink of sleep; not to

sleep a wink.

manjō (満場), *n.* the whole house [assembly]; the whole audience (聴衆全部). —満場一致の, unanimous. —満場一致で, unanimously; by common consent; with one consent.

manjū (饅頭), *n.* ❶ a (bean-jam) bun. ❷【棘皮】the cake-urchin.

mankai (満開), *n.* full bloom; bloom. —満開の, full-blown. —満開する, to be in full bloom [blossom]; be at their best; be all [fully] out.

Mankan (満韓), *n.* Chosen [Korea] and Manchuria. ¶ 満韓地方, the Chosen [Korean] and Manchurian districts.

mankanshoku (満艦飾), *n.* rainbow-dressing. —満艦飾を施す, to dress ship rainbow fashion; full dress ship.

manki (満期), *n.* expiry; maturity; expiration [completion] of a term. —満期になる, ① to expire (期間が終る); complete one's term of service (服務が). ② (手形などが) to mature; fall [become] due. —満期出獄する, to be discharged upon expiration of the term; be released from prison after serving out a term. ¶ 満期日, due date; maturity. —満期兵, a time-expired [disbanded] soldier. —満期手形, a bill on maturity; a matured bill.

mankō (満腔の), *a.* hearty; heartfelt; full [whole]-hearted. —満腔の誠意を以て, with all one's heart; from the bottom of one's heart. —満腔の同情を表す, to feel sincere [deep] sympathy (for another); tender one's fullest sympathy *to*.

manmaku (幔幕), *n.* a curtain tapestry. ☞ ***maku*** (幕).

manman (漫漫たる), *a.* vast; boundless.

manman (満満たる), *a.* full of; brimming (cup など); overflowing. —満々たる野心, overflowing ambition.

manmaru (真圓な), *a.* perfectly round.

manmato (甘甘と), *ad.* successfully; artfully; fairly. —まんまと逃げのびる, to make good one's escape.

manmen (満面), *n.* the whole face. —満面朱を濺いで, with a face flushed with anger. —満面に笑を湛へて, with a face beaming [radiant] with a smile.

Manmō (満蒙), *n.* Manchuria and Mongolia.

manmosu (マンモス), *n.*【古生】the mammoth.

mannaka (眞中), *n.* ❶ (中程) the middle. ❷ (中心) the middle; the midst; the centre; the heart; the core. —森の眞中に, in the midst of a forest. —眞中から二つに折れる, to break in two in the middle; part amidships (船). —髪を眞中で分る, to have one's hair parted in the middle.

mannen (萬年), *n.* ten thousand years; a great age. ¶ 萬年暦, a perpetual calendar. —萬年筆, a fountain-pen.

manoatari (目のあたり), *ad.* ❶ before one's eyes (眼前); in one's presence (面前); to one's face (面と向って). ❷ (直接) directly; personally (自身で); with one's own eyes. —目のあたり之を責める, to blame a person to his face. —まのあたり見るが如き心地す, ① I feel as if it occurred before my eyes. ② I feel as if he were here in the flesh.

manowarui (間の悪い), *a.* malapropos; unseasonable.

manpai (満杯), *n.* a brimming glass; a full cup; a bumper; a brimmer. —満杯を傾ける, to drain a bumper of wine.

manpitsu (漫筆), *n.* stray notes: (random) jottings.

manpuku (満腹), *n.* a full stomach. —満腹する, to eat one's fill; eat to one's heart's content.

manpyō (漫評), *n.* literary gossip.

manriki (萬力), *n.* a vice.

manroku (漫録), *n.* =***manpitsu, mangen.***

manryō (硃砂根), *n.*【植】Ardisia crispa (spear-flower の一種學名).

manryō (満了), *n.* expiration. —満了する, to expire; come to an end: fulfil (a term of office).

mansai (満載する), *v.* ❶ (貨物を) to be full-laden *with*; be loaded to capacity; be laden with a full cargo. ❷ (記事を) to be full *of*. —茶を満載して, with [having] a full cargo of tea on board.

mansei (慢性の), *a.* chronic. —慢性になる, to become chronic. ¶ 慢性胃病, chronic dyspepsia. —慢性患者, a chronic (invalid).

mansen (満船), *n.* a full ship.

manshin (満身), *n.* the whole body. —満身の力をこめて, putting out all one's strength; with one's whole strength.

manshin (慢心), *n.* self-conceit. —慢心する, to be proud [self-conceited]; be puffed up *with*.

Manshū (満洲), *n.* Manchuria. ¶ 満洲人, a Manchu.

manten (満點), *n.* a full mark. —満點を取る, to get [obtain] a full mark.

mantenka (満天下), *n.* the whole world 《realm》. —満天下に, throughout the world; all over the country.

Mantetsu (満鐵), *n.* (南満洲鐵道株式會社の略) the South Manchurian Railway Company.

manto (マント), *n.* a cloak; a mantle (婦人用); a manteau (同上); a capote (將校·婦人などの頭巾ある) ⌈mantle (瓦斯燈の).

mantoru (マントル), *n.* a (gas-)

manukareru (免れる), *v.* ❶ (危難などを) to escape; be relieved *of*; get off. ❷ (義務·責任などを免除さる) to be discharged *from*; be released *from*; be exempted *from*. ❸ (回避する) to avoid; evade; escape. ☞ ***nogareru***. —免れ難い, unavoidable; inevitable. —免れて恥なき徒, those fellows who feel no shame if they keep clear of the law. —危險を免れる, to escape danger. —罰金《稅》を免れる, to be exempted from a fine 《taxes》. —債務を免れる, to be discharged from one's liability —危い所を免れる, to have a narrow escape; escape by a hair's breadth.

manuke (間拔), *n.* ❶ stupidity; a blunder (失策). ❷ (人) a blockhead; a dunce; an ass. —間拔けた事を云ふ, to say stupid things.

mañyū (漫遊), *n.* a tour; a trip; a pleasure-trip. —漫遊する, to make a tour [trip] *round*; travel *in*; travel [tour] *through* [*about*]. ¶ 世界漫遊, a trip [tour] round the world. —漫遊者, a tourist.

manza (満座), *n.* the whole company. —満座の中で恥をかかす, to put another to shame before the whole company.

manzai (萬歲), *n.* ❶ a strolling clown. ❷ =***banzai***.

manzara (満更), *ad.* (not) entirely; (not) altogether. —満更いやでもないらしい, He does not appear to be wholly averse to it.

manzen (漫然), *ad.* heedlessly; thoughtlessly; at random; without a definite object in view.

manzoku (満足), *n.* satisfaction; gratification; contentment (知足). —満足な解決, a satisfactory conclusion. —満足に, satisfactorily. —満足する, to be satisfied [gratified] *with*; be contented *with*. —欲望を満足さす, to gratify [satisfy] a want. ⌈-grass.

mao (麻苧), *n.* 【植】 the rhee-

mappadaka (眞裸), *n.* stark-nakedness; nudity. —眞裸になる, to strip oneself stark-naked; strip off one's clothes. —眞裸にする, to strip another naked (of his clothes) [to the skin]. —眞裸で駈け出す, to rush out naked.

mappira (眞平), *ad.* earnestly; flatly. —そんな話は眞平だ, No such talk for me, please.

mappiruma (眞晝間), *ad.* in broad daylight; in the daytime.

mapputatsu (眞二つに), *ad.* ☞ ***mafutatsu***.

marariya (マラリヤ熱), *n.* malaria; malarial fever; marsh-fever.

marason (マラソン競走), *n.* a Marathon race.

mare (稀な), *a.* ❶ (少ない) rare· scarce; few. ❷ (珍しい) rare; uncommon. —稀に, seldom; rarely; seldom; if ever. (稀に見る大漁, a rare take of fish.)

Marei (馬來半島), *n.* the Malay Peninsula. ¶ 馬來語, Malay; Malayan. —馬來人, a Malay.

mari (鞠, 毬), *n.* a ball. —鞠をつく, to play (at) ball. ¶ 鞠唄, a hand-ball song. ⌈turn.

marobasu (轉ばす), *vt.* to roll;

maru (丸), *n.* a circle. ——, *a.* (満) full; whole; complete; clean; good. —丸一年, a whole year. —丸五日, five full [whole] days; all these five days. ⌈column.

marubashira (圓柱), *n.* a

marubocha (丸ぼちゃ), *n.* a chubby face; a chubby-faced [-cheeked] woman.

marubushukan (枸櫞), *n.* 【植】 the median lemon.

marudashi (丸出しの), *a.* ❶ exposed; uncovered; undisguised. ❷ (そっくり) just [exactly] like. —田舍者丸出しである, to be undisguisedly rustic.

marude (丸で), *ad.* ❶ (全然) completely; entirely; altogether. ❷ (宛然) at all; so to speak; as it were. —まるで違ふ, to be nothing of the kind; differ entirely. —まるで知らない, to know nothing *of*; be completely in the dark *about*.

marudori (丸取する), *v.* to take all to oneself; take exclusive possession *of*.

marugao (丸顔), *n.* a round face.

marui (圓·丸い), *a.* round. ❶ (平面の) circular; ring-like. ❷ (球形の) spherical; globular. —丸い頭, a bullet-head.

marujōgi (丸定木), *n.* a round [circular] ruler. ⌈-bridge.

marukibashi (獨木橋), *n.* a log-

marukibune (獨木舟), *n.* a canoe; a log-canoe; a dug-out.

marukkiri (丸っきり), *ad.* Ⓢ

丸ッきし, absolutely; completely; entirely. ☞ *marude*.

maruku (圓く), *ad.* ❶ round; roundly; circularly. ❷ (圓滿に) peacefully; amicably; harmoniously. —眼を圓くして, with surprised eyes. —圓く納める, to smooth over [away] (quarrels).

maruku (馬克), *n.* a mark.

marumage (丸髷), *n.* a round chignon (of a married woman).

marumaru (○○), *n.* ❶ (言ふを憚ること又は物) blank-blank. ❷ (互に了解さるゝ或る事物) so and so; such and such. ¶ ○○事件, the — affair. (—は blank 又は blanked などと讀む)

marumaru (圓圓, 丸丸), *ad.* ❶ plumply; fatly. ❷ =*marukkiri*. —豚のやうに圓々肥えてる, to be fat as a pig; be plump as a dumpling.

marumero (榲桲), *n.* 【植】the quince-tree: (實) a quince.

marumeru (圓·丸める), *vt.* ❶ (圓くする) to make round; roll; round (up; off). ❷ (籠絡する) to dupe; delude; manage. —手の内に丸め込む, to twist a person round one's little finger.

marumi (圓味ある), *a.* roundish.

marumōke (丸儲), *n.* a complete gain. —丸儲けする, to realize a complete gain; make a good haul.

marunomi (丸呑にする), *vt.* to swallow (whole); gulp; bolt; cram. —學科を丸呑みにする, to cram a whole course.

marunomi (圓鑿), *n.* a gouge; a round chisel; a scauper (彫刻用).

maruobi (丸帶), *n.* a belt made of one piece of cloth.

marusa (圓·丸さ), *n.* roundness. —二錢銅貨大の丸さ, the size of a two-*sen* copper.

maruta (丸太), *n.* a log. —松の丸太, a pine log.

marutenjō (圓天井), *n.* a dome; a vault.

marutsubure (全潰), *n.* collapse; dead failure. —全潰れになる, to be completely ruined.

maruyake (丸燒になる), *vi.* ❶ to be burnt out by a fire. ❷ to be completely burnt; be burnt down; be laid in [reduced to] ashes; be burnt to the ground.

maruyaki (丸燒), *n.* barbecue (豚·牛等の); roasting whole.

maruzon (丸損), *n.* a dead loss; a complete [clear] loss. —丸損になる, to turn out a clear loss. —丸損をする, to meet a dead loss.

maryoku (魔力), *n.* charm; spell; bewitching power.

masa (柾), *n.* ❶ shingles. ❷ (柾目) straight grain (of wood).

masaka (豈夫), *ad.* improbably; unlikely. —まさかの時の用意をする, to prepare for the worst; lay up against a rainy day (貯蓄); provide against the time of need. —まさかと思ッた, I thought it unlikely. —まさかそんな事は云ふまい, He can scarcely have said so.

masakari (鉞), *n.* a broad-axe; a battle-axe; a halberd (斧の戈).

masaki (正木), *n.* 【植】the Japanese spindle-tree.

masani (正·方に), *ad.* exactly; just; surely. —正に其人である, He is the very man.

masani (將·且に), *ad.* nearly; almost; about. —將に...せんとする, to be on the point [verge; brink] *of*; be going [about] to. —將に行かんとす, to be about to go; be going.

masaru (優·勝る), *v.* to surpass; excel; be superior *to*.

masashiku (正しく), *ad.* certainly; exactly; precisely.

masatsu (摩擦), *n.* friction; rubbing; chafing. —摩擦する, to rub; chafe. ¶ 摩擦電氣, frictional electricity. —靜止《運動》摩擦, statical 《dynamic》 friction.

masayume (正夢), *n.* a true dream; a dream which proves [turns out] true.

maseta (ませた), *a.* precocious; forward. —ませた子, a precocious child. —年の割にませてゐる, to be wise above one's age; be old for one's age.

mashaku (間尺), *n.* Ⓢ ましゃく. a *ken* measure; a carpenter's measure. —間尺にあはぬ, ① (作事の寸法に合はぬ) not to agree with the measure. ② (割に合はぬ) not to pay; be unprofitable.

mashi (増, 優), *n.* addition; increase. —無いよりましだ, It is better than nothing. —郵劵代用一割増の事, Ten per cent. extra, if postage stamps are sent instead.

mashimasu (坐す), *vi.* to be; live; dwell. —天に坐す, to dwell in heaven.

mashin (痲疹), *n.* 【醫】morbilli; measles.

mashin (魔神), *n.* a demon; a devil.

mashini (增しに), *ad.* more and more. —日増しに, day by day [daily] more. —一年増しに, year after year [yearly] more.

mashiro (眞白の), *a.* pure [snowy] white; whiter than snow.

mashita (眞下の), *a.* directly down. —眞下に, directly below 《downward》; right under.

mashite (況して), *ad.* much more; still more; how much more. ☞ *iwañya.*

mashō (魔性), *n.* devilishness. —魔性の女, an abandoned woman. —魔性の者, a spirit; a spectre.

mashō (ませう), *v. aux.* shall; will; may. —太郎さん, 遊びませう, Let us play, Tarō.

mashōmen (眞正面), *n.* a position directly opposite; the direct [right] front. —眞正面の家, a house in front; a house just opposite. —眞正面に坐る, to sit in front.

mason (磨損), *n.* attrition; wear (and tear). —磨損する, to be frayed; wear.

massai (秣菜), *n.* green fodder.

massaichū (眞最中に), *ad.* in the midst *of*; in [at] the height *of*. —暴風雨の眞最中に, in the height of the storm. —演説の眞最中に, in the heat of a speech.

massāji (按摩), *n.* massage. ¶ マッサージ師, a massagist; a masseur; a masseuse (女).

massakari (眞盛), *n.* ❶ (花の) full bloom. ❷ (物の) the zenith; the meridian; the noon (of life).

massakasama (眞逆様に), *ad.* headlong; head-foremost; head over heels.

massaki (眞先の), *a.* ❶ ahead; foremost; headmost. ❷ first; initial. **—— -ni,** *ad.* ❶ at the very first; first and foremost. ❷ at the very beginning. —眞先に進む, to take the lead.

massao (眞青な), *a.* deep blue; deadly [ghastly] pale; livid. —眞青な顔, a pallid [wan; cadaverous] face. —眞青になる, to turn deadly pale.

massatsu (抹殺), *n.* cancellation; obliteration; erasure. **—— -suru,** *vt.* to cancel; strike [rub] out; erase. —數行抹殺する, to expunge several lines.

masse (末世), *n.* ❶ (末法) a corrupt generation; a degenerate age. ❷ (後世) future ages [generations].

masseki (末席), *n.* =*basseki.*

massetsu (末節), *n.* trifles; triviality. —末節に拘泥する, to stick [adhere] to trifles.

masshigura (驀地に), *ad.* precipitately; impetuously; at full speed. —驀地に進む, to go right on; advance impetuously.

masshō (抹消), *n.* cancellation; erasure. ☞ *massatsu.*

masshōjiki (眞正直な), *a.* straightforward. —眞正直に, straightforwardly.

masshō-shinkei (末梢神經), *n.* the peripheric nerve; the nerve-ending.

massugu (眞直), *n.* ❶ straight. ❷ (正直) uprightness; integrity. **—— -na,** *a.* ❶ straight. ❷ upright; honest. —眞直な道, a straight road. **—— -ni,** *ad.* straightly; directly; in a bee [straight] line. —眞直に白狀する, to confess straightforwardly. —眞直に世を渡る, to live honestly; lead an honest life.

masu (鱒), *n.* 【魚】 the salmon-trout; the trout 【俗】. ¶ 紅鱒, the blue-back [sawqui] salmon.

masu (枡), *n.* ❶ a measure; a dry 《liquid》 measure. ❷ (枡目) measure. ❸ 【劇】 a box. ❹ (商標) a square. ❺ (樋の) a joint-box (of a water-pipe). ¶ 不正枡, an illegal measure.

masu (增す), *vt.* to increase (增加); extend (擴大); raise (高める). **——,** *vi.* to increase (*in*); multiply; add *to*; rise (高まる); swell; grow (more; *in*). —賃錢を增す, to raise wages. —勢力を增す, to extend one's influence.

masugata (枡形), *n.* a square.

masui (痲醉), *n.* (*a*) 【醫】 anæsthesia; narcosis: (*b*) stupor; stupefaction; numbness. —痲醉さす, to narcotize; anæsthetise; stupefy. ¶ 痲醉劑, a narcotic; an anæsthetic; an opiate.

masuku (マスク), *n.* a mask. —マスクをかける, to put on a mask; mask oneself.

masumasu (益), *ad.* still (more); more and more. —益〻惡くする, to make still worse. —益〻御勝健奉賀候, I beg to congratulate you on your good health.

masume (枡目), *n.* measure. —枡目を誤魔化す, to give short measure.

masunosuke (鱒之介), *n.* 【魚】 the quinnat [king]-salmon.

masurao (益荒男, 丈夫), *n.* ❶ (勇者) a brave man. ❷ (男) a man; a manly person. ❸ (戰士) a warrior; a soldier.

masuto (檣), *n.* a mast.

masuuri (枡賣する), *v.* to sell by the measure.

mata (又), *ad.* ❶ (其上に) moreover; besides; further. ❷ (亦) also; too. ❸ (復) again; another time; afresh. ❹ (矢張) as well as; yet (nor と共に). **——,** *conj.* and. —又一方では, on the other hand; while. —山又山の險路, the steep paths of one mountain after another. —またいらっしゃい, Please come again.

mata (叉), *n.* a fork; a tine (角などの); a prong (同上).
mata (胯, 股), *n.* the crotch; the thigh; the fork (ズボンの). —大《小》股に歩く, to walk with long 《short》 strides [steps]. —日本中を股にかける, to roam all over Japan.
matadanomi (又頼), *n.* an indirect request.
matadonari (又隣), *n.* next door but one.
matagari (又借), *n.* ❶ borrowing second-hand. ❷ under-tenancy. —又借りする, to borrow at second-hand.
matagaru (跨る), *v.* ❶ (跨り乗る) to stride; straddle; sit *on* (馬に); sit [stand] astride. ❷ (亙る) to extend over; stretch over; spread over; cover. ❸ (架す) to span; bridge; \be laid across.
matagashi (又貸する), *vt.* to underlet; sublet.
matagerai (復家來), *n.* a rear-vassal; a servant's servant.
matagiki (復聞する), *v.* to know by hearsay; hear at second hand; learn indirectly.
matagu (跨ぐ), *vt.* to straddle; stride. —溝を跨ぐ, to step over a ditch.
mataitoko (再從兄弟), *n.* a second cousin.
matamata (又又), *ad.* Ⓢ 又もや, 又候. again; once more.
mataseru (待たせる), *vt.* to keep (a person) waiting; detain.
matatabi (木天蓼), *n.* 【植】 Actinidia polygama (學名).
matataki (瞬), *n.* an eye-blink; a wink; a twinkle.
matataku (瞬く), *vi.* to wink; blink; twinkle. —雲間にまたゝく, to twinkle among the clouds. —瞬く間に, in the twinkling of an eye; in a moment [an instant]; in the twinkling of a bedpost.
mata-to-nai (復と無い), *a.* unique; matchless; unequalled. —復とない好機會, a golden opportunity which will never come [present itself] again; a unique opportunity.
mataukeoi (又請負), *n.* a sub-contract. —又請負する, [*vt.*] to subcontract.
matawa (又は), *conj.* or; either or.
matazure (股擦), *n.* a thigh-sore.
matcha (抹茶), *n.* powdered tea; ground tea.
matchi (燐寸), *n.* a match. —燐寸をつける, to strike [light] a match. ¶ 燐寸箱, a match-box.
mate (竹蟶), *n.* 【貝】 the razor-shell.
matenkaku (摩天閣), *n.* a sky-scraper; a lofty building.
mato (的), *n.* ❶ a mark; a target; a butt. ❷ (目標) an object; an aim. —的なきに矢を放つ, to shoot an arrow at random. —的を外れる, to miss the mark.
matoi (纏), *n.* a fireman's standard.
matomari (纏り), *n.* ❶ (統一) uniformity; symmetry; coherence. ❷ (落著) settlement; conclusion; arrangement (整理). ❸ (集團) group. —纏りをつける, to settle.
matomaru (纏る), *vi.* ❶ (統一) to be unified. ❷ (整ふ) to be arranged; be in order. ❸ (決定) to be settled; be decided; come to a conclusion. ❹ (集まる) to be collected; be brought together. —纏った意見, a definite view [opinion]. —纏った金, a round sum. —話が纏る, The negotiations come to a conclusion.
matomeru (纏める), *vt.* ❶ (統一) to unify; systematize. ❷ (整へる) to arrange; dispose; put in order. ❸ (決定) to settle; decide; bring to terms. ❹ (集める) to collect; gather; bring together. —纏めて買ふ, to buy in a lump. —材料を纏める, to collect the materials. —相談をまとめる, to bring the matter to a settlement.
matomo (正面), *n.* the front. —風を正面に受けて, in the teeth of the wind.
matou (纏ふ), *vt.* ❶ (著る) to wear; put on (動作); have on (狀態). ❷ (捲きつける) to entwine; twist about; coil [wind] round. ❸ (つきまとふ) to follow about. ❹ (包む) to wrap in. —喪服を纏ふ, to wear mourning.
matsu (松), *n.* the pine; the pine-tree. —松の嫩(みどり), young pine-needles.
matsu (末), *n.* ❶ (粉末) powder. ❷ (すゑ) an and. ¶ 硼酸末, borax powder.
matsu (待·竢·俟·須つ), *vt.* ❶ (待受ける) to wait *for*; await. ❷ (待窺ふ) to watch *for*; bide; abide. ❸ (期待, 期望) to expect; hope *for*; look forward *to*. ❹ (待遇する) to treat; use. —待て!, Hold on!; Wait! —今か今かと待つ, to wait impatiently; expect every moment. —お待ち申します, I shall expect you. —君の言を須つまでもない, It is plain enough without your saying so. —待つ間程なくやって來た, I had not waited long before he came.
matsuba (松葉), *n.* a pine-needle.
matsubabotan (松葉牡丹), *n.*

【植】 the large-flowered purslane; the sun-plant.

matsubara (松原), *n.* a pine-grove.

matsubaudo (石刀柏), *n.* 【植】 the asparagus.

matsubazue (松葉杖), *n.* crutches. —松葉杖に縋って歩く, to walk on crutches.

matsubayashi (松林), *n.* a pine forest [wood].

matsubi (末尾), *n.* the end; the tail; the finish; the termination; the finis (書物の終に書く).

matsudai (末代), *n.* ❶ (永久) eternity. ❷ (未來) the future ages. ❸ (澆季) a degenerate age. —末代までの恥辱である, It is an eternal shame.

matsudake (松茸), *n.* 【植】 Armillaria edodes (mushroom の一種·學名).

matsuge (睫毛), *n.* 【解】 eyelashes; cilium [*pl.* cilia].

matsugo (末期), *n.* the last moment [hour]; the hour of death. —末期の水, water given to the dying. —末期の苦み, the last gasp [agonies]; the agony of death.

matsuji (末寺), *n.* a branch temple.

matsujitsu (末日), *n.* the last day; the end. ¶ 末日審判, 【神】 the Great Assize; doom. (末日審判の日, the Day of Doom.)

matsukasa (松子, 松毬), *n.* a pine-cone; a fir-cone.

matsukazari (松飾), *n.* the New-Year's pine decoration. —松飾りをする, to decorate for the New Year with pine branches; set pine-branches for the New Year's decoration.

matsukaze (松風), *n.* soughing of the wind among pine-trees.

matsumushi (松蟲), *n.* 【昆】 Calyptotryphus marmoratus (cricket 一種·學名).

matsunouchi (松の内), *n.* the pine-decoration season; the first seven days of the New Year.

matsuri (祭), *n.* a festival; a fête; a holiday.

matsuriageru (祭上げる), *vt.* to set up. —會長に祭り上げる, to set him up as chairman.

matsurigoto (政), *n.* government; administration; state [political] affairs. —政を聽く, to hold court.

matsurikomu (祭込む), *vt.* ❶ to canonize; worship as a deity. ❷ to relegate; send up; kick upstairs 【卑】. —名譽職に祭込む, to relegate to an honorary post.

matsuringo (鳳梨), *n.* 【植】 the pine-apple.

matsuro (末路), *n.* the evening [last part; end] of one's life.

matsuru (祭·祀る), *vt.* ❶ (神に) to deify; (offer) worship. ❷ (祭式を行ふ) to celebrate; hold a mass *for*; observe the anniversary of the death. ❸ (祠を建てる) to enshrine; dedicate a shrine *to*. —神に祀る, to honour a person as a *kami*; deify him; dedicate a shrine to him.

matsuryū (末流), *n.* ❶ (後裔) descendants. ❷ (門下) disciples; followers. ❸ (下流) the lower stream.

matsuwaru (纏る), *v.* ❶ (纏綿) to be entangled; get caught *on*. ❷ (纏繞) to coil; twine.

matsuyani (松脂), *n.* pine-resin; pitch; turpentine.

matsuyō (末葉), *n.* ❶ the last period of an age. ❷ (子孫) a descendant. —十八世紀の末葉に, at the end of the eighteenth century.

matsuza (末座), *n.* the last seat.

matta (待った), *vt.* wait! ; not yet! —待ったなしに, without saying "not yet."

mattadanaka (眞直中), *n.* the centre; the middle; the midst. —敵の眞直中に, in the midst of the enemy.

mattaki (全き), *a.* ❶ (完全) perfect; complete; entire; whole. ❷ (安全) safe; unhurt; undamaged. —全きを望む, to expect perfection.

mattaku (全く), *ad.* ❶ (全然) quite; perfectly; entirely. ❷ (少しも) (not) at all; in the least. ❸ (實際) truly; really; certainly. —全く知らぬ, to know nothing *of*. —全くの紳士, a perfect gentleman. —全くの浪費, sheer waste. —全くの嘘, a downright [plump] lie.

mattan (末端), *n.* an end; a tip.

matto (マット), *n.* ❶ (靴拭) a shoe [door]-mat. ❷ (艶消) mat.

mattō-suru (全·完うする), *vt.* to complete; fulfil; bring to perfection [completion]. —任務を全うする, to discharge one's duties; carry out one's mission (使節などの). —身を全うする, to save one's life; escape death. —終を全うする, ① to remain happy to the end of one's life. ② to bring it to a happy end.

mau (舞ふ), *vi.* ❶ to dance. ❷ (空中に翻り飛ぶ) to flutter about (蝶·小鳥などが); be driven (木葉などが). ❸ (旋回する) to gyrate; turn; revolve; whirl (渦などが). —舞を舞ふ, to dance;

perform a dance.

maue (眞上), *ad.* right overhead.

mawari (廻), *n.* ❶ (回轉) revolution; rotation. ❷ (周圍) a circumference; a perimeter; girth. ❸ (一巡) a round; a turn; a tour (巡回). ❹ (附近) surrounding places; neighbourhood. ——, *ad.* about; around; in the neighbourhood [vicinity]. —家の周りに, about a house; in one's neighbourhood (近所). —一周りして來る, to take a turn (庭など); go one's rounds (巡回). —錢の廻りが良い《惡い》, to be well《badly》off. —年賀廻りをする, to pay a round of the New Year's calls.

mawariawase (廻合せ), *n.* luck; fortune; chance; fate (運命). —廻り合はせる, to happen; chance *upon.* (飛んだ所へ廻り合はせた, I happened upon an awkward occasion.)

mawaributai (廻舞臺), *n.* a revolving stage.

mawaridōi (廻遠い), *a.* roundabout; devious; circuitous (道などの). —廻り遠く, circuitously; deviously; roundabout.

mawaridōrō (走馬燈), *n.* a revolving lantern.

mawarikudoi (廻りくどい), *a.* circumlocutory; roundabout; periphrastic. —廻りくどい話, a tedious talk; long-winded talk.

mawarimichi (廻路), *n.* a roundabout way; a detour; a circuitous route. —廻り路をする, to go round; take a roundabout way; make a detour.

mawarimochi (廻持), *n.* taking a duty by turns.

mawaru (廻る), *vi.* ❶ (廻轉) to turn round; revolve; rotate; wheel. ❷ (巡回) to go one's rounds; patrol. ❸ (迂回) to go round; take a roundabout way. ❹ (循環) to circulate. —廻れ右, Right about turn! —筆が廻る, to have a facile pen. —舞臺が廻る, The stage turns [revolves]. —敵の側面に廻る, to turn the flank of the enemy.

mawashi (廻し), *n.* ❶ (廻すこと) passing. ❷ (褌) a loin-cloth. ❸ (締込) an ornamental apron.

mawashimono (廻者), *n.* a spy; a secret agent; an emissary. ☞ *kanchō* (間諜).

mawasu (廻す), *vt.* ❶ (回轉) to turn; wheel; roll. ❷ (轉送) to forward (手紙を行先へ); send round; circulate (回狀など). —次へ廻す, to pass it on. —手紙を廻す (回章), to send round [circulate] a letter. —ハンドルを廻す, to turn a handle.

mawata (眞綿), *n.* floss-silk; silk-wadding; filoselle.

mayakashi (まやかし), *n.* a fraud; cheat; hocus-pocus; humbug. ¶ まやかし物, a forgery; a sham; a bogus (いかさま物); 【商】 meretricious goods.

mayakasu (まやかす), *vt.* to cheat; swindle; hocus.

mayaku (麻藥), *n.* a narcotic; an anæsthetic. —麻藥をかゞせる [かける], to administer an anæsthetic; drug.

mayoi (迷), *n.* ❶ (當惑) perplexity; bewilderment; puzzle. ❷ (迷誤) delusion; fallacy; illusion (錯覺). ❸ (迷信) superstition. ❹ (惑溺) infatuation; captivation. —迷が覺める, to recover from a delusion; be disillusioned; come to one's senses. —迷を覺ます, to disillusion him from his day-dreams; bring him to his senses.

mayoke (魔除), *n.* a charm (against ill-luck); a talisman (護符).

mayonaka (眞夜中に), *ad.* at midnight; at dead of night.

mayou (迷ふ), *vi.* ❶ (當惑) to be puzzled [perplexed]; be at a loss; be bewildered. ❷ (惑溺) to be infatuated; be fascinated; be captivated *by.* ❸ (正道より) to stray *from*; deviate [swerve] *from* (a just course). ❹ (迷信) to be superstitious; be fanatic (狂信). ❺ (成佛せぬ) to haunt; be restless in one's grave; linger in the world. —迷へる群集, stray sheep. —女に迷ふ, to be infatuated with a woman; be captivated by a woman. —取捨に迷ふ, to be puzzled which alternative to choose; be perplexed in making a selection. —方角に迷ふ, to lose one's bearings (船など); not to know which road to take (四辻等で). —邪道に迷ひ入る, to stray from the path of duty; stray from virtue.

mayowasu (迷はす), *vt.* ❶ (當惑) to puzzle; perplex; bewilder. ❷ (混亂) to delude; cheat; beguile. ❸ (岐路又は邪道に) to lead astray; mislead; misguide. ❹ (惑溺) to fascinate; captivate; infatuate. ——, *a.* ❶ (誤解) delusive; illusive; misleading. ❷ (誘惑) tempting; bewitching.

mayu (眉), *n.* the eyebrow; the brows. —眉を落す, to shave off one's eyebrows. —眉をつくろふ, to pencil [paint] the eyebrows. —眉を顰める, to knit the brows.

mayu (繭), *n.* a cocoon; a follicle. —繭から絲を取る, to

reel silk cocoons. [-puff.]
mayubake (眉刷), *n.* a powder-
mayuge (眉毛), *n.* the eyebrow. ☞ *mayu* (眉).
mayuzumi (眉墨, 黛), *n.* eyebrow-paint; blackened eyebrows.
mazamaza (まざまざと), *ad.* plainly; clearly; vividly.
mazari (雜, 混), **mazarike** (混氣), *n.* mixture; impurity. ☞ *majiri* (雜).
mazaru (雜ざる), *vi.* to be [get] mixed *with*; mingle *with*; be adulterated.
mazekaesu (雜返す), *vt.* ❶ (攪亂) to stir; confuse; interrupt; obstruct; disturb. ❷ (嘲弄) to jeer [chaff; scoff] *at*; banter; rally.
mazekoze (まぜこぜの), *a.* mixed; confused; disorderly. —まぜこぜに, ① (雜多) mixedly. ② (雜然) disorderly; promiscuously; pell-mell.
mazemono (雜物), *n.* ❶ a mixture; a hotch-potch; a jumble; a medley. ❷ an ingredient. —雜ぜ物する, to adulterate; mix.
mazeru (混·雜·交ぜる), *vt.* to mix; mingle; adulterate. —茶に牛乳を混ぜる, to put milk into one's tea. —酒に水を混ぜる, to dash *sake* with water.
mazu (先づ), *ad.* ❶ (第一に) first, in the first place [instance]; to begin with. ❷ (凡そ) about; some; almost; nearly. —先づ第一に, to begin [start] with.
mazui (まづい), *a.* ❶ (不味) unsavoury; tasteless; disagreeable. ❷ (拙い) awkward; clumsy; unskilful. —拙い文章, a clumsy [an unrefined] style; unpolished writing. —拙い細工, clumsy workmanship.
mazushii (貧しい), *a.* poor; destitute; indigent. —貧しく, poorly; penuriously; meagrely.
me (目), *n.* ❶ (眼) the eye. ❷ (眼球) the eyeball. ❸ (視力) sight; eyesight; vision. ❹ (經驗) experience. ❺ (鑑識) an eye; judgment. ❻ (骰子の) a spot; a pip. ❼ (碁盤等の) a square; a checker. ❽ (織目) texture; fabric. ❾ (其他) (*a*) a mesh (網目); grain (木理): (*b*) a tooth (鋸の); a ridge (鑢の). —目の上の瘤, an eye-sore. —目で知らせる, to wink *at*; make a sign with the eye. —目で解[わか]る (人の意中など), to see from a person's looks. —目が廻る, to feel dizzy; one's head swims; one's eyes swim [dance]. —目が覺める, ① to awake; wake up. ② to awake *to*; come to one's senses. —目が早い, to be quick of sight; be quick-sighted. —を見る目がある, to have an eye *for*. —に目がくれる, to be blinded *by*. —目が見えなくなる, to become blind; lose one's eyesight. —日本人の目から見ると, in the eyes of a Japanese. —目も當てられぬ, too pitiful [terrible, *etc.*] to look *at*. —目に見えぬ, [*a.*] invisible; imperceptible; unseen. —目につく [立つ], ① [*v.*] to catch the eye; attract [draw] attention. ② [*a.*] conspicuous; striking; attractive. —眼に惡い, bad for [trying to] the eyes. —目に觸れる, to catch the eye. —目に見る如し, to be as if one saw it with one's own eyes. —米人の眼に映じた日本, Japan as Americans see it. —眼の屆かぬ所に, beyond eyeshot; beyond one's vision. —目を拭ふ, to wipe one's eyes. —目を潰す, to put out a person's eyes. —目を離す, ① to take one's eyes off. ② to slacken one's attention. —目を樂します, to amuse [delight] one's eyes. —目を盜む, to do by stealth. —目を廻す, ① (氣絶する) to fall into a swoon; swoon; faint. ② (呆氣にとられる) to be bewildered. —目を奪ふ, to dazzle one's eyes. —目をかける, to favour; patronize; have pity [compassion] *on*; treat affectionately. —目をつぶる, ① to shut [close] one's eyes. ② (死ぬ) to close one's eyes. (目をつぶって聽く, to listen with closed eyes.) —目を側てる, to look askance *at*. —(鋸の) 目を立てる, to set the teeth.
me (目), *n.* ❶ =*monme* (匁). ❷ =*kakeme* (掛目). —秤の目, ① notches of a beam. ② weight.
me (牝, 雌), *n.* a female. ¶ 牝山羊, a she-goat. —牝鯨, a cow-whale. —雌雀, a hen-sparrow.
me (芽), *n.* ❶ a bud. ❷ (芽枝) a sprout; a shoot. ❸ (幼芽, 胚種) a germ; an ovule. —芽が出る, ① to sprout; bud out; shoot forth. ② to burgeon, bourgeon; pullulate. —芽を出す [吹く], to put forth leaves [buds].
-me (目), *suf.* (序數を作る). —三年目, the third year. —五日目の朝, the morning of the fifth day. —角から二軒目の店, the shop next to the corner.
meaki (目明), *n.* ❶ (物を見得る人) one who has eyes. ❷ (事理を解する人) one who can see things. ❸ (文字を解する人) the lettered; the literate.

meatarashii (目新らしい), *a.* new; fresh; novel.

meate (目當), *n.* ❶ =*mokuteki*. ❷ =*mokuhyō*. —目當てにする, to aim *at*; keep in view; have in one's eye. —持參金を目當てに結婚する, to marry a girl for her dowry.

meawaseru (妻せる), *vt.* to marry; give in marriage.

mebachi (雌蜂), *n.* 【昆】 the queen-bee; a female bee.

mebae (芽生), *n.* a bud; a sprout; a young shoot [leaf].

mebana (雌花), *n.* a female [fertile; pistillate] flower.

mebari (目張する), *vt.* to paste paper over; seal.

mebaru (眼張, 鮴), *n.* 【魚】 the black rockfish.

mebayai (目早い), *a.* sharp-sighted; quick-sighted; keen-sighted. —目早く見つける, to notice with sharp [quick] eyes.

meberi (量減), *n.* ullage.

meboshi (目星), *n.* ❶ (狙) an aim. ❷ 【醫】 (角膜斑點) leucoma; macula corneæ. —犯人と目星をつける, to scent [spot] a person as the culprit.

meboshii (目ぼしい), *a.* important; chief; noteworthy; attractive.

mebunryō (目分量), *n.* judging by the eye. —目分量で量る, to measure by the eye.

mecha (滅茶・苦茶, ·滅茶), *n.* confusion; disorder; mess. —滅茶な, confused; disordered; at sixes and sevens. —滅茶滅茶の大安賣, a rummage-sale. —滅茶に, ① in confusion; in disorder; pell-mell. ② (取捨せずに) indiscriminately; promiscuously. —滅茶滅茶に引裂く, to tear up; tear to pieces [ribbons]. —滅茶苦茶に押込む, to huddle together.

mechiru (メチル), *n.* 【化】 methyl. —メチル·アルコール, methyl alcohol; wood-spirit.

medaka (目高), *n.* 【魚】 Pœcilia latipes (killifish の一種·學名).

medake (雌竹), *n.* the medake [metake] bamboo

medama (目玉, 眼球), *n.* the eye-ball. —お目玉を頂戴する, to be rebuked [scolded]; catch it.

medatsu (目立つ), *vi.* to be conspicuous; be striking [prominent]; attract attention. ——, *a.* prominent; striking; conspicuous; noticeable; flaring. —目立つ色, a striking colour. —目立たぬ服裝で, in plain clothes. —目立たぬ樣に, in a quiet way; in a modest manner. —一際目立って美しい, to be strikingly beautiful.

mederu (愛でる), *vt.* to love; be fond *of*; delight *in*. —...に愛でて, in acknowledgment [recognition] *of*.

medetai (目出度い), *a.* happy; fortunate; auspicious. —目出度く解決する, to be happily concluded [settled]; be brought to a happy conclusion. —改暦の御慶目出度申納候, I wish you a happy New Year.

medo (針眼), *n.* ❶ the eye (of a needle). ❷ =*meate*.

medōri (目通り), *n.* ❶ (面前) one's presence. ❷ (謁見) an audience; an interview. —目通りする, ① to come into a superior's presence. ② to be received in audience. —目通りを許さる, to be received *by*; be received in audience; be admitted into another's presence.

megafon (メガフォン), *n.* a megaphone.

megakeru (目掛ける), *vt.* ❶ (狙ふ) to aim *at*; point *at*; level *at*. ❷ (選ぶ) to single out; mark out. —...目掛けて發砲する, to fire *at*.

megami (女神), *n.* a goddess.

megane (眼鏡), *n.* spectacles; eye-glasses. —八度の眼鏡, spectacles of 8 degrees. —眼鏡を掛ける, to put on 《wear》 spectacles. —眼鏡を掛けて, with spectacles on. —眼鏡を外す, to take off spectacles. —眼鏡越しに人を見る, to look at another over one's spectacles. ¶ 眼鏡商, an optician.

megane (眼鑑), *n.* judgment; discernment. —主人のお眼鑑に叶ふ, to find favour with one's master; stand high in one's master's estimation.

megeru (負げる), *vi.* to be affected *by*; suffer *from*; wither; droop. —...にもめげず, notwithstanding [in spite *of*] (the rain); unaffected *by* (the cold season).

megumi (惠), *n.* ❶ (天惠) blessing; grace. ❷ (恩惠) favour; kindness; benevolence. —神の惠により, by (the) grace of god. —惠を受ける, to receive kindness; be favoured with kindness *by*.

megumibukai (惠深い), *a.* gracious; benevolent (主人など).

megumu (萌む), *vi.* to bud; sprout; shoot; germinate.

megumu (惠む), *v.* ❶ to bless (神が); favour; show kindness. ❷ (與へる) to give; send. —金を惠む, to give money.

megurasu (廻らす), *vt.* ❶ (圍繞) to surround; encircle. ❷ (轉回) to turn; revolve. ❸ (運) to think out; plan out. —梱を廻

[繞] らす, to fence around; surround with fences; palisade. —踵を旋らす, to turn on one's heels. —一頭を廻らす, to look back. —思慮を運らす, to ponder *over* [*on*]; meditate *on*.

meguri (廻), *n.* ❶ (循環) circulation. ❷ =***mawari***. ❸ (遍歴) going [travelling] round [about]; pilgrimage. ❹ =***gekkei*** (月經).

meguriau (廻合ふ), *vt.* to come across; meet *with*; light *on*.

meguru (廻る), *v.* ❶ (循環) to circulate. ❷ (廻轉) to revolve (round); turn (round). ❸ (遍歴) to go round; travel about; make a pilgrimage.

megusa (薄荷), *n.* 【植】the corn-mint.

megusuri (目藥), *n.* eye-wash; eye-water; eye-lotion. —目藥をさす, to apply eye-lotion; drop eye-water *into*.

mehachibun (目八分に), *ad.* a little above [higher than] the eyes.

mehana (目鼻), *n.* eyes and a nose. —目鼻をつける, to lick into shape; bring into order. ¶ 目鼻立, countenance; features.

mehashi (目端が利く), to be quick to perceive; be acute; be sharp-headed.

mei (銘), *n.* ❶ a name (刀劍等の); an inscription (碑·器物等の). ❷ (自警の辭) a precept; a motto.

mei (命), *n.* ❶ (命令) an order; a command. ❷ (壽命) life. ❸ (運命) fate; destiny. —命に背く, to disobey the orders *of*. —命を奉じて, in obedience to [in execution of] a command. —命は天に在り, To be is fixed by Heaven.

mei (明), *n.* ❶ (視力) eyesight. ❷ (鑑識) discernment; discrimination; penetration. ❸ (光) light; glitter; sheen. —明を失する, to lose one's eyesight. —人を見るの明がある, to be a shrewd judge of character.

mei (姪), *n.* a niece.

mei- (名), *a.* fine; noted; famous; celebrated; precious.

meian (名案), *n.* a good [capital] plan; a bright [happy; fine] idea. —名案を考へつく, to hit upon a capital idea.

meian (明暗), *n.* ❶ light and darkness; light and shade. ❷ 【繪畫】*chiaroscuro* 〔伊〕.

meibi (明媚な), *a.* picturesque; picture-like; scenic.

meibin (明敏な), *a.* clear; bright; sagacious; penetrating. —明敏な頭腦, a clear head.

meibo (名簿), *n.* a register of names; a (name-)list; a roll (學校·軍隊等の); a matricula (大學などの). —名簿に載せる, to register [enroll; enlist] (one's name) *in*. —名簿より削る, to strike [take] a person's name off the list 「books」. ¶ 會員名簿, a list of members.

meibō (名望), *n.* reputation; repute; popularity. —名望ある紳士, a gentleman of repute. —名望を失墜する, to fall in public estimation; dwindle in the public eye. ¶ 名望家, a man of repute; a man of high reputation.

meibō (明眸), *n.* bright eyes.

meibun (名文), *n.* a fine [an excellent] composition. ¶ 名文家, a fine writer.

meibun (名分), *n.* relation (關係); justification (名義). —君臣の名分を明かにする, to make clear the relation of lord and retainer.

meibun (明文), *n.* an express provision. —法律に明文がある, to be provided for in the law; be expressly determined by law.

meibutsu (名物), *n.* a noted product; a speciality. —倫敦名物の霧, the notorious London fog. —大阪名物の煤煙, soot, characteristic of Ōsaka. ¶ 名物男, a lion; a celebrity; a man whose name is in everybody's mouth.

meicho (名著), *n.* a fine work; a masterpiece.

meichū (命中), *n.* direct shot [hit]; hitting the mark. ——**suru**, *v.* to hit (the mark); tell; take effect. —司令塔に命中する, to strike (the ship on) the conning tower. ¶ 命中彈, a hit.

meidai (命題), *n.* 【論】a proposition. ¶ 肯定《否定》命題, an affirmative 《a negative》 proposition.

meidan (明斷), *n.* a clear [just] decision; a sound judgment.

meido (冥途, 冥土), *n.* the other world; the Hades. —冥土の旅, a journey to the other world.

meidō (鳴動する), *vi.* to rumble.

meifuku (冥福), *n.* a blessing; happiness in a future existence. —死者の冥福を祈る, to pray for the happiness of the dead.

meiga (螟蛾), *n.* 【蛾】Chilo simplex (pearl-moth の一種·學名).

meiga (名畫), *n.* a fine picture; a masterpiece (of painting).

meigara (銘柄), *n.* 【商】a brand; a chop 〔印度支那〕.

meigen (名言), *n.* a wise [golden] saying; a true saying. —千古の名言, an immortal saying.

meigen (明言する), *vt.* to declare; announce; affirm; say definitely.

meigetsu (明月), *n.* ❶ a bright

moon. ❸ (十五夜の月) a full moon. ❹ (仲秋の) the harvest-moon.

meigi (名義), *n.* name. —名義上の主權者, a titular sovereign. —僕の《自分の》名義で, in my《one's own》name. ¶ 名義書換簿 a transfer-book. —名義人, a nominal person. —名義社員, an ostensible partner.

meigo (冥護), *n.* God's blessing; divine protection [care].

meihaku (明白な), *a.* clear; obvious; plain. —極めて明白な, plain as a pike-staff. —明白な證據, a clear proof. —明白になる, to become clear.

meihangan (名判官), *n.* a wise judge.

meihitsu (名筆), *n.* ❶ (筆蹟) a fine hand [handwriting] (書); a fine [good] painting (畫) ❷ (書畫) a masterpiece of pen《brush》.

meihyō (名標), *n.* a tally.

meii (名醫), *n.* an expert [excellent] physician; a famous doctor.

Meiji (明治), *n.* the Meiji era. ¶ 明治維新, the Restoration of Meiji. —明治天皇祭, the Anniversary of the Death of the Emperor Meiji.

meiji (名辭), *n.* 【論】a term.

meijin (名人), *n.* a master; a master [an experienced] hand; a past master. —テニスの名人, an expert tennis-player.

meijitsu (名實), *n.* name and fact [reality]. —名實共に, both in name and reality; not only in name, but also in fact.

meijo (冥助), *n.* divine help.

meijō (名狀する), *vt.* to describe; draw. —名狀すべからず, to begger [be beyond] description.

meika (名家), *n.* ❶ (名門) an illustrious family; a noble family. ❷ (大家) an authority; a great master. ❸ (著名の人) a man of distinction; a famous person.

meikai (明快な), *a.* clear; plain. —明快な答辯をする, to give an explicit answer. —明快に說明する, to give a lucid explanation *of*.

meikaku (明確な), *a.* clear and exact; distinct; unquestionable; undoubted; definite.

meikan (名鑑), *n.* a list. ¶ 畫家名鑑, a list of artists.

meiki (銘記する), *v.* to impress upon one's mind [memory]; engrave [stamp] on one's heart [memory]; fix on the mind.

meiki (銘旗), *n.* a bannerol (高貴の人の); a banneret (小形); a funeral-banner (葬禮の).

meiki (明記する), *vt.* to specify; state clearly; mention expressly. —記錄に明記する, to enter in a record; put upon record.

meikin (鳴禽), *n.* a song-bird; a singing-bird; a singer. ¶ 鳴禽類, 【鳥】Oscines (學名); the singing birds.

meikō (名工), *n.* a master(-hand); a good [practised] hand; a skilful [an experienced] artisan.

meiku (名句), *n.* ❶ (散文の) a fine expression; an exquisite passage. ❷ (詩歌の) a fine poem [verse]; a famous [celebrated] stanza. ¶ 名句集, an anthology; a golden treasury of thoughts; a chrestomathy.

meikun (名君), *n.* a wise ruler; a good king.

meikyō (名敎), *n.* social [public] morals.

meikyū (迷宮), *n.* a maze; a labyrinth. —迷宮に入る, to be lost in mystery; be classed with unsolved mysteries.

meimei (命名する), *vt.* to name; give a name *to*; christen. ¶ 命名式, the naming; the christening. —命名者, a namer; a nomenclator (特に博物學上の); a godfather《godmother》(名親).

meimei (銘銘), *ad.* each (one); every one; separately. —銘々の each; several; respective. ¶ 義士銘々傳, the Lives of the Loyal Retainers.

meimetsu (明滅する), *vi.* to flicker; glimmer; shimmer.

meimoku (瞑目する), *vi.* ❶ (目を塞ぐ) to close [shut] the eyes. ❷ (死す) to close one's eyes; pass away; sleep in peace.

meimon (名門), *n.* a noted family; noble descent; blue blood. —名門の出である, to be born [come] of a good family.

meimu (迷夢), *n.* delusion; fallacy; misconception. —迷夢が醒める, to come to one's senses; come to oneself. —迷夢を醒ます, to bring a person to his senses; disillusion a person of his day-dreams; wake him up.

meimyaku (命脈), *n.* ❶ (命の綱) the thread of life; the breath of life. ❷ (其物の運命·命數) destiny; fate; life. —僅かに命脈を保つ He has only a spark of life le

meinichi (命日), *n.* the death-day; the anniversary of a death.

meinu (牝犬), *n.* a lady-dog; a female dog; a bitch.

meirei (命令), *n.* an order; a command; bidding; 【法】an ordinance. —命令する, to order; command; bid; give an order. ¶ 命令文 【文】an imperative sen tence. —命令法, 【文】the imperative mood.

meiri (名利), *n.* wealth and fame; honour and profit. —名利の外に超然たり, to be above the temptation of worldly fame and gain.

meiron (名論), *n.* a sound argument. ¶ 名論卓説, sound arguments and opinions.

meiru (滅入る), *vi.* to be depressed.

meiryō (明瞭な), *a.* clear; distinct; plain. —明瞭な筆蹟, clear handwriting. —明瞭に說明する, to explain clearly.

meisai (明細), *n.* details; particulars. —明細な, particular; minute; detailed. —明細に亙る, to enter [go] into details; go into [descend to] particulars. —明細に說明する, to explain in detail. ¶ 明細書, a detailed account.

meisaku (名作), *n.* a masterpiece; a fine work.

meisan (名產), *n.* a noted [famous] product.

meisatsu (明察する), *v.* to observe sharply; discern clearly; penetrate *into*.

meisei (名聲), *n.* fame; repute; renown. —名聲を博する, to win a reputation [fame].

meiseki (明晰), *n.* clearness; plainness. —明晰な, clear; plain; perspicuous.

meisha (目醫者), *n.* an oculist; an opnthalmologist.

meishi (名士), *n.* a man of distinction [note; rank; mark]; a notable (person). ¶ 現代名士錄, a who's who.

meishi (名刺), *n.* a card; a visiting card; a name-card. —名刺を出して面會を求める, to send in a card and ask for an interview.

meishi (名詞), *n.* 【文】the noun. ¶ 普通《固有》名詞, the common 《proper》 noun. —抽象《具象》名詞, the abstract 《concrete》 noun. —物質《集合》名詞, the material 《collective》 noun.

meishi (明示), *n.* clear statement. —明示の, express. —明示する, to state clearly; point out clearly.

meishin (迷信), *n.* superstition. —迷信的信仰, superstitious belief. ¶ 迷信家, a superstitious person.

meisho (名所), *n.* a famous [noted; celebrated] place; a show-place; a sight. ¶ 名所案內, a guide-book. —名所舊蹟, famous places and historic sites.

meishō (名匠), *n.* a master; a master-hand.

meishō (名將), *n.* a famous general; a great general.

meishō (名勝), *n.* famous views.

meishō (名稱), *n.* a name; a title; a designation.

meishu (銘酒), *n.* superior *sake*. ¶ 銘酒屋, a dram [grog]-shop; a pothouse; a saloon 〔米〕; an *assommoir* 〔佛〕.

meishu (盟主), *n.* the chief [leader] of confederate states; the leading power.

meisō (迷想), *n.* fancy; illusion.

meisō (瞑想), *n.* meditation; contemplation; speculation. —瞑想する, to meditate *on*; contemplate *on*; ponder [brood] *over*. —瞑想に耽る, to be lost in thought.

meisū (名數), *n.* 【數】a concrete number.

meisū (命數), *n.* ❶ (壽命) one's life; one's days. ❷ (運命) fate; destiny; predestination. —命數が盡きる, to end one's days; one's days are numbered.

mei-suru (銘する), *vt.* ❶ (金石に) to inscribe (*on*); engrave (*on*). ❷ (心に) to stamp (*on*); impress (*on* or *in*); imprint (*on* or *in*). —肝に銘する, to write on the heart; impress on one's mind.

mei-suru (瞑する), *vi.* to close one's eyes; sleep in peace; rest in peace. —地下に瞑せよ, *requiescat in pace*! 〔羅〕(往々墓石に R. I. P. と略して); may he 《she》 rest in peace!

meitatsu (明達の), *a.* wise; sagacious; talented. —明達の士, a man of wisdom [talent].

meitei (酩酊), *n.* drunkenness, intoxication. —酩酊さす, to intoxicate; inebriate. —酩酊する, to be intoxicated; be overcome with liquor.

meitō (名刀), *n.* a fine blade; a noted sword. —名刀正宗, a fine blade by Masamune; a fine Masamune.

meitō (明答), *n.* a plain answer; a definite reply. —明答する, to answer plainly; reply definitely.

meiwaku (迷惑), *n.* trouble; inconvenience; embarrassment. —迷惑さす, to trouble; inconvenience; embarrass. —迷惑する, to be troubled; be put to inconvenience; be embarrassed. —人に迷惑をかける, to put a person to trouble; put a person to inconvenience; embarrass another.

meiyaku (盟約), *n.* ❶ (誓約) pledge; covenant; pact. ❷ (同盟) alliance; league. —盟約する, ① to covenant; pledge oneself *to*. ② to league; form an alliance; make a league. ¶ 盟約書, a covenant.

meiyo (名誉), *n.* honour; reputation; repute; good [fair] name. —名誉にかけて, upon my honour; honour bright 〔俗〕. (名誉にかけての誓, a word of honour.) —名誉とする, to consider it honour *to*; esteem it an honour *to*. —名誉の戦死を遂げる, to die a glorious [an honourable] death in battle. ¶ 名誉博士, an honorary doctor; a doctor *honoris causa*. —名誉會長, an honorary president [chairman]. —名誉恢復, rehabilitation (of character). —名誉毀損, defamation. —名誉教授, an honorary [emeritus] professor. —名誉心, ① (高名心) desire for fame; ambition. ② (廉恥心) sense of honour. —名誉賞牌, a medal of honour. —名誉職, an honorary post; an unpaid post.

meiyū (名優), *n.* a famous actor [(actress)]; a star.

meizan (名山), *n.* a celebrated [noted] mountain.

mei-zuru (命ずる), *vt.* ❶ (命令する) to order; give orders; command. ❷ (任命する) to appoint; nominate. —酒を命ずる, to order [call for] *sake*. —良心の命ずる所に從って行動する, to act in accordance with the dictates of one's conscience.

meji(gatsuo) (鯤鰹), *n.* 【魚】 a young tunny.

mejika (牡鹿), *n.* the doe; the hind.

mejiri (眼尻, 眥), *n.* the corner [tail] of the eye; the outer [external] canthus. —釣上った眼尻, upturned eyes.

mejiro (目白), *n.* 【鳥】 the Japanese white-eye [silver-eye].

mejirushi (目標), *n.* ❶ a mark; a guide; a guide [finger; sign] -post (道標). ❷ (記號) a sign; a mark. —白墨で目標をつける, to chalk a mark.

mekake (妾), *n.* a concubine; a mistress.

mekakushi (目隠), *n.* ❶ 【建】 a blind; a screen. ❷ (衝立) a (board-)screen. ❸ (馬の) a blind; blinkers; blinders 〔米〕. ❹ (迷藏戯) blindman's buff. —目隠しする, ① to put up a board-screen. ② to blindfold a person.

mekashiya (めかし屋), *n.* ❶ (男) a fop; a dandy; a swell. ❷ (女) a dressy woman.

mekasu (めかす), *vi.* to dress finely; be in full toilet; adorn [beautify] oneself.

mekata (目方), *n.* weight. —一噸の目方がある, to weigh a ton. —目方が超過してゐる, to exceed in weight; be over weight.

mekiki (目利), *n.* ❶ (事) judging; criticism. ❷ (人) a judge; a connoisseur (美術品の); a virtuoso (同上). —目利きする, to judge; criticize.

mekimeki (めきめき), *ad.* rapidly; markedly. —めきめき上達する, to make rapid progress.

Mekishiko (墨其西哥), *n.* Mexico. ¶ 墨其西哥人, a Mexican.

mekkachi (隻眼), *n.* a one-eyed man.

mekki (鍍金), *n.* ❶ gilding; plating; coating. ❷ (鍍金物) plated ware. —鍍金する, to gild; plate; coat (with gold leaf). ¶ 鍍金工, a gilder; a plater.

mekkiri (めっきり), *ad.* markedly; remarkably; noticeably.

mekkyaku (滅却する), *vt.* to efface; sink; ruin; destroy; extinguish.

mekubari (目配), *n.* watch; overseeing; superintendence.

mekubase (眴, 目配せ), *n.* winking; wink. —目配せする, to wink *at*; make a sign with the eye; tip another the wink.

mekugi (目釘), *n.* a pin; a rivet (of a sword-hilt).

mekura (盲), *n.* ❶ (盲目) (*a*) (事) blindness: (*b*) (人) a blind man; the blind (集合的). ❷ (文盲) (*a*) (事) illiteracy: (*b*) (人) an illiterate; the unlettered. —盲の, ① blind. ② illiterate; unlettered; ignorant. —盲になる, to become blind; go blind; lose one's sight. —盲蛇に怯ぢず, "Nothing so bold as a blind man."

mekuraban (盲判を押す), ❶ (日本) to stamp [affix; put] one's seal blindly on. ❷ (西洋) to sign without perusing the contents; sign unread.

mekurasagashi (盲探), *n.* groping. —盲探しする, to grope *for* [*after*]; grabble *for*; search blindly. —盲探しに歩く, to feel one's way; grope one's way.

mekureru (目眩れる), *vi.* to be blinded *by*. —金に目(が)眩れる, to be blinded by gold; be tempted by the golden bait.

mekuru (捲る), *vt.* ❶ (ひっくり返す) to turn over; turn up (トランプなど). ❷ (剝ぎ取る) to tear off; strip off; uncover. —頁をめくる, to turn over leaves. —床板をめくる, to tear off the floor-boards.

mekusare (目腐れ), *n.* ❶ (眼瞼縁炎) blepharitis marginalis [ciliaris]; inflammation of the ciliary border of the eyelids. ❷ (眼瞼軟骨炎) tarsitis; imflammation of the tarsal cartilage. ¶ 目腐れ金, a paltry [beggarly] sum; a mere

pittance (給料などの). 「gum.」
mekuso (目糞), *n.* eye-wax;
memagurushii (目まぐるしい), *a.* dizzy; giddy; vertiginous. —目まぐるしい變化, dizzy changes.
memai (眩暈), *n.* dizziness; giddiness; vertigo. —眩暈がする, to be dizzy; get giddy. (眩暈がして倒れる, to swoon down; faint away.)
memeshii (女女しい), *a.* womanish; effeminate. —女々しく振舞ふ, to play the woman; behave like a woman.
memie (目見), *n.* ❶ (謁見) audience. ❷ (僕婢の) a trial service. —お目見中である, to be on trial.
memo (便箋), *n.* a memo; a memorandum.
memori (目盛), *n.* ❶ (目分量で盛ること) filling by the eye. ❷ calibration; graduation (寒暖計などの); scale (尺度の). —目盛りする, to calibrate; graduate.
memoto (目許), *n.* the eye; expression of the eyes. —目もと涼しく鼻筋通る, to have bright eyes and a shapely nose.
men (面), *n.* ❶ (顔) the face. ❷ (假面) a mask. ❸ (表面) the surface; the face. ❹ (平面) a plane. ❺ (立體面) a side. ❻ (撃劍の面) a face-guard. —面と向って, face to face (顔つき合せて); to one's face (面前で) (面と向って惡口を云ふ, to abuse another to his face.) —面を被る, to put on [wear] a mask. (正義の面を被って, under the pretence [mask] of justice.) —面を脱ぐ, to unmask; take one's mask off.
men (綿), *n.* cotton. ¶ 綿羅紗, cotton-mixed woollen cloth. —綿セル, cotton-mixed serge.
menareru (目馴れる), *vi.* to get accustomed [used] to the sight.
menba (面罵する), *v.* to blame a person to his face; cast a reproach into a person's teeth.
menbō (麪棒), *n.* a rolling-pin; a roller.
menboku (面目), *n.* ❶ (顔) countenance. ❷ (名譽) honour; reputation; credit. ❸ (樣子) an appearance; an aspect. —身に餘る面目, an honour more than one deserves. —面目に關する, to affect one's dignity; be a point of honour. —面目を施す, to get credit; gain honour. —面目を失ふ, to lose countenance; be disgraced; be discredited. —面目を失はす, to put a person out of countenance; disgrace. —面目を改める, to alter the aspect *of*; put on a new face; assume a new aspect. —面目を保たせる; 面目を立てる, to keep a person in countenance (積極的に); save another's face (消極的に).
menchi (メンチ), *n.* 【料理】 mincemeat. —メンチ·ボール, a mincemeat ball.
mendan (面談), *n.* an interview; a talk. —面談する, to talk *with*; have an interview *with*; speak *to*. —委細面談の事, Particulars to be given personally. —御主人に面談したい, I wish to speak to your master.
mendō (面倒), *n.* ❶ (手數, 厄介, 迷惑) trouble. ❷ (困難) difficulty. ❸ (錯綜) complication. —面倒な, ① troublesome. ② (むづかしい) difficult. ③ (入りくんだ) complicated. —御面倒ながら, I am sorry to give you trouble, but.... —面倒にする, to complicate; embarrass. —面倒を見る, to see [look] *after*; take care *of*. —他人に面倒をかける, to trouble a person; give [cause] a person trouble; put a person to trouble. —それでは事が面倒になる, That will complicate matters.
mendori (牝鷄), *n.* a hen.
meṅeki (免役), *n.* ❶ (兵役免除) exemption from military service. ❷ (放免) discharge from penal service. —免役になる; 免役される, ① to be exempted from military service. ② to be discharged [released] from prison; be set free.
meṅeki (免疫 -性), *n.* immunity. —免疫になる, to become immune *from*. —免疫する, to immunize; render immune *against*. ¶ 免疫注射, immunization injection. —免疫者, an immune.
meneko (牡猫), *n.* a she-cat; a female cat.
meṅetsu (面謁), *n.* an audience; an interview. —面謁する, to have an audience *with*; be received in audience *by*; have an interview *with*.
men-furanneru (綿フランネル), *n.* cotton flannel; flannelette.
men-jiru (免じる), *vt.* to excuse. —君に免じて, for your sake; out of consideration for your feelings. —地位に免じて, respecting a person's position; in deference to his position.
menjo (免除), *n.* exemption; remissior release. —免除する, to exem *from*; remit; release *from*.
menjō (免狀), *n.* a certificate; a licence. —免狀を下附する, to license; grant [give] a licence.
menka (棉花), *n.* raw cotton.

menkai (面會), *n.* an interview; a meeting. —面會する, to meet; see; have an interview *with.* ¶ 面會日, a reception-day; an at-home day; a visiting-day. —面會者, a visitor; a caller. —面會謝絕, visits [interviews] declined; not at home.

menkan (免官), *n.* dismissal (from office). —依願免官となる, to be relieved from one's post at one's own request.

menkayaku (綿火藥), *n.* gun-cotton; cotton.

menko (めんこ), *n.* 【遊戲】chuck-farthing.

menkurau (面喰ふ), *vi.* to be confused; be flustered; be bewildered; be taken aback; lose one's head.

menkyo (免許), *n.* ❶ licence; permission. ❷ (傳授) certification of proficiency (in an art). —免許する, ① to license; permit. ② to certify a person's proficiency in an art. ¶ 免許醫, a licensed physician. —免許狀, a licence; a certificate; a permit; a diploma (學位等). —免許皆傳, instruction in all the mysteries of an art.

menma (牝馬), *n.* a mare.

menmitsu (綿密な), *a.* nice; minute (詳密); close (嚴密); scrupulous (周到). —綿密な頭, a head for details. —綿密な調査, a thorough investigation. —綿密な注意, scrupulous care. —綿密に檢査する, to examine minutely.

menmō (綿毛), *n.* mixture of cotton and wool. ¶ 綿毛交織, domett; woolsey.

menmoku (面目), *n.* =*menboku.*

men-neru (綿ネル), *n.* cotton flannel; flannelette.

menō (瑪瑙), *n.* 【鑛】agate.

menoko-kanjō (目子勘定), *n.* ⑤ 目子算. counting by tens.

menomae (目前に), *ad.* before [under] one's eyes; under one's (very) nose.

meṅorimono (綿織物), *n.* cotton cloth; cotton tissues.

menotama (目の玉), *n.* an eye-ball. —目の玉の飛び出る程とられる, to pay through the nose.

menpi (面皮), *n.* reputation; honour. —面皮を剝ぐ, to take the shine out of him.

menpu (綿布), *n.* ❶ (綿服) cotton clothes. ❷ (織物) cotton tissue; cotton stuff.

menpuku (綿服), *n.* cotton clothes; a cotton garment.

menrui (麪類), *n.* vermicelli

menseki (面責), *n.* personal reproof [reproach]. —面責する, to reprove a person to his face; cast a reproach in a person's teeth.

menseki (面積), *n.* area; dimensions. —面積百方里ある, to cover 100 sq. *ri* (in area.)

mensha (面謝する), *v.* ❶ to call on a person and tender one's thanks. ❷ to visit a person to make an apology *for.*

menshi (綿絲), *n.* cotton thread; cotton yarn. ¶ 綿絲紡績會社, a cotton-spinning company.

menshiki (面識), *n.* acquaintance. —面識ある人, a personal acquaintance. —面識が無い, to have no acquaintance *with*; be quite a stranger *to.*

menshoku (免職), *n.* dismissal (from office); discharge; deposition. —免職する, to dismiss; discharge; depose (特に高官を).

menshoku (面色), *n.* complexion; look; appearance. —面色土の如く, as pale as ashes [death].

menshū (免囚), *n.* a released prisoner.

menso (免租), *n.* remission of [exemption from] tax. ¶ 免租地, land exempted from tax.

menso (免訴), *n.* dismissal of a (law) case; discharge; acquittal. —免訴となる, The case is dismissed [dropped]; (人が) to be acquitted; be released.

mensō (面相), *n.* a countenance; features; the physiognomy.

men-suru (面する), *vt.* to face; front on; look [open] on. —四方海に面する, to face the sea on all sides.

mentarutesuto (精神檢査), *n.* mental test.

mentei (面體), *n.* looks; countenance.

menuki (目拔の), *a.* important; conspicuous; busy; flourishing. —目拔きの場所, important quarters; busy quarters.

meṅyō (緬羊), *n.* a sheep.

meṅyō (面妖な), *a.* strange; uncanny; wonderful.

menyū (獻立表), *n.* a menu; a bill of fare.

menzei (免稅), *n.* exemption [immunity] from taxes; remission of taxation. ¶ 免稅品, free goods. —免稅輸入品, duty-free imports.

menzen (面前), *n.* one's presence. —面前で, before; in the presence *of*; to one's face. (公衆の面前で, in public; before company. —面前で惡口する, to abuse a person to his face.)

men-zuru (免ずる), *vt.* ❶ (職を) to dismiss (from office). ❷ (免除) to discharge *from*; exempt *from*; remit. ❸ (免じる) to excuse.

meppō (滅法な), *a.* ⑤ 滅法界

な. extraordinary; extravagant; preposterous. —滅法に, extraordinarily; extravagantly; awfully.

merigo (廻轉木馬), *n.* a merry-go-round.

merikenko (米利堅粉), *n.* American flour.

merikomu (めり込む), *vi.* to cave in; stave in; sink in.

merinsu (メリンス), *n.* muslin; muslin-de-laine; mousseline-de-laine. ¶ 絹メリンス, mousseline-de-soie.

meriyasu (莫大小), *n.* knitted [knit] goods; hosiery. ¶ 莫大小工場, a knitting-factory; a hosier-manufactory. —莫大小商人, a hosier.

meruton (メルトン), *n.* melton.

mesaki (目先), *n.* before one's eyes; before one; the present. —目先の早い, quick-sighted. —目先の變ッた, novel. —目先の利く, far-sighted [-seeing]; foresighted; sagacious; shrewd. —目先の利かぬ, short [near]-sighted; without foresight. —目先にちらつく, to flitter before one; appear before one's eyes; see it before one's eyes. —目先ばかりを考へる, to think only of the present. —目先をかへる, to change a plan.

meshi (召), *n.* summons; call; calling (神の).

meshi (飯), *n.* ❶ boiled [cooked] rice. ❷ (食事) a meal. —三度の飯, three meals. —飯を炊く, to boil [cook] rice. —他人の飯を食ふ, to eat another's salt; share a corner at another's table.

meshiagaru (召上る), *vt.* to take; have.

meshibe (雌蕊), *n.* 【植】 the pistil.

meshibitsu (飯櫃), *n.* a boiled-rice box; a rice-tub.

meshidoki (飯時), *n.* meal-time; dinner-time.

meshikakaeru (召抱へる), *vt.* to take into service; engage.

meshimono (召物), *n.* ❶ (召上り物) food. ❷ (著物) (one's) clothes.

meshita (目下), *n.* one's inferiors; one's subordinates (部下); one's juniors (後輩). —目下に見る, to look down upon a person. —目下の者に目をかける, to treat one's inferiors with kindness; be sympathetic to one's inferiors.

meshitaki (飯炊), *n.* ❶ (事) rice-cooking. ❷ (人) a cook; a cooky 【俗】.

meshitoru (召捕る), *vt.* to arrest; apprehend.

meshitsubu (飯粒), *n.* a boiled rice-grain.

meshitsukai (召使), *n.* a servant; a domestic.

meshiya (飯屋), *n.* an eating-house; a chop-house.

Mesojisuto (メソヂスト敎), *n.* Methodism. —メソヂスト敎派の人, a Methodist.

mesomeso (めそめそ泣く), *vi.* to sob.

messhitsu (滅失), *n.* loss. —滅失する, to be lost; be destroyed.

messō (滅相な), *a.* extraordinary; extravagant; unreasonable. —滅相もない, far from it.

mes-suru (滅する), *vt.* ❶ (亡ぼす, 絕やす) to destroy; ruin; extinguish; put an end *to*; exterminate. ❷ (消す) to put out; extinguish. —, *vi.* ❶ (亡ぶ, 絕ゆ) to be destroyed [ruined]; be extinguished; die out; perish; cease to exist; become extinct. ❷ (消ゆ) to go out; be extinguished; be put out.

mesu (牝, 雌), *n.* 【動】 a female.

mesu (召す), *vt.* ❶ (呼び寄す) to summon; call. ❷ (著る, 穿く) to wear; put on. ❸ (食ふ, 飮む) to take; have. ❹ (乘る) to ride; take. ❺ (買ふ) to buy. —お氣に召す, to suit your fancy. —お風呂を召す, to take bath. —お年を召す, to grow old [in age]; advance in years.

mesu (メス), *n.* 【獨 messer】 a knife.

mētā (メーター), *n.* a meter; a taximeter.

metaru (メタル), **medaru** (メダル), *n.* a medal.

metate (目立する), *vt.* to set.

mete (右手, 馬手), *n.* the right hand; the sword-hand.

metoru (娶る), *vt.* to marry; take in marriage; take to wife.

mētoru (メートル), *n.* ❶ (米突) a metre. ❷ (計器) a meter. ❸ (晴雨計) a barometer. —千米突, a kilometre. —メートルが上がる《下がる》, The barometer is rising 《falling》. —盃を重ねながらメートルを上げる, to talk big [tall] over one's cups. ¶ メートル尺, a metric scale. —米突法, the metric system.

metsubō (滅亡), *n.* ruin; fall; downfall; destruction. —滅亡する, to fall; be ruined; be destroyed; come to an end. —滅亡に瀕してゐる, to be on the verge of destruction.

metsubushi (目潰), *n.* a blinder; a thing thrown to blind the eye. —灰を投げて目潰しをする, to throw ashes to blind another's eyes.

metsugi (芽接 -法), *n.* 【園】 bud-grafting; inoculation. —芽接する, to bud; inoculate.

metsuki (目附), *n.* eyes; expression of the eyes; look.

metta (滅多な), *a.* thoughtless; reckless; rash. **——-ni,** *ad.* ❶ thoughtlessly; recklessly; rashly. ❷ (稀に) seldom; rarely; scarcely [hardly] ever. —そんな事は滅多にない, It rarely [seldom] happens. —夕方には滅多に外出しません. I hardly ever go out of an evening.

metta-mushō (滅多無性に), *ad.* Ⓢ 滅多矢鱈に. at random; at hazard; without choice. —滅多無性に打つ, to shoot [hit; fire] at random.

meuchi (目打), *n.* perforation. —目打ちする, to perforate.

meue (目上), *n.* one's superiors; one's betters; one's seniors (先輩).

meushi (牝牛), *n.* a cow.

meutsuri (目移がする), *vi.* to be drawn alternately; be perplexed in making a choice.

meyani (目脂), *n.* eye-wax.

meyasu (目安), *n.* ❶ (算盤の) (*a*) (減) a subtractor: (*b*) (乘) a multiplier: (*c*) (除) a divisor. ❷ (標準) standard. ❸ (目的) an aim; an object; a goal. —目安を立てる, to fix one's aim. —*a* を目安にして *b* を割る, to divide *b* with *a* as the divisor.

mezamashi (目覺), *n.* ❶ (目を覺すこと) rousing from sleep. ❷ (目を覺すもの) an eye-opener. ❸ ＝目覺時計. —目覺しをかける, to set the alarm. ¶ 目覺時計, an alarm [alarum]-clock.

mezamashii (目覺しい), *a.* ❶ (驚くべき) astonishing; striking; surprising; wonderful. ❷ (立派な) splendid; brilliant; grand. —目覺しい早業, a lightning feat. —目覺しい發展, a wonderful [surprising] development. —目覺しい働をする, to do splendid work; perform astonishing deeds; perform wonders.

mezamasu (目覺す), *vt.* to awaken; wake up; rouse from sleep.

mezameru (目覺める), *vi.* ❶ to wake; awaken; waken. ❷ (迷を啓く) to come to one's senses. —人生の現實に目覺める, to awake to the realities of life.

mezashi (目刺), *n.* sardines dried on a skewer.

mezasu (目指す), *vt.* to aim *at*; have an eye *to*. —目指す敵, the enemy one aims at.

mezatoi (目敏い), *a.* ❶ (覺め易い) easily awakened. ❷ (目早い) quick-sighted; keen-eyed; sharp-sighted. —目敏い人, a light sleeper. —目ざとく見附ける, to detect with sharp eyes.

mezawari (目障), *n.* an eyesore; an obstruction to the view. —目障りになる, to be offensive to the eye [sight]; offend the eye; obstruct the view.

mezurashii (珍しい), *a.* ❶ (稀有) rare; scarce. ❷ (新奇) new; novel. ❸ (異常) unusual; uncommon; extraordinary. ❹ (奇異) queer; curious; strange. —珍しいもの, ① a novelty; a rarity; an oddity. ② (土產など) a nice present. —近年珍しい, rarely experienced [seen] in recent times. (こんな大雪は近年珍らしい, Such a heavy snow has not been known for years.) —別段珍らしい事も出てゐない, There is nothing particularly new in the papers.

mezurashigaru (珍しがる), *v.* to deem it a novelty; esteem it as a treasure (珍重する).

mezurashiku (珍しく), *ad.* unusually; uncommonly; strangely; wonderfully. —珍しくも可成りの身なりをして來た, He came, for a wonder, in decent clothes.

mi (身), *n.* ❶ (身體) the body; the person. ❷ (自身) oneself. ❸ (生命) life. ❹ (肉) flesh. ❺ (心) heart. ❻ (樹心) heart; pith. ❼ (刃) a blade. ❽ (中味) contents. ❾ (蓋に對し) a vessel. —身の程を知らぬ, to forget one's social position; not to know one's position in life. —身に沁みてる, to be deeply impressed *with*; be indelibly engraved on the heart. —身につまされて, compared with one's own miserable lot. —身にあまる光榮, an honour more than one deserves [merits]; an honour beyond one's desert. —身を切るやうな風, a cutting [biting; sharp] wind. —身を捨てて, at the risk of one's life. —...に身を入れる, to put one's heart *into*; go heart and soul *into*. —身を入れて働く, to work with all one's heart; work with a will. —身を亡ぼす, to ruin oneself; bring about one's own ruin. —身を任せる, to place oneself in another's keeping. —身を全うする, to save oneself. —身を賣る, to sell oneself. —身を誤る, to go astray; take a wrong course; wreck oneself. —身を以て免れる, to escape with life and limb [with bare life]. —身を殺して仁を爲す, to lay down one's life for the cause of humanity.

mi (實), *n.* ❶ (果實) a fruit. ❷

(實質) substance; matter —汁の實, the garniture of a soup. —實の無い話, a gassy talk. —實が入る, to fill; grow ripe. (話に實が入る, to become absorbed in the talk.) —實を持つ [結ぶ], to bear fruit.

mi (箕), *n.* a winnow; a fan. —箕で簸る, [*vt.*] to winnow; fan.

-mi (味), tint; tinge; tincture; flavour; taste. —甘味, a sweet flavour. —靑味, blue tint. —人間味の乏しい, lacking humanity. —可笑味のある作風, a style tinged with humour.

miageru (見上げる), *v.* ❶ (仰ぎ見る) to look up *at*; raise one's eyes; lift up the eyes; turn one's face upward. ❷ (感服する) to admire; respect. —見上げた精神, an admirable [a noble] spirit.

miai (見合), *n.* seeing each other with a view to marriage; a formal interview before marriage.

miakiru (見飽きる), *v.* to be tired of seeing; see enough *of*.

miarawasu (見露はす), *vt.* to detect; discover; find out.

miataru (見當る), *v.* to come *across*; find. ☞ *mitsukaru*.

miawasu (見合す), *v.* ❶ (相見る) to look at each other; exchange looks. ❷ (延期す) to postpone; put off; defer; suspend (中止).

miba, mibae, (見榮), *n.* show; appearance; effect. —見榮えがする, to look fine; make a good show; be effective. —見榮えがしない, to make a poor show.

mibō (未萌), *n.* an undeveloped state; early stage. —未萌に防ぐ, to nip in the bud.

mibōjin (未亡人), *n.* a widow.

mibun (身分), *n.* ❶ social position [standing]; station in [of] life; social status. ❷【法】status. —身分ある人, a man of position [condition; standing; rank]. —身分の低い人, a man of low standing [birth]; a man low in social rank. —身分を忘れる《知る》, to forget 《know》 one's station. —身分相應の暮しをする, to live in accordance with one's station in life. ¶ 身分證明書, an identification card.

miburi (身振), *n.* gesture; gesticulation. —身振りする, to (make) gesture; gesticulate.

miburui (身震), *n.* shudder; shiver; tremble. —身震ひする, to shudder; tremble; shiver. —考へても身震ひがする, to tremble [shudder] at the thought *of*.

michi (道, 路, 途), *n.* ❶ (道路) a road; a way. ❷ (道程) distance; way. ❸ (方法) a way; means; a course. ❹ (方面, むき) the line; the way. ❺ (順路) a route; a course. ❻ (條理) reason; right. ❼ (行ひの道) a path; a way; the right way; the path of righteousness; justice (正義); morality (道德); moral principles (同上); teachings (敎へ). —道ならぬ戀, illicit love. —その道の人, one versed in the matter; an expert; a specialist. —その道に明るい, to be in the line. —此處へ來る道で, on my way here. —道に迷ふ, to lose one's way. —外に途がない, to have no alternative left. (...するより外に道がない, to have no choice [option] but to....) —道を敎へる《尋ねる》, to show 《ask》 the way. —道を間違へる, to take a wrong road. —途を開く, ① (讓る) to make way *for*. ② to pave the way *for*. —後進の路を塞ぐ, to stand in the way of those coming after.

michi (未知の), *a.* unknown; undiscovered. ¶ 未知量《數》,【數】an unknown quantity 《number》.

michiannai (道案內), *n.* a guide. —道案內をする, to act as guide; guide.

michiashi (途步), (號令) March { at ease! }

michibata (路傍), *n.* the wayside; the roadside. —路傍の茶屋, a wayside teahouse.

michibiku (導く), *vt.* to lead; guide; show [usher] *into* (案內); conduct *to* (同上). —惡人を善道に導く, to lead a wicked man into the path of righteousness.

michibushin (道普請), *n.* road-repair; road-mending. —道普請をする, to repair [mend] a road.

michigaeru (見違へる), *vt.* to take *for*; mistake *for*. —見違へるほど大きくなる, to grow almost beyond recognition.

michihi (滿干), *n.* ebb and flow; rise and fall; tide.

michijun (道順), *n.* a route.

michikake (盈虧), *n.* phase; waxing and waning.

michikusa (道草を喰ふ), to loiter on the road; tarry on one's way.

michinarashi (道均し), *n.* ❶ (器械) a road-roller; a road-leveller; a steam-roller (蒸氣力の). ❷ (事) road-levelling. —道均しをする, to level a road.

michinori (道程), *n.* distance; way.

michiru (滿ちる), *vi.* ❶ (充滿) to become full; fill; be full *of*; to filled *with*; abound *in*. ❷ (滿

了) to expire; run out; come to an end. ❹ to wax (月); flow (潮). —歓喜に滿ちた, filled with joy. —涙に滿ちた眼, eyes brimming [filled] with tears. —滿つれば虧く, "A flow will have an ebb." —聽衆堂に滿つ, The audience filled the hall. —任期が滿ちた, His term of office has expired [run out]. ⌈[water].⌉

michishio (滿潮), *n.* high tide

michishirube (道しるべ), *n.* ❶ (道標) a finger [guide]-post. ❷ (手引) a guide.

michisugara (途上), *ad.* (while) on the way; as one goes along.

michisuji (道筋), *n.* a route; a course.

michiyuki (道行), *n.* ❶ (徑路) the (natural) course; process. ❷ (駆落) elopement.

michizure (道伴), *n.* a fellow-traveller; a companion in travelling. —道伴れになる, ① to join a person in travelling. ② to travel together.

Mida (彌陀), *n.* Amitabha [梵]

midara (淫な), *a.* immoral; unchaste; obscene (猥褻).

midarebako (亂箱), *n.* a clothes-box.

midaregami (亂髮), *n.* dishevelled hair; ruffled hair.

midareru (亂れる), *vi.* ❶ (混亂) to be out of order [in disorder]; be confused; be thrown into confusion [disorder]; become disorganized (國家·社會など) ❷ (紊亂) to be disarranged (財政など); be deranged (同上); be disturbed (治安など). ❸ (敗頽) to be demoralised; be corrupted. —亂れた風俗, corrupt morals. —一絲亂れず, well regulated; in perfect trim [order]. —足並が亂れる, to be out of step.

midarigawashii (淫りがはしい), *a.* =*midara* (淫な).

midarini (濫·漫·妄·猥に), *ad.* ❶ (無斷で) without permission [leave]. ❷ (故なく) without sufficient cause [good reason]. ❸ (擅に) freely; arbitrarily; wantonly. ❹ (無暗に) lavishly; at random. —猥りに立入るべからず, "No admittance without leave." ⌈arbitrary.⌉

midarino (猥の), *a.* random;

midashi (見出), *n.* ❶ (標題) a title; a head-line; a heading (新聞紙の). ❷ (索引) an index; a guide (帳面の). ¶ 見出地圖, a key-map. —見出語, a catchword (辭書の); a key-word (杜).

midasu (亂·紊す), *vt.* ❶ (混亂) to disturb; derange; throw into confusion [disorder]. ❷ (壞亂) to demoralize; corrupt; break. ❸ (動搖) to agitate; unsettle. ❹ (縺れさす) to dishevel; tumble (衣服·髮等を). —列を亂す, to break square [squares]; break the ranks. —風儀を亂す, to corrupt public morals.

midokoro (見所), *n.* ❶ the most interesting sight ⟪part⟫. ❷ (見込み) promise; hope. —見所のある青年, a promising youth.

midori (綠), *n.* ❶ green; verdure (草木の). ❷ (松の若葉) a a pine-shoot. —綠の黑髮, raven hair. —綠する, to green.

midorigo (嬰兒), *n.* a baby.

-midoro (塗), *suf.* covered *with.* —汗みどろになって, covered with sweat.

mie (見え), *n.* (外觀) an appearance; show; display. —見え(のため)にする, to do it for show. (家柄を見えにする, to boast of one's lineage.) —見えを張る, ① [*v.*] to cut a dash [figure]; make a show [display]. ② [*a.*] ostentatious; showy. ⌈fop; a swell.⌉

miebō (見榮坊), *n.* a dandy; a

miegakure (見え隱れに), *ad.* appearing at times. —見え隱れに跡をつけて行く, to follow a person without being observed; shadow a person.

mieru (見える), *vi.* ❶ to see; catch sight *of* (見とめる); be in sight (見えてゐる). ❷ (らしい) to seem; look; appear. ❸ (來る) to be here; come; turn up. —見えなくなる, to go out of sight; vanish; disappear. (列車は見えなくなった, The train passed from our view.) —見え出す; 見えて來る, to come in sight. —さも…の如く見える, to look as if....

miesuku (見透く), *vi.* to be transparent [pellucid]; be seen through. ——, *a.* thin; obvious. —見え透いた嘘, a glaring [transparent] lie.

mifutatsu (身二つになる), *v.* to be delivered of a child; give birth to a child.

migaki (磨き), *n.* polish; burnishing. —磨きをかける, to polish; burnish.

migakigami (磨紙), *n.* emery-paper; glass-paper.

migakiko (磨粉), *n.* polishing-powder; plate-powder (金物の).

migaku (磨く), *vt.* ❶ (艶を出す) to polish; rub; burnish; brush (up) (刷毛で). ❷ (練る) to refine; improve; cultivate. —磨き上げる, to polish up; burnish up;

finish up (仕上げる). —靴を能く磨く, to put a good shine on boots. —レンズ《金剛石》を磨く, to grind lenses 《diamonds》.

migamae (身構), *n.* attitude; position; posture. —身構へする, ① (闘の用意する) to prepare (oneself) for a fight; stand up *to*; show fight (敵意を示す). ② (防がんとする) to stand on the defensive; place oneself on one's guard; guard *against*.

migaru (身輕な), *a.* agile; nimble; light. —身輕な服裝, a light dress. **—— - ni,** *ad.* lightly; nimbly. —身輕になる, to be eased [relieved] of a burden (重荷を下して): be delivered of a child (子を生んで).

migawari (身代), *n.* a substitute; a scapegoat. —身代りに立つ, to serve as another's substitute; take the place *of*.

migi (右), *n.* the right; the right side. —右隣, the right-hand neighbour; next door on the right. —右の腕, the right arm. —右の者, the above-mentioned. —右の品, the aforesaid article. —右の如き, such. —右に出る, to have the upper hand *of*; take precedence *of*; be superior *to*; surpass.

migigawa (右側), *n.* the right; the off side.

migiri (砌), *n.* occasion; time. **——,** *ad.* when. —嚴寒の砌, in this severe cold season.

migiwa (水際, 汀), *n.* the water's edge. ☞ *nagisa* (渚).

migoro (見頃である), to be at its 《their》 best; be in full bloom.

migoroshi (見殺しにする), *v.* to let a person die before one's very eyes; leave him to fate.

migoshirae (身拵する), *v.* to prepare [equip] oneself; dress oneself.

migoto (見事な), *a.* ❶ (巧妙) dexterous; adroit; expert. ❷ (立派) beautiful; fine; splendid; capital. —見事に勝つ, to win fairly. —見事に咲いた花, a flower in fine bloom.

migurushii (見苦しい), *a.* ❶ unsightly; unseemly; indecent; objectionable (態度); homely (女). ❷ (不面目な) disgraceful; dishonourable; shameful. ❸ (見すぼらしい) shabby; mean. ❹ (不格好な) awkward; clumsy; uncouth. —見苦しい最期, a dishonourable death. —見苦しい敗北, a shameful defeat.

mihakarai (見計), *n.* discretion (裁量); selection (選擇). —見計らふ, to use discretion; act as one thinks best.

mihakken (未發見の), *a.* undiscovered. ¶ 未發見地, the unknown land; *terra incognita* [羅].

mihanasu (見放す), *vt.* to forsake; desert; abandon. —醫者に見放される, to be given up by the doctor.

miharai (未拂の), *a.* unpaid; outstanding. —未拂の利子, the interest in arrears. ¶ 未拂勘定, unpaid [unsettled] account. —未拂金, arrears; arrearage. —未拂込資本, unpaid capital.

miharashi (見晴し), *n.* a view; a prospect; outlook. —見晴しのよい家, a house with [commanding] a fine view. —見晴らす, to command a view *of*; look out *on* [*over*]; overlook.

mihari (見張), *n.* ❶ (張番) a watch; a lookout; picket-duty. ❷ (番人, 見張番) a watchman; an outlook; a picket. —見張りをして, on the watch *for*; on the alert. ¶ 見張所, a lookout.

miharu (見張る), *v.* ❶ [睜] (眼を見開く) to open one's eyes wide. ❷ (張番をする) to watch *for*; guard *against*; keep watch [guard]; look out *for*; be on the lookout. —驚きの眼を睜る, to stare in amazement.

mihatsu (未發の), *a.* not yet come to pass. —前人未發の, undiscovered. —未發に防ぐ, to nip in the bud; destroy in the egg.

mihon (見本), *n.* ❶ (商品) a sample; a specimen; a specimen copy (本の). ❷ (雛形) a pattern; a model. —見本を取る; 見本を試驗する, [*vt.*] to sample. —見本通り《以下》である, to be up to 《below》 the sample. —見本通りに作る, to make after a sample. ¶ 進呈見本, a presentation sample. —見本帳, a sample-book. —見本市, a sample market. —見本切れ [切地], sample clippings [cuttings]. —見本室, a sample-room.

miidasu (見出す), *vt.* to find; discover; catch; spy.

miira (木乃伊), *n.* a mummy.

miiri (實入), *n.* ❶ (利得) profit; gains; earnings. ❷ (收入) an income. ❸ (收穫) harvest; crop. —實入がよい《少ない》, to have a good 《poor》 income.

miiru (魅る), *vt.* to possess (憑く); bewitch (魅する).

miitsu (稜威), *n.* the glory [influence] of the Imperial throne.

mijikai (短い), *a.* short; brief (簡單); simple (同上).

mijikaku (短く), *ad.* short

briefly (簡單に). —短くする, to shorten; make [cut] short.

mijimai (身仕舞する), *v.* to dress oneself; smart oneself up (めかす); make one's toilet (化粧する).

mijime (不見目な), *a.* miserable; pitiful; cruel. —みじめな生活, a wretched [sad] life; a dog's life. —みじめを見る, to suffer from a wretched life; fall into distress.

mijin (微塵), *n.* atoms; pieces; fragments. —微塵もない, to have not a bit [an atom; a spark] *of* (sense; conscience). —微塵に毀す, to smash into [to] smithereens; break [crush] into pieces; crush [knock] to atoms. —微塵に壞れる, to fly in pieces; be broken to pieces.

mijinko (微塵子), *n.* 【甲殼】 the water-flea.

mijiroku (身動く), *vi.* to stir; budge.

mijitaku (身支度), *n.* equipment; outfit; making [getting] ready. ☞ *migoshirae*.

mijuku (未熟), *n.* unripeness; greenness; inexperience (特に技術の). —— -**na**, *a.* unripe; immature; green. —未熟な果實, a green fruit. —未熟な腕前, prentice hand.

mikado (帝), *n.* the Mikado 【日】; the Emperor of Japan.

mikaerihin (見返品), *n.* collateral security.

mikaeru (見返る), *v.* to look back; turn one's head; look over one's shoulder.

mikaeshi (見返), *n.* ❶ (本の) the inside of a cover (of a book); backing; a fly-leaf. ❷ (洋服の) a lappet.

mikaesu (見返す), *v.* ❶ (振向く) to look back. ❷ (再び見る) to look at again [once more]; see over again. ❸ to look down upon in turn.

mikageishi (御影石), *n.* granite.

mikagiru (見限る), *v.* to abandon; give up; forsake; desert.

mikai (未開の), *a.* ❶ barbarous; savage; uncivilized. ❷ (未開墾の) uncultivated. ¶ 未開(墾)地, uncultivated land; virgin soil.

mikake (見掛), *n.* appearance; looks. —見掛倒しの, showy; trumpery; gimcrack. —人は見掛けによらぬもの, "Appearances are deceptive"; "Beauty is but skin-deep."

mikakeru (見掛ける), *vt.* ❶ to see; notice; catch sight *of*. ❷ (見ようとする) to be about to see.

mikakō (未加工の), *a.* unwrought; raw; crude.

mikaku (味覺), *n.* the sense of taste; gustation. ¶ 味覺神經, the gustatory nerve.

mikan (蜜柑), *n.* the mandarin orange.

mikan (未完), to be continued (續く). —未完の, unfinished; incomplete.

mikaneru (見兼ねる), *v.* to be unable to bear to see. —見るに見兼ねて, being unable to look on any longer.

mikanryō (未完了の), *a.* 【文】 imperfect.

mikata (見方), *n.* a view-point; a point of view; way of looking at (things).

mikata (味方), *n.* a supporter; a partisan [-zan]; an adherent; one's side. —味方する, to take the side *of*; side *with*; range oneself *with* [on the side *of*]; support. —味方に引入れる, to gain [win; bring] *over*; make an ally *of*.

mikawasu (見交す), *v.* to look at each other; exchange looks.

mikazuki (三日月), *n.* the new moon; the crescent moon; the sickle-moon. —三日月形の, crescent-shaped; sickled.

miken (未見の), *a.* unseen; undiscovered; unknown.

miken (眉間), *n.* 【解】 glabella; glabellum: the middle of the forehead. —眉間を割られる, to be cut between the eye-brows.

mikeneko (三毛猫), *n.* a tortoise (-shell) cat.

miketsu (未決), *n.* undecidedness; indeterminateness; 【法】 pendency. —未決の, ① undecided; unsettled; unconvicted (罪人の). ② (問題) pending; open; moot. ¶ 未決事件, a pending case. —未決問題, an open question; a pending question (懸案); a moot point (論點). —未決囚, an unconvicted prisoner; a prisoner awaiting trial.

miki (幹), *n.* a trunk; a body; a stock.

miki (神酒), *n.* a libation; wine offered at a Shintō shrine.

mikiri (見切), *n.* abandonment; relinquishment. —見切りを附ける, to give up; get rid *of*. ¶ 見切品, clearance goods. —見切賣, a clearance sale; a bargain.

mikiru (見切る), *vt.* ❶ (見終る) to have seen; see through. ❷ (見限る) to abandon; give up. ❸ (安賣する) to clear off; sell at a bargain; bargain away.

mikiwameru (見極める), *vt.* ❶ (確認する) to ascertain; make sure [certain]. ❷ (深く探る) to probe to the bottom.

mikka (三日), *n.* ❶ three days. ❷ (月の) the third (day). —三日置きに, every fourth day. —

三日天下, "three days' rule"; ephemeral grandeur.

mikkai (密會), *n.* a secret [clandestine] meeting; a stolen interview. —密會する, to meet secretly [in secret]; have a secret meeting; have a stolen interview. ¶ 密會所, a secret meeting-place.

mikkei (密計), *n.* a secret plan [plot]; an underplot; an intrigue.

mikkō (密行), *n.* secret going (密に行くこと); secret patrol (秘密巡回). —密行する, to go secretly [in secret]: patrol secretly; prowl. ¶ 密行巡査, a policeman in plain clothes; a detective (刑事).

mikkō (密航), *n.* secret passage. —密航する, to go abroad without licence. ¶ 密航者, a stowaway.

mikkoku (密告), *n.* secret information; betrayal. —其筋に密告する, to inform the authorities; denounce to the government. ¶ 密告者, a betrayer; an informer; a peach [卑] (特に裏切して).

miko (巫女), *n.* ❶ (市子) a witch. ❷ a young woman serving in a shrine; a dancing girl.

mikomi (見込), *n.* ❶ (考) opinion; judgment (判斷). ❷ (望, 有望) prospect; hope; promise (有望). ❸ (めあて, あてこみ) anticipation; expectation; speculation (思惑). —見込ある事業, a promising business. —見込が外れる, to go amiss; come short of expectation; be baulked in one's expectations. —少しも見込なし, to have no chance *of*; there is no prospect [hope; probability] *of*. —見込をつける (意見を定める), to form an opinion [a judgment; an estimate] *of*.

mikomu (見込む), *vt.* ❶ (有望と考ふ) to consider (a person) of promise. ❷ (豫期) to expect; anticipate. ❸ (期待, 信用) to rely [count] *upon*; reckon *upon*; calculate *upon*; place confidence *in* (信用). ❹ to possess (魅す); spot (目星をつける). —人を見込む, to place [put; repose] confidence in a person. —人に見込まれる, to be considered of high promise by another; win another's confidence. —刑事に見込まれる, to be spotted by a detective.

mikon (未婚の), *a.* single; unmarried. ¶ 未婚者, an unmarried person; a bachelor (男); an old maid (女); a spinster (女).

mikoshi (御輿), *n.* ❶ (輿) an Imperial palanquin (天皇の). ❷ (神輿) a shrine carried at festivals; a sacred car.

mikoshi (見越), *n.* anticipation (豫期): foresight (先見); speculation (投機). ¶ 見越輸入, anticipatory importation.

mikosu (見越す), *vt.* ❶ to anticipate (豫期); know beforehand (豫知); foresee (先見). ❷ (望見) to look across; overlook. —平和を見越して, in anticipation [expectation] of peace.

mikotonori (詔), *n.* an Imperial edict [decree]; an Imperial mandate. —詔する, to decree.

mikubiru (見縊る), *vt.* ❶(輕蔑) to despise; think meanly *of*. ❷ (安ッぽく見る) to undervalue; underrate; depreciate. —相手を見縊る, to hold a person cheap [in contempt]; look down upon a person.

mikudarihan (三行半), *n.* a letter of divorce.

mikudasu (見下す), *vt.* ❶ (見おろす) to look down. ❷ (輕蔑する) to despise; look down *upon* [*on*]; hold in contempt. —人を眼下に見下す, to look down upon a person; lord it over another.

mikuji (神籤), *n.* a written oracle; a sacred [pious] lot. —神籤を抽く, to receive a written oracle.

mikuraberu (見較べる), *vt.* to compare; bring into comparison; estimate relatively.

mimai (見舞), *n.* ❶ (*a*) (病氣の) inquiry after another's health: (*b*) (訪問) a visit; a call; a friendly visit. ❷ (見舞品) a present (taken [sent] when inquiry is made). ¶ 見舞狀, a letter of sympathy; a letter of friendly inquiry. —見舞金, a present of money (to a sick person); a solatium. —見舞人, a visitor; a caller.

mimamoru (見守る), *vt.* ❶ to gaze *at*; stare *at*; look steadily. ❷ (守護) to watch *over*.

miman (未滿), *a.* less than. —, *prep.* under; below. —平均點未滿, below the average mark. —二十歲未滿の者, persons under twenty years of age.

mimau (見舞ふ), *vt.* to visit; call (*on*, 人; *at*, 家) inquire after (another's health) (病氣を).

mimawari (見廻り), *n.* ❶ going around; inspection (視察). ❷ (巡査·兵卒などの) a round of watch; a patrol. —見廻る, ① (巡回) to patrol; see over; make [go] one's rounds. ② (視察) to inspect; make a tour of inspection.

mimawasu (見廻す), *vt.* to look round [about]; survey; take a glance round. —あたりを見廻す,

to look about one.

mime (眉目よき), *a.* comely; well-favoured; well-featured.

mimei (未明に), before dawn [daybreak]; in the grey of the morning.

mimi (耳), *n.* ❶ the ear. ❷ (物の端) (*a*) the edge; the end: (*b*) (織物の) the selvedge; the loop; the list (羅紗などの). —耳の練習, ear-exercise. —耳癖となる, to become familiar to the ear. —耳が遠い《早い》, to be hard 《quick》 of hearing. —耳が鳴る, to have a singing [ringing] in one's ears; one's ears sing. —耳に逆ふ, to sound harsh to the ear. —耳にはさむ, ① to put a thing behind the ear. ② (耳にする) to hear; learn. —耳に入る, to reach a person's ear; come to the ear *of*. —耳を掩ふ, to close [cover] one's ears. —耳を傾ける, to listen *to*; give ear *to*. —耳を欹てる, to prick up one's ears; strain one's ears; cock the ears. —耳を折る (書物などの), to dog-ear; dog's-ear. —一寸耳を貸せ, A word in your ear.

mimiaka (耳垢), *n.* ear-wax.

mimiana (耳孔), *n.* the ear-hole; the auditory canal.

mimiatarashii (耳新らしい), *a.* novel; strange; new.

mimidare (脖耳), *n.* 【醫】 otorrhœa: discharge from the ears.

mimikaki (耳掻), *n.* an ear-pick; an auriscalp.

mimikosuri (耳擦りする), *vi.* to speak in the ear; whisper in another's ear.

mimikuso (耳糞), *n.* ear-wax; cerumen. —耳糞を取る, to clean one's ears.

miminareru (耳慣れる), *vi.* to be used to hearing; become familiar to the ear.

miminari (耳鳴), *n.* 【醫】 tinnitus: drumming in the ears; ringing [singing] in the ear. —耳鳴がする, My ears are singing; My ears ring.

mimitabu (耳朶), *n.* the ear-lobe; the ear-lap.

mimiwa (耳環), *n.* an ear-ring.

mimiyori (耳寄の), *a.* desirous of hearing; welcome. —耳寄りの話, welcome intelligence [news].

mimizawari (耳障な), *a.* harsh; grating; jarring; discordant; dissonant. —耳障りになる, to offend the ear; be offensive to the ear; jar [grate] upon the ear.

mimizu (蚯蚓), *n.* 【環蟲】 the earthworm.

mimizubare (蚯蚓脹れ), *n.* a stripe; a wale; a wheal. —蚯蚓脹れになってゐる, to leave a wale on the skin.

mimizuku (角鴟), *n.* 【鳥】 the feathered-toed scops-owl.

mimochi (身持), *n.* ❶ (行爲) conduct; behaviour; way. ❷ =*ninshin*. —身持ちが善い, to be well-behaved; be well-conducted. —身持ちが惡い, to be ill-behaved; misconduct oneself.

mimono (觀物), *n.* a sight (worth seeing); a grand sight (壯觀); an attraction (人氣物).

mimoto (身元), *n.* ❶ (素性) one's antecedents; one's previous history; one's character and qualification (人物資格). ❷ (社會的地位) one's social position; one's status. —身元の確かな男, a man of good references. ¶ 身元引受人, a surety. —身元保證金, guaranty money for conduct; caution-money. —身元問合せ先, a reference.

mimuku (見向く), *v.* to look towards; turn one's face; look round. —見向きもせずに, without even glancing at it.

mina, minna, (皆), *pron.* all; every one; everything. —, *ad.* one and all; without exception. —彼等は皆, all [every one] of them. —他の者は皆, all the others. —皆殘らず, all without exception. —皆で二十, twenty in all. —皆さんに宜しく, Please remember me to all your family.

minage (身投する), *v.* to throw oneself into the water.

minagirasu (漲らす), *vt.* to inundate; overrun.

minagiru (漲る), *v.* ❶ (氾濫) to overflow; inundate; rise high. ❷ (充滿) to be filled *with*. ❸ (瀰漫) to pervade; spread *through*; permeate.

minagoroshi (鏖にする), *vt.* to massacre; exterminate; cut to pieces; cut up. —敵を鏖にする, to annihilate the enemy.

minakami (水上), *n.* ❶ (上流) the upper stream; the upper course of a river. ❷ (水源) the source; the head-water.

minakuchi (水口), *n.* the inlet for irrigation water. —水口をせきとめる, to stop up the inlet for water.

minami (南), *n.* ❶ south. ❷ (南風) the south wind. ☞ *higashi*. —南向きの家, a house with a southern aspect [exposure]; a house facing [open to] the south.

minamoto (源), *n.* ❶ (水源) the source; the (fountain-)head; the spring. ❷ (起源) the origin; the beginning; the source (淵源). —源を發する, to come *from*; originate *from* [*in*]; have its origin *in*. —河の源を探る, to trace a river to its source.

minaosu 見直す), *v.* ❶ (再び見る) to look at again; see over again. ❷ (病人·形勢など) to take a turn for the better; improve; rally.

minarai (見習), *n.* ❶ apprenticeship; probation. ❷ (人) an apprentice (商工徒弟); a cadet; an improver (商業見習). —行儀見習に奉公する, to enter service to learn manners. —見習書記《運轉手見習》として奉職する, to serve as an articled clerk《an apprentice engine-driver》. ¶ 見習生, an apprentice-student; a probationer. —見習士官, a probational officer.

minarau (見習ふ), *v.* ❶ (修業) to learn; receive training; practise oneself *in*. ❷ (眞似) to follow another's example; follow suit; take another for a model. —上を見習ふ下, "Like master, like man."

minareru (見慣れる), *vi.* to get used to seeing; become familiar *with*. —見慣れぬ人, a stranger; a strange gentleman《lady》.

minari (服裝, 身裝), *n.* dress; clothing; appearance. —服裝に構はぬ, to be careless [indifferent] about appearance.

minashigo (孤兒), *n.* an orphan.

minasu (看做す), *vt.* ❶【法】to deem; presume conclusively. ❷ to deem; consider; regard.

minato (港), *n.* a harbour; a (sea-)port; a haven (多く避難所の意味で). —港に寄る, to call at a port. —港を出る, to leave [clear] port; sail from a port.

mine (峰), *n.* ❶ (竪に高い) the peak; the summit; the crest. ❷ (横に長い) the back (of a hill); the mountain ridge (山の背). —刀の峰, the back of a sword; a false edge (of a sword). —峰打ちを喰はす, to give a blow with the sword-back.

miṅei (民營), *n.* private management.

mingyō (民業), *n.* a private enterprise.

miṅi (民意), *n.* the public [popular] will; public opinion. —民意を尊重する《せぬ》, to pay due respect to《make light of》public opinion.

minikui (見惡い), *a.* ❶ (不明瞭) indistinct; illegible (讀み惡い). ❷ (醜い) unsightly; ugly; plain; homely. ❸ (不面目な) disgraceful; shameful. —こゝからぢゃ見惡い, It is hard to see from here.

minji (民事), *n.* ❶ civil matters. ❷ (民事事件) a civil case. ❸ (非商事) non-mercantile affairs. —民事上の責任, civil responsibility. ¶ 民事原告人《被告人》, a plaintiff《defendant》. —民事局, the Bureau of Civil Matters. —民事訴訟, a civil case [suit; action; cause]. (民事訴訟法, the code of civil procedure.)

minjō (民情), *n.* the condition of the people. —民情を察する, to observe the condition of the people.

minka (民家), *n.* a house; a farm house; a peasant's cottage.

minkan (民間), amongst [among] the people. ¶ 民間飛行家, a civilian airman. —民間事業, a popular [private] enterprise.

minken (民權), *n.* popular rights; the people's rights.

minmin (みんみん蟬), *n.*【昆】Pomponia maculaticollis (cicada の一種·學名).

mino (蓑), *n.* a straw rain-coat; a straw-coat.

minō (未納の), *a.* unpaid. ¶ 未納金, arrears. —未納者, a defaulter; a person who has failed to pay.

minogasu (見逃す), *vt.* ❶ (見落す) to overlook; miss; pass by. ❷ (咎めぬ) to wink *at*; overlook; pass over; shut one's eyes *to*.

minokedatsu (身毛立つ), *vi.* ❶ (寒さで) to shiver with cold. ❷ (恐れて) to shudder *at*; shiver *at*; tremble *with*.

minokoshi (見殘), *n.* a thing overlooked《left unseen》; an oversight. —見殘す, to overlook; leave unseen.

minomawari (身の廻り), *n.* ❶ personal ornaments (裝身具); personal articles; one's things. ❷ (みなり) one's person; dress.

minomushi (蓑蟲), *n.* the case-weaver; the basket-worm.

minori (實), *n.* crop; harvest; yield. —實りがよい, to be fruitful [fertile]; have《yield》good crops fill well (玉蜀黍など).

minoru (實る), *vi.* ❶ (實が入る) to fill. ❷ (熟す) to ripen; become [grow] ripe.

minoshiro (身の代-金), *n.* ❶ (身賣金) the price for the possession of a person. ❷ (身受金) ransom; the price paid for the release of a person.

minotake (身の丈), *n.* stature; height. —身の丈五尺五寸, to measure [stand] five feet and a half (high).

minoue (身の上), *n.* ❶ (境遇) one's condition of life; one's lot.

● (經歷) one's history; one's personal career. ● (運命) one's fortunes; one's fate. —哀れな身の上, a poor lot; a miserable life. —身の上判斷をする, to tell a person's fortune; divine the future *of*. —弟の身の上を案じる, to be anxious about one's brother's fate. ¶ 身の上噺, the story of one's life.

minpō (民法), *n.* the civil law; the civil code (法典).

minpon (民本的), *a.* democratic. ¶ 民本主義, democracy.

minpuku (民福), *n.* the welfare [happiness] of the people. —民福を圖る, to take measures for the welfare of the people.

minryoku (民力), *n.* national resources.

minsei (民政), *n.* civil administration. ¶ 民政廳, a civil administration office. —關東都督府民政長官, the civil governor of the Government-General of Kwantung.

minsen (民選), *n.* popular election.

minshin (民心), *n.* popular sentiment [feelings]. —民心を收攬する, to gain popular favour; go to the bottom of the people's heart.

minshu (民主的), *a.* democratic. ¶ 民主政體, democracy; democratic government. —民主主義, democracy; democratism. —民主黨, the Democratic Party 【米】.

minshū (民衆), *n.* people; the populace; the masses. —藝術の民衆化, democratization of art. —民衆化する, to popularize. ¶ 民衆藝術, popular arts. —民衆運動, a popular movement [agitation].

mintō (民黨), *n.* the people's party; the Popular Party.

minufuri (見ぬ振する), *v.* to wink *at*; overlook; pretend not to see. —見ぬ振して見る, to steal a glance *at*; look stealthily. —見て見ぬ振する, to wink *at*; pretend not to see.

minuku (見拔く), *vt.* ❶ (洞察) to see [look] *through*; have an insight *into*; penetrate *into*. ❷ (選出) to select. —腹の中を見拔く, to see into a peron's mind.

miṅyaku (民約), *n.* social contract.

miṅyō (民謠), *n.* a folk-song; a popular song.

miṅyū (民有), *n.* the people's possession; private possession [ownership]. ☞ *shiyū* (私有). ¶ 民有地, private land.

minzoku (民俗), *n.* folk-customs; the manners and customs of the people.

minzoku (民族), *n.* a nation; folk; a race (人種). ¶ 民族傳說, folk-lore. ¶ 民族自決, self-determination of nations.

mio (澪), *n.* a waterway; a fairway; a tideway; a channel.

mioboe (見覺), *n.* remembrance; recognition. —見覺える, to recognize; remember; learn by sight. —見覺えがある, to recognize. —見覺えのある, ① remembered; recognizable. ② which I recognize; whom I remember to have seen.

miokuri (見送), *n.* a send-off; seeing off. —見送りに行く, to go to see a person off. ¶ 見送人, a person come to see another off; senders-off.

miokuru (見送る), *vt.* ❶ (出立を) to see off; give a send-off; send off. ❷ (目送する) to follow with the eyes. ❸ (家まで送る) to see (a person) home; see (another) to his door. —玄關まで見送る, to see another to the porch.

miorosu (見下す), *vt.* to look down; command (a view *of*); command a bird's-eye view *of*.

miosame (見納), *n.* the last look. —見納めをする, to see the last *of*; have a last look *at*.

miotori (見劣がする), to look inferior; show to disadvantage.

miotoshi (見落), *n.* oversight. —見落す, to overlook; pass over; miss seeing.

miotsukushi (澪標), *n.* Ⓢ 澪杭. a boom; a channel-mark.

mippei (密閉する), *vt.* to cover up tightly; seal hermetically; shut close.

mippu (密夫), *n.* a paramour; a lover.

mippū (密封する), *vt.* to seal hermetically [tightly].

mirai (未來), *n.* ❶ (將來) the future; the time to come. ❷ (來世) the future state [life]; the next world. ❸ 【文】 the future tense. —未來の夫《妻》, the future husband《wife》. —未來の大家, a coming man. —未來を信ずる, to believe in future life. ¶ 未來派, 【藝術】 futurism; futurists.

miren (未練), *n.* ❶ (諦め得ざる) regret. ❷ (卑怯) cowardice; timidity; pusillanimity; poltroonery. —未練が殘る, to have regrets *for*. —未練がある, to feel regret *for*.

miriamētoru (ミリアメートル), *n.* a myriametre.

miriguramu (ミリグラム), *n.* a milligramme.

mirimētoru (ミリメートル), *n.* a millimetre.

mirin (味醂), *n.* sweet *sake*.

miru (海松), *n.* 【植】 Codium mucronatum (學名).

miru (見·観·視·看る), *v.* ❶ to see; look *at*; take [have] a look *at* (一寸見る); observe. ❷ (検する) to inspect; examine. ❸ (讀む) to read. ❹ (會ふ) to meet; experience. ❺ (試みる) to try. —見た所, to all appearances; to outward seeming. —見るに足る, [*a.*] worth seeing; sightworthy. —外國の例に見る, to compare cases in foreign countries. —私の視る所では, im my opinion; from my point of view; as I take it. —時計を見る, to consult the watch. —上衣を著てみる, to try on a coat. —空模様の變るのを見る, to observe the sky change. —今に見ろ, ① (今に解る) You shall soon see. ② (覺えてゐろ) I'll soon be even with you. —それ見給へ, There! Didn't I tell you so? —あんな奴は見るもいやだ, I cannot bear the sight of that man. —なかなか世間を見てる, He has seen much of life.

miruku (ミルク), *n.* milk. ¶ ミルク·ホール, a milk-hall. —ミルク·セーキ, milkshake [米].

mirumiru (見る見る), *ad.* in a moment; in an instant.

miryō (未了の), *a.* unfulfilled; unfinished; incomplete.

miryoku (魅力), *n.* charm; fascination; witchery. —魅力ある眼, a fascinating eye.

misadameru (見定める), *vt.* to make sure *of*. —天氣を見定める, to make sure of the weather. —形勢を見定めた上で, after I have made sure of the situation.

misageru (見下げる), *vt.* to look down *upon*; despise; disdain; hold in contempt. —見下げた, despicable; contemptible. —見下げはてた奴だ, He is a most despicable fellow.

misago (鶚), *n.* 【鳥】 the osprey; the fish-hawk.

misai (未濟の), *a.* ❶ unfinished. ❷ (未拂の) outstanding; unpaid; unsettled. ¶ 未濟勘定, an outstanding [unpaid; unsettled] account. —未濟試驗, an unfinished [a pending] examination.

misakai (見境), *n.* distinction; discrimination; difference. —見境のない, undiscriminating; without discrimination.

misaki (岬), *n.* a cape; a headland; a promontory.

misao (操), *n.* ❶ (貞操) chastity; constancy; virtue. ❷ (節操) fidelity to one's principle. —操正しい女 a woman of virtue; a virtuous woman. —操を守る, to observe chastity. —操を立て通す, to remain chaste to the end.

misasagi (陵), *n.* an Imperial tomb; an Imperial mausoleum.

mise (店), *n.* a shop [英]; a store [米]; a firm (商館). —店を張る (經營), to keep a shop [store [米]] —店を疊む, to shut up a shop.

miseban (店番), *n.* a salesman; a shopman.

misebaya (みせばや), *n.* 【植】 Siebold's stonecrop (學名).

misebirakasu (見せびらかす), *vt.* to display; parade; show off.

misebiraki (店開), *n.* opening of a business [shop]. —店開きをする, to open a shop; start [set up] in business; set up a shop [a store].

misegane (見せ金), *n.* show money.

misei (未成の), *a.* unfinished; unmade; crude; raw. ¶ 未成品, an unmanufactured [a crude; an unfinished] article. —未成線, an uncompleted line.

miseinen (未成年), *n.* minority; being under age. ¶ 未成年者, 【法】 an infant; a minor: a person under age.

misejimai (店仕舞), *n.* closing business.

misekake (見せかけ), *n.* ❶ (外見) (outward) show; external appearance. ❷ (假面) guise; pretension. —見せかける, to pretend; make believe; make a show [pretence] *of*.

misekazari (店飾), *n.* decoration of a shop; window-dressing.

misemono (見世物), *n.* a show; a spectacle; a circus (巡業の). —見世物にする, to exhibit; make a show *of*. ¶ 見世物小屋, a show-booth. —見世物師 (旅廻りの), a travelling showman; a stroller.

miseru (見せる), *v.* to show; let see [look *at*]; exhibit (公開する). —一寸お見せ, Let me have a look at it.

misesaki (店先), *n.* the shop-front.

miseshime (見せしめ), *n.* an example; a lesson; a warning. —見せしめに, as a warning (to others); for a lesson. —見せしめにする, to punish for discipline; make an example [a lesson] *of*.

misetsukeru (見せつける), *vt.* to show off; make a display *of*; show by practical demonstration.

mishimishi (みしみし), *ad.* ❶ (音) creakily. ❷ (容赦なく) without compunction; relentlessly.

mishin (ミシン), *n.* a sewing-machine. —ミシン縫ひの, machine-sewed. ¶ ミシン絲 machine-thread.

mishinkei (味神經), *n.* 【解】 a taste-nerve; a gustatory nerve.

mishiranu (見知らぬ), *a.* unacquainted; strange; unknown. —見知らぬ人, a stranger.
mishiru (見知る), *v.* ❶ (認知) to know by sight; recognize. ❷ (知人となる) to get acquainted *with*.
mishō (未詳の), *a.* unknown; uncertain; not exactly known.
mishō (實生), *n.* a seedling.
miso (味噌), *n.* bean-paste. —味噌をつける, to get into a mess *over*; make a mess of it. ¶ 味噌汁, *miso* soup; bean-paste soup.
misohagi (千屈菜), *n.* 【植】 the (common) purple loosestrife; the willow-weed.
misoka (晦日), *n.* the last day of the month. ¶ 晦日拂ひ, month--end payment.
misokonai (見損), *n.* misjudgment; misapprehension; mistaken impression. —見損ふ, ① (見附け得ぬ) to miss; lose. ② (見誤る) to mistake in seeing; misjudge; misapprehend.
misomame (黄大豆), *n.* 【植】 the soja [soy] bean.
misomeru (見初める), *vt.* to fall in love at first sight.
misoppa (味噌齒), *n.* a decayed (milk-)tooth.
misoreru (見外れる), *v.* to fail to recognize; miss. —お見それ致しました, You have the advantage of me.
misosazai (鷦鷯), *n.* 【鳥】 the Japanese wren.
misou (未曾有の), *a.* =***mizou***.
missei (密生する), *vi.* to grow thickly; grow in clusters.
missetsu (密接な), *a.* close; intimate. —密接する, to be 《come》 close together. —兩者間に密接な關係がある, There is a close connection between the two.
misshi (密旨), *n.* a secret order.
misshi (密使), *n.* a secret envoy [messenger]; an emissary.
misshiri (みっしり), *ad.* ❶ (嚴に) strictly; severely. ❷ (密に) closely. ❸ (熱心に) (*a*) earnestly; intently; singly: (*b*) (注意して) carefully; attentively. ❹ (澤山に) in abundance; in a large amount. —みっしり意見をする, to reprove severely. —みっしり積込む, to load [take in] heavily.
misshitsu (密室), *n.* a solitary cell; a secret room; a closet. ¶ 密室監禁, solitary confinement.
missho (密書), *n.* a secret [confidential] letter.
misshō (密商), *n.* smuggling (事); a smuggler (人).
misshū (密集する), *vi.* to mass; crowd; swarm. ¶ 密集部隊, 【軍】 a massed body; a force in close order.
misu (御簾), *n.* a bamboo blind; a bamboo screen.
misuborashii (みすぼらしい), *a.* shobby; seedy; miserable —みすぼらしい姿[なり]で, in shabby [seedy] clothes.
misue (見据), *n.* ❶ =***misakai***. ❷ (希望) hope.
misueru (見据ゑる), *v.* to set [keep] one's eyes *on*; stare *at*; fix [rivet] one's eyes *on* [*upon*].
misugosu (看過す), *v.* ❶ (見落す) to overlook; pass over; miss seeing. ❷ (見遁す) to overlook; pass by; let pass.
misui (未遂), *n.* an attempt. ¶ 放火未遂, attempted arson. —未遂犯人, an attempter. —未遂罪, criminal attempt.
misukasu (見透す), *vt.* to see *through*; penetrate; discern.
misumasu (見澄す), *vt.* to observe carefully; make sure (確む).
misumisu (見す見す), *ad.* while looking on; before one's very eyes.
mi-suru (魅する), *vt.* to captivate; fascinate; bewitch.
misuteru (見棄てる), *vt.* to forsake; abandon; throw over.
mitama (御靈), *n.* one's soul; one's spirit. ¶ 御靈屋, a mausoleum.
mitaosu (見倒す), *vt.* ❶ (見下げる) to depreciate; undervalue. ❷ (素見[ひやか]す) to have a look at ...and merely ask the price; amuse oneself by looking *at*.
mitarashi (御手洗), *n.* holy water for washing hands.
mitasu (滿·充す), *vt.* ❶ (充滿さす) to fill up; pack (詰込む); stuff (同上). ❷ (滿足さす) to satisfy. ❸ (位置を) to occupy. —需要を滿す, to supply a demand. —希望を滿す, to satisfy one's desire; gratify another's wishes (人の).
mitate (見立), *n.* ❶ (選定) choice; selection. ❷ (判斷) judgment; estimation. ❸ (診斷) diagnosis. —醫者の見立によれば, according to the doctor; in the doctor's opinion. —見立違ひをする, to judge 《dignose》 erroneously. —この柄は僕の見立だ, This pattern was my choosing [chosen by me].
mitateru (見立てる), *vt.* ❶ (見送) to see off. ❷ (選定) to choose; select. ❸ (判斷) to judge. ❹ (診察) to diagnose. ❺ (擬する) to put down for; liken *to*; take *as*.
mitchaku (密著する), *v.* to adhere closely; stick *to*; glue (膠著).
mitei (未定の), *a.* undecided;

undetermined; unsettled. ¶ 演題未定, subject undecided. —未定稿, an unfinished manuscript; a rough draft. [☞ *miseinen*.]

miteinen (未丁年), *n.* minority.

mitetoru (見て取る), *vt.* to perceive; see through.

mitodokeru (見屆ける), *vt.* ❶ (確める) to ascertain; make sure [certain]. ❷ (目擊する) to witness; find out (發見). —現場を見屆ける, to inspect the spot. —君の先途を見屆ける, to make sure of [ascertain] one's lord's fate.

mitogameru (見咎める), *vt.* ❶ (咎める) to rebuke; find fault *with*. ❷ (誰何する) to question; challenge. ❸ (見附ける) to detect.

mitomein (認印), *n.* a private seal; a signet.

mitomeru (認める), *vt.* ❶ (目に留める) to notice; note; observe. ❷ (認識する) to recognize; appreciate (價値などを). ❸ (承認する) recognize (獨立·政府などを); acknowledge. ❹ (可とする) to approve; recognize. ❺ (看做す) to consider; regard; deem. —至當と認める, to think fit [good] *to*. —(しかするを)必要と認めたるときは, if he considers it necessary (to do so).

mitomonai (見ともない), *a.* Ⓢ みッともない. indecent; unseemly; shabby (汚い).

mitoreru (見惚れる), *v.* to be lost in admiration; be fascinated [charmed] *by*.

mitorizu (見取圖), *n.* an outline; a sketch. —見取圖を取る, to sketch.

mitoru (見取る), *vt.* ❶ (看取る) to perceive; see though; take in. ❷ (見て寫取る) to sketch. ❸ =*kanbyō* (看病する).

mitōshi (見通), *n.* ❶ (通景) a vista; a perspective. ❷ (豫見) foresight. ❸ (洞察) insight; penetration. —見通す, ① (端から端まで見る) to see [look] through. ② (豫見する) to foresee; anticipate. ③ (見拔く) to penetrate into; see through.

mitsu (蜜), *n.* honey.

mitsuba (三葉), *n.* ❶ a trefoil. ❷ 【植】(野蜀葵) the American honewort (Japanese variety).

mitsubachi (蜜蜂), *n.* 【昆】the Japanese honey-bee; the honey-bee 〔俗〕 —蜜蜂の巢, a beehive.

mitsubai (密賣-買), *n.* illicit sale. —密賣する, to sell secretly; smuggle. ¶ 密賣品, a secretly-sold article; smuggled goods.

mitsuban (三つ半), *n.* (三つ半鐘の略) a treble-peal fire-alarm.

mitsubō (密謀), *n.* an intrigue; a secret plot; a conspiracy.

mitsudan (密談), *n.* secret [private] conversation; confidential talk. —密談する, to talk [speak] *to* in private; have a secret interview; consult [confer] privately.

mitsudo (密度), *n.* 【理】density.

mitsuga (密畫), *n.* an elaborate drawing; a minutely-painted picture.

mitsugi (貢), *n.* a tribute.

mitsugi (密議), *n.* a private [closet] consultation; a secret conference [sitting; deliberation]. ☞ *mitsudan*. —密議を凝らす, to discuss with closed doors [in secret].

mitsugo (三つ子), *n.* ❶ (同時に生れた) triplets. ❷ (幼兒) a child; a baby. —三つ兒の魂百まで, "What is learned in the cradle lasts till the grave."

mitsugu (貢ぐ), *v.* ❶ (貢納) to pay tribute. ❷ (仕送り) to support; supply with money.

mitsugumi (三つ組), *n.* a triad; a set of three pieces. —三つ組の洋服, a suit of foreign clothes.

mitsuji (密事), *n.* a secret.

mitsukado (三角), *n.* (三辻) a three-cornered [Y-shaped] crossing. ☞ *sankaku*.

mitsukaru (見附かる), *vi.* to be found out; be discovered; be caught; be detected.

mitsuke (見附), *n.* 【築城】a guarded castle-gate.

mitsukeru (見附ける), *vt.* ❶ =*minareru*. ❷ (發見) to find (out); discover; detect. ❸ (探す) to look *for*; search *for*. —盜む所を見附ける, to detect a person in the act of stealing.

mitsuki (見附), *n.* ❶ (見掛) appearance. ❷ (最初に眼に入ること) first sight. —見附きのよい家, a pretty-looking house.

mitsukuchi (缺脣), *n.* a hare-lip.

mitsukurou (見繕ふ), *v.* to do at discretion. ☞ *mihakarau*.

mitsukusu (見盡す), *v.* to see all; exhaust in seeing.

mitsumata (三椏), *n.* 【植】Edgeworthia chrysantha (學名).

mitsumata (三叉), *n.* a three-pronged fork; a trident.

mitsumegiri (三稜錐), *n.* a triangular drill [bit].

mitsumeru (見詰める), *v.* to gaze; stare; fix [rivet] one's eyes *on*. —顏を見つめる, to stare a person in the face.

mitsumori (見積), *n.* ❶ (目測) measurement by sight. ❷ (概算) estimate; calculation; valuation;

【商】 quotation. —大體の見積, rough estimation. ¶見積價格, estimated value [cost] —見積書, an estimate.

mitsumoru (見積る), *vt.* ❶ (目分量) to measure by the eye. ❷ (概算) to estimate; calculate; appraise. —五百圓と見積る, to estimate it at ¥500.

mitsu-na (密な), *a.* ❶ (親密) intimate; familiar. ❷ (稠密) dense; compact; crowded. ❸ (精密) minute; precise. ❹ = *himitsu*.

mitsu-ni (密に), *ad.* ❶ =*hisokani*. ❷ thickly (接近して); closely (精密に).

mitsuori (三折にする), *v.* to fold in three.

mitsurin (密林), *n.* a dense forest; a thick wood.

mitsurō (蜜蠟), *n.* beeswax; wax.

mitsuryō (密獵, 密漁), *n.* poaching. —密獵する, to poach. ¶密獵船, a poaching-schooner. —密獵者, a poacher.

mitsuun (密雲), *n.* a dense [thick] cloud.

mitsuyaku (密約), *n.* a secret treaty [understanding]; a secret promise (個人間の). —密約する, to make a secret treaty.

mitsuyunyū (密輸入), *n.* smuggling; running. —密輸入する, to smuggle (in); run. ¶密輸入船[者], a smuggler.

mitsuyushutsu (密輸出), *n.* smuggling.

mitsuzō (密造), *n.* illicit manufacture. —密造する, to manufacture clandestinely.

mitsuzuki (蜜月), *n.* a honeymoon. —蜜月の旅, a honeymoon trip.

mitto (ミット), *n.* 【野球】 a mitten; a mitt.

mittsū (密通), *n.* ❶ (姦通) adultery. ❷ =*naitsū*. —密通する ① to commit adultery *with*. ② to communicate secretly *with*.

miuchi (身內), *n.* ❶ (親戚) one's relations; one's relatives. ❷ (子分) a follower; a dependant.

miugoki (身動), *n.* movement. —四方から押されて身動きがならない, Being pressed on all sides, I cannot move.

miuke (身受), *n.* redemption; ransom. —身受する, to ransom; redeem. ¶身受金, a ransom.

miukeru (見受ける), *vt.* to see; observe; notice; catch sight *of*. —よ見受け申した處, to all appearance; to outward seeming.

miushinau (見失ふ), *vt.* to lose sight *of*; lose; miss.

miwake (見分), *v.* discrimination; distinction. —見分けのつかぬ, indistinguishable.

miwakeru (見分ける), *vt.* to distinguish; discriminate; discern.

miwasureru (見忘れる), *vt.* to forget the face *of*; not to recognize.

miwatasu (見渡す), *vt.* to overlook; see far; look around (見廻す); command (見下ろす). —見渡す限り, as far as the eye can reach [sweep]; as far as one can see. —海を見渡す, to look out over the sea.

miya (宮), *n.* ❶ (神社) a *Shintō* shrine. ❷ (御殿) a palace; the court (宮廷); the Imperial Palace (皇居). ❸ (皇族) an Imperial [a royal] prince (princess, 姫宮).

miyabiyaka (雅かな), *a.* Ⓢ 雅びた. refined; elegant; courtly.

miyaburu (看破る), *vt.* to see *into*; penetrate *into*; see *through* (洞察する). ☞ *kanpa*. —祕密を看破る, to pierce into a secret; detect another's secret.

miyage (土產), *n.* a souvenir (記念の); a present (進物); a gift. ¶洋行土產, a present made as a souvenir of one's stay abroad. —土產話, a story heard in one's travels; a traveller's tale.

miyake (宮家), *n.* a prince of the Blood.

miyako (都), *n.* a capital; a metropolis; the chief city [town].

miyakodori (都鳥), *n.* 【鳥】 the Japanese oyster-catcher.

miyama (深山), *n.* (山) a mountain; (奥山) a deep mountain.

miyamairi (宮參), *n.* a new-born baby's visit to its tutelary shrine.

miyameguri (宮巡), *n.* to pilgrimage to shrines.

miyasudokoro (御息所), *n.* the consort of an Imperial prince; a princess (consort).

miyasui (見易い), *a.* visible; obvious; plain (平明な). —見易い道理, a reason easy to understand.

miyazukae (宮仕する), *v.* to serve in the court.

miyo (御代), *n.* a reign.

miyō (見樣), *n.* way of seeing; point of view; sight. ☞ *mikata* (見方). —見樣見眞似で覺える, to learn by sight.

miyoi (見よい), *a.* ❶ (見やすい) convenient to see. ❷ (美しい) beautiful [pretty] to see. —見よい場所, a place [position] favourable for seeing.

miyori (身寄), *n.* a relation; kindred. ☞ *miuchi*.

miyoshi (舳), *n.* the bow; the prow.

mizame (見醒がする), *v.* to tire of seeing.

mizen (未然に), *ad.* before materializing; in the bud.

mizeni (身錢を切ッて), with one's own money.
mizo (溝), *n.* ❶ (下水) a ditch; a drain; a gully; a gutter; a kennel. ❷ (小濠) a ditch. ❸ (閾などの) a groove; a channel. —溝を掘る, ① (閾などの) to channel [*vt.*]; groove [*vt.*]. ② to make [dig] a ditch [drain].
mizore (霙), *n.* sleet. —霙降る, It sleets.
mizou (未曾有の), *a.* unprecedented; unheard-of; unparalleled. —未曾有の事變, an unprecedented [unparalleled] affair.
mizu (水), *n.* ❶ water; cold water (冷水). ❷ (洪水) a flood; an inundation. —水だらけの, watery; sloppy (床·机など). —水が出る, to flood; inundate. —水の漏らない, water-tight. —水に流す, to consign to [bury in] oblivion. —水を離れた魚, a fish out of the water. —水を向ける, ① (ホースを) to turn a hose *on*. ② to draw out; fish for. —水をさす, ① to pour water *into*. ② to cause ill-feeling between; make bad blood between. —朝顔に水をやる, to water a morning-glory.
mizuabi (水浴), *n.* ❶ bathing; a cold-water bath. ❷ (水泳) a bathe.
mizuabura (水油), *n.* oil; toilet oil; hair-oil.
mizuage (水揚), *n.* (陸揚) landing [discharging] cargo. —水揚げする, to unlade [unload] (a ship); discharge cargo.
mizuame (水飴), *n.* millet-jelly.
mizuasagi (水淺葱), *n.* light blue (色).
mizuasobi (水遊), *n.* ❶ dabbling in water. ❷ (水上戲) water sports; aquatics.
mizuatari (水中), *n.* an ailment caused by drinking water.
mizubana (水洟), *n.* watery mucus (from the nose); snivel. —水洟を垂らす, to run at the nose; snivel.
mizubashira (水柱), *n.* a water-spout (龍卷); a water-column.
mizubukure (水腫), *n.* ❶【醫】a bleb; a water-blister. ❷ (水氣で全身脹れること) dropsy. —水腫れが出來る, to have a water-blister.
mizubune (水船), *n.* ❶ (給水船) a water-boat; a watering-ship (大形の). ❷ (水槽) a cistern; a water-tank; a water-trough.
mizuchi (蛟蛟), *n.* a sea-dragon.
mizudeppō (水鐵砲), *n.* a squirt; a squirt-gun.
mizue (水繪), *n.* a water-colour picture. =***suisaiga***.
mizuenogu (水繪具), *n.* water-colours.
mizugame (水瓶), *n.* a water-pot; a water-jar; a water-pitcher.
mizugashi (水菓子), *n.* fruits. ¶ 水菓子屋, a fruiterer (人): a fruit-shop (店).
mizugiwa (水際), *n.* ❶ (水陸の境目) the water's edge; the brink [edge; margin; verge] of the water. ❷ (水の邊) the waterside; the shore. —水際立ッた, fine; splendid; conspicuous. (水際だッた美人, a woman of superior beauty.)
mizugori (水垢離), *n.* purification by [with] water; ablution. —水垢離をとる, to purify one's self with water.
mizuguki (水莖の跡), *n.* hand-writing.
mizuguruma (水車), *n.* a water-wheel [-mill]; an irrigation-wheel (灌水用の).
mizugusa (水草), *n.* a water-plant; an aquatic plant.
mizugusuri (水藥), *n.* a liquid medicine; a wash (外用水藥); a lotion (洗滌劑).
mizuhake (排水), *n.* drainage; sewerage; a drain (溝). —水排けが惡い《よい》, to drain badly 《well》; run badly 《well》 (水が).
mizuhiki (水引), *n.* ❶ a fine paper-cord for tying presents. ❷ (水引幕) a sky-curtain. ❸【植】(金線草) the Virginian knot-grass.
mizuhiyashi (冷水壜), *n.* a goglet; a gurglet.
mizuijiri (水弄), *n.* playing with water.
mizuirazu (水入らずの), *a.* pure; unmixed; undisturbed.
mizuire (水入), *n.* a pitcher (瓶); a water-holder.
mizuiro (水色), *n.* light blue.
mizukagami (水鏡), *n.* a water-mirror; a reflection in the water. —水鏡で見る, to look at one's shadow in the water.
mizukakeron (水掛論), *n.* a fruitless [an endless] argument.
mizukaki (水搔), *n.* ❶【禽】a web; a web-foot. ❷ a blade (橈の); a paddle-board (汽船外輪の).
mizukara (自·親ら), *n.* self. ☞ ***jibun*** (自分). —, *ad.* (身自ら) personally; in person; (獨力で) for oneself; (獨りでに) of itself 《oneself》. —自ら進んで, voluntarily; of one's free will; of one's own choice [accord]. —自らやる, to do it oneself.
mizukasa (水嵩), *n.* the volume of water; the water.
mizukau (飲ふ), *vt.* to water.
mizuke (水氣), *n.* moisture; dampness (濕氣); juice (果實等

の). 一水氣ある《なき》果實, a juicy 《husky》 fruit.
mizukemuri (水烟), *n.* spray; watery mist.
mizukiri (水切), *n.* 【遊戯】 ducks and drakes.
mizukoboshi (水翻), *n.* a slop-basin [-bowl]; a slop-jar.
mizukoshi (水漉), *n.* a filter; a colander; a strainer.
mizukumi (水汲), *n.* drawing water.
mizukusai (水臭い), *a.* ❶ (水ッぽい) watery; washy. ❷ (隔意ある) indifferent; cold-hearted [-blooded]; reserved.
mizumaki (水撒), *n.* ❶ (事) watering; sprinkling. ❷ a sprinkler (人及び器); a street waterman. 一水撒きする, to sprinkle water; water [*vt.*]. ☞ *sansui*.
mizumakura (水枕), *n.* a water-pillow.
mizumawashi (水廻), *n.* = *amenbō*.
mizumizushii (水水しい), *a.* fresh; green; young and beautiful; ruddy.
mizumori (水盛), *n.* 【機】 a (water-)level.
mizumushi (水蟲), *n.* ❶ a water-insect. ❷ (掌內鱗屑癬) palmar psoriasis.
mizuna (水菜), *n.* 【植】 Brassica japonica (cabbage の一種・學名).
mizunomi (水呑), *n.* a tumbler; a glass (コップ); a dipper (携帶用). ¶ 水呑百姓, a petty [small] farmer; a poor peasant.
mizuochi (鳩尾), *n.* Ⓢ みぞおち. 【解】 the pit (of the stomach); the wind.
mizuoke (水桶), *n.* a pail.
mizuoshiroi (水白粉), *n.* a liquid face-paint.
mizuppoi (水ッぽい), *a.* watery; washy (液體の).
mizurai (見づらい), *a.* ❶ (見難い) hard [difficult] to see. ❷ (見るに忍びぬ) unbearable to see [look upon].
mizusabi (水銹), *n.* scum.
mizusakazuki (水盃をする), to take cups of water at the final parting.
mizusaki (水先), *n.* ❶ (水の流れる方向) the direction of a current. ❷ (船の進む水路) a ship's course. ❸ =水先案內. ¶ 水先案內, pilotage (事); a pilot (人). (水先案內料, pilotage. 一水先案內船, a pilot-boat. 一水先案內をする, to pilot.)
mizusashi (水差), *n.* a pitcher; a water-jug; a carafe.
mizushirazu (不見不知の), *a.* strange; quite unknown. 一見ず知らずの人, a perfect [an utter] stranger.
mizusumashi (水澄), *n.* ❶ 【昆】 (豉豆蟲) the whirligig; the whirlwig. ❷ =*amenbō*.
mizuta (水田), *n.* a paddy-field.
mizutade (みづたで), *n.* 【植】 the water pepper; the lakeweed.
mizutamari (水溜), *n.* a pool (自然の); a puddle (雨後の); a plash (沼様の).
mizutame (水溜), *n.* a reservoir (池又は水槽); a cistern (桶); a water-tank (汽船等の); a rain-tub (用水桶); a water-butt.
mizutori (水鳥), *n.* a water-bird; a water-fowl.
mizuumi (湖), *n.* a lake.
mizuzeme (水攻), *n.* ❶ (水責) torture by water. ❷ (洪水) a flood. 一敵の陣を水攻めにする, to flood the enemy's camp.
mo (藻), *n.* a water-weed.
mo (喪), *n.* mourning; the period of mourning (喪期). 一喪が明ける, to be out of mourning. 一喪に服する, ① to mourn *for*; be in mourning *for*. ② (新に) to go into mourning *for*. 一喪を發する, to announce the mourning.
mo (も), *conj.* ❶ (及び) and; as well as; both...and; neither...nor (否定). ❷ (孰れにしても) either...or; whether ...or not. ❸ (とも, 雖も) even if; even though; although. ❹ (程も) as many 《much》 as; no less than; as far as (距離). **—**, *ad.* ❶ (竝に) besides; moreover. ❷ (でも) even. ❸ (も亦) too; also; either (not と用ふ). 一遲く《善く》も, at (the) latest 《best》. 一高くも, (even) at the dearest. 一十日も, as long as ten days. 一五人も, no less than five persons. 一私も亦(然り), so am 《do》 I. 一見も知らぬ人, a perfect stranger. 一止まるも進むも, whether we stay or (whether we) go. 一行くも行かぬも, whether you go or not. 一一月も經たない中に, in less than a month; before a month had passed. 一三度も呼んだけれども, I called three several times, but.... 一一錢もない, I have not even a *sen*. 一晴れさうもない, There is no promise of clearing up. 一善くもなければ惡くもない, It is neither good nor bad.
mo (も), **mō** (もう), *ad.* ❶ (既に) already. ❷ (今頃) by this time. ❸ (今) now. ❹ (程なく) shortly; soon; before [ere] long. ❺ (更に) more; again; another [*pron.*] 一もう一度, once more [again]; yet once (more); over again; a second time. 一もう...なし, no more (數量); no longer (時間).

—もう澤山, No, thanks. —もう濟んだ, It is now over. —もう一杯やれ, Try another cup. —もう今ぢゃ行かぬ, I go there no longer.

mō (毛), *n.* ❶ (錢) a *mō*; one-tenth of a *rin*. ❷ (髮) hair.

mō (蒙を啓く), *v.* to enlighten; open another's eyes.

mō (網), *n.* a network. —通信網を張る, to spread a network of communication.

mō (もーと鳴く), *vi.* to moo; low.

mōa (盲啞), *a.* blind and dumb [deaf-mute] ¶ 盲啞學校, a blind and deaf-mute school.

mōaku (猛惡な), *a.* brutal; savage; ferocious.

mochi (餅), *n.* rice-cake; rice-dumpling. —餅を搗く, to pound rice (for rice-cake). ¶ 餅屋, a rice-pounder. (餅は餅屋, "Every one has his speciality.")

mochi (黐), *n.* ❶【植】=*mochinoki*. ❷ (鳥黐) bird-lime[-glue].

mochi (持), *n.* ❶ (耐久力) wear; durability. ❷ (所有) ownership; possession. ❸ (擔任, 負擔) charge. —當方 (の) 持ちで, at our cost [expense]. —持ちのよい, durable. —持ちが善い《惡い》, to wear well 《ill》. (A は B よりも持ちがよい, A lasts longer [is more durable] than B.)

mochiagaru (持上る), *vi.* ❶ to be lifted up. ❷ (起る) to arise (相談·事件·問題など); come up (問題); happen; take place.

mochiageru (持上げる), *vt.* ❶ to raise; lift up; take [hold; bear] up. ❷ (煽てる) to belaud; laud to the skies; load with praise.

mochiagumu (持あぐむ), *vt.* to be sick of holding; be tired of keeping. —品を持ちあぐんで居る, The goods lie heavy on their hands.

mochiau (持合ふ), *v.* to help each other (共助); maintain equilibrium (均衡を保つ); remain steady (相場が); hold in common. —持合ひで, on joint account.

mochiawase (持合せ), *n.* things on hand; stock on hand (商品の); ready money (金の). —持合せる, ① (手許に) to have on hand (金·商品を); have in stock (商品を). ② (携帶) to have about [with] one. —丁度金の持合せがなかった, I happened to have no money with me.

mochiba (持場), *n.* ❶ (部署) a post; a station. ❷ (巡囘區) the round; the beat; the walk (行商人等の). —持場に就く, to take up one's station.

mochibun (持分), *n.* a share; an interest.

mochidasu (持出す), *vt.* ❶ to bring [take] out; carry out [away]. ❷ (提出) to propose; offer; bring forward.

mochigashi (餅菓子), *n.* a bean-jam cake.

mochigome (糯米), *n.* glutinous rice.

mochigusa (餅草), *n.* young mugwort leaves.

mochigusare (持腐れ), *n.* possession without use.

mochihakobi (持運び), *n.* portage; carriage; conveyance. —持運ぶ, to carry; convey; transport. —持運びに便利な道具, a portable utensil.

mochiiru (用ひる), *vt.* ❶ (使用) to use; make use *of*; put to use. ❷ (採用) to adopt; take. ❸ (適用) to apply. —用ひ盡す, to use up. —用ひられなくなる, to go out of use. —主人に重く用ひられる, to be highly trusted by the employer. —人の言を用ひる, to act on another's advice.

mochikaeru (持換へる), *vt.* to shift from one hand to the other.

mochikaeru (持歸る), *vt.* to carry back; bring back with one; bring [take] home (家へ).

mochikakeru (持掛ける), *vt.* ❶ (吹っかける) to make; force. ❷ (仄かす) to suggest; propose (提言). ❸ (言ひ寄る) to make advances; make up *to*.

mochikata (持方), *n.* the manner of holding; the way to hold.

mochikiru (持切る), *vt.* ❶ (維持) to hold [stand] out; maintain. ❷ (專有) to occupy exclusively; possess solely. —その話で持切ってる, The matter is in everybody's mouth.

mochikitasu (持來す), *vt.* to bring (on).

mochikomu (持込む), *vt.* ❶ (搬入) to carry [bring] in; carry [take] *to*. ❷ (申出) to propose; offer; make; enter (抗議を). —不平を持込む, to make complaints to a person. ¶ 持込賃, porterage; carriage (運賃). —持込値段, free of charges.

mochikosu (持越す), *vt.* ❶ to hold over; bring [carry] over; carry on (株式にて次の立會日まで). ❷ (もちこたへる) to last [hold] *through*. —冬を持越す, to last through the winter. —春まで (物を) 持越す, to hold it over till spring.

mochikotaeru (持堪へる), *v.* ❶ (維持) to maintain; sustain; hold [stand; stick] out. ❷ (長

くもつ) to last; endure.

mochikuzusu (持崩す), *vt.* to ruin; wreck. —身を持ち崩す, to ruin [wreck] oneself; degenerate.

mochimae (持前), *n.* ❶ (天性) nature. ❷ (特色, 特質) a characteristic; an idiosyncrasy (人の); peculiarity; quality (物質の); property (同上). ❸ (持分, 分前) a share. —持前の性質, intrinsic nature (生來の); proper quality (本來の); one's own character (特有の); characteristic traits. —持前の病氣, ① one's inherent disease. ② (例の癖) an inveterate habit.

mochimawaru (持廻る), *vt.* to take round; hand round (手渡し).

mochimono (持物), *n.* ❶ (所有物) one's property; a possession. ❷ (携帶品) things carried by one; one's luggage; one's belongings; one's things.

mochinaosu (持直す), *v.* ❶ to recover; restore; rally; revive (天氣など) ❷ =*mochikaeru*.

mochinige (持逃する), *v.* to run away [make off; abscond] *with*.

mochinoki (黐木), *n.* 【植】 Ilex integra (holly の一種·學名).

mochinushi (持主), *n.* an owner; a proprieter [*fem.* -tress]; a possessor.

mochiron (勿論), *ad.* of course; certainly. ☞ *muron*. —は勿論の事だ, It is certainly understood that...; It goes without saying that....

mochiryō (持料), *n.* a thing in one's use; an article for one's personal use.

mochisaru (持去る), *v.* to go away *with*; carry away; walk off [away] *with*.

mochitsuki (餅搗), *n.* (事) rice-pounding: (人) a rice-pounder.

mochizuki (望月), *n.* the full moon.

mōchō (盲腸), *n.* 【解】 the cæcum; the blind gut. ¶ 盲腸炎, 【醫】 typhlitis; cæcitis.

mochū (喪中), *n.* the period of mourning. —喪中である, to be in mourning.

modae (悶), *n.* ❶ (心身の) agony; pain. ❷ (主として心の) pang; anguish.

modaeru (悶える), *vi.* to be [writhe] in agony; be tortured. ☞ *mogaku*.

modashi (もだし難く), hard to remain silent [keep silence; hold one's tongue] (默し難く); unable to refuse (拒絶し難く); hard to disobey (背き難く).

moderu (モデル), *n.* a model. —彫刻家のモデルになる, to become a model for a sculptor.

mōderu (詣でる), *v.* to go out to worship; visit (a temple or shrine).

modokashii (もどかしい), *a.* impatient; irritating; tedious (のろくて). —もどかしがる, to feel [become] impatient [irritated]; be fretful.

modori (戻), *n.* ❶ =*kaeri*. ❷ (商品) returns. ¶ 戻り路, the way back [home].

modoru (戻る), *vi.* ❶ (歸る) to return; come [get] back. ❷ =*atomodori* (後戻する). ❸ (縒が) to unwind; untwine. —話が元に戻る, to resume the thread of one's discourse. —來た路を戻る, to return the way one came; retrace one's steps.

modoshizei (戻稅), *n.* a drawback. ¶ 戻稅證明書 (稅關の), a debenture.

modosu (戻す), *vt.* ❶ (返す) to return; give back; pay back (返濟); restore (還附). ❷ (送り返す) to send back. ❸ (もとの所へ) to put back. ❹ (却下) to reject. ❺ (嘔く) to throw [bring] up; vomit; spew. —撚りを戻す, to untwine. —時計の針を戻す, to put back a watch. —(港へ)船を戻す, to put back (to port).

moeagaru (燃上る), *vi.* to blaze up; kindle; blare up.

moegara (燃殼), *n.* cinders.

moegi (萌黃), *n.* (色) light [yellowish] green.

moeru (萌える), *vi.* to sprout; shoot; spring up; come out.

moeru (燃える), *vi.* ❶ (火が) to burn; blaze. ❷ (情が) to burn; blaze up; kindle. —燃える思, an ardent passion. —燃えて居る炭, live charcoal. —燃えきる, to burn (itself) out; be burnt out. —嫉妬心に燃える, to burn with jealousy.

moesashi (燃えさし), *n.* embers; a half-burnt stump.

moetatsu (燃立つ), *vi.* to burst into flames; burn [blaze] up. ☞ *moeagaru*.

moetsuku (燃附く), *vi.* to catch [take] fire; inflame; kindle.

moeutsuru (燃移る), *vi.* to spread *to* (擴がる).

mōfu (毛布), *n.* a blanket; a rug; a woollen cloth.

mofuku (喪服), *n.* mourning dress [clothes]; black sables.

mogaku (踠く), *vi.* to struggle; wriggle; writhe. —手足を踠く, to struggle with one's limbs.

mogeru (捥げる), *vi.* to be wrenched [twisted] off; come off.

mogi (摸擬), *n.* imitation; mimicry. —摸擬する, to imitate. ¶ 摸擬戰, a sham fight. —摸擬試驗, a test examination. —摸擬店, an imitation shop.

mogidō (沒義道な), *a.* inhuman; heartless; hard-hearted.

mogitoru (捥取る), *vt.* to wrest [wrench] off; pluck [tear; break] off; pick off (果物など).

mogu (捥ぐ), *vt.* to pull; pick; pluck. ☞ *mogitoru.*

mogumogu (もぐもぐ噛む), *vi.* to mumble; munch [& *vt.*].

mogura (**mochi**) (土龍), *n.* 【哺乳】 the mole.

moguri (潜り), *n.* ❶ (潜水) dive (事); a diver (水). ❷ (無免許) an unlicensed practitioner.

moguru (潜る), *vi.* ❶ (水中に) to dive (*into*; *beneath*; *under*); dip *into* (ちょいと). ❷ (這入る) to creep [crawl] *in*; slip *into.* —水底に潜る, to dive to the bottom; sound (鯨等が). —泥の中へ潜り込む, to creep into the mud.

mogusa (艾), *n.* moxa.

mohan (模範), *n.* a model; a pattern; an exemplar (手本). —模範とすべき人物, a man to be taken as a model. —模範を示す, to set an [a good] example. ¶ 模範村《學生》, a model village 《student》.

mōhatsu (毛髮), *n.* hair.

mohaya (最早), *ad.* already (既に); now (今や); any longer. ☞ *mō* (もう).

mōhi (毛皮), *n.* fur; pelt (羊等の). ¶ 毛皮商, a furrier; a pelt-monger.

mōhitsu (毛筆), *n.* a hair-pencil. ¶ 毛筆畫, a hair-pencil picture.

mohō (摸倣), *n.* imitation. —摸倣する, to imitate; simulate; model; copy. ¶ 摸倣者, an imitator.

mōi (猛威), *n.* fierceness; ferocity; fury; overwhelming power. —猛威を逞しうする, to display ferocity; show fierce power; rage.

mōja (亡者), *n.* the dead (死者); a ghost (幽靈).

mojamoja (もぢゃもぢゃ), *ad.* shaggily. —もぢゃもぢゃ(した)髭, a frowzy beard.

moji, monji, (文字), *n.* ❶ (字) a letter; a character; an ideograph (表意字). ❷ (言葉) a word; a term. ❸ (學問) learning; literacy (讀み書き). —文字上の意味, literal meaning. —文字通りに譯する, to translate literally [word for word].

mojimoji (もぢもぢする), *vi.* to fidget; be uneasy [restless].

mōjin (盲人), *n.* a blindman; the blind (集合的).

mōjin (蒙塵する), *v.* to fly from the palace.

mojiru (捩ぢる), *vt.* ❶ (ねぢる) to twist; distort; crook. ❷ (他人の文を) to parody; travesty.

mōjū (盲從), *n.* blind obedience [adherence; submission]; implicit obedience. —盲從する, to follow like sheep; follow [obey; submit] blindly

mōjū (猛獸), *n.* a beast of prey; a savage beast; a fierce animal.

mōka (猛火), *n.* ❶ raging blame; furious [fierce] fire. ❷ (猛烈な砲火) a heavy fire. —猛火の中に包まれる, to be wrapped in blazing flames.

mōkaru (儲かる), *vi.* ❶ (物·事業が) to be profitable [lucrative]; pay (引合ふ). ❷ (〃) to profit; make a profit; make [*vt.*]. ——, *a.* profitable; lucrative; paying.

mōke (設), *n.* ❶ (設備) accommodation; an establishment. ❷ (仕度) preparation. —...の設けがある, to be provided [furnished] *with*.... —設けの席に著く, to take the seat provided.

mōke (儲), *n.* profit; gains; earnings (稼高); makings (同上). —儲けの薄い商賣, a trade with small profit. —儲け口を見つける, to find out a paying job. —大した儲けはあるまい, It will not yield much profit. ¶ 儲け物, a windfall.

mokei (模型), *n.* a model; a mould (型); a pattern (同上). —模型圖を引く, to draw a model. ¶ 軍艦《人體》模型, a model of a warship 《the human body》. —模型地圖, a relief map.

mōken (猛犬), *n.* a ferocious [fierce] dog.

mōkeru (設ける), *vt.* ❶ (建設) to build; construct. ❷ (設置, 設立) to establish; institute; set up; create; form. ❸ (制定) to make; enact; frame. —規則を設ける, to lay down a rule. —規定を設ける, to provide *for*. —子を設ける, to get a child.

mōkeru (儲ける), *vt.* to profit; gain; make. —儲けて賣る, to sell at a profit.

mōkin (猛禽), *n.* a bird of prey; a rapacious bird. ¶ 猛禽類, 【鳥】 Raptores, Raptatores (學名); the raptorial birds.

mokka (目下), *ad.* now; at present; for the present. —目下の狀態では, according to the present conditions; as the matters

stand.
mokka (默過する), *vt.* to overlook; wink *at*; pass over [by].
mokke (勿怪の幸), *n.* unexpected fortune; a godsend; a windfall.
mokkei (默契), *n.* tacit understanding.
mokko (畚), *n.* a straw mat for carrying earth; a mat earth-carrier.
mokkō (木工), *n.* a woodworker; a carpenter; 【軍】 an army carpenter.
mokkō (沐猴), *n.* a painted ape.
mokkō (默考), *n.* meditation; contemplation; musing. —默考する, to meditate; contemplate; muse.
mokkoku (木斛), *n.* 【植】 Ternstrœmia japonica (scarlet-seed の一種·學名).
mokkyo (默許), *n.* tacit consent; implicit permission. —默許する, to permit tacitly; give an implicit consent.
moko (模糊たる), *a.* dim; hazy; indistinct.
Mōko (蒙古), *n.* Mongolia. ¶ 蒙古人種, the Mongolian race.
mōkon (毛根), *n.* the root of a hair.
moku (藻), *n.* a water-weed.
moku (目), *n.* ❶ (項目) an item. ❷ (碁石) a piece (石); a cross (盤目). ❸ =*mokume*.
mokuba (木馬), *n.* ❶ a wooden horse; a hobby-horse (玩具); a rocking-horse (前後に搖れる玩具). ❷ 【體操】 a horse; a vaulting-horse. —木馬を跳ぶ, to vault over a horse.
mokudaku (默諾), *n.* tacit consent; acquiescence. —默諾する, to acquiesce *in*; consent tacitly *to*; give a tacit consent *to*.
mokudō (木道), *n.* a wood (-block) pavement (木塊鋪道).
mokugeki (目撃する), *vt.* to witness; see; observe. ¶ 目撃者, a witness; an eye-witness; a spectator.
mokugeki (默劇), *n.* a pantomime; a dumb-show; a mummery.
mokugū (木偶), *n.* ❶ (木の人形) a wooden image. ❷ (傀儡) a puppet; a dummy.
mokugyo (木魚), *n.* a wooden gong.
mokuhai (木杯), *n.* a wooden cup; a noggin.
mokuhan (木版), *n.* wood-engraving; woodcutting; block-printing. ¶ 木版畫, a woodcut; a wood-engraving; a block-print. —木版師 [屋], a block-cutter; a wood-engraver.
mokuhen (木片), *n.* a bit [chip] of wood; a splinter (薄く細長い).
mokuhi (木皮), *n.* the bark; the cortex (外皮).
mokuhon (木本), *n.* 【植】 a woody plant; a tree.
mokuhyō (目標), *n.* a mark; a landmark (陸標); a guide(-post) (道路標).
mokuji (目次), *n.* the contents; a table of contents.
mokujiki (木食), *n.* fruit diet.
mokujū (默從), *n.* acquiescence; passive obedience. —默從する, to acquiesce *in*; obey passively; follow tacitly.
mokume (木理), *n.* the grain (of wood).
mokumoku (默默), *ad.* silently; in silence; mutely. —默々の裡に, tacitly; implicitly.
mokuneji (木螺旋), *n.* a screw; a wood-screw (木材締に用ひる).
mokunin (默認), *n.* =*mokkyo*.
mokurei (目禮する), *vi.* to salute [greet] with the eyes.
mokurei (默禮), *n.* nodding. —默禮する, to nod.
mokurenge (木蓮, 木蘭), *n.* 【植】 the purple flowered magnolia.
mokurenga (木煉瓦), *n.* a nog; a wood [wooden] brick; a wooden [wood-] block (鋪道用の).
mokuroku (目錄), *n.* ❶ (商品·圖書の) a catalogue; (財產·屬具などの) an inventory; (索引) an index. ❷ =*mokuji*. ❸ (進物·人名等の) a list of presents 《names》. —目錄を作る, to make a catalogue 《an inventory》 *of*. ¶ 分類目錄, a classed catalogue. —著者《件名》目錄, an author 《a title》-catalogue. —カード式目錄, a card-catalogue. —免稅品目錄, a free list.
mokuromi (目論見), *n.* a design; a plan. —目論見が外れる, to go off against one's plan. ¶ 目論見書, a prospectus.
mokuromu (目論む), *vt.* to design; plan; project.
mokusan (目算), *n.* ❶ (見積) a rough estimate [calculation]. ❷ (企畫) a plan. ☞ *mokuromi*.
mokusatsu (默殺する), *vt.* to ignore (取上げぬ); take no notice *of* (同上); shelve (討議を永久に延期する); smother (討議させぬ樣に); leave unanswered (返事せずに). —委員の勸說を默殺する, to smother the recommendations of the committee.
mokusei (木犀), *n.* 【植】 the fragrant olive.
mokusei (木星), *n.* 【天】 Jupiter.
mokusei (木精), *n.* ❶ 【化】 wood-spirit; methyl(-ic) alcohol. ❷ a wood-nymph; a dryad.
mokusei (木製の), *a.* wooden; made of wood.

mokusen (木船), *n.* a wooden vessel.

mokushi (目示する), *vi.* to wink; give a wink.

mokushi (默止する), *vt.* ❶ to keep silent *about.* ❷ to remain silent.

mokushi (默示), *n.* revelation; apocalypse. —默示の, implied (expressed の對). —默示する, to reveal (啓示); imply (明示の對). ¶ 默示錄, the (Book of) Revelations; the Apocalypse.

mokushi (默視する), *vt.* to look indifferently *on*; overlook; wink *at*.

mokushō (目睫の間に迫る), to be near [close] at hand; be imminent.

mokusō (目送する), *vt.* to look [gaze] *after*; follow with the eyes.

mokusō (默想), *n.* contemplation; meditation; reflection. —默想する, to meditate; ponder *on* [*over*]; contemplate.

mokusoku (目測する), *vt.* to measure with the eye.

moku-suru (目する), *vt.* to regard [consider] (*as*); look upon (*as*); think (him to be).

moku-suru (沐する), *vi.* ❶ to bathe; wash. ❷ to be exposed (to rain).

moku-suru (默する), *vi.* to be silent; keep silent; hold one's tongue.

mokutan (木炭), *n.* ❶ (wood-) charcoal. ❷ (畫用) a charcoal (-pencil). ¶ 木炭畫, charcoal drawing.

mokuteki (目的), *n.* ❶ (目あて) an object; an end; an aim. ❷ (意圖) a purpose; an intention; a design. ❸ subject; subject-matter (目的物). —…の目的で, for the purpose [end] *of*; with the object [intention] *of*; with a view *to*. —目的とする, to aim *at*; have in view. (本會は…するを以て目的とす, The society has for its object….) —目的を果す [達する], to attain one's object; accomplish [effect; execute] one's purpose; carry one's point. ¶ 目的地, the destination (行先); 【軍】 the objective; an object-point (地點). —目的格, 【文】 the objective (case); the accusative.

mokutō (默禱), *n.* mental prayer; silent prayer. —默禱する, to pray in silence.

mokuyaku (默約), *n.* tacit agreement [understanding].

mokuyōbi (木曜日), *n.* Thursday.

mokuyoku (沐浴), *n.* bathing (入浴); ablution (齋戒沐浴). —沐浴する, to bathe; take a bath; wash oneself; do ablution.

mokuzai (木材), *n.* wood; timber (築材); lumber (挽材). ¶ 木材商, timber-trade (事): a timber-merchant (人).

mokuzen (目前), *n.* the immediate present. —目前のみを考へる, to take short views; think of the present only. —目前の小利に走る, to run after small gains before one's eyes. —目前に迫る, to be imminent; be close at hand.

mokuzen (默然), *ad.* silently; in silence. ☞ *mokumoku.*

mokuzō (木造の), *a.* wooden; of wood; built [made] of wood. ¶ 木造家屋, a frame-house. —木造建築, a wooden building.

mokuzō (木像), *n.* a wooden image [statue; idol].

mokuzu (藻屑), *n.* seaweed. —海底の藻屑となる, to be drowned at sea; find a watery grave.

mōmai (蒙昧な), *a.* dark; ignorant; benighted.

mōmaku (網膜), *n.* 【解】 omentum (腹膜の); retina (眼の). ¶ 網膜炎, 【醫】 omentitis; retinitis.

mome (揉め), *n.* Ⓢ 揉め事. (葛藤) dissension; discord; difference; a disturbance (騷擾).

momen (木綿), *n.* cotton (cloth). ¶ 木綿絲, a cotton thread; sewing-cotton. —木綿織, a cotton fabric; cotton goods (織ったもの); cotton (cloth).

momeru (揉める), *v.* ❶ (悶着) to have troubles *with*; dispute; have a quarrel. ❷ (氣が) to be anxious *about*; be disquieted; be uneasy (落著かぬ).

momi (樅), *n.* 【植】 Abies firma (fir-tree の一種學名). ¶ 樅材, fir; deal.

momi (籾), *n.* ❶ (籾殼) chaff; rice hull. ❷ (籾ある米) unhulled [rough] rice. ¶ 籾種, seed-rice.

momi (紅絹, 紅絹), *n.* scarlet silk (cloth).

momiage (揉上げ), *n.* a tuft of hair under the temple.

momiau (揉合ふ), *v.* to jostle *with* [*against*]; struggle [push] together.

momide (揉手する), *v.* to rub one's hands.

momigiri (錐錐), *n.* a hand drill.

momiji (紅葉), *n.* ❶ red [crimson] leaves; autumn leaves; autumnal tints (秋色). ❷ (楓) the (Japanese) maple. ¶ 紅葉狩, an excursion for viewing crimson maple-leaves; maple-viewing.

momikesu (揉消す), *vt.* ❶ (火を) to put out; smother. ❷ (事件などを) to suppress; smother [stifle] up; hush up. —醜聞を揉み消す, to smother (up) a scandal. —火を揉み消す, to stifle a fire.

momiryōji (揉療治), *n.* massage; shampooing. ☞ *anma*.

momo (桃), *n.* 【植】 the peach.

momo (股, 腿), *n.* the thigh.

mōmō (濛濛), *ad.* mistily; dimly. —濛々たる, mistful; foggy; dim. —濛々と立ち昇る, to rise in thick clouds.

momohiki (股引), *n.* drawers (ズボン下); close-fitting trousers (職人などの); pants 【俗】. ¶ 半股引, breeches (膝の下までの); trunk-drawers.

momoiro (桃色), *n.* peach [rose] colour; pink.

mōmoku (盲目), *n.* blindness. ☞ *mekura*. —盲目的, blind.

momonga (鼯鼠), *n.* 【哺乳】 the Japanese assapan.

momu (揉む), *v.* ❶ (皺にする) to crumple; rumple; rub (こする). ❷ (氣を) to fret [worry] oneself about; be restless [uneasy] about (落着かぬ). ❸ (肩等を) to knead; shampoo. ❹ (錐を) to work (a gimlet). ❺ (稽古) to train; drill. —浪に揉まれる, to be buffeted [tossed about] by the waves. —世の波風に揉まれる, to be buffetted by the world; taste the sweets and bitters of life (辛酸を嘗める). —肩を揉ませる, to have one's shoulders shampooed.

mon- (紋), *n.* ❶ =*monshō* (紋章). ❷ (定紋) a family crest [badge]. ❸ (模様) a pattern; a design. —五つ紋の羽織, a *haori* with five crests. —紋を附ける, to put on a crest.

mon (門), *n.* ❶ a gate. ❷ (部門) class; order. ❸ (砲數) a piece. ❹ =*juku* (塾). —砲二門, two guns. —...の門に醫學を研究する, to study medicine under....

monaka (最中), *n.* ❶ (さいちう) the middle; the midst; the depth. ❷ (菓子) a bean-jam wafer.

monban (門番), *n.* a gate-keeper; a gateman; a porter [*fem.* portress]. ¶ 門番所, a gate-house; a (gate) lodge; a porter's [gate-keeper's] lodge.

monbashira (門柱), *n.* a gate-post.

monbatsu (門閥), *n.* ❶ (系統) lineage; line. ❷ (名門) a good family; good lineage. ☞ *iegara*. —門閥の出なる, coming of a good family. ¶ 門閥家, a person of high [noble] birth [descent].

monbu (文部省), *n.* the Department of Education; the Education(-al) Department. ¶ 文部大臣, the Minister of (State for) Education; the Minister of Public Instruction (佛國等の). —文部次官, the Vice-Minister of Education.

monchaku (悶著), *n.* difficulties; (紛議) dissension; complications.

mondai (問題), *n.* a question; a problem; a subject. —問題外!, (議論の脱線せる時の叫) Question! (問題外に走る, to deviate from the point [subject]. —それは問題外だ, That is not [beside] the question.) —事實《法律》問題, a question of fact 《law》. —時日《趣味》の問題, a question of time 《taste》. —問題の核心, the nucleus of a problem. —問題になる, to come into question.

mondō (問答), *n.* questions and answers; interlocution (對話); catechism (禪宗等の).

mondori (翻筋斗), *n.* a somersault. —翻筋斗打って倒れる, to turn a somersault and fall on the ground.

mōnen (妄念), *n.* ❶ heretical thoughts; evil [immoral; impure] thought. ❷ (執念) a ghost; an uneasy spirit.

mongaikan (門外漢), *n.* an outsider; the man in the street; a stranger (第三者); the laity (素人). —門外漢の意見, lay opinion.

mongen (門限), *n.* the closing-time. —門限に遲れる, to stay away beyond the closing-time; break leave.

mongon (文言), *n.* the contents of a letter; wording.

mōningukōto (モーニング・コート), *n.* a morning coat.

monjin (門人), *n.* a disciple; a pupil; a follower.

monka (門下-生), *n.* a pupil; a disciple. —象山門下の傑物, the ablest of Shōzan's disciples.

monkan (門鑑), *n.* a gate-pass.

monkirigata (紋切形), *n.* ❶ a fixed form; conventionality. ❷ (文句) a set [stereotyped] phrase. —紋切形の嚇文句, a stereotyped form of threat.

monko (門戶), *n.* a gate; a door; an entrance. —滿洲の門戶を開放する, to open the door in Manchuria. ¶ 門戶開放主義, the open-door principle 《policy》.

monku (文句), *n.* ❶ (句) a phrase; an expression; wording (文言). ❷ (言ひぶん) complaint; grievance. —文句を言ふ, to complain *of*; grumble *at*.

monme (匁), *n.* (重量) *monme*; a measure of weight (=.1325 ounces; 3.7565 grammes).

monmō (文盲), *n.* ❶ (文字を知らぬこと) illiteracy; ignorance. ❷ (同上の人) an illiterate.

monnai (門内に), *n.* within a gate. —門内に入る可からず, "No admittance."

mono (もの), *n.* ❶ 〔物〕 a thing; an object. ❷ (物質) matter; substance. ❸ 〔者〕 a person; a man; one. —物の分かる人, a sensible man; a man of sense. —物にならぬ, to come to nothing. —これでどうやら物になった, This is something like. —此は學校の物だ, This belongs to the school. ¶ 大阪者, a man from Ōsaka.

monoageba (物揚場), *n.* a landing-stage [-place].

monoanji (物案じ), *n.* anxiety; pensiveness.

monoarasoi (物爭), *n.* a quarrel; a squabble; a brawl.

monoganashii (物悲しい), *a.* sad; pensive; melancholy.

monogatai (物堅い), *a.* honest; strict; conscientious.

monogatari (物語), *n.* ❶ (話) talking (事); a story; a narration (說話). ❷ a legend (傳說); a fable (寓話); a romance (傳奇). —哀れな《面白い》物語, a sad 《an interesting》 story. ¶ 浦島物語, the Legend of Urashima. —源氏物語, the Genji Romance.

monogataru (物語る), *vt.* to relate; narrate; give an account *of*.

monogokoro (物心), *n.* discretion; sound [mature] judgment. —物心ついてから此方, since I was old enough to know things.

monogoto (物事), *n.* things; an affair; a matter. —物事を苦にする, to take things too seriously.

monogusa (物臭な), *a.* lazy; indolent; sluggish; slothful. ¶ 物臭もの, a lazybones.

monohoshi (物干), *n.* a clothes-dryer; a clothes-horse. —物干に乾す, to hang out on a clothes-dryer. ¶ 物干場, a drying-place. —物干繩《竿》, a clothes-line 《-pole》.

monoii (物言), *n.* ❶ speaking; address; the way of speaking. ❷ (物爭) a quarrel; a dispute; an objection (反對). —物言ひをつける, to object *to*; start an objection; claim a foul (勝負に).

monoimi (物忌する), *vi.* to fast.

monoiri (物入), *n.* expenses; outlay. —物入りが多い, to require great expenses.

monoiu (物言ふ), *v.* to speak; talk. —物言ふ花, a speaking flower; a beautiful young woman.

monokage (物蔭) *n.* a shadow.

monomane (物眞似), *n.* mimicry. —物眞似する, to mimic; ape.

monomi (物見), *n.* ❶ (望樓) a look-out; a watch-tower. ❷ (見物) sight-seeing. —物見高い, curious to see.

monomochi (物持), *n.* a rich person; a man of wealth.

monomonoshii (物物しい), *a.* ❶ (尊大な) stately; imposing; lordly. ❷ (仰山な) pompous; ostentatious. —物々しく警戒する, to guard with great display.

monomorai (物貰), *n.* ❶ (乞食) a beggar; a mendicant. ❷ (麥粒腫) a hordeolum; a sty.

mononareru (物馴れる), *vi.* to get used *to*. ☞ *nareru*. —物馴れた人, a man of experience.

monono (物の), (約) about; some. —ものの半時, for half an hour. —ものの三分も經たぬ内に, in less than three minutes.

monono (ものの), *conj.* though; although. —とは言ふものの, though I say so.

mononofu (武士), *n.* a warrior; a soldier.

monooboe (物覺), *n.* memory.

monooki (物置), *n.* ❶ (部屋) a lumber-room; a store-room; a closet. ❷ (獨立の建物) a warehouse; a shed. ¶ 物置臺, a stand.

monoomoi (物思), *n.* ❶ (心配) anxiety; concern; apprehension. ❷ (思案) thought; meditation. —物思はしげな, pensive. —物思ひに沈む, to muse *on* [*upon*]; brood *on* [*over*]; be sunk [deep; lost] in thought(s).

monooshimi (物吝みする), *a.* stingy; niggardly.

monooto (物音), *n.* a noise; a sound.

monosabishii (物淋しい), *a.* lonely; dreary. —物淋しい夕暮, a lonely evening.

monosashi (物差), *n.* a foot-rule; a rule; a measure.

monosawagashii (物騷しい), *a.* noisy; tumultuous; boisterous.

monoshirazu (物識らず), *n.* an ignorant person; an ignoramus.

monoshiri (物識), *n.* a learned man; a scholar; a man of general information. ¶ 物識り顏, a pedantic air; a knowing look.

monosugoi (物凄い), *a.* ❶ (凄い) ghastly; uncanny; weird. ❷ (恐しい) dreadful; horrible; terrible. —物凄く, weirdly; uncannily; horribly; terribly. —物凄い光景, a terrible [horrible] sight [scene]. —物凄い光を投げる, to cast a lurid light (*on*).

monotaranu (物足らぬ), *vi.* to feel dissatisfied; be unsatisfactory; feel something lacking [wanting].

monotomosenu (物ともせぬ), *vt.* to make nothing *of*; make no account *of*; set at defiance. —…を物ともせずに, despite; in spite *of*; in defiance *of*; in the teeth *of*; making no account *of* (a great enemy).

monouge (慵げな), *a.* indolent; sluggish.

monoui (物憂い), *a.* dreary; indolent; languid. —何をするのも物憂い, to feel too indolent to do anything.

monowakare (物別れになる), ❶ to fail to reach understanding. ❷ to part with enmity [grudge].

monowarai (物笑), *n.* a laughing-stock; ridicule; mockery. —世間の物笑ひとなる, to become the laughing-stock of the world.

monowasure (物忘する), *vi.* to be forgetful; have a short [poor] memory.

monoyawaraka (物柔かな), *a.* soft; mild; gentle. —物柔かに, gently; softly; mildly.

monozuki (物好), *n.* curiosity; inquisitiveness. —物好きな, curious (好奇心); inquisitive (聞きたがり); whimsical. —物好き半分に, just [merely] from curiosity.

Monrō-shugi (モンロー主義), *n.* the Monroe doctrine; Monroeism.

monrui (門壘), *n.* 【蹴球】 the goal. ¶ 門壘手, the goal-keeper.

monsatsu (門札), *n.* (門鑑) a (gate-)pass; (表札) a name-plate.

monseki (問責する), *vt.* to censure; call to account; call in question.

monshi (門齒), *n.* an incisor (tooth).

monshō (紋章), *n.* a crest; a badge; a coat of arms. —菊花の御紋章, the Imperial crest of the chrysanthemum. ¶ 紋章學, heraldry.

montei (門弟), *n.* Ⓢ 門徒. a disciple; a follower; an adherent.

montsuki (紋附), *n.* a garment with the family crest.

monuke (蛻脱の殼), *n.* ❶ exuviæ; a slough. ❷ an empty bed.

monzai (問罪), *n.* accusation; arraignment. —問罪の師, a punitive force. —問罪的態度, an accusatory attitude.

monzeki (門跡), *n.* an Imperial prince in holy orders.

monzen (門前), *n.* the front of a gate. —門前拂ひを食ふ, to be sent away from the door. —門前拂ひを食はす, to refuse to see a caller; drive from the door. —毎朝門前を通る, to pass a person's door every morning.

monzetsu (悶絶する), *vi.* to swoon; faint under mortification.

moppara (專), *ad.* ❶ (主として) chiefly; mainly; principally. ❷ (一心に) intently; devotedly; whole-heartedly. ❸ (全然) wholly; completely; entirely; exclusively. —專らにする, ① (專一にする) ot devote [apply] oneself *to*; be intent *on*. ② (恣にする) to abuse; be despotic *in*. —專ら…を勉强する, to devote oneself to the study *of*; study with all one's heart.

mōra (網羅する), *vt.* to include; comprise; comprehend.

moraigo (貰兒), *n.* an adopted child; a foster-child.

moraimono (貰物), *n.* a present; a gift.

morainaki (貰泣する), *vi.* to weep for company.

moraite (貰手), *n.* a recipient; a suitor (嫁の).

morasu (漏す), *vt.* ❶ (水等を) to let leak; discharge. ❷ (祕密等を) to reveal; divulge; let out. ❸ (脫漏) to omit; skip; forget. —書き洩らす, to forget to write. —口から洩らす, to let anything pass one's lips.

moratoryūmu (支拂延期令), *n.* 【法】 moratorium.

morau (貰ふ), *vt.* ❶ (受ける) to get; receive; obtain. ❷ (…してもらふ) to get [have] a thing done *by*; get another to do a thing *for*; have another do a thing *for*. —妻を貰ふ, to get a wife. —勳章を貰ふ, to be decorated with an order. —靴を修繕して貰ふ, to have [get] one's shoes mended. —私も貰ひたいな, I should like to have it, too.

more (漏), *n.* ❶ (脫落) an omission; an oversight; a slip (手落). ❷ =*mori* (漏). —漏れなく, one and all; all without exception; without any omission. (漏れなく通知する, to leave no person uninformed.)

morekiku (漏聞く), *v.* to overhear; hear casually; hear it said.

moreru (漏·洩れる), *v.* ❶ (水等が) to leak; escape; come in through (光等が). ❷ (祕密が) to leak [ooze] out; transpire; be disclosed [revealed]. ❸ (脫漏) to be omitted; be left out; be neglected. ❹ (感情が) to be expressed; be given vent; appear. —恩賞に漏れる, to be left out in the distribution of rewards.

mōretsu (猛烈), *n.* violence; ferocity; vehemence. **—— -na,** *a.* violent; ferocious; vehement. —猛烈な攻擊, fierce attack. —猛烈な疫病, raging plague. —猛烈な勢で, with terrible energy 《force》. —猛烈に攻撃する, to attack furiously.

mori (守), *n.* ❶ (子の) a nurse; a nursery-maid (保姆). ❷ (番人) a keeper; a care-taker. —子供をよく守する, to take great care of a child.

mori (森), *n.* a wood; a grove (小森).

mori (盛), *n.* filling; swelling (盛上ってゐること). —盛りが宜《惡》い, to give full 《scanty》 measures.

mori (銛), *n.* a harpoon. —銛で突く, [*vt.*] to harpoon.

mori (漏), *n.* leak; leakage. —漏(口)を止める, to stop a leak.

moriagaru (盛上る), *vi.* to rise up; bulge [swell] out.

moriageru (盛上げる), *vt.* ❶ to emboss; relieve. ❷ (物を) to heap up; pile up; accumulate.

moribana (盛花), *n.* flowers arranged in a basket [bowl, &c.].

morikaesu (盛返す), *vt.* to revive; rally; retrieve (身代等を). —勇氣を盛り返す, to regain courage.

moriuta (守唄), *n.* a lullaby; a nursery song; a cradle-song.

moriyaku (守役), *n.* attendance: (人) an attendant; a tutor.

moro (諸), *n.* ❶ (各) each; each one. ❷ (一雙) both; two; double.

mōrō (朦朧と), *ad.* dimly; mistily; indistinctly. —朦朧たる, dim; misty; indistinct; vague.

moroha (諸刃の), *a.* two-edged; double-edged.

morohada (諸肌), *n.* the upper half of the body. —諸肌脱ぐ, to strip oneself to the waist.

moroi (脆い), *a.* ❶ (物の) fragile; brittle; flimsy. ❷ (情の) tender; easily moved; sensitive. —脆い命, frail [fleeting] life. —脆くなる, to become brittle [fragile].

morokko-gawa (モロッコ革), *n.* morocco.

morokoshi (蜀黍), *n.* 【植】 the East Indian millet; the durra.

mōroku (耄碌), *n.* dotage; senility; second childhood. —耄碌する, to dote; be in one's dotage [second childhood]; enter upon one's dotage. ¶ 耄碌婆, a doting old woman.

moromoro (諸の), *a.* ❶ all; every. ❷ (色々の) various; diverse; different.

morote (諸手), *n.* ❶ (左右の手) both hands. ❷ (諸方面) all directions.

morotomo (諸共), *ad.* together *with*; all together.

moru (盛る), *vt.* ❶ (器物に) to help; serve. ❷ (うづ高く) to heap; pile up. ❸ (藥を) to administer. —碁盤の目を盛る, to cut the lines on a checker-board.

moru (漏·洩る), *vi.* to leak; ooze (out). ——, *a.* leaky. —盥が漏る, The tub leaks. —瓦斯が漏れてる, There is a leak of gas.

moruhine (モルヒネ), *n.* morphia; morphine. ¶ モルヒネ注射, a morphine injection.

Morumon (モルモン宗), *n.* Mormonism; the Mormon Church.

morumotto (豚鼠), *n.* 【哺乳】 the marmot.

mosa (猛者), *n.* ❶ a man of courage; a valiant man; a lion. ❷ (田夫) a rustic; a countryman; a peasant.

mōsaikan (毛細管), *n.* a capillary tube; a capillary (vessel).

mosaku (摸索する), *v.* to grope.

mōseiyaku (毛生藥), *n.* a hair-grower.

mōsen (毛氈), *n.* a carpet; a rug. ¶ 毛氈苔, the sundew.

mosha (摸寫), *n.* a facsimile; a copy; a reproduction (複製); a replica (繪畫などの). —摸寫する, to copy; reproduce; make a facsimile *of*. ¶ 摸寫物, a copy; a facsimile.

moshi (若), ❶ (ひょっと) if; in case; in case *of*. ❷ (假りに) supposing that; provided that. —若し失敗したら, if I (should) fail. —若し雨天ならば, in case of bad weather; if it rains.

moshi, moshimoshi (もしもし), *int.* hallo; halloa; I say; please; if you please. —もしもし本局の三百三十三番, Hullo, No. 333, Central.

Mōshi (孟子), *n.* Mengtze; Mencius.

mōshiageru (申上げる), *vt.* ❶ to tell; relate; state. ❷ (白狀) to confess. —申上げます, please, sir; please your honour. —厚く御禮申上げます, I beg to tender my best thanks.

mōshiawase (申合せ), *n.* mutual agreement [arrangement]; mutual [common] consent; appointment. —申合せる, to arrange; agree *upon*; consent; appoint. —申合せた樣に, as if by common consent [by previous arrangement].

mōshibun (申分), *n.* ❶ (申條) an objection. ❷ (缺點) a defect; a blemish; a flaw. —申分のない婿, an ideal son-in-law. —これなら申分がない, This would leave nothing to be desired.

mōshide (申出), *n.* an offer; a proposal; an application (出願).

mōshideru (申出る), *vt.* ❶ (言ひ出る) to claim; ask *for*; apply *for* (願出る). ❷ (提議) to propose; offer (申込); tender; bring forward (提出). —警察へ申出る, to inform [report to] the police. —異議を申出る, to offer an objection *to*.

mōshigo (申兒), *n.* a child born in answer to prayer.

mōshihiraki (申開), *n.* ❶ (辯明) explanation; answer (答辯); excuse (言譯). ❷ (辯護) vindication; defence. —申開きをする, to explain; answer; justify [clear] oneself (*of*); vindicate oneself *from*. —申開きが立つ《立たぬ》. An excuse is admitted 《rejected》.

mōshikaneru (申兼ねる), hard to say. —誠に申兼ねますが, I am really sorry to trouble you, but....

moshikasuruto (若しかすると), *ad.* possibly. —若しかするとさうかも知れぬ, It may possibly be so.

mōshikomi (申込), *n.* 【法】 an offer: a proposal (縁談等の); an application (株式・保險・就職などの); a notice (通告). —株式の申込, an application for shares. —決闘の申込, a challenge (to a duel). —申込に應ずる, to accept a proposal [an offer]; close with an offer. ¶ 申込期限, the last day for application. —申込人, an offerer; a subscriber (株などの); an applicant; a proposer (提案者). —申込書, an application; a letter of application; a request note. —申込用紙, an application form; an application-blank.

mōshikomu (申込む), *v.* to offer; propose; apply *for*; subscribe *for* (株など); enter (抗議). —十株申込む, to subscribe for 10 shares. —試合を申込む, to send a challenge *to*. —會見を申込む, to ask for an interview.

moshikuwa (若くは), *conj.* or.

moshimo (若しも), if; in case. —若しもの場合には, should emergency arise; in case of accident; if the worst [unexpected] should happen. —若しもの覺悟をする, to be prepared for the worst.

mōshin (猛進する), *v.* to rush in; dash forward; push forward.

mōshiokuru (申送る), *v.* to send word; write a letter *to*.

mōshitate (申立), *n.* statement; declaration; testimony (證言). —虛僞の申立, false statement. ¶ 申立人, a declarant. —申立書, a declaration; an account.

mōshitateru (申立てる), *vt.* to state; declare; testify (證言する). —故障を申立てる, to raise an objection; enter a protest. —犯罪の事實を申立てる, to state the facts of a crime.

mōshitsuke (申附), *n.* an order; a command; an appointment (任命). —申附ける, to order; command; appoint.

mōshiukeru (申受ける), *vt.* to receive; accept; have; take; charge. —茶代は一切不申受候, "No gratuities accepted."

mōshiwake (申譯), *n.* ❶ (詫) an excuse; an apology. ❷ (口實) a plea; a pretext. ❸ (辯解) an explanation. —申譯する, to make an excuse; apologize; explain. —申譯ばかりの鼻, an apology for a nose. —ほんの申譯に, as a matter of form. —申譯が立たぬ, not to admit of any excuse. —申譯のない過ち, an inexcusable mistake.

mōshiwatashi (申渡), *n.* a sentence (宣告); a pronouncement (同上); a judgment (判決). —死刑の申渡を受けてゐる, to be under sentence of death.

mōshiwatasu (申渡す), *vt.* ❶ (言渡す) to pronounce [give] (sentence or judgment); pass (judgment or sentence); sentence (a person to imprisonment). ❷ (命ずる) to give order (that); order; bid; tell; announce (告げる). —判決を申渡す, to give judgment.

moshiya (若しや), *ad.* perhaps; perchance; by chance. —若しや…するといけないから, lest; for fear that. (もしや雨が降るといけないから, lest it should rain.)

moshō (喪章), *n.* a mourning-band [badge]; a crape. —喪章をつける, to wear a crape; pin a mourning-band.

mōshō (猛省する), *vt.* to reflect [consider] carefully.

moshu (喪主), *n.* the chief mourner.

mōshū (妄執), *n.* deep resentment.

mōsō (孟宗竹), *n.* 【植】 Phyllostachys mitis (wanghee-cane の類).

mōsō (毛瘡), *n.* 【醫】 sycosis; the barber's itch; chin-whelk.

mosshokushi (沒食子), *n.* a gall-nut. ¶ 沒食子酸, gallic acid.

mosu (燃す), *vt.* ☞ *moyasu*.

mōsu (申す), *vt.* ❶ (言ふ) to say; tell; speak. ❷ (名づける) to name; call. ☞ *iu* (言ふ).

mosukoshi (も少し), *ad.* a little more (分量); a little longer (時間). —も少しで, all but; almost; nearly.

mosurin (モスリン), *n.* mousseline; muslin.

mo-suru (摸する), *vt.* to imitate; model; counterfeit.

mosuso (裳), *n.* the skirt of a

garment; a train (婦人服の).

mōtā (發動機), *n.* a motor. ¶ モーター・ボート, a motor-boat.

motageru (擡げる), *vt.* to uplift; lift; raise. ☞ *taitō* (擡頭).

motarasu (齎す), *vt.* to bring; carry; bear. —好結果を齎す, to bring [lead to] a good result.

motareru (もたれる), *vi.* ❶ (凭る) to lean *against* [*on*]; rest *against*; recline *on*. ❷ (食物が) to sit [lie] heavy (on the stomach). —ソーファに凭れかゝる, to loll on a sofa.

motaseru (持たせる), *vt.* ❶ (取らせる) to give; let a person have [take]. ❷ (携へさす) to make a person carry. ❸ (凭れかく) to lean [rest] *against* [*on*]; loll *on* (頭・四肢等を). ❹ (保持) to keep; preserve. —店を持たせる, to set a person up in business [trade]. —魚を鹽で保たせる, to preserve a fish with salt. —土産物を持たせて (使に) やる, to send a person with a present *to*.

moteamasu (持餘す), *v.* to be unable to manage; cannot do *with*; be worried [embarrassed] *with*. —仕事を持餘す, to have more work on hand than one can manage. ¶ 持餘し者, a source of trouble; a troublesome person.

moteasobi (玩, 弄), *n.* ❶ (玩具) a plaything; a toy. ❷ (弄み) mockery; ridicule; amusement.

moteasobu (玩・弄ぶ), *vt.* ❶ (手に) to play *on*; twiddle (*with*). ❷ (遊物にする) to play *with*; make sport [plaything] *of*. ❸ (愚弄する) to trifle *with*; make a fool *of*. ❹ (なぐさむ) to amuse oneself *with*. ❺ (自由に扱ふ) to handle easily. —學問を玩ぶ, to make a plaything of learning. —法を弄ぶ, to make a bad use of law. —婦人の貞操を玩ぶ, to trifle with a woman's virtue.

motehayasu (持囃す), *vt.* to belaud; sing [chant] the praises *of*; extol. —其の功をもて囃す, to sing a person's merits.

motenashi (持成), *n.* ❶ (待遇) treatment. ❷ (饗應) entertainment; a dinner. —懇ろな待遇(もてなし), a warm [kind] treatment. —もてなしのよい女主人, a hospitable hostess.

motenasu (持成す), *vt.* ❶ to treat; receive; welcome. ❷ (馳走) to entertain; regale; fête.

moteru (持てる), *vi.* ❶ (保つ) to keep; last; continue. ❷ (はやさる) to be praised; be talked much *of*; be popular. ❸ (優遇さる) to be welcome; get into favour. —女に持てる, to be popular with women. —非常に持てる, to be welcome as the flowers in May.

moto (本, 元, 原, 基), *n.* ❶ the origin (起り, 素性); the source (源); the root (根原); the cause (原因); the beginning (初). ❷ (根柢) the basis; the base. ❸ the capital (資本); the principal (元金). ❹ (元價) the cost [prime] price. —, *ad.* formerly. —禍の元, the root of all evil. —元から, from the beginning [the first; the outset]. —元の通り, as before. —元の儘に, as it was. —原狀(もと)へ戻す, to restore to the original state. —元を糺す, to go to [get at] the root. **—-no,** *a.* ❶ (原初の) original. ❷ (故の) the late. ❸ (從來の) the old. ❹ (以前の) former; ex- [*prep.*]; late (前). —元の京都府知事, the ex-governor of Kyōto Prefecture. —故の中江先生, the late Mr. Nakae. —まだ元の所に居る, to be still at the old place.

moto (許), under. —親の許で, under one's parents.

moto (釀母), *n.* yeast; ferment.

mōto (毛頭), *ad.* =***sukoshimo***.

motochō (元帳), *n.* a ledger. —元帳へ移記する, to enter in a ledger; post up accounts.

motode (元手, 資本), *n.* capital; funds.

motodori (髻), *n.* a knot (of hair).

motogome (後裝銃), *n.* a breech-loader; a breech-loading rifle.

motoharai (元拂), *n.* advance payment. ¶ 元拂運賃, advance freight.

motoi (基), *n.* ❶ (基礎) the basis; the foundation. ❷ (根元) the origin; the source; the root; the bottom; the cause (原因). —富國强兵の基, the basis of national wealth and military strength.

motoire (元入する), *vt.* to invest *in*. ☞ *tōshi* (投資する).

motokata (元方), *n.* ❶ (資本主) a financier. ❷ (製造元) a producer; a manufacturer. ❸ (卸屋) a wholesale dealer [merchant]; a wholesale store (店).

motokin (元金), *n.* the principal (貸借の); the capital (資本).

motome (求, 需), *n.* ❶ a demand (要求); a request (要請). ❷ (註文) an order. —需に應ずる, to meet a demand; comply with a request. —需に應じて, by request.

motomeru (求・需める), *vt.* ❶ (要求) to demand; claim; require. ❷ (追求) to seek; search *after* [*for*]; pursue (知識等). ❸ (希求) to ask *for*; wish *for*; beg; want;

desire; request. ❹ (購求) to buy; purchase; obtain (獲る). ❺ (見出す) to find. —再考を求める, to ask for reconsideration. —…の和を求める, to find the sum *of*. —求めて事を破る, to break it up on purpose.

motomoto (もともと), *ad.* from the first; originally.

motone (元價), *n.* the cost [prime; original] price.

motoni (下に), *prep.* under; at. —一撃の下に, at a blow. —號令の下に, at the word of command. —彈丸雨飛の下に, under a shower of bullets.

motoru (悖·戻る), *vi.* to be contrary *to*; go [run] counter *to*; depart [deviate] *from*. —正義に戻る, to deviate from justice.

motoyori (素·固より), *ad.* ❶ (元來) originally; from the first [outset]. ❷ (無論) of course; certainly; as a matter of course [fact].

motoyui (元結), *n.* a paper-string (for tying the hair); a paper-fillet.

motozuku (基く), *vi.* ❶ (起因) to originate *in*; come [spring; rise] *from*; be due *to*. ❷ (基礎となる) to be founded [based; grounded] *on* [*upon*]. ❸ (準據) to conform *to*; act *on*. —天佑に基く, to owe it [to be due] to God's protection. —事實に基いて, based on fact.

motsu (持つ), *vt.* ❶ (手に) to have; take; hold. ❷ (所有) to have; possess; own. ❸ (携帶) to carry; bear; have *with* [*about*]. ❹ (受持つ) to take [have] charge *of*; take in one's charge; bear (負擔). ——, *vi.* (保つ) to keep; hold; last. —十年間保つ, to keep [be good] for ten years. —株を持つ, to hold shares. —費用の半分を持つ, to bear [stand] half the expenses. —天氣がこれで持てばよい, I hope the weather will keep like this. —油は今夜中はもたう, The oil will last through the night. —病人は夏中もたうか, Can the invalid hold out through the summer?

motsurasu (縺らす), *vt.* ❶ (物を) to tangle; knot; mat (毛等を). ❷ (紛糾) to entangle; perplex; complicate.

motsure (縺), *n.* ❶ (亂雜) tangle. ❷ (紛糾) entanglement; complication; perplexity. ¶ 縺れ髮, tangled [tousled; matted] hair.

motsureru (縺れる), *vi.* ❶ to be in a tangle; be knotted. ❷ (紛糾) to be entangled; be complicated. —絲が縺れる, The thread [string] gets tangled. —話が縺れる, The story becomes complicated.

mottai (勿體), *n.* an air of importance; airs; pompousness; haughtiness. —勿體ぶる, to stand upon one's dignity; give oneself airs; assume [put on] an air of importance. —勿體をつける, to attach importance.

mottainai (勿體ない), *a.* ❶ (不敬) impious; profane; unthankful. ❷ (不經濟) wasteful; uneconomical. —あら勿體ない, Oh, what a waste!

motte (以て), *prep.* ❶ (道具) with. ❷ (方便) by; by means [dint] *of*; through; per. ❸ (理由) for; on account of. —使を以て, per messenger. —人を以て賴む, to ask a person through another. —千を以て數へる, to count by the thousand.

mottekoi (持ってこいの), *a.* ideal; suitable *for*; the very. —市長に持ってこいである, He is the very man for a mayor. —持って來いの船日和だ, It is the ideal weather for sailing.

mottekuru (持って來る), *vt.* to bring; fetch (取って); get (同上).

mottemawatta (持って廻った), *a.* ❶ (迂遠) roundabout; circuitous. ❷ (附會の) distorted; far-fetched; forced. —持って廻った解釋, a far-fetched interpretation.

motte-no-hoka (以ての外), *ad.* ❶ unexpectedly; contrary to one's expectation; against one's anticipation. ❷ (思ひもよらぬ) out of the question. —以ての外の, ① (意外) unexpected; unanticipated; unusual (異常). ② (不條理の) unreasonable; absurd; preposterous; most reprehensible (不都合).

motteyuku (持って行く), *vt.* ❶ (携帶) to take with one; carry with one. ❷ (さらって行く) to carry off [away]; take off. ❸ (物をどこへ) to take *to*.

motto (もっと), *ad.* more; much [still] more; any longer (時間). —もっとゐらっしゃい, Stay a little longer. —昨日はもっと暖かでした, It was still warmer yesterday.

mottō (標語), *n.* a motto.

mottomo (尤も), (併し) but; however; though; (如何にも) indeed. —尤もな, reasonable; natural; right. —尤もらしい議論, a plausible argument. —尤もである, to be quite reasonable [natural; right]. —尤もらしく話す, to talk plausibly. —尤もらしい虚言をつく, to tell specious lies. —成程御尤もです, Well, you are right.

—君のさう云ふのも尤もだ, You may well say so.

mottomo (最も), *ad.* most; extremely. —最も遠い, most distant; remotest; farthest.

moya (靄), *n.* a mist; a haze.

moya (母屋), *n.* the principal building; the main house; the homestead.

moyai (催合), *n.* undertaking in common; being joint: a joint enterprise. —催合ひで買ふ, to buy jointly. —催合ひでする, to hold [have] in common; share *with*; pool. ¶ 催合井戸, a common well; a well for common use. —催合壁, 【建】 a party-wall.

moyaizuna (舫索), *n.* a mooring [slip]-rope; a painter (端舟の).

moyashi (萌), *n.* ❶ (麥芽) malt; grist (釀造用の). ❷ (季節外發芽の) artificially-grown vegetables.

moyasu (燃す), *v.* ❶ to burn. ❷ (點火) to kindle; light; fire. —火を燃す, to make the fire burn. —嫉妬《怒》の焰を燃す, to burn with jealousy 《wrath》.

moyau (舫ふ), *vt.* ❶ (舟と舟を) to connect (a ship) to another. ❷ (舟をつなぐ) to moor; secure a vessel *in* 《*to*》.

moyō (模樣), *n.* ❶ (彩紋) a pattern; a design; a figure. ❷ (樣子) look; aspect; signs. ❸ (狀態) state; condition; circumstances; situation. —模樣のある, marked with pattern; inwrought (織物の). —模樣を置く, to put on a pattern; pattern [*vt.*]; print [*vt.*]. —降りさうな模樣だ, It threatens to [looks like] rain. ¶ 古代模樣, an ancient design.

moyogi (萌黃), *n.* light [yellowish] green.

moyori (最寄), *n.* the neighbourhood; the vicinity. —最寄りの交番, the nearest police-box.

moyōshi (催), *n.* ❶ (會) a meeting; an entertainment (餘興); a reception (歡迎會). ❷ (主催) auspices; instance. ❸= *chōkō* (徵候). —報知新聞社の催で, under the auspices of the *Hōchi Shinbun*.

moyōsu (催す), *v.* ❶ (開催) to hold; give. ❷ (促す) to threaten; brew; call. ❸ (感ず) to feel. ❹ (兆す) to show signs *of*. —會を催す, to hold a meeting. —眠氣を催す, to feel drowsy [sleepy].

mōzen (猛然), *ad.* dashingly; resolutely; determinedly.

mozō (摸造), *n.* imitation; reproduction (複製). —摸造する, to imitate; model; counterfeit (贋造); reproduce (複製). ¶ 摸造品, an imitation; a counterfeit; a spurious article (僞造品). —摸造革, imitation leather; leatherette. —摸造者, an imitator; a counterfeiter. —摸造紙, Japanese vellum.

mōzō (妄想), *n.* chimera; fancy; delusion. ¶ 妄想家, a dreamer.

mozu (百舌), *n.* 【鳥】 the (bull-headed) shrike.

mozuku (海蘊), *n.* 【植】 Cladosiphon decipiens.

mu (無), *n.* nothing; naught; non-existence. ☞ *mu-nisuru*.

mube (宜), *a.* natural (當然); right (正當); well. —宜なり其美を天下に擅にするや, Well may its beauty be the greatest in the country. —むべこそ彼等の末斯くなるは, No wonder that they should come to such an end.

mubi (夢寐), *n.* sleep. —夢寐の間も忘れぬ, not to forget even in sleep.

mubō (無謀), *n.* indiscretion; imprudence; thoughtlessness. ——**na**, *a.* indiscreet; imprudent; thoughtless. —無謀な事をする, to leap in the dark; play with edged tools (未熟の身で).

mubyō (無病の), *a.* healthy; sound. —無病息災の, in sound health; healthy and sound; hale and hearty.

mucha (無茶な), *a.* ❶ (不道理) unreasonable; absurd; nonsensical. ❷ (無秩序) disordered; confused; topsyturvy. —無茶苦茶になる, ① to turn topsyturvy; be out of order. ② to become rude. —無茶苦茶に擲る, to strike wildly.

muchakuriku (無著陸で), without landing [alighting]. ¶ 無著陸飛行, a no-stop flight.

muchi (鞭), *n.* ❶ a whip; a lash (索の); a horse-whip (馬の). ❷ (笞) a rod; a ferule; a pointer (物を指す). ☞ *muchiutsu*.

muchi (無智), *n.* ignorance; illiteracy (無學). —無智の, ignorant; illiterate; simple (單純); unenlightened (蒙昧の).

muchi (無恥), *n.* impudence; immodesty; shamelessness. —無恥の, shameless; immodest; unashamed.

muchikaku (無知覺), *n.* insensibility; non-perception.

muchin (無賃の), *a.* free; free of charge. —無賃で, rent-free; without charge; gratis. ¶ 無賃乘車券, a free pass. —無賃制限外手荷物, excess luggage.

muchitsujo (無秩序), *n.* disorder; confusion; chaos.

muchiutsu (鞭つ), *vt.* ❶ to whip; lash; flog (罪人等を). ❷ (折檻) to castigate; chastise; trounce. ❸ (鞭撻) to lash; spur [goad] on; urge; encourage.

muchū (夢中), *n.* ❶ (熱中) absorption; engrossment; immersion. ❷ (無我) ecstasy (嬉しくて); delirium (同上); intoxication (心酔). —夢中になる, ① to become absorbed *in*; be engrossed [immersed] *in*; be transported. ② to lose one's senses; be beside oneself. (喜んで夢中になる, to become delirious with joy. —夢中になって聴く, to listen with rapt attention.)

muda (無駄な), *a.* unavailing; futile; ineffectual. —無駄にする, to render useless; throw away. —無駄骨を折る, to labour in vain; exert oneself to no purpose. —無駄足を踏む, to go on a fool's [sleeveless] errand; call on a person in vain. —無駄話をする, to talk idly; gossip; tattle. —無駄口を叩く, to spend [waste] one's breath.

mudabana (空花), *n.* Ⓢ あだ花. a fruitless [an abortive] flower; a neuter flower.

mudai (無代で), free of charge [cost]; cost-free; gratis.

mudan (無斷), *ad.* ❶ (無通知) without notice. ❷ (無許可) without permission [leave]. —無斷で使ふ, to make free *with*. ¶ 無斷缺席, absence without notice.

mudazukai (浪費), *n.* waste of money; useless expense.

muden (無電), *n.* radio. ☞ *musen*. ¶ 無電愛好者, a radio-fan.

mudō (無道), *n.* wickedness.

mueki (無益な), *a.* useless; of no use; unserviceable. —無益に爭ふ, to fight to no purpose.

muen (無煙の), *a.* smokeless. ¶ 無煙火藥, smokeless powder. —無煙炭, smokeless coal; anthracite.

muen (無緣の), *a.* ❶ (緣のない) without relation. ❷ (弔ふ者のない) neglected; deserted. ¶ 無緣墓, a neglected gravestone.

mufū (無風), *n.* a dead calm; 【氣象】 calm. ¶ 無風帶, calm latitudes; doldrums.

mufunbetsu (無分別), *n.* indiscretion; inconsideration; rashness (向見ず). —…する樣な無分別ではない, to know better than to…; be too prudent to. **——-na,** *a.* indiscreet; inconsiderate; rash. —無分別な男, an indiscreet fellow.

muga (無我), *n.* ❶ (私なきこと) non-ego; unselfishness; disinterestedness. ❷ (無心) absent-mindedness; absence of mind; absorption (夢中). —無我無中で, in a trance; in ecstasies.

mugai (無蓋の), *a.* open; uncovered; roofless. ¶ 無蓋馬車, an open carriage.

mugai (無害の), *a.* harmless; innocent; innocuous; inoffensive.

mugaku (無學), *n.* ignorance; illiteracy. ¶ 無學者, an illiterate. —無學文盲 (人), the ignorant and unlettered.

mugei (無藝の), *a.* unaccomplished.

mugen (夢幻), *n.* dreams and phantasms; visions. ¶ 夢幻樂, 【音】 fantasia; fantasy. —夢幻劇, a fantastic play; an extravaganza. —夢幻境, ecstasy.

mugen (無限の), *a.* infinite; (無制限の) unlimited; boundless; (無盡藏の) inexhaustible; (永遠の) eternal; endless. —無限大の, infinite; infinitely great. —無限小の, infinitesimal; infinitely small. —無限に, infinitely; boundlessly; unlimitedly.

mugessha (無月謝の), *a.* free. —無月謝で, tuition free; free of tuition-fee. ¶ 無月謝學校, a free school.

mugi (麥), *n.* the wheat (小麥); the corn (同上); the barley (大麥); the oat (燕麥); the rye (裸麥). ¶ 麥畑, a wheat-field; a corn-field. —麥の穗, a barley (wheat) ear.

mugiko (麥粉), *n.* wheat flour; barley flour.

mugiwara (麥稈), *n.* wheat (barley) straw. ¶ 麥藁帽子, a straw hat. —麥稈眞田, straw-plait; straw-braid.

mugiyu (麥湯), *n.* hot barley water.

mugiwaratonbo (紅蜻), *n.* 【昆】 Orthetrum japonicum.

mugoi (酷い), *a.* ❶ (殘酷な) cruel; merciless; brutal. ❷ (痛はしい) pitiful.

mugoku (酷く), *ad.* ❶ cruelly; mercilessly; brutally. ❷ pitifully.

mugon (無言), *n.* silence; muteness. —無言の行, silent austerities. ¶ 無言劇, a pantomime.

mugotarashii (酷たらしい), *a.* shocking; horrible; cruel; pitiful.

mugura (土龍), *n.* the mole.

mugura (葎), *n.* the burweed; the goose-grass.

muhaitō (無配當), *n.* non-dividend.

muhi (無比の), *a.* matchless; unparalleled; unequalled. —世界無比の國體, a national constitution unparalleled in the world. —東洋無比の良港, the finest harbour in the East.

muhitsu (無筆), *n.* illiteracy.

muhō (無法の), *a.* (亂暴) lawless; outrageous; (無理, 法外) unreasonable; (法外) extravagant; exorbitant. —無法な行爲, a lawless act. —無法な事をいふ, to say something unreasonable; talk unreasonably. ¶ 無法者, an outrageous fellow; a rowdy.

muhon (謀叛), *n.* ❶ (叛亂) revolt; rebellion; insurrection. ❷ (反逆) treason. ❸ (陰謀) conspiracy. —謀叛する; 謀叛を起す, to rebel [revolt] *against*; rise in revolt; raise a rebellion; conspire *against*. ¶ 謀叛人, a traitor; a rebel; an insurgent.

muhōshin (無方針の), *a.* unplanned; unprincipled.

muhōshū (無報酬の), *a.* gratuitous; gratis. —無報酬で, gratuitously; gratis; without recompense [consideration].

mui (無位), *n.* having no rank. —無位無官の, plain.

mui (無異), *n.* =*bui* (無異).

muimi (無意味の), *a.* meaningless; senseless; insignificant; nonsensical; absurd. —無意味な事をいふ, to talk nonsense. —無意味の生活を送る, to lead a senseless life.

muin (無韻の), *a.* unrhymed. ¶ 無韻詩, a blank verse.

muishiki (無意識の), *a.* unconscious. —無意識に, unconsciously. ¶ 無意識行動, an unconscious action.

mujaki (無邪氣な), *a.* innocent; artless; naïve.

muji (無地の), *a.* plain; unfigured. ¶ 無地羅紗, plain (woollen) cloth.

muji (無事), *n.* =*buji*.

mujihi (無慈悲な), *a.* merciless; pitiless; heartless.

mujin (無盡), *n.* ❶ (無限) inexhaustibleness. ❷ (頼母子) mutual credit. —無盡に當る, to gain a prize in the mutual credit lottery. ¶ 無盡講, a mutual credit [loan] society.

mujina (狢), *n.* the (Japanese) raccoon-dog (with a black tail-tip in summer). —一つ穴の狢, birds of a feather.

mujinzō (無盡藏の), *a.* inexhaustible; unfailing.

mujitsu (無實の), *a.* false; untrue. —無實の罪に陷[おとしい]れる, to bring a false charge *against*. —無實の罪を被せられる, to be falsely charged.

mujō (無上の), *a.* the supreme; the highest; consummate. —無上の幸福, supreme happiness. —人生無上の快樂, the foremost of all human pleasures.

mujō (無常), *n.* uncertainty; transiency; frailty. —無常の人世, a frail life. —世の無常を悟る, to feel [awake to] the transiency of the world.

mujō (無情の), *a.* heartless; unfeeling; cold [hard]-hearted.

mujōken (無條件の), *a.* unqualified; unconditional; absolute.

mujōyaku (無條約國), *n.* a non-treaty country.

mujun (矛盾), *v.* contradiction; inconsistency. —— **-suru**, *v.* to conflict *with*; be contradictory; be inconsistent *with*. —矛盾せる, contradictory; inconsistent; illogical. —陳述と矛盾する, to conflict with a statement. ¶ 矛盾律, the law of contradiction.

mukachi (無價値の), *a.* worthless; valueless; paltry.

mukade (蜈蚣), *n.* the centipede.

mukae (迎), *n.* ❶ going to meet [receive]. ❷ (人) a person sent to meet 《invite》 another. —迎へにやる, to send a person for (him). —迎へに行く, to go to meet (him).

mukaeru (迎へる), *vt.* ❶ (出迎ふ) to go out to meet. ❷ (歡迎する) to welcome; receive; greet. ❸ (招待) to invite. ❹ (聘する) to engage. —新年を迎へる, to greet the New Year. —妻を迎へる, to take a wife. —夫の歸りを迎へる, to welcome a husband home.

mukaezake (迎酒), *n.* a drink in the morning after a debauch; a hair of the dog that bit one.

mukai (向), *n.* the opposite side [place]. ☞ *mukō*.

mukaiau (向合ふ), *vi.* to be opposite *to*; face each other. ☞ *mukiau*. —向ひ合って, *vis-à-vis*; face to face.

mukaiawase (向合せ), *n.* facing each other. —向合せの席, *vis-a-vis* seats. —向合せに坐る, to sit *vis-à-vis*; sit opposite him.

mukaikaze (逆風), *n.* a head [contrary; an adverse] wind.

mukamuka (むかむかする), *vi.* ❶ (吐氣) to feel sick [nausea]. ❷ (怒氣) to get excited; swell with anger.

mukan (無冠の), *a.* uncrowned.

mukankaku (無感覺の), *a.* insensitive; callous; numb. —無感覺になる, to become numb.

mukankei (無關係の), *a.* unrelated; unconcerned; unconnected. —無關係である, to have no connection [relation] *with*; have nothing to do *with*; have no hand *in*. —問題と無關係の議論, an argument foreign [irrelevant] to the question.

mukanshin (無關心の), *a.* disinterested; unconcerned; indifferent.

mukanshō (無干涉), *n.* non-interference; non-intervention; *laissez-faire* 〔佛〕. ¶ 無干涉主義, *laissez-faire* [let-alone] policy.

mukappara (むかッ腹), *n.* anger; passion; rage. —むかッ腹を立てる, to take offence; fly into a passion; cut up rough.

mukashi (昔), *n.* ancient [old] times; remote ages; antiquity. —, *ad.* once upon a time; long, long ago; in the days of yore. —昔々; 今は昔, once upon a time; long, long ago. —昔ながらの小漁村, a small fishing village as it was long ago.

mukashibanashi (昔噺), *n.* an old tale; a fairy-tale (お伽噺); a fable (寓話).

mukashifū (昔風の), *a.* old-fashioned; antiquated.

mukashikatagi (昔氣質の), *a.* of the old school; old-fashioned. —昔氣質の親爺, an old fogy.

mukashimono (昔者), *n.* ❶ (老人) an old person. ❷ (昔氣質の) an old-spirited [-fashioned] person; a fogy.

mukashinajimi (昔馴染), *n.* one's old crony (友人); one's old love (情人).

mukatsuku (むかつく), *vi.* to feel [turn] sick; retch; revolt (at sight of). —, *a.* nauseous; queasy; sick. —見た丈けでもむかつく, The sight turns my stomach; My stomach turns at the sight.

mukatte (向って), *prep.* ❶ (指して) towards; for; in the direction of; to. ❷ (逆って) against; in the teeth of. ❸ (對して) at; to; before (前で); opposite (向合って). —...へ向って行く, to set one's face *to* [*towards*]; make *for*. —主に向って弓を引く, to rebel against one's master. —風に向って航行する, to sail in the wind's eye [teeth of the wind]; run against the wind. —向って右から三番目, the third on the right as you face it.

mukau (向ふ), *v.* ❶ (面す) to face [front] (*towards*); be opposite; look upon. ❷ (抗す) to face; oppose. ❸ (赴く) (*a*) to proceed *to*; go *to*; start *for*; 【航】 sail [steer; bear up] *for*: (*b*) to turn; tend. ❹ (近づく) to approach; draw [come] near. ☞ *mukō* (向). —向ふ所敵なし, to carry all before one. — 人心の嚮ふ所を察する, to observe the trend of the popular mind.

mukei (無形の), *a.* abstract (抽象的); spiritual (精神的); incorporeal (無體の); formless (同上). —無形の財產, incorporeal property.

mukei (無稽の), *a.* unfounded; groundless; baseless; absurd. —無稽の談, an unfounded story; a fabrication.

mukeiken (無經驗), *n.* inexperience; want of experience. —無經驗の爲に失敗する, to fail through lack of experience. ¶ 無經驗者, an inexperienced person; a green hand.

mukekka (無結果), *n.* resultlessness; fruitlessness; failure.

mukeru (向ける), *vt.* ❶ (振向ける) (*a*) to turn *to*; direct *to*; bend *to*: (*b*) (充當) to appropriate. ❷ (差向ける) to send *to*; direct *to*. ❸ (銃砲を) to aim *at*; point *at*; train *upon*. —歩を向ける, to direct [bend; turn] one's steps *to* [*towards*]. —ピストルを向ける, to point a pistol *at*. —大砲を向ける, to train a gun *upon*.

mukeru (剝ける), *vi.* to come off; peel off.

mukesseki (無缺席), *n.* regular attendance; non-absence. ¶ 無缺席者, an non-absentee; one regular in attendance.

muketsu (無缺の), *a.* perfect; whole.

muki (向), *n.* ❶ (方向) direction. ❷ (家の) aspect; exposure. ❸ (適合性) suitableness; adaptability. ❹ (性向) turn; inclination. —向きのよい《惡い》(商品の), marketable; salable 《unmarketable; unsalable》. —田舍向きの, suitable [fit] for the country. —北向きの家, a house with a northern aspect; a house facing the north. —右に向きをかへ!, (號令) Right form!

muki (異氣になる), to become excited. —異氣になって怒る, to be hot with anger.

muki (無期の), *a.* unlimited; indefinite. ¶ 無期延期, indefinite postponement; adjournment *sine die.*

muki (無機の), *a.* inorganic. ¶ 無機化學, inorganic chemistry. —無機體, an inorganic body.

mukiau (向合ふ), *v.* ❶ to be opposite *to*; face each other. ❷ (對坐) to sit face to face. —向合はす, to set [lay] opposite each other; confront.

mukidashi (剝出しの), *a.* ❶ (裸) naked; bare. ❷ (露骨)

open; frank; unreserved. —事實を剝出しに述べる, to state a fact without reserve.

mukidasu (剝出す), *vt.* to show; lay bare. —歯をむきだす, to show one's teeth.

mukigen (無期限の), *a.* limitless; unlimited; indefinite.

mukimei (無記名の), *a.* unregistered; uninscribed; unsigned (投票); secret (同上).

mukimi (剝身), *n.* stripped shellfish.

mukin-gyūnyū (無菌牛乳), *n.* sterilized milk.

mukiryoku (無氣力の), *a.* spiritless; nerveless; languid.

mukitsuke (向附けに), *ad.* to one's face; in one's presence.

mukizu (無瑕の), *a.* flawless; spotless; perfect.

mukkuri (むっくり), *ad.* (突然) suddenly. —むっくりした, (丸々した) plump. (むっくりした顔, a plump face.)

muko (婿), *n.* a son-in-law.

muko (無辜の), *a.* innocent; harmless. —無辜の民, innocent people.

mukō (向), *n.* ❶ (向う側) the other [opposite] side. ❷ (先方) the other party. —向う一年間, for a year to come; for the next year [twelvemonth]. —向う三軒兩隣, the houses in the immediate neighbourhood; neighbouring houses; opposite and next door neighbours. —向うの丘, that [the] hill over there; yonder hill. —遙か向うに, in the distance; far off [away]. —海の向うに, across [over] the ocean [sea]. —向うを張る, to set up *against*; vie *with*; compete *with*. —向う三日間臨時休業, "Closed for the next three days." ¶ 向河岸, the opposite bank.

mukō (無效), *n.* 【法】 invalidity; nullity. —— **-no**, *a.* 【法】 void; invalid; null: inoperative; of no effect. —無效の契約, a void agreement [contract]. —無效にする《なる》, to make 《become》 void; invalidate 《be invalidated》.

mukōhachimaki (向鉢卷), *n.* a rolled towel tied round the head with the knot in front. —向鉢卷する, to tie a rolled towel round the head. —向鉢卷になる, to brace oneself for an effort; gird up the loins.

mukōkizu (向傷), *n.* a wound in front [on the forehead]

mukōmizu (向見ずの), *a.* rash; headlong; reckless. —向見ずの事をする, to act rashly; commit a rash act.

mukon (無根の), *a.* groundless; baseless; unfounded.

mukōzune (向脛), *n.* the shin.

muku (無垢の), *a.* pure; spotless; innocent.

muku (向く), *v.* ❶ (轉向) to turn. ❷ (傾く) to tend *towards*. ❸ (面す) to face; front; look *upon* 《*towards*》. ❹ (適す) to suit; be suitable *for*. —軍人に向く, to be suited [cut out] for the military profession. —向いて來る (運が), to turn round; turn in one's favour.

muku (剝く), *vt.* to peel; skin; pare (刃物で); husk (籾など); strip off.

mukuchi (無口の), *a.* taciturn; reticent; silent.

mukudori (椋鳥), *n.* ❶【鳥】 the grey starling. ❷ (田舍者) a bumpkin; a pigeon.

mukuge (木槿), *n.* 【植】 the rose of Sharon; the althæa-frutex.

mukuge (毳毛), *n.* down; fluff.

mukui (報, 酬), *n.* ❶ (報復) retribution; punishment. ❷ (報償) recompense; compensation; reward. —惡行の報い, the fruit of evil deeds. —報いとして, ① in retribution *for*. ② in reward *for*; in requital *of*.

mukuinu (尨犬), *n.* a shaggy dog.

mukuiru (報·酬いる), *v.* ❶ (返報) to retaliate (報復); requite; return. ❷ (報償) to recompense; compensate; reward.

mukumi (浮腫), *n.* dropsy; œdema. —浮腫が全身に出る, to suffer from dropsy all over.

mukumu (浮腫む), *vi.* to swell; become dropsical [bloated].

mukumuku (尨尨), *ad.* ❶ (肥えた狀) buxomly. ❷ (うごめく狀) squirmingly; wrigglingly; ❸ (毳などの) shaggily. —むくむくした, plump.

mukyōiku (無教育の), *a.* uneducated; illiterate. ¶ 無教育者, an illiterate; uneducated people.

mukyū (無給の), *a.* unpaid; unsalaried; non-stipendiary.

mukyū (無窮の), *a.* eternal (時); infinite (時·空間·數量など); boundless.

mumei (無名), *n.* ❶ (名なし) namelessness; bearing no name; anonymity (又不明). ❷ (有名でない) obscurity; insignificance. —無名の手紙, an anonymous letter. —無名の一青年, a youth to fame unknown. —無名の作家, a nameless novelist; an obscure writer. —金五圓無名氏寄贈, 5 *yen* contributed anonymously. ¶ 無名兵士, unknown warriors. —

無名指, the ring-finger.

mumei (無銘の), *a.* unsigned; without the maker's name.

mumenkyo (無免許の), *a.* unlicensed; without a licence [diploma]. —無免許の歯醫者, an unlicensed dentist.

mumi (無味の), *a.* tasteless; flat; uninteresting; dry (as dust) (乾燥の); prosaic; insipid.

mumyō (無明の), *a.* lightless; obscure; dark. —無明の暗, dark ignorance.

munadaka (胸高に), *ad.* breast-high. —帶を胸高に締める, to tie a sash about the breast.

munage (胸毛), *n.* breast-hairs; hairs on the breast; feathers on the breast (鳥の).

munagi (棟木), *n.* a ridge-timber [-beam]; a roof-timber.

munagura (胸倉), *n.* the breast of a coat. —胸倉を取る, to seize a person by the breast of his coat.

munagurushii (胸苦しい), *a.* oppressed in one's breast; hard to breathe (息苦しい).

munahaba (胸幅), *n.* breadth of the chest. —胸幅が廣い《狹い》, to be broad 《narrow》 in the chest.

munaita (胸板), *n.* a breast-bone (胸骨).

munasaki (胸先), *n.* the breast; the chest; the pit (of the stomach). —胸先へ差し込む, to feel oppressed in the chest.

munasawagi (胸騒ぎする), *v.* to feel uneasy; be in a flutter; feel fluttered.

munashii (空しい), *a.* ❶ (空虛) empty; vacant; blank. ❷ (無痕) without any trace [vestige; evidence]; traceless. ❸ (無駄) useless; ineffectual; void. ❹ (缺乏) destitute *of*; in want *of*; short. ❺ (死亡) dead; lifeless; breathless.

munashiku (空しく), *ad.* in vain; to no end [purpose]; fruitlessly. —手を空しくして, with empty hands; without any business. —空しく日を送る, to spend one's days in idleness.

munayake (胸燒), *n.* 【醫】heartburn; hot coppers (酒後の). —胸燒けがする, to have heartburn.

munazan (胸算 -用), *n.* mental arithmetic [calculation]; rough estimation (概算).

mune (旨), *n.* ❶ (心, 意思) intention; mind. ❷ (趣, 趣旨) the effect; the purport; the point. ❸ (命令) command; order. ❹ (主義) principle; an object (目的). —…の旨を報告する, to report to the effect that....

mune (胸), *n.* ❶ (胸部) the breast; the chest; the bosom (懷). ❷ (心中) the heart; the mind; conscience (良心). ❸ (度量) generosity. —胸が惡い, to feel sick *at*; keck *at* (えづく). —胸がすく, ① to feel refreshed. ② to feel relieved. —胸がやける, to have heartburn. —胸も張り裂けさうな, heart-breaking [-rending]. —胸に浮ぶ, to come to mind; enter one's head; cross one's mind. —しみじみ胸にこたへる, to come home to one's heart. —ぎくりと胸にこたへる, to be touched on the raw; pierce one's heart. —胸を撫で下ろす, to feel relieved; breathe again [freely]. —胸をひやりとさせる, to strike terror into one's heart.

mune (棟), *n.* the ridge (of a roof). —一棟三戸建の長屋, a block of three houses.

muneage (棟上), *n.* the fixing of the ridge-pole.

munekazari (胸飾), *n.* a brooch.

munekuso (胸糞の惡い), *a.* nauseating; disgusting; vexing.

munen (無念), *n.* regret; mortification; chagrin. —無念の涙, tears of mortification. —無念に思ふ, to regret; be mortified; be chagrined. —無念を晴らす, to revenge oneself; have [take] revenge; pay off old scores.

muni (無二の), *a.* unique; matchless; unequalled. —無二の親友, one's second self; *alter ego* 【羅】; the most intimate [a bosom] friend.

munimusan (無二無三に), *ad.* desperately; furiously; precipitately. —無二無三に亂入する, to rush violently *into*. —無二無三に攻め立てる, to precipitate oneself upon the enemy.

muninsho (無任所の), *a.* without portfolio; unattached. ¶ 無任所大臣, a minister without portfolio.

mu-nisuru (無にする), *vt.* to undo; nullify; bring to naught; vitiate; make ineffectual. —人の深切を無にする, to bring another's kindness to naught; abuse [disregard] another's kindness. —深切が無になる, Kindness is thrown away.

munō (無能), *n.* inefficiency; incompetence; incapacity. —無能の, incapable; incompetent; of no ablity.

munōryoku (無能力), *n.* 【法】 incompetence; incapacity; disability. ¶ 無能力者, 【法】an

incompetent person; a person without legal capacity.
muon (無音の), *a.* silent; mute; unvoiced; quiet.
mura (村), *n.* a village. ¶ 村人, the village (全體); the village folk (同上); a villager. ¶ 村外れ, the outskirts of a village. —村役場, a village office.
mura (斑), *n.* ❶ (色の) blotch; blot. ❷ (不揃) inequality; unevenness; irregularity. ❸ (氣の) caprice; whim; fitfulness. —斑なく染める, to dye evenly.
mura (叢), *n.* a cluster; a clump.
muragaru (群る), *vi.* to crowd; assemble; throng (人); flock together (鳥); swarm (蟲); cluster (樹). **——,** *a.* crowding; thronging; flocking.
muraki (斑氣の), *a.* capricious; whimsical; skittish.
murakumo (叢雲), *n.* a cluster of clouds.
murasaki (紫), *n.* ❶【植】the gromwell. ❷ (色) purple.
murasame (村雨), *n.* a shower.
mure (群), *n.* ❶ =*gun* (群). ❷ (仲間) associates; companions. —少女の群, a bevy of girls.
murekusai (蒸臭い), *a.* close; stuffy; fusty.
mureru (蒸れる), *vi.* ❶ to grow musty; ferment; mould. ❷ (むしあつく感じる) to be sultry; be close; be stuffy.
muri (無理), *n.* irrationality; unreasonableness; force (暴力). —無理算段をする, to make a shift. —無理ではない, to be reasonable; may well; no wonder. (彼が怒ッたのも無理ではない, No wonder he was angry.) **—— - na,** *a* irrational; unreasonable; unnatural (不自然な); forced (牽强の). —私には無理な仕事である. It is too hard a task for me. **—— - ni,** *ad.* unreasonably (不法に); by force [violence]. —無理に...さす, to force [compel] a person to do. —無理に割り込む, to squeeze oneself by force *into.*
muridori (無理取りする), *vt.* to screw; extort; exact.
muriōjō (無理往生に), *ad.* by force. —無理往生させる, to compel [force] to consent; screw consent *from*; coerce into submission.
murishinjū (無理心中), *n.* double suicide by coercion.
murisoku (無利息で), *ad.* without interest. —無利息の, passive; non-interest-bearing.
muro (室), *n.* a hot-house (溫室); a green-house (同上); a drying-room (乾燥室). —室咲きの花, a hot-house flower.
muroaji (室鰺), *n.* Decapterus muroadsi (學名).
muron (無論), *ad.* of course; unquestionably; beyond dispute. —それは無論のことだ, That is a matter of course.
murui (無類の), *a.* unique; unparalleled; unequalled. —無類飛切りの品, an article of the finest quality; an A 1 article.
muryo (無慮), *ad.* about; in round numbers; approximately. —無慮八百人, about eight hundred men.
muryō (無料の), *a.* free (of charge); gratuitous. —無料で, freely; free of charge; charge free; gratis. ¶ 無料觀覽者, a dead-head. —無料宿泊所, a free lodginghouse.
muryō (無聊の), *a.* weary; dull; ennuyé. —無聊に苦しむ, to be terribly ennuyé; be overcome with ennui.
muryō (無量の), *a.* innumerable; infinite; immeasurable. —無量の感慨, profound emotion.
muryoku (無力の), *a.* powerless; incapable;【醫】atonic.
musaboru (貪る), *vt.* to devour; covet (慾張る); crave *for* (切望する). —俥賃を貪る, to charge excessive *jinrikisha* fare.
musai (無妻), *n.* celibacy; bachelorhood. ¶ 無妻者, a bachelor. —無妻主義 celibacy.
musai (穢い), *a.* foul; filthy; dirty.
musakuroshii (むさくろしい), *a.* dirty; shabby.
musan (無產), *n.* proletarianism. ¶ 無產階級, the proletariat, proletariate. —無產政黨, the proletariat party. —無產者, a proletarian. —無產主義, proletariatism.
musasabi (鼯鼠), *n.* the Japanese flying squirrel.
musebu (咽ぶ), *vi.* to suffocate; be choked. —淚《煙》に咽ぶ, to be choked with tears《by smoke》.
musei (無性の), *a.* sexless; asexual; agamous; neutral.
museibutsu (無生物), *n.* dead matter; stocks and stones.
museifu (無政府), *n.* anarchy. ¶ 無政府主義, anarchism. —無政府黨, the anarchists.
museigen (無制限の), *a.* limitless; unrestricted. —無制限に, unrestrictedly; without restriction.
museiryoku (無勢力), *n.* powerlessness; being without influence.
museki (無籍), *n.* absence of registered domicile; homelessness. ¶ 無籍者, a person without a (registered) domicile; a vagrant

(浮浪人).

musekinin (無責任の), *a.* irresponsible *for* [*to*]; unaccountable *for* [*to*]. —無責任な言論, an irresponsible opinion.

musekitsui (無脊椎動物), *n.* an invertebrate animal; the invertebrates; Invertebrata (學名)

musen (無線の), *a.* wireless. ¶ 無線電報, a wireless (telegram); a marconigram; a radiogram; an aerogram. —無線電信 wireless telegraphy; radiography. (無線電信機, a wireless telegraph (apparatus); an aerograph. —無線電信局, a wireless station. —無線電信で, wirelessly. —船中から無線電信をかける, to wireless on board the ship [from a ship].) —無線電話, ① wireless (message). ② (術) wireless telephony; radiotelephony. (無線電話機, a radiophone; a wireless telephone; an aerophone; a radiotelephone.) —無線放送, wireless [radio-] broadcasting. (無線放送機〔者〕, a radio-broadcaster. —無線放送局, a radio-broadcasting station.)

musen (無錢の), *a.* moneyless; penniless; impecunious. ¶ 無錢旅行, travelling without money.

museru (噎る), *vi.* =*musebu*.

musessō (無節操な), *a.* unprincipled; inconstant; unchaste.

musha (武者), *n.* a warrior; a soldier. —武者振りつく, to seize [catch] hold *of*; dash [spring] *upon* (とびかゝる). ¶ 武者修業, knight-errantry.

mushabetsu (無差別), *n.* indiscrimination. —無差別な, indiscriminate. —無差別に, indiscriminately; without discrimination [distinction].

mushaku (無爵の), *a.* untitled.

mushakusha (むしゃくしゃする), *vi.* to be irritated [vexed]; be fretful.

mushamusha (むしゃむしゃ食ふ), *vi.* to munch (音立てて).

mushi (蟲), *n.* ❶ an insect (昆蟲); a worm (腸蟲, 蠕蟲); a caterpillar (芋蟲類). ❷ =*kan* (癇). —蟲のよい話, selfish talk; a selfish proposal. —蟲のよい男, an impudent fellow. —蟲の息でゐる, to breathe faintly; be on the point of death. —蟲が起る, to become irritable. —蟲が知らす, to have a presentiment; have a foreboding. —蟲が好かぬ, ① [*a.*] disagreeable; offensive; sickening. ② [*vi.*] to have an antipathy *to*. ——寸の蟲にも五分の魂, "Even a fly hath its spleen."

mushi (無私の), *a.* impartial; unselfish; disinterested. ☞*kōhei*.

mushi (無視する), *vt.* to disregard; ignore; set at naught.

mushiatsui (蒸暑い), *a.* sultry; close; oppressive (息詰るやうな).

mushiba (齲齒), *n.* a decayed tooth. —齲齒を塡充する, to plug a decayed tooth.

mushibamu (蝕む), *vi.* to be eaten by worm.

mushiboshi (蟲干), *n.* airing. —什器を蟲干する, to air the furniture [utensils].

mushiburo (蒸風呂), *n.* a hot-air [vapour; steam]-bath; a Turkish bath.

mushigashi (蒸菓子), *n.* steamed cake.

mushikaeshi (蒸返し), *n.* ❶ re-steaming. ❷ repetition; revival; an after-clap.

mushikago (蟲籠), *n.* an insect-cage.

mushikaku (無資格の), *a.* unqualified. ¶ 無資格教員, an unqualified teacher.

mushike (蟲氣), *n.* nervous irritation.

mushiken (無試驗で), without examination. —無試驗入學を許す, to admit without examination. ¶ 無試驗入學者, a student admitted without examination.

mushiki (無識), *n.* ignorance.

mushikudashi (蟲下し), *n.* a vermifuge; an anthelminthic.

mushikui (蟲食ひの), *a.* worm-eaten; moth-eaten.

mushimegane (蟲眼鏡), *n.* a a hand-glass; a magnifying-glass.

mushi-mushū (無始無終の), *a.* eternal; without beginning or end.

mushin (無心), *n.* ❶ (無邪氣) innocence. ❷ (懇願) solicitation. —無心の, innocent; involuntary (無意). —無心する, to beg; ask (earnestly) *for*; solicit *for*. —金の無心を言ふ, to ask for money.

mushinja (無信者), *n.* an unbeliever; an infidel.

mushinkei (無神經), *n.* insensibility; apathy; impassiveness (無覺). —無神經の, insensible; apathetic.

mushinkō (無信仰), *n.* unbelief; unfaith; unreligiousness.

mushinron (無神論), *n.* atheism. ¶ 無神論者, an atheist.

mushiritoru (捥取る), *vt.* to tear off; pluck [pick] off.

mushiro (筵, 蓆), *n.* ❶ a straw-mat; mat; matting. ❷ (席) a seat. —筵を布く, to spread a mat.

mushiro (寧ろ), *ad.* rather; sooner; better; before [*conj.* & *prep.*] —恥かく位なら寧ろ死ぬ, I should choose death before disgrace; I should prefer death to dishonour; I shoud rather die than disgrace myself. —寧ろ言はない方がよい. Better leave it unsaid.

mushiru (挘る), *vt.* to pluck; tear; pick. —鳥の羽を挘る, to pluck feathers off a bird; pick a fowl.

mushisha (無死者), *n.* 【野球】 a non-out.

mushiryoku (無資力の), *a.* without capital [fund].

mushitoriami (蟲取網), *n.* a sweep-net.

mushitoriko (除蟲粉), *n.* in-sect powder.

mushitorisumire (蟲取菫), *n.* the bog-violet; the butterwort.

mushiuri (蟲賣), *n.* Ⓢ 蟲屋. a hawker of chirping insects.

mushiyoke (蟲除け), *n.* a vermifuge (驅蟲藥).

mushiyokegiku (除蟲菊), *n.* 【植】 a vermifuge-chrysanthemum.

mushizu (蟲酸, 呑酸), *n.* 【醫】 water-brash. —蟲酸が走る, (*a*) to have a water-brash: (*b*) to loath; The stomach [gorge] rises.

mushō (無性に), *ad.* ❶ (過度に) extremely; exceedingly. ❷ = *midari* (猥に).

mushō (無償で), *ad.* 【法】 without consideration; without indemnity; gratis. ☞ *muhōshū*.

mushoku (無色の), *a.* colourless; uncoloured (無著色); achromatic (光の).

mushoku (無職-業), *n.* unemployment; unoccupation. —無職の, unemployed; unoccupied.

mushozoku (無所屬の), *a.* independent. ¶ 無所屬團, the independent group. —無所屬代議士, an independent (member).

mushū (無臭の), *a.* odourless; scentless; inodorous.

mushugi (無主義の), *a.* without [destitute of] any definite principle; unprincipled.

mushuku (無宿の), *a.* homeless; vagrant; vagabond. ¶ 無宿者, a tramp; a vagabond; a vagrant.

mushūkyō (無宗教の), *a.* without religion; irreligious. ¶ 無宗教者, an irreligionist.

mushumi (無趣味の), *a.* tasteless; insipid. —無趣味な人, a prosaic person; a man of no taste.

musō (夢想), *n.* a day-dream; vision; reverie (妄想). —夢想する, to dream *of*; indulge in reverie.

musō (無雙の), *a.* =*busō*.

musochi (無租地), *n.* land free from tax; tax-free land.

musu (蒸す), *vt.* ❶ (ふかす) to steam; warm with steam. ❷ (罨布する) to foment; embrocate. **—,** *vi.* (氣温が) to be sultry; be muggy; be oppressive; be stuffy. —痛み所を蒸す, to foment a sore. —轉石苔蒸さず, "A rolling stone gathers no moss."

musū (無數の), *a.* numberless; innumerable; countless.

musubi (結), *n.* ❶ (結ぶこと) tying; binding. ❷ (結目) a knot; a tie. ❸ (終結) an end; a close; a conclusion. ❹ (連結) connection. ❺ (握飯) a rice-ball; a roasted rice-ball (燒飯).

musubiawasu (結合す), *vt.* to join; link; piece [tie] together.

musubime (結節), *n.* a knot; a tie; 【航】 a bend.

musubitsukeru (結附ける), *vt.* to tie (up); attach *to*; fasten together.

musuboreru (結ぼれる), *vi.* ❶ to be (en-)tangled; be in a tangle; be knotted. ❷ (氣が) to despond; be dejected; be depressed.

musubu (掬ぶ), *vt.* to scoop. —水を掬ぶ, to scoop up water with a hand.

musubu (結ぶ), *v.* ❶ (物を) to tie; knot; join. ❷ (實を) to bear. ❸ (文等を) to conclude; close. ❹ (約束等を) to contract; enter *into*; make; conclude. —蝶形に結ぶ, to tie in a bow. —實を結ぶ, to bear a fruit. —交りを結ぶ, to contract a friendship.

musubu-no-kami (結ぶの神), *n.* Hymen (希臘神話).

musui (無水の), *a.* waterless; 【化】 anhydrous.

musuko (息子), *n.* a son; a boy (男兒).

musume (娘), *n.* a daughter (息女); a girl (娘); a *musume* 【日】. —娘らしいつゝましやかさ, maiden modesty. ¶ 娘盛り, the flower [prime] of girlhood.

mutai (無體の), *a.* ❶ (無理) compulsory. ❷ (無禮) insolent; rude; improper; impertinent. ❸ (無形) incorporeal; intangible. —無理無體に, by force. ¶ 無體物, incorporeal things; intangible [immaterial] things.

mute (無手で), *ad.* ❶ (空手) empty-handed. ❷ (武器なし) unarmed; without arms. ❸ (無資) without capital.

muteikei (無定形の), *a.* amorphous; formless.

muteiken (無定見の), *a.* without a fixed view.

muteikō (無抵抗), *n.* non-resistance. —無抵抗の抵抗, passive resistance. ¶ 無抵抗主義, non-resistance principle.

muteki (無敵の), *a.* invincible.

muteki (霧笛), *n.* a fog-whistle.

muteppō (無鐵砲), *n.* rashness;

recklessness. —無鐵砲な男, a rash fellow; a hotspur.

mutodoke (無屆で), *ad.* without notice (leave). ¶ 無屆遲參, being late without leave.

mutonjaku (無頓著な), *a.* indifferent; careless; unconcerned; nonchalant. —服裝に無頓著である, to be indifferent [careless] about one's dress.

mutsu (鯥), *n.* 【魚】 Scombrops boops (學名).

mutsu (六つ), *n.* six.

mutsugoto (睦言), *n.* soft whispers; soft nothings; lovers' talk.

mutsuki (襁褓), *n.* a swaddling-clothes [-bands]; a diaper.

mutsumajii (睦じい), *a.* harmonious; intimate; friendly. —睦じく交はる, to be on familiar [intimate] terms *with.* —睦じく暮す, to live in harmony.

mutto (むッとする), *v.* ❶ (怒る) to take huff; take offence. ❷ (息苦しい) to be stuffy; be fusty; be close. —むッとして口をつぐむ, to purse one's lips sullenly.

muttsuri (むッつりした), *a.* sullen; sombre. —むッつりして居る, to remain sullen.

muyami (無暗な), *a.* ❶ (輕率な) indiscreet; careless. ❷ (無茶な) rash; reckless. ❸ (過度な) excessive; immoderate. —無暗に, indiscreetly; carelessly; rashly; recklessly; excessively; immoderately.

muyō (無用), *n.* ❶ (役に立たぬ) uselessness; futility; inutility. ❷ (不必要) needlessness; unnecessariness. —開放し無用, "Shut the door after you." ——**-no,** *a.* ❶ useless; futile; unserviceable. ❷ needless; unnecessary. ❸ having no business; without business. —無用の者入るべからず, "No admittance except on business."

muyoku (無慾な), *a.* unavaricious; unselfish. —大慾は無慾に似たり, "Avarice overreaches itself."

muyūbyō (夢遊病), *n.* sleep [night]-walking; somnambulism. ¶ 夢遊病者, a sleep [night]-walker; a somnamblist.

muzai (無罪), *n.* innocence; guiltlessness. —無罪の, innocent. guiltless; ¶ 無罪放免, acquittal (and discharge).

muzamuza (むざむざ), *ad.* ❶ (情氣なく) recklessly; lavishly. ❷ (徒に) in vain; uselessly; easily (容易に).

muzan (無慙な), *a.* ❶ (慘酷な) merciless; relentless; cruel. ❷ (憐な) pitiful; piteous; sad; poor. —無慙の最期を遂げる, to die a miserable death; come to a tragical end.

muzei (無稅の), *a.* (tax-)free; duty-free; untaxed. ¶ 無稅品, (duty-)free goods; non-dutiable goods. (無稅品目錄, a free list.)

muzōsa (無造作な), *a.* easy; ready. —— **-ni,** *ad.* easily; with ease; readily. —無造作に仕事を引受ける, to undertake work without due consideration.

muzukaru (むづかる), *vi.* to fret; be in a pet; be peevish.

muzukashii (むづかしい), *a.* ❶ (困難な) difficult; hard; laborious (骨の折れる). ❷ (顏附の) stern; severe; sullen (陰氣). ❸ (氣の) ill to please. ❹ (病氣の) serious (重い); incurable (不治の); hopeless (絕望的). —難しい試驗, a stiff examination.

muzumuzu (むずむずする), *vi.* ❶ (體が) to itch; feel itchy [creepy]. ❷ (氣等が) to be impatient; itch *to* [*for*]; fidget. ——, *a.* itchy; creepy; impatient; uneasy.

muzuto (無手と), *ad.* with all one's might. —むずと組み附く, to come to grips with all one's might.

myakkan (脈管), *n.* 【解】 a (blood-)vessel.

myaku (脈), *n.* ❶ (血脈) = *myakkan.* ❷ (脈搏) pulse; pulsation. ❸ 【鑛·地質】 a vein. —まだ脈がある, ① (生きてゐる) The pulse still beats. ② (望がある) to give a faint gleam of hope. —脈を診[ミ]る[とる], to feel the pulse *of.*

myakudō (脈動), *n.* pulsation. —脈動する, to pulsate.

myakuha (脈波), *n.* pulse wave [undulation].

myakuhaku (脈搏), *n.* pulse; 【醫】 sphygmus. ☞ *myaku.*

myakuraku (脈絡), *n.* a line of connection; a chain; a thread.

myō (妙), *n.* ❶ (不思議) wonderfulness; strangeness. ❷ (玄妙) mystery. ❸ = *kōmyō* (巧妙). ❹ (美) beauty. —…に妙を得てる, to be the master *of.* —— **-na,** *a.* ❶ strange; queer; odd; singular. ❷ (巧な) admirable; excellent; dexterous; subtle. —妙に, strangely; singularly. —妙なことを云ふ, to say strange things.

myōan (妙案), *n.* an excellent device; a bright [happy] idea; a capital idea; a skilful plan.

myōban (明晚), *n.* & *ad.* to-morrow evening [night].

myōban (明礬), *n.* alum. ¶ 明

礬石, alum-stone.
myōchō (明朝), *n.* & *ad.* to-morrow morning.
myōdai (名代), *n.* ❶ (代理) agency; proxy. ❷ (代理人) an agent; a proxy. —名代として, on behalf of another; as a substitute.
myōga (茗荷), *n.* 【植】 Zingiber mioga (ginger の一種·學名). —茗荷の子, a ginger flower.
myōga (冥加), *n.* ❶ (冥護) divine protection. ❷ (神恵) blessing of God; providence; divine grace [favour]. —冥加に餘る, to be more than one deserves.
myōgi (妙技), *n.* ❶ (技) a wonderful performance; a splendid [brilliant] feat. ❷ (工) dexterous craft; skilful workmanship; delicate touch. —妙技を振ふ, to exhibit one's brilliant feats.
myōgonen (明後年), *n.* the year after next.
myōgonichi (明後日), *n.* & *ad.* the day after to-morrow.
myōji (名字, 苗字), *n.* a surname; a family name.
myōjō (明星), *n.* ❶ Venus. ❷ (傑出した人) a star. —文壇の明星, a star in the literary world.
myōkyoku (妙曲), *n.* a charming melody; a melodious time.
myōmi (妙味), *n.* a fine point; charm; beauty. —其の妙味を味ふ, to appreciate its charm.
myōmoku (名目), *n.* ❶ (稱號) a name; a title; a designation. ❷ (口實) a pretext; an excuse. —病氣と云ふ名目で, under the pretext of illness. ¶ 名目値段《賃銀》, nominal price 《wages》.
myōmon (名聞), *n.* reputation; fame. ☞ ***meibun***.
myōmyōgonichi (明明後日), *n.* & *ad.* three days hence.
myōnen (明年), *n.* & *ad.* next [the coming] year.
myōnichi (明日), *n.* & *ad.* to-morrow.
myōon (妙音), *n.* sweet music.
myōrei (妙齡), *n.* youth; the flower of youth. —妙齡に達する, to arrive at puberty.
myōri (冥利), *n.* ❶ = ***myōga*** (冥加). ❷ (行ひの應報) retribution. —冥利が盡きる, to forfeit divine protection.
myōsen-jishō (名詮自性), *nomen atque omen* 【羅.=a name and also an omen】.
myōsho (妙所), *n.* a fine point; a secret. ☞ ***myōmi***.
myōshu (妙手), *n.* a skilful person; an expert; an adept. —ヴァイオリンの妙手, an expert [skilful] violinist.
myōtei (妙諦), *n.* mystic truth; mystery; secrets.
myōyaku (妙藥), *n.* a specific; a sovereign remedy.
myōyō (妙用), *n.* ❶ (巧な應用) skilful use. ❷ (妙な作用) mystery.

N

na (名), *n.* a name; a Christian [personal] name (人の); a title (書物·官職等の): a good [fair] name (名聲); fame (同上); a pretext (口實, 名義). —名ある作家, a widely [well-] known novelist. —名ばかりの王, a titular king; a king in name only. —名もなき一介の書生, a mere nameless student. —名にふさはしい, worthy of the name. —名を揚げる, to win [make] a name for oneself; win fame [renown], distinguish oneself; make [get] oneself a name; make one's mark. —名をなす, to achieve meritorious deeds; distinguish oneself *in*. —人の名を騙る, to assume another's name. —大酒を以て名ある, known as a hard drinker.
na (菜), *n.* ❶ (野菜) greens; vegetables. ❷ =***aburana***. —菜の花, a rape-flower.
na (な), *v.* do not; don't; do not be. ☞ ***nakare***.
na (な), **nā** (なあ), you know; I should say; what? —隨分むづかしいですからなあ, Rather difficult, I should say.
nā (なあ), (嘆噫) how; what; how I wish (願望); I wish (同上). —綺麗な月だなあ, What a beautiful moon!
naate (名宛), *n.* an address; a direction. ☞ ***atena***. ¶ 名宛人, an addressee.
nabe (鍋), *n.* a pot (深い); a pan (淺い). ¶ 鍋蓋, a pot lid.
nabete (なべて), *ad.* on the whole. —老いも若きもなべて, young and old alike.
nabezuru (鍋鶴), *n.* 【鳥】 the white-headed crane.
nabiku (靡く), *vi.* ❶ (風·流水に) to bend; bow; wave; sway. ❷ (從ふ) to submit; be swayed. —風に靡く, to bend before the wind. —黄金に靡く, to bow to money.
naburigoroshi (嬲殺にする), *vt.* to butcher; kill by inches; torture to death (いぢめ殺す).
naburimono (嬲物), *n.* a play-

thing; a toy; a sport; a laughing-stock (笑草). 一嬲り物にする, to make sport [a game; a plaything] *of*.

naburu (嬲る), *vt.* to banter; chaff; play [sport] *with*. —お前はなぶられたのだ, You have been played with.

nada (灘), *n.* an open sea (外海); a sea.

nadai (名題), *n.* ❶ (表題) a name; a title. ❷ 【名代】 (著名) fame; celebrity; notoriety (惡しき意味で). —名題の; 名代の, famous; noted; notorious (惡黨など).

nadakai (名高い), *a.* ❶ (有名) famous; noted; celebrated; well-known; notorious (惡い意味で). ❷ (卓越) distinguished; eminent; prominent.

nadameru (宥める), *vt.* (和げる) to soothe; pacify; appease. —怒りを宥める, to soothe [appease] another's anger.

nadaraka (なだらかな), *a.* ❶ (穩かな) smooth; calm; gentle. ❷ (緩やかな) even; slow. ❸ (流暢な) fluent; flowing.

nadare (なだれ), *n.* ❶ (傾斜) slope; declivity (下向の). ❷ (雪崩) a snow-slip [-slide]; an avalanche. ❸ =*jisuberi*. —なだれを打てる群集, a surging crowd. —なだれをうって進む《退く》, to surge forward 《backward》.

nadareru (なだれる), *vi.* to slope *to*; incline *to*; slide down (辷り落つ).

nadataru (名だたる), *a.* famous; noted; celebrated.

nadegiri (撫斬にする), *v.* ❶ to slash; kill at random; kill one after another in one's way. ❷ to sweep; make a clean sweep.

naderu (撫でる), *vt.* to stroke; rub; comb (梳る). —髪を撫で上げる《下げる》, to comb up 《down》 one's hair. —子供の頭を撫でる, to stroke [pat] a child on the head.

nadeshiko (撫子), *n.* 【植】 the fringed pink.

nadetsukeru (撫附ける), *vt.* to comb down (髮を); smooth down.

nado (など, 等, 抔), and so on [forth]; and the like; such like 《as》; etcetera (&c., etc. と略す).

nae (苗), *n.* a seedling; a young shoot. ¶ 稻苗, a rice-seedling.

naedoko (苗床), *n.* a seed-plot; a nursery.

naegi (苗木), *n.* a sapling; a young plant.

naeru (萎・痿える), *vt.* ❶ (しをれる) to wither; droop; hang down (たれる). ❷ (力失す) to droop; weaken; lose strength.

nafuda (名札), *n.* a name-plate; a door-plate; a name-card (名刺).

nafukin (ナフキン), *n.* ☞ *napukin*.

nafutarin (ナフタリン), *n.* 【化】 naphthaline.

nagaame (霖雨), *n.* a continual rain; a long spell of rain.

nagabanashi (長話, 長談), *n.* a long tiresome [tedious] talk.

nagabikasu (長引かす), *vt.* to protract; prolong; drag out (飽々する迄). —戰爭を長引かす, to protract a war.

nagabiku (長引く), *vi.* to be protracted; be prolonged; drag on. —長引ける病氣, a prolonged [protracted] illness.

nagadangi (長談義), *n.* a long tiresome story; a long-winded speech; a tedious discourse.

nagae (轅), *n.* a shaft (馬車の); a thill (車及び馬車の).

nagae (長柄), *n.* a long handle; a long shaft.

nagagutsu (長靴), *n.* wellingtons; jack boots; top-boots.

nagahibachi (長火鉢), *n.* an oblong brazier.

nagai (長・永い), *a.* long; lengthy. —長い間, for a long time [while]. —長い內には, in the long run.

nagai (長居する), *v.* to stay long; outstay (他の客より).

nagaiki (長生), *n.* longevity; long-living. —長生する, to live long; live to a great age; outlive (他より).

nagaimo (長芋), *n.* 【植】 the (Chinese) yam.

nagaisu (長椅子), *n.* a sofa; a lounge; a bench (ベンチ).

nagajuban (長襦袢), *n.* a long under-garment.

nagaku (長・永く), *ad.* long; for a long time [an age]; for a great [good] while; lengthily (話・文體等). —長くとも十日, ten days at the longest. —長くなる, to lengthen; draw out (日が); lie down (寢ころぶ). —長くする, to prolong; lengthen.

nagame (眺), *n.* a view; a sight; a prospect.

nagameru (眺める), *vt.* to see; look at [on]; view. —遠く眺められる, to command a distant view *of*. —ぼんやり眺める, to look vacantly *at*.

nagamichi (長途をする), to make a long journey; go a long road [way].

nagamochi (永持する), *vi.* to wear well; last; keep [last] long. ☞ *motsu* (持つ).

nagamochi (長持), *n.* a long chest.

naganaga (永永, 長長), *ad.* very long; for a long time [while]. —長々しい說明, a long-winded explanation. —長々しい夜《日》, the livelong night 《day》. —長々と橫たはる, to lie at (full) length.

naganen (永年), *n.* many years. ☞ ***tanen***.

nagaoi (長追する), *v.* to pursue long; give a long chase.

nagara (ながら, 乍ら), ❶ (同時行爲, つゝ) (*a*) [*prep.*] over; with: (*b*) [*conj.*] as; while: (*c*) [*ad.*] at the same time. ❷ (とは言へ, なれども) (*a*) [*conj.*] though; yet; notwithstanding: (*b*) [*prep.*] in spite *of*; with: (*c*) [*ad.*] even. ☞ ***iedomo*** (雖も). ❸ (孰れも) [*conj.*] all; each; both. ❹ (通り) [*conj.*] as. —厭々ながら, against one's will; reluctantly. —二つながら, both ...and; both together. —生れながらの詩人, a born poet. —臥[*]ながら讀む, to read lying down. —飲みながら話す, to talk over a bottle. —歩きながら讀む, to read walking. —貧しい暮しをしてゐながら, notwithstanding one's life of poverty; while living in poverty.

nagaraeru (存らへる), *vi.* = ***ikinagaraeru***.

nagaraku (長らく), *ad.* (very) long; for a long time [while].

nagare (流), *n.* ❶ (水流) a current; a water-course; running water (流水). ❷ (小川) a stream; a brook; a rivulet. ❸ (系統) lineage; stock. ☞ ***kettō*** (血統). ❹ (學派, 流派) a school. ❺ (傾向) a current; a tendency; a trend. ❻ (中止) suspension; cessation. —抵當流れ, a forfeited mortgage. —時の流れ, the current of the times; the tendency of the age. —雨でお流れになる, to be given up on account of the rain. —流れのまにまに漂ふ, to float down with the stream. —千家の流れを汲む, to follow the Senke school.

nagaredama (流彈), *n.* = ***ryū-dan*** (流彈).

nagarederu (流出る), *vi.* to flow out; ooze out (だらだら出る); gush out (迸る).

nagarekomu (流込む), *vi.* ❶ (流入) to flow in; pour in. ❷ (人が) to wander into; drift into. ❸ (抵當物が) to be forfeited. —海へ流れ込む, to run [flow] into a sea. —大阪へ流れ込む, (漂浪) to drift [wander] into Ōsaka.

nagareru (流れる), *vi.* ❶ (液體が) to flow; stream; run (down). ❷ (蠟が) to run down; gutter. ❸ (漂ふ) to drift; float; wander about. ❹ (傾く) to fall into; lapse into; run to; incline to. ❺ (質物が) to be forfeited; be foreclosed. ❻ (中止) to be suspended; be given up. —流るゝが如き辯舌, fluent speech. —奢侈(放縦; 懶惰)に流れる, to lapse into luxury (profligacy; idleness). —市中を流れる, to run through the city. —洪水で橋が流された, The bridge was carried away by the flood.

nagaretsuku (流着く), *vi.* to drift *to* [ashore]; be driven *to* [ashore]; be cast ashore.

nagareya (流矢), *n.* a stray arrow. —流矢に中る, to be struck by a stray arrow.

nagasa (長さ), *n.* length. —長さいくらだ, What is the length? —長さ五呎だ, It is five feet long; It measures five feet in length.

nagashi (流し), *n.* ❶ (臺所の) a scullery; a sink (箱或は桶). ❷ (湯屋の) washing. ❸ (門附) a strolling musician.

nagashiami (流網), *n.* a drift(-net).

nagashime (流眄に見る), *v.* to look askance *at*; cast a sidelong glance *at*; look at from the corner of one's eye.

nagashizuri (流釣), *n.* whiffing; surface-fishing.

nagasu (流す), *vt.* ❶ (流下) to let run out; let flow; pour (注ぐ). ❷ (漂流) to float; drift; set adrift [afloat]. ❸ (滴す) to drop; spill (血など); shed (血·涙など). ❹ (流失) to carry away; wash away. ❺ (流謫) to exile; transport; banish. ❻ (質物を) to forfeit; foreclose. —汗を流す, ① to run with sweat; perspire. ② (洗浴) to wash off sweat; take a bath. —筏を流す, to flow down a raft. —汚物を川へ流す, to throw garbage into the river.

nagatabi (長旅), *n.* a long journey (voyage).

nagatarashii (長たらしい), *a.* tedious; prolix; lengthy.

nagawazurai (長患), *n.* a protracted illness; a lingering disease. —長患ひをする, to suffer from a long illness.

nagaya (長屋), *n.* a tenement-house; a block of houses. —長屋建ての, built in the tenement style. ¶ 長屋住居, the life in a tenement [the slum].

nageageru (投上げる), *vt.* to throw up; cast up; fling up; toss.

nagedasu (投出す), *vt.* ❶ (放り出す) to throw out; throw [lay] aside; fling away. ❷ (放棄する) to abandon; give up; throw up. —馬車から投げ出される, to be thrown out of a carriage. —足を投げ出す, to spread [stretch] out one's legs. —内閣を投げ出す, to give up a cabinet. —命を投げ出して, at the risk of one's life.

nagee (投餌), *n.* ground-bait.
nageire (投入花), *n.* a flower thrown in.
nagekawashii (歎はしい), *a.* ❶ (慨歎) deplorable; regrettable. ❷ (悲歎) lamentable; mournful.
nageki (歎), *n.* lamentation; grief; sorrow. —歎きの餘り, in the excess of one's grief. —深き歎きに沈む, to be overcome with deep sorrow; sink [fall] into extreme grief.
nagekomu (投込む), *vt.* to throw [cast; fling] *into*; throw overboard (船上より). —人を河に投げ込む, to pitch a person into a river.
nageku (歎く), *v.* ❶ (歎息する) to sigh; give [fetch] a sigh. ❷ (悲歎する) to lament; moan *for* (*over*); bewail. ❸ (慨歎する) to deplore; regret. —身の不運を歎く, to bewail one's ill fortune.
nageni (投荷), *n.* ❶ (投げること) jettison. ❷ (荷) jetsam.
nageru (投げる), *vt.* ❶ to throw; cast; fling; hurl; pitch (球を). ❷ (放棄) to throw up; give up. ☞ *nagedasu.* —投げ返す, to throw back. —球を投げる, to throw [pitch] a ball; deliver a ball (狙って). —影を投げる, to cast [throw] a shadow.
nageshi (長押), *n.* a lintel-joist.
nagesuteru (投棄てる), *vt.* to throw off [away].
nagetsukeru (投附ける), *vt.* ❶ to throw [cast; fling; hurl] *at*. ❷ (投倒す) to fling [throw] down.
nageuri (投賣), *n.* selling at a sacrifice; dumping.
nageutsu (擲つ), *vt.* to cast aside; throw [give] up; abandon; lay down (生命など). —職を擲つ, to throw [give] up one's office.
nageyari (投遣), *n.* letting alone; neglect. —仕事を投遣りにする, to work carelessly; leave one's work unfinished (未了に).
nagi (凪), *n.* calmness; calm; a lull (暴風雨中一時の).
naginata (薙刀), *n.* a halberd.
naginatahōzuki (薙刀酸漿), *n.* the brood-pouch of the *Rapana bezoar.*
nagisa (渚), *n.* a beach; a shore; [a strand (修・詩).]
nagori (名殘), *n.* ❶ (殘餘) the rest; remains (殘跡); vestiges (形跡). ❷ (殘懐) reminiscence; remembrance. ❸ (別離) farewell; parting; leave-taking. —榮華の名殘, a shadow of one's former prosperity. —名殘惜しげに, looking reluctant [unwilling] to part; with reluctant steps (足重げに). —名殘を惜む, to be loath [reluctant] to part; be sorry to take leave; hesitate to bid farewell. ¶ お名殘狂言, a farewell performance.
nagu (凪ぐ), *vi.* to (become) calm; fall; subside; die away.
nagu (薙ぐ), *vt.* to mow; cut down; sweep (一掃). —草を薙ぐ, to cut down the grass.
naguriai (毆合), *n.* blows; a hand-to-hand fight; fisticuffs. —毆り合ふ, to fight (with fists); exchange blows.
nagurigaki (擲書), *n.* scribble; scrawl. —擲書きする, to scribble; scrawl; dash off.
naguru (毆・擲・撲る), *vt.* to beat; thrash; give a blow [thrashing]. —撲り返す, to return a blow. —毆り殺す, to beat to death; kill with a blow; strike dead. —毆り倒す, to knock [strike] down [to the ground].
nagusame (慰), *n.* comfort; consolation; solace. ☞ *ian.*
nagusameru (慰める), *vt.* to console; comfort; solace. —耳(目)を慰める, to delight the ears (eyes) (物が); feast the ears (eyes) *on* (見聞く事物に). —人の悲みを慰める, to console a person in his sorrow. —讀書で心を慰める, to take comfort in reading.
nagusami (慰み), *n.* ❶ (鬱散) diversion; recreation; distraction. ❷ (娛樂) amusement; pleasure; pastime; entertainment; sport (遊戯). —慰み半分にする, to do partly for fun [sport]. —慰みに繪を描く, to paint for (one's own) amusement.
nagusamu (慰む), *vi.* to take comfort *in* [*from*] (自ら).
nahen (那邊に), *ad.* where.
nai (内に), *ad.* within (a week); in (the city); inside (the gate).
nai (無い), *v.* ❶ (存せず) not to be; not to exist. ❷ (有せず) not to have; be without. ❸ (盡きる) to be out *of*; run short *of*. ❹ (缺く) to be wanting [lacking] *in*; be devoid *of*; be deficient *in*. ❺ (でない) to be anything but; be far *from*. **——,** *ad.* not; never. **——,** *a.* no. —無いも同樣, next to nothing. —...のない時は, in default *of*; in the absence *of*. —勇氣が無い, to be deficient [lacking; wanting] in courage. —少し[毫]も...でない, not at all; not the least. —決して學者ではない, He is anything but a scholar. —インキはすっかり無くなった, My ink is all gone. —缺點の無い人はない, No man is without

his faults. —成功の見込がない, There is no hope of success.

naibu (内部), *n.* the interior; the inner part; the inside; within. —内部の, inner; inside; internal; interior. —室の内部, the inside [interior] of a room. —會社の内部での噂さ, a rumour prevailing in the firm. ¶ 内部關係, internal relation.

naibun (内分), *n.* a secret; secrecy.

naibun (内聞する), *v.* to hear privately.

naichi (内地), *n.* ❶ (奥地) the inland; the interior of a country. ❷ home (内國, 本國); Japan Proper (朝鮮·臺灣等に對して). —内地へ歸る, to return home. ¶ 内地人, the people in the interior; the people at home; an inlander. —内地米, home-grown rice. —内地(製)品, home-made articles.

naichi (内治), *n.* home administration; internal government.

naidaijin (内大臣), *n.* the Keeper of the Privy Seal. ¶ 内大臣府, the office of the Keeper of the Privy Seal.

naidaku (内諾), *n.* private [informal] consent.

naidan (内談する), *vi.* to talk privately; have a confidential talk [conversation].

naiden (内殿), *n.* ❶ (神社) the sanctum of a shrine; a sanctuary. ❷ (宮中) the inner hall [chamber].

naido (内帑), *n.* the Privy Purse. —内帑金を下賜さる, to donate out of the Privy Purse.

naien (内宴), *n.* a private dinner.

naien (内縁), *n.* unregistered marriage. —内縁の妻, a wife who is not legally recognized; a brevet-wife 【俗】.

naietsu (内謁), *n.* a private audience. —内謁を賜はる, to be granted a private audience.

naifu (内府), *n.* =*naidaijin*.

naifu (小刀), *n.* a knife; a penknife (鉛筆などを削る).

naifuku (内服), *n.* internal use. ¶ 内服薬, an internal medicine.

naigai (内外), *n.* ❶ (うちとそと) in and out; inside and outside. ❷ (内部と外部) within and without; interior and exterior; internal and external. ❸ (内國と外國) domestic and foreign; at home and abroad. ❹ (大約) about; thereabouts; more or less; or so. —百圓内外, about 100 *yen*; a hundred *yen* or so. —一週間内外, a week or thereabouts [so]. —内外多事である, to be busy [eventful] (both) at home and abroad. ¶ 内外人, natives and foreigners.

naigan (内願), *n.* a private request [petition].

naigashiro (蔑にする), *vt.* to despise; look down *upon*; hold in contempt; make light *of*; slight. ☞ *besshi* (蔑視する).

naihō (内方に), *ad.* inwards; inside.

naihō (内包), *n.* 【論】 intension; connotation.

naihō (内報), *n.* secret [confidential] information [report].

naii (内意), *n.* private [personal] opinion [intention; wishes]; one's intention (意中).

naiji (内事), *n.* internal affairs; private [personal] affairs. ¶ 内事課, the section of internal affairs.

naijien (内耳炎), *n.* 【醫】 otitis interna; inflammation of the internal ear.

naijitsu (内實), *n.* the truth; the fact; the real state [condition]; the true fact. —内實は, in reality [fact]; really.

naijo (内助), *n.* private aid. —内助の功によって, through one's wife's assistance.

naijō (内情), *n.* the private circumstances; the internal conditions; the real state [conditions]. —内情に通ずる, to be acquainted with the actual condition; be behind the scene.

naika (内科), *n.* internal treatment of a disease; (practical) medicine. ¶ 内科醫, a physician; an internalist.

naikai (内界), *n.* the internal world.

naikai (内海), *n.* an inland sea; an arm of the sea (入江). ¶ 瀬戸内海, the Inland Sea (of Japan).

naikaku (内角), *n.* 【數】 an internal [interior] angle.

naikaku (内閣), *n.* the cabinet; the ministry. —内閣の交迭, a ministerial [cabinet] change. —内閣を乗取る, to take over a cabinet. ¶ 責任内閣, a responsible cabinet. —内閣會議, a cabinet council. —内閣書記官長, the chief secretary of the cabinet. —内閣總辭職, resignation of the whole cabinet; resignation *en bloc*. —内閣總理大臣, the Prime Minister; the Premier; the Minister-President (of State).

naikan (内觀), *n.* introspection.

naiki (内規), *n.* a private rule; a customary rule.

naikin (内勤), *n.* indoor service.

naiko (内顧), *n.* household cares. —内顧の憂なからしむ, to relieve of household [domestic] cares.

naikō (内攻する), *vi.* to retrocede; 【醫】 strike in.

naikō (内訌), *n.* an internal disturbance [disorder]; domestic discord [disunion].

naikoku (内國), *n.* home. —内國製の, domestic; home-made; of home manufacture. ¶ 内國爲替, an inland [domestic] exchange. —内國船舶, vessels flying the national flag. —内國市場, home market. —内國郵便, domestic mail.

naikun (内訓), *n.* private [secret] instructions.

naimaku (内幕), *n.* private circumstances.

naimaku (内膜), *n.* 【解】 the lining membrane.

naimei (内命), *n.* a secret order.

naimen (内面), *n.* ❶ the inside; the interior. ❷ =*rimen* (裏面). ¶ 内面生活, inner life.

naimu (内務), *n.* home [internal] affairs. ¶ 内務部長, the chief of the department of internal affairs (of a prefecture). —内務大臣; 内務卿, the Minister (of State) for Home Affairs; the Minister of the Interior; the Secretary (of State) for the Home Affairs (英. the Home Secretary と略す); the Secretary of the Interior (米). —内務監察官, an administrative inspector. —内務省, the Department of Home Affairs; the Home Office; the Department [Ministry] of the Interior.

nainai (内内), *ad.* privately; secretly; confidentially. —内々で式を擧げる, to hold privately a wedding ceremony.

nainenki (内燃機), *n.* an internal-combustion engine.

naiō (内應), *n.* betrayal; secret communication. ☞ *naitsū*.

nairan (内亂), *n.* a civil war; an internal disturbance.

nairan (内覽), *n.* a private view [inspection]. —内覽に供する, to submit for a person's private inspection.

naisai (内債), *n.* a home debt; a domestic loan.

naisai (内濟), *n.* compromise; private settlement. —内濟にする, to compromise; compound; settle privately [out of court].

naisei (内省), *n.* introspection; reflexion. —内省する, to introspect; reflect.

naisei (内政), *n.* domestic [home] administration (affairs). —内政に干渉する, to interfere in the domestic affairs.

naisetsu (内接する), *v.* 【數】 to be inscribed; touch internally. ¶ 内接圓, an inscribed circle.

naishi (乃至), *prep.* from...to; between...and. ——, *conj.* or.

naishi (内示する), *vt.* to show privately [confidentially].

naishidokoro (内侍所), *n.* the hall where the Yata Mirror is installed.

naishin (内心), *n.* ❶ (心底) real intention; inner [inmost] heart; the state of one's mind. ❷ 【數】 the inner centre. ——, *ad.* at heart; inwardly; secretly (内々).

naishin (内診), *n.* ❶ (體内診察) endoscopy. ❷ office consultation.

naishinnō (内親王), *n.* a [an Imperial; a royal] princess; princess of the Blood.

naishō (内證), *n.* ❶ (秘密) secrecy. ❷ (身上) one's private circumstances. —父に内證で, without one's father's knowledge. ¶ 内證話, whispering; secret talk.

naishōgan (内障眼), *n.* a cataract.

naishoku (内職), *n.* a private work [occupation]; job-work; by-work [-business]. —内職の口を探す, to search for job-work.

naishūgen (内祝言), *n.* a private marriage; a family celebration of marriage.

naisō (内奏する), *v.* to report privately to the Emperor; make an informal representation to the Throne.

naitan (内探), *n.* a secret investigation [inquiry].

naitatsu (内達), *n.* private [secret] instructions.

naitei (内定する), *v.* to decide unofficially [privately].

naitei (内偵する), *vt.* to investigate secretly; make private inquiries.

naiteki (内的), *a.* inner (生活等).

naitsū (内通する), *v.* to communicate secretly [betray] to the enemy. ¶ 内通者, a betrayer.

naiya (内野), *n.* 【野球】 the infield; the diamond.

naiyaku (内約), *n.* a private [secret] contract [agreement]; a secret understanding. —内約する, to make a private contract; enter into a secret understanding.

naiyō (内用), *n.* (内服) internal use [application]. ¶ 内用藥, a medicine for internal use.

naiyō (内容), *n.*. contents; substance; matter. —書物の内容, the contents of a book. ¶ 内容見本, a specimen copy (一冊の); sample pages (或部分). —内容證明 (郵便), certification of contents.

naiyū (内憂), *n.* domestic troubles; internal difficulties. ¶ 内憂外患, troubles both at home and abroad; domestic troubles and external disasters.

naizō (内臟), *n.* 【解】 the splanchna; the entrails; the intestines; the viscera.

najimi (馴染), *n.* ❶ (親密) familiarity; intimacy; acquaintance. ❷ (知人) an acquaintance; an intimate.

najimu (馴染む), *vi.* to become familiar *with*; be attached *to*; take *to*; be domesticated (馴れる). —乳母に馴染む, to take to one's (wet-)nurse. —仕事に馴染む, to become [grow] used to the work.

najiru (詰じる), *vt.* to twit; taunt.

naka (中), *n.* (內部) the interior; the inside. —中三日, three clear days. —町の中で, in [on (米)] the street. —箱の中を搜す, to search the inside of a box. **——e, ——-ni,** *prep.* (*a*) in; into: (*b*) (兩者の中) between: (*c*) (多數の中) among; amongst: (*d*) (眞只中) amid; amidst; in the midst *of*: (*e*) (內部) within; inside. —火の中へ投げ込む, to throw it into the fire.

naka (仲), *n.* relations; terms. —仲が惡い, to be on bad terms *with* (a person; each other). —仲に入る, to mediate *between*; act as go-between. —仲のよい友達, an intimate friend. —仲を裂く, to part [sever] the couple ((two lovers)).

nakaba (半), *n.* ❶ (半分) half. ❷ (中程) middle; midst. **——,** *ad.* partly; in part; half. —討論半ばに, in the course of debate. —半ば隱れてゐる, to be half concealed.

nakabataraki (仲働), *n.* a parlour-maid; a housemaid.

nakadachi (仲立), *n.* agency; medium; good offices. —仲立する, to intermediate *between*; mediate *between*; act as go-between. ¶ 仲立人, a broker; a middleman.

nakadaka (凸の), *a.* convex.

nakagai (仲買), *n.* brokerage. —仲買する, to act as broker; job (株式・貨物を). ¶ 仲買人, a broker; a commission agent; a middleman; a jobber. —仲買手數料, brokerage.

nakagoro (中頃), *ad.* about the middle *of*.

nakahodo (中程), *n.* the middle; midway. ☞ *chūto* (中途).

nakairi (中入), *n.* a recess.

nakakubo (凹の), *a.* concave.

nakama (仲間), *n.* ❶ (朋輩) a comrade; a companion; a mate. ❷ (同業者) a fellow-trader [craftsman]; a *confrère* (佛). ❸ (協力者) a partner; an associate; a co-partner. ❹ (徒黨) a company; a set; a circle. —仲間に入る, to take stock [part] *in*; join. —仲間を離れて, separated from one's fellows. —仲間外れにされる, to be treated as an outsider. ¶ 仲間贔屓, partiality to one's own party. —仲間喧嘩, a quarrel among a party.

nakamaku (中幕), *n.* an interact; an interlude; an *entr'acte* (佛); an intermezzo.

nakami (中實), *n.* contents; inside; substance.

nakanaka (中中), *ad.* ❶ (餘程) very; quite; exceedingly. ❷ (容易) easily; readily. —中々怒らぬ, [*a.*] slow to anger. —中々骨が折れる, to require no slight trouble. —中々承知しない, He will not readily consent.

nakanaori (仲直り), *n.* reconciliation. —仲直りする, to become reconciled; make it up *with*; make one's peace *with*; be friends again.

nakaniwa (中庭), *n.* a courtyard; a court.

nakanzuku (就中), *ad.* especially; particularly; above all.

nakaore (中折-帽子), *n.* a soft hat.

nakare (勿れ), *v.* be not; do not; have not; must [should; ought] not; never....

nakariseba (なかりせば), if there be not; but for; were it not for.

nakashi (仲仕), *n.* a cargo coolie; a stevedore; a longshoreman.

nakasu (中洲), *n.* a holm, holme; a delta (河口の三角洲).

nakasu (泣かす), *vt.* ❶ to make ((let)) (a person) cry. ❷ (感動) to move (a person) to tears. ❸ (迷惑) to bother; put (a person) to trouble. —親を泣かす, to bother one's parents.

nakatagai (仲違ひ), *n.* discord; disagreement; dissension. —仲違ひする, to disagree; quarrel; fall out *with*.

nakatsugi (仲次, 仲繼), *n.* brokerage; agency; an agent (人); a relay (驛馬などの). ¶ 仲繼港, a transit port.

nakayasumi (中休), *n.* a recess; breathing time. —中休みする, to take rest [breath]; take [have] a recess; lie [rest] on one's oars.

nakayoku (仲好く), *ad.* intimately; harmoniously; on good [intimate; friendly] terms. —仲よくする, to get on [stand] well *with*; get on friendly terms *with*; agree together.

nakayoshi (仲好), *n.* ❶ (親密) familiarity; intimacy. ❷ (親友) an intimate [a bosom] friend; a (an old) chum.

nakayubi (中指), *n.* the middle finger; the long finger.

nakenashi (なけなしの金), what little money one has.

nakereba (なければ), ❶ if there

[it] be not; but for. ❷ =*ara-zareba*. —助がなければ, without the aid *of*; but for the aid *of*. —品格が伴はなければ, unless accompanied by character.

naki (泣), *n.* weeping; crying. —泣きの涙で, in bitter tears; crying mournfully. —泣きを入れる, ① (賣買解約を懇願する) to beg for the cancellation of a contract. ② (愁訴する) to cry mercy.

naki (なき), *a.* ❶ (無き) devoid *of*; destitute *of*; wanting [lacking] *in*. ☞ *nai* (無い) の❶ ❷ (亡き) deceased; dead; late. —亡き父, one's deceased [late] father.

nakiakasu (泣明かす), *vt.* to weep [cry] all night (through); weep the night out.

nakiato (亡き後), after one's death. —亡き後を弔ふ, to hold a religious service for the dead; console the spirit of the deceased.

nakidasu (泣出す), *vi.* to begin to cry [weep]; give way to tears; fall to crying 《sobbing》. —…を見て泣き出す, to cry out at the sight *of*. —わッと泣き出す, to burst into tears; burst out crying.

nakifusu (泣伏す), *vi.* to throw oneself down in tears.

nakigao (泣顔), *n.* a tearful face; a crying [weeping] face; a tear-stained face. —泣顔を隠す, to hide one's tears; turn aside one's tear-stained face (反ける).

nakigara (遺骸), *n.* the dead body; the remains.

nakigoe (泣聲), *n.* a tearful voice; cry; whine (哀聲).

nakigoe (鳴聲), *n.* a cry; a call; a song; moo (牛の); neigh (馬の); whinny (同上); wee-wee (豚の); baa (羊の); bow-wow (犬の); mew (猫·鷗の); howl (狼の); roar (獅子·虎等の); (小鳥の) twit-twit; chirping; piping (高鳴); coo (鳩の); cock-a-doodle-doo (鷄の); quack (家鴨の); caw (鴉の); cuckoo (杜鵑の); chirp (蟀蟋の); croak (蛙の).

nakigoto (泣言), *n.* a complaint; a grievance. —泣事を言ふ, to complain *of*; grumble *at*; murmur *at*; croak *at*.

nakiharasu (泣腫らす), *v.* to have (one's eyes) swollen with tears.

nakijakuri (嘘唏, 歔欷), *n.* a sob; sobbing. —嘘唏する, to sob; sigh convulsively.

nakijōgo (泣上戸), *n.* a maudlin person; a sentimental drunkard.

nakikurasu (泣暮す), *vi.* to spend one's days in tears; weep the day away; live in sorrow.

nakikuzureru (泣崩れる), *vi.* to abandon oneself to tears; cry one's heart out.

nakimane (泣眞似する), *vi.* to shed false [sham] tears; feign weeping; shed crocodile tears.

nakimushi (泣蟲), *n.* Ⓢ 泣みそ. a blubberer; a cry-baby.

nakineiri (泣寐入), *n.* ❶ (子等が) crying oneself to sleep. ❷ (しぶしぶ往生すること) reluctant submission. —泣寐入りになる, to be obliged to pass it over; give it up reluctantly. —彼等はたうとう泣寐入りになった, They ended by letting the matter drop.

nakisakebu (泣叫ぶ), *vi.* to shriek; scream; howl.

nakitsubusu (泣潰す), *vt.* to cry (one's eyes) out; cry [weep] (oneself) blind.

nakitsuku (泣附く), *vt.* to entreat [implore; beseech].

nakitsura (泣面), *n.* a tearful face. —泣面に蜂, "Misfortunes seldom come singly."

nakiwakare (泣別), *n.* tearful parting; parting in tears.

nakiwarai (泣笑), *n.* a tearful smile; smiling through one's tears.

nakōdo (媒介), *n.* a go-between; a match-maker: match-making (媒妁). —媒介役をつとめる, to play the part of a match-maker.

naku (泣く), *v.* to cry (聲を立てて); weep (聲を潛めて); sob (啜泣く); shed tears (流涕する). —泣き止む, to stop crying. —心行く迄泣く, to have a good cry; weep oneself out. —泣きながら物語る, to tell a story with tears. —泣いて乳を求める, to cry for milk. —死骸に縋って泣く, to weep over a person's remains.

naku (鳴·啼く), *vi.* ❶ (獸類) to cry: (犬) bark; bay; howl: (猫) mew: (牛) low; moo (牝); bellow (牡): (馬) neigh; whinny (低聲で): (驢馬) brag: (豕) grunt; squeak; squeal: (羊·山羊等) bleat; baa (小羊): (獅子·虎等) roar; growl: (狼) howl: (熊) growl: (猿) gibber; chatter: (兎·鼠等) squeal; squeak: (象) trumpet. ❷ (鳥) to cry; sing; chant; chirp (小鳥): (鷄) crow (雄); cockadoo (時を告げる); cackle (雌); cluck (同上); pip (雛); peep (同上): (家鴨) quack: (鵞鳥) cackle; gabble; gaggle; hiss: (七面鳥) gobble: (鶴) whoop: (鷲·鷹·孔雀等) scream; screech: (鶫·つぐみ等) pipe; whistle: (鶯·カナリヤ等) sing; warble; pipe: (郭公) cuckoo: (鴉) caw; croak (大鴉): (鳩) coo: (鸚鵡) talk: (梟) hoot; whoop;

scream; screech: (雀·燕·目白等) chirp; twitter. ❷ (蟲) chirp; chirrup; stridulate: (蜂·蚊等) hum; buzz; boom: (蟋蟀) chirp: (蟬) sing: (蛙) croak.

nakunaku (泣く泣く), *ad.* ❶ with tears; weeping. ❷ (澁々) reluctantly; unwillingly.

nakunaru (無·失くなる), *vi.* to be gone. ❶ (紛失) to be lost; be missing. ❷ (消滅) to disappear; vanish; be lost. ❸ (盡きる) to be exhausted; be used up; run out. ❹ (死亡) to die; pass away.

-nakunaru (なくなる), *vi.* to cease to (fear, 恐[こ]く); come not to (be novel, 珍らしく).

nakusu (無·失くす), *vt.* Ⓢ 無くなす. to lose. —子をなくす, to lose a child; have a child dead. —酒で財産をなくす, to drink away one's property.

nakute (無くて), *prep.* for want [lack] of. —常識がなくては, without [lacking; wanting] common sense. —無くて困る, to suffer from want *of*. —無くてはならぬ, ① [*a.*] indispensable; necessary; vital. ② [*vi.*] to be unable to do without; cannot be dispensed with; be unable to spare. —蝙蝠傘がいるか. なくてもよい, Do you need an umbrella? No, I can do without it.

nama (生の), *a.* ❶ (調理せざる) raw; uncooked. ❷ (不熟) unripe; green; crude. ❸ (新鮮) fresh; new. ¶ 生欠[なまあくび], stifled yawn. —生ビール, draught-beer. —生バタ(鯡), fresh butter (herrings). —生血, fresh blood. —生米, raw [uncooked] rice. —生卵, a raw egg.

namaatatakai (生暖かい), *a.* lukewarm; tepid.

namabyōhō (生兵法), *n.* ❶ superficial knowledge of military tactics; crude tactics. ❷ (半可通の知識) smattering; little knowledge; sciolism. —生兵法は大怪我の基, "A little knowledge is a dangerous thing."

namae (名前), *n.* a name. ☞ *na* (名).

namagakumon (生學問), *n.* superficial [slight; little] knowledge; smattering; sciolism.

namagawa (生皮), *n.* a (raw) hide; a pelt; a raw [untanned] skin.

namagiki (生聞), *n.* smattering; half knowledge.

namagoroshi (生殺し), *n.* being half-killed. ☞ *hangoroshi* (半殺し). —蛇の生殺し, ① a half-killed snake. ② (いづれとも決せぬ) being unsettled; hanging in the balance; being in suspense.

namagusa (腥·物), *n.* animal food. ¶ 腥坊主, a depraved priest.

namagusai (腥い), *a.* fishy (魚の); bloody (血腥い); smelling of blood (同上).

namahanka (生半可の), *a.* ❶ (不完全) incomplete; imperfect; done by halves. ❷ (淺薄) superficial; shallow. —生半可の英語, superficial knowledge of English. —生半可で止める, to leave it half-done.

namahenji (生返事), *n.* ❶ (不確定の) a vague [half] answer. ❷ (不承不承の) a reluctant answer. —生返事をする, to give a vague answer; answer reluctantly; give a reluctant answer.

namaiki (生意氣), *n.* ❶ (氣取り) affectation. ❷ (差出る事) impertinence; sauciness. ❸ (自惚) conceit; self-conceit. ❹ (鐵面皮) impudence. ——**-na**, *a.* ❶ affected. ❷ saucy; impertinent. ❸ conceited; self-conceited. ❹ impudent; cheeky. —生意氣な事を云ふ, to give cheek. —生意氣云ふな, Don't be impertinent!; None of your impertinence!

namajikka (憖ッか), *ad.* thoughtlessly; inconsiderately; half-heartedly (本氣でなく). —憖ッかな計畫, a half-hearted attempt.

namajiroi (生白い), *a.* pale; wan; sickly. —生白い月, a sickly [pale] moon.

namakajiri (生噛り), *n.* superficial learning; little [slight] knowledge; smattering. —英語を生噛りする, to get a smattering of English.

namakemono (怠惰者), *n.* an idler; an idle fellow; a dawdler; a lazybones. —このなまけものめ, You lazy hound [beggar]!

namakeru (怠ける), *v.* to idle; dawdle; neglect (怠る). ——, *a.* idle; indolent; lazy. —怠け暮らす, to idle away one's life [time]. —仕事を怠ける, to neglect one's work; idle over one's work.

namaki (生木), *n.* a live tree; green wood; unseasoned wood (生乾きの木材).

namakizu (生傷), *n.* a green [fresh] wound.

namako (海鼠), *n.* 【棘皮】 the trepang; the sea-slug; the *bêche-de-mer* 【佛】. ¶ 生子鐵板, corrugated iron.

namakubi (生首), *n.* a head recently cut off [severed] from the body.

namakura (なまくら), *n.* a blunt sword; a dull blade.

namamekashii (艶しい), *a.* ❶ (婀娜) beautiful; charming; fascinating. ❷ (艶媚) coquettish; amorous.

namamizu (生水), *n.* unboiled water.

namamono (生物), *n.* ❶ the raw [uncooked] food. ❷ (肴) fish.

namamonoshiri (生物識), *n.* a smatterer; a sciolist.

namanaka (生中, 生半), *ad.* imperfectly; incompletely; by halves. —生半な金ぢゃすむまい, No little money will be required.

namanamashii (生生しい), *a.* fresh; green; immature.

namanie (生煮の), *a.* half-cooked [-done; -boiled]; underdone.

namanurui (生温い), *a.* lukewarm; tepid; mild.

namari (鉛), *n.* lead. —鉛色の, lead (-coloured); livid; lead-gray.

namari (訛), *n.* ❶ an (a provincial) accent; brogue. ❷ a corruption (轉訛). ¶ お國訛, one's native brogue.

namari (生節), *n.* a half-dried bonito.

namaru (訛る), *v.* to speak with a provincial accent.

namasu (膾), *n.* raw fish and vegetables seasoned in vinegar; fish salad.

namauo (生魚), *n.* Ⓢ 生肴. a raw fish.

namayake (生燒の), *a.* half-roasted; half-baked (パン等); half-done; underdone.

namayoi (生醉), *n.* ❶ slight intoxication. ❷ (半醉客) a half-drunken man. —生醉ひ本性たがはず, "There is truth in wine."

namazu (鯰), *n.* 【魚】the sheat-fish; the wels.

namazu (癜風), *n.* 【醫】pityriasis [tinea] versicolor.

namazume (生爪を剝がす), to tear a nail to the quick; sever a nail *from.*

namekuji (蛞蝓), *n.* 【腹足】Philomycus (slug の一種·學名).

nameraka (滑かな), *a.* ❶ (平滑) smooth; slippery; glib (表面等の). ❷ (つるつるした) glossy; sleek; velvety. ❸ (平坦) even; smooth; flat. —滑かな毛皮, a glossy fur. —滑かな雪の肌, a white smooth skin. ——**-ni,** *ad.* smoothly; 【音】*legato* 【伊】. —滑かにする, to (make) smooth.

nameru (舐·嘗める), *vt.* ❶ (ねぶる) to lick. ❷ (味ふ) to taste. ❸ (經驗) to taste; experience; suffer. ❹ (あなどる) to slight; make light of. —あらゆる困難を嘗める, to experience all kinds of hardships. —火が江戸の大半を舐めた, The fire licked up a greater part of Yedo.

nameshigawa (鞣皮), *n.* a leather; a tanned skin; a chamois-leather (羊·山羊·鹿等の).

namesu (鞣す), *vt.* to tan; taw (特に明礬と食鹽との溶液で).

nami (波), *n.* a wave; a billow (大濤); a ripple (小波); a breaker (岸に碎ける波); a surge (うねり). —浪と闘ふ, to buffet the waves. —浪を浴びる (端艇等が), to ship a sea. —世と共に波を揚げる, to swim with the tide [stream].

nami (竝), *n.* the medium [common] quality; the average. ☞ *futsū* (普通), *tsūjō* (通常). ——**-no,** *a.* common; ordinary; average. —竝の容色[きりょう]《丈》, the average personal appearance 《height》. —普通の人, an average [ordinary] man; a man of average [ordinary] talents [intelligence].

namiashi (竝足), *n.* a slow step; a foot-pace; a walking pace. —竝足!, (號令) Keep step!

namida (涙), *n.* a tear; a tear-drop. —せきくる涙, gushing tears. —涙なき人, a stone-hearted man. —涙に咽ぶ, to be choked with tears. —涙を流《滴ら》す, to shed 《drop》 tears. —涙を拭ふ, to dry [wipe] one's tears [eyes]. —涙を呑む, to choke down tears; gulp down sobs. —涙片手に物語る, to narrate with tears.

namidagumu (涙含む), *vi.* to be filled with [full of] tears. —涙ぐましい, sad; tragic; tearful.

namidappoi (涙ッぽい), *a.* maudlin; over-emotional; easily moved to tears.

namidakin (涙金), *n.* consolation money; a solatium (慰藉料).

namidatsu (波立つ), *vi.* to billow; swell (大波が); ripple (小波が); surge (海又は麥畑が). —波立てる水面, the broken water.

namigata (波形の), *a.* wavy; undulate.

namihazure (竝外れの), *a.* out of the common; out of [beyond] the ordinary; extraordinary.

namiji (波路), *n.* a (sea-)voyage. —波路遙かに, across 《over》 the sea.

namikaze (波風), *n.* winds and waves; disturbance (不和).

namiki (竝木), *n.* a row of trees. ¶ 竝木街道, an avenue.

naminami (波波と), *ad.* to the full [brim]; brimfully; overflowingly. —波々と酒を注ぐ, to fill the glass to the brim.

namisuru (蔑する), *vt.* to slight. ☞ *naigashiro.*

namiuchigiwa (波打際), *n.* a beach.

namiutsu (浪打つ), *vi.* to beat; dash, undulate; surge (群衆·麥畑など); wave (麥畑が)

namiyoke (波除), *n.* ❶ (防波堤) a mole; a breakwater. ❷ (汽船の) a bulwark; a dasher【米】; a dash-board.

namu (南無), *int.* 【梵】 Namo; save us.

namusan (南無三-寶), *int.* O heavens!; (By) heavens!

nan (男), *n.* a son.

nan (難), *n.* ❶ (困難) difficulty; trouble; hardship (艱難). ❷ (災難) a danger (危難); a calamity; a disaster; an accident. ❸ (缺點) a defect; a blemish. ❹ (非難) censure; charge. —難に遭ふ, to meet a disaster; encounter a danger; meet with an accident. —難を避ける, to fly [flee] from danger. ¶ 經營難, difficulty of management.

Nana (南阿), *n.* South Africa. ¶ 南阿聯邦, the Union of South Africa.

nanafushigi (七不思議), *n.* the seven wonders.

nanako (斜子), *n.* ❶ (彫刻物などが表面に打出す細點) the spawn [ovum]-like figure [pattern]. ❷ (織方) a silk stuff woven with threads of three strands. —斜子側の時計, a twilled-case watch.

nanakusa (七草), *n.* ❶ the seven herbs (of spring 《autumn》). ❷ the festival on the seventh day of January.

naname (斜), *n.* obliquity; slant. —斜の, oblique; diagonal; slanting. —御機嫌斜ならず, to be exceedingly [highly] pleased. ——**ni,** *ad.* obliquely; diagonally; aslant. —斜になる《する》, to cant; bevel; slant. —帽子を斜に被る, to cock one's hat.

nanashi (無名の), *a.* nameless; anonymous. ☞ ***mumei***.

nanatsu (七つ), *n.* seven.

nanba (難場), *n.* predicament. —難場を切り抜ける, to come out of the predicament.

nanban (何番), *n.* ❶ (番號) what number. ❷ (大さ) what size.

Nanbei (南米), *n.* South America.

nanben (何遍), *ad.* how many times; how often. ☞ ***ikudo***.

nanboku (南北), *n.* north and south. ¶ 南北朝, the Northern and Southern Dynasties. —南北戰爭, the American Civil War.

nanbu (南部), *n.* the southern part.

nanbutsu (難物), *n.* ❶ (人) an awkward customer; a (hard) nut to crack (又は物); a puzzler (同上). ❷ (物) a thing hard to dispose *of*; a puzzle; a crux. ❸ =***nanmon*** (難問).

nanbyō (難病), *n.* a serious disease; a difficult case; a disease hard to cure.

nanda (何だ), *pron.* what. ——, *int.* why; what. —何だ, この野郎, What! you wretch. —なあんだ, つまらない, Humbug!; Bah!

nanda (軟打), *n.* 【野球】 the band.

nandai (難題), *n.* ❶ (難問) a difficult [hard; knotty] problem [question]. ❷ (難件) a difficult matter [affair]; a difficulty. —難題を吹きかける, to bring up a difficult matter [affair].

nandaka (何だか), *ad.* somehow. ——, *pron.* something.

nandatte (何だって), ❶ (何で) why; for what reason. ❷ (どんなでも) what; whatever. ——, *int.* why; what.

nande (何で), *ad.* why. ☞ ***naniyue***.

nandei (軟泥), *n.* watery mud; slush; sludge; ooze (河等の).

nandemo (何でも), *pron.* ❶ any; anything; whatever. ❷ (悉く) everything. ——, *ad.* ❶ (是非とも) by all means; anyhow; at any cost [risk]. ❷ (兎にも角にも) at any rate; at all events. ❸ probably; perhaps. —何が何んでも, at all events. —何んでも彼んでも, ① anything and everything; all sorts of things. ② by all means; at any cost. —何んでもない, It is nothing [no matter].

nando (何度), *ad.* ❶ (幾たび) how often; how many times. ❷ (度盛りが) what degree.

nando (納戶), *n.* a dressing room; a closet.

nandoki (何時), *ad.* what time; what o'clock; when (いつ). —何時でも, at any time; whenever.

nangi (難儀), *n.* distress; hardship; difficulty; trouble; adversity (逆境). —難儀な仕事, a laborious work; an arduous task; a tough job. —難儀する, to meet with trouble; suffer hardships; pass through a hard experience. —人に難儀をかける, to cause a person distress; put a person in a difficulty.

nangyō-kugyō (難行苦行), *n.* penance; ascetic practices; religious austerities. —難行苦行をする, to do penance; suffer many hardships.

nani, nan, (何), *pron.* Ⓢ なーに. what; anything; something. ——, *a.* what; any; some. ——, *int.* what!; why!; well!; oh! —何とかして, somehow; in some way or other. —あの何とか云った人《物》, what-d'ye-call-him 《it》; the thingumbob. —何よりも, above all; first of all; of all things; before everything else.

—何のあてもなく, without any definite object; at random [hazard]. —何から何まで, all things; everything. —何は扨措き, above all; first of all. —何をするにも, whatever one may do; in doing anything. —何にもならぬ, to come to nothing [naught]. —何の役にも立たぬ, to be of no use [good]; be good for nothing. —心配するな, 何とかなるよ, Never mind, it will mend itself. —なに, かまふものか. Oh, I don't care.

nāni (何有に), *int.* no; why. ☞ *nani* (何).

nani (南緯), *n.* the south latitude; the south parallel. —南緯三十度二十分に, in 30° 20′ S. Lat.

nani (難易), *n.* hardness (or easiness); difficulty. —難易に關はらず, whether difficult or easy.

nanibun (何分), *ad.* in any way (是非); by all means (同上); please (何卒); anyway (どうも). —何分景氣がよいので, anyway, owing to the briskness of business.

nanigashi (某), *pron.* & *n.* a certain person; somebody; (Mr.) So-and-so.

nanigenaku (何氣なく), *ad.* unintentionally; undesignedly; casually (不圖). —何氣なき樣子で, pretending not to know; composedly (平然と); unconcernedly.

nanigoto (何事), *pron.* what; what matter 《business》; something (何か). —何事か. What's up?; What's the matter? —何事によらず, no matter what; everything (萬事). —何事が起らうとも, come what will [may]; whatever may happen. —何事を措いても, before anything else.

nanihodo (何程), *ad.* how much 《many》. ☞ *ikahodo* (いか程).

nanika (何か), *pron.* something; anything. ——, *a.* some; any. —何か(彼か)惡戯をする, to do some mischief or other. —何か食物が欲しい, I want something to eat. —何か御用ですか. Can I do anything for you? —何か氣に入らぬと見える, Something seems to disgruntle him.

nanika-kaka (何か彼か), some or other; this or that.

nanikato (何かと), *ad.* Ⓢ 何くれと. in various ways; one way or another. —何くれとなく, in various ways; in all sorts of things. —何くれと注意する, to give a person every precaution; take every care (of). —何かと云ふと國自慢をする, to take every opportunity to boast of his native place.

nanikuso (何糞), *int.* damn [dash; confound] it!

nanikuwanu (何喰はぬ顔して), looking as if nothing had happened; pretending not to know [see]; with an unconcerned air. —何喰はぬ顔する, to feign innocence (潔白を裝ふ); pretend ignorance (知らぬ振する); assume an unconcerned air (平氣を裝ふ).

nanimo-kamo (何も彼も), *pron.* & *n.* everything; all; one and all. —何もかも承知で, knowing what one is about; knowing the time of day. —何もかも一人でやる, to do everything by oneself.

nanimono (何もの), *pron.* ❶ (何者) who; what: some one: no one (打消). ❷ (何物) something; nothing (打消). —相手は何者か. What is the other party?

nanira (何等の), *a.* any; no; little. ☞ *nanra* (何等の).

nanishiro (何しろ), *ad.* Ⓢ 何せよ. anyhow; anyway; at any rate.

nanitozo (何卒), *ad.* please; pray; I pray you. ☞ *dōzo.*

naniyori (何よりな), *a.* most desirable; nicest; most charming.

naniyue (何故), *ad.* why; for what reason.

nanjaku (軟弱な), *a.* weak; feeble; effeminate. ☞ *jūjaku.*

nanji (汝), *pron.* you; thou (古體).

nanji (何時), *ad.* what time [o'clock]; when. —何時ですか. what time [o'clock] is it now?

nanji (難治の), *a.* ❶ (醫し難い) incurable; inveterate; fatal. ❷ (馭し難い) ungovernable.

nanji (難事), *n.* a difficult matter; a troublesome affair; a tough work.

nanjū (難澁), *n.* sufferings; distress; hardship. ☞ *nangi.*

nanka (南下する), *vi.* to go [advance; march] southward; turn to the south.

nanka (軟化), *n.* mollification (物又は意見); softening (同上); mitigation (緩和). —軟化する, to soften; yield; give ground.

nanka (何箇), *a.* how many. —何箇月, how many months.

nankai (難解の), *a.* hard to make out; difficult to understand; unintelligible; abstruse (晦澁な).

nankan (難關), *n.* a barrier; a bar. —難關を突破する, to surmount a difficulty; cut one's way through a barrier.

Nankin (南京), *n.* ❶ Nanking. ❷ [俗] (支那人) a Chinaman. ¶ 南京珠, a glass-bead. —南京花火, a cracker. —南京米, China rice. —南京鼠, the white mouse.

nankinmame (落花生), *n.* 【植】 the pea [ground]-nut.

nankinmushi (南京蟲), *n.* 【昆】 the (bed) bug.

nankitsu (難詰する), *vt.* to twit; taunt; reproach.

nankō (軟膏), *n.* a salve; an unguent; an ointment.

nankō-furaku (難攻不落の), *a.* impregnable.

nankotsu (軟骨), *n.* a cartilage.

nanku (難句), *n.* a difficult phrase; hard passages.

nankuse (難癖), *n.* a bad name; a fault (缺點). —難癖をつける, to give a bad name; find fault *with*; pick holes in another's coat.

nankyoku (南極), *n.* the south pole. ¶ 南極圈, the Antarctic circle. —南極探檢, an Antarctic expedition [exploration].

nankyoku (難局), *n.* a difficult [grave; serious] situation; a crisis. —難局に當る, to deal with [take charge of] a difficult situation; stand in the bre[illegible]

nankyū (軟球), *n.* 【庭球】 a soft ball.

nanmon (難問 -題), *n.* a difficult [hard] question; a knotty problem; a hard nut to crack. —難問を出す《に答へる》, to put 《answer》 a difficult question.

nan-naku (難なく), *ad.* with ease; without difficulty; without any trouble [effort].

nannan (垂とする), *vi.* to be approaching; be close [near] *upon*; be on the verge [point; brink] *of*. —死に垂んとして, lying at death's door; on the point [verge] of death. —七十に垂んとする, to be close upon seventy.

nannen (何年), *n.* what year; how many years (期間). —何年か前, some years ago.

nannichi (何日), *n.* what day of the month; how many days (期間). —今日は何日ですか, What day of the month is this?

nanno (何の), *a.* ❶ (種類·性質等を問ふ) what kind of; what. ❷ =*nanra* (何等の). **——**, *ad.* (強語的否定) never; not at all. —何んの益もない, to bring no profit whatever. —何んの斯のと言って, by using every pretext. —何んの, お安い御用です, Not at all; it is no trouble.

nannyo (男女), *n.* =***danjo***.

Nanō (南歐), *n.* South Europe; the southern part of Europe.

nanori (名乘を揚げる), to declare one's own name. —立候補の名乘を揚げる, to announce oneself [come forward] as a candidate.

nanoru (名乘る), *v.* to discover oneself *to*; introduce oneself *to*; give [declare] one's name *to*. —警察へ名乘り出る, to give oneself up to the police.

nanpa (軟派), *n.* the moderate party; the moderates. ¶ 軟派議員, a moderate member; a moderatist.

nanpa (難破), *n.* shipwreck. ☞ ***nansen.***

nanpū (軟風), *n.* ❶ a breeze; a light [soft] wind. ❷ 【氣象】 a gentle breeze.

Nanpyōyō (南氷洋), *n.* the Antarctic Ocean.

nanra (何等の), *a.* no; any; what (何んたる). —何等の價値なき, of no value whatever. —何等の理由《故障》もなく, without any cause 《obstacle》 whatever.

nansai (何歲), how old; what age.

nansen (難船), *n.* ❶ (難破) wreck; shipwreck. ❷ (難破船) a wreck; a wrecked ship; a ship in a distress. —難船さす, to wreck a ship. —難破する, to be shipwrecked; be wrecked. —難船を救ふ, to rescue a ship in distress. ¶ 難船者, a castaway.

Nanshi (南支), *n.* South China.

nansho (難所), *n.* a place hard to pass; a perilous [dangerous] path.

nanshoku (難色), *n.* disapprobation; disapproval; displeasure. —難色あり, ① to show disapprobation. ② to look doubtful [dubious] of success.

nansui (軟水), *n.* soft water.

nansurezo (何爲ぞ), *ad.* why; wherefore.

nantai-dōbutsu (軟體動物), *n.* 【動】 Mollusca (學名); the molluscs.

nantan (南端), *n.* the southern extremity.

nanten (南天), *n.* 【植】 the nandina; the sacred bamboo.

nanten (難點), *n.* a difficult [knotty] point.

nanto (何と), *pron.* & *ad.* what; how. **——**, *int.* I say; well.

nantomo (何とも), nothing; not at all. —何んとも思はぬ, not to care a fig *for*; care nothing *for*. —何とも言へぬ悲しさ, unspeakable sorrow. —何とも云はずに, without any word. —何とも申譯がありません, I do not know how to apologize to you.

nantonaku (何となく), *ad.* somehow; in some way. —何となく物悲しい, to feel vague sorrow.

nantonareba (何となれば), *conj.* for; because.

Nanyō (南洋), *n.* the South Seas. ¶ 南洋諸島, the South Sea Islands.

nanzan (難產), *n.* a difficult delivery [childbirth]. —難產する, to be delivered of a child with difficulty; have a difficult delivery.

nanzo (何ぞ), *ad.* why; how. ☞ ***izukunzo.***

nao (猶,尙), *n.* ❶ (尙一層) more; further. ❷ =***naosara*** (尙更). ❸ [猶] (未だ) still; yet. ❹ (丁度) just like; no more...than; might as well. —尙熟考の爲めに, for further consideration. —尙困ッたことには, what is worse; to make the matter worse. —それなら尙結構だ, So much the better.

naomata (尙又), *ad.* ❶ (且又) moreover; besides. ❷ (加之) in addition *to*; into the bargain. ——, *conj.* not only [merely]... but (also).

naonao (尙尙), *ad.* more and more; still [far] more; much more. ☞ ***naosara.***

naore (名折), *n.* disgrace; dishonour; blot; reproach.

naoru (直·治る), *vi.* ❶ (矯正) to be corrected [reformed]; grow out *of*; get rid *of* (脫す). ❷ (修繕) to be mended [repaired]; be set to rights. ❸ (治癒) to be cured *of*; recover *from*; be healed (傷). ❹ (復舊) to be restored. —直れ!, (號令) Eyes front! —とても直らぬ, ① (修復·矯正し難い) to be past mending《praying for》. ② (不治) to be beyond recovery; be incurable. —齒痛《腹痛》が治る, to get rid of [get over] one's tooth-ache《stomachache》.

naosara (尙更), *ad.* still more 《less》; all the more; yet again.

naoshi (直し), *n.* ❶ (訂正) correction; 【印】alterations [author's corrections]. ❷ (修繕) mending; repairing. ❸ (直す人) a mender; a repairer. —靴を直しにやる, to send boots for repair.

naosu (直す), *vt.* ❶ (訂正) to correct; revise; put right. ❷ (修繕) to mend; repair. ❸ (治療) to cure; heal; remedy. ❹ (矯正) to correct; rectify; put [set] right. ❺ (復舊) to restore; recover; bring to the former condition. ❻ (變更) to alter; change. ❼ (整頓) to adjust; set; set [put] to rights; put in order. —數へ直す, to count over again; recount. —直して惡くする, to change for the worse. —惡癖を直す, to break oneself of a bad habit; give up a bad habit. —病氣を治す, to cure a person of his disease. —時計の針を直す, to put [set] right the hand of a clock.

naoya (名親), *n.* a sponsor; a godfather; a godmother.

naozari (等閑にする), *vt.* to neglect. —職務を等閑にする, to neglect [slight; make light of] one's duties.

napukin (拭布), *n.* a (table-) napkin; a table-linen; a serviette (食卓の); a paper-napkin (紙の).

nara (楢), *n.* 【植】Quercus glandulifera (oak の一種·學名).

nara (なら), *conj.* if; in case *of*; provided (that); when. —必要なら, if (it is) necessary; ¨ need be. —雨天なら延期する, It will be put off in case of rain.

naraba (ならば), ❶ =***nara*** (なら). ❷ (出來るなら) if possible.

naraberu (竝べる), *vt.* ❶ (整列) to arrange; range; line. ❷ (列擧) to enumerate; count [reckon] up. —きちんと竝べる, to put [arrange; place] in good order. —店に商品を竝べる, to arrange goods in a shop. —反對理由を竝べる, to enumerate one's reasons *against*.

narabi (竝,列), *n.* ❶ [竝] (順) arrangement; order; rank. ❷ [列] (線) a line; a row; a side (側). ❸ =***hirui.*** —竝びなき, unequalled; unrivalled; peerless. —竝に, [*conj.*] and (also); both... and; both together; as well as.

narabu (竝·列ぶ), *vi.* ❶ (連なる) to be (arranged; drawn up) in a row; lie in a row; (stand in a) line. ❷ (竝行する) to be parallel; stand side by side. —竝んで, in a row; side by side; abreast. (人と竝んで步む, to walk abreast with a person.)

naradewa (ならでは), Ⓢ でなくては. unless; but; except.

narai (習), *n.* a custom; a usage; practice. —これが浮世の習ひだ, This is the way of the world.

naraikomu (習込む), *vt.* to study [learn] well; learn thoroughly; gain a thorough knowledge *of*.

naraku (奈落), *n.* ❶ [梵 Naraka] a hell; an abyss. ❷【劇場】a trap(-cellar). —奈落の底に陷る, to fall into an abyss [the bottomless deep].

naranu (ならぬ), Ⓢ ならない. ❶ (...せねばならぬ) must; to have to; be obliged to; be compelled [forced] to. ❷ (當然である,べきである) ought to; should; shall. ❸ (...してはならぬ) must not; should not. ❹ (出來ぬ) can not. —長者は尊敬せねばならぬ, You should respect your seniors. —此の室へ這入ッてはならぬ, You must not enter this room.

narashi (均), *n.* =***heikin.***

narasu (均す), *vt.* ❶ (平にする) to level; smooth; flatten; make flat. ❷ (平均する) to average.

—道を均らす, to level the road.

narasu (鳴す), *vt.* ❶ to ring; chime (調子よく); toll (同上); tang (高く); clink (パチリと, カチリと); clank (ガチャリと); toot (吹きならす). ❷ (不平を) to express [give vent to] (one's dissatisfaction). ❸ (有名) to be well-known; be famous; flourish (榮える). —手を鳴らす, to clap one's hands. —呼鈴を鳴らす, to ring the (call-)bell; pull the bell; press the (electric) button.

narasu (馴す), *vt.* to tame; train; break. —馬を馴らす, to break in a horse. —野獣を馴らす, to tame a wild animal.

narasu (慣·熟す), *vt.* to accustom; inure; season (氣候に). —勞働に慣らす, to accustom a person to labour. —困難に慣らす, to inure a person to hardships.

narau (習ふ), *v.* ❶ to learn; study (研究). ❷ (教はる) to be taught [instructed *in*]; take lessons *in*; get training *in*. ❸ (練習する) to practise; exercise. —繪を習ふ, to practise painting. —ピアノを習ふ, to take lessons in piano; practise on the piano.

narau (倣ふ), *vt.* to imitate; follow; take *after*. —…に倣って, after; in imitation *of*. —例に倣ふ, to follow another's example.

narawashi (習慣), *n.* the habit; the usage. ☞ ***shūkan***.

narazumono (ならず者), *n.* a rascal; a rogue.

nareai (馴合), *n.* ❶ (通謀) collusion; conspiracy. ❷ (私通) fornication. —馴合ひで, in collusion (*with*). ¶ 馴合ひ夫婦, an unmarried couple. —馴合ひ勝負, a made-up match; a cross.

nareau (馴合ふ), *vi.* ❶ (私通) to become intimate *with*. ❷ (共謀) to collude *with*; intrigue *with*; conspire together. —馴れ合って事を計る, to plot together.

naredomo (なれども), *conj.* ❶ (さり乍ら) but; however. ❷ (と雖も) though; as; although.

narekko (馴れっこになる), to get used to it.

narenareshii (狎狎しい), *a.* familiar; intimate; free —狎々しく話し掛ける, to talk to a person in a familiar tone [in a friendly manner].

nare-no-hate (成れの果), one's ruined state; the wreck [ruin; shadow] of one's former self.

nareru (慣·馴·狎れる), *vi.* ❶ 〔慣〕 to get used; be habituated; be inured. ❷ 〔馴〕 to become tame [domesticated]. ❸ 〔狎〕 to get [become] familiar [intimate] *with*. ❹ to be seasoned (氣候等に); be naturalized (土地に); become acclimatized (動植物が風土に); become acclimated (人が風土に). ❺ 〔熟〕 (食物) to be seasoned (鮨·漬物等); be matured (酒等). —慣れた土地, a locality with which one has grown familiar. —熟れた漬物, seasoned pickles. —慣れぬ商賣, a trade in which one is inexperienced. —恩に狎れる, to come to look upon a person's favour as a matter of course. —貧乏に慣れる, to get used to poverty.

nari (形), *n.* ❶ (形狀) a form; a figure; a shape. ❷ (柄) size; stature. ❸ (服裝) dress; costume. —弓なりの, bow-shaped. —V字形に, in V-shape. —大きな態をして, while you are a big boy ((girl)); in spite of his great size. —彼は形には一向無頓著だ, He is quite indifferent about his dress.

nari (鳴), *n.* sound; ring; ringing; stroke (時計の). —鳴りを靜める, to become silent.

nari (なり), ❶ (するや否や) on; as soon as; when. ❷ (孰れなりと) whether...or. ❸ (…の儘) as it is ((was)).

nariagari (成上り-者), *n.* an upstart; a parvenu. —成上る, to rise in the world.

narifuri (形振), *n.* appearance; costume; dress. ☞ ***nari*** (形).

narihateru (成果てる), *vi.* to come to (one's fate); be reduced to (a wretched condition).

narihibiku (鳴響く), *vi.* to resound echo; reverberate.

narikawaru (成代る), *v.* to take the place *of*. —…に成り代って, on behalf *of*; in the place *of*.

narikin (成金), *n.* ❶ 【將棋】 a promoted man. ❷ (俄分限) a parvenu; a *narikin* 〔日〕; a *nouveau riche* 〔佛〕; the new rich 〔俗〕. ¶ 戰爭成金, a war-profiteer. —成金根性, a parvenu spirit.

narimono (鳴物), *n.* a musical instrument. —鳴物入りで, ① with a musical accompaniment. ② with a great deal of trumpeting. ¶ 鳴物停止, suspension of musical performances.

narinbō (癩病), *n.* leprosy; a leper (人).

narisagaru (成下る), *vi.* to become; be reduced *to*; degrade [degenerate] *into*.

narisokonau (成損ふ), *v.* to fail to be [become]; miss becoming [being], miss one's chance of becoming.

naritachi (成立), *n.* ❶ (組織)

formation; organization. ❷ (由來) history; origin. —成立ちから考へると, if we consider how it came into being.

naritatsu (成立つ), *vi.* ❶ (成立する) to come into being [existence]; be reached [arrived at] (了解など); be materialized. ❷ (より成る) to consist *of*; be formed [made up] *of*; be composed *of*.

nariwai (生業), *n.* ❶ (生計) livelihood; living. ❷ (職業) calling; employment; occupation.

nariwataru (鳴渡る), *vi.* to sound; resound; re-echo. —天下に鳴り渡る, to spread throughout the country.

nariyuki (成行), *n.* the course (of events); the development (of affairs); the progress; a result (結果). —自然の成行, the course of nature; a natural result. —成行に委す, to leave a thing to take its own [natural] course; let things run their course.

naru (生る), *v.* to bear; (bear) fruit; produce. —此木には實が澤山生る《餘り生らぬ》, This tree bears much 《little》 fruit. —林檎が澤山なってる, There are many apples (growing) on the trees.

naru (爲·成る), *v.* ❶ to become; grow; turn. ❷ (成就) to succeed; be completed [finished]. ❸ (達す) to reach; attain; come *to*. ❹ (變移) to pass *into*; change *into*; lead *to*. ❺ (扮裝) to act *as*; take the part *of*. —成り行く, to turn out; take a turn; become *of*; end. —事成る, to succeed in the attempt. —暗くなる, to grow [get] dark. —段々强くなる, to grow in strength. —都合が惡くなる, to go wrong. —癖になる, to grow into a habit. —病氣《滿期》になる, to fall ill 《due》. —大暴風になる, to pass into a great storm. —回々敎徒になる, to turn Mohammedan. —總額千圓になる, to amount [come (up)] to 1000 *yen*. —豪[?]い人になる, to grow up to be a great man. —十五歲になる, to reach the fifteenth year. —人の身に成って見る, to put oneself in another's place. —纖維より成る, to be com[posed] of fibres. —多くの成分より to consist of many ingred[ients]. —雪が雨となる, The snow melts into rain. —七つになるかならずである, He is scarcely seven years old. —も一つで十になる, One more will make ten.

naru (鳴る), *vi.* ❶ to sound; ring (鐘·鈴など); sing (耳); rumble (腹); roar (海など). ❷ (反響) to resound; echo. ❸ (聞える) to resound; ring; be celebrated; be well-known. —今三時が鳴った, It has just struck three. —ドンはまだ鳴らない, The noon-gun is not yet fired. —其の名天下に鳴る, His fame resounds throughout the world; The world rings with his fame.

narubeku (可成), *ad.* =*narutake*.

naruhodo (成程), indeed; to be sure; just so; That accounts for it (道理で).

naruko (鳴子), *n.* a (bird-)clapper.

narutake (成丈), *ad.* as...as possible; as...as one can. —成るたけなら, if circumstances permit; if possible. —成るたけ早く, at your earliest convenience; with all convenient speed; as quickly as possible [may be].

nasake (情), *n.* ❶ (愛情) affection. ❷ (慈悲, 憐み) mercy; pity; benevolence; compassion; sympathy (同情). —お情け及第, promotion from compassion. —情ある人, a man of feeling; a soft [tender; warm]-hearted man. —情の籠った言葉, tender words. —情を知らぬ, unfeeling; hard. —情をかける, to be kind [compassionate] *to*; show sympathy *for*.

nasakebukai (情深い), *a.* kind; merciful; compassionate.

nasakenai (情ない), *a.* ❶ (無情) merciless; unkind; cold-hearted. ❷ (憫然) miserable; pitiful; sorry. ❸ (蔑むべき) despicable; shameful. ❹ (慨すべき) deplorable. —情なくも, sorry to say: I grieve to say. —情ないことだが, to my shame I must say....

nasanunaka (生さぬ中の), *a.* not of one's blood; not born of one [one's womb].

nasasō (無さそうである), not to appear [seem]. —たいした金もなさそうだ, He does not appear to have much money.

nashi (梨), *n.* 【植】 the (Chinese) pear. ¶ 西洋梨, the choke apple.

nashi (無し), ☞ *nai* (無い). —無しに, without.

nashiji (梨子地), *n.* aventurine ground. ¶ 金梨子地, gold aventurine.

nashikuzushi (濟崩), *n.* payment by instalments. —濟崩しで返濟する, to pay back by instalments.

nashitogeru (成遂げる), *vt.* to accomplish; complete; achieve.

nashiuri (梨瓜), *n.* a cantaloup(e).

nassen (捺染), *n.* textile printing.

nassho (納所), *n.* ❶ (事務所)

a temple office. ❷ (納所坊主) a priestling.

nasu, nasubi, (茄子), *n.* ❶【植】 the egg-plant. ❷ (實) an egg--apple; a mad-apple.

nasu (爲·成·作す), *vt.* ❶ (する, 行ふ) to do; act; perform. ❷ (遂げる) to accomplish; finish; complete. ❸ (拵へる) to make; form; obtain (得る). ❹ (作[おこ]す) to rouse; stir up. —なすこともなく, doing nothing. —爲さざるを得ない, to be under the necessity of doing a thing; cannot but do [help doing] a thing. —害を爲す, to work mischief; do harm. —名を成す, to make one's name; win fame. —事を爲す, to achieve something. —產をなす, to make a fortune. —の一部をなす, to form a part *of*. —の用をなす, to serve *for* [*as*]; do duty *for*. —王となす, to make him king.

nasu (濟す), *vt.* to pay back [off]; return.

nasuritsukeru (擦附ける), *vt.* to impute (a blame) to another; lay (the blame) on a person. —自分の失策を人に擦り附ける, to lay one's own fault to another's charge [at another's door].

nasuru (擦る), *vt.* ❶ (塗る) to smear; daub (泥など); rub *against*. ❷ (嫁す) to lay (a blame) on a person [at another's door]; impute (a blame) to another. —罪をなすり合ふ, to recriminate each other.

nata (鉈), *n.* a hatchet.

natamame (刀豆), *n.* 【植】 the Jamaica horse-bean.

natane (菜種), *n.* the rape; rape--seed; cole-seed.

natoryūmu (ナトリウム), *n.* sodium.

natsu (夏), *n.* summer; summer--time. —夏らしい, summerly. —夏向きの, for summer use [wear]; summer (他の名詞と合して).

natsuba (夏場), *n.* the summer--time; the summer season.

natsubō (夏帽-子), *n.* a summer hat.

natsufuku (夏服), *n.* summer clothes [suit].

natsuin (捺印), *n.* seal; signet. —捺印する, to seal; put [affix; set] one's seal; attach a seal *to*.

natsukashigaru (懷しがる), *vt.* to yearn [long] *for*; feel yearning *for*; pine *for*. ☞ *shitau*.

natsukashige (懷しげな), *a.* yearning; longing. —懷かしげに見返《眺め》る, to look back 《on》 with longing eyes.

natsukashii (懷しい), *a.* dear; longed-for; dear to one's memory. —懷しい我が幼年時代, the dear old days of my childhood.

natsukeru (懷ける), *vt.* ❶ (動物を) to tame; domesticate. ☞ *narasu* (馴らす). ❷ (人を) to make familiar; attach (a man) *to*; gain over; conciliate. —子供を懷ける, to make children take to one; win children's hearts.

natsuku (懷く), *vi.* to take to; become attached *to*; become familiar *with*; be tamed (馴れる).

natsume (棗), *n.* 【植】 the jujube--tree; a jujube (實).

natsumikan (夏蜜柑), *n.* ❶ 【植】 the (sweet) orange-tree. ❷ (實) a (sweet) orange.

natsumono (夏物), *n.* summer clothing [wear].

natsuyase (夏痩), *n.* loss of flesh in summer. —夏痩する, to fall away in summer.

natsuyasumi (夏休), *n.* a summer vacation; the summer holidays; the long vacation.

natteru (成ってる), *vi.* to be pretty [tolerably] well. —成ってない, [*a.*] not worthy of criticism; awkward; clumsy.

nattō (納豆), *n.* steamed beans.

nattoku (納得), *n.* ❶ (了解) understanding. ❷ (承諾) assent; consent. —納得する, ① to understand. ② to assent; consent. —納得させる, ① to make a person understand; convince him *of*; bring a thing home to a person. ② to make a person consent; win a person's consent.

nau (綯ふ), *vt.* to twist; twine.

nawa (繩, 索), *n.* a rope; a cord; a straw rope. —繩を掛ける, to bind with a rope; rope. —繩を解く, to unbind. —繩を綯ふ, to twist [make] a rope.

nawabari (繩張), *n.* ❶ (繩圍) an enclosure; a space enclosed with rope. ❷ (勢力範圍) one's beat.

nawabashigo (索梯子), *n.* a ropel-adder.

nawame (繩目), *n.* bonds; fetters. —繩目の恥, the disgrace of arrest.

nawanoren (繩暖簾), *n.* ❶ a rope-curtain. ❷ =*izakaya*.

nawashiro (苗代-田), *n.* a rice--bed; a rice-nursery.

nawate (畷), *n.* a path through rice-fields.

nawatsuki (繩附), *n.* a person in bonds; a criminal.

nawatobi (繩跳), *n.* 【遊戲】 skipping; rope-skipping. —繩跳びをする, to skip; skip with a rope.

naya (納屋), *n.* an outhouse; a shed; a barn.

nayamasu (惱ます), *vt.* to trouble; annoy; worry; harass.

nayami (惱み), *n.* ❶ (懊惱)

trouble; worry; qualm. ❷ (難澁) suffering; distress. ❸ (苦痛) pain; agony. —心の惱みとなる, to lie heavy [hard] on [upon] one's mind.

nayamu (惱む), *vi.* to be troubled [annoyed; tormented]; be worried *about*; be afflicted [distressed] *with*. —戀に惱む, to be tormented by love. —神經痛を惱む, to be tortured with neuralgia.

nazasu (名指す), *v.* to call a person by name; nominate.

naze (何故), *ad.* why; on what ground; what for.

nazo (謎), *n.* ❶ a riddle; an enigma; puzzle. ❷ (暗示) a hint; a suggestion. —謎を掛ける, ① to propose [put; give] a riddle; riddle. ② (誘言) to drop a hint. —謎を解く, ① to solve a puzzle [riddle]; unriddle. ② (暗示を) to take the hint. ¶ 謎掛け, (遊び) a puzzle-game.

nazoraeru (擬へる), *vt.* to compare [liken] *to*.

nazukeru (名附ける), *vt.* to call; name; term.

nazumu (泥む), *vi.* ❶ (拘泥する). to adhere *to*; stick *to*. ❷ (澁る) to hesitate; stay.

nazuna (薺), *n.* 【植】 the mother's heart; the pickpurse; the shepherd's purse [scrip]; the toothwort.

ne (ね), **nē** (ねえ), *particle.* you see; isn't it?; do you?; don't you?; you know.

ne (音), *n.* a sound (響); a tone (調子); a note (樂器·鳥の); a voice (聲); a strain (管弦樂の).

ne (根), *n.* ❶ (草木の根) a root. ❷ (根元) the root; the origin; the source; the cause. ❸ (腫物の) a nucleus. —根も葉もない噂, a groundless rumour; a false report. —根に持つ, to owe [bear] a person a grudge; have a spite against a person. —根を張る, to spread the root.

ne (値), *n.* price; cost. —値が上る, to rise [advance] in price. —値が下る, to fall [come down] in price. —値を附ける, to bid; make a bid; give [set] a price *on*. —値を上《下》げる, to raise 《lower》 the price.

ne (寢), *n.* sleep. ☞ ***suimin.***

neage (値上), *n.* ❶ advance [rise] in price 《fare, 賃錢》. ❷ (事) price 《fare》-raising. —勞銀の値上げ, an increase in wages. —値上げする, to raise [advance; enhance] the price 《fare》.

nease (盜汗), *n.* night-sweat. —盜汗をかく, to have night-sweat.

nebaneba (粘粘する), *a.* sticky; greasy (脂·汗等); tough (土等).

nebari (粘), *n.* ❶ stickiness; tack (ワニス·インキ等の). ❷ (執着) tenacity; perseverance. —粘り氣がなくなる, to lose viscidity.

nebarizuyoi (粘强い), *a.* tenacious; persevering.

nebaru (粘る), *vi.* to be 《become》 sticky. —口が粘る, to feel sticky in one's mouth.

nebatsuchi (粘土), *n.* clay; slime.

nebatsuku (粘つく), *vi.* to adhere; stick; be sticky.

nebie (寢冷), *n.* a cold [chill] caught in sleep. —寢冷えする, to catch cold [chill] in sleep.

nebiki (値引する), *vi.* to reduce the price; allow some discount [reduction].

nebō (寢坊), *n.* a late riser; a sleepyhead (眠がり). —寢坊する, to oversleep oneself; rise late.

nebokeru (寢惚ける), *vi.* to be dazed with sleep; be half asleep.

nebukai (根深い), *a.* deep-rooted [-seated]; ingrained.

nebumi (價踏), *n.* valuation; appraisement; estimation.

neburu (舐る), *vt.* to lick.

nebuto (瘤瘡), *n.* a (blind) boil; a furuncle.

neda (根太), *n.* a (floor-)joist. —根太を張る, to joist; floor.

nedai (寢臺), *n.* a bedstead. ☞ ***shindai.***

nedan (値段), *n.* price. ☞ ***ne*** (値). —現金《小賣; 卸》値段, cash 《the retail; wholesale》 price.

nedaru (强請る), *vt.* to importune; solicit; ask importunately.

nedayashi (根絶), *n.* extermination; eradication. —根絶しする, to eradicate; stamp out; root [weed] out.

nedoko (寢床), *n.* a bed; a bedstead (寢臺); a berth (船·汽車等の棚寢床).

negaeri (寢返), *n.* ❶ turning in sleep [bed]. ❷ (離反) betrayal. —寢返りする, to turn (over) in sleep [bed]. —寢返りを打つ, to turn one's back *on* [*upon*]; betray; change sides; turn traitor *to*; change [turn] one's coat (改黨).

negai (願), *n.* request (要求); entreaty (懇願); petition (請願); desire (願望); wish (同上). —願ひがかなふ, to have one's desire fulfilled; have one's request heard (要求が); have one's petition granted (歎願が); have one's prayer answered (祈願が). —願ひに依り本官を免ぜらる, to be relieved from office at one's own request. —願ひを聞き屆ける, to grant a request. ¶ 願事, a request; a desire. —願人, a petitioner; an applicant (出願者). —願書, a written application.

negaideru (願出る), *vt.* to apply to a person *for*; make an application *to.* ☞ ***shutsugan.***

negaisage (願下), *n.* withdrawing a suit 《petition; application》. —願下げする, to withdraw a suit 《application; petition》.

negan (寝棺), *n.* a coffin.

negao (寝顔), *n.* the expression of the face in sleep; a face in sleep.

negau (願ふ), *vt.* ❶ to beg; wish; request. ❷ (切願) to beseech; entreat; implore; pray.

negawakuwa (願くは), would that; may; I wish [pray; hope].

negawashii (願はしい), *a.* desirable.

negi (葱), *n.* 【植】 the stone leek; the Welsh onion.

negi (禰宜), *n.* a *Shintō* priest of low rank.

negirau (犒ふ), *vt.* to entertain (もてなす); return thanks *for.*

negiru (値切る), *v.* to beat [cut] down the price; haggle with a person over the price; chaffer with a person. —五圓(に)値切る, to beat down (the price to) five *yen.*

negokochi (寝心地のよい), *a.* comfortable to sleep *in.* —寝心地がよい, to enjoy sleep; lie snug in bed; sleep comfortably.

negoto (寝言), *n.* ❶ talking in sleep. ❷ (愚言) nonsense; silly talk; rot 【卑】. —寝言を言ふ, ① to talk in sleep. ② to talk nonsense [rot].

negura (塒), *n.* a roost. —塒に歸る, to roost; go to roost.

negurushii (寝苦しい), *a.* unable to sleep well. —寝苦しい夜, a wakeful night.

nehan (涅槃), *n.* 【梵】 Nirvâna. —涅槃に入る, to enter into Nirvâna. ¶ 涅槃像, the image of the dying Buddha.

nehori-hahori (根掘り葉掘り尋ねる), to ask inquisitively [to the minutest details]; inquire minutely; ask persistently (しつこく); go to the root *of* (調べる).

neiben (佞辯), *n.* adulation; cajolery; flattery.

neijin (佞人), *n.* a flatterer; a sycophant; an adulator.

neijitsu (寧日), *n.* a peaceful day.

neiki (寝息), *n.* breathing in sleep. —寝息を覗ふ, to ascertain whether a person is asleep.

neimō (獰猛な), *a.* = ***dōmō.***

neiribana (寝入端), *n.* the time when one has just gone to sleep.

neiro (音色), *n.* tone; quality of a sound.

neiru (寝入る), *vi.* ❶ to fall asleep; go to sleep; sink into sleep. ❷ (相場) to become dull; slacken. —ぐッすり寝入る, to fall into a profound sleep; fall fast asleep.

neji (螺旋), *n.* ❶ a screw. ❷ (栓) a stop-cock. —螺旋を締める, to tighten [fasten] a screw. ¶ 雄《雌》螺旋, a male 《female》 screw. —螺旋廻し, a screw-key [-driver]; a wrench; a spanner (雌螺旋廻し).

nejikeru (拗ける), *vi.* ❶ (拗曲) to be distorted [twisted]. ❷ (邪僻) to be 《become》 perverse; be crooked. —拗けた心, twisted mind; distorted character (性質).

nejikiru (捩切る), *vt.* to wrench off; twist off [apart].

nejikomu (捩込む), *vt.* ❶ (螺旋) to screw in. ❷ (押込む) to thrust in; force in; stuff in. ❸ (詰る) to press for (an explanation).

nejime (音締), *n.* the tune.

nejire (捩れ), *n.* twist; contortion; wryness.

nejireru (捩れる), *vi.* to be twisted; be contorted [distorted]; be crooked.

nejiro (根城), *n.* the main castle; the headquarters (本營): the base (本據). —根城を構へる, to set up the base.

nejiru (扭・捩ぢる), *vt.* to wrench; wring; twist; screw. —右へ捩ぢる, to screw [wind] to the right. —腕を捻ぢ上げる, to wrench up a person's arm.

nejitoru (扭取る), *vt.* to wrench off. ☞ ***mogitoru.***

nekashimono (寝かし物), *n.* drugs in the market; dead stock.

nekasu (寝かす), *vt.* Ⓢ 寝さす, 寝せる. ❶ (眠らす) to put to sleep [bed]. ❷ (横へる) to lay down; lay on the side. ❸ (死藏) to let lie idle.

nekirimushi (根切蟲), *n.* 【昆】 the cutworm.

nekkara (根ッから), *ad.* (not) at all; (not) a bit [whit]; in the least. ☞ ***mattaku.***

nekketsu (熱血), *n.* hot blood; zeal; ardour; fervour. —熱血を注いで, with zeal; with one's heart's blood. ¶ 熱血漢, a hot-blooded man; an ardent spirit.

nekkyō (熱狂), *n.* (great) enthusiasm; (wild) excitement; fanaticism (狂信). —熱狂的歡迎, an enthusiastic welcome [ovation]. —熱狂せる群衆, an excited crowd. —熱狂さす, to excite; stir [fire] the blood. —熱狂する, to grow excited; become wild [mad] (with enthusiasm).

neko (猫), *n.* 【哺乳】 ❶ a cat; a house-cat; puss (愛し呼ぶ語). ❷ (行火) a foot-warmer. —猫に小判, to cast pearls before swine. —猫も杓子も, one and all; every man Jack; all the world and his wife. —猫をかぶる, to hide her claws; play the hypocrite; sail under false colours 【俗】. ¶ 牡《牝》猫, a tom 《she》-cat. —虎[斑] 猫, a tabby (cat).

neko (葇荑花), *n.* 【植】 a catkin.

nekogi (根扱にする), *v.* to up-root; root up [out; away]; pull [tear] up by the roots.

nekoirazu (猫いらず), *n.* a ratsbane; a rat-poison.

nekomu (寢込む), *vi.* ❶ (寢入る) to fall asleep. ❷ (病氣で) to be laid up *with*; take to one's bed; be confined to bed.

nekonadegoe (猫撫聲で話す), to speak [talk] in an insinuating voice [a coaxing tone].

nekorobu (寢轉ぶ), *vi.* to lie down; lay [throw] oneself down.

nekosoge (根こそげ), *ad.* Ⓢ 根こそぎ. root and branch; completely; entirely. —根こそぎ持って行く, to carry away everything.

nekoyanagi (猫柳), *n.* 【植】 Salix Thunbergiana (willow の一種學名).

nekoze (猫背), *n.* a stoop; a hump-back.

nekutai (ネクタイ), *n.* a necktie.

nema (寢間), *n.* ❶ a bedroom; a bedchamber. ❷ (床) a bed.

nemaki (寢衣), *n.* a night-shirt [-gown; -dress]; night-clothes.

nemeru (睨る), *vt.* to glare *at*.

nemimi (寢耳に水), to be a great surprise *to*; come like a thunderclap.

nemonogatari (寢物語), *n.* talking in bed.

nemoto (根元), *n.* the root.

nemugari (睡がり), *n.* a sleepy-head 【俗】.

nemui (睡い), *vi.* to be sleepy [drowsy]. ——, *a.* ❶ sleepy; drowsy. ❷ (退屈な) dull; sluggish; tedious. —睡くなる, to become [feel] sleepy [drowsy].

nemuke (睡氣), *n.* sleepiness; drowsiness. —頻に睡氣が催す, The eyes gather [draw] straws. —眼をこすって睡氣を覺ます, to rub [wipe; shake] the sleep out of one's eyes. ¶ 睡氣覺し, something to keep one awake; a cure for drowsiness.

nemunoki (合歡木), *n.* 【植】 the silk-tree.

nemuri (眠), *n.* a sleep; a slumber. —深い眠り, a deep [sound] sleep. —眠りに就く, to go to sleep.

nemurigusa (含羞草), *n.* 【植】 the sensitive [humble] plant.

nemuru (眠る), *vi.* ❶ to sleep; slumber; have a sleep. ❷ (寢入る) to fall asleep. ❸ (ゐねむる) to doze; nap. ❹ 【養蠶】 to moult. —よく眠る《れない》, to have a good 《bad》 sleep [night]. —少しも眠れない, not to get a wink of sleep. —右《左》を下にして眠る, to sleep on the right 《left》 ear. —眠るが如く死ぬる, to die a peaceful death; pass away quietly.

nemusō (睡さうな), *a.* sleepy; drowsy; sluggish (だらけた). —睡さうな眼, heavy eyes.

nen (年), *n.* ❶ (とし) a year. ❷ (年季) a term of service. —年百年中, from year [year's end] to year [year's end]; all the year round; year in and year out. —年に七分, seven per cent. per annum.

nen (念), *n.* ❶ (觀念) idea; thought. ❷ (注意) attention; care. ❸ (感) sense. ❹ (願) wish; desire; hope (希望). —感謝の念, sense of gratitude. —念の爲め, to make sure; by way of precaution. —念を入れて, with great care. —念を押す, to make sure.

neñake (年明), *n.* expiration of the term of service.

nenbangan (粘板岩), *n.* 【地質】 clay-slate.

nenbutsu (念佛), *n.* a Buddhist invocation. —念佛を唱へる, to pray to Amidha Buddha; say one's prayer.

nenchaku (粘著), *n.* cohesion; adhesion. —粘著性の sticky; adhesive; tenacious (粘り强い). —粘著する, to cohere; adhere.

nenchō (年長), *n.* seniority. ¶ 年長者, a senior; an elder.

nendai (年代), *n.* an age; an era; a period. —千八百五十年代, the (eighteen) fifties. ¶ 年代順, chronological order. —年代史, a chronicle; annals.

nendo (年度), *n.* a year; a financial year (會計年度). —年度初《末》に, at the beginning 《end》 of the financial year. ¶ 年度替り, change of the financial year.

nendo (粘土), *n.* clay; slime. ¶ 粘土細工, a clay-work.

nendo (粘度), *n.* viscosity.

neñeki (粘液), *n.* (animate) mucilage; mucus. ¶ 粘液質, phlegmatic temperament.

nenga (年賀), *n.* the New Year's greetings [call]. —年賀に廻る, to make [pay] a round of the New Year's calls; pay the New Year's (complimentary) visits. ¶

年賀客, a New Year's caller [visitor]. —年賀狀, a letter greeting the New Year; a New Year's card.

nengaku (年額), *n.* a yearly amount; an annual sum.

nengen (年限), *n.* a term of years; a period.

nengetsu (年月), *n.* years and months; time.

nengō (年號), *n.* the name of an era.

nengoro (懇な), *a.* ❶ (慇懃) polite; courteous; (深切) kind; obliging; (懇篤) cordial; hospitable: careful. ❷ (昵懇) intimate; familiar. —— **-ni,** *ad.* politely; courteously: kindly: hospitably; with cordiality: carefully. —懇ろにもてなす, to treat hospitably; give a warm reception. —懇ろにして居る, to be on intimate terms *with.*

nengu (年貢), *n.* ❶(年々の貢物) an annual tribute. ❷ (小作料) farm-rent.

neñiri (念入の), *a.* thoughtful; deliberate; elaborate (細工等の).

nenjū (年中), *n.* the whole year; all the year. ——, *ad.* all the year round; throughout the year. ¶ 年中行事, rites and ceremonies of the year; annual observances [functions].

nenkan (年間), *ad.* during the period. —明治年間, the Meiji era.

nenkan (年鑑), *n.* a year-book; an annual. ¶ 野球年鑑, the Baseball Annual.

nenki (年忌), *n.* Ⓢ年囘. an anniversary of a person's death; an anniversary (祭).

nenki (年期), *n.* a term of years; a term of service (奉公などの); prentice years (同上). ¶ 年期奉公, apprenticeship. (年期奉公をさせる, to apprentice [indent] *to*; bind [put] (a person) apprentice *to.*) —年期小僧, an apprentice; a prentice boy.

nenkin (年金), *n.* an annuity; a pension (恩給). ¶ 年金受領者, an annuitant; a pensioner.

nenkō (年功), *n.* ❶ (年來の功勞) long service. ❷ (年來の熟練) long [many years'] experience. ¶ 年功加俸, an additional salary for long service.

nenkyū (年級), *n.* a year grade. ¶ 五年級, the fifth-year grade.

nenmaku (粘膜), *n.* a mucous membrane.

nenmatsu (年末), *n.* the end [close] of the year; the year-end. ¶ 年末賞與, the year-end bonus.

nennai (年內に), *ad.* within the year.

nenneko (ねんねこ -半纏), *n.* a nursery gown.

nennen (年年), *ad.* yearly; annually; year by [after] year; every year. ☞ *mainen.* —年々の, yearly; annual.

nenpai (年配), *n.* age; years of age. —五十年配の人, a man of about fifty.

nenpō (年俸), *n.* an annual [yearly] salary.

nenpō (年報), *n.* an annual (report); an annual return (統計).

nenpu (年賦), *n.* an yearly instalment; an annual payment. ¶ 年賦償還, amortization.

nenpyō (年表), *n.* a chronological table; a chronology (年代記).

nenrai (年來), *ad.* years past; for years (past). —六十年來稀に見る暴風雨, the most violent storm known for the past sixty years.

nenrei (年齡), *n.* age; years of age.

nenri (年利), *n.* annual [yearly] interest. —年利五分, five per cent. per annum.

nenryō (燃料), *n.* fuel. ¶ 液《氣》體燃料, liquid《gaseous》fuel. —燃料節約器, a fuel-economizer.

nensha (念寫), *n.* spirit photography; a spirit photograph.

nenshi (年始), *n.* the New Year's greetings. ☞ *nenga.*

nenshō (年少の), *a.* young; little; juvenile. ¶ 年少者, a youth; a junior.

nenshō (燃燒), *n.* combustion; burning. —燃燒する, to burn.

nenshū (年收), *n.* an annual [yearly] income.

nenshutsu (捻出する), *vt.* to think out. —財源を捻出する, to think out sources of revenue.

nensū (年數), *n.* years; the number of years.

nentō (念頭), *n.* mind; thought. —念頭に置く, to bear in mind. —寸時も念頭を離れない, not to leave one's mind even for a moment.

neñyu (燃油), *n.* fuel oil.

nenzu (念珠), *n.* beads.

nen-zuru (念ずる), *vt.* to pray; make a prayer; invoke a god's help [protection] (冥助を祈る). ☞ *inoru.*

neoki (寢起する), *vi.* to lie down and get up. —寢起きを共にする, to live under the same roof; live [stay] *with.*

neppū (熱風), *n.* a hot wind; a sirocco (リビア沙漠の); a simoon (アラビア沙漠の).

nerai (狙), *n.* aim. —狙が外れる, to miss one's aim [the mark]; shoot wide《short》of the mark.

—狙を定める[すます], to take a steady [good; deliberate] aim *at*. ¶ 狙ひ所, the point aimed at.

nerau (狙ふ), *vt.* ❶ to aim *at*; take aim *at*; level (a gun) *at* [*against*] (銃を向ける). ❷ (窺ふ) to watch; shadow (尾行す). —此地位を狙ってる者が澤山ある, There are many after this post.

neriko (捏粉), *n.* dough.

nerimono (煉物), *n.* paste; temper (漆喰等); fictile wares.

neriyaku (煉藥), *n.* an electuary; an eclegma.

neru (寢る), *vi.* ❶ (就眠) to sleep; go to bed; retire; turn in. ❷ (横臥) to lie down; throw [lay] oneself down. ❸ (病臥) to take [keep] to one's bed. ❹ (商品が) to remain unsold; be dead stock. —寢飽きる, to tire of sleep ⦅lying in bed⦆. —寢た振りする, to sham [feign] sleep.

neru (錬·練·煉·捏る), *vt.* ❶ to knead (捏る); gloss (絹等を) temper (金·土等を). ❷ (訓練) to train; drill; exercise. ❸ (練磨) to polish; refine; file (文を). —練り歩く, to parade; go in procession. (市内を練り歩く to parade [march through] the city. —膽を練る, to cultivate one's courage.

neru (ネル), *n.* flannel.

nesage (値下げ), *n.* reduction of the price. —値下げする, to cheapen; reduce [lower] the price; mark down the price.

neshizumaru (寢靜まる), *vi.* to be buried in sleep.

neshōben (寢小便), *n.* bed-wetting. —寢小便をする, to wet the bed.

nesobireru (寢そびれる), *vi.* to fail to sleep.

nessei (熱誠), *n.* enthusiasm; zeal; ardour. —熱誠なる歡迎を受ける, to meet with a warm [enthusiastic] reception.

nesshabyō (熱射病), *n.* heat-stroke; heat-apoplexy.

nesshin (熱心), *n.* eagerness; ardour; enthusiasm. —熱心な, eager; ardent; enthusiastic. —熱心に, eagerly; with all one's heart and soul (熱誠に). ¶ 熱心家, an enthusiast; an ardent lover (*of*); a keen hand (*at*).

nes-suru (熱する), *vi.* ❶ to heat; be heated; be hot. ❷ to be heated [excited; kindled]. ——, *vt.* to heat; make hot. —熱し易い人, an excitable person.

nesugosu (寢過す), *vi.* to oversleep (oneself); sleep too long; sleep beyond the time.

netamashii (妬·嫉ましい), *a.* ❶ (嫉妬) jealous *of*. ❷ (羨望) enviable; envious *of*.

netami (妬,嫉), *n.* Ⓢ妬心. envy (羨望); jealousy (嫉妬).

netamu (妬·嫉む), *vt.* to envy; be envious ⦅jealous⦆ *of*; grudge. —他人の名聲を妬む, to grudge a person his fame.

netchū (熱中する), *vi.* to be eager [crazy] (to do); be enthusiastic *over*; be absorbed [engrossed] *in*. —仕事に熱中する, to be absorbed in one's work.

netori (寢鳥), *n.* a bird at roost.

netsu (熱), *n.* ❶ heat. ❷ temperature (體溫); fever (病熱). ❸ (流行) mania; craze; fever; fad (一時の). ❹ =***netsujō***. —熱がある, to be [feel] feverish; have a fever. —熱が出る, to become feverish; bring on a fever; have an attack of a fever. —熱が下る, One's fever abates [falls]. ¶ 野球熱, baseball mania.

netsuben (熱辯), *n.* a fiery speech. —熱辯を揮ふ, to speak with fervency; make a fiery speech.

netsubō (熱望), *n.* ardent wish; vehement desire; hunger. —熱望する, to desire eagerly; be anxious to; crave for.

netsubyō (熱病), *n.* a fever; 【醫】pyrexia.

netsudenki (熱電氣), *n.* thermoelectricity.

netsudo (熱度), *n.* (degree of) heat; temperature (體溫).

netsugaku (熱學), *n.* thermotics.

netsui (拗い), *a.* obstinate; persistent. ☞ ***shitsukoi***.

netsujō (熱情), *n.* fervour; ardour; passion.

netsukagaku (熱化學), *n.* thermochemistry; thermal chemistry.

netsukasu (寢附かす), *vt.* to put (a child) to sleep; lull (a child) to sleep (すかして).

netsuke (根附), *n.* a button (for suspending a pouch).

netsuku (寢附く), *vi.* to go off; go [get] to sleep; fall asleep.

netsuretsu (熱烈な), *a.* fervent; ardent; vehement; fiery.

netsurikigaku (熱力學), *n.* thermodynamics.

netsurui (熱涙), *n.* burning [hot; scalding] tears.

netsuryō (熱量), *n.* calorie, calory; quantity of heat. ¶ 熱量計, a calorimeter.

netsusamashi (解熱劑), *n.* an antifebrile; a febrifuge.

netsuzō (捏造), *n.* fabrication; falsehood; invention. —捏造する, to fabricate; invent; forge. ¶ 捏造者, a forger.

nettai (熱帶), *n.* the torrid zone; the tropics. ¶ 熱帶地方, the tropical region; the hot climates; the tropics. —熱帶產動植物, tropical fauna and flora [animals and plants].

nettō (熱湯), *n.* hot [boiling] water.

nettō (熱鬧), *n.* bustle; hubbub. —熱閙の, bustling; crowded.

neuchi (値打), *n.* ❶ (價値) value; worth. ❷ (品格) dignity; grace. —値打のある, valuable; worthy; worth. —値打のない, valueless; worthless; of no value. —百圓の値打は十分ある, to be well worth 100 *yen*. —博士の値打はない, not to be worthy of being a doctor.

nezake (寢酒), *n.* a nightcap [俗].

nezame (寢覺), *n.* awaking from sleep. —寢覺が惡い, to sleep badly; be unable to sleep in peace; feel remorse (at night).

nezasu (根差す), *vi.* ❶ (根づく) to strike [take] root. ❷ (由來する) to result *from*; be traceable (*to*); come out of. —深く國民性に根ざしてる, to be deeply rooted in the national character.

nezaya (値鞘), *n.* 【商】margin.

nezō (寢相), *n.* sleeping posture. —寢相が惡い, to be ungraceful in one's sleeping posture.

nezu (杜松), *n.* 【植】Juniperus rigida (juniper の一種·學名).

nezuban (不寢番), *n.* vigil; an all-night watch: a night-watchman (人). —不寢番をする, to keep vigil; keep watch during the night.

nezuku (根づく), *vi.* to strike [take] root; root.

nezumi (鼠), *n.* ❶ a rat. ❷ (色) grey, gray.

nezumiirazu (鼠入らず), *n.* a cupboard; a meat-safe (蠅帳).

nezumitori (鼠捕), *n.* ❶ (鼠おとし) a rat-trap. ❷ (藥) a ratsbane; a rat-poison; ratin. ❸ (人) a rat-catcher.

nezuyoi (根强い), *a.* strong (-rooted); firm; on a sure ground.

ni (に), *n.* 【音】D; re 〔伊〕; 2.

ni (に), *conj.* ❶ and. ❷ (のに) though. —五呎に三呎, 5 feet by 3. —朝に夕に, morning and evening; day and night.

ni (に), *prep.* ❶ (時間) at (小時間), on (日及特定の朝夕); in (週·月·年など). ❷ (場所) at; in; on. ❸ (位置) on (表面); in (中); at (側). ❹ (方角) to; in; on. ❺ (方向) to; for (へ); into (中へ); at (目がけて). ❻ (關係など) to; for; of; with. ❼ (受身) by. —北に, in the north (北部に); on the north (北側に); to the north (北に當って); northward (北に向って). —正午に, at noon. —月曜の朝に, in the morning on Monday; on Monday morning. —八月三日に, on the 3rd of August. —八歲の時に, in one's eighth year; at seven years of age; at the age of seven. —十錢に五つ, five for ten *sen*. —月に二回, twice a month. —...に劣《優》る, inferior 《superior》 *to*.

ni (二), *n.* two. ☞ ***ichi*** (一).

ni (荷), *n.* a burden (荷,重荷,厄介物,責任); goods (貨物); load (積荷); freight (同上); cargo (船荷); a pack (包); luggage (手荷物). —彼には荷が勝ち過ぎる, It will be too great a burden for him.

niage (荷揚), *n.* landing; unloading; discharging. —荷揚げする, to unload; unlade; discharge (a cargo from a ship; a ship of her cargo); clear a ship. —荷揚げを始める, to break bulk. ¶ 荷揚場, a landing (-place); a wharf. —荷揚料, landing charges.

niashi (荷足), *n.* ❶ (船の) ballast. ❷ (賣行) sale; salability.

niau (似合ふ), *v.* to become; suit; fit; match. —似合った夫婦, a well-matched couple. —顏に似合はぬ, in spite of one's looks; gentle 《lovely, *etc.*》 as one is.

niawashii (似合はしい), *a.* suitable; becoming; well-matched.

nibai (二倍), double; twice; twofold; two times.

nibako (荷箱), *n.* a packing box [case].

niban (二番), *n.* ❶ (回數) twice; two times. ❷ (順番) the second; number two. ¶ 二番草, aftermath.

nibana (煮端), *n.* the first infusion of tea. ☞ ***debana*** (出花).

nibasha (荷馬車), *n.* a dray; a cart; a waggon (四輪の).

nibe (魚膠), *n.* fish-glue; isinglass (特に蝶鮫の).

nibu (二部), *n.* ❶ two parts 《copies》. ❷ (第二部) the second part; the second section. ¶ 二部合奏, a duet. —二部敎授, a half-time school system.

nibui (鈍い), *a.* dull; slow; blunt (刃物). —鈍くなる, to become dull; blunt.

nibune (荷船), *n.* a cargo boat [ship]; a lighter (艀); a barge (主に河川·運河の).

niburasu (鈍らす), *vt.* to dull; blunt; turn [blunt] the edge *of*. —決心を鈍らす, to blunt one's resolution.

niburu (鈍る), *vi.* to (become) blunt [dull]. —決心が鈍る, to become enervated in one's resolution.

nichanicha (にちゃにちゃする), *vi.* to be slimy [sticky]. ——, *a.* slimy; gummy; sticky.
Nichibei (日米), *n.* Japan and America. ¶ 日米協會, the America-Japan Society.
nichibotsu (日沒), *n.* sunset; sundown; night-fall (薄暮).
Nichidoku (日獨), *n.* Japan and Germany.
Nichiei (日英), *n.* Japan and England. ¶ 日英條約, the Anglo-Japanese treaty.
Nichifutsu (日佛), *n.* Japan and France. ¶ 日佛協約, the Franco-Japanese agreement.
nichigen (日限), *n.* time (期限); a term (期間); a date (日次); a fixed [an appointed] day. —日限迄には, by the day [time].
Nichiin (日印), *n.* Japan and India. —日印の, Indo-Japanese. ¶ 日印協會, the Indo-Japanese Association.
nichijō (日常), *ad.* everyday; always. —日常の, daily; usual. ¶ 日常生活, everyday life.
nichinichi (日日), *ad.* everyday; daily; day by [after] day.
Nichiren (日蓮宗), *n.* the Nichiren Sect. ¶ 日蓮主義, Nichirenism.
Nichiro (日露), *n.* Japan and Russia. ¶ 日露戰爭, the Russo-Japanese war.
nichiya (日夜), *ad.* day and night; by day and by night; always; constantly.
nichiyō (日用の), *a.* daily; of daily necessity [use]. ¶ 日用文, a social letter. —日用語, everyday language; everyday words. —日用品, an article o' daily necessity; daily necessaries; necessaries of life.
nichiyō (日曜 -日), *n.* Sunday. ¶ 日曜學校, a Sunday school.
nido (二度), *ad.* twice; again. —二度目, the second time.
nie (贄), *n.* an offering (to God or the Emperor); a victim; a tribute.
niekaeru (煮返る), *vi.* to boil up; seethe; be in a ferment (國內など).
niekiranu (煮切らぬ), *a.* ❶ (優柔不斷の) undetermined; irresolute; ❷ (曖昧な) vague. —煮えきらぬ返辭, a vague answer; a reluctant answer (澁々).
nieru (煮える), *vi.* to boil; be boiled [cooked]. —煮えこぼれる, to boil over. —煮え過ぎる, to overboil; be overdone.
nietatsu (煮立つ), *vi.* to boil; boil up.
nieyu (煮湯), *n.* boiling water.
nifuda (荷札), *n.* a label; a tag.
nigai (苦い), *a.* bitter; disagreeable (不快). ——, *vi.* to taste bitter. —苦い顏をする, to look sullen; make a sour [sulky; wry] face. —苦い經驗をなめる, to undergo a bitter experience.
nigami (苦味), *n.* bitterness; a bitter taste; gall. —苦味走った, bitter; galling; sour.
niganigashii (苦苦しい), *a.* bitter; disgusting. —苦々しい振舞, loathsome manners; hateful conduct.
nigao (似顏), *n.* a portrait; a likeness. ¶ 似顏繪, a portrait.
nigari (滷汁), **nigashio** (苦鹽), *n.* bittern.
nigasu (逃す), *vt.* ❶ (放つ) to let go [out; fly (鳥など)]; set free (釋放する). ❷ (取逃がす) to let escape; miss (機會を); let slip (同上). —犯人を逃がす, ① (取逃がす) to let the criminal escape. ② (故意に逃がす) to make the criminal escape. —逃がした魚は大きい, "A thing is bigger for being spared."
nigate (苦手), *n.* a person hard to contend with; a pet aversion.
nigatsu (二月), *n.* February.
nigawarai (苦笑), *n.* a bitter smile. =*kushō*. —苦笑ひする, to smile a bitter smile.
nigawase (荷爲替), *n.* a documentary bill [draft].
nigayomogi (にがよもぎ), *n.* 【植】 the wormwood.
nigeashi (逃足), *n.* preparation for flight. —逃げ足になる, to prepare for flight; be ready for escape [to run away]; show the white feather.
nigeba (逃場), *n.* ❶ (避難場) a shelter; a place of refuge [safety]. ❷ (逃路) a way 《means》 of escape. —逃場を失ふ, to lose means of escape; have one's escape cut off (逃路を斷たれる).
nigedasu (逃出す), *vi.* to run away; take to one's heels.
nigejitaku (逃仕度する), *v.* to prepare [make ready] to run away.
nigekaeru (逃歸る), *v.* to escape and come back.
nigekakureru (逃隱れる), *vi.* to escape and conceal oneself; run [flee] out of sight.
nigekōjō (逃口上), *n.* an excuse; an evasion; a subterfuge.
nigekomu (逃込む), *vi.* to take refuge *in*; run in for safety.
nigemawaru (逃廻る), *vi.* to run about. —恐れて逃げ廻る, to avoid another's sight from fear.
nigemichi (逃路), *n.* a way 《means》 of escape; escape.

nigenai (似氣無い), *a.* unbecoming; unlike; unworthy. —女に似氣ない力, great strength unusual in a woman.
nigenkin (二絃琴), *n.* a two-stringed *koto.*
nigeru (逃げる), *vi.* to run (away; off); get away [off]; take to flight [one's heels; one's legs]; (make one's) escape. **——,** *vt.* (避ける) to avoid; evade; escape. —逃げ損ふ, to fail to escape.
nigirasu (握らす), *v.* to bribe (a man); grease another's palm; oil another's hand; slip (a coin) into another's hand.
nigiri (握), *n.* ❶ (把握) a grip; a grasp. ❷ (掌長〔ﾃﾅｶﾞ〕) a palm (四吋); a hand (同上). ❸ (掌量) a handful. ❹ (把手) a handle; a knob; a hand.
nigirikobushi (握拳), *n.* a fist; a clenched fist.
nigirimeshi (握飯), *n.* a rice-ball.
nigirishimeru (握締める), *vt.* to grasp tightly; hold fast; clinch, clench (手等を).
nigiritsubusu (握潰す), *vt.* ❶ to crush in the hand. ❷ (默殺) to ignore; take no notice *of*; burke. ☞ *mokusatsu.*
nigiru (握る), *vt.* to clasp; grasp; clutch; lay hold *of* [*on*]. —實權を握ってる, to have the real power in one's hands.
nigiwai (賑ひ), *n.* ❶ (繁榮) prosperity. ❷ (雜沓) bustle; stir. —お祭のやうな賑ひ, great bustling like a fête day.
nigiwashii (賑しい), *vi.* to be crowded; be bustling. **——,** *a.* =*nigiyaka.*
nigiwasu (賑はす), *vt.* ❶ to make prosperous. ❷ (賑恤) to give alms *to.*
nigiwau (賑ふ), *vi.* ❶ (繁榮) to thrive; prosper; flourish. ❷ (人出) to be crowded; be bustling. —人出に賑ふ場所, a place of great resort.
nigiyaka (賑かな), *a.* ❶ (雜沓) bustling; thronged. ❷ (陽氣) lively; merry; gay. ❸ (繁昌) prosperous; thriving. —賑かに, gayly; lively.
nigon (二言), *n.* duplicity. = *nimai* (二枚舌).
nigorasu (濁らす), *vt.* ❶ (汚濁) to make impure [turbid; muddy]; soil. ❷ (曖昧) to make ambiguous. —言葉を濁(ら)す, to speak ambiguously; equivocate; shuffle; prevaricate.
nigoru (濁る), *vi.* ❶ to be (become; grow) muddy [turbid; impure]. ❷ (濁音) to have a flat sound. —濁った, muddy; turbid; thick; cloudy (酒など); impure (不純な).
nigosu (濁す), *vt.* =*nigorasu.*
nigura (荷鞍), *n.* a pack-saddle.
niguruma (荷車), *n.* a cart; a hand-cart (手挽の). ¶ 荷車挽, a cart-puller.
Nihon, Nippon, (日本), *n.* Japan. —日本化する, to Japonicise. ¶ 表《裏》日本, the Pacific 《Japan-Sea》 side of Japan. —日本銀行, the Bank of Japan. —日本語, (the) Japanese (language). —日本人, the Japanese; a Japanese; a Jap 〔俗〕. —日本海, the Japan Sea; the Sea of Japan.
nihonbō (二本棒), *n.* a spoony; a hen-pecked husband.
nihyakutōka (二百十日), *n.* the two-hundred-and-tenth day.
Niinamesai (新嘗祭), *n.* the Harvest Festival.
niin-seido (二院制度), *n.* the bicameral system.
niji (虹), *n.* a rainbow. —虹の如き氣焔を吐く, to draw [shoot] the long bow.
niji (二次の), *a.* 【數】 quadratic. ¶ 二次方程式, a quadratic equation. —二次會, an after-meeting; a second sitting; an after-feast.
nijiki (二食主義), *n.* the two-meal principle.
nijimu (滲・鈍染む), *vi.* to spread; run; blur. —血が滲む, Blood curdles.
nijiriyoru (膝行り寄る), *vi.* to draw near; approach closely; press *upon.*
nijirushi (荷印), *n.* a mark; a brand.
nijō (二乘), *n.* square; self-multiplication. ☞ *jijō* (自乘).
niju (二豎), *n.* a malady; a disease. —二豎の冒す所となる, to be attacked by illness.
nijū (二十), *n.* twenty; a score; the twentieth (第二十). —二十代, the twenties. —二十分の一, a twentieth.
nijū (二重), *n.* doubleness; duplication. —二重の, double; duplex; duplicate; twofold. —二重生活をする, to lead a double life. **—— - ni,** *ad.* doubly; twofold. —二重にする, to double; duplicate; reduplicate. ¶ 二重廻し, an inverness.
nikaesu (煮返す), *vt.* Ⓢ 煮直す. to reboil.
nikagetsugoto (二箇月毎の), *a.* bimonthly.
nikai (二回), *n.* twice; two times.
nikai (二階), *n.* the second stor(e)y; the first floor; upstair. —二階に上る《から下りる》, to go upstairs 《downstairs》. ¶ 二階家, a two-storied house.

nikata (煮方), *n.* cookery; a way of cooking (方法).

nikawa (膠), *n.* glue. —膠でつける, [*vt.*] to glue.

niki (二季), *n.* two periods [seasons].

nikibi (面皰), *n.* a pimple; (粉刺) milium: (痤瘡) a whelk; stone-pock; acne.

nikka (日貨), *n.* Japanese goods. ¶ 日貨排斥, boycotting of Japanese goods.

nikka (日課), *n.* a daily lesson; daily work [routine task].

Nikkan (日韓), *n.* Japan and Korea. ¶ 日韓併合, the Japanese annexation of Korea.

nikkan (日刊), *n.* daily issue; daily publication: a daily.

nikkan (肉感), *n.* sexual feeling; carnal passion. —肉感的, sensual; fleshly.

nikkei (肉桂), *n.* 【植】Cinnamomum Soureirii (cinnamon の一種. 學名); the cinnamon (俗稱).

nikkeru (ニッケル), *n.* nickel. ¶ ニッケル鍍金, nickel-plating.

nikki (日記), *n.* a diary; a journal. —日記をつける, to keep [write up] a diary. ¶ 日記帳, ① a diary. ②【簿記】a day-book; a journal.

nikkō (日光), *n.* sunlight; sunshine; sunbeam (射光). ¶ 日光療法, sun-bath; insolation; heliotherapy. —日光消毒, disinfection by exposure to the sun [by sunlight].

nikkori (莞爾する), *vi.* to smile.

nikkyū (日給), *n.* daily wages; a day's wage. —日給で働く, to work by the day.

nikō (二項の), *a.* binomial. ¶ 二項式定理, the binomial theorem.

nikochin (ニコチン), *n.* 【化】nicotine. ¶ ニコチン中毒, nicotinism.

nikoge (毳毛, 氄), *n.* (鳥の) down (feather).

nikoniko (にこにこ), *ad.* smilingly; beaming with a smile; cheerfully. —にこにこする, to smile; look cheerful [happy]. ¶ にこにこ顔, a cheerful countenance; a beaming face.

nikoyaka (にこやかな), *a.* ❶ (溫容で愛嬌ある) affable; gentle. ❷ (莞爾たる) smiling; cheerful.

niku (肉), *n.* ❶ flesh; meat (食用). ❷ (肉體) the flesh; the body. ❸ (印肉) sealing-ink; an ink [inking]-pad. ❹ (肉慾) sensual pleasures.

nikudan (肉彈), *n.* a human bullet.

nikugan (肉眼), *n.* the naked eye. —肉眼に見えぬ, to be invisible to the naked eye.

nikuge (憎氣な), *a.* hateful. —憎氣のない, innocent; simple.

nikuhaku (肉薄する), *v.* to press (a competitor) hard [close]; close *with*; run (a competitor) hard [close]. —敵の牙城に肉薄する, to press hard upon the enemy's headquarters.

nikuhen (肉片), *n.* Ⓢ 肉切れ. a piece [chop] of meat.

nikuhiki (碎肉器), *n.* a meat-chopper.

nikuhitsu (肉筆), *n.* handwriting (書); original drawing (畫); autograph (直筆).

nikui (憎い), *a.* ha'eful; odious; abominable.

-nikui (難い), *a.* difficult; hard. —扱ひ難い, hard [difficult] to deal with.

nikuiro (肉色), *n.* flesh-colour; carnation. —肉色の, flesh-coloured; carnation(-ed).

nikujiki (肉食), *n.* flesh-eating; sarcophagy.

nikujū (肉汁), *n.* meat-juice; gravy.

nikujuban (肉襦袢), *n.* (flesh) lights; fleshings.

nikukai (肉塊), *n.* a piece of flesh.

nikumareguchi (憎まれ口), *n.* offensive language; abusive language; satirical remarks. —憎まれ口を利く, to talk abusively; use offensive language.

nikumareru (憎まれる), *vi.* to be hated [disliked; detested]; be (held) in detestation.

nikumareyaku (憎まれ役), *n.* a villain's part [rôle].

nikumu (憎む), *vt.* to hate; abhor; detest. —憎むべき, hateful; detestable; odious.

nikurashii (憎らしい), *a.* provoking; detestable.

nikurui (肉類), *n.* meat (食用); flesh.

nikusashi (肉叉), *n.* a fork.

nikushimi (憎み), *n.* hatred. —人の憎しみを受ける, to incur others' hatred.

nikushin (肉親), *n.* blood relationship; kinship; a blood relation (人); one's (own) flesh (人).

nikushoku (肉色), *n.* 【繪畫】flesh-tint: carnation; flesh-colour.

nikushoku (肉食), *n.* meat-diet; flesh-feeding (特に動物); sarcophagy; animal food. —肉食する, to eat meat; feed on [upon] flesh. ¶ 肉食鳥《獸》, a bird《beast》of prey. —肉食動物, a carnivorous animal.

nikushu (肉腫), *n.* Ⓢ 肉瘤. 【醫】a sarcoma; a fungus [*pl.* -i].

nikutai (肉體), *n.* the flesh; the (human) body. ¶ 肉體美, physical beauty.

nikuya (肉屋), *n.* (人) a butcher: (店) a butcher's (shop); a meat-

-shop: (業) the butcher's trade.
nikuyoku (肉慾), *n.* sensual pleasures.
nikuzuki (肉附よき), *a.* fleshy; plump.
nikuzuku (肉豆蔻), *n.* 【植】 the nutmeg-tree; the nutmeg.
nikuzuku (肉づく), *vi.* to get [gain; put on] flesh.
nimai (二枚の), *a.* two-leaved. ¶ 二枚舌, a double tongue; duplicity. (二枚舌を使ふ, ① [*v.*] to use a double tongue. ② [*a.*] double-tongued.)
nimame (煮豆), *n.* boiled beans. ¶ 煮豆屋, boiled-bean seller.
nimo (にも), *ad.* also; too; even (でも). ——, *conj.* both...and.
nimono (煮物), *n.* cooked food; cookery (調理).
nimotsu (荷物), *n.* a pack; a load; goods.
nin (人), *n.* a man; a person.
nin (仁), *n.* 【植】 a kernel; a core.
nin (任), *n.* office; post; charge (擔任); duties (任務). —任に當る, to take the duties upon oneself; take a trust on oneself. —任に堪へる《堪へない》, to be competent 《incompetent》 for the task; be equal 《unequal》 to the task.
ninau (擔ふ), *vi.* to shoulder; bear; take 《carry》 on one's shoulder. —銃を擔ふ, to slope arms. —大なる使命を擔ふ, to be entrusted with a great mission.
ninawa (荷繩), *n.* a packing rope [cord].
ninbetsu (人別), *n.* ❶ (各人) everybody. ❷ (人別調べ) census; census-taking.
ninbu (人夫), *n.* a coolie. ☞ *ninpu.*
ninchi (任地), *n.* one's post.
ninchi (認知), *n.* acknowledgment; recognition. —私生子を認知する, to acknowledge a child as one's own.
nindaku (認諾), *n.* assent; approval; admission. —相手方の請求を認諾する, to admit the other party's claim.
nindō (忍冬), *n.* 【植】 the Japanese honeysuckle.
ningen (人間), *n.* man; a human being [creature]; mankind (全體). —人間萬事金の世の中, "Money moves the world."
ningyo (人魚), *n.* a mermaid (女); a merman (男).
ningyō (人形), *n.* a doll; a puppet (操り人形). —人形のやうに可愛い, as sweet as a cherub. ¶ 人形芝居, a puppet-show[-play]. —人形使ひ, a puppet-man [-player]; a puppet-showman.
nini (任意の), *a.* voluntary; optional; permissive; arbitrary; discretionary. —任意の自白, voluntary confession. —任意の一點Aより, from an arbitrary point A. —— **-ni,** *ad.* voluntarily; at will; of one's own free will; as one pleases. —任意に處置する, to dispose at will [discretion]. ¶ 任意法, permissive law. —任意組合 a voluntary association.
ninin (二人), *n.* two men. ¶ 二人乘り, a double-seated *jinrikisha*; a two-seater (自動車·飛行機等の). —二人三脚 (遊戲) a three-legged race.
ninjin (人參), *n.* 【植】 ❶ the ginseng(-plant). ❷ 〔胡蘿蔔〕 the bees' [birds'] nest; the wild carrot; the carrot (通稱).
ninjō (人情), *n.* ❶ (人の情) humanity; feeling (情). ❷ (人性) (human) nature. —人情のない, inhumane; unfeeling; cold-hearted. —人情に引かされる, to be driven by humanity. —人情の機微に觸れる, to touch a string of the human heart. ¶ 人情噺, a love-story.
ninjū (忍從), *n.* passivity; passiveness; resignation. —忍從する, to resign oneself *to*; submit calmly *to*; yield *to.*
ninka (認可), *n.* sanction; authorization; approval. —認可する, to authorize; sanction; approve. ¶ 認可證, a certificate; a licence.
ninkan (任官), *n.* an appointment (to a government post).
ninki (人氣), *n.* ❶ (人望) popularity; popular favour. ❷ (氣性) the temper of the people. ❸ (市場景氣) market; popular spirit. —人氣に投ずる, to make a great sensation; catch the public fancy. —人氣の裏を行く, to act contrarily to the tendency of the market. —人氣を得る [博する], to win popularity [popular favour]; get into favour (氣に入る). —人氣を煽る, to make a market. ¶ 人氣役者, a popular actor.
ninki (任期), *n.* a term of office [service]; the tenure (of office).
ninkyo (認許), *n.* approval. ☞ *ninka.*
ninkyō (任俠), *n.* chivalry; manly spirit.
ninmei (任命), *n.* appointment; instalment. —任命する, to appoint *to*; nominate *to*; designate *to* [*as*; *for*]; install [place; put] *in.*
ninmen (任免), *n.* appointment and dismissal.
ninmen-jūshin (人面獸心), *n.* =***jinmen-jūshin.***
ninmu (任務), *n.* ❶ (使命) a mission. ❷ (職務) office; duty; function. —任務を果す, to dis-

charge one's duties; carry out one's mission.

ninniku (葫), *n.* 【植】the Spanish garlic; the sand-leek.

ninniku (忍辱), *n.* endurance; fortitude; forbearance.

ninoashi (二の足を踏む), to hesitate; vacillate.

ninoku (二の句), *n.* another word. —二の句が出ぬ, to be unable to utter another word; be struck dumb (呆然として); be dumbfounded (同上).

ninomai (二の舞を演ずる), to repeat the folly 《failure》.

ninoude (二の腕), *n.* the upper arm.

ninpinin (人非人), *n.* an inhuman fellow; a (human) monster.

ninpu (人夫), *n.* a coolie; a porter; a navvy (土工). ¶ 人夫頭, a coolie-foreman. —人夫賃, coolie-hire; porterage.

ninpu (妊婦), *n.* a pregnant woman; a woman with child. ¶ 妊婦預り所, a maternity-home; a lying-in house.

ninsen (人選), *n.* selection (of a person). ☞ *jinsen*.

ninshiki (認識), *n.* cognition; recognition; cognizance. —認識する, to cognize; recognize. ¶ 認識論, 【哲】epistemology; theory of cognition.

ninshin (妊娠), *n.* pregnancy; conception (受胎). —妊娠する, to conceive; become pregnant.

ninshō (人稱), *n.* 【文】person. ¶ 第一《二; 三》人稱, the first 《second; third》 person.

ninshō (人證), *n.* 【法】testimony of witnesses.

ninshō (認證), *n.* authentication; certification. —認證する, to authenticate; certify.

ninsō (人相), *n.* features; lineaments; the cut of one's face; physiognomy (人相學上の). —人相のよくない男, a fellow of evil physiognomy; a suspicious-looking person (胡散な). —人相を見る, to judge [read] (a person's) character 《tell fortune》 by his face; physiognomize. ¶ 人相書, a (personal) description; a written description. —人相學, physiognomy.

ninsoku (人足), *n.* a coolie. ☞ *ninpu* (人夫).

nintai (忍耐), *n.* patience; endurance; perseverance (堅忍). —忍耐力のある, patient; persevering. —忍耐する, to be patient; endure; persevere.

nintei (認定), *n.* ❶ acknowledgment; conclusion; recognition. ❷ (認可) authorization; sanction. —認定する, ① to acknowledge; conclude; recognize. ② to authorize; sanction.

ninushi (荷主), *n.* a cargo-owner; a consignor (荷送人); a shipper (荷積出人).

ninyō (任用), *n.* appointment; official employment. —任用する, to appoint; employ in an official capacity.

ninyō (認容する), *vt.* to admit; tolerate.

ninzu (人數), *n.* number of persons; strength (兵力).

nin-zuru (任ずる), *vt.* ❶ (任命) to appoint; nominate. ❷ (自任) to profess [claim] to be; call oneself. —知事に任ずる, to appoint a person governor. —藝術家を以て任ずる, to set up for an artist.

niō (二王), *n.* the two Deva Kings. ¶ 二王門, the Deva gate.

nioi (香, 匂), *n.* ❶ odour; smell; scent. ❷ (芳香) fragrance; perfume; aroma. —匂の善い, sweet-smelling; fragrant. —匂の惡い, foul-smelling; stinking.

nioibukuro (匂袋), *n.* a scent-bag.

niokurinin (荷送人), *n.* a shipper; a consignor.

nioroshi (荷卸), *n.* discharge; unloading. —荷卸しする, to discharge; unload; unburden.

niou (香-匂ふ), *vi.* ❶ (香る) to scent; smell; be fragrant. ❷ (鮮かに映える) to be bright; be splendid.

niowasu (香-匂はす), *vt.* ❶ (薫らす) to perfume; scent; let smell. ❷ (仄めかす) to hint (*at*).

nippō (日報), *n.* a daily report [bulletin].

nira (韮), *n.* 【植】the fragrant-flowered garlic.

nirami (睨), *n.* a glare; a stare. —睨みが利く, to be weighty [dignified] enough; possess sufficient dignity.

niramiau (睨合ふ), *vi.* ❶ (互に睨む) to glare at each other; look daggers [fiercely] at each other. ❷ (機を窺合ふ) to watch each other; be on guard against each other. ❸ (反目) to be at odds [variance; feud; daggers drawn] *with*.

niramikura (睨競), *n.* a staring match.

niramu (睨む), *vt.* ❶ to glare *at*; glower *at*; stare *at*. ❷ (眼をつける) to set one's eyes *upon*; keep a watchful eye *on*; watch [view] suspiciously. —睨み返す, to stare [glare] back. —俺が睨んでるからには, as I keep my eyes open.

nire (楡), *n.* 【植】Ulnus parvifolia (elm-tree の類-學名).

nirenpatsu (二連發), *n.* a double-barrelled gun.
niretsu (二列), *n.* a double rank; two rows. —二列に竝ぶ, to form two ranks.
nirinsha (二輪車), *n.* a two-wheeled vehicle; a two-wheeler; a bicycle (自轉車).
niru (似る), *v.* to resemble; look like; take *after*.
niru (煮る), *vt.* to boil; cook (料理).
nisan (二三の), *a.* two or three; a few; some. —二三遍[度], two or three times. —言を二三にする, to use a double tongue.
nisankabutsu (二酸化物), *n.* 【化】 a dioxide.
nise (贋), *n.* a sham; a counterfeit (贋造物); a forgery (同上). ¶ 贋金, a false [bad; counterfeit; spurious] coin. —贋印, a forged seal. —贋物, a sham; an imitation; a counterfeit. —贋札, counterfeit [forged] paper-money; flash money. —贋證文, a forged bond. —贋手紙, a forged letter.
nise (二世), *n.* the present and the future; this world and the next. —二世を契る, to pledge [plight] one's troth for this world and the next.
niseru (似·擬·贋せる), *vt.* to imitate; counterfeit; forge.
nishi (西), *n.* west; westward (西方): the west (西風). —西の, west; western; westerly. —西に, in the west (西部); to [towards] the west (西をさして); westwards (同上); on the west (西側に).
nishibi (西日), *n.* the westering sun.
nishiki (錦), *n.* brocade; cloth of gold. —錦を飾って故郷に歸る, to return to one's birthplace in splendour [glory].
nishikie (錦繪), *n.* a chromoxylograph; a *nishikie* 【日】.
nishime (煮染), *n.* vegetable hotchpotch. —煮染める, to boil 《simmer》 down.
nishin (鯡), *n.* 【魚】 the herring.
nishin (二伸), *n.* postscript (P. S. と略す).
nishitewa (にしては), *prep.* considering; for. —子供にしては, for a child; considering he is a mere child.
nishū (二週), *n.* two weeks; a fortnight. —二週每の《に》, fortnightly.
nisoku-sanmon (二束三文に), *ad.* dirt [dog]-cheap. —二束三文に賣る, to sell for an old song; sell dirt-cheap.
nissan (日參する), *v.* ❶ to visit a temple daily. ❷ to pay a daily visit *to*; frequent.
Nissen (日鮮), *n.* Japan and Chōsen [Korea].
nisshabyō (日射病), *n.* 【醫】 sunstroke; siriasis.
Nisshi (日支), *n.* Japan and China. —日支の, Sino-Japanese. ¶ 日支親善, the friendly relations between Japan and China.
nisshi (日誌), *n.* a diary; a daily record. ☞ *nikki* (日記).
nisshin-geppo (日進月步の), *a.* ever-progressing; ever-improving.
nisshōki (日章旗), *n.* the Sun-flag; the flag of the Rising Sun; the national flag of Japan.
nisshoku (日蝕), *n.* a solar eclipse; an eclipse of the sun.
nisshutsu (日出-時), *n.* sunrise.
nissū (日數), *n.* a number of days; days.
nisu (假漆), *n.* varnish.
nitaki (煮焚), *n.* cooking.
nitanita (にたにた笑ふ), *vi.* to grin; make a grin.
nitari (荷足-船), *n.* a barge; a lighter.
nitari-yottari (似たり寄ったり), *a.* six of one and half a dozen of the other; little to choose between the two; much of a muchness.
nitate (煮立ての), *a.* fresh from the pot; hot and hot (熱々の).
nitatsu (煮立つ), *vi.* to boil up.
nitchimo-satchimo (二進も三進も行かぬ), to be in a tight place; be in a (tight) box; be in a (nice) fix; be at a fix; be driven to the wall.
nitchū (日中), *n.* the daytime; the midday. ——, *ad.* during the day; in the daytime.
nite (にて), *particle.* =*de* (で). —郵便にて, per post.
nitehinaru (似而非なる), *a.* false; sham. ☞ *ese.*
nito (二兎), *n.* two hares [rabbits]. —二兎を追ふ者は一兎を得ず, "He who pursues two hares, catches neither."
nitō (二等), *n.* the second; the second class. ☞ *ittō* (一等).
nitōbun (二等分する), *vt.* to bisect.
nitōhen (二等邊の), *a.* 【數】 isosceles (三角形の). ¶ 二等邊三角形, an isosceles triangle.
nitsuke (煮附), *n.* hard-boiling.
nitsuku (似附く), *v.* to become; suit. ☞ *niau.*
nitsumeru (煮詰める), *vt.* to boil down; boil dry; simmer down (じりじりと).
nittei (日程), *n.* a day's programme; the order of the day (議事日程又は其の日の仕事). —

日程を變更する, to change [alter] the order of the day.

nittō (日當), *n.* daily allowance; daily pay.

niukenin (荷受人), *n.* a consignee.

niwa (庭), *n.* a garden; a court (-yard) (中庭); a yard (同上); grounds (構內). —庭を作る, to lay out a garden.

niwa (には), *prep.* in; for; to.

niwaka (俄の), *a.* sudden; abrupt. —俄の出立, sudden departure. —— **-ni**, *ad.* suddenly; abruptly. —俄に死ぬ, to die suddenly.

niwaka (仁和賀), *n.* a farce; a mime.

niwakaame (俄雨), *n.* a shower (of rain).

niwakabenkyō (俄勉强), *n.* cramming.

niwakabungen (俄分限), *n.* an upstart; a mushroom. = *narikin*.

niwaki (庭木), *n.* a garden plant [tree].

niwashi (庭師), *n.* a (landscape-) gardener.

niwatashi (荷渡し), *n.* delivery.

niwatoko (接骨木), *n.* 【植】 the hart's elder.

niwatori (鷄,雞), *n.* the (domestic) fowl; a hen (雌); a cock (雄). —鷄を割くに牛刀を用ひる, to break [crush] a fly [butterfly] on the wheel; take a spear to kili a fly.

niyaku (荷役), *n.* landing and loading.

niyaniya (にやにや笑ふ), *vi.* to grin.

niyō (二樣の), *a.* two; double. —二樣の解釋が出來る, It may be interpreted in two ways; It bears [admits of] two different interpretations.

niyori (似寄の), *a.* like; similar.

nizakana (煮肴), *n.* boiled fish.

nizukuri (荷造), *n.* packing; package. —荷造りする, to pack goods. ¶ 荷造費, packing charges.

no (の), *prep.* of; in; at; with; to. —籠の鳥, a bird in a cage. —家の譽れ, a credit to one's family. —日本の地位, Japan's position. —五十圓の小切手, a cheque for fifty *yen*.

no (野), *n.* a field; a plain (平原); a wilderness (荒野).

nō (能), *n.* ability (力量); faculty (能力); talent (才能). —能ある鷹は爪を隱す, "Cats hide their claws." —遊んでる計りが能でない, It won't do to be always idle. ¶ 能不能, merits and demerits. —能なし, a good-for--nothing.

nō (能), *n.* *Nō*; a *Nō* dance [play]. ¶ 能舞臺, a *Nō* stage.

nō (腦), *n.* the brain; brains (知力). ☞ *atama* (頭).

nō (農), *n.* husbandry; agriculture; farming (耕作). ☞ *nōgyō*.

nō (膿), *n.* pus; (purulent) matter. —膿を持つ, to become purulent; come to a head; suppurate.

nobanashi (野放し), *n.* pasturage; putting to pasture.

nobara (野薔薇), *n.* 【植】 the many-flowered rose.

nobasu (延·伸ばす), *vt.* ❶ (引伸ばす) to stretch; lengthen; extend. ❷ (期間を) to lengthen; prolong; protract. ❸ (延期す) to postpone; defer; put off. ❹ (薄める) to dilute. —他日に延ばす, to put off to another day. —枝を伸ばす, to spread the branches. —日限を延ばす, to extend the time. —足を伸ばす, to stretch one's legs. —才を伸ばす, to give full scope to one's talents. —髮を長く伸ばす, to let one's hair grow long.

nobato (野鳩), *n.* the blue rock-pigeon.

nobe (延べ), *n.* ❶ (延長) stretching; lengthening; extending. ❷ =*nobetorihiki*. ——一日五人宛十日間の延人員五十人, the total number of attendances in ten days at five men per day is fifty.

nobe (野邊), *n.* a field; a moor. —野邊送りをする, to perform the last office to the deceased.

nōben (能辯), *n.* eloquence; fluency. ☞ *yūben*.

noberu (述べる), *vt.* ❶ (陳述) to state; relate. ❷ (表白) to express. ❸ (話す) to tell; narrate. —事情を述べる, to relate the circumstances. —理由を述べる, to state [give] the reason.

noberu-shōkin (ノーベル賞金), *n.* a Nobel prize.

nobetorihiki (延取引), *n.* a time-bargain; a transaction in futures.

nobetsu (のべつに), *ad.* continuously; incessantly; without interval. —のべつに喋る, to talk without a pause; wag one's tongue.

nobi (伸), *n.* ❶ (背のび) stretching oneself. ❷ (成長) growth. —伸びをする, to stretch oneself.

nobi (野火), *n.* a wild fire.

nobiagaru (伸上る), *vi.* to stretch oneself up; straighten up; stand on tiptoe (爪先で).

nobichijimi (伸縮), *n.* expansion and contraction; elasticity.

nobinobi (のびのび), *ad.* ❶ (のんびり) cheerfully; comfortably. ❷ (延引して) being gradually postponed [deferred; put off]. —氣が伸び伸びする, to feel quite relieved [easy].

nobiru (山蒜), *n.* 【植】 Allium nipponicum (garlic の一種·學名).

nobiru (延·伸びる), *vi.* ❶ (延長) to extend; stretch; lengthen. ❷ (延引) to be put off. ❸ (增大) to increase; grow (成長). ❹ (進步) to (make) progress. ❺ (皺など) to be smoothed [flattened].

nobori (幟), *n.* a banner; a flag. ¶ 五月幟, a flag of the May fête. —幟竿, a flag-staff.

nobori (上·昇), *n.* ascent; rise; going up. —それから道は次第に上りになる, There the road begins to ascend gradually. ¶ 上り列車, an up-train.

noborimichi (上道), *n.* an up-hill road; an up-hill journey.

noborizaka (登坂), *n.* an ascent; a slope; an up-hill road.

noboru (上·昇·登る), *vt.* ❶ (昇る) to rise; go up; ascend. ❷ (攀登る) to climb. ❸ (達す) to reach; come up *to*; amount *to*. ☞ *agaru* (上る). —都へ上る, to go up to town. —教育會議に上る, to be brought before the educational conference.

nobose (逆上), *n.* ❶ dizziness. ❷ (熱中) eagerness.

noboseru (上·登せる), *vt.* ❶ (上ぐ) to raise; elevate. ❷ (記載する) to enter; register; publish; insert. ❸ (出す) (*a*) to bring up (a matter for discussion): (*b*) to serve up (so many dishes).

noboseru (逆上せる), *vi.* ❶ (眩暈) to have a rush of blood to the head; become dizzy. ❷ (熱中) to have on the brain; be enthusiastic *over*; be beside oneself *with*. —試驗に逆上せる, to have the examination on the brain.

nobudō (蛇葡萄), *n.* 【植】 the variegated Virginian creeper.

nōbyō (腦病), *n.* a brain disease. ¶ 腦病院, a hospital for brain diseases.

nochi (後), *n.* ❶ future; next time. ❷ (子孫) a descendant; posterity. —後の世, future life: the later generations. —四五日の後に, four or five days later [after]. —後の事を託す, to leave one's affairs after death in a person's hands.

nochihodo (後程), *ad.* later on; afterwards; by and by.

nochinochi (後後), *n.* the future. ——, *ad.* in the future; afterwards.

nōchū (嚢中), *n.* ❶ (嚢の中) the inside of a bag. ❷ (所持金) the contents of a purse. —嚢中無一物で, without a penny in one's pocket. —嚢中に物を探るが如し, to be as easy as searching the inside of a bag.

nodate (野立), *n.* a rest in the fields. ¶ 御野立所, the resting-place of an emperor.

nodatsu (野立つ), *vi.* to grow tall; grow up (成長する).

node (ので), *prep.* because of; on account of. ——, *conj.* as; since; now that.

noden (野天で), in the open air; under the blue sky. ¶ 野天興行, an outdoor performance.

nodo (咽, 喉), *n.* the throat; the gullet. —喉が渇く, to feel thirsty.

nōdo (濃度), *n.* density; shade (of colour) (色の); concentration (溶液の).

nōdō (能動的), *a.* active. ¶ 能動調 [態], 【文】 the active voice.

nodobiko (咽喉垂), *n.* 【醫】 the uvula.

nodobotoke (咽佛), *n.* Adam's apple.

nodobue (喉笛), *n.* the wind-pipe; the trachea [*pl.* -æ].

nodoka (長閑な), *a.* Ⓢ 長閑けき. calm; mild; genial. —長閑な天氣, a pleasant [genial] weather.

nodokubi (喉頸), *n.* the throat; the neck.

nōdokushō (膿毒症), *n.* 【醫】 pyæmia.

nōen (農園), *n.* a garden; a farm; a plantation (栽植地).

nōen (濃艶な), *a.* ❶ lovely; charming; coquettish (仇っぽい). ❷ (色の) rich; heavy.

nōfu (納付する), *vt.* Ⓢ 納入する. to pay (in); supply.

nōfu (農夫), *n.* a farmer; a husbandman.

nogai (野飼), *n.* pasturing on the moor.

nōgaki (能書), *n.* ❶ (效能書) a statement of the virtues (of a medicine). ❷ (吹聽) self-advertisement; a puff (誇大の廣告).

nōgakkō (農學校), *n.* an agricultural school 《college》.

nōgaku (農學), *n.* (the science of) agriculture. ¶ 農學士《博士》, a bachelor 《doctor》 of agriculture. —農學者, an agriculturist.

nogareru (逃·免れる), *vi.* to escape; get off; get rid of. —逃れられぬ運命, an inevitable [unavoidable] fate.

nogasu (逃がす), *vt.* to let escape; let slip; miss. ☞ *nigasu.*

nōgei (農藝), *n.* agricultural technology.

nogeshi (苦菜), *n.* 【植】 the sow-thistle; the milk-weed.

nogi (芒), *n.* 【植】 an awn; an arista.

nogiku (野菊), *n.* the wild camomile [chamomile].

nōgu (農具), *n.* farm [agricultural] implements; farming tools; agricultural machinery (機械類).

nōgyō (農業), *n.* agriculture; husbandry; farming. ¶ 農業國《銀行》, an agricultural country 《bank》. —農業家, an agriculturist; a farmer (百姓).

nohara (野原), *n.* a field.

nōhinketsu (腦貧血), *n.* cerebral anæmia. —腦貧血を起す, to have a fit of cerebral anæmia.

nōhitsu (能筆), *n.* ❶ good penmanship. ❷ (人) a good penman; a skilled calligrapher.

nōhon (納本), *n.* ❶ presentation of copies to the authorities. ❷ a presented copy.

nōikketsu (腦溢血), *n.* cerebral hæmorrhage; apoplexy.

nōji (能事), *n.* work; proper work.

nōji (農時), *n.* farming season.

nōji (農事), *n.* agriculture; agricultural affairs. ¶ 農事試驗場, an agricultural experimental station; an experimental farm.

nōjō (農場), *n.* a farm; a plantation.

nōjūketsu (腦充血), *n.* cerebral hyperæmia; congestion of the brain.

nojuku (野宿する), *vi.* to camp out; bivouac; sleep in open air [in a field; under the blue sky].

nōka (農科), *n.* an agricultural department.

nōka (農家), *n.* ❶ (家) a farmer's house [cottage]; a farmhouse; a farm-stead. ❷ (人) a farmer.

nōkai (農會), *n.* an agricultural society.

nōkai (膿潰), *n.* 【醫】 ulceration; suppuration; fester. —膿潰する, to ulcerate; suppurate; fester.

nōkan (納棺する), *vt.* to encoffin; enclose in a coffin. ¶ 納棺式, the ceremony of encoffinment.

nokemono (除物にする), *v.* to leave out in the cold; exclude.

nokeru (除ける), *vt.* ❶ (移す) to remove; put [take] out of the way; put aside [away]. ❷ (除く) to get rid *of*; remove. ❸ (省く) to omit.

noki (軒, 檐), *n.* the eaves. —軒を竝べる, to stand in a row [side by side].

nōki (納期), *n.* the term for payment.

nokinami (軒竝に), *ad.* at every house [door].

nōkinshō (腦焮衝), *n.* phrenitis; inflammation of the brain.

nōkō (農工), *n.* agriculture and industry. ¶ 農工銀行, an agricultural and industrial bank.

nōkō (濃厚な), *a.* thick; dense; rich (色·風味など). —濃厚な食物, a rich food.

nokogiri (鋸), *n.* a saw.

nokogirizame (鋸鮫), *n.* 【魚】 the saw-shark.

nokonoko (のこのこ), *ad.* nonchalantly (平氣で); coolly; obtrusively (無遠慮に).

nokorazu (殘らず), *ad.* all; altogether; entirely. —彼等は一人も殘らず殺された, They were killed every one of them.

nokori (殘), *n.* the rest; the remainder; the balance (差引殘高). —殘りの人々, the rest of the people.

nokorimono (殘物), *n.* remains; leavings; remainders (商品等の).

nokorioshii (殘惜しい), *a.* regrettable; much regretted. —殘惜しさうに, with a regretful look.

nokoru (殘る), *vi.* ❶ (殘留) (*a*) to remain: (*b*) to remain behind; stay. ❷ (餘る) to remain over; be left over. —記憶に殘る, to remain in one's memory. —七時まで殘ッてゐる, to remain till seven. —殘る隈なく捜す, to search everywhere; look in every nook and corner. —十から七引いて三殘る, Seven from ten leaves three. —痘瘡は痕が殘る, The small-pox leaves scars behind.

nokosu (殘·遺·貽す), *vt.* to leave behind. ❶ [殘] (後に留む) to leave (to); leave over; keep back (取ッて置く); save (ためる). ❷ [貽] (後に傳へる) to bequeath. —名を殘す, to leave a name behind one; bequeath a name. —誤を後世に貽す, to mislead posterity. —少なからぬ金を殘す, to save (up) a large sum of money. —大勢の家族を殘した, He left a large family.

nōkotsudō (納骨堂), *n.* a charnel(-house).

noku (退く), *vi.* to move off; stand [move] aside; get out of the way; make way for.

nōkyōgen (能狂言), *n.* a *Nō* farce; *Nō* plays and farces.

nōmaku (腦膜), *n.* meninx [*pl.* -ninges]; the membrane of the brain. —¶ 腦膜炎, brain-fever; meningitis. (急性腦膜炎, acute meningitis.)

nomareru (呑まれる), *vi.* ❶ to be swallowed. ❷ (威壓) to be overwhelmed.

nomaseru (飲ませる), *vt.* Ⓢ 飲ます. to let 《make》 drink; give a drink; water (馬に); dose (藥を).

nomeru (のめる), *vi.* to fall forward [on one's face].

nomeru (飲める), *a.* good to

drink; drinkable.

nomi (蚤), *n.* 【昆】 the flea. —蚤に喰はれた痕, a fleabite. —蚤に喰はれる, to be bitten by a flea.

nomi (鑿), *n.* a chisel; a tooler (石工用). —鑿で彫る, to chisel.

nomi (而已, 耳), *ad.* only; alone; merely. ——, *prep.* except; but. ☞ ***dake, bakari.***

nomichi (野道), *n.* a path through a field [moor].

nomiguchi (呑口), *n.* a tap; a faucet; a cock; a spigot. —樽に呑口を附ける, to tap a cask.

nomigusuri (飲藥), *n.* an internal medicine.

nomihosu (飲干す), *vt.* to drain (a cup); drink up [off]; drink [drain] to the lees [dregs]; toss off; drink (a cup) clean (綺麗に).

nomikake (飲掛けの), *a.* half--drunk (酒など); half-smoked (煙草など). —飲み掛けの盃, an unfinished glass.

nomikkura (飲競), *n.* a drinking match [bout]; a carouse. —飲競をする, to have a drinking-bout; carouse.

nomikomi (呑込), *n.* understanding; comprehension; grasp. —呑込みが善い [早い] 《惡い [遅い]》, to be quick 《slow》 to understand.

nomikomu (呑込む), *vt.* ❶ (嚥下) to swallow. ❷ (會得) to understand; comprehend; grasp; take in. —仕事の呼吸を呑み込む, to get the knack [the hang] of one's business.

nomikui (飲食), *n.* eating and drinking.

nomimizu (飲水), *n.* drinking water.

nomimono (飲物), *n.* a drink; a beverage.

nōmin (農民), *n.* the peasantry (階級); a peasant (個人); a farmer (同上). ¶ 農民黨, the agrarian party.

nominakama (飲仲間), *n.* a bottle [boon]-companion.

nominarazu (のみならず), not only [merely]...but (also); moreover (加之).

nomishiro (飲代), *n.* drink--money; *pourboire* 【佛】.

nomisugiru (飲過ぎる), *v.* to overdrink oneself; drink too much; drink to excess.

nomite (飲手), *n.* a hard [great] drinker.

nomitoriko (蚤取粉), *n.* flea--powder; insect-powder.

nomitorimanako (蚤取眼で), with sharp [keen] eyes.

nomitsubusu (飲潰す), *vt.* ❶ (相手を) to drink (one's companion) down [under the table]. ❷ (財産を) to drink away.

nomu (飲·呑む), *vt.* ❶ to drink; take; have. ❷ (吸ふ) to smoke (煙草); suck (乳等). ❸ (呑込む) to swallow. ❹ (倂呑) to swallow up. ❺ (侮る) to despise; slight; make light of. —飲み明かす, to drink the night out; drink away the night; make a night of it. —飲み廻る, to drink about; drink at more than one place. —人を呑んで掛かる, to make light of another; put a slight upon a person; look down upon another. —聲を飲んで泣く, to cry in a muffled voice. —まだ飲み足りないと見える, He appears not to have had enough drink.

nōmu (農務), *n.* agricultural affairs. ¶ 農務局, the Bureau of Agriculture.

nōmu (濃霧), *n.* a dense [thick] fog.

nonbiri (のんびりした), *a.* calm; gentle; mild. —のんびり育つ, to grow up gentle. —氣がのんびりする, to feel easy.

nondakure (大酒者), *n.* a drunkard; a sot; a toper.

noni (のに), *conj.* (*a*) (拘らず) though; although: (*b*) (一方では) when; while. ——, *prep.* (*a*) (拘らず) in spite of; notwithstanding: (*b*) (爲には) for. —ここへ來いってるのに, Come here, I tell you. —私の云ふ通りにすればよかったのに, You had better have done as I told you.

nonki (暢氣な), *a.* easy-going; free and easy; happy-go-lucky. —暢氣な人, an easy-going man; a happy-go-lucky fellow; a light--hearted person. —暢氣に暮す, to lead an easy life.

nonoshiru (罵る), *vi.* ❶ (叫〔?〕く) to shout; yell. ❷ (謗〔?〕る) to talk abusively. ——, *vt.* ❶ (謗る) to abuse; revile; rail *at.* ❷ (叱る) to scold. —口を極めて [散々] 罵る, to shout all kinds of abuses.

nopperi (のっぺり), *ad.* smoothly; flat. —のっぺりした顔, a flat face.

noppiki (退引ならぬ), *a.* unavoidable; inevitable; impossible to escape. —退引きならぬ用事で, through unavoidable business. —退引きならないので, as it is absolutely necessary; having no alternative; admitting of no excuse [escape].

noppō (のっぽう), *n.* a tall clown; a strapper 【俗】; a lamp-post.

nora (野良), *n.* a field; a moor. ¶ 野良犬, a masterless [homeless] dog.

norakura (のらくらと), *ad.* idly;

lazily; indolently. —のらくらする, to idle; drone. ¶ のらくら者, an idler; a loafer; a lounger.

noren (暖簾), *n.* ❶ (帳[とばり]) a curtain; a screen; a shop-curtain (店用). ❷ (商家の名聲) the credit of a shop; the good name of a firm. —暖簾を汚す, to impair the credit of one's shop; discredit one's firm.

nori (海苔), *n.* 【植】 the laver. ¶ 乾《味附け》海苔, dried 《seasoned》 laver.

nori (法), *n.* ❶ (大道) the way; the divine law. ❷ (規則) a law; a rule; regulation.

nori (乘), *n.* ❶ riding. ❷ (塗りつくこと) painting ❸ 【商】(乘合) joint account 《partnership》.

nori (糊), *n.* paste; starch. —糊のきいたシャツ, a well-starched shirt. —糊張りする, to starch; paste.

nōri (腦裏), *n.* the brain. —深く腦裏に印する, to be deeply impressed *with*.

noriageru (乘上げる), *v.* to run on; run ashore [aground]; strand. —船を乘り上げる, to drive a ship on shore.

noriai (乘合), *n.* ❶ (事) riding together. ❷ (人) a fellow-passenger. ❸ (共同) joint partnership. —乘合はす, to happen to ride (in the same car, *etc.*) *with*. —乘合ひで買ふ, to buy on joint account. ¶ 乘合馬車, a (stage-)coach; an omnibus (bus, と略す). —乘合船, a passenger-boat.

noribake (糊刷毛), *n.* a paste-brush.

noribera (糊篦), *n.* a starch-spatula.

noridasu (乘出す), *vi.* ❶ (出帆) to put to sea; put off; set sail. ❷ (出發) to start; go on. ❸ (入る) to enter on; embark upon. ❹ (前進) to move forward. —沖へ乘り出す, 【航】 to stand to [make for] sea. —實業界へ乘り出す, to enter on a business career.

norikae (乘換, 乘替), *n.* ❶ (船汽車の) a change; transfer. ❷ (取引市場) carrying over; continuation. —乘り換へる, to change (car; ship); transfer [*vi.*]. —品川方面行は乘換へ, "Change here for Shinagawa." ¶ 乘換場, a place for changing; a junction; a transfer. —乘換驛, a station for changing; a junction (station). —乘換切符, a transfer-ticket; a transfer.

norikakeru (乘掛ける), *vi.* ❶ to begin to get in. ❷ (乘上げる) to run aground.

noriki (乘氣になる), *vi.* to take a fancy *to*; have keen interest *in*.

norikoeru (乘越える), *vt.* to get *over*; cross *over*; ride *over*. —垣を乘り越える, to get over a fence.

norikomu (乘込む), *vt.* ❶ to get *in*; go on board (船); catch (乘る); take (同上). ❷ (繰込む) to proceed *to*; make an entry; parade [march] *into* (華々しく).

norikosu (乘越す), *v.* to ride past. ¶ 乘越賃銀, excess fare (on railway).

norikumi (乘組 -員), *n.* crew; ship's company. —乘り組む, to ship. —乘組員を雇入れる, to ship a crew.

norimawaru (乘廻る), *vi.* to ride round [about]; drive around.

norimodosu (乘戻す), *vt.* to ride 《drive》 back.

norimono (乘物), *n.* a vehicle; a palanquin (轎[かご]).

nōrin (農林), *n.* agriculture and forestry. ¶ 農林大臣, the Minister of (State for) Agriculture and Forestry. —農林學校, an agricultural and dendrological [forestry] school. —農林省, the Department of Agriculture and Forestry.

norinige (乘逃する), *vi.* to steal a ride; run away without paying the fare; run away on another's bicycle (自轉車の).

noriokureru (乘後れる), *v.* to miss [lose] (the train; boat, &c.).

noriori (乘降), *n.* getting in and out. ¶ 乘降場, ① (汽車の) a platform; a landing. ② (電車の) a station.

norisugiru (乘過ぎる), *vt.* to ride too much; ride past (乘越す).

norisuteru (乘捨てる) *vt.* to get off. —車を乘り捨てて徒步で行く, to alight from *jinrikisha* and go on foot.

norite (乘手), *n.* ❶ (乘客) a passenger. ❷ (騎者) a rider.

norito (祝詞), *n.* a *Shintō* ritual; *Shintō* prayers.

noritoru (乘取る), *vt.* to take possession *of*; seize; capture.

nōritsu (能率), *n.* efficiency; 【機】 a moment. —能率をあげる, to raise efficiency. ¶ 勞働能率, efficiency of labour. —能率增進法, the method of increasing efficiency.

noritsubusu (乘潰す), *vt.* (馬を) to ride down; ride [run] to death.

noritsukeru (乘附ける), *vi.* ❶ to ride up *to*. ❷ (乘慣れる) to get used to riding.

noriutsuru (乘移る), *v.* to change (car; ship, *etc.*).

noriutsuru (憑移る), *v.* to

possess; bewitch.

norizuke (糊著), *n.* pasting; starching. —糊著けする, to paste; starch.

nōrō (膿漏), *n.* 【醫】 catarrh of the frontal sinuses (前頭竇加答兒).

noroi (呪), *n.* curse; imprecation; execration.

noroi (のろい), *a.* ❶ (遲い) slow; tardy. ❷ (鈍い) dull. —仕事がのろい, to be slow [dull] in one's work; be tardy at business.

noroma (野呂間), *n.* a slow-coach; a simpleton; a blockhead. —野呂間な, stupid; blunt; slow-witted.

noronoro (のろのろ), *ad.* slowly; sluggishly; at snail's pace.

noroshi (狼煙), *n.* a signal-fire; a rocket; a beacon(-fire). —狼煙を揚げる, to fire a rocket; raise a signal-fire.

norou (呪ふ), *vt.* to curse; imprecate; execrate. —呪はれた, accursed; cursed. —人を呪ふ, to imprecate [invoke] evil upon a person.

noru (乘·載る), *v.* ❶ (乘物に) to ride; take; go on board (船に). ❷ (物の上に) to mount (*on*); get *upon*. ❸ (仲間に入る) to join; take part 《stock》 *in*. ❹ (記載さる) to appear; be written [recorded]; be put on. ❺ (塗りつく) to spread (白粉など). ❻ (欺かる) to fall into (a trap). —飛行機に乘る, to get on an air-plane. —歷史に載る, to be recorded in history. —相談に乘る, ① to give one's opinion *about*; accept a person's offer (應ずる). ② to take part in an enterprise; share with another in some undertaking. —計略に乘る, to fall into a person's snare [trap].

noruka-soruka (伸るか反るか), *ad.* hit or miss; sink or swim; victory or death. —のるかそるかやって見る, to try one's luck; stake all on chance.

Noruwei (諾威), *n.* Norway. ¶ 諾威人, a Norwegian.

nōryō (納涼), *n.* enjoying the cool breeze; cooling and refreshing oneself. ¶ 納涼博覽會, an evening fair. —納涼客, a cool-breeze hunter.

nōryoku (能力), *n.* ❶ (力量) ability; capacity; talent (才能). ❷ 【法】 (legal) capacity; competence. —能力ある, able; capable; competent. ¶ 能力者, 【法】 a person of full legal capacity; a competent person.

nōsaku (農作), *n.* tillage; husbandry; farming. ¶ 農作物, a crop.

nōsan (農產 -物), *n.* agricultural products; farm produce [products]. ¶ 農產物種子, seed-grains.

nōsatsu (惱殺する), *vt.* to fascinate; charm; enchant; captivate.

nōsekizui (腦脊髓), *n.* cerebrospinal medulla. ¶ 腦脊髓膜炎, cerebrospinal meningitis [fever].

noseru (乘せる), *vt.* ❶ (置く) to put [place; lay] on. ❷ (積む) to load; take [get] on board (船に); give a person a lift (人を車に). ❸ 〔載〕 (記す) to record; mention; publish (公表). ❹ (はめる) to take in; impose upon. —馬車に乘せてやる (助けて), to help a person into a carriage.

noshi (熨斗), *n.* ❶ a *noshi*; a miniature [symbolic] piece of dried sea-ear. ❷ (熨斗鮑) a thin strip of dried sea-ear.

nōshinkei (腦神經), *n.* a cranial nerve.

nōshintō (腦震盪), *n.* concussion of the brain.

nōsho (能書), *n.* fine penmanship; calligraphy. ¶ 能書家, a skilful penman; a calligrapher; a calligraphist.

nōshō (農相), *n.* =*nōrin* (農林大臣).

nōshō (腦漿), *n.* the brain. —腦漿を絞る, to cudgel [beat] one's brains.

nōshōmu (農商務 -省), *n.* the Department of Agriculture and Commerce. ¶ 農商務大臣, the Minister of (State for) Agriculture and Commerce.

nōshu (膿腫), *n.* 【醫】 an abscess.

nōshukketsu (腦出血), *n.* cerebral hæmorrhage.

nosodachi (野育の), *a.* wild; uneducated (特に無教育). —野育ちにする, to allow to run wild; allow to grow as they will.

nōson (農村), *n.* a farm-village. ¶ 農村改革, agrarian reform. —農村振興策, policy for the prosperity of the farm-villages.

nōsotchū (腦卒中), *n.* (cerebral) apoplexy.

nosonoso (のそのそ), *ad.* Ⓢ のそりのそり. slowly; sluggishly; in a heavy manner. —のそのそ歩く, to walk heavily; jog.

nosu (伸す), *v.* ❶ =*nobasu* (延す)の ❶. ❷ (出世する) to rise [get up] in the world.

nōsuishu (腦水腫), *n.* 【醫】 hydrocephalus; water on the brain.

nosuri (のすり), *n.* 【鳥】 the buzzard.

notakuru (のたくる), *vi.* to wriggle; writhe; squirm.

nōtan (濃淡), *n.* shade; light and shade (明暗).

notarejini (野倒死する), *vi.* to die on the roadside; die in a ditch.
nōten (腦天), *n.* the scalp; the top [crown] of head; the pate【俗】.
nōto (ノート), *n.* ❶ (標註) a note. ❷ (控) a note; a note-book (控帳). —ノートに取って置く, to write [set] down in a note-book.
notto (浬, 節), *n.* a knot. —一時間三十五節出る, to make 35 knots an hour.
nottoru (則る), *vt.* ❶ (從ふ) to follow; conform *to*; act on. ❷ (倣ふ) to imitate; model after [*on*]. —先例に則って, acting on [following] the precedents.
nottoru (乘取る), *vt.* =***noritoru***.
nousagi (野兎), *n.*【哺乳】a hare.
nōzei (納稅), *n.* payment of a tax; tax-paying; rate-paying (地方稅). ¶ 納稅義務, liability to pay taxes. —納稅階級, the tax ⦅rate⦆-paying classes. —納稅期限, the period of tax-payment. —納稅告知書, notice of tax-paying; tax-papers. —納稅者, a taxpayer; a ratepayer. —納稅資格, tax [rate] qualification.
nozoite (除いて), *prep.* except; but; with the exception *of*. —小數の例外を除いては, saving rare exceptional cases. —居合はす人人を除いて, the present company excepted.
nozoki (覗き), *n.* ❶ (覗くこと) a peep. ❷ (覗機關〔カラクリ〕) a peep-show. ¶ 覗き孔, a peep-hole.
nozoku (除く), *vt.* ❶ (除外) to exclude; except. ❷ (除去) to do away with; remove. ❸ (省略) to omit; leave out. —組合から除く, to exclude a person from the association. —通路の邪魔物を除く, to clear the road of obstacles.
nozoku (覗·覘く), *v.* to peep *through* [*into*]; take a peep *at*. —鍵穴から覗く, to peep at the key-hole. —窓から覗く, to peep through a window; look in at a window (內を). —室の內を覗き込む, to peep into a room. —活動(寫眞)を覗く, to have a look at the movies.
nozomashii (望ましい), *a.* desirable; advisable. ——, *v.* it is to be desired [wished]; it is desirable that....
nozomi (望), *n.* ❶ desire (願望); wish (同上); hope (希望). ❷ (抱負) aspiration; ambition. ❸ (好み) preference; choice. ❹ (見込) promise; prospect. —望みの品, the desired article. —大に望みのある男, a man of great promise. —お望みによ り, at [in compliance with] your request. —成功の望みがある, to be hopeful of success; bid fair to succeed; promise well. —成功の望みがない, to be ⦅have⦆ no prospect of success. —多年の望みが叶ふ, to attain one's long-cherished desire. —望みを掛ける, ① (囑望) to put hope *in*; expect (something) of [from] a person. ② (得んと欲す) to have [set] one's mind *on*.
nozomite (望手), *n.* ❶ (申込人) an applicant. ❷ (買手) a buyer; a purchaser. ❸ (求婚者) a suitor.
nozomu (望む), *vt.* ❶ (欲求) to desire; wish. ❷ (希望) to hope; expect (期待). ❸ (選擇) to prefer; choose. ❹ (眺める) to look *at*; see. —望んでゐる, to be desirous.
nozomu (臨む), *v.* ❶ (面す) to look over; look out upon; face. ❷ (臨場) to be present *at*; attend. —海に臨む, to face the sea. —開場式に臨む, to be present at the opening ceremony. —死に臨んで, in face [the presence] of death.
nozomurakuwa (望むらくは), it is to be desired that...; would that.
nōzui (腦髓), *n.* the brain.
nu (ぬ), *ad.* (打消し) not.
nūbō (ヌーボー), *n.* & *a.* *nouveau*【佛】. ¶ ヌーボー式, ① (藝術) an art *nouveau*. ② (大きくぼーっとした) vagueness.
nue (鵺, 鵼), *n.* ❶【鳥】(とらつぐみ) the White's (ground-)thrush. ❷ a monster with a monkey's head, a tiger's body, and a serpent's tail; a chimera.
nugasu (脫がす), *vt.* to undress; unclothe; strip *of*. —上衣を脫がしてやる, to help a person off with his coat.
nugu (脫ぐ), *vt.* to take [put] off; pull off (引脫ぐ); remove. —著物を脫ぐ, to take [throw; cast] one's clothes off; slip one's garment off. —帽子を脫ぐ, to take off one's hat (挨拶の爲に).
nuguiotosu (拭落す), *vt.* to wipe off [out]; scrape away [off] (靴の泥など).
nuguu (拭ふ), *vt.* to wipe; give (it) a wipe. —拭ふべからざる, indelible; ineffaceable. —淚を拭ふ, to wipe the tears away.
nui (縫), *n.* ❶ (裁縫) sewing; a stitch (一針). ❷ =***nuitori***.
nuiage (縫揚), *n.* a tuck.
nuiawasu (縫合す), *vt.* to sew [stitch] together; quilt.
nuibari (縫針), *n.* a (sewing-) needle.
nuihaku (縫箔), *n.* embroidery.
nuikomu (縫込む), *vt.* ❶ to tuck. ❷ to sew [stitch] *into*.

nuime (縫目), *n.* a seam. —縫目無しの蚊帳, a seamless mosquito-net.

nuimono (縫物), *n.* sewing; needlework.

nuitori (縫取), *n.* embroidery. ☞ *shishū* (刺繡).

nuitsukeru (縫附ける), *vt.* to sew on. —ボタンを縫ひ附ける, to sew on a button.

nuka (糠), *n.* ❶ bran; rice-bran (米の). ❷ [稃] chaff. —糠に釘, to pour water into a sieve.

nukaame (糠雨), *n.* a drizzle; a mizzle; a misty [fine] rain.

nukamiso (糠味噌), *n.* a mixture of rice-bran and salt.

nukarimichi (泥濘道), *n.* a muddy road.

nukaru (泥濘る), *vi.* to become [be] muddy.

nukarumi (泥濘), *n.* mire; mud; slough (雪等の).

nukasu (抜かす), *vt.* to omit; leave out; drop.

nukazuku (額づく), *vi.* to bow; kotow.

nukeana (抜穴), *n.* an underground passage; a tunnel (獸の).

nukederu (抜出る), *vi.* ❶ (忍び出る) to steal out; slip out. ❷ (動物が) to get loose [out of]; come out. —家を抜け出る, to steal out of the house.

nukegake (抜駈をする), *vi.* to forestall; steal a march *on*. —抜駈けの功名, a meritorious feat in advance of others.

nukegara (脱殻), *n.* a cast-off skin; exuviæ; a casting (蛇等の).

nukege (抜毛), *n.* fallen hair; shed plume (鳥の).

nukekawari (脱換), *n.* moult; moulting. —脱け換はる, to moult; shed [change] feathers.

nukeme (抜目なき), *a.* cautious; prudent; shrewd. —抜目のない男, a knowing man [card]; a wide-awake person.

nukemichi (抜路), *n.* ❶ a secret path; a by path [-road; -way]. ❷ =*nigemichi*.

nukeru (脱·抜·貫ける), *v.* ❶ (脱す) to come out (栓·釘·歯·汚點等); come off; fall off; fall away. ❷ (脱出) to steal out; slip out; escape *from*. ❸ (脱漏) to be omitted [dropped]; be left out. ❹ (消滅) to be gone (香氣等が); escape. ❺ (貫通) to go [pass; run] through. ❻ (脱退) to secede [withdraw] *from*. ❼ (陷る) to fall. —力が脱ける, strength leaves [fails] one. —香《鹽氣》が拔ける, to lose aroma《saltiness》. —氣が拔ける, ① (酒類) to become stale [flat]. ② (氣落ち) to be dispirited. —繩目を脱ける, to slip the bonds. —森を貫ける, to go [pass] through the wood. —彼は少し抜けてゐる, He is a little wanting. —あいつ何處か抜けてゐる, There is something fatuous [stupid] about him. —汚點[しみ]は中々抜けない, The stain will not come out.

nuki (抜), *n.* omission. —抜きにする, to leave out; omit; skip.

nuki (貫, 貫材), *n.* a brace.

nukiashi (抜足で), *ad.* with stealthy steps; walking on tip-toe.

nukidasu (抜出·抽出す), *vt.* to pick [take; pull; draw] out; select; extract.

nukide (抜手), *n.* 【游泳】 an overhand stroke. —抜手を切る, to swim hand over hand; swim with above-water strokes. ¶ 小抜手, Australian crawl. —片抜手, over-arm stroke.

nukigaki (抜書), *n.* an extract; a selection; an abstract. —抜書きする, to extract; select.

nukimi (抜身), *n.* a drawn sword; a naked blade.

nukinderu (抽んでる), *vt.* to excel; surpass. —抽んでた, eminent; prominent; distinguished. —嶄然抽んでる, to be far above the common run; stand out conspicuous.

nukinderu (擢んでる), *vt.* to select. ☞ *nukidasu*.

nukisashi (抜差), *n.* ❶ (ぬくとさす) taking out and putting in; extracting and inserting. ❷ (とりかへ) alteration; rearrangement (整理). —抜差しならぬ, inalterable; unalterable.

nukitoru (抜取·抽取る), *vt.* to extract; select; pick out.

nuku (抜く), *vt.* ❶ (引抜く) to draw (a sword; a cork; a tooth; a spike); take out (a stain); pull out (a tooth; a nail; a tree); pluck (a hair; a feather); extract (a tooth); uncork (a bottle). ❷ (抽んでる) to excel; surpass. ❸ (抜萃) to extract; select; quote (引用). ❹ (抜除) to remove; get rid of. ❺ (省略) to omit; leave off [out]. ❻ (攻落) to carry; capture; seize. ❼ (追ひ抜く) to outstrip; outrun; speed ahead *of*. —五人抜く, to defeat five adversaries in succession. —空氣を抜く, to let air off; squeeze out air (絞って); pump out air (ポンプで). —汚點を抜く, to take out [remove] a stain. —風を抜く, to get rid of cold. —鹽を抜く, to extract [take out; remove] salt. —敵の陣地を抜く, to carry [capture] the enemy's position. —抜く手も見せず切り附ける, to give

a stroke at a flash.
nukui (温い), *a.* warm; mild; genial (氣候等の).
nukumeru(暖める), *vt.* to warm.
numa (沼), *n.* a marsh; a swamp; a bog; a morass.
nume (絖), *n.* white satin.
nuno (布), *n.* cloth; drapery.
nunome (布目), *n.* texture.
nurakura (ぬらくら), *ad.* Ⓢ ぬらりくらり. ❶ slipperily; smoothly. ❷ (のらくら) idly; indolently.
nuranura(滑滑する), *a.* slippery; slimy; clammy.
nurasu (濡らす), *vt.* ❶ to wet; dip (浸す). ❷ (浸透す) to soak; drench. ❸ (濕らす) to moisten; damp(-en). —著物を濡らす, to have one's clothes wet.
nureginu (濡衣), *n.* ❶ (濡れた衣) wet clothes. ❷ (無實の罪科) a false charge. —人に濡衣を著せる, to make a false charge against another.
nuremono (濡物), *n.* ❶ wet things. ❷ (濡らすべからざる品) dry goods. ¶ 濡物無用, "Keep dry." (荷印).
nurenezumi(濡鼠になる), *vi.* to be wet [soaked; drenched] to the bone [skin].
nureni (濡荷), *n.* sea-damaged goods.
nureru (濡れる), *vi.* to be 《get》 wet; be drenched. —濡れた, wet.
nurete (濡手), *n.* a wet hand. —濡手で粟の攌取り, making money without any exertion [with a wet finger].
nuri (塗り), *n.* coat; coating; lacquering (漆の); varnishing (ニスの); painting (ペンキの). ¶ 塗盆《箸》, a lacquered tray 《chop--sticks》.
nurigusuri (塗藥), *n.* 【醫】 a liniment (液); an ointmnet (膏).
nuriita (塗板), *n.* a blackboard (黑板); a lacquered board (漆塗).
nurikaeru (塗替へる), *vt.* to recoat; repaint (ペンキを); revarnish (ニスを).
nurimono (塗物), *n.* a lacquerware; a japanned article. ¶ 塗物師, a lacquerer; a japanner.
nuritate (塗立の), *a.* freshly--painted 《-plastered》. —ペンキ塗立, "Wet paint!"
nuru (塗る), *vt.* to paint (ペンキ·繪具等を); plaster (壁を); coat (繪具·錫等を); lacquer (漆を); varnish (ニスを); apply (藥を). —塗り消す, to paint out. —壁を塗る, to plaster a wall. —顔に墨を塗る, to smear one's face with black ink. —罪を人に塗り附ける, to lay the blame upon another.
nurude (塩膚木), *n.* 【植】 the Chinese [Japanese] nut-gall-tree.
nurui (ぬるい), *a.* lukewarm; tepid; dull (火).
nurumayu (微温湯), *n.* ❶ lukewarm [tepid] water. ❷ (浴) a tepid bath.
nurumu (温む), *vi.* to become lukewarm.
nurunuru(滑滑する), *a.* slippery; slimy; clammy.
nusa (幣), *n.* cut-paper, *etc.* offered to a *kami.*
nushi (主), *n.* ❶ (持主, 飼主) the owner; the master. ❷ (あるじ) the master; the spirit (精). —主のない; 主の知れぬ, ownerless.
nushi (塗師 -屋), *n.* a lacquerer.
nusubito (盗人), *n.* a thief. —盗人に追銭, "Throwing good money after bad."
nusumi (盗み), *n.* theft; stealing.
nusumigiki (竊聞する), *vt.* to overhear; eavesdrop [*vi.*] (立聞き).
nusumigui (盗食する), *vt.* to eat by stealth.
nusumimi (偸見する), *vt.* to steal a glance *at*; cast a sidelong glance *at*; take a peep *at.*
nusumimono (盗物), *n.* stolen goods.
nusumiwarai (偸笑), *n.* stealthy laugh. —偸笑ひする, to laugh in one's sleeve.
nusumu (盗·竊·偸む), *vt.* to steal; purloin; filch. —名爵を竊む, to hold a high position without deserving it. —暇を偸む, to snatch a moment's leisure.
nuta (饅), *n.* 【割烹】 a fish-salad.
nutto (ぬッと), *ad.* suddenly; unexpectedly; abruptly.
nuu (縫ふ), *vt.* to sew; stitch. —三針縫ふ, to put in three stitches in the wound; give three stitches. —森の中を縫って流れる, to run winding through the forest. —人込の中を縫って歩く, to thread one's way through the crowd.
nyānyā (にゃーにゃー), *n.* ❶ (猫の聲) mew. ❷ 〔小兒〕 puss; pussy.
nyō (尿), *n.* urine. —尿を檢査する, to inspect the urine.
nyōbo, nyōbō, (女房), *n.* a wife; one's mate. —女房の尻に敷かれる, to be pinned to one's wife's apron-strings.
nyōdō (尿道), *n.* 【解】 urethra; the urinary passage. ¶ 尿道炎, urethritis; inflammation of the urethra. —尿道結石, a urinary [urethral] calculus. —尿道狹窄, stricture of the urethra.
nyōdokushō (尿毒症), *n.* 【醫】 uræmia.
nyōhachi (鐃鈸), *n.* cymbals.
nyoi (如意), *n.* 〔梵〕 Anụruddha (阿那律).
nyojitsu (如實に), *ad.* as it is; just like.

nyokan (女官), *n.* a maid of honour; a court lady.

nyonin (女人), *n.* women. ¶ 女人禁制, "Women forbidden to enter"; "Closed to women."

nyoō (女王), *n.* =*joō*.

nyoronyoro (にょろにょろ), *ad.* with a sluggish [loitering] motion.

nyōsan (尿酸), *n.* uric acid.

nyoshin (女神), *n.* a goddess; a deess; a female deity.

nyōso (尿素), *n.* 【化】 urea.

nyozōchū (女像柱), *n.* 【建】 a caryatid.

nyūbachi (乳鉢), *n.* a glass-[-mortar; a mortar.]

nyūbai (入梅), *n.* ❶ the rainy season. ❷ the first day of the rainy [wet] season.

nyūbi (乳糜), *n.* chyle. ¶ 乳糜管, 【解】 a lacteal duct.

nyūbo (乳母), *n.* a (wet-)nurse; a milk-nurse.

nyūbō (乳房), *n.* 【解】 a breast. ¶ 乳房炎, 【醫】 mastitis.

nyūbō (乳棒), *n.* a pestle.

nyūchō (入超), *n.* excess of imports over exports.

nyūchō (入朝), *n.* visiting the Imperial Palace: visiting Japan.

nyūden (入電), *n.* a received telegram.

nyūdō (入道), *n.* a lay-bonze [-priest]. ¶ 大入道, a giant; a huge demon.

nyūei (入營する), *vi.* to enter barracks; join the army.

nyūfu (入夫), *n.* =*irimuko*.

nyūgaku (入學), *n.* entrance into a school. —入學する, to enter a school. —入學試驗を受ける, to take [try; sit for] an entrance examination. ¶ 入學願書, an application for admission. —入學金, an entrance-fee. —入學志願者, an applicant [a candidate] for admission. —入學試驗問題, entrance examination questions.

nyūgan (乳癌), *n.* 【醫】 mammary carcinoma [cancer]; the cancer of the breast.

nyūgoku (入獄する), *vi.* to be imprisoned; be sent to prison [gaol]; be cast [put] into prison.

nyūgyo (入御あらせらる), *vi.* to enter into the (inner) palace.

nyūgyū (乳牛), *n.* a milch-cow.

nyūhaku (乳白 -色), *n.* milk-white.

nyūhi (入費), *n.* expenses; ex-[penditure.]

nyūin (入院), *n.* admission into [entering] a hospital. —入院する, to enter a hospital; be sent [removed] to (a) hospital. ¶ 入院患者, an in-patient. —入院料, accommodation charge in a hospital.

nyūjaku (柔弱), *n.* feebleness; weakness; effeminacy.

nyūji (乳兒), *n.* a suckling; a baby; an infant at the breast.

nyūjō (入場), *n.* entrance; admission. ¶ 入場券, a ticket (of admission); an admission [entrance] ticket · a platform ticket (驛の). (無料入場券, a free pass.) —入場料, the charge for admission; admission(-fee); gate-money; door-money. (半額入場料, admission-charge at half-price.) —入場隨意 [無料], free to all; admission free.

nyūjū (乳汁), *n.* milk.

nyūka (乳菓), *n.* an emulsion.

nyūkai (入會), *n.* entrance; entry. —入會する, to join [associate oneself with] a society; enter a society. ¶ 入會金, entrance fee. —入會者, an entrant; a person admitted into a society.

nyūkaku (入閣する), *vi.* to enter [join] a cabinet; become a cabinet member.

nyūkan (入監する), *vi.* to be im-[prisoned.]

nyūkin (入金), *n.* ❶ (收入) receipt (受領); money received (受領さる金); money due (受取るべき金). ❷ (支拂) payment; part payment (内金拂); money paid (支拂へる金). —入金する, to pay in part [on account].

nyūkō (入校), *n.* entrance into a [school.]

nyūkō (入港), *n.* entrance; entering a port. —入港する, to enter a port [harbour]; put into a port; make a port.

nyūkō (入寇), *n.* invasion; inroad; raid. —入寇する, to invade; (make a) raid *into*.

nyūkō (乳香), *n.* ❶ 【植】 (*a*) the frankincense-tree; the olibanum-tree: (*b*) the mastich-tree. ❷ 【化】 mastic.

nyūkoku (入國する), *vi.* to enter a country. ¶ 入國禁止《許可》, prohibition 《permission》 of entry.

nyūkyo (入渠), *n.* entering a dock; docking. —入渠する, to dock; come into a dock.

nyūkyō (入京), *n.* entering the capital. —入京する, to come to the capital.

nyūmon (入門), *n.* ❶ entering a private school. ❷ (手引) an introduction; a primer; an A B C. —入門する, to enter a private school; become —'s pupil.

nyūnen (入念の), *a.* elaborate; careful. —入念に, carefully; elaborately.

nyūraku (乳酪), *n.* butter.

nyūsan (乳酸), *n.* lactic acid. ¶ 乳酸鹽, 【化】 a lactate.

nyūsatsu (入札), *n.* a tender; a written bid. —入札する, to (make a) tender *for*; (make a) bid *for*. ¶ 競爭入札, a public tender. —指名入札, tenders by specified bidders; private tenders.

nyūseki (入籍), *n.* entry in a family register. —入籍する, to have one's name entered in a family register.

nyūsen (入選する), *v.* to be selected.

nyūsen (乳腺), *n.* 【解】a lacteal [mammary] gland.

nyūsha (入社), *n.* entering a society (company, *etc.*); initiation. —入社する, to enter a society; join the editorial staff (新聞社へ).

nyūshakaku (入射角), *n.* 【理】an angle of incidence.

nyūshi (乳歯), *n.* a milk-tooth; a temporary [deciduous] tooth.

nyūshin (入神の), *a.* inspired; divine.

nyūshū (乳臭), *n.* ❶ the odour of milk. ❷ (經驗の足りぬこと) callowness; inexperience. ¶ 乳臭兒, a fledgling.

nyūtai (入隊する), *vt.* to join the army (a regiment). ¶ 入隊者, a recruit.

nyūtō (入黨する), *vi.* to join [enter] a political party.

nyūtō (乳頭), *n.* ❶【解】a nipple; a mammilla; a teat. ❷【動·植】a papilla.

nyūtō (乳糖), *n.* milk-sugar; sugar of milk; 【化】lactose.

nyūwa (柔和), *n.* gentleness; mildness. —柔和な, gentle; mild; meak.

nyūyō (入用), *n.* need; necessity; want. —入用の, necessary; requisite; needful. —小僧入用, "Wanted, boys." —御入用の節は何時たりとも, whenever you want it.

nyūyō (乳養する), *vt.* to nurse (on); bring up from the bottle (ミルクで育てる); bring up by hand.

nyūyoku (入浴), *n.* bathing. —入浴する, to take a bath; bathe. ¶ 入浴者, a bather.

nyūzai (乳劑), *n.* an emulsion. ¶ 石油乳劑, kerosene emulsion.

O

o (を), *particle.* at; for; in; on; with; of. 【註】名詞及び同代用詞を目的格に置く時は動詞との關係上邦語助辭「を」は當然此格に使用せられた語の中に含まれるものであるから譯出するを要せぬ.

o (尾), *n.* a tail; a trail (長く引ける尾); a brush (狐などの); a train (孔雀の). —尾を垂れる, to have one's tail between one's legs. —尾を振る, to wag the tail.

o (苧), *n.* hemp.

o (牡, 雄), *n.* a male.

o (緒), *n.* a string; a cord; a thong (皮の鼻緒など).

ō (大), *a.* large; great; big; heavy (雨·雪など). ¶ 大河, a large river.

ō (王), *n.* ❶ a king; a monarch; a prince (皇族中の王·小國の王). ❷ (將棋) a king. —百獸(鳥)の王, the king of beasts (birds). ¶ 鐵道王, a railway king.

ō (おう), *int.* O, oh; ah. —おう痛い, Ouch, it hurts.

Ōa (歐亞の), *a.* Europeo-Asiatic.

ōame (大雨), *n.* a heavy [pelting] rain; a downpour.

ōarashi (大暴風雨), *n.* a tempest; a severe [violent] storm; a hurricane (颶風); a typhoon (颱風).

oashi (お錢), *n.* 〔卑〕brass; tin.

oashisu (オアシス), *n.* an oasis.

ōatama (大頭), *n.* Ⓢ 首領. a leader; a leading figure; a chief.

ōatari (大當), *n.* a bonanza; a (great) hit [success].

ōawa (粱), *n.* 【植】the Italian millet; the Bengal grass.

oba (叔母, 伯母), *n.* an aunt. —叔母ちゃん, aunty, auntie —小母さん, aunt; aunty.

ōbā (オーヴァー), *n.* an overcoat.

obake (お化), *n.* ❶ a ghost; a spectre. ❷ (怪物) a monster; a fright. ☞ ***bakemono.***

obako, ōbako, (車前草), *n.* 【植】the greater plantain.

ōban (骨頂), *n.* 【鳥】the coot.

ōban (大判), *n.* (紙の) large size [sheet]; folio size.

obāsan (お婆さん), *n.* ☞ ***baba*** (婆).

Ōbei (歐米), *n.* Europe and America. ¶ 歐米漫遊, a tour through [in] Europe and America.

obekka (おべっか), *n.* flattery; adulation. —おべっかを言ふ[する; 使ふ], to flatter; fawn *upon*; curry favour *with*.

obi (帶), *n.* an *obi* 〔日〕; a belt; a sash; a girdle (腰帶); a band (胴締). —帶を締める, to do up a sash; put on an *obi*. —帶を解く, to untie [undo] a sash.

obidome (帶留), *n.* a sash-band.

obieru (怯える), *vi.* ❶ (恐怖) to fear; be afraid of; be frightened (喫驚する). ❷ (夢におそはれる) to have a nightmare.

obifū (帶封), *n.* Ⓢ 帶紙. a wrapper.

obigane (帯金), *n.* an iron tape; a hoop iron.
obikawa (帯革), *n.* a leather belt [girdle]; 【軍】 a cartridge-belt.
obikidasu (誘出す), *vt.* to decoy out; entice out; lure out.
ōbira (大披露に), *ad.* openly; publicly; in public; to the view.
obiru (帯びる), *v.* ❶ (有す, 含む) to have; wear (様子など); bear (稱號など); partake of (性質など). ❷ (任務を) to be charged [entrusted] *with*; be assigned. ❸ (佩) to wear; gird *on*; carry in the belt. —黄味を帯びた, yellowish. —喜色を帯びる, to wear a face of joy. —特別任務を帯びる, to be invested with a special duty.
obitadashii (夥しい), *a.* ❶ (數多) a great many [deal of]; numerous; abundant. ❷ (甚しい) most; violent; severe. —夥しく, ① abundantly. ② very; exceedingly; most.
obiyakasu (脅す), *vt.* to threaten; intimidate; scare. —殺すぞと脅かす, to threaten [menace] a person with death.
ōbo (應募), *n.* subscription (豫約・公債などの); application (志願, 申込); enlistment (募兵に). —應募する, to subscribe *to*; apply for; enlist (募兵に). ¶ 應募價格, subscription price. —應募者, an applicant; a subscriber.
ōbō (往訪する), *vt.* to visit; make [pay] a visit; call *on* (*at*, 家).
ōbō (横暴な), *a.* tyrannical; oppressive; arbitrary.
oboe (覺), *n.* ❶ (感覺) feeling. ❷ (了解) understanding; apprehension. ❸ (記憶) memory; recollection (回想); experience (經驗). ❹ (控へ) a memorandum; a memo. ❺ (信用) favour; confidence (信任). —覺えがよい, to be ready to acquire; be quick of apprehension; have a good [retentive] memory (記憶). —覺えが惡い, to be dull of apprehension; be slow in understanding; have a bad [poor] memory. —覺え目出度し, to stand high in a person's estimation [favour]. —そんな事云った覺えはない. I do not recollect having said so.
oboechō (覺帳), *n.* a memorandum-book; a minute [note]-book.
oboegaki (覺書), *n.* a note; a memorandum [*pl.* -da]; a minute.
oboeru (覺える), *vt.* ❶ (習得) to learn; study; acquire. ❷ (記憶) to keep [have; bear] in mind; commit to memory; remember. ❸ (感覺) to feel. ❹ (思ふ) to think. —空で覺える, to learn [get] by heart. —腕に痛みを覺える, to feel pain in one's arm. —むづかしくて覺えられない, It is too difficult to remember.
oboezu (覺えず), *ad.* unconsciously; without knowing it; in spite of oneself.
oboko (初心, 未通), *n.* ❶ (狀態) artlessness; simplicity. ❷ (人) an artless [a mere] child; an unsophisticated girl; a babe (ねんね). —おぼこな, naïve; innocent; artless.
oborasu (溺らす), *vt.* to drown.
oboreru (溺れる), *vi.* ❶ (溺沒) to be drowned. ❷ (耽溺) to give oneself up *to*; be addicted *to*. —妻子の愛に溺れる, to dote on one's wife and children.
oboro (朧), *n.* vagueness; faintness; dreaminess.
oboroge (朧氣な), *a.* vague; faint; dim; hazy (霞める). —朧氣に, vaguely; faintly. —朧氣な記憶を辿る, to trace back a vague memory.
oborozuki (朧月), *n.* a clouded moon; the moon behind a cloud. ¶ 朧月夜, a dim moonlit night.
oboshii (覺しい), *vi.* to appear; seem; be taken to be; look like.
oboshimeshi (思召), *n.* ❶ (意見) an idea; an opinion; a thought. ❷ (志望) wish; desire; intention. ❸ (好み) fancy; choice. —思召に適ふ, to suit [please] a person's fancy; take [catch] a person's fancy.
oboshimesu (思召す), *vt.* to think; consider; deem. ☞ *omou* (思ふ).
obotsukanai (覺束ない), *a.* ❶ (疑はしい) doubtful; uncertain; questionable. ❷ (心もとない) uneasy; anxious. —生命覺束なし. There is little hope of his recovery.
ōbun (歐文), *n.* European writing (language). ¶ 歐文電報, a Romanized telegram.
ōbun (應分), *ad.* according to one's means (station; ability). —應分の寄附をする, to contribute according to one's means.
oburāto (オブラート), *n.* 【獨 oblate】 a wafer.
ōburi (大降), *n.* a heavy rain; a downpour.
ōburoshiki (大風呂敷), *n.* big talk; exaggeration. —大風呂敷を擴げる, to talk big.
obusaru (負さる), *vi.* ❶ (背に) to get [ride] on the back; ride pickaback. ❷ (依賴) to depend *upon*; rely *on*.

obutsu (汚物), *n.* dirt; filth; garbage (塵所); sewage (下水).

obuu (負ふ), *vt.* to take on one's back. ☞ *ou* (負ふ).

ōchaku (横著), *n.* ❶ (図々しさ) effrontery; impudence; cheekiness. ❷ (なまけ) negligence; idleness. —横著な, impudent; shameless; idle; shirking.

ochi (落), *n.* ❶ (落ちること) a fall. ❷ (遺脱) omission; slip. ❸ (落語の下げ) the point. ❹ (終結) the end. ❺ (株券等) ex [*prep.*] —落ちなく, =*more* (漏なく). —話の落ちが分る《分らぬ》, to see [catch] 《miss》 the point of a story. —落を取る, to take the best part.

ochiai (落合), *n.* (川の) confluence; junction of two rivers.

ochiau (落合ふ), *vi.* to meet; come together [upon]. —偶然落合ふ, to fall in with; stumble [come] across [on; upon].

ochiba (落葉), *n.* fallen leaves. —落葉を掻く, to rake the fallen leaves together.

ochibureru (零落れる), *vi.* to be ruined [impoverished]; run [go; come] to ruin; sink [come down] in the world.

ochido (越度), *n.* ❶ (過失) a fault; a slip; an error. ❷ (罪) blame. —私の越度です, I am to blame for it.

ōchigai (大違ひ), *n.* ❶ (差) a great difference. ❷ (謬) a blunder; a gross [grand] mistake.

ochiho (落穂), *n.* gleanings. —落穂を拾ふ [集める], to glean.

ochiiru (陥る), *vi.* ❶ (はまる) to fall *into*; sink *into*; run *into*. ❷ (陥落) to fall; surrender. ❸ =*ochikomu*. ❹ (引掛かる) to fall *into*. —悲運に陥る, to come to misfortune. —危險に陥る, to run into danger; be in danger. —絶望狀態に陥る, to be reduced to despair.

ochikasanaru (落重なる), *vi.* to fall one upon another; fall upon; fall in a heap.

ochikochi (遠近), *ad.* far and near; hither and thither; here and there.

ochikomu (落込む), *vi.* to fall *in* 《*into*》; collapse (凹む); sink (土地が). —落込んだ目, sunken eyes. —落込んだ頰, hollow cheeks.

ochime (落目), *n.* the decline of fortune; sinking fortune. —落目になってゐる, to be on the decline; be at the ebb of fortune.

ochimusha (落武者), *n.* ❶ (落人) a refugee; a fugitive. ❷ (落第坊主) a plucked student.

ochinobiru (落延びる), *vi.* to run away; escape; make one's escape (to a distance).

ochiochi (落落), *ad.* calmly; peacefully; quietly; comfortably. —おちおち夜も眠れぬ, I cannot sleep quietly at night.

ochiru (落·墜·墮ちる), *vi.* ❶ (落下, 墜落) to fall (down); have a fall; drop down; give way (橋·二階·棧敷など重さで). ❷ (滴下) to drop; drip. ❸ (陥る) to fall; be captured. ❹ =*otoru*. ❺ (落第) to fail; be plucked. ❻ (墮落) to degenerate; plunge *into*. ❼ (死ぬ) to drop; cease to breathe (絶息す). ❽ (脫漏) to be omitted; be left out. ❾ (遁逃) to run away; escape; flee; take flight. ❿ (沒する) to sink; set; go down. —品が落ちる, to be inferior in quality. —手中に落ちる, to fall into another's hands. —馬から落ちて死ぬ, to be killed by a fall from a horse.

ochitsukasu (落著かす), *vt.* Ⓢ 落著ける. to calm; quiet; set a person at ease. —氣を落ち著ける, to gather oneself (together); collect [compose] oneself.

ochitsuki (落著), *n.* calmness; composure; self-possession.

ochitsuku (落著く), *vi.* ❶ (定まる) to settle. ❷ (行き著く) to reach; arrive *at* [*in*]. ❸ (心が) to calm down. ❹ (風が) to become calm; fall. ❺ (調和) to be suitable; be in harmony *with*. —落著いた; 落著きのある, calm; composed; self-possessed. —落著いた色, quiet colours. —落著いて, calmly; with composure; in peace. —落著き拂ふ, to remain [look] cool as a cucumber. —氣が落著いて我に返る, to grow calmer and recover one's senses.

ochiudo (落人), *n.* a fugitive; a refugee.

ochiyuku (落行く), *vi.* to escape; take flight *to*. —落行く先, one's destination; the place to which one is bound.

ōchō (王朝), *n.* a dynasty.

ōda (毆打), *n.* assault; assault and battery. —毆打する, to (commit) assault; hit; assail with blows. —毆打して殺す, to knock a person to death. ¶ 毆打致死, an assault resulting in death. —毆打創傷, assault and wounding.

ōdai (鯛), *n.* 【魚】the porgy; the sea-bream.

odake (雄竹), *n.* 【植】Phyllostachys bambusoides (whangee cane の類·學名).

odamaki (苧環), *n.* ❶ (絲卷) a spool. ❷【植】Aquilegia flabellata (columbine の一種學名).

ōdan (黄疸), *n.* ❶【醫】icterus; jaundice. ❷ (膽石病) biliary calculus.

ōdan (横斷する), *vt.* to intersect; cross; go 《sail; travel; swim》 across; lie 《run》 across. ¶ 横斷面, a cross-section; a transverse section; a transection. —横斷線, a transversal (line). —大陸横斷鐵道, the trans-Continental Railway. —英佛海峡横斷遠泳, the cross-Channel swim.

odate (煽), *n.* instigation; incitement. —煽てに乗る, to let oneself be egged on.

odateru (煽てる), *vt.* to instigate; incite; egg on.

ōdatemono (大立物), *n.* a leading figure; a protagonist; a star (俳優等). —文壇の大立物, a lion in the literary world.

ōdatsu (横奪する), *vt.* to dispossess; usurp; plunder.

odawarahyōjō (小田原評定), *n.* an endless talk resulting in nothing; an inconclusive discussion.

odayaka (穩な), *a.* calm; tranquil; moderate. —穩かな海, a calm [smooth; level] sea. —穩かな性質, a quiet disposition. —穩かならぬ振舞, improper behaviour; overbearing demeanour. —穩かに, quietly; calmly. —穩かになる, to quiet [calm] down.

ōde (大手を振る), to swing one's arms. —大手を振って歩く, to strut; swagger about.

ōdeki (大出來), *n.* a great success; 「an éclat

odeko (お出額), *n.* beetle-brows; a projecting forehead.

ōdō (黄銅), *n.* brass.

ōdōgu (大道具), *n.* 【劇】stage-setting. ¶ 大道具方, a scene-man.

odokashi (嚇し), *n.* a threat; a menace. ¶ おどかしもの, a scarecrow.

odokasu (嚇す), *vt.* ❶ (威迫する) to threaten; menace. ❷ (こはがらす) to frighten; startle; scare; terrify. —嚇かして金を取る, to rob a person of money with threats. —嚇して子供を逐っ拂ふ, to scare away children.

odoke (滑稽), *n.* joke; jest; drollery. ☞ *kokkei*.

odokeru (おどける), *v.* to joke; make [cut] a joke; jest. —おどけた, funny; joking; humorous. —おどけて, in fun; in joke. ¶ 滑稽話, a joke; a jest; a witty talk. —滑稽者, a joker; a clown; a buffoon.

odomi (澱), *n.* sediment; lees; 「dregs.

odomu (澱む), *vi.* to fall [settle] to the bottom; be deposited.

odoodo (悚悚する), *v.* to be nervous; look timid. —おどおどして, in fear; timidly; nervously.

odori (踊), *n.* a dance; dancing. —踊の師匠, a dancing-master 《-mistress》. ¶ 踊場, a dancing-room. —踊屋臺, a dancing-platform. 「a high road.

ōdōri (大通), *n.* the main street;

odoriagaru (躍上がる), *vi.* to jump [spring] up; leap. —躍上って喜ぶ, to jump for joy.

odoriko (踊子), *n.* a dancing-girl; a dancer.

odorikomu (躍込む), *vi.* to jump *into*; rush *into*; burst *into*.

odorokasu (驚かす), *vt.* to surprise; astonish; startle. —世を驚かす, to startle the world.

odoroki (驚), *n.* surprise; astonishment; wonder; fright; alarm.

odoroku (驚く), *vi.* ❶ (驚異) to wonder *at*; marvel *at* [that]. ❷ (驚愕) to be surprised; be astonished; be startled (吃驚). —驚くべき, wonderful; marvellous; astonishing. —驚いて眼を丸くする, to stare with astonishment. —驚いて物が言へぬ, to be struck dumb with astonishment.

odoru (踊·跳る), *vi.* ❶ (跳躍する) to jump; leap; skip; prance (馬が). ❷ (舞踏する) to dance; foot; foot it. ❸ (胸騒ぐ) to throb; palpitate; go pit-a-pat; jump. ——, *vt.* to dance. —ヂッグを踊る, to dance a jig. —嬉しくて躍り立つ, to jump for joy. —躍る胸を撫で下ろす, to stroke into calm one's fluttering breast.

odoshi (威·嚇), *n.* a threat; a menace. ¶ 嚇し文句, threatening language; menacing words.

odoshi (縅), *n.* thread (of an armour). —黒絲縅の鎧, a black-threaded armour.

odosu (威·嚇す), *vt.* to threaten; menace; browbeat; frighten. —殺すぞと嚇す, to threaten [menace] with death. —刀を以て威す, to threaten with a sword. —威して白狀さす, to awe into confession.

ōen (應援), *n.* ❶ (援助) aid; assistance; help. ❷ (聲援) encouragement; backing; support. —應援する, to aid; assist; help; (give) support; back; encourage; cheer; root *for* [米·卑]. —應援に行く, to go to the aid *of*. —應援演說をする, to make a speech in support of a candidate. ¶ 應援團, a cheering party; fans; rooters [米·卑]. —應援者, a supporter;

a backer; a fan; a rooter 〔米〕.
oenai (おへない), *a.* Ⓢ おへぬ. unmanageable; hard to deal with. ☞ *te* (手におへない).
oeru (終·卒へる), *vt.* to end; finish; go [do] through. **——,** *vi.* to be over. —會を終へる, to break up [close] a meeting. —仕事が終へない内に, before the work was over. —業を卒へる, to complete a course.
oetsu (嗚咽する), *vi.* to sob.
ōfū (大風, 横風), *n.* arrogance; haughtiness. **——-na,** *a.* proud; arrogant; haughty. —横風な口の利き方をする, to have an arrogant way of speaking. 「style.
ōfū (歐風の), *a.* in European
ofuda (お札), *n.* a charm; an amulet; a talisman.
ōfuku (往復), *n.* going and returning; intercommunication; correspondence (文書の). —往復する, ① to go and return; ply (*between*) (舟が); run (*between*) (舟·車が). ② (往來) to communicate *with*; hold intercourse *with*; keep company *with*. —手紙の往復をする, to carry on correspondence *with*; correspond *with*; exchange letters *with*. —往復いくらだ, What is your charge for going there and back? ¶ 往復葉書, a return postcard. —往復切符, a return ticket. —往復運賃, freight on and home.
oga, ōga, (大鋸), *n.* a large saw. ¶ 大鋸屑, saw-dust.
ōga (横臥する), *vi.* to lie (down).
ōgama (大釜), *n.* a cauldron.
ogami (男神), *n.* a god.
ogamitaosu (拜倒す), *vt.* to entreat (a person) into consent; win over with entreaties.
ogamu (拜む), *vt.* ❶ (禮拜) to worship; adore; bow *to*. ❷ (拜見) to witness with respect; look *at* reverently. —伏し拜む, to adore [implore] on one's knees; fall down in adoration 《entreaty》 before a god 《a person》.
ōgane (大金), *n.* a great sum of money. ¶ 大金持, a very rich [wealthy] man; a millionaire.
ōgankyō (凹眼鏡), *n.* a concave glass. 「[boon].
ogara (苧幹), *n.* a hemp reed
ōgara (大柄), *n.* ❶ (身體の) a large build; a large body. ❷ (模樣の) large figure 《stripes》.
ōgata (大形), *n.* a large size.
ogawa (小川), *n.* a brook; a rivulet; a rill; a runnel; a runlet.
ōgesa (大袈裟な), *a.* exaggerated; inflated (言語につき); highly-coloured. —大袈裟な仕掛, work on a large scale. —大袈裟に話す, to exaggerate; overstate; overdraw; draw a [the] long bow.
ogi (荻), *n.* 【植】 Miscanthus sacchariflorus (學名).
ōgi (扇), *n.* a (folding-)fan; an *ōgi* 〔日〕. —扇の要, the rivet of a fan. —扇を使ふ, to fan oneself; use a fan. 「*okugi*.
ōgi (奥義), *n.* the secrets. ☞
oginai (補), *n.* ❶ (補充) supplement; complement. ❷ (囘復) recuperation; retrieval; reparation.
oginau (補ふ), *vt.* ❶ to supplement; complement; supply; make up; make good. ❷ to recuperate; retrieve; repair. —損失を補ふ, to make good the loss. —缺員を補ふ, to fill up the vacancies.
ōgiri (大切), *n.* ❶ (演技等の) an after-piece; a *finale* 〔伊〕. ❷ (事物の) a close; an end.
ōgoe (大聲), *n.* a loud voice. —大聲で, in a loud voice; loudly; aloud.
ōgon (黄金), *n.* gold (きん); money (かね). ¶ 黄金萬能主義, mammonism; the almighty dollar principle. (黄金萬能主義者, a mammonist; a mammonite.) —黄金時代, the golden age.
ogori (奢), *n.* ❶ (奢侈) luxury; extravagance. ❷ (驕傲) pride; haughtiness. —奢りに耽る, to be given [addicted] to luxury; roll in luxury
ogoru (奢·驕る), *v.* ❶ (贅澤) to be extravagant; live in luxury. ❷ 〔驕〕 to be proud [arrogant; haughty]. ❸ (振舞ふ) to treat *to*; entertain; stand 〔俗〕 ❹ (買ふ) to buy. —口が奢る, to have a pampered taste. —驕る者久しからず, "Pride will have a fall."
ōgosho (大御所), *n.* the abdicant [retired] *shōgun*. —實業界の大御所, the father [grand old man] of the business world.
ogosoka (厳かな), *a.* solemn; stately; grave. —厳かに, solemnly; gravely; in state.
ōgoto (大事), *n.* a serious affair [matter]; a grave matter. —大事になる, to become serious.
ōguchi (大口), *n.* ❶ (口) an open mouth (開口); a splay-mouth (廣口). ❷ (大言) a boastful speech; a big [tall] talk; bragging. ❸ (纏まって大きな) a large sum; a big mass. —大口の註文, a large [big] order. —大口を開く, to open the mouth wide.
ōgui (大食), *n.* =*taishoku.*
oguruma (旋覆花), *n.* 【植】 Inula britannica (fleabane の一種·學名)
ōguruma (土木香), *n.* 【植】 the elecampane; the elf-dock.

ōgyō (大仰な), *a.* exaggerated.
ōgyoku (黄玉), *n.* topaz.
oha (尾羽打枯らして), in shabby clothes.
ohachi (お鉢), *n.* (飯櫃) a rice tub. —お鉢が此方へ廻って来た, It has come to our turn.
ohaguro (鐵漿), *n.* black tooth-dye. ☞ *kane.*
ohako (十八番), *n.* a hobby; a speciality. —おはこの, favourite; pet (a pet theory; a pet plan, *etc.*) —おはこを出す, to ride [mount on] one's horse [hobby].
ōharai (大祓), *n.* great (ceremony of) exorcism.
oharaibako (お祓箱になる), to get the sack [bag; boot]; be dismissed; be sent packing.
ohari (お針), *n.* ❶ (裁縫) sewing; needlework. ❷ (裁縫女) a seamstress; a sempstress; a needle-woman.
ohayō (お早う), *int.* Good-morning.
ōhei (横柄), *n.* arrogance; haughtiness; insolence. —横柄な, arrogant; haughty; high-handed. —横柄に振舞ふ, to behave haughtily; ride over people; ride people down.
ōhi (王妃), *n.* ❶ a queen; a queen-consort. ❷ a princess.
ohire (尾鰭), *n.* ❶ the tail and the fin. ❷【動】the caudal fin. —尾鰭をつける, to exaggerate.
ōhiroma (大廣間), *n.* a hall; a saloon; a large room.
ohitoyoshi (好人物), *n.* a good-natured man (woman); an accommodating man.
ohitsu (御櫃), *n.* a rice-tub.
ohiya (お冷), *n.* ❶ (冷水) cold water. ❷ (冷飯) cold boiled rice.
ōhō (應報), *n.* retribution; requital. —應報する to requite.
ohyakudo (お百度を踏む), *v.* ❶ (神社佛閣で) to walk round a shrine (temple) a hundred times and worship before the idol at each turn; make the hundred tramps. ❷ (度々人を訪問する) to visit a person frequently [heaps of times] for a request.
oi (老), *n.* old age; hoary age. —老いの繰言, the tedious talk of old people; the complaint of the aged (愚痴).
oi (甥), *n.* a nephew.
oi (おい), *int.* hey!; hi!; hallo!; I say!
ōi (覆, 蓋, 蔽, 被), *n.* a cover; a shade (日覆); a tilt (車用).
ōi (王位), *n.* the throne. —王位に卽く, to come to [accede to; ascend] the throne; set oneself as a king. —王位を繼ぐ(奪ふ), to succeed to (usurp) the throne.
ōi (多い), *a.* ❶ (數) many; numerous. ❷ (量) much; a great [good] deal of. ❸ (數量) abundant; plentiful; copious. —誤が多い, to be full of errors; teem with blunders. —顧客が多い, to have a large number of customers.
oibore (老耄), *n.* decrepitude; dotage; a dotard (人). —老耄れる, to dote; become decrepit. —老耄れた, decrepit; worn with age; infirm through age.
oichirasu (追散らす), *vt.* to dispel; scatter; disperse.
oidasu (追出す), *vt.* to drive out; turn out; oust; expel (放逐). —女房を追ひ出す, to send away [turn out] a wife.
oiesōdō (お家騒動), *n.* a disturbance in a *daimyō's* (noble; rich) family.
oihagi (追剝, 路賊), *n.* a footpad; a highwayman; highway robbery (行爲).
oihago (追羽子), *n.* battledore and shuttlecock.
oiharau (追拂ふ), *vt.* to drive away [off]; expel; sweep (一掃す); disperse (追散らす).
oikaesu (追返す), *vt.* to drive back; send away; repel.
oikakeru (追掛ける), *vt.* to run [start] after; pursue. —追ひ掛けて手紙を出す, to send another letter immediately after.
oikaze (追風), *n.* a fair [favourable] wind. ☞ *oite* (追風).
oikomu (老込む), *vi.* to advance in age; grow old and feeble.
oikomu (追込む), *vt.* to drive in; shut in (閉ぢ込む); pen up [in] (家畜を).
oikosu (追越す), *vt.* to outrun; outstrip; get ahead *of*.
oimawasu (追廻す), *vt.* to run after [about]; drive round [about]; tread on (another's heels) (附纏ふ). —追ひ廻はさす, to lead one a dance.
ōin (押印する), *vt.* to seal; imprint; impress.
ōin (押韻する), *v.* to rhyme.
ōinaru (大いなる), *a.* great; large; big.
ōini (大いに), *ad.* very; (very) much; greatly; largely; exceedingly.
oioi (追追), *ad.* gradually; by degrees; little by little.
ōiri (大入), *n.* a large [full; crowded] house. —溢れる程の大入, an overflowing house. ¶ 大入場, a gallery.
oiru (老いる), *v.* to grow old. —老いた, aged; old; advanced in years.
oisaki (生先), *n.* future (career); remaining years.
oishigeru (生茂る), *vi.* to grow in abundance; grow luxuriantly.

oishii (旨しい), *a.* delicious; palatable; toothsome. —おいしくない, unsavoury; unpalatable.

ōisogi (大急ぎの), *a.* hurried; urgent (火急). —大急ぎで, in a great hurry; in great haste.

oisore (おいそれと), *ad.* readily; at a moment's notice; easily.

oitachi (生立), *n.* ❶ (生長) growth; bringing up; breeding. ❷ (閲歴) career; personal history.

oitate (追立), *n.* ❶ chase; driving away. ❷ (立退) eviction; ejection. —追立てる, ① to drive away; chase. ② to evict; eject; turn out.

oitatsu (生立つ), *vi.* to grow up; be brought up.

oite (於て), *prep.* in; at; upon; on. —東京に於て, in Tōkyō.

oite (追風), *n.* a fair [favourable] wind. —追風に帆を揚げる, to set a sail in a fair wind.

oitekebori (置いてけぼりにする), *vt.* to leave behind; abandon; desert. —置いてけぼりを食ふ, to be left behind (alone).

oitsukau (追使ふ), *v.* to drive to work; order about

oitsuku (追つく), *vt.* Ⓢ 追ッつく. to overtake; catch up; come up *with*. —今にも追ひつきさう, to run another hard [close].

oitsumeru (追詰める), *vt.* to drive [get] into a (tight) corner; run [hunt] down; drive [bring] to bay.

oiwake (追分, 岐路), *n* a forked road.

oiyaru (追遣る), *vt.* to drive away; send away.

ojan (おじゃんになる), *vi.* to come to naught; go to the ground; be given up. —おじゃんにする, to bring to naught; give up.

oji (伯父, 叔父), *n.* an uncle.

ōji (王子, 皇子), *n.* a Royal 《an Imperial》 prince; a prince.

ōji (王事), *n.* the king's service; the affairs of the emperor.

ōji (往事), *n.* past events; the past; bygones. —往事を追懐すれば, if we retrace the past.

ōji (往時), *n.* the old [past] times; the days gone by. ——, *ad.* of old; in old [former] times; formerly; long ago.

ojigisō (含羞草), *n.* 【植】 the sensitive plant; the humble plant.

ōjikake (大仕掛で·に), *ad.* on a large scale; in large.

ojike (怖氣), *n.* fear; dread; timidity. —怖氣がつく, to be seized with fear.

ojikeru (怖ける), *vi.* to fear; be afraid of; shrink *from*; funk 【卑】.

ojime (緒締), *n.* a string-fastener (of a pouch [bag]).

ojioji (怖怖), *ad.* in fear; timidly; nervously; timorously. —おぢおぢ進み出る, to come forward timidly.

ō-jiru (應じる), *v.* ❶ (應答) to reply; answer. ❷ (應諾) to accept; comply *with*; listen *to*. ❸ (應募) to subscribe *for*; apply *for*. ❹ (滿足) to fulfil; satisfy; meet. ❺ (應變す) to adapt; meet. —招きに應ずる, to accept an invitation. —挑戰に應ずる, to take up the glove; accept the challenge. —申出に應ずる, to assent to a proposal.

ō-jite (應じて), *ad.* ❶ (從って) in obedience *to*; in compliance *with*. ❷ (答へて) in response *to*. ❸ (割合) in proportion *to*. ——, *prep.* according *to*. —聲に應じて, in response to the voice [call]. —分に應じて, according to one's means. —御申越に應じて, in answer to your letter.

ōjo (王女, 皇女), *n.* an Imperial 《a Royal》 princess; a princess.

ōjō (王城, 皇城), *n.* an Imperial 《a Royal》 castle.

ōjō (往生), *n.* ❶ (淨土に生れること) rebirth in paradise. ❷ (死去) death; extinction of life. ❸ = *akirame*. —往生さす, ① to do to death; cook a person's goose; settle a person's hash. ② to make (a person) give up. (無理に往生させる, to force consent from a person; compel a person to consent). —往生する, ① (淨土に生る) to be reborn in paradise. ② (死ぬ) to die; pass away. ③ =*akirameru*. —鐵道往生をする, to die by being run over by a train.

ojoku (汚辱), *n.* disgrace; dishonour; shame.

ojōsan (お孃さん), *n.* a young lady; your 《his》 daughter (人の娘); miss (呼稱).

oka (岡, 丘), *n.* a hill; a hillock (小丘); a mound (塚).

oka (陸), *n.* land; the shore.

ōka (歐化する), *vt.* to Europeanize. ¶ 歐化主義, Europeanism; Westernism; Occidentalism. (歐化主義者, an Occidentalist.)

ōka (謳歌する), *vt.* to sing; admire; glorify; applaud. ¶ 謳歌者, an admirer; a worshipper.

okabo (陸稻), *n.* upland rice.

okabore (傍惚する), *v.* to take a fancy to; fancy.

okage (お蔭), *n.* kindness; favour; patronage; help. —お蔭で, by your help; through your kind influence. —僕の今日あるは君のお蔭だ, I owe you [You have made me] what I am.

okai (汚穢), *n.* filth; dirt; night-soil (糞尿). —飲料水を汚穢する, to pollute [muddle] drinking water.

ōkakumaku (横隔膜), *n.* 【解】 the diaphragm; the midriff.

okame (お亀), *n.* ❶ (面) a moon-face. ❷ (女) an ill-favoured woman; a jade.

okame (岡目), *n.* a looker-on; a bystander. —岡目八目, "Lookers-on see more than players."

ōkami (狼), *n.* the wolf.

okamochi (岡持), *n.* a wooden carrying-box.

okan (惡寒), *n.* the chill; the cold; 【醫】 rigor. —惡寒を覺える, to catch a chill; shiver.

ōkan (王冠), *n.* the crown.

ōkan (往還), *n.* ❶ (往復) going and returning. ❷ (公道) a highway; a (public) road.

okāsan (お母さん), *n.* mother; mamma; mammie, ma (かあ).

okashii (可笑しい), *a.* Ⓢ 可笑な. ❶ (笑ふべき) laughable; funny; droll. ❷ (面白い) amusing; interesting. ❸ (滑稽な) ridiculous; comic. ❹ (變な) strange; absurd (不條理). —可笑しな風俗, funny customs. —可笑しさをこらへる, to suppress one's laughter.

okasu (犯す), *vt* ❶ (罪惡を) to commit; perpetrate. ❷ (法律·規則を) to violate; break; infringe. ❸ (暴行) to violate; outrage; defile. —罪を犯す, to commit a crime.

okasu (侵す), *vt.* ❶ (侵入) to invade; intrude *on*; break *into* (闖入). ❷ (侵害) to violate; encroach *on*. —霜に侵される, to be damaged by frost. —領域を侵す, to invade a territory.

okasu (冒す), *vt.* ❶ (敢てす) to dare; venture; risk. ❷ (瀆す) to profane; desecrate. ❸ (病が) to attack; affect. —寒氣に冒される, to take [catch] cold. —雨を冒して進む, to march in the rain. —彈丸雨飛の間を冒す, to face the showering bullets. —外家の姓を冒す, to assume the name of the maternal house.

ōkata (大方), *ad.* ❶ =*tabun*. ❷ (大半) almost; mostly; for the most part.

okawari (お替り), *n.* another helping; a second help. —お替する, to ask for a second help.

okayu (陸湯), *n.* hot tank-water.

ōkaze (大風), *n.* a strong [violent] wind; a gale. ☞ *kaze*. —大風の吹いた後のやう, as calm as a lull after a storm.

okazu (お菜), *n.* a relish; side-dishes.

oke (桶), *n.* a tub; a pail; a coop. ¶ 桶屋, a cooper.

ōken (王權), *n.* the royalty; the royal [king's] authority; the crown.

okeru (於ける), *prep.* in; to.

ōkesutora (オーケストラ), *n.* an orchestra.

oki (沖), *n.* the offing; the open sea. ¶ 沖人足, a cargo coolie (日本專用の); an off-coolie.

oki (置, 隔), *ad.* at intervals *of*. —二日置きに, every third day. —一行置きに書く, to write on every other line [on alternate lines].

oki (燠), *n.* embers.

okiagarikoboshi (不倒翁), *n.* a tumbler.

okiagaru (起上がる), *vi.* to get up; rise (up); stand up (起立); pick oneself up (轉んで); recover one's legs (同上).

okiba (置場), *n.* a place for [of] deposit; a yard; a shed. ¶ 材木置場, a timber-yard.

okichigaeru (置違へる), *vt.* to misplace; mislay.

okidokei (置時計), *n.* a table-clock.

okifushi (起臥), *n.* getting up [rising] and lying down.

ōkii (大きい), *a.* big; large; great. ☞ *kyodai*, *kōdai* (廣大).

okikaeru (置換へる), *vt.* ❶ (交互に) to interchange; transpose. ❷ (代用) to put *for*; substitute *for*.

okikorobi (起轉び), *n.* rising and falling; vicissitudes; ups and downs.

ōkiku (大きく), *ad.* large; in large size; on a large scale (大規模に). —大きくなる, ① (成大) to grow [get] big [large]; be enlarged [increased]. ② (成長) to grow (up); become tall [big]; become a man (大人になる). ——·**suru**, *vt.* to enlarge; increase (增加); expand (膨脹); extend (擴張). —騷ぎを大きくする, to pour oil on the fire; add fuel to the fire.

okimiyage (置土産), *n.* a souvenir [a keepsake; a present] left behind.

okimono (置物), *n.* an ornament for the alcove.

okina (翁), *n.* an old [aged] man.

okinaosu (置直す), *vt.* to rearrange; relay; replace.

ōkini (大きに), *ad.* ❶ (大いに) very much; greatly. ❷ (成程) indeed.

okiru (起きる), *vi.* ❶ (起床) to get up; rise; get out of bed; turn out. ❷ (眼覺め) to awake; wake up. ❸ (起座) to sit up; be up. —火が起きた, The fire has kindled.

ōkisa (大きさ), *n.* size; measure; bulk. —犬程の大きさの, about

as large as [about the size of] a dog. —大きさが違ふ, to be of a different size.

okite (掟), *n.* law; rule; regulations. ☞ *hōritsu*.

okitegami (置手紙), *n.* a letter [note] left behind.

okiwasureru (置忘れる), *vt.* to mislay; leave (forgetfully); forget.

okizari (置去), *n.* desertion; abandonment. —置去りにする, to leave behind; desert; abandon.

okkakeru (追掛ける), *vt.* =*oikakeru* (追掛ける).

okkanai (怖い), *n.* fearful; dreadful. ☞ *kowai*.

okkō, okkū, (億劫), *n.* ❶ (永劫年) æon; eternity. ❷ (面倒) trouble; annoyance; a bother. —億劫な, troublesome; annoying.

okō (惡行, 汚行), *n.* loose conduct; misconduct; profligacy (放蕩); a disgraceful [shameful] act.

ōko (往古), *n.* antiquity; ancient times.

ōkō (往航), *n.* an outward voyage [[passage].

ōkō (横行する), *vi.* ❶ (横様に歩む) to walk sideways; go sidewise. ❷ (跋扈する) to go freely; be rampant; overrun (a district). —横行濶歩する, to stride; strut.

okogamashii (烏滸がましい), *a.* ❶ (可笑しい) ridiculous. ❷ (生意氣な) conceited; insolent; impudent.

ōkoku (王國), *n.* a kingdom; a [monarchy.

okomori (お籠する), *v.* to confine oneself in a shrine for prayer.

okonai (行), *n.* ❶ (所行) an act (-ion); a deed. ❷ (品行) conduct; behaviour; deportment. ❸ (戒行) religious austerities.

okonau (行ふ), *vt.* ❶ (爲す) to perform (擧行); practise (實行); exercise (行使). ❷ (振舞ふ) to behave; carry oneself. —結婚式を行ふ, to solemnize a marriage.

okonawareru (行はれる), *vi.* ❶ (擧行) to take place; be held; come off. ❷ (實行) to be put in practice. ❸ (流行) to prevail; be in vogue [fashion]. —行はれなくなる, to go out of force [fashion]; fall into disuse.

okorasu (怒らす), *vt.* to make angry; enrage; provoke.

okori (起), *n.* ❶ (起原) the origin; the source. ❷ (元始) the beginning; the rise; the cause (原因).

okori (瘧), *n.* ague. —瘧を患ふ, to have a fit of ague.

okorijōgo (怒上戸), *n.* one who loses his temper over his cups.

okorippoi (怒りっぽい), *a.* irritable; quick [hasty; hot]-tempered; testy.

okoru (起る), *vi.* ❶ (出來) to happen; occur; take place; arise; break out (戰爭·火事等). ❷ (起因) to arise [rise] *from*; spring *from*; follow *from*. ❸ (興) (榮える) to rise; become prosperous. —何事が起らうとも, whatever may happen; come what may.

okoru (怒る), *vi.* to become [get] angry; be angry. ☞ *ikaru*. —怒って, in anger. —ぷんぷん怒って居る, to be in a fume.

okosu (起す), *vt.* ❶ (立たす) to raise up; set upright; help a person up. ❷ (開始) to commence; begin; set on foot. ❸ (設立) to establish; set up; found. ❹ (惹起) to provoke; give rise [birth] *to*; rouse. ❺ (醒起) to wake; awake; rouse; arouse. ❻ (興起) to revive; regain; resuscitate. ❼ (發生) to produce; generate; make [build] (a fire) (火を). —疑ひ《野心》を起す, to harbour suspicion《ambition》. —新事業を起す, to start [launch] a new enterprise. —騷動を起す, to create a commotion. —爭を起す, to stir up a strife. —寢て居る人を起す, to awake a person from his sleep; wake up a sleeper.

okotari (怠), *n.* neglect; negligence; idleness; remissness. —怠り勝ちの, neglectful; apt to be neglected《to neglect》.

okotaru (怠·懈る), *vt.* to neglect; be neglectful *of*; slight. —病怠る, to be [get] better. —職務を怠る, to neglect one's duty; fail in one's duty.

okoze (䲃), *n.* 【魚】 Minous [Adamsi (學名).

oku (奧), *n.* the recesses (山·心などの); the interior (内部); the heart (中央部). —森の奧, the depth of a forest. —山の奧, the heart of a mountain. —客を奧へ通す, to show a visitor into the parlour.

oku (億), *n.* a hundred millions.

oku (置く), *vt.* ❶ (場所におく) to put; place; lay (横に); set (立てて); rest *on* (安置する); station (駐屯). ❷ (設ける) to establish (設置); appoint (任命). ❸ (犬·召使·下宿人·食物等) to keep. ❹ (捨て置く) to leave; let. ❺ (殘し置く) to leave. ❻ (除外) to set [put] aside; except. ❼ (やめる) to give up; cease; discontinue. —爲さずに置く, to leave undone. —テーブルの上に置く, to put it on the table. —愛惜措かざる所である, to be never tired of admiring.

ōku (多く), *ad.* much; greatly; mostly. —多くて; 多くとも, at

most. —多くは, for the most part; mostly; mainly; generally. —多くの場合に於ては, as a rule; in many cases [instances].

okuba (奥歯), *n.* an axle-tooth; a molar (tooth); a grinder. —奥歯に物が挟まったやうな, as if he were not quite candid with me.

okubi (噯氣), *n.* beiching; eructation. —噯氣にも出さぬ, to keep mum *about*; breathe not a syllable of it.

okubukai (奥深い), *a.* deep; profound. —奥深く, deep; deeply; profoundly.

okubyō (臆病), *n.* cowardice; timidity; pusillanimity —臆病な, cowardly; timid; faint-hearted. —臆病神にとりつかれる, to be possessed by cowardice. ¶ 臆病者, a coward; a poltroon; a funk.

okudan (臆斷), *n.* a conjecture; a supposition; an opinion; an inference. —臆斷する, to conjecture; guess; infer.

okugai (屋外), *n.* the exterior of a house; the open air. —屋外に, outdoors; in the open air. ¶ 屋外演說, an open-air speech. —屋外勞働, outdoor labour. —屋外遊戲, outdoor games [sports].

okugi (奥義), *n.* the secrets; the mystery. —奥義を究める, to master the secrets.

okujō (屋上), on the house-top. —屋上屋を架す, to gild refined gold. ¶ 屋上制限法, a roof-restriction law. —屋上庭園, a roof-garden.

okumen (臆面なく), *ad.* unblushingly; boldly; audaciously.

okumi (衽), *n.* a gore; a gusset.

okunai (屋内), *n.* the interior of a house. —屋内の, indoor. —屋内に, indoors.

okunoin (奥の院), *n.* a sanctum.

okunote (奥の手), *n.* ❶ =*okugi.* ❷ (最後の手段) the best card. —奥の手を出す, to play one's best cards [trump card]; show one's hand.

ōkura (大藏省), *n.* the Finance Department; the Department of Finance; the Treasury Department (米); the Exchequer (英). ¶ 大藏大臣, the Minister of (State for) Finance.

okurasu (後らす), *vt.* to retard; delay; defer. —時計を後らす, to put back a clock.

okure (後), *n.* ❶ (時間に) lateness. ❷ (人に) defeat; failure. ❸ (時代・期節・流行等に) backwardness. —人に後れを取る, to be beaten *by*; be defeated; be outstripped.

okurebase (後馳に), *ad.* late. —後れ馳せに駆けつける, to come [run] up late.

okureru (後れる), *vi.* ❶ (時間に) to be late; be behind time; be delayed. ❷ (時計が) to be slow; lose. ❸ (時勢・流行等に) to be behind; fall [get; hang] behind; drop [fall] behind [to the rear]. —(時計) が毎日十分後れる, to lose ten minutes every day.

okuridasu (送出す), *vt.* ❶ to send out; forward. ❷ (客を) to show out. —人を送り出す, to show [usher] a person out.

okurijō (送狀), *n.* 【商】an invoice.

okurimono (贈物), *n.* a present; a gift; a donation. —贈物をする, to make a present.

okurina (諡), *n.* a posthumous name.

okurinin (送人), *n.* a sender; a mourner (會葬者).

okurisaki (送先), *n.* the destination.

okuru (送る), *vt.* ❶ to send; forward; convey (運送). ❷ (派遣) to send; despatch. ❸ (過ごす) to pass; spend. —代表者を送る, to send delegates (*to*).

okuru (贈る), *vt.* ❶ (贈呈) to present; send; make a present *of*. ❷ (授與) to confer; bestow. —博士號を贈る, to confer the title of doctor.

okusama (奥樣), *n.* your lady; missis, missus; mistress (召使から); madam, ma'am (呼び掛け語).

okusetsu (臆說), *n.* an opinion; a conjecture; a supposition.

okusoko (奥底), *n.* the bottom; the depth. —奥底のない, open, frank; open-hearted.

okusoku (臆測), *n.* a guess; a surmise; a conjecture. —臆測する, to guess; surmise; conjecture. —臆測に過ぎぬ, to be no more than [nothing but] a surmise; be a mere conjecture.

oku-suru (臆する), *vi.* to fear; be afraid; be timid; be shy. —危險に臆せぬ, undaunted by dangers.

okute (晩稻), *n.* late rice; a late crop.

okuyama (奥山), *n.* a deep mountain.

okuyukashii (奥床しい), *a.* refined; graceful; elegant.

okuyuki (奥行), *n.* depth; the distance from front to rear. —奥行三間間口五間の家, a house three *ken* in depth and five in frontage.

okuzashiki (奥座敷), *n.* a back-room [-parlour]; an inner room.

okuzuke (奥附), *n.* (本の) a colophon.

ōkyō (凹鏡), *n.* oxeyes; a concave mirror (鏡).

ōkyū (應急の), *a.* emergent; temporary. —應急策を取る, to take emergency measures. ¶ 應急舵(修理), temporary rudder (repairs). —應急手當, first aid; emergency treatment. (應急手當を施す, to give first aid.)

ōma (黄麻), *n.* jute.

ōmachigai (大間違), *n.* a great [gross] mistake [blunder].

ōmaka (大まかな), *a.* ❶ (大體の) rough. ❷ (腹の大きい) generous; liberal; open-handed (物惜みせぬ). —大まかに, roughly; generously; liberally.

omake (お負), *n.* an addition; an extra. —お負けに, over and above; into the bargain; to boot; to make the matter worse. —お負けをつけて話す, to talk big; colour highly. —お負けに雪が降ってる, To make the matter worse, the snow falls.

ōmake (大負), *n.* ❶ (大敗) a severe [heavy] defeat. ❷ (減價) a great bargain [rebate]; a great reduction in price.

omamori (お守), *n.* a charm; a talisman; an amulet.

omaru (虎子), *n.* a chamber-pot; a (close)-stool; a commode.

ōmata (大跨, 大股), *n.* a (long) stride. —大股に歩く, to walk with great strides; walk at a great pace; walk with long steps.

omatsurisawagi (お祭騒ぎ), *n.* bustle and confusion as at a fête.

omawari (お廻り), *n.* a policeman; a bobby 〔卑〕; a copper 〔卑 cop と略す〕; a peeler 〔卑〕.

ome (お目), your [his; her, *etc.*] eyes. —お目に掛かる, to meet; see; have the pleasure [honour] of seeing. —お目に掛ける, ① to show; submit for another's inspection. ② (贈與) to present; make a present *of*.

ōme (大目に見る), *v.* to overlook; wink *at*; pass over; look through one's fingers *at*.

omedama (お目玉), *n.* scolding; reprimand (公務上の). —お目玉を頂戴する, to be scolded; catch it hot.

omedeta (お目出度), *n.* a happy event; a matter for congratulation.

omedetai (お目出度い), *a.* ❶ =*medetai*. ❷ (お人よしの) good-natured.

omedetō (お目出度う), I congratulate you *upon*; (accept my) congratulations; I wish you joy. —新年お目出度う, I wish you a happy New Year; A happy New Year to you!

omei (汚名), *n.* a bad name [repute]; stigma; a stain on one's good name. —汚名を被せる, to cast a slur upon a person; give a person a bad character. —汚名を雪ぐ, to vindicate one's honour; clear one's reputation [name].

omeku (喚く), *v.* to yell; bawl; shout.

ōmen (凹面の), *a.* concave.

omeome (阿容阿容), *ad.* shamelessly; unblushingly.

omeshi (御召), *n.* ❶ (衣服) a dress; clothes. ❷ (召喚) summons. ¶ 御召馬車, an Imperial [Emperor's] coach. —御召艦, the warship with His Majesty on board.

omezu-okusezu (怯めず臆せず), *ad.* undauntedly; boldly; fearlessly.

omiki (お神酒), *n.* sacred wine; libation; wine (酒).

ominaeshi (女郎花), *n.* 【植】 Patrinia scabiosæfolia (學名).

ōmisoka (大晦日), *n.* the old year's day; the last day of the year; the New-year's Eve.

ōmizu (大水), *n.* a flood; an inundation; a deluge.

omocha (玩具), *n.* a plaything; a toy; a knick-knack. —玩具の様な大砲, a toy of a gun. —玩具の熊, a toy bear. —人を玩具にする, to make fun [sport] of a person; play [toy] with a person. ¶ 玩具箱, a toy-box. —玩具屋, a toy-shop.

omodaka (澤瀉), *n.* 【植】 the arrow-head; the arrow-leaf.

omodatta (重立った), *a.* principal; chief. —重立った役員, the leading members of a staff.

omoeraku (以爲), *ad.* in one's opinion; in one's judgment; methinks [*v.*].

omogai (絡頭, 羈), *n.* a head-stall.

omoi (思), *n.* ❶ (思念) thinking. ❷ (思想) thought; mind; idea. ❸ (感情) feeling. ❹ (情緒) sentiment; emotion. ❺ (願望) a desire; a wish. ❻ (心) mind; sense; heart. ❼ (愛慕) love; affection. ❽ (心配) care. ❾ (想像) imagination. ❿ (執念) a revengeful spirit. —思ひが届く, to attain one's wishes [desire]; have one's desire satisfied. —思ひの儘に, freely; as one thinks [pleases; wishes]. —思ひを寄せる, to give [lose] one's heart *to*; set one's affections [heart] *on*; take a fancy *to*. —思ひを遂げる, to satisfy one's desire.

omoi (重い), *a.* heavy. ❶ (重量) weighty. ❷ (重大) important; weighty; serious; grave. —重い病氣, a serious illness. —重い責

任 (税金) heavy responsibility (taxes) —口が重い, to have a heavy tongue. —頭が重い, My head feels heavy.

omoiataru (思當る), *v.* ❶ (思附く) to occur to one's mind; flash on one's mind. ❷ (思出す) to call [bring] to mind; recollect; recall (to one's mind)

omoiau (思合ふ), *v.* to love each other; think of each other.

omoiawasu (思合す), *vt.* to consider [put] together. —彼れ此れ思ひ合はす, to put two and two together.

omoichigai (思違ひ), *n.* mistake; misapprehension; misunderstanding. —僕の思違ひでした, It was misapprehension on my part.

omoidasu (思出す), *vt.* to recollect; recall; call [bring] to mind; think *of*. —思ひ出させる, to call to a person's mind; recall to a person; remind a person *of*. —故郷を思ひ出す, to think of one's old home.

omoide (思出), *n.* recollections; memories; reminiscence. —故郷の思ひ出, memories of one's native country [land]. —思ひ出多き秋の夜, an autumnal night suggestive of the past.

omoidōri (思通り), *ad.* as one pleases [thinks fit; desires]; to one's fancy [satisfaction]; to one's heart's content. —思ひ通りの貸家, a house to let that satisfies one in every respect. —思ひ通りにする, to have one's own way; take one's own course.

omoigake (思掛けない), *a.* unthought of; unexpected; unlooked-for. —思ひ掛けなく, unexpectedly; unawares.

omoikaesu (思返す), *v.* to think (over) again; reconsider.

omoikiri (思切), *n.* ❶ (あきらめ) resignation; abandonment. ❷ (決心) resolution; determination. ——, *ad.* to one's heart's content; to excess (素敵に). —思切りがよい, to be resolute; readily resign oneself. —思ひ切る, to resign oneself *to*; abandon; give up; give up all thoughts *of*. —思ひ切って, ① daringly; boldly; resolutely. ② (極度に) exceedingly; to excess.

omoikogareru (思焦れる), *vi.* to yearn *after*; long [sigh] *for*.

omoikomu (思込む), *v.* ❶ to be strongly impressed *with*; believe firmly *in*; be possessed *with*. ❷ (一心) to set one's heart *upon*; resolve.

omoimadou (思惑ふ), *vi.* to be perplexed (*at*); be at a loss.

omoimawasu (想廻す), *vt.* ❶ (回想) to reflect (*on*). ❷ (沈思) to ponder; meditate; revolve [turn over] in mind.

omoimiru (想見る), *vt.* to image to oneself; imagine; think over.

omoimōkeru (思設ける), *vt.* to anticipate; expect; presuppose.

omoimoyoranu (思ひも寄らぬ), *a.* unlooked-for; unexpected; unforeseen. ——, *v.* to be out of the question; not to be thought of; (I) had no thought [idea] *of*; (I) had never thought *of*.

omoinaosu (思直す), *vt.* to reconsider; think over again; think better of.

omoinashi (思做), *n.* fancy.

omoinayamu (思惱む), *vi.* to be depressed with thought.

omoinohoka (思の外), *ad.* unexpectedly; beyond one's expectation. ☞ ***angai***.

omoinokosu (思殘す), *vt.* Ⓢ 思置く. to regret. —思ひ殘す所は何もない, to have nothing to regret; have no regret.

omoiokosu (想起す), *vt.* to recollect; call to mind. ☞ ***omoidasu***.

omoiomoi (思思に), *ad.* each according to his wish; each in his own way; as they please. —思ひ思ひの事を言ふ, to say each what he pleases.

omoitatsu (思立つ), *vt.* to take into one's head (思ひつく); think *of*; resolve (決心).

omoitomaru (思止まる), *vt.* to give up (something; the idea of...); abandon; desist *from*. —思ひ止まらす, to dissuade him *from* (doing something).

omoitsuki (思附), *n.* an idea; a plan; a suggestion. —一寸した思附き, an idea which crosses one's mind [occurs to one]. —好い思ひつき, a happy thought; a capital idea; a good plan.

omoitsuku (思附く), *vt.* to hit *upon*; think *of*; conceive. ——, *vi.* to occur to [flash on] one [one's mind].

omoitsumeru (思詰める), *vt.* to think earnestly *of*; brood *over*; think continuously.

omoitsunoru (思募る), *vt.* to think more and more.

omoiukabu (思浮ぶ), *vi.* to occur to one; flash on one's mind [upon one]. ☞ ***omoitsuku***.

omoiwazurau (思煩ふ), *vt.* Ⓢ 思佗びる. to feel very anxious *about*; be perplexed *about* [*for*; *at*, *etc.*]

omoiyari (思遣り), *n.* fellow-feeling; sympathy; consideration. —思遣りのない, inconsiderate; unsympathetic; unkind; cold. —思遣る, ① to enter into a person's feelings; sympathize *with*; feel *for* [*with*]. ② (想像) to imagine.

omokage (俤, 面影), *n.* ❶ (面相) a figure; a face. ❷ (幻影) a phantom; a vision. ❸ (痕跡) a trace; vestiges. —政治家の面影, a dash of statesman. —在りし昔の面影, the ruin [shadow] of what it was.

omokaji (面舵), *n.* 【航】 port-helm: (命令) port the helm! —面舵を取る, to port the helm.

ōmōke (大儲), *n.* a large profit. —大儲けをする, to make a good haul; realize a huge profit.

omoki (重き), *a.* heavy; weighty; serious; important. ☞ *omoi.* —重きをなす, to carry weight; count for much. (重きをなす人, a man of account [consequence; importance].) —重きを置く, to put [set] value; attach importance [weight] *to*; set great store *by*; lay stress *on*. —重きを置かれる《置かれぬ》, to be much 《little》 accounted of.

omoku (重く), *ad.* heavily; seriously (事を). —重くなる, to become heavy (責任が); become [grow] serious (病が). —重くする, to make heavy; aggravate (病氣·罪などを). —重く視る, to attach importance *to*. —重く用ひる, to give an important position.

omokurushii (重苦しい), *a.* heavy; ponderous (文體等の); oppressive (空氣等の). —重苦しい外套, a cumbrous overcoat.

omomi (重み), *n.* ❶ (物の) weight. ❷ (人物·言葉の) weight; importance; authority (權威); dignity (威厳). ❸ (語·文·事實の) emphasis. —重みある, weighty; ponderous; dignified (人).

omomochi (面持), *n.* countenance; looks; expression (of the face). —怪訝な面持ちで, with a doubtful look.

omomuki (趣), *n.* ❶ (趣意) meaning; effect; purport. ❷ (趣致) taste; flavour; elegance (雅趣). ❸ (風) air; appearance; aspect. —書面の趣, the tenor of a letter. —全體の趣, general effect. —趣ある, elegant; tasteful. —趣なき, tasteless; inelegant.

omomuku (赴く), *vi.* ❶ to go; proceed; make *towards.* ❷ (なる) to grow; get. ❸ (傾く) to tend *towards.* —快方に赴く, to get [become] better.

omomuro (徐に), *ad.* slowly; by slow degrees; gently; deliberately.

omona (重な), *a.* principal; chief; leading; important. —重な成分, principal ingredients. —重な産物, the chief products.

omonaga (面長), *n.* a long face. —少し面長の, oval-faced.

omoneru (阿る), *v.* to flatter; fawn *upon*; cringe *to.* —世に阿る, to truckle to the times.

omoni (重荷), *n.* a (heavy) load [burden]; encumbrance. —精神上の重荷, spiritual burden. —重荷を下ろす, to throw off a burden; relieve [ease] oneself of a burden; disburden oneself.

omonmiru (惟る), *vt.* to think; reflect. —熟〻惟るに, it seems to me upon careful reflection.

omonpakari (慮), *n.* ❶ (思慮) thought; consideration. ❷ (計畫) a plan.

omonpakaru (慮る), *vt.* to think [ponder] *on* [*over*]; take thought *of.* —遠く慮る, to dip deep [see far] into the future.

omon-zuru (重んずる), *vt.* ❶ (尊重) to respect; honour; regard. ❷ (重要視する) to esteem; value; set store *by.* —重んぜぬ, to make little *of*; have no regard *for*; make light *of.* —友情を重んずる, to set store by friendship. —職を重んずる, to regard one's duties seriously.

omoomoshii (重重しい), *a.* ❶ heavy; ponderous; weighty. ❷ (厳かな) grave; serious; solemn (莊重); dignified (威厳のある). —重々しい足取り, a heavy [leaden] step; a solemn pace. —重重しい口調で, in a grave tone.

omori (錘), *n.* ❶ (秤の) a weight. ❷ (測鉛) a plumb; a plummet; a (sounding-)lead. ❸ (釣絲の) a sinker. —錘を附ける, to weight.

omoru (重る), *vi.* to grow serious.

omosa (重さ), *n.* weight. —重さ五封度ある, It weighs five pounds.

omoshi (壓石), *n.* a weight (-stone).

omoshirogaru (面白がる), *vi.* to be amused; be delighted (悦ぶ); be interested *in* (興がる). —面白がらす, to amuse; entertain a person *with* (興を與へる); interest a person *in* (同上).

omoshirohanbun (面白半分に), *ad.* half in fun [joke]; half for fun; partly for amusement (樂みに).

omoshiroi (面白い), *a.* ❶ (興味ある) amusing; interesting; delightful. ❷ (滑稽な) funny;

droll. ❸(奇妙な) queer; singular. —面白い話, an amusing story. —面白く, gaily; funnily; interestingly; pleasantly. —面白くない, unamusing; uninteresting; dull. —面白くなくなる, to lose interest. —いと面白げに語る, to tell it in a very interesting tone.

omoshiromi (面白味), *n.* interest; fun; pleasure.

omoshirosō (面白さうな), *a.* seeming (to be) pleasant. —面白さうに, merrily; pleasantly; like fun.

omote (表), *n.* ❶(表面) a surface; a face. ❷(前面) a front. ❸(戸外) outside. ❹(街路) a street. ❺(表口) a front-door. —布の表, the right side of cloth. —五回の表 (野球の), the first half of the fifth inning.

omote (面), *n.* a face. —砲火の面に立つ, to stand fire. —面を伏せる, to hang one's head.

omotedatsu (表立つ), *vi.* ❶(公になる) to become public. ❷(表沙汰) to be brought to law.

omotedōri (表通り), *n.* a main street; a street.

omoteguchi (表口), *n.* a street-door; a front-door.

omotemon (表門), *n.* a front-gate.

omotemuki (表向), *n.* publicity (公); appearance (外見). ——, *ad.* publicly; openly; formally; officially. —表向きの, public; official; formal; outward; ostensible (用事など). (表向きの理由《目的》, an ostensible reason《purpose》.) —表向きは, outwardly; ostensibly.

omotezata (表沙汰にする), *v.* ❶(訴訟) to bring before the court; appeal to the law; go to law. ❷(公表) to make public; bring to light.

omoto (萬年青), *n.* 【植】Rhodea japonica (學名).

ōmoto (大本), *n.* foundation; source.

omou (思·惟·想·懷ふ), *v.* ❶(考ふ) to think *of* [*about*]; consider; meditate *on* (沈思). ❷(感じる) to feel. ❸(想像) to suppose; imagine; fancy. ❹(信じる) to believe. ❺(願望) to wish; want; desire. ❻(豫期) to expect. ❼(戀愛) to love; take fancy *to*; yearn [sigh] *for*; fall in love *with*. —よく思ふ, to think well *of*. —己の名譽を思うて, for (one's) name's sake. —思ふ事を直言する, to speak one's mind. —何とも思はぬ, to make little account *of*; think nothing *of*; make nothing *of*. —憎からず思ふ, to be far from hating.

omoumama (思ふ儘に), *ad.* as one pleases [wishes]. —思ふ儘にする, to have one's (own) way.

omoutsubo (思ふ局に嵌る), to turn out according to one's wish.

omouzonbun (思ふ存分), *ad.* Ⓢ 思ふ樣. to one's heart's content.

omowaku (思惑), *n.* ❶ thought; intention; view. ❷(株式相場) speculation (spec. と略す). —思惑通り, according to one's mind [intention]. —思惑が違ふ, to be out of reckoning; fall short of one's expectation.

omowareru (思はれる), *vi.* ❶(考へらる) to be thought; be regarded; appear. ❷(思慕) to be loved; be yearned for. —私には…思はれる, I believe; I fancy; it seems to me; I feel (感じる).

omowaseburi (思はせ振), *n.* playing with another's fancy [feelings]. —思はせ振りをする [云ふ], to play with another's fancy [feelings].

omowaseru (思はせる), *vt.* to make (another) think; put in mind *of* (想起せしむ).

omowashii (思はしい), *a.* satisfactory; desirable. —思はしくない, unsatisfactory; disappointing.

omowazu (思はず), *ad.* undesignedly; unconsciously; unintentionally. —思はず (知らず) 噴き出す, to laugh in spite of oneself.

omoya (母屋), *n.* 【建】the main house [building].

omoyatsure (面窶), *n.* Ⓢ 面痩. emaciation of a face. —苦勞で面窶れのした, care-worn. —病氣で面窶れのした, emaciated by disease.

omoyu (重湯), *n.* rice-gruel; 【醫】rice-water. —重湯を啜る, to sip rice-gruel.

omozashi (面差), *n.* countenance; feature.

ōmu (鸚鵡), *n.* 【鳥】the grey parrot; the parrot (通稱). —鸚鵡返しする, to repeat what another says; reecho.

ōmugi (大麥), *n.* 【植】the (six-rowed) barley.

ōmukashi (太古), *n.* great [remote] antiquity; the ancient times. —大昔より, from time immemorial; time out of mind.

ōmukō (大向), *n.* 【劇】the gallery. —大向を當てこむ, to play to the gallery. ¶ 大向連, the gods【卑】.

ōmune (大概), *ad.* ☞ *taigai.*

omuretsu (オムレツ), *n.* omelet, omelette.

ōmyō (奥妙), *n.* secret; mystery; profoundness. —奥妙な, profound; mysterious.

on (音), *n.* a sound; pronunciation (發音).

on (恩), *n.* kindness; favour; grace. —恩を賣る, to take advantage of one's past favours [kindness]. —恩を施す, to do a person a kindness. —…の恩を受けて, under an obligation *to*. —恩を仇で返す, to requite kindness [good] with evil; return evil for good.

on (溫), *n.* warmth.

onabe (お鍋), *n.* a (female) cook; a cookee【俗】.

onagabachi (尾長蜂), *n.*【昆】the ichneumon-wasp.

onagadori (尾長鳥), *n.*【鳥】the Eastern blue magpie.

onagazaru (尾長猿), *n.*【哺乳】Cercopithecus (學名); the monkey.

ōnagi (大凪), *n.* dead calm.

oṅai (恩愛), *n.* affection; love; tender feeling. —恩愛の絆, the bond of affection; the link of love.

onaji (同じ), *a.* ❶ (同一) the same; one and the same; identical. ❷ (類似) similar; like; analogous. ❸ (均等) equal; equivalent. —同じ程に, to the same extent. —…の場合も亦之に同じ, the same rule applies to the case of….

onajiku (同じく), *ad.* ❶ the same; in the same way [manner]. ❷ (等しく) likewise; ditto (同上の意); as well. ❸ (平等) equally. —感を同じくする, to feel the same; have the same feeling.

onaka (腹), *n.* the stomach; the belly.

onami (男波), *n.* an advancing wave.

ōnami (大浪), *n.* a b[illegible] [high] wave; a surge; a bil[illegible]

onando (お納戸-色), *n.* greyish-blue.

onari (御成), *n.* the visit (of august personages). —御成りになる, to visit; honour with his visit.

onashizaru (無尾猿), *n.*【哺乳】the ape.

ōnatsu (押捺する), *vt.* to stamp; put on; affix; set.

onba (乳母), *n.* a nurse; a wet-nurse. —乳母日傘で育つ, to be nursed in luxury.

onbin (音便), *n.* euphony; an euphonical change.

onbin (穩便の), *a.* peaceful. —穩便の沙汰を乞ふ, to beg for a quiet [peaceable] settlement. —穩便に濟ます, to settle the matter privately [in peace].

onbō (隱亡), *n.* a firer [burner] at a crematory; a cremator.

onchō (音調), *n.* tune; tone; measure.

onchō (恩寵), *n.* favour; grace.

onchū (御中), Messieurs. —日本郵船會社御中, Messrs. the Nippon Yūsen Kaisha.

ondan (溫暖な), *a.* genial; mild; warm.

ondo (音頭), *n.* lead; leading (in singing). —合唱の音頭を取る, to lead the chorus. ¶ 音頭取, ① (歌の) the leading singer. ② (首唱者) a leading spirit; a leader.

ondo (溫度), *n.* temperature. —溫度を計る, to take the temperature.

ondoku (音讀), *n.* reading aloud; vocal reading. —音讀する, to read aloud.

ondori (牡鷄), *n.* a cock; a rooster【米】.

oneji (雄ねぢ), *n.* a male [an internal] screw.

onga (溫雅な), *a.* gentle; refined; graceful.

ongaeshi (恩返), *n.* returning favours. —恩返しをする, to requite a kindness [an obligation]; repay a debt of gratitude.

ongaku (音樂), *n.* music. —音樂の教師, a music master [*fem.* mistress]. ¶ 音樂堂, a band-stand. —音樂學校, a musical school; a music academy. —音樂家, a musician. —音樂會, a concert; a musical society (協會). (音樂會を開く, to give a concert.)

ongi (恩義), *n.* favour; obligation. —恩義に酬いる, to repay an obligation. —恩義に感ずる, to be moved with gratitude; appreciate kindness.

ongyoku (音曲), *n.* music; song.

oni (鬼), *n.* ❶ (亡靈) a ghost; a departed spirit. ❷ (惡神) a devil; a demon; a genius. ❸ (妖魔) a bogy, bogey; a goblin. an ogre (食人鬼). ❹ (鬼事の) a tagger; a hoodman (目隱しの). ❺ (債鬼) a creditor; a dun. —鬼の夫婦, a devilish pair; a cruel couple. —鬼のやうな, fiendish; devilish; demoniac(-al); diabolic; cruel; inhuman. —心を鬼にして, steeling oneself [one's heart] (against pity). ¶ 鬼婆, a hag.

oṅi (恩威), *n.* kindness and dignity; justice and mercy; sternness and magnanimity.

onibasu (鬼蓮), *n.*【植】the prickly water-lily; the gorgon-plant.

onibi (鬼火), *n.* the will-o'-the-wisp; Jack-o'-lantern; a corpse-candle (【英】墓地等の).

onibishi (おにびし), *n.*【植】the water-chestnut [-caltrops].

onigawara (鬼瓦), *n.* a ridge-end tile.

onigokko, onigoto, (鬼事), *n.* tag; blindman's buff (目隱し). —鬼事する, to play catch who catch can; play tag (blindman's buff).

oṅin (音韻), *n.* a vocal sound.

oniyuri (卷丹), *n.*【植】the tiger-

-lily. [-warmer.]

onjaku (溫石), *n.* a pocket-

onjin (恩人), *n.* a benefactor [*fem.* -tress]; a patron [*fem.* -oness].

onjō (溫情), *n.* warm-heartedness; kindness. —溫情ある友人, a warm friend. ¶ 溫情主義, paternalism.

onjun (溫順), *n.* ❶ (溫和) gentleness; mildness. ❷ (從順) obedience. —溫順な, gentle; mild; meek; obedient. [scale.]

onkai (音階), *n.* 【音】 a (musical)

onkei (恩惠), *n.* favour; beneficence; grace. —恩惠を施す, to bestow favours. ¶ 恩惠日, 【商】 days of grace.

onken (穩健な), *a.* moderate; reasonable; sensible. —穩健な說, a moderate view. —穩健な處置, a moderate measure. ¶ 穩健派, the Moderates [Moderatists]; Mensheviki (露國の).

onketsu-dōbutsu (溫血動物), *n.* a warm-blooded animal.

onko (恩顧), *n.* special favours; patronage.

onkō (溫厚な), *a.* gentle; mild.

onkyō (音響), *n.* a sound; an echo. ¶ 音響學, acoustics.

onkyū (恩給), *n.* a pension. —恩給で暮す, to live on a pension. ¶ 恩給受領者, a pensioner. —恩給局, the pension bureau.

onna (女), *n.* ❶ a woman; a female. ❷ (下婢) a maid-servant. ❸ (情婦) a mistress; a sweetheart. —醒めた女, the awakened woman. —暗い女, a woman with a past. —女の樣な, effeminate; womanish. —女に迷ふ, to be infatuated with a woman. ¶ 女醫者, a woman doctor.

onnaaruji (女主人), *n.* a mistress; a landlady.

onnagata (女形), *n.* 【劇】 an actor who takes female parts.

onnagirai (女嫌ひ), *n.* a misogynist; a woman-hater.

onnakamiyui (女髮結), *n.* a female hair-dresser.

onnamochi (女持の), *a.* a lady's. —女持ちの蝙蝠傘, a lady's umbrella.

onnanoko (女の子), *n.* a baby girl; a female child; a girl.

onnarashii (女らしい), *a.* ❶ womanly; womanlike; ❷ (めめしい) womanish; effeminate.

onnashashō (女車掌), *n.* a girl conductor; a conductress.

onnashibai (女芝居), *n.* a performance given by actresses.

onnatenka (女天下), *n.* petticoatism; petticoat government; female home rule.

onnayakusha (女役者), *n.* an actress.

ono (斧), *n.* an ax, axe; a hatchet (手斧); a chopper.

ōnō (懊惱), *n.* chagrin; agony; anguish (of mind). ☞ ***modae***. —懊惱さす, to mortify (他人を); chagrin. —懊惱する, to groan in the mind.

ononoku (戰く), *vi.* to quiver; shudder; tremble. —恐れをのゝく, to shudder for fear; tremble with fear.

onoono (各), *pron.* each; every one; one and all. ——, *ad.* individually; respectively; each (二者又は以上); either (二者); every (數者各ゝ). —各の, every; respective; each.

onore (己), *pron.* ❶ (自己) I; self; oneself. ❷ (對者) you; yourself. —己を抑へる, to deny oneself. —己を棄てる, to rise above self. —己を以て人を量る, to judge of others by oneself; measure another's corn by one's own bushel.

onozukara (自ら), *ad.* Ⓢ 自づと. naturally; of itself; spontaneously.

onpa (音波), *n.* a sound-wave.

onpu (音符), *n.* 【音】 a note.

onpu (音譜), *n.* ❶ = ***gakufu*** (樂譜). ❷ (蓄音機の) a record.

onpyō-moji (音標文字), *n.* a phonogram; a phonetic character.

onryō (音量), *n.* volume.

onryō (怨靈), *n.* a revengeful ghost. [able; meek.]

onryō (溫良な), *a.* gentle; ami-

onsa (音叉), *n.* a tuning fork.

onsei (音聲), *n.* voice; sound.

onsen (溫泉), *n.* hot-springs. ¶ 溫泉場, a spa; a hot-spring resort; a watering-place. —溫泉宿, a hotel [an inn] at hot-springs.

onsetsu (音節), *n.* a syllable.

onsha (恩赦), *n.* amnesty; pardon.

onshi (恩師), *n.* one's kind teacher; a (respected) teacher.

onshi (恩賜), *n.* an Imperial donation [gift]. —恩賜の銀時計, a silver watch as an Imperial gift. ¶ 恩賜金, an Imperial bounty.

onshin (音信), *n.* a message; communication. ☞ ***inshin***.

onshirazu (恩知らず), *n.* ❶ (忘恩) ingratitude. ❷ (背恩者) an ungrateful person; an ingrate. —恩知らずの, ungrateful.

onshitsu (溫室), *n.* a hothouse; a greenhouse; a conservatory. ¶ 溫室植物, a hothouse plant.

onshō (恩賞), *n.* a reward. —厚き恩賞に與(アズ)かる, to receive a large reward.

onshō (溫床), *n.* a hotbed.
onshoku (溫色), *n.* a warm colour (cold colour の對).
onshū (溫習), *n.* review; exercise; rehearsal (技藝の). —溫習する, to review; go over; rehearse.
onsu (オンス, 兩), *n.* an ounce.
ontai (御大), *n.* a boss; a governor; a guvnor 【卑】.
ontai (溫帶), *n.* the temperate zone. ¶ 溫帶植物, the flora of the temperate zone.
ontaku (恩澤), *n.* beneficence; favour. —恩澤に浴する, to receive favours.
onten (恩典), *n.* grace; special favour; an act of grace. —特別の恩典を以て, by special favour; as a special act of grace.
ontō (穩當な), *a.* ❶ (妥當) proper; appropriate; reasonable. ❷ (溫和) mild; gentle; moderate.
onwa (溫和な), *a.* mild; gentle; genial. —溫和な性質, good [sweet] temper.
onwa (穩和な), *a.* moderate; pacific; temperate. ¶ 穩和派, ①【露】Mensheviki; the minimalist party. ② a moderate party; the Moderates. —穩和黨員, a moderatist; a moderate; a minimalist (露國の).
on̓yoku (溫浴), *n.* a warm bath. —溫浴する, to take a warm bath.
on̓yō (溫容), *n.* a kindly look.
ōō (往往), *ad.* ❶ (時々) sometimes; occasionally; now and then. ❷ (度々) often; frequently.
ōō (怏怏), *ad.* joylessly; in low spirits; despondently. —怏々としてゐる, to be disconsolate; be despondent.
ōoba (大叔母, 大伯母), *n.* a great-aunt; a grand-aunt.
ōoji (大叔父, 大伯父), *n.* a great-uncle; a grand-uncle.
ōoji (大祖父), *n.* a great-grandfather.
ooshii (雄雄しい), *a.* manly; valiant; heroic.
ōotoko (大男), *n.* a big man; a giant.
opera (歌劇), *n.* an opera. ¶ オペラバック, an opera-bag. —オペラグラス, an opera-glass.
ōrai (往來), *n.* ❶ (交通) traffic; intercourse (交際); communication (通信). ❷ (道路) a road; a street; a thoroughfare. —往來で, on the road [street]. —往來する, to go about; come and go; keep company *with* (交る). (往來する人, passers-by.) —(片側) 往來止, "No thoroughfare (on this side)."
ōrai (宜しい), all right.
Oranda (和蘭), *n.* Holland; the Netherlands. ¶ 和蘭語, Dutch. —和蘭人, a Dutchman; a Hollander; a Netherlander.
orekugi (折釘), *n.* a hooked nail; a clench nail; a broken nail (折れた釘).
oreme (折目), *n.* ❶ a mark of breaking. ❷ a folding mark; a crease.
orenji (オレンヂ), *n.* an orange.
ōrenzu (凹レンズ), *n.* a concave lens.
oreru (折れる), *vi.* ❶ (摧け切れる) to break; be broken; give way. ❷ (疊める) to be doubled; be folded. ❸ (轉向) to turn. ❹ (屈する) to yield; give in. —折れて出る, to sing another song. —左に折れる, to turn to the left.
ori (折), *n.* ❶ fold; double. ❷ (折箱) a chip-box; a small wooden box (菓子入など). ¶ 折詰, (food) packed in a chip-box.
ori (折, 機), *n.* an occasion; an opportunity (機會); a moment (瞬間). —この宴會の折に, on this festive occasion. —折にふれて, occasionally; at times; now and then. —折もあらば, if I find an opportunity.
ori (檻), *n.* ❶ a cage; a pen (家畜の); a corral (同上). ❷ (監房) a cell; a cage; a prison.
ori (滓澤), *n.* dregs; lees; settlings.
oriai (折合), *n.* relations (仲); concord (和合); compromise (妥協). —折合ひが惡い, to be at odds *with*; be on bad terms *with*. —折合ひがつく, to come to terms.
oriashiku (折惡く), *ad.* unfortunately; unluckily; as (ill) luck would have it.
oriau (折合ふ), *vi.* ❶ (調和) to agree *with*; get on *with*; pull together *with*. ❷ (妥協) to come to [make] terms *with*; compromise *with*. —人と折り合って行く, to get along with a person. —夫婦仲が折り合はぬ, The couple cannot hit it off together.
oridashi (織出し), *n.* ❶ woven figures. ❷ (織始め) a selvedge.
oridehon (折手本), *n.* a folding copy-book.
orido (折戸), *n.* a folding-door.
orieri (折襟), *n.* a turn-down collar; a lapel.
orifushi (折節), *ad.* ❶ (時々) sometimes; occasionally; now and then. ❷ (丁度其時) just then; at that moment [juncture].
origami (折紙), *n.* ❶ (鑑定書) a certificate. ❷ (手工用の) a folding paper. —折紙附きの, certified; authorized.
orihon (折本), *n.* a folding book; a folder.
oriitte (折入って), *ad.* earnestly;

fervently; zealously. —折入って賴む, to ask earnestly; entreat.
orikaban (折鞄), *n.* a folding bag; a portfolio.
orikaeshi (折返し), *n.* ❶ (物) the lappet. ❷ a burden (詩歌等の); refrain. ❸ (襟の) a lapel; a turn-down. ❹【商·俗】double. ——, *ad.* by return (of post).
orikara (折柄), *ad.* just then; just at the time; at the time when. —折から御多忙中の處, at the time when you are so busy. —氣候不順の折柄, at this unseasonable time of the year. —折柄の烈風に煽られて, fanned by a violent wind then blowing.
orikasanaru (折重なる), *vi.* to overlap; interlap; lie [be folded] one upon another. —折り重って倒れる, to fall down one upon another.
oriko (織子), *n.* a weaver.
orikomu (折込む), *vt.* to turn in; tuck in; make a tuck in.
orikomu (織込む), *vt.* to interweave; weave *into.*
orime (折目), *n.* a fold; a crease (著物などの). —折目をつける, to crease.
orimono (下物), *n.* excretion; discharge.
orimono (織物), *n.* woven goods; cloth; a textile fabric. ¶ 織物市場, cloth-market. —織物消費稅, textile consumption tax.
orinpikku (オリンピック), *n.* Olympic games; Olympiad. —東洋オリンピック大會, the Far Eastern Olympic Meeting.
oriori (折折), *ad.* sometimes; occasionally; now and then; every now and then [again]; from time to time; at intervals; once in a while.
oriru (下·降りる), *vi.* ❶ (降る) to get down; come [go] down; descend. ❷ (下車) to alight *from*; get off; get [step] out *of*. ❸ (霜などが) to fall (霜); settle down (露). ❹ (流產) to miscarry; be delivered prematurely. ❺ (排泄) to be discharged; be excreted. —電車から下りる, to get off a street-car. —山を降りる, to descend a mountain.
orishimo (折しも), *ad.* at that instant [moment]; just then.
oritatamu (折疊む), *vt.* to fold; lap; double up. —折疊みの出來る, collapsible; folding.
oriyu (橄欖), *n.* 【植】 the olive.
oriyoku (折好く), *ad.* fortunately; luckily; happily.
oroka (愚), *n.* foolishness; dulness (遲鈍); illiteracy (無教育). —愚かな, foolish; silly; dull; ignorant. ¶ 愚者, a fool.
oroka (おろか), *ad.* not to mention; to say nothing *of*. —無殘といふもおろかなり, Cruel is too light a word for it.
oroorogoe (おろおろ聲で), in a trembling [broken] voice; in a tearful tone.
oroshi (卸·賣), *n.* wholesale. —卸で, by the gross; (by) wholesale. —卸直段で, at trade [wholesale] price. ¶ 卸店, a wholesale store. —卸商, ① (業) wholesale trade [business]. ② (人) a wholesale-dealer [-merchant].
oroshi (颪), *n.* a wind blowing down a hill.
oroshi (銼器), *n.* a grater.
orosoka (疎な), *a.* negligent; careless; remiss. —疎かに, negligently; carelessly; heedlessly. —疎かにする, to neglect; slight.
orosu (下す), *vt.* ❶ (高所より) to take down; bring down; put down. ❷ (幕等を) to drop; let down; let fall. ❸ (錨を) to drop. ❹ (船を) to launch. ❺ (積荷を) to unload; dismount (馬より); discharge (船荷を). ❻ (帆·旗等を) to douse; lower; take [let] down. ❼ (枝を) to prune off [away]; trim off [away] (下枝を). ❽ (著物の揚げを) to let out (a tuck). ❾ (大根等を擦る) to grate. ❿ (墮胎さす) to procure miscarriage [abortion]. ⓫ (膽石を下す) to pass (a gall-stone). ⓬ (新に使用する) to use for the first time. —旗を下ろす, to dip [lower; strike] a flag. —荷物《乘客》を降[おろ]す, to set a load 《passenger》 down; drop a passenger.
orosu (卸す), *vt.* to sell (by) wholesale.
oru (折る), *vt.* ❶ (枝等を) to break; snap (ぽきりと); fracture (骨を). ❷ (疊む) to fold; double. ❸ (曲げる) to bend. —我を折る, to yield; give in. —頁の端を折る, to dog-ear a page.
oru (居る), *vi.* =*iru* (居る).
oru (織る), *vt.* to weave.
ōru (橈), *n.* an oar.
orugan (オルガン), *n.* an organ.
ōryō (橫領), *n.* embezzlement; misappropriation; dispossession; usurpation. —橫領する, to misappropriate; embezzle; dispossess; seize; usurp.
osa (筬), *n.* a reed; the dents of a reed.
osaeru (抑·押·壓へる), *vt.* ❶ (抑へつける) to press (傷·頭など); hold (頭など); hold down (物の端·人); get under (人). ❷ (抑制) to keep down; keep under; repress; restrain; control; sup-

press; keep [hold] back. ❸ (抑留) to detain; hold. ❹ (差押へる) to seize; attach. ❺ (捕へる) to take; seize; catch. —抑へ難き, uncontrollable; irrepressible. —抑へ附ける, to press [hold] down; keep under; dominate *over*. —目《口》を押へる, to cover one's eyes《mouth》. —馬を押へる, to stop a horse.

osagame (をさがめ), *n.* 【爬蟲】 the leathery turtle.

osaki (お先), *n.* ❶ future. ☞ *saki* (先). ❷ (先棒) a cat's paw; a puppet. —人をお先に使ふ, to make a cat's paw of a man. —どうぞお先へ, After you.

osamari (收り), *n.* settlement; conclusion. —收りをつける, to settle; bring to a conclusion; put an end *to*.

osamaru (收·納まる), *vi.* ❶ (平靜) to calm [quiet] down; settle (down); fall [drop] (風など); be over (すむ). ❷ (解決) to be settled. ❸ (納入) to be paid (in). ❹ (はいる) to be put *into*. ❺ (火事が) to be put out; be got under control. —椅子に納まる, to settle oneself in a chair.

osamaru (治·鎮まる), *vi.* ❶ (國等が) to be peaceful; enjoy peace; be ruled. ❷ (騷動などが) to settle (down); calm down. ❸ (痛みなど) to abate; be soothed; be cured. —よく治まった家庭, a well-regulated family.

osameru (收·納める), *vt.* ❶ (收得) to gain; obtain; take; bring (もたらす); accept (受納). ❷ (納入) to pay (支拂); dedicate (奉納); supply (供給); furnish (同上). ❸ (收藏) to put *in*; store *in*. ❹ (終る) to finish; end. —元へ納める, to replace; put back (a thing in《into》its place). —藏に收める, to store in a godown.

osameru (治める), *vt.* ❶ (統治) to govern; rule (over) (君臨); reign over (同上); manage (a household or a state). ❷ (平定) to quiet; settle; pacify; put down. —家を治める, to manage one's house. —自ら產を治める, to manage one's own affairs.

osameru (修める), *vt.* to study; learn. —身を修める, to become steady; regulate one's conduct. —各國語を修める, to master various languages.

osanagao (幼顏), *n.* the face in childhood; a child's face.

osanago (幼兒), *n.* an infant; a child.

osanagokoro (幼心), *n.* a child's mind.

osanai (幼い), *a.* ❶ (幼年) infant; young; juvenile. ❷ (未熟) green; inexperienced; childish (子供じみた). —幼い頃に, in one's childhood; when infant.

osandon (お爨どん), *n.* a (female) cook; a cookee【俗】.

osaosa (をさをさ), *ad.* ❶ hardly; scarcely. ❷ carefully; diligently.

osaraba (をさらば), *int.* farewell; adieu.

osarai (溫習), *n.* a review.

osato (お里), *n.* nursery. —お里が知れる, to savour of the pan; betray one's origin.

ōsawagi (大騷), *n.* a great uproar; a fuss; a bustle. ☞ *sawagi*. —大騷ぎする, to make a fuss *over*; kick up a row; raise the devil [Cain]. —大騷ぎして, with much ado.

ōse (仰), *n.* a command (命令); an order (同上); words (話). —仰せに從ひ, according to your command; in obedience to your orders.

ōsei (王政), *n.* ❶ royal [imperial] government. ❷ (王國の) monarchy. ¶ 王政復古, the Restoration.

ōsei (旺盛), *n.* a flourishing [prosperous] condition [state]. —旺盛な, vigorous; prosperous. —元氣旺盛である, to be in high spirits. —賣行き頗る旺盛である, to have a very large sale.

ōseishi (王世子), *n.* a crown prince; the heir to the throne.

osekkai (お切匙), *n.* ❶ (事) meddlesomeness; officiousness. ❷ (人) a busybody; a meddler. —お切匙をする, to have [put; shove] one's [an] oar in a person's boat; poke [put; thrust] one's nose into (an affair).

ōsen (橫線), *n.* 【數】 an abscissa; a horizontal line; a cross line. ¶ 橫線引小切手, a crossed check.

ōsen (應戰する), *vi.* to reply [respond] to a fire; accept a battle.

ōseru (終せる), *vi.* to be able *to*; can; succeed (*in*). —隱しおほせぬ, to be unable to keep it secret to the end.

ōsetsu (應接), *n.* ❶ (もてなし) reception. ❷ (面會) audience. —應接する, to receive; meet. ¶ 應接室, a drawing-room; a reception-room; a lobby (議會などの). —應接時間, a call-hour; an at-home hour.

ōsetsukeru (仰附ける), *vt.* to order; command.

oshaberi (お饒舌, お喋), *n.* ❶ (事) chatter; prattle; idle talk.

❷ (人) a chatterbox; a tattler; a rattler. —お饒舌する, to chatter; rattle; wag one's chin. —お喋りはやめなさい, Hold your jaw [tongue]!

oshi (押, 壓), *n.* ❶ (押, 壓) push; pressure. ❷ (重み, 貫祿) authority; weight. ❸ (圖々しさ) hardihood; audacity. ❹ (取引市場) a fall. —押しの强い, = ***oshizuyoi***. —押しが利[*]く, to be able to exercise one's authority. — 一押し押す, to give a push *at*.

oshi (啞), *n.* ❶ dumbness; muteness. ❷ (啞者) a dumb; a mute; a deaf-mute (聾啞者).

ōshi (橫死), *n.* a violent [an unnatural] death. —橫死を遂げる, to die a violent death.

oshiageru (押上げる), *vt.* to push [force] up; throw up.

oshiau (押合ふ), *vi.* to jostle [push] one another; hustle.

oshiakeru (押開ける), *vt.* to fling open; push [force] open.

oshibe (雄蕊), *n.* a stamen.

oshibotan (押釦), *n.* a push-button.

oshidashi (押出し), *n.* ❶ (突出し) pushing out of the ring. ❷ (衆人の中へ出ての態度·風采) appearance; presence. —押出しのいい人, a man of fine [commanding] presence. —押し出す, to push out; force out; thrust out; elbow out; push forward.

oshideru (押出る), *vi.* to force one's way out.

oshidori (鴛鴦), *n.* 【鳥】 the mandarin duck.

oshie (敎), *n.* teaching; instruction; a precept (敎訓). —敎を受ける, to be taught *by*; receive one's lesson; take lesson *in* (*of*).

oshie (押繪), *n.* a pasted rag-picture.

oshiego (敎子), *n.* one's pupil.

oshiekata (敎方), *n.* a method [manner] of teaching.

oshieru (敎へる), *vt.* ❶ to teach; instruct; give lesson (*in*). ❷ (敎示) to tell; inform; show. —道を敎へる, to show a person the way. —場所を敎へる, to point a place to a person. —本を敎へる, to read a book with one's pupils.

oshigaru (惜しがる), *vt.* to grudge. ☞ ***oshimu***.

oshige (惜氣なく), *ad.* unsparingly; ungrudgingly; without stint. —惜氣も無く金を使ふ, to squander money ungrudgingly.

oshihakaru (推量る), *vt.* ❶ to conjecture; infer. ❷ to enter into (another's feelings).

oshihiromeru (推弘める), *vt.* ❶ (弘める) to spread; extend; propagate. ❷ (敷衍) to amplify; enlarge *on*.

oshii (惜しい), *a.* ❶ (殘念) regrettable. ❷ (大切) precious; worthy; ill-spared. —惜しいことには, it is a pity that...; it is to be regretted that... —命が惜しいなら, if you value your life.

oshiire (押入), *n.* a closet; a wardrobe

oshiiru (押入る), *vi.* to break into.

oshikakeru (押掛ける), *vt.* to force oneself *into*; go uninvited; force one's company *upon*. ¶ 押掛客, an unbidden [uninvited] guest; a surprise party. —押掛女房, a woman who forces herself into a house as wife.

oshikiri (押切), *n.* a straw-cutter. ¶ 押切帳, a receipt-book.

oshikomeru (押込める), *vt.* ❶ (詰める) to press [force; push] *in*. ❷ (禁錮する) to shut [pent] up; imprison; confine. —やたらに押込める, to overcrowd.

oshikomi (押込), *n.* ❶ (押入) a closet; a wardrobe. ❷ (强盜) a robber; a burglar.

oshikomu (押込む), *vt.* to press *into*; force *into*; push *into*. —抽斗に押し込む, to shove it into the drawer.

oshikorosu (壓殺す), *vt.* to press [squeeze] to death.

oshikowasu (押毀す), *vt.* to break by pushing; burst in (押し毀して入る).

oshime (襁褓), *n.* a diaper. ☞ ***mutsuki***.

oshimodosu (押戾す), *vt.* to push back.

oshimondō (押問答), *n.* repeated questions and answers.

oshimu (惜む), *vt.* ❶ (重んず) to value; esteem. ❷ (悲む) to regret; lament (哀悼). ❸ (吝) to grudge; be chary (*of*); stint. —惜むべき人, a person whom one can ill spare. —惜みても餘りある, never-enough-to-be-regretted. —費用を惜まず, without regard to the expense. —寸陰を惜む, to value time. —勞を惜む, to grudge pains; stint labour.

ōshin (往診), *n.* a visit to a patient. —往診する, to attend a patient at his house. ¶ 往診料, the doctor's fee for a visit.

oshinabete (押竝べて), *ad.* generally; in general; on the whole [an average].

oshinagasu (押流す), *vt.* to wash [carry; sweep] away.

oshinokeru (押退ける), *vt.* to push away [aside]; thrust aside [off]; elbow aside (肘で). —一人

を押しのけて通る, to elbow [force] one's way through the crowd.

ōshio (大潮), *n.* a spring-tide.

oshiroi (白粉), *n.* (toilet) powder; face-paint. ¶ 水白粉, liquid face-paint. —煉白粉, face-paste. —紙白粉, *papier poudre* 【佛】. —白粉をつける, to paint; powder.

oshiroibana (紫茉莉), *n.* 【植】 the marvel-of-Peru; the false jalap.

oshisōni (惜しさうに), *ad.* stintingly; grudgingly.

oshisusumeru (押進める), *vt.* to push; impel; drive.

oshitaosu (押倒す), *vt.* to push [force] down; bear down.

oshitateru (押立てる), *vt.* to hoist; set up. —旗を眞先に押し立てる, to put up a flag at the head [van].

oshite (押して), *ad.* ❶ (拘らず) in spite of. ❷ (たって) insistently; importunately; earnestly. —病を押して, in spite of one's illness. —押して頼む, to press a request; importune.

oshite (推して), judging *from*; inferring *from*. ☞ *osu* (推す). —餘は推して知るべし, The rest may be inferred.

oshitōsu (押通す), *vt.* ❶ (貫徹) to push through; carry through. ❷ (主張) to insist *on*; persist to the end [last] *in*. ❸ (我慢) to endure through. ☞ *tōsu* (通す). —其の心掛で押し通すがよい, You had better keep that spirit to the end.

oshitsubusu (壓潰す), *vt.* to crush; squeeze to pieces.

oshitsukeru (押附ける), *vt.* ❶ (壓迫) to press *against*; push [thrust] *against*. ❷ (强ひる) to force *upon*. ❸ (掴ます) to impose *upon*; palm off. —押し附けがましい話ですが, though I may appear to wish to have my own way. —壁へ押しつける, to press against the wall. —金を押し附ける, to force [press] money upon a person.

oshitsumaru (押詰まる), *vi.* to be close *upon*; be near at hand; be near its [the] close.

oshiuri (押賣する), *vt.* to press (a person) to buy; thrust (a thing) *on* (a person); force (goods) *upon* (a person).

oshiutsuru (推移る), *vi.* to pass away; elapse; change.

oshiwakeru (押分ける), *vt.* to push apart; push through. —人込を押し分けてゆく, to push [force; elbow] one's way through the crowd.

oshiyaburu (押破る), *vt.* to force [push] open (戸等を); break by pushing. —戸を押し破る, to burst the door open.

oshiyoseru (押寄せる), *v.* ❶ to press [push] near; push [press] forward; advance [march] *on*; come dashing (浪など). ❷ (物を) to push *into* (a corner).

oshizuyoi (押强い), *a.* ❶ (しつこい) pertinacious; stubborn. ❷ (大膽な) audacious; bold.

oshō (和尙), *n.* an abbot; a Buddhist priest; a bonze.

ōsho (凹所), *n.* a pit; a hollow; a depression; a concavity.

ōshō (鞅掌する), *v.* ❶ to be engaged *in*; be busy *with*; be occupied *in* [*with*]. ❷ (司る) to manage; administer.

Ōshū (歐洲), *n.* Europe. ¶ 歐洲大陸, the continent of Europe.

ōshū (押收する), *vt.* to seize; impound.

ōshū (應酬する), *vt.* to reply; respond (應答); retaliate (返報).

ōsōdō (大騷動), *n.* a great confusion; a riot; a serious disturbance. ☞ *sōdō*.

ōsō (押送する), *vt.* to send under guard.

osoi (遲い), *a.* ❶ (時間) late; behind time (遲刻). ❷ (遲鈍, 緩慢) slow; tardy; dull. —歸りが遲い, to be long in coming home; be a long time gone.

ōsōji (大掃除), *n.* general cleaning. —大掃除をする, to carry out general cleaning.

osokare-hayakare (晚かれ早かれ), *ad.* =*sōban*.

osoku (遲く), *ad.* ❶ (時間) late. ❷ (緩慢) slowly; tardidly. —こんなに遲く, so late; at this time of day 《night》. —遲くとも, at (the) latest [farthest]. —遲くなる, to be [get] late; be behind time; slow down (速力等が).

osomaki (遲蒔), *n.* ❶ (種の) late-sown seeds. ❷ (事の) a day after the fair. —今更遲蒔だが, it is late now; but....

osorakuwa (恐らくは), *ad.* perhaps; probably; possibly. —恐らくは本當でせう, I am afraid that it is true.

osore (恐, 懼, 畏, 虞), *n.* ❶ 【恐】 fear; terror; dread. ❷ 【懼】 = *ojike*. ❸ 【畏】 fear; fright. ❹ apprehension; anxiety; concern. —...の虞あり, to be menaced [threatened] *with*; be in danger *of*. —將來紛議を醸す虞あり, to promise future troubles. —風をひく虞がある, There is the risk of his catching cold.

osoreiru (恐入る), *vi.* ❶ (恐縮)

to feel small; be abashed (恥入る); be filled with awe. ❷ (服罪) to plead guilty; acknowledge one's guilt. ❸ (多謝) to be very sorry; be greatly obliged. ❹ (閉口) to be embarrassed; be troubled [annoyed]. —毎度恐れ入りますが, sorry to trouble you so often, but.... —恐れ入りました, ① (服罪) I throw myself on your mercy; I plead guilty. ② (降參) I throw up the sponge; I give in; You have me! —どうも恐れ入ります, (I am) much obliged to you.

osorenagara (恐れ乍ら), *ad.* most humbly [respectfully]; I beg to state.

osoreōi (畏多い), *a.* august; awe-inspiring. —畏多くも, graciously. —申すも畏多いことである, It is to be said with due reverence.

osoreononoku (恐戰く), *vi.* to shudder for [tremble with] fear.

osoreru (恐れる), *v.* to fear; be afraid *of*; dread. —畏れしめる, to keep [hold] in awe; terrify; appal. —山なす浪をも恐れず, fearless of high waves.

osoroshii (恐しい), *a.* ❶ (恐い) fearful; dreadful; terrible. ❷ (猛しい) fierce; ferocious; savage. ❸ (非常な) very; tremendous; formidable; awful 【俗】. ❹ (凄じい) formidable; appalling. —恐しい力, stupendous power. —恐しい險幕, black looks; a threatening attitude. —恐しい人出, a tremendous turn-out of people. —恐しい勢で, with terrible [furious] energy [force].

osoroshiku (恐しく), *ad.* fearfully; terribly; dreadfully; awfully 【俗】. 「—或は恐る, I fear.」

osoru (恐る), *v.* =*osoreru.*

osorubeki (恐るべき), *a.* dreadful; terrible. ☞ *osoroshii.*

osou (襲ふ), *vt.* ❶ (攻める) to attack; assail; assault. ❷ (繼ぐ) to succeed; inherit. —沿岸を襲ふ, to come down [descend] upon the coast. —魔窟を襲ふ (巡査が), to make a raid on a suspected den. —城を襲ひ取る, to take a fort by assault.

osowareru (襲はれる), *vi.* ❶ (襲擊) to be attacked [assailed]. ❷ (惡夢に) to have [be oppressed by] (a nightmare). —恐怖に襲はれる, to be seized with a panic. —暴風雨に襲はれる, to be caught in a storm (逢ふ); be visited by a storm.

osowaru (敎はる), *vi.* to be taught; learn; take lessons *in.*

osozaki (遲咲), *n.* blooming late; a late flower.

osu (牡, 雄), *n.* a male.

osu (押す), *vt.* ❶ (突押) to push; thrust; shove; jostle. ❷ (押壓) to press; compress; squeeze. ❸ =*ōnatsu* (押捺する). —押し伏せる, to force (a man) down on the face. —後から押す, to push from behind. —押しも押されもせぬ商人, a respectful [wealthy] merchant; a merchant of established fame.

osu (推す), *vt.* ❶ (推擧) to recommend; elect; choose. ❷ (推測) to guess; infer [deduce] *from*; judge *from*; gather *from*. ☞ *oshite*. —推されて議長となる, to be put in the president's chair.

ōsugiru (多過ぎる), *a.* too many; excessive. ,—, *vi.* to be in excess; be too many 《much》.

osui (汚水), *n.* foul water; sewage. ¶ 汚水管, a soil pipe.

osuramu (オスラム燈), *n.* an osram-lamp.

otafuku (お多福), *n.* a moon-faced woman; an ugly woman (醜女). ¶ おたふく風, 【醫】 parotitis; mumps.

ōtai (應對), *n.* an interview (面接); a conference (面談); a reply (應答). —應對する, to interview; receive; confer *with*. —應對振りの旨い人, a man of good address.

ōtai (橫隊), *n.* a line; a rank.

otamajakushi (お玉杓子), *n.* ❶ a wooden table-spoon. ❷ (蝌蚪) a tadpole.

otamaya (お靈屋), *n.* a mausoleum.

otamegokashi (お爲ごかしに), *ad.* under the cloak of kindness; with a show of kindness; with simulated kindness. —お爲ごかしにする, to do a thing for a man under the cloak of kindness.

ōtatemono (大立物), *n.* =*ōdatemono*.

otazunemono (お尋者), *n.* a person sought by the police; a fugitive from justice.

ōte (大手), *n.* ❶ the front castle-gate. ❷ (取引市場) a large speculator.

ōte (王手), *n.* & *int.* check. —王手をする, to check; checkmate (最後の王手をする); mate (同上).

ōtei (押丁), *n.* a jailer, gaoler; a turnkey.

otemotokin (御手許金), *n.* the Privy Purse (皇室の).

oten (汚點), *n.* a blot; a taint; a stain. —拭ふべからざる汚點, an ineffaceable blot. —汚點をつける, to spot; fleck.

ōten (橫轉する), *vi.* to turn sideways.

otenba (お轉婆な), *a.* romping; pert; forward. ¶ お轉婆娘, a romping girl; a tomboy; a hoyden.

otenomono (お手の物), *n.* one's forte; one's speciality; something in one's line.

oteyawaraka (お手柔かに), *ad.* gently; leniently. —お手柔かに願ひます, Don't be hard on me!

oto (音), *n.* ❶ (音響) a sound; a noise (騒音). ❷ (音調) tone; tune. ❸ =*otosata*. —鐵砲の音, a report of a gun. —音を立てる, to make sounds; make a noise.

ōto (嘔吐), *n.* vomiting. —嘔吐する, to vomit; turn up. —嘔吐を催さす, ① to make sick. ② [*a.*] (*a*) (食物) mawkish; queasy: (*b*) (嫌惡) nauseating; disgusting; loathsome.

ōtō (王黨), *n.* the Royalists; the monarchical party.

ōtō (應答), *n.* a reply; an answer. —應答する, to reply; answer; make an answer [a reply].

ōtobai (オートバイ), *n.* an autocycle; a motor-cycle; an autobi.

otogai (頤), *n.* the chin; the lower jaw. —人の頤を解く, to make a person laugh.

otogi (お伽), *n.* =*togi* (伽). ¶ お伽噺, a fairy tale; a nursery [household] tale; a juvenile story.

otoko (男), *n.* ❶ (男子) a man; a male. ❷ (一個の男子) a man. ❸ (大人) manhood; an adult; a full man. ❹ (男の意氣) manhood; manliness. ❺ (下男) a man-servant; a man. ❻ (情夫) a lover; a paramour (密夫). ❼ (奴) a fellow; a chap. —面白い男, a jolly fellow. —男になる, ① to become a man. ② to come of age; arrive at manhood. —一人前の男にする, to make a man *of*. —男と見こんで頼む, to ask by relying on another's manly spirit; appeal to another as a man. —男(振)を上げる, to look handsome: raise one's reputation.

otokoburi (男振), *n.* Ⓢ 男前. (personal) appearance; looks. —男振りのよい人, a good-looking man; a handsome man.

otokodate (男伊達), *n.* ❶ (俠氣) chivalry; gallantry. ❷ (人) a chivalrous man.

otokogi (俠氣), *n.* chivalry; gallantry; manly spirit. —俠氣のある, chivalrous; gallant; manly.

otokogirai (男嫌), *n.* a man-hater.

otokomasari (男優りの), *a.* manly; manlike; strong-minded; stout-hearted. —男優りの女, a woman of masculine spirit; a spirited woman.

otokonoko (男の子), *n.* a boy-child; a boy.

otokorashii (男らしい), *a* manly; manlike; virile. —男らしく振舞ふ, to play the man; behave oneself like a man.

otokoyamome (鰥), *n.* ❶ a widower. ❷ (獨身者) a bachelor; a single man.

otome (少女, 乙女), *n.* a maiden; a damsel; a virgin (處女).

ōtomiru (オートミル), *n.* oatmeal.

otona (大人), *n.* manhood; an adult; a grown-up person; a full man. —大人になる, to arrive at manhood; grow up to a man; come of age (丁年に達する).

otonaburu (大人振る), *vi.* to assume a grown-up person's airs.

otonagenai (大人げない), *a.* unmanly; childish; puerile.

otonashii (おとなしい), *a.* quiet; gentle; tractable; well-behaved (行儀のよい). —おとなしく, gently; quietly. —おとなしくせよ, Be a good child!; Behave yourself!; Be quiet! (靜に).

ōtoporo (自動車打球), *n.* auto-polo.

otori (媒鳥, 囮), *n.* a call-bird; a decoy(-bird). —囮になる, to play booty.

otoroeru (衰へる), *vi.* ❶ (衰弱) to become [grow] weak; languish; fall (元氣が); fail (健康·視力など). ❷ (衰微) to decline; wane; decay; wither (凋落); fade (同上). —氣力が衰へる, to become low in spirit. —店が衰へる, The shop goes down.

otoru (劣る), *vi.* to be inferior *to*; be worse than; fall behind. —劣らぬ, to be as good as; compare favourably *with*. —誰にも劣らない, to be second to none; fall behind none.

otōsan (お父さん), *n.* father; papa; dad, dada, daddy.

otosata (音沙汰), *n.* news; tidings; information. —何の音沙汰もなく, without news of any kind: without any notice.

otoshi (落し), *n.* ❶ (火鉢の) a false bottom. ❷ [阱] a trap. = *otoshiana*. ❸ = *ochi* (落).

otoshiana (陷穽), *n.* a (pit) fall; a pit; a trap.

otoshibanashi (落話), *n.* a story ending in a word-play. ☞ *rakugo*.

otoshiireru (陷れる), *vt.* ❶ to entice [decoy] *in*; entrap; ensnare. ❷ (陷落) to capture; take. —人を陷れんとして自ら陷る, to be hoist with one's own petard.

otoshimono (落物), *n.* a thing dropped [lost] on the road.

otosu (落す), *vt.* ❶ (墜落) to drop; let fall; throw down. ❷ (脱漏) to omit; leave out; pass over (見落す). ❸ (失ふ) to lose; drop. ❹ (貶する) to reduce; degrade. ❺ (攻略) to capture; take. —聲を落す, to drop [lower] one's voice. —信用を落す, to sink in another's estimation; shake one's credit; lose one's credit. —紙入を落す, to lose a pocket-book.

otōto (弟), *n.* a (younger) brother.

ototoi (一昨日), *n.* the day before yesterday.

ototoshi (去去年), *n.* the year before last.

ōtotsu (凹凸), *n.* unevenness; irregularity; raggedness. —凹凸ある, ragged; uneven; irregular.

otozure (音信), *n.* news; tidings; message. —喜ばしい音信, joyful [glad] tidings. —音信がない, to have no news *from*; receive no tidings *from*. —音信をする, to write (a letter) *to*.

otozureru (訪る), *vt.* to call *on* (a person); call *at* (a place); visit; drop in (不意に).

otsu (乙), *n.* ❶ (順序の第二) the second; B. ❷【音】(低音) bass. —おつな, ① (奇態な) strange; odd. ② (妙味ある) smart; spicy. —おつに, strangely; stylishly; smartly. (おつにすまし込む, to look strangely prim.)

otsuge (お告), *n.* an oracle; a revelation. —神のお告を蒙る, to receive a divine revelation.

otsuki (お附), *n.* a person in waiting (侍者); an attendant (從者); a page; a squire.

otsukuri (化粧), *n.* toilet; make-up. —化粧をする, to make one's toilet.

otsuya (乙夜の覽), ☞ *itsuya*.

otte (追手), *n.* a pursuer; a chaser; a pursuing party [force].

otte (追て), *ad.* later on; in a little while; by and by. —追ッて命令《通知》するまで, until further order 《notice》. ¶ 追て書《P》, a postscript [PS.; P.S.].

otto (夫), *n.* a husband. —夫ある身, a married woman. —夫を迎へる, to get [take] a husband.

otto (おッと), *int.* oh. —おッと危い, Oh, look out.

ottori (おッとりした), *a.* ❶ (膽汁質の) phlegmatic; dull. ❷ (大様な) generous. ❸ (落著ある) calm; quiet; reposeful (檢など).

ottosei (膃肭獸), *n.* 【哺乳】 the (northern) fur-seal.

ottsu-kattsu (追ッつ勝ッつ), *ad.* ❶ (似たり寄ッたり) closely; much the same; almost equal. ❷ (際どい時間に) in the nick of time. —おッつかッつの勝負, a close contest. —おッつかッつの年頃, about the same age.

ottsuke (おッつけ), *ad.* soon; presently; before long.

ou (生ふ), *vi.* to grow.

ou (負ふ), *vt.* ❶ (背負ふ) to bear; carry on one's back. ❷ (受ける) to receive; sustain; suffer. ❸ (負ふ所あり) to owe *to*; be indebted *to*; be in debt *to*. ❹ (引受ける) to bear; assume; take upon oneself; take upon one's shoulders. —國家に對して負へる義務, the duty which one owes to one's country. —に負ふ所多大なり, to owe in great part *to*. —重荷《責》を負ふ, to bear a burden 《the blame》. —借財を負ふ, to be burdened with debts.

ou (追·逐ふ), *vt.* ❶ (逐拂ふ) to drive away; turn out. ❷ (驅る, 馭す) to drive. ❸ (追掛ける) to pursue; run after; chase. —國外に追ふ, to banish from the country. —日を逐うて, in course of time. —快樂を追ふ, to pursue pleasure. —名利を追ふ, to run after wealth and fame.

ōu (蔽·覆·掩·被·蓋ふ), *vt.* ❶ (蓋ふ) to cover; veil; overspread. ❷ (遮る) to screen; shade. ❸ (匿す) to hide; conceal; dissemble. ❹ (包む) to wrap; envelop; mantle. —掩ふべからざる事實, a patent [broad] fact; a stern reality. —雲に覆はれる, to be overspread with clouds. —事實を掩ふ, to disguise a fact. —人の目を覆ふ, to hoodwink. —顏を掩ふ, to cover one's face.

ouma (牡馬), *n.* a horse; a stallion (種馬).

ōumi (大海), *n.* Ⓢ 大海原. a great sea; an ocean.

ōurisabaki (大賣捌), *n.* wholesale; a wholesale dealer 《shop》.

ōuridashi (大賣出), *n.* a great opening sale. —大賣出をする, to open a great sale.

oushi (牡牛), *n.* a bull; an ox.

outadokoro (御歌所), *n.* the Imperial Poetry Bureau. ¶ 御歌所寄人, a Commissioner of the Imperial Poetry Bureau.

outakai (御歌會), *n.* a poetical party at the Palace. ¶ 新年御歌會, the Imperial Poetical Party for the New Year.

ōvākōto (外套), *n.* an overcoat.

ōvāshūsu (外靴), *n.* overshoes.

owai (汚穢), *n.* night-soil. ¶ 汚穢屋, a nightman.
owareru (追はれる), *v.* ❶ (追迫) to be pursued; be chased; be pressed. ❷ (追放) to be expelled; be driven out. —事務に追はれる, to be pressed with business.
owari (終), *n.* end; close; conclusion. —終まで, to the last; to the end; to the bitter end. (芝居を終りまで見る, to sit out a play.) —終に臨んで, in conclusion. —終に近づく, to draw to a close. —終を告げる, to come to the end; wind up.
owaru (終る), *vi.* to (come to an) end; close; be over. ☞ *oeru*. —失敗に終る, to end in failure.
ōwashi (羌鷲), *n.* 【鳥】 Steller's sea-eagle.
owasu (負はす), *vt.* ❶ (擔はす) to make a person bear. ❷ (負擔さす) to burden *with*; charge *with*; impose *upon*. ❸ (被せる) to charge *on*; impose *on*; lay [put; fix] *on*; lay at a person's door. ❹ (蒙らす) to inflict; give. —重傷を負はせる, to inflict a severe wound *on*.
oya (親), *n.* ❶ parents. ❷ (骨牌の) the dealer; a banker. —親の威光, parental authority. —親の脛をかじる, to depend on one's father. —此親にして此子あり, "Like father, like son." —親の因果が子に報ふ, "The sins of the father are visited on the children."
oya (おや), *int.* oh!; dear me!; oh dear! —おやまあ (驚いた), well, to be sure!; well, I declare!
ōya (大屋), *n.* a landlord; the owner of a rented house.
oyabun (親分), *n.* the boss; the chief; the master.
oyadama (親玉), *n.* the chief; the ringleader (暴動等の); the boss [卑].
oyafune (親船), *n.* a depot-ship; a parent ship.
oyagakari (親がかり), *n.* dependence on one's father.
oyaginkō (親銀行), *n.* the parent bank.
oyagokoro (親心), *n.* a parent's heart [feelings].
oyaji (親父), *n.* ❶ (父) father; governor (guvnor と略す); pater [學生語]. ❷ (老爺) an old man [boy; fellow]; an elderly man.
oyakabu (親株), *n.* ❶ (母樹(ぼじゅ)) a stool. ❷ (株式の) the parent stock.
oyakata (親方), *n.* a master; a chief; a boss.
ōyake (公の), *a.* public; open; official (公式の, 官廳に關はる). —公の場所で, in public; in a public place. —— -**ni**, *ad.* publicly; openly; in public. —公にする, to make public; bring to light; announce. —(財政上)の意見を公にする, to ventilate one's opinion on (finance).
oyako (親子), *n.* parent and child; father and son. ¶ 親子喧嘩, a quarrel between parent and child.
oyakoroshi (親殺し), *n.* a parricide; a patricide 《matricide》.
oyamoto (親元), *n.* parental roof; home. —親元の善い人, a man of good parentage.
oyanashi (親無の), *a.* parentless; orphan. ¶ 親無し子, an orphan
oyaomoi (親思), *n* ❶ (事) filial affection. ❷ (人) a good [dutiful] son 《daughter》.
oyashio (親潮), *n.* the Kurile Current.
oyashirazu (親知らず, 智齒), *n.* a wisdom-tooth.
ōyasuuri (大安賣), *n.* a great bargain; selling at a bargain. ¶ 大安賣日, a bargain day.
oyatsu (お八), *n.* afternoon refreshment 《tea》.
oyayubi (拇指), *n.* the thumb; the big toe (拇趾).
oyayuzuri (親讓りの), *a.* hereditary; inherited; patrimonial. —親讓りの財產, a patrimony.
ōyō (應用), *n.* application. —應用する, to apply; put in practice. ¶ 應用科學, applied science. —應用問題, a problem for application.
ōyō (大樣·鷹揚な), *a.* generous; magnanimous; large-hearted. —大樣に, generously; open-handedly; magnanimously.
oyobanai (及ばない), *vi.* ❶ (匹敵せぬ) to be inferior *to*; not to match; be short *of*. ❷ (達せぬ) not to reach; not to come up *to*. ❸ (必要なし) not to need; be unnecessary; be needless. —遠く及ばない, to be behind (another); be nothing like [near] as good as (another). —言ふに及ばない, It need scarcely be said that; It goes without saying; needless to say (多く插句的に). —是非に及ばぬ, There is no help for it. —筆にも口にも及ばぬ, to beggar description. —急ぐには及ばぬ, There is no occasion [need] for haste [hurry].
oyobazunagara (乍不及), *ad.* with my poor ability [power]. —及ばず乍ら御盡力致しませう, I will do what little I can.
oyobi (及び), *conj.* and; as well as.
oyobosu (及ぼす), *vt.* ❶ (感化·

影響などを) to have *upon*; exercise; work. ❷ (擴める) to extend. —衆に及ぼす, to extend to all. —に影響を及ぼす, to have influence *upon*; affect; influence; act [work; operate] *upon*. —人に感化を及ぼす, to work upon a person 《his mind》.

oyobu (及ぶ), *v.* ❶ (達する) to attain *to*; reach; come *to*; extend *to*; stretch *to*; turn *on* (談が). ❷ (匹敵する) to be equal *to*; match; compare *with*; touch *in*. ❸ (能ふ) to be able *to*; lie in [be within] one's power [ability]. —及ぶかぎり, to the utmost [best] of one's ability; as much as one can do. —及びもつかぬ, to be beyond one's reach 《power》. —調査するに及んで, on examination. —海外に及ぶ (勢力など), to extend beyond the seas.

oyogi (游泳), *n.* swimming.

oyogu (泳ぐ), *vi.* to swim; sail (魚·水鳥等の). —泳ぎ著く, to swim to a point. —伏して《仰向に; 横に》泳ぐ, to swim on one's chest 《back; side》. —よく泳ぐ者はよく溺る, "Good swimmers are oftenest drowned."

oyoso (凡), *ad.* ❶ (おしなべて) generally; usually; on the whole. ❷ (約) about; almost; approximately; roundly; in round numbers. —凡その, rough; approximate; general. —凡そ一千磅, something like £1000.

ōyuki (大雪), *n.* a heavy (fall of) snow; a heavy snowfall.

ōzakenomi (大酒飲), *n.* a strong [heavy] drinker.

ozanari (お座なりを云ふ), *v.* to tune one's talk to the company.

ōzappa (大ざっぱの), *a.* ❶ (物惜みせぬ) profuse; lavish; unstinting. ❷ (大凡の) rough; loose. —大ざっぱに, ① profusely; lavishly; unstintingly. ② roughly.

ōzei (大勢), *n.* a multitude; a large force; a large crowd (群集); a large company. —大勢の, a large [great] number *of*; large. (大勢の家族, a large family.) —大勢でやって來る, to come [appear] in force.

ōzeki (大關), *n* a head-wrestler.

ōzoku (王族), *n.* the royal family.

ozōn (オゾーン), *n.* 【化】 ozone.

ōzora (大空), *n.* the sky; the heavens. ☞ ***sora.***

ōzukami (大掴みに), *ad.* roughly; in gross. —大掴みに言へば, roughly speaking.

ōzume (大詰), *n.* the end; the conclusion; 【劇】 the catastrophe.

ozuozu (怯怯), *ad.* timidly; with fear; trembling with fear.

ō-zuru (應ずる), *v.* =***ō-jiru.***

P

pachin (ぱちんと), *ad.* with a snap [click; crack].

pachipachi (ぱちぱち), *n.* crick-crack; crackle. —ぱちぱちはねる, to crack and snap.

pai (パイ), *n.* a pie.

painappuru (鳳梨), *n.* a pine-apple.

paipu (管), *n.* a pipe; a cigarette 《cigar》-holder (煙管).

pakuri (ぱくりと), *ad.* Ⓢ ぱっくりと. with a snap. —ぱくりと食ふ《喰ひつく》, to snap up 《at》.

pan (麵麭), *n.* bread. —パンの爲に働く, to work for bread. —パンを奪ふ, to take the bread out of a person's mouth. ¶ 軍用パン, ammunition bread. —パン粉, dough; flour; breadstuff. —麵麭屋, a baker (人); a bakery (場所).

Panama (パナマ), *n.* Panama. ¶ パナマ帽, a Panama-hat; a Panama.

panfuretto (小冊子), *n.* a pamphlet.

panku (パンクする), *vi.* to puncture; suffer [sustain] a puncture; punk 【卑】.

panorama (パノラマ), *n.* a panorama.

pantogurafu (圖畫伸縮器, 寫圖器), *n.* a pantograph.

papa (父), *n.* papa.

pappu (罨布), *n.* a poultice; a cataplasm.

parachibusu (パラ窒扶斯), *n.* 【醫】 paratyphus.

paradaisu (極樂, 樂園), *n.* a paradise.

parafin (パラフィン), *n.* Ⓢ パラピン. paraffine.

parapara (ぱらぱら降る), *vi.* to sprinkle; fall in drops. —雨がパラパラと窓にあたる, The rain patters on the window. ¶ パラパラ雨, a sprinkle.

parashūto (落下傘), *n.* a parachute.

parasoru (日傘), *n.* a parasol.

Paresutina (パレスティナ), *n.* Palestine.

Pari (巴里), *n.* Paris. —巴里の, Parisian. ¶ 巴里人, a Parisian.

paripari (ぱりぱり), *n.* a man of influence; the best. —江戸ッ子のぱりぱり, a true *Yedokko*; a typical man of *Yedo*.

pāru (眞珠), *n.* pearl.

parupu (パルプ), *n.* pulp.

pāsento (パーセント), per cent.

pasha (總督), *n.* 【土耳其】 a pasha.

passēji-sutoa (通拔店), *n.* a

passage store.
pasu (パス), *n.* a (free) pass (無賃乘車券, 無料入場券); a season ticket (定期乘車券). **—— -suru** *vt.* (合格, 通過) to pass.
pasuteru (パステル), *n.* pastel. ¶ パステル畫, a pastel.
patan (ばたん), *n.* bang. —戶がバタンと締まる, A door shuts with a bang.
patchiri (ぱっちり), *ad.* wide; bright. —眼をパッチリ開ける, to open one's eyes wide.
patē (油灰), *n.* putty.
pattari (ぱったり), *ad.* ❶ (突然) suddenly; all of a sudden. ❷ (全く) completely. —ぱったり泣き止む, to stop crying abruptly. —ぱったり出會ふ, to chance *upon*. —商賣がぱったり止った, Business came to a standstill.
patto (ぱっと), *ad.* ❶ with a flash. ❷ (突然) suddenly. ❸ (速に) rapidly; in a flash. —ぱッと燃える, to flare up.
pedaru (踏子), *n.* a pedal.
peipei (ぺいぺい), *a.* inferior; low-class; green. ¶ ぺいぺい役者, a utility-man; a super 〔卑〕.
pējento (公共劇), *n.* a pageant.
pēji (頁), *n.* a page.
peke (ぺけ), no use; no go.
pekopeko (ぺこぺこする), *vi.* to bow frequently; truckle.
pen (ペン), *n.* a pen. ¶ ペン畫, a pen and ink drawing. —ペン軸, a penholder. —ペン尖, a pen-point; a nib. —ペン習字, lessons in penmanship (for writing Japanese characters).
pengin (ペンギン), *n.* 【鳥】 the penguin.
penki (ペンキ), *n.* Ⓢ ペーント. paint. —ペンキを塗る, to paint. ¶ ペンキ屋, a painter.
penpengusa (ぺんぺんぐさ), *n.* 【植】 the mother's-heart.
pēpā (ペーパー), *n.* ❶ (磨紙) sand-paper; emery-paper. ❷ (貼附紙) a label (商品などの). ❸ = *kami* (紙).
perikan (ペリカン), *n.* 【鳥】 the pelican.
perori (ぺろりと), *ad.* easily; readily. —ペロリと舌を出す, to slap out one's tongue.
Perū (秘露), *n.* Peru. ¶ 秘露人, a Peruvian.
Perusha (波斯), *n.* Persia. ¶ 波斯語 〔人〕, Persian 〔a Persian〕. —波斯國皇帝, the Shah of Persia.
pesuto (黑死病), *n.* 【醫】 the black death; bubonic plague; pest.
petan (ぺたんと), *ad.* flatly; with a flap.
peten (ぺてん), *n.* trickery; fraud; a trick. —ぺてんに掛ける, to swindle; hoax; take in. ¶ ぺてん師, an impostor; a sharper; a swindler.
pettari (ぺったり), *ad.* flat. —壁にペったりと著く, to stick flat against the wall.
pianisuto (洋琴家), *n.* a pianist.
piano (洋琴), *n.* a piano; a pianoforte.
pichapicha (ぴちゃぴちゃと), *ad.* with splashing sounds.
pikapika (ぴかぴか), *n.* glitter; flash; flare. —ピカピカする, to glitter; flash; flare.
pikari (ぴかりと), *ad.* with a flash. —ピカリと光る, to flash; give out a flash.
pikunikku (ピクニック), *n.* a picnic.
pin (留針), *n.* a pin. —ピンで留める, to (fasten with a) pin. ¶ ヘヤピン, a hair-pin.
pinpin (ぴんぴん), *ad.* in a lively manner. —ピンピンしてゐる, to be in good [excellent; robust] health; be hale and hearty [well and sound].
pinpon (卓球戲), *n.* ping-pong.
pinsetto (鑷子), *n.* a pincette.
pinto (ピント), *n.* focus. —ピントを合はす, to focus.
pinto (ぴんと), *ad.* Ⓢ ぴーんと. stiffly. —指でピンと彈く, to flip with a finger. —繩をピンと張る, to stretch a rope tight.
pīpī (ぴーぴー), *n.* cheep (雛の鳴聲); peep (同上); chirp (小鳥). —ピーピー鳴く, to cheep; peep.
piramiddo (金字塔), *n.* a pyramid. —金字塔の, pyramidal.
piririto (ぴりりと), *ad.* Ⓢ ぴりッと. spicily; poignantly; sharply. —ピリッとする, spicy; racy.
piritsuku (ぴりつく), *vi.* ❶ (ぴりぴり痛む) to smart; tingle; prick. ❷ (畏怖する) to shrink; shrivel; recoil.
pishari (ぴしゃりと), *ad.* Ⓢ ぴしゃん. with a bang [slam]; with a slap (平手で). —ピシャリと打つ, to flap; whack; slap (掌で). —ピシャンと戶を締める, to shut a door with a bang.
pisuton (吸鍔), *n.* 【機】 a piston.
pisutoru (拳銃), *n.* a pistol; a revolver (連發の). ¶ ピストル强盜, a robber 〔burglar〕 armed with a revolver.
pitchā (投手), *n.* 【野球】 a pitcher.
pitchi (ピッチ), *n.* pitch.
pitarito (ぴたりと), *ad.* Ⓢ ぴッたり. precisely; to a hair [T]; exactly.
pochapocha (ぽちゃぽちゃ), *n.* ❶ (水を弄ぶ音) splashes. ❷ (肥滿のさま) chubbiness. —ポチャポチャした顏, a chubby face. —ポチャポチャ水遊びする, to amuse

oneself by splashing.

pochi (點), *n.* a dot; a jot; a point. —ポチを打つ, to dot.

pochi (狗兒), *n.* a pup, puppy.

pointā (ポインター犬), *n.* a pointer.

pointo (ポイント), *n.* ❶【印】point (活字の大さを計る單位). ❷ (小數點) a decimal point [sign]; a point. ❸【鐵道】points (轉轍器). ¶ ポイントマン, a pointsman.

pokan (ぽかんと), *ad.* vacantly; with open mouth. —ポカンとしてゐる, to look blank [absent-minded]. —ポカンと毆る, to hit [give] a person a crack.

pokapoka (ぽかぽか), —ぽかぽか毆る, to give a person repeated whacks. —ぽかぽか暖くなる, to grow warm.

poketto (衣兜), *n.* a pocket. ¶ ポケットマネー, pocket-money.

poki (ぽき), *n.* Ⓢ ぽきん, ぽきり. snap. —ポキッと枝を折る, to break a branch with a snap; snap a branch off.

pokkuri (木履), *n.* hollow-soled clogs.

ponchi (ポンチ), *n.* punch. ¶ ポンチ畫, a caricature; a comic picture.

pondo (磅), *n.* ❶【磅】(金) a pound (略符 £). ❷【封度】(量) a pound (略符 lb.).

ponhiki(ぽん引), *n.* ❶ (事) bunco. ❷ (人) a bunco-steerer; a confidence-man. —ぽん引にひッかゝる, to fall victim to a bunco-steerer.

ponpon (腹), *n.*【小兒】tummy.

ponpu (喞筒), *n.* a pump; an inflator (タイヤに空氣を入れる). —ポンプでかへ出す, to pump out. ¶ 自動車ポンプ, a motor fire-truck; a motor fire-engine. —蒸氣ポンプ, ① a steam-pump. ② a steam fire-engine. —手押ポンプ, a hand-pump. —消火用ポンプ, a fire-pump. —吸上ポンプ, a suction-pump. —水管ポンプ, a fire-tender.

pon-to (ぽんと), *ad.* with a pop. 德利の栓をポンと拔く, to uncork the bottle with a pop.

poppo (ぽッぽ), *n.* puffing; a puff. —ポッポと湯氣《煙》を出す, to puff steam 《smoke》.

Pōrando (波蘭), *n.* Poland. ¶ 波蘭語《人》, Polish 《a Pole》.

poroporo (ぽろぽろ), *ad.* in drops. —ぽろぽろ涙をこぼして泣く, to weep with tears falling in drops.

pōru (桿), *n.* a (trolley-)pole. —ポールが外れた, The trolley is off the wire.

Porutogaru (葡萄牙), *n.* Portugal. ¶ 葡萄牙語《人》, Portuguese 《a Portuguese》.

posutā (ポスター), *n.* a poster.

posuto (郵便函), *n.* a post-box; a pillar(-box).

potapota (ぽたぽた), Ⓢ ぽたりぽたり. tap-tap; drip-drop; spatter. —ポタポタ滴る, to trickle; drip; fall in drops.

potchiri (ぽッちり), *ad.* a little *of*; a bit *of*; a drop *of*. —ほんのぽッちり, only a little.

potsupotsu (ぽつぽつ), *n.* specks (斑點); dots. ——, *ad.* in small numbers 《drops》; little by little (少しづつ); gradually (段々).

puden (プデン), *n.* pudding.

pūdo (プード), *n.* a pood (露國の重量·約 36 封度).

puito (ぷいと), *ad.* suddenly; abruptly.

punpun (ぷんぷん), *ad.* ❶ (香) sweetly; fragrantly; poignantly. ❷ (怒) wrathfully; in a rage; furiously. —ぷんぷん匂はす, to scent strongly. —ぷんぷんしてゐる, to be in a wild rage.

pūnto (ぷーんと), *ad.* ❶ (香) softly; sweetly. ❷ (むッつり) in bad temper; in a huff.

purachina (白金), *n.*【化】platinum.

puraido (自負心, 矜恃), *n.* pride.

puraiuddo (合板), *n.* ply-wood.

purasu (加), *n.* plus.

purattofōmu (プラットフォーム), *n.* a platform.

puremia(mu) (割增金), *n.* premium. —プレミアム附で, at a premium. ¶ プレミアム·システム, the premium system.

purēto (板), *n.* ❶ plate. ❷ (投手板) a pitcher's plate.

purizumu (三稜鏡), *n.*【理】a prism.

puro (プロ), *n.* a proletarian; the proletariat (無產階級).

purodakushon (プロダクション), *n.* production.

puroguramu (プログラム), *n.* a program(-me).

puropaganda (宣傳), *n.* propaganda.

puroperā (推進機), *n.* a propeller.

puroretaria (無產階級), *n.* the proletariat.

Purosha (普魯西), *n.* Prussia. ¶ 普魯西人, a Prussian.

pūru (水泳池), *n.* a (swimming-)pool.

putomain (死體毒), *n.* ptomaine.

putto (ぷッと), *ad.* with a puff. —灯をプッと吹き消す, to blow out a light.

pyoipyoi (ぴょいぴょい), *ad.* Ⓢ ぴょんぴょん. with a hop. —ぴょいぴょい跳ぶ, to leap; hop; skip.

pyū (ぴゅー), *n.* phew.

pyūpyū (ぴゅーぴゅー), *n.* whistle. ☞ *hyūhyū*. —ピューピュー吹く風, piping winds.

R

raba (騾馬), *n.* 【哺乳】 the mule.
rachi (埒), *n.* ❶ (馬埒) a (picket) fence; a pale. ❷ (限度) limit; bound. —埒をあける, to bring to a settlement; settle; finish off.
rai (來), *n.* coming. ——, *a.* next; coming. ——, *suf.* since. ☞ *irai.* —來春, next spring. —舊冬來, since last winter.
rai (雷), *n.* a thunder.
raibyō (癩病), *n.* leprosy; lepra. ¶ 癩病患者, a leper; a lazar.
raichaku (來著), *n.* arrival; coming. ☞ *tōchaku.*
raichō (雷鳥), *n.* 【鳥】 the ptarmigan.
raichō (來朝する), *vi.* to come to Japan 《the Emperor's Court》.
raiden (來電), *n.* a (received) telegram. —桑港來電, a telegram from San Francisco; a San Francisco telegram. —...旨來電あり, a telegram has been received (to the effect) that....
raiden (雷電), *n.* a thunderbolt; thunder and lightning.
raidō (雷同する), *vt.* to echo. ——, *vi.* to follow another [the lead] blindly. —他人の說に雷同する, to chime in with another's view. ¶ 雷同者, a blind follower; a servile imitator.
raigetsu (來月), *ad.* & *n.* next month; proximo (prox. と略す) —來月三日, the 3rd of next month; the 3rd prox.
raihin (來賓), *n.* a guest; a visitor. ¶ 來賓競走《席》, the visitors' race 《seats》.
raihō (來訪), *n.* a visit; a call. —來訪する, to visit; pay [make] a visit *to*; call on. ¶ 來訪者, a caller; a visitor.
raii (來意), *n.* the object of one's visit.
raikai (來會する), *vi.* to come and meet; attend [be present at] a meeting. ¶ 來會者, a person attending a meeting; attendance.
raikan (雷管), *n.* a (percussion-) cap; a detonator.
raikan (來觀する), *v.* to come and see; inspect. ¶ 來觀者, a spectator; a visitor.
raikō (來航する), *vi.* to come (by sea).
raikyaku (來客), *n.* a visitor; a guest; a caller; company. —來客中ですから少々お待ち下さい, As he has company now, please wait a while.
raimei (雷名), *n.* a (world-wide) fame.
raimei (雷鳴), *n.* a thunder; a thunder-clap; a peal of thunder.
rai-mugi (ライ麥), *n.* rye.
rainen (來年), *n.* & *ad.* next year; the coming year.
rairaku (磊落な), *a.* open-hearted [-minded]; large-minded; ingenuous; free and easy. —磊落な人, a large-minded person.
raireki (來歷), *n.* (經歷) a history; one's past life [career]; one's antecedents; (由來) origin.
rairin (來臨), *n.* presence; attendance. —...の御來臨を忝うす, to be honoured [favoured] with the presence *of*.
raisan (禮讃), *n.* worship.
raise (來世), *n.* the world [life] to come; the other [next] world; after [future] life.
raishin (來信), *n.* a letter (received; from).
raishin (來診を求める), to ask a doctor to come; send for a doctor (迎へにやる).
raishinshi (賴信紙), *n.* a telegram-form; a message-form.
raishū (來週), *n.* & *ad.* next week. —來週土曜日, Saturday (next) week.
raishū (來襲), *n.* an attack; an assault; an invasion; a raid. —敵の來襲に備へる, to provide against the enemy's attack.
raisukarē (ライス・カレー), *n.* curried rice.
raiu (雷雨), *n.* a thunder-storm.
raiyoke (雷除), *n.* ❶ (呪符) a charm against lightning. ❷ = *hiraishin.*
raiyū (來遊), *n.* a visit. —我國へ來遊する, to visit our country. ¶ 來遊者, a visitor; a tourist (觀光客).
rajio (無電), *n.* radio 【俗】 (radio-telephone, 無線電話; radio-telegraph, 無線電信; radio-telegram, 無線電報の略).
rajō (螺狀), *n.* a spiral [helical] form; a spiral; a helix.
rajūmu (ラヂゥム), *n.* radium.
rakan (羅漢), *n.* 【梵】 Arhan.
rakan (臘乾), *n.* bacon.
raketto (ラケット), *n.* 【庭球】 a racket.
rakka (落下), *n.* descent; drop; downfall. —落下する, to fall down. ¶ 落下傘, a parachute.
rakka (落花), *n.* fallen flowers; falling of blossoms (落ちること). —落花狼藉, fallen flowers scattered in disorder.
rakkan (落款), *n.* a writer's 《painter's》 signature and seal.
rakkan (樂觀), *n.* optimism. —樂觀的, optimistic. —樂觀する, to take a hopeful [an optimistic]

view *of*. ¶ 樂觀者, an optimist.

rakkasei (落花生), *n*. 【植】 the peanut; the groundnut.

rakko (臘虎), *n*. 【哺乳】 the sea-otter.

rakkyō (薤), *n*. 【植】 Allium Bakeri (garlic の一種·學名).

raku (樂), *n*. ❶ (安樂) ease. ❷ (安靜) repose; calmness. ❸ (安慰) comfort. ❹ (快樂) pleasure. **—— - na,** *a*. easy; comfortable. —樂な仕事, an easy work [task]; a soft job 〔卑〕. **—— - ni** *ad*. ❶ (安樂) easily; at ease; comfortably. ❷ (寬いで) at home [one's ease]. ❸ (容易) easily; with ease; without (any) difficulty. —樂になる, to ease off (負擔など); feel relief (苦みなど); get rid *of* (痛みなど); be mitigated (同上). —樂に暮す, to live in comfort [at ease]; lead a comfortable life.

rakuba (落馬する), *vi*. to fall off a horse; be thrown from a horse; be floored.

rakubaku (落寞たる), *a*. lonely; solitary.

rakuchaku (落著), *n*. (final) settlement; conclusion; ending. —落著する, to be settled [concluded]; come to a conclusion [settlement].

rakuchō (落丁), *n*. a missing page.

rakuchū (洛中), *n*. the capital; the city. **——,** *ad*. in the capital [city]. —洛中洛外, in and out of the capital.

rakuda (駱駝), *n*. 【哺乳】 the camel. ¶ 單峰駱駝, the Arabian camel; the dromedary. —雙峰駱駝, the Bactrian camel; the two-humped camel. —駱駝絨, vicugna-cloth.

rakudai (落第), *n*. failure in an examination. —落第する, to fail in an examination; get plucked. ¶ 落第生, a plucked student.

rakueki (絡繹), *ad*. uninterruptedly; in endless succession; without intermission. —絡繹として績るが如し, to pass by in an uninterrupted succession.

rakuen (樂園), *n*. paradise; Eden; the Elysian Fields.

rakugaki (樂書する), *v*. to scribble.

rakugo (落伍する), *vi*. to straggle; drop out of ranks; be left behind. ¶ 落伍者, a straggler; a failure (失敗者). (生存競爭の落伍者, a failure in the struggle for existence; a social failure.)

rakugo (落語), *n*. a comic story; a story ending in a word-play. ¶ 落語家, a story [tale]-teller.

rakuhaku (落魄), *n*. ruin; fall. ☞ *reiraku*.

rakuin (烙印), *n*. a brand; a brand-iron; a brand-mark.

rakuin (落胤), *n*. a bastard of a noble.

rakujitsu (落日), *n*. the setting [sinking] sun.

rakujō (落城), *n*. ❶ (城の陷ること) fall of a castle; surrender of a fort. ❷ (沒落) fall; ruin. —落城する, to fall; surrender.

rakunōjō (酪農場), *n*. a dairy.

rakurai (落雷), *n*. a thunderbolt. —落雷する, to be struck by lightning; a thunderbolt falls.

rakuraku (樂樂と), *ad*. ❶ (安樂) in greatest comfort. ❷ (容易) with the greatest ease; without any effort. —樂々する, to feel relieved.

rakurui (落涙する), *vi*. to drop [shed] tears; be moved to tears.

rakusatsu (落札), *n*. fall of the hammer; awarding of a contract. —その請負は僕に落札した, The contract was awarded to me. ¶ 落札者, a successful bidder.

rakusei (落成), *n*. completion. —落成する, to be completed; be finished. ¶ 落成式, the completion ceremony.

rakusen (落選), *n*. ❶ (選擧に落ちること) defeat in an election. ❷ (入選せぬこと) rejection. —落選する, to be defeated [rejected]; fail. ¶ 落選者, an unsuccessful candidate.

rakushu (落手する), *v*. to receive; be in receipt *of*; come to hand (物が).

rakushu (落首), *n*. a squib; a lampoon; a pasquinade.

rakutan (落膽), *n*. despondency; dejection. —落膽さす, to discourage; deject; cast [strike] a damp *over* [*into*]. —落膽する, to despond; be dejected; be disheartened. —落膽するな, Don't despair; [Cheer up].

rakuten (樂天 -主義), *n*. optimism. —樂天的, optimistic. ¶ 樂天家, an optimist; a happy-go-lucky person.

rakuyō (落葉), *n*. ❶ fall of leaves. ❷ fallen leaves. —落葉する, to cast [drop] leaves. ¶ 落葉松, the larch.

Rama (喇嘛), *n*. the Lama. ¶ 喇嘛教, lamaism. —喇嘛僧, a Lama.

ramune (ラムネ), *n*. lemonade.

ran (蘭), *n*. 【植】 the orchid.

ran (欄), *n*. ❶ (手すり) railings; a balustrade. ❷ (檻) a pen; a corral. ❸ (新聞·用紙の) a column.

ran (亂), *n*. a rebellion; an insurrection; a war (戰亂). —亂をなす, to rise in revolt; raise a rebellion.

ranbatsu (濫伐する), *vt.* to cut down recklessly; disforest indiscriminately.

ranbiki (蘭引, 蒸溜器), *n.* 〔葡 lambique〕 an alembic; a retort; a still.

ranbō (亂暴), *n.* violence; outrage; excesses; a lawless act (行); unruly conduct (行). —亂暴な, violent; outrageous; rough. —亂暴する, to act violently [in an unruly manner]; behave roughly. —亂暴に取扱ふ, to handle roughly. ¶ 亂暴者, a disorderly person; a rowdy.

ranchi (ランチ), *n.* ❶ (汽艇) a (steam) launch. ❷ (晝食) a lunch.

ranchikisawagi (亂痴氣騷をする), to make a racket; raise a rough-house.

ranchū (蘭鑄), *n.* 【魚】 the telescope-carp [-fish]; the scarlet fish.

randa (亂打する), *vt.* to batter; belabour; strike recklessly. —半鐘を亂打する, to strike the fire-bell furiously; ring the fire-bell violently. ☞ *taida.*

randa (懶惰), *n.* laziness; indolence.

randoku (濫讀), *n.* desultory reading. —濫讀する, to read at random [desultorily].

randoseru (背嚢), *n.* 〔蘭 randsel〕 a knapsack; a satchel.

rangai (欄外), *n.* the margin (of a book; newspaper). —欄外記事, stop-press news. ¶ 欄外記載事項, marginal notations. —欄外見出し, a running title.

rangaku (蘭學), *n.* Dutch learning; study of the Dutch language. ¶ 蘭學者, a Dutch scholar.

rangoku (亂國), *n.* a country disturbed by war.

rangui (亂杙), *n.* pickets; palisade.

rangun (亂軍), *n.* confused fighting; a *mêlée* 〔佛〕; an army in confusion (軍隊).

rangyō (亂行), *n.* violence; profligacy (放蕩); dissipation (同上).

ranjuku (爛熟の), *a.* overripe. —爛熟の境に入る, to reach full maturity.

ranjushō (藍綬章), *n.* a Blue Ribbon Medal.

rankaku (卵殼), *n.* an egg-shell.

rankaku (濫獲する), *vt.* to overfish (魚介を).

rankan (欄干), *n.* a railing; a (hand-)rail; a balustrade.

rankei (卵形の), *a.* oval; ovoid.

ranma (亂麻), *n.* great disturbance; chaos; a chaotic condition.

ranma (欄間 -窓), *n.* a transom window; a fan-light (扇形の).

ranman (爛漫として), *ad.* in full bloom; in splendour.

ranmyaku (亂脈), *n.* disarrangement; disorder; confusion. ☞ *ranzatsu.* —內部の亂脈, an internal disorder.

ranningu (ランニング), *n.* running.

rannyū (亂入する), *v.* to break *into*; burst into; force way *into.*

ranō (卵黃), *n.* the yolk; the yellow; the vitellus [*pl.* -li].

ranpaku (卵白), *n.* the white (of an egg); the albumen.

ranpatsu (亂髮), *n.* dishevelled [unkempt; shaggy] hairs.

ranpatsu (濫發), *n.* overissue; indiscriminate issue. —濫發する, to issue excessively [recklessly]; overissue.

ranpatsu (亂發する), *v.* to fire at random.

ranpi (濫費), *n.* waste; extravagance. —濫費する, to dissipate; waste; squander.

ranpitsu (亂筆), *n.* a scribble; a scrawl; hasty writing.

rampu (洋燈), *n.* a lamp. —ランプを點ける《消す》, to light 《put out》 a lamp.

ranru (襤褸), *n.* ragged clothes; rags; tatters. ☞ *boro.*

ransei-dōbutsu (卵生動物), *n.* the oviparous animals; Ovipara.

ransei (亂世), *n.* warlike ages; troubled [turbulent] times.

ransha (亂射する), *v.* to fire at random.

ranshi (亂視), *n.* astigmatism.

ranshin (亂心する), *vi.* to go out of one's mind; become mad [insane].

ranshō (濫觴), *n.* origin; beginning; source.

ransō (卵巢), *n.* 【解】 the oophoron; the ovary.

rantō (亂鬪する), *vi.* to engage in a mixed fighting; scuffle.

ranyō (濫用), *n.* abuse; misuse; misappropriation (私用). ——**suru**, *vt.* to abuse; misuse; misappropriate. —特權を濫用する, to abuse one's privilege.

ranzatsu (亂雜), *n.* disorder; disarrangement; confusion. —亂雜な, disorderly; confused; irregular. —亂雜に, confusedly; irregularly; pell-mell.

ranzō (濫造), *n.* ❶ (多產) overproduction; excessive manufacture. ❷ (粗製) careless manufacture. —濫造する, to manufacture [produce] excessively [recklessly]; overproduce.

rao (羅宇), *n.* a stem; a bamboo pipe-stem. —羅宇をすげ換へる, to stem; put in a new stem.

rappa (喇叭), *n.* a trumpet; a bugle; a horn. —喇叭の聲, blare; bray; toot. —喇叭を吹く, to blow a trumpet [bugle]. (進軍《退却》喇叭を吹く, to trumpet [sound] the march 《retreat》. ¶ 空氣喇叭, a siren (自動車などの). —喇叭長, a trumpet-major. —喇叭管, 【解】 the oviduct; the salpinx; the Fallopian tube. —喇叭手, a trumpeter; a bugler.

-rareru (られる), ❶ (受身) to be —ed. ❷ (可能) can; be able *to*. ❸ (敬語) graciously; be pleased *to*.

raretsu (羅列する), *vt.* to arrange.

rasen (螺旋), *n.* a screw; a spiral. —螺旋狀の, spiral.

rasha (羅紗), *n.* woollen cloth. ¶ 羅紗商, a woollen draper.

rashii (らしい), *v.* to look; appear; seem. —利口らしい, to look clever. —雨《君》らしい, It looks like rain 《you》. —女《紳士》らしい, womanly 《gentlemanly》; womanlike 《gentlemanlike》. —正直《餘程惡い》らしい, to appear to be honest 《very ill》. —その家の主人らしい人, a person, apparently the master of the house.

-rashiku, *ad.* like; as if. —男らしく, manly; like a man. —紳士らしくもない, unbecoming [unworthy of] a gentleman.

rashinban (羅針盤), *n.* a compass. —學海の羅針盤, a guide to the literary [scientific] world. —羅針盤で方位を測定する, to set by the compass. ¶ 航海用羅針盤, a mariner's compass.

rashutsu (裸出する), *vt.* to expose; uncover. ——, *vi.* to be exposed; be naked.

rasuto (ラスト), *n.* one's last.

ratai (裸體), *n.* nakedness; nudity; a naked body; 【美】 the nude. —裸體の, naked; nude. —裸體になる, to strip off one's clothes; strip oneself naked; become stark-naked. ¶ 裸體畫, a nude picture.

Raten (羅典, 拉丁), *n.* Latin. ¶ 羅典語, Latin.

ratsuwan (辣腕), *n.* astuteness; shrewdness. ¶ 辣腕家, an astute man.

ravu (愛), *n.* love.

redēmēdo (出來合服), *n.* a ready-made (clothing).

rei (令), *n.* 【法】 an ordinance: an order; a command.

rei (例), *n.* ❶ (慣例) a custom: a usage; a precedent (先例). ❷ (例證, 實例) an illustration; an instance; an example. ❸ (場合) a case. —例に倣ふ, to take example *by*; follow in the wake *of*; follow suit; take the cue from others. —例になる, to become a usage 《precedent》. —例として, for example; by way of example. —例をあげて, by illustration [example]. ——-**no,** *a.* usual; customary. —例の如く, usually; as usual.

rei (零), *n.* 【數】 a zero; a cipher; nought.

rei (禮), *n.* ❶ (敬禮) salutation; salute; bow. ❷ (禮儀) courtesy; civility; etiquette (作法). ❸ (謝禮) (*a*) (謝意) thanks; an acknowledgment (of another's favour): (*b*) (禮金) a fee; an honorarium; a reward. —禮をする, ① (叩頭) to bow down. ② (返禮) to make a return present. —禮を述べる, to express one's thanks. —禮を失する, to be impolite; act discourteously. —禮を厚くして人を招く, to invite a man with great courtesy.

rei (靈), *n.* ❶ (靈魂) the soul; the spirit; 【宗】 the inner man. ❷ (亡靈) a spirit; a ghost; a wraith. ❸ =*reimyō* (靈妙). —靈的生活, spiritual life.

reibō (禮帽), *n.* a silk hat; a top hat.

reibun (令聞), *n.* fame; repute; a fair name.

reibyō (靈廟), *n.* a mausoleum.

reichi (靈地), *n.* a sacred [holy] place.

reichi (靈智), *n.* wisdom; intellect; intellectuality.

reidai (例題), *n.* an example; an exercise.

reido (零度), *n.* zero; the zero point.

reifujin (令夫人), *n.* a 《your; his》 wife; Mrs....; Lady...; her 《your; their》 ladyship.

reifuku (禮服), *n.* a dress coat; dress-clothes; a *robe décolletée* (婦人用): 【宗】 vestments. ¶ 通常禮服, a dress; dress-clothes.

reigai (例外), *n.* an exception. —例外を設ける, to make an exception.

reigen (靈驗), *n.* a miracle; the efficacy of prayer; a miraculous virtue (efficacy) (藥等の).

reigi (禮儀), *n.* ❶ (禮儀作法) (good) manners; etiquette; decorum. ❷ (禮) courtesy; propriety; politeness. —禮儀正しい, [*a.*] courteous; decorous; polite; well-mannered.

reigū (冷遇), *n.* cold treatment. —冷遇する, to treat coldly; give the cold shoulder *to*.

reigū (禮遇), *n.* respectful treatment; courteous [cordial] reception. —禮遇する, to receive courteously [warmly]; treat respectfully. —禮遇停止を解く, to remove the suspension of treatment (as a peer). —特に前官の禮遇を賜ふ, to accord specially the treatment due to his late office.

reihai (禮拜), *n.* worship; church-service; service. —禮拜する, to worship; bow *to*. ¶ 禮拜堂, a chapel. —礼拝式,【宗】office; divine office [service; worship]; liturgy (希臘敎の).

reihai (零敗 -戰), *n.* a shut-out; a skunk [卑]. —零敗さす, to shut-out. —零敗する, to fail to score.

reihō (禮法), *n.* courtesy; etiquette. ☞ *reigi* (禮儀).

reihō (禮砲), *n.*【陸海】a salute (gun). —禮砲を發する, to salute; fire a salute.

reihyō (冷評), *n.* a sarcastic [bitter] criticism. —冷評する, to criticize sarcastically.

reiji (零時), *n.* twelve o'clock; midday (晝の); midnight (夜の).

reijin (伶人), *n.* a (court) musician; a minstrel.

reijitsu (例日), *n.* the usual days.

reijō (令狀), *n.*【法】a warrant; a writ. —令狀を送達《執行; 發》する, to serve《execute; issue》a warrant.

reijō (令孃), *n.* a daughter; a young lady; miss.

reijō (禮狀), *n.* a letter of thanks [acknowledgment].

reikai (例會), *n.* a regular [an ordinary] meeting.

reikan (靈感), *n.* inspiration.

reiketsu (冷血動物), *n.* ❶【動】a cold-blooded [hematocryal] animal; Hæmatocrya (學名). ❷ (冷血漢) a cold-blooded man; a stony-hearted man.

reiki (冷氣), *n.* cool; coolness.

reiki (例規), *n.* established rules.

reikin (禮金), *n.* a recompense; a remuneration; an honorarium; a fee; a reward (懸賞金).

reikō (勵行する), *vt.* to enforce; carry out [execute] strictly; put into force.

reikōjutsu (靈交術), *n.* spiritualism.

reikoku (冷酷, 冷刻), *n.* cruelty; heartlessness; cold-heartedness. —冷酷な, cruel; cold-hearted; unfeeling.

reikoku (例刻), *n.* the usual hour [time].

reikon (靈魂), *n.* a soul; a spirit. —靈魂の不滅を信ずる, to believe in the immortality of the soul. ¶ 靈魂不滅論, immortalism.

reikyaku (冷却する), *vi.* to cool (down). —, *vt.* to refrigerate; cool. ¶ 冷却器, a refrigerator.

reimawari (禮廻りする), *vi.* to make a round of visits to return thanks.

reimei (黎明), *n.* break of day; daybreak. —, *ad.* at dawn [daybreak]; in the grey of the morning; at peep of day. ¶ 黎明運動, an awakening movement.

reimyō (靈妙), *n.* miraculousness; wonder. —靈妙な, miraculous; wonderful; mysterious.

reinen (例年), *n.* & *ad.* the ordinary [normal] year; every year. —例年の通り, as usual.

reiraku (零落), *n.* ruin; fall; downfall. —零落する, to go to ruin; come down in the world; fall low.

reireishiku (麗麗しく), *ad.* glaringly; ostentatiously.

reiri (怜悧な), *a.* clever; smart; intelligent.

reirō (玲瓏たる), *a.* fair; clear; bright; mellow (人格など). —八面玲瓏の人, a man of clear character.

reisai (零碎な), *a.* trifling; fragmental; small. —零碎な義捐金を集める, to collect trifling subscriptions.

reisei (冷靜), *n.* calmness; composure; coolness. —**-na**, *a.* calm; cool; self-possessed. —極めて冷靜な, cool as a cucumber.

reisei (勵精する), *vi.* to labour; be assiduous; strive.

reisetsu (禮節), *n.* propriety; decorum. ☞ *reigi* (禮儀).

reishi (茘枝), *n.*【植】the litchi.

reishi (令旨), *n.* Her Majesty's 《His Highness's》 address.

reishiki (禮式), *n.* formality; etiquette; manners. ☞ ***reigi***.

reishō (冷笑), *n.* a sneer; a sardonic laugh; a derisive smile. —冷笑する, to sneer *at*; smile *at*.

reishō (例證), *n.* an exemplification; an illustration. —例證する, to exemplify; illustrate.

reisoku (令息), *n.* a son; your son; his son.

reisui (冷水), *n.* cold water. —冷水浴をする, to take a cold bath. ¶ 冷水摩擦, cold-water massage.

reitan (冷淡), *n.* ❶ (無情) coldness; cold-heartedness. ❷ (無頓着) indifference; nonchalance. ❸ (不熱心) lukewarmness; perfunctoriness. —冷淡な, cold; cold-hearted; indifferent; nonchalant; perfunctory. —冷淡に, coldly; indifferently. —金錢に冷淡である, to be careless about money.

reiten (零點), *n.* ❶ (零度) the zero point. ❷ (無點) the zero; a duck [學生]; a round o [學生].

reiyaku (靈藥), *n.* a wonderful medicine; a panacea.

reitō (冷凍), *n.* congealment; congelation. —冷凍する, to congeal. ¶ 冷凍魚, a congealed fish.

reiyō (羚羊), *n.* =***kamoshika***.

reizen (靈前), before the ancestral tablet. —靈前に供へる, to offer before the ancestral tablet; dedicate to the memory *of*.

reizō (冷藏する), *vt.* to refrigerate; freeze; ice (氷漬). ¶ 冷藏庫, a refrigerator; an ice-safe. —冷藏貨車, a refrigerator-car. —冷藏室, a refrigerating-chamber; a cold-storage room.

reizoku (隸屬する), *vi.* to be subject [subordinate] *to*; be under the jurisdiction [authority] *of*; be under the control *of*.

reki (曆), *n.* a calendar; an almanac.

rekidai (歷代), *n.* successive generations. —歷代の首相, the successive prime ministers.

rekidan (轢斷する), *vt.* to cut off by running over.

rekihō (歷訪する), *vt.* to make a round *of* (government offices; calls on noted persons).

rekijitsu (曆日), *n.* a civil day; a calendar day.

rekinen (曆年), *n.* a legal [civil; calendar] year.

rekireki (歷歷), *n.* ❶ (身分高い人) men of high standing [rank]; men of (exalted) station; personages; men of worth. ❷ (門閥家) men of good family; men of birth. **——,** *ad.* distinctly; vividly; clearly. **—— - no,** *a.* prominent; eminent; distinguished.

rekisatsu (轢殺する), *vt.* to kill by running down [over].

rekisei (瀝靑), *n.* 【鑛】 asphalt; bitumen.

rekishi (歷史), *n.* (a) history. —歷史的, historic(-al). (歷史的光景, a historic scene.) —長く歷史に殘る, to remain long in history. ¶ 歷史畫《小說》, a historical picture [painting] 《novel》. —歷史家, a historian.

rekishi (轢死する), *vi.* to be run over and killed; be killed by a train. ¶ 轢死者, a person run over and killed.

rekiyū (歷遊する), *v.* to itinerate; travel (from place to place); tour (about).

rekizen (歷然), *ad.* clearly; vividly; distinctly. —歷然たる, clear; evident; vivid; distinct.

rekka (烈火), *n.* a blazing [raging] fire. —烈火の如く憤る, to flare up like a blazing fire.

rekkaku (劣角), *n.* 【數】 a minor (conjugate) angle.

rekkoku (列國), *n.* all the countries; the nations; the powers (列强). ¶ 列國會議, a conference of the Powers [nations].

rekkyo (列擧する), *vt.* to enumerate; particularize.

rekkyō (列强), *n.* the (great) powers; world-powers.

rekōdo (レコード), *n.* ❶ (記錄) a record. ☞ *kiroku.* ❷ (蓄音器音譜) a record. —レコードを破る, to break [beat; cut] the record. —レコードを作る, to create [establish] a record.

remon (檸檬), *n.* 【植】 the (common) lemon-tree (木): a lemon (果實). ¶ レモン水, lemonade.

ren (連), *n.* ❶ =*renjū*. ❷ (印刷紙の) a ream.

ren'ai (戀愛), *n.* love; the tender passion. ¶ 戀愛小說, a love-story; an erotic [a love] novel.

renbai (廉賣), *n.* selling cheap; bargain [cheap] sale. ¶ 廉賣市, a bargain market.

renban (連判), *n.* joint signature; joint seal. —連判する, to sign 《seal》 jointly. ¶ 連判狀, a compact under joint signature.

renbei (聯袂して), *ad.* jointly; in a body; *en masse* 【佛】. —聯袂辭職する, to resign in a body.

renbo (戀慕する), *vt.* to love; fall in love *with*; give one's heart *to*. ☞ *renbo*.

renchaku (戀著する), *vt.* to love.

renchi (廉恥), *n.* integrity; uprightness; honour. —廉恥心なき人, a person without [lost to] shame.

renchoku (廉直な), *a.* honest; upright; chaste.

renchū (連中), *n.* =*renjū*.

rendai (輦臺), *n.* a litter.

rendō (聯動), *n.* gearing. —聯動する, to move in gear; work by gearing. ¶ 聯動機, 【機】 a gear, gearing.

renga (煉瓦), *n.* a brick. —煉瓦を積む, to lay the courses. —煉瓦を燒く, to burn [bake] bricks. ¶ 化粧煉瓦, a dressed brick; a faced brick. —燒過ぎ煉瓦, an overburnt brick. —煉瓦鋪裝《鋪道》, brick pavement. —煉瓦工場, a brick-yard [-field]. —煉瓦製造人, a brick-burner; a brickmaker. —煉瓦職, a brick-layer; a brick-mason.

renge (蓮華), *n.* the lotus flower.

rengesō (蓮華草), *n.* 【植】 = *genge*.

rengō (聯合, 連合), *n.* combination; union; alliance; federation; confederation; association (特に觀念の); coalition (政黨の提携). **—— - suru,** *v.* to combine; unite; confederate; federate; join; associate (oneself) *with*. —聯合して, conjointly; in combination [alliance] *with*. ¶ 物上《身上》聯合; 物《人》的聯合, real 《personal》 union. —聯合軍, the allied forces [armies]; the allies. —聯合艦隊, a combined fleet. —聯合國, ① the allies. ② (歐洲大戰中の) the Allies; the Entente

Powers; the Allied and Associated Powers (米國加入後の公稱). —聯合運動會, a joint athletic meeting. —聯合賣出, a joint bargain sale.

rengyō (連翹), *n.* 【植】 the Japanese golden-ball tree.

reñin (連印), *n.* joint seal and signature.

renji (連字), *n.* 【印】 a ligature (æ, fi の如き); a diphthong.

renji (櫺子), *n.* lattice. ¶ 櫺子窓, a lattice window.

renjitsu (連日), *n.* day after day; a series of days; consecutive days. —連日の降雨で, by continued rain.

renjū (連中), *n.* a party; a company; a set.

renka (廉價), *n.* a low price; cheapness. —廉價の, cheap; low-priced.

renketsu (廉潔), *n.* integrity; uprightness; probity. —廉潔な, honest; upright; righteous.

renketsu (聯結; 連結), *n.* combination; connection. —連結する, to combine; connect; link (汽車等を); couple. ¶ 自動聯結機, an automatic coupler.

renkinjutsu (錬金術), *n.* alchemy; hermetic art; transmutation.

renki-tōhyō (連記投票), *n.* a general ticket; a plural vote.

renkoku (輦轂の下で), in the capital.

renkon (蓮根), *n.* the lotus root [rhizome].

renku (聯句), *n.* 【詩】 a couplet.

renma (練磨), *n.* exercise; training; drilling. **—— - suru,** *vt.* to exercise; cultivate; train. —知識を練磨する, to polish one's knowledge.

renmei (連名), *n.* joint signature. —連名で抗議を申込む, to make a joint protest.

renmei (聯盟), *n.* ❶ a league; a federation. ❷ (國際聯盟) the League of Nations. ¶ 勞働聯盟, Federation of Labour [Workers].

renmen (連綿), *ad.* continuously; in an unbroken line; in an uninterrupted succession. —連綿として限なし, to continue for ever.

renmin (憐愍), *n.* compassion; pity; commiseration. —憐愍を垂れる, to pity; commiserate.

rennen (連年), *n.* year after year; successive years; a series of years.

rennyū (煉乳), *n.* condensed milk.

renpatsu (連發), *n.* running fire; a volley (飛道具·惡口等の). **—— - suru,** *vt.* to volley; fire [discharge] in volleys. —質問を連發する, to volley out questions; put questions one after another. ¶ 連發銃, a magazine-gun [-rifle]; a repeating rifle; a repeater.

renpei (練兵), *n.* military drill; military exercise. —練兵する, to drill; exercise the troops. ¶ 練兵場, a parade ground; a drill-ground.

renpō (聯邦), *n.* a confederation; a confederation of states; a federation (結合の度は前者よりも緊密). ¶ 獨逸聯邦, German(-ic) confederation. —濠洲聯邦, the Commonwealth of Australia. —聯邦政府, the federal government (米國·濠洲·瑞西等の).

renraku (聯絡, 連絡), *n.* ❶ (接續) connection; junction. ❷ (交通) communication; correspondence (通信). ❸ (關係) relation; connection. —聯絡ある, connected. —聯絡する, ① [*vt.*] to connect; interlink. ② [*vi.*] to connect. —連絡をつける [通ずる], to establish a connection *with*. —後方との連絡を斷つ, to cut off the communications with the rear. ¶ 連絡切符, a coupon ticket (他線への [米]); a joint ticket; a through ticket (通し切符); a railway and steamship combination-ticket (汽車·汽船の). —連絡船《線》, a connecting steamer《line》.

renren (戀戀たる), *a.* ardently attached; very affectionate; very reluctant (to part; to part *with* something; to resign one's post).

renritsu (聯立), *n.* coalition; alliance. ¶ 聯立方程式, simultaneous equations. —聯立內閣, a coalition cabinet [ministry].

renrui (連累), *n.* implication (in a crime); involvement; complicity. —連累になる, to be implicated [involved] in a crime. ¶ 連累者, an accomplice; a confederate.

rensa (連鎖), *n.* ❶ (鎖) a chain; a link. ❷ (連り) a series; connection. ¶ 連鎖劇, a film and stage combination play; a play connected with the kinematograph. —連鎖法, 【數】 the chain-rule.

rensai (連載する), *vt.* to publish serially. —連載される, to appear in the serial form.

rensen (連戰), *n.* successive battles; a series of battles; battle after battle. —連戰連勝《敗》する, to gain《sustain》 a succession [a series] of victories《defeats》; win《lose》 every battle.

rensetsu (連接, 聯接), *n.* connection. —連接する, to connect;

join; link; switch on (電話を). ¶ 連接電話, indirect telephone connection.

renshaku (連借), *n.* a joint debt; a debt on joint security. ¶ 連借人, joint debtors.

rensho (連署), *n.* joint signature. —連署する, to sign jointly. —保證人連署を以て, with the joint signature of the surety.

renshō (連勝, 連捷), *n.* successive victories. ☞ *rensen.*

renshū (練習), *n.* practice; exercise; training. —練習する, to practise; exercise; train. ¶ 練習航海, practice-cruise; training navigation [cruise]. —練習艦《船》, a training ship; a school-ship. —練習問題, an exercise; a practice question. —練習所, a seminary; a training school. —練習生, a training student; a cadet (海軍).

rensō (聯想), *n.* association; 【心】association of ideas. —聯想さす, to associate (one thing) *with* (another); remind one *of*; suggest the idea *of*. —聯想する, to think of. (フランクリンと云へば電氣を聯想する, The name of Franklin is associated with [reminds us of] electricity.)

rentai (連帶), *n.* solidarity. —連帶で, jointly and severally. ¶ 社會連帶, social solidarity. —連帶責任, joint and several responsibility [liability].

rentai (聯隊), *n.* a regiment. ¶ 聯隊長, a regimental commander. —聯隊旗, the regimental colours. —聯隊區司令官, the commander of a regimental district.

rentan (煉炭), *n.* a briquette, [briquet.]

rentetsu (鍊鐵), *n.* wrought iron; tempered [wrought] steel.

rentogen (レントゲン), *n.* 【理】Roentgen rays; X-rays.

renza (連坐), *n.* implication; complicity. —連坐する, to be involved [implicated] (in a crime).

renzan (連山), *n.* a range [chain] of mountains; a (mountain) range.

renzoku (連續), *n.* continuity; succession. —連續する, to continue; last; go on. —連續せる, continuous; successive; consecutive; unbroken; serial (小說など). —三日間連續して, for three days running [in succession].

renzu (レンズ), *n.* a lens. —レンズに收める, to get into a camera.

reppai (劣敗する), *vi.* to be defeated; be left behind. ¶ 劣敗者, a failure.

reppu (烈婦), *n.* a heroine; a heroic woman; a chaste woman.

reppū (烈風), *n.* 【氣象】a strong gale; a violent wind.

rēru (軌條), *n.* a rail.

reshīvā (受話器), *n.* a receiver.

resseki (列席), *n.* attendance; presence. —— **-suru,** *v.* to attend; be present *at*; assist *at*; sit *at*. —會議に列席する, to attend a conference. ¶ 列席者, those present; attendants.

ressha (列車), *n.* a (railway) train. ¶ 貸切列車, a reserved train. —汽船聯絡列車, a boat-train. —特別(仕立)列車, a special (train); a limited mail. —列車渡船, a ferry-bridge.

Resshi (烈氏寒暖計), *n.* a Réaumur thermometer.

resshin (烈震), *n.* 【地文】a violent shock (地面の龜裂崩壞を起す程度).

resshō (裂傷), *n.* a laceration.

res-suru (列する), *v.* ❶ (出席) to attend; be present *at*. ❷ (授爵) to be ranked; be created. ❸ (伍する) to rank *with*; rank *among*. —公爵に列する, to be ranked as [raised to] a prince. —會議に列する, to attend a meeting; assist at a conference. —華族に列せられる, to be created a peer; attain (to) a peerage.

rēsu (レース), *n.* ❶ lace; lacing. ❷ (競走, 競漕) a race.

retsu (列), *n.* a line; a rank; a row; a file (縦の). —列をなして, in rows [a row]; in a line; in file. —列を作る, to form a line. —列を正す, to dress the ranks. —列を離れる《詰める》, to leave 《close》 the ranks.

retsuza (列坐), *n.* the (whole) company; those present. —列坐する, to sit in a row; attend. —列坐の中で, in company.

retteru (レッテル), *n.* a label.

rettō (劣等の), *a.* inferior; low; of lower quality [grade]. ¶ 劣等品, goods of inferior quality.

rettō (列島), *n.* a chain of islands.

ri (利), *n.* ❶ (利益) profit (儲け); gain (同上); advantage (利害·便利·地の利等の利); interests (ため). ❷ (利子) interest. ❸ (勝利) victory. —利がつく, to draw [bear] interest. —利に迷ふ, to be led astray by gain. —利の爲には, for the sake of gain. —利を見るに敏なり, to have a quick eye for the main chance.

ri (里), *n.* a *ri* (=2.44 miles); 【支】a *li* (=0.36 mile; 五町十六間).

ri (理), *n.* reason (道理); truth (眞理); principle (原理). —理に適ふ, to accord with [stand to]

reason. —理を非に枉げる, to pervert reason.
ribetsu (離別), *n.* ❶ (別離) parting. ❷ (離婚) divorce. —離別する, ① to part *from.* ② to divorce.
ribon (リボン), *n.* a ribbon.
richaku (離著), *n.* leaving and landing. ¶ 離著甲板, a flying-off deck.
richi (理智), *n.* 【哲】 intellect.
richigi (律義), *n.* ❶ (實直) uprightness; honesty. ❷ (質朴) simplicity. —律義な, ① upright; honest. ② simple.
rīdā (リーダー), *n.* ❶ (讀本) a reader. ❷ 【印】 a leader (點線).
rīdo (リードする), *v.* to lead.
rieki (利益), *n.* ❶ (利得) profit; gain; returns. ❷ (利害關係上の利益) interest(s). ❸ (裨益) benefit; good. ❹ (利害得失上の利益) advantage. ❺ (誰の利不利の利益) favour. —日本の滿洲に於ける特殊利益, Japan's special interests in Manchuria. —利益のある, ① (利潤ある) profitable; lucrative; remunerative. ② (裨益) beneficial. ③ (便益) advantageous. —利益が少い《多い》, to bring [yield] little 《great》 profit; be of little 《great》 benefit [advantage]. ¶ 利益配當, division of profits. (利益配當制度, the profit-sharing system.)
rien (離緣), *n.* ❶ 【法】 dissolution of adoption. ❷ (離婚) divorce. —離緣する, to divorce. ¶ 離緣狀, a letter of divorce.
rifuda (利札), *n.* a coupon. ¶ 利札落債券, an ex-coupon bond.
rifujin (理不盡な), *a.* unreasonable; lawless; violent. —理不盡にも, unreasonably; lawlessly; without any justification. (理不盡にも僕を打った, He was so lawless [violent] as to strike me; He has struck me without provocation.)
rigai (利害), *n.* ❶ (利害關係) interest; concern. ❷ (利害得失) advantages and disadvantages. —利害關係を有する, to have a concern [an interest] *in*; be interested [concerned] *in.* ¶ 利害關係人, the party interested; the interested party; the person concerned.
rigaku (理學), *n.* physical science. ¶ 理學博士, a doctor of science (D. Sc. と略す). —理學者, a scientist. —理學士, a bachelor of science (B. Sc. と略す).
rigen (利源), *n.* natural resources.
rigen (俚諺), *n.* a proverb; a common saying.
rigō (離合), *n.* parting and meeting.
rihan (離畔), *n.* disaffection; estrangement; alienation. —離畔する, to be estranged; be alienated: (叛く) to revolt (*against*).
rihatsu (理髮), *n.* hair-cutting; hair-dressing. ¶ 理髮師, a barber; a hair-dresser. —理髮店, a barber's shop; a hair-dresser's shop; a tonsorial saloon (誇張的).
rihi (理非), *n.* rights and wrongs. —理非曲直を明かにする, to make clear its rights and wrongs.
rihō (理法), *n.* a law.
rīgu-sen (リーグ戰), *n.* a baseball league.
riin (吏員), *n.* an official; an employee.
riji (理事), *n.* a director; a trustee (學校·敎會などの); a judge advocate (軍法會議の). ¶ 理事長, the head-director; the managing director. —理事會, a board of directors 《trustees》. —理事官, a procurator.
rijun (利潤), *n.* profit; gain. ☞ *rieki.*
rika (理科), *n.* science. ¶ 理科大學, the College of Science.
rikai (理解, 理會), *n.* understanding; comprehension; apprehension. —理解する, to understand; comprehend; perceive; make out. ¶ 理解力, understanding; comprehensive faculty; apprehensive power.
rikaku (離隔), *n.* isolation. ☞ *kakuri.*
rikan (離間), *n.* estrangement; alienation; separation. —日支間を離間する, to alienate [estrange; separate] Japan from China.
riken (利權), *n.* rights (and interests); a concession. —利權を獲得する, to acquire a right.
riki (利器), *n.* ❶ (武器) a weapon. ❷ (刃物) an edged tool; a sharp instrument. ❸ (便利なもの) a convenience.
rikigaku (力學), *n.* dynamics.
rikimu (力む), *vi.* ❶ (力を入れる) to strain (oneself). ❷ (威張る) to bluster; swagger. —力んで, with all one's might; with an effort; strenuously. —一人で力む, to bluster by oneself.
rikiryō (力量), *n.* ❶ (腕力) (physical) strength [power]. ❷ (器量) ability; talent; capacity. —力量ある, able; capable; talented.
rikisaku (力作), *n.* a painstaking work; a work written with great pains.
rikisetsu (力說する), *vt.* to emphasize; accentuate; lay stress [emphasis] *on.*
rikishi (力士), *n.* a wrestler.
rikisō (力走する), *vi.* to spurt.
rikisō (力漕する), *vi.* to row

harder.

rikkaigun (陸海軍), *n.* the army and navy; the (fighting) services. —陸海軍の軍人, military and naval men; soldiers and sailors.

rikken (立憲的), *a.* constitutional. ¶ 立憲君主政體, constitutional monarchy. —立憲政治[體], constitutional government.

rikkyaku (立脚する), *vt.* to take one's ground *on*. —立脚點を異にす, to take a different position. ¶ 立脚地, a standpoint; a footing; a foothold; stand; ground. (立脚地を失ふ, to lose one's footing; lose ground.)

riko (利己), *n.* self-interest; selfishness. —利己的, selfish; self-seeking; self-interested. ¶ 利己主義, egoism. (利己主義者, an egoist.)

rikō (利口), *n.* cleverness; sagaciousness, sagacity. —利口な, clever; sagacious; shrewd. —利口ぶる, to be conceited; try to look clever. —利口さうな, clever [intelligent]-looking. —利口に立廻る, to move about with adroitness; act smartly.

rikō (履行), *n.* 【法】performance; discharge. —履行する, to perform; discharge; make good. ¶ 履行者, a performer; a discharger.

rikon (離婚), *n.* divorce. —離婚する, to divorce. —離婚の訴を起す, to sue for a divorce.

rikonbyō (離魂病), *n.* sleep-walking; night-walking; somnambulism.

riku (陸), *n.* land.

rikuage (陸揚), *n.* landing; unloading; discharge of cargo. —陸揚げする, to land; unload; unship; discharge. ¶ 陸揚場, a landing-place. —陸揚港, a port of discharge.

rikuchi (陸地), *n.* land.

rikugun (陸軍), *n.* the army. ¶ 陸軍大學校, the military staff college. —陸軍大臣, the War Minister; the Minister of State for War. —陸軍軍人, a soldier; a military man. —陸軍士官學校, the military academy. —陸軍省, the Department of War; the War Office.

rikujō (陸上), *n.* land; shore. ¶ 陸上勤務, shore-service. —陸上競技, athletic sports.

rikuro (陸路), *n.* a land route; a land journey. ——, *ad.* by land; overland.

rikusen (陸戰), *n.* a land-battle; land-warfare; a war on land. ¶ 陸戰隊, a landing-party.

rikutsu (理窟), *n.* argument (議論); reason (道理); theory (理論); logic (論理); pretext (口實); quibbling (詭辯). —理窟上, rationally; in reason. —理窟を捏ねる, to chop logic; cavil.

rikuun (陸運), *n.* land-carriage [-transportation]; carriage [transportation] by land.

rikuzoku (陸續), *ad.* successively; consecutively; one after another.

rikyū (離宮), *n.* a detached palace.

rimawari (利廻), *n.* yield.

rimen (裏面), *n.* ❶ (裏側) the inside; the back; the reverse; the other side. ❷ (内幕) secrecy. —裏面で, in secret; behind one's back; behind the scene. —その裏面に, behind it; at the back of it. —裏面を見よ, "Please turn over" (P. T. O. と略す); "See the back page" (廣め札等).

rin (厘), *n.* one-tenth of a *sen* (*fun*).

rin (鈴), *n.* a bell; a hand-bell.

rin (輪), *n.* ❶ (圏) a circle; a ring; an annulus. ❷ (車輪) a wheel.

rin (燐), *n.* phosphorus.

rinban (輪番), *n.* turns; rotation. ☞ *kōtai*. —輪番に, by turns; by rotation.

rinchi (隣地), *n.* adjoining land.

rinchi (私刑), *n.* lynch law.

rine, rinne, (輪廻), *n.* metempsychosis; transmigration of the soul.

ringaku (林學), *n.* forestry; dendrology (樹木學).

ringen (綸言汗の如し), The Emperor's orders can never be recalled.

ringetsu (臨月), *n.* the month of parturition.

ringo (林檎), *n.* the apple-tree (樹): an apple (菓果).

ringoku (隣國), *n.* a neighbouring country (province); adjoining states.

ringyo (臨御), *n.* an Imperial visit; the Imperial presence.

ringyō (林業), *n.* forestry.

rinji (臨時), *a.* temporary; special; extraordinary. —— -**ni**, *ad.* temporarily; specially. —臨時に生徒を募集する, to admit students specially. ¶ 臨時代理公(大)使, the chargé d'affaires *ad interim* of a legation (an embassy). —臨時議會, a special session of the Diet. —臨時費, extraordinary expenses; casual expenses. —臨時會, a special [an extraordinary] meeting. —臨時列車, an extra train. —臨時支出, extraordinary disbursement. —臨時雇, a temporary employee; an extra hand. —臨時增刊, an extra (edition).

rinjin (隣人), *n.* a neighbour; people in one's neighbourhood.

rinjō (臨場), *n.* attendance; presence. —臨場する, to attend;

visit; be present *at*.

rinjū (臨終), *n.* the point [moment] of death; the [one's] last moment; one's dying hour. —臨終に, at the point of death; *in articulo mortis* 【羅. =at the moment of death】. —臨終の遺言, a dying wish. —只今御臨終です, He is now passing away.

rinka (隣家), *n.* a neighbouring house; the next door [house]; the adjoining houses.

rinka (燐火), *n.* phosphorus light; phosphorescence.

rinkai (臨海), *a.* seaside. ¶ 夏期臨海學校, a summer seaside school.

rinkaku (輪郭), *n.* ❶ an outline; the contour. ❷【製本】fillet (表紙に押した). —輪郭のはっきりした顔, a clear-cut face; chiselled features.

rinkan (輪奐), *n.* magnificence [splendour] (of a building).

rinkan-gakkō (林間學校), *n.* a forest-school; an open-air school.

rinken (臨檢), *n.* a visitation; a visit of inspection; personal inspection. —臨檢する, to visit; inspect.

rinki (悋氣), *n.* jealousy. —悋氣する, to be jealous *of*.

rinki (臨機の), *a.* Ⓢ 臨機應變の. expedient; suitable. —臨機應變の才, the talent of adapting oneself to circumstances. —臨機應變の處置をする, to act according to circumstances; act as the occasion demands 【may demand】.

rinkō (臨幸), *n.* an Imperial visit. —臨幸を仰ぐ, to beg to be honoured with an Imperial visit.

rinkō (輪講), *n.* reading by turns; alternate explanation [exposition; interpretation]. —輪講する, to construe (a book) in turn.

rinkō (燐光), *n.* phosphorus light; phosphorescence.

rinkō-tetsudō (臨港鐵道), *n.* a harbour railway.

rinmō (釐毛), *n.* ❶ a farthing; the smallest sum. ❷ (微塵) an atom; a jot; a bit.

rinmukan (林務官), *n.* a forester; a forest officer; an inspector of state forests.

rinneru (リンネル), *n.* linen; linen cloth.

rinpa (淋巴), *n.* 【解】lymph. ¶ 淋巴管〘腺〙, a lymphatic vessel 〘gland〙.

rinraku (淪落), *n.* ❶ (零落) ruin. ❷ (墮落) degeneration. —淪落の女, a ruined [fallen; lost] woman.

rinretsu (凜冽), *ad.* intensely; severely; rigorously. —凜冽たる, intense; severe; rigorous.

rinri (淋漓), *ad.* profusely; freely.

rinri (倫理), *n.* ethics; morals. ¶ 倫理學, ethics; moral philosophy; ethical [moral] science. (倫理學者, a moral philosopher; an ethicist; a moralist (道學者).)

rinrin (凜凜), *ad.* ❶ (勇氣) imposingly; with dashing spirit. ❷ (寒氣) severely; rigorously; intensely. —凜々たる, ① awe-inspiring; imposing. ② severe; biting; rigorous.

rinritsu (林立する), *vi.* to stand close together; be like a forest; bristle *with* (masts, *etc.*).

rinsan (燐酸), *n.* 【化】phosphoric acid.

rinseki (臨席), *n.* presence; attendance. —臨席する, to attend; be present *at*.

rinseki (隣席), *n.* the next seat.

rinsen (臨戰), *n.* presence in a battle; going into battle. ¶ 臨戰準備, preparation for action.

rinsetsu (隣接せる), *a.* neighbouring; adjacent; adjoining; contiguous *to*.

rinshi (綸旨), *n.* a commission [written order] from the Emperor.

rinshitsu (隣室), *n.* the next [adjoining] room.

rinshō (臨床の), *a.* clinical. ¶ 臨床講義, a clinic; a clinical lecture.

rinshoku (吝嗇), *n.* stinginess; parsimony; niggardliness. —吝嗇な, stingy; parsimonious; niggardly. ¶ 吝嗇家, a miser; a niggard.

rinten (輪轉), *n.* rotation; revolution. —輪轉する, to rotate; revolve. ¶ 輪轉機, a roller; a cylinder-press.

rinu (霖雨), *n.* a long-continued rain; a long spell of rain.

rinyō (利尿), *n.* 【醫】diuresis.

rinzu (綸子), *n.* figured satin.

rippa (立派な), *a.* fine; splendid; magnificent. —立派な人, a worthy man; a man of fine character. —立派な商人, a respectable merchant. —立派に, finely; beautifully; admirably; in grand style; with a good grace (潔く).

rippō (立方), *n.* cube. —三呎立方, a three-foot cube. —一立方呎の瓦斯, a cubic foot of gas. ¶ 立方根, a cube root. —立方體, a cube.

rippō (立法), *n.* legislation; law-making. ¶ 立法部, the legislature; the legislative chamber [body]. —立法權, legislative [law-making] power.

rippuku (立腹), *n.* anger; wrath; displeasure. —立腹する, to get [become; grow] angry; be enraged; take offence. —大に立腹して, in high [great] dudgeon.

rireki (履歴), *n.* a personal history; antecedents; one's career. —官途の履歴, an official career. ¶ 履歴書, a record (of one's life); a *curriculum vitæ* 【羅. =course of life】.

rirē-rēsu (リレーレース), *n.* 【競技】 a relay race.

ririku (離陸する), *vi.* to leave [rise from] the ground.

ririshii (凛凛しい), *a.* gallant; manly; majestic; imposing.

riritsu (利率), *n.* the rate of interest.

riron (理論), *n.* theory. —理論的, theoretical.

risai (罹災), *n.* suffering (from a calamity). ¶ 罹災地, the districts affected; the afflicted district. —罹災者, the sufferers; the victims. (罹災者救助金, the sufferers relief fund.)

risan (離散), *n.* dissolution; dispersion. —離散する, to scatter; disperse.

risei (理性), *n.* reason. —理性に訴へる, to appeal to reason.

riseki (離籍する), *vi.* to erase a person's name from a family register.

rishi (利子), *n.* interest. ☞ *ri* (利). —利子のつく, interest-bearing. ¶ 利子早見表, an interest ready-reckoner [reckoning table].

rishin (離心), *n.* 【天】 eccentricity; disloyalty; defection. ¶ 離心率, 【數】 eccentricity.

rishō (離礁する), *vi.* to get off the rock; float; be refloated.

rishoku (利殖), *n.* money-making. ☞ *kashoku.*

risō (理想), *n.* an ideal. —理想の夫《妻》, an ideal husband 《wife》. —理想の低い人, a man of low ideals. ¶ 理想主義, idealism.

risoku (利息), *n.* interest. ☞ *ri, rishi.*

risshiden (立志傳), *n.* biographies of self-made men.

risshin (立身), *n.* rise (in the world); advancement in life. ☞ *shusse* (出世).

risshō (立證), *n.* proof. —立證する, to prove; establish.

risshoku (立食), *n.* a stand-up collation; a stand-up luncheon.

risshū (立秋), *n.* the Beginning of Autumn, August 7.

risshun (立春), *n.* the Beginning of Spring, Feb. 5.

rissui (立錐の地), *n.* a small space. —立錐の地もない, there is no standing-room left.

ris-suru (律する), *vt.* ❶ (はかる) to judge; measure. ❷ (規律する) to regulate.

risu (栗鼠), *n.* 【哺乳】 the squirrel.

risu (離洲する), *vi.* to refloat; float.

risui (利水), *n.* irrigation.

risui (離水する), *vi.* to rise from [leave] the water.

risurin (リスリン), *n.* glycerine.

ri-suru (利する), *vt.* (を裨益する) to profit; benefit; advantage. ——, *vi.* (が得る所あり) to profit *by*; benefit *by*; advantage *by*; gain *in* 《*from*》; derive benefit *from*. —經驗によって利する, to benefit by experience. —その本を讀んで利する所があった, I have read the book to my benefit.

rita (利他), *n.* altruism. ¶ 利他主義者, an altruist.

ritei (里程), *n.* Ⓢ 里數. mileage; distance. ¶ 里程標, a mile-post 《-stone》.

ritoku (利得), *n.* gains; profit. ☞ *rieki.* ¶ 利得税, excess-profits tax.

ritsu (律), *n.* ❶ (法) a law (因果律·道德律·成文律の律). ❷ (戒律) commandments. ❸ (律呂) rhythm. ❹ (標準) a standard; a rule.

ritsu (率), *n.* rate (割合); ratio (比率); 【數】 index.

ritsuan (立案), *n.* a plan; a device; a draft. —立案する, to make [draw; form; frame] a plan; draft a bill; devise.

ritsudō (律動), *n.* 【理·生】 rhythm.

ritsuron (立論), *n.* argument; proposition. —立論する, to argue; make [put forward] an argument.

ritsuzen (慄然), *ad.* tremblingly; with a shudder.

ritsuzō (立像), *n.* a statue.

rittai (立體), *n.* 【數】 a solid (body). ¶ 立體派, 【美】 cubism; a cubist (畫家). —立體幾何學, solid geometry.

rittaishi (立太子), *n.* proclamation of an Heir (Apparent) to the Throne.

rittō (立黨式), *n.* the inauguration of a party. —立黨の精神に悖る, to be contrary to the spirit underlying the formation of the party.

rittoru (立), *n.* a litre (我が五合五勺强).

riyaku (利益), *n.* divine favour. —御利益があった, My prayer was answered.

riyō (利用), *n.* use; utilization. ——**-suru**, *vt.* to utilize; make use *of*; turn to account [one's advantage]; avail oneself *of*. —機會を利用する, to take advantage of an opportunity; take [embrace] an opportunity; improve the occasion.

riyoku (利慾), *n.* avarice; greed; covetousness. —利慾に趨る, to be tempted by gain; be swayed by avarice.

riyū (理由), *n.* reason; cause; ground. —…の理由で, on the score [ground] *of*. —如何なる理由で, on what grounds; for what reason; why. —理由なく, without reason. —十分理由がある, to have a good [sufficient] reason. —理由が立たぬ, to be without reason.

rizai (理財), *n.* economy (經濟); finance (財政). ¶ 理財學, economics; political economy. —理財局, the Financial Bureau.

rizume (理詰), *n.* force of reason [argument]. —理詰めの言葉, reasonable words. —理詰めにする, to reason a person down (*into*; *out of*).

ro (ろ), *n.* 【香】B; si【伊】; 7.

ro (絽), *n.* silk gauze.

ro (櫓, 艪), *n.* an oar.

ro (爐), *n.* ❶ (圍爐裏) a fire-place; a hearth. ❷ (熔鑛爐) a furnace.

rō (牢), *n.* =*rōgoku*.

rō (勞), *n.* trouble; pains; service (勤勞); labour (勞働). —勞を惜む(まぬ), to spare oneself trouble (spare no pains). —人の勞を省く, to save a person trouble.

rō (樓), *n.* ❶ a tower; a hall. ❷ the upper floor (of a house).

rō (蠟), *n.* wax. —蠟が垂れる, The candle runs down [gutters].

rō (聾), *n.* deafness. —聾する, to deafen.

rō (隴を得て蜀を望む), "The more one has, the more one desires."

rōa (聾啞), *n.* ❶ deaf-dumbness. ❷ the deaf and dumb; a deaf-mute.

roba (驢馬), *n.* a donkey; an ass.

rōba (老婆), *n.* an old woman; a grandam; a grandmother (祖母). ¶ 老婆心, grandmotherliness; grandmotherly notions; excessive solicitude (for another's welfare). (老婆心から, out of [from motives of] kindness.)

rōbai (狼狽), *n.* disconcertment; dismay; consternation; confusion. —狼狽する, to be disconcerted; be panic-stricken; lose one's head [presence of mind]. —狼狽して, in confusion; confusedly; in a panic.

rōban (牢番), *n.* a gaoler; a jailer.

robo (鹵簿), *n.* an Imperial cortège [procession].

robō (路傍), *n.* roadside; wayside. ¶ 路傍說敎者(演說者), a street preacher (speaker).

rochō (顱頂), *n.* the scalp; the skull-cap; 【解】the calvarium. ¶ 顱頂骨, the parietal bone.

rodai (露臺), *n.* a balcony.

rōdan (壟斷), *n.* engrossment; monopolization. —壟斷する, to engross; monopolize; take exclusive possession *of*; have to oneself.

rōden (漏電), *n.* electric leakage. —漏電する, Electricity leaks.

rōdō (勞働), *n.* labour; toil. —勞働する, to labour; work. ¶ 八時間勞働, eight-hour labour. —精神(筋肉)勞働, mental [brain] (physical; manual; muscular) labour. —勞働團體, a labour organization. —勞働(者)保險, workingmen's [labourers'] insurance. —勞働時間, working hours. —勞働(者)階級, the labouring [working] class. —勞働組合, a trade-union; a (labour) union (米). (勞働《非勞働》組合員, a union (non-union) man (米); a unionist (non-unionist) (英). 勞働組合員のみを傭ふ工場を a closed [union] shop と云ひ兩者を傭ふ工場を an open shop と云ふ). —勞働問題, a labour question [problem]. —勞働祭, the May Day; the Labour Day (米). —勞働者, a labourer; a worker; work [working]-people. (組合《非組合》勞働者, a union (non-union) labourer (米); a union (non-union) man (米); a unionist (non-unionist; free labourer) (英). —組合勞働者の手になれる品 union-made articles.) —萬國勞働者協會, The International Working Men's Association; Industrial Workers of the World (I. W. W. と略す). —勞働市場, the labour market. —勞働爭議, labour dispute [conflict]. —勞働黨, the labour party; a labourite (一員).

rōdoku (朗讀), *n.* reading aloud; recitation (暗誦). —朗讀する, to read aloud; recite; give recitation. ¶ 朗讀演說, a written speech; a speech read from notes. (朗讀演說をする, to read an address.)

roei (露營), *n.* bivouac; camping-out; encampment. —露營する, to bivouac; encamp.

rōei (漏洩), *n.* leakage. ——**suru**, *v.* ❶ [*vi.*] to leak out; be out. ❷ [*vt.*] to let out; disclose. —祕密を漏洩する, to let the secrets leak out.

rōeki (勞役), *n.* labour; toil; hard labour (特に囚人の). —勞役する, to labour; work hard. ¶ 勞役者, a labourer.

rōgan (老眼), *n.* 【醫】 presbyopia; far-sightedness. ☞ *enshigan.* ¶ 老眼鏡, convex glasses [spectacles]; spectacles for the aged.

rōgin (勞銀), *n.* wages. ☞ *chingin.*

rōgin (朗吟), *n.* recitation; recital.

rōgo (老後の), *a.* in [of] old age. —老後の思ひ出に, as the last effort of an old man.

rōgoku (牢獄), *n.* a prison; a gaol; a jail.

roha (ロハで), *ad.* for nothing; gratis (無代で); free of charge (無料で).

rōha (綠礬), *n.* 【化】 sulphate of iron; ferrous sulphate; copperas.

rōhai (老廢する), *v.* to become superannuated; be in one's dotage.

rōhi (浪費), *n.* waste; extravagance; prodigality. **—— - suru,** *vt.* to waste; squander; lavish. —時間を浪費する, to waste time; spend time to no purpose; loaf time away (のらくらとして). ¶ 浪費者, a squanderer; a prodigal; a spendthrift.

rōjaku-danjo (老弱男女), *n.* young and old, men and women. —老弱男女の區別無く, without distinction [irrespective] of age or sex.

roji (路地), *n.* an alley; a lane. —行止り《通拔け自由》の路地, a blind 《open》 alley.

rōjin (老人), *n.* an old man; the old; the aged.

rōjo (老女), *n.* a matron; an old woman.

rōjō (籠城), *n.* ❶ a siege; beleaguerment. ❷ (閉居) confinement. —籠城する, ① to be besieged. ② to be shut up; be confined; be kept in. —籠城に堪へる, to stand a long siege.

rōjuku (老熟する), *vi.* to be experienced (in); be mature.

roka (濾過), *n.* filtration. —濾過する, to filter; filtrate; strain. ¶ 濾過地, a filter-bed. —濾過器, a strainer; a filter.

rōka (廊下), *n.* a gallery; a corridor; a passage. —廊下傳ひに, along a corridor.

rokai (蘆薈), *n.* 【植】 Aloë vera (aloe の一種·學名).

rōkai (老獪), *n.* craftiness; astuteness. —老獪な, crafty; astute; shrewd; cunning.

rokaku (鹵獲), *n.* capture. —鹵獲する, to capture. ¶ 鹵獲品, a booty.

rōkaku (樓閣), *n.* a palace; a mansion; a tower.

rōkei (蠟型), *n.* a wax figure [model]; a ceroplastic.

roken (露見), *n.* discovery; disclosure; detection. **—— - suru,** *vi.* to come [be brought] to light; come out; be discovered; be detected. —惡事が露見した, Evil deeds came to light.

rokēshon (出張撮影), *n.* location.

rokkaku (六角 -形), *n.* a hexagon.

rokkotsu (肋骨), *n.* ❶ a rib; a costa. ❷ (船の肋材) a rib; the frame.

rōko (牢乎), *ad.* firmly; steadily. —牢乎たる, firm; steadfast; strong.

rōkō (老功の), *a.* veteran; experienced; practised.

rōkō (漏口), *n.* a leak; a vent.

Rokoku (露國), *n.* Russia.

rokotsu (露骨の), *a.* blunt; candid; free-spoken; plain-spoken. **—— - ni,** *ad.* bluntly; candidly; frankly. —露骨に言ふと, to be plain [frank] with you; to say openly.

roku (六), *n.* six; the sixth (第六).

roku (祿), *n.* a fief; a feud. —祿を食む, to receive a feud; serve a feudal lord. —祿を盜む, to receive a feud without rendering a service.

rōku (勞苦), *n.* trouble; toil; labour. —勞苦する, to toil.

rokubu (六部), *n.* a Buddhist pilgrim.

rokubungi (六分儀), *n.* a sextant.

rokudenashi (碌でなし), *n.* ❶ (役に立たず) a worthless fellow; a good-for-nothing. ❷ (無賴漢) a wretch; a villain; a ruffian.

rokugatsu (六月), *n.* June.

rokujū (六十), *n.* sixty; threescore; the sixtieth (第六十). —六十代の人, a sexagenarian.

rokumai-byōbu (六枚屏風), *n.* a six-leafed screen.

rokumaku (肋膜), *n.* the pleura [*pl.* -æ]. ¶ 肋膜炎, pleurisy; pleuritis. —肋膜肺炎, pleuropneumonia.

roku-na (陸碌な), *a.* ❶ (正しい, 良い) right; good; proper. ❷ (價値ある) worthy. ❸ (滿足な) satisfactory. —碌なものにならない, He will never come to anything. **—— - ni,** *ad.* ❶ properly; worthily; satisfactorily. ❷ hardly; scarcely. —碌に手紙も書けない癖に, when he cannot even write a letter properly. —碌に顏を見せたこともない I have hardly seen his face.

rokuro (轆轤), *n.* ❶ a lathe; a pulley (滑車). ❷ (絞盤[ｷｬﾌﾟ]) a capstan; a windlass. ¶ 轆轤師, a turner. —轆轤細工, turnery.

rokuroku (碌碌, 陸陸), *ad.* ❶ (碌々として) idly. ❷ =*roku-ni.*

rokusai (鹿砦), *n.* an abatis.

rokushō (綠靑), *n.* 【化】 verdigris; copper-rust.

roku-suru (錄する), *vt.* to record; put on record; register.

rōkyō (老境), *n.* declining years; old age. —老境に入る, to enter upon one's declining years.

rōkyū (老朽), *n.* ❶ superannuation; decrepitude. ❷ a superannuated man 《employé; official》. —老朽の, superannuated; old; decrepit. —老朽する, to become superannuated. —老朽淘汰を行ふ, to superannuate; weed out decrepit ones. ¶ 老朽船《船員》, a superannuated ship 《seaman》.

Rōma (羅馬), *n.* Rome. —羅馬は一日にして成らず, "Rome was not built in a day." ¶ 羅馬法, Roman law. —羅馬法王, the Pope; the Supreme Pontiff; the Holy Father. (羅馬法王の宮殿, the Vatican. —羅馬法王の使節, a legate; a nuncio.) —羅馬字, Roman letters. (羅馬字綴りの日本語, Romanized Japanese.) —羅馬敎, the Roman Catholic Church; Roman-Catholicism; the Church of Rome. (羅馬敎徒, a papist; a (Roman) Catholic.) —羅馬數字, Roman numerals.

rōman-shugi (浪漫主義), *n.* romanticism.

rōmansu (ローマンス), *n.* romance; a love story (戀愛談).

rōmantikku (浪漫的), *a.* romantic.

rōmatchi (蠟燐寸), *n.* a vesta; a wax match.

romei (露命), *n.* transitory [fleeting] life. —僅に露命をつなぐ, just to manage to keep body and soul together.

romen (路面), *n.* road surface.

rōmō (老耄), *n.* dotage; decrepitude; senility; anility. —老耄する, to dote; be in one's dotage.

rōmu (勞務), *n.* (personal) service. ¶ 勞務出資社員, a working [an active] partner.

ron (論), *n.* argument (議論); a discussion (論議, 審議); debate (討論); dispute (論爭); a theory (學說, 理論); a treatise (秩序立ッた論文); an essay (短い論文). —論を待たぬ, to be beyond discussion. —論より證據, "The proof of the pudding is in the eating."

ronbaku (論駁する), *vt.* to refute; dispute; confute; rebut.

ronbun (論文), *n.* a thesis (論說, 卒業又は學位請求などの); an essay (文學上の短い); a treatise (纏った專門的の).

ronchō (論調), *n.* the tone of argument; the tone of the press (新聞の).

rondai (論題), *n.* a subject; a theme; a topic.

rondan (論斷する), *vt.* to conclude.

Rondon (倫敦), *n.* London. ¶ 倫敦兒, a Londoner; a cockney.

rōnen (老年), *n.* old [advanced] age; a ripe age; declining years.

rongai (論外の), *a.* out of the question; beside the question.

rongi (論議する), *vt.* to discuss; talk about.

Rongo (論語), *n.* the Analects of Confucius.

rōnin (浪人), *n.* ❶ a *rōnin*; a discharged *samurai*; a masterless *samurai*. ❷ (失職者) a person out of employment. —浪人する, to become *rōnin*: lose [get out of] employment (失業). —職を失ッて浪人してゐる, He has lost his position and is out of employment.

ron-jiru (論じる), *vt.* ❶ to argue; discuss; debate. ❷ to treat *of*; discourse *on*; deal *with*. —論じ詰めると, when argued to the end. —論ずるに及ばぬ, to be beyond [without; out of] controversy; be out of the question. —男女を論ぜず, irrespective [regardless] of sex. —當日晴雨を論ぜず, on the day wet or fine.

ronketsu (論結), *n.* conclusion; peroration (演說の). —論結する, to conclude; perorate.

ronkō-kōshō (論功行賞), bestowal of rewards (after inquiry into services). —論功行賞を行ふ, to bestow rewards for meritorious services.

ronkyo (論據), *n.* the basis [ground] of one's argument; the ground [principle] of proof. —確實な論據によって, on the sound basis of argument.

ronkyū (論及する), *vt.* to refer *to*; enter upon the discussion *of*.

ronkyū (論究する), *vt.* to discuss thoroughly; canvass; investigate; inquire *into*.

rōnō (勞農-會), *n.* Ⓢ 勞兵會. a soviet. ¶ 勞農露西亞, Soviet Russia. —勞農制《政府》, the Soviet system 《Government》.

ronpa (論破する), *vt.* to refute; disprove; overcome by argument.

ronpō (論法), *n.* reasoning; logic.

ronpō (論鋒), *n.* the force of argument [reasoning].

ronpyō (論評), *n.* criticism; review; comment. —論評する, to criticize; review.

ronri (論理-學), *n.* logic. —論理的に, logically. —論理に背く, to be against logic; be illogical.

ronsen (論戰), *n.* disputation;

a controversy; a passage-at [of] -arms; a paper-war.

ronsetsu (論說), *n.* ❶ an essay; a discourse; a treatise. ❷ (社說) an editorial; a leading article; a leader.

ronsha (論者), *n.* ❶ a disputant; a debater; a speaker (演說の). ❷ (賛成論者) an advocate (of peace など).

ronshi (論旨), *n.* the point of an argument; 【論】 issue.

ronshō (論證), *n.* proof; 【論】 demonstration. —論證する, to prove; demonstrate.

ronsō (論爭), *n.* a disputation; a contention; a controversy; a dispute; a contest. **—— -suru,** *vt.* to dispute; contest; controvert. —人と論爭する, to argue with a person.

ronten (論點), *n.* a point at issue [in question].

rōntenisu (庭球), *n.* lawn-tennis.

ron-zuru (論ずる), *vt.* =*ronjiru.*

roppō (六法-全書), *n.* a collection of the six laws.

roppyakurokugō (六百六號), *n.* 606; salvarsan; kharsivan (英國での商標名).

rōrā (ローラー), *n.* an inker (印肉棒); a roller (同上·修道轆[ポテト?]など). ¶ ローラー·スケート, a roller-skate.

rōraku (籠絡), *n.* inveiglement; cajolement. **—— -suru,** *vt.* to inveigle; cajole; wheedle. —賄賂を使って籠絡する, to ensnare a person with a bribe.

rōren (老練な), *a.* skilled; old; veteran. ¶ 老練家, a veteran; a skilled man; an old hand.

roretsu (呂律がまはらぬ), to be unable to talk coherently.

rōretsu (陋劣な), *a.* mean; vile; base. —陋劣な手段を弄する, to resort to vile means.

rōrō (朗朗), *ad.* ❶ (音色) sonorously; mellowly. ❷ (光) brightly. —朗々と誦讀する, to read clearly.

rōryoku (勞力), *n.* labour. ☞ *rō* (勞). —勞力を節約する, ① [*v.*] to save labour. ② [*a.*] labour-saving.

rōsei (狼星), *n.* Sirius; the Greater Dog; the dog-star.

rōseki (蠟石), *n.* marble.

Rosha, Roshia, (露西亞), *n.* Russia. ¶ 露西亞語, Russian. —露西亞人, a Russian.

rōsha (聾者), *n.* the deaf.

Roshi (露支), *a.* Russo-Chinese.

rōshi (勞資), *n.* capital and labour.

rōshi (老死する), *vi.* to die of old age.

rōshigan (老視眼), *n.* 【醫】 presbyopia; old sight.

rōshō (勞症), *n.* consumption; phthisis.

roshuku (露宿), *n.* bivouac; camping out. ☞ *nojuku.*

roshutsu (露出), *n.* exposure; disclosure; outcrop (鑛脈). —露出する, ① [*vt.*] to disclose; expose; lay bare. ② [*vi.*] to be exposed; be disclosed; 【地質】 crop out [up] (地上に).

rōshutsu (漏出), *n.* leakage; escape. —漏出する, to leak out; ooze out; escape.

rōsō (狼瘡), *n.* 【醫】 lupus.

rōsoku (蠟燭), *n.* a candle; a wax-candle; a taper (細い).

rōsu (ロース), *n.* roast; sirloin (牛肉の).

rōsui (老衰), *n.* senility; dotage; decrepitude. —老衰する, to become decrepit from age. —老衰せる, decrepit; senile.

rō-suru (弄する), *vt.* to play with; trifle with. ☞ *moteasobu.* —諧謔を弄する, to crack a joke.

rō-suru (勞する), *vi.* to labour; toil; take pains. **——,** *vt.* to trouble (煩はす). —勞して功無し, to work in vain [to no purpose].

rō-suru (聾する), *vt.* to deafen.

rotei (路程), *n.* distance (距離); journey (旅行).

roten (露天), *n.* the open air. —露天の, out-of-door(s); open-air.

roten (露店), *n.* a street-stall; a booth. ¶ 露天商人, a pitcher; a street-vendor.

rotō (路頭), *n.* the roadside; the wayside. —路頭に迷ふ, to be turned into the street; be reduced to beggary.

rotō (路燈), *n.* a road [street]-lamp.

rōto (漏斗), *n.* ❶ a funnel. ❷ 【解】 an infundibulum. —漏斗狀の, funnelled; funnel-shaped; infundibular.

rōya (牢屋), *n.* a prison; a jail.

royō (路用), *n.* travelling expenses.

rōzeki (狼藉), *n.* ❶ (混亂) disorder; confusion. ❷ (亂暴) violence; outrage. ¶ 狼藉者, a disorderly person; a ruffian.

rōzu (玷貨), *n.* waste.

rufu (流布), *n.* currency; dissemination; circulation. —流布する, ① [*vt.*] to circulate; disseminate; spread. ② [*vi.*] to be prevalent; get abroad; take the air; go the round.

ruhō (屢報する), *vi.* to report repeatedly [more than once].

rui (累), *n.* trouble (迷惑); implication (掛り合ひ). —累を他に

及ぼす, to bring trouble upon others.

rui (壘), *n.* ❶ (壘塞) a rampart; a fort. ❷【野球】a base. ——《二;三》壘手, the first 《second; third》 baseman. —壘を摩す, to rival (a person *in*); touch (a person *in*); vie *with* (a person *in*).

rui (類), *n.* ❶ (種類) a kind; a sort; a class. ❷ (比類) a parallel; an equal; a rival. ❸【博物】a family; an order. —他に類のない, unique; of its own kind. —類は友を呼ぶ, "Like will to like." —類を以て集る, "Birds of a feather flock together."

ruibetsu (類別), *n.* classification. —類別する, to classify; make into [reduce to] classes.

ruidai (累代), *n.* successive generations.

ruidan (涙彈), *n.* 【軍】a tear-shell [-bomb]; a lachrymatory shell.

ruigo (類語), *n.* a synonym.

ruihan (累犯), *n.* 【法】repeated offence; recidivism. ¶ 累犯者, an old offender; a recidivist.

ruiheki (壘壁), *n.* a rampart; a wall.

ruiji (累次), *ad.* successively; consecutively; repeatedly.

ruiji (類似), *n.* resemblance; similarity; likeness. —類似する, to resemble; be similar *to*. ——**no**, *a.* like; similar; akin to; kindred; analogous. —其の他之に類似の器械, and other apparatuses of like nature.

ruijinen (類人猿), *n.* 【哺乳】an anthropoid ape.

ruijō (累乘する), *v.* to practise involution. ¶ 累乘法,【數】involution.

ruikan (涙管), *n.* 【解】the lachrymal duct.

ruikei (累計), *n.* the total; the total sum; the sum total.

ruikei (類型), *n.* type.

ruinen (累年), *n.* successive years. ——, *ad.* every year; year after year.

ruiran (累卵), *n.* a pile of eggs. —累卵の如く危い, as hazardous as a pile of eggs.

ruirei (類例), *n.* a similar case [instance; example]. —類例なき, unexampled; unique.

ruireki (瘰癧), *n.* scrofula; the royal [king's] evil.

ruirui (累累), *ad.* in a pile; in heaps. —死屍累々たり, Corpses [Bodies] lay in heaps.

ruiseki (累積), *n.* accumulation; cumulation; a heap. —累積する, to be piled up; lie in heaps; accumulate.

ruisen (涙腺), *n.* 【解】the lachrymal gland.

ruisetsu (縲絏), *n.* fetters; bonds; shackles. —縲絏の辱めを受ける, to be exposed to the disgrace of bonds; become a prisoner.

ruishin (累進), *n.* successive promotion. —累進する, to be promoted successively; rise from grade to grade. ¶ 累進税, progressive [graduated] taxes (degressive taxes の對).

ruisho (類書), *n.* books of the (same) kind.

ruishō (類症の), *a.* of similar diseases.

ruishō (類燒する), *vi.* to be burnt down by a spreading fire. —類燒を免れる, to escape the fire. ¶ 類燒者, a person burnt out; a sufferer from [a victim of] a fire.

ruishu (壘手), *n.* a baseman.

ruisui (類推), *n.* analogy; analogism. —類推する, to analogize.

rui-suru (累する), *vt.* to plague; annoy; trouble; involve (連累).

rui-suru (類する), *vt.* to resemble; be similar *to*; be analogous *to*.

rujutsu (縷述する), *vt.* to detail; particularize; dwell *on*. —事情を縷述する, to give a full account of the circumstances.

runessansu (ルネッサンス), *n.* 【文藝】Renaissance.

runin (流人), *n.* ❶ (放浪者) a vagabond. ❷ (流者) an exile; a person transported.

rurā (ルラー), *n.* ❶ =*rōrā*. ❷ (簿記棒) a ruler.

ruri (瑠璃), *n.* ❶ lapis lazuli. ❷【鳥】(大瑠璃) the Japanese blue flycatcher.

rurō (流浪), *n.* vagrancy. —流浪する, to wander about; roam; rove. ¶ 流浪人, a vagabond; a tramp; a wanderer.

ruru (縷縷), *ad.* in particular; in detail; minutely. —縷々陳述する, to explain in detail [at length]; go into particulars.

rusu (留守), *n.* absence. —留守中に, in one's absence. —留守である, to be out; be not at home; be (away) from home. (學校へ行って《旅行して》留守です, He is away at school 《on a journey》.) —留守を使ふ, to pretend to be out; be not at home (to another). ¶ 留守番, a care-taker. (留守番をする, to take care [charge of the house]/during another's absence.)

ruten (流轉), *n.* ❶ (佛教) transmigration. ❷ (遷移) fluxion; continuous change; vicissitude. ❸ (流浪) wandering. —流轉する, ① to transmigrate. ② to change in continuous succession. ③ to wander [roam] about.

rutsubo (坩堝), *n.* a crucible; a (melting) pot.

ruzai (流罪), *n.* exile; banishment. ¶ 流罪人, an exile.

rūzu-rīfu (加除式), *n.* 【簿記】 loose-leaf system.

ryakkai (略解), *n.* a rough explanation; a brief note.

ryakki (略記する), *vt.* to write briefly; make [give] a sketch; give an outline.

ryaku (略), *n.* ❶ =*ryakuji* (略字). ❷ (概略) an outline; a sketch. ❸ (策略) a stratagem; a policy.

ryakudatsu (掠奪, 略奪), *n.* plunder; pillage; depredation. —掠奪する, to plunder; pillage; despoil [deprive] *of*; loot [sack] (占領した都市を). ¶ 掠奪者, a plunderer; a pillager.

ryakuden (略傳), *n.* a short life; a short biography; a biographical sketch.

ryakufuku (略服), *n.* an undress (uniform); an ordinary dress; a mufti (軍人の).

ryakuga (略畫), *n.* a (rough) sketch.

ryakugen (略言する), *vt.* to summarize; state concisely [briefly]. —略言すれば, in short [brief]; to be brief; in a word; to make a long story short.

ryakugi (略儀), *n.* informality. —略儀ながら, informal as it is.

ryakugo (略語), *n.* an abbreviation; an abbreviated word; a grammalogue (速記の).

ryakugō (略號), *n.* a code address; a telegraphic (code) address (電信の).

ryakuhyō (略表), *n.* an abridged table.

ryakuji (略字), *n.* an abbreviation (Am.; S. O. S. の類); a contraction (約字 ne'er; can't の類).

ryakureki (略歴), *n.* a sketch of a person's life.

ryakusetsu (略說), *n.* an outline; a summary; a condensed 《rough》 account. —略說する, to summarize; give an outline *of*.

ryakushiki (略式), *n.* informality. —略式の, informal; 【法】 summary. —略式に, informally; without formality [ceremony]. ¶ 略式裁判, a summary conviction [trial].

ryakushō (略章), *n.* a rosette.

ryakushu (略取), *n.* ❶ (攻略) capture. ❷ (かっさらひ) kidnapping. —略取する, ① to capture; carry; seize; take; occupy. ② to kidnap; take [carry] away.

ryaku-suru (略する), *vt.* ❶ (省略) to abbreviate; curtail; abridge; omit; dispense *with* (formalities). ❷ (略取) to capture; seize; take. —略して言へば, in short; in brief; in a word; to make a long story short. —詳細の事は略す, to omit the details. —名前を略さずに書く, to write one's name in full.

ryakuzu (略圖), *n.* a sketch; a rough plan; an outline-map (輪郭地圖). —略圖を取る, to sketch; take a rough sketch *of*.

ryō (兩), *n.* (貨幣) a tael 〔支〕. ——, *a.* two; both (banks; sides など). —兩三度, two or three times; a few times.

ryō (料), *n.* ❶ (材料) materials. ❷ (料金) charge; fee.

ryō (漁), *n.* ❶ fishing; fishery. ❷ (漁獲高) a catch; a haul. —漁に行く, to go (a-)fishing.

ryō (領), *n.* ❶ (所領) a possession. ❷ (領土) a dominion; a territory. ¶ 英領, British possessions. (英領印度, British India.)

ryō (寮), *n.* ❶ (寄宿舍) a dormitory. ❷ (別莊) a villa. ❸ (官寮) a bureau; a department.

ryō (龍), *n.* a dragon.

ryō (獵), *n.* ❶ (狩) hunting; shooting (銃獵); sporting (遊獵). ❷ (獲物) a take; a game; a bag. —獵に行く, to go (out) hunting [shooting]; follow the hounds.

ryōan (諒闇), *n.* national [court] mourning; an interregnum (特に天皇崩御の).

ryōba (獵場), *n.* ❶ (陸) a hunting place [ground]. ❷ (海) a fishing station [ground].

ryōben (兩便), *n.* both calls of nature.

ryōbun (領分), *n.* ❶ (領域) (*a*) (學問の) domain; province; region: (*b*) (管轄の) jurisdiction. ❷ (領土) a dominion; a territory. ❸ (所領) a possession. —他人の領分を犯す, to encroach [trespass] upon another's domain.

ryōchi (了知する), *vt.* to know; understand; comprehend.

ryōchi (領地), *n.* ❶ (采邑) a fief; a feud. ❷ a domain.

ryodan (旅團), *n.* a brigade. ¶ 混成旅團, a mixed [composite] brigade. —旅團長, a brigade commander; a brigadier(-general).

ryōdo (領土), *n.* a dominion; a territory; a possession (屬領).

ryōdō (糧道), *n.* supply of provisions. —糧道を絶つ, to cut off the enemy's supplies.

ryōdōtai (良導體), *n.* 【理】 a good conductor.

ryōen (良緣), *n.* a suitable [good] match.

ryōen (遼遠なる), *a.* distant. —遼遠なる前途, a distant hope. —前途遼遠である, We are still far

[a long way] from our object.
ryōfu (獵夫), *n.* a hunter; a huntsman.
ryōfū (涼風), *n.* a refreshing [cool] breeze.
ryōga (凌駕する), *vt.* to surpass; be superior *to*; exceed; outstrip.
ryōgae (兩替), *n.* exchange; change. —兩替する, to exchange [change] (money). ¶ 兩替屋, a money-changer; an exchange-broker [-shop (店)].
ryogai (慮外), *n.* ❶ (意外) unexpectedness. ❷ (失禮) rudeness; discourtesy. —慮外の, rude; discourteous.
ryōgan (兩眼), *n.* two [both] eyes. ¶ 兩眼鏡, a binocular.
ryohi (旅費), *n.* travelling expenses.
ryōgen (燎原の火), *n.* wild-fire. —燎原の火の如く擴まる, to spread like wild-fire.
ryōhi (良否), *n.* good or bad. —品質の良否, the quality of an article.
ryōhō (兩方), *n.* both; both sides [parties]; the one and the other.
ryōhō (療法), *n.* cure; remedy; (a method of) treatment; means of remedy; therapy (主として複合詞として用ひる).
ryōhoñi (兩本位-制), *n.* bimetallism; bimetallic system.
ryōi (良醫), *n.* a good physician; a skilful doctor.
ryōiki (領域), *n.* a domain; a territory; a region; a sphere. ☞ *ryōbun.*
ryōin (兩院), *n.* both Chambers [Houses]. ¶ 兩院協議會, a conference of the two Houses. —兩院協議委員會, a joint committee.
ryōji (領事), *n.* a consul. ¶ 副領事, a vice-consul. —領事代理, an acting-consul. —領事團, consular corps [body]. —領事館, a consulate.
ryōji (療治), *n.* (surgical) operation (外科); (medical) treatment. —療治する, to treat (medically); perform surgical operation. —療治を受ける, to undergo medical treatment 《an operation》.
ryojin (旅人), *n.* a traveller; a tourist (觀光の). ¶ 旅人宿, an inn; a tavern.
ryōjitsu (良日), *n.* a good [an auspicious] day; a red-letter day.
ryōjō (旅情を慰める), to divert the monotony of one's travel; cheer the heart of a traveller.
ryōjoku (凌辱), *n.* insult (侮辱); outrage (暴行). —凌辱する, to insult; affront; outrage. —凌辱を受ける, to be subjected to insult.
ryōjū (獵銃), *n.* a hunting gun; a sporting gun; a fowling-piece (鳥銃).
ryōjū (獵獸), *n.* game.
ryōka (良家), *n.* a good [respectable] family.
ryōkai (了解), *n.* understanding; apprehension; comprehension. —了解する, to understand; comprehend; apprehend. —了解出來ない, to be beyond one [one's comprehension]. —當局の了解を得て, with the aquiescence of the authorities.
ryōkai (領海), *n.* territorial waters; closed sea.
ryokaku (旅客), *n.* a passenger; a traveller. ¶ 旅客驛《飛行; 運送》, passenger station 《flight; traffic》. —旅客名簿, a list of passengers.
ryokan (旅館), *n.* a hotel; an inn. —旅館の主人, a landlord [*fem.* -lady]; a host [*fem.* -ess].
ryōkan (獵官), *n.* place-hunting. ¶ 獵官者, a place-hunter [-seeker]; an office-hunter [-seeker] 〔米〕.
ryōkan (僚艦), *n.* a consort.
ryōkei (菱形), *n.* a rhomb.
ryoken (旅券), *n.* a passport. —旅券を査證《下附》する, to visé 《issue》 a passport. —旅券の下附を願出る, to apply for a passport.
ryōken (料簡, 了見, 量見), *n.* ❶ (考) an idea; a thought; a notion. ❷ (分別) discretion; judgment (判斷). ❸ (意向) an intention. ❹ (堪忍) pardon; forgiveness. —惡い了見を起す, to be tempted to an evil thought. ¶ 料簡違ひ, ① (誤解) misunderstanding; misjudgment; misconception. ② (過誤) an error; a fault.
ryōken (獵犬), *n.* a hunting-dog; a hound; a hunter.
ryōki (量器), *n.* a meter (メーター, メートル); a measure.
ryōki (獵期), *n.* the hunting season; the open season.
ryōkin (料金), *n.* charge; fee; fare.
ryokkō (力行する), *vi.* to make strenuous [great] efforts; exert oneself.
ryokō (旅行), *n.* a travel; a journey; a voyage (海旅). —旅行する, to travel; make a journey; make a voyage. —旅行で不在です, He is away on his journey. ¶ 旅行案內, a guide-book. —旅行家, a traveller; a tourist. —旅行免狀, a passport. ☞ *ryoken.* —旅行者, a passenger; a traveller; a voyager (海上旅行者).
ryōkō (良好なる), *a.* good; satisfactory; successful; favourable. —良好なる結果を齎す, to produce a good [satisfactory] result.
ryōkū (領空), *n.* territorial air.
ryokuban (綠礬), *n.* sulphate of

iron; copperas; green vitriol.
ryokucha (緑茶), *n.* green tea.
ryokugyoku (緑玉), *n.* emerald.
ryokuin (緑蔭), *n.* the shade of a tree; a green shade.
ryokumon (緑門), *n.* an arch (of green leaves).
ryokunaishō (緑内障), *n.* 【醫】 glaucoma (硝子液不透明症).
ryokusen (力戰する), *vi.* to fight desperately; struggle.
ryokushoku (緑色), *n.* greenness; green colour.
ryokusō (力爭する), *vi.* to dispute [quarrel] violently.
ryokyaku (旅客), *n.* a passenger. ☞ *ryokaku*.
ryōkyakuki (兩脚規), *n.* 【數】 dividers; compasses.
ryōkyō (稜鏡), *n.* 【理】 a prism.
ryōkyoku (兩極), *n.* the two poles.
ryōmae (兩前), *a.* double-breasted.
ryōmatsu (糧秣), *n.* provisions and fodder; provisions. ¶ 糧秣廠, the provisions department.
ryōmen (兩面), *n.* two [both] faces; two sides [aspects] (of a thing).
ryōmin (良民), *n.* peaceful people; law-abiding citizens. —良民を苦しめる, to oppress peaceful people.
ryōmoku (量目), *n.* measure.
ryonō (旅嚢), *n.* a travelling-bag; a knapsack; a rucksack (背嚢).
ryōō (兩凹の), *a.* concavo-concave; biconcave.
ryōri (料理), *n.* ❶ (割烹) cooking; cookery; cuisine. ❷ (料理品) dishes; fare. ❸ (處辨) management; administration. ——suru, *vt.* ❶ to manage; administer; conduct. ❷ to cook; dress; prepare. —國政を料理する, to put the national administration straight. ¶ 料理人, a cook; a *cuisinier* 【佛】. —料理店, a restaurant; a cook-shop; an eating-house.
ryōritsu (兩立する), *vi.* to stand [consist] together; coexist *with*; stand *with*; consist *with*; be compatible *with*. —兩立せぬ信條, warring creeds.
ryōsai (良妻), *n.* a good wife.
ryōsaku (良策), *n.* a good plan; a fine device.
ryōsatsu (諒察), *n.* sympathy; consideration. —諒察する, to sympathize *with*; feel *for* [*with*]; take into consideration [account]. —御諒察を乞ふ, I appeal to your sympathy.
ryōsei (兩性), *n.* the (two) sexes; both sexes. —兩性の, bisexual; androgynous.
ryōseirui (兩棲類), *n.* 【動】 Amphibia.
ryōsen (獵船), *n.* a fishing-boat [-vessel].
ryōsha (兩者), *n.* both; both parties.
ryōshi (獵師, 漁夫), *n.* ❶ (獵夫) a huntsman; a hunter. ❷ (漁夫) a fisherman.
ryōshin (兩親), *n.* the parents; both parents.
ryōshin (良心), *n.* conscience. —良心のある〘ない〙人, a man of 〘without〙 conscience. —良心の苛責, the pangs [qualms; pricks] of conscience; compunction. —良心に背く, to go against one's conscience. —良心に恥ぢる, to have pangs of conscience. —良心が麻痺してゐる, His conscience is numb.
ryōsho (良書), *n.* a good book.
ryōshoku (糧食), *n.* food; provisions; victuals.
ryōshu (領主), *n.* a (feudal) lord; the lord of a manor.
ryōshū (領收), *n.* receipt. —領收する, to receive. —右正に領收候也, Received with thanks. ¶ 領收書, a receipt.
ryōshū (領袖), *n.* a leader (of a party).
ryoshuku (旅宿), *n.* ❶ (旅の宿り) stopping; putting up. ❷ (宿屋) an inn; a tavern.
ryosō (旅裝), *n.* a kit; a travelling suit; travelling outfit. —旅裝を調へる, ① to get together travelling outfit. ② to dress [equip] oneself for a journey.
ryōsuikei (量水計), *n.* a water-meter.
ryō-suru (了する), *vt.* ❶ (終る) to end; finish; complete. ❷ (了承する) to accept; acknowledge. ❸ (了知する) to understand. —手續を了する, to have gone through formalities.
ryō-suru (諒する), *v.* to sympathize *with*; appreciate; approve *of*; enter into another's feeling.
ryō-suru (領する), *vt.* (領有する) to be lord *of*; possess; be in possession *of*.
ryōte (兩手), *n.* both [two] hands; right and left hands. —兩手に花, good fortune [success] on both hands. ¶ 兩手利き, ambidexterity; an ambidexter (人).
ryotei (旅程), *n.* a journey; an itinerary (旅行のプログラム).
ryōtei (料亭), *n.* a restaurant.
ryōtei (涼亭), *n.* a summer-house.
ryōtenbin (兩天秤), *n.* double-dealing; alternatives; two strings to one's bow. —兩天秤にかける, to have two strings to one's bow.
ryōtō (兩刀), *n.* two swords; the long and short swords. ¶ 兩刀

論法,【論】a dilemma.
ryō-tosuru (諒とする), *vt.* to appreciate; sympathize. ☞ *ryō-suru.* —彼の言を諒とする, to approve of [appreciate] his views.
ryōtotsu (兩凸の), *a.* biconvex; convexo-convex; lenticular. ¶ 兩凸鏡, biconvex lens.
ryōyaku (良藥), *n.* an efficacious [good] medicine.
ryōyō (療養), *n.* medical treatment; recuperation. —療養する, to recuperate oneself; recruit (one's health).
ryōyū (良友), *n.* a good companion.
ryōyū (兩雄), *n.* the two heroes. —兩雄並び立たず, "Two cocks in one yard do not agree."
ryōyū (僚友), *n.* a colleague; a fellow(-worker); a co-worker.
ryōyū (領有する), *vt.* to possess; hold.
ryōzai (良材), *n.* ❶ a good timber. ❷ a man of talent (有材の人).
ryōzen (兩全の), *a.* mutually advantag[eous] [complete]. —兩全の道を講じる, to make a plan advantageous to both.
ryōzen (瞭然), *ad.* apparently; obviously; clearly. ☞ *ichimoku.*
ryōzō (兩造), *n.* both parties. ¶ 原被兩造, the plaintiff and defendant.
ryōzoku (僚屬), *n.* the staff; the personnel (人員).
ryū (流), *n.* ❶ (流儀) a style; a fashion; a manner; a school (派). ❷ (等級) rank; rate; class. —佛國流に, in the French style. —日本流の英語の發音, the Japanized pronunciation of English.
ryū (龍), *n.* a dragon.
ryūbetsu (留別), *n.* farewell; parting; separation. —留別の辭, a valediction; a valedictory (speech). ¶ 留別會, a farewell dinner (given by a person leaving).
ryūboku (流木), *n.* a driftwood.
ryūchi (留置), *n.* detention. —留置する, to detain; hold; retain. ¶ 留置場, a lock-up; a police cell. —留置權,【法】lien; right of retention [lien]; a possessory lien.
ryūchō (流暢な), *a.* fluent; easy; flowing. —辯舌が流暢だ, He has a silver tongue.
ryūdan (流彈), *n.* a stray bullet (shell).
ryūdan (榴彈), *n.* a shell.
ryūden (流電), *pref.* volta. —, *a.* voltaic; galvanic. ¶ 流電氣, voltaic electricity.
ryūdō (流動的), *a.* fluid; liquid. —流動する, to flow; float. ¶ 流動物, a fluid; a liquid; liquid food. —流動資本, floating [circulating] capital.
ryūdosui (龍吐水), *n.* a syringe; a squirt(-gun).
ryūgaku (留學), *n.* studying abroad. —留學する, to go abroad for study; study abroad. —留學を命ぜられる, to be ordered to study abroad. ¶ 留學生, students sent abroad to study. (在日本支那留學生, Chinese students in Japan.)
ryūgan (龍顏), *n.* the Imperial countenance.
ryūganniku (龍眼肉), *n.* a longan; a dragon's eye.
ryūgen (流言), *n.* a rumour. —流言を放つ, to set a rumour going [afloat]; circulate [spread] a rumour. ¶ 流言浮說 [蜚語], groundless rumours.
ryūgi (流儀), *n.* a style; a fashion; a way. —...の流儀によって, after the fashion [manner] *of.*
ryūgū (流寓する), *vi.* to roam about; drift about; live in exile.
ryūgū (龍宮), *n.* the Dragon Palace.
ryūho (留保), *n.* reserve; reservation; retention. —留保する, to reserve; retain.
ryūhyō (流氷), *n.* drift-ice; drifting [sailing]-ice.
ryūi (留意する), *vt.* to heed; notice; pay attention *to.*
ryūiki (流域), *n.* a catchment (-area; -basin);【地】a basin.
ryūin (溜飲), *n.* 【醫】pyrosis; water-brash. —やッと溜飲が下ッた, I feel relieved at last.
ryūka (硫化), *n.* 【化】sulphuration; sulphurization. ¶ 硫化物, a sulphide.
ryūkai (流會になる), *v.* to fail to be held; be given up.
ryūkan (流感), *n.* influenza; (*la*) *grippe* 【佛】.
ryūkei (流刑), *n.* exile; banishment; transportation.
ryūki (隆起), *n.* (an) upheaval 【地質】; swelling up. —隆起する, to heave up; rise; swell up.
ryukkusakku (背嚢), *n.* a rucksack (登山又は徒步旅行用の).
ryūkō (流行), *n.* ❶ fashion; vogue. ❷ (病氣の) prevalence. —最新流行, the latest fashion. —流行性の,【醫】epidemic; pandemic. —流行後れの, out of fashion; behind the fashion; old-fashioned; obsolete. —流行する, to be in fashion [vogue]; be popular; be prevalent; prevail. —流行となる, to come into fashion [vogue]. —それが大流行だ, It is all [quite] the go. ¶ 流行物, a fashion; a vogue. —流行病, an epidemic. —流行性感冒, influenza; (*la*) *grippe* 【佛】. —流行社會, fashionable society; the *beau monde* 【佛】.

—流行唄, a popular song.
ryūkotsu (龍骨), *n.* 【造船】a keel.
Ryūkyū (琉球), *n.* the Loochoo Islands.
ryūmachisu (僂麻質斯), *n.* 【醫】rheumatism. ¶ リウマチス患者, a rheumatoid; a rheumatic 〔俗〕.
ryūniku (隆肉), *n.* a hunch; a hump (駱駝等の).
ryūnin (留任する), *vi.* to remain [continue] in one's post. ¶ 留任運動, a movement for retaining a person in his post. (留任運動をする, to make an effort to induce a person to remain in his office.)
ryūnō (龍腦), *n.* ❶【植】the camphor-tree of Borneo. ❷ Borneo [Sumatra] camphor; borneol; camphol.
ryūnyū (流入), *n.* indraught; influx; inflow. —流入する, to flow in.
ryūrei (流麗な), *a.* smooth and elegant; mellifluous.
ryūro (流露), *n.* an outflow (of good feeling など).
ryūryō (劉喨たる), *a.* melodious; clear.
ryūryū (隆隆), *ad.* flourishing; thrivingly; in great force. —隆隆たる, high; prosperous; flourishing; thriving; ascendant.
ryūsan (硫酸), *n.* 【化】sulphuric acid; vitriol. ¶ 硫酸銅, copper sulphate. —硫酸鹽, a sulphate.
ryūsandan (榴散彈), *n.* a shrapnel (shell).
ryūsei (流星), *n.* a meteor; a shooting star; a bolide.
ryūsei (隆盛), *n.* prosperity. —隆盛に赴く, to flourish; prosper.
ryūsetsu (流說), *n.* a rumour; a current report.
ryūshitsu (流失する), *vi.* to be carried [swept; washed] away; drift away.
ryūshitsu (流出), *n.* outflow; efflux. —正貨の流出, efflux of species. —流出する, to flow [stream] out; run out.
ryūsui (流水), *n.* running water.
ryūtai (流體), *n.* a fluid.
ryūtō-dabi (龍頭蛇尾に終る), to go up like a rocket and come down like the stick.
ryūtsū (流通), *n.* ❶ (通用) circulation; negotiation. ❷ (通氣) ventilation. —流通する, to circulate; pass. —空氣の流通をよくする, to have the room well ventilated. ¶ 流通貨幣, money in circulation; currency. —流通手形《證券》, a negotiable bill《instrument》.
ryūyō (流用), *n.* diversion. —流用する, to divert *to*.
ryūzan (流產), *n.* miscarriage. —流產する, to miscarry.
ryūzetsuran (龍舌蘭), *n.* 【植】the American aloe; the century-plant.
ryūzu (龍頭), *n.* the stem (of a watch). —龍頭卷きの時計, a stem-winder; a keyless watch.

S

sa (左), *n.* ❶ (ひだり) the left. ❷ (次, 下) the following. —左の如く, as follows; in the following manner.
sa (差), *n.* ❶ (相違) difference; disparity; dissimilarity. ❷ the remainder (殘り); 【商】a margin (差額, 開き). —少しの差で, with a small difference. —五票《分; 艇身》の差で, by five votes《minutes; lengths》. —差を求める, to find the remainder.
sā (さあ), *int.* Ⓢ さあさあ. ❶ (驚愕を表す發聲) ah!; oh!; O dear! ❷ (同意を示す發聲) come!; now; well. ❸ (威歎, 命令) come! —さあ來い, Come on! —さあ是からだ, Here goes! —さあ大變だ, Oh, Heavens!
saba (鯖), *n.* 【魚】the chub [Spanish] mackerel; the mackerel.
sabakeru (捌ける), *vi.* ❶ (解ける) to be disentangled; be loosed. ❷ (世なれる) to grow worldly; be sociable [accessible]. ❸ (賣れる) to sell [be sold] off; be salable [merchantable]. —捌けた人, a sociable person; a man of the world. —品がずんずん捌ける, The articles [goods] find a ready sale.
sabaki (捌), *n.* ❶ (解き分けること) disentanglement; clearing. ❷ 〔裁〕(裁斷) judgment; decision. ❸ (賣行) sale; market; demand. ❹ (物事の取扱) management; treatment. —裁きをする, to judge; decide the case.
sabaku (沙漠), *n.* a desert.
sabaku (捌く), *vt.* ❶ (分ける) to disentangle; hackle (麻等を); comb (梳る). ❷ 〔裁〕(裁斷) to judge; decide. ❸ (こなす) to handle; treat; manage. ❹ (商ふ) to sell; dispose *of*.
sāberu (軍刀), *n.* a sabre; a cavalry sword. ¶ サーベル內閣, a militarist cabinet.
sabetsu (差別), *n.* distinction; discrimination; difference (差異). —差別する, to distinguish *between* 《*from*》; discriminate *between*. —

差別がつかぬ, to be unable to distinguish *between*; cannot tell the one from the other. —差別を立てる, to make a discrimination *between*. —差別を撤廢する, to do away with discrimination; make odds even. —誰彼の差別なく, without distinction of person. ——**-teki,** *a.* differential; discriminative; discriminatory. —差別的待遇をする, to treat discriminatingly; make a discrimination (*against*). ¶ 差別關稅, differential [discriminating] duties.

sabi (銹, 銹, 鏽), *n.* ❶ rust; rustiness. ❷ (古雅) patina; antiquated appearance. ❸ (老熟して味あること) matureness. —寂ある聲, a mellow voice. —銹がつく, to be rusted; become patinated. ☞ *sabiru*. —銹を止める《落す》, to prevent 《remove》 rust.

sabireru (寂·荒れる), *vi.* to be desolated; decline; go down.

sabiru (銹·銹·鏽びる), *vi.* ❶ (銹を生じる) to rust; grow rusty; be patinated. ❷ (古色を帶びる) to age; have an antique look [patina]. ❸ (枯れる) to become mature. —銹びた rusty; patinated. —銹びさす, to rust; oxidize.

sabishii (淋しい), *a.* ❶ (孤獨) lonely; solitary. ❷ (寂寥) desolate; dismal; dreary. ❸ (心細さ) lonesome; lonely; cheerless. ——, *vi.* to feel lonely. —淋しい山家, a solitary house in the mountains. —懐中が淋しい, to have a light purse. —淋しく暮す, to lead [pass] a a lonesome life. —今夜は何だか淋しい晩だ, To-night I feel somehow lonely.

saboru (サボる), *vi.* to go on a sabotage; sabotage; go slow.

sabotāju (怠業), *n.* sabotage 【佛】; go slow; ca' canny.

saboten (仙人掌; 覇王樹), *n.* 【植】 the cochineal cactus.

sābu (サーブ), *n.* 【庭球】 serve; service.

sāchiraito (探照燈), *n.* a search-light.

sadamaru (定る), *vi.* ❶ (きまる) to be settled; be decided. ❷ (鎮定) to be quelled; be subjugated. —定まった, decided; settled; definite. —定まれる住所, settled habitation. —定まれる命, fated life.

sadame (定), *n.* ❶ (規定) law; rule; regulation. ❷ (決定) decision. —定めなき, unsettled; irregular (不規則); mutable (敢果なき); changeable (同上). (定めなき世, an uncertain [a changeable] world.)

sadameru (定める), *vt.* ❶ (きめる) to decide; fix; set. ❷ (制定) to establish; set [lay] down; enact. ❸ (鎮定) to subjugate; subdue; conquer. —別に定むる規則, the rules specially provided. —日を定める, to settle [fix] the day. —方針を定める, to decide the line of action. —法律を以て之を定む, to determine it by law.

sadameshi (定めし), *ad.* ❶ (多分) probably; perhaps; I dare say. ❷ (乾度) surely; no doubt; undoubtedly. —定めし御疲れでせう, You must surely be tired.

sadeami (叉手網), *n.* a dip-net; a scoop-net.

sae (さへ), even (...でさへ); only. —只さへ寒いのに, when the weather is cold enough as it is. —此の缺點さへなければ, but [if it were not] for this defect. —あゝ! 金さへあれば, Alas! if only I had money.

saegiru (遮る), *vt.* ❶ to obstruct (the way or view) (阻碍); interrupt (the view or communication) (遮斷); bar (the way) (妨げ); shut out (the view) (遮閉); screen (something from view) (蔽ふ); cut off (the enemy's retreat) (遮斷). ❷ (口を挾む) to interpose [cut in] [*vi.*]; cut short. —人の話を遮る, to choke off a person's talk; cut a person short. —目を遮るものなし, There is nothing to interrupt my sight.

saeki (差益), *n.* difference; margin.

saeru (冴える), *vi.* ❶ (冷ゆ) to be keenly cold. ❷ (澄む) to be bright (and clear); be clear [transparent]; mellow (光·色·音に言ふ). ❸ (熟達する) to be skilled; become dexterous. —冴えた, ① keenly cold. ② clear; bright (and clear). ③ skilled; dexterous; accomplished. (冴えた音色, a clear note.) —冴えない, ① (色) dull; sombre. ② melancholy; depressed.

saezuru (囀る), *vi.* to sing; chirp (鋭聲で); twitter (雀等が); warble (鶯等が); chirrup.

safuran (泊夫藍), *n.* 【植】 the saffron-plant; the saffron.

sagaku (差額), *n.* balance; difference. —差額を拂ふ, to pay [meet] the difference.

sagan (沙岩), *n.* 【地質】 sandstone; gritstone (理[きめ]の粗い).

Sagaren (薩哈連), *n.* Saghalien, Sakhalin.

sagaru (下る), *vi.* ❶ (降下) to fall; come down; descend. ❷ (懸垂) to hang down. ❸ (下落)

to fall; decline; sink. ❹ (退出) to leave; retire; withdraw. ❺ (後退) to go backward. ❻ (衰退) to decline; go [come] down; wane. —鑑札が下る, to obtain a licence; be licensed. —値打が下る, to fall in one's estimation. —一歩後へ下る, to take a step backward; retire a step.

sagashidasu (捜出す), *vt.* to find [search; seek; hunt] out; rummage out (かき廻して). —罪人《秘密》を捜し出す, to search [ferret] out a criminal 《secret》.

sagashimawaru (捜廻る), *vt.* to search about; ferret up and down; look in every nook and corner.

sagashimono (探物), *n.* a thing searched [sought after].

sagasu (捜·探す), *vt.* to seek; search (*for; after*); look *for*; hunt (up); rummage. —手探りで捜す, to feel about; grope about. —鉦や太鼓で探す, to search with hue and cry. —人を探す, to look for a person. —職を探す, to look about for an employment. —何を探してゐるのか, What are you looking for?

sagefuda (下札), *n.* a label; a tag.

sagefuri (垂準), *n.* a pendulum.

sagegami (下髪), *n.* the hair hanging down the back; a cue, queue; a pigtail.

sagen (左舷), *n.* 【航】 the port; the larboard.

sageru (下げる), *vt.* ❶ (垂下) to hang down. ❷ (低下) to lower; let [bring] down; reduce; degrade (地位等を). ❸ = *orosu*. ❹ (佩用) to wear; gird. ❺ (片づける) to clear; take away. —物價を下げる, to depress [lower] the price of goods. —階級を下げる, to reduce a person to a lower grade. —眼尻を下げる, to lower the corner of one's eye. —男を下げる, to lower one's reputation.

sageru (提げる), *vt.* to carry; take *with*.

sageshio (下潮), *n.* ebb-tide.

sagesumu (蔑む), *vt.* to despise; look down *upon*; slight. —人を蔑む, to look down upon a man; put a slight upon a man.

sagi (鷺), *n.* 【鳥】 the heron. —鷺を烏と云ひくろめる, to talk black into white; talk wrong into right. ¶ 白鷺, the little egret.

sagi (詐欺, 詐僞), *n.* fraud; swindling; imposture. —詐欺的, fraudulent. —詐欺を働く, to commit a fraud. ¶ 詐欺師, a swindler; an impostor; a sharper. —詐欺取財, obtaining goods by fraud [false pretences].

saguri (探り), *n.* ❶ (探ること) searching; a feeler; a *ballon d'essai* 【佛】. ❷ (間諜) a spy. ❸ 【探針】 (醫療具) a sound; a probe; a searcher. —探りを入れる, ① (探索) to pry *into*; feel the pulse; throw out a feeler. ② (探針を) to sound; probe; explore. ③ (間諜を) to send out a spy.

saguriashi (探足で進む), to grope one's way with the feet.

saguridasu (探出す), *vt.* to pump; grope [pry] out; smell out (秘密等を).

saguru (探る), *vt.* ❶ (手探) to grope [feel] *for*. ❷ (探索) to search; look *for*; ransack. ❸ (推測) to sound; fathom; search. ❹ (按診) to probe; sound; explore. —傷を探る, to probe a wound. —懐中を探る, to search [feel for] in the pocket; feel the pocket; fumble in one's pocket. —名所を探る, to visit famous places; make an excursion for viewing the sights. —人の心を探る, to search men's hearts; sound a person. —敵の動靜を探る, to reconnoitre the enemy's movements.

sagyō (作業), *n.* work (仕事); operation(s) (工事, 操業). ¶ 作業時間, work-hours. —帝國鐵道作業局, the Imperial Railway Working Bureau. —作業服, a working-dress; 【軍】 a fatigue-dress.

sahai (差配), *n.* management (管理); agency (代辨); a house 《land》-agent (人). —差配する, to have the management *of*; act as an agent. ¶ 差配人, a house-agent (家の); a land-agent (土地の). —差配所, an agency.

sahanji (茶飯事), *n.* a trifle; a trivial thing; a commonplace. —日常茶飯事, a matter of daily occurrence; an everyday affair.

sahō (左方), *n.* the left side.

sahō (作法), *n.* manners; etiquette; propriety. ☞ *gyōgi*. —それは作法に合はぬ, It is a breach of etiquette.

sahodo (左程, 然程), *ad.* so much; so; much; very (餘り); particularly (さして). —然程の事はない, It is not so serious.

sai (犀), *n.* 【哺乳】 the rhinoceros.

sai (才), *n.* ability; talent; wit (頓智); sagacity (穎才). —の才がある, to have an ability [a genius; turn] *for*. —才のある人, a man of talent; a talented man. —才を恃み過ぎる, to rely too much upon one's talents.

sai (妻), *n.* a wife.

sai (菜), *n.* food taken with rice; side-dishes. —飯の菜にする, to take with rice.
sai (祭), *n.* a fête; a festival; an anniversary (週年祭).
sai (際), *n.* the occasion; the time; the juncture. ——, *ad.* as; when; at the time [juncture]; on the occasion. —出發の際は, when I left the place; at the time of departure. —此際だから, the time being what it is.
sai (歳), *n.* a year; years of age. —十歳の男兒, a boy of ten years; a boy ten years old. —二十一歳の時に, at the age of twenty-one; at one and twenty.
sai (釆, 骰子), *n.* a die [*pl.* dice]. ☞ *sainome*. —骰子を投げる, to throw [cast] a die.
sai (差異, 差違), *n.* difference. ☞ *sa* (差) の ❶.
saiai (最愛の), *a.* most dear; dearest; beloved. —最愛の妻, the wife of one's bosom.
saiaku (最惡の), *a.* worst.
saibai (栽培), *n.* plantation; cultivation; culture. —栽培する, to grow; cultivate. ¶ 栽培者, a cultivator; a grower.
saiban (裁判), *n.* hearing; trial; judgment. —裁判する, to judge; sit in judgment *upon*; pass judgment *on*; hear [try] (the causes). —裁判に勝つ《負ける》, to win 《lose》 a suit. ¶ 巡回裁判, assizes. —裁判長, the chief justice; the presiding judge. —裁判官, a judge; the bench (全體); the judicature [judiciary] (同上). —裁判權, jurisdiction. —裁判所, a court (of justice); a law-court; a court-house [building] (建物). (調停裁判所, a court of conciliation. —巡回裁判所, a circuit court. —下級裁判所, a lower [inferior] court. —裁判所書記, a clerk of the court.)
saibetsu (細別), *n.* subdivision.
saibun (祭文), *n.* an address of condolence (弔詞); a funeral oration.
saichi (才智), *n.* ❶ (才と智慧) ability and intelligence. ❷ (利口) sagacity; cleverness. —才智のある, intelligent; sagacious.
saichiku (再築), *n.* reconstruction; rebuilding. —再築する, to reconstruct; rebuild.
saichō (再調する), *vt.* to reinvestigate; re-examine; review.
saichū (最中), *ad.* in the course *of*; in the midst [middle] *of*; in the height *of*. —雨の降る最中に, in the midst of a pouring rain.
saidā (サイダー), *n.* cider, cyder.
saidai (細大), *n.* the great and small. —細大洩らさず, to the smallest details.
saidai (最大の), *a.* greatest; maximum. ¶ 最大級, 【文】 superlative degree. —最大公約數, the greatest common measure (G. C. M. と略す).
saidan (祭壇), *n.* an altar.
saidan (裁斷), *n.* decision; judgment; discretion (裁量). —裁斷する, to decide; judge.
saido (再度), *n.* a second time. ——, *ad.* twice; again; anew.
saido (濟度), *n.* salvation; redemption (贖罪); reclamation (矯正). —濟度する, to save; redeem; reclaim. —濟度し難い, to be irredeemable; be past [beyond] redemption; be past saving.
saidoku (再讀する), *v.* to re-read; read again.
saieki (再役), *n.* a second service; re-engagement; re-enlistment. —再役する, 【軍】 to re-enlist.
saien (才媛), *n.* an able [talented] woman; a woman of genius.
saien (再演), *n.* an *encore* 【佛】. —再演する, to give an *encore*.
saien (再緣), *n.* remarriage; a second marriage. —再緣する, to remarry; marry again; be married again.
saien (菜園), *n.* a kitchen-garden; a vegetable-garden; a market-garden.
saiensu (科學), *n.* science.
saifu (財布), *n.* a purse; a pocket-book; a *porte-monnaie* 【佛】. —財布の底をはたく, to clear [empty] the purse. —財布の紐を握る《寛める; 緊める》, to hold 《loosen; tighten》 the purse-strings.
saifuku (祭服), *n.* a priests' ritual robe; a vestment.
saigai (災害), *n.* a calamity; a disaster; sufferings. —災害を蒙る, to suffer from a disaster. ¶ 災害地, the suffering district; the district affected.
saigai (際涯なき), *a.* limitless; boundless.
saigei (才藝), *n.* accomplishments. —才藝ある, accomplished.
saigen (再現), *n.* reappearance; 【心】 reproduction. —基督の再現, the Second Advent. —再現する, ① [*vi.*] to reappear. ② [*a.*] reappearing; reproductive.
saigen (際限), *n.* a limit; an end; a bound. —際限なき, interminate; limitless; boundless; endless.
saigetsu (歳月), *n.* time. —歳月人を待たず, "Time and tide wait for no man."

saigi (再議), *n.* reconsideration. —再議する, to reconsider. —再議に付する, to bring it up for reconsideration.

saigi (猜疑), *n.* suspicion; distrust. —猜疑する, to suspect; distrust —猜疑心の强い, suspicious. —猜疑の眼を以て, with suspicious eyes.

saigo (最後), *n.* the last; the end; the conclusion (結了). —最後に, finally; lastly; in the end. **—— - no,** *a.* final; last; ultimate. —最後の手段をとる, to play one's last card; resort to the last expedient. —最後の通牒を發する, to send an ultimatum. —彼奴につかまったが最後離しっこない, If the fellow catches me, all is over, for he'll never let go.

saigo (最期), *n.* the time of death; the last moment; death. —華々しい《悲慘な》最期, a glorious death《a sad end》. —最期を遂げる, to meet one's end.

saihai (采配), *n.* ❶ (指揮幣) a baton of command. ❷ (塵はたき) a duster. ❸ (指圖) command.

saihan (再犯), *n.* a second offence.

saihan (再版), *n.* reprint; republication; the second edition (第二版). —再版出來, the second edition ready [just out]. —再版する, to republish; reprint.

saihatsu (再發), *n.* recurrence; relapse (病の). —再發する, to recur; relapse; return.

saihen (災變), *n.* a disaster; an accident. ☞ *saigai.*

saihen (碎片), *n.* fragments; splinters; a broken piece. —硝子の碎片, a piece of broken glass.

saihi (採否), *n.* adoption or rejection. —採否を決する, to decide the adoption or rejection; vote *on* (議會などで).

saihi (歲費), *n.* ❶ (一年間の費用) annual expenditure. ❷ (議員の) an annual allowance.

saihō (細胞), *n.* a cell; cellule. ¶ 細胞分裂, cell-division. —細胞組織, cellulation; cellular tissue.

saihō (裁縫), *n.* needlework; sewing; tailoring. ¶ 裁縫科, a needlework course. —裁縫師, a seamstress, sempstress (女); a sewer; a tailor [*fem.* -ress].

saihoken (再保險), *n.* reinsurance.

saihyō (碎氷), *n.* breaking ice (事); broken ice (物). ¶ 碎氷船, an ice-breaker; an ice-boat.

saiji (細字), *n.* small letters; fine print.

saiji (細事), *n.* small matters.

saijitsu (祭日), *n.* a (national) holiday; a fête day; a festival day.

saijitsu (齋日), *n.* a fasting-day; a fast-day.

saijō (最上), *n.* ❶ the prime; the first class [grade; rate]. ❷ supremacy. —最上の, best; supreme; highest. ¶ 最上級, the highest class [grade]; 【文】the superlative degree.

saijō (齋場), *n.* the place for religious service.

saika (裁可), *n.* sanction; approval; assent. —裁可する, to sanction; give sanction *to*; approve. —御裁可を經る, to obtain the Imperial sanction.

saika (最下の), *a.* lowest; bottom; worst (最惡). —最下級, the lowest grade.

saikachi (皂莢), *n.* 【植】Gleditschia japonica (honey-locust の一種·學名).

saika (西下する), *vi.* to go westward; go west.

saikai (再開する), *v.* to reopen.

saikai (再會する), *vi.* to meet again. —再會を期す, to have an opportunity of meeting again.

saikai (際會する), *vi.* to meet by chance; happen [chance] upon.

saikai (齋戒), *n.* purification. —齋戒する, to purify oneself. ¶ 齋戒沐浴, purification by ablution.

saikaku (才覺), *n.* ❶ (機轉) wit. ☞ *sai* (才). ❷ (工面) a plan; a scheme; a scheme for raising money. —才覺する, to plan; raise (money).

saikan (才幹), *n.* talent; ability.

saikatsu (催滑), *n.* lubrication. ¶ 催滑料, a lubricant.

saikei (歲計), *n.* an annual [a yearly] account. ¶ 歲計豫算, annual estimates.

saikeikoku (最惠國), *n.* the most favoured nation. ¶ 最惠國條款, the most-favoured-nation clause.

saikeirei (最敬禮), *n.* the most respectful salutation.

saiken (債券), *n.* a debenture; a (loan) bond. —債券を發行する, to issue bonds. ¶ 債券額, the face-value of a bond.

saiken (債權), *n.* 【法】obligation; obligatory right. ¶ 債權國, a creditor nation. —債權者, 【法】an obligee; a creditor. (債權者集會, a meeting of creditors.)

saiketsu (採決), *n.* division (會議にての). **—— - suru,** *v.* to divide; take a vote. —投票によって採決する, to decide by vote.

saiketsu (裁決), *n.* decision; judgment; verdict (陪審官の). —裁決する, to give a decision [judgment] *on*; decide.

saiki (才氣), *n.* wit; smartness; sagacity; cleverness.

saiki (才器), *n.* ❶ (才) ability; talent. ❷ (人) an able man; a man of talent.

saiki (再歸), *n.* recurrence. —再歸する, to recur. ¶ 再歸動詞, 【文】 a reflexive verb. —再歸熱, recurrent [relapsing] fever.

saiki (再起), *n.* ❶ (病氣恢復) recovery. ❷ (再擧) rising again; another [second] attempt. —再起不能の敗北, a crushing defeat.

saiki (猜忌), *n.* jealousy; envy. —猜忌の眼で見る, to look on with jealous eyes.

saikin (細菌), *n.* a bacillus [*pl.* -li]; a bacterium [*pl.* -ia]. ¶ 細菌學, bacteriology.

saikin (細瑾), *n.* a small defect; a slight fault.

saikin (最近), *ad.* recently; lately; of late. —最近の, most recent; latest; nearest.

saikō (再考), *n.* reconsideration; reflection; second thought. —再考する, to reconsider; give a second thought. —再考を促す, to urge him to reconsider it.

saikō (再校), *n.* second proof; revisal.

saikō (再興), *n.* restoration (復興); revival (同上); re-establishment (事業等の). —再興する, to restore; revive; re-establish.

saikō (採光), *n.* lighting. ¶ 採光權, 【法】 light.

saikō (採鑛), *n.* mining. —採鑛する, to mine. ¶ 採鑛冶金學, mining and metallurgy.

saikō (最高の), *a.* highest; supreme; superlative; maximum. ¶ 最高學府, the highest seat of learning. —最高顧問府 (最高會議), the supreme council.

saikoku (催告), *n.* 【法】 notification; demand. —催告する, to demand; call upon; notify.

saikon (再婚), *n.* a second marriage; remarriage. —再婚する, to marry [be married] again; remarry.

saikon (再建), *n.* reconstruction; re-erection; rebuilding. —再建する, to reconstruct; re-erect; rebuild.

saiku (細工), *n.* ❶ work; workmanship; -work (複合用). ❷ (策略) tact; makeshift. —細工する, to work; make shift. —餘り細工をし過ぎる, to elaborate too much. ¶ 浮彫細工, relief-work.

saikun (細君), *n.* a wife; one's better half.

saikutsu (採掘), *n.* mining. —採掘する, to mine (gold, *etc.*); work (a mine). ¶ 採掘權, mining right.

saikyo (再擧), *n.* a second attempt; beginning [rising] again. —再擧する, to attempt again; begin afresh.

saimatsu (細末), *n.* ❶ (細事) a trifle. ❷ (細粉) powder. —細末にする, to powder; pulverise; reduce to powder.

saimin (細民), *n.* the poor; pauperdom; a pauper. ¶ 細民窟, a slum; a poor quarter.

saimin (催眠さす), *vt.* to hypnotize; mesmerize. ¶ 自己催眠, self-hypnosis. —催眠術, hypnotism; mesmerism. (催眠術に罹る, to be hypnotized; be mesmerized. —催眠術師, a hypnotist.) —催眠劑, a soporific.

saimitsu (細密な), *a.* minute; detailed; elaborate.

saimoku (細目), *n.* details; particulars; items. —細目に涉りて, in detail.

saimu (債務), *n.* a debt; an obligation; liabilities. —債務を履行する, to discharge one's liabilities; settle one's debt. ¶ 債務者, 【法】 an obligor; a debtor.

sainamu (さいなむ), *vt.* ❶ (訶[さい]る) to scold; rebuke. ❷ (苛[さい]める) to torture; torment.

sainan (災難), *n.* a calamity; a disaster; an accident (椿事). —災難に罹る, to meet with a mishap. —とんだ御災難でしたね, What a terrible mishap!

sainen (再燃), *n.* ❶ rekindling. ❷ (復活) revival; resuscitation. —再燃する, to rekindle; revive; come to the fore again.

sainin (再任), *n.* reappointment. —再任する, to be reappointed.

sainō (才能), *n.* talent; ability; capacity. —才能ある, able; gifted; capable.

sainokawara (賽の河原), *n.* the Children's Limbo.

sainome (采目, 賽目), *n.* ❶ (賽の點) a pip; a cast (投げて出た目). ❷ (賽形の物) a small cube; a die. —賽の目に刻む, to cut into small cubes.

sainyū (歳入), *n.* annual revenue (國家の); annual receipts [income] (個人の). ¶ 歳入超過額, surplus; excess of revenue over expenditure.

saiō (再應), *ad.* again; over again; once more; repeatedly.

saiō-ga-uma (塞翁が馬), *n.* unexpected turns of the world's affair. —人間萬事塞翁が馬, "A joyful evening may follow a sorrowful morning."

sairai (再來), *n.* the second coming.

sairei (祭禮), *n.* a festival; a fête.

sairi (犀利な), *a.* keen; sharp; penetrating.

sairō (豺狼), *n.* ❶ (山犬と狼) a wild dog and a wolf. ❷ (貪慾無道の者) a wolf; a rapacious [greedy] person.

sairoku (再錄する), *vt.* to report again (再報); re-record.

sairuidan (催涙彈), *n.* =*ruidan.*

sairyaku (才略), *n.* resources.

sairyō (宰領), *n.* ❶ (司宰) superintendence; supervision. ❷ a supervisor; a manager. ❸ (旅行團の取締) the manager of a tourist party. —宰領する, to superintend; supervise.

sairyō (最良), *n.* the best. —最良の, best; superfine; first-rate.

sairyō (裁量), *n.* discretion. —人の自由裁量にまかす, to leave to a person's discretion.

sairyoku (才力), *n.* ability; talent.

saisa (歲差), *n.* 【天】 precession (of the equinoxes).

saisai (再再), *ad.* Ⓢ 再三. again and again; over and over (again); repeatedly; frequently.

saisaki (幸先よき), *a.* lucky; auspicious; favourable; propitious.

saisan (採算), *n.* paying. —採算不能に陷る, to bring the balance on the wrong side.

saisei (再生), *n.* ❶ (蘇生) revival; resuscitation. ❷ 【心】 =*saigen* (再現). ❸【神】 regeneration; rebirth. —再生する, to revive; return to life; be born again. ¶ 再生同路, a regenerative circuit.

saisei (再製), *n.* remanufacture. —再製する, to remake; remanufacture. ¶ 再製鹽, refined salt.

saisei (祭政), *n.* the church and state.

saisei (催靑), *n.* 【養蠶】 incubation.

Saiseikai (濟生會), *n.* the Imperial Charity Association.

saisen (再選), *n.* re-election. —再選する, to re-elect.

saisen (賽錢), *n.* an offering of money; an offertory. ¶ 賽錢箱, an offertory-chest.

saisetsu (細說する), *vt.* to explain minutely; give a detailed account; detail.

saishi (才子), *n.* a man of talent [ability]; a clever person; a genius (天才の人). —才子短命, "Whom the gods love, die young."

saishi (妻子), *n.* wife and children; one's family (一家族).

saishi (祭司), *n.* a priest; an officiating priest; a celebrant.

saishi (祭祀), *n.* religious celebration; fête; divine service.

saishiki (彩色), *n.* painting; colouring; colour. —彩色する, to paint; colour. ¶ 彩色畫, a coloured picture; a painting.

saishin (再審), *n.* 【法】 rehearing; retrial; revision; re-examination. —再審する, to retry; re-examine; rehear; reconsider; review.

saishin (最新の), *a.* latest; newest. ☞ *saikin*. —最新式の, up-to-date 〔俗〕.

saishin (細心の), *a.* cautious; careful; scrupulous; prudent. —細心の注意を拂ふ, to pay the most scrupulous attention *to*; use the greatest care; use the utmost prudence.

saishinrei (再浸禮), *n.* rebaptism; anabaptism.

saishiryō (祭粢料), *n.* a grant of money for funeral service.

sai-shite (際して), *prep.* in; at; in the case of; in the event of. —此時に際して, at this juncture.

saisho (最初), *n.* the beginning; the commencement; the outset. ——, *ad.* at first; at the outset; at the beginning. —最初の, first; original. —先づ最初に, first; in the first place.

saishō (宰相), *n.* the Premier; the Prime Minister; the Chancellor (獨·墺); the Minister President.

saishō (最小, 最少), *n.* minimum; the least; the smallest. —最小の, smallest; least; minimum (最小限度の).

saishoku (才色), *n.* wit and beauty. —才色兼備の婦人, a wise and beautiful woman.

saishoku (菜食), *n.* green food; vegetable diet. —菜食する, to live on vegetables. ¶ 菜食家, a vegetarian.

saishu (祭主), *n.* the chief mourner (喪主); the master of funeral rites.

saishu (齋主), *n.* the chief officiating *Shintō*-priest.

saishū (採集), *n.* collecting; gathering; picking. —採集する, to gather; collect.

saishū (最終の), *a.* final; ultimate; last; terminal. ¶ 最終列車 (電車), the last train (tram).

saishutsu (再出), *n.* reappearance; reproduction.

saishutsu (歲出), *n.* annual expenditure.

saisō (再送), *n.* resending; re-forwarding; redirecting. —再送する, to resend; reforward; redirect.

saisoku (細則), *n.* detailed rules [regulations].

saisoku (催促), *n.* pressing; urging; calling upon. ——-**suru**, *vt.* to urge (a person) *for* [to do]; press (a person) *for*. —賃金を催促する, to dun for a debt; press for the payment of a debt.

saita (最多の), *a*. maximum; most. ¶ 最多數, the maximum [*pl*. -ma]; the greatest number.

saitai (妻帶する), *v*. to marry; become a married man. ¶ 妻帶者, a married man.

saitaku (採擇する), *vt*. to adopt.

saitan (載炭), *n*. coaling. ¶ 載炭量, coal-capacity.

saitan (採炭), *n*. coal-mining; output of coal (採炭額).

saitei (再訂), *n*. revision.

saitei (裁定), *n*. arbitration; adjudication; decision. —裁定する, to adjudicate; decide; judge. ¶ 裁定取引, 【商】 arbitrage.

saitei (最低の), *a*. lowest; lowermost; minimun (賃銀など). ¶ 最低價格, the lowest [bottom] price; the reserve price (競賣等の場合).

saiten (採點), *n*. marking; giving marks. —採點する, to give marks; mark (papers); score. ¶ 採點表, a score-list.

saiten (祭典), *n*. a festival; a fête; festivity.

saitori (才取), *n*. a middleman; a broker.

saiu (細雨), *n*. a mizzle; a drizzle; a fine [thin; misty] rain.

saiwai (幸), *n*. ❶ (幸福) happiness; blessing; felicity. ❷ (幸運) a good luck; fortune; a happy turn. —幸な, happy; fortunate; lucky; blessed; felicitous. —幸に [にも; にして], happily; fortunately; luckily; by good luck. —不幸中の幸だ, It was a piece of fortune in misfortune.

saiwaribiki (再割引), *n*. 【商】 rediscount.

saiyō (採用), *n*. ❶ (用ふること) adoption. ❷ (任用) appointment. —採用する, ① to adopt; take up; accept. ② to appoint; take into service. ¶ 採用試驗, an examination for service.

saiyunyū (再輸入), *n*. reimportation. —再輸入する, to reimport.

saiyushutsu (再輸出), *n*. re-exportation. —再輸出する, to re-export.

saizen (最善), *n*. the best; the utmost (極力). —最善の努力をなす, to do one's utmost [best].

saizen (最前), *ad*. a little while ago; a few minutes ago.

saizuchi (木槌), *n*. a mallet.

saji (匙), *n*. a spoon. —匙を投げる, to abandon the case (醫者が); give up (放棄する).

saji (些事, 瑣事), *n*. a trifle; a trivial matter; a matter of detail; small things.

sāji (サージ), *n*. serge. —紺サージの洋服, a navy-blue serge suit.

sajikagen (匙加減), *n*. ❶ compounding [making up] of medicine. ❷ (手心) discretion; management. —匙加減をする, to moderate; modify; make allowance.

sajiki (棧敷), *n*. an upper box (芝居の); a stand (壇の); a gallery (高き).

saka (阪, 坂), *n*. a slope; an incline; a hill. —阪を上《下》る, to go uphill 《downhill》. —四十の阪を越えてゐる, to be on the shady [wrong; other] side of forty.

sakaba (酒場), *n*. a bar; a bar-room; a tap-room.

sakadachi (逆立する), *v*. ❶ to stand on one's head. ❷ 【航空】 to land on the nose; remain tail high.

sakadaru (酒樽), *n*. a wine-cask; a wine-barrel; a wine-keg.

sakadatsu (逆立つ), *vi*. to stand [erect] on end; bristle [stick] up.

sakae (榮), *n*. prosperity (繁榮); welfare (福祉); glory (光榮).

sakaeru (榮える), *vi*. to prosper; thrive; flourish. —榮え行く, to make one's own way.

sakai (境), *n*. a boundary; a border; the frontier (國境). —境する, to border *on*; be contiguous *to*.

sakaki (榊), *n*. 【植】 Eurya ochnacea (學名).

sakamaku (逆卷く), *vi*. to surge; roll back; rage. —逆卷く浪, the surging [boiling] waves.

sakamata (逆戟鯨), *n*. 【哺乳】 the grampus.

sakamise (酒店), *n*. a sake-shop; a tap-house. ☞ *sakaba*.

sakamogi (逆茂木), *n*. an abatis [又 *pl*.]; *chevaux de frise* 【佛】.

sakamori (酒盛), *n*. a feast; a banquet; a drinking-bout.

sakan (左官), *n*. a plasterer.

sakan (佐官), *n*. 【陸】 a field-officer; 【海】 a captain or commander.

sakan (盛な), *a*. prosperous; thriving; vigorous. ——**-ni**, *ad*. prosperously; vigorously; furiously (猛烈に). —盛になる, to prosper; flourish; become active; become furious (猛烈). —盛に燃えて居る, to be burning furiously. —あの店は中々盛だ, His shop is doing fine trade. —雨が盛に降ッてゐる, It is raining cats and dogs.

sakana (肴), *n*. ❶ (肴) a relish with wine. ❷ (魚) fish. ☞ *uo*. ¶ 肴屋, a fishmonger's (shop) (店): a fishmonger (人).

sakaneji (逆捩), *n.* ❶ (詰問) retort; retaliation; counter-argument; counterblast. ❷ (逆に捩ぢること) twisting back. —逆捩ぢを食はす, to turn the tables (on a person); retort.

sakanoboru (溯る), *vt.* ❶ to go up (a stream). ❷ (既往に) to go back (to the past); trace back; retrace. ❸ (原因に) to retrace (a thing) to its cause [origin]. —流を溯る, to go up the stream.

sakaotoshi (逆落し), *n.* 【飛】 nose dive.

sakarau (逆ふ), *vt.* to oppose; disobey; go *against*; run counter *to*. —に逆って, against; contrary to; in the teeth of. (風に逆って, against [in the teeth of] the wind.) —運命に逆ふ, to strive against fate. —世の風潮に逆ふ, to swim against the stream.

sakari (盛), *n.* the bloom; the prime; the flower; the palmy days. —盛りの, prime; blooming. (盛りの花を散らす, to be cut off in the flower of one's youth.) ¶ 盛り場, the busy haunts of men; a holiday resort; a fashionable quarter.

sakasa, sakasama, (倒, 逆), *n.* inverse; topsyturvy. —逆様に, head foremost [first]; upside-down; topsyturvy. —其では持方が逆様だ, You are holding it upside-down.

sakashii (賢しい), *a.* clever; sharp; sagacious.

sakatazame (犂頭鮫), *n.* 【魚】 the guitar-fish.

sakate (逆手に持つ), to hold (a thing) the point downward.

sakate (酒代), *n.* drink-money; a tip (心附). —酒代をやる, to tip; give drink-money.

sakaya (酒屋), *n.* (店) a wine-shop; a grog-shop; a tap-room; (造酒屋) a brewery: (人) a wine-dealer; a wine-merchant.

sakayaki (月代), *n.* the shaven part of the head.

sakazuki (杯, 盃), *n.* a wine-cup; a wine-glass (コップ); a goblet; a tankard (大きな). —一杯を廻す, to pass the wine-cup. —一杯を差す, to offer a cup.

sake (鮏, 鮭), *n.* ❶ 【魚】 the dog-salmon; the salmon (俗稱). ❷ (電車の釣革に下る人) a strap-hanger.

sake (酒), *n.* *sake* 〔日〕; wine; drink. —酒の勇氣, Dutch courage; pot-valour. —酒びたりになる, to be drowned in wine; be steeped in liquor. —酒は百藥の長, "Good wine makes good blood."

sakebi (叫), *n.* a cry; a shout; a shriek (悲鳴). —自由の叫び, the cry for liberty.

sakebu (叫ぶ), *vi.* to cry; shout; shriek. —喜び叫ぶ, to shriek with joy.

sakei (左傾する), *v.* to radicalize. —左傾的, radical.

sakeme (裂目), *n.* a rent; a split; a rip (衣服の); a tear (同上).

saken (差遣する), *vt.* to send; despatch.

sakenomi (飲酒家), *n.* a drinker; a tippler; a wine-bibber.

sakeru (裂ける), *vi.* to tear; rip; crack; split.

sakeru (避ける), *vt.* to avoid; shun; evade; elude; get out of the way (よける). —人目を避ける, to shun [avoid] others' notice. —危險を避ける, to ward off [avert] danger. —困難を避ける, to elude [get round] a difficulty.

saki (先, 前), *n.* ❶ (前途) the future. ❷ (先位) priority; precedency. ❸ (到達地) the destination. ❹ (先方) the other party. ❺ (續き) the sequel. ❻ (前面) the front. ❼ (第一) the first. —先の, ① (未來の) future; coming. ② (以前の) previous; former (元の). —先に, ① (時) before; beforehand; formerly (以前). ② (所) ahead; in front; away; off. —先に立って, at the head *of*. (先に立って…する, to take the lead *in*.) —先を爭って進む, to vie with one another in advancing. —どうぞお先へ, After you, please. —君はまだ先が長い, You have a long future before you. —一寸先は闇の世の中, An inch before us, all is darkness.

saki (先, 尖端), *n.* a point; a tip; the end (端).

saki (崎, 岬), *n.* a cape; a headland.

saki (左記の), *a.* undermentioned; the following. —左記の通り, as undermentioned; as follows; as given [mentioned] hereunder.

sakibarai (先拂), *n.* ❶ (前金拂) prepayment; payment in advance. ❷ (屆先拂) payment on delivery; carriage forward (運賃の). —先拂する, to pay in advance. ¶ 先拂運賃, freight payable at destination [on delivery].

sakibashiru (先走る), *vi.* ❶ to run forward [ahead]. ❷ = *desugiru* の ❶.

sakibō (先棒), *n.* ❶ (輿舁の先きに立つ者) the forward [foremost] bearer. ❷ (人の手先となる者) a cat's paw. —先棒に使はれる, to be made a cat's paw *of*.

sakibure (前觸), *n.* ❶ (人) a harbinger; a forerunner. ❷ (事)

preliminary announcement. ☞ *maebure*. —前觸れする, to harbinger; announce beforehand; herald; forerun (先驅).

sakidatsu (先立つ), *v.* to go [come] before; precede; go in advance *of*. —子に先立たれる, to be left behind by one's child; survive one's child. —先立つものは金. The first thing needed is money.

sakitori (先取する), *vt.* to take in advance.

sakigake (魁), *n.* lead (事); a leader (人); the first (人,物); a pioneer (人). —魁する, to be the first; take the lead *of*; steal a march *on* [*upon*] (出し拔く). —流行の魁をする, to lead [set] the fashion.

sakigari (前借), *n.* borrowing in advance.

sakigashi (前貸), *n.* lending in advance; advance.

sakigoro (先頃), *ad.* the other day; some time ago; some time since.

sakihodo (先程), *ad.* a little while ago; a little before.

sakimawari (先廻りする), *v.* to forestall another; steal a march on a person.

sakimidareru (咲亂れる), *vi.* to bloom all over; be resplendent with flowers; blossom luxuriantly.

sakimono (先物), *n.* 【商】 futures; a third-month option.

sakin (砂金), *n.* gold dust; alluvial gold.

sakin (差金), *n.* difference; margin; balance.

sakinzuru (先んずる), *vt.* to forestall; anticipate; steal a march *on* [*upon*]; have [get] the start *of*. —衆に先んずる, to anticipate [have the start of] others.

sakiototoi (一昨昨日), *ad.* three days back; the day but one before yesterday.

sakite (先手), *n.* =*sente*.

sakiwakeru (咲分ける), *vi.* to bloom in different colours.

sakka (作家), *n* a writer.

sakka (作歌), *n.* ❶ (作る事) versification; composing poems; writing songs. ❷ (歌) an ode; a verse. —B氏作歌, composed by Mr. B.

sakka (蒴果), *n.* 【植】 a capsule.

sakka (擦過する), *vt.* to graze; abrade. ¶ 擦過傷, an abrasion.

sakkaku (錯角), *n.* 【數】 alternate angles.

sakkaku (錯覺), *n.* illusion.

sakkarin (サッカリン), *n.* saccharine.

sakki (殺氣立つ), *v.* to look ferocious [threatening; menacing]. —殺氣を帶びる, to look eerie [ghastly].

sakkin (殺菌する), *vt.* to sterilize. ¶ 殺菌牛乳, sterilized milk. —殺菌劑, a bactericide; a bacillicide.

sakkon (昨今), *ad.* of late; nowadays. —昨今の, recent; late. —つい昨今のことである, It was but recently.

sakku (サック), *n.* a sack.

sakkyoku (作曲), *n.* composition. ¶ 作曲家, a composer.

sakkyū (早急), *n.* hurry; haste; precipitation. —早急に, in a hurry; in hot haste; precipitately.

sakō (鎖港), *n.* closing the ports.

sakoku (鎖國), *n.* the closing of the country; national isolation. —鎖國する, to close the country; close the door to foreign countries.

sakotsu (鎖骨), *n.* 【解】 the clavicle; the collar-bone.

saku (作), *n.* ❶ (製作) production; composition; workmanship. ❷ (製作品) a work; a composition. ❸ (農作物) a harvest; a crop; a yield. —當り作, a full harvest; a heavy crop. —左甚五郎作, a work by Hidari Jingorō.

saku (柵), *n.* ❶ 【軍】 a barricade; a stockade; a palisade. ❷ 【建】 a picket fence. —柵を結ふ, to erect a stockade.

saku (策), *n.* ❶ a policy; a plan; a stratagem. ❷ (鞭) a whip. —策を運らす, to devise a scheme; think out a plan.

saku (咲く), *vi.* to flower; bloom; blossom. —咲き揃ふ, to be in full bloom.

saku (裂·割く), *vt.* to tear; rend; split. —二つに《半分に》裂く, to tear it in two 《half》. —著物を裂く, to rend one's garments. —仲を裂く, to estrange one person from another; set one person against another.

sakuban (昨晩), *n.* & *ad.* last evening; last night (昨夜).

sakubun (作文), *n.* composition; a theme (課題に對して書ける). ¶ 作文課題, exercise.

sakuchō (昨朝), *n.* & *ad.* yesterday morning.

sakudō (策動する), *vi.* to act in concert [coordination]; cooperate.

sakudō (索道), *n.* a cableway; a ropeway; a cable [rope] railway.

sakugara (作柄), *n.* a crop; a harvest.

sakugen (削減), *n.* curtailment; reduction. —削減する, to reduce; curtail; cut down.

sakugenchi (策源地), *n.* the base of operations.

sakugo (錯誤), *n.* an error; a mistake.

sakugu (索具), *n.* 【航】 rigging; tackle; cordage.

sakuheki (作癖), *n.* 【文學】 mannerism.

sakuhin (作品), *n.* a work of art; a production; a work.

sakui (作爲), *n.* 【法】 a commission; an action; a positive act.

sakui (作意), *n.* ❶ fancy; conceit. ❷ (製作の意匠) design; conception; *motif* 【佛】.

sakui (窄衣), *n.* a strait-jacket.

sakuin (作因), *n.* an agent.

sakuin (索引), *n.* an index. —索引を附ける, to index.

sakuji (作事), *n.* building; construction.

sakujitsu (昨日), *n.* & *ad.* yesterday.

sakujo (削除する), *vt.* to erase; cancel; strike out; delete; remove; eliminate.

sakujō (銖條), *n.* a cable. ¶ 銖條鐵道, a cable-railway; a rope-railway; a funicular railway.

sakujō (槊杖), *n.* a wiper; a wiping-rod.

sakumotsu (作物), *n.* a crop; a harvest; raw produce.

sakunen (昨年), *n.* & *ad.* last year.

sakunyū (搾乳), *n.* milking. —搾乳する, to milk. ¶ 搾乳場, a dairy.

sakuō (策應する), *vi.* to follow a concerted plan; cooperate *with*; act in concert *with*.

sakuotoko (作男), *n.* a farm-servant [-hand].

sakura (櫻), *n.* the cherry-tree (樹); the cherry-blossoms (花). ¶ 櫻時, the cherry-blossom season. —櫻狩, an excursion for viewing cherry-blossoms.

sakurairo (櫻色), *n.* pink; cerise; roseate.

sakuran (錯亂), *n.* derangement; disorder; aberration. —錯亂さす, to derange. —錯亂する, to be deranged; be out of order.

sakuranbo (櫻桃), *n.* a cherry.

sakurasō (櫻草), *n.* 【植】 the (Cortusa-leaved) primrose.

sakurei (作例), *n.* a composition model; an example.

sakuretsu (炸裂する), *vi.* to burst; explode.

sakuretsu (錯列), *n.* 【數】 combination.

sakuri (吃逆), *n.* hiccough, hiccup.

sakuryaku (策略), *n.* a scheme; a stratagem; a ruse. ☞ *saku* (策). —策略を運らす, to resort to schemes. ¶ 策略家, a strategist; a man of resources.

sakusan (醋酸), *n.* 【化】 acetic acid.

sakusei (作成), *n.* drawing up; formation. —作成する, to draw up; make out; frame.

sakusei (鑿井), *n.* well-boring; well-sinking.

sakusen (作戰), *n.* military (naval) operations. ¶ 作戰地, a field of operations. —作戰計畫, a plan of campaign [operations]; a problem (將棋などの).

sakusha (作者), *n.* a writer; an author; a dramatist (脚本家); a maker (製作者).

sakushi (策士), *n.* a tactician; a schemer; a man of resources.

sakushu (搾取する), *vt.* to extract; squeeze; press; exact; exploit. —葡萄から液汁を搾取する, to squeeze [press] the juice from [out of] grapes.

sakusō (錯綜), *n.* entanglement; intrication; complication.

sakuya (昨夜), *n.* & *ad.* last night; last evening (昨夕).

sakuyaku (炸藥), *n.* bursting-charge.

sakuzatsu (錯雜), *n.* complexity; complication; intricacy. —錯雜せる, complicated; complex; intricate. —錯雜さす, to perplex; complicate; confuse. —錯雜する, to be complicated; be confused; be mixed together.

sama (樣), *n.* ❶ (有樣) condition; state. ❷ (體裁) appearance; form (形狀); shape (同上).

sama (樣), (敬稱語) Mr. (Mister の略); Mrs. (Mistress の略); Esq. (Esquire の略); Mdme (Madame の略); Master (男兒); Miss (孃); Messrs. (Messieurs の略. Mr. の複數).

samade (さまで), *ad.* so; so much; to that extent. —さまでの事でもない, It is not so serious.

samasu (冷す), *vt.* ❶ (冷えさす) to cool; chill; bring down (熱等を). ❷ (殺ぐ) to spoil (興味など); damp(en) (熱心など). —熱を冷ます (病の), to bring down a fever. —興を冷ます, to spoil a person's amusement; mar the enjoyment *of*.

samasu (覺・醒ます), *vt.* ❶ (眠より) to awaken; arouse. ❷ (悟らす) to convince; undeceive. ❸ (醉を) to make sober; sober. —迷ひを醒ます, to disillusion a person. —目を覺ます (自分で), to wake up.

samasu (褪す), *vt.* to fade; subdue.

samatage (妨), *n.* obstacle; obstruction; hindrance; impediment. ☞ *bōgai*. —勉强 (睡眠) の妨げをする, to disturb a person's study (sleep).

samatageru (妨げる), *vt.* to obstruct; hinder; impede; retard (阻害); disturb (安眠·勉强など).

—他人の仕事を妨げる, to interfere with another's work. —計畫を妨げる, to counteract [thwart] one's plan [design].

samayou (彷徨ふ), *vi.* to wander about; roam about. —市中をうろうろ彷徨ふ, to roam about the city.

samazama (樣樣の), *a.* various; diverse; of many kinds. ☞ *shuju.* —樣々に, in many ways; in various ways; variously; diversely. —人の心は樣々だ, "Many men, many minds."

same (鯊, 鮫), *n.* 【魚】 the shark. ¶ 鮫革, shagreen.

samehada (鮫肌), *n.* goose-flesh; goose-skin.

sameru (冷める), *vi.* ❶ (熱去る) to cool; get cold. ❷ (減退) to subside; abate; be spoilt (興が). —冷めぬ樣に, to keep it hot.

sameru (覺·醒める), *vi.* ❶ (眠より) to awake; become awake; wake (up). ❷ (迷より) to awake; be disillusioned [undeceived]; come to one's senses. ❸ (酒より) to sober; become sober. —お座が醒める, The company is chilled.

sameru (褪める), *vi.* to fade (away); fly. —褪め易い, fugitive.

samezame (潸潸と), *ad.* bitterly; unrestrainedly.

samidare (五月雨), *n.* early summer rain.

samisen (三味線), *n.* the *samisen*; the three-stringed guitar. —三味線を彈く, to thrum [play] the *samisen.*

samo (さも), *ad.* as if [though]; just; just like. —さも嬉しさうに, as if he were greatly pleased. —さも有りなん, That may well be.

samoaraba-are (遮莫), be it as it may.

samon (査問), *n.* inquiry; investigation. ☞ *torishirabe.*

samonakuba (さもなくば), *conj.* or; (or) else; otherwise.

samoshii (さもしい), *a.* ❶ (見すぼらしき) poor; wretched. ❷ (心根賤しき) mean; base. —さもしい根性を出す, to show one's base spirit.

samui (寒い), *a.* cold; chilly. —寒がる, to feel chilly; feel cold; complain of the cold. —寒くなる, to grow [get] cold. ¶ 寒がり, a person sensitive to the cold.

samuke (寒氣), *n.* ❶ (さむさ) a chill; chilliness; cold. ❷ (惡寒) a cold fit. —寒氣立つ; 寒氣がする, to feel a chill; have a chill.

samurai (士, 侍), *n.* a *samurai.*

samusa (寒さ), *n.* cold; coldness. —寒さ凌ぎに, to keep off the cold.

san (三), *n.* three; the third (第三).

san (產), *n.* ❶ (出產) delivery; labour; parturition. ❷ (產出) production; a product (產物). ❸ (財產) a fortune; property. —產が輕い《重》い, to have an easy 《a difficult; laborious》 delivery. —產をする, to give birth to a child; be delivered of a child.

san (棧), *n.* ❶ (細き材) a cross-piece; a cleat. ❷ =*neda* (根太). ❸ (障子等の骨) a frame; a batten (戶などの).

san (算), *n.* a number. —算を亂して, in confusion.

san (酸), *n.* 【化】 an acid.

san (贊), *n.* eulogy; praise. —畫に贊をする, to add a eulogy to a picture.

sanada (眞田), *n.* a braid; a plait. —眞田に編む, to braid. ¶ 眞田紐, a (flat) braid; narrow goods.

sanadamushi (條蟲), *n.* 【蠕形】 the tapeworm.

sanae (早苗), *n.* a rice-sprout.

sanagara (宛然), *ad.* as it were; exactly; just. —宛然…の如く, as if; as though.

sanagi (蛹), *n.* a pupa; a chrysalis; a nymph.

sanba (產婆), *n.* a midwife. ¶ 產婆術, midwifery.

sanbai (三倍), *n.* thrice; three times. —三倍の, treble; three-fold.

sanbashi (棧橋), *n.* a pier; a jetty.

sanbasō (三番叟), *n.* ❶ 【劇】 the prelude to a theatrical performance. ❷ (始) the prelude; the beginning.

sanbi (酸鼻), *n.* piteousness. —酸鼻の極である, to be horrible; be a piteous sight to see.

sanbi (讃美する), *vt.* to praise (神等を); laud; extol; glorify; chant [sing] the praise *of.* ¶ 讃美歌, a hymn. —讃美者, an admirer.

sanbō (三方), *n.* ❶ the three sides [directions]. ❷ (器具) a wooden stand; a *sanbō.*

sanbō (參謀), *n.* the staff. ¶ 參謀長, the chief of staff; a flag-captain (艦隊の). —參謀本部, the General Staff Office. —參謀將校, a staff officer. —參謀總長, the Chief of the General Staff.

sanbukutsui (三幅對), *n.* a set of three *kakemono*; a set of three; a trio. —三幅對の, triplicate.

sanbun (散文), *n.* prose. ¶ 散文家, a prose writer.

sanbutsu (產物), *n.* a product; a production; a produce.

sanbyaku (三百), *n.* three hundred. ¶ 三百代言, a pettifogger. —三百年祭, a tercentennial; a tricentenary; a tercentenary.

sanbyōshi (三拍子), *n.* a time played with three instruments; a trio.

sanchaku (參着), *n.* arrival. ¶ 參着拂爲替手形, a sight-draft; a bill on demand [presentation].

sanchi (山地), *n.* a mountainous district; upland; highland.

sanchi (產地), *n.* the place of production; a habitat (動·植物の).

sanchi (珊), *n.* a centimetre.

sanchō (山頂), *n.* the top [summit] of a mountain; a peak; a crest.

sanchūmon (三柱門), *n.* (クリケット戯) a wicket.

sandai (參內する), *v.* to go to Court; repair to the (Imperial) Palace.

sandai (散大), *n.* dilatation.

sandan (算段), *n.* a device; an expedient; contrivances. ☞ *kumen.* ——**-suru,** *vt.* to contrive; manage. —金を算段する, to raise money.

sandan (霰彈), *n.* case-shot; (canister-)shot.

sandan-ronpō (三段論法), *n.* 【論】 syllogism.

sandatsu (簒奪する), *vt.* to usurp; seize. ¶ 簒奪者, a usurper.

sandayū (三太夫), *n.* a steward.

sandō (山道), *n.* a mountain-road [-path].

sandō (棧道), *n.* a bridge over a ravine.

sandō (參道), *n.* the road to a shrine (temple).

sandō (贊同), *n.* approval; support. =*sansei.*

sandowitchi (サンドウィッチ), *n.* sandwich.

sandoku (慘毒), *n.* poison.

sane (核), *n.* ❶ a stone; a a kernel. ❷ 【建】 a tongue.

sanga (參賀する), *v.* to go and congratulate.

sangai (三階), *n.* the second floor; the third storey 【米】. ¶ 三階建, a three-storied house.

sangai (慘害), *n.* disastrous damages; ravages; devastation.

sangaku (山嶽), *n.* a mountain. ¶ 山嶽會, the mountaineers' association.

sangaku (產額), *n.* the amount of production; yield; output.

sangatsu (三月), *n.* March.

sangeki (慘劇), *n.* a terrible tragedy.

sango (珊瑚), *n.* 【腔腸】 the coral. ¶ 珊瑚蟲, a coral-polyp; a coral-insect. —珊瑚珠, a coral. —珊瑚島 (礁), a coral-island (-reef).

sangoku-dōmei (三國同盟), *n.* a Triple Alliance.

sangū (參宮), *n.* a visit [a pilgrimage] to the Ise Shrine.

sangyō (產業), *n.* industry. ¶ 基本 (幼稚) 產業, key (infant) industries.

sangyō (蠶業), *n.* sericulture.

sañ-ittai (三位一體), *n.* the Trinity.

sañitsu (散逸する), *vi.* to be scattered and lost.

sanji (三次), *n.* the third time; 【數】 the three dimensions. ¶ 三次方程式, a cubic equation.

sanji (參事), *n.* a secretary. ¶ 參事會, a council. (參事會員, a member of a council; a councillor.) —參事官, a councillor; an adviser.

sanji (產兒), *n.* a new-born baby; a new arrival. ¶ 產兒制限, birth control.

sanji (慘事), *n.* a tragedy; a disaster; a calamity; a catastrophe.

sanji (讃辭), *n.* words of praise; a eulogy.

sanjo (贊助), *n.* support; help. —贊助する, to support; help.

sanjō (三乘), *n.* 【數】 cube.

sanjō (參上する), *vi.* to call on you; go to see you; visit you.

sanjō (慘狀), *n.* a pitiful condition [plight]; misery; wretched state. —慘狀を極める, to be in a miserable [pitiful] condition.

sanjoku (產褥), *n.* a childbed. —產褥に就く, to be confined (in the childbed). ¶ 產褥熱, 【醫】 puerperal fever.

sanjū (三十), *n.* thirty; the thirtieth (第三十).

sanjū (三重の), *a.* threefold; triple; treble.

sanjutsu (算術), *n.* arithmetic.

sanka (傘下に), under one's umbrella. —彼の傘下に馳せ參じる, to gather [flock] to his standard; rally round his standard.

sanka (參加), *n.* participation. —參加する, to participate *in*; take part *in*; join; make one of (the party, *etc.*). ¶ 參加引受, acceptance for honour; supraprotest.

sanka (產科 -學), *n.* obstetrics. ¶ 產科醫, an obstetrician. —產科病院, a maternity [lying-in] hospital.

sanka (酸化), *n.* 【化】 oxid(-iz)-ation; oxygenation; acidification. —酸化する, to oxidize. ¶ 酸化物, an oxide.

sankai (山海), *n.* mountain and sea; land and water.

sankai (參會する), *v.* to attend a meeting; be present at a meeting.

sankai (散開), *n.* extension; dispersion. —散開する, to extend; disperse.

sankai (散會), *n.* dispersion. —

散會する, to break up; disperse; rise.

sankaku (三角), *n.* three angles [corners]; a triangle; triangularity. —戀の三角關係, a triangle of love; the Eternal Triangle. —三角同盟を作る, to form a triangular alliance. ¶ 三角術, trigonometry. —三角洲, a delta. —三角測量, trigonometrical survey.

sankan (山間に), *ad.* amongst mountains [hills].

sankan (參觀), *n.* visit; inspection. —參觀する, to visit; inspect. ¶ 參觀人, a visitor; an inspector.

sanke (產氣づく), *vi.* to begin to labour.

sankei (三景), *n.* the three famous views.

sankei (山系), *n.* a mountain system.

sankei (參詣), *n.* a visit to a temple 《shrine》; a pilgrimage (巡拜). —參詣する, to visit [go to] a temple 《shrine》; worship *at.* ¶ 參詣人, a worshipper; a pilgrim.

sankei (繖形の), *a.* umbellate.

sanken (散見する), *vi.* to come across in places.

sankō (三更), *n.* midnight.

sankō (參考), *n.* reference; personal information. —參考の爲に, for the purpose of reference; for personal information. —參考する, to refer *to*; compare *with* (參照). —參考になる, to serve as a reference. ¶ 參考人, 【法】a referee. —參考書, a reference book; a book of reference.

sankōchō (三光鳥), *n.* 【鳥】the Japanese paradise flycatcher.

sankyaku (三脚), *n.* three legs. ¶ 三脚器, a tripod. —三脚競走, a three-legged race.

sanma (秋刀魚), *n.* 【魚】the skipper; the saury(-pike).

sanmai (三昧), *n.* 〔梵 Samadhi, 三摩提〕 ❶ (靜觀) meditation. ❷ (夢中) devotion; absorption. —一念佛三昧で暮す, to pass one's days in prayers to Amida Buddha.

sanman (散漫な), *a.* loose; scattered; discursive. —散漫な頭腦, a scattered [loose] brain.

sanmi (酸味), *n.* sourness; acidity.

sanmi-ittai (三位一體), *n.* = *sańi-ittai.*

sanmon (山門), *n.* a temple-gate.

sanmon-bunshi (三文文士), *n.* a hack [hedge]-writer; a literary hack; a penny-a-liner.

sanmyaku (山脈), *n.* a mountain-range [-chain]; a ridge.

sannengoto (三年毎の), *a.* triennial.

sannyū (算入する), *vt.* to reckon (a thing) *among* [*in*]; include *in.*

sa-no (些の), *a.* the least.

sanomi (さのみ), *ad.* so much; such; particularly.

sanpai (參拜する), *vt.* to visit (and worship). ☞ *sankei.*

sanpai (慘敗), *n.* a crushing defeat; a complete defeat. —慘敗する, to suffer a heavy [crushing] defeat; be beaten to the ground.

sanpai (酸敗), *n.* acidification.

sanpan (三板, 舢舨), *n.* 〔支那〕 a sampan (小舟).

sanpasen (三巴戰), *n.* a triangular [three-cornered] contest.

sanpatsu (散髮), *n.* ❶ (理髮) hair-cutting. ❷ (ざんぎり) cropped hair. ❸ (ちらし髮) dishevelled hair. ¶ 散髮屋, a barber (人); a barber's shop (店).

sanpei (散兵), *n.* a skirmisher; a tirailleur. ¶ 散兵線《演習》, a skirmishing line《drill》.

sanpi (贊否), *n.* yes or no; ayes or noes. —贊否の論, arguments for and against; pros and cons.

sanpitsu (算筆), *n.* arithmetic and writing [penmanship].

sanpo (散步), *n.* a walk; an airing; a stroll. —散步する, to walk (about); take a walk; stroll. —散步がてら, during a walk.

sanpō (山砲), *n.* a mountain-gun. ¶ 山砲隊, a mountain artillery.

sanpō (算法), *n.* arithmetic.

sanpu (產婦), *n.* a lying-in woman; a woman in childbed [labour]. ¶ 產婦預所, a maternity; a maternity hospital.

sanpu (散布, 撒布), *n.* diffusion; distribution; dispersion. —撒布する, to distribute; diffuse; disperse.

sanpuku (三伏), *n.* the dog-days.

sanpuku (山腹), *n.* a hillside; a mountain-side [-belly]; a flank.

sanpuru (見本), *n.* a sample.

sanran (產卵する), *vi.* to lay eggs; spawn (魚に言ふ). ¶ 產卵期, a breeding-season.

sanran (散亂する), *vi.* to disperse; be scattered about.

sanran (燦爛), *n.* brilliancy; brightness; glitter. —燦爛たる, brilliant; bright; dazzling.

sanran (蠶卵), *n.* silkworm-eggs. ¶ 蠶卵紙, a silkworm-egg card.

sanretsu (參列), *n.* attendance; presence. —參列する, to attend; be present *at.*

sanrin (山林), *n.* a forest. ¶ 山林局, the Forestry Bureau.

sanrinsha (三輪車), *n.* a tricycle.

sanroku (山麓), *n.* the foot of a mountain. ☞ *fumoto.*

sanryō (山陵), *n.* an Imperial tomb [tumulus].

sanryō (三稜-形), *n.* 【數】a prism.

sansa (三叉), *n.* trifurcation.
sansaku (散策), *n.* =*sanpo*.
sansan-gogo (三三五五), *ad.* in small numbers [groups]; by twos and threes. —三々五々歸路に就く, to go home by twos and threes; straggle home.
sansankudo (三三九度), *n.* the nuptial drinking ceremony. —三三九度の盃をする, to drink the nuptial cup.
sanseiken (參政權), *n.* the right of participation in the government; political rights; suffrage (選擧權). ¶ 女子參政權, ☞ *joshi*.
sansei (酸性), *n.* acidity.
sansei (贊成), *n.* agreement; support; seconding. **——-suru,** *vt.* to agree *with*; support; approve *of*; favour. —君が贊成するなら, if you are agreeable. —贊成! 贊成!, Yes, yes. —僕は改革に贊成だ, I am in favour of a reform. ¶ 贊成者, a supporter; a seconder. —贊成投票, ayes; votes in the affirmative.
sanseki (山積する), *v.* ❶ (積上げる) to load [heap; pile] high up. ❷ (堆くなる) to form a mountain; be piled up in a heap.
sansen (山川), *n.* mountains and rivers.
sansha (三舍), *n.* three postal stations. —...をして三舍を避けしむ, to overshadow; throw into the shade.
sanshaku (參酌する), *vt.* to take into consideration; consult.
sanshi (蠶絲), *n.* silk; silk-thread; silk-yarn.
sanshi-kyōsō (撒紙競走), *n.* the hare and hounds; a paper chase.
sanshin (三振), *n.* 【野球】 three strikes; struck out.
sanshitsu (蠶室), *n.* a silkworm rearing-room.
sanshō (秦椒, 山椒), *n.* 【植】 the Chinese [Japanese] pepper.
sanshō (三唱), *n.* ❶ three cheers. ❷ singing 《reciting》 three times. —萬歲を三唱する, to give three cheers [banzais].
sanshō (參照), *n.* reference; comparison. —參照する, to refer *to*; consult. ¶ 相互參照, cross reference.
sanshoku (三色の), *a.* three-coloured; tricoloured. ¶ 三色版, three-coloured printing. —三色旗, a tricolour. —三色菫, 【植】 the heart's-ease.
sanshoku (蠶食する), *vt.* to encroach *upon.*
sanshōuo (山椒魚), *n.* 【兩棲】 the (giant) salamander.
sanshū (參集する), *vi.* to assemble; gather.
sanshutsu (產出), *n.* production; yield; output. —產出する, to produce; turn out; yield. ¶ 產出高, output; outturn; yield.
sanshutsu (算出する), *v.* to calculate; compute.
sanso (酸素), *n.* oxygen. ¶ 酸素吸入器, a lung-motor.
sansui (山水), *n.* a landscape; scenery. —山水の美, scenic beauty. ¶ 山水畫, a landscape.
sansui (撒水), *n.* watering. —撒水する, to water; sprinkle. ¶ 撒水車, a watering-cart; a water-cart; a (water-)dray. —撒水自動車, a watering motor-car.
sansuke (三助), *n.* a bath-man [-boy]; a bath-room attendant.
Sansukuritto (梵語), *n.* Sanskrit, Sanscrit.
san-suru (產する), *vt.* to produce; yield; turn out (製品など).
san-suru (算する), *vt.* to number; amount to; come up to.
san-suru (贊する), *vt.* to support. ☞ *sansei* (贊成する).
Santakurōzu (サンタクロース), *n.* Santa Claus.
santan (三嘆する), *vt.* to admire highly.
santan (慘憺たる), *a.* miserable; wretched; tragic(-al). —苦心慘憺して, with great pains. —慘憺たる光景を呈する, to present a tragical [pathetic] scene.
santan (讚嘆する), *vt.* to admire; praise; extol.
santō (三等), *n.* third class; third rate. —三等で行く, to go third class.
santōbun (三等分する), *vt.* to trisect; divide into three equal parts.
sanyaku (散藥), *n.* a powder (medicine).
sanyo (參與), *n.* participation (in public affairs). —參與する, to take part *in*; participate *in*. ¶ 參與官, a councillor.
sanyō (算用), *n.* calculation; reckoning; computation. ☞ *kanjō*. ¶ 算用數字, the Arabic figures [characters].
sanzai (散在する), *vi.* to be [lie] scattered; lie here and there. —散在せる, sporadic; scattered.
sanzai (散財), *n.* expense; dissipation. —散財する, to spend money; squander; be put to expense. —人に散財をかける, to put a man to expense.
sanzan (散散), *ad.* severely; harshly; badly; soundly. —散々に負ける, to be utterly defeated. —散々な目に逢ふ, ① to be treated very harshly. ② to have a bitter experience; have a hard time of it. —人を散々なぐる, to give a

person a sound thrashing; thrash a man; beat a man soundly. —人に散々迷惑をかける, to give [put] a man to so much trouble.

sanzoku (山賊), *n.* a brigand; a bandit; a highwayman (追剝). —山賊に遭ふ, to fall among highway robbers.

sanzu-no-kawa (三途の川), *n.* the (River) Styx. —三途の川の渡守, the Stygian ferry-man; Charon.

san-zuru (散ずる), *v.* to disperse; dissipate; scatter; spend (費す).

sao (竿, 桿, 棹), *n.* ❶ a pole; a rod; a staff. ❷ (衡桿) a beam.

saobakari (桿秤), *n.* a steelyard [beam; Roman] balance.

saosasu (棹さす), *vt.* to pole; push with a pole; punt. —順潮に棹さす, to row with the tide.

saotobi (竿跳), *n.* pole-jump(-ing); pole-vault.

saō-uō (左往右往に), *ad.* right and left; about. —左往右往に逃げ亂れる, to scatter right and left.

sappa (拶雙魚), *n.* 【魚】 the scalloped-sardine.

sappari (さっぱり), *ad.* ❶ (全然) quite; entirely; at all; in the least. ❷ (清楚) neatly; cleanly; nattily. ❸ (淡白) frankly; candidly; open-heartedly. —氣がさっぱりする, to feel refreshed. —さっぱり譯が解らぬ, to make nothing *of*; cannot make head or tail *of*; do not know what to make *of*. ——**-shita**, *a.* ❶ (清楚) neat; tidy. ❷ (淡白) (*a*) (性質) frank; candid: (*b*) (食物) plain; light; refreshing (飲料). —さっぱりした身裝をしてゐる, to be neatly dressed. —さっぱりした人だ, He is a man of frank disposition.

sappitsuga (擦筆畫), *n.* a stump drawing.

sappūkei (殺風景な), *a.* tasteless; dry; prosaic; ungraceful.

sara (皿), *n.* ❶ a plate (平皿); a dish (深皿); a sauce (下皿); a scale (秤の). ❷ (皿盛り肴の稱) a dish. —目を皿のやうにして驚いた, He opened his eyes wide with surprise.

saraba (さらば), *ad.* (左様なら) farewell; adieu; good-bye. ——, *conj.* (それならば) then; well (then); in that case; if (it is) so; now.

sarabakari (皿秤), *n.* a balance; scales.

sarada (サラダ), *n.* salad.

sarai (浚), *n.* dredging; scraping; clearing [cleaning] out.

sarai (復習), *n.* ❶ review. ❷ (遊藝の) rehearsal.

saraigetsu (再來月), *n.* the month after next; next month but one.

sarainen (再來年), *n.* the year after next; next year but one.

sarakedasu (さらけ出す), *vt.* to reveal; disclose; expose; lay bare.

sarani (更に), *ad.* ❶ (重ねて) again; once more; over again; afresh. ❷ (絶えて) (not) at all; (not) in the least. —更に頓著しない, not to care a rush [bit].

sarari (さらりと), *ad.* ❶ (全く) all; entirely; completely. ❷ (障りなく) without a hitch; smoothly (さらさらと). ❸ (未練なく) without regret. ❹ (爽快に) refreshingly. —さらりと諦める, to give up all hopes 《thoughts》 *of*.

sarari (月給), *n.* salary. ¶ サラリメン階級, the salariat. —サラリメン組合, the Salaried Men's Union.

sarasa (更紗), *n.* (cotton) print; chintz. ¶ 更紗工場, a print-works.

sarasara (さらさら), *ad.* ❶ (すらすら) smoothly; without hindrance. ❷ (流水·木葉の戰ぐ貌) rustlingly; murmuring (流れ). ❸ (爽快) refreshingly. —さらさらと鳴る, to rustle.

sarashi (晒), *n.* ❶ (漂白) bleaching. ❷ 【暴】 (暴露) exposure. ❸ (晒木綿) bleached cotton. ¶ 晒粉, bleaching-powder. —晒屋, a bleacher (人): a bleachery (業).

sarasu (晒す), *vt.* ❶ (漂白) to bleach. ❷ 【暴】 to expose. ❸ 【梟】 to expose (the head of a criminal). —風雨に暴す, to expose to the weather. —内の恥を外に晒す, to wash one's dirty linen in public. —暴者にする, to expose (a criminal) to public disgrace.

sarau (浚ふ), *vt.* to dredge; clear; clear [clean] out; scrape.

sarau (攫ふ), *vt.* ❶ (持逃げする) to make off *with*; run away *with*. ❷ (略取する) to kidnap; carry away [off]; take away. ❸ (波·流が押流す) to sweep [carry] away; wash overboard (甲板から). —(鷹が) 雛を攫ふ, to make a pounce upon a chicken. —(波に) 足を攫はれる, to be carried off one's legs.

sarau (復習ふ), *v.* =*fukushū* (復習する).

sareba (されば), *ad.* & *conj.* on that account; then; so; therefore; hence.

saredo (されど-も), *conj.* however; but.

sareki (沙礫), *n.* grit; pebbles; gravel.

sarekōbe (髑髏), *n.* the skull.

sarichiru-san (サリチル酸), *n.* 【藥】 salicylic acid.

sarinagara (さりながら), *ad.* & *conj.* nevertheless; notwithstanding; however.

saritowa (さりとは), *ad.* in that case; then. —さりとは餘り酷い, In that case it is too cruel.

saron (サロン), *n.* ❶ (客間) a *salon* 【佛】. ❷ [S-] (巴里美術展覽會) the *Salon*.

saru (猿), *n.* ❶【哺乳】the monkey; the ape. ❷【建】(戸じまり具) a bolt. —猿の人眞似, an ape's mimicry of man. —猿も木から落ちる, "A good marksman may miss."

saru (さる), *a.* a certain. —さる人, a certain person.

saru (去·距る), *v.* ❶ (離れる) to leave; go away [off]; depart. ❷ (除去) to remove; get rid of. ❸ (離縁する) to divorce. ❹【距】to be distant [remote]; be separated. —去る三月, last March. —職を去る, to resign one's post; retire from one's post. —此世を去る, to depart from (this) life; depart this life; pass away. —去る者日に疎し, "Out of sight, out of mind."

saru (然る), *a.* ❶ such; of the sort [kind]; that. ❷ (尤もな) reasonable; right; natural.

sarugutsuwa (猿轡), *n.* a gag. —猿轡を嵌める, to gag.

sarujie (猿智慧), *n.* shallow cunning [craftiness].

sarumata (猿股), *n.* short drawers; bathing-drawers.

sarumawashi (猿廻し), *n.* a monkey-leader.

sarusuberi (百日紅), *n.*【植】the Indian lilac; the crape-myrtle.

saruvarusan (サルヴァルサン), *n.*【藥】salvarsan.

sasa (笹), *n.*【植】the bamboo-grass; the dwarf bamboo.

sasae (支), *n.* ❶ (支ふること) support; maintenance. ❷ (支棒) a prop; a support; a stay.

sasaeru (支へる), *vt.* ❶ (維持する) to support; sustain; maintain; keep up. ❷ (重い物を) (*a*) (柱が屋根などを) to support; sustain: (*b*) (支柱などで) to prop up; stay. ❸ (喰ひ止める) to (hold in) check; stay; defend. ❹ (耐へる) to bear; stand; sustain. —一家を支へる, to support a family. —生活を支へる, to sustain [hold up] life. —騎兵の突撃を支へる, to sustain [bear] the shock of a cavalry charge. —あの銀行は最早支へ切れぬ, That bank cannot hold out any longer.

sasage (大角豆), *n.*【植】the Chowtee-plant; the cow-pea.

sasagemono (捧物), *n.* an offering; a present; a sacrifice (神の).

sasageru (捧げる), *vt.* ❶ (手で) to lift up; hold up. ❷ (獻上する) to offer; present; tender. —捧げ銃をする, to present arms. —君國に生命を捧げる, to lay down one's life for one's country.

sasaheri (笹縁), *n.* edging; lace.

sasai (些細な), *a.* trivial; petty; insignificant. —些細な事に拘泥する, to stick to trifles.

sasameki (私語), *n.* a whisper; a murmur.

sasameku (私語く), *vi.* to whisper.

sasara (簓), *n.* a whisk.

sasayabu (笹藪), *n.* a bamboo-jungle.

sasayaka (細かな), *a.* small; little.

sasayaki (囁), *n.* whispering; whisper; murmur.

sasayaku (囁く), *vi.* to whisper; murmur; ripple (流などが). ——, *vt.* to whisper; speak in the ear [under one's breath].

sasen (左遷), *n.* relegation; degradation. —左遷する, to relegate; degrade.

saseru (爲せる), *vt.* ❶ (消極的に) to let (one do); allow (one to do). ❷ (積極的に) to make (one do); get (something done); have (him do it). —勝手にさせておく, to let one do as one pleases. —君を虐待させはせぬ, I will not allow you to be ill-treated.

sashi (差, 尺), *n.* a measure; a rule.

sashiageru (差上げる), *vt.* ❶ (高くあげる) to lift up; hold up. ❷ (進上する) to present; offer. —お茶を差上げませうか, May I offer you a cup of tea?

sashiai (差合), *n.* an obstacle; a hindrance; an appointment [engagement] (先約). —差し合ふ, to be hindered.

sashiashi (差足), *n.* stealthy [soft] steps. —差し足抜き足で忍び寄る, to approach with soft, stealthy steps.

sashiatari (差當り), *ad.* ❶ (當分) for the present; for the time being; for the nonce. ❷ (目下) at present; at the present moment; for the moment.

sashichigaeru (刺違へる), *vi.* to stab [thrust] each other.

sashidashinin (差出人), *n.* a sender; a remitter (爲替の).

sashidasu (差出す), *vt.* ❶ (提出) to present; offer; tender; produce (證據物を). ❷ (發送) to send; deliver; post (投函). ❸ (伸す) to stretch [hold] out (手を). —願書を差出す, to send in an application.

sashidegamashii (差出がましい), *a.* intrusive; meddlesome; impertinent.

sashideguchi (差出口する), *vi.* to make an uncalled-for-remark; interfere. —差出口をするな, Mind your own business.

sashideru (差出る), *v.* to put [poke; thrust] one's nose *into*; obtrude oneself; meddle.

sashie (插繪), *n.* an illustration; a book-illustration.

sashieda (插枝), *n.* a slip; a scion; a graft.

sashigami (差紙), *n.* a written summons; a writ of the court.

sashigane (差金), *n.* ❶ (曲尺) a carpenter's [an L] square; a metal foot-measure. ❷ (指揮) direction; instructions; instigation (使嗾). —彼の差金で, at his instigation.

sashigusuri (差藥), *n.* an injection (注射); an eye-lotion (目藥).

sashihasamu (挾む), *vt.* ❶ (插入する) to insert; put in; stick. ❷ (左右より挾む) to hold *between*. ❸ (抱懷する) to hold; cherish; harbour. —河を挾んで, with a river between. —勢を挾む, to presume upon one's power. —怨を挾む, to harbour a grudge.

sashihikaeru (差控へる), *v.* to forbear *from*; refrain *from*; keep back *from*. ☞ ***hikaeru***.

sashihiki (差引), *n.* ❶ (差引くこと) subtraction; deduction. ❷ (差引計算) balance; the net result. ❸ (潮の進退) ebb and flow. ❹ (熱の增減) rise and fall. —差引勘定する, to reckon *with*; settle accounts *with*. —差引君の方が得だ, The balance of advantage lies with you.

sashihiku (差引く), *vt.* to discount; deduct; subtract. —費用を俸給から差引く, to stop the cost out of his salary.

sashiire (差入), *n.* ❶ (差込むこと) insertion. ❷ (差入物) a present to a prisoner. —差入れする, to make a present to a prisoner. ¶ 郵便物差入口, a letter-drop.

sashiireru (差入れる), *v.* ❶ (插入) to insert; put *in*. ❷ to make (a prisoner) a present *of*.

sashikae (差替, 插替), *n.* ❶ replacement; rearrangement; substitution. ❷【印】amendment. —差替へる, to replace; substitute; rearrange; amend.

sashikakaru (差掛·差懸る), *vi.* ❶ (上より掩ふ) to hang [impend] over; overhang. ❷ (通りかゝる) to come near; approach. —差掛かった用も無い, I have no business on hand.

sashikake (差掛-小屋), *n.* 【建】 a lean-to [-roof]; a pentice; a pent-house [-roof].

sashikakeru (差掛ける), *vt.* to hold over. —傘を差掛ける, to hold an umbrella over a person.

sashiki (插木), *n.* a cutting; a slip; a scion. —插木する, to plant a cutting in the earth.

sashikomi (差込), *n.* ❶ (插入) insertion. ❷ (痙攣) convulsion; spasm; a griping pain. ❸ (一種の簪) a bodkin.

sashikomu (差込む), *v.* ❶ (插入) to insert *in*; put in; thrust *in*; wedge *in*. ❷ (射入る) to shine in; stream in; enter; come in. ❸ (潮が) to flow in. ❹ (劇痛) to have the gripes [a griping pain]; have spasms in one's side. —月影の射し込む窓, the window which lets in the moonlight.

sashikorosu (刺殺す), *vt.* to stab to death; sting to death (蜂等が).

sashikuru (差繰る), *vi.* to make shift; shift.

sashimaneku (麾く), *vt.* ❶ to beckon *to*. ❷ (指圖) to command; direct.

sashimawasu (差廻す), *vt.* to send round; send.

sashimi (刺身), *n.* 【料理】slices of raw fish.

sashimo-no (さしもの), *a.* even such. —さしもの大帝國も, a great empire as it was.

sashimono (指物), *n.* joinery-work; joinery; cabinet-work. ¶ 指物師, a joiner; a cabinet-maker.

sashimukai (差向ひで), *ad.* face to face; *tête-à-tête* 【佛】. —差向ひで話す, to talk face to face [*tête-à-tête*].

sashimukau (差向ふ), *v.* ❶ (其方に向く) to face; turn *to*. ❷ (相對する) to be face to face.

sashimukeru (差向ける), *vt.* ❶ (遣す) to send; despatch (派遣). ❷ (差附ける) to point [present] *at*. —僕に鐵砲を差向ける, to point a gun at me.

sashine (指直), *n.* (取引市場) limit.

sashioku (差措く), *vt.* to set [put; lay] aside; leave. —彼をさし措いて, leaving him out. —何を差措いても, by all means; even setting everything else aside; first of all.

sashiosae (差押), *n.* 【法】seizure; attachment; distraint; distress. —動產《不動產》差押, personal 《real》 distress. ¶ 差押物件, seized goods; distress.

sashisawari (差障), *n.* an obstacle; an impediment. —差障る, to obstruct; impede.

sashisemaru (差迫る), *vi.* to press; approach; be close at hand. —差迫った, pressing; imminent;

impending.

sashishimesu (指示す), *vt.* to point (out); indicate.

sashishio (差潮), *n.* a flood-tide; a rising tide; a flow.

sashisoeru (差添へる), *vt.* to add *to.*

sashitaru (左したる), *a.* particular; special; serious (重大).

sashitate (差立), *n.* despatch; forwarding. —差立てる, to despatch; send; forward.

sashite (さして), *ad.* (格別) particularly; specially. ——, *prep.* (に向って) for; toward; in the direction *of*.

sashitome (差止), *n.* ❶ (禁止) prohibition; forbidding. ❷ (抑止) stopping; suspension. ❸ (抑留) detention.

sashitomeru (差止める), *vt.* ❶ (禁止) to prohibit; forbid. ❷ (抑止) to stop; suspend; restrain (制止). ❸ (抑留) to detain. —出入を差止める, to forbid him the house. —小切手の支拂を差止める, to stop a cheque.

sashitōsu (刺通す), *n.* to pierce; thrust; stab.

sashitsukae (差支), *n.* ❶ (故障) obstacle; hindrance; an appointment [engagement] (先約). ❷ (異議) objection. ❸ (缺乏) want; lack. —差支無くば, if there is no objection [hindrance]; if you have no objection. —差支へる, ① to be hindered; be prevented; be engaged (用事·先約等にて). ② to stand in need *of*; be hard up *for*. —と云ふも差支ない, we may say that.... —何時でも差支無し, Any time will suit me [will do]. —私しは少しも差支ない, There is no objection on my part. —少々金に差支へた, I am a little pressed for money.

sashitsukawasu (差遣はす), *vt.* to send; dispatch. —御用の節は店員差遣はし可申候, "Customers attended at their own houses."

sashitsukeru (差附ける), *vt.* ❶ (拳銃など) to point [present] (a pistol at a person); push *against*. ❷ (證據など) to confront (a person with proofs).

sashitsumaru (差詰まる), *vi.* to be embarrassed; be pressed; be hard up; come to an extremity.

sashiwatashi (差渡), *n.* ❶ (直徑) the diameter; the calibre (口徑). ❷ (差渡した長さ) the distance across; the direct distance. ——, *ad.* across; in a bee-line; as the crow flies.

sashizoe (差添), *n.* the smaller [shorter] sword. ¶ 差添人, an attendant; a chaperon (婦人への).

sashizu (指圖), *n.* order; direction; instructions. —指圖する, to order; direct; instruct; give orders; give instructions. —人の指圖などは受けぬ, I will not be dictated to. ¶ 指圖人拂, payable to order. —指圖式小切手, an order cheque; a cheque to order. —指圖書, directions.

sashizume (差詰), *ad.* for the present; for the time being; firstly (第一に); immediately (すぐに).

sashō (些少), *n.* a few (數); a little (量); a trifle. —些少の, ① little; few; scanty. ② slight; trifling. —些少ながら, slight as it is; such as it is, though of little worth.

sashō (査證), *n.* visé, visa. —旅券に査證を受ける, to have one's passport viséed [visaed].

sashō (詐稱), *n.* false personation. —詐稱する, to personate (a prince, 皇族と); represent oneself as [to be] (a judge, 判事と); assume (another's name, 人の名を).

sashu (詐取する), *vt.* to swindle [defraud; cheat] (a person of a thing); obtain by false pretences.

sashū (沙洲), *n.* a sand-bar; a spit.

sashū (査收する), *vt.* to receive.

sasoku (左側), *n.* the left side; the left hand; the near side (馬車等の). ¶ 左側通行, "Keep to the left."

sasori (蠍), *n.* 【蟲】the scorpion.

sasou (誘ふ), *vt.* to call (*for*) (立寄る). ☞ *izanau*. —誘ひ出す, to decoy out; entice out; draw out.

sassato (さっさと), *ad.* quickly; promptly; speedily. —さっさと去る (出て行く), to go quick; fling out. —さっさと云へ, Out with it.

sassatsu (颯颯たる), *a.* murmuring; rustling; whistling.

sasshi (察), *n.* sympathy; consideration. —察しがよい, to be sympathizing [sympathetic]. —お察しのよいことね, How considerate!; What a good guess!. —お察しの通りです, It is as you have conjectured.

sasshi (冊子), *n.* a book; pamphlet; a brochure (假綴の).

sasshin (刷新), *n.* reform; innovation; renovation. —刷新する, to reform; renovate.

sasshō (殺傷), *n.* killing and wounding; butchery (虐殺). —殺傷する, to kill and wound; butcher.

sassō (颯爽たる), *a.* gallant. —颯爽たる英姿, a gallant figure.

sassoku (早速), *ad.* at once; immediately; directly; promptly. —早速ですが, excuse my suddenness, but…; I will come to the point at once.

sas-suru (察する), *vt.* ❶ (察知) to understand; perceive; see. ❷ (推量) to guess; conjecture; judge. ❸ (思ひやる) to sympathize *with*. —察するに, I suppose that; I dare say; I conjecture that.

sasu (差す), *vi.* ❶ (潮が) to rise. ❷ (射る) to shine *into* 《*upon*》. —魔が差す, to be possessed by a devil. —夕日が窓にさす, The evening sun shines upon the window. —彼は少し氣がさしてる, He is a little out of his wits.

sasu (差す), *vt.* ❶ 【指】 (指示する) to point; point out; indicate; direct. ❷ (注ぐ) to pour *into*; drop *upon*. ❸ (杯をさす) to pass (*to*); give; offer. —油をさす, to oil; drop oil *into*. —眼薬をさす, to drop eye-lotion into the eyes. —箱を指す, to make [join] a box. —日傘をさす, to put up a parasol. —將棋をさす, to play chess; move a man. —脣に紅をさす, to rouge the lips.

sasu (刺す), *vt.* ❶ (突き込む) to thrust (through); stab; pierce. ❷ (縫ふ) to sew. ❸ (插む) to insert *in*; put between [into]. ❹ 【螫】 (蟲が) to bite; sting. —刺すが如き, cutting; piercing; prickly. —雀を刺す, to catch a sparrow with a limed pole. —走者を刺す (野球), to catch the base runner.

sasuga (流石), *ad.* as one might have expected; truly; indeed. —流石賢明の彼も, wise as he was. —流石日本の首府だけあって, like the capital of Japan that it is.

sasumata (刺股), *n.* a pitchfork (二叉); a trident (三叉).

sasurai (流離, 漂浪), *n.* wandering; roaming; roving. —流離ふ, to wander about; roam; ramble.

sasuru (擦る), *vt.* to rub; stroke; shampoo (按摩をする).

sata (沙汰), *n.* ❶ (官府の指令) order; instructions. ❷ (たより, 報道) notice; a report; a news. ❸ (噂, 評判) a rumour; town-talk. —特別の沙汰 (恩惠), a special favour. —沙汰する, to report; inform; give notice *of*; write *to*; let (a person) know. ——向沙汰が無い, I have not heard from him at all. —實に沙汰の限りだ, It is really amazing [intolerable].

satan (左袒する), *v.* to side [hold] *with*; espouse; stand by; take the part *of*.

satan (嗟歎する), *v.* to sigh; deplore; lament.

satchū (殺蟲する), *a.* insecticidal. ¶ 殺蟲劑, 【醫】 a vermifuge; an insecticide; insect-powder (粉).

sate (偖, 扨), now; well; so. —さてどうしたものだらう, Well, what had we better do? —さては汝であったよな, Oh, was it you?

satei (查定), *n.* assessment (評價); revision (修正). —查定する, to examine and decide; assess; revise. ¶ 查定案, a revised budget.

satemo-satemo (扨も扨も), *int.* Dear me!; Oh, dear!; O my!

sateoki (扨措き), *ad.* ❶ (云ふに及ばず) not to mention; to say nothing *of*; let alone. ❷ (よしにして) setting [putting] aside; apart *from*. —冗談は扨措き, jesting apart; apart from joking; and now to be serious. —何は扨措き, above all things; before everything.

satetsu (蹉跌), *n.* miscarriage; failure; a setback. —蹉跌する, to miscarry; fail; break down. —大蹉跌を來す, to meet with a great setback.

sato (里), *n.* ❶ (村落) a village; a hamlet. ❷ (生地) one's native place; home. ❸ (生家) one's home. —子を里に出す, to send the child out to nurse.

satō (左黨), *n.* the Left.

satō (砂糖), *n.* sugar. ¶ 白《赤; 黑》砂糖, white 《brown; raw》 sugar. —砂糖大根, the sugar-beet. —砂糖黍, a sugar-cane. —砂糖漬, sugar-candy (菓子); conserves; a candied fruit.

satogo (里子), *n.* a child sent out to nurse; a foster child. —里子にやる, to put [send] out a baby to nurse.

satoi (敏い), *a.* sharp; quick; intelligent.

satoimo (里芋), *n.* 【植】 the taro.

satori (覺, 悟), *n.* perception; understanding; enlightenment. —悟りが早い, to be clever; be quick-witted; be quick to understand [of apprehension]. —悟りを開く, to see (it) through; attain higher perception; attain to enlightenment.

satoru (悟·覺る), *vt.* to apprehend; perceive; discern. ——, *vi.* to become enlightened. —死期を覺る, to see that one's hour of death has come. —それと覺って, on discerning it. —それと覺った時は, when I perceived it. —誤を悟らせる, to convince a person of his error.

satoshi (諭), *n.* admonition; instruction; counsel.

satosu (諭す), *vt.* to admonish; warn; counsel; instruct. —懇々諭す, to talk [speak] seriously to a person.

satsu (札), *n.* ❶ (札) a card; a ticket. ❷ (紙幣) paper money; a note; a bank-note. —札びらを切る, to flash one's rags. ¶ 十圓札, a ten-*yen* note.

satsu (冊), *n.* a volume (卷); a copy (部).

satsubatsu (殺伐な), *a.* brutal; barbarous; murderous; bloodthirsty. ¶ 殺伐時代, a bloody age.

satsuei (撮影), *n.* photography. —撮影する, to photograph; take a photograph *of*; film (活動寫眞を). ¶ 撮影場 (活動寫眞の), a studio (for the production of pictures). —撮影監督, a movie [film]-director.

satsugai (殺害), *n.* murder; killing. —殺害する, to murder; slay; kill.

satsui (殺意), *n.* murderous intent; intent to kill.

satsuire (札入), *n.* a pocket-book; a *porte-monnaie* 【佛】.

satsujin (殺人-犯), *n.* homicide; murder (謀殺); manslaughter (故殺). —殺人罪を犯す, to commit murder. ¶ 殺人光線, a death-ray. —殺人者, a murderer; a homicide.

satsuki (杜鵑花), *n.* 【植】 Rhododendron indicum (rhododendron の一種·學名); the azalea (俗稱).

satsumaimo (甘藷), *n.* 【植】 Ipomæa edulis (morning-glory の一種·學名): (俗稱) a sweet-potato; a batata.

satsuriku (殺戮), *n.* massacre; slaughter; carnage. —殺戮する, to massacre; slaughter.

satto (颯と), *ad.* suddenly; quickly. —颯と吹き來る風, a sudden blast [gust] of wind. —さッと顏を赤らめた, Her face flushed up on a sudden.

sattō (殺到する), *vi.* to pour in; rush *to*; press upon (us) in swarms; come down upon. —註文が殺到した, Orders poured in from all quarters; We had an enormous number [a flood] of orders from all quarters.

sāvu (サーヴ), *n.* 【庭球】 serve; service; delivery; a server (人).

sawa (澤), *n.* a swamp; a marsh.

sawagashii (騷しい), *a.* ❶ (騷騷しい) noisy; boisterous; uproarious. ❷ (穩かならぬ) turbulent; agitated; excited.

sawagasu (騷がす), *vt.* to disturb; agitate; stir; alarm. —議場を騷がす, to create a disturbance in the House. —(事件·噂などが) 世間《市中》を騷がす, to create a sensation [stir] among the people 《in town》.

sawagi (騷), *n.* ❶ (騷々しい) noise; clamour; uproar; a din. ❷ (騷動) tumult; excitement; disturbance; stir; fuss; flurry. ❸ (遊興) revelry; a spree; high jinks. —非常な騷ぎ, a hell of a noise; a great excitement. —賃銀値上の騷ぎ, clamour for higher wages.

sawagitateru (騷立てる), *v.* to raise an uproar; make a fuss (about); be excited.

sawagu (騷ぐ), *vi.* to make a noise [disturbance]; be noisy; make merry (酒宴で騷ぐ). —胸が騷ぐ, to feel uneasy; be agitated. —酒を呑んで騷ぐ, to be on the spree. —彼は少しも騷がなかった, He did not show the least agitation.

sawara (鰆), *n.* 【魚】 Scombremorus niphonium (學名).

sawara (花柏), *n.* 【植】 the Japanese cypress.

sawari (障), *n.* ❶ (邪魔) a hindrance; an obstruction. ❷ (病氣) sickness. ❸ (影響) harm; affection. —何等の障りもなく, without any hitch.

sawari (觸), *n.* ❶ (觸感) feeling; touch. ❷ (鼓の響紋) snares. ❸ (義太夫の) the singing passages; the impassioned passages. —觸りがよい, to feel smooth; be pleasant to the touch.

sawaru (障る), *vt.* ❶ to obstruct; hamper; interfere *with*. ❷ (影響) to affect; do one harm (害になる); be injurious [harmful] *to* (health) (同上). —健康に障る, to affect a person's health.

sawaru (觸る), *vt.* to touch; feel; meddle *with* (いぢる). —觸るべからず, "Hands off!"

sawayaka (爽な), *a.* ❶ (爽快な) refreshing; agreeable; pleasant; (新鮮な) fresh. ❷ (明晰な) clear; distinct. ❸ (流暢な) fluent (tongue). —爽かな聲, a clear [silvery] voice.

saya (莢), *n.* 【植】 a pod; a hull; a shell; a husk. ¶ 莢豆, a legumen, legume.

saya (鞘), *n.* ❶ a sheath; a scabbard (刀劍等の); a case (小刀·眼鏡等の); a cap (萬年筆の). ❷ (賣買價の差) a margin. —刀の鞘を拂ふ, to unsheathe a sword; draw a sword out of its scabbard. —刀を鞘に納める, to sheathe a sword; put up one's sword. ——もとの鞘に納まる, to be reconciled.

sayaku (鎖鑰), *n.* the key (of a position).

sayatori (鞘取), *n.* 【商】 arbitrage.

sayō (左樣), ❶ (然り) yes; so; all right. ❷ (共通り) Just so;

you are right; That's it. —左様左様, quite so; just so. —左様な, such. —左様ならば, then; now.

sayō (作用), *n.* ❶ (方法) a process. ❷ (働き) an action; an operation. ❸ (機能) a function. —作用する, to act *upon*; work *upon*; operate *on*. —電氣の作用で, by the action of electricity.

sayoku (左翼), *n.* 【軍】 the left wing. ¶ 左翼打手,【野球】a left-field batter.

sayōnara (左様なら), *int.* good-bye; *adieu* 【佛】; so long 【俗·男子間】; farewell (永別).

sayori (針魚), *n.* 【魚】 Hyporamphus sajori (half-beak の一種).

sayu (白湯), *n.* hot water.

sayū (左右), *n.* the right and left. —左右する, to control; dominate; overrule; command. —左右されて, at the mercy *of*. —言を左右に託する, to talk ambiguously; equivocate. (言を左右に託して, on one pretext or another.)

sazae (蠑螺), *n.* 【貝】 the top-shell; the wreath-shell.

sazameki (さざめき), *n.* whispering; murmur.

sazanami (漣, 小波), *n.* ripples; wavelets; dimples. —漣立つ, to ripple.

sazanka (山茶花), *n.* 【植】Thea sasanqua (tea-tree の一種·學名); the tea-oil plant.

sazareishi (細石), *n.* a pebble; gravel.

sazo (嘸), *ad.* Ⓢ 嘸かし. ❶ (大に) how; what; much. ❷ (定めし) indeed; surely. —嘸...でせう, I dare say; I am sure; it must be.

sazukaru (授かる), *v.* ❶ (受ける) to receive; be given; be endowed *with*. ❷ (敎はる) to be taught; take lessons *in* (課目) (under, 敎師). ¶ 授り物, a gift; a godsend.

sazukeru (授ける), *vt.* ❶ (與へる) to give; confer (a degree, a title, a favour, *etc.*) *on*; invest (a person) *with* (authority, rank, virtues, *etc.*) ☞ ***fuyo, juyo***. ❷ (敎へる) to teach; impart; give lessons in; initiate *into* (祕訣などを). —勳章を授ける, to decorate a person with an order.

se (畝), *n.* *se* (=30 *tsubo*).

se (背, 脊), *n.* ❶ the back; the ridge (山の). ❷ =***sei*** (丈).

se (瀨), *n.* (早瀨) the current; rapids: (淺瀨) a shoal; shallows.

sebameru (狹める), *vt.* to narrow; straiten; reduce.

sebiro (脊廣 -服), *n.* a lounge-suit; a cutaway; a sack-coat.

sebiru (强びる), *vt.* to tease (a person) *for*; importune (a person) *for*. ☞ ***nedaru***.

sebone (脊骨), *n.* the backbone; the spine.

sebumi (瀨踏), *n.* ❶ wading to try the depth. ❷ (探り) a previous trial; sounding. —瀨踏みする, ① to try the depth. ② to throw out a feeler; sound his views; sound him (about it).

sechi (世智), *n.* worldly wisdom. —世智に長けた, worldly-wise; prudent.

sechigarai (世智辛い), *a.* hard to live in. —世智辛い世の中, a hard world; a world hard to live in.

sedō (世道 -人心), *n.* public morals [morality].

segaki (施餓鬼), *n.* mass for the dead. —川施餓鬼をする, to hold mass for those drowned in the river.

segamu (强請む), *vt.* to tease *for*; importune *for*.

segare (忰, 倅), *n.* a son; my son.

segawa (背革), *n.* a leather-back. ¶ 背革綴, half-binding.

segyō (施行), *n.* charity; alms. —施行する, to dispense charities.

sehi (施肥), *n.* manuring.

sehire (脊鰭), *n.* the dorsal fin.

sehyō (世評), *n.* the (public) opinion; the public sentiment [feeling]; a rumour (噂). —世評に上る, to be in everyone's mouth; be talked about.

sei (丈, 脊), *n.* height; stature. —丈が立つ, to touch the ground [bottom]. —丈がのびる, to grow taller; grow in height. —丈が六尺ある, to stand six feet; measure six feet in height.

sei (正), *n.* ❶ right; righteousness; correctness. ❷ (資格の) regularity.

sei (世), *n.* a generation; an age.

sei (生), *n.* life; existence.

sei (性), *n.* ❶ (男女の) sex; 【文】 gender. ❷ (本性) nature. ❸ (品性) character. —人の性は善なり, Man is by nature good. ¶ 性教育, sex training [education].

sei (姓), *n.* a family name; a surname (Christian name の對).

sei (制), *n.* ❶ (支配) sway; rule. ❷ (制御) command; control. ❸ (制度) a system.

sei (精), *n.* ❶ (精力) energy; force; strength. ❷ (出精) diligence; exertion. ❸ (精髓) essence. ❹ (精靈) a spirit. —精が盡きる, to be exhausted. —精を出す, =***seidasu***.

sei (製), *n.* make; manufacture.

—英國製の, of English make [manufacture].

sei (勢), *n.* force; vigour; strength.

sei (所爲), *n.* ❶ (原因) cause. ❷ (陽氣などの影響, 加減) effects; influence. ❸ (誰の罪) fault; blame. —…のせゐである, to be due *to*; be owing *to*. —の所爲にする, to ascribe [attribute] it *to*.

seia (井蛙の見), a narrow [biassed; prejudiced] view.

seian (成案), *n.* a plan; a design; a draft (草案).

seibai (成敗), *n.* ❶ (裁き) judgment. ❷ (處罰) punishment. —成敗する, to judge; punish.

seiban (生蕃), *n.* the savages [aborigines] (of Formosa).

seibatsu (征伐), *n.* expedition (遠征); chastisement (問罪); subjugation (征服). —征伐する, to subjugate; chastise; make war *upon*.

seibetsu (生別), *n.* a life-long parting [separation]. —生別する, to part forever [for life].

seibo (生母), *n.* the real mother.

seibo (聖母), *n.* the Holy Mother; Our Lady; Madonna.

seibo (歲暮), *n.* ❶ (年末) the end of the year. ❷ (進物) a year-end present.

seibō (正帽), *n.* a full-dress [ceremonial] head-dress.

seibō (制帽), *n.* a regulation [uniform] cap.

seibō (聲望), *n.* popularity (人氣); high reputation (名聲). —聲望ある人, a man of high reputation.

seibun (成文の), *a.* written. ¶ 成文律 [法], a written law; a statute (law).

seibun (成分), *n.* an ingredient; a component; a constituent.

seibun (精分), *n.* vigour; strength; vitality. —精分をつける, to invigorate; give energy *to*.

seibutsu (生物), *n.* a living thing; a creature; a thing of life. ¶ 生物學, biology. (生物學者, a biologist.)

seibutsuga (靜物畫), *n.* a still life.

seibyō (聖廟), *n.* the temple of Confucius.

seicha (製茶), *n.* tea-manufacture; manufactured tea. ¶ 製茶業, tea-manufacture.

seichi (生地), *n.* a birthplace; one's native place [soil].

seichi (聖地), *n.* the holy land; a sacred place.

seichō (生長, 成長), *n.* growth. —生長する, to grow; grow up.

seichō (政廳), *n.* a government office.

seichō (整調), *n.* ❶ tuning. ❷ 【競漕】 a stroke-oar; the stroke. —整調する, 【音】 to tune.

seichō (聲調), *n.* a voice; a tone (of voice).

seichoku (正直), *n.* =***shōjiki***.

seichōseki (正長石), *n.* 【鑛】 orthoclase.

seichū (成蟲), *n.* 【昆】 the imago.

seichū (掣肘する), *vt.* to hamper; restrain.

seidai (世代), *n.* succession; generations.

seidai (正大な), *a.* just; impartial.

seidai (聖代), *n.* the age of a virtuous Emperor; a glorious reign.

seidai (盛大), *n.* ❶ (繁榮) prosperity. ❷ (壯大) grandeur. —盛大な, ① prosperous; thriving. ② grand; splendid. —盛大に, prosperously; on a grand scale.

seidaku (清濁), *n.* the clear and turbid; the pure and impure; purity and impurity. —清濁併せ呑む, to admit men of all shades.

seidan (政談), *n.* a political talk; a political lecture. ¶ 政談演說《演說會》, a political speech 《meeting》.

seidan (聖壇), *n.* an altar.

seidan (聖斷), *n.* an Imperial decision. —聖斷を仰ぐ, to submit a case to the Emperor for decision; appeal to Imperial decision.

seidasu (精出す), *vi.* to toil [work] hard; put out efforts; exert [strain] oneself. —精出して, industriously; assiduously; diligently. —課業に精出す, to study one's lessons with diligence; be diligent at one's study.

seiden (世傳の), *a.* hereditary.

seido (制度), *n.* a system; an institution; a regime. ¶ 敎育制度, the educational system.

seidō (生動する), *vi.* to be animated.

seidō (正道), *n.* justice; righteousness; the right way. —正道を踏む, to follow the right way; act with justice.

seidō (制動), *n.* a check; a hold. —制動する, to trig; skid (制輪子石等で). ¶ 制動機, a brake. —制動手, a brakesman.

seidō (青銅), *n.* bronze.

seidoku (精讀する), *vt.* to peruse; read carefully.

seiei (精英), *n.* essence; flower; *élite* 【佛】. ☞ ***sui*** (粹). —精英を抽く, to pick out the best.

seiei (精銳), *n.* the pick; the flower. —聯合軍の精銳, the picked [best] troops of the allies; the pick of the allies. —精銳な, picked; efficient; highly trained.

seien (製鹽), *n.* salt manufacture. ¶ 製鹽業者, a salter. —製鹽所, a salt-works; a saltern; a salt-manufactory.

seien (聲援), *n.* encouragement; support. —聲援する, to encourage; support; cheer.

seifu (政府), *n.* the government; the ministry. ¶ 政府案《委員》, a government bill《delegate》. —政府黨, the government party; the ministerialists.

seifuku (正服), *n.* a full dress; a dress; a court dress. ¶ 正服巡査, a full-dress constable; a policeman in full dress.

seifuku (正副), *n.* the chief and vice-chief; original and copy (書類の). —正副二通を作る, to make in duplicate.

seifuku (征服), *n.* conquest; subjection; subjugation. —征服する, to conquer; subdue; subjugate. ¶ 征服者, a conqueror.

seifuku (制服), *n.* a uniform.

seifun (製粉), *n.* milling. ¶ 製粉機械, a mill. —製粉所, a (flour-)mill; a grinding-mill.

seiga (聖駕), *n.* the Imperial palanquin.

seigaku (星學), *n.* astronomy.

seigaku (聲樂), *n.* vocal music. ¶ 聲樂家, a vocalist.

seigan (誓願), *n.* a vow.

seigan (請願), *n.* petition; application; memorial. —請願する, to petition; apply; memorialize. ¶ 請願委員, the petitions committee. —請願者, a petitioner; an applicant; a memorialist.

seigen (正弦), *n.* 【數】a sine.

seigen (西諺), *n.* a Western proverb [saying].

seigen (制限), *n.* limit; limitation; restriction. —制限ある, [*a*] limited; restricted; qualified. —制限する, to limit; restrict; put bounds [limit] *to*; qualify; confine. —適當の制限を加へる, to impose suitable restriction *upon*. —制限外發行高, the amount of excess-issue. —制限外手荷物, an excess luggage.

seigen, seigon, (誓言), *n.* a pledge; a vow; an oath. —誓言する, to take an oath [pledge]; make a vow [an oath]; pass one's word.

seigi (正義), *n.* justice; righteousness. —正義の, just; righteous.

seigo (正誤), *n.* a correction; an emendation (修正). —正誤する, to correct an error; rectify. ¶ 正誤表, (a table of) errata; corrigenda.

seigo (成語), *n.* a phrase.

seigō (正號), *n.* 【數】the positive sign.

seigyo (制御, 制馭), *n.* control; governing; management. —制御する, to control; govern; manage. —制御し難き, unmanageable; intractable.

seigyō (正業), *n.* a respectable calling; a legitimate [legal] occupation. ¶ 正業者, a man of respectable profession [calling].

seigyō (成業), *n.* completion of work《studies》.

seihai (成敗), *n.* success (and failure); victory (and defeat).

seihakumai (精白米), *n.* refined rice.

seihan (正犯), *n.* ❶ the principal offence. ❷ (人) the principal offender; the principal in the first degree.

seihan (製版), *n.* founding.

seihantai (正反對), *n.* direct opposition; the very opposite [reverse]. —正反對の, diametrically [direct] opposite [opposed]. —實際は正反對です, The very contrary is the case.

seihatsu (齊發), *n.* a volley; a salvo. —齊發する, to volley; fire a salvo.

seihei (精兵), *n.* picked troops; the pick.

seiheki (性癖), *n.* propensity; inclination; predisposition.

seihen (政變), *n.* a political change; the change of government (政府の更迭); political disturbances (政治的動亂).

seihi (成否), *n.* success or failure; issue. —(事の)成否を決する, to decide the fate.

seihin (正賓), *n.* the chief guest; the guest of honour.

seihin (清貧), *n.* honest poverty.

seihin (製品), *n.* manufactured goods [articles]; a manufacture.

seihirei (正比例), *n.* 【數】direct proportion. —...と正比例する, it is in direct proportion to....

seihō (成法), *n.* 【法】positive law; written law.

seihō (製法), *n.* the method《process》of manufacture; manufacture.

seihōkei (正方形), *n.* a square; a quadrate.

seihoku (西北), *n.* the north-west.

seihon (正本), *n.* an exemplification; an exemplified copy; an authentic writing.

seihon (製本), *n.* book-binding. —製本する, to bind. —製本頗る堅牢, It is very strongly bound. ¶ 製本屋, a (book-)binder; a book-bindery (製本工場).

seihyō (星標), *n.* an asterisk; a star.

seihyō (製氷), *n.* artificial ice: ice-manufacture (製造).
seii (誠意), *n.* sincerity; faith. —誠意がない, to lack sincerity. —誠意を披瀝する, to open one's bosom.
seii (聖意), *n.* Imperial will; an Imperial order.
seiiku (生育, 成育), *n.* ❶【成育】growth. ❷【生育】bringing up; rearing; upbringing.
seiippai (精一杯), *ad.* to the full extent of one's power; to the utmost; with all one's might.
seija (正邪), *n.* right and wrong; good and evil. —正邪を辨ずる, to know right from wrong.
seiji (青磁), *n.* a celadon; a porcelain.
seiji (政治), *n.* politics; government (治國); political affairs (政務). —政治的生涯, a political life [career]. ¶ 政治團體, a political association; a political body. —政治學, political science; politics. —政治家, a politician; a statesman. —政治運動, political agitations.
seiji (政事), *n.* political affairs.
seijin (成人), *n.* an adult; a grown-up person. ¶ 成人教育, adult education. ☞ *otona.*
seijin (聖人), *n.* a sage; a wise man; a saint.
seijitsu (誠實), *n.* sincerity; honesty; rectitude. —誠實な人, a man of sincerity. —誠實に, sincerely; faithfully; honestly.
seijō (正條), *n.* the definite articles; an express provision.
seijō (性情), *n.* ❶ (性質) nature; disposition (氣質). ❷ (心情) heart; feeling; sentiment.
seijō (清淨), *n.* purity; cleanliness (清潔). ☞ *shōjō.*
seijō (聖上), *n.* His Majesty (the Emperor).
seijōki (星條旗), *n.* the Stars and Stripes.
seiju (聖壽), *n.* the age of an Emperor. —聖壽萬萬歲, Long live the Emperor!
seijū (製絨), *n.* wool-weaving. ¶ 製絨所, a (woollen-)cloth factory [manufactory].
seijuku (成熟), *n.* ripeness; maturity; full growth. —成熟する, to ripen; mature. —成熟せる, ① ripe; mature; mellow. ② adult; mature; full-grown. ¶ 成熟期, the adult stage. (成熟期に達する, to reach maturity.)
seika (生家), *n.* one's parents' house; one's home.
seika (正貨), *n.* specie; coin; metallic currency. ¶ 正貨準備, specie [cash] reserve.
seika (正價), *n.* net price.
seika (成果), *n.* fruit; result.
seika (盛夏), *n.* midsummer; the height of summer.
seika (精華), *n.* essence; flower.
seika (製菓), *n.* confectionery.
seika (請暇), *n.* furlough; a leave of absence. —二週間の請暇を得て, on a fortnight's leave of absence [furlough].
seika (聲價), *n.* reputation; popularity; name; credit.
seikai (政界), *n.* political world [arena]; political circles. —政界を退く《に入る》, to quit 《enter》 the political world [arena].
seikai (盛會), *n.* a successful meeting.
seikaiken (制海權), *n.* command of the sea.
seikaku (正格な), *a.* regular; correct; right.
seikaku (正確·精確な), *a.* exact; accurate; correct. —正確な時計, a punctual watch. **—— -ni,** *ad.* exactly; correctly; accurately; punctually (時間の). —正確に言ふ, to speak by the card.
seikaku (性格), *n.* character; individuality (個性); personality (爲人). —性格の人, a man of character. ¶ 性格俳優, a character actor.
seikaku (政客), *n.* a politician.
seikaku (製革), *n.* tanning. ¶ 製革所, a tan-yard; a tannery.
seikan (生還), *n.* ❶ returning alive. ❷【野球】home in. —生還する, ① to return [come back] alive. ②【野球】to get home.
seikan (盛觀), *n.* pomp; magnificence; grandeur. —盛觀を呈する, to make a splendid [fine] sight.
seikan (精悍な), *a.* energetic; courageous.
seikan (製罐), *n.* tin-manufacturing.
seikan (製艦), *n.* naval construction.
seikatsu (生活), *n.* ❶ life; living. ❷ (生計) living; livelihood. —私《公》的生活, one's private 《public》 life. —生活の安定《標準; 態樣》, the security 《standard; mode》 of living. —生活する, to live; get one's living [livelihood]; support oneself. —生活を一新する, to give a new turn to one's life; put on the new man. —生活狀態を改善する, to improve the living conditions. ¶ 都市《田園》生活, city 《country》 life; urban 《rural》 life. —生活賃銀, living wage. —生活費, cost of living. —生活難, the difficulties of living; the high cost of living.
seikei (生計), *n.* livelihood; living; subsistence. —其日の生

計に追はれる, to live from hand to mouth. —生計を立てる, to get [earn] a livelihood; get one's living; support oneself.

seikei (世系), *n.* ❶ (世統) a family line; lineage. ❷ (系圖) a genealogical table; family tree.

seikei (西經), *n.* west longitude. —西經三十度, thirty degrees West longitude (30° W. Long.)

seikei (整形の), *a.* plastic. ¶ 整形藝術, the plastic [glyptic] art. —整形外科, plastic surgery.

seiken (政見), *n.* a political view. —政見を發表する, to declare one's political views.

seiken (政權), *n.* political power. —政權を離れる《てる》, to go 《be》 out of power. —政權を握る, to come into power; assume the reins of government.

seiken (聖賢), *n.* a sage; a man of wisdom.

seiketsu (清潔), *n.* cleanness; purity. —清潔な, clean; cleanly; pure. —清潔にする, to clean; cleanse; purge. ¶ 清潔屋, a W. C. cleaner; a night-man.

seiki (正規の), *a.* regular; legitimate. ¶ 正規軍, a regular army.

seiki (生氣), *n.* animation; life; vitality. ☞ ***kakki.***

seiki (世紀), *n.* a century.

seiki (成規の), *a.* regular; prescribed; legal. —成規の手續をする, to go through the regular procedure.

seiki (政機), *n.* the political situation (政局); the opportunity for political change (政變の機).

seiki (旌旗), *n.* a flag; a banner; the colours.

seiki (精氣), *n.* ether; spirit; essence.

seikin (生擒), *n.* =***ikedori.***

seikin (精勤), *n.* diligence; industry; regular attendance. —精勤する, to work diligently [hard; strenuously]; be diligent. ¶ 精勤者, a hard worker; one diligent in his duties; a person regular in attendance.

seikō (生硬な), *a.* immature; indigested; raw.

seikō (正鵠), *n.* the mark; the point. —正鵠を得る, to hit it [the mark]; hit the (right) nail (on the head). —正鵠を失する, to miss it [the mark].

seikō (成功), *n.* (a) success. —成功を祈る, to wish a person success. —成功する, to succeed *in*; be successful; win [attain] success; achieve; turn out well. —成功の見込がない, There is no prospect of success. ¶ 成功者, a successful man.

seikō (性行), *n.* character and conduct.

seikō (政綱), *n.* platform; political programme; policy.

seikō (精巧), *n.* excellent [perfect] skill; subtlety; ingenuity. —精巧な, delicate; ingenious; exquisite; elaborate (緻密な).

seikō (製鋼), *n.* steel manufacture. ¶ 製鋼所, the steel-works; the steel-mill.

seikōkai (聖公會), *n.* the Episcopal(-ian) [Holy Catholic] Church (米國派); the Church of England; the English Church; the Anglican Church.

seiku (成句), *n.* a phrase; an expression.

seikūken (制空權), *n.* command of the air.

seikun (請訓する), *vt.* to ask for instructions.

seikyo (逝去する), *vi.* to pass away; die.

seikyō (正敎), *n.* orthodoxy. ¶ 正敎會, the Orthodox [Greek] Church; the Russian church.

seikyō (政況), *n.* the political outlook [aspect]; the political situation [condition].

seikyō (政敎), *n.* the church and state; the government and religion. ¶ 政敎分離《一致》, the separation 《union》 of church and state.

seikyō (盛況), *n.* a brilliant [splendid] condition; great prosperity.

seikyōin (正敎員), *n.* a regular teacher.

seikyoku (政局), *n.* the political situation.

seikyōto (清敎徒), *n.* 【宗·史】 a puritan.

seikyū (性急な), *a.* quick-tempered. ☞ ***kimijika.***

seikyū (請求), *n.* claim; demand; call (拂込の); application (免狀·見本などの). —請求次第, at call; on demand; on application (申込次第). —請求に應ずる, to meet another's demand. —支拂を請求する, to claim [demand] payment of a person; call upon a person to pay his debt; ask for payment. ¶ 請求權, (right of) claim. —請求者, a claimant; a demandant; an applicant (申請人, 申込人). —請求書, a bill; a written demand; an application.

seima (製麻), *n.* dressing of hemp (行爲); dressed hemp.

seimai (精米), *n.* cleaned rice. ¶ 精米所《機械》, a rice-cleaning mill 《machine》.

seimei (生命), *n.* ❶ (いのち) life. ❷ (たましひ) the life; the soul. —貞操は女の生命である, Chastity is the life and soul of women. ¶ 生命保險, life insurance [assurance]. (簡易生命保險, industrial life insurance (勞働

者の); post-office life insurance (郵便局取扱の). —生命保險會社, a life insurance [assurance] company; a life office.)

seimei (姓名), *n.* a full name; a name. ¶ 姓名判斷, onomancy.

seimei (聲明), *n.* declaration; announcement; proclamation. —聲明する, to declare; announce; proclaim. —反對(の旨)を聲明する, to declare oneself against it. —聲明書を發する, to issue a (written) statement.

seimen (正面), *n.* the front; the face.

seimen (生面), *n.* a new phase; a new departure.

seimitsu (精密な), *a.* accurate (精確); detailed (詳細); minute (細密). —精密に, minutely; precisely; accurately.

seimon (正門), *n.* the main [front] gate.

seimon (聲門), *n.* 【解】glottis.

seimu (政務), *n.* government affairs [business]; political affairs. ¶ 政務委員, a political committee. —政務官, an executive [a political] officer. (政務次官, a parliamentary undersecretary.)

seinan (西南), *n.* the southwest.

seinen (生年), *n.* the year of birth.

seinen (成年), *n.* majority; full age; lawful age. —成年に達する, to come of age; attain one's majority. ¶ 成年者, an adult; a full-grown person.

seinen (青年), *n.* a young man; a youth; the rising [younger] generation (總稱). ¶ 青年男女, the youth; young men and women. —青年時代[期], adolescence; youth. —地方《中央》青年團, a local《the central》Young Men's Association.

seinen (盛年), *n.* the prime of manhood.

seinobi (脊伸する), *vi.* to stretch oneself.

seion (清音), *n.* 【聲音】a surd; a non-vocal (s, p, f, t, k, の如き).

seion (聖恩), *n.* Imperial favours. —聖恩の厚きに感泣する, to weep with gratitude at the greatness of Imperial favours.

seion (靜穩な), *a.* calm; quiet; tranquil.

seion (聲音), *n.* a sound; a vocal sound. ¶ 聲音學, phonetics.

seirai (生來), *ad.* naturally; by nature [birth]. —生來の, natural; inborn; born; congenital.

seirei (生靈), *n.* ❶ (人民) the people. ❷ (魂,人命) soul. —三百の生靈を犧牲にして, at the sacrifice of 300 souls.

seirei (聖靈), *n.* the (Holy) Ghost [Spirit].

seirei (精靈), *n.* the soul; the spirit.

seireki (西暦), *n.* the Christian Era. —西暦千年, the 1000th year of the Christian Era [of grace; of our Lord]; 1000 A. D.

seiren (清廉の), *a.* pure; honest; white-handed; incorruptible. —清廉の士, a man of integrity.

seiren (精錬), *n.* refinement; tempering. —精錬する, to refine; temper. ¶ 精錬所, a refinery.

seiren (精練), *n.* full training.

seiretsu (整列), *n.* parade; alignment. —整列する《さす》, to line up; draw up; form in line; fall in [*vi.*]. —途の兩側に整列する, to line both sides of the road.

seiri (正理), *n.* reason; truth.

seiri (生理-學), *n.* physiology. —生理的, physiological. ¶ 生理學者, a physiologist.

seiri (整理), *n.* arrangement; readjustment; consolidation. —— **suru**, *vt.* to (re-)adjust; put [set] in order; consolidate (公債を). —財政を整理する, to adjust [readjust] finance. ¶ 整理委員, an adjustment committee. —整理公債, a consolidated public loan; consols【英】.

seiritsu (成立), *n.* existence; formation; establishment. —成立さす, to bring [call] into existence [being]. —成立する, to come into being [existence]; be established (設立); consist [composed; be made] *of* (より成る).

seiro (正路), *n.* the right road [path; way].

seirō (晴朗な), *a.* fine; unclouded; clear.

seirō (蒸籠), *n.* a steamer; a steaming basket.

seiron (正論), *n.* sound argument.

seiron (政論), *n.* political arguments; politics; publicism.

seiryaku (政略), *n.* policy; statecraft.

seiryaku (征略する), *vt.* to conquer; capture (略取).

seiryo (聖慮), *n.* Imperial thought; the Emperor's mind.

seiryō (正量), *n.* positive quantity.

seiryō (清涼な), *a.* cool; refreshing. ¶ 清涼飲料水, a (refreshing) beverage; a cooling-drink.

seiryoku (勢力), *n.* ❶ influence; power; authority. ❷【理】energy. —勢力ある, influential; powerful; authoritative. —勢力を揮ふ, to exercise influence [authority] over. ¶ 勢力範圍, the sphere of influence. —勢力家, a man of influence.

seiryoku (精力), *n.* energy; strength; vigour. —彼は精力絶倫である, He has unparalleled energy. ¶ 精力家, a man of energy [pith]; a strenuous person; a hard-working man (努力家).

seisai (制裁), *n.* penalty; sanction; restraint (抑制). —社會の制裁, social restraint. —制裁を加へる, to bring [place] under restraint; punish.

seisaku (政策), *n.* a policy. ¶ 商業《工業》政策, commercial 《industrial》 policy.

seisaku (製作), *n.* manufacture; fabrication; production. —製作する, to manufacture; make; produce. ¶ 製作品, a product; a manufactured article; a work. —製作所, a workshop; a manufactory; a works.

seisan (正餐), *n.* dinner.

seisan (生產), *n.* production. —生產する, to produce. ¶ 生產地, the land of origin (原產地); the place of production. —生產高, an output; an outturn; a turnout. —生產費, cost of production. —生產過剩, overproduction. —生產力, productive power; producing capacity (生產能力). —生產者, a producer.

seisan (成算), *n.* a plan sure of success; a promising plan. —僕にはちゃんと成算がある, I have already a plan up my sleeve.

seisan (清算), *n.* 【法】liquidation. ¶ 清算人, a liquidator.

seisan (精算), *n.* ❶ exact calculation. ❷ settlement of accounts. —精算する, to settle [square] accounts.

seisan (聖餐), *n.* 【宗】Holy Communion; the Lord's Supper.

seisan (製產), *n.* manufacture; production. ¶ 製產物, manufactured goods; manufactures.

seisatsu (生殺與奪の權), *n.* the power of life and death.

seisatsu (制札), *n.* a notice-board; an edict-board.

seisei (正正の), *a.* fair; just. —正々堂々たる, fair and honourable; fair and square; stand-up (戰). (正々堂々たる勝負, a fair fight [match]. —正々堂々と戰ふ, to fight 《play》 fair).

seisei (淸淸する), *a.* refreshing. ——, *vi.* to feel refreshed. —ああこれで淸々した, Well, I feel refreshed now.

seisei (精製), *n.* refinement; purification. —精製する, to refine; purify; work (raw materials). —精製せる, refined; purified. ¶ 精製品, a refined article; a finished article (加製品).

seiseki (成績), *n.* result; achievement. —成績順に, in the order of merit. —成績が惡い, to be poor in result. ¶ 成績表, a merit-roll.

seisekkai (生石灰), *n.* quicklime.

seisen (政戰), *n.* a political campaign.

seisen (精選する), *vt.* to choose [select] with care; pick out carefully.

seisha (政社), *n.* a political association [society].

seisha (聖者), *n.* a saint.

seishi (生死), *n.* life and death. —生死不明である, to be missing. —生死の巷に出入する, to enter the jaws of death.

seishi (世子, 世嗣), *n.* the heir apparent.

seishi (正使), *n.* the senior envoy.

seishi (正視), *n.* ❶ (視力の完全なこと) normal vision. ❷ (對視) a direct [straight] view. —正視する, to look straight; look in the face. ¶ 正視眼, 【醫】 emmetropia.

seishi (制止), *n.* restraint; check; repression. —制止する, to restrain; check; repress.

seishi (製紙), *n.* paper manufacture; paper-making. ¶ 製紙原料, pulp; paper stock (襤褸等の) —製紙會社, a paper-mill company. —製紙場, a paper-mill [-manufactory].

seishi (製絲), *n.* reeling; filature. ¶ 製絲場, a filature(-mill). —製絲器械, a filatory; a reeling machine.

seishi (聖旨), *n.* Imperial command [will]. —聖旨を奉じて, in obedience to His Majesty's command.

seishi (誓紙), *n.* a written oath [pledge].

seishi (靜思する), *v.* to meditate.

seishiki (正式), *n.* formality. **—— - ni**, *ad.* formally; in due form. —正式に申込む, to make a formal application. ¶ 正式裁判, a formal trial.

seishiki (整式), *n.* an integral expression.

seishin (星辰), *n.* a star.

seishin (淸新の), *a.* fresh; new.

seishin (精神), *n.* soul; spirit; mind. ☞ ***kokoro*** (心). —犧牲的精神, the spirit of self-sacrifice. —精神的勝利, moral victory. —精神に異狀がある, to be mentally deranged. —精神に異狀無し, to be in (full) possession of one's faculties. ¶ 精神病, mental disorder [trouble]; a mental disease. (精神病醫, an alienist. —精神病院, an insane asylum.) —精神狀態, state of mind. —精神檢查[考查], mental test. —精神療法, psychotherapy; mind-cure. —精神錯亂, delirium; lunacy;

insanity. —精神生活, ① (精神的生活) inner [spiritual] life. ② (精神の活動) mental life [activity]. —精神修養 mental training [culture].

seishin-seii (誠心誠意), *n.* sincerity; whole [single]-heartedness. —, *ad.* sincerely; from the bottom of one's heart; with all one's heart.

seishitsu (性質), *n.* ❶ (性向) disposition; turn. ❷ (氣質) temper; temperament. ❸ (性格) character. ❹ (本質) nature. ❺ (品質) quality. ❻ (種類) kind; sort; stamp. —の性質上, in [by; from] the nature *of*. —性質のよい《惡い》人, a man of good 《evil》 disposition; a well 《ill》-disposed person. —の性質を帶びる, to partake of the nature *of*.

seisho (清書), *n.* a fair [clean] copy. —清書する, to write out fair; make a fair copy *of*.

seisho (聖書), *n.* the (Holy) Bible; the Scripture.

seisho (誓書), *n.* an affidavit; a written oath.

seishoku (生色), *n.* vivid appearance; animation. —生色なき, unearthly pale; livid.

seishoku (生食), *n.* predacity. ¶ 生食動物, a predacious animal.

seishoku (生殖-作用), *n.* generation; reproduction. —生殖する, to reproduce. ¶ 生殖器, reproductive [generative] organs. —生殖機能, reproductive [generative] function.

seishu (清酒), *n.* refined *sake*.

seishuku (星宿), *n.* a constellation.

seishuku (靜肅), *n.* quiet; stillness; silence. —靜肅な, quiet; still; calm. —靜肅に!, Be quiet!; Keep quiet!

seishun (靑春), *n.* ❶ (春季) spring; springtime; spring-tide. ❷ (若い時代) youth; adolescence. —靑春の男女, young men and women.

seishutsu (製出), *n.* manufacture; production. ☞ *seisaku*.

seiso (淸楚な), *a.* neat; tidy.

seiso (精粗), *n.* fineness (and coarseness).

seisō (正裝), *n.* full dress; full uniform (軍人など). —正裝する, to be in full dress 《uniform》.

seisō (政爭), *n.* political contest; party strife. —政爭の具に供する, to make it a matter for political contest.

seisō (星霜), *n.* years; time.

seisō (盛裝), *n.* full dress. —盛裝する, to be in full dress; dress fully; dress in one's best. —盛裝を凝らして, dressed in one's best.

seisōgaku (性相學), *n.* physiognomy.

seisoku (正則), *n.* normalness; regularity. —正則の, regular; normal. —正則の敎育, public education.

seisoku (棲息する), *v.* to live; inhabit.

seison (生存), *n.* existence; life; survival (生殘). —生存する, to live; exist; survive. ¶ 生存權, the right to live. —生存競爭, struggle for existence. (生存競爭場裏, the arena of life.) —生存者, a survivor; a survival.

seisū (正數), *n.* 【數】 a positive number.

seisū (整數), *n.* 【數】 an integer; an integral number.

seisui (淸水), *n.* clean [pure] water.

seisui (精粹), *n.* essence; quintessence; marrow. ☞ *sui* (粹).

seisui (盛衰), *n.* prosperity and adversity; rise and fall; vicissitudes. —盛衰する, to wax and wane; rise and fall.

sei-suru (制する), *vt.* ❶ (制御する) to control; master; govern; dominate. ❷ (制止する) to check; restrain; repress; rein. ❸ (節制する) to moderate. —制し難き, uncontrollable; unrestrainable. —情慾を制する, to keep one's passions under control.

sei-suru (製する), *vt.* to make; manufacture (製造する); prepare (調製する). —…から何を製する, to make a thing *of*; make a thing *from* (特に物質の變る場合).

seitai (政體), *n.* the form [system] of government.

seitai (聲帶), *n.* 【解】 the vocal cord.

seitai (臍帶), *n.* 【解】 the umbilical cord; the navel-string.

seitaku (請託), *n.* petition; entreaty. —請託を容れる, to grant [comply with] his request.

seitei (制定), *n.* enactment; establishment; institution. —制定する, 【法】 to enact; establish. ¶ 制定法, artificial law.

seitei (製釘), *n.* nail-manufacture; nail-making. ¶ 製釘所, a nailery.

seiteki (政敵), *n.* a political opponent [enemy; adversary].

seiteki (性的), *a.* sexual.

seiteki (靜的), *a.* static.

seiten (靑天), *n.* a blue sky; a cloudless sky. —靑天の霹靂, a bolt from the blue. —靑天白日の身となる, to have one's innocence clearly proved.

seiten (晴天), *n.* fine weather; a cloudless sky. —晴天ならば, weather permitting.

seitetsu (西哲), *n.* a Western philosopher [man of learning].
seitetsu (製鐵), *n.* iron manufacture. ¶ 製鐵所, an ironworks.
seito (生徒), *n.* a student (高等學校程度の); a pupil (中學程度の); a school-boy (-girl) (同上); a school-child (小學校の); a scholar (一般の).
seito (征途に上る), *vi.* go to the front; go on an expedition.
seito (聖徒), *n.* a saint.
seitō (正當な), *a.* legal; lawful; right; rightful. —正當な手段を以て, by fair means. ¶ 正當防衞, self-defence; legal defence.
seitō (正統の), *a.* legitimate; lineal; orthodox (宗教信仰の).
seitō (征討), *n.* punitive expedition. ☞ *seibatsu.*
seitō (政黨), *n.* a political party. ¶ 政黨員, a member of a political party; a party man. —政黨政治, party government.
seitō (青踏), *n.* a blue-stocking.
seitō (製陶), *n.* pottery-manufacture. ¶ 製陶家, a pottery-manufacturer; a potter.
seitō (製糖), *n.* sugar manufacture. ¶ 精(粗)製糖, refined (coarse) sugar. —製糖會社, a sugar-refining company. —製糖所, a sugar-refinery.
seiton (整頓), *n.* arrangement; orderliness; adjustment. —**-suru**, *vt.* to arrange; adjust; put [set] in order [to rights]. —整頓した, orderly; tidy (室など). —よく整頓してゐる, to be in good order.
seitsū (精通), *n.* complete knowledge; mastery; conversance. —**-suru**, *v.* to master; be well-versed [at home] *in*; be conversant *with.* —事情に精通してゐる, to be well acquainted with the affairs.
seiu (晴雨), *n.* fair or rainy [foul] weather; (the condition of the) weather. —晴雨に拘らず, rain or shine; wet or fine. ¶ 晴雨計, a barometer.
seiuchi (海象), *n.* 【哺乳】 the walrus.
seiun (青雲), *n.* a blue cloud; high rank [office] (高位). —青雲の志を抱く, to harbour high ambition.
seiun (星雲), *n.* 【天】 a nebula.
seiun (盛運), *n.* prosperity; good fortune.
seiyaku (制約), *n.* condition.
seiyaku (製藥), *n.* pharmacy; medicine manufacture. ¶ 製藥業(所), (a) pharmacy.
seiyaku (誓約), *n.* an oath; a vow; a pledge. ☞ *chikai.*

seiyō (西洋), *n.* the West; Western countries; the Occident. ☞ *Ōshū.* —西洋かぶれする, to occidentalize; Europeanize. ¶ 西洋人, a westerner; a European; a foreigner. —西洋家具, foreign household goods. —西洋料理, foreign food [dishes]; European cookery (法); a foreign restaurant (店). —西洋紙, foreign paper.
seiyō (靜養する), *vi.* to take a rest; recruit oneself; recuperate oneself.
seiyoku (性慾), *n.* sexual desire [appetite].
seiyoku (制慾), *n.* self-control; self-denial; control of passion.
seiyu (製油), *n.* oil-manufacture.
seiyū (政友), *n.* a political friend.
seiyū (淸遊を試みる), to make an excursion *to.*
seiza (正坐する), *vi.* to sit straight.
seiza (星座), *n.* 【天】 a constellation.
seiza (靜坐する), *vi.* to sit still [quietly].
seizai (製材), *n.* sawing. ¶ 製材所, a lumber-mill; a sawing-mill.
seizei (精精), *ad.* to the utmost; at the most (多くとも); at best (よくとも); at the highest (高くとも). —精々速く, as fast [quickly] as one can. —精々勉强する, ① to study with all one's might. ② (最大減價) to make the largest possible reduction.
seizen (生前), *n.* lifetime. —生前に, during one's life; while living; before one's death.
seizen (整然, 井然), *ad.* in good [fine] order; in are gular manner; systematically. —整然として一絲亂れぬ, to be in perfect order. —秩序整然たり, Strict order is maintained.
seizō (製造), *n.* manufacture; fabrication; making. ¶ 製造品, manufactures; products; manufactured goods. —製造者, a manufacturer; a maker; a producer. —製造所, a manufactory; a factory; a works; a mill.
seizoroi (勢揃する), *v.* to appear in full force; assemble together; line up (蹴球戯等の).
seizu (製圖), *n.* drawing; map-drawing (地圖). —製圖する, to draw (a map); chart. ¶ 製圖器械, a drawing instrument. —製圖者, a drawer; a delineator; a draughtsman. —製圖室, a drawing-room.
seizui (精髓), *n.* essence; pith and marrow; the pick.
seji (世事), *n.* worldly affairs; the world; common business. —世事に長けた人, a man of the

world ; a worldly-wise person.

seji (世辭), *n.* a compliment ; a complimentary speech ; fair words ; delicate flattery. —お世辭に, in compliment ; out of courtesy [politeness] (善い意味で). —そらぞらしいお世辭, empty compliments. —お世辭を云ふ, to pay compliments ; flatter. —お世辭を使ふ, to flatter ; carry favour *with.*

sejin (世人), *n.* people ; the world ; the public.

sejō (世上), *n.* the world. —世上の物議を醸す, to give birth to public controversy.

sejō (世情), *n.* worldly [social] life ; the world. —世情に明るい (疎い), to be versed in (ignorant of) worldly affairs.

sekai (世界), *n.* the world ; the earth (地球) ; the globe (同上). —世界中, (all) the world over ; throughout the world. —世界的人物, a world figure. —世界的名聲, a world-wide fame. —世界の果まで, to the uttermost ends of the world ; through all the world ; to the world's end. —世界廣しと雖も, wide as the world is. —世界を一週する, to go round the world ; circumnavigate. —今日は電氣の世界だ, Now is the age of electricity. ¶ 世界漫遊, globe-trotting ; a trip round the world. (世界漫遊者, a globe-trotter.) —世界主義, cosmopolitanism ; internationalism. —世界大戰, the Great [World] War.

sekaseka (せかせかする), *vi.* to fidget ; have the fidgets ; bustle. —彼はいつもせかせかしてゐる, He is always in a fidget.

sekasu (急かす), *vt.* to hurry. ☞ *isogasu.*

seken (世間), *n.* the world ; the public ; people (人々). —世間並の, common ; average ; ordinary. —世間に出る, to begin the world ; go out. —世間を見る, to see [know] the world ; see life [the ways of the world]. —彼は世間が狹い, His experience of the world is narrow. ¶ 世間話, gossip ; small talk ; society conversation.

seki (咳), *n.* a cough. —咳する, to cough.

seki (席), *n.* ❶ (座所) a seat ; one's place ; room (場所). ❷＝*sekitei* (席亭). —席に著く (復る), to take (resume) one's seat. —席を起つ, to leave [quit] one's seat [place]. —席を讓る, to make room *for* ; give place [one's seat] *to.* —席を蹴って去る, to fling out of the room.

seki (堰), *n.* a dam ; a weir.

seki (積), *n.* ❶【數】(相乘) a product. ❷ (地面の坪數) area.

seki (關), *n.* a barrier.

seki (籍), *n.* a census register ; a domicile. —籍を移す, to transfer a name *from.*

sekiageru (迫上げる), *vi.* to sob ; be choked.

sekiageru (咳上げる), *vi.* to have severe fits of cough.

sekiaku (積惡), *n.* accumulation of wickedness.

sekibaku (寂寞), *n.* loneliness ; desolateness ; solitariness. —寂寞たる, lonesome ; desolate ; solitary.

sekiban (石版), *n.* a lithograph ; lithography (術).

sekiban (石盤, 石板), *n.* a slate. —石盤拭, a slate-wiper. —石板屋根, a slated roof.

sekibarai (咳拂), *n.* hem ; clearing the throat. —咳拂ひする, to hem ; haw ; clear one's throat.

sekiboku (石墨), *n.* 【鑛】graphite ; plumbago ; black-lead.

sekibokushitsu (赤木質), *n.* heart-wood.

sekibun (積分-學), *n.* 【數】the integral calculus.

sekichi (瘠地), *n.* barren [unfertile ; unproductive] land [soil].

sekichiku (石竹), *n.* 【植】the Chinese [Indian] pink.

sekichū (脊柱), *n.* 【解】the spine ; the spinal [vertebral] column.

sekidō (赤道), *n.* the equator. —赤道直下の, equatorial ; on the (equatorial) line. —赤道を橫切る, 【航】to cross [pass] the line.

sekidōkō (赤銅鑛), *n.* 【鑛】cuprite ; the red copper ore.

sekidoku (尺牘), *n.* an epistle ; a letter. ☞ *shokan.*

sekidome (咳止), *n.* a cough medicine. ¶ 咳止ボンボン, a cough bonbon ; a cough-drop [-lozenge].

sekiei (石英), *n.* 【鑛】quartz(-ite).

sekiei (隻影), *n.* a single shadow.

sekifu (石斧), *n.* 【考古】a stone-axe.

sekifu (責付), *n.* bail.

sekiga (席畫), *n.* a picture dashed off on the spot ; a lightning [an off-hand ; impromptu] picture. —席畫を描く, to dash off a picture on the spot.

sekigaku (碩學), *n.* a profound [great] scholar ; a man of erudition [great learning].

sekigun (赤軍), *n.* Ⓢ 赤衞軍. the Red Army [Guard] (the White Army [Guard], 白軍の對).

sekihan (赤飯), *n.* steamed rice mixed with red beans.

sekihei (積弊), *n.* a deep-rooted evil.

sekihi (石碑), *n.* a tombstone ; a gravestone ; a tomb. —石碑を

建てる, to raise a tombstone (*for*).
sekihin (赤貧), *n.* extreme [abject] poverty; utter destitution; beggary; penury.
sekihitsu (石筆), *n.* a slate-pencil.
sekiji (席次), *n.* the order of seat. ¶ 宮中席次, precedence at court.
sekijitsu (積日の), *a.* long-standing; many days'. —積日の雨, many days' rain.
sekijō (席上), *ad.* at the meeting [assembly]; in company; extempore (其場で). ¶ 席上演說, an extempore [impromptu] speech.
sekijūji (赤十字), *n.* the Red Cross. ¶ 赤十字病院, the Red Cross Hospital. —赤十字社, the Red Cross Society.
sekijun (石筍), *n.* 【地質】 stalagmite.
sekijun (席順), *n.* the order of seat.
sekika (赤化), *n.* Bolshevization. —赤化する, to Bolshevize.
sekikō (石工), *n.* a stone-cutter; a (stone-)mason.
sekikomu (急込む), *vi.* to be excited; be [get] flurried. —急込んで, impatiently; in excitement.
sekikotsu (脊骨), *n.* =***sebone***.
sekimatsu (席末), *n.* the last [back] seat. =***basseki***.
sekimen (石綿), *n.* 【鑛】 asbestos.
sekimen (赤面する), *vi.* to blush; flush [be red] with shame; turn red. —赤面さす, to put a person to the blush.
sekimon (石門), *n.* a stone-gate.
sekimu (責務), *n.* duty; obligation; responsibility.
sekinen (積年の), *a.* long-standing; many years'; inveterate.
sekinin (責任), *n.* ❶ (負ふべき) responsibility; liability. ❷ (爲すべき) duty; obligation. —責任の(ある)地位, a responsible post; a position of trust. —に對し責任がある, to be liable [responsible] *for*. —責任を果す, to discharge [fulfil] one's duty. —責任を問ふ, to call a man to account. —責任を重んずる, to have a deep sense of responsibility; attach importance to responsibility. —責任を回避する, to shirk [evade] one's responsibility. —責任を雙肩に擔ふ, to bear responsibility on one's shoulders; shoulder the responsibility. —特定額に對し責任を負ふ, to make oneself responsible for a specified sum. ¶ 無限《有限》責任, unlimited 《limited》 liability. —責任保險, liability insurance. —責任準備金, legal reserve. —責任內閣, a responsible cabinet. —責任者, a responsible person.
sekirara (赤裸裸の), *a.* ❶ (すッぱだかの) stark-naked. ❷ (*a*) (有の儘の) naked; bare: (*b*) (率直な) outspoken; plain-spoken; frank. —赤裸々に云ふ, to tell the naked facts.
sekirei (鶺鴒), *n.* 【鳥】 the wag-tail.
sekiri (赤痢), *n.* 【醫】 dysentery.
sekirin (赤燐), *n.* red [amorphous] phosphorus.
sekiro (赤露), *n.* Red Russia.
sekiryō (脊梁), *n.* 【解】 the vertebral [spinal] column.
sekiryō (席料), *n.* the charge for [hire of] a room.
sekiryō (積量), *n.* carrying [loading] capacity.
sekisai (積載), *n.* lading; carrying. —積載する, to load; carry. ¶ 積載噸數, freight [capacity] tonnage (船); loading capacity of a car in tons (貨車).
sekisei (赤誠), *n.* sincerity; singleness of heart. —赤誠を盡す, to labour with singleness of heart.
sekisetsu (積雪), *n.* deep snow. —積雪五寸に及んだ, The snow accumulated five inches deep.
sekishin (赤心), *n.* the single [true] mind.
sekisho (關所), *n.* a barrier.
sekishō (石菖蒲), *n.* 【植】 the grass-leaved sweet-flag.
sekishoku (赤色), *n.* red; red colour. —赤色の, red; ruddy.
sekishu (赤手), *n.* an empty hand.
sekishu (隻手), *n.* one [a single] hand.
sekitan (石炭), *n.* coal. —石炭積込の爲め寄港する, to enter the port to coal. ¶ 石炭瓦斯, coal-gas. —石炭庫, a coal-cellar (窖); a coal-hole (小窖); a coal-bunker (船の). —石炭坑, a coal-mine; a coal-pit; a colliery. —石炭船, a collier; a coal-ship. —石炭車, a coal-truck; a coal-waggon (貨車). —石炭商, a coal-merchant; a coaler.
sekitansan (石炭酸), *n.* 【化】 carbonic acid; phenol. ¶ 石炭酸水, carbonic acid solution; liquefied phenol.
sekitateru (急立てる), *vt.* to hurry; urge; press.
sekitei (席亭), *n.* a story-tellers' hall; a variety-hall.
sekitekkō (赤鐵鑛), *n.* (red) hæmatite, hematite; red oxide of iron.
sekiten (釋奠), *n.* a festival in honour of Confucius.
sekitō (石塔), *n.* ❶ (石造りの五輪塔) a stone pagoda of five stories. ❷ (墓碑) a gravestone.
sekitomeru (堰止める), *vt.* to

dam (up); stem; block up.

sekitori (關取), *n.* a wrestler of the first grade; a wrestler (力士).

sekitsui (脊椎), *n.* 【動】a vertebra [*pl.* -ræ]; a backbone. ¶ 脊椎動物, Vertebrata (學名); the vertebrates. (無脊椎動物, Invertebrata; the invertebrates.)

sekiutsu (積鬱), *n.* melancholy.

sekiwaki (關脇), *n.* the second head-wrestler.

sekiyō (夕陽), *n.* the setting [sinking; declining] sun.

sekiyu (石油) *n.* petroleum; rock-oil. ¶ 石油發動機, an oil-engine; a petroleum motor [engine]. —石油槽, an oil-tank. —石油運搬車 (運送船), a tank-car (-vessel).

sekizai (石材), *n.* stone; building-stone.

sekizen (積善), *n.* accumulated virtuous deeds.

sekizō (石造の), *a.* stone; built of stone. ¶ 石造建築, a stone building; a stone(-built) house.

sekizō (石像), *n.* a stone image [statue].

sekizui (脊髓), *n.* 【解】the spinal cord; the pith. ¶ 脊髓神經, a spinal nerve.

sekkachi (性急の), *a.* hasty; impetuous; impatient. —性急な男, a hasty-tempered person; an impetuous man.

sekkai (石灰), *n.* lime. ¶ 石灰石, 【地質】limestone.

sekkai (切開), *n.* 【醫】incision; dissection; operation. —切開する, to incise; operate *upon*; open.

sekkaku (折角), *ad.* ❶ (苦勞して) with great pains; with much trouble. ❷ especially (特に); earnestly (切に); pressingly (達って). —折角の, earnest (切なる); pressing (達っての). —折角ですが, though you kindly say so. —折角だから, since you are so pressing. —折角お大事になさいまし, Take great care of yourself.

sekkaku (刺客), *n.* an assassin.

sekkaku (接角), *n.* 【數】an adjacent [contiguous] angle.

sekkan (切諫する), *vt.* to remonstrate *with*; expostulate *with*.

sekkan (折檻), *n.* chastisement; castigation. —折檻する, to chastise; castigate; chasten; reprove.

sekkei (設計), *n.* a plan; a design. —設計する, to plan; draw a plan (*for*); scheme. ¶ 設計者, a planner; a designer. —設計圖, a plan.

sekkekkyū (赤血球), *n.* red blood-corpuscles.

sekken (石鹼), *n.* soap.

sekken (接見), *n.* a reception; an audience (特に高貴の). —接見する, to receive; receive in audience. ¶ 接見日, a reception day; an at-home day.

sekken (節儉), *n.* frugality; thrift (勤儉). ☞ *kenyaku*. —節儉する, to practise economy [thrift]; economize. ¶ 節儉家, an economist; a frugal [thrifty] person.

sekki (赤旗), *n.* a red flag.

sekki (石器), *n.* a stone implement; stoneware. ¶ 石器時代, the stone age.

sekki (節季), *n.* the end of the year.

sekkin (接近), *n.* contiguity; proximity; approach. —接近する, to approach; draw near. —接近してゐる, to stand close *to*; be adjacent [contiguous] *to*. —兩國間の接近を圖る, to bring about rapprochement between the two countries. —彼は接近し難い, He is difficult of approach [access].

sekkō (石膏), *n.* 【鑛】gypsum; plaster. ¶ 石膏像, a plaster figure (bust).

sekkō (斥候), *n.* 【軍】a patrol; a scout. ¶ 斥候隊, a patrol party.

sekkotsu (接骨), *n.* bone-setting. ¶ 接骨醫, a bone-setter.

sekku (節句), *n.* one of the five annual feasts. -雛の節句, The Feast of Dolls; the Dolls' Festival.

sekkyaku (隻脚), *n.* one [a single] leg.

sekkyō (說敎), *n.* ❶ (說話) a sermon. ❷ (お叱) a sermon; a lecture. —說敎する, to preach *to*; preach a sermon. —お說敎を聞かせる, to read (one) a lecture; give a sermon *to*. ¶ 說敎師, a preacher.

sekkyoku (積極), *n.* ❶ the positive pole. ❷ positiveness. —積極的政策, a positive policy. ¶ 積極主義, positivism.

seko (世故), *n.* worldly affairs. —世故に長けた, worldly-wise.

seko (勢子), *n.* a beater.

sekondo (セコンド), *n.* ❶ (秒) a second. ❷ (秒針) a second hand. ❸【野球】the second (base).

seku (咳く), *vi.* to cough.

seku (急く), *vt.* (促す) to hurry; urge; press. ——, *vi.* to hurry (急ぐ); be impatient (待遠しい). —氣がせく, to feel impatient. —せいては事を仕損じる, "Haste makes waste."

seku (堰く), *vt.* to dam (up); (防遏) check; keep in check.

semai (施米), *n.* a dole of rice.

semai (狹い), *a.* narrow; close; limited. —狹苦しい部屋, a narrow room.

semaru (迫る), *vi.* to be on the brink [verge] *of* (瀕する); draw near [close] (近づく); be near at hand (同上); become close [narrow] (つまる); press (切迫する, 肉薄する). ——, *vt.* to press; urge; compel [force] (强制する). —時日が迫る, Time presses. —呼吸が迫る, to become hard of breathing. —饑餓に迫る, to be on the verge of starvation; be driven [pressed] by hunger. —敵城に薄る, to press on the enemy's castle. —返事を迫る, to press a man for an answer.

seme (責), *n.* ❶ (責任) liability; responsibility; blame (罪). ❷ (責苦) torture. —責を負ふ, to answer *for*; bear the responsibility *for*; hold oneself responsible *for*.

semedōgu (責道具), *n.* ❶ the instruments of torture. ❷ (攻具) the weapons of attack.

semegu (鬩ぐ), *vi.* to quarrel; wrangle; dispute. —今は兄弟牆に鬩ぐの時に非ず, This is no time for quarrelling among ourselves.

semeiri (攻入), *n.* an invasion; an inroad. —攻め入る, to invade; make an inroad *upon*; make a raid *on*.

semeku (責苦), *n.* torture. —責苦に逢うて白狀する, to be tortured into confession.

semento (洋灰), *n.* cement.

semeotosu (攻落す), *vt.* to take; carry; reduce; take [carry] by assault [storm].

semeru (攻める), *vt.* to attack; assault; assail. —攻め合ふ, to attack each other. —攻め圍む, to besiege; lay siege *to*. ☞ *kōi*. —攻め寄せる, to advance *upon*; march *on*; press *on*.

semeru (責める), *vt.* ❶ (非難) to blame; censure; bring [take] to task. ❷ (呵責) to torture. —責めさいなむ, to ill-treat; treat with cruelty. —責め立てる, to urge [press] hard. —人の不信を責める, to take a person to task for his disloyalty.

semete (攻手), *n.* an assailant; an attacking party ⟪force⟫.

semete (切て), *ad.* at least; even if (たとへ).

semi (蟬), *n.* 【昆】 the cicada. —蟬の脫殼, casting of a cicada.

semi (滑車), *n.* a pulley; a block.

semikujira (脊美鯨), *n.* 【哺乳】 the right whale.

semotsu (施物), *n.* an alms; a charity; a dole.

semushi (傴僂), *n.* a humpback, hunchback.

sen (千), *n.* a thousand.

sen (先), *a.* former (以前の); previous (先だっての); late (故); first (最初の). —先主君, one's former lord. —先に, formerly. —先を越す, to get the start *of*; steal a march *on*; forestall.

sen (栓), *n.* a spigot (小さき); a cork (コルク栓); a plug (流出を止める栓); a bung (樽の); a stopper (德利の). —栓を拔く, to uncork; unstop. —栓をする, to cork; bung; put a stopper *on*.

sen (腺), *n.* 【生】 a gland.

sen (線), *n.* a line; a wire (針金). —線を引く, to draw a line. ¶ 中央線, the Central Line.

sen (選, 撰), *n.* ❶ selection; choice. ❷ (選集) compilation. —選に入る, to be selected. ☞ *nyūsen*. —選を異にする, to be (entirely) different *from*; not to be compared [classed] *with*.

senaka (背中), *n.* the back. ☞ *se*. —背中合せに寢る, to sleep back to back.

senbai (專賣), *n.* monopoly. ☞ *tokkyo* —專賣する, to monopolize; make a monopoly *of*. ¶ 專賣局, the Monopoly Bureau. —專賣特許, patent (專賣特許品, a patented article.)

senbaiken (先買權), *n.* preemption.

senban (千萬), *ad.* extremely; very much; most.

senban (旋盤), *n.* a lathe. ¶ 旋盤工, a turner. —旋盤工場, a turnery.

senbatsu (選拔), *n.* selection; picking out. —選拔する, to select; single out; choose. ¶ 選拔試驗, a selective examination.

senbei (煎餅), *n.* cracknel (of wheaten flour); rice-cracker.

senben (先鞭を著ける), to forestall; steal a march *upon*; get ahead *of*.

senbetsu (餞別), *n.* a farewell gift; a parting present.

senbi (船尾), *n.* the stern. —船尾に, astern.

senbi (戰備), *n.* war preparations; preparations for war; warlike preparations.

senbō (羨望), *n.* envy. —羨望する, to envy. —羨望の的となる, to become the object of envy.

senbōkyō (潛望鏡), *n.* a periscope.

senburi (胡黃蓮), *n.* 【植】 Swertia chinensis (marsh felwort の類).

senbyō (腺病), *n.* 【醫】 scrofula; gland-disease. —腺病質の, scrofulous.

sencha (煎茶), *n.* tea for boiling; an infusion of tea.

sencha (磚茶), *n.* brick [tile] tea.

senchaku (先著), *n.* first arrival.

senchi (戰地), *n.* the front; the

seat [theatre] of war.

senchō (船長), *n.* a captain; a ship-master; a master mariner; a skipper (小商船·漁船の). ¶ 船長室, the (captain's) cabin.

senchū (船中に), in a ship; on (ship)board; aboard.

sendai (先代), *n.* ❶ (以前の代) the former [last] generation. ❷ (先の主人) the predecessor (in the family line).

sendan (楝), *n.* 【植】 Melia japonica (bead-tree の一種·學名).

sendan (專斷, 擅斷), *n.* arbitrary decision. —專斷に, arbitrarily.

sendatsu (先達), *n.* ❶ (先進) a leader; a pioneer. ❷ (案內者) a guide; a leader.

sendatte (先達), *ad.* the other day; some days ago.

sendeki (洗滌), *n.* washing; cleansing; 【醫】 ablution; catharsis. —洗滌する, to wash; scour. ¶ 洗滌藥, an abluent; a detersive; an abstergent; a cathartic; a wash.

senden (宣傳), *n.* propaganda; propagandism. —宣傳する, to propagandize. ¶ 宣傳戰, a propaganda warfare. —宣傳者, a propagandist.

sendō (先導), *n.* guidance; leadership. —先導する, to guide; lead the way. ¶ 先導者, a guide; a leader.

sendō (船頭), *n.* a boatman; a sailor; a seaman. —船頭多くして船山に上る, "Too many cooks spoil the broth."

sendō (煽動), *n.* instigation; incitement. —煽動する, to instigate; incite; egg on; foment. ¶ 煽動(的)演說, an incendiary speech. —煽動者, an instigator; an exciter; a fomenter.

sendō (顫動する), *vi.* to vibrate.

seṅeki (戰役), *n.* a war; a campaign.

seṅen (遷延), *n.* delay; deferment; procrastination. —遷延する, to be put off; be deferred; be shifted off.

seṅetsu (僭越), *n.* presumption; impertinence. —僭越な, presumptuous; impertinent; forward.

sengaku (淺學), *n.* superficial learning [knowledge]; sciolism. —淺學の徒, a sciolist.

senge (遷化), *n.* the death of a high Buddhist priest. —遷化する, to die; pass away.

sengen (宣言), *n.* declaration; proclamation. —宣言する, to declare; proclaim. ¶ 宣言書, a manifesto; a declaration.

sengetsu (先月), *n.* & *ad.* last month; ultimo (ult. と略す) [*ad.*]. —先月廿八日, on the 28th ult.

sengi (詮議), *n.* ❶ (審議) consideration. ❷ (取調) inquiry; examination; investigation. —詮議する, ① to consider; deliberate *upon.* ② to investigate; inquire *into.* —詮議中である, to be on the carpet [tapis]; be on [upon] the anvil; be under consideration.

sengiken (先議權), *n.* prior right of debate.

sengo (戰後の), *a.* after-war; post-war. —戰後の經濟策, post-bellum economic policy.

sengoku (戰國), *n.* a country in the state of war.

sengu (船具), *n.* ship's fittings; tackle (檣桁等の); the rigging (of a ship) (索具). ¶ 船具商, ship-chandlery; a ship-chandler (人).

sengū (遷宮), *n.* removal to a shrine.

senguri (先繰に), *ad.* successively; in succession. —先繰りに出て行く, to go out one after another [in succession].

sengyo (鮮魚), *n.* fresh fish.

sengyō (專業), *n.* special [principal] occupation; speciality.

sengyō (賤業), *n.* a mean occupation; a shameful trade.

seṅi (纖維), *n.* fibre; staple; filament (特に植物組織中の). —纖維質の, fibrous; filamented.

seṅi (戰意), *n.* intention of fighting; fighting spirit (軍隊の).

seṅin (船員), *n.* the crew (of a ship); the ship's company.

seṅitsu (專一に), *ad.* specially; whole-heartedly; with heart and soul.

senja (選者), *n.* a selector.

senjaku (纖弱な), *a.* fragile; frail; delicate.

senji (戰時), *n.* war-time; time of war. ¶ 戰時保險, insurance for war risk; war insurance. —戰時手當, war bonus. —戰時稅, a war tax. (戰時利得稅, a war-profit tax.)

senjigusuri (煎藥), *n.* a (medical) decoction.

senjin (先陣), *n.* the van of an army; the forefront of a battle; the advanced guards.

senjin (鮮人), *n.* a Korean, Corean.

sen-jiru (煎じる), *vt.* to boil; decoct; make a decoction *of.* —煎じ出す, to extract by boiling; prepare an infusion *of.* —茶を煎じる, to draw the tea.

senjitsu (先日), *n.* & *ad.* the other day.

senjitsumeru (煎詰める), *vt.* to boil down. —煎じ詰めると, in the end; ultimately.

senjō (洗淨), *n.* washing; ablution; abstersion. ☞ *sendeki*. —洗浄する, to wash; cleanse by ablution.

senjō (戰場), *n.* a battle-field; a field of battle.
senjō (煽情的), *a.* sensational.
senjōjū (旋條銃), *n.* a rifle.
senjutsu (戰術), *n.* tactics.
senka (專科), *n.* a special course.
senka (戰禍), *n.* war disasters [evils]; dogs of war.
senka (選科), *n.* an elective course.
senkai (旋囘), *n.* revolution; gyration. —旋囘する, to revolve; rotate; gyrate. ¶ 旋囘軸, 【機】 a pivot; the axis of revolution.
senkaku (先覺-者), *n.* a luminary; a shining light; a pioneer. —時代の先覺者, the enlightened man of the age.
senkan (專管), *n.* exclusive jurisdiction. ¶ 專管居留地, an exclusive settlement.
senkan (潛函), *n.* Ⓢ 潛水函. a caisson.
senkata (詮方), *n.* means; resource; expedient (術計). —詮方なく, unavoidably; having no other plan; driven to one's last resource. —...より外に詮方なし, there is nothing for it but....
senken (先見), *n.* foresight; prescience. —先見の明がある, to be far-sighted; have a long head; be a man of foresight.
senken (淺見), *n.* a shallow view; a superficial idea.
senken (專權), *n.* dictatorship (獨裁); an exclusive right (排他).
senketsu (先決), *n.* previous decision. ¶ 先決問題, a previous question.
senketsu (鮮血), *n.* fresh blood. —鮮血淋漓たり, to drip with fresh blood.
senki (疝氣), *n.* enteralgia; colic.
senki (船旗), *n.* a bunting.
senki (戰機), *n.* the time for fighting [battle]. —戰機の熟するを待つ, to await the time for battle to arrive.
senkin (千鈞の重みがある), to have great weight; have the weight of authority.
senko (千古), *n.* ❶ (太古) remote antiquity. ❷ (永遠) eternity; all ages. —千古の英雄, the greatest hero of all ages. —千古の名言, an eternal truth; an unchangeable maxim.
senkō (先行する), *vt.* to precede. ¶ 先行詞, 【文】 the antecedent.
senkō (先攻する), *v.* 【野球】 to go to bat first.
senkō (染工), *n.* a dyer; a stainer.
senkō (閃光), *n.* a flash.
senkō (穿孔), *n.* a hole; boring; perforation.
senkō (船工), *n.* a shipwright; a ship's carpenter.
senkō (專攻), *n.* special study; post-graduate study. —專攻する, to study specially; make a special study *of*. ¶ 專攻生, a post-graduate student.
senkō (銓衡), *n.* choice; selection. —銓衡する, to select; choice; make one's choice. ¶ 銓衡委員, a qualification-committee.
senkō (線香), *n.* a joss-stick; an incense-stick.
senkō (戰功), *n.* military merit; military exploits; distinguished war service.
senkō (潛航する), *vi.* to move under water. ¶ 潛航艇, a submarine (boat); a submergible; a diver 〔俗〕. (潛航艇狩《戰》, submarine hunting 《warfare》.)
senkoku (先刻), *ad.* just; just now; a little while ago. —先刻御承知だ, I know all about it.
senkoku (宣告), *n.* ❶ (判決の言渡) 【法】 sentence; judgment; adjudication. ❷ (宣言) declaration; pronouncement. —宣告する, to sentence; adjudge; adjudicate; declare; pronounce. ¶ 宣告書, a written sentence.
senkotsu (薦骨), *n.* 【解】 the sacrum; a sacral bone.
senku (先驅), *n.* an outrider; a forerunner. —文明の先驅, the van of civilization. —先驅する, to forerun; ride in advance. ¶ 先驅者, a forerunner; a precursor; a leader; a pioneer; a herald.
senkuchi (先口), *n.* prior claim.
senkyaku (先客), *n.* the first comer; a comer before one.
senkyaku (船客), *n.* a (ship-) passenger. ¶ 一等船客, a cabin [first-class; saloon] passenger. —三等船客, a steerage passenger.
senkyo (船渠), *n.* a dock.
senkyo (選擧), *n.* election; poll. —選擧する, to elect. ¶ 總選擧, a general election. —選擧法違反, violation of the election law. —選擧事務所, an election office. —選擧場, the poll. —選擧權, suffrage; franchise. —選擧區, an election [electoral] district; a constituency. —選擧人, a voter; an elector; a constituent. —選擧投票, an election vote. —選擧運動, electioneering; canvassing for votes. (選擧運動者, an electioneerer; a canvasser for votes.)
senkyō (仙境), *n.* a fairy [an elf] -land; an enchanted land [place].
senkyō (戰況), *n.* the progress of a battle; the condition of a war.
senkyō (船橋), *n.* ❶ 【航】 a

bridge. ❷ 【軍】 a pontoon (bridge).

senkyoku (戰局), *n.* the situation of war. —戰局に影響を及ぼす, to affect the situation of war.

senkyōshi (宣敎師), *n.* a missionary.

senmaidōshi (千枚通し), *n.* a bodkin.

senmanchōja (千萬長者), *n.* a multi-millionaire.

senmei (鮮明な), *a.* clear; lucid; plain. —旗幟を鮮明にする, to show one's colours.

senmen (洗面), *n.* washing one's face. ¶ 洗面器, a wash-basin. —洗面所, a lavatory; a toilet (-room); a retiring-room.

senmin (賤民), *n.* the humble; the common [vulgar] breed; the proletariat (無產階級).

senmon (專門), *n.* a specialty. —專門の, professional; special; technical. —專門違ひである, to be out of one's beat. —英語を專門に硏究する, to make a special study of English. ¶ 專門學校, an academy; a college. —專門語, a technic; a technical term. —專門家, an expert; a specialist; a professional.

senmu (專務), *n.* duty; principal business. ¶ 專務取締役, a managing director.

sen-naki (詮なき), *a.* useless; unavailing; of no use; of no avail. —今更悔んでも詮無いことだ, It is useless to cry over spilt milk.

sennarihōzuki (千成酸漿), *n.* 【植】 the toothed-leaved winter-cherry; the ground-cherry.

sennen (先年), *ad.* some years ago; a few years ago; the other year.

sennetsu (潛熱), *n.* latent heat; dormant temperature.

sennichisō (千日紅), *n.* 【植】 the globe-amaranth.

sennin (仙人), *n.* a hermit; an anchorite.

sennin (先任), *n.* seniority. ¶ 先任者, a senior; a senior official [member].

sennin (專任), *n.* special duty; sole duty; full service.

sennin (選任する), *vt.* to appoint (任命); elect (選擧); nominate (指名).

sennuki (栓拔), *n.* a cork-screw; a cork extractor.

sennyo (仙女), *n.* a fairy.

sennyūshu (先入主), *n.* preconception; preoccupation; prepossession. —先入主となる, to preoccupy; prepossess.

senō (專橫), *n.* despotism; arbitrariness. **——-no,** *a.* high-handed; arbitrary; despotic. —專橫の振舞ひ, high-handed conduct.

senobi (背伸する), *vi.* to stretch oneself.

senpai (先輩), *n.* a senior; an elder; a superior.

senpaikoku (戰敗國), *n.* a vanquished nation; the vanquished.

senpaku (船舶), *n.* a vessel; a ship; shipping. ¶ 船舶管理人, a ship's husband. —船舶局, a ship-station (海岸局の對). —船舶國籍證書, the certificate of a ship's nationality.

senpaku (淺薄な), *a.* superficial; shallow. —淺薄な議論, a shallow argument.

senpan (先般), *ad.* the other day; some time ago; previously.

senpatsu (先發する), *vi.* to start in advance.

senpatsu (閃發する), *vi.* to sparkle.

senpen-banka (千變萬化), *n.* innumerable changes; infinite variety; kaleidoscopic(-al) changes. —千變萬化の, versatile; kaleidoscopic(-al).

senpen-ichiritsu (千篇一律の), *a.* monotonous. —彼のやる事は千篇一律だ, He runs in a groove.

senpi (先非), *n.* a past fault [error]. —先非を悔いる, to repent (of) one's past errors.

senpō (先方), *n.* ❶ (對手) the other party [side]. ❷ (到著地) the destination.

senpō (先鋒), *n.* the van; the forefront; the vanguard; the advanced guards. —先鋒となる, to lead the van. —タンクが先鋒となって前進した, Tanks moved forward in the van.

senpu (宣布する), *vt.* to propagate.

senpū (旋風), *n.* a whirlwind; an eddy-wind; a wind-spout; 【地】 a cyclone. —一陣の旋風, a whirl-blast.

senpūki (扇風機), *n.* an electric fan; a fan-motor.

senpuku (船腹), *n.* space; bottom; tonnage. —船腹の不足, the scarcity [shortage] of bottoms.

senpuku (潛伏), *n.* ❶ (匿れひそむ) ambush; concealment. ❷ (病の) incubation. —潛伏せる, latent; dormant; incubative; incubatory. —潛伏する, ① to conceal oneself; lie hidden. ② to lie latent. ¶ 潛伏期 (病の), the latent period; the period of incubation.

senran (戰亂), *n.* wars; disturbances. —戰亂の巷, the seat of hostilities.

senrei (先例), *n.* a precedent; an example; an authority. —先例なき, unprecedented, unexampled. —先例を作る《に從ふ》, to create 《follow》 a precedent.

senrei (洗禮), *n.* baptism; christening. —洗禮を受ける, to be baptized; be christened. (砲火の洗禮を受ける, to receive baptism of fire.)

senren (洗練), *n.* refinement. —洗練する, to refine *upon*; polish up. —文章はよく洗練されてゐる, The style is highly polished.

senretsu (戰列), *n.* a line of battle. ¶ 戰列艦, ships of the line.

senrigan (千里眼), *n.* ❶ clairvoyhnce; the second sight. ❷ far-sightedness. ¶ 千里眼者, a clairvoyant; a seer.

senrihin (戰利品), *n.* spoils; booty; a trophy.

senrin (線輪), *n.* 【電】a coil.

senritsu (旋律), *n.* 【音】melody.

senritsu (戰慄), *n.* shivering; shudder; thrill. —戰慄さす, to horrify; freeze one's blood; make one's flesh creep. —戰慄する, to shudder; shiver; tremble with fear; thrill; shake for fear.

senro (線路), *n.* 【鐵道】a line; a track. ¶ 線路工夫, a plate-layer (布設工); a track-layer (同上); a lineman (特に修繕工); a trackman (見廻工).

senryaku (戰略), *n.* strategy; stratagem. ¶ 戰略家, a strategist.

senryo (淺慮の), *a.* shallow-brained; shallow-minded. ☞ *asahaka*.

senryō (占領), *n.* occupation; capture; possession. **——-suru,** *vt.* to occupy; capture; take (possession *of*). —廣い部屋を一人で占領する, to keep a large room to oneself. ¶ 占領地, an occupied territory. —占領軍, an army of occupation.

senryō (染料), *n.* dye-stuff; dyes.

senryō (選良), *n.* ❶ selectness; choiceness. ❷ the choice; the élite; a representative.

senryō-yakusha (千兩役者), *n.* an actor of the highest grade; a star.

sensabanbetsu (千差萬別の), *a.* multifarious.

sensai (先妻), *n.* a former wife; the first wife.

sensaku (穿鑿, 詮索), *n.* search; inquiry; investigation. **——-suru,** *vt.* to search [look] *for* (探す); search [look] *into* (取調べる); investigate; inquire *into*. —何處までも穿鑿する, to probe a matter to the bottom.

sensei (先生), *n.* ❶ a teacher; an instructor; a master. ❷ (敬稱) my respected teacher; sir (呼掛). —英語の先生, a teacher of English; an English master. —先生知ってゐます, Sir, I know.

sensei (宣誓), *n.* an oath; parole. —新入大學生の宣誓式, a matriculation ceremony. —宣誓する, to swear; plight; take [make; swear] an oath. ¶ 宣誓書, 【法】an affidavit; a written oath.

sensei (專制的), *a.* despotic(-al); absolute; autocratic(-al). ¶ 專制國, an absolute monarchy. —專制君主, a despot; an absolute ruler; an autocrat. —專制政治, autocracy; absolutism; despotism.

senseiryoku (潜勢力), *n.* potential [static; latent] energy; potency.

senseki (船籍), *n.* a ship's nationality.

sensen (宣戰), *n.* a declaration of war; a proclamation of war. —宣戰する, to declare war *upon*.

sensen (戰線), *n.* the fighting line; the front. —戰線に立つ, to be at the front; take part in a battle; be brought into action.

sensengetsu (先先月), *n.* & *ad.* the month before last.

sensen-kyōkyō (戰戰兢兢), *ad.* tremblingly; shiveringly; with fear and trembling. —戰々兢々たる, trembling; nervous.

sensha (戰車), *n.* ❶【陸】a tank. ❷ (古代の) a chariot.

senshi (戰士), *n.* a warrior; a fighting man; a champion.

senshi (戰史), *a.* a military history; a history of wars.

senshi (戰死), *n.* death in battle. —戰死する, to die [fall] in battle; be killed in battle. ¶ 戰死者名簿, a roll of honour.

senshin (先進の), *a.* senior; advanced. —歐洲の先進國, the advanced countries in Europe.

senshin (專心に), *ad.* intently; concentratingly; whole-heartedly. —事業の經營に專心沒頭する, to concentrate one's whole mind upon one's business.

senshin-banku (千辛萬苦), *n.* innumerable hardships; intense application. —千辛萬苦する, to suffer [experience; go through] many hardships.

senshitsu (船室), *n.* a cabin; a state-room (二人寢室). ¶ 一(二)等船室, a first-(second-class) cabin. —三等船室, the steerage.

senshō (戰勝, 戰捷), *n.* a victory. ¶ 戰勝國, a victorious power. —戰勝記念日, the victory day. —戰勝者, a victor.

senshō (僭稱する), *vt.* to arrogate the name *of*; assume the title *of*.

senshoku (染織), *n.* dyeing and weaving. ¶ 染織學校, a textile school.

senshu (先取), *n.* priority; preference. ¶ 先取特權, 【法】 preferential right; priority.
senshu (船主), *n.* a shipowner.
senshu (船首), *n.* the bow; the prow; the head; the stem.
senshu (僭取する), *vt.* to usurp.
senshu (選手), *n.* a champion; a picked team (一團). ¶ 世界選手權, the world's championship.
senshū (先週), *n.* & *ad.* the last week. —先週の火曜日, last Tuesday; Tuesday last; last week's Tuesday.
senshū (專修する), *v.* to study exclusively. ☞ *senkō*. ¶ 法律專修科, a special law course.
senshūraku (千秋樂), *n.* a close; an end.
senshutsu (選出), *n.* election; return. —B縣選出代議士, a member of the Diet for B Prefecture. —選出する, to elect; return.
sensō (船窓), *n.* a port-hole.
sensō (船艙), *n.* 【航】 the hold (of a ship); a ship's hold.
sensō (戰爭), *n.* ❶ (戰役) a war; warfare. ❷ (合戰) a battle; a combat; a fight. —戰爭する, to wage war; go to [make] war (*with*); fight (a battle). —戰爭に勝つ《負ける》, to gain [win] 《lose》 a battle. —...と戰爭して居る, to bė at war *with*.
sensoku (洗足), *n.* a foot-bath; washing the feet.
sensoku (船側), *n.* a broadside; a side of a ship.
sensu (扇子), *n.* a (folding) fan.
sensube (詮術), *n.* =*senkata*.
sensui (泉水), *n.* an artificial pond; a fountain (噴水).
sensui (潛水), *n.* dive; diving. ¶ 潛水夫, a diver. —潛水服, a diving [submarine] armour; a diving-dress. —潛水艇, a submarine boat. (潛水艇攻擊艇, a submarine chaser. —潛水艇欺擊艇, a hush-boat; a mystery ship.) —潛水器, a diving-bell; a diving apparatus [machine].
sentai (蘚苔), *n.* 【植】 moss.
sentai (船體), *n.* the hull.
sentaku (洗濯), *n.* wash; washing. —洗濯する, to wash. —洗濯がきく, to stand wash. —命の洗濯をする, to feed [nourish] one's energy. ¶ 洗濯板《盥》, a wash-board 《-tub》. —洗濯シャボン, wash [washing; laundry] soap. —洗濯曹達, washing soda. —洗濯屋, ① (店) a laundry; a wash-house. ② (人) a washer; a laundryman.
sentaku (選擇), *n.* selection; option; choice. —選擇する, to select; choose; make choice. —選擇は君に一任する, I will leave the choice to you.
sentan (尖端), *n.* a point; an extremity.
sentan (戰端を開く), to open hostilities; take up arms (*against*).
sente (先手), *n.* ❶ (さきて) the van. ❷ (機先を制すること) forestalling. ❸ (勝負事) the first move (將棋); the first putting of a *go*-stone (圍碁). —先手を打つ, ① (圍碁, 將棋) to take the lead. ② (機先を制す) to forestall; steal a march *on*.
sentei (先帝), *n.* the late Emperor.
sentei (選定), *n.* selection; choice. ☞ *sentaku*.
senten (先天的), *a.* inborn; *a priori*; innate; inherent; congenital (病氣等の). —先天的不具, a congenital deformity.
senten (旋轉), *n.* rotation; revolution. —旋轉する, ① [*vi.*] to rotate; revolve; gyrate. ② [*a.*] rotary; rotatory; gyratory.
sentetsu (銑鐵), *n.* pig(-iron).
sentō (先登する), *v.* ❶ to scale first the enemy's wall. ❷ to arrive first.
sentō (先頭), *n.* the first; the head; the lead; the van. —先頭に立つ, to be at the head *of*; be in the lead [van]; lead the others.
sentō (尖塔), *n.* a spire; a pinnacle.
sentō (錢湯), *n.* a public bath; a bath-house.
sentō (戰鬪), *n.* a battle; a fight; an action; hostilities. —戰鬪する, to fight; battle; combat. —戰鬪を開始する, to open fire; open hostilities; go into action. ¶ 戰鬪員, a combatant. —戰鬪準備, preparation for action; clearing for action (軍艦の). —戰鬪艦, a battle-ship. —戰鬪機, a fighter; a fighting aeroplane. —戰鬪力, fighting power; fight. (戰鬪力を失はせる, to disable; cripple; put (a ship) out of action.)
señun (船暈), *n.* sea-sickness.
señun (戰雲), *n.* war-clouds.
señya (先夜), *ad.* the other night; a few nights ago.
señyaku (仙藥), *n.* ❶ (特效ある藥) a medicine of great virtue. ❷ (不老不死の藥) the elixir of life.
señyaku (先約), *n.* a previous engagement (會合の); a prior contract [promise]. —先約する, to preengage; contract previously
señyaku (煎藥), *n.* a (medical) decoction; a decoctum.
señyō (宣揚する), *vt.* to enhance; raise; promote; increase.
señyō (專用), *n.* exclusive 《private》 use. —專用の, exclusive;

private. —専用する, to use exclusively; be for private use. ¶ (水道)専用栓, a private stop-cock.

seṅyū (占有), *n.* 【法】possession; occupation; occupancy. —占有する, to take possession *of*; possess; occupy. ¶ 占有者, a possessor; a man in possession; an occupant.

seṅyū (専有), *n.* monopoly; exclusive possession. —専有する, to have by oneself; take sole possession *of*. ¶ 専有權, exclusive right.

seṅyū (戰友), *n.* a brother-in--arms; a comrade(-in-arms).

senzai (千載), *n.* a thousand years. —千載一遇(の好機), a golden opportunity.

senzai (前栽), *n.* ❶ (庭木) a garden-plant [-tree]. ❷ (庭) a garden. ❸ (前栽物) vegetables; greens.

senzai (潜在する), *vi.* to lurk; be latent; be [lie] dormant. ¶ 潜在意識, subconsciousness.

senzen (戰前の), *a.* pre-war. —戰前に, in pre-war times.

senzo (先祖), *n.* an ancestor; a forefather.

senzoku (專屬の), *a.* exclusive (管轄など); attached *to*; solely belonging. —帝劇專屬の女優, an actress attached to the Imperial Theatre. —專屬する, to belong exclusively *to*; be under the exclusive control *of*.

sen-zuru (詮ずる所), *ad.* Ⓢ 詮じつめると. in the long run; in the end; after all.

seou (背負ふ), *vt.* to carry on the back (shoulder).

seppa (說破する), *vt.* to refute (a person's argument or opinion; an accusation); confute (a person; a person's argument or opinion); silence (a person) (沈默さす); persuade (a person) (說伏する).

seppaku (切迫), *n.* imminence; impendence; approach; tension (緊張). —切迫せる, urgent; pressing; imminent; impending. —切迫する, to be close [near] at hand; be imminent; impend; press (時日).

seppaku (雪白の), *a.* snow-white; white.

seppan (折半する), *vt.* to halve; go shares.

seppan (接伴), *n.* reception. ¶ 接伴艦隊, the reception squadron.

seppatsumaru (切羽詰まる), *vi.* to be driven into a corner; be put in a fix; come to the end of one's tether.

seppō (說法), *n.* a sermon. ☞ *sekkyō*.

seppuku (切腹), *n.* *harakiri* [日]; the happy dispatch. —切腹する, to commit *harakiri*; disembowel oneself.

seppuku (說服する), *vt.* to persuade; convince *of*; prevail *on*.

seppun (接吻), *n.* a kiss; kissing. —接吻する, to kiss.

seri (水芹), *n.* 【植】Œnanthe stolonifera (marsh-parsley の一種).

seri (糶, 競), *n.* auction. —糶にかける, to bring under the hammer; put to the hammer.

seriau (競合ふ), *vi.* to struggle; vie *with*; scramble (for seats).

seridashi (迫出), *n.* emergence; pushing out; 【劇】emergence from the cellar. —迫り出す, to push out [up]; expel from a place; 【劇】emerge from the cellar.

serifu (臺詞), *n.* 【劇】words; speech.

seriichi (糶市), *n.* auction sale; an auction market.

serimochi (迫持), *n.* 【建】an arch.

seriuri (糶賣, 競賣), *n.* auction; sale by auction. —糶賣りする, to sell by auction; auctioneer. ¶ 糶賣場, an auction-room. —糶賣人, an auctioneer.

sero (セロ), *n.* a cello; a violoncello.

seron (世論), *n.* public opinion.

seru (糶·競る), *vt.* ❶ (競ふ) to compete *with*; vie *with*. ❷ to bid; hold an auction. —競り上げる, to bid up the price. —十圓で競り落す, to knock down [off] at ten *yen*.

seru (セル), *n.* serge.

seruroido (セルロイド), *n.* celluloid.

seryō (施療), *n.* gratuitous treatment. —施療する, to treat (a patient) gratis [gratuitously]; give a free medical treatment. ¶ 施療院, a charity hospital.

sesai (世才), *n.* worldly [practical] wisdom. —世才に長けた人, a man of the world; a worldly-wise person.

sesekomashii (せせこましい), *a.* Ⓢ せせッこましい. ❶ (こせこせ) fussy; narrow-minded. ❷ (狭苦しき) crowded; narrow. ❸ (餘りに綿密な) hair-splitting. —せゝこましい人, a fussy [narrow-minded] man. —せゝこましく, fussily; narrow-mindedly; by hair-splitting.

seserawarai (嘲笑), *n.* a laugh of derision; a sardonic laugh. —嘲笑ふ, to laugh with derision *at*; laugh sardonically; scorn.

seseru (せせる), *vt.* ❶ (弄ぶ) to play [toy] *with*. ❷ (ほじくる) to peck.

sesesshon (セセッション式), *n.* secessionism.

seshimeru (せしめる), *vt.* to

appropriate (to oneself); help oneself *to*; extract [draw; get] out of. 一奴から之をせしめてやった, I have done him out of this.
seshu (施主), *n.* ❶ (喪主) the chief mourner. ❷ (施しをする人) a benefactor; a donor.
seshū (世襲の), *a.* hereditary. ¶ 世襲財産, hereditary property.
sessa (切磋), *n.* assiduity; diligence. —切磋琢磨する, to polish; work hard.
sessaku (拙策), *n.* a poor [awkward] plan; a poor shift; a poor policy.
sessei (節制), *n.* temperance (飲食等の); moderation (適度); self-control (抑制); self-restraint (同上). —節制する, to be temperate; abstain *from*; be continent; be moderate; control oneself.
sessei (攝生), *n.* hygiene; care [preservation] of health. —攝生する, to take care of one's health. ¶ 攝生法, hygiene.
sessen (切線), *n.* 【數】 tangent (曲線の).
sessen (接戰), *n.* a hand-to-hand fight; a fight at close quarters; a close combat; a close game (競技の); a close contest (競爭); a close election (選擧). —接戰する, to come to a close fight [combat]; fight hand to hand [at close quarters]; fight a close game; contest evenly.
sesseto (切切と), *ad.* diligently; assiduously; hard. —セッセと働く, to work with diligence.
Sesshi (攝氏), *n.* Celsius. ¶ 攝氏寒暖計, a centigrade [Celsius] thermometer.
sesshi (切歯する), *v.* to set one's teeth; gnash the teeth.
sesshō (折衝), *n.* negotiations. —折衝する, to negotiate *with*; carry on negotiations *with*.
sesshō (殺生), *n.* the taking of life; killing. —殺生禁斷の地, a place where killing is forbidden. —殺生する, to take life; destroy living beings; kill. —無益の生殺するな, Do not take life wantonly.
sesshō (攝政), *n.* ❶ (事) regency. ❷ (人) a regent. ¶ 攝政宮, the Prince Regent.
sesshoku (接觸), *n.* contact; touch; kiss (球突の). —接觸する, to touch; be in contact *with*; come into [in] contact *with*. —接觸を保つ, to keep in touch *with* (a person). ¶ 接觸電氣《角》, contact electricity 《angle》.
sesshoku (節食する), *vi.* to be temperate in eating.
sesshu (接手する), *vt.* to receive.
sesshu (接種), *n.* inoculation. —接種する, to inoculate *with*.
sesshu (節酒), *n.* temperance; moderation in drink. —節酒する, to be moderate in drinking.
sesshu (攝取), *n.* taking; 【生】 intussusception. —攝取する, to take.
sesshu (竊取する), *vt.* to steal; purloin.
sessō (節奏), *n.* rhythm; accentuation.
sessō (節操), *n.* principle; honour; constancy. —節操の無い人, a man without principle.
sessoku (拙速), *n.* being quick but unskilful. ¶ 拙速工《訓練》, rough-and-ready workmen 《training》.
ses-suru (接する), *v.* ❶ (接觸) to touch; be in contact *with*. ❷ (隣接) to adjoin; border; be next *to*. ❸ (引見) to receive; meet; have an interview *with*. ❹ (受領) to receive; be in receipt *of*. —人家に接せる野原, a field adjacent to the house. —吉報に接する, to receive [hear] good news. —婦人に接する, to become intimate with a woman.
ses-suru (節する), *v.* ❶ (適度にする) to moderate. ❷ (節約) to economize; save. ❸ (飲食を) to be temperate. ❹ (情慾を) to restrain [control] oneself.
sesuji (背筋), *n.* the line over the backbone; the seam over the back.
setai (世態), *n.* the condition of the world; the social condition. —世態人情に通じる, to see much of the world.
setchi (接地), *n.* 【電】 earth; ground.
setchi (設置), *n.* establishment (設立); organization (組織); creation (創設). —設置する, to establish; organize; create; form.
setchin (雪隠), *n.* a privy; a water-closet. ☞ *benjo*.
setchū (折衷), *n.* compromise; the middle course [way]. —折衷する, to compromise; blend. ¶ 折衷説, eclecticism.
seto (瀬戸), *n.* a strait; a channel.
setogiwa (瀬戸際), *n.* a crisis; a critical moment.
setomono (瀬戸物), *n.* china-ware; crockery; pottery. ¶ 瀬戸物屋, a china-shop.
setsu (說), *n.* ❶ (意見) an opinion; a view. ❷ (學說) a theory. ❸ (教理) a doctrine. ❹ (風說) a rumour. —說を同じうする, to be of the same opinion. —說を異にする, to differ in opinion.
setsu (節), *n.* ❶ (季節) season. ❷ (時期) time; an occasion (折). ❸ (文章の) a paragraph; a clause (一文の). ❹ (節操) principle;

faith; honour. —第二章第一節, Chapter II, Section I. —其の節は, on that occasion. —こちらへお出の節は, when you come this way. —節を賣る, to sell one's honour. —節を變ずる, to desert one's colours; turn one's coat.

setsubi (設備), *n.* equipment; accommodation (收容設備). —旅館の設備, hotel accommodation (設け); the appointments of a hotel (裝備). —設備する, to provide; equip; furnish; appoint; set out. —設備の整った, well-equipped; well-appointed.

setsubigo (接尾語), *n.* 【文】 a suffix.

setsubō (切望), *n.* earnest desire. —切望する, to entreat; hunger *for* [*after*]; hanker *after*.

setsubun (節分), *n.* the change of season.

setsudan (切斷), *n.* cutting; amputation (肢の). —切斷する, to cut off; sever; amputate.

setsuen (雪寃する), *v.* to clear oneself of a false charge.

setsugan (切願する), *vt.* to implore; entreat. ☞ *setsubō*.

setsugen (切言する), *v.* to emphasize (力說); speak emphatically; put (it) strongly; urge (切りに說く).

setsugen (節減), *n.* retrenchment; reduction; curtailment. **—-suru,** *vt.* to reduce; cut down; retrench. —經費を節減する, to curtail expenditures.

setsugi (節義), *n.* principle; constancy; faith. —節義を重んじる, to prize [value] principle.

setsugō (接合), *n.* union; junction; connection; 【醫】 commissure. —接合する, to connect; unite; join.

setsugosen (攝護腺), *n.* 【解】 the prostate (gland).

setsuji (綴字), *n.* spelling. ¶ 綴字法, orthography.

setsujitsu (切實な), *a.* close; pertinent (適切な); practical (實際的); urgent (焦眉の); sincere (誠實な); faithful (忠實な); true (眞實の). —切實な問題, a close question.

setsujokusen (雪辱戰), *n.* ❶ a battle for recovery of one's honour [to wipe out a former shame]. ❷ (競技の) a return match [game].

setsuju (接受する), *vt.* to receive.

setsujutsu (說述), *n.* mention; statement. —說述する, to state; mention.

setsuku (迫つく), *vt.* to press; urge; hurry.

setsumei (說明), *n.* explanation; elucidation; exposition. —說明する, to explain; elucidate; expound. —說明の限りに非ず, There is no need to explain. —事實は說明を要せぬ, The fact will explain itself. ¶ 說明書, an explanation.

setsuna (刹那), *n.* 【梵】 Kṣaṇa; the moment; the instant. —其の刹那, at the very moment; at that juncture. —刹那の歡, a momentary joy [delight].

setsu-na (切な), *a.* eager; earnest; ardent.

setsu-na (拙な), *a.* poor; awkward; clumsy; inexpert; unskilful; bungling.

setsunai (切ない), *a.* oppressive; painful. **—,** *v.* to feel pain. —切ない私の心, my painful heart.

setsu-ni (切に), *ad.* eagerly; earnestly; fervently. —それは私の切に望む處だ, It is what I fervently desire.

setsuretsu (拙劣な), *a.* =*setsu-na* (拙な).

setsuri (攝理), *n.* Providence.

setsuritsu (設立), *n.* foundation; establishment; creation. —設立する, to establish; found; create. ¶ 設立者, a founder; an organizer (創立者).

setsuryaku (節略する), *vt.* to abridge; omit; shorten. ☞ *shōryaku*.

setsuyaku (節約), *n.* saving; economy; frugality. **—-suru,** *vt.* to save; economize. —費用を節約する, to save expenses. —時間を節約する, to economize [save] time.

setsuyō (節用), *n.* ❶ =*setsuyaku*. ❷ a digest; a manual; a handbook; a thesaurus (寶典).

setsuyu (說諭), *n.* admonition; gentle reproof. **—-suru,** *vt.* to admonish; reprove gently. —懇々說諭する, to admonish carefully; speak [talk] seriously *to*.

setsuzoku (接續), *n.* connection; joining; 【音】 break. —接續する, to connect; join; adjoin. ¶ 接續町村, adjoining towns and villages. —接續詞, 【文】 the conjunction.

setta (雪駄), *n.* leather-soled sandals.

settai (接待), *n.* ❶ reception; entertainment. ❷ charity. —接待する, ① to receive; entertain. ② to give in charity; serve (tea) free. ¶ 接待係, a reception committe.

settei (設定), *n.* establishment; institution; creation (權利の). —設定する, to establish; institute; create.

settō (竊盜), *n.* ❶ theft; larceny. ❷ (人) a thief. —竊盜する, to thieve · steal; commit a theft.

settōgo (接頭語), *n.* 【文】a prefix.

settoku (說得する), *vt.* to persuade; convince *of*; prevail *on*. —爲る《止める》やう說得する, to argue a person *into* 《*out of*》.

sewa (世話), *n.* ❶ (助力) aid; help; assistance. ❷ (斡旋) good [kind] offices; services. ❸ (面倒) care (監督); trouble (手數). —世話好きの, officious. —世話の燒ける子, a troublesome child. —に世話を燒かす, to give trouble *to*. —人の世話になる, to be (under) a person's care (監督下にあり); be an inmate of a person's house (同居); be dependent upon another (食客). —いらぬ御世話だ, Thank you for nothing. —大きなお世話だ, Mind your own business. —大きにお世話様でした, Much obliged to you.

—— - suru, *vt.* ❶ to help; aid; assist. ❷ to do [render] (a person) a service; get [procure] (得てやる); find (見つけてやる). ❸ (面倒を見る) to take care *of*; look *after*. —地位を世話する, to get [procure] a person a place [position]. —女中を世話する, to find a person a maidservant. ¶ 世話物, a domestic play. —世話人, a committee (委員); a go-between (媒介人). —世話役, a manager; a person in charge *of*.

sewashii (忙しい), *a.* busy.

seyaku (施藥), *n.* charity administration; medicines dispensed gratuitously. —施藥する, to dispense (gratuitously).

seyo (施與する), *vt.* to give in charity.

sezoku (世俗), *n.* common [popular] customs [manners]; the world (世間). —世俗の, worldly; popular; earthly.

sha (社), *n.* ❶ (神社) a shrine. ❷ (結社) an association; a society. ❸ (商社) a firm; a company (會社); an office (事務所). ❹ (蕃社) a tribe.

sha (斜の), *a.* slant; oblique. —斜に構へる, to hold aslant.

sha (紗), *n.* (silk) gauze; tiffany.

shaba (車馬), *n.* horses and vehicles. —車馬通行止, No thoroughfare for horses and vehicles.

shaba (娑婆), *n.* 【梵】Sabā; this [the] world (現世); worldly life (現世生活). ¶ 娑婆ッ氣, an earthly [a worldly] desire.

shaberu (喋る), *vi.* ❶ (饒舌) to chatter; prattle; wag one's chin [tongue]. ❷ =*iu* (言ふ). —よく喋る女, a talkative woman. —くだらぬ事を喋る, to gabble [chatter] nonsense.

shaberu (シャベル), *n.* a shovel.

shabetsu (差別), *n.* =*sabetsu*.

shabon (石鹼), *n.* soap. ¶ シャボン玉, a soap-bubble.

shaboten (仙人掌, 覇王樹), *n.* =*saboten*.

shaburu (舐る), *vt.* to suck; lick.

shachi(hoko) (鯱), *n.* 【魚】the grampus; the killer-whale. ¶ 鯱立ち, standing on one's head.

shachikobaru (鯱子張る), *vi.* ❶ (剛張る) to be stiff [rigid]. ❷ (儀式張る) to stand on ceremony. ❸ (威張る) to stand upon one's dignity; be haughty.

shachō (社長), *n.* a president; a senior partner.

shachū (社中), *n.* a company; a society; a coterie (仲間).

shadai (車臺), *n.* a car [carriage] -body [-trunk]; a chassis (自動車).

shadan (社團), *n.* an association; a corporation. ¶ 社團法人,【法】a juridical [incorporated] association; a corporation aggregate; a corporate juridical person.

shadan (遮斷する), *vt.* to intercept; interrupt; cut [shut] off. —交通を遮斷される, to be cut off from communication.

shaden (社殿), *n.* a shrine.

shadō (車道), *n.* a carriageway; a carriage-road; a roadway.

shaei (舍營), *n.* 【軍】cantonment; billets. —舍營する, to be billeted *upon*.

shafu (車夫), *n.* a *jinrikisha*-man [-drawer].

shafutsu (煮沸する), *v.* to boil.

shagamu (蹲む), *vi.* to squat (on the heels); crouch.

shagaregoe (嗄聲), *n.* a hoarse [husky] voice.

shagareru (嗄れる), *vi.* to become hoarse.

shageki (射擊), *n.* shooting; firing; gunning (特に遊獵の). —射擊する, to shoot; fire *at* [*on*; *upon*]. ¶ 實彈《空砲》射擊, ball 《blank》-firing. —射擊演習, target [rifle] practice.

shagi (謝儀), *n.* a present; a fee (謝禮金).

shahan (這般の), *a.* the; this; such (斯樣な).

shahei (遮蔽する), *vt.* to cover; defilade.

shahen (斜邊), *n.* 【數】a hypotenuse.

shahōkei (斜方形), *n.* a rhombus; a lozenge.

shahon (寫本), *n.* a written copy; a manuscript (book); a transcript.

shai (謝意), *n.* thanks; (a sense of) gratitude. —謝意を表する, to tender thanks; express one's gratitude.

shain (社員), *n.* a partner (組合員); a member (會員); a member of the staff; an employé (雇). ¶ 終身社員, a life-member.

shaji (社寺), *n.* shrines and temples. ¶ 古社寺保存會, a society for the preservation of old shrines and temples.

shaji (寫字), *n.* copying; transcription. ¶ 寫字生, a copyist; a a transcriber; an amanuensis.

shaji (謝辭), *n.* ❶ (感謝の詞) thanks; an address of thanks. ❷ (謝罪の詞) an apology.

shajiku (車軸), *n.* an axle. —雨車軸を流す, to rain in torrents; rain cats and dogs.

shajitsu (寫實的), *a.* realistic. ¶ 寫實主義, realism.

Shaka (釋迦), *n.* Sakya; Gautama.

shakai (社會), *n.* ❶ (一般社會) society; community. ❷ (何々社會) circles; world; classes (階級). —資本主義の社會, capitalist society. —社會に對する義務, social duties. —社會的, social. (社會的地位, social position; social status; a station in life.) —社會の爲に, for the public interest; for the welfare of society. —社會の一員として, as a member of society. —吾々社會では, in our circle. ¶ 軍人社會, military circles. —社會道徳, social morality. —社會學, sociology; social science. —社會奉仕, social service. —社會事業《改良》家, a social worker《reformer》. —社會契約, social compact [contract]. —社會局, the Bureau of Social Welfare [Service]. —社會問題, a social problem. —社會政策, social politics. —社會組織, social constitution. —社會主義, socialism. (社會主義者, a socialist.) —社會黨, the socialists. (社會民主黨, the Social Democratic party.)

shakaku (射角), *n.* the angle of fire.

shakan (左官), *n.* a plasterer.

shakan (舎監), *n.* a dormitory-inspector; a house-master【英】.

shakin (砂金), *n.* gold dust; placer gold. ¶ 砂金採集, placer-mining.

shakka (借家), *n.* a rented house; a hired house. —借家する, to rent [hire; lease] a house. ¶ 借家人, a tenant; a lessee. —借家法, law relating to the hiring of houses.

shakkan (借款), *n.* a loan. ¶ 四國借款團, the Quadruple Loan Group; the Four-Power Group. —借款團契約, a consortium.

shakkin (借金), *n.* a debt; a loan; borrowed money; (pecuniary) liabilities. —借金がある, to have debts; be in debt; owe to a person. —借金を返す, to pay a debt. —借金で首が廻らぬ, to be up to ears in debt; be deep in debt. —— **-suru**, *vi.* to run [fall; get] into debt; contract [incur] a debt; borrow money. —借金せぬ様にする, to keep one's head above water; keep out of debt. —向見ずに借金する, to rush into debt. ¶ 借金取り, a dun.

shako (蝦蛄), *n.* 【甲殼】 the mantis-shrimp; the quill.

shako (鷓鴣), *n.* 【鳥】 the partridge.

shako (車庫), *n.* a coach-house (馬車の); a car-shed (電車·汽車の); a garage (自動車の).

shakō (社交), *n.* society; social intercourse. —社交的手腕, social talent. —社交界の花形, the queen [shining star; *belle*【佛】] of society; a society leader. —社交界に出る, to enter [go into] society. ¶ 社交期, the season.

shakō (藉口する), *v.* to make it an excuse; take advantage *of*.

shakōshin (射倖心), *n.* a speculative [gambling] spirit [mind].

shaku (尺), *n.* ❶ (尺度) the Japanese foot [=.994 foot]. ❷ (長さ) length; measure.

shaku (杓), *n.* a ladle; a scoop.

shaku (酌をする), *v.* to serve a person with *sake*. —一つお酌をしませう, Let me serve you a cup.

shaku (笏), *n.* a sceptre; a mace.

shaku (爵), *n.* =*shakui*.

shaku (癪), *n.* ❶ gastrospasm (胃痙攣); hysterospasm (子宮痙攣). ❷ (不快) displeasure; indignation; anger. —癪に障る, ① [*vi.*] to be displeased; stir one's bile. ② [*a.*] provoking; offensive; offending. —癪を起す, to have a spasmodic attack. —全く癪ぢゃないか, That's enough to make a saint swear.

shakuchi (借地), *n.* rented [leased] ground; lease. —借地する, to lease [rent] ground. ¶ 借地法, law relating to the lease of land. —借地權, lease; leasehold. —借地人, a tenant; a lessor; a leaseholder. —借地料, ground-rent.

shakudo (尺度), *n.* a (linear) measure; a rule; a scale.

shakudō (赤銅), *n.* *shakudō*【日】; an alloy of copper and gold.

shakufu (酌婦), *n.* a waitress.

shakugi (釋義), *n.* a commentary; an exposition.

shakuhachi (尺八), *n.* *shakuhachi*【日】; a bamboo flute.

shakuhō (釋放), *n.* discharge; liberation; release. —釋放する,

to discharge; release; set free.

shakui (爵位), *n.* peerage and court rank; peerage; title.

shakujō (錫杖), *n.* a pikestaff; a priest's staff.

shakumei (釋明), *n.* an explanation; an apology. —釋明する, to elucidate; explain.

shakunage (石楠花), *n.* 【植】 Rhododendron hymenanthes (rhododendron の一種·學名).

shakunetsu (灼熱), *n.* glow; incandescence; 【化】 ignition. —灼熱せる, incandescent. —灼熱する, to ignite.

shakuri (吃逆, 噦), *n.* hiccup; hiccough. —吃逆する, to hiccup, hiccough.

shakuryō (酌量), *n.* consideration; allowance; extenuation. —酌量する, to consider; take into consideration [account]; make allowances *for*. —情狀を酌量して, in consideration of extenuating circumstances. ¶ 酌量減刑 reduction of penalty on account of extenuating circumstances.

shakushaku (綽綽), *a.* free and easy (無拘束); free and unconstrained (同上); calm (ゆったり); ample (十分). —餘裕綽々たり, to have much in reserve.

shakushi (杓子), *n.* a wooden spoon. —杓子定規にやる, to adhere to hard and fast rules.

shakutori (尺蠖), *n.* 【蟲】 the looper; the geometer; the measuring-worm.

shakuu (掬ふ), *vt.* to ladle; dip up.

shakuya (借家), *n.* = ***shakka***.

shakuyaku (芍藥), *n.* 【植】 the herbaceous [white-flowered] peony.

shakuyō (借用), *n.* borrowing. —借用する, to have the loan *of*; borrow. ¶ 借用證書, a bond of debt [loan]; an IOU (I owe you の略. I. O. U. とも書く).

shakuzai (借財), *n.* a loan; a debt; liabilities. ☞ ***shakkin***.

shamen (斜面), *n.* a slope; a slanting surface; an inclined plane.

shamen (赦免), *n.* pardon; absolution; amnesty (大赦). —赦免する, to pardon; let a person off (a penalty); absolve a person *from*.

shamo (軍鷄), *n.* ❶ 【鳥】 the cochin(-china). ❷ = ***keiniku*** (鷄肉).

Shamu (暹羅), *n.* Siam. ¶ 暹羅人, a Siamese.

shamusho (社務所), *n.* a shrine-office.

shanikusai (謝肉祭), *n.* the carnival.

shanimuni (遮二無二), *ad.* forcibly; by force; recklessly. —遮二無二突き進む, to force one's way.

shanpan, shanpen, (三鞭酒), *n.* champagne.

shaon (謝恩), *n.* gratitude. ¶ 謝恩會, a thanksgiving dinner (in honour of former teachers).

sharaku (洒落), *n.* frankness; open-heartedness. —風流洒落の人, a refined and open-hearted man.

sharakusai (洒落臭い), *a.* ❶ (衒學的) pedantic; scholastic; bookish. ❷ (虛飾) ostentatious; vain. —洒落臭いことを言ふ, to talk pedantically.

share (洒落), *n.* ❶ (諧謔) a witticism; a joke; a word-play (言語上の); a pun (同上). ❷ (おしゃれ) dandyism; foppishness; smartness. —洒落がうまい, to be good at jokes. —あの人はお洒落だ, He is quite a dandy. ¶ 洒落者, a dandy; a swell; a fop.

sharei (謝禮), *n.* ❶ (感謝) thanks. ❷ (報酬) remuneration; a fee (醫師·辯護士等專門家への); an honorarium (同上); a premium (弟子などの); a reward (懸賞金). —謝禮する, ① (謝意を述べる) to give one's thanks. ② (報酬する, *vt.*) to remunerate; fee; reward.

shareru (洒落る), *v.* ❶ (言葉) to play upon words; crack [cut] a joke; pun; joke. ❷ (おしゃれ) to beautify oneself; dandify [adonize] oneself; be stylish [dandy]. —洒落た, ① (諧謔) witty; humorous. ② (おつな) stylish; smart; good. (洒落た事をぬかすな, None of your sauce!) —此本の裝幀は一寸洒落てる, This book is bound in a pretty style.

shari (射利), *n.* speculation; love of gain. —射利的, mercenary, mercantile; speculative.

sharibetsu (舍利別), *n.* syrup.

sharien (舍利鹽), *n.* 【化】 Epsom salts; sulphate of magnesia.

shariki (車力), *n.* ❶ (人) a carter; a cart-coolie; a cartman. ❷ (車) a hand-cart; a cart.

sharikōbe (髑髏), *n.* the skull.

sharin (車輪), *n.* a wheel.

sharyō (車輛), *n.* cars; vehicles; rolling-stock (鐵道の).

shasai (社債), *n.* a debenture; debenture debt. —社債を發行する, to issue debentures.

shasatsu (射殺する), *vt.* to shoot dead; kill by shooting.

shasei (寫生), *n.* sketching; drawing from life [nature]. —寫生する, to sketch; make a sketch; draw 《paint》 from life [nature]. ¶ 寫生文, a realistic writing. —寫生帖, a sketch-book

[-block]. —写生畫, a sketch; a picture drawn from nature.
shasen (斜線), *n.* an oblique line.
shasetsu (社說), *n.* an editorial; a leader; a leading article.
shāshā (洒蛙洒蛙), *ad.* composedly; without shame. —洒蛙洒蛙してゐる, to be composed.
shashi (斜視), *n.* a squint; squinting; 【醫】 strabismus. ¶ 斜視眼, a squint [cross; gimlet] eye.
shashi (奢侈), *n.* luxury; luxuriousness; extravagance. —奢侈の, luxurious; extravagant. —奢侈に耽る, to be addicted to extravagance; live in the lap of luxury; be luxurious [extravagant]. ¶ 奢侈品, an article of luxury; luxuries. (奢侈品稅, tax on luxuries; luxuries tax.)
shashin (寫眞), *n.* a photograph; a photo; a portrait (肖像). —寫眞を撮る, to photograph (自分で); take a photograph (同上); have a photograph taken (寫してもらふ). ¶ 光澤《艶消》寫眞, a glazed 《matted》 photograph. ¶ 寫眞愛好家, a camera-man. —寫眞版, a photogravure; a heliogravure. —寫眞帖, a photograph album. —寫眞道樂, a photograph [camera] hobby. —寫眞班, a photographic section. —寫眞術, photography. —寫眞器, a photographic apparatus; a (photographic) camera; a kodak (手提). —寫眞師, a photographer.
shashō (車掌), *n.* a conductor; a guard (汽車の) 【英】. ¶ 車掌臺, a dicky, dickey; a conductor's platform.
shashu (射手), *n.* a shooter; a marksman; an archer (弓の).
shashū (沙洲), *n.* a sand-bar; a bar; a bank.
shashutsu (射出する), *v.* to project; shoot; radiate; shed.
shasoku (社則), *n.* the regulations of a company [an association].
shasuiro (射水路), *n.* a water-shoot.
sha-suru (謝する), *vt.* ❶ (わぶ) to apologize; make an excuse. ❷ (謝絕) to decline; refuse. ❸ (感謝) to thank; acknowledge. —厚意を謝する, to thank a person for his good-will.
shataku (舍宅), *n.* a house; a residence. ¶ 舍宅料, house-allowance.
shataku (社宅), *n.* a company's residences (for its members and employees).
shatei (射程), *n.* a gun-shot; a shooting [rifle]-range.
shateki (射的), *n.* target-practice; shooting. ¶ 射的場, a rifle-ground; a target-practice ground; a rifle [shooting] range.
shatsu (襯衣), *n.* a shirt; an undershirt; a camisole (婦人常用).
shattā (シャッター), *n.* a shutter.
shayū (社友), *n.* a friend [well-wisher] of a firm.
shazai (謝罪), *n.* apology. —謝罪する, to apologize; acknowledge one's fault. ¶ 謝罪廣告, an apology published in newspaper.
shazetsu (謝絕), *n.* declining; refusal (拒絕). —謝絕する, to decline; refuse.
shi (士), *n.* a gentleman; a man; a *samurai*.
shi (氏), *n.* ❶ (氏族) a family. ❷ (敬語) Mr. ❸ he.
shi (史), *n.* history.
shi (四), *n.* four; the fourth (第四).
shi (市), *n.* a city; a municipality. ¶ 市行政機關, municipal corporation. —市當局, municipal authorities.
shi (死), *n.* death; decease; departure; demise (崩御, 薨去). —死に就く, ① to meet one's death. ② to commit suicide. —死に至るまで, to one's dying day. —死に至らしめる, to prove fatal; cause the death *of*.
shi (刺), *n.* a card. —刺を通ずる, to send in a card.
shi (師), *n.* ❶ (軍隊) an army; forces. ❷ (師匠, 先生) a master; a teacher. —ジョーゼフ師, Abbé Joseph.
shi (詩), *n.* a poem; a verse; poetry (總稱). —詩に作る, to versify; verse.
shi (資), *n.* ❶ capital (資本); funds (同上); means (資力); resources (資源). ❷ (資質) quality.
shi (叱), *int.* ❶ (靜まれの發聲) hush!; whist!; hist! ❷ (馬を進める發聲) gee!; gee-ho!; gee-up!; gee-wo! ❸ (家禽を追ふ發聲) shoo! —こん畜生, しっしっ, You beast, shoo, shoo!
shiagaru (仕上がる), *vi.* to be finished; be completed.
shiage (仕上げ), *n.* finish; touch; dressing. ¶ 仕上勘定, payment by the piece. —仕上工場, finishing-shop.
shiageru (仕上げる), *vt.* to finish; complete; perfect. —小僧から仕上げる, to rise from a shop-boy.
shiai (試合), *n.* a game; a match; a contest (競爭). —試合する, to play a match; have a bout. —試合を申込む《承知する》, to send 《accept》 a challenge. ¶ 對校試合, an inter-school

match; a school match.

shian (思案), *n.* thought; meditation (沈思); consideration (熟慮). —思案に餘る, to beat one's wits' end; be at a loss (what to do). —思案に暮れる, to be lost [sunk] in thought. —茲が思案のしどころ, This is the point for consideration.

shiasatte (明明後日), *n.* & *ad.* two days after to-morrow; three days hence.

shiau (仕合ふ), *v.* ❶ (試合ふ) to have a match [bout]. ❷ (爲合ふ) to do each other.

shiawase (仕合), *n.* fortune (運); good luck (幸運); happiness (幸福). ☞*kōfuku*. ¶ 仕合せ者, a fortunate [lucky] man.

shiba (芝), *n.* 【植】 Zoisia pungens (學名).

shiba (柴), *n.* brushwood; fire-wood.

shibahara (芝原), *n.* a sward; a greensward; a lawn; a turf.

shibai (四倍), *n.* four times; quadruple. —四倍にする, to quadruplicate; quadruple.

shibai (芝居), *n.* ❶ a play. ❷ (劇場) a theatre; a play-house. —芝居に仕組む, to dramatize. —芝居を打つ, ① (芝居興行) to run a play. ② (世間の耳目を驚かすことをする) to play a great rôle. —彼は餘りに芝居をし過ぎる, He is too theatrical. ¶ 芝居行き, theatre-going; play-going. —芝居好き, a theatre-goer.

shibakari (柴刈), *n.* firewood-gathering: a firewood-gatherer.

shibaraku (少暫く), *ad.* ❶ (暫時) a little while; for a while; for a time (一時). ❷ (稍久しく) for some time; a good while; for a long time [while]. ❸ (姑) for the present. —暫くありて, after a little while. —その問題は姑く措き, setting [putting] aside for the moment the question. —やあ, 暫くだったね, Oh, you are quite a stranger.

shibaru (縛る), *vt.* ❶ (くゝる) to bind; tie. ❷ (捕縛) to arrest. ❸ (拘束) to bind; fetter. —縛りつける, to tie up; bind up; make fast. —細引で人を縛る, to bind [tie] a person with a cord. —契約に縛られる, to be bound to an agreement.

shibashi (暫時), *ad.* =*zanji*.

shibashiba (屢), *ad.* often; frequently; repeatedly. —…に屢ゝ行く, to frequent; visit frequently; haunt.

shibataku (繁叩, 瞬く), *vt.* to wink.

shibau (芝生), *n.* a lawn; a turf; a grass(-plot); a greensward.

shiben (支辨), *n.* defrayment; payment. —支辨する, to defray; disburse; pay.

Shiberia (西伯利), *n.* Siberia.

shibetsu (死別), *n.* separation by death.

shibi (鮪), *n.* 【魚】 the tunny.

shibin (溲瓶), *n.* a urine glass; a chamber-pot.

shibire (痺), *n.* numbness; paralysis; pins and needles. —痺が切れる, to have one's legs numbed. ¶ 痺藥, an anæsthetic.

shibireru (痺れる), *vi.* to be 《become》$_0$ numb. —痺れた, numb; paralytic. —痺れさす, to numb; stupefy; paralyze.

shibito (死人), *n.* a corpse; a dead body.

shibō (子房), *n.* 【植】 an ovary.

shibō (死亡), *n.* death; decease. —死亡する, to die; pass away; expire. ¶ 死亡率, death-rate; mortality. —死亡診斷書, a certificate of death [decease]. —死亡者, the dead; the deceased. —死亡屆, a notice of death.

shibō (志望), *n.* desire; aspiration. —志望する, to wish; desire; aspire *after*. ¶ 志望者, an aspirant; a candidate.

shibō (脂肪), *n.* fat. —脂肪質の, fatty; sebaceous. ¶ 脂肪物, a fatty [sebaceous] substance; fatty matter.

shibomu (萎·凋む), *vi.* to fade; wither.

shibori (絞), *n.* ❶ (寫眞器の) a diaphragm. ❷ =*shiborizome*.

shiborikasu (絞糟), *n.* lees; refuse.

shiborizome (絞染), *n.* dyeing in the skein.

shiboru (絞る), *vt.* to press; squeeze; wring (clothes in washing; water out of a wet garment). —聲を絞って, at the top [highest pitch] of one's voice. —涙を絞る, to shed tears in torrents. —金を絞り取る, to wring [squeeze] money *from*. —葡萄から汁を絞る, to press [squeeze] the juice from [out of] grapes. —勞働者の膏血を絞る, to sweat the workmen in one's employ.

shibu (澁), *n.* the juice of astringent persimmons (柿澁).

shibu (支部), *n.* a branch.

shibui (澁い), *a.* ❶ astringent. ❷ (地味な) quiet (色合など); tasty. ❸ (氣むづかしい) sullen; glum. ❹ (吝嗇) stingy; niggardly. —澁い柄, a tasty pattern. —澁い顏をする, to look glum; put on sulky [sullen; glum] looks. —中々澁い身裝(なり)をしてゐる, He is dressed quite in elegant taste.

shibukami (澁紙), *n.* *shibu*-paper.

shibuki (飛沫, 繁吹), *n.* a spray.
shibuku (繁吹く), *vi.* to spray; break in sprays.
shibun (四分), *n.* quartering. —四分する, to quarter; quadrate (圓など). —四分五裂する, to be divided into parts; be broken up; be disrupted. ¶ 四分儀, a quadrant.
shibun (死文), *n.* dead letter.
shiburu (澁る), *vi.* ❶ to be reluctant [unwilling]. ❷ (腹が) to be constipated. —金を出し澁る, to be unwilling to give money. —澁って返事をしない, to look sullen and give no reply.
shibushibu (澁澁), *ad.* reluctantly; unwillingly; against one's will. ☞ *iyaiya*. —澁々返事する, to give a reluctant reply.
shibutoi (しぶとい), *a.* obstinate; stubborn. —しぶとい奴だ, You stiff-necked fellow!
shibutsu (死物), *n.* a lifeless thing; an inanimate object.
shibyō (死病), *n.* a fatal disease.
shichi (七), *n.* seven; the seventh (第七).
shichi (質), *n.* a pawn; a pledge. —質に取る, to take in pledge [pawn]. —質に入れる; 質入れする, to pledge; pawn. —質受けする, to redeem; take out of pawn. ¶ 質物, a pledge; a pawn; the thing pledged. —質流れ, a forfeited pawn. —質屋, a pawnbroker (人): a pawnshop (店).
shichi (死地), *n.* the jaws of death; a fatal position.
shichigatsu (七月), *n.* July.
shichijū (七十), *n.* seventy; the seventieth (第七十). —七十代の人, a septuagenarian.
shichikaku (七角-形), *n.* a heptagon.
shichiken (質權), *n.* 【法】 (right of) pledge.
shichimenchō (七面鳥), *n.* ❶ 【鳥】 the turkey. ❷ (變化多きもの) a chameleon.
shichin (繻珍), *n.* figured satin.
shichirin (七厘), *n.* a (small portable) furnace.
shichiten-battō (七顚八倒する), *vi.* to writhe with pain. —七顚八倒の苦み, agonizing pain.
shichō (支廳), *n.* a branch-office; a prefectural office (臺灣の).
shichō (市長), *n.* a mayor. —東京市長, the Mayor of Tōkyō.
shichō (市廳), *n.* a municipal office; a city hall; an *hôtel de ville* 〔佛〕.
shichō (思潮), *n.* the current idea [thought]; the current of thought.
shichō (紙帳), *n.* a paper mosquito-net.
shichō (視聽), *n.* sight and hearing. —天下の視聽を聳動する, to electrify the world; take the public by surprise. —天下の視聽を一身に集める, to make oneself the focus of public interest.
shichō (輜重), *n.* 【軍】 military stores. ¶ 輜重監, a commissary. —輜重隊, Army Service Corps (A. S. C. と略す). —輜重輸卒, a driver of a military train; a transport auxiliary.
shichoku (司直), *n.* ❶ (裁判) judgment. ❷ (判事) a judge.
shichōson (市町村), *n.* cities, towns, and villages.
shichū (仔蟲), *n.* a larva.
shichū (支柱), *n.* a support; a prop; a stay; a stanchion; bracing tube (飛行機の); a strut (同上).
shichū (市中), *n.* the city; the town; streets.
shichū (シチウ), *n.* 【料理】 stew.
shida (羊齒), *n.* 【植】 Gleichenia glauca (net-fern の一種·學名); a fern (俗稱).
shidai (至大の), *a.* remarkable; very great.
shidai (次第), *n.* ❶ (順序) order. ❷ (事情) circumstances; the state of things. ❸ (理由) reason; cause. —, *ad.* as soon as; no sooner than. —申込次第, on application. —到著次第, upon arrival. —御勝手次第, as you please. —機會のあり次第, on the first opportunity. —當人が歸り次第, as soon as he comes home. —次第に, gradually; by degrees; little by little.
shidan (史談), *n.* historical stories (anecdotes).
shidan (師團), *n.* a division. ¶ 留守師團, a depôt division. —師團長, a divisional commander.
shidara (しだらない), *a.* disorderly; slovenly.
shidare (枝垂), *a.* weeping; pendulous. ¶ 枝垂柳, the weeping-willow.
shidareru (枝垂れる), *vi.* to droop; weep; hang down.
shidashi (仕出), *n.* a meal [dishes] supplied. ¶ 仕出屋, a caterer; a cook-shop which supplies meals to order.
shidasu (仕出す), *vt.* ❶ (爲し始む) to begin to do. ❷ =*dekasu*. ❸ (料理を) to prepare and supply to order.
shiden (史傳), *n.* a history; biography; a biographical story.
shide-no-tabi (死出の旅), *n.* a journey to one's last home.
shido (示度), *n.* reading; record; registered [recorded] degrees.
shidō (士道), *n.* ❶ (武士道) chivalry; knighthood. ❷ (士た

る の 道) gentlemanliness; manliness.

shidō (支道), *n.* a by-path; a by-way; a by-road.

shidō (私道), *n.* a private road [path].

shidō (指導), *n.* leading; guidance; direction (指圖). —指導する, to lead; guide. —教授の指導の下に, under (the guidance of) a professor.

shidō (斯道), *n.* (斯の道) one's line of study. —斯道に通じてゐる, to be in the line. —彼は斯道の達人であった, He was an expert in his own line.

shidomi (矢獨密), *n.* 【植】 the Japan quince.

shidoro (四途亂に), *ad.* in confusion; disorderly. —しどろもどろになる, to be thrown into great confusion.

shiei (市營), *n.* municipal management; municipalization (市有). —市營にする, to municipalize; transfer to municipal management. ¶ 市營事業, a municipal undertaking [enterprise].

shieki (私益), *n.* personal gain [profit]; private interest.

shieki (使役), *n.* employment; work; service; 【軍】 fatigue duty. —使役する, to employ; put to work. ¶ 使役動詞, 【文】 the causative verb.

shien (賜宴), *n.* an Imperial dinner.

shietageru (虐げる), *vt.* to oppress; tyrannize; ill-treat.

shifu (師傅), *n.* a tutor; a mentor.

shifuku (私腹), *n.* one's own pocket. —私腹を肥やす, to feather one's nest.

shifun (私憤), *n.* personal spite.

shigā (葉卷煙草), *n.* a cigar.

shigai (市外), *n.* the suburbs; the outskirts; the environs. —市外の電車線, a suburban electric-car line.

shigai (市街), *n.* a town; a city; a (city-)street (通). ¶ 市街電車, a tram-car 【英】; street-car 【米】. —市街戰, street fighting. —市街鐵道, a tramway 【英】; a street-railway 【米】.

shigai (死骸), *n.* a corpse; a dead body; remains.

shigaisen (紫外線), *n.* 【化】 ultra-violet rays.

shigaku (史學), *n.* historiology; history.

shigaku (視學), *n.* a school-inspector (人): school inspection (事). ¶ 視學官, a government school-inspector.

shigaku (詩學), *n.* poetry; prosody.

shigamitsuku (獅噛みつく), *vt.* to clasp; cling *to*.

shigan (志願), *n.* desire (志望); application (申込); volunteering (特志の). —志願する, to desire; apply *for*; volunteer *for*; go in *for*. ¶ 志願兵, a volunteer. —志願者, a volunteer; a candidate; an applicant.

shigarami (柵, 梱), *n.* a stockade; wattled work; a hurdle.

shigaretto (紙卷煙草), *n.* a cigarette.

shigatsu (四月), *n.* April.

shigeki (史劇), *n.* a historical play [drama].

shigeki (刺戟, 刺激), *n.* stimulation; incentive; incitement. —刺激する, to stimulate; excite; irritate; incite; jar; give an impetus *to*. ¶ 刺戟物, a stimulus; a stimulative; an irritant.

shigeki (繁き), *a.* ❶ (繁茂) dense; thick. ❷ (頻繁) frequent; repeated; incessant (絶えざる).

shigeku (繁く), *ad.* ❶ (繁茂) densely; thickly. ❷ (頻繁) frequently; often; repeatedly; incessantly (絶えず). —足繁く通ふ, to visit a person [repair to a place] frequently.

shigemi (繁み), *n.* a thicket; a bush.

shigen (資源), *n.* resources.

shigeru (茂·繁る), *vi.* to thicken; be thick; be dense. —茂った, dense; thick; luxuriant. (葉の繁った木, a tree thick with leaves.)

shigeshige (繁繁), *ad.* frequently; very often; again and again.

shigi (鴫), *n.* 【鳥】 the snipe (俗稱).

shigi (私議), *n.* ❶ (私見) personal opinion [views]. ❷ (陰口) backbiting. —私議する, to criticize in secret; speak ill of a person behind his back; backbite.

shigi (思議する), *vi.* to think; conceive. —思議すべからざる, unthinkable. ☞ *fushigi*.

shigo (死語), *n.* a dead language; an obsolete word (廢語).

shigo (死後), *ad.* after one's death; posthumously; post-mortem 【羅】. —死後の名を成す, to die a glorious death.

shigo (私語), *n.* secret talk; mutter; whisper. —私語する, to whisper; mutter; talk in a low voice.

shigoken (子午圈), *n.* 【天】 a meridian circle.

shigoki (扱帶), *n.* a waistband; an under-sash.

shigoku (至極), *ad.* very; extremely; exceedingly.

shigoku (扱く), *vt.* to draw [work] through the hand.

shigosen (子午線), *n.* 【天】 the meridian.

shigoto (仕事), *n.* work; task; job (賃仕事); labour (勞役);

needlework (針仕事). —仕事してゐる, to be at work. —仕事を始める [に取掛かる], to set to (work); go to business. —近頃仕事が急がしい, I am now kept pretty busy. ¶ 仕事師 ① (勞働者) a labourer; a workman. ② (消防夫) a fireman.

shigure (時雨), *n.* a drizzle; a drizzling shower.

shigureru (しぐれる), *vi.* to drizzle.

shigusa (科), *n.* 【劇】an action; a gesture; business.

shigyō (始業), *n.* commencement [outset] of work. —始業する, to commence work (a lessons); open school. ¶ 始業式, the opening ceremony (學校等の).

shiha (支派), *n.* a branch.

shihai (支配), *n.* management (處理); government (統治); rule (同上); control (管理); jurisdiction (管轄). —支配する, to manage; govern; rule; reign *over*; dominate (*over*). —情に支配される, to be influenced by passion. ¶ 支配人, a manager. (總支配人, a general manager.)

shihajimeru (仕始める), *vt.* to commence; set to (work). ☞ *chakushu* (着手する).

shihan (師範), *n.* ❶ (人) a master; a teacher. ❷ (事) teaching; instruction. ¶ 師範學校, a normal school; a training school.

shihan (紫斑), *n.* 【醫】petechia [*pl.* -æ]; petechial spots.

shiharai (支拂), *n.* payment; discharge (返濟); settlement (勘定). —支拂期限を過ぎた, [*a.*] overdue. —支拂不能に陷る, to become insolvent. —支拂を停止する, to suspend [stop] payment. ¶ 支拂日, the pay-day. —支拂高, amount paid (due). —支拂延期令, moratorium. —支拂期日, the date of payment; the due date; usance (外國爲替の). —支拂命令, an order for payment. —支拂人, a payer. —支拂能力, solvency. —支拂請求書, a demand-note.

shiharau (支拂ふ), *vt.* to pay; honour (手形を); cash (小切手を); defray (支辨). —手形を支拂ふ, to meet a note; pay a bill.

shihei (紙幣), *n.* paper-money; paper currency; a (bank-)note; a bill (米). ¶ 十圓紙幣, a ten-*yen* note.

shihen (四邊), *n.* the four sides. ¶ 四邊形, a quadrilateral.

shihi (市費), *n.* municipal expenses.

shihi (私費), *n.* private expense [cost]; private fortune (私財).

shihitsu (試筆), *n.* the first writing of the year.

shiho (試補), *n.* a probationer. ¶ 司法官試補, a judicial probationer.

shihō (四方), *n.* four sides [quarters]; all sides [directions]; the cardinal points (東西南北). —五尺四方, five feet square. —四方に, on all sides [hands]; on every side [hand]; all around [about]. —四方八方から攻める, to attack an enemy from all quarters.

shihō (司法), *n.* the judicature; administration of justice. ¶ 司法部, the judicature. —司法大臣, the Minister of (State for) Justice. —司法官, a judicial officer; the judiciary (全體). —司法警察, the judicial police. —司法權, judicial power; jurisdiction. —司法省, the Department of Justice; the Judicial Department.

shihō (私法), *n.* private law.

shihō (私報), *n.* a private report (telegram, 電報).

shihōdai (仕放題に), *ad.* as one pleases [wishes]. —彼は我儘の仕放題だ, He does whatever he pleases.

Shihōhai (四方拜), *n.* the worship of the gods in all quarters.

shihon (資本), *n.* capital; capital fund. —資本を集注する, to invest capital solely *on*. ¶ 資本家, a capitalist. (資本家階級, the capitalist classes.) —資本主義, capitalism. —資本稅, a capital levy; a levy on capital.

shihyō (指標), *n.* an index; 【數】a characteristic.

shihyō (師表), *n.* a model; a pattern, a mirror.

shii (椎), *n.* 【植】Pasania cuspidata (oak の一種·學名).

shii(undō) (示威-運動), *n.* a demonstration.

shii (私意), *n.* self-will; one's own will.

shii (思惟する), *vt.* to think; consider.

shiiku (飼育する), *vt.* to rear; breed; raise. ¶ 飼育場, a breeding ground.

shiin (子音), *n.* a consonant.

shiin (死因), *n.* the cause of death. —死因を確める, to ascertain [find out] the cause of death.

shiin (私印), *n.* a private seal.

shiina (粃), *n.* a blasted ear (of corn).

shiira (しいら), *n.* 【魚】the dolphin.

shiire (仕入), *n.* laying [buying] in; stocking; purchase. ¶ 仕入帳, an invoice [a bought] book. 仕入物, stock-in-trade; ready-made goods.

shiireru (仕入れる), *vt.* to buy; lay in (goods; a stock); stock a shop *with.*

shiiru (强ひる), *vt.* to press; force; compel. —寄附を强ひる, to lay a person under contribution. —人に酒を强ひる, to force [press] wine upon a person; press a person to drink; ply a person with *sake.*

shiiru (誣ひる), *vt.* to lay a false charge; slander; defame.

shiisuru (弑する), *vt.* to murder (one's lord or father).

shiitake (椎茸), *n.* ❶【植】Cortinellus shiitake (fungus の一種·學名). ❷ dried mushrooms.

shiite (强ひて), *ad.* by force; by compulsion; forcibly; insistently (しつこく). —强ひて言へば, if I insist on it. —强ひてなさしむ to force [compel; drive; impel] to do [into action]. —强ひてなすには及ばない, You need not compel yourself to do it. —强ひて御賛成を求める譯ではありません, I do not mean to force my opinion upon you.

shiji (支持), *n.* support; maintenance. —支持する, to support; keep; maintain; sustain; uphold. ☞ *sasaeru.*

shiji (四時), *n.* the four seasons; the whole year. —, *ad.* all the year round; at all seasons.

shiji (私事), *n.* personal [private] affairs; a private matter. —人の私事に立入る, to enter into another's private affairs.

shijimaru (窘まる), *vi.* to diminish; dwindle. ☞ *chijimaru.*

shijimi (蜆), *n.* 【貝】Corbicula leana (學名).

shijin (私人), *n.* an (a private) individual; a private person.

shijin (詩人), *n.* a poet. ¶ 女流詩人, a poetess. —平凡(な)詩人, a verse-monger; a poetaster.

shijitsu (史實), *n.* a historic(-al) fact [truth].

shijo (士女), *n.* men and women.

shijō (市場), *n.* a market; a market-place. —市場で賣買する, to market. ¶ 公開市場, a market overt.

shijō (至情), *n.* deep feeling [affection]; one's true heart.

shijō (私情), *n.* personal feelings; personal affection [regard].

shijō (紙上の), *a.* paper. —紙上の空論, an academical argument. —紙上を以て, through the press.

shijū (四十), *n.* forty; the fortieth (第四十). —四十代の人 a quadragenarian.

shijū (四重), *n.* fourfold.

shijū (始終), *ad.* ❶ (始から終迄) (*a*) from beginning to end; all along: (*b*) all the time [while]; early and late (旦暮). ❷ (いつも) always; at all times. ❸ (絕えず) constantly; perpetually. —始終お世話樣です, Thank you for your frequent kindness.

shijūgara (四十雀), *n.* 【鳥】the Manchurian great-tit (big oxeye の一種·學名).

shijuku (私塾), *n.* a private school.

shijun (諮詢), *n.* inquiry. —諮詢する, to consult; make inquiry. ¶ 諮詢機關, an advisory organ; a consultative body.

shijutsu (施術), *n.* an operation; a surgical operation.

shika (鹿), *n.* the Japanese deer; the deer: a stag (赤牡鹿); a doe (牝鹿); a hind (赤牝鹿).

shika (しか), *ad.* only; but. —これしか外に何もない, That is all there is. —一度しか見たことない, I have only seen it once.

shika (市價), *n.* market-price [-value]; quotations (相場).

shika (紙價), *n.* the price of paper. —洛陽の紙價を高からしむ, to raise the price of paper in the city.

shika (翅果), *n.* 【植】a samara.

shika (詩化する), *vt.* to poetize; poeticize.

shika (詩歌), *n.* poetry; Chinese poems and Japanese odes; a poetical composition.

shika (齒科), *n.* dentistry; dental surgery. ¶ 齒科醫, a dentist; a dental surgeon. —齒科術, dentistry.

shika (賜暇), *n.* a leave (of absence); furlough. —一週間の賜暇を得て, on a week's leave (of absence).

shikabane (屍), *n.* a corpse; a dead body.

shikaeru (仕替へる), *vt.* to make [change] anew; do over again (し直す).

shikaeshi (仕返し), *n.* revenge; retaliation; tit for tat. —仕返しする, to return; revenge; retaliate.

shikai (四海), *n.* the four seas; the (whole) world (天下).

shikai (司會), *n.* chairmanship; the chair. —司會する, to preside *over*; take the chair. —A 氏の司會で, under Mr. A's chairmanship. ¶ 司會者, the chairman; the toast-master (饗宴の).

shikai (市會), *n.* a city [municipal] assembly. ¶ 市會議員, a member of a municipal assembly. —市會議事堂, a city [town] hall.

shikai (死灰), *n.* ashes; cinders.

shikai (視界), *n.* the field of vision; eyeshot; view.
shikajika (爾爾), *a.* such (and such). ——, *ad.* so and so.
shikake (仕掛), *n.* ❶ (仕組) device; contrivance; works. ❷ (半途) being half-done. ❸ = *shihajime*. ❹ (規模) a scale. ¶ 電氣仕掛, electric device. —仕掛花火, a set piece; set fireworks.
shikakeru (仕掛ける), *vt.* ❶ =*chakushu*. ❷ (設備) to set up; frame; lay. ❸ (挑む) to challenge; force *upon*. —喧嘩を仕掛ける, to pick a quarrel *with*; force a quarrel *upon*. —人に話を仕掛ける, to accost [speak to] a person. —しかけた仕事がある, I have a work on hand.
shikaku (四角), *n.* a square; a quadrangle. —四角の, square. —四角四面な, stern; staid; stiff. (四角四面な人, a square-toes; a square-toed person.)
shikaku (刺客), *n.* an assassin. =*sekikaku*.
shikaku (視角), *n.* an optic [a visual] angle.
shikaku (視覺), *n.* the sense of sight; sight; vision. ¶ 視覺器, a visual organ; an organ of vision.
shikaku (資格), *n.* qualification; capacity; competence. —資格ある, qualified; competent; able; capable. (資格ある教師, a certificated [qualified] teacher.) —資格を與へる, to qualify; capacitate. —資格を失ふ, to be disqualified *from*. ¶ 資格檢定試驗, a qualifying examination. —資格證明書, a certificate of qualification.
shikaku (爾く), *ad.* so; so much.
shikakubaru (四角張る), *vi.* to be formal; be stiff; be starchy. —四角張ッた, stiff; starchy; ceremonious.
shikameru (顰める), *vt.* to wrinkle. —顔を顰めて, with drawn [frowning] face; with knitted brows.
shikamezura (顰面), *n.* a grimace; a frown (眉をひそめた); a wry face. —顰面する, to make [cut; pull] a face [faces]; make grimaces; pucker up the face.
shikamo (而も), *ad.* ❶ (其上に) moreover; furthermore; too; yet; and more. ❷ (それにも係らず) with all; notwithstanding; for all that. ——, *conj.* and; yet; but. —富貴にして而も樂しからざる人, those who are wealthy and yet unhappy. —深くして而も澄んでゐる, to be both [at once] deep and clear. —僕がそれを手に入れた, 而も安く, I got [bought] it, and that, too, at a low price.
shikan (士官), *n.* a regimental [company] officer; an officer. ¶ 士官學校, the military academy. —士官候補生, an officer candidate.
shikan (齒冠), *n.* 【齒科】a crown.
shikaneru (仕兼ねる), *vi.* to hesitate [scruple; be reluctant] to do.
shikanominarazu (加之), *ad.* moreover.
shikansetsu (指關節), *n.* 【解】 a phalangeal joint.
shikaraba (然らば), *conj.* and (then); (but,) then; if so; if it be so; in the case; now. —求めよ然らば與へられん, Ask, and it shall be given you.
shikarashimuru (然らしむる), *v.* to cause to be so; make it so. —境遇の然らしむる所, the outcome of the circumstances. —怠慢の然らしむる所である, to be due to negligence; come of [result from] negligence.
shikarazareba (然らざれば), *conj.* or; else; or else; otherwise; if not so. —吾に自由を與へよ然らざれば死を與へよ, Give me liberty or give me death. —孜々として勉めよ, 然らざれば失敗せん, Work hard, otherwise [or else] you will fail.
shikarazu (然らず), *vi.* not to be so. ——, *ad.* no. —大に然らず, far from it; anything but.
shikaredomo (然れども), *conj.* however; nevertheless.
shikari (然り), *ad.* yes; so; certainly. —然り大に然り, I quite agree with you.
shikaru (叱る), *vt.* to scold; rate; chide. —叱り飛ばす, to blow up; rate roundly; storm *at*. —ひどく叱りつける, to rebuke sharply; give a severe scolding.
shikarubeki (然るべき), *a.* proper; suitable; due. —萬事然るべくお頼み申します, I beg you to settle the matter as you may think best.
shikaruni (然るに), *conj.* but; however; nevertheless; and yet; while (on the contrary).
shikarunochi (然る後に), *ad.* then; and then.
shikashi (然·併し), *conj.* Ⓢ 乍併. but; however; though; nevertheless; (and) yet. —多くの缺點はあるが然し尙紳士たるを失はない, He has many faults, but still he is a gentleman.
shikata (仕方), *n.* ❶ (方法) a method; a way. ❷ (手段, 方策)

a way; means; help. ❷ (身振) gesture. —仕方を示す, to show the way [how to do it]. —仕方がないと諦める, to abide by the inevitable; be resigned to fate; accept the situation. —今となっては仕方がない, There is, indeed, no help for it now. —さう怒ッたって仕方がない, It is no use getting so angry.

shikato (確と), *ad.* for certain; exactly; definitely. —手をしかと握る, to take firm hold of a hand. —僕には確とは言へない, I cannot say for certain.

shikatsu (死活), *n.* life and death. ¶ 死活問題, a vital question; a question of vital importance [life and death].

shikatsume (鹿爪らしい), *a.* serious; staid; prim; consequential. —鹿爪らしく, seriously; consequentially.

shikazu (如かず), *v.* ❶ (及ばぬ) not to be better than. ❷ (如くはない, 越したことはない) to be best (to do); be most advisable (to do). —百聞一見に如かず, "One eye-witness is better than ten hearsays."

shike (時化), *n.* ❶ (暴風雨) stormy [inclement; rough] weather; stress of weather. ❷ (不漁) scarcity of fish; poor fishery [catch]. —時化を喰ふ, to be driven by stress of weather.

shikei (死刑), *n.* death; capital punishment; death penalty. —死刑に處する, to condemn to death; put to death; send to the scaffold. ¶ 死刑執行, execution. (死刑執行命令, a death-warrant. —死刑執行者, an executioner; a hangman.)

shikei (私刑), *n.* lynch, lynching.

shikei (紙型), *n.* 【印】 a papier-maché mould; a (paper) matrix.

shikekomu (しけこむ), *vi.* to slip *into* (for a stay).

shiken (私見), *n.* ❶ a personal view. ❷ (卑見) one's (humble) view.

shiken (私權), *n.* 【法】 private right.

shiken (試驗), *n.* an examination; a test; an experiment (實驗); a trial (ためし). —試驗の準備をする, to make preparations for examination. —試驗を受ける, to sit for an examination; uudergo an examination; go in for examination. —悉く試驗問題に答へる, to answer all the questions; clear an examination paper. —— **-suru,** *vt.* to examine; test; try; make a trial; 【化】 test (試藥で). —英語の試驗する, to examine in English. ¶ 人物試驗, a character test. —試驗賣買, trial sales. —試驗委員, an examiner. —試驗所, an experiment station. —試驗管, a test-tube. —試驗紙, 【化】 test-paper. —試驗答案, an examination-paper.

shikeru (濕ける), *vi.* to be moist; be wet; damp.

shikeru (時化る), *vi.* to storm; rage; be disturbed.

shiki (式), *n.* ❶ (儀式) a ceremony; rites. ❷ (形式) a form; a style; a type (型式); a pattern. ❸ 【數】 an expression; 【理】 a formula; 【論】 a mood. —式を學げる, to hold [perform] a ceremony. ¶ 純日本式, an orthodox Japanese style [fashion].

shiki (敷), *n.* ❶ (下敷) a stand. ❷ (敷蒲團) a mattress. ❸ = *shikikin.*

shiki (士氣), *n.* martial spirit; military spirit; morale of troops.

shiki (四季), *n.* the four seasons. —四季の眺め, views of the four seasons. ¶ 四季拂, quarterly payment.

shiki (死期), *n.* the last hour; the hour of death.

shiki (指揮), *n.* command; order; direction. —指揮する, to command; order; direct. —指揮の下にある, to be under the command [direction] *of.* ¶ 指揮棒, a baton (樂長の). —指揮官, a commander; an officer in command. —指揮者, a director; a conductor.

shiki (しき), only; such. —それしきの怪我で, at such a slight injury.

shikibetsu (識別), *n.* discrimination; discernment. —識別する, to discriminate; discern; distinguish.

shikibu (式部), *n.* the Board of Ceremonies. ¶ 式部長, the Grand Master of Ceremonies. —式部官, a master of ceremonies.

shikibuton (敷蒲團), *n.* ❶ a mattress. ❷ (座蒲團) a cushion.

shikichi (敷地), *n.* a site; a ground.

shikichō (色調), *n.* the tone of colour; tonality (繪畫の).

shikifu (敷布), *n.* a sheet; a bed-sheet.

shikigawa (敷皮), *n.* a fur-skin cushion.

shikii (敷居, 閾), *n.* the threshold (入口の); the door-sill (戶の). —二度とこの家の敷居を跨ぐな, Never darken these doors again.

shikiishi (鋪石), *n.* a paving-stone.

shikiji (式辭), *n.* an address at a ceremony.

shikijitsu (式日), *n.* a day of celebration.

shikijō (式場), *n.* a ceremonial hall; the place where the ceremony is held.

shikijō (色情), *n.* sexual passion; carnal desire.

shikiken (識見), *n.* knowledge; discernment. ☞ *kenshiki*.

shikikin (敷金), *n.* deposit; caution-money; margin.

shikima (色魔), *n.* a Lothario; a libertine.

shikimi (樒), *n.* 【植】 the star-anise tree; the star-aniseed tree.

shikimō (色盲), *n.* 【醫】 colour-blindness.

shikimono (敷物), *n.* ❶ (絨毯) a rug; a carpet. ❷ a matting (莫蓙); a cushion (座蒲團). —敷物を布く, to lay a carpet.

shikin (試金する), *vt.* to assay. ¶ 試金石, a touchstone.

shikin (資金), *n.* capital (資本); funds; money; a fund (基金). —資金缺乏の爲め, for want [lack] of funds.

shikin (賜金), *n.* a government grant.

shikiri (仕切), *n.* ❶ (區劃) partition; boundary. ❷ (決算) settlement of accounts.

shikiri (頻·切に), *ad.* ❶ (間斷なく) continually; incessantly; constantly. ❷ (度々) frequently; at frequent intervals. ❸ (切に) eagerly; intently; persistently (しつこく); urgently. ❹ (ひどく) hard; very much. —切りに勉强する, to work hard. —切りに或る方針を勸める, to urge a person to a course of action. —雪が頻りに降ってゐる, It snows thick and fast.

shikiru (仕切る), *vt.* ❶ (區劃) to divide with a partition; partition. ❷ (決算) to settle accounts.

-shikiru (頻る), *vi.* to do much; do continuously (絕えず). —吹き(降り)頻る, to blow (rain) hard; blow (rain) incessantly.

shikisai (色彩), *n.* colouring; coloration.

shikise (仕着せ), *n.* clothes given by an employer; a livery.

shikisha (識者), *n.* an intellectual man; a learned man.

shikishi (色紙), *n.* thick fancy paper (for writing or painting).

shikiso (色素), *n.* ❶ colouring-matter; pigment. ❷【生】 pigment.

shikitaku (色澤), *n.* lustre; gloss.

shikitari (慣例), *n.* =*kanshū*.

shikiutsushi (敷寫), *n.* tracing. —敷寫しする, to trace *over*; make a tracing *of*.

shikka (失火), *n.* an accidental fire. —昨夜失火あり, An accidental fire broke out last night.

shikka (膝下), *ad.* below [at] the knee. —父母の膝下を辭してより, since I left my parents.

shikkai (悉皆), *ad.* all; entirely; wholly. ☞ *mina, zenbu*.

shikkari (しっかり), *ad.* ❶ (確實に) certainly; surely. ❷ (堅固に) firmly; fast; tight(-ly); steadfastly. —しっかりした, ① (確實な) certain. ② (堅固な) strong; firm; steady. —しっかり握ってゐる, to take fast hold *of*. —人物がしっかりしてる, to be a man of firm [steady] character. —しっかりしろ (氣絕者に言ふ), Keep up your spirits. —しっかりしろ, もう子供ぢゃあるまい, Act firmly; you are no longer a child.

shikke (濕氣), *n.* =*shikki*.

shikkei (失敬), *n.* ❶ (無禮) disrespect; impoliteness; rudeness. ❷ (別れの挨拶) good-bye. —失敬な, disrespectful; impolite; rude. —これで失敬します, I will now take my leave.

shikken (失權), *n.* loss of right.

shikki (漆器), *n.* a lacquer (-ware); a lacquered ware.

shikki (濕氣), *n.* dampness; humidity; moisture. —濕氣ある, damp; humid; moist.

shikkirinashi (しっきりなしに), *ad.* continuously; uninterruptedly. —しっきりなしに喋る, to talk incessantly.

shikko (疾呼する), *vi.* to call out (loudly); shout; yell.

shikkō (執行), *n.* execution; performance (遂行); discharge (同上); enforcement (實行). —三年間の執行猶豫附で, with three years' grace. —刑の執行を猶豫する, to postpone the execution of a sentence. **—— -suru**, *vt.* to execute; carry into execution; perform; enforce. —令狀を執行する, to execute a warrant. —死刑を執行する, to execute the sentence of death. ¶ 執行委員, an executive committee. —執行官, an executive officer; an executor. —執行機關, an executive organ. —執行令狀, a writ of execution; *fieri facias* 【羅】. —執行者, an executor; a performer.

shikkoku (漆黑の), *a.* jet-black.

shikku (疾苦), *n.* affliction; distress; suffering.

shikku (疾驅する), *vi.* to run swiftly; run hard; spur on; drive at high speed.

shikkui (漆喰), *n.* mortar; plaster; 【建】stucco.

shikkuri (しっくり), *ad.* exactly; to a nicety; to a T. —しっくりと合ふ, to agree to a T (氣心が); fit to a nicety (衣服が).

shikkyaku (失脚), *n.* failure; fall. —失脚する, to fall; fail.

shiko (四股), *n.* the limbs. —四股を踏む, to stamp (to begin wrestling).

shiko (指呼の間にある), to lie within hail.

shikō (私交), *n.* private intercourse (relations). —私交上で, from private relations.

shikō (私行), *n.* private conduct.

shikō (伺候する), *v.* to visit; wait *on* [*upon*]; pay respects (*to*).

shikō (祗候), *n.* a lord-in-waiting. ¶ 錦鷄間祗候, a Lord-in-waiting of the Hall of the Golden Pheasant.

shikō (思考), *n.* thinking; consideration; contemplation (熟考). —思考する, to think; consider.

shikō (施行), *n.* enforcement; carrying out. —施行する, to enforce; put in force [operation]; carry out. —發布の日より施行す, to come into force on the day of its promulgation.

shikō (嗜好), *n.* taste; liking; fancy. —嗜好に適する, to suit one's taste. ¶ 嗜好物, table-luxuries.

shikomi (仕込), *n.* ❶ (教育) education; tuition. ❷ (訓練) training; breeding. ❸ =*shiire*.

shikomizue (仕込杖), *n.* a sword-stick; a sword-cane.

shikomu (仕込む), *vt.* ❶ (教育) to teach; educate. ❷ (訓練) to train; breed. ❸ =*shiireru*. ❹ (刀などを) to fit (a sword) into a cane. —馬を仕込む, to train [break in] a horse. —音樂家に仕込む, to bring him up as a musician. —辯護士として仕込まれる, to be bred a lawyer.

shikon (紫紺), *n.* purple-blue.

shikon (齒齦), *n.* 【解】the gingiva; the gum. ¶ 齒齦炎, 【醫】gingivitis.

shikonashi (しこなし), *n.* bearing; carriage: management (處理). —しこなす, ① to act gracefully; bear decently. ② to carry out; manage.

shikori (凝), *n.* an induration; a node.

shikoro (錣), *n.* neck-plates.

shikoru (凝る), *vi.* to get [have] a node [an induration].

shikotama (しこたま), *ad.* much; a great deal *of*; lots [heaps] *of*. ☞ *takusan*.

shikotsu (趾骨, 指骨), *n.* 【解】a phalange, phalanx.

shiku (市區), *n.* a municipal [an urban] district; streets. ¶ 市區改正, street [city] improvement.

shiku (死苦), *n.* the agony of death.

shiku (詩句), *n.* a verse; a stave.

shiku (如く), *v.* to be equal *in*; be no less...than; equal [rival] (a person) *in*. ☞ *shikazu*. —斯くするに如くはない, Nothing is better than to do so; There is nothing better than doing so.

shiku (敷·布く), *vt.* ❶ (擴げ敷く) to spread (a carpet); lay (the floor) *with* (a carpet); cover (the bottom) *with* (paper). ❷ (下に敷く) to sit *on*. ❸ (敷設) to lay. ❹ (鋪裝) to pave (a street) *with* (bricks). ❺ (發布) to promulgate. ❻ (陣地·砲列を) to take up (a position); range (guns). —道路に砂利を敷く, to gravel the road; cover the road with gravel. —鐵道を敷いて交通に便する, to facilitate communication by laying a railway. —さあどうぞお敷き下さい, Come, sit on the cushion, please.

shikujiri (縮尻), *n.* a failure; a blunder; a mistake.

shikujiru (しくじる), *vi.* ❶ (失敗す) to fail; make [commit] a mistake; make a blunder. ❷ (失職す) to be cashiered; be dismissed; be sacked. —またしくじった, Another blunder!

shikumi (仕組), *n.* ❶ (計畫) a design; a plan; a plot. ❷ (劇·小說の) a plot. —仕組む, ① to design; plan. ② to plot; set up a plot.

shikushiku (しくしく), *ad.* ❶ (泣く貌) bitterly. ❷ (痛む貌) painfully. —しくしく泣く, to weep bitterly; sob. —腹がしくしく痛む, to have a pricking pain in the stomach.

shikutsu (試掘), *n.* prospecting. —試掘する, to prospect; work experimentally.

shikyo (死去), *n.* death; decease. —死去する, to die; pass away.

shikyō (市況), *n.* the condition [tone; state] of a market.

shikyō (司教), *n.* a bishop.

shikyō (示教), *n.* advice; opinion; guidance; showing.

shikyoku (支局), *n.* a branch office.

shikyoku (私曲), *n.* jobbery; graft 【米·俗】.

shikyū (子宮), *n.* 【解】the uterus; the matrix; the womb. ¶ 子宮痙攣, uterine spasm. —子宮內膜炎, endometritis.

shikyū (支給), *n.* supply; provision. —支給する, to supply; provide (*with*).

shikyū (止球), *n.* 【野球】a block-ball.

shikyū (死球), *n.* 【野球】a dead ball.

shikyū (至急), *n.* urgency. —至急の, urgent; pressing; immediate. —至急に, urgently; with all speed [haste]; immediately. —至急お目にかゝりたい, I want to see you as soon as possible. ¶ 至急親展, urgent and personal.

shikyūshiki (始球式), *n.* 【野球】 opening the game; pitching the first ball.

shima (島), *n.* an island. —取り附く島もない, to have no one to turn *to*. ¶ 島人, an islander.

shima (縞), *n.* stripes; striped pattern. —縞の服, a dress of striped cloth.

shima (揣摩), *n.* conjecture; surmise. —揣摩する, to conjecture; surmise; (make a) guess.

shimagara (縞柄), *n.* pattern; marking.

shimaguni (島國), *n.* an insular country; an island-empire [-kingdom]. ¶ 島國根性, an insular spirit; insularism.

shimai (仕舞), *n.* end; close; finish (完成). —仕舞まで, to the end; to the last. (仕舞まで聞く, to hear him out. —仕舞まで見る, to sit out a play, game, *etc.*) —仕舞になる, to come to an end (終る); be out (つきる); be finished (仕事など); be all gone (品物); be sold out (賣切れる). —仕舞には解る, to come to light in the end. —もう是でお仕舞よ, Let us leave off now.

shimai (姉妹), *n.* sisters. ¶ 姉妹語《艦》, a sister language《warship》. —姉妹篇, a companion volume.

shimanagashi (島流), *n.* exile [banishment] to an island.

shimanezumi (花金鼠), *n.* 【哺乳】 the chipmunk, chipmuck; the chipping squirrel.

shimari (締), *n.* ❶ (緊縮) tightness. ❷ (戸締) locking; fastening the doors. ❸ (心の) prudence; thrift (節約). —締りのない, loose (build); lax (government); thriftless. —締りのある, compact [well-knit] (body or frame); thrifty. —財布の締りがない to have no control over his pursestrings. —窓の締りをする, to secure [fasten] a window. —彼は締りがない, He needs [wants] screwing [winding] up.

shimaru (締る), *vi.* ❶ (戸が) to shut; close; be closed [shut]. ❷ (人が) to become sober; become thrifty. —締ッた口元, a well-knit mouth.

shimatsu (始末), *n.* ❶ (次第) circumstances; facts; the particulars. ☞ *tenmatsu*. ❷ (結末) settlement; decision. ❸ (處置) management. ❹ (節約) thrift. —始末する, to manage; settle; economize (儉約); be frugal (同上). —始末に負へぬ, unmanageable; unruly; incorrigible. —何とか始末をつける, to settle the matter somehow. —始末書を取られる, to have to hand in an account (of one's failure; blunder, &c.) —あとの始末は誰がする, Who is to set it to rights after?

shimatta (失策ッた), *int.* hang it; the deuce; Heavens!

shimau (仕舞ふ), *vt.* ❶ [終, 了] to end; close; finish. ❷ [藏] to put away; lock up (錠を下ろして); store (貯藏). ❸ (取引市場) to undo (a bargain); close (an account). —店を仕舞ふ, ① (閉店) to shut up [close] shop. ② (廢業) to close [give up] business; shut up shop. —今日は之で了ひませう, We will now finish up for to-day.

shimauma (斑馬), *n.* 【哺乳】 the zebra.

shime (蠟嘴), *n.* 【鳥】 the Eastern (common) hawfinch.

shime (締, 〆), *n.* ❶ (合計) the total; the sum-total. ❷ (紙十束の締) a bundle; a ream of a hundred *jō*. —〆金五十圓也, total...fifty *yen*.

shime (七五三 -繩), *n.* a rope with tufts of straw《paper》.

shimedaka (締高), *n.* the total amount; the sum-total.

shimedasu (閉出す), *vt.* to shut [lock] (a person) out.

shimegane (締金), *n.* a buckle.

shimegi (締木), *n.* a press; a wedge. —締木に掛ける, to put to a press.

shimei (氏名), *n.* the full name.

shimei (死命), *n.* death. —死命を制する, to spell death *to*; have a grip [hold] *upon*.

shimei (使命), *n.* a mission. —使命を果す, to perform one's mission.

shimei (指名), *n.* nomination; naming. —指名する, to nominate; name; designate. ¶ 指名入札, tenders by specified bidders; private tenders.

shimekasu (搾糟), *n.* oil-cake.

shimekiri (締切), *n.* close;

"closed." (貼紙). ¶ 締切時間, the closing-time.

shimekiru (締切る), *vt.* to close. —あの門はいつも締切ってある, That gate is always kept shut.

shimekorosu (絞殺す), *vt.* to strangle [throttle] to death; string up【俗】.

shimekukuru (締括る), *vt.* ❶ (緊束) to bind; tie up. ❷ (監督) to supervise; superintend. ❸ (支配, 管理) to manage; control; regulate.

shimen (四面), *n.* the four sides; all quarters [directions]. —四面楚歌の聲, to be invested by the enemy; be surrounded on every side by the enemy.

shimen (死面), *n.* a death-mask.

shimen (紙面), *n.* space; paper. —紙面の都合で, for want of space. ¶ 紙面經濟, economy of space.

shimeri (濕), *n.* ❶ moisture; dampness. ❷ (降雨) a rain.

shimeru (占める), *vt.* ❶ (座席等を) to take; hold; fill (地位を). ❷ (占有) to occupy; possess; take into one's possession. —好地位を占める, to occupy a good position. —上席を占める, to take the top seat.

shimeru (締める), *vt.* ❶ (緊締する) to tighten; fasten; brace; tie closely. ❷ (閉ぢる) to shut [close] (the door or gate); shut up (shop); lock [fasten] (the door) (締りをする). ❸ (捩る) to wring; screw up. ❹ (合計する) to count up (the items); cast up (accounts); sum up (the gains). —〆て, altogether; in all; in the total; to sum up. (〆て百圓になる, to come to ¥100 in all [altogether].) —螺旋を締める, to tighten a screw. —鷄を締める, to wring a fowl's neck. —帶を締める, to put on [wear] a sash. —喉を締める, to grip a person's throat.

shimeru (濕る), *vi.* to moisten; dampen. —濕っぽい, wet; moist; damp.

shimeshi (示), *n.* ❶ (示すこと) showing. ❷ an example (手本); a warning (戒め); a lesson (教訓, 懲しめ). —下々に示しがつかぬ, cannot keep those under one in order; cannot keep the subordinates under control.

shimeshi (襁褓), *n.* a diaper.

shimeshiawasu (諜合す), *vi.* to prearrange; preconcert; agree beforehand.

shimesu (示す), *vt.* to indicate; show; point out (指示). —模範を示す, to set a person an example. —抵抗の氣勢を示す, to show fight.

shimesu (濕す), *vt.* to wet; moisten; dampen. —喉を濕す, to wet one's whistle; moisten the throat.

shimeta (占めた), *int.* Ⓢ 占め占め, capital!; all right!; I've got it. —占めた, もうこっちのものだ, Capital, we've got it now.

shimeyaka (しめやかに), *ad.* gently; quietly; lonely. —しめやかな話, a quiet talk.

shimi (衣魚), *n.*【蟲】the walking-fish; the silver-fish [-moth; -tail; -watch].

shimi (汚點), *n.* a stain; a blot; a smear; a smudge. —汚點ある, stained; spotted; smeared.

shimideru (滲出る), *vi.* to ooze; exude.

shimijimi (染染), *ad.* fully; quite; thoroughly. —しみじみ言って聞かせる, to explain [admonish] carefully.

shimikomu (染込む), *vi.* to soak *into*; sink *into*; penetrate (*into, through*, to). —舊道徳の染み込んだ頭, a brain imbued with old morals. —紙にインキが染み込む, The ink soaks into paper.

shimin (市民), *n.* citizens; townspeople; townsmen.

shimin-jōtai (嗜眠狀態), *n.*【醫】sopor; lethargy.

shimiru (染みる), *v.* ❶ (滲透) to penetrate; percolate *through*. ❷ (感動) to come to heart; sink into the mind; pierce. ❸ (痛を感ず) to smart. —身に沁む風, a cutting [biting] wind. —仕事に身が染まない, to have no interest in one's work. —社會全般に染み渡る, to spread over [pervade] the whole society.

shimittare (しみったれ), *n.* ❶ (吝嗇) (*a*) (事) stinginess; niggardliness: (*b*) (人) a miser; a stingy fellow. ❷ (意氣地なし) (*a*) (事) spiritlessness: (*b*) (人) a poor-spirited person. —しみったれた, sordid; shabby. —そんなしみったれを言ふな, Don't say such sordid things.

shimizu (清水), *n.* spring water.

shimo (下), *n.* ❶ (下ナ) the lower part; the foot (席の); the bottom (等級の). ❷ (被治者) the governed; the people. ❸ (下層社會) the lower classes. ❹ (目下) one's inferiors; one's men (部下); a servant (召使). —下に, ① [*ad.*] under; below; downward. ② [*prep.*] under; below; down. —下を憐む, to be con-

siderate to one's inferiors. ¶ 下半期, the latter half-year.
shimo (霜), *n.* frost; white frost; hoar-frost. —霜が降る, It frosts.
shimobashira (霜柱), *n.* rime; hoar-frost. —霜柱が立つ, Rime forms (*on*).
shimobe (僕), *n.* a (man-)servant; a servant.
shimodoke (霜解), *n.* frost thaw; thawing. —霜解けがする, It thaws; The frost breaks.
shimofuri (霜降), *n.* & *a.* pepper-and-salt.
shimogare (霜枯の), *a.* withered by the frost; frost-nipped; wintry. —霜枯れの空, a wintry sky. ¶ 霜枯時, the dull winter season.
shimogeru (霜萎る), *vi.* to be frost-bitten.
shimogoe (下肥), *n.* night-soil.
shimojimo (下下), *n.* the common people; the populace; the masses.
shimon (指紋), *n.* a finger-print. ¶ 指紋法, the finger-print method [system]; dactylology.
shimon (諮問), *n.* question; inquiry, enquiry. ☞ ***shijun.*** ¶ 諮問案, a draft submitted for opinion; a *questionnaire* [佛].
shimotaya (仕舞家), *n.* a family living in ease without any trade.
shimoyake (凍瘡), *n.* a chilblain; a frost-bite. —凍瘡にかかった, chilblained; frost-bitten.
shimoyōke (霜除), *n.* a frost-shed; a protection against frost.
shimuke (仕向), *n.* ❶ (待遇) treatment; usage. ❷ (發送) forwarding. —仕向ける, ① to treat; deal *with*; behave [act; conduct] *towards.* ② to forward. ¶ 仕向先, the destination.
shimyaku (支脈), *n.* ❶ (鑛山の) a shoot. ❷ (山脈) a spur; an offset; a branch.
shin (心), *n.* ❶ (こゝろ) the heart. ☞ ***shinsoko.*** ❷ (中心) the centre; the heart. ❸ (木髓) pith; heartwood. ❹ (果心) a core. ❺ (燈火の) a wick. —帶の心, the padding of a sash. —心のある飯, half-boiled rice.
shin (臣), *n.* ❶ (臣下) a subject. ❷ (家來) a retainer; a vassal.
shin (信), *n.* ❶ (信義) faith; fidelity; sincerity. ❷ =***onshin.*** ❸ (信仰) faith; belief. ❹ (信任) credit; trust. —信を置く, to trust; believe; put trust [faith] *in.* —朋友に信を失ふ, to lose credit with one's friend.
shin (神), *n.* a god; a deity; a spirit.
shin (眞), *n.* ❶ (眞實) truth. ❷ (眞正) genuineness. ☞ ***shinno.*** —眞の友, one's true friend. —眞に迫る, to be true to nature; be the very picture *of*; be lifelike; be vivid. (描寫眞に迫る, to be painted 《described》 to life.)
shin (新), *a.* new; novel; fresh.
shin (箴), *n.* a warning; a counsel.
shin (親), *n.* ❶ a relative; a kinsman; a consanguinity (血緣). ❷ =***washin*** (和親).
shin (寢に就く), to go to sleep; retire (for rest).
Shina (支那), *n.* China. ☞ ***chūka*** (中華). ¶ 支那語, (the) Chinese (language). —支那人, a Chinese. —支那料理, Chinese cookery; a Chinese dinner.
shina (品), *n.* an article (品物); goods (同上); stuff (地質); quality (品質).
shina (科), *n.* ❶ =***shigusa.*** ❷ (事情) circumstances. ❸ (嬌態) an affected pose; attitudinization; coquetry. —嬌態[しな]をつくる, to pose affectedly; attitudinize; strike an attitude; coquet.
-shina (しな), when; at the moment *of.* —出しなに, when one is about to start [leave].
shinabiru (凋びる), *vi.* to wither; wilt; shrivel. —しなびた蜜柑, a shrivelled orange.
shinadareru (しなだれる), *vi.* ❶ (萎び垂れる) to droop down. ❷ (媚び寄る) to nestle up *to.*
shinagire (品切), *n.* being out of stock; being sold out (賣切). ¶ 品切値段, famine prices.
shinai (市內), *n.* the city. —市內に, in the city; within the city limits. —市內及び市外線, urban and suburban lines.
shinai (竹刀), *n.* a bamboo-sword; a fencing-stick.
shinai (親愛な), *a.* dear; beloved.
shinamono (品物), *n.* an article; goods.
shinan (指南), *n.* teaching; instruction. —指南する, to teach; instruct; give lessons *in.* ¶ 指南車, a compass (vehicle).
shinan (新案), *n.* a new [novel] idea; a new [fresh] design; a novelty. ¶ 新案意匠登錄, registration of a new design. —新案特許, a utility model patent.
shinaoshi (仕直し), *n.* doing over again; renewal. —仕直す, to do over again; renew.
shinasadame (品定), *n.* criticism. ☞ ***hinpyō.***
shinau (撓ふ), *vi.* to bend; be pliant.
shinawake (品別), *n.* assortment.
shinayaka (嫋かな), *a.* ❶ (柔軟な) pliant; supple; lithe. ❷ (纖細な) slender; delicate. ❸ (優美な) graceful; elegant. —しなや

かな手, slender hand.
shinbari (心張-棒), *n.* a prop; a bar; a fastening.
shinbei (親米), *n.* pro-Americanism.
shinbi (審美), *n.* æsthetic beauty. —審美的, æsthetic(-al). ¶ 審美學, æsthetics.
shinbō (心棒), *n.* an axle; an axis (軸); a mandrel (旋盤の); a piston-rod (活塞桿); a stem (獨樂〔こま〕の).
shinbō (辛抱), *n.* ❶ (忍耐) patience; endurance. ❷ (堅忍) perseverance; fortitude. ❸ (勘辨) forbearance. —辛抱强い, patient; persevering; indefatigable. —辛抱する, to endure; bear; stand; forbear; put up *with*; persevere *in*. —もう少しの辛抱です, Put up with it a little longer.
shinbō (深謀-遠慮), *n.* profound design and far-sightedness.
shinboku (神木), *n.* a sacred tree.
shinboku (親睦), *n.* friendliness; intimacy; friendly [intimate] relations. —會員相互の親睦を圖る, to promote the mutual intimacy of its members. ¶ 親睦會, a friendly meeting; a social meeting [gathering].
shinbun (新聞-紙), *n.* a newspaper; a paper; a journal; the press (總稱). —今日の新聞に, in to-day's paper. —新聞の報ずる所に依れば, according to the papers; the paper says; it says in the papers that.... —新聞を取る, to take in a newspaper【英】; take a newspaper【米】; subscribe to a newspaper. ¶ 新聞業, journalism. —新聞配達人, a newsman. —新聞縦覽室, a newsroom. —新聞記者, a journalist; a newspaperman; a pressman; a news-writer; the members of the press (記者連). (新聞記者席 (特に衆議院の), a press-gallery.) —新聞購讀者, a newspaper reader. —新聞社, a newspaper office. —新聞賣子, a newsboy. —新聞賣捌所[取次所], a newspaper-agency.
shincha (新茶), *n.* new [first] tea.
shinchaku (新著), *n.* a new [fresh] arrival. ¶ 新著書籍, newly-arrived books.
shinchi (新地), *n.* land newly laid out; reclaimed land (埋立地).
shinchiku (新築), *n.* building; construction. —新築の, new-built; newly-built. —新築する, to build (newly).
shinchin-taisha (新陳代謝), *n.* ❶ renewal; replacement; substitution. ❷【生】metabolism; anagenesis.
shinchō (身長), *n.* stature; height.
shinchō (伸長), *n.* elongation; prolongation. —伸長する, to elongate; prolong; extend.
shinchō (伸張), *n.* stretch; expansion; extension. —伸張する, to stretch (四肢など); expand (國威·民權など); extend (同上).
shinchō (深長な), *a.* deep; profound. —意味深長である, to be pregnant with meaning; have a deep meaning [significance].
shinchō (新調の), *a.* new; newly-made 〘-bought〙; spick and span.
shinchō (愼重な), *a.* prudent; careful; cautious; circumspect. —愼重の言葉, guarded language. —愼重な態度を執る, to use prudence. —愼重に審議する, to discuss with great care.
shinchoku (進捗する), *vi.* to make progress; proceed.
shinchū (心中), *n.* the heart; the mind. —心中平かならず, to be ill at ease. —心中で嗤ふ, to laugh to oneself.
shinchū (眞鍮), *n.* brass. —眞鍮製の, brazen; brass.
shindai (身代), *n.* property; fortune. —身代を拵へる, to make [amass] a fortune; build up a [one's] fortune. —身代を潰す, to run [go] through one's fortune.
shindai (寢臺), *n.* a bedstead; a sleeping-berth (汽車の); a truckle-bed (輪附寢臺). ¶ 寢臺車, a sleeping-car; a sleeper; a sleeping saloon.
shindaikagiri (身代限), *n.* = *hasan*. —身代限をする, to become bankrupt [insolvent]; be ruined; be brought to ruin.
shindan (診斷), *n.* medical examination;【醫】diagnosis. —診斷する, to diagnose; examine. ¶ 診斷書, a medical certificate.
shinden (神殿), *n.* a sanctuary.
shinden (新田), *n.* a newly-reclaimed rice-field.
shindō (神童), *n.* an infant prodigy; a phenomenon.
shindō (新道), *n.* a newly-made [-opened] road.
shindō (震動, 振動), *n.* ❶ (振動) oscillation; vibration; swing. ❷ (震動) vibration; tremor; shock. —震動する, to shake; tremble; quake; vibrate; swing (振動); oscillate (同上).
shindoku (親獨), *n.* Germanophilism; pro-Germanism.
shin'ei (眞影), *n.* a photograph; a portrait.
shin'ei (親英), *n.* Anglophilism.
shin'en (神苑), *n.* a sacred garden

within the precincts of a shrine.
shiñen (深淵), *n.* a deep abyss; a bottomless gulf; the depths.
shiñen (深遠な), *a.* profound; abstruse; unfathomable (意味などの); recondite (教義などの).
shinfutsu (親佛), *n.* Francophilism; Gallophilism.
shingai (心外な), *a.* regrettable; mortifying. —とは心外の至りだ, It is to be deeply regretted that...
shingai (侵害), *n.* encroachment; invasion; infringement. —侵害する, to encroach *upon*; invade; infringe. ¶ 侵害者, an invader; a trespasser.
shingai (震駭する), *v.* to be struck with terror.
shingaku (心學), *n.* ethics; moral philosophy. ¶ 心學道話, talks [chats] on morals.
shingaku (神學), *n.* theology. ¶ 神學校, a theological school. --神學博士, a doctor of divinity. (D. D. と略す).
shingan (心眼), *n.* the mind's eye.
shingan (心願), *n.* the heart's desire; an earnest wish (prayer).
shingao (新顏), *n.* a new-comer; a new face.
shingara (新柄), *n.* a new pattern [design].
shingari (殿, 殿軍), *n.* the rear; the rear guard. —殿する, to bring up the rear.
shingeki (進擊), *n.* an assault; a charge; an attack. —進擊する, to charge; assault; storm; (make an) attack; advance to the attack.
shingen (森厳な), *a.* solemn; grave; awe-inspiring.
shingen (箴言), *n.* a maxim; an aphorism; an apothegm.
shingen (震源), *n.* 【地文】 the centrum; the focus; the seismic centre [focus]; the centre of disturbance; the epicentre (震央).
shingenbukuro (信玄袋), *n.* a reticule; a cloth-pouch.
shingetsu (新月), *n.* a new moon; a crescent moon; the prime of the moon.
shingi (信義), *n.* faith; faithfulness; fidelity.
shingi (眞僞), *n.* genuineness; truth; authenticity.
shingi (審議), *n.* discussion; deliberation; consideration. —審議する, to discuss; deliberate; consider. —審議中である, to be on the *tapis*; be under discussion. —審議を遂げる, to bring a discussion to a close.
shingin (呻吟する), *vi.* to groan; howl; utter a cry of pain.
shingo (新語), *n.* a new word.
shingō (信號), *n.* a signal; signalling. —信號する, to signal; make [give] a signal. ¶ 信號旗, a signal flag; 【航】 a jack. —信號機, a semaphore (特に鐵道の). —信號手, a signalman; a signaller.
shingu (寢具), *n.* bedding.
shingun (進軍), *n.* march; advance. —進軍する, to march; advance. ¶ 進軍喇叭, a marching bugle.
shiñi (心意), *n.* mind; spirit; soul. ☞ *seishin.*
shiñi (神意), *n.* divine will; providence.
shiñi (眞意), *n.* ❶ real intention [motive]; underlying motive. ❷ (眞の意味) true meaning.
shinibana (死花を咲かす), to die a glorious death.
shinigami (死神), *n.* the god of death. —死神に憑(つ)かれる, to be possessed by the god of death.
shinigane (死金), *n.* ❶ (葬禮金) money laid by for one's funeral expenses. ❷ (使用して效力なき金) money spent to no purpose. ❸ (利用せぬ金) unutilized money. —死金を遣ふ, to spend money to no purpose.
shinigao (死顏), *n.* a dead face.
shinigiwa (死際に), *ad.* at the point [time; hour] of death; in the article of death; at one's last moment.
shinihaji (死恥を曝す), to die a shameful death.
shiñiki (震域), *n.* earthquake-area; seismic area.
shinikui (仕惡い), *a.* hard; difficult.
shinime (死目), *n.* the moment of death. —親の死目に會ふ, to attend one's parent's death-bed; be at one's parent's death-bed.
shinimizu (死水をとる), ❶ to give a person water to drink at the point of his death. ❷ to nurse the dying as one's last duty.
shinimonogurui (死物狂), *n.* desperate struggle. —死物狂ひで, desperately; with desperation; for soul and body (一生懸命で). (死物狂ひで戰ふ, to fight with desperation.) —死物狂ひになる, to be driven to desperate struggle.
shinin (死人), *n.* a dead person; the dead. —死人に口なし, "A dead man does not speak."
shiniokureru (死後れる), *v.* to outlive; survive.
shinise (老舗), *n.* a shop of long standing; an old-established shop.
shinisokonau (死損ふ), *vi.* to fail to die; outlive one's time.
shinitaeru (死絶える), *vi.* to die out; become extinct.
shiniwakareru (死別れる), *v.* to be parted [separated] by death *from*; be bereaved by death *of*;

lose. ⌈devotee; the faithful.⌉
shinja (信者), *n.* a believer; a⌋
shinji (心事), *n.* the mind; one's heart; one's motive (動機). —心事を吐露する, to open oneself [one's heart] *to.* ⌈[epoch].⌉
shinjidai (新時代), *n.* a new age⌋
shinjikēto (シンヂケート), *n.* 【經】 a syndicate.
shinjin (信心), *n.* faith; devotion (歸依); piety (敬神). —信心する, to believe *in* (god); be devout. ¶ 信心家, a pious man; a man of piety; a believer (信者).
shinjin (神人), *n.* ❶ (神と人) gods and men. ❷ (神の如き人) a godlike man.
shinjin (新人), *n.* ❶ a new man; an ultramodernist. ❷ (悔改めて新生命を得たる人) a regenerate.
shinjitsu (信實), *n.* sincerity; faithfulness; integrity. —信實な, sincere; faithful.
shinjitsu (眞實), *n.* truth; reality. —眞實の, real; true. ⌈sentiment.⌉
shinjō (心情), *n.* feeling; heart;⌋
shinjō (信條), *n.* creed; credendum; an article of faith.
shinjotai (新世帶), *n.* new housekeeping; a new home.
shinju (樗), *n.* 【植】 the ailanto; the false [Japan] varnish-tree; the tree of Heaven [the Gods].
shinju (眞珠), *n.* a pearl. ¶ 摸造眞珠, olivet. —眞珠母, a pearl-shell. —眞珠採取, pearl-fishery. (眞珠採取業者, a pearl-fisher; a pearl-diver.)
shinjū (心中), *n.* a suicide of lovers; a double suicide. —心中する, to commit a double suicide. ¶ 合意心中, a double suicide by mutual consent. —無理心中, a forced double suicide.
shinjutsu (心術), *n.* mind; heart.
shinjutsu (賑恤する), *v.* to give alms; give a thing in charity.
shinjutsu (鍼術), *n.* acupuncture.
shinka (神化), *n.* deification.
shinka (眞價), *n.* the intrinsic [true; real] value. —眞價を認める, to appreciate the true value.
shinka (進化), *n.* evolution; development. —進化する, to evolve; develop. ¶ 進化論, evolutionism; the theory of evolution. (進化論者, an evolutionist.)
shinkai (新開), *n.* new reclamation. ¶ 新開地, ① a newly-reclaimed land; newly-reclaimed rice-fields. ② newly-opened streets (quarters); a new town (village).
shinkan (信管), *n.* a fuse.
shinkan (神官), *n.* a *Shintō* priest.
shinkan (宸翰), *n.* an Imperial letter [epistle].
shinkan (新刊), *n.* a new publication. ¶ 新刊紹介, announcement of new books; a book-notice.
shinkara (心から), *ad.* heartily; from (the bottom of) one's heart.
shinkei (神經), *n.* a nerve. —神經を尖らす, to become nervous. —そりや神經のせゐでせう, I think that is owing to your nerves. ¶ 神經病, neurosis; a nervous disease; neuropathy. —神經中樞, a nerve-centre. —神經家, a nervous man. —神經過敏, hyperæsthesia. (神經過敏になる, to have a bit of nerves.) —神經質, nervous temperament. (神經質の人, a man of nervous temperament; a nervous man; a sensitive person.) —神經衰弱, neurasthenia; nervous prostration [debility]. (神經衰弱になる, to suffer from nervous debility.) —神經痛, neuralgia.
shinken (眞劍), *n.* ❶ a real sword. ❷ (本氣) earnestness; seriousness. —眞劍で, ① with a (real) sword. ② in sober [dead] earnest. —眞劍の勝負をする, to fight hilt to hilt [with swords].
shinken (親權), *n.* 【法】 parental power [authority].
shinken (審檢), *n.* examination; inquiry. —審檢する, to examine; inquire *into.*
shinketsu (心血を濺ぐ), to devote one's whole self *to*; go heart and soul *into.*
shinki (心氣, 神氣), *n.* the spirit. —心氣頓に爽快を覺える, to feel suddenly refreshed.
shinki (心機), *n.* the mind; mental attitude. —心機頓に一轉せり, My mind suddenly took a new turn.
shinki (辛氣臭い), *a.* tedious; fretful. ——, *vi.* to feel fretful.
shinki (神器), *n.* the sacred [holy] treasures. ⌈奇の, novel.⌉
shinki (新奇), *n.* novelty. —新⌋
shinki (新規の), *a.* fresh; new. —新規に, freshly; newly. —新規蒔直しする, to begin the world anew; make a fresh start; do a thing over again.
shinki (振起する), *vt.* to encourage; stimulate; shake up; stir up; spur (*to*).
shinkigen (新紀元), *n.* a new era. —新紀元を開く [劃する], to make an epoch; mark a new era.
shinkijiku (新機軸), *n.* a new device [departure]; originality. —新機軸を出す, to strike out a line for oneself.
shinkin (宸襟), *n.* the heart of the Emperor. —宸襟を安じ奉る, to ease the heart [mind] of the

Emperor; set the heart of the Emperor at ease.
shinkin (親近の), *a.* intimate.
shinkirō (蜃氣樓), *n.* a mirage; *fata Morgana* 【伊】.
shinko (糝粉), *n.* rice-dough. ¶ 糝粉細工, figures made with rice-dough.
shinkō (信仰), *n.* 【神】 faith; belief; devotion. ¶ 信仰治療, faith-cure [healing]. —信仰箇條, the articles of faith. —信仰者, a believer.
shinkō (深更に), *ad.* at dead of night; at midnight; in the small hours of the morning.
shinkō (深厚な), *a.* deep; profound; great. —深厚の同情を寄せる, to show deep sympathy.
shinkō (振興), *n.* encouragement; rousing; promotion. —振興する, to rouse; stir up; promote; encourage; help forward.
shinkō (親交), *n.* (close) friendship; intimacy.
shinkō (進行), *n.* progress; advance; course. —事件の進行, the progress of the case [matter]. —進行する, to advance; progress; move on. —進行中, in [going on] progress; under way (船·汽車·事件の); under steam (特に汽船の). (進行中の汽車から飛降りる, to jump down from a moving [running] train.) ¶ 進行係, one charged with the task of carrying a bill through. —進行曲, the march.
shinkō (進講する), *v.* to give a lecture in the presence of a high personage.
shinkoku (申告), *n.* statement; declaration; report. —申告する, to state; declare; report. —選擧費用の虛僞の申告, false declaration of election expenses. ¶ 申告者, reporter. —申告書, a declaration (稅關への); a report.
shinkoku (深刻な), *a.* deep; profound; penetrating. —深刻に描出する, to describe with great penetration.
shinkoku (親告), *n.* ❶ (自ら告ぐること) personal information. ❷ 【法】 (被害者の告訴) the sufferer's complaint. —親告する, to inform ⟪complain⟫ personally; send in a personal letter of complaint. ¶ 親告罪, an offence punishable on the lodgment of complaint.
shinkokyū (深呼吸する), *vi.* to draw a deep breath; breathe hard.
shinkon (新婚), *n.* a new marriage [wedding]. ¶ 新婚夫婦, a newly-wedded couple. —新婚旅行, a honeymoon trip; a wedding tour [trip].
shinkōshoku (深紅色), *n.* scarlet; deep crimson; burning-red.
shinku (辛苦), *n.* hardship; trial.
shinkū (眞空), *n.* vacuum. ¶ 眞空管 [球], a vacuum tube. —眞空療法, vacuum-treatment.
shinkuimushi (果蠹蟲), *n.* 【蛾】 the codling-moth (苹樹等の).
shinkyō (心境), *n.* the heart; the inner world.
shinkyō (信敎), *n.* religious belief. —信敎の自由, the liberty of conscience [religious belief].
Shinkyō (新敎), *n.* 【基督】 Protestantism. ¶ 新敎徒, a Protestant.
shinkyokumen (新局面), *n.* a new phase [situation; aspect]. —新局面を展開する, to develop a new phase; take a fresh course.
shinkyū (新舊の), *a.* old and new.
shinkyū (進級), *n.* promotion; preferment. —進級する, to be promoted; be raised in rank.
shinmai (新前, 新參), *n.* a green hand; a new hand [comer]; a novice.
shinme (新芽), *n.* a sprout; a shoot; a flush.
shinmei (身命), *n.* life. —身命を賭して, at the risk of one's life. —身命を抛つ, to lay down one's life.
shinmei (神明), *n.* a divinity; a deity; Heaven.
shinmenboku (眞面目), *n.* earnestness; seriousness. ☞ *majime*.
shinmi (親身), *n.* a blood-relation; a relative; a kindred; kinsfolk. —親身に世話する, to look after with sincerity.
shinmichi (新道), *n.* ❶ a new road; a newly-built highway (街道). ❷ a narrow street; an alley.
shinmin (臣民), *n.* a subject; the people.
shinmiri (しんみり), *ad.* heartily; seriously; closely.
shinmitsu (親密), *n.* intimacy; familiarity (*with*); closeness. —親密な, intimate; close; familiar.
shinmon (審問), *n.* inquiry, enquiry; trial; examination. —審問する, to try; inquire, enquire; examine.
shinmotsu (進物), *n.* a present; a gift.
shinmyō (神妙な), *a.* praiseworthy; admirable. —神妙に, praiseworthily; admirably; quietly (おとなしく). —御用だ, 神妙にしろ, You are wanted; obey quietly.
shinnen (信念), *n.* faith; belief.
shinnen (新年), *n.* a new year; the New Year's Day. —新年の賀狀, the New Year's letter of greetings. —新年お目出度う, I wish you a Happy New Year.

¶ 新年宴會, a New Year dinner-party; a New Year's feast [banquet].

shinneri-muttsuri (しんねりむッつりの), *a.* morose; surly; crusty.

shin-ni (眞に), *ad.* truly; in truth [fact]; really. ☞ ***makotoni.***

shinnichi (親日), *n.* pro-Japan; Japanophilism. —親日的, pro-Japanese. ¶ 親日家, a Japanophile.

shinnin (信任), *n.* confidence; trust; credit. —信任する, to confide *in* (a person); place confidence *in* (a person). —厚く陛下の御信任を得る, to enjoy the great confidence of His Majesty. ¶ 信任狀, credentials; a letter of credence. —信任投票, vote of confidence.

shinnin (信認), *n.* acknowledgment. —信認する, to acknowledge; accept as true.

shinnin (新任), *n.* new appointment. ¶ 新任披露, announcement of an appointment.

shinnin (親任), *n.* a direct Imperial appointment. —親任する, to appoint directly [personally]. ¶ 親任官, an official directly appointed by His Majesty. —親任式, the installation ceremony.

shin-no (眞の), *a.* ❶ (本當の) true; real; genuine. ❷ (全くの) utter; perfect.

shinnō (親王), *n.* an Imperial (a Royal) prince; a prince of the Blood.

shinnyo (眞如), *n.* absolute [fundamental] truth.

shinnyū (侵入), *n.* ❶ (侵略) invasion; raid. ❷ (闖入) intrusion; trespass. —侵入する, ① to invade; encroach *on*; raid *into*. ② to intrude; break [force] *into*. ¶ 侵入者, ① an invader. ② an intruder.

shinnyū (新入), *n.* new arrival. ¶ 新入生, a new student; a fresh(-man) (大學一年の).

shinnyū (滲入), *n.* infiltration; percolation; endosmosis. —滲入する, to infiltrate *into*; percolate *through*; permeate.

shinnyū (進入), *n.* penetration; ingress; entry. —進入する, to penetrate *into*; enter.

shino (篠), *n.* 【植】 a bamboo-bush. —篠突く雨, a heavy rain; a downpour.

shinō (震央), *n.* 【地文】 the epicentre, epicentrum; the seismic vertical.

shinobi (微行), *n.* walking in disguise; going incognito.

shinobideru (忍出る), *vi.* to steal out; go out secretly; slip out (of the house); slip off [away].

shinobikomu (忍込む), *vi.* to steal [slip; creep] *into*; enter secretly.

shinobishinobi (忍忍), *ad.* secretly; quietly; surreptitiously.

shinobiwarai (忍笑), *n.* a suppressed laughter; a silent [secretive] laugh; a giggle; a titter. —忍笑ひする, to giggle; titter; laugh in one's sleeve.

shinobu (葱), *n.* 【植】 Davallia bullata (hare's foot fern の一種).

shinobu (忍ぶ), *vt.* ❶ (忍耐) to bear; endure; suffer (insolence); put up *with*; pocket [stomach; swallow] (an insult). ❷ (潜伏) to conceal [hide] oneself. —忍んで, ① patiently; with patience. ② stealthily; by stealth. —世を忍ぶ, to live in concealment [hiding]; lie [fly] low. —苦痛を忍ぶ, to stand [endure] pain; bear one's cross. —爲す《云ふ》に忍びない, I cannot bear to do《mention》it. —私は去るに忍びなかった, I could not tear myself away.

shinobu (偲ぶ), *vt.* to think *of*; reflect *on* (the past); yearn after (慕ふ). —古を偲びて, for old sake's sake.

shinogi (鎬を削る), to cross [measure] swords *with*; fight each other with desperation.

shinogu (凌ぐ), *vt.* ❶ (凌駕) to surpass *in*; exceed in; excel *in*; tower [rise] *above*; outdo (one's opponent). ❷ (切拔ける) to tide [bridge; get] over (a difficulty); stand [hold] out (a crisis); ride out (the storm) (船が). ❸ (輕視) to slight [put a slight upon] (one's superiors). ❹ (我慢) to bear (the heat; hunger); endure. ❺ (防ぐ) to keep off (the cold); take shelter (from the rain). —雨露を凌ぐに足る小屋, the cottage which can shelter us from the rain. —高さ富士を凌ぐ, to surpass Mt. Fuji in height; rise above Mt. Fuji. —一時凌げる[凌ぎがつく], We can bridge it over for a while.

shinōkōshō (士農工商), *n.* the military, agricultural, industrial, and mercantile classes; the soldier, farmer, artificer, and merchant.

shinonome (東雲), *n.* dawn; daybreak. —紅染むる東雲の空, the deep-red morning sky.

shinpa (新派), *n.* a new school.

shinpai (心配), *n.* ❶ (憂慮) anxiety; solicitude. ❷ (配慮) care; concern. ❸ (不安) uneasiness; disquiet. ❹ (危惧) fear; apprehension; misgiving. ❺ (心勞, 氣苦勞) worry; trouble. —心配な,

anxious; uneasy; apprehensive. —金の心配で, through pecuniary troubles. —心配の餘り, in the excess of care. —心配でたまらぬ, to be tormented [oppressed] with anxiety; be harassed with apprehension. —心配なく暮す, to live at ease; dwell secure. —心配御無用, never mind [fear]. **—— -suru,** *v.* to be anxious [solicitous]; care; feel concern; be concerned; fear; be afraid *of*; feel [be] uneasy; be ill at ease; worry oneself; be worried; be troubled. —人に心配させる, to keep a person in suspense; cause anxiety to another. —心配すると頭が禿げる, "Many cares make the head white."

shinpan (新版), *n.* a new edition [publication].

shinpan (審判), *n.* judgment; decision; award; trial (審問); umpireship (競技の). —審判する, to judge; try; act as an umpire [a referee]; umpire (in a game). ¶ 審判官, a judge; an umpire. —審判者, an umpire (野球); a referee (蹴球). (壘審判者, a field umpire).

shinpatsu (進發), *n.* march-off; march. —進發する, to march off [away]; leave camp.

shinpei (新兵), *n.* a (raw) recruit; a newly-levied soldier.

shinpenfushigi (神變不思議の), *a.* miraculous; supernatural.

shinpi (眞皮), *n.* 【解】the corium; the derma; the true skin.

shinpi (神祕), *n.* mystery; mysteriousness; miraculousness. —神祕な, mysterious; mystic; miraculous.

shinpi (深祕な), *a.* secret; strictly confidential.

shinpitsu (眞筆), *n.* a genuine writing; an autograph (自筆).

shinpitsu (親筆), *n.* an autograph, autography.

shinpo (進歩), *n.* progress; advance; improvement. —進歩的, progressive. —進歩する, to (make) progress; advance; improve. —長足の進歩をなす, to make rapid progress (*in*); advance by [take] long strides (*in*). ¶ 進歩黨, the progressives; the progressive party.

shinpu (新婦), *n.* a bride.

shinpuku (心服する), *vi.* to submit completely; bear obedience *to*; serve faithfully.

shinpuku (臣服する), *v.* to pay homage *to*; submit; be subject *to*.

shinpuku (振幅), *n.* amplitude.

shinpuku (震幅), *n.* the amplitude of an earthquake.

shinpyō (信憑する), *vt.* to rely *on* [*upon*]; believe; place confidence *in*. —信憑すべき, reliable; authentic; trustworthy. ¶ 信憑力, authenticity; reliability.

shinra-banshō (森羅萬象), *n.* universe; (universal) nature; all things.

shinrai (信賴), *n.* ● (賴り) reliance; dependence. ● (信任) confidence; trust. —信賴する, ① to rely [depend; count] *upon*; place reliance *on*. ② to confide *in*; trust; put [place] trust [confidence] *in*. —信賴すべき, reliable; trustworthy; faithful. —信賴し難い友, a dubious friend.

shinrai (神來), *n.* inspiration; a divine voice [whisper]. —神來の作, an inspired work.

shinrai (新來の), *a.* new-come; newly-arrived.

shinratsu (辛辣), *n.* bitterness; harshness; acrimony. **—— -na,** *a.* bitter; harsh; acrid. —辛辣な批評, a caustic criticism.

shinrei (心靈), *n.* a spirit; a soul.

shinrei (振鈴), *n.* ringing a bell; a hand-bell.

shinrei (浸禮), *n.* baptism (by immersion); immersion. ☞ *senrei*. 浸禮教會, the Baptist Church.

shinri (心理), *n.* mind; mental phenomena (心理現象); the condition of the mind (心理狀態); mental state (同上). —心理的, psychological; psychic(-al). ¶ 心理學, psychology; mental philosophy [science]. (心理學者, a psychologist.) —心理療法, psychotherapy, psychotherapeutics.

shinri (眞理), *n.* truth. —眞理の, true; truthful. —眞理を探求する, to search after truth.

shinri (審理), *n.* examination; trial. —審理する, to examine; sit *on* [*upon*]; try (事件·論點等).

shinrin (森林), *n.* a forest; a wood. ¶ 森林地方, a wooded country; a woodland. —森林保護, protection of forest; forest conservancy. —森林開拓, disafforestation.

shinrin (親臨), *n.* personal attendance of Emperor; Imperial visit. —親臨する, to be present in person; attend personally; pay a personal visit. —陛下の親臨を忝うする, to be honoured with an Imperial visit.

shinro (針路), *n.* a course; a direction. —針路を西に取る, to take a westerly course.

shinro (進路), *n.* a course; a path; an approach. —進路を開く, ① to open a way [path;

passage]. ② to make room; give way.

shinro (親露), *n.* pro-Russian- ⌈ism; Russophilism.

shinrō-shinpu (新郎新婦), *n.* a bride and a bridegroom; a newly-married couple.

shinrui (親類), *n.* a relation; a relative; a kindred. —親類である, to be related *to*.

shinryaku (侵略), *n.* invasion; aggression; raid. —經濟的侵略, economic invasion. —侵略する, to invade; encroach *upon*. ¶ 侵略戰, an aggressive war. —侵略者, a raider; an aggressor.

shinryo (深慮), *n.* deep thought; prudence; discretion. —深慮ある人, a deep thinker; a man of great discretion.

shinryō (臣僚), *n.* subjects. ¶ 内外臣僚, chief officers of the country and the chiefs [heads] of foreign missions.

shinryoku (新綠), *n.* fresh ver- ⌈dure.

shinsa (審査), *n.* ❶ (檢査) examination; inspection; inquiry. ❷ (判定) judgment. —審査する, to examine; inquire; inspect. ¶ 審査委員, a committee of inquiry; a hanging-committee (美術展覽會の); a jury (展覽會·共進會などの). —審査官, a juror; a judge; an examiner.

shinsai (震災), *n.* an earthquake disaster [calamity]. —震災を一層慘烈たらしめた大火災, the ravages of a great fire which aggravated the earthquake disaster. ¶ 震災地[區域], a district damaged by earthquake.

shinsai (親裁), *n.* Imperial decision [judgment]. —陛下の親裁を仰ぐ, to submit for Imperial decision.

shinsan (心算), *n.* mental calculation (あて); intention (積り). —心算が外れる, One's calculation goes wrong.

shinsan (辛酸), *n.* bitterness; hardship; sufferings. —世の辛酸を嘗める, to go through [suffer] many hardships; taste the bitters of life.

shinsatsu (診察), *n.* 【醫】 diagnosis; medical examination; consultation (患者から言ふ). —診察する, to examine (a patient); give an advice; diagnose. —診察を受ける, to consult a physician; be diagnosed; take medical advice. ¶ 診察日, a consultation day. —診察時間, consulting [consultation] hours. —診察料, consultation-fee; doctor's fee.

shinsei (申請), *n.* application; petition; 【法】 motion (裁判所へ). —申請する, to apply *for*; make application; move *for* (裁判所へ). ¶ 申請人, an applicant; a petitioner. —申請書, an application; a written application.

shinsei (神聖), *n.* holiness; sacredness; sanctity. —神聖な, holy; sacred; divine. —神聖にする, to consecrate; sanctify. —神聖を汚す, to desecrate. —神聖にして犯すべからず, to be sacred and inviolable.

shinsei (眞正の), *a.* true (courage; pest); genuine (article; courage; disease; letters; money); authentic (record; history); real (value).

shinsei (新製の), *a.* new-made.

shinseimen (新生面を開く), to put a new phase *on*; break new ground; open a new field.

shinsekai (新世界), *n.* a new world; the New World (西半球).

shinseki (臣籍), *n.* status of a subjects.

shinseki (親戚), *n.* a relation [relative]; relationship (親戚關係).

shinsen (神仙), *n.* a fairy. ¶ 神仙譚, a fairy-tale.

shinsen (神饌), *n.* an offering (to a god); oblation.

shinsen (浸染する), *vi.* to be infected *with* (a bad habit); be imbued [permeated] *with* (dangerous thoughts). ——, *vt.* to imbue; infect (the tissue, 病毒が); soak; saturate.

shinsen (深淺), *n.* shallowness and deepness; depth (深さ).

shinsen (新鮮), *n.* freshness. **—— -na**, *a.* fresh; new. —新鮮な空氣を入れる《吸ふ》, to let in 《breathe》 fresh air.

shinsetsu (深切, 親切), *n.* kindness; goodness; friendliness. —深切な, kind; friendly; obliging. —深切に, kindly; heartily; in a friendly manner.

shinsetsu (新設の), *a.* newly--established; newly-organized. —新設する, to establish [organize] newly; create.

shinsha (辰砂), *n.* 【鑛】 cinnabar.

shinsha (親炙する), *v.* to be brought up at another's feet.

shinshaku (斟酌), *n.* consideration; allowance; qualification. —斟酌する, to consider; take into consideration [account]; make allowances *for*.

shinshi (簎簇), *n.* a temple; a tenter; a tenter-hook.

shinshi (振子), *n.* 【理】 a pen- ⌈dulum.

shinshi (紳士), *n.* a gentleman; a man of position. —紳士淑女諸君, Ladies and Gentlemen! —紳士の體面を汚す, to disgrace one's position as a gentleman. ¶ 紳士道, gentlemanhood; gentlemanship. —紳士契約, a gentleman's agreement. —紳士錄, a directory; who's who; a court-guide [英].

shinshi (眞摯な), *a.* sincere; earnest; eager sober.

shinshi (參差), *ad.* irregularly; ruggedly; intricately (錯綜). —參差する, to be irregular.

shinshi (震死する), *vi.* ❶ (落雷で) to be killed [struck dead] by lightning. ❷ (地震で) to be killed by an earthquake.

shinshiki (神式), *n.* the *Shintō* rites [ritual].

shinshiki (新式), *n.* a new pattern [style]. —新式の, of a new pattern [style]; new-fashioned.

shinshin (心身), *n.* mind and body. —…に心身を委ねる, to put body and heart *into*.

shinshin (心神), *n.* mind. —心神喪失, mental derangement [unsoundness].

shinshin (津津), *ad.* brimmingly.

shinshin (深深), *ad.* ❶ deeply. ❷ chilly. —(夜が) 深々と更け渡る, to advance into deathlike silence.

shinshin (新進の), *a.* new; rising. ¶ 新進作家, a rising writer.

shinshitsu (心室), *n.* 【解】 the ventricles of the heart.

shinshitsu (寢室), *n.* a bedroom; a bedchamber; a cubicle (分劃寢室).

shinsho (信書), *n.* a letter. —信書の祕密, privacy of correspondence.

shinshō (心象), *n.* 【心】 images; imagery.

shinshō (心證), *n.* 【法】 free conviction; impression. —心證を害する, to make a bad impression.

shinshō (身上), *n.* ❶ (財產) a fortune; property. ☞ *shindai*. ❷ (とりえ) a merit; a forte. —身上持の上手な女, a good house-keeper; a frugal [thrifty] woman. ¶ 身上道具, household goods.

shinshō (眞症), *n.* a genuine disease.

shinshō (紳商), *n.* a merchant of position.

shinshō-bōdai (針小棒大の), *a.* exaggerated. —針小棒大に言ふ, to make a mountain (out) of a molehill; make an elephant of a fly.

shinshōgai (新生涯に入る), to enter upon a new life.

shinshoku (神色), *n.* the countenance; expression of the face. —神色自若として, with imperturbable calmness.

shinshoku (神職), *n.* a *Shintō* priest.

shinshoku (侵蝕, 浸蝕), *n.* 【地質】 erosion; corrosion; denudation. —浸蝕する, to denude; erode; bite in.

shinshoku (寢食), *n.* sleep and food; eating and sleeping. —寢食を共にする, to live in the same house [under the same roof] with a person. —寢食を忘れて看護する, to nurse a person regardless of oneself.

shinshu (進取の), *a.* progressive. —進取の氣象ある, pushing; go-ahead; enterprising.

Shinshū (眞宗), *n.* the *Shin* Sect; the Shin Shu.

shinshuku (伸縮), *n.* expansion and contraction; elasticity. ☞ *nobichijimi*. —伸縮自在の, elastic. —伸縮する, to expand or contract; be elastic.

shinshuku (振肅), *n.* strict enforcement. —振肅する, to enforce strictly. ¶ 官紀振肅, strict enforcement of government discipline.

shinshutsu (進出する), *vi.* to advance; make an advance (of three miles); debouch (into the open plain).

shinshutsu-kibotsu (神出鬼沒), *n.* sudden appearance and disappearance; miraculous swiftness. —神出鬼沒の怪賊, a robber who appears and disappears with amazing suddenness.

shinso (親疎), *n.* (the degree of) intimacy.

shinsō (神葬にする), *v.* to bury with the *Shintō* rites.

shinsō (眞相), *n.* the true [actual] state [condition]; real facts; bottom facts. —眞相を明かにする, to make the real state of affairs clear. —眞相を究める, to get at the root [bottom] of things; reach the truth.

shinsō (深窓), *n.* a most secluded chamber. —深窓の處女, a virgin living in seclusion.

shinsoko (心底), *n.* the bottom of one's heart; one's inmost heart; the heart of hearts. —心底から, whole-heartedly; from (the bottom of) one's heart.

shinsoku (神速な), *a.* swift; speedy; rapid.

shinsotsu (眞率な), *a.* simple (-hearted); frank; sincere.

shinsui (心醉する), *v.* to be charmed *with*; be fascinated *by*; be intoxicated *with*. —歐洲文明に心醉する, to be intoxicated with [be under the fascination of] European civilization.

shinsui (浸水), *n.* ❶ inundation; submersion. ❷ (船の) leakage; leaking. —浸水する, ① to be flooded; be submerged; be inundated. ② (船が) to leak; make water. ¶ 浸水家屋, submerged [flooded] houses; houses under water.

shinsui (薪水), *n.* firewood and water. —薪水の勞を取る, to do menial labour *for.*

shinsui (進水), *n.* launch; launching. —進水する, to launch (船を); be launched (船が). —進水式を擧げる, to hold the launching ceremony.

shintai (身體), *n.* the body; the person. —身體の構造, bodily structure. ¶ 身體檢査, physical examination.

shintai (神體), *n.* the image of a god.

shintai (進退), *n.* ❶ advance and retreat. ❷ (掛引) tact. ❸ (動作) movement; behaviour; manner. —進退する, to move. —進退谷まる; 進退兩難に陷る, to find oneself in an inextricable difficulty; be driven from post to pillar; be between the devil and the deep sea. —進退を共にする, to throw [cast] in one's lot *with.*

shintaku (信託), *n.* trust. —信託する, to entrust *with*; trust *to.* —人の信託に背く, to betray another's trust. ¶ 信託會社, a trust company.

shintaku (神託), *n.* an oracle; inspiration; a divine message [revelation]. —夢に神託を蒙る, to receive a divine message in a dream.

shintan (心膽), *n.* heart; courage. —心膽を練る, to foster courage.

shintan (薪炭), *n.* wood and charcoal; fuel; firing. ¶ 薪炭商, a wood and charcoal dealer; a fuel merchant.

shintei (心底), *n.* the bottom of the heart; the real intention (眞意). (—心底を見拔く, to see through a person's inmost heart.

shintei (進呈), *n.* presentation. —進呈する; to give; offer; present a (person with a thing; a thing to a person); make a present *of.* ¶ 進呈本, a presentation copy.

shinteki (心的), *a.* mental; psychial. ¶ 心的狀態, mentation; mental state.

shinten (進展), *n.* progress; development. —進展する, to progress; proceed; develop.

shinten (親展の), *a.* private; confidential; personal. ¶ 親展書, a confidential [personal] letter.

shinto (信徒), *n.* a believer.

shinto (森と), *ad.* still; in silence. —森とした, still; silent.

shintō (心頭), *n.* the heart; mind.

shintō (神道), *n.* Shintoism; the *Shintō* religion; the Way of the Gods. —神道の信者 [研究者], a Shintoist.

shintō (震盪, 振盪), *n.* concussion; shock. —震盪する, to shake; give a shock.

shintō (親等), *n.* degree of relationship [kinship].

shintō (滲透), *n.* 【理】 osmosis; permeation. —滲透する, ① [*vi.*] to permeate. ② [*a.*] osmotic; permeant.

shintsū (心痛), *n.* anxiety; concern; care; trouble; mental suffering; heart-ache. —心痛する, to be anxious [concerned] *about*; be troubled about; be grieved; feel uneasy.

shintsū (神通), *n.* communication of God; inspiration; afflatus. ¶ 神通力, divine power.

shinu (死ぬ), *vi.* Ⓢ 死する. to die; expire; pass away. —死せる, deceased; dead; departed. —死ぬまで, to the death [very last]; to the last hour of one's life; as long as any breath is left in one. —死んだ者と諦める, to give up a person for lost.

shiṅun (進運), *n.* advance; progress. —世の進運に伴ふ, to keep pace with the progress of the world.

shinwa (神話), *n.* a myth; mythology. ¶ 自然神話, nature myth. —神話時代, the mythical age.

shinwa (親和), *n.* ❶ affinity. ❷ [=*washin* (和親).]

shiṅya (深夜), *n.* midnight; the dead of night; the deep night. —深夜に, late at night; at midnight; at dead of night.

shiṅyaku (神藥), *n.* an elixir; a wonderful medicine; a sovereign remedy.

shiṅyaku-zensho (新約全書), [*n.* the New Testament.]

shiṅyō (信用), *n.* credit; confidence; trust. —信用する, to trust; give credit [credence] *to*; put trust *in*; have [place; repose] confidence *in.* —信用の出來る [置ける], trustworthy; creditable; reliable. —信用がある, to be trusted [credited]; have credit [influence] *with.* —世間の信用が薄い, to have little credit in the world. —信用に關はる, to affect one's credit. —信用を害する, to impair a person's credit. —彼の信用を失ふ, to lose credit with him. ¶ 信用借, credit debt. —信用保險, ① (身元) fidelity insurance. ② (資力) credit insurance. —信用狀, a letter of credit. —信用組合, a credit-union. —信用詐欺, a confidence trick.

shiṅyū (親友), *n.* an intimate [a bosom] friend; a chum.

shinzai (心材), *n.* heart-wood.

shinzan (深山), *n.* a deep mountain. ¶ 深山幽谷, deep mountains and dark valleys.

shinzan (新參-者), *n.* a new comer; a novice; a fresh blood.

shinzen (親善), *n.* friendship; friendly relations; close relationship. —親善な, intimate; familiar; close. —日支親善の實を擧げる, to realize close relationship between Japan and China.

shinzō (心臟), *n.* the heart. —心臟の鼓動, heart-throbs; beating [palpitation] of the heart. ¶ 心臟瓣膜, a valve of the heart; a cardiac valve. —心臟病, a heart-disease [-trouble]. —心臟肥大, dilatation of heart; 【生】diastole. —心臟麻痺, heart-failure; the failure [paralysis] of the heart.

shinzō (心像), *n.* an image; semblance.

shinzō (新造の), *a.* newly [lately]-built; new-coined (特に語句). —新造する, to make [build; construct] anew; coin (新語を); mint (同上).

shinzoku (親族), *n.* a relation; a relative. ☞ *shinrui*. ¶ 親族會,【法】a family council. —親族關係, relationship.

shinzui (眞髓), *n.* the pith; the essence; the soul. —武士道の眞髓, the essence of *Bushidō*.

shin-zuru (信ずる), *vt.* ❶ (確信) to believe; credit; give credit *to*. ❷ (信用) to trust; confide *in*; put trust *in*. ❸ (信仰) to believe *in*. —信じ難き, incredible; unreliable; hard to believe. —信ずべき筋より出でたる報知, a report from a reliable source.

shio (潮), *n.* ❶ tide. ❷ (機會) an opportunity; an occasion; a chance. ❸ (海水) sea water. —潮が滿ちる, The tide flows [rises]. —潮が退く, The tide ebbs [falls].

shio (鹽), *n.* (common) salt. —鹽按排する, to give the right flavour. ¶ 鹽製造《販賣》人, a salter.

shiō (雌黃), *n.* gamboge.

shiobiki (鹽引), *n.* a salted fish.

shiobuta (鹽豚), *n.* salted pork.

shiode (牛尾菜), *n.* 【植】 the carrion flower.

shiodoki (汐時), *n.* ❶ a tidal hour. ❷ (好機會) a good chance [opportunity].

shiofuki (汐吹貝), *n.* 【貝】Mactra veneriformis (trough-shell の一種·學名).

shiogama (鹽竈), *n.* a salt-pan; a brine-pan.

shiohi (汐干), *n.* the ebb tide; low tide. ¶ 汐干狩, fishing [shell-gathering] at low tide.

shioire (鹽入), *n.* a salt-cellar (食卓用の).

shiokara (鹽辛), *n.* salted fish-intestines.

shiokarai (鹽辛·鹹い), *a.* salty; saline; briny.

shiokaze (潮風), *n.* a sea-wind; a sea-breeze.

shioke (鹽氣), *n.* saltness; saltiness; salinity.

shioki (仕置), *n.* punishment; execution (死刑).

shiokuri (仕送), *n.* supply; remittance. —仕送する, to supply [send] money regularly; remit money.

shiomizu (潮水), *n.* salt water; sea water; brine.

shiomizu (鹽水), *n.* saline water; salt water.

shion (紫苑), *n.* 【植】Aster tataricus (starwort の一種·學名).

shion (子音), *n.* a consonant (sound.)

shion (私恩), *n.* personal obligations. —私恩を賣る, to bring another under obligation for ulterior purposes.

shion (齒音), *n.* a dental.

shioppai (鹽ッぱい), *a.* salty; briny; saline.

shiorashii (悄らしい), *a.* ❶ pitiful. ❷ delicate; tender; pretty. —しをらしい事を云ふ, to say tender things.

shioreru (萎れる), *vi.* ❶ (萎む) to wither; droop. ❷ (悄げる) to be out of spirits; be dejected [depressed]; be cast down. —萎れた, ① withered; faded. ② dispirited; dejected.

shiori (栞), *n.* ❶ (書物の) a book-mark; a book-marker. ❷ (案內) a guide.

shiosashi (潮差), *n.* flood-tide.

shiotareru (汐垂れる), *vi.* ❶ (汐に濡る) to be drenched with salt water. ❷ (涙に濡る) to be wet with tears.

shioyaki (鹽燒), *n.* roasting《fish roasted》with salt.

shiozuke (鹽漬), *n.* salted food; preservation with salt (事).

shippai (失敗), *n.* failure; miscarriage; ill success; defeat (敗亡). —失敗に歸する, to end in failure; prove a failure [abortive]; come to nothing [naught]. —する事なす事失敗する, to be defeated at every turn. ¶ 失敗者, a failure.

shippei (竹篦), *n.* ❶ (笞) a ferule. ❷ (手背打) a back-hander. —竹篦返しをする, to retort *on*;

retaliate; pay another in his own coin. ☞ *byōki.*

shippei (疾病), *n.* illness; disease.

shippi (失費), *n.* expense.

shippi (櫛比する), *vi.* to stand in a long row; line closely.

shippo (尻尾), *n.* a tail; a tag. ☞ *o* (尾). —尻尾を出す, to show the cloven foot [hoof]; show one's colours. —尻尾を押へる, to catch a person on the hip.

shippōyaki (七寳燒), *n.* cloisonné (enamel); cloisonné ware; *shippō.*

shippu (濕布), *n.* 【醫】 a stupe; a (wet) pack. —濕布する, to stupe; pack.

shippū (疾風), *n.* ❶ 【氣象】 a strong wind. ❷ a gale. —疾風迅雷の勢で, with lightning speed.

-shira (知ら), I wonder. —人がどう思ふか知ら, I wonder what people think of me.

shirabakureru (しらばくれる), *vi.* to dissemble; feign [pretend] ignorance; brazen (it) out.

shirabamu (白ばむ), *vi.* to become whitish; whiten.

shirabe (調), *n.* ❶ inquiry; investigation; examination. ☞ *chōsa.* ❷ (音樂) music; melody; tune. ¶ 調革, a belt; a band. —調車, a pulley.

shiraberu (調べる), *vi.* ❶ (調査) to examine; investigate; inquire *into*; look *into.* ❷ (搜索) to search; consult (辭書など). ❸ (整調) to tune. ❹ (奏でる) to play. —調べ出す, to find out; take out. —書類を檢べる, to look over [up] the document [the papers]. —人數を調べる, to count [find out] the number of persons. —箱の中を調べる, to search [look into] a box.

shiracha (白茶-色), *n.* light yellow; straw colour.

shirafu (素面), *n.* soberness; sobriety. —素面でそんな事は切り出せない, I cannot broach such a thing when I am sober.

shiraga (白髮), *n.* white hair; hoary hair. —白髮交りの頭, a grizzly-haired head; a gray head. ¶ 白髮頭, a hoary head. —白髮染, a hair-dye.

shirageru (精げる), *vt.* to refine.

shirahada (白癜風), *n.* 【醫】 vitiligo; piebald skin.

shiraji (白地), *n.* ❶ unbaked earthenware. ❷ blankness. —白地の, blank.

shirajirashii (白白しい), *a.* unconcerned; brassy. —白々しい虚言をいふ, to tell a transparent lie.

shirakami (白紙), *n.* ❶ white paper. ❷ blank paper. —白紙の答案を出す, to send in blank paper.

shirakanba (白樺), *n.* 【植】 the Japanese birch.

shirakeru (白ける), *vi.* to be spoiled; be deprived of interest. —座がしらけた, A chill fell on the company.

shiraki (白木), *n.* plain wood.

shirako (魚精), *n.* milt; soft roe.

shirakumo (白雲), *n.* ❶ white [fleecy] clouds. ❷ (白癬) favus; tinea favosa; scald-head.

shirami (虱, 蝨), *n.* 【昆】 the louse [*pl.* lice]. —虱潰しに, one by one. ¶ 頭蝨, the head-louse. —衣蝨, the body-louse; the gray-back.

shiramu (白む), *vi.* ❶ to become white; whiten. ❷ (東雲する) to grow light [bright]; it [the morning; the day] dawns; the dawn approaches.

shiranai (知らない), *vt.* Ⓢ 知らぬ. not to know; be ignorant *of.* ☞ *shiru.* ——, *a.* unknown; strange. —恐れを知らぬ人, a stranger to fear. —知らぬ振りする, to pretend to be ignorant *of*; feign [pretend] ignorance. —知らぬが佛, "Ignorance is bliss."

shirasagi (白鷺), *n.* 【鳥】 the little egret.

shirase (知らせ), *n.* ❶ (通知) information; intelligence; tidings. ❷ (前兆) an omen; a presentiment (豫感); a sign. —知らせを遣る, to send a message; send a messenger.

shiraseru (知らせる), *vt.* to let know; make it known *to*; inform. —眞相を知らしめる, to make the truth known. —威力を知らしめる, to make one's power felt.

shirasu (しらす), *n.* 【魚】 Leucopsarion Petersii (學名). ¶ 白子乾, dried leucopsarion.

shirasu (白洲), *n.* ❶ (洲) a sand-bar; a shoal. ❷ (法廷) the court; the tribunal; the bar. —白洲へ引出される, to be brought into court.

shirata (白木質, 白太), *n.* sap-wood; sap; alburn, alburnum.

shirauo (白魚), *n.* 【魚】 the whitebait.

shirazu-shirazu (不知不識), *ad.* unawares; unconsciously; unwittingly.

shirei (司令), *n.* ❶ command. ❷ (人) a commander. ¶ 司令部, 【軍】 headquarters. —司令官, a commandant; a commander; a commanding officer. (司令長官, 【海】 a commander-in-chief.) —司令塔, a conning-tower.

shirei (指令), *n.* instructions; an order; a notice. —指令する, to order; instruct; give instructions.
shirekitta (知れきった), *a.* well-known; obvious; self-evident (自明). —知れきった虚言, an evident [transparent] falsehood [lie].
shiren (試錬), *n.* a test; a trial; an ordeal. —試錬する, to try; test; put to test. —誘惑《戰爭》の試錬に堪へる, to stand the test of temptation 《war》.
shireru (知れる), *v.* to become known; come to one's knowledge [one's ears]; come to light.
shirewatatta (知れ渡った), *a.* well-known; wide-spread; notorious. —知れ渡った醜聞, an open scandal.
shiri (尻), *n.* ❶ (臀部) the buttocks; the rump; the bottom. ❷ (衣類などの) the seat; the buttocks. ❸ (底部) the bottom; the base; the end (先端). —尻から一番, the first from the bottom. —尻が輕い, ① to be wanton [light-heeled]. ② to be active. —尻が長い, to stay too long. —尻が重い, to be indolent. —尻が落ちつかぬ, to change often one's business 《master; employer》; not to stay long in a place 《at one's post》. —夫を尻に敷く, to wear the breeches. —妻の尻に敷かれる, to be tied to the wife's apron-strings. —尻を拭ふ, to pay for a person's blunder; pay the piper. —尻食へ觀音, "The river past, and God forgotten."
shiri (私利), *n.* private [personal] gain; self-interest. —私利を謀る, to look after one's own interests; look to the main chance.
shiriai (知合), *n.* ❶ (面識) acquaintance. ❷ (知人) an acquaintance. —知合になる, to become acquainted *with*; make the acquaintance *of*; come to know.
shirie (後方), *n.* the back; the rear. —後へに, behind; backwards.
shirigomi (尻込する), *vi.* to recoil; shrink back; back.
shirime (尻目), *n.* a side-glance; looking aslant [askant]. —尻目にかける, to look askance at a person; look at a person contemptuously; see out of the corner of one's eye.
shiri-metsuretsu (支離滅裂の), *a.* incoherent; inconsistent.
shirimochi (尻餅舂く), *v.* to fall on one's seat [bottom; buttocks].
shiringu (志), *n.* a shilling (英貨, s. と略す. 我が約五十錢).
shirinuke (尻拔), *n.* ❶ (物忘れ) forgetfulness (事); a forgetful person (人). ❷ (締無し) looseness (事); a sloven (男); a slut (女); an improvident person (金錢上). —學ぶそばから尻拔けする, to forget as soon as one learns.
shirio (尻尾), *n.* =*shippo*.
shirioshi (尻押), *n.* ❶ backing; supporting; seconding. ❷ (人) a backer; a supporter; an instigator. —尻押しする, to back (up); support; bolster up.
shiritsu (市立の), *a.* municipal. ¶ 市立病院, a municipal hospital.
shiritsu (私立の), *a.* private. ¶ 私立學校, a private school.
shiriuma (尻馬に乘る), (人後につく) to follow another blindly.
shirizokeru (退·斥·黜ける), *vt.* ❶ (拒絶) to refuse; reject; repel. ❷ (排斥) to expel. ❸ (擊退) to drive back; repulse. —要求を斥ける, to reject [repel] a person's demand.
shirizoku (退く), *v.* ❶ (退却) to retreat; withdraw; fall back. ❷ (引退) to retire; resign (辭職). —官を退く, to retire from office. —一步退いて考へる, to reconsider; think again; stop to think.
shiro (白), *n.* ❶ (白色) white. ❷ (空白) blank. ☞ *shiroi*.
shiro (城), *n.* a castle; a citadel (市砦); a fortress (要塞). ¶ 城明渡し, surrender (of a castle).
shiroari (白蟻), *n.* 【昆】 the white ant; the termite.
shiroato (城跡), *n.* ruins [remains] of an ancient castle.
shiroeri-montsuki (白襟紋附), *n.* a white-banded and crested dress.
shiroi (白い), *a.* white; hoar; hoary (髮など); blank (何も書いてない). —白くなる《する》, to whiten; become 《make》 white.
shirokuban (四六版), *n.* a duodecimo (米. 4.27 寸×6.4 寸); crown octavo (4.2 寸×6.25 寸).
shirokuma (白熊), *n.* 【哺乳】 the white [polar] bear.
shirome (白眼), *n.* the white of the eye. —白眼勝ちの目, eyes in which the white predominates.
shirome (白鑞), *n.* solder.
shiromi (白味), *n.* a white tinge [tint] (色の); the white (卵の).
shiromono (代物), *n.* ❶ (物品) goods; merchandise (商品). ❷ (材料) material; stuff. ❸ (人間) a fellow; a character. —喰へない[始末にをへない]代物, an awkward [ugly] customer.
shiromuku (白無垢), *n.* a white dress.
shironuri (白塗の), *a.* white-

-plastered [-washed]; stuccoed.
shirotae (白妙の), *a.* white. —白妙の富士の高根, the snow-clad peak of Mt. Fuji.
shirōto (素人), *n.* an amateur; a non-professional; a layman; laity (全體を言ふ). ¶ 素人藝, amateur accomplishments. —素人劇, amateur theatricals. —素人下宿, a private lodging-house.
shirouri (白瓜, 越瓜), *n.* 【植】the melon; the connemon (of Japan).
shiru (汁), *n.* ❶ (液) sap (樹液); juice (果汁). ❷ (吸物) soup. ❸ (水漿) fluid; discharge. —汁の多い, juicy; succulent; mellow.
shiru (知る), *vt.* ❶ (聞知する) to know; learn; feel (感知する). ❷ (解る) to know; understand; see. ❸ (構ふ) to care; be concerned *with.* ❹ (知合になる) to know; make another's acquaintance. ☞ *shiranai.* —知って ゐる, ① to know; be aware *of* (心得てゐる). ② (知合となって) to be acquainted *with*; be familiar [intimate] *with.* (一通り知ってゐる, to have a fair knowledge *of.* —文法をよく知ってゐる, to be well up in grammar.) —私の知る限りでは, as far as I know; to the best of my knowledge. —少しも知らぬと言ふ, to deny any knowledge *of.*
shirube (知邊), *n.* ❶ (相識) an acquaintance; a friend. ❷ a clue (手がかり); a guide (案内).
shiruko (汁粉), *n.* red-bean soup with rice-cake.
shirukuhatto (絹高帽), *n.* a silk hat.
shirushi (印), *n.* ❶ (記號) a mark; a sign; a badge (徽章). ❷ (徴候) a symptom; an indication; a sign. ❸ (記念) memory. ❹ (證據) a proof. ❺ (效驗) efficacy; effect. —ライオン印, the lion brand. —效驗がない, to be of no effect. —印をつける, to mark; tick; make a mark [sign].
shirusu (記す), *vt.* ❶ (書附ける) to write down; note; put [jot] down. ❷ (敍述する) to describe; give an account *of.* ❸ (印をつける) to mark; make a mark [sign]. —其槪略を記す, to give a general account of it.
shiryo (思慮), *n.* consideration; discretion (分別). —思慮ある, thoughtful; considerate; discreet. —思慮のない事をする, to act thoughtlessly.
shiryō (史料), *n.* materials for history; historical materials.
shiryō (死靈), *n.* the spirit of a dead person; a ghost.
shiryō (思料する), *vt.* to think; consider. ☞ *kangaeru.*
shiryō (資料), *n.* materials; matter; data.
shiryoku (死力), *n.* a desperate effort. —死力を盡す, to do [exert oneself to] the utmost; make desperate efforts.
shiryoku (視力), *n.* sight; eyesight; (power of) vision. ¶ 視力試驗, examination of eyesight.
shiryoku (資力), *n.* funds; resource; capital. —資力ある, resourceful; sound.
shiryū (支流), *n.* a branch (stream); a tributary (stream); an affluent; a feeder.
shisa (示唆する), *t.* to suggest.
shisai (仔細), *n.* ❶ (理由) account; reason; circumstances. ❷ (委細) details; particulars. —仔細あって, for certain reasons. —仔細に點檢する, to examine minutely [closely].
shisai (市債), *n.* a municipal loan; a city bond.
shisaku (思索), *n.* thinking; contemplation. —思索する, to think out.
shisaku (試作), *n.* trial manufacture (製造); trial rearing (栽培); an essay (試圖); an attempt (同上). —試作する, to plant on trial.
shisaku (詩作), *n.* writing poems; versification.
shisan (四散する), *vi.* to disperse (in every direction); go to the winds.
shisan (試算), *n.* trial. ¶ 試算表, a trial balance.
shisan (資產), *n.* assets; property; fortune. —五萬圓の資產がある, to be worth ¥50,000. ¶ 資產家, a man of property [means; wealth]. —資產階級, the propertied class.
shisanjikai (市參事會), *n.* a municipal [city] council. ¶ 市參事會員, a municipal [city] councillor; an alderman.
shisañyo (市參與), *n.* a municipal adviser [counsellor].
shisatsu (視察), *n.* inspection; observation. —視察する, to inspect; observe. —視察(旅行)の途に上る, to go on a tour of inspection [an observation trip]. ¶ 高等視察(警視廳の), a political inspector. —視察談, an account of one's tour of inspection. —視察員, an inspector.
shisei (市井), *n.* streets; a town. —市井の徒, the blackguards [hooligans] of the town.
shisei (市政), *n.* municipal government [administration].

shisei (市制), *n.* law relating to a municipality; municipal organization [system].

shisei (死生), *n.* life and death.

shisei (至誠), *n.* sincerity; loyalty; faithfulness.

shisei (私製の), *a.* private; of private manufacture.

shisei (施政), *n.* administration; government. ¶ 施政方針, an administrative policy.

shisei (姿勢), *n.* a posture; an attitude; a pose. —姿勢を正す, to sit upright; draw oneself up; straighten up one's person.

shisei (紙製の), *n.* paper; made of paper.

shisei (詩聖), *n.* a great poet.

shisei (資性), *n.* nature; composition; disposition (氣質).

shisei-chōsa (市勢調査), *n.* (municipal) census.

shiseiji (私生兒), *n.* an illegitimate [a natural] child; a bastard.

shiseki (咫尺), *n.* a very short distance. —黒闇咫尺を辨ぜず, It is so dark that we cannot see an inch before us.

shisekiei (紫石英), *n.* 【鑛】 amethyst.

shisen (支線, 枝線), *n.* a branch (line); a feeder (培養線).

shisen (死戰), *n.* a desperate fight. —死戰する, to fight a desperate battle [with desperation].

shisen (死線), *n.* the dead-line.

shisen (視線), *n.* the visual line; the line of vision [sight]; visual rays; 【理】 the line of collimation.

shisetsu (使節), *n.* an envoy; a legate; a mission (使節團).

shisetsu (私設の), *a.* private.

shisetsu (施設), *n.* institution; equipment (設備); facilities (便宜); plans. —施設する, to institute.

shisetsu (指節), *n.* 【解】 an internode; a phalange, phalanx.

shisha (支社), *n.* a branch (office).

shisha (死者), *n.* ❶ (死んだ人) the dead; the deceased. ❷ (殺された人) the slain; the killed.

shisha (使者), *n.* a messenger; an envoy.

shishagonyū (四捨五入), counting 1/2 and higher fractions as units and disregarding the rest.

shishaku (子爵), *n.* a viscount. ¶ 子爵夫人, a viscountess.

shishi (獅子), *n.* 【哺乳】 the lion (牡); the lioness (牝). —獅子身中の蟲, a snake in one's bosom; a canker at the core. ¶ 獅子鼻, a snub-nose; a pug-nose. —獅子吼, a (lion's) roar. (獅子吼する, to make a fiery speech; harangue.)

shishi (四肢), *n.* the limbs; the arms and legs; the extremities.

shishi (死屍), *n.* a corpse; a dead body. —死屍に鞭つ, to denounce the dead.

shishi (志士), *n.* a patriot (愛國家); a public-spirited man (篤志家); a man of high purpose (同).

shishi (孜孜として), *ad.* assiduously; diligently; strenuously.

shishi (指示する), *vt.* to point *to*; point out (指摘); indicate; denote. ¶ 指示形容詞, 【文】 the demonstrative adjective.

shishi (嗣子), *n.* an heir [*fem.* -ess]; an heir apparent.

shishin (私心), *n.* the selfishness; private interest; a selfish motive.

shishin (私信), *n.* a private letter (手紙); private communication (同上); private message (手紙·報道等の).

shishin (使臣), *n.* an envoy; the chief of a mission.

shishin (指針), *n.* ❶ (磁石の針) a compass-needle. ❷ (諸器機の) an index. ❸ (嚮導) a guide.

shishinkei (視神經), *n.* 【解】 an optic nerve.

shishinkei (齒神經), *n.* 【解】 a dental nerve.

shishitsu (資質), *n.* nature; quality; temperament.

shisho (四書五經), *n.* the four classics and the five canons.

shisho (司書), *n.* a librarian.

shisho (私書), *n.* a private letter; 【法】 a private document. ¶ 郵便私書函, a post-office box; P. O. box; P. O. B.

shishō (支障), *n.* hitch; hindrance; impediment. ☞ *sashitsukae*. —支障なく, without hindrance [a hitch]; smoothly.

shishō (死傷-者), *n.* the killed and wounded; persons killed and wounded; casualties. —(戰爭の)死傷數, the losses in killed and wounded.

shishō (私消), *n.* embezzlement; peculation. —私消する, to embezzle; peculate.

shishō (師匠), *n.* a teacher; a master; an instructor.

shishu (四手類), *n.* 【動】 Quadrumana (學名).

shishu (死守する), *v.* to defend desperately [to the death; to the last]; die in the last ditch.

shishu (旨趣), *n.* the import; the gist; the point.

shishu (詩趣), *n.* poetical interest; poetical taste.

shishū (刺繡), *n.* embroidery; piqué-work. —刺繡する, to embroider; lace.

shishū (詩集), *n.* a collection of poems; an anthology.

shishuku (止宿する), *vi.* to lodge *at* [*in*]; put up *at*; take up one's quarters *in*. ¶ 止宿人, a lodger. —止宿所, lodgings; quarters.

shishuku (私淑する), *v.* to model oneself *upon*; take pattern *by*; take *after*.

shishutsu (支出), *n.* ❶ (事) payment; defrayment; disbursement. ❷ (金錢又は物) expenditure; expense; outlay. —支出する, to pay; defray; disburse; expend.

shiso (紫蘇), *n.* 【植】 Perilla nankinensis (學名).

shiso (私訴), *n.* a civil action; a civil suit.

shiso (始祖), *n.* the progenitor; an ancestor; a founder (元祖).

shisō (志操), *n.* ❶ (意志) will; mind. ❷ (節操) constancy; principle.

shisō (使嗾, 指嗾), *n.* instigation. —指嗾する, to instigate; abet; stir up; egg on.

shisō (思想), *n.* thought; idea. ¶ 思想家, a thinker.

shisō (詩宗), *n.* a great [master] poet; a poet laureate (桂冠詩宗).

shīsō (シーソー戯), *n.* seesaw.

shisokonau (仕損ふ), *v.* to fail; mismanage; make a mistake.

shisoku (四則), *n.* 【數】 the four rules (of arithmetic).

shisoku (四足類), *n.* the quadrupeds.

shison (子孫), *n.* descendants; posterity.

shison (至尊), *n.* ❶ sovereignty. ❷ (天子) His Majesty.

shisonjiru (仕損じる), *v.* = *shisokonau*.

shissaku (失錯, 失策), *n.* a blunder; an error; failure. —失策をする, to commit an error; blunder; fail.

shissei (失政), *n.* maladministration; misrule.

shissei (執政), *n.* a dictator.

shisseki (叱責), *n.* reproof; rebuke; reprimand. —叱責する, to reprove; rebuke; reprimand.

shisshi (嫉視する), *vt.* to regard with jealousy; keep a jealous eye *on*.

shisshin (失心, 失神), *n.* swoon; a fainting-fit; 【醫】 vertigo. —失神さす, to petrify; stupefy. —失神する, to swoon (away); fall into a swoon; lose one's senses.

shisshin (濕疹), *n.* 【醫】 eczema.

shisshō (失笑する), *vi.* to burst out laughing; burst into laughter.

shisshoku (失職), *n.* unemployment. —失職する, to be (thrown) out of work [employment]. ¶ 失職者, an unemployed person; a person out of work; the unemployed (集合).

shisso (質素), *n.* modesty; plainness; simplicity. —質素な, modest; plain; simple. —質素に暮らす, to live in a small way.

shissō (失踪), *n.* 【法】 disappearance; missing. —失踪する, to disappear. ¶ 失踪者, a person missing.

shissō (疾走する), *vi.* to scamper; scud.

shissō (濕瘡), *n.* 【醫】 scabies.

shis-suru (失する), *vt.* to lose; miss; let slip (機會等). —寬に失する, to be too lenient. —火を失する, to cause a fire through carelessness. —禮を失する, to be impolite; act against etiquette.

shīsu (シース), *n.* a sheath.

shisū (指數), *n.* 【數】 an index; an exponent; an index-number. ¶ 物價指數, 【經】 index-numbers of prices.

shisugiru (仕過ぎる), *vt.* to overdo; do too much; go too far. —仕事を仕過ぎる, to overwork oneself.

shisui (止水, 死水), *n.* dead [still; standing] water.

shi-suru (資する), *v.* to be a help [an aid] *for*; be of help *to*; contribute *to*; conduce [be conducive] *to*; serve *as*. —參考に資する, to serve as a reference.

-shi-suru (視する), *vt.* to regard ...*as*...; look upon...*as*...; consider ...*as*...; reckon...*as* [*for*]....

shita (下), *n.* ❶ (下方) the bottom; the foot; the lower part. ❷ (下民) the people; the governed. ❸ (目下) one's inferior. ❹ (代金の代りに渡す物) a thing offered in part-payment. —下から二番目の抽斗, the second drawer from the bottom. —橋の下を通る, to pass under a bridge. **—— -ni**, *ad.* & *prep.* down; beneath; under; below. —下に置く, to lay down.

shita (舌), *n.* ❶ the tongue. ❷ (舌狀物) a tongue; a clapper (鐘の). —舌を捲く, to be stumped *by*. —舌を出す, to put out [protrude] one's tongue. —舌をふるふ, to wag one's tongue. —舌の根がまだ渴かぬ中に, while yet the words are fresh from one's mouth.

shitabataraki (下働), *n.* ❶ (事) subordinate work; yeoman work. ❷ (人) an under-worker; an under-servant; an under-maid (特に下女の).

shitabi (下火), *n.* a smouldering fire; a fire under control. —下

火になる, A fire gets under.
shitabirame (したびらめ), *n.* 【魚】 the sole.
shitae (下繪), *n.* a design (for a picture); a draught; an outline sketch; 【美】 a study.
shitagaeru (從へる), *v.* ❶ (隨) (同伴する) to be attended [followed; accompanied] *by.* ❷ (服從せしむ) to bring to subjection [under one's control].
shitagaki (下書), *n.* a rough copy [draught]; an outline sketch (繪). 一下書きする, to draught.
shitagatte (隨ッて), *ad.* accordingly; consequently; hence. —, *prep.* in proportion *to*; according *to*; as. —, *conj.* according as. 一人文の發達に隨ッて, keeping pace with the advance of civilization. 一流に順ッて下る, to run down with a stream.
shitagau (從ふ), *vt.* ❶ (服從) to obey; submit *to*; bend *to.* ❷ (從事) to engage *in*; pursue; follow. ❸ (隨從) to follow (忠言·先例·指導に); act *upon* (忠言に); accompany (隨行). ☞ *shitagatte.* 一彼に從へば, according to him. 一人の意見に遵ふ, to bow to another's opinion. 一規則《條件》に從ふ, to comply with the rules 《conditions》.
shitageiko (下稽古), *n.* rehearsal (演劇などの); preparation (學課の).
shitagi (下衣), *n.* an underwear; underclothes; an undershirt.
shitagokoro (下心), *n.* intention; design; view (目的).
shitagoshirae (下拵), *n.* preliminary preparations [arrangements]. 一下拵へする, to make preliminary preparations [arrangements] *for*; prepare *for*; make ready *for.*
shitahara (下腹), *n.* the lower part of the abdomen [belly].
shitai (死胎), *n.* a dead fœtus. ¶ 死胎分娩, still birth.
shitai (死體, 屍體), *n.* a dead body; a corpse; a carcass (動物の); a cadaver (解剖用). 一死體檢案をする, to make a post-mortem examination. ¶ 屍體毒, ptomaine. 一死體强直, 【醫】 rigor mortis.
shitai (枝隊), *n.* 【軍】 a detachment.
shitai (仕度い), *vt.* to wish (to do); want (to do); be inclined (to do).
shitaji (下地), *n.* ❶ (根基) the foundation; the basis; the ground. ❷ (氣) inclination. ❸ (醬油) soy. 一下地を作る, to lay the foundation of the future.
shitajiki (下敷), *n.* a thing laid under; a stand (釜などの). 一下敷きになる, to be under.
shitajoku (下職), *n.* an under-workman; a subordinate.
shitakensa (下檢査), *n.* a previous [preliminary; preparatory] examination.
shitaku (支度), *n.* ❶ (準備) preparation; arrangement; outfit. ❷ (裝束) dressing; attire. ❸ (途中の食事) a lunch, luncheon. 一支度をする, to prepare (*for*); make preparations (*for*); get ready. 一朝飯《食事》の支度をする, to lay breakfast 《table》. ¶ 支度料, outfit allowance.
shitaku (私宅), *n.* a private house.
shitamachi (下町), *n.* down-town.
shitamae (下前), *n.* the under fold of clothes.
shitamawari (下廻り), *n.* ❶ petty work. ❷ (人) an underling; an under-servant.
shitame (下目), *n.* casting down the eyes. 一下目に見る, to look down *on* [*upon*].
shitami (淸), *n.* drops.
shitami (下見), *n.* ❶ (板壁) weather-boarded wall. ❷ (賣立てなどの) preliminary inspection. ❸ =*shitashirabe.*
shitamu (淸む), *vt.* to let drop [drip].
shitamuki (下向), *n.* ❶ bending downwards. ❷ (相場) downward tendency. 一下向く, to look downward; cast one's eyes down; bend one's head down: show a downward tendency.
shitan (紫檀), *n.* 【植】 the Burmese rosewood; the lingo-tree.
shitanamezuri (舌舐めずりする), *vi.* to lick one's chaps.
shitanuri (下塗), *n.* first coating; undercoating; ground. 一下塗りする, to prime; give the first coating.
shitaobi (下帶), *n.* ❶ an under-sash. ❷ (褌) a loin-cloth.
shitasaki (舌端), *n.* ❶ the tip of the tongue. ❷ (巧言) fair words.
shitashii (親しい), *a.* intimate; friendly; familiar. 一親しく, ① intimately. ② (親ら) personally; in person. ③ (實地に) actually.
shitashimi (親み), *n.* intimacy; friendship; familiarity.
shitashimu (親む), *v.* to strike friendship *with*; become intimate [friendly; familiar] *with.*
shitashirabe (下調), *n.* ❶ (豫審) a preliminary inquiry; a preliminary examination. ❷ (下

調査) a preliminary investigation. ❷ (豫習) preparation; prep 〖學生・卑〗. ―下調べする, to inquire beforehand; examine previously; prepare (a lesson); make preparations *for*.

shitataka (健か, 强か), *ad.* a great deal; very much; greatly; heavily. ―强か肋を打ちつける, to get a terrible blow on the ribs. ¶ 剛者, a rascal; a villain; an abandoned woman (女).

shitatameru (認める), *vt.* ❶ (書く) to write (a letter); draw up (a report). ❷ (食べる) to take [have] (breakfast; meals); eat (dinner). ―書面に認める, to commit to [put in] writing.

shitatari (滴), *n.* a drop; a drip; dripping.

shitataru (滴る), *vi.* to drop; drip; dripple.

shitate (下手), *n.* ❶【相撲】a grip under the arms. ❷ (服從) deference. ―下手に出る, to treat a person with deference; sing small; adopt a humble attitude.

shitate (仕立), *n.* ❶ (裁縫) tailoring; sewing. ❷ (作爲) making up. ¶ 仕立物, tailoring; needlework. ―仕立屋, a tailor [*fem.* -ess]; a dress-maker.

shitateru (仕立てる), *vt.* ❶ (衣服を) to make (clothes). ❷ (船車・飛脚など) *(a)* (立てる) to despatch; send: *(b)* (用意する) to make ready; get ready. ❸ (仕込む) to train; bring up. ―別列車を仕立てる, to provide a special train.

shitazutsumi (舌鼓を打つ), to click the tongue.

shitau (慕ふ), *vt.* to pine [yearn] *after* [*for*]; long *for*.

shitauchi (舌打), *n.* ❶ (舌鼓) click of the tongue. ❷ (揞癡の) a tut. ―舌打ちする, to click one's tongue; tut.

shitaukeoi (下請負), *n.* a subcontract (下請契約): a subcontractor (下請人).

shitauma (下馬), *n.* a jackal; a lion's provider. ―下馬になる, to follow another; play second fiddle to a person.

shitayaku (下役), *n.* an underling; a satellite; a subordinate (official).

shitayomi (下讀), *n.* preparation (of lessons).

shitazumi (下積み), *n.* a lower [an under] layer.

shitchi (濕地), *n.* a marsh; a morass; damp ground.

shite (して), *conj.* and.

shitei (子弟), *n.* sons and young brothers; children; youth.

shitei (使丁), *n.* an errand-boy; a messenger; a runner.

shitei (師弟), *n.* teacher and pupil.

shitei (指定), *n.* appointment; designation; indication. ―指定する, to designate; appoint; indicate.

shiteki (史的), *a.* historic(-al).

shiteki (私的), *a.* private.

shiteki (指摘する), *vt.* to show; indicate; point out. ―誤譯を指摘する, to point out mistranslation.

shiteki (詩的), *a.* poetic(-al). ¶ 詩的感興, poetical inspiration.

shitemo (しても), *conj.* granting (that); even supposing (that); even if [though] allowing for. ―何れにしても, any way; in any case.

shiten (支店), *n.* a branch (shop; house; office; establishment). ―支店詰になる, to be transferred to a branch office. ¶ 支店長, a manager of a branch; a branch-manager.

shiten (支點), *n.* 【理】the fulcrum.

shiten (死點), *n.* 【機】a dead-point [-centre].

shiten (視點), *n.* the visual point; the point of vision.

shitewa (しては), ❶ (にしては) for (a boy); considering (his age). ❷ (としては) as (a statesman); considered as (a teacher). ―君にしては上出來だ, It is well done for you.

shiteyaru (してやる), *vt.* to take in; hoodwink; play a trick *upon*.

shito (使徒), *n.* an apostle; a disciple.

shito (支途), *n.* outlay; expenses.

shitō (至當), *n.* reasonableness. ―至當な, reasonable; fair; deserving. ―至當の罰, merited punishment.

shitō (私黨), *n.* a faction.

shitogeru (仕遂げる), *vt.* to accomplish; finish; achieve.

shitomi (蔀), *n.* 【建】breast-summer; a shutter.

shitone (褥), *n.* a mattress; a cushion; a bed.

shitoron (シトロン), *n.* citron.

shitoshito (しとしと), *ad.* ❶ (靜かに) gently; lonesomely. ❷ (濕っぽく) dampishly. ―しとしと降る雨, a soft rain; a drizzling rain.

shitoyaka (しとやかな), *a.* gentle; suave; graceful. ―しとやかな振舞, suave [soft] manners.

shitsu (失), *n.* ❶ a disadvantage (不利益); a loss (損失). ❷ (過失, 失策) an error; a mistake; a fault.

shitsu (室), *n.* a room; a

chamber; a compartment (分室). ―二等室(汽車の), a second--class compartment.

shitsu (質), *n.* nature (天性); disposition (性向); temperament (氣質); constitution (體質); quality (品質). ―質が良い《惡い》, to be of good 《bad》 quality; be superior 《inferior》 in quality. ¶ 動《植》物質, animal 《vegetable》 matter.

shitsu (疥癬), *n.* the itch; scabies. ¶ 疥癬かき, a scabious person.

shitsū (齒痛), *n.* toothache; 「【醫】odontalgia.」

shītsu (敷布, 上敷), *n.* a sheet.

shitsubō (失望), *n.* disappointment. ―失望さす, to disappoint. ―失望する, to be disappointed *at* [*in*; *of*]

shitsuboku (質朴), *n.* simplicity; plainness. ―質朴な, simple; simple-minded; plain.

shitsudo (濕度), *n.* 【理】humidity. ¶ 濕度計, a hygrometer; a hygroscope.

shitsugaikotsu (膝蓋骨), *n.* 【解】the patella; the knee-pan [-cap]; the stifle-bone (馬の).

shitsugen (失言), *n.* a slip of the tongue; *lapsus linguæ* 【羅】; a misstatement. ―失言する, to make a slip of the tongue. ―失言を責める, to call a man to account for a slip of the tongue. ―失言を取消す, to take back hasty words.

shitsugi (質疑), *n.* question; inquiry, enquiry; interrogation.

shitsugyō (失業), *n.* unemployment. ―失業する, to be out of employment [work]; be unemployed. ¶ 失業調查, unemployment census ―失業保險, unemployment insurance. ―失業者, the unemployed (persons); a person out of work. (失業勞働者, unemployed workmen [labour].) ―失業救濟事業, relief-works. ―失業手當[給付], unemployment benefit. ―失業統計, statistics of unemployment.

shitsui (失意), *n.* disappointment; discouragement. ¶ 失意時代, one's dark days.

shitsuji (執事), *n.* a private secretary; a clerk; a steward (華族等の); a deacon (寺の).

shitsukansetsu (膝關接), *n.* 【解】the knee-joint.

shitsuke (仕附), *n.* ❶【裁縫】baste; tack. ❷【躾】training; education; breeding. ❸ (田植) implantation. ―躾の惡い, ill--bred. ―躾のよい, well-bred.

shitsukeru (仕附ける), *vt.* ❶ (田植) to implant. ❷【躾】to train; educate; breed. ❸ (し慣れる) to be accustomed [used] to do; be in the habit of doing. ―行儀よく躾ける, to bring up in good manners.

shitsukoi (しつこい), *a.* ❶ (執拗) persistent; obstinate. ❷ (うるさい) troublesome; tiresome. ❸ (濃厚) heavy; oily. ―しつこい料理, heavy cookery. ―しつこい程の甘さ, sickly sweetness. ―しつこく, obstinately; persistently; heavily.

shitsukusu (仕盡す), *vt.* to exhaust; do everything possible. ―道樂を仕盡す, to drain the cup of pleasure to the dregs.

shitsumei (失明), *n.* blindness; loss of sight. ―失明する, to lose one's eyesight; become blind.

shitsumon (質問), *n.* a question; interrogation; an interpellation (議會等の). ―急所を衝いた質問, a question which goes to the point [which thrusts home]. ―質問する, to make [put] a question *to*; interrogate; interpellate. ¶ 質問書, a written inquiry; a *questionnaire* 【佛】.

shitsumu (執務), *n.* business; official duties; office routine. ―執務する, to attend to one's business [official duties]. ¶ 執務時間, official [business] hours; hours of business [duty]. (執務時間中面會謝絕, All visits declined during office hours.)

shitsunai (室內), *n.* the interior of a room. ――, *ad.* in a room; within [inside] a room. ¶ 室內旅行, fireside travels. ―室內射的, gallery shooting. ―室內運動, indoor exercise 《gymnastics》. ―室內遊戲, indoor games [sports; amusements].

shitsunen (失念する), *v.* to forget. ☞ *wasureru*.

shitsurei (失禮), *n.* discourtesy; impoliteness; incivility. ―失禮な, discourteous; impolite; uncivil. ―失禮ながら, excuse me, but...; pardon me, but...; may I ask....; if you please; I beg your pardon; forgive me for saying so, but...; give me leave to say; by your leave. ―ではこれで失禮いたします, Now I will take my leave.

shitsuren (失戀), *n.* disappointed love; disappointment in love. ―失戀する, to be disappointed [crossed] in love; be lovelorn.

shitsuryō (質量), *n.* 【理】mass.

shitsuyō (執拗), *n.* obstinacy; persistency; stubbornness.

shitta (叱咤), *n.* a shout of anger

an angry shout. —叱咤する, to scold; rate; storm *at*; lash.

shittai (失態), *n.* ❶ (失策) a fault; a mistake; a blunder. ❷ (不爲態) misconduct; miscarriage; mismanagement. ❸ (不面目) disgrace; ignominy. ❹ (不謹愼) indiscretion. —失態を演ずる, to bring ignominy upon oneself; commit a blunder.

shittatsuri (執達吏), *n.* a bailiff; a process-server.

shitten (質點), *n.* 【理】 a particle.

shitten-battō (七顚八倒), *n.* writhing with pain [*in* agony]. —七轉八倒の苦しみをする, to writhe in deepest agonies.

shitto (嫉妬), *n.* jealousy. —嫉妬する, to be jealous *of*; regard with jealousy. —嫉妬心を起す, to feel jealous *of*.

shittō (失當の), *a.* undeserved; improper; unfair; wrong.

shittsui (失墜する), *vt.* to lose; destroy. ——, *vi.* to fall (off); sink.

shiuchi (仕打), *n.* bearing [behaviour; action] *to* [*against*]; treatment.

shiunten (試運轉), *n.* a trial-trip [-run] (船車とも).

shiwa (皺), *n.* wrinkles (特に顏の); creases; crinkles; furrows (深き). —皺にする, to wrinkle; crumple; crease; ruffle. —皺をのばす, to smooth away [over; out] creases. —額に皺を寄せる, to wrinkle (up) one's forehead; pucker (up) one's brow.

shiwabuki (咳嗽), *n.* tussis; cough.

shiwagareru (嗄れる), *vi.* to become hoarse. —しはがれた, hoarse; husky.

shiwai (吝い), *a.* miserly; niggardly; stingy. ☞ *rinshoku*.

shiwake (仕分, 仕譯), *n.* division; classification; assortment (組合せ); journalizing (帳簿の). —仕分けする, to divide; classify; assort; journal. ¶ 仕譯帳, a journal (複式簿記); a stock-account. —仕譯日記帳, a journal day-book.

shiwakucha (皺くちゃの), *a.* ruffled; wrinkled; rumpled; crumpled. —皺くちゃにする, to crumple; rumple; ruffle.

shiwamu (皺む), *vi.* Ⓢ 皺よる. to wrinkle; crinkle.

shiwanbō (吝坊), *n.* a stingy person; a miser; a niggard.

shiwasu (師走), *n.* the twelfth month (of the lunar calendar).

shiwaza (仕業), *n.* act; deed; work.

shiya (視野), *n.* a visual field; a field of vision.

shiyaku (試藥), *n.* 【化】 a test; a reagent.

shiyakusho (市役所), *n.* the municipal [city] office.

shiyō (子葉), *n.* 【植】 a cotyledon; a seed-leaf (發達せる); a seed-lobe (未發の).

shiyō (仕樣), *n.* method; way; means. —仕樣のない, (役立たぬ) worthless; useless; good-for-nothing. ¶ 仕樣書, specifications.

shiyō (至要の), *a.* most important; essential; vital.

shiyō (私用), *n.* ❶ (使用) private [personal] use. ❷ (用事) private business. —私用する, to turn to private use; appropriate.

shiyō (使用), *n.* use; employment; application (充用, 應用). —使用する, to use; employ; put to use; make use *of*; apply. ¶ 使用法, use; direction for use; how to use. —使用人, an employee. —使用料, rent; rental. —使用者, ① (雇主) an employer. ② (物の) a user; a hirer (賃借人).

shiyō (枝葉), *n.* ❶ branches and leaves. ❷ unnecessary particulars; unimportant details; minor details. —枝葉の問題, a subordinate problem. —枝葉に涉る, to diverge; make a digression; digress from the subject.

shiyō (試用), *n.* trying; trial. —試用する, to try; employ on trial.

shiyō (飼養する), *vt.* to raise; rear; breed; keep. ¶ 飼養者, a breeder; a rearer; a fancier (犬·鳥などの).

shiyoku (私慾), *n.* self-interest; selfish desire; selfishness. —私慾に趨る, to pursue one's self-interest.

shiyū (市有), *n.* municipal ownership. —市有にする, to municipalize. ¶ 市有財產, municipal property.

shiyū (私有), *n.* private ownership [possession]. ¶ 私有物, private goods. —私有地, private land. —私有財產制度, the private property system.

shiyū (雌雄), *n.* ❶ male and female. ❷ (勝敗) victory or defeat; mastery; superiority. —雌雄を決する, to decide a contest; try conclusions *with*. ¶ 雌雄淘汰, sexual selection.

shizai (支材), *n.* a prop; a support; a set (炭坑の).

shizai (死罪), *n.* ❶ (死刑) capital punishment; death penalty. ❷ a capital crime [offence].

shizai (私財), *n.* a private fortune; private property; private funds. —私財を投じて設ける, to establish at one's own expense.

shize (市是), *n.* municipal policy.

shizei (市稅), *n.* a municipal tax

[duty; rate].
shizeikan (司税官), *n.* a surveyor [comptroller] of taxes.
shizen (自然), *n.* ❶ (天然) nature. ❷ (自發) spontaneity. ❸ (無技巧) artlessness; simplicity. ❹ (無理のないこと) naturalness. ——, *ad* naturally; spontaneously; by itself. —自然の, natural; spontaneous. (自然の趨勢, the course of nature.) —自然に還る, to return to nature. ¶ 自然發火, spontaneous combustion. —自然發生, spontaneous generation; abiogenesis. —自然法 [律], ①【法】(性法) a natural law. ② (自然界の法則) laws of nature. —自然人,【法】a natural person. —自然科學, natural science; physical science. —自然界, the natural world; the world of nature. —自然經濟, natural economy. —自然療法, nature-cure. —自然力, natural forces; natural agencies. —自然主義,【文藝】naturalism. —自然崇拜, nature-worship. —自然淘汰, natural selection.
shizen (至善), *n.* the highest [chief; supreme] good.
shizetsu (死絶), *n.* extinction.
shizō (死藏する), *vt.* to let lie idle; keep idle.
shizoku (士族), *n.* the *samurai* family.
shizui (雌蕊), *n.*【植】a pistil.
shizui (齒髓), *n.*【解】dental pulp.
shizuka (靜な), *a.* still; tranquil; quiet; calm. ——**-ni**, *ad.* gently; softly; calmly; quietly. —靜かにしろ!, Hush!; Silence!; Be silent!; Be quiet!
shizuku (雫), *n.* a drop; a drip. —雫が垂れる, to drip; drop; trickle down.
shizumaru (靜鎭まる), *vi.* to become quiet; calm [settle; cool] down; subside (暴風·暴動等が).
shizumeru (沈める), *vt.* to sink; send to the bottom. ——, *a.* deep (音の); grave (同上); sunken.
shizumeru (靜鎭める), *vt.* ❶ (鎭定) to subdue; pacify; suppress. ❷ (鎭靜) to quiet; calm; compose (落ちつける). ❸ (緩和) to moderate; soothe; allay. —氣を鎭める, to collect [compose] oneself. —騷擾を鎭める, to quell a disturbance.
shizumu (沈む), *vi.* ❶ (沈沒) to sink; go to the bottom; go down. ❷ (日沒) to sink; set; go down. ❸ (沈鬱) to be downcast; be crest-fallen; be depressed. —沈んだ調子, a low tone. —思に沈む, to be buried in thought. —社會のどん底に沈む, to sink to the lowest stratum [depth] of society.
sho (書), *n.* ❶ (書法) calligraphy; handwriting; penmanship. ❷ (手紙) a letter. ❸ (書類) a document. ❹ (書物) a book. —書を能くする, to write a good hand.
sho (暑), *n.* ❶ (暑氣) the heat. ❷ (暑中) the hot season.
sho (署), *n.* an office; a station.
sho (諸), *a.* many; various.
shō (小), *n.* ❶ smallness. ❷ (月の) a month of thirty days; twenty-nine days (陰曆). ——, *a.* little; small; slight; minor. —小デューマ, Alexandre Dumas, fils (父に對し). —小ジョウンズ, Jones minor (長者に對し). ¶ 小修繕, minor repairs.
shō (少), *a.* ❶ (少き) little (量); few (數). ❷ (若き) young.
shō (省), *n.* ❶ (官省) a department; an office. ❷ (行政區劃) a province.
shō (升), *n.* a measure of capacity (=1.588 quart; 0.48 standard gallon; 1.804 litre).
shō (正), *n.* (位階の) the first grade (從に對す). ——, *a.* genuine (眞正の). ——, *ad.* just (時間の); punctually (同上). —正二時, just two; two sharp.
shō (症), *n.* a disease.
shō (生), *n.* life. —生ある物, living things.
shō (性), *n.* ❶ (氣質) temperament; disposition; character. ❷ =*shōai*. ❸ (品質) quality. —性の[に]合った友《仕事》, a congenial friend《work》. —性の知れない品, goods of unknown character. —性も懲りもない男, an incorrigible fellow.
shō (笙), *n.* a reed-organ.
shō (床), *n.* a bed.
shō (商), *n.* ❶ (商業) trade; commerce. ❷ (商人) a merchant; a dealer. ❸【數】the quotient.
shō (祥), *n.* a good omen; a happy [an auspicious] sign.
shō (章), *n.* ❶ (章句) a chapter (cap. 又は c., ch. と略す); section. ❷ (印章) a sign; a symbol; an emblem.
shō (將), *n.* the commander of an army《a fleet》; a general (將軍).
shō (稱), *n.* a name; a title; a designation.
shō (賞), *n.* a prize; a reward. —勤勉の賞として, as reward for diligence. —賞を受くべき, deserving a reward; meritorious. —人の首に賞を懸ける, to set a price on a person's head.
shō (衝), *n.* ❶【天】opposition. ❷ (通路) a main road. ❸ (要所) an important position. —攻擊の衝に當る, to stand in the breach;

bear the brunt of the attack. —交通の衝に當る, to form a centre of communication. —責任の衝に當る, to take up a responsible post.

shōai (性合), *n.* ❶ (性質) nature; character; quality (品質). ❷ (貨幣などの純分) standard; fineness.

shōaku (掌握する), *vt.* to hold; grasp; seize; take. —政權を掌握する, to take [assume] the reins of government; come in power.

shōbai (商賣), *n.* ❶ (商法) trade; business. ❷ (職業) occupation. —商賣する, to engage in business; transact business. —商賣換へする, to change one's trade. —商賣を始める, to open a shop; set up in business; start [go in for; go into] business. —商賣をしてゐる, to be engaged in business; deal [trade; traffic] *in* (何商賣). —商賣を止める, to give up [wind up] business; retire from business (退隠する); shut up shop 〔俗〕. ¶ 商賣敵, a trade rival; a rival in trade. —商賣人, a merchant; a trader; a professional (黒人). (商賣人根性, tradesman spirit.)

shōban (相伴する), *vt.* to partake *of*; share. ¶ 相伴者, a sharer.

shobatsu (處罰), *n.* punishment. —處罰する, to punish. —...の廉で處罰される, to be punished *for*.

shōbatsu (賞罰), *n.* rewards and penalties; sanction. —賞罰を明かにする, to reward or punish with an even hand.

shoben (處辨する), *vt.* to manage; deal *with*; transact.

shōben (小便), *n.* urine; stale (牛馬の). —小便する, ① to make [pass] water; urinate; pump ship 〔俗〕. ② (破約) to back out (of a contract); withdraw [recede] from an agreement. ¶ 小便無用, "Decency forbids"; "Commit no nuisance." —小便所, a urinal; a latrine.

shōbi (薔薇), *n.* 【植】 the rose. 「☞ *bara*.」

shōbi (焦眉の), *a.* urgent; impending; pressing. —焦眉の問題, a burning [an urgent] question. —焦眉の急, the most urgent needs. (焦眉の急を救ふ, to deal with an emergency.)

shōbi (稱美, 賞美), *n.* praise; applause; admiration. —食用として賞美さる, to be prized [valued] for food.

shōbin (魚狗), *n.* 【鳥】 the Eastern [Indo-Malay] kingfisher.

shōbō (消防), *n.* the prevention and extinction of fires. ¶ 消防出初式, the New Year's review of fire-brigades. —消防演習, a fire-drill. —消防組, a fire-brigade. —消防署, a fire-brigade station; a fire-department. —消防手, a fireman. —消防隊, a fire-brigade; a fire-company; a fire-band.

shōbu (菖蒲), *n.* 【植】 the sweet flag; the myrtle flag [grass].

shōbu (尙武の), *a.* militaristic; warlike. —尙武の氣象, military spirit; militarism.

shōbu (勝負), *n.* ❶ (勝敗) victory or defeat; final (決勝). ❷ (試合) a match; a contest; a bout. —面白い勝負, an exciting match. —勝負する, to try a fall; have a match [game; bout]; fight. ¶ 勝負事, game; gambling.

shobun (處分), *n.* ❶ (處置) settling; disposition. ❷ (處罰) punishment. ——**-suru**, *vt.* to dispose of (賣拂ふ); settle (解決); deal *with* (扱ふ); punish (處罰する). —刑法に照らして處分する, to deal with (a criminal) according to the provisions of the Criminal Code.

shōbun (性分), *n.* temperament; natural disposition.

shōbyōhei (傷病兵), *n.* the sick and wounded (soldiers).

shochi (處置), *n.* measures; management; disposition. —處置する, to manage; dispose *of*; take measures [steps] (手段を講じる); 【化】 treat *with*. —斷乎たる處置を執る, to take strong measures [decisive steps].

shōchi (承知), *n.* ❶ (承諾) consent; assent. ❷ (存知) knowledge. —御承知の通り, as you see; as you are aware. —互に承知の上で, by mutual consent. —承知する, ① (承諾する) to consent *to*; agree *to*; accede *to*. ② (知る) to know; understand; be aware *of*. ③ (勘辨する) to pardon; forgive.

shōchi (勝地), *n.* a place noted for its scenery; a famous view.

shōchin (銷沈する), *vi.* to despond; be dejected; be in low spirits.

shochō (署長), *n.* the head of a government office.

shōchō (小腸), *n.* 【解】 the small intestine.

shōchō (消長), *n.* prosperity and decay; rise and fall; the vicissitudes of fortune.

shōchō (象徵), *n.* a symbol. —象徵する, to symbolize. ¶ 象徵主義, symbolism.

shōchoku (詔勅), *n.* an Imperial Edict [Proclamation; Rescript].

shochū (暑中), *n.* midsummer; the hot season. ¶ 暑中休暇, a

summer vacation [holidays]; a long vacation (法廷·大學の). —暑中見舞, a visit during the hot season; a midsummer present.

shōchū (掌中の), *a.* in one's grasp. —掌中に歸する, to fall into the power [clutches] *of*; fall into one's hands. —掌中の珠と愛で育てる, to love and foster it as the apple [light] of one's eye. —決定權は君の掌中にある, The decision lies [rests] with you. —僕を殺すも活かすも君の掌中にある, I am at your mercy; I am in your power.

shōchū (燒酎), *n.* distilled spirit.

shōdai (昭代), *n.* a brilliant period [era]; a peaceful reign. —昭代の恨事, a blot on the bright page of the reign.

shōdai (招待), *n.* invitation. —招待する, to invite (a person to a party); ask (a person to dinner). —招待に應ずる《を斷る》, to accept《decline》an invitation. —園遊會へ招待を受ける, to receive an invitation to a garden party. ¶ 招待狀, an invitation-card; a letter of invitation. —招待券, a complimentary ticket.

shōdaku (承諾), *n.* consent; assent; compliance. —承諾する, to consent *to*; assent *to*; comply *with*. —承諾を得て, with a person's consent. —承諾を與へる, to give consent *to*.

shodan (處斷), *n.* judgment; decision. —處斷する, to judge; decide.

shodana (書棚), *n.* a book-shelf; a book-case.

shōden (小傳), *n.* a short biography; a biographical notice.

shōdo (焦土), *n.* burnt ground. —焦土と化す, to be burnt [levelled] to the ground.

shōdō (唱道する), *vt.* to advocate; preach; put [set] forth. —社會改造の唱道者, an advocate of social reconstruction. —自由を唱道する, to preach liberty.

shōdō (衝動), *n.* impulse; impulsion; shock. —衝動を與へる, to give a shock.

shōdō (聳動する), *vt.* to startle; electrify. —世界の耳目を聳動する, to electrify the world.

shōdoku (消毒), *n.* disinfection; fumigation (燻蒸). —消毒する, to disinfect; fumigate (燻蒸); sterilize (殺菌); boil (煮て). —消毒を施す, to subject to disinfection. —消毒法を施行する, to carry out disinfection. ¶ 消毒衣, disinfected clothes. —消毒室《所》, a disinfecting room《station》. —消毒藥, a disinfectant; an alexipharmic.

shōekichi (承役地), *n.* 【法】the servient land.

shōen (硝煙), *n.* powder smoke. —硝煙彈雨の中, amid the powder smoke and hail of shells.

shōfu (生麩), *n.* dried starch.

shōfuda (正札), *n.* a price-card; a price-mark. —正札附の詐僞師, an unadulterated swindler. —正札附懸値無し, one-price marked and no overcharge made.

shoga (書畫), *n.* pictures and writings; painting and calligraphy. ¶ 書畫屋, a dealer in pictures and writings.

shōga (生薑), *n.* 【植】the ginger.

shōgai (生涯), *n.* whole life; lifetime; all one's life [days]. —生涯の, lifelong. (生涯の事業とする, to make it one's lifework.)

shōgai (障害, 障碍, 障礙), *n.* an obstacle; a hindrance; an impediment. —障害を一掃する, to sweep [remove] all obstacles. ¶ 障碍物, an obstacle; a hindrance. (障碍物競走, an obstacle-race; a hurdle-race. —高《低》障碍物競走, a high《low》hurdle-race.)

shōgai (傷害), *n.* injury; harm; lesion. —傷害する, to injure; inflict an injury *upon*. ¶ 傷害保險, accident insurance.

shōgai-chōsa (涉外調査), *n.* investigation of [inquiry into] foreign affairs.

shogakari (諸掛), *n.* expenses; 【商】charges.

shōgakkō (小學校), *n.* an elementary [a primary; a common] school. ¶ (尋常《高等》小學校, an ordinary《a higher》primary [elementary] school.

shogaku(sha) (初學 -者), *n.* a beginner. —初學の書, an elementary book; a primer.

shōgaku (小學), *n.* an elementary course of study. ¶ 小學教育, elementary [primary] education. —小學教師, a primary school teacher a primary schoolmaster. —小學生, primary school children; a primary scholar.

shōgaku (小額), *n.* a small sum. ¶ 小額紙幣, a small bank-note.

shōgaku (商學), *n.* Ⓢ 商業學. commercial science. ¶ 商學士, a bachelor of commercial science.

shōgaku (獎學), *n.* encouragement of learning [study]. ¶ 獎學資金, a fund for encouragement of study.

shōgakubō (正覺坊), *n.* 【爬蟲】the green turtle.

shōgan (賞翫), *n.* appreciation. —賞翫する, to appreciate.

shōgatsu (正月), *n.* January; the New Year (新年).

shōgeki (衝擊), *n.* impingement;

percussion; shock.

shōgen (詳言する), *vt.* to state fully; give a full account *of*.

shōgen (證言), *n.* 【法】 deposition; testimony; evidence. —證言する, to testify *to*; bear witness *to*; depose; give evidence. ¶ 證言者, 【法】 a deponent.

shogeru (悄げる), *vi.* to despond; be dejected; be cast down.

shōgi (床几), *n.* a stool; a bench; a camp-stool.

shōgi (商議), *n.* consultation; negotiation; conference. —商議する, to consult *about*; negotiate; confer. ¶ 商議員, a negotiator; a councillor; a trustee (學校等の).

shōgi (將棋), *n.* Japanese chess. —將棋をさす, to have a game of chess; play at chess. ¶ 將棋盤, a chess-board.

shōgo (正午), *n.* noon; 【天】 mean noon.

shōgō (商號), *n.* a firm-name; a trade-name.

shōgō (承合する), *v.* to apply (*at* some place *for* details).

shōgō (照合), *n.* collation; comparison. —照合する, to collate; compare.

shōgō (稱號), *n.* appellation; designation; a title. —理學博士の稱號, the degree of D. Sc.

shōgun (將軍), *n.* *Shōgun* 【日】; a general (軍將).

shogyō (所業), *n.* conduct; action; doings.

shogyō (諸行, 所行), *n.* all earthly [worldly] things; all things.

shōgyō (商業), *n.* commerce; trade; (mercantile) business. —商業道德を重んずる, to set value upon commercial morality. ¶ 商業帳簿, a trade-book. —商業學校, a commercial school. —商業銀行, a commercial bank. —商業實務, commercial practice. —商業巡囘員, a commercial traveller. —商業家, a merchant; a trader. —商業會議所, a chamber of commerce. —商業區域, commercial quarters. —商業資本, trading capital. —商業使用人, trade assistants. —商業手形, a commercial bill. —商業登記簿, a commercial register.

shōhai (勝敗), *n.* victory or defeat; the issue (of the war; of the day). —勝敗を決する, to settle the day. —勝敗は時の運, Victory or defeat depends upon chance.

shōhai (賞杯), *n.* a prize-cup; a challenge cup.

shōhai (賞牌), *n.* a (prize-)medal; a medallion (大形の). ¶ 賞牌受領者, a medallist.

shohan (初犯), *n.* a first offence; a first offender (人).

shohan (諸般の), *a.* various; all every. —諸般の準備, every preparation [arrangement].

shōhei (招聘), *n.* engagement. —招聘する, to engage. —招聘に應じる, to accept another's engagement.

shōhei (哨兵), *n.* 【軍】 a sentinel; a sentry; a picket. ¶ 哨兵線, a picket [sentry]-line; lines of sentry; a cordon.

shōheki (峭壁), *n.* a precipice; a cliff.

shōheki (障壁, 墻壁), *n.* a wall; a barrier; a bar. —間に障壁を築く, to raise a barrier *between*.

shōhi (消費), *n.* 【經】 consumption; spending. —消費する, to consume; spend; use up; waste. ¶ 消費組合, a consumers' cooperative society. (消費組合員, a cooperative.) —消費者, a consumer. —消費稅, consumption-duty; excise (duty).

shōhin (小品), *n.* a short piece. ¶ 小品文, a sketch; a short piece; a morceau.

shōhin (商品), *n.* merchandise; commodities; goods; stock (總稱). ¶ 商品陳列窓, a show-window. —商品陳列室, a show-room. —商品學, a study of articles of commerce. —商品切手, a presentation-ticket. —商品目錄, a catalogue; an inventory (of stock). —商品取引所, a produce(s) exchange.

shōhin (賞品), *n.* a prize.

shoho (初步), *n.* the first step; rudiments; elements.

shohō (書法), *n.* the art of handwriting; penmanship; calligraphy.

shohō (處方), *n.* 【醫】 (medical) preparation. —處方を書く, to prescribe; write a prescription. ¶ 處方箋, a prescription; a recipe.

shohō (諸方), *n.* all directions; various quarters. —諸方から集まる, to gather from all quarters.

shōhō (商法), *n.* ❶ 【法】 the commercial law 《code》. ❷ (商賣の道) commercialism. ❸ (商賣) business; trade.

shōhō (捷報), *n.* the news [report] of a victory.

shōhō (詳報), *n.* a detailed [full] report [account]; details; particulars. —詳報を發する, to despatch a full report; report in full [detail].

shōhon (抄本), *n.* an extract; an abstract.

shōhyō (商標), *n.* a trade-mark; a brand; a stamp. ¶ 商標名, a trade(-mark)-name. —商標侵害, piracy of trade-marks.

shōhyō (證憑), *n.* testimony; a

voucher (證據となるもの).

shoi (所爲), *n.* conduct; an act; proceedings; doings; performance.

shōi (小異), *n.* minor difference. —小異を捨てて大同を取る, to disregard the minor differences and take the general similarity.

shōi (少尉), *n.* 【陸】 a second lieutenant: 【海】 a sublieutenant, 2nd class; a sublieutenant 【英】.

shoikomu (背負込む), *v.* ❶ (賣殘る) to overstock; remain unsold. ❷ (負擔する) to encumber oneself; be saddled *with*.

shoin (所員), *n.* a member of a staff.

shoin (書院), *n.* ❶ (學舍) a lecture-hall. ❷ (書齋) a study; a reading room. ❸ (貴人の客間) a parlour; a reception-room; a guest-chamber [-room].

shōin (證印), *n.* a seal affixed to a document.

shoinage (背負投を喰はす), to throw a person over after having encouraged him; (play the) jilt (女が男に).

shōja (生者必滅), The living must surely die.

shōja (盛者必衰), The prosperous must decline.

shojaku (書籍), *n.* =*shoseki*.

shoji (所持), *n.* possession. —所持の金子, money in one's possession; money one has about one. —所持する, to possess; be possessed *of*. ¶ 所持人, a holder (株式などの); a bearer (特に持參人拂小切手の); a possessor.

shōji (小事), *n.* a trifle; a trivial [small; petty] matter; a matter of little importance.

shōji (商事), *n.* commercial matters; business. ¶ 商事會社, a commercial [trading] company.

shōji (障子), *n.* a paper sliding-door; a sliding-screen. —障子越しに, through [on the other side of] a paper sliding-door. ¶ 硝子障子, a glazed sliding-screen.

shōjiki (正直), *n.* honesty; rectitude; uprightness. —正直な, honest; upright; square. —正直に云へば, to be candid; to tell the truth; candidly speaking. ¶ 正直者, an honest man.

shōjin (小人), *n.* ❶ (下劣な人) a mean person; a small man; an insignificant man. ❷ (狹量者) a narrow-minded person. ❸ (矮人) a pigmy; a Lilliputian. —小人閑居して不善を爲す, "An idle man tempts the devil."

shōjin (精進), *n.* ❶ 【佛】 devotion; assiduity (精勵). ❷ (潔齋) religious purification. ❸ (肉食を斷つこと) abstinence from animal food; vegetable diet. —精進する, ① to pursue assiduously; advance courageously (奮進). ② to exercise religious purification. ③ to abstain from animal food. ¶ 精進日, a fast-day; a day of abstinence. —精進料理, vegetable cooking [food].

shojo (處女), *n.* a virgin; a maiden. —處女性を失ふ, to lose her maidenhood. ¶ 處女地, virgin soil. —處女作, a maiden work.

shojō (書狀), *n.* a letter; an epistle; correspondence.

shōjo (少女), *n.* a young [little] girl; a maiden; a lass.

shōjō (猩猩), *n.* ❶ 【哺乳】 the orang-outang. ❷ (大酒家) a hard drinker.

shōjō (症狀), *n.* a symptom.

shōjō (清淨), *n.* purity; cleanness; immaculateness. ——**-na,** *a.* pure; clean; undefiled; immaculate. —清淨無垢な少女, a pure and innocent maiden.

shōjō (賞狀), *n.* a certificate of merit. —賞狀を授與する, to hand [confer] a certificate of merit.

shōjū (小銃), *n.* a rifle; a musket.

shojun (初旬), *n.* the first ten days of a month. —來月初旬, early next month.

shōjun (照準), *n.* aim; laying. —照準する, to (take) aim [sight]; lay (a gun); collimate (望遠鏡·顯微鏡等を).

shoka (書家), *n.* a calligraphist, calligrapher.

shōka (上下), *n.* the high and low; the governing and the governed (官民). ☞ *jōge*. —上下する, to move up and down; rise and fall; heave and set (船, 波); fluctuate (相場).

shōka (昇華), *n.* 【化】 sublimation. ¶ 昇華物, a sublimate.

shōka (消火), *n.* extinguishing of fire. ¶ 消火ポンプ, a fire-engine. —消火器, a fire-extinguisher; an extinguisher. —消火栓, a fire-plug (F. P. と略す); a fire-hydrant.

shōka (消化), *n.* ❶ (食物の) digestion. ❷ (知識の) mental assimilation; digestion. —消化する, to digest. —消化し易き, easy of digestion. ¶ 消化不良, indigestion; dyspepsia, dyspepsy. —消化器, the digestive organs; the organs of digestion.

shōka (商家), *n.* a commercial [mercantile] house; a shop.

shōka (唱歌), *n.* a song; singing; vocal music. —唱歌を歌ふ, to sing (a song). ¶ 唱歌敎室, a singing-room.

shōka (漿果), *n.* a berry.

shōkachi (消渴), *n.* 【醫】 diabetes insipidus (單尿崩); diabetes mellitus (糖尿病). 「pany.

shōkai (商會), *n.* a firm; a com-

shōkai (紹介), *n.* introduction; presentation. —H氏の紹介で, by Mr. H's introduction. —外國に紹介する, to introduce to foreign countries. ¶ 紹介狀, a letter of introduction. —紹介者, an introducer.

shōkai (詳解), *n.* exposition; detailed explanation 《introduction》. —詳解する, to explain minutely; introduce in detail.

shōkai (照會), *n.* inquiry [communication] by letter; reference; inquiry. —照會する, to communicate (*with*); refer *to* (his former employer for his character (人物の如何を前主人に).

shōkaku (昇格), *n.* promotion of status [rank]. **—— - suru,** *v.* to raise 《be raised》 in status. —大學に昇格する, to raise 《be raised》 to the status of a university. ¶ 昇格運動, movement for the promotion of the school status.

shokan (所管), *n.* 【法】 competency; jurisdiction. ¶ 所管廳, the proper [competent] authorities; the authorities concerned.

shokan (所感), *n.* impression; thought. —所感を述べる, to give one's impressions; express one's thoughts; give expression to one's opinion.

shokan (書翰), *n.* a letter; an epistle; correspondence. ¶ 書翰文, a composition in epistolary style.

shōkan (召喚), *n.* 【法】 citation; summons; call. —召喚する, to cite; summon; call (up); subpœna. ¶ 召喚狀, a writ of [written] summons; a citation; a subpœna.

shōkan (召還する), *vt.* to recall.

shōkan (哨艦), *n.* a look-out ship.

shōkan (商館), *n.* a firm; a concern; a mercantile [commercial] house. ¶ 外國商館, a foreign firm [mercantile house]; a hong (支那の).

shōkan (將官), *n.* ❶ 【陸】 a general officer. ❷ 【海】 an admiral; a flag officer. ¶ 將官相當官, an officer ranking with a general 《flag》 officer. 「☞ *kanshō*.

shōkan (賞鑑), *n.* appreciation.

shōkan (償還), *n.* payment; repayment; redemption. —償還する, to redeem; pay; repay. ¶ 償還期限, the term [period] of redemption. —償還基金, an amortization [a sinking] fund.

shōkanshū (商慣習), *n.* commercial [mercantile; business] usage (事實たる); usage of trade (同上); a commercial custom (法律たる).

shokatsu (所轄), *n.* competency; jurisdiction. ¶ 所轄警察署, the competent police(-station).

shoke (所化), *n.* a priestling.

shokei (處刑), *n.* punishment. —處刑する, to punish.

shōkei (少憩), *n.* a recess; a short rest. 「*keishō*.

shōkei (承繼), *n.* succession. ☞

shōkei (捷徑), *n.* a short cut; a royal road *to*.

shōkei (象形-文字), *n.* a hieroglyph; hieroglyphics.

shōkei (晶形), *n.* crystal.

shōkei (憧憬する), *vt.* to long [yearn] *for*. ☞ *akogareru*.

shoken (所見), *n.* one's view [opinion]. ☞ *iken*. —所見を異にする, to differ in opinion.

shōken (商權), *n.* commercial right [power]. —商權を握る, to hold the commercial right.

shōken (證劵), *n.* an instrument; a bond; a bill. ¶ 假證劵, a scrip. —證劵取引, stock negotiations.

shoketsu (處決), *n.* ❶ (裁決) decision. ❷ (覺悟) resolution. ☞ *ketsudan*. —處決する, to decide; determine; resolve.

shōketsu (猖獗なる), *a.* violent; virulent; vehement. —猖獗なる勢を以て, with great violence.

shoki (初期), *n.* the first [initial] stage; the beginning; the early days [period] (時代).

shoki (所期), *n.* expectation; anticipation. —所期に反する, to be contrary to (one's) expectation.

shoki (書記), *n.* a clerk; a writer; a secretary. ¶ 郡書記, a clerk of a district office. —裁判所監督書記, a superintending [chief] clerk of a court. —書記長, a head clerk; a chief clerk. —書記課, a section of clerks. —書記官, a secretary. (書記官長, a chief secretary.) —外務書記生, a chancellor of the Foreign Office.

shoki (暑氣), *n.* the heat; hot weather. ¶ 暑氣中(ア), suffering from the heat; heat-stroke.

shōki (正氣), *n.* right senses; sobriety; right mind. —正氣にかへる, to recover oneself; come to oneself; come to one's senses. —正氣を失ふ, to lose one's senses [mind]; faint (氣絶する).

shōki (商機), *n.* business opportunity. —商機を失する[逸する], to miss a business opportunity.

shōki (燒棄する), *vt.* to burn; commit to the flames; reduce to ashes. ¶ 塵芥燒棄場, a place for burning garbage.

shōkin (正金), *n.* specie; hard cash; real money. —正金で支拂ふ, to pay in specie. —正金に引換へる, to cash; convert [turn] into cash; realize. ¶ 正金銀行, a specie bank.

shōkin (賞金), *n.* a prize in money; a cash prize; a reward. —賞金をかけて…を募集する, to offer prizes in money *for*....

shōkin (償金), *n.* indemnity (特に媾和の一條件としての); compensation. —償金を課する, to charge with indemnity.

shōkinrui (涉禽類), *n.* 【動】 Grallatores (學名); the waders.

shokkaku (食客), *n.* a hanger-on; a dependant; a parasite.

shokkaku (觸角), *n.* 【動】 a palp, palpus; a feeler; an antenna.

shokkaku (觸覺), *n.* (the sense of) touch; feel; a tactile sense. ¶ 觸覺器, a touch [tactile] organ.

shokkan (觸感), *n.* touch.

shokke (食氣), *n.* appetite.

shokken (職權), *n.* authority; official powers. —職權外の, extra-official. —職權を以て, of one's [its] own motion; on one's own authority. —職權を濫用する, to abuse one's authority; override one's commission; act *ultra vires.*

shokki (食器), *n.* table-ware.

shokki (織機), *n.* a loom; a weaving machine.

shokkō (燭光), *n.* candle-power (光力); candle-light (蠟燭の光). —五十燭光, fifty candle-power.

shokkō (職工), *n.* a workman; a mechanic (機械工); an artisan (匠工); a craftsman (職人). ¶ 職工長, a foreman. —職工學校, an artisan school; a technical school.

shokku (衝動), *n.* shock.

shoko (書庫), *n.* a library.

shokō (諸侯), *n.* feudal lords; territorial barons.

shokō (曙光), *n.* ❶ dawn; morning twilight; aurora. ❷ (徵候) a symptom. —平和の曙光, a prospect of peace.

shōko (尙古), *n.* classicolatry.

shōko (稱呼), *n.* name; nomination; appellation; designation.

shōko (證據), *n.* proof; evidence; testimony. —證據十分なる, well-authenticated. —證據立てる, to prove; testify; authenticate; bear witness *to.* —此を證據として, on this authority [evidence]; with this as proof. —證據として提出する to produce in evidence. —證據不十分で放免になる, to be acquitted on account of insufficiency of evidence. ¶ 證據物件, an evidence; a corroboration; an exhibit. —證據金, warrant-money; deposit in security; margin (取引所の).

shōkō (小康), *n.* temporary ease; brief tranquillity; a lull (病·戰爭などの). —小康を得る, to come to a state of lull.

shōkō (昇汞), *n.* 【化】 corrosive sublimate; bichloride of mercury; mercuric chloride. ¶ 昇汞水, a solution of corrosive sublimate.

shōkō (昇降), *n.* ascent and descent; rise and fall; fluctuation (動搖). —昇降する, to go down and up; ascend and descend; fluctuate. ¶ 昇降舵, 【飛】 an elevator. —昇降口, an entrance; 【航】 a hatch; a hatchway. —昇降機, a lift (英); an elevator (米).

shōkō (症候), *n.* symptoms.

shōkō (消光する), *v.* to spend one's time; pass time.

shōkō (商工-業), *n.* commerce and industry. —商工業の發達に俟つ, to depend upon the development of commerce and industry. ¶ 商工大臣, the Minister of (State for) Commerce and Industry. —商工省, the Ministry [Department] of Commerce and Industry.

shōkō (商港), *n.* a commercial port; a trade port.

shōkō (將校), *n.* an (a commissioned) officer. ¶ 將校集會所, an officers' mess-hall.

shōkō (燒香する), *vi.* to burn incense (before a coffin).

shōkōdenpō (照校電報), *n.* a collated telegram (T C と略す).

shōkōi (商行爲), *n.* a commercial act [transaction.]

shōkoku (生國), *n.* one's native country 《province》; one's native land. ☞ *kokyō.*

shokon (初婚), *n.* the first marriage.

shōkōnetsu (猩紅熱), *n.* scarlet fever; scarlatina.

shōkon-sai (招魂祭), *n.* a memorial service for those killed in war. ¶ 招魂社, a shrine dedicated to those who died for their country; a pantheon.

shōkotsu (掌骨), *n.* 【解】 the metacarpus; a metacarpal bone.

shoku (食), *n.* ❶ (食物) food; victuals. ❷ (食事) eating; meal. ❸ (食慾) an appetite. —食が進まない, to have a poor appetite. —食を取る, to take [eat] something.

shoku (蝕), *n.* 【天】 eclipse; occultation.

shoku (職), *n.* ❶ (任務) duty; function. ❷ (職業) an occupation; a calling. ☞ *shokugyō.* —職に就く, to find [get] a position; assume the post *of.* —職を求め

る, to seek [apply] for employment; search after a position. —職を失ふ, to lose one's position; be out of employment [work]; lose one's job 【俗】. —職を解く, to relieve a person of his post.

shokuatari (食あたり), *n.* Ⓢ 急性胃加答兒. acute catarrhal gastritis; indigestion.

shokubō (囑望する), *vt.* to put hopes *in* [*on*]; expect *of* [*from*].

shokubun (職分), *n.* functions; duties; mission (天職). —職分を盡す, to discharge one's duties [functions].

shokubutsu (植物), *n.* a plant; vegetation; flora (一地方又は一時代の). —植物性の, vegetal; vegetable; vegetative. ¶ 植物園, a botanical garden. —植物標本, a botanical specimen. —植物採集, herborization; plant-collecting. (植物採集者 [家], a herborist; a plant-collector.) —植物帶, a floral zone; a zone of vegetation.

shokuchi (諸口), *n.* sundries.

shokuchi (觸知する), *vt.* to feel.

shokuchō (職長), *n.* a foreman; a chief workman.

shokuchū (植蟲), *n.* 【動】 the zoophyte; the phytozoon.

shokuchūrui (食蟲類), *n.* 【動】 Insectivora (學名); the insectivores.

shokudai (燭臺), *n.* a candle-stick; a chandelier.

shokudō (食堂), *n.* a dining-room; a dining hall; a refreshment-room (停車場等の). ¶ 簡易食堂, the people's dining saloon. —食堂車, a dining-car; a dining-saloon; a buffet-car.

shokudō (食道), *n.* 【解】 the œsophagus; the gullet. ¶ 食道炎, œsophagitis. —食道癌, cancer of the œsophagus.

shokuen (食鹽), *n.* (common) salt; table salt. ¶ 食鹽注射, salt injection. —食鹽灌腸, salt clyster.

shokugen (食言する), *vi.* to eat one's words; break one's word; go back on one's word.

shokugo (食後), *ad.* after a meal.

shokugyō (職業), *n.* an occupation; a profession (知識的); a calling; a vocation; a trade (職商賣). ☞ *shoku*. —職業とする, to make it one's business to.... ¶ 職業案內 (新聞の廣告), advertisements for situations. —職業婦人《政治家》, a professional woman 《politician》. —職業教育, professional education. —職業紹介所, an employment exchange; an employment office.

shokuhatsu-suirai (觸發水雷), *n.* a contact mine.

shokuhi (食費), *n.* charge for board.

shokuhi (植皮 -法), *n.* skin-grafting [-planting]; transplantation of skin. —植皮する, to graft skin *in* [*on*, *etc.*].

shokuhin (食品), *n.* eatables; an article of food; provisions.

shokuin (職員), *n.* the staff; personnel; faculty (學校等の). ¶ 職員錄, a list of government officials.

shokuji (食事), *n.* meal; diet. —食事中, at meals [table]. —食事する, to dine; take a meal.

shokuji (植字), *n.* type-setting; typography. —植字する, to compose; set type; set up (an MS). ¶ 植字工, a compositor; a type-setter.

shokujin-jinshu (食人人種), *n.* a cannibal race; the anthropophagi.

shokujo (織女), *n.* 【天】 Vega; α [alpha] Lyra.

shokuken (食券), *n.* ❶ (食堂で割引して賣る) a meal ticket. ❷ (食糧引換券) a food coupon.

shokumin (植民, 殖民), *n.* colonization; colonists. —植民する, to colonize; settle. ¶ 植民地, a colony; a settlement. —植民政策, colonial policy.

shokumō (觸毛), *n.* a feeler; 【動】 a palp, palpus; a cirrus.

shokumoku (囑目する), *vt.* to pay close attention *to*.

shokumotsu (食物), *n.* food; eatables; fare; victuals; diet (規定の); an article of food. ¶ 食物 [食餌] 療法, diet-cure.

shokumu (職務), *n.* duties; service; functions. —職務上の, official. —職務勉勵の廉を以て, for diligence in the discharge of his duties. ¶ 職務俸, a salary attached to a post.

shokun (諸君), gentlemen; you.

shokunin (職人), *n.* a workman; an artisan (工匠); a mechanic (機械工); an operative; a hand. —職人體の怪しい男, a suspicious-looking man in a workman's clothes.

shōkunkyoku (賞勳局), *n.* the Bureau [Board] of Decorations.

shokunō (職能), *n.* function.

shokupan (食麵麭), *n.* bread.

shokurai (觸雷する), *vi.* to touch a mine; strike a mine.

shokurin (植林, 殖林), *n.* afforestation.

shokuryō (食料), *n.* ❶ food; food-stuffs; victuals. ❷ (賄料) the charge for boarding; board. ¶ 食料品, food-stuffs. (食料品屋, a victualler.)

shokuryō (食糧), *n.* provisions.

☞ *ryōshoku*. ¶ 食糧管理, food control. (食糧管理官, the food controller. —食糧管理を行ふ, to exercise control of the nation's food supplies.) —食糧局《省》, the food bureau 《ministry》.

shokusan (殖產), *n.* increase of productions; industry.

shokuseki (職責), *n.* duty; responsibility. —職責を重んずる, to be attentive to one's duty.

shokusetsu (觸接), *n.* contact. ¶ 觸接傳染, contagion.

shokushi (食指), *n.* the forefinger; the index finger. —食指大に動く, to be itching to do it.

shokushi (喞子), *n.* 【機】 a piston; a sucker (吸上ポンプの).

shokushō (食傷), *n.* surfeit (過食); indigestion (不消化). —食傷する, to be surfeited; suffer indigestion.

shokushō (職掌), *n.* (official) duties; functions.

shokushu (觸手), *n.* 【動】 a tentacle; a feeler.

shokushu (觸鬚), *n.* 【動】 a palp, palpus (昆蟲の); a wattle (魚の); a feeler.

shoku-suru (食する), *vt.* =*kuu*.

shoku-suru (蝕する), *v.* to eclipse.

shokutaku (食卓), *n.* a dining-table; a table; a board. —食卓を圍める人々, the table. —食卓に就く, to sit at table. —食卓の用意する, to lay the cloth; set the table. ¶ 食卓料, board; table-money (將校などに給する).

shokutaku (囑託), *n.* ❶ a person not on the regular staff. ❷ = *irai* (依賴). —內務省囑託某氏, a certain person commissioned by the Home Department. ¶ 囑託敎師, a teacher not on the regular staff.

shokuyasumi (食休), *n.* mid-day recess.

shokuyō (食用), *n.* use for food. —食用に適する, to be eatable [edible; esculent]; be good to eat.

shokuyoku (食慾), *n.* appetite; 【醫】 orexis. —食慾がある《無い》, to have an 《no》 appetite. —食慾を滿たす, to satisfy one's appetite. —食慾を進める, to whet [sharpen] one's appetite.

shokuyu (職由する), *vi.* to be chiefly due *to*; be mainly owing *to*; be mostly caused *by*.

shokuzai (贖罪), *n.* atonement; expiation. —贖罪する, to atone for a crime; expiate one's sin. ¶ 贖罪金, ransom.

shokuzen (食前), *ad.* before meal. —每日三回食前服用, to be taken before meals three times a day.

shōkyaku (消却), *n.* 【商】 amortization. —消却する, to amortize. ¶ 減價消却勘定, 【商】 depreciation account.

shōkyaku (銷却する), *vt.* to withdraw.

shōkyaku (償却), *n.* repayment; redemption; refundment. ☞ *shōkan*. —**-suru**, *vt.* to repay; redeem; pay [clear] off; amortize. —公債を償却する, to redeem a public loan. ¶ 買入償却, redemption by purchase.

shōkyō (商況), *n.* the condition [state] of trade [market]; trade; the market; business. —商況不振なり, The trade [market] is dull [heavy; depressed].

shōkyoku (消極), *n.* the negative pole; the negative. —消極的財政策, a negative financial policy.

shokyū (初給), *n.* the first pay; the pay to begin *with*; the entrance [starting] salary.

shōkyū (昇給), *n.* increase [rise; raise 【米】] of salary. —昇給する, to have one's salary increased; get an increase of salary.

shōkyū (陞級), *n.* promotion; advance; rise. ☞ *shōshin*.

shōkyū (撞球), *n.* billiards. ¶ 撞球臺, a billiard-table. —撞球者, a billiard-player.

shōma (しょうま), *n.* 【植】 the bugbane.

shōmakyō (照魔鏡), *n.* a magic mirror. —照魔鏡に照される, to be exposed to the search-light.

shomei (署名), *n.* signature; sign manual. —署名する, to sign (one's name); set one's hand *to*. —署名捺印する, to sign and seal; set one's hand and seal *to*. ¶ 署名發行人, the nominal publisher. —署名國, a signatory power. —署名者, a signatory; a signer.

shōmei (照明), *n.* illumination. ¶ 照明彈, a flare-bomb. —照明器, an illuminator.

shōmei (證明), *n.* verification; attestation; authentication; 【數】 demonstration. —證明する, to verify; testify *to*; attest; bear witness *to*; demonstrate (學理など). ¶ 證明者, a certifier; a demonstrator; a verifier. —證明書, a certificate; a testimonial (性格·行爲·資格の); a voucher. (在學證明書, a school-certificate. —身元證明書, a reference.)

shomen (書面), *n.* ❶ (手紙) a letter. ❷ (文書) a document; a writing. —御書面の趣, the contents [purport] of your letter.

shōmen (正面), *n.* ❶ the front; the face; 【建】 a façade. ❷ (正面棧敷) a seat facing the stage. —(汽船·汽車など) 正面衝突をな

す, to collide head on. —(汽船·飛行機が) 正面遭遇をなす, to meet end on. ¶ 正面攻撃, a frontal attack. ¶ 正面圖, a front view.
shōmetsu (生滅), *n.* appearance and disappearance; life and death.
shōmetsu (消滅), *n.* disappearance; extinction; lapse. —權利の消滅, lapse of right. —消滅する, to disappear; cease; lapse.
shōmi (正味), *n.* ❶ (風袋を取除いた目方) net weight. ❷ (眞の事物) the truth; the real case. —正味三日, three clear days.
shōmi (賞味する), *vt.* to relish; taste; appreciate.
shomin (庶民), *n.* the common people; the masses; the populace.
shomō (所望), *n.* desire; wish; hope. ☞ *nozomi*. —所望する, to hope; desire; wish *for*.
shōmō (消耗), *n.* consumption; exhaustion; wear and tear. —消耗する, to consume; waste; use up. ¶ 消耗費, wear and tear expenses. —消耗品, an article of consumption.
shomoku (書目), *n.* a catalogue [of books.]
shōmon (證文), *n.* a bond; a deed; an instrument.
shomotsu (書物), *n.* a book. 【註】書物の天即ち上端を top edge, 地を bottom edge, 開くべき小口を fore edge, 背を back と云ふ.
shomu (庶務), *n.* general affairs. ¶ 庶務課, the section of general affairs. —庶務係, an official (a clerk) in charge of general affairs.
shōmu (商務), *n.* commercial affairs. ¶ 商務官, a commercial commissioner. ¶ 商務局, the Bureau of Commerce.
shomu-kitei (處務規程), *n.* regulations for the conduct of business; proceedings; regulations.
shōmyō (唱名), *n.* reciting Amitabha Buddha's name.
shōne (性根), *n.* natural disposition; temper; mind; the core (心底). —性根の腐った男, a fellow of bad disposition; a corrupt man.
shonen (初年), *n.* the first year; the early years. ¶ 初年兵, 【軍】 new recruits. ☞ *shinpei*.
shōnen (少年), *n.* a child; a boy; a lad. ¶ 少年(義勇)團, boy scouts. (少年團員, a (boy) scout.) —少年文學, juvenile literature. —少年時代, childhood; boyhood. —少年裁判所, a juvenile court.
shōni (小兒), *n.* an infant; a child. ¶ 小兒科, pædiatrics, pædiatry.
shōnin (上人, 聖人), *n.* a saint; a father; a holy priest.
shōnin (商人), *n.* a merchant; a tradesman (特に店商人); a shopkeeper (店主). ¶ 商人氣質, mercantilism; trade-spirit.
shōnin (承認), *n.* recognition; acknowledgment; approval; acceptance. —承認する, to recognize; acknowledge; approve.
shōnin (證人), *n.* 【法】 a witness: an attestor; a certifier. —證人に立つ, to bear witness *to*. ¶ 證人旅費, conduct-money.
shōnō (小農), *n.* ❶ a small [petty] farmer; a peasant-proprietor (自作小農). ❷ (小農法) *petite culture*.
shōnō (小腦), *n.* 【解】 the cerebellum.
shōnō (樟腦), *n.* camphor; Japan [[Dutch] camphor.]
shōnyūdō (鐘乳洞), *n.* a stalactite grotto.
shōnyūseki (鐘乳石), *n.* 【鑛】 [stalactite.]
shōō (照應), *n.* correspondence; concurrence; accordance. —照應する, to correspond *with* [*to*]; concur; accord *with*.
shōrai (招來する), *vt.* to bring [(about).]
shōrai (將來), *n.* the future; the time to come. —, *ad.* in future; for the future; hereafter (今後); some day (他日). —近き將來に, in the near future. —將來有望である, to be promising; have bright prospects. —將來を誡める, to warn a person for the future.
shōrei (省令), *n.* a departmental ordinance.
shōrei (奬勵), *n.* encouragement; stimulation; patronage (文學者·美術家などの). —奬勵する, to encourage; stimulate; patronize. ¶ 奬勵金, a bounty; a subsidy (補助金); a subvention (同上).
shori (處理), *n.* treatment; management; dealing. ☞ *shochi*. —處理する, to treat *with*; manage; deal *with*.
shōri (小利), *n.* small profit [gain].
shōri (勝利), *n.* victory; win; triumph. ☞ *kachi*. —華々しい勝利, a splendid [glorious] victory. —日本の勝利に歸する, to end in a victory for Japan. ¶ 勝利者, a conqueror; a victor; a winner.
shorō (所勞), *n.* illness; ailment; [indisposition.]
shōro (衝路), *n.* ❶ a main road. ❷ (場所の) the centre. —東海の衝路に當る, to be on the main roadway of the Tōkaidō.
shōrō (檣樓), *n.* 【航】 a top; a crow's nest; a lookout.
shōrō (鐘樓), *n.* a belfry; a bell-tower; a campanile.
shōroku (抄錄), *n.* an abstract; an extract; an epitome. —抄錄する, to make an abstract *of*; extract; quote *from* (引用する).

shōru (肩 掛), *n.* a shawl.
shorui (書 類), *n.* documents; papers; instruments. ¶ 一件書類, documents relating to the matter. 一哲學書類, philosophical works.
shōryaku (省略), *n.* ❶ (略除) omission. ❷ (要 約) abridgment; abbreviation; contraction. 一省略する, to omit; pass over; abridge; abbreviate. ¶ 省略符, 【文】 an apostrophe.
shōryaku (商略), *n.* ❶ (商業上の駈引) commercial [business] policy. ❷ (謀) policy; tact.
shōryō (小量, 少量), *n.* ❶ 【少】 a small quantity; a modicum. ❷ 【小】 (狹量) a small [narrow] mind; narrow-mindedness.
shōryō (涉獵する), *vt.* to read *through*; look *through*; range *over* [scamper *through*] (many books).
shōryō (精靈), *n.* the spirit (of the dead).
shoryō-no-kami (諸陵頭), *n.* the Chief Keeper of Imperial Mausolea.
shoryōryō (諸陵寮), *n.* the Bureau of Imperial Mausolea.
shosa (所 作), *n.* ❶ (所行) conduct; deed; action. ❷ (こなし) demeanour; behaviour; deportment. ❸ (踊) dance. ¶ 所作事, (mimetic) posture-dances.
shōsa (少佐), *n.* ❶ 【陸】 a major. ❷ 【海】 a lieutenant-commander.
shōsa (照查), *n.* examination by reference. 一照査する, to examine by reference.
shosai (書 齋), *n.* a study.
shōsai (詳細), *n.* details; particulars; minutiæ. 一詳細を極めた説明, full and particular account. 一詳細な, minute; detailed; circumstantial. 一詳細に, minutely; in detail; in full.
shōsan (消 散), *n.* dissipation; evanescence; 【醫】 resolution (腫物の). 一消散さす, to dissipate; scatter; disperse. 一消散する, to dissipate; scatter; resolve; lift (雲·霧等が).
shōsan (硝酸), *n.* 【化】 nitric acid. ¶ 硝酸銀, nitrate of silver; caustic silver; lunar caustic.
shōsan (勝算), *n.* calculating upon a victory; prospects of success [victory]. 一勝算あり, to stand a good chance of victory.
shōsan (稱讚, 賞讚), *n.* praise; admiration; approbation. 一稱讚を博する, to win (high) praise; meet with approbation. —— -**suru**, *vt.* to praise; admire; extol. 一稱讚するに言葉なし, to be above praise [beyond all praise].
shōsasshi (小冊子), *n.* a pamphlet.
shōsatsu (笑殺する), *v.* ❶ (大に笑はせる) to cause a great laughter. ❷ (あざ笑ふ) to laugh away [*at*]; pooh-pooh away.
shosei (初生), *n.* first birth; first formation. ¶ 初生兒, a first child.
shosei (書 生), *n.* ❶ (學生) a student; a scholar. ❷ (玄關番) a student-servant. ❸ (門 生) a pupil; a disciple.
shosei (處世), *n.* conduct in life; living. 一處世の方針として, as one's guiding principle in life. 一處世術に拙い, to be inept in the art of *savoir-vivre*.
shōsei (小成), *n.* small success; small accomplishment. 一小成に安んずる, to be contented with small success.
shōsei (笑聲), *n.* a sound of laughter; laughter; laugh.
shōsei (照星), *n.* a foresight; a muzzle-sight; a front sight.
shoseki (書 籍), *n.* books; literature. 一書籍上の知識, book-learning; book-lore; book knowledge. ¶ 書籍出版業者, a publisher.
shōseki (硝 石), *n.* 【化】 nitre; saltpetre.
shōseki (證 跡), *n.* evidence; proof.
shōsekkai (消石灰), *n.* slaked lime.
shōsekkō (燒石膏), *n.* plaster of Paris.
shosen (所詮), *ad.* after all; in the end; eventually.
shōsen (省線), *n.* =*kansen* (官線). ¶ 省線電車, an electric car on a government line.
shōsen (商 船), *n.* a merchant ship [vessel]; a merchantman; a trader; the mercantile marine. ¶ 商船學校, a mercantile marine school; a nautical college [school].
shōsen (商戰), *n.* a commercial campaign.
shosetsu (諸 說), *n.* various [different] views; varied accounts; various theories.
shōsetsu (小說), *n.* a novel; fiction; a story. ¶ 滑稽小說, a humorous story. 一戀愛小說, a love [an erotic] novel. 一寫實小說, a realistic novel. 一小說本, a story-book; a novel. 一小說家, a novelist; a story-writer; a fictionist.
shōsetsu (詳說する), *v.* to explain in detail; dwell [expatiate] *upon*; give full account.
shōsha (商 社), *n.* a company; a firm; a concern; a trading [mercantile] company [firm].
shōsha (瀟 洒), *n.* nattiness; neatness; cleanliness. 一瀟洒たる, natty; neat; clean.

shōshaku (照尺), *n.* the back-sight.

shōshaku (燒灼), *n.* 【醫】 cautery; cauterization. ―燒灼する, to cauterize.

shoshi (書肆), *n.* a book-shop; a book-store 〔米〕; a bookseller's.

shoshi (庶子), *n.* a legitimized child.

shōshi (硝子), *n.* glass. ¶ 硝子樣液, 【解】 vitreous humour.

shōshi (將指), *n.* the middle finger.

shōshi (燒死する), *vi.* to be burnt to death; perish in a [by] fire.

shoshiki (書式), *n.* a form; an established form. ―規定の書式通りに, according to the form provided.

shoshiki (諸色, 諸式), *n.* (all kinds of) goods; all merchandise; commodities. ―諸式が高くて, with the prices high up.

shoshin (初心), *n.* ❶ (未熟) inexperience. ❷ (うぶ) naïveté.

shoshin (初審), *n.* the first hearing [instance].

shoshin (所信), *n.* belief; opinion; principle (主義).

shoshin (書信), *n.* ❶ (文通) communication; correspondence. ❷ (書翰) a letter.

shōshin (小心), *n.* ❶ (細心) cautiousness; carefulness; prudence. ❷ (臆病) timidity; timorousness. ―小心翼々として, very cautiously [carefully]; scrupulously; with circumspection. ―小心なる, ① cautious; careful; prudent. ② timid; timorous; faint-[chicken-]hearted. ¶ 小心者, a faint-heart; a timid person.

shōshin (昇進), *n.* promotion; advancement; rise. ―昇進さす, to promote; advance; raise. ―少將に昇進する, to be promoted to (the rank of) major-general.

shōshitsu (消失), *n.* disappearance. ―消失する, to vanish; disappear.

shōshitsu (燒失する), *vi.* to be burnt up [out; down]; be destroyed [consumed] by fire.

shosho (處處), *ad.* at [in] several places; here and there. ―處々を彷徨[さまよ]ふ, to wander from place to place.

shōsho (詔書), *n.* an Imperial edict [rescript].

shōsho (證書), *n.* a bond (債務の); a deed (讓渡の); a voucher (支拂受取等の); a certificate (證明の); a diploma (卒業證書等). ―證書を作成する, to draw up a deed. ¶ 證書書換, renewal of a deed [bond].

shōshō (少少), *ad.* little (量); few (數). ☞ *sukoshi*.

shōshō (少將), *n.* ❶ 【陸】 a major-general. ❷ 【海】 a rear-admiral.

shōshō (商相), *n.* *shōkō* (商工大臣).

shōshoku (小食), *n.* spare diet. ¶ 小食家, a spare eater.

shōshū (召集), *n.* call; convocation; 【軍】 levy; muster. ―― -**suru**, *vt.* to call out; convene; convoke; levy (兵士·軍隊等を); muster (同上). ―帝國議會は每年召集される, The Imperial Diet is convoked every year. ¶ 召集令狀, an order to join the colours.

shōso (勝訴), *n.* winning a case. ―勝訴になる, to win a suit; result [be decided] in favour *of*.

shōsō (少壯), *n.* youth; the young. ―少壯の, young.

shōsō (尙早), *n.* prematurity. ―出兵尙早論を唱へる, to pronounce the expedition premature.

shōsō (焦燥), *n.* irritation; fretfulness.

shōsoku (消息), *n.* ❶ (變遷) change. ❷ (動靜) movement; condition; state. ❸ (報道) news; tidings; information. ―實業界の消息に通ずる, to be posted in the news of the business world. ―消息を傳へる, to bring tidings; inform *of*; bring word. ¶ 消息文, a letter of personal inquiry [intelligence]. ―消息通, a well-informed person; well-informed quarters; those in the know.

shoson (書損), *n.* an error [a mistake] in writing; a clerical error; a slip of the pen.

shōsū (小數), *n.* 【數】 a decimal; a decimal fraction. ¶ 小數點, a decimal point [sign]; a point. (小數點を打つ, to point off.) 【註】 7·53 は seven point five three と讀む.

shōsū (少數), *n.* a small number; a minority. ¶ 少數派, a minority party; the minority.

shōsui (將帥), *n.* a commander; a commandant; a general.

shōsui (憔悴), *n.* emaciation; haggardness; tabefaction. ―憔悴する, to be emaciated; be haggard; tabefy.

sho-suru (書する), *vt.* to write; copy (寫す).

sho-suru (處する), *v.* ❶ (處理する) to manage; deal *with*; treat. ❷ (住む) to live; get on. ❸ (一身を) to conduct oneself; decide by oneself (自決). ❹ (處罰する) to punish; condemn; sentence (宣告). ―世に處するの道, the way to get on in the world. ―罰金に處せらる, to be punished with a fine; be condemned to a fine.

shō-suru (稱する), *vt.* ❶ (呼稱する) to call; name; entitle. ❷ (詐る) to plead; pretend; feign. ❸ =*shō-suru* (賞する) の ❶. —病氣と稱して, on the pretext of illness.

shō-suru (賞する), *vt.* ❶ (賞讃) to praise; applaud; admire. ❷ (賞與) to reward.

shō-suru (證する), *vt.* to prove. ☞ *shōmei* (證明する).

shotai (所帶, 世帶), *n.* housekeeping; household; an establishment. —所帶を持つ, to keep (a) house; set up a house; settle down. —所帶を疊む, to wind up one's affairs; break up a house. ¶ 所帶道具, household furniture; kitchen utensils.

shōtai (小隊), *n.* 【軍】a section. ¶ 半箇小隊, a subsection; a half section. —小隊長, a section leader [commander].

shōtai (正體), *n.* ❶ (本質) the real form; the natural [original] shape; the true character. ❷ (正氣) consciousness; sense. —正體を現はす, to show one's true colours; throw off [pull off; drop] the mask; reveal its real form (化物など). —前後正體なし, to be utterly senseless.

shōtai (招待), *n.* =*shōdai*.

shōtaku (沼澤), *n.* a swamp; a bog; a marsh. ¶ 沼澤地, a fenland; a marsh; a swamp.

shōtan (小膽), *n.* timidity; cowardice; pusillanimity. ☞ *okubyō*. —小膽な, timid; cowardly; pusillanimous.

shōtan (賞嘆する), *vt.* to admire. —賞嘆に値する, to be worthy of admiration.

shōtchū (始終), *ad.* all the time; constantly. ☞ *shijū* (始終).

shote (初手), *n.* the first; the beginning; the outset; the start.

shōtei (哨艇), *n.* a patrol-vessel.

shoten (書店), *n.* a book-shop; a book-store [米]; a bookseller's.

shōten (昇天), *n.* ascension (基督の); assumption (聖母の). —昇天する, to ascend to heaven.

shōten (商店), *n.* a shop; a store; a firm; a mercantile [business] house.

shōten (焦點, 燒點), *n.* 【理】a focus. —非難の焦點となる, to become the focus [centre] of censure [a target for censure].

shotō (初等), *n.* the first grade. ¶ 初等科, an elementary course. —初等教育, elementary education.

shotō (蔗糖), *n.* 【化】sucrose; saccharose.

shotō (諸島), *n.* islands.

shōtō (消燈する), *v.* to put out lights. ¶ 消燈喇叭, "lights out." —消燈時間, the hour for putting out lights.

shotoku (所得), *n.* income; revenue; incomings. ¶ 超過所得, excess income. —所得稅, income tax.

shōtoku (生得), *n.* ❶ innateness. ❷ nature. —生得の, inborn; innate; congenital.

shōtoku (頌德する), *vt.* to praise; eulogize. ¶ 頌得表, a eulogy; a laudatory address.

shōtorihiki (商取引), *n.* commercial transaction.

shotōsū (諸等數), *n.* 【數】a compound number.

shō-tosuru (將とする), *vt.* to put in command. —…に將として, in command *of*; at the head *of*.

shōtotsu (衝突), *n.* ❶ (船·車等の) collision. ❷ (軍隊等の) conflict; encounter. ❸ (意見·感情等の) collision; conflict; contradiction (撞著). —意見《思想》の衝突, conflict [collision] of opinions 《ideas》. —又々汽車の衝突, another railway collision. —衝突する, ① to collide *with*; come into collision *with*; run *into* 《down》; run foul [aboard] *of* (船). ② to encounter; have a skirmish *with*. ③ to conflict *with*; run counter *to*; be in conflict *with*.

shōtsuki (祥月), *n.* the month of the anniversary of a person's death. ¶ 祥月命日, the anniversary of a person's death.

shou (背負ふ), *vt.* ❶ to carry on one's back. ❷ (負擔する) to shoulder; take on one's back. —背負はす, to saddle (upon [on] a person).

shōwa (笑話), *n.* ❶ (をかしい話) a funny story; a joke. ❷ (笑ひつゝ話す) a chat.

shōya (庄屋), *n.* a village head-man.

shoyaku (抄譯), *n.* translation of an extract. —抄譯する, to translate extracts *of*.

shōyaku (硝藥), *n.* gunpowder.

shoyō (所用), *n.* ❶ (使用する所) use; employment. ❷ (用件) business; engagement. —所用ありて外出中, out on business.

shoyō (所要の), *a.* necessary; required.

shōyo (賞與), *n.* a reward; a prize; a bonus. —賞與を與へる, to reward; give a prize. ¶ 年末賞與, a year-end bonus. —賞與金, a bonus; a reward.

shōyō (商用), *n.* (commercial)

business. ¶ 商用文, commercial correspondence.

shōyō (逍遙 徜徉), *n.* a walk; a stroll; a saunter. —逍遙する, to walk; stroll; saunter.

shōyō (從容), *ad.* composedly; calmly; with composure [calmness]. —從容迫らざる態度で, with an easy self-possessed air.

shōyō (慫慂する), *vt.* to encourage. ☞ *susumeru.*

shōyō (稱揚, 賞揚), *n.* praise; approbation.

shoyū (所有), *n.* possession. —所有する, ① (所有權を有す) to own. ② (現在持つ) to possess; hold; be in possession *of*; be possessed *of*. —所有に歸する, to come into one's possession; fall into one's hand. ¶ 所有地, an estate; a landed property; land in one's possession. —所有品, belongings; personal effects. —所有權, ownership; possession; proprietary rights. —所有者, an owner; a possessor; a proprietor.

shōyu (醬油), *n.* soy.

shōyūsei (小熊星), *n.* 【天】 Ursa Minor 【羅】; the Little Bear.

shōza (正座), *n.* the front; the stage. —正座に控へる, to occupy the highest seat.

shozai (所在), *n.* whereabouts. ☞ *kyosho* (居所). —所在を晦ます, to conceal one's whereabouts; hide oneself. ¶ 所在地, the seat; the position; the station; the locality.

shōzen (承前), continued (from...).

shōzen (悄然), *ad.* dispiritedly; despondently; with a heavy heart. —悄然たる, dispirited; down-hearted; crest-fallen.

shōzō (肖像), *n.* a portrait; a likeness; a statue (彫像). —肖像を畫く, to portray a person; take a person's likeness. ¶ 肖像畫, a portrait; portrait-painting.

shozoku (所屬の), *a.* belonging *to*; attached *to*.

shōzoku (裝束), *n.* ❶ (正裝) a court robe; a full dress. ❷ (衣服) a dress. ❸ (裝) costume.

shozon (所存), *n.* ❶ (意見) view; opinion. ❷ (考) thought; idea; intention (意向). —所存を述べる, to give one's opinion; give one's mind.

shō-zuru (生ずる), *vt.* ❶ (產出) to produce; yield; beget. ❷ (惹起) to cause; occasion. ❸ (發生) to bring forth; give rise [birth] *to*. ——, *vi.* ❶ (發生) to arise; come *of*. ❷ (物發) to occur; happen. ❸ (由來) to grow *out of*; result *from*. —種々の噂を生ずる, to give occasion to various rumours.

shu, shū, (主), *n.* ❶ (主人) a master. ❷ (主君) a lord; a master. ❸ (神) the Lord. ❹ (眼目) the main point.

shu (朱), *n.* cinnabar.

shu (種), *n.* a sort; a kind; a race; 【博·論】 a species. —種の起源, the origin of species —斯の種の物, things of this nature; a thing of the kind.

shū (州), *n.* a province; a county (英); a shire (英); a state (米); a canton (瑞西).

shū (洲), *n.* a continent.

shū (宗), *n.* a sect; a denomination; a religion.

shū (週), *n.* a week. ☞ *shū-kan* (週間).

shū (衆), *n.* the multitude; the people. —衆を以て寡を擊つ, to fight a few with many.

shū (集), *n.* a collection.

shūaku (醜惡), *n.* ugliness; villainy (心の). —醜惡な, ugly; foul; villainous.

shuba (種馬), *n.* a stud(-horse); a stallion. ¶ 種馬飼養所, a stud-farm.

shūban (週番), *n.* weekly duty. ¶ 週番士官, the officer of the week; an orderly officer.

shubetsu (種別), *n.* classification; assortment. ☞ *ruibetsu.*

shubi (守備), *n.* defence; defensive preparations; fielding (野球の). —守備する, to garrison; field (野球の). —守備に就く, 【野球】 to take the field. ¶ 守備隊, garrison; the guards.

shubi (首尾), *n.* ❶ (始終) beginning and end; the alpha and the omega. ❷ (成行) course; development; circumstances (事情). ❸ (結果) the result; the end. —首尾一貫せる行動, an action consistent throughout. —首尾よく, successfully; fortunately; happily. —首尾がよい, to be lucky [fortunate]; It fares well *with*. —首尾が惡い, to be unlucky; go amiss [wrong]; It fares ill *with*.

shūbi (愁眉), *n.* contracted brows; an anxious look. —愁眉を開く, to feel relieved; recover from anxiety.

shūbō (首謀-者), *n.* a ringleader; a leader; a principal.

shūbō (衆望), *n.* popularity; public expectation. —衆望を負ひて, with the support of the public. —衆望を一身に集める, to become the centre of popularity; become a popular hero.

shubu (主部), *n.* ❶ (要部) the

principal [main] part. ❸【文】the subject.
shubun (主文), *n.* 【文】the principal sentence; 【法】the subject.
shūbun (秋分 -點), *n.* the autumnal equinox; September 23rd.
shūbun (醜聞), *n.* a scandal; an evil [infamous] report.
shubyō (種苗), *n.* a seedling.
shūchaku (執著), *n.* ❶ adhesion; adherence. ❷ attachment. —執著する, ① to stick [cling] *to*; be wedded *to*; hug (偏見等); adhere *to*; cleave *to*. ② (愛著) to be attached *to*; love.
shūchi (周知), *n.* publicity. —世間周知の事實, a well-known fact; a fact widely known to the public; a matter of common knowledge.
shūchi (羞恥), *n.* shame; shyness; coyness. —羞恥の念, a sense of shame.
shūchikan (集治監), *n.* a convict prison.
shūchiku (修築), *n.* repair; repairing. ☞ *shūzen.*
shuchin (稀珍), *n.* =*shichin*.
shūchin (袖珍本), *n.* a pocket-book. ¶ 袖珍版, a pocket edition.
shuchō (主張), *n.* advocacy (唱道); assertion (權利·意見などの); maintenance (同上); claim (權利·存在の). —主張する, to advocate; assert; maintain; claim. —自己の主張を通す, to carry [gain] one's point. ¶ 主張者, an advocate; a claimant (權利などの).
shūchō (酋長), *n.* a chief; a headman; a chieftain [*fem.* -ness].
shuchū (主廚), *n.* a cook.
shūchū (集中), *n.* concentration. **——-suru,** *vt.* to concentrate; centre; focus. —精力を集中する, to concentrate one's energy. ¶ 集中點, the centre; the focus; the cynosure (衆目の).
shudai (主題), *n.* ❶ subject. ❷【音】thema; theme.
shudan (手段), *n.* means; ways; measures. —手段を選ばずに, by any means; by hook or by crook. —手段を執る, to take means [steps; measures]; resort [have recourse] to some means. —手段をあやまる, to take wrong measures.
shūdan (集團), *n.* a group; a mass; a body. ¶ 集團競技, a mass-game. —集團生活, gregarious life.
shudō (主動 -者), *n.* the prime mover; the originator; the animating [ruling] spirit.
shudō (首導の), *a.* initiative.
shudoku (酒毒), *n.* alcoholic poisoning.

shuei (守衞), *n.* ❶ (守護) guard; watch. ❷ (人) a guard; a guardsman; a sergeant-at-arms (議會の).
shūeki (收益), *n.* earnings; takings; proceeds.
shuen (酒宴), *n.* a banquet; a feast.
shūen (終焉), *n.* the end (of life); death. —終焉を告げる, to come to the end of one's life.
shufu (主婦), *n.* a mistress; a matron; a hostess; a landlady (宿屋の).
shufu (首府), *n.* the capital; the metropolis.
shūfu (醜婦), *n.* an ugly [a plain] woman; a fright.
shufuku, shūfuku, (修復), *n.* repair. ☞ *shūzen.*
shūgaku (修學), *n.* learning; study. ¶ 修學旅行, a school excursion; a tour of study.
shūgaku (就學), *n.* school attendance; entering a school. —就學する, to attend school; enter a school; study [learn] under a teacher. ¶ 就學兒童《年齡》, a school child 《the school age》.
shugan (主眼 -點), *n.* ❶ the (important; main) point; the essential feature; the essence. ❷ (目的) the principal object; the aim.
shugei (手藝), *n.* manual arts; handicraft. ¶ 女子手藝學校, a girls' handicraft school.
shūgeki (襲擊), *n.* attack; assault; raid. —襲擊する, to attack; assault; raid. —不意に襲擊される, to be taken by surprise. ¶ 襲擊機, a raider. —襲擊隊, an attacking force.
shūgen (祝言), *n.* ❶ (祝辭) a congratulatory address; congratulation; greetings. ❷ (婚禮) a marriage [wedding] (ceremony); nuptials; marriage rites. ❸ (祝) congratulation.
shugi (主義), *n.* principle; doctrine; one's rules. —主義を實行する, to act upon principle.
shūgi (祝儀), *n.* ❶ (祝賀) congratulation; felicitation. ❷ (心附) a tip; a gratuity. —祝儀をやる, to give a tip; tip.
shūgi (衆議), *n.* general consultation [deliberation]. —衆議に從ふ, to follow the decision reached upon general consultation.
shūgiin (衆議院), *n.* the House of Representatives (日·米); the House of Commons (英); the Chamber of Deputies (伊·佛). ☞ *gikai.* ¶ 衆議院議長, the President of the House of Representatives; the Speaker of the House of Commons (英). —衆議院議員, a member of the House of Representatives; a Representative; a

member of Parliament; an M. P.
shugo (主語), *n.* 【文·論】 the subject.
shugo (守護), *n.* protection; guard; watch. —守護する, to protect; guard; watch *for*. ¶ 守護神, the genius; the guardian [tutelary] deity.
shūgō (聚合, 集合), *n.* collection; meeting; gathering. —集合的, collective; aggregate. —聚合する, to throng; gather; assemble. ¶ 聚合果, 【植】 multiple fruits.
shugū (殊遇), *n.* special treatment.
shūgu (衆愚), *n.* the vulgar; the mob.
shugyō (修行), *n.* ascetic practices; practice of religious austerities. —修行する, to practise religious austerities.
shūgyō (修業), *n.* training; discipline; study (學問の). —修業する, to train oneself; study. ¶ 修業證書, a certificate of completion of a course; a licence.
shūgyō (終業), *n.* the end [conclusion] of work.
shūgyō (就業), *n.* engagement in work; commencement of work (始業). ¶ 就業時間, working hours.
shugyoku (珠玉), *n.* a jewel; a gem; a precious stone.
shūha (宗派), *n.* a sect; a denomination; a connection.
shuha (周波), *n.* 【電】 a cycle. ¶ 高《低》周波, high 《low》 frequency; radio 《audio》 frequency.
shūha (秋波), *n.* an amorous glance [look]; a love glance; an ogle. —秋波を送る, to ogle; cast sheep's eyes [an amorous glance] *at*; make eyes *at*.
shūhai (崇拜), *n.* worship; veneration (尊崇); adoration (嘆美). —崇拜する, to worship; venerate; adore.
shūhai (集配), *n.* collection and delivery. ¶ 集配人, a postman.
shuhan (主犯), *n.* the principal offender.
shūheki (習癖), *n.* habit; mannerism.
shuhi (種皮), *n.* 【植】 a testa; a spermoderm: a seed-coat.
shuhin (主賓), *n.* the guest of honour.
shuhitsu (主筆), *n.* the chief editor.
shuho (酒保), *n.* 【軍】 a canteen.
shuhō (手法), *n.* (way of) treatment; manner; technic.
shūho (襲歩), *n.* *pas-de-charge* 〔佛〕, gallop.
shūhō (週報), *n.* a weekly report; a weekly (paper, 新聞).
shūhyō (衆評), *n.* general [public] opinion [judgment].
shui (主位), *n.* ❶ =*shuseki* (首席). ❷ 【論】 the subject.
shui (趣意), *n.* ❶ (旨意) the purport; the import. ❷ (要旨) the point; the gist; the effect. ❸ (意味) sense; meaning. ¶ 趣意書, a prospectus.
shūi (周圍), *n.* ❶ (周邊) circumference; circuit; perimeter. ❷ (環境) the environment; the circumstances; the surrounding; the neighbourhood. —周圍の感化, the influence of environment.
shūitsu (秀逸), *n.* super-excellence; the first-class; a masterpiece (傑作). —秀逸の, (most) excellent; supreme; perfect.
shuji (主治の), *a.* principal; in charge. ¶ 主治醫, a physician in charge. —主治效能, the principal effects; the chief virtue.
shuji (主辭), *n.* 【論·修】 a subject.
shūji (習字), *n.* penmanship; handwriting; the art of handwriting. ¶ 習字帳, a copy-book.
shūji (修辭-學), *n.* rhetoric. —修辭的, rhetorical.
shujin (主人), *n.* a master; a householder (一家の); a host (客に對し); a landlord (旅館の); an employer (雇主); one's husband (夫). —主人役を勤める, to act as host. ¶ 主人公, 【文藝】 a hero.
shūjin (囚人), *n.* a prisoner.
shūjin (衆人), *n.* ❶ a crowd of people [men]. ❷ the people; the public; the multitude.
shūjitsu (終日), *ad.* all day (long); the whole day; throughout the day.
shūjō (主上), *n.* the Emperor; His Majesty.
shujō (衆生), *n.* 【梵 Sattva】 【佛】 living beings; creatures. ¶ 衆生濟度, salvation of the world.
shuju (侏儒), *n.* a dwarf; a pygmy; a hop-o'-my-thumb.
shuju (種種), *n.* all sorts; various kinds; variety. ☞ *iroiro* (色色). —種々手を盡す, to try every means. —種々の, various; multifarious; all sorts *of*. —種々に, in various ways; multifariously.
shūjū (主從), *n.* master and servant; lord and retainer.
shūjuku (習熟する), *v.* to master; acquire; become expert [skilful] *in*. —習熟さす, to make a person expert [skilful; proficient] *in*.
shujutsu (手術), *n.* an (a surgical) operation; surgical treatment; surgery. ¶ 手術臺, an operating-table. —手術衣, an operating-dress. —手術者, an operator.
shūka (臭化), *n.* 【化】 bromination. ¶ 臭化銀, silver bromide.
shūka (衆寡), *n.* odds. —衆寡敵せず, There is no fighting a-

gainst such odds.
shūka (瘦果), *n.* an achene.
shukai (首魁), *n.* a ringleader.
shūkai (集會), *n.* a meeting; a gathering; an assembly. —集會する, to meet together; gather; assemble. ¶ 集會所, a meeting-place; an assembly-hall; a rendezvous.
shūkai (澁晦な), *a.* abstruse; recondite; obscure.
shūkaidō (秋海棠), *n.* 【植】 the beefsteak-plant; the begonia (俗稱).
shukaku (主格), *n.* 【文】 the nominative (case); the subject.
shukaku (主客), *n.* ❶ (主人と客) host and guest. ❷ (主と副) subject and object. —主客顚倒する, to put the cart before the horse.
shūkaku (收穫), *n.* harvest; crop; yield. —收穫する, to harvest; crop; reap (and gather). ¶ 收穫時, the harvest (time; season).
shukan (主幹), *n.* the chief editor.
shukan (主管), *n.* ❶ (事) superintendence; management. ❷ (人) a superintendent; a supervisor; a manager. —主管する, to superintend; supervise; have charge *of*.
shukan (主觀), *n.* 【哲】 subject. —主觀的に云へば, from a subjective point of view.
shūkan (收監する), *vt.* to imprison; put in jail; commit to prison.
shūkan (習慣), *n.* ❶ (習癖) a habit. ❷ (慣例) a custom; usage. —習慣的, habitual; customary; conventional. —惡い習慣がつく, to contract a bad habit. —習慣を破る, to break off a habit; break oneself of a habit. ¶ 習慣法, a common law; a consuetudinary [customary] law.
shūkan (週刊), *n.* weekly publication; a weekly edition; a weekly.
shukei (主刑), *n.* 【法】 the principal penalty.
shūkei (主計), *n.* ❶ (會計) accounts; finance. ❷ (會計官) an accountant. ❸【海】a paymaster; 【陸】 an intendant. ¶ 陸軍主計總監, an intendant-general.
shuken (主權), *n.* sovereignty; the sovereign power; supremacy. ¶ 主權者, the sovereign; the ruler.
shūken (集權), *n.* concentration of power.
shūketsu (終結), *n.* conclusion; termination; completion. —終結する, to determine; terminate; be concluded. —討論終結を動議する, to move the closure.
shuki (手記), *n.* ❶ (控帖) a note-book; a pocket-book. ❷ (覺書) a note; a memorandum; private paper. —手記する, to note down; jot down; write down.
shuki (酒氣), *n.* the smell [fumes] of wine. —酒氣を藉りて罵る, to abuse a person under the influence of wine.
shūki (週忌), *n.* an anniversary (of death).
shūki (秋期, 秋季), *n.* autumn; autumn season.
shūki (臭氣), *n.* an offensive [a bad] smell; a stench; a stink. —臭氣を發する, to reek; stink; emit an offensive smell.
shūki (終期), *n.* termination.
shūki (週期), *n.* a periodic time; a (period of) revolution; a cycle.
Shūkikōreisai (秋季皇靈祭), *n.* the Feast of the Autumnal Equinox.
shūkin (集金), *n.* collection of money; bill-collection. —集金に廻る, to go round to collect money. ¶集金人, a (bill-)collector. —集金郵便, collection-post.
shukka (出火), *n.* outbreak of fire; a fire. —出火の原因, the cause of a fire.
shukkan (出棺), *n.* leaving of a coffin.
shukke (出家), *n.* ❶ (遁世) retirement; reclusion. ❷ (僧侶) a Buddhist priest; a bonze; a monk. —出家する, to retire from the world [into a cloister]; become a bonze.
shukketsu (出血), *n.* bleeding; effusion of blood; hemorrhage, hæmorrhage. —出血する, to bleed. —出血を止める, to arrest the flow of blood; stop bleeding.
shukkin (出金), *n.* ❶ (投資) investment. ❷ (寄附) contribution. ❸ (支出) payment; disbursement. —出金する, ① to invest money. ② to contribute. ③ to defray; pay; disburse. ¶ 出金者, a contributor; an investor (投資者); a financier (金主).
shukkin (出勤), *n.* attendance (at office). —出勤する, to attend one's office; go to office; go on duty. ¶ 出勤簿, an attendance-book; a time-book. —出勤時間, the hour for attending office.
shukkō (出校する), *vi.* to attend school; go to school.
shukkō (出港), *n.* departure; clearance. —出港する, to leave port; clear (out); put (out) to sea. ¶ 出港免狀, a clearance-permit; a chop.
shukkon (宿根の), *a.* perennial. ¶ 宿根草, a perennial; a perennial plant.
shukkyō (出京する), *vi.* to come [go] to town [the capital].

shukō (手工), *n.* manual training; manual labour [work]; handwork. ¶ 手工業, handicraft; handwork. (手工業者, a manual labourer; a handicraftsman; a craftsman.) —手工科, a manual training course.

shukō (首肯する), *vi.* to nod; nod one's assent; assent [consent] *to*; approve.

shukō (殊功), *n.* special merit; distinguished services.

shukō (酒肴), *n.* wine and food; viands and beverages. ¶ 酒肴料, an allowance for an entertainment.

shukō (趣向), *n.* ❶ (仕組) a plot; 【美】 a conduct. ❷ (計畫) a plan; a project. ❸ (意匠) a design. ❹ (工夫) a contrivance; a device. 一旨い趣向, a happy thought; a capital idea. —趣向を凝らす, to cudgel one's brains for a plan.

shūkō (周航), *n.* circumnavigation; sailing round. —周航する, to circumnavigate; sail round.

shūkō (修好), *n.* amity; contracting of friendly relations. ¶ 修好條約, a treaty of amity [friendship].

shūkō (崇高なる), *a.* lofty; sublime; majestic.

shūkō (醜行), *n.* ignominy; scandal; disgraceful [ignominious; scandalous] conduct.

shūkoroshi (主殺し), *n.* ❶ (事) murder of one's master. ❷ (人) the murderer of his master.

shuku (宿), *n.* a post-town; a stage; a relay-station.

shuku (主句), *n.* 【文】 a principal clause.

shūku (秀句), *n.* ❶ (秀逸なる句) an excellent poem. ❷ (洒落) a play upon words.

shukua (宿痾), *n.* a chronic [lingering] disease; a deep-rooted [an obstinate] illness; an inveterate disease. ¶ 宿痾再發, recrudescence of a chronic disease.

shukubō (宿望), *n.* a cherished desire [hope]; the heart's desire. —宿望を達する, to attain a cherished desire; obtain one's heart's desire.

shukubun (祝文), *n.* a congratulatory address.

shukuchoku (宿直), *n.* night-duty; keeping night-watch. —宿直する, to keep night-watch [vigil]; be on night-duty. ¶ 宿直番, one's turn for night-duty. —宿直員, a person on night-duty; an officer on duty.

shukudai (宿題), *n.* a home task [lesson; work]; a holiday task (休暇中の). —宿題を出す, to set [give] a home lesson.

shukuden (祝電), *n.* a congratulatory telegram.

shukuei (宿營), *n.* 【軍】 quarters; encampment; cantonment. ☞ *shaei* (舍營). —宿營する, to quarter; (en-)camp; take up one's quarters.

shukuen (祝宴), *n.* a feast (in celebration of an event); a banquet; a congratulatory entertainment. —祝宴を張る, to give a feast in celebration of an event.

shukuen (宿怨), *n.* an old grudge; a score; long-harboured resentment. —宿怨を晴らす, to pay off old scores; quit scores *with*; gratify an old grudge.

shukuen (宿緣), *n.* preestablished relations; karma-relations.

shukufuku (祝福), *n.* a benediction; a benedictory; a blessing. —祝福する, to bless; pronounce a benediction *upon*; invoke (a) blessing *upon*.

shukuga (祝賀), *n.* ❶ (人に對して) congratulation; felicitation. ❷ (事に對して) celebration. —祝賀する, to congratulate [felicitate] a person *upon* [*on*]; celebrate an event. ¶ 祝賀會, a celebration; a reunion in celebration of an event.

shukugan (宿願), *n.* cherished wish [desire]; the heart's desire.

shukuhai (祝杯), *n.* a toast; a pledge; a congratulatory [wassail] cup. —祝杯を擧げる, to toast; pledge (wine cups); drink a toast.

shukuhaku (宿泊), *n.* lodging; putting up; stopping. —宿泊さす, to lodge; put up; accommodate with lodgings. —宿泊する, to lodge; stop; put up; stay (at hotel); take lodgings. ¶ 宿泊人, a lodger; a boarder; a guest (客). —宿泊料, lodging-charge; bed and board; board and lodging.

shukuhei (宿弊), *n.* an inveterate vice; a deep-rooted [-seated] evil; a long-standing evil.

shukuhō (祝砲), *n.* 【陸海】 a salute (of guns); *feu de joie* 【佛】. —祝砲を放つ, to fire a salute.

shukui (祝意), *n.* congratulations; felicitations; celebration. —祝意を表する, to offer [present; tender] one's congratulations [felicitations]; congratulate; wish a person joy. —祝意を表して, in honour of (the day or occasion).

shukuji (祝辭), *n.* a congratulatory [complimentary] address;

congratulations; greetings. —祝辭を代讀する, to read a congratulatory address in the name of....

shukujitsu (祝日), *n.* a day of rejoicing; a holiday; a fête [gala] day.

shukujo (淑女), *n.* ❶ (貞女) a woman of virtue; a virtuous woman. ❷ (婦女の尊稱) a lady; a gentlewoman.

shukumei (宿命), *n.* predestination; destiny; fatality. —宿命を信ずる, to believe in fate. ¶ 宿命論, fatalism.

shukun (主君), *n.* one's lord; one's master.

shukun (殊勳), *n.* special merit; distinguished [conspicuous] services. ¶ 殊勳者, one who has rendered distinguished service.

shūkurīmu (シュークリーム), *n.* cream-cake.

shukuryō (宿料), *n.* lodging-charge.

shukusai (祝祭), *n.* a festival; a fête; a commemoration. ¶ 祝祭日, a holiday; a gala day.

shukusatsu (縮刷), *n.* a small--type edition; a pocket edition.

shukuse (宿世), *n.* a former [previous] world [life; existence].

shukusha (宿舍), *n.* a lodging; a billet; quarters.

shukusha (縮寫), *n.* drawing [copying] on a small scale; a reduced copy; a miniature. —縮寫する, to copy [draw; represent] on a smaller scale; make a reduced copy; miniature.

shukushaku (縮尺), *n.* scale; reduced scale. —縮尺十萬分の一, scale 1-100,000.

shukushi (宿志, 夙志), *n.* a cherished ambition [intention; desire; hope]. —宿志を遂げる, to attain one's cherished ambition; gain one's heart's desire.

shukusho (宿所), *n.* an address; a dwelling-place; a residence. —宿所を移す, to change one's address; remove.

shukushō (祝勝, 祝捷), *n.* celebration of a victory.

shukushō (縮少), *n.* reduction; retrenchment; curtailment. ——**suru,** *vt.* to reduce; curtail; cut down; contract. ——, *vi.* to become smaller; dwindle; shrink (收縮). —經費を縮少する, to cut down the expenses. —規模を縮少する, to reduce the plan.

shukushu (宿主), *n.* 【生物】 a host. Ⓢ 寄主.

shukushuku (肅肅), *ad.* ❶ (靜かに) quietly; in solemn silence. ❷ (嚴に) solemnly; imposingly.

shukusui (宿醉), *n.* =*futsukayoi*.

shuku-suru (祝する), *vt.* to congratulate; celebrate.

shukuten (祝典), *n.* celebration; gaiety; a commemoration (記念祭). —祝典を擧げる, to celebrate; commemorate.

shukutoku (淑德), *n.* chastity; high virtue; female virtue.

shuku-toshite (肅として), *ad.* silently; in solemn silence; in deep [perfect] silence. —場內肅として聲なし, The place is in deep silence; A perfect silence reigns over the scene; Even the fall of a pin could be heard.

shukuzu (縮圖), *n.* a reduced drawing; a map on reduced scale; an epitome.

shukyō (主教), *n.* 【宗】 a primate; a bishop; an eparch (希臘敎の).

shukyō (酒興), *n.* ❶ (酒に醉うた面白味) conviviality; exhilaration from drink. ❷ (酒の時の座興) an entertainment at a feast.

shūkyō (宗敎), *n.* religion. —宗敎に依って慰を得る, to find solace in religion. ¶ 宗敎(的)團體, a spiritual [religious] corporation [body]. —宗敎家, a religionist. —宗敎改革, religious reformation; 【史】 the Reformation. —宗敎局, the Bureau of Religious Affairs. —宗敎心, a religious spirit; piety.

shūkyoku (終局), *n.* end; conclusion; termination. —終局の勝利, the final victory. —終局を告げる, to come to an end; reach conclusion; terminate.

shūkyoku (終極), *n.* finality; extremity; end. —終局の, ultimate; final; last.

shukyū (守舊), *n.* conservation; conventionality. ☞ *hoshu*.

shūkyū (蹴球), *n.* (a) football. ¶ ア式《ラ式》蹴球, Association 《Rugby》 football.

shumeryō (主馬寮), *n.* the Bureau of Imperial Mews.

shūmei (醜名), *n.* infamy; an ill-name; disrepute.

shūmei (襲名), *n.* succession to a name. —襲名する, to succeed to a name.

shūmen (澁面), *n.* =*jūmen*.

shumi (趣味), *n.* taste; interest (興味). —趣味を持つ, to have a taste [turn; fancy] *for*; like; be fond *of*. (詩には全然趣味を持たぬ, to have no relish for poetry.) —趣味津々として盡きず, It is ever brimming with interest.

shūmi (臭味), *n.* ❶ (臭と味) smell and taste. ❷ (臭氣) odour; stench. —同臭味の輩(ﾊｲ),

those of the same party. —毫も公役所風の臭味がない, not to have the least taint of officialism.

shūmin (就眠する), *vi.* to go to bed; turn in. ☞ *neru* (寝る). ¶就眠時間, bedtime; the hour of rest; the hour for going to bed [for turning in].

shūmitsu (周密な), *a.* minute; [precise.]

shumō (蛛網), *n.* a cobweb; a web; a gossamer.

shumoku (種目), *n.* an item.

shumoku (撞木), *n.* a wooden bell-hammer. ¶撞木杖, a crutch; a staff with a T-handle.

shūmoku (衆目), *n.* eyes of the multitude; public attention [eyes].

shūmon (宗門), *n.* religion: (宗派) a sect; a denomination.

shumotsu (腫物), *n.* 【醫】 a tumour; an ulcer; a sore.

shumu (主務の), *a.* competent. ¶主務官廳《省》, the competent authorities 《department of state》.

shun (旬), *n.* season. —旬の, in season. —旬外れの, out of season.

shunba, shunme, (駿馬), *n.* a gallant horse [steed]; a fine horse; a courser.

shunbun (春分), *n.* the vernal equinox; March 20th 《21st》.

shundan (春暖), *n.* warm spring weather.

shundō (蠢動する), *vi.* to wriggle. —裏面に蠢動する, to be agitated behind the scenes.

shūnen (執念), *n.* implacability; a spite; a grudge. —執念深い, vindictive; implacable; spiteful.

shunga (春畫), *n.* an obscene [indecent] picture.

shungen (峻嚴な), *a.* strict; rigid; severe; austere. —檢事の峻嚴な論告, the procurator's severe statement.

shuniku (朱肉), *n.* cinnabar [stamp-ink.]

shunin (主任), *n.* a person in charge; a responsible official; a superintendent. ¶主任技師, a chief [supervising] engineer. —主任教師, a teacher in charge.

shūnin (就任), *n.* assumption of office; entrance into office. —就任する, to assume an office; enter into [upon] an office; take up a position. —就任挨拶をする, to make an inaugural address.

shunji (瞬時), *n.* a moment; a second; an instant. —瞬時にして, in a moment; in the twinkling of an eye. —瞬時と雖も, even for a moment.

shunjū (春秋), *n.* ❶ (春と秋) spring and autumn. ❷ (年月) years. ❸ (年齢) age; summers (少年に言ふ); winters (老年に言ふ). —春秋に富む, to have a long future before one.

shunjun (逡巡する), *vi.* to hesitate; be irresolute; vacillate. —逡巡して進まず, to hesitate to advance.

shunkan (瞬間), *n.* a moment; an instant; a twinkle. —丁度其の瞬間に, just at that moment.

shunken (峻險, 峻嶮), *n.* a precipice; a cliff. —峻險な, precipitous; steep; abrupt.

shunketsu (俊傑), *n.* a great man; a man of talent; a hero.

shunki (春季), *n.* the spring; the springtime; the springtide. ¶春季運動會, a spring athletic meeting [sports].

Shunkikōreisai (春季皇靈祭), *n.* the Feast of the Vernal Equinox.

shunkō (竣功), *n.* completion; accomplishment. —竣功する, to be completed; be finished.

shunkyo (峻拒する), *vt.* to rebuff; repulse; refuse flatly [bluntly]; give a flat refusal.

shunō (主腦), *n.* the brain; the head; the animating [ruling] spirit. —主腦となる, to take the lead. ¶主腦部, the managing staff; the management; the directorate.

shūnō (收納), *n.* a harvest; the (corn-) crop; receipt (金錢の). —收納する, to gather [take] in; harvest; receive.

shunpū (春風), *n.* spring [vernal] breeze.

shunsai (俊才), *n.* a superior intellect; a man of talent (人).

shunsetsu (浚渫), *n.* dredging; scour. —浚渫する, to dredge; scour. ¶浚渫機, a dredge(r); a dredging-machine. (掬桶《梯狀》浚渫機, a bucket 《ladder》-dredge(r).) —浚渫船, a dredge-boat; a dredger.

shunshoku (春色), *n.* spring scenery; vernal atmosphere; vernal array; nature in spring.

shunsoku (駿足), *n.* ❶ (速歩) swift feet; fleetness. ❷ (駿馬) a swift horse. ❸ (駿才) a man of talent. —門下の駿足, the pick of one's pupils.

shunuri (朱塗の), *a.* lacquered [with cinnabar.]

shūnyū (收入), *n.* an income (所得); receipts (受取金); revenue (歲入); earnings (儲け高); proceeds (賣上). —收入内で《以上に》暮す, to live within 《beyond》 one's income. ¶收入印紙, a revenue-stamp. —收入關稅, revenue tax. —收入役, a cashier; a revenue-officer.

shuppan (出帆), *n.* sailing; setting sail; departure. —出帆する, to sail; set sail; put to sea. ¶ 出帆日, the sailing-day. —出帆旗, the blue peter.

shuppan (出版), *n.* publication; edition; issue. —出版の自由, the liberty of the press. —出版する, to issue; publish; put out. —出版した許りの, fresh from the press. ¶ 出版部, the publishing department. —出版業者, a publisher. —出版界, the publishing interests [world].

shuppatsu (出發), *n.* starting; departure (特に汽車の). —出發する, to start; leave; set out; take one's departure. ¶ 出發點, a start (競走の); a base (同上); a starting point (線路·競走·旅行).

shuppei (出兵), *n.* despatch of troops; an expedition (遠征). —出兵する, to despatch troops; send an expedition.

shuppi (出費), *n.* expense; outlay; expenditure.

shuppin (出品), *n.* an exhibit; exhibition. —出品する, to exhibit. ¶ 出品人, an exhibitor.

shuppon (出奔する), *vi.* to abscond; decamp; run away. ¶ 出奔者, an absconder; a runaway.

shurajō (修羅場), *n.* Ⓢ 修羅の巷. shambles.

shūrai (襲來), *n.* an invasion; raid; visitation (天災の). —襲來する, to come down upon; make a descent *upon*; visit (暴風など).

shuran (酒亂), *n.* drunken frenzy. —酒亂の癖がある, to have the habit of becoming frenzy by drink.

shūran (收攬する), *vt.* to grasp; have in one's grasp [at one's command]. —人心を收攬する, to draw the people's hearts to oneself; capture hearts; win the people's hearts.

shūrei (秋冷), *n.* autumn chill.

shūrei (秀麗な), *a.* beautiful; excellent; fine.

shūrei (秀靈な), *a.* sublime.

shuren (手練), *n.* skill; dexterity; proficiency. —手練の早業, a sleight of hand.

shūren (收斂), *n.* ❶ (納收) harvest. ❷ (誅求) exaction of taxes. ❸【醫】astringency. ❹【理】convergence. —收斂する, ① to harvest. ② to exact. ③ to converge. ¶ 收斂劑, an astringent.

shūressha (終列車), *n.* the last train.

shūri (修理), *n.* repair; mending. ☞ *shūzen*. —修理する, to repair; mend. ¶ 修理工場, a repair-shop.

shuriken (手裏劍), *n.* a dart.

shuro (棕櫚), *n.*【植】the hemp-palm. ¶ 棕櫚箒《繩》, a hemp-palm broom《rope》.

shurochiku (棕櫚竹), *n.*【植】Rhapis humilis (ground-rattan の類·學名).

shūrō (醜陋), *n.* ugliness; foulness. ☞ *rōretsu*. —醜陋な, ugly; foul; mean; base.

shurui (酒類), *n.* liquors; drinks; spirits (火酒).

shurui (種類), *n.* kind; sort; species; variety. —種類分けする, to classify; sort (over; out).

shūrui (醜類), *n.* vicious company; rascals; corrupt elements.

shuryō (首領), *n.* a leader; a chief; a head.

shuryō (狩獵), *n.* hunting; hunt; shooting; the chase. ☞ *ryō*. ¶ 狩獵法, the game law; the hunting law. —狩獵家, a hunter; a sportsman. —狩獵免狀 [鑑札], a shooting licence.

shūryō (修了する), *vt.* to complete (one's study [course] *of*).

shūryō (終了), *n.* the end; the conclusion; completion; expiry (滿期). —— **-suru,** *vt.* to conclude; complete; bring to a close. ——, *vi.* to end; complete; come to an end; expire.

shuryōkan (主獵官), *n.* a grand veneur; a chief huntsman.

shuryoku (主力), *n.* a main force [body]. —主力を注ぐ, to concentrate one's powers [energies] *on*. ¶ 主力艦, a capital ship. (主力艦隊, the main squadron.)

shusa (主査), *n.* a subcommittee with a special charge.

shusabi (酒齄鼻), *n.*【醫】(acne) rosacea; a brandy [whisky] nose.

shusai (主宰-者), *n.* a president; a governor; a chairman. —主宰する, to preside *over*; superintend.

shusai (主催), *n.* auspices. —萬朝報主催の下に, under the auspices of Yorozu Chōhō.

shūsai (秀才), *n.* a talented person.

shūsaku (習作), *n.*【美】a study.

shusan (珠算), *n.* calculation with the abacus.

shūsan (集散, 聚散), *n.* gathering and dispersion. —集散する, to gather and disperse. ¶ 集散地《市場》, a distributing centre《market》.

shūsan (蓚酸), *n.*【化】oxalic acid.

shūsan-shugi (集產主義), *n.* collectivism.

shūsatsu (愁殺する), *v.* to make a person extremely melan-

choly. ⌈preservation.⌉
shusei (守成), *n.* maintenance;⌋
shusei (守勢), *n.* defence; defensive. —守勢的, defensive. —守勢を取る, to act on [take] the defensive. —攻勢から守勢に轉ずる, to change from the offensive to the defensive.
shusei (酒精), *n.* alcohol; spirits (of wine). ¶ 酒精中毒,【醫】alcoholism; alcoholic poisoning.
shūsei (修正), *n.* amendment (法案など); revision (條約·本など). —修正する, to amend; revise.
shūsei (修整), *n.* dressing (服裝など); retouching (寫眞). —修整する, to dress; retouch.
shūsei (終生), *n.* all lifetime; all one's life. ——, *ad.* all one's life; to the end of one's life; for life. —終生の, lifelong; perpetual; for life.
shūsei (習性), *n.* ❶ an (acquired) habit. ❷【生物】habit.
shūsei (集成する), *vt.* to collect (together); compile.
shūsei (醜聲), *n.* scandal; a scandalous report. ☞ *shūbun*. —醜聲外に漏る, The scandal got out [abroad].
shuseki (手跡, 手蹟), *n.* handwriting; hand; autography (眞筆).
shuseki (首席), *n.* the chief [head; first] seat. —首席を占める, to occupy the head seat; be at the head. ¶ 首席領事, the doyen [dean] of the consular body.
shuseki (酒石), *n.*【化】(crude) tartar. ¶ 酒石英, the cream of tartar. —酒石酸, tartaric acid.
shusen (酒饌), *n.* wine and delicacy; a banquet. ¶ 酒饌料, entertainment money.
shūsen (周旋), *n.* agency (仲介); intermediation (同上); good offices (好意, 盡力); recommendation (推薦). —— - **suru**, *vt.* to aid; render service *to*; find [get] anything *for*; recommend. —就職口を周旋する, to find [get; procure] another a situation [place]. —賣家, 但周旋謝絶, A house for sale; agents declined. ¶ 周旋業, brokerage; commission agency. —周旋料, brokerage; commission. —周旋屋, ① (仲介業者) a broker; a commission agent. ② (桂庵) an employment-office; a servants' registry (office) (英); a register office (米); an intelligence office.
shusendo (守錢奴), *n.* a miser; a niggard; a skinflint.
shusenron (主戰論), *n.* jingoism; advocacy of war. ¶ 主戰論者, those for war; war advocates; jingoists.
shusha (取捨), *n.* selection; choice; option. —取捨する, to take or leave; select; choose. —取捨に迷ふ, to be at a loss which to take.
shūshabachin (舟車馬賃), *n.* conveyance expenses.
shūshaku (襲爵), *n.* succession to a peerage. —襲爵仰附けらる, to be ordered to succeed to the peerage.
shushi (主旨), *n.* the subject (-matter); a (principal) object.
shushi (種子), *n.* a seed.
shushi (趣旨), *n.* the purport; the effect; the substance.
shūshi (收支), *n.* receipts and disbursements; revenue [income] and expenditure. —收支償はしめる, to make both ends meet; meet one's expenses. ¶ 收支決算, settled accounts of revenue and expenditure.
shūshi (宗旨), *n.* a sect; a denomination; a religion (宗敎).
shūshi (終始), *n.* the beginning and the end. ——, *ad.* throughout; constantly. ☞ *shijū*. —終始一貫せる, consistent; coherent (筋路の立った). —主義と終始する, to adhere to one's principle to the end.
shūshin (修身), *n.* ❶ (修德) moral training; cultivation of morality. ❷ (倫理) ethics; moral philosophy.
shūshin (終身), *n.* lifetime; all one's life. ☞ *shūsei*. ¶ 終身官, an official for life.
shūshin (終審), *n.* a final examination. ¶ 終審裁判所, the court of the last resort.
shūshin (執心), *n.* devotion; attachment. ☞ *shūchaku*. —執心する, ① to be devoted *to*. ② to be attached *to*; set one's mind *on*.
shusho (手書), *n.* an autograph (自筆); a chirograph (自筆證書).
shusho (朱書する), *vt.* to write in red.
shushō (主將), *n.* a general; a commander-in-chief; 【野球】a captain.
shushō (首相), *n.* the premier; the prime minister.
shushō (首唱), *n.* promotion; advocacy. —首唱する, to promote; advocate; propose; take the lead. ¶ 首唱者, a promoter; an advocate; a prime mover.
shushō (殊勝な), *a.* laudable; praiseworthy; admirable.
shūshō (周章·狼狽), *n.* alarm and confusion; bewilderment;

panic. —— -**suru,** *vi.* to be bewildered; lose one's presence of mind; lose one's head; be panic-stricken. —周章狼狽して, in great confusion; in utter bewilderment.

shūshō (愁傷), *n.* grief; deep sorrow; lamentation. —愁傷する, to grieve; lament; mourn. —御愁傷樣です, I am very sorry for you.

shushoku (主食), *n.* the staple food; the principal dish.

shushoku (酒色), *n.* sensual pleasures; dissipation. —酒色に耽る, to be addicted to sensual pleasures; give oneself up to dissipation.

shūshoku (修飾), *n.* ornamentation; ornament; embellishment (文の). —修飾する, to ornament; adorn; embellish (文を); 【文】 modify. ¶ 修飾語, 【文】 a modifier; an adjunct.

shūshoku (就職), *n.* entering official service; obtaining an employment. —就職する, to enter into service; take up an official post. —就職口を世話する, to find a situation for a person. ¶ 就職難, the difficulty of securing employment.

shūshu (袖手する), *vi.* to fold arms. —袖手傍観する, to look on unconcernedly [with indifference]; look on with folded arms.

shūshū (收拾する), *vt.* to adjust; arrange; save. —時局を收拾する, to save the situation.

shūshū (蒐集), *n.* collection; gathering; gleaning. —蒐集する, to collect; gather; glean.

shūshuku (收縮), *n.* contraction; constriction; shrinking. —收縮性の, contractive; contractile. —收縮する, to contract; constrict; shrink.

shūso (宗祖), *n.* the founder of a sect.

shūso (臭素), *n.* 【化】 bromine. ¶ 臭素紙, bromide paper.

shūso (愁訴), *n.* an appeal; petition; supplication. —愁訴する, to appeal; make one's moan; supplicate.

shusoku (手足), *n.* hands and feet; the limbs; the extremities. —手足を延ばす, ① to stretch one's limbs; make oneself easy. ② to extend one's influence.

shūsoku (終熄する), *vi.* to come to an end; end.

shuso-ryōtan (首鼠兩端), *n.* vacillation; irresolution; hesitancy. —首鼠兩端を持す, to be irresolute; hesitate; vacillate.

shussan (出產), *n.* birth; childbirth; delivery. —出產する, to give birth *to*; be delivered *of*. ¶ 出產率, birth-rate. —出產屆, the report of a birth.

shussatsu-gakari (出札係), *n.* a booking-clerk (英); a ticket-clerk (米). ¶ 出札所, a booking-office (英); a ticket-office(米).

shusse (出世), *n.* rise in the world; making one's way; advancement [success] in life. —出世する, to rise in the world; get on in the world; make one's way in life [in the world]; come to the front. —出世が早い, to rise rapidly in the world. —出世の機會を得る, to get a chance in life.

shussei (出征), *n.* departure for the front; expedition. —出征する, to depart for [go to] the front; take part in war (參加). ¶ 出征軍人, soldiers [men] at the front.

shussei (出精), *n.* diligence; industry; assiduity. —出精する, to be diligent [industrious]; exert oneself; work strenuously.

shusseki (出席), *n.* attendance; presence. —出席する, to attend; be present *at*; put in [make] an appearance. ¶ 出席簿, an attendance-book. —出席者, an attendance (總體); an attendant; persons present. —出席數, (the number of) attendances.

shusshi (出資), *n.* contribution; investment (投資). —出資する, to contribute; invest; financier. ¶ 出資者, a contributor; an investor.

shusshin (出身), *n.* ❶ (學校の) graduation. ❷ (土地の) birth; extraction. —帝大出身者, an Imperial University man. —彼は信州出身である, He comes from Shinshū; He is of Shinshū extraction. ¶ 出身地, one's native place.

shussho (出所), *n.* the origin; the source; the derivation (語の). —報告の確なる出所, a reliable source of information.

shusshō (出生), *n.* birth. ☞ *shussan*. —出生する, to be born. ¶ 出生地, one's birth-place.

shusshoku (出色の), *a.* excellent; prominent; distinguished.

shusso (出訴する), *v.* to bring a suit [an action]; sue; go to law.

shussui (出水), *n.* a flood; an inundation. —出水する, to overflow; flood; inundate.

shusu (繻子), *n.* satin.
shutai (主體), *n.* 【法·哲】 subject.
shūtai (澁滞), *n.* delay; retardation; procrastination. —澁滞する, to be delayed [retarded]; procrastinate. —事件の進行に澁滞を來す, to retard the progress of the event.
shūtai (醜態), *n.* an offensive [a disagreeable] appearance [condition], offensive [unsightly] behaviour; an unseemly sight. —醜態を顯はす, to present an offensive appearance. —醜態を演じる, to behave oneself shamefully; make an exhibition of oneself.
shūtan (愁嘆), *n.* grief; lamentation; sorrow. —愁嘆する, to grieve; lament. ¶ 愁嘆場《話》, a pathetic scene 《story》.
shūtaneki (終端驛), *n.* a (railway) terminus; a terminal station.
shu-taru (主たる), *a.* principal; chief.
shutchō (出張), *n.* an official tour. —出張する, to go [proceed] on official business. ¶ 出張所, an agency.
shūteki (讐敵), *n.* an enemy; a foe; an adversary. —相視る讐敵の如し, to be at daggers drawn with each other.
shūten (終點), *n.* the terminus; the terminal point.
shuto (首都), *n.* the capital; the metropolis.
shutō (種痘), *n.* vaccination; inoculation. —種痘する, ① [*vt.*] to vaccinate; inoculate. ② [*vi.*] to be vaccinated (して貰ふ). —種痘濟 (醫師の證明), vaccinated.
shūto (舅), *n.* a father-in-law.
shūto (囚徒), *n.* a prisoner; a convict.
shūtō (周到な), *a.* careful; thorough; exhaustive. —周到な注意を以て, with scrupulous [sedulous] care.
shūtō (襲踏する), *vt.* to follow (an example); imitate.
shutoku (主徳, 首徳), *n.* cardinal virtues.
shutoku (取得), *n.* acquisition. —取得する, to acquire; obtain. ¶ 繼受的取得, derivative acquisition.
shūtoku (拾得する), *vt.* to find; pick up. ¶ 拾得物, a find; a found article. —拾得者, a finder.
shūtoku (習得する), *vt.* to acquire; learn (學ぶ); obtain.
shūtome (姑), *n.* a mother-in-law.
shu-toshite (主として), *ad.* mainly; chiefly; principally; primarily.
shu-tosuru (主とする), *vt.* to emphasize; put stress [emphasis] on; set value *on* (重んずる). —自己の幸福を主とする, to set value on one's own happiness.
shutsuba (出馬する), *vi.* to go out on horseback; go [proceed] *to*: come forward.
shutsubotsu (出沒), *n.* appearing and disappearing. —出沒する, to make its 《one's》 appearance; come and go; haunt (a place); infest (a place) (山賊などが荒す).
shutsudō (出動する), *vi.* to put out to sea (出港); proceed *to* (出向く); turn out; be called out. —軍隊の出動を要する, to require the despatch of troops. —命令一下出動の準備が出來てる, (軍艦) to be ready for sea at a moment's notice. ¶ 出動命令, sailing orders (出港命令).
shutsuen (出演する), *vi.* ❶ (演技) to appear (出る); perform (演ずる). ❷ (演説) to make a speech; address; speak.
shutsuga (出芽), *n.* 【植】 sprouting; germination.
shutsugan (出願), *n.* application. —出願する, to apply *for*; make an application *for*. —專賣特許出願中, patent applied for. ¶ 出願者, an applicant.
shutsugen (出現), *n.* appearance; arrival. —出現する, to appear; make an appearance.
shutsugoku (出獄), *n.* discharge from prison. —出獄する, to be discharged from prison; be released. ¶ 出獄人保護, protection of discharged prisoners.
shutsugyo (出御), *n.* going out of the Emperor.
shutsugyo (出漁する), *vi.* to go out fishing.
shutsujin (出陣する), *vi.* to go to the front; take the field.
shutsujō (出場する), *v.* to appear; be present *at* (臨む); participate *in* (參加).
shutsumon (出門), *n.* leaving.
shutsunyū (出入), *n.* ❶ coming and going; entrance and exit; ingress and egress. ❷ (收支) receipts and disbursements. ☞ *deiri*. —出入する, to go in and out; enter and leave; haunt; call frequently *on* [*at*].
shutsuran (出藍の譽あり), to be famed as surpassing one's teacher in ability.
shutsuro (出路), *n.* an outlet.
shutsuro (出廬する), *vi.* to come out of one's retirement; come forward to take office.
shuttai (出來), *n.* ❶ (完成) finish; completion. ❷ (發生) occurrence. —出來する, ① to be done

[finished; accomplished]. ② to happen; take place; occur.

shuttatsu (出立), *n.* departure. ☞ *shuppatsu*.

shuttei (出廷), *n.* 【法】 appearance in a law-court. —出廷する, to appear in court; make one's appearance at the court; appear before a judge.

shutten (出典), *n.* the origin; the source; the authority.

shuttō (出頭), *n.* appearance; attendance; presence. ——**suru,** *v.* to appear; attend; present oneself; put in an appearance. —本人[自身]出頭する, to appear in person.

shūu (驟雨), *n.* a shower. —驟雨に逢ふ, to be caught in a shower. —驟雨の兆あり, It threatens to shower.

shūwai (收賄), *n.* corruption; bribery. —收賄する, to take [receive] a bribe. ¶ 收賄事件, the bribery affair [case]; a case of official corruption; a graft case. —收賄者, a briber.

shuwan (手腕), *n.* ability; capacity; tact. —遺憾なく手腕を發揮する, to give ample scope to one's ability. ¶ 手腕家, a man of ability [parts].

shūya (終夜), *n.* all night; the whole night. ¶ 終夜運轉, all-night service.

shūyaku (集約的), *a.* 【經·農】 intensive. ¶ 集約農業, intensive cultivation.

shuyō (主要な), *a.* chief; principal; leading. ¶ 主要驛, principal stations.

shūyō (收用する), *vt.* 【法】 to expropriate (土地等を).

shūyō (收容する), *vt.* to take in; receive *into*; accommodate. —患者を收容する, to receive [take in] patients. ¶ 收容所, a camp; barracks; quarters.

shūyō (修養), *n.* culture; cultivation. —修養する, to cultivate.

shūyō (執拗), *n.* obstinacy; stubbornness. —執拗な, obstinate; stubborn.

shuyu (須臾も), *ad.* (even) for a moment.

shūyū (舟遊), *n.* boating; boat-excursion. —舟遊する, to go boating; go in a pleasure-boat.

shūyū (周遊), *n.* an excursion; a tour; a pleasure-trip. —周遊する, to make an excursion 《a tour》; take a pleasure-trip.

shuzei (酒稅), *n.* a tax on *sake*; a *sake*-tax.

shūzei (收稅), *n.* tax-collection; collection of taxes. —收稅する, to collect taxes. ¶ 收稅吏, a tax-collector [-gatherer]; an exciseman (内國消費稅の); a revenue officer (關稅の).

shuzeikyoku (主稅局), *n.* the Revenue [Taxation] Bureau.

shūzen (修繕), *n.* repair; mending; renovation (建築物などの). —修繕する, to repair; mend; renovate. —修繕が行屆いてゐる《行屆かない》, to be in good 《bad》 repair.

shūzen (愁然), *ad.* mournfully; sorrowfully; plaintively.

shuzō (酒造), *n.* *sake*-brewing. ¶ 酒造場, a *sake*-brewery; a distillery. —酒造家, a *sake*-brewer.

shuzoku (種族), *n.* a race (人種); a tribe (酋長下の部族); a species (生物學上の).

shūzoku (習俗), *n.* customs; usage; convention. —習俗に囚はれる, to be slave to conventions.

shuzumi (朱墨), *n.* red ink; a cinnabar-stick.

so (祖), *n.* ❶ (祖先) an ancestor; a progenitor. ❷ (始祖) the founder; the father; the pioneer. —蘭學の祖, the pioneer of Dutch studies.

so (疽), *n.* necrosis.

so (疎·粗なる), *a.* ❶ (粗雜) coarse; rough. ❷ (疎野) rude; wild. ❸ (疎遠) estranged.

sō (壯), *n.* ❶ (壯健) strong health. ❷ (さかり) the prime (of life). ❸ (立派) magnificence.

sō (相), *n.* ❶ (貌) appearance; countenance (顏色). ❷ (人相) physiognomy. ❸【電】phase. ❹【文】the voice.

sō (想), *n.* idea; conception. ☞ *shisō*.

sō (僧), *n.* =*sōryo*.

sō (層), *n.* ❶【建】(重屋) a course. ❷ (かさね) a layer; a seam; a bed; a region (空氣·海洋等の); 【地質】a stratum. —層をなしてゐる, to be formed in layers.

sō (總), *a.* ❶ gross; total; aggregate; all. ❷ general (attack; election; strike, *etc.*).

sō (左樣), *ad.* ❶ so. ❷ yes. ——, *int.* well. —さうですとも, So it is; Indeed it is; Yes, indeed. —彼奴はいつでもさうだ, That is always the case with him.

-sō (さう), to seem; look; be [look] likely *to*. —嚙みつきさうである, to look like biting. —好い結果になりさうである, to promise good results. —米人のやりさうな事だ, That is just like an American.

soaku (粗惡な), *a.* crude; inferior; coarse. ¶ 粗惡品, inferior articles.

sōan (草案), *n.* a draft; a rough cast. ¶ 民法草案, the draft civil code.

soba (蕎麥), *n.* ❶【植】the buckwheat. ❷ (蕎麥切) buckwheat vermicelli.

soba (側, 傍), *n.* side; vicinity (附近). 一側を通る人, a passer-by. 一積み上げるそばから崩れる, to come down as fast as one piles them up. **——-ni,** *ad.* & *prep.* by (the side of); beside; close; alongside; near; near by; hard [close] by. 一私の側に, beside me; at my side. 一傍にある机, the table near a person [at one's elbow].

sōba (相場), *n.* ❶ (價) a price; a market-price; a quotation; market. ❷ (投機) speculation. ❸ (評判) public estimation. 一米の小賣相場, the retail price of rice. 一相場で儲ける, to make money by speculation. 一相場が上り下りする, The market rises and falls. 一相場に手を出す, to speculate *in* (*on*); engage in speculation; have a flutter [俗]. ¶ 相場表, a list of quotations; a price-list. 一相場師, a speculator.

sobadateru (欹てる), *vt.* to perk; prick up (耳などを). 一枕を欹てて聞く, to listen with the head raised from the pillow.

sobadatsu (峙つ), *vi.* to stand high; tower up.

sobakasu (雀斑), *n.* freckles. 一雀斑のある顔, a freckled face.

sōban (早晚), *ad.* sooner or later; early or late; in time (其内に).

sōbana (總花), *n.* presents made all round. ¶ 總花政策, the all-prizes-and-no-blank policy.

sōbatō (走馬燈), *n.* a revolving lantern. 一走馬燈的變動, a kalëidoscopic change.

sobazue (傍杖), *n.* injury received in another's quarrel; a by-blow. 一喧嘩の傍杖を食ふ, to get [receive] a by-blow in another's quarrel.

sōbetsu (送別), *n.* farewell; send-off; speeding. 一送別の辭, a farewell speech [address]. 一送別會を開く, to hold a send-off dinner. 一盛んな送別をする, to give an enthusiastic [a splendid] send-off.

sōbi (壯美), *n.* the sublime (beauty); sublimity. 一壯美なる, sublime; grand.

sōbi (裝備), *n.* equipment; equipage; outfit. 一裝備する, to equip; fit out; mount (大砲等を).

sobieru (聳える), *vi.* to rise; tower; soar. 一雲表に聳える, to soar above the clouds.

sobireru (そびれる), *v.* to lose [slip] the chance *of*. 一寢そびれる, to fail to sleep.

sobo (祖母), *n.* a grandmother.

sobō (粗暴), *n.* roughness; rudeness; violence. **——-na,** rough; rude; violent. 一粗暴な擧動, rough behaviour.

sōbō (相貌), *n.* physiognomy; face; countenance. ☞ *sō*.

sōbō (僧帽), *n.* a mitre; a hood; a cowl. ¶ 僧帽瓣, 【解】 the mitral valve.

soboku (素朴な), *a.* simple; ingenuous; unaffected.

soburi (素振), *n.* behaviour; bearing; manner. 一意味ありげな素振をする, to bear oneself in a significant manner.

sobyō (素描), *n.* dessin [佛]; drawing.

sōbyō (宗廟), *n.* an Imperial ancestral mausoleum.

sochi (素地), *n.* ❶ (地) ground. ❷ (素質) nature; making.

sochi (措置), *n.* measure; management. ☞ *shochi*.

sōchi (送致する), *vt.* to send; despatch forward.

sōchi (裝置), *n.* gear; installation; equipment. 一裝置する, to fit up *with*; install; set up; equip *with*.

sōchitsuryō (宗秩寮), *n.* the Bureau of Peerage.

sōchō (早朝), *n.* early morning. **——,** *ad.* early in the morning; at daybreak; bright and early; in the fresh of the morning.

sōchō (莊重), *n.* solemnity; dignity; gravity. **——-na,** *a.* solemn; grave; dignified. 一莊重典雅の文體, a solemn and refined style of writing.

sōchō (曹長), *n.* a sergeant-major.

sōchō (總長), *n.* ❶ the president; the general director; the superintendent. ❷ [支那] (各部長官) a minister. 一東京帝國大學總長, the President of the Tōkyō Imperial University.

soda (粗朶), *n.* brushwood; faggot (薪).

sōda (曹達), *n.* 【化】 soda. ¶ 曹達水, soda-water.

sodachi (育), *n.* ❶ (成長) growth. ❷ (養育) breeding; bringing up; training (躾). 一育ちが善い, ① to be well-bred. ② (成長) to grow rapidly; be of rapid growth. 一育ちが惡い, ① to be ill-bred. ② (成長) to grow poorly; be of slow growth.

sodai (粗大の), *a.* gross; coarse; rough.

sōdai (壯大), *n.* magnificence; grandeur. 一壯大な, grand; magnificent; imposing.

sōdai (總代), *n.* a representative; a spokesman; a delegate. 一卒業生の總代として答辭を讀む, to read out the reply as the spokesman of the graduates [on behalf of the graduates].

sōdaka (總高), *n.* the total sum; the total amount; the sum-total.

sōdan (相談), *n.* consultation; conference (會議). —出來ない相談, an impracticable proposal. —相談する, ① to consult a person (又は with a person about a matter); confer *with*; talk over *with*. ② (意見を求める) to seek advice; take counsel —相談が纏まる, to come to an agreement [understanding]; come to terms. —相談に乘る, to become party to a consultation. ¶ 相談役, an adviser; a counsellor.

sodateru (育てる), *vt.* ❶ to bring up; nurse; foster; rear (動·植物など); raise (植物·家畜など). ❷ (しこむ) to train; educate. —牛乳で育てる, to bring up a child on bottle [cow's milk]. —少年を法律家に育てあげる, to breed a boy a lawyer [to the law].

sodatsu (育つ), *vi.* to grow; grow up; thrive; be brought up. —よく育つ, to grow up well; flourish (草木).

sōdatsu (爭奪), *n.* scramble. —爭奪する, to scramble *for*; contest [struggle] *for*.

sōdatsu (送達), *n.* ❶ delivery; conveyance. ❷【法】service (令狀等の). —送達する, ① to deliver; convey. ② to serve.

sode (袖), *n.* a sleeve; an arm; an undersleeve (下著などの). —袖に縋る, ① to hang on a person's sleeve. ② to cry mercy. —袖をしぼる, to wet [stain] one's sleeve with tears. —袖を聯ねて, in a body; *en masse* (佛).

sōde (總出), *n.* turning out in full force; a full company; the full troupe (役者等の).

sodeguchi (袖口), *n.* ❶ the opening of a sleeve. ❷ (袖口用の布切) the cuff; the wristband (シャツ等の).

sōden (相傳の), *a.* hereditary; inherited. —相傳する, to inherit; hand down; transmit.

sōden (送電), *n.* power-transmission; transmission of electricity [electric power]. —送電する, to transmit electricity.

sodenoshita (袖の下), *n.* a bribe. —袖の下を使ふ, to bribe a person; grease a person's palm.

sōdō (騷動), *n.* confusion; disorder; disturbance; tumult (大騷). —騷動を起す, to raise a disturbance; give rise to confusion [disorder]. ¶ 米騷動, a rice-riot. —御家騷動, family strife.

sodoku (素讀), *n.* reading Chinese characters (without construing).

soegaki (添書), *n.* a postscript; an addendum.

soen (疎遠), *n.* estrangement; alienation; long negligence [silence] (無沙汰). —疎遠になる, to be estranged; be alienated.

sōen (蒼鉛), *n.*【化】bismuth.

soeru (添へる), *vt.* ❶ (添加) to add. ❷ (附屬) to attach; affix; annex. ❸ (添附) to append; accompany. —お負けに添へる, to throw in something; throw it into the bargain. —興味を添へる, to add zest *to*. —力を添へる, to help; aid; assist; give an aid *to*. —譯文を添へて送付する, to send it accompanied by a translation.

sofu (祖父), *n.* a grandfather.

sōfu (送付する), *vt.* to send; forward; consign (商品).

sofuku (粗服), *n.* coarse clothing; plain dress. —粗服を著 [纏う] てゐる, to be plainly dressed.

sofuto (柔), *a.* soft. ¶ ソフト帽, a soft hat. —ソフトカラー, a soft collar.

soga (粗畫), *n.* a rough picture; a rude [rough] drawing.

sōga (爪牙), *n.* ❶ claws and teeth. ❷ (手先) a tool; a cat's paw. ❸ (股肱) a right-hand man; a henchman. —他人の爪牙となる, to be used as a tool; be made a cat's paw of. —高利貸の爪牙にかゝる, to fall into the clutches of a usurer.

sōga (插畫), *n.* an illustration.

sogai (阻害), *n.* obstruction; hindrance; impediment. ☞ *jama*. —阻害する, to hinder; obstruct; impede. ☞ *samatageru*.

sogai (疎外する), *vt.* to estrange; keep [hold] off; keep [hold] at a distance.

sōgai (霜害), *n.* damage [injury] done [caused] by frost. —霜害を受けた, [*a.*] frost-bitten.

sōgakari (總掛), *n.* ❶ (總費用) the total cost. ❷ (一同の人) full force; all hands. —總掛りで, in full force; all hands.

sōgaku (奏樂), *n.* music; a musical performance. —奏樂する, to play [perform] music. ¶ 奏樂者, a performer; a player.

sōgaku (總額), *n.* the total amount [sum]; the sum total. ¶ 資本總額, the aggregate capital.

sogan (訴願), *n.* appeal; petition. —訴願する, to appeal; petition. ¶ 訴願人, a petitioner; an appellant.

sōgankyō (雙眼鏡), *n.* a binocular; a glass; a field-glass (陸

上用); a marine-glass (海上用); an opera-glass (劇場用); a stereoscope (實體雙眼鏡).

sōgawa (總革), *n.* full-leather binding (書物の). ¶ 總革金文字製本, a full-leather binding with gilt letters.

soge (竹木刺), *n.* a splinter; a splint.

sōgei (送迎する), *vt.* to see off and welcome. ¶ 送迎委員, a reception committee.

sogeki (狙擊), *n.* shooting; sharp-shooting. —狙擊する, to aim and shoot; fire *at*; shoot; pick off.

sogen (溯源する), *vi.* to trace to the source; inquire into the origin.

sogi (枌), *n.* splits; shingles.

sōgi (爭議), *n.* a dispute; a conflict; a trouble; controversy. —爭議を仲裁する, to arbitrate a dispute. ¶ 爭議團本部, the headquarters of the strikers.

sōgi (葬儀), *n.* a funeral; funeral service [rites]. ¶ 葬儀馬車《自動車》, a 《motor》 hearse. —葬儀係, persons in charge of a funeral. —葬儀社; 葬儀屋, an undertaker's office; an undertaker.

sogo (齟齬), *n.* ❶ disagreement; discrepancy. ❷ failure; miscarriage. —齟齬する, to disagree; be contrary *to*; go wrong; come to grief; fall to the ground.

sōgo (壯語), *n.* gasconade; spirited language; big words. —壯語する, to talk big; talk with spirit.

sōgo (相互の), *a.* mutual; reciprocal. ¶ 相互扶助, mutual aid. —相互保險, mutual insurance. —相互契約, mutual contract. —相互主義, reciprocity.

sōgō (相好), *n.* the face; countenance; features. —顏の相好を崩す, to pucker one's face with joy.

sōgō (綜合), *n.* aggregation; colligation; synthesis. —綜合する, to synthesize, synthetize; colligate; collate; aggregate.

sōgōkei (總合計), *n.* the grand total.

sōgon (莊嚴), *n.* magnificence; sublimity; grandeur; stateliness. —莊嚴な, magnificent; sublime; stately. ¶ 莊嚴美, the sublime (beauty).

sogu (殺·削ぐ), *vt.* ❶ (斜に削る) to cut off aslant [obliquely]. ❷ (切取る) to chip; cut off; mutilate (耳·鼻等を). ❸ (減殺する) to diminish; reduce; lessen; deaden. —病勢を殺ぐ, to deprive a disease of its virulence. —興を殺ぐ, to diminish one's enjoyment; spoil [damp] one's pleasure.

sōgu (爭具), *n.* the subject of dispute; the bone of contention. —爭具に供する, to make it the subject of dispute; bring it forward as the bone of contention.

sōgu (葬具), *n.* funeral articles. ¶ 葬具屋, =*sōgi* (葬儀屋).

sōgū (遭遇する), *vt.* to encounter; meet *with*; come *upon*; fall in *with*. ¶ 遭遇戰, an encounter.

sōgyō (創業), *n.* the commencement [starting] of an enterprise; initiation. —創業の際, at the commencement of an enterprise. —創業する, to commence; start; establish; initiate. ¶ 創業費, preliminary (and flotation) expenses.

sōgyō (操業), *n.* operations. —操業を短縮する, to curtail [cut down] operations.

sohai (鼠輩), *n.* contemptible fellows; the small fry.

sōhai (崇拜), *n.* =*shūhai.*

sōhaku (蒼白の), *a.* pale; pallid; livid. —蒼白な顏色, a sickly complexion; pale countenance.

sōhaku (糟粕), *n.* dregs; leavings; sediment. —古人の糟粕を嘗める, to lick the leavings of old writers.

sōhasen (爭霸戰), *n.* a contest for supremacy [mastery] 《championship》; a decisive fight 《match》. —早明野球の爭霸戰, a baseball champion match between Waseda and Meiji.

sōheki (雙璧), *n.* two jewels; two geniuses 《stars; flowers》 *of*.

sohō (粗放な), *a.* rough; inconsiderate; heedless.

sōhō (雙方), *n.* both sides; both parties; each side. —雙方(的)行爲, a bilateral act. —雙方合意の上, by mutual agreement [consent]. **——-no,** *a.* both; either; mutual. —雙方の言分を聞く, to hear both sides. **——-ni,** *ad.* on both sides; on either side. —雙方に言分がある, Much might be said on both sides.

sohōka (素封家), *n.* a wealthy person; a man of wealth.

sohon (粗笨), *n.* crudeness; artlessness; coarseness. —粗笨な, crude; coarse; artless; 【經·農】 extensive. ¶ 粗笨農業, extensive cultivation [farming; culture].

sōhon (草本), *n.* a herb.

sōhonke (總本家), *n.* the head-family.

sōhonten (總本店), *n.* the general head-shop.

sōhonzan (總本山), *n.* the head-temple of a sect.

sōi (相異, 相違), *n.* ❶ (差異) difference. ❷ (齟齬) disagreement; discrepancy; contradiction (矛盾). ❸ (懸隔) a gap; a distance; disparity. ❹ (不同) dissimilitude. —相違する, to be different *from*; discord (*with*; *from*); differ *from*; be at variance *with*; contradict. —— **-naku,** *ad.* without fail; undoubtedly; certainly. —相違無し, There is no doubt; I am sure *of* [sure that]; It is beyond doubt. —相違無く返金する, to repay without fail. —良い醫者になるに相違無い, He is sure to become a skilful doctor.

sōi (創意), *n.* an original thought; originality. —創意に富んだ, original; full of originality.

sōi (創痍), *n.* a wound.

soin (素因), *n.* a predisposition; a predominant cause; a material cause. ☞ *genin*.

soin (疎音), *n.* failure [neglect] to write 《call; visit》. —平素の疎音を謝す, I beg to apologize for my long silence.

sōin (總員), *n.* all the party; all hands (船の); the whole [all] number; full force. —總員百二十名, 120 persons in all.

sōiu (さういふ), such; like that. —さういふ人, a person of that name. —さういふ譯ですから, as such were the circumstances.

soji (措辭), *n.* diction; phraseology; wording.

sōji (相似), *n.* similarity; similitude; resemblance. ¶ 相似形, 【數】similar figures.

sōji (掃除), *n.* cleaning; sweeping; dusting. —— **-suru,** *vt.* to clean; sweep; dust; wash (水で); scavenge (市街を). —雪を掃除する, to sweep away the snow. —部屋を掃除させる, to have a room cleaned. ¶ 掃除夫, a scavenger (市街の); a dustman (芥屋). —掃除屋, a nightman (肥取人).

sōjishoku (總辭職), *n.* general resignation; resignation in a body. —總辭職をする, to resign in a body; resign *en masse*.

sō-jite (總じて), *ad.* generally; in general; as a general rule.

sojō (訴狀), *n.* a written complaint; a petition.

sōjō (相乘), *n.* 【數】multiplication. —相乘する, to multiply. ¶ 相乘比《平均》, geometrical ratio 《mean》. —相乘積, product.

sōjō (奏上する), *vt.* to report [submit] to His Majesty.

sōjō (僧正), *n.* a bishop.

sōjō (騷擾), *n.* a disturbance; a riot; a tumult. —騷擾を來たす, to create [cause] disturbances.

sōjōden (葬場殿), *n.* a funeral service hall.

sōjū (操銃), *n.* musketry. ¶ 操銃教練, musket-drill.

sōjū (操縱), *n.* management; manipulation; manœuvre. —— **-suru,** *vt.* to handle; manage; manipulate; pilot (飛行機を); manœuvre. —機械《舵》を操縱する, to work a machine 《rudder》. ¶ 操縱桿, a control stick [lever]. —操縱(者)席, the pilot's cockpit. —(飛行機)操縱士, a pilot.

sōjuku (早熟の), *a.* premature; precocious. —早熟の少年, a precocious boy.

sojutsu (祖述する), *vt.* to comment [explain] (on another's doctrine; on a basis); follow. ¶ 祖述者, a commentator; a follower.

sōjutsu (蒼朮), *n.* 【植】Atractylis ovata (spindlewort の類·學名).

sōka (桑果), *n.* sorosis.

sōka (想化する), *vt.* to idealize.

sokai (租界), *n.* a (foreign) settlement; a concession.

sōkai (壯快), *n.* liveliness; animation. —壯快な, lively; animating; grand.

sōkai (爽快な), *a.* refreshing; exhilarating; enlivening. —爽快な空氣, bracing [crisp] air.

sōkai (蒼海), *n.* the blue sea. —蒼海の一粟を探る, to look for a needle in a bottle of hay.

sōkai (掃海する), *vi.* to sweep the sea (for mines). ¶ 掃海艇, a mine-sweeper; a mine-dredger; a drifter.

sōkai (總會), *n.* a general meeting; 【宗】a synod. —總會を開く, to hold a general meeting. ¶ 定期《臨時》總會, an ordinary 《extraordinary》 general meeting.

sokaku (疎隔), *n.* estrangement; alienation; a gap.

sōkakurui (雙殼類), *n.* the bivalves.

sōkan (壯漢), *n.* a big fellow; a gigantic fellow.

sōkan (壯觀), *n.* a fine [grand] sight [view]; a magnificent sight [scene]; a striking demonstration. —自然の壯觀, the grandeur of nature. —壯觀を呈する, to make a magnificent appearance.

sōkan (相關的), *a.* relative; correlative; mutually related [connected].

sōkan (送還する), *vt.* to send back; return.

sōkan (創刊), *n.* the first publication; starting (of a periodical). —創刊する, to start. ¶ 創刊號, the first number (of a magazine).

sōkan (總監), *n.* an inspector [a superintendent; a commissioner]-general; a chief commissioner.

sōkanjō (總勘定), *n.* settlement of accounts. —總勘定する, to settle an account [accounts].

sōkatsu (總括), *n.* (wide) generalization; recapitulation; summary. —総括的, recapitulatory; summary. —— **-suru,** *vt.* to generalize; summarize; recapitulate. —総括して云へば, in (the) gross; generally speaking; in substance.

sōkatsu (總轄), *n.* general control [supervision]. —總轄する, to have general control; superintend; preside *over*.

sōke (宗家), *n.* the head family.

sōkedatsu (總毛立つ), *v.* to have the goose-flesh; make hair stand on end. —總毛立って身震ひする, to tremble with goose-flesh all over one's body.

sokei (鼠蹊), *n.* 【解】the inguen; the groin. ¶ 鼠蹊腺, an inguinal gland.

sokei (麁景, 粗景), *n.* Ⓢ 粗品. a slight [trifling] present.

sōkei (早計), *n.* over-hastiness; precipitance; prematurity. —早計に失する, to be far too hasty.

sōkei (總計), *n.* the sum (total); the total (amount or number); the aggregate; the grand total (總合計). ——, *ad.* in all; in the aggregate; in the gross. —總計する, to sum (up); total; totalize; count up (計算する). —總計千圓となる, to amount [come up] to ¥1000 altogether. —彼の債務は總計五千弗であった, His debts aggregated 5000 dollars.

soken (訴權), *n.* the right of action.

sōken (壯健な), *a.* healthy; sound; robust; stout. —壯健である, to be in good health; be very well.

sōken (創見), *n.* discovery; originality; an original view [remark]. —創見に富む, to have an original mind.

sōken (創建する), *vt.* to establish; found; build.

sōken (雙肩), *n.* both shoulders. —雙肩に責任を荷ふ, to take the responsibility on one's shoulders.

soketto (承口), *n.* a socket.

sōki (槍旗), *n.* a pennon, pennant.

sōkihei (槍騎兵), *n.* a lancer; an uhlan (獨·墺·露の).

sōkin (送金), *n.* remittance. —送金する, to remit [send] money. ¶ 送金手形, a remittance draft. —送金手數料, remittance charge.

sōkinrui (走禽類), *n.* 【鳥】Cursores (學名); the runners.

sokka (足下), *pron.* you. —足下に, at one's feet (足もと); under one's feet (足の下).

sokkenai (素氣ない), *a.* blunt; curt; brusque. —素氣ない挨拶, a curt answer; a cold answer.

sokketsu (卽決), *n.* 【法】summary judgment [decision]: immediate decision. —卽決する, 【法】to pass a summary judgment: make a prompt decision; decide on the spot. ¶ 卽決裁判, summary trial; summary conviction (陪審官なき).

sokki (速記), *n.* shorthand; stenography; phonography (聲音の). —議事の速記錄, a shorthand [stenographic] record of the proceedings. —速記する, to take down in shorthand; stenograph. ¶ 速記術, stenography. —速記者, a stenographer; a stenographist; a shorthand writer. —速記タイプライター係, a shorthand typist.

sokkin (卽金), *n.* cash; cash [ready] payment. —卽金で拂ふ, to pay in cash [ready money].

sokkin (側近), *n.* attendance, being about another's person. ¶ 側近者, attendants; persons in attendance *on*.

sokkō (卽效), *n.* immediate effect. ¶ 卽效紙, a sticking-plaster; the gold-beater's skin.

sokkoku (卽刻), *ad.* this moment; instantly; immediately.

sokkōsho (測候所), *n.* a meteorological station [observatory]; a weather-station.

sokkuri (そっくり), *ad.* ❶ (その儘) just as it is. ❷ (正しく) exactly; just like. ❸ (悉皆) all; altogether; entirely. —そっくりの, intact (手のつかぬ); exact (そのまゝの). —そっくりして置け, Let it alone. —あの娘の顏は母親そっくりだ, Her face is her mother's to a hair; She is the very image of her mother.

sokkyō (卽興), *n.* improvised amusement. —卽興の, offhand; impromptu; extemporaneous.

sokkyū (速球), *n.* 【野球】a fast ball.

soko (底), *n.* the bottom; the entrails (地の); the floor (海·洞穴等の); the sole (靴などの); the depth (水·心の). —底に屆く, to touch the bottom. —心の底をうちあける, to open one's mind [heart]; speak frankly.

soko (其處), *n.* that place; there. —其處へ, there. —其處から, thence. —そこだて, That's the point (要點); That's the question (問題).

sokō (素行), *n.* behaviour; conduct. —素行が修らぬ, to be profligate; be loose in one's conduct.

sokō (溯航する), *v.* to go up (against a stream).

sōko (倉庫), *n.* a warehouse; a store-house; a godown 【印度】. —倉庫に入れる, to warehouse; deposit in a warehouse; store. ☞ *kurani* (倉荷). ¶ 倉庫預證券, a warehouse receipt. —倉庫帳, a warehouse-book. —倉庫業, warehousing. (倉庫業者, a warehouseman.)

sōko (操觚), *n.* literature. ☞ *bunpitsu*. ¶ 操觚者, a man of letters; a writer; a journalist (新聞記者); literati (總稱).

sōkō (奏功), *n.* success. —奏功する, ① to succeed. ② to tell; be effective.

sōkō (草稿), *n.* a draft; a copy; a rough sketch. —草稿を作る, to make a draft; draft (an address); make notes *of*. —草稿演說をする, to speak from notes.

sōkō (倉皇, 蒼皇), *ad.* hurriedly; hastily; in a hurry.

sōkō (艙口), *n.* 【航】 a hatch; a hatchway.

sōkō (裝甲の), *a.* ironclad; armour-clad; armoured. —裝甲する, to armour. ¶ 裝甲自動車《巡洋艦; 列車》, an armoured automobile 《cruiser; train》.

sōkō (操行), *n.* conduct; behaviour; deportment. ☞ *hinkō*.

sōkō (糟糠), *n.* rice-bran (ぬか); coarse food (粗食); poverty (貧乏). —糟糠の妻, a wife wed amid difficulties.

sokobie (底冷する), *v.* to feel cold to the core.

sokode (そこで), *ad.* ❶ (場合) there. ❷ (其の時) then; thereupon; at that [that time].

sokohi (內障眼), *n.* 【醫】 cataract (白內障).

sokoi (底意), *n.* ❶ an underlying motive; an ultimate motive; a true meaning [intention]. ❷ (取引市場) under tone.

sokoiji (底意地), *n.* spite; malice. —底意地の惡い人, a spiteful man.

sokoku (祖國), *n.* the fatherland; one's country; home.

sokomame (底豆), *n.* a clavus; a corn (on the sole of the foot).

sōkon (早婚), *n.* early marriage.

sōkon (草根), *n.* the root of a plant.

sōkon (創痕), *n.* 【醫】 a cicatrice, cicatrix; a scar (刀傷の).

sokonau (損·害ふ), *v.* ❶ (損傷) to harm; hurt; injure; break. ❷ (駄目にする) to spoil; ruin; mar. ❸ (仕損ふ) to fail; mistake; make a mistake. —見損ふ, to fail to see. —擊ち損ふ, to make a bad shot; miss. —人の感情を損ふ, to hurt another's feelings. —健康を害ふ, to impair one's health.

sokoni (底荷), *n.* 【航】 ballast. —底荷を積む, to ballast.

sokonuke (底拔け), *n.* ❶ bottomlessness. ❷ (心のしまりのなきこと) instability of mind; unstable mind. —底拔け騷をする, to revel; paint the town red; go on a racket. ¶ 底拔け上戶, an insatiable [a hard] drinker; a guzzler.

sokora (其處邊), *n.* thereabout (-s); about there. ——, *ad.* or so; about; thereabout(s); about as much as. —二ガロンかそこら, two gallons or thereabouts. —其處ら中に散らかす, to scatter all over the place.

sokosoko (そこそこ), *ad.* ❶ = *sokora*. ❷ (急ぎて) hastily; hurriedly. —そこそこに引揚げる, to beat a hasty retreat.

sōkō-suru (左樣斯樣する), *vt.* to do this or that. —さうかうする中に, meanwhile; meantime; in the meantime.

sokotsu (粗忽), *n.* ❶ (不注意) carelessness; heedlessness. ❷ (粗放) rashness; imprudence. ❸ (あやまち) a blunder; a mistake. —粗忽な, careless; heedless; rash; imprudent. —粗忽を謝する, to beg pardon [apologize] for one's carelessness. ¶ 粗忽者, a careless fellow; a heedless fellow.

sokozumi (底積), *n.* stowing away in the bottom; ballast (船の底荷).

soku (束), *n.* a bundle (*of*); a sheaf (*of*) (藁などの).

-soku, -zoku, (足), a pair (*of*). —靴五足, five pair [pairs] of shoes.

sōku (挿句), *n.* a parenthesis.

sōku (走狗), *n.* a cat's paw.

sokubai (卽賣), *n.* spot sale. —卽賣する, to sell on the spot.

sokubaku (束縛), *n.* binding; restriction; restraint. —束縛を脫する, to shake off one's yoke; get rid of restraints. —— **-suru,** *vt.* to bind; restrict; restrain. —條件を附して束縛する, to tie a person (down) to conditions.

sokubu (足部), *n.* the foot. —足部に負傷する, to be injured in the foot.

sokubu (側部), *n.* a lateral part; a side.

sokubun (仄聞する), *vt.* to hear say; hear indistinctly; know through a rumour; get an inkling *of*.

sokuchi (測地), *n.* land surveying. ¶ 測地學, geodesy.

sokudai (卽題), *n.* a problem [subject] for immediate (class) work.

sokudan (卽斷), *n.* decision on the spot; immediate decision. —卽斷する, to decide on the spot; give an immediate decision.

sokudan (速斷), *n.* immediate (hasty) conclusion. —速斷する

to come to an immediate (hasty) conclusion; jump [rush] to a conclusion; draw a hasty inference.

sokudo (速度), *n.* speed; velocity; the rate of speed [progress]; 【音】*tempo* 〔伊〕. —高(低)速度, high (low) speed. —一時間十哩の速度で, at the speed of ten miles per hour.

sokuen (測鉛), *n.* a sounding-lead; a plumb; a lead. ¶ 測鉛線, a lead-line.

sokuhatsu (束髮), *n.* a foreign style of hair-dressing. —束髮に結ふ, to have one's hair done in foreign style. ¶ 束髮止, a hair-pin.

sokuheki (側壁), *n.* 【建】a side-wall; 【動】a theca.

sokuhō (速報する), *vt.* to report promptly. ¶ 速報臺, a bulletin-board.

sokui (卽位), *n.* accession (to the throne); succession to the throne. —神武卽位紀元二千五百八十六年, the year 2586 from the Accession of the Emperor Jinmu. —卽位する, to accede to [ascend] the throne; succeed to the throne; come to the throne. ¶ 卽位式, an accession ceremony; a coronation (ceremony).

sokui (續飯), *n.* rice-paste.

sokuin (惻隱の情に動かされる), to be touched with the feeling of commiseration.

sokuji (卽時), *ad.* immediately; in an instant; at once. ¶ 卽時拂, prompt payment. —卽時渡, spot delivery.

sokujitsu (卽日), *n.* the same day. ——, *ad.* (on) the same day; (on) the very day.

sokujo (息女), *n.* a daughter.

sokumen (側面), *n.* a side; 【軍】a flank; 【數】a lateral face. —日本歷史側面觀, a side-view of Japanese history. ¶ 側面攻擊, a flank attack. —側面圖, a side-view; a lateral plan.

sokuniku (息肉), *n.* 【醫】a polypus; a polyp.

sokurō (足勞), *n.* trouble to walk. —御足勞を掛ける, to trouble you to come.

sokuryō (測量), *n.* survey; measurement; sounding (水深などの). ——**-suru**, *vt.* to survey; measure; sound; take sounding. —海深を測量する, to sound the depth of a sea. —鐵道敷設地を測量する, to survey the land for railway. ¶ 陸地測量部, the land-survey department. —測量技師, a surveyor. —測量班, a surveying corps. —測量標, a levelling-pole [-staff]. —測量術, surveying; mensuration. —測量竿, a staff. —測量器械, a surveying instrument. —測量圖, a survey-map.

sokuryoku (速力), *n.* speed; velocity. —速力を出す, to put on speed; speed up; 【航】gather way. —速力を緩める, to slow down [off]; slack off (汽車). —速力三十二節の驅逐艦, a torpedo-destroyer of thirty-two knots speed. ¶ 速力試驗, speed-trial.

sokusa (測鎖), *n.* Gunter's [the surveyor's] chain.

sokusai (息災な), *a.* in good [sound] health; healthy; well; safe.

sokusan (速算), *n.* rapid calculation.

sokusei (促成する), *vt.* to encourage; urge; hurry. ¶ 促成栽培, hot-house rearing.

sokusei (速成), *n.* rapid completion (execution); quick mastery. ¶ 速成科, a rapid course.

sokuseki (足跡), *n.* a footprint; a foot-mark.

sokuseki (卽席の·に), *a.* & *ad.* offhand; extemporaneous; impromptu. —卽席には間に合せかねます, We cannot have it ready at a moment's notice. ¶ 卽席演說, an extempore [extemporaneous] speech. —卽席御料理, "Cooking done while you wait."

sokusen (側線), *n.* 【鐵道】a side-track; a siding.

sokusenki (測線器), *n.* a wire-gauge.

sokusha (速射), *n.* snap-shot; quick firing. ¶ 速射砲, a quick-firing [rapid-fire] gun; a quick-firer; a rapid-firer.

sokusha (側射), *n.* flanking fire.

sokushi (卽死), *n.* instantaneous death. —卽死する, to die on the spot; die an instant death.

sokushin (促進する), *vt.* to accelerate; quicken; hasten; further. —平和を促進する, to hasten peace. —食慾を促進せしめる, to edge [sharpen; whet] one's appetite.

sokushū (束脩), *n.* an entrance-fee.

sokusui (測錘), *n.* 【航】a sounding-lead.

soku-suru (卽する), *v.* to stick *to*; adhere *to*; hold *to*. —現實に卽する, to cling to the reality; adhere to actual facts.

sokutatsu (速達), *n.* express (delivery); dispatch. ¶ 速達郵便, an express mail

sokutei (測定), *n.* measurement; survey. —測定する, to measure; survey.

sokutō (卽答), *n.* a prompt [an immediate] reply [answer]; a ready answer. —即答する, to answer [reply] at once [promptly; immediately; instantly]; make a prompt answer.

sokutsū (足痛), *n.* a foot-sore; a pain in the foot.

sōkutsu (巣窟), *n.* a resort; a den; a nest. —盗賊の巣窟, a thieves' den; a flash-house [卑].

sokuya (卽夜), *ad.* (on) the same [very] night.

sokuza (卽座に), *ad.* immediately; instantly; offhand.

sōkuzure (總崩), *n.* collapse; rout. —總崩れになる, to collapse; be routed.

sōkyo (壯擧), *n.* a daring [bold] enterprise; a fine undertaking.

sōkyōiku (早敎育), *n.* early education.

sokyū (遡及する), *v.* to retroact; trace *to*.

sōkyū (躁急な), *a.* hasty; impatient; impetuous.

soma (杣), *n.* ❶ a timber forest; a timber mountain. ❷ (材木) timber. ❸ (杣人) a woodcutter; a woodman; a lumberer; a lumberman.

sōmai (草昧), *n.* primitiveness.

somaru (染まる), *vi.* ❶ (色にしむ) to be dyed; be coloured; be stained. ❷ (感化を受く) to be influenced; be imbued *with*.

somatsu (粗末な), *a.* humble; coarse; crude. —お粗末ながら, such as it is. —金錢を粗末にする, to be careless of money.

some (染), *n.* dyeing; colouring.

somegusuri (染藥), *n.* a dye; dyestuff.

sōmei (聰明な), *a.* wise; sagacious; clear-headed.

someiro (染色), *n.* colour; dye-colour.

somekaesu (染返す), *vt.* to re-dye; dye again [anew].

someko (染粉), *n.* a dye.

somemono (染物), *n.* dyed goods. ¶ 染物屋, a dyer (人); a dye-house (店).

somemoyō (染模樣), *n.* a dyed pattern.

sōmen (索麵), *n.* wheat vermicelli.

sōmen (層面), *n.* ❶ the layer-face. ❷【地質】strikes; the stratification plane.

somenuki (染拔), *n.* ❶ (染め拔くこと) dyeing (*through*). ❷ (そめぬきたる模樣) dyed patterns [figures]. —定紋を染め拔いた幔幕, a curtain with the family crest dyed on it.

someru (染める), *vt.* to dye; colour; ingrain. —指を染めるを許さぬ, not to allow a person put his finger on it.

somewake (染分の), *a.* parti-coloured; motley; medley. —赤に白の染分けの襷, a *tasuki* dyed in red and white.

somitsu (疎密), *n.* density.

sōmō (草莽), *n.* a bush; a jungle. —草莽の臣, your humble subject.

sōmoku (草木), *n.* plants; plants and trees; vegetation. —草木の繁茂せる, thick with trees and bushes; overgrown with vegetation.

sōmon (奏聞する), *v.* to report to the Emperor. ☞ *sōjō*.

somosomo (抑), now; then; well. —抑〻から, from its (very) beginning.

sōmu (總務), *n.* ❶ general business [affairs]. ❷ = 總務委員. ¶ 總務長官, a director-general; a vice-minister. —總務委員, the managers.

sōmu (雙務-的), *a.* bilateral; synallagmatic.

somukeru (背ける), *vt.* to turn away; turn one's back *to* [*on*]. —顏を背ける, to turn away one's face; look the other way.

somuku (背く), *vt.* ❶ (違背) to break; infringe; contravene. ❷ (不從順) to disobey. ❸ (叛逆) to rebel [revolt] *against*; rise *against*. —期待に背く, to be contrary to one's expectation. —國法に背く, to offend against the law (of the realm). —前例に背く, to be against [contrary to] the precedents. —母の意に背いて上京する, to go to the capital against one's mother's wishes.

son (損), *n.* loss (損失); damage (損害); disadvantage (不利益). —重ね重ねの損, losses upon losses. —損な立場, a disadvantageous position. —損をする, to lose; suffer [sustain; incur] a loss; suffer [meet] with a loss; lose money. —他人に損をかける [させる], to inflict loss upon another; put another to a loss.

sonae (備), *n.* ❶ (用意) preparation. ❷ (防禦) defences; preparations for defence. ❸ (陣立) battle array [formation]. ❹ (供給) supply. ❺ (豫備) provision. —不時の備, provision for [against] emergencies.

sonaemono (供物), *n.* an offering; religious offering.

sonaeru (供へる), *vt.* to offer; sacrifice; dedicate (奉納). —神前に供へる, to offer to a god.

sonaeru (備へる), *vt.* ❶ (準備) to prepare *for*; provide *for*; make preparations *for*. ❷ (供給) to supply *with*; furnish *with*. ❸ (具備) to possess; equip. —萬一 [不慮] に備へる, to provide against accidents [emergencies; eventualities]. —完全なる人格を具へ

る, to possess a perfect personality. —來訪者名簿を備へる, to keep a visitors' book.

sonaetsuke (備附の), *a.* provided; furnished.

sonaetsukeru (備附ける), *vt.* to provide *with*; furnish *with*; equip *with*. —巨砲が備附けてある, to be equipped with gigantic guns.

sōnan (遭難), *n.* a disaster; an accident; a casuality. —遭難する, to meet with a disaster [an accident]. ¶ 遭難地, the place [locality] of a disaster. —遭難船, a ship in distress. —遭難者, a sufferer (by an accident); a victim. —遭難信號, a signal of distress.

sonarematsu (磯馴松), *n.* ❶【植】(はひびゃくしん) the procumbent Chinese juniper. ❷ (なれふした松) a pine-tree with trailing branches.

sonawaru (備はる), *vi.* to be furnished [equipped] *with*; be supplied *with*; be endowed [blessed] *with* (天然に).

sonbō (存亡), *n.* existence; fate; life or death. —存亡に關する, to affect one's fate. —存亡の危機に迫る, to be at the crisis of its existence.

sonchō (村長), *n.* a village headman.

sonchō (尊重する), *vt.* to respect; esteem; value. —尊重すべき, respectable; estimable.

sondai (尊大な), *a.* haughty; arrogant; pompous. —尊大振る, to bear oneself haughtily; stand on one's dignity; put on airs.

soṅeki (損益), *n.* profit and loss; loss and gain. ¶ 損益表, a statement of profit and loss; a profit and loss account (損益計算書).

sonemashii (嫉·猜ましい), *a.* envious; jealous.

sonemi (嫉), *n.* jealousy; envy.

sonemu (嫉む), *vt.* to envy; be jealous *of*. ☞ *netamu.*

sōnen (壯年), *n.* the prime of manhood; the meridian of life.

sōnen (想念), *n.* notion.

songai (損害), *n.* ❶ (損傷) damage; injury (傷害). ❷ (損失) loss. —損害を與へる, to damage; inflict damage *on*. —多大の損害を蒙る, to sustain a great [heavy] loss; suffer seriously [heavily]. ¶ 損害賠償, compensation for damage. (損害賠償の訴を起す, to sue a person for damages.) —損害要償, claim for damages.

songen (尊嚴), *n.* dignity; majesty.

sōnin (奏任), *n.* the *sōnin* rank; an appointment made with His Majesty's approval. ¶ 奏任官, a *sōnin* official; an official of the *sōnin* rank; an official appointed with His Majesty's approval. —奏任待遇, treatment of the *sōnin* rank.

son-jiru (損じる), *vt.* to injure; damage. ——, *vi.* to be injured (damaged); be broken. —損じ易い, fragile; easily broken; perishable. —健康を損じる, to impair one's health.

sonkai (村會), *n.* a village assembly.

sonkei (尊敬), *n.* respect; honour; esteem. —萬人の尊敬を受けて居る, to command the respect of all people. **—-suru,** *vt.* to respect; esteem; revere; honour; regard with reverence; have a respect *for*; have a high regard *for*; hold in respect [reverence]. —尊敬すべき, estimable; honourable; worthy of respect [esteem].

sonmin (村民), *n.* villagers.

sonmō (損耗), *n.* loss; damage. ☞ *son, sonshitsu.*

sonna (其樣な), *a.* such; of the sort [kind]. —そんな筈はない, It cannot be so. —そんなに急ぐな, Don't be in such a hurry. —そんな事ぢゃない, It is nothing of the sort.

sonnara (其樣なら), *ad.* in the case; if so; if that is the case.

sono (其), *pron.* that [*pl.* those]; its; his; her; their.

sono (園), *n.* a garden.

sonō (嗉囊), *n.* 【動】the crop.

soṅō (尊王), *n.* loyalism; reverence for the Emperor. ¶ 尊王攘夷, reverence for the Emperor and expulsion of foreigners. —尊王家, a loyalist.

sonoba (其場), *n.* that place; the spot. —其場で, then and there; on the spot; at once (卽刻).

sonogo (其後), *ad.* afterwards; after that; subsequently. —其後の通信によれば, according to a later report. —其後逢ひません, I have not seen him since.

sonohen (其邊), *ad.* somewhere about there; thereabout(s).

sonohi (其日), *n.* that day. ——, *ad.* (on) that day; the very [same] day; on the day in question. —どうかかうか其日を送る, to manage just to live on from day to day; pick up a scanty [bare] livelihood. ¶ 其日暮し, living from hand to mouth; a hand-to-mouth life.

sonohito (其人), *n.* the person himself. —王其人であった, It was no other than the king; It was the king himself.

sonohō (其方), *n.* ❶ (方向) that

direction [way]. ● (仕事) that; that one.
sonohoka (其外), *ad.* besides; else; moreover. —其外の人, the rest; the others. —其外の理由, a further reason. —其外あらゆるもの, and all others.
sonokoro (其頃), *ad.* those times; about that time. ☞ *tōji.* —其頃の東京, the Tōkyō of those days.
sonokurai (其位), *ad.* as much; as many (數). (度,量)
sonokuse (其癖), *ad.* nevertheless; none the less; all the same.
sonomama (其儘), *ad.* as it is [stands]; in that condition. —其儘で喰べる, to eat it as it is. —其儘にしておく, to let alone; leave...as it is.
sonomichi (其道), *n.* the line; the profession. ☞ *shidō.* —其道の人, a professional; a specialist; a man in the line.
sonomono (其物), *n.* the very [same] thing. ——, *pron.* itself; himself; hereself; themselves. —文學其物を愛する, to love literature itself [for its own sake]. —彼は愛國心其物[の權化]であった, He was patriotism itself.
sonomukashi (其昔), *ad.* ❶ (當時) in those days [times]; at that time; when. ● (昔) once; once upon a time; in ancient times.
sonosuji (其筋), *n.* the authorities; the authorities concerned. —其筋の命により, by order of the authorities.
sonota (其他), *ad.* besides. ☞ *sonohoka.* —其他總て, and (all) the rest of it. —其他一切の手段, every other means. —其他の事は何にも知りません, I know nothing else.
sonotame (其爲に), *ad.* so; therefore; for that reason. —其爲め上京する, to go up to Tōkyō for that purpose.
sonotoki (其時), *ad.* then; at that [the] time; in those days. —丁度その時, just then; at the very time. —其時迄に, by then.
sonouchi (其中に), *ad.* some day; before long; in a few days. ——, *prep.* amid; among; in.
sonoue (其上), *ad.* moreover; over and above; in addition *to*; into the bargain. —其上の說明, further explanation. —其上困ッた事には, to make matters worse; what is worse.
sonpai (存廢), *n.* existence.
sonpi (存否), *n.* existence.
sonpūshi (村夫子), *n.* a country scholar; a pedagogue.
sonraku (村落), *n.* a village; a hamlet (小村).
sonritsu (存立), *n.* existence. —存立する, to exist. —存立を危くする, to imperil the existence *of*.
sonritsu (村立の), *a.* established by a village. ¶ 村立小學校, a village primary school.
sonryō (損料), *n.* hire. —損料で, for hire; on hire. —損料貸する, to lend for hire; hire out. —損料借する, to hire; borrow on hire.
sonsha (村社), *n.* a village shrine.
sonshitsu (損失), *n.* loss; damage. ☞ *son.*
sonshō (尊稱), *n.* a title (of honour).
sonshō (損傷), *n.* injury; damage; casualties. —損傷する, to damage; injure; break (こはす); stain (汚損).
sonshoku (遜色), *n.* humiliation; inferiority. —遜色がある, to be inferior *to*. —毫も遜色が無い, to be by no means inferior *to*; have nothing to fear from comparison *with*; stand comparison *with*.
sonso (樽俎の間), *n.* a ceremony; a ceremonial occasion. ¶ 樽俎折衝, diplomatic negotiations; a conference.
sonsō (尊崇), *n.* adoration; veneration. ☞ *shūhai* (崇拜).
son-suru (存する), *vi.* ❶ (存在) to exist. ● (殘存) to remain. ——, *vt.* (保存) to preserve; retain. —今猶心に存する, to ring [remain] in one's heart.
son-suru (損する), *v.* to lose; suffer [sustain] loss. ☞ *son.*
sontaku (忖度する), *vt.* to conjecture; surmise; guess.
sontoku (損得), *n.* loss and gain; profit and loss; advantage and disadvantage (利害).
sōnyū (插入), *n.* insertion; interpolation. —插入する, to insert; put *in*; introduce.
sonzai (存在), *n.* existence; subsistence; being (實在). —存在する, to be; exist; subsist.
sonzei (村稅), *n.* a village rate.
sonzoku (存續), *n.* continuance; duration. —存續する, to continue; last; endure; stand.
sonzoku (尊屬), *n.* an ascendant. ¶ 尊屬親, an ascendant relative.
sōō (相應), *n.* fitness; suitability; correspondence (對應). —相應の資產, competence. —相應する, to be suitable; suit; be fit *for*. —身分相應の生活をする, to live according to one's means. —佛語も相應に話す, to speak French tolerably well.
sōon (噪音), *n.* a noise; disso-

nance; discord.

soppa (反歯), *n.* projecting teeth; buck-teeth.

sora (空, 天), *n.* ❶ the heavens; sky; the air. ❷ (空惚) feigning ignorance. —空行く雲, a cloud flying across the sky. —空高く, high up in the sky. —虚託[ソラ]を使ふ, to pretend ignorance. **—— -de,** *ad.* by heart; by rote; without book. —空で讀む, to recite from memory; say by heart; say by rote.

sora (そら), *int.* there; here; look!; see! ☞ *sore* (其). —そら見ろ, There! You see. —そらあぶないよ, Look out, there!

soradanomi (空頼), *n.* a vain hope; an empty hope.

soragoto (虚事, 空言), *n.* a lie (虚言); a falsehood (同上); a fabrication (虚構).

sorairo (空色), *n.* ❶ (空模様) the weather. ❷ (うす藍色) sky-blue; azure; blue.

sorajini (空死), *n.* feigned death. —空死にする, to pretend to be dead; sham death.

sorajō (空錠), *n.* a draw-bolt lock. —空錠を下ろす, to fasten with a draw-bolt lock.

soramame (蠶豆), *n.* 【植】 the straight bean.

soramimi (空耳), *n.* ❶ (聞違ひ) mishearing. ❷ (聞きて聞かぬさまをすること) pretended deafness. —空耳を潰す, to turn a deaf ear *to*; pretend not to hear.

soramoyō (空模樣), *n.* ❶ (天候) the weather; the look [aspect] of the sky. ❷ (事件) the look [aspect] of affairs.

soranaki (空泣する), *vi.* to pretend to cry [weep]; shed sham [false] tears; weep crocodile tears.

soranamida (空涙), *n.* false tears; crocodile tears.

sorane (空寢), *n.* fox-sleep; sham [pretended] sleep.

sorani (空似), *n.* accidental resemblance.

soranzuru (諳んずる), *vt.* to learn by heart; commit to memory. ☞ *anki* (諳記する).

soraosoroshii (空恐しい), *vi.* to have vague fear.

soraseji (空世辭), *n.* mock courtesy; flummery; empty compliments.

sorasu (反らす), *vt.* to curve [bend] backwards.

sorasu (逸·外らす), *vt.* to turn aside; draw off (心などを); divert (流·心などを); deflect (飛來物などを). —目を外らす, to look away; turn one's eyes away. —球を外らす, 【擲球】 to break the balls. —質問を外らす, to parry a question.

soratoboke (空惚), *n.* feigning ignorance. —空惚ける, to pretend not to know; pretend to be ignorant (*of*).

soratsunbo (空聾), *n.* sham [feigned] deafness; deafness.

sorausobuku (空嘯く), *vi.* to turn a deaf ear *to*; pretend not to hear.

sorawarai (空笑), *n.* feigned laugh; forced laugh. —空笑ひする, to force a laugh; laugh a forced laugh.

sorayomi (空讀), *n.* recitation.

sorazorashii (空空しい), *a.* feigned; false; obvious (見えすいた). —空々しい虚言をつく, to tell a palpable lie.

sore (其), *pron.* it; that; he; she. **——,** *int.* there!; now!; see!; look! ☞ *sora* (そら). —それの, its. —それ以後, since then; afterwards. —それはそれとして, be it as it may. —それかあらぬか, whether that was the reason or not. —それだ, それだ, That's the very thing; That's it. —それ逃すな, There, don't let him slip away.

sore (逸·外れ), *n.* divergence; swerve; deflection.

soredake (其丈), *ad.* that much; so much; as many as; so far as. —それ丈でも, even with that alone. —それ丈しかありません, That's all I have [there is].

soredama (逸丸, 流彈), *n.* a stray bullet [ball].

soredanoni (其だのに), yet; in spite of that; notwithstanding.

sorede (其で), *ad.* ❶ (かくて) so. ❷ therefore; accordingly. ☞ *soreyue*. —それでよい, That will do; That's right. —それで譯が判った, That explains it [makes it clear].

soredekoso (其でこそ), that, indeed...; that, really... —それでこそ君だ, That would show your true self.

soredemo (其でも), still; yet; but; however; nevertheless; though.

soredewa (其では), *ad.* then; in that case; if it is the case; if so.

soregashi (某), *n.* ❶ a Mr.; Mr. So-and-so; a certain one. ☞ *nanigashi*. ❷ (我) I. —田中某, a certain (Mr.) Tanaka.

sorehodo (其程), *ad.* so much; so; much; so much as that. —それ程の病氣でもない, It is not such a serious illness.

sōrei (壯麗), *n.* splendour; pompousness; magnificence. —壯麗な, splendid; magnificent; pompous.

sōrei (葬禮), *n.* funeral rites; obsequies; burial service.

sorekara (それから), *ad.* then; next; after that; since then. —それからどうした, What happened after that?; Well, then?

sorekkiri (それっきり), *pron.* all. —それっきりです, That's all there is. —それっきり會った事がない, I have not seen him since.

sorekoso (それこそ), *pron.* that; it. —それこそ大變な事になる, That would certainly be a serious matter.

soremade (其迄), *ad.* till then; till that time; so long. —それまでに, ① by then; by that time. ② so; so much; so far.

sōren (操練), *n.* drill; training; exercises. —操練する, to drill; train; exercise.

sorenara (其なら), *ad.* then; if so; if that is the case.

sorenari (其なり), *ad.* as it is. ☞ *sonomama.*

sorenishitemo (其にしても), *ad.* (even) though. ☞ *soredemo.*

soreniwa (其には), *ad.* for that. —それには及ばない, There is no need for it.

soreru (逸·外れる), *vi.* ❶ to stray; diverge; glance off [aside]. ❷【野球】to shoot; swerve. —話が横道へ逸れる, The talk goes astray.

soresōō (其相應の), *a.* suitable; appropriate. —それ相應に體面を保つ, to keep up an appearance suited to one's position.

soretomo (それとも), *conj.* or.

soretonaku (それとなく), *ad.* indirectly; in a casual manner.

sōretsu (壯烈な), *a.* heroic; daring; gallant.

sōretsu (葬列), *n.* a funeral procession.

sorewasateoki (閑話休題), be that as it may; to return to our subject.

soreya (流矢), *n.* a stray arrow. —流矢に中る, to be struck by a stray arrow.

soreyue (其故), *ad.* Ⓢ それだから. therefore; for that reason; on that account. —それ故辭職する, That is why I resign.

sorezore (夫夫), *ad.* each; severally; respectively. —夫々の, several; each; respective. —夫々その位置に配置する to put them in their respective places.

sori (反), *n.* warp; curve; bend. —…と反りが合はぬ, not to hit it off *with.*

sori (橇), *n.* a sled, sledge; a sleigh (大形); a toboggan (長形).

sōri (總理), *n.* ❶ presidency. ❷ (人) the president; the leader; the chief. ¶ 總理大臣, the Prime Minister; the Premier; the Minister President (of State).

sorihashi (反橋), *n.* an arched bridge.

sorikaeru (反返る), *vi.* to warp (挽材など); bend backward; throw back one's head.

sorimi (反身), *n.* bending back the body. —反身になる, to throw out one's chest.

sōritsu (創立), *n.* establishment; foundation; organization. —創立する, to establish; organize; constitute; found; institute. ¶ 創立委員, the organizing committee. —創立事務所, the organization office.

soro (獨唱), *n.* solo. —ソロの大家, a great soloist.

sorō (疎漏), *n.* carelessness; heedlessness; inadvertence. —疎漏な, careless; heedless; inadvertent. —校正が疎漏だから, as the proof-reading was carelessly done.

sōrō (層樓), *n.* a storied building. ¶ 三層樓, a three-storied building.

soroban (算盤), *n.* an abacus. —算盤が取れる, to pay; be remunerative. —算盤を彈く, ① to use an abacus. ② to calculate. ¶ 算盤珠, a counter.

soroeru (揃へる), *vt.* ❶ (整理する) to put [arrange] in order; adjust. ❷ (纏める) to complete (the number). ❸ (品別する) to assort; sort. —口を揃へて, with one voice. —足並を揃へて進む, to march keeping pace.

soroi (揃), *n.* a set; a suit; an assortment (組合せ). —揃ひの, uniform; of the same pattern.

sōron (爭論), *n.* controversy; difference; dispute. —爭論中, in dispute. —と爭論する, to dispute *with*; have words *with.* —爭論を始める, to enter into a controversy *with.*

sōron (總論), *n.* introduction; general remarks. —總論より各論に入る, to descend from generals to particulars.

sorosoro (そろそろ), *ad.* ❶ (徐々) slowly; softly; gently. ❷ (次第次第) gradually; little by little. —そろそろ歩く, to walk at a slow pace.

sorou (揃ふ), *vi.* ❶ (合致) to agree; accord. ❷ (集合) to gather; assemble. ❸ (整頓) to be arranged in order; assort (組合ッて); become complete (纏まる). —揃ッた, even; equal; complete. (大さの揃ッた, of a size; of even size.) —兄弟が揃ひも揃ッて博士になッた, The brothers have all become doctors.

soru (反る), *vi.* to bend backwards; spring (木が); cast (同上); warp (同上).

soru (剃る), *vt.* to shave. —顔剃金三十錢, Shaving, thirty *sen.* —顔を剃らせる, to get [have] one's face shaved.

sōrui (走壘), *n.* 【野球】 base run. ¶ 走壘者, a base-runner.

soryaku (疎略), *n.* negligence; neglect; carelessness. ☞ *somatsu*. —疎略にする, to neglect; treat carelessly ⦅contemptuously⦆; manage neglectfully.

sōryo (僧侶), *n.* a priest; a bonze; a clergyman (牧師); a minister (英國國敎外の牧師); the clergy (緇徒); the cloth (同上).

sōryō (送料), *n.* postage (郵税).

sōryō (總量), *n.* gross weight.

sōryō (總領), *n.* the eldest son [child]; the first-born. ¶ 總領息子 ⦅娘⦆, the eldest son ⦅daughter⦆.

sōryōji (總領事), *n.* a consul-general. ¶ 總領事館, a consulate-general.

sosai (蔬菜), *n.* greens; vegetables; garden products.

sōsai (相殺), *n.* a set-off. —相殺する, to set off; cancel each other.

sōsai (總裁), *n.* a president; a director; a governor. —總裁となる, to assume the presidency *of*. ¶ 日本銀行總裁, the Governor of the Bank of Japan. —憲政會總裁, the President of the Kenseikai.

sōsaku (創作), *n.* creation; origination; an original work. —創作する, to originate; create; call into being. ¶ 創作家, an original writer. —創作者, an originator; a creator.

sōsaku (搜索), *n.* search; quest; hunting. —— **-suru,** *vt.* to search *for* [*after*]; look *for*; hunt (犯人·獵物などを). —身體を搜索する, to search the person *of*. ¶ 搜索隊, a search-party.

sosan (粗餐), *n.* poor meal.

sōsan (早產), *n.* premature birth.

sosei (粗製), *n.* coarse manufacture. —粗製する, to scamp; make coarsely. ¶ 粗製品, a crude article; a shoddy; an article of inferior make.

sosei (組成), *n.* composition; constitution; formation. —組成する, to compose; form; constitute. ¶ 組成物, a composite; a composition.

sosei (蘇生), *n.* resuscitation; revival; reanimation. —蘇生さす, to resuscitate; reanimate; bring back to life; bring to life. —蘇生する, to revive; recover; return to life. —蘇生の思をした, I feel as if I had come to life again.

sōsei (早世), *n.* early [untimely] decease [death]; premature death. —早世する, to die young; die an early death.

sōsei (奏請する), *vi.* to petition the Emperor.

sōsei (創世), *n.* the creation (of the world). ¶ 創世紀, the (Book of) Genesis (舊約全書の).

sōsei (叢生する), *vi.* to grow in clusters [bundles]; cluster.

sōsēji (腸詰), *n.* a sausage.

sōseki (送籍), *n.* a transfer of domicile. —送籍する, to transfer one's domicile.

sōseki (踪跡), *n.* a trace; whereabouts. —踪跡を晦ます, to leave no trace behind; cover one's traces. —踪跡を失する, to lose sight *of*; be at fault.

sosen (祖先), *n.* an ancestor; a progenitor; a forefather. —祖先を祭る, to worship one's ancestors. —祖先の祭をする, to hold a memorial service for one's ancestors. ¶ 祖先崇拜, ancestor-worship.

sōsenkyo (總選擧), *n.* a general election. ¶ 總選擧期日, the (general) election day.

sōsetsu (創設), *n.* establishment; creation; institution. ☞ *sōritsu* (創立).

sōsha (走者), *n.* a runner.

sōsha (壯者), *n.* a healthy man; a vigorous person; a man in the prime of life.

sōsha (掃射する), *vt.* to sweep with fire.

soshaku (咀嚼), *n.* manducation; mastication. —咀嚼する, to manducate; masticate; digest.

soshaku (租借), *n.* lease. —租借する, to lease. ¶ 租借地, a leased ground; a lease.

soshi (阻止), *n.* obstruction; impediment; interception. —— **-suru,** *vt.* to obstruct; impede; check. —水流を阻止する, to obstruct the stream.

soshi (祖師), *n.* the founder of a sect.

soshi (素志), *n.* a (long-)cherished design; a cherished desire; one's heart's desire. —素志を果す, to gain one's heart's desire. —素志を覆さぬ, to remain faithful to one's cherished design.

sōshi (壯士), *n.* a bravo; a political bully; a rowdy.

sōshi (相思), *n.* mutual love [affection].

sōshi (草紙), *n.* ❶ (稿) a draft. ❷ (冊子) a book; a story-book. ❸ (手習草紙) a copy-book.

soshiki (組織), *n.* ❶ organization; constitution; system (體系). ❷【生物】(細胞組織) the tissue;【解】the tela;【植】the texture (稀). —組織的, systematic; organic. —組織する, to compose; organize; constitute. —合資組織を株式組織に改める, to change a partnership into a joint-stock system. ¶ 組織學, histology. —組織者, a systematizer; an organizer; a constitutor.

sōshiki (相識), *n.* acquaintance.

sōshiki (葬式), *n.* a funeral (ceremony); the burial [funeral] rites [service]; the obsequies.

sōshin (總身), *n.* the whole body.

soshina (粗品), *n.* a slight present. —粗品ながら, slight as it is.

sōshingu (裝身具), *n.* personal ornaments; trinkets; *bijouterie* (佛).

soshiranu (素知らぬ), *a.* feigning ignorance. —素知らぬ顔をする, to dissemble; feign ignorance.

soshiri (譏), *n.* censure; slander; defamation. —後世の譏を免る, to escape the censure of posterity.

soshiru (譏る), *vt.* to slander; defame; censure.

sōshirui (雙翅類), *n.*【昆】Diptera (學名).

soshite (そして), *conj.* and; and then.

soshitsu (素質), *n.* ❶ nature; disposition; temperament;【醫】diathesis. ❷ (傾向) tendency; bent; turn. —遺傳的素質, inherited temperament. —君には詩人の素質がある, You have the making of a poet.

sōshitsu (喪失), *n.* loss; forfeiture; deprivation. —權利の喪失, loss (lapse) of a right. —喪失する, to lose; forfeit; be deprived *of*.

sōshiyō (雙子葉), *n.*【植】a dicotyledon. ¶ 雙子葉植物, Dicotyledoneæ (學名).

soshō (訴訟), *n.* a suit; an action; a lawsuit; a case. —訴訟する, to sue; bring suit [an action] *against*; go to law *with*. —訴訟に負ける, to lose a lawsuit. ¶ 訴訟代理人, a counsel; a process-attorney; an attorney-at-law. —訴訟費用, law costs; the costs) of legal proceeding). —訴訟事件, a lawsuit; a (judicial) case; a cause. —訴訟鑑定(事務), chamber-practice. —訴訟人, a suitor; an impleader; a plaintiff. —訴訟手續, judicial [legal] procedure.

sōsho (草書), *n.* a running hand; a grass hand.

sōsho (叢書), *n.* a library; a series. ¶ 日本文學叢書, the library of Japanese literature.

sōshō (爪床), *n.*【解】a nail-bed.

sōshō (宗匠), *n.* a master; a teacher; an expert.

sōshō (相稱), *n.* symmetry.

sōshō (創傷), *n.*【醫】trauma; a wound; an incised wound.

sōshō (總稱), *n.* a general name [term];【博】a generic name. —總稱する, to name generically.

soshoku (粗食), *n.* coarse food [fare]; simple [plain] diet; hard [rough] fare. —粗食する, to live plainly [on coarse food].

sōshoku (草食), *n.* feeding upon grass. ¶ 草食類,【動】Herbivoræ (學名).

sōshoku (裝飾), *n.* ornament (-ation); adornment; embellishment; decoration. —裝飾する, to decorate; adorn; ornament; dress (船舶·店頭等を); upholster (室內を). —裝飾と實用とを兼ねる, to combine use with ornament. ¶ 裝飾美術, decorative art. —裝飾品, fancy goods; a trinket (裝身具); upholstery (室內の). —裝飾屋, an upholsterer.

sōshu (宗主), *n.* suzerainty. ¶ 宗主權, suzerain rights; suzerainty.

sōshu (漕手), *n.* a rower; an oarsman; a puller.

sōshu (雙手), *n.* both hands. —雙手を擧げて贊成する, to second [support] with all one's heart.

sosō (沮喪), *n.* dispiritedness; dejection; despondency. —沮喪さす, to discourage; dispirit; dishearten. (士氣を沮喪さす, to break the spirit of the army.) —沮喪する, to despond; be dejected [dispirited; disheartened]; be cast down.

sosō (祖宗), *n.* ancestors; forefathers.

sosō (粗相), *n.* ❶ (不注意) carelessness; heedlessness. ❷ (過誤) a fault; a blunder; a careless mistake. —粗相をする, to make a mistake; commit a blunder. —粗相な, heedless; careless; inadvertent. ¶ 粗相火, an accidental fire.

sōsō (早早, 匆匆), *ad.* ❶ quickly; promptly; in [with] haste; ❷ (手紙の結句) yours truly. —五月早々, early in May. —歸ると早々, immediately he got home.

sōsō (草創), *n.* beginning; commencement.

sōsō (錚錚たる), *a.* conspicuous; surpassing. ―錚々たる人物, a prominent [conspicuous] figure; a man of high reputation.

sōsō (さうさう), *ad.* like that; so often; so frequently.

sōsobo (曾祖母), *n.* a great-grandmother.

sōsofu (曾祖父), *n.* a great-grandfather.

sosogu (注ぐ), *v.* ❶ (撒水) to pour *over*; sprinkle *on*; water. ❷ (注込む) to pour *into*; instil *into*. ❸ (流入) to pour [flow; run; empty] *into*. ❹ (集中) to fix; rivet; concentrate. ❺ (灌漑) to water; irrigate. ―利根川に注ぐ, to empty itself into the River Tone. ―燒家へ水を注ぐ(喞筒で), to turn a hose upon a burning house; play a stream of water on a house in flames. ―淚を注ぐ, to shed [drop] tears. ―全力を注いでやれ, Do it with all your might.

sosokkashii (そそっかしい), *a.* ❶ (不注意) heedless; careless; thoughtless. ❷ (性急) rash; hasty; precipitate.

sōsoku (總則), *n.* general provisions [rules].

sōson (曾孫), *n.* a great-grandchild.

sosonokasu (唆す), *vt.* ❶ (誘惑) to entice; allure; tempt. ❷ (煽動) to instigate; incite; egg on. ―人を唆して道樂をさせる, to lure a person into profligacy.

sosoru (唆る), *vi.* to stimulate; excite; stir. ―血を唆る, to stir one's blood. ―淚を唆る, to draw tears from a person.

sōsotsu (匆卒, 倉卒), *n.* suddenness (突然); precipitation (匆々). ―匆卒の, abrupt; sudden; precipitate. ―匆卒に, abruptly; of [on] a sudden; precipitately.

sossen (率先する), *vi.* to take the lead; lead off; be a pioneer [the first man]. ¶ 率先者, a leader; a pioneer.

sosū (素數), *n.* 【數】 a prime (number).

sōsu (ソース), *n.* sauce. ―ソースを掛ける, to sauce. ¶ ソース容器[入], a sauce-tureen [-boat].

sōsū (總數), *n.* the total [whole] number; the total. ――, *ad.* in the aggregate; in all.

sosui (疏水), *n.* drainage; water-drainage. ―疏水工事を起す, to commence drainage work.

sōsui (送水する), *vi.* to supply with water. ¶ 送水管, a water-pipe. (送水本管, a water-main.)

sō-suru (奏する), *vt.* ❶ (奏上) to report to the Emperor; submit to the Throne. ❷ (演奏) to play; perform. ❸ (奏功) to take (effect); have (effect) *on*; succeed *in* (an attempt). ―何等の功を奏せぬ, to be of no avail; be without avail [success]. ―注射が功を奏した, The inoculation took.

sōtai (早退), *n.* early retirement [leaving of office].

sōtai (相對), *n.* relativity. ―相對的, relative. ―相對の善, a relative good. ¶ 相對(的)義務, 【法】 reciprocal obligation. ―相對性原理, the theory of relativity; the Einstein theory.

sōtai (總體), *n.* the whole; all; the mass; the entirety. ―總體の, general; whole; total.

sōtan (爭端), *n.* a dispute; a quarrel. ―爭端を開く, to commence a dispute.

sōtatsu (送達), *n.* ❶ conveyance; delivery; despatch. ❷ 【法】 service. ―送達する, to send; convey; deliver; serve.

sotchi (其方), *pron.* (口語) that; you. ――, *ad.* there.

sotchinoke (そっち除けにする), *vi.* to ignore; neglect; leave out of consideration.

sotchoku (率直), *n.* plainness; frankness; simplicity. ―率直な, plain; frank; straightforward; simple(-hearted; -minded). ―率直に言ふ, to speak plainly [bluntly].

sotchū (卒中), *n.* fulminant apoplexy. ―卒中の發作, an apoplectic attack [fit]. ―卒中で頓死する, to die suddenly of apoplexy.

sōte (沿うて), *prep.* & *ad.* along. (☞ sou (沿ふ).)

sōtei (壯丁), *n.* an able-bodied man (壯男); a full-grown person (成人); an adult (同上); a youth of conscription age (適齡者). ¶ 壯丁檢査, physical examination of men of conscription age. ―壯丁名簿, a list of persons of conscription [military] age.

sōtei (裝釘), *n.* the binding; the get-up. ―裝釘する, to bind.

sōtei (想定的), *a.* imaginary. ―想定する, to suppose; imagine. ¶ 想定敵國, an imaginary enemy.

sōteihō (漕艇法), *n.* oarsmanship; the art of rowing.

sōten (爭點), *n.* a point of [in] dispute; a point in question [at issue]. ―事實上の爭點, an issue of fact. ―爭點となる, to be at issue.

sōten (裝塡), *n.* the charge (of a gun); loading. ――-**suru**, *vt.* to charge (gun); load; cap (雷管を). ―實彈を裝塡する, to load with ball cartridges.

sōten (操典), *n.* a drill-book. ¶ 步兵操典, a manual of infantry drill.
sotetsu (蘇鐵), *n.* 【植】 the fern palm; the sago-palm (of Japan).
soto (外), *n.* the outside (外側); the exterior (外界); the open (air) (戶外). —外の, outer; out (-ward); outdoor. —外に, outside; out; without; out of doors.
sotō (粗糖), *n.* raw sugar.
sōto (壯圖), *n.* a daring [bold] enterprise. ☞ *sōkyo.*
sōto (僧徒), *n.* priests; the priesthood. ☞ *sōryo.*
sōtō (爭鬪), *n.* a struggle; a strife; a conflict. —爭鬪する, to struggle; fight.
sōtō (相當な), *a.* ❶ (適當) suitable; proper; adequate. ❷ (至當) reasonable; due. ❸ (程合) moderate. ❹ (釣合) proportionate. ❺ (可成) fair; respectable; pretty. ❻ (該當) corresponding. —相當な資產家, a man of competent fortune. —腕前相當の給料, a salary proportionate to ability. —相當する, ① [*vi*] to be appropriate *to*; correspond *to* (該當); match (釣合). ② [*vt.*] to suit; fit; befit; become; deserve [merit] (賞罰). —相當の條件で, on fair terms [conditions]. —相當に繁昌する, to be fairly prosperous. ¶ 相當官, a ranking officer [official]; a departmental officer. (陸軍少將相當官, an officer ranking with a major-general.)
sōtō (掃蕩する), *vt.* to sweep; clear *of*. —海上の敵を掃蕩する, to sweep (the enemy from) the seas.
sōtō (雙頭の), *a.* double-headed. —雙頭の鷲, a double eagle.
sotoba (卒塔婆), *n.* 【梵】 a stupa.
sotobako (外箱), *n.* a packing-case.
sotobori (外濠), *n.* the outer [outside] moat. ¶ 外濠線, the tramway along the outer moat.
sotogamae (外構), *n.* ❶ (外觀) the outward [outer] aspect; the external appearance. ❷ (外砦) the outworks; the outer wall.
sotogawa (外側), *n.* ❶ the outside; the exterior. ❷ a case (時計等の).
sōtoku (總督), *n.* a governor-general; a viceroy (植民地などの). ¶ 印度總督, the Viceroy of India.
sō-tosuru (壯とする), *vt.* to admire. ☞ *sō* (壯). —其の擧を壯とする, to admire the undertaking.
sotoumi (外海), *n.* an open [outer] sea.
sotowa (**ni**) (外鰐), *n.* bandy [bow] legs. —外鰐に步く, to walk with the legs bowed.
sotsū (疏通), *n.* ❶ (疏水) drainage. ❷ (理解) understanding. —疏通する, to come to a mutual understanding; understand each other. —意志の疏通を圖る, to bring about mutual understanding.
sotsugyō (卒業), *n.* graduation; completion of a course of study. —— **-suru**, *v.* to graduate *at* 〔英〕; be graduated *from* 〔米〕; complete a course. —卒業すると直ぐ, immediately upon completing [as soon as one had completed] one's school course. —大學を優等で卒業する, to graduate at a college with honours. ¶ 卒業論文, a graduation thesis. —卒業生, a graduate; an alumnus 〔羅〕. —卒業試驗, a graduation examination. —卒業證書, a diploma; a certificate of the completion of a school course.
sotsuji (卒爾な), *a.* abrupt. —卒爾ながら, excuse my abruptness, but....
sotto (そッと), *ad.* ❶ (ひそかに) stealthily. ❷ (靜かに) quietly; gently; softly. ❸ (輕く) lightly; softly. —そッと覗く, to peep *at* stealthily. —そッと置く, to lay gently.
sottō (卒倒する), *vi.* to swoon; faint away; fall down senseless.
sou (沿ふ), *vi.* to be in touch [contact] *with*. —河に沿うて, along the river. —海岸に沿うて進む, to skirt along the coast; go along by the coast.
sou (添·副ふ), *v.* ❶ (附き添ふ) to accompany; go *with* (同行する). ❷ (夫婦になる) to be married *to*; be united in marriage. ❸ (副) (一致) to accord *with*; be in accordance *with*; satisfy.
sōun (層雲), *n.* 【氣象】 a stratus.
sōwa (送話), *n.* transmission of speech [a telephonic message]. ¶ 送話口, a mouthpiece; a transmitter. —送話器, a transmitter; a microphone (無線電話の). (炭素送話器, a carbon microphone.)
sōwa (插話), *n.* an episode.
sowasowa (そはそは), *ad.* restlessly; uneasily; in a fidget. —そはそはする, to be restless; be uneasy; be fidgety.
soya (粗野), *n.* rusticity; coarseness; rudeness. —粗野な, rude; rustic; coarse.
sōyaku (裝藥), *n.* priming. —裝藥する, to prime.
soyō (素養), *n.* knowledge; acquirement; attainment. —素養

のない, without knowledge *of*; having no knowledge *of*.

soyogu (戦ぐ), *vi.* ❶ (風が) to breathe; fan; sigh. ❷ (木等が) to stir; tremble; quiver; rustle. —風に戦ぐ, to tremble [quiver] in the breeze; rustle in the wind.

soyokaze (微風), *n.* a breeze; a gentle [soft; light] breeze [wind]; a breath of air [wind].

soyosoyo (そよそよ), *ad.* gently; softly. —そよそよと吹く, to breathe; blow gently [softly].

sōzai (総菜), *n.* food for the whole household; household fare; plain food. ¶ 総菜料理, plain cookery.

sozatsu (粗雑), *n.* rudeness; coarseness; crudeness. —粗雑な, rough; coarse; crude.

sozei (租税), *n.* taxes. —租税の徴收, levying of taxes; collection of taxes. —租税の轉嫁, shifting of a tax. —租税を課する, to impose a tax.

sōzei (總勢), *n.* the whole number (of persons); the whole army.

sōzen (蒼然), *ad.* ❶ (樹木に言ふ) in green; verdantly. ❷ (暮色に言ふ) dimly; in grey.

sōzen (騒然), *ad.* noisily; clamorously. —騒然たり, to be in an uproar [a clamour; a tumult].

sōzetsu (壯絶), *n.* sublimity; grandeur; magnificence. —壯絶な, sublime; grand; magnificent.

sozō (粗糙の), *a.* rough; coarse.

sozō (塑像), *n.* a clay [an earthen] figure; a plaster image.

sōzō (創造), *n.* creation. —— -**suru**, *vt.* to create. —天地を創造せる神, God who created the universe. ¶ 創造物, a (fellow-) creature; the creation.

sōzō (想像), *n.* ❶ imagination. ❷ (幻想) fancy. ❸ (推定) conjecture; surmise. ❹ (假想, 豫想) supposition; preconception. —想像する, to imagine; conceive; fancy; conjecture. —想像し難き, unthinkable; unimaginable; inconceivable. ¶ 想像畫, a fancy picture. —想像力, imaginative power. (豐富なる想像力, a fertile imagination.)

sozoku (鼠賊), *n.* a petty thief; a sneak-thief; a pilferer.

sōzoku (相續), *n.* 【法】 inheritance; succession. —— -**suru**, *vt.* to inherit; succeed. —父の跡を相續する, to succeed one's father. ¶ 相續權, the right of succession [inheritance]. —相續人, an heir; a successor. (法定相續人, a legal heir; an heir at law. —推定相續人, an heir presumptive.) —相續稅, 【法】 succession duty [tax].

sōzoku (僧俗), *n.* the priest and layman; the priesthood [clergy] and laity.

sozoro (漫に), *ad.* involuntarily; unaccountably. —漫に悲しい, to feel unaccountably sorrowful.

sōzōshii (騒騒しい), *a.* noisy; clamorous; boisterous.

su (洲), *n.* a sand-bank; a shoal; a spit.

su (巢), *n.* ❶ (鳥の) a nest; an aerie (鷲などの). ❷ (蜘蛛の) a web; a cobweb. ❸ (蜂の) a comb; a hive. ❹ (獸の) a lair; a den. ❺ (巢窟) a den. —盗賊の巢, a den [nest] of robbers. —巢に歸る, to go to roost; home (特に鳩に云ふ). —巢に就く, [*vi.*] to brood; sit on eggs; incubate. —巢をつくる [かける], to build a nest; nest; spin a web (蜘蛛).

su (酢), *n.* vinegar. ¶ 酢牡蠣, oyster seasoned with vinegar.

su, suaki, (鬆), *n.* a pore. —鬆のある大根, a porous radish.

su (簀), *n.* =*sudare* (簾).

sū (數), *n.* ❶ a number. ❷ (數字) figures. ❸ (運命) one's destiny; one's fate. ❹ (理法) the law of the universe. —數に顯はす, to express in figures. —自然の數である, It stands to reason that...; It is natural that....

su-, sū-, (數), several; some. —數人, several persons; some people. (數十人, some tens of persons. —數百人, several hundred men; hundreds of men.)

suashi (素足), *n.* barefoot; naked feet. —素足の, barefooted. —素足で, barefoot; without stockings 《socks》 (足袋なしで).

subako (寸白), *n.* woman's colic; verminous [worm] colic.

subarashii (素晴しい), *a.* grand; splendid; magnificent. —素晴らしい出來, a phenomenal success. —素晴しく澤山な金, a stupendous sum [an awful lot] of money.

subashikoi (素敏こい), *a.* ❶ (性質) sharp; smart; keen. ❷ (動作) quick; nimble.

subayai (素早い), *a.* quick; rapid; nimble; deft.

sube (術), *n.* a way; a means. —逃れ出でん術もなく, with no means of escape.

subekaraku (須らく), *ad.* by all means; under any circumstances.

subekkoi (滑っこい), *a.* smooth; slippery.

subekukuru (總括る), *vt.* to control; oversee.

suberasu (辷·滑らす), *vt.* to slip; let slip. —口を辷らす, to make a slip of the tongue; blurt out the truth.

suberu (辷·滑る), *vi.* ❶ to slide; glide; slip; skate (氷靴にて); be slippery (すべッこい). ❷ (落第) to be plucked [ploughed; degraded] 〔學生·俗〕. —滑り易い, [*a.*] slippery; eely. —崖から滑り落ちる, to slip down the cliff. —第二壘に滑り込む, to slide into the second base. —氷上を滑る, to skate [slide] on the ice.

suberu (統·總べる), *vt.* to reign *over*; superintend; preside *over*.

subesube (滑滑した), *a.* = *subekkoi*.

subete (凡·總て), *ad.* ❶ (凡そ) generally; in general; on the whole. ❷ (全く) all; entirely; wholly; altogether. —總ての, all; whole; entire.

subomeru (窄める), *vt.* to pucker; shut; make narrower. ☞ *tsubomeru*. —肩をすぼめる, to shrug one's shoulders.

suchīmu (蒸氣), *n.* steam.

sudachi (巣立), *n.* ❶ (鳥が) leaving a nest. ❷ (人が) standing on one's own legs. ❸ (産婦が) leaving one's bed after confinement. —巣立つ, ① to leave a nest. ② to become independent; stand on one's own legs.

sudaku (集く), *vi.* to gather; crowd together.

sudare (簾), *n.* a bamboo-blind. —簾を懸ける, to hang a bamboo-blind. —簾を捲上げる《下ろす》, to roll up《let down》a bamboo-blind.

sude (素手), *n.* an empty hand; an uncovered [ungloved] hand. —素手で, empty-handed; unarmed (寸鐵を帶びず); with bare hands (同上).

sudeni (已·既·業に), *ad.* ❶〔既〕(既往に屬す) already. ❷〔已〕(現今に屬す) now. ❸〔業〕(未來に屬す) on the point *of*. —既に危く見えたところを救はれる, to be rescued from imminent danger. —已に業に晩い. Now it is too late.

sudōri (素通する), *v.* to pass by without calling.

sudōshi (素透の), *a.* plain. —素透しの眼鏡, plain-glass spectacles.

sue (末), *n.* ❶ (終尾) end; close. ❷ (未來) the future. ❸ (子孫) a descendant. ❹ (末世) a degenerate [corrupt] age. —多年苦心の末, after many years' efforts. —末頼もしき少年, a boy with a hopeful future; a promising youth. —末の末まで, till [to] the very end of one's life. —末は野となれ山となれ, "After us the deluge."

suefuro (据風呂), *n.* a stationary bath with a stove.

suehiro (末廣), *n.* a fan; a folding-fan. —末廣形の, fan-shaped.

suekko (末子), *n.* =*basshi*.

sueoki (据置の), *a.* unredeemed; deferred. —据ゑ置く, to leave as it is; leave it intact; leave unredeemed (公債など). ¶ 据置貯金, fixed deposit. —据置年金, deferred annuity.

sueru (据ゑる), *vt.* ❶ (置く) to set; place; lay. ❷ to fix; fit up; install. —膳を据ゑる, to set a table. —眼を据ゑて私を見てゐた. He was looking at me with set [fixed] eyes.

sueru (饐ゑる), *vi.* to rot; corrupt; putrefy. ☞ *kusaru* (腐る). —飯が饐ゑた. The boiled rice has turned sour.

sueshijū (末始終), *ad.* eternally; for ever; to [till] the end.

suetsuke (据附), *n.* fitting out; installation; mounting; setting. —機械の据附, fitting up of machinery. —据ゑ附ける, to fix; fit up; install; mount (砲を).

suēta (スエータ), *n.* a sweater.

suezen (据膳), *n.* a table set before a person.

sufinkusu (スフィンクス), *n.* a sphinx.

sugaito (絓絲), *n.* unglossed silk.

sūgaku (數學), *n.* mathematics. —數學の, mathematical. ¶ 數學家, a mathematician. —數學敎師, a mathematical teacher; a mathematics master.

sugame (眇), *n.* ❶ (片目) a one-eyed man. ❷ (藪睨) a squint.

sugao (素顏), *n.* an unpainted face.

-sugara (すがら), all through; throughout. —夜(も)すがら, all night through. —道すがら, on one's way; all the way; as one goes along.

sugaru (縋る), *vt.* ❶ (取すがる) to cling *to*; hold on *to*. ❷ (依賴する) to depend *on*; hang on *to*; resort *to*. —膝に縋る, to lean on a person's knees. —杖に縋って歩く, to walk leaning on a stick.

sugata (姿), *n.* a figure (姿勢); a form (形); a shape (同上); appearance (風體); a condition (狀態). —昔の姿, one's old [former] self.

sugatami (姿見鏡), *n.* a large looking-glass; a cheval-glass; a pier-glass (壁鏡).

suge (菅), *n.* 【植】 the sedge.

suge-nai (素氣ない), *a.* brusque;

curt (そっけない); blunt (ぶっきらぼうの). 一すげない返事, a curt reply. **—— - naku,** *ad.* bluntly; curtly; brusquely. 一素氣なく斷[ﾄﾜ]る, to give a rebuff; give a flat [abrupt; square] refusal: refuse pointblank.

sugeru (据げる), *vt.* to put in; insert; tie. 一下駄の鼻緒を据げる, to tie the thong to a clog.

sugi (杉), *n.* 【植】 the cryptomeria; the Japanese cedar. ¶ 杉箸, cedar chopsticks. 一杉垣, a cedar hedge. 一杉山 (並木), a hill (row) of cryptomeria.

sugi (過), *prep.* past; after. **——,** *ad.* over; too. 一十二時過ぎ, past twelve (o'clock). 一食ひ過ぎ, surfeit; excessive eating.

sugigoke (土馬鬃), *n.* 【植】 the hair-moss; the golden maidenhair; the goldilocks.

sugiita (杉板), *n.* a cryptomeria board [plank].

sugikawa (杉皮), *n.* a cryptomeria-bark.

sugina (杉菜), *n.* 【植】 the bottle-brush; the false horsetail.

suginari (杉形), *n.* a cone. 一杉形に盛上げる, to heap in a conical form.

sugiru (過ぎる), *v.* ❶ (通過) to pass by; go past. ❷ (經過) to pass; elapse. ❸ (過度) to go beyond; exceed; carry [go] too far. 一に過ぎない, to be no more than; be nothing but. 一仲が好過ぎる, to be too intimate. 一寛大過ぎる, to be too generous; be generous to a fault. 一私には過ぎた光榮, an honour beyond my deserts. 一春が過ぎた, The spring is over.

sugisaru (過去る), *vi.* to pass (away); elapse. 一過ぎ去った, past; past and gone; overpast. (過ぎ去った事は仕方が無い, "Let bygones be bygones.")

sugiyuku (過行く), *vi.* ❶ (通過) to go past; pass away. ❷ =*sugisaru*.

sugizai (杉材), *n.* a cedar.

sugoi (凄い), *a.* uncanny; weird; dreadful. 一凄い顏, a dreadful face. 一凄い腕, singular [wonderful] ability; amazing artifice; uncommon shrewdness. 一凄い程いい女, a woman whose beauty is chilling.

sugomi (凄味), *n.* uncanniness; weirdness.

sugomoru (巣籠る), *vi.* ❶ (巣に籠る) to nest. ❷ (冬眠する) to hibernate.

sugoroku (雙六), *n.* the Japanese backgammon. ¶ 雙六盤, a backgammon-board.

sugosu (過す), *vt.* ❶ (時を送る) to pass; spend; get *through*. ❷ (過度) to exceed; go *beyond*. 一酒を過ごす, to drink (wine) to excess. 一空しく時を過ごす, to pass time idly; waste time.

sugosugo (悄悄), *ad.* despondently; dejectedly. ☞ *shōzen*.

sugu (直ぐ), *ad.* Ⓢ 直に. immediately; instantly; at once. 一すぐ近くに, hard by; close by. 一直ぐ目の前に [鼻先に], just before one's nose. 一直ぐ覺える, to be quick to learn. 一門が閉ぢると直ぐ…, as soon as the gate was closed.

sugureru (勝·優れる), *v.* to surpass; excel. 一優れた, excellent; surpassing; preeminent. 一顏が勝れない, to look poorly. 一健康が勝れない, to be in poor health; be out of sorts. 一人並勝れて大きい, to be superior in size to most men.

suguri (すぐり), *n.* 【植】 Ribes grossularioides (currant の一種·學名). 一まるすぐり, the gooseberry. 一ふさすぐり, the red currant; the raisin-tree.

suguru (選る), *vt.* to select; choose; pick.

sugusama (直樣), *ad.* immediately; at once. ☞ *sugu*.

suhada (素肌), *n.* the bare [naked] body.

sūhai (崇拜), *n.* =*shūhai*.

suhamasō (獐耳細辛), *n.* 【植】 the hepatica; the noble liverwort.

sui (粋), *n.* ❶ (精華) essence; cream; pink; flower. ❷ (精英) choice; flower; *élite* 【佛】. ❸ (意氣) fashionableness; stylishness. 一粋な, refined; stylish; smart; *chic* 【佛】. 一粋を集める, to take the essence *of*.

sui (膵), *n.* 【解】 the pancreas; the sweetbread (動物の).

sui (酸い), *a.* sour; acid; tart. 一酸いも甘いも知って居る, to have tasted the sweets and bitters of life.

sūi (趨異), *n.* 【生物】 variation.

suiageru (吸上げる), *vt.* to suck up; draw [pump] up. ¶ 吸上ポンプ, a suction-pump.

suiatsu (水壓), *n.* water pressure; hydraulic pressure. ¶ 水壓計, a piezometer; a hydraulic gauge. 一水壓機, 【理】 a hydraulic press [compressor]; a Bramah press. 一水壓試驗, a hydraulic test.

suiban (水盤), *n.* a basin.

suibi (衰微), *n.* decline; decay; decadence. 一衰微する, to decline; decay; sink. 一衰微に向ふ, to begin to decline; go down hill; be on the down grade.

suibō (水防), *n.* defence [protec-

tion] against water.
suibō (衰亡), *n.* decline and fall; ruin; downfall.
suibun (水分), *n.* moisture; humidity. —水分の多い, watery; humid. —水分のある, wet; moist; humid.
suichi (推知), *n.* inference. —推知する, to infer.
suichō (水鳥), *n.* a water-bird; a water-fowl. [☞ *sonchō*.]
suichō (推重), *n.* respect.
suichoku (垂直), *n.* verticality; perpendicularity. —垂直の, vertical; perpendicular; plumb. —垂直に, vertically; perpendicularly; plumb. ¶ 垂直角《面; 線》, a vertical angle《plane; line》.
suichū (水中の), *a.* submarine; subaquatic; under-water. —水中に沒する, to disappear in the water; sink. ¶ 水中爆彈, depth charge [bomb]. —水中防禦物《信號器》, a submarine defence《signal》.
suidashi (吸出), *n.* an epispastic; a blister-paper (膏藥). —吸出す, to draw (out); suck up.
suiden (水田), *n.* a paddy-field.
suidō (水道), *n.* ❶ (水路) water-course. ❷ (海峽) a channel. ❸ (上水) waterworks; an aqueduct. —水道を引く, to have water-pipes laid; have water supplied from the waterworks. ¶ 對島水道, the Tsushima Channel. —水道部, the waterworks department. —水道工事, water-supply works. —水道栓, a hydrant. —水道(使用)料, water-rate.
suiei (水泳), *n.* swimming; natation. ¶ 水泳服, a swimming-dress. —水泳場, a swimming-place; a swimming-bath (屋內); a swimming-pool (池).
suifu (水夫), *n.* a sailor; a seaman; a mariner. —水夫となる, to go to sea; follow the sea. ¶ 水夫長, a boatswain. —水夫宿泊所, a sailors' home.
suifu (炊夫), *n.* a cook.
suifuku (推服する), *vt.* to respect; admire.
suifukube (吸瓢), *n.* a cupping-glass; a cup. —吸瓢をかける, to apply a cupping-glass; cup.
suigai (水害), *n.* damage by water [flood]. —水害を蒙る, to suffer damage by flood; suffer from flood. ¶ 水害地, a district damaged by flood; a flooded district.
suigan (醉眼), *n.* drunken eyes. —醉眼朦朧として, with heavy eyes; with dull drunken eyes.
suigara (吸殼), *n.* a cigar [cigarette]-end; fag-ends (卷煙草の); tobacco-ashes (煙管の).
suigen (水源), *n.* the source of water; a head-water; a well-head. ¶ 水源地, the gathering-ground; the catchment-area.
suigin (水銀), *n.* mercury; quick-silver. ¶ 水銀丸《軟膏》, blue pills《ointment》.
suigō (水鄉), *n.* a riverside [waterside] village.
suigyo (水魚の交をする), to be in close intimacy *with*; be great friends *with*; be hand and glove *with*.
suigyū (水牛), *n.* 【哺乳】 the Indian buffalo; the arna.
suihei (水兵), *n.* 【海】 a marine; a seaman; a blue-jacket. ¶ 一等水兵, a first-class marine; a seaman, 1st class; a seaman. —二等水兵, a second-class marine; a seaman, 2nd class; an ordinary seaman. —三等水兵, a seaman, 3rd class; an apprentice seaman. —水兵服, a seaman's uniform.
suihei (水平), *n.* the water-level. —水平の, level; horizontal. —水平にする, to level. —水平に線をひく, to draw a line horizontally. ¶ 水平動, (地震) horizontal motion. —水平面, 【數】 a horizontal plane. —水平線, the horizon; a horizontal line. —水平運動, (社會的) the *Suiheisha* movement; the movement for the abolition of the *eta* caste.
suihō (水泡), *n.* a foam; a bubble. —水泡に歸する, to come to naught; end in smoke [a fiasco; failure]. [bleb; a blister.]
suihō (水疱), *n.* 【醫】 a bulla; a
suii (推移), *n.* transition; change; movement (文藝の). —推移する, to change; undergo changes; pass away; elapse. —時勢の推移に伴うて, with the changes of the times.
suijaku (衰弱), *n.* weakness; enervation; exhaustion; 【醫】 asthenia. —衰弱する, to be weakened [wasted; debilitated]; be exhausted.
suiji (炊事), *n.* cooking; cookery. —炊事する, to cook. ¶ 炊事場, a kitchen; a cook-room; a cook-house (船の); a gallery (同上); a field-kitchen (野營の); a cook-camp (同上).
suijihō (水治法), *n.* 【醫】 hydrotherapy; water cure.
suijin (水神), *n.* the water-god; the god of water; the river-god.
suijin (粹人), *n.* a man about town [of the world].
suijō (水上), *n.* surface of the

water. ¶ 水上艦, a surface ship; surface craft. —水上警察署, a water-police office; harbour-police. —水上競技, aquatic sports. —水上運動會, an aquatic sports meeting.

suijōka (穗狀花), *n.* 【植】 a spica; a spike.

suijōki (水蒸氣), *n.* aqueous vapour.

suijun (水準), *n.* water-level. ¶ 水準器, a (water-)level. (水準器で測る, to level.) —水準線, a horizontal line.

suijun (垂準, 錘準), *n.* a plummet.

suika (水火), *n.* fire and water. —水火も啻ならぬ間柄である, to be on very bad terms with each other.

suika (西瓜), *n.* 【植】 the water-melon.

suika (垂下), *n.* flaccidity; drooping. —垂下する, to hang down; droop.

suika (誰何), *n.* challenge. —番兵の誰何, a sentry's challenge. —誰何する, to challenge.

suikan (水管), *n.* ❶ a water-pipe; a spout; a hose. ❷【動】 a siphon; a siphuncle.

suikan (吹管), *n.* a blowpipe. ¶ 吹管分析, 【化】 blowpipe analysis.

suikan (醉漢), *n.* a drunken fellow [man]; a drunkard; a sot.

suiki (水氣), *n.* ❶ (みづけ) moisture; damp; humidity. ❷ (水腫) dropsy. —足に水氣が來る, Dropsy comes on in the leg.

suikin (水禽), *n.* a water-fowl [-bird]; an aquatic bird. ¶ 水禽類, 【動】 Natatores; the swimmers.

suikō (推考), *n.* inference; deduction. —推考する, to infer; deduce.

suikō (推敲), *n.* polish; elaboration. —推敲する, to polish; refine; elaborate.

suikō (遂行), *n.* execution; prosecution; accomplishment. —遂行する, to execute; carry out; accomplish.

suikomi (吸込), *n.* ❶ inhalation (吸氣); draught; absorption (吸收). ❷ (放水の) drainage. —吸ひ込む, ① (氣體を) to inhale; breathe in; imbibe. ② (液體を) to suck in; imbibe; absorb. ③ (卷込む) to engulf; gulp; suck in.

Suikōsha (水交社), *n.* the Naval Club.

suikuchi (吸口), *n.* a mouthpiece.

suikyo (推擧), *n.* recommendation. —推擧する, to recommend. —推擧されて, upon recommendation.

suikyō (水鄉), *n.* =*suigō*.

suikyō (醉狂), *n.* ❶ (酒狂) frenzy of drunkenness; frenzy caused by drink. ❷ (ものずき) vagary; whim; freak. —醉狂な, eccentric; whimsical. —醉狂で, out of (mere) freak.

suikyū (推究する), *vt.* to infer; deduct.

suima (睡魔), *n.* ❶ the spirit of sleep; Morpheus. ❷ (睡) sleepiness; drowsiness. —睡魔に襲はる, to be overcome by drowsiness.

suimen (水面), *n.* surface of water; water-level. —水面に浮び出る, to come up to the surface of the water.

suimi (酸味), *n.* acid taste.

suimin (睡眠), *n.* sleep; slumber. —睡眠する, to sleep; slumber; rest. —睡眠不足で疲れる, to be fatigued through want of sleep; be worn out from insufficient sleep. ¶ 睡眠時間, hours of sleep.

suimitsutō (水蜜桃), *n.* a peach.

suimon (水門), *n.* Ⓢ 水閘, a sluice (-gate); a water [flood]-gate.

suimono (吸物), *n.* soup. ¶ 吸物椀, a soup-bowl.

suimyaku (水脈), *n.* ❶ (澪) a channel. ❷ (水筋) a vein of water; a (subterranean) channel of water.

suinan (水難), *n.* an accident by water; a casualty [disaster] at sea (海難). ¶ 水難救助, rescue at sea. —水難救濟所, a life-saving station. —帝國水難救濟會, the Imperial Life-boat Association.

suinō (水囊), *n.* ❶ a water-bag; a water-skin. ❷ =*mizukoshi*.

suirai (水雷), *n.* a torpedo. —水雷に觸れる, to strike a mine. ¶ 沈設水雷, a submarine mine. —觸發水雷, a contact-mine. —機械水雷, a mechanical mine. —水雷防禦網, a torpedo-net. —水雷母艦, a torpedo-boat depôt-ship; a torpedo-vessel. —水雷團, a torpedo-division; a torpedo-station. —水雷敷設艇, a mine-layer. —水雷發射管, a torpedo-tube. —水雷驅逐艦, a (torpedo-boat)destroyer. —水雷驅逐隊, a torpedo flotilla. —水雷艇, a torpedo-boat. (水雷艇隊, a torpedo-boat flotilla.)

suiren (水練), *n.* =*suiei* (水泳).

suiri (水利), *n.* ❶ (水の便利) (facilities of) water transportation. ❷ (水の利用) utilization of water; irrigation (灌漑). —水利を便にする, to facilitate the use of water. ¶ 水利權, water-privilege. —水利組合, a water-utilization association.

suiri (推理), *n.* reasoning; inference; ratiocination; 【論】 induction. —推理する, to reason (*on*; *about*; *of*); ratiocinate; infer. ¶ 推理力, rationality; reasoning power [faculty].

suirikigaku (水力學), *n.* hydro-dynamics.

suiro (水路), *n.* ❶ (水脈) a vein of water. ❷ (航路) a waterway; a water-route; a channel(-way); a passage. ¶ 水路部, the hydrographical department 〔英〕; a hydrographic office 〔米〕. —水路測量, hydrographical surveying.

suiron (推論), *n.* reasoning; ratiocination; deduction. —推論する, to reason; theorize; ratiocinate; deduct (*from*). ¶ 推論式, a syllogism.

suiryō (水量), *n.* the quantity [volume] of water. ¶ 水量計, a water-meter; a water-gauge.

suiryō (推量), *n.* ❶ (想像) guess; conjecture; presumption. ❷ (諒察) sympathy; compassion. —推量する, to guess; conjecture; presume; sympathize; feel *for*. ¶ あて推量, a random guess.

suiryoku (水力), *n.* water-power; hydraulic power. ¶ 水力電氣, hydroelectricity. —水力機械, hydraulic machinery.

suisai (水災), *n.* ❶ (水害) damage by water [flood]. ❷ (水患) calamity by water [flood].

suisaiga (水彩畫), *n.* a water-colour (painting); water-colours; an *aquarelle* 〔佛〕. ¶ 水彩畫家, a water-colourist; an aquarelliste.

suisan (水產 -物), *n.* aquatic [marine] products. ¶ 水產業, aquatic [marine] products industry. —水產講習所, a fisheries institute; a marine products school. —水產試驗所, a fisheries experimental station.

suisan (推參), *n.* ❶ (推しかけること) a call; a visit. ❷ (不禮) insolence; impudence; obtrusiveness. —推參する, to call *on*; pay a visit.

suisan (推算), *n.* ❶ calculation; prediction. ❷ (推考) inference; deduction.

suisanka (水酸化), *n.* 【化】 hydroxide. ¶ 水酸化物, a hydrate; a hydroxide.

suisatsu (推察), *n.* ❶ (想像) guess; conjecture; presumption. ❷ (諒察) sympathy; compassion. —推察する, to guess; conjecture; presume; sympathize; enter into another's feelings.

suisei (水星), *n.* Mercury.

suisei (水棲の), *a.* aquatic; marine. ¶ 水棲動物, an aquatic (animal).

suisei (水勢), *n.* the force of water (a current).

suisei (衰勢), *n.* declining tendency. —衰勢を挽回する, to recover from a declining tendency.

suisei (彗星), *n.* a comet.

suiseigan (水成岩), *n.* 【地質】 sedimentary [aqueous] rocks.

suisen (水仙), *n.* 【植】 the French daffodil; the daffodil (俗稱).

suisen (水線), *n.* the water-line.

suisen (垂線), *n.* a perpendicular.

suisen (推薦), *n.* recommendation. —推薦する, to recommend; nominate (指名). —會長の推薦に依り, on the recommendation of the president. ¶ 推薦狀, a letter of recommendation.

suisha (水車), *n.* a water-mill; a mill; an irrigation-wheel (灌水用の); a water-wheel (車輪). ¶ 水車場, a mill; a water-mill.

suishi (水死), *n.* drowning; death by drowning. —水死する, to be drowned; drown oneself (身投).

suishi (水師), *n.* the navy; the marine forces. ¶ 水師提督, the commander of naval forces; an admiral. ☞ *teitoku*.

suishi (出師), *n.* despatch of troops; an expedition (出征). ¶ 出師準備, mobilization.

suishi (錘子), *n.* a plumb-bob.

suishin (水深), *n.* the depth of water.

suishin (垂心), *n.* 【數】 an orthocentre.

suishin (推進), *n.* propulsion; push. —推進する, to propel; drive; push. ¶ 推進機, a propeller; an aeropropeller (飛行機の); a screw-propeller (汽船等の).

suishō (水晶), *n.* (rock-)crystal. ¶ 水晶體, 【解】 the (crystalline) lens.

suishō (推奬), *n.* recommendation. —推奬する, to recommend.

suishoku (翠色), *n.* green; verdure; viridity.

suishu (水腫), *n.* 【醫】 œdema; hydrops; dropsy.

suiso (水素), *n.* 【化】 hydrogen.

suisō (水草), *n.* ❶ (水と草) water and grass. ❷ a water-plant; an aquatic plant. —水草を逐うて移轉する, to wander about (after water and grass); lead a nomadic life.

suisō (水槽), *n.* a water-tank.

suisō (水葬), *n.* burying in water; burial at sea. —水葬にする, to bury in water [at sea].

suisō (吹奏), *n.* piping; blowing; blow. —吹奏する, to blow; pipe. ¶ 吹奏樂器, a wind-instrument. —吹奏者, a piper; a flutist; a player.

suisoku (垂足の), *a.* 【數】 pedal.

suisoku (推測), *n.* ❶ conjecture; presumption; inference. ❷ (推理) reasoning; ratiocination. —

推測する, ① to conjecture; presume; infer. ② to ratiocinate.

Suisu (瑞西), *n.* Switzerland. ¶ 瑞西人, a Swiss.

suitai (水體), *n.* a body of water.

suitai (衰頽), *n.* decay; decline; degeneration. —衰頽する, to decline; decay; degenerate.

suitai (推戴する), *vt.* to install; look up as the chief. —會長に推戴する, to install as president.

suitai (醉態), *n.* drunken state [condition].

suitchi (開閉器), *n.* 【電】switch.

suitei (水底), *n.* the bottom of the water. —水底に沈む, to sink [go] to the bottom of the water.

suitei (推定), *n.* presumption; conclusion; inference. —事實の推定, presumption of fact. —推定する, ① 【法】(看做すの對) to presume. ② to presume; conclude; infer.

suiten (水天), *n.* the sky and sea; the sky reflected in water.

suitetsu (水蛭), *n.* the leech (特に醫療用の); the blood-sucker.

suitō (水筒), *n.* a flask; a canteen (軍人用の).

suitō (水痘), *n.* varicella; chicken-pox.

suitō (水塔), *n.* a water-tower.

suitō (出納), *n.* receipts and disbursements. ¶ 出納係, a cashier; a treasurer. —出納官吏, an official in charge of accounts; an accounts official.

suitorigami (吸取紙), *n.* blotting-paper; a blotter.

suitoru (吸取る), *vt.* ❶ (吸收) to suck up (吸盡す); suck out (吸出す); absorb; soak in [up]; draw up. ❷ (絞取る) to suck; extort; squeeze. —吸取紙で吸ひ取る, to absorb with blotting-paper. —水氣を吸ひ取る, to extract the moisture.

suitsuku (吸附く), *vi.* to adhere to; stick fast to.

Suittsuru (瑞西), *n.* Switzerland.

suiun (水運), *n.* water-carriage; transportation by water.

suiun (衰運), *n.* declining fortune; decay. —衰運に向ふ, to begin to decline; tend towards decline. —衰運を挽回する, to recover from decline.

suiyaku (水藥), *n.* a liquid medicine; a medicinal draught [potion].

suiyōbi (水曜日), *n.* Wednesday.

suiyōeki (水様液), *n.* 【解】 aqueous humour.

suiyoku (水浴), *n.* a cold-water bath; (water-)bathing.

suiyū (睡遊), *n.* somnambulism; night [sleep]-walking.

suizen (垂涎), *n.* slobberiness; running saliva. —垂涎する, ① to slobber, slabber; drivel; water. ② (羨む) to gloat on [upon]; lust *for*; long *for*. —垂涎せしむ, to bring water into one's mouth; make one's mouth water.

suizoku (水族), *n.* aquatic animals. ¶ 水族館, an aquarium.

suji (筋, 系, 條), *n.* ❶ (線) a line. ❷ (筋) a sinew. ❸ (腱) a tendon. ❹ (纖維) a string. ❺ (條) a stripe; a streak. ❻ (皺) a wrinkle. ❼ (脈管) a vein. ❽ (家系) lineage. ❾ (條理) reason. ❿ (要點) the point. ⓫ (大要) the outline. ⓬ (仕組) a plot. ⓭ (方面) a quarter. —或筋への情報, a report received in certain quarters —條の立たぬ, absurd; incoherent (支離滅裂の). —筋を引く, ① (線を) to draw a line. ② (遺傳) to be hereditary; be inherited. —筋だけ知るために讀む, to read only for the plot.

sūji (數字), *n.* a figure (特にアラビア數字); a numeral. —數字で示す, [*vt.*] to figure. ¶ 數字値, digit value.

sujibaru (筋張る), *vi.* to become stringy. —筋張った手, a stringy [horny] hand.

sujichigai (筋違), *n.* ❶ (筋かひ) obliquity. ❷ (不條理) unreasonableness; absurdity. —筋違ひの, oblique; unreasonable; absurd.

sujigaki (筋書), *n.* ❶ (劇の) the plot [argument] of a play; a scenario (活動の) ❷ (目論見) a plot; a programme.

sujikai (筋違), *n.* obliquity. —筋かひに切る, to cut aslant.

sujiko (筋子), *n.* salmon-roe; spawn of salmon.

sūjiku (樞軸), *n.* ❶ (要部) the pivot; the centre; the heart. ❷ (羅盤の) a pivot; a centre-pin.

sujime (筋目), *n.* ❶ (條理) reason. ❷ (血統) lineage; a family line. ❸ (線) a line. —筋目の正しい家, a house of good lineage.

sujimichi (筋道), *n.* ❶ (條理) reason. ❷ (手續) procedure; channel. —筋道の立った, coherent; consistent; reasonable. —筋道を立てて言ふ, to speak methodically.

sujimukō (筋向), *n.* Ⓢ 筋向ひ. standing obliquely opposite *to*.

sujō (素性), *n.* ❶ (血統) a family line; lineage. ❷ (性質) character. ❸ (由緒) origin; antecedents. —素性卑しき《良き》, low 《high》 -born. —素性の知れぬ人間, a man of unknown antecedents. —素性をただす, to ascertain a man's character.

sūkai (數回), *n.* & *ad.* several times.

sukanpin (素寒貧), *n.* a penniless fellow (人); an empty purse [pocket]; impecuniosity.

sukareru (好かれる), *vi.* to be liked [loved]; be popular *with.*

sukaru (スカル), *n.* a scull.

sukashi (透し), *n.* ❶ (紙の) a watermark. ❷ (細工の) openwork. ❸ =*kūgeki* (空隙). —透し入の吸取紙, blotting paper with watermarks. —透しを入れる, to watermark.

sukashibori (透彫), *n.* an ornamental openwork; an openwork.

sukashiji (透字の), *a.* perforated. ¶透字小切手, a perforated cheque.

sukashiyaki (透燒陶器), *n.* (日本·支那の) grain-of-rice porcelain.

sukasu (透す), *vt.* ❶ (明ける) to leave an opening; thin out; 【印】space. ❷ (透見る) to look through; hold to the light; peep [peer] *into* (覗く). —間を透かして植ゑる, to plant trees sparsely [at intervals]. —暗い中を透かして見る, to peep into the darkness.

sukasu (賺す), *vt.* to cajole; coax. —賺して止めさす, to cajole a person out of doing. —機嫌を賺し直す, to coax a person into good temper.

sukāto (スカート), *n.* a skirt.

suke (助), *n.* ❶ (助力) help; aid; assistance. ❷ (すけて) an assistant. ❸ =*sasae* (支) の ❸. —助に行く, to go and help; go to the rescue.

sukedachi (助太刀をする), *v.* to assist in a fight; back [support] in a duel.

sukeru (助ける), *vt.* to help; assist; aid.

suketchi (スケッチ), *n.* a sketch. ¶スケッチブック, a sketch-book.

sukēto (スケート), *n.* ❶ (*a*) a skate; a pair of skates: (*b*) a roller-skate: (*c*) skating. ❷ (玩具) a scooter. —スケートする, to skate. ¶スケート(練習)場, a skating-rink.

suketōdara (介黨鱈), *n.* 【魚】 the pollack.

suki (好), *n.* pleasure; fancy; taste (嗜好); liking. —好きな樣にする, to have one's own way [will]; do as one pleases [likes]; suit oneself. —好きなやうにさせる, to leave it to a person's choice; indulge a person in his taste. —甘い物が好きである, to have a liking for sweet things; have a sweet tooth. ¶猫好き, a person fond of cats.

suki (隙), *n.* ❶ =*sukima* (隙間). ❷ (手すき) leisure; spare time. ❸ (機會) a chance; an opportunity. ❹ (不用意) an unguarded point (moment); a blind side. —隙漏る風, a draught. —隙漏る月の光, the moonlight breaking through the crevices. —隙がない, ① to have no time to spare. ② to be on the alert. —隙に乘ずる, to catch [take] a person napping. —隙を狙ふ, to watch for a chance.

suki (犂), *n.* a plough.

suki (鋤), *n.* a spade; a hoe.

suki (數寄), *n.* artistic taste; beauty. —數寄を凝らした, elaborate; refined; dainty.

suki (雪艇), *n.* a ski, skee; a pair of skis. —スキーで走る, to ski; run [slide] on skis. ¶スキー家, a ski-runner; a skier.

sūki (樞機), *n.* ❶ =*kururu* (樞). ❷ a secret. ❸ the helm of the state; the important affairs of state. —國務の樞機に參する, to take part in important state affairs; be at the helm of the state.

sūki (數奇), *n.* succession of misfortunes. —運命の數奇に弄ばれる, to be at odds with fate.

sukiabura (梳油), *n.* pomade; pomatum; hair-oil.

sukigaeshi (漉反し), *n.* remanufactured paper.

sukige (梳毛), *n.* the combings of the hair.

sukihara (空腹), *n.* an empty stomach.

sukikirai (好嫌), *n.* likes and dislikes.

sukima (隙間), *n.* a crack; a crevice; an opening; an interval (合間); leisure (手すき). ☞ *suki* (隙). —壁の隙間, chinks in the wall.

sukimi (剝身), *n.* a slice.

sukimi (隙見する), *vi.* to peep *into*; peep *through* [*at*]; pry *into.* —隙見する人, a peeper; a peeping Tom.

sukitōru (透通る), *vi.* to be transparent; be seen through.

sukiutsushi (透寫), *n.* tracing. —透寫しする, to trace.

sukiya (透綾), *n.* diaphanous silk.

sukiya (數寄屋), *n.* a dainty little house; a tea-cottage.

sukizuki (好好), *n.* taste; fancy.

sukkari (悉皆), *ad.* completely; entirely; wholly; quite; all.

sukku (すっくと), *ad.* straight; erect; upright.

sūkō (崇高な), *a.* =*shūkō*.

sūkō (數行), *n.* several lines (streaks). —數行の涙, streaks of tears. —數行の過雁, wild-geese flying in several lines.

sukoburu (頗る), *ad.* extremely; exceedingly; highly. —頗る上等の, remarkably good; of high quality.

sukoshi (少し), *n.* ❶ (量) a small quantity. ❷ (數) a small number. ❸ (度) a bit. ❹ (時) a moment; a little while. ❺ (距離) a short distance; a little way. ☞ *mosukoshi.* —少しづつ, by piecemeal; inch by inch; little by little. —少しでも, any; even a little. (少しでも深切氣があれば, if you have a spark of kindness in you.) —少しも屈せず, nothing daunted. —少しも劣らない, no way inferior. —少しも知らぬ, not to have the slightest knowledge *of*. —ブランデーを少し入れる, to infuse a dash of brandy. —今日は少しよい, I am a shade better to-day. —少しも常識がない, He has not an atom [a bit] of sense. —もう少しで殺される所だった, I was nearly [all but; almost] killed.

sukotchi (スコッチ), *n.* Scotch. ¶ スコッチ帽, a Scotch cap.

Sukottorando (蘇格蘭), *n.* Scotland. ¶ 蘇格蘭人, a Scot; a Scotchman, Scotsman; the Scotch (全體); a Sandy (綽名).

sukoyaka (健な), *a.* healthy; robust; hale. ☞ *sōken.*

suku (好く), *vt.* to like; be fond *of*; delight *in*; prefer (選り好む).

suku (犂く), *vt.* to break ground; plough, plow; furrow.

suku (結く), *v.* to net; make. —網をすく, to make a net.

suku (梳く), *vt.* to comb; card; dress. —髮を梳く, to comb the hair.

suku (透く), *vi.* ❶ =*sukitōru.* ❷ (疎になる) to become thin. ❸ (空いてる) to be empty. ❹ (手が) to be at leisure. —前の方は隙いてる, There is room in front.

suku (漉く), *vt.* to make.

suku (鋤く), *vt.* to hoe; spade; dig with a spade.

sukui (救), *n.* ❶ (救助) rescue; relief. ❷ (助力) help; assistance. ❸ (救世) salvation; redemption (贖罪). —聲を限りに救を求める, to cry for help at the top of one's voice.

sukuiami (掬網), *n.* a dip-net; a scoop-net.

sukuidasu (救出す), *vt.* to rescue *from* [*out of*]; disembarass; deliver. —子供を火焰の中から救ひ出す, to rescue a child from flames.

sukuinushi (救主), *n.* ❶ a rescuer. ❷ (救世主) the Saviour.

sukumo (泥炭), *n.* 【地質】 peat.

sukumo (稃皮), *n.* chaff; rice-hulls.

sukumu (竦窘む), *v.* ❶ (畏縮) to shrink; feel small. ❷ (蹲る) to crouch; cringe; cower. —足が竦む, to have cramp in one's legs. —恐がってすくむ, to crouch in fear.

sukūna (スクーナ), *n.* 【航】 a schooner.

sukunai (少い), *a.* ❶ (數) few; of small number. ❷ (量, 度) little; scanty; meagre. ❸ (稀有) rare; scarce. ❹ (不足) wanting; short of.

sukunakarazu (尠·鮮からず), not a little (few).

sukunakutomo (少くとも), *ad.* at least; at the (very) least; at (the) fewest.

sukurīn (映寫幕), *n.* a screen.

sukurappu (斷片, 切拔), *n.* a scrap. ☞ *kirinuki.*

sukuu (救ふ), *vt.* to save; help; rescue. —敵手より救ふ, to rescue a person from the enemy. —人の困難を救ふ, to help a person out of a difficulty.

sukuu (掬ふ), *vt.* to scoop (up); ladle (杓で). —杓子で掬ふ, to ladle with a dipper. —網で魚を掬ふ, to scoop [catch] a fish with a net.

sukuu (巣構ふ), *vi.* to (build a) nest.

sumai (住居), *n.* a house; a dwelling(-house); a residence. —都の住居, urban [city] life.

sumanai (濟まない), *a.* unpardonable; unjustifiable; regrettable. ☞ *sumu* (濟む). —濟まない事を仕出來かす, to commit an unpardonable mistake.

sumasu (澄ます), *v.* ❶ (氣取る) to keep one's countenance; look wise; look composed (平氣を裝ふ). ❷ (清める) to clear; clarify; purify. —すました顏で, with a demure face; demurely. —耳を澄して聞く, to listen with the closest attention [with both ears].

sumasu (濟ます), *vt.* ❶ (なし遂ぐ) to finish; conclude; close. ❷ (返濟) to pay; settle; clear off. —なしで濟ます, to do [manage] *without*; dispense *with*; spare. —朝飯を食はずに濟ます, to go without one's breakfast. —勘定を濟ます, to pay [settle] an account. —この儘には濟ませない, I cannot let the matter rest here.

sumau (住ふ), *vi.* to live *in*; dwell *in*; reside *in*. ☞ *sumu.*

sumen (素面), *n.* soberness; a sober face.

sumi (炭), *n.* charcoal. —炭をつぐ, to feed with [put .....on] charcoal. ¶ 炭火, charcoal fire. —炭俵, a charcoal sack.

sumi (隅), *n.* a corner; a nook; an angle (角). —隅から隅まで, in every nook and corner. —隅に置かれぬ, to be too acute to be left in the cold.

sumi (墨), *n.* Indian [Chinese] ink; an ink-stick; ink. —墨だらけの手, a hand smeared all over with ink. —墨を流したやうな空, a sky as black as ink; an inky-black sky. —墨を磨る, to rub an ink-stick. —墨をつける, to smear with ink (物に); dip in ink (筆に).

sumi (酸味), *n.* acidity; sourness. —酸味ある, sour; acid.

sumiishi (隅石), *n.* a corner-stone.

sumika (住家), *n.* ❶ a house; a dwelling(-house). ❷ a dwelling-place; a den (巣窟).

sumikomi (住込), *n.* living in (one's master's house). —住み込む, to enter service; be an inmate *of*; live in one's employer's house. ¶ 住込制度, living-in system.

suminareru (住慣れる), *vi.* to become accustomed to live *in*. —住慣れた故郷, one's old home where one had lived so long.

sumire (菫菜), *n.* 【植】 Viola Patrinii (學名); the violet (俗稱). —すみれ色の, violet. ¶ 三色菫, the pansy; the heart's ease.

sumitori (炭斗), *n.* a charcoal-scuttle; a coal-box (石炭箱); a scuttle (同上).

sumitsubo (墨斗), *n.* an ink-stand; an ink-bottle; an ink-pot (大工用の).

sūmitsuin (樞密院), *n.* the Privy Council. —樞密院の諮詢を經たる勅令, an order in council. ¶ 樞密顧問官, a Privy Councillor (P. C. と略す).

sumiya (炭屋), *n.* a charcoal-dealer.

sumiyaka (速に), *ad* ❶ (速度) fast; quickly; rapidly; speedily. ❷ (直に) at once; immediately; directly. —速な, speedy; quick; rapid; fast. —速なること風の如し, to be as fast as a wind.

sumiyaki (炭燒), *n.* charcoal-burning. a charcoal-burner (人).

sumizome (墨染の衣), *n.* a black robe.

sumizumi (隅隅), *n.* all the corners; every corner; every nook and corner.

sumō (相撲, 角力), *n.* wrestling; a wrestling-match. —角力の手, chips [throws] in wrestling. —相撲を一番取る, to try a fall; have a bout. ¶ 花相撲, an ordinary wrestling-match. —贔屓相撲, one's favourite wrestler. —相撲協會, the Wrestlers' Association. —相撲取, a wrestler.

sumomo (李), *n.* 【植】 Prunus communis (學名). ¶ 西洋李, the plum-tree.

sumu (住・棲む), *v.* to live *in*; dwell *in*; reside *in*. —只今どちらにお住みですか, Where do you live now?

sumu (澄む), *vi.* to become clear; settle (澱む); sleep (獨樂が). —澄んだ, clear; bright; lucid; limpid; serene.

sumu (濟む), *vi.* ❶ (終る) to end; come to an end; close; be over. ❷ (事ずみになる) to be settled (解決); be let off. —首尾よく《無事に》濟む, to go off very well 《without a hitch》. —氣がすむ, to feel at ease; be appeased. —仕事が濟んでから, after office-hours; after I have done my work. —濟まぬ事とは知り乍ら, knowing that it was inexcusable. —罰金で濟んだ, I was let off with a fine. —濟まない事をした, I am sorry for what I have done. —御面倒かけて濟みません, I am sorry to trouble you. —夜分遲く上って濟みません, Excuse me for coming so late at night. —濟みませんが戸を締めてくださいませんか, May I trouble you to shut the door? —それでは彼に濟まない, In that case I should not be able to excuse myself before him.

sun (寸), *n.* ❶ (單位) the Japanese inch (=1.193 inches). ❷ (寸法) length.

suna (砂, 沙), *n.* sand.

sunabokori (砂埃), *n.* a cloud of sand.

sunabukuro (砂嚢), *n.* ❶【動】 a gizzard. ❷ a sand-bag.

sunaburui (砂篩), *n.* a sand-sieve; a sand-sifter; a sand-screen.

sunachi (砂地), *n.* sands; sandy soil.

sunadokei (砂漏), *n.* a sand-glass; an hour-glass.

sunadoru (漁る), *v.* Ⓢ 漁りする. to fish; net.

sunahama (砂濱), *n.* sands; sandy coast.

sunagami (砂紙), *n.* sand-paper.

sunagawara (砂磧), *n.* sands.

sunago (砂子), *n.* sand; silver 《gold》 powder.

sunagoshi (砂漉), *n.* filtration through sand; a thing sand-filtered.

sunakemuri (砂烟), *n.* a cloud of sand; sand-cloud (沙漠の). —砂烟を起てる, to raise dust.

sunao (素直な), *a.* good (特に兒童の); meek; mild; gentle; tractable (御し易い); docile (同上). —素直に云ふことを聽く, to listen meekly to a person.

sunawachi (則, 卽, 乃), *conj.* ❶ 【則】 (ならば, すれば) when; if. ❷ 【卽】 (それが, それは) namely;

viz. (videlicet の略); that is (to say); or. ❷ 〔乃〕(そこで) and then. —失敗は卽ち破滅. Failure spells [means] ruin.

sunayama (砂山), *n.* a sand-hill; a dune (海岸の).

sundan (寸斷する), *vt.* to hackle; lacerate; cut ⟪tear⟫ in pieces; tear to shreds.

sune (脛, 臑), *n.* a shank; a shin (向脛); a leg (脚). —脛に傷持ちゃ笹原走る. "The thief is frightened even by a mouse." ¶ 脛嚙り, a sponge; a sponger; a hanger-on.

sunemono (拗者), *n.* a peevish [sulky; petulant] fellow; a malcontent; a cynic.

sūnen (數年), *n.* several [some] years; a number of years.

suneru (拗ねる), *vi.* to sulk; be peevish; be sulky; be in sulks.

sungō (寸毫も), *ad.* =*gō-mo.*

sunin (寸陰), *n.* a moment.

sunji (寸時), *n.* a moment; an instant. —寸時も早く, without a moment's delay.

sunka (寸暇), *n.* a moment's leisure; the least spare time. —一寸暇を惜んで讀書する, to read whenever he has time.

sunoko (簀子), *n.* a hurdle.

sunpō (寸法), *n.* measure; size; dimension(s). —寸法を取る, to measure a person; take (a person's) measure. ¶ 寸法書, measurements; specifications.

sunpun (寸分), *n.* the least; a bit. —寸分違はぬ, to be absolutely identical; not to differ in the least; be exactly the same *with*; be exactly alike.

suntetsu (寸鐵), *n.* ❶ an inch of steel. ❷ a weapon. —身に寸鐵を帶びず, to be unarmed; not to have a single weapon about one. —寸鐵人を殺す, to thrust home with incisive language.

suō (蘇方), *n.* 【植】 the bukkum-wood: sappan-wood (木材, 木).

supaiku (スパイク), *n.* ❶ spikes. ❷ (運動靴) spiked shoes.

supāku (火花), *n.* spark.

supana (雌捻子廻し), *n.* a spanner.

supasupa (すぱすぱ), *ad.* with a puff. —すぱすぱ吸ふ, to puff at one's pipe.

supekutoru (スペクトル), *n.* 【理】 spectrum.

Supēn (西班牙), *n.* Spain. ¶ 西班牙語, Spanish; the Spanish language. —西班牙人, a Spaniard.

supoito (スポイト), *n.* 〔蘭 spuit〕 a syringe; a spurt.

supōtsu (競技), *n.* sports. ☞ *kyōgi.*

suppadaka (素裸), *n.* stark-nakedness. —素裸になる, to become stark-naked; strip oneself completely. —素裸にする, to strip a person naked [to the skin].

suppai (すっぱい), *a.* =*sui.*

suppanuku (素破拔く), *vt.* to expose; disclose; lay bare. —秘密を素破拔く, to expose [reveal] a secret.

suppari (すっぱり), *ad.* ❶ cleanly. ❷ =*sukkari.*

suppon (すっぽん), *n.* 【爬蟲】 the snapping-turtle; the Japanese soft tortoise. —月とすっぽんほど違ふ, to be as different as chalk from cheese [light from darkness].

sūpu (スープ), *n.* Ⓢ ソップ. soup.

supurintā (スプリンター), *n.* a sprinter (短距離力走者).

sura (すら), *ad.* even; so much as. ☞ *sae, dani.* —挨拶すらせずに, without so much as saying good-bye.

surari (すらりと), *ad.* smoothly; easily (容易に); without trouble (滯なく). —背のすらりとした女, a slim [slender-figured] woman.

surasura (すらすら), *ad.* smoothly; swimmingly; without a hitch (滯なく); fluently (流暢に). —すらすらした文體, smooth style. —佛語をすらすら話す, to speak French fluently. —事がすらすらと運んだ. The matter went on swimmingly.

sureau (擦合ふ), *vi.* ❶ to rub [chafe] against each other. ❷ to be in discord; be at strife. —人と擦れ合ふ, to rub shoulders with another.

surechigau (擦違ふ), *v.* to pass by each other; cross each other; go past. —人とすれ違ふ, to cross a person.

surekkarashi (擦枯し), *n.* a forward person; a fast woman.

sureru (擦れる), *vi.* ❶ to be rubbed; be chafed; be worn (磨滅); rustle (葉·絹布など). ❷ (世になれて人惡くなる) to grow vicious [sophisticated].

surēto (スレート), *n.* slate.

suri (掏摸), *n.* a pickpocket; a cutpurse; a pickpurse. —紳士風の掏摸, a swell-mob; a swell-mobsman. —掏摸にすられる, to be robbed by a pickpocket.

sūri (數理), *n.* a mathematical principle.

suribachi (擂鉢), *n.* an earthenware mortar; a mortar.

suriban (擦半), *n.* rapid peals of the fire-bell.

surigarasu (擂硝子), *n.* frosted [ground] glass.

suriherasu (擦減らす), *vt.* to wear down [away]; rub off.

surikaeru (掏替へる), *vt.* to substitute; change secretly (密かに).

surikesu (擦消す), *vt.* to rub out; erase.

surikireru (擦切れる), *vi.* to be worn through [out]; become threadbare (著物など).

surikogi (擂木), *n.* a pestle.

surikomu (刷込む), *vt.* to enface.

surikomu (擦込む), *vt.* to rub in; stencil.

surimigaku (擦磨く), *vt.* to polish; rub; scour.

surimuke (擦剝傷), *n.* an excoriation; a graze; an abrasion.

surimuku (擦剝く), *vt.* to graze; rub, abrade.

surippa (スリッパ), *n.* a pair of slippers.

surisokonai (刷損ひ), *n.* misprint; spoilage. —刷り損ふ, to misprint.

suritsukeru (擦附ける), *vt.* to rub *against* [*on*]; nuzzle (鼻を).

suriyoru (擦寄る), *vi.* to sidle (up); snuggle; nestle close *to.*

suru (する), *v.* ❶ (行ふ) to do; act. ❷ (作る) to make; turn *into* (變成). ❸ (價する) to cost. ☞ *nasu* (爲す). —せずして, instead of. —…せざるを得ず, cannot but do; cannot help doing. —する事なす事旨くゆかぬ, Everything I do goes wrong.

suru (擦·摩·磨る), *vt.* ❶ to rub; chafe; file. (鑢で). ❷ 【磨】 to grind. ☞ *hiku* (挽く). ❸ (失ふ) to lose. ❹ (刷る) to print; put in print; print [strike] off. —色刷に刷る, to print in colours. —硝子を磨る, to frost glass. —マッチを擦る, to strike a match. —資本[?]を磨る, to lose one's capital. —身代をすってしまふ, to run through [squander away] one's fortune.

suru (掏る), *vt.* to pick (a pocket); rob (a person of his purse); steal.

surudoi (鋭い), *a.* ❶ (鋭利) sharp; keen; pointed. ❷ (味·臭の) stinging; poignant; pungent. ❸ (さとい) smart; sharp; shrewd. ❹ (きつい) acute; sharp; shrewd; piercing (眼光など).

surume (鯣), *n.* dried cuttle-fish.

sururi (するりと), *ad.* in a slippery manner. —するりと嵌まる《外れる》, to slip into 《out of》 a place. —するりと抜ける, to slip right through.

suruto (すると), *conj.* whereupon; when; and just then. ——, *ad.* then.

sūryō (數量), *n.* quantity; number.

susa (寸莎), *n.* straw [rags] used for compo [cob].

susamu (荒む), *vi.* to grow wild; increase in violence; decline (衰へ行く); be addicted [abandoned] *to* (耽る). —藝が荒む, His art deteriorates. —風が吹き荒ぶ, The wind blows violently [heavily].

susamajii (凄じい), *a.* terrible; fearful; dreadful. —凄じい勢で, with terrific energy [force].

sūsei (趨勢), *n.* trend; tendency; drift. —世界の趨勢を察する, to perceive the trend of the world.

sushi (鮨, 鮓), *n.* *sushi*; boiled rice flavoured with vinegar and mixed with other food.

sūshi (數詞), *n.* 【文】 the numeral.

suso (裾), *n.* ❶ the skirt; the train (引摺). ❷ (麓) the foot. ❸ (ズボンの) the bottom.

susomawashi (裾廻し), *n.* the lining of a skirt.

susomoyō (裾模樣), *n.* a skirt-pattern; a design on the skirt; a patterned skirt.

susono (裾野), *n.* the skirts of a mountain. —富士の裾野, the skirts of Mt. Fuji.

susu (煤), *n.* soot. —煤を拂ふ, to dust away.

susugu (濯·嗽·雪ぐ), *vt.* to wash (洗ふ); rinse (ゆすぐ): wipe out. —口を嗽ぐ, to rinse the mouth.

susuhaki (煤掃), *n.* Ⓢ 煤拂. house-cleaning. —煤掃をする, to set to house-cleaning.

susukeru (煤ける), *vi.* to become sooty; be smoked. —煤けた, smoky; dirty; sooty.

susuki (芒, 薄), *n.* 【植】 Miscanthus sinensis (學名).

susume (勸), *n.* advice (助言, 忠言); recommendation (勸告, 勸說); encouragement (奬勵).

susumeru (進める), *vt.* ❶ (進級) to promote; raise. ❷ (前進) to advance; put forward [on]; progress; push on. ❸ (進呈) to present; offer. ❹ (はかどらす) to expedite; speed up; hasten. —交渉を進める, to push the negotiations. —食慾を進める, to whet [sharpen; stimulate] one's appetite. —兵を敵地に進める, to march an army against the enemy.

susumeru (勸める), *vt.* ❶ (助言, 忠告) to advise; counsel; exhort. ❷ (奬勵) to encourage; get. ❸ (强勸) to urge; press; force. —善を勸める, to exhort a person to virtue. —何と勸めても聽かない, He is deaf to all advice.

susumeru (薦める), *vt.* to recommend (推薦); introduce (紹介); invite (勸誘).

susumu (進む), *vi.* ❶ (前進) to advance; march; go forward [ahead]. ❷ (進步) to progress; make progress. —眞直に二哩進む, to keep straight on for two miles. —末座より進み出る, to come forward from the last seat

—困難を排して進む, to make head against difficulties.

susurinaki (啜泣, 歔欷), *n.* sob; sobbing; whimper. —啜泣きする, to sob; whimper.

susuru (啜る), *vt.* to sip; sup. —粥を啜る, to sip rice-broth.

susunde (進んで), *ad.* of one's own accord [will]; voluntarily.

sutā (花形), *n.* a star.

sutairu (姿, 恰好), *n.* style.

sutajio (スタヂオ), *n.* a studio (美術家の仕事場).

sutajūmu (運動競技場), *n.* a stadium.

sutando (スタンド), *n.* a stand (観覧席又は賣品臺).

sutanpu (スタンプ), *n.* a stamp. —スタンプを押す, to stamp. ¶ 記念スタンプ, a commemoration stamp.

sutareru (廢れる), *vi.* ❶ (物が) to go out of use; fall into disuse; go [run] to waste. ❷ (流行が) to go out of fashion [vogue; favour; date]. —次第に廢れる, to pass into disuse.

sutāto (スタート), *n.* start. —スタートを切る, to start off.

sutebachi (捨鉢), *n.* despair; self-abandonment. —捨鉢な態度, a desperate attitude. —捨鉢になる, to yield to despair; be driven to despair.

sutego (棄兒), *n.* ❶ child desertion. ❷ an abandoned [a deserted] child; a foundling; a waif.

suteki (素敵な), *a.* fine; remarkable; capital. —素敵に, exceedingly; remarkably; wonderfully.

sutekki (洋杖), *n.* ❶ (杖) a stick; a walking-stick; a cane. ❷【印】a setting-stick; a composing-stick. —ステッキをつく, to walk with a cane. —ステッキを振り廻す, to flourish a walking-stick.

sutemi (捨身), *n.* ❶ risk of life; self-sacrifice. ❷ (柔道) a somersault trick. —捨身になる, to risk one's life.

sutene (捨値), *n.* a ridiculously low price. —捨値同様に, practically for an old song. —捨値で賣る, to sell for an old song.

suteoku (捨置く), *vt.* to leave untouched [as it is]; let alone. —なすがまゝに捨て置く, to leave a person to do as he pleases.

sutero-ban (ステロ版), *n.* stereotype; stereo.

suteru (捨·棄てる), *vt.* ❶ (投棄てる) to throw [fling; cast] away. ❷ (顧みぬ) to abandon; desert; discard; forsake; renounce; relinquish; cast away. —捨てて顧みぬ, to turn one's back *on*. —世に捨てられる, to be overlooked by society. —子を棄てる, to abandon a child. —名譽を捨てる, to give up honour [fame]. —戀人を捨てる, to discard [cast off; jilt] a lover.

sutēshon (停車場, 驛), *n.* a station.

sutētomento (陳述書), *n.* a statement.

suteuki (捨浮), *n.*【游泳】floating; a dead man's float.

suteuri (捨賣), *n.* selling at a loss [sacrifice]. —捨賣りにする, to sell at a sacrifice; sell for an old song; sell dog-cheap.

sutoppuwotchi (ストップウォッチ), *n.* a stop-watch.

sutoraiki (ストライキ), *n.* ❶ (同盟罷業) a strike. ❷【野球】a strike. —ストライキを起す, to go on strike; strike (work). ¶ ストライキ·ブレーカー (罷工破り), a strike-breaker.

sutorikinīne (斯篤里規尼涅), *n.*【化】strychnia, strychnine.

sutōvu (ストーヴ), *n.* a stove.

suu (吸ふ), *vt.* ❶ (呼吸) to breathe; inhale. ❷ (啜る) to sip; suck. ❸ (吸收) to absorb; imbibe. ❹ (吸引する) to draw; attract. —汁を吸ふ, to sip soup. —頬を吸ふ, to kiss another's cheeks. —不潔な空氣を吸ふ, to breathe foul [unwholesome] air.

suwa (すは), *int.* (警告の發聲) great Heavens!; good gracious! —すはといふ時には, in the moment of danger; in the hour of peril.

suwaru (坐·据る), *vi.* ❶ to sit; be seated; squat. ❷ =*zashō* (坐礁する). —坐り勝ちの人, a man of sedentary habits. —樂に坐る, to sit at one's ease. —目が据る, One's eyes set.

Suwēden (瑞典), *n.* Sweden. ¶ 瑞典語, Swedish. —瑞典人, a Swede.

suwitchi (開閉器), *n.*【電】switch. —スウィッチを捻る, to turn a switch.

suyaki (素燒), *n.* unglazed pottery. ¶ 素燒瓶, a porous pot.

suyasuya (すやすや), *ad.* quietly; calmly; soundly. —すやすや眠る, to sleep calmly.

sūyō (樞要な), *a.* important; weighty; momentous. —樞要の地位, an important post.

suzu (鈴), *n.* a bell; a tinkler (小鈴). —鈴の音, the tinkle of a bell. —鈴を振る, to swing a bell. —鈴をならす, to ring a bell; tinkle a bell.

suzu (錫), *n.* tin.

suzukakenoki (篠懸の木), *n.*【植】the Eastern [Oriental] plane-tree; the platan.

suzuki (鱸), *n.* 【魚】Lateolabrax japonicus (學名).
suzume (雀), *n.* 【鳥】the tree-sparrow; the sparrow (俗稱).
suzume (天蛾), *n.* 【蛾】the sphinx.
suzumi (納涼), *n.* cooling oneself; enjoying the evening breeze. ☞ *nōryō*. ¶ 納涼舟, a boat for enjoying the evening cool. — 納涼客, a cool-breeze hunter.
suzumu (涼む), *vi.* to cool oneself; enjoy the cool breeze. —木蔭で涼む, to cool oneself in the shade of a tree.
suzumushi (鈴蟲), *n.* 【昆】Homœogryllus japonicus (cricket の一種·學名).
suzuran (鈴蘭), *n.* 【植】❶ (君影草) the (common) lily of the valley; the conval [May] lily. ❷ (かきらん) Epipactis Thunbergii (helleborine の一種·學名).
suzuri (硯), *n.* an ink-slab; an ink-stone. ¶ 硯箱, an ink-case. —硯石, an ink-stone.
suzushii (涼しい), *a.* cool; refreshing. ——, *vi.* to be cool. 一目もとの涼しい, bright-eyed.

T

ta (田), *n.* a rice-field; a paddy-field. —田に水を引く, to irrigate a rice-field. (我が田に水を引く, to draw water to one's own mill; rake the fire under one's own pot.)
ta (他), *n.* other; another; the rest. ☞ *sonota*. —之を他に舍[措]き, setting this aside; putting this apart. —他は推して知るべし, The rest may be inferred. —他に餘罪ある見込みである, He is believed to have committed other offences.
taba (束), *n.* a bundle; a sheaf (藁の); a coil (一卷); a tuft (秣·草·羽等の). —繩一束, a coil of rope. —束にする, to tie up in a bundle; make into a bundle; make up (秣等を).
tabakaru (誑る), *vt.* to cheat; deceive; impose *on* [*upon*].
tabako (煙草), *n.* [葡 tabaco] ❶ 【植】the Virginian tobacco-plant. ❷ tobacco. —煙草に酔ふ, to smoke oneself sick. —煙草に火を附ける, to light a cigar; light up. —煙草の火を借りる, to light a pipe by another's fire. —煙草を呑む [吸ふ], to smoke (a pipe 《cigar; cigarette》). ¶ 煙草盆, a tobacco-tray. —煙草屋, a tobacconist.
tabaneru (束ねる), *vt.* to tie up in a bundle; make into a bundle. —髮を束ねる, to tie up the hair.
tabeakiru (食飽きる), *vi.* to be tired of eating; be surfeited *with*.
tabemono (食物), *n.* food; fare; diet. ☞ *kuimono*.
taben (多辯), *n.* talkativeness; verbosity; loquacity. ——**-na**, *a.* talkative; voluble; verbose; loquacious; garrulous. ¶ 多辯な人, a great talker; a chatterbox; a prattler; a man of many words.
tabenareru (食慣れる), *vi.* to get used to eating.
taberu (食べる), *vt.* to eat. ☞ *kuu* (食ふ). —食べたい程食べる, to eat to one's heart's content.
tabesasu (食べさす), *vt.* to support; feed. —家族を食べさせて行く, to support one's family.
tabezugirai (食べず嫌ひ), *n.* disliking without tasting.
tabi (度), *n.* ❶ (折, 時) time; occasion. ❷ (回數) time. —度に, 度毎に, every time; whenever; as often as.
tabi (旅), *n.* travel; a journey. ☞ *ryokō* (旅行). —歸らぬ旅, a journey to one's long home; a journey to the next world; one's last journey. —旅に出る, to go on a journey. —旅をする, to travel; make a journey. —旅は道連れ, "No road is long with good company."
tabi (足袋), *n.* Japanese socks. —足袋跣足で駆け出す, to run out in one's socks. ¶ 紺《白》足袋, deep blue《white》socks. —護謨底足袋, rubber-soled socks.
tabiakinai (旅商), *n.* peddling in the country.
tabiakindo (旅商人), *n.* a travelling merchant; a pedlar; a packman.
tabibito (旅人), *n.* a traveller; a wayfarer.
tabidachi (旅立), *n.* departure; setting out on a journey. —旅立する, to set out [start] on a journey; depart; set forward.
tabiji (旅路), *n.* ❶ (旅行の道途) a journey. ❷ = *tabisaki* (旅先). —長の旅路を經て, after a long journey.
tabijitaku (旅仕度), *n.* preparations for a journey. —旅仕度をする, to prepare [equip] (oneself) for a journey.
tabikasanaru (度重なる), *vi.* to occur several times; be frequently repeated.
tabikasegi (旅稼), *n.* working away from home; working in other

parts; itinerancy.
tabikōgyō (旅興行), *n.* provincial [local] performances.
tābin (タービン), *n.* a turbine. ¶ 蒸氣《瓦斯》タービン, a steam 《gas》 turbine.
tabinareru (旅慣れる), *vi.* to get used to travelling.
tabisaki (旅先), *n.* ❶ (目的地) the destination. ❷ =*taizai* (滯在地). —旅先で死ぬ, to die on one's journey.
tabitabi (度度), *ad.* often; frequently; repeatedly. —度々の災難, frequent calamities. —度々の催促で, being repeatedly pressed.
tabiyakusha (旅役者), *n.* a strolling player; a stroller.
tabiyatsure (旅窶れの), *a.* Ⓢ 旅疲れの. travel-worn.
tabizure (旅連れ), *n.* a travelling companion; a fellow-traveller.
tabo (髱), *n.* the back-hair. ¶ 髱どめ, a hairpin for the back-hair.
tabō (多忙), *n.* press [pressure] of business. —多忙を極める, to be pressed [driven] by business; have one's hands full.
tabō (多望な), *a.* hopeful. —多望な前途, a bright future; a hopeful outlook.
tabun (他聞), *n.* reaching others' ears; publicity. —他聞を憚る, to be afraid of publicity.
tabun (多分), *n.* (澤山) a great deal. —, *ad.* ❶ (大抵) probably; in all likelihood [probability]; maybe; likely; most likely. ❷ (大部分) mostly; for the most part. ❸ (十中八九) ten to one; in nine cases out of ten. —多分…だらう, it is most likely that …; it is more than probable that …; the odds are that….
taburakasu (誑かす), *vt.* to cheat; defraud; deceive; seduce; impose *on*.
taburetto (タブレット), *n.* 【鐵道】 a tablet. ¶ タブレット式, the tablet system.
tabyō (多病の), *a.* sickly; infirm; of delicate health.
tachi (質), *n.* ❶ (品質) quality. ❷ (性質) nature; character; (natural) disposition; temperament. ❸ (體質) constitution. —質のよい, well-disposed; of good quality (品質). —質の惡い, ill-disposed; ill-natured; of coarse [inferior] quality (品質). —學問の質がよい, to have an aptitude for study.
tachi (太刀), *n.* a long sword.
tachiagaru (立上る), *vt.* ❶ (座を起つ) to stand [rise] up; rise [get] to one's feet. ❷ (格闘を始めんとして起立する) to stand up for fight. —後足で立上る, to stand up on its hind legs.
tachiai (立會), *n.* ❶ (臨席) presence; attendance. ❷ (取引市場) market. —警官立會の上で, in the presence of the police. —醫者の立會で手術する, to operate in the presence of doctors. ¶ 立會官吏, an official in attendance. —立會人, a witness.
tachiaoi (蜀葵), *n.* 【植】 the hollyhock.
tachiau (立會ふ), *v.* ❶ to attend; be present *at*. ❷ to rise together.
tachiba (立場), *n.* a standpoint (立脚點); situation (境遇); ground (地步). —立場がない, not to have a leg to stand on. —立場を失ふ, to lose one's standpoint [ground]. —自己の立場を明かにする, to make clear one's standpoint.
tachiban (立番), *n.* a sentry; a sentinel; a picket. ☞ *mihari*. —立番する, to stand on guard (見張する); be on sentry (歩哨に立つ); be on point-duty (交通巡査の); picket (罷業の際の).
tachibana (橘), *n.* 【植】 Citrus nobilis (orange の一種·學名).
tachibanashi (立話する), *vi.* to talk standing.
tachidokoro (立所に), *ad.* instantly; on the spot; outright; offhand (卽席に).
tachidomaru (立止る), *vi.* to stop (short); stand (still); pause; come to a halt. —立止ってはいかん, Move on (巡査の命令).
tachifusagaru (立塞がる), *vi.* to stand in another's way; bar the way.
tachigie (立消えになる), ❶ (火が) to go out half-burnt. ❷ to be dropped; end in smoke.
tachigiki (立聞する), *v.* to eavesdrop; listen secretly.
tachigui (立食), *n.* a stand-up meal; eating while on one's legs. —立食ひする, to eat standing.
tachigurami (立眩), *n.* dizziness; vertigo. —立眩みがする, to feel dizzy.
tachiha (立端), *n.* an opportunity of quitting 《standing》.
tachii (起居), *n.* movement. ¶ 起居振舞, behaviour; deportment.
tachiiru (立入る), *vt.* ❶ (入る) to enter (*into*); go *into*. ❷ (たづさはる) to meddle *with*; interfere *in*; thrust one's nose *into*. —人の内事に立入る, to thrust one's nose into another's private affairs.
tachiita (裁板), *n.* a tailor's board.
tachikata (裁方), *n.* cut. —衣服の裁方を敎へる, to teach how to cut out cloth.
tachikawaru (立代る), *v.* to take another's place; change

places with another. 一立代り入代り, one after another; in rapid succession. 一本人に立代ッて謝罪する, to apologize in his place.

tachiki (立木), *n.* a standing [growing] tree.

tachikuzu (裁屑), *n.* scraps; shreds; cuttings (切地などの).

tachimachi (忽ち), *ad.* ❶ (卽座に) at once; immediately; instantly; in a moment; in a twinkling. ❷ (突然) suddenly; all of a sudden.

tachimawari (立廻り), *n.* ❶ 【劇】 a fighting scene. ❷ (摑合) a scuffle; fighting; scrimmage. ❸ (行動) action; motion. 一大立廻りを始める, to make a scene; have a rough-and-tumble.

tachimawaru (立廻る), *vi.* to move about; act. 一如才なく立廻る, to act with great tact.

tachimi (立見), *n.* ❶ seeing at the gallery. ❷ =立見場. ¶ 立見場, 【劇】 the gallery.

tachimodoru (立戻る), *vi.* to come back; return *to*.

tachimono (裁物), *n.* cutting out cloth. ¶ 裁物庖丁, a tailor's knife.

tachimono (斷物), *n.* food abstained from; a forbidden food. 一斷物をする, to abstain from certain food.

tachimukau (立向ふ), *vi.* to stand *against*; stand up to fight *against*; confront; face.

tachinarabu (立竝ぶ), *vi.* to stand in a row.

tachinbō (立坊), *n.* a street tout.

tachinoboru (立昇る), *vi.* to rise; ascend.

tachinoki (立退), *n.* removal; vacation (明渡). 一立退を命ずる, to order to remove; give notice to quit. ¶ 立退料, compensation for removal. 一立退先, one's refuge [shelter].

tachinoku (立退く), *v.* to quit; leave; remove (移轉); vacate.

tachinouo (太刀魚), *n.* 【魚】 the hair-tail; the ribbon-fish.

tachiōjō (立往生する), ❶ to die in a standing posture. ❷ (立ッたまゝ) to be kept standing; remain [stay] on one's feet. ❸ (當惑する) to be embarrassed [nonplussed]; be in a fix.

tachiokureru (立後れる), *vi.* ❶ (後れて立つ) to be delayed in standing. ❷ (爲すべき時機を失す) to lose the chance at the outset; be left behind at the start. 一立後れを取る, to be forestalled.

tachioyogi (立泳), *n.* treading water.

tachisaru (立去る), *v.* to quit; leave; depart *from*; go away.

tachisukumi (立竦), *n.* standstill; dead-lock. 一立竦む, to stand and shudder; be petrified with fear; cower.

tachiuchi (太刀打する), *vi.* to cross [measure] swords *with*; compete [vie] *with* (競爭する). 一太刀打ちは出來ぬ, to be no match *for*.

tachiwakare (立別), *n.* =**mo-nowakare.**

tachiwaru (斷割る), *vt.* to cut straight; cut open; cleave.

tachiyaku (立役), *n.* 【劇】 a male character (役); an actor who takes male parts (人).

tachiyoru (立寄る), *v.* to call *on* (a person); call *at* (a house); look in; look up; stop *at*.

tachiyuku (立行く), *vi.* to get along. 一かう不景氣では立ち行かぬ, We cannot make both ends meet in this time of depression. 一あの銀行はもう立ち行かない, That bank cannot hold out any longer.

tachizukumeru (立ちづくめる), *v.* to keep [remain] standing; keep on one's legs.

tada (只), *ad.* ❶ 〔唯〕 (單に) merely; simply; only. ❷ 〔但〕 (外のものをのけて) solely; exclusively. ❸ 〔徒〕 (無駄に) in vain. ❹ (無代) gratis; gratuitously; for nothing; free (of charge). 一只同樣で買ふ《賣る》, to buy 《sell》 for a song [an old song]. 一只一つの, sole; only; single. 一只の人, an ordinary man; a common man. 一只の一度も…しない, never once. 一只さへ寒いのに, when it is cold enough as it is.

tadachini (直に), *ad.* ❶ (直接に) directly; direct. ❷ (すぐに) immediately; at once; instantly; directly.

tadagoto (唯事, 徒事), *n.* a trivial matter; a commonplace.

tadai (多大の), *a.* great; serious; heavy. 一多大の損害, a heavy loss; a great deal of damage. 一多大の人命を犧牲にして, at a great sacrifice of life.

tadaima (唯今), *ad.* ❶ (目下) now; at present; just now (たった今). ❷ (直ぐに) soon; presently; in a minute. 一只今の所, at present; for the present. 一只今お話申上げた通り, as I have just told you. 一只今參ります, I am coming, sir.

tadanaka (直中, 只中), *n.* the centre; the middle. 一的の(眞)只中を射貫く, to hit the very centre of a target.

tadanaranu (只ならぬ), *a.* unusual; uncommon; extraordinary.

tadani (啻に), *ad.* only; merely.

tadanori (只乗する), *v.* to steal a passage 《ride》; bilk.

tadare (糜爛), *n.* a sore; an inflammation.

tadareru (爛れる), *vi.* to fester; be sore; be inflamed.

tadashi (但), *conj.* provided that; however; but. ¶ 但書, a proviso; a provisory clause. (但書附の, conditional.)

tada-shii (正しい), *a.* ❶ (心の) righteous; just; honest (正直). ❷ (行爲の) right; just; proper (當を得た); correct. ❸ (正確の) correct; proper (適當). —正しい人, a just [an honest; righteous] man. —正しい道を履む, to take [tread] the right path. **—— - shiku,** *ad.* right, rightly; correctly; properly; exactly. —正しく發音する, to pronounce correctly. —ペンを正しく持つ, to hold one's pen right.

tadasu (正す), *vt.* ❶ (訂正) to correct; rectify. ❷ (矯正) to correct; amend; reform. ❸ (調整) to adjust. —誤を正す, to correct an error. —時間を正す, to set a clock 《watch》.

tadasu (董す), *vt.* to superintend. ☞ *kantoku* (監督する).

tadasu (質·糺す), *vt.* ❶ (質問) to question; inquire; ask. ❷ (糺明) to examine; inquire. ❸ (確める) to ascertain. —罪を糺す, to inquire into a person's offence. —實否を糺す, to ascertain the truth; inquire into the truth of an affair.

tadayou (漂ふ), *vi.* ❶ (漂流) to drift; be adrift; float. ❷ (流浪) to wander about.

tade (蓼), *n.* 【植】the knotweed.

taderu (たでる), *vt.* to foment.

tadō (他動的), *a.* 【文】transitive. ¶ 他動詞, the transitive verb.

tadon (炭團), *n.* a charcoal ball. ¶ 炭團屋, a charcoal-ball maker 《dealer》.

tadoru (辿る), *vt.* to go along; plod along; grope one's way (搜り進む). —山道を辿る, to grope one's way through [plod along] a mountain-path.

taedae (絶絶), *ad.* gaspingly (息など); almost exhausted; faintly. —絶え絶えに流れる, to flow at intervals. —息も絶え絶えになる, His breathing becomes laboured.

taegatai (堪難い), *a.* intolerable; unbearable; insufferable. —堪へ難い侮辱, an intolerable affront.

taehateru (絶果てる), *vi.* to become extinct.

taema (絶間), *n.* intermission; an interval. —絶え間なき, endless; ceaseless; incessant. —絶え間なく降り頻る雨, the rain falling without intermission.

taeru (堪·耐へる), *vt.* ❶ (忍ぶ) to bear; endure; put up with. ❷ (さゝへる) to support; bear; stand. ❸ (使用に) to be fit *for*; be good *for*. —堪へ得る限り, as long as one can endure. —熱に堪へる, to stand heat. —試練に堪へる, to bear test; stand a trial [severe proof]. —汗顏に堪へず, to feel greatly ashamed.

taeru (絶える), *vi.* ❶ (絕滅) to become extinct; die out; die. ❷ (終止) to (come to an) end; cease. —息が絶える, to breathe one's last; expire. —人跡が絶える, to be untrodden by men.

taeshinobu (堪忍ぶ), *vt.* to endure; bear patiently. ☞ *shinbō* (辛抱する).

taete (絕えて), *ad.* quite; entirely. —絶えて久しく, for a long time. —絶えて…せず, [*ad.*] never.

taezu (絶えず), *ad.* continually; incessantly; constantly (恆に); uninterruptedly (途絶えずに).

taga (箍), *n.* a hoop. —箍がゆるむ, ① The hoop becomes loose. ② (精力を失ふ) to lose one's energy [spirit]. —箍をかける, to hoop; bind with hoops. —箍を外す, to unhoop (a barrel); take off hoops.

tagaeru (違へる) *vt.* to break; violate; infringe.

tagai (互の), *a.* mutual; reciprocal; each other's; one another's. **—— - ni,** *ad.* each other; with each other; with one another (三人); mutually; reciprocally. —互に證書を取交はす, to exchange bonds with each other. —互に心を打明かす, to unbosom each other's mind.

tagaichigai (互違に), *ad.* alternately. —互違にする, to alternate.

tagaku (多額), *n.* =*takaku*.

tagane (鏨刀), *n.* a graver; a burin; a cold chisel.

-tagaru (たがる), *vi.* to want *to*; wish *to*. —見たがる, to be curious [eager] to see. —爲したがる, to want to do.

tagau (違ふ), *v.* ❶ (異る) to differ *from*. ❷ (違反) to break; infringe; violate. ❸ (道に外れる) to deviate *from*; depart *from*. —約束に違ふ, to break a promise; go back on one's word.

tagayasan (鐵刀木), *n.* 【植】the East Indian ironwood; the Chinese fan-palm.

tagayasu (耕す), *vt.* to cultivate;

till; plough.

tagei (多藝の), *a.* versatile; highly accomplished; many-sided; all-round. —多藝は無藝, "Jack of all trades and master of none."

tagen, tagon, (他言), *n.* divulgation. —他言する, to tell (others); let out (a secret); divulge.

tageri (田鳧), *n.* 【鳥】the lapwing.

tagi (多義), *n.* ambiguity.

tagiru (滾る), *vi.* to boil. —湯が滾ってゐる, The (hot) water is seething.

tagui (類, 比), *n.* ❶ (同等なるもの) a match; an equal. ❷ (種類) kind; sort. ☞ *rui* (類). —類稀なる, of a rare kind. —外に類のない品, a unique article.

taguru (手繰る), *vt.* to haul in (a rope) hand over hand. —手許へ手繰り込む, to haul into one's hands.

tahenkei (多邊形), *n.* 【數】a [polygon.]

tahibari (田鷚), *n.* 【鳥】the Japanese alpine pipit.

tahō (他方), *n.* ❶ another side; another quarter; a different direction. ❷ the other; the other side; the other party. ☞ *ippō.*

tahōmen (多方面), *n.* versatility; many-sidedness (趣味ある); variety; many directions (方面). —多方面な, many-sided; versatile. (趣味の多方面な人, a man of versatile tastes.)

tai (鯛), *n.* 【魚】the sea-bream. ¶ 黑鯛, the gilthead.

tai (帶), *n.* 【地】a zone; a region; a belt; 【解】a girdle.

tai (隊), *n.* a company (of soldiers); a body (of troops); a band; a party (一行). —隊を組む, to form a company.

tai (對), *prep.* against; toward; between; versus (v. と略す); *vis-à-vis.* ——, *n.* ❶ the opposite. ❷ (五分五分) a tie (同點); a draw (無勝負); a drawn game (同上). —國家主義對社會主義, nationalism versus socialism. —三對零の勝, winning by three goals to nil (蹴球); winning by the score of three to nought (野球). ¶ 對支關係, Chinese relations; relations with China.

tai (體), *n.* ❶ (身體) a body. ❷ (樣式, 形式) style; form. ❸ (姿勢) posture. —體を退(ひ)く, to draw back (one's body).

tai (他意), *n.* another intention; another purpose; ill-will. —他意なく, friendlily; with singleness of purpose; single-mindedly.

-tai (度い), (希望の意) to wish *to*; want *to*; be anxious *to*.

taian (對案), *n.* a counter-proposal (-draft).

taiban (胎盤), *n.* 【解】the pla-[centa.]

taibatsu (體罰), *n.* corporal punishment.

taibetsu (大別する), *vt.* to make a general classification; classify roughly.

taibi (大尾), *n.* the end; finis【羅】.

taibu (大部の), *a.* voluminous; large. ¶ 大部の書, a voluminous work.

taibutsu (對物的), *a.* real. ¶ 對物信用, real credit. —對物擔保, security against a thing.

taibyō (大病), *n.* a serious [dangerous] illness. ¶ 大病人, a patient in a serious condition.

taibyō (大廟), *n.* a great shrine; the Imperial mausoleum.

taichō (退潮), *n.* reflux; ebb-tide.

taichō (退廳する), *vi.* to leave one's office. —退廳の時間は四時, The Office closes at 4.

taichō (隊長), *n.* a commanding officer; a commander; a captain; a chief; a leader.

taida (怠惰), *n.* indolence; idleness; laziness. —怠惰な, idle; indolent; lazy.

taidan (對談), *n.* conversation; talk; an interview; *tête-à-tête* 【佛.=head to head】. —對談する, to converse [talk] *with.*

taiden (帶電), *n.* electrification.

taido (大度), *n.* generosity; magnanimity; high-mindedness. —大度な, magnanimous; high-minded; generous.

taido (態度), *n.* attitude; posture; position. —態度を明かにする, to make clear one's position. —態度を一變する, to change one's tune [tone].

taidoku (胎毒), *n.* hereditary [[congenital] syphilis.]

taiei (退嬰), *n.* retrogression. —退嬰的, passive (受動的); conservative (保守的). —退嬰する, to retrogress; shrink.

taieki (退役), *n.* retirement. —退役する, 【陸】to retire (from the army). ¶ 退役士官, a retired officer.

taifū (大風), *n.* a hurricane; a gale.

taifū (颱風), *n.* a typhoon.

taigai (大概), *ad.* ❶ (大抵) generally; in general; for the most part. ❷ (多分) probably; in all probability.

taigai (對外の), *a.* foreign; external. ¶ 對外關係, foreign relations. —對外硬派, a vigorous foreign policy party.

taigaku (退學する), *vi.* to leave a school. —退學を命ぜらる, to be expelled [dismissed] from a school; be sacked 【俗】. ¶ 事故

《論旨》退學, leaving a school for private reasons (by the advice of the principal).

taigan (對岸), *n.* the opposite bank [shore]. —對岸の火災視する, to look on unconcerned.

taigen (大言), *n.* tall [big] talk; boast; magniloquence. —大言する, to talk big; boast; draw the long bow. ¶ 大言家, a braggart; a boaster.

taigen (體現), *n.* personification; embodiment; realization. —體現する, to embody; personify; realize.

taigi (大義), *n.* great moral obligation; loyalty and patriotism; righteousness. —大義名分を明かにする, to make clear the relations of lord and retainer.

taigi (大儀), *n.* (疲勞) fatigue; weariness; languidness (無氣力). —大儀ながら, though I am sorry to trouble you. —大儀さうに歩む, to toil on; walk with heavy steps.

taigo (大悟), *n.* =*daigo.*

taigo (隊伍), *n.* the ranks. —隊伍を亂し《整へ》て, in confused (regular) ranks; in disorder (order).

taigū (待遇), *n.* treatment; usage; reception. —前官の待遇, the treatment due to one's late office. —待遇する, to treat; usage; serve; receive. —奏任待遇を受ける, to be treated as a *sonin* official; be accorded treatment as a *sonin*-official. —好い《惡い》待遇を受ける, to receive good (ill) treatment.

taigun (大軍), *n.* a large force; a great [strong] army.

taigyō (大業), *n.* a great enterprise; a great work.

taigyō (怠業), *n.* go slow; ca' canny.

taiha (大破), *n.* serious injury; great damage; great dilapidation; ruin. —大破する, to be seriously injured [damaged]; be greatly dilapidated.

taihai (大敗), *n.* a heavy [signal; great; crushing] defeat. —大敗する, to be heavily defeated; suffer a serious defeat.

taihai (頽廢), *n.* deterioration; corruption; decay. —頽廢せる, deteriorated; corrupted; decayed. (頽廢せる風儀, corrupt morals.) -頽廢する, to be deteriorated; be corrupted; decay.

taihan (大半), *n.* the majority; the most (part); a greater part. ☞ *taigai.* —大半は, mostly; for the most part.

taihei (太平 泰平), *n.* peace; tranquillity; profound peace. —泰平の世, the piping time [times] of peace; peaceful times.

taiheiraku (太平樂), *n.* the time of Blessed Peace (曲名); the fool's paradise. —太平樂をならべる, to say whatever one pleases.

taiheiyō (太平洋), *n.* the Pacific (Ocean). —太平洋橫斷の, trans-Pacific. ¶太平洋沿岸, the Pacific coast.

taihen (大變), *n.* a serious affair. —大變な, serious; terrible; dreadful. —大變に, seriously (重大); very (非常); exceedingly; remarkably. —さあ大變だ, Good Heavens!

taihi (貸費), *n.* loaned expenses. —貸費する, to loan expenses; advance expenses. ¶ 貸費生, a student whose expenses are advanced; a loan student

taiho (退步), *n.* retrogradation; retrogression. —退步する, ① [*vi.*] to retrograde; fall backward. ② [*a.*] retrograde; retrogressive.

taiho (逮捕), *n.* arrest; apprehension. —逮捕する, to arrest; apprehend. ¶ 逮捕狀, a warrant (of arrest).

taihō (大砲), *n.* a gun; a cannon [*pl.* cannon]; artillery; ordnance. —大砲を放つ, to fire a gun. ¶ 三十三珊大砲, a 33-centimetre gun.

taihō (對方), *n.* 【簿記】 contra. —對方で, per contra.

taihon (大本), *n.* the great foundation [basis].

taii (大尉), *n.* 【陸】 a captain; 【海】 a lieutenant.

taii (大意), *n.* the purport; the substance; the outline. —演說の大意を筆記する, to note down the substance of a speech. ¶ 物理學大意, the outline of physics.

taiiku (體育), *n.* physical education [training; culture]. ¶ 日本體育協會, the Japan Physical Education Society. —體育家, a physical educator.

taiin (太陰), *n.* the moon. ¶ 太陰曆, the lunar calendar.

taiin (退院する), *vi.* to leave hospital.

taiin (退隱), *n.* retreat; retirement; seclusion. —退隱する, to retire; seclude [sequester] oneself. ¶ 退隱料, a retiring allowance. —退隱生活, a retired [sequestered] life.

taiji (大事), *n.* a serious affair (大事件); a great work (大事業). —大事を託する, to entrust a serious affair.

taiji (胎兒), *n.* a child in the womb; a fœtus; an embryo.

taiji (退治), *n.* subjugation; subdual; suppression. —退治する, to subjugate; subdue; suppress.

taiji (對峙), *n.* standing face to face; confrontation. —對峙する, to stand face to face; confront each other.

taijin (大人), *n.* ❶ (成人) an adult; a man; a grown-up man. ❷ (大人物) a great man; a superior man.

taijin (退陣), *n.* decampment; retreat.

taijin (對人的), *a.* 【法】personal. ¶ 對人擔保《信用》, personal security 《credit》.

taijin (對陣), *n.* confrontation. —對陣する, to confront [face] each other.

taijō (退場), *n.* exit; leaving; going away. —退場さす, to expel (a person from); send a person out of a room. —退場を命ずる, to order (a person) to leave a hall.

taijō (退讓), *n.* deference; diffidence. ☞ *kenson* (謙遜). —退讓する, to defer; show diffidence.

taijū (體重), *n.* =*tairyō* (體量).

taika (大火), *n.* a conflagration; a great [big] fire.

taika (大家), *n.* ❶ (學術·技藝等の) a master; a distinguished scholar 《artist》; the great masters (繪畫·彫刻·音樂の); an authority. ❷ (大家屋) a great house [building]. —文章の大家, a master of style. —音樂の大家, a great musician.

taika (大過), *n.* a great error [mistake]; grave faults. —...と云ふも大過なからん, It would be no great error to say that....

taika (大廈), *n.* a large house; an edifice. ¶ 大廈高樓, a great edifice; large and imposing buildings.

taika (耐火の), *a.* fire-proof. ¶ 耐火煉瓦, a fire-brick. —耐火家屋《金庫》, a fire-proof building 《safe》.

taika (退化), *n.* 【生物】degeneration; devolution. —退化する, to degenerate.

taika (滯貨), *n.* congested freights. —滯貨を一掃する, to clear [sweep] the station of congested freights.

taikai (大海), *n.* the great sea; the ocean.

taikai (大塊), *n.* a hunk; a great lump 《mass; piece; block》.

taikai (大會), *n.* a great 《mass》 meeting. ¶ 春季大會, the great spring meeting.

taikai (退會), *n.* secession [withdrawal] from a party [society]. —退會する, to secede [resign] from a party [society]. ¶ 退會者, a seceder; a withdrawing [seceding] member. —退會屆, a notice of withdrawal.

taikaku (對角), *n.* 【數】opposite angle(s). ¶ 對角線, a diagonal.

taikaku (體格), *n.* physique; build; frame; constitution. —體格のよい, of fine physique; fine-built; stout-built; well-knit. —體格がよい, to have a good [fine] physique. ¶ 體格檢査, physical examination.

taikan (大旱), *n.* a severe [great] drought. —大旱の雲霓を望むが如し, It is like espying a rain-cloud during a great drought.

taikan (大患), *n.* ❶ (大なる憂) great troubles. ❷ (大病) a serious [dangerous] illness.

taikan (大觀), *n.* a bird's-eye view (概察, 鳥瞰圖); a grand view (壯觀); a comprehensive view (達觀). —大觀する, to have a general view; take in the whole situation.

taikan (退官), *n.* retirement from office; resignation. —退官する, to retire from office; resign. ¶ 退官賜金, a retiring allowance.

taikanshiki (戴冠式), *n.* coronation (ceremony).

taikatsu (大喝), *n.* ❶ thunderbolt. ❷ cry; shout. —大喝する, to shout; thunder.

taikasshoku (帶褐色の), *a.* brownish.

taikei (大計), *n.* a far-reaching policy. —國家百年の大計, a fundamental state policy.

taikei (隊形), *n.* 【軍】formation.

taikei (體刑), *n.* corporal punishment. —體刑に處する, to inflict corporal punishment.

taikei (體系), *n.* a system.

taiken (大權), *n.* ❶ (憲法上の大權) the Royal [Imperial] prerogatives. ❷ (統治權) supreme power.

taiken (帶劍), *n.* wearing a sword: a sword (by one's side).

taiken (體驗する), *vt.* to experience; pass through; undergo.

taiketsu (對決), *n.* confrontation. —對決さす, to confront (the accuser with the accused).

taiki (大氣), *n.* atmosphere; the air.

taiki (大器), *n.* ❶ (大なる器) a large vessel. ❷ (大器量, 大器量ある人) great talent. —大器晩成. Great talents mature late.

taikin (大金), *n.* a large sum (of money); a sight of money. —大金を投じて購ふ, to pay a large sum of money for it.

taiko (太古), *n.* remote ages [antiquity]; high antiquity. ¶ 太古の民, ancient peoples; people in ancient times.

taiko (太鼓), *n.* ❶ a tambour (特に低音の); a drum. ❷ (幇間) sycophancy; fawning: a toady; a led captain. —太鼓を敲く, ① to beat a drum; drum. ② (調子を合はす) to chime in *with*. ③ (おだてる) to instigate; incite. ¶ 團扇太鼓, a (fan-shaped) flat drum. —太鼓橋, a semicircular bridge. —太鼓桴(ぢ), drum-sticks. —太鼓敲き, ① a drummer. ② (ごますり) a flatterer; a toady; an instigator.

taikō (太公), *n.* an archduke (墺地利皇子の稱); a grand duke.

taikō (大功), *n.* great merit; eminent service; distinguished service.

taikō (大行), *n.* great actions [deeds]. —大行は細瑾を顧みず, In great undertakings slight faults are overlooked.

taikō (大綱), *n.* generality; fundamental principles; an outline.

taikō (太后), *n.* the Empress (Queen) Dowager.

taikō (退校), *n.* ❶ (學校の處分) dismissal from a school. ❷ (自分より) leaving a school; removal from a school. —退校する, to leave school; go away from school.

taikō (對抗), *n.* emulation; confrontation; opposition. —對抗する,【法】to set up *against*: confront; stand up *to*; counter; cope *with*. —獨逸の宣傳に對抗せんが爲め, to counter German propaganda. ¶ 對抗演習, manœuvres (between two sides). —對抗運動, a counter-movement.

taikō (對校の), *a.* inter-school; intercollegiate (專門學校程度以上の). ¶ 對校試合, an inter-school match; a school match.

taikomochi (幇間), *n.* a professional jester; a buffoon.

taikon (大婚), *n.* the Imperial wedding.

taikōshoku (褪紅色), *n.* deep orange.

taikōtaikō (太皇太后), *n.* the grand Empress Dowager.

taikouchi (紅娘華), *n.* 【蟲】the water-scorpion.

taiku (體軀), *n.* the body.

taikū (大空), *n.* the sky.

taikunsha (帶勳者), *n.* the holder of a decoration.

taikutsu (退屈), *n.* ennui; tedium; tediousness. —退屈な, weary; tedious; wearisome. —退屈する, to weary; feel ennuyé; be tired; be bored. —退屈を凌ぐ, to kill time; while away tedium; drive away ennui.

taikyaku (退却), *n.* retreat; retirement. —豫定の退却, pre-arranged retreat. —退却する, to retreat; retire; fall back.

taikyo (大擧), *n.* a great enterprise (大事業). —大擧して, in a body; in a large force.

taikyo (退去), *n.* leaving; withdrawal. —退去する, to depart; leave; withdraw.

taikyō (胎教), *n.* antenatal training; antenatal puericulture.

taikyō (滯京する), *v.* to remain [stay] in the capital. —滯京中に, during one's stay in the capital.

taikyoku (大局), *n.* the general situation; the issue. —大局を制する, to be predominant over the general situation. —大局を定める, to decide the issue *of*.

taikyū (耐久), *n.* durability. —耐久力ある, lasting; durable; persistent.

taima (大麻), *n.* 【植】hemp.

taimai (瑇瑁), *n.* 【動】the hawk's-bill turtle; the hawkbill; the caret.

taiman (怠慢), *n.* negligence; neglect; inadvertence. —怠慢な, negligent; neglectful; inadvertent; remiss.

taimatsu (松明, 炬火), *n.* a (pine-)torch; a link; a fire-brand; a flambeau. ¶ 松明行列, a torch-light procession.

taimei (大命), *n.* an Imperial command; an Imperial mandate.

taimei (待命), *n.* awaiting orders. —待命仰附けらる, to be ordered to await further orders. ¶ 待命公使館書記官, an unattached secretary of legation.

taimen (對面), *n.* interview; meeting. —對面する, to interview; meet.

taimen (體面), *n.* honour (名譽); dignity (威嚴); appearance (體裁); reputation (名聲). —體面に關はる, to affect one's reputation [honour]. —學生の體面を汚す, to impair the honour of students. —國家の體面を毀損する, to impair the national dignity. —身分相當の體面を保つ, to maintain an appearance appropriate to one's position.

taimō (大望), *n.* ambition; a great ambition [desire]; aspiration. —大望ある, ambitious.

tainai (胎內), *n.* the interior of the womb.

tainai (對內的), *a.* domestic; interior. ¶ 對內政策, domestic policy.

tainin (大任), *n.* a heavy task; an important charge [service];

an important position (重職). —大任を完うする, to perform the great task.

tainin (耐忍), *n.* endurance; forbearance. =***nintai***.

tainō (大腦), *n.* =***dainō***.

tainō (滯納), *n.* non-payment [arrearage] (of taxes); default; neglect to pay taxes. —滯納する, to fail to pay; default; neglect to pay. ¶ 滯納者, a defaulter; a delinquent taxpayer. —滯納處分, a disposition for the recovery of taxes in arrears.

tainō-kyōsō (戴嚢競爭), *n.* a bag-on-the-head race.

taiō (對歐), *a.* for [toward; against] Europe. ¶ 對歐政策, a European policy.

taiō (對應), *n.* correspondence; homology; symmetry (雙方の調和). —對應する, ① [*v.*] to answer; correspond; match. ② [*a.*] corresponding; coincident; symmetrical; homologous. ¶ 對應策, a plan to meet a case.

taion (體溫), *n.* the temperature (of the body); the bodily [animal; blood] heat. —體溫を計る, to take the temperature of the body. ¶ 體溫器, a clinical thermometer.

taipisuto (タイピスト), *n.* a typist.

taipu (タイプ), *n.* type (型, 型式; 活字).

taipuraitā (印字機), *n.* a typewriter.

taira (平), *n.* Ⓢ 平か. ❶ (平滑, 水平) plainness; evenness; flat; level. ❷ (靜平) calmness; composure (泰然). —平らな; 平かな, ① plain; even; flat; level. ② calm; tranquil; composed. —平らに, flatly; calmly; equably. (地面を平らにする, to level the ground. —どうぞ平らに, Please make yourself at home.)

tairageru (平げる), *vt.* ❶ (平定する) to subjugate; subdue; suppress; quell. ❷ (食盡す) to eat up; punish 【俗】.

tairagi (玉珧), *n.* 【貝】 the sea-wing.

tairan (台覽), *n.* inspection.

taireifuku (大禮服), *n.* court [full] dress; uniform. —大禮服を著用して, in full dress.

tairetsu (隊列), *n.* ranks; a line; formation.

tairiku (大陸), *n.* a continent; a mainland. ¶ 大陸橫斷鐵道, a transcontinental railway. —大陸的氣候, continental climate.

tairitsu (對立), *n.* ❶ opposition; confrontation. ❷ 【論】 coordination. —對立する, to oppose; confront; stand face to face; face.

tairo (退路), *n.* the retreat. —退路を斷つ, to cut off the retreat.

tairu (瓦), *n.* a tile.

tairyaku (大略), *n.* ❶ (槪略) outline; résumé; summary. ❷ (大なる才略) great ability. —, *ad.* ❶ (大凡) about; approximately; almost (殆ど). ❷ (一般に) in general; generally.

tairyō (大量), *n.* ❶ (數量の) a large quantity. ❷ (大度, 寛大) generosity; magnanimity; large-mindedness. —大量の人, a generous person; a large-minded man. ¶ 大量[數]觀察, quantitative observation. —大量生產, large-scale production.

tairyō (大獵, 大漁), *n.* a large catch; a large take.

tairyō (體量), *n.* the weight of a body. —體量が增す〘減る〙, to gain 〘lose〙 weight. —體量が十五貫ある, to weigh fifteen *kan*.

tairyoku (體力), *n.* physical strength; (bodily) strength. —體力を養ふ, to develop one's physical strength.

tairyū (滯留), *n.* =***taizai***.

taisa (大佐), *n.* 【陸】 a colonel; 【海】 a captain. ¶ 海軍大佐參謀, a flag-captain.

taisa (大差), *n.* a great [marked] difference. —殆ど大差なきに至る, to come up to nearly the same level.

taisai (大祭), *n.* a great fête; a great festival. ¶ 大祭日, a great national holiday.

taisaku (對策), *n.* a counter-plot [-measure].

taisan (退散), *n.* dispersion; flight (逃げる); rout (敗走). —退散する, ① to disperse; break up. ② to flee; run away; be routed.

taisanboku (たいさんぼく), *n.* 【植】 the large-flowered magnolia.

taisei (大成), *n.* a complete success; completion. —大成する, to complete successfully; be crowned with success; be successfully completed.

taisei (大勢), *n.* the general trend [tendency; current]. —大勢に順應する, to adapt oneself to (the tendency of) the times.

taisei (大聲), *n.* a loud voice; a stentorian voice. —大聲疾呼する, to harangue; shout.

taisei (胎生), *n.* 【生物】 viviparity ¶ 胎生動物, a viviparous animal.

taisei (泰西), *n.* the Occident; the Western countries; the West. ☞ *Ōshū* (歐洲). —泰西文物の輸入, the introduction of

Western civilization.
taisei (頽勢), *n.* declining [downward] tendency; decline.
taisei (對生の), *a.* 【植】opposite; symmetric; dichotomic. ¶ 對生葉, opposite leaves.
taisei (體制), *n.* organization; organism; system. —體制的, organic.
Taiseiyō (大西洋), *n.* the Atlantic (Ocean).
taiseki (退席する), *vi.* to leave one's seat.
taiseki (堆積), *n.* accumulation; pile; deposit. —堆積する, to pile; deposit; accumulate.
taiseki (對席), *n.* ❶ (相對する席) opposite seats. ❷ (向ひ合ふこと) sitting face to face (*with*); sitting opposite *to*.
taiseki (體積), *n.* 【數】solidity; volume; capacity.
taisen (苔蘚), *n.* =*sentai*.
taisetsu (大切な), *a.* important; valuable (貴重な); precious (同上). 一何よりも大切である, to be more important than anything else. **——-ni**, *ad.* carefully. —身體を大切にする, to take great care of oneself.
taisha (大赦), *n.* general pardon; amnesty. —大赦する, to amnesty. —大赦を行ふ, to grant amnesty.
taisha (代赭-色), *n.* red ochre
taisha (退社), *n.* retirement from [leaving] a company [society]. —退社の辭, a retiring address. —退社する, to retire from [leave] a company [society].
taishaku (貸借), *n.* a loan. —帳簿上の貸借勘定, book-account. ¶ 貸借對照表, a balance-sheet.
taishi (大志), *n.* great ambition; high aspiration. ☞ *taimō*.
taishi (大使), *n.* an ambassador; an envoy. ¶ 駐英大使, an ambassador to the Court of St. James's. —《特命》全權大使, an ambassador 《extraordinary and》 plenipotentiary. —大使夫人, an ambassadress. —大使館, an embassy. (在米日本大使館, the Japanese embassy at Washington. —大使館員, the embassy staff.)
taishi (太子), *n.* the Prince Imperial; the Crown Prince; the Prince Royal. —太子に立つ, to be proclaimed Crown Prince.
taishi (對支), for [towards; against] China. —米國の對支活動, American activities in China.
taishin (耐震の), *a.* earthquake-proof. ¶ 耐震家屋, an earthquake-proof building.
taishin (對審), *n.* 【法】confrontation.
taishita (大した), *a.* ❶ (非常な) very; extraordinary; extreme. ❷ (多くの) much; many; a lot *of*. ❸ (重大な) important; serious. ❹ (偉大な) great. 一大したことはない, There [It] is nothing serious.
taishite (大して), *ad.* so; (so) much; greatly; very.
tai-shite (對して), *prep.* for; by; to; toward; with; against. **——**, *ad.* in comparison *with* (と比較して); in [with] relation *to* (の關係で); in regard *to* (に關して); opposite (向って).
taishitsu (對質), *n.* confrontation.
taishitsu (體質), *n.* constitution.
taishō (大笑), *n.* loud laughter; a horse-laugh; a roar of laughter. —大笑する, to laugh loud; burst into [roar with] laughter.
taishō (大將), *n.* ❶【陸】a general; 【海】an admiral. ❷ (首領) a head; a chief; a master.
taishō (大捷), *n.* a great [signal] victory. —大捷を得る, to gain a great victory.
taishō (對消する), *vt.* 【數】to cancel.
taishō (對象), *n.* an object.
taishō (對照), *n.* contrast; comparison (比較); collation (引合はせ). **——-suru**, *vt.* to contrast; compare; collate. —原本と對照する, to compare [collate] with the original.
taishō (對稱), *n.* ❶ (釣合) symmetry; balance; counterpoise. ❷【文】(第二人稱) the second person. ❸【數】symmetry.
taishō (隊商), *n.* a caravan.
taishōgun (大將軍), *n.* a commander-in-chief; a generalissimo.
taishoku (大食), *n.* gluttony; gourmandise. —大食する, to eat much; gormandize; gorge. ¶ 大食家, a hard [great] eater; a glutton; a gormand(-izer).
taishoku (退職), *n.* retirement. —退職する, to retire from one's post [duties]. ¶ 退職年齢, disqualifying age. —退職手當, a retiring allowance.
taishoku (褪色), *n.* =*tonshoku*.
taishō-ryōhō (對症療法), *n.* 【醫】allopathy; symptomatic treatment.
taishu (大酒), *n.* heavy [hard] drinking; intemperance. ¶ 大酒家, a great [heavy; hard; deep] drinker; a toper.
taishu (太守), *n.* a governor; a governor-general; a viceroy; a sirdar 〔英印度〕.
taishu (退守), *n.* the defensive. —退守する, to keep on the defensive.
taishu (對手), *n.* an opponent; an adversary; a rival; a match.

taishū (大衆), *n.* a large crowd (群衆); the multitude (民衆).

taishukubo (大叔母), *n.* a great aunt.

taishukufu (大叔父), *n.* a great uncle.

taishutsu (退出), *n.* leaving; exit. —退出する, to leave; withdraw; retire. ¶ 退出時刻 the closing hour.

taishutsu (帶出する), *v.* to carry out. ¶ 圖書帶出許可證, a book-loan certificate.

taisō (大層), *ad.* very; much; greatly; highly; extremely.

taisō (體操), *n.* gymnastics. —體操をする, to exercise gymnastics. ¶ 體操器具, gymnastic appliances. —體操教師, a gymnastics teacher.

taisobo (大祖母), *n.* a great-grandmother.

taisofu (大祖父), *n.* a great-grandfather.

taisoku (大息), *n.* a sigh; a long breath. —大息する, to heave a (deep) sigh; draw a long breath.

taisū (對數), *n.* 【數】 a logarithm. ¶ 對數表, a table of logarithms.

taisui (大醉), *n.* intoxication. —大醉する, to get dead drunk; get quite intoxicated; fuddle.

taisui (耐水の), *a.* waterproof. ¶ 耐水布, waterproof cloth.

tai-suru (對する), *vt.* ❶ (向合ふ) to front; face; be opposite *to*; 【數】 subtend. ❷ (應ずる) to correspond *to*. ❸ (抗する, 當る) to oppose; face. ——, *prep.* for; to; toward; against. —賓客に對する禮を失する, to act impolitely towards the guest. —三十に對する百五十票の多數, a majority of 150 votes against 30.

tai-suru (體する), *vt.* to understand; comprehend: obey; comply *with*.

taitei (大抵), *ad.* generally; mostly; on the whole. —大抵の人, most men. —大抵の辭書, almost every dictionary.

taitei (退廷する), *vi.* to leave the court.

taiteki (大敵), *n.* a powerful enemy.

taiteki (對敵), *n.* an adversary; an antagonist; an enemy: hostility (敵對). ¶ 對敵取引禁遏, prohibition of trade with the enemy.

taiten (大典), *n.* a great ceremony: a great code.

taiten (退轉する), *vi.* ❶ to retrograde; change for the worse. ❷ to remove upon bankruptcy.

taito (泰斗), *n.* an authority; a star; a leading light. —泰斗と仰がれる, to be looked upon as the leading light *of*.

taitō (駘蕩たる), *a.* calm; genial. —春色駘蕩たる花の都, a city of flowers in its vernal array.

taitō (對當), *n.* ❶ (當り合ふこと) equivalence, equivalency. ❷ (相當) homology. ❸ 【論】 opposition. ❹ counterpart.

taitō (對等), *n.* equality; equal footing; parity. —對等に, on a level [plane; par; an equal footing] *with*; on equal terms; on even ground. ¶ 對等條約, a treaty on an equal footing.

taitō (擡頭する), *v.* ❶ (頭を擡げる) to raise one's head. ❷ (勢力を得來る) to become powerful; come to the front [fore].

taitoku (體得する), *vt.* to acquire; comprehend; realize.

taiu (大雨), *n.* a heavy rain [rainfall]; torrents of rain.

taiwa (對話), *n.* conversation; colloquy; dialogue. —對話する, to converse *with*; talk face to face *with*.

Taiwan (臺灣), *n.* Taiwan; Formosa. ¶ 臺灣坊主, 【醫】 alopecia. —臺灣人, a Formosan. —臺灣總督, the Governor-General of Formosa. (臺灣總督府, the Government-General of Formosa.)

taiya (逮夜), *n.* the eve of the anniversary of a death.

taiyaku (大役), *n.* a great office; an important duty.

taiyaku (對譯), *n.* a translation side by side with the original.

taiyo (貸與する), *vt.* to lend; let; loan 〔米〕.

taiyō (大要), *n.* summary; outline (槪要); epitome (提要).

taiyo (大洋), *n.* the ocean; the main (sea) ¶ 大洋航路線, an ocean line.

taiyō (太陽), *n.* the sun. —太陽の黑點, 【天】 a sun-spot. ¶ 太陽系, 【天】 the solar system. —太陽曆, the solar calendar. —太陽崇拜, sun-worship; heliolatry.

taiyoku (大慾), *n.* ❶ (極めて慾深き) avarice; avidity; covetousness. ❷ (大望) a great ambition. —大慾は無慾, "Avarice overreaches itself."

Taiyōshū (大洋洲), *n.* Oceania.

taiyū (大勇), *n.* moral courage; great [cool] courage.

taiyūsei (大熊星), *n.* 【天】 Ursa Major 〔羅〕. ☞ *hokutosei*.

taiza (對坐する), *vi.* to sit opposite to each other; sit face to face; sit *vis-a-vis*.

taizai (大罪), *n.* a serious crime (法律上の); a grand sin (道德上の). ¶ 大罪人, a great sinner

(道徳上の); a great criminal [offender] (法律上の).

taizai (滯在), *n.* sojourn; stay. **—— -suru,** *vi.* to stay [stop] *at* [*in*]; make a stay; sojourn. —一週間滯在する, to stay a weak. ¶ 滯在地, the place of sojourn. —滯在日當, a daily allowance for sojourn.

taizan (大山), *n.* a great mountain. —大山鳴動して一鼠出づ, "The mountain is in labour and brings forth a mouse."

taizei (大勢), *n.* a large number of persons; a large force.

taizen (泰然), *ad.* calmly; with the utmost calmness; with composure. —盤石の如く泰然と, as fast as a mountain [rock]. —泰然として死に就く, to face death calmly.

taizuki (隊附の), *a.* regimental. ¶ 隊附將校, a regimental officer.

taji (多事の), *a.* busy; eventful. —天下多事の秋に於て, in these eventful days.

tajirogu (退避ぐ), *vi.* to flinch; shrink back; start back.

tajitsu (他日), *n.* one day; another day; some day. —他日を期する, to put it off to another occasion; expect it another time.

tajō (多情), *n.* ❶ (浮氣) amorousness. ❷ (多感) sensibility.

taka (鷹), *n.* 【鳥】 the hawk; the falcon (特に鷹狩用の).

taka (高), *n.* ❶ quantity; amount; a sum. ❷ (收穫高) the amount of rice-crop.

taka (多寡), *n.* quantity; amount. —多寡の知れた, inconsiderable; trifling; not worth considering. —多寡を括る, to underestimate; make light *of*. **—— -ga,** *ad.* merely; after all. —多寡が五圓ばかりだ, It is worth no more than 5 *yen*.

takabisha (高飛車に), *ad.* coercively; oppressively; high-handedly. —高飛車に出る, to act high-handedly (高壓的に).

takabō (高帽), *n.* a tall [silk] hat; a dress-hat; a chimney-pot.

takabōki (竹箒), *n.* a bamboo-broom.

takabori (高彫), *n.* high relief; alto-relievo 【伊】.

takaburu (驕ぶる), *vi.* ❶ to be proud [haughty; pompous]; hold up one's head; be stuck-up. ❷ 〔亢〕 = *kōfun* (興奮する).

takadai (高臺), *n.* an upland; a height; a terrace.

takadaka (高高), *ad.* at (the) most; at the highest.

takahari (高張-提燈), *n.* a lantern hung on a pole.

takai (高い), *a.* ❶ (高低の) high; lofty; tall (身長などの). ❷ (地位の) high; elevated. ❸ (聲の) loud; high-pitched (高調子の). ❹ (價の) dear; expensive. ❺ (品格の) high-toned.

takaibiki (高鼾), *n.* a loud snore. —高鼾をかく, to snore loudly; snore like thunder.

takaku (多角の), *a.* polygonal. ¶ 多角形, 【數】 a polygon.

takaku (多額), *n.* a large [great] sum. ¶ 多額納稅議員, a representative of the highest tax-payers. —多額納稅者, the highest tax-payer; the payer of the largest amount of taxes.

takaku (高く), *ad.* up; high; aloft; eminently; soaringly. —高くなる, ① to rise; become higher; swell (土地など). ② (成長する) to grow tall. ③ (騰貴する) to rise; become dear. —高くとまる, to look big; hold one's head high. —少し調子を高くする, to raise the tune a little more.

Takamagahara (高天原), *n.* the Japanese Olympus; the Heavens.

takamakura (高枕), *n.* sleeping free from care; the sleep of the just.

takamaru (高まる), *vi.* to rise; go up; swell.

takameru (高める), *vt.* to raise; elevate; improve (改善). —品性《趣味》を高める, to elevate [improve] a person's character《taste》. —勞働者の地位を高める, to improve the condition of labourers.

takami (高み), *n.* a height; an eminence; an elevation. —高みで見物する, to look on unconcernedly [with indifference]; look on with folded arms.

takan (多感), *n.* sensibility; sentimentality; susceptibility. —多感の, sensitive; sentimental; susceptible.

takane (高値), *n.* high price. —高値を唱へる, to be quoted high.

takara (寶), *n.* ❶ a treasure; a highly-prized article. ❷ (金錢) money. —寶の持腐れ, a white elephant. —寶の山に入りながら手を空しうして歸る, to return empty-handed from a mountain of treasures. ¶ 寶貝, 【貝】 the tiger cowry. —寶探し, treasure-hunting.

takaraka (高らかに), *ad.* loud; loudly; aloud.

takaru (集る), *vi.* to swarm; gather; crowd; flock together; collect. —虱がたかってる著物, a dress infested with vermin.

takasa (高さ), *n.* height; elevation; altitude (高度); pitch (調子の); loudness (音聲の).

takate-kote (高手籠手に), *ad.* firmly; tightly. —高手籠手に縛る, to bind a person tightly.
takatobi (高跳), *n.* 【競技】 high jump.
takatobi (高飛する), *vi.* to levant; decamp. —亞米利加へ高飛びする, to levant to America.
takaukibori (高浮彫), *n.* high relief; alto-relievo.
takawarai (高笑), *n.* a loud laugh; a hee-haw (笑聲).
take (竹), *n.* 【植】 the bamboo. ¶ 竹の節, a bamboo-knot. —竹垣, a bamboo fence. —竹簾, bamboo-blinds. —竹屋, a bamboo-dealer. —竹竿, a bamboo-pole. —竹細工, bamboo-ware; bamboo-work. —竹筒, bamboo-tube.
take (丈), *n.* ❶ (身長) height; stature. ❷ (長さ) length. ❸ (寸法) measure. ☞ *se* (背). —丈の高い, tall. —身の丈六尺に餘る大男, a big man over six feet in height. —君は丈いくらあるか, How many feet do you stand?
take (茸), *n.* the mushroom (菌). ☞ *kinoko.*
takedakeshii (猛猛しい), *a.* ❶ (甚だ猛き) fierce; ferocious. ❷ (圖太き) audacious.
takekago (竹籠), *n.* a bamboo basket.
takeki (猛き), *a.* ❶ (勇猛) brave; valiant; dauntless; intrepid; bold; fearless. ❷ (猛烈) fierce.
takenawa (闌, 酣), *ad.* at the height. —宴酣なる時, when the feast was at its height.
takenokawa (籜), *n.* a bamboo-sheath.
takenoko (筍, 笋), *n.* a bamboo-shoot. ¶ 筍醫者, an unskilled doctor.
takenosonō (竹の園生), *n.* Imperial princes. —竹の園生の御身にて, though born in the purple.
takeru (長ける), *vi.* ❶ (酣になる) to reach the height; be far advanced (夜が). ❷ (盛を過ぐ) to wane; decline.
takeru (哮る), *vi.* to roar; bellow.
takeru (猛る), *vi.* to become furious; grow rowdy. —猛り狂ふ, to rush about in frenzy; be on the rampage; run amuck.
taketsu (多血), *n.* ❶【醫】(體内の血液多量) plethora. ❷ (性質の) sanguineness. ¶ 多血質, sanguine temperament.
takeuma (竹馬), *n.* stilts. —竹馬に乘る, to walk on stilts.
takeyabu (竹藪), *r.* a bamboo-grove; a bamboo-jungle.
takeyari (竹槍), *n.* a bamboo-spear.
taki (瀧), *n.* a waterfall; falls; a cataract (大); a cascade (小).
taki (多岐), *n.* many branches [side-roads]. —多岐に別る, to branch off in various directions.
takibi (焚火), *n.* bonfire; wood-fire. —焚火する, to light a fire.
takidashi (焚出), *n.* boiling rice at an emergency. —罹災者のため焚出をする, to boil rice for the sufferers.
takigi (薪), *n.* firewood; faggot, fagot (束ねた); stick. ☞ *maki.*
takimono (焚物), *n.* ❶ fuel; firewood. ❷ (薰物) incense.
takishīdo (タキシード), *n.* a tuxedo (coat).
takitsubo (瀧壺), *n.* the basin of a waterfall.
takitsuke (焚附), *n.* a fire-lighter; kindling-wood 《coal》.
takitsukeru (焚附ける), *v.* ❶ (火を) to light; kindle; make [build] a fire. ❷ (唆す) to incite; enkindle; add oil to the fire.
takkan (達觀する), *vt.* to grasp comprehensively; take a wide view *of.*
takken (卓見), *n.* foresight; clear-sightedness; an excellent view.
takkyū (卓球), *n.* table-tennis; ping-pong.
tako (蛸, 章魚), *n.* the octopus.
tako (凧), *n.* a kite. —凧を上げる, to fly a kite. ¶ 凧上げ, kite-flying.
tako (胼胝), *n.* a callosity. —足に胼胝が出來る, to get a callosity on one's foot.
tako (撞槌), *n.* a rammer; a stamper; a pile-driver. —大撞槌で衝く, to drive in with a great pile-driver.
takō (多幸), *n.* great happiness; great fortune; blissfulness. —多幸の, lucky; fortunate; blissful.
takōshiki (多項式), *n.* a polynomial [multinomial] expression.
takobune (紅魚), *n.* 【貝】 the argonaut; the paper-nautilus.
takoku (他國), *n.* a strange land. ❶ (外國) another [a foreign] country; a foreign [an alien] land. ❷ (國内の) another province. ¶ 他國人, a foreigner; an alien; a stranger.
takon (多恨), *n.* many regrets; great discontent.
taku (宅), *n.* ❶ home; a house; a residence. ❷ my husband (我夫).
taku (卓), *n.* a table.
taku (炊く), *vt.* to boil; cook. —飯を炊く, to boil rice.
taku (焚く), *v.* to burn; kindle. —火を焚く, to kindle a fire; make [build] a fire.
takuan (澤庵), *n.* pickled radish.
takuchi (宅地), *n.* building lot; residential land.
takuetsu (卓越する), *v.* to excel;

surpass; outrun; stand high [out]. —卓越せる, prominent; distinguished; pre-eminent.
takuhatsu (托鉢), *n.* mendicancy. —托鉢する, to go about as a mendicant priest. ¶ 托鉢僧, a mendicant friar [priest]; a calender (回々敎の).
takujisho (託兒所), *n.* a public [day-]nursery; a *crèche* 【佛】.
takujō (卓上), *ad.* on the table.
takuma (琢磨する), *vt.* to polish; scour. ☞ *migaku*.
takumashii (逞しい), *a.* strong; robust; stout. —筋骨の逞しい靑年, a sturdy [stalwart] lad.
takumi (巧), *n.* ❶ (考案) art; plan. ❷ (巧妙) skill; dexterity. ❸ =*takurami*. —巧な, skilful; clever; ingenious; masterly. ——**ni,** *ad.* skilfully; finely; subtly; craftily (こすく); diplomatically (同上). —巧に飛行機を操縱する, to work an aeroplane skilfully.
takumiryō (內匠寮), *n.* the Bureau of Construction.
takumu (企む) *vt.* to devise; contrive; plan. —彼が企んだ謀計, a scheme of his contrivance. —惡い事を企む, to plan a wicked affair.
takurami (企み), *n.* a design; a plot; a scheme.
takuramu (企む), *vt.* to plan; devise; plot. ☞ *takumu*.
takusan (澤山), *n.* ❶ (多數) a great many; a large [great] number; a lot *of*. ❷ (多量) a great deal; a large [great] quantity; plenty *of*. —澤山の人, lots of people. —澤山の仕事, plenty of work. —澤山に, enough; plentifully; abundantly; in abundance. —もう澤山, Enough!; No (more), thank you. —それ丈で澤山だ, That will be enough.
takusen (託宣), *n.* an oracle; a divine message. ☞ *shintaku*.
takusetsu (卓說), *n.* an excellent opinion; enlightened views.
takushi (卓子), *n.* a table.
takushī (辻自動車), *n.* a taxi; a taxi-cab. —タクシーで行く, to taxi; go by taxi(-cab).
takushiki (卓識), *n.* acute discernment. ¶ 卓識の士, a clear-sighted person.
takushin (宅診), *n.* office consultation. —午前宅診午後往診, "Hours of Consultation: before noon, at Office; after noon, at Residences."
takushoku (拓殖), *n.* colonization. ☞ *shokumin*. ¶ 北海道拓殖銀行, the Hokkaidō Colonial Bank.
takusō (託送する), *vt.* to send by; send under the care *of*.
taku-suru (託する), *vt.* ❶ (依託) to trust; entrust, intrust; give in charge; commit to the care *of*; charge *with*. ❷ (口實) to make a pretext *of*; pretend. —A君に託す (封筒に書く), (kindly) favoured by Mr. A; kindness of Mr. A; per favour of Mr. A. —病氣に託して辭職する, to resign on the pretext [under (the) pretence] of illness. —事件を友人に託する, to put the matter in a friend's hands; commit the affair to a friend's care.
takuwae (貯へ), *n.* ❶ (貯金) savings. ❷ (貯藏) store (物品); reserve (豫備); stock (原料, 製品).
takuwaeru (貯へる), *vt.* to save; amass; lay by; hoard; store.
takuyō (托葉), *n.* 【植】 a stipule.
takuzetsu (卓絕), *n.* superexcellence; pre-eminence; superiority. —卓絕する, to surpass; be pre-eminent.
tama (玉, 球, 丸), *n.* ❶ (球) a ball; a globe; a bulb (植物の根, 寒暖計・電燈の球). ❷ (彈丸) a bullet (小銃彈); a ball; a shot. ☞ *dangan* (彈丸). ❸ (寶玉) a gem; a jewel; a *bijou* [*pl. bijoux*] 【佛】. —眼鏡の玉, a lens. —玉に瑕, a fly in ointment. —玉に使ふ, to make use of as a decoy. —掌中の珠と慈しむ, to love a person as the apple of one's eye. —球を打つ, to bat; drive. —球を受ける, to catch a ball. —彈丸を込める, to load [charge] (a gun).
tama (手網), *n.* a spoon-net; a scoop-net.
tamabuchi (玉緣), *n.* 【建】 an astragal; a bead.
tamagaki (玉垣), *n.* a shrine-fence.
tamageru (魂消る), *vi.* to be horror-struck; be thunderstruck; wonder (*at*). ☞ *odoroku*.
tamago (卵, 玉子), *n.* an egg (特に鷄卵); spawn (魚介類の); spat (特に牡蠣の卵). —卵を抱く, to brood: sit on eggs. —玉子を抱かせる, to set a hen on eggs. —玉子をかへす, to hatch an egg. ¶ 玉子燒, an omelet; fried eggs: an egg-frying-pan (道具) —玉子色, a yellowish colour. —卵の蛋白(しろみ) (蛋黃(きみ)), the white (yolk) of an egg.
tamagushi (玉串), *n.* a branch of Eurya ochnacea offered to a god.
tamaki (環), *n.* a ring; a circle.
tamakizu (彈疵), *n.* a bullet-wound; a gunshot-wound.
tamakorogashi (球轉し), *n.* bowling.

tamamayu (玉繭), *n.* a double cocoon.

tamamono (賜物), *n.* ❶ a present; a gift (from a superior); a donation. ❷ (恩惠) goodness. ❸ (結果) result. —天の賜物, a gift from Heaven. —の賜物である, to be due *to*. ☞ *okage*.

tamamushi (吉丁蟲), *n.* 【昆】 Chrysochroa elegans (學名). ¶ 玉蟲色, iridescence.

tamana (甘藍), *n.* the (garden) cabbage; the colewort.

tamanashi (玉無にする), *vt.* to lose entirely; spoil.

tamanegi (玉葱), *n.* 【植】 the onion.

tamani (偶に), *ad.* ❶ (時には) at times; occasionally; sometimes. ❷ (稀) seldom; rarely. —偶には喧嘩することもあるよ, It happens sometimes that we have a quarrel.

tama-no-o (玉の緒), *n.* the thread of life; the life-strings; life.

tamanori (玉乘), *n.* walking on a ball. ¶ 娘玉乘, a girl-dancer on a ball.

tamaranai (堪らない), *a.* intolerable; unbearable; unendurable. —可笑しくて堪らない, I cannot help laughing. —痒《痛》くてたまらない, It itches《pains me》 beyond endurance.

tamari (溜), *n.* (控所) a lobby; a waiting-room; a stand (馬車等の). ¶ 溜水, standing [stagnant] water; puddle; pool.

tamaru (溜る), *vi.* ❶ to collect; accumulate. ❷ (水が) to stand; stay. —金は中々溜らぬ, Money is very hard to save.

tamashii (魂), *n.* ❶ (靈魂) a soul. ❷ (精神) a spirit. ❸ (生命) the life (and soul). —魂天涯に飛ぶ, to go off into ecstasies. —魂を吹き込む, to breathe life *into*. —魂を入れ替へて勉强する, to reform oneself and study. ¶ 獨逸魂, the German spirit.

tamatama (偶), *ad.* ❶ (偶然) by chance; accidentally. ☞ *gūzen*. ❷ = *tamani*. —たまたま訪ねたら, when I happened to call on him.

tamatebako (玉手箱), *n.* a casket.

tamatsubaki (玉椿), *n.* 【植】 the Japanese privet.

tamatsuki (球突), *n.* billiards. —球突をする, to play (at) billiards. ¶ 球突棒, a (billiard-)cue. —球突臺, a billiard-table.

tamau (給ふ), *v.* to deign *to*; be pleased *to*.

tamau (賜ふ), *vt.* to grant; bestow; award; confer *upon*. —拜謁を賜ふ, to grant an audience *to*. —陪食の榮を賜はる, to have the honour of lunching with His Majesty.

tamaya (玉屋), *n.* a jeweller.

tamaya (靈屋), *n.* a mausoleum.

tamazan (珠算), *n.* calculation with an abacus.

tame (爲), *n.* ❶ (利益) advantage; benefit; good. ❷ (結果) consequence; effect. **——-ni**, *ad.* consequently; in consequence. **——**, *conj.* because; for; as; for as much as. **——**, *prep.* ❶ (利益·便益の爲) for; for the sake [benefit] *of*; in [on] behalf *of*; in favour *of*; in the interest *of*. ❷ (目的の爲) for the purpose [sake] *of*; with a view *to*; in order *to*. ❸ (原因·理由よりして) on account *of*; in consequence *of*; owing *to*; because *of*; for; through; from. ❹ (力で, 所爲で) by; thanks *to*. —保養の爲に, for one's health. —天候險惡の爲に, owing to [on account of] threatening weather. —不景氣の爲に, in consequence of the trade depression. —事變があった爲に, as [because] there was an accident. —此佳節を祝する爲に, in honour of the occasion. —爲になる, to benefit; be beneficial *to*; profit. —爲にならぬ, to be uninstructive; do one harm; be against one's interests.

tame (溜), *n.* ❶ (物を溜め置く處) a depository. ❷ (汚水溜) a cesspool.

tameike (溜池), *n.* a reservoir; an irrigation pond.

tameiki (溜息), *n.* a sigh. —溜息する[をつく], to sigh; heave [fetch] a sigh.

tamen (他面), *n.* another side [face]; the other side.

tamen (多面の), *a.* polyhedral; many-sided. ¶ 多面體, 【數】 a polyhedron.

tame-nisuru (爲にする), *v.* to do for one's own purpose; have an ulterior purpose. —何等か爲にせんとする者の說, the view of one with an ulterior motive.

tamerau (ためらふ), *vi.* to hesitate; waver; pause.

tameru (溜める), *vt.* ❶ (貯蓄) to save; lay up; hoard (溜込む). ❷ (蓄積) to accumulate; amass. ❸ (集める) to collect; gather. —働いて貯める, to work and scrape.

tameru (矯める), *vt.* ❶ (直くす) to straighten; make straight. ❷ (撓·曲げる) to bend; twist; bow. ❸ (矯正) to correct; reform; amend. ❹ (曲解) to strain; stretch. ❺ (僞る) to feign; pretend. —情を矯める, to restrain one's emotion. —癖を矯める, to correct one's bad habit; break a person of a bad habit.

tameshi (例), *n.* an instance; an example; a case (場合); a precedent (先例). —例のない, unprecedented; unexampled; without example.

tameshi (試), *n.* a trial; an attempt (企); an experiment (實驗); an experience (經驗). —試斬りをする, to try a sword on a person. —試に使って見る, to take a person on trial; make a trial of it (物を).

tamesu (試す), *vt.* ❶ to try; attempt; make a trial *of*. ❷ (試驗する) to put [bring; submit] to the test; put to the touch [touchstone]; test. ❸ (實驗する), to experiment; make an experiment. —腕をためす, to try one's hand. (人の腕を試す, to put another's ability to the test.)

tami (民), *n.* the people (人民); the subjects (臣民).

tamoto (袂), *n.* ❶ (袖) a sleeve; the bag of a sleeve. ❷ (麓) the foot. ❸ (際[きわ]) the edge; the brink; the side. —橋の袂, the edge [foot; end] of a bridge; the approach to a bridge. —惜しき袂を別つ, to tear oneself from one's companion.

tamotsu (保つ), *vt.* ❶ (保有) to possess; hold; keep. ❷ (保存) to keep; preserve. ❸ (維持) to hold (out); maintain; sustain; retain. ——, *vi.* to keep; last; wear (著物などが). —命を保つ, to preserve life. —平均を保つ, to balance; keep [maintain] equilibrium. —威嚴を保つ, to maintain one's dignity.

tamuke (手向), *n.* ❶ (神·佛への供物) an offering; a tribute. ❷ (はなむけ) a farewell present. —香華を手向ける, to offer incense and flowers.

tamuro (屯), *n.* ❶ (警官屯所) a police station. ❷ (軍隊の) a camp; barracks; quarters. ❸ (集合所) a rendezvous. —屯する, to encamp; be stationed; be quartered.

tamushi (輪蝨), *n.* a ringworm.

tan (反), *n.* (反物の) a piece [roll] of cloth (=about 12½ yards). —反で買ふ, to buy by the roll.

tan (段, 反), *n.* a superficial measure (=about .245 acres).

tan (短), *n.* ❶ shortness. ❷ (缺點, 過失) a fault; a defect. —短を補ふ, to remedy a defect.

tan (痰), *n.* phlegm; sputum. —痰を吐く, to cough up sputum.

tan (歎), *n.* ❶ (悲歎) regret; grief. ❷ (慨歎) deploration.

tan (膽), *n.* ❶ (膽嚢) the gall-bladder. ❷ (膽力) spirit; courage. —膽を練る, to foster courage. —膽を奪ふ, to frighten; frighten another out of his wits; terrify.

tana (店), *n.* ❶ (みせ) a shop; a store. ❷ (借家) a rented house.

tana (棚), *n.* a shelf; ledge (壁などから出張った). —棚から牡丹餅, an unexpected piece of good luck. —棚に上げる, ① to put on a shelf. ② (さし措く) to set aside; leave out.

tanaami (棚網), *n.* (列車の) a net; a rack.

tanabata (七夕), *n.* the seventh day of the seventh month (of the lunar calendar); 【天】the Weaver; the star Vega.

tanabiku (棚引く), *vi.* to tail.

tanachin (店賃), *n.* a house-rent; a shop-rent.

tanadate (店立), *n.* eviction; ejection. —店立てを食はせる, to evict (a person) from a house; turn out.

tanagari (店借), *n.* ❶ tenancy (of a house). ❷ (借家人) a tenant.

tanago (たなご), *n.* 【魚】 Acheilognathus limbata (學名).

tanagokoro (掌), *n.* the palm; the hollow of the hand. —掌を反す樣に, as readily as one might turn one's hand.

tanako (店子), *n.* a tenant.

tanaoroshi (棚卸, 店卸), *n.* ❶ 【商】 stock-taking. ❷ (あら探し) fault-finding. —棚卸しする, ① to take stock; take account of stock. ② to run down; pick a hole *in*; find fault *with*. ¶ 棚卸表, an inventory.

tanazarashi (店晒), *n.* ❶ soiling by exposure in a shop. ❷ (店晒品) shop-worn [shop-soiled] articles; slug goods; old stock. —店晒しになる, to soil by exposure in a shop.

tanbetsu (反別), *n.* the area of land; acreage.

tanbi (嘆美する), *vt.* to admire; praise; extol.

tanbo (田圃), *n.* rice-field; a paddy-field. ¶ 田圃道, a path through a rice-field; a farm road.

tanbō (探訪), *n.* private inquiry. —探訪する, to make private inquiry *into*. ¶ 探訪記者, a (newspaper-)reporter; an interviewer. (朝日の探訪記者をしてゐる, to report for the Asahi.)

tanbun (單文), *n.* 【文】 the simple sentence.

tanchi (探知), *n.* detection; finding out by inquiry. —探知する, to find out by inquiry; detect; ferret out.

tancho (端緒), *n.* =*tansho*.
tanchō (單調), *n.* monotony; flatness; simplicity. ――**-na,** *a.* monotonous; flat; simple (簡單). ―單調な日を送る, to lead a monotonous (humdrum) life.
tanchō-no-tsuru (丹頂の鶴), *n.* the sacred crane.
tandeki (耽溺する), *vt.* to indulge *in*; be given up *to*; abandon oneself *to*. ¶ 耽溺家, a debauchee; a libertine. ―耽溺生活, a voluptuous life; a life given to pleasure.
tanden (炭田), *n.* a coal-field.
tandoku (丹毒), *n.* 【醫】 erysipelas.
tandoku (單獨), *n.* singleness; single-handedness. ―單獨の, single; single-handed; independent. ―單獨でやる, to do single-handed. ¶ 單獨行爲, 【法】 a unilateral (juristic) act. ―單獨講和, a separate peace.
tane (種), *n.* ❶ (種子) a seed; a stone (桃類の); a kernel (核); a pip (橙類の). ❷ (產種) breed. ❸ (胤, 血筋) blood; lineage. ❹ (原因) a source; a cause; an origin. ❺ (手段) means. ❻ (主題) a subject; a topic (話の). ❼ (資本) capital. ❽ (菓子等の) stock. ―不和の種, an apple of discord; a bone of contention. ―間違ひ(心配)の種, a source of error (anxiety). ―種を明かす, to show how the trick is done. ―噂の種を蒔く, to give a handle for a rumour.
taneabura (種油), *n.* rape-oil; colza-oil (菜牡丹の).
tanechigai (胤違), *n.* ❶ a half-blood. ❷ (兄弟) a (uterine) half-brother (sister). ―胤違ひの, born from a different father. (胤違ひの兄, one's elder half-brother.)
tanegami (蠶卵紙), *n.* a silkworm-egg card.
tanegawari (種變), *n.* a variety. ¶種變りの朝顔, a variety of the morning-glory.
tanegire (種切), *n.* out of resources; exhaustion. ―話が種切れになった, The topics for conversation were exhausted.
tanehon (種本), *n.* the original.
taneita (種板), *n.* 【寫眞】 negative; a dry-plate (乾板); a magic lantern slide (幻燈の).
tanemaki (種蒔き), *n.* sowing; the seed-time (時).
tanemonoya (種物屋), *n.* a seed-store (店): a seedsman (人).
tanen (多年), *n.* many [long] years. ―多年の希望, one's long-cherished desire [ambition]. ―多年の經驗により, from many years' experience. ¶ 多年生草本, a perennial herb.
tanetamago (種卵), *n.* a nest-egg.
taneuma (種馬), *n.* a stud-horse; a stallion. ☞ *shuba*.
taneushi (種牛), *n.* a bull for breeding. ¶ 種牛牧場, a cattle-farm.
tangan (歎願), *n.* entreaty; petition; supplication. ―歎願する, to entreat; petition; supplicate; implore.
tangei (端倪する), *vt.* to conjecture; guess. ―端倪すべからず, to be beyond conjecture.
tango (單語), *n.* a word. ¶ 單語集, a vocabulary; a glossary.
tango (端午), *n.* the fifth day of the fifth month (of the lunar calendar); the Feast of Flags.
tangusuten (タングステン), *n.* tungsten; wolfram. ¶ タングステン電球, a tungsten lamp.
tangutsu (短靴), *n.* shoes.
tanhoṅi (單本位), *n.* 【經】 single standard; monometallism.
tani (谷), *n.* ❶ a valley; a glen (小谷); a dell (樹木ある小谷). ❷【建】 valley. ¶ 谷川, a mountain-stream; a rill. ―谷間, a ravine; a gorge; a dell. (谷間の姫百合, the lily of the valley.)
ta-ni (他に), *ad.* else. ―他に望なし, I have no other hope.
taṅi (單位), *n.* a unit.
taṅi (單衣), *n.* an unlined dress.
tanikuka (多肉果), *n.* succulent fruit.
tanin (他人), *n.* ❶ (血緣なき人) an unrelated person. ❷ (我以外の人) another person; others. ❸ (未知人) a stranger. ―赤の他人 an entire stranger. ―他人がましく, like a stranger; reservedly. ―他人扱ひする, to treat like a stranger.
tanishi (田螺), *n.* 【腹足】 the river snail.
taṅitsu (單一), *n.* unity; singleness; simplicity. ―單一な, unique; single; simple.
tanjō (誕生), *n.* birth; nativity. ―誕生を祝ふ, to celebrate a birth. ¶ 誕生日, a birthday. ―誕生祝, a birthday celebration.
tanjū (短銃), *n.* a pistol; a revolver (連發の).
tanjū (膽汁), *n.* bile; gall. ¶ 膽汁質, a bilious temperament.
tanjun (單純), *n.* simplicity; simpleness. ―單純な, simple; pure (純一); absolute (引受·承認など). ―單純化する, to simplify.
tanka (炭化), *n.* carbonization. ¶ 炭化水素, carburetted hydrogen; hydrocarbon.
tanka (短歌), *n.* ❶ an ode; a song; a ditty. ❷ =*waka*.

tanka (單價), *n.* a simple [unit] price. —單價五圓にて, at ¥5 apiece.

tanka (痰呵を切る), *v.* to talk [speak] caustically [with a caustic tongue]

tanka (擔架), *n.* a stretcher; a litter. —擔架で負傷者を運ぶ, to convey the wounded on stretchers. ¶ 擔架卒, a stretcher-bearer.

tankaitō (探海燈), *n.* a search--light.

tankasshoku (淡褐色), *n.* drab; light brown colour; biscuit.

tan-kawa (タン皮), *n.* a tan (皮を鞣すに用ひる槲の樹等の皮).

tanken (探檢, 探險), *n.* expedition; exploration. —探檢する, to explore. ¶ 北極探檢, an Arctic expedition. —探檢隊, a party of explorers; an expeditionary party.

tanken (短見), *n.* short-sightedness; short sight; a shallow view.

tanken (短劍), *n.* ❶ a short sword; a small sword; a dirk. ❷ (匕首) a dagger; a poniard; a hanger; a rapier (細身の); a cutlass (少しく曲れる水兵用の).

tanki (短氣), *n.* quick [short; hasty] temper; impatience; hastiness (性急). —短氣な, quick--tempered; impatient; hasty. —短氣を起す, to become impatient [irritated]; lose one's temper. —短氣は損氣, "Haste makes waste." ¶ 短氣者, a short-tempered [choleric] person; a spitfire.

tanki (短期), *n.* a short term; a short period; a short date (手形の). ¶ 短期公債, a short(-term) loan. —短期戰, a short war. —短期手形, a short(-dated) bill.

tanki (單記), *n.* 【簿記】 single entry. ¶ 單記投票, single vote.

tanki (單騎), *n.* a single horseman. ¶ 單騎旅行, a solitary journey on horseback.

tanki (膽氣), *n.* courage; boldness; intrepidity.

tankō (炭坑), *n.* a coal-mine; a colliery; a coal pit. ¶ 炭坑夫, a collier. —炭坑主, a coal-owner; a coal-master.

tankō (炭鑛), *n.* coal.

tankō (探鑛する), *vi.* to prospect *for* (gold, *etc*). ¶ 探鑛家, a prospector.

tankō (堪航-性), *n.* 【飛】 airworthiness; 【航】 seaworthiness. ¶ 堪航證, 【飛】 a certificate of airworthiness.

tankō (單行する), *vi.* to go alone. ¶ 單行本, a separate [special] volume. (單行本として出版する, to publish in book form.)

tankō (鍛工), *n.* a blacksmith; a smith; a metal-worker.

tankobu (痰瘤), *n.* a wen; a bunch. —目の上の痰瘤, a great nuisance [encumbrance].

tankōshiki (單項式), *n.* 【數】 a uninomial [monomial] expression.

tankōshoku (淡紅色), *n.* pink; rose-pink; blush-tint.

tanku (短句), *n.* a phrase.

tanku (タンク), *n.* a tank (槽; 戰車). ¶ 瓦斯タンク, a gas-tank.

tankyori (短距離), *n.* a short range [distance]. ¶ 短距離競走, a short-distance race; a sprint--race. (短距離競走者, a sprinter.)

tankyū (探求), *n.* search. —探求する, to search *after* [*for*]; seek. ¶ 探求者, a seeker.

tankyū (探究), *n.* investigation; research; exploration. —探究する, to investigate; make researches; explore. ¶ 探究者, an investigator.

tankyū (單級), *n.* a single class. ¶ 單級組織, a single-class [ungraded] system.

tanmei (短命), *n.* a short life; an ephemeral life. —短命な, short-lived; ephemeral.

tanmono (反物), *n.* piece-goods; drapery; dry goods 【米】; textiles (織物); cloth (布帛). ¶ 反物屋, ① (人) a draper. ② (店) a draper's (shop); a dry-goods store 【米】.

tan-naru (單なる), *a.* mere; simple; sheer.

tannen (丹念な), *a.* assiduous; painstaking; careful (念入). —丹念に, with utmost care; painstakingly.

tan-ni (單に), *ad.* only; merely; simply.

tannin (單寧), *n.* 【化】 tannin. ¶ 單寧酸, tannic acid.

tannin (擔任), *n.* taking charge *of*; charge. —擔任する, to take charge *of*. ¶ 擔任教師, the teacher in charge.

tannō (堪能な), *a.* proficient; skilful. —音樂に堪能である, to be highly proficient in music.

tannō (膽嚢), *n.* 【解】 the gall--bladder; the gall.

tanō (多能), *n.* many accomplishments; versatility. ¶ 多能な人, a talented [versatile; many-sided] person.

tanō (蛋黃), *n.* yolk; vitellus.

ta-no-kuro (田畔), *n.* a ridge (between rice-fields).

tanomi (賴), *n.* ❶ (依賴) request; solicitation. ❷ (信賴) confidence; trust. ❸ (依賴心) reliance; dependence. —賴みになる; 賴み甲斐ある, reliable; trustworthy. —賴みの綱が切れる, One's last hope is gone. —君に一つ賴みが

ある, I have a request to make you.

tanomoshikō (頼母子講), *n.* a mutual credit society.

tanomoshii (頼もしい), *a.* ❶ (見込ある) promising; hopeful. ❷ (頼りになる) reliable; trusty. —頼もしい人, a promising person; a reliable person.

tanomu (頼·恃む), *vt.* ❶ (依頼する) to ask; request; desire. ❷ (依託する) to trust *to*; entrust (a person) *with*; entrust (a matter) *to*; charge (a person) *with*. ❸ (雇ふ) to engage; employ; hire (船·車·馬など). ❹ (信頼する) to trust *to*; rely *on*; depend *on*; confide *in*; count *on*. —恃み難き, unreliable; untrustworthy. —恃み過ぎる, [*a.*] overconfident. —僥倖を恃む, to trust to chance. —演説を頼む, to call upon a person for [to make] a speech. —多數黨を恃む, to rely upon the majority (party). —人にものを頼む, to ask a person a favour; ask a favour of a person; make a request to a person. —辯護士を頼む, to engage a lawyer. —頼まれて一場の演説をした, I obliged them with a speech; I made a speech at their request.

tanoshii (樂しい), *a.* pleasant; joyful; happy. —樂しく暮らす, to pass one's days pleasantly; lead a happy life.

tanoshimasu (樂ます), *vt.* to please; amuse; feast; entertain.

tanoshimi (樂), *n.* ❶ (娛樂) amusement; entertainment. ❷ (愉快) pleasure; delight; enjoyment. ❸ (幸福) happiness.

tanoshimu (樂む), *v.* to take pleasure [delight] *in*; enjoy (oneself); amuse oneself *with*. —獨り樂む, to enjoy oneself alone. —畫を見て樂む, to feast on pictures; take pleasure in pictures. —將來を樂み待つ, to look forward to the future with pleasure.

tanpaku (淡白), *n.* ❶ (性質の) frankness; candour; unaffectedness (飾氣なきこと). ❷ (食物の) plainness. ——**-na**, *a.* ❶ frank; candid; unaffected. ❷ plain. —淡白な料理, plain cookery. —金錢に淡白な人, a man careless about money.

tanpaku (蛋白), *n.* albumen; glair (卵の白味). ¶ 蛋白石, 【鑛】 opal. —蛋白質, albumen; protein.

tanpan (膽礬), *n.* ❶【化】 blue vitriol; sulphate of copper. ❷【鑛】 chalcanthite.

tanpei (短兵), *n.* a short sword. —短兵急に, impetuously; suddenly; precipitately. ¶ 短兵戰, fighting at close quarters; a hand-to-hand fight.

tanpen (短篇), *n.* a short piece; a sketch. ¶ 短篇小說, a short story; a novelette; a storiette. —短篇集, a collection of short pieces [stories].

tanpi (單比), *n.* 【數】 simple ratio.

tanpirei (單比例), *n.* 【數】 simple proportion.

tanpo (擔保), *n.* security; collateral securities; guarantee. —擔保に入れる, to give [lay; put] in security. ¶ 擔保貸附, loan on security.

tanpopo (蒲公英), *n.* 【植】 the dandelion.

tanpyō (短評), *n.* short criticism. —短評を下す, to criticize briefly.

tanran (貪婪), *n.* avarice; rapacity; cupidity. —貪婪の, avaricious; rapacious.

tanrei (端麗な), *a.* graceful; elegant; handsome.

tanren (鍛練), *n.* ❶ (鐵等の) forge; temper. ❷ (訓練) drilling; discipline; training. —鍛練の足らぬ, under-trained. —鍛練する, to forge; temper; drill; train; discipline.

tanretsu (單列), *n.* a line.

tanri (單利), *n.* simple interest. ¶ 單利法, the method of simple interest.

tanryaku (膽略), *n.* courage and resourcefulness.

tanryo (短慮), *n.* quick [hot] temper; impatience; shallow-mindedness (淺慮).

tanryoku (膽力), *n.* cool courage; mettle; pluck 【俗】. —膽力ある, courageous; plucky.

tansa (探査), *n.* secret inquiry [investigation]. —探査する, to make secret inquiry; investigate secretly.

tansai (淡彩), *n.* light [thin] colouring.

tansai (短才), *n.* small [little] ability [talent].

tansaibō (單細胞), *n.* one [a single] cell. ¶ 單細胞動物, a unicellular [one-celled] animal.

tansaku (探索する), *vt.* ❶ (探す) to search *for*; look *for*. ❷ (探究) to make researches; investigate; inquire *into*.

tansan (炭酸), *n.* 【化】 carbonic acid. ¶ 炭酸鹽, a carbonate. —炭酸瓦斯, carbonic acid gas. —炭酸紙, carbon paper. —炭酸曹達, sodium carbonate; carbonate of soda. (重炭酸曹達, bicarbonate of soda). —炭酸水, aerated water.

tansei (丹靑), *n.* a picture; a painting.

tansei (丹誠), *n.* ❶ (誠實

sincerity; faithfulness; honesty. ❷ (努力) industry; assiduity; painstaking. —丹誠する, to be assiduous; apply oneself closely; take pains. —丹誠して育てる, to bring up with great care.

tansei (單性), *n.* unisexuality; one sex. ¶ 單性花, a unisexual flower.

tansei (端正なる), *a.* upright; just; virtuous.

tansei (歎聲), *n.* a plaint; a groan; a wail. —歎聲を洩らす, to deplore; heave a deep sigh.

tanseki (旦夕), *n.* morning and evening; day and night. —命旦夕に迫る, to be on the brink of death; lie at death's door; One's life hangs by a thread.

tanseki (痰咳), *n.* 【醫】 mucous cough; moist cough.

tanseki (膽石), *n.* 【醫】 a gall-stone. ¶ 膽石病, cholelithiasis, cholelithias.

tansen (單線), *n.* 【鐵道】 a single track. ¶ 單線式, the earth-return system (電氣鐵道の). —單線鐵道, a single-tracked railway. —單線運轉, single-track operation (of trains).

tansha (丹砂), *n.* cinnabar.

tanshiki (單式), *n.* 【簿記】 single entry. ¶ 單式簿記, book-keeping by single entry.

tanshin (丹心), *n.* a sincere heart; sincerity; singleness of heart.

tanshin (單身), *n.* single-handedness; a single individual. —, *ad.* single-handed; alone. —單身敵地に入る, to enter the enemy's territory alone.

tanshin (誕辰), *n.* a birthday.

tansho (短所), *n.* a defect; a shortcoming; a demerit; a failing.

tansho (端緒), *n.* commencement; beginning; the first step (第一步); a clue (手掛り). —端緒を開く, to pave the way *for*; enter *on* [*upon*]; commence.

tanshō (嘆賞する), *vt.* to admire; praise; extol.

tanshōtō (探照燈), *n.* a search-light.

tanshuku (短縮), *n.* shortening; contraction; abridgment; condensation. —短縮する, to shorten; cut short; contract; abridge.

tanso (炭素), *n.* 【化】 carbon. ¶ 炭素線 (弧光燈の), a carbon-point; a crayon.

tansō (炭層), *n.* a coal seam; coal measures.

tansoku (歎息), *n.* sigh; lamentation. —歎息する, to sigh; heave a sigh.

tansu (箪笥), *n.* a chest of drawers. ¶ 用箪笥, a cabinet. —總桐重ね箪笥, a double chest of drawers made entirely of paulownia-wood.

tansū (單數), *n.* 【文】 the singular (number). —單數の, singular.

tansui (炭水), *n.* ❶ coal and water. ❷ (炭素と水素) carbon and hydrogen. ¶ 炭水化物, a carbohydrate. —炭水車, a tender.

tansui (淡水), *n.* fresh water. ¶ 淡水魚, a fresh-water fish. —淡水湖, a fresh lake.

tantai (單體), *n.* ❶ 【化】 a simple substance [body]. ❷ 【建】 a monolith.

tantan (坦坦たる), *a.* smooth; level; even.

tantan (淡淡), *ad.* ❶ (冷淡) indifferently. ❷ (無味) tastelessly. ❸ (色彩の) lightly; faintly. —淡々たる, indifferent; tasteless; light; pale; faint.

tantei (探偵), *n.* ❶ (事) secret inquiry [investigation]; espionage. ❷ (人) a detective. —探偵する, to spy; inquire secretly; ferret out. —探偵をつける, to set a detective *upon*. ¶ 探偵吏, a secret policeman. —私立探偵所, a private detective agency.

tantei (單蹄), *n.* a solid hoof. ¶ 單蹄獸, 【動】 a soliped; a solid-ungulate.

tantei (端艇), *n.* a boat; a rowboat. ¶ 端艇競漕, a boat-race; a regatta.

tanteki (端的に), *ad.* ❶ (的然) plainly; evidently. ❷ (手短に) shortly; directly (直接に); hastily (急いで).

tantetsu (鍛鐵), *n.* ❶ (鍛ひたる鐵) wrought iron. ❷ (鐵を鍛ふること) temper; forge.

tantō (短刀), *n.* a short sword; a dagger (匕首); a dirk (同上); a poniard (同上).

tantō (擔當), *n.* charge. ☞ *tannin* (擔任). —擔當する, to take charge *of*.

tantōchokunyū (單刀直入), *ad.* directly; precipitantly; straightforward. —單刀直入する, to go full-tilt.

tantsuba (痰唾), *n.* spittle.

tantsubo (唾壺), *n.* a spittoon; a spit-box; a cuspidor 〔米〕.

tanuki (狸), *n.* ❶ 【哺乳】 the Japanese raccoon-dog. ❷ (狸寢入) a sham sleep; fox-sleep; cat's [cat]-sleep. —狸をつかふ, to play the fox. —捕らぬ狸の皮算用する, "to count the chickens before they are hatched."

tanyō (單葉), *n.* ❶ 【植】 a simple leaf. ❷ (單葉飛行機) a monoplane.

tanyū (膽勇), *n.* intrepidity;

dauntlessness; fearlessness.

tanza (端坐する), *vi.* to sit straight; sit up.

tanzaku (短冊), *n.* a strip of paper for an ode. ¶ 短冊形, rectangle. —短冊掛け, a frame for ode-paper.

tanzan (炭山), *n.* a colliery; a coal-mine. ☞ ***tankō*** (炭坑).

tanzeisha (擔稅者), *n.* a tax-bearer; a bearer of tax.

tanzen (端然), *ad.* solemnly; seriously; with gravity. ⌈***zuru.***

tan-zuru (彈ずる), *vt.* =***dan-***⌋

tan-zuru (歎ずる), *v.* ❶ (慨歎) to lament; deplore; regret. ❷ (嘆賞) to admire.

taore (倒), *n.* ❶ a fail. ❷ (貸金·賣掛代金等の) bad debts.

taoreru (倒る), *vi.* ❶ (轉倒) to fall (down); tumble down; come down. ❷ (倒產) to be ruined; break down. ❸ (殪, 斃) to fall; die; perish. —倒れかゝった家, a tumble-down house. —病で斃れる, to succumb to a disease. —地面に倒れる, to fall on the ground. —斃れて後止む, to strive ⦅fight⦆ to the last; give up [leave off] only when one falls down dead. —內閣は偶然倒れた, The cabinet was accidentally turned over.

taoru (手折る), *vt.* to break off; pluck off. ☞ ***oru*** (折る).

taoru (タオル), *n.* a towel.

taosu (倒す), *vt.* ❶ (覆へす) to throw down; bring down; fell (伐り倒す); overthrow (顚覆). ❷ (殺す) to kill. ❸ (破る) to defeat; beat. ❹ (借金など) to evade payment *of*; shirk. ☞ ***fumi-taosu***. —幕府を倒す, to bring down the feudal government.

taoyaka (嫋かな), *a.* ❶ (しなやか) gentle; delicate; slender. ❷ (みやびやか) graceful.

taoyame (手弱女), *n.* a gentle [graceful] woman.

tappitsu (達筆), *n.* ❶ a ready [facile] pen. ❷ (人) a ready writer.

tappuri (たっぷり), *ad.* fully; amply; abundantly. —たっぷり一時間, for a full hour. —…に色氣たっぷりである, to have a full [great; good] mind *to*…; have a great desire *for*….

tara (鱈), *n.* 【魚】 the cod(-fish). ¶ 鱈の油, cod-liver oil. —鱈の糟漬, the cod(-fish) preserved in *sake*-lees.

tara (たら), **dara** (だら), *particle.* ❶ (假定條件のとき) if; in case. ❷ (旣定條件のとき) when.

tarafuku (鱈腹), *ad.* fully; to one's heart's content. —たらふく食ふ, to eat one's fill; gorge oneself. ⌈wash-basin.

tarai (盥), *n.* a tub; a basin; a⌋

tarasu (垂らす), *vt.* ❶ to hang down; let fall. ❷ (滴) to drop; dribble; spill. ⌈cajole; wheedle.

tarasu (蕩す), *vt.* to coax;⌋

taratara (滴滴), *ad.* dripping.

tarazu (足らず), *ad.* nearly; not quite; inside of 【米】. ——, *prep.* less than; close upon. —百圓足らずの金, a sum less than one hundred *yen*. —一哩 ⦅時間⦆ 足らず, less than a mile ⦅an hour⦆; a short mile ⦅hour⦆.

tare (誰), *pron.* ❶ who (が); whose (の); whom (に, を). ❷ (誰か) some one; any one. ☞ ***dare*** (誰). —誰も彼も, one and all; every individual; all the world and his wife. ⌈excrete.

tareru (放れる), *v.* to let off;⌋

tareru (垂れる), *vt.* ❶ (垂下) to hang down; droop. ❷ (賜與) to confer; grant; bestow. ❸ (遺す) to bequeath; leave. ——, *vi.* to hang; droop (首など); trail (長髮など). ☞ ***sagaru*** (下がる). —洟 ⦅涎⦆ が垂れる, to run at the nose ⦅mouth⦆. —簾を垂れる, to hang down the bamboo blind. —憐を垂れる, to have compassion *on*; take pity *on*. —功名を竹帛に垂れる, to leave one's name on record. —範を後世に垂れる, to leave an example to the world. ⌈drop; dribble.

tareru (滴れる), *vi.* to drip;⌋

tari (たり), *particle.* and; or; now…now. —見たり聞いたり, what with seeing and what with hearing. —立ったり坐ったりする, to stand now and now sit. —降ったり照ったりする, to rain and shine in turn.

tariki (他力), *n.* the power of another; intercession. ¶ 他力本願, salvation worship.

taritsu (他律), *n.* heteronomy.

taru (樽), *n.* a cask; a barrel; a butt (大樽); a keg (小樽). —樽に詰める, to barrel [*vt.*]; put in a barrel. ¶ 樽口, a bung-hole; a bung (栓).

taru (足る), *v.* Ⓢ 足りる. ❶ (十分) to be enough; be sufficient; suffice. ❷ (價値ある) to be worth [worthy *of*]. —云ふに足らぬ, not worth mention(-ing). —…と言へば足る, suffice it to say that…. —手 ⦅金⦆ が足らぬ, to be short of hands ⦅money⦆. —取るに足らぬ人, a fellow not worth serious consideration; a person beneath notice.

-taru (たる), *suf.* 「とある」の省略, である. —臣民たる本分, one's duty as a subject. —何人たるを問はず, no matter who; irrespective of persons.

tāru (タール), *n.* tar. —タールを塗る, [*vt.*] to tar.

tarugaki (樽柿), *n.* persimmons seasoned in a *sake*-cask.

taruki (垂木, 桷), *n.* 【建】 a rafter.

tarumi (弛), *n.* ❶ (ゆるみ) loosening; slackening; sag. ❷ (懈怠) remissness; dulness (無活氣).

tarumu (弛む), *vi.* ❶ (ゆるむ) to slacken; become loose; sag. ❷ (撓む) to be relaxed; become dull (だれる). ❸ (怠ける) to become remiss. ¶ 弛んだ綱, a slack rope.

taryō (多量), *n.* a great [large] quantity; a great deal. —多量の, much; plentiful.

taryū (他流), *n.* another [a different] style; another school. ¶ 他流試合, a contest between followers of different schools.

tasai (多才), *n.* many-sidedness; versatility. —多才の, talented; versatile; many-sided.

tasatsu (他殺), *n.* murder; foul play. —他殺の疑あるを以て, being suspected of foul play.

tasei (多勢), *n.* =*tazei* (多勢).

tasha (多謝), *int.* ❶ (忝し) many [hearty] thanks. ❷ (あやまる時) a thousand apologies. —多謝多謝!, thanks, thanks; many thanks. —多謝する, to thank heartily.

tashi (足し), *n.* making up; supply. —何かの足しになる, to be good for something; serve some purpose. —これ丈けあれば餘程費用の足しになる, This money will go a long way towards paying my expenses.

tashi (たし), **tai** (たい), (I) wish; (I) should like to.

tashi (多士), *n.* many talents [intellects]. ¶ 多士濟々, full of talents.

tashika (確), *ad.* probably; perhaps. ☞ *tabun*.

tashika (確な), *a.* ❶ (確實) certain; sure. ❷ (確定) firm; definite; positive. ❸ (信賴すべき) reliable; trustworthy; authentic (典據ある). ❹ (安全) safe; secure. ❺ (分明) clear; evident. ❻ (強固) sound; firm. ❼ (腕の) able; competent. —確な人, a reliable person. —確な證人, a trustworthy witness. —確な證據, positive proof. —確な所から聞く, to hear from a reliable source. **—— -ni,** *ad.* ❶ (確實) certainly; for certain; to be sure; positively. ❷ (疑なく) undoubtedly; assuredly. ❸ (誓って) on [upon] my word [honour]; my life for it. ❹ (間違なく) without fail; at all events (どうなっても).

tashikameru (確める), *vt.* to ascertain; make sure (*of*); convince [assure] oneself *of*.

tashiki (多識), *n.* wide [extensive] knowledge; erudition. —多識の, well-informed; of wide knowledge.

tashimu (嗜む), *vt.* =*tashinamu* の ❶.

tashimae (足前), *n.* supply; boot; supplement. —足し前にする, to supply [supplement] the deficit; help [eke] out *with*.

tashinameru (窘める), *vt.* to reprove; reprimand; blame.

tashinami (嗜), *n.* ❶ (嗜好) relish; taste; fondness. ❷ (心掛) prudence; providence. ❸ (愼み) self-denial; self-constraint. ❹ (技藝) accomplishments. —嗜のよい女, a prudent woman.

tashinamu (嗜む), *v.* ❶ (好む) to be fond *of*; like; relish. ❷ (愼む) to be prudent; deny oneself.

tashinkyō (多神教), *n.* polytheism.

tashō (他生), *n.* a previous state of existence. —他生の緣, karma-relations from a previous state of existence.

tashō (多少), *ad.* more or less; large or small; in some measure; to a certain degree. **—— -no,** *a.* some; more or less. —多少の損失は覺悟してゐる, I am prepared for more or less loss.

tashū (他宗), *n.* another religion; another sect (of religion).

tashutsu (他出), *n.* going out. ☞ *gaishutsu*.

tasogare (黄昏), *n.* dusk; nightfall; gloaming.

tasokurui (多足類), *n.* 【蟲】 Myriapoda (學名); the millipeds.

tassha (達者な), *a.* ❶ (壯健) healthy; strong; robust. ❷ (巧者) skilful; expert; adept. —足が達者である, to have strong legs. —口が達者である, to be talkative [loquacious]; have a fluent [glib; long] tongue.

tasshi (達), *n.* a public [government] notification [proclamation]. ¶ 達書き, a notice; a notification.

tasshiki (達識), *n.* great insight; long sight.

tas-suru (達する), *v.* ❶ (遂げる) to attain; accomplish (成就); carry out (實行). ❷ (布達する) to notify. ❸ (熟達) to become proficient [versed] *in*. ❹ (到著) to reach; arrive *at*; get *to* (*at*). ❺ (數量の) to reach; amount *to*;

come *to*; run *to*. —武藝に達する, to be accomplished in military arts. —頭蓋骨に達する傷, a wound reaching [penetrating to] the skull. —十哩の速さに達する, to reach as far as ten miles.

tasu (足す), *vt.* ❶ (加へる) to add. ❷ (補ふ) to append; supplement.

tasu (達す), *vt.* to do. —用を達す, ① to do one's business; serve others (他人の). ② (便所で) to ease oneself [nature].

tasū (多數), *n.* a large [great] number; the many; the majority. —僅少の多數で, by bare [narrow] majority. —多數の力で勝つ, to win by (force of) number. —多數決で極める, to decide by majority. —多數を占める, to command a majority. ¶ 絶對多數, an absolute majority (投票の). ¶ 多數黨, a majority party.

tasukaru (助かる), *vi.* ❶ (危難より) to be saved [rescued; delivered] *from*. ❷ (勞力が省ける) to be relieved *of*; save one trouble. —やッと助かる, to have a narrow escape. —助からぬ者と諦める, to give oneself up for lost.

tasuke (助), *n.* ❶ (助力) aid; help; assistance; support (後援). ❷ (救助) rescue; relief. —...の助を藉りて, aided by; by the help of. —聲を揚げて助を呼ぶ, to cry aloud for help.

tasukebune (助船), *n.* a life-boat; a rescue-boat. —助船を出す, to put out a rescue-boat.

tasukeru (助ける), *vt.* ❶ (助力) to help; aid; assist. ❷ (救助) to save; rescue; succour. —助け合ふ, to help each other (one another). —病を扶けて出勤する, to go to office in spite of one's illness.

tasuki (襷), *n.* a cord used for girding up the sleeves. —襷掛けで働く, to work girded up with a *tasuki*.

tata (多多), *ad.* more and more. —多々益〻辨ずる, The more work one has, the more speedily one disposes of it. —かゝる例は他にも多々ある, There are many other instances of this kind.

tataeru (湛へる), *vt.* to fill; brim. —顔中に笑を湛へる, to clothe the face in smiles.

tatakai (戰), *n.* ❶ (合戰) a fight; a battle. ❷ (戰役) a war; a campaign. ❸ (闘爭, 競爭) a struggle; a strife; a contest. —戰を始める, to open hostilities; draw the sword. —闘を挑む, to fling [throw] down the gauntlet; challenge to battle; provoke war. —戰を宣する, to declare war.

tatakau (戰ふ), *v.* to fight *with*; combat *with* (格闘); struggle *with* (困難などと). —誘惑と闘ふ, to fight against temptation.

tatakawasu (闘はす), *vt.* to fight; make a person fight. —論を闘はす, to join issue *with*; engage in wordy warfare.

tataki (敲・叩き), *n.* ❶ (たゝく事) pat; knock. ❷ (笞刑) whipping. ❸ (鳥獣肉の) mince-meat. ❹ (甃石) pavement; concrete facing.

tatakiageru (叩上げる), *v.* ❶ (急造する) to knock up. ❷ (練り鍛へる) to train oneself; work one's way up. —小僧から叩上げる, to work one's way up from an apprentice.

tatakiai (敲合), *n.* a scuffle; a fight; exchange of blows. —敲き合ふ, to fight; scuffle; exchange blows.

tatakidasu (敲出す), *vt.* ❶ to turn [put] out; drive out; expel. ❷ (打擲して去らす) to knock out; beat off.

tatakikomu (叩込む), *vt.* to strike *into*; hammer *into* (槌で); drive *into*; tamp (道路に砂利を). —本場で叩込んだ腕, skill acquired in the real place. —頭へ叩込む, to bang [beat] into another's head.

tatakikorosu (敲殺す), *vt.* to beat [flog] to death; thrash the life out of a person; strike dead.

tatakitsukeru (叩附ける), *vt.* to throw a thing (against a thing; at a person).

tataku (叩・敲く), *vt.* ❶ to strike; beat; knock; tap (輕打); rap (ことこと); clap (手を); slap (平手で). ❷ (烈しく攻撃する) to lash; attack; condemn. —叩き倒す, to knock down. —叩き落す, to knock [beat; strike] down. —敲き壊す, to knock to pieces; smash. —意見を敲く, to sound another's views. —新聞で叩かれる, to be lashed in the papers.

tatami (疊), *n.* ❶ (座敷の) a mat. ❷ (下駄・雪駄などの) a sole matting. —疊の上の水練, swimming on one's table. —疊附きの下駄, matted clogs. —疊を敷く, to lay mats. —疊換へをする, to reface a mat.

tatamibōshi (疊帽子), *n.* a gibus(-hat); an opera hat (高い).

tatamiisu (疊椅子), *n.* a camp-chair; a folding-chair.

tataminaifu (疊ナイフ), *n.* a clasp-knife; a folding-knife; a jack-knife (大形の).

tatamu (疊む), *vt.* ❶ (折返して重ね) to furl (帆等を); fold up; double over [up]; lap. ❷ (閉ぢる) to shut up; shut; close. ❸ (殺す) to settle another's hash [卑]. —著物の疊み方, a way of folding clothes. —布團を疊む, to fold the bedding. —世帶を疊む, to shut up one's house.

tatan (多端), *n.* ❶ (件數多し) many items; eventfulness (多事). ❷ (多忙) business. —多端の, busy; having one's hands full.

tatara (踏鞴), *n.* foot-bellows.

tatari (祟), *n.* a curse; malediction. —祟りある, accursed.

tataru (祟る), *v.* to incur a curse; be cursed *with*; haunt (怨靈が). —怨靈に祟られる, to be haunted by a vindictive spirit.

tatazumu (彳·佇む), *vi.* to stand; stop. —門口に彳む, to stand at the entrance.

tate (楯), *n.* a shield; a buckler (手楯). —楯に取って, on the authority *of*; under. —楯の半面を見る, to look only on one side of the shield. —楯をつく, to oppose; defy.

tate (縱, 竪), *n.* ❶ length (長さ); height (高さ). ❷ = ***tateito*** (經絲). ❸ (時間) time (space の對). —縱の, longitudinal; lengthwise; perpendicular. —縱に, lengthwise; longitudinally. (縱に列べる, to range one behind another; place end to end.)

-tate (たての), fresh *from*; hot *from*. —買ひ立ての, [*a.*] newly-bought. —學校出たての青年, a youth fresh from school. —生み立ての玉子, a new-laid egg.

tateami (建網), *n.* a set-net.

tateba (立場), *n.* ❶ (驛) a stand; a stage; a stopping place. ❷ (屑屋の市場) a ragmen's stand.

tateeri (立襟), *n.* a stand-up collar. —立襟の洋服, a coat with a stand-up collar.

tatefuda (立札), *n.* a notice-board.

tategami (鬣), *n.* a mane.

tategoto (竪琴), *n.* a harp.

tategu (建具), *n.* fittings; fixtures. ¶ 建具屋, a joiner.

tatehiza (立膝をする), to sit with one knee erect.

tateito (經絲), *n.* abb; warp.

tatejima (竪縞), *n.* vertical stripes; striped fabric. —竪縞の, striped.

tatekae (立替), *n.* advance (前拂); payment for another. —立替へる, to advance; pay for another. ¶ 立替金, advance. —立替料, charges forward.

tatekae (建替), *n.* reconstruction; re-erection; rebuilding. —建て替へる, to rebuild; reconstruct; re-erect.

tatekakeru (立掛ける), *vt.* to lean [rest; stand] *against*.

tatekata (建方, 立方), *n.* structure; build. ¶ 議論の立て方, the way of putting an argument.

tatekomoru (立籠る), *vi.* to shut oneself up; be confined; coop up [in]. —城中に立籠る, to shut oneself up in a castle; entrench oneself.

tatekomu (立込む), *vi.* to be pressed with business; be busy; be crowded (人で).

tatekomu (建込む), *vi.* (土地が) to be crowded with buildings; be built up.

tatemae (建前), *n.* house-raising; building the framework: celebration of the completion of the framework.

tatemashi (建增), *n.* an annexe; extension of a building. —建增しする, to add; extend; build an annexe.

tatematsuru (奉る), *vt.* to offer (to a superior); make an offering *of*.

tatemono (立物), *n.* a leading actor; a star; a lion; a leading [conspicuous] figure.

tatemono (建物), *n.* a building; a structure; an edifice (大建築).

taten (他店), *n.* another shop.

tatenaosu (立直す), *v.* ❶ (勢を盛返す) to recover one's energy; pull oneself together. ❷ (亂れた軍勢を) to rally; rearrange (the disposition of troops).

tateoyama (立女形), *n.* 【劇】 the leading actor [the star] in female parts.

tateru (立·建てる), *vt.* ❶ (竪にす) to stand. ❷ (起す) to erect; set up; raise. ❸ (建築) to build; construct; erect. ❹ (設立) to establish; found; organize (組織). ❺ (樹立) to pitch. ❻ (閉ぢる) to close; shut up. —保證人に立てる, to appoint a person one's surety. —新說を立てる, to set up a new theory. —會社を立てる, to establish a company. —身を立てる, to establish oneself in the world. —策を樹てる, to lay down a plan; form a plan. —噂を立てる, to set afloat a rumour. —煙を起てる, to emit smoke. —男を立てる, to show one's manliness; maintain one's dignity. —鋭を立てる, to stand a glass on end. —鋸の目を立てる, to sharpen the teeth of a saw. —指に棘[とげ]を立てる, to run a thorn into one's finger.

tatetōsu (立通す), *vt.* to retain [keep; maintain] to the end. ——, *vi.* to remain to the last. —後家を立て通す, to remain a widow till death.

tatetsubo (建坪), *n.* a building area.

tatetsuke (建附), *n.* shutting; fitting (備附け). —建附けがよい《惡い》, to shut well《badly》.

tateya (建家), *n.* a building.

tateyaku (立役), *n.* the leading part [business].

tateyakusha (立役者), *n.* the leading actor (*of*; *in*); the star (of a theatre).

tateyoko (縱橫), *n.* length and breadth; warp and woof (織物の). —縱橫に, lengthwise and breadthwise; crosswise (十文字に).

tatō (疊紙), *n.* a folding paper-case.

tatoe (譬), *n.* ❶ (諺) a proverb; a saying. ❷ (比喩) a parable; an allegory. ❸ (例) an illustration; an example. ❹ (比較) comparison.

tatoe (假令), *ad.* =*tatoi*.

tatoeba (例へば), *ad.* for example; for instance; *e. g.* [羅 exempli gratia の略].

tatoeru (譬へる), *vt.* ❶ (或事物を引きて說く) to illustrate. ❷ (或事物に比して說く) to liken *to*; compare *to*; use a simile《metaphor》. —人生を航海に譬へる, to compare [liken] life to a voyage.

tatoete (譬へて), *ad.* figuratively; metaphorically; by way of illustration.

tatoi (假令), *ad.* even if; although; admitting [granting] that. —假令死んでも, even if I died. —假令如何に貧乏でも, however poor I may be. —たとひ大臣であらうと何であらうと共分にして置かない, Minister or no minister, he shall smart for it.

ta-tosuru (多とする), *vt.* to be thankful [grateful] to a person *for*; appreciate.

tatsu (龍), *n.* a dragon.

tatsu (立·起·建つ), *v.* ❶ (立上る) to rise; stand up. ❷ (奮起) to gird up; come forward. ❸ (建設) to be built [erected]; be established; be founded. ❹ (出立) to start; leave; set off. —立ち乍ら, while standing; in a standing posture. —(病人など) 立って步く, to get on one's legs. —立ち詰める, to keep on one's legs; keep standing. —立っても居てもゐられない, to be unable to remain still (for excitement, anxiety, &c.) —よく立つ聲だ, He has a sonorous voice. —指に刺が立つ, A thorn runs into my finger. —君の說は立たぬ, Your view will not hold water. —九を三で割れば三が立つ, Nine by three makes three.

tatsu (裁つ), *vt.* to cut up; cut off. —此寸法で著物を裁って下さい, Please cut out the dress to this measure.

tatsu (絕·斷つ), *vt.* ❶ (斷截する) to cut off; break off; sever. ❷ (止める) to give up; leave off; abstain *from*. ❸ (遮斷·中斷する) to interrupt; intercept; cut off. —糧道を斷つ, to cut off supplies. —交際を絕つ, to cut off social relations (*with*); break off with a person. —酒と煙草を絕つ, to abstain from wine and tobacco.

tatsu (たつ), *vi.* ❶ (經) to pass; elapse; fly. ❷ (火·蠟燭が) to be burnt out. ——一月も經たぬに, in less than a month.

tatsugan (達眼), *n.* piercing eyes; far-sightedness. —達眼の士, a man with piercing eyes; a far-sighted man.

tatsujin (達人), *n.* ❶ (熟練家) an expert; an adept; a master. ❷ (悟道に入りし人) a past master.

tatsukuri (田作), *n.* =*gomame*.

tatsumaki (龍卷), *n.* a water-spout (海上); a sand-pillar (沙漠).

tatsunohige (龍の髯), *n.* 【植】 Diarrhena japonica (學名).

tatsunootoshigo (海馬), *n.* the hippocampus; the sea-horse.

tatta (只), *ad.* merely; only; but. —たった十, no more than ten; only ten. —たった今, (only) just (現在完了に伴ふ); just now (過去に伴ふ); this moment.

tatte (達て), *ad.* earnestly; importunately. —達ての望, an earnest desire.

tattobu (尊·貴ぶ), *vt.* ❶ (敬ふ) to respect; honour; hold in respect; revere. ❷ (重んず) to value highly; esteem; prize. —尊ぶべき, estimable; respectable. —武を尙ぶ, to hold militarism in high esteem.

tattoi (貴·尊い), *a.* ❶ (尊敬すべき) honourable; respectable; venerable. ❷ (高貴の) noble; exalted; high. ❸ (貴重の) valuable; precious. ❹ (高價の) dear. —金よりも貴い, more precious than money.

taue (田植), *n.* rice-transplantation. —田植する, to transplant rice. ¶ 田植時, the rice-planting season.

taukogi (田五加木), *n.* 【植】 the

bur-marigold; the water-agrimony.

tawainai (たわいない), *a.* ❶ (馬鹿げた) idle; stupid; senseless. ❷ (無邪氣な) innocent; childish; puerile. —たわいない話, prattle; nonsense; idle talk.

tawainaku (たわいなく), *ad.* ❶ (容易に) easily; without effort. ❷ (無心に) innocently. —たわいなく眠る, to sleep forgetful of all around. —たわいなく負ける, to be easily defeated; be defeated without difficulty.

tawake (戯), *n.* ❶ foolishness; stupidity. ❷ (馬鹿者) a dunce; a fool; an idiot; an ass. —此戯者め, You ass [idiot]. [foolery.]

tawakoto (戯事), *n.* a folly;

tawakoto (譫語), *n.* ❶ (たはけたる言語) silly talk; twaddle; nonsense. ❷ =*uwakoto*.

tawameru (撓める), *vt.* to bend. ☞ *tameru* (矯める).

tawamure (戯), *n.* ❶ (戯談) trifling; joke; jest; fun. ❷ (遊戯) a sport; play. ❸ (男女の) dalliance. —造化の戯れ, a freak of nature. —戯れの, sportive; playful. ——**-ni**, *ad.* for sport; for fun; in play; in jest. —戯れに言ふ, to say for fun.

tawamureru (戯れる), *vi.* ❶ (遊び) to play; sport. ❷ (戯謔) to sport; trifle *with*; make sport [fun] *of* (からかふ); make jokes (ふざける); frolic (同上). [bale.]

tawara (俵), *n.* a straw-bag; a

tawaramugi (たはらむぎ), *n.* 【植】 the pearl-grass.

tawashi (把蒭), *n.* a scrubbing-brush; a swab; a wisp.

tayasu (絶やす), *vt.* to eradicate; extirpate; put an end *to*. —菫の種を絶やす, to let the seed of the violet go out of stock.

tayasui (容易い), *a.* easy; simple.

tayasuku (容易く), *ad.* with ease; easily; readily.

tayō (多用), *n.* much business. —多用の, busy.

tayō (多様の), *a.* diverse; various.

tayō-hikōki (多葉飛行機), *n.* a multiplane.

tayoku (多慾), *n.* avarice; covetousness; greediness. —多慾の, greedy; avaricious; covetous.

tayori (便), *n.* ❶ news; tidings; intelligence. ❷ (寄邊) reliance; confidence; trust. —便りがない, to hear nothing *from*; have no tidings *from*. —便をする, to write (a letter) *to*. —…を便りとして, on the strength *of*; relying *on*.

tayoru (頼る), *vi.* ❶ to depend [rely; lean] *upon*; place reliance *on*. ❷ (當にする) to count [reckon; calculate] *on*. ❸ (助を求めて) to turn [look] to a person for help [assistance]. ❹ (信を置く) to trust *to*; put one's trust *in*.

tayū (大夫), *n.* ❶ (官職の) a lord-steward; a grand-master. ❷ (藝人の) a performer.

tayumu (撓む), *vi.* ❶ (弛む) to flag; relax (in one's effort). ❷ (弱る) to yield; give way *to*. ❸ (曲る) to bend.

tazei (多勢), *n.* a great number; great odds; a large company. —多勢を恃んで, relying upon numbers [their greater number].

tazuna (手綱), *n.* a rein; a bridle. —手綱を執る, to handle [take] the ribbons. —手綱を引締める《緩める》, to tighten 《slacken》 the reins.

tazuneru (訪ねる), *vt.* to call (*on* a person; *at* a house); visit; pay a visit *to*; inquire *for* (a person).

tazuneru (尋ねる), *vt.* ❶ (探す) to seek; search *for*; look *for*. ❷ (聞き質す) to ask; inquire; make inquiry. —尋ね出す, to seek and find out; seek out. —道を尋ねる, to ask [inquire] one's way. —眞理をたづねる, to search for truth. —安否を尋ねる, to inquire after a person [his health]. —理由を尋ねる, to inquire the reason of him. —草を分けても尋ね出さずには置かぬ, I will leave no stone unturned to hunt him out.

tazusaeru (携へる), *vt.* to carry (something) in one's hand (提げる); carry (something) with one (携帶); take [bring] (a person or something) with one (同上). —妻子を携へて旅行する, to go on a journey with one's family; take one's family for a journey.

tazusawaru (携はる), *vi.* to concern oneself *in*; be concerned *in*; have a hand [concern] *in*.

te (て), *particle.* and (例, deep and clear); as (例, as it is too difficult); for (例, for want of money).

te (手), *n.* ❶ (人の上肢) the hand (手); the arm (腕); the paw (猫などの). ❷ (手段) a way; a means; a trick (奸計). ❸ (手蹟) handwriting; writing; penmanship. ❹ (器具の把手) a handle. ❺ (種類) description; kind; sort. ❻ (方向) direction; quarter. ❼ (技倆) skill; art. ❽ (人手) a hand. ❾ (手札) a hand (骨牌戯). —手が上る, to become skilful [expert] *in*. —手が下る, to become poor *at*; get out of practice (不練習のため). —手が長い, to have light fingers; be light-fingered. —手が

廻る, ① to be well prepared *for*; be ready *for*. ② to go smoothly; get on without a hitch. —手が明いてゐる, to be disengaged [free; at leisure]; have no work in hand; have spare time. —手が塞がってゐる, to be busy [engaged]; have one's hands full. —手が足りない [廻り兼ねる], to be short of hands; be short-handed. —手も無く, without much trouble [any difficulty]. —手に乗る, to fall into a trap; play into the enemy's hand. —手にかける, ① (自らなす) to do oneself. ② (殺す) to kill by one's own hand. ③ (育てる) to bring up. —手に合はぬ [餘る; おへぬ], ① (制御し難い) to be above [beyond] control; be ungovernable [unmanageable; intractable]. ② (敵はぬ) to be more than one's match. ③ (力及ばぬ) to be beyond one's power [ability; capacity; control]. —手に入れる, to get [obtain]; get [gain] possession *of*; become master *of*. —手に汗を握って, with suppressed excitement; with breathless interest. —手に唾して起つ, ① to spit into one's hands and stand up. ② (蹶起) to rouse oneself; brace oneself up. —敵の手に落ちる, to fall into the enemy's hand. —手に手を執って, hand in hand. —手に手を盡す, to try every (possible) means; leave no stone unturned. —手を束ねて, with folded arms. —手を抜く, to do carelessly; scamp one's work. —手を離れる, to leave one's hand; go out of hand. —手を拍く, to clap one's hands. —手を出す, ① to put [hold] out a hand. ② (事業に) to try one's hand *in*; dabble *in* (相場に). (何にでも手を出す, to have a finger in every pie.) —手を下す, ① (着手) to put one's hand (to the plough). ② (從事) to get one's hand *in*; engage *in*. —手を燒く, to singe one's feathers [wings]; burn one's fingers. —手をつく, ①【相撲】(地に手をつく) to touch the ground with a hand. ② (あやまるとき) to be down on one's knees. —手を擴げる, ① to spread out one's arms. ② (事業など手廣くする) to extend one's business. —手を引く, ① to lead a person by the hand. ② (後へ) to back one's hand. ③ (關係を絕つ) to withdraw [retire] *from*; back out *of*; cry off. —手を切る, to wash one's hand(s) *of*; break *with*; severe one's connection *with*. —手を易へ品を易へて, by every imaginable means. —掌を合せて拜む, to pray with joined hands. —朝顏の手を遣る, to prop up the morning-glory plant. —村役場の手を經て, through the village office. —女の手一つで育てる, to bring up by the weak hand of a woman.

teaburi (手焙), *n.* a small brazier; a hand-warmer.

teaka (手垢), *n.* hand-soil; thumb-mark. —手垢のついた本, a hand-soiled book; a thumb-marked book.

teaki (手明の), *a.* disengaged; leisured.

teami (手編), *n.* knitting by hand. —手編みの靴下, hand-knit socks.

tearai (手洗), *n.* ❶ hand-washing. ❷ (手洗鉢) a wash-basin. ¶ 手洗水, water for hand-washing.

tearai (手荒い), *a.* rough; rude. —手荒いことをする, to act violently; resort to force [violence].

tearaku (手荒く), *ad.* roughly; in a rough manner; ruggedly. —手荒く取扱ふ, to handle in a rough manner.

teashi (手足), *n.* hands and feet; the limbs.

teatari (手當り), *n.* ❶ (手ざはり) feel. ❷ (手に觸ること) coming to hand. —手當り次第持ち出す, to carry away everything within reach [whatever comes to hand].

teate (手當), *n.* ❶ (給與金) an allowance. ❷ (準備) preparation; provision. ❸ (傷病者の) treatment; dressing (傷などの). —手當をする, ① (準備) to provide *for*; make provision. ② (傷病の) to treat; dress. —手當が行屆いたので助かった, As he was properly treated, he was saved from death. ¶ 戰時手當,【軍】field (service) allowance.

teatsui (手厚い), *a.* courteous; hospitable; cordial.

teatsuku (手厚く), *ad.* hospitably; with cordiality; courteously. —手厚く待遇する, ① to treat with great hospitality; give a warm [cordial] treatment. ② (報酬) to give handsome treatment; treat handsomely.

teawase (手合) *n.* ❶ (勝負) a game; a bout (擊劍). ❷ (商の) a sale; a bargain. —手合せする, ① to have a game. ② to strike a bargain.

tebako (手箱), *n.* a toilet-case; a casket (寶玉などの).

tebanasu (手放す), *v.* ❶ (手を放す) to remove the hand; quit [let go] hold *of*. ❷ (賣却, 讓與) to dispose *of*; part *with*; make away *with*. ❸ (手許を離れさす) to let go; dismiss. ❹ (監視せぬ)

to leave unlooked-after. 一愛児を手放す, to send away [part with] one's dear child.

tebaru (手張る), *vi.* to be too much for one to do; be more than one can manage.

tebashikoi (手捷い), *a.* nimble; quick; adroit.

tebataki (手拍), *n.* ❶ (拍手) clapping one's hands. ❷ (全部を盡す) being exhausted; having no more on hand.

tebayai (手早い), *a.* nimble; quick; adroit.

tebikae (手控), *n.* ❶ (覺帳) a note-book; a memorandum-book. ❷ (事業などの範圍縮少) curtailment; reduction; contraction. —手控を取る, to note; note [jot] down; make a note *of*.

tebikaeru (手控へる), *vt.* ❶ to note. ❷ to withhold; hold off; keep back *from*.

tebiki (手引), *n.* ❶ (指導) guidance; a guide (案内人, 栞). ❷ (紹介) introduction. ❸ =*tezuru* (手蔓). —手引する, ① (手を引く) to lead a person by the hand. ② (指導する) to guide; lead.

tebiroi (手廣い), *a.* ❶ (構廣き) roomy; wide; spacious. ❷ (範圍の廣き) extensive. —手廣く商賣する, to do extensive trade; carry on business on a large scale.

tebukuro (手袋), *n.* a glove; a mitten (半手袋); kids (仔山羊革製の); a muffle [muffler] (拳闘用の). —手袋をはめる《とる》, to put on 《take off》 one's gloves.

tebunko (手文庫), *n.* a hand-box; a casket.

tebura (素手, 空手), *n.* an empty hand.

tēburu (テーブル), *n.* a table. ¶ テーブル掛, a table-cloth (食卓用); a table-cover (裝飾用).

tebyōshi (手拍子をとる), to beat time with the hands.

techigai (手違), *n.* a mistake; a blunder; a mishap. —手違ひになる, to go wrong with one.

techō (手帳), *n.* a note-book; a memorandum-book.

tedai (手代), *n.* a clerk; a shop-assistant; a shopman; a salesman.

tedama (手玉), *n.* (玩具) dib-stones; jackstones; chuckstones. —手玉をとる, to play at dibs. —大の男を手玉にとる, to keep a fellow under one's thumbs; turn a man round one's little finger.

tedashi (手出し), *n.* meddling; interference. —手出しする, to put one's hand *to*; meddle *in*; strike the first blow (先に手出しする).

tedasuke (手助), *n.* help; aid; assistance. —手助けになる, to be helpful; be a help *to*; be of service *to*.

tedate (手段), *n.* a means; a measure.

tedōgu (手道具), *n.* utensils.

tedorikin (手取金), *n.* net receipt [proceeds]; balance in hand.

tefuda (手札), *n.* a visiting-card; a card; a hand (骨牌戯). ¶ 手札形寫眞, a *carte-de-visite* 〔佛〕.

tefūkin (手風琴), *n.* an accordion; a concertina; a hand-organ.

tegai (手飼の) *a.* pet; reared [fed] by oneself.

tegakari (手掛り), *n.* ❶ (手を懸ける所) a hold. ❷ (搜索の便宜) a clue. —手掛りになる, to give the clue. —まだ何の手掛りもない, There is as yet no clue whatever.

tegami (手紙), *n.* a letter; a note (尺牘); favour (敬語, 特に商用). —昨日《本日》の御手紙, your letter of yesterday's date 《of even date》. —人に手紙を出す, to send a letter to a person.

tegara (手柄), *n.* an exploit; an achievement; a meritorious deed. ☞ *kō*. —…手柄にする, to make a merit *of*. —手柄をする, to distinguish oneself *in*.

tegaru (手輕の), *a.* light; easy; simple; plain. —手輕に, easily; off-hand. ¶ 御手輕料理, a (quick) lunch; a light meal; plain cooking. —手輕料理店, a buffet; a refreshment bar.

tegata (手形), *n.* ❶ (手に墨をつけて押す形) a hand-mark; a hand-print. ❷ a bill; a note; a draft. —手形に裏書する, to back [indorse] a bill. —手形を振出す, to draw a bill *on*. —手形を更新する, to renew a bill. —手形を切る, to discount a bill. —手形を支拂ふ, to take up [receive] a bill. ¶ 持參人《指圖人》拂手形, a note to bearer 《order》. —手形帳, a bill-book. —手形振出人, the drawer (of a bill). —手形引受人, an acceptor. —手形交換所, a (bankers') clearing-house. (手形交換所組合銀行, a clearing bank; an associated bank 〔米〕.) —手形受取人, the payee (of a bill). —手形割引, discounting of a bill.

tegatai (手堅い), *a.* firm; secure; steady; trustworthy. —手堅く營業をやる, to carry on business steadily.

tegawari (手代), *n.* one who relieves another at work; a substitute.

tegire (手切), *n.* severing of relations; rupture. —手切れにする, to sever one's relations *with*; break *with*. ¶ 手切れ金, a solatium for severing relations.

tegiwa (手際), *n.* skill; dexterity; workmanship (細工). —見事な手際, a clever stroke; a master-stroke. —手際よく片附ける, to settle tactfully [skilfully]. —手際を見せる, to display one's skill [dexterity]; execute skilfully.

tegokoro (手心), *n.* discretion. ☞ ***tekagen***. —手心を用ひる[加へる], to use one's discretion.

tegome (手込), *n.* Ⓢ 手込み. outrage; violation; doing by force. —手込めにする, to violate; outrage; do violence *to*.

tegoro (手頃の), *a.* handy; moderate (値段). —手頃の辭書, a handy dictionary.

tegotae (手應), *n.* rebound; kick. —手應へがある, to feel the kick; offer resistance (抵抗する); have effect (效果ある).

tegowai (手剛い), *a.* tough; hardy; unyielding. ☞ ***tezuyoi***.

teguruma (手車), *n.* ❶ (手押車) a hand-cart; a barrow; a truck (トロッコ); a trolley (物資の曳く). ❷ (自家用人力車) a private *jinrikisha*.

tegusu (天蠶絲), *n.* wild-cocoon silk.

tegusune (手藥煉引いて待つ), to wait fully prepared *for*.

tehai (手配), *n.* =***tekubari***.

tehajime (手初め), *n.* the outset; the commencement; the beginning. —手初めに, at the outset [beginning]; to begin [start] with.

tehazu (手筈), *n.* arrangement; order. —手筈を定める, to arrange beforehand.

tehidoi (手酷い), *a.* severe; violent. —手ひどい打擊を受ける, to suffer a heavy blow; be hard hit.

tehodoki (手解), *n.* ❶ teaching of introduction; instruction in the rudiments. ❷ (初步) ABC; introduction; rudiments (初步). —手ほどきする, to teach [instruct] rudiments *of*; initiate a person *into*.

tehon (手本), *n.* ❶ (習字の) a copy-book. ❷ (型,見本) a pattern; a model. ❸ (模範) a model; an example. —手本にしてよい行ひ, exemplary conduct. —手本とする, to follow another's example; take a leaf out of another's book. —よい手本を示す, to set a good example.

tei (邸), *n.* a mansion. —邸內に, on the premises; in the compound; in the grounds.

tei (帝), *n.* an emperor; an empress (女帝).

tei (體), *n.* ❶ (外觀) appearance. ❷ (狀態) condition. —體のよい免職, virtual dismissal. —體のよい事を云ふ, to say fine things to keep up appearances.

teian (提案), *n.* a proposal; overtures; a proposition. —提案する, to propose; make overtures; put forward a proposal. ¶ 提案者, a proposer.

teiatsu (低壓), *n.* low pressure; low tension.

teibō (堤防), *n.* a bank; an embankment; a dike, dyke (和蘭海岸などの). —堤防を築く, to construct an embankment; embank.

teichaku (定著), *n.* settlement; fixation; fixing (寫眞の). —定著する, to fix (色・寫眞などを); take [strike] root; be attached *to* (land, 土地に). ¶ 定著物, 【法】a fixture. (土地の定著物, things fixed to land.) ¶ 定著液, 【寫眞】a fixer; a fixing solution.

teichi (低地), *n.* lowlands; low ground; low-lying land.

teichi (定置の), *a.* stationary; fixed.

teichō (低潮), *n.* the neap; the neap-tide.

teichō (艇長), *n.* a coxswain (短艇の).

teichō (鄭重), *n.* courtesy; civility. ☞ ***teinei***. —鄭重な, courteous; civil; polite. —鄭重に取扱ふ(人を), to treat with consideration.

teiden (停電), *n.* ❶ the stoppage of electric current; the giving out of the electric power. ❷ (電車の) a tie-up. —停電する, ① The electric current is (cut) off. ② (電車が) to be tied up.

teido (程度), *n.* standard; degree; extent (範圍). —入學試驗の程度, the standard of the entrance-examination. —中等程度の學校, a school of the middle-school standard [grade]. —或程度までは讓步する, to concede [yield] to a certain extent.

teien (邸園), *n.* a (private) garden.

teien (庭園), *n.* a (flower) garden.

teigaku (定額), *n.* a fixed amount [sum]. ¶ 定額戾入, refunding the appropriations.

teigaku (停學), *n.* rustication; suspension from attendance. —停學する, to rusticate; suspend from school; send down. —停學を命ぜらる, to be suspended from attendance at school.

teigen (低減), *n.* ❶ (縮少) reduction. ❷ (低落) fall; depreciation. —低減する, ① to reduce; cut [bring] down; make a reduction *of*. ② to fall; depreciate.

teigen (定限), *n.* limit; bound; restriction (制限). —定限する, to limit; restrict.

teigen (遞減), *n.* decrease in order; retardation (遠力). —遞減する, ① [*vt.*] to decrease in order; scale down. ② [*vi.*] to diminish gradually.

teigi (定義), *n.* a definition. —定義を下す, to give a definition; define.

teigi (提議), *n.* a proposal; a proposition; an overture. —政府の提議にて, at the instance of the authorities. —提議する, to propose; make a proposal.

teigin (低吟), *n.* singing in a low voice; humming.

teigyō (定業), *n.* a regular employment [occupation].

teihaku (碇泊), *n.* anchoring; anchorage; mooring. —碇泊する, to anchor; come to anchor; cast [drop] anchor (投錨). —碇泊してゐる, to be [lie; ride] at anchor. ¶ 碇泊料, demurrage (滯船料) —碇泊所, an anchor; a moorage; a berth.

teihatsu (剃髮), *n.* tonsure; shaving the head. —剃髮する, to shave the head; tonsure; enter the Buddhist priesthood.

teihen (底邊), *n.* 【數】the base.

teihyō (定評), *n.* a settled opinion.

teii (帝位), *n.* the (Imperial) Throne; emperorship. —帝位に上る, to ascend the Throne.

teiin (定員), *n.* full [fixed; regular] number (of persons); full personnel; regular strength (of a staff); regular staff; 【軍·航】complement. —定員に達する, to reach [come up to] regular number. ¶ 平《戰》時定員, 【軍】 peace 《war》 establishment.

teiji (呈示), *n.* presentation. =「*teishi*.」

teiji (定時), *n.* a fixed time 《period》. ¶ 定時刊行物, a periodical. —定時總會, an ordinary general meeting.

teiji (遞次), *ad.* successively; in order; gradually.

teijitsu (定日), *n.* a fixed date; an assigned [appointed] day (指定の日).

teijo (貞女), *n.* a chaste [virtuous] woman.

teijū (定住する), *vi.* to domicile; settle (down); reside permanently.

teika (低下), *n.* lowering; fall; sinking; depression. —低下する, to sink; fall; go down.

teika (定價), *n.* a fixed [set] price. —定價通りに賣る, to sell at the fixed price. —半定價で賣る, to sell at half the price [half-price]. ¶ 定價表, a price-list; a priced catalogue.

teika (遞加), *n.* successive addition; increasing; acceleration. —遞加する, to add successively; increase; accelerate.

teikai (低回する), *vi.* to roam [wander; loiter] (about).

teikai (停會), *n.* suspension of a meeting. —停會する, to suspend a meeting.

teikan (定款), *n.* articles of association; a company contract.

teike (手活), *n.* arrangement in a vase by oneself. —手活の花と眺める, to look at as one's own.

teikei (定形), *n.* a fixed form.

teikei (定型), *n.* a type.

teikei (定繫する), *v.* to anchor at the usual place. ¶ 定繫場, a fixed moorage [anchorage].

teikei (梯形), *n.* ❶【數】a trapezoid. ❷【軍】an echelon formation (二梯陣).

teikei (提携), *n.* alliance; concert; coalition. —相提携して, in concert [union] *with*. —ある政黨と提携する, to identify one's interests with a certain political party.

teiken (定見), *n.* a definite opinion [view]; conviction (確信). —定見が無い, to have no fixed view of one's own.

teiketsu (締結), *n.* conclusion. —締結する, to conclude; enter into; make.

teiki (定期), *n.* ❶ (定まれる期限) a fixed [stated] period [term]. ❷ (投機) dealing in futures. —定期に, at stated periods [intervals]. ¶ 定期航海, 【航】regular service. —定期米, rice sold on time. —定期船, 【航】a (regular) liner. —定期試驗《改選》, a periodical examination 《re-election》. —定期預金, a fixed deposit.

teiki (提起する), *vt.* to institute; present; lodge. —訴訟を提起する, to institute [lodge] a lawsuit; bring an action *against*; prepare a charge *against*.

teikiatsu (低氣壓), *n.* low (atmospheric) pressure; (atmospheric) depression.

teikin (提琴), *n.* a fiddle. —提琴を彈奏する, to fiddle; play on a fiddle. ¶ 提琴弓, a fiddle-bow; a fiddle-stick.

teiko (艇庫), *n.* a boat-house.

teikō (抵抗), *n.* resistance; opposition; defiance. —抵抗する, to resist; stand (up) *against*; offer resistance; defy. —抵抗し得る《難き》, resistible 《irresistible》. —抵抗を受ける, to encounter [meet with] resistance. ¶ (加減)抵抗器, a rheostat. —抵抗力, power of resistance; resisting power. —最小抵抗線, the line of least resistance.

teikoku (定刻), *n.* the regular [fixed] time [hour]; the appointed time [hour] (指定の時刻). —定刻迄に, by the appointed [regular] hour.

teikoku (帝國), *n.* ❶ an empire. ❷ (日本國) the Empire of Japan; the Japanese Empire. ¶ 帝國大學, the Imperial University. —帝國議會, the Imperial Diet. —帝國主義, imperialism. (帝國主義者, an imperialist.)

teikū (低空), *n.* a low altitude.

teikyō (提供), *n.* offer; tender; proffer. —辨濟の提供を受領する, to accept the tender of performance. **——-suru,** *vt.* to offer; tender; proffer. —有利の條件を提供する, to offer advantageous conditions.

teikyū (低級), *n.* low standard [grade]; inferiority. ¶ 低級讀者, a low-grade reader. —低級趣味, low taste.

teikyū (庭球), *n.* (lawn-)tennis. —庭球用の球, a tennis-ball. ¶ 庭球場, a tennis-court; a lawn-tennis ground. —庭球單《複》試合, a tennis single 《double》 match [game].

teikyū (涕泣する), *vi.* to weep.

teikyūbi (定休日), *n.* regular holidays.

teimei (低迷する), *vi.* to hang low.

teimei (締盟), *n.* conclusion of a treaty. —締盟する, to conclude a treaty. ¶ 締盟國, a treaty power (條約國); a signatory power (署名國).

teimen (底面), *n.* (砲眼の) the sole; 【數】 the base.

teinei (丁寧), *n.* ❶ (丁重) politeness; courteousness; civility. ❷ (注意) care; carefulness. —丁寧な, polite; civil; courteous. **——ni,** *ad.* politely; courteously. —丁寧に挨拶する, to greet politely.

teinen (丁年), *n.* majority; full age; lawful age; manhood. —丁年に達する, to come of age; attain [reach] one's majority. ¶ 丁年者, a major; an adult.

teinen (停年), *n.* age limit; seniority. —停年に達する, to reach the age limit. ¶ 陸軍停年名簿, an army list (with the names of officers in order of seniority).

teinō (低能), *n.* a weak head [mind; intellect]; weak-mindedness; feeble-mindedness. ¶ 低能兒, a feeble [weak]-minded child.

teiō (帝王), *n.* an emperor; a sovereign.

teion (低音), *n.* 【音】 bass; a low-pitch sound.

teippai (手一杯), *n.* a handful; the utmost of one's power (力一杯). —手一杯に暮らしてゐる, to be living to the limit of one's means. —手一杯の仕事をしてゐる, to be working with one's hands full.

teiraku (低落), *n.* fall; decline; depreciation. —低落する, to fall; decline; go down; depreciate.

teirazu (手不入), *n.* ❶ (手數なきこと) no trouble. ❷ (手を加へざること) being untouched.

teire (手入), *n.* ❶ (修理) repairing; mending. ❷ (世話) taking care (*of*); trimming (樹·庭等の). ❸ (警官の) raid. —博奕場の手入, a raid on a gambling-den. —手入の屆いた庭, well-kept grounds. —手入をする, to repair; mend; take care *of.*

teirei (定例), *n.* established usage; established rule.

teiren (低廉な), *a.* cheap; of low price.

teiri (低利), *n.* low interest. ¶ 低利貸金, a low-interest loan. —低利資金, a low-interest fund: cheap money 【俗】.

teiri (定理), *n.* 【數】 a theorem.

teiritsu (定律), *n.* ❶ (定法) a fixed law. ❷ 【數·理】 a law. ❸ 【音】 fixed rhythm.

teiritsu (定率), *n.* a fixed rate.

teiritsu (鼎立), *n.* a triangular position; taking a triangular position. —鼎立する, to take a triangular position; make a triangle.

teiron (定論), *n.* a fixed opinion; a fixed theory (學術上の).

teiryō (定量), *n.* a fixed quantity. ¶ 定量分析, quantitative analysis.

teiryū (停留), *n.* stoppage; stop. —停留する, to stop; halt. ¶ 停留場, a stopping-place; a stop; a station.

teisai (體裁), *n.* style; form; show; appearance; make-up (衣服·本等の); set-up (同上); format (本の). —體裁のよい, decent; seemly; graceful; decorous; plausible. —體裁の惡い, awkward; unseeming. —體裁を裝ふ, to keep up appearances.

teisatsu (偵察), *n.* reconnaissance; scout; patrol. —偵察する, to reconnoitre; scout; patrol. ¶ 偵察(飛行)機, a scout; a scouting plane; a scout-plane. —偵察巡洋艦, a scout-cruiser. —偵察將校 [兵], a scout. ¶ 偵察隊, a reconnoitring-party; a patrol.

teisei (低聲に), *ad.* in a low voice; under one's breath; in a whisper.

teisei (定性), *n.* a fixed quality. ¶ 定性分析, 【化】 qualitative analysis.

teisei (訂正), *n.* revision; correction; rectification; amendment. —訂正する, to revise; correct; rectify; amend. ¶ 訂正增補, revised and enlarged.

teisei (帝政), *n.* imperial government [rule; regime]

teisen (汀線), *n.* 【地】 beach (line).

teisen (停船), *n.* stopping (of a

vessel); stoppage; detention (抑留). —停船する, to heave to; bring a ship to; stop. —停船を命ずる, to order the stopping of a ship; order a ship to heave to.

teisetsu (貞節), *n.* chastity; constancy; virtue.

teisha (停車), *n.* stoppage; stop. —停車する, to stop [halt] *at*. ¶ 普通停車, a service stop. —非常停車, an emergency stop. —停車場, a station; a railway station; a depot 〔米〕. (停車場構內, a station yard).

teishi (呈示), *n.* presentation. —呈示次第, 【商】 at presentation. —呈示する, to present; show.

teishi (底止する), *v.* to come to an end [a stop]; cease.

teishi (停止), *n.* ❶ stop; halt; standstill. ❷ (中止) suspension; stoppage; discontinuance. —— **-suru,** *v.* to stop; halt; suspend; discontinue. —仕拂を停止する, to suspend [stop] payment.

teishiki (定式), *n.* a formula; regularity. ¶ 定式總會, a regular general meeting.

teishin (挺身·挺進する), *vi.* to go [advance] ahead of the others.

teishin (遞信), *n.* communications. ¶ 遞信大臣, the Minister of Communications; the Postmaster-General 〔英〕. —遞信省, the Department of Communications; the Communications Department.

teishitsu (帝室), *n.* the Imperial House [Family]; the Imperial Household. ¶ 帝室技藝員, the court artist; the art committee to the Imperial Household. —帝室博物館, the Imperial Museum.

teishō (提唱する), *vt.* to advocate; advance; bring forward; introduce; lecture on (講義).

teishō (遞相), *n.* = *teishin* (遞信大臣).

teishōgai (低障害), *n.* 【競技】 a low hurdle(-race).

teishoku (定食), *n.* diet; ration (一日の); table d'hôte (料理店の).

teishoku (定職), *n.* a regular occupation [employment].

teishoku (停職), *n.* suspension from office. —停職を命ぜらる, to be suspended from office.

teishoku (牴觸), *n.* collision; conflict; contradiction. —— **-suru,** *vi.* to collide *with*; conflict *with*; be in conflict *with*; be contradictory [contrary] *to*. —法律に牴觸する to be contrary to law.

teishu (亭主), *n.* ❶ (夫) a husband. ❷ (主人) a master; a host (客に對して). ❸ (宿の) a landlord; a host.

teishuku (貞淑な), *a.* chaste; virtuous; modest.

teishutsu (提出), *n.* presentation; lodgement (抗議·問題等); introduction. —— **-suru,** *vt.* to present; offer; lodge; introduce (議案); produce (證據); bring forward (同上). —辭表を提出する, to tender [send in] one's resignation. —法律案を提出する, to initiate projects of law; file a bill. —議會に豫算を提出する, to introduce the Budget to the Diet. ¶ 提出者, a presenter; a proposer; a mover (動議の).

teisō (貞操), *n.* chastity; virtue; faithfulness. —貞操を守る, to remain faithful [chaste]. —貞操を破る, to break one's chastity; stray from the path of virtue. —貞操を蹂躙する, to defile [trifle with] a woman's chastity.

teisō (遞送), *n.* conveyance; forwarding. —遞送する, to convey; forward; send by post.

teisoku (定則), *n.* 【數】 a law; a rule; an established rule.

teisokusū (定足數), *n.* a quorum. —定足數に達する, to come up to the quorum.

teisoshiki (定礎式), *n.* 【建】 laying of the foundation-stone.

teisū (定數), *n.* ❶ a fixed [full] number; a quorum (定足數); 【數】 a constant. ❷ (運命) fate.

tei-suru (呈する), *vt.* to present. ❶ (贈る) to make a present *of*; offer. ❷ (表はす) to show; display. —赤色を呈する, to turn [come out] red. —奇怪な現象を呈する, to exhibit strange phenomena. —精神に異狀を呈する, to show a deranged condition of mind.

teitai (停滯), *n.* ❶ stagnation; accumulation (堆積). ❷ (食物の) retention in the stomach. —停滯せる, stagnant (水など); sluggish; stationary (文明·人口等). —— **-suru,** *vi.* to be stagnant; be sluggish; accumulate. —貨物が停滯してゐる, Goods remain undelivered. —食物が胃に停滯してゐる, Food is retained in the stomach.

teitai (梯隊), *n.* 【軍】 echelon.

teitai (艇隊), *n.* a flotilla.

teitai (手痛い), *a.* heavy; severe. —手痛い打擊を受ける, to suffer a heavy blow; be hard hit.

teitaku (邸宅), *n.* a mansion; a residence.

teitaraku (爲體) *n.* a condition;

a state of things; plight.

teitei (廷丁), *n.* a crier; a court-attendant.

teitetsu (蹄鐵), *n.* a horseshoe; a shoe. —蹄鐵形の, horseshoe; U-shaped. —蹄鐵を打つ, to shoe (a horse). ¶ 蹄鐵工, a farrier. —蹄鐵所, a farriery.

teito (帝都), *n.* the Imperial capital.

teitō (低頭する), *vi.* to bow; droop one's head.

teitō (抵當), *n.* ❶ (行爲) mortgage; security (擔保). ❷ (物) a mortgage; a security. —抵當に入れる, to mortgage; put [lay] in mortgage. ¶ 抵當權, mortgage. (抵當權者, a mortgagee. —抵當權設定者, a mortgagor.)

teitoku (提督), *n.* a squadron commander; an admiral 〔英〕; a commodore 〔米〕.

teiton (停頓), *n.* standstill. —(談判など) 停頓する, to come to a standstill.

teiyō (提要), *n.* an outline; an epitome; a summary; a gist.

teiyoku (體よく), *ad.* plausibly. —體よく斷る《返す》, to decline 《return》 with thanks.

teiza (鼎坐する), *vi.* to sit in a triangle.

tejaku (手酌で飲む), to drink *sake* by helping oneself to it.

tejika (手近な), *a.* close by; near by; hard by. —手近な例, a familiar example. —手近に, close by; (near; close) at hand; within reach.

tejina (手品), *n.* ❶ jugglery; sleight of hand; conjuring tricks. ❷ (欺瞞) cheating; deceit; a trick (狡猾な手段). —手品を使ふ, to make the pass; juggle; do conjuring tricks; play a person a trick (瞞す). ¶ 手品師, a conjuror; a juggler.

tejō (手錠), *n.* a handcuff; manacles; a wristlet; irons. —手錠を嵌める, [*vt.*] to handcuff; manacle; put (a person) in irons.

tejun (手順), *n.* ❶ (順序) order. ❷ (手筈) arrangements. ❸ (手續) procedure; routine. ❹ (過程) process; course. —手順が狂ふ, to get out of order. —手順を定める, to prepare a programme; make arrangements.

tekagen (手加減), *n.* discretion (裁量); allowance (斟酌); knock (こつ). —手加減する, to make allowance *for*; take into consideration.

tekagi (手鉤), *n.* a hook; a stevedore's hook.

tekase (手械), *n.* handcuffs; manacles; irons. —手械をかけられる, to be handcuffed.

tekazu (手數), *n.* trouble. ☞ *tesū.*

teki (滴), *n.* a drop. —香水二三滴たらす, to let fall a few drops of scent.

teki (敵), *n.* ❶ (仇敵) an enemy; a foe (仇者); a foeman (同上). ❷ (遊戲·討論·政治上等の) an opponent; an antagonist; an adversary. —敵の, enemy; hostile. —敵に後を見せる, to turn the back on [show one's back to] the enemy.

tekichi (敵地), *n.* the enemy's land [territory].

tekibishii (手嚴しい), *a.* severe; hard. —手嚴しく返金を催促する, to press severely for payment.

tekichū (的中), *n.* hit; hitting the mark. —時弊に的中する, to strike home the abuses of the time.

tekichūrui (滴蟲類), *n.* 【動】 Infusoria.

tekidan (敵彈), *n.* the enemy's shell 《bullets》.

tekidan (擲彈), *n.* 【軍】 a grenade. ¶ 擲彈兵, a grenadier.

tekido (適度), *n.* moderation; proper degree; measure. —適度の, moderate; temperate; reasonable. —適度にする, to moderate; keep within limits.

tekigaishin (敵愾心), *n.* a hostile feeling; hostility; enmity. —敵愾心を起す, to give rise to hostile feelings.

tekigi (適宜), *n.* fitness; suitableness; convenience (便宜); discretion (裁量). —適宜の, ① fitting; suitable; appropriate; convenient. ② discretionary. —適宜に取計ふ, to manage at one's discretion; do [act] as one thinks fit. ¶ 適宜處分, a suitable measure [disposition].

tekigō (適合する), *vi.* to fit (*for*); conform *to*; accord *with*. —適合さす, to make fit *for* [equal *to*]; shape (a man; a thing); adapt.

tekigun (敵軍), *n.* the enemy's [hostile] army [troops; force]; the enemy.

tekihatsu (摘發する), *vt.* to expose; disclose; reveal. —人の惡事を摘發する, to expose a man's misdeeds.

tekihei (敵兵), *n.* a soldier of the enemy; the enemy's troops (敵軍).

tekihi (適否), *n.* propriety; suitability.

tekihō (適法の), *a.* legal; lawful; legitimate. —適法(の)行爲, a lawful act.

tekihon-shugi (敵本主義), *n.* a blind; a make-believe; a feint.

tekihyō (適評), *n.* just criticism.

tekii (敵意), *n.* hostility; hostile feeling; animosity. —敵意を挾

む, to harbour hostility.

tekijin (敵陣), *n.* ❶ (敵營) the enemy's [hostile] camp; the position of the enemy. ❷ (敵の隊) the ranks of the enemy; the enemy's line.

tekijō (敵情), *n.* the condition; movement (動靜); position (and strength) of the enemy. 一敵情を偵察する, to feel the enemy.

tekikaku (的確な), *a.* accurate; precise; exact.

tekikan (敵艦), *n.* an enemy ship.

tekiki (手利), *n.* ❶ expertness; adroitness. ❷ a master-hand; an expert person.

tekiki (敵機), *n.* an enemy [a hostile] plane [machine; craft].

tekikoku (敵國), *n.* a hostile power [country]; the enemy.

tekimen (覿面), *ad.* at once; immediately; swiftly. 一因果は覿面, Retribution comes swiftly.

tekimikata (敵味方), *n.* friend and foe; both sides.

tekin (手金), *n.* earnest [bargain] money. 一手金を打つ, to deposit earnest money.

tekinin (適任の), *a.* competent; well-fitted; well-qualified. ¶ 適任者, a well-qualified [fit] person; the right man in the right place. (彼は最適任者だ, He is most fitted to the post; He is the very man for the post.) 一適任證, 【軍】 a certificate of efficiency [fitness; competence].

tekiō (適應), *n.* adaptation; accommodation; appropriateness. **—— - suru**, *a.* adaptative; correspondent; appropriate. ——, *vi.* to fit; suit; be adaptable; correspond *with*. 一環境に適應する, to adapt oneself to environment. ¶ 適應性, adaptability.

tekipaki (てきぱき), *ad.* briskly; quickly; alertly; spiritedly.

tekirei (適例), *n.* a case in point; a good example [illustration].

tekirei (適齡), *n.* military age; conscriptive [conscription] age. ¶ 適齡者, a person of conscription age.

tekiryō (適量), *n.* a proper quantity.

tekiryō (滴量), *n.* 【藥】 drops.

tekisei (敵勢), *n.* ❶ (敵の軍勢) enemy's force [troops]. ❷ (敵の威勢) the enemy's spirit.

tekisetsu (適切な), *a.* fit; relevant; appropriate.

tekisha-seizon (適者生存), *n.* the survival of the fittest.

tekishi (敵視する), *v.* to regard with hostility; regard as enemy; be hostile *to*.

tekisho (適所), *n.* a right [proper] place. 一適材を適所に置く, to put the right man in the right place.

tekishu (敵手), *n.* (相手) a match; an opponent; an adversary; an enemy. 一敵手に落ちる, to fall into one's opponent's hand.

tekishutsu (摘出する), *vt.* ❶ (拔萃) to quote; extract. ❷ (摘發) to expose; point out openly. ❸ (剔出) to extract; remove.

teki-suru (敵する), *v.* ❶ (敵對する) to oppose; resist; stand against; antagonize. ❷ (匹敵する) to match; be a match *for*.

teki-suru (適する), *v.* to fit; suit; be (well) adapted. ——, *a.* fitting; suitable; adaptative. 一健康に適せる, favourable to health. 一飲《食》用に適する, to be good to drink 《eat》; fit for drinking 《eating》.

tekitai (敵對), *n.* hostility; antagonism. 一敵對する, =*teki-suru* の ❶. ¶ 敵對行動, hostilities; a hostile act; an act of hostility.

tekitei (滴定), *n.* 【化】 titration.

tek'itō (適當の), *a.* suitable; proper; appropriate; fitting. 一適當に, properly; suitably; befittingly; appropriately. 一適當な時に, in proper [good] time.

tekiyaku (適役), *n.* a post suited to one; an office fit for one.

tekiyaku (適譯), *n.* a good translation.

tekiyaku (適藥), *n.* a specific.

tekiyō (適用), *n.* application; adaptation. 一適用する, to apply; adapt.

tekiyō (摘要), *n.* a summary; a digest; an outline; an epitome. 一摘要する, to summarize; epitomize; sum up.

tekizai (適材), *n.* a man suitable for a post.

tekizu (手傷), *n.* a wound.

tekkai (撤回), *n.* withdrawal. **—— - suru**, *vt.* to withdraw; recall; take back; retract. 一議案を撤回する, to withdraw a bill. 一要求を撤回する, to recede from one's demand.

tekkan (鐵管), *n.* an iron tube; an iron pipe (大なる).

tekken (鐵拳), *n.* a fist; a clenched hand. 一鐵拳を加へる, to hit with a fist.

tekketsu (鐵血), *n.* blood and iron.

tekki (摘記する), *vt.* Ⓢ 摘錄. to summarize.

tekki (鐵器), *n.* ironware; hardware; iron (utensils). ¶ 鐵器時代, the iron age. 一鐵器商, an ironmonger; a hardwareman.

tekkin-konkurīto (鐵筋コンクリート), *n.* 【建】 steel concrete; concrete-steel; ferro-concrete.
tekkiri (てっきり), *ad.* certainly; surely; evidently.
tekkō (手甲), *n.* mittens.
tekkō (鐵工), *n.* an ironsmith; an iron-founder. ¶ 鐵工所, an iron-foundry; an ironworks.
tekkō (鐵坑), *n.* an iron mine.
tekkō (鐵鑛), *n.* an iron ore.
tekkotsu (鐵骨), *n.* an iron frame. ¶ 鐵骨建築, a steel-skeleton building. —鐵骨コンクリート, ferro [steel]-concrete.
tekkyo (撤去), *n.* removal; withdrawal; evacuation. —撤去する, to remove; withdraw (撤退); evacuate (明渡し).
tekkyō (鐵橋), *n.* an iron bridge.
tekkyū (鐵灸), *n.* a gridiron; a grid; a grill.
teko (梃子, 槓子), *n.* a lever; a handspike. —槓子で持上げる, to raise with a handspike.
tekozuru (手古摺る), *vi.* to be puzzled; be embarrassed; be gravelled.
tekubari (手配), *n.* arrangements (手筈); disposition (配置); preparation (準備). —手配りする, to arrange *for*; prepare *for*; make preparations *for*; dispose.
tekubi (手首), *n.* the wrist; the carpus.
tekuda (手管), *n.* a trick; trickery; an artifice; wiles.
tekuse (手癖), *n.* a characteristic of penmanship; mannerism. —手癖の惡い, thievish; light-fingered.
tema (手間), *n.* ❶ (時) time. ❷ (勞力) labour; work. ¶ 手間賃[代], wages; pay for job-work.
temadoru (手間取る), *vi.* to be delayed; be long *over* (*in*); take time.
temae (手前), *n.* ❶ (自分) I ❷ (相手に對する賤稱) you. ❸ (此方) this side. —橋の手前に, this side (of) the bridge. —手前味噌を竝べる[いふ], to praise oneself; sing [sound] one's own praise; blow one's own trumpet.
temakura (手枕), *n.* making a pillow of the arm; resting the head on the arm. —手枕する, to lay the head on the forearm.
temane (手眞似), *n.* a gesture; gesticulation; a sign (合圖). —手眞似をする, to gesticulate; make gestures; make a sign (合圖する).
temaneki (手招きする), *vt.* to beckon.
temari (手鞠), *n.* a hand-ball; a small ball. —手鞠をつく, to play at hand-ball.
temawashi (手廻し), *n.* preparation; arrangements. —手廻しする, to prepare *for*; make [get] ready *for*.
temijika (手短な), *a.* brief; short; simple (平易). ☞ *kantan*. —手短かに, briefly; shortly. (手短かに云へば, in short.)
temo (ても), *conj.* but; however; (even) if; (even) though. —降ッても照ッても, rain or shine. —どんなに金が掛かッても, no matter how much it costs.
temochi-busata (手持無沙汰である), to feel awkward [embarrassed]; be ill at ease.
temonaku (手もなく), *ad.* easily; with ease; without difficulty.
temoto (手許に), *ad.* at hand; within reach; on [in] hand (持合せて). —手許不如意である, to be short of money. ¶ 御手許金, the Privy Purse. —手許有金, 【商】 cash in [on] hand.
temukai (手向ひ), *n.* resistance; opposition. ☞ *teikō*.
temukau (手向ふ), *vt.* Ⓢ 手向ひする. to resist; oppose; stand up *against*; raise one's hand *against*.
ten (貂), *n.* 【哺乳】 Mustela melampus (marten の一種·學名).
ten (天), *n.* ❶ heavens. ❷ (空) the sky; the upper region. ❸ (天上界) Heaven; Paradise. ❹ (自然の道) nature; the course of nature. ❺=*tenmei*. ❻ (天道, 神) Heaven; Providence. ❼ (上部) top. —天に沖する, to soar into the sky (火焔等); run sky-high (意氣等). —天にも昇る心地する, to be transported with joy; feel like going to Heaven.
ten (典), *n.* a ceremony.
ten (點), *n.* ❶ a point (幾何學上·出發點·沸騰點の點); a dot (點線などの點); pip (トランプ面の) ❷ (斑點) a spot; a speck. ❸ (評點) a mark. ❹ (競技·遊戲の得點) a score; a point. ❺ (論點) a point. ❻ =*shōsūten* (小數點). —點が甘い (辛い), to be liberal (severe) with one's marks. —...の點より見れば, from the view-point *of*; viewed in the light *of*. —一點とる, to make a point. —點をつける, ① [*vt.*] (句讀點) to punctuate. ② (採點) to mark; give marks. —選擧で最高點を得る, to poll the highest at an election. —その點では一致する. We agree on that point.
tenaga (手長な), *a.* having long limbs; long-armed.
tenagazaru (手長猿), *n.* 【哺乳】

the gibbon; the long-armed ape.

tenaishoku (手内職), *n.* manual [light] home-occupation.

tenami (手並), *n.* skill; dexterity.

tenarai (手習), *n.* penmanship; learning to write. ☞ *shūji.* —手習する, to learn writing. —八十の手習, beginning to learn in old age. ¶ 手習草紙, a copy-book.

tenareru (手馴れる), *vi.* to get used *to.* —手馴れた, ① tame; trained. ② accustomed; used.

tenazukeru (手懐ける), *vt.* ❶ (馴らす) to tame; domesticate. ❷ (懐ける) to attach *to*; make familiar; conciliate; gain over.

tenbai (轉賣), *n.* resale. —轉賣する, to resell.

tenbatsu (天罰), *n.* retribution; vengeance [punishment] of Heaven; Nemesis (應報). —天罰を蒙る, to be punished by Heaven; incur Heaven's retribution.

tenbin (天秤), *n.* ❶ (衡) a balance; (a pair of) scales; a steelyard (桿秤). ❷ (棒) a pole. —天秤にかける, to weigh with a steelyard. ¶ 天秤棒, a pole.

tenbō (展望), *n.* a view; a prospect. —展望する, to view; look *upon*; have a view *of.* —展望がきく, to command a view (*of*). ¶ 展望鏡, a periscope; a kleptoscope. —展望車, an observation-car.

tenbun (天分), *n.* nature (天性); mission (天職); natural gifts. —天分に富む, to be highly gifted.

tenbutsu (典物), *n.* a pledge; a pawn. =***shichimotsu.***

tenchi (天地), *n.* ❶ (天と地) Heaven and Earth. ❷ (宇宙) the universe. ❸ (上下) top and bottom. —天地を震撼する, to shake the world. —自己の天地を開拓する, to cultivate one's own sphere [field].

tenchi (轉地), *n.* a change of air. —轉地する, to move; change; change one's abode. ¶ 轉地療養, treatment by change of air. (轉地療養をする, to try a change of air for one's health.)

tenchō (天頂), *n.* zenith.

tenchō (天聽に達する), to reach His Majesty's ears.

Tenchōsetsu (天長節), *n.* the Emperor's Birthday. —天長節祝日, the Imperial Birthday Celebration Day.

tenchū (天誅), *n.* the punishment of heaven; divine retribution. —天誅を加へる, to inflict Heaven's vengeance *on.*

tende (てんで), *ad.* at all; altogether. —てんで話にならぬ, to be altogether out of question.

tendeni (各自に), *ad.* Ⓢ てんでんに. each; severally; respectively. —てんでんに勝手な方へ行く, to go each his own way. —てんでんばらばらになる, to be scattered in all directions.

tendō (天道), *n.* the way of Heaven; Providence.

tenga (典雅), *n.* refinement; elegance. —典雅な, refined; elegant; graceful.

tengai (天外の), *a.* supercelestial. —魂天外に飛ぶ, to be transported to the seventh heaven; go off into ecstasies.

tengai (天涯), *n.* ❶ (水平線) the horizon; the sky-line. ❷ (遠地) a far country.

tengai (天蓋), *n.* ❶ (佛像等の) a silk parasol. ❷【建】a canopy; a baldachin; a ciborium (祭壇の).

tengaku (轉學), *n.* Ⓢ 轉校. change of school. —轉學する, to change [remove] to another school.

tengan (天顔), *n.* the Emperor's countenance. —天顔に咫尺する, to appear before His Majesty; present oneself before the Emperor.

tengansui (點眼水), *n.* an eye-lotion.

tengantsū (天眼通), *n.* supernatural vision.

tengi (轉義), *n.* Ⓢ 轉意. figurative meaning.

tengoku (天國), *n.* Heaven; Paradise.

tengoku (典獄), *n.* a prison governor.

tengu (天狗), *n.* ❶ a long-nosed goblin. ❷ (高慢な人) a braggart; a boaster. —天狗になる, to give oneself high airs; be stuck-up.

tengyō (轉業する), *vi.* to change one's employment [trade].

teni (天意), *n.* providence; the will of Heaven.

tenimotsu (手荷物), *n.* (personal) luggage【英】; baggage【米】; traps【俗】. ¶ 手荷物一時預所, a left-luggage office; a cloak-room. —手荷物取扱所, a luggage-office【英】; a baggage-office【米】.

tenin (店員), *n.* a clerk; a shop-assistant; a shopman; a shop-woman (女). ¶ 小店員, a shop-boy; a shop-girl (女).

tenioha (てにをは), *n.*【文】the particle; the post position (後置詞).

tenisu (庭球), *n.* a (lawn-)tennis.

tenji (典侍), *n.* a maid of honour.

tenji (點字), *n.* braille points [types]; the braille.

Tenjiku (天竺), *n.* ❶ (印度の古稱) India. ❷ (天) the heavens. ¶ 天竺牡丹,【植】the dahlia. —

天竺金巾；天竺木綿, T-cloths.

tenjin (天神), *n.* heavenly gods. ¶ 天神地祇, the gods of heaven and earth.

tenjō (天上), *n.* ❶ (天) heavens. ❷ (天國) Heaven; Paradise. ❸ =*shōten* (昇天). —天上より, from above [a high].

tenjō (天井), *n.* a ceiling. —天上知らずの相場, the ever-rising market. ¶ 天井裏, the rafters.

tenjō (天壤無窮の), eternal as heaven and earth; coextensive with heaven and earth.

tenjō (纏繞), *n.* twine. —纏繞する, to entwine; twine (round) (植物·蛇に云ふ); creep (植物). ¶ 纏繞植物, a creeper; a winder.

tenju (天授の), *a.* heaven-sent; gifted (by nature).

tenju (轉手), *n.* a peg; a tuning-peg; tuning-pin (ピアノの).

tenjū (塡充), *n.* filling; plugging; tamping. —塡充する to stuff; plug; tamp.

tenka (天下), *n.* ❶ (世界) the world. ❷ (全國) the whole country. ❸ =*chisei* (治世). —天下分目の戰, a decisive battle. —天下晴れての夫婦, husband and wife before all the world. —天下を取る[統一する], to bring the world [the whole country] under one's rule [sway]. ¶ 天下泰平, The country is in peace.

tenka (添加), *n.* annexing; addition. —添加する, to annex; affix; append. ¶ 添加物, an annexe; an appendix.

tenka (點火), *n.* ignition; firing. —點火する, to light; fire; kindle; ignite.

tenka (轉化), *n.* ❶ change; transformation; inversion. ❷【哲】becoming. —轉化する, to change; be transformed; be inverted.

tenka (轉訛), *n.* corruption.

tenka (轉嫁), *n.* ❶ (再度の嫁入) one's second marriage. ❷ (罪過·責任の塗附) imputation; shifting (責任·租税など). —轉嫁する, to impute *to*; shift (*on* another's shoulders).

tenkai (展開), *n.* ❶ development; evolvement. ❷【數】development; expansion. ❸【軍】deployment. —局面の展開, development of the situation. —展開する, ① [*vi.*] to develop; evolve; spread out (擴がる). ② [*vt.*] to expand; deploy (隊列を).

tenkai (轉回), *n.* 【音】inversion; *volta* 【伊】; revolution. —轉回する, ① [*vi.*] to revolve; rotate. ② [*vt.*]【音】to invert.

tenkan (轉換), *n.* conversion; turn. —轉換する, to convert; switch (電流を). ¶ 轉換期, a turning-point.

tenkan (癲癇), *n.* 【醫】epilepsy; falling sickness. —癲癇を起す, to have an epileptic fit; have a fit of epilepsy. ¶ 癲癇患者, an epileptic.

tenkei (天啓), *n.* (divine) revelation; revelation from heaven. —天啓の, apocalyptic(-al); revealed. ¶ 天啓敎, a revealed religion.

tenkei (典型), *n.* a type; a model; an ideal. —典型的, typical; model; representative.

tenken (天險), *n.* a natural fastness.

tenken (點檢), *n.* inspection. —點檢を受ける, to undergo an inspection. —機體を點檢する, to examine the machine.

tenki (天氣), *n.* ❶ (空模樣) the weather. ❷ (好天氣) fair [fine] weather. —上天氣, good [splendid; charming] weather. —嫌な天氣, wretched [nasty] weather. ¶ 天氣豫報, a weather-forecast.

tenki (天機), *n.* ❶ secrets of nature. ❷ (機密) a profound secrets. ❸ (天子の御機嫌) health of the Emperor. —天機を奉伺する, to pay one's respects to His Majesty.

tenki (轉記), *n.* 【簿記】posting.

tenki (轉機), *n.* a turning-point.

tenkin (天金), *n.* 【製本】gilt top.

tenkin (轉筋), *n.* cramp.

tenkin (轉勤する), *vi.* to change one's office; be transferred to another office.

tenko (點呼), *n.* roll-call; call-over. —點呼する, to call the roll; call over.

tenkō (天候), *n.* weather. ☞ *tenki*. ¶ 天候險惡, threatening weather; rough weather.

tenkō (轉向), *n.* angular turning. —轉向する, to slew, slue; turn.

tenkoku (篆刻), *n.* seal-engraving.

tenkū (天空), *n.* the sky; the air; the firmament.

tenkyo (典據), *n.* authority.

tenkyo (轉居), *n.* (house) removal; change of residence [abode]. —轉居する, to remove *to*; move *into*. ¶ 轉居先, the place to which one has removed.

tenma (天魔), *n.* a demon; a devil. —天魔に魅られる, to be tempted by a devil; be possessed by [of] a demon.

tenma (傳馬), *n.* ❶ a post-horse. ❷ (傳馬船) a barge; a sampan; a junk's boat.

tenmado (天窓), *n.* a skylight;

a scuttle; a dormer-window.
tenmaku (天幕), *n.* a tent.
tenmatsu (顚末), *n.* the details; an account; the circumstances.
tenmei (天命), *n.* destiny; providence; the will of Heaven.
tenmen (纏綿たる), *a.* clinging; entangled (纏れ); involved (同上).
tenmō (天網), *n.* the net of Heavens; providence. —天網恢恢疎にして漏さず, "The mills of the gods grind slowly but surely."
tenmon (天文-學), *n.* astronomy. ¶ 天文臺, an (astronomical) observatory. —天文學者, an astronomer.
tenmondō (天門冬), *n.* 【植】 Asparagus lucidus (asparagus の一種·學名).
tennen (天然), *n.* ❶ (自然) nature. ❷ (自生) spontaneity. ☞ *shizen*. —天然の, ① (人工を加へざる) natural; unartificial; native (金屬等の). ② (自生) spontaneous. ③ (生得の) natural; innate. —天然に, naturally; innately; spontaneously. ¶ 天然物, a natural object. —天然色寫眞, a photograph in natural colour; a chromophotograph. —天然水, natural water. —天然痘, 【醫】 smallpox.
tennin (轉任), *n.* change of post [office; service]; transfer. —轉任する, to be removed [transferred] to another post.
tennō (天皇), *n.* the Emperor. ¶ 天皇旗, the Imperial standard.
tennyo (天女), *n.* a maid of heaven; a houri.
tenohira (掌), *n.* 【解】 the palm [flat] (of the hand).
tenokō (手の甲), *n.* the back of a hand.
tenomono (手のもの), *n.* ❶ (得意) specialty; something in one's line. ❷ (掌中の物) a thing in one's hand. ❸ =*buka* (部下).
teṅon (天恩), *n.* ❶ (造化の恵) blessing of Heaven. ❷ (天子の恩) the benevolence of the Emperor.
teṅōsei (天王星), *n.* 【天】 Uranus.
tenosuji (手の筋), *n.* the lines of the palm. ☞ *tesō*.
tenpan (典範), *n.* ❶ (法式) a law. ❷ =*mohan* (模範).
tenpen (天變), *n.* ❶ (天災) a natural calamity [disaster]. ❷ an extraordinary sign in the heavens. ☞ *chii* (地異).
tenpen (轉變), *n.* transition; chops and changes.
tenpi (天日), *n.* the sun; sunlight. —天日で干す, to dry in the sun. ¶ 天日製鹽, bay-salt; salt obtained by spontaneous evaporation. 「[米].」
tenpo (店舗), *n.* a shop; a store
tenpo (塡補) *n.* filling (塡充); making up (補償). —塡補する, to fill; make good [up]; cover.
tenpu (天賦の), *a.* natural; innate; inherent.
tenpu (添附), *n.* ❶ affixture; annexing. ❷ 【法】 accession; accretion. —添附する, to append; affix; annex; add. ¶ 添附書類, appended papers; annex(e).
tenpu (轉付), *n.* ❶ transference. ❷ 【法】 assignment. —轉付する, to transfer *to*; assign *to*. ¶ 轉付命令, an order of assignment.
tenpuku (顚覆), *n.* ❶ (顚倒) upset; overturn; overthrow. ❷ (破滅) collapse; overthrow. —顚覆する, to upset; overturn; fall (政府·國家など); collapse (同上); overthrow (同上); 【航】 capsize; turn turtle.
tenpura (天麩羅), *n.* fried food. —天麩羅の金時計, a gold-plated watch. 「inspired.」
tenrai (天來の), *a.* heavenly;
tenran (天覧), *n.* the Emperor's inspection. —天覧を賜はる, to be honoured with His Majesty's inspection.
tenran (展覽), *n.* ❶ (陳列) exhibition; display; show. ❷ (披き見る事) seeing something by unfolding. ¶ 展覽會, an exhibition; an exposition; a show.
tenri (天理), *n.* nature; a natural law [principle]; a law of nature.
tensai (甜菜), *n.* 【植】 the red beet.
tensai (天才), *n.* (才) a genius; a natural talent [gift]: (人) a (man of) genius.
tensai (天災), *n.* an act of God [nature]; a natural calamity.
tensai (轉載), *n.* reproduction; quotation. —轉載する, to reproduce; quote *from*. —轉載を禁ず, "Reproduction prohibited."
tensaku (添削, 點刪), *n.* correction; revision. —添削する, to correct; revise; touch up.
tensan (天蠶), *n.* 【蛾】 the Japanese oak silk-moth.
tensanbutsu (天產物), *n.* natural produces [products].
tensei (天性), *n.* nature; natural disposition. ——, *ad.* by nature; naturally; constitutionally. —習慣は第二の天性, "Habit is a second nature."
tensei (展性), *n.* malleability.
tenseki (轉籍), *n.* transfer of one's domicile. —轉籍する, to transfer one's (permanent) domicile.

tensen (點線), *n.* a dotted line.
tensen (轉戰する), *v.* to fight in one place after another; shift operations.
tensetsu (點綴), *n.* interspersion. —點綴する, to intersperse; dot; stud.
tensha (轉寫), *n.* transcription; transference. —轉寫する, to transcribe; transfer (圖形を, 特に轉寫紙にて石版に).
tenshadai (轉車臺), *n.* 【鐵道】a turntable.
tenshaku (轉借), *n.* subtenancy; under-tenancy; borrowing at second hand. —轉借する, to borrow [rent] at second hand.
tenshi (天使), *n.* an angel; a seraph. ¶ 天使長, an archangel.
tenshi (天資), *n.* nature; constitution; natural quality.
tenshin (天眞), *n.* naïveté; simplicity; artlessness. —天眞爛漫な, open-hearted; simple-minded; straightforward. (天眞爛漫の人, a simple soul; an open-hearted man.)
tensho (添書), *n.* ❶ (紹介狀) a letter of introduction. ❷ (推薦狀) a letter of recommendation.
tensho (篆書), *n.* a seal-character.
tenshō (天象), *n.* an astronomical phenomenon.
Tenshōkōdaijin (天照皇太神), *n.* the Sun-Goddess.
tenshoku (天職), *n.* a mission (in life); a vocation; a calling. —天職を全うする, to fulfil [carry out] one's mission.
tenshoku (轉職する), *vt.* to change one's employment [trade].
tenshu (天主), *n.* God; the Lord of Heaven; Jehovah. ¶ 天主教, the Roman Catholic Church; Roman Catholicism.
tenshu (天守 -閣), *n.* a castle-tower.
tenshu (店主), *n.* a shopkeeper; a storekeeper【米】; the head of a firm.
tenshuku (轉宿する), *vi.* to change one's lodgings; change one's boarding house.
tensō (轉送), *n.* transmission; transference: translation (電信の中繼). —轉送する, to transmit; forward (郵便等); transfer: translate (電信を).
tensoku (天則), *n.* law of nature; natural law.
tensoku (纏足), *n.* foot-binding.
tenson (天孫), *n.* the Emperor's grandson; the Sun-Goddess's grandson (天照太神の孫).
tensū (點數), *n.* (the number of) marks; score (遊戲の); the number of articles (品物の). ☞ *ten.*
tensui (天水), *n.* rain-water. ¶ 天水桶, the rain-tub; a rain-water tank.
tentai (天體), *n.* a heavenly [celestial] body. —天體の運動, movements of heavenly bodies. —天體を觀測する, to observe heavenly bodies; make an astronomical observation.
tentai (轉貸), *n.* sublease; underlease; subletting. —轉貸する, to underlet; sublet; subrent.
tentan (恬淡), *n.* indifference; simplicity; disinterestedness. —恬淡な, indifferent; simple; disinterested.
tentei (天帝), *n.* God; Heaven.
tenteki (點滴), *n.* a drop; dripping; rain-drops (雨滴).
tentekomai (天手古舞), *n.* ❶ (狼狽) topsyturvydom. ❷ (欣喜雀躍) dancing with joy. —天手古舞する, ① to be in confusion; go topsyturvy. ② to dance with joy; be in raptures.
tenten (輾轉), *n.* rolling and tumbling; jactation. —輾轉する, to roll and tumble; wallow.
tenten (轉轉), *ad.* ❶ (所有主を轉ず) by changes; changing hands; from hand to hand. ❷ (轉がる) rolling. ❸ (居所を轉ず) from place to place. —轉々する, ① to change hands; pass through many hands; go round from hand to hand. ② to go rolling. ③ to wander about from place to place.
tentetsu (轉轍する), *vt.* to switch (汽車を). ¶ 轉轍手, a switchman; a pointsman; a shunter.
tento (天幕), *n.* a tent; an awning. —天幕を張る《取外す》, to pitch 《strike》 a tent.
tento (奠都), *n.* establishment of the capital.
tentō (天道), *n.* ❶ (自然) nature. ❷ (太陽) the sun. ❸ Heaven; providence. ☞ *tendō.* —天道生[ぇ]の, self-sown; unplanted.
tentō (店頭), *n.* a shop-front; shop. —店頭の裝飾陳列, window-display. ¶ 店頭裝飾術, window-dressing.
tentō (點燈), *n.* lighting. —點燈する, to light a lamp. ¶ 點燈夫, a lamp-lighter. —點燈料, light-charge.
tentō (顚倒), *n.* ❶ (顚覆) overturning; inversion; reversal (逆倒). ❷ (狼狽) topsyturvydom; bewilderment; confusion. —顚倒する, ① to overturn; capsize; tumble; reverse. ② to be confused; be bewildered.
tentō (纏頭), *n.* a gratuity; a perquisite (慣習的). ☞ *shūgi.*
tentōmushi (瓢蟲), *n.* 【昆】 Ptychanatis oxyridis (ladybird の一種·學名)

tentori (點取), *n.* competition for marks. ¶ 點取表, a score; a score-sheet.

ten-toshite (恬として), *ad.* with composure; coolly; indifferently. —恬として恥ぢず, not to feel any disgrace [shame]; be barefaced.

tenugui (手拭), *n.* a towel; a hand-towel. ¶ 手拭掛, a towel-horse [-rack]; a towel-roller (roller-towel, 卷手拭の).

tenukari (手拔り), *n.* an oversight; an omission; a slip. ☞ *teochi*.

tenukume (手煖套), *n.* a muff (婦人の).

teṅun (天運), *n.* destiny; fate; fortune; lot. ☞ *unmei*.

tenurui (手緩い), *a.* ❶ (緩慢) slack; lax; tardy. ❷ (やさしい) mild; gentle.

teṅyo (天與), *n.* a gift of Heaven. —天與の, natural; heaven-sent.

teṅyu (諂諛), *n.* flattery; adulation; obsequiousness.

teṅyū (天佑), *n.* the grace of Heaven; special Providence. —天佑に依り, by the grace of God.

ten-zuru (點ずる), *vt.* to light; switch (電燈): drop (滴らす).

ten-zuru (轉ずる), *v.* ❶ (變轉) to change; turn; divert. ❷ (廻轉) to rotate; revolve. ❸ =*iten* (移轉). —針路を轉ずる,【航】to go [put] about. —話頭を轉ずる, to change the subject [topic].

teochi (手落), *n.* a slip; an oversight; an omission. —手落ちなく, thoroughly; perfectly; without any slip.

teodori (手踊), *n.* dancing; posture-dancing.

teoi (手負), *n.* a wound; a wounded person (人).

teoke (手桶), *n.* a pail; a bucket.

teokure (手後れになる), to be too late; be delayed.

teomoi (手重い), *a.* ❶ (取扱の鄭重な) courteous. ❷ (容易ならぬ) serious; grave.

teono (手斧), *n.* a hatchet; an adze.

teori (手織の), *a.* home-woven; homespun. —手織の著物, homespun clothes.

teppai (撤廢), *n.* removal; abolition (廢止). **—— - suru,** *vt.* to remove; abolish (廢止). —差別を撤廢する, to do away with the discrimination.

teppei (撤兵), *n.* withdrawal of troops; evacuation. —撤兵する, to withdraw troops; evacuate.

teppeki (鐵壁), *n.* an iron wall.

teppen (天邊, 天頂), *n.* the top; the summit; the crown. —頭の天邊から足の爪先まで, from the crown of the head to the tip of the toe.

teppitsu (鐵筆), *n.* ❶ (印刻用小刀) a seal-graver; a burin. ❷ (鐵の筆) an iron stylus. ❸ a steel pen.

teppō (鐵砲), *n.* ❶ (小銃) a gun; a musket; a rifle. ❷ (据風呂の釜) a bath-furnace. —鐵砲に彈を塡(ツ)める, to load a gun. ¶ 鐵砲玉, ① (彈丸) a bullet; a ball; a gunshot. ② (菓子) a bull's-eye. ¶ 鐵砲鍛冶, a gunsmith.

teppu (テップ), *n.* a tape. —テップを切る,【競技】to breast the tape.

tera (寺), *n.* a Buddhist temple [monastery]; an abbey. —寺へ參詣する, to visit [go to worship at] a temple. ¶ 寺守, a sexton.

teranpu (手洋燈), *n.* a hand-lamp.

terasu (照らす), *vt.* ❶ (光を映ず) to shine *upon*; shed light *on*; cast [throw] a light *on*. ❷ (燭らす) to lighten; illuminate. ❸ (比較, 參照) to compare *with*; collate. —肝膽相照らす, to know [understand] each other thoroughly. —法律に照らして處分する, to deal *with* according to law.

terau (衒ふ), *vt.* to boast *of*; parade; flaunt. —學識を衒ふ, to be pedantic; exhibit [parade; display] one's learning.

terepin (テレピン), *n.* turpentine. ¶ テレピン油, (oil of) turpentine; oil of terebinth; turps.

tereru (てれる), *vi.* ❶ (興さめる) to lose interest. ❷ (跋が惡い) to feel awkward; be ashamed. —てれ隱しに, in order to hide [cover up] one's awkward position.

teriame (照雨), *n.* the devil beating his wife.

terikaeshi (照返し), *n.* (反射) reflection: (反照器) a reflector.

teritsukeru (照附ける), *vi.* to shine *upon*; blaze *upon* (燒附ける).

teriyaki (照燒), *n.* fish broiled with sauce.

teru (照る), *vi.* to shine.

tēru (兩), *n.* 〔支那〕a tael.

teryōji (手療治する), *v.* to use self-treatment; doctor oneself.

teryōri (手料理), *n.* home-cookery.

tesage (手提-袋), *n.* a reticule (婦人の); a lady's bag. ¶ 手提鞄, a hand-bag; a hand-satchel; a valise. —手提籠, a hand-basket. —手提金庫, a portable [handy] cash-box.

tesaguri (手探), *n.* feeling; groping. —手探りで行く, to feel [grope] one's way.

tesaki (手先), *n.* ❶ the hand; the fingers. ❷ =*teshita*. ❸ (お先) a tool; a cat's paw. —手先の器

用な, dextrous, dexterous. —手先に使ふ, to make a cat's paw of a person; use as a tool.
tesei (手製の), *a.* ❶ hand-made. ❷ domestic; home-made[-spun].
teshita (手下), *n.* a follower; an adherent; a following (集合的).
teshoku (手燭), *n.* a candlestick; a hand-lamp.
teshoku (手職), *n.* a handicraft; a handiwork.
tesō (手相), *n.* the lines of the hand; palmistry (手相術). —手相を見る, to see the lines of the hand; tell fortunes by the palm of the hand; practise chiromancy. ¶ 手相術, palmistry; chiromancy. —手相見, a palmist; a chiromancer.
tessaku (鐵柵), *n.* an iron railing; an iron fence.
tesseki (鐵石), *n.* ❶ (鐵と石) iron and stone; adament (堅石). ❷ (甚だ堅きこと) firmness. —鐵石の如くである, to be firm as adamant. ¶ 鐵石心, an iron will.
tessen (鐵泉), *n.* a ferruginous [chalybeate] spring.
tessenka (鐵線花), *ad.* 【植】 the large-flowered clematis.
tesshō (徹宵), *n.* all night; throughout the night; all the night through.
tessō (鐵窓), *n.* ❶ (鐵格子窓) an iron window. ❷ (獄屋) a prison. —鐵窓の下に呻吟する, to pine in prison.
tes-suru (徹する), *v.* to pierce; penetrate. —夜を徹して, throughout the night; all night. —心魂に徹する, to come home to one's heart. —怨み骨髓に徹する, to be penetrated with resentment.
tes-suru (撤する), *vt.* to withdraw (兵・議案等); remove (撤去); strike (陣・天幕等). —橋を撤する, to demolish a bridge.
tesū (手數), *n.* trouble. ☞ *mendō*. ¶ 手數料, ① (公務) a fee. ② (口錢) a commission; percentage; brokerage (仲立の).
tesuji (手筋), *n.* ❶ (手の筋) the lines of the hand. ❷ (手蹟) hand.
tesuki (手隙), *n.* leisure; leisure moments; spare time. —お手隙なら, if you have spare time; if you are free [disengaged].
tesuri (手欄), *n.* a hand-rail; a railing; a balustrade.
tetenashigo (父無兒), *n.* a bastard; a love-child; a natural [an illegitimate] child.
tetsu (轍), *n.* a rut; a track. ☞ *fukutetsu*. —…の轍を履む, to follow [tread] in the steps [footsteps; wake] of.
tetsu (鐵), *n.* iron. —鐵製の, iron.
tetsuan (鐵案), *n.* an immutable decision.
tetsubin (鐵瓶), *n.* an iron pot.
tetsudai (手傳), *n.* ❶ (事) help; assistance. ❷ (手傳ひ人) a help; a helper; an assistant.
tetsudau (手傳ふ), *vt.* to help; assist; lend a hand [helping hand].
tetsudō (鐵道), *n.* a railway; a railroad 【米】. —鐵道便で, per rail. —鐵道往生する, to die by being run over by a train. —鐵道を敷設する, to lay [construct; build] a railway. ¶ 地表鐵道, a surface-road. —市街《市外》鐵道, a street 《suburban》 railway. —鐵道案内所, a railway inquiry office. —鐵道大臣, the Minister of Railways. —鐵道從業員, a railway operative. —鐵道管理局, the Railway Superintendence Bureau. —鐵道作業局, the Railway Construction Bureau. —鐵道線路, a railway (line); a (railway) track (軌道). —鐵道省, the Department of Railways; the Railway Department. —鐵道隊, railway corps. —鐵道運賃, railway fares 《rates, 荷物の》; freight-tax 【米】. —鐵道輸送, transportation by rail.
tetsugaku (哲學), *n.* philosophy. ¶ 哲學者, a philosopher.
tetsuiro (鐵色), *n.* iron-blue.
tetsujin (哲人), *n.* a sage; a wise man; a philosopher.
tetsujōmō (鐵條網), *n.* barbed-wire entanglements (棘あるもの). —鐵條網を張る, to set wire entanglements.
tetsuke (手附-金), *n.* earnest-money; bargain money; deposit. —手附をうつ, to pay [advance] earnest-money; make a deposit.
tetsumenpi (鐵面皮), *n.* (brazen) face; impudence; effrontery. —鐵面皮な, impudent; brazen-faced; barefaced. —鐵面皮にも…する, to have the impudence [face; cheek] *to*.
tetsuran (鐵欄), *n.* an iron railing. —鐵欄で圍む, [*vt.*] to rail in.
tetsuri (哲理), *n.* philosophy; philosophical principles.
tetsya (徹夜), *n.* sitting up all night; vigil. —徹夜する, to sit up [stay up] all night; keep vigil (不寢番して).
tetsuzuki (手續), *n.* procedure; formalities; process. —手續をする, to take steps; go through the procedure. —相當の手續を經る, to pass [go] through proper formalities.
tettai (撤退する), *vt.* to withdraw *from*; evacuate (a place; a position, *etc.*).
tettei (徹底), *n.* thoroughness;

completeness. —徹底的, thorough; complete; exhaustive. —徹底さす, to bring it home to their hearts. —徹底する, to be thorough-going ⦅exhaustive⦆; reach [go to] the bottom *of*; get at the root *of*.

tettoribayai (手取早い), *a.* prompt; rough and ready.

tettō-tetsubi (徹頭徹尾), from beginning to end; from first to last; from top to bottom; throughout; thoroughly.

tettsui (鐵鎚), *n.* an iron hammer; a sledge-hammer (大鎚). —一大鐵槌を下す, to deal a heavy blow *on*. ¶ 鐵鎚投げ,【競技】throwing the hammer.

teuchi (手打), *n.* ❶ (和解) reconciliation. ❷ (取引成立) striking a bargain.

teue (手植), *n.* personal plantation. —皇太子殿下御手植の松, the pine-tree planted by the Crown Prince.

teusui (手薄い), *a.* (薄い) thin; weak: (乏しい) scanty; slender.

tewake (手分), *n.* forming into parties; dividing; allotment. —手分けして探す, to separate and make search; seek in parties.

tewatashi (手渡), *n.* delivery; handing over. —手渡しする, to hand over; hand personally.

tewaza (手技, 手業), *n.* ❶ (手業) manual labour [work]; hand work. ❷ (手技) skill; feat. ☞ *waza*.

tezawari (手觸), *n.* feel; touch. —手觸りのよい, silky; velvety. —手觸りが柔い, to feel soft; be soft to the feel [touch].

tezei (手勢), *n.* one's body of troops.

tezema (手狹な), *a.* narrow; small; confined.

tezukami (手掴), *n.* seizing [taking] with the fingers. —手掴みで物を食べる, to eat a thing with one's fingers.

tezukara (手づから), *ad.* with one's own hand; oneself; personally (親しく).

tezuma (手妻), *n.* = *tejina*.

tezume (手詰の), *a.* pressing; decisive (決定的); final (最後の). —手詰めの談判, an ultimatum; a final move.

tezuri-kikai (手刷機械), *n.* a hand-press.

tezuru (手蔓), *n.* a means (手段); influence [interest] (つて); connection (緣故); a clue (手掛り).

tezusabi (手遊), *n.* diversion; pastime.

tezuyoi (手强い), *a.* firm; resolute; severe. —手强く刎ね附ける, to reject firmly.

to (と), *n.* 【音】G; sol【伊】; 5.

to (と), *conj.* ❶ (及び) and. ❷ (日時) when; as; as soon as. ❸ (假定) if. ❹ (といふ事) that. —, *prep.* ❶ (共に) with. ❷ (交換) for; with. ❸ (間違) for. ❹ (目的) to. ❺ (變化) into. —, *ad.* ❶ (及び) as well as. ❷ (共に) along with; accompanied *by*. ❸ (目的) with intention; in order to; (so) that...may.

to (戶), *n.* a door; a shutter (窓の); a sliding-door (引戶). —戶を開ける⦅閉める⦆, to open ⦅shut; close⦆ the door.

to (堵), *n.* a fence; an enclosure. —堵に安んずる, to live in peace.

to (途), *n.* a way; a road. ☞ *michi*. —上京の途に上る, to start on a journey to the capital.

tō (十), *n.* ten; half a score.

tō (刀), *n.* a sword; a sabre (軍刀); a knife (小刀). ☞ *katana*.

tō (塔), *n.* a tower; a pagoda; a steeple (會堂の); a tope (墓石); an obelisk (方尖塔).

tō (等), *n.* grade; class; degree. —一⦅二⦆等星, star of the first ⦅second⦆ magnitude. —罪一等を減ず, to reduce a penalty by one degree.

tō (等), and so on [forth]; and others; *et cetera* 【羅. =and the rest.】 (etc. 又は &c. と略す).

tō (當), *n.* justice; propriety. —當を失する, to be unfair; be unjust; be improper.

tō (當), ❶ (當該) in question; the said. ❷ (現今の) this. —當の敵, the enemy aimed at.

tō (頭), *n.* a head. —牛十二頭, twenty head of cattle.

tō (黨), *n.* a party; a league (徒黨); a clique (同類). —黨を組む, to form a league [party]; clique together. —黨內黨を立てる, to form a faction [a party within a party].

tō (薹), *n.* a spike. —薹が立つ, to go [run] to seed; pass [have passed] her bloom (女).

tō (籐), *n.* ❶ 【植】 the chair-bottom cane. ❷ rattan; cane.

tōa (東亞), *n.* East [Eastern] Asia. —東亞の, East-Asian [-Asiatic].

toami (投網), *n.* a casting-net; a cast-net. —投網を打つ, to shoot a fishing-net; throw a cast-net.

tōan (答案), *n.* an answer (答); an examination-paper (答を書けるもの); a paper (同上). —答案を調べる, to look over examination-papers. ¶ 答案用紙, an examination-paper.

tōan (偸安), *n.* idleness; procrastination. —偸安する, to temporize; procrastinate.

toaru (とある), *a.* a; a certain.

tōasa (遠淺), *n.* a shoal (of great width); a shallow.

tobae (鳥羽繪), *n.* a caricature; a comic picture. ¶ 鳥羽繪師, a caricaturist.

tobaku (賭博), *n.* gambling; play; gaming. ☞ *bakuchi*. —賭博する, to gamble; play dice 《card》. ¶ 賭博者, a gambler.

tōban (當番), *n.* ❶ (番に當ること) being on duty; one's turn for duty; the person on duty (其人). ❷ (宿直) a person on night-duty. ¶ 掃除當番, one's turn for sweeping. —當番士官, 【海】 an officer of the deck.

tobari (帷, 帳), *n.* a curtain; a hanging; hangings; a screen (帳).

tobashiri (飛沫), *n.* ❶ (しぶき) splash; spatter. ❷ (傍杖) a by-blow.

tobashiru (迸る), *vi.* to splash; spatter.

tobasu (飛ばす), *vt.* ❶ (放鳥) to let fly. ❷ (飛揚) to fly. ❸ (省略) to skip; leave out; jump over. ❹ (水を) to splash; spatter. —鳩を飛ばす, to let a dove fly. —馬を飛ばす, to gallop a horse. —自動車を飛ばして驅けつける, to fly to the spot in a motor-car.

tōbatsu (討伐する), *vt.* to subjugate; subdue. ¶ 討伐隊, a punitive force [expedition].

tobei (渡米), *n.* visit [going] to America. —渡米する, to visit [go to] America. ¶ 渡米實業團, a party of business men visiting America.

tōben (答辯), *n.* 【法】 plea; an answer; a reply. —答辯する, to answer; reply; plead. ¶ 答辯書, a written reply.

tōbeni (唐紅), *n.* fuchsine.

tobi (跳), *n.* jump; spring; leap.

tobi (鳶), *n.* 【鳥】 the black kite.

tobiagaru (飛上る), *vt.* ❶ (飛上る) to fly; soar up. ❷ (跳り上る) to jump [spring; start] up. ❸ (間を踰えて昇る) to jump over. —驚いて跳び上る, to start up to one's feet.

tobiaruku (飛歩く), *vi.* to gad about.

tobichiru (飛散る), *vi.* to fly about; scatter about; fly asunder.

tobidasu (跳出す), *vt.* to jump out; rush [dash] out; burst out (破って). —一室を跳び出す, to rush [bounce] out of a room.

tobideru (飛出る), *vi.* to project; protrude; goggle (眼が).

tobidōgu (飛道具), *n.* a missile.

tobiguchi (鳶口), *n.* a hook; a fire-hook; a fireman's hook.

tobihanareru (飛放れる), *vi.* ❶ (退く) to fly apart. ❷ (隔つ) to be far apart; differ greatly. —飛放れた業をする, to do an extraordinary trick.

tobihi (飛火), *n.* ❶ sparks from a fire. ❷ (大水泡疹) pemphigus. —飛火で燒ける, to be burnt by sparks from a fire.

tobiiri (飛入), *n.* jumping *into*; entry. —飛入り勝手次第, open to all comers.

tobiiro (鳶色), *n.* brown.

tobiishi (飛石), *n.* a stepping-stone.

tobikakaru (跳掛る), *vi.* to spring [jump; throw oneself] *upon*; fly *at*; fall *upon* (喧嘩などして).

tobikau (飛交ふ), *vi.* to fly about (飛び廻る); fly past each other (飛び違ふ).

tobikiri (飛切の), *a.* first-class [-rate]; crack; tiptop. —飛切り上等品, an A1 article.

tobikoeru (跳越える), *vi.* to jump [leap] *over* [*across*]; clear. ☞ *tobikosu*.

tobikomu (跳込む), *vi.* to jump [spring; leap] *into*; rush [dash] *into*; plunge *into*. —瀧の中へ跳び込む, to throw oneself into a waterfall.

tobikosu (跳越す), *v.* ❶ to jump [leap] *over*; clear; vault (木馬等を). ❷ (順を越える) to skip over; overjump. —門を跳び越す, to clear [jump over] a gate.

tobimawaru (飛廻る), *vi.* ❶ (飛翔して) to fly [flutter] about. ❷ (跳躍して) to jump [dance] about; skip; gambol (ふざけて). ❸ (放浪) to wander about. ❹ (奔走) to go about busily; bustle about.

tobimushi (跳蟲), *n.* 【蟲】 the spring-tail.

tobinori (飛乘する), *vi.* to jump into a running car (電車); vault upon a horse (馬へ).

tobinouo (文鰩魚), *n.* 【魚】 the flying-fish.

tobiokiru (跳起きる), *vi.* ❶ to spring [jump] to one's feet. ❷ to start from one's sleep; jump out of bed.

tobioriru (跳下·飛下りる), *vi.* to jump [leap] down. —馬から跳び下りる, to leap from a horse. —電車から跳び下りる, to jump off a running car.

tobira (扉), *n.* ❶ a door; a leaf; a door-leaf. ❷ (書物の) a title-leaf; a title-page.

tobitatsu (跳立つ), *vi.* to jump [spring; start] up (to one's feet). —跳び立つやうに嬉しい, to jump for joy.

tobitobi (飛飛に), *ad.* at intervals; sparsely; scatteredly. —飛び飛びに讀む, to read desultorily; skip through.

tobitsuku (跳附く), *vt.* to run

[rush] *at*; spring *at* [*on*]; fly [hawk] *at*. —跳びつかんとして居る, on the pounce.

tōbo (登簿), *n.* registration; entry. —登簿する, to register; enter. ¶ 登簿料, registration-fee. —登簿噸數, registered tonnage.

tōbō (逃亡), *n.* flight; desertion; decampment. —逃亡する, to fly; flee; run away. ☞ *nigeru*. ¶ 逃亡者, a fugitive; a runaway; an absconder; a deserter.

tōboe (遠吠), *n.* bay. —遠吠えする, to bay.

tobokeru (恍ける), *vi.* ❶ to be absent-minded; look blank. ❷ to dissemble; pretend [feign] ignorance: sham innocence. ❸ (耄碌する) to dote; be silly with age. —恍けた振りをする, to pretend to be out of wits.

toboru (點る), *vi.* to burn; light; (flame.)

toboshii (乏しい), *a.* ❶ (僅少) scanty; meagre; scarce. ❷ (不足) lacking [wanting; deficient] *in*; short *of*. —滋養に乏しい食物, lean food; food deficient in nutrition. —世の經驗に乏しい, to be little experienced in life.

tobosu (點す), *vt.* to light; kindle.

tobotobo (とぼとぼ), *ad.* ❶ (蹌踉) in a hobbing manner; totteringly. ❷ =*yoboyobo*. —とぼとぼ歩く, to hobble along; plod [jog] on [along]; trudge.

tobu (飛ぶ), *vi.* ❶ (飛翔) to fly; soar (舞上る); hover (飛舞ふ). ❷ (跳) to jump; leap; spring; vault (竿で); bound (鞠・兎等が); gambol (ふざけて); frisk (同上). ❸ =*tobichiru*. ❹ (拔く) to skip over; leave off. —飛び去る, to fly away; take wing. —空を飛ぶ, to fly in the air. —飛ぶ鳥を落す勢である, to nod and shake the sphere; have all at one's nod [beck]. —三年飛ばず鳴かず, to remain quiet [in seclusion] for three years. —飛んで火に入る夏の蟲, "The fly flutters about the candle till at last it gets burned."

tōbu (頭部), *n.* the head.

tobukuro (戸袋), *n.* 【建】 the door-boxing; the boxing (鎧戸の).

tōbun (當分), *ad.* for the present [nonce]; for the time being; for some time.

tōbun (等分), *n.* ❶ (等量で分つ) division into equal parts. ❷ (等量) equal proportions; same quantity. —等分する, to halve; share equally; go halves; divide into equal parts.

tōbun (糖分), *n.* quantity [percentage] of sugar.

tōbutsu (唐物), *n.* foreign goods [articles]; imported goods. ¶ 唐物屋, a foreign-goods store (店): a foreign-goods dealer (人).

tōbyō (投錨する), *vi.* to (cast; drop) anchor; come to an anchor. ¶ 投錨地, an anchorage; an anchor-ground.

tōbyō (痘苗), *n.* vaccine; (vaccine) lymph.

tōchaku (到著), *n.* arrival. —到著する, to arrive *at* [*in*]; arrive *upon* (臨場); reach; get [come] *to*; land (著港, 著陸).

tochi (橡), *n.* 【植】 Æsculus turbinata (horse-chestnut の一種・學名).

tochi (土地), *n.* ❶ (地面) earth; land; ground. ❷ (地所) an estate; (a piece of) land; (a lot of) ground. ❸ (領地) territory; fief. ❹ (土壤) soil; earth. ❺ (地方) a district; a locality; a region; a place (所). —土地を分譲する, to transfer [convey] land in lots. ¶ 土地賣買, land-jobbing. —土地臺帳, a cadastre; a land-register. —土地國有, land-nationalization. —土地所有權, land-ownership. —土地所有者, a land-owner. —土地收用法, the law for expropriation of land.

tōchi (統治), *n.* rule; reign; government. —統治する, to rule; rule [reign] over; govern. —統治權を行ふ, to exercise sovereign authority. ¶ 統治機關, 【法】 government organs [machinery]; sovereignty organs. —統治者, a ruler; a sovereign.

tōchi (當地), *n.* this place [region]; this locality.

tochiku (屠畜), *n.* butchery; slaughter. ¶ 屠畜業, butchery trade [business]. —屠畜場, a slaughter-house; an *abattoir* 【佛】.

tōchirimen (唐縮緬), *n.* = *mosurin*.

tōchō (島廳), *n.* an island office.

tōchoku (當直), *n.* 【航】 watch; duty. —當直する, 【航】 to keep the watch. ¶ 當直員, a watch-keeper. —當直將校, the officer of the watch [guard].

tochū (途中), *n.* ❶ (途上) way. ❷ =*chūto*. —話の途中で, in the midst of a conversation. —學校への途中で, on the road [one's way] to school. —途中で止める, to stop short. —途中から引返す, to retrace one's steps while on the road. —途中行列を廢する, to dispense with a procession.

todaeru (跡絶える), *vi.* to cease; stop; disappear. —往き來の人が全くとだえた, The street was absolutely deserted.

todai (渡臺する), *vi.* to go [cross]

over to Formosa; visit Formosa.

tōdai (當代), *n.* ❶ (現代) the present age [generation]; the present. ❷ (その時代) those days. —當代の, present; contemporary.

tōdai (燈臺), *n.* a lighthouse; a fire-tower; lights. ¶ 燈臺守, a lighthouse [light]-keeper. —燈臺船, a light-ship.

tōdan (登壇する), *vi.* to go on the platform; take the rostrum. —辯士の登壇を促す, to call the speaker to the platform.

tōden (答電), *n.* a reply telegram. —答電する, to answer [reply] by telegram 《cable》.

tōdo (陶土), *n.* potter's clay.

tōdō (東道する), *vt.* to guide. —東道の主となる, to guide; conduct another in the capacity of a host.

todoke (屆), *n.* ❶ a report; a notice; notification. ❷ (送致) sending.

todokeru (屆ける), *vt.* ❶ (送致) to send; forward; deliver. ❷ (通告) to report; notify; give [send a] notice *of*. —口頭で屆ける, to make a verbal report. —小荷物を屆ける, to forward a parcel.

todokōri (滯り), *n.* ❶ (滯納) arrearage; arrears. ❷ (停滯) stagnation; stoppage. ❸ (遲滯) delay. ❹ (支障) a hitch; a hindrance. —地代《家賃》の滯り, back rent. —滯りなく, without a hitch; without accident; duly. (式が滯りなく濟んだ, The ceremony was performed without a hitch.) ¶ 滯貸, a loan in arrears.

todokōru (滯る), *vi.* ❶ (滯納) to be in arrears; be back *on*. ❷ (停滯) to stagnate; be stagnant. ❸ (遲滯) to be delayed; be retarded. ❹ (支障) to be impeded; be hindered.

todoku (荼毒), *n.* injury; harm. —社會に荼毒を流す, to poison [bring harm upon] society.

todoku (屆く), *v.* ❶ (到著) to arrive *at*; come to hand (品物が). ❷ (到達) to reach; get *at*. ❸ (充足) to be fulfilled [realized; attained]. ❹ (聽許) to be heard; be granted. ❺ (成就) to succeed. ❻ (注意が) to be attentive [careful; scrupulous]. —屆いた人, a careful [scrupulous] man. —屆かぬ《屆く》所に, above [out of; beyond] 《within》 (one's) reach. (大砲の屆く《屆かぬ》所に, within 《out of》 range of the guns.) —眼の屆く限り, as far as the eye can reach [sweep]. —標準《標的》に屆かぬ, to fall short of the mark.

todomaru (止·停·留まる), *vi.* ❶ (止まる) to stop. ☞ *tomaru*. ❷ (逗留) to stay. ❸ (居殘る) to remain behind. ❹ (限定) to be limited [confined]. —一局部に止まる, to be confined to a single part.

todomatsu (椴松), *n.* 【植】Abies sachalinensis (fir-tree の一種·學名).

todome (止を刺す), to give a person the *coup de grâce* [the finishing stroke].

todomeru (止·停·留める), *vt.* to restrain (抑制); stop (休止); leave (殘す). ☞ *tomeru*. —大要を述ぶるに止める, to give only the outline. —...と云ふに止めん, Suffice it to say that....

todonotsumari (とどのつまり), *ad.* at last [length]; in the end [long run]; finally; after all.

tōdori (頭取), *n.* a president (銀行の); a director; a chief (頭領).

todorokasu (轟かす), *vt.* to rumble; peal. —世界に名を轟かす, to win a world-wide fame; be known the world over; make a noise in the world.

todoroki (轟), *n.* roll (雷); roar (大砲); palpitation (胸の).

todoroku (轟く), *vi.* to roar; roll; rumble; beat (胸が); be well known (名が). —山河に轟く, to reverberate over hill and river. —轟く胸を押し靜める, to soothe one's mental agitation; collect oneself. —雷鳴が轟く, The thunder rolls. —名聲世界に轟く, His fame resounds throughout [all over] the world.

tōei (冬營), *n.* 【軍】winter-quarters; wintering. —冬營する, to winter.

tōei (投影), *n.* 【數】projection; a (cast) shadow. ¶ 投影畫, a projection.

tofu (都府), *n.* a city; a town.

tofu (塗布), *n.* suffusion. —塗布する, to suffuse; apply (an ointment). ¶ 塗布藥, 【醫】liniment; ointment.

tōfu (豆腐), *n.* *tōfu* [日]; bean-curd. ¶ 豆腐屋, a *tōfu*-dealer; a bean-curd seller.

toga (栂), *n.* 【植】Tsuga Sieboldi (hemlock-spruce の一種·學名).

toga (科, 咎), *n.* ❶ (あやまち) a fault; blame (責). ❷ (罪科) a crime; an offence; a charge (廉).

toga (都雅), *n.* urbanity; elegance; polish. —都雅な, urbane; elegant; polished.

toga (渡河する), *vi.* to cross a river.

tōga (冬瓜), *n.* 【植】the wax-gourd; the white gourd.

tōgai (當該), *a.* competent; proper; concerned; in charge *of*. ¶ 當該官廳, the proper [competent] authorities; the authorities concerned. —當該官吏, the official concerned [in charge]; a competent official.

togame (咎め), *n.* rebuke; reproof; blame; censure. —自ら咎めを引く, to take the blame upon oneself. —天の咎めを受ける, to be reproved by Heaven.

togameru (咎める), *vt.* ❶ (非難) to censure; disapprove; condemn. ❷ (叱責) to rebuke; reprove. ❸ (糺す) to call (a person) to account; bring (a person) to book. ❹ (焮衝を起し又は化膿さす) to inflame; irritate. ——, *vi.* ❶ (心が) to be conscience-stricken; be smitten by one's conscience. ❷ (腫物が) to inflame; get angry; suppurate (化膿). —咎められる, to bear the blame; meet a rebuke; get it (hot). (巡査に咎められる, to be questioned by a policeman.) —人の言ふことを咎める, to take a person up short.

tōgan (冬瓜), *n.* =*tōga.*

toganin (咎人), *n.* an offender; a criminal. ☞ *zainin.*

tōgarashi (蕃椒), *n.* 【植】 the Cayenne [Guinea] pepper; the bird's-eye pepper. ¶ 干蕃椒 (藥味用), chilli, chilly. —獅子蕃椒 the bell-pepper.

togarasu (尖らす), *vt.* to sharpen; point.

togari (尖り), *n.* a point; a tip; a peak. ¶ 尖り鼻, a hawk-nose.

togaru (尖る), *vi.* to be sharp [pointed]; sharpen; come to a point. —尖った, sharp; pointed; peaked. (先の尖った指, taper fingers.)

toge (刺), *n.* ❶ (草木の) a thorn; a spine; a prickle (草の); a sting (いらぐさ等の); an own (麥の穗の). ❷ (そげ) a splinter. ❸ (魚の) a spine; a spike. —刺のある言葉, stinging words; harsh language. —刺の多い枝, a thorny [prickly] branch. —指に刺が立つ, to have a thorn 《splinter》 in one's finger; A thorn runs into one's finger.

tōge (峠), *n.* a (mountain-)pass; a defile (狹き山道); a crisis (危機); a climax (絕頂). —峠を越す, to cross [leave behind] a pass; pass the crisis (病氣); turn [go round] the corner (同上).

togenuki (刺拔), *n.* a pair of tweezers; a volsella (藥).

togeru (遂げる), *vt.* ❶ (完成) to complete; finish. ❷ (成就) to accomplish; achieve. ❸ (實現) to realize; attain. ❹ (履行) to fulfil; perform. ❺ (貫徹) to carry through [out]; make through with. —思を遂げる, to realize one's desire; have one's will. —自殺を遂げる, to commit suicide.

togi (伽), *n.* ❶ (侍坐) attendance; an attendant (人); an entertainer (人); a companion (貴婦人等の). ❷ (看護) nursing; a (sick-)nurse (人). ❸ =*yotogi.* —伽をする, to attend; wait on; keep company *with*; nurse.

tōgi (討議), *n.* discussion; debate; deliberation. —討議する, to discuss; debate [deliberate] *upon* [*on*]. —討議に付する, to bring under deliberation.

tōgi (黨議), *n.* a party decision (議決); a party assembly (會議).

tōgi (闘技), *n.* athletic competition; contest; match. ¶ 闘技場, a (prize) ring; a competition-ground; an arena. —闘技者, a competitor; a contestant.

togire (途切, 跡切), *n.* a pause; a break; a gap; stoppage. —途切れる, to pause; cease for a while; be interrupted.

togiri (頳桐), *n.* 【植】 Clerodendron squamatum (glory-tree の一種·學名).

togishi (研師, 磨師), *n.* a grinder; a sharpener; a polisher.

tōgō (投合), *n.* agreement; coincidence; unity. —投合する, to agree [coincide; concur] *with*; conform *to* (迎合).

tōgoku (島國), *n.* an island country; a sea-girt country. ☞ *shimaguni.*

tōgoma (蓖麻), *n.* 【植】 the castor-bean; the castor-oil-plant.

togu (研磨ぐ), *vt.* ❶ (刃物を) to grind; sharpen; whet. ❷ (滑にす) to polish; burnish; scour. ❸ (米を) to wash. —刀を研ぐ, to whet [sharpen] a sword. —米を淅(ト)ぐ, to wash rice.

tōgū (東宮), *n.* the Crown Prince; the Prince Imperial. ¶ 東宮武官, an Aide-de-camp to H. I. H. Crown Prince. —東宮御學問所, the lecture-hall of the Crown Prince. —東宮御所, H. I. H. the Crown Prince's Palace. —東宮御用掛, an official in service of H. I. H. the Crown Prince. —東宮妃, the Crown Princess. —東宮職, H. I. H. the Crown Prince's Household; Services to H. I. H. the Crown Prince. (東宮職主事, the Senior Steward to H. I. H. the Crown Prince.)

toguchi (戶口), *n.* the door; the doorway; the entrance.

toguro (蜷局), *n.* coiling; a coil (卷). —蜷局を卷く, to coil round; wind. (蛇が草叢で蜷局を卷いて

ゐる, The snake has coiled itself in the grass.)

tōguwa (唐鍬), *n.* an iron-headed hoe.

togyo (蠹魚), *n.* a bookworm. ☞ *shimi* (衣魚).

tōgyo (統御, 統馭), *n.* rule; reign; control. —統御する, to rule [reign] over; govern; control.

tōgyō (糖業), *n.* sugar industry.

tōgyū (屠牛), *n.* =*tochiku*.

tōha (黨派), *n.* a party; a league (徒黨); a faction (黨類). ☞ *tō* (黨). —黨を立てて爭ふ, to dispute in factions. ¶ 黨派心, party spirit.

tōhatsu (頭髮), *n.* the hair of the head; locks; tresses (婦人·少女等の); a head of hair (豐かな).

tōheki (盜癖), *n.* mania for stealing; kleptomania.

tōhen (等邊の), *a.* equilateral. ¶ 等邊三角形, an equilateral triangle. —等邊六邊形, a regular hexagon.

tohi (徒費), *n.* waste of money; useless expenditures [expenses]. —徒費する, to waste; squander; dissipate.

tohi (都鄙), *n.* city [town] and country. —都鄙の別なく, irrespectively of town or country.

tōhi (當否), *n.* right or wrong [not]; propriety; justice.

tōhi (等比), *n.* ratio of equality. ¶ 等比級數, 【數】 geometric(-al) progression.

tōhi (逃避する), *vt.* to escape; flee; fly; avoid.

tōhi (橙皮), *n.* the rind of the bitter orange.

toho (徒步), *n.* pedestrianism; walk. —徒步で, on foot; on one's own feet. —徒步する, to walk; go [tramp along] on foot; foot it; take to one's feet. —徒步旅行をする, to travel on foot; tramp (a journey). ¶ 徒步競走, a walking [foot] race.

tohō (途方), *n.* ❶ (方向, 方針) a direction; a course. ❷ (手段) a way; a means. ❸ (道理) reason; right. —途方もない, absurd; preposterous; unreasonable. —途方に暮れる, to be puzzled; be at sea [one's wits' end].

tōhō (東方), *n.* the east; the eastward; the Orient; ¶ 東方問題, the Eastern question.

tōhoku (東北), *n.* north-east. ¶ 東北地方, the north-east; the north-eastern provinces.

tōhon (唐本), *n.* a book printed in China.

tōhon (謄本), *n.* a (an attested) copy; a duplicate; an exemplar. —謄本を取る, ① (作る) to make an attested copy. ② (もらふ) to get [obtain] an attested copy.

tōhon-seisō (東奔西走する), *vi.* to visit here and there; busy oneself about; be constantly on the move.

tōhoshu (投捕手), *n.* 【野球】 battery.

tōhyō (投票), *n.* ❶ (採決) vote. ❷ (行爲) voting; poll; ballot. ❸ (票札) a vote; a ticket; a ballot (無記名). —投票する, to vote; ballot; give [cast] a vote. —投票に付する, to put to vote. —多數の投票を得て, by a majority of votes. ¶ 浮動投票, the floating vote. —祕密投票, a vote by ballot; a secret ballot. —決定投票, a casting vote (議長の). —記名《無記名》投票, a closed 《an unsigned》 ballot; an open 《a secret》 ballot. —投票函, a ballot-box. —投票者, a voter. (不在投票者, absent voters.) —投票所, a poll; a voting-place; a polling-place [-station]. —投票數, poll. —投票用紙, voting-paper.

toi (問), *n.* a question; an inquiry. —人に問をかける, to put a question to a person; ask a person a question.

toi (樋), *n.* a water-pipe; a (conduit-)pipe; a gutter (雨樋).

tōi (遠い), *a.* far; distant; remote. —遠い昔, a distant [remote] age; an age long past. —最も遠い, remotest; farthest; furthest; furthermost. —耳が遠い, to be hard [slow] of hearing.

toiawase (問合), *n.* inquiry; reference; communication. —問合はす, to inquire *of*; make inquiry *of*; communicate *with*. (友人の安否を問合はす, to inquire after a friend's welfare.)

toiki (吐息), *n.* a long breath; a sigh. —吐息つく, to sigh; have [fetch] a sigh; draw a long [deep] breath.

toishi (砥石), *n.* a whetstone; a grindstone; a hone. —砥石にかける, to whet; grind; sharpen on a stone.

tōi-sokumyō (當意卽妙の), *a.* witty; ready-witted; smart. —當意卽妙の答をする, to make repartees [witty retorts]; give a smart reply.

tōisu (籐椅子), *n.* a cane-chair; a rattan chair.

toita (戶板), *n.* a door used as a stretcher.

tōitsu (統一), *n.* unity; unification; consolidation (整理). —統一する, to unify; bring under single control [rule]; consolidate. —統一がない, to lack unity.

toitsumeru (問詰める), *vt.* to question closely; press hard with questions; cross-question [-examine]. —如何に問ひ詰めても, cross-question him how one may.

toiya (問屋), *n.* a commission merchant [agent]; a factor; a wholesale merchant [dealer]; a wholesale house [firm] (店). —病の問屋, a storehouse of diseases. ¶ 乾物問屋, a wholesale grocer. —砂糖問屋, a sugar merchant. —問屋業, commission agency; wholesale agency. —問屋口錢, factorage.

toji (綴), *n.* binding (製本); sewing (縫ひつづり).

toji (刀自), *n.* a madame; a matron; a housekeeper (主婦). —雪子刀自, Madame Yuki-ko.

tōji (冬至), *n.* the winter solstice, Dec. 22.

tōji (答辭), *n.* a reply; an answer; a response; an address in response [reply]. —答辭を述べる, to make an address in response; speak in reply.

tōji (當時), *n.* ❶ (現今) the present time; these days. ❷ (其頃) that time; those days. ——, *ad.* at present; at the present time; in these days; nowadays: at that time; in those days. —鎌倉幕府の當時, the days [times] of the Kamakura Shogunate. —當時の公爵, the then Duke. —當時の科學者, the scientists of the time.

tōji (湯治), *n.* hot-spring cure [treatment]; hydrotherapy (水治); hydropathy (同上). —湯治に行く, to go to the baths [a watering-place]. ¶ 湯治場, a watering [bathing]-place; a spa; the springs; the baths. —湯治客, visitors at a spa.

tojigame (とぢがめ), *n.* 【爬蟲】 the snapping turtle.

tojigane (綴金), **tojiito** (綴絲), *n.* a file.

tojikomeru (閉込める), *vt.* to confine; shut [lock] *in*; encage, incage. —雪に閉ぢ込められた, snow-bound.

tojikomi (綴込), *n.* a file. ¶ 新聞の綴込み, a newspaper file.

tojikomoru (閉籠る), *vi.* to confine oneself [be confined] within [*in*; *to*]; shut oneself up (*in*); keep the house.

tojikomu (綴込む), *vt.* to bind together (一緒に); file (後から). —新聞を綴ぢ込んで置く, to keep the newspapers on file.

tojimari (戸締), *n.* closing; fastening; locking. —戸締りする, to fasten [shut (up); bolt] a door. —戸締りを嚴重にする, to fasten the doors very carefully.

tojime (綴目), *n.* ❶ (とぢた所) a seam. ❷ (終局) the end; the close. ❸ (末期) an end of one's life; the last moment.

tojin (都人), *n.* a citizen; a townsman; city people; townsfolk.

tōjin (唐人), *n.* a foreigner (外人); a Chinese, Chinaman (支那人). —唐人の寢言, gibberish; double Dutch.

tōjin (黨人), *n.* a partisan, partizan; a party-man; a member of a party (黨員). ¶ 黨人根性, party spirit.

tōjin (蕩盡する), *vt.* to exhaust; dissipate; squander. —家產を蕩盡する, to squander the family property.

tojiru (閉ぢる), *vt.* to close; shut; 【航】 douse (舷窓など). —會を閉ぢる, to close a meeting. —通路を閉ぢる, to shut up [block] the passage.

tojiru (綴ぢる), *vt.* ❶ (重ね綴ぢる) to bind; fasten together; file (綴込む). ❷ (縫合はす) to sew together; stitch. —本を綴ぢる, to sew a book. —玉子を綴ぢる, to poach eggs.

tōjisha (當事者), *n.* the party; 【法】 the person concerned.

tōjitsu (當日), *n.* that [the] day; the day above-mentioned; the appointed day (約束の日). ——, *ad.* on that day; on the occasion.

tōjō (搭乘する), *vi.* to ride; go on board (汽船に); embark (同上). —飛行機に搭乘する, to get on [board] a plane.

tōjō (筒狀の), *a.* tubular; tubiform; tubulate. ¶ 筒狀花, 【植】 a tubular flower.

tōjō (登場), *n.* entrance. —登場する, to enter [appear on] the stage. ¶ 登場人物, *dramatis personæ* 〔羅〕; cast.

tōjōka (頭狀花), *n.* 【植】 a capitate flower.

tōjusu (唐繻子), *n.* silk satin.

toka (都下), *n.* the capital; the metropolis. —都下の名所, the famous places in [of] the capital; the sights of the capital.

tōka (投下する), *vt.* to throw [fling] down; drop; invest (投資). —爆彈を投下する, to drop bombs. ¶ 投下資本, invested capital.

tōka (透過する), *vt.* to permeate; pass *through*.

tōka (糖化), *n.* saccharification; saccharization. —糖化する, to saccharify; saccharize.

tōka (糖菓), *n.* sugar-candy; sweet-meats [-stuff]; sweets.

tōka (燈火), *n.* a lamp [candle]-light; a light. —燈火親しむべきの候となれり, The season has set in for reading by lamp-light.

tōkaede (三角楓), *n.* 【植】 the trifid-leaved maple.

tokage (蜥蜴), *n.* 【爬蟲】 the

skink; the lizard. ¶ 足無蜥蜴, the slow [blind]-worm.

tokai (都會), *n.* a city; a town. ¶ 都會生活, city [town; urban] life.

tokaki (槪), *n.* a strickle.

tokaku (兎角), *ad.* ❶ (かれこれ) in one way or another; in this way or that. ❷ (ともすれば) frequently (往々); too often. —兎角する中, in the mean time [while]; meanwhile; meantime. —兎角の評がある, to be often subjected to criticism.

tōkaku (統覺), *n.* 【心】 apperception. —統覺する, to apperceive.

tōkaku (頭角), *n.* the top (of a head); one's head. —頭角を見[げ]す, to stand head and shoulder above one's fellows; cut [make] a figure; make oneself prominent [conspicuous].

tōkan (投函する), *vt.* to post; drop into a letter 《ballot》-box.

tōkan (等閑), *n.* neglect; negligence; slight. —等閑に付する, to neglect; slight; make light *of*.

tōkan (統監), *n.* ❶ (監督) supervision. ❷ (官吏) a resident-general.

tōkara (疾から), *ad.* for a long time; a long time since; long since [ago].

tōkarazu (遠からず), *ad.* soon; shortly; in the near future.

tokasu (溶·鎔かす), *vt.* ❶ 〔溶〕 to melt; dissolve (水中に); liquefy (液化). ❷ 〔鎔〕 to melt; fuse (强熱で). —氷を溶かす, to melt ice. —金を鎔かす, to fuse [melt] metals.

tokasu (解かす), *vt.* to comb. —髮[かみ]を解かす, to comb one's hair.

tōkatsu (統轄), *n.* government; rule; superintendence. —統轄する, to govern; rule; superintend.

tokei (時計), *n.* a time-piece [-keeper]; a watch (懷中用); a clock (振子時計). —時計を卷く, to wind (up) a watch 《clock》. —時計を進める, to put the clock on; put forward the watch; flog the clock (特に船中にて當番時間を減ずるため). —時計を戻す, to set the clock back. —時計を直す, ① to regulate the clock; put [set] the clock right. ② to have one's watch mended (人に賴んで); mend a watch. —時計を合はす, to set a clock. —時計を見る, to look at a clock; consult one's watch (出して). —時計が鳴る, A clock strikes. —時計がよく合ふ《合はぬ》, A watch keeps good 《bad》 time. —此の時計は進む《遲れる》, This watch gains 《loses》. —君の時計は合ってゐるか, Is your watch right? ¶ 時計臺, a clock-tower. —時計屋, a watch-shop; a clock-shop.

tōkei (刀圭), *n.* a medicine spoon. ¶ 刀圭家, a physician. —刀圭界, the medical world.

tōkei (統計), *n.* statistics. —統計的, statistic(-al). —統計を取る, to take statistics. ¶ 統計學, (science of) statistics. (統計學者, a statist; a statistician.) —統計表, a statistical table; a return. —統計年鑑《年報》, a year-book 《an annual report》 of statistics.

tōkei (鬪鷄), *n.* ❶ (仕合) cock-fighting; a cock-fight. ❷ (鷄) a fighting-cock; a game-cock. ¶ 鬪鷄場, a cockpit; a pit.

tokeisō (西蕃蓮), *n.* 【植】 the blue passion-flower.

token (杜鵑), *n.* 【鳥】 the little cuckoo. ☞ *hototogisu*.

tōken (刀劍), *n.* a sword; a cold steel (firearm の對); side-arms.

tōken (鬪犬), *n.* ❶ (仕合) dog-fighting; a dog-fight. ❷ (犬) a fighting-dog.

tokeru (溶·鎔·融ける), *vi.* to melt; fuse (强熱で); dissolve (溶解); thaw (氷·雪が). —鎔け難い, [*a.*] infusible. —溶け去る, to melt away; clear (off). —火に鎔ける, to melt in the fire.

tokeru (解ける), *vi.* to be unloosed [untied; disentangled]; be solved (問題が); be dispelled [cleared] (疑が). —怒りが解ける, His anger melts away.

toketsu (吐血), *n.* hæmoptysis; vomiting of blood. —吐血する, to vomit [spit] blood; expectorate [cough up] blood.

toki (朱鷺), *n.* 【鳥】 the Japanese crested ibis. ¶ 朱鷺色; 鴇色, pink; rose-pink.

toki (時), *n.* time; hour (時刻); age (時代); season (季節); opportunity (好機). —時の人, one's contemporaries; the people of that time. —時の總理大臣, the then Premier. —時の鐘, an hour-bell. —時ならぬ雪, unseasonable snowfall. —時に臨んで, on the occasion *of*; at the time *of*. —帝の時に當り, in the days of the Emperor. —私が子供の時に, when I was a little boy. —丁度よい時に, in the nick (of time) (きはどい時); in time *for*; just at the right moment. —時の拍子で, on the spur of the moment. —時をつくる, to crow. —時を移さず, immediately; at once; without losing a moment. —時を同じうする, to contemporize; agree in time. —時を切って, periodically; at regular [certain] intervals. —時を得た忠告, a well-timed advice. —失敗した時は, in case of failure. —まさかの時には, in the hour of need. —時としては, sometimes; at times; occasionally. —時は金なり, (諺) "Time is money."

toki (鬨 -聲), *n.* Ⓢ 鯨波. a war [battle]-cry; a cry (叫). —鬨の聲を揚げる, to raise a (war-)cry.

tōki (冬期), *n.* the winter season [months]; the winter-time. ¶ 冬期休暇, the winter vacation [holidays].

tōki (投機), *n.* speculation; stock-jobbing (相場); a venture. —投機的, speculative; risky; adventurous. (投機的事業, speculative business; an adventure; a risky undertaking; a gambling venture. —投機的にやる, to risk; venture.) —投機する, to speculate. ¶ 投機師, a speculator.

tōki (陶器), *n.* pottery (不透明なもの); faience; ceramic ware (燒物). —陶器製の, china; ceramic, keramic. ¶ 陶器師, a potter; a ceramist. —陶器商, a dealer in earthenware; a crockery-dealer; a china-shop (店).

tōki (登記), *n.* registration; entry; record. ¶ 身分登記, registration of one's status. —登記簿, a register (book). —登記料, registration fee. —登記所, a registry; a register [registration] office.

tōki (騰貴), *n.* rise; appreciation. —騰貴する, to rise; advance; appreciate.

tokiakasu (說明す), *vt.* to explain; elucidate.

tokidoki (時時), *ad.* occasionally; at times; from time to time; now and then.

tōkibi (蜀黍), *n.* 【植】 the East Indian millet; the durra.

tokifuseru (說伏せる), *vt.* to defeat [win over] in argument; reduce to silence (沈默せしむ); convince (說服する). —說伏せて味方にする, to gain over.

tokigashi (時貸する), *v.* to accommodate a person with a temporary loan.

tokihogosu (解きほごす), *vt.* to pick to pieces; unravel (編物を); unsew (縫物を).

tokimeku (時めく), *vi.* to enjoy great prosperity; prosper; flourish. **——,** *a.* prosperous; thriving. —時めく大官, a high dignitary of great estate.

tokimeku (悸めく), *vi.* to beat; palpitate. —ときめく胸を押し鎮める, to calm one's agitated breast.

tokitsukeru (說きつける), *vt.* to persuade; talk over; win over.

tokiwa (常盤の), *a.* firm as a rock: everlasting; eternal; evergreen (常綠の). ¶ 常盤木, an evergreen.

tokka (特價), *n.* a special price; a reduced price (割引値). ¶ 特價販賣, sale at a reduction [at reduced prices]. —特價提供, a special offer.

tokkaku (凸角), *n.* a salient angle; a jag (岩角); 【數】 a convex angle.

tokkan (吶喊), *n.* =*toki* (鬨).

tokkan (突貫), *n.* dash; rush; fierce charge; sortie (城内より). **—— -suru,** *vi.* to dash [rush] *at*; charge *on* [*upon*]; make a rush *for*. —敵陣に突貫する, to rush upon the enemy's position.

tokkei (特惠的), *a.* preferential. ¶ 特惠稅率, preferential tariff.

tokken (特權), *n.* a privilege; a special right; a prerogative (特に國王等の). —特權ある, privileged. ¶ 特權階級, a privileged class.

tokki (突起), *n.* 【解】 a process; an appendix: a protuberance. —突起する, to project; protrude.

tokko (獨鈷), *n.* a dorjé 【佛】.

tokkō (特效), *n.* special virtue [efficacy; effect]. ¶ 特效藥, a specific (medicine [remedy]).

tokkō (德行), *n.* moral [virtuous] conduct; well-doing; virtue.

tokkuni (夙・疾に), *ad.* long ago [since]; already (既に). —疾ッくの昔, long, long ago; ages ago.

tokkuri (德利), *n.* a bottle; a *sake*-bottle.

tokkyo (特許), *n.* a special permission [licence]; a concession (鑛山採掘・鐵道敷設等の); a patent (專賣の). —特許する, to patent; privilege; concede [grant] a special permission; charter. —特許になる, to be specially permitted [licensed]; be chartered; A patent is granted. —特許を得る, to obtain a special permission; obtain a patent. ¶ 特許品陳列所, a patent museum. —特許狀, letters patent; a patent (licence); a letter of patent; a charter. —特許局, the patent office [bureau]. (特許局長, the Director of the Patent Bureau; the Comptroller-General of Patents 【英】; the Commissioner of Patents 【米】) —特許料, patent fee. —特許出願人, an applicant for a patent. —特許登錄簿, a patent-roll.

tokkyō (凸鏡), *n.* a convex lens [(mirror)].

tokkyū (特急 -列車), *n.* a limited express [train]; a special express. ¶ 電話特急架設, urgent installation of a telephone.

toko (床), *n.* ❶ (寢床, 苗床, 河床) a bed. ❷ (ゆか) a floor. ❸ (床の間) an alcove. ❹ (髮床) a hair-dresser's. ❺ (疊の心) the body of mat. —床に就く, ① (就眠) to go [retire] to bed [rest]; turn in. ② (病で) to take to one's bed; be laid up. —床を離れる, ① (起床) to get up; turn out; get out of bed. ② =*tokoage* (床揚する). —床を取る, to make a bed. —床を揚げる, to put away a bed.

tokō (渡航), *n.* a passage; a voyage. —渡航する, to make a voyage *to*; cross a sea; go over *to*.

tōkō (投降する), *vi.* to surrender; submit.

tōkō (投稿する), *v.* to contribute to a periodical; send a contribution. ¶ 投稿者, a contributor; an outside writer.

tōkō (登校する), *vi.* to go to school; attend school.

tokoage (床揚), *n.* recovery from illness. —床揚げの祝, celebration of one's recovery from illness. —床揚げする, to rise from a sick-bed; recover from illness; leave one's bed.

tokogae (床替), *n.* transplanting.

tokojirami (床蝨), *n.* the bed-bug; the house-bug.

tokokazari (床飾), *n.* an alcove ornament.

tokomise (床店), *n.* a stall; a lockup shop.

tokon (吐根), *n.* 【植】Uragoga Ipecacuanha (學名); 【藥】ipecacuanha.

tōkon (痘痕), *n.* pock-marks.

tōkon (當今), *n.* nowadays; the present [these] times. ——, *ad.* nowadays; in these times; at the present time; now. —當今の學生, students of the day.

tokonatsu (常夏), *n.* 【植】the fringed pink.

tokonoma (床の間), *n.* an alcove; a recess.

tokoro (處, 所), *n.* ❶ (場所) a place; a room (餘地). ❷ (住所) a residence; an address. ❸ (位置) situation; position. ❹ (土地) a place; a locality; a region. ❺ (箇處) a point; a passage; a part. ——, *conj.* that; which. —所で, ① (假定) though; even if. ② (發語) well; then. —所では, so (as) far as; in so far as. (余の知るところでは, for aught [as far as] I know. —僕の見る所では, in my opinion [eyes].) —かゝる所へ, at this juncture. —己の欲せざる所, which one does not desire [wish for oneself]. —處嫌はずぶん撲る, to thrash him all over. —所變れば品變る, "So many countries, so many customs."

tokorodokoro (所所, 處處), *ad.* here and there; in various places; at [in] places. —所々讀む, to read different parts of a book.

tokoroegao (所得顏), *n.* a triumphant look; a proud countenance. —所得顏に咲く, to bloom with pride.

tokoroga (ところが), *conj.* ❶ (にしても) even if; though. ❷ but (然るに); and (そして); as (所へ); when (同上).

tokorogaki (所書), *n.* an address.

tokoroten (心太), *n.* gelidium jelly.

tokoshie (永に), *ad.* eternally; perpetually.

tōkōshoku (橙黃色), *n.* orange (colour); orange-yellow.

tokoya (床屋), *n.* ❶ a barber's shop; a hair-dresser's saloon. ❷ (人) a barber; a hair-dresser. —床屋の看板, the barber's pole.

tokoyami (常闇), *n.* everlasting darkness.

tokozure (床擦, 褥瘡), *n.* a bed-sore.

toku (得), *n.* ❶ (利潤) profit; gains; profitableness. ❷ (利便) advantage; benefit; advantageousness. —得な, profitable; lucrative; advantageous. —得になる, to turn [prove] to one's profit.

toku (德), *n.* ❶【倫】(道德的力) virtue; morality. ❷ (恩惠) grace; favour. ❸ (效能) virtue; merit. —德のある, virtuous; worthy. —德の高い人, a man of high virtue [noble character]; a high-minded person. —德とする, to be grateful *for*. —德を養ふ, to cultivate one's character.

toku (疾く), *ad.* rapidly; swiftly; early (時間). ☞ *hayaku*. —疾く走る, to run rapidly.

toku (解く), *vt.* ❶ (ほどく) to untie; unbind; unloose. ❷ (解釋) to interpret; (re-)solve (問題を); work out (同上). ❸ (解除) to relieve; release; rescind (契約を). ❹ (釋放) to (set) free; liberate; release. ❺ (分離) to disjoin; disunite; take to pieces (解體). ❻ (氷解) to disperse; dispel. —小包を解く, to undo [unwrap] a parcel. —髮を解く, to (un-)loose [undo] the hair. —禁を解く, to remove a prohibition. —疑ひを解く, to dispel a doubt. —任を解く, to discharge a person from office; relieve a person of a post. —人の迷を解く, to open another's eyes.

toku (溶く), *vt.* =*tokasu* (溶かす).

toku (說く), *vt.* ❶ (說明) to explain; interpret; elucidate. ❷ (說

述) to state; expatiate. ❷ (說得) to talk over [round]; persuade. ❸ (說教) to preach. —說き出す, to begin to state [tell]. —說き及ぶ, to touch *on* [*upon*]; refer *to*. —說き落す, to persuade into compliance; win over; preach down. —道を說く, to preach the path of morality. —敎育の必要を說く, to expatiate upon the necessity of education.

tōku (遠く), *ad.* (a-)far; far off [away]; distantly; remotely. —遠く慮る, to take a long view; consider remote effects. —遠く及ばない, to be far inferior *to*. —氣が遠くなる, to feel faint; faint. —遠くに見える山, a mountain in the distance. —遠く神代より, from the remote age of the gods.

tokubai (特賣), *n.* ❶ (競爭入札によらぬ賣渡し) sale by private contract. ❷ (特價で賣る) a special offer; sale at special prices. —特賣する, to sell by private contract; sell at special prices.

tokubetsu (特別), *n.* particularity; extraordinariness; exception (例外). —特別の, special; particular (特殊の); express; limited (鐵道・郵便等の). **—— - ni,** *vd.* specially; particularly; in particular; exceptionally. —特別に取扱ふ, to give special treatment. ¶ 特別委員, an extraordinary committee [commission]. —特別上等, super-excellence; an extra fine article (品物). —特別會計, special finance; special account. —特別及第, passing on special considerations. —特別任用, special appointment. —特別席, a special [reserved] seat.

tokubō (德望), *n.* moral repute; a fair name (令聞). ¶ 德望家, a man of moral repute; a man of fair name.

tokubun (得分), *n.* ❶ (まうけ) profit; gains. ❷ (とりまへ) share.

tokuchō (特長), *n.* a strong point; a forte; special talent.

tokuchō (特徵), *n.* a (special) feature [trait]; a (special) characteristic; a mark; 【生物】 diagnosis. —特徵的, characteristic.

tokudatsu (得脫さす), *vt.* to save; redeem.

tokuden (特電), *n.* a special telegram.

tokudo (得度する), *vi.* ❶ to be saved. ❷ (出家する) to become a priest; enter the priesthood.

tokugakkan (督學官), *n.* a school-inspector.

tokugaku (篤學), *n.* ❶ (博學) (profound) erudition; wide learning [knowledge]. ❷ (學事に精勵) studiousness; diligence; assiduous study. —篤學の士, a scholar of profound erudition; a learned person; a diligent student.

tokugi (德義), *n.* morality; virtue; moral duties. —德義上, morally; in honour (義理上). (德義上の, moral. —德義上…すべきなり, to be bound in honour *to*.) —德義に背く, to be contrary to morality; go against moral duties. ¶ 德義心, a moral sense [spirit].

tokugyōshi (得業士), *n.* a graduate of a special ⦅medical⦆ college; a licentiate.

tokuha (特派), *n.* special despatch [dispatch]; 【軍】 detail. **—— - suru,** *vt.* to despatch [send off] specially; 【軍】 detail; tell off. —使者を特派する, to despatch a messenger. ¶ 特派員, a special mission [delegate]; a specially-despatched person; a special correspondent (新聞の). —特派大使, an ambassador extraordinary.

tokuhitsu (特筆する), *vt.* to write in large character; record in golden letters. —特筆すべき事件, events worthy of special mention. —特筆大書する, to write in large and plain characters.

tokuhon (讀本), *n.* a reader; a reading book. ¶ 第四讀本, the fourth reader. —小學讀本, a primary school reader.

tokuhyō (得票), *n.* the number of votes obtained [gained].

tokui (特異の), *a.* distinctive; peculiar; differential.

tokui (得意), *n.* ❶ (喜悅) exaltation; elation. ❷ (自慢) pride. ❸ (顧客) a customer; a patron; custom. ❹ (得手) a forte; speciality; merits. —大事なお得意, one's best customer. —得意の說, a stock argument. —得意の境遇, a favourable position. —得意滿面の, proud; elated; triumphant. —…が得意である, to be good [expert; skilful] *at*; be at home *in*. —得意になる, ① (自慢) to be elated [exalted]; be proud *of*; take a pride *in*; pride oneself *on*. ② (顧客になる) to become a customer [patron]. (得意になって歸る, to go home in triumph.) —得意廻りをする, to go round asking for orders. ¶ 得意時代, one's bright days. —得意先, a customer; a connection.

tokuiku (德育), *n.* moral education [culture; training].

tokujitsu (篤實), *n.* honesty; sincerity; faithfulness. —篤實な, honest; sincere; faithful.

tokumei (特命), *n.* special command; special appointment.

tokumei (匿名), *n.* anonymity; anonymousness. —匿名の手紙, an anonymous letter. ¶ 匿名組合, 【法】 an anonymous association; a *société anonyme* 【佛】.

tokumu (特務), *n.* special duty [service]. ¶ 特務巡査, a policeman on special service; a special (constable). —特務艦, a special service ship. —特務曹長, a special sergeant-major.

tokuni (特に), *ad.* (e-)specially; particularly; by (way of) eminence; *par excellence* 【佛】. —特に重大なる事柄, a thing of especial importance.

tokurei (督勵する), *vt.* to encourage; stimulate; urge.

tokuri (德利), *n.* =***tokkuri***.

tokusa (木賊), *n.* 【植】 the Dutch rush; the scouring rush.

tokusaku (得策), *n.* the best plan [policy]; advisability. —得策の, expedient; politic; advisable; wise.

tokusan (特產 -物), *n.* a special product.

tokusei (特性), *n.* special [peculiar] character [quality]; distinctive nature; 【生物】 diagnosis.

tokusei (特製の), *a.* specially-made; of special manufacture [make].

tokusei (得性), *n.* an acquired character.

tokusei (德性), *n.* morality; virtue; moral sense [spirit] (德義心).

tokusen (特選), *n.* special choice.

tokusha (特赦), *n.* (a special) amnesty [pardon]. —特赦を行ふ, to grant [give] an amnesty; grant dispensation. —特赦で出獄を許される, to be released from prison on amnesty.

tokushi (特旨), *n.* special grace. ¶ 特旨敍任, conferment and appointment by special grace.

tokushi (特使), *n.* an envoy; a special messenger; an express (messenger).

tokushi (篤志), *n.* ❶ benevolence; charity; kindness. ❷ (熱心) ardour; zeal. ¶ 篤志家, a benevolent [charitable] person. —篤志看護婦會, the (Ladies') Volunteer Nurse Society.

tokushin (得心), *n.* ❶ (承諾) consent. ❷ (納得) satisfaction. ❸ (會得) appreciation; understanding. —得心さす, to make (a person) consent; convince (a person) *of*; satisfy (a person) *of*. —得心する, to consent; understand; be convinced *of*; be satisfied.

tokushitsu (特質), *n.* special [peculiar] character [quality]; peculiarity; distinctive nature; property (物質の).

tokushitsu (得失), *n.* advantages and disadvantages; merits and demerits; relative merits [advantages]. —得失を考究する, to estimate relative advantages; weigh pros and cons.

tokusho (讀書), *n.* reading. —讀書三昧に耽る, to be devoted to reading; be immersed in books. ¶ 讀書家, a great reader; a book-reader. —讀書界, the reading public.

tokushō (特稱), *n.* a specific name.

tokushoku (特色), *n.* special [peculiar] character [features; quality]; a special characteristic; a trait. —特色を發揮する, to display a special character; exhibit a peculiar trait.

tokushoku (瀆職), *n.* (official) corruption; graft. ¶ 瀆職事件, an official corruption case; a graft case. —瀆職行爲, corrupt practices.

tokushu (特殊), *n.* specificness; particularity. **—— -no**, *a.* specific; (e-)special; distinctive; characteristic. —特殊の目的, a particular object. ¶ 特殊學校, a ragged school; a special school. —特殊銀行《會社》, a chartered bank 《company》.

tokusō (德操), *n.* morality; chastity.

tokusoku (督促), *n.* =***saisoku***. ¶ 督促手數料, (稅金などの) a fee for urging payment (of a tax).

tokusū (得數), *n.* a result.

tokutai (特待), *n.* special treatment; distinction. —特待する, to treat a person specially; give a special treatment; receive a person with distinction. ¶ 特待券, a complimentary ticket. —特待生, an honours student; a scholar; an exhibitioner.

tokutaku (德澤), *n.* grace; favour; benevolence.

tokutei (特定の), *a.* fixed; special; specified. —少數の特定の場合を除いて, except in a few specified cases. ¶ 特定物, 【法】 a specific thing. —特定賃銀, fixed fares.

tokuten (特典), *n.* a special favour; a privilege.

tokuten (特點), *n.* a characteristic [distinctive] point; a salient feature; a virtue. ☞ ***tokuchō***.

tokuten (得點), *n.* the marks [points] obtained; the score. —得點數を記入する, 【野球】 to score the runs. —雙方共まだ得點なし, 【庭球】 love all. ¶ 得點球, a game-ball (其一點で勝を得る球).

tokuto (篤と), *ad.* thoroughly (十分に); carefully (注意して);

attentively (同上); seriously. —篤と考へてから, after mature consideration. —篤と事實を調査する, to make thorough inquiry into the facts.

tokutō (禿頭), *n.* =*hageatama.* ¶ 禿頭病, alopecia.

tokutō (特等), *n.* a special grade [class]. ¶ 特等席, a special seat; a box (劇場).

tokutoku (得得と), *ad.* proudly; boastfully; triumphantly.

tokuyaku (特約), *n.* (特別な條件附隨の契約) special contract [agreement]. —特約を結ぶ (する), to enter into special contract; make special agreement. ¶ 特約一手販賣, sole agents by special contract. —特約店, a firm under special contract.

tokuyō (徳用の), *a.* economical; serviceable; advantageous. ¶ 徳用品, an economical article.

tokuyū (特有 -性), *n.* speciality; peculiarity. —— **-no,** *a.* ❶ (獨得の) special; specific; peculiar. ❷ (別有の) separate; private-owned. —日本特有の技術, Japan's characteristic art. —日本民族特有の精神, a spirit peculiar to the Japanese race. ¶ 特有財產, separate estate (妻の).

tōkyaku (等脚の), *a.* 【數】 isosceles (三角形の). ¶ 等脚三角形, an isosceles triangle.

tōkyoku (當局 -者), *n.* the authorities (concerned); the powers that be.

tōkyū (投球), *n.* bowling (クリケットの); pitch (野球の); delivery.

tōkyū (討究), *n.* investigation; inquiry; research. —討究する, to investigate; inquire [search] *into.* ¶ 討究者, an investigator.

tōkyū (等級), *n.* degree; rank; class; grade; rating (船員の); 【天】 magnitude. —等級を附ける, to classify; grade; rank; rate.

tōkyū (闘球), *n.* =*tamatsuki.*

toma (苫), *n.* a rush-mat. —苫を掛ける, to cover with rush-matting.

tomadoi (戸惑する), *vi.* to be bewildered; go to a wrong place [house]; lose one's way.

tōmaki (遠卷にする), *vt.* to surround at a distance; close in.

tomari (止, 留), *n.* ❶ (休止) stop; stopping; stoppage. ❷ (終端) an end; a termination; a terminus (終點).

tomari (泊), *n.* ❶ (港) a port; a harbour. ❷ (宿り) putting up; lodging. ❸ (宿屋) an inn; a hotel. ❹ (宿直) night-watch [-duty].

tomariawaseru (泊合せる), *vi.* to put up [stop] at the same inn. —火事の晩に泊り合せる, to happen to stop there on the night (when) there was a fire.

tomariban (泊番), *n.* a turn for night-duty [-watch].

tomarigi (棲木), *n.* a perch; a roost (塒).

tomariyado (泊宿), *n.* an inn; a hotel.

tomaru (止·留·泊る), *vi.* ❶ (休止) to stop; come to a stop; stand still. ❷ (佇立) to halt; stand (still). ❸ (終止) to end; come to an end; cease. ❹ (中止) to be suspended [interrupted]. ❺ (留) (滯在) to stay; sojourn; remain behind (居殘る). ❻ (宿泊) to lodge; take up one's lodgings; put up. ❼ (鳥が) to perch; alight; sit [settle] *on.* —ぴったり止まる, to come to a full [dead] stop. —出血が止る, to stop bleeding. —宿屋に泊る, to stop at an inn; put up at a hotel. —(人の)眼に留まる, to meet a person's eye; catch [attract] another's eye. —時計が止った, The clock has run down (卷かぬため); The clock has stopped.

tomasu (富ます), *vt.* to make wealthy [rich]; enrich.

tomato (トマト), *n.* 【植】 the tomato.

tomatsu (塗沫), *n.* erasure. —塗沫する, to erase; efface; blot out; obliterate; paint.

tōmawari (迂回), *n.* a détour; a roundabout [circuitous] way. —遠廻りする, to make a détour; take a circuitous route [roundabout way]; go round.

tōmawashi (遠廻しに), *ad.* indirectly; in a roundabout way; circuitously. —遠廻しに言ふ, to use circumlocution; say in a roundabout way; throw out a hint (仄めかす). —遠廻しに意中を探る, to feel another's pulse; beat about the bush.

tome (止, 留), *n.* a stop; an end (終); 【建】 a mitre.

tōme (遠目), *n.* long sight; far-sightedness; a distant view (遠見).

tomebari (留針), *n.* a (fastening-) pin. ☞ *pin.*

tōmegane (遠眼鏡), *n.* a telescope; a spy-glass (小形).

tōmei (透明), *n.* transparency. —— **-na,** *a.* transparent; limpid; clear. —透明な水, crystal water.

tōmen (當面の), *a.* present; urgent; pressing; of the hour. —當面の問題, a matter in hand; an urgent problem.

tomeoki (留置), *n.* ❶ (抑留) detention ❷ (郵便の) leaving until called for; "to be called for." ¶ 留置電報, *telegraphe restante.* — 留置郵便, *poste restante* 〔佛〕; "to be called for" (郵便物の上書).

tomeoku (留置く), *vt.* ❶ (抑留) to detain; lock up; retain; hold. ☞ *ryūchi.* ❷ (郵便を) to leave until called for. ❸ (終とす) to put an end *to*; stop; leave off. ❹ (記し置く) to write down; make a note *of.*

tomeru (止·留·泊める), *vt.* ❶ (休止) to stop; put [bring] to a stop; turn off (捻って); switch off (同上). ❷ (終止) to end; put [bring] to an end. ❸ (禁止) to forbid; prohibit. ❹ (抑制) to check; restrain; control. ❺ (防止) to hold back [in check]; arrest; stay. ❻ (抑留) to detain; keep in custody. ❼ (宿泊) to lodge (a person) overnight; give (a person) a night's lodging. ❽ (結附) to fasten *to* [*on*; *upon*]. —氣を止めて, with attention. —馬を留める, to rein [pull] up a horse; draw bit [bridle; rein]. —喧嘩を止める, to put a stop to quarrelling. —痛みを止める, to put an end to pain. —出血を止める, to staunch (the flow of) blood. —腐敗を止める, to arrest decay. —ピンで襟を止める, to fasten the neck-band with a pin.

tomeru (富める), *a.* rich; wealthy; affluent. —産物に富める國, a country rich in natural products. —魚に富める川, a river teeming with fish. —慾にも思はれなかッた程富める, rich beyond the dreams of avarice.

tomi (富), *n.* ❶ wealth; riches; affluence. ❷ (富籤) a lottery. —巨萬の富を作る, to make a large fortune [great wealth]. —富王侯を凌ぐ, to be above a prince in wealth.

tōmi (唐箕), *n.* a winnower; a winnowing-machine; a fanning--machine[-mill].

tōmi (遠見), *n.* ❶ (遠景) a distant view. ❷ (遠物見) watch [look-out] in a tower.

tōmichi (遠路), *n.* ❶ (長途) a long way; a great distance. ❷ =*tōmawari.* —遠路をする, to take a long road; go a long way.

tomikuji (富籤), *n.* a lottery--ticket.

tōmimi (遠耳), *n.* ❶ (聞えぬ) a deaf ear; an ear hard of hearing. ❷ (耳敏い) a sharp ear; an ear quick of hearing.

tōmin (島民), *n.* islanders.

tōmitsu (糖蜜), *n.* molasses; treacle; syrup.

tomo (友, 伴, 侶), *n.* ❶ (朋友) a friend. ❷ (仲間) a comrade; a mate; a fellow. ❸ (伴侶) a companion. ❹ 〔供〕(從者) an attendant; a servant; an escort (護衛の). —眞の友, a true [tried] friend. —友を擇ぶ, to choose a friend. —友を棄てる, to forsake [abandon] one's friend. —供を連れてゆく, to go with [be accompanied by] attendants. —旅の伴をする, to accompany a person on a journey. —自然を友とする, to make a friend of Nature.

tomo (共), with; together with; and; including.

tomo (艫), *n.* the stern.

tomo (とも), *conj.* ❶ (雖も) although; though (...yet); even if; if. ❷ (或は又) whether...or; or. ——, *ad.* ❶ (勿論) certainly; indeed; of course. ❷ (又) also. —...とも云ふべし, it may be said to be...; it may be called...; it is, in a sense [manner].... —善く《惡く》とも, at the best《worst》. —お前が何と云はうとも, whatever you may say; no matter what you say. —いか程金があらうとも, however rich you may be. —親を親とも思はぬ, He does not look upon his parents as such.

tomoare (兎もあれ), *ad.* however that may be; be that as it may; at any rate. ☞ *tomokaku.*

tomodachi (友達), *n.* a friend. ☞ *tomo.* —酒飲み[遊び]友達, a good [jolly] fellow; a boon companion. —女の友達, a female [lady] friend.

tomodaore (共倒れ), *n.* falling together; being ruined together [with a person]. —共倒れになる, to fall with another.

tomodomo (共共), *ad.* together; in company (組んで); mutually (互に).

tomoe (巴, 鞆繪), *n.* a whirl; an eddy.

tomogara (輩), *n.* fellows; comrades; a company. —斯る輩, such [these] people.

tomogui (共食する), *vi.* ❶ to eat [feed upon] another of one's own species. ❷ to make an internecine struggle.

tomokaku (兎も角 -も), *ad.* at any rate; at all events; in any case; anyhow; anyway. —昔は兎も角 (今では)..., whatever it may formerly have been....

tomokasegi (共稼), *n.* working together for a living.

tōmoku (頭目), *n.* a chief; a leader; a headman.

tomonau (伴ふ) *v.* ❶ (連れて

行く) to be accompanied *by*; be attended *by*. ● (随伴する) *,* accompany; attend; follow. —時勢に伴ふ, to keep abreast of the times. —文明の進歩に伴うて, with the progress of civilization. —妻子を伴うて, with wife and children.

tomoni (共·倶·與に), *ad.* ❶ (一緒に) together (*with*); along *with*; in company *with*; hand in hand. ❷ (同時に) at the same time. **——,** *prep.* with. —男女共に, men and women alike; irrespective of (the) sex. —夏冬共に, in both summer and winter. —運命を共にする, to cast in one's lot *with*. —苦樂を共にする, to share one's joys and sorrows *with*.

tōmorokoshi (玉蜀黍), *n.* 【植】 the (Indian) corn; the maize.

tomoshiabura (燈油), *n.* = *toboshiabura*.

tomoshibi (燈), *n.* a lamp; a light; lamplight.

tomoshiraga (倶白髮), *n.* aging together. —倶白髮の後まで, until we both grow gray-haired.

tomosureba (ともすれば), Ⓢ ともすると. apt [liable; prone] to; frequently (往々); too often.

tomozuna (纜), *n.* a stern-cable [-hawser]; a land-tie.

tomu (富む), *v.* ❶ (富裕) to become ⟪be⟫ rich [wealthy]. ❷ (豐富) to have plenty *of*; abound *in*; be rich *in*; teem *with*. —文才に富む, to be rich in literary talent. —經驗に富む, to have much experience. —魚族に富む, to teem with fish.

tomurai (弔), *n.* ❶ (送葬) a funeral; burial (埋葬). ❷ (哀悼) condolence. ❸ (追福) mass for the dead. —弔の行列, a funeral procession. —弔をする, to hold a funeral. ¶ 弔合戰, a battle to revenge the death of comrades-in-arms; a revenge.

tomurau (弔ふ), *v.* ❶ to mourn *for* (追悼); condole *with*... (on the death of) (弔意を述ぶ); say mass *for* (追福). ❷ (會葬) to attend a funeral. —死者を弔ふ, to mourn for the dead; say mass for the dead. —後を弔ふ, to hold mass for the soul of the dead.

tōmyō (燈明), *n.* a light ⟪candle⟫ offered. ¶ 燈明臺, a lighthouse.

tōmusha (當務者), *n.* the person in charge.

ton (噸), *n.* a ton. —二千噸積の船, a two-thousand-tonner; a ship of 2000 tons. ¶ 呎噸, foot-ton. —容積噸, measurement ton; 40 cubic feet.

tōna (菘菜), *n.* 【植】 the Chinese cabbage; the pak-choi.

tonaeru (唱へる), *v.* ❶ (讀誦) to recite; chant. ❷ (吟唱) to chant; sing. ❸ (唱道) to advocate; preach. ❹ (主張) to insist; maintain; raise (異議を). ❺ (叫ぶ) to cry; shout. —神の御名を唱へる, to call on the name o God. —新說を唱へ出す, to advance [put forward] a new theory. —自由民權の說を唱へる, to preach liberty and people's rights.

tonaeru (稱へる), *vt.* to call; name.

tonakai (馴鹿), *n.* 【哺乳】 the reindeer.

tōnan (盗難), *n.* robbery; burglary; loss from robbery. —盗難に罹る, to be robbed of things.

tonari (隣), *n.* neighbourship; the next door [house]; the neighbouring house. —隣の, neighbouring; next; next-door; adjacent (近くの); adjoining (隣接せる). —隣に坐る, to sit next to a person. —隣に引越す, to move into the next door to a person.

tonariau (隣合ふ), *v.* to neighbour; live next door to each other.

tonarizashiki (隣座敷), *n.* the next parlour; an adjoining room.

tōnasu (南瓜), *n.* 【植】 the pumpkin; the (summer) squash.

tonbi (鳶), *n.* ❶ =*tobi* (鳶). ❷ (外套) a cloak; a paletôt. ❸ (攫拂ひ) a filcher; a sneak-thief; a pilferer.

tonbo (蜻蛉, 蜻蜓), *n.* 【昆】 the dragon-fly. ¶ 蜻蛉返り, a somersault, somerset; a loop (飛行機の). (蜻蛉返りする, to somersault, somerset; turn somersault [head over heels]; make a somersault.)

tonchi (頓智), *n.* wit; ready [quick; sharp] wit. —頓智の利く [のよい; のある], witty; ready [quick; sharp]-witted.

tonchinkan (頓珍漢な), *a.* inconsistent; self-contradictory; incoherent. —頓珍漢な事を云ふ, to say things that are not on all fours.

tonda (とんだ), *a.* Ⓢ とんでもない. unexpected; extraordinary; surprising (驚くべき). —とんだ災難, an unexpected calamity. —とんでもない失策をする, to make a mess of it.

tonden (屯田), *n.* a military colony; military colonization. ¶ 屯田兵, colonial troops [militia].

tōne (遠音), *n.* a distant sound; a voice in the distance.

tonei (屯營), *n.* ❶ (行爲) quartering; encampment. ❷ (宿所) barracks; quarters; a garrison; a military station. —屯營する, to be quartered [stationed]; encamp.

tōnen (當年), *n.* ❶ (今年) this [the current] year. ❷ (其年) that year. —當年の鬼將軍, the dare--devil general of those days. —當年取って十六歲, sixteen years old this year.

tōni (疾に), *ad.* =*tokkuni*.

tonikaku (兎に角), *ad.* anyhow; at any rate. ☞ *tomokaku*.

tōnin (當人), *n.* the said person; the person in question; the person concerned.

tonjaku (頓著), *n.* care; respect; heed. —誰彼の頓著なく, regardless of person. —— **-suru**, *v.* to regard; mind; heed; pay attention *to*; care *about*. —身形に頓著する, to trouble oneself about one's appearance. —時間に頓著しない, to pay no attention to time.

tonji (遁辭), *n.* an excuse; an evasion; a subterfuge. —遁辭に窮する, to be at a loss for an excuse. —遁辭を設ける, to make an excuse; resort to subterfuges; evade a question.

tonko (頓呼-法), *n.* 【修】apostrophe.

tonkyō (頓狂な), *a.* freakish; blighty; giddy. —頓狂な聲を出す, to speak in a blighty voice. ¶ 頓狂者, a harum-scarum.

tonma (頓間), *n.* ❶ (性質) idiocy; stupidity; foolishness. ❷ (人) an idiot; an ass; a booby. —— **-na**, *a.* foolish; stupid; block--headed. —此頓間奴, idiot!; you booby! —頓間な事をする, to do silly things; make a fool of oneself; make a blunder [mess].

tonneru (隧道), *n.* a tunnel. —トンネルを掘る, to cut [drive] a tunnel; (mine a) tunnel.

ton-ni (頓に), *ad.* suddenly; abruptly; all at once. ☞ *niwaka*.

tonniku (豚肉), *n.* pork.

tō-no (當の), *a.* in question; concerned. ☞ *tō* (當). —當の仇, one's foe; the enemy himself.

tōnoimo (唐芋, 紫芋), *n.* (a kind of) taro.

tōnoku (遠退く), *vi.* to fall off; withdraw [recede] far *from*.

tonomo-no-kami (主殿頭), *n.* the Director of the Bureau of Imperial Palaces.

tonomoryō (主殿寮), *n.* the Bureau of Imperial Palaces.

tōnori (遠乘する), *vt.* to ride a long distance; make [have] a long ride.

tonosama (殿様), *n.* a lord; a prince; a feudal lord.

tonosamagaeru (金線蛙), *n.* 【兩棲】the edible [green] frog.

tonpuku (頓服-藥), *n.* 【醫】a draught. —頓服する, to take (a draught *of*).

tonsai (頓才), *n.* =*tonchi*.

tonsei (遁世), *n.* seclusion; retirement. —遁世する, to seclude oneself; retire from [renounce] the world; become a recluse. ¶ 遁世者, a recluse; a hermit; an anchoret(-rite); an anc(ho)ress [*fem.*].

tonshi (頓死), *n.* sudden death. —頓死する, to die suddenly; fall down dead.

tonsho (屯所), *n.* a post; a (military) station; quarters; an encampment.

tonshu (頓首する), *vi.* to bend one's head; do [pay; make] obeisance; bow. —頓首再拜, yours very respectfully; your obedient [humble] servant.

tonsō (遁走する), *vi.* to take [betake oneself] to flight; run away; abscond.

tonsū (噸數), *n.* tonnage. ¶ 排水噸數, displacement tonnage. —(貨物)積載噸數, freight [capacity] tonnage.

ton-to (頓と), *ad.* wholly; entirely; (not) at all. —頓と構はぬ, not to care a farthing [pin; straw; bit].

tonton (とんとん), *n.* ❶ (叩く音) a rap; a tap; a rat-tat. ❷ (相子) even; quits; equal. ——, *ad.* rapidly; quickly; swiftly. —トントン戸を叩く, to rap at the door. —トントン拍子で成功する, to win rapid success. —トントン拍子で出世する, to advance by leaps and bounds.

tōnyōbyō (糖尿病), *n.* glycosuria, glucosuria; diabetes (mellitus).

tonza (頓挫), *n.* a sudden check; a standstill; a rebuff. —頓挫する, to sustain a sudden check; come to a standstill; come to a sudden stop. —頓挫を來す, to come [be brought] to a standstill.

tonzei (噸稅), *n.* tonnage (dues); tonnage-duty.

tōonsen (等溫線), *n.* 【地文】an isotherm; an isothermal (line).

toppa (突破する), *vt.* to break *through*; rush *through* (驅け拔ける); rise *above* (値段が). —敵陣を突破する, to break the enemy's line. —五十圓臺を突破する, to go above the 50 *yen* level.

toppan (凸版), *n.* ❶ (銅又は亞鉛に凸起せる畫版) a relief. ❷ (インキの附く部が他より突起したる版式) relief [anastatic] printing; surface-printing (特に木版の).

toppatsu (突發する), *vi.* to break out; occur suddenly. —突發的, unforeseen; unexpected; sudden.

toppi (突飛な), *a.* extraordinary; extravagant; exorbitant; wild (投機·空想など); reckless (向見ずの)

—突飛な計畫, a queer plan; an adventurous scheme. —突飛な事をする人, a romantic person; a reckless fellow.

toppū (突風), *n.* a gust; a squall. —突風を喰ふ, to meet with a gust.

tora (虎), *n.* 【哺乳】 the tiger; a tigress (牝). —虎の子, ① a cub (of a tiger); a tiger kitten. ② (大事にするもの) one's treasure. —虎の威を藉る狐, an ass in the lion's skin. —虎の尾を履む心地する, to feel as if one were treading on the lion's tail.

toradishon (傳統), *n.* tradition.

toraeru (捕·捉へる), *vt.* to catch; take; seize (つかまへる); arrest (捕縛す); capture (生捕にす). —襟首を捕へる, to catch a person by the neck. —捉へ所がない, There is nowhere to catch him.

torafu (虎斑), *n.* tiger-like stripes. —虎斑の, brindle(d); striped like a tiger; tabby (猫に云ふ).

torahōmu (トラホーム), *n.* trachoma.

torai (渡來する), *vi.* ❶ (來航する) to come over [across] the sea. ❷ (文物が) to be brought over; be introduced (傳來).

tōrai (到來), *n.* coming; arrival; advent. —到來する, to come; arrive; present itself (機會が).

torakku (トラック), *n.* ❶ (競走路) a (race-)track. ❷ (運搬自動車) a (motor-)truck.

torakutā (牽引機, 牽引車), *n.* a tractor.

toraneko (虎猫), *n.* a tiger-cat (山猫の一種); a tabby, tabby-cat.

toranku (旅行鞄), *n.* a trunk.

toranomaki (虎の卷), *n.* a book of the secret. —受験生の虎の卷, a good reference book for examinees.

toranoo (とらのを), *n.* 【植】 ❶ (珍珠菜) the clethra-leaved loosestrife. ❷ (莩蕈) Panicum Matsumuræ (panic-grass の一種·學名).

toranpu (トランプ), *n.* (trump, trump-card は切札) card-playing; cards; whist (普通四人にてなす).

torasuto (企業同盟), *n.* 【商】 a trust. ¶ 石油トラスト, a petroleum [an oil] trust. —トラスト征伐, an anti-trust agitation.

torawareru (捕·囚はれる), *v.* ❶ (捕縛) to be caught [arrested; seized]. ☞ *tsukamaru*. ❷ (拘泥) to be wedded *to*; adhere *to*; stick *to*. —習慣に囚はれる, to fall victim to a habit. —恐怖に囚はれたる, ridden by fears. —傳統に囚はれない, to be free from traditions.

tōrei (答禮), *n.* a return salute (敬禮の); return call (訪問の). —答禮の爲め, to return courtesies. —答禮する, to take the salute (特に軍人に言ふ); return a salute [call; courtesies; compliment]. —…發の答禮砲を放つ, to return a salute of…guns.

toreru (取·採·捕れる), *v.* ❶ to be caught [taken] (物がとられる); be able to catch (人が物を). ❷ (放れる) to come off; get out *of*; be detached. ❸ (痛が) to leave; go off. ❹ (要す) to take; require. ❺ (產出) to yield; produce; bring. —大分手間が取れる, to take a considerable time. —この土地からよい作物がとれる, The land yields good crops.

toretsu (堵列する), *vi.* to be drawn up. —兩側に堵列する, to line both sides; form a lane.

tori (鳥), *n.* a bird; a fowl (家禽); a hen (鷄); chicken (鷄肉). —空飛ぶ鳥, a bird in the sky [on the wing]. —鳥の巢, a bird('s)-nest. —鳥なき里の蝙蝠, "In the country of the blind, the one-eyed man is king."

tōri (通), *n.* ❶ (街路) a street; a road. ❷ (往來) coming and going; traffic. ❸ (疏通) passage; drainage (水の). ❹ (了解) understanding. ❺ (種類) a kind; a sort; a way (方法). ❻ (評判) favour; repute; credit (信用). —通りがよい, ① (下水·煙管など) to run [pass] well; draw well (煙管, 煙筒). ② (早く分る) to be easily understood. —大きな通へ出る, to come to a wide road. —此通りの箱が欲しい, I want a box just like this (one). —その通りだ, Just so! ——**-ni**, *ad.* as. ——, *prep.* according *to*; in accordance *with*; after (則って). —常の通りに, (the same) as usual. —豫想の通りに, as one expected. —手本の通りに書く, to write after a copy-book.

toriaezu (取敢へず), *ad.* at once; immediately; first of all (何よりも). —取敢へず知らす, to hasten to inform a person that….

toriage (取上), *n.* ❶ (沒收) confiscation. ❷ (受理) acceptance. ❸ (剝奪) deprivation; expropriation. ❹ (助産) midwifery. ¶ 取上婆, a midwife.

toriageru (取上げる), *vt.* ❶ (手に) to take up; take in one's hand. ❷ (容れる) to accept; take; adopt. ❸ (氣に留める) to notice [heed], take notice [heed] *of*; listen to. ❹ (沒收する) to confiscate. ❺ (剝奪する) to deprive (a person) *of*; take away *from*; expropriate (收用). —取上げな

い, to ignore; take no notice [heed] *of*; pay [give] no notice *to*; reject. —勳章を取上げる, to deprive a person of his decoration. —子供を取上げる, to midwife; assist in childbirth; deliver a woman of a child.

toriai (取合), *n.* scramble. —取合ひする, =**toriau** の ❷.

tōriame (通雨), *n.* a shower; a passing rain. —通り雨が降る, to shower.

toriami (鳥網), *n.* a fowler's [fowling] net.

toriatsukai (取扱), *n.* ❶ (人又は物の) treatment; handling; usage; use (使用); entertainment (もてなし). ❷ (事務の) conduct; management; transaction. —取扱注意, with care. —取扱ひに便である, to be convenient to manage. —生徒に對する公平な取扱ひ, impartial treatment of pupils. ¶ 局長事務取扱, an acting director of a bureau. —取扱方, the method of treatment; the usage (使用法). —取扱人, a manager; a person in charge; an agent.

toriatsukau (取扱ふ), *vt.* ❶ (人又は物) to treat; handle; deal *with* (問題·事件·人等); manipulate (機械·問題·人を巧に); deal [trade; traffic] *in* (商品を). ❷ (事務) to conduct; manage; transact. —取扱ひ易い, ① [*a.*] manageable; handy; tractable (素直な). ② [*vi.*] to be easy to deal with. —取扱ひ惡い, ① [*a.*] unmanageable; unwieldy; awkward. ② [*vi.*] to be difficult to treat; be hard to deal with. —公平に取扱ふ, to deal justly with a person. —事務を取扱ふ, to manage the affairs; conduct [transact] business.

toriatsume (取集), *n.* collection; gathering. —取集める, to collect; gather. ¶ 取集人, a collector.

toriau (取合ふ), *vt.* ❶ (互に取る) to take each other. ❷ (爭奪する) to scramble [struggle] *for*. ❸ (相手にする) to deal *with* (人); take notice [heed] *of* (苦情など). —取合はぬ, to ignore; take no notice [heed] *of*; pay no heed [attention] *to*; not to give ear *to*. —人氣を取合ふ, to bid for popularity.

toriawase (取合), *n.* combination; arrangement; assortment. —色の取合せ, combination of colours. —この箱にはキャンディーの上等の取合せが入ってゐる, The box contains a choice assortment of candy.

toriawaseru (取合せる), *vt.* to group; combine; arrange; match (他と). —酢五勺と醬油三合とを取合はせる, to take five *shaku* of vinegar and three *gō* of soy.

tōriawaseru (通合せる), *vi.* to happen to pass by.

torichigaeru (取違へる), *v.* ❶ (間違へる) to mistake; take (a person) for another (人を); take a wrong one (物を). ❷ (誤解する) to misunderstand; misapprehend.

torichirasu (取散す), *vt.* to scatter about (散亂); put out of order (亂雜); put in disorder (同上). —取散してある, to be out of order; be in disorder.

toridaka (取高), *n.* income (收入); fee (大名の); crop (取入高).

toride (砦, 寨, 壘), *n.* a fort; a fortification; a fortress (城寨). —砦を築く, to build a fort; fortify.

toridori (取取), *ad.* variously; diversely; differently. —噂とりどりにして, as the rumours are diverse. —色とりどりに咲き出でる, to flower in various colours.

torie (取得), *n.* Ⓢ 取所. ❶ (價値) worth; merit; value. ❷ (效用) use; utility; a useful point. ❸ (特徵) a strong point; a forte. —取得のない, worthless; of no use [value]; good-for-nothing. —何の取得もない男だ, He has nothing to recommend him.

torigai (鳥貝), *n.* 【貝】the cockle.

tōrigakari (通掛りの), *a.* Ⓢ 通掛けの. passing; chance; casual. —通りがかりの人, a passer-by. —通掛けに立寄る, to drop in as one passes the house.

tōrigakaru (通掛る), *vi.* to happen to pass by; come along.

torige (鳥毛), *n.* a feather; a plume; an aigrette (裝飾の).

torigoya (鳥小屋), *n.* an aviary; a hen-house [cote] (鷄の).

torihada (鳥肌), *n.* goose-skin; goose-flesh.

torihakarai (取計), *n.* management; arrangement; disposition.

torihakarau (取計ふ), *v.* to manage; take measures [steps]; arrange; dispose *of*. —よい樣に取計ふ, to put a matter right. —然るべく取計ふ, to dispose of it as one thinks best.

toriharai (取拂), *n.* clearing away; removal; pulling down.

toriharau (取拂ふ), *vt.* to remove; clear away; pull down (こはす). —煉瓦塀を取拂ふ, to pull down a brick wall.

torihazushi (取外), *n.* ❶ taking apart [to pieces]. ❷ (取外し得る裝置) dismantlement.

torihazusu (取外す), *vt.* to take apart [away]; dismantle (設備を); take to pieces (解體する). —取

外しの出來る, sectional (組立式); removable. (取外しの出來る様に造られてゐる (汽船など), to be built in sections.) —船の索具を取外す, to strip a ship.

torihiki (取引), *n.* transaction; business; dealing. —取引する, ① (人と) to trade *with* (a firm *for* some goods); transact [do] business *with*; have dealings *with*. ② (品の) to traffic [trade; deal] *in* (some goods). —取引關係がない, to have no dealings (to do) *with*. —取引を初める, to open an account (*with*); enter into a connection. —取引を止める, to close an account *with*; break off a connection. —取引を申込む, to propose to open business (*with*). ¶ 地方取引, local transaction. —直(延)取引, immediate (future) delivery. —取引銀行, a bank with which the credit is opened. —取引所, an exchange; a 'change (exchange の略). (商品取引所, a produce exchange.) —取引先, a customer; a connection; a correspondent (特に外國の).

torihirogeru (取擴げる), *vt.* to widen; enlarge; extend.

torihishigu (取挫ぐ), *vt.* to defeat; crush; destroy; push to the wall. —鬼をも取挫ぐ元氣, a spirit that would even defeat demons.

torii (鳥居), *n.* a *torii* [日]; a shrine-entrance.

tōriippen (通一遍の), *a.* formal; indifferent (冷淡な); casual (其場限りの). —通り一遍の客, a casual guest. —通り一遍の挨拶, formal compliments.

toriire (取入), *n.* crop; harvest. —秋の取入れ, an autumn harvest. ¶ 取入れ時, harvest-time [season].

toriireru (取入れる), *vt.* ❶ (取込む) to take in [into]; adopt (採用); introduce (輸入); borrow (借りる). ❷ (收穫) to harvest; crop; get (in).

toriiru (取入る), *v.* to work [worm; insinuate] into another's favour; wind oneself into another's affection; flatter. —權那に取入る, to ingratiate oneself with one's master; win one's master's good graces. —上役に取入る, to curry favour with one's superiors.

toriisogu (取急ぐ), *vi.* to hurry up; make haste; hasten. —取急いで, in haste; hastily; in one's hurry.

torikabuto (鳥頭), *n.* 【植】 the Japanese monk's-hood.

torikae (取換, 取替), *n.* ❶ (交換) exchange. ❷ =*kakegae*.

torikaeru (取換へる), *vt.* ❶ (代用) to replace (one thing for another); renew (更新する); substitute (one for another). ❷ (交換) to exchange [change] (one thing for another); barter (物物交易). —取替へ引替へ, one after another; successively; continuously.

torikaekko (取換へっこ), *n.* exchange; swop. —此と彼と取換へっこする, to exchange [swop] this for that.

torikaeshi (取返し), *n.* recovery; restitution. —取返しのつかぬ, irretrievable; irredeemable; past [beyond] retrieve [recovery].

torikaesu (取返す), *vt.* ❶ (恢復する) to restore; recover; bring back. ❷ (回收する) to regain; repossess; take [get] back [again]. ❸ (償ふ) to compensate; make up for; make good. —城を取返す, to recover a castle. —身代を取返す, to retrieve one's fortune.

torikago (鳥籠), *n.* a bird-cage; a hen-coop (鷄の).

torikai (鳥飼), *n.* a bird-fancier.

torikaji (取舵), 【航】 (命令) starboard (the helm)! —取舵一杯, hard a starboard!

torikakaru (取掛かる), *vt.* to commence; begin; set about; set the hand *to* (企てる). —仕事に取掛かる, to commence work *on*; set [go; proceed; turn] to work. (仕事に取掛からせる, to set a person to work. —註文に取掛からせる, to put an order in hand.)

torikakomu (取圍む), *vt.* to surround; encircle; besiege; hem in. —海に取圍まれた國, a sea-girt country. —火に取圍まれる, to be hemmed in by fire.

torikata (取方), *n.* the manner [way; method] of taking. —歌留多の取方, the way of taking ode-cards. —寫眞の撮方, how to take a photograph [portrait].

torikatazukeru (取片附ける), *vt.* to put in order; tidy up. ☞ *katazukeru*.

torikawasu (取交はす), *vt.* to exchange. —指環を取交はす, to exchange rings. —手を取交はす, to grasp each other's hand.

torikeshi (取消), *n.* ❶ 【法】 cancellation; revocation; rescission (解除). ❷ (撤回) withdrawal; retraction; recantation. ❸ (判決の) reversal; recall; repeal. ❹ (命令等の) countermand; annulment. —取消を申込む, to require retraction.

torikesu (取消す), *vt.* ❶ 【法】 to cancel; revoke; rescind (解除). ❷ (撤回する) to withdraw; recall;

retract; take back. ❷ (判決等を) to repeal; revoke; recall; set aside. ❶ (命令等を) to countermand; annul. —約束を取消す, to declare off a promise. —前判決を取消す, to revoke a former decision. —免許を取消す, to revoke a licence.

toriki (壓枝, 壓條), *n.* a layer. —壓條する, to layer.

torikime (取極), *n.* arrangement; decision (決定); settlement (解決); agreement (契約). —取極める, to arrange; decide; settle; fix. ☞ *kimeru.* ¶ 取極書, a written contract.

torikiru (取切る), *vt.* ❶ =*toritsukusu* (取盡す). ❷ (一人でする) to do [manage] by oneself. —取切って世話をする, to look after a person by oneself.

toriko (俘, 虜, 擒), *n.* a captive; a prisoner of war: the prisoner's base (遊戲). —虜になる, to be taken prisoner; be led captive. —虜にする, to capture; take [lead] a person captive [prisoner].

torikobotsu (取毀つ), *vt.* to pull [tear; break; take] down; demolish; destroy. —古家を取毀つ, to pull down an old house.

torikomi (取込), *n.* ❶ (混雜) confusion; being busy ❷ (著服) embezzlement; appropriation. —取込み最中に, in the midst of confusion.

torikomu (取込む), *v.* ❶ (取入れる) to take in; harvest. ❷ = *toriiru.* ❸ (著服する) to appropriate; embezzle; pocket. —取込んで居る, to be in confusion (混雜); be busy (いそがしい).

torikorosu (取殺す), *vt.* to kill (a person) by possessing him; curse (a person) to death.

torikoshi (取越), *n.* anticipation. ¶ 取越苦勞, anxiety [worry] in anticipation; over-anxiety for the future; borrowed trouble. (取越苦勞をする, to trouble [worry] oneself for the future; anticipate with fear; meet trouble half-way.

tōrikosu (通越す), *vt.* to go [walk] beyond; pass; give the go-by *to*; pass over; walk past.

tōrikotoba (通言葉), *n.* a cant; a catchword (政治上·宗敎上の).

torikowasu (取毀す), *vt.* to pull down. ☞ *torikobotsu.*

torikumi (取組), *n.* ❶ (角力の) a match; a bout; pairing (顏合). ❷ (爲替の) drawing. —大錦と鳳との取組, a wrestling-bout [match] between Ōnishiki and Ōtori. ¶ 好取組, a well-paired [-matched] wrestle [bout]. —取組番附, a wrestling p.ogramme.

torikumu (取組む), *vi.* ❶ (組附く) to wrestle [grapple; close] *with.* ❷ (爲替等を) to draw. —四つに取組む, to grip each other crosswise. —手形を取組む, to draw a bill *on.*

torikuzusu (取崩す), *vt.* to pull down. ☞ *torikobotsu.*

torimagireru (取紛れる), *vi.* ❶ =*magireru.* ❷ to be taken up [occupied] *with.* —用事に取紛れる, to be taken up with business.

torimaku (取卷く), *vt.* to surround; encircle; engirdle. ☞ *torikakomu.*

torimatomeru (取纏める), *vt.* ❶ (集合す) to collect; gather all together. ❷ (整へる) to arrange; put in order; dispose; adjust. ❸ (決定する) to decide; settle. —一つに取纏める, to collect into a lump; gather into a whole. —家財道具をすっかり取纏める, to collect all furniture and utensils.

torimawashi (取廻し), *n.* management; entertainment (應待振); treatment (もてなし).

torimawasu (取廻す), *v.* ❶ (巧にとりなす) to manage; deal with a person tactfully. ❷ (順に廻す) to pass round a thing after taking up one's portion of it.

torimaze (取交ぜ), *ad.* all together; together *with*; in mixture *with.* —取交ぜる, to mix; put [throw] together. —大小取交ぜ十ある, They are ten altogether, large and small.

torime (鳥目, 雀目, 夜盲), *n.* ❶ night-blindness. ❷ (人) a night-blind man.

tōrimichi (通路) *n.* a passage; a path; a thoroughfare (往來).

torimidasu (取亂す), *vt.* to confuse; disorder; put out of order. —取亂した姿, a disordered form.

torimochi (取持), *n.* ❶ (待遇) treatment; entertainment. ❷ (周旋) intermediation (仲介); recommendation (推擧).

torimochi (鳥黐), *n.* bird-lime.

torimodoshi (取戻), *n.* recovery; repossession. —取戻す, to recover; repossess; take [get] beck. ☞ *torikaesu.*

torimonaosazu (取りも直さず), *ad.* nothing but; nothing more [less] than; that is to say (卽ち).

torimotsu (取持つ), *v.* ❶ (待遇する) to treat; entertain. ❷ (周旋する) to intermediate; act as (a) go-between [an agent]. ❸ (推擧する) to recommend.

torinashi (執成), *n.* mediation (調停); recommendation (推擧).

torinasu (執成す), *v.* ❶ (推擧) to recommend. ❷ (調停) to mediate *between.* ❸ to plead [intercede] (with the father) for [in behalf of] (the son) (詫びてやる); smooth over (a fault) (言ひ繕ふ); say good things *for* (よいやうに云ふ). —よいやうに執成す, to mediate for a person to his advantage.

torinawa (捕繩), *n.* a cord.

torinoichi (酉の市), *n.* the bird-day fair (held on the bird-days of November).

torinoke (取除), *n.* removal; an exception (除外例).

torinokeru (取除ける), *vt.* ❶ (取去る) to remove; take away [off]; clear away. ❷ (横へやる) to put [set; lay] aside. ❸ (除外する) to except *from.*

torinokosu (取殘す), *vt.* to leave behind; leave a portion behind (一部分殘す).

torinozoku (取除く), *vt.* to take away [off]; remove. ☞ ***torinokeru.*** —危險物を取除く, to remove a danger.

tōrinuke (通拔), *n.* passing through; a through passage (道路). —通拔無用, "No thoroughfare." —通り拔ける, to pass [go; run; get] *through.*

toriodoshi (鳥威), *n.* a scarecrow; a bogle; a (bird-)clapper (鳴子).

toriokonau (執行ふ), *vt.* to hold; perform; carry out.

toriosaeru (取押へる), *vt.* ❶ (抑へ止む) to hold back; prevent. ❷ (からめ捕る) to arrest; seize; take; catch.

toriotosu (取落す), *vt.* to let fall; let slip; leave behind (遺脫する); omit (同上).

torisage (取下), *n.* withdrawal. —告訴を取下げる, to withdraw a complaint.

torisaru (取去る), *vt.* to remove; take off [away].

torisashi (鳥刺), *n.* birding (事); a bird-catcher (人).

torisata (取沙汰), *n.* a (current) rumour [report]; town-talk. —…の取沙汰, it is rumoured that…; a rumour is afloat that….

torishimari (取締), *n.* ❶ (管理) management; direction; control. ❷ (監督) supervision; superintendence; oversight. ❸ (監督者, 監理者) a supervisor; an overseer; a director; a manager. ¶ 取締規則, regulations for the control (of). ¶ 取締役, a director; a manager. (取締役會, a board of directors; a directorate.)

torishimaru (取締る), *vt.* to control; manage; supervise; superintend; oversee. —嚴重に取締まる, to maintain strict order; supervise strictly. —規則を以て取締まる, to control with regulations.

torishirabe (取調), *n.* examination; investigation; inquiry, enquiry. ¶ 特別取調委員 (各派の代表者より成る), a select committee.

torishiraberu (取調べる), *vt.* to examine; investigate; go *into.* —由來を取調べる, to go [inquire] into the origin. —目下取調中である, to be under investigation.

torisoroeru (取揃へる), *vt.* to assort; put together; complete; keep an assortment.

torisugaru (取縋る), *v.* to cling *to.* ☞ ***sugaru.***

tōrisugiru (通過ぎる), *vi.* to pass by; go past; blow over (危險などが).

toritadasu (取糺す), *vt.* to inquire; examine. ☞ ***tadasu.***

toritate (取立), *n.* ❶ (徵收) collection (債權·稅の); levy (稅の); ❷ (引立) patronage (愛顧); appointment (任命); adoption (採用). —年貢の取立, collection of land tax. —手形の取立を他行に委任する, to appoint another bank to collect the bill. ¶ 取立金, collection; money collected; levy; exaction. —取立人, a collector. —取立手形, a bill of collection.

toritate (取立ての), *a.* fresh; fresh-caught. —取立ての果物, a fresh fruit.

toritateru (取立てる), *vt.* ❶ (徵收する) to collect; levy; exact. ❷ (引立てる) to patronize; appoint; adopt; raise; push forward. —後輩を取立てる, to promote one's junior. —取立てて云ふ程のものでない, It is not worth mentioning [worthy of mention].

toritomenaki (取留なき), *a.* uncertain; foolish; unintelligible. ¶ 取留めのない話, gibberish; jargon; silly talk; rambling talk.

toritomeru (取留める), *vt.* to save; rescue. —漸く一命を取りとめた, We just managed to save his life.

toritsugi (取次), *n.* ❶ (仲立) (commercial) agency; intermediation; mediation; an agent (人). ❷ (玄關の) answering the door; an usher (人). —取次に出る, to answer the door [knock; call; bell]. —取次を賴む, to knock [call] at the front door. ¶ 取次人, an agent; an intermediary; an usher. —取次所; 取次店, an agency. (書籍雜誌大取次店, a wholesale store of books and magazines.)

toritsugu (取次ぐ), *v.* ❶ (仲立する) to act as agent; mediate. ❷ (客を) to announce (告げる); usher (案内); introduce (同上). ❸ (傳達する) to convey; transmit.

toritsuke (取附), *n.* ❶ (据附) installation. ❷ (銀行の) a run on the bank. ❸ (預金の) drawing; cashing. —造作の取附け, equipment of a house with fixtures. —取附けの店, a shop one always goes to [orders from]; one's shop. —取附けに會ふ, to have a run.

toritsukeru (取附ける), *vt.* ❶ (据附る) to install; fit up; set. ❷ (銀行に) to run on [upon] a bank. ❸ (預金を) to draw; cash. ❹ (買附ける) to be accustomed to buy; buy usually. —造作を取附ける, to set fixtures; furnish a house.

toritsuki (取附), *n.* ❶ (憑依) possession. ❷ (著手) commencement; beginning. ❸ (入口) an approach; the foot (麓). —夏の取附きに, in the early part of summer; when the summer begins.

toritsuku (取附く), *v.* to cling [hang on] *to*; hold fast. —漸く商賣に取附く, to come [enter] upon a trade at last. —取附く島もない, to have no one to turn to.

toritsuku (取憑く), *vt.* to possess; take possession *of*.

toritsukurou (取繕ふ), *vt.* ❶ (修繕) to mend; repair. ❷ (彌縫) to smooth [gloss] over; temporize; patch up. —人前を取繕ふ, to keep up appearances; put a good face on the matter.

toritsumeru (取詰める), *v.* ❶ (嚴しく迫る) to press urgently; persecute. ❷ (思詰める) to think persistently; brood over.

toriuchi (鳥撃), *n.* ❶ (鳥獵) fowling; bird-shooting. ❷ (銃) a fowling-piece.

toriuchibō (鳥打帽), *n.* a hunting-cap.

toriwake (取分), *ad.* ❶ (特に) particularly; in particular; (e-)specially. ❷ (中でも) above all; of [before] all things; first of all.

toriwakeru (取分ける), *vt.* to divide; distribute; assort (類別する). ☞ *wakeru*.

toriya (鳥屋), *n.* a bird-fancier (飼鳥者); a poulterer (鳥肉屋).

toriyari (取遣り), *n.* exchange; reciprocation. —手紙の取遣り, exchange of letters.

toriyoseru (取寄せる), *vt.* to get; obtain; procure. —外國から取寄せる, to procure from abroad.

torizao (鳥竿), *n.* a limed fowling-rod.

toro (吐露する), *vt.* to utter; give utterance [vent] *to*; express; set forth. —意見を吐露する, to set forth one's views [opinions]; give expression to one's views.

torō (徒勞), *n.* vain labour [efforts; attempt]; a sterile effort; useless labour. —徒勞に歸する, to prove unavailing [abortive]; come to nothing [naught].

tōro (當路), *n.* =*tōkyoku*.

tōrō (蟷螂), *n.* 【昆】 the praying-mantis; the soothsayer. —隆車に向ふ蟷螂, "a fly on the (coach) wheel."

tōrō (燈籠), *n.* a lantern; a dedicatory lantern (奉燈); a hanging lantern (吊燈籠); a garden-lantern (庭燈籠). —唐金の燈籠, a bronze-lantern.

torobi (文火), *n.* a slow [gentle; dull] fire. —文火に掛ける, to hang over a slow fire.

torofi (戰勝標), *n.* a trophy.

torokasu (盪かす), *vt.* ❶ (金屬を) to melt; fuse; liquefy. ❷ (心を) to melt; fascinate; charm.

torokeru (盪ける), *vi.* ❶ (物が) to melt; dissolve; fuse. ❷ (心が) to be fascinated [charmed]; be enraptured.

torokko (トロッコ), *n.* a truck; a trundle.

tōroku (登錄), *n.* registration; entry; record. —登錄する, to register; record. ¶ 登錄商標, a registered trade-mark. —登錄稅, registration-fee. —登錄濟, "registered."

tōron (討論), *n.* debate; discussion. —討論する, to debate; discuss. —討論終結の動議を提出する, to move [report] progress; bring a motion for closure. ¶ 討論會, a debating society; a hall-exercise (大學の). —討論者, a debater.

tororo (とろろ), *n.* 【植】 Dioscorea japonica (yam の一種·學名).

torōru (トロール), *n.* a trawl. ¶ トロール網, a trawl(-net). —トロール漁業, trawling. (トロール漁業者, a trawler.) —トロール船, a trawl-boat; a trawler; a steam-trawler (汽船).

torotoro (とろとろ), *ad.* ❶ (やはやは) slowly; dully; gently. ❷ (眠けを催すさま) drowsily. —とろとろ睡る, to doze off. —とろ火がとろとろ燃えてゐる, A dull fire is burning.

toru (取·捕·採·把·執る), *vt.* to take. ❶ (喫する) to have. ❷ (摑む, 握る) to hold; grasp; take [catch] hold *of*. ❸ (捕獲) to catch; seize; capture. ❷ (獲得) to get; gain; obtain. ❸ (盗む) to steal; rob [deprive] *of*. ❹ (占む) to occupy; take possession *of* (占領). ❺ (除去) to remove; take off [away]. ❻ (選取る) to prefer; choose [select] out; pick out. ❼ (採用) to adopt. —よく取る力士, a skilful wrestler. —取ッて逃げる, to run [get] away *with*. —取りにやる, to send a person *for*. —取りにゆく, to go *for*. —取りに來る, to come *for*. —善《惡》く取る, to put a good 《bad》 construction *upon*; take in good 《ill》 part. —武器を執る, to take up arms. —毒を取る, to extract poison *from*. —異名を取る, to get a nickname; be nicknamed. —勘定を取る, to collect a bill; have a bill brought. —利を取る, to charge interest. —宿を取る, to take lodgings. —流動物を攝る, to take liquid food. —菜種から油を取る, to extract oil from rape-seeds. —道を西に取る, to take the road to the west. —君の爲に取らぬ, I do not consider it to your advantage. —取らんとする者は先づ與へよ, "He who would take, must give." —取ることにかけては拔目がない, If there is anything to be got, he will not let it go.

tōru (通·徹·透る), *v*. ❶ (通行) to pass (one's door 門前を); pass by (通掛る); pass along (a street, 往來を); pass through (a tunnel, トンネルを). ❷ (通用) to pass *for* [*as*]; go by (the name *of*, の名で). ❸ (通過) to pass; go through. ❹ (貫通) to go through; pierce; penetrate. ❺ (透過) to pass through; permeate. ❻ (屆く) to be realized; be satisfied. ❼ (鳴響く) to resound. —筋の徹ッた議論, a logical argument. —隅から隅まで通る (聲が), to reach every nook and corner of the place. —應接室に通る, to enter a drawing-room. —橋を通らせる, to let a person cross a bridge. —左《右》側を通る, to keep to the left 《right》. —そんな理窟は通らぬ, Such an argument cannot be admitted.

tōrui (盗壘), *n*. 【野球】 stealing a base.

tōrui (黨類), *n*. partisans; confederates; a set; a gang.

Toruko (土耳其), *n*. Turkey. ¶ 土耳其帽, a fez; a Turkish cap. —土耳其語, Turkish. —土耳其人, a Turk; an Ottoman. —土耳其皇帝, the Sultan of Turkey. —土耳其政府, the Sublime Porte; the Turkish Government.

torunitaranu (取るに足らぬ), *a*. not worth one's consideration; not worth taking up. —取るに足らぬ人, a nobody; a non-entity. —取るに足らぬ物《事》, a trifle; a triviality; a thing of little value. —取るに足らない, to be beneath notice.

tōryaku (黨略), *n*. party policy.

toryō (塗料), *n*. paints; foil (鏡裏の).

tōryō (頭領, 統領), *n*. ❶ (國家の重鎭) a support; a pillar of the state. ❷ (首領) a chief; a head; a leader; a manager. ❸ 【棟梁】 (親方) a master; a boss; a master-builder.

tōryū (逗留), *n*. stay; sojourn; visit. **——-suru**, *vi*. to stay; sojourn; stop (暫時); remain (殘留する). —人の家に逗留する, to abide [stay] with a person. ¶ 逗留人, a sojourner.

tōsa (等差), *n*. ❶ (等しき差) equal difference. ❷ (等位, 差別) grade; class; discrimination (差別). ¶ 等差級數, 【數】 arithmetical [arithmetic] progression [series].

tōsa (踏査), *n*. exploration; survey. **——-suru**, *vt*. to explore; survey. —實地を踏査する, to go over the ground.

tōsai (搭載する), *vt*. ❶ (荷を積込む) to load; lade; take on board; entrain (特に軍隊を汽車に). ❷ (軍艦が砲·飛行機を, 飛行機が砲を) to carry; mount; have. —船に貨物を搭載する, to load a ship with goods; get [take] goods on board. —小麥を搭載してゐる, to be laden with wheat; have wheat on board.

tōsai (統裁する), *v*. to preside over.

tōsai (當歳), *n*. this year; the present year. ¶ 當歳兒, a child under a year.

tosaka (鳥冠), *n*. the cock's comb; the crest.

tōsan (倒產, 蕩產), *n*. ❶【倒, 蕩】 (破產) bankruptcy; failure; insolvency (支拂不能). ❷【倒】 (逆產) cross-birth. —倒產する, ① to fail; become a [turn] bankrupt; become insolvent. ② to give cross-birth *to*. —倒產に瀕してゐる, to be on the verge of bankruptcy; become insolvent.

tosatsu (屠殺), *n*. ❶ slaughter; butcher. ❷ (虐殺) massacre. —屠殺する, to slaughter; butcher; massacre.

tosatsu (塗擦), *n*. embrocation; inunction. —塗擦する, to embrocate. ¶ 塗擦劑, an embrocation; 【醫】 a liniment.

tosei (渡世), *n*. ❶ (生業) living; livelihood; subsistence. ❷ (職業)

a calling; an occupation; a trade. —渡世する, to live *upon* [*by*]; earn one's living [livelihood]; walk [go] through the world. —渡世を始む, to start a business; enter [go] into business.

tōsei (當世), *n.* ❶ (今の世) the present time [age; day]; the period. ❷ =當世風. —當世に向かない人, a man out of the time. ¶ 當世風, the latest [up-to-date] fashion; the new fashion; the fashionable style; modernism (近代風). (當世風の, fashionable; up-to-date; modern. —當世風に, after the fashion; in the latest fashion.) —當世男, a man of fashion; a fashionable man.

tōsei (統整的), *a.* systematic. ☞ *keitō* (系統的).

tōsei (黨勢), *n.* party influence; the condition of a state (黨狀). —黨勢が甚だ振はない, The party is at a low ebb.

tōseki (投石する), *vi.* to throw [cast] stones *at*.

tōseki (透析), *n.* 【化】 dialysis.

tosen (渡船), *n.* ferrying (事); a ferry-boat (舟). ¶ 渡船場, a ferry (station).

tōsen (當選する), *vi.* to be elected; be returned; win a prize (懸賞に). —當選の見込ある候補者, a strong candidate. —評議員に當選する, to be elected a councillor. —最高點《次點》で當選する, to be returned with the largest [second largest] number of votes. ¶ 當選人, the elected; a successful candidate. —當選訴訟, an election suit.

tōsen (當籤する), *vi.* to win a prize; draw a lottery-prize. —第一等に當籤する, to win the first class prize. ¶ 當籤番號, a winning number. —當籤者, a winner.

tōsetsu (當節), *ad.* now; nowadays; of late; at the present time; in these days.

tosha (吐瀉する), *vi.* to vomit and purge. ¶ 吐瀉物, vomit; vomitted matter.

tōsha (投射), *n.* 【數】 projection; 【理】 incidence. —投射する, to project.

tōsha (謄寫), *n.* copy; transcription; facsimile. —謄寫する, to copy; transcribe; manifold (複寫). ¶ 謄寫版, a mimeograph; a papyrograph; a manifolder; a manifold writer. —謄寫料, copying-fee.

toshi (年, 歲), *n.* ❶ (年齡) age; years; time of life. ❷ (一年) a year. —次の年, the following year. —其次の年, the next year. —年が經つうちに, in the course [process] of years. —年の暮《暮頃》に, at《towards》the end [close] of the year. —年の加減で, on account of one's age; from age; because of one's age. —年の割りに若い, to be young for one's years [age]. —年甲斐もなく, in spite of one's age. —年を取る, to age; grow in years; advance in age [years]; grow [become] old. (一つ年を取る, to grow a year older. —かなり年を取った人, persons of fairly ripe years.) —年を迎へる, to welcome the New Year. —年を送る, ① to pass years. ② to speed the parting year; see the old year out. —年を越す, to pass into the new year; keep over the winter (植物などが). —年が年だから無理はない, It is but natural, considering his age. —歲寒うして松柏の凋むに後るゝを知る, "A hero is only known in time of misfortune."

toshi (徒死する), *vi.* to die to no purpose; die in vain.

toshi (都市), *n.* a city; (cities and) towns. ¶ 大都市, a large [great] city. —都市計畫, city-planning; town-planning. —都市問題, municipal problems. —都市生活, city [municipal] life.

tōshi (篩), *n.* a sieve.

tōshi (投資), *n.* investment. —最確實なる投資物, the safest investment. **——-suru,** *vi.* to invest (capital) *in*; put money *in*; place money; lay out capital *in*. —石油株に投資する, to invest [put one's money] in oil stock. ¶ 投資者, an investor; a capitalist (資本家).

tōshi (唐紙), *n.* rice-paper; pith paper; Chinese paper.

tōshi (島司), *n.* the governor of an island.

tōshi (通し), *n.* going direct [straight; without stopping]; a direct route. —通しで行く, to go direct [without stopping on the way]. ¶ 通し汽車, a through-train. —通し切符, a through-ticket.

tōshi (凍死する), *vi.* to freeze [be frozen] to death; die of [from] cold. ¶ 凍死者, a person frozen to death.

tōshi (透視), *n.* clairvoyance. —透視する, to telepathize (人の心を); discern; see through. ¶ 透視畫, a diorama; a perspective drawing; perspective representation. —透視家, a clairvoyant(e).

toshidama (年玉), *n.* a New Year's gift [present]; a hansel, handsel. —年玉を與へる, to hansel, handsel; give a New Year's present.

toshigoro (年頃), *n.* ❶ (齡の程度) age; time of life. ❷ (嫁娶期) nubility; nubile [marriageable] age. ❸ (一人前の年) maturity; adolescence (青年期); puberty (懷春期). 一年頃の娘, a girl of nubile age; a girl on the threshold of womanhood. 一同じ年頃の, of about the same age.

toshikasa (年嵩の), *a.* older (in years). ☞ *toshiue.*

tōshiki (等式), *n.* 【數】 equality.

toshikoshi (年越), *n.* ❶ = *etsunen.* ❷ (大晦日) the last day of the year. ❸ (節分の夜) the first night of the spring.

toshima (年增), *n.* ❶ (年齡) adult age. ❷ (女) an adult woman; a woman in maturity.

toshimawari (年廻), *n.* the luck [fortune] of one's years. 一今年は年廻りが善い《惡い》, I am of lucky 《unlucky》 age this year.

tōshin (盗心), *n.* thieving propensity.

tōshin (等身), *n.* & *a.* life-size. 一等身大の, as large as life. ¶ 等身像, a life figure.

tōshin (燈心), *n.* a wick. ¶ 燈心草, 【植】 Juncus effusus (rush の一種.學名). = *i* (藺).

toshinoichi (年の市), *n.* a year-end fair.

toshishita (年下), *n.* juniority. 一年下の, junior; younger (in years; in age).

toshite (として), as; by way *of*; in token *of* (印として); in capacity *of* (資格で). 一祝の印として, in token of one's congratulations. 一總裁として, in the capacity of president. 一としても, if; though; granted that; supposing that. (彼の言葉が眞實としても, even if his words were true.) 一としては, for; considered as. (私《子供》としては, for my part 《a child》.)

toshiueno (年上の), *a.* elder; senior; older (in years [age]). 一年上の人, elders; seniors.

toshiwakano (年若の), *a.* youthful; young.

toshiyori (年寄), *n.* an old [aged] person; the aged; old age (老齡). 一年寄の物忘れ若い者の物知らず, "The old forgets, the young doesn't know."

toshiyoru (年寄る), *vi.* to age; grow [become] old; advance in age. 一年寄った, old; aged. 一彼は年寄らぬ, He wears his years [age] well.

toshizakari (年盛), *n.* the prime [bloom] of life; the flower of one's age.

tosho (屠所), *n.* a slaughter-house; a butchery; an *abattoir* 【佛】. 一屠所の羊, the sheep led to the slaughter-house.

tosho (圖書), *n.* books. ¶ 圖書閲覽室, a reading-room. 一圖書係, a librarian. 一圖書館, a library. (圖書館長, the chief librarian.) 一圖書目錄, catalogues of books. 一圖書頭, the Director of the Bureau of Libraries.

tōsho (投書), *n.* a contribution. 一投書する, to contribute (an article) *to.* ¶ 投書家, a contributor. 一投書欄, the contributor's column.

tōsho (島嶼), *n.* islands; islets.

tōsho (當初), *n.* ❶ (初手) the first; the beginning; the outset. ❷ (當時) those days; that time. ——, *ad.* originally; at first [the beginning; commencement; the outset]; in those days; at that time.

tōshō (凍傷), *n.* 【醫】 pernio; frost-bite; chilblain. 一凍傷に罹る, to be frost-bitten; get a chilblain.

tōshō (湯傷), *n.* scald. ☞ *ya-kedo.*

toshu (徒手), *n.* an empty hand. 一徒手空拳にて, empty-handed; without any capital (無資本で); unarmed (素手で). ¶ 徒手體操, free gymnastics.

tōshu (投手), *n.* 【野球】 a pitcher; a twirler; a hurler; a bowler (クリケットの). 一左利の投手, a left-hand(-ed) pitcher; a southpaw 【俗】. 一投手として働く, to work on the pitcher's-box. ¶ 投手板, 【野球】 the pitcher's-plate.

tōshū (蹈襲, 踏襲), *n.* adoption (採用); imitation (摸倣). 一奴隸的踏襲, slavish imitation. 一蹈襲する, to adopt; follow; imitate; follow [tread] in the footsteps [steps] *of.*

tōshuku (投宿する), *vi.* to put up [stay; lodge] *at*; stop *in.*

toso (屠蘇), *n.* spiced *sake.*

tōsō (逃走), *n.* flight; escape. 一逃走する, to run [get] away; take flight; abscond; escape. ¶ 逃走者, a runaway; a fugitive.

tōsō (痘瘡), *n.* 【醫】 smallpox; variola.

tōsō (黨爭), *n.* party strife [rivalry].

tōsō (鬪爭), *n.* a struggle; a fight; a combat. 一鬪爭する, to struggle [fight; combat] *with.*

tōsokurui (頭足類), *n.* 【動】 Cephalopoda (學名); the cephalopods.

tōsotsu (統率), *n.* leadership; generalship. —— - **suru,** *vt.*

to lead; command (指揮); direct (支配). 一部下を統率する, to lead one's men. ¶ 統率者, a leader; a head (頭).

tossa (咄嗟), *n.* an instant; a moment. 一咄嗟の間に, ① (瞬く間に) in an instant; in a moment [minute]. ② (卽座に) at once; on the spot; on the spur (of the moment).

tosshin (突進), *n.* dash; rush; charge. 一突進する, to rush [dart; dash] *at*; advance headlong; sally out [forth] (城中より). 一列車が向うから突進して來た, A train came dashing along.

tosshutsu (突出, 凸出), *n.* ❶ (凸起) projection; prominence; convexity. ❷ =*tosshin* (突進). **—— - suru,** *v.* to shoot [jut; stand; run] out; project; protrude. 一河中に突出する, to project [jut out] into the river.

tōsu (通·徹·透す), *vt.* ❶ (入れる) to pass; admit. ❷ (貫通する) to pass [thrust] through; let pass; pierce. ❸ (貫徹する) to carry through; accomplish. ❹ (滲透する) to soak [wet; permeate] *through*. ❺ (濾過する) to filter; filtrate; percolate. ❻ (招じる) to show in. 一堪へ通す, to get through *with*; stand out; endure to the end. 一なくて通す, to do [go] without. 一紐を通す, to pass a cord through. 一主義を通す, to carry one's principle through to the end. 一孔に繩を通す, to put a rope through a hole. 一客を座敷へ通す, to show a person into the parlour. 一仲人を通して掛合ふ, to negotiate through a mediator.

tōsui (陶酔する), *vi.* to be intoxicated; be charmed.

tōsui (統帥), *n.* ❶ =*tōsotsu*. ❷ (天皇の) supreme command. ¶ 統帥權, 【法】(prerogative of) supreme command.

tōsumitonbo (豆娘), *n.* 【昆】 Agrion quadrigerum (學名).

to-suru (賭する), *vt.* to risk; stake; hazard; bet (賭ける). 一戰を賭する, to risk a battle. 一萬事を賭して, at all hazards [risks].

tō-suru (黨する), *v.* to make common cause *with.*

tōta (淘汰), *n.* ❶ (自然の) selection. ❷ (黜陟) dismissal; discharge. **—— - suru,** *vt.* to select; eliminate: dismiss; discharge; 【鑛】 concentrate. 一冗員を淘汰する, to weed out [dismiss] superfluous officials.

totan (亞鉛), *n.* zinc. 一亞鉛で葺く, to roof with zinc. ¶ 亞鉛板, sheet-zinc.

totan (途端), *n.* chance; time. 一途端に, just as; in the act *of*; at the moment. (駈出す途端に, just as I ran out.)

totan (塗炭), *n.* ❶ (泥と炭) mud and charcoal. ❷ (汚穢物) dirt; dust; filth. ❸ (難儀) distress; misery; wretchedness. 一塗炭の中に苦む, to live in abject misery.

tōtatsu (到達), *n.* arrival. 一到達する, to arrive *at* [*in*]; reach. ¶ 到達地, the destination.

tote (とて), ❶ (「と言ひて」又は「と思ひて」等の省約) saying that; thinking that; in order *to* [that] (目的で); for the purpose *of* (同上). ❷ (とも) even if [though]. ❸ (ので) as; because; on the ground. 一今も今とて, this very moment; just now. 一逃げようとて, even though you tried to escape.

totei (徒弟), *n.* ❶ (門人) a disciple; a pupil. ❷ (丁稚) an apprentice. 一寫眞師の徒弟となる, to become a photographer's pupil; be apprenticed to a photographer. ¶ 徒弟學校, an apprentices school. 一徒弟教育, education of apprentices.

tōtei (到底), *ad.* ❶ after all; in the end. ❷ (どうしても) possibly; by no means; not at all.

totemo (迚も), *ad.* by no means; not at all. 一とても有り得べからざる, [*a.*] highly improbable; absolutely impossible.

tōten (唐天), *n.* velveteen; cotton velvet.

tōten (沼天の), *a.* rising to the sky. 一沼天の勢, overwhelming force; ascendancy.

totetsu (途轍もない), *a.* absurd; unreasonable; monstrous. 一途轍もない野心, an inordinate ambition. 一途轍もない話, a monstrous story; a fish-story [米·俗].

tōtetsu (透徹する), *vi.* to be transparent [clear].

totō (徒黨), *n.* a league; a faction; a confederacy; a band (盗賊等の). 一徒黨を組む, to band [league; combine] together; form a faction. (徒黨を組んで, in faction.)

tōtō (到頭), *ad.* ❶ (遂に) at last; finally; in the end. ❷ (結局) after all; in the long run.

tōtō (滔滔), *ad.* ❶ (盛んに流る る貌) in a large stream; rapidly (速に). ❷ (流暢に) eloquently; fluently; volubly. ❸ (相率ゐて) generally; in general. 一滔々たる, fluent; eloquent; voluble; vast (洋々たる). 一滔々懸河の辯, a flood of words. 一滔々と流れる, to flow in a large stream; rush in torrents.

tōtoi (尊・貴い), *a.* ❶ 〔尊〕(品位高き) noble; high; august. ❷ 〔貴〕(價値高き) precious; valuable; of great value [price]. —尊き方, an august personage.

totoku (都督), *n.* ❶ =*tōsotsu* (統率). ❷ (人) a chief commander (總大將); a governor-general (總督); a *tutu* 〔支那〕. ¶ 關東都督《府》, the Governor-General《Government-General》of Kwantung.

tōtomu (尊・貴む), *vt.* ❶ 〔尊〕(あがめる) to respect; honour; venerate. ❷ (尊重する) to esteem; hold in esteem [estimation]; set store *by* [a high value *on*]. —尊むべき, honourable; venerable; precious; valuable.

totonoeru (調・整・齊へる), *vt.* ❶ 〔調〕(整調する) to attune; adjust; accord. ❷ 〔調〕(準備する) to prepare *for*; make [get] ready; procure. ❸ 〔整, 齊〕(整頓する) to fix; arrange; put [bring; set] in order. ——, *a.* orderly; arranged; tidy; neat; in order; straight; trim. —夕食を調へる, to get supper ready; spread for supper. —金を調へる, to get money ready. —部屋をきちんと整へる, to tidy up a room; put a room in order. —用意を調へる, to make preparations [arrangements]; complete preparations. —家を齊へる, to manage household affairs.

totonou (調・整・齊ふ), *vi.* ❶ 〔調〕(調子が) to be attuned; (準備が) be prepared [ready]. ❷ 〔整, 齊〕(整頓する) to be put in order. ❸ (揃ふ) (*a*) to be made even: (*b*) 〔整〕 to be completed. ❹ 〔調〕(纏まる) to be settled; come to conclusion.

tōtotsu (唐突に), *ad.* suddenly. 「☞ *totsuzen*.」

totsu (咄), *int.* ❶ (輕侮・叱責の聲) pooh; tut; pshaw. ❷ (驚き怪む聲) what; oh; dear; dear me; well. ❸ (呼びかく聲) holla; hullo. —咄何事ぞ!, Fie upon it!

tōtsū (疼痛), *n.* pain; ache; irritation. ☞ *itami* (痛).

totsuben (訥辯の), *a.* slow of speech; unfluent; awkward. ¶ 訥辯家, an unfluent [awkward; a poor] speaker.

totsugeki (突撃), *n.* a charge; an assault (强襲); a sally (城中よりの); a sortie (同上). ——-**suru**, *v.* to advance to attack; charge; sally out; make a sortie. —敵を目掛けて突撃する, to make a dash at the enemy. ¶ 騎兵突擊, a cavalry charge.

totsugu (嫁ぐ), *vi.* to marry; get married.

totsuji (凸字), *n.* a raised type (活字); braille (points) (點字).

totsumen (凸面), *n.* a convex surface. ¶ 凸面鏡, a convex mirror.

totsunen (突燃), *n.* 【化】 deflagration.

totsuō (凸凹), *n.* convexity and concavity; convexo-concavity. ¶ 凸凹鏡, a convexo-concave lens.

totsuzen (突然), *ad.* suddenly; all of a sudden; abruptly. —突然の死, a sudden death. —突然の御來訪, your unexpected visit.

totte (把手), *n.* a handle (柄); a knob (戶・抽斗等の); a button (抽斗の); a pull (引手); an ear (水差等の). —把手を附ける, to fix a handle; (furnish a) knob.

tottekaesu (取って返す), *vi.* to come back; retrace one's steps.

tottekawaru (取って代る), *vt.* to supplant; (oust and) take the place *of*.

totteoki (取って置きの), *a.* Ⓢ 取っときの. reserved; in reserve; highly prized. —取って置きの計策, a card up one's sleeve.

totteoku (取って置く), *vt.* Ⓢ 取っとく. ❶ (保留) to reserve. ❷ (除外) to set aside [apart; by]; lay aside; put by. ❸ (貯藏) to keep in; store; preserve.

tottewa (取っては), *prep.* to; for; with. ☞ *tai-shite*.

tou (問ふ), *vt.* ❶ (質問する) to ask; question; put a question *to*. ❷ (糺す) to inquire; cross-question (詰問する). —罪を問ふ, to inquire into another's crime; cross-examine a person on his crime. —問ふは一時の恥, 問はぬは末代の恥, "He who is afraid of asking is ashamed of learning."

tou (訪ふ), *vt.* to visit; pay [make] a visit *to*; call *on* (人); call *at* (家). ☞ *hōmon*. —人を事務所に訪ふ, to call on [ask for] a person at his office.

towa (とは), ❶ 「と云ふは」の意. ❷ (意外を示す) should. —とは意外だ, I cannot think *of*.... —人生とは何ぞ, What is life? —とは又どうして?, Why do you say so? —とは誰の事?, Whom do you refer to? —事玆に到らんとは, That it should have come to this!

towaie (とはいへ), Ⓢ とは言ふものの. though; even though [*if*]; admitting [granting] that.

tōwaku (當惑), *n.* perplexity; bewilderment; embarrassment. —當惑する, to be perplexed [nonplussed]; be at a loss [fault; one's wits' end]. —當惑した樣子

をして, with a puzzled air.

towazu (問はず), *ad.* without discrimination; without regard *to*; irrespective *of*. —誰彼を問はず, irrespective of persons.

towazugatari (不問語), *n.* telling unasked. —問はずがたりに語る, to tell unasked.

toya (鳥屋), *n.* an aviary; a roost (塒); a (hen-)coop; a hen-house. —鳥屋に就く, ① (鳥が) to go to roost. ② (卵子を抱く) to sit on eggs; brood.

tōya (陶冶), *n.* (薫陶) education; cultivation; discipline (訓練). —品性の陶冶, the formation of character. —— **-suru,** *vt.* to educate; cultivate; discipline. —品性を陶冶する, to cultivate one's character.

toyakaku (兎や角), Ⓢ 兎や斯う. this and that; with one thing or another. —兎や角言はずに, without saying this and that; without murmuring —兎や角と迷った末, after being perplexed by this or that.

tōyaku (當藥), *n.* 【植】Swertia chinensis (felwort の一種·學名).

tōyo (黨與), *n.* ❶ adherents; followers; supporters. ❷ a faction; a set; a league.

tōyō (東洋), *n.* the East; the Orient; the Far East (極東). —東洋の覇權を握る, to have the hegemony of the East. ¶ 東洋風, Orientalism. —東洋人, an Oriental; the Eastern people. —東洋問題, the Eastern question. —東洋思想, Orientalism; Eastern thought. —東洋諸國, the Orient; the Eastern countries [nations].

tōyō (登庸, 登用), *n.* promotion; advancement; preferment; appointment (任用). —— **-suru,** *vt.* to promote; advance; prefer (to a higher office); appoint. —人材を登庸する, to take men of talent into service.

tōyō (盗用), *n.* peculation; embezzlement; appropriation. —盗用する, to peculate; embezzle; appropriate. —電流を盗用する, to tap electric current.

tōyō (當用), *n.* present [temporary] use: a matter [work] in hand; business at present. ¶ 當用日記, a commonplace book; a memorandum book.

tōyu (桐油), *n.* oil-paper; oil-cloth; tarpaulin (タール引の防水帆布).

tōza (當座), *n.* ❶ (一時) the present (time). ❷ (銀行の) current deposit. —當座の小使, pocket-money for the present. —當座凌ぎに, as a temporary expedient; as a makeshift. —當座へ預け入れる, to deposit it on current account. ¶ 小口當座, petty current account. —當座貸越, overdraft; overdrawn account. —當座貸附金, call-money [-loan]. —當座預金; 當座預け, a current deposit [account]. (特別當座預金, special current account; a savings deposit.)

tozai (吐劑), *n.* an emetic.

tozai (塗劑), *n.* an ointment; an unguent; a liniment (液體); an embrocation (同上).

tōzai (東西), *n.* ❶ (東と西) east and west. ❷ (事物) thing. —東西も知らぬ幼兒, an infant which does not know its right hand from its left. —東西を失ふ, to lose one's bearings; be at a loss. —東西東西, Ladies and Gentlemen! ¶ 東西南北, the cardinal points; north, east, south and west.

tōzaiku (籐細工), *n.* rattan work.

tōzakaru (遠ざかる), *vi.* ❶ to go far *from*; get away; recede *from*. ❷ ☞ *hanareru*. —遠ざかってゐる, to remain at a distance; stand aloof [away; clear *of*].

tōzakeru (遠ざける), *vt.* ❶ (斥ける) to keep [hold] off [at a distance; at arm's length]. ❷ (よそよそしくする) to alienate; estrange. —敬して遠ざける, to keep a person at a respectful distance. —惡友を遠ざける, to shun bad company. —酒を遠ざける, to abstain from liquor.

tozan (登山), *n.* mountaineering; mountain-climbing; ascent of a mountain. —登山する, to ascend [go up; climb] a mountain; mount a hill. ¶ 登山者, a mountain-climber; a mountaineer. —富士登山, the ascent of Mt. Fuji.

tozasu (閉·鎖す), *vt.* to shut; close; bar. —窓を鎖す, to close a window.

tozen (徒然), *n.* tedium; ennui; wearisomeness. —徒然に堪へかねる, to be overcome with ennui. —徒然を慰める, to cheer one's dull hours.

tōzen (東漸), *n.* eastward penetration [permeation]. —東漸する, to spread [penetrate; permeate] eastward (東進). ¶ 佛教東漸, the eastward extension of Buddhism.

tōzen (陶然とする), *v.* to be elevated with liquor; become mellow.

tōzen (當然), *ad.* justly; naturally; reasonably. —— **-no** *a.* proper; natural; reasonable.

一當然の事, a matter of course. 一當然の賞罰を受ける, to get [have; meet with] one's deserts.

tozetsu (杜絶), *n.* stoppage; cessation; blockade (閉塞). 一杜絶する, to be stopped; be blockaded; be intercepted; be cut off.

tōzoku (盗賊), *n.* a thief; a robber.

tō-zuru (投ずる), *vt.* to throw; cast; fling. ——, *vi.* ❶ (赴く) to run *to*; go over; join; strike in *with*. ❷ (投合す) to agree; coincide; accord. 一海に投じて死する, to throw oneself into the sea and die. 一賊軍に投ずる, to go over to the rebel army. 一獄に投ずる, to cast [put] into a prison. 一大金を投じて買ふ, to pay a large sum of money *for*. 一不良少年の群に投ずる, to join a band of depraved youths.

tsepperin (ツェッペリン), *n.* a Zeppelin (飛行船).

tsu (津), *n.* ❶ (港) a port; a harbour. ❷ (渡し) a ferry.

tsū (通), *n.* ❶ (事) knowledge (of the world); authority. ❷ (人) an authority. ❸ a man about town. 一通がる, to set up for an authority; fancy oneself an authority. ¶ 支那通, an authority on China. 一骨董通, an authority on [a connoisseur of] bric-à-brac.

-tsū (通), copy. 一正副二通を提出する, to send [present] in duplicate.

tsuba, tsubaki, (唾), *n.* spittle; 【醫】saliva. 一唾する, to spit. 一人の顔へ唾を吐き掛ける, to spit on another's face.

tsuba (鍔), *n.* ❶ a sword-guard. ❷ (釜·帽子などの) the brim. 一鍔際で失敗する, to fail at the critical moment.

tsūba (痛罵), *n.* harsh abuse [criticism]; vituperation. 一痛罵する, to abuse harshly; vituperate; tear to pieces.

tsubaki (山茶, 椿), *n.* 【植】the camellia; the Japan rose.

tsubame (燕), *n.* 【鳥】the eastern chimney-swallow; the swallow (俗稱).

tsubana (白茅, 茅花), *n.* 【植】the Lalong-grass.

tsubasa (翼, 翅), *n.* the wings. 一翼を擴げる, to spread wings. 一翼を搏つ, to flap (the wings).

tsūben (通辯), *n.* ❶ (事) interpretation. ❷ (人) an interpreter.

tsuberukurin (ツベルクリン), *n.* tuberculin.

tsubo (坪), *n.* ❶ (六尺平方) a six-*shaku* square; four square yards. ❷ (六尺立方) a six-*shaku* cube. ¶ 坪數, area.

tsubo (壺), *n.* a pot (土製·金屬製·硝子等の); a crock (土製の).

tsūbō (痛棒を食はす), *v.* to rail at; make a severe criticism.

tsubogane (壺金), *n.* a staple.

tsubokugi (雀耳釘), *n.* a staple.

tsubomeru (窄める), *vt.* to shut (閉める); close (同上); gather (絲を通して). 一傘を窄める, to shut [fold up] an umbrella. 一目を窄める, to screw up one's eyes.

tsubomi (蕾, 莟), *n.* ❶ (花の) a bud; a flower-bud; a button. ❷ (青春) the youth. 一莟を持つ, to have [bear] buds. ¶ 蕾の花 a bud of promise (少女).

tsubomu (蕾む), *vi.* ❶ (蕾をもつ) to bud; have [bear] buds. ❷ (窄む) to be shut; be closed.

tsubone (局), *n.* ❶ (宮女の部屋) the apartment of a court-lady. ❷ (部屋を有する女官) a court-lady having her own apartment.

tsubu (粒), *n.* a grain; a drop (液體). 一大粒の雨 heavy drops of rain. 一粒揃ひの豆, beans of even size.

tsūbun (通分), *n.* 【數】reduction of fractions to a common denominator. 一通分する, to reduce (fractions) to a common denominator.

tsūbunbo (通分母), *n.* 【數】a common denominator.

tsubure (潰), *n.* ❶ (崩解) collapse; crush; smash. ❷ (磨滅) obliteration; defacement. ❸ (破產) bankruptcy; failure. ¶ 潰家, a broken [tumble]-down house.

tsubureru (潰れる), *vi.* ❶ (崩解) to fall down; collapse; be crushed [smashed]. ❷ (磨滅) to be worn down; be effaced; be obliterated. ❸ (破產) to be [become] bankrupt; be ruined. 一眼が潰れる, to become blind; lose one's sight.

tsubusani (具に), *ad.* minutely; fully; in detail [full]. 一具に陳述する, to describe minutely; talk minutely [at length]; dwell *on*. 一具に艱難を嘗める, to go through many hardships.

tsubushi (潰し), *n.* ❶ (潰すこと) crush. ❷ (潰して地金にする事) reduction. ❸ (融通) adaptability; versatility. 一潰しが利く, to be of service elsewhere. 一暇潰しに碁を打つ, to play *go* to kill time. 一潰し値で賣る, to sell at the price of broken metal. 一潰しの利かぬ職業, a blind-alley occupation.

tsubusu (潰す), *vt.* ❶ (破壞) to crush; destroy; demolish. ❷ (觸

潰) to reduce; melt down. ❸ (料る) to dress; kill (殺す). ❹ (消費) to waste; consume. ❺ (破產) to bankrupt; ruin; break. —玉子を潰す, to crush an egg. —牛を潰す, to slaughter an ox. —顏を潰す, ☞ *kao*.

tsubute (飛礫), *n.* a (thrown) stone; a pebble. —飛礫を打つ, to throw [hurl] a pebble *at*.

tsubuyaku (呟く), *v.* to grumble (*at; about; over*); murmur (*at; against*); mutter [complain] to oneself. —口の中で呟く, to grumble to oneself.

tsuchi (土), *n.* earth; soil; clay. —土を埋める, to fill up with earth. —異國の土となる, to die in a foreign [strange] land.

tsuchi (槌), *n.* a hammer; a mallet (木製の); a sledge(-hammer) (鍛冶の); a gavel (石工·議長の). —槌で打つ, to hammer; beat with a mallet; maul.

tsūchi (通知), *n.* report; information; intelligence; notice (通告); a note (同上); communication (通信); advice (商業上の通信). —通知する, to inform; give notice of the matter; communicate. —通知を受ける, to be informed; have a notice. ¶ 通知書, a notice.

tsuchibachi (土蜂), *n.* 【昆】 the digger-wasp.

tsuchifumazu (土不踏), *n.* Ⓢ 脚心. the plantar arch.

tsuchigumo (土蜘蛛), *n.* ❶ 【節足】 Stypus kaishi (學名). ❷ (穴居の夷族) a cave-dweller; a cave-man.

tsuchihori (土掘り), *n.* digging.

tsuchiiro (土色), *n.* earth colour. —土色の, sallow; pale. —顏が土色になる, to turn pale.

tsuchikau (培ふ), *vt.* to cultivate. ☞ *baiyō* (培養する).

tsuchikemuri (土煙), *n.* a cloud of dust. —土煙を立てる, to raise thick dust.

tsuchikujira (槌鯨), *n.* 【哺乳】 the bottle-nose whale.

tsuchikure (土塊), *n.* a clod; a lump of clay [earth]. —土塊の如き, cloddy.

tsuchikusai (土臭い), *n.* ❶ (土の匂ひある) smelling of earth. ❷ (鄙びた) rustic; boorish; countrified. —土臭い百姓娘, a rustic peasant-girl.

tsuchiyaki (土燒), *n.* an (unglazed) earthenware.

tsūchō (通牒), *n.* a notification; a despatch; communication. —通牒する, to communicate; notify. —通牒を發する, to issue [send] a notification.

tsudo (都度), *ad.* each [every] time; whenever. —事故ある都度, whenever anything happens. —其の都度檢査を受ける, to be examined each time.

tsūdoku (通讀), *n.* through reading. —通讀後の感, the impression after reading to the end. —通讀する, to read [look] through.

tsudou (集ふ), *vi.* ❶ (集合) to come [get] together; crowd (群る). ❷ (會合) to meet; assemble.

tsue (杖), *n.* ❶ a cane; a (walking-)stick; a staff. ❷ (笞) a rod. —杖に縋る, to lean upon a stick. —杖(とも)柱とも賴む, to depend upon as the staff of one's life. —杖をつく, to walk with a cane. —筇を郊外に曳く, to take a walk in the suburbs.

tsūfū (通風), *n.* ventilation; draught. ¶ 通風機, a ventilator.

tsūfū (痛風), *n.* 【醫】 arthritis; gout; podagra (脚痛風). ¶ 痛風患者, a martyr to gout.

tsuga (栂), *n.* 【植】 the Japan hemlock-spruce.

tsugai (番), *n.* ❶ (對) a pair; a couple; a doublet; a joint (關節). ❷ (雌雄) a couple; a pair.

tsūgaku (通學), *n.* attending school. —通學する, to attend school; go to school. ¶ 通學生, a day-scholar; a day-boy.

tsugau (番ふ), *vt.* ❶ (組, 對) to be in couple. ❷ (つるむ) to pair *with*; couple. —番はせる, to pair; cover. —矢を番ふ, to fix [fit; notch] an arrow.

tsuge (黃楊), *n.* 【植】 the Japanese box; the box-tree (俗稱): box-wood (材).

tsugeguchi (告口), *n.* tale-bearing. —告口する, to tell tales; peach (密告) 【卑】; squeal *on* (同上) 【卑】; round *on*. ¶ 告口屋, a sneak; a tell-tale; an informer.

tsugeru (告げる), *vt.* ❶ (知らせる) to inform; tell. ❷ (公告する) to announce; advertise. —天下に告げる, to announce to the public.

tsugi (次), *n.* the next. —次に, in the second place; secondly; secondarily; next; after; (and) then. ——**·no**, *a.* ❶ (時間·場所の) next; following; ensuing. ❷ (等級の) second(-ary). —次の日, the following [next] day. —一軒置いて次の家, next door but one. ¶ 東海道五十三次, the fifty-three stages [postal towns] of the Tōkaidō.

tsugi (繼), *n.* ❶ a joint; a seam (縫目). ❷ (補布) a patch; a clout. —補布を當てる, to patch; put a patch *on*; sew (in) a patch.

tsūgi (通義), *n.* ❶ general [universal] principle; common sense (常識). ❷ (普通の解釋·意義) usual interpretation 《meaning》.

tsūgiawase (接合せ), *n.* joint; splicing (木·繩·布等を). —接ぎ合はす, to join together; splice together (木·繩·布を); patch (布を).

tsugiki (接木), *n.* grafting. —接木する, to graft; ingraft.

tsugikomu (注込む), *vt.* ❶ to pour [instil] *into*. ❷ (金を費す) to spend money *on*; sink money *on* (價なき企業などに).

tsugime (接目), *n.* a junction; a juncture; a joint; a seam (縫目). —接ぎ目が離れる, to be put out of joint.

tsuginoma (次の間), *n.* an antechamber; an anteroom; the next [adjoining] room.

tsugitasu (繼足す), *vt.* to add; lengthen (長くする). —繩を繼ぎ足す, to splice a rope.

tsugite (繼手), *n.* ❶ (接ぎ目) a joint; a juncture. ☞ *tsugime*. ❷ (つぐ人) a joiner.

tsugō (都合), *n.* ❶ (便宜) convenience; advantage. ❷ (事情, 成行) circumstances; occasion (場合); opportunity (機會). ——, *ad.* in all. —都合五圓, five *yen* in all. —都合惡しき, inconvenient; unfavourable; inexpedient. —都合よき, convenient; favourable; expedient. (何時にても御都合よき時に, whenever convenient to you; at your convenience.) —都合に依り, for certain [private] reasons; for reasons of one's own; owing to circumstances. —其時の都合で, as it may chance. —御都合つき次第, at your earliest convenience. —都合が好い, to suit one's convenience. (都合が好かッたら, if circumstances permit; if (it is) convenient. —御都合がよければ, if (it is) convenient to you.) —萬事都合よく行く, Everything goes well with one; Everything turns out as it should. —都合する; 都合をつける, ① (手筈, 處置) to arrange; manage; facilitate (便宜ならしめる) ② (調金) to raise; find.

tsūgo (通語), *n.* =*tōrikotoba*.

tsugu (次·亞ぐ), *vt.* ❶ [次] (後に續く) to succeed *to*; follow. ❷ [亞] (次に位す) to come after [next]; rank next [second] *to*. —倫敦に亞ぐ大都會, a great city next to London.

tsugu (注ぐ), *vt.* ❶ to pour out (in); fill (a cup) *with*; put in (油などを). ❷ (酌をする) to help.

tsugu (接ぐ), *vt.* ❶ (接合) to join (together); connect; cement (瀨戶物·ガラス等を). ❷ (接木する) to graft; ingraft. —骨を接ぐ, to set a fracture.

tsugu (繼·嗣·續ぐ), *vt.* ❶ (繼承) to succeed *to*; inherit (家を). ❷ (布を) to splice; patch; sew together. ❸ (取次ぐ) to transmit. ❹ =*tsugitasu*. —父の名を繼ぐ, to succeed to one's father's name. —夜を日に繼いで勉强する, to study day and night in succession.

tsugumi (鶫), *n.* 【鳥】 the dusky ouzel; the Eastern fieldfare.

tsugumu (噤む), *v.* to be silent; close [shut] (one's mouth); hold (one's tongue).

tsugunai, tsugunoi, (償), *n.* ❶ (報償) compensation; recompense. ❷ (賠償) indemnity; indemnification; compensation. ❸ (贖罪) atonement; expiation. —...の償として, in compensation for....

tsugunau, tsugunou, (償ふ), *vt.* ❶ (賠償) to indemnify; retrieve; compensate *for*. ❷ (補ふ) to make up *for*; make good [amends]; cover. ❸ (消す) to atone (罪を); expiate (同上). —償ひ得べき, reparable; retrievable; expiable. —償ひ難き, irreparable; irretrievable; inexpiable. —損害を償ふ, to make good [compensate for] a damage [loss]. —出費を償ふ, to cover the expenses [costs].

tsūgyō (通曉する), *vi.* to be versed *in*; be (well) posted up *in*; be at home (*on* [*with*] a subject; *in* English).

tsūhatsu (通發 -作用), *n.* 【植】 transpiration.

tsūhō (通法), *n.* 【數】 reduction.

tsūhō (通報), *n.* a report; an advice; information.

tsui (對), *n.* a couple; a pair; a set (一組). —對の衣裳, the dress of the same design.

tsui (つい), *ad.* ❶ (僅々) just; only; but. ❷ (圖らず) unintentionally; inadvertently. —つい此間, only the other day. —つい先程, just now; but a few minutes ago. —つい近所に居る, to live close by.

tsuibamu (啄む), *vt.* to peck; pick.

tsuibi (追尾する), *vt.* to shadow; follow; dog the steps *of*.

tsuibo (追慕する), *vt.* to hold in reverence; revere [cherish] the memory *of*.

tsuichō (追徵する), *vt.* to collect (the balance or the whole sum) afterwards. ¶ 追徵金, the balance (or the sum) to be collected afterwards.

tsuide (序), *n.* ❶ (順序) order; arrangement. ❷ (折) occasion; opportunity; convenience. —お序の節に, at your convenience; when you have occasion. ——**-ni,** *ad.* by the bye [by]; by the way; while you are about it. —筆の序に, while one is writing. —話の序に, in the course of a conversation.

tsuide (尋・次で), *ad.* ❶ (次に) next; secondly; in the second place. ❷ (其後) then; subsequently; after that. —相次いで, one after another; in succession.

tsuie (費), *n.* ❶ (入費) expense; expenditure. ❷ (冗費) waste.

tsuieru (費える), *vi.* to be wasted [squandered]; be thrown away.

tsuieru (潰える), *vi.* to be routed; be put to rout; be utterly defeated.

tsuigeki (追擊), *n.* pursuit; chase; 【海】 stern-chase (敵艦の艦尾に從ひて). —追擊する, to pursue; chase; give chase *to.* ¶ 追擊機, a chaser. —追擊戰, a running fight.

tsuihō (追放), *n.* expulsion; deportation; ostracism. ——**-suru,** *vt.* to expel; deport. —國外に追放する, to expel out of the country; expatriate. ¶ 追放人, a deportee.

tsuika (追加), *n.* an appendix; an addendum [*pl.* -da]; a supplement (補足). —追加する, to append; add; subjoin; supplement. ¶ 追加番號, a supplementary number. —追加約款, an additional article. —追加豫算, a supplementary budget; supplementary estimates.

tsuika (墜下), *n.* precipitation; fall. ☞ *tsuiraku.*

tsuikai (追懷), *n.* =*tsuisō.*

tsuikotsu (椎骨), *n.* 【解】 the vertebra.

tsuikotsu (槌骨), *n.* 【解】 the malleus.

tsuiku (對句), *n.* an antithesis.

tsuikyū (追及する), *vt.* ❶ (追ひつく) to overtake; take up; overhaul. ❷ (溯る) to retrace; trace back.

tsuikyū (追求), *n.* pursuit; hunting. —追求する, to pursue; chase; seek [run] after.

tsuikyū (追窮), *n.* close inquiry; cross-examination [-question]. —追窮する, ① to inquire thoroughly; search to the bottom; cross-examine. ② to pursue to the extreme.

tsūin (痛飲する), *v.* to drink deep [hard; like a fish].

tsuini (遂・終に), *ad.* ❶ (仕舞に) at last; in the end; finally; at length (漸く). ❷ (結局) ultimately; after all; in the long run.

tsuinin (追認), *n.* ratification; confirmation. —追認する, to ratify; confirm.

tsuiraku (墜落), *n.* a fall; a drop. —墜落する, to fall; fall [come down] to the ground; come to grief (飛行機). (甲板から墜落する, to fall overboard.)

tsuiseki (追跡), *n.* pursuit; chase. —追跡する, to pursue; follow up; trace; give chase *to.* ¶ 追跡者, a pursuer; a follower; a tracer.

tsuishin (追伸), *n.* a postscript (P. S. と略す).

tsuishō (追從), *n.* flattery; sycophancy; adulation. —追從する, to flatter; adulate; ingratiate oneself *with.* ¶ 追從輕薄, flattery and insincerity. —追從者, a flatterer; a sycophant; an adulator. —追從笑ひ, flattering laugh.

tsuishō (追蹤・追躡する), *vt.* to follow; pursue; chase. —追蹤を許さない, to be unequalled [unrivalled]; excel by far; tower above others.

tsuishu (堆朱), *n.* carved [embossed] cinnabar lacquer.

tsuisō (追想), *n.* recollection; retrospection; reminiscence. ——**-suru,** *vt.* to recollect; call to mind [memory]; look back *upon.* —往事を追想する, to look back upon the bygone days; carry one's thoughts to the past; run back over the past.

tsuitachi (朔日), *n.* the first day (of a month).

tsuitake (衝丈), *n.* the length of one's body.

tsuitate (衝立), *n.* a screen.

tsuite (就いて), *prep.* ❶ (關して) of; about; concerning; respecting; regarding; with [in] regard [respect] *to*; with [in] reference *to.* ❷ (替) per. ❸ (沿うて) along. ❹ (指導下に) under (the guidance of). —就ては, in this connection. —此事に就いて, in connection with this matter. —師に就いて學ぶ, to learn under a teacher. —賃錢に就いての小喧嘩, a trivial dispute about fares.

tsuitō (追討), *n.* chastisement; subjugation. —追討する, to chastise; subjugate; hunt down.

tsuitō (追悼), *n.* mourning; lamentation. —追悼する, to mourn *for*; lament [regret] (the death). ¶ M氏追悼會, the memorial service [meeting] for the late Mr. M.

tsuitotsu (追突する), *v.* to collide with [run against] another car from behind.

tsuiyasu (費す), *vt.* ❶ to spend; expend; use (使用). ❷ (消費) to spend; use up; consume. ❸ (浪費) to waste; squander; spend to no purpose. —多大の歳月と勞力とを費して, at a great cost of time and labour.

tsuizen (追善), *n.* praying for the happiness of the dead; mass. —追善をする[營む], to pray for the happiness of the dead; hold a memorial service. ¶ 追善興行, a memorial performance. —追善供養, a memorial service; mass.

tsuizui (追隨する), *vt.* to follow. —斷じて他の追隨を許さず, to be positively without a rival (in its field). ¶ 追隨外交, passive diplomacy.

tsuji (辻) *n.* ❶ (十字街) a crossing; cross-roads; a street corner (町角). ❷ (巷) a street.

tsūji (通じ), *n.* ❶ passage. ☞ *bentsū* (便通). ❷ (感應) effect; efficacy. —通じがない, ① to be costive [constipated]. ② (無效) to have no effect. —通じがある, to have a passage; The bowels move. —通じをつける, to loosen [move] the bowels. (通じをつけて置く, to keep the bowels open.) —通じは如何ですか, How are the bowels? ¶ 通じ藥, a lenitive; an aperient; a laxative.

tsujiakindo (辻商人), *n.* a street-vendor; a kerb-stone hawker.

tsujibasha (辻馬車), *n.* a cab; a hackney (coach).

tsujidō (辻堂), *n.* a wayside shrine.

tsujigiri (辻斬), *n.* cutting down with a sword in a street.

tsujiguruma (辻車), *n.* a public *jinrikisha.*

tsūjin (通人), *n.* ❶ one familiar with the *demi-monde.* ❷ (粹人) a man of the world.

tsū-jiru (通じる), *vi.* ❶ (通過) to pass. ❷ (精通) to be deeply versed *in*; be well acquainted *with.* ❸ (疏通, 了解) to be understood. ❹ (內應) to communicate secretly *with.* ❺ (道路がどこへ) to lead *to.* ❻ (室と室·海と湖水など) to communicate *with.* ❼ (通用) to go [pass] current. ❽ (鐵道など復舊) (the line) is reopened; (the traffic) is re-established. ❾ (關係) to become intimate *with*; have intimate relations *with.* ——, *vt.* ❶ (通過さす) to pass (an electric current; gas) *through.* ❷ (鐵道·運河を) to construct (a railway or canal) *between*; connect (the two cities by a railway, *etc.*) ❸ (知らせる) to inform (a person of [that]...); make known; communicate (it) *to*; communicate *with* (the other party, *etc.*). ❹ to send in (one's card, 刺を); announce (a guest, 客來を). —電話が通じない, The telephone does not communicate. —人情に通じる, to be deep in the human heart. —事情に通じる, to become familiar with the conditions. —意志を通じる, to make known one's intention. —橋を通じる, to connect by a bridge. —電氣を通じる, to pass an electric current *through*; close [switch on] an electric current [circuit].

tsū-jite (通じて), *ad.* throughout; all over. ——, *prep.* ❶ (介して) through (Mr. A); through the medium *of* (the governor); through [by] the agency [instrumentality] *of* (England). ❷ (全體に亙って) throughout (the country; the year; the whole of one's life); all over (the country).

tsujitsuma (辻褄), *n.* consistency; coherence. —辻褄が合ふ, to be consistent; agree *with*; hang together [俗]. —辻褄のあはぬ, [*a.*] self-contradictory; incoherent; inconsistent. —話の辻褄を合はす, to make a story consistent.

tsujiura (辻占), *n.* ❶ a slip of paper with a motto; fortune-telling by *tsujiura.* ❷ (兆) an omen. ¶ 辻占賣, a *tsujiura*-hawker.

tsūjō (通常), *ad.* usually; ordinarily; generally; as a rule. ☞ *futsū* (普通). —通常の日, an ordinary day; a working day. ¶ 通常會員, an ordinary member. —通常禮服, a dress-coat; a swallow-tail.

tsuka (束), *n.* ❶ (一握) hand-breadth; a palm. ❷ (たば) a bundle. ❸ (束柱) a pop.

tsuka (柄, 欛), *n.* a hilt (刀の); a haft (刃物の); a grip (武器の); a holder; a handle.

tsuka (塚), *n.* a mound; a hillock; a barrow; a tumulus (墳丘); a grave (墓). —塚を築く, to pile up a tumulus.

tsūka (通貨), *n.* a current coin; currency; a circulating medium. ¶ 通貨膨脹, inflation of currency. 通貨流出, efflux of currency.

tsūka (通過), *n.* passage; transit (天體, 貨物); carriage (議案など).

—— -**sasu,** *vt.* to pass (議案·貨物·受驗者を); carry (議案·動議など). —動議《議案》を通過させる, to carry a motion 《bill》.
—— -**suru,** *v.* to pass (試驗·稅關·議會などを); be carried (議案などが); be put through (同上). —(議案が)下院を通過する, to pass [get through] the Lower House. ¶ 通過貿易, transit trade. —通過驛, a non-stop station. —通過貨物, transit goods; goods of transit; "Transit" (包裝表記). —通過稅, transit-duty [-dues].

tsukaeru (仕·事へる), *vt.* ❶ to serve; enter (another's) service; take service *with.* ❷ (かしづく) to attend [wait] *on*; minister *to.* —夫に貞實に仕へる, to serve one's husband faithfully.

tsukaeru (支·閊へる), *vi.* to be obstructed; be stopped up; be blocked (up); be choked (up); stick *in* (the throat, 喉に). —先が支へてゐる, The upper ranks are full. —溝が支へてゐる, The ditch is choked with mud. —前に電車が何臺も支へてゐる, Several tram-cars are at a standstill before us.

tsukai (使), *n.* ❶ a message; an errand. ❷ (使者) a messenger; a runner. —使に遣る, to send a person on an errand. —使に行く, to go on an errand [a message]; take a message. —使を以て, per bearer. —使をやる, to send *for*; send a messenger *to.* —使をする, to do errands; run (on) errands. ¶ 使賃, errand charge; a tip to a messenger.

tsūkai (痛快), *n.* keen pleasure. —痛快に, vehemently. —あゝ痛快だ, How pleasant (it is)!

tsukaidokoro (使處), *n.* employment; use. ☞ *tsukaimichi* (使途). —使處が無い, to be unfit for any employment; be good for nothing; be of no use.

tsukaihatasu (費果す), *vt.* to use up; exhaust; consume. —金を費ひ果たす, to go [run] through one's money.

tsukaikata (使方), *n.* use; how to use; the way of using.

tsukaikomi (使込み), *n.* peculation; defalcation; embezzlement.

tsukaikomu (使込む), *vt.* ❶ (私消) to peculate; defalcate; embezzle. ❷ (道具等を) to be accustomed to use. —主人の金を使ひ込む, to make free with one's master's money.

tsukaimichi (使途), *n.* use; application. —使途のある, of use; useful; serviceable. —使途のない, of no use; useless; good-for-nothing.

tsukaimono (遣物), *n.* a present; a gift; a bribe (賄賂). —遣物にする, to make a present *of.*

tsukainarasu (使馴らす), *vt.* to break in by use; make docile.

tsukainareru (使馴れる), *vi.* to be accustomed to use; get used [accustomed] *to.* —使ひ馴れた机, a table which one is accustomed to use.

tsukaisaki (使先), *n.* a messenger's destination. —使先で, at one's destination; at the place where one is sent (to).

tsukaisugi (使過), *n.* ❶ overspending; overusing. ❷ =*karō.*

tsukaisugiru (使過ぎる), *vt.* to overuse; use in excess [too much]; overspend; overwork (過勞). —頭を使ひ過ぎる, to use one's head too much; tax one's brains. —金を使ひ過ぎる, to spend too much money. —身體を使ひ過ぎる, to overwork oneself.

tsukaite (使手), *n.* ❶ (使用者) a user. ❷ (雇主) an employer. ❸ (消費者) a consumer; a spendthrift (浪費者); a squanderer.

tsukaiwakeru (使分ける), *vt.* to use (each) in its proper place.

tsukamaedokoro (捉へ所), *n.* a hold; a grip. —捉へ所のない, slippery; vague; elusive.

tsūkamaeru (摑へる), *vt.* to catch; seize; catch [take] hold *of.* ☞ *toraeru.* —人の頸玉を摑へる, to seize a person by the neck.

tsukamaru (つかまる), *v.* ❶ (捕まへらる) to be seized [be caught; be taken] *by.* ❷ (物に倚って體を支へる) to hold on *to.* —摑まらぬ樣にする, to keep out of a person's clutches.

tsukamasu (摑ます), *vt.* ❶ to let grasp. ❷ (鼻藥を) to grease [gild] another's palm; slip into another's hand. ❸ (僞物等を) to palm off *on*; foist *on.*

tsukamiai (摑合), *n.* a scuffle; a tussle; a grapple. —摑み合ふ, to grapple; scuffle; be at 《come to》 grips *with.*

tsukamikorosu (摑殺す), *vt.* to crush with the hand; squeeze to death.

tsukamu (摑む), *vt.* to seize; grip; grasp; clutch. —摑み取る, to snatch. —急所を摑む, to seize his vulnerable point.

tsūkan (通關する), *v.* to pass the custom-house. ¶ 通關手續, clearance. (通關手續濟, "Examined.") —通關手數料,【商】clearing; passing customs.

tsūkan (通觀する), *vt.* to survey; run one's eyes *through*; glance *through*.

tsūkan (痛感する), *vt.* to feel acutely.

tsukaneru (束ねる), *vt.* to bind; tie in a bundle; make into sheaves.

tsukanoma (束の間), *n.* a moment; a twinkle; a jiffy. —束の間の, short-lived; transient; momentary. —束の間に, in a moment; in the twinkling of an eye; in a jiff [jiffy] 【俗】.

tsukanu (つかぬ), *a.* abrupt; unexpected. —つかぬ事を伺ひますが, this is an abrupt question, but…

tsukarasu (疲らす), *vt.* to tire; weary; fatigue. —精神を疲らす, to weary one's spirit.

tsukare (疲), *n.* weariness; fatigue; exhaustion. ☞ *hirō*. —疲れを休める, to rest one's wearied limbs; rest from fatigue.

tsukareru (疲れる), *vi.* to get tired; become fatigued. —疲れ果てた, dead-tired. —疲れ易い (仕事など), wearisome; tiresome. —旅行で疲れた, [*a.*] worn with travel; travel-worn; way-worn.

tsukareru (魅かれる), *v.* to be possessed *by* [*of*; *with*].

tsukaru (浸·漬かる), *vi.* ❶ to get into (water); be soaked; be steeped. ❷ (漬物が) to be seasoned.

tsukasa (司), *n.* ❶ (官廳) a government office. ❷ (官職) office; official duties. ❸ (長官) the head official.

tsukasadoru (司·掌る), *vt.* ❶ (管掌) to officiate; take charge *of* (擔當); conduct; direct. ❷ (支配) to govern; rule; administer. —國政を司る, to administer the affairs of state. —事務を掌る, to conduct business.

tsukatsuka (つかつか), *ad.* straight; bluntly —つかつかと進む, to walk straight up to a person.

tsukau (使ふ), *vt.* ❶ (使用) to use; put in use. ❷ (雇用) to employ; take into one's service. ❸ (消費) to spend; consume. —使ひへらす, ① to diminish [wear out] by use. ② to lessen (money) by spending. —辨當を使ふ, to take tiffin [luncheon]. —柔術《魔法》を使ふ, to practise *jūjitsu* 《sorcery》. —金を上手に使ふ, to spend money skilfully; make effective use of one's money. —英語を使ふ, to speak [use] English. —使ふ者は使はれる, "Masters are mostly the greatest servants in the house."

tsukawasu (遣はす), *vt.* ❶ to send; despatch. ❷ (與へる) to give; bestow *on*. —使を遣はす, to send a messenger.

tsuke (附), *n.* an account; a bill.

tsukeagaru (つけあがる), *vi.* to presume *on*; take advantage *of*.

tsukeawase (附合), *n.* vegetables taken with meat; relish.

tsukebi (附火), *n.* incendiarism; arson; an incendiary fire.

tsukebumi (附文), *n.* a love-letter; a *billet-doux* 【佛】. —附文をする, to send a love-letter.

tsukebusoku (附不足), *n.* 【簿記】 undercharge.

tsukedashi (附出し), *n.* an incidental item; an extra. —勘定に附出す, to charge [put down] to one's account.

tsukefuda (附札), *n.* a label; a tag; a docket (貨物の).

tsukegenki (附元氣), *n.* false courage; Dutch courage.

tsukegi (附木), *n.* a match; a spill.

tsukegusuri (附藥), *n.* medicine for external application.

tsukehige (附髯), *n.* a false [artificial] moustache 《beard》. —附け髯をする, to stick [put] on a false moustache.

tsukehimo (附紐), *n.* cords for children's clothes.

tsukeiru (附入る), *v.* to take advantage *of*. ☞ *tsukekomu*.

tsukejie (附智慧), *n.* borrowed [second-hand] wisdom; suggestion (暗示); instigation (敎唆). —附智慧をする, to prompt *to*; put up *to*; instigate. (少し附智慧をする, to give a person a wrinkle or two.)

tsukekaeru (附換へる), *vt.* to renew; replace; change for a new one. —電球を附換へる, to change an electric lamp.

tsukekake (附掛), *n.* overcharge; surcharge. —附掛けする, to overcharge.

tsukekomu (附込む), *vt.* ❶ (帳簿に) to enter in a ledger; note down; inscribe. ❷ (弱點に) to take advantage *of*; profit by; trade *on*. ❸ 【劇】 (豫約) to engage; book. —弱點に附け込む, to take advantage of another's weak points.

tsukemawasu (附廻す), *vt.* to follow on the heels *of*; shadow; dangle *about* [*after*]. —人の後を附け廻す, to follow on another's heels; dog another's steps.

tsukemono (漬物), *n.* pickles;

salted greens.

tsūken (通劵), *n.* a pass.

tsukene (附値), *n.* a price offered [bid]; a bid (price).

tsukene (附根), *n.* a joint. —耳の附根, the root of an ear. —股の附根, the groin.

tsukenerau (附狙ふ), *vt.* to prowl *after*; dog; hang *about*. —...の後を附け狙ふ, to hang on another's rear.

tsukeru (附·著ける), *vt.* ❶ (添加, 接合) to attach; affix; set; stick. ❷ (裝備) to equip; mount; harness (馬具を). ❸ (點火) to light; kindle; apply. ❹ (尾行) to follow; trace; shadow. ❺ (値を) to put; offer. ❻ to put on (著用); apply (塗布); enter (記入); keep (a diary, 日記を); charge (to a person's account, の勘定に附出す). —身に附ける, to carry about one [on the body]. —元帳につける, to put down [enter] in a ledger. —巡査につけられてゐる, to have the police after one; be shadowed by the police. —景品を附ける, to give a premium with an article. —目藥をつける, to apply an eye-medicine. —糊を附ける, to put paste on a thing. —ジョンと云ふ名を附ける, to name a person John. —ペンにインキを附ける, to dip a pen in ink. —砂糖を附けて食ふ, to eat with sugar. —卓子に脚を附ける, to fix the legs to a table.

tsukeru (漬ける), *vt.* ❶ (浸す) to soak; steep; immerse. ❷ (漬物にする) to pickle; salt; season.

-tsukeru (つける), *vi.* to be accustomed *to*; be habituated *to*; be used *to*. —歩きつけない道, a strange road. —仕つけない仕事, unfamiliar work. —聞きつけない聲, an unfamiliar [a strange] voice.

tsuketari (附けたり), *n.* an addition; an accessory; an appendage. —つけたりの, odd; additional; accessory.

tsuketodoke (附屆), *n.* a present.

tsuketsuke (つけつけ), *ad.* rudely; without reserve. —つけつけ物を云ふ, to speak roughly

tsukeyakiba (附燒刃), *n.* borrowed wisdom (入れ智慧).

tsuki (月), *n.* ❶ (太陰) the moon. ❷ (一箇月) a month; a moon [古]. —十日の月, a ten-day-old moon. —大〔小〕の月, a month of 31 〔30〕 days. —月に一度, once a month. —月に三十圓, thirty *yen* per month.

tsuki (付, 附), ❶ (附屬) attached *to*. ❷ (毎に) per; for. ❸ (故に) on account *of*. ☞ *tsuite* (就いて). —聯隊附の, attached to a regiment. —若樣附の女中, the young lord's waiting-maid. —一人に付一志, a shilling per man. —三箇に付十錢, ten *sen* for three. ¶ 五分利附公債, public bonds at 5 per cent.; the five-per-cents; the fives.

tsuki (衝, 突), *n.* ❶ (擊劍) a thrust; a pass; a lunge. ❷ (其他の武器) a stab; a push (角にも言ふ); a prod (尖ったもの). —突と受 (劍), thrust and parry. —衝を入れる, to pass; lunge (擊劍にて); give a thrust. —一突きに突き倒す, to bring a person down with a thrust.

tsūki (通氣), *n.* ventilation. ☞ *tsūfū* (通風). ¶ 通氣孔, a vent; an air-trunk (敎會堂などの).

tsukiageru (突上げる), *vt.* to push up; thrust up.

tsukiageru (築上げる), *vt.* to build up; pile [heap] up.

tsukiai (附合), *n.* association; friendship; keeping company. ☞ *kōsai* (交際). —附合ひのよい人, a sociable person; a jolly fellow [dog]. —附合ひの惡い人, a man hard to get on with; a hedgehog.

tsukiatari (突當), *n.* ❶ =*shōtotsu* (衝突). ❷ (終點) the end of a street (lane; passage, *etc.*).

tsukiataru (突當·衝當る), *vi.* ❶ (衝突) to run [strike; dash; knock; bump] *against*; collide *with*. ❷ (行詰る) to come to the end *of*. —電信柱に突當って倒れる, to run against a telegraph pole and fall down. —突當って左へ曲る, to turn to the left at the end of the road.

tsukiau (附合ふ), *vi.* ❶ (交際) to keep company *with*; associate *with*; have intercourse *with*. ❷ (同行) to go *with*; keep [bear] company. —親しく附合ってる, to be on intimate terms *with*. —廣く附合ふ, to have a wide circle of acquaintances.

tsukiau (突合ふ), *vi.* to push each other.

tsukiawase (突合せ), *n.* ❶ (顏の) confronting; facing each other. ❷ =*taishō* (對照). —突合はす, ① (顏を) to confront; bring (persons) face to face; meet (a man) face to face; face (a person) *with*. ② (對照) to compare; check; collate *with*. ③ (對決) to confront.

tsukiban (月番), *n.* monthly duty.

tsukibarai (月拂), *n.* monthly

payment [instalment]. —三月拂で, by three monthly instalments.

tsukibito (附人), *n.* an attendant.

tsukidasu (突出す), *vt.* to thrust [push; stick] out; protrude. —家の外へ突き出す, to push a person out of a house. —胸を突き出す, to stick [throw] out one's chest. —手を突き出す, to thrust one's hand.

tsukideru (突出る), *vi.* to project; jut [stand] out; run [shoot] out. —大洋に突き出る, to run out into the ocean.

tsukige (月毛), *n.* (馬) a light cream-coloured horse.

tsukigime (月極の), *a.* monthly. —月極めで, by the month. —月極の讀者, a monthly subscriber.

tsukigome (搗米), *n.* cleaned [polished] rice.

tsukihajime (月始), *n.* the beginning of a month.

tsukihanasu (突放す), *vt.* ❶ to throw [thrust] away. ❷ (相手にせず) to defy.

tsukihi (月日), *n.* ❶ (月と日) month and day; date (日附). ❷ (光陰) time.

tsukiii (築地), *n.* reclaimed land.

tsukikaesu (突返す), *vt.* ❶ to thrust [push] back. ❷ (贈物などを) to send back; reject; refuse to accept.

tsukikage (月影), *n.* ❶ (月光) moonlight; moonbeam. ❷ (月光で映る影) a moonlit shadow.

tsukikatameru (突固める), *vt.* to strengthen; harden; ram (撞槌(ﾄﾞｳ)で).

tsukikiri (附切), *n.* constant attendance. —病人に附切りである, to be in constant attendance upon the patient.

tsukikizu (突傷), *n.* a stab.

tsukikomu (突込む), *vt.* = *tsukkomu.*

tsukikorobasu (突轉ばす), *vt.* to push over; knock down.

tsukikorosu (突殺す), *vt.* to stab [pierce] to death.

tsukimatou (附纏ふ), *vt.* Ⓢ 附纏はる. to follow about; hang *about* [*around*]; shadow (尾行). —うるさく附纏ふ, to hang about to one's annoyance.

tsukimazeru (つきまぜる), *vt.* ❶ (搗いて) to pound together. ❷ (混淆) to mix (*with*); throw *into.*

tsukimi (月見), *n.* viewing the moon; enjoying the moonlight.

tsukimigusa (月見草), *n.* 【植】 the evening primrose.

tsukimono (附物), *n.* an accessory; an appendage; garniture (料理の). —薔薇に刺は附物, No rose without a thorn. —怠惰に貧乏は附物, Idleness and poverty go together.

tsūkin (通勤), *n.* attending [going to] office. —通勤する, to attend [go to] office; live out (店員が). ¶ 通勤時間, rush-hour (通勤のため電車などの込合ふ時間). —通勤制度, living-out system.

tsukinami (月並), *n.* ❶ (毎月) every month. ❷ (平凡) commonplace. **——-no,** *a.* ❶ monthly. ❷ commonplace; hackneyed; stale. —月並の洒落, a hackneyed joke.

tsukinokeru (突退ける), *vt.* to thrust [push] aside.

tsukinuke (突拔け), *n.* ❶ (突き通ること) piercing *through.* ❷ (通り拔け) a through passage. —突き拔ける, ① (突き通る) to thrust [pierce; pass] *through*; penetrate. ② (通り拔ける) to pass *through.*

tsukinuku (突拔く), *vt.* to thrust [pierce; run; pass] *through.*

tsukiokure (月後れの), *a.* of the previous [preceding] month. ¶ 月後れの雜誌, the back numbers (of a magazine).

tsukiotosu (突落す), *vt.* to push [thrust] down; precipitate (高所より).

tsukiru (盡きる), *vi.* ❶ (無くなる) to be exhausted; go [run] out; be gone. ❷ (終る) to come to an end; be at an end; expire (期限). —手段が盡きる, to come to the end of one's means [of one's tether]. —彈藥將に盡きんとす, We ran short of ammunition. —盡きぬ名殘を惜む, to feel an endless sorrow at parting.

tsukisasu (突刺す), *vt.* to thrust [pierce; run] *through* (劍などを); stab (短刀などで).

tsukisoi (附添-人), *n.* ❶ (從者) an attendant: (隨行員全體) a suite; a retinue; an attendance. ❷ (子供·病人の) a nurse. ❸ = *kaizoenin* (介添人).

tsukisou (附添ふ), *vt.* ❶ to attend; be in attendance *upon*; escort (警護して). ❷ (女に) to escort; chaperon (社交界で若き娘等に).

tsukitaosu (突倒す), *vt.* to push [thrust] over; knock down.

tsukitarazu (月不足), *n.* premature birth. ¶ 月不足の子, a prematurely-born child.

tsukitobasu (突飛ばす), *vt.* to send flying; push [thrust] away.

tsukitomeru (突留める), *vt.* ❶ (さし殺す) to stab to death. ❷

(究め確める) to ascertain; make sure *of*. —住所を突き留める, to ascertain a person's address. —噂の出所を突き留める, to trace the source of a rumour.

tsukitōsu (突通す), *vt.* to pierce [thrust; run; drive] *through*; transfix.

tsukitsukeru (突附ける), *vt.* to present (a pistol) at a person; flash (a sword) before a person's face; thrust (one's fist) into a person's face; confront (a person with proofs). —證據を突附けて, with the proofs before him. —白刃を鼻先へ突附ける, to thrust a blade under a person's nose.

tsukiyaku (月經), *n.* the menses; the monthlies. ☞ ***gekkei.***

tsukiyama (築山), *n.* an artificial [miniature] hill; a rockery; a rock-work. —築山を築く, to build an artificial hill.

tsukiyo (月夜), *n.* a moonlight [moonlit] night. —月夜に釜を抜かれる, to be given the go-by.

tsukizue (月末), *n.* the end of the month.

tsukkai (支柱), *n.* Ⓢ つっかひぼう. a prop; a support; a strut. —支柱する, to prop (up); support; stick (植物を).

tsukkakaru (突掛かる), *v.* ❶ (喰って掛る) to fly out *at*; run amuck *at*. ❷ (突當る) to strike [knock] *against*. ❸ (突かんとする) to stab *at*; thrust *at*.

tsukkendon (突慳貪な), *a.* sharp; snappish; tart. —つっけんどんにものを言ふ, to speak snappishly.

tsukkiru (突切る), *vt.* to cross; make [force] one's way *through*. —線路を突ッ切る, to cross the line. —水を突ッ切って進む, to cleave one's way through the water.

tsukkomi (突込), *n.* (突撃) a charge. ——, *ad.* =***komi.***

tsukkomu (突込む), *vt.* ❶ (差込む) to put [thrust] *into*; plunge *into*; thrust *through*; run *through*; pierce. ❷ (乘じる) to catch [have] a person on the hip. ❸ (突撃す) to charge (*at*). —一本突ッ込む, to return a retort. —も一歩突ッ込んで, a step further; still further. —衣兜に手を突ッ込んで, diving into one's pockets; with one's hands in one's pockets. —柄(ツカ)も通れと突ッ込む, to thrust a dagger home. —頭を水中に突ッ込む, to duck one's head into the water. —人を水中に突ッ込む, to plunge a man into the water.

tsūkō (通行), *n.* passage; transit; traffic. —通行する, to pass (through); go past. ¶ 通行止, stoppage of traffic; "No thoroughfare." —通行劵, a pass; a safe-conduct. —通行權, right of way; (right of) passage. —通行人, a passer-by; a foot-passenger. —通行稅, transit tax; travelling-tax.

tsūkō (通航), *n.* navigation; sailing; communication by sea. —通航する, to navigate; sail.

tsūkoku (通告), *n.* notice; notification; communication. —— -**suru**, *vt.* to notify; inform. —人に通告する, to notify [inform] a person of a thing; notify a person that….

tsūkon (痛恨), *n.* deep resentment [mortification]; deep regret; ruefulness.

tsuku (吐く), *v.* to utter (云ふ); heave [fetch] (a sigh, 溜息を). ☞ ***haku*** (吐く). —虛言をつく, to tell a lie; utter a falsehood. —惡口をつく, to use abusive language.

tsuku (附く), *v.* ❶ (附著, 粘著) to stick; adhere. ❷ (集る) to gather. ❸ (味方す) to join; take the side *of*. ❹ (價す, 當る) to cost; be worth. ❺ (根づく) to take root. ❻ (習癖が) to contract [acquire] (a habit *of*); get [fall] into (the habit *of*). ❼ (火が) to catch [take] fire; be ignited. ❽ (痕が) to be marked [impressed]. ❾ (利息が) to accrue; bear (interest at five per cent); yield (5%). ❿ (附隨する) to follow. —…に附いてゐる, to be attached *to* (附屬, なつく); be annexed *to* (附屬). —判斷が附く, to come to judgment. —一年七分の利が附く, to yield [give] an interest of 7 per cent. per annum. —味方に附く, to join our party; take our side; take our course. —兄について行く, to follow [accompany; go with] one's brother. —後れずについて行く, to keep up with another. —砂糖に蟻がつく, Ants gather upon sugar. —借金には利子が附く, Loans carry interest.

tsuku (卽く), *v.* to accede *to*; ⌈ascend.⌉

tsuku (就く), *v.* ❶ (席に) to take (a seat); sit down. ❷ (職に) to take up (a calling). ❸ (師に) to study *under*; follow. —席につく, to take one's seat; sit down. —歸途に就く, to direct one's steps towards home; leave [start; set out] for home; make for home. —一定まった職に就く, to take up a definite calling. —教師に就いて英語を學ぶ, to study

English under a teacher. —水の低きに就くが如く, as water seeks a lower level.

tsuku (著く), *v.* to arrive *at* (*in*); reach; get *to*. —目的地に著く, to reach one's destination. —四時までに家に著いた, He got home by four.

tsuku (搗く), *vt.* to pound; mill; hull. —米を舂く, to hull rice.

tsuku (撞く), *vt.* to strike; toll. —鐘を撞く, to strike [toll] a bell. —球を撞く, to strike a ball; play billiards (ゲームする).

tsuku (築く), *vt.* =*kizuku*.

tsuku (衝·突く), *vt.* ❶ to spear (槍で); bayonet (銃劍で); lunge (劍で); stick (短刀などで); butt (角·頭で); prick (刺·針で); gore (角·牙で); poke (棒で); prod (尖ったもので). ❷ =*tsukisasu*. ❸ (押す) to push; thrust; give a push [thrust]. ❹ (突撃する) to charge *at*. —咽喉を突く, to stab one's throat. —中堅を衝く, to charge at the centre; attack the centre. —風雨を衝いて進む, to march in the face of wind and rain.

tsuku (憑く), *vt.* to possess; take possession *of*; obsess.

tsūku (痛苦), *n.* acute pain (痛み); severe torment (惱み); heavy trouble (難). —痛苦を忍ぶ, to bear acute pain.

tsukubane (つくばね), *n.* 【植】 Buckleya quadriala (學名).

tsukubau (蹲ふ), *vi.* to squat down. ☞ *shagamu*.

tsukudani (佃煮), *n.* food boiled down in soy; *tsukudani*-cooking.

tsukue (机), *n.* a desk; a writing-desk; a table (テーブル). ¶ 机掛, a desk-cover.

tsukuimo (佛掌藷), *n.* Ⓢつくねいも. 【植】 the Japanese yam; the Chinese yam.

tsukumo (太藺), *n.* 【植】 the bulrush; the mat-rush.

tsukunen (つくねんと), *ad.* listlessly; in a fit of abstraction; absent-mindedly.

tsukuneru (捏ねる), *vt.* ❶ to knead. ❷ to fold (one's arms).

tsukuri (造, 作), *n.* ❶ (構造) make; construction; workmanship (細工). ❷ (化粧) toilet; make-up (俳優の). ❸ (體格) build.

tsukuribana (造花), *n.* artificial flowers.

tsukuribanashi (作話), *n.* ❶ (讀物の) a fable; a fiction. ❷ (虛構の) a made-up story; a cock-and-bull story; a fabrication.

tsukuridaka (造高), *n.* ❶ (製造高) output; outturn. ❷ (產出高) yield. ❸ (釀造高) the amount brewed.

tsukuridasu (作出す), *vt.* to make; manufacture; turn out.

tsukurigoe (作聲), *n.* a feigned voice. —作り聲で, in a feigned voice.

tsukurigoto (作事), *n.* a fabrication; an invention; a put-up job; a made-up story (作り話).

tsukurikae (作替), *n.* ❶ (改作) adaptation. ❷ (改造) remaking; reconstruction; remodelling. —作替へる, ① to adapt. ② to remake; reconstruct; remodel.

tsukurikata (作方), *n.* ❶ (製法) the way of making; how to make (construct). ❷ (構造) make; construction; structure; workmanship (細工).

tsukurinaosu (造直す), *vt.* to remake; reconstruct; remodel.

tsukuritsuke (造附), *n.* a fixture (物): being fixed (事). —造り附ける, to fix.

tsukuriwarai (作笑), *n.* a forced [strained] laugh; a feigned smile; a simper.

tsukurou (繕ふ), *vt.* ❶ (修繕) to mend; repair; patch up (つゞる); tinker (同上). ❷ (調製) to trim; adjust. ❸ (彌縫) to gloss [gloze; smooth] over; patch up. —所々繕った上衣, a coat patched in places. —衣紋を繕ふ, to adjust one's dress; trim oneself up. —體裁を繕ふ, to save [keep up] appearances.

tsukuru (作る), *vt.* ❶ (製作) to make; manufacture. ❷ (構成) to make; compose; form. ❸ (建設) to build; erect; construct. ❹ (耕作) to plough; till. ❺ (栽培) to cultivate; raise; grow; rear. —木で造る, to make with wood. —眞鍮で作る, to work in brass. —田を作る, to till a rice-field. —野菜を作る, to raise [grow] vegetables. —財產を作る, to make [build up] a fortune. —多くの人物を作る, to bring up many men of talent.

tsukushi (筆頭菜), *n.* 【植】 the bottle-brush; the false horsetail.

tsukusu (盡す), *v.* ❶ (使ひ盡す) to exhaust; consume; use up. ❷ (果す) to discharge; fulfil. ❸ (盡力する) to exert oneself *for* [in behalf of]; do [render] him service. —論じ盡す, to exhaust [work out] a subject. —言語に盡し難い, to be beyond description [the power of speech]. —資力を盡す, to exhaust one's means. —深切を盡す, to show every kindness. —百方手を盡す, to try every means; leave no stone unturned. —己の

分を能く盡す, to acquit oneself well; perform one's duties fully; discharge one's duties.

tsukutsukubōshi (つくつくぼふし), *n.* 【昆】 Cosmopsaltria colorata (學名).

tsukuzuku (熟), *ad.* ❶ (全然) thoroughly; quite; utterly. ❷ (注意して) attentively; eagerly. ☞ *shimijimi.* —つくづく眺める, to look with fixed eyes. —つくづく厭になる, to become utterly disgusted *with.*

tsuma (妻), *n.* a wife; a married woman. —妻を迎へる, to take a wife; marry.

tsuma (褄を取る), to take [tuck] up one's skirts.

tsumabiraka (詳・審かな), *a.* particular; detailed; minute. ——**ni,** *ad.* ❶ in detail; minutely; fully; at length. ❷ 〔審〕 carefully. —詳かに書く, to write fully. —事實を審かにする, to make the matter clear.

tsumadatsu (爪立つ), *vi.* to stand on tiptoe.

tsumado (妻戸), *n.* a side-door.

tsumaguru (爪繰る), *vt.* to finger; roll between the thumb and the fingers.

tsumahajiki (爪彈), *n.* ❶ fillip; flick. ❷ (擯斥) rejection; abhorrence (嫌惡). ☞ *shidan.* —爪彈きする, ① to fillip; flick. ② to reject; abhore; despise.

tsumakawa (爪革), *n.* Ⓢ 爪掛. a toe-cover (of a clog).

tsumako (妻子), *n.* one's family. —妻子を養ふ, to support [provide for] one's family.

tsumamareru (撮まれる), *vi.* to be charmed; be bewitched.

tsumami (撮, 摘), *n.* ❶ (つまむこと) pinch. ❷ (摘みたる量) a pinch (of). ❸ (把手) a knob. —鹽一摘み, a pinch of salt.

tsumamidasu (撮出・摘出す), *vt.* ❶ (つまみて出す) to pick out; take out. ❷ (無造作に提〔*〕げ出す) to chuck out; turn out.

tsumamigui (摘食する), *v.* ❶ (摘んで食ふ) to eat with fingers. ❷ (ぬすみ食する) to eat by stealth.

tsumamu (撮・摘む), *vt.* ❶ (指にて) to pinch; pick. ❷ (撮要) to summarize; sum up; abstract; abridge; condense. —撮み取る, to pinch off; pick off; clip (剪み取る). —撮み込む, ① (撮入れる) to pick in; pinch *into.* ② (無造作に入れる) to throw in; thrust *into.* —摘んで言へば, to make a long story short; in brief [short].

tsumaranai (詰らない), *a.* Ⓢ つまらぬ. ❶ (やくざな) worthless; useless; valueless.. ❷ (けちな) petty; trivial; insignificant. ❸ (無趣味) uninteresting. ❹ (馬鹿げた) stupid; foolish. —(何だ)詰らない!, (What) nonsense!; Humbug! —詰らぬ奴, a sorry [worthless] fellow; a scrub; a nobody. —詰らない本, a book of no value. —詰らない贈物, a worthless present. —詰らぬ事に騒ぐ, to make a fuss about nothing [trifles]; raise a storm in a teacup. —詰らぬ事をする, to play the fool. —つまらない目に逢ふ, to have one's expectation betrayed; do a thing to no purpose. —詰らなく日を送る, to live an unhappy life.

tsumari (詰り), *n.* the close; the conclusion. ——, *ad.* ❶ (結局) in the end; finally; eventually; in the long run; after all (畢竟). ❷ (要するに) in short; in a word. —詰りは, in the end; finally; in the long run. —身の詰り, the end of one's fortune; one's last lot; one's ruin. (惚れられた《贅澤した》のが身の詰り, Her love 《His extravagance》 was his ruin [undoing].)

tsumaru (詰る), *vi.* ❶ (塞がる) to be stopped up; be clogged; be choked up. ❷ (充滿する) to be full; be packed full. ❸ (窮する) (*a*) (金に) to be pinched *for*; be hard up *for*; be straitened *for*: (*b*) (返事に) be at a loss *for.* ❹ (短縮する) to shrink; contract; shorten [draw in; grow short] (日が). —金に詰ッて惡事をする, to do wrong [evil] for want of money. —日が詰ってくる, The days begin to shorten.

tsumasaki (爪先, 趾頭), *n.* the tip of a toe; tiptoe; the toe (靴の). —頭から爪先まで, from head to foot; from top to toe. ¶ 爪先上り, gradual ascent; an uphill [ascending] path.

tsumasareru (つまされる), *vi.* to be moved; be struck with. —情につまされる, to be touched *with.* —身につまされる, to be moved by comparison of another's situation 《feelings》.

tsuma-shii (儉しい), *a.* frugal; economical; thrifty. —儉しい暮し, frugal life. ——**-shiku,** *ad.* frugally; economically. —儉しくする, to use economy; be frugal.

tsumayōji (爪楊枝), *n.* a toothpick.

tsumazuku (躓く), *vi.* ❶ to stumble (*over*; *against*); trip (*over*); make [take] a false step. ❷ (蹉跌する) to stumble; fail. —石に躓く, to stumble over [against] a stone; trip over a stone.

tsume (爪), *n.* a nail (人の); a

claw (禽獸·蟹等の); a hoof (蹄); a talon (猛禽の); a fluke (錨の). —爪で引搔く, to scratch with nails (claws). —爪を咬む, ① to bite one's nails. ② to be ashamed; be in fidgets. —爪を研ぐ, to sharpen the claws. —爪に火を點[とも]す, to lead a stingy life; skin a flint [俗]; whip the cat.

tsume (詰), *n.* ❶ (塡充物) a stuffing; stopper (栓). ❷ (端) the end. ❸ (將棋の) checkmating. ❹ (勤務) appointment. —半打詰一箱, a box of a half-dozen. —本社詰になる, to be transferred to the head office.

tsumeato (爪痕), *n.* a nail-mark.

tsumeban (詰番), *n.* ❶ (番をすること) watch. ❷ (詰番の順) the order [turn] for watch.

tsumebara (詰腹を切らす), ❶ to compel another to commit *harakiri*. ❷ to compel another to resign.

tsumeeri (詰襟), *n.* a stand-up collar; a buttoned-up front (of a jacket). —詰襟の洋服, a jacket with a stand-up collar; a close-buttoned jacket.

tsumein (爪印), *n.* a thumb-mark [-print] (for a seal).

tsumekae (詰替), *n.* refilling. —詰め替へる, to restuff; repack (荷物など); rebottle (瓶).

tsumekake (爪掛), *n.* (辭書などの) thumb notch; thumb index.

tsumekiri (詰切), *n.* constant attendance.

tsumekiribasami (爪切剪刀), *n.* nail-scissors.

tsumekiru (詰切る), *v.* to be in constant attendance; attend constantly.

tsumekomi (詰込), *n.* stuffing; packing; cramming. ¶ 詰込み學問, cram.

tsumekomu (詰込む), *vt.* to cram; stuff; pack (荷物·人を); crowd (人を); gorge (食物を口へ). ——, *vi.* (大食) to stuff; tuck in; gorge. —詰め込める丈け詰め込む, to cram as much as possible [to its utmost capacity]. —試驗前に無暗に詰め込む, to cram indiscriminately before examination. —鞄に詰め込む, to pack a trunk. —穴に綿を詰め込む, to stuff a hole with cotton. —人を一室に詰め込む, to crowd [pack] a room with people; crowd [pack] people into a room.

tsumekusa (漆姑草), *n.* 【植】 Sagina Sinnaei (pearlwort の一種).

tsumemono (詰物, 塡物), *n.* stuffing; pad(-ding) (綿·ボロ·藁など); wad(-ding) (同上); a plug (孔などの).

tsumeru (抓る), *vt.* Ⓢ つねる. to pinch; give a pinch; nip.

tsumeru (詰·塡める), *vt.* ❶ (閉塞する) to close; block. ❷ (容れる) to fill in; put in; stuff; pack; plug (詰物する). ❸ (間を) to put closely; put near (近づける). ❹ (迫る) to press (on). ❺ (短縮) to shorten; cut down; reduce; abridge. —詰めて書く, to write close(-ly). —鑵へ詰める, to can; fill in a can. —列を詰める, to close the ranks. —期間を詰める, to shorten [reduce] the period.

-tsumeru (詰める), *v.* to keep up; go on with; attend constantly. —泣きつめる, to keep crying. —此道を行きつめる, to go to the end of this road.

tsumesho (詰所), *n.* a station; an office; a guard-room (番人の).

tsumetai (冷たい), *a.* cold; chill(-y) (氣溫に就て). —冷たい風, a chilly [cold] wind [blast].

tsumeyoru (詰寄る), *v.* to draw close *to*; press on; approach (closely); close. —ぢりぢりと詰め寄る, to draw closer and closer *to*.

tsumi (罪), *n.* ❶ (罪惡) a sin. ❷ (犯罪) a crime; an offence. ❸ (咎め) blame. ❹ (過失) a fault. ❺ (罰) punishment; penalty. —罪のない虛言, a white lie. —罪のない子供, an innocent child. —罪を作る, to commit a sin. —罪を負はす, to impose (a man) with a crime; impose a crime on (a man); incriminate; lay the blame on (a person). —罪を免れる, ① to evade punishment. ② be acquitted of a crime; be absolved from sin. —罪を鳴らす, to call to account; accuse of a fault; bring to book.

tsumi (積), *n.* ❶ (積込) shipment; loading. ❷ (積量) (carrying) capacity. ¶ 汽車積, shipment [forwarding] by rail. —千石積, a junk of a thousand *koku* capacity. —六噸積貨車, a six-ton freight-car.

tsumiageru (積上げる), *vt.* to heap up; pile up; accumulate. —山の様に積み上げる, to heap [pile] high as a hill.

tsumibito (罪人), *n.* ❶ (宗教·道德上の) a sinner; a transgressor. ❷ (法律上の) a criminal; a culprit; an offender.

tsumidashi (積出), *n.* shipment.

tsumidasu (積出す), *vt.* to ship (off); send off; forward. —汽車で積み出す, to ship goods by rail. —横濱から積み出す, to ship at Yokohama. ¶ 積出港, the port of shipment.

tsumihoroboshi (罪滅), *n.* atonement of sins; expiation. —罪滅しに寺を建立する, to erect a temple in atonement for [in expiation of] one's sins.

tsumikae (積換), *n.* transhipment; reshipment. —積み換へる, to tranship; reship.

tsumikasanaru (積重なる), *vi.* to be piled up; be accumulated.

tsumikasaneru (積重ねる), *vt.* to pile up; heap (up); accumulate.

tsumiki (積木), *n.* 【玩具】 toy-blocks; building-blocks.

tsumikin (積金), *n.* ❶ (積立金) a (reserve) fund. ❷ (貯金) saving. —積金する, ① to put into a fund. ② to save up; lay [put] by.

tsumikiru (積切る), *vt.* ❶ to ship completely (船に); load completely (車に). ❷ to pile completely.

tsumikomi (積込), *n.* shipment (船舶·汽車に); stowage (船舶); loading (汽車·荷車等に).

tsumikomu (積込), *vt.* to ship; take on board; stow; load (a car). —石炭を積み込む, to ship coal; take in coal (船が).

tsumikusa (摘草する), *v.* to gather young plants [herbs].

tsumimodoshi (積戻), *n.* reshipment. —積み戻す, to reship.

tsumini (積荷), *n.* ❶ (荷物) load; freight; cargo (船貨). ❷ (荷役) loading; shipping. —積荷を下す, to unload. ¶ 積荷案內, advice of shipment. —積荷口, 【航】 the cargo-port (商船の). —積荷目錄, a manifest. —積荷料, stowage.

tsumiokuri (積送), *n.* consignment; shipment. —積み送る, to consign; send off (by ship, *etc.*) ¶ 積送品, a consignment. —積送人, a consignor; a shipper.

tsumioroshi (積卸), *n.* shipping and discharging; loading and unloading.

tsumitate (積立), *n.* reserving; laying [putting] by. —積立てる, to reserve; lay [put] by; amass. ¶ 積立金, a reserve (fund); a rest (銀行の).

tsumitsukuri (罪作), *n.* ❶ (罪惡を犯すこと) sinfulness. ❷ (人) a sinner. —罪作をする, ① to commit a sin. ② (無慈悲なことをする) to act cruelly.

tsumori (積), *n.* ❶ (考) intention (意嚮); purpose (目的); expectation (豫期). ❷ (見積) calculation; estimation. —...の積りで, with a view *to*; with the intention *of*; for the purpose *of*; in expectation *of*. —惡い積りではなかった, I meant no harm. —僕等を欺く積りだ, He thinks to deceive us. —私は彼を辯護士にする積りだ, I intend him to be a lawyer; I intend to make a lawyer of him. —冗談の積りで云ったんだ, My remark was intended for a joke.

tsumorichigai (積違), *n.* miscalculation; a wrong estimate.

tsumorigaki (積書), *n.* an estimate; a written estimate.

tsumoru (積る), *vi.* (積堆する) to accumulate; be piled up; be amassed. ——, *vt.* (見積る) to estimate; calculate. —積る話, accumulating subjects of talk. —雪が地上に深く積った, The snow lay thick on the ground.

tsumu (詰む), *vi.* ❶ (つまる) to be pressed; be hard up. ❷ (緻密になる) to become fine [close]. ❸ 【將棋】 to take the mate.

tsumu (摘·剪む), *vt.* to pluck; pick; nip (剪む); snip (同上); gather (採集する). —茶を摘む, to pick tea-leaves; engage in tea-picking.

tsumu (積む), *vt.* ❶ (積重ねる) to pile up; heap (up); lay; stack. ❷ (積載) to load (船·車に); lade (同上); ship (船); take on board (船). ❸ (蓄積) to accumulate; cumulate; amass. ❹ (貯蓄) to lay [put] by; save. ——, *vi.* = *tsumoru*. —山の如く積む, to heap up high. —馬に荷を積む, to pack a horse; load a horse (with goods).

tsumu (紡錘子), *n.* a spindle. —錘數を減ずる, to reduce the number of spindles.

tsumugi (絅, 紬), *n.* pongee.

tsumugu (紡ぐ), *vt.* to spin.

tsumuji (旋毛), *n.* the whirl of hair on the head. ¶ 旋毛曲り, ① (事) perversity; crotchetiness. ② (人) a crank; a crotchety [an eccentric] man; a wayward man.

tsumujikaze (旋風), *n.* a whirl-wind; a cyclone; an eddy-wind.

tsuna (綱, 索), *n.* a line; a rope; a cord (細引); a hawser (大綱, 小錨條); a cable (周圍十吋以上, 麻·針金製の).

tsunagi (繋ぎ), *n.* ❶ (事) connection; joining; dove-tailing. ❷ (物) a bond; a tie; a link. —時間繋ぎに, to fill up the time. —繋ぎに入れる, to put something to fill up a gap.

tsunagu (繋ぐ), *vt.* ❶ (結ぶ) to tie; fasten; chain (鎖で); moor (船を); tether (獣を). ❷ (繋合す) to tie [fasten] together; link together; join (ladders or tables) end to end. —電話を繋ぐ, to connect; switch *on*; put a person through to another. 一舟を岸に繋ぐ, to moor a ship to the bank. 一犬を繋いでおく, to tether [tie up] a dog.

tsunahiki (綱引), *n.* 【遊戯】 a tug of war.

tsunami (津浪), *n.* ❶【地文】 sea-quake. ❷ (海嘯) a tidal wave; a storm-wave. 一津浪に攫はれる, to be swept away by a tidal wave.

tsunaso (黄麻), *n.* 【植】 the jute plant; the gunny-bag plant.

tsunawatari (綱渡り), *n.* (事) rope-dancing: (人) a rope-dancer; a rope-walker. 一綱渡りする, to walk on a rope.

tsunbo (聾), *n.* ❶ (事) deafness. ❷ (人) a deaf man. 一聾になる, to become deaf; be deafened. 一聾にする, to deafen.

tsune (常), *n.* ordinary [usual] times (ふだん); usual state [condition] (平素の狀態); an ordinary course of things (尋常の成行). 一常なき, unstable; transitory; changeable. 一常ならぬ, unusual; out of common; out of sorts (氣分の). 一常に, always; at all times; usually; habitually. 一常の如く, as usual; according to wont.

tsunezune (常常), *ad.* always; usually. ☞ *tsune* (常に).

tsuno (角), *n.* a horn; an antler (鹿の); a feeler (觸角); an antenna [*pl.* -næ] (同上). 一角を生やす, to get angry (怒る); feel jealous *of* (嫉妬). 一角を立てる, to raise its horn.

tsunomata (鹿角菜), *n.* 【植】 Chondrus ocellatus (Irish moss の一種·學名).

tsunoru (募る), *vt.* ❶ (徵募) to levy; enlist; recruit. ❷ (募集) to raise; invite; collect. ☞ *boshū*. —, *vi.* (劇烈になる) to grow violent [intense]; grow [gain] upon one (癖·感情など). 一病勢が募る, Illness becomes serious [worse].

tsunozaiku (角細工), *n.* a horn-work.

tsunozukiai (角突合する), *v.* ❶ (獸などが) to push each other with horns; fight with horns. ❷ to be at discord with each other; be at daggers drawn with each other.

tsunto (つんと), *ad.* ❶ (澄まして愛想なきさま) stiffly; primly; haughtily. ❷ (嗅覺を甚しく刺戟するに云ふ) piercingly; poignantly. 一つんと澄ます, to assume a stiff attitude; prim.

tsunzaku (劈く), *vt.* to break; tear; rend. 一耳を劈く, to burst the ear-drum.

tsupparu (突張る), *vt.* ❶ (押す, 突く) to push; thrust. ❷ (支へる) to prop (up); support. ❸ (押通す) to insist (on); carry out. 一仕舞まで突ッ張る, to persist to the end.

tsura (面), *n.* a face; a mug [卑]; a phiz [俗].

tsuraate (面當), *n.* an indirect hit [cut]; an allusive remark; an innuendo. 一面當に, allusively; by innuendo; out of spite. 一散散面當を云ふ, to say all sorts of things in allusion *to*; make many allusive remarks.

tsuragamae (面構), *n.* Ⓢ 面附. a cast of countenance; the cut of the face; expression of the face; a look.

tsurai (辛い), *a.* ❶ (むごい) bitter; cruel. ❷ (苦しい) hard; trying; painful; bitter. 一つらい目に逢ふ, to have a hard [pretty] time of it; go through hardship; have bitter experiences. 一つらい思をする, to feel bitterly.

tsuraku (辛く), *ad.* painfully; bitterly; harshly. 一辛く當る, to treat harshly; be hard on a person.

tsuramaeru (捕まへる), *vt.* to catch; seize; capture; cop [俗].

tsuranaru (連る), *v.* ❶ (連續) to connect; join. ❷ (整列) to stand [lie] in row. ❸ (參列) to be present; attend. ❹ (關係) to be connected *with*. 一席に連る, to attend. 一南北に連る, to range north and south. 一其事業に連る, to be connected with that business.

tsuraneru (連ねる), *vt.* to link; connect; combine (合する); join (同上). 一…と手を連ねる, to join hands *with*. 一手を連ねて, hand in hand. 一翼を連ねて飛ぶ, to fly abreast.

tsuranikui (面憎い), *a.* abominable; detestable; hateful.

tsuranokawa (面皮), *n.* the skin of the face. 一面の皮の厚い, brazen-faced. 一面の皮を剝く, to put a person to shame; take him down a peg or two.

tsuranuku (貫く), *vt.* ❶ (貫通) to pierce (*through*); pass through; penetrate; run through (主義·鐵道·河が). ❷ (貫徹) to accomplish; carry through. 一主張を貫く, to carry one's point. 一的を貫く, to pierce the mark.

tsurara (氷柱), *n.* an icicle.

tsuratsura (熟), *ad.* deeply; attentively; carefully. 一つらつら惟ふに, upon careful consideration.

tsurayogoshi (面汚し), *n.* shame; disgrace. 一貴樣は親の面汚しだ, You are a shame to your parents.

tsure (連), *n.* a companion; a partner; company (數人); party

(同上)); a fellow-traveller (旅の). —連れになる, to become a companion. —連れに外れる, to stray [get separated] from one's companions.

tsureai (連合), *n.* a spouse; a helpmate; a partner.

tsureau (連合ふ), *v.* ❶ (伴ふ) to accompany; go together. ❷ =*tsuresou*.

tsuredasu (連出す), *vt.* to take [bring] out; entice [decoy] out (おびき出す); draw a person *from*.

tsuredatsu (連立つ), *v.* to accompany; go in company *with*; go (along) *with*.

tsūrei (通例), *ad.* ❶ (普通) usually; commonly; ordinarily. ❷ (概して, 一般に) mostly; on the whole; as a rule; generally. ❸ (習慣上) customarily.

tsureko (連子), *n.* a child brought into a family by its parent's marriage.

tsurekomu (連込む), *vt.* to take [bring; lead] *into*.

tsurenai (强顔い), *a.* heartless; unfeeling; cold(-hearted). —つれなく, heartlessly; coldly.

tsureru (連れる), *vt.* to bring [take] *with*; accompany. —連れに行く, to go *for*; go to fetch. —連れて來る, to bring. —連れて行く, to take [carry] away. —戰爭の進展するにつれて, as the war progressed; with the progress of the war.

tsuresou (連添ふ), *v.* to be man and wife; mate *with*; marry.

tsurezure (徒然), *n.* =*tozen*. —徒然なる儘に, as I feel lonely.

tsuri (釣), *n.* ❶ (釣魚) angling; fishing. ❷ (釣錢) change; broken money. —釣をする, to fish with rod and line; angle. ¶ 釣仲間, a brother of the angle.

tsuriageru (釣上げる), *vt.* ❶ to hang up; suspend (吊す). ❷ (魚を) to fish up; draw out; catch (a fish) with rod and line. ❸ (相場を) to bull (the market); raise (the prices) by manipulation.

tsuriai (釣合), *n.* balance; equilibrium; harmony (調和); symmetry (左右均齊); proportion (比準); match (對當). —安定の釣合, stable equilibrium of forces. —釣合よき, well-balanced; harmonious; well-proportioned; well-matched. —釣合よく, proportionately; in trim (船). —釣合が取れぬ, to bear no relation *to*; be out of (all) proportion; be out of trim (船). —釣合を取る, to balance oneself (身體の); trim a ship (乘客·荷物等を適當に配置して).

tsuriau (釣合ふ), *v.* ❶ (平均する) to balance; go together. ❷ (均等を保つ) to be in equilibrium. ❸ (恰好よし) to be in proportion *to*; be in harmony *with*; be in keeping *with*. ❹ (對當する) to match.

tsuribari (釣針), *n.* a fish-hook; a hook.

tsuribashi (吊橋), *n.* a suspension-bridge.

tsuribori (釣堀), *n.* a fishing [angling] pond.

tsuridai (釣臺), *n.* a litter; a stretcher.

tsuridana (吊棚), *n.* a hanging shelf.

tsuridasu (釣出す), *vt.* to decoy [entice] out; lure away; draw. —相手の言葉を釣り出す, to draw a person out into speaking; draw words out of a person.

tsuridōgu (釣道具), *n.* fishing-tackle; fishing-gear.

tsuridoko (釣床), *n.* a hammock; a hanging-bed; a cot (船の).

tsurigane (釣鐘), *n.* a temple bell. ¶ 釣鐘堂, a belfry; a bell-tower; a campanile.

tsuriganesō (山小菜), *n.* 【植】 the spotted bell-flower.

tsurihimo (吊紐), *n.* 【建】 a sash-cord; a sash-line.

tsuriito (釣絲), *n.* a fishing-line.

tsurikago (吊籃), *n.* a hanging basket; a car (氣球·飛行船の); a gondola (飛行船の).

tsurikawa (吊革), *n.* a strap. —吊革につかまる, to hang on to a strap. (吊革につかまる人, a strap-hanger.

tsūriki (通力), *n.* supernatural power.

tsurikomu (釣込む), *vt.* ❶ (引込む) to take *in*; draw *into*. ❷ (誘ひ入る) to entice; decoy; inveigle. —話に釣り込まれる, to be drawn into talk.

tsuriranpu (吊洋燈), *n.* a hanging-lamp.

tsurisageru (吊下げる), *vt.* to hang (down); suspend.

tsurisen (釣錢), *n.* change. —釣錢お斷り, "No change given."

tsurishi (釣師), *n.* an angler; a rodman.

tsurite (釣手), *n.* ❶ (釣する人) an angler. ❷ (蚊帳など) a mosquito-net hanger.

tsuritenjō (釣天井), *n.* a hanging-ceiling.

tsurizao (釣竿), *n.* a rod; a fishing-rod; an angling rod.

tsūro (通路), *n.* a passage; a way; a path. —通路を開く, ① to clear the passage. ② to open the way.

tsūron (通論), *n.* ❶ (通說) common opinion. ❷ (概論) outline; first principles; general principles.

tsuru (鶴), *n.* 【鳥】 the crane. —鶴の一聲, a cry of a crane; the voice of one in authority. ¶ 白鶴, the Siberian white crane.

tsuru (弦), *n.* a string; a bowstring (弓の); a chord (樂器の).
tsuru (蔓), *n.* ❶ a vine (葡萄などの); a tendril (卷鬚); a runner (薯の). ❷ [鉉] (鐵瓶等の) a haddle.
tsuru (吊る), *v.* ❶ (物をつるす) to hang; suspend. ❷ (目尻が) to be turned up. —蚊帳を吊る, to put up a mosquito-net. —棚を吊る, to fix a shelf. —吊床を吊る, to swing a hammock.
tsuru (釣る), *vt.* ❶ (魚を) to angle; fish. ❷ (騙る) to decoy; ensnare; entrap. —魚を釣る, to angle for fish.
tsuru (痙る), *vi.* to be cramped; be contracted; have a cramp [spasm.] —筋が痙る, to have a cramp in the muscle.
tsurube (釣瓶), *n.* a well-bucket. ¶ 釣瓶井戸, a draw-well. —釣瓶擊ち, a volley; rapid firing.
tsurugi (劍, 劍), *n.* a sword.
tsuruhashi (鶴嘴), *n.* a pick; a pick-axe; a mattock.
tsurureishi (苦瓜), *n.* 【植】the balsam-pear.
tsurushigaki (吊柿), *n.* a dried persimmon.
tsurusu (吊す), *vt.* to hang; suspend. ☞ *tsuru* (吊る).
tsurutsuru (つるつる), *ad.* slipperily; smoothly. —つるつるした禿頭 a smooth bald head.
tsūsan (通算), *n.* summing up. ——-**suru**, *vt.* to sum up; cast up; total. —刑期を通算する, to add up the terms of punishment.
tsūsei (通性), *n.* =***tsūyūsei***.
tsūseki (痛惜する), *vt.* to sorrow greatly; regret deeply; lament.
tsūsetsu (通說), *n.* the current [common] opinion.
tsūsetsu (痛切な), *a.* acute; poignant; exquisite. —痛切に, acutely; poignantly; keenly.
tsūshin (通信), *n.* an advice; a news; correspondence; communication. —通信する, to correspond [communicate] *with*; report. ¶ 通信簿, a school report-book. —通信學校, a correspondence school. —通信販賣, mail-order business. (通信販賣店, a mail-order house.) —通信員, a correspondent. (本社紐育通信員, our New York correspondent.) —通信事務官, a communication secretary. —通信機關, means of communication. —通信教授, teaching by correspondence; correspondence lessons. —通信局 the Direction General [Bureau] of Post and Telegraphs. —通信社, a news-agency. —通信手, a post-office clerk.
tsūshō (通商), *n.* commerce; trade. ¶ 通商條約, a commercial treaty; a treaty of commerce. —通商禁止, embargo; suspension of commerce. —通商航海條約, a treaty of commerce and navigation. —通商局, the Bureau of Commercial Affairs.
tsūshō (通稱), *n.* a common [popular] name; a private name.
tsūsoku (通則), *n.* a general rule.
tsuta (蔦, 地錦), *n.* 【植】the Japanese ivy.
tsutaeru (傳へる), *vt.* ❶ (傳達) to convey; carry; report (報知); inform (同上); transmit (傳送); deliver (傳言を). ❷ (傳授) to teach; initiate (祕訣など); impart (知識を). ❸ (世々に, 後世に) to hand down; transmit. —傳へ言ふ, tradition says. —報を傳へる, to carry news. —道を傳へる, to hand down the precepts. —人から人へ傳へる, to hand on from one to another. —上海來電の傳ふる所に依れば, according to a message from Shanghai; a Shanghai telegram reports that....
tsutanai (拙い), *a.* ❶ (拙) awkward; clumsy; unskilful. ❷ (不運) unlucky; ill-fated.
tsutau (傳ふ), *vi.* to go *along*; climb *by* (the help *of*). —堤を傳って行く, to go along the embankment.
tsutawaru (傳はる), *vi.* ❶ (傳承) to be handed down; be transmitted. ❷ (傳來) to be brought over; be introduced. ❸ (傳播) to spread; go (the) round. ❹ =***tsutau***. —昔から傳はった話, a story handed down from old times. —音響の傳はる時間, the time required for transmission of a sound. —父より子に傳はる, to pass [descend] from father to son. —先祖から傳はる, to be handed down from one's ancestors.
tsute (傳), *n.* ❶ =***tayori***. ❷ (手蔓) an intermediary; an introducer (紹介者); interest; influence. —A氏の傳で, through Mr. A's kind [good] offices; through Mr. A's influence. —Aに傳手がある, to have interest [influence] with A. —宜い傳がないから, as one has no good supporter [backer].
tsuto (苞苴), *n.* ❶ a straw-wrapper. ❷ (いへづと) a souvenir.
tsūtō (痛悼する), *vt.* to lament; regret.
tsutomaru (勤まる), *v.* to be equal *to*; be fit *for*; be fit for the duties *of*.
tsutome (務, 勤), *n.* ❶ 勤勞) service; business (仕事). ❷ (本務) duty; office. ❸ (勤行) divine) service; church-service. —務を

大事にする, to attend faithfully to one's duties. —日々の勤をする, to perform daily service.

tsutomeageru (勤上げる), *vt.* to serve out (one's time [term]).

tsutomenin (勤人), *n.* a salaried man. ¶ 勤人階級, the salariat.

tsutomeru (力·努·勉·務める), *v.* to try; endeavour; strive. —目的を達せんと努める, to endeavour to attain one's object.

tsutomeru (勤める), *v.* ❶ (勤務) to hold a post [an office] *in*; be employed; serve (役·年期など). ❷ (演ずる) to act; play. ❸ (盡す) to do; attend *to* (身を入れる). —大藏省へ勤めてゐる, to hold a post [serve] in the Finance Department. —通譯を勤める, to act as interpreter. —懲役を勤める, to serve a term of penal servitude.

tsutomesaki (勤先), *n.* one's office; one's business. —勤先をしくじる, to fail to discharge one's duties; lose one's employment; be discharged in disgrace.

tsutomete (勉めて), *ad.* to the best of one's power [ability]; as far as one can; assiduously; diligently.

tsutoni (夙に), *ad.* ❶ (朝早く) early in the morning. ❷ (幼時に) in childhood; at an early age. ❸ (早く) early. —夙に起き晩く寝ね, to rise [get up] early and retire [go to bed] late.

tsutsu (筒), *n.* ❶ (管) a pipe; a tube; a case (長目の). ❷ (銃身) a gun-barrel. ❸ (銃砲) a gun.

tsutsu (つつ), *particle.* ❶ 現在進行を示す. ❷ 同時行爲を表す. —頭を掻きつゝ引さがる, to withdraw scratching one's head. —知りつゝ出掛ける, to go out though well aware of it.

tsutsudori (筒鳥), *n.* 【鳥】 the Himalayan cuckoo.

tsutsuganaku (恙なく), *ad.* safely; in safety; in good health. (健康にて). —當方一同恙なく暮し居候, We are all in good health.

tsutsuguchi (筒口), *n.* the muzzle.

tsutsuji (躑躅), *n.* 【植】 the Indian azalea [rhododendron].

tsutsujiri (筒尻), *n.* a breach; the butt(-end of a gun).

tsutsuku (つつく), *vt.* ❶ (突く) to thrust in; poke. ❷ (啄む) to peck *at*; pick. ❸ (唆す) to instigate; egg on. ❹ (水をさす) to try to alienate. —餌を啄く, to nibble at a bait. —木を啄く, to peck a tree. —陰で突附く人があるから, as there is someone to egg him on.

tsutsumashii (愼しい), *a.* Ⓢ 愼しやかな. ❶ (淑かな) modest. ❷ (約しい) frugal. —愼しやかに, modestly: frugally; in a small way.

tsutsumi (包), *n.* ❶ (包みたるもの) a package; a packet; a bundle; a parcel (小包); an envelope (金などの); a bale (梱). ❷ (包むもの) a wrapper; a covering; a case (外包).

tsutsumi (堤), *n.* ❶ =*teibō* (堤防). ❷ (塘) (溜池) a reservoir; a pond; a dam.

tsutsumigami (包紙), *n.* a packing-sheet; wrapping-paper; parcel-paper; an envelope; a wrapper; a jacket (本の表紙の).

tsutsumikakushi (包隱), *n.* concealment; hiding. —包み隱しのない話, a round unvarnished tale.

tsutsumikakusu (包隱す), *vt.* to hide; conceal. —包み隱さず話す, to speak without disguise; tell candidly. —事實を包み隱す, to conceal the truth; cover [wrap] up the truth; smother [stifle] up facts.

tsutsumotase (美人局), *n.* the badger game.

tsutsumu (包む), *vt.* ❶ (くるむ) to wrap; do up; lap about; pack (荷造する). ❷ (圍む) to envelope; surround. ❸ (覆ふ) to cover; mantle; veneer (良材で). ❹ (かくす) to conceal; hide. —紙に包む, to fold in paper. —火焰に包まれて, enveloped in flames. —濃霧に包まる, to be enshrouded in a thick fog. —包まず白狀する, to confess without concealment; make a clean breast of it.

tsutsusaki (筒先), *n.* ❶ (筒の先) the end [tip] of a tube [pipe]. ❷ (銃口) the muzzle. ❸ (ホースの先) a nozzle. —筒先を向ける, to turn the muzzle; point [level] a gun *at*; turn the hose *upon*.

tsutsushimi (愼, 謹), *n.* ❶ (謙遜) modesty. ❷ (愼重) prudence; discretion. ❸ (抑制) self-restraint [-control]; continence (色慾の). ❹ (用心) caution; circumspection. —愼ある; 愼深い, ① modest. ② prudent; discreet. ③ self-restraining. ④ cautious; scrupulous; wary.

tsutsushimu (謹·愼む), *v.* ❶ (愼重) to be prudent; be discreet (思慮ある). ❷ (控へる) to restrain oneself; refrain [abstain] *from*; be continent (色慾を). ❸ (用心) to be cautious; be circumspect; be careful. —將來を愼む, to be circumspect for the future. —言行を謹む, to be cautious in speech and action. —嫉妬を愼む, to be careful not to be jealous.

tsutsushinde (謹んで), *ad.* (恭しく) reverently; respectfully. —謹んで承る, to listen to a person with respect.

tsutsusode (筒袖), *n.* a tight [round] sleeve; a tight-sleeved dress (衣服).

tsuttatsu (衝立つ), *vi.* ❶ (眞直に立つ) to stand up [straight]; rise upright. ❷ (急に立つ) to jump [spring] to one's feet.

tsūun (通運), *n.* transportation; forwarding. ¶ 通運會社, a transport [an express] company; a parcels delivery company; a forwarding [transport] agency.

tsūwa (通話), *n.* message. ¶ 通話料(電話の), message rate.

tsuwabuki (槖吾), *n.* 【植】 the Japanese silver-leaf.

tsuwamono (兵), *n.* a soldier; a warrior.

tsuwari (惡疽), *n.* 【醫】 vomitus gravidarum; morning-sickness.

tsuya (艶), *n.* gloss; lustre; polish. —艶のある, glossy; polished; sleek. —艶のない, lustreless; mat; dull. —艶のよい顔, a bright [clear] (-complexioned) face. —艶のない顔, a bad [dull] (-complexioned) face. —艶を出す [附ける], to bring out the lustre; polish; glaze; calender (布·紙に). —艶を消す, to take the lustre [shine] out *of*; mat (硝子·金屬·寫眞などを); frost (硝子などを).

tsuya (通夜), *n.* a wake; a death-watch. —通夜する, to wake; hold a wake.

tsuyabukin (艶布巾), *n.* a polishing-cloth.

tsuyagami (艶紙), *n.* glazed [ivory] paper.

tsuyagawa (艶革), *n.* patent leather.

tsuyakeshi (艶消しの), *a.* ❶ ground; frosted; matted. ❷ (色消) unelegant. ¶ 艶消硝子, ground [frosted; obscured] glass.

tsūyaku (通約), *n.* 【數】 commensuration; reduction to a common measure. —通約する, to commensurate. —通約し得べき, 【數】 commensurable.

tsūyaku (通譯), *n.* ❶ (事) interpretation. ❷ (人) an interpreter. —通譯する, to interpret; act as (an) interpreter. ¶ 通譯官, a secretary-interpreter; an official interpreter.

tsuyatsuya (艶艶と), *ad.* brightly; lustrously. —艶々した, glossy; polished; sleek.

tsūyō (通用), *n.* ❶ common use; current use. ❷ (流通) circulation; currency. —通用する, ① (貨幣など) to pass (*for*; *as*); circulate; pass current. ② (切符など) to be available [good] (for some days). ③ (議論など) to pass; pass current. ¶ 通用貨幣, current coins; currency. —通用門, a side-gate. —切符通用期限, the term [time] for which a ticket is available.

tsūyō (痛痒), *n.* (痛と痒と) pain and itch. ❷ (利害) interest. —痛痒を感じない, not to be affected [concerned].

tsuyoi (强い), *a.* strong. ❶ (强健) robust (壯健); sturdy (頑丈). ❷ (堅牢) solid. ❸ (力の) powerful; mighty; muscular (筋骨の). (勇壯) brave; courageous. ❹ (激烈) violent; severe. —强い印象, a strong impression. —非常に力の强い人, a man of great force. —强いは勝, "The battle is to the strong."

tsuyoki (强氣), *n.* (取引市場) firmness. —强氣の, firm; strong.

tsuyoku (强く), *ad.* ❶ (烈しく) hard; violently. ❷ (力强く) strongly; powerfully. ❸ (强度に) vigorously; intensely; keenly. ❹ 【音】 *vigoroso* (=violently) 【伊】. —强く打つ, to strike hard [vigorously]; slog. —風が一層强くなる, The wind freshens still more.

tsuyomeru (强める), *vt.* to make strong; strengthen; invigorate; confirm (確實); increase (增加); emphasize (語を); lay stress *on* (同上). —調子を强める, to strengthen the tone. —少しく語を强めて云へば, to put the matter a little stronger.

tsuyomi (强み), *n.* strength; superiority; a strong point.

tsuyosōna (强さうな), *a.* strong-looking.

tsuyu (汁), *n.* soup; broth.

tsuyu (露), *n.* the dew. —露の珠, a dewdrop. —露けき草原, a dewy meadow; a dew-laden grass field. —露に濡れた, wet with dew. —露程も疑はぬ, I have not a shadow of a doubt.

tsuyu (梅雨), *n.* the rainy [wet] season. —梅雨の入, the setting-in [the first day] of the rainy season. —梅雨の明, the passing of the rainy season.

tsuyuharai (露拂), *n.* a herald; a forerunner.

tsuyukusa (鴨跖草), *n.* 【植】 the day flower. ¶ ひらさきつゆくさ, the virgin-spiderwort; the flower-of-a-day.

tsūyūsei (通有性), *n.* common property; generality; community.

tsūzoku (通俗), *n.* popularity. —通俗に書く, to write in a popular style. —通俗化する, to popularize. ¶ 通俗文, a popular composition. —通俗文學《科學》, popular literature 《science》. —通俗語, a colloquialism; a colloquial word. —通俗講話, a popular lecture.

tsuzukeru (續ける), *vt.* to continue; keep on; proceed [go on] *with* (やめたことを再び). —叫び《泣き》續ける, to keep on crying 《weeping》. —進行を續ける, to go on [hold on] one's way.

tsuzukete (續けて), *ad.* ❶ (繼續して) continuously; uninterruptedly. ❷ (連續して) successively; in succession; one after another (相次いで). ❸ (休まずに) without resting [stopping]; at a stretch (一氣に). —三日續けて, for three days running [in succession; on end]; for three consecutive days.

tsuzukesama (續様に), *ad.* ❶ (續けて) continuously; successively; in succession. ❷ (一氣に) at a stretch; at one effort. —續け様に撲る, to give successive [repeated] blows; hail down a shower of blows.

tsuzuki (續), *n.* continuation; a succession (一聯); a sequel (話の續き). —幸運《不幸》續き, a train [series; succession; run; streak] of fortunes 《misfortunes》. —二軒續きの家, a block of two houses; a pair of semi-detached houses.

tsuzukiai (續合), *n.* a relation; a connection.

tsuzukimono (續物), *n.* a serial (story); a story given serially.

tsuzuku (續く), *vi.* ❶ (繼續) to continue; last; hold out (持續). ❷ (後に續く) to succeed; follow; ensue. ——, *a.* continuous; continual; successive. —前頁より續く, "continued from the preceding page." —此稿尙續く, "to be continued." —一者共續け, Follow me all. —山又山と續く, Hill succeeds hill. —葬式は十町も續いた, The funeral procession ran more than ten *chō*.

tsuzuite (續いて), *ad.* continually; successively; in succession. —大洪水に續いて疫病が起った, Pestilence came close on the heels of the great flood.

tsuzumayaka (約やかな), *a.* thrifty; frugal; simple (簡易な). —約やかな暮し, a simple living.

tsuzumeru (約める), *vt.* to shorten. ❶ (文章·書物などを) to curtail [cut down] (an essay); condense (an essay; a paragraph); epitomize (a discourse); abridge (a book; a dictionary). ❷ (語句などを) to abbreviate [contract] (a word; a phrase).

tsuzumi (鼓), *n.* a long snare-drum beaten with the hand.

tsuzura (葛籠), *n.* a bamboo trunk; a clothes-box.

tsuzuraori (九十九折), *n.* a winding pass; meanders. —つゞら折の山路, a winding mountain path.

tsuzure (襤褸, 綴), *n.* rags; tatters. ¶ 綴の錦, Gobelin tapestry; figured brocade.

tsuzuri (綴), *n.* a syllable; spelling (綴字).

tsuzuriji (綴字), *n.* spelling.

tsuzurikata (綴方), *n.* ❶ spelling. ❷ (作文) composition.

tsuzurikomi (綴込), *n.* a file.

tsuzuru (綴る), *vt.* ❶ (字を) to spell. ❷ (文を) to compose; write. ❸ (とぢる) to bind; patch (綻など); sew (縫ふ). —文字を綴る, to spell a word. —帳面を綴る, to bind a book. —シユッドと云ふ字はどう綴るか, How do you spell the word "shōōd"? —b-e-a-u-x と綴って何と讀むか, What does "b-e-a-u-x" read?

tsū-zuru (通ずる), *v.* = *tsū-jiru*.

U

u (鵜), *n.* 【鳥】 the cormorant.

u (有), *n.* being; existence.

uba (うば), *n.* ❶ (姥) an old woman. ❷ (乳母) a nurse; a wet-nurse; a milk-nurse. ¶ 乳母車, a perambulator; a baby-carriage; a pram (俗). —乳母不要(ウイズ ベラ), a feeding-bottle; a sucking-bottle.

ubagai (姥貝), *n.* 【貝】 Trigonella sacchalinensis (學名).

ubau (奪ふ), *vt.* ❶ (ひったくる) to snatch *from*; wrest *from*; take away. ❷ (剝奪) to deprive *of*; divest *of*. —光を奪ふ, to take the shine *out of*. —敵の陣地を奪ふ, to carry [capture] the enemy's position. —遊びに心を奪はれる, to be absorbed in play 《pleasures》.

uboku (烏木), *n.* 【植】 the ebony.

ubu (初心), *n.* naïveté; simplicity; inexperience (未熟). —初心な, simple; naïve; inexperienced; green.

ubuge (產毛), *n.* down. —產毛の樣な, downy.

ubugi (產衣), *n.* the first-worn swaddling-clothes.

ubugoe (產聲), *n.* vagitus; the first cry of a new-born baby.

ubusuna (產土), *n.* the birth-place. ¶ 產土神, the tutelary deity; one's genius (守本尊).

ubuyu (產湯), *n.* the baby's first

bath.

uchi (内, 中), *n.* ❶ (内部) inside; interior. ❷ (家宅) a house; one's home. ❸ (我夫) my husband; my old man; Mr.... —内で, ① (家で) at home; indoors; within doors. ② (中で) between (二つの); among (二つ以上の); of. —我々の中の二人, two of us. —一週間の中に, within a week. —朝の中に, in (the course of) the morning. —晝の中に, in the day-time. —夜の中に, during the night. —あらゆる危險の中に, amidst all dangers. —二つの中孰かを選ぶ, to choose between the two. —若い中に勉强する, to study while young [in one's youth]. —内も外も眞黒である, to be black in and out. —内に省みて疚しからず, As I look into my heart, I feel no shame.

uchiageru (打上げる), *vt.* ❶ (打ちて上げる) to strike [knock] up; shoot [send] up (花火等を); let [set] off (同上). ❷ (酒宴など) to bring to a close; finish up; end. ❸ (興行を終へる) to finish up [off]; close (a run). ❹ (波が物を) to throw (a ship) on shore; wash (a corpse) ashore. ——, *vi.* ❶ (擱坐) to run aground [ashore]; strand; be stranded. ❷ (波が) to dash *upon*. —花火を打上げる, to set off [let off] fire-works. —波に打ちあげられる, to be washed up by the sea.

uchiakeru (打明ける), *vt.* to throw open; reveal; disclose; confess (自白). —祕密を打明ける, to entrust a person with one's secret; confide the secret to a person. —內事を打明ける, to take a person into one's confidence. —打明けて言へば, to be frank [candid] with you; to speak frankly. ¶ 打明け話, an unreserved talk.

uchiami (打網), *n.* =*toami*.

uchiau (打合ふ), *v.* ❶ (毆合) to exchange blows; strike each other. ❷ (射擊を交換す) to exchange shots [fire].

uchiawase (打合せ), *n.* previous arrangement; preliminaries. —打合せる, to arrange [confer] beforehand; preconcert; make a previous arrangement *with*. —時間の打合せをする, to make arrangements as to time. ¶ 打合せ會, a preliminary meeting.

uchiba (內端), *n.* moderation. ☞ *uchiwa* (內輪).

uchibori (內濠), *n.* the inner ditch [moat].

uchibu (打步), *n.* 【商】agio; premium.

uchibutokoro (內懷), *n.* ❶ the bosom under the folds of the dress. ❷ (內心) one's heart; one's intention. —內懷に入れる, to put in the bosom under the dress.

uchidashi (打出し), *n.* ❶ (はね) the closing hour; the close. ❷ (模様などの) repoussage; embossment. ❸【庭球】serve; service; delivery. ¶ 打出し細工, a repoussé (work); a chasing; embossed [raised] work.

uchidasu (打出す), *v.* ❶ (打ちて出だす) to strike out. ❷ (打ち始む) to begin to beat. ❸ (興行を終る) to end; close. ❹ (模様などを) to emboss; chase; raise. ❺ (鐵砲を) to open fire.

uchide-no-kozuchi (打出の小槌), *n.* (Daikoku's) mallet of luck.

uchideshi (內弟子), *n.* a home-pupil; a private pupil.

uchigari (內借), *n.* advance loan. —內借する, to get [receive] part of...in advance; draw in advance.

uchigawa (內側), *n.* the inside. —外套の內側の衣嚢に, in the inside pocket of the greatcoat.

uchiharau (打拂ふ), *vt.* ❶ (拂落す) to beat off [away]; shake off. ❷ (追拂ふ) to drive away; beat off.

uchihimo (打紐), *n.* a braid; a braided cord.

uchiiri (討入), *n.* forcible entry; breaking in; a raid (襲擊). —四十七士の吉良邸討入, the forty-seven *rōnin's* entry into Kira's mansion.

uchijini (討死), *n.* death in battle. —討死する, to die [fall] in battle; be killed in battle; die fighting.

uchikabuto (內兜を見透かす), to discern a person's weakness.

uchikaesu (打返す), *vt.* ❶ to strike back; return a blow; counter (拳鬪). ❷ (反覆) to repeat. ❸ (打直す) to rewhip (古綿を). —球を打返す, to return a ball. —花々しい打返しをする, to practise a good return.

uchikake (裲襠, 打掛), *n.* a long over-dress.

uchikata (打方), *n.* firing; shooting. —打方止め!, Stop [Cease] firing!

uchikatsu (打勝・打克つ), *vt.* to overcome; get over; surmount; conquer; get the better *of*. ☞ *katsu* (勝つ). —打勝ち難き, insurmountable (困難·障碍等); unsurpassable; invincible.

uchikeshi (打消), *n.* denial; negation; *dementi* 【佛】(特に政府の). —打消の, 【文】negative.

uchikesu (打消す), *vt.* to deny; contradict. —風說を打消す, to contradict the rumours.

uchiki (内氣), *n.* retiring disposition; diffidence; shyness. 一内氣な, diffident; bashful; shy.

uchikin (内金), *n.* part of a price; money paid on account; part payment. 一内金として渡す《受取る》, to pay 《receive》 money on account. ¶ 内金支拂, part payment; payment on account.

uchikiri (打切), *n.* closing; the close; the end. 一打切る, to bring to a close; finish; leave off. (交渉を打切る, to close negotiations.)

uchikizu (打傷), *n.* a bruise; a contusion.

uchikomu (打込む), *vt.* ❶ (杭など) to drive in; beat *into.* ❷ (砲を) to shoot [fire] *into.* ❸ (庭球で球を) to smash. ❹ (仕事などに) to devote oneself *to*; put one's heart *into.* 一一太刀打込む, to slash with a sword. 一杭を深く打込む, to drive a pile deep *into.* 一仕事に魂を打込む, to go [enter] heart and soul into one's work.

uchikorosu (打殺す), *vt.* ❶ (毆殺) to beat [knock] to death; strike dead; deal a death-blow. ❷ (銃殺) to shoot to death; shoot dead [down].

uchimaku (内幕), *n.* ❶ (幕の一種) an inner curtain. ❷ (内部の事情) one's private circumstances; one's family condition. 一内幕に立入る, to get behind the scenes. 一内幕を知ってる, to be well acquainted with a person's private circumstances.

uchimata (内股), *n.* the inside of the thigh; the twister (馬背に跨るが故); the crutch. ¶ 内股膏藥(人), a Jack of [o'; on] both sides; a trimmer. (内股膏藥をする, to hold [run] with the hare and run [hunt] with the hounds).

uchimi (打身), *n.* a bruise; a contusion.

uchimono (打物), *n.* ❶ (太刀·槍の類) a weapon; a sword (刀劍). ❷ (鍛へ打ちて作りたる金屬の器) forged work. ❸ (菓子の) moulded cake. ❹ (樂器の) percussive instruments.

uchimorasu (討漏らす), *vt.* to let escape; miss killing.

uchimurasaki (内紫), *n.* ❶【貝】 Saxidomus purpuratus (學名). ❷【植】(香欒) the shaddock-tree.

uchini (打荷), *n.* jetsam; jettison; jettisoned cargo.

uchiniwa (内庭), *n.* an inner court; a *patio* 【西】.

uchinobasu (打展す), *vt.* to beat out.

uchinomesu (打ちのめす), *vt.* to beat [strike] down; beat to a mummy [jelly]; maul.

uchinori (内法), *n.* the inner [inside] dimensions; inside measure.

uchinuku (打貫く), *vt.* ❶ (穿孔) to punch; perforate. ❷ (射貫く) to pierce; penetrate; shoot *through.* ¶ 打拔切手, a perforated stamp.

uchiotosu (打落す), *vt.* to strike [knock] down; shoot down. 一首を打落す, to cut off a head. 一鳥を打落す, to shoot down a bird.

uchishiki (打敷), *n.* an altar-cloth; a cloth-cover.

uchisueru (打据ゑる), *vt.* to knock down; strike down.

uchisuteru (打捨てる), *vt.* ❶ (捨置く) to leave as it is; leave alone. ❷ (切棄てる) to cut off; cut down.

uchitaosu (打倒す), *vt.* to knock [strike] down; strike to the ground.

uchitokeru (打解ける), *vi.* to be frank [candid]; be unreserved; unbosom oneself. 一打解けて話す, to talk unreservedly; have a familiar talk *with*; have a chat *with.* ¶ 打解け話, a familiar [an unrestrained] talk; an intimate conversation.

uchitomeru (打留める), *vt.* ❶ to kill. ❷ to shoot to death; shoot dead. 一一發で擊留める, to bring down with a single shot.

uchitoru (打取る), *vt.* ❶ = ***toru*** (取る). ❷ (捕へる) to catch; arrest. ❸ (討伐する) to conquer. ❹ (斬殺す) to kill.

uchitsuke (打附に), *ad.* bluntly; flatly. ☞ ***buttsuke.*** 一打附ける, ① (釘などで) to nail on [down]; rivet (鋲などで); fix. ② (投げつける) to throw *at*; shy *at.* ☞ ***buttsukeru.***

uchitsuzukeru (打續ける), *vt.* ❶ (打擲) to strike successively; give repeated blows. ❷ (發砲) to fire without intermission; batter. ❸ (興行) to perform successively.

uchitsuzuku (打續く), *vi.* to continue [last] long. ☞ ***tsuzuku*** (續く). 一打續く不幸, a train [series; succession; run] of misfortunes. 一打續く炎天, a long spell of hot weather.

uchiuchi (内内の), *a.* private; informal (略式). 一内々で, in one's family; among one's people.

uchiumi (内海), *n.* an inland sea; a gulf (灣).

uchiwa (内輪), *n.* ❶ (家族間) one's family; one's people. ❷ (控目) moderation. ❸ = ***uchiwani.*** 一内輪の恥, a family skeleton; a skeleton in the cupboard. —内輪喧嘩する, to quarrel among themselves. —— -ni, *ad.* ❶ (控目に) moderately; in moderation; in a small way. ❷ with turned-in toes. —内輪に歩く, to walk with turned-in toes; walk pigeon-toed; toe in. ¶ 内輪揉め, family dissension; domestic discord.

uchiwa (團扇), *n.* a round fan. —團扇を使ふ, to fan oneself. —團扇を擧げる, ① (勝方を示す) to show which side has won. ② (裁決する) to judge. —甲に團扇が擧がる, to be decided in favour of A.

uchiwake (内譯), *n.* the items (of an account). —内譯をする, to state the items of an account.

uchiwani (内鰐), *n.* knock-knee; in-knee.

uchiwari (内割), *n.* the rate of bank discount.

uchiwaru (打割る), *vt.* ❶ (打ちて割る) to break [split] open. ❷ (打明ける) to unbosom.

uchiwata (打綿), *n.* ❶ (繰綿を綿弓にて打ちたるもの) whipped cotton. ❷ (古綿をうちかへしたるもの) rewhipped old cotton.

uchiwatashi (内渡), *n.* part delivery; part payment.

uchiyoseru (打寄せる), *vi.* ❶ (波が) to roll towards. ❷ (敵が) to come on; come down *upon*; march *against*; rush *at* (突擊).

uchōten (有頂天), *n.* ecstasy; rapture; entrancement. —有頂天になる, to go off into ecstasies [raptures]. (嬉しくて有頂天になってゐる, to be in the seventh heaven with joy; be transported with joy; be in an ecstasy of joy.)

uchū (宇宙), *n.* the universe; the cosmos. —宇宙間に於て, in the whole universe; in all the round of nature. ¶ 宇宙引力《重力》, universal attraction《gravitation》. —宇宙神教, universalism.

uchū (雨注), *n.* a shower; a hail. —矢を雨注する, to send a shower of arrows; shower arrows.

udatsu (梲), *n.* a short post. —一生梲が上らぬ, never to rise in the world.

ude (腕), *n.* ❶ (肢體) the arm. ❷ (伎倆) ability; capacity; skill. —腕に抱ける小兒, a child [an infant] in arms. —腕試しをする, to test one's strength《ability》. —腕に撚をかける, to strain every nerve. —腕をまくる, to roll up the sleeves. ¶ 腕時計, a wrist [strap] watch. —腕飾, an armlet; a bracelet. —腕競べ, a trial of strength《ability》.

udegi (腕木), *n.* a putlog; a bracket; a roof-truss (軒の); a bridge-truss (橋の); a cross-arm (電柱等の); a cross-piece (同上); an arm.

udegumisuru (腕組する), *vi.* to fold one's arms. —腕組みして, with folded arms.

udekiki (腕利), *n.* a man of ability; an able man.

udemae (腕前), *n.* ❶ (力量) ability; capacity. ❷ (手練) dexterity; skill. —腕前を顯はす, to show one's ability; give a taste of one's quality.

udemakuri (腕捲する), *vi.* to roll [tuck] up one's sleeves.

udeppushi (腕節), *n.* physical strength [power]. —腕ッ節の强い男, a man of great strength.

uderu (茹でる), *vt.* =*yuderu*.

udewa (腕環), *n.* a bracelet; an armlet; an arm-ring; a wristlet.

udezuku (腕盡で), *ad.* by sheer strength; by (main) force.

udo (獨活), *n.* 【植】 Aralia cordata (Hercules's club の類·學名); the *udo* [日].

udon (饂飩), *n.* wheat vermicelli.

udonge (優曇華), *n.* ❶ [梵] Udanbara (靈瑞). ❷ the eggs of the lace-wing fly.

ue (上), *n.* the top (頂); the upper part (上の方, 上部); upside (上邊, 上側, 上面); surface (表面). —上から九行目, the ninth line from the top. —五つから上の子供, children of five and upwards. —この上もない喜び, the greatest joy. —酒の上で, under the influence of *sake*. —再考の上で, after reconsideration. —一應取調の上で, after I have made inquiry. —丘の上に, up the hill. —…の上に出る, to be above; be over; exceed; be more than. —上に置く, to put [set] on; superpose; superimpose (*on*). —地面の上に現はれてゐる, to appear above the ground. —かくなる上は, now that it has come to this pass. —上を下への大騷ぎだ, They are all turned upside down.

ue (飢, 饑), *n.* hunger; starvation. —飢を凌ぐ, to ward [stave] off starvation; keep the wolf from the door.

uebōsō (種疱), *n.* inoculation; vaccination. —種痘する, to vaccinate.

uejinisuru (餓死する), *vi.* to starve (oneself) to death; die of [from] hunger.

uekae (植換), *n.* transplantation. —植ゑ換へる, to transplant; replant; reset (活字等を).

ueki (植木) *n.* a pot-plant (鉢植);

a garden plant (庭木); a plant; a tree. ¶ 植木鉢, a flower pot; a pot. —植木棚, a pot-plant shelf [stand]. —植木屋, a gardener (園丁); a nursery-man (養樹家).

uekomi (植込), *n.* plantation; a thick growth of plants.

uen (迂遠), *n.* ❶ (廻り遠い) circuitousness; circumlocution. ❷ (うとい) dulness; stupidity. —迂遠な, ① roundabout; circuitous; circumlocutory. ② dull; stupid; silly.

ueru (飢ゑる), *vi.* ❶ to be hungry; starve; hunger; famish. ❷ (渇望する) to crave (*for*); hunger *for* [*after*]; hanker *for* [*after*]. —飢ゑた, hungry; starving; keen [sharp]-set. —飢ゑしめる, to hunger; famish.

ueru (植ゑる), *vt.* to plant (草木を); set up (type, 活字を).

ueshita (上下), up and down; above and below (位置の). ☞ *jōge* (上下).

uetsuke (植附), *n.* ❶ (植附けること) plantation; implantation. ❷ (田植) rice-transplantation. —植ゑ附ける, to plant; implant. ¶ 植附時, the transplanting season.

ufuku (雨覆), *n.* (鳥の) a covert. ¶ 大《中; 小》雨覆, greater《median; lesser》coverts. —初列《次列》雨覆, primary《secondary》coverts.

ugachi (穿ち), *n.* ❶ (穿掘) perforation. ❷ (見拔くこと) penetration; insight. ❸ (諷刺) satire.

ugai (含嗽), *n.* gargling; rinsing the throat. —含嗽する, to gargle; rinse one's mouth. ¶ 含嗽藥, a gargle.

ugai (鵜飼), *n.* =*ukai*.

ugarasu (うがらす), *n.* 【鳥】 the resplendent shag.

ugatsu (穿つ), *v.* ❶ (掘る) to dig; perforate; pierce. ☞ *horu* (掘る). ❷ (眞を寫す) to be true to nature [life]. ❸ (諷刺) to satirize. ❹ (著ける) to put on; wear. —穿った言葉, a good hit. —地を穿つ, to dig in the ground. —靴を穿つ, to wear [put on] boots. —よく人情を穿ってる, to be true to human nature.

ugen (右舷), *n.* 【航】 the starboard.

ugō (烏合-の衆), *n.* a rabble; a disorderly crowd; a mob.

ugokasu (動かす), *vt.* ❶ to move; stir; budge (固定した物を); shift [change the position *of*]; remove (移す). ❷ (搖り動かす) to rock; swing; shake. ❸ (運轉) to operate; work; set in motion. ❹ (變更) to change; alter. ❺ (感動) to move; touch; affect; influence; work [act; operate] (upon the mind). —動かすべからざる, unchangeable (一定不變の); fixed (同上); established (確定の); indisputable (爭ふべからざる). —兵を動かす, ① to mobilize troops (動員する); take up arms (戈を執って起つ). —天下を動かす, to arouse the world. —決心を動かす, to shake one's resolution. —市會を動かす, to influence the city assembly.

ugoki (動き), *n.* motion; movement. —動きが取れぬ, ① to be unable to move [stir]; stick fast [in the mud] (泥中で). ② (板挾みになる) to be in dilemma.

ugoku (動く), *vi.* ❶ to move; stir; budge; shift [change position]. ❷ (運轉) to operate; work; go; run. ❸ (變化) to change; alter. ❹ (搖ぐ) to swing; shake; joggle. —意頻りに動く, to be itching; be extremely inclined *to*. —ピクとも動かない, not to stir a peg. —さう易くは動くまい, He will not be influenced so easily.

ugomeki (蠢き), *n.* wriggle; squirm. —蠢めく, to wriggle; squirm; twitch.

ugui (うぐひ), *n.* 【魚】 the dace.

uguisu (鶯), *n.* 【鳥】 the large Japanese bush-warbler; the Japan nightingale.

uguisugai (鶯貝), *n.* 【貝】 Pteria breviolata (wing-shellの一種·學名).

uhi (雨飛する), *vi.* to shower. —彈丸雨飛の下に, under a shower [hail] of bullets.

uhyō (雨氷), *n.* glazed frost.

uijin (初陣), *n.* a maiden battle.

uisukī (ウィスキー), *n.* whisky. —ウィスキーを生[*]で飲む, to take whisky short.

ui-tenpen (有爲轉變), *n.* ❶ (變り易き事) incessant change; mutability. ❷ (盛衰) vicissitudes; ups and downs; shifts and changes.

uizan (初產), *n.* the first parturition [child-birth].

ujakeru (邕ける), *vi.* Ⓢ うじゃじゃける. to rot; decay; decompose; grow sodden (ふやける).

ujauja (うじゃうじゃ), *ad.* in swarms; in packs.

uji (蛆), *n.* 【蟲】 a worm; a grub; a maggot.

uji (氏), *n.* ❶ (家名) a family name; a surname. ❷ (家系) family stock. ❸ (尊稱) Mister; Mr. —氏より育ち, "Birth is much, but breeding is more."

ujigami (氏神), *n.* a tutelary deity [god].

ujiko (氏子), *n.* the protégés of a tutelary deity.

ujiuji (うじうじ), *ad.* ❶ (蛆などの群る) in swarms. ❷ (逡巡)

hesitatingly.
ujō (有情の), *a.* animate; sentient.
uka (雨下する), *v.* to rain; pour down; shower.
ukaberu (浮べる), *vt.* ❶ (水に) to float; launch (進水); sail (玩具の船を). ❷ (引揚げる) to refloat; raise. —顔に喜色を浮べる, to wear a joyful look. —目に涙を浮べて, with tears in her eyes.
ukabu (浮ぶ), *vi.* ❶ (水に) to float; swim; rise to the surface (浮上る). ❷ (心に) to occur *to*; suggest itself to one's mind; come to one's mind; cross one's mind. ❸ (成佛) to rest in peace. —浮べる舟《城》, a floating vessel 《castle》. —浮ばれまい, will be unable to rest in peace; will turn in the grave. —浮び出る, to come to the surface. —一生浮ぶ瀬が無い, never to be able to live decently. —急に胸に浮んだ, A sudden idea struck me.
ukagai (伺), *n.* ❶ (訪問) a call; a visit. ❷ (尋問) a question; an inquiry. ¶ 暑中伺, an inquiry after another's health [a formal call] in midsummer.
ukagau (伺ふ), *vt.* ❶ (尋問) to ask; inquire; question. ❷ (訪問) to visit; call *on* (人を); call *at* (家を). ❸ (聞く) to hear.
ukagau (窺ふ), *vt.* ❶ (機會を) to watch [look] *for*. ❷ (様子を) to pry *about*; peep *into* (覗く). ☞ *nozoku* (覗く). —隙を窺ふ, to watch for an unguarded moment. —形勢を窺ふ, to see how the wind blows; see the turn of events.
ukai (迂回), *n.* circuitousness; deviousness; a détour. —迂回する, to make a détour; go round; take a roundabout [circuitous] route.
ukai (鵜飼), *n.* fishing with a cormorant.
ukareru (浮れる), *vi.* to become giddy [gay]; give away to merriment. —浮れてゐる, to be in high spirits; be on a spree.
ukasareru (浮される), *vi.* to be carried away; be made delirious; be affected; be bewitched [fascinated]. —熱に浮される, to be made delirious by fever. —茶に浮される, to be kept awake through drinking tea.
ukasu (浮す), *vt.* ❶ to refloat; raise. ❷ (水・コルク等が物を) to float; buoy up; support. ❸ (彫りて) to emboss; raise.
ukato (浮と), *ad.* ❶ (不注意に) carelessly; inattentivly. ❷ (考なく) thoughtlessly. ❸ (茫然と) in abstraction; absent-mindedly. —うかと口車に乗る, to allow oneself thoughtlessly to be wheedled.
ukatsu (迂濶), *n.* ❶ (不注意) inattention; thoughtlessness; imprudence. ❷ (迂愚) stupidity; dulness. —迂濶な, careless; thoughtless; inattentive; stupid; dull. ¶ 迂濶者, a scatter-brains; a stupid [dull] person.
ukauka (浮浮), *ad.* ❶ (心の落著かぬ貌) fidgetily; restlessly. ❷ (何の思慮もなき貌) carelessly; heedlessly; unconsciously; absently. —うかうか過ごす, to dream [idle] away (one's time); doze away (one's time). —うかうかする, ① (なまける) to idle about. ② (ぼんやりする) to be in abstraction; be careless. ③ (浮れる) to become gay [giddy].
uke (受), *n.* ❶ (受器) a receiver; a bearer. ❷ (支へ) a holder. ❸ (承諾) consent; acceptance. ❹ (氣受) reputation; popularity. —受がよい《惡い》, to be popular 《unpopular》. ¶ 油受, an oil-receiver.
uke (浮), *n.* =*uki*.
uke (有卦), *n.* a period of luck; a stroke of luck. —有卦に入る, to come into luck; be in luck [clover]; have a good luck.
ukeai (請合), *n.* guarantee; assurance; security.
ukeau (請合ふ), *vt.* ❶ (身に引受ける) to undertake; take upon oneself; contract. ❷ (保證する) to guarantee; warrant; assure; answer *for*; vouch *for*. —請合って, assuredly; securely. —身元を請合ふ, to go security for a person.
ukedachi (受太刀), *n.* ❶ (守勢) being on the defensive ❷ a parry. —受太刀になる, to be [stand] on the defensive.
ukedasu (受出・請出す), *vt.* (質物を) to redeem; take out. —質物を請出す, to redeem [take out] a pawn.
ukeireru (受入れる), *vt.* to accept.
ukemi (受身), *n.* acting on the defensive; 【文】 the passive. —— **no,** *a.* passive; defensive. —受身の動詞, a verb in the passive.
ukemochi (受持), *n.* charge; duty. —受持つ, to have [take] charge *of*; take in one's charge. ¶ 受持時間, one's hours in class. —受持教員, a class-teacher.
ukemodosu (請戻す), *vt.* to redeem.
ukenagasu (受流す), *vt.* to parry; ward off; evade; turn aside. —厳しい質問を受流す, to parry a prying question.
ukeoi (請負, 受負), *n.* a contract

(for work); an undertaking. ¶ 土木請負業, engineering contract business. —請負契約, an agreement [a contract] for work. —請負入札, a contract tender. —請負師, a contractor. —請負仕事, a task-work; a contract work; the work contracted for.

ukeou (請負ふ), *vt.* to contract *for*; undertake.

ukeru (受ける), *vt.* ❶ (受納) to receive; accept; take. ❷ (受止める) to catch; stop; receive; prop up (支へる); support (同上). ❸ (應試) (*a*) (課せらる) to be subjected *to*; undergo: (*b*) (應じる) to take; try; sit *for*. ❹ (蒙る) to receive; suffer; sustain; be subjected *to*. —受け損ふ, to muff (球などを); miss. —俸給を受ける, to draw one's salary. —訪問を受ける, to have a visit *from*.

ukesho (請書), *n.* a receipt; a written acknowledgment; a letter of acceptance (就任の).

uketamawaru (承る), *vt.* to hear; learn; listen *to* (傾聽); receive (a command) (命を).

uketomeru (受止める), *vt.* to stop; catch; parry; ward. —球を受止める, to stop [catch] a ball.

uketori (受取, 請取), *n.* ❶ (受取ること) acceptance. ❷ (請取書) a receipt; a quittance. ¶ 受取人, a receiver; a recipient; a remittee. —受取手形, bills receivable.

uketoru (受取る), *vt.* to receive; accept; take. —右正に受取申候也, "Received with thanks."

uketsugi (受繼), *n.* succession (繼承); inheritance (相續). —受け繼ぐ, to succeed; take over; inherit.

uketsuke (受附), *n.* ❶ an office. ❷ (受理) acceptance; receipt. ¶ 受附係, an usher; a janitor 〔米〕.

uketsukeru (受附ける), *vt.* to accept (a petition; an apology; a proposal); take up (a case; an appeal); receive (a petition; an application); entertain (a request; a proposal).

ukeuri (請賣, 受賣), *n.* ❶ retail; sale and [or] return (殘品引取の約束の). ❷ (學說などを我物顔に述べること) giving second-hand; borrowing. —受賣する, to retail; tell second-hand (話を); borrow *from* (學說など). ¶ 受賣知識, second-hand knowledge. —賣藥請賣業, retail trade in patent medicines.

ukewatashi (受渡), *n.* transfer; delivery. ¶ 受渡日, a settling [delivery] day.

uki (浮), *n.* ❶ (釣に用ひる) a float; a cork; a quill. ❷ (浮標) a buoy. ❸ (浮袋) a life-preserver; a life-belt; a life-buoy.

uki (雨季, 雨期), *n.* the rainy [wet] season. —雨期に入る, The rainy season sets in.

ukiagaru (浮上る), *vi.* to refloat; float (off); rise [come] to the surface (*of*).

ukiashi (浮足), *n.* ❶ (そっと踏みて行くこと) soft tread. ❷ (落着かぬこと) waver; falter; swaying. —浮足になる, to begin to falter; become half-hearted.

ukibori (浮彫), *n.* a relief; an embossed carving; raised work; an alto-relievo 〔伊〕. —浮彫を施す, to emboss; chase; carve in relief. ¶ 浮彫細工, relief [raised] work; an embossment.

ukibukuro (浮袋), *n.* ❶ (水泳·救護用の) a life-buoy. ☞ *uki* の ❸. ❷ (魚鰾) an air-bladder; a swimming [swim]-bladder.

ukigumo (浮雲), *n.* a floating cloud; a cloud-drift.

ukihashi (浮橋), *n.* a float-bridge; a pontoon(-bridge).

ukihōjiro (うきほうじろ), *n.* 【鳥】 the snow-bunting; the snowflake.

ukiishi (浮石), *n.* a pumice-stone.

ukiko (浮粉), *n.* a fine rice-powder.

ukikusa (浮草, 萍), *n.* 【植】 the duckweed.

ukime (憂目), *n.* affliction; misery; hardships; sorrows. —憂き目を見る, to suffer affliction; have a hard time of it; go through hardships.

ukimi (憂身を窶す), to devote oneself heart and soul *to*.

ukimo (浮藻), *n.* the floating weed.

ukina (浮名を流す), to become the talk of the town for one's love-affairs.

ukini (浮荷), *n.* a flotsam; a floatage.

ukiori (浮織), *n.* being woven with raised figures.

ukishima (浮島), *n.* a floating island.

ukishizumi (浮沈), *n.* ❶ (浮沈) floating and sinking. ❷ (盛衰) ups and downs; rise and fall; vicissitudes.

ukisu (浮洲), *n.* a sand-bank.

ukitatsu (浮立つ), *vi.* to become buoyant [volatile; gay-spirited]; enliven. —浮立たせる, to enliven; cheer (up); exhilarate.

ukiuki (浮浮した), *a.* cheerful; light-hearted; sprightly. —浮々と, cheerfully; light-heartedly; in good spirits.

ukiyo (浮世), *n.* the world; the fleeting [transitory] world. —浮世の絆, worldly bonds [fetters].

—浮世の塵, dust of the world; the things of this world; worldly affairs. —浮世の情, worldly feelings. —浮世の榮華, the pomps and vanities of the world. —浮世を遠ざかる, to live out of the world; keep aloof from the world. —浮世を捨てる, to forsake [renounce] the world.

ukiyoe (浮世繪), *n.* a genre-painting [picture]; an *ukiyoe.* ¶ 浮世繪板畫, a printed genre-picture; a colour print.

ukkari (うっかり-と), *ad.* carelessly; thoughtlessly; in an unguarded moment. —うっかり秘密を洩らす, to blunder out a secret.

ukketsu (鬱血), *n.* engorgement; congestion (of blood).

ukki (鬱氣), *n.* ❶ (こもりたる氣) close air; foul air. ❷ (心のふさぐこと) gloom; melancholy. —鬱氣を散ずる, ① (こもりたる氣を) to ventilate (a room). ② (心の鬱を) to drive away melancholy.

ukkonkō (鬱金香), *n.* 【植】 the garden tulip; the tulip.

ukon (鬱金), *n.* ❶ 【植】 the turmeric-plant; the turmeric. ❷ (根) turmeric. ¶ 鬱金色, saffron. —鬱金粉, turmeric.

uku (浮く), *vi.* ❶ to float; swim. ❷ (浮き上る) to (re-)float; come to the surface *of.* ❸ (浮彫のやうに) to be relieved [set] *against*; be seen distinctly; loom. —氣が浮いてゐる, to be in good spirits [humour].

ukyoku (紆曲), *n.* ❶ (くねり) wind; turning; crookedness. ❷ (紆回) roundabout; circumvolution. —紆曲する, ① to wind; turn; crook. ② to make a circuit [roundabout].

uma (馬), *n.* ❶ a horse. ❷ (桂馬) a knight (將棋の). ❸ (臺) an andiron (薪架); a (fire-)dog. (同上); a saw-horse (挽臺); a (vaulting-)horse (木馬); a stool (踏臺); a step (同上). ❹ (附馬) a tout who accompanies the guest for payment. —玩具の馬, a hobby-horse. —馬から下りる, to dismount; alight from a horse. —馬から落ちる, to fall off a horse. —馬から落す, to dismount (敵などを). —馬に乘る, to mount a horse; ride on horseback. —馬に乘って來る, to come on horseback. —馬を止める, to draw rein [bit; bridle]; rein in [up] a horse. —馬を走らす, to course a horse. —馬を急がす, to spur (on; forward); spur a horse (into gallop); urge a horse on [forward]. —車に馬をつける, to horse a cart. —五十哩を馬で行く, to ride 50 miles. —馬の耳に念佛, "It is like water off a duck's back." —此の馬は乘り好い《難い》, This horse rides well 《hard》.

umabae (馬蠅), *n.* 【昆】 the horse bat-fly.

umabiru (馬蛭), *n.* 【蟲】 the horse-leech.

umagoyashi (苜蓿), *n.* 【植】 the denticulate medic [medick]; the snail-clover.

umai (旨い), *a.* ❶ (味が) delicious; nice; palatable. ❷ (上手) good; skilful; clever; happy (適切な). ❸ (首尾よき) splendid; grand; successful. —飜譯が旨い, to be good [clever] at translation. —旨い香がする, to smell nice. —うまい事を言ふ, to oil one's tongue (世辭); say clever things. —旨い汁を吸ふ, to squeeze [suck] the orange. —話があまり旨すぎる, His story is too good to be true.

umaichi (馬市), *n.* a horse-market [-fair].

umajirushi (馬印), *n.* ❶ a brand(-mark) on a horse. ❷ (馬の象標) a mark of a horse.

umakata (馬方), *n.* a pack-horse driver [man] (荷馬曳き); a cartman, carter (馬車追ひ).

umaku (旨く), *ad.* ❶ (味よく) deliciously; toothsomely. ❷ (上手に) skilfully; well; finely. ❸ (首尾よく) successfully; happily; satisfactorily.

umami (旨味), *n.* deliciousness; flavour; gusts; zest. —旨味のない文章, an insipid composition. —旨味をつけて話す, to add a zest to one's story; speak with zest.

umanoashi (馬の脚), *n.* 【劇】 a super; a utility (man).

umanoashigata (毛茛), *n.* 【植】 the butter-daisy; the buttercup.

umanokuso (馬糞), *n.* horse-dung.

umanori (馬乘), *n.* ❶ (馬に乘る人) a (horse-)rider. ❷ (馬に乘ること) (horse-)riding; equitation. ❸ (馬に乘る如く物に跨がること) sitting astride. ❹ 【裁縫】 (一方を存して裁ち割ること) slit.

umanosu (馬尾), *n.* horsehair.

umaoi (馬追), *n.* ❶ (駄馬等を追ふ人) the driver of a pack-horse; a horse-driver; a carter. ❷ (牧場にて野馬を追ひ込め捕へる人) a catcher of a wild horse.

umare (生れ), *n.* ❶ (出生) birth. ❷ (生れ故郷) one's native place; one's birthplace. ❸ (家系) lineage; birth. ❹ (資性) nature. —微賤の生れ, low birth. —東京生れの, Tōkyō-born. ¶ 生れ年, the year of one's birth.

umarekawari (生變り), *n.* ❶ (再生) rebirth; regeneration (新生活に入る); new birth. ❷ (輪廻) transmigration of the soul; metempsychosis.

umarekawaru (生變る), *vi.* ❶ to be reborn; be regenerated; become a new man. ❷ to transmigrate (靈魂が). —生れ變り死に變りて, through changes by birth and death. —生れ變った人間にする, to make a new man of another.

umarenagara (生れながら), *ad.* by nature; congenitally; naturally. **—-no,** *a.* natural; born; congenital. —生れながらの盲目である, to be born blind.

umareru (生れる), *vi.* to be born; be brought forth; come into [to] the world; see the light. —生れ落ちてこの方, in all my born days. —富家に生れる, to be born rich; be born with a silver spoon in one's mouth. —悧潑に生れる, to be born clever. —聖代に生れ合はす, to be born in a brilliant reign.

umaretate (生立ての), *a.* new-born; newly born. —生れたての子, a new-born baby.

umaretsuki (生附), *n.* nature; character; temperament. —生附きの, natural; inborn; innate; congenital.

umaretsuku (生附く), *v.* to be inborn; be innate [congenital]; be endowed *with*. —生れもつかぬ不具になる, to become a cripple by force of circumstances.

umaya (廐·厩), *n.* a stable. —厩に入れる, to stable [put up] (a horse).

umazume (石女), *n.* a barren [sterile] woman.

ume (梅), *n.* ❶ (樹) the mume-plum; the plum-tree (俗稱). ❷ (實) a plum. —梅の花, plum-blossoms. —梅を探る, to stroll to see plum-blossoms. ¶ 梅屋敷, a plum-garden.

umeawase (埋合), *n.* amends; compensation; recompense.

umeawaseru (埋合せる), *vt.* to make amends *for*; make up *for*; compensate *for*; make good. —損失を埋合はせる, to make up [compensate] for a loss; make good a loss.

umeboshi (梅干), *n.* pickled plums. ¶ 梅干婆, a crone; a wrinkled old woman.

umeku (呻く), *vi.* to groan; moan.

umekusa (埋草), *n.* fill-space; padding (新聞·著述等の); balaam (新聞紙の). —城の埋草となる, to fill up the castle-moats; become food for powder.

umemi (梅見), *n.* plum-blossom viewing; an excursion for seeing plum-blossoms.

umemodoki (落霜紅), *n.* 【植】 Ilex Sieboldi (holly の一種·學名).

umeru (埋める), *vt.* ❶ to bury. ❷ (埋葬) to bury; inter. ❸ (塡充) to plug; fill up [in]; inlay (象眼する). —遺骸を埋める, to bury [inter] another's remains. —空所を埋める, to fill up a space. —齲歯を金で埋める, to plug a decayed tooth with gold.

umeru (うめる), *vt.* to pour in. —風呂に水をうめる, to pour cold water into a bath.

umetate (埋立), *n.* reclamation; reclaim. —埋立てる, to reclaim; fill in. ¶ 埋立地, reclaimed land [ground]; polder (海濱の). —埋立工事, reclamation work.

umezu (梅酢), *n.* plum vinegar.

umi (海), *n.* the sea; the ocean (大洋). —火の海, a sea of flame. —海に圍まれた國, a sea-girt country. —海へ乘り出す, to put (out) to sea.

umi (膿), *n.* pus; (purulent) matter. —膿を持つ, ① [*vi.*] to suppurate; gather; come to a head. ② [*a.*] purulent; suppurative.

umibe (海邊), *n.* the coast; the sea-beach; the seashore. ☞ *kaihen*.

umidanuki (海狸), *n.* 【哺乳】 the beaver.

umidasu (產出す), *vt.* to bring forth; produce; give birth *to*. —利が利を產み出す, Interest brings forth interest.

umigame (海龜), *n.* 【爬蟲】 the (sea-)turtle.

umigiwa (海際), *n.* the seaside; the seashore.

umigusa (海草), *n.* a seaweed.

umihōzuki (海酸漿), *n.* the brooch-pouch of the Hemifusus ternatanus.

umioso (海獺), *n.* 【哺乳】 the sea-otter [-beaver].

umisuzume (海雀), *n.* 【鳥】 the Bering's murrelet.

umitsubame (海燕), *n.* 【鳥】 the petrel. ¶ 嵐海燕, the stormy petrel; Mother Cary's chicken.

umitsukeru (產附ける), *vt.* to blow; deposit (*on*); spawn (魚が).

umō (羽毛), *n.* feathers; plumage; a plumelet (小羽毛); a down (毱); feathering (全體の).

umoregi (埋木), *n.* ❶ bog-wood; lignitized wood. ❷ (世に捨てられたこと) living in obscurity. ¶ 埋木細工, lignitized-wood work.

umu (生·產む), *vt.* ❶ to bring forth; give birth *to*; be delivered *of*; bear. ❷ (生ずる) to bring forth; produce; yield; bear. ❸ (卵を) to lay (鳥など); spawn (魚); spat (貝など); breed. —男子を産む, to give birth to a boy. —利子を産む, to produce [yield; bear] interest.

umu (有無), *n.* ❶ (存否) existence (or non-existence). ❷ (諾否) yes or no. —御出席の有無, whether you will attend or not. —有無を言はせず, without giving a person time to protest; allowing no time for answer; willy-nilly.

umu (倦む), *vi.* to get tired [weary]; be wearied; tire; weary. —倦ます, to weary; tire. —倦まずに, tirelessly; untiringly. —仕事に倦む, to get [become] tired of the work.

umu (熟·膿む), *vi.* ❶ (熟す) to get ripe; ripen. ❷ (化膿する) to gather; suppurate; draw to a head.

umu (績む), *vt.* to spin.

un (運), *n.* fortune; luck; lot (命數); fate (宿命); destiny (天命). ☞ *unmei.* —運の盡, the end of one's luck. —運惡く, unluckily; by ill luck; by mischance. —運よく, fortunately; luckily; by good fortune [luck]; by a lucky chance. (運よくば, if Fortune smiles upon one.) —運が向く, Fortune smiles upon one; Luck turns in one's favour. —運が向かぬ, to have no luck; be out of luck; Fortune is against one. —運が盡きる, One's star sinks [is set]; One's doom is sealed. —運を天に任せて, leaving one's fate to Heaven; trusting to fate. —運を試す, to try one's luck [chance]; take one's chance.

un (うん), *int.* ❶ (承諾の時) yes; oh yes; all right. ❷ (思ひ出した時) h'm. —うんと云って氣絶する, to swoon with a groan. —うんな様か, H'm, indeed?

u-na (迂な), *a.* roundabout; devious.

unabara (海原), *n.* the ocean; the sea; a wide expanse of water.

unadareru (項垂れる), *vi.* to hang down the head; droop (one's head).

unagasu (促す), *vt.* to urge; press; stimulate. —注意を促す, to call attention *to.* —進歩を促す, to quicken [accelerate] the progress.

unagi (鰻), *n.* 【魚】 the eel. ¶ 鰻飯, eel and rice. —鰻上り, steady promotion. —鰻屋, an eel-restaurant.

unaji (項) *n.* the nape (of the neck); the back of the neck.

unari (唸), *n.* ❶ (呻き聲) a groan; a moan. ❷ (怒りの) a growl; a snarl. ❸ (獸の) a roar; a growl; a bellow. ❹ (風箏) the bow of the kite (紙鳶の). ❺ (獨樂·車輪等の) hum.

unaru (唸る), *vi.* ❶ (うめく) to groan; moan. ❷ (怒りほざく) to growl; snarl. ❸ (咆哮する) to roar; bellow; growl; snarl. ❹ (其他) to roar (風など); hum (獨樂·車輪など); hiss (矢など).

unasare (魘れ), *n.* a nightmare.

unasareru (魘される), *vi.* to have [be troubled with] a nightmare; be hag-ridden.

unau (耡ふ), *vt.* to plough, plow; cultivate.

unazuku (頷く), *vi.* to nod; noddle (續けて).

unchiku (蘊蓄), *n.* deep learning; a great stock of knowledge. —蘊蓄のある, well-stored; of profound knowledge.

unchin (運賃), *n.* carriage; freight; porterage; portage; cartage. ¶ 旅客運賃, passenger fare; passage-money. —運賃拂濟, carriage paid. —運賃元拂, payment of freight in advance. —運賃先拂, carriage forward; carriage payable on delivery; freight payable at destination.

undameshi (運試し), *n.* cast. —最後の運試し, the last cast. —運試しに, for trial of one's luck.

undei (雲泥の差), *n.* a wide difference; a violent discrepancy; the difference *toto cælo.* —兩者の意見には雲泥の差がある, Their opinions are wide as the poles asunder.

undō (運動), *n.* ❶ (動くこと) movement; motion. ❷ (散步) a walk. ❸ (身體の) exercise; athletics (運動競技). ❹ (奔走) a canvass; an agitation; a movement. —東都の運動界, the athletic world of Tōkyō. —運動に出掛ける, to go out for a walk; go for a trot. —運動が足りないので, through insufficient exercise.

—— **-suru,** *vi.* ❶ to move; be in motion. ❷ to walk. ❸ to take exercise. ❹ to canvass *for*; agitate *for.* —知事に運動する, to make interest with the governor. —醜聞の揉消運動する, to make an effort to hush up a scandal. —改革の爲めに運動する, to agitate for reform. —就職のため運動する, to run for an office. ¶ 運動中樞, the centre of motion. —運動費, a canvassing fund (資金); canvassing expenses (費用); expenditures to influence (officials, *etc.* 買收費). —運動員, a canvasser. —運動場, a playground; an exercise-ground; a recreation-ground (遊園地); a promenade; a gymnasium (體操場); a crush-room (芝居等の). —運動會, athletic sports; an athletic meeting. —運動者, an agitator (政治上の); a canvasser (選擧の); an electioneerer (同上); an election agent (同上). —運動神經, 【解】 a motor nerve.

une (畦, 畝), *n.* ❶ a ridge (in a field); rib (織物, 莫大小などの); a cord (同上). ❷ =*uneri*.

unen (雲煙), *n.* ❶ clouds and smoke. ❷ (山水畫) a landscape. —雲煙過眼視する, to give no thought to a thing (after looking at it); look abstractly *at*.

uneri (うねり), *n.* ❶ (うねること) undulation; winding; meandering. ❷ (膨浪) a swell; a ground-swell (底浪).

uneritatsu (畝立つ), *v.* to ridge.

uneru (うねる), *vi.* ❶ (波動) to undulate. ❷ to wind; meander. —うねりくねる, to turn and twist. —うねりくねッた, serpentine; winding; meandrous; tortuous.

uneune (うねうね), *ad.* windingly; zigzag; in zigzags. —うねうねする, winding; meandering; zigzag.

unga (運河), *n.* a canal. —運河を開く, to dig [build] a canal; canalize [*vt.*]. ¶ スウェズ運河, the Suez Canal. —水閘式運河, a locked canal. —海平式運河, a sea-level canal.

uni (海膽), *n.* 【棘皮】 the sea--urchin; the sea-egg [-hedgehog].

unka (浮塵子), *n.* 【昆】 the true leaf-hopper.

unka (雲霞), *n.* clouds and haze. —雲霞の如き大軍, an enormous army. —雲霞の如く群り來る, to come in swarms.

unkō (運行), *n.* revolution. —運行する, to revolve (around).

unmei (運命), *n.* destiny; fate; doom; lot; fortune. ☞ *un*. —運命の寵兒, fortune's favourite; the child of fortune. —運命づける, to destine. —運命に支配されて, controlled by fate. —運命に任せる, to abandon oneself to fate; leave to fate. —運命に飜弄される, to become the sport of fortune. —運命と諦める, to accept as fate; resign [bend] to fate. —國民の運命を支配する, to sway the destinies of a nation. —その運命を定める, to decide [fix; seal] the fate. ¶ 運命論, fatalism. (運命論者, a fatalist.)

unmo (雲母), *n.* 【鑛】 mica; 【商】 talc (特に窓用の) 〔俗〕. ¶ 雲母片岩, mica-schist; mica-slate.

unmon (雲紋), *n.* moire 〔佛〕.

unnun (云云), *ad.* ❶ (しかじか) so and so. ❷ (等) and so on; and so forth; et cetera (etc.; &c. と略す). —云々[云爲] する, to say something or other *of*; criticize.

unō (蘊奥), *n.* mysteries. —蘊奥を究める, to master the most abstruse principles *of*; reach the mysteries *of*.

unohana (卯の花), *n.* ❶ (うつぎの花) the flower of the Deutzia scabra. ❷ 〔雪花菜〕 (豆腐の) bean-curd refuse.

unome (鵜目鷹目で), with keen [sharp] eyes; with vigilant eyes.

unomi (鵜呑にする), *vt.* to swallow whole; bolt; gulp down.

unpan (運搬), *n.* conveyance; carriage; portage (水路間の). ☞ *unsō*. —運搬する, to carry; convey; transport. ¶ 運搬費, the carriage; the portage.

unpitsu (運筆), *n.* calligraphy; the use of the brush.

unpu-tenpu (運賦天賦), *n.* hazard; chance. —運賦天賦でやッて見る, to take the chance; try one's luck [fortune]; run the hazard.

unsaiori (雲齋織), *n.* (cotton) drill.

unsei (運勢), *n.* ❶ (運の勢ひ) one's current of fortune. ❷ (運) one's fortune; one's star. —運勢を卜する, to tell a person's fortune; cast a horoscope.

unshū (溫州-蜜柑), *n.* the Satsuma orange 〔米〕.

unshū (雲集する), *vi.* to swarm; crowd; come in swarms. —雲集霧散する, to come and go in swarms.

unsō (運送), *n.* carriage; transportation. —運送中に停滯せる貨物, goods delayed in transit. —運送する, to transport; convey; carry; rail (鐵道で); ship (船で). ¶ 運送業, transportation business; carrying-trade. —運送人; 運送業者, a carrier; a common carrier. —運送取扱人, a forwarding agent; a forwarder.

unsō (運漕), *n.* marine transportation; shipping; freighting. ¶ 運漕店, a freight agency.

unsui (雲水), *n.* (行脚僧) an itinerant priest.

unten (運轉), *n.* working; motion; operation; running (汽車等の). —運轉を止める, to stop the engine. **—— -suru,** *vt.* to work; operate; run; put [set] in motion; employ (運用). —電氣にて運轉する, to be worked by electricity. —資本を巧みに運轉する, to employ one's capital skilfully. 一資本を迅速に運轉する, to turn over capital quickly. ¶ 運轉系統, the tram system. 一運轉士,【航】a mate. (一等運轉士, a first [chief] mate [officer]. 一二等《三等》運轉士, a second《third》mate.) 一運轉資本, working capital.

untenshu (運轉手), *n.* ❶ (電車の) a (tram-car) driver; a motor-man; a trolley-man. ❷ (自動車の) a chauffeur.

unto (うんと), *ad.* ❶ (一生懸命に) with great force [might]. ❷ (澤山) abundantly. ❸ (したゝか) severely; roundly; soundly. 一うんと毆る, to give a good [sound] drubbing. 一うんと力を入れて押す, to push with all one's strength.

unubore (自惚), *n.* self-conceit; overconfidence; vanity. 一自惚の强い, self-conceited; overconfident; vain. (自惚の强い人, a very self-conceited fellow; a fly on a wheel.)

unuboreru (自惚れる), *vi.* to be vain [conceited]; fancy oneself; have a high opinion of oneself. 一自惚れ過ぎる, to have too high an opinion of oneself.

unyō (運用), *n.* employment; use; administration; working. —— **-suru,** *vt.* to employ; use; work. 一船舶を運用する, to work [manage; navigate] a vessel.

unyu (運輸), *n.* traffic; transport; conveyance. ☞ *unsō*. ¶ 運輸會社, a transportation company. 一運輸局, the traffic departmet. (運輸局長, the traffic manager.)

unzan (運算), *n.*【數】operation.

unzari (うんざりする), *vi.* to be disgusted *with*; be sick *of*; be wearied *with*. 一喋〔ﾁ〕り立てて人をうんざりさす, to weary a person with lengthy talk; talk a person's head off.

uo (魚), *n.* fish. 一魚を取り盡す, to fish out. ¶ 魚問屋, a fish-factory; a wholesale fish-dealer.

uogashi (魚河岸), *n.* a riverside fish-market.

uoichiba (魚市場), *n.* a fish-market.

uonome (魚目, 鷄眼), *n.* a corn.

uō-saō (右往左往に), *ad.* right and left; this way and that; hither and thither. 一火の子を冒して右往左往する, to rush about among the sparks.

uppun (鬱憤), *n.* anger; rancour; resentment. 一鬱憤を漏らす, to wreak one's wrath. 一鬱憤を晴らす, to give vent to one's anger; satisfy one's resentment.

ura (浦), *n.* ❶ (入江) a creek; a bight; a bay. ❷ (海邊) the seacost; the seashore.

ura (裏), *n.* ❶ (裏面) the reverse side; the wrong side; the back-side. ❷ (後部) the back; the rear. ❸ (反對) the reverse; the contrary; the opposite;【數】the obverse. ❹ (衣服等の) the lining. 一貨幣〔ﾍｲ〕の裏, the reverse (side) [tail] of a coin; verso. 一裏をつける, to line. 一裏をかく; 裏を行く, to defeat [upset; frustrate; baffle] another's plan; take the wind out of another's sails. (言葉の裏をかく, to go behind one's words.)

urabon (盂蘭盆), *n.* the Feast of Lanterns.

uradana (裏店), *n.* a tenement-house in the slums; a house in an alley. ¶ 裏店住居《借人》, life《a tenant》in the slums.

uradōri (裏通), *n.* a back street [road].

uragaeshi (裏返し), *n.* turning inside out; eversion. 一著物を裏返しする, to turn the dress. 一服を裏返しに著る, to wear a coat the wrong side out.

uragaesu (裏返す), *vt.* to turn inside out; turn out. 一袋を裏返す, to turn out a bag.

uragaki (裏書), *n.* indorsement, endorsement. —— **-suru,** *vt.* to endorse, indorse; back. 一B氏の說に裏書する, to indorse the opinion of Mr. B. ¶ 裏書人, an indorser, endorser. (被裏書人, an indorsee.)

uragiku (金盞菜), *n.*【植】the blue [purple] chamomile; the blue daisy; the tripoly.

uragiri (裏切), *n.* betrayal; treachery; foul play. 一裏切をする, to go over to the enemy (敵につく); turn one's coat (變節する); betray a person. ¶ 裏切者, a betrayer; a traitor; a turncoat; an informer.

uragiru (裏切る), *vt.* to betray; play (a person) foul [false]; sell. 一豫想を裏切る, to betray one's expectation. 一世間の同情を裏切る, to betray public sympathy.

uraguchi (裏口), *n.* a backdoor; a back-entrance.

urahara (裏腹), *n.* oppositeness; contrariness; the reverse [opposite; contrary]. ☞ *hantai*.

uraita (裏板), *n.* ❶【建】(屋根裏に張り著けた板) a roof-plate; a roof-board. ❷ (天井) ceiling. ❸ (裏目の板) a cross-grained board.

uraji (裏地), *n.* the lining; the backing.

urajiro (裏白), *n.*【植】Gleichenia glauca (net-fern の一種·學名).

urakaidan (裏階段), *n.* backstairs; a backstair case.

uramachi (裏街), *n.* a back-street; the slums (細民窟).

urameshii (怨しい), *a.* hateful; odious. —怨しく思ふ, to have a grudge *against*.

urami (怨, 恨, 憾), *n.* ❶ (怨恨) resentment; grudge; animosity; rancour. ❷ (憎惡) spite; hatred; ill-will; malice. ❸ (遺憾) regret. —怨深き, spiteful; resentful; vengeful. —怨重なる親の仇, my father's murderer, the object of my long resentment. —怨を懷く, to have [bear] a grudge [an animosity] against a person; bear [own] a person a grudge. —怨を晴らす, to satisfy one's resentment; take one's revenge *on*. —怨を報いる, to pay [wipe] off old scores; quit scores with a person. —怨に報いるに德を以てする, to heap coals of fire on another's head.

uramichi (裏道), *n.* ❶ (裏通) a back road [street]. ❷ (間道) a secret path; a path of escape.

uramon (裏門), *n.* a back [rear; postern] gate.

uramu (怨·恨·憾む), *vt.* ❶ (無念とす) to bear (a person) an ill-will [a grudge]; show resentment *at*. ❷ (憎む) to hate; spite. ❸ (遺憾とす) to regret. —無情を怨む, to resent a person's want of feeling.

uranagaya (裏長屋), *n.* a tenement-house in the slums. ☞ *uradana*.

uranai (卜, 占), *n.* fortune-telling; divination (神易); augury (兆を見ての占). ¶ 獨占, self-divination. —卜者, a fortune-teller; a diviner; a soothsayer.

uranau (占·卜ふ), *v.* to divine; tell fortune. —卜者にトッて貰ふ, to consult a fortune-teller. —身の上をトふ, to divine another's fortune for him.

uraniwa (裏庭), *n.* a backyard; a back-court.

uraomote (裏表), *n.* the face [front] and the back; the surface and its lining. ☞ *hyōri*. —紙の裏表, two sides of a sheet of paper.

uraraka (麗かな), *a.* serene; clear; bright; fine.

urate (裏手), *n.* the back; the rear. —裏手へ廻る, to go round to the back of the house.

urauchi (裏打する), *vt.* to back; line; paper (紙で).

uraya (裏屋), *n.* =*uradana*.

urayamashii (羨しい), *a.* enviable; desirable; to be envied.

urayami (羨), *n.* envy; jealousy.

urayamu (羨む), *vt.* to envy; be envious *of*; be jealous (妬む). —羨ませる, to make a person's nose swell; make a person envious.

ure (賣), *n.* sale; demand; market. —賣れがよい《惡い》, to meet a good 《bad》 market; sell well.

uredaka (賣高), *n.* the amount sold; sales; proceeds; circulation (新聞·雜誌の).

uree, urei, (愁, 憂, 患), *n.* ❶ (心配) anxiety; concern; worry. ❷ (悲しみ) sorrow; grief; distress. ❸ (虞[ｵｿﾚ]) fear; apprehension; risk (危險); danger (同上). —愁に沈む, to be oppressed by sorrow; be overcome [pressed] with grief; be sunk in grief. —攻擊の憂なき, free from [without fear of] attack.

ureeru (愁·憂·患へる), *v.* ❶ (悲しむ) to feel sorrow *for*; grieve; mourn; be distressed. ❷ (心配す) to be troubled [worried] *about*; be anxious [solicitous] *about*. ❸ (虞れる) to fear; apprehend; have fear *for*. —憂へしめる, to inspire uneasiness [fear]; trouble; distress. —國事を憂へる, to be anxious about the state affairs.

urekko (賣ッ子), *n.* =***hayarikko*** (流行兒).

urekuchi (賣口), *n.* sale; demand; market; outlet (捌口). —賣口のよい, salable; marketable; in good demand. —賣口の遲い品, slow-moving goods. —賣口を見附ける, to find a sale *for*.

urenokori (賣殘), *n.* remainders. —賣殘る, to lie [be left unsold] on one's hands; remain unsold.

ureru (賣れる), *vi.* ❶ (品物が) to sell; have a demand. ❷ (名が) to be well known; be popular. —よく賣れる, to have a good [large] sale [demand]; sell well; meet a good market; command a sale; have a large circulation (新聞·雜誌など). —どんどん[飛ぶやうに]賣れる, to sell like wild-fire [hot cakes].

ureshigarasu (嬉しがらす), *vt.* to please; gladden; delight.

ureshigaru (嬉しがる), *vi.* to rejoice; be delighted [glad]; hug oneself *on* [*for*]. —躍り上って嬉しがる, to jump [dance] with joy.

ureshige (嬉しげな), *a.* Ⓢ 嬉しさうな. delightful; joyful; glad. —嬉しげな様子, a delighted air.

ureshii (嬉しい), *a.* joyful; glad; happy. ——, *vi.* to be glad [delighted; rejoiced; pleased]. —やれ嬉しや, Thank God [Heaven]! —嬉しくて嬉しくて物が言へぬ, I am speechless with joy.

ureshinaki (嬉泣する), *vi.* to

weep for joy.

ureshinamida (嬉涙), *n.* tears of joy. —嬉し涙を流す, to shed tears of joy; weep for joy.

ureyuki (賣行), *n.* Ⓢ 賣足. sale; demand; salability.

uri (瓜), *n.* a melon. —瓜二つのやうな, as like as two peas [eggs]. —瓜の蔓に茄子はならぬ, "An onion will not produce a rose."

uri (賣), *n.* sale; selling. ¶ 玉子賣, an egg-seller. —花賣女, a flower-girl.

uriage (賣上), *n.* closing sale; sale. ¶ 賣上歩合, selling [sale] commission. —賣上高, the amount sold; the sales; the proceeds (of a sale). —賣上勘定, account sales (A/S と略す).

uriba (賣場), *n.* a sales-counter; a shop (店). ¶ 賣場監督係, a floor manager. —賣場見廻役, a shop-walker; a floor-walker.

uridame (賣溜-金), *n.* money in a till; the proceeds of a sale.

uridashi (賣出), *n.* sale; selling; the bargain sale (安賣); clearance sale (藏拂ひ). —夏物の賣出し, the sale of summer wear; summer sale. —若手の賣出し, a rising young man. —今賣出しの小說家, a novelist of rising popularity. ¶ 賣出し廣告, advertising the special sale.

uridasu (賣出す), *v.* ❶ (發賣する) to begin to sell; sell; place on sale [on the market] (公債·債券など). ❷ (名を賣り始む) to make one's name popular; become popular.

urigoe (賣聲), *n.* a cry of wares; a hawker's [pedlar's] cry.

uriharau (賣拂ふ), *vt.* to sell off; clear off; dispose *of*; get rid *of*. —家屋敷を賣り拂ふ, to sell one's house with the grounds.

urihiromeru (賣擴める), *vt.* to extend the market [sale] *of*; capture a new market *for*; spread by selling.

uriie (賣家), *n.* a house to sell; a house for sale.

urikai (賣買), *n.* buying and selling.

urikake (賣掛), *n.* credit sales. ¶ 賣掛代金, money due for goods sold on credit. —賣掛勘定, account of credit sales.

urikashiie (賣貸家), *n.* "house to sell or let."

urikata (賣方), *n.* ❶ (販賣法) the art [method] of selling; salesmanship. ❷ (人) a seller; (株式市場の) a bear 【英】; a short 【米】.

urikireru (賣切れる), *vi.* to be sold [closed] out; go out of stock; be cleared out.

uriko (賣子), *n.* a salesman; a saleswoman; a shopman; a shop-woman; a shop-boy; a shop-girl [-maid]; a news-boy (新聞の); a hawker (行商人).

urikomishō (賣込商), *n.* a commission seller.

urikomu (賣込む), *v.* to sell; extend the market. —多年賣込んだ小間物店, an old-established fancy-goods store.

urikotoba (賣言葉), *n.* offensive speech; provoking words. —賣言葉に買言葉, tit for tat; retaliation; a Roland for an [one's] Oliver.

urimono (賣物), *n.* an article for sale; (貼札) "for sale." —賣物に出す, to put [set] on sale; put [place] on the market; put to sale. —賣物に出る, to come into the market. —賣物に出てゐる, to be offered for sale; be on the market; be on sale. —賣物に花を飾る, to bedeck an article for sale.

urine (賣値), *n.* a sale-price; a selling-price.

urioshimi (賣惜みする), to be indisposed to sell.

urisabaki (賣捌), *n.* sale. ¶ 賣捌所, a shop; a store; an agency (代理店). (郵便切手收入印紙賣捌所, "Postage and revenue stamps on sale"; a place for the sale of postage and revenue stamps.) —賣捌人, a salesman. (大賣捌人, a wholesale dealer.)

urisabaku (賣捌く), *vt.* to sell; deal *in*.

urite (賣手), *n.* a seller; a vendor.

uritobasu (賣飛す), *vt.* to sell (off); dispose *of*. —二足三文に賣り飛ばす, to sell for a song.

uritsukeru (賣附ける), *vt.* to force (an article) *upon*; press (a person) to buy; impose (a sham) *upon* (僞物を). —僞物を賣り附ける, to impose [foist; palm off] a false article upon a person.

uritsukusu (賣盡す), *vt.* to sell out [off]; clear out.

uriwatashi (賣渡), *n.* sale and delivery; sale. —賣り渡す, to sell over; negotiate (手形等を). ¶ 賣渡人, a vendor 【法】; a seller. —賣渡證, a bill of sale.

uriya (賣家), *n.* a house for sale; a house to sell.

urizanegao (瓜實顏), *n.* an oval face.

urizome (賣初), *n.* opening the sale *of*.

urizuru (瓜蔓), *n.* a melon-vine.

uro (虛), *n.* a cavity; a hollow; a hole (穴).

uro (迂路), *n.* a roundabout way; a *détour* 【佛】. —迂路を取る, to go a long way round.

uro (雨露), *n.* rain and dew. —雨露を凌ぐ, to have a roof over one. —雨露を凌ぐ小舍, a hut

which shelters us from the rain.
uroko (鱗), *n.* a scale; a scutellum (鳥の脚部の). —魚の鱗を落す, to scale fish; remove the scales from fish.
urokogata (鱗形), *n.* a triangle.
uron (胡亂な), *a.* suspicious (-looking); questionable; doubtful. —胡亂な奴, a suspicious-looking man; a bad character. —胡亂に思ふ, to have suspicions *of*.
uronuku (虚抜く), *vt.* to thin.
urooboe (空覺), *n.* imperfect remembrance; half-learning. —空覺えに覺えて居る, to have a faint recollection of it.
urotaeru (うろたへる), *vi.* to be confused [agitated; flurried; flustered; bewildered]; lose one's presence of mind. —うろたへて, in confusion [bewilderment]; confusedly. ¶ 狼狽者, one easily bewildered.
urotsuku (うろつく), *vi.* to prowl about; wander about; hang [loiter; rove] about (ぶらつく).
urouro (うろうろ), *ad.* ❶ (ぶらぶら) loiteringly; indolently. ❷ (うろたへて) in confusion [bewilderment].
uru (得·獲る), *vt.* (獲得) to take; have; get; gain; obtain; acquire; procure; come by; take [gain] possession *of*; earn; win. ——, *vi.* (出來る) to be able to; be possible to; be capable *of*. ——, *v. aux.* can; may. —支那語を話し得る者, a person who can speak Chinese. —後援者を得る, to find a supporter. —糊口の資を得る, to win [earn] one's bread.
uru (賣る), *vt.* ❶ (販賣す) to sell; deal *in* (商ふ); dispose *of* (所持品等を). ❷ (反く) to sell; betray. —賣らせる, to make another sell. —友を賣る, to sell [betray; dupe] one's friend. —金錢の爲め名譽《節操》を賣る, to sell one's honour 《one's chastity》. —名を天下に賣る, to win a world-wide reputation.
uruchi (粳), *n.* cultivated rice.
urumi (潤み), *n.* opacity (不透明); cloudiness (曇り); dulness (光澤なきこと); moisture (濕潤).
urumu (潤む), *vi.* to be clouded (曇る); be dull (光澤がない); be bleared (眼が); be black and blue (捻ねられて).
uruoi (潤), *n.* ❶ (しめり) dampness; moisture. ❷ (利潤) gain; profit. ❸ (恩澤) benefaction; favour. —潤ひある, ① bright; lustrous; tasteful. ② moist; fresh; sweet.
uruosu (濕·潤す), *vt.* ❶ (ぬらす) to moisten; wet; damp(-en); make moist [damp]. ❷ (富ます) to profit; benefit; enrich; make prosper. ❸ (恩澤を受けしむ) to give benefaction. —口《喉》を潤す, to moisten one's lips 《throat》. —袖を濕す, to wet one's sleeves with tears.
uruou (濕·潤ふ), *vi.* ❶ (水氣を含む) to be moist [damp; wet]. ❷ (富む) to be enriched; become prosperous; make a profit. ❸ (惠を受ける) to receive benefaction [benefits].
urusai (うるさい), *a.* ❶ (厄介な) annoying; troublesome. ❷ (嫌な) tiresome; wearisome; irksome. ❸ (しつこい) importunate; pertinacious. —うるさい奴, a gadfly; a bore. —うるさい質問, a troublesome question. —うるさがる, to feel annoyed.
urusaku (うるさく), *ad.* irksomely; tiresomely; importunately (しつこく). —うるさく催促する, to press a person tiresomely. —うるさく附き纏ふ, to stick by a person to his annoyance; follow a person obstinately.
urushi (漆), *n.* ❶ lacquer; japan. ❷【植】(漆樹) the Japan lacquer-tree [varnish-tree]. —漆にかぶれる, to be poisoned with lacquer. —漆を塗る, [*vt.*] to japan; lacquer. ¶ 漆毒疹[ｼﾝ], lacquer-poisoning. —漆屋, a lacquer-dealer; a lacquer-shop. —漆細工, (器物) a lacquer; a japan; a lacquered [japanned] ware [work].
urushizuta (漆蔦), *n.* 【植】 the American poison ivy [oak].
uruu (閏), *n.* embolism. ¶ 閏月, an intercalary month. —閏年, a leap-year.
uruwashii (麗しい), *a.* beautiful; fine; lovely.
uryō (雨量), *n.* rainfall. ¶ 雨量計, a rain-gauge; a hyetometer; an udometer.
usa (憂), *n.* ❶ gloom; melancholy. ❷ =*monoomoi.*
usagi (兎), *n.* 【哺乳】 the rabbit (飼兎); the hare (野兎); the bunny〔俗〕. ¶ 兎狩, hare-hunting.
usagiuma (驢馬), *n.* 【哺乳】 an ass; a donkey.
usaharashi (憂晴), *n.* dispelling melancholy; diversion.
usaikaku (烏犀角), *n.* a rhinoceros horn.
usan (胡散な), *a.* suspicious-looking; questionable.
usemono (失物), *n.* a lost article; a lost property.
useru (失せる), *vi.* ❶ (消失) to disappear; vanish. ❷ (紛失) to be lost.

ushi (牛), *n.* ❶【哺乳】(black) cattle; a cow (牝); a bull (牡); an ox (去勢の); a calf (犢[こうし]). ❷ (のそのそ者) a sluggard; a dullard. —牛を馬に乗りかへる, to change for the better. —牛は牛づれ馬は馬づれ, "Every Jack must have his Jill."

ushiguruma (牛車), *n.* an ox-cart.

ushikai (牛飼), *n.* a cowherd; an oxherd; a cowboy【米】.

ushinau (失ふ), *vt.* to lose; part *with*; be deprived [bereft] *of*. —子を失ふ, to lose [be bereaved of] a child. —財産を失ふ, to lose one's fortune. —光を失ふ, to be deprived of light. —立脚地を失ふ, to lose ground. —この發明のために命《財產》を失ッた, The invention cost him his life《property》.

ushio (潮), *n.* = *shio* (潮). —潮の如く押し寄せる, to come on like a flooding tide.

ushioi (牛追ひ), *n.* ❶ (牛を扱ふ人) an ox driver. ❷ (牛車力) an ox-cart driver.

ushiro (後), *n.* the back; the rear. —後へ廻る, to get the back *of*; get behind. —直ぐ後から, at one's heels [skirt]. —後から襲ふ, to attack a person from behind; take a person in the rear. —(敵に) 後を見せる, to fly before an enemy; turn one's back *on*; show one's heels.

ushirodate (後楯), *n.* ❶ (背面の防禦となるもの) rear defences. ❷ (後援) backing; support: (人) a backer; a supporter. —後楯になる, to back up; support; be at the back *of*.

ushirode (後手), *n.* the back; the rear. —後手に縛る, to tie [bind] a person's hand behind him [his back].

ushirogami (後髮), *n.* the back-hair. —後髮ひかるゝ思がする, to feel reluctant to part *with* [tear oneself away *from*]; feel as if one's heart were left behind; feel oneself pulled by the hair from behind.

ushirogurai (後暗い), *a.* suspicious; shady; remorseful (後悔すべき). ☞ *yamashii*.

ushirokage (後影), *n.* a retreating figure. —後影を見送る, to gaze at a person's retreating figure; follow a departing person with one's eyes; gaze after a person.

ushiromuki (後向), *n.* backwardness. —後向きに坐る, to sit with one's back to the front《to a person》.

ushirosugata (後姿), *n.* the sight of another's back [of another from behind].

ushiroyubi (後指を指す), to point the finger of scorn; point at a person.

uso (鷽), *n.*【鳥】the Oriental bulfinch.

uso (噓, 虛), *n.* ❶ (虛言) a lie; a falsehood; an untruth. ❷ (實ならざる事) untruth. ❸ (誤謬) an error. —噓云ふ癖, mendacity. —噓をつく [言ふ], to lie; tell a lie [falsehood]; tell a story. —誠らしい噓を言ふ, to tell a specious lie. —噓は後から剝げる, "Lies melt like snow"; "A lie has short legs."

usobuku (嘯く), *vi.* ❶ to roar; whistle (風); howl (同上). ❷ (吟ず) to sing.

usotsuki (虛言者), *n.* a liar; a story-teller; a fibber.

ussan (鬱散), *n.* recreation; diversion; relief. —鬱散する, to recreate oneself; divert oneself.

usseki (鬱積), *n.*【醫】colluvies.

ussōtaru (鬱蒼たる), *a.* luxuriant; dense. ¶鬱蒼たる森林, a thick [dense] forest.

ussura (うッすら), *ad.* Ⓢ うッすり. thinly; lightly; dimly.

us-suru (鬱する), *vi.* to feel gloomy; be despondent; be in low spirits.

usu (臼), *n.* a hand-mill (挽臼); a mortar (搗臼).

usuakai (薄赤い), *a.* pale red; light red.

usuakari (薄明), *n.* ❶ (微明) a dim light. ❷ (日出前又は日沒後の) twilight.

usuba (薄刃), *n.* a thin-bladed kitchen-knife.

usubakagerō (うすばかげろふ), *n.*【昆】the ant-lion.

usuberi (薄緣), *n.* a bordered matting.

usubi (薄日), *n.* soft sun-beams.

usubikari (うすびかりの), *a.* lambent; softly radiant.

usucha (薄茶), *n.* ❶ a weak infusion of powdered tea. ❷ (薄茶色) light tea-colour.

usude (薄手), *n.* ❶ (器物の薄きもの) a thin article. ❷ (輕傷) a slight cut [wound]. —薄手の茶碗, a tea-cup of thin make. —薄手を負ふ, to suffer a slight wound.

usufujiiro (薄藤色), *n.* lilac.

usugeshō (薄化粧), *n.* light toilet. —薄化粧する, to make one's toilet lightly; powder the face lightly.

usugi (薄著), *n.* thin clothing. —薄著する, to be thinly-clothed; be thinly clad.

usuginu (薄絹), *n.* light silk.

usugireru (薄切れる), *vi.* to rive; be rent.

usugurai (薄暗い), *a.* dim; dusky; gloomy; sombre. —薄暗くなる, to become [grow] dim [dusky]; dusk. —薄暗い内に出立する, to start in morning twilight.

usuguroi (薄黒い), *a.* dingy; dusky; umber; dark.

usuhiki (臼挽), *n.* milling (事); a miller (人).

usui (薄い), *a.* ❶ (厚さの) thin. ❷ (濃厚ならぬ) light; weak (茶など); thin (髪·粥など). ❸ (色の) light; pale; faint; watery; washy.

usukawa (薄皮), *n.* a thin skin; a film; a membrane.

usukimiwarui (薄氣味惡い), *a.* uncanny; eerie; weird. ☞ *kimi* (氣味惡い). —薄氣味惡い笑ひ方, an uncanny laugh.

usuku (薄く), *ad.* ❶ (厚さを) thinly. ❷ (濃度を) lightly. ❸ (色を) faintly; lightly. —薄くする, to thin; weaken (茶など); lighten. (色を薄くする, to lighten the colour; tone down.)

usukuragari (薄暗がり), *n.* dim light; twilight; dusk.

usumekura (薄盲の), *a.* gravel-blind; sand-blind.

usumono (薄物, 羅), *n.* light [thin] stuff.

usuppera (薄ッぺらな), *a.* ❶ thin. ❷ (淺薄) superficial; shallow; shallow-minded. ☞ *kei-haku*. —薄ッぺらな學問《理窟》, a shallow learning 《argument》.

usurageru (薄らげる), *vt.* to lighten; thin; tone down (色など).

usuragu (薄らぐ), *vi.* to lighten; become thin 《dim, vague; faint, 記憶など》; fade (色が); abate (痛が); lessen; decline (興味が).

usurai (薄氷), *n.* thin ice.

usutsuku (舂く), *v.* to pound [beat] in a mortar. —日既に西山に舂く, The sun was about to sink behind the western hills.

usuusu (薄薄), *n.* ❶ (うッすり) dimly. ❷ (すこし) a little; slightly. —うすうす知ッてゐます, I have an inkling of it.

usuzuki (薄月), *n.* the moon behind a cloud. ¶ 薄月夜, a night with a misty moon.

usuzumi (薄墨), *n.* thin ink. —薄墨を流した樣である, to be dark as ink.

uta (歌), *n.* ❶ (歌謠) a song; a ballad. ❷ (詩歌) an ode; a poem; poetry. ❸ =*waka*.

utagai (疑), *n.* ❶ (疑念) doubt; distrust (不信認); mistrust (同上). ❷ (嫌疑) suspicion. ❸ (疑問) a question. —疑もなく, undoubtedly; without [beyond] doubt; no doubt; out of [beyond] question. —疑の目で見る, to view with suspicious glance; look askance *at*; look with suspicion *on*. —疑を抱く, ① (疑問·疑念を) to doubt; harbour [entertain] doubt. ② (嫌疑を) to suspect; harbour [entertain] suspicion. —疑を晴らす, to disillusion(-ize); clear away [dispel] suspicion. —疑を容れず, to admit of no doubt.

utagaibukai (疑深い), *a.* distrustful; suspicious; doubting.

utagaruta (歌骨牌), *n.* playing cards containing odes: ode-cards.

utagau (疑ふ), *vt.* ❶ (疑念) to doubt; call in question. ❷ (不信) to distrust; have [lay] no confidence *in*. ❸ (嫌疑) to suspect. —疑ふべき點, a disputable point. —疑ふ餘地がない, to be above suspicion; admit of no doubt.

utagawashii (疑はしい), *a.* ❶ (不慥な) doubtful; uncertain; questionable. ❷ (怪しい) suspicious. —疑はしげに, ① doubtfully; dubiously. ② suspiciously.

utaguchi (歌口), *n.* a mouthpiece; a mouth-hole. —歌口を濕す, to wet the mouthpiece.

utai (謠), *n.* *utai*; a lyrical play. —謠曲を謠ふ, to sing a lyrical play. ¶ 謠本, an *utai* libretto.

utaime (歌女), *n.* a singing-girl; a chantress; a songstress; a *chanteuse* [佛].

utata (轉), *ad.* ❶ (愈ゝ) more and more; ncreasingly; deeply. ❷ (何となく) somehow; in some way. —轉た追懷の念に堪へず, Recollections come rushing upon one; Recollections crowd upon one's mind.

utatane (轉寢, 假眠), *n.* a nap; a snooze; forty winks. —轉寢する, to take a nap; nap; doze.

utau (歌ふ), *vt.* to sing; chant; carol. —名將と謳はれてる彼, he who is known [talked of] as a great commander.

utayomi (歌人), *n.* a poet.

utcharakasu (打棄らかす), *vt.* to lay [cast] aside; toss aside; leave alone. ☞ —仕事をうッちゃらかして, neglecting one's duty; tossing aside one's work.

utcharu (打棄る), *vt.* to throw [cast] away; reject; throw to the dogs [winds]. —うッちゃッて置く, to let [leave] alone.

uten (雨天), *n.* rainy [bad] weather; a rainy day; rain. —雨天順延のこと, to be postponed to [be held on] the first fine day in case of rain. ¶ 雨天體操場, a covered drill-ground; a gymnasium. —雨天續き, continued rainy weather; a spell of rain.

utena (臺), *n.* ❶ a hall; a tower (塔). ❷ 〔蕚〕【植】the calyx.

utō (善知鳥), *n.* 【鳥】the rhinoceros-auk.

utoi (疎い), *a.* ❶ (疎音) distant; estranged. ❷ (迂遠) roundabout. ❸ (不案内) unacquainted; ignorant. 一時勢に疎くなる, to lose touch with the world. 一去る者は日に疎し, "Lost to sight, lost to mind."; "Out of sight, out of mind."

utonzuru (疎んずる), *vt.* Ⓢ 疎む. to keep at arm's length; be cool *towards*; give the cold shoulder *to*; alienate; estrange. 一人を疎んずる, to treat a person coldly.

utouto (うとうと), *ad.* drowsily. 一うとうとする, to nod; doze; snooze; fall dozing. (いつの間にかうとうとして來た, A drowsy feeling crept over me.)

utsu (打·擊·討·射·拍·搏つ), *vt.* ❶ (たゝく) to strike; beat; hit; knock; thrash; toll (鐘を). ❷ (うち込む) to drive in; strike into. ❸ (發射) to fire; shoot; discharge. ❹ (攻擊) to attack; assault. ❺ (拍つ) to clap (one's hands). ❻ (發する) to send [despatch] (a telegram). **——,** *vi.* ❶ 〔打〕to gamble. ❷ 〔搏〕to beat (脈が); fight (組打する). 一打ち固める, to beat [pound] hard. 一めちゃめちゃに打ち据ゑる, to pound a man into a jelly. 一五時を打つ, to strike five. 一網を打つ, to cast a net. 一刀を鍛つ, to temper a sword. 一彈丸を擊ち盡す, to shoot away all one's ammunition.

utsu (鬱), *n.* melancholy; gloom; depression. 一鬱を散ずる, to drive away [dispel] melancholy; divert one's mind.

utsubari (梁), *n.* a beam; a timber.

utsubo (靫), *n.* a quiver.

utsubotsu (鬱勃たる), *a.* pent-up; constrained. 一鬱勃たる元氣, pent-up energy.

utsubuku (俯伏く), *vi.* =*utsumuku.*

utsubushi (俯伏に), *ad.* =*utsumuki* (俯向に).

utsugi (溲疏), *n.* 【植】Deutzia scabra (Japanese snowflower の類).

utsuke (空), *n.* ❶ (うつろ) hollow; emptiness; vacancy. ❷ (間拔け) stupidity; empty-headedness. ¶ うつけ者, a fool; a simpleton; a blockhead; an abstracted person (うっかり者).

utsuku-shii (美しい), *a.* beautiful; handsome; fair (特に容貌の); lovely (可愛らしい). 一心の美しい, pure; pure-minded. 一美しい顏, a fair face. **—— - shiku,** *ad.* beautifully; handsomely; finely. 一美しく著飾る, to dress oneself beautifully; dress up.

utsumi (内海), *n.* =*uchiumi.*

utsumuki (俯向に), *ad.* upside down (顚倒に); face downward (顏を); with one's face on the ground (同上). 一俯向に寢る, to lie on one's face.

utsumuku (俯向く), *vi.* to bend forward; bend [droop; bow] one's head.

utsurautsura (うつらうつら), *ad.* =*utouto.*

utsuri (映), *n.* ❶ (うつること) reflection. ❷ (配合) harmony; match.

utsurigi (移氣), *n.* fickleness; capriciousness; light-mindedness. **—— - na,** *a.* fickle; capricious; light-minded. 一移氣な人, an inconstant [a capricious; a fickle] person; a weather-cock.

utsurikawari (移變), *n.* change; transition; vicissitude. 一移り變る, to change; alter.

utsuro (うつろ), *n.* hollowness; emptiness; void; a hollow; a cavity. ¶ 獨木舟, a canoe; a dugout; a pirogue.

utsuru (映る), *vi.* ❶ (光·影が) to be reflected; be thrown *upon*; fall upon; take (寫眞が). ❷ (調和) to suit; match; harmonize.

utsuru (移る), *vi.* ❶ (移轉) to remove; move. ❷ (變) to change; alter. ❸ (過行く) to pass away. ❹ (燃移る) to spread *to.* ❺ (傳染する) to be infected; catch. **——,** *a.* catching; infectious (間接); contagious (接觸). 一移り易い, [*a.*] ① (變り易い) changeable; transient; mutable. ② (感染し易い) infectious. 一時の移るを知らず, to be unaware of the passing [flight] of time.

utsushi (寫), *n.* a copy; a transcript; a duplicate (副本). 一寫をとる, to copy; make a duplicate.

utsushie (寫繪), *n.* a shadow-graph.

utsushimono (寫物), *n.* ❶ (謄寫) copying; transcription. ❷ (謄寫したる物) a copy; a transcript.

utsusu (移す), *vt.* ❶ (移轉) to remove; move; transfer. ❷ (傳染さす) to infect. ❸ (液體を) to pour *into*; empty *into*; transfuse *from...to....* ❹ (時を) to pass; lose. 一怒を移す, to turn one's anger upon another. 一時を移さず準備する, to lose no time in making preparations.

utsusu (寫·映す), *vt.* ❶ (謄寫) to copy; transcribe; reproduce;

trace (引寫). ❷ (摸寫) to copy; imitate; facsimile; reproduce. ❸ (投影) to reflect; mirror (鏡などの). ❹ (寫眞を) to photograph; take; have one's photograph taken (寫してもらふ). ❺ (描寫) to represent; draw; depict.

utsutsu (現), *n.* ❶ (現實) reality; the actual. ❷ (夢見心地) reverie; trance; absent-mindedness. —現になって居る, to be in a reverie. —女に現をぬかす, to be stuck on a woman.

utsuutsu (鬱鬱), *ad.* ❶ melancholily; gloomily; despondingly. ❷ thickly; densely. —鬱々日を送る, to mope one's time away.

utsuwa (器), *n.* ❶ (容器) a vessel; a receptacle. ❷ (器具) an instrument; an implement. ❸ (才能, 器量) capacity; calibre; ability. —その器にあらず, not to be qualified for it. —器が大きい, to be large-minded; be a man of great capacity.

uttae (訴), *n.* ❶ an appeal; a complaint (愁訴). ❷ (訴訟) a suit; a lawsuit; an action. ❸ (告訴) complaint; accusation; information. ❹ (訴願) a petition. —訴を聽く, to hear a case [suit]. —訴を起す, to go to law; bring an action *against*. ¶ 訴へ人, an informer (告訴人); an accuser (同上); a plaintiff (原告).

uttaeru (訴へる), *vt.* ❶ to appeal *to*; complain *of* (不平·苦痛を). ❷ (依賴す) to appeal *to*; resort *to*; have recourse *to*. ❸ (訴訟) to sue; go to law; bring an action [a suit] *against*; accuse. ❹ (訴願) to petition; appeal. —法律に訴へる, to appeal to the law. —天に訴へる, to cry to heaven for a thing. —腕力[暴力]に訴へる, to resort to force [violence]. —武力[干戈]に訴へる, to appeal to arms.

utte (討手), *n.* an attacking party [force]; a pursuer (追手). 討手を差向ける, to send a punitive force.

uttederu (打って出る), *vi.* ❶ (軍勢が) to sally out; make a sally. ❷ (議員の候補者などに) to stand *for*; run *for*. —議員の候補者として打って出る, to run for parliament; come forward as candidate for representation.

uttekawaru (打って變る), *vi.* ❶ (急變する) to change suddenly. ❷ (全然變る) to change utterly; undergo a complete change. —打って變って, on the contrary; in an entirely different manner. —打って變った態度に出る, to take a completely changed [an entirely different] attitude.

uttori (うっとり), *ad.* ❶ (恍惚と) with rapture; absorbedly; infatuatedly. ❷ (ぼんやりと) absent-mindedly; absently; vacantly; dimly (霞などの); faintly (同上). —うっとりした, ① absorbed; enraptured; infatuated. ② absent-minded; absent; vacant; blank; dim; misty; faint.

uttō-shii (鬱陶しい), *a.* gloomy; depressing; dull; cloudy (曇れる); unpleasant (不快な). —鬱陶しい空, a heavy [cloudy] sky. —鬱陶しく, gloomily; depressingly; unpleasantly.

uun (雨雲), *n.* 【氣象】a nimbus; a rain-cloud.

uwa (上), *a.* upper (上方); outer (外方); outward (同上).

uwaago (上顎), *n.* the upper jaw; the palate (口蓋).

uwaba (上齒), *n.* the upper (set of) teeth.

uwabami (蟒蛇), *n.* 【爬蟲】the boa(-constrictor).

uwabataraki (上働き), *n.* a parlour-maid.

uwabe (上邊, 上面), *n.* ❶ (外部) surface; exterior. ❷ (外見) appearance; show. —上邊だけの友達, a seeming friend. —上邊を飾る, to make outward show; put a good face on (a matter).

uwabyōshi (上表紙), *n.* a wrapper; a jacket; a cover.

uwachōshi (上調子), *n.* ❶【音】a high pitch. ❷ (輕薄) superficiality; flippancy; frivolity; levity. —上調子な, frivolous; flippant.

uwae (上繪), *n.* crest-painting. ¶ 上繪師, a crest-painter.

uwagaki (上書), *n.* superscription; address (手紙の); direction (同上). —上書する, to superscribe; address; direct.

uwagi (上著), *n.* an upper garment; a coat; a cloak; an overcoat (外套); overclothes (外衣類).

uwagusuri (釉藥), *n.* glaze. —釉藥をかける, to glaze.

uwagutsu (上沓), *n.* ❶ (床沓) slippers. ❷ (靴のカヴァー) overshoes; goloshes.

uwakawa (上皮), *n.* ❶ (表皮) the epidermis; the cuticle; the scarf-skin. ❷ (外被) the cream (液體); the film (同上); the crust (堅い). ❸ =*uwabe*.

uwaki (浮氣), *n.* dissipation; unchastity; unfaithfulness. —浮氣な, unchaste; dissipated; wanton; fickle; skittish; light. ¶ 浮氣者, a Don Juan (男); a gay Lothario (男); a light-o'-love (女); a loose-kirtle (女).

uwakoto (譫言), *n.* talk in delirium. —譫言を云ふ, to talk in delirium.
uwamae (上前), *n.* ❶ (衣服の) the outer skirt. ❷ (金銭上の) a percentage; a commission. —上前を刎ねる, to take a commission.
uwame (上目), *n.* an upward glance. —上目を使ふ, to glance upward; turn up the eyes.
uwamuki (上向), *n.* ❶ =*aomuki*. ❷ (外見) appearance; show. ❸ (相場の騰貴に傾くこと) upward tendency. —上向きの, apparent (外見); turned-up (鼻); *retroussé* (同上) 【佛】; upward. —物價は上は向き, The prices are looking up; Prices tend upwards.
uwanori (上乘), *n.* a supercargo.
uwanosora (上の空), *n.* absent-mindedness; abstraction; inattention. —上の空で, inattentively; absent-mindedly; absently.
uwanuri (上塗), *n.* ❶(壁等の) set; final [last] coating; facing; hard finishing. ❷ (惡しき事の) making worse; aggravation. —上塗りをする, ① to give the final [last] coating. ② to make worse; aggravate. ☞ *haji* (恥).
uwappari (上張), *n.* overwear.
uwasa (噂), *n.* a rumour; a talk; a report; hearsay. —噂が立つ, to take [get] wind. —噂によれば, according to the rumour; they say; it is said; the report goes. —噂する, to rumour; talk *about*. —噂をすれば影とかや, "Talk of the devil and he will appear."
uwashiki (上敷, 表敷), *n.* ❶ (物の上に敷くもの) a carpet (絨毯); a sheet (敷布); a mat (莫蓙). ❷ (鞍敷) a saddle-cloth.
uwate (上手), *n.* ❶ (上の方) the upper part. ❷ (上手) the upper stream. ❸ (風上) the windward. ❹ (優越) more skill; comparative superiority. ❺ (相撲) catching by the shoulders. —上手に出る, to preponderate [outdo] (a person); get the upper hand.
uwatsuku (浮つく), *vi.* to be fickle; be restless; have bees in the head [brains]; have a bee in one's bonnet. ☞ *uwabe*.
uwatsura (上面), *n.* surface.
uwaya (上屋), *n.* ❶ a shed. ❷ (稅關の) a customs shed.
uwayaku (上役), *n.* a superior [senior] official.
uwazōri (上草履), *n.* indoor sandals.
uwazumi (上積), *n.* upper load: deck cargo.
uwazuru (上擦る), *vi.* ❶ (うはすべりする) to slide [slip] (on a thing). ❷ (浮く) to buoy up. ❸ (輕薄である) to be flippant.
uwazutsumi (上包), *n.* ❶ (包む物) a packing-sheet; a cover; an envelope. ❷ (書物の帙) a case [cover] for books.
uyamau (敬ふ), *vt.* to respect; honour; revere; venerate. —神の様に敬ふ, to revere a person like a god; regard a person with reverence; hold a person in reverence.
uyamuya (有耶無耶), *n.* ambiguity; ambiguousness; haziness. 有耶無耶の裏に葬る, to bury in vagueness; suppress. —有耶無耶になる, to become hazy [ambiguous].
uyauyashii (恭しい), *a.* respectful; reverential; reverent; deferential. —恭しく, respectfully; reverentially; devoutly (神に); with honour [reverence; awe].
uyo (紆餘), *n.* ❶ (うねりまがり) crook; bend; winding; meanders (河·道などの). ❷ (婉曲) euphemism. —紆餘曲折を經て, after many complications.
uyoku (右翼), *n.* the right flank [wing; column]; 【野球】 the right field. —敵の右翼を衝く, to attack the enemy's right flank. ¶ 右翼打手, a right-field batter. —右翼手, the right-fielder.
uyoku (羽翼), *n.* ❶ feathers and wings. ❷ (輔佐) aid; help; assistance; the right arm.
uyouyo (うようよ), *ad.* in swarms; squirmingly. —うようよする, to squirm [wriggle about] in swarms.
uyū (烏有), *n.* ❶ (燒滅) being burnt down. ❷ (皆無) nothingness; naught. —烏有に歸する, to be consumed by fire; be reduced to ashes; become the prey of the flames.
uzō-muzō (有像無像), *n.* ❶ matter and spirit. ❷ (雜多の人物) all sorts and conditions of men.
uzudakai (堆い), *a.* high; heaped. —堆く積む, to pile up (high); heap up.
uzuku (疼く), *vi.* to tingle; ache; pain one.
uzukumaru (蹲る), *vi.* to squat down; crouch.
uzumaki (渦卷), *n.* an eddy; a whirlpool; a whirl; a vortex. —渦卷の中へ卷き込まれる, to be drawn into the vortex.
uzumaku (渦卷く), *vi.* to eddy; swirl; whirl.
uzumaru (埋まる), *vi.* to be buried (filled up).
uzumeru (埋める), *vt.* ❶ (地中に) to bury. ❷ (空所を) to fill up; fill in. —餘白を埋める, to

fill up the blank space.

uzumoreru (埋れる), *vi.* to be buried. 一世に埋れる, to be buried in oblivion; live unknown [in obscurity]. 一田舎に埋れてゐる, to live in obscurity in the country.

uzura (鶉), *n.* ❶【鳥】the quail. ❷【劇場】a lower box.

uzuragai (鶉貝), *n.* 【貝】the tun-shell.

uzuramame (鶉豆), *n.* a mottled kidney-bean.

V

vaiorin (四弦提琴), *n.* a violin; a fiddle. ¶ ヴァイオリン弾き, a violinist.

vaioretto (菫菜), *n.* ❶【植】= *sumire.* ❷ (色) violet (colour).

vājin (處女), *n.* a virgin.

vāchū (德), *n.* virtue.

veniya (ヴェニヤ板, 被板), *n.* veneer(-wood).

veranda (椽側), *n.* a veranda(h).

vēru (面網), *n.* a veil. 一面網を被る, to veil; cover with a veil.

verumotto (ヴェルモット酒), *n.* vermouth, vermuth.

veruvetto (天鵞絨), *n.* velvet.

vikutori (勝利), *n.* victory.

Vinasu (愛の女神), *n.* Venus.

viora (大提琴), *n.* a viola.

vitāmin (ヴィターミン), *n.* vitamine. ¶ ヴィターミン缺乏症, a (vitamine) deficiency disease.

voisu (ヴォイス), *n.* ❶ (聲) voice. ❷【文】(態) the voice.

vokaburari (語彙), *n.* vocabulary.

vōrē (ヴォーレー), *n.* 【庭球】volley. 一ヴォーレー・ボール [排球], 【競技】a volley-ball.

voruto (ヴォルト), *n.* 【電】(電壓の單位) a volt. ¶ ヴォルト計, a voltaelectrometer; a voltameter.

vui-jikei (ヴイ字形の), *a.* V-shaped.

W

wa (は), *particle.* ❶ 主格の働きをなす. ❷ 用言に附屬して意味を强める. 一名は太郎, Tarō by name; whose name is Tarō. 一生れは猶太人, a Jew by birth.

wa (和), *n.* ❶ (平和,和睦) peace; reconciliation (和解). ❷【數】the sum. ❸ (和合) harmony. 一和を結ぶ, to make peace; conclude peace.

wa (輪, 環), *n.* a circle (圓); a ring (環); a loop (絲の); a wheel (車輪); a hoop (子供の轉し遊ぶ). 一輪になって坐る, to sit in a circle. 一輪に輪をかける, to exaggerate. 一環を作る, to make a circle; loop; coil. 一環を嵌める, to ring.

wa (把, 束), *numeral.* a bundle; a faggot; a sheaf. ☞ *taba.*

wabi (詫), *n.* apology; intercession (人の爲の). ¶ 詫狀, a letter of apology; a written apology.

wabiru (侘びる), *vi.* ❶ (思ひわづらふ) to be worried *about.* ❷ (賴りなく淋しく思ふ) to feel forlorn [solitary]. ❸ (見すぼらしくある) to be miserable. 一待ち侘びる, to long *for.* 一世を侘びる, to renounce the world.

wabiru (詫びる), *v.* to apologize; make an apology; beg [ask] pardon. 一頭を下げて詫びる, to make a humble apology. 一人に詫びて貰ふ, to get another to plead for one.

wabishii (侘しい), *a.* ❶ (心細く淋しい) desolate; solitary; lonely. ❷ (見すぼらしい) poor; miserable. 一侘しい暮しをする, to live a lonely life.

wabizumai (侘住居), *n.* lonely [solitary; retired] life.

waboku (和睦), *n.* peace (親和, 講和); reconciliation (和解). 一和睦さす, to reconcile; reunite. 一和睦する, to make peace *with*; be reconciled; come to terms.

wabun (和文), *n.* Japanese; Japanese writing 《composition》. ¶ 和文電報, a telegram in Japanese. 一和文英譯, translation from [of] Japanese into English.

wachū (和衷), *n.* harmony; concord. 一和衷協同して, in full concord and harmony.

wadachi (轍), *n.* a rut; a furrow; a wheel-track.

wadai (話題), *n.* a topic; a subject. 一話題に上る, to be made a topic; be talked about.

wadakamari (蟠), *n.* ❶ (蟠居) coiling. ❷ (心中の) troubles. 一心に蟠りがある, to have something on one's mind; be troubled in one's mind.

wadakamaru (蟠る), *vi.* ❶ (蟠踞) to be coiled; wind; meander. ❷ (心中に) to be rooted; be harboured; lie hidden; lie heavily on one's mind.

wadome (輪止), *n.* ❶ a linchpin (輪の脱出を止める). ❷ =*hadome* (齒止め).

waei (和英), *a.* Japanese-English.

waffuru (ワッフル), *n.* (菓子) a waffle.

wafuku (和服), *n.* Japanese clothes; *kimono.*

waga (我が), *pron.* my; our; one's own. —我が皇帝陛下, His Majesty my August Master [Sovereign] (公文例). —我が國, our country; my country (他國人の中に居て). —我が物《身》, one's (own) property 《body》.

wagahai (我輩), *pron.* we; I.

wagamama (我儘), *n.* waywardness; wilfulness; selfishness; self-indulgence; caprice (氣紛れ). —我儘な, wayward; wilful; self-indulgent. —我儘に, wilfully; selfishly; capriciously. —我儘をする, to act wilfully; have one's own way. ¶ 我儘者, a wayward 《selfish》 person; an egotist.

waganeru (綰ねる), *vt.* to bend into a hoop [circle].

wagi (和議), *n.* ❶ peace; peace negotiations (談判); a conference for peace (會議). ❷【法】(settlement by) composition.

wagiri (輪切), *n.* ❶ (事) cutting in round slices. ❷ (物) a round slice. —輪切りにする, to cut into round slices; ring (玉葱·林檎等を).

wagō (和合), *n.* harmony; concord; union. —和合する, to harmonize; accord; agree.

wahei (話柄), *n.* a topic; a subject; talk.

wahō (話法), *n.* parlance;【文】narration.

wahon (和本), *n.* a Japanese book; a book bound in Japanese style.

waidan (猥談), *n.* a foul talk; an indecent talk; a filthy tale.

waijin (矮人), *n.* a dwarf; a pigmy; a midget.

wain (和韻), *n.* bouts-rimés verses.

wairo (賄賂), *n.* ❶ (事) bribery; corruption. ❷ (物) a bribe; a sop; the golden key; boodle【米】. —賄賂の利く, bribable; corruptible. —賄賂の利かぬ, incorruptible; proof against corruption. —賄賂を取る, to take [accept] a bribe. —賄賂を使ふ, to bribe; corrupt; oil another's hand [fist]; grease [gild] another's palm [fist]. (賄賂を使ってさせる《内證にする》, to bribe a person into doing it 《into silence》.)

wairushibyō (ワイル氏病), *n.*【醫】Weil's disease.

wairyoku (歪力), *n.*【理】stress.

waisetsu (猥褻), *n.* obscenity; indecency; indelicacy. —猥褻な話, a foul talk; a filthy tale. —猥褻な小說《畫》, an indecent [obscene] novel 《picture》.

waishatsu (ワイシャツ), *n.* a white shirt.

waishō (矮小の), *a.* dwarfish; diminutive; pigmy; stunted (いぢけた).

waiwai (わいわい), *ad.* noisily; clamorously. —わいわい騒ぐ, to be noisy. ¶ わいわい連, the rabble; the riff-raff; ragtag and bobtail; the rowdy element.

waiyā (針金), *n.* wire. ¶ ワイヤーロープ, a wire-rope.

waka (和歌), *n.* a Japanese ode.

wakaba (若葉, 嫩葉), *n.*【植】young leaves; new foliage; leaflets.

wakagaeri (若返り), *n.* rejuvenescence; rejuvenation. ¶ 若返り法, rejuvenation treatment.

wakagaeru (若返る), *vi.* to renew one's youth; grow young again; rejuvenesce; be rejuvenated. ——, *a.* juvenescent.

wakage (若氣), *n.* youthful spirit [vigour]; ardour [sap] of youth. —若氣の至りで, through exuberance of youthful spirits.

wakai (和解), *n.* reconciliation (仲直り); friendly [amicable] settlement (圓滿解決); composition (債權者との妥協);【法】compromise (原被間の). —和解さす, to reconcile; conciliate; reunite. —和解する, to be reconciled *with*; make up *with*; reach a friendly settlement; compound *with* (one's creditor *for*); compromise *with* (a person); compromise a lawsuit.

wakai (若い), *a.* ❶ (弱年) young; youthful. ❷ (年下) younger; junior. ❸ (未熟) inexperienced; green; immature. —若い時から, from one's youth up [upwards]; from early youth. —若い時には嘸美しかったらう, She must have been very beautiful in her day. —あの女は恐しく若く見える, She carries her age wonderfully well. —私は彼より三つ若い, I am his junior by three years.

wakajini (若死·夭折する), *vi.* to die young; die an early death; come to an untimely death; die in the prime of one's life.

wakakusa (若草), *n.* young [fresh] grass. —若草萌ゆる春の野邊, the spring field with (sprouting) young grass.

wakame (若布), *n.*【植】Undaria pinnatifida (學名).

wakamiya (若宮), *n.* the son of an Imperial prince; a young [younger] prince. —伏見若宮殿下, H. I. H. Prince Fushimi, Junior.

wakamono (若者), *n.* a young man; a youth; a lad; a stripling.

wakan (和漢), *n.* Japan and China. —和漢洋の學に通ずる, to be

versed in Japanese, Chinese and Western literature.

wakarazuya (沒分曉漢), *n.* an obstinate person; a blockhead; a beetle-head.

wakare (別, 分), *n.* ❶ (分離) separation; disjunction. ❷ (別離) farewell; parting; leave-taking. ❸ (分出) a branch; an offshoot. —別れの辛さ, the tug at parting; the sorrow of parting. —別れを告げる, to bid farewell [adieu]; say good-bye; take leave of a person.

wakareji (別路), *n.* ❶ a branch-road; the parting of the ways. ❷ (別離) parting.

wakareru (別·分れる), *vi.* ❶ (分離) to separate; segregate; disunite. ❷ (別離) to part *from*; separate *from*; bid farewell; part company *with* (仲間などから). ❸ (岐出) to fork; part. ❹ (解散) to break up. ❺ (分裂) to split *into*; be divided (意見など). —別れ!, (號令) Break ranks! —…から別れ出る, to branch off *from*; diverge *from*. —親に早く分れる, to part from one's parents in one's early days. —二派に分れる, to divide itself into two groups; split [take sides] *on* (a question, ある問題で).

wakari (解, 理解) *n.* understanding; comprehension; apprehension. —解りの早い, quick of apprehension; quick-witted; nimble. —解りの遲い, slow of apprehension; thick-witted; thick-headed. —解りの惡い, unintelligent; dull-witted; hard of understanding.

wakarikitta (解り切った), *a.* obvious; evident; palpable; self-evident (自明の); self-explaining (合成語など). —解り切った嘘, a palpable [glaring] lie.

wakarinikui (解り難い), *a.* ❶ (難解なる) hard to understand; puzzling. ❷ (會得し難い) incomprehensible. ❸ crabbed (文體の); cramp (筆跡の); illegible (筆跡·印刷等の); hard to make out; unintelligible. —解り難い手跡, cramp handwriting.

wakariyasui (解り易い), *a.* easy (to understand); simple (簡單); plain (平易); intelligible (明瞭).

wakariyoi (解りよい), *a.* easy to understand; intelligible.

wakaru (解る), *v.* ❶ (解する) to understand; catch; make out; see. ❷ (知る) to know; tell; say. ❸ (判明する) to prove [turn out] to be; become plain. ❹ (露見する) to come to light. ❺ (事理が) to have sense; be sensible. —解って來る, to come to know; dawn upon one [one's mind]; open to one's mind (同上). —意味が分る, to pick [make] out the meaning *of*. —迚も解らぬ, to pass one's comprehension; be above one's comprehension. —もう分った, I understand now: Enough!; Say no more. —それで解った, That accounts for it. —漸く解りました, I see it at last. —道が分ってるか, Do you know your way? —確な處は分らぬ, I can't say for certain. —言はんでも分ってゐる, The matter speaks for itself. —あの人は譯が分ってる, He has good sense. —君の家は分らなかった, I could not find out your house. —いくら嘘ついても直ぐ解るよ, Whatever lie you may tell, it will soon be found out. —人間には分らぬことが澤山ある, There are many things above [beyond] human perception. —どんな事になるか分らない, There is no saying [knowing] what may become of it.

wakasa (若さ), *n.* youth; youthfulness.

wakasagi (公魚), *n.* 【魚】 the pond-smelt.

wakashiraga (若白髮), *n.* gray hair in youth.

wakasu (沸かす), *vt.* to boil; heat. —湯を沸かす, to boil water. —青年の血を沸かす, to stir [turn] the blood of the youth.

wakate (若手), *n.* a young man; young blood.

wakatō (若黨), *n.* a young attendant [retainer].

wakatsu (分つ), *vt.* to divide; share; part; separate. ☞ *wakeru* (分ける).

wakawakashii (若若しい), *a.* young-looking; juvenescent; fresh.

wakazakari (若盛り), *n.* the prime [flower; May] of life; the vigour [flush] of youth.

wakazukuri (若作り), *n.* toilet which makes one look younger.

wake (分), *n.* division (分配); sharing (同上); a draw (引分). —分けになる, to end in a draw.

wake (譯), *n.* ❶ (理由) reason; ground. ❷ (原因) cause. ❸ (意味) meaning; sense. ❹ (仔細) circumstances. —譯の解らぬ人, an unreasonable man; a person deaf to reason. —譯の分らぬ話, a gabbling talk; a blind story; gibberish. —譯ない, easy; simple. —譯なく, ① (容易に) easily; with ease. ② (不條理に) without reason《cause》; wantonly. —かう云ふ譯で, for this reason; on this account; such being the case. —どういふ譯で, why; for what reason; on what ground. —どう

いふ譯だか, from some unknown cause; somehow or other; for some reason or other; I don't know how it is, but.... —譯を質す, to inquire into the reason. —腹を立てる譯はない, There is no occasion to be angry. —それはかういふ譯だ, The case stands thus. —そいつは又譯が違ふよ, That's quite another thing. —これには深い譯がある, There is a deep cause for it. —僕に何も異議があるといふ譯でない, Not that I have any objection.

wakedori (分取), *n.* partition; sharing. —分取りする, to partition; share; divide.

wakegara (譯柄), *n.* =***wake.***

wakehedate (分隔, 別隔), *n.* discrimination; distinction. —分隔てなく, without discrimination. —分隔てする, to make distinctions *between*; discriminate *between*.

wakemae (分前), *n.* a share; a portion. —不當の分前, an excessive [unfair] share; a lion's share. —利益の分前を貰ふ, to share in the profits.

wakeme (別目), *n.* ❶ (別けたる所) a dividing line; a partition (仕切); parting (髮などの). ❷ (成敗を定むる機會) a decisive point; a crisis. —天下分目の戰, a decisive battle.

wakeru (分ける), *vt.* ❶ (分割) to divide; part. ❷ (分配) to give a share *of*; divide [share; portion; distribute] *between* 《*among*》; deal (骨牌札等を). ❸ (引分く) to part; draw apart. ❹ (擇分, 分類) to sort out; classify (分類). ❺ =***kubetsu*** (區別する). —分けて置く, to set apart. —額を分ける, to split the sum. —人と物を分ける, to break [share] a thing with a person. —組を分けて賣る, to break a set and sell. —人込の中を分ける, to push [force] one's way through the crowd. —髮を眞中から分ける, to part the hair in the middle. —一部わけて吳れんか, Can you spare me a copy?

wakete (別けて), *ad.* ❶ (特に) especially; specially; in particular. ❷ (就中) above all.

waki (脇), *n.* ❶ (腋, 掖) the side of the chest; flank (禽獸の). ❷ (側) the side. ❸ (餘所) another place. —脇へ向く, to turn aside. —脇へ寄れ, Stand aside. —包を脇に抱へる, to have a package under one's arm. —話を脇へそらす, to turn aside the conversation.

waki (和氣), *n.* harmony; concord. —和氣靄々たる間に, in perfect harmony.

wakiake (腋明), *n.* an arm-hole.

wakibara (脇腹), *n.* the side.

wakibasamu (脇挾む), *vt.* to have [hold] under arm.

wakideru (湧出る), *vi.* to gush out [forth]; spout; well.

wakiga (腋臭), *n.* smell of the armpits.

wakige (腋毛), *n.* hair of the armpit.

wakikaeru (沸返る), *vi.* ❶ (煮へ返る) to boil up. ❷ (洶涌) to boil up; bubble; seethe. ❸ (群集などが騷ぎ立つ) to ferment; be excited. —沸き返る樣な騷ぎ, seething commotion.

wakimae (辨), *n.* ❶ (辨別) discernment; discrimination; discretion; judgment. ❷ (心得) knowledge; understanding. —辨への無い, undiscerning; indiscreet. —前後の辨へもなく, without a thought of the consequences.

wakimaeru (辨へる), *vt.* to discern; understand; bear in mind. ☞ ***benbetsu.*** —己の利害はよく辨へてゐる, to know on which side one's bread is buttered.

wakimi (脇見する), =***yosomi.***

wakimichi (脇道), *n.* a by-road; a bypath; a byway; a branch-road. —脇道に這入る, ① to go astray; wander into a by-road. ② (話が) to digress; make a digression. —議論が脇道へそれた, The discussion ran into a side issue.

wakinoshita (腋下, 腋窩), *n.* 【醫】 the axilla; the armpit. —腋の下を擽ぐる, to tickle under the arm.

wakitatsu (沸立つ), *vi.* to boil up; seethe; ferment.

wakizashi (脇差), *n.* a short sword; a dirk.

wakōhō (和較法), *n.* 【數】 alligation alternate.

waku (枠, 籰), *n.* ❶ (絡車) a reel; a spool. ❷ (木框) a frame; a framework; a picture-frame (額の); a tambour (刺繡の).

waku (沸・涌く), *vi.* ❶ (沸騰) to boil; ferment. ❷ (湧出) to gush forth [out]; spout. ❸ (發生) to grow; breed. —沸き溢れる, to boil over. —風呂が沸きました, The bath is ready. —希望は絕えず人の胸の中に湧く, "Hope springs eternal in the human breast."

wakuchin (ワクチン), *n.* 【醫】 vaccine. ¶ ワクチン注射, vaccine-injection.

wakudeki (惑溺する), *vi.* to be addicted *to*; be infatuated *with*; overindulge *in*.

wakuran (惑亂する), *vt.* =***madowasu.***

wakusei (惑星), *n.* 【天】 a planet.

wakuwaku (わくわく), *ad.* in agony. —わくわくする, to tremble. 一わくわく日を送る, to pass one's days in agony.

wakyō (和協), *n.* ❶ (親和) harmony; concord; amicability. ❷ (音聲の調和) harmony; concord. ☞ *wachū* (和衷協同). 一意見の不折合を和協する, to smooth over [away] differences. ¶ 和協音, 【音】 concert.

wakyoku (和局), *n.* an amicable settlement. 一和局を結ぶ, An amicable settlement was reached.

wameku (喚く), *vi.* to scream; shriek; yell.

wan (椀), *n.* a wooden bowl; a bowl. 一椀に盛る[よそる], to fill a bowl *with*; serve in a bowl (盛って出す).

wan (灣), *n.* a gulf; a bay (小なる). 一灣をなす, to form a bay. ¶ 東京灣, Tōkyō Bay; the Bay of Tōkyō.

wana (罠, 係蹄), *n.* a trap; a snare; a gin. 一係蹄にかける, to catch in a trap [snare]; trap; snare; noose; gin. 一罠に落ちる, to fall into a snare. 一罠をかける, to lay a snare; set a trap.

wanage (輪投), *n.* 【遊戲】 quoits.

wananaku (戰慄く), *vi.* to tremble; shudder. ☞ *senritsu* (戰慄する).

wanari (輪狀の), *a.* ring-shaped; annular.

wanchin (腕枕), *n.* a guiding-stick; a maulstick; a rest-stick.

wani (鰐魚), *n.* 【爬蟲】 the crocodile; the alligator; the caiman. 一鰐の口をのがれる, to escape from the jaws of death.

waniashi (鰐足), *n.* a bent knee. 一鰐足の, ① (外鰐) bandy-legged; bow-legged. ② (內鰐) knock-kneed. 一內《外》鰐足で步く, to toe in《out》.

wanisu (假漆), *n.* varnish.

wanizame (鰐鮫), *n.* 【魚】 Carcharias japonicus (blue-shark の類).

wankansetsu (腕關節), *n.* 【解】 the radiocarpal articulation; the wrist-joint.

wankotsu (腕骨), *n.* 【解】 the carpus.

wankyoku (彎曲), *n.* curvature; inflexion; flexure; curve; bow; bend. 一彎曲する, to curve; bend.

wanpaku (腕白), *n.* naughtiness. 一腕白な, naughty; mischievous; wilful (我儘な). ¶ 腕白小僧, an urchin; an imp; a naughty child.

wanryoku (腕力), *n.* physical [brute] force; force; muscular strength. 一腕力沙汰になる, to come to blows. 一腕力で勝つ, to subdue by the strong hand; win [gain] by force. ¶ 腕力家, a strong man.

wanryū (灣流), *n.* (the) Gulf Stream.

wanshō (腕章), *n.* a brassard.

wanwan (喧喧), *n.* ❶ (犬の鳴聲) bow-wow. ❷ (犬) a bow-wow; a puppy-dog; a pup. 一わんわん吠える, to bow-wow; bark.

wanzenkotsu (腕前骨), *n.* 【解】 the metacarpus; a metacarpal bone (五骨の一).

wappu (割賦), *n.* allotment. 一割賦する, to allot; apportion; share. ¶ 割賦金, an allotment; a share; a dividend (配當金).

wappuru (ワップル), *n.* (菓子) a waffle.

wara (藁), *n.* straw.

warabai (藁灰), *n.* straw-ashes.

warabe (童), *n.* a child.

warabi (蕨), *n.* 【植】 the brake; the bracken; the eagle-fern; the adder's spit.

warabuton (藁蒲團), *n.* a paillasse; a straw mattress.

waragami (藁紙), *n.* rice-paper.

warai (笑), *n.* ❶ (聲出しての笑) laughter; a laugh. ❷ (聲出さぬ笑) a smile. ❸ (嘲笑) ridicule; derision. 一大きな笑聲, a roar of laughter. 一世人の笑を招く, to bring [incur] public derision; become an object of public derision. ¶ 笑話, a funny story.

waraigusa (笑草), *n.* a laughing-stock; a standing jest [joke]; a butt for ridicule. 一笑草になる, to become a laughing-stock.

waraijōgo (笑上戶), *n.* ❶ one who laughs in his cups. ❷ (よく笑ふ人) a ticklish person; one easily given to laughter.

waraji (草鞋), *n.* straw-sandals. 一草鞋穿きで, in straw-sandals.

waranawa (藁繩), *n.* a straw-rope.

waraningyō (藁人形), *n.* a jack-straw; a straw-figure [-effigy]; a straw man.

warau (笑·嗤ふ), *v.* ❶ (聲を出して) to laugh. ❷ (聲を出さずに) to smile. ❸ (嘲笑) to laugh *at*; ridicule; jeer [sneer] *at*. ❹ (蕾開く) to bloom. 一笑ひ轉げる, to roll with laughter. 一笑って迎へる, to smile welcome. 一苦々しく笑ふ, to smile bitterly. 一キャッキャと笑ふ, to be convulsed with laughter. 一大きな聲で笑ひ出す, to burst into a loud laugh. 一笑はずに居られぬ, (One) cannot help laughing. 一笑ふ門には福來る, "Fortune comes to a merry home."

waraya (藁家), *n.* a straw-thatched house.

warazōri (藁草履), *n.* straw-sandals.

warazuto (藁包), *n.* a straw-wrapper.

ware (我, 吾), *pron.* ❶ (我國, 我味方) we. ❷ (自分) I. ❸ (自我)

[*n.*] self; ego. —我勝ちに, each taking no heed of others; each striving to be first. (我勝ちに出口を爭ふ, to make a scramble to reach the door.) —我先に席をとる《錢を拾ふ》, to scramble for seats《coins》. —我に返る, to become conscious; come to oneself [one's senses]. —我を忘れて喜ぶ, to forget oneself in one's joy.

waregane (破鐘), *n.* a broken bell; a cracked bell. —破鐘のやうな聲を出す, to roar in a cracked voice.

wareme (割目), *n.* a crack; a crevice; a fissure; a rift.

warenabe (破鍋), *n.* a cracked pot; a broken pot. —破鍋に綴ぢ蓋, "No pot is so ugly as not to find a cover."

wareru (割れる), *vi.* ❶ (龜裂) to crack; split; fissure. ❷ (破壞) to break; smash. —割れ易い, cracky; frail; fragile.

wareshirazu (我不知), *ad.* unconsciously; involuntarily; in spite of oneself. —我知らず叫ぶ, to cry in spite of oneself.

wareware (我我), *pron.* Ⓢ 我等. we. —我々の《に; を》, our《us》.

wari (割), *n.* ❶ (割合) rate; proportion. ❷ (利益) profit. ❸ (比較) comparison. ❹ =*wariate* (割當). —五割引, fifty per cent. discount [reduction]. —俸給割で, proportionately to the salary. —割のよい, profitable; lucrative; remunerative. (割のよい商賣, a lucrative trade.) —割の惡い, unprofitable; disadvantageous. —年一割の利息で, at the interest of ten per cent. per annum. —割に合はぬ, ① [*a.*] unremunerative; unprofitable. ② [*vi.*] not to pay; not to be worth one's while. —一時間九哩の割で走る, to run at the rate [speed] of nine miles an hour. **——-ni,** *ad.* (比較的) comparatively; relatively. **——,** *prep.* (...の割に) for; considering. —其割に proportionally; proportionately. —大きい割に輕い, to be light for its size.

wariai (割合), *n.* rate; proportion. ratio. —五對二の割合, the ratio of five to two. —...の割合で, in the proportion *of*; at the rate *of* (ten miles per hour); at the ratio *of* (3 to 5, 3:5, 3/5). **——-ni,** *ad.* =*wari* (割に).

wariate (割當), *n.* allotment; assignment; allocation.

wariateru (割當てる), *vt.* to allot [assign; apportion] *to*; parcel [portion] out; apportion; share [divide; distribute] *among*. —仕事を割當てる, to parcel out [apportion] work. —それを五人に割當てる, to divide [share] it among five (persons). —時間に割當てる, to divide by the hours.

waribiki (割引), *n.* discount; rebate; reduction. **——-suru,** *vt.* to discount; rebate; reduce; abate; take off; make discount [a reduction]. —割引して聞く, to hear with some reduction [qualification]; take with a grain of salt. ¶ 割引步合, discount rate; rate of discount. —割引賃錢, reduced fare. —割引電車, a cheap car. —割引時間, reduced-fare hours. —割引乘車券, a cheap ticket. —割引列車, a parliamentary train [英]. —割引手形, a bill discounted; a discounted bill.

waridasu (割出す), *vt.* ❶ (算出) to calculate; compute. ❷ (推斷) to deduce *from*; conclude *from*.

warifu (割符, 割札), *n.* ❶ (分割したる符) a tally; a score; a tally-sheet (紙の). ❷ (切符) a check. —割符を合せる, to tally.

wariguriishi (割栗石), *n.* broken stone; road-metal. ¶ 割栗石鋪道, a macadamized road; a macadam.

wariin (割印), *n.* an impression of a seal over two edges; a tally. —割印を押す, to affix a seal over two edges.

warikireru (割切れる), *vi.* to be divisible (without a remainder). **——,** *a.* divisible.

warikomu (割込む), *vi.* to squeeze (oneself) *into* [*in*]; wedge oneself *into*; force oneself in. —內閣に割込む, to take a seat in the cabinet.

warimae (割前), *n.* a share; a proportion; a snack [俗]. —割前を拂ふ, to pay one's share [shot].

warimashi (割增-金), *n.* a premium; a bonus. ¶ 割增賃銀《運賃》extra wages《freight》. —割增金附勸業債券, premium-bearing hypothec debentures (日本專用).

warimodoshi (割戾), *n.* a drawback; a rebate. ¶ 割戾稅, a drawback.

warimodosu (割戾), *vt.* to rebate.

warinaki (別なき仲になる), to become intimate *with*.

waritsuke (割附), *n.* allotment; distribution; assessment (租稅の). —割附ける, to allot; assign; divide; distribute; assess. ¶ 割附金, a dividend; a share; an allotment; an assessment.

warizan (割算), *n.* 【數】division.

waru (割る), *vt.* ❶ (分ける) to divide; portion; distribute. ❷ (離す) to part; separate; sever. ❸

(裂く) to cut; chop; cleave; split. ❹ (壞す) to break; smash; crack. ❺【數】(除する) to divide. ❻ (混入する) to mix; dilute; adulterate. —割って入る, to push one's way *into*. —木《石》を割る, to split wood 《stone》. —胡桃を割る, to crack a nut. —九を三で割る, to divide nine by three.

waruasobi (惡遊), *n.* ❶ (いたづら) a prank; a practical joke; a mischievous play. ❷ (よからぬ遊興) evil [vicious] pleasures; scandalous amusements.

warubireru (惡怯れる), *vi.* to fear; be afraid *of*; feel abashed. —惡怯れず言ふ, to outspeak; speak out. —少しも惡びれたる態なく, without the least fear; without the slightest appearance of shame.

warudakumi (惡企をする), *v.* to make evil designs; form a plot; plot.

warufuzake (惡巫山戯する), *v.* to play a prank [trick; practical joke] *on*; play [serve] a person a trick.

warugashikoi (惡賢い), *a.* wily; cunning; artful; crafty.

warugi (惡氣), *n.* ill will; evil intention; malicious intent; malice; spite. —惡氣のない, without malice. —何等惡氣はない, He intends you [means] no harm.

warui (惡い), *a.* ❶ bad (good の對); wrong (right の對); ill (well の對). ❷ (非道な) immoral; wrong; sinful. ❸ (不法な) illegal; unlawful. ❹ (邪惡な) ill-natured; wicked; malicious. ❺ (いたづらな) mischievous; prankish. ❻ (不吉な) evil; ill; ominous. ❼ (不運な) ill; unlucky; sad. ❽ (有害な) harmful; injurious; hurtful. ❾ (不健全な) sickly; unsound; unwholesome; unhealthy. —惡い天氣, bad [nasty] weather. —惡い風, an unfavourable wind: a bad cold (風邪). —より惡い, worse. —最も惡い, worst. —顏色が惡い, to be off colour. —胸が惡い, to feel sick. —惡い事をする, to do wrong [evil]; commit a crime 《sin》; work ill. —惡い事は出來ぬもの, "Murder will out."

warujie (惡智慧), *n.* wiles; craft; cunning. —惡智慧を附ける, to put a person up *to*.

waruku (惡く), *ad.* badly; wrongly; ill. —惡く言ふ, to speak ill [evil] *of*. —惡くなる, to become bad; go [turn out] bad; spoil; turn sour. (惡くなる一方である, to grow only worse and worse.) —惡くすると, (may) possibly.

warukuchi (惡口), *n.* abuse; abusive [foul] language; detraction. ☞ *akkō*. ¶ 惡口屋, a clash-bag [俗]; a scandal-monger.

warumono (惡者), *n.* a bad fellow; a rogue; a rascal. ☞ *akkan*.

wasabi (山葵), *n.* 【植】Eutrema wasabi (學名).

wasan (和算), *n.* calculation with the abacus.

wase (早稻), *n.* ❶ (稻の一種) early rice. ❷ (早熟) precociousness; precocity; prematurity. ¶ 早稻田, an early-rice field.

wasei (和製の), *a.* Japan-made; of Japanese make; home-made (內國製の). ¶ 和製品, Japan-made articles; goods of Japanese make.

wasen (和戰), *n.* peace and war. —和戰兩樣の準備, preparation both for peace and war.

washa (話者), *n.* the speaker; the teller; the narrator.

washi (鷲), *n.* ❶【鳥】the eagle. ❷【天】(星座) Aquila; the Eagle. ¶ 鷲印鉛筆, a pencil with the eagle brand; an eagle-brand pencil.

washin (和親), *n.* friendly relation; amity; friendship. —和親を結ぶ, to enter into friendly relations with another.

washiru (走る), *vi.* = ***hashiru***.

wasuregachi (忘れ勝ちの), *a.* forgetful; oblivious.

wasuregatami (忘形見), *n.* ❶ (遺孤) a posthumous child. ❷ (記念物) a memento; a souvenir; a keepsake.

wasuremono (忘物), *n.* things left behind. —忘物をする, to leave a thing behind.

wasurenagusa (勿忘草), *n.* 【植】the forget-me-not.

wasureppoi (忘れっぽい), *a.* forgetful; oblivious. ——, *vi.* to be apt to forget. —忘れっぽい男, a forgetful man; a man of short [bad; poor] memory.

wasureru (忘れる), *vt.* to forget; let slip from the memory; efface from one's memory; leave behind (置き忘れる). —忘るべからざる, never-to-be-forgotten; memorable. —忘れてしまふ, to think no more *of*. —片時も忘れずに, always present to one's mind. —世間から忘れられる, to be forgotten by the world.

wa-suru (和する), *vi.* ❶ (親む) to become intimate *with*. ❷ (調和する) to harmonize *with*. ❸ (和睦する) to make peace *with*. ❹ (唱和する) to respond; follow. —和せず, to discord; be out of tune [harmony].

wata (綿), *n.* ❶ cotton. ❷【植】(棉) the cotton-plant. ❸ (草綿)

the (common) herbaceous cotton-plant. —綿一枚, a roll of cotton. —綿を打つ《摘む》, to willow 《pick》 cotton. —着物に綿を入れる, to wad clothes with cotton. ¶ 綿商, cotton trade; a cotton-dealer; a cotton-broker (仲買).

wata (腸), *n.* the intestines; the entrails; the bowels. —の腸を抜く, to remove [extract; take out] the entrails *of*; draw (a fowl).

watage (綿毛), *n.* down; pile (羊の); floccus (羽毛なき幼鳥の).

wataire (綿入), *n.* a wadded garment; padded clothes.

watakuri (綿繰), *n.* ❶ (事) ginning. ❷ (人) a ginner. ¶ 綿繰車, a cotton-gin.

watakushi (私), *pron.* I. —私の《に; を》, my 《me》.

watakushi (私), *n.* ❶ (公の對) privacy; privateness. ❷ (秘密) secrecy; secrets. ❸ (不公平) partiality; unfairness. ❹ (私利) self-interest; selfishness. —私なき, impartial; disinterested: unselfish. —私の, private; personal; secret. —私に, privately; in private; secretly. **—— - suru,** *vt.* to embezzle; appropriate. —寸毫も私せず, not to appropriate the least thing.

watariau (渡合ふ), *vi.* to cross swords *with*; fight *with*.

wataridori (渡鳥, 候鳥), *n.* a bird of passage; a migratory bird; a migrant.

watarimono (渡者, 渡物), *n.* a wandering labourer; a journey-worker; a rolling stone.

watarizome (渡初), *n.* the first crossing of a new bridge; the opening ceremony of a newly-built bridge.

wataru (渡·済·渉·亙る), *v.* ❶ (越え行く) to cross [pass] over. ❷ (通る) to go [walk; run; fly] across. ❸ (渡來する) to be imported [introduced]; come over. ❹ (及ぶ) to range; extend; cover; last (繼續). ❺ (通ずる) to be well versed; be at home. ❻ (暮す) to get along; live. ❼ (水を) to wade; ford; ferry. —他人の手に渡る, to change hands; pass into another's hands. —二時間に亙る, to last two hours. —數哩に亙る, to cover [extend over] several miles. —廊下を渡る, to go along a corridor. —川を渡《渉》る, to cross 《ford; wade》 a river. —渡る世間に鬼はない, "There is kindness to be found everywhere."

watashi (渡), *n.* ❶ (渡すこと) conveyance; ferrying over. ❷ (受渡, 交付) delivery; transfer. ❸ (請負) contract. ❹ = 渡船. ❺ (渡船場) a ferry. —矢口の渡し, the Yaguchi Ferry. ¶ 渡船, a ferry-boat; a wherry. —渡守, a ferryman. —渡錢, ferriage; a death-penny (三途川の).

watasu (渡す), *vt.* ❶ (彼岸へ) to pass *across* [*over*]; take *over*; ferry *over* (渡船で). ❷ (架する) to lay; span; build (建造). ❸ (交付する, 引渡す) to hand (over); deliver; transfer; make over. ❹ (請負はす) to contract *for*. —物品を渡す, to deliver goods. —橋を渡す, to span a bridge *over*. —板を渡す, to lay [set] a plank *across* [*over*]. —河を渡す, to convey a person across a river. —鑑札を渡す, to grant a licence.

watasuge (わたすげ), *n.* 【植】 the globe cotton-grass.

watauchi (綿打), *n.* ❶ (事) willowing. ❷ (人) a willower.

wataya (綿屋), *n.* a cotton shop (店); a cotton-dealer (人).

watō (話頭), *n.* the topic [subject] of conversation. —話頭を轉ずる, to change one's subject.

watto (わッと), *ad.* with a loud cry; loudly. —わッと泣出す, to burst into tears; burst out crying.

watto (ワット), *n.* 【電】 watt.

wayaku (和譯), *n.* translation [rendering] into Japanese. —和譯する, to translate [render] into Japanese. ¶ 英文和譯法, how to translate from English into Japanese.

wayō-setchū (和洋折衷), *n.* a compromise between Japanese and European styles; a blending of Japanese and foreign styles.

waza (業, 技), *n.* ❶ (所業) an act; a deed; work. ❷ (職業) occupation; calling. ❸ (技術) art; a trick. —人間の業, the work of man; human handwork.

wazato (態と), *ad.* purposely; on purpose; intentionally. —態と知らぬ振をする, to pretend ignorance. **—— - rashii,** *a.* artificial; affected. —態とらしい笑, a forced smile. —態とらしい様子, an artificial manner,

wazawai (禍, 災), *n.* a disaster; a calamity; a misfortune. —禍に遭ふ [罹る], to have [meet] a misfortune. —自ら禍を招く, to bring calamity upon oneself. —禍を未然に防ぐ, to take preventive measures against a calamity.

wazawaza (態態), *ad.* ❶ (殊更に) specially; expressly. ❷ (故意に) purposely; on purpose; intentionally; by design. —遠方の

所を態ゝ御出でになったのだから, since you have been at the trouble of coming all this way. —態ゝ見に行く値打はない, It is not worth going all the way to see it. —態ゝさうするには及ばない, You need not go to the trouble of doing so; You need not take the trouble to do so.

wazuka (僅, 纔), *n.* ❶ (僅少) a small quantity [amount]; a little ((few)). ❷ (短少) a short while ((distance)). ——, *ad.* =*wazuka-ni* の ❶. —僅か五年で, in the short space of five years; in only five years. —僅か十歳で, when he was only ten years old. **—— - no,** *a.* ❶ (數, 量, 度) few; little; small; short. ❷ (瑣細な) slight; mere; trifling. ❸ (取るに足らぬ) insignificant; inconsiderable. —僅の收入, a slender income. —僅の入り, a thin house. —僅の時間で, in a short space of time. **—— - ni,** *ad.* ❶ [僅] (少し) only; merely; little; slightly. ❷ [纔] (辛じて) barely. —纔に暮しを立てる, just to keep the pot boiling.

wazurai (煩, 患), *n.* ❶ (病) affliction; an illness; a disease. ❷ (惱み) worry; sufferings; anxiety. ❸ (面倒) a trouble.

wazurau (患·煩ふ), *vi.* ❶ (思ひ惱む) to worry [trouble] oneself; be anxious. ❷ (病む) to suffer *from*; be afflicted; be sick *of*; be ill *with*. —患ひつく, to fall ill. —氣管を患ふ, to have something the matter with the trachea.

wazurawashii (煩しい), *a.* ❶ (厄介な) vexatious; troublesome; annoying. ❷ (氣懸りな) anxious; uneasy; solicitous. ❸ (繁雑な) complicated; intricate; confused. —煩しい手數, troublesome labour; complicated formalities (手續).

wazurawasu (煩はす), *vt.* to annoy; worry; trouble (手數をかける). —心を煩はす, to worry oneself; cause anxiety. —君を煩はしては濟まないが, I am sorry to trouble you, but.... —此事に就いて君の手を煩はしたいのだ, I should like to have your help in this matter.

Y

ya (や), *particle.* ❶ 用言を根幹とする文末に附し疑問を示す. ❷ 反語に用ひる. ❸ 命令又は希望の意を表はす. ❹ 主格に附して「は」の代用を爲し其意を强める. ❺「…すると直に」の意を表はす. ❻「…する時は」の意を示す. —聞けや革命の鐘の響を, Hark! There goes the tocsin of revolution. —聞くや否や駈け出した, No sooner did he hear it than he ran out.

ya (や), *int.* ❶ (驚唉の發聲) oh!; ah!; dear me! ❷ (呼掛の發聲) hallo!, halloo! ☞ *yā* (やあ). —したりやしたりや, Bravo!; Well done!

ya (や), *conj.* and; or. —何や彼やで, with one thing or another.

ya (矢), *n.* ❶ (箭) an arrow; a shaft; a bolt. ❷ (楔) a wedge. —矢狀の, sagittate. —矢を射る, to shoot [let fly; let off] an arrow. (矢を射る如く, as swift as an arrow.) —矢の催促する, to press a person hard [urgently] *for*.

ya (野), *n.* a field. —野に下る, to go out of office; resign one's (government) post.

ya (輻), *n.* a spoke (車輪の).

ya (やッ), **yā** (やあ), *int.* ❶ (呼掛) hallo!, halloo! ❷ (驚の聲) oh!; ah!; dear me! —やあ之は驚いた, God bless me!; my life!; my soul! —やあしくじッた, Oh dear! I have failed!

yaba (矢場), *n.* an archery-ground; an archery-gallery.

yaban (野蠻), *n.* savageness; barbarism; barbarousness. —野蠻な, barbarous; savage; rude; wild. —野蠻の域を脫する, to emerge from savagery. ¶ 野蠻人, a barbarian; a savage; a wild man. (野蠻人の如き, barbaric.) —野蠻時代, the age of barbarism; rude times.

yabo (野暮), *n.* boorishness (無粋); rusticity (粗野). **—— - na,** *a.* unrefined; boorish; uncouth. —野暮な男, a boorish [an uncouth] fellow; an unlicked cub. —野暮な事をいふ, to say boorish [uncouth] things.

yabu (藪, 薮), *n.* a thicket; a jungle; a bush (小藪); a bamboo-jungle (竹藪). —藪から棒に云ふ, to say abruptly [without notice]. —藪をつゝいて蛇を出す, to bring a hornet's nest about one's ears; poke one's head into a hornet's nest. ¶ 藪地, a jungle-land; a jungle.

yabuhebi (藪蛇), *n.* waking a sleeping dog. —藪蛇を出すな, Let well alone; Let the sleeping dogs lie.

yabuiri (藪入), *n.* the servants'

holiday; the apprentices' holiday.

yabuisha (藪醫者), *n.* an unskilled doctor; a medicaster.

yabuka (藪蚊), *n.* 【昆】 Culex dives (gnat の一種學名).

yabukeru (破ける), *vi.* to break; be torn; burst. ☞ *yabureru.*

yabukōji (紫金牛), *n.* 【植】 Ardisia japonica (spear-flower の一種學名). ☞ *yaburu.*

yabuku (破く), *vt.* to break; tear.

yabumi (矢文), *n.* ❶ (矢に結びて敵に送る書) a letter fixed to an arrow. ❷ (續けさまの手紙) a succession of letters.

yabun (夜分), *n.* night; night-time; evening. —夜分晩く, late at night.

yabunirami (藪睨), *n.* 【醫】 strabismus: squint; a squint-eye. —藪睨みの人, a squint-eyed man; a squinter.

yabure (破), *n.* ❶ (破綻) breach; breaking; failure (失敗). ❷ (裂隙) a tear; a rent.

yaburekabure (やぶれかぶれ), *n.* desperation; despair. ——, *ad.* desperately; in desperation; with the courage of despair. —やぶれかぶれになる, to become desperate.

yabureme (破目), *n.* a rent; a tear.

yabureru (破れる), *vi.* ❶ to break; be torn [rent] (裂ける); burst (破壞する); rupture (同上); ❷ (敗北) to be defeated; suffer a defeat; lose a battle. ❸ (失敗) to fall through; fail *in*; come [go] to the ground; be frustrated. —各部に敗れた軍, an army defeated in detail. —協調が破れる, An agreement falls through. —腫物が破れる, A tumour collapses [bursts].

yabureta (破れた), *a.* broken; torn; ragged (ぼろぼろの); worn out (擦切れた); defeated (負けた). —破れた軍旗, a tattered ensign. —破れた著物, worn-out clothes.

yaburu (破る), *vt.* ❶ (裂く) to tear; rend; rupture. ❷ (破壞) to break. ❸ (犯す) to violate; infringe; break. ❹ (負かす) to defeat; outrival. ❺ (計畫など) to frustrate; checkmate; bring to naught. —未だ破られざりしレコード, an unbroken record. —牢を破る, to break jail [prison]; break out of prison. —敵を破る, to defeat the enemy. —家憲を破る, to infringe the rules of one's family. —敵の計畫を破る, to baffle [foil] the enemy's plan.

yabusaka (吝な), *a.* stingy; parsimonious; niggardly. —他人の說を容るゝに吝ならぬ, to be open to conviction. —過を改むるに吝ならぬ, to be not slow to correct one's errors.

yachin (家賃), *n.* a house-rent; a rent. —家賃の滯り, rent-arrear.

yacho (野猪), *n.* a wild boar.

yachoku (夜直), *n.* night-duty; night-watch. ☞ *shukuchoku.*

yachū (夜中), *n.* night; night-time. ——, *ad.* at night (午後六時より夜半に至る間に); in the night. ¶ 夜中郵便箱, a letter-box (for night use).

yado (宿), *n.* ❶ (家) home; a house. ❷ (宿り) lodging. ❸ (宿屋) a lodging-house. ❹ (夫) my husband; my good man; Mr.—. —宿をとる, to put up *at*; stay *at* [*in*]; take up one's lodgings [quarters] *in*; lodge *at*. —宿を貸す, to give a lodging; accommodate a person with a lodging.

yādo (碼), *n.* a yard. ¶ 碼尺, a cloth-measure; a yardstick; a yard-wand. —百碼競走, a 100 yards; a 100-yd race.

yadochin (宿賃), *n.* =*yadosen.*

yadochō (宿帳), *n.* a hotel register.

yadogae (宿替), *n.* a change of residence; removal. ☞ *iten.*

yadoguruma (宿車), *n.* a *jinrikisha* at a *jinrikisha*-house.

yadohiki (宿引), *n.* a hotel-runner; a tout.

yadokari (寄居蟹), *n.* 【節足】 the hermit crab.

yadomoto (宿許), *n.* a (servant's) surety's house.

yadonashi (宿無), *n.* a homeless person; a vagrant; a waif. —宿無しの, homeless; houseless; vagrant. ¶ 宿なし子, a homeless child; a street arab; a gutter-child [-snipe]; a mud-lark.

yadonushi (宿主), *n.* a landlord; a landlady (女); a host; a hostess (女).

yadori (宿), *n.* lodging.

yadorigi (寄生木), *n.* ❶ a parasite; a parasitic plant. ❷ 【植】 (槲寄生) the mistletoe.

yadoru (宿る), *v.* ❶ (宿泊) to lodge *at*; put up *at*; stay *at* [*in*]; take up one's lodgings *in*. ❷ (寄生) to live *in* (*upon*). ❸ (精神など) to lodge; dwell *in*; inhabit. ❹ (子が) to be conceived.

yadosen (宿錢), *n.* hotel (inn) charges.

yadosu (宿す), *vt.* ❶ =*tomeru* (泊める). ❷ (懐姙) to conceive; become pregnant *with*.

yadoya (宿屋), *n.* a [an] hotel; an inn; a tavern. —宿屋の主人, a landlord; a landlady; an inn-keeper; an *aubergiste* 【佛】. —宿屋をする, to run a hotel.

yae (八重の), *a.* ❶ (八つ重なれ

る) eightfold; octuple. ❸ (數多く重なれる) multiple; multifold. ❹【植】(重瓣) double; double-petalled. ―八重咲きつ躑躅, a double-flowered azalea.

yaeba (八重齒), *n.* double teeth.

yaei (野營), *n.* a camp; an encampment; camping (事). ―野營する, to encamp camp (out); bivouac. ¶ 野營地, a camping-ground.

yaen (夜宴), *n.* an evening party; a banquet at night.

yaen (野猿), *n.* a wild monkey.

yaenari (綠豆), *n.* 【植】 the hairy-podded kidney-bean.

yaeyamagame (八重山龜), *n.* 【爬蟲】 the box-tortoise.

yaezakura (八重櫻), *n.* 【植】 Prunus pseudo-cerasus (wild cherry の一種·學名).

yaga (夜蛾), *n.* 【蛾】 the owlet-moth.

yagai (野外), *n.* ❶ (原野) a field. ❷ (郊外) the outskirts [environs] of a town. ―野外の, field; open-air; outdoor. (野外の景色, a rural scene.) ¶ 野外演習, field-practice. (野外演習日, 【軍】 a field-day.) ―野外劇, an open-air theatre. ―野外競馬, a steeple-chase. ―野外寫生, outdoor sketching. ―野外遊戯, field-sports.

yagakkō (夜學校), *n.* a night-school; an evening-school.

yagaku (夜學), *n.* learning at night; night study. ―夜學に行く [通ふ], to attend a night-class [night-school].

yagate (軈て), *ad.* presently; shortly; before long; in due time.

yagen (藥研), *n.* a druggist's mortar; a muller.

yagi (山羊), *n.* the goat; a he [billy]-goat (牡); a she-goat (牝). ¶ 山羊皮, a goatskin; a kid (手袋·靴用); a chevrette (手袋用). (山羊皮の手袋, kid gloves; kids.)

yagō (屋號), *n.* a shop-name; a firm-name; a trade-name.

yagu (夜具), *n.* bedclothes; bedding.

yagura (櫓), *n.* ❶ (矢倉) (武庫) an armoury. ❷ (城樓) a castle-tower; a turret; a keep. ❸ (火見櫓) a fire-tower. ❹ (相撲櫓) a tower at a wrestling-booth. ❺ (炬燵櫓) a foot-warmer frame.

yagurumagiku (矢車菊), *n.* 【植】 the blue corn-flower; the corn-bottle.

yagyō (夜業), *n.* night-work. ―夜業する, to work at night. ―夜業をやめる《始める》, to give up 《commence》 night-work. ¶ 夜業組, a night shift (day shift の對).

yagyū (野牛), *n.* the buffalo; the wild ox.

yahan (夜半), *n.* midnight; noon of night. ―夜半前の眠, beauty-sleep. ―夜半に, at midnight; at dead of night.

yahari (矢張), *ad.* ❶ (亦) too; also; as well; likewise (同樣). ❷ (猶) still; all the same; none the less; after all (結局). ―私も矢張りさう, So am [do] I.

yahi (野鄙な), *a.* vulgar; low-bred; rude; boorish. ―野卑な言葉を使ふ, to use vulgar [gross] language.

yahō (野砲), *n.* a field-gun; a field-piece. ¶ 野砲兵, a field-artillery. (野砲兵隊, a field-battery.)

yai (やい), *int.* hi; hey. ―やい待て, Hi, I say, wait. ―やい, 何をしやがる, Hey! What are you up to?

yaiba (刃), *n.* the blade; the steel; a sword (刀). ―刃にかゝって死する, to die by another's sword. ―刃を交へる, to cross swords [one's steel] *wit.*.

yain (夜陰), *n.* night; night-shade. ―夜陰に乘じて, under cover [screen] of night; by night.

yaito (灸), *n.* =*kyū* (灸).

yaiyai (やいやい), *ad.* hard; urgently; pressingly. ―やいやい迫附〔ツ〕く, to press hard.

yaji (彌次), *n.* ❶ (人) (*a*) (應援) supporters; rooters 〔米·卑〕; barrackers: (*b*) (わいわい連の) busybodies. ❷ (事) (*a*) hooting; barracking: (*b*) mocking; disturbing (演說等の); catcalling (芝居等の). ―野球の彌次, a baseball-fan〔米〕. ¶ 彌次馬連, busybodies; a mob; a rabble.

yajin (野人), *n.* a rustic; a boor; a bumpkin; a yokel. ―野人禮に嫺〔ナラ〕はず, A boor does not observe etiquette.

yajiri (鏃), *n.* an arrow-head; the barb of an arrow; a pile.

yajiru (彌次る), *vt.* to hoot; barrack; deride; jeer *at*; catcall.

yajū (野獸), *n.* a wild beast.

yakai (夜會), *n.* an evening party [reception]; a soirée; a ball (舞踏會). ―天長節の夜會, the Emperor's Birthday Ball. ―夜會を催す, to give [hold] an evening party. ¶ 夜會服, an evening dress.

yakamashii (喧しい), *a.* ❶ (騷騷しい) noisy; uproarious; turbulent. ❷ (小言多き) fault-finding; captious; carping. ❸ (嚴格な) strict; severe; hard. ❹ (むづかしい) particular; nice; fastidious. ―やかましい主人, a hard master. ―喧しい問題, a subject of much discussion. ―政府の處置に喧しく反對する, to cry out clamorously

against governmental measures.
yakan (夜間), *n.* night-time; night. ——, *ad.* at 《by》 night. ¶ 夜間開場, opening at night. —夜間撮影, night photographing.
yakan (藥鑵), *n.* a (tea-)kettle. ¶ 藥鑵頭, a bald head; a pate as bald as an egg [a coot].
yakara (族), *n.* ❶ (一族) a family. ❷ (手合) a set.
yakata (館), *n.* a mansion; a castle.
yakatabune (屋形船), *n.* a house-boat; a pleasure-boat.
yakazu (家數), *n.* = ***kosū***.
yake (燒), *n.* ❶ (燒ける事) burning. ❷ (空の) glow. ❸ 【自暴】 desperation; despair. —自暴で, from despair. —やけに熱い, [*a.*] awfully hot. —やけに降る, to rain cats and dogs. —自暴になる; 自暴を起す, to become [grow] desperate; give oneself up to despair; be driven to desperation *by*. (失敗の結果自暴になった, Failure drove him to despair.)
yakeato (燒跡), *n.* the site of a fire; a burnt place; a burn.
yakebokkui (燒木杭), *n.* a charred pile. —燒木杭には火がつき易い, "Charred wood soon takes fire."
yakebokori (燒埃), *n.* dusts rising from a burnt place.
yakebutori (燒太り), *n.* Ⓢ 燒起り. prosperity after a fire.
yakedasareru (燒出される), *vi.* to be burnt out; be burnt out of house and home.
yakedo (火傷, 湯傷), *n.* a burn (火傷); a scald (湯傷). —火傷の痕, a scar left by a burn 《scald》. —火傷する, to burn 《scald》 oneself; get burnt. (手を湯傷する, to scald one's hand.)
yakehibashi (燒火箸), *n.* red-hot tongs.
yakei (夜警), *n.* night-guard (事); a night-watchman (人). —夜警をする, to mount night-guard; keep night-watch. ¶ 夜警團, a group of night-watchmen.
yakei (夜景), *n.* a night-view; a night-scene. ¶ 夜景畫, a night-piece; a nocturne.
yakeishi (燒石), *n.* a hot stone; lava (熔岩). —燒石に水, "All is lost that is put in a riven dish."
yakekoge (燒焦), *n.* a burnt spot; a burn. —著物に燒焦げをこしらへる, to burn a hole in one's clothes.
yaken (野犬), *n.* an ownerless dog; a homeless [pariah] dog; a wild dog. ¶ 野犬狩, the hunting up of homeless dogs.
yakeno (燒野), *n.* a burnt field; a burnt prairie.
yakenokori (燒殘), *n.* remains after a fire. —燒け殘る, to remain unburnt; escape a fire.
yakeochiru (燒落ちる), *vi.* to burn and fall; be burnt down.
yakeru (燒ける), *vi.* ❶ to burn. ❷ (變色) to be discoloured. ❸ (嫉妬) to be envious 《jealous》. ❹ (空が) to glow. —眞赤に燒けた, red-hot. —燒けて堪らぬ, to be bursting with envy 《jealousy》.
yakeshini (燒死), *n.* death by fire. —燒死する, to be burnt to death; perish in the fire [flames].
yaketsuchi (燒土), *n.* burnt earth [soil]; burnt ground.
yaketsuku (燒附く), *vi.* to burn; scorch. —燒け附く様な太陽, the burning [scorching] sun.
yakeyama (燒山), *n.* a burnt hill; a dormant volcano (休火山); an extinct volcano (死火山).
yakezake (自暴酒), *n.* drinking out of despair; drowning one's grief in cups. —やけ酒を飲む, to drink out of despair; drown one's grief in cups.
yaki (燒), *n.* roasting; toasting baking (パン・粘土など); tempering (刃など). ¶ 九谷燒, Kutani wares. —伊太利《印度》燒, Italian 《Indian》 pottery.
yakiba (燒刃), *n.* ❶ (燒いた刃) a tempered edge. ❷ (刃の上にある波紋の如き模様) a cloud.
yakiba (燒場), *n.* (火葬場) a crematory; a crematorium.
yakiban (燒判), *n.* ❶ a brand. ❷ a brand; a brand-iron; a branding-iron.
yakie (燒畫), *n.* a poker-work; a pyrogravure.
yakigote (燒鏝), *n.* a hot-iron a smoothing iron; a cautery iron (醫療用); a searing iron (同上).
yakigushi (炙串), *n.* a spit; a skewer.
yakiharau (燒拂ふ), *vt.* to burn away [down]; destroy by fire lay in ashes. —市街を燒き拂ふ, to lay a city in ashes; raze a city to the ground.
yakiimo (燒芋), *n.* baked potatoes. ¶ 燒芋屋, a potato-baker a baked-potato shop.
yakikorosu (燒殺す), *vt.* to burn to death.
yakimashi (燒增), *n.* (寫眞の) further copies of a photograph.
yakimochi (燒餅), *n.* ❶ (炙りたる餅) roast rice-cake. ❷ (嫉妬) jealousy. —燒餅が燒ける, to burn with jealousy. —燒餅を燒く, to be jealous. ¶ 嫉妬喧嘩, a quarrel caused by jealousy. —燒餅燒き, a jealous woman 《man》.

yakimodosu (燒戻す), *vt.* to anneal; attemper.

yakimoki (焦思する), *vi.* to be [feel] impatient; worry oneself; be in suspense. —やきもきさす, to keep a person in suspense.

yakimono (燒物), *n.* ceramic ware (土器·陶器·磁器等); pottery (陶器). ¶ 燒物師, a potter.

yakin (冶金學), *n.* metallurgy. ¶ 冶金學者, a metallurgist.

yakin (夜勤), *n.* night-duty.

yakinaoshi (燒直し), *n.* ❶ rebaking; warming over. ❷ (改鬪) a (literary) rehash. —燒き直す, ① to rebake; warm over. ② to rehash.

yakiniku (燔肉), *n.* steak; roast (meat); broil.

yakishio (燒鹽), *n.* baked salt.

yakisugiru (燒過ぎる), *vt.* ❶ to overbake; overroast; overdo. ❷ (寫眞を) to overprint; solarize (曝光のため).

yakisuteru (燒棄てる), *vt.* to burn up; commit to the flames.

yakitsugi (燒接), *n.* cementing broken china by baking. ¶ 燒接屋, a china-mender.

yakitsuke (燒附), *n.* ❶ (陶器の) enamelling. ❷ (鍍金) plating. ❸【寫眞】printing.

yakitsukeru (燒附ける), *vt.* ❶ to fix by baking. ❷ (陶器) to enamel. ❸ (鍍金) to plate. ❹【寫眞】to print.

yakitsukusu (燒盡す), *vt.* to burn up [away]; consume by fire; lay in ashes.

yakiuchi (燒打), *n.* attacking and burning; burning. —燒打ちをする, to burn down; attack and set on fire.

yakka (藥價), *n.* the price of medicine; the charge for medicines; a medical fee (藥禮).

yakkai (厄介), *n.* ❶ (面倒) trouble; annoyance. ❷ (世話) dependence: care; charge. —厄介な, troublesome; annoying; burdensome. —厄介になる, ① (邪魔) to be a trouble [burden] *to*. ② (世話) to be under the care of; be dependent *upon*; be a burden *on*. —厄介を掛ける, to give trouble *to*. —厄介拂ひをする, to get rid of some trouble ((a nuisance)); see the back *of*.

yakkan (約款), *n.* a stipulation; an article; a clause. ¶ 保險約款, policy conditions [clauses].

yakkan (譯官), *n.* an official interpreter.

yakki (躍氣), *n.* zeal; enthusiasm; eagerness. —躍氣になる, to be excited; become [glow] eager; get warm; be furious. (躍氣になって運動する, to canvass with great zeal.)

yakko (奴), *n.* ❶ (下部, 下男) a servant. ❷ (やつ) a fellow; a chap.

yakkyoku (藥局), *n.* a dispensary; a pharmacy; an apothecary's [a chemist] shop. ¶ 藥局方, pharmacopœia. (日本藥局方, Pharmacopœia Japonica.)

yakō (夜光の), *a.* noctilucent; noctilucid. —夜光の玉, a noctilucent gem. ¶ 夜光蟲,【纖毛】Noctiluca (學名).

yakō (夜行), *n.* ❶ going by night. ❷ (夜行列車) a night-train. —夜行する, to go [travel] by night. —夜行で行く, to go by a night-train.

yaku (厄), *n.* ❶ (災難) a misfortune; a calamity. ❷ =*yakudoshi* (厄年).

yaku (役), *n.* ❶ (官職) an office; a post. ❷ (職務) duty; function. ❸ (芝居の) a character; a part; a rôle. ❹ (效用) use; utility; service. —役に立つ, ① [*a.*] useful; serviceable; efficient (腕のある); able (同上). ② [*v.*] to be useful [serviceable]; be of use [service]; answer the ((one's)) purpose; be good *for*. —役に立たぬ, ① [*a.*] useless; unserviceable; good-for-nothing. ② [*v.*] to be useless; be of no use; be of no avail; count for nothing. —ハムレットの役を勤める, to play [act] Hamlet. —通辯の役を務める, to act as interpreter.

yaku (約), *n.* a promise; an engagement; a pledge (誓). ☞ *yakusoku* (約束).

yaku (約), *ad.* about; some. ☞ *ōyoso*.

yaku (葯), *n.*【植】an anther.

yaku (譯), *n.* ❶ (飜譯) translation; rendering; version. ❷ (通譯) interpretation.

yaku (燒く), *vt.* ❶ (燒失) to burn. ❷ (放火) to set on fire; set fire *to*. ❸ (焦がす) to scorch. ❹ (炙る) to roast; broil; toast (狐色に); bake (パン·煎餠·燒芋など). ❺ (陶器·煉瓦を) to bake; burn; fire. ❻ (炭を) to make; produce. ❼ (寫眞を) to print. ❽ (死骸を) to cremate. ❾ (妬む) to be jealous ((envious)) *of*. ❿【醫】to cauterize; burn. —燒くが如き炎天に曝される, to be exposed to the burning [parching; scorching] sun. —鳥を燒く, to broil [roast] fowl. —パンを燒く, to bake ((toast)) bread.

yakuba (役場), *n.* a village ((town)) office.

yakubi (厄日), *n.* ❶ (魔日) an

unlucky day; a black day. ❷ (農家等にて天候等の厄難多しとする日) a critical day.

yakubun (約分), *n.* 【數】 abbreviation; reduction of a fraction. —約分する, to abbreviate.

yakubun (譯文), *n.* a translated sentence; a translation; a version; a rendering.

yakubutsu (藥物), *n.* medicines; medicament; *materia medica* 【羅】. ¶ 藥物學, pharmacology; *materia medica* 【羅】.

yakubyō (疫病), *n.* a pestilence; a plague. ☞ *ekibyō*. ¶ 疫病神, the god of plague.

yakudoku (譯讀), *n.* translation. —譯讀する, to translate *into*.

yakudoshi (厄年), *n.* an unlucky year; a critical age; a climacteric. ¶ 大厄年, the grand climacteric (西洋にては滿六十三歲).

yakugaku (藥學), *n.* pharmacy; pharmacology; pharmaceutics. ¶ 藥學士《博士》, a master 《doctor》 of pharmacology. —藥學校, a school of pharmacy; a pharmaceutical school.

yakugen (約言), *n.* ❶ summary; summing up. ❷ =*yakusoku*. —約言する, to speak briefly; sum up; summarize.

yakugo (譯語), *n.* words [terms] used in a translation.

yakuharai (厄拂ひ), *n.* ❶ (厄落し) exorcism. ❷ (人) an exorcist; a beggar who exorcises.

yakuhin (藥品), *n.* medicines; drugs; chemicals. ⌈ry's shop.⌉

yakuho (藥舖), *n.* an apotheca-

yakuin (役員), *n.* an officer; an official; the staff (總員); a person in charge (當務者). ¶ 役員賞與金, bonuses to officials.

yakujo (躍如たる), *a.* vivid. —躍如たらしむ, to vivify.

yakujō (約定), *n.* a contract; an agreement; a covenant; a promise; an engagement. —約定する, to promise; agree; contract; make a contract; enter into an agreement. ¶ 約定利率, the agreed rate of interest. —約定書, a written contract; a deed of contract; a bond. (假約定書, an *ad referendum* contract.)

yakume (役目), *n.* duty; function; office; a rôle; a part. —お役目的に, perfunctorily. —...するのは動脈の役目である, It is the function of the arteries to.... —役目を果す, to discharge one's duties [functions].

yakumi (藥味), *n.* spices; condiments; seasoning; flavouring. ¶ 藥味入れ, a castor; a cruet.

yakunin (役人), *n.* an (a government) official; an officer; a placeman (屢々輕蔑的に). ☞ *kanri* (官吏). —役人風を吹かす, to stand on one's official authority. ¶ 同役人, fellow-officials. —役人根性, an official spirit; bumbledom.

yakuotoshi (厄落し), *n.* exorcism. ⌈fee.⌉

yakurei (藥禮), *n.* a medical

yakurō (藥籠), *n.* ❶ (藥箱) a medicine chest. ❷ =*inrō*. —自家藥籠中の物とする, to get a person under one's thumb.

yakuseki (藥石), *n.* medicines; medical treatment. —藥石效なく今朝死去仕候, (In spite of medical treatment) he passed away this morning.

yakusha (役者), *n.* a player; an actor; an actress (女). —役者になる, to go on the stage; walk the boards; tread the stage [boards]. —役者をやめる, to retire from the stage; leave the boards.

yakusha (譯者), *n.* a translator.

yakushin (躍進する), *vi.* to advance by rushes; rush on.

yakushitsu (藥室), *n.* a powder [cartridge]-chamber; a chamber.

yakusho (役所), *n.* a public office; an office.

yakushu (藥種), *n.* drugs. ¶ 藥種屋, a druggist; a drug-store (店).

yakusō (役僧), *n.* an inferior priest; an assistant-priest.

yakusō (藥草), *n.* a medicinal herb; a simple.

yakusoku (約束), *n.* ❶ a promise; an agreement; an engagement; an appointment; a pledge. ❷ (條件) condition. —約束の堅い人, a man of his word. 前世からの約束事, a predestined event; one's fate decreed from a former life. —約束通り, as promised; true to one's word [promise]. —約束の時までに, by the appointed time. —約束する, to promise; agree; make a promise [an engagement]; give [pledge, pass] a person one's word; enter into an agreement. —約束を守る, to keep one's promise; keep one's word; be as good as one's word. —約束を破る, to break one's promise. —約束を果す, to fulfil one's promise; make good one's word; meet one's engagement; redeem one's pledge. ¶ 約束手形, a promissory note; a note of hand; a note. —約束郵便, contract mail; second-class postal matter 【米】.

yakusū (約數), *n.* 【數】a measure; an exact measure [divisor].

yaku-suru (扼する), *vt.* ❶ (制する) to command; have the command *of*. ❷ (取挫ぐ) to defeat; crush; conquer. —敵の咽喉を扼する, to have the enemy by the throat.

yaku-suru (約する), *v.* ❶ (約束) to promise; agree. ❷ (省略) to abbreviate; contract; omit (省く). ❸【數】to abbreviate.

yaku-suru (譯する), *vt.* to translate; render; metaphrase (逐語的に). —佛蘭語に譯する, to translate [turn; render] it into French.

yakutō (藥湯), *n.* a medical bath.

yakutoku (役得), *n.* a perquisite; an apanage, appanage.

yakuwan (扼腕する), *vi.* to roll up the sleeves (with chagrin).

yakuwari (役割), *n.* ❶ (分擔) allotment of parts [duties]. ❷【劇】cast. ❸ (役) a rôle; a part. —役割を定める, to allot duties; design parts; cast.

yakuyō (藥用), *n.* medical use. ¶ 藥用葡萄酒《石鹼》, medicated wine 《soap》. —藥用植物, a medical plant; a simple.

yakuyoke (厄除の), *a.* protecting against misfortune. —厄除けの御符, a charm against misfortune.

yakuza (やくざな), *a.* useless; worthless; good-for-nothing; scrub-by (つまらぬ); trashy. ¶ やくざ者, ① (人) a good-for-nothing (fellow); a ne'er-do-well; a bad egg【俗】. ② (物) coarse things; a trash; wretched stuff.

yakuzai (藥劑), *n.* a medicine. ¶ 藥劑官, a pharmacist; an army 《a naval》 pharmacist. —藥劑師, a pharmacist.

yakyū (野球), *n.* baseball. ¶ 野球部, the baseball department. —野球團, a baseball team; a nine. —野球場, a baseball ground; a field. —野球狂, a baseball fan. —野球リーグ, a baseball league. —野球選手, a (picked) baseball player. —野球試合, a baseball match. (野球試合をする, to hold a baseball match.)

yama (山), *n.* ❶ a mountain (普通五千呎以上); a hill (普通五千呎以下); a mount; a peak (峯); a height (高地). ❷ (山林) a forest. ❸ (鑛山) a mine. ❹ (堆積) a pile; a heap. ❺ (投機) speculation; spec; adventure (冒險). ❻ (絶極) the climax. —帽子の山, the crown. —山の樣な大浪, a mountainous wave; a mountain of a wave. —山の多い國, a mountainous [rough] country. —やまで買ふ, to buy on speculation. —山が當る, to turn out a good spec; strike oil; hit the mark. —山が外れる, to miss the mark. —山の如く積上げる, to pile in a heap.

yamaai (峽), *n.* a gorge.

yamaarashi (豪猪), *n.* 【哺乳】 the porcupine.

yamabato (やまばと), *n.* 【鳥】 the turtle(-dove).

yamabiko (山彥), *n.* an echo. —山彥が響く, Echoes resound.

yamabiraki (山開), *n.* ❶ (山道をつくること) making a road through a mountain. ❷ (その年に始めて登山を許すこと) the first permission of the year for ascending a mountain.

yamabuki (棣棠花, 山吹), *n.* 【植】Kerria japonica (學名). ¶ 山吹色, bright yellow.

yamabushi (山伏), *n.* ❶ (山中に宿る) taking one's abode in a mountain; retiring into a mountain 《forest》. ❷ (修驗者) an itinerant priest.

yamadaka (山高帽), *n.* a derby; a bowler. —山高の, high crowned.

yamadashi (山出し), *n.* ❶ (山より出すこと) sending from a mountain. ❷ (產地よりの新來) new arrivals from the habitat. ❸ (ぽっと出) a rustic; a bumpkin. —山出しの下女, a maid newly come from the country.

yamadera (山寺), *n.* a temple in a mountain.

yamadori (山鳥), *n.* 【鳥】 the Hondo copper pheasant

yamaga (山家), *a.* a house 《village》 in a mountain.

yamagara (山雀), *n.* 【鳥】 the Japanese tit.

yamagarasu (山烏), *n.* ❶ (山にをる烏) a mountain crow. ❷【鳥】(はしぶとがらす) the oriental raven. ❸【鳥】(みやまがらす) the eastern rook.

yamagi (山氣), *n.* speculative spirit. —山氣ある, speculative. —山氣を出す, to be tempted to speculate; become speculative.

yamagobō (商陸), *n.* 【植】 the Indian poke.

yamagoshi (山越), *n.* crossing a mountain 《hill》.

yamaguni (山國), *n.* a mountainous [hilly; rough] country.

yamai (病), *n.* ❶ (疾病) illness; sickness; a disease; a disorder. ❷ (癖) a habit. —病に罹る, to fall [get; be taken] ill. —病を推して働く, to work in spite of one's illness. —病には勝たれぬ,

"Sickness is every man's master."

yamaimo (薯蕷), *n.* 【植】 Dioscorea japonica (yam の一種·學名).

yamainu (山犬), *n.* ❶【哺乳】 the Japanese wolf. ❷ (野犬) a wild dog.

yamaji (山路), *n.* a mountain-path. —山路を辿る, to trace [go along] a mountain-path.

yamakagashi (赤棟蛇), *n.* 【爬蟲】 Natrix tigrina (學名).

yamakaji (山火事), *n.* a forest (hill) fire.

yamakujira (山鯨), *n.* (猪肉) the wild boar's flesh.

yamakuzure (山崩), *n.* a landslip; a landslide; a landfall.

yamame (やまめ), *n.* Ⓢ やまべ. 【魚】 the trout; the *yamabe* 【日】.

yamamayu (天蠶蛾), *n.* ❶【昆】 the Japanese oak silk-moth (蛾); the *yamamai* silkworm (蛆). ❷ (繭) the cocoon of a wild silkworm; the *yamamai*.

yamamichi (山道), *n.* a mountain-path; a pass.

yamamomo (山桃), *n.* 【植】 the red candleberry-myrtle.

yamamori (山盛), *n.* a high pile [heap]; brimfulness (液體). —枡に山盛りにする, to fill up a measure; pour into a measure to the brim (液體を).

yamaneko (山猫), *n.* the wild cat.

yamanokami (山の神), *n.* ❶ the god of a mountain. ❷ (妻) an old woman; a Xanthippe.

yamanote (山の手), *n.* a hilly district; the suburbs (郊外); a bluff (海河を見下す所). ¶ 山の手線, a suburban line; a hilly district line

yamaoku (山奥), *n.* the depth [recess] of a mountain.

yamaoroshi (山颪), *n.* a wind blowing down a hill.

yamasemi (山翡翠), *n.* 【鳥】 the Oriental spotted kingfisher.

yamashi (山師), *n.* ❶ =*kōzan* (鑛山師). ❷ (投機師) a speculator; an adventurer (冒險家). ❸ (山木賣買業者) a dealer in forest wood. ❹ (野師) a quack; a charlatan; a mountebank. ¶ 山師會社, a wild-cat company.

yamashii (疚しい), *vi.* to have a guilty conscience; have qualms of conscience; be ashamed *of* (恥ぢる). ——, *a.* guilty; painful.

yamate (山手), *n.* =*yamanote*. —横濱山手十五番, No. 15, the Bluff, Yokohama.

Yamato (大和, 倭), *n.* Japan. ¶ 大和魂, the Japanese spirit; the soul of Japan. —大和民族, the Japanese [Yamato] race.

yamatsunami (山津浪), *n.* a landslip; a landslide.

yamatsutsuji (山躑躅), *n.* 【植】 the Indian rhododendron [azalea].

yamawake (山分にする), *v.* to divide equally; go halves (*with*); go shares [share and share alike].

yamayoi (山醉), *n.* mountain-sickness.

yamayuri (山百合), *n.* 【植】 the gold-stripe lily.

yamazakura (山櫻), *n.* the wild cherry.

yamazato (山里), *n.* a mountain village; a village in a mountain.

yame (止·罷·廢め), *n.* stop. ❶ (廢止) abolition. ❷ (中止) cessation; discontinuance. ❸ (終止) end. ❹ (絶つこと) abstention. ❺ (斷念, 拋棄) abandonment.

yameru (止·罷·止める), *vt.* to stop. ❶ (廢止) to abolish. ❷ (終止) to stop; discontinue; cease; desist *from*; end; bring to an end; put an end [a stop] *to*; terminate. ❸ (絶つ) to abstain *from*; give up. ❹ (斷念, 放棄) to abandon; give up. —止め!, (號令) Stop!; Easy all! (漕方など). —止めろ!, Drop it! —急に止める, to stop short; stop suddenly. —官[職]を罷める, to retire from office; resign one's post. —業を罷める, to discontinue one's occupation. —目論見を止める, to lay aside a design. —仕事を止める, to leave off work. —酒を止める, to give up drinking; abstain from wine. —商賣《教師》をやめる, to give up business 《teaching》. —こゝで止めにしませう, Let us leave off here!

yamesaseru (止·罷·廢めさせる), *vt.* to stop (another) *from*; dismiss (解職). —惡行を止めさせる, to turn another away from evil practices. —煙草を止めさせる, to stop his smoking; stop him from smoking. —說論して爭を罷めさせる, to reason persons out of a quarrel.

yami (闇), *n.* dark(-ness). —子故の闇に迷ふ, to be led astray by love for one's child. —事件を闇から闇に葬る, to dispose of a matter in ambiguous circumstances.

yamiagari (病上り), *n.* (事, 時) convalescence: (人) a convalescent. —病上りの, convalescent.

yamikumo (闇雲), *ad.* at random; at hazard; rashly.

yamitsuku (病附く), *v.* ❶ (罹病) to be taken ill; fall ill [sick]. ❷ (心醉し始める) to take fancy *to*; be infatuated *with*.

yamiuchi (闇討), *n.* ❶ an attack in the dark. ❷ =*fuiuchi*. —

闇討を喰はす, to attack in the dark; attack from ambush.

yamiyo (闇夜), *n.* a dark [moonless] night. ☞ *anya.*

yamō (夜盲-症), *n.* 【醫】 nyctalopia; night-blindness.

yamome (寡婦), *n.* a widow; a relict.

yamoo (鰥夫), *n.* a widower.

yamori (守宮), *n.* 【爬蟲】 the Japanese gecko (學名).

yamu (止·已·罷む), *vi.* to stop; cease; come to stop; die (out) (風·聲等が); end (終る). 一雨が止む, It stops [leaves off] raining; The rain stops [leaves off]. 一風が止む, The wind goes down [dies away].

yamu (病む), *vi.* to be taken ill; fall ill. 一病める, diseased; sick.

yamunaki (已むなき), *a.* Ⓢ 已むを得ぬ. unavoidable; inevitable. 一已むを得ない事情, unavoidable circumstances.

yamunaku (已むなく), *ad.* Ⓢ 已むを得ず. unavoidably; inevitably. 一已むなくば, if need be; if unavoidable.

yana (魚簗), *n.* a kiddle; a lasher; a weir, wear; a fish-trap.

yanagi (柳), *n.* 【植】 the willow. 一柳に風と受け流す, to parry a question. ¶ 柳行李, a wicker trunk.

yanase (簗瀬), *n.* a shallow current where a weir is set.

yanchan (やんちゃん), *n.* mischievousness; naughtiness; wantonness (我儘): a wanton fellow; a naughty [mischievous] boy. 一やんちゃんな, mischievous; naughty; unruly.

yane (屋根), *n.* a roof; a roofing; the house-top. 一屋根裏の部屋, an attic; a garret. 一屋根傳ひに行く, to walk from roof to roof. 一瓦《藁》で屋根を葺く, to roof a house with tiles 《straw》. ¶ 屋根船, a house-boat. 一屋根替, re-roofing. 一屋根瓦, a roof [roofing] tile. 一屋根板, a shingle. 一屋根屋, a roofer; a thatcher (藁葺の).

yangotonaki (やんごとなき), *a.* noble; exalted; august. 一やんごとなき御方, an exalted personage.

yani (脂), *n.* ❶ (樹の) resin; gum. ❷ (煙草の) nicotine. ❸ (眼の) eye-wax. 一脂の强い煙草, tobacco with strong nicotine.

yanikkoi (やにっこい), *a.* weak; delicate; frail.

yaniwa (矢庭に), *ad.* suddenly; all of a sudden; abruptly. 一矢庭におッとる, to snatch; seize. 一矢庭に飛びつく, to fly *at*; pounce.

Yankī (洋鬼), *n.* a Yankee.

yanma (やんま), *n.* a dragon-fly.

yanoasatte (明明後日), *n.* three days hence [from to-day]; next day but one after to-morrow; two days after to-morrow.

yanone (矢根), *n.* an arrow-head. ¶ 矢根石, a flint arrow-head.

yanushi (家主), *n.* a landlord (of a house); the owner of a house.

yaṅyato (やんやと), *ad.* with applause. 一やんやと賞める, to give hearty cheers.

yaochō (八百長), *n.* a got-up affair; a (double-)cross. 一八百長をやる, to fight a cross; play a prize. ¶ 八百長競技, a hippodrome 【米·卑】. 一八百長相撲, a double-cross wrestling-match.

yaomote (矢面), *n.* the front line of archers. 一矢面に立つ, to stand before a bowman's mark. (攻撃の矢面に立つ, to stand exposed to abuse; bear the brunt of an attack; stand in the breach.)

yaora (やをら), *ad.* ❶ (靜かに) quietly; gently. ❷ (徐に) slowly; deliberately.

yaoya (八百屋), *n.* ❶ a green-grocer. ❷ (萬屋) Jack of all trades; a dabbler in all kinds of knowledge (學問の). ¶ 八百屋物, green stuff; vegetables.

yaoyorozuno (八百萬の), *a.* numberless; innumerable; countless. 一八百萬の神, myriads of deities.

yara (やら), *conj.* (また, 或は) and; or. ——, (噂) they say; it is said; I am told; I hear.

yarai (矢來), *n.* a palisade; a stockade; a picket-fence. 一矢來を結ふ, to set up a palisade. ¶ 竹矢來, a bamboo-palisade.

yarai (夜來), *ad.* since last night; throughout the night; overnight. 一夜來の雨で, by the rain which has fallen since last night.

yare (やれ), **yareyare** (やれやれ), *int.* o!; oh!; well! 一やれ嬉しや, Oh! How glad I am!; Oh! How delightful. 一やれやれと胸撫で下ろす, to feel a sense of relief. 一やれ嬉しやと思ふ間もなく, no sooner did the first flush of joy was over than.... 一やれやれこれでやッと一安心だ, Now I feel relieved by this.

yari (槍), *n.* (武器) a spear; a lance; a pike; a dart (投槍); a javelin(同上). 一十文字槍, a cross-headed spear. 一槍の穗, a spear-head. 一槍の柄, a spear-handle [-shaft]; a pikestaff. 一槍で突く, to spear; lance; tilt.

yariau (遣合ふ), *vi.* ❶ to operate [manage] mutually; cooperate (共

同作業). ❷ =*arasou* (爭ふ).

yaribanashi (遣放し), *n.* leaving unfinished [half-done] (半途); leaving in disorder (不始末); non-interference (無干渉). —遣放しにする, to leave unfinished [half-done]; leave in disorder; leave [let] alone.

yaridama (槍玉にあげる), ❶ to spit on a spear. ❷ to make a victim for an attack (a rebuke).

yarihago (遣羽子), *n.* battledore and shuttlecock.

yarikake (遣掛), *n.* ❶ (起首) beginning; opening; commencement; outset. ❷ (未了) being unfinished. ☞ *shikake*. —遣り掛けの, ① first; early; incipient. ② unfinished; half-done (半やりの). —遣り掛ける, to begin (to do); commence; set about (著手); set *to* (同上). (やりかけた事をうッちゃッて置く, to leave unfinished what one has begun.)

yarikata (遣方), *n.* a manner (of acting); a way (of doing); a method; a course.

yarikiru (遣切る), *vt.* to finish; complete; go through *with*; carry out. —遣り切れない, to be unable to get along (遣ッて行けない); be too much [hard] *for*; be unable to stand [bear] (耐へられない); be intolerable (同上).

yarikomeru (遣込める), *vt.* to confute; (put to) silence; put down; floor.

yarikuri (遣繰), *n.* shifting; makeshift; tiding(-over). —財政の遣繰り, financial makeshift. —遣繰りする, to make (a) shift; shift; tide over; temporize. —遣繰りが旨い (拙い), to be skilful (poor) at shifting. ¶ 遣繰算段, cutting and contriving; contrivances. —遣繰身代, a fortune kept by makeshifts.

yarinage (槍投), *n.* 【競技】 throwing the javelin.

yarinaosu (遣直す), *vt.* to do again [over; over again; once more]; try again; have another try [go]; begin again [anew].

yarisaki (槍先), *n.* a spear-head. —槍先の功名, exploits [deeds] of arms.

yarisokonai (遣損), *n.* failure; miscarriage; a bungle; a miss. —遣り損ふ, to fail *in*; mismanage; bungle.

yarisugiru (遣過ぎる), *v.* ❶ (仕過ぎる) to do too much; overdo; go too far. ❷ (與へ過ぎる) to give too much.

yarisugosu (遣過ごす), *vt.* to let pass a person ahead of one. —機會を遣り過ごす, to miss [let slip] an opportunity.

yarite (遣手), *n.* ❶ (手腕家) an able man; a man of ability. ❷ (仕手) a performer; a doer. ❸ (與へる人) a giver; a donor.

yaritori (遣取), *n.* exchange; give and take. —遣取りをする, to give and take; exchange. (書面の遣取りをする, to write to each other; exchange letters with each other.)

yaritōsu (遣通す), *vt.* to carry through; go through *with*; follow out.

yaritsuzukeru (遣續ける), *vt.* to do (anything) uninterruptedly [continuously]; keep on [up]; follow out.

yarō (野郎), *n.* a fellow; a rustic. —この野郎, You rascal!

yaru (やる), *vt.* ❶ 【與】 (與へる) to give; present. ❷ 【遣, 行】 (爲る) to do; commit; perform; practise (實行する又は營む). —旨く (拙く) 行る, to do well (ill; badly). —同じ筆法で行る, to do [dispose of] in a similar way. —手紙を遣る, to send [write] a letter *to*. —醫者をやる, to practise medicine. —醫者を呼びにやる, to send for a doctor. —毎月五十圓宛やる, to allow a person fifty *yen* a month. —君のやりさうなことだよ, That is just like you. —やるぞ! さあ, やれ! "Ready!" "All right, come on!" —少ないが君にこれをやる, Here is something for you. —此本は誰にやるのだ, Whom [Who] is this book (intended) for?

yāru (ヤール), *n.* a yard (yd. と「略す).

yarusenai (遣瀬ない), *a.* inconsolable.

yasagashi (家探), *n.* searching a house; domiciliary search. —家探しをする, to search a house; make domiciliary search.

yasagata (優形), *n.* a thin [slender; spare; delicate] figure [form]; a graceful figure.

yasai (野菜), *n.* vegetables; greens. ¶ 野菜ソップ, a vegetable soup.

yasaki (矢先), *n.* ❶ (鏃の) an arrow-point. ❷ =*yaomote* (矢面). ❸ (間際) the point; the moment. —思ッた矢先, just at the moment when I thought so.

yasa-shii (優しい), *a.* ❶ (柔和) gentle; tender; quiet. ❷ (優雅) delicate; graceful. ❸ (深切) kind; kind-hearted. —優しい言葉 (眼; 聲), soft [tender] words (eyes; voice). —氣立のやさしい娘, a sweet-tempered girl. ——**-shiku**, *ad.* ❶ gently; tenderly. ❷ delicately. ● kindly. —やさしくしてやる, to show a person kindness; be gentle *to*.

yasashii (容易しい), *a.* easy; simple; plain. ☞ *heii*.

yasasugata (優姿), *n.* a graceful figure; a delicate appearance.

yasechi (瘠地), *n.* barren [sterile; poor] soil; unproductive land; worn land.

yasegaman (痩我慢), *n.* strained endurance. —痩我慢にも, for the life of me. —痩我慢する, to endure from pride [self-will].

yasei (野生の), *a.* wild; uncultivated; ferine; feral; undomesticated. —野生の狀態,【動·植】state of nature. —野生する, to grow wild; grow without cultivation. ¶ 野生動物, wild animals; ferine beasts; animals.

yasei (野性), *n.* unpolished nature.

yasejotai (痩世帶), *n.* a poor household; small means; straitened circumstances. —痩世帶を張る, to keep up one's poor household; live in straitened circumstances.

yasen (野戰), *n.* a plain battle; field operations; field warfare. ¶ 野戰病院, a field-hospital. —野戰電信《電話》, a field-telegraph 《-telephone》. —野戰衛生隊, a field-bearer company; an ambulance corps. —野戰砲兵, a field--artillery. —野戰鐵道, a field--railway. —野戰郵便, field-post [-mail]. (野戰郵便局, a field post--office.)

yaseru (瘠·痩せる), *v.* ● (身體が) to become thin [lean]; lose flesh; dwindle; be emaciated. ● (土地が) to become sterile; be impoverished. —瘠せた, ① thin; lean; spare; lank; gaunt; skinny; meagre; tabid (病氣で). ② sterile; infertile; barren. —痩せさす, to emaciate; let down [reduce] flesh; impoverish (地味を). —痩せ衰へる, to become emaciated; waste [pine] away. —痩せ衰へた, emaciated; peaked. —痩せても枯れても一城の主である, Poor as he may be, he is the lord of a castle.

yaseude (痩腕), *n.* ● a thin arm. ● (鈍腕) poor ability; poor earning power. —痩腕には苦しい, to be too much for one's limited capacity.

yasha (夜叉), *n.* 【梵】Yaksa; a demon; a devil.

yashago (玄孫), *n.* a great-great--grandchild 《-grandson; -granddaughter》.

yashi (椰子), *n.* 【植】the cocoa--nut palm; (實) a cocoa-nut.

yashi (香具師, 野師), *n.* a show-man; a mountebank; a quack; a charlatan. —野師的, quackish; charlatanic(-al).

yashiki (屋敷), *n.* ● (邸地) a compound; premises; the grounds. ● (館) a mansion; a residence. ● (外人商館) a foreign firm. ¶ 屋敷町, residential quarters.

yashin (野心), *n.* ● ambition. ● (陰謀) designs. ● (逆心) treachery; treason. —野心勃々たり, to burn with ambition. —野心に驅られる, to be egged on by ambition. —野心を抱く, to be ambitious; fly high; have ambition. (ヤップ島に野心がある, to have designs upon Yap.) ¶ 野心家, an ambitious 《a treacherous》 person; a high-flier.

yashinau (養ふ), *vt.* ● (養育) to bring up; foster; rear. ● (給養) to support; maintain; provide *for* (糧を與ふ); keep (飼ふ); feed (飼養). ● (滋養) to nourish.

yashino (箭竹), *n.* 【植】Arundinaria japonica (Ningala bamboo の類·學名).

yashiro (社), *n.* a *Shintō* shrine.

yashoku (夜色), *n.* night scenery.

yashoku (夜食), *n.* supper. —夜食をたべる, to take supper.

yashu (野手), *n.* 【野球】a fielder; a fieldsman. ¶ 內《外》野手, an in 《out》-fielder.

yashu (野趣), *n.* rusticity; rurality; rural taste. ——**-aru**, *a.* rural; rustic; pastoral. —野趣ある畫, a pastoral picture.

yashū (夜習), *n.* night-study. —夜習する, to study at night.

yashū (夜襲), *n.* a night attack. —夜襲する, to make a night attack [assault] *on*.

Yaso (耶蘇), *n.* Jesus. ☞ *Kirisuto*.

yasu (魚扠), *n.* a fish-spear; a leister; a harpoon. —魚扠で突く, to leister; harpoon.

yasubushin (安普請), *n.* jerry--building; flimsy building. —安普請の, jerry-built; flimsily built.

yasude (馬陸), *n.* 【多足】the myriapod; the milliped.

yasudomari (安泊), *n.* a cheap inn; a common lodging-house; a doss-house (木賃宿). —安泊りに寢る, to doss.

yasui (安·廉い), *a.* ● (安意) peaceful; quiet; tranquil. ● (廉價) cheap; inexpensive; low; low--priced. —安き心地する, to feel easy 《peaceful》.

yasui (易い), *a.* ● (容易) easy; simple; light. ● (傾向を有す, …し勝ち) apt to; liable to; prone to; ready to. —お易い御用, It is no trouble. —初心の人は間違

をし易い, Beginners are liable to make mistakes.

yasuku (安く), *ad.* cheaply; cheap; at a low price [figure]. —安く積る, to value at a low rate. —安く見る, to underrate; value low.

yasumaru (休まる), *vi.* ❶ (心) to be set at ease [rest]; feel relieved. ❷ (休息) to repose.

yasumaseru (休ませる), *vt.* to suspend; make a pause; give a rest; give person a holiday; excuse a person from his duties. —人《馬; 機械》を休ませる, to give a person 《horse; machine》 a rest. —今日は休まして頂きたい, I wish to be excused from my duties to-day.

yasumeru (休める), *vt.* ❶ (休息) to repose; rest; give a rest. ❷ (安神) to ease; set at ease [rest]. —腦を休める, to rest one's brains. —骨を休める, to rest from one's labour; rest oneself. —身體を休める, to give one's body a rest. —氣を休める, to relieve a person's mind.

yasumi (休), *n.* ❶ (休息) rest; recess; repose. ❷ (休日) a holiday; a vacation (休暇). ❸ (中止) suspension; pause. ❹ (缺席) absence. ❺ (ストライキにて職工の) a play. ❻ (蠶眠) moulting.

yasumono (安物), *n.* ❶ (安價な物) a low-priced [cheap] article. ❷ (粗惡な物) an inferior article. —安物買ひの錢失ひ, "Cheap bargains are dear."

yasumu (休む), *vi.* ❶ (休憩) to rest; take a rest; take a breath; pause. ❷ (缺席) to be absent *from*; not to attend; stay away *from*. ❸ (就寢) to go to bed; turn in. ——, *vt.* (中止) to suspend; discontinue. —休め, (號令) Stand at ease! —お休みなさい, Good night. —休む間もない, to have no time to rest. —仕事を休む, to rest from one's labours [work]. —學校を休む, to absent oneself from school; stay away from school.

yasunjiru (安んじる), *vi.* ❶ (滿足) to be contented *with*; be satisfied *with*; content oneself *with*; rest satisfied *with*. ❷ (安心) to be at ease [rest]; rest assured. ——, *vt.* to set at ease [rest]; relieve. —安んじて, contentedly; trustingly; at ease; in peace. —宸襟を安んじ奉る, to relieve the Emperor's heart; set the Emperor's heart at ease. —人の心を安んぜしむる, to set a person's heart at rest.

yasuppoi (安っぽい), *a.* (安價) cheap: (價値·重み少き) mean; insignificant; paltry. —人を安っぽく見る, to hold a man cheap.

yasuraka (安らかな), *a.* ❶ (安穩) peaceful; tranquil; calm; restful. ❷ (安意) free from trouble [care]; easy. —安らかな御代, a peaceful reign. —安らかな眠, a calm slumber; a quiet sleep.

yasuri (鑢), *n.* a file; a rasp (大目の); a grail (櫛屋用). —鑢をかける, to file; rasp away [off]. ¶ 鑢紙, emery-paper; sand-paper. —鑢工, a filer. —鑢布, emery-cloth.

yasuri (安利), *n.* low interest.

yasuukeai (安請合), *n.* a ready [light-hearted] promise. —安請合をする, ① to undertake light-heartedly; make a promise without deliberation. ② (しがち) to be too ready to promise. —安請合の尻拔け, "A man apt to promise is apt to forget."

yasuuri (安賣), *n.* selling cheap; sacrifice (捨賣). —安賣をする, to sell cheap [at a low price]; sell at a bargain [sacrifice]. —大見切大安賣, great bargains.

yasuyasu (易易, 安安), *ad.* with ease; without difficulty (難なく); without effort (苦も無く). —易々と成功する, to win success with ease; accomplish without effort.

yatai (屋臺), *n.* ❶ a roofed car. ❷ (踊屋臺) a dancing-car.

yataimise (屋臺店), *n.* a (an open air; a street) stall; a booth.

yatara (矢鱈に), *ad.* ❶ (無差別) indiscriminately; promiscuously. ❷ (亂暴) wildly; recklessly; amuck. ❸ (無考へ) heedlessly; thoughtlessly. ❹ (澤山) profusely; prodigally (浪費). ❺ (過度に) excessively; immoderately. —矢鱈に褒める, to be ready to praise; praise ungrudgingly. —無暗矢鱈に撃つ, to fire at randon [haphazard]; shoot recklessly.

yatate (矢立), *n.* a portable ink and pen case; an inkhorn.

yatō (野黨), *n.* the opposition; a non-ministerialist party; the outs.

yatoi (雇), *n.* ❶ (雇傭) employment; hire. ❷ (雇人) an employé, employee. ❸ (雇職員) a government employé. ¶ 文部省御雇敎師, an instructor in the employ of the Educational Department. —雇外國人, a foreign employé. —雇ひ婆, a charwoman.

yatoiire (雇入), *n.* engagement; employment. —雇入れる, to engage; take (into one's service); charter (船を); ship (海員を).

yatoinin (雇人), *n.* an employee, employé; a servant; a hired man 《woman》; a domestic (家僕). ¶ 雇人口入所, a servant's registry office; a register-office 【米】; an intelligence office 【米】.

yatoinushi (雇主), *n.* an employer; a master; a hirer; a governor 【俗】.

yatou (雇ふ), *vt.* to engage; employ; take; hire (一時的); retain (辯護士等を). 一雇はれてゐる, to be in another's employ [service; pay]. 一下女《下男》を雇ふ, to take [engage] a maid 《man》. 一船を雇ふ, to hire a boat [sampan].

yatsu (奴), *n.* a fellow; a creature; a chap; a thing. ——, *pron.* he; she; one.

yatsuatari (八當りする), *vi.* to run amuck *at* [*against*]; fly out *at* [*against*]; run foul all around *at*; vent one's anger at random.

yatsubo (矢壺, 矢坪), *n.* ❶ (矢筒) a quiver. ❷ (矢を放つ覘場所) the aim of an arrow.

yatsude (八手, 八角金盤), *n.* 【植】 Fatsia japonica (學名).

yatsugashira (八頭), *n.* 【植】 (a variety of) the taro.

yatsugashira (戴勝), *n.* 【鳥】 the hoopoe.

yatsugibaya (矢繼早に), *ad.* in rapid [quick] succession.

yatsukuchi (八口), *n.* the open part of the sleeve under the arm.

yatsumeunagi (八目鰻), *n.* 【魚】 the small lamprey [lampern]; the sand-piper. ¶ 川八目鰻, the river lamprey; the lampern.

yatsureru (窶れる), *vi.* to become emaciated; pine away; waste away; be worn out. 一窶れた, gaunt; haggard; emaciated; care-worn; worn-out. 一見る影もなく窶れる, to be worn to a shadow.

yatsushirosō (やつしろさう), *n.* 【植】 the clustered bell-flower.

yatsusu (俏·窶す), *v.* ❶ (化粧) to adorn oneself. ❷ (扮裝) to disguise oneself *as*. ❸ (身心を砕く) to give oneself up *to*; devote oneself *to*. ❹ (行儀をくづす) to make oneself at home. ❺ (字體をくづす) to write a character in a simplified form. 一乞食に身を窶して, under the disguise of a beggar.

yattekuru (やって來る), *vi.* to come (along); make one's appearance; put in an appearance. 一やって來たぞ (朋輩などに長上の來たことを警告する語), [*int.*] *cave* 【羅.=beware】. 一そらやって來た, There, it has come. 一少しやって來給へ, Come and see me sometimes. 一向から A 君がやって來た, Here comes Mr. A.

yattemiru (やってみる), *v.* to try; have a try; attempt; make an attempt [trial]; venture *upon*; try one's hand *at*; have a go [fling] *at*.

yattenokeru (やって退ける), *vt.* to finish; accomplish; make out. 一立派にやって退ける, to accomplish splendidly; perform one's part to one's credit; acquit oneself to one's credit.

yatto (やっと), *ad.* ❶ (漸く, 遂に) at last; at length; finally. ❷ (骨折りて) with difficulty; laboriously. ❸ (辛うじて, 纔に) barely; narrowly; just; only. 一やっと及第する, to scrape through the examination; manage barely to pass. 一やっと逃れる, to have a narrow escape; escape barely. 一やっと分った, I see it now. 一やっと十三歲位です, He is barely [scarcely] thirteen. 一彼はやっと當選した, He was elected by a narrow majority.

yattoko (鋏), *n.* pincers, pinchers; nippers (小さき); pliers.

yattsukeru (やっつける), *vt.* ❶ (行ふ, 遣る) to do; go at. ❷ (負かす) to beat; put down (やりこめる); floor (同上); silence (默らす). ❸ (殺す) to do *for*; settle another's hash; despatch. 一やっつけろ!, ① (續けて, 盛に) Go it (while you are young)! ② (倒せ) Down with him 《the tyrant; the aristocrats》!

yawa (夜話), *n.* a talk at night; a night talk. ¶ 亞剌比亞夜話, the Arabian Nights' Entertainments; the Thousand and One Nights.

yawarageru (和げる), *vt.* ❶ (柔にする) to soften; temper; moderate; qualify; dilute (水など割る); dulcify (性質など); subdue (光線·色など). ❷ (緩和) to pacify; appease; palliate. 一言葉を和げる, to soften one's voice. 一苦痛を和げる, to palliate [relieve] pain.

yawaragu (和ぐ), *vi.* ❶ (柔になる) to soften; moderate; be tempered. ❷ (緩和) to be alleviated; be palliated; abate. ❸ (穩になる) to calm [cool] down; relent.

yawaraka (柔かな), *a.* ❶ (柔軟) soft; tender (肉など); downy; ductile (展性ある). ❷ (穩·軟な) gentle; mild. ❸ (色·音など) mellow; lambent; light. 一柔かな皮膚, a soft skin. 一柔かい煙草, mild tobacco. 一軟かい感じ, a soft touch. ——-**ni**, *ad.* ❶

(柔かく) softly; downily. ❷ (靜かに) gently; mildly; meekly; 【音】*piano* 【伊】. —柔かにな《す》る, to become 《make》 soft; soften. —柔かに煮る, to boil tender; braise (野菜を肉と). —お手やはらかに, Don't be too hard on me.

yawatashirazu (八幡知らず), *n.* a maze; a labyrinth.

yawayawa (柔柔), *ad.* softly (軟かに); gently (靜かに); pliantly (しなやかに); slowly (徐々に). —柔々した, soft; gentle; pliant.

yaya (稍, 較), *ad.* ❶ (多少) more or less; in some degree [measure]; something; somewhat; in a certain degree. ❷ (少し) a little; a bit. —良[や]ありて, after a while; a little after. —良久しく, for a good while; for a long time. —彼の謠は稍ゝ物になってる, His *utai* is something like.

yāyā (やあやあ), *int.* ❶ (やや) oh!; dear me! ❷ (呼かけ) hallo!; hear me!; listen!

yayamosureba (動もすれば), apt *to*; liable *to*; prone *to*. —動もすれば怒る人だ, He is a man prone to anger.

yayu (揶揄する), *vt.* to banter; chaff; play *with*; make fun *of*.

yayū (野遊), *n.* an excursion; a picnic. —學校生徒の野遊, a school-treat; a school-excursion.

yazen (夜前), *n.* & *ad.* last night 《evening》.

yazukuri (家作), *n.* ❶ (家屋建築) building a house. ❷ (家の建て方) the style of a building.

yen (圓), *n.* (日本貨幣) *yen.*

yo (世), *n.* ❶ (世間) the world. ❷ (時代) an age; an era; a period; lifetime (生涯). ❸ (あの世·この世などの世) life; world. ❹ (時勢) the times; the days. —大正の世, the era of Taishō. —世の塵, worldly affairs. —世に聞えた, well known in the world; famous. —世に知られぬ, obscure; unknown. —世に逆ふ, to go against the stream [tide; times]. —世に容れられぬ, to be forsaken by the world; be shut out of society. —世に後れる, to fall behind the times. —世に媚びる[阿[おもね]る], to truckle to the times. —世に出る, ① (出世) to rise in the world; come to the front. ② (生れ出る) to see the light of the world. ③ (世間に現はる) to appear before the public. —世を渡る, to get along; walk through life [the world]. —世を厭ふ, to get weary of life [the world]. —世を捨てる, to forsake [renounce] the world. —世を益する, to benefit the world [public]. —世を憚る, to shun public notice. —世を知る, ① to know men. ② to see the world; see life. —世を去る, to leave [depart] this world.

yo (代), *n.* ❶ (世代) generation; time. ❷ (時代) an age; a period. ❸ (治世) a reign; a dynasty (王朝). —帝の代に, in [during] the reign of the Emperor.

yo (余, 予), *pron.* I; we (記者); the present writer (著者).

yo (夜), *n.* night. —夜晚く迄, till late at night. —夜が明ける, It dawns; Day breaks; Morning dawns. —夜になる, It becomes dark; Night falls [comes on]. —夜に入りて, after dark; after night 【俗】. —夜に紛れて, under cover of night. —夜を日に繼いで, night and day; day and night; at all hours. —夜を明かす, to pass a night. —心配で夜の目も合はぬ, Anxiety keeps me awake all night.

yo (餘), *n.* ❶ =*zanyo* (殘餘). ❷ (ほか) the rest; the others. **—**, *ad.* ❶ (以上, 餘り) above; over; and over; more than; upwards *of*. ❷ (後) after. —十里餘, over ten *ri*. —六萬餘, sixty thousand and odd [more]. —三十餘圓, thirty-odd *yen*. —病餘の身, a body recovered from an illness. —餘の, other.

yō (用), *n.* ❶ (用事) business. ❷ (役) use; service. ❸ (入費) expenses. —試驗用に, for experimental use. —用に立つ, ① (間に合ふ) to do; serve one's purpose. ② (有用) to be of use; be useful [serviceable]. —用に立てる, to make use of; put to use [service]. —用に立たぬ, to be useless; be of no use; be unserviceable. —用を足す, ① (便所) to wash one's hands; ease nature; obey the call of nature. ② (用事) to do one's business. —宣傳用に使ふ, to use for propaganda purposes. —何か御用が御座いますか, What can I do for you? —何の御用でお見えになりました, What business has brought you here? —用があったら呼んでくれ, Call me if I am wanted. —雜貨屋から御用を聞きに來ました, The grocer's man has come for orders.

yō (洋), *n.* an ocean; the main 【詩】.

yō (要), *n.* ❶ (要點) the main [important] point. ❷ (精髓) the essence. ❸ (必要) need; necessity. —簡にして要を得て居る, to be short [brief] and to the point.

yō (陽), *n.* ❶ (支那哲學) positive. ❷ (山南) the south of a mountain. ❸ (表面) openness.

yō (様), *n.* ❶ (様式) mode; way; manner. ❷ (種類) kind; sort. ❸ (外觀) appearance. **—-na,** *a.* like; such as; such (...as). —慈母の様な愛情, affection like a mother's. —佛の様な人, a saint of a man. —獅子や虎のやうな猛獸, beasts of prey, such as lions and tigers. —眼が痛くなるやうな緋色, such a scarlet as makes the eyes ache. **—-ni,** *ad.* & *conj.* ❶ (の如く) like; as. ❷ (爲に) so as *to*; so that...may. ❸ (恰も) as if. —常時[ﾌﾞﾝ]の様に, as usual. —若く見える様に, so as to look younger; so that I may look younger. —怪我をせぬ様に注意なさい, Take care not to get hurt. —誰も居ない様だ, No one appears to be there.

yō (癰), *n.* 【醫】 a carbuncle; an anthrax.

yō (よう), *particle.* 意志又は未來を表はす. —明日又來よう, I will come again to-morrow.

yō (よう), **yōyō** (ようよう), *int.* (褒める發聲) bravo! —よう, 大出來, Bravo! Well done.

yō (よう), *int.* (物を乞ふ時·返事を催促する時など) do; please. —よう, 空氣銃を買って頂戴よう, Please, do buy me an air-gun.

yō (能う), *ad.* =*yoku* (能く). —ようこそお出でなさい, Very glad to see you.

-yō (様), *suf.* -form; -shaped; -like.

yoakashi (夜明し), *n.* =*tetsuya.*

yoake (夜明), *n.* dawn; daybreak; break [dawn] of day. —夜明前, before daylight. —夜明に, at dawn; at daybreak; at break of day; at peep of day.

yoakindo (夜商人), *n.* a night--tradesman [pedlar].

yoarashi (夜嵐), *n.* a night-storm.

yoaruki (夜歩), *n.* a night-walk; walking about at night; a nocturnal stroll. —夜歩きをする, to walk about at night.

yoasobi (夜遊), *n.* night amusement [pleasure]. —夜遊びの好きな人, a fly-by-night. —夜遊びする, to go out for amusement at night; fly with the owl.

yōba (用場), *n.* a privy; a water--closet; one's office.

yōbai (溶媒), *n.* Ⓢ 溶劑. a solvent.

yoban (夜番), *n.* ❶ night-watch; night-guard. ❷ (人) a night--watchman; a night-porter (旅館·邸宅などの). —夜番をする, to keep night-watch; mount night--guard.

yobi (豫備), *n.* ❶ (豫備物, 隊, 兵) reserve. ❷ (豫備役) *yobi* 【日】; service in the first reserve. ❸ (準備) preparation. —豫備の, ① reserve; spare. ② preparatory; preliminary. —豫備に持ってゐる, to have anything in reserve. —豫備役に編入せらる, to be placed [put] in [be transferred to] the first reserve list; pass [go] into the reserve. ¶ 豫備判事, a deputy judge. —豫備兵, the first reserve; *landsturm* 【獨】; a first reservist [reserve]. —豫備艦, a reserve--ship; a ship in the reserve. —豫備金, an emergency fund (政府の豫備費); a contingent fund (一般商人の不時に備へる); a reserve (fund) (銀行などの支拂準備金); a rest (同上). —豫備選手, a reserve; an emergency man 【英】 (野球·クリケット戲の). —豫備試驗, a preliminary examination; preliminaries. —豫備少尉, a sub-lieutenant in the first reserve list. —豫備將校, an officer of the (first) reserve; an officer on the (first) reserve list. —豫備隊, the reserve forces; the reserves.

yobiatsumeru (呼集める), *vt.* to call together; assemble (集める); rally (再び糾合する).

yobidashi (呼出), *n.* call; calling out; summons (召喚). —呼出電話をかける, to telephone to a non-subscriber. ¶ 呼出狀, a written summons; a subpœna; a writ of subpœna.

yobidasu (呼出す), *vt.* ❶ to call; call out; summon. ❷ (召喚) to summons; cite; subpœna. ❸ (電話) to call up; ring up. ❹ (誘出) to decoy out; draw out. —電話口へ呼び出す, to ring up to the telephone.

yobigoe (呼聲), *n.* ❶ (呼ぶ聲) a call; a cry. ❷ (賣聲) a street--call; a street cry; hawker's cries. ❸ (評判) report; rumour. —一番呼聲が高い, to be considered the most promising (candidate).

yobiireru (呼入れる), *vt.* Ⓢ 呼込む. to call in.

yobikake (呼掛), *n.* calling out; accosting; addressing. —呼び掛ける, to call (out) *to*; cry *to*; address; accost.

yobimodosu (呼戻す), *vt.* Ⓢ 呼び返す. to call back; recall.

yobimono (呼物), *n.* ❶ the chief attraction [feature]. ❷【商】 leading articles; the catch.

yobimukaeru (呼迎へる), *vt.* to send *for.*

yobine (呼價), *n.* 【商】 a nominal price.

yobiokosu (呼起·喚起す), *vt.* ❶ (眠れる人を) to wake up; arouse. ❷ (感情などを) to awaken; arouse; excite. ❸ (記

憶を) to refresh [jog; touch up] (one's memory). —記憶を喚び起す, to call to memory; call [bring; recall] to mind.

yobirin (呼鈴), *n.* a (call-)bell. —呼鈴を鳴らす, to ring the bell.

yobisute (呼捨にする), *vt.* to call another's name without any honorific.

yobitateru (呼立てる), *vt.* ❶ (大聲に呼ぶ) to call out. ❷ (呼寄せる) to call [summon] a person; ask a person to come; send *for* (迎へにやる).

yobitomeru (呼止める), *vt.* to call and stop.

yobitsukeru (呼附ける), *vt.* to call; summon; send *for*.

yobiuri (呼賣), *n.* ❶ hawking; huckstery. ❷ a hawker; a huckster (特に八百屋). —呼賣りする, to hawk (about).

yobiyoseru (呼寄せる), *vt.* ❶ (招來) to summon; send *for* (使で). ❷ (呼集める) to call together; assemble. —手紙《電報》で人を呼び寄せる, to write 《wire》 for a person.

yobō (豫防), *n.* prevention; precaution. —豫防する, to prevent; keep [ward] off; take preventive measures; provide *against*; take precautions *against*. ¶ 豫防注射, preventive injection. —豫防法, a precautionary [preventive] measure; 【醫】 prophylaxis. —豫防策, a precaution. —豫防接種, 【醫】 preventive vaccination. —豫防劑, a prophylactic; a preventive; a preservative.

yobō (輿望), *n.* popularity; public credit [trust]. —國民の輿望を荷ふ, to take the nation's trust on oneself; have the support of the whole nation.

yōbo (養母), *n.* an adoptive mother; a foster-mother.

yōbō (要望), *n.* a claim; a demand. —多年の要望に應ずる, to meet [supply] a long-felt want.

yōbō (容貌), *n.* countenance; appearance; features.

yoboyobo (よぼよぼ) *ad.* totteringly; unsteadily; infirmly. —よぼよぼ歩く, to walk with tottering [unsteady; faltering] steps.

yobu (呼ぶ), *vt.* ❶ (呼掛ける) to call; call (out) *to*. ❷ (招致) to summon; bring (つれてくる); send *for* (呼びにやる). ❸ (招待) to invite; ask. ❹ (稱する) to call; name. ❺ (引きつける) to draw; attract. —呼べば聞える處に, within call [ear-shot; hail]. —呼んで來る, to bring; fetch. —醫師を呼ぶ, to send for a doctor. —醫者を呼びに行く, to go for the doctor. —名を呼ぶ, to call a person by name; call out his name. —名前を呼び上げる, to call out a person's name; call the roll. —(顧)客を呼ぶ, to draw [attract] customers. —後から聲をかけて呼ぶ, to call out to a person from behind.

yōbu (要部), *n.* the principal [important] part; the essential [vital] parts; part and parcel.

yōbu (腰部), *n.* the lumbar region; the loins.

yobuko (呼子), *n.* ❶ a bird-call. ❷ a whistle; a call. —呼子を吹く, to blow a whistle.

yobun (餘分), *n.* excess; surplus; superfluity. —餘分になる, to become superfluous. **—— -no,** *a.* excessive; surplus; extra; superfluous; spare. —餘分の仕事, extra work.

yōbun (養分), *n.* nourishment; nutriment. ☞ ***eiyōbun.***

yobyō (餘病), *n.* 【醫】 *sequela* [*pl.* -*æ*] 【羅】; a secondary disease. —餘病を併發せざる限り, unless complications set in.

yōbyōki (揚錨機), *n.* 【航】 a capstan; a windlass; a winch.

yochi (餘地), *n.* room; place; space; scope (活動·發展の); margin (同上). —議論《疑》の餘地がない, to admit [allow; permit] of no dispute 《doubt》; There is no room for dispute 《doubt》.

yochi (豫知する), *vt.* to foreknow; know beforehand; foresee; forebode (凶事を).

yōchi (幼稚), *n.* infancy. **—— -na,** *a.* infant; puerile; childish; immature (未熟な); primitive (原始的). —幼稚な考, a childish idea. ¶ 幼稚園, a kindergarten; an infant-school. (幼稚園教師, a kindergartner.) —幼稚產業, infant industries.

yōchi (用地), *n.* land (for use); land (allotted for...).

yochiyochi (よちよち), *ad.* totteringly; unsteadily.

yōchō (羊腸たる), *a.* winding; mazy.

yōchō (窈窕たる), *a.* charming; [elegant; beautiful.]

yōchō (膺懲する), *vt.* to punish; chastise. —膺懲の師, a punitive force.

yōchū (幼蟲), *n.* 【昆】 a larva [[*pl.* -æ].]

yōdai (容態, 樣態), *n.* the condition of a patient. —容體(書)を發表する, to issue a bulletin. **—— -buru,** *vi.* to give oneself airs; assume an air of importance. —容態ぶって步く, to walk with a swagger; stalk; strut;

prance. —容態ぶッた物の言ひ方をする, to have an affected [a high and mighty] way of speaking.

yodan (餘談), *n.* ❶ (話の續き) the sequel (of a story or talk). ❷ (枝話) a digression. ❸ = ***zatsudan***. —餘談は姑く措き, setting aside other matters. —餘談に亙る, to wander [digress] from the subject; make a digression.

yodan (豫斷), *n.* prejudgment; forecast (豫想). —豫斷する, to prejudge; decide previously; forecast (豫想).

yōdan (用談), *n.* business-talk. —用談があって參りました, I have come as I have some business to talk over with you.

yōdansu (用簞笥), *n.* a cabinet; a chest of drawers.

yodare (涎), *n.* slaver; slabber, slobber. —涎を流す, ① (涎をくる) to slaver; run slobber; drivel. ② (欲しがる) to gloat *on* [*upon*]; lust *for*. —聞いた丈けでも涎が出る, The very mention of it makes one's mouth water. ¶ 涎掛, a bib; a dicky; a pinafore. —涎繰り, a slabberer; a slaverer; a driveller.

yōdateru (用立てる), *vt.* to lend; advance; accommodate (a person) *with*.

yodatsu (彌立つ), *vi.* to bristle; stand on end. ☞ ***minoke***.

yodo (淀), *n.* a pool (of a river).

yōdo (用度), *n.* expenses; expenditure; outlay. ¶ 用度課, the stores department; the supply section.

yōdo (沃度), *n.* 【化】iodine. ¶ 沃度丁幾, tincture of iodine. —沃度ホルム, iodoform.

yodomi (澱, 淀), *n.* ❶ (淀) a pool. ❷ (停滯) stagnation; faltering (口籠り). ❸ (沈澱) sedimentation; settling (at the bottom); deposit (沈澱物). —淀みなく述べる, to state without stumbling [stammering; a hitch].

yodomu (澱む), *vi.* ❶ (停滯) to stagnate; be sluggish. ❷ (沈澱) to settle; deposit; subside. ❸ (口籠る) to falter; stumble.

yodōshi (夜通), *ad.* all night; throughout the night; during the whole night.

yoei (餘榮), *n.* posthumous honours.

yōeki (溶液), *n.* a solution.

yōekichi (要役地), *n.* 【法】dominant land [tenement].

yōfu (養父), *n.* an adoptive father; a foster-father.

yōfū (洋風), *n.* foreign style 《manner》; European fashion. ¶ 洋風菓子, foreign cake [confectionery].

yofukashi (夜深しする), *vi.* to keep late hours; sit up late at night; stay up till late.

yofuke (夜更に), late at night; midnight; at the dead of night.

yōfuku (洋服), *n.* foreign clothes [dress]; European clothes [costume]. ¶ 洋服地, cloth; stuff. —洋服細民, poor salaried men; the respectable poor. —洋服屋, a tailor (人); a tailor's (shop) (店).

yofune (夜船), *n.* a night-boat.

yōga (洋畫), *n.* a Western painting. ¶ 洋畫家, an oil-painter.

yōgai (要害), *n.* a stronghold; a fortress. —要害の地, a strong 《strategical》 position [place; point]; a place of strategic importance; the key of a position.

yōgaku (洋學), *n.* Western learning.

yōgaku (洋樂), *n.* Western music.

yōgan (熔岩), *n.* 【地質】lava.

yōgeki (要擊する), *vt.* to ambush; ambuscade.

yogen (餘弦), *n.* 【數】a cosine.

yogen (豫言), *n.* prophecy; prediction; prognostication. —豫言する, to foretell; predict; prophesy; prognosticate; vaticinate. ¶ 豫言者, a prophet; a seer; a soothsayer.

yōgen (揚言する), *v.* to shout out; profess; proclaim; declare openly.

yogi (夜著), *n.* bed-clothes; bed-covering.

yōgi (容儀), *n.* deportment; demeanour; manners.

yōgin (洋銀), *n.* German [nickel] silver.

yoginai (餘儀ない), *a.* = ***yamunaki***.

yoginakusuru (餘儀なくする), *vi.* (已むなく…する) to be obliged (to do); be compelled (to do). —, *vt.* (已むを得ざらしめる) to compel [force] (a person to do); oblige (a persod to do); drive (a person to do).

yogiru (過ぎる), *vt.* ❶ (通過) to pass by; go by. ❷ (横切る) to cross. ❸ (立寄る) to drop in; look in; go round.

yogisha (夜汽車), *n.* a night-train.

yogo (豫後), *n.* 【醫】prognosis. ¶ 豫後佳良《不良》, favourable 《unfavourable》 prognosis.

yōgo (用語), *n.* ❶ (術語) a term; terminology. ❷ (語法) phraseology.

yōgo (洋語), *n.* a foreign language 《word》.

yōgo (擁護), *n.* protection; defence; vindication. **—-suru**, *vt.* to defend; protect; vindicate.

—憲政を擁護する, to defend the constitutional government. ¶ 擁護者, a champion; a defender; a protector; a vindicator.

yogore (汚), *n.* a spot; a stain; a soil; a smudge; a blot.

yogoreppoi (汚れッぽい), *a.* easily soiled.

yogoreru (汚れる), *vi.* to become dirty [filthy]; be soiled; be stained; be blemished (美點が). —汚れた體, a defiled body. —汚れた著物, soiled clothes. —汚れた手で, with dirty hands.

yogosu (汚す), *vt.* to stain; soil; blot.

yōgu (用具), *n.* a tool; an instrument; implements; an appliance.

yōguruto (ヨーグルト), *n.* 〔土耳古〕 yoghoort, yoghurt, yogourt.

yōgyo (養魚), *n.* fish-farming; fish-culture; pisciculture. ¶ 養魚池, a breeding-pond. —養魚場, a breeding-place; a fish-farm; a feeding-ground.

yōgyō (窯業), *n.* ceramics, kerамics. ¶ 窯業家, a ceramist.

yoha (餘波), *n.* a secondary effect; an after-effect; a sequel. —金融逼迫の餘波で, as a secondary effect of the tightness of money.

yōhai (遙拜する), *vt.* to worship from a distance. —遙拜式を行ふ, to hold the ceremony of worshipping from a distance.

yohaku (餘白), *n.* blank (空欄); (blank) space (同上); margin (紙端の). —餘白を殘して置く, to leave blanks.

yōhei (傭聘する), *vt.* to engage.

yōhin (用品), *n.* articles (for the use of...). ¶ 學校用品, school articles.

yōhin (洋品), *n.* Ⓢ 洋物. a foreign article. ¶ 洋品店, a foreign-goods store.

yohō (豫報), *n.* preannouncement (豫告); forecast (豫想); prediction (豫言). —豫報する, to preannounce; forecast; predict.

yōhō (用法), *n.* how to use; use; directions for use.

yōhō (養蜂), *n.* bee-keeping; bee-culture; apiculture. ¶ 養蜂所, a bee-yard; a bee-garden; an apiary. —養蜂家, a bee-keeper; a bee-master; an apiculturist.

yohodo (餘程), *ad.* very; much; very much; greatly; highly; far (遙か); by far (同上); well (可なり). —餘程の, many (數); much (量); great (數量); considerable; exceeding; a great [good] deal *of*; serious (ひどい).

yōhon (洋本), *n.* a foreign book. ¶ 洋本仕立, foreign binding.

yohyō (豫表する), *vt.* to foreshow; foreshadow; betoken; forebode.

yoi (宵), *n.* an evening; the early hours of a night.

yoi (善·好·良い), ❶ (善良) good; fine; nice. ❷ (比較して) better; superior *to*. ❸ (美なる) fine; beautiful; pretty. ❹ (好ましい) pleasing; desirable. ❺ (健全) well. ❻ (十分) enough; sufficient. ❼ (正しい) all right. ❽ (許可) may. ❾ (願望) I wish; I hope. ❿ (構はぬ) not to mind; may as well; not to care. ☞ *ii* (いい). —しよい, to be easy to do. —仕なくともよい, need not do; there is no need to do [of doing]. —よい樣にする, to do as one pleases [likes] (好きな樣に); do at one's (own) discretion (考へ通り). —よいか, Ready? (支度); Understand?; See? —よし來た, All right! —歸ってもよい, You are at liberty to go home. —よい氣味だ, Serve [It serves] him (you) right. —何時でもよい, Any time will do. —行かない方が宜い, You had better not go. —外出してもよいか, May I go out? —乞食といってもよい位だ, He is little better than a beggar.

yoi (醉), *n.* intoxication; tipsiness. —醉が廻る, to grow tipsy. —醉を醒ます, to sober.

yoi (餘威), *n.* influence. —成功の餘威を以て, elated with success.

yōi (用意), *n.* ❶ (支度) preparation; arrangement; outfit (旅などの); provision (貯へ). ❷ (用心) precaution; caution; prudence. —用意!, (號令) Stand by!; Ready! —用意周到な, prudent; careful; exhaustive. —蟻は冬の用意に食物を蓄へる, Ants store up food against the winter. ——**-suru**, *v.* ❶ to prepare [arrange; provide] *for*; get [make] ready; equip oneself *for*. ❷ to take care [precaution]. —飯の用意する, to get dinner ready; serve [set] up dinner. —いざと言ふ時の用意する, to provide against the time of need; set by (money) against a rainy day.

yōi (容易), *n.* ease; facility; readiness; simplicity. —容易な, easy; ready; simple (簡易); plain (平易). —容易ならぬ件, a serious [grave] matter. ——**-ni**, *ad.* easily; with ease; without difficulty; readily. —容易に怒らぬ, to be slow to anger. —容易にヤってのける, to make a short work *of*. —さうすれば事が容易になる, That will simplify matters.

yoigoshi (宵越), *n.* being left overnight. —宵越しの錢を持たぬ, not to keep one's money overnight.

yōiku (養育), *n.* bringing up; breeding; nurture; education. —養育する, to bring up; foster; breed; nurture; educate. ¶ 御養育係, the guardian of a young prince 《princess》. —養育院, a poor-house; an asylum; an almshouse. —養育者, a fosterer; a fostress (女); a rearer; a breeder.

yoimatsuri (宵祭), *n.* the eve of a festival.

yoin (餘韻, 餘音), *n.* reverberation (音); an aftertaste; after-sensation.

yoi-no-myōjō (宵の明星), *n.* the evening-star; Hesperus; Venus.

yoippari (宵張り), *n.* sitting up late at night: a night-owl 【卑】. —宵張りの朝寢坊, late to bed and late to rise.

yoiyami (宵闇), *n.* dusk; gloaming; darkness of evening.

yoiyoi (脹腿風), *n.* 【醫】 tabes (dorsalis); locomotor ataxia.

yoizame (醉醒), *n.* recovering from intoxication. —醉醒の水を飲む, to take water to cool one's coppers 【卑】.

yoji (餘事は扨措き), setting aside other matters [things].

yōji (用事), *n.* business; errand (使の).

yōji (幼兒), *n.* a baby; an infant (七歳未滿の小兒); a nursling (乳母に對して). ¶ 幼兒預所, a *crèche* 【佛】.

yōji (幼時), *n.* childhood; infancy.

yōji (楊枝), *n.* ❶ (小楊子) a toothpick. ❷ (齒磨楊子) a tooth-brush. —楊枝を使ふ, ① to pick the teeth. ② to brush the teeth.

yōjin (用心), *n.* ❶ (注意) heed; carefulness; thoughtfulness. ❷ (警戒) caution; precaution; vigilance. ❸ (愼重) prudence; circumspection; discretion. —用心深い, ① careful; thoughtful; scrupulous. ② cautious; vigilant; watchful. ③ prudent; circumspect. —用心過ぎる, overcareful; overscrupulous; overcautious. —用心する, ① to take precautions *against*; guard *against*. ② to be prudent [circumspect]; use prudence. —用心させる, to put another on his guard *against*; warn him *against*. —用心して居る, to be on one's guard; be on the alert; be on the *qui vive*.

yojireru (捩れる), *vi.* =*nejireru*.

yojirōbe (與次郎兵衞), *n.* (翫具) a balancer.

yojiru (捩ぢる), *vt.* *nejiru*.

yojiru (攀ぢる), *v.* Ⓢ 攀上る. to climb (up); clamber; scale (城壁など梯子にて). —山を攀ぢる, to clamber up a hill.

yojitsu (餘日), *n.* days remaining; time left. —もう今年も餘日幾何もない, There are now but a few days left of this year.

yojō (餘剩), *n.* remainder; surplus; residue. ¶ 餘剩價値, 【經】 surplus value.

yōjo (養女), *n.* an adopted daughter; a foster-daughter.

yōjō (洋靛), *n.* Prussian-blue.

yōjō (養生), *n.* care [preservation] of health; sanitation; recuperation. —養生の爲に, for (the benefit of) one's health. —養生する, to take care of one's health; recuperate oneself. ¶ 養生法, sanitation; hygiene. —養生院, a sanatorium, sanitarium.

yojū (夜中), *n.* all night (long) ☞ *shūya, yodōshi*.

yōjutsu (妖術), *n.* magic; witchcraft; sorcery; black art. —妖術を使ふ, to practise sorcery; exercise witchcraft. ¶ 妖術者, a magician; a sorcerer; a wizard; a witch (女).

yoka (餘暇), *n.* leisure (hours); spare time; time to spare. —少しも餘暇が無い, I have no time to spare.

yoka (豫科), *n.* a preparatory course.

yōka (養家), *n.* an adoptive family.

yokai (豫戒), *n.* premonition; preadmonition; preliminary caution [warning] (警告). —豫戒する, to give admonition [caution; warning] beforehand. ¶ 豫戒令, a premonitory order.

yōkai (妖怪), *n.* a ghost; an apparition; a phantom; a spectre.

yōkai (容喙), *n.* interference; meddling. —容喙する, to interfere *in*; meddle *in*; put in a word; put in one's oar; interpose. —他人の容喙を許さぬ, not to allow another's interference.

yōkai (溶解, 鎔解), *n.* ❶ (固體より液體に) fusion (鎔解); liquefaction; deliquescence (潮解). ❷ (液體中に) solution; dissolution. —溶解性の, soluble. ——**-suru**, *v.* ❶ to melt; fuse; liquefy; deliquesce. ❷ to solve; dissolve. ——, *a.* liquefacient; deliquescent; dissoluble; soluble.

yokaku (餘角), *n.* 【數】 the complement (of an angle); a complementary angle.

yokan (豫感), *n.* preperception; presentiment.

yokan (餘寒), *n.* the lingering cold after the winter.

yōkan (羊羹), *n.* a fine sweet paste.

yōkan (洋館), *n.* a house built in foreign style; a European-style building.

yokare-ashikare (善かれ惡かれ), *ad.* good or bad; right or wrong; for better or (for) worse; for good or (for) evil.

yokatsu (餘割), *n.* 【數】a cosecant.

-yoke (除), protection; shelter. —鬼門除けをする, to erect a temple 《a shrine》 in the north-eastern direction 《corner》 of the site for protection against evil spirits. ¶ 風《霜》除け, a shelter [protection] against wind 《frost》.

yokei (餘計な), *a.* needless (不必要な); superfluous (餘分な); gratuitous (故なき); uncalled-for (賴まれもせぬ); unasked (同上); spare (なくてすむ). —餘計に, excessively; to excess; too much 《many》; more; superabundantly; abundantly; much. —餘計な世話を燒く, to give uncalled-for assistance. —餘計な心配をする, to borrow trouble; be gratuitously anxious *about*. —この言は餘計のものだ, The remark was uncalled-for. —餘計な口を出すな, Don't poke your nose into another man's affairs. —餘計なお世話だ, Mind your own business.

yokei (餘慶), *n.* happiness given by great virtue.

yōkei (養鷄-業), *n.* poultry-farming [-keeping]. ¶ 養鷄場, a poultry-farm. —養鷄家, a poulterer.

yōken (要件), *n.* ❶ (必要な用事) an important business; a necessary matter. ❷ (必要條件) a necessary condition; essentials; 【論】a postulate.

yōken (洋犬), *n.* a foreign dog; a dog of foreign breed.

yokeru (避ける), *v.* to avoid; shun; keep [hold] aloof; keep (away) *from*. —車を避ける, to get out of the way of a cart; make way for a cart.

yoki (豫期), *n.* ❶ (期待) expectation; expectancy; anticipation. ❷ (豫見) foresight; forecast. —豫期に反して, contrary to expectation. —豫期の如く, as one expected; as had been expected. **—— -suru,** *vt.* ❶ to expect; anticipate; calculate *on*. ❷ to foresee; forecast. —豫期して, in expectation *of*. —豫期せざる, unexpected; unlooked-for.

yōki (容器), *n.* a receptacle; a repository; a vessel.

yōki (陽氣), *n.* ❶ (時候) season; weather (天候). ❷ (春の時候) spring weather. ❸ (賑か) gaiety; merriment. ❹ (活氣) liveliness; cheerfulness; vivacity. —陽氣な, merry; gay; lively; cheerful. —陽氣になる, to wax merry; become lively [cheerful]. —陽氣に騷ぐ, to make merry. —陽氣の加減で, under the influence of the weather.

yōkiga (用器畫), *n.* geometrical [mechanical] drawing.

yokin (預金), *n.* deposit (money); money on deposit. —預金する, to deposit (money in a bank); bank. ¶ 定期預金, a fixed [time] deposit. —通知預金, deposit at notice [call]. —預金銀行, a deposit bank; a bank of deposit. —預金者, a depositor. —預金證書, a deposit receipt 〔英〕; a certificate of deposit 〔米〕. —預金通帳, a deposit pass-book.

yōkin (洋琴), *n.* a piano; a pianoforte. ¶ 洋琴家, a pianist.

yokkaku (浴客), *n.* a visitor to a spa [hot springs]; a bathing-guest; a bather.

yokkyū (欲求), *n.* desire; will. —欲求する, to desire; will.

yoko (横), *n.* ❶ (幅) width; breadth. ❷ (側面) a side; a flank. ❸ (水平) horizontality. ❹ (方向) traverse direction. ❺ (空間) space. —横二尺の箱, a box two *shaku* in width. —横の, transverse; sidelong; sideward; lateral. —横へ, ① [*prep.*] beside. ② [*ad.*] sidelong; sidewards. —横から, sideward(s); from the flank. (横から口を出す, to put in one's oar [nose]. —横から見ても縱から見ても, from all appearances; from top to toe.) **—— -ni,** *ad.* in width [breadth]; sideways; sidewards; sidewise; sidelong; laterally; horizontally; transversely. **——,** *prep.* (側に) by; beside. —横になる, to lie (down). —横に歩く, to side; walk sideways. —横に線を引く, to draw a horizontal line.

yokō (豫行), *n.* preliminary performance; a rehearsal. ¶ 豫行演習, preliminary exercises.

yōkō (洋行), *n.* ❶ (外國行) going abroad. ❷ (支那人の又は支那人と取引する店舗) a hong; a firm (商館). —私費《官費》で洋行する, to go abroad at one's private 《government》 expense.

yōkō (洋紅-色), *n.* carmine; cochineal.

yōkō (要港), *n.* a secondary

naval port. ¶ 要港部, a secondary naval station; a naval depôt.

yokoai (横合), *n.* ❶ (横手) the side; the flank. ❷ (局外) the outside. —横合へ外れる, to fly sidewards. —横合から口を出す, to interfere *in*; put in one's oar; cut in; interpose; put in a word.

yokobai (横這する), *vi.* to crawl sidewards.

yokobue (横笛), *n.* a flute; a fife.

yokoburi (横降), *n.* a driving [slanting] rain. —横降りに降る, to rain aslant.

yokochō (横町), *n.* a by-street; a side-street; an alley.

yokodaore (横倒), *n.* falling sideways [sidelong].

yokode (横手), *n.* the side. —横手を打って喜ぶ, to clap one's hands with joy.

yokodori (横取), *n.* assumption; usurpation. —横取りする, to usurp; assume; dispossess; snatch; intercept (a letter, 途中で).

yokogamiyaburi (横紙破), *n.* ❶ (事) perverseness; perversity; waywardness. ❷ (人) a perverse man; a wayward man.

yokogao (横顔), *n.* a side [half]-face; a profile; a silhouette (影の). —横顔を覗く, to look sideways into another's face.

yokogi (横木, 軫), *n.* a cross-piece; a bar (閂); a cross-bar; a cross-tree (檣頭の); a splinter-bar (軫); a ledger (足場の).

yokogiru (横切る), *vt.* to cross; go [cut] across; intersect. —横切って, across; over; athwart. —川を横ぎる, to cross a river. —線路を横切る, to go across a railway [track].

yokoguruma (横車を押す), to act wilfully [waywardly]; endeavour to have one's own way.

yokohaba (横幅), *n.* width; breadth.

yokoito (緯絲, 横絲), *n.* the weft; the woof.

yokoku (與國), *n.* an allied power; an ally.

yokoku (豫告), *n.* (a previous) notice; warning; a preliminary announcement. —豫告の通り, as already announced. **—— -suru,** *v.* to notify [announce; inform] beforehand; give notice beforehand. —一箇月前に解雇を豫告する, to give a month's notice [warning].

yokome (横目), *n.* ❶ (横見) a side glance. ❷ (秋波) sheep's eyes; ogle; leer; an amorous glance. —横目で見る, to look [eye; view] askance *at*; cast a side glance *upon*; squint *at*; leer *at* (いやらしく, 憎氣に); look out of the corner of one's eye. —横目を使ふ, to cast sheep's eyes *at*; leer *at*; ogle *at*. —横目も振らず仕事を勵む, to work hard without looking aside.

yokomi (横見), *n.* a side [sidelong] glance. ☞ *yokome.*

yokomichi (横道), *n.* ❶ (枝道) a branch road; a side road; a by-street; a side street; a byway. ❷ (議論などの) a side-issue; a byway. ❸ (邪道) wrong (way); injustice. —横道へ入る, ① to digress [wander] (from the main subject); branch out. ② (邪道に入る) to deviate [swerve] from the right way [path].

yokomoji (横文字), *n.* letters written sideways: a European letter [writing] (歐洲文字).

yokomuki (横向), *n.* turning sidewards. —横向に坐る, to sit sideways.

yokone (横痃), *n.* 【醫】 bubo; inguinal adenitis.

yokoppara (横腹), *n.* the side; the flank. —人の横腹をつゝく, to give a person a poke [dig] in the ribs. ¶ 船の横腹, the ship's side.

yōkōro (鎔鑛爐), *n.* a blast-furnace; a smelting-furnace; a furnace.

yokoshima (邪), *n.* injustice; wrong; wickedness (邪惡). —邪な, unjust; wrong; wicked.

yokosoppō (横外方), *n.* ❶ (他方面) another side [direction; quarter]. ❷ (横顔) a side-face. —横外方のことを言ふ, to speak beside the point.

yokosu (遣す), *vt.* to send; forward (送致); hand (over) (渡す); give (與へる). —今晩使を遣して下さい, Let your messenger call this evening. —今來ると云ってよこした, He has sent me word that he is coming.

yokotaeru (横へる), *v.* to lay [put; place] sideways [athwart; across]; lay; traverse.

yokotate (横縦), *n.* length and breadth. ☞ *tateyoko.*

yokotaoshi (横倒), *n.* bringing sideways down. —横倒しにする, to bring [throw] down sideways.

yokotawaru (横はる), *vi.* ❶ (横になる) to lie down; lay oneself down. ❷ (如何なる方向に) to lie. ❸ (横斷して) to lie across [athwart]. —道に横はる, to lie across the road. —南北に横はる, to lie from south to north; lie north and south.

yokotoji (横綴), *n.* oblong book-binding.

yokoyari (横槍を入れる), to put

in one's oar [nose]; chop in (with an objection).

yokozuke (横附けにする), *vt.* to put [lay; bring] alongside (船を). —玄關に橫附けにする, to bring alongside the porch.

yokozuna (横綱), *n.* ❶ (綱) a champion's belt. ❷ (人) a champion wrestler.

yokozura (横面), *n.* ❶ (顔) a side-face. ❷ (側面) the side; the flank. —横面を張る, to give a slap in the face.

yoku (翌), *a.* the next [following].

yoku (慾), *n.* ❶ (慾張) avarice; covetousness; greed. ❷ (欲望) want; desire; appetite. ❸ (情慾) passions. —慾の深い女, an avaricious woman. —慾を云へば, if I could have my wish. —慾に目がくらむ; 慾に目がない, to be blind with avarice. —慾を制する, to control one's passions. —慾を離れて考へる, to consider apart from avarice.

yoku (翼), *n.* ❶ (つばさ) a wing (鳥·飛行機の); a plane (飛行機の). ❷【軍】a flank; a wing.

yoku (良·善·能·好·宜く), *ad.* ❶ well. ❷ (立派に) nicely; splendidly. ❸ (巧に) skilfully; ably. ❹ (注意して) carefully; with care; elaborately (入念に). ❺ (深切に) kindly; cordially. ❻ (忠實に) faithfully. ❼ (屢々) often; frequently. ❽ (傾向) aptly. ❾ (一般に) generally; in general. —よくあることだが, as often happens. —良くも考へないで, without thinking it over carefully. —よく入らっしゃいました, You are welcome; How good of you to come! —よく戯談を云ふ人だね, What a man you are for jokes! —能く言ふ者能く行はず, "The greatest talkers are always the least doers."

yokuasa (翌朝), *n.* the next [following] morning. —, *ad.* on the next morning; next morning.

yokuatsu (抑壓), *n.* restraint; check; suppression; oppression. —抑壓する, to check; restrain; suppress; oppress.

yokuban (翌晩), *n.* the next evening; the following night. —, *ad.* next evening; next night.

yokubari (慾張), *n.* ❶ (事) avarice; greed; covetousness. ❷ (人) a screw; a rapacious [grasping] man; a money-grabber. ¶ 慾張り根性, greedy disposition; cupidity.

yokubaru (慾張る), *vi.* to be avaricious; be covetous; be greedy. —慾張ッた, greedy; covetous; avaricious. —慾張ッて, greedily; covetously; avariciously.

yokubō (欲望), *n.*【經】want: desire; wish. —欲望を滿たす, to satisfy [gratify] one's desire [want].

yokuchi (沃地), *n.* Ⓢ 沃土. a fertile land [soil]; a rich soil.

yokufuka (慾深), *n.* ❶ avarice; greed; covetousness. ❷ (人) a grasping man. —慾深をすると爪が抜ける, "He that grasps at too much, holds nothing fast."

yokugi (欲氣, 慾氣), *n.* avarice; greed.

yokujitsu (翌日), *n.* the next [following] day. —, *ad.* on the next day.

yokujō (沃饒), *n.* fertility; fecundity; fruitfulness. —沃饒なる, fertile; fecund; fruitful.

yokujō (浴場), *n.* a bath-room [-place]; a bath-house. ¶ 公設浴場, a public bath-house.

yokume (慾目), *n.* partial eyes; partiality. —親の慾目, a parent's partial eye. —所謂惚れた慾目で, as the proverb says "Love is blind."

yokunen (翌年), *n.* the following [next] year; the year after. —, *ad.* next year; in the year following.

yokuryū (抑留), *n.* detention; internment; confinement. —抑留する, to detain; intern; keep back; keep in custody.

yokusan (翼賛), *n.* assistance; help; support; protection. —翼賛する, to assist; help; support; protect.

yokusei (抑制), *n.* control; restraint; suppression. —**-suru**, *vt.* to control; restrain; suppress. ☞ ***sei-suru*** (制する). —欲情を抑制する, to control [restrain] one's appetite.

yokushitsu (浴室), *n.* a bath-room.

yokushurui (翼手類), *n.*【動】Chiroptera (學名).

yokusō (浴槽), *n.* a bath-tub; a bath-tank.

yoku-suru (浴する), *vi.* ❶ (あびる) to bathe *in*. ❷ (受ける, 蒙る) to be favoured; be honoured. —恩澤に浴する, to be honoured with another's favour.

yoku-suru (能·善くする), *v.* ❶ to be able. ❷ to be skilful. —字を善くする, to be good at handwriting; be clever with one's pen. —能くする所にあらず, to be beyond one's power; be too much for one.

yokutoku (慾得), *n.* mercenariness; self-interest; selfishness. —慾得づくの戀, interested [cupboard] love.

yokuya (沃野), *n.* a fertile [fat; rich] plain.

yokuyō (抑揚), *n.* ❶ (音調の) intonation; modulation; 【音】swell; rhythm. ❷ (褒貶) praise and censure.

yokuyoku (よくよく), *ad.* ❶ very carefully (注意); elaborately (入念). ❷ very (大に); exceedingly (非常に); heartily (心から). —よくよくの馬鹿者, the veriest simpleton; an unmitigated fool.

yokuyokujitsu (翌翌日), *n.* the next day but one. ——, *ad.* next day but one; two days later [after].

yokyō (餘饗), *n.* after-effect; influence.

yokyō (餘興), *n.* entertainments.

yōkyoku (陽極), *n.* 【電】a positive pole; an anode.

yōkyoku (謠曲), *n.* *utai.* ☞ *utai.*

yōkyū (要求), *n.* ❶ claim (權利に基く); demand; requirement (又必要). ❷ (要請) request. —要求する, ① to claim; demand; require; request. ② (要する, 必要とする) to demand; require; call for. —要求に應じる, to admit another's claim (許容する); comply with [meet] another's demand; accede to [comply with] another's request (頼みを聞入れる). (時代の要求に應じる, to meet the requirements of the times.) —要求を斥ける, to reject a claim. ¶ 要求者, a claimant; a demandant.

yōkyū (揚弓), *n.* a toy [miniature] bow.

yomaigoto (世迷言を云ふ), *v.* to murmur; grumble; mutter.

yōmaku (羊膜), *n.* 【解】the amnion.

yomawari (夜廻), *n.* ❶ (事) night-watch. ❷ (人) a night-watchman.

yome (嫁), *n.* ❶ (息子の妻) a daughter-in-law. ❷ (新婦) a young wife; a bride (花嫁). ❸ (妻) a wife. —嫁に貰ふ, to take in marriage. —嫁にやる, to give in marriage; espouse *to.* —嫁に行く, to marry; get married.

yome (夜目), *n.* seeing at night [in the dark].

yomeiri (嫁入), *n.* marriage; wedding.

yomena (嫁菜), *n.* 【植】Aster indicus (starwort の一種.學名).

yomenokasa (嫁の笠), *n.* 【貝】the limpet.

yomeru (讀める), *v.* ❶ (明瞭) to be legible; be decipherable. ❷ (讀み得る) to be able to read. ❸ (讀む價値ある) to be worth reading; be readable.

yomiageru (讀上げる), *v.* to read out; read aloud. —名前を讀み上げる, to read the roll.

yomiawase (讀合せ), *n.* collation by reading out. —讀み合はす, to read out for collation; check.

yomiayamari (讀誤), *n.* misreading; mispronunciation (發音誤り). —讀み誤る, to misread; read wrong.

yomichi (夜道), *n.* going by night; a night-journey.

yomigaeri (甦り), *n.* revival; resuscitation; return to life.

yomigaeru (甦る), *vi.* to come to life [oneself]; return to life; rise from the dead; revive. —甦らす, to raise from the dead; restore [recall; bring] to life; resuscitate; revive.

yomiji (黃泉), *n.* Hades.

yomikaesu (讀返す), *v.* to read over again.

yomikaki (讀書), *n.* reading and writing. —讀書き算用, reading, writing, and arithmetic; the three R's.

yomikata (讀方), *n.* (the way of) reading; pronunciation (發音); a reading lesson (學課).

yomikikasu (讀聞かす), *vt.* to read *to.*

yomikiri (讀切), *n.* ❶ (讀み終ること) finishing reading; reading through. ❷ (句讀) punctuation. ❸ (完結) completion.

yomikuse (讀癖), *n.* ❶ one's peculiarity in reading. ❷ corrupt pronunciation.

yomimono (讀物), *n.* reading; reading matter.

yominareru (讀馴れる), *vi.* to be used to reading; be familiar *with.*

yominikui (讀難い), *a.* illegible; indecipherable; hard [difficult] to read.

yomise (夜見世), *n.* a night-stall; a night-booth. —夜見世を張る, to open a night-stall. ¶ 夜店商人, a night-stall seller.

yomisu (嘉す), *vt.* to approve; appreciate; esteem.

yomite (讀手), *n.* a reader.

yomiuri (讀賣), *n.* a ballad-monger (俗謠の); a hawker of ballads (同上).

yomiya (宵宮), *n.* the eve of a festival; a vigil.

yomiyasui (讀易い), *a.* readable; easy to read (易い); legible (筆蹟).

yomo (四方), *n.* ❶ (東西南北) the four quarters. ❷ (諸方) all parts; all directions. —四方の, of all parts [quarters]. —四方に, in all directions [quarters]; on all sides.

yōmō (羊毛), *n.* wool. —羊毛製の, woollen.

yomogi (艾), *n.* 【植】 the felon-herb; the mugwort; the wormwood.
yomosugara (通宵), *ad.* all night (long); the whole night; all the night through.
yomoya (よもや), *ad.* probably; possibly; perhaps. ☞ *masaka*. —よもや見捨てはなさるまい, Surely you will not desert me.
yomoyama (四方山), *n.* ❶ (世間) the world. ❷ (雜多) all sorts. —四方山の話, gossip; small talk; desultory chat [talk].
yomu (讀む), *vt.* ❶ (讀書) to read. ❷ (吟唱) to recite. ❸ (了解) to understand; see; make out. ❹ (吟詠) to compose; indite; sing. ❺ (數へる) to count. —讀み直す, to read over again; reread. —讀落しの無い樣に, not to miss in reading. —讀みながら寢附く, to read oneself to sleep. —顏色を讀む, to read another's face. —小說を讀んで泣く, to cry over a novel. —中々英書を讀んでゐる, He is well read in English books.
yōmu (用務), *n.* business; affairs.
yōmu (要務), *n.* an important affair [business]. —要務を帶びて, on an important business《mission》.
yonabe (夜なべ), *n.* night-work. ☞ *yagyō*.
yonageru (淘げる), *vt.* ❶ to wash. ❷ =*tōta* (淘汰する).
yonaka (夜半に), *ad.* at the dead of night; at midnight.
yonaki (夜泣, 夜啼), *n.* night cry. —夜啼きする, to cry at night.
yonareru (世馴れる), *vi.* to grow used to the world; grow worldly. —世馴れた人, a man of experience.
yōnashi (用無し), *n.* ❶ (不用) disuse. ❷ (閑散) want of business. —君にはもう用無しだ, I have done with you for the future.
yondokoronai (據所ない), *a.* unavoidable; inevitable; necessary; imperative. —據所なく, unavoidably; inevitably; perforce. —據所ない事情で, for unavoidable reasons; driven by circumstances.
yonen (餘念なき), *a.* absorbed; intent; innocent (無邪氣). —餘念なく, intently; absorbedly; with the whole heart; innocently.
yōnen (幼年), *n.* infancy; childhood. ¶ 地方《中央》幼年學校, a local《central》military preparatory school. —幼年工, a child (worker).
yō-ni (陽に), *ad.* openly; ostensibly.
yonige (夜逃), *n.* moonlight-flitting (借家人の); flight by night. —夜逃げする, to flee by night; shoot the moon【卑】. ¶ 夜逃げ人, a fly-by-night.
yōniku (羊肉), *n.* mutton.
yōnin (容認する), *vt.* to admit; allow; permit; tolerate. ☞ *ninyō* (認容する).
yonō (豫納), *n.* prepayment. —豫納する, to prepay. ¶ 豫納金, prepayment money.
yononaka (世の中), *n.* the world; the public; the times (時代). —世の中に出る, to start in life.
yōon (拗音), *n.* a contracted sound.
yōon (揚音), *n.* accent.
yopparai (醉漢), *n.* a drunken man; a drunkard.
yopparau (醉ッぱらふ), *vt.* to get tipsy [drunk; intoxicated]. ☞ *you* (醉ふ).
yōraku (瓔珞), *n.* a diadem (頭の).
yōran (搖籃), *n.* a cradle. —文明《自由》の搖籃, the cradle of civilization《liberty》.
yori (撚), *n.* twist. —撚を戾す, to untwine; untwist. ¶ 三本撚, three-ply.
yori (より), *prep.* ❶ (から) from; of; off; since (以來). ☞ *kara*. ❷ (よりも) than; before. —花より外に…ない, nothing but a flower. —今日只今より, from this day, this hour. —人より物を買ふ, to buy a thing of a man. —部屋より飛出す, to rush out of a room. —日は東より出る, The sun rises in the east. —死ぬより外に途はない, There is no other way but death. —降伏するよりは寧ろ死ぬ, I would die, rather than surrender; I should prefer death to surrender.
yori (依·據り -て), ☞ *yoru*.
yoriai (寄合), *n.* ❶ =*yoriatsumari*. ❷ (集合) a meeting; an assembly.
yoriatsumari (寄集り), *n.* a group; a crowd; a gathering. —寄集まる, to gather; assemble; throng; rally; flock together.
yoridasu (選出す), *vt.* to pick out. ☞ *erabidasu*.
yoridokoro (據所), *n.* authority; a foundation; a ground; a basis. —據所のある, authorized; authenticated; reliable (確な). —據所のない, unauthentic; groundless; baseless; uncertain.
yoridori (選取), *n.* choice; picking out. —選取り一錢, one *sen* the pick. —選取りする, to pick out; choose; take one's choice.
yoriito (撚絲), *n.* twisted thread; thrown silk (絹の); singles (同上).
yorikakaru (凭掛かる), *vi.* to lean *against* [*on*; *upon*]; rest *against*; recline *on*. —壁に凭りかかる, to lean against the wall.

—机に凭りかゝる, to lean on the table.

yorikonomi (選好する), *v.* to be particular [fastidious; nice] *about*.

yorimichi (寄道する), *vi.* to call on the way; make a call on the way.

yorinuki (選抜), *n.* the choice; the pick; the selection. —選抜きの品, a select [choice] article. —選抜きの俳優, picked actors. —選り抜く, to choose; pick out; sift out.

yorisou (寄添ふ), *vi.* to go beside another; approach; draw near [close].

yōritsu (擁立する), *vt.* to support (a person in a position).

yoritsuku (寄附く), *vi.* ❶ to come near; approach. ❷ (訪れる) to come; call on 《at》.

yoriwakeru (選分ける), *vt.* to sort out; winnow; sift; assort.

yōro (要路), *n.* ❶ (肝要の道筋) an important road. ❷ (重位) an important position; the authorities (當局). —要路の顯官, high officials in important positions. —要路に立つ, to occupy an important position.

yōrō (養老), *n.* ❶ (老人を勞はり養ふこと) caring for the aged. ❷ (老後を安樂に送ること) passing one's last years free from care. ¶ 養老保險, an endowment insurance. —養老院, an asylum for the aged; an old people's home. —養老金, a retiring pension (年金); a lump sum given for past services (一時贈與金); an old-age pension (每週又は每月交付).

yoroi (鎧), *n.* an armour.

yoroido (鎧戶), *n.* a shutter; a louvre.

yoroimushi (鎧蟲), *n.* a beetle.

yorokeru (よろける), *vi.* to stagger. ☞ *yoromeku.*

yorokobashii (喜ばしい), *a.* joyful; glad; happy; delightful.

yorokobasu (喜·悅ばす), *vt.* to delight; gladden; give pleasure *to*. —…で眼《耳》を悅ばす, to feed one's eyes 《ears》 *with*.

yorokobi (喜, 悅), *n.* ❶ (喜悅) joy; gladness; rejoicing; delight. ❷ (祝意) congratulation. —心よりの喜びを述べる, to express one's heart-felt pleasure.

yorokobu (喜·悅·歡ぶ), *v.* to be glad; rejoice *at*; be delighted *by* [*with*]; be pleased *with*. —喜び輝ける顏, a radiant [beaming] face. —跳上って喜ぶ, to jump up with joy. —喜び勇む, to bustle with joy; be in the best of spirits. —喜んで, ① joyfully; with joy; gladly; delightedly. ② with pleasure; willingly; with all one's heart.

yoromeku (蹣跚く), *vi.* to stagger; reel; totter; falter. —, *a.* tottering; unsteady; groggy. —よろめき倒れる, to topple (down; over). —よろめき立つ, to stagger to one's feet.

yoron (輿論), *n.* public opinion; the popular voice. —輿論に抗する, to defy public opinion. —輿論の制裁を受ける, to be tried at the bar of public opinion.

Yōroppa (歐羅巴), *n.* Europe. ☞ *Ōshū.*

yoroshii (宜しい), *a.* ❶ (善良) good; fair. ❷ (適當) proper; fit; suitable. ❸ (可) right. ☞ *yoi.* —, *ad.* well; all right. —, *int.* all right; all serene 〔俗〕. —貴下が宜しければ, if you don't mind. —御都合宜敷候はば, if it suits your convenience; if (it is) convenient to you. —どうでも宜しい, It makes no difference [is all the same] to me.

yoroshiku (宜しく), ❶ (適宜に) suitably; properly. ❷ (須らく) should. —どうぞ皆さんによろしく, Please remember me [give my kind regards] to them; Present (to) them my compliments [respects]. —今後共何分宜しく, I beg for your further acquaintance. —よろしく召上れ, I wish you a good appetite.

yoroyoro (蹣跚, 蹌踉), *ad.* staggeringly; totteringly; falteringly. —よろよろする, =*yoromeku.*

yorozu (萬), *n.* ❶ (數) a myriad; ten thousand. ❷ (許多) a large number; a great many [deal]; myriads. ❸ (萬事) all; everything. —, *ad.* in everything; in all things. —よろづ賣典, "What's what"; "Inquire within for everything."

yorozuya (萬屋), *n.* ❶ (百貨商) (人) a general dealer; a universal provider: (店) a general shop; a jumble shop. ❷ (何でも屋) a Jack of all trades; a dabbler in all kinds; a pantologist (學問の).

yoru (夜), *n.* night. —, *ad.* at night; by night. —夜になる, The Night falls [comes].

yoru (由·依·據·因·賴る), *v.* ❶ 〔由〕 to be based [founded] *on*. ❷ 〔因〕 to be due *to*; be caused *by*. ❸ 〔據〕 to take a stand; occupy. ❹ 〔賴〕 to rely *on* [*upon*]; depend *upon*. **yori** (に據·依り-て), *prep.* ❶ (基きて) on; under; by reason *of*; on account *of*; on the ground *of*. ❷ (從って) at; with; according *to*; in accordance [compliance] *with*. ❷ (手段で) by; with; by means *of*; through (the medium *of*). —御示敎に依り, on your kind suggestion. —御依賴に依り, at your request. —貴下の御助力に依り, through your kind help. —最近の調査に據れば, according to the latest investigation. —規則に依って罰する, to punish a person according to law. —いや事に依ったら死んだかも知れぬ, Why, for all I know, he may be dead. [☞ *yorikakaru*.]

yoru (凭る), *vi*. to lean *against*.

yoru (寄る), *vi*. ❶ (近寄る) to approach; draw near. ❷ (集まる) to meet; assemble; come together. ❸ (立寄る) to look in (立寄る); drop [step] in (同上); stop *at* (汽車など); touch [call] *at* (船が); put in *at* (同上). —寄ると觸ると, whenever they meet. —片一方へ寄る, to draw to one side. —寄ってたかって打擲する, to crowd and beat him.

yoru (撚·縒る), *vt*. twist; twine; kink; throw (絹を).

yoru (選る), *vt*. to choose; pick out; single out.

yorube (寄邊), *n*. one to depend on; a friend (知己); a relative (親戚); a helper (助力者); a protector (保護者); a shelter (庇護者·所). —寄邊なき孤兒, a helpless orphan.

yoruhiru (夜晝), *n*. day and night. **——**, *ad*. night and day; always.

yorui (餘類), *n*. accomplices; confederates. [measure of capacity.]

yōryō (容量), *n*. capacity; volume;

yōryō (要領), *n*. ❶ (要點) the point; the pith; the gist. ❷ (摘要) a compendium; an epitome; a summary; an abstract. ❸ (用法) use; the knack (骨). —要領を得てゐる, to be to the purpose [point]. —要領を得ない, pointless; irrelevant; inconclusive. —要領を得た演說, a speech to the point [of pith and point].

yōryō (養療), *n*. recuperation of health. ¶ 養療院, a sanatorium, sanitarium.

yoryoku (餘力), *n*. remaining [surplus] power [strength]; reserve of energy; spare time 《money》; time 《money》 to spare. ¶ 發行餘力, margin of the issuing power. [chlorophyll.]

yōryokuso (葉綠素), *n*. 【植】

yōsai (要塞), *n*. 【軍】 a fortress; a stronghold; fortifications. ¶ 要塞地帶, the strategic zone. —要塞砲兵, garrison [fortress] artillery. —要塞司令官, a fortress commandant.

yosan (豫算), *n*. an estimate; an estimated cost; a budget (特に政府の). —豫算が狂ふ, One's estimates go wrong [amiss]. —豫算を立てる, to make an estimate. ¶ 總豫算, the general budget; the total estimates. —追加豫算, a supplementary budget. —豫算案, a budget. —豫算超過, the excess over the estimates; the budget deficit. —豫算不成立, rejection of the budget. —豫算外支出, defrayment unprovided for in the budget. —豫算委員, a budget committee.

yōsan (養蠶), *n*. sericulture; silkworm culture. ¶ 養蠶家, a sericulturist; a silk-grower. [-out.]

yōsatsu (要殺), *n*. 【野球】 force-

yose (寄席), *n*. a story-tellers' hall; a variety hall.

yoseatsume (寄集め), *n*. ❶ collection; gathering; gleaning (拾集). ❷ (混淆) medley; mixture. —寄せ集める, to collect; gather; glean.

yosegi (寄木), *n*. marquetry; a parquet. ¶ 寄木細工, ① (細工) mosaic work; marquetry; parquetry. ② (物) a marquetry [parquetry] ware; a wooden mosaic.

yosegire (寄切), *n*. odd ends [pieces] of cloth; jumble cloth. ¶ 寄切れ賣出し, a remnants bargain.

yosei (餘生), *n*. the remainder [rest] of one's life [days]; one's remaining years. —餘生を送る, to spend [pass] one's remaining years.

yosei (餘勢), *n*. force; momentum.

yōsei (要請), *n*. a request; a demand.

yōsei (養成), *n*. cultivation; training; education. **——-suru**, *vt*. to cultivate; educate; train. —人物を養成する, to cultivate men of character 《talent》. —自由の精神を養成する, to foster the spirit of liberty. ¶ 敎員養成所, a teachers' training school.

yōseki (容積), *n*. contents. ❶ (容量) capacity. ❷ (體積) volume. ¶ 容積[輕量]貨物, measurement goods [cargo] (heavy goods, 重量貨物の對). —容積量, the measure of capacity. —容積噸, measurement ton.

yosen (豫選), *n*. provisional selection [election]; preelection; primary election 〔米〕. —豫選する, to select [elect] provisionally; preelect. ¶ 豫選會, a primary (meeting) 〔米·政〕. —豫選競技, (trial) heats; trials; preliminary contests (次は semi-final, 準決勝

又は final, 決勝が行はれる).
yōsen (用箋), *n.* a blank (form); a form.
yōsen (傭船), *n.* ❶ (事) charterage. ❷ (船) a chartered ship. —傭船する, to charter a ship; hire a ship. ¶ 傭船契約 (書), a charter-party. —傭船料, charterage. —傭船者, a charterer.
yoseru (寄せる), *vt.* ❶ (片よせる) to bring [draw; put] near; bring [put] aside (傍へ). ❷ (加へる) to add (together); sum up. ❸ (集める) to collect; call together (呼び集める). ❹ (寄せつける) to let (a person) come. ❺ (書を) to send; write (a letter) *to*. —寄せ來る敵, the surging enemy. —思を寄せる, to give one's heart *to*. —身を寄せる, to become dependent *on*; shelter oneself under another's protection.
yosetsu (餘切), *n.* 【數】 a cotangent.
yōsetsu (夭折), *n.* Ⓢ 夭死. early death; premature death. —夭折する, to die young; die an early death; die prematurely.
yosetsukeru (寄附ける), *vt.* to let approach [come near]; let come; make company *with* (交る). —追手を寄せ附けぬ, to keep the pursuers at bay.
yosezan (寄算), *n.* 【數】 addition.
yōsha (幼者), *n.* an infant; a child; a minor (未丁年者).
yōsha (容赦), *n.* ❶ (赦すこと) pardon; forgiveness; forbearance. ❷ (控目にすること) reserve; restraint. —容赦する, to pardon; forgive; be reserved; keep oneself back. ——**-naku**, *ad.* unsparingly; mercilessly; unrelentingly; unforgivingly; without reserve. —容赦なく取扱ふ, to handle without reserve [gloves].
yoshi (蘆, 葦), *n.* 【植】 the (ditch) reed.
yoshi (由), *n.* ❶ (理由) reason. ❷ (趣旨) the effect; the purport; the point. ❸ (手段) a means; a way. ❹ (…の由) it is said that; I 《we》 hear that; they say that; I am 《we are》 told that. —其の由を通知する, to inform to that effect. —本日歸京の由, He is expected to return to Tōkyō to-day.
yōshi (用紙), *n.* a blank form; a blank. ¶ 申込《註文》用紙, an application 《order》 blank.
yōshi (洋紙), *n.* foreign paper; European paper
yōshi (要旨), *n* the purport; the substance; the gist; the points.
yōshi (容姿), *n.* figure; form.
yōshi (養子), *n.* an adopted child 《daughter; son》; a foster-child. —養子にゆく, to be adopted; become an adopted child *of*. —養子にする, to adopt as one's son 《daughter》.
yoshiashi (善惡), *n.* ❶ good and bad; good and wrong [evil]; right and wrong; quality (品質). ❷ (一得一失) merit and demerit. —…するのも善し惡しだ, It is doubtful whether it is good to do….
yōshiki (樣式), *n.* a mode; a form; a formula; a style; 【論】 a mood; 【建】 an order. —一定の樣式, a fixed form.
yoshikiri (葦切), *n.* 【鳥】 the eastern reed-thrush.
yoshimi (誼), *n.* intimacy; friendship. —朋友の誼を以て, for friendship's sake.
yoshin (餘震), *n.* 【地文】 the after-shocks.
yoshin (豫審), *n.* 【法】 preliminary examination. ¶ 豫審調書, the protocol of preliminary examination. —豫審判事, an examining [preliminary] judge; a *juge d'instruction* 【佛】. —豫審決定書, the written finding [decision in writing] upon preliminary examination. —豫審廷, the preliminary court of inquiry.
yōshin (養親), *n.* adoptive parents; foster-parents.
yoshinba (よしんば), *conj.* though; if; even if [though]; even supposing that. —よしんば行けたとしても何事もなし得なかったのだ, Supposing I could have gone there, nothing could have been done.
yōshinkei (腰神經), *n.* 【解】 a lumbar nerve.
yoshiya (よしや), *conj.* though; if; even if. ☞ *yoshinba*.
yoshizu (葦簀), *n.* a reed-screen; a reed-blind. —葦簀張りの茶店, a resting booth sheltered with reed.
yōsho (要處), *n.* an important point; an important position.
yōsho (洋書), *n.* a foreign [European] book.
yōshō (幼少), *n.* childhood; infancy; boyhood. —幼少の頃に, in one's infancy; in childhood. —幼少(の頃)から, from childhood [infancy]; from a child [an infant].
yōshō (要衝), *n.* an important place [position]; a focus; a point of strategic importance [advantage] (軍事上の). ☞ *yōro*.
yōshō (要償), *n.* a claim (for compensation). —要償する, to claim compensation [damages]; lay damages.
yoshoku (餘色), *n.* 【理】 a complementary colour.
yōshoku (要職), *n.* an important post; a responsible post.

yōshoku (洋食), *n.* European [Western] food. ¶ 洋食屋, a restaurant; a café.

yōshoku (容色), *n.* the face and form [figure]; the complexion (顔ばせ); figure (姿); appearance (外貌). —容色を失ふ, to lose one's rose(s); lose one's good looks.

yōshoku (養殖する), *vt.* to cultivate; rear; raise.

yoshū (豫習), *n.* preparation; rehearsal. —豫習する, to prepare lessons; rehearse.

yōshu (洋酒), *n.* foreign wine [liquors; drinks].

yoso (餘所), *n.* another place; a strange quarter. —餘所に, elsewhere; in another place. —餘所を見る, to look away [off; aside]. —人の苦勞を餘所に見る, to look unconcernedly on other's troubles. —餘所の見る目も羨し, to make even onlookers envy them. —ここには居ない, どこか餘所を探しなさい, He is not here; you should look elsewhere for him.

yosō (豫想), *n.* ❶ (豫期) expectation; anticipation; forecast. ❷ (推測) presumption; conjecture; surmise. —豫想外の, unexpected; unanticipated; unlooked-for. —豫想外に, unexpectedly; contrary to expectation (豫想に反して); beyond expectation (豫想以上に). —豫想する, to expect; forecast; presume. —豫想通りになる, to come up to one's expectation. ¶ 豫想高, estimates.

yōso (沃素), *n.* 【化】 iodine.

yōso (要素), *n.* an element; a constituent; a factor.

yōso (養素), *n.* 【生】 a nutritious [nutritive] substance; a nutrient.

yōso (癰疽), *n.* 【醫】 an anthrax; a carbuncle.

yōsō (洋裝), *n.* ❶ (書物の) foreign binding. ❷ (服裝の) foreign [Western] style of dress. —洋裝する, to be dressed in foreign style; be dressed after Western fashion. ¶ 洋裝婦人, a lady in foreign dress.

yōsobo (養祖母), *n.* an adoptive grandmother.

yōsofu (養祖父), *n.* an adoptive grandfather.

yosogoto (餘所事), *n.* another's affairs (他人事); another matter (他事). —餘所事を云ふ, to say things irrelevant to the matter; talk irrelevantly.

yosoku (豫測), *n.* estimate; forecast; presumption. —豫測する, to estimate; forecast; presuppose.

yosome (餘所目), *n.* ❶ (盗見) a stealthy look [glance]; a glance. ❷ (餘所見) looking away. ❸ (傍觀) looking-on; the eyes of others. —餘所目で見る, to steal a glance *at*. —餘所目が恥しい, to feel ashamed to be seen by others.

yosomi (餘所見する), *vi.* to look away [aside]; have one's eyes off.

yosonagara (餘所ながら), *ad.* by a hint; in a casual manner; indirectly. —餘所ながら暇乞ひをする, to take a final leave without saying so.

yosooi (裝, 粧), *n.* ❶ (身支度) equipment; outfit. ❷ (扮裝) make-up; dressing up; adornment (飾). ❸ (樣子) appearance.

yosoou (裝ふ), *vt.* ❶ (扮する) to dress up. ❷ (佯る) to feign; affect; pretend; assume; make pretence *of*. —…を裝うて, under pretence [colour; the cover] *of*…, —恐を裝ふ, to feign fear; pretend to be afraid. —船を艤ふ, to rig [equip; fit out] a ship. —平氣を裝ふ, to assume [put on] an air of indifference.

yosoyososhii (餘所餘所しい), *a.* unconcerned; indifferent; cold. —餘所々々しくする, to make a stranger of a man; treat a man with indifference; keep one's distance.

yosu (止す), *vt.* to stop; give up; leave off. ☞ *yameru*. —止せ, Don't!; Drop it! —馬鹿な事はよせ, Stop that nonsense! —よしたがよからう, I advise you to give it up. —よせばよいのに, He should have given it up [refrained from it]; He might have spared himself the trouble.

yosū (餘數), *n.* 【數】 remainder; a complement of a number.

yōsu (樣子), *n.* ❶ (狀態) state; condition; position (of affairs). ❷ (姿態) look; appearance; air; mien; attitude (態度). ❸ (徴候) a sign; an indication; a symptom. —樣子ぶって歩く, to walk affectedly; strut. —樣子を窺ふ, to see how the position is [the land lies]. —樣子が大變可笑しい, He is very strange in his manners. —彼の樣子は何だか怪しい, There is something suspicious about him. —樣子が段々よくなり始めた, Things began to look brighter. —今にも降って來さうな樣子だ, It looks as if it were going to rain every moment.

yōsui (用水), *n.* rain-water (caught in a cistern) (天水); city [service] water (水道の); water for irrigation (灌漑水). ¶ 用水池, a reservoir. —用水權, water-right. —用水渠, a mill-race (水車場の). —用水桶, a rain-tub; a rain-water tank. —用水路, a flume (工業用) [米].

yosumi (四隅), *n.* four corners.

yō-suru (要する), *vt.* ❶ (必要とする) to need; require; demand; call for; want; take (時日・人手など). ❷ (待伏する) to waylay; lie in ambush [wait]. —絶對安靜を要する, to need absolute rest. —婦女子を途に要する, to lie in wait for women. —此等の事は時間を要する, These things take time. —會員は入場料を要せず, Members admitted free.

yō-suru (擁する), *vt.* ❶ (抱擁) to embrace; take into one's arms. ❷ (擁護) to support; protect. ❸ (持つ) to possess; hold. ❹ (引率) to lead; command. —巨富を擁する, to possess an enormous wealth. —爐を擁して語る, to talk with one's hands over a brazier.

yō-suruni (要するに), *ad.* in a word; in short; in brief; to sum up; the long and short of it is that. —要するに斯うなんだ, In brief, the matter stands thus.

yosutebito (世捨人), *n.* ❶ (僧) a monk; a priest. ❷ (隱遁者) a hermit; a recluse. —世捨人となる, to renounce [retire from] the world.

yota (與太), *n.* 【卑】 ❶ (愚人) a fool; a dunce. ❷ (虛言家) a liar. —與太を飛ばす, ① (話) to speak at random. ② (仕事) to do a thing perfunctorily; scamp work.

yotaka (夜鷹, 蚊母鳥), *n.* 【鳥】 the Japanese goatsucker.

yotaku (餘澤), *n.* blessings.

yōtashi (用達), *n.* ❶ business; an errand (使ひあるき). ❷ (御用商人) a government contractor 《purveyor》. ❸ (御用聞) a roundsman. ¶ 陸軍御用達, an army-contractor. —鐵道御用達, a purveyor to the Railway Department.

yotei (豫定), *n.* ❶ prearrangement; previous arrangement. ❷ (豫想) expectation; anticipation. ❸ (豫算) estimation. —豫定の行動, preconcerted operations. —豫定の退却, a prearranged retreat. —豫定通り, as previously arranged; according to previous arrangement. —豫定する, ① to prearrange; arrange previously. ② to estimate. —豫定を變じて, changing the programme.

yōten (要點), *n.* the gist; the pith; the main [essential] point. —要點を摑む, to seize [grasp] the essence of the matter.

yotō (夜盜), *n.* (事) burglary: (人) a burglar; a night-thief.

yotō (與黨), *n.* ❶ a league; a party. ❷ (政府黨) the government party; the ministerialists.

yōto (用途), *n.* use.

yōtō (羊頭), *n.* a sheep's-head. —羊頭を懸けて狗肉を賣る, "to cry up wine, and sell vinegar."

yotogi (夜伽する), *vi.* to attend on a person at night; sit up with a person.

yotoku (餘得), *n.* Ⓢ 役得. perquisites.

yotoku (餘德), *n.* the influence of great virtue; the benefits of great merits.

yotōmushi (夜盜蟲, 地蟲), *n.* 【蛾】 the cabbage moth.

yōton (養豚), *n.* swine-keeping; hog-raising. ¶ 養豚場, a piggery. —養豚者, a swineherd.

yotsu (四つ), *n.* four.

yōtsū (腰痛), *n.* 【醫】 lumbago; crick in the back.

yotsuashi (四足), *n.* a quadruped; a four-footed animal.

yotsubai (四這ひで), *ad.* on all fours. —四這ひになる, to crawl on all fours.

yotsugi (世嗣), *n.* ❶ (相續) succession. ❷ (相續人) a successor; an heir; an heiress (女).

yotsukado (四角), *n.* cross-roads. —四角を左へ曲る, to turn the cross-roads to the left.

yotsume (四目), *n.* 【紋】 four squares. ¶ 四目錐, a square drill. —四目格子, a lattice.

yotsuori (四折の), *a.* folded in four; quarto. —四折りにする, to fold in four.

yotsuwari (四割), *n.* ❶ (四分の一) a quarter. ❷ (四分する事) quartering.

yotsuyu (夜露), *n.* the night dew.

yotte (仍・因・依って), *ad.* consequently; hence; therefore. ☞ *yori.* —依って其名あり, Hence (comes) its name.

yotto (快走船), *n.* a yacht.

you (醉ふ), *vi.* ❶ (酒等に) to get drunk; get tipsy. ❷ (恍惚となる) to be intoxicated [drunk]; be elated; be in raptures. —魚に醉ふ, to be poisoned by fish. —煙草に醉ふ, to become sick from smoking. —汽車《人》に醉ふ, to feel sick from the jarring of a train 《from the jostling of a crowd》. —人生の歡喜に醉ふ, to become drunk with the joy of life.

youchi (夜討), *n.* a night attack. —夜討をする, to attack by night.

youn (餘蘊なき), *a.* exhaustive (researches or treatment). —餘蘊なく研究する, to exhaust (a subject).

yowai (齡), *n.* age. ☞ *toshi.*

yowai (弱い), *a.* ❶ (虛弱, 薄弱) weak; delicate; feeble. ❷ (微弱)

faint. ● (脆弱) frail. ● (酒など) weak; light; thin. —弱い身體, a weak [delicate] constitution. —船に弱い人, a poor sailor.

yowaimono (弱者), *n.* a man of feeble strength; a weak person; the weak. —弱い者いぢめする, to bully the weak.

yowaisuru (齢する), *v.* to rank *with* (伍する); associate *with* (交はる).

yowaku (弱く), *ad.* weakly; feebly; faintly.

yowameru (弱める), *vt.* to weaken; enfeeble; impair; dilute (薄くする); make low (調子を).

yowami (弱味), *n.* a weakness; a weak point; a weak side. —弱身に附込んで, taking advantage of another's weak point [weakness]. —弱味を見せる, to betray cowardice; show the white feather.

yowamiso (弱味噌), *n.* Ⓢ 弱蟲. a weakling; a coward; a week [feeble] fellow.

yowane (弱音), *n.* weakness. —弱音を吹く, to draw in one's horns; say die.

yowarime (弱目), *n.* weakness; the decline of fortune (運命の). —弱り目に祟り目, "Misfortunes come one after another."

yowaru (弱る), *vi.* ● (衰弱) to weaken; grow weak [feeble]. ● (閉口) to be troubled [annoyed]; be perplexed [harassed]; be at a loss. ● (銷沈) to be downcast; be dejected. —弱り果てる; 弱りきる, to be utterly exhausted. —病氣で弱る, to be shaken [be pulled down] by one's illness. —彼奴には弱ッた, I am stumped by that fellow. —汽車の速力が弱ッた, The train slowed down. —何をそんなに弱ってゐる, What are you so downcast about?

yowasu (酔はす), *vt.* to make drunk [tipsy]; intoxicate.

yowatari (世渡), *n.* going through the world; a living; a livelihood. —世渡りする, to live; go [walk] through the world; push one's way in the world. —世渡りが上手だ, He knows how to get on in life [the world].

yowayowashii (弱弱しい), *a.* weak-looking; slender; delicate.

yoyaku (豫約), *n.* (provisional) promise; precontract; subscription (出版物の); an engagement (婚姻の). —豫約する, to precontract; subscribe *for* (books); reserve (場席·室·船腹などを); book (同上). ¶ 豫約者, a subscriber. —豫約出版, publication by subscription.

yōyaku (漸く), *ad.* ● (段々) gradually; little by little; by degrees. ● (辛うじて) hardly; barely; with difficulty. ☞ *yatto* (やッと). —漸くの事で, with difficulty; after a great deal of trouble. —漸く歩けるやうになる, to be able at last to walk.

yoyo (代代), *ad.* =*daidai*.

yōyō (漸う), *ad.* =*yōyaku*.

yōyō (要用), *n.* ● (必要, 肝要) necessity; need. ● (要件) an important matter. —要用な, ① necessary; essential; indispensable. ② important; of importance.

yōyō (洋洋たる), *a.* wide; vast; boundless. —前途洋々たり, The prospects are boundless.

yōyō (揚揚), *ad.* loftily; proudly; triumphantly; wit'. an air of self--sufficiency. —揚々として濶歩する, to prance; swagger; strut.

yoyū (餘裕), *n.* ● (剩餘) surplus; margin; play; room (餘地). ● (時日) time; time to spare. ● (平氣) composure; placidity. —餘裕がある, to have time (money; energy, *etc.*) in reserve [to spare]. —十人を容れる餘裕は十分ある, There is plenty of room for ten persons.

yozai (餘罪), *n.* another crime; other crimes; further crimes. —他に餘罪ある見込, to be suspected of other crimes.

yōzai (用材), *n.* materials; timber (材木). ¶ 建築用材, building materials.

yōzan (洋算), *n.* foreign arithmetic.

yozen (餘喘), *n.* ● (蟲のいき) faint breathing. ● (餘生, 餘命) the (few) remaining years [days]. —辛うじて餘喘を保つ, to keep barely alive in one's last days.

yu (油), *n.* oil.

yu (湯), *n.* ● hot water. ● (風呂) a hot bath; a bath-house (湯屋). ● (溫泉) a hot spring; a spa (溫泉, 溫泉場). —有馬の湯, the spa of Arima. —湯に行く, to go to a bath-house. —湯を沸かす, to boil water.

yū (尤なる), *a.* best; most excellent; prominent (顯著なる).

yū (有), *n.* ● being; existence. ● (所有) possession; ownership. —の有に歸する, to fall [come] into a person's hands [possession].

yū (勇), *n.* courage; bravery; valour. ☞ *yūki* (勇氣). —勇を鼓する, to rally [summon; pluck; screw up] one's courage; take heart.

yū (雄), *n.* ● (牡) a male. ● (英雄) a hero. ● (猛) valour; courage; bravery. ● (優越) superiority; excellence; mastery

(勝). —雄を争ふ, to contend for supremacy [mastery].

yūai (友愛), *n.* friendship; fellowship; fraternity. —友愛の, friendly; fraternal.

yuaka (湯垢), *n.* scale; fur.

yūaku (優渥なる), *a.* gracious. —優渥なる勅語を賜はる, to be honoured with a gracious speech from the Emperor.

yuba (湯葉), *n.* the bean-curd skin.

yubana (湯花), *n.* ❶ (硫黄末の結晶) incrustations in a hot spring; hot spring crystals; flowers of sulphur (硫黄華). ❷ =*yuaka*. ❸ (湯玉) a boiling-bubble.

yūbe (夕), *n.* evening; eventide.

yūbe (昨夜), *n.* & *ad.* last night; yesterday evening.

yūben (雄辯), *n.* eloquence; fluency. —雄辯なる, eloquent; fluent. —雄辯を振ふ, to speak eloquently. ¶ 雄辯術, oratory. —雄辯家, an eloquent speaker; an orator.

yubi (指, 趾), *n.* ❶ 【指】 a finger; a digit. ❷ 【趾】 a toe. —指にはめる, to put (a ring, *etc.*) on a finger. —指を染める, to put [lay; set] one's hand to the plough; take in hand; try; make an attempt. —指を銜へて見て居る, to look on with a finger in one's mouth; look with envy *at*; remain a mere looker-on (空しく傍観する). —指を折って數へる, to count on the fingers. ¶ 指サック, a finger-stall.

yūbi (幽微な), *a.* subtle; mysterious; abstruse.

yūbi (優美), *n.* grace; elegance; refinement. ——-**na**, *a.* graceful; elegant; refined. —優美な意匠, an elegant design.

yubiato (指痕), *n.* a finger-mark; a thumb-mark. —指痕をつける, to leave finger-marks; thumb (the leaves of a book).

yubihajiki (指彈), *n.* fillip; flip. —指彈きする, to fillip; flip.

yubihame (指嵌), *n.* a ring.

yūbin (郵便), *n.* post; mail. ¶ 郵便箱, a post-box; a pillar-box; a post. —郵便馬車, a mail-coach; a mail-cart. —郵便物, a postal [mail-] matter. (第一種郵便物, first-class mail-matter.) —郵便貯金, post deposit; postal savings. —郵便葉書, a postcard; a postal card. —郵便配達, ① mail delivery. ② (人) a postman; a letter [mail]-carrier. —郵便飛行, postal aviation. —郵便自動車, a motor mail-van. —郵便爲替, a post-office order; a (postal) money order. (郵便小爲替, a postal order.) —郵便禁制品, a prohibited mail-matter. —郵便切手, a postage stamp. (郵便切手蒐集, stamp collection; philately.) —郵便行嚢, a mail [post]-bag; a mail-pouch (革製); a mail-sack (布製). —郵便局, a post-office. (郵便局長, a postmaster.) —郵便列車, a mail-train. —郵便船, a mail-boat; a mail-steamer; a packet-boat. —郵便線路圖, a mail-road chart; a postal map. —郵便車, a mail-car. —郵便締切日, a mail-day. —郵便受函, a letter-box. —郵便受取所, a mail receiving office.

yubinuki (指貫), *n.* a thimble.

yubiori (指折の), *a.* prominent; eminent; leading. ☞ *kusshi*. —指折り數へる, to count on [with] one's fingers.

yūbirui (有尾類), *n.* 【動】 Caudata (學名); the tailed amphibians.

yubisaki (指先), *n.* the tip of a finger; the finger-tip. —指先の器用な人, a deft-fingered man.

yubisashi (指差), *n.* ❶ pointing with the finger. ❷ (指差札) a finger-post; an index. ❸ (印刷の) an index; a fist.

yubisasu (指す), *vt.* to point (to); point with a finger. —指して笑ふ, to laugh *at*; point *at*.

yubiwa (指環), *n.* a ring; a finger-ring. —指環をはめる, to put a ring on one's finger. —指環をはめてゐる, to have a ring on one's finger.

yubizaru (指猿), *n.* 【哺乳】 the aye-aye.

yūbō (有望), *n.* hopefulness; favourableness; high [great] promise; bright prospects. —有望の, hopeful; promising; favourable. (有望の青年, a promising youth.) ☞ *zento*.

yūboku (遊牧), *n.* nomadism. —遊牧する, to nomadize. ¶ 遊牧民, nomads.

yubune (湯槽), *n.* a bath-tub; a bath-tank; a hot-water tank.

yūbutsu (尤物), *n.* ❶ (すぐれたるもの) the best. ❷ (美婦) a beauty; a *belle* 【佛】.

yūchaku (癒著), *n.* 【醫】 adhesion; union. ☞ *yugō* (癒合). —癒著する, to adhere; heal up.

yūchi (誘致する), *vt.* ❶ (誘起) to induce; bring on; lead *to*. ❷ (おびく) to lure; decoy; entice.

yūchō (優長な), *a.* leisurely; slow; deliberate. —優長な人, a leisurely [an easy-going] person.

yūda (遊惰), *n.* indolence; laziness; sloth. —遊惰の, indolent; lazy; slothful. —遊惰に日を送る, to eat the bread of idleness; idle away one's time.

yūdachi (夕立), *n.* an evening shower; a shower (驟雨); a thunder-shower (雷を伴ふもの). —夕立がする《來る》, It showers. —途中で夕立に遇ふ, to be caught in a shower on the way.

yūdai (雄大), *n.* grandeur; magnificence. —雄大な, grand; magnificent.

yudaki (湯瀧), *n.* a hot shower-bath; a hot douche.

yudan (油斷), *n.* ❶ (不注意) inattention; incautiousness; imprudence. ❷ (怠慢) negligence; remissness. —油斷なく, attentively; watchfully; alertly. —油斷する, to be off one's guard; relax one's attention. —油斷させる, to throw [put] a person off his guard; lull another to sleep. —油斷に乘ずる, to take a person off his guard; catch another napping [asleep].

yudaneru (委ねる), *vt.* to entrust; charge a person *with*; leave to another's care. —身を委ねる, to devote oneself *to*; apply [commit] oneself *to*.

yudaru (煠·茹る), *vi.* to boil; seethe.

Yudaya (猶太), *n.* Judea; the Holy Land. ¶ 猶太人, a Jew; a Hebrew; Jewry (總稱). —猶太教, Judaism. —猶太民族, the Jewish race.

yuden (油田), *n.* an oil-field; a petroleum field.

yuderu (煠·茹でる), *vt.* to boil; seethe.

yūdō (遊動), *n.* play. ¶ 遊動病院, an ambulance hospital. —遊動圓木, a swinging-pole.

yūdō (誘導), *n.* induction; introduction; leading; 【化】 derivation; 【電】 influence. —誘導する, to induce; introduce; lead; 【化】 derive. ¶ 自己誘導, self-inductance. —誘導電氣, induced electricity. —誘導線輪, an induction-coil.

yūdoku (有毒の), *a.* poisonous; baneful; noxious; virulent; venomous; toxic.

yudono (湯殿), *n.* a bath-room.

yue (故), *n.* ❶ (理由) reason; cause (原因). ❷ (事情) circumstances. —故ありて, for certain reasons; through circumstances. —故なく, without (any) reason [cause]; gratuitously.

yuei (輸贏), *n.* victory (or defeat). ☞ *shōhai*. —輸贏を決する, to contend (with each other) for victory [mastery].

yūei (游泳), *n.* swimming; natation. —游泳する, to swim. ¶ 游泳服, a bathing-dress; a swimming-dress. —游泳場, a swimming-place [-pool]; a natatorium (室內の). —游泳者, a swimmer.

yūeki (有益な), *a.* useful; serviceable; beneficial; instructive. —有益な話, an instructive story. —金を有益に使ふ, to get the money's worth; make the best use of one's money.

yuen (油煙), *n.* lamp-soot; lamp-black.

yuen (所以), *n.* why; reason. —是れその名ある所以なり, This is the reason why it is so named.

yūen (有煙の), *a.* smoky. ¶ 有煙炭, bituminous coal; soft coal.

yūenchi (遊園地), *n.* a pleasure-garden; a pleasure-ground; a recreation-ground.

yueni (故に), *ad.* therefore; hence; consequently. ——, *conj.* because; as; for; since. ——, *prep.* on account *of*; by reason *of*; because *of*; for.

yūetsu (優越), *n.* predominance; superiority; supremacy. —優越せる, predominant; surpassing; superior. —優越する, to surpass; predominate *over*. —滿洲に於ける日本の優越(權)を確立《承認》する, to establish 《recognize》 Japan's pre-eminence in Manchuria.

yūfu (有夫の), *a.* married. ¶ 有夫の婦, a married woman.

yufuda (湯札), *n.* a bath-ticket.

yūfukuna (裕福な), *a.* rich; wealthy; well-off; opulent.

yūga (優雅), *n.* grace; elegance; refinement. —優雅な, graceful; elegant; refined.

yūgai (有害の), *a.* harmful (*to*); injurious (*to*); noxious. ¶ 有害鳥獸, noxious birds and animals.

yūgai (有蓋の), *a.* covered; closed. ¶ 有蓋貨車, a covered waggon.

yugaku (湯掻く), *vt.* to scald.

yūgaku (遊學), *n.* study. —遊學する, to study away from home; go to some place for study (どこへ).

yugameru (歪める), *vt.* to distort; bend; warp. —口を歪める, to screw up one's mouth; make a mouth.

yugami (歪み), *n.* distortion; contortion; crookedness; wryness.

yugamu (歪む), *vi.* to crook; warp; be distorted; be out of shape.

yūgao (夕顏), *n.* 【植】 the bottle-gourd. ¶ 夕顏棚, a bottle-gourd trellis.

yūgata (夕方), *n.* evening. ——, *ad.* in the evening; towards evening [the sunset; the close of the day]; at dusk.

yuge (湯氣), *n.* steam; vapour. —湯氣を立てる, to reek; steam.

yūgei (遊藝), *n.* a light accomplishment.

yūgeki (遊擊), *n.* 【軍】 a raid; diversion. ¶ 遊擊手, 【野球】 a short stop. —遊擊隊, ① 【陸】 a flying army [corps; party]. ② 【海】 a flying squadron.

yūgen (有限の), *a.* limited; terminable; finite. ¶ 有限年金, a terminable annuity. —有限責任, limited liability (Ltd. と略す). (有限責任社員, a special partner (a general partner の對).)

yūgen (幽玄な), *a.* profound; occult; mysterious.

yūgeshiki (夕景色), *n.* evening scenery.

yūgi (友誼), *n.* friendship; fellowship; neighbourliness; friendly relations. ☞ *kōgi*. —友誼に厚い, to be tender in friendship.

yūgi (遊戲), *n.* play; a sport; amusement; a game. —遊戲的氣分, a playful mood. ¶ 遊戲本能, a sportive instinct. —遊戲場, a playground; a play-court; a field.

yūgiri (夕霧), *n.* evening mist.

yugō (癒合), *n.* agglutination; adhesion. ☞ *yuchaku*.

yūgō (融合), *n.* fusion; melting down; harmony. —融合する, to fuse; melt down; be harmonious *with*.

yūgū (優遇), *n.* warm treatment; cordial [hearty] reception. —優遇する, to treat well; treat with respect; receive kindly.

yūgun (遊軍), *n.* a flying army.

yūgure (夕暮), *n.* evening. ☞ *yūgata*.

yūhan (夕飯), *n.* a supper; an evening meal.

yūhei (幽閉), *n.* confinement; incarceration; imprisonment. —幽閉する, to confine; incarcerate; imprison.

yūhen (雄篇), *n.* a great work; a masterpiece.

yūhi (夕日), *n.* the setting [westering] sun; the evening sun.

yūhi (雄飛する), *vi.* to take a great leap; soar up. —實業界に雄飛する, to take a great leap in the business world.

yūho (遊步), *n.* a saunter; a walk; a stroll. ¶ 遊步場, a recreation-ground; a promenade; an esplanade.

yūhō (友邦), *n.* a friendly nation [country].

yūi (有爲の), *a.* able; capable; efficient. —有爲の靑年, a promising [hopeful] youth.

yuibutsu (唯物的), *a.* material; materialistic. ¶ 唯物論, 【哲】 materialism. (唯物論者, a materialist.) —唯物史觀, the materialistic conception of history; historical materialism.

yūigi (有意義の), *a.* significant.

yuigon (遺言), *n.* a will; a testament; death-bed injunctions. —遺言する, to leave [make] a will. —遺言に依って, under a person's will; in conformity with his will. ¶ 遺言狀, a will; a testament; one's last will and testament. (遺言狀を作る, to make one's will.) —遺言者, 【法】 a testator; a testatrix (女). —遺言執行者, an executor [*fem.* -trix].

yuiitsu (唯一の), *a.* only; sole; single. —唯一の手段, the only measure left; one's only resource. —唯一の望, one's sole wish.

yuiitsushinkyō (唯一神敎), *n.* 【宗】 monotheism; Unitarianism.

yuimotsu (遺物), *n.* a bequest; a relic; a souvenir.

yūin (誘引), *n.* invitation; allurement; enticement. —誘引する, to invite; entice; allure.

yuinō (結納), *n.* a betrothal present. —結納を取り交す, to exchange betrothal presents.

yuiriron (唯理論), *n.* 【哲】 rationalism.

yuishin (唯心的), *a.* spiritual. ¶ 唯心論, 【哲】 spiritualism. (唯心論者, a spiritualist.)

yuisho (由緒), *n.* ❶ (來歷) history. ❷ (家系) lineage; blood; pedigree. —由緒ある, ① historic. ② of good lineage.

yuitsu (唯一の), *a.* = *yuiitsu*.

yūji (有事), *n.* emergency. —有事の日には, in case of emergency; when an emergency arises.

yūjin (友人), *n.* a friend; a companion. ☞ *tomodachi*.

yūjo (宥恕), *n.* pardon; forgiveness. —宥恕する, to pardon; excuse; forgive; condone.

yūjō (友情), *n.* friendliness; friendship; fellowship. —友情を溫める, to strengthen [promote] friendship.

yūjū (優柔), *n.* effeminacy; enervation. —優柔不斷の, irresolute; indecisive; vacillating.

yuka (床), *n.* ❶ a floor. ❷ (高座) a dais; a (temporary) platform. ¶ 床板, floor-boarding.

yūka (有價の), *a.* valuable. ¶ 有價物, valuables. —有價證券, documentary [valuable] securities.

yukai (愉快), *n.* pleasure; enjoyment; merriment. —— **-na**, pleasant; delightful; merry; exhilarating. —愉快な春, merry spring. —愉快に過ごす, to have a good [fine] time; pass one's time pleasantly. —愉快, 愉快, How pleasant, how delightful!

yūkai (誘拐), *n.* abduction; kidnapping. ——-**suru,** *vt.* to abduct (a woman); kidnap (a man or child); carry off. ¶ 誘拐者, an abductor; a kidnapper.

yūkai (融解), *n.* fusion; melting; dissolution. —融解する, to fuse; melt; dissolve.

yukan (湯灌する), *v.* to wash a dead body (with hot water).

yūkan (夕刊), *n.* ❶ an evening edition [issue]. ❷ an evening paper [press].

yūkan (勇敢), *n.* bravery; daring; dauntlessness; intrepidity. —勇敢な, brave; daring; dauntless; intrepid.

yūkan (勇悍), *n.* daring; intrepidity.

yūkan-kaikyū (有閑階級), *n.* the leisured [idle] class.

yukari (緣), *n.* relation; connection; affinity. —何の緣もない人, an utter stranger.

yukashii (懷·床しい), *a.* ❶ = *okuyukashii.* ❷ (慕はしい) lovely; sweet; charming.

yukata (浴衣), *n.* a bath-dress [-robe]; a coarse unlined garment.

yūkata (夕方), *n.* =*yūgata.*

yūkei (有形), *n.* materiality; corporeality. —有形の, material; corporeal; concrete. ¶ 有形物, a concrete (object). ☞ *yūtai.*

yūken (雄健な), *a.* stout; sturdy; vigorous. —雄健な文章, a vigorous composition.

yūken (郵券), *n.* a postage stamp. —郵券代用一割增, ten per cent. increase when paid in stamps.

yūken-gakki (有鍵樂器), *n.* a keyed instrument.

yūkensha (有權者), *n.* a voter [英]; an elector [米]: a person entitled *to*; a person qualified *for*; a person possessing the right *of*.

yuketsu (輸血), *n.* 【醫】 transfusion of blood.

yuki (行), *n.* going. —青森行手荷物, a luggage booked for Aomori. —歐洲行汽船, a steamer (bound) for Europe. —この汽車は東京行です, This train is for Tōkyō. —行きは電車で歸りは汽車でした, I went by tram and came back by train.

yuki (裄), *n.* the length of sleeves.

yuki (雪), *n.* snow; snows (積れる雪). —大雪がふる, It snows heavily; It snows thick and fast. —雪に閉ぢ[降り]込められた, snow-bound. —雪を戴ける, snow-capped. —雪の明日は裸蟲の洗濯, "After snow comes fair weather."

yūki (有期の), *a.* terminable; for a time. ¶ 有期刑, penalty for a term. —有期公債【年金】, a terminable loan 《annuity》.

yūki (有機的), *a.* organic. ¶ 有機物, an organism; organic matter. —有機化學, organic chemistry. —有機體, an organic body.

yūki (勇氣), *n.* courage; bravery; valour. —勇氣ある, courageous; brave; valiant. —勇氣づく, to hearten up; cheer up; take heart. —勇氣づける, to encourage; nerve; hearten [spirit] up. —勇氣を振ひ起す, to pluck up one's heart; summon [screw up] one's courage. —勇氣を挫く, to discourage; dispirit; dishearten.

yukiau (行合ふ), *vi.* to meet on the way; come *across.*

yukiakari (雪明), *n.* snow-blink; snow-light.

yukibakama (雪袴), *n.* snow-trousers.

yukichigai (行違), *n.* ❶ crossing. ❷ (間違) misunderstanding (誤解); a quarrel (爭ひ). —行き違ふ, to pass each other; cross. —君の手紙は僕のと行違ひになッた, Your letter crossed mine.

yukidaore (行倒), *n.* ❶ (事) dying on the road. ❷ (人) a man dying 《dead》 on the road. —行倒れになる, to fall on the road [in the street].

yukidaruma (雪達磨), *n.* a snow-man; a snow image of Dharma.

yukidoke (雪解), *n.* the thawing of snow; snow-break. —雪解けする, It thaws. —雪解で道が惡い, The thaw has made roads muddy.

yukidokoro (行所), *n.* ❶ (行方) whereabouts; the place where a person has gone. ❷ (目的地) the destination; the place to go to.

yukidomari (行止), *n.* ❶ (袋小路) a blind alley; a *cul-de-sac* 【佛】; an *impasse* 【佛】. ❷ (限點) the limit. —行止まる, to come to the end; come to an *impasse.*

yūkifuri (雪降), *n.* a snowfall.

yukigakari (行掛り), *n.* the circumstances. —行掛り上餘儀なくされる, to be compelled by force of circumstances to do so.

yukigake (行掛けに), *ad.* on one's way there [to...].

yukigata (行方), *n.* the place where a person has gone; whereabouts. ☞ *yukue* (行方). —行方知れずになった, He has gone no one knows where.

yukigakoi (雪圍), *n.* a snow-shed.

yukige (雪氣), *n.* weather threatening snow. ☞ *yukimoyō.*

yukigeshiki (雪景色), *n.* a snow-scene [-landscape]; a snow-covered landscape.

yukiguni (雪國), *n.* a snowy

country; snowy districts. [-shoes.]
yukigutsu (雪靴), *n.* snow-
yukikaeri (往復), *n.* =*ōfuku*.
yukikai (行交), *n.* going and coming. —行き交ふ, to come and go; go to and fro.
yukikaki (雪掻), *n.* ❶(道具) a snow-shovel; a snow-plough (汽車の). ❷(事) snow-raking; shovelling away snow. ❸(人) a snow-raker. —庭の雪掻きをする, to clear the garden of snow.
yukikata (行方), *n.* ❶=*yukigata*. whereabouts. ❷(方法) a manner; a method; a way.
yukiki (往來), *n.* ❶(ゆきかひ) going and coming; passing to and fro; traffic. ❷(交際) friendly intercourse. —往來する, ① to come and go; pass. ② to hold intercourse *with*; associate *with*.
yukikorogashi (雪轉), *n.* rolling a snowball.
yukikureru (行暮れる), *vi.* to be overtaken by night on the road. —行き暮れた旅人, a benighted traveller.
yukikuzure (雪崩), *n.* a snowslip; an avalanche (大なるもの).
yukimi (雪見), *n.* snow-viewing.
yukimoyō (雪模様), *n.* ❶(雪氣) foreboding of snow; a sign of snow. ❷(雪輪模様) a figure of snowflakes.
yūkin (遊金), *n.* spare money; money to spare; idle [unemployed] money.
yukinadare (雪崩), *n.* a snowslip; a snowslide.
yukinage (雪投), *n.* snowballing. —雪投げする, to play (at) snowballing.
yukinari (行成), *n.* leaving a thing to itself. ☞ *nariyuki*. —, *ad.* =*ikinari*.
yukinayami (行惱), *n.* a deadlock; a standstill; a tie-up. —行き惱む, to come to a deadlock; be brought to a standstill.
yukinoshita (虎耳草), *n.* 【植】 the creeping [strawberry] saxifrage; the strawberry geranium.
yūkinrui (游禽類), *n.* 【鳥】 Natatores (學名); the swimmers.
yukisaki (行先), *n.* ❶(行方) the place where a person has gone. ❷(目的地) the destination.
yukisugiru (行過ぎる), *v.* ❶ to go too far; go [walk] past [beyond]. ❷ to overshoot the mark; outstop (想像が事實より).
yukitodoku (行屆く), *vi.* to be scrupulous; be careful; be thorough. —行屆いた人, a man of scrupulous care. —何から何までもよく行屆く, to be careful even to the minutest details. —手入れが行屆いてゐる, The garden is well kept (庭の); The house is kept in good repairs (家の). —皆私が行屆かないからです, It is all due to my unworthiness [want of care].
yukitsuke (行つけの), *a.* favourite; accustomed.
yukitsuku (行著く), *v.* to arrive *at* [*in*]; reach; get *to*; reach one's destination; find one's way (漸く辿り著く).
yukiwataru (行渡る), *v.* to extend over; spread over [all over; throughout]; pervade (the country, *etc.*); go round (食物など). —皆に行き渡るだけスープがない, There is not enough soup to go round.
yukizora (雪空), *n.* a snowy sky.
yukizumari (行詰), *n.* a deadlock; a standstill; a stalemate (將棋); an *impasse* 【佛】. —政策の行詰り, an impasse of the ministerial policy. —行き詰る, to come to a deadlock [standstill]; stick; be brought to a standstill. (返事に行き詰る, to be stuck for an answer.)
yukkuri (ゆっくり), *ad.* slowly; leisurely; in a leisurely manner. —氣がゆっくりする, to be at ease; feel easy. —ゆっくり旅をする, to travel by easy stages. —ゆっくりやれ, Take your time. —ゆっくりでよい, You may take your time. —ゆっくり見て行きませう, Let us take our time looking at it. —ゆっくりして居られない, We've no time to lose. —まあいいぢゃありませんか. ごゆっくりなさい, Oh, don't hurry away.
yūkō (有功), *n.* meritoriousness; merit. ¶ 有功賞牌, a medal for merit.
yūkō (有效), *n.* efficiency; efficacy; 【法】 validity. —有效である, to be effective; hold good; be valid. —有效になる, to come into effect; take effect. —有效にする, to give effect; validate. —本切符は五日間有效である, This ticket is available for five days. ——**na**, *a.* effective; effectual; available; valid. —有效な手段を執る, to take effective measure. ¶ 有效期間, the term of validity.
yukoku (諭告), *n.* instructions; counsel; admonition. —諭告する, to give instructions; issue an admonition.
yūkoku (夕刻), *n.* =*yūgata*.
yūkoku (幽谷), *n.* a deep ravine; a dingle; a glen.
yūkoku (憂國), *n.* patriotism. ¶ 憂國の情, patriotic spirit. —憂國

の士, a patriot.

yuku (行く), *vi.* ❶ (赴く) to go [repair] to (a place); proceed to (a place); go over *to*. ❷ (逝く) to die; pass away. ❸ (首尾, 成行) to go [fare] (well or ill). —往くもの來るもの, comers and goers. —行きつ戻りつする, to linger about a place; walk up and down. —二哩行く, to cover [go over] two miles; fly two miles (彈丸が). —運動に行く, to go out for exercise. —見に行く, to go and see. —本通りを行く, to go along the main street. —同じ《最も近い》道を行く, to go the same《shortest》way. —眞直に行け, Follow your nose!; Go straight on! —さう旨くは行くまい, I am not so certain of success. —うまく行きましたか, Has it gone well?

yukue (行方), *n.* whereabouts. —行方を晦ます, to cover one's traces; conceal oneself. ¶ 行方不明, missing; whereabouts unknown. (行方不明の人, a missing man.)

yukurinaku (ゆくりなく), *ad.* unexpectedly; accidentally; by chance; by accident. ☞ *gūzen*. —ゆくりなく出逢ふ, to meet a person accidentally.

yukusaki (行先), *n.* ❶ = *yukisaki*. ❷ (將來) the future.

yukusue (行末), *n.* the future. —行末を案じる, to feel anxious about another's future.

yukute (行手), *n.* one's way. —行手を遮る, to close another's path; stand in another's way.

yukuyuku (行行), *ad.* ❶ (行きながら) on the way [road]; as we went along. ❷ (終には, 後には) in the future; in the end; in course of time.

yūkyō (遊興), *n.* pleasures; amusements; diversion. —遊興する, to amuse [divert] oneself. ¶ 遊興費, the expenses of pleasures. —遊興税, tax on amusements.

yūkyū (有給の), *a.* paid; salaried; stipendiary.

yumaki (湯卷), *n.* a loin-cloth.

yume (夢), *n.* ❶ a dream. ❷ (幻想) a day-dream; a vision; an illusion. ❸ (眠) a sleep. —夢ともなく現ともなく, half asleep and half awake; in the borderland of dream. —夢が覺める, to awake from a dream; wake up; be disillusioned (迷夢より); come to one's senses (同上). —とは夢にも思はなかった, little did I dream of ever —ing; I never thought of —ing even in a dream. —夢に現れる, to appear to a person in a dream. —夢を見る, to dream a dream; have a dream. (故郷の夢を見る, to dream of [about] home.) —夢を驚かす, to awake a person from his sleep. —夢を驚かされる, to start from one's sleep. —夢ではないかと思った, I could not believe my eyes; I fancied myself in a dream.

yumehandan (夢判斷), *n.* oneiromancy; interpretation of a dream. —夢判斷をする, to interpret [read] a dream.

yūmei (有名な), *a.* famous; noted; well-known; celebrated. —有名な泥棒, a notorious burglar. —大きいので有名な, famous for its (large) size. —有名になる, to become famous; acquire fame.

yūmei (幽明), *n.* ❶ (明暗) darkness and brightness. ❷ (冥土と現世) this and the other world. —幽明境を異にする, to live in the other world.

yūmei-mujitsu (有名無實の), *a.* nominal; titular.

yumeji (夢路を辿る), to follow the road in dreamland.

yumemakura (夢枕に立つ), to appear to a person in a dream.

yumemiru (夢みる), *v.* ❶ (夢を見る) to dream; have a dream. ❷ (夢想する) to dream *of*.

yūmeshi (夕飯), *n.* a supper; an evening meal.

yume-utsutsu (夢現), *n.* ❶ (夢と現) the dream and the reality. ❷ (夢心地) dreaminess; trance; ecstasy. ☞ *yume* (夢). —夢現で聞く, to listen to dreamily [half asleep].

yumi (弓), *n.* a bow. —弓を引く, to draw [bend] a bow.

yumihari (弓張-提燈), *n.* a paper-lantern with a bow-handle.

yūmin (遊民), *n.* idle people; non-workers; idlers; drones. ¶ 高等遊民, educated idlers.

yuminari (弓形の), *a.* curved; bowed. —弓形に曲げる, to bow; bend; hunch.

yumiya (弓矢), *n.* bow and arrow. ¶ 弓矢の神, the war-god; Mars.

yumizu (湯水), *n.* hot and cold water. —金錢を湯水の樣に使ふ, to spend money like water; squander one's money; make ducks and drakes of one's money.

yumizuru, yuzuru, (弓弦), *n.* a bowstring.

yūmō (勇猛), *n.* intrepidity; valour; bravery. —勇猛な, intrepid; valiant; brave.

yūmoa (ユーモア), *n.* humour.

yumoji (湯文字), *n.* a loin-cloth.

yūmon (幽門), *n.* 【解】 the pylorus.
yumoto (湯元), *n.* the source of a hot-spring.
yūnagi (夕凪), *n.* an evening calm.
yunde (弓手, 左手), *n.* the left hand.
yū-ni (優に), *ad.* ❶ (しとやかに) gently; quietly; calmly. ❷ (裕) (十分に) enough; sufficiently; easily (容易に). —優にやさしき姿, a gentle and elegant form. —それは優に一番だ, It is out of sight [by far] the best.
yunomi (湯呑 -茶碗), *n.* a mug; a cup.
yunoshi (湯熨), *n.* smoothing cloth with steam. —湯熨しする, to smooth with steam.
yunyōkan (輸尿管), *n.* 【解】 the ureter.
yunyū (輸入), *n.* importation; import; introduction (文物·制度等の). —輸入する, to import; introduce. ¶ 輸入貿易, import trade. —輸入品, imports; imported goods [articles]. —輸入港, an import port. —輸入者, an importer (輸入商); an introducer. —輸入申告書, a declaration for importation. —輸入税, import duty.
yuō (硫黄), *n.* 【化】 sulphur; brimstone. ¶ 硫黄華, flowers of sulphur; sublimed sulphur. —硫黄燻蒸, sulphuration. —硫黄泉, a sulphur-spring; a sulphuretted spring.
yūō (勇往する), *vi.* to advance courageously. —勇往邁進する, to dash [push] undauntedly.
yūō (雄黄), *n.* 【鑛】 orpiment.
yuoke (湯桶), *n.* a bath-tub.
yurai (由來), *n.* ❶ origin; derivation (出源); cause (原因). ❷ (來歷) history. ——, *ad.* naturally; originally; essentially; from the first (初めから). —由來する, to originate *in* [*from*; *with*]; result *from*; be derived *from*. —由來を尋ねる, to trace [enquire *into*; look *into*] a source [an origin].
yūraku (遊樂), *n.* amusement; pleasure; enjoyment; diversion.
yurameku (搖めく), *vi.* to flicker; waver to and fro.
yūran (遊覧), *n.* excursion; sightseeing; a round-trip; a pleasure-trip (觀光旅行) —遊覧する, to go sightseeing; do the sights. ¶ 遊覧地, a pleasure resort; a tourist point. —遊覧切符, a tourist ticket; an excursion-ticket; a round-trip ticket. —遊覧客, sightseers; excursionists; tourists. —遊覧列車, an excursion-train. —遊覧船, an excursion ship; a yacht.
yurankan (輸卵管), *n.* 【解】 the Fallopian tube.
yurayura (搖搖), *ad.* swingingly; swayingly; waveringly. —搖々する, to rock; swing; sway; waver.
yure (搖れ), *n.* jolt; joggle; jumble; shake. ☞ *yurugi*.
yureru (搖れる), *vi.* to shake; quake; swing; rock; roll (横に); pitch (縦に). —左右に搖れる, to rock from side to side; roll. —前後左右に搖れる, to pitch and roll (船など).
yuredoko (搖床), *n.* a cradle; a swinging cot; a hammock.
yūrei (幽靈), *n.* a ghost; a spectre; a spook. —幽靈の如き, ghostly; ghostlike; spookish. —あの家は幽靈が出る, A ghost haunts [appears in] the house; The house is haunted. ¶ 幽靈番號, a bogus number.
yūreki (遊歴), *n.* tour; itinerancy. —遊歴する, to tour [make a tour] about; roam; rove; travel about; itinerate. ¶ 遊歴者, a tourist; a rover; a roamer.
yūretsu (勇烈な), *a.* brave; intrepid; daring; dauntless.
yūretsu (優劣), *n.* superiority and inferiority; quality. —優劣なき, level; close. —優劣を爭ふ, to try conclusions with a person; vie for superiority with a person. —兩者の優劣如何, What are the relative merits of the two?; Which is the better of the two?
yuri (百合), *n.* 【植】 the lily.
yūri (有利), *n.* profitableness; lucrativeness; advantageousness. ——**-na**, *a.* profitable; lucrative; advantageous (好都合の). —有利な事業, a profitable enterprise. —有利な位置を占める, to occupy a point of vantage. —被告に有利な證言をなす, to give testimony favourable to [in favour of] the accused.
yūri (游離, 遊離), *n.* 【化】 isolation. —遊離せる, isolated; free. —遊離さす, to isolate; free.
yuriisu (搖椅子), *n.* a rocking chair; a rocker.
yurikaeshi (搖返), *n.* an after-shock.
yurikago (搖籃), *n.* a cradle.
yuriokosu (搖起す), *vt.* to wake by shaking; shake up; shake (another) out of his sleep.
yuriugokasu (搖動かす), *vt.* to sway. ☞ *yurugasu*.
yuru (搖る), *v.* to swing; sway; shake; rock.
yurugasu (搖がす), *vt.* to swing; sway; shake.
yurugu (搖ぐ), *vi.* to swing; waver; shake.
yurui (緩い), *a.* ❶ (緊縮ならぬ) loose; slack; lax. ❷ (寛大な) lenient; generous. ❸ (緩調な) slow. —寛[ゆる]い半股引, wide

knickerbockers. —緩い勾配, gentle slope. —緩くなる, to come [get] loose.

yurukase (忽にする), *vt.* to neglect; disregard; slight. ☞ *naozari*. —寸毫も忽にせぬ, not to neglect in the least.

yurumeru (緩める), *vt.* to loosen; loose; slack(-en) (速力·綱など); relax (氣·努力·攻撃など). —手を緩める, to loose hold (of); relax one's grasp. —帶を緩める, to loosen the belt. —歩調を緩める, to slacken one's pace. —汽船《汽車》の速力を緩める, to slow a steamer 《train》. —船《汽車》が速力を緩めた, The boat 《train》 slowed up [down]; The boat 《train》 slacked up (停止前).

yurumi (緩み), *n.* looseness; relaxation; slackness. —心に緩みが出る, to be relieved from a mental strain; One's mind is relaxed.

yurumu (緩·弛む), *vi.* to loosen; relax; slack(-en); become remiss (氣が). —腹が緩む, to have loose bowels.

yurushi (許, 宥, 赦), *n.* ❶ (許可) permission; leave; licence (免許). ❷ (宥恕) forgiveness; pardon. ❸ (放免) release; remission; acquital. —許を得て, with permission. —許を取る, to be specially taught [instructed].

yurusu (許·宥·赦す), *vt.* ❶ (許可) to permit; grant; approve (認可); license (免許). ❷ (許容) to admit; permit; allow. ❸ (宥恕) to forgive; pardon; excuse. ❹ (放免) to release; let off [go]; remit (制裁を加へない); acquit (無罪とす). ❺ (緩くする) to relax; slacken; remit. —許すべからざる, impermissible; unpardonable; inexcusable. —其筋から許される, to be sanctioned by the (proper) authorities. —心を許す, to remit [relax] one's caution *against* (油斷); admit into confidence (腹心). —願を許す, to grant a request. —猶豫を許さぬ, to permit [admit] of no delay. —時間の許す限り, so far as time permits. —事情が之を許さぬ, Circumstances do not admit [allow] of this.

yuruyaka (緩·寬かな), *a.* ❶ (緊縮ならぬ) loose; slack. ❷ (寬大な) lenient; generous. ❸ (遲い) slow. ❹ (靜かな) gentle. ☞ *yurui* (緩い). —寬かな規則, a moderate rule [regulation].

yuruyuru (緩緩), *ad.* = *yukkuri*.

yūryo (憂慮), *n.* anxiety; apprehension; solicitude. ☞ *shinpai*. —憂慮する, to be anxious *about*; apprehend; be solicitous [concerned] *about*.

yūryō (有料の), *a.* charged. ¶ 有料郵便物, chargeable mail-matter.

yūryō (遊獵), *n.* sport; sporting; hunting; shooting. —遊獵する, to sport; hunt. ¶ 遊獵家, a sportsman. —遊獵期, the shooting season. ☞ *shuryō*.

yūryō (優良な), *a.* superior; excellent; choice. ¶ 優良品, an excellent [a fine] article.

yūryoku (有力な), *a.* powerful; strong; influential. —有力な證據, a strong [valid] evidence. ¶ 有力者, an influential person; a man of influence.

yusan (遊山), *n.* a picnic; an excursion; a jaunt. —遊山する, to picnic; take [make; go on] an excursion; jaunt. ¶ 遊山船, an excursion-barge; a pleasure-boat; a barge; a yacht. —遊山地, a pleasure resort; a recreation-ground. —遊山客, a pleasure-seeker; a holiday-maker.

yūsan-kaikyū (有產階級), *n.* the propertied class; the property-owning class.

yūsei (遊星), *n.* 【天】 a planet.

yūsei (優勢), *n.* superiority; preponderance; ascendency; predominance. —優勢な敵, a strong [superior] enemy force. —優勢を占める, to prevail *over* [*against*]; predominate [preponderate] *over*. —漸次優勢となる, to gain ground; gain in strength.

yūseigaku (優生學), *n.* Ⓢ 優種學. eugenics.

yūseki-dōbutsu (有脊動物), *n.* = *sekitsui-dōbutsu*.

yusen (湯錢), *n.* bath-money.

yūsen (有線の), *a.* wire.

yūsen (郵船), *n.* a mail-steamer; a packet-boat [ship]; a mail-boat. ¶ 日本郵船會社, the Japan Mail Steamship Company; the Nippon Yūsen Kaisha (N. Y. K. と略す).

yūsen, yusen, (遊船), *n.* a yacht; a pleasure-boat.

yūsen (優先·權), *n.* preference; priority. —優先權を得る, to acquire preferential rights. —...に優先する, to take precedence *of*. ¶ 優先株, preference shares; preferred stocks. —優先債權者, a preferred creditor.

yūsha (勇者), *n.* a man of courage; the brave. the strong.

yūsha (優者), *n.* a superior;

yūshaku (有爵の), *a.* noble. ¶ 有爵者, a nobleman; a peer; the peerage (階級).

yushi (諭示), *n.* admonition; injunction; instructions. —諭示する, to issue admonition [instructions].

yushi (諭旨), *n.* official advice (to a subordinate). ¶ 諭旨免官, resignation by the advice of a superior; resignation officially prompted. —諭旨退學, leaving school by the advice of the principal. (諭旨退學される, to be asked to leave school.)

yūshi (有司), *n.* the powers that be; the constituted authorities.

yūshi (有史前の), *a.* prehistoric. —有史以來, since the dawn of history. (有史以來の大戰爭, the greatest war in history [on record].)

yūshi (有志), *n.* (有志者) a volunteer (篤志家); a person interested (關係者); a sympathizer (共鳴者); men of the same mind (同志の士). ¶ 有志看護婦, a volunteer sick-nurse.

yūshi (勇士), *n.* the brave; a brave warrior; a hero.

yūshi (雄姿), *n.* a gallant [brave] figure (雄々しい); a splendid [grand] figure (壯大, 壯麗); a sublime figure (山などの壯嚴).

yūshi (雄視する), *vi.* to predominate *over*; preponderate *over*; cut a conspicuous figure. —政界の一方に雄視する, to be predominant in some quarter of the political world; take a leading part in the political world.

yūshi (遊資), *n.* idle funds [capital]; unemployed capital.

yūshikakusha (有資格者), *n.* a properly qualified person.

yūshikisha (有識者), *n.* a learned man; a man of general information; a man of light and leading.

yūshinron (有神論), *n.* 【哲】 theism. ¶ 有神論者, a theist.

yūshō (有償), *n.* a consideration. ¶ 有償契約, 【法】 a contract made for a consideration.

yūshō (優詔), *n.* a gracious Imperial message.

yūshō (優勝), *n.* ❶ (優勢) predominance; superiority. ❷ (優者の勝利) victory; championship. —優勝旗を取る, to carry off a champion-flag. —優勝の地位を占める, to get to the windward *of*; occupy a vantage-ground. ¶ 優勝劣敗, the survival of the fittest.

yūshoku (夕食), *n.* supper; the evening meal. —夕食を認める, to take supper; sup.

yūshoku (憂色), *n.* a worried [an anxious] look. —憂色を帶びる, to wear a worried look.

yūshoku (遊食する), *vi.* to live an idle life; vegetate; loaf. ¶ 遊食者, a drone; a loafer; an idler.

yūshoku-jinshu (有色人種), *n.* the coloured race.

yūshū (有衆), *n.* the people; the multitude; the many.

yūshū (有終の), *a.* crowning. —有終の美を濟[ナ]す, to crown with perfection.

yūshū (憂愁), *n.* melancholy; gloom; grief. —憂愁を帶びた顏, a face as long as a fiddle; a melancholy look. —邸內は憂愁に閉されて居た, Melancholy reigned over the premises.

yūshū (優秀の), *a.* superior; excellent.

yūshūkan (遊就館), *n.* the Military Museum.

yushutsu (輸出), *n.* export; exportation. —輸出する, to export. ¶ 輸出品, exports; an exported article. —輸出港, an export port. —輸出戾稅, export drawback. —輸出奬勵, encouragement of exportation. (輸出奬勵金, an export bounty.)

yūshutsu (涌出, 湧出), *n.* gush; eruption. —湧出する, to gush out; well; erupt (噴出).

yusō (油槽), *n.* an oil-tank.

yusō (輸送), *n.* transport(-ation); conveyance. —輸送する, to transport; convey. ¶ 陸上〔海上〕輸送, transportation by land 〔sea〕. —輸送力, transport capacity; carrying power.

yūsō (勇壯な), *a.* brave; heroic; gallant; valiant; (soul-)stirring.

yūsō (郵送), *n.* post; mail. —郵送する, to send by post (內地); post; send by mail (外國); mail. ¶ 郵送料, postage.

yusotsu (輸卒), *n.* a transport soldier.

yūsū (有數の), *a.* (pre-)eminent; prominent; distinguished. —有數の英學者, one of the best English scholars. —日本有數の工業地として知らる, to be known as a great industrial centre in Japan.

yusuburu (搖ぶる), *vt.* to shake; rock; swing; jog; joggle. —實を搖ぶり落す, to shake down fruits from a tree. —赤兒を搖ぶり寢かす, to rock a baby to sleep.

yusugu (ゆすぐ), *vt.* to rinse. —手拭を濯ぐ, to rinse a towel.

yusuri (强請), *n.* ❶ (事) extortion; exaction; blackmail. ❷ (人) a blackmailer; an extortioner.

yusuru (强請る), *v.* to extort; exact; blackmail. —金を强請る, to blackmail a person; extort money from a person.

yusuru (搖する), *vt.* to shake; rock; swing; sway; jog. —搖すり起す, to shake a person awake.

yu-suru (輸する), *v.* ❶ (送る)

to transport. ❷ (劣る, ひけをとる) to be inferior *to*; be second *to*.

yū-suru (有する), *vt.* to have; possess; own; be possessed *of*. ☞ *motsu, aru.*

yūsuzumi (夕涼をする), *vi.* to enjoy the cool of the evening; cool oneself in the evening breeze.

yūtai (有體の), *a.* material; substantial; corporeal. ¶ 有體動產,【法】corporeal movables; goods and chattels.

yūtai (勇退する), *vi.* to retire *from.*

yūtai (優待), *n.* generous [courteous; warm] treatment; welcome; hospitality. —優待する, to welcome; treat handsomely [with courtesy]; receive hospitably. ¶ 優待券, a complimentary ticket.

yutaka (豐·裕な), *a.* ❶ plentiful; ample; abundant. ❷ wealthy; rich; affluent; opulent. —— **-ni,** *ad.* abundantly; plentifully; amply; in affluence; opulently. —豐に暮す, to live in affluence; be in comfortable [affluent; easy] circumstances.

yutan (油單), *n.* ❶ an oil-cloth. ❷ (簞笥·長持等の被布) an oil covering [cloth covering] (for a chest of drawers, *etc.*).

yutanpo (湯湯婆), *n.* a (foot-) warmer; a hot-water bottle.

yutatsu (諭達), *n.* official instructions.

yutō (湯桶), *n.* a hot-water jug.

yūtō (遊蕩), *n.* dissipation; profligacy; debauchery. ¶ 遊蕩兒, a dissipated person; a rake; a man of pleasure.

yūtō (優等), *n.* excellence; high-class; superiority; honours (學生). —優等の, excellent; high-class; superior; first. —優等で(大學を)卒業する, to graduate at a college with honours. ¶ 優等品, a thing of the first quality. —優等賞, an honours prize.

yūtoku, utoku, (有德の), *a.* virtuous; good.

yuton (油團), *n.* an oiled-paper cushion; linoleum (敷物).

yūtopia (理想鄕), *n.* Utopia.

yutori (遊隙), *n.* play; room. ☞ *yoyū.* —多少のゆとりを取って置く, to give some play to the rope.

yuttari (寛り), *ad.* easily; composedly; leisurely. —寛りした, easy; composed; calm; sedate.

yuu (結ふ), *vt.* ❶ (紐など) to tie. ❷ (髮を) to dress; do (up).

yūutsu (憂鬱), *n.* melancholy; dejection; low spirits; depression. —憂鬱な, melancholy; dejected; dispirited; out of spirits. ¶ 憂鬱症, melancholia; a fit of the blues; hypochondria.

yūwa (融和), *n.* melting; softening; soothing; reconciliation; harmony (調和). —融和する, ① [*vt.*] to melt; soften; soothe; reconcile. ② [*vi.*] to soften; melt; harmonize *with.*

yuwaeru (結へる), *vt.* to tie; fasten; bind.

yuwakashi (湯沸), *n.* a kettle.

yūwaku (誘惑), *n.* temptation; enticement; allurement; seduction. —大首府の誘惑, the seductions of a great capital. —誘惑と戰ふ, to wrestle with [fight against] temptation. —誘惑する, to tempt; entice; allure; seduce. ¶ 誘惑者, a tempter; an enticer; a seducer.

yuya (湯屋), *n.* a public bath; a bath; a bath-house.

yūyake (夕燒), *n.* evening glow; after-glow; the sunset colour.

yūyaku (勇躍する), *vi.* to be animated; be spirited.

yūyaku (釉藥, 泑藥), *n.* enamel.

yūyo (有餘), *a.* more (than). ——, *prep.* over; above; upwards *of.* —八百有餘の兵, over eight hundred soldiers.

yūyo (猶豫), *n.* ❶ (延期) delay; postponement; deferment; extension of time; grace. ❷ (躊躇) hesitation. —猶豫なく, without giving grace; without hesitation. —猶豫する, ① (延期す) to grant grace; give time; respite. ② (躊躇す) to hesitate. —寸時も猶豫せず, without a moment's delay. —一日の支拂豫猶を與へる, to give a day's grace. ¶ 猶豫期間, a postponement period; 【法】 a legal delay; days of grace (手形の); a renewal period (保險).

yūyō (有用), *n.* usefulness; subservience. —有用の, useful; of use. (國家有用の材, a man of service to the country.)

yūyoku (遊弋·游弋する), *vi.* to cruise; range; sail to and fro.

yūyū (悠悠), *ad.* ❶ (ゆるゆる) in a leisurely manner; slowly; deliberately. ❷ (落ついて) calmly; quietly. ❸ (無限) (*a*) (時間) eternally; endlessly: (*b*) (空間) boundlessly; vastly. —悠々閑々と日を送る, to pass one's days in indolence.

yuyushiki (由由しき), *a.* serious; grave; fatal. —由々しき事件, a serious [grave] affair.

yūzai (有罪), *n.* guiltiness; guilt; culpability. —有罪の評決を下す, to give [bring in] a verdict of guilty. —有罪の宣告を受ける, to be adjudged guilty; be found guilty.

yuzame (湯冷), *n.* feeling cold after a bath.

yūzei (有税の), *a.* dutiable; taxable. ¶ 有税品, dutiable goods; goods subject to duty.

yūzei (郵税), *n.* postage. —郵税先拂の, paid on delivery. —郵税前拂で, with postage prepaid. —郵税拂濟の, post-paid. ¶ 郵税不足, insufficient postage. —郵税無料, post-free.

yūzei (遊說), *n.* stumping; political speech-making; a speaking tour. —遊說する, [*vi.*] to stump; canvass. —遊說中である, to be on the stump【俗】. —遊說の途に上る, to start on a speaking [canvassing] tour. ¶ 遊說員, a stump speaker; a stumper.

yūzen (悠然), *ad.* ❶ (平靜に) calmly; composedly; with (perfect) composure. ❷ (悠長に) leisurely; deliberately. —悠然たる, ① calm; composed. ② leisurely; deliberate.

yūzenikkusu (優生學), *n.* eugenics.

yuzu (柚), *n.*【植】the true citron.

yūzū (融通), *n.* ❶ (流通) circulation. ❷ (用立) accommodation. ❸ versatility (多才); elasticity (伸縮自在); adaptability (變通). —融通の利く, versatile; elastic; adaptable. —融通の利かぬ, unadaptable; lacking in versatility. —融通を利かす, to adapt oneself *to*. —彼は千圓の融通が利く, His credit is worth [good for] 1000 *yen*. ——**-suru**, *vt.* to accommodate; lend; advance. —金を融通する, to accommodate a person with money. ¶ 融通力, credit; borrowing power. —融通手形,【商】an accommodation-bill; a kite【卑】.

yūzui (雄蕊), *n.*【植】a stamen.

yuzuriai (讓合), *n.* mutual concession. —讓り合ふ, to make mutual concessions; meet halfway.

yuzurimono (讓物), *n.* a concession; something obtained by transfer.

yuzuriuke (讓受), *n.* taking over; inheritance. ¶ 讓受人, a transferee; an assignee; a grantee.

yuzuriukeru (讓受ける), *vt.* to obtain by transfer; take over; inherit. —親の財產を讓受ける, to inherit one's father's property.

yuzuriwatashi (讓渡), *n.* transfer; assignment; conveyance; negotiation (手形の). —讓渡の出來る, transferable; negotiable (手形). ¶ 讓渡人, a granter; a transferor; an assignor; a conveyer.

yuzuriwatasu (讓渡す), *vt.* to hand [make; turn] over (*to*); transfer (*to*); convey (*to*); assign.

yuzuru (讓る), *v.* ❶ =*yuzuriwatasu*. ❷ (讓步) to concede; give way; yield. ❸ (劣る) to yield; fall below; be inferior *to*. —一步讓る, to yield a step; make a concession. —座を讓る, to make room *for*; give place *to*; resign one's seat *to*. —權利を讓る, to make over rights to a person. —店を讓る, to turn over one's business *to*. —忠實の點では誰にも讓らぬ, He yields to none in fidelity; He is second to none in faithfulness.

Z

za (座), *n.* ❶ (座席) a seat. ❷ (劇場) a theatre. ❸ (座金) a (metal) washer. ❹ (腫物の) a seat. —座に就く, to take one's seat. —座を賑はす, (宴席などで) to keep the table amused. ¶ 歌舞伎座, the Kabukiza Theatre.

zā (ザー), *n.* the Czar, Tzar (露西亞皇帝).

zabon (朱欒), *n.* =*jabon*.

zabun (潑然と), *ad.* with a splash. —ザブンと水中に跳び込む, to plunge into water with a splash [a sound].

zabuton (座蒲團), *n.* a cushion.

zabuzabu (ざぶざぶ), *ad.* in plenty. —ザブザブと水を掛ける, to pour plenty of water *on*.

zachō (座長), *n.* a chairman.

zadan (座談), *n.* conversation; table-talk. —座談に長ずる, to be good at conversation; be a good talker.

zadoru (痣取る), *vi.* to become black and blue.

zagyō (坐業), *n.* sedentary occupation. ¶ 坐業者, a sedentary.

zagashira (座頭), *n.*【劇】the leading actor (of a theatrical company).

zaguri (坐繰), *n.* ❶ (事) re-reeling. ❷ (機械) a re-reel machine; a hand-reeling instrument. ¶ 坐繰絲, re-reels; hand-filature; re-reeled raw silk.

zai (在), *n.* suburbs; outskirts; neighbouring districts; the country (田舍). —京都の在, a suburb of Kyōto. ——, *prep.* in. —在英中に, while in England; during one's stay in England.

zai (材), *n.* ❶ (木材) timber; lumber. ❷ (材料) material. ❸ (器量) ability; talent.

zai (財), *n.* ❶ (金) money; riches (富); wealth (同上). ❷【經】

goods (財物).

zaiaku (罪惡), *n.* ❶ (道德·宗教上の) a sin; an iniquity; a vice (惡德). ❷ (法律上の) a crime. ☞ *tsumi.*

zaibatsu (財閥), *n.* plutocrats; plutocracy.

zaibutsu (財物), *n.* goods.

zaichō (在朝の), *a.* government (-al); in office [power].

zaichū (在中), *n.* being inside; being closed in. —寫眞在中, "photographs"; "photos only." —原稿在中, "manuscripts"; "MSS."

zaidan (財團), *n.* ❶ (財團法人) a foundation; a foundational juridical person. ❷ (全資産) assets. ❸ (金融團) a financial group; a syndicate. ¶ 破産財團, assets (資産); a bankrupt's estate (資産+負債).

zaieki (在役), *n.* ❶ (兵役) being in arms; being in military ⟪naval⟫ service. ❷ (軍艦の) being in commissioned service. ❸ (犯罪人の) being in penal servitude. —在役中, ① in one's military service; during one's naval service. ② in prison. ¶ 在役艦, a ship in commission.

zaigai (在外の), *a.* stationed [resident] abroad. ¶ 在外公館, embassies, legations, and consulates abroad; government offices abroad. —在外正貨, specie deposited abroad.

zaigaku (在學する), *vi.* to be in school. ¶ 在學期間, school-days; school-period. —在學生, the students; the scholars. —在學證明書, a school certificate.

zaigen (財源), *n.* resources; a source of revenue; financial resources; (ways and) means. —財源が涸渇する, The resources are exhausted. —財源を求める, to look for a source of revenue.

zaigō (在鄉), *n.* the country; the country-side. ¶ 在鄉軍人, ex-soldiers; ex-service-men; military men in their homes. (在鄉軍人會, an ex-service-men's association.)

zaigō (罪業), *n.* a sin; a sinful act.

zaihō (財寶), *n.* treasures; riches; wealth.

zaii (在位), *n.* being on the throne; a reign.

zaijō (罪狀), *n.* the nature of a crime [an offence]. —彼の罪狀は明白だ, He stands confessed of a crime.

zaijū (在住), *n.* residence; dwelling. —神戶在住の英國人, Englishmen (resident) in Kōbe; English residents in Kōbe.

zaika (財貨), *n.* 【經】 goods; commodities.

zaika (罪科), *n.* ❶ an offence; a crime. ❷ (處刑) punishment.

zaikai (財界), *n.* ❶ (經濟界) the economic world; economic circles. ❷ (金融界) the money-market; the financial world; financial circles.

zaikansha (在監者), *n.* a prisoner.

zaikata (在方), *n.* rural districts; the country; the country-side.

zaikin (在勤する), *vi.* to hold a post; hold office. —芝警察署に在勤してゐる, to hold a post at the Shiba Police Station. —倫敦在勤を命ぜらる, to be appointed to a post at London. ¶ 海外在勤俸, a foreign service allowance.

zaikohin (在庫品), *n.* goods in a storehouse; stored goods; stock in store.

zaikyō (在京する), *vi.* to reside [be] in Tōkyō. —在京中, during one's stay in Tōkyō.

zaimoku (材木), *n.* wood; timber; lumber. ¶ 材木置場, a lumber [timber]-yard. —材木屋, a timber dealer [merchant].

zaimu (財務), *n.* financial affairs. ¶ 財務官, a financial agent [commissioner].

zainin (罪人), *n.* ❶ (法律上の) a criminal; an offender; a culprit. ❷ (道德·宗教上の) a sinner; a transgressor.

zainō (財嚢), *n.* a purse; a money-bag; money-bags (富).

zairai (在來), *ad.* hitherto; until now; up to this time. —在來の, usual; customary; ordinary (普通の); conventional (習俗的の).

zairyō (材料), *n.* material; stuff; raw material (原料). —材料を供給する, to supply with materials.

zairyoku (財力), *n.* wealth.

zairyū (在留の), *a.* resident; living. —在留する, to reside; dwell; stay. ¶ 在留外人, foreign residents. —桑港在留邦人, Japanese residents in San Francisco.

zaisan (財産), *n.* an estate; fortune; property; assets. ☞ *shisan.* —財産を作る, to make [amass] a fortune. —財産を相續する, to succeed to a property. ¶ 財産家, a man of property [substance; means]. —財産權, 【法】 property right; right of property. —財產目錄, an inventory (of a property); a general inventory.

zaisei (財政), *n.* finance. —財政に窮する, to be embarrassed in one's finances; be in financial difficulties; be in pecuniary distress. 財政計畫を定める, to decide on a financial programme. ¶ 財政學, the science of finance. —財政狀態, the financial condition. —財政家, a financier. —財政困難, financial difficulties; pecuniary embarrassments. —財政整理, financial readjustment [reform]; reorganization of the finances; adjustment of finances. —財政政策, financial policy.

zaiseki (罪跡), *n.* traces [proofs] of a crime; evidence of a crime. —罪跡を晦ます, to destroy proofs of guilt.

zaishō (罪障), *n.* a sin; a vice. —罪障を消滅する, to expiate [blot out] past sins.

zaishō (罪證), *n.* traces of crime [guilt].

zaishoku (在職する), *v.* to hold an office [post]. ¶ 在職期間, (the period of) one's tenure of an office.

zaitaku (在宅する), *vi.* to be at home; be in. —御主人は御在宅ですか. Is Mr.— at home?

zaiya (在野), *n.* non-officialdom; being out of office; not being in office. —在野當時に, when out of power. ¶ 在野黨, a non-government party; a party out of office [power]; the non-ministerial party.

zajō (坐乘する), *vi.* to be on board. ——, *vt.* to get on board. —旗艦に坐乘する, to board the flag-ship.

zakka (雜貨), *n.* miscellaneous goods; general merchandise; groceries (荒物). ¶ 雜貨商, a grocer; a general dealer. —雜貨店, a grocery; a chandlery; a general shop [store].

zakki (雜記), *n.* miscellanea; miscellaneous notes. ¶ 雜記帳, a note-book; a commonplace book; 【簿記】 a waste-book.

zakkoku (雜穀), *n.* cereals. ¶ 雜穀商, a corn-chandler. —雜穀問屋, a dealer in cereals; a corn merchant.

zakkyo (雜居), *n.* mixed residence. —雜居する, to reside together.

zako (雜魚), *n.* small fish.

zakotsu (坐骨), *n.* 【解】 ischium. ¶ 坐骨神經, the sciatic nerve. (坐骨神經痛, 【醫】 sciatica; sciatic gout.)

zakuro (安石榴), *n.* 【植】 the pomegranate(-tree).

zakurobana (柘榴鼻), *n.* a grog-blossom 【卑】; (acne) rosacea.

zakuroishi (柘榴石), *n.* 【鑛】 garnet.

zakyō (座興), *n.* an amusement (for a company); a fun. —座興に, as amusement; for entertainment; for fun.

zama (樣, 態), *n.* a state; a plight; a condition. —見られた態でない, not fit to be seen. —態見ろ, Serve you right!

zanbō (讒謗), *n.* slander; calumny; libel; defamation. —讒謗する, to slander; calumniate; libel; defame. ¶ 讒謗者, a slanderer; a calumniator; a scandal-monger.

zanbu (殘部), *n.* the remainder; the remnant; the rest.

zanbu (ざんぶと), *ad.* Ⓢ ざんぶりと. with a plunge [splash]; plump. —ザンブと海中へ跳び込む, to jump plump into the sea.

zanbutsu (殘物), *n.* remnants; remains; leavings.

zandaka (殘高), *n.* 【簿記】 balance. —殘高を繰越す, to have the balance carried forward to the next term.

zangai (殘骸), *n.* a carcass; the remains; ruins; wreck.

zangai (慘害), *n.* serious damage; disasters; ravages.

zangaku (殘額), *n.* the remainder; the balance.

zangan (嶄岸), *n.* an overhanging precipice; a sheer cliff.

zange (懺悔), *n.* penitence (後悔); contrition (同上); confession (告白). —懺悔の涙《生活》, penitential tears 《life》. —懺悔する, to confess (one's guilt; to a priest). —人を懺悔さす, to draw a confession from a person. ¶ 懺悔者, a confessor (する人); a confessed penitent (した人).

zangen (讒言), *n.* false charge; slander; calumny; defamation.

zangetsu (殘月), *n.* the moon in the morning sky.

zangiriatama (散切頭), *n.* a crop-haired head.

zangō (塹壕), *n.* 【軍】 a trench. —塹壕を掘進する, to advance the trenches. —塹壕を掘り始める, to open the trenches. ¶ 交通塹壕, communication trenches. —塹壕熱, trench fever. —塹壕戰《生活》, trench warfare 《life》.

zangyaku (殘虐), *n.* (a) cruelty; (a) brutality; (an) atrocity; (an) inhumanity. —殘虐な, cruel; outrageous; atrocious; brutal.

zanji (暫時), *n.* a short time [while]; a (little) while; a space of time. ——, *ad.* for a while; a little; a little while; a while.

zankanjō (斬奸狀), *n.* a declaration of reasons for assassination.

zanki (慚愧), *n.* shame; humiliation. —慚愧させる, to put [bring] to shame. —慚愧に耐へぬ, to writhe with shame.

zankin (残金), *n.* the balance: the surplus (money) (剩餘金).

zankoku (殘刻, 殘酷), *n.* cruelty; mercilessness; ruthlessness. —殘酷な, cruel; merciless; ruthless. —殘酷に取扱ふ, to treat a person cruelly [with brutality].

zanmu (殘務), *n.* remaining business. ¶殘務整理, adjustment of remaining business; winding up of pending business.

zannen (殘念), *n.* regret; mortification; chagrin. —殘念な, regrettable. —殘念ながら, to my regret; I am sorry to say. —殘念がる, to regret; be mortified; be chagrined; show one's regret. (殘念がって地團駄を踏む, to stamp on the ground with chagrin.)

zannin (殘忍), *n.* savageness; brutality; atrocity. ☞ *zankoku*. —殘忍な, brutal; merciless; atrocious.

zanninki (殘任期), *n.* the remaining term of one's office; the remainder of one's term of office.

zanpai (慘敗する), *vi.* to suffer a heavy [crushing] defeat; be beaten all to sticks.

zanpan (殘飯), *n.* the remains of boiled rice.

zanpei (殘兵), *n.* the remnant of a defeated army.

zanpin (殘品), *n.* goods [the stock] left; the remaining stock.

zansatsu (殘殺), *n.* cruel murder; massacre. —殘殺する, to slaughter; massacre; butcher; slay.

zanshi (慘死する), *vi.* to be killed (by a disaster).

zanshi (慙死する), *vi.* to die of [from] shame.

zanshin (斬新), *n.* novelty; unconventionality; originality. —斬新な, new; novel; unconventional; original.

zansho (殘暑), *n.* lingering summer heat.

zanso (讒訴), *n.* slander; a false charge. ☞ *zangen*.

zanson (殘存する), *v.* ❶ (生殘る) to survive; subsist. ❷ (殘留する) to remain; be left. ¶殘存者, a survivor.

zansū (殘數), *n.* the remnant; the remainder; the rest.

zantei (暫定的), *a.* provisional. ¶暫定條約, a provisional treaty; a *modus vivendi* [佛].

zantō (殘黨), *n.* the remnant of a (defeated) party.

zanushi (座主), *n.* the proprietor [owner] of a theatre.

zan'yo (殘餘), *n.* the remainder; the remnant; the rest. —殘餘の, remaining.

zanzai (斬罪), *n.* decapitation.

zanzen (嶄然), *ad.* prominently; (pre-)eminently; conspicuously. —嶄然頭角を見はす, to cut a brilliant figure; be conspicuous.

zappai (雜輩), *n.* small fry.

zappaku (雜駁な), *a.* ❶ (不純) impure; mixed. ❷ (不統一) unsystematic; inconsistent; confused; incoherent; loose.

zappi (雜費), *n.* miscellaneous expenses; incidental [sundry] expenses; petty charges; petty expenses; sundries.

zappō (雜報), *n.* general news; miscellaneous paragraphs; newspaper paragraphs. ¶雜報欄, the general news column.

zarame (粗目), *n.* crystallized sugar.

zarani (ざらに), *ad.* everywhere. —ざらにある, to be very common; be met with everywhere.

zarazara (ざらざらする), *vi.* to feel rough; be rough to the feel [touch]. ——, *a.* rough; coarse; harsh; granular.

zarigani (ざりがに), *n.* 【甲殼】 the crayfish, crawfish.

zaru (笊), *n.* a basket; a crate (大きな).

zaseki (座席), *n.* a seat; room (餘地).

zasetsu (挫折), *n.* ❶ (計畫など) set-back; breakdown. ❷ (氣力の) collapse; disheartenment. —挫折する, ① (計畫など) to be frustrated; break down; suffer a set-back. ② (氣力が) to be disheartened; collapse.

zashi (坐視する), *v.* to remain unconcerned; look on with indifference [idly].

zashiki (座敷), *n.* ❶ (部屋) a room; an apartment. ❷ (客間) a drawing-room; a parlour [米]. ❸ (酒席) a banquet-hall. —座敷へ通す, to show [take] a person into the drawing-room. —座敷牢に入れる, to confine a person in a room.

zashō (坐礁する), *vi.* to run on the rocks (擱岩); strand [ground] (擱岸); run aground [ashore] (同上). —船を坐礁さす, to run a ship on a rock; strand a ship.

zashō (挫傷), *n.* a sprain.

zashoku (坐食する), *vi.* to eat the bread of idleness; live without work; live idly [in idleness]; vegetate. ¶坐食階級, the idle classes.

zasshi (雜誌), *n.* a magazine; a journal. ¶文藝雜誌, a literary magazine. —同窓會雜誌, an alumni bulletin.

zassho (雜書), *n.* a pamphlet; miscellaneous books (色々の書).

zasshu (雜種), *n.* ❶ (色々の種

類) variety; various kinds. ❷ (あひのこ) a mixed breed; a cross (-breed); a mongrel; a hybrid; a half-caste (特に父が歐人母が印度人). —雜種の, ① miscellaneous; various. ② cross-bred; half-bred; hybrid; mongrel. ¶ 雜種馬, a cross-bred horse.

zasshūnyū (雜收入), *n.* miscellaneous receipts [income]; sundry receipts.

zassō (雜草), *n.* a weed. —雜草を除く, to weed; hoe. ¶ 雜草地, a weed-grown land; a place overgrown with weeds.

zassoku (雜則), *n.* miscellaneous rules [regulations].

zasu (座主), *n.* the chief abbot.

zasu (坐洲する), *vi.* to strand; ground; run aground [ashore].

za-suru (坐する), *vi.* ❶ to sit down; take a seat. ❷ (連坐する) to be involved *in.* —罪に坐する, to be brought up for a crime.

zatō (座頭), *n.* a blind man; a blind ministrel (盲樂師); a blind shampooer (按摩).

zatōkujira (座頭鯨), *n.* 【哺乳】 the humpback whale.

zatsu (雜な), *a.* ❶ (粗雜) rude; rough; coarse. ❷【數】adfected; mixed. —雜な言葉, a rude language. —雜に, rudely; roughly; coarsely.

zatsudan (雜談), *n.* gossip; idle [small; desultory] talk; tittle-tattle; chit-chat. —雜談する, to gossip; have an idle talk; tittle-tattle. —雜談に時を過ごす, to waste time in idle talk.

zatsueki (雜役), *n.* ❶ (事) odd jobs; 【軍】 fatigue-duty. ❷ (人) odd men; fatigues (兵士の). ¶ 雜役婦, a maid-of-all-work; a charwoman (日給の).

zatsugu (雜具), *n.* various tools.

zatsuki (座附), *n.* (芝居の) being attached to a theatre. ¶ 座附俳優, an actor attached to the theatre.

zatsumu (雜務), *n.* miscellaneous business [duties]. —雜務に追はれる, to be pressed with miscellaneous business.

zatsuroku (雜錄), *n.* a miscellany; miscellanea; a medley.

zatsuwa (雜話), *n.* desultory talk. ☞ *zatsudan.*

zatsuyō (雜用), *n.* miscellaneous business.

zatsuzen (雜然と), *ad.* in confusion; out of order; promiscuously; desultorily.

zatta (雜多の), *a.* various; miscellaneous; sundry. ☞ *shuju.* —雜多の物, all sorts of things.

zatto (ざっと), *ad.* ❶ (粗末に, 手輕に) roughly; cursorily ❷ (大略) roughly; in the rough; approximately; in round numbers. —ざっと言へば, roughly speaking. —ざっと目を通す, to run *over*; glance over; skim; give a cursory reading.

zattō (雜沓), *n.* bustle; crowd; press; crush. **—— -suru,** *vi.* to bustle; crowd together; be thronged; be congested. —雜沓せる群集, a thick crowd; a crowded mass.

zawazawa (ざわざわ), *ad.* murmuringly; noisily; rustlingly. —ざわざわする, to be noisy; be agitated; rustle.

zayaku (坐藥), *n.* 【醫】 a suppository; a collyrium.

zayoku (坐浴), *n.* a sitz-bath; a hip-bath.

zayū (座右), *n.* the right side of one's seat. —座右の銘, a watch-word; a constant guide; a maxim. —座右の友, a constant companion.

zazen (坐禪), *n.* an umbilical contemplation; a self-contemplation; 【梵】 Dhyāna Pāramitā (禪定波羅密). —坐禪する, to sit in umbilical contemplation [religious meditation].

zazō (坐像), *n.* a sedentary statue; a sitting image.

ze (是), *n.* the right; righteousness. —是は是とし非は非とする, to consider what is right right and wrong wrong.

zegahidemo (是が非でも), *ad.* whether right or wrong; by any manner of means; by hook or by crook.

zehi (是非), *n.* right and wrong. **——,** *ad.* by all means; in any case; at any cost [price]; anyhow; positively; certainly; without fail. —是非なき, inevitable; unavoidable. —是非なく, by force; perforce; by compulsion. —是非を辨ずる, to make distinction between right and wrong; tell the good from the bad. —是非もない, There is no help for it. —是非彼を連れて來い, Bring him by all means. —是非と云ってきかない, He will take no refusal.

zei (稅), *n.* a tax (人又は財產に課す); a duty (關稅, 消費稅, 行爲稅); a rate (地方稅); a toll (道路稅·橋稅など). —稅をかける, to impose [levy] a tax *upon*; tax. —稅を取り立てる, to draw a tax *from*; collect a tax.

zeibutsu (贅物), *n.* ❶ (無用物) a superfluous [useless] thing; unnecessaries. ❷ (贅澤品) a luxury.

zeigen (贅言), *n.* a pleonasm; a redundancy; a redundant expression; superfluous words.

zeihi (贅費), *n.* superfluous expenses.

zeihō (税法), *n.* a tax law; a law of taxation.

zeijaku (脆弱), *n.* fragility; frailty. —脆弱な, fragile; frail; delicate; brittle; flimsy; tender.

zeikan (税關), *n.* a custom-house; the customs. ¶ 税關長, the superintendent [controller] of customs; the director [commissioner] of customs. —税關貨物取扱人, a customs [custom-house]-broker. —税關監吏, a land [tide]-waiter; a customs inspector; a customs-officer; a revenue-officer. —税關假置場, a customs free dépôt. —税關上屋, a customs shed.

zeikin (税金), *n.* a tax. ☞ *zei.*

zeimu (税務), *n.* taxation business. ¶ 税務官吏, a revenue officer. —税務監督局, a taxation superintendence office. —税務署, a taxation office. (税務署長, the superintendent of a taxation office.)

zeiniku (贅肉), *n.* 【醫】 condyloma; a fungus [*pl.* -gi]; proud flesh.

zeiritsu (税率), *n.* tariff; the rate of a tax.

zeisei (税制), *n.* the system of taxation; a tax system. ¶ 税制整理案, a bill for the readjustment of the taxation system.

zeitaku (贅澤), *n.* luxury; extravagance; sumptuousness. —贅澤三昧をする, to indulge in luxury; be satiated with luxury. ——**-na,** *a.* luxurious; extravagant; sumptuous. —贅澤な暮し, a high living; an extravagant life. ¶ 贅澤品, a luxury.

zekkai (絶海), *n.* the farthest seas. —絶海の孤島, a lonely [solitary] island in the farthest sea. —絶海の無人島に上陸する, to land on a desert island in the distant sea.

zekke (絶家), *n.* an extinct family. ¶ 絶家再興, revival of an extinct family.

zekkei (絶景), *n.* a masterpiece of nature; an indescribably fine view; a scene beautiful beyond description.

zekkō (絶交), *n.* breach; rupture; breaking off friendship. —絶交する, to break off friendship *with*; sever [cut] acquaintance *with*; break *with*. —君とは絶交だ, I have done with you.

zekkō (絶好の), *a.* the best; capital; golden. —絶好の機會, a golden [the best] opportunity.

zekkotsu (舌骨), *n.* 【解】 the hyoid bone; the tongue-bone.

zekkyō (絶叫する), *vi.* to exclaim; ejaculate; yell; shout.

zen (全), *a.* whole; total; all; entire; complete; full; pan-[*pref.*]. ¶ 全獨主義, pan-Germanism. —全生涯, one's whole life. —全財產, one's all; the entire property.

zen (前の), *a.* ❶ (以前の) former; late; previous; ex-[*pref.*]. ❷ (上記の) above; preceding. ☞ *mae* (前の). ¶ 前代議士, an ex-member of the Diet; an ex-M.P. —前電, a previous telegram. —前國務卿, the late Secretary of State. —前半, the first half.

zen (善), *n.* good(-ness); virtue (德). —善は急げ, Do quickly what is good.

zen (膳), *n.* ❶ (器具) a small dining-table; a table. ❷ (膳部) a meal set on a table. ——, *numeral.* ❶ (一椀) a bowl (of soup, *etc.*). ❷ (一對) a pair (of chopsticks).

zen (漸を追うて), gradually; by degrees.

zenaku (善惡), *n.* good and (or) bad [evil]; virtue and vice (德不德); right and wrong (正邪).

zenbi (全備), *n.* perfection; completion; consummation.

zenbi (善美), *n.* ❶ the good and beautiful. ❷ (贅美) sumptuousness. —善美を盡した, superb; exquisite. —善美を盡す, to equip gorgeously; adorn sumptuously.

zenbin (前便), *n.* one's last (letter).

zenbu (全部), *n.* the whole; all; all parts. ——, *ad.* wholly; all; entirely; altogether; thoroughly; completely. —全部で, in all. —全部揃って, in its entirety; in a complete set.

zenbun (全文), *n.* the complete sentence; the full text (條約などの). —手紙の全文を掲げる, to give the letter in full.

zenchi (全知), *n.* omniscience. —全知全能の神, the Almighty; Almighty God.

zenchi (全治), *n.* complete recovery; perfect cure. —全治する, to recover completely; be completely cured.

zenchishi (前置詞), *n.* 【文】 the preposition.

zenchō (全長), *n.* the whole length: spread; span (飛行機の).

zenchō (前兆), *n.* an omen; a presage; a sign. —目出度い前兆, a good omen; a happy augury. —前兆する, to foretell; foretoken; presage; augur.

zenchū (蠕蟲), *n.* the worm.

zendai (前代), *n.* ❶ (前の代) former ages; the last generation. ❷ =*sendai*. —前代未聞の, unprecedented; unheard-of.

zendate (膳立), *n.* ❶ (食事の) setting dining-tables in order; spreading the table (for dinner).

❷ (仕事の準備) preparations; arrangements. —膳立する, to lay the table [cloth]; spread the table (for dinner); serve (up) dinner.

zendo (全土), *n.* the whole (of Europe, Japan, *etc.*) —歐洲全土に亙って, all over Europe.

zendō (善導する), *vt.* to instruct; enlighten; guide properly; lead to the right path [path of virtue]. —國民の思想を善導する, to lead public thought properly.

zendō (蠕動), *n.* 【蟲】 peristalsis; vermiculation. —蠕動する, to worm; creep.

zenei (全英の), *a.* all-red (全部英領を通過する); imperial (大英帝國の). ¶ 全英會議, an Imperial Conference. —全英航空路, an all--red air-route.

zenei (前衛), *n.* ❶ the advanced--guards; the vanguard; the van. ❷ an up-player (庭球の); a forward (蹴球の).

zengaku (全額), *n.* the sum (total); the total; the total amount. ¶ 全額支拂, payment in full.

zengaku (禪學), *n.* the *Zen* doctrine.

zengen (前言), *n.* previous words. —前言を食む《取消す》, to eat 《take back》 one's word.

zengen (漸減), *n.* decrease; gradual diminution. —漸減する, to decrease; diminish gradually.

zengo (前後), *n.* (順序) order; sequence. ——, *ad.* ❶ (位置の) before and behind. ❷ (時間の) before and after [since]. ❸ (殆ど, 大略) about; some; thereabout; or so; more or less. —前後の考へもなく, without considering the consequences. —前後を通じて, from the first to the last; throughout; first and last. —前後を忘れて怒る, to become blind with rage. —話が前後した, The talk has got out of order.

zengosaku (善後策), *n.* remedial [relief] measures; remedies. —善後策を講じる, to work out a relief measure.

zeni (錢), *n.* money; a coin. ☞「*kane* (金).」

zeni (善意), *n.* ❶ good intent. ❷【法】good faith; *bona fides*【羅】. —善意の第三者,【法】third person acting in good faith. —善意の相手方, the innocent party. —善意の買得者, a *bona-fide* purchaser. —善意に解釋する, to take [construe] matter with good intent; put a good construction on another's remark.

zeniaoi (錦葵), *n.* 【植】 the「marsh-mallow.」

zenibako (錢箱), *n.* a cash-box; a (money-)box (貯金又は寄附金等の); a money-drawer (抽斗).

zenigame (錢龜), *n.* 【爬蟲】 the Japanese terrapin.

zenigoke (地錢), *n.* 【植】 the liverwort.

zeniire (錢入), *n.* a pocket-book;「a purse.」

zenin (是認する), *vt.* to approve *of*; indorse; admit; countenance.

zenin (全院), *n.* the whole House (議會の). ¶ 全院委員長, the chairman of committees; the chairman of the committee of the whole House; the chairman of Ways and Means 【英】. —全院委員會, a meeting of the committee of the whole House; a sitting of the whole House in committee.

zenji (善事), *n.* ❶ a good [happy] thing. ❷ (善行) a virtuous deed [act]; a good deed [action].

zenji (漸次), *ad.* gradually; by degrees; little by little.

zenjin (前人), *n.* a predecessor; former people (昔の人). —前人未發の言, words never spoken by our predecessors.

zenjitsu (前日), *n.* ❶ the preceding [previous] day; the day before. ❷ (曩日) the former [past] day.

zenjō (前條), *n.* the preceding [foregoing] article.

zenjutsu (前述の), *a.* above--mentioned [-referred to]; foregoing; the said. —前述の通り, as has been previously mentioned [referred to].

zenka (全科), *n.* the whole curriculum [course]. ¶ 全科卒業證書, a certificate of the completion of the whole course.

zenka (前科), *n.* a previous offence [conviction]. —前科八犯の曲者, a villain who has already been convicted eight times. ¶ 前科者, an ex-convict; an old offender.

zenkai (全快), *n.* complete recovery (from illness). —全快する, to be perfectly cured; recover completely (from an illness); be restored to health. —全快の見込は全然ない, His recovery is beyond all hope; There is no hope of his recovery. ¶ 全快祝, a celebration of one's restoration to health.

zenkai (全會), *n.* the whole meeting; the whole assembly. —全會一致で, unanimously; with one consent [accord].

zenkan (善感), *n.* effectiveness of vaccination. —種痘が三顆善感した, Three inoculations took (effect).

zenkei (全景), *n.* a complete view; a panorama; a bird's-eye view.

zenken (全權), *n.* full [plenipotentiary] powers; absolute [plenary; full] authority; *carte blanche* 〔佛〕 —全權を持つ, to have absolute authority (*in*). ¶ 全權委員, a plenipotentiary.

zenki (前記の), *a.* foregoing; the said; above [fore]-mentioned; above referred to. —前記の金額, the said sum (of money).

zenki (前期), *n.* ❶ the first [former] period [term]. ❷ (前の期間) the last [previous] period. ¶ 前期議會, last session. —前期繰越金, the sum brought over from the preceding term. —前期試驗, a preliminary examination; the preliminaries.

zenkin (前金), *n.* payment in advance; an advance. —前金で支拂ふ, to pay in advance.

zenkō (善行), *n.* good conduct [action]; good deeds. —善行を表彰する, to show appreciation of another's good conduct. ¶ 善行章, a good-conduct badge; a good-conduct stripe.

zenkoku (全國), *n.* the whole country [state]. —全國に, over the whole country; throughout [all over] the country. (日本全國に, throughout [all over] Japan; in every part of Japan; in all Japan.)

zenku (前驅), *n.* an outrider; the van; the vanguard; a precursor; a forerunner. ☞ *senku*. ¶ 前驅症, 【醫】 prodrome.

zenkyaku (前脚), *n.* forelegs.

zenkyoku (全局), *n.* the whole aspect [field] (of affairs); the whole situation. —全局に眼を注ぐ, to keep an eye upon the whole field of affairs.

zenmai (薇), *n.* 【植】 the osmund royal; the flowering fern.

zenmai (發條), *n.* a spring; a mainspring (主要なる). ☞ *bane*. —發條を卷く, to wind a spring. ¶ 發條仕掛, clockwork; an apparatus worked by a spring.

zenmen (前面), *n.* front; the front-face; the façade (正面).

zenmetsu (全滅する), *vi.* to be annihilated; be destroyed; be extirpated; be stamped out. —全滅さす, to annihilate; destroy; wipe out —全滅するまで戰ふ, to fight to the last man.

zenmon (前門), *n.* a front gate. —前門に虎, 後門に狼, "A precipice in front, a wolf behind."

zennin (前任の), *a.* former. ¶ 前任知事, the former governor. —前任者, the predecessor (in a post).

zennin (善人), *n.* a good [virtuous] man.

zennō (全能), *n.* omnipotence, almightiness. —全能の, almighty; omnipotent; all-powerful.

zennō (前納), *n.* advance payment; prepayment. —前納する, to pay beforehand [in advance].

zenpai (全敗する), *vi.* to be utterly [totally] defeated; sustain a complete defeat.

zenpai (全廢する), *vt.* to abolish totally; do away with; put out of existence.

zenpan (全般の), *a.* whole; general; universal.

zenpi (前非), *n.* one's former misconduct; one's past misdeeds. —前非を悔いる, to repent of one's former misconduct; repent of one's past misdeeds.

zenpō (前方), *n.* the front. —前方に, ahead; forward; in front *of*.

zenpuku (全幅の), *a.* implicit; full; utmost; greatest; whole-hearted. —全幅の信任を置く, to repose implicit confidence *in*.

zenpyō (全豹), *n.* the whole; the general state; the whole situation. —一斑を以て全豹を斷ずる, to judge of the whole from a part.

zenraku (漸落), *n.* a gradual fall (物價などの).

zenrei (前例), *n.* a precedent; a previous example; an example. —前例なき出來事, an unprecedented [unexampled] event. —前例に依って, in accordance with the precedent; following the previous example [instance].

zenretsu (前列), *n.* the front rank.

zenritsu (前率), *n.* 【數】 an antecedent (a consequent の對).

zenryō (善良), *n.* goodness; virtuousness (有德). —— -**na**, *a.* good; right; virtuous; excellent. —善良の風俗に反する行爲, acts against [contrary to] good morals.

zenryoku (全力), *n.* all one's strength [energies]; one's best [utmost]. —全力を盡して, with all one's strength [might]; with might and main; with all one's heart; with one's whole heart.

zense (前世), *n.* a previous life; a prenatal existence [life]; a former world; pre-existence. —前世の約束, 〔梵〕 Karma; predestination; pre-established relations.

zensei (全盛), *n.* the height of prosperity [fortune]. —全盛時代に, in the days of one's prosperity; in its palmiest days. —全盛を極めてゐる, to be at the zenith of one's prosperity. —全盛の, the most prosperous [flourishing; thriving]; meridian; at its height.

zensei (善政), *n.* good government. —善政を施く, to rule wisely.

zensekai (前世界), *n.* the prehistoric age.

zensen (全線), *n.* all lines; the whole line. —全線を通じて, all along the lines.

zensen (前線), *n.* 【軍】the front line.

zensen (善戰する), *vi.* to fight bravely [well]; fight one's good fight.

zensha (前車), *n.* ❶ (砲車の) a limber. ❷ (前の車) the front cart [carriage]. —前車の覆るは後車の戒, "Learn wisdom from the follies of others."

zensha (前者), *n.* the former; the first; 【法】the prior party.

zenshaku (前借), *n.* advance; borrowing in advance. —前借する, to borrow (money) in advance.

zenshi (前肢), *n.* 【動】anterior [fore] limbs.

zenshi (前齒), *n.* a front tooth.

zenshin (全身), *n.* ❶ the whole body. ❷【寫】the full length. **——**, *ad.* all over the body; from top to toe; from head to foot. ¶ 全身病, a general [constitutional] disorder. —全身像, a full [whole]-length portrait [figure].

zenshin (前身), *n.* antecedents; the past: a precursor.

zenshin (前進), *n.* advance; progress. —前進する, to advance; progress; march on; go ahead; make headway.

zenshin (漸進的), *a.* gradual; moderate. —漸進する, to advance [progress] gradually. ¶ 漸進主義, gradual advance principle.

zensho (善處する), *vi.* to act judiciously; deal judiciously *with*; rise to the occasion.

zenshō (全勝), *n.* a complete victory; a clean record (野球などにて). —全勝する, to gain a complete victory (*over*); sweep the field (戰爭で).

zenshō (全燒), *n.* complete destruction by fire. —全燒する, to be completely destroyed by fire; be entirely burnt down.

zenshō (前哨), *n.* 【軍】an outpost; an advanced-post.

zenshū (全集), *n.* one's complete works; a complete collection.

zenshū (前週), *n.* last week; the preceding week; the week before.

zenshū (禪宗), *n.* the *Zen* Sect.

zensoku (喘息), *n.* 【醫】asthma. —喘息を病む, to suffer from asthma.

zensokuryoku (全速力), *n.* full [top; all] speed. —全速力で走る, to run at full speed.

zenson (全損), *n.* total loss.

zentai (全體), *n.* the whole; all (parts); the sum total (合計). **——**, *ad.* ❶ (元來) originally; from the first; naturally. ❷ (一體全體) (who; what; where, why に伴ふ) ever; on earth; in the world. ☞ *ittai*. —全體の, all; whole; entire. —全體で, in all; altogether. —全體から見れば, on the whole; taken altogether. **——-ni**, *ad.* in general; generally. —歐洲全體に, all over Europe; throughout the European countries. —全體に行き渡る, to pervade; spread all over: (物が) be distributed to all; go round. —全體なぜそんな事をしたのか, Why ever did you do such a thing?

zentei (前程), *n.* the journey before one.

zentei (前提), *n.* 【論】a premise, premiss. —誤った前提で推論する, to reason from false premises. ¶ 大(小)前提, a major (minor) premise.

zentetsu (前轍), *n.* another's experience [example]. —前轍を踏む, to tread in a person's steps; follow in the wake of another.

zenteki (全的), *a.* ☞ *zen.*

zento (前途), *n.* future career; (future) prospects; outlook; the future. —前途に橫はる困難, the difficulties lying before one; rocks ahead; Alps in the way. —前途有望の作家, a writer of great promise. —彼の前途は多望である, His prospects are bright; He has a great [brilliant] future before him.

zentokin (前渡金), *n.* money paid in advance.

zentō (前燈), *n.* a head-light.

zentō (漸騰), *n.* a gradual rise (相場·物價の).

zentōkotsu (前頭骨), *n.* 【解】a frontal bone.

zentoruman (紳士), *n.* a gentleman.

zentsū (全通する), *vi.* to be opened throughout for traffic; be completely opened for traffic.

zenwan (前腕), *n.* the forearm.

zenyaku (前約), *n.* pre-engagement; a previous engagement [agreement]. ☞ *senyaku, yoyaku.*

zenyō (善用する), *vt.* to make a good use *of*; put (anything) to a good use.

zenzen (全然), *ad.* entirely; wholly; totally; completely.

zenzen (漸漸), *ad.* gradually; by degrees; little by little.

zenzu (全圖), *n.* an unabridged [a complete] map. ¶ 日本(世界)全圖, a map of Japan (the world).

zeppan (絶版), *n.* being out of print. —絶版になる(である), to go (be) out of print.

zeppeki (絶壁), *n.* a precipice;

a steep; a cliff.

zeppin (絶品), *n.* a rare thing; a phenomenon. —天下の絶品, a work of greatest rarity in the world.

zeppitsu (絶筆), *n.* one's last writing 《painting》.

zerachin (ゼラチン), *n.* 【化】 gelatine.

zero (零), *n.* zero; nought. ¶ ゼロ·ゲーム, 【庭球】 a love game.

zessei (絶世の), *a.* peerless; matchless; unique. —絶世の美人, a woman of peerless beauty; the fairest of her sex.

zessen (舌戰), *n.* a war of words; a wordy dispute; a verbal contest; a passage of [at] arms. —舌戰する, to bandy words; have a verbal contest.

zesshō (絶勝), *n.* ❶ (最優) superexcellence; superiority. ❷ (絶景) a masterpiece of nature; a fine view. —東海の絶勝, the most beautiful scenery in the Eastern provinces.

zesshoku (絶食), *n.* abstinence from food. —— **-suru**, *vi.* to fast; abstain from food. —絶食して死ぬ, to starve oneself to death. ¶ 絶食同盟, a hunger strike. —絶食療法, 【醫】 fast-cure.

zessoku (絶息), *n.* expiration. —絶息する, to cease to breathe; breathe one's last; expire.

zes-suru (絶する), *vi.* ❶ (絶ゆ) to become extinct. ❷ (卓絶す る) to exceed; surpass; surmount. —言語に絶する, to be beyond description [the power of language].

zetchō (絶頂), *n.* ❶ (山巓) the highest point; the top; the summit; the crown. ❷ (極點) the climax; the zenith; the height; the pinnacle. —得意の絶頂にゐる, He is at the height of his pride.

zetsubi (絶美), *n.* superexcellence; exquisite [extraordinary] beauty.

zetsubō (絶望), *n.* hopelessness; despair; desperation. —絶望的, hopeless; desperate. —絶望する, to lose hope; despair; fall into despair; give up hope. —彼(の生命)は絶望だ, His life is despaired of.

zetsudai (絶大な), *a.* enormous; the largest [greatest]; gigantic.

zetsuen (舌炎), *n.* 【醫】 glossitis.

zetsuen (絶縁), *n.* ❶ (縁切) severing of relations. ❷ 【電】 isolation; insulation. —絶縁する, ① to sever relations; break off connection. ② to isolate; insulate. ¶ 絶縁線, an insulated wire. —絶縁體, an insulator.

zetsugan (舌癌), *n.* 【醫】 the cancer of the tongue.

zetsumei (絶命する), *vi.* to expire; breathe one's last; die.

zetsumu (絶無), *n.* nothing; nil; zero. —絶無である, there is no such...; it is impossible....

zetsumyō (絶妙の), *a.* super-excellent; exquisite.

zetsurin (絶倫の), *a.* matchless; peerless; unrivalled. —精力絶倫の人, a man of unequalled energy.

zettai (舌苔), *n.* fur.

zettai (絶對), *n.* absoluteness. —絶對的, absolute; positive. —絶對に無效である, to be void for all purposes. —絶對反對である, to be absolutely opposed *to*. ¶ 絶對服從, absolute obedience. —絶對權, 【法】 absolute right. —絶對命令, imperative; absolute imperative (良心の).

zettai-zetsumei (絶體絶命), *n.* the last extremity. —絶體絶命になる, to be driven to the last extremity [one's last resources]; be put to one's trumps [one's (last) shifts].

zettō (絶東), *n.* the Far East. 「☞ *kyokutō*.」

zettō (絶島), *n.* an isolated island.

zettō (絶倒する), *vi.* to shake one's sides; split [burst] one's sides. ☞ *hōfuku*.

zezehihi-shugi (是是非非主義), *n.* the clear-cut principle; the principle of impartial treatment.

zō (象), *n.* 【哺乳】 the elephant.

zō (像), *n.* ❶ (肖像) a figure; an image; a portrait; a likeness; a statue (立像). ❷ 【理】 an image.

zōbutsu (贓物), *n.* stolen goods; a pilferage; a swag 【卑】. —贓物の收受《故買; 牙保》, receiving 《buying; broking》 of stolen goods. ¶ 贓物故買者, a fence.

zōbutsusha (造物者), *n.* the Creator (of the world); God.

zōchiku (增築), *n.* the extension [enlargement] of a building. —增築する, to extend [enlarge] a building; build an annex [extension; addition] *to*.

zōchō (增長する), *vi.* to become puffed up [self-conceited]; grow presumptuous.

zōdai (增大), *n.* enlargement; increase; augmentation; enhancement. —增大する, ① [*vt.*] to enlarge; increase; swell; augment. ② [*vi.*] to increase; swell.

zōei (造營), *n.* building; erection; construction. —造營する, to build; construct; erect.

zōen (增援), *n.* reinforcement. —增援する, to reinforce.

zōfu (臟腑), *n.* viscera; entrails; intestines.
zōfukuki (増幅器), *n.* an amplifier (ラヂオの).
zōgaku (増額), *n.* the increase; the increased amount; the increment. —増額する, to increase; augment; raise.
zōgan (象眼, 象嵌), *n.* inlaid work; inlaying; damascene. —象眼する, to inlay; set; damascene, damaskeen. —鍔に金の象眼をする, to inlay a sword-guard with gold. ¶ 象眼細工, inlaid work; inlay; marquetry, marqueterie.
zōge (象牙), *n.* ivory. ¶ 摸造象牙, imitation [artificial] ivory. —象牙細工, ivory-work.
zōgen (増減), *n.* increase and decrease; addition and reduction; rise or fall. —増減する, to increase and decrease; add and reduce. —正比例に増減する, to vary directly. —年により多少の増減がある, to vary with the year. —實收穫は豫想に比し多少の増減を免れない, The actual yield cannot but vary [differ more or less] from the estimate.
zōgon (雜言), *n.* abusiveness; abusive [foul] language. —惡口雜言を云ひ散らす, to indulge in most abusive language.
zōhan (藏版), *n.* copyright.
zōhei (造兵), *n.* arms-manufacture; manufacture of arms and ammunition. ¶ 造兵官, a naval ordnance officer. —造兵廠, an arsenal; an arms-manufactory; an armoury 【米】. (海軍造兵廠, the naval arsenal.)
zōhei (造幣), *n.* mintage; coinage. ¶ 造幣局, the mint. (造幣局長, the mint-master; the treasurer of the mint 【米】.)
zōhei (増兵する), *v.* to reinforce; send [despatch] more troops.
zōhibyō (象皮病), *n.* 【醫】 elephantiasis.
zōho (増補), *n.* supplement; enlargement. —増補する, to enlarge; supplement; make addition *to*.
zōhō (増俸), *n.* increase [rise] of salary. —増俸する, to increase [raise] a salary.
zōhyō (雜兵), *n.* common soldiers; the ranks; the rank and file; the privates.
zōi (贈位), *n.* conferment of a posthumous (court) rank.
zōi (贈遺), *n.* a gift or a legacy; a present; a gift.
zōka (造化), *n.* ● creation; nature. ● (造物者) the Creator. —造化の妙, the wonder of nature. —造化の戯, a freak of nature.
zōka (造花), *n.* artificial flowers.
zōka (増加), *n.* increase; addition; increment; gain. —増加に向ってゐる, to be on the increase. ——**suru**, *v.* to increase; augment; multiply (倍加). —三割方増加する, to increase by about thirty per cent.
zōkan (増刊), *n.* a special number (of a magazine). ¶ 臨時増刊, an extra special number.
zōkei (造詣), *n.* profound knowledge; attainment; scholarship. —造詣がある, to be at home *in*; be well versed *in*; have a profound knowledge *of*.
zōken (増遣する), *vt.* Ⓢ 増派する. to dispatch [send] in addition.
zōki (雜木), *n.* small trees; inferior wood [timber] (粗材). ¶ 雜木林, a copse(-wood). —雜木山, a copsy hill.
zōki (臟器), *n.* viscera; intestines.
zōkin (雜巾), *n.* a house-cloth; a dust-cloth; a floor-cloth. —雜巾がけする, to wipe with a house-cloth.
zokka (俗化), *n.* vulgarization; popularization. —俗化する, to be vulgarized; become degenerated.
zokka (俗歌), *n.* a popular song; a folksong; a ballad.
zokkai (俗界), *n.* the (common) world; the earth; secular[earthly] life. —俗界の, worldly; earthly; temporal; secular. —俗界の快樂を追ふ, to pursue worldly pleasures.
zokkan (俗間), *n.* the world; the public; the people. —俗間傳ふる所に據れば, according to the town-talk.
zokkan (屬官), *n.* a petty official; a clerk; a subordinate (official).
zokki (俗氣), *n.* earthly desire; worldly ambition. —俗氣ある人, a worldly-minded man. —俗氣が拔けない, ① [*a.*] worldly; earthly; of worldly ambition. ② [*v.*] to be still haunted by ambition.
zokkō (續行), *n.* pursuance; continuance. —續行する, to pursue; continue; carry on.
zokkoku (屬國), *n.* a dependency; a subject state; a tributary. —屬國になる, to pass under the sway of some power.
zokkyoku (俗曲), *n.* =***zokka***.
zōkokudaka (造石高), *n.* brewage. ¶ 造石稅, tax on brewage.
zoku (俗), *n.* ● (風俗) custom; manners. ● (俗人) a lay man; the laity. ● (野卑) vulgarity; coarseness. —俗に媚びる, to cater to the public. —俗をな

す, to become a custom. ——**na,** *a.* ❶ (現世的) worldly-minded; earthly; worldly; mundane; lay (僧に對す). ❷ (野卑の) vulgar; coarse; low; base; unrefined. ❸ (通俗の) common, popular. 一俗な飾, vulgar finery. ——**ni,** *ad.* ❶ (普通) commonly; popularly. ❷ (野卑に) vulgarly; coarsely. 一俗に言へば, in common [vulgar] parlance; to use a common phrase (獨立句).

zoku (族), *n.* ❶ (家族) family; kinsmen; relations (親族); one's people (やから). ❷ (種族) a tribe. ❸ (博物學の) a family; 【動·植】 a tribe; 【動】 a series.

zoku (賊), *n.* ❶ (賊徒) rebels; traitors. ❷ (盜賊) a robber; a thief; a burglar (夜盜). 一賊を討つ【平げる】, to attack【subjugate】 rebels.

zoku (屬), *n.* ❶ (屬官) a petty official. ☞ *zokkan* (屬官). ❷ (分類上の) 【生·動·植】 genus. ¶ 大藏省屬, a clerk of the Finance Department.

zokuaku (俗惡な), *a.* vulgar; base; unrefined.

zokubun (俗文), *n.* colloquial style.

zokubungaku (俗文學), *n.* popular literature.

zokubutsu (俗物), *n.* a worldling; a vulgar [worldly-minded] person; a man of low taste.

zokuchi (屬地), *n.* a dependency; a possession; a territory.

zokuchō (族長), *n.* the head of a family; the father; the patriarch. ¶ 族長時代, the patriarchal age.

zokuga (俗畫), *n.* a cad-catcher.

zokugaku (俗樂), *n.* popular music; folk-music.

zokugan (俗眼), *n.* a common [vulgar] eye; an ordinary view.

zokugo (俗語), *n.* colloquial language; a colloquialism; the vulgar tongue; a vulgarism (卑語).

zokugu (屬具), *n.* appurtenances; equipment (船舶の).

zokugun (賊軍), *n.* rebels; a rebel army.

zokuhatsu (續發する), *vi.* to happen [occur] in succession; come out one after another.

zokuhen (續編), *n.* a sequel; a supplementary volume; a continuation.

zokuji (俗事), *n.* temporal interests; temporal [worldly; earthly] affairs; common [everyday] business [affairs]. 一俗事に關らない, to keep aloof from common affairs. 一俗事にかまける, to be occupied with everyday affairs.

zokujin (俗人), *n.* ❶ (俗物) a worldling. ❷ (在家の人) a lay man; the laity.

zokujin (俗塵), *n.* the world. 一俗塵を避ける, to keep aloof from earthly affairs.

zokumoku (屬目する), *v.* = *shokumoku.*

zokumu (俗務), *n.* secular affairs; earthly affairs. ☞ *zokuji.* 一俗務多端, to have plenty of worldly business; be in a whirl of business.

zokumyō (俗名), *n.* a common name; an ordinary name.

zokunen (俗念), *n.* worldy mind; earthly desire. 一俗念を去る, to free oneself from earthly desires.

zokuri (俗吏), *n.* ❶ (小役人) a petty official; a subordinate official. ❷ (凡俗官吏) a consequential petty official; a Jack-in-office; a bumble. ¶ 俗吏根性, bumbledom; beadledom.

zokuri (屬吏), *n.* ❶ (配下の吏) a subordinate (official); an inferior official. ❷ (小吏) a petty official.

zokuron (俗論), *n.* vulgar opinion.

zokuryō (屬僚), *n.* a subaltern; subordinates; the staff. 一大【公】使の屬僚, the diplomatic staff.

zokusai (俗才), *n.* worldly wisdom; practical wisdom. 一俗才に長ける, to have seen much of life. (俗才に長けた人, a worldly-wise person.)

zokusai (續載する), *vt.* to bring out in succession; give in the sequel.

zokusei (簇生), *n.* gregarious growth 一簇生する, ① to grow gregariously; grow in clusters. ② (簇出) to spring into existence in great numbers【one after another】.

zokusei (屬性), *n.* 【哲】 attribution; an attribute: a predicate. 一神の屬性, an attribute of God.

zokuseki (族籍), *n.* social status and domicile.

zokusen (賊船), *n.* a pirate-ship; a sea-rover.

zokusetsu (俗說), *n.* a common [vulgar] saying; folk-lore (口碑). 一俗說に曰く, it is said popularly; tradition says.

zokushin (俗心), *n.* worldliness; earthliness; a worldly mind.

zokushō (俗稱), *n.* a common name (特に植物學で); a popular designation.

zokushū (俗臭), *n.* low [vulgar] taste.

zokushū (俗習), *n.* vulgar practice [manners].

zokushutsu (續出する), *vi.* to appear【occur】 in succession [one after another].

zoku-suru (屬する), *vi.* to belong *to*; appertain *to* (權利上); reside [rest; inhere; be vested] *in* (權利·權力等が); be subject *to*

(隷屬する). ——, *vt.* (託する) to charge *with*; intrust *to*; put in another's care. —政友會に屬する, to attach oneself to the Seiyūkai; join the Seiyūkai: be a Seiyūkai man. —英國に屬してゐる, to be under English rule. —眼を屬する, to have [keep] an eye *on*. —大事を屬する, to charge with important affairs. —望を屬する, to put hopes *upon*.

zokutaku (囑託する), *vt.* to charge; commission. ☞ ***shokutaku*** (囑託する).

zokuto (賊徒), *n.* ❶ (賊群) a gang of robbers. ❷ (朝敵) traitors; rebels.

zokuuke (俗受), *n.* popularity. —俗受けのする畫家, an artist popular among undiscriminating persons. —俗受けがする, to appeal [be] to the popular [common] taste.

zokuwa (俗話), *n.* town-talk; gossip; vulgar talk.

zokuyō (俗謠), *n.* a ballad; a folk-song; a popular song.

zokuzoku (續續), *ad.* in rapid succession; one after another; continuously. —續々詰め掛ける, to come in rapid succession.

zokuzoku (ぞくぞくする), *vi.* ❶ (寒くて) to feel chilly; shiver. ❷ (情が激發して) to thrill; shudder. —ぞくぞくする程嬉しがる, to tremble [thrill] with joy. —一寸見ただけでぞくぞくした, A mere glance made me feel creepy. —嬉しくてぞくぞくした, It sent a thrill of joy to my heart.

zōkyū (增給), *n.* increase [rise] of wages. ☞ ***zōhō***.

zōmotsu (雜物), *n.* sundries.

zōmotsu (臟物), *n.* guts; pluck (牛·羊等の); giblets (禽類の).

zonbun (存分), *ad.* without reserve; to one's heart's content. —思ふ存分泣く, to weep one's fill.

zōnen (雜念), *n.* various ideas; wild fancies.

zongai (存外), *ad.* beyond (one's) expectation; contrary to (one's) expectation (期待と反對の場合).

zonjinagara (存じ乍ら), *ad.* consciously; knowingly.

zonjō (存生), *n.* Ⓢ 存命. existence; living. —存生する, to live; survive; be alive.

zonnen (存念), *n.* thought; an idea.

zonzai (ぞんざいな), *a.* rough; rude; slovenly; careless (不注意). —ぞんざいな口のききやう, a rude way of speaking. ——**-ni,** *ad.* roughly; in a rude manner; carelessly. —ぞんざいに扱ふ, to handle [use] roughly [carelessly].

zon-zuru (存ずる), *vt.* ❶ (知る) to know; be aware. ❷ (思ふ) to think; feel; intend. ❸ (知己) to be acquainted *with*. —私は…と存じます, I think that…; my idea is that….

zōo (憎惡), *n.* hatred; detestation; abhorrence. —憎惡すべき, hateful; detestable; execrable.

zōri (草履), *n.* straw sandals. —草履を穿く, to wear sandals.

zōrimushi (草履蟲), *n.* 【昆】 Paramœcium; the slipper-animalcule.

zōrin (造林), *n.* afforestation. —造林する, to afforest. ¶ 造林法, forestry; sylviculture; forest management.

zorozoro (ぞろぞろ), *ad.* in succession; one after another.

zōsaku (造作), *n.* ❶ fixtures; appointments. ❷ (顏の) countenance; features. —造作を附ける, to furnish a house. ¶ 造作附貸家, a house to let with fixtures.

zōsanai (造作ない), *a.* easy. —造作なく, easily; readily; with) out trouble [difficulty].

zōsen (造船), *n.* shipbuilding. ¶ 造船學, naval architecture; shipbuilding. —造船術, shipbuilding. —造船監督官, a shipbuilding inspector. —造船計畫, a shipbuilding programme. —造船所, a dockyard; a shipyard; a shipbuilding yard.

zōshi (增師), *n.* an increase of divisions. ¶ 增師案, a bill for an increase of divisions. —增師問題, the divisions increase question.

zōshin (增進), *n.* promotion; increase. —能率增進を計る, to take measures for promoting efficiency. ——**-suru,** *v.* to promote; increase. —健康を增進する, to build up one's health.

zōsho (藏書), *n.* a book in one's possession; a library. ¶ 藏書家, the owner of a well-stocked [large] library. —藏書目錄, a library catalogue.

zōshō (藏相), *n.* the Minister of Finance; the Finance Minister.

zōshoku (增殖), *n.* multiplication; increase. —增殖する, to increase; multiply.

zōshū (增收), *n.* an additional income; increase of receipts.

zōsui (增水), *n.* the rise of a river; a freshet. —增水する, to rise; swell. ¶ 增水標, a flood-mark.

zōsui (雜炊), *n.* a medley soup; a chowder; a lobscouse (海員の).

zō-suru (藏する), *vt.* to have; keep. —萬卷の書を藏する, to

have a large library.

zōtei (贈呈), *n.* presentation; offer. —贈呈する, to present a person with a thing; make a person a present of a thing; offer. ¶ 贈呈本, a presentation copy.

zōtō (贈答), *n.* exchange. —進物の贈答, an exchange of presents. —贈答する, to exchange.

zōtoku (藏匿), *n.* shelter; concealment; secretion. **——-suru,** *vt.* to shelter; harbour; conceal. —犯人を藏匿する, to harbour a culprit [criminal].

zotto (ぞッとする), *vi.* to shudder; shiver; be struck with terror; feel a chill (寒け). **——,** *a.* thrilling; frightful; horrible; dire. —ぞッとする程の恐しさ, a thrill of horror. —ぞッとするやうなよい聲, a thrilling voice. —見ただけでぞッとする, to shudder [tremble] at the mere sight of it. —想像するだにぞッとする, I shudder at the bare idea. —餘りぞッとしない品だ, It is not an article that I fancy much.

zōwai (贈賄), *n.* bribery; corruption. ☞ *wairo*. —贈賄する, to bribe; corrupt; give a bribe. ¶ 贈賄事件, a bribery case. —贈賄者, a briber.

zōyo (贈與), *n.* dona ion; presentation; gift. —贈與する, to give; donate; present a thing to a person; present a person with a thing.

zōyō (雜用), *n.* (種々の費用) miscellaneous outlay; various [sundry] expenses.

zōzei (增稅), *n.* increase of taxation; increased tax. —增稅する, to increase taxes. ¶ 增稅案, an increased taxation bill.

zu (圖), *n.* ❶ (地圖) a map. ❷ (繪圖) a picture; a drawing. ❸ (圖面) a plan; a drawing. ❹ (插畫) an illustration; a cut. ❺ (數學の) a diagram. ❻ (思ふ壺) the aim; the mark. —圖で示す, to show by diagrams [graphically]. —圖で說明する, to illustrate; explain with diagrams. —圖に當る, to hit the mark. —圖に乘る, ① (得意, 自惚) to be puffed up *with*; be elated *with*; let oneself go (調子づく). ② to presume *upon* (つけ上る). —圖を引く, to draw a plan; draw.

zuan (圖案), *n.* a design; a sketch; a device. ¶ 衣裳圖案, a dress design. —圖案家, a designer; a draughtsman. —圖案科, the design course.

zubon (ズボン), *n.* trousers; breeches; pantaloons [米]. ¶ ズボン下, drawers; pants. —ズボン吊り, braces [英]; suspenders [米].

zubora (ずぼらな), *a.* slovenly; idle; negligent. —ずぼらな男, a sloven; an idle fellow.

zuboshi (圖星), *n.* the bull's eye; the mark. —圖星を中てる, to hit the mark; hit the right nail on the head.

zubunure (ずぶ濡), *n.* being drenched; being wet to the skin. —ずぶ濡れになる, to get soaked; be wet to the skin.

zuburi (ずぶりと刺す), to stab [pierce] through.

zuburoku (圖部六に醉ふ), to be dead [blind] drunk; be beastly drunk; be drunk as a fish.

zubutoi (圖太い), *a.* bold; daring; impudent; audacious. —圖太い事をする, to act audaciously.

zudabukuro (頭陀袋), *n.* a wallet; a scrip.

zudon (づどんと), *ad.* ❶ with a bang. ❷ with a thud; plump. —ヅドンと落ちる, to fall with a thud; plump down. —ヅドンと一發, Bang! went the gun (pistol).

zudori (圖取), *n.* sketching; a diagram; a plan. —圖取りする, to sketch; figure; draw a plan [diagram].

zuga (圖畫), *n.* (a) drawing. ¶ 圖畫用紙, drawing-paper.

zugai (頭蓋), *n.* 【解】the cranium; the brain-pan. ¶ 頭蓋骨, the cranium; the skull.

zuhiki (圖引), *n.* ❶ (圖を引くこと) drawing. ❷ (圖を引く人) a draughtsman. ¶ 圖引器械, drawing instruments.

zuhō (圖法), *n.* drawing; draughtsmanship. ¶ 平面圖法, projection.

zui (髓), *n.* ❶ 【解】 the marrow. ❷ 【植】 the pith. ❸ (心髓) the core.

zui (蕊), *n.* 【植】 a stamen (雄); a pistil (雌).

zuibun (隨分), *ad.* ❶ (可なり) fairly; pretty; tolerably. ❷ (非常に) very; extremely; seriously. —隨分な, (反語) nice; fine. (隨分な人だ, He is a nice fellow.) —隨分年寄ってゐる, He is well advanced in years. —あら隨分だわ, Oh, that's too bad.

zuichō (瑞兆), *n.* a good [happy; an auspicious] omen.

zuihan (隨伴する), *vt.* to accompany; follow; attend *upon*.

zuihitsu (隨筆), *n.* jottings; stray notes; miscellaneous writings; a sketch; a miscellany; a medley. ¶ 隨筆家, a miscellanist; a rambler.

zuihōshō (瑞寶章), *n.* the Order

of the Sacred Treasure.

zuii (隨意), *n.* freedom; voluntariness; option (任意). —— **-ni,** *ad.* freely; at liberty; at (one's) will; without restraint. —隨意にさす, to let a person have his way. —人の隨意に任す, to leave a thing to a person [person's option]; place [put] a thing at another's disposal. —隨意に歸宅してよろしい, You are free to go home ¶ 隨意科, an optional course. —隨意契約, a private contract. —隨意筋, 【解】 a voluntary muscle.

zuiichi (隨一の), *a.* the best; the first; the greatest. —天下隨一, the best in the world. —東北隨一の名勝, the most famous place in the North-eastern provinces.

zuiji (隨時), *ad.* at any time. —必要に應じ隨時, on occasion; whenever need arises. ¶ 隨時收入, an extra receipt.

zuikan (隨感), *n.* occasional thoughts. ¶ 隨感隨筆, occasional writings; stray notes.

zuiki (隨喜), *n.* idolization; adoration; gratification. —隨喜する, to idolize; adore. —隨喜の涙を流す, to shed tears of joy.

zuikō (隨行), *n.* attendance on a journey. —隨行する, to attend *upon*; accompany; follow. ¶ 隨行員, a suite; a retinue; a train (of attendants).

zuimushi (螟蟲), *n.* 【昆】 the pearl-moth.

zuisho (隨處に), *ad.* everywhere.

zuishō (瑞祥), *n.* =*zuichō*.

zuishō (瑞相), *n.* ❶ (瑞兆) a good omen. ❷ (福々しき人相) a face betokening good fortune. —泰平の世の瑞相, a happy sign of the peaceful reign.

zuiun (瑞雲), *n.* lucky [auspicious] clouds.

zukai (圖解), *n.* an explanatory diagram; an illustration; a figure. —圖解する, to illustrate.

zukazuka (づかづか), *ad.* straight; without leave; without a word. —づかづか物を言ふ, to speak bluntly. —僕の前をづかづか通った, He went past me without a word.

-zuke (附), dated; under date. —先月十日附御書面, your letter dated [under date of] the 10th ult.

-zuki (好), -phil, -phile; philo-; mania; a lover. ¶ 學問好き, a philomath. —本好き, a bibliophil(-e). —芝居好き, a playgoer; a frequenter of theatres. —運動好き, a lover of exercise.

-zuki (附の), with; furnished; attached *to*. —景品附の, with a premium. —湯殿附の家, a house furnished with a bath-room.

zukin (頭巾), *n.* a hood; a skull-cap (室內用); a gorget (婦人用); a wimple (尼の); a cowl (僧の).

zukizuki (づきづきする), *vi.* to throb with pain; smart; rankle.

zukku (ヅック), *n.* cotton duck; canvas. ¶ ヅック靴, canvas-shoes.

zukotsu (頭骨), *n.* the skull.

zuku (木菟), *n.* 【鳥】 the feather-toed scops-owl.

-zukude (づくで), by; by means *of*; by dint *of*; by force *of*. —力づくで, by sheer [main] force. —腕づくでさせる, to make a person do something by force. —金づくでも何づくでも得られない, It is not to be had for love or money.

zukutetsu (銑鐵), *n.* pig-iron; pig.

-zume (詰), ❶ (任命) appointment. ❷ (塡充) packing. ❸ (繼續) keeping. —行李詰の, basketed; packed in a basket. —一行二十字詰, twenty characters to a line. —終日立詰めでした, I kept on my legs all day. ¶ 本省詰, service at the head department.

zumen (圖面), *n.* a drawing; a plan; a map.

-zumi (積), burden; lading. —下積(の荷物), (goods in) the lower layer. —百噸積の船, a ship of 100 tons burden.

zunō (頭腦), *n.* the head; the brain. —頭腦明晰な, clear-headed; astute.

zunukete (圖抜けて), *ad.* extraordinarily; exceptionally; out of the common [ordinary].

zunzun (ずんずん), *ad.* rapidly (速に); by leaps and bounds (とんとん拍子に); swimmingly (すらすら). —(仕事など) ずんずん進行する, to go on swimmingly.

zurari (ずらりと), *ad.* in a (long) line; in a row. —ずらりと竝ぶ, to form a line; stand in a row.

zurasu (ずらす), *vt.* to shift; move aside.

-zure (擦), sore; graze. ¶ 鞍擦れ, a saddle gall. —靴擦れ, a boot-sore. —床擦れ, a bed-sore.

zureru (ずれる), *vi.* to slip; 【機】 shear.

zurideru (滑出る), *vi.* to slip out; glide out.

zuriochiru (滑落ちる), *vi.* to slip down; glide down.

zuriotosu (滑落す), *vt.* to let (a thing) slip off.

zurō (杜漏な), *a.* careless; negligent; slovenly.

zuru (ずる), *n.* ❶ (事) craftiness; cunning. ❷ (行爲) a trick; a foul play; a guile. ❸ (人) a crafty person: a shirk; a slacker 〔俗〕. —ずるを極める, to play truant (學校を休む); shirk one's duty.

zuru (滑る), *vi.* to slide; slip; skid (車輪など横に); shift (移動).

zurui (ずるい), *a.* sly; cunning; crafty.

zurukeru (ずるける), *v.* to be idle [lazy]; shirk. —仕事をずるける, to shirk work.

zuruzuru (ずるずる), *ad.* ❶ (物を引ずる樣) trailingly. ❷ (滑かな樣) slipperily. —ずるずるべッたりになる, ① to remain unsettled. ② to stay on.

zushi (廚子), *n.* a small shrine (in a temple); a sanctuary.

zushiki (圖式), *n.* a diagram; 【論】 a figure.

zusho (圖書), *n.* =***tosho*** (圖書). ¶ 圖書頭, the Director of the Library Bureau.

-zutai (傳ひに), along. —川傳ひに行く, to go on along the river.

zūtai (圖體), *n.* a body; a frame; physique.

zutazuta (寸斷に), *ad.* to pieces; into strips; into shreds. —ずたずたに切る, to cut into strips [pieces]; tear to ribbons.

-zutsu (宛), apiece [*ad.*]; by [*prep.*]. —一人に一箇づつ, one apiece. —二人に一箇づつ, one to every two persons. —一日に三回宛, three times a day. —二つ宛數へる, to count two by two.

zutsū (頭痛), *n.* a headache; a racking headache (割れさうに痛む). —頭痛がする, to have a headache; have a pain in one's head; One's head aches. ¶ 頭痛鉢卷, racking one's brain. —頭痛膏, a sticking-plaster for headaches. —頭痛持, a person subject to headaches.

zutto (ずッと), *ad.* ❶ (眞直に) directly; straight. ❷ (遙に) very much; far and away; by far; far; vastly. ❸ (通して) all the time; through. —ずッと以前に, a long while ago; many years ago. —ずッと北の方に, away (to the) north. —春からずッと, ever since last spring. —ずッと這入る, to go straight on.

zuzan (杜撰な), *a.* careless; slipshod; inaccurate. —杜撰な豫算案, a carelessly-got-up budget.

zuzu (珠數), *n.* =***juzu***.

zuzugo (川穀), *n.* 【植】 Job's tears; the gromwell-reed.

zuzukakebato (斑鳩), *n.* 【鳥】 the (common) Indian dove.

zūzūshii (圖圖しい), *a.* impudent; cool; brazen [bold]-faced. —圖々しい奴, an impudent fellow; a cool hand. —圖々しくも…する, to have the face [impudence; cheek] to. —圖々しくやり通す, to carry it off; brazen it out; face through.

附録

不規則動詞表

下表中イタリックにしたる語はその古體なるを示す.

現在	過去	過去分詞
abide	abode	abode
arise	arose	arisen
awake	awoke, awaked	awaked
be	was	been
bear[1]（生む）	bore, *bare*	born
bear[2]（負ふ）	bore, *bare*	borne
beat	beat	beaten, beat
begin	began	begun
behold	beheld	beheld
belay	belaid, *belayed*	belaid, *belayed*
bend	bent, bended	bent, bended
bereave	bereft, bereaved	bereft, bereaved
beseech	besought	besought
bet	bet, betted	bet, betted
bid	bad, bade, *bid*	bidden, *bid*
bind	bound	bound
bite	bit	bitten, bit
bleed	bled	bled
blend	blent, blended	blent, blended
bless	blest, blessed	blest, blessed
blow	blew	blown
break	broke, *brake*	broken
breed	bred	bred
bring	brought	brought
build	built, *builded*	built, *builded*
burn	burnt, *burned*	burnt, *burned*
burst	burst	burst
buy	bought	bought
can	could	——
cast	cast	cast
catch	caught, *catched*	caught, *catched*
chide	chid, *chode*	chidden, *chid*
choose	chose	chosen
cleave[1]（割る）	clove, cleft	cloven, cleft
cleave[2]（固著する）	cleaved, *clave*	cleaved
climb	climbed, *clomb*	climbed
cling	clung	clung
clothe	clothed, clad	clad, clothed
come	came	come
cost	cost	cost
creep	crept	crept
crow	crew, crowed	crowed
cut	cut	cut
dare	durst, dared	dared
deal	dealt, *dealed*	dealt, *dealed*
dig	dug, *digged*	dug, *digged*
do	did	done
draw	drew	drawn
dream	dreamt, dreamed	dreamt, dreamed
dress	dressed, *drest*	dressed, *drest*
drink	drank, *drunk*	drunk, *drunken*
drive	drove	driven
dwell	dwelt, *dwelled*	dwelt, *dwelled*
eat	ate, *eat*	eaten, *eat*
fall	fell	fallen
feed	fed	fed
feel	felt	felt

現在	過去	過去分詞
fight	fought	fought
find	found	found
flee	fled	fled
fling	flung	flung
fly	flew	flown
forbear	forbore	forborne
forget	forgot	forgotten, *forgot*
forsake	forsook	forsaken
freeze	froze	frozen
get	got	got, gotten
gild	gilt, gilded	gilt, gilded
gird	girt, girded	girt, girded
give	gave	given
go	went	gone
grave	graved	graven, graved
grind	ground	ground
grow	grew	grown
hang	hung, hanged	hung, hanged
have	had	had
hear	heard	heard
heave	hove, heaved	hove, heaved
hew	hewed	hewn, hewed
hide	hid	hidden, hid
hit	hit	hit
hold	held	held, *holden*
hurt	hurt	hurt
keep	kept	kept
kneel	knelt, kneeled	knelt, kneeled
knit	knit, knitted	knit, knitted
know	knew	known
lade	laded	laded, laden
lay	laid	laid
lead	led	led
lean	leant, leaned	leant, leaned
leap	leapt (lept), leaped	leapt (lept), leaped
learn	learnt, learned	learnt, learned
leave	left	left
lend	lent	lent
let	let	let
lie（横はる）	lay	lain
light	lit, lighted	lit, lighted
lose	lost	lost
make	made	made
may	might	——
mean	meant	meant
meet	met	met
melt	melted	molten, melted
mow	mowed	mown, mowed
pass	past, passed	past, passed
pay	paid	paid
pen（囲ひ）	pent, penned	pent, penned
prove	proved	proven, proved
put	put	put
quit	quitted, *quit*	quitted, *quit*
rap	rapt, rapped	rapt, rapped
read	read (red)	read (red)
reeve	rove, reeved	rove, reeved
rend	rent	rent
rid	rid	rid
ride	rode, *rid*	ridden, *rid*
ring	rang, *rung*	rung
rise	rose	risen
rive	rived	riven, *rived*

現　　在	過　　去	過去分詞
run	ran	run, *runned*
saw	sawed	sawn, *sawed*
say	said	said
see	saw	seen
seek	sought	sought
seethe	seethed, *sod*	seethed, *sodden*
sell	sold	sold
send	sent	sent
set	set	set
sew	sewed	sewn
shake	shook	shaken
shall	should	——
shape	shaped	shaped, *shapen*
shave	shaved	shaven, shaved
shear	sheared, *shore*	shorn, *sheared*
shed	shed	shed
shine	shone, *shined*	shone, *shined*
shoe	shod	shod
shoot	shot	shot
show	showed	shown, *showed*
shred	shred	shred
shrink	shrank, *shrunk*	shrunk, *shrunken*
shut	shut	shut
sing	sang, *sung*	sung
sink	sank, *sunk*	sunk
sit	sat	sat
slay	slew	slain
sleep	slept	slept
slide	slid	slid, *slidden*
sling	slung, *slang*	slung
slink	slunk, *slank*	slunk
slit	slit, slitted	slit, slitted
smell	smelt, *smelled*	smelt, *smelled*
smite	smote, *smit*	smitten, *smit*
sow	sowed	sown, sowed
speak	spoke, *spake*	spoken
speed	sped, speeded	sped, speeded
spell	spelt, spelled	spelt, spelled
spend	spent	spent
spill	spilt, spilled	spilt, spilled
spin	spun, span	spun
spit	spat, *spit*	spat, *spit*
split	split, *splitted*	split, *splitted*
spoil	spoilt, spoiled	spoilt, spoiled
spread	spread	spread
spring	sprang, *sprung*	sprung
stand	stood	stood
stave	stove, staved	stove, staved
steal	stole	stolen
stick	stuck	stuck
sting	stung	stung
stink	stank	stunk
strew	strewed	strewn, strewed
stride	strode	strid, *stridden*
strike	struck	struck, stricken
string	strung	strung
strive	strove	striven
strow, strew	strowed, strewed	strown, strowed
swear	swore, *sware*	sworn
sweep	swept	swept
swell	swelled	swollen, swelled
swim	swam, *swum*	swum
swing	swung, *swang*	swung

現在	過去	過去分詞
take	**took**	**taken**
teach	**taught**	**taught**
tear	**tore,** ***tare***	**torn**
tell	**told**	**told**
think	**thought**	**thought**
thrive	**throve, thrived**	**thriven, thrived**
throw	**threw**	**thrown**
thrust	**thrust**	**thrust**
tread	**trod,** ***trode***	**trodden, trod**
wake	**woke, waked**	**woke, woken, waked**
wax	**waxed**	**waxen, waxed**
wear	**wore**	**worn**
weave	**wove**	**woven**
wed	**wed, wedded**	**wed, wedded**
weep	**wept**	**wept**
wend	**went**	**went**
wet	**wet, wetted**	**wet, wetted**
whet	**whet, whetted**	**whet, whetted**
will	**would**	——
win	**won**	**won**
wind	**wound,** ***winded***	**wound**
work	**wrought, worked**	**wrought, worked**
wring	**wrung**	**wrung**
write	**wrote,** ***writ***	**written**
writhe	**writhed**	**writhen, writhed**

複合不規則動詞表

下表各語中イタリックにしたる部分は變化の生ずべき本語を示すものにして其變化は各語に就き前表を見るべし.

- be*come*
- be*fall*
- be*get*
- be*gird*
- be*set*
- be*speak*
- be*spit*
- be*strew*
- be*stride*
- be*take*
- be*think*
- brow*beat*
- en*gird*
- en*grave*
- for*bid*
- for*do*
- fore*cast*
- fore*go*
- fore*know*
- fore*run*
- fore*see*
- fore*show*
- fore*tell*
- or*go*
- for*swear*
- ham*string*
- in*lay*
- inter*breed*
- inter*weave*
- inter*wind*
- mis*become*
- mis*deal*
- mis*give*
- mis*hear*
- mis*lay*
- mis*lead*
- mis*read*
- mis*spell*
- mis*spend*
- mis*take*
- misunder*stand*
- off*drive*
- on*drive*
- out*bid*
- out*eat*
- out*fight*
- out*fly*
- out*grow*
- out*ride*
- out*run*
- out*shine*
- out*shoot*
- out*sing*
- out*sit*
- out*spend*
- out*stink*
- out*swim*
- out*think*
- out*wear*
- over*bear*
- over*blow*
- over*build*
- over*buy*
- over*cast*
- over*come*
- over*do*
- over*draw*
- over*drink*
- over*drive*
- over*eat*
- over*feed*
- over*flow*
- over*gild*
- over*grow*
- over*hang*
- over*hear*
- over*lay*
- over*leap*
- over*lie*
- over*pass*
- over*read*
- over*ride*
- over*run*
- over*see*
- over*sell*
- over*sew*
- over*shoot*
- over*spend*
- over*spill*
- over*spread*
- over*stay*
- over*take*
- over*throw*
- over*wind*
- over*work*
- par*take*
- re*bind*
- re*build*
- re*cast*
- re*do*
- re*gild*
- re*hang*
- re*hear*
- re*make*
- re*pass*
- re*pay*
- re*read*
- re*seck*
- re*set*
- re*spell*
- re*take*
- re*tell*
- re*tread*
- re*win*
- re*write*
- thunder*strike*
- un*bear*
- un*bend*
- un*bind*
- under*bid*
- under*cut*
- under*do*
- under*draw*
- under*go*
- under*lay*
- under*let*
- under*lie*
- under*pay*
- uuder*run*
- nnder*sell*
- under*set*
- under*stand*
- under*stay*
- under*take*
- under*write*
- un*do*
- un*gild*
- un*gird*
- un*hang*
- un*lay*
- un*lead*
- un*learn*
- un*make*
- un*ring*
- un*say*
- un*set*
- un*speak*
- un*spell*
- un*string*
- un*swear*
- un*think*
- un*weave*
- un*wind*
- un*work*
- up*bear*
- up*bind*
- up*rise*
- up*set*
- way*lay*
- wire*draw*
- with*draw*
- with*hold*
- with*stand*

年號索引

年號及年數	紀元	西曆
Aṅei (安永 9)	2432—2440	1772—1780
Angen (安元 2)	1835—1836	1175—1176
Ansei (安政 6)	2514—2519	1854—1859
Antei (安貞 2)	1887—1888	1227—1228
Anwa (安和 2)	1628—1629	968— 969
Buṅan (文安 5)	2104—2108	1444—1448
Bunchū (南朝, 文中 3)	2032—2034	1372—1374
Buṅei (文永 11)	1924—1934	1264—1274
Bunji (文治 5)	1845—1849	1185—1189
Bunka (文化 14)	2464—2477	1804—1817
Bunki (文龜 3)	2161—2163	1501—1503
Bunkyū (文久 3)	2521—2523	1861—1863
Bunmei (文明 18)	2129—2146	1469—1486
Buṅō (文應 1)	1920	1260
Bunpō (文保 2)	1977—1978	1317—1318
Bunroku (文祿 4)	2252—2255	1592—1595
Bunryaku (文曆 1)	1894	1234
Bunsei (文政 12)	2478—2489	1818—1829
Bunshō (文正 1)	2126	1466
Bunwa (北朝, 文和 4)	2012—2015	1352—1355
Chōgen (長元 9)	1688—1696	1028—1036
Chōhō (長保 5)	1659—1663	999—1003
Chōji (長治 2)	1764—1765	1104—1105
Chōkan (長寬 2)	1823—1824	1163—1164
Chōkyō (長享 2)	2147—2148	1487—1488
Chōkyū (長久 4)	1700—1703	1040—1043
Chōroku (長祿 3)	2117—2119	1457—1459
Chōryaku (長曆 3)	1097—1699	1037—1039
Chōshō (長承 3)	1792—1794	1132—1134
Chōtoku (長德 4)	1655—1658	995— 998
Chōwa (長和 5)	1672—1676	1012—1015
Daidō (大同 4)	1466—1469	806— 809
Daihō (大寶 3)	1361—1363	701— 703
Daiji (大治 5)	1786—1790	1126—1130
Eichō (永長 1)	1756	1096
Eien (永延 2)	1647—1648	987— 988
Eihō (永保 3)	1741—1743	1081—1083
Eiji (永治 1)	1801	1141
Eikan (永觀 2)	1643—1644	983— 984
Eikyō (永享 12)	2089—2100	1429—1440
Eikyū (永久 5)	1773—1777	1113—1117
Eiman (永萬 1)	1825	1165
Einin (永仁 6)	1953—1958	1293—1298
Eiroku (永祿 12)	2218—2229	1558—1569
Eiryaku (永曆 1)	1820	1160
Eishō (永承 7)	1706—1712	1046—1052
Eishō (永正 17)	2164—2180	1504—1520
Eiso (永祚 1)	1649	989
Eitoku (北朝, 永德 3)	2041—2043	1381—1383
Eiwa (北朝, 永和 4)	2035—2038	1375—1378
Ėnbun (北朝, 延文 5)	2016—2020	1356—1360
Enchō (延長 8)	1583—1590	923— 930
Engen (南朝, 延元 4)	1996—1999	1336—1339
Engi (延喜 22)	1561—1582	901— 922
Enkei (延慶 3)	1968—1970	1308—1310
Enkyō (延享 4)	2404—2407	1744—1747
Enkyū (延久 5)	1729—1733	1069—1073
Eṅō (延應 1)	1899	1239

年號及年數	紀元	西暦
Enpō (延寶 8)	2333—2340	1673—1680
Enryaku (延暦 24)	1442—1465	782— 805
Entoku (延德 3)	2149—2151	1489—1491
Genbun (元文 5)	2396—2400	1736—1740
Genchū (南朝, 元中 9)	2044—2052	1384—1392
Geṅei (元永 2)	1778—1779	1118—1119
Genji (元治 1)	2524	1864
Genkei (元慶 8)	1537—1544	877— 884
Genki (元龜 3)	2230—2232	1570—1572
Genkō (元弘 3)	1991—1993	1331—1333
Genkyō (元享 3)	1981—1983	1321—1323
Genkyū (元久 2)	1864—1865	1204—1205
Geṅō (元應 2)	1979—1980	1319—1320
Gennin (元仁 1)	1884	1224
Genroku (元祿 16)	2348—2363	1688—1703
Genryaku (元暦 1)	1844	1184
Gentoku (元德 2)	1989—1990	1329—1330
Genwa (元和 9)	2275—2283	1615—1623
Hakuchi (白雉 5)...	1310—1314	650— 654
Hakuhō (白鳳 15)	1332—1346	672— 689
Heiji (平治 1)...	1819	1159
Hōan (保安 4)	1780—1783	1120—1123
Hōei (寶永 7)...	2364—2370	1704—1710
Hōen (保延 6)	1795—1800	1135—1140
Hōgen (保元 3)	1816—1818	1156—1158
Hōji (寶治 2)	1907—1908	1247—1248
Hōki (寶龜 11)	1430—1440	770— 780
Hōreki (寶暦 13)	2411—2423	1751—1763
Hōtoku (寶德 3)	2109—2111	1449—1451
Jian (治安 3)	1681—1683	1021—1023
Jingokeiun (神護景雲 3)	1427—1429	767— 769
Jinki (神龜 5)...	1384—1388	724— 728
Jiryaku (治暦 4)	1725—1728	1065—1068
Jishō (治承 4)	1837—1840	1177—1180
Jōei (貞永 1)	1892	1232
Jōgan (貞觀 18)	1519—1536	859— 876
Jōgen (貞元 2)	1536—1537	976— 977
Juei (壽永 2)	1842—1843	1182—1183
Kaei (嘉永 6)...	2508—2513	1848—1853
Kagen (嘉元 3)	1963—1965	1303—1305
Kahō (嘉保 2)	1754—1755	1094—1095
Kakei (北朝, 嘉慶 2)	2047—2048	1387—1388
Kakitsu (嘉吉 3)...	2101—2103	1441—1443
Kanbun (寛文 12)	2321—2332	1661—1672
Kaṅei (寛永 20)	2284—2303	1624—1643
Kaṅen (寛延 3)	2408—2410	1748—1750
Kangen (寛元 4)	1903—1906	1243—1246
Kanji (寛治 7)	1747—1753	1087—1093
Kanki (寛喜 3)	1889—1891	1229—1231
Kankō (寛弘 8)	1664—1671	1004—1011
Kannin (寛仁 4)	1677—1680	1017—1020
Kaṅō (北朝, 觀應 2)	2010—2011	1350—1351
Kanpō (寛保 3)	2401—2403	1741—1743
Kanpyō (寛平 9)	1549—1557	889— 897
Kansei (寛政 12)	2449—2460	1789—1800
Kanshō (寛正 6)	2120—2125	1460—1465
Kantoku (寛德 2)	1704—1705	1044—1045
Kanwa (寛和 2)	1645—1646	985— 986
Kaō (嘉應 2)	1829—1830	1169—1170
Kareki (嘉暦 3)	1986—1988	1326—1328
Karoku (嘉祿 2)	1885—1886	1225—1226
Kashō (嘉祥 3)	1508—1510	848— 850
Kashō (嘉承 2)	1766—1767	1106—1107

年號及年數	紀元	西暦
Katei (嘉禎 3)	1895—1897	1235—1237
Keian (慶安 4)	2308—2311	1648—1651
Keichō (慶長 19)	2256—2274	1596—1614
Keiō (慶應 3)	2525—2527	1865—1867
Keiun (慶雲 4)	1364—1367	704— 707
Kenchō (建長 7)	1909—1915	1249—1255
Keṅei (建永 1)	1866	1206
Kengen (乾元 1)	1962	1302
Kenji (建治 3)	1935—1937	1275—1277
Kenkyū (建久 9)	1850—1858	1190—1198
Kenmu (建武 2)	1994—1995	1334—1335
Kennin (建仁 3)	1861—1863	1201—1203
Kenpō (建保 6)	1873—1878	1213—1218
Kenryaku (建暦 2)	1871—1872	1211—1212
Kentoku (南朝, 建德 2) ...	2030—2031	1370—1371
Kōan (弘安 10)	1938—1947	1278—1287
Kōan (北朝, 康安 1)	2021	1361
Kōchō (弘長 3)	1921—1923	1261—1263
Kōei (北朝, 康永 3)	2002—2004	1342—1344
Kōgen (康元 1)	1916	1256
Kōhei (康平 7)	1718—1724	1058—1064
Kōhō (康保 4)	1624—1627	964— 967
Kōji (康治 2)	1802—1803	1142—1143
Kōji (弘治 3)	2215—2217	1555—1557
Kōka (弘化 4)	2504—2507	1844—1847
Kōkoku (南朝, 興國 6)	2000—2005	1340—1345
Kōnin (弘仁 14)	1470—1483	810— 823
Kōō (北朝, 康應 1)	2049	1382
Kōryaku (北朝, 康曆 2) ...	2039—2040	1379—1380
Kōshō (康正 2)	2115—2116	1455—1456
Kōwa (康和 5)	1759—1763	1099—1103
Kōwa (南朝, 弘和 3)	2041—2043	1381—1383
Kyōhō (享保 20)	2376—2395	1716—1735
Kyōroku (享祿 4)	2188—2191	1528—1531
Kyōtoku (享德 3)	2112—2114	1452—1454
Kyōwa (享和 3)	2461—2463	1801—1803
Kyūan (久安 6)	1805—1810	1145—1150
Kyūju (久壽 2)	1814—1815	1154—1155
Maṅen (萬延 1)	2520	1860
Manji (萬治 3)	2318—2320	1658—1660
Manju (萬壽 4)	1684—1687	1024—1027
Meiji (明治 44)	2528—2571	1868—1911
Meiō (明應 9)	2152—2160	1492—1500
Meireki (明曆 3)	2315—2317	1655—1657
Meitoku (明德 4)	2050—2053	1390—1393
Meiwa (明和 8)	2424—2431	1764—1771
Niṅan (仁安 3)	1826—1828	1166—1168
Ninji (仁治 3)	1900—1902	1240—1242
Ninju (仁壽 3)	1511—1513	851— 853
Ninpyō (仁平 3)	1811—1813	1151—1153
Ninwa (仁和 4)	1545—1548	885— 888
Ōan (北朝, 應安 7)	2028—2034	1368—1374
Ōchō (應長 1)	1971	1311
Ōei (應永 34)	2054—2087	1394—1427
Ōhō (應保 2)	1821—1822	1161—1162
Ōnin (應仁 2)	2127—2128	1467—1468
Ōtoku (應德 3)	1744—1746	1084—1086
Ōwa (應和 3)	1621—1623	961— 963
Reiki (靈龜 2)	1375—1376	715— 716
Ryakunin (曆仁 1)	1898	1238
Ryakuō (北朝, 曆應 4)	1998—2001	1338—1341
Saikō (齊衡 3)	1514—1516	854— 856
Shitoku (北朝, 至德 3)	2044—2046	1384—1386

年號及年數	紀元	西暦
Shōan (承安 4) … … … …	1831—1834	1171—1174
Shōan (正安 3) … … … …	1959—1961	1299—1301
Shōchō (正長 1) … … … …	2088	1428
Shōchū (正中 2) … … … …	1984—1985	1324—1325
Shōgen (承元 4) … … … …	1867—1870	1207—1210
Shōhei (南朝, 正平 24) … …	2006—2029	1346—1369
Shōhō (承保 3) … … … …	1734—1736	1074—1076
Shōhō (正保 4) … … … …	2304—2307	1644—1647
Shōhyō (承平 7) … … … …	1591—1597	931— 937
Shōji (正治 2) … … … …	1859—1860	1199—1200
Shōka (正嘉 2) … … … …	2917—1918	1257—1258
Shōkei (北朝, 正慶 2) … …	1992—1993	1332—1333
Shōkyū (承久 3) … … … …	1879—1881	1219—1221
Shōō (正應 5) … … … …	1948—1952	1288—1292
Shōō (承應 3) … … … …	2312—2314	1652—1654
Shōryaku (正曆 5) … … …	1650—1654	990— 994
Shōryaku (承曆 4) … … …	1737—1740	1077—1080
Shōtai (昌泰 3). … … …	1558—1560	898— 900
Shōtoku (承德 2, … … …	1757—1758	1097—1098
Shōtoku (正德 5)… … …	2371—2375	1711—1715
Shōwa (承和 14) … … …	1494—1507	834—847
Shōwa (正和 5) … … …	1972—1976	1312—1316
Shōwa (昭和) … … …	2586—	1926—
Shuchō (朱鳥 10)… … … …	1347—1356	687— 696
Taiei (大永 7) … … … …	2181—2187	1521—1527
Taika (大化 5) … … … …	1305—1309	645— 649
Taishō (大正 14) … … … …	2572—2585	1912—1925
Teiji (北朝, 貞治 6) … …	2022—2027	1362—1367
Teikyō (貞享 4) … … … …	2344—2347	1684—1687
Teiō (貞應 2) … … … …	1882—1883	1222—1223
Teiwa (北朝, 貞和 5) … …	2005—2009	1345—1349
Teṅan (天安 2) … … … …	1517—1518	857— 858
Tenchō (天長 10)… … … …	1484—1493	824— 833
Teṅei (天永 3) … … … …	1770—1772	1110—1112
Teṅen (天延 3) … … … …	1633—1635	973— 975
Tengen (天元 5)… … … …	1538—1642	978— 982
Tenji (天治 2) … … … …	1784—1785	1124—1125
Tenju (南朝, 天授 6) … …	2035—2040	1375—1380
Tenki (天喜 5) … … … …	1713—1717	1053—1057
Tenkyō (天慶 9) … … … …	1598—1606	938— 946
Tenmei (天明 8) … … … …	2441—2448	1781—1788
Tenmon (天文 23) … … …	2192—2214	1532—1554
Tennin (天仁 2) … … … …	1768—1769	1108—1109
Tenō (天應 1) … … … …	1441	781
Tenpō (天保 14)… … … …	2490—2503	1830—1843
Tenpuku (天福 1) … … …	1893	1233
Tenpyō (天平 20)… … … …	1389—1408	729— 748
Tenpyōhōji (天平寶字 8) … …	1417—1424	757— 764
Tenpyōjingo (天平神護 2) …	1425—1426	765— 766
Tenpyōshōhō (天平勝寶 8) …	1409—1416	749— 756
Tenroku (天祿 3) … … …	1630—1632	970— 972
Tenryaku (天曆 10) … … …	1607—1616	947— 956
Tenshō (天承 1) … … … …	1791	1131
Tenshō (天正 19)… … … …	2233—2251	1573—1591
Tentoku (天德 4)… … … …	1617—1620	957— 960
Tenwa (天和 3) … … … …	2341—2343	1681—1683
Teṅyō (天養 1) … … … …	1804	1144
Tokuji (德治 2) … … … …	1966—1967	1306—1307
Wadō (和銅 7) … … … …	1368—1374	708— 714
Yōrō (養老 7)… … … …	1377—1383	717— 723
Yōwa (養和 1) … … … …	1841	1181

歷代年表

表中 * は南朝，× は北朝を示す

天皇	年號	在位	紀元	西曆
Ankan (安閑) … … … …	… … … …	2	1194	534 A.D.
Ankō (安康) … … … …	… … … …	3	1114	454 „
Annei (安寧) … … … …	… … … …	38	113	548 B.C.
Antoku (安德)… … …	養和，壽永	3	1841	1181 A.D.
Bitatsu (敏達)… … …	… … … …	14	1232	572 „
Buretsu (武烈) … … …	… … … …	8	1159	499 „
Chūai (仲哀) … … …	… … … …	9	852	192 „
Chūkyō (仲恭)… … …	承久	2	1880	1220 „
Daigo (醍醐) … … …	昌泰，延喜，延長	33	1558	898 „
Enyū (圓融) … … …	天祿，天延，貞元，天元，永觀	15	1630	970 „
Fushimi (伏見) … … …	正應，永仁	11	1948	1288 „
Genmyō (元明) … … …	和銅	7	1368	708 „
Genshō (元正) … … …	靈龜，養老	9	1375	715 „
Godaigo (後醍醐) … …	元應，元亨，正中，嘉曆，元德，元弘，建武	17	1979	1319 „
* Godaigo (後醍醐) … …	延元	3	1996	1336 „
×Goenyū (後圓融) …	應安，永和，康曆，永德	11	2032	1372 „
Gofukakusa (後深草) … …	寶治，建長，康元，正嘉，正元	13	1907	1247 „
Gofushimi (後伏見) … …	正安	3	1959	1299 „
Gohanazono (後花園)… …	永亨，嘉吉，文安，寶德，享德，康正，長祿，寬正	36	2089	1429 „
Gohorikawa (後堀河) … …	貞應，元仁，嘉祿，安貞，寬喜，貞永	11	1882	1222 „
Goichijō (後一條) … … …	寬仁，治安，萬壽，長元	20	1677	1017 „
* Gokameyama (後龜山) …	正平，建德，文中，天授，弘和，元中	24	2029	1369 „
Gokashiwabara (後柏原) …	文龜，永正，大永	26	2161	1501 „
×Gokōgon (後光嚴) … …	文和，延文，康安，貞治，應安	20	2012	1352 „
Gokomatsu (後小松) … …	明德，應永	20	2053	1393 „
×Gokomatsu (後小松) …	永德，至德，嘉慶，康應，明德	10	2043	1383 „
Gokōmyō (後光明) … …	正保，慶安，承應	11	2304	1644 „
Gomizunoo (後水尾) … …	慶長，元和，寬永	18	2272	1612 „
Gomomozono (後桃園) …	明和，安永	9	2431	1771 „
* Gomurakami (後村上) …	興國，正平	30	1999	1339 „
Gonara (後奈良) … … …	大永，享祿，弘治	31	2187	1527 „
Gonijō (後二條) … … …	乾元，嘉元，德治，延慶	7	1962	1302 „
Goreizei (後冷泉) … … …	永承，天喜，康平，治曆	23	1706	1046 „
Gosaga (後嵯峨) … … …	寬元	4	1903	1243 „
Gosaiin (後西院) … … …	明曆，萬治，寬文	8	2315	1655 „
Gosakuramachi (後櫻町)…	寶曆，明和	8	2423	1763 „
Gosanjō (後三條) … … …	延久	4	1729	1069 „
Goshirakawa (後白河)… …	保元	3	1816	1156 „
Goshujaku (後朱雀) … …	長曆，長久，寬德	9	1697	1037 „
Gotoba (後鳥羽) … … …	元曆，文治，建久	15	1844	1184 „
Gotsuchimikado (後土御門)	寬正，文正，應仁，文明，長享，延德，明應	36	2125	1465 „
Gouta (後宇多) … … …	建治，弘安	13	1935	1275 „
Goyōzei (後陽成) … … …	天正，文祿，慶長	25	2247	1587 „

天　皇	年　號	在位	紀元	西曆
Hanazono (花園)	延慶, 應長, 正和, 文保	10	1969	1309 A.D.
Hanshō (反正)	... ...	6	1066	406 "
Heizei (平城)	大同	4	1466	806 "
Higashiyama (東山)	貞享, 元祿, 寶永	24	2346	1686 "
Horikawa (堀河)	寬治, 嘉保, 永長, 承德, 康和, 長治, 嘉承	21	1747	1087 "
Ichijō (一條)	永延, 永祚, 正曆, 長德, 長保, 寬弘	25	1647	987 "
Inkyō (允恭)	... ...	42	1072	412 "
Itoku (懿德)	... ...	34	151	510 B.C.
Jinmu (神武)	... ...	76	1	660 "
Jitō (持統)	朱鳥	10	1347	687 A.D.
Jomei (舒明)	... ...	13	1289	629 "
Junnin (淳仁)	天平寶字	6	1419	759 "
Juntoku (順德)	建曆, 建保, 承久	10	1871	1211 "
Junwa (淳和)	天長	10	1484	824 "
Kaika (開化)	... ...	60	504	157 B.C.
Kameyama (龜山)	文應, 弘長, 文永	15	1920	1260 A.D.
Kanmu (桓武)	延暦	24	1442	782 "
Kazan (花山)	寬和	2	1645	985 "
Keikō (景行)	... ...	60	731	71 "
Keitai (繼體)	... ...	25	1167	507 "
Kensō (顯宗)	... ...	3	1145	485 "
Kinjō (今上)	昭和	—	—	—
Kinmei (欽明)	... ...	32	1200	540 "
Kōan (孝安)	... ...	102	269	392 B.C.
Kōbun (弘文)	白鳳	1	1332	672 A.D.
Kōgen (孝元)	... ...	57	447	214 B.C.
× **Kōgon** (光嚴)	正慶	2	1992	1332 A.D.
Kōkaku (光格)	安永, 天明, 寬政, 享和, 文化	37	2440	1780 "
Kōken (孝謙)	天平勝寶, 天平寶字	10	1409	749 "
Kōkō (光孝)	仁和	4	1545	885 "
Kōkyoku (皇極)	... ...	3	1302	642 "
Kōmei (孝明)	弘化, 嘉永, 安政, 萬延, 文久, 元治, 慶應	20	2507	1847 "
× **Kōmyō** (光明)	曆應, 康永, 貞和	11	1998	1338 "
Kōnin (光仁)	寶龜, 天應	12	1430	770 "
Konoe (近衛)	康治, 天養, 久安, 仁平, 久壽	14	1802	1142 "
Kōrei (孝靈)	... ...	76	371	290 B.C.
Kōshō (孝昭)	... ...	83	186	475 "
Kōtoku (孝德)	大化, 白雉	10	1305	645 A.D.
Meiji (明治)	慶應, 明治	46	2527	1867 "
Momozono (桃園)	寬延, 寶曆	15	2408	1748 "
Monmu (文武)	太寶, 慶雲	11	1357	697 "
Montoku (文德)	仁壽, 齊衡, 天安	8	1511	851 "
Murakami (村上)	天曆, 天德, 應和, 康保	21	1607	947 "
Myōshō (明正)	寬永	14	2290	1630 "
Nakamikado (中御門) ...	寶永, 正德, 享保	26	2370	1710 "
Nijō (二條)	平治, 永曆, 應保, 長寬, 永萬	7	1819	1159 "
Ninken (仁賢)	... ...	11	1148	488 "
Ninkō (仁孝)	文化, 文政, 天保, 弘化	30	2477	1817 "
Ninmyō (仁明)	承和, 嘉祥	17	1494	834 "
Nintoku (仁德)	... ...	87	973	313 "
Ōgimachi (正親町)	永祿, 元龜, 天正	29	2218	1558 "
Ōjin (應神)	神功攝政 ... 69	110	861	201 "
Reigen (靈元)	寬文, 延寶, 天和, 貞享	23	2323	1663 "

天皇	年號	在位	紀元	西曆
Reizei (冷泉) … … … …	安和	2	1628	968 A.D.
Richū (履仲) … … … …	… … … …	6	1060	400 „
Rokujō (六條) … … … …	仁安	3	1826	1166 „
Saga (嵯峨) … … … …	弘仁	14	1470	810 „
Saimei (齊明) … … … …	… … … …	7	1315	655 „
Sakuramachi (櫻町) …	元文, 寬保, 延享	12	2396	1736 „
Sanjō (三條) … … … …	長和	5	1672	1012 „
Seimu (成務) … … … …	… … … …	60	791	131 „
Seinei (淸寧) … … … …	… … … …	5	1140	480 „
Seiwa (淸和) … … … …	貞觀	18	1519	859 „
Senka (宣化) … … … …	… … … …	4	1196	536 „
Shirakawa (白河) … … …	延久, 承保, 承曆, 永保, 應德	14	1733	1073 „
Shōkō (稱光) … … … …	慶永, 正長	16	2073	1413 „
Shōmu (聖武) … … … …	神龜, 天平	25	1384	724 „
Shōtoku (稱德) … … …	天平神護, 神護景雲	5	1425	755 „
Shujaku (朱雀) … … …	承平, 天慶	16	1591	931 „
Suiko (推古) … … … …	… … … …	36	1253	593 „
Suinin (垂仁) … … … …	… … … …	99	632	29 B.C.
Suisei (綏靖) … … … …	… … … …	33	80	581 „
Sujin (崇神) … … … …	… … … …	68	564	97 „
×**Sukō** (崇光) … … … …	貞和, 觀應	3	2009	1349 A.D.
Sushun (崇峻 … … … …	… … … …	5	1248	588 „
Sutoku (崇德) … … … …	天治, 大治, 天承, 長承, 保延, 永治	18	1784	1124 „
Taishō (大正) … … … …	大正	14	2572	1912 „
Takakura (高倉) … … …	嘉應, 承安, 安元, 治承	12	1829	1169 „
Tenchi (天智) … … … …	… … … …	10	1322	662 „
Tenmu (天武) … … … …	… … … …	14	1333	673 „
Toba (鳥羽) … … … …	天仁, 天永, 永久, 元永, 保安	16	1768	1108 „
Tsuchimikado (土御門) …	正治, 建仁, 元久, 建永, 承元	12	1859	1199 „
Uda (宇多) … … … …	寬平	9	1549	889 „
Yojō (四條) … … … …	天福, 文曆, 嘉禎, 曆仁, 延應 仁治	10	1893	1233 „
Yōmei (用明) … … … …	… … … …	2	1246	586 „
Yōzei (陽成) … … … …	元慶	8	1537	877 „
Yūryaku (雄略) … … …	… … … …	23	1117	457 „

度量衡換算表

度

日本		英國	メートル法
分		.11931 in.	.0030303 metre
寸	10分	1.1931 in.	.030303 "
尺	10寸	11.931 in.; .9942 ft.	.30303 "
間	6尺	1.9884 yd.; 5.9652 ft.	1.81818 "
町	60間	5.423 ch., 119.304 yds; .5426 fur.	109.0909 metres
里	36町; 2160間	2.4403 miles	3.9273kilometres

英國		日本	メートル法
inch (in.)		0.8382 寸	.02540 metre
foot (ft.)	12 in.	1.00584 尺	.30479 "
yard (yd.)	3 ft.; 36 in.	3.01752 尺	.91438 "
rod[pole; perch]	5½ yds; 16½ ft.	2間4尺5.9625 寸	5.02911 metres
link	7.92 in.	6.63854 寸	.20116 metre
chain ch.)	100 links; 22yds.	11 間 3 尺 8.538 寸	20.11644 metres
furlong (fur.)	220yds.; 10ch.	1 町 50 間 3 尺 8.538 寸	201.1644 "
mile (m.)	8 fur.; 1760 yds.; 80 ch.	14 町 45 間 8.35 寸; .40973 里	1,609.315 "
league	3 m.	1 里 8 町 15 間 2 尺 5.05 寸; 1.22919 里	4,827.945 "

link と chain とは測量に用ひる。

nautical mile (海哩) は 6,080 ft. で普通の mile (又は statute mile と稱す) は 5,280 ft. で前者は後者より 800 ft. 長く，一nautical mile は一statute mile の 1.1515 に當り後者は前者の .86842 に當るより x statute miles を nautical miles に換算する時には x×.86842 とすれば良い，又 y nautical miles を statute miles に換算するには y×1.1515 とする，卽ち 1000 nautical miles は 1,151.5 statute miles に當り 1000 statute miles は 868.42 nautical miles に當る。

メートル法		日本	英國
millimetre	1/1000 metre	.033 寸	.03937 in.
centimetre	1/100 metre	.33 寸	.3937 in.
decimetre	1/10 metre	3.3 寸	3.937 in.; 3.28 ft.
metre		3 尺 3 寸	39.3708 in.; 3.2809 ft.; 1.0936 yd.
decametre	10 metres	3 丈 3 尺; 5½ 間	32.809 ft.; 10.936 yds.
hectometre	100 metres	55 間; .9166 町	328.09 ft.; 109.36 yds.
kilometre	1,000 metres	550間; 9町 10間; .2546 里	1093.6 yds.; .62138 m.
myriametre	10,000 metres	2 里 19 町 40 間	6.2138 miles

面積

日本		英國	メートル法
平方寸		1.42349 sq. in.	.0000091827 are
平方尺	100 方寸	142.349 sq. in; .98813 sq. ft.	.00091827 „
			.00330577 „
合	1/10 坪; 3.6 方尺	3.55871 sq. ft.; .39531 sq. yd.	
坪, 歩	36 方尺	35.5871 sq. ft.; 3.9531 sq. yds.	.0330577 „
畝	30 歩	118.593 sq. yds.	.991731 „
段, 反	10 畝; 300 歩	1185.93 sq. yds.	9.91731 ares
町	10 段; 3000 歩	2.4503 ac.; 2ac. 2221 sq. yds.	99.1731 „
方里	1,552.2 町	5.9551 sq. miles	153,936.486 „
英國		**日本**	**メートル法**
square inch (sq. in.)		.70258 方寸	.000006451 are
square foot (sq. ft.)	144 sq. in.	1.01171 方尺	.000929 „
square yard (sq. yd.)	9 sq. ft.	9.10539 方尺; .25293 歩	.008361 „
square rod [perch]	30¼ sq. yds.	7.65107 歩	.25292 „
rood	40 sq. rods; 1,210 sq. yds.	306.043 歩; 一段 6.043 歩	10.11678 ares
acre (ac.)	4 roods; 4,840 sq. yds.	1,224.172 歩; 4 段 24.172 歩	40.4671 „
square mile	640 acres; 3,097,600 sq. yds.	261 町 1 段 5 畝 20.8 歩; .16792 方里	25,898.945 „
メートル法		**日本**	**英國**
milliare	1/1000 are	1.089 方尺; .3025 合	155 sq. in.; 1.076 sq. ft.
centiare	1/100 are; 1 sq. metre	10.89 方尺; 3.025 合	10.76 sq. ft.; 1.19 sq. yd.
deciare	1/10 are; 10 sq. metres	108.9 方尺; 3 歩 0.25 合	107.64 sq. ft.; 11.96 sq. yds.
are	100 sq. metres	1 畝 0.25 歩	119.6 sq. yds.
decare	10 ares; 1000 sq. metres	1 段 2.5 歩	1,196 sq. yds.; .2471 acre
hectare	100 ares; 10,000 sq. metres	1 町 25 歩	2.471 acres

立方

日本		英國	メートル法
立方寸		1.6984 cub. in.	.00002782 stere
立方尺	1000 立方寸	1698.4 cub. in.; .98285 cub. ft.	.02782 „
英國		**日本**	**メートル法**
cubic inch		.5819 立方寸	.000016386 stere
cubic foot	1,728 cub. in.	1.0052 立方尺	.0283153 „
cubic yard	27 cub. ft.	27 立方尺; 140.4 立方寸	.764513 „

メートル法		日　本	英　國
millistere	1/1000 stere, 1 cubic decimetre	35.937 立方寸	61.028 cub. in.
centistere	1/100 stere	.35937 立方尺	610.28 „
decistere	1/10 stere	3.5937 „	3.5317 cub. ft.
stere	1 cubic metre	35.937 „	35.317 cub. ft.; 1.308 cub. yd.
decastere	10 steres	359.37 „	13.08 cub. yds.
hectostere	100 „	3593.7 „	130.802 cub. yds.

量

日　本		英　國	メートル法
合		1.26976 gills; .31744 pint	.18039 litre
升	10 合	3.1744 pints	1.8039 „
斗	10 升	31.744 pts.; 3.968 gallons	18.039 litres
石	10 斗	317.44 pts.; 4.96 bushels	180.39 „
英　國		**日　本**	**メートル法**
gill		.78779 合	.141983 litre
pint (pt.)	4 gills	3.15017 合	.56793 „
quart (qrt.)	2 pints	6.30034 合	1.13586 „
gallon (g.)	4 qrts; 8 pts	2 升 5.316 合	4.543457 litres
peck	2 g.; 8 qrts; 16 pts	5 升 0.6272 合	9.086915 „
bushel	4 pecks; 8 g.; 64 pts	2 斗 2.5 合	36.34766 „
quarter	8 bushels; 64 g.	1 石 6 斗 2 升 0.70 合	290.7813 „

gill と gallon は液量に用ひ其他は液量・穀量共に用ひる.

メートル法		日　本	英　國
millilitre	1/1000 litre	.0055435 合	.00176 pt.; .00704 gill
centilitre	1/100 litre	.055435 合	.0176 pt.; .0704 gill
decilitre	1/10 litre	.55435 合	.176 pt.; .704 gill
litre	=1 cubic decimetre	5.5435 合	1.76 pt.; .22 gallons
decalitre	10 litres	5 升 5.43 合	2.2 gallons; .275 bushels
hectolitre	100 litres	5 斗 5 升 4.35 合	22 gallons; 2.75 bushels
kilolitre	1,000 litres=1 cubic metre=1 stere	5 石 5 斗 4 升 3.5 合	220 gallons; 27.5 bushels
myrialitre	10,000 litres	55 石 4 斗 3 升 5 合	275.121 bushels

衡

日本		英國	メートル法
厘		.5787 gr.	.0375 gramme
分	10 厘	5.787 grs.	.375 "
匁	10 分	57.87 grs ; .14028 oz. av.	3.75 grammes
斤	160 匁	1.322 lbs. av.	540 "
貫	1,000 匁	8.2673 lbs. av.	3750 "

英國		日本	メートル法
dram avoirdupois (dr. av.)		4.72492 分	1.771836 gramme
ounce " (oz. av.)	16 drachms	7 匁 5.5987 分	28.349375 grammes
pound " (lb. av.)	16 oz.; 7,000 grains	120 匁 9.579 分	453.59265 "
stone (st.)	14 lbs.	1 貫 693.41 匁	6,350.29 "
quarter (qr.)	(英) 2 stones ; 28 lbs.	3 貫 386.82 匁	12,700.58 "
	(米) 25 lbs.	3 貫 23.95 匁	11,339.816 "
hundredweight (cwt.)	4 qrs. (英) ; 112 lbs.	13 貫 547.28 匁	50,802.38 "
	4 qrs. (米) ; 100 lbs.	12 貫 95.8 匁	45,359.265 "
ton	20 cwt. (英) 2240 lbs.	270 貫 945.6 匁	1,016,047.5 "
	" (米) 2000 lbs.	241 貫 916 匁	907,185.3 "
grain		1.72799 厘	.064799 "
pennyweight (dwt.)	24 grains	4.14712 分	1.55517 "
ounce troy	20 dwt.	8.29426 匁	31.10346 "
pound troy	12 oz. troy ; 5760 grains	99.53114 匁	373.2419 "

troy weight は金銀寶石等を秤るに用ひるので其他は一般に avoirdupois を用ひる.

メートル法		日本	英國
milligramme	1/1000 gramme	.02667 厘	.015 grain
centigramme	1/100 "	.2667 厘	.154 "
decigramme	1/10 "	2.6667 厘	1.543 "
gramme		2.66667 分	15.432 grains
decagramme	10 grammes	2.66667 匁	.35 oz. av.
hectogramme	100 "	26.6667 匁	3.527 oz.; .22046 lb.
kilogramme	1,000 "	266.667 匁	35.27 oz.; 2.2046 lbs.
myriagramme	10,000 "	2 貫 666.67 匁	22.046 lbs.
quintal	100,000 "	26 貫 666.7 匁	220.46 lbs.; 1.9684 cwt. (英)
millier, metric ton.	1,000,000 "	266 貫 667 匁	2204.62 lbs.; 19.684 cwt.; .9842 ton

英文手紙の書方

手紙には我々が日常生活上に用ひる普通の社交文 (Social letter) と，營業上に用ひる商用文 (Business letter) と，官公署の用ひる公用文 (Official letter) との區別はあるが，玆には主として社交文に就て述べる．

I. 一般の心得

(A). インキと用紙と封筒——手紙を書くには普通黑インキと稱するもの，卽ち writing ink 又は office ink を用ふべきである．赤色や紫色のものは成るべく避けねばならぬ．書簡紙は多少大小の相違はあつても，一般には note-paper 又は letter-paper と稱する白色のものを用ひる．罫の引いたものや色紙は用ひないのが普通である．但し婦人は淡靑や淡桃色の紙を用ひても差支へない．封筒は其の長さが用紙の幅と同じか心持ち長いもので且つ用紙と同質のものを用ふべきである．形は正方形でも長方形でもよいが，普通には長方形のものが用ひられる．若し用紙に色紙を用ひる時は封筒も同色のものを用ひる方がよいのである．

(B). 封入の仕方——手紙が書けたら書き違ひなど無いかどうか一應讀み直した上，下の端を大凡用紙の三分の一位の處まで折上げ，更に封筒の幅より少し狹くなるやう上端から下方に折下げる．すべて封筒の出し入れに便利なるやう心すべきである．之を封筒に入れるには，先づ封筒の裏を上向きにして封じ口を右手に向け，書簡箋を疊んだまゝに上前の折目を先にして插入する．次にゴム糊の部分を濕して封をすることは日本風の封筒と同樣であるが，其の封じ目に〆や封や緘など書かないのが一般の風習である．(注意．紹介狀や推薦狀は封をせぬこと)

II. 封筒面の書方

封筒は上下轉倒せぬやう，日本の封筒と同じく封じ目を上にし，表面の受信人・住所姓名は特に書き誤りなきやう十分注意して丁寧に明瞭に認めねばならぬ．

(A). 宛名と敬稱——受信人の氏名敬稱は封筒表面の中央部に書く．氏名は名を先にし姓を後にすること勿論であるが，名を全部書く時は次に **,** も **.** も用ひず，頭字だけ書く時には **.** を附ける．姓の終りには **,** を附す．

普通用ひられる敬稱は次の通りである．

Mr.	Mister の略字．樣，殿，君．(男子)
.... Esq.,	Esquire の略字．樣，殿．(男子)
Master	樣，君．(少年)
Miss	(子) 樣．(未婚の女子)

Mrs. .... Mistress の略字. 樣, 奥樣, 令夫人. (既婚の婦人)

Messrs......... Mr. の複數 (佛蘭西語 Messieurs の略). 各位, 御中. (團體, 會社, 商店)

Esq., は英國に於て紳士間には一般に用ひられるが, 正式の文書には略字を用ひず Esquire と書く. 米國に於ては Esquire は普通法律家だけに用ひられて居る. Miss は未婚の娘に用ひるのであるが, 單に Miss Wilson と書くと Wilson 家の長女のことになるから, 次女乃至三女宛の時はそれぞれに Christian name を Miss と Wilson との間に插入せねばならない. Mrs. の次には夫たる人の名と姓とを書くのであるが, 若し未亡人であれば夫人自身の名と夫の姓とを書かねばならない.

敬稱を二つ以上用ひることは勿論出來ないのであるが, 若し名宛人が稱號を有つて居るならばそれをも書き加へねばならない. 此時は例へば「法學博士坂東太郎殿」ならば Dr. T. Bando. とするか T. Bando, Esq., LL.D. とする. Dr. T. Bando, LL.D. とすることは出來ないのである.

(B). 住所——住所は宛名の下へ少し右寄りに書く. 二行乃至三行に亙る時は段々右方へ少しづつ引込めながら書く. 順序は番地, 町村名, 郡區名, 市府縣名といふ風に下から書き上げる形式になる. 例へば「東京市神田區美土代町百八十番地」は

180 Mitoshiro-cho,
Kanda-ku,
Tokyo.

と書く. 180 の前へ番地の No. (伊太利語の Numero = Number の略字) を置いてもよいのであるが, 普通には之を略する. 番地の次には , を入れることがあるが普通は無くてよい. 然し町名や區名などの次にはそれぞれに , を附け, 住所の最後には . を附ける. ....樣方, ...樣氣附 など書くには, 初めに c/o (care of の略) を置き次に配達先の名前を書き, 前述の通りに住所を書けばよい. 同市內, 同一府縣下へ出す時は府縣市名を省略する.

(C). 發信人の住所姓名——封筒には表裏とも自分の住所姓名を書かないのが普通である. (外國では中の手紙の初めに書き入れることになつて居る. 之は後に說明する) ただ受信人の住所が不確かで, 配達不能の懸念があるなどの場合には,「...........へ御返送を乞ふ」といふ意味で封筒の左の上隅に If undelivered, please return to 又は單に Please return to として其の次に發信人の氏名住所を書いて置く. 但し商業上の手紙には之を書いてあるのが多い.

(D). 指定語——外國へ發送する手紙には其の經路を指定するために, 封筒の左上隅若しくは少し右寄りに次の如き語を書く

ことがある．若し左上隅に發信人の住所姓名を書いた時は左下隅若しくは少し右寄りに書いてもよい．

Via Seattle　(シャトル經由)
Via Siberia　(シベリア經由)
Per s/s "Minnesota"　(汽船ミネソウタ號便にて)

尙左の下隅には次の如き語を書いて差支ない．

Private (親展)	Personal (親展)	Confidential (祕密)
In Haste (至急)	Immediate (至急)	Urgent (急用)
Photos only (寫眞在中)	Strictly confidential (極祕)	
With compliments (進呈)	Registered 又は Reg'd (書留)	
Poste restante (局留)	Printed matter only (印刷物在中)	
Please forward (轉居先へ廻送を乞ふ)		

(E)．切手——切手は封筒の右上隅へ貼附する．二枚乃至三枚用ひる時は横に竝べて貼る．先方で不足税を徵收せられないやう注意すべきは言ふまでもない．

以上は葉書の上書にも共通するが上に述べたところを形式に示すと下の如き體裁になる．

Stamp

Master K. Katsura,
c/o Juntendo,
Ochanomizu,
Hongo-ku.

Via Seattle

Stamp

Mr. George Tennyson,
42 Rector Street,
New York,
U. S. A.

If undelivered, please
return to K. Sato,
32 Kikui-cho, Ushigome,
Tokyo, Japan.

Stamp

______________,

______________,

__________.

III. 手紙の組立

手紙は普通次の四部分から成立つて居る.

A. Heading (標記) { Sender's Address (發信人住所) / Date (日附)

B. Introduction (前置) { Recipient's Name and Address (受信人住所氏名) / Salutation (挨拶の辭)

C. Body (本文)

D. Conclusion (結末) { Complimentary Close (結末の辭) / Signature (署名)

(A). Heading は書輸箋の上部右寄りに書く. 住所は一行で濟む場合もあり又二行になることもあるが, 三行では少し長過ぎる嫌ひがある. 書き方は封筒住所の書き方と同じであるから省く. ただ住所の最後に . を附けないのが通則である.

日附は住所の最後の行より更に右に引込めて書く. その書き方は例へば千九百三十六年八月一日ならば Aug. 1, 1936. の如く月日年の順序で書く. 米國では之を 1 Aug., 1936. と書くこともある. 一日は first であるから 1st と書く人もあるが必ずしも st を附ける要はない. 又之を 1/8/'36 など書くのは先方に對して禮を缺くことになるから避けねばならぬ. 月の長いものは January (一月) を Jan. February (二月) を Feb. August (八月) を Aug. September (九月) を Sept. October (十月) を Oct. November (十一月) を Nov. December (十二月) を Dec. と略して書くが, 短いもの March (三月), April (四月), May (五月) June (六月), July (七月) などは略さないで書く.

以上のことを例示すると次の如きものとなる.

325 Zoshigaya, Takata-machi,
Toshima-ku, Tōkyō
Aug. 1, 1936.

(B). Introduction は本文の初め左寄りに本文より少し引込めて書く. 受信人の氏名住所 (Address) と挨拶の辭 (Salutation) とに分れるが氏名住所の書き方は封筒の上書と凡て同様である. ただこゝでは住所の最後に . を附けないでよい. 此の氏名住所は公用文・商用文又は普通文でも目上の人に出す場合には書くのが正式であるが, 友人間や家族に出す手紙には之を書く要はない. 又之を Introduction として書かないで手紙の終りの署名より低く左側に書くこともある.

Salutation は Address のすぐ下に Address の初めの行と同じ高さに書く. 若し Address を書かない時はその位置に書く. これは我國の「拜啓」「手紙を以て申上候」などに當るもので, 宛名に相當する敬語を附けて書くものであるから, 手紙の終りに「…………様」など別に書くに及ばないのである. 次にその主なるものを掲げる.

1. 近親者には
   - My dear Father, 父上様
   - My dear Mother, 母上様
   - My dear Brother, 兄上様
2. 友人には
   - My dear Taro, 太郎君
3. 餘り親密でない友人には
   - Dear Hayashi, 林様
   - Dear Mr. Hayashi, 林様 (男)
   - Dear Miss Hayashi, 林様 (娘)
4. 形式的には
   - Dear Sir, (男子一人の時)
   - Dear Sirs, (男子二人以上の時)
   - Sir, (やゝ四角張つたもの)
   - Dear Madam, (夫人又は少女以上の婦人)
   - Gentlemen, (男子二人以上又は會社, 團體宛)
   - My Lord, (華族宛)

尙此の外親子夫婦間の如く極めて親密なものには My dearest …………, My darling, など書くこともある. すべて Salutation の終りには , を附けて次の本文に移る.

以上 Introduction を例示すると次の如き形になる.

Taro Katsura, Esq.,
15 Wakamatsu-cho,
Ushigome-ku, Tokyo
My dear Katsura,

(C). Body は手紙の本體である. すべて手紙は普通の談話體を以て要領よく書くべきもので, むづかしい語句は成るべく避けねばならぬ. 書き初めは Salutation の二語目の初め位の高さから書く. 本文の左右餘白は大凡半インチ位あける. 餘り端へ寄ると全體の體裁が惡くなる. 文例は最後に添へてあるから玆には省くが, 今之を形式に示すと次の通りである.

My dear Hayashi,

I am very sorry..............................

....

....

(D). Conclusion は本文の次へ中央より少し右寄りに書く. Complimentary Close と Signature との二部に分れる. Complimentary Close は結末の辭で, 我國の「早々」「頓首」「敬具」などに當るべきものである. 之は頭字で書き始めて , で切る. 一般に多く用ひられて居るものを次に示す.

1. 子から父母へ

Your affectionate [loving] son, あなたの愛する息子より

Your affectionate [loving] daughter, あなたの愛する娘より

2. 父母から子へ

Your affectionate [loving] father, お前の愛する父より

Your affectionate [loving] mother, お前の愛する母より

3. 友人間には

Yours (very) truly, Yours (very) sincerely,

Yours faithfully, Your (sincere) friend,

Ever (faithfully) yours,

4. 敬意を表すべき場合には

Yours (very) respectfully, Respectfully yours,

Your (most humble,) obedient servant, (强き敬意)

Body と結末の辭との間に動詞句を挾むことがある. その主なるものは Believe me, 又は I remain, であるが, 後者は以前から情誼の繼續して居る者へでなければ用ひられない. 尙兩者とも其の次へ my dear James, dear John, などと先方の名を加へることもある. 又 Your obedient servant, の如き敬意を表する句の前には I have the honour to be なる句を加へる. すべて動詞句を插入する時は結末の辭より少し高く書き始める.

Signature は發信人の署名で結末の辭より少し引込めて書き, 終りに . を附ける. 親しい間柄の者には名を頭字だけに略しても差支ないが, 普通は略さず全部書いた方がよい.

以上述べた Conclusion を例示すると次の如きものになる.

a. Believe me, (dear John),

Yours very sincerely,

Kiyomasa Kato.

b. I remain, (my dear James),
Yours faithfully,
M. Miyamoto.

c. I have the honour to be
Your obedient servant,
Hideyoshi Toyotomi.

以上手紙の組立を說明し終つたが，今之を更に取纏めて例示すると次の通りである．

10 Imagawa Koji,
Kanda-ku, Tokyo
Feb. 15, 1936.

Jiro Okabe, Esq.,
8 Takehaya-cho,
Koishikawa-ku, Tokyo

My dear Jiro,

I am very sorry I was out when you favoured me with a call this morning. We have not met for a long time; and I am very anxious to see you. Will you be at home next Sunday afternoon? If you are not then engaged, I shall call and apologize for my absence this morning.

Yours very sincerely,
Taro Hamada.

IV. 作　　例

普通の社交的書簡の中日常最も多く用ひられるのは次の四種類である．

1. Familiar Letters (普通の日用文)
2. Letters of Congratulation (慶賀文)
3. Letters of Condolence (弔慰文)
4. Letters of Introduction (紹介狀)

今此等に就て數例を擧げる. Heading と Recipient's Name and Address とは既に說明したところで別に變化がないから省くことにする.

拜啓　其後御無沙汰致居候. 昨今は殊の外寒氣酷敷候處御兩親初め皆々樣御變り無之候や御伺ひ申上候. 私方一同無事消光罷在候に付御安心下され度候. 御暇の節にはちと御遊びに 越し下され度先は寒中御見舞まで. 敬具

田中一郎

中山二郎様

My dear M. Nakayama,

I must apologize for my long neglect to write to you. It has lately grown very cold; but I sincerely hope that your parents, yourself, and all your family are in good health. I am glad to say that we are all quite well. Please favour us with a call whenever you have time to spare.

With sincere wishes for the continued good health of yourself and your family,

I am, dear Mr. Nakayama,
Yours very sincerely,
Ichiro Tanaka.

拜啓　先日は御訪ね下され有難く存候. 其節一寸御話申上候遠足の儀, 太田君と相談の結果次の日曜日に高雄山へ登ることと相成申候に付, 辨當御持參同日午前七時までに新宿驛まで御出で下され度, 此段御通知申上候. 草々

小川新太郎

山田登兄

Dear Mr. Yamada,

Many thanks for your call the other day. With respect to the tour we talked about on that occasion, we have decided after consultation with Mr. Ota to go up Mt. Takao on Sunday next. We hope, therefore, you will be at Shinjuku Station by seven o'clock on the morning of that day. Please bring your luncheon with you.

Yours very truly,
Shintaro Ogawa.

拜啓　貴堂益々御隆盛奉賀候．陳ば御發行の賀川豊彦氏著「死線を越えて」一冊，大至急御郵送下され度，定價並に送料二圓八十錢也郵便爲替同封右御註文に及び候．草々

井上敬二

改造社御中

Messrs. Kaizosha.

Dear Sirs,

I shall be obliged if you will forward me as soon as possible a copy of Toyohiko Kagawa's "Beyond the Death-line," published by your firm.

I enclose herewith a P.O.O. for ¥2.80, postage included.

Yours respectfully,

Keiji Inouye.

(註)　P.O.O. は Post Office Order (郵便爲替) の略．

謹呈　昨日は男子御出生の趣慶賀の至に奉存候．其後御母子共に御壯健に御肥立ちの事と存居り申し候．早速御祝に參るべき筈の處，目下田舍より來客有之手放し兼ね候に付，取あへず書中を以て御賀び申述べ候．草々

岩崎久雄

鈴木米太郎様

My dear Mr. Suzuki,

Allow me to congratulate you on the birth of a son yesterday. I trust both mother and child are doing well. I should have offered my congratulations in person; but as I have at present visitors from the country whom I cannot leave, you will, I hope, pardon my expressing my congratulations by letter.

Yours very faithfully,

Hisao Iwasaki.

拜啓　過日は御近所より出火御類燒の趣新聞紙上にて拜承驚入申候．御家族様には何の御怪我も無之候哉御伺申上候．不慮の御災難とて差當つての御不自由幾重にも御察し申上候．別便小包を以て反物三反御送り致し候に付御受納下され度，取あへず御見舞申上候．頓首

水谷岩吉

風間淑雄殿

Dear Mr. Kazama,

I was very much shocked when I saw in the papers that you had suffered from the fire which broke out in your neighbourhood a few days ago. I hope, however, that no one of your family has been injured. I can well imagine to what inconvenience you are put by this unlooked-for misfortune. I have forwarded by parcel post three *tan* of cloth which I beg you will accept as a slight token of my deep sympathy in the great calamity to which you have been exposed.

I remain, dear Mr. Kazama,

Yours very faithfully,

Iwakichi Mizutani.

拜啓　小生知人西村孃を御紹介申上候．御多忙中恐縮に候へ共御引見下され，本人滯在中何分の御配慮賜はり候はば光榮の至に存申し候．敬具

大澤行雄

村山樣

Dear Mr. Murayama,

I have the pleasure to introduce to you a young lady friend Miss Nishimura. I shall esteem it a personal favour if you will see her and help her during her stay in your town.

Yours very sincerely,

Yukio Osawa.
